AP® EDITION

The Earth and Its Peoples
A Global History   Seventh Edition

Richard W. Bulliet
Columbia University

Steven W. Hirsch
Tufts University

Lyman L. Johnson
University of North Carolina—Charlotte

Pamela Kyle Crossley
Dartmouth College

Daniel R. Headrick
Roosevelt University

David Northrup
Boston College

CENGAGE

Australia • Brazil • Mexico • Singapore • United Kingdom • United States

ARCTIC OCEAN

ALASKA RANGE

60°N

ROCKY MOUNTAINS

CANADIAN SHIELD

NORTH AMERICA

40°N

APPALACHIAN MTS.

Mississippi R.

NORTH PACIFIC OCEAN

NORTH ATLANTIC OCEAN

Rio Grande

Tropic of Cancer

20°N

0° Equator

Amazon R.

SOUTH AMERICA

ANDES MOUNTAINS

20°S

Tropic of Capricorn

SOUTH PACIFIC OCEAN

SOUTH ATLANTIC OCEAN

40°S

Cape Horn

60°S

Antarctic Circle

80°S

180°

Sea ice
Ice cap
Tundra
Forest
Grassland
Desert
Mountains

180° 150°W 140°W 120°W 100°W 80°W 60°W 40°W 20°W

80°N

ARCTIC OCEAN

80°N

60°N

URAL MTS.

Volga R.

Ob R.

EUROPE

40°N

ASIA

GOBI

HINDU KUSH

HIMALAYA MTS.

Indus R.

Ganges R.

SYRIAN DESERT

Tropic of Cancer

20°N

HARA

Niter R.

AFRICA

DECCAN PLATEAU

PACIFIC OCEAN

0°

INDIAN OCEAN

NAMIB DESERT

KALAHARI DESERT

GREAT SANDY DESERT

20°S

Tropic of Capricorn

AUSTRALIA

Cape of Good Hope

0   1,000   2,000 Km.

0   1,000   2,000 Mi.

60°S

Antarctic Circle

TARCTICA

80°S

180°

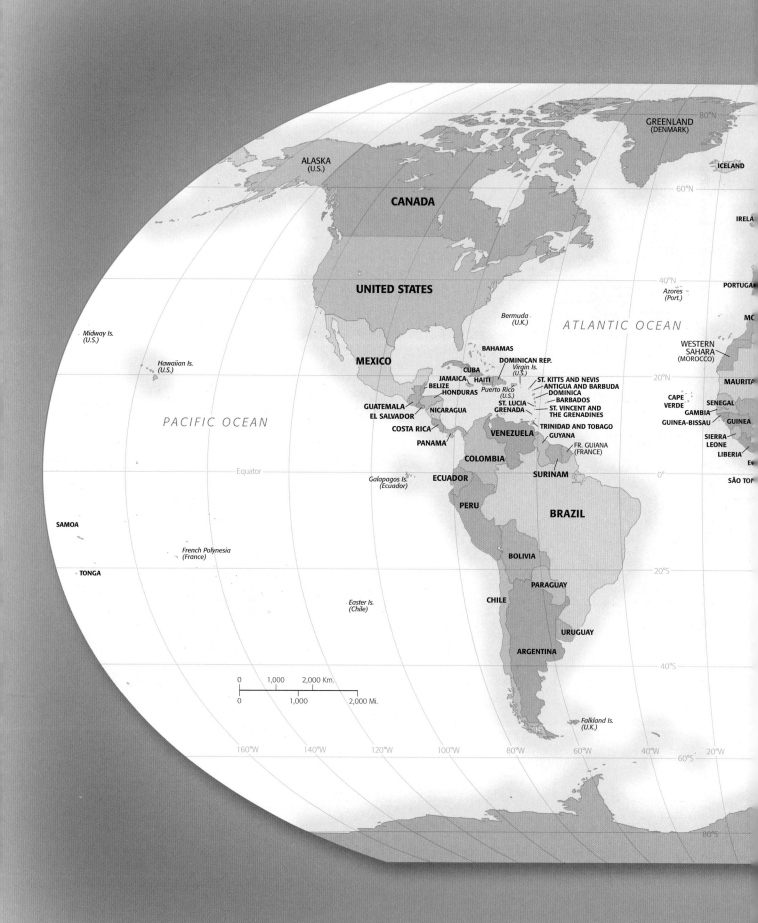

GREENLAND
(DENMARK)

ICELAND

ALASKA
(U.S.)

CANADA

60°N

IRELA

80°N

UNITED STATES

40°N

Azores
(Port.)

PORTUGA

Bermuda
(U.K.)

ATLANTIC OCEAN

MO

Midway Is.
(U.S.)

WESTERN
SAHARA
(MOROCCO)

BAHAMAS

Hawaiian Is.
(U.S.)

MEXICO

DOMINICAN REP.
CUBA

20°N

MAURITA

Virgin Is.
(U.S.)

ST. KITTS AND NEVIS
ANTIGUA AND BARBUDA
DOMINICA

JAMAICA HAITI

BELIZE

HONDURAS

Puerto Rico
(U.S.)

CAPE
VERDE

SENEGAL

PACIFIC OCEAN

GUATEMALA
EL SALVADOR

NICARAGUA

ST. LUCIA
GRENADA

BARBADOS
ST. VINCENT AND
THE GRENADINES

GAMBIA

GUINEA-BISSAU

GUINEA

COSTA RICA

TRINIDAD AND TOBAGO
GUYANA

SIERRA
LEONE

PANAMA

VENEZUELA

FR. GUIANA
(FRANCE)

LIBERIA

E

COLOMBIA

Equator

Galapagos Is.
(Ecuador)

ECUADOR

SURINAM

0°

SÃO TO

SAMOA

PERU

BRAZIL

French Polynesia
(France)

BOLIVIA

TONGA

20°S

PARAGUAY

Easter Is.
(Chile)

CHILE

URUGUAY

ARGENTINA

40°S

0   1,000   2,000 Km.

0   1,000   2,000 Mi.

Falkland Is.
(U.K.)

60°S

160°W   140°W   120°W   100°W   80°W   60°W   40°W   20°W

80°S

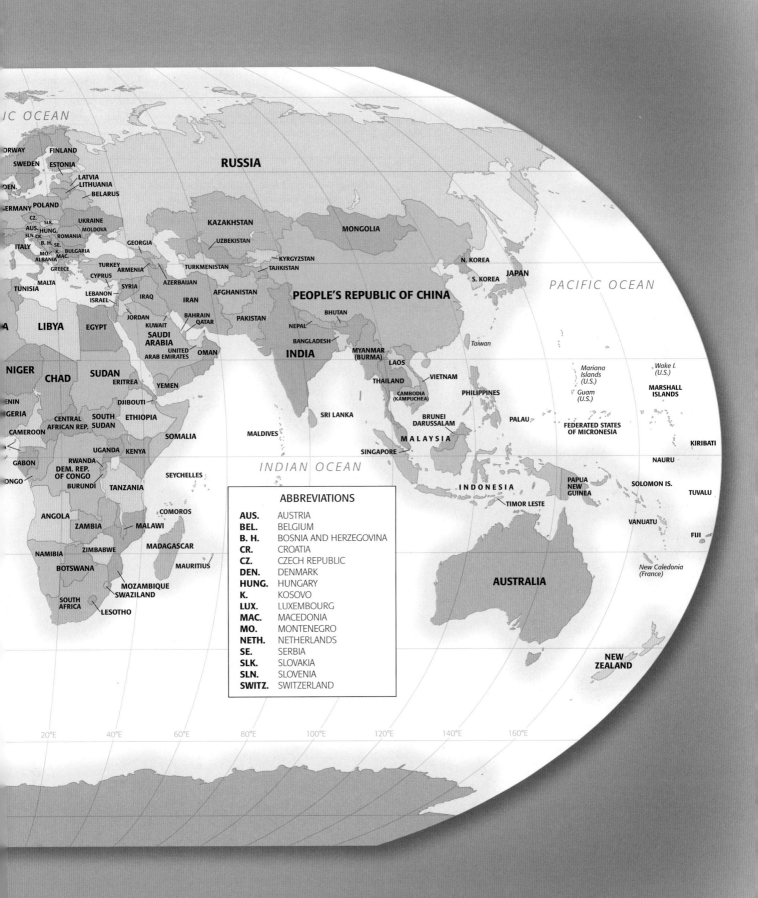

The Earth and Its Peoples: A Global History, **Seventh Edition, AP® Edition**

Richard W. Bulliet / Steven W. Hirsch / Lyman L. Johnson / Pamela Kyle Crossley / Daniel R. Headrick / David Northrup

Product Manager: Richard Lena

Content Developer: Sarah Edmonds

Associate Content Developer: Emma Guiton

Product Assistant: Sayaka Kawano

Senior Product Marketing Manager: Valerie Hartman

Senior Content Project Manager: Carol Newman

Manufacturing Planner: Julio Esperas

IP Analyst: Alexandra Ricciardi

IP Project Manager: Betsy Hathaway

Production Service: SPi Global

Senior Art Director: Cate Barr

Text Designer: Jeanne Calabrese

Cover Designer: Wing Ngan of Ink Design, Inc.

Cover Image: Volcanic tufa formations, known as fairy chimneys. Pasbag, near Zelve, Cappadocia, Anatolia, Turkey. Robert Harding/Superstock

Product Director, Advanced and Elective Products Program: Dawn Giovanniello

Product Manager, Advanced and Elective Products Program: Jeff Werle

Executive Product Marketing Manager, Advanced and Elective Products Program: Andrea Kingman

Content Developer, Advanced and Elective Products Program: Julie Allen

Product Assistant, Advanced and Elective Products Program: Emma Collins

For product information and technology assistance, contact us at **Cengage Customer & Sales Support, 1-888-915-3276 or SchoolCustomerService@cengage.com**
To locate your sales consultant, go to **NGL.Cengage.com/RepFinder.**
For permission to use material from this text or product, submit all requests online at **www.cengage.com/permissions**.

Library of Congress Control Number: 2017950429

Student Edition ISBN: 978-1-337-40150-0

Cengage
20 Channel Center Street
Boston, MA 02210
USA

Cengage is a leading provider of customized learning solutions with employees residing in nearly 40 different countries and sales in more than 125 countries around the world. Find your local representative at **www.cengage.com.**

Cengage products are represented in Canada by Nelson Education, Ltd.

To learn more about Cengage platforms and services, visit **www.cengage.com.**

Printed in the United States of America
Print Number: 03   Print Year: 2019

Brief Contents

Contents

PART I The Emergence of Human Communities, to 500 BCE **2**

AP® is a trademark registered by the College Board, which is not affiliated with, and does not endorse, this product.

Maps

Features

Environment & Technology

Diversity & Dominance

Material Culture

Issues in World History

Preface

The overall goal of *The Earth and Its Peoples, AP® Edition,* remains as it has been since its first edition: to be a textbook that speaks not only for the past but also to today's student and teacher. Students and instructors alike should take away from this text a broad and flowing impression of human societies beginning as sparse and disconnected communities reacting creatively to local circumstances; experiencing ever more intensive stages of contact, interpenetration, and cultural expansion and amalgamation; and arriving at a twenty-first-century world in which people increasingly visualize, and sometimes challenge, a single global community.

Process, not progress, is the keynote of this book: a steady process of change over time, at first experienced differently in various regions but eventually connecting peoples and traditions from all parts of the globe. Students should come away from this book with a sense that the problems and promises of their world are rooted in a past in which people of every sort, in every part of the world, confronted problems of a similar character and coped with them as best they could. We believe that our efforts will help students see where their world has come from and thereby learn something useful for their own lives.

Central Themes and Goals

We subtitled *The Earth and Its Peoples* "A Global History" because the book explores the common challenges and experiences that unite the human past. Although the dispersal of early humans to every livable environment resulted in a myriad of different economic, social, political, and cultural systems, all societies displayed analogous patterns in meeting their needs and exploiting their environments. Our challenge was to select the particular data and episodes that would best illuminate these global patterns of human experience.

To meet this challenge, we adopted two themes for our history: "technology and the environment" and "diversity and dominance." The first theme represents the commonplace material bases of all human societies at all times. It grants no special favor to any cultural group even as it embraces subjects of the broadest topical, chronological, and geographical range. The second theme expresses the reality that every human society has constructed or inherited structures of domination. We examine practices and institutions of many sorts: military, economic, social, political, religious, and cultural, as well as those based on kinship, gender, and literacy. Simultaneously we recognize that alternative ways of life and visions of societal organization continually manifest themselves both within and in dialogue with every structure of domination.

With respect to the first theme, it is vital for students to understand that technology, in the broad sense of experience-based knowledge of the physical world, underlies all human activity. Writing is a technology, but so is oral transmission from generation to generation of lore about medicinal or poisonous plants. The magnetic compass is a navigational technology, but so is Polynesian mariners' hard-won knowledge of winds, currents, and tides that made possible the settlement of the Pacific islands.

All technological development has come about in interaction with environments, both physical and human, and has, in turn, affected those environments. The story of how humanity has changed the face of the globe is an integral part of our first theme. Yet technology and the environment do not explain or underlie all important episodes of human experience. The theme of "diversity and dominance" informs all our discussions of politics, culture, and society. Thus when narrating the histories of empires, we describe a range of human experiences within and beyond the imperial frontiers without assuming that imperial institutions are a more fit topic for discussion than the economic and social organization of pastoral nomads or the lives of peasant women. When religion and culture occupy our narrative, we focus not only on the dominant tradition but also on the diversity of alternative beliefs and practices.

Organization

The *Earth and Its Peoples, AP® Edition,* uses eight broad chronological divisions to define its conceptual scheme of global historical development.

In **Part I: The Emergence of Human Communities, to 500 BCE**, we examine important patterns of human communal organization primarily in the Eastern Hemisphere. Small, dispersed human communities living by foraging spread to most parts of the world over tens of thousands of years. They responded to enormously diverse environmental conditions, at different times in different ways, discovering how to cultivate plants and utilize the products of domestic animals. On the basis of these new modes of sustenance, population grew, permanent towns appeared, and political and religious authority, based on collection and control of agricultural surpluses, spread over extensive areas.

Part II: The Formation of New Cultural Communities, 1000 BCE–400 CE introduces the concept of a "cultural community," in the sense of a coherent pattern of activities and symbols pertaining to a specific human community. While all human communities develop distinctive cultures, including those discussed in Part I, historical development in this stage of global history prolonged and magnified the impact of some cultures more than others. In the geographically contiguous African-Eurasian landmass, as well as in the Western Hemisphere, the cultures that proved to have the most enduring influence traced their roots to the second and first millennia BCE.

Part III: Growth and Interaction of Cultural Communities, 300 BCE–1200 CE deals with early episodes of technological, social, and cultural exchange and interaction on a continental scale both within and beyond the framework of imperial expansion. These are so different from earlier interactions arising from more limited conquests or extensions of political boundaries that they constitute a distinct era in world history, an era that set the world on the path of increasing global interaction and interdependence that it has been following ever since.

In **Part IV: Interregional Patterns of Culture and Contact, 1200–1550**, we look at the world during the three and a half centuries that saw both intensified cultural and commercial contact and increasingly confident self-definition of cultural communities in Europe, Asia, Africa, and the Americas. The Mongol conquest of a vast empire extending from the Pacific Ocean to eastern Europe greatly stimulated trade and interaction. In the West, strengthened European kingdoms began maritime expansion in the Atlantic, forging direct ties with sub-Saharan Africa and entering into conflict with the civilizations of the Western Hemisphere.

Part V: The Globe Encompassed, 1500–1750 treats a period dominated by the global effects of European expansion and continued economic growth. European ships took over, expanded, and extended the maritime trade of the Indian Ocean, coastal Africa, and the Asian rim of the Pacific Ocean. This maritime commercial enterprise had its counterpart in European colonial empires in the Americas and a new Atlantic trading system. The contrasting capacities and fortunes of traditional land empires and new maritime empires, along with the exchange of domestic plants and animals between the hemispheres, underline the technological and environmental dimensions of this first era of complete global interaction.

In **Part VI: Revolutions Reshape the World, 1750–1870**, the word *revolution* is used in several senses: in the political sense of governmental overthrow, as in France and the Americas; in the metaphorical sense of radical transformative change, as in the Industrial Revolution; and in the broadest sense of a perception of a profound change in circumstances and worldview. Technology and environment lie at the core of these developments. With the rapid ascendancy of the Western belief that science and technology could overcome all challenges—environmental or otherwise—technology became an instrument not only of transformation but also of domination, to the point of threatening the integrity and autonomy of cultural traditions in nonindustrial lands and provoking strong movements of resistance.

Part VII: Global Diversity and Dominance, 1750–1945 examines the development of a world arena in which people conceived of events on a global scale. Imperialism, international economic connections, and world-encompassing ideological tendencies, such as nationalism and socialism, present the picture of a globe becoming increasingly involved with European political and ideological concerns. Two world wars arising from European rivalries provide a climax to these developments, and European exhaustion affords other parts of the world new opportunities for independence and self-expression.

For **Part VIII: Perils and Promises of a Global Community, 1945 to the Present**, we divide the period since World War II into three time periods: 1945–1975, 1975–2000, and 2000 to the present. The challenges of the Cold War and postcolonial nation building dominate much of the period and unleash global economic, technological, and political forces that become increasingly important in all aspects of human life. With the end of the Cold War, however, new forces come to the fore. Technology is a key topic in Part VIII because of its integral role in both the growth and the problems of a global community. However, its many benefits in improving the quality of life become clouded by negative impacts on the environment. Other negative impacts come from the spread of instability, terrorist disruption, and military intervention in many troubled parts of the globe along with a growth of animosity toward groups that are suspected of supporting such disruptions.

Features and AP® Pedagogical Aids

As with previous editions, the seventh edition offers, in addition to enhanced visual design, a number of valuable features and pedagogical aids designed to pique student interest in specific world history topics and help them process and retain key information. Challenging questions designed to prompt inquiry into historical processes have been added to each map, to every feature box, and to the end of every chapter. And each of the eight parts now climaxes in two essays called Issues in World History and Material Culture. These are specifically designed to alert students to broad and recurring conceptual issues that are of great interest to contemporary historians. The Issues in World History essay for Part VIII, "Popular Culture: Words of Warning," is entirely new; "Religious Conversion" has been restored from an earlier edition; and "Little Ice Age" has been substantially updated. A Material Culture essay on "Roads" is also new. The Environment & Technology feature, which has been a valuable resource in all prior editions of *The Earth and Its Peoples, AP*®*Edition*, serves to illuminate the major theme of the text by demonstrating the shared material bases of all human societies across time. Eight of the features are new with this edition: "Nomad Homes," "Roads," "Stained Glass Windows," "The West African Voyage of Hanno the Carthaginian," "East Asian Transportation," "Persian Rugs," "New Wars, New Tools," and "Intelligence and Technology." Finally, there are six new or heavily revised Diversity & Dominance features containing primary source readings that bring a myriad of real historical voices to life in the age-old tug-of-war between power and autonomy: "Poetry and Society in Early China and Greece," "Becoming Muslim," "Justice and Kingship," "Understanding Cross-Cultural Encounters," "The Manchu Moment from Ming to Ching," and "Madame de Staël Remembers Napoleon."

Pedagogical aids include:

- **AP® Tips** In the margins of each chapter, AP® test-taking tips, updated for the redesigned course, offer candid advice to students about events and topics that they will need to know for the exam.
- **AP® Review Questions** At the end of each chapter, AP® multiple-choice and short-answer review questions, formatted like the questions that appear on the real exam, offer additional practice for students and a useful means of evaluation for teachers.
- **Part Openings** These introductions include, for each of the eight parts, the titles of the chapters in that part, a list of the AP® Key Concepts (expressed as questions) covered in the chapter, a table showing how each of the five AP® themes is referenced in the chapter, and a brief introduction to the content of the part.
- **Chapter Openings** These introductions include a list of the terms, events, and names that appear on the content outline of the course and a set of "overarching questions" that direct students' attention to the thematic learning objectives of the course.
- **Focus Questions** These questions are keyed to every major subdivision of the chapter and serve to help students focus on the core chapter concepts.
- **Section Reviews** Short bullet-point reviews summarize each major section in every chapter and remind students of key information.
- **Chapter Conclusions** Every chapter ends with a comparative conclusion that helps students better synthesize chapter material and understand how it fits into the larger picture.
- **Marginal Key Term with Definitions** Students can handily find key term definitions on the same page where the term first appears.

- **Pronunciation Guide** Hard-to-pronounce words are spelled phonetically for students throughout the text.
- **Suggested Readings** These have been expanded and resituated from the end of each chapter to the Teacher's Resource Guide.

Changes in This Edition

In addition to the pedagogical aids outlined above, numerous chapter-by-chapter changes have been made, including new illustrations, new maps, streamlining of the textual discussion, and updates to many of the boxed feature essays. Here are a few highlights:

- Chapter 1 includes new discussion of the recent discovery of *Homo naledi* (now a key term) in South Africa, with a new photo of the skeleton of the hand and foot.
- Chapter 3 contains a new Environment & Technology feature, "The West African Voyage of Hanno the Carthaginian," and includes new Map 3.6 depicting the path of Hanno's expedition. Crucial information from the previous edition's feature, "Ancient Textiles and Dyes," has been incorporated into the section on Phoenician city-states.
- Chapter 4 has a new Diversity & Dominance feature, "Poetry and Society in Early China and Greece," that compares outlooks on Chinese society through poems from the Chinese *Book of Songs*, with Greek poems by Sappho and Tyrtaeus.
- Chapter 7 includes new art, including a new chapter-opening photo of the exterior of the Temple of Minakshi at Madurai, a sculpture depicting Buddha at the moment he achieves enlightenment, and a new wall painting from the caves at Ajanta that reflects members of different castes and ethnic groups.
- Chapter 10 includes a new subsection, "Marginal Communities," as well as a Diversity & Dominance feature, "Becoming Muslim," that gives firsthand accounts of conversions to the faith.
- Chapter 12 has changed the title and all internal references from "Inner Asia" to "Central Asia." The introduction has also been heavily updated.
- Chapter 14 contains new discussion of the coach's introduction to western Europe from Hungary in the late 1400s. It also includes a new Environment & Technology feature, "Stained Glass Windows."
- Chapter 15 includes revisions to the introduction to the section "Tropical Africa and Asia" and the subsection "The Tropical Environment in Africa and Asia." The Diversity & Dominance feature contains a new excerpt from *The Tale of the Anklet*.
- In addition to several new illustrations, Chapter 17 contains added discussion of the Catholic Church's council meetings between 1545 and 1563 and of Phillip II.
- Chapter 18 contains new discussion of the application of the label "Indian" and the position of native elites, as well as new coverage of the hundreds of distinct native peoples in the English and French colonies in North America.
- Chapter 19 contains updates to the modern conversions of a planter's expenses and a rural laborer and wealthy noble family's incomes and provides the most recent research and statistics on the importation of African slaves into Islamic regions.
- Chapter 22 includes several new illustrations, as well as updated and expanded subsections on "Changes in Society," "Protests and Reforms," "India," and the "Conclusion."
- Chapter 23 contains new coverage of the baroness Germaine de Staël, including a portrait and a new Diversity & Dominance feature that uses an excerpt from de Staël's memoir to shed light on Napoleon's character.
- Chapter 24 includes an updated Environment & Technology feature, "The Web of War," with the addition of a firsthand account of the siege of Sevastopol (the Crimean capital) from the *Times* of London.
- Chapter 27 includes revisions to several sections, including "The New Power Balance, 1850–1900," "Nationalism and the Rise of Italy, Germany, and Japan," and "China, Japan, and the Western Powers."
- Chapter 28 includes a new Environment & Technology feature, "New War, New Tools," that describes the technological advances of World War I including chemical warfare, flamethrowers, concertina wire, radios, food rations, and camouflage.

- In this edition, the chapter "The Collapse of the Old Order, 1929–1949" (now Chapter 29) appears before the chapter "Revolutions in Living, 1900–1950" (now Chapter 30).
- Chapter 31 contains an updated introduction to Part VIII that adds insight about industrial and economic recovery after the end of World War II, as well as additions about global famine.
- Chapter 32 contains new and updated statistics throughout that reflect the most recent research, including data through 2000 in Table 32.1. The chapter also notes the recent violence and civil wars in Syria and Libya.
- Chapter 33 covers updates in world affairs through the first half of 2017, including the 2016 terror attacks in Paris and Brussels; the elevation of Pope Francis I; Brexit; the abortive military coup in Turkey in 2016; and the election of Donald Trump and the early acts of the new administration. The section "The Question of Values" has been moved and is now the first section in the chapter.

MindTap

MindTap for *The Earth and Its Peoples*, 7e, AP® Edition, is a flexible, online learning platform that provides students with an immersive learning experience to build and foster critical thinking skills. Through a carefully designed chapter-based learning path, MindTap allows students to easily identify learning objectives; draw connections and improve writing skills by completing unit-level essay assignments; read short, manageable sections from the e-book; and test their content knowledge with map- and timeline-based critical thinking questions.

MindTap allows instructors to customize their content, providing tools that seamlessly integrate YouTube clips, outside websites, and personal content directly into the learning path. Instructors can assign additional primary source content through the Instructor Resource Center and Questia primary- and secondary-source databases that house thousands of peer-reviewed journals, newspapers, magazines, and full-length books.

The additional content available in MindTap mirrors and complements the authors' narrative, but also includes primary-source content and assessments not found in the printed text. To learn more, contact your sales representative.

Supplements

Teacher Resources

Instructor's Companion Website   The Instructor's Companion Website, accessed through the Instructor Resource Center (*login.cengage.com*), houses all of the supplemental materials you can use for your course. This includes a Test Bank, Teacher's Resource Guide, and PowerPoint Lecture Presentations. The Test Bank, offered in Cognero® formats, contains multiple-choice, short-answer, document-based, and long-essay questions in AP® format. Cognero® is a flexible, online system that allows you to author, edit, and manage test bank content for *The Earth and Its Peoples*, 7e, AP® Edition. Create multiple test versions instantly and deliver through your LMS from your classroom, or wherever you may be, with no special installs or downloads required. Finally, the PowerPoint lectures are ADA-compliant slides that collate the key takeaways from the chapter in concise visual formats perfect for in-class presentations or for student review.

Teacher's Resource Guide for the Advanced Placement® Program   Based on the college Instructor's Manual, this resource is designed to help teachers make optimal use of *The Earth and Its Peoples, AP® Edition*, in preparing for the AP® exam. The manual includes chapter summaries, suggested lecture topics, map exercises, discussion questions for the primary sources, topics for student research, relevant websites, suggestions for additional videos, and online resources for information on historical sites. This content has been updated to reflect the latest changes to the AP® World History course.

Student Resources

Reader Program   Cengage Learning publishes a number of readers. Some contain exclusively primary sources, others are devoted to essays and secondary sources, and still others provide a combination of primary and secondary sources. All of these readers are designed to guide students through the process of historical inquiry. Visit *www.cengage.com/history* for a complete list of readers.

Fast Track to a 5: Preparing for the AP® World History Examination [ISBN: 9781337401814] This test-prep manual, written by Dawn Bolton, Eric Hahn, Jonathan Henderson, Amie La Porte, and Kristin Taylor, includes an introduction for students on taking the AP® Exam; a diagnostic test to help students assess their level of preparedness; review chapters following the AP® topic list, with content review questions for each chapter and AP® format multiple-choice, short-answer, and long-essay questions for each part; and two complete practice tests. *Fast Track to a 5* may be purchased either with the text or separately.

Acknowledgments

In preparing the seventh edition, we benefited from the critical readings of many colleagues. We are also indebted to the following instructors who lent their insight over various editions: Waitman Beorn, University of Nebraska Omaha; Anna Biel, Fulton-Montgomery Community College; Michael Brooks, Bowling Green State University; Lucien Frary, Rider University; Yan Gao, University of Memphis; Thomas Laub, Delta State University; Dennis Laumann, University of Memphis; Christina Mehrtens, University of Massachusetts Dartmouth; Catherine Phipps, University of Memphis; Jonathan Robins, Michigan Tech University; Martina Saltamacchia, University of Nebraska Omaha; Bianka Stumpf, Central Community College; Hedrick Alixopuilos, Santa Rosa Junior College; Hayden Bellenoit, U.S. Naval Academy; Dusty Bender, Central Baptist College; Cory Crawford, Ohio University; Adrian De Gifis, Loyola University New Orleans; Peter de Rosa, Bridgewater State University; Aaron Gulyas, Mott Community College; Darlene Hall, Lake Erie College; Adrien Ivan, Vernon College; Vic Jagos, Scottsdale Community College; Andrew Muldoon, Metropolitan State College of Denver; Percy Murray, Shaw University; Dave Price, Santa Fe College; Anthony Steinhoff, University of Tennessee—Chattanooga; Anara Tabyshalieva, Marshal University; Beatrice Manz, Tufts University.

When textbook authors set out on a project, they are inclined to believe that 90 percent of the effort will be theirs and 10 percent that of various editors and production specialists employed by their publisher. How very naive. This book would never have seen the light of day had it not been for the unstinting labors of the great team of professionals who turned the authors' words into beautifully presented print and supplied a marvelous set of visual accompaniments. Our debt to the staff of Cengage Learning remains undiminished in the seventh edition. Scott Greenan helped shape this edition as Product Manager for Western Civilization and World History. Sarah Edmonds, our Content Developer, has been an extraordinarily helpful and multitasking manager for the project. Phil Scott has overseen the technical side of things as Project Manager from SPi Global. Carol Newman, our coworker for several editions, has again kept us on schedule. And Charlotte Miller continues to do her wonderful work on maps.

We also thank the many students whose questions and concerns, expressed directly or through their instructors, shaped much of this revision. We continue to welcome all readers' suggestions, queries, and criticisms. Please contact us at our respective institutions.

Correlation of Key Concepts for the AP® World History Course to *The Earth and Its Peoples: A Global History, Seventh Edition, AP® Edition*

Key to Thematic Learning Objectives:
ENV — Interaction Between Humans and the Environment
CUL — Development and Interaction of Cultures
SB — State Building, Expansion, and Conflict
ECON — Creation, Expansion, and Interaction of Economic Systems
SOC — Development and Transformation of Social Structures

World History Curriculum	Section and Page References
Period 1: Technological and Environmental Transformations, to c. 600 BCE	**Chapters 1, 2, 3, 4, 5, 8**

- **Key Concept 1.1 The Paleolithic Era**

  Throughout the Paleolithic era, humans developed sophisticated technologies and adapted to different geographical environments as they migrated from Africa to Eurasia, Australasia, and the Americas.

  Chapter 1

  I. Archeological evidence indicates that during the Paleolithic era, hunter-forager bands of humans gradually migrated from their origin in East Africa to Eurasia, Australia, and the Americas, adapting their technology and cultures to new climate regions. **[ENV-1, 2| CUL-3 | ECON-2, 7]**

  1.1 African Genesis (p. 5)
  1.2 Technology and Culture in the Ice Age (p. 11)

- **Key Concept 1.2 The Neolithic Revolution and Early Agricultural Societies**

  Chapters 1, 2, 3, 4, 8

  Beginning about 10,000 years ago, some human communities adopted sedentism and agriculture, while others pursued hunter-forager or pastoralist lifestyles—different pathways that had significant social and demographic ramifications.

  I. The Neolithic Revolution led to the development of more complex economic and social systems. **[ENV-1, 2, 3| SB-5 | ECON-2, 7]**

  1.3 The Agricultural Revolution (p. 16)
  1.4 Life in Neolithic Communities (p. 21)
  2.1 Mesopotamia (p. 27)
  2.2 Egypt (p. 39)
  2.3 The Indus Valley Civilization (p. 45)
  3.1 The Cosmopolitan Middle East, 1700–1100 BCE (p. 51)
  3.2 The Aegean World, 2000–1100 BCE (p. 57)
  3.3 The Assyrian Empire, 911–612 BCE (p. 62)
  3.4 Israel, 2000–500 BCE (p. 64)
  3.5 Phoenicia and the Mediterranean, 1200–500 BCE (p. 69)
  4.1 Early China, 2000–221 BCE (p. 81)
  4.2 Nubia, 2300 B.C.E – 350 C.E (p. 93)
  4.3 Pastoral Nomads of the Eurasian Steppes, 1000–100 BCE (p. 96)
  4.4 Celtic Europe, 1000–50 BCE (p. 100)
  8.1 Formative Civilizations of the Olmec and Chavín, 1200–200 BCE (p. 194)

World History Curriculum	Section and Page References
II. Agriculture and pastoralism began to transform human societies. **[ENV-1, 2	SB-1, 4, 5	ECON-2, 5, 7	SOC-1, 4]**	1.4 Life in Neolithic Communities (p. 16) 2.1 Mesopotamia (p. 27) 2.2 Egypt (p. 39) 2.3 The Indus Valley Civilization (p. 45) 3.1 The Cosmopolitan Middle East, 1700–1100 BCE (p. 51) 3.2 The Aegean World, 2000–1100 BCE (p. 57) 3.3 The Assyrian Empire, 911–612 BCE (p. 62) 3.4 Israel, 2000–500 BCE (p. 64) 3.5 Phoenicia and the Mediterranean, 1200–500 BCE (p. 69) 4.1 Early China, 2000–221 BCE (p. 81) 4.2 Nubia, 2300 BCE – 350 CE (p. 93) 4.3 Pastoral Nomads of the Eurasian Steppes, 1000–100 BCE (p. 96) 4.4 Celtic Europe, 1000–50 BCE (p. 100) 8.1 Formative Civilizations of the Olmec and Chavín, 1200–200 BCE (p. 194)
• **Key Concept 1.3 The Development and Interactions of Early Agricultural, Pastoral, and Urban Societies** The appearance of the first urban societies 5,000 years ago laid the foundations for the development of complex civilizations; these civilizations shared several significant social, political, and economic characteristics.	Chapters 1, 2, 3, 4, 5, 8
I. Core and foundational civilizations developed in a variety of geographical and environmental settings where agriculture flourished, including Mesopotamia in the Tigris and Euphrates River Valleys, Egypt in the Nile River Valley, Mohenjo-Daro and Harappa in the Indus River Valley, Shang in the Yellow River (Huang He) Valley, Olmec in Mesoamerica, and Chavín in Andean South America. **[ENV-1, 2]**	2.1 Mesopotamia (p. 27) 2.2 Egypt (p. 39) 2.3 The Indus Valley Civilization (p. 45) 3.1 The Cosmopolitan Middle East, 1700–1100 BCE (p. 51) 3.2 The Aegean World, 2000–1100 BCE (p. 57) 3.3 The Assyrian Empire, 911–612 BCE (p. 62) 3.4 Israel, 2000–500 BCE (p. 64) 3.5 Phoenicia and the Mediterranean, 1200–500 BCE (p. 69) 4.1 Early China, 2000–221 BCE (p. 81) 4.3 Pastoral Nomads of the Eurasian Steppes, 1000–100 BCE (p. 96) 8.1 Formative Civilizations of the Olmec and Chavín, 1200–200 BCE (p. 194) 8.2 Classic-Era Culture and Society in Mesoamerica, 200–900 (p. 199)
II. The first states emerged within core civilizations in Mesopotamia and the Nile River Valley. **[ENV-1, 2	SB-1, 2, 3, 4, 5	ECON-2, 3, 5, 7	SOC-4]**	2.1 Mesopotamia (p. 27) 2.2 Egypt (p. 39) 4.3 Pastoral Nomads of the Eurasian Steppes, 1000–100 BCE (p. 96)

World History Curriculum	Section and Page References
III. Culture played a significant role in unifying states through laws, language, literature, religion, myths, and monumental art. **[ENV-1	CUL-1, 2, 3, 5, 6	SB-1, 2, 3, 4	ECON-7	SOC-2, 3, 5]**	2.1 Mesopotamia (p. 27) 2.2 Egypt (p. 39) 2.3 The Indus Valley Civilization (p. 45) 3.2 The Aegean World, 2000–1100 BCE (p. 57) 3.3 The Assyrian Empire, 911–612 BCE (p. 62) 3.4 Israel, 2000–500 BCE (p. 64) 4.1 Early China, 2000–221 BCE (p. 81) 5.1 Ancient Iran, 1000–500 BCE (p. 113) 5.2 The Rise of the Greeks, 1000–500 BCE (p. 120) 8.1 Formative Civilizations of the Olmec and Chavín, 1200–200 BCE (p. 194)

Period 2:   Organization and Reorganization of Human Societies, c. 600 BCE to c. 600 CE   **Chapters 3, 4, 5, 6, 7, 8, 9, 10**

- **Key Concept 2.1 The Development and Codification of Religious and Cultural Traditions**

As states and empires increased in size and contacts between regions intensified, human communities transformed their religious and ideological beliefs and practices.	Chapters 3, 4, 5, 6, 7, 8
I. Codifications and further developments of existing religious traditions provided a bond among people and an ethical code to live by. **[CUL-1, 2	SB-4	SOC-2, 5]**	3.4 Israel, 2000 – 500 BCE (p. 64) 7.1 Foundations of Indian Civilization, 1500 BCE–300 CE (p. 169) 7.2 The Imperial Expansion and Collapse, 324 BCE–650 CE (p. 172) 9.5 The Spread of Ideas (p. 240) 10.1 The Sassanid Empire, 224–651 (pp. 246–248)
II. New belief systems and cultural traditions emerged and spread, often asserting universal truths. **[ENV-1	CUL-1, 2, 5, 6	ECON-6	SOC-2, 3, 5]**	4.1 Early China, 2000–221 BCE (p. 81) 5.2 The Rise of the Greeks, 1000–500 BCE (p. 120) 6.1 Rome's Creation of a Mediterranean Empire, 753 BCE–330 CE (p. 143) 6.2 The Origins of Imperial China, 221 BCE–220 CE (p. 158) 7.1 Foundations of Indian Civilization, 1500 BCE–300 CE (p. 169) 10.2 The Origins of Islam (p. 248)
III. Belief systems generally reinforced existing social structures while also offering new roles and status to some men and women. **[CUL-1, 2	SOC-1, 5]**	5.3 The Struggle of Persia and Greece, 546–323 BCE (p. 130) 6.1 Rome's Creation of a Mediterranean Empire, 753 BCE–330 CE (p. 143) 6.2 The Origins of Imperial China, 221 BCE–220 CE (p. 158) 7.1 Foundations of Indian Civilizations, 1500 BCE–300 CE (p. 169) 7.2 Imperial Expansion and Collapse, 324 BCE–650 CE (p. 172) 9.5 The Spread of Ideas (p.240) 10.4 Islamic Civilization (p. 259)

World History Curriculum	Section and Page References
IV. Other religious and cultural traditions continued and in some places were incorporated into major religious traditions. **[ENV-1]**	4.4 Celtic Europe, 1000–50 BCE (p. 100) 5.3 The Struggle of Persia and Greece, 546–323 BCE (p. 130) 6.1 Rome's Creation of a Mediterranean Empire, 753 BCE–330 CE (p. 143) 6.2 The Origins of Imperial China, 221 BCE–220 CE (p. 158) 7.1 Foundations of Indian Civilization, 1500 BCE–300 CE (p.169) 8.2 Classic-Era Culture and Society in Mesoamerica, 200–900 (p. 199) 8.5 Andean Civilizations, 200–1400 (p. 211)
• **Key Concept 2.2 The Development of States and Empires** As the early states and empires grew in number, size, and population, they frequently competed for resources and came into conflict with one another.	Chapters 4, 5, 6, 7, 8, 10
I. The number and size of key states and empires grew dramatically as rulers imposed political unity on areas where previously there had been competing states. **[ENV-2	SB-2, 3, 5, 6]**	4.3 Pastoral Nomads of the Eurasian Steppes, 1000–100 BCE (p. 96) 5.3 The Struggle of Persia and Greece, 546–323 BCE (p. 130) 6.1 Rome's Creation of a Mediterranean Empire, 753 BCE–330 CE (p. 143) 6.2 The Origins of Imperial China, 221 BCE–220 CE (p. 158) 7.2 Imperial Expansion and Collapse, 324 BCE–650 CE (p. 172) 7.3 Southeast Asia, 50-1025 CE (p. 186) 8.5 Andean Civilizations, 200–1400 (p. 211) 10.1 The Sasanid Empire, 224–651 (p. 246)
II. Empires and states developed new techniques of imperial administration based, in part, on the success of earlier political forms. **[ENV-1, 3, 5	SB-1, 2, 3, 4, 5, 6	ECON-2, 3]**	5.1 Ancient Iran, 1000–500 BCE (p. 113) 5.3 The Struggle of Persia and Greece, 546–323 BCE (p. 130) 6.1 Rome's Creation of a Mediterranean Empire, 753 BCE–330 CE (p. 143) 7.2 Imperial Expansion and Collapse, 324 BCE–650 CE (p. 172) 7.3 Southeast Asia, 50-1025 (p. 186) 8.2 Classic-Era Culture and Society in Mesoamerica, 200–900 (p. 199) 8.5 Andean Civilizations, 200–1400 (p. 211) 10.4 Islamic Civilization (p. 259)

World History Curriculum	**Section and Page References**
III. Unique social and economic dimensions developed in imperial societies in Afro-Eurasia and the Americas. **[CUL-5 | SB-1, 2, 3, 4, 5, 6 | ECON-2, 3, 5 | SOC-1, 2, 3, 5]**	4.4 Celtic Europe, 1000–50 BCE (p. 100) 5.1 Ancient Iran, 1000–500 BCE (p. 113) 5.2 The Rise of the Greeks, 1000–500 BCE (p. 120) 5.3 The Struggle of Persia and Greece, 546–323 BCE (p. 130) 5.4 The Hellenistic Synthesis, 323–30 BCE (p. 135) 6.1 Rome's Creation of a Mediterranean Empire, 753 BCE–330 CE (p. 143) 6.2 The Origins of Imperial China, 221 BCE–220 CE (p. 158) 7.2 Imperial Expansion and Collapse, 324 BCE–650 CE (p. 172) 8.2 Classic-Era Culture and Society in Mesoamerica, 200–900 (p. 199) 8.4 Northern Peoples (p. 207) 8.5 Andean Civilizations, 200–1400 (p. 211)
IV. The Roman, Han, Persian, Mauryan, and Gupta Empires encountered political, cultural, and administrative difficulties that they could not manage, which eventually led to their decline, collapse, and transformation into successor empires or states. **[ENV-1, 2, 3 | SB-2, 3, 4, 5 | SOC-3, 5]**	5.3 The Struggle of Persia and Greece, 546–323 BCE (p. 130) 5.4 The Hellenistic Synthesis, 323–30 BCE (p. 135) 6.1 Rome's Creation of a Mediterranean Empire, 753 BCE–330 CE (p. 143) 6.2 The Origins of Imperial China, 221 BCE–220 CE (p. 158) 7.2 Imperial Expansion and Collapse, 324 BCE–650 CE (p. 172)
• **Key Concept 2.3 Emergence of Interregional Networks of Communication and Exchange** With the organization of large-scale empires, transregional trade intensified, leading to the creation of extensive networks of commercial and cultural exchange.	Chapters 5, 6, 7, 8, 9
I. Land and water routes became the basis for interregional trade, communication, and exchange networks in the Eastern Hemisphere. **[ENV-1, 2 | CUL-3 | SB-6 | ECON-7]**	6.1 Rome's Creation of a Mediterranean Empire, 753 BCE–330 CE (p. 143) 6.2 The Origins of Imperial China, 221 BCE–220 CE (p. 158) 9.1 The Silk Road (p. 226) 9.2 The Indian Ocean Maritime System (p. 230) 9.3 Routes Across the Sahara (p. 234)
II. New technologies facilitated long-distance communication and exchange. **[ENV-1, 2 | CUL-3 | SB-6 | ECON-7]**	8.1 Formative Civilizations of the Olmec and Chavín, 1200–200 BCE (p. 194) 9.1 The Silk Road (p. 226) 9.2 The Indian Ocean Maritime System (p. 230) 9.3 Routes Across the Sahara (p. 234)

World History Curriculum	**Section and Page References**
III. Alongside the trade in goods, the exchange of people, technology, religious and cultural beliefs, food crops, domesticated animals, and disease pathogens developed across extensive networks of communication and exchange. **[ENV-1, 2, 3, 5 | CUL-1, 3 | SB-3 | ECON-2, 6, 7]**	5.3 The Struggle of Persia and Greece, 546–323 BCE (p. 130) 6.1 Rome's Creation of a Mediterranean Empire, 753 BCE–330 CE (p. 143) 6.2 The Origins of Imperial China, 221 BCE–220 CE (p. 158) 7.2 Imperial Expansion and Collapse, 324 BCE–650 CE (p. 172) 7.3 Southeast Asia, 50–1025 CE (p. 186) 8.1 Formative Civilizations of the Olmec and Chavín, 1200–200 BCE (p. 194) 9.1 The Silk Road (p. 226) 9.2 The Indian Ocean Maritime System (p. 230) 9.3 Routes Across the Sahara (p. 234) 9.4 Sub-Saharan Africa (p. 237) 9.5 The Spread of Ideas (p. 240)

Period 3: Regional and Interregional Interactions, c. 600 CE to c. 1450	**Chapters 8, 9, 10, 11, 12, 13, 14, 15, 16**

- **Key Concept 3.1 Expansion and Intensification of Communication and Exchange Networks**

A deepening and widening of networks of human interaction within and across regions contributed to cultural, technological, and biological diffusion within and between various societies.	Chapters 8, 9, 10, 11, 12, 13, 14, 15, 16
I. Improved transportation technologies and commercial practices led to an increased volume of trade and expanded the geographical range of existing and newly active trade networks. **[ENV-2, 3, 5 | CUL-3 | SB-1, 2, 3, 4, 5, | ECON-3, 5, 7]**	8.3 The Postclassic Period in Mesoamerica, 900–1300 (p. 205) 11.5 Western Europe Revives, 1000–1200 (pp. 287–289) 12.2 China and Its Rivals (p. 300) 13.1 The Rise of the Mongols, 1200–1260 (p. 319) 13.4 Mongol Domination in China, 1271–1368 (p. 332) 14.1 Rural Growth and Crisis (p. 345) 14.2 Urban Revival (p. 349) 15.3 Indian Ocean Trade (p. 378) 16.1 Global Maritime Expansion Before 1450 (p. 394) 16.2 European Expansion, 1400–1550 (p. 400)
II. The movement of peoples caused environmental and linguistic effects. **[ENV-2, 3, 5 | CUL-3 | SB-3]**	8.5 Andean Civilizations, 200–1400 (p. 211) 9.4 Sub-Saharan Africa (p. 237) 10.2 The Origins of Islam (p. 248) 10.4 Islamic Civilization (p. 259) 11.2 Early Medieval Europe, 600–1000 (p. 273) 12.1 The Sui and Tang Empires, 581–755 (p. 294) 13.2 The Mongols and Islam, 1260–1500 (p. 326) 13.3 Regional Responses in Western Eurasia (p. 330) 13.4 Mongol Domination in China, 1271–1368 (p. 332) 15.1 Tropical Africa and Asia (p. 367) 15.3 Indian Ocean Trade (p. 378) 15.4 Social and Cultural Change (p. 383)

World History Curriculum	Section and Page References
III. Cross-cultural exchanges were fostered by the intensification of existing, or the creation of new, networks of trade and communication. **[CUL-1, 2, 3, 4, 5, 6	SB-3, 6	ECON-7	SOC-1, 2, 5, 6]**	8.3 The Postclassic Period in Mesoamerica, 900–1300 (p. 205) 10.4 Islamic Civilization (p. 259) 11.1 The Byzantine Empire, 600–1200 (p. 270) 11.5 Western Europe Revives, 1000–1200 (p. 286) 11.6 The Crusades, 1095–1204 (p. 288) 12.1 The Sui and Tang Empires, 581–755 (p. 294) 12.2 China and Its Rivals (p. 300) 13.1 The Rise of the Mongols, 1200–1260 (p. 319) 13.2 The Mongols and Islam, 1260–1500 (p. 326) 13.4 Mongol Domination in China, 1271–1368 (p. 332) 13.5 The Early Ming Empire, 1368–1500 (p. 335) 13.6 Centralization and Militarism in East Asia, 1200–1500 (p. 339) 14.1 Rural Growth and Crisis (p. 345) 14.2 Urban Revival (p. 349) 14.3 Learning, Literature, and the Renaissance (p. 355) 15.1 Tropical Africa and Asia (p. 367) 15.2 New Islamic Empires (p. 372) 15.3 Indian Ocean Trade (p. 378) 15.4 Social and Cultural Change (p. 383) 16.1 Global Maritime Expansion Before 1450 (p. 394) 16.2 European Expansion, 1400–1550 (p. 400)
IV. There was continued diffusion of crops and pathogens, including epidemic diseases like the bubonic plague, along trade routes. **[ENV-3, 5	ECON-7]**	13.1 The Rise of the Mongols, 1200–1260 (p. 319) 14.1 Rural Growth and Crisis (p. 345) 14.2 Urban Revival (p. 349)
• **Key Concept 3.2 Continuity and Innovation of State Forms and Their Interactions**	
State formation and development demonstrated continuity, innovation, and diversity in various regions.	Chapters 8, 10, 11, 12, 13, 14, 15
I. Empires collapsed in different regions of the world, and in some areas were replaced by new imperial states or political systems. **[CUL-1, 2	SB-1, 2, 3, 4, 5, 6	ECON-2, 3, 7	SOC-1, 3, 5]**	8.3 The Postclassic Period in Mesoamerica, 900–1300 (p. 205) 8.5 Andean Civilizations, 200–1400 (p. 211) 10.3 The Rise and Fall of the Caliphate, 632–1258 (p. 252) 11.1 The Byzantine Empire, 600–1200 (p. 270) 11.4 Kievan Russia, 900–1200 (p. 283) 12.1 The Sui and Tang Empires, 581–755 (p. 294) 12.2 China and Its Rivals (p. 300) 12.3 New Kingdoms in East Asia (p. 307) 13.1 The Rise of the Mongols, 1200–1260 (p. 319) 13.2 The Mongols and Islam, 1260–1500 (p. 326) 13.3 Regional Responses in Western Eurasia (p. 330) 13.4 Mongol Domination in China, 1271–1368 (p. 332) 13.5 The Early Ming Empire, 1368–1500 (p. 335) 13.6 Centralization and Militarism in East Asia, 1200–1500 (p. 339) 14.4 Political and Military Transformations (p. 359) 15.2 New Islamic Empires (p. 372) 15.5 The Western Hemisphere (p. 385)

World History Curriculum	**Section and Page References**
II. Interregional contacts and conflicts between states and empires encouraged significant technological and cultural transfers. **[CUL-3 | SB-3, 4, 5, 6 | ECON-7]**	10.3 The Rise and Fall of the Caliphate, 632–1258 (p. 252) 11.5 Western Europe Revives, 1000–1200 (p. 286) 11.6 The Crusades, 1095–1204 (p. 288) 12.1 The Sui and Tang Empires, 581–755 (p. 294) 13.1 The Rise of the Mongols, 1200–1260 (p. 319) 13.2 The Mongols and Islam, 1260–1500 (p. 326) 13.3 Regional Responses in Western Eurasia (p. 330) 13.4 Mongol Domination in China, 1271–1368 (p. 332) 13.5 The Early Ming Empire, 1368–1500 (p. 335) 13.6 Centralization and Militarism in East Asia, 1200–1500 (p. 339) 15.2 New Islamic Empires (p. 372) 15.3 Indian Ocean Trade (p. 378) 15.4 Social and Cultural Change (p. 383)
• **Key Concept 3.3 Increased Economic Productive Capacity and Its Consequences** Changes in trade networks resulted from and stimulated increasing productive capacity, with important implications for social and gender structures and environmental processes.	Chapters 8, 10, 11, 12, 13, 14, 15
I. Innovations stimulated agricultural and industrial production in many regions. **[ENV-3, 4, 5 | ECON-2, 3, 5, 7]**	8.5 Andean Civilizations, 200–1400 (p. 211) 12.2 China and Its Rivals (p. 300) 13.4 Mongol Domination in China, 1271–1368 (p. 332) 14.1 Rural Growth and Crisis (p. 345) 15.1 Tropical Africa and Asia (p. 367) 15.5 The Western Hemisphere (p. 385)
II. The fate of cities varied greatly, with periods of significant decline and periods of increased urbanization buoyed by rising productivity and expanding trade networks. **[ENV-2, 3, 5 | SB-2, 3, 4 | ECON-2, 3, 5, 7]**	8.2 Classic-Era Culture and Socie-ty in Mesoamerica, 200–900 (p. 199) 8.3 The Postclassic Period in Mes-oamerica, 900–1300 (p. 205) 10.4 Islamic Civilization (p. 259) 11.1 The Byzantine Empire, 600–1200 (p. 270) 15.5 Western Europe Revives, 1000–1200 (p. 286) 12.1 The Sui and Tang Empires, 581–755 (p. 294) 13.1 The Rise of the Mongols, 1200–1260 (pp. 324–330) 13.3 Regional Responses in Western Eurasia (p. 330) 13.4 Mongol Domination in China, 1271–1368 (p. 332) 14.2 Urban Revival (p. 349) 14.3 Learning, Literature, and the Renaissance (p. 355) 15.2 New Islamic Empires (p. 372) 15.3 Indian Ocean Trade (p. 378) 15.5 The Western Hemisphere (p. 385)

World History Curriculum	Section and Page References
III. Despite significant continuities in social structures and in methods of production, there were also some important changes in labor management and in the effect of religious conversion on gender relations and family life. **[CUL-2	SB-2, 3, 4, 5, 6	ECON-2, 3, 5	SOC-1, 3, 4, 5, 6]**	10.4 Islamic Civilization (p. 259) 11.1 The Byzantine Empire, 600–1200 (p. 270) 11.2 Early Medieval Europe, 600–1000 (p. 273) 11.3 The Western Church (p. 278) 12.1 The Sui and Tang Empires, 581–755 (p. 294) 12.2 China and Its Rivals (p. 300) 14.1 Rural Growth and Crisis (p. 345) 14.2 Urban Revival (p. 349) 15.2 New Islamic Empires (p. 372) 15.4 Social and Cultural Change (p. 383)

Period 4: Global Interactions, c. 1450 to c. 1750	Chapters 14, 16, 17, 18, 19, 20, 21

- **Key Concept 4.1 Globalizing Networks of Communication and Exchange**

The interconnection of the Eastern and Western Hemispheres, made possible by transoceanic voyaging, transformed trade and religion and had a significant economic, cultural, social, and demographic impact on the world.	Chapters 14, 16, 17, 18, 19, 20, 21
I. Existing regional patterns of trade intensified in the context of the new global circulation of goods. **[SB-3	ECON-2, 3, 7]**	16.2 European Expansion, 1400–1550 (p. 400) 16.3 Encounters with Europe, 1450–1550 (p. 406) 18.2 Spanish America and Brazil (p. 456) 18.3 English and French Colonies in North America (p. 467) 19.1 Plantations in the West Indies (p. 479) 19.2 Plantation Life in the Eighteenth Century (p. 482) 19.3 Creating the Atlantic Economy (p. 490) 19.4 Africa, the Atlantic, and Islam (p. 495) 20.1 The Ottoman Empire, to 1750 (p. 508) 20.2 The Safavid Empire, 1502–1722 (p. 515) 20.3 The Mughal Empire 1526–1739 (p. 519) 20.4 The Russian Empire, 1500–1725 (p. 522) 20.5 The Maritime Worlds of Islam, 1500–1750 (p. 527) 21.1 East Asia and Europe (p. 533) 21.4 From Ming to Qing (p. 542)
II. European technological developments in cartography and navigation built on previous knowledge developed in the Classical, Islamic, and Asian worlds. **[ENV-2	CUL-3	ECON-7]**	16.2 European Expansion, 1400–1550 (p. 400) 16.3 Encounters with Europe, 1450–1550 (p. 406) 17.1 Culture and Ideas (p. 426) 18.2 Spanish America and Brazil (p. 456) 18.3 English and French Colonies in North America (p. 467) 20.5 The Maritime Worlds of Islam, 1500–1750 (p. 527)
III. Remarkable new transoceanic maritime reconnaissance occurred in this period. **[ENV-2	CUL-3	ECON-2, 3, 7]**	16.2 European Expansion, 1400–1550 (p. 400) 16.3 Encounters with Europe, 1450–1550 (p. 406) 20.5 The Maritime Worlds of Islam, 1500–1750 (p. 527)

World History Curriculum	Section and Page References
IV. The new global circulation of goods was facilitated by chartered European monopoly companies and the flow of silver from Spanish colonies in the Americas to purchase Asian goods for the Atlantic markets. Regional markets continued to flourish in Afro-Eurasia by using established commercial practices and new transoceanic shipping services developed by European merchants. **[SB-3, 5, 6	ECON-2, 5, 6, 7	SOC-1, 3, 4, 5, 6]**	16.2 European Expansion, 1400–1550 (p. 400) 16.3 Encounters with Europe, 1450–1550 (p. 406) 17.1 Culture and Ideas (p. 426) 18.2 Spanish America and Brazil (p. 456) 18.4 Colonial Expansion and Conflict (p. 474) 19.1 Plantations in the West Indies (p. 479) 19.2 Plantation Life in the Eighteenth Century (p. 482) 19.3 Creating the Atlantic Economy (p. 490) 19.4 Africa, the Atlantic, and Islam (p. 495) 20.5 The Maritime Worlds of Islam, 1500–1750 (p. 527)
V. The new connections between the Eastern and Western hemispheres resulted in the Columbian Exchange. **[ENV-3, 5	ECON-2, 5, 7	SOC-1, 3, 4, 5, 6]**	18.1 The Columbian Exchange (p. 454) 18.4 Colonial Expansion and Conflict (p. 474) 19.1 Plantations in the West Indies (p. 479) 19.2 Plantation Life in the Eighteenth Century (p. 482)
VI. The increase in interactions between newly connected hemispheres and intensification of connections within hemispheres expanded the spread and reform of existing religions and contributed to both religious conflicts and the creation of syncretic belief systems and practices. **[ENV- 2, 3	CUL-1, 2	ECON-6]**	17.1 Culture and Ideas (p. 426) 19.3 Spanish America and Brazil (p. 456) 19.4 English and French Colonies in North America (p. 467) 19.5 Africa, the Atlantic, and Islam (p. 495) 20.1 The Ottoman Empire, to 1750 (p. 508) 20.2 The Safavid Empire, 1502–1722 (p. 515) 20.3 The Mughal Empire, 1526–1739 (p. 519) 20.4 The Russian Empire, 1500–1750 (p. 522) 20.5 The Maritime Worlds of Islam, 1500–1750 (p. 527) 21.1 East Asia and Europe (p. 533)
VII. As merchants' profits increased and governments collected more taxes, funding for the visual and performing arts, even for popular audiences, increased along with an expansion of literacy and increased focus on innovation and scientific inquiry. **[CUL- 5, 6	SB-1, 3]**	14.3 Learning, Literature, and the Renaissance (p. 355) 17.1 Culture and Ideas (p. 426) 17.2 Social and Economic Life (p. 434) 17.3 Political Innovations (p. 439) 20.2 The Safavid Empire, 1502–1722 (p. 515)

- **Key Concept 4.2 New Forms of Social Organization and Modes of Production**

Although the world's productive systems continued to be heavily centered on agriculture, major changes occurred in agricultural labor, the systems and locations of manufacturing, gender and social structures, and environmental processes.	Chapters 16, 17, 18, 19, 20, 21
I. Beginning in the 14th century, there was a decrease in mean temperatures, often referred to as the Little Ice Age, around the world that lasted until the 19th century, contributing to changes in agricultural practices and the contraction of settlement in parts of the Northern Hemisphere. **[ENV-2, 3, 5,	ECON-2]**	16.5 Climate and Population to 1500 (Issues in World History) (pp. 420–421) 20.4 The Russian Empire, 1500–1725 (p. 522) 21.5 The Little Ice Age (Issues in World History) (pp. 552–553)

World History Curriculum	Section and Page References
II. Traditional peasant agriculture increased and changed, plantations expanded, and demand for labor increased. These changes both fed and responded to growing global demand for raw materials and finished products. [SB-3 | ECON-2, 3, 5, 7 | SOC-1, 3, 4, 5, 6]	17.2 Social and Economic Life (p. 434) 17.3 Political Innovations (p. 439) 18.2 Spanish America and Brazil (p. 456) 18.3 English and French Colonies in North America (p. 467) 18.4 Colonial Expansion and Conflict (p. 474) 19.1 Plantations in the West Indies (p. 479) 19.2 Plantation Life in the Eighteenth Century (p. 482) 19.3 Creating the Atlantic Economy (p. 490) 19.4 Africa, the Atlantic, and Islam (p. 495) 20.1 The Ottoman Empire, to 1750 (p. 508) 20.4 The Russian Empire, 1500–1725 (p. 522)
III. As social and political elites changed, they also restructured ethnic, racial, and gender hierarchies. [SB-3 | ECON-2, 5 | SOC-1, 3, 4, 5, 6]	16.3 Encounters with Europe, 1450–1550 (p. 406) 17.2 Social and Economic Life (p. 434) 18.2 Spanish America and Brazil (p. 456) 18.4 Colonial Expansion and Conflict (p. 474) 19.1 Plantations in the West Indies (p. 479) 19.2 Plantation Life in the Eighteenth Century (p. 482) 19.4 Africa, the Atlantic, and Islam (p. 495) 20.1 The Ottoman Empire, to 1750 (p. 508) 20.2 The Safavid Empire, 1502–1722 (p. 515) 20.4 The Russian Empire, 1500–1725 (p. 522) 21.3 Tokugawa Japan and Cho-son Korea to 1800 (p. 539)

- **Key Concept 4.3 State Consolidation and Imperial Expansion**

Empires expanded around the world, presenting new challenges in the incorporation of diverse populations and in the effective administration of new coerced labor systems.	Chapters 16, 17, 18, 19, 20, 21
I. Rulers used a variety of methods to legitimize and consolidate their power. [CUL- 2, 5 | SB-1, 2, 3, 4, 5, 6 | ECON-2, 3, 6, | SOC-1, 2, 3, 5, 6]	16.3 Encounters with Europe, 1450–1550 (p. 406) 17.1 Culture and Ideas (p. 426) 17.3 Political Innovations (p. 439) 18.2 Spanish America and Brazil (p. 456) 18.3 English and French Colonies in North America (p. 467) 18.4 Colonial Expansion and Conflict (p. 474) 19.1 Plantations in the West Indies (p. 479) 19.2 Plantation Life in the Eighteenth Century (p. 482) 19.4 Africa, the Atlantic, and Islam (p. 495) 20.3 The Mughal Empire, 1526–1739 (p. 519) 20.4 The Russian Empire, 1500–1725 (p. 522) 21.4 From Ming to Qing (p. 542)
II. Imperial expansion relied on the increased use of gunpowder, cannons, and armed trade to establish large empires in both hemispheres. [ENV-2 | SB-1, 2, 3 | ECON-2, 3, 7]	16.3 Encounters with Europe, 1450–1550 (p. 406) 17.3 Political Innovations (p. 439) 18.3 English and French Colonies in North America (p. 467) 20.1 The Ottoman Empire, to 1750 (p. 508) 20.4 The Russian Empire, 1500–1725 (p. 522) 20.5 The Maritime Worlds of Islam, 1500–1750 (p. 527) 21.2 The Imjin War and Japanese Unification (p. 537)

World History Curriculum	Section and Page References
III. Competition over trade routes, state rivalries, and local resistance all provided significant challenges to state consolidation and expansion. **[SB-2, 3, 4, 5, 6	ECON-2, 3]**	16.2 European Expansion, 1400–1550 (p. 400) 16.3 Encounters with Europe, 1450–1550 (p. 406) 17.3 Political Innovations (p. 439) 18.3 English and French Colonies in North America (p. 467) 19.1 Plantations in the West Indies (p. 479) 19.3 Creating the Atlantic Economy (p. 490) 19.4 Africa, the Atlantic, and Islam (p. 495) 20.1 The Ottoman Empire, to 1750 (p. 508) 20.3 The Mughal Empire, 1526–1739 (p. 519) 20.4 The Russian Empire, 1500–1725 (p. 522) 20.5 The Maritime Worlds of Islam, 1500–1750 (p. 527) 21.4 From Ming to Qing (p. 542)
Period 5: Industrialization and Global Integration, c. 1750 to c. 1900	**Chapters 17, 19, 22, 23, 24, 25, 26, 27, 28**

- **Key Concept 5.1 Industrialization and Global Capitalism**

The process of industrialization changed the way in which goods were produced and consumed, with far-reaching effects on the global economy, social relations, and culture.	Chapters 22, 23, 24, 25, 26, 27
I. Industrialization fundamentally changed how goods were produced. **[ENV-4, 5	SB-2	ECON-1, 3, 5, 6	SOC-1, 2, 3, 4]**	22.1 Causes of the Industrial Revolution (p. 558) 22.2 The Technological Revolution (p. 563) 22.3 The Impact of the Early Industrial Revolution (p. 571) 22.5 The Limits of Industrialization Outside the West (p. 580) 25.3 The Challenge of Social and Economic Change (p. 650) 27.1 New Technologies and the World Economy (p. 698) 27.2 Social Changes (p. 703)
II. New patterns of global trade and production developed and further integrated the global economy as industrialists sought raw materials and new markets for the increasing amount and array of goods produced in their factories. **[ENV-4, 5	CUL-3	SB-3	ECON-1, 2, 3, 7]**	22.1 Causes of the Industrial Revolution (p. 558) 22.2 The Technological Revolution (p. 563) 22.3 The Impact of the Early Industrial Revolution (p. 571) 22.4 New Economic and Political Ideas (p. 576) 22.5 The Limits of Industrialization Outside the West (p. 580) 24.3 The Qing Empire (p. 623) 25.3 The Challenge of Social and Economic Change (p. 650) 26.1 Changes and Exchanges in Africa (p. 670) 26.2 India Under British Rule (p. 679) 26.5 The World Economy and the Global Environment (p. 691) 27.1 New Technologies and the World Economy (p. 698)

World History Curriculum	**Section and Page References**
III. To facilitate investments at all levels of industrial production, financiers developed and expanded various financial institutions. **[CUL-1 | ECON-1, 2, 3, 6, 7]**	22.1 Causes of the Industrial Revolution (p. 558) 22.4 New Economic and Political Ideas (p. 576) 26.5 The World Economy and the Global Environment (p. 691) 27.1 New Technologies and the World Economy (p. 698)
IV. There were major developments and innovations in transportation and communication, including railroads, steamships, telegraphs, and canals. **[ENV-2 | ECON-7]**	22.2 The Technological Revolution (p. 563) 27.1 New Technologies and the World Economy (p. 698)
V. The development and spread of global capitalism led to a variety of responses. **[CUL-1 | SB-1, 2, 3, 4 | ECON-2, 3, 4, 6 | SOC-1, 2]**	19.3 Creating the Atlantic Economy (p. 490) 23.4 New Economic and Political Ideas (p. 576) 23.5 The Limits of Industrialization Outside the West (p. 580) 24.1 The Ottoman Empire (p. 611) 24.3 The Qing Empire (p. 623) 25.3 The Challenge of Social and Economic Change (p. 650) 26.1 Changes and Exchanges in Africa (p. 670) 27.3 Socialism and Labor Movements (p. 708)
VI. The ways in which people organized themselves into societies also underwent significant transformations in industrialized states due to the fundamental restructuring of the global economy. **[ENV-3, 4, 5 | SB-3 | ECON-5 | SOC-1, 2, 4]**	22.3 The Impact of the Early Industrial Revolution (p. 571) 23.1 Prelude to Revolution: The Eighteenth-Century Crisis (p. 586) 24.1 The Ottoman Empire (p. 611) 24.2 The Russian Empire (p. 619) 24.2 The Qing Empire (p. 623) 26.5 The World Economy and the Global Environment (p. 691) 27.2 Social Changes (p. 703) 27.3 Socialism and Labor Movements (p. 708)
• **Key Concept 5.2 Imperialism and Nation-State Formation**	
As states industrialized, they also expanded existing overseas empires and established new colonies and transoceanic relationships.	Chapters 23, 24, 25, 26, 27
I. Industrializing powers established transoceanic empires. **[ENV-4, 5 | SB-1, 2, 3, 6 | ECON-2, 3 | SOC-3, 5, 6]**	23.5 The Limits of Industrialization Outside the West (p. 580) 24.3 The Qing Empire (p. 623) 26.1 Changes and Exchanges in Africa (p. 670) 26.2 India Under British Rule (p. 679) 26.3 Southeast Asia and the Pacific (p. 683) 26.4 Imperialism in Latin America (p. 686) 27.4 Nationalism and the Rise of Italy, Germany, and Japan (p. 710) 27.6 China, Japan, and the Western Powers (p. 722)

World History Curriculum	Section and Page References

II. Imperialism influenced state formation and contraction around the world. **[CUL-1 | SB-1, 2, 3, 5, 6 | ECON-1 | SOC-3, 5, 6]**

23.4 Revolution Spreads, Conservatives Respond, 1789–1850 (p. 604)
24.1 The Ottoman Empire (p. 611)
24.2 The Russian Empire (p. 619)
24.3 The Qing Empire (p. 623)
26.1 Changes and Exchanges in Africa (p. 670)
26.3 Southeast Asia and the Pacific (p. 683)
26.4 Imperialism in Latin America (p. 686)
27.4 Nationalism and the Rise of Italy, Germany, and Japan (p. 710)
27.6 China, Japan, and the Western Powers (p. 722)

III. In some imperial societies, emerging cultural, religious, and racial ideologies, including social Darwinism, were used to justify imperialism. **[CUL-1, 2 | SB-3 | ECON-6 | SOC-5]**

24.3 The Qing Empire (p. 623)
25.2 The Problem of Order, 1825–1890 (p. 640)
26.1 Changes and Exchanges in Africa (p. 670)
26.2 India Under British Rule (p. 679)
26.3 Southeast Asia and the Pacific (p. 683)
27.4 Nationalism and the Rise of Italy, Germany, and Japan (p. 710)

- **Key Concept 5.3 Nationalism, Revolution, and Reform**

The 18th century marked the beginning of an intense period of revolution and rebellion against existing governments, leading to the establishment of new nation-states around the world.

Chapters 17, 19, 22, 23, 24, 25, 26, 27, 28

I. The rise and diffusion of Enlightenment thought that questioned established traditions in all areas of life often preceded revolutions and rebellions against existing governments. **[CUL-1, 2, 4 | SB-3, 4 | ECON-4 | SOC-1, 2, 3, 4, 5, 6]**

17.1 Culture and Ideas (p. 426)
23.1 Prelude to Revolution: The Eighteenth-Century Crisis (p. 586)
23.2 The American Revolution, 1775–1800 (p. 590)
23.3 The French Revolution, 1789–1815 (p. 595)
23.4 Revolution Spreads, Conservatives Respond, 1789–1850 (p. 604)
25.1 Independence in Latin America, 1800–1830 (p. 636)
25.3 The Challenge of Social and Economic Change (p. 650)
26.2 India Under British Rule (p. 679)
26.4 Imperialism in Latin America (p. 686)
27.2 Social Changes (p. 703)
27.5 The Great Powers of Europe, 1871–1900 (p. 719)

II. Beginning in the 18th century, peoples around the world developed a new sense of commonality based on language, religion, social customs, and territory. These newly imagined national communities linked this identity with the borders of the state, while governments used this idea of nationalism to unite diverse populations. In some cases, nationalists challenged boundaries or sought unification of fragmented regions. **[CUL-1, 2, 4 | SB-3 | SOC-1, 2, 3, 5, 6]**

23.2 The American Revolution, 1775–1800 (p. 590)
23.4 Revolution Spreads, Conservatives Respond, 1789–1850 (p. 604)
24.1 The Ottoman Empire (p. 611)
24.2 The Russian Empire (p. 619)
25.1 Independence in Latin America, 1800–1830 (p. 636)
26.2 India Under British Rule (p. 679)
26.4 Imperialism in Latin America (p. 686)
27.3 Socialism and Labor Movements (p. 708)
27.4 Nationalism and the Rise of Italy, Germany, and Japan (p. 710)

World History Curriculum	**Section and Page References**
III. Increasing discontent with imperial rule propelled reformist and revolutionary movements. **[SB-1, 2, 3, 4, 5, 6	ECON-4	SOC-1, 3, 5, 6]**	23.1 Prelude to Revolution: The Eighteenth-Century Crisis (p. 586) 23.2 The American Revolution, 1775–1800 (p. 590) 23.3 The French Revolution, 1789–1815 (p. 595) 23.4 Revolution Spreads, Conservatives Respond, 1789–1850 (p. 604) 24.1 The Ottoman Empire (p. 611) 24.3 The Qing Empire (p. 623) 25.1 Independence in Latin America, 1800–1830 (p. 636) 26.2 India Under British Rule (p. 679) 26.4 Imperialism in Latin America (p. 686) 27.4 Nationalism and the Rise of Italy, Germany, and Japan (p. 710) 27.6 China, Japan, and the Western Powers (p. 722)
IV. The global spread of European political and social thought and the increasing number of rebellions stimulated new transnational ideologies and solidarities. **[CUL-1, 2	SB-3, 4	ECON-4	SOC-1, 2, 3, 4, 5]**	23.1 Prelude to Revolution: The Eighteenth-Century Crisis (p. 586) 23.2 The American Revolution, 1775–1800 (p. 590) 23.3 The French Revolution, 1789–1815 (p. 595) 23.4 Revolution Spreads, Conservatives Respond, 1789–1850 (p. 604) 24.1 The Ottoman Empire (p. 611) 24.3 The Qing Empire (p. 623) 25.1 Independence in Latin America, 1800–1830 (p. 636) 25.2 The Problem of Order, 1825–1890 (p. 640) 25.3 The Challenge of Social and Economic Change (p. 650) 26.4 Imperialism in Latin America (p. 686) 27.3 Socialism and Labor Movements (p. 708) 27.5 The Great Powers of Europe, 1871–1900 (p. 719) 28.4 China, Japan, and the Western Powers (p. 740)
• **Key Concept 5.4 Global Migration** As a result of the emergence of transoceanic empires and a global capitalist economy, migration patterns changed dramatically, and the numbers of migrants increased significantly.	Chapters 19, 22, 25, 26, 27
I. Migration in many cases was influenced by changes in demographics in both industrialized and unindustrialized societies that presented challenges to existing patterns of living. **[ENV-2, 3, 5	SB-2	ECON-1, 3, 7	SOC-6]**	19.3 Creating the Atlantic Economy (p. 490) 22.1 Causes of the Industrial Revolution (p. 558) 22.3 The Impact of the Early Industrial Revolution (p. 571) 25.3 The Challenge of Social and Economic Change (p. 650) 26.3 Southeast Asia and the Pacific (p. 683) 27.2 Social Changes (p. 703)

World History Curriculum	Section and Page References
II. Migrants relocated for a variety of reasons. **[ENV-2, 3 | ECON-5 | SOC-1, 4, 6]**	19.3 Creating the Atlantic Economy (p. 490) 22.3 The Impact of the Early Industrial Revolution (p. 571) 25.3 The Challenge of Social and Economic Change (p. 650) 26.3 Southeast Asia and the Pacific (p. 683) 26.5 The World Economy and the Global Environment (p. 691) 27.2 Social Changes (p. 703)
III. The large-scale nature of migration, especially in the 19th century, produced a variety of consequences and reactions to the increasingly diverse societies on the part of migrants and the existing populations. **[ENV-2 | CUL-6 | SOC-1, 6]**	22.3 The Impact of the Early Industrial Revolution (p. 571) 25.3 The Challenge of Social and Economic Change (p. 650) 26.3 Southeast Asia and the Pacific (p. 683) 26.5 The World Economy and the Global Environment (p. 691) 27.2 Social Changes (p. 703)

Period 6: Accelerating Global Change and Realignments, 1900 to the Present	Chapters 27, 28, 29, 30, 31, 32, 33

- **Key Concept 6.1 Science and the Environment**

Rapid advances in science and technology altered the understanding of the universe and the natural world and led to advances in communication, transportation, industry, agriculture, and medicine.	Chapters 27, 29, 30, 31, 32, 33
I. Researchers made rapid advances in science that spread throughout the world, assisted by the development of new technology. **[ENV-2, 3, 4, 5 | CUL-3, 4 | ECON-2, 7]**	27.1 New Technology Outside the Industrialized World (p. 698) 29.6 The Character of Warfare (p. 769) 30.2 New Ways of Living in the Industrialized World (p. 782) 32.5 Technological and Environmental Change (p. 857) 33.3 Global Culture (p. 883)
II. During a period of unprecedented global population expansion, humans fundamentally changed their interactions with the environment. **[ENV-2, 3, 4, 5 | SB-3 | ECON-1]**	27.1 New Technology Outside the Industrialized World (p. 698) 29.6 The Character of Warfare (p. 769) 30.2 New Ways of Living in the Industrialized World (p. 782) 31.3 Beyond a Bipolar World (p. 827) 32.3 The Challenge of Population Growth (p. 848) 32.4 Unequal Development and the Movement of Peoples (p. 852) 32.5 Technological and Environmental Change (p. 857) 33.3 Global Culture (p. 883)
III. Disease, scientific innovations, and conflict led to demographic shifts. **[ENV-3 | CUL-4 | SB-3, 6 | SOC-5]**	29.6 The Character of Warfare (p. 769) 30.2 New Ways of Living in the Industrialized World (p. 782) 32.3 The Challenge of Population Growth (p. 848) 32.4 Unequal Development and the Movement of Peoples (p. 852) 33.3 Global Culture (p. 883)

World History Curriculum	Section and Page References
Key Concept 6.2 Global Conflicts and Their Consequences	
Peoples and states around the world challenged the existing political and social order in varying ways, leading to unprecedented worldwide conflicts.	Chapters 28, 29, 30, 31, 32, 33
I. Europe dominated the global political order at the beginning of the 20th century, but both land-based and transoceanic empires gave way to new states by the century's end. [SB-2, 3, 4, 6 | ECON-1]	28.1 Origins of the Crisis in Europe and the Middle East (p. 727) 28.5 The New Middle East (p. 743) 29.6 The Character of Warfare (p. 769) 30.3 A New India, 1905–1947 (p. 787) 30.5 Sub-Saharan Africa, 1900–1945 (p. 797) 31.1 The Cold War (p. 810) 31.2 Decolonization and Nation Building (p. 819) 31.3 Beyond a Bipolar World (p. 827) 32.1 Postcolonial Crises and Asian Economic Expansion (p. 836) 32.2 The End of the Bipolar World (p. 845) 33.1 The Question of Values (p. 866) 33.2 Globalization and Economic Crisis (p. 877)
II. Emerging ideologies of anti-imperialism contributed to the dissolution of empires and the restructuring of states. [CUL-1, 2, 6 | SB-1, 2, 3, 4, 6, | ECON-4, 6 | SOC-1, 2, 3, 5, 6]	28.5 The New Middle East (p. 743) 29.3 The Rise of Fascism (p. 757) 30.3 A New India, 1905–1947 (p. 787) 31.2 Decolonization and Nation Building (p. 819) 31.3 Beyond a Bipolar World (p. 827) 32.1 Postcolonial Crises and Asian Economic Expansion (p. 836) 32.2 The End of the Bipolar World (p. 845) 33.1 The Question of Values (p. 866) 33.2 Globalization and Economic Crisis (p. 877)
III. Political changes were accompanied by major demographic and social consequences. [SB-3, 4, 6 | ECON-3 | SOC-6]	28.1 Origins of the Crisis in Europe and the Middle East (p. 727) 28.4 China and Japan: Contrasting Destinies (p. 740) 28.5 The New Middle East (p. 743) 29.1 The Stalin Revolution (p. 752) 29.3 The Rise of Fascism (p. 757) 29.4 East Asia, 1931–1945 (p. 760) 29.6 The Character of Warfare (p. 769) 30.3 A New India, 1905–1947 (p. 787) 30.4 Mexico, Argentina, and Brazil, 1917–1949 (p. 794) 30.5 Sub-Saharan Africa, 1900–1945 (p. 797) 32.1 Postcolonial Crises and Asian Economic Expansion (p. 836) 32.2 The End of the Bipolar World (p. 845) 32.3 The Challenge of Popula-tion Growth (p. 848) 32.4 Unequal Development and the Movement of Peoples (p. 852) 33.2 Globalization and Economic Crisis (p. 877)

World History Curriculum	**Section and Page References**
IV. Military conflicts occurred on an unprecedented global scale. **[CUL-1, 5 | SB-1, 2, 3, 4, 6| ECON-1, 2, 3, 6 | SOC-3, 6]**	28.1 Origins of the Crisis in Europe and the Middle East (p. 727) 28.2 The "Great War" and the Russian Revolutions, 1914–1918 (p. 729) 28.4 China and Japan: Contrasting Destinies (p. 740) 29.3 The Rise of Fascism (p. 757) 29.4 East Asia, 1931–1945 (p. 760) 29.5 The Second World War (p. 763) 29.6 The Character of Warfare (p. 769) 31.1 The Cold War (p. 810) 32.1 Postcolonial Crises and Asian Economic Expansion (p. 836) 32.2 The End of the Bipolar World (p. 845) 33.1 The Question of Values (p. 866)
V. Although conflict dominated much of the 20th century, many individuals and groups—including states—opposed this trend. Some individuals and groups, however, intensified the conflicts. **[CUL-1, 5, 6 | SB-1, 2, 3, 4, 6 | ECON-2 | SOC-1, 2, 3, 5]**	28.1 Origins of the Crisis in Europe and the Middle East (p. 727) 28.2 The "Great War" and the Russian Revolutions, 1914–1918 (p. 729) 28.4 China and Japan: Contrasting Destinies (p. 740) 29.3 The Rise of Fascism (p. 757) 29.4 East Asia, 1931–1945 (p. 760) 29.5 The Second World War (p. 763) 29.6 The Character of Warfare (p. 769) 30.3 A New India, 1905–1947 (p. 787) 31.1 The Cold War (p. 810) 31.2 Decolonization and Nation Building (p. 819) 31.3 Beyond a Bipolar World (p. 827) 32.1 Postcolonial Crises and Asian Economic Expansion (p. 836) 33.1 The Question of Values (p. 866) 33.2 Globalization and Econom-ic Crisis (p. 877)

- **Key Concept 6.3 New Conceptualizations of Global Economy, Society, and Culture**

The role of the state in the domestic economy varied, and new institutions of global association emerged and continued to develop throughout the century	Chapters 28, 29, 30, 31, 32, 33
I. States responded in a variety of ways to the economic challenges of the 20th century. **[CUL-1 | SB-1, 2, 3, 4 | ECON-1, 2, 3, 6]**	28.3 Peace and Dislocation in Europe, 1919–1929 (p. 737) 28.4 China and Japan: Contrasting Destinies (p. 740) 28.5 The New Middle East (p. 743) 29.1 The Stalin Revolution (p. 752) 29.2 The Depression (p. 754) 29.3 The Rise of Fascism (p. 757) 30.4 Mexico, Argentina, and Brazil, 1917–1949 (p. 794) 31.1 The Cold War (p. 810) 31.2 Decolonization and Nation Building (p. 819) 31.3 Beyond a Bipolar World (p. 827) 32.1 Postcolonial Crises and Asian Economic Expansion (p. 836) 32.5 Technological and Environmental Change (p. 857) 33.2 Globalization and Economic Crisis (p. 877)

World History Curriculum	Section and Page References
II. States, communities, and individuals became increasingly interdependent— a process facilitated by the growth of institutions of global governance. **[ENV-2, 4, 5	CUL-1| SB-2, 3, 4, 5, 6	ECON-1, 2, 3, 6, 7| SOC-5]**	28.3 Peace and Dislocation in Europe, 1919–1929 (p. 737) 31.1 The Cold War (p. 810) 31.3 Beyond a Bipolar World (p. 827) 33.1 Religion and Politics (p. 866) 33.2 Globalization and Economic Crisis (p. 877) 33.3 Global Culture (p. 883)
III. People conceptualized society and culture in new ways; rights-based discourses challenged old assumptions about race, class, gender, and religion. In much of the world, access to education, as well as participation in new political and professional roles, became more inclusive in terms of these factors. **[CUL-1, 2, 5, 6	SB-3| ECON-1| SOC-1, 2, 5]**	30.2 New Ways of Living in the Industrialized World (p. 782) 30.3 A New India, 1905–1947 (p. 787) 31.2 Decolonization and Nation Building (p. 819) 33.1 The Question of Values (p. 866) 33.3 Global Culture (p. 883)
IV. Political and social changes of the 20th century led to changes in the arts and literature. In the second half of the century, popular and consumer culture became more global. **[CUL-5, 6	ECON-1, 3]**	30.2 New Ways of Living in the Industrialized World (p. 782) 32.5 Technological and Environmental Change (p. 857) 33.3 Global Culture (p. 883)

About the Authors

Richard W. Bulliet   Professor of Middle Eastern History at Columbia University, Richard W. Bulliet received his Ph.D. from Harvard University. He has written scholarly works on a number of topics: the social and economic history of medieval Iran (*The Patricians of Nishapur and Cotton, Climate, and Camels in Early Islamic Iran*), the history of human–animal relations (*The Camel and the Wheel and Hunters, Herders, and Hamburgers*), the process of conversion to Islam (*Conversion to Islam in the Medieval Period*), the overall course of Islamic social history (*Islam: The View from the Edge and The Case for Islamo-Christian Civilization*), and the history of transportation (*The Wheel: Inventions and Reinventions*). Dr. Bulliet is the editor of the *Columbia History of the Twentieth Century*. He has published six novels, coedited the *Encyclopedia of the Modern Middle East*, and hosted an educational television series on the Middle East. He was awarded a fellowship by the John Simon Guggenheim Memorial Foundation and was named a Carnegie Corporation Scholar. The Richard W. Bulliet Chair in Islamic History has been established in his honor at Columbia University.

Steven W. Hirsch   Steven W. Hirsch holds a Ph.D. in Classics from Stanford University and is currently Associate Professor of Classics and History at Tufts University. He has received grants from the National Endowment for the Humanities and the Massachusetts Foundation for Humanities and Public Policy. Dr. Hirsch's research and publications include *The Friendship of the Barbarians: Xenophon and the Persian Empire*, as well as articles and reviews in the *Classical Journal, the American Journal of Philology*, and the *Journal of Interdisciplinary History*. He is about to publish a comparative study of ancient Greco-Roman and Chinese civilizations.

Lyman L. Johnson   Professor Emeritus of History at the University of North Carolina at Charlotte, Lyman L. Johnson earned his Ph.D. in Latin American History from the University of Connecticut. A two-time Senior Fulbright-Hays Lecturer, he also has received fellowships from the Tinker Foundation, the Social Science Research Council, the National Endowment for the Humanities, and the American Philosophical Society. Dr. Johnson's recent books include *Workshop of Revolution: Plebeian Buenos Aires and the Atlantic World, 1776–1810*; *Death, Dismemberment, and Memory*; *The Faces of Honor* (with Sonya Lipsett-Rivera); *Aftershocks: Earthquakes and Popular Politics in Latin America* (with Jürgen Buchenau); *Essays on the Price History of Eighteenth-Century Latin America* (with Enrique Tandeter); and *Colonial Latin America* (with Mark A. Burkholder). He also has published in journals, including the *Hispanic American Historical Review*, the *Journal of Latin American Studies*, the *International Review of Social History, Social History*, and *Desarrollo Económico*. Dr. Johnson has served as president of the Conference on Latin American History and recently received its Distinguished Service Award.

Pamela Kyle Crossley   Pamela Kyle Crossley received her Ph.D. in Modern Chinese History from Yale University. She is currently the Robert and Barbara Black Professor of History at Dartmouth College. Dr. Crossley's books include *The Wobbling Pivot: An Interpretive History of China Since 1800; What Is Global History?; A Translucent Mirror: History and Identity in Qing Imperial Ideology; The Manchus; Orphan Warriors: Three Manchu Generations and the End of the Qing World*; and (with Lynn Hollen Lees and John W. Servos) *Global Society: The World Since 1900*.

Daniel R. Headrick   Daniel R. Headrick received his Ph.D. in History from Princeton University. Professor of History and Social Science, Emeritus, at Roosevelt University in Chicago, he is the author of several books on the history of technology, imperialism, and international relations, including *The Tools of Empire: Technology and European Imperialism in the Nineteenth Century; The Tentacles of Progress: Technology Transfer in the Age of Imperialism; The Invisible Weapon: Telecommunications and International Politics; Technology: A World History; Power Over Peoples: Technology, Environments and Western Imperialism, 1400 to the Present*; and *When Information Came of Age: Technologies of Knowledge in the Age of Reason and Revolution, 1700–1850*. Dr. Headrick's articles have appeared in the *Journal of World History* and the *Journal of Modern History*, and he has been awarded fellowships by the National Endowment for the Humanities, the John Simon Guggenheim Memorial Foundation, and the Alfred P. Sloan Foundation.

David Northrup   David Northrup earned his Ph.D. in African and European History from the University of California, Los Angeles. He has published scholarly works on African, Atlantic, and world history. Dr. Northrup's most recent books are *How English Became the Global Language*, the third edition of *Africa's Discovery of Europe, 1450–1850*, and the *Diary of Antera Duke, an Eighteenth-Century African Slave Trader*. He taught at a rural secondary school in Nigeria, Tuskegee Institute in Alabama, Boston College, and Venice International University and is a past president of the World History Association.

Note on Spelling and Usage

Where necessary for clarity, dates are followed by the letters CE or BCE. The abbreviation CE stands for "Common Era" and is equivalent to AD (anno Domini, Latin for "in the year of the Lord"). The abbreviation BCE stands for "before the Common Era" and means the same as BC ("before Christ"). In keeping with our goal of approaching world history without special concentration on one culture or another, we chose these neutral abbreviations as appropriate to our enterprise. Because many readers will be more familiar with English than with metric measurements, however, units of measure are generally given in the English system, with metric equivalents following in parentheses.

In general, Chinese has been Romanized according to the pinyin method. Exceptions include proper names well established in English (e.g., Canton, Chiang Kaishek) and a few English words borrowed from Chinese (e.g., kowtow). Spellings of Arabic, Ottoman Turkish, Persian, Mongolian, Manchu, Japanese, and Korean names and terms avoid special diacritical marks for letters that are pronounced only slightly differently in English. An apostrophe is used to indicate when two Chinese syllables are pronounced separately (e.g., Chang'an).

For words transliterated from languages that use the Arabic script—Arabic, Ottoman Turkish, Persian, Urdu—the apostrophe indicating separately pronounced syllables may represent either of two special consonants, the hamza or the ain. Because most English-speakers do not hear the distinction between these two, they have not been distinguished in transliteration and are not indicated when they occur at the beginning or end of a word. As with Chinese, some words and commonly used place-names from these languages are given familiar English spellings (e.g., Quran instead of Qur'an, Cairo instead of al-Qahira). Arabic romanization has normally been used for terms relating to Islam, even where the context justifies slightly different Turkish or Persian forms, again for ease of comprehension.

Before 1492 the inhabitants of the Western Hemisphere had no single name for themselves. They had neither a racial consciousness nor a racial identity. Identity was derived from kin groups, language, cultural practices, and political structures. There was no sense that physical similarities created a shared identity. America's original inhabitants had racial consciousness and racial identity imposed on them by conquest and the occupation of their lands by Europeans after 1492. All of the collective terms for these first American peoples are tainted by this history. *Indians*, *Native Americans*, *Amerindians*, *First Peoples*, and *Indigenous Peoples* are among the terms in common usage. In this book the names of individual cultures and states are used wherever possible. Amerindian and other terms that suggest transcultural identity and experience are used most commonly for the period after 1492.

There is an ongoing debate about how best to render Amerindian words in English. It has been common for authors writing in English to follow Mexican usage for Nahuatl and Yucatec Maya words and place-names. In this style, for example, the capital of the Aztec state is spelled Tenochtitlán, and the important late Maya city-state is spelled Chichén Itzá. Although these forms are still common even in the specialist literature, we have chosen to follow the scholarship that sees these accents as unnecessary. The exceptions are modern place-names, such as Mérida and Yucatán, which are accented. A similar problem exists for the spelling of Quechua and Aymara words from the Andean region of South America. Although there is significant disagreement among scholars, we follow the emerging consensus and use the spellings *khipu* (not *quipu*), *Tiwanaku* (not *Tiahuanaco*), and *Wari* (not *Huari*). In this edition we have introduced the now common spelling *Inka* (not *Inca*) but keep *Cuzco* for the capital city (not *Cusco*), since this spelling facilitates locating this still-important city on maps.

Preparing for the AP® World History Exam

Advanced Placement® is a challenging yet stimulating experience. Whether you are taking an AP® course at your school or you are working on AP® independently, the stage is set for a great intellectual journey. As the school year progresses and you burrow deeper and deeper into the coursework, you can see the broad concepts, events, conflicts, resolutions, and personalities that have shaped the history of our complex world. Examining the cultural, political, and economic developments that have brought great change while acknowledging the continuities that remain throughout world history is a thrilling task. Fleshing out those forces of change and continuity in world history is exciting. More exciting still is recognizing references to those forces in the media and how history has shaped current world events.

But as spring approaches and the College Board examination begins to loom on the horizon, Advanced Placement® can seem quite intimidating, given the enormous scope and extent of the information you need to know. If you are intimidated by the College Board examination, you are certainly not alone.

The best way to approach an AP® examination is to master it, not let it master you. If you manage your time effectively, you will eliminate one major obstacle—learning a considerable amount of factual material along with the analytical skills needed to be a true world historian. In addition, if you can think of these tests as a way to show off how your mind works, you have a leg up: attitude *does* help. If you are not one of those students, there is still a lot you can do to sideline your anxiety. Focused review and practice time will help you master the examination so that you can walk in with confidence and get a 5.

Before the Exam

By February, long before the exam, you need to make sure that you are registered to take the test. Many schools take care of the paperwork and handle the fees for their AP® students, but check with your teacher or the AP® coordinator to make sure that you are on the registration list. (This is especially important if you have a documented disability and need test accommodations.) If you are studying AP® independently, call AP® Services at the College Board for the name of the local AP® coordinator, who will help you through the registration process.

The evening before the exam is not a great time for partying. Nor is it a great time for cramming. If you like, look over class notes or drift through your textbook, but concentrate on the broad outlines, not the small details, of the course. You might also want to skim through this book and read the AP® tips. Then relax. Get your things together for the next day. Sharpen a fistful of no. 2 pencils with good erasers for the multiple-choice section of the test, and set out several black or dark-blue ballpoint pens for the free-response questions. You should bring a watch in order to pace yourself since you will not be allowed to use the clock or timer functions on your smartphone. Get a piece of fruit or a snack bar and a bottle of water for the break. Depending on your testing site, you may need your Social Security number, photo identification, and an admission ticket. After you have set aside all of those items, put your mind at ease, go to bed, and get a good night's sleep. An extra hour of sleep is more valuable than an extra hour of study.

On the day of the examination, make certain to eat breakfast—fuel for the brain. Studies show that students who eat a hot breakfast before testing get higher grades. You will be given a 10-minute break between Section I and Section II; the World History exam lasts for over three hours, so be prepared for a long morning. You do not want to be distracted by a growling stomach or hunger pangs. Be sure to wear comfortable clothes, taking along a sweater in case the heating or air-conditioning is erratic. When you get to the testing location, make certain to comply with all security procedures. Cell phones are not allowed, so leave yours at home or in your locker if at all possible. Be careful not to drink a lot of liquids, necessitating trips to the bathroom, which take up valuable test time.

Remember, preparation is key! Best wishes on your journey to success—go out and get that 5.

Taking the AP® World History Exam

The AP® World History exam consists of four parts in two sections. Section I includes Parts A and B. Section I Part A consists of 55 multiple-choice questions that you will have 55 minutes to answer; all questions will be organized into sets of two to five questions that follow an item of stimulus material (a primary or secondary source). Section I Part B consists of three short-answer questions that you will answer in 40 minutes. Section II includes its own Part A and Part B. Section II Part A is the document-based question (DBQ) assessing your ability to apply your understanding of the documents while using history reasoning skills. You will be given 60 minutes to read the documents and answer the question. Section II Part B consists of three long-essay questions that both focus on the same history reasoning skill as it applies to different time periods; you will choose to respond to one of these in the allotted 40 minutes. Both Part A and Part B of Section II require students to develop a thesis supported by relevant evidence and strengthened with analysis and synthesis. Your proctor will monitor the time, but you need to keep an eye on your watch and pace yourself so you can do your best on all parts of the exam. Remember that smart watches, watch alarms, and smartphones are not allowed.

Here is a chart to help you visualize the breakdown of the exam:

Section	Multiple-Choice Questions	Short-Answer Questions	Document-Based Question (Essay)	Long Essay Question (Essay)
Weight	40% of exam	20% of exam	25% of exam	15% of exam
Number of Questions	55	3	1	Choose 1 of the 3 question options
Time Allowed	55 minutes	40 minutes	100 minutes for reading and writing	
Suggested Pace	Approx. 1 minute per question	Approx. 13 minutes per question	15 minutes for reading and planning and 45 minutes to write	40 minutes to plan and write

The Themes, Disciplinary Practices, and Reasoning Skills

In order to be successful on the exam, the AP® World History course requires you to use all of the disciplinary practices and reasoning skills that you have worked all year in class to develop. These skills are essential for any historian, but they are particularly critical in world history because of the large amount of content in the course. The themes, disciplinary practices, and reasoning skills were created to provide a framework upon which you can hang all of the information you have learned throughout the year. Additionally, the College Board has developed thematic learning objectives that aid students in identifying broad historical trends and offer students the opportunity to develop history disciplinary practices and reasoning skills in the process of traversing through the themes. All questions on the AP® World History Exam will require students to apply one or more history reasoning skills to at least one of the thematic learning objectives, so it is a good idea to familiarize yourself with both.

A practical exercise that should become a habit is to ask yourself, "What theme does this piece of historical information fall under?" "What disciplinary practice or reasoning skill am I using right now to process this information and make meaning out of it?" This will help you to see the larger historical trends and global connections that twine through our past and present and into the future.

Below are the themes, disciplinary practices, and reasoning skills for the AP® World History course. Please examine them carefully and use them throughout this review book as an essential reference tool and guideline.

Themes

1. Interaction Between Humans and the Environment (ENV)
   - Demography and disease
   - Migration
   - Patterns of settlement
   - Technology
   - Use of natural resources
2. Development and Interaction of Cultures (CUL)
   - Religions
   - Belief systems, philosophies, and ideologies
   - Science and technology
   - The arts and architecture
3. State Building, Expansion, and Conflict (SB)
   - Political structures and forms of governance
   - Empires
   - Nations and nationalism
   - Revolts and revolutions
   - Regional, transregional, and global structures and organizations
   - Diplomacy
4. Creation, Expansion, and Interaction of Economic Systems (ECON)
   - Agricultural and pastoral production
   - Trade and commerce
   - Labor systems
   - Industrialization
   - Capitalism and socialism
5. Development and Transformation of Social Structures (SOC)
   - Gender roles and relations
   - Family and kinship
   - Racial and ethnic constructions
   - Social and economic classes

These themes are constant topics throughout the course, and you should be working with them from the beginning of the year. Throughout the course keep asking yourself where you see elements of both continuity and change—in particular societies, across regions, and throughout time—as they relate to each of these themes. It is also a good idea to begin using the themes as a way to make comparisons between societies over the course of human history.

AP® History Disciplinary Practices and Reasoning Skills

One of the broader goals of AP® World History is to train you to think like a historian. That begs the question, "How do historians think?" The answer is found in the AP® History Disciplinary Practices and Reasoning skills. As a student in any rigorous history course, you should be able to do the following:

Disciplinary Practices: Analyzing Historical Evidence and Argument Development
- Practice 1—Analyzing Historical Evidence: Make conclusions about the past by using a variety of diverse sources.
- Practice 2—Argument Development: Answer a question by making a clear and persuasive argument.

Reasoning Skills: Making Historical Connections and Chronological Reasoning
- Skill 1—Contextualization: Connect large historical processes to individual situations in history.
- Skill 2—Comparison: View the similarities and differences among societies or among developments within one society.

- Skill 3—Causation: Evaluate the causes and effects for what has occurred in the past.
- Skill 4—Continuity and Change Over Time: Analyze history through an investigation of what has stayed the same and what has changed.

To be successful on the AP® World History exam, you need to master these disciplinary practices and reasoning skills as well as the content. The history reasoning skills are the tools you need to unlock the meaning from the content in the multiple-choice section as well as in the free-response portions of the exam. For example, on the DBQ you will use several different history reasoning skills, from analyzing primary documents to understanding diverse interpretations. Any time you write a thesis you are constructing an argument. Long-essay questions may ask you to demonstrate your ability to assess continuity and change or to compare societies in a variety of ways. In the multiple-choice section, you will apply the disciplinary practice and reasoning skills when you examine graphs, maps, and primary source information and you will often deal with multiple-choice questions that require an understanding of diverse interpretations or ask you to address an author's point of view.

The history disciplinary practices and reasoning skills are also the tools you use in the classroom every day to think critically about the content of the course. These are the tools of historians that you train with all year; by the time of the exam you should be ready to demonstrate your understanding of these historical thinking skills as well as the content of the AP® World History course.

Strategies for the Multiple-Choice Section

As mentioned in the chart above, the multiple-choice section of the test makes up 40% of your total score. Thus, it is important that you spend time learning how to master this section—especially its timing. Here are some rules of thumb to help you work your way through the multiple-choice questions:

- **Read the question carefully.** Pressured for time, many students make the mistake of reading the questions too quickly or merely skimming them. By reading a question carefully, you may already have some idea about the correct answer. You can then look for it in the responses. Careful reading is especially important in EXCEPT or NOT questions because, unlike the typical multiple-choice question, all the answers are right except for one.
- **Eliminate any answer you know is wrong.** You can write on the multiple-choice questions in the test book. As you read through the responses, draw a line through any answer you know is wrong.
- **Read all of the possible answers, then choose the most accurate response.** AP® exams are written to test your precise knowledge of a subject. Sometimes there are a few probable answers but one of them is more accurate.
- **Mark and skip tough questions.** If you are hung up on a question, mark it in the margin of the question book. You can come back to it later if you have time. Make sure you skip that question on your answer sheet too.
- **Apply the history reasoning skills and the course themes to help you answer stimulus-based questions.** All of the multiple-choice questions will ask you to use a primary source, a secondary source, or a historical issue, including a document, an image, a map, a graph, or a chart to help answer the question. Examine the wording of the question for clues as to what reasoning skill and theme you should be using.
- **Watch your time carefully!** You can spend too much time pondering potential answers—especially when you have multiple sources to synthesize. Watch the time and don't get bogged down. Instead, mark the best answer and then flag the question for review should you have time remaining at the end.

Types of Multiple-Choice Questions

Although you will encounter various types of multiple-choice questions in Section I Part A of the exam, one characteristic they all have in common is that each question is tied to some type of stimulus. The answer to each question may not come directly from the stimulus, in which case you will need to combine your knowledge of the content of the course (thematic learning objectives and concept outline) with your ability to apply history disciplinary practices and reasoning skills. Additionally, although the stimulus will typically represent one period (or one region or society) in world history, the questions accompanying the stimulus may ask you to make connections to information from a different time period (or region).

Here are some suggestions for how to approach each kind of stimulus you are likely to encounter on the exam.

Photograph/Illustration/Cartoon Questions

These questions require you to interpret a picture to answer the question. A good approach is to examine the picture and any given source information before you read the question and possible responses. Look for symbolism in the image; symbols are especially used in cartoons and paintings. Ask yourself what the artist or photographer is trying to convey. After you have read the question, re-examine the image for clues to answer correctly.

▲ **Gandhi's Salt March to the Sea** Dinodia Photos/Alamy Stock Photo

41. The people in the image above would most likely support which of the following?

   (A) Continued monopoly of a natural resource
   (B) A civil war
   (C) Manufacturing salt in Great Britain
   (D) Nonviolent civil disobedience

ANSWER: D. The above photo shows Mohandas K. Gandhi and his supporters marching to the sea to make salt from ocean water. The act portrayed nonviolent civil disobedience, since the manufacture of salt was a legal monopoly of the British Indian government.

History Disciplinary Practice: Analyzing Historical Evidence
Themes: Creation, expansion, and interaction of economic systems; Development and transformation of social structures; Development and interaction of cultures; State building, expansion, and conflict

Chart/Graph Questions

These questions require you to examine the data on a chart or graph. Although these questions are not difficult, spending too much time interpreting a chart or graph can slow you down. Therefore, for these kinds of stimuli, it is preferable to read the question and all of the possible answers first so that you know what you are looking for as you look over the stimulus. Often, you can even eliminate obviously incorrect responses quickly by reading the question first, making the final answer selection easier.

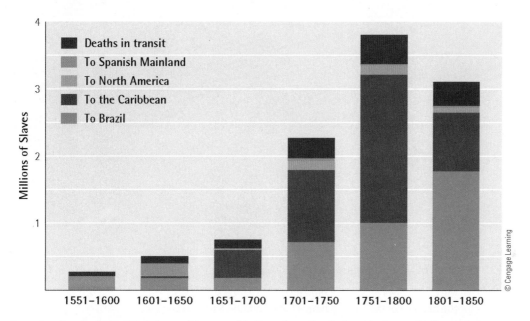

Source: Data from David Eltis, "The Volume and Structure of the Transatlantic Slave Trade: A Reassessment," *William and Mary Quarterly,* 3rd Series, 58 (2001), tables II and III.

2. Which of the following statements does the above table best support?

    (A) The transatlantic slave trade remained at the same level from 1551 to 1850.
    (B) The period 1801–1850 witnessed the largest forced migration of African slaves.
    (C) Most slaves came from East Africa.
    (D) Beginning in 1651, the majority of slaves were brought to the Caribbean and Brazil.

ANSWER: D. After analyzing the table, Option A can be eliminated because the measurement bars are not level in any period. Option B is incorrect because the total number of Africans in transit was highest in the period 1751–1800 and declined some in the period 1801–1850. Option C is incorrect in that there is no way to tell from the table what percentage of the slaves came from a specific region in Africa. Because the bars for transit of slaves to the Caribbean and Brazil are longest beginning in 1651, Option D is the correct answer.
History Disciplinary Practice: Analyzing Historical Evidence
Themes: Interaction between humans and the environment; Creation, expansion, and interaction of economic systems

Interpreting a Map

For history students, maps are used to describe not only geography, but also to convey information about the social, political, cultural, and/or economic organization of human societies. When you are asked to interpret a map, your best bet is to read the title and the key to the map first, to get an idea of what information you will find on the map. Then, read through the questions and the answer choices before going back to the map to find the correct answer.

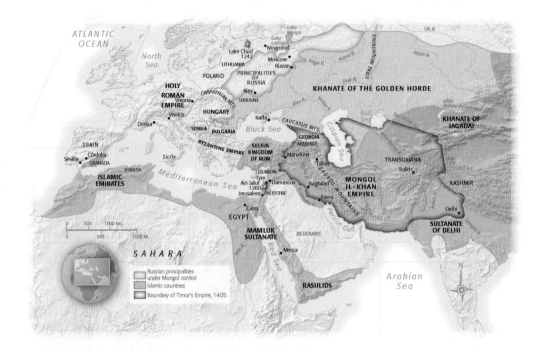

3. This map of western Eurasia in the 1300s shows

    (A) the coexistence of Mongol domains and Islamic sultanates.
    (B) the khanate of the Great Khan, which Khubilai Khan ruled.
    (C) the Mongol takeover of all of western Eurasia.
    (D) the Mongol takeover of all of the Islamic world.

ANSWER: A. The map shows both Mongol khanates and Islamic kingdoms. The answer cannot be B because the domains of the Great Khan were in Central and East Asia. It cannot be C or D because we see other kingdoms that the Mongols did not control, including those of western Europe.
History Disciplinary Practice and Reasoning Skill: Analyzing Historical Evidence; Contextualization
Theme: State building, expansion, and conflict

Interpreting a Primary Source

Historians rely on primary sources to gather information about the past. When presented with primary sources on the AP® World History Exam, be sure to note the origin of the source (both time and place) in order to help you situate the source within your knowledge of history. Although authors' names are cited whenever possible, it is likely that you won't be familiar with the author, so attention to the details of the time and place in which the source was created can help you better understand the source itself. For these kinds of questions, you should look over the source information first. Next, read through each multiple-choice question before thoroughly reading the entire source carefully. Because textual sources often accompany a longer set of multiple-choice questions (three to five per source), it will save time if you consider the questions first so that you know what information to focus on from the source. Sometimes, you might be presented with two short sources and may be asked to compare or identify the reason for differences between the two.

> **Code of Nesilim 8.** If anyone blind a male or female slave or knock out their teeth, he shall give ten half-shekels of silver, he shall let it go to his home.
>
> —Hittite legal code from ca. 1650–1500 BCE
>
> **Hammurabi's code 17.** If any one find runaway male or female slaves in the open country and bring them to their masters, the master of the slaves shall pay him two shekels of silver.
>
> —Babylonian law code from ca. 1750 BCE

4. It appears from the above excerpts of two ancient law codes that

    (A) slaves were considered property.
    (B) male and female slaves were considered equal in value.
    (C) slaves had legal rights.
    (D) silver was a common medium of exchange for slaves.

ANSWER: B. Although answers A, C, and D are also partially evident from the textual evidence, it is evident from the excerpts that both societies viewed the value of male and female slaves equally. Thus, B is the best answer.

History Disciplinary Practice and Reasoning Skills: Analyzing Historical Evidence; Comparison; Contextualization

Theme: Development and transformation of social structures

Interpreting a Secondary Source

Secondary sources reveal the work historians do to interpret and develop analytical theories about the past. A secondary source presents the historian's argument along with the historical evidence to support it. You might be asked to identify appropriate historical evidence to either support or challenge the argument presented in the source. Sometimes, you will be presented with two short excerpts from two historians that might present opposing views or interpretations of the same topic and then be asked to compare the two and/or identify the differences between the authors' interpretations. As with primary source–based multiple-choice questions, a strategy to help you use your time effectively is to read the questions first to get an idea of what to look for in the source excerpts. Be sure to read the entire excerpt carefully before selecting an answer.

Short-Answer Questions

You are required to write responses to a total of three short-answer questions (SAQs) in 40 minutes for Part B of Section I of the AP® World History Exam. Your score on this portion will count for 20% of your final exam score. Each SAQ will have three tasks and the first two questions will require using or interpreting a stimulus (the same types of stimulus material seen in the multiple-choice sections: primary and secondary sources, graphs, charts, maps, images, etc.). You will choose a third question to answer from Question 3 and Question 4. Neither of these will utilize a stimulus. Furthermore, each SAQ will focus on a chronological range using the AP® World History Curriculum Framework as a guide. The chart below will help you visualize the SAQ section of the exam:

Short-Answer Questions	Primary Practice or Skill Assessed	Source Type	Periods Assessed
Questions 1 AND 2 are mandatory			
1	Analyzing Secondary Sources	Secondary Source	Periods 3-6 (c. 1450 CE to Present)
2	Comparison OR Continuity and Change over Time	Primary source text or visual source	Periods 3-6 (c. 1450 CE to Present)
Students choose Question 3 OR Question 4			
3	Comparison OR Continuity and Change over Time (Different skill from SAQ #2)	No Stimulus	Periods 1-3 (to c. 1450 CE)
4			Periods 4-6 (c. 1750 CE to Present)

As you can see, each SAQ will also directly assess one of the disciplinary practices or reasoning skills. In addition, each question will also assess one or more of the thematic learning objectives.

Although you do not need to develop and defend a thesis for these types of questions, you may not simply write a "bulleted" response. Instead, word your responses to each part of each short-answer question in a complete sentence (or a few concise sentences) that respond directly to the question. Take care to also fit your entire response within the indicated space (a lined box) in the response booklet. Be sure to include the correct number of clear and relevant examples as required by the question in your response. The scoring for the short-answer questions is fairly straightforward: you earn one point for each successfully answered part of each question.

Considering the following example of a short-answer question:

3. Answer all parts of the question that follows.

   a) Identify ONE way in which Christianity influenced the development of Islam in the period 600 CE to 1450 CE.
   b) Explain ONE similarity between the diffusion of Christianity and the diffusion of Islam in the period 600 CE to 1450 CE.
   c) Explain ONE difference between the diffusion of Christianity and the diffusion of Islam in the period 600 CE to 1450 CE.

ANSWER: For Part A, there are several ways that Christianity influenced Islam, from monotheism, the incorporation of Jesus of Nazareth as a prophet, or the impact of the Crusades. A good response would not only identify one of these reasons but also directly connect and thoroughly explain how the reason identified actually contributed to the development of Islam.

A good response to Part B could include a discussion of how both Christianity and Islam were adapted by the various cultures that converted to each religion or how both religions were spread in part by the work of missionaries. Regardless of the identified similarity, a good response would need to directly address the similarity and provide specific evidence to bolster the argument.

A good response to part C could include the role of military conquest in the spread of Islam versus Christianity's more gradual spread throughout western Europe, or the role of the Roman Catholic bureaucracy in the spread of Christianity versus the role of the caliphates. Again, the response would need to directly address the difference and provide specific evidence to support it.

Strategies for Section II

In Section II of the AP® World History exam, you are required to write essays for one document-based question (DBQ) and one long-essay question. Part A of Section II is the DBQ, and it represents 25 percent of your final score. For the DBQ, you are given 15 minutes for reading the documents and organizing and outlining your material, and 45 minutes for writing the essay. The DBQ is scored out of 7 points.

Part B of Section II is the long-essay question, and it represents 15 percent of your final score. For Part B, you will be presented with two questions that assess the same history disciplinary practice or reasoning skill as applied to different time periods, so you will have to choose which question you will answer. You will have 40 minutes to plan and respond to whichever of the three long-essay questions you choose. The long-essay question is scored out of 6 points.

The key to success on each of these essays is understanding and internalizing the components of each type of essay's scoring rubric. That's what we will focus on here.

★ **AP® Exam Tip** For each essay in Section II, the AP® examination has built in time for you to develop an outline. Time spent on an outline is important for a number of reasons:

- It prevents you from writing an essay that is unorganized because you begin writing whatever comes into your head at the moment.
- It allows you to determine your analytical thesis after seeing the evidence you can gather to support your argument.
- It provides you with an opportunity to brainstorm before writing the essay.

Once you have outlined your essay, it is time to put pen to paper. Remember that examination readers are looking for a clear thesis backed up with specifics. Concentrate on setting out accurate information in straightforward, concise prose. You cannot mask vague information with elegant prose.

The Document-Based Question (DBQ)

As its name implies, the DBQ presents you with a variety of primary-source information in the form of seven documents. Primary sources are original material created during the time period under study, and they include everything from maps, photographs, and illustrations to excerpts of speeches, essays, books, and personal letters. Furthermore, the DBQ will only assess periods 3-6, or c. 1450 CE to the present.

All free-response questions require you to utilize your knowledge of the topic, but with the DBQ your essay must additionally be based on the documents provided. Your goal is to link each document to the question and then use that information in an analytical and evaluative essay. Thus, the following are necessary for a quality DBQ essay according to the AP® World History rubric:

- **Thesis/Claim (0-1 point):** One point is earned for the presentation of a thesis that makes a historically defensible claim. The thesis must respond specifically to all parts of the question and must do more than restate or rephrase the question. The thesis must consist of at least one sentence located in either the introduction or conclusion.
- **Contextualization (0-1 point):** One point is earned for relating the topic of the prompt to broader historical events, developments, or processes that occur before, during, or continue after the time frame of the question. Merely a phrase or reference will not count here; you must illustrate a specific relationship.
- **Evidence (0-3 points):** One point is earned for accurately describing the content from at least three of the documents. Quotes are not appropriate and will not be sufficient to earn this point.

  To earn two points, your essay must accurately describe the content from at least six documents. Again, quotes will not be sufficient. In addition, your essay must also use the content of the documents to support an argument in response to the prompt.

  To earn the third point for Evidence, you must use at least one piece of specific historical evidence not found in the documents. You will need to describe the evidence and use it to support an argument about the prompt. Furthermore, this piece of evidence may not be the same evidence used to earn the Contextualization point.
- **Analysis and Reasoning (0-2 points):** One point is earned for explaining how or why the document's point of view, purpose, historical situation, or audience is relevant to an argument about the prompt for at least three documents.

  The second point is earned by demonstrating a good understanding of the historical development that is the focus of the prompt and using evidence to corroborate, qualify, or modify an argument that addresses the prompt. There are several ways to demonstrate this, such as:
  - Explaining nuance of an issue by analyzing multiple variables
  - Explaining both similarity and difference, or explaining both continuity and change, or explaining multiple causes, or explaining both cause and effect
  - Explaining relevant and insightful connections within and across periods
  - Confirming the validity of an argument by corroborating multiple perspectives across themes
  - Qualifying or modifying an argument by considering diverse or alternative views or evidence

Take a look at this sample DBQ:

1. **Using the following documents, analyze the extent to which technology has led to the formation of the global marketplace in the period 1750–1900.**

Document 1

> Source: *Sketch of the Progress of the Human Mind*, written by the Marquis de Condorcet in 1793. The Marquis de Condorcet was a mathematician, philosopher and educational reformer in France.
>
> If we were to limit ourselves to showing the benefits derived from the immediate applications of the sciences, or in their application to man-made devices for the well-being of individuals and the prosperity of nations, we would be making known only a slim part of their benefits. The most important, perhaps, is having destroyed prejudices and re-established human intelligence, which until then had been forced to bend down to false instructions instilled in it by absurd beliefs passed down to the children of each generation by terrors of superstition and the fear of tyranny...

Document 2

Source: Joseph Dupleix, Memorandum to the Directors of the French East India Company, written in 1753

All the Company's commerce in India is shared with the English, Dutch, Portuguese and Danes. The division of trade, or rather this rivalry, has served to raise considerably the price of merchandise here and has contributed quite a little toward cheapening the quality – two unfortunate circumstances which further reduce the price and profits in Europe... Our Company can hope for no monopoly in the Indian trade.

Document 3

Source: Richard Guest, *A Compendious History of the Cotton Manufactory*, published in 1823

The present age is distinguished beyond all others by the rapid progress of human discovery... One, however, which would seem to merit the attention of the Englishman from its having brought an immense increase of wealth and population to his territory, has obtained comparatively little attention. While admiration has been unboundedly lavish on other triumphs of the mind, the successive inventions and improvements of the Machinery employed in the Cotton Manufacture have [not] obtained the notice... their national importance required...

Under the influence of the manufacture of which they have been the promoters, the town of Manchester has, from an unimportant provincial town, become the second in extent and population in England, and Liverpool has become in opulence, magnitude, elegance and commerce, the second Seaport in Europe...

Document 4

Source: Excerpt from a booklet published by the Liverpool and Manchester Railway Company to publicize the opening of its railroad in 1830.

During the last fifty years, the transit of goods between Liverpool and Manchester has taken place on the Mersey and Irwell Navigation or the Duke of Bridgewater's canal. These in their day, were great works... but they cease to be adequate to the conveyance of goods...it was recommended in 1832 to diminish the distance between these two great towns by the means of a Rail-road... Speed – despatch – distance – are still relative terms, but their meaning has been totally changed within a few months, what was quick is now slow, what was distant is now near, and this change in our ideas will not be limited to the environs of Liverpool and Manchester – it will pervade society at large...

Document 5

Source: Advertisement for Lipton Teas, published in the *Illustrated London News*, 1890s

Document 6

Source: Map of the expansion of the United States, 1850–1920

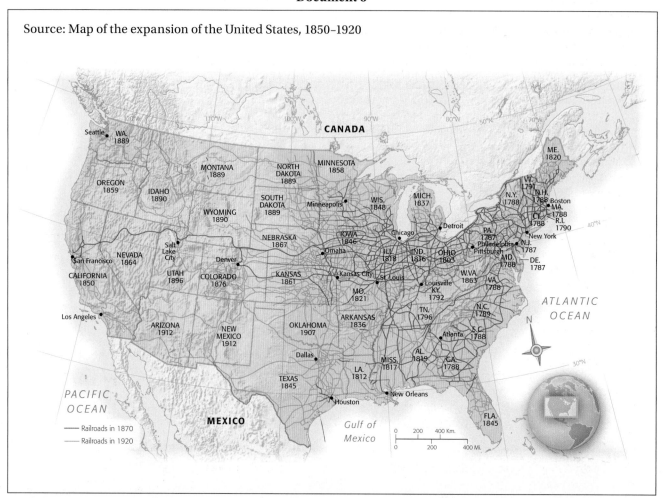

Document 7

Source: Excerpt from a letter by Iwasaki Mitsubishi to his employees in 1876

Many people have expressed differing opinions concerning the principles and advantages of engaging foreigners or Japanese in the task of coastal trade... Looking back into the past... when we abandoned the policy of seclusion and entered into an era of friendly commerce with foreign nations, we should have been prepared for this very task. However, due to the fact that our people lack knowledge and wealth, we have yet to assemble a fleet sufficient to engage in coastal navigation. Furthermore, we have neither the necessary skills for navigation nor a plan for developing maritime transportation industry. This condition is the cause of attracting foreign shipping companies to occupy our major maritime transportation lines... I now propose... to recover the right of coastal trade in our hands.

The first step is an analysis of each document in order to come up with evidence in order to create your thesis. What is the meaning of the document? What or who is the source, and how does that affect their point of view? The source provides important clues in the position being put forth in the document. As you analyze the meaning or significance of the document, jot down margin notes—generalizations that relate to the document and the prompt. For example:

- **Margin note for Document 1** *Human intellect should be praised over technology for creating progress.*

- **Margin note for Document 2** *National rivalries drove the need for new technology, which allowed for competition in the global marketplace.*

- **Margin note for Document 3** *Technological advancements in cotton allowed English cities to be prominent in global trade.*
- **Margin note for Document 4** *Railroads increased the speed and volume of trade.*
- **Margin note for Document 5** *Technology allowed easier access to raw materials.*
- **Margin note for Document 6** *Technology increased participation in the global marketplace.*
- **Margin note for Document 7** *Nationalism fueled technological development.*

Once you have done this, you should consider the information you know about the prompt outside of the information presented in the documents. Combine the evidence from the documents with the outside information to create your thesis and the main points you are going to use to prove your thesis (your arguments). Each argument should specifically connect evidence from the document back to your main thesis, while incorporating outside information and analysis of the purpose, intended audience, historical context of the document, and/or author's point of view. For example, your thesis might argue that while technology improved the volume and number of participants in the global marketplace, other factors were also at work. Competition between states was also a driving force behind developing the marketplace between 1750 and 1900. Throughout your essay, you will provide evidence to support this claim. Decide which documents are best for showing your analysis and reasoning skills. You may want to explain that document 4 is an advertisement – a brochure touting the marvels of the company's product to encourage future investors. Consider mentioning America's arrival in Japan and the subsequent Meiji Restoration as historical context for document 7. To decide on additional historical examples that would be helpful, look at the sources that are provided. Think about other information you know that could help corroborate your argument that isn't already in any of these sources. Make sure your outside evidence is specific and includes an explanation of how it is relevant to your argument.

As part of your planning, you will also want to consider broader historical events or processes that may have influenced the topic to use for your contextualization. Finally, write your thesis, making sure it answers the prompt and shows your argument. Make sure your thesis has an argument and does not just repeat the prompt. With good planning at the beginning, your DBQ should be in great shape!

There are twelve DBQs in the appendix of this book. Use these DBQs to practice going through the process of writing a DBQ, and you will feel very comfortable and confident on the exam!

Long–Essay Questions

The AP® World History exam concludes with the essay question. You will be required to choose to respond to one of the three possible prompts. The prompts assess the same theme and the same reasoning skill but from different time periods. The first prompt deals with periods 1–2, the second with periods 3–4, the third with periods 5–6. The option you choose really depends on how much accurate, relevant historical evidence you can confidently include in your essay given that you should spend no more than 40 minutes on planning and writing it.

Your essay for this question must come entirely from your knowledge of world history—you will not be provided with any information outside of the prompts themselves. However, the topics of the questions are limited to topics or examples detailed in the concept outline developed by the College Board for AP® World History. Again, the prompt will assess your ability to demonstrate one of the history reasoning skills, such as comparison, causation, or continuity and change over time. Long-essay questions are graded with a 6-point rubric as follows:

- **Thesis (0–1 point)** An acceptable thesis must make a historically defensible claim and directly and specifically address all parts of the question. Simply restating or rephrasing the prompt is unacceptable. The thesis must consist of at least one sentence located in either the introduction or the conclusion.
- **Contextualization (0–1 point)** One point is earned for relating the topic of the prompt to broader historical events, developments, or processes that occur before, during, or continue after the time frame of the question. Merely a phrase or reference will not count here; you must illustrate a specific relationship.
- **Evidence (0–2 points)** In order to earn one point, your essay must contain specific historical examples of evidence relevant to the prompt. To earn the second point, you must use specific historical examples to support an argument in response to the prompt.

- **Analysis and Reasoning (0–2 points)** To earn the first point, you must demonstrate the reasoning skills (comparison, causation, continuity and change over time) by framing or structuring your argument with them. The skill assessed will be apparent based on the prompt. The second point is earned by demonstrating a good understanding of the historical development that is the focus of the prompt and using evidence to corroborate, qualify, or modify an argument that addresses the prompt. There are several ways to demonstrate this, such as:
  - Explaining nuance of an issue by analyzing multiple variables.
  - Explaining both similarity and difference or explaining both continuity and change, or explaining multiple causes, or explaining both cause and effect.
  - Explaining relevant and insightful connections within and across periods.
  - Confirming the validity of an argument by corroborating multiple perspectives across themes.
  - Qualifying or modifying an argument by considering diverse or alternative views or evidence.

Be sure that in your preparation you practice a few times with each type of skill so that you will feel confident applying any of the skills. You will find practice LEQ prompts in the appendix of the textbook.

To conclude, here are some tips for writing AP® World History essays:

- **Thesis** Be sure that your thesis statement is in either the introduction or the conclusion of your essay. You need to present your main argument in the first paragraph or the last paragraph so it is clear what you are proving in your essay.
- **Grammar** You will not lose points for spelling or grammar errors as AP® exam essays are essentially rough drafts, but it is important to write as coherently as possible. Remember, if the reader is unable to follow your arguments because of excessively poor grammar and/or spelling, it will be harder to get the necessary information across and earn points. It is also important to write as legibly as possible so all of your good ideas can be understood. An illegible essay struggles to earn points.
- **Dates** Do not panic if you cannot remember a specific date; try to use a broader description such as "early nineteenth century" or "around the sixth century" if you cannot remember the exact date.
- **Quality over quantity** Remember: quality, not quantity. Writing a great deal does not mean you are writing what needs to be in your essay. Focus on making sure you are hitting all the rubric points rather than writing long introductions or conclusions. Make your argument, support it with relevant and accurate historical evidence, and wrap up. You want to have time to do both essays well.

The Earth and Its Peoples

PART I

The Emergence of Human Communities, to 500 BCE

▲ **Babylonian Map of the World, ca. 600 BCE** This map on a clay tablet, with labels written in Akkadian cuneiform, shows a flat, round world with the city of Babylon at the center. Nearby features of the Mesopotamian landscape include the Euphrates River, mountains, marshes, and cities. Beyond the great encircling salt sea are seven islands. Like many ancient peoples, the Babylonians believed that distant lands were home to legendary beasts, strangely formed peoples, and mysterious natural phenomena. The Trustees of the British Museum/Art Resource, NY

About 10,000 years ago, early humans began to cultivate plants, domesticate animals, and make pottery vessels for storage, which led to permanent settlements. The earliest complex societies arose in the great river valleys of Mesopotamia, Egypt, Pakistan, and northern China. Kings and priests dominated these early urban centers by controlling access to water; they were assisted in this domination by individuals in a variety of other specialized positions. Peasants living outside the urban centers grew the food necessary for survival, and artisans made weapons, tools, and ritual objects from bronze, giving rise to unique cultures.

Kingdoms grew as their rulers sought to control access to raw materials, especially metals; this growth stimulated long-distance trade and diplomatic relations between major powers as well as the spread of culture and technology to neighboring regions, such as southern China, Nubia, Syria-Palestine, Anatolia, and the Aegean.

Early civilizations of the Western Hemisphere (located in southern Mexico and the Andean region of South America) faced different challenges and are discussed in Part II. ●

Environment	Culture	State Building	Economics	Social Structure
• Variety of responses to environment by different types of societies	• Origins, beliefs, development, economic/social/political impact, and spread of major religions, philosophies, and belief systems (Judaism, Confucianism, Daoism)	• Creation and maintenance (changes and continuities) of forms, functions, and institutions of governance	• Causes/effects of economic strategies of different types of communities, states, and empires (Neolithic Revolution)	• Impact of kinship, ethnicity, class, gender, and race on social hierarchies (patriarchy)
• Impact of environmental factors, disease, and technology on migration and settlement	• Effect of cross-cultural interactions on diffusion of technology and scientific knowledge	• Impact of economic, social, cultural, and geographical factors on state building, expansion, and dissolution	• Development and change of modes and locations of production over time	• Impact of ideologies, philosophies, and religions on social hierarchies (Confucianism, Daoism, Judaism)
• Impact of migration, population, and urbanization on environment (Neolithic Revolution)	• Reflection and impact of society in the arts	• Influence of varied economic organizations on state formation and expansion	• Development and change of labor systems over time	• Challenges and confirmations of legal systems, colonialism, nationalism, and independence movements on class, gender, and racial hierarchies over time
	• Impact of expanding exchange networks on transregional culture such as music, literature, and visual art	• Impact of internal/external political factors on state building, expansion, and dissolution • Interaction between states and state-less societies	• Influence and impact of local, regional, and global economic systems and exchange networks on each other	• Interaction between specialized labor systems and social hierarchies

Key Concept 1.1

• How does archaeological evidence show the gradual migration and adaptation of early hunting-foraging bands?

Key Concept 1.2

• How did the Neolithic Revolution lead to the development of complex economic and social systems?
• How did agriculture and pastoralism transform human societies?

Key Concept 1.3

• How did geography and environment affect the foundation of the following civilizations: Mesopotamia, Egypt, Mohenjo-daro, Shang, Olmec, Chavín?
• What were the roles of civilizations in Mesopotamia and the Nile River Valley in the early creation of society?
• What elements of culture (such as language, religion, myth, law codes, literature, and monumental art) began to emerge, giving each civilization a unique identity and footprint?

Key Concept 2.1

• How did the compilation of the Hebrew scriptures and the growth of the Jewish Diaspora create a bond among people and an ethical code to live by?
• How did the codification of Confucianism form a foundation for social relationships and behaviors of all classes in China?
• How did the core beliefs of Daoism influence the development of Chinese culture?
• How did belief systems such as shamanism, animism, and ancestor veneration continue and evolve as they were incorporated into other religious traditions?

Nature, Humanity, and History, to 3500 BCE

1

AP® Framework Terms

Paleolithic Era
Fire
Neolithic Revolution
Mesopotamia
Nile River Valley (Egypt)
Sub-Saharan Africa
Mesoamerica
Andes
Pastoralism

Overarching Questions

1 How have different types of societies adapted to and affected the environment as they have settled? (ENV)

2 How have religions, belief systems, philosophies, and ideologies affected the political, economic, and social development of societies? (CUL)

3 In what ways do cultural artifacts reflect innovation, adaptation, and creativity of specific societies? (CUL)

4 How have different forms of governance been constructed and maintained over time? (SB)

5 How have distinctions based on kinship, ethnicity, class, gender, and race influenced the development and transformations of social hierarchies? (SOC)

Paintings and engravings on stone created tens of thousands of years ago by early humans have been found on every continent. Someone in Central Africa carved this image of cattle around 5000 bce, when the Sahara was not a desert but a verdant savanna supporting numerous species of wildlife. Why the image was carved and what significance it originally held will likely remain a mystery, but for us it is a beautiful work of art that reveals much about our human ancestry.

Long before the invention of writing, societies told themselves stories about how human beings and the natural world were created. Some, like the Yoruba (**yoh-roo-bah**) people of West Africa, related that the first humans came down from the sky; others, like the Hopi of southwest North America, claimed that they emerged out of a hole in the earth. Although such creation myths typically explain how a people's way of life, social divisions, and cultural system arose, historical accuracy in the modern sense was not their primary purpose. As with the story of Adam and Eve in the Hebrew Bible, their goal was to define the moral principles that people thought should govern their dealings with the supernatural world, with each other, and with the rest of nature.

In the nineteenth century evidence began to accumulate about the actual

▲ **Engraving of Two Cattle in the Sahara, ca. 5000 BCE** Around 10,000 people settled in the central Sahara and began to engrave rocks with pictures of animals. The engravings display an expert knowledge of animal stance, movement, and anatomy.
David Coulson/Robert Estall Photo Agency

origins of humanity. Natural scientists were finding remains of early humans who resembled apes. Other discoveries suggested that the familiar ways of life based on farming and herding did not arise within a generation or two of creation, as many myths suggested, but tens of thousands of years after humans first appeared. This evidence provides insights into human identity that are as meaningful as those propounded by the creation myths. ●

1-1 **African Genesis**

In light of scientific advances in our understanding of human origins, what have we learned about our relationship to the earth and other living species?

The discovery in the mid-nineteenth century of the remains of ancient creatures that had both humanlike and apelike features generated excitement and controversy. The finds upset many people because they challenged religious beliefs about human origins. Others welcomed the new evidence for what some had long suspected: that the physical characteristics of modern humans had evolved over incredibly long periods of time.

1-1a **Interpreting the Evidence**

In 1856 in the Neander Valley of Germany, laborers discovered fossilized bones of a creature with a body much like that of modern humans but with a face that had heavy brow ridges and a low forehead, like the faces of apes. Although we now know these were Neanderthals, a type of human common in Europe and the Middle East from 135,000 to 25,000 years ago, in the mid-nineteenth century the idea of humans that different from modern people was so novel that some scholars thought they must be deformed individuals from recent times.

Three years after the Neanderthal finds, Charles Darwin, a young English *naturalist* (student of natural history), published *On the Origin of Species*, in which he argued that the time frame for all biological life was far longer than most people supposed. Darwin based his conclusion on the pioneering research of others and on his own investigations of fossils and living plant and animal species in Latin America. He proposed that the great diversity of living species and the profound changes in them over time could be explained by natural selection, the process by which biological variations that enhance a population's ability to survive become dominant in that species. He theorized that, over long periods of time, the changes brought about by this process could lead to the **evolution** of distinct new species.

Turning to the sensitive subject of human evolution in *The Descent of Man* (1871), Darwin summarized the growing consensus among naturalists that human beings had come into existence through the same process of natural selection. Because humans shared so many physical similarities with African apes, he proposed Africa as the home of the first humans, even though there was no fossil evidence at the time to support his hypothesis.

The next major discoveries pointed to Asia, rather than Africa, as the original human home. On the Indonesian island of Java in 1891, Eugene Dubois uncovered an ancient skullcap of what was soon called Java man. In 1929 near Peking (an old form of Beijing [**bay-jeeng**]), China, W. C. Pei discovered a similar skullcap of what became known as Peking man.

By then, even older fossils had been found in southern Africa. In 1924 Raymond Dart found the skull of a creature that he named *Australopithecus africanus* (**aw-strah-loh-PITH-uh-kuhs ah-frih-KAH-nuhs**) (African southern ape), which he argued was transitional between apes and early humans. For many years most specialists disputed Dart's idea because, although *Australopithecus africanus* walked upright like a human, its brain was the size of an ape's.

Since 1950, Louis and Mary Leakey and their son Richard, along with many others, have discovered a wealth of early human fossils in the exposed sediments of the Great Rift Valley of eastern Africa. These finds are strong evidence for Dart's hypothesis and for Darwin's guess that the tropical habitat of the African apes was the cradle of humanity.

The development of modern archaeological techniques has added to our knowledge. Rather than collect isolated bones, researchers sift the neighboring soils to extract the fossilized remains of other creatures, seeds, and even pollen existing at the time, documenting the environment in which early humans lived. They can also measure the age of most finds by the rate of molecular change in potassium, contained in minerals in lava flows, or in carbon from wood and bone.

A major new approach was made possible by the full decipherment of the human genetic code in 2003. Researchers have been able to extrapolate backward from genetic differences among contemporary human populations to answer such questions as when language first emerged; the approximate size and location in northeast Africa of the ancestral human population and the date when some of its members moved out of the continent; the paths taken by migrating groups as humans ultimately spread to all habitable parts of the planet; and when the skin color of the various human populations developed.

By combining these forms of evidence with the growing understanding of how other species adapt to their natural environments, researchers can trace the evolutionary changes that produced modern humans over the course of millions of years.

1-1b Human Evolution

Biologists classify **australopithecines** (**aw-strah-loh-PITH-uh-seen**) and humans as members of a family of primates known as **hominids** (**HOM-uh-nid**). Primates are members of a class of warm-blooded, four-limbed, social animals known as mammals that came to prominence about 65 million years ago. The first hominids are now dated to about 7 million years ago.

Among living primates, modern humans are most closely related to the African apes—chimpanzees and gorillas. Since Darwin's time it has been popular (and controversial) to say that we are descended from apes. In fact, apes and humans share a common ancestor. Over 99 percent of human deoxyribonucleic acid (DNA), the basic genetic blueprint, is identical to that of the great apes. But three traits distinguish humans from apes and other primates. The earliest of these traits to appear was **bipedalism** (walking upright on two legs). Being upright frees the forelimbs from any role in locomotion and enhances an older primate trait: a hand with a long, opposable thumb that can work with the fingers to manipulate objects skillfully. Modern humans' second distinctive trait is a very large brain. Besides enabling humans to think abstractly, experience profound emotions, and construct complex social relationships, this larger brain controls the fine motor movements of the hand and of the tongue, increasing humans' tool-using capacity and facilitating the development of speech. The physical possibility of language, however, depends on a third distinctive human trait: the location of the *larynx* (voice box). In humans it lies much lower in the neck than in any other primate.

evolution The biological theory that, over time, changes occurring in plants and animals, mainly as a result of natural selection and genetic mutation, result in new species.

australopithecines The several extinct species of humanlike primates that existed from about 4.5 million years ago to 1.4 million years ago (genus Australopithecus).

hominids The biological family that includes humans and humanlike primates.

bipedalism The ability to walk upright on two legs, characteristic of hominids.

CHRONOLOGY

	Geological Epochs	Species and Migrations	Technological Advances
7,000,000 BCE		7,000,000 BCE Earliest hominids	
4,000,000 BCE		4,500,000 BCE Australopithecines 2,300,000 BCE Early *Homo habilis*	2,600,000 BCE Earliest stone tools; hunting-and-gathering (foraging) societies
2,000,000 BCE	2,000,000–9000 BCE Pleistocene (Great Ice Age)	1,800,000–350,000 BCE *Homo erectus*	2,000,000–8000 BCE Paleolithic (Old Stone Age)
1,000,000 BCE			500,000 BCE Use of fire
200,000 BCE		200,000–100,000 BCE Anatomically modern *Homo sapiens* in Africa 80,000–50,000 BCE Behaviorally modern *Homo sapiens* possessing language; migrations to Eurasia 46,000 BCE Modern humans in Australia 18,000 BCE Modern humans in Americas	30,000 BCE First cave paintings
10,000 BCE	9000 BCE–present Holocene		8000–2000 BCE Neolithic (New Stone Age); earliest agriculture

These critical biological traits are due to natural selection, the preservation of genetic changes that enhanced the ability of the ancestors of modern humans to survive and reproduce. Major shifts in the world's climate led to evolutionary changes in human ancestors and other species. Falling temperatures culminated in the **Great Ice Age**, or Pleistocene (**PLY-stuh-seen**) epoch, extending from about 2 million to about 9000 BCE (see Chronology). These temperature changes and altered rainfall and vegetation imposed great strains on plant and animal species, causing large numbers of new species to evolve.

Beginning approximately 4.5 million years ago, several species of australopithecines evolved in southern and eastern Africa. In northern Ethiopia in 1974, Donald Johanson unearthed a well-preserved skeleton of a twenty-five-year-old female, whom he nicknamed Lucy. Mary Leakey's discovery of fossilized footprints in Tanzania in 1977 provided spectacular visual evidence that australopithecines walked on two legs.

Bipedalism evolved because it provided australopithecines with some advantage for survival. Some studies suggest that walking and running on two legs is very energy efficient. Another theory is that bipeds survived better because they could carry armfuls of food back to their mates and children.

Climate changes between 2 and 3 million years ago led to the evolution of a new species, the first to be classified in the same genus (*Homo*) with modern humans. At Olduvai (**ol-DOO-vy**) Gorge in northern Tanzania in the early 1960s, Louis Leakey discovered the fossilized remains of a creature that he named *Homo habilis* (**HOH-moh HAB-uh-luhs**) (handy human). What most distinguished *Homo habilis* from the australopithecines was a brain that was nearly 50 percent larger. Greater intelligence may have enabled *Homo habilis* to locate things to eat throughout the seasons of the year. Seeds and other fossilized remains found in ancient *Homo habilis* camps indicate that the new species ate a greater variety of more nutritious foods than did australopithecines.

By 1 million years ago *Homo habilis* and all the australopithecines had become extinct. In their habitat lived a new hominid, *Homo erectus* (**HOH-moh ee-REK-tuhs**) (upright human), which first appeared in eastern Africa about 1.8 million years ago. (It is uncertain whether *Homo erectus* evolved from *Homo habilis* or both species descended from *Australopithecus*.) These creatures possessed brains a third larger than those of *Homo habilis*, which presumably accounted for their better survivability. A nearly complete skeleton of a twelve-year-old male of the species discovered by Richard Leakey in 1984 on the shores of Lake Turkana in Kenya shows

AP® Exam Tip Consider how environmental changes impacted the development of human civilization.

Great Ice Age Geological era that occurred between about 2 million and 11,000 years ago.

Homo habilis The first human species (now extinct). It evolved in Africa about 2.3 million years ago.

Homo erectus An extinct human species. It evolved in Africa about 1.8 million years ago.

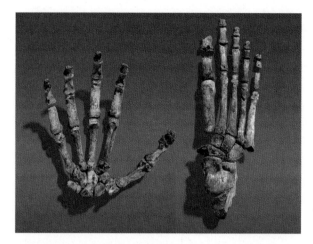

▲ **Hand and Foot of *Homo naledi*** The foot is designed for walking upright, while the hand combines more modern features with curved fingers for climbing trees. Stefan Fichtel/National Geographic Creative

▲ **Skull Casts of Early Hominids** These skulls show the extensive cranial changes associated with the increase in brain size during 2.5 million years of evolutionary change. *Australopithecus* on the left, *Homo erectus* in the middle, *Homo sapiens* on the right. Smithsonian Institution

that *Homo erectus* closely resembled modern people from the neck down. *Homo erectus* was very successful in dealing with different environments and underwent hardly any biological changes for over a million years.

A recent discovery in South Africa both complicates our understanding of human evolution and challenges a number of conventional beliefs. Over 1,500 bone fragments from fifteen or more individuals have been excavated from a remote and not easily accessible cave floor. *Homo naledi*, as the new species has been called, displays a curious mix of more and less primitive features. The skull and small brain are similar to those of australopithecines, but other features are like those of more advanced hominids, including feet designed for walking upright and long, curved hands that would have made it adept at climbing trees. There is still much controversy about the dating of this species, based largely on comparing its skeletal features with those of other hominid types, with suggested dates ranging between 2 million and 900,000 years ago. Experts are also still debating whether the bones were purposely deposited deep in the cave as a kind of burial and whether this would have required the use of torches. Even on the later proposed dating, this would attest to the use of fire and the existence of social rituals long before these behaviors existed according to the conventional view.

Sometime between 200,000 and 100,000 years ago, a new human species emerged: *Homo sapiens* **(HOH-moh SAY-pee-enz)** (wise human). The brains of *Homo sapiens* were a third larger than those of *Homo erectus*, whom they gradually superseded. Although this species was anatomically similar to people today, archaeological and genetic evidence suggest that a further development sometime between 80,000 and 50,000 years ago produced the first behaviorally modern humans, with the intellectual and social capabilities that we have.

There is no scholarly consensus on when, why, or how humans developed the capacity to speak. In the absence of tangible evidence, this question has even been labeled "the hardest problem in science." Assuming that the shape of the throat and low position of the larynx are essential to vocalizing a wide range of sounds, it ought to be relevant that these features were still evolving in *Homo habilis* and *Homo erectus*. Some scholars link the development of language in the fullest sense to the period around 70,000 years ago when *Homo sapiens* began to migrate out of Africa and employed a larger, more sophisticated set of tools that can be sorted into functional categories.

This slow but remarkable process of physical evolution, which distinguished humans from other primates, was one part of what was happening. Equally remarkable was the way in which humans were extending their habitat.

1-1c **Migrations from Africa**

Early humans first expanded their range in eastern and southern Africa. Then they ventured out of Africa, perhaps following migrating herds of animals or searching for more abundant food supplies in a time of drought. The reasons are uncertain, but the end results are vividly clear: humans successfully colonized diverse environments, including deserts and arctic lands (see Map 1.1). This dispersal demonstrates early humans' talent for adaptation.

Homo erectus was the first human species to inhabit all parts of Africa and to be found outside Africa. Java man and Peking man were members of this species. At that time, Java was

Homo naledi A recently discovered early hominid with a puzzling mix of primitive and more advanced features.

Homo sapiens The current human species. It evolved in Africa sometime between 400,000 and 100,000 years ago.

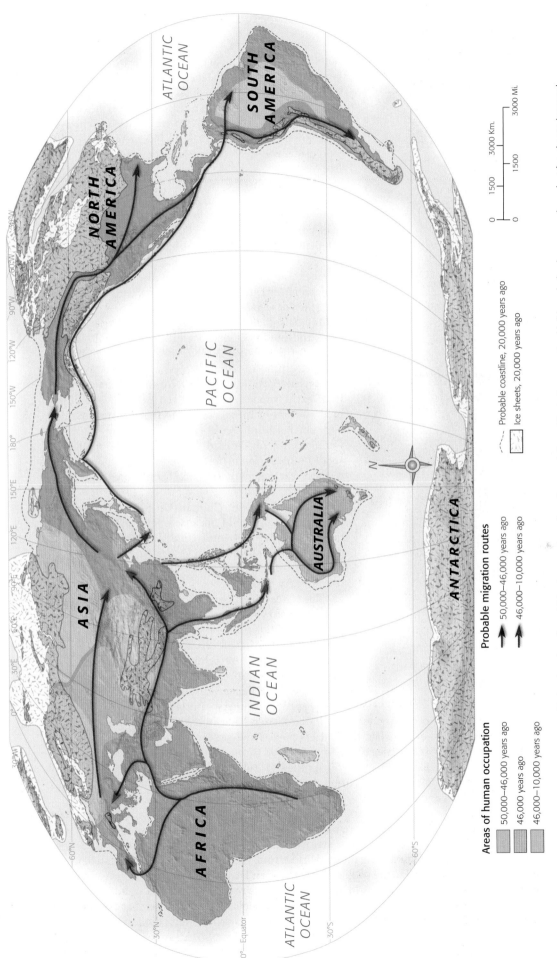

MAP 1.1 Human Dispersal to 10,000 Years Ago Early migrations from Africa into southern Eurasia were followed by treks across land bridges during ice ages, when giant ice sheets lowered ocean levels. Boats may also have been employed.

Which regions of human settlement could only have been reached by boat?

▲ **Fossilized Footprints** Archaeologist Mary Leakey (shown at top) found these remarkable footprints of a hominid adult and child at Laetoli, Tanzania. The pair had walked through fresh volcanic ash that solidified after being buried by a new volcanic eruption. Dated to 3.5 million years ago, the footprints are the oldest evidence of bipedalism yet found. John Reader/Science Source

not an island but was part of the Southeast Asian mainland. During the Pleistocene, massive glaciers of frozen water spread out from the poles and mountains. At their peak such glaciers covered a third of the earth's surface and contained so much frozen water that ocean levels were lowered by over 450 feet (140 meters), exposing land bridges between many places now isolated by water (see Map 1.1).

DNA and fossil evidence suggest that *Homo sapiens* also first evolved in Africa. The ancestral group from which all modern humans are descended may have comprised as few as 5,000 individuals. From this population, a band of several hundred people initially moved out of northeast Africa, crossing the strait between the horn of Africa and the Arabian peninsula, sometime between 80,000 and 50,000 years ago, and their descendants rapidly spread across the planet (although some scientists dispute this "African Genesis" and hold that distinct groups of *Homo sapiens* evolved from *Homo erectus* populations in Africa, Europe, China, and Southeast Asia).

Recent excavations and DNA analysis have shown that early modern humans co-existed and interbred with other species of *Homo* that are now extinct: Neanderthals and Denisovans (whose bone fragments were recently discovered in Siberia). The small and small-brained *Homo floresiensis*, whose remains were recently excavated in Indonesia, only died out about 12,000 years ago.

Ultimately modern humans displaced older human populations, probably because they were better able to survive environmental conditions in the Ice Age, though some scholars believe the Neanderthals were absorbed into the *Homo sapiens* population through interbreeding.

The Great Ice Age enabled modern humans to penetrate into the Americas and even the Arctic. During glacial periods, people would have been able to cross a land bridge from Siberia to Alaska, perhaps beginning around 18,000 BCE, though some scholars believe that the first migrations occurred as early as 35,000 to 25,000 BCE. Scholars are also investigating the possibility that people from Asia initially explored and settled the western coast of North America by boat, but there is little archaeological evidence because these areas were submerged when the glaciers melted and sea levels rose. Over thousands of years the population of the Americas grew and spread throughout the hemisphere, penetrating southern South America by 10,500 BCE. As they spread, these humans adapted to environments that included polar extremes, tropical rain forests, and high mountain ranges as well as deserts, woodlands, and prairies.

About 46,000 years ago, modern humans, traveling by boat from Java, colonized New Guinea and Australia when both were part of a single landmass, and others crossed the land bridge then existing between the Asian mainland and Japan. When global temperatures rose and the glaciers melted, submerging the land bridges and increasing the extent of ocean between Southeast Asia and Australia, the peoples of the Western Hemisphere and Australia were virtually isolated from the rest of the world for at least 15,000 years.

As populations migrated, they underwent minor evolutionary changes that helped them adapt to extreme environments. One such change was in skin color. The deeply pigmented skin of today's indigenous inhabitants of the tropics (and presumably of all early humans) reduces harmful effects of the harsh tropical sun such as sunburn and skin cancer. At some point between 20,000 and 5,000 years ago, pale skin became characteristic of Europeans living in northern latitudes with far less sunshine, especially during winter months. The loss of pigment enabled their skin to produce more vitamin D from sunshine.

As distinctive as skin color seems, it represents a very minor biological change. What is far more remarkable is that widely dispersed human populations vary so little in their genetic makeup. Whereas other species need to evolve physically to adapt to new environments, modern humans have been able to adapt technologically, changing their eating habits and devising new forms of tools, clothing, and shelter. As a result, human communities have become culturally diverse while remaining physically homogeneous.

Section Review

- Nineteenth-, twentieth-, and twenty-first-century discoveries of hominid fossil remains upset traditional beliefs about human origins.

- In Charles Darwin's theory of evolution, natural selection of traits that promote survival and reproduction accounts for the gradual development of modern humans from primate ancestors.

- Bipedalism, a large brain, and a lower location of the larynx that enables speech are advantages that humans have over other primates.

- Africa is the place of origin of the earliest hominids, about 7 million years ago, and of modern humans between 200,000 and 100,000 years ago. Sometime between 80,000 and 50,000 years ago they began to migrate to the other continents, using land bridges during glacial periods with low sea levels.

1-2 Technology and Culture in the Ice Age

How did the evolution of early humans enable them to adapt to new environments during the Great Ice Age?

Evidence of early humans' splendid creative abilities came to light in 1940 near Lascaux in southern France. Youths who stumbled onto the entrance to a vast underground cavern found its walls covered with paintings of animals, including many that had been extinct for thousands of years. Other ancient cave paintings have been found in Spain, Africa, Australia, and elsewhere. The artistic quality of ancient cave art is vivid evidence that the biologically modern people who made such art were intellectually modern as well (see Diversity & Dominance: Cave Art).

The production of similar art and specialized tools over wide areas and long periods of time demonstrates that skills and ideas were deliberately passed along within and between societies. These learned patterns of action and expression constitute **culture**. Culture includes both material objects, such as dwellings, clothing, tools, and crafts, and nonmaterial values, beliefs, and languages. While some animals also learn new ways, their activities are determined primarily by inherited instincts. Among humans, instincts are less important than the cultural traditions that each generation learns from its elders.

AP® Exam Tip
Explain how the development of diverse and sophisticated tools, including multiple uses of fire, helped humans adapt to new environments.

1-2a Food Gathering and Stone Tools

When archaeologists examine the remains of ancient human sites, the first thing that jumps out at them is the abundant evidence of human toolmaking. Because the tools that survive are mostly made of stone, the extensive period of history from the appearance of the first fabricated stone tools around 2.6 million years ago until the appearance of metal tools around 6,000 years ago has been called the **Stone Age**.

The name can be misleading because not all tools were made of stone. Early humans also made useful objects out of bone, skin, wood, plant fibers, and other materials less likely than stone to survive the ravages of time. Early scholars recognized two phases of the Stone Age: the **Paleolithic (pay-lee-oh-LITH-ik)** (Old Stone Age), down to 8000 BCE, and the **Neolithic (NEE-OH-LITH-IK)** (New Stone Age), which is associated with the rise of agriculture. Modern scientists have developed more complex schemes with many subdivisions.

Most early human activity centered on gathering food. Like the australopithecines, early humans depended heavily on vegetable foods such as leaves, seeds, and grasses, but during the Ice Age the consumption of highly nutritious animal flesh increased. Moreover, unlike australopithecines, humans regularly made tools. These two changes—increased meat eating and toolmaking—appear to be closely linked.

culture Socially transmitted patterns of action and expression.

Stone Age The historical period characterized by the production of tools from stone and other nonmetallic substances.

Paleolithic The period of the Stone Age associated with the evolution of humans.

Neolithic The period of the Stone Age associated with the ancient Agricultural Revolution(s).

Were the people who lived tens of thousands of years ago different from people today? Biologically, members of *Homo sapiens* have not changed much over time. But what were our ancestors like inside—in their thoughts, imaginations, and emotions? Did their eyes see beauty, their ears hear music, and their minds wonder at the meaning of the world around them and the celestial bodies above them? One way to approach this difficult question is to look at the earliest art.

The oldest recognizable human art, a carefully crosshatched bone from Blombos Cave east of Cape Town, South Africa, dates from over 70,000 years ago. When the first painted cave was discovered at Altamira in Spain in the later nineteenth century, many people refused to believe that the images were the work of prehistoric people. The quality of the art was too high, the skill of the artists too impressive, to reconcile with conventional conceptions of "cavemen." Scientists calculated that the paintings in Lascaux, the most famous of the caves, discovered in southwestern France in 1940, date to about 15,000 BCE. Then in 1994 the discovery of Chauvet (sho-VAY) Cave, in southeastern France, pushed back the evidence for painting by humans to a much earlier time. Jean-Marie Chauvet and two companions discovered a small cliffside entrance into a vast cave complex. The original entrance to the cave had been closed off long before by a rock slide, thereby sealing and preserving not only the magnificent paintings on the walls of the cave, but also animal bones, human and animal footprints, and other artifacts. The Chauvet Cave paintings are currently dated to between 30,000 and 35,000 years ago. The cave has been put off-limits by the French government to preserve it from human and environmental damage, and even scholars are only allowed in for short periods of time. (However, a nearby replica of the cave was opened for visitors in 2015.)

The prehistoric artists of Chauvet lived during the Ice Age, when glaciers covered much of France. The Ardèche River Gorge, where the cave is located, was teeming with life—modern humans, Neanderthals, and animals of all sorts, both those that humans hunted and dangerous predators. The cave paintings depict the animals of that epoch: cave lions, cave bears, rhinoceroses, wild horses, bison, reindeer, aurochs (wild oxen), and mammoths. The only representations of humans are the silhouettes of hands, made by blowing paint around them (experts can identify one particular individual whose handprint is found at several cave locations by a distinctively curling little finger), and a large stalactite projection, near the back of the cave, painted to represent the lower half of a woman. Scholars have noted the similarity of this figure to a multitude of small female statuettes, often called Venuses (after the Roman goddess of sex and love) because of the exaggerated genitalia, found throughout Europe from as early as 35,000 to as late as 11,000 years ago. This similarity suggests a continuity in representation throughout the Paleolithic and, presumably, a continuity in the thoughts behind it, that may have to do with promoting reproduction.

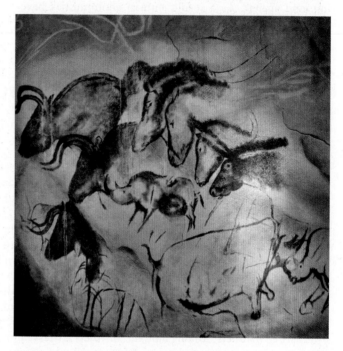

▲ **Painted Animals in Chauvet Cave, France**   HIP/Art Resource, NY

Specimens of crude early tools found in the Great Rift Valley of eastern Africa reveal that *Homo habilis* made tools by chipping flakes off the edges of volcanic stones. The razor-sharp edges of such flakes are highly effective for skinning and butchering wild animals.

Lacking the skill to hunt and kill large animals, small-brained *Homo habilis* probably obtained animal protein by scavenging meat from kills made by animal predators or resulting from accidents. This species probably used large stone "choppers" for cracking open bones to get at the nutritious marrow. The fact that such tools are found far from the volcanic outcrops where they were quarried suggests that people carried them long distances for use at kill sites and camps.

Members of *Homo erectus* were also scavengers, but their larger brains made them more clever. They made more effective tools for butchering large animals, including a hand ax formed by removing chips from both sides of a stone to produce a sharp outer edge. The hand ax was an efficient multipurpose tool, suitable for skinning and butchering animals, for scraping skins clean for use as clothing and mats, for sharpening wooden tools, and for digging up edible roots. Since a hand ax can also be hurled accurately for nearly 100 feet (30 meters), it might also have been used as a projectile to fell animals. *Homo erectus* even hunted elephants by driving them into swamps, where they became trapped and died.

The walls of the cave are not flat, but rather full of projections and indentations, and the artists have skillfully incorporated these natural features into the paintings, as well as etched the outlines of some figures to give them a startling three-dimensional quality. Besides having a rough sense of perspective, they used sophisticated techniques to represent motion and multiplicity, such as a bison with eight legs to indicate rapid motion. Sometimes new figures were painted over earlier figures, suggesting that the activity of painting may have gone on over a long period of time.

No traces of human habitation have been found in the cave, so it evidently had a different purpose. One can only marvel at the effort that must have gone into illuminating the deep recesses of the cave so that the artists could see what they were doing. There are black smudge marks on the walls where torchbearers wiped off excess carbon to keep the torches lit. There is also an altar-like stone platform on which a cave bear's skull had been purposefully set.

The scene reproduced here, depicting a woolly rhinoceros, aurochs, and wild horses, shows the skill and techniques of the artists and the variety of subject matter, and it has been noted that the artists cleverly incorporated clefts, bumps, and other natural features of the rock into their tableau.

Why did the prehistoric artists of Chauvet and other caves draw what they did? And why in caves? It is a huge challenge for us to understand the meaning and purpose of these cave paintings. Prehistory is, by definition, a time before there were written texts that can tell us about ancient humans' lives and thoughts. For such periods we primarily depend on archaeology, but while excavated artifacts can tell us about the material culture of a society—their tools, weapons, jewelry, food, burial practices, and the physical spaces in which they operated—it is much harder to infer from physical objects the social institutions, customs, beliefs, and values of the people who made and used them. However, we can regard these paintings as a kind of text because the artists were trying to communicate something to their fellows. Modern scholars, operating across a vast cultural divide between us and the Paleolithic people of Chauvet, can only speculate about the meaning of the paintings to the artists and their contemporaries and the cultural function of the caves.

Commentators often start with the context in which the art was made. Given that humans did not live in Chauvet Cave, what might have been its function? It was no accident that they went to such trouble to work inside dark caves that could be illuminated only with crude torches. However, they probably did not do so with the goal of protecting and preserving their art for tens of thousands of years. Rather, the artists may have gone deep underground "to feel the power of the earth"—they may have believed that the wild animals and the earth itself were full of spiritual energy. (Indeed, many of the archaeologists who have worked in Chauvet and other caves have commented on the mysterious, spiritual feeling induced by being deep inside the earth.) It is thus possible that the artists were the spiritual guides of their communities, and the decorated caverns were holy places where religious ceremonies were performed and where those present would have had powerful religious experiences.

One must also consider the subject matter of the paintings, the preponderance of animals, and the absence (with the exceptions already noted) of humans. The animals represented include both those that humans hunted and those they did not, and the artists had a fund of knowledge about the appearance, movement, and behavior of those animals, derived, no doubt, from close observation. It has been suggested that ancient cave art may have expressed the mystical relationship of humans with the animals with whom they shared the world. Perhaps humans could absorb something of the power of the bears, antelope, bison, or other animals depicted in the caves by viewing or touching them.

AP® History Reasoning Skills

Comparison *What similarities and differences are suggested about the societies involved when you compare this cave painting with the cattle carvings at the beginning of the chapter?*

Contextualization *What details about the society that created this image can be supported by details from the image?*

Members of *Homo sapiens* were far more skillful hunters. Using their superior intelligence and an array of finely made tools, they tracked and killed large animals. Sharp stone flakes chipped from carefully prepared rock cores were used in combination with other materials. Attaching a stone point to a wooden shaft made a spear. Embedding several sharp stone flakes in a bone handle produced a sawing tool.

Indeed, members of *Homo sapiens* were so successful as hunters that they may have caused a series of ecological crises. Between 40,000 and 13,000 years ago the giant mastodons and mammoths gradually disappeared from Africa, Southeast Asia, and northern Europe. In North America around 11,000 years ago, three-fourths of the large mammals became extinct, including giant bison, camels, ground sloths, stag-moose, giant cats, mastodons, and mammoths. In Australia there was a similar event. However, since these extinctions occurred during severe cold spells at the end of the Ice Age, it is difficult to distinguish the effects of climate change and human predation.

Despite the evidence for hunting, anthropologists do not believe that early humans depended primarily on meat for their food. The few surviving present-day **foragers** (hunting and food-gathering peoples) in Africa derive the bulk of their day-to-day nourishment from wild vegetable foods, with meat reserved for feasts. The same was probably true for Stone Age peoples, even though tools for gathering and processing vegetable foods have left few traces

foragers People who support themselves by hunting wild animals and gathering wild edible plants and insects.

because they were made of perishable materials. Ancient humans would have used skins and mats woven from leaves for collecting fruits, berries, and wild seeds. They would have dug edible roots out of the ground with wooden sticks.

Both meat and vegetables become tastier and easier to digest when they are cooked. The first cooked foods were probably found by accident after wildfires. Humans may have been setting fires deliberately as early as 1.4 million years ago and maintaining hearths around 500,000 years ago. However, only with the appearance of clay cooking pots some 18,000 years ago in East Asia is there hard evidence of cooking.

1-2b Gender Roles and Social Life

AP® Exam Tip

Consider the roles of gender and social hierarchies on human civilization.

Researchers have studied the behavior and organization of nonhuman primates for clues about very early human society. Gorillas and chimpanzees live in groups consisting of several adult males and females and their offspring. Status varies with age and sex, and a dominant male usually heads the group. Sexual unions between males and females generally do not result in long-term pairing. Instead, the strongest ties are those between a female and her children and among siblings. Adult males are often recruited from neighboring bands.

Very early human groups likely shared some of these primate traits, but long before the advent of modern *Homo sapiens* the two-parent family would have been common. We can only guess how this change developed, but it is likely that physical and social evolution were linked. Big-headed humans with large brains have to be born in a less mature state than other mammals so that they can pass through the narrow birth canal. Other large mammals are mature at two or three years of age; humans are not able to care for themselves until the age of twelve to fifteen. The need of human infants and children for much longer nurturing makes care by mothers, fathers, and other family members a biological imperative.

The human reproductive cycle also became unique. In many other species sexual contact is biologically restricted to a special mating season of the year or to the fertile part of the female's menstrual cycle. Moreover, among other primates the choice of mate is usually not a matter for long deliberation. To a female baboon in heat any male will do, and to a male baboon any receptive female is a suitable sexual partner. In contrast, adult humans can mate at any time and are much choosier about their partners. Once they mate, frequent sexual contact promotes deep emotional ties and long-term bonding.

An enduring bond between human parents made it much easier for vulnerable offspring to receive the care they needed during the long period of their childhood. Working together, mothers and fathers could nurture dependent children of different ages at the same time, unlike other large mammals, whose females must raise their offspring nearly to maturity before beginning another reproductive cycle. Spacing births close together also would have enabled humans to multiply more rapidly than other large mammals.

Researchers studying present-day foragers infer that Ice Age women would have done most of the gathering and cooking (which they could do while caring for small children). Older women past childbearing age would have been the most knowledgeable and productive food gatherers. Men, with stronger arms, would have been more suited than women to hunting, particularly for large animals. Since the male hunters will only occasionally have succeeded in bringing down their prey, while the women gatherers provided the bulk of the band's daily diet, it is likely that women held a respected position in early human societies.

All recent foragers have lived in small bands. The community has to have enough members to defend itself from predators and

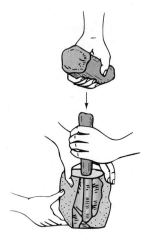

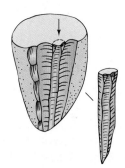

◀ **Making Stone Tools** About 35,000 years ago the manufacture of stone tools became highly specialized. Small blades chipped from a rock core were mounted in a bone or wooden handle. Not only were such composite tools more varied than earlier all-purpose hand axes, but the small blades also required fewer rock cores—an important consideration where suitable rocks were scarce. From Jacques Bordaz, Tools of the Old and New Stone Age. Copyright 1970 by Jacques Bordaz. Redrawn by permission of Addison-Wesley Educational Publishers, Inc.

divide responsibility for collection and preparation of foods. However, too many members would exhaust the food available in its immediate vicinity. The band has to move at regular intervals to follow migrating animals and take advantage of seasonally ripening plants in different places. Archaeological evidence from Ice Age campsites suggests that early humans, too, lived in highly mobile bands.

1-2c Hearths and Cultural Expressions

Because frequent moves were necessary, early hunter-gatherers did not lavish much time on housing. Natural shelters under overhanging rocks or in caves were favorite camping places to which bands returned at regular intervals. Where the climate was severe or where natural shelters did not exist, people erected huts of branches, stones, bones, skins, and leaves. Large, solid structures were common in fishing villages that grew up along riverbanks and lakeshores, where the abundance of fish permitted people to occupy the same site year-round.

Animal skin cloaks were probably an early form of clothing. Although the oldest evidence of fibers woven into cloth dates from about 26,000 years ago, the appearance of the body louse around 70,000 years ago has been linked to people beginning to wear close-fitting garments. An "Iceman" from 5,300 years ago, whose frozen remains were found in the European Alps in 1991, was wearing many different garments made of animal skins sewn together with cord fashioned from vegetable fibers and rawhide (see Environment & Technology: The Iceman).

Although accidents, erratic weather, and disease might take a heavy toll on a foraging band, day-to-day existence was probably not particularly hard or unpleasant. Studies suggest that, in plant- and game-rich areas, obtaining necessary food, clothing, and shelter would have occupied only from three to five hours a day. This would have left a great deal of time for artistic endeavors, toolmaking, and social life.

The foundations of science, art, and religion were built during the Stone Age. Basic to human survival was extensive knowledge about the natural environment. Gatherers learned which local plants were best for food and when they were available, and hunters gained intimate knowledge of the habits of game animals. People learned how to use plant and animal parts for clothing, twine, building materials, and dyes; minerals for paints and stones for tools; as well as natural substances effective for medicine and consciousness altering. It is very likely that the transmission of such knowledge involved verbal communication, even though direct evidence for language appears only in later periods.

Early music and dance have left no traces, but there is abundant evidence of painting and drawing (see Diversity & Dominance: Cave Art). Because many cave paintings feature wild animals that were hunted for food, some believe they were meant to record hunting scenes or formed part of magical and religious rites to ensure successful hunting. However, the recently discovered Chauvet Cave in southern France features rhinoceroses, panthers, bears, and other animals that probably were not hunted. Other drawings include people dressed in animal skins and smeared with paint. In many caves there are stencils of human hands. Are these the signatures of the artists or the world's oldest graffiti? Some scholars suspect that other marks in cave paintings and on bones from this period may represent efforts at counting or writing. Other theories suggest that cave and rock art represent concerns with fertility, efforts to educate the young, or elaborate mechanisms for time reckoning.

Without written texts it is difficult to know about the religious beliefs of early humans. Sites of deliberate human burials from about 100,000 years ago give some hints. The fact that an adult was often buried with stone implements, food, clothing, and red-ochre powder suggests that early people revered their leaders, relatives, and companions enough to honor them after death and may imply a belief in an afterlife where such items would be useful.

Today we recognize that the Old Stone Age, whose existence was scarcely dreamed of two centuries ago, was a formative period. Important in its own right, it also laid the foundation for major changes ahead as human communities passed from being food gatherers to food producers.

Section Review

- Unlike other animals, humans have used the learned patterns of culture to adapt to and occupy very diverse environments.

- Early humans made tools, foraged for food, and hunted. They found natural shelters or built temporary shelters, and they provided themselves with clothing.

- In early hunter-gatherer societies, women gathered the plant foods that provided most of the band's diet, while men did the hunting. The two-parent family offered children protection and a long period to mature.

- This lifestyle left them leisure to develop art and religion. Although the remains of their art and religion are difficult to interpret, it is clear that early modern humans had the mental capabilities that we have.

Environment & Technology
The Iceman

The discovery of the well-preserved remains of a man at the edge of a melting glacier in the European Alps in 1991 provided detailed information about everyday technologies of the fourth millennium BCE. Not just the body of this "Iceman" was well preserved, but also his clothing, his tools, and even the food in his stomach survived in remarkably good condition.

Dressed from head to toe for the cold weather of the mountains, the fifty-year-old man was wearing a fur hat fastened under the chin with a strap, a vest of different-colored deerskins, leather leggings and loincloth, and a padded cloak made of grasses. His calfskin shoes were also padded with grass for warmth and comfort. The articles of clothing had been sewn together with fiber and leather cords. He carried a birch-bark drinking cup.

In a leather fanny pack he carried small flint tools for cutting, scraping, and punching holes, as well as some tinder for making a fire. He also carried a

leather quiver with flint-tipped arrows, but his 6-foot (1.8-meter) bow was unfinished, lacking a bowstring. In addition, he had a flint knife and a tool for sharpening flints. His most sophisticated tool, indicating the dawning of the age of metals, was a copper-bladed ax with a wooden handle.

His death was violent, caused either by a small arrowhead lodged in his shoulder or a blow to the head. In his stomach, researchers found the remains of the meat-rich meal he had eaten not long before he died.

▲ **The Iceman**   This is an artist's rendition of what the Iceman might have looked like. Notice his clothing and tools, remarkable evidence of the technology of his day.
MARKA/Alamy Stock Photo

Questions for Analysis

1. Based on his clothing and the food in his stomach, what kinds of animals did the Iceman encounter and make use of?

2. What were the purposes of the various tools and weapons found with the Iceman?

3. What do you think the Iceman was doing so high up in the mountains?

1-3 The Agricultural Revolutions

After nearly 2 million years of physical and cultural development, how did human communities in different parts of the world learn to manipulate nature through agriculture and the domestication of animals?

For most of human existence people ate only wild plants and animals. But around 10,000 years ago global climate changes seem to have induced some societies to enhance their food supplies with domesticated plants and animals. More and more people became food producers over the following millennia. Although hunting and gathering did not disappear, this transition from foraging to food production was one of the great turning points in history because it fostered a rapid increase in population and greatly altered humans' relationship to nature (see Map 1.2).

Because agriculture arose in combination with new kinds of stone tools, archaeologists called this period the Neolithic, or New Stone Age, and the rise of agriculture the Neolithic Revolution. But that name can be misleading: first, stone tools were not its essential component, and second, it was not a single event but a series of separate transformations in different parts of the world. A better term is **Agricultural Revolutions**, which emphasizes that the central change was in food production and that agriculture arose independently in many places. In most cases agriculture included the domestication of animals as well as the cultivation of new food crops.

AP® Exam Tip

Understand how the Neolithic Revolution led to the development of more complex economic and political systems.

Agricultural Revolutions
The change from food gathering to food production that occurred between about 8000 and 2000 BCE. Also known as the Neolithic Revolution.

1-3a The Transition to Plant Cultivation

Food gathering gave way to food production in stages spread over hundreds of generations. The process may have begun when forager bands, returning year after year to the same seasonal camps, deliberately scattered the seeds of desirable plants in locations where they

▲ **A Neolithic House**   This reconstruction of an early permanent human habitation has a single door and no windows. Simple dwellings were constructed of mud brick over a timber frame or of wattle and daub, a lattice of branches covered with a sticky composite of mud, straw, and other materials. The roof is thatched, a layering of dried vegetation that sheds water.   Herv Champollion/akg-images/Newscom

would thrive and discouraged the growth of competing plants by clearing them away. Such semicultivation could have supplemented food gathering for many generations. Eventually, families choosing to concentrate on food production would have settled permanently near their fields.

The presence of new, specialized tools for agriculture first alerted archaeologists to the beginning of a food production revolution. These included polished stone heads to work the soil, sharp stone chips embedded in bone or wooden handles to cut grain, and stone mortars to pulverize grain. Since stone axes were not very efficient for clearing away shrubs and trees, farmers used fire to get rid of unwanted undergrowth (the ashes were a natural fertilizer).

The transition to agriculture occurred first in the Middle East. By 8000 BCE humans, by selecting the highest-yielding strains, had transformed certain wild grasses into the domesticated grains now known as emmer wheat and barley. They also discovered that alternating the cultivation of grains and *pulses* (plants yielding edible seeds such as lentils and peas) helped maintain soil fertility. Women, the principal gatherers of wild plant foods, had the expertise to play a major role in this transition to plant cultivation, but the heavy work of clearing the fields would have fallen to men.

Plants domesticated in the Middle East spread to Greece as early as 6000 BCE, to the light-soiled plains of central Europe and along the Danube River shortly after 4000 BCE, and then to other parts of Europe over the next millennium (see Map 1.2). Early farmers in Europe and elsewhere practiced shifting cultivation, also known as swidden agriculture. After a few growing seasons, the fields were left *fallow* (abandoned to natural vegetation) for a time to restore their fertility, and new fields were cleared nearby. From around 2600 BCE people in central Europe began using ox-drawn wooden plows to till heavier and richer soils.

Wheat and barley could not spread farther south because the rainfall patterns in most of Africa were unsuited to their growth. Instead, separate Agricultural Revolutions took place in Saharan and sub-Saharan Africa, beginning almost as early as in the Middle East. During a particularly wet period after 8000 BCE, people in what is now the eastern Sahara began to cultivate sorghum, a grain derived from wild grasses they had previously gathered. Over the next 3,000 years the Saharan farmers domesticated pearl millet, black-eyed peas, a kind of peanut, sesame, and gourds. In the Ethiopian highlands, farmers domesticated finger millet and a grain

AP® Exam Tip
Understand how the domestication of plants and animals affected both the humans and the environments involved.

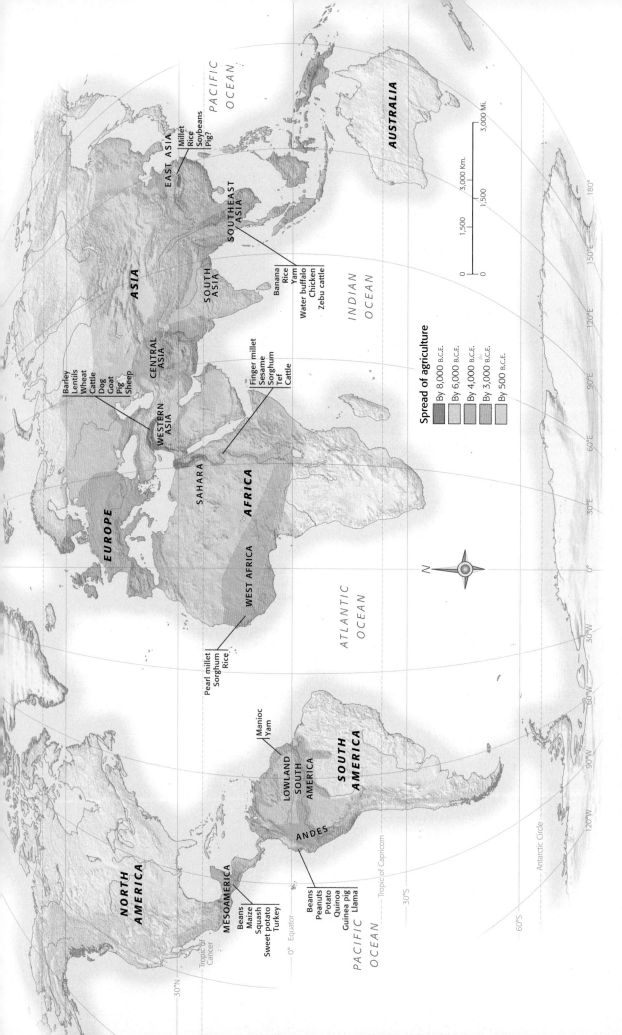

MAP 1.2 Early Centers of Plant and Animal Domestication Many different parts of the world made original contributions to domestication during the Agricultural Revolutions that began about 10,000 years ago. Later interactions helped spread these domesticated animals and plants to new locations. In lands less suitable for crop cultivation, pastoralism and hunting remained more important for supplying food.

Why are most of the regions where crops were first domesticated relatively close to the Equator?

called tef. The return of drier conditions about 5000 BCE led many Saharan farmers to move to the Nile Valley, where the annual flooding of the river provided moisture for farming. People in the rain forests of equatorial West Africa domesticated rice and yams.

Rice, which thrives in warm and wet conditions, was probably first domesticated in the Yangzi River Valley in central China, possibly as early as 10,000 BCE, and by 3000 BCE it had made its way to Southeast Asia and India. In India several pulses domesticated about 2000 BCE (including hyacinth beans, green grams, and black grams) were cultivated along with rice.

The inhabitants of the American continents were domesticating other crops; potatos in the Andes, perhaps as early as 7000 BCE; by about 5000 BCE, maize (**mayz**), or corn, in Mexico, manioc in Brazil and Panama, and beans and squash in Mesoamerica. By 4000 BCE, the inhabitants of Peru were developing quinoa (**kee-NOH-uh**), a protein-rich seed grain. Insofar as their climates and soils permitted, other farming communities throughout the Americas adopted these crops, along with tomatoes and peppers.

1-3b Domesticated Animals and Pastoralism

The first domesticated animals were probably dogs descended from wolves that were used initially to help hunters track game and later to herd other domesticated animals as well as provide protection and companionship. There is much debate about the place, date, and process of domestication. Experts have argued for Siberia, the Middle East, and Europe as the site of the first domestication. The time of domestication may go back 30,000 years or more, though the first known burial of a dog with a human—a sure sign of the relationship—is from around 14,000 BCE.

The domestication of animals expanded rapidly during the Neolithic period, as other animals were domesticated to provide meat, milk, and energy. Refuse heaps outside some Middle East villages during the centuries after 7000 BCE show that sheep and goat bones gradually replaced gazelle bones. As wild sheep and goats scavenged for food scraps around villages, the tamer animals probably accepted human control and protection in exchange for a ready supply of food. Selective breeding for desirable characteristics such as high milk production and long wooly coats eventually led to distinct breeds of sheep and goats.

AP® Exam Tip
Understand how pastoralism and cooperative work led to significant impacts on environmental diversity.

▼ **Ancient Dog Burial** This husky-like dog, buried 7,000 years ago in Siberia, was interred along with, and in the same manner as, humans. This, and the fact that he ate the same food as humans, suggests that he was seen as a companion and helper. Skeletal damage has also been interpreted as showing that he carried heavy loads and may have been repeatedly injured on hunts. Vladimir Bazaliiskii/Robert Losey/Sandra Garvie-Lok/Mietje Germonpre/Jennifer Leonard/Andrew Allen/Anne Katzenberg/ Mikhail Sablin

Elsewhere, other animal species were domesticated during the centuries before 3000 BCE: wild cattle in northern Africa or the Middle East; donkeys in northern Africa; water buffalo in China; and humped-back Zebu (**ZEE-boo**) cattle in India. Varieties of domesticated animals spread from one region to another.

Once cattle became tame enough to be yoked to plows, they became essential to grain production. In addition, animal droppings provided valuable fertilizer. In the Americas, however, comparatively few species of wild animals were suitable for domestication, and domesticated animals could not spread from elsewhere because the land bridge to Asia had been submerged by raised sea levels. In the Western Hemisphere, therefore, domesticated llamas provided transport and wool, while guinea pigs and turkeys furnished meat. Hunting remained the most important source of meat for Amerindians.

In the more arid parts of Africa and in some regions of western and Central Asia, pastoralism, a way of life dependent on large herds of small and large stock, predominated. As the Sahara approached its maximum dryness around 2500 BCE, pastoralists replaced farmers, who migrated southward (see Chapter 9). Moving their herds to new pastures and watering places throughout the year made pastoralists almost as mobile as foragers and discouraged accumulation of bulky possessions and construction of substantial dwellings. Early herders probably relied more heavily on milk than on meat, since killing animals reduced their herds. During wet seasons, they may also have done some hasty crop cultivation or bartered meat and skins for plant foods with nearby farming communities.

1-3c Agriculture and Ecological Crisis

AP® Exam Tip
Consider how pastoralism and agriculture led to demographic changes and the specialization of labor.

Why did the Agricultural Revolutions occur? Some theories assume that people were drawn to food production by its obvious advantages, such as the promise of a secure food supply. It has recently been suggested that people in the Middle East might have settled down so they could grow enough grains to ensure themselves a ready supply of beer.

However, most experts believe that climate change drove people to abandon hunting and gathering in favor of agriculture or pastoralism. With the end of the Great Ice Age, the temperate lands became exceptionally warm between 6000 and 2000 BCE, the era when people in many parts of the world adopted agriculture. The precise nature of the crisis probably varied. Shortages of wild food in the Middle East caused by a dry spell or population growth may have prodded people to take up food production. Elsewhere, a warmer, wetter climate could turn grasslands into forest, reducing supplies of game and wild grains.

In many drier parts of the world, where wild food remained abundant, people did not take up agriculture. The inhabitants of Australia continued to rely exclusively on foraging until recent centuries. Many Amerindians in the arid grasslands from Alaska to the Gulf of Mexico hunted bison, others in the Pacific Northwest took up salmon-fishing, and east of the Mississippi River food gatherers thrived on abundant supplies of fish, shellfish, and aquatic animals. In Africa, in the equatorial rain forest and in the southern part of the continent, conditions favored retention of the older ways. The reindeer-based societies of northern Eurasia were also unaffected by the spread of farming.

Whatever the causes, the gradual adoption of food production transformed most parts of the world. A hundred thousand years ago there were fewer than 2 million people, and their range was largely confined to the temperate and tropical regions of Africa and Eurasia. The population may have fallen even lower during the last glacial epoch, between 32,000 and 13,000 years ago. Then, as the glaciers retreated and people took up agriculture, their numbers rose. World population may have reached 10 million by 5000 BCE and then mushroomed to between 50 million and 100 million by 1000 BCE.[1] This increase led to important changes in social and cultural life.

Section Review

- Around 10,000 years ago humans began to cultivate plants, selecting for those with the highest nutritional yield, and to domesticate animals. These Agricultural Revolutions arose in various parts of the world.

- Climate change at the end of the last Ice Age is probably the major reason for the switch from food gathering to food production.

- Agriculturalists gradually spread across much of the planet, but in certain environments pastoralism, the dependence of people on herd animals, prevailed.

- The more secure food supply made possible by agriculture led to a great increase in human population.

---

[1]Colin McEvedy and Richard Jones, *Atlas of World Population History* (New York: Penguin Books, 1978), 13–15.

1-4 **Life in Neolithic Communities**

What cultural and social consequences of sedentary agriculture differentiated life in the Neolithic period from the hunter-gatherer lifestyle of earlier periods?

Evidence that an ecological crisis may have driven people to food production has prompted a reexamination of the assumption that farmers enjoyed better lives than foragers. Modern studies demonstrate that food producers have to work much harder and for much longer periods than do food gatherers, clearing and cultivating land, guiding herds to pastures, and guarding them from predators.

Although early farmers were less likely to starve because they could store food between harvests, their diet was less varied and nutritious than that of foragers. Skeletal remains show that Neolithic farmers were shorter on average than earlier food-gathering peoples. Farmers were also more likely to die at an earlier age because people in permanent settlements were more exposed to diseases. Their water was contaminated by human waste; disease-bearing vermin and insects infested their bodies and homes; and they could catch new diseases from their domesticated animals.

1-4a **The Triumph of Food Producers**

So how did farmers displace foragers? Some researchers have envisioned a violent struggle between practitioners of the two ways of life; others have argued for a more peaceful transition. In most cases, farmers seem to have displaced foragers by gradual infiltration rather than by conquest.

The key to the food producers' expansion may have been the fact that their small surpluses gave them a long-term advantage in population growth by ensuring higher survival rates during times of drought or other crisis. Archaeologist Colin Renfrew argues that over a few centuries farming population densities in Europe could have increased by a factor of 50 to 100. As population rose, individuals who had to farm far from their native village would have formed a new settlement close to their fields. A steady, nonviolent expansion of only 12 to 19 miles (20 to 30 kilometers) a generation could have repopulated the whole of Europe between 6500 and 3500 BCE.[2] So gradual a process need not have provoked sharp conflicts with existing foragers, who simply could have stayed clear of the agricultural frontier or gradually adopted agriculture themselves. New studies that map genetic changes also attest to a gradual spread of agricultural people across Europe from southeast to northwest.[3]

The expanding farming communities were organized around kinship and marriage. *Nuclear families* (parents and their children) probably lived in separate households but felt solidarity with all those related to them by descent from common ancestors. These kinship units, known as lineages (**LIN-ee-ij**) or clans, acted together to defend their common interests and land. Some societies trace descent equally through both parents, but most give greater importance to descent through either the mother (matrilineal [**mat-ruh-LIN-ee-uhl**] societies) or the father (patrilineal [**pat-ruh-LIN-ee-uhl**] societies). It is important not to confuse tracing descent through women (matrilineality) with the rule of women (matriarchy [**MAY-tree-ahr-key**]).

1-4b **Cultural Expressions**

Kinship systems influenced early agricultural people's outlook on the world. Burials of elders might be occasions for elaborate ceremonies expressing their descendants' group solidarity. Plastered skulls found in the ancient city of Jericho (**JER-ih-koh**) (see Map 2.1) may be evidence of such early ancestor reverence or worship.

AP® Exam Tip

Explain how technological innovations led to improvements in agricultural production, trade, and transportation.

---

[2]Colin Renfrew, *Archaeology and Language: The Puzzle of Indo-European Origins* (New York: Cambridge University Press, 1988), 125, 150.

[3]Cavalli-Sforza, L. Luca, Paolo Menozzi, and Alberto Piazza, *The History and Geography of Human Genes* (Princeton, NJ: Princeton University Press, 1994).

A society's religious beliefs tend to reflect its relations to nature. The religion of food gatherers centered on sacred groves, springs, and wild animals, while pastoralists worshiped the sky-god who controlled the rains and guided their migrations. In contrast, the religion of many farming communities centered on the Earth Mother; since women bear children, a female deity was logically believed to be the source of all new life.

The worship of ancestors, gods of the heavens, and earthly nature and fertility deities varied from place to place, and many societies combined the different elements. A recently discovered complex of stone structures in the Egyptian desert that was in use by 5000 BCE includes burial chambers presumably for ancestors, a calendar circle, and pairs of upright stones that frame the rising sun at the summer solstice. The builders must have been deeply concerned with the cycle of the seasons and how they were linked to the movement of heavenly bodies. Other **megaliths** (meaning "big stones") were erected elsewhere. Observation and worship of the sun are evident at the famous Stonehenge site in England, constructed about 2000 BCE. Megalithic burial chambers dating from 4000 BCE are evidence of ancestor rituals in western and southern Europe. The early ones appear to have been communal burial chambers, erected by descent groups to mark their claims to farmland. In the Middle East, the Americas, and other parts of the world, giant earth burial mounds may have served similar functions.

Another fundamental contribution of the Neolithic period was the dissemination of the large language families that form the basis of most languages spoken today. The root language of the giant Indo-European language family arose around 5000 BCE, probably in the region north of the Black and Caspian Seas. Its spread to the south and west across Europe and south and east into Anatolia (modern Turkey), Iran, and the Indian subcontinent may have been the work of pioneering agriculturalists. In the course of this very gradual expansion, Celtic, Germanic, Romance, Slavic, Iranian, and Indian languages developed. Similarly, the Afro-Asiatic language family of the Middle East and northern Africa may have been the result of food producers' expansion, as might the spread of the Sino-Tibetan family in East and Southeast Asia.

1-4c Early Towns and Specialists

Most early farmers lived in small villages, but in some parts of the world a few villages grew into more densely populated towns that were centers of trade and specialized crafts. These towns had grander dwellings and ceremonial buildings, as well as large structures for storing surplus food until the next harvest. Farmers could make most of the buildings, tools, and containers they needed in their spare time, but in large communities some craft specialists devoted their full time to making products of unusual complexity or beauty.

Two early towns in the Middle East that have been extensively excavated are Jericho on the west bank of the Jordan River and Çatal Hüyük (**cha-TAHL hoo-YOOK**) in central Turkey

megaliths Structures and complexes of very large stones constructed for ceremonial and religious purposes in Neolithic times.

◀ **The Stone Alignments at Carnac**   In the vicinity of the village of Carnac, in Brittany, France, over 3,000 stones were erected by the Neolithic population between 5000 and 3000 BCE. Especially intriguing are the so-called alignments of single stones (*menhirs*) that fan out for almost a mile. Some scholars think they served as an astronomical observatory, while others think they pointed to burials or sacred spaces.   age fotostock/Alamy Stock Photo

◀ **Model of the Early Town at Çatal Hüyük** Note the buildings directly abutting one another, with main access by rooftop entrance, and the outermost structures serving as a defensive wall. Cultivated fields lay outside the city perimeter. De Agostini Picture Library/Getty Images

(Map 2.1 shows their locations). Jericho, located near a natural spring, was an unusually large and elaborate agricultural settlement around 8000 BCE whose round, mud-brick dwellings may have been modeled on hunters' tents. A millennium later, rectangular buildings with finely plastered walls and floors and wide doorways opened onto central courtyards. A massive stone wall surrounding the 10-acre (4-hectare) settlement defended it against attacks.

The ruins of Çatal Hüyük, an even larger town, date to between 7000 and 5000 BCE and cover 32 acres (13 hectares). Its residents also occupied plastered mud-brick rooms with elaborate decorations, but Çatal Hüyük had no defensive wall. Instead, the walls of the town's outermost houses formed a continuous barrier without doors or large windows. Residents entered their house by means of ladders through holes in the roof.

Çatal Hüyük prospered from long-distance trade in obsidian, a hard volcanic rock that craftspeople made into tools, weapons, mirrors, and ornaments. Other residents made fine pottery, wove baskets and woolen cloth, made stone and shell beads, and worked leather and wood. House sizes varied, but there is no evidence of a dominant class or centralized political structure. Fields around the town produced crops of barley and emmer wheat, as well as vegetables. Pigs were kept along with goats and sheep. Yet wild foods—acorns, wild grains, and game animals—still featured prominently in the residents' diet.

Wall paintings, remarkably similar to earlier cave paintings, reveal the continuing importance of hunting. Scenes depict people adorned with the skins of wild leopards, and men were buried with weapons of war and hunting, not the tools of farming.

There is a religious shrine for every two houses. Many rooms contain depictions of horned wild bulls, female breasts, goddesses, leopards, and handprints. Rituals involved burning grains, legumes, and meat as offerings, but there is no evidence of live animal sacrifice. Statues of plump female deities far outnumber statues of male deities, suggesting that the inhabitants primarily venerated a goddess of fertility. According to the site's principal excavator, "it seems extremely likely that the cult of the goddess was administered mainly by women."[4]

---

[4]James Mellaart, *Çatal Hüyük: A Neolithic Town in Anatolia* (New York: McGraw-Hill, 1967), 202.

Section Review

- The lives of farmers are, in many respects, harder and more hazardous than those of hunter-gatherers.

- Because of their capacity to increase their population, agriculturalists expanded across much of the planet at the expense of hunter-gatherers. The process was gradual and largely peaceful.

- Megaliths and other monumental structures are products of the diverse religious beliefs and practices of Neolithic societies.

- The spread of several large language families, including the Indo-European family, may have been linked to the spread of agriculture.

- In some places small agricultural villages developed into towns that were centers of trade and home to sophisticated craftspeople and people in other specialized professions. Farmers had to produce surpluses to feed nonfarming specialists.

- Jericho and Çatal Hüyük are two excavated sites that give us vivid glimpses of early Neolithic towns.

Metalworking became an important specialized occupation in the late Neolithic period. At Çatal Hüyük objects of copper and lead—metals that occur naturally in a fairly pure form—date to about 6400 BCE. In many parts of the world silver and gold were also worked at an early date. Because of their rarity and softness, those metals did not replace stone tools and weapons but were used primarily to make decorative or ceremonial objects. The discovery of many such objects in graves suggests they were symbols of status and power.

The emergence of towns and individuals engaged in crafts and other specialized occupations added to the workload of agriculturalists. Extra food had to be produced for nonfarmers such as priests and artisans. Added labor was needed to build permanent houses, town walls, and towers, not to mention religious structures and megalithic monuments. It is not known whether these tasks were performed freely or coerced.

1-5 Conclusion

The theory of evolution, supported by an enormous body of evidence, leads to far-reaching conclusions. Every living species evolved from a common ancestor. Humans are descended from earlier hominid species that evolved in Africa beginning about 7 million years ago, and every modern human being is descended from communities that evolved in Africa sometime between 80,000 to 50,000 years ago, with some groups then migrating to the other habitable continents. However diverse their cultures became, all human communities are directly related—to each other, to all other living species, and to the earth.

More than 2 million years ago there was a dramatic increase in the variety of tools early humans made—above all from stone, but also from bone, skin, wood, and plant fiber. Paleolithic families enjoyed a primarily vegetarian diet, though their skill at making weapons also made them effective hunters. Work was divided along gender lines, with women responsible for food gathering, cooking, and childrearing, and men for activities such as hunting because of their greater upper-body strength. Humans acquired a profound knowledge of the natural world that helped them create clothing, medicine, and other useful products. Cave and rock art opens a tantalizing window onto their imaginative and spiritual lives.

Research suggests that climate change drove the first human communities to abandon hunting and gathering and adopt the practices of agriculture and pastoralism. In the warmer era following the Great Ice Age around 9000 BCE, populations on every major continent except Australia underwent this great transformation, selecting high-yield strains of plants for cultivation and breeding livestock for the consumption of meat and dairy products. By 5000 BCE wheat and barley had been domesticated in the Middle East; sorghum in Africa; rice in India and Southeast Asia; and corn, beans, and squash in Mesoamerica. After the dog, the first animals to be domesticated were sheep, goats, and cattle. Many people living in far northern and southern latitudes never adopted agriculture, but for those who did the consequences were enormous. In less than 10,000 years the global human population increased from 2 to 10 million.

Farming and settled life in the Neolithic period brought plagues of animal-borne diseases and a more labor-intensive way of life, but also the prosperity that gave rise to the first towns, trade, and specialized occupations. Human beings' intimate relationship to their ancestors, the earth, and seasonal cycles of death and rebirth is revealed by archaeological sites with a clearly religious significance—from the megalithic monuments of northern Europe to the household shrines at Çatal Hüyük. However foreign the world of our ancestors may seem, the scientific study of prehistory has brought us much closer to understanding it.

Key Terms

evolution p. 6	*Homo habilis* p. 7	Stone Age p. 11	Agricultural Revolutions
australopithecines p. 6	*Homo erectus* p. 7	Paleolithic p. 11	p. 16
hominid p. 6	*Homo naledi* p. 8	Neolithic p. 11	megaliths p. 22
bipedalism p. 6	*Homo sapiens* p. 8	foragers p. 13	
Great Ice Age p. 7	culture p. 11		

Review Questions

1. The agricultural revolutions led to a large increase in the human population. What do you think were some of the consequences of that vastly increased population?

2. The change from hunting and gathering to agriculture meant that men replaced women as the major providers of food. How did this change the activities, social status, and interactions of men and women?

3. As people became sedentary agriculturalists, they acquired fixed residences where they could accumulate and store more possessions. How might that affect the social and economic organization of human communities?

 MindTap® is a fully online, personalized learning experience built upon Cengage Learning content. MindTap® combines student learning tools—readings, multimedia, activities, and assessments—into a singular Learning Path that guides students through the course and helps students develop the critical thinking, analysis, and communication skills that are essential to academic and professional success.

Multiple-Choice Questions

Questions 1–3 refer to the image below.

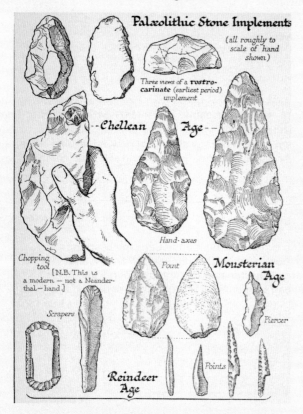

▲ **Paleolithic Stone Tools** Private Collection/Ken Welsh/Bridgeman Images

1. The Paleolithic tools in the picture can be used to provide evidence of which of the following?

    (A) Paleolithic people used tools that they found when scavenging.

    (B) Paleolithic people needed sophisticated tools to survive.

    (C) Paleolithic people needed tools to plant and harvest crops.

    (D) Paleolithic people used their tools primarily for protection against hostile groups.

2. As early humans migrated out of East Africa in the Paleolithic era, why was it necessary for them to develop diverse technologies?

    (A) The new regions were populated by dangerous tribes making weapons of defense necessary.

    (B) Trade with other nomadic groups led to the development of new tools of communication.

    (C) Fertile land reduced the need for hunting tools and required farm implements.

    (D) Adaptation to new climatic regions required a new range of tools and clothing.

3. Which of the following statements best describes the social structure of most humans during the Paleolithic era?

    (A) Isolated large groups with an elected leader who made all major decisions

    (B) Family units that usually did not interact with other groups

    (C) Small groups that exchanged ideas and goods with other clans

    (D) Large villages that relied on both hunting and cultivation for survival

Questions 4–7 refer to the image below.

▲ **Settlement plan discovered in Çatal Hüyük excavations, Anatolian Civilization Museum, Ankara, Turkey** Images & Stories/Alamy Stock Photo

4. The map of Çatal Hüyük provides evidence of which of the following characteristics of urban life after the Neolithic Revolution?

    (A) Urban communities had to work cooperatively to establish ordered settlements for large groups to inhabit.

    (B) Religious belief systems led to patriarchal domination, which resulted in most of the power concentrated in elder males.

    (C) Urban areas were overpopulated, which led to violence and frequent revolts.

    (D) Urban areas rivaled modern cities in size and influence.

5. The Neolithic Revolution led to the development of sedentary agriculturalist communities like Çatal Hüyük and was responsible for all of the following changes in society EXCEPT

    (A) a more reliable food supply.

    (B) a heavy influence of religion.

    (C) specialized labor.

    (D) population growth.

6. Pastoral groups were less likely to develop sedentary societies like Çatal Hüyük for which of the following reasons?

(A) They tended to develop in river valleys where there was an abundance of fertile soil.

(B) They were forced into uninhabitable areas by conflicts that marginalized some groups.

(C) They survived on a diet of only animal-based food.

(D) They lived on arid grasslands that provided fodder for domesticated animal herds.

7. What did the locations of early civilizations like Çatal Hüyük all have in common?

(A) They were located in arid areas with little rainfall.

(B) They were able to support flourishing agricultural settlements.

(C) They were able to access large reserves of iron needed for toolmaking.

(D) They were in temperate zones with seasonal rains.

Questions 8–10 refer to the image below.

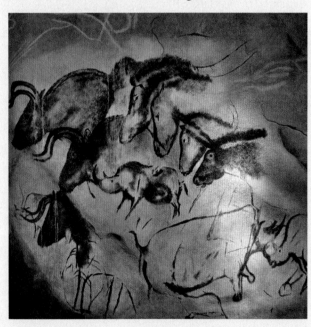

▲ **Painted Animals in Chauvet Cave, France** HIP/Art Resource, NY

8. Which of the following allowed for the development of artwork like that seen in the cave painting above?

(A) Increasing understanding of the environment passed down orally

(B) Creation of early schools and educational facilities

(C) Gender-diversified social settings allowing women to focus on creating art

(D) Development of stone tools to carve into the cave walls

9. Realistic images like the ones in the cave painting could be used to reaffirm which of the following assertions about early humans?

(A) Early communities remained nomadic because of a lack of food sources.

(B) Artists and storytellers were the lowest level of the social hierarchy.

(C) Early images may have had a religious or magical purpose.

(D) Development of stone tools that were used to carve into the cave walls.

10. In addition to artistic development, early human societies before 5000 BCE demonstrated what other advancements?

(A) Gender-neutral societies where all individuals were equal

(B) Monotheistic religions

(C) Legal advancement such as early law codes

(D) Technological innovations such as pottery and the wheel

Short-Answer Questions

1. Answer all parts of the question that follows.

(A) Identify ONE way environmental factors influenced early migration and settlement.

(B) Explain ONE way early humans used technology to overcome geographic barriers to migration.

(C) Explain ONE ADDITIONAL way early humans used technology to overcome geographic barriers to migration.

2. Answer all parts of the question that follows.

(A) Identify ONE cause of the Neolithic (Agricultural) Revolution.

(B) Explain ONE way the Neolithic (Agricultural) Revolution CHANGED the economic or social systems of humans.

(C) Explain ONE way the economic or social systems of humans CONTINUED despite the Neolithic (Agricultural) Revolution.

2 The First River-Valley Civilizations, 3500–1500 BCE

AP® Framework Terms

Mesopotamia
Nile River Valley (Egypt)
Indus River Valley (Mohenjo-Daro)
Monumental architecture

Overarching Questions

1 How have environmental factors shaped the development of diverse technologies, industrialization, transportation methods, and exchange and communication networks? (ENV)

2 How have religions, belief systems, philosophies, and ideologies affected the political, economic, and social development of societies? (CUL)

3 In what ways do cultural artifacts reflect innovation, adaptation, and creativity of specific societies? (CUL)

4 How have different forms of governance been constructed and maintained over time? (SB)

5 How have distinctions based on kinship, ethnicity, class, gender, and race influenced the development and transformations of social hierarchies? (SOC)

The *Epic of Gilgamesh*, whose roots date to before 2000 BCE, defines *civilization* as the people of ancient Mesopotamia (present-day Iraq) understood it. Gilgamesh, an early king (who may be depicted on the sculpture shown here), sends a temple prostitute to tame Enkidu (**EN-kee-doo**), a wild man who lives like an animal in the grasslands. Using her sexual charms to win Enkidu's trust, the temple prostitute tells him:

> Come with me to the city, to Uruk (**OO-rook**), to the temple of Anu and the goddess Ishtar . . . to Uruk, where the processions are and music, let us go together through the dancing to the palace hall where Gilgamesh presides.[1]

She clothes Enkidu and teaches him to eat cooked food, drink beer, and bathe and oil his body. Her words and actions signal the principal traits of civilized life in ancient Mesopotamia.

---

[1]David Ferry, *Gilgamesh: A New Rendering in English Verse* (New York: Noonday Press, 1992).

▲ **Gilgamesh Strangling a Lion** This eighth-century BCE sculpture of a king, possibly Gilgamesh, from the palace of the Assyrian king Sargon II, represents the magical power and omnipotence of kingship. The Gilgamesh story was still popular in Mesopotamia twenty centuries after the king of Uruk's lifetime. DeAgostini/DeAgostini/Superstock

The Mesopotamians, like other peoples throughout history, equated civilization with their own way of life, but *civilization* is an ambiguous concept, and the charge that a particular group is "uncivilized" has been used throughout human history to justify many distressing acts. Thus it is important to explain the common claim that the first advanced civilizations emerged in Mesopotamia and Egypt sometime before 3000 BCE.

Certain political, social, economic, and technological traits are usually seen as indicators of **civilization**: (1) cities as administrative centers, (2) a political system based on control of a defined territory rather than kinship connections, (3) many people engaged in specialized, non-food-producing activities, (4) status distinctions based largely on accumulation of substantial wealth by some groups, (5) monumental building, (6) a system for keeping permanent records, (7) long-distance trade, and (8) major advances in science and the arts. The earliest societies exhibiting these traits developed in the floodplains of great rivers: the Tigris (**TIE-gris**) and Euphrates (**you-FRAY-teez**) in Iraq, the Indus in Pakistan, the Yellow (Huang He [**hwang huh**]) in China, and the Nile in Egypt (see Map 2.1). The periodic flooding of the rivers deposited fertile silt and provided water for agriculture, but it also threatened lives and property. To protect themselves and channel the forces of nature, people living near the rivers created new technologies and forms of political and social organization.

In this chapter we trace the rise of complex societies in Mesopotamia, Egypt, and the Indus River Valley from approximately 3500 to 1500 BCE (China, developing slightly later, is discussed in Chapter 4.) Our starting point roughly coincides with the origins of writing, allowing us to observe aspects of human experience not revealed by archaeological evidence alone. ●

2-1 **Mesopotamia**

How did Mesopotamian civilization emerge, and what technologies promoted its advancement?

Mesopotamia means "land between the rivers" in Greek. The name reflects the centrality of the Euphrates and Tigris Rivers to the way of life in this region (see Map 2.2). Mesopotamian civilization developed in the plain alongside and between the rivers, which originate in the mountains of eastern Anatolia (modern Turkey) and empty into the Persian Gulf. This is

civilization An ambiguous term often used to denote more complex societies but sometimes used by anthropologists to describe any group of people sharing a set of cultural traits.

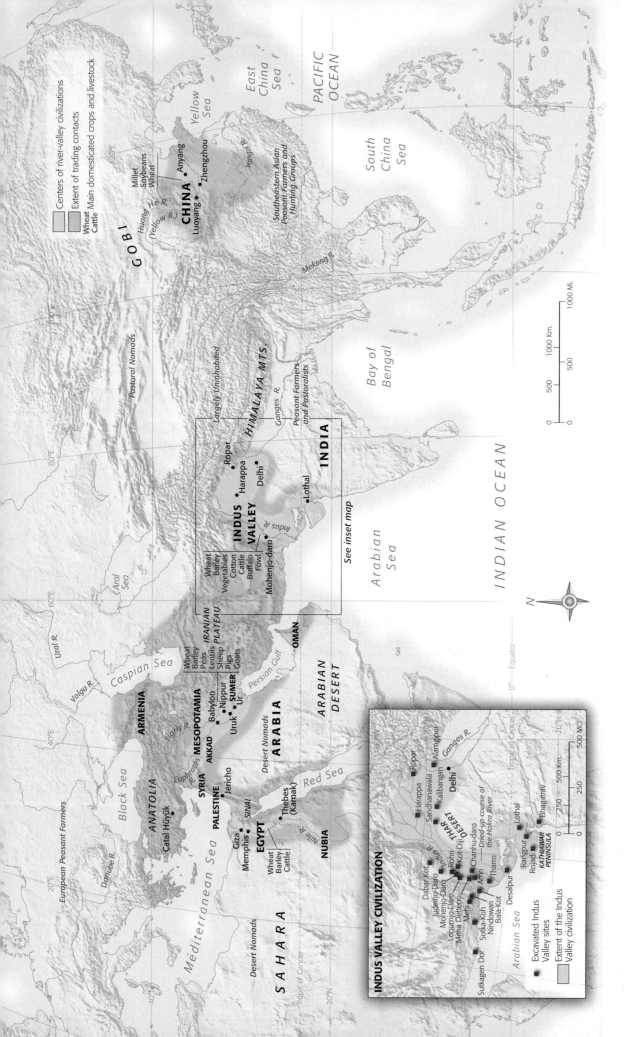

MAP 2.1   River-Valley Civilizations, 3500–1500 BCE The earliest complex societies arose in the floodplains of large rivers: in the fourth millennium BCE in the valley of the Tigris and Euphrates Rivers in Mesopotamia and the Nile River in Egypt, in the third millennium BCE in the valley of the Indus River in Pakistan, and in the second millennium BCE in the valley of the Yellow River in China.

Which geographical features are common to the three early civilizations covered in this chapter?

CHRONOLOGY

	Mesopotamia	Egypt	Indus Valley
3500 BCE		3100–2575 BCE Early Dynastic	
3000 BCE	3000–2350 BCE Early Dynastic (Sumerian)		
2500 BCE	2350–2230 BCE Akkadian (Semitic)	2575–2134 BCE Old Kingdom	2600 BCE Beginning of Indus Valley civilization
	2112–2004 BCE Third Dynasty of Ur (Sumerian)	2134–2040 BCE First Intermediate Period	
		2040–1640 BCE Middle Kingdom	
2000 BCE	1900–1600 BCE Old Babylonian (Semitic)	1640–1532 BCE Second Intermediate Period	1900 BCE End of Indus Valley civilization
1500 BCE	1500–1150 BCE Kassite	1532–1070 BCE New Kingdom	

an alluvial plain—a flat, fertile expanse built up over many millennia by silt that the rivers deposited.

Mesopotamia lies mostly within modern Iraq. To the north and east, an arc of mountains extends from northern Syria and southeastern Anatolia to the Zagros (**ZAG-ruhs**) Mountains, which separate the plain from the Iranian Plateau. The Syrian and Arabian deserts lie to the west and southwest, the Persian Gulf to the southeast.

AP® Exam Tip
Know where the core foundational civilizations developed and explain how agriculture helped those regions mature into states.

2-1a Settled Agriculture in an Unstable Landscape

Although the first domestication of plants and animals took place in the "Fertile Crescent" region of northern Syria and southeastern Anatolia around 8000 BCE, agriculture did not come to southern Mesopotamia until approximately 5000 BCE. Lacking adequate rainfall (at least 8 inches [20 centimeters] is needed annually), farming in hot, dry southern Mesopotamia depended on irrigation—the artificial provision of water to crops. At first, people probably took advantage of the occasional flooding of the rivers into nearby fields, but the floods could be sudden and violent and tended to come at the wrong time for grain agriculture—in the spring when the crop was ripening in the field. Moreover, the floods sometimes caused the rivers to suddenly change course, cutting off fields and population centers from water and from travel and transport of trade goods on the river. Shortly after 3000 BCE the Mesopotamians learned to construct canals to carry water to more distant fields.

By 4000 BCE farmers were using ox-drawn plows to turn over the earth. An attached funnel dropped a carefully measured amount of seed into the furrow. Barley was the main cereal crop because of its ability to tolerate hot, dry conditions and withstand the salt drawn to the surface by evaporation. Fields were left fallow (unplanted) every other year to replenish the nutrients in the soil. Date palms provided food, fiber, and wood, while garden plots produced vegetables. Reed plants, which grew on the riverbanks and in the marshy southern delta, could be woven into mats, baskets, huts, and boats. Fish was a dietary staple. Herds of sheep and goats, which grazed on fallow land or beyond the zone of cultivation, provided wool, milk, and meat. Donkeys, originally domesticated in northeast Africa, and cattle carried or pulled burdens; in the second millennium BCE they were joined by newly introduced camels from Arabia and horses from the mountains.

2-1b Sumerians and Semites

The people living in Mesopotamia at the start of the "historical period"—the period for which we have written evidence—were the **Sumerians**. Archaeological evidence places them in southern Mesopotamia by 5000 BCE and perhaps even earlier. The Sumerians created the framework of civilization in Mesopotamia during a long period of dominance in the fourth and third

Sumerians The people who dominated southern Mesopotamia through the end of the third millennium BCE.

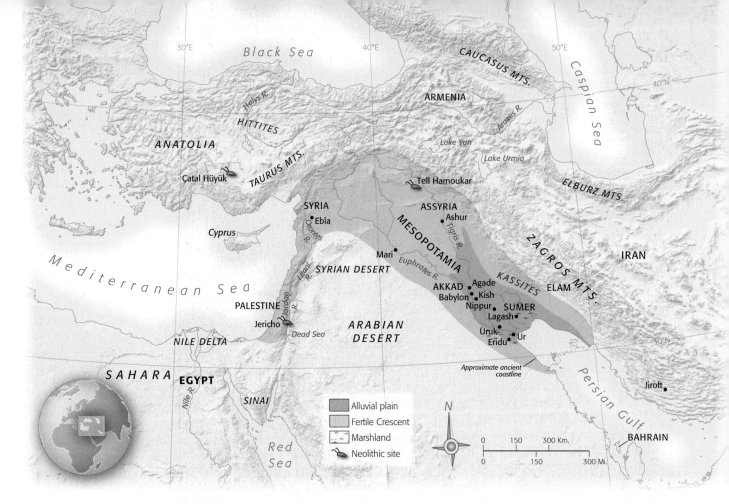

MAP 2.2   Mesopotamia   In order to organize labor resources to create and maintain an irrigation network in the Tigris-Euphrates Valley, a land of little rain, the Sumerians of southern Mesopotamia developed new technologies, complex political and social institutions, and distinctive cultural practices.

Why was Mesopotamia more vulnerable to migrations and invasions than Egypt or the Indus Valley?

millennia BCE. Other peoples lived in Mesopotamia as well. Personal names recorded in inscriptions from northern cities from as early as 2900 BCE reveal the presence of people who spoke a **Semitic (suh-MIT-ik)** language. (*Semitic* refers to a family of languages spoken in parts of western Asia and northern Africa, including ancient Hebrew, Aramaic [**ar-uh-MAY-ik**], Phoenician [**fi-NEE-shuhn**], and modern Arabic.) Possibly the descendants of nomads who had migrated into the Mesopotamian plain from the western desert, these Semites seem to have lived in peace with the Sumerians, adopting their culture and sometimes achieving positions of wealth and power.

By 2000 BCE the Semitic peoples had become politically dominant, and from this time forward the Semitic language Akkadian (**uh-KAY-dee-uhn**) supplanted Sumerian, although the Sumerian cultural legacy was preserved. Sumerian-Akkadian dictionaries were compiled, Sumerian literature was translated, and the gods, mythology, and religious practices of the Sumerians were adopted and adapted by the Semitic peoples of the region. This cultural synthesis parallels a biological merging of Sumerians and Semites through intermarriage. Other ethnic groups, including mountain peoples such as the Kassites (**KAS-ite**) as well as Elamites (**EE-luh-mite**) and Persians from Iran, played a part in Mesopotamian history. But not until the arrival of Greeks in the late fourth century BCE was the Sumerian-Semitic cultural heritage of Mesopotamia fundamentally altered.

2-1c   Cities, Kings, and Trade

Mesopotamia was a land of villages and cities. Groups of farming families banded together in villages to protect one another; work together at key times in the agricultural cycle; and share tools, barns, and threshing floors. Village society also provided companionship and a pool of potential marriage partners.

Semitic Family of related languages long spoken across parts of western Asia and northern Africa. In antiquity these languages included Hebrew, Aramaic, and Phoenician. The most widespread modern member of the Semitic family is Arabic.

Most cities evolved from villages. When a successful village grew, small satellite villages developed nearby and eventually merged with the main village to form an urban center. Historians use the term **city-state** to designate these self-governing urban centers and the agricultural territories they controlled.

Scholars have long believed that the earliest cities and complex societies arose in southern Mesopotamia in the fourth millennium BCE, as a result of the need to organize labor to create and maintain irrigation channels. However, recent archaeological discoveries in northern Mesopotamia, where agriculture first developed in this part of the world and was sustained by rainfall, are suggesting a more complicated picture, as a number of sites in northeast Syria appear to have developed urban centers, bureaucracy, and other elements of social complexity at roughly the same time.

Cities needed food, and many Mesopotamian city dwellers went out each day to labor in nearby fields. However, some urban residents did not engage in food production but instead specialized in crafts, manufacturing pottery, artwork, and clothing, as well as weapons, tools, and other objects forged out of metal. Others served the gods or carried out administrative duties. These urban specialists depended on the surplus food production from the villages in their vicinity. In return, the city provided rural districts with military protection against bandits and raiders and a market where villagers could acquire manufactured goods produced by urban specialists.

Stretches of uncultivated land, either desert or swamp, served as buffers between the many small city-states of early Mesopotamia. Nevertheless, disputes over land, water rights, and movable property often sparked hostilities between neighboring cities and prompted most to build protective walls of sun-dried mud bricks.

Southern Mesopotamians opened new land to agriculture by building and maintaining irrigation networks. Dams raised the level of the river so that water could flow by gravity into canals, which brought water to fields far from the rivers. Drainage ditches carried water away from flooded fields before evaporation could draw salt and minerals harmful to crops to the surface. Dikes protected fields near the riverbanks from floods. Because the rivers carried so much silt, clogged channels needed constant dredging.

Successful construction and maintenance of these irrigation systems required leaders who were able to organize large numbers of people to work together. Other projects called for similar coordination: the harvest, sheep shearing, the construction of fortification walls and large public buildings, and warfare. Little is known about the political institutions of early Mesopotamian city-states, although there are traces of a citizens' assembly that may have evolved from the traditional village council. The two centers of power attested in written records are the temple and the palace of the king.

AP® Exam Tip
Understand how specialization of labor developed in core civilizations and compare labor organization across different societies.

AP® Exam Tip
Explain how early civilizations developed monumental architecture and urban planning.

city-state A small independent state consisting of an urban center and the surrounding agricultural territory; a characteristic political form in early Mesopotamia, Archaic and Classical Greece, Phoenicia, and early Italy.

▼ **Law Code of Hammurabi**   The relief sculpture at the top of the black basalt stele shows Hammurabi facing the seated Sun-god, Shamash, who is associated with the concept of Justice. The laws, written in Akkadian cuneiform, fill the rest of the monument. Roman Milert/Alamy Stock Photo, jsp/Shutterstock.com

Each city had one or more centrally located temples that housed the *cult* (a set of religious practices) of the deity or deities who watched over the community. The temples owned extensive agricultural lands and stored the gifts that worshipers donated. The leading priests, who controlled the shrines and managed their wealth, played prominent political and economic roles in early communities.

In the third millennium BCE the *lugal* (**LOO-gahl**), or "big man"—we would call him a king—emerged in Sumerian cities. A plausible theory maintains that certain men chosen by the community to lead the armies in time of war extended their authority in peacetime and assumed key judicial and ritual functions. The location of the temple in the city's heart and the less prominent location of the king's palace attest to the later emergence of royalty.

The priests and temples retained influence because of their wealth and religious mystique, but they gradually became dependent on the palace. Normally, the king portrayed himself as the deity's earthly representative and saw to the upkeep and building of temples and the proper performance of ritual. Other royal responsibilities included maintaining city walls and defenses, extending and repairing irrigation channels, guarding property rights, warding off outside attackers, and establishing justice.

AP® Exam Tip
Identify and explain how core civilizations unified their regions.

Some city-states became powerful enough to dominate others. **Sargon** (**SAHR-gone**), ruler of the city of Akkad (**AH-kahd**) around 2350 BCE, was the first to unite many cities under one king and capital. Sargon and the four family members who succeeded him over a period of 120 years secured their power in several ways. They razed the walls of conquered cities and installed governors backed by garrisons of Akkadian troops, and they gave land to soldiers to ensure their loyalty. Being of Semitic stock, they adapted the cuneiform (**kyoo-NEE-uh-form**) system of writing used for Sumerian (discussed later in the chapter) to express their own language.

For reasons that remain obscure, the Akkadian state fell around 2230 BCE. The Sumerian language and culture became dominant again in the cities of the southern plain under the Third Dynasty of Ur (2112–2004 BCE). Through campaigns of conquest and marriage alliances, this dynasty of five kings flourished for a century. Although not controlling territories as extensive as those of the Akkadians, they maintained tight control by means of a rapidly expanding bureaucracy of administrators and obsessive record keeping. Messengers and well-maintained road stations enabled rapid communication, and an official calendar, standardized weights and measures, and uniform writing practices increased the efficiency of the central administration.

In the northwest the kings erected a great wall 125 miles (201 kilometers) in length to keep out the nomadic Amorites (**AM-uh-rite**), but in the end nomad incursions combined with an Elamite attack from the southeast toppled the Third Dynasty of Ur. The Semitic Amorites founded a new city at **Babylon**, not far from Akkad. Toward the end of a long reign, **Hammurabi** (**HAM-uh-rah-bee**) (r. 1792–1750 BCE) launched a series of aggressive military campaigns, and Babylon became the capital of what historians call the "Old Babylonian" state, which stretched beyond Sumer and Akkad into the north and northwest from 1900 to 1600 BCE. Hammurabi's famous Law Code, inscribed on a polished black stone pillar, provided judges with a lengthy set of examples illustrating principles to use in deciding cases (and thereby left us a fascinating window on the activities of everyday life). Many offenses were met with severe physical punishments and, not infrequently, the death penalty. Penalties for crimes prescribed in the Law Code depended on the class of the offender, with the most severe punishments reserved for the lower orders.

Sargon The first Mesopotamian ruler to gain control of multiple city-states, as the Semitic-speaking peoples began to dominate the region.

Babylon The largest and most important city in Mesopotamia. It achieved particular eminence as the capital of the Amorite king Hammurabi in the eighteenth century BCE.

Hammurabi Amorite ruler of Babylon (r. 1792–1750 BCE). He conquered many city-states in southern and northern Mesopotamia and is best known for a code of laws, inscribed on a black stone pillar, illustrating the principles to be used in legal cases.

Hammurabi's approach to justice is clear in the following set of related laws:

196. If a free person puts out the eye of another free person, that person's eye shall be put out.
197. If a free person breaks the bone of another free person, that person's bone shall be broken.
198. If a free person puts out the eye or breaks the bone of a civil-servant, that person shall pay one-half kilogram of silver.
199. If a free person puts out the eye or breaks the bone of another free person's slave, that person shall pay half the value of the slave.[2]

We see here a simple formula for restitution when one free person has been physically injured by another, with the offender forced to suffer the same loss. This "eye for an eye" principle can then be extended to any body part. But we also see that some people are considered more important than others, based on social standing, with the punishment for injuring a person of a lower order stipulated as a mere monetary penalty.

---

[2]See https://history.hanover.edu/courses/excerpts/165hammurabi.html.

The far-reaching conquests of some states were motivated, at least in part, by the need to obtain vital resources. The alternative was to trade for raw materials, and long-distance commerce flourished in most periods. Evidence of boats used in river and sea trade appears as early as the fifth millennium BCE. Recent archaeological discoveries outside the core zone in southern Mesopotamia—in Anatolia, northern Mesopotamia, and Iran—are demonstrating that cities and complex societies were evolving across western Asia, probably as a consequence of the long-distance trade networks. Wool, barley, and vegetable oil were exported in exchange for wood from cedar forests in Lebanon and Syria, silver from Anatolia, gold from Egypt, copper from the eastern Mediterranean and Oman (on the Arabian peninsula), and tin from Afghanistan. Precious stones used for jewelry and carved figurines came from Iran, Afghanistan, and Pakistan.

In the third millennium BCE merchants were primarily employed by the palace or temple, the only two institutions with the financial resources and long-distance connections to organize the collection, transport, and protection of goods. Merchants exchanged surplus food from the estates of kings or temples for raw materials and luxury goods. In the second millennium BCE more commerce came into the hands of independent merchants, and *guilds* (cooperative associations formed by merchants) became powerful forces in Mesopotamian society. Items could be bartered—traded for one another—or valued in relation to fixed weights of precious metal, primarily silver, or measures of grain.

2-1d Mesopotamian Society

Urbanized civilizations generate social divisions—variations in the status and legal and political privileges of certain groups of people. The rise of cities, specialization of labor, centralization of power, and the use of written records enabled some groups to amass unprecedented wealth. Temple leaders and kings controlled large agricultural estates, and the palace administration collected taxes from subjects. An elite class acquired large landholdings, and soldiers and religious officials received plots of land in return for their services.

The Law Code of Hammurabi in eighteenth-century BCE Babylonia reflects social divisions that may also have been valid at other times. Society was divided into three classes: (1) the free, landowning class, largely living in the cities, which included royalty, high-ranking officials,

AP® Exam Tip
Understand the relationship between legal codes and existing hierarchies in core civilizations.

▼ **Mesopotamian Cylinder Seal** Seals indicated the identity of an individual and were impressed into wet clay or wax to "sign" legal documents or to mark ownership of an object. This seal, produced in the period of the Akkadian Empire, depicts Ea (second from right), the god of underground waters, symbolized by the stream with fish emanating from his shoulders; Ishtar, whose attributes of fertility and war are indicated by the date cluster in her hand and the pointed weapons showing above her wings; and the sun-god Shamash, cutting his way out of the mountains with a jagged knife, an evocation of sunrise. The Trustees of the British Museum/Art Resource, NY

warriors, priests, merchants, and some artisans and shopkeepers; (2) the class of dependent farmers and artisans, whose legal attachment to royal, temple, or private estates made them the primary rural workforce; and (3) the class of slaves, primarily employed in domestic service. As we have seen, penalties for crimes prescribed in the Law Code depended on the class of the offender, with the most severe punishments reserved for the lower orders.

Slavery was not as prevalent and fundamental to the economy as it would be in the later societies of Greece and Rome (see Chapters 5 and 6). Many slaves came from mountain tribes, either captured in war or sold by slave traders. Others were people unable to pay their debts. Normally slaves were not chained, but they were identified by a distinctive hairstyle; if given their freedom, a barber shaved off the telltale mark. In the Old Babylonian period, as the class of people who were not dependent on the temple or palace grew in numbers and importance, the amount of land and other property in private hands increased, and the hiring of free laborers became more common. Slaves, dependent workers tied to a particular plot of land, and hired laborers were all compensated with commodities such as food and oil in quantities proportional to their age, gender, and tasks.

The daily lives of ordinary Mesopotamians, especially those in villages or on large estates in the countryside, left few archaeological or written remains. Peasants built houses of mud brick and reed, which quickly disintegrate, and they had few metal possessions. Being illiterate, they left no written record of their lives.

It is likewise difficult to discover much about the experiences of women. The written sources were produced by male **scribes**—trained professionals who applied their reading and writing skills to tasks of administration—and for the most part reflect elite male activities. Anthropologists theorize that women lost social standing and freedoms in societies where agriculture superseded hunting and gathering (see Chapter 1). In hunting-and-gathering societies women provided most of the community's food from their gathering activities, and this work was highly valued. But in Mesopotamia food production depended on the heavy physical labor of plowing, harvesting, and digging irrigation channels, jobs usually performed by men. Since food surpluses permitted families to have more children, bearing and rearing children became the primary occupation of many women, preventing them from acquiring the specialized skills of the scribe or artisan. However, women could own property, maintain control of their *dowry* (a sum of money given by the woman's father to support her in her husband's household), and even engage in trade. Some worked outside the household in textile factories and breweries or as prostitutes, tavern keepers, bakers, or fortunetellers. Nonelite women who stayed at home helped with farming, planted vegetable gardens, cooked, cleaned, fetched water, tended the household fire, and wove baskets and textiles.

The standing of women seems to have declined further in the second millennium BCE, perhaps because of the rise of an urbanized middle class and an increase in private wealth. The laws favored the rights of husbands. Although Mesopotamian society was generally monogamous, a man could take a second wife if the first gave him no children, and in later Mesopotamian history kings and wealthy men had several wives. Marriage alliances arranged between families made women into instruments for preserving and increasing family wealth. Alternatively, a family might decide to avoid a daughter's marriage—and the resulting loss of a dowry—by dedicating her to the service of a deity as a "god's bride." Constraints on women's lives that eventually became part of Islamic tradition, such as largely confining themselves to the home and wearing veils in public (see Chapter 9), may have originated in the second millennium BCE.

2-1e Gods, Priests, and Temples

The Sumerian gods embodied the forces of nature: Anu was the sky, Enlil the air, Enki fresh water, Ninhursag the earth, and Inanna presided over warfare, fertility, and sex. When the Semitic peoples became dominant, they either took over Sumerian deities or equated their deities with those of the Sumerians (e.g., Ea was correlated with Sumerian Enki, Ishtar with Inanna). Myths of the Sumerian gods were transferred to their Semitic counterparts, and many of the same rituals continued to be practiced. People imagined the gods as *anthropomorphic* (**an-thruh-puh-MORE-fik**)—like humans in form and conduct. They thought the gods had bodies and senses, sought nourishment from sacrifice, enjoyed the worship and obedience of humanity, and were driven by lust, love, hate, anger, and envy. The Mesopotamians feared their gods, believing them responsible for the natural disasters that occurred without warning in their environment, and sought to appease them.

The public, state-organized religion is most visible in the archaeological record. Cities built temples and showed devotion to the divinities who protected the community. The temple

AP® Exam Tip
Compare the development of new religious beliefs during this time period and how these beliefs influenced society and culture.

scribes In the governments of many ancient societies, a professional position reserved for men who had undergone the lengthy training required to be able to read and write using cuneiform, hieroglyphics, or other early, cumbersome writing systems.

▲ **Model of Babylon in Sixth Century BCE** Note the central location of the religious precinct and ziggurat. The function of ziggurats is unknown. Balage Balogh/Art Resource, NY

precinct, encircled by a high wall, contained the shrine of the chief deity; open-air plazas; chapels for lesser gods; housing, dining facilities, and offices for priests and other temple staff; and craft shops, storerooms, and service buildings. The most visible part of the temple compound was the **ziggurat (ZIG-uh-rat)**, a multistory, mud-brick, pyramid-shaped tower approached by ramps and stairs. Scholars are not certain of the ziggurat's function and symbolic meaning.

A temple was considered the god's residence, and the statue in its interior shrine was believed to be occupied by the deity's life force. Priests anticipated and met every need of the divine image in a daily cycle of waking, bathing, dressing, feeding, moving around, entertaining, soothing, and revering. These efforts reflected the claim of the Babylonian Creation Myth that humankind had been created from the blood of a vanquished rebel deity in order to serve the gods. Several thousand priests may have staffed a large temple like that of the chief god Marduk at Babylon.

Priests passed their hereditary office and sacred lore to their sons, and their families lived on rations of food from the deity's estates. The amount a priest received depended on his rank within a complicated hierarchy of status and specialized function. The high priest performed the central acts in the great rituals. Certain priests made music to please the gods. Others exorcised evil spirits. Still others interpreted dreams and divined the future by examining the organs of sacrificed animals, reading patterns in the rising incense smoke, or casting dice.

Harder to determine are the everyday beliefs and religious practices of the common people. Scholars do not know how much access the general public had to the temple buildings, although individuals did place votive statues in the sanctuaries, believing that these miniature replicas of themselves could continually seek the deity's favor. The survival of many **amulets** (small charms meant to protect the bearer from evil) and representations of a host of demons suggests widespread belief in magic—the use of special words and rituals to manipulate and control the forces of nature. For example, people believed that a headache was caused by a demon that could be driven out of the ailing body. In return for a gift or sacrifice, a god or goddess might reveal information about the future. We do know that elite and common folk came together in great festivals such as the twelve-day New Year's Festival held each spring in Babylon to mark the beginning of a new agricultural cycle (see Diversity & Dominance: Violence and Order in the Babylonian New Year's Festival).

ziggurat A massive pyramidal stepped tower made of mud bricks. It is associated with religious complexes in ancient Mesopotamian cities, but its function is unknown.

amulets Small charms meant to protect the bearer from evil. Found frequently in archaeological excavations in Mesopotamia and Egypt, amulets reflect the religious practices of the common people.

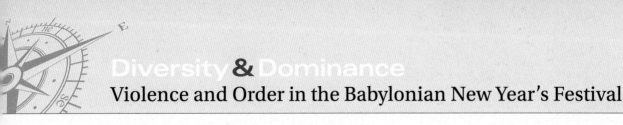
The twelve-day Babylonian New Year's Festival was one of the most important religious celebrations in ancient Mesopotamia. Fragmentary documents of the third century BCE (1,500 years after Hammurabi) provide most of our information, but because of the continuity of culture over several millennia, the later Babylonian New Year's Festival preserves many of the beliefs and practices of earlier epochs.

In the first days of the festival, most activities took place in inner chambers of the temple of Marduk, patron deity of Babylon, attended only by high-ranking priests. A key ceremony was a ritualized humiliation of the king, followed by a renewal of the institution of divinely sanctioned kingship:

On the fifth day of the month Nisannu . . . they shall bring water for washing the king's hands and then shall accompany him to the temple Esagil. The urigallu-priest shall leave the sanctuary and take away the scepter, the circle, and the sword from the king. He shall bring them before the god Bel [Marduk] and place them on a chair. He shall leave the sanctuary and strike the king's cheek. He shall accompany the king into the presence of the god Bel. He shall drag him by the ears and make him bow to the ground. The king shall speak the following only once: "I did not sin, lord of the countries. I was not neglectful of the requirements of your godship. I did not destroy Babylon. The temple Esagil, I did not forget its rites. I did not rain blows on the cheek of a subordinate." . . . [The urigallu-priest responds:] "The god Bel will listen to your prayer. He will exalt your kingship. The god Bel will bless you forever. He will destroy your enemy, fell your adversary." After the urigallu-priest says this, the king shall regain his composure. The scepter, circle, and sword shall be restored to the king.

Also in the early days of the festival, a priest recited the entire Babylonian Creation Epic to the image of Marduk. After relating the origins of the gods from the mating of two primordial creatures, Tiamat, the female embodiment of the salt sea, and Apsu, the male embodiment of fresh water, the myth tells how Tiamat gathered an army of older gods and monsters to destroy the younger generation of gods.

All the Anunnaki [the younger gods], the host of gods gathered into that place tongue-tied; they sat with mouths shut for they thought, "What other god can make war on Tiamat? No one else can face her and come back." . . . Lord Marduk exulted, . . . with racing spirits he said to the father of gods, "Creator of the gods who decides their destiny, if I must be your avenger, defeating Tiamat, saving your lives, call the Assembly, give me precedence over all the rest; . . . now and for ever let my word be law; I, not you, will decide the world's nature, the things to come. My decrees shall never be altered, never be annulled, but my creation endures to the ends of the world." . . . He took his route towards the rising sound of Tiamat's rage, and all the gods besides, the fathers of the gods pressed in around him, and the lord approached Tiamat. . . . When Tiamat heard him her wits scattered, she was possessed and shrieked aloud, her legs shook from the crotch down, she gabbled spells, muttered maledictions, while the gods of war sharpened their weapons. . . . The lord shot his net to entangle Tiamat, and the pursuing tumid wind, Imhullu, came from behind and beat in her face. When the mouth gaped open to suck him down he drove Imhullu in, so that the mouth would not shut but wind raged through her belly; her carcass blown up, tumescent. She gaped. And now he shot the arrow that split the belly, that pierced the gut and cut the womb. . . .

He split it apart like a cockle-shell; with the upper half he constructed the arc of sky, he pulled down the bar and set a watch on the waters, so they should never escape. . . . He projected positions for the Great Gods conspicuous in the sky, he gave them a starry aspect as constellations; he measured the year, gave it a beginning and an end, and to each month of the twelve three rising stars. . . . Through her ribs he opened gates in the east and west, and gave them strong bolts on the right and left; and high in the belly of Tiamat he set the zenith. He gave the moon the luster of a jewel, he gave him all the night, to mark off days, to watch by night each month the circle of a waxing waning light. . . . When Marduk had sent out the moon, he took the sun and set him to complete the cycle from this one to the next New Year. . . .

Then Marduk considered Tiamat. He skimmed spume from the bitter sea, heaped up the clouds, spindrift of wet and wind and cooling rain, the spittle of Tiamat. With his own hands from the steaming

AP® Exam Tip

Explain how systems of record keeping arose independently in early civilizations, and compare the methods of writing and record keeping used by different societies.

2-1f Technology and Science

The term *technology*, from the Greek word *techne*, meaning "skill" or "specialized knowledge," normally refers to the tools and machines that humans use to manipulate the physical world. Many scholars now use the term more broadly for any specialized knowledge used to transform the natural environment and human society.

An important example of the broader type of technology is writing, which first appeared in Mesopotamia before 3300 BCE. The earliest inscribed tablets, found in the chief temple at Uruk, date from a time when the temple was the most important economic institution in the community. According to a plausible recent theory, writing originated from a system of tokens used to keep track of property—such as sheep, cattle, or wagon wheels—when increases in the amount of accumulated wealth and the complexity of commercial transactions strained people's memories. The tokens, made in the shape of the commodity, were sealed in clay envelopes, and pictures of the tokens were incised on the outside of the envelopes as a reminder of what was inside. Eventually, people realized that the incised pictures were an adequate record, making

mist he spread the clouds. He pressed hard down the head of water, heaping mountains over it, opening springs to flow: Euphrates and Tigris rose from her eyes, but he closed the nostrils and held back their springhead. He piled huge mountains on her paps and through them drove water-holes to channel the deep sources; and high overhead he arched her tail, locked-in to the wheel of heaven; the pit was under his feet, between was the crotch, the sky's fulcrum. Now the earth had foundations and the sky its mantle. . . .

Marduk considered and began to speak to the gods assembled in his presence. This is what he said, "In the former time you inhabited the void above the abyss, but I have made Earth as the mirror of Heaven, I have consolidated the soil for the foundations, and there I will build my city, my beloved home. A holy precinct shall be established with sacred halls for the presence of the king. When you come up from the deep to join the Synod you will find lodging and sleep by night. When others from heaven descend to the Assembly, you too will find lodging and sleep by night. It shall be BABYLON the home of the gods. The masters of all crafts shall build it according to my plan." . . . Now that Marduk has heard what it is the gods are saying, he is moved with desire to create a work of consummate art. He told Ea the deep thought in his heart.

"Blood to blood
I join,
blood to bone
I form
an original thing,
its name is MAN,
aboriginal man
is mine in making.
"All his occupations
are faithful service. . . ."

Ea answered with carefully chosen words, completing the plan for the gods' comfort. He said to Marduk, "Let one of the kindred be taken; only one need die for the new creation. Bring the gods together in the Great Assembly; there let the guilty die, so the rest may live."

Marduk called the Great Gods to the Synod. . . . The king speaks to the rebel gods, "Declare on your oath if ever before you spoke the truth, who instigated rebellion? Who stirred up Tiamat? Who led the battle? Let the instigator of war be handed over; guilt and retribution are on him, and peace will be yours for ever."

The Great Gods answered the Lord of the Universe, the king and counselor of gods, "It was Kingu who instigated rebellion, he stirred up that sea of bitterness and led the battle for her." They declared him guilty, they bound and held him down in front of Ea, they cut his arteries and from his blood they created man; and Ea imposed his servitude.

Much of the subsequent activity of the festival, which took place in the temple courtyard and streets, was a reenactment of the events of the Creation Myth. The festival occurred at the beginning of spring, when the grain shoots were beginning to emerge, and its essential symbolism concerns the return of natural life to the world. The Babylonians believed that the natural world had an annual life cycle consisting of birth, growth, maturity, and death. In winter the cycle drew to a close, and there was no guarantee that life would return to the world. Babylonians hoped proper performance of the New Year's Festival would encourage the gods to grant a renewal of time and life, in essence to re-create the world.

AP® History Reasoning Skills

Contextualization *To what extent does the violent nature of the Creation Epic reveal details about the Mesopotamian view of the physical world and the role of the Mesopotamian gods?*

Continuity and Change Over Time *In what ways did the events of the New Year's Festival reinforce the social structure and governmental system of the Babylonians, allowing the festival to last for millennia?*

Source: Pritchard, James, *Ancient Near Eastern Texts Relating to the Old Testament.* © 1969 by Princeton University Press. Reprinted by permission of Princeton University Press.

the tokens inside the envelope redundant. These pictures were the first written symbols. Each symbol represented an object, and it could also stand for the sound of the word for that object if the sound was part of a longer word.

The usual method of writing involved pressing the point of a sharpened reed into a moist clay tablet. Because the reed made wedge-shaped impressions, the early realistic pictures were increasingly stylized into a combination of strokes and wedges, a system known as **cuneiform** (Latin for "wedge-shaped") writing. Mastering this system required years of training and practice. Several hundred signs were in use at any one time, as compared to the twenty-five or so signs in an alphabetic system. The prestige and regular employment that went with their position may have made scribes reluctant to simplify the cuneiform system. In the Old Babylonian period, the growth of private commerce brought an increase in the number of people who could read and write, but only a small percentage of the population was literate.

The earliest Mesopotamian documents are economic, but cuneiform came to have wide-ranging uses. Written documents marked with the seal of the participants became the primary proof of legal actions. Texts were written about political, literary, religious, and scientific topics.

cuneiform A system of writing in which wedge-shaped symbols represented words or syllables. It originated in Mesopotamia and was used initially for Sumerian and Akkadian but later was adapted to represent other languages of western Asia. Literacy was confined to a relatively small group of administrators and scribes.

Section Review

- Mesopotamia was home to a complex civilization that developed in the plain of the Tigris and Euphrates Rivers, beginning in the fourth millennium BCE.

- The elements of civilization initially created by the Sumerians, the earliest known people to live in Mesopotamia, were later taken over and adapted by the Semitic peoples who became dominant in the region.

- City-states, centered on cities that coalesced out of villages and controlled rural territory, were initially independent.

- The temples of the gods, the earliest centers of political and economic power, became subordinate to kings.

- Mesopotamian society was divided into three classes: free landowners and professionals in the cities, dependent peasants and artisans on rural estates, and slaves in domestic service.

- Mesopotamians feared their gods, who embodied the often-violent forces of nature.

- Cuneiform writing evolved from a system of tokens used for economic records, but it came to have a wide range of uses.

- A range of technologies (metallurgy, ceramics, transportation, and engineering) and sciences (mathematics and astronomy) enabled Mesopotamians to meet the challenges of their environment.

AP® Exam Tip Understand how technological innovations led to improvements in agriculture, trade, and transportation.

Cuneiform is not a language but rather a system of writing. Developed originally for the Sumerian language, it was later adapted to the Akkadian language of the Mesopotamian Semites as well as to other languages of western Asia, such as Hittite, Elamite, and Persian.

Other technologies enabled the Mesopotamians to meet the challenges of their physical environment. Wheeled carts and sledlike platforms dragged by cattle were used to transport goods in some locations. In the south, where numerous water channels cut up the landscape, boats and barges predominated. In northern Mesopotamia, donkeys were the chief pack animals for overland caravans before the advent of the camel around 1200 BCE (see Chapter 9).

The Mesopotamians had to import metals, but they became skilled in metallurgy, refining ores containing copper and alloying them with arsenic or tin to make **bronze**. Craftsmen poured molten bronze into molds to produce tools and weapons. The cooled and hardened bronze took a sharper edge than stone, was less likely to break, and was more easily repaired. Stone implements remained in use among poor people, who could not afford bronze.

Widely available clay was used to make dishware and storage vessels. By 4000 BCE the potter's wheel, a revolving platform spun by hands or feet, made possible the rapid production of vessels with precise and complex shapes. Mud bricks, dried in the sun or baked in an oven for greater durability, were the primary building material. Construction of city walls, temples, and palaces required practical knowledge of architecture and engineering. For example, the reed mats that Mesopotamian builders laid between the mud-brick layers of ziggurats served the same stabilizing purpose as girders in modern high-rise construction.

Early military forces were nonprofessional militias of able-bodied men called up for short periods when needed. The powerful states of the later third and second millennia BCE built up armies of well-trained and well-paid full-time soldiers. In the early second millennium BCE horses appeared in western Asia, and the horse-drawn chariot came into vogue. Infantry found themselves at the mercy of swift chariots carrying a driver and an archer who could easily run them down. Mesopotamian soldiers also used increasingly effective siege machinery that enabled them to climb over, undermine, or knock down the walls protecting the cities of their enemies.

Mesopotamians used a base-60 number system in which numbers were expressed as fractions or multiples of 60 (in contrast to our base-10 system; this is the origin of the seconds and minutes we use in calculating time today). Advances in mathematics and careful observation of the skies made the Mesopotamians sophisticated practitioners of astronomy. Priests compiled lists of omens or unusual sightings on earth and in the heavens, together with a record of the events that coincided with them. They consulted these texts at critical times, for they believed that the recurrence of such phenomena could provide clues to future developments. The underlying premise was that the elements of the material universe, from the microscopic to the macrocosmic, were interconnected in mysterious but undeniable ways.

bronze An alloy of copper with a small amount of tin (or sometimes arsenic), which is harder and more durable than copper alone. The term Bronze Age is applied to the era—the dates of which vary in different parts of the world—when bronze was the primary metal for tools and weapons.

2-2 Egypt

What role did the environment and religion play in the evolution of Egyptian civilization?

No place exhibits the impact of the natural environment on the history and culture of a society better than ancient Egypt. Located at the intersection of Asia and Africa, Egypt was protected by surrounding barriers of desert and a harborless, marshy seacoast. Whereas Mesopotamia was open to migration or invasion and was dependent on imported resources, Egypt's natural isolation and material self-sufficiency fostered a unique culture that for long periods had relatively little to do with other civilizations.

2-2a The Land of Egypt: "Gift of the Nile"

The fifth-century BCE Greek traveler Herodotus (**he-ROD-uh-tuhs**) justifiably called Egypt the "gift of the Nile." The world's longest river, the Nile flows northward from Lake Victoria and several large tributaries in the highlands of tropical Africa, carving a narrow valley between a chain of hills on either side, until it reaches the Mediterranean Sea (see Map 2.3). Though bordered mostly by desert, the banks of the river support lush vegetation. About 100 miles (160 kilometers) from the Mediterranean, the Nile divides into channels to form a triangular delta. Most of the population, then as now, lived on the twisting, green ribbon of land alongside the river or in the Nile Delta. The rest of the country, 90 percent or more, is a bleak and inhospitable desert of mountains, rocks, and dunes. The ancient Egyptians distinguished between the low-lying, life-sustaining dark soil of the "Black Land" along the river and the elevated, deadly "Red Land" of the desert.

The river was the main means of travel and communication, with the most important cities located upstream away from the Mediterranean. Because the river flows from south to north, the Egyptians called the southern part of the country "Upper Egypt" and the northern delta "Lower Egypt." In most periods the southern boundary of Egypt was the First Cataract of the Nile, the northernmost of a series of impassable rocks and rapids below Aswan (**AS-wahn**) (about 500 miles [800 kilometers] south of the Mediterranean). At times Egyptians' control extended farther south into what they called "Kush" (later Nubia, today part of southern Egypt and northern Sudan). The Egyptians also settled a chain of large oases west of the river, green and habitable "islands" in the midst of the desert.

While the hot, sunny climate favored agriculture, rain rarely falls south of the delta, and agriculture was entirely dependent on river water. Each September the river overflowed its banks, spreading water into the bordering basins, and irrigation channels carried water farther out into the valley to increase the area suitable for planting. Unlike the Tigris and Euphrates, the Nile flooded at exactly the right time for grain agriculture. When the waters receded, they left behind a moist, fertile layer of mineral-rich silt in which farmers could easily plant their crops. An Egyptian creation myth featured the emergence of a life-supporting mound of earth from a primeval swamp.

The level of the flood's crest determined the abundance of the next harvest. "Nilometers," stone staircases with incised units of measure placed along the river's edge, gauged the flood surge. When the flood was too high, dikes protecting inhabited areas were washed out, and much damage resulted. When the floods were too low for several years, less land could be cultivated, and the country experienced famine and decline. The ebb and flow of successful and failed regimes seems to have been linked to the cycle of floods. Nevertheless, remarkable stability characterized most eras, and Egyptians viewed the universe as an orderly and beneficent place.

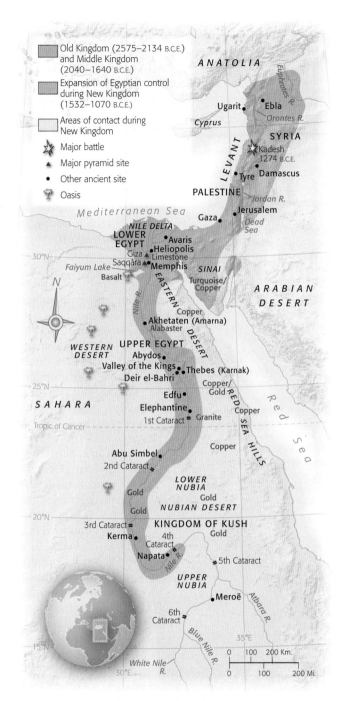

MAP 2.3   Ancient Egypt The Nile River, flowing south to north, carved out of the surrounding desert a narrow green valley that became heavily settled in antiquity.

What might be the political and economic consequences of the fact that almost the entire population of ancient Egypt lived near the Nile River?

AP® Exam Tip
Be ready to explain the impact of the environment on the development of Egyptian civilization.

Egypt was well endowed with natural resources and far more self-sufficient than Mesopotamia. Egyptians used papyrus reeds growing in marshy areas to make sails, ropes, and a kind of paper. Hunters pursued the abundant wild animals and birds in the marshes and on the edge of the desert, and fishermen netted fish from the river. Building stone was quarried and floated downstream from southern Egypt. Clay for mud bricks and pottery could be found almost everywhere. The state organized armed expeditions and forced labor to exploit copper and turquoise deposits in the Sinai Desert to the east and gold from Nubia to the south.

The farming villages that appeared in Egypt as early as 5500 BCE relied on domesticated plant and animal species that had originated several millennia earlier in western Asia. Egypt's emergence as a focal point of civilization stemmed, at least in part, from a gradual change in climate from the fifth to the third millennium BCE. Until then, the Sahara, the vast region that is now the world's largest desert, had a relatively mild and wet climate, and its lakes and grasslands supported a variety of plant and animal species as well as populations of hunter-gatherers (see Chapter 9). As the Sahara became a desert, displaced groups migrated into the Nile Valley, where they developed a sedentary way of life.

2-2b Divine Kingship

The increase in population led to more complex political organization, including a form of local kingship. Later generations of Egyptians saw the conquest of these smaller units and the unification of all Egypt by Menes (**MEH-neez**), a ruler from the south, as a pivotal event. Kings of Egypt bore the title "Ruler of the Two Lands"—Upper and Lower Egypt—and wore two crowns symbolizing the unification of the country. In contrast to Mesopotamia, Egypt was unified early in its history.

Historians organize Egyptian history using the system of thirty dynasties (sequences of kings from the same family) identified by Manetho, an Egyptian from the third century BCE. The rise and fall of dynasties often reflect the dominance of different parts of the country. More generally, scholars refer to the "Old," "Middle," and "New Kingdoms," each a period of centralized political power and brilliant cultural achievement, punctuated by "Intermediate Periods" of political fragmentation and cultural decline. Although experts debate the specific dates for these periods, the chronology on page 29 reflects current opinion.

The Egyptian state centered on the king, often known by the New Kingdom term **pharaoh**, from an Egyptian phrase meaning "palace." From the time of the Old Kingdom, if not earlier, Egyptians considered the king to be a god sent to earth to maintain **ma'at** (**muh-AHT**), the divinely authorized order of the universe. He was the indispensable link between his people and the gods, and his benevolent rule ensured the welfare and prosperity of the country.

So much depended on the kings that their deaths called forth elaborate efforts to ensure the well-being of their spirits on their perilous journey to rejoin the gods. Massive resources were poured into the construction of royal tombs, the celebration of elaborate funerary rites, and the sustenance of the kings' spirits in the afterlife by perpetual offerings in funerary chapels attached to the royal tombs. Early rulers were buried in flat-topped, rectangular tombs made of mud brick. Around 2630 BCE Djoser (**JO-sur**), a Third Dynasty king, constructed a stepped **pyramid** consisting of a series of stone platforms laid one on top of the other at Saqqara (**suh-KAHR-uh**), near Memphis. Rulers in the Fourth Dynasty filled in the steps to create the smooth-sided, limestone pyramids that have become the most memorable symbol of ancient Egypt. Between 2550 and 2490 BCE the pharaohs Khufu (**KOO-foo**) and Khafre (**KAF-ray**) erected huge pyramids at Giza, several miles north of Saqqara.

pharaoh The central figure in the ancient Egyptian state. Believed to be an earthly manifestation of the gods, he used his absolute power to maintain the safety and prosperity of Egypt.

ma'at Egyptian term for the concept of divinely created and maintained order in the universe. The divine ruler was the earthly guarantor of this order.

pyramid A large, triangular stone monument, used in Egypt and Nubia as a burial place for the king. The largest pyramids, erected during the Old Kingdom near Memphis, reflect the Egyptian belief that the proper and spectacular burial of the divine ruler would guarantee the continued prosperity of the land.

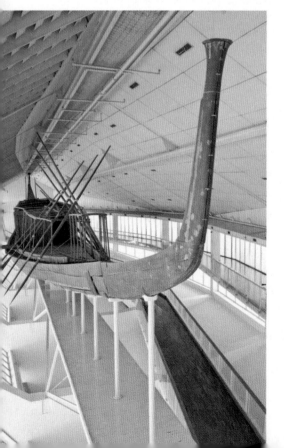

◄ **Solar Ship of King Khufu**   This full-size ship (143 feet [43.6 meters] long and 19.5 feet [5.9 meters] wide) was buried in a pit at the base of the Great Pyramid ca. 2500 BCE. While it was probably intended to carry the resurrected king along with the sun-god Ra across the sky, it may also have been used to transport Khufu's embalmed body to Giza. Ships equipped with sails and oars were well suited for travel on the peaceful Nile and sometimes were used for voyages on the more turbulent Mediterranean and Red Seas. Andrea Thompson Photography/Getty Images

▲ **Pyramids of Menkaure, Khafre, and Khufu at Giza, ca. 2500 BCE** With a width of 755 feet (230 meters) and a height of 480 feet (146 meters), the Great Pyramid of Khufu is the largest stone structure ever built. The construction of these massive edifices depended on relatively simple techniques of stonecutting, transport (the stones were floated downriver on boats and rolled to the site on sledges), and lifting (the stones were dragged up the face of the pyramid on mud-brick ramps). However, the surveying and engineering skills required to level the platform, lay out the measurements, and securely position the blocks were very sophisticated and have withstood the test of time. Michele Burgess/Michele Burgess/Superstock

Egyptians accomplished this construction with stone tools (bronze was still expensive and rare) and no machinery other than simple levers, pulleys, and rollers. What made it possible was almost unlimited human muscle power. Calculations of the human resources needed to build a pyramid within the lifetime of the ruler suggest that large numbers of people must have been pressed into service for part of each year, probably during the flood season when no agricultural work could be done. Although this labor was compulsory, the Egyptian masses probably regarded it as a kind of religious service that helped ensure prosperity. The age of the great pyramids lasted only about a century, although pyramids continued to be built on a smaller scale for two millennia.

AP® Exam Tip
Explain why rulers of early states often claimed divine connections to power.

2-2c **Administration and Communication**

Ruling dynasties usually placed their capitals in the area of their original power base. **Memphis**, near the apex of the delta (close to Cairo, the modern capital), held this central position during the Old Kingdom. **Thebes**, far to the south, supplanted it during the Middle and New Kingdom periods (see Map 2.3).

The extensive administrative system began at the village level and progressed to the districts into which the country was divided and, finally, to the central government in the capital city. Bureaucrats kept track of land, products, and people, extracting as taxes a substantial portion of the country's annual revenues—at times as much as 50 percent. This income supported the palace, bureaucracy, and army, as well as the construction and maintenance of temples and great monuments celebrating the ruler's reign. The government maintained a monopoly over key sectors of the economy and controlled long-distance trade, unlike in Mesopotamia, where commerce increasingly fell into the hands of an acquisitive urban middle class.

The hallmark of the administrative class was literacy. A writing system had been developed by the beginning of the Early Dynastic period. **Hieroglyphics (high-ruh-GLIF-iks)**, the earliest form of this system, were picture symbols standing for words, syllables, or individual sounds. Hieroglyphic writing long continued to be used on monuments and ornamental inscriptions. By 2500 BCE, however, a cursive script, in which the original pictorial nature of the symbol was less apparent, had been developed for the everyday needs of administrators and copyists. The Egyptians used writing for many purposes other than administrative record keeping. Their written literature included tales of adventure and magic, love poetry, religious hymns, and instruction

Memphis The capital of Old Kingdom Egypt, near the head of the Nile Delta. Early rulers were interred in the nearby pyramids.

Thebes Capital city of Egypt and home of the ruling dynasties during the Middle and New Kingdoms. Monarchs were buried across the river in the Valley of the Kings.

Hieroglyphics A system of writing in which pictorial symbols represented sounds, syllables, or concepts. It was used for official and monumental inscriptions in ancient Egypt. Because of the long period of study required to master this system, literacy in hieroglyphics was confined to a relatively small group of scribes and administrators.

manuals on technical subjects. Scribes in workshops attached to the temples made copies of traditional texts. They worked with ink on a writing material made from the **papyrus (puh-PIE-ruhs)** reed. The plant grew only in Egypt but was in demand throughout the ancient world and was exported in large quantities.

When the monarchy was strong, officials were appointed and promoted on the basis of ability and accomplishment. The king gave them grants of land cultivated by dependent peasants. Low-level officials were assigned to villages and district capitals, while high-ranking officials served in the royal capital. When Old Kingdom officials died, they were buried in tombs around the monumental tomb of the king so that they could serve him in death as they had in life.

Throughout Egyptian history there was an underlying tension between the centralizing power of the monarchy and the decentralizing tendencies of the bureaucracy. One sign of the breakdown of royal power in the late Old Kingdom and First Intermediate Period was the placement of officials' tombs in their home districts, where they spent much of their time and exercised power more or less independently, rather than near the royal tomb. Another sign was the tendency of administrative posts to become hereditary. The early monarchs of the Middle Kingdom restored centralized control by reducing the power and prerogatives of the old elite and creating a new class of loyal administrators.

It has often been said that Egypt lacked real cities because the political capitals were primarily extensions of the palace and central administration. Compared to Mesopotamia, a far larger percentage of Egyptians lived in rural villages and engaged in agriculture, and Egypt's wealth derived to a higher degree from the land and its products. But there were towns and cities in ancient Egypt, although they were less crucial to the economic and cultural dynamism of the country than were Mesopotamian urban centers. Unfortunately, archaeologists have been unable to excavate many ancient urban sites in Egypt because they lie beneath modern communities.

During the Old and Middle Kingdoms, Egypt's foreign policy was essentially isolationist. Technically, all foreigners were considered enemies. When necessary, local militia units backed up a small standing army of professional soldiers. Nomadic groups in the eastern and western deserts and Libyans to the northwest were a nuisance rather than a real danger and were readily handled by the Egyptian military. Egypt's interests abroad focused on maintaining access to valuable resources rather than on acquiring territory. Trade with the coastal towns of the Levant **(luh-VANT)** (modern Israel, the Palestinian territories, Lebanon, and Syria) brought in cedar wood. In return, Egypt exported grain, papyrus, and gold.

In all periods the Egyptians had a particularly strong interest in goods from the south. Nubia had rich sources of gold (Chapter 4 examines the rise of a civilization in Nubia that, though considerably influenced by Egypt, created a vital and original culture that lasted for more than 2,000 years), and the southern course of the Nile offered the easiest passage to sub-Saharan Africa. In the Old Kingdom, Egyptian noblemen led donkey caravans south to trade for gold, incense, and products of tropical Africa such as ivory, dark ebony wood, and exotic jungle animals. A line of forts along the southern border protected Egypt from attack. In the early second millennium BCE Egyptian forces struck south into Nubia, extending the border to the Third Cataract of the Nile and taking possession of the gold fields. Still farther to the south, perhaps in the coastal region of present-day Sudan or Eritrea, lay the fabled land of Punt **(poont)**, source of the fragrant myrrh resin burned on the altars of the Egyptian gods.

2-2d The People of Egypt

The million to million and a half inhabitants of Egypt included various physical types, ranging from dark-skinned people related to the populations of sub-Saharan Africa to lighter-skinned people akin to the populations of North Africa and western Asia. Although Egypt did not experience the large-scale migrations and invasions common in Mesopotamia, settlers periodically trickled into the Nile Valley and assimilated with the people already living there.

Although some Egyptians had higher status and more wealth and power than others, in contrast to Mesopotamia no formal class structure emerged. At the top of the social hierarchy were the king and high-ranking officials. In the middle were lower-level officials, local leaders, priests and other professionals, artisans, and well-to-do farmers. At the bottom were peasants, who made up the vast majority of the population.

Any account of the lives of ordinary Egyptians is largely conjectural; the villages of ancient Egypt, like those of Mesopotamia, left few traces in the archaeological or literary record. In tomb

AP® Exam Tip
Compare the way different early societies used legal codes to facilitate the role of the government.

papyrus A reed that grows along the banks of the Nile River in Egypt. From it was produced a coarse, paperlike writing medium used by the Egyptians and many other peoples in the ancient Mediterranean and Middle East.

paintings of the elite, artists indicated status by pictorial conventions, such as obesity for their wealthy and comfortable patrons, baldness and deformity for the working classes. Egyptian poets frequently used metaphors of farming and hunting, and papyrus documents preserved in the hot, dry sands tell of property transactions and legal disputes among ordinary people.

Peasants living in rural villages engaged in the seasonally changing tasks of agriculture: plowing, sowing, tending emerging shoots, reaping, threshing, and storing grain or other products of the soil. They maintained and extended the irrigation network of channels, basins, and dikes. Meat from domesticated animals—cattle, sheep, goats, and poultry—and fish supplemented a diet based on wheat or barley, beer, and vegetables. Villagers shared implements, work animals, and storage facilities and helped one another at peak times in the agricultural cycle and in the construction of houses and other buildings. They prayed and feasted together at festivals to the local gods. Periodically they had to contribute labor to state projects. If taxation or compulsory service was too great a burden, flight into the desert was the only escape.

Some information is available about the lives of women of the upper classes, but it is filtered through the brushes and pens of male artists and scribes. Tomb paintings show women of the royal family and elite classes accompanying their husbands and engaging in typical domestic activities. They are depicted with dignity and affection, though they are clearly subordinate to the men. The artistic convention of depicting men with a dark red and women with a yellow flesh tone implies that the elite woman's proper sphere was indoors, away from the searing sun. In the beautiful love poetry of the New Kingdom, lovers address each other in terms of apparent equality and express emotions of romantic love.

Legal documents show that Egyptian women could own property, inherit property from their parents, and will their property to whomever they wished. Marriage, usually monogamous, was not confirmed by any legal or religious ceremony and essentially constituted a decision by a man and woman to establish a household together. Either party could dissolve the relationship, and the divorced woman retained rights over her dowry. At certain times queens and queen-mothers played significant behind-the-scenes roles in the politics of the court, and priestesses sometimes supervised the cults of female deities. In general, the limited evidence suggests that women in ancient Egypt were treated more respectfully and had more legal rights and social freedom than women in Mesopotamia and other ancient societies.

AP® Exam Tip
Consider the ways Egyptian society exemplified and challenged the patriarchal social structures common in early civilizations.

2-2e Belief and Knowledge

Egyptian religion was rooted in the landscape of the Nile Valley and the vision of cosmic order that it evoked. The consistency of their environment—the sun rose every day in a clear and cloudless sky, and the river flooded on schedule every year, ensuring a bounteous harvest—persuaded the Egyptians that the natural world was a place of recurrent cycles and periodic renewal. The sky was imagined to be a great ocean surrounding the inhabited world. The sun-god Re **(ray)** traversed this blue waterway in a boat by day, then returned through the Underworld at night, fighting off the attacks of demonic serpents so that he could be born anew in the morning. In one especially popular story Osiris **(oh-SIGH-ris)**, a god who once ruled Egypt, was slain by his jealous brother Seth, who then scattered the dismembered pieces. Isis, Osiris's devoted sister and wife, found and reconstructed the remnants, and Horus, his son, took revenge on Seth. Osiris was restored to life and installed as king of the Underworld, and his example gave people hope of a new life in a world beyond this one.

The king, who was seen as Horus and as the son of Re, was thus associated with both the return of the dead to life and the life-giving and self-renewing sun-god. He was the chief priest of Egypt, intervening with the gods on behalf of his land and people. Egyptian rulers zealously built new temples, refurbished old ones, and made lavish gifts to the gods. Much of the country's wealth was directed to religious activities in a ceaseless effort to win the gods' favor, maintain the continuity of divine kingship, and ensure the renewal of the life-giving forces that sustained the world.

The many gods of ancient Egypt were diverse in origin and nature. Some were normally depicted with animal heads; others were always given human form. Few myths about the origins and adventures of the gods have survived, but there must have been a rich oral tradition. Many towns had temples for locally prominent deities. When a town became the capital of a ruling dynasty, the chief god of that town became prominent across the land. Thus did Ptah **(puh-TAH)** of Memphis, Re of Heliopolis **(he-lee-OP-uh-lis)**, and Amon **(AH-muhn)** of Thebes become gods of all Egypt, serving to unify the country and strengthen the monarchy. As in Mesopotamia,

AP® Exam Tip
Compare the development of early Egyptian religion with that of other early societies.

▶ **Scene from the Egyptian Book of the Dead, ca. 1300 BCE** The mummy of a royal scribe named Hunefar is approached by members of his household before being placed in the tomb. Behind Hunefar is jackal-headed Anubis, the god who will conduct the spirit of the deceased to the afterlife. The Book of the Dead provided Egyptians with the instructions they needed to complete this arduous journey and gain a blessed existence in the afterlife. The Trustees of the British Museum / Art Resource, NY

mummy A body preserved by chemical processes or special natural circumstances, often in the belief that the deceased will need it again in the afterlife.

some temples possessed extensive landholdings worked by dependent peasants, and the priests who administered the deity's wealth were influential locally and sometimes even throughout the land.

Cult activities were carried out in the inner reaches of the temples, off limits to all but the priests who served the needs of the deity by attending to his or her statue. During great festivals, the priests paraded a boat-shaped litter carrying the shrouded statue and cult items of the deity around the town, an event that brought large numbers of people into contact with the deity in an outpouring of devotion and celebration. However, little is known about the day-to-day beliefs and practices of the common people. In the household family members made small offerings to Bes, the grotesque god of marriage and domestic happiness, to local deities, and to the family's ancestors. They relied on amulets and depictions of demonic figures to protect the bearer and ward off evil forces. In later times Greeks and Romans commented that the devotion to magic was especially strong in Egypt.

Egyptians believed in the afterlife and made extensive preparations for safe passage to the next world and a comfortable existence once they arrived there. A common belief was that death was a journey beset with hazards. The Egyptian Book of the Dead, present in many excavated tombs, contained rituals and spells to protect the journeying spirit. The final challenge was the weighing of the deceased's heart in the presence of the judges of the Underworld to determine whether the person had led a good life and deserved to reach the ultimate blessed destination.

Obsession with the afterlife led to great concern about the physical condition of the cadaver, and Egyptians perfected techniques of mummification to preserve the dead body. The idea probably grew out of the early practice of burying the dead in the hot, dry sand on the edge of the desert, where bodies decomposed slowly. The elite classes utilized the most expensive kind of mummification. Vital organs were removed, preserved, and stored in stone jars laid out around the corpse. Body cavities were filled with various packing materials. The cadaver, immersed for long periods in dehydrating and preserving chemicals, eventually was wrapped in linen. The **mummy** was then placed in one or more decorated wooden caskets and deposited in a tomb.

The form of the tomb reflected the wealth and status of the deceased. Common people made do with simple pit graves or small mud-brick chambers. The privileged classes built larger tombs. Kings erected pyramids and other grand edifices, employing subterfuge to hide the sealed chamber containing the body and treasures, as well as curses and other magical precautions to foil tomb robbers. Rarely did they succeed, however, and archaeologists have seldom discovered an undisturbed royal tomb. The tombs, usually built at the edge of the desert so as not to tie up valuable farmland, were filled with pictures, food, and the objects of everyday life to provide whatever the deceased might need in the next life. Small figurines called *shawabtis* (**shuh-WAB-tees**) were included to play the part of servants and take the place of the deceased in case the afterlife required periodic compulsory labor. The elite classes attached chapels to their tombs and left endowments to subsidize the daily attendance of a priest and offerings of foodstuffs to sustain their spirits for all eternity.

The ancient Egyptians made remarkable advances in many areas of knowledge. The process of mummification taught them about human anatomy, and Egyptian doctors were in demand in the courts of western Asia. They developed mathematics to measure the dimensions of fields and to calculate the quantity of agricultural produce owed to the state. Through careful observation of the stars they constructed the most accurate calendar in the world, and they knew that the appearance of the star Sirius on the horizon shortly before sunrise meant that the Nile flood surge was imminent. Pyramids, temple complexes, and other monumental building projects called for great skill in engineering. Long underground passageways were excavated to connect mortuary temples by the river with tombs near the desert's edge. On several occasions Egyptian kings dredged out a canal more than 50 miles (80 kilometers) long in order to join the Nile Valley to the Red Sea and expedite the transport of goods.

Section Review

- Most of the population of ancient Egypt lived alongside the river or in the delta.
- Egypt was well endowed with natural resources and largely self-sufficient.
- Because the king was the essential link between the people of Egypt and their gods, lavish resources were poured into the construction of pyramids and other royal tombs.
- Hieroglyphic and other systems of writing were used by administrators, but also for many genres of literature.
- The population of Egypt was physically diverse, and there was no formal system of classes.
- The status and privileges of Egyptian women were superior to those of their Mesopotamian counterparts, and poetry reveals an ideal of romantic love.
- Obsessed with the afterlife, Egyptians used mummification to preserve dead bodies, constructed elaborate tombs, and employed the Book of the Dead to navigate the hazardous journey to a comfortable final destination.
- Egyptians acquired substantial knowledge about medicine, mathematics, astronomy, and engineering.

2-3 The Indus Valley Civilization

What does the material evidence tell us about the nature of the Indus Valley civilization, and what is the most likely reason for its collapse?

Civilization arose almost as early in South Asia as in Mesopotamia and Egypt. In the fertile floodplain of the Indus River, farming created the food surplus essential to urbanized society.

2-3a Natural Environment

A plain of more than 1 million acres (400,000 hectares) stretches from the mountains of western Pakistan east to the Thar (**tahr**) Desert in the Sind (**sinned**) region of modern Pakistan (see Map 2.1). Over many centuries silt carried downstream and deposited by the Indus River has elevated the riverbed and its banks above the level of the plain. Twice a year the river overflows and inundates surrounding land as far as 10 miles (16 kilometers). In March and April melting snow from the Pamir (**pah-MEER**) and Himalaya (**him-uh-LAY-uh**) mountain ranges feeds the floods. In August, the great monsoon (seasonal wind) blowing off the ocean to the southwest brings rains that cause a second flood. Farmers in this region of little rainfall are thus able to plant and harvest two crops a year. In ancient times the Hakra (**HAK-ruh**) River (sometimes referred to as the Saraswati), which has since dried up, ran parallel to the Indus about 25 miles (40 kilometers) to the east and supplied water to a second cultivable area.

Adjacent regions shared many cultural traits with this core area. To the northeast is the Punjab, where five rivers converge to form the main course of the Indus. Lying beneath the towering Himalaya range, the Punjab receives considerably more rainfall than the central plain but is less prone to flooding. Settlements spread as far east as Delhi (**DEL-ee**) in northwest India. Settlement also extended south into the great delta where the Indus empties into the Arabian Sea, and southeast into India's hook-shaped Kathiawar (**kah-tee-uh-WAHR**) Peninsula, an area of alluvial plains and coastal marshes. The Indus Valley civilization covered an area much larger than the zone of Mesopotamian civilization.

2-3b Material Culture

The Indus Valley civilization flourished from approximately 2600 to 1900 BCE. Although archaeologists have located several hundred sites, the culture is best known from the remains of two great cities first discovered eighty years ago. Since the ancient names of these cities are unknown, they are referred to by modern names: **Harappa** and **Mohenjo-Daro** (**moe-hen-joe–DAHR-oh**). Unfortunately, the high water table at these sites makes excavation of the earliest levels of settlement nearly impossible.

Settled agriculture in this region dates back to at least 5000 BCE. The precise relationship between the Indus Valley civilization and earlier cultural complexes in the Indus Valley and in the hilly lands to the west is unclear. Also unclear are the forces that gave rise to urbanization, population increase, and technological advances in the mid–third millennium BCE. Nevertheless, the case for continuity with the earlier cultures seems stronger than the case for a sudden transformation due to the arrival of new peoples.

This society produced major urban centers. Harappa, 3.5 miles (5.6 kilometers) in circumference, may have housed a population of 35,000. Mohenjo-Daro was several times larger. High, thick brick walls surrounded each city, and the streets were laid out in a rectangular grid. Covered drainpipes carried away waste. The consistent width of streets and length of city blocks and the uniformity of the mud bricks used in construction suggest a strong central authority. The seat of this authority may have been the citadel—an elevated, enclosed compound containing large buildings. Scholars think the well-ventilated structures nearby were storehouses of grain for feeding the urban population and for export. The presence of barracks may point to some regimentation of skilled artisans.

Different centers may have had different functions. Mohenjo-Daro dominates the great floodplain of the Indus. Harappa, which is nearly 500 miles (805 kilometers) to the north, is on a frontier between farmland and herding land, and it may have served as a "gateway" for procuring the copper, tin, and precious stones of the northwest. Coastal towns in the south gathered fish and highly prized seashells and engaged in seaborne trade with the Persian Gulf.

Mohenjo-Daro and Harappa have been extensively excavated, and published accounts of the Indus Valley civilization tend to treat them as the norm. Most people, however, lived in smaller settlements, which exhibit the same artifacts and the same standardization of styles and shapes as the large cities. Some scholars attribute this standardization to extensive exchange of goods within the zone of Indus Valley civilization, rather than to the urban centers' control of the smaller settlements.

There is a greater quantity of metal in the Indus Valley than in Mesopotamia and Egypt, and most metal objects are utilitarian tools and other everyday objects. In contrast, more jewelry and other decorative metal objects have been unearthed in Mesopotamia and Egypt. Apparently metals were available to a broad cross-section of the population in the Indus Valley, while primarily reserved for the elite in the Middle East.

Technologically, the Indus Valley people showed skill in irrigation, used the potter's wheel, and laid the foundations of large public

Harappa Site of one of the great cities of the Indus Valley civilization of the third millennium BCE. It was located on the northwest frontier of the zone of cultivation (in modern Pakistan).

Mohenjo-Daro Largest of the cities of the Indus Valley civilization, centrally located in the extensive floodplain of the Indus River in contemporary Pakistan.

◀ **Man from Mohenjo-Daro, ca. 2600–1900 BCE** This statue of a seated man wearing a cloak and headband was carved from a soft stone called steatite. It is often called the "Priest-King" because some scholars believe it may represent someone with religious and secular authority, but the true identity and status of this person are unknown. Scala/Art Resource, NY

The three river-valley civilizations discussed in this chapter were located in arid or semiarid regions. Such regions are particularly vulnerable to changes in the environment. Scholars' debates about the existence and impact of changes in the climate and landscape of the Indus Valley illuminate some of the possible factors at work, as well as the difficulties of verifying and interpreting such long-ago changes.

One of the points at issue is climate change. Earlier scholars believed the climate of the Indus Valley was considerably wetter during the height of that civilization than it is now. They pointed to the enormous quantities of timber needed to bake the millions of mud bricks used to construct the cities (see photo), the distribution of human settlements on land now unfavorable for agriculture, and the representation of jungle and marsh animals on decorated seals. They maintained that the growth of population, prosperity, and complexity in the Indus Valley in the third millennium BCE required wet conditions, and they concluded that the change to a drier climate in the early second millennium BCE pushed this civilization into decline.

Other experts, skeptical about radical climate change, offered alternative calculations of the amount of timber needed and pointed to the evidence of plant remains—particularly barley, a grain that is tolerant of dry conditions. However, recent studies of the stabilization of sand dunes, which occurs in periods of heavy rainfall, and analysis of the sediment deposited by rivers and winds have strengthened the view that the Indus Valley used to be wetter and that in the early- to mid–second millennium BCE it entered a period of relatively dry conditions that have persisted to the present.

A clearer case can be made for changes in the landscape caused by shifts in the courses of rivers. These shifts are due, in some cases, to tectonic forces such as earthquakes. Dried-up riverbeds can be detected in satellite photographs or by on-the-ground inspection. It appears that a second major river system, the Hakra, once ran parallel to the Indus some distance to the east. The Hakra, with teeming towns and fertile fields along its banks, appears to have been a second axis of this civilization. Either the Sutlej, which now feeds into the Indus, or the Yamuna, which now pours into the Ganges, may have been the main source of water for the Hakra before undergoing a change of course. The consequences of the drying-up of this major waterway must have been immense—the loss of huge amounts of arable land and the food it produced, the abandonment of cities and villages and migration of their populations, shifts in trade routes, and desperate competition for shrinking resources.

As for the Indus itself, the present-day course of the lower reaches of the river has shifted 100 miles (161 kilometers) to the west since the arrival of the Greek conqueror Alexander the Great in the late fourth century BCE and the deposit of massive volumes of silt has pushed the mouth of the river 50 miles (80 kilometers) farther south. A similar shift of the riverbed and buildup of alluvial deposits may have occurred in the third and second millennia BCE and played a role in the decline of the Indus civilization.

As was pointed out earlier in this chapter, climate change between the fifth and third millennia BCE led to the formation of the vast Sahara Desert in northern Africa and the migration of people into the Nile River valley. The extreme consequences of climate change in northern Africa and the Indus River valley should serve as a salutary warning to us today, as we face potentially disastrous consequences from global warming. While climate change in antiquity was due to natural causes, most contemporary scientists are convinced that current changes are being caused by the accumulation of greenhouse gases in the atmosphere produced by human activities. Will we, with our advantages in knowledge and technology over ancient humans, use those advantages to forestall further damaging changes?

▲ **Mud-Brick Construction at Mohenjo-Daro**   View of the excavated remains of houses in the Lower Town, with the elevated Citadel in the background. Flood-resistant reddish-colored baked bricks were used for the foundations and lower levels, with unbaked bricks above. Construction of fortification walls and buildings required large numbers of bricks, ample fuel to bake the bricks, and enormous man-hours of labor. Globuss Images/Alamy Stock Photo

Questions for Analysis

1. What environmental changes have been proposed as the cause of the decline of the Indus Valley civilization?

2. What might have been the consequences of the drying up of the Hakra River?

3. What do you think happened to the people of the Indus Valley when that civilization failed?

Section Review

- The Indus Valley civilization occupied a large territory, including the fertile Indus floodplain as well as adjacent regions.

- Both the major urban centers and smaller settlements exhibit a uniformity of techniques and styles that indicates either strong central control or extensive communication between different regions.

- The Indus Valley people were technologically advanced in irrigation, ceramics, and construction. Metals were more widely available than in Mesopotamia and Egypt. The writing system has not been deciphered.

- The Indus Valley had widespread trading contacts, reaching as far as Mesopotamia.

- Cities were abandoned and the civilization declined after 1900 BCE, probably as a result of natural disasters or environmental changes.

buildings with mud bricks fired to rocky hardness in kilns (sun-dried bricks would have dissolved quickly in floodwaters). They had a system of writing with more than 400 signs. Archaeologists have recovered thousands of inscribed seal stones and copper tablets, but no one has been able to decipher these documents.

The people of the Indus Valley had widespread trading contacts. They had ready access to the metals and precious stones of eastern Iran and Afghanistan, as well as to ore deposits in western India, building stone, and timber. Goods were moved on rivers within the zone of Indus Valley culture. Indus Valley seal stones have been found in the Tigris-Euphrates Valley, indicating that Indus Valley merchants served as middlemen in long-distance trade, obtaining raw materials from the northwest and shipping them to the Persian Gulf. The undeciphered writing on seal stones may represent the names of merchants who stamped their wares.

We know little about the political, social, economic, and religious institutions of Indus Valley society. Attempts to link artifacts and images to cultural features characteristic of later periods of Indian history (see Chapter 7)—including a system of hereditary occupational groups with priests predominating, bathing tanks like those later found in Hindu temples, depictions of gods and sacred animals on seal stones, a cult of the mother-goddess—are highly speculative. Further knowledge about this society awaits additional archaeological finds and the deciphering of the Indus Valley script.

2-3c Transformation of the Indus Valley Civilization

The Indus Valley cities were abandoned sometime after 1900 BCE. Archaeologists once thought that invaders destroyed them, but they now believe this civilization suffered "systems failure"—a breakdown of the fragile interrelationship of political, social, and economic systems that sustained order and prosperity. The cause may have been one or more natural disasters, such as an earthquake or massive flooding. Gradual ecological changes may also have played a role as the Hakra river system dried up and salinization (an increase in the amount of salt in the soil, inhibiting plant growth) and erosion increased (see Environment & Technology: Environmental Stress in the Indus Valley).

Towns no longer on the river, ports separated from the sea by silt deposits in the deltas, and the loss of fertile soil and water would have necessitated the relocation of populations and a change in the livelihood of those who remained. The causes and pace of change probably varied in different areas. The urban centers eventually succumbed, however, and village-based farming and herding took their place. As the interaction between regions lessened, regional variation replaced the standardization of technology and style of the previous era. It is important to keep in mind that in most cases like this the majority of the population adjusts to the new circumstances. But members of the elite, who depend on the urban centers and complex political and economic structures, lose the source of their authority and are merged with the population as a whole.

2-4 Conclusion

It is no accident that the first civilizations to develop high levels of political centralization, urbanization, and technology were situated in river valleys where rainfall was insufficient for reliable agriculture. Dependent on river water to irrigate the cultivated land that fed their populations, Mesopotamia, Egypt, and the Indus Valley civilization channeled considerable human resources into the construction and maintenance of canals, dams, and dikes. This effort required the formation of political centers that could organize the necessary labor force.

In both Egypt and Mesopotamia, kingship emerged as the dominant political form. The Egyptian king's divine origins and symbolic association with the forces of renewal made him central to the welfare of the entire country and gave him religious authority superseding the temples and priests. Egyptian monarchs lavished much of the country's wealth on their tombs, believing that a proper burial would ensure the continuity of kingship and the attendant blessings that it brought to the land and people. Mesopotamian rulers, who were not normally regarded as divine but still dominated the religious institutions, built new cities, towering walls, splendid palaces, and religious edifices as lasting testaments to their power.

The unpredictable and violent floods in the Tigris-Euphrates Basin were a constant source of alarm for the people of Mesopotamia. In contrast, the predictable, opportune, and gradual Nile floods were eagerly anticipated events in Egypt. The relationship with nature stamped the religious outlooks of both peoples, since their gods embodied the forces of the environment. Mesopotamians nervously tried to appease their harsh deities so as to survive in a dangerous world, whereas Egyptians largely trusted in and nurtured the supernatural powers that, they believed, guaranteed orderliness and prosperity. The Egyptians also believed that, although the journey to the next world was beset with hazards, the righteous spirit that overcame them could look forward to a blessed existence. In contrast, Gilgamesh, the hero of the Mesopotamian epic, is tormented by terrifying visions of the afterlife: disembodied spirits of the dead stumbling around in the darkness of the Underworld for all eternity, eating dust and clay and slaving for the heartless gods of that realm.

Although the populations of Egypt and Mesopotamia were ethnically heterogeneous, both regions experienced a remarkable degree of cultural continuity. New immigrants readily assimilated to the dominant language, belief system, and lifestyles of the civilization. Mesopotamia developed sharp social divisions that were reflected in the class-based penalties set down in the Law Code of Hammurabi, whereas Egyptian society was less urban and less stratified. Mesopotamian women's apparent loss of freedom and legal privilege in the second millennium BCE also may have been related to the higher degree of urbanization and class stratification in this society. In contrast, Egyptian pictorial documents, love poems, and legal records indicate respect and greater equality for women in the valley of the Nile.

Because of the lack of readable texts, we can say very little about the political institutions, social organization, and religious beliefs of the Indus Valley people. However, they clearly possessed technologies on a par with those found in Mesopotamia and Egypt—a writing system, irrigation, bronze-casting, and techniques for producing monumental architecture. The striking uniformity in the planning and construction of cities and towns and in the shapes and styles of artifacts argues for easy communication and some kind of interdependence among the far-flung Indus Valley settlements, as does the relatively rapid collapse of this civilization as a result of ecological changes.

Key Terms

civilization p. 27	**Hammurabi** p. 32	**pharaoh** p. 40	**papyrus** p. 42
Sumerians p. 29	**scribe** p. 34	**ma'at** p. 40	**mummy** p. 44
Semitic p. 30	**ziggurat** p. 35	**pyramid** p. 40	**Harappa** p. 46
city-state p. 31	**amulet** p. 35	**Memphis** p. 41	**Mohenjo-Daro** p. 46
Sargon of Akkad p. 32	**cuneiform** p. 37	**Thebes** p. 41	
Babylon p. 32	**bronze** p. 38	**hieroglyphics** p. 41	

Review Questions

1. How might political and social organization differ in societies that received enough rainfall to grow crops as opposed to those of the river-valley civilizations?

2. How was the worldview of the different societies treated in this chapter affected by their beliefs about the character of the gods and the fate of the dead?

3. How were women regarded and treated as societies became increasingly urbanized and materialistic?

 MindTap® is a fully online, personalized learning experience built upon Cengage Learning content. MindTap® combines student learning tools–readings, multimedia, activities, and assessments–into a singular Learning Path that guides students through the course and helps students develop the critical thinking, analysis, and communication skills that are essential to academic and professional success.

Multiple-Choice Questions

Questions 1–3 refer to the image below.

▲ **Mud-Brick construction at Mohenjo-Daro** View of the excavated remains of houses in the Lower Town, with elevated Citadel in the background. Globuss Images/Alamy Stock Photo

1. The use of mud to build the city of Mohenjo-Daro supports which of the following claims made by historians?

   (A) The city was built on land that was once under water, a result of significant climate change.

   (B) Where agriculture flourished, early civilizations were able to grow in a variety of environmental areas.

   (C) A lack of farmable land led early Indus River civilizations to center around commerce and trade instead.

   (D) Indus River Valley use of slave labor was necessary to build such detailed buildings.

2. Which of the following might have been a cause for the building of a citadel on higher land in the center of the city?

   (A) Social hierarchies were powerful in Mohenjo-Daro, and the central location of the citadel was reserved for lower-class citizens.

   (B) This central, large building was used as housing, with the remaining buildings used mainly for trade.

   (C) Mohenjo-Daro was a highly religious city with early roots of Hinduism found throughout the remains.

   (D) Central buildings, like this one in Mohenjo-Daro, were often built by early rulers to gain the support of specialized military and religious elites.

3. The discovery of precious stones from Iran and Afghanistan in the ruins of Harappa and Mohenjo-Daro serves as evidence of which of the following?

   (A) Indus Valley's widespread trading contacts allowed for interregional cultural and technological exchange.

   (B) The Indus Valley civilizations were highly militaristic and pillaged conquered people's treasures.

   (C) The Indus Valley civilizations remained geographically isolated until later conquered by expanding European civilizations.

   (D) The Indus Valley civilizations were technologically far behind their Mesopotamian rivals.

Questions 4–7 refer to Map 2.3 Ancient Egypt on page 39.

4. By examining the map, which of the following conclusions can be reached?

   (A) Though Egypt's empire expanded over time, it remained closely tied to the Nile because of its impact on agriculture.

   (B) Egypt's empire was largely unchanged, but they transferred from an agriculture economy to a strict trade-based economy.

   (C) Environmental factors like the Nile's flow (south to north) and the surrounding desert kept Egypt largely isolated.

   (D) Egyptian society had few natural resources and had to rely on trade with other nations for basic needs.

5. All of the following led to the change in the Egyptian empire indicated on the map EXCEPT

   (A) favorable location on the Nile River.

   (B) growing population thanks to good food production.

   (C) consistency of the harsh, dry Sahara climate for protection.

   (D) access to more resources for both trade and growth.

6. Egyptian pharaohs used which of the following methods to consolidate and affirm their power?

   (A) Economic gifts to the people to gain favor

   (B) Military purges designed to inspire fear

   (C) Use of early stages of democracy as people chose the new leader

   (D) Claims to divinity as the "divine link" between the people and the gods

7. Which of the following is a good comparison of Egypt and the Indus River Valley civilizations based on archaeological evidence?

(A) The highly developed religious iconography of the Egyptian civilization indicates Egypt was more highly favored by the gods than the Indus River Valley.

(B) The use of metal in utilitarian objects in Mohenjo-Dara indicates the resource was far more present in the Indus River Valley than in Egypt.

(C) Papyrus writing found in tombs in Egypt indicates that Egypt was far more technologically advanced than the Indus River Valley civilizations.

(D) The use of mud bricks to build towns like Mohenjo-Daro indicates that the Indus River Valley civilizations were far more closely tied to the river than the Egyptians.

Questions 8–10 refer to the passage below.

"#6. If anyone steal the property of a temple or of the court, he shall be put to death, and also the one who receives the stolen thing from him shall be put to death.

#8. If anyone steal cattle or sheep, or an ass, or a pig or a goat, if it belong to a god or to the court, the thief shall pay thirtyfold therefor; if they belonged to a freed man of the king he shall pay tenfold; if the thief has nothing with which to pay he shall be put to death.

#29. If [when a chieftain or a man be caught in the misfortune of a king, (captured in battle)] his son is still young, and cannot take possession, a third of the field and garden shall be given to his mother, and she shall bring him up.

#130. If a man violate the wife (betrothed or child-wife) of another man, who has never known a man, and still lives in her father's house, and sleep with her and be surprised, this man shall be put to death, but the wife is blameless.

#175. If a State slave or the slave of a freed man marry the daughter of a free man, and children are born, the master of the slave shall have no right to enslave the children of the free."

The Code of Hammurabi, a Babylonian law code promulgated in ancient Mesopotamia, ca 1754 BCE

8. When examining the passages from the Code of Hammurabi, which of the following statements is most accurate?

(A) The laws only applied to a small sector of the population and were designed to punish the less important subjects.

(B) The legal code concerned only the rights of men, as Mesopotamia was a patriarchal society.

(C) The laws were open to interpretation depending on the social class of the plaintiff.

(D) The legal code was designed to provide clear examples and ensure a uniformity of decision making in lawsuits.

9. The law code provided supports which characteristic of Mesopotamian society that also appears to have been present in nearly all of the other early civilizations?

(A) Lack of trade guidelines

(B) Some form of social hierarchy, typically patriarchy

(C) Equality of all citizens under the law

(D) Extensive bureaucracies to facilitate government

10. Legal codes like the Code of Hammurabi had which of the following effects on the relationship between government and the individual?

(A) They replaced governmental power over people with religious ties.

(B) Law codes prevented the fall of autocratic governments.

(C) They facilitated the rule of governments over people.

(D) Law codes reinforced the role of women who were the chief scribes.

Short-Answer Questions

1. Answer all parts of the question that follows.

(A) Identify ONE specific early city that exemplifies the River Valley civilizations.

(B) Explain ONE way culture played a significant role in unifying states in the early River Valley civilizations.

(C) Explain ANOTHER way culture played a significant role in unifying states in the early River Valley civilizations.

2. Answer all parts of the question that follows.

(A) Identify ONE way the emergence of cities affected social hierarchies in early civilizations before 600 BCE.

(B) Explain ONE way the emergence of cities affected economic activities in early civilizations before 600 BCE.

(C) Explain ONE way the emergence of cities affected political hierarchies in early civilizations before 600 BCE.

The Mediterranean and Middle East, 2000–500 BCE

3

AP® Framework Terms

Hebrew monotheism
Judaism
Hebrew scriptures
Jewish Diaspora
Assyrian Empire
Babylonian Empire
Phoenicia

Overarching Questions

1 How and to what extent have environmental factors, disease, and technology affected patterns of human migration and settlement over time? (ENV)

2 How have religions, belief systems, philosophies, and ideologies affected the political, economic, and social development of societies? (CUL)

3 How and why have economic, social, cultural, and geographic factors influenced the process of state building, expansion, and dissolution? (SB)

4 How have economic systems and the development of ideologies, values, and institutions influenced each other over time? (ECON)

5 How have social categories, roles, and practices been maintained or challenged over time? (SOC)

Ancient peoples' stories—even when not historically accurate—provide valuable insights into how they thought about their origins and identity. One famous story concerned the founding of the city of Carthage (**KAHR-thuhj**) in present-day Tunisia, which for centuries dominated the waters and waterborne commerce of the western Mediterranean. Tradition held that Dido and her supporters fled the Phoenician city-state of Tyre (**tire**) in southern Lebanon after her husband was murdered by her brother, the king. Landing on the North African coast, they made contact with local people, who offered them as much land as a cow's hide could cover. Cleverly cutting the hide into narrow strips, they marked out a substantial territory for Kart Khadasht, the "New City" (called *Carthago* by their Roman enemies). The painting at the beginning of this chapter envisions the construction of the city.

This story highlights the spread of cultural patterns from older centers to new regions, as well as the migration of Late Bronze Age and Early Iron Age peoples in the Mediterranean lands and western Asia. Trade, diplomatic contacts, military conquests, and the relocation of large numbers of people spread knowledge, beliefs, practices, and technologies.

By the early first millennium BCE many societies of the Eastern Hemisphere were entering the **Iron Age**, using iron in addition to bronze for tools and weapons. Iron offered several advantages. It was a single metal rather than an alloy, and there were many sources of iron ore. Once the technology had been mastered—iron has to be heated to a higher temperature than bronze, and its hardness depends on the amount of carbon added during the forging process—iron tools were found to have harder, sharper edges than bronze tools.

▲ **Dido Building Carthage** This 1815 CE painting by British artist J. M. W. Turner shows the construction of the newly founded city of Carthage by Dido (seen on the left), a story familiar from the Roman poet Vergil's epic *Aeneid*. Heritage Image Partnership Ltd/Alamy Stock Photo

The first part of this chapter resumes the story of Mesopotamia and Egypt in the second millennium BCE: their relations with neighboring peoples; the development of a prosperous, "cosmopolitan" network of states in the Middle East; and the period of destruction and decline that set in around 1200 BCE. We also look at how the Minoan and Mycenaean civilizations of the Aegean Sea were inspired by the technologies and cultural patterns of the older Middle Eastern centers and prospered from participation in long-distance trade networks. The remainder of the chapter examines the resurgence of this region in the Early Iron Age, from 1000 to 500 BCE. The focus is on three societies: the Assyrians of northern Mesopotamia; the Israelites of Israel; and the Phoenicians of Lebanon and their colonies in the western Mediterranean, mainly Carthage. After the decline of the ancient centers dominant throughout the third and second millennia BCE, these societies evolved into new political, cultural, and commercial centers. ●

3-1 The Cosmopolitan Middle East, 1700–1100 BCE

How did a cosmopolitan civilization develop in the Middle East during the Late Bronze Age, and what forms did it take?

Both Mesopotamia and Egypt succumbed to outside invaders in the seventeenth century BCE. Eventually the outsiders were either ejected or assimilated, and conditions of stability and prosperity were restored. Between 1500 and 1200 BCE a number of large states dominated the Middle East (see Map 3.1), controlling the smaller states and *kinship groups* (peoples with simple political structures living in relatively small groups based on perceived descent from common ancestors) as they interacted, competed with, and sometimes fought against one another for control of valuable commodities and trade routes.

The Late Bronze Age in the Middle East was a "cosmopolitan" era of widely shared cultures and lifestyles. Diplomatic relations and commercial contacts between states fostered the flow of goods and ideas, and elite groups shared similar values and enjoyed a relatively high standard of living. The peasants in the country-side, who constituted the majority of the population, saw some improvement in their standard of living but reaped fewer benefits from the increasing contacts and trade.

Iron Age Historians' term for the period during which iron was the primary metal for tools and weapons. The advent of iron technology began at different times in different parts of the world.

3-1a Western Asia

By 1500 BCE Mesopotamia was divided into two distinct political zones: Babylonia in the south and Assyria in the north (see Map 3.1). The city of Babylon had gained political and cultural ascendancy over the southern plain under the dynasty of Hammurabi in the eighteenth and seventeenth centuries BCE (see Chapter 2). Subsequently Kassites (**KAS-ite**) from the Zagros (**ZAH-groes**) Mountains to the east migrated into southern Mesopotamia, and by 1460 BCE a Kassite dynasty ruled in Babylon. The Kassites retained names in their native language but otherwise embraced Babylonian language and culture and inter-married with the native population. During their 250 years in power, the Kassite rulers of Babylonia defended their core area and traded for raw materials, but they did not pursue territorial conquest.

The Assyrian kingdom in northern Mesopotamia was more ambitious. As early as the twentieth century BCE (the "Old Assyrian" period) the city of Ashur (**AH-shoor**) on the northern Tigris anchored a busy trade route stretching across the northern plain to the Anatolian Plateau. Assyrian merchant families settled outside the walls of Anatolian cities and exchanged textiles and tin (a component of bronze) for Anatolian silver. After 1400 BCE a resurgent "Middle Assyrian" kingdom engaged in campaigns of conquest and expansion of its economic interests.

Other dynamic states emerged on the periphery of the Mesopotamian heartland, including Elam in southwest Iran and Mitanni (**mih-TAH-nee**) in the broad plain between the upper Euphrates and Tigris Rivers. Most formidable of all were the **Hittites** (**HIT-ite**), who became the foremost power in Anatolia from around 1700 to 1200 BCE. From their capital at Hattusha (**haht-tush-SHAH**), near present-day Ankara (**ANG-kuh-ruh**) in central Turkey, they deployed

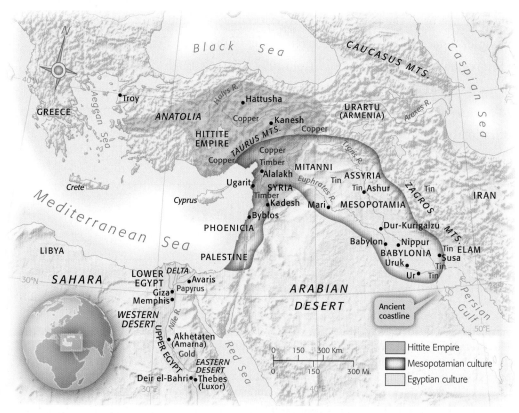

Hittites A people from central Anatolia who established an empire in Anatolia and Syria in the Late Bronze Age. With wealth from the trade in metals and military power based on chariot forces, the Hittites vied with New Kingdom Egypt for control of Syria-Palestine before falling to unidentified attackers ca. 1200 BCE.

MAP 3.1 The Middle East in the Second Millennium BCE Although warfare was not uncommon, treaties, diplomatic missions, and correspondence in Akkadian cuneiform fostered cooperative relationships between states. All were tied together by extensive networks of exchange centering on the trade in metals, and peripheral regions, such as Nubia and the Aegean Sea, were drawn into the web of commerce.

Given the relative locations of the three major cultural zones shown on this map and the technology of the time, how do you think trade goods may have been transported between these regions?

CHRONOLOGY

	Western Asia	Egypt	Syria–Palestine	Mediterranean
2000 BCE	2000 BCE Horses in use 1700–1200 BCE Hittites dominant in Anatolia	2040–1640 BCE Middle Kingdom 1640–1532 BCE Hyksos dominate northern Egypt 1532 BCE Beginning of New Kingdom	1800 BCE Abraham migrates to Canaan	2000 BCE Rise of Minoan civilization on Crete; early Greeks arrive in Greece 1600 BCE Rise of Mycenaean civilization in Greece
1500 BCE	1500 BCE Hittites develop iron metallurgy 1460 BCE Kassites assume control of southern Mesopotamia 1200 BCE Destruction of Hittite kingdom	1470 BCE Queen Hat-shepsut dispatches expedition to Punt 1353 BCE Akhenaten launches reforms 1290–1224 BCE Reign of Ramesses the Great 1200–1150 BCE Sea Peoples attack Egypt 1070 BCE End of New Kingdom	1500 BCE Early "alphabetic" script developed at Ugarit 1250–1200 BCE Israelite occupation of Canaan 1150 BCE Philistines settle southern coast of Israel	1450 BCE Destruction of Minoan palaces in Crete 1200–1150 BCE Destruction of Mycenaean centers in Greece
1000 BCE	1000 BCE Iron metallurgy begins 911 BCE Rise of Neo-Assyrian Empire 744–727 BCE Reforms of Tiglathpileser 668–627 BCE Reign of Ashurbanipal 626–539 BCE Neo-Babylonian kingdom 612 BCE Fall of Assyria	750 BCE Kings of Kush control Egypt 671 BCE Assyrian conquest of Egypt	1000 BCE Jerusalem made Israelite capital 969 BCE Hiram of Tyre comes to power 960 BCE Solomon builds First Temple 920 BCE Division into two kingdoms of Israel and Judah 721 BCE Assyrian conquest of northern kingdom 701 BCE Assyrian humiliation of Tyre	1000 BCE Iron metallurgy 814 BCE Foundation of Carthage
600 BCE			587 BCE Capture of Jerusalem 515 BCE Deportees from Babylon return to Jerusalem 450 BCE Completion of Hebrew Bible	550–300 BCE Rivalry of Carthaginians and Greeks in western Mediterranean ca. 500 BCE Hanno the Carthaginian explores West Africa

the fearsome new technology of horse-drawn war chariots. The Hittites exploited Anatolia's rich metal deposits to play a key role in international commerce.

The Hittites also first developed a technique for making tools and weapons of iron. Heating the ore until it was soft enough to shape, they pounded it to remove impurities and then plunged it into cold water to harden. They kept knowledge of this process secret because it provided military and economic advantages. In the disrupted period after 1200 BCE, blacksmiths from the Hittite core area may have migrated and spread iron technology.

During the second millennium BCE Mesopotamian political and cultural concepts spread across western Asia. Akkadian (**uh-KAY-dee-uhn**) became the language of diplomacy and correspondence between governments. The Elamites (**EE-luh-mite**) and Hittites, among others, adapted the cuneiform system to write their own languages. In the Syrian coastal city-state of Ugarit (**OO-guh-reet**), thirty cuneiform symbols were used to write consonant sounds, an early use of the alphabetic principle and a considerable advance over the hundreds of signs required in conventional cuneiform and hieroglyphic writing. Mesopotamian myths, legends, and styles of

▲ **Remains of a Sunken Cargo Ship from the Late Bronze Age** Underwater archaeologists excavate a merchant vessel that went down off the coast of southern Turkey ca. 1300 BCE. To the left of the wooden keel and planking is a stone anchor, to the right a row of copper ingots. The vessel was carrying a cargo of copper and tin ingots, as well as Canaanite pots that probably contained incense, fine pottery from Cyprus, sub-Saharan ebony wood and elephant tusks, and some Mycenaean Greek objects, illustrating the wide-ranging seaborne trade in the eastern Mediterranean in that era. Institute of Nautical Archaeology

art and architecture were widely imitated. Newcomers who had learned and improved on the lessons of Mesopotamian civilization often put pressure on the old core area. The small, fractious city-states of the third millennium BCE had been concerned only with their immediate neighbors in southern Mesopotamia. In contrast, the larger states of the second millennium BCE interacted politically, militarily, and economically in a geopolitical sphere encompassing all of western Asia.

3-1b New Kingdom Egypt

After flourishing for nearly 400 years (see Chapter 2), the Egyptian Middle Kingdom declined in the seventeenth century BCE. As officials in the countryside became increasingly independent and new groups migrated into the Nile Delta, central authority broke down and Egypt entered a period of political fragmentation and economic decline. Around 1640 BCE northern Egypt came under foreign rule for the first time, at the hands of the Hyksos (**HICK-soes**), or "Princes of Foreign Lands."

Historians are uncertain who the Hyksos were and how they came to power. Semitic peoples had been migrating from the Syria-Palestine region (present-day Syria, Jordan, Lebanon, Israel, and the Palestinian territories) into the eastern Nile Delta for centuries. In the chaotic conditions of this time, various groups may have cooperated to establish control, first in the delta and then in the middle of the country. The Hyksos possessed advantageous military technologies, such as the horse-drawn war chariot and a composite bow, made of wood and horn, that had greater range and velocity than the simple wooden bow. They intermarried with Egyptians, used the Egyptian language, and maintained Egyptian institutions and culture. Nevertheless, in contrast to the easy assimilation of outsiders such as the Kassites in Mesopotamia, the Egyptians, with their strong ethnic identity, continued to regard the Hyksos as "foreigners."

As with the formation of the Middle Kingdom 500 years earlier, the reunification of Egypt under a native dynasty was accomplished by princes from Thebes. After three decades of warfare, Kamose (**KAH-mose**) and Ahmose (**AH-mose**) expelled the Hyksos from Egypt and inaugurated the New Kingdom, which lasted from about 1532 to 1070 BCE.

A century of foreign domination had injured Egyptian pride and shattered the isolationist mindset of earlier eras. New Kingdom Egypt was an aggressive and expansionist state. By extending its territorial control north into Syria-Palestine and south into Nubia, Egypt won access to timber, gold, and copper (bronze metallurgy took hold in Egypt around 1500 BCE), as well as taxes and tribute payments from the conquered peoples. The occupied territories provided a buffer zone, protecting Egypt from attack. In Nubia, Egypt imposed direct control and pressed the native population to adopt Egyptian language and culture. In the Syria-Palestine region, in contrast, the Egyptians stationed garrisons at strategically placed forts and supported cooperative local rulers.

In this period of innovation, Egypt fully participated in the diplomatic and commercial networks linking the states of western Asia. Egyptian soldiers, administrators, diplomats, and merchants traveled widely, bringing back new fruits and vegetables, new musical instruments, and new technologies, such as an improved potter's wheel and weaver's loom.

Hatshepsut Queen of Egypt (r. 1473–1458 BCE). She dispatched a naval expedition to Punt (possibly northeast Sudan or Eritrea), the faraway source of myrrh. There is evidence of opposition to a woman as ruler, and after her death her name and image were frequently defaced.

One woman held the throne of New Kingdom Egypt. When her husband died, Queen Hatshepsut (**hat-SHEP-soot**) claimed the royal title for herself (r. 1473–1458 BCE). In inscriptions she often used the male pronoun for herself, and drawings and sculptures show her wearing the long, conical beard of the Egyptian ruler.

▲ **The Mortuary Temple of Queen Hatshepsut at Deir el-Bahri, Egypt, ca. 1460 BCE** This beautiful complex of terraces, ramps, and colonnades featured relief sculptures and texts commemorating the famous expedition to Punt. Hatshepsut, facing resistance from traditionalists opposed to a woman ruling Egypt, sought to prove her worth by publicizing the opening of direct contact with the source of highly prized myrrh. eugen_z/Shutterstock.com

Around 1470 BCE Hatshepsut sent a naval expedition down the Red Sea to the fabled land of Punt **(poont)**, probably near the coast of eastern Sudan or Eritrea. Hatshepsut was seeking the source of myrrh **(murr)**, a reddish-brown resin from the hardened sap of a local tree, which the Egyptians burned on the altars of their gods and used in medicines and cosmetics. When the expedition returned with myrrh and sub-Saharan luxury goods—ebony, ivory, cosmetics, live monkeys, panther skins—Hatshepsut celebrated the achievement in a great public display and in words and pictures on the walls of her mortuary temple at Deir el-Bahri **(DARE uhl–BAH-ree)**. She may have used the success of this expedition to bolster her claim to the throne. After her death, her image was defaced and her name blotted out wherever it appeared, presumably by officials opposed to a woman ruler.

A century later another untraditional ruler ascended the throne as Amenhotep **(ah-muhn-HOE-tep)** IV, but he soon began to refer to himself as **Akhenaten (ah-ken-AHT-n)** (r. 1353–1335 BCE), meaning "beneficial to the Aten" **(AHT-n)** (the disk of the sun). Changing his name was one way to spread his belief in Aten as the supreme deity. He closed the temples of other gods, challenging the age-old supremacy of the chief god Amon **(AH-muhn)** and the power and influence of his priests. Some scholars have credited Akhenaten with the invention of *monotheism*—the belief in one exclusive god. It is likely, however, that Akhenaten was attempting to reassert the superiority of the king over the priests and to renew belief in the king's divinity. Worship of Aten was confined to the royal family: the people of Egypt were pressed to revere the divine ruler.

Akhenaten built a new capital at modern-day Amarna **(uh-MAHR-nuh)**, halfway between Memphis and Thebes (see Map 3.1). He transplanted thousands of Egyptians to construct the site and serve the ruling elite. Akhenaten and his artists created a new style that broke with the conventions of earlier art: the king, his wife Nefertiti **(nef-uhr-TEE-tee)**, and their daughters were depicted in fluid, natural poses with strangely elongated heads and limbs and swelling abdomens.

AP® Exam Tip
Know examples of monumental architecture developed by early civilizations.

Akhenaten Egyptian pharaoh (r. 1353–1335 BCE). He built a new capital at Amarna, fostered a new style of naturalistic art, and created a religious revolution by imposing worship of the sun-disk.

Akhenaten's reforms were strongly resented by government officials and priests whose privileges and wealth were linked to the traditional system. After his death the temples were reopened; Amon was reinstated as chief god; the capital was returned to Thebes; and the institution of kingship was weakened to the advantage of the priests. The boy-king Tutankhamun (**tuht-uhnk-AH-muhn**) (r. 1333–1323 BCE), famous solely because his was the only royal tomb found by archaeologists that had not been pillaged by robbers, reveals both in his name (meaning "beautiful in life is Amon") and in his insignificant reign the ultimate failure of Akhenaten's revolution.

The rulers of a new dynasty, the Ramessides (**RAM-ih-side**), returned to the policy of conquest and expansion that Akhenaten had neglected. The greatest of these monarchs, **Ramesses II** (**RAM-ih-seez**), ruled for sixty-six years (r. 1290–1224 BCE) and dominated his age. Ramesses undertook monumental building projects all over Egypt. Living into his nineties, he had many wives and may have fathered more than a hundred children. Since 1990 archaeologists have been excavating a network of corridors and chambers carved deep into a hillside near Thebes, where many sons of Ramesses were buried.

3-1c Commerce and Communication

Early in his reign Ramesses II fought the Hittites to a draw in a major battle at Kadesh in northern Syria (1285 BCE). Subsequently, diplomats negotiated a treaty, which was strengthened by Ramesses's marriage to a Hittite princess. At issue was control of Syria-Palestine, strategically located between the great powers of the Middle East and at the end of the east–west trade route across Asia. Inland cities—such as Mari (**MAH-ree**) on the upper Euphrates and Alalakh (**UH-luh-luhk**) in western Syria—received overland caravans. Coastal towns—particularly Ugarit and the Phoenician towns of the Lebanese seaboard—extended commerce to the lands ringing the Mediterranean Sea.

Any state seeking to project its power needed metals for tools, weapons, and ornamentation, and commerce in metals energized the long-distance trade of the time. Assyrians were interested in silver from Anatolia (discussed previously), and the Egyptians had a passion for Nubian gold (see Chapter 4). Copper came from Anatolia and Cyprus, tin from Afghanistan and possibly the British Isles. Both ores had to be carried long distances and pass through a number of hands before reaching their final destinations.

Ramesses II A long-lived ruler of New Kingdom Egypt (r. 1290–1224 BCE). He reached an accommodation with the Hittites of Anatolia after a standoff in battle at Kadesh in Syria. He built on a grand scale throughout Egypt.

▲ **Ramesses II in a War Chariot Attacks Nubian Enemies**   This is a restoration of a thirteenth century BCE painting on the wall of a temple at Beit el Wali. Other paintings depict the pharaoh attacking Asiatic enemies and making offerings to the high god Amon. www.BibleLandPictures.com / Alamy Stock Photo

New modes of transportation expedited communications and commerce across great distances and inhospitable landscapes. Horses, domesticated by nomadic peoples in Central Asia, were brought into Mesopotamia through the Zagros Mountains around 2000 BCE and reached Egypt before 1600 BCE. The speed of travel and communication made possible by horses contributed to the creation of large states and empires, enabling soldiers and government agents to cover great distances quickly. Swift, maneuverable horse-drawn chariots became the premier instrument of war. The team of driver and archer could run up and unleash a volley of arrows or trample terrified foot-soldiers.

Sometime after 1500 BCE in western Asia, but not for another thousand years in Egypt, people began to make common use of camels, though the animal may have been domesticated a millennium earlier in southern Arabia. Thanks to their strength and ability to go long distances without water, camels were able to travel across barren terrain. Their physical qualities eventually led to the emergence of a new kind of desert nomad and the creation of cross-desert trade routes (see Chapter 9).

Section Review

- In the Late Bronze Age trade and diplomatic contacts between states fostered the flow of goods and ideas, and elite groups enjoyed similar lifestyles and a relatively high standard of living.

- Immigrant groups that came to power in Babylonia (Kassites) and Egypt (Hyksos) assimilated to Babylonian and Egyptian language and culture.

- New peoples in western Asia who learned and improved on the technologies and culture of Mesopotamian civilization challenged the old core area.

- The Hittites used the technologies of chariot warfare and iron metallurgy to dominate Anatolia.

- New Kingdom Egypt abandoned traditional isolationism and extended control over Syria-Palestine and Nubia. The era was marked by rulers who challenged tradition—Hatshepsut, Akhenaten, and Ramesses.

- Long-distance trade networks were based on metals and expedited by the advent of horses and camels.

3-2 The Aegean World, 2000–1100 BCE

What civilizations emerged in the Aegean world, and what relationship did they have to the older civilizations to the east?

The influence of Mesopotamia, Syria-Palestine, and Egypt was felt as far away as the Aegean Sea, a gulf of the eastern Mediterranean. The emergence of the Minoan **(mih-NO-uhn)** civilization on the island of Crete and the Mycenaean **(my-suh-NEE-uhn)** civilization of Greece is another manifestation of the fertilizing influence of older centers on outlying lands and peoples, who then struck out on their own unique paths of cultural evolution. With few deposits of metals and little timber, Aegean peoples had to import these commodities, as well as additional food supplies, from abroad. As a result, the rise, success, and eventual fall of the Minoan and Mycenaean societies were closely tied to their commercial and political relations with other peoples in the region.

3-2a Minoan Crete

By 2000 BCE the island of Crete (see Map 3.2) was home to the first European civilization to have complex political and social structures and advanced technologies like those found in western Asia and northeastern Africa. Archaeologists named this civilization **Minoan** after King Minos, who, in Greek legend, ruled a naval empire in the Aegean and kept the monstrous *Minotaur* **(MIN-uh-tor)** (half-man, half-bull) in a mazelike labyrinth built by the ingenious inventor Daedalus **(DED-ih-luhs)**. Thus later Greeks recollected a time when Crete had been home to many ships and skilled craftsmen.

The ethnicity of the Minoans is uncertain, and their writing has not been deciphered. But the distribution of Cretan pottery and other artifacts around the Mediterranean and Middle East testifies to widespread trading connections. Egyptian, Syrian, and Mesopotamian influences can be seen in the design of the Minoan palaces, centralized government, and system of writing. The absence of identifiable representations of Cretan rulers, however, contrasts sharply with the grandiose depictions of kings in the Middle East and suggests a different conception of authority. Also noteworthy is the absence of fortifications at the palace sites and the presence of high-quality indoor plumbing.

Minoan Prosperous civilization on the Aegean island of Crete in the second millennium BCE. The Minoans engaged in far-flung commerce around the Mediterranean and exerted powerful cultural influences on the early Greeks.

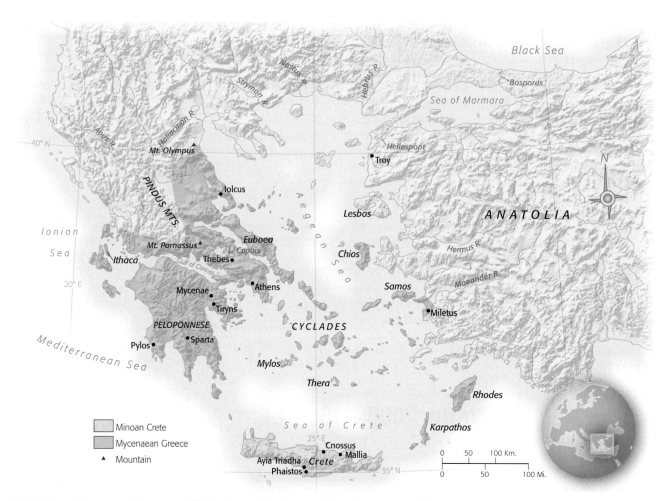

MAP 3.2 **Minoan and Mycenaean Civilizations of the Aegean** The earliest complex civilizations in Europe arose in the Aegean Sea. The Minoan civilization on the island of Crete evolved in the later third millennium BCE and had a major cultural influence on the Mycenaean Greeks. Palaces decorated with fresco paintings, a centrally controlled economy, and the use of writing for record keeping are conspicuous features of these societies.

What factors might have limited the expansion of the Minoans and Mycenaean Greeks into neighboring areas?

Statuettes of women with elaborate headdresses and serpents coiling around their limbs may represent fertility goddesses. Colorful frescoes (paintings done on the moist plaster surfaces of walls) in the palaces portray groups of women in frilly skirts conversing or watching performances. We do not know whether pictures of young acrobats vaulting over the horns and back of an onrushing bull show a religious activity or mere sport. The stylized depictions of scenes from nature on vases—plants with swaying leaves and playful octopuses winding their tentacles around the surface of the vase—communicate a delight in the beauty and order of the natural world.

All the Cretan palaces except at Cnossus (**NOSS-suhs**), along with the houses of the elite and peasants in the countryside, were deliberately destroyed around 1450 BCE. Because Mycenaean Greeks took over at Cnossus, most historians regard them as the culprits.

3-2b **Mycenaean Greece**

Speakers of an Indo-European language ancestral to Greek migrated into the Greek peninsula around 2000 BCE. Through intermarriage, blending of languages, and melding of cultural practices, the indigenous population and the newcomers created the first Greek culture. For centuries this society remained simple and static. Farmers and shepherds lived in Stone Age conditions, wringing a bare living from the land. Then, sometime around 1600 BCE, life changed relatively suddenly.

In 1876 a German businessman, Heinrich Schliemann (**SHLEE-muhn**), discovered a circle of graves at **Mycenae** (**my-SEE-nee**), in southern Greece. These deep, rectangular **shaft graves** contained the bodies of men, women, and children and were filled with gold jewelry and ornaments, weapons, and utensils. Clearly, some people in this society had acquired wealth, authority, and the capacity to mobilize human labor. Subsequent excavation uncovered a large palace complex, massive walls, more shaft graves, and other evidence of a rich and technologically advanced civilization that lasted from around 1600 to 1150 BCE.

How can the sudden rise of Mycenae and other centers in mainland Greece be explained? These early Greeks were clearly influenced by the Minoan palaces, centralized economy, and administrative bureaucracy, as well as the writing system. They adopted Minoan styles of architecture, pottery, and fresco and vase painting. The sudden accumulation of power and wealth may have resulted from the profits from trade and piracy and perhaps also from pay and booty brought back by *mercenaries* (soldiers who served for pay in foreign lands).

This first advanced civilization in Greece is called "Mycenaean" because Mycenae was the first site excavated. Other excavated centers reveal similar features: a hilltop location and high, thick fortification walls made of stones so large that later Greeks believed the giant, one-eyed Cyclopes (**SIGH-kloe-pees**) of legend had lifted them into place. The fortified citadel provided refuge for the entire community in time of danger and contained the palace and administrative complex. A large central hall with an open hearth and columned porch was surrounded by courtyards, living quarters for the royal family and their retainers, offices, storerooms, and workshops. Palace walls were covered with brightly painted frescoes depicting scenes of war, the hunt, and daily life, as well as decorative motifs from nature.

Nearby lay the tombs of the rulers and leading families: shaft graves at first; later, grand beehive-shaped structures made of stone and covered with a mound of earth. Large houses belonging to the aristocracy lay just outside the walls. The peasants lived on the lower slopes and in the plain below, close to the land they worked.

Additional information is provided by over 4,000 baked clay tablets written in a script called **Linear B**, which uses pictorial signs to represent syllables and is an early form of Greek. Palace administrators kept track of people, animals, and objects in exhaustive detail, listing the number of chariot wheels in storerooms, the rations paid to workers, and the gifts dedicated to various gods. The government exercised a high degree of control over the economy, organizing grain production and the wool industry from raw material to finished product. The tablets reveal little, however, about the political and legal system, social structure, gender relations, and religious beliefs. They tell nothing about historical figures (not even the name of a single Mycenaean king), particular historical events, or relations with other Mycenaean centers or foreign peoples.

Long-distance contact and trade were made possible by the seafaring skill of Minoans and Mycenaeans. Commercial vessels depended primarily on wind and sail. In general, ancient sailors preferred to sail in daylight hours and keep the land in sight. Their light, wooden vessels with low keels could run up onto the beach, allowing the crew to go ashore to eat and sleep at night.

Cretan and Greek pottery and crafted goods are found not only in the Aegean but also in other parts of the Mediterranean and Middle East. The oldest artifacts are Minoan; then Minoan and Mycenaean objects are found side by side; and eventually Greek wares replace Cretan goods altogether. Such evidence indicates that Cretan merchants pioneered trade routes and established trading posts and were later joined by Mycenaean traders, who supplanted them in the fifteenth century BCE.

The numerous Aegean pots found throughout the Mediterranean and Middle East once contained such products as wine and olive oil. Other possible exports include textiles, weapons, and other crafted goods, as well as slaves and mercenary soldiers. Aegean sailors also may have transported the trade goods of other peoples.

As for imports, *amber* (a translucent, yellowish-brown fossilized tree resin used for jewelry) from northern Europe and ivory carved in Syria have been discovered at Aegean sites, and the large population of southern Greece may have relied on imports of grain. Above all, the Aegean lands needed metals, both gold and the copper and tin needed to make bronze. Several sunken ships carrying copper ingots have been found on the floor of the Mediterranean. Only the elite classes owned metal goods, which may have been symbols of their superior status, as well as equipping them with superior weapons.

AP® Exam Tip
Be familiar with the development and diffusion of several systems of record keeping from this time period.

Mycenae Site of a fortified palace complex in southern Greece that controlled a Late Bronze Age kingdom. In Homer's epic poems, Mycenae was the base of King Agamemnon, who commanded the Greeks besieging Troy. Contemporary archaeologists call the complex Greek society of the second millennium BCE "Mycenaean."

shaft graves A term used for the burial sites of elite members of Mycenaean Greek society in the mid-second millennium BCE. At the bottom of deep shafts lined with stone slabs, the bodies were laid out along with gold and bronze jewelry, implements, weapons, and masks.

Linear B A set of syllabic symbols, derived from the writing system of Minoan Crete, used in the Mycenaean palaces of the Late Bronze Age to write an early form of Greek. It was used primarily for palace records, and the surviving Linear B tablets provide substantial information about the economic organization of Mycenaean society and tantalizing clues about political, social, and religious institutions.

▲ **Fresco from the Aegean Island of Thera, ca. 1650 BCE**   This picture shows the arrival of a fleet in a harbor as people watch from the walls of the town. The Minoan civilization of Crete was famous in legend for its naval power. The fresco reveals the appearance and design of ships in the Bronze Age Aegean. In the seventeenth century BCE, the island of Thera was devastated by a massive volcanic explosion, thought by many to be the origin of the myth of Atlantis sinking beneath the sea.   Dea/G Nimatallah/De Agostini Editore/Age Fotostock

Mycenaeans were tough, warlike, and acquisitive, trading with those who were strong and taking from those who were weak. In the fourteenth and thirteenth centuries BCE these qualities led them into conflict with the Hittite kings of Anatolia. Documents in the archives at the Hittite capital refer to the king and land of Ahhijawa (**uh-key-YAW-wuh**), most likely a Hittite rendering of *Achaeans* (**uh-KEY-uhns**), a term used by Homer for the Greeks. They indicate that relations were sometimes friendly, sometimes strained, and that the people of Ahhijawa took advantage of Hittite preoccupation or weakness. The *Iliad*, Homer's tale of the Achaeans' ten-year siege and eventual destruction of Troy, a city on the fringes of Hittite territory controlling the sea route between the Mediterranean and Black Seas, should be seen against this backdrop of Mycenaean belligerence and opportunism. Archaeology has confirmed a destruction at Troy around 1200 BCE.

3-2c The Fall of Late Bronze Age Civilizations

Hittite difficulties with Ahhijawa and the attack on Troy foreshadowed the troubles that culminated in the destruction of many of the old centers of the Middle East and Mediterranean around 1200 BCE. In this period, for reasons not well understood, large numbers of people were on the move. As migrants swarmed into one region, they displaced other peoples, who then joined the tide of refugees.

Around 1200 BCE unidentified invaders destroyed the Hittite capital, Hattusha, and the Hittite kingdom in Anatolia came crashing down. The tide of destruction moved south into Syria, and the great coastal city of Ugarit was swept away. Egypt managed to beat back two attacks: an assault on the Nile Delta around 1220 BCE by "Libyans and Northerners coming from all lands" and a major invasion by the "Sea Peoples" about thirty years later. Although the Egyptian ruler claimed a great victory, the Philistines (**FIH-luh-steen**) occupied the coast of Palestine (this is the origin of the name subsequently used for this region). Egypt soon surrendered all its territory in Syria-Palestine and lost contact with the rest of western Asia. The Egyptians also lost their foothold in Nubia, opening the way for the emergence of the native kingdom centered on Napata (see Chapter 4).

Among the invaders listed in the Egyptian inscriptions are the Ekwesh (**ECK-wesh**), who could be Achaeans—that is, Greeks. In these troubled times it is easy to imagine the participation of opportunistic Mycenaeans. The Mycenaean centers also saw trouble coming; at some sites they began to build more extensive fortifications and took steps to guarantee the water supply of the citadels. But their efforts were in vain, and nearly all the palaces were destroyed in the first half of the twelfth century BCE.

How these events came about is unclear. The archaeological record contains no trace of foreign invaders. An attractive explanation combines external and internal factors, since it is likely to be more than coincidence that the demise of Mycenaean civilization occurred at roughly the same time as the fall of other great civilizations in the region. Since the Mycenaean ruling class depended on the import of vital commodities and the profits from trade, the destruction of major trading partners and disruption of trade routes would have weakened their position. Competition for limited resources may have led to internal unrest and, ultimately, political collapse.

The end of Mycenaean civilization illustrates the interdependence of the major centers of the Late Bronze Age. It also highlights the consequences of political and economic collapse. The destruction of the palaces ended the domination of the ruling class. The massive administrative apparatus revealed in the Linear B tablets disappeared. The technique of writing was forgotten, since it had been known only to palace officials and was no longer useful. Archaeological studies indicate the depopulation of some regions of Greece and an inflow of people to other regions that had escaped destruction. The Greek language persisted, and a thousand years later people were still worshiping gods mentioned in the Linear B tablets. People also continued to make the vessels and implements that they were familiar with, although with a marked decline in artistic and technical skill in a much poorer society. The cultural uniformity of the Mycenaean Age gave way to regional variations in shapes, styles, and techniques, reflecting increased isolation of different parts of Greece.

Thus perished the cosmopolitan world of the Late Bronze Age in the Mediterranean and Middle East. Societies that had long prospered through complex links of trade, diplomacy, and shared technologies now collapsed in the face of external violence and internal weakness, and the peoples of the region entered a centuries-long "Dark Age" of poverty, isolation, and loss of knowledge.

Section Review

- The Minoan civilization on the island of Crete and the Mycenaean civilization of Greece were strongly influenced by the older centers in Egypt, Syria, and Mesopotamia, yet they followed unique paths of cultural evolution.

- By 2000 BCE Crete was home to the first European civilization, with complex political and social structures and advanced technologies.

- The sudden rise to wealth and power of Mycenae and other centers in mainland Greece ca. 1600 was due to the influence of Minoan Crete and the Mycenaeans' insertion into trade networks.

- The Linear B tablets reveal how the Mycenaean palaces exerted centralized control over the economy, and Hittite documents show the Mycenaeans to be aggressive and acquisitive.

- The economic interdependence of Late Bronze Age states increased their vulnerability to attacks by migrating peoples ca. 1200 BCE. The region descended into a centuries-long "Dark Age."

3-3 The Assyrian Empire, 911–612 BCE

How did the Assyrian Empire rise to power and eventually dominate most of the ancient Middle East?

A number of new centers emerged in western Asia and the eastern Mediterranean in the centuries after 1000 BCE. The most powerful and successful was the **Neo-Assyrian Empire** (911–612 BCE). Compared to the flat expanse of Babylonia to the south, the Assyrian homeland in northern Mesopotamia is hillier and has a more temperate climate and greater rainfall.

Peasant farmers, accustomed to defending themselves against raiders from the mountains to the east and north and the arid plain to the west, provided the foot-soldiers for the revival of Assyrian power. The rulers of the Neo-Assyrian Empire led a ceaseless series of campaigns: westward across the plain and desert as far as the Mediterranean, north into mountainous Urartu (**ur-RAHR-too**) (modern Armenia), east across the Zagros range onto the Iranian Plateau, and south along the Tigris River to Babylonia. These campaigns provided immediate booty and the long-term prospect of tribute and taxes. They also secured access to vital resources such as iron and silver and gave the Assyrians control of international commerce. Driven by pride, greed, and religious conviction, the Assyrians defeated the other great kingdoms of the day. At

Neo-Assyrian Empire An empire extending from western Iran to Syria-Palestine, conquered by the Assyrians of northern Mesopotamia between the tenth and seventh centuries BCE. They used force and terror and exploited the wealth and labor of their subjects. They also preserved and continued the cultural and scientific developments of Mesopotamian civilization.

its peak their empire stretched from Anatolia, Syria-Palestine, and Egypt in the west, across Armenia and Mesopotamia, and as far as western Iran. The Assyrians created a new kind of empire, larger in extent than anything seen before (see Map 3.3) and dedicated to the enrichment of the imperial center at the expense of the subjugated periphery.

3-3a God and King

The king was literally and symbolically the center of the Assyrian universe. All the land belonged to him, and all the people, even the highest-ranking officials, were his servants. Assyrians believed that the gods chose the king as their earthly representative. Normally the king selected one of his sons to succeed him, then had the choice confirmed by divine oracles and the Assyrian elite. In the revered ancient city of Ashur the high priest anointed the new king's head with oil and gave him the insignia of kingship: a crown and scepter. The kings were also buried in Ashur.

Messengers and spies brought the king information from every corner of the empire. The king appointed officials, heard complaints, dictated correspondence to an army of scribes, and received foreign envoys. He was the military leader, responsible for planning campaigns, and was often away from the capital commanding operations in the field.

The king also devoted much of his time to supervising the state religion, attending elaborate public and private rituals, and overseeing the upkeep of the temples. He made no decisions of state without consulting the gods through rituals of divination, and all actions were carried out in the name of Ashur, the chief god. Military victories were cited as proof of Ashur's superiority over the gods of the conquered peoples.

Relentless government propaganda secured popular support for military campaigns that mostly benefited the king and the nobility. Royal inscriptions posted throughout the empire catalogued recent victories, extolled the unshakeable determination of the king, and promised ruthless punishments to anyone who resisted. Relief sculptures depicting hunts, battles, sieges, executions, and deportations covered the walls of the royal palaces. Looming over most scenes was the king, larger than anyone else, muscular and fierce. Few visitors to the Assyrian court could fail to be awed and intimidated.

3-3b Conquest and Control

Superior military organization and technology lay behind Assyria's unprecedented conquests. Early armies consisted of men who served in return for grants of land and peasants and slaves contributed by large landowners. Later, King Tiglath-pileser (**TIG-lath-pih-LEE-zuhr**) (r. 744–727 BCE) created a core army of professional soldiers made up of Assyrians and the most formidable subject peoples. At its peak the Assyrian state could mobilize a half-million troops, including light-armed bowmen and slingers who launched stone projectiles, armored spearmen, cavalry equipped with bows or spears, and four-man chariots.

Iron weapons gave Assyrian soldiers an advantage over many opponents, and cavalry provided speed and mobility. Assyrian engineers developed machinery and tactics for besieging fortified towns. They dug tunnels under the walls, built mobile towers for archers, and applied battering rams to weak points. Couriers and signal fires provided long-distance communication, while a network of spies gathered intelligence.

The Assyrians used terror tactics to discourage resistance and rebellion, inflicting harsh punishments and publicizing their brutality: civilians were thrown into fires, prisoners

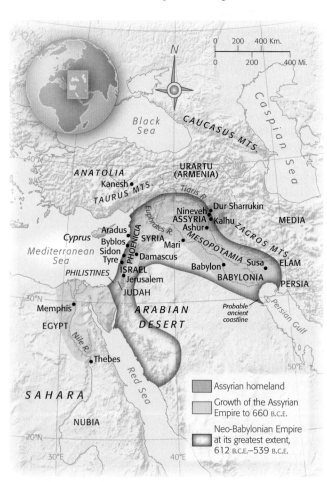

MAP 3.3 **The Assyrian Empire** From the tenth to the seventh century BCE the Assyrians of northern Mesopotamia created the largest empire the world had yet seen, extending from the Iranian Plateau to the eastern shore of the Mediterranean and containing a diverse array of peoples.

What geographical factors facilitated and blocked the expansion of the Assyrian Empire?

were skinned alive, and the severed heads of defeated rulers hung on city walls. **Mass deportation**—the forced uprooting of entire communities and resettlement elsewhere—broke the spirit of rebellious peoples. Although this tactic had a long history in the ancient Middle East, the Neo-Assyrian monarchs used it on an unprecedented scale, and up to 4 million people may have been relocated. Deportation also shifted human resources from the periphery to the center, where the deportees worked on royal and noble estates, opened new lands for agriculture, and built palaces and cities.

The Assyrians never discovered an effective method of governing an empire of such vast distances, varied landscapes, and diverse peoples. Control tended to be tight at the center and in lands closest to the core area, and less so farther away. The Assyrian kings waged many campaigns to reinstate control over territories subdued in previous wars. Provincial officials oversaw the collection of tribute and taxes, maintained law and order, raised troops, undertook public works, and provisioned armies and administrators passing through their territory. Provincial governors were subject to frequent inspections by royal overseers.

The Assyrians ruthlessly exploited the wealth and resources of their subjects. Military campaigns and administration were funded by plunder and tribute. Wealth from the periphery was funneled to the center, where the king and nobility grew rich. Triumphant kings expanded the ancestral capital and religious center at Ashur and built magnificent new royal cities encircled by high walls and containing ornate palaces and temples. Dur Sharrukin (**DOOR SHAH-roo-keen**), the "Fortress of Sargon," was completed in a mere ten years by a massive labor force composed of prisoners of war and Assyrian citizens who owed periodic service to the state.

Nevertheless, the Assyrian Empire was not simply parasitic. There is some evidence of royal investment in provincial infrastructure. The cities and merchant classes thrived on expanded long-distance commerce, and some subject populations were surprisingly loyal to their Assyrian rulers.

3-3c Assyrian Society and Culture

The Assyrian elite class was bound to the monarch by oaths of obedience, fear of punishment, and the expectation of rewards, such as land grants or shares of booty and taxes. Skilled professionals—priests, diviners, scribes, doctors, and artisans—were similarly bound.

Surviving sources primarily shed light on the deeds of kings and elites, and only a little is known about the lives and activities of the millions of Assyrian subjects. The government did not distinguish between native Assyrians and the increasingly large number of immigrants and deportees in the Assyrian homeland. All were referred to as "human beings," entitled to the same legal protections and liable for the same labor and military service. Over time the inflow of outsiders changed the ethnic makeup of the core area.

The vast majority of subjects worked on the land. The agricultural surpluses they produced allowed substantial numbers of people—the standing army, government officials, religious experts, merchants, artisans, and other professionals in the towns and cities—to engage in specialized activities.

▲ **Wall Relief from the Palace of Sennacherib at Nineveh** Assyrian soldiers leading prisoners with bound hands and holding up the heads of slain enemies. Such depictions were probably intended to intimidate visitors to the palace. www.BibleLandPictures.com/Alamy Stock Photo

Mass deportation The forcible removal and relocation of large numbers of people or entire populations. The mass deportations practiced by the Assyrian and Persian Empires were meant as a terrifying warning of the consequences of rebellion. They also brought skilled and unskilled labor to the imperial center.

Section Review

- Tough farmers in northern Mesopotamia provided the foot-soldiers for the rise of the Neo-Assyrian Empire, which dominated western Asia from the late tenth to seventh centuries BCE.

- Ceaseless campaigns of conquest brought booty, tribute and taxes, and control of international commerce and valuable resources.

- The all-powerful Assyrian king, claiming the support of the god Ashur, was at the center of government and the state religion.

- The Assyrians employed military might, propaganda, and state terrorism to intimidate their subjects, but they never developed an effective system of political control and frequently had to reconquer territory.

- The Assyrians ruthlessly funneled the wealth and resources of their subjects to the center, where the king and nobility grew rich. Frequent mass deportations provided manpower to build royal cities and work the lands of the elite.

- Assyrian scholars preserved and added to the long intellectual and scientific legacy of Mesopotamian civilization.

Individual artisans and small workshops in the towns manufactured pottery, tools, and clothing, and most trade took place at the local level. The state fostered long-distance trade, since imported luxury goods—metals, fine textiles, dyes, gems, and ivory—brought in substantial customs revenues and found their way to the royal family and elite classes. Silver was the basic medium of exchange, weighed out for each transaction in a time before the invention of coins.

Assyrian scholars preserved and built on the achievements of their Mesopotamian predecessors. When archaeologists excavated the palace of Ashurbanipal **(ah-shur-BAH-nee-pahl)** (r. 668–627 BCE), one of the last Assyrian kings, at Nineveh **(NIN-uh-vuh)**, they discovered more than 25,000 tablets or fragments. The **Library of Ashurbanipal** contained official documents as well as literary and scientific texts. Some were originals that had been brought to the capital; others were copies made at the king's request. The "House of Knowledge" referred to in some documents may have been an academy that attracted learned men to the imperial center. Much of what we know about Mesopotamian art, literature, science, and earlier history comes from discoveries at Assyrian sites.

3-4 Israel, 2000–500 BCE

How did the civilization of Israel develop, following both cultural patterns typical of other societies and its own unique ways?

The small land of Israel probably appeared insignificant to the Assyrian masters of western Asia, but it would play an important role in world history. Two interconnected dramas played out here between around 2000 and 500 BCE. First, a loose collection of nomadic groups engaged in herding and caravan traffic became a sedentary, agricultural people, developed complex political and social institutions, and became integrated into the commercial and diplomatic networks of the Middle East. Second, these people transformed the austere cult of a desert god into the concept of a single, all-powerful, and all-knowing deity, in the process creating ethical and intellectual traditions that underlie the beliefs and values of Judaism, Christianity, and Islam.

The land and people at the heart of this story have gone by various names: Canaan, Israel, Palestine; Hebrews, Israelites, Jews. For the sake of consistency, the people are referred to here as *Israelites*, the land they occupied in antiquity as **Israel**.

Israel is a crossroads, linking Anatolia, Egypt, Arabia, and Mesopotamia (see Map 3.4). Its natural resources are few. The Negev Desert and the vast wasteland of the Sinai **(SIE-nie)** lie to the south. The Mediterranean coastal plain was usually in the hands of others, particularly the Philistines, throughout much of this period. Galilee to the north, with its sea of the same name, was a relatively fertile land of grassy hills and small plains. The narrow ribbon of the Jordan River runs down the eastern side of the region into the Dead Sea, so named because its high salt content is toxic to life.

3-4a Origins, Exodus, and Settlement

Information about ancient Israel comes partly from archaeological excavations and documents such as the royal annals of Egypt and Assyria. Fundamental, but also problematic, are the texts preserved in the **Hebrew Bible** (called the Old Testament by Christians), a compilation of several collections of materials that originated with different groups and advocated particular interpretations of past events. Traditions about the Israelites' early history were long transmitted orally. Not until the tenth century BCE were they written down in a script borrowed from the Phoenicians. The text that we have today dates from the fifth century BCE, with a few later additions, and reflects the point of view of the priests who controlled the Temple in Jerusalem. The Hebrew language of the Bible reflects the speech of the Israelites until about 500 BCE, when it was supplanted by Aramaic. Although historians disagree about how accurately this document represents Israelite history, it provides a foundation to be used critically and tested against archaeological discoveries.

The history of ancient Israel follows a familiar pattern in the ancient Middle East: nomadic pastoralists, occupying marginal land between the inhospitable desert and settled agricultural

AP® Exam Tip Understand how Jewish monotheism influenced religions in later periods.

Library of Ashurbanipal A large collection of writings drawn from the ancient literary, religious, and scientific traditions of Mesopotamia. It was assembled by the seventh-century BCE Assyrian ruler Ashurbanipal. The many tablets unearthed by archaeologists constitute one of the most important sources of present-day knowledge of the long literary tradition of Mesopotamia.

Israel In antiquity, the land between the eastern shore of the Mediterranean and the Jordan River, occupied by the Israelites from the early second millennium BCE. The modern state of Israel was founded in 1948.

Hebrew Bible A collection of sacred books containing diverse materials concerning the origins, experiences, beliefs, and practices of the Israelites. Most of the extant text was compiled by members of the priestly class in the fifth century BCE and reflects the concerns and views of this group.

areas, sometimes engaged in trade and sometimes raided the farms and villages of settled peoples, but eventually they settled down to an agricultural way of life and later developed a unified state.

The Hebrew Bible tells the story of Abraham and his descendants. Born in the city of Ur in southern Mesopotamia, Abraham rejected the idol worship of his homeland and migrated with his family and livestock across the Syrian Desert. Eventually he arrived in the land of Israel, which had been promised to him and his descendants by the Israelite god, Yahweh.

These "recollections" of the journey of Abraham (who, if he was a real person, probably lived around 1800 BCE) may compress the experiences of generations of pastoralists who migrated from the grazing lands between the upper reaches of the Tigris and Euphrates Rivers to the Mediterranean coastal plain. They camped by a permanent water source in the dry season, then drove herds of sheep, cattle, and donkeys to a well-established sequence of grazing areas during the rest of the year. The animals provided them with milk, cheese, meat, and cloth.

The nomadic Israelites and the settled peoples were suspicious of one another. This friction between herders and farmers permeates the biblical story of the innocent shepherd Abel, who was killed by his farmer brother Cain, and the story of Sodom (**SOE-duhm**) and Gomorrah (**guh-MORE-uh**), two cities that Yahweh destroyed because of their wickedness.

In the Hebrew Bible, Abraham's son Isaac and then his grandson Jacob became the leaders of this migratory group of herders. In the next generation the squabbling sons of Jacob's several wives sold their brother Joseph as a slave to passing merchants heading for Egypt. Through luck and ability Joseph became a high official at the pharaoh's court. Thus he was in a position to help his people when drought struck and forced the Israelites to migrate to Egypt. The sophisticated Egyptians looked down on these rough herders and eventually enslaved them and put them to work on royal building projects.

Several points need to be made about this biblical account. First, the Israelite migration to Egypt and later enslavement may have been connected to the rise and fall of the Hyksos. Second, although surviving Egyptian sources do not refer to Israelite slaves, they do complain about Apiru (**uh-PEE-roo**), a derogatory term applied to

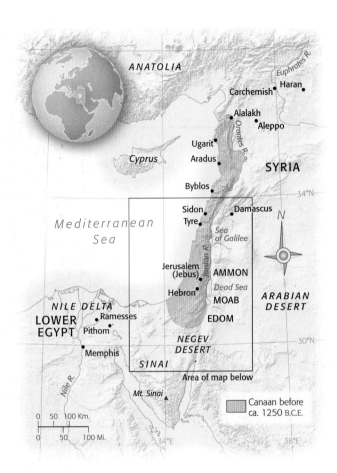

MAP 3.4 Phoenicia and Israel The lands along the eastern shore of the Mediterranean Sea—sometimes called the Levant or Syria-Palestine—have always been a crossroads, traversed by migrants, nomads, merchants, and armies moving between Egypt, Arabia, Mesopotamia, and Anatolia.

How did the arrival of the Israelites and Philistines impact the Canaanites already occupying the region?

caravan drivers, outcasts, bandits, and other marginal groups. Some scholars believe there may be a connection between the similar-sounding terms *Apiru* and *Hebrew*. Third, the period of alleged Israelite slavery coincided with the ambitious building programs launched by several New Kingdom pharaohs. However, there is little archaeological evidence of an Israelite presence in Egypt.

According to the Hebrew Bible, the Israelites were led out of captivity by Moses, an Israelite with connections to the Egyptian royal family. The narrative of their departure, the Exodus, is overlaid with folktale motifs, including the ten plagues that Yahweh inflicted on Egypt to persuade the pharaoh to release the Israelites and the miraculous parting of the waters of the Red Sea that enabled the refugees to escape. Oral tradition may have embellished memories of a real emigration from Egypt followed by years of wandering in the wilderness of Sinai.

During their forty years in the desert, as reported in the Hebrew Bible, the Israelites entered into a "covenant" or pact with their god, Yahweh: they would be his "Chosen People" if they promised to worship him exclusively. This covenant was confirmed by tablets that Moses brought down from the top of Mount Sinai, inscribed with the Ten Commandments that set out the basic tenets of Jewish belief and practice. The Commandments prohibited murder, adultery, theft, lying, and envy and demanded respect for parents and rest from work on the Sabbath, the seventh day of the week.

The biblical account proceeds to tell how Joshua, Moses's successor, led the Israelites from the east side of the Jordan River into the land of Canaan **(KAY-nuhn)** (modern Israel and the Palestinian territories), where they attacked and destroyed Canaanite **(KAY-nuh-nite)** cities. Archaeological evidence confirms the destruction of some Canaanite towns between 1250 and 1200 BCE, though not precisely the towns mentioned in the biblical account. Shortly thereafter, lowland sites were resettled and new sites were established in the hills. The material culture of the new settlers was cruder but continued Canaanite patterns. Most scholars doubt that Canaan was conquered by a unified Israelite army. In a time of widespread disruption, movements of peoples, and decline and destruction of cities throughout this region, it is more likely that Israelite migrants took advantage of the disorder and were joined by other groups and even refugees from the Canaanite cities.

The new coalition of peoples invented a common ancestry. The "Children of Israel," as they called themselves, were divided into twelve tribes supposedly descended from the sons of Jacob and Joseph. Each tribe was installed in a different part of the country and led by one or more chiefs. Such leaders usually had limited power and were primarily responsible for mediating disputes and seeing to the welfare and protection of the group. Certain charismatic figures, famed for their daring in war or genius in arbitration, were called "Judges" and enjoyed a special standing that transcended tribal boundaries. The tribes also shared access to a shrine in the hill country at Shiloh **(SHIE-loe)**, which housed the Ark of the Covenant, a sacred chest containing the tablets that Yahweh had given Moses.

3-4b Rise of the Monarchy

The troubles afflicting the eastern Mediterranean around 1200 BCE also brought the Philistines to the coastal plain of Israel, where they came into frequent conflict with the Israelites. Their wars were memorialized in Bible stories about the long-haired strongman Samson, who toppled a Philistine temple, and the shepherd boy David, whose slingshot felled the towering warrior Goliath. A religious leader named Samuel recognized the need for a strong central authority and anointed Saul as the first king of Israel around 1020 BCE. When Saul perished in battle, the throne passed to David (r. ca. 1000–960 BCE). Many scholars regard the biblical account for the period of the monarchy as more historically reliable than the earlier parts, although some maintain that the archaeological record still does not match up very well with that narrative and that the wealth and power of the early kings have been greatly exaggerated.

A gifted musician, warrior, and politician, David oversaw Israel's transition from tribal confederacy to unified monarchy. He strengthened royal authority by making the captured hill city of Jerusalem his capital. Soon after, David brought the Ark to Jerusalem, making the city the religious as well as political center of the kingdom. A census was taken to facilitate the collection of taxes, and a standing army, with soldiers paid by and loyal to the king, was established. These innovations enabled David to win military victories and expand Israel's borders.

▲ **The Western Wall in Jerusalem** The sole remaining remnant of King Herod's magnificent Second Temple, the religious center of ancient Judaism. It replaced Solomon's Temple, destroyed in the Babylonian conquest of 586 BCE, but was destroyed by the Romans in 70 CE in the course of suppressing a revolt in Judaea. The site is also sacred to Islam, with the golden Dome of the Rock in the background. Protasov AN/Shutterstock.com

The reign of David's son Solomon (r. ca. 960–920 BCE) marked the high point of the Israelite monarchy. Alliances and trade linked Israel with near and distant lands. Solomon and Hiram, the king of Phoenician Tyre, dispatched a fleet into the Red Sea to bring back gold, ivory, jewels, sandalwood, and exotic animals. The story of the visit to Solomon by the queen of Sheba may be mythical, but it reflects the reality of trade with Saba (**SUH-buh**) in south Arabia (present-day Yemen) or the Horn of Africa (present-day Somalia). The wealth gained from military and commercial ventures supported a lavish court life, a sizable bureaucracy, and an intimidating chariot army that made Israel a regional power. Solomon undertook an ambitious building program employing slaves and the compulsory labor of citizens. To strengthen the link between religious and secular authority, he built the **First Temple** in Jerusalem. The Israelites now had a central shrine and an impressive set of rituals that could compete with other religions in the area.

The Temple priests became a powerful and wealthy class, receiving a share of the annual harvest in return for making animal sacrifices to Yahweh on behalf of the community. The expansion of Jerusalem, new commercial opportunities, and the increasing prestige of the Temple hierarchy changed the social composition of Israelite society. A gap between urban and rural, rich and poor, polarized a people that previously had been relatively homogeneous. Fiery prophets, claiming revelation from Yahweh, accused the monarchs and aristocracy of corruption, impiety, and neglect of the poor (see Diversity & Dominance: Protests Against the Ruling Class in Israel and Babylonia).

The Israelites lived in extended families, several generations residing together under the authority of the eldest male. Male heirs were of paramount importance, and first-born sons received a double share of the inheritance. If a couple had no son, they could adopt one, or the husband could have a child by the wife's slave attendant. If a man died childless, his brother was expected to marry his widow and sire an heir.

In early Israel, because women provided vital goods and services that sustained the family, they were respected and had some influence with their husbands. Unlike men, however, they could not inherit property or initiate divorce, and a woman caught in extramarital relations could be put to death. Peasant women labored with other family members in agriculture or

First Temple A monumental sanctuary built in Jerusalem by King Solomon in the tenth century BCE to be the religious center for the Israelite god Yahweh. The Temple priesthood conducted sacrifices, received a tithe or percentage of agricultural revenues, and became economically and politically powerful.

herding in addition to caring for the house and children. As the society became urbanized, some women worked outside the home as cooks, perfumers, wet nurses, prostitutes, and singers of laments at funerals. A few women reached positions of power, such as Deborah the Judge, who led troops in battle against the Canaanites. "Wise women" composed sacred texts in poetry and prose. This reality has been obscured, in part by the male bias of the Hebrew Bible, in part because the status of women declined as Israelite society became more urbanized.

3-4c Fragmentation and Dispersal

After Solomon's death around 920 BCE, resentment over royal demands for money and labor and the neglect of tribal prerogatives split the monarchy into two kingdoms: Israel in the north, with its capital at Samaria (**suh-MAH-ree-yuh**), and Judah (**JOO-duh**) in the southern territory around Jerusalem (see Map 3.4). The two were sometimes at war, sometimes allied.

This period saw the final formulation of **monotheism**, the belief in Yahweh as the one and only god. Nevertheless, many Israelites were attracted to the ecstatic rituals of the Canaanite storm-god Baal (**BAHL**) and the fertility goddess Asherah (**uh-SHARE-uh**). Prophets condemned the adoption of foreign ritual and threatened that Yahweh would punish Israel severely.

The two Israelite kingdoms and other small states in the region laid aside their rivalries to mount a joint resistance to the Neo-Assyrian Empire, but to no avail. In 721 BCE the Assyrians destroyed the northern kingdom of Israel and deported much of its population to the east. New settlers were brought in from Syria, Babylon, and Iran, changing the area's ethnic, cultural, and religious character. The kingdom of Judah survived more than a century longer, sometimes rebelling, sometimes paying tribute to the Assyrians or the Neo-Babylonian kingdom (626–539 BCE) that succeeded them. When the Neo-Babylonian monarch Nebuchadnezzar (**NAB-oo-kuhd-nez-uhr**) captured Jerusalem in 587 BCE, he destroyed the Temple and deported to Babylon the royal family, the aristocracy, and many skilled workers such as blacksmiths and scribes.

The deportees prospered so well in their new home "by the waters of Babylon" that half a century later most of their descendants refused the offer of the Persian monarch Cyrus (see Chapter 5) to return to their homeland. This was the origin of the **Diaspora** (**die-ASS-peh-rah**)—a Greek word meaning "dispersion" or "scattering." This dispersion outside the homeland of many Jews—as we may now call these people, since an independent Israel no longer existed—continues to this day. To maintain their religion and culture, the Diaspora communities developed institutions like the synagogue (Greek for "bringing together"), a communal meeting place that served religious, educational, and social functions.

Several groups of Babylonian Jews did make the long trek back to Judah in the later sixth and fifth centuries BCE. They rebuilt the Temple in modest form and edited the Hebrew Bible into roughly its present form.

The loss of political autonomy and the experience of exile had sharpened Jewish identity. With an unyielding monotheism as their core belief, Jews lived by a rigid set of rules. Dietary restrictions forbade the eating of pork and shellfish and mandated that meat and dairy products not be consumed together. Ritual baths were used to achieve spiritual purity. The Jews venerated the Sabbath (Saturday, the seventh day of the week) by refraining from work and from fighting, following the example of Yahweh, who, according to the Bible, rested on the seventh day after creating the world (this is the origin of the concept of the week and the weekend). These strictures and others, including a ban on marrying non-Jews, tended to isolate the Jews from other peoples, but they also fostered a powerful sense of community and the belief that the Jews were protected by a watchful and beneficent deity.

AP® Exam Tip
Understand how the conquest of the Jewish state by the Assyrians, Babylonians, and Romans led to the Diaspora.

monotheism Belief in the existence of a single divine entity. Some scholars cite the devotion of the Egyptian pharaoh Akhenaten to Aten (sun-disk) and his suppression of traditional gods as the earliest instance. The Israelite worship of Yahweh developed into an exclusive belief in one god, and this concept passed into Christianity and Islam.

Diaspora Greek word meaning "dispersal," used to describe the communities of a given ethnic group living outside their homeland. Jews, for example, spread from Israel to western Asia and Mediterranean lands in antiquity and today can be found throughout the world.

Section Review

- Because of its strategic location, the small, resource-poor land of Israel has played an important role in world history.

- The history of the ancient Israelites can be reconstructed by critically comparing information in the Hebrew Bible with archaeological discoveries.

- The early Israelites were nomadic pastoralists, but eventually they settled down as farmers and herders in Canaan.

- As a result of their rivalry with the coastal Philistines, the once loosely organized Israelite tribes united under a monarchy, with Jerusalem as the capital.

- Urbanization, wealth from trade, and the status of the Temple priesthood created divisions within Israelite society. Fiery prophets railed against the greed and corruption of the elite.

- Following conquests by the Assyrian Empire and Neo-Babylonian kingdom, many Israelites were taken from their homeland. Diaspora communities created new institutions, a distinctive way of life, and a strong Jewish identity.

3-5 Phoenicia and the Mediterranean, 1200–500 BCE

How did the Phoenicians rise to commercial dominance over much of the Mediterranean world?

While the Israelite tribes were forging a united kingdom, the people who occupied the Mediterranean coast to the north were developing their own distinctive civilization. Historians follow the Greeks in calling them **Phoenicians** (**fi-NEE-shun**), though they referred to themselves as "Can'ani"—Canaanites. Despite few written records and archaeological remains disturbed by frequent migrations and invasions, some of their history can be reconstructed.

3-5a The Phoenician City-States

When the eastern Mediterranean was disturbed by violent upheavals and mass migrations around 1200 BCE, many Canaanite settlements in the Syria-Palestine region were destroyed. Aramaeans (**ah-ruh-MAY-uhn**)—nomadic pastoralists similar to the early Israelites—migrated into the interior portions of Syria. Farther south, Israelite herders and farmers settled in the interior of present-day Israel. The Philistines occupied the southern coast and introduced iron-based metallurgy to this part of the world.

By 1100 BCE Canaanite territory had shrunk to a narrow strip of present-day Lebanon between the mountains and the sea (see Map 3.4). Rivers and rocky spurs of Mount Lebanon sliced the coastal plain into a series of small city-states, chief among them Byblos (**BIB-loss**), Berytus (**buh-RIE-tuhs**), Sidon (**SIE-duhn**), and Tyre. The inhabitants of this densely populated area adopted new political forms and turned to seaborne commerce and new kinds of manufacture for their survival.

A thriving trade in raw materials (cedar and pine, metals, incense, papyrus), foodstuffs (wine, spices, salted fish), and crafted luxury goods (carved ivory, glass, and textiles) brought considerable wealth to the Phoenician city-states and gave them an important role in international politics. Fine textiles with bright, permanent colors became a major export product. Most prized was the red-purple known as Tyrian purple because Tyre was the major source. Persian and Hellenistic kings wore robes dyed this color, and a white toga with a purple border was the sign of a Roman senator. The production of Tyrian purple was an exceedingly laborious process. The spiny dye-murex snail lives on the sandy Mediterranean bottom at depths ranging from 30 to 500 feet (10 to 150 meters). Nine thousand snails were needed to produce 1 gram (0.035 ounce) of dye. Huge mounds of broken shells on the Phoenician coast are testimony to the ancient industry. The snail may have been rendered nearly extinct at many locations, and some scholars speculate that Phoenician colonization in the Mediterranean was motivated in part by the search for new sources of snails.

AP® Exam Tip
Be familiar with Phoenicia and its colonies as an example of the growth of empires through political unity.

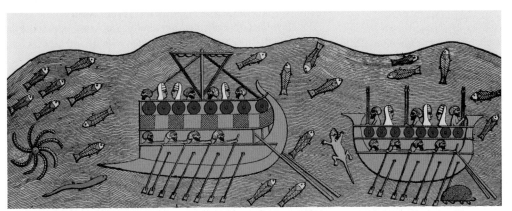

▲ **Phoenician Warships** Wall relief from Assyrian palace ca. 700 BCE depicting Phoenician warships. These "biremes," with two rows of oars, were later superseded by "triremes," utilized by the Phoenicians and their Greek rivals, equipped with three banks of oars and capable of attaining higher speeds. Photo Researchers, Inc/Alamy Stock Photo

Phoenicians Semitic-speaking Canaanites living on the coast of modern Lebanon and Syria in the first millennium BCE. From major cities such as Tyre and Sidon, Phoenician merchants and sailors explored the Mediterranean, engaged in widespread commerce, and founded Carthage and other colonies in the western Mediterranean.

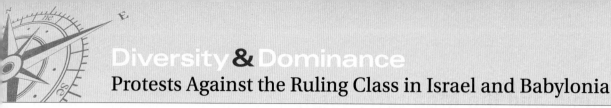
Israelite society underwent profound changes in the period of the monarchy, and the new opportunities for some to acquire considerable wealth led to greater disparities between rich and poor. A series of prophets publicly challenged the behavior of the Israelite ruling elite. They denounced the changes in Israelite society as corrupting people and separating them from the religious devotion and moral rectitude of an earlier, better time. The prophets often spoke out on behalf of the uneducated, illiterate, and powerless lower classes, and they thus provide valuable information about the experiences of different social groups. Theirs was not objective reporting, but rather the angry, anguished visions of unconventional individuals.

The following excerpt from the Hebrew Bible is taken from the book of Amos. A herdsman from the southern kingdom of Judah in the era of the divided monarchy, Amos was active in the northern kingdom of Israel in the mid-eighth century BCE, when Assyria threatened the Syria-Palestine region.

1:1 *The following is a record of what Amos prophesied. He was one of the herdsmen from Tekoa. These prophecies about Israel were revealed to him during the time of King Uzziah of Judah and King Jeroboam son of Joash of Israel....*

3:1 *Listen, you Israelites, to this message which the Lord is proclaiming against you. This message is for the entire clan I brought up from the land of Egypt:*

3:2 *"I have chosen you alone from all the clans of the earth. Therefore I will punish you for all your sins."...*

3:9 *"Gather on the hills around Samaria! [capital of the northern kingdom] Observe the many acts of violence taking place within the city, the oppressive deeds occurring in it."...*

3:11 *"Therefore," says the sovereign Lord, "an enemy will encircle the land. Your power, Samaria, will be taken away; your fortresses will be looted."*

3:12 *This is what the Lord says: "Just as a shepherd salvages from the lion's mouth a couple of leg bones or a piece of an ear, so the Israelites who live in Samaria will be salvaged. They will be left with just a corner of a bed, and a part of a couch."...*

4:1 *Listen to this message, you "cows of Bashan" who live on Mount Samaria! You oppress the poor; you crush the needy. You say to your husbands, "Bring us more to drink so we can party!"*

4:2 *The sovereign Lord confirms this oath by his own holy character: "Certainly the time is approaching! You will be carried away in baskets, every last one of you in fishermen's pots.*

4:3 *Each of you will go straight through the gaps in the walls; you will be thrown out toward Harmon."...*

5:11 *"Therefore, because you make the poor pay taxes on their crops and exact a grain tax from them, you will not live in the houses you built with chiseled stone, nor will you drink the wine from the fine vineyards you planted.*

5:12 *Certainly I am aware of your many rebellious acts and your numerous sins. You torment the innocent, you take bribes, and you deny justice to the needy at the city gate. ...*

5:21 *I absolutely despise your festivals. I get no pleasure from your religious assemblies.*

5:22 *Even if you offer me burnt and grain offerings, I will not be satisfied; I will not look with favor on the fattened calves you offer in peace.*

5:23 *Take away from me your noisy songs; I don't want to hear the music of your stringed instruments."...*

6:4 *They lie around on beds decorated with ivory, and sprawl out on their couches. They eat lambs from the flock, and calves from the middle of the pen.*

6:5 *They sing to the tune of stringed instruments; like David they invent musical instruments.*

6:6 *They drink wine from sacrificial bowls, and pour the very best oils on themselves.*

6:7 *Therefore they will now be the first to go into exile, and the religious banquets where they sprawl out on couches will end.*

7:10 *Amaziah the priest of Bethel sent this message to King Jeroboam of Israel: "Amos is conspiring against you in the very heart of the kingdom of Israel! The land cannot endure all his prophecies.*

7:11 *As a matter of fact, Amos is saying this: 'Jeroboam will die by the sword and Israel will certainly be carried into exile away from its land.'"*

7:12 *Amaziah then said to Amos, "Leave, you visionary! Run away to the land of Judah! Earn money and prophesy there!*

7:13 *Don't prophesy at Bethel any longer, for a royal temple and palace are here!"*

7:14 *Amos replied to Amaziah, "I was not a prophet by profession. No, I was a herdsman who also took care of sycamore fig trees.*

7:15 *Then the Lord took me from tending flocks and gave me this commission, 'Go! Prophesy to my people Israel!'"...*

8:8 *"Because of this the earth will quake, and all who live in it will mourn. The whole earth will rise like the River Nile, it will surge upward and then grow calm, like the Nile in Egypt.*

8:9 *In that day," says the sovereign Lord, "I will make the sun set at noon, and make the earth dark in the middle of the day.*

8:10 *I will turn your festivals into funerals, and all your songs into funeral dirges. I will make everyone wear funeral clothes and cause every head to be shaved bald. I will make you mourn as if you had lost your only son; when it ends it will indeed have been a bitter day."...*

9:8 *"Look, the sovereign Lord is watching the sinful nation, and I will destroy it from the face of the earth. But I will not completely destroy the family of Jacob," says the Lord. …*

9:11 *"In that day I will rebuild the collapsing hut of David. I will seal its gaps, repair its ruins, and restore it to what it was like in days gone by."*

A document from Babylon, which may have been composed around 1000 BCE, reveals the prevalence of similar inequities and abuses in that society. It is presented as a dialogue between a man in distress (who, despite his claim of low status, is literate and presumably comes from the urban middle class) and his compassionate friend.

Sufferer

I have looked around in the world, but things are turned around.

The god does not impede the way of even a demon.

A father tows a boat along the canal,

While his son lies in bed.

The eldest son makes his way like a lion,

The second son is happy to be a mule driver.

The heir goes about along the streets like a peddler,

The younger son (has enough) that he can give food to the destitute.

What has it profited me that I have bowed down to my god?

I must bow even to a person who is lower than I,

The rich and opulent treat me, as a younger brother, with contempt. …

Friend

O wise one, O savant, who masters knowledge,

Your heart has become hardened and you accuse the god wrongly.

The mind of the god, like the center of the heavens, is remote;

Knowledge of it is very difficult; people cannot know it …

In the case of a cow, the first calf is a runt,

The later offspring is twice as big.

A first child is born a weakling,

But the second is called a mighty warrior.

Sufferer

… People extol the words of a strong man who has learned to kill

But bring down the powerless who has done no wrong.

They confirm (the position of) the wicked for whom what should be an abomination is considered right

Yet drive off the honest man who heeds the will of his god.

They fill the [storehouse] of the oppressor with gold,

But empty the larder of the beggar of its provisions.

They support the powerful, whose … [text uncertain] is guilt,

But destroy the weak and trample the powerless.

And, as for me, an insignificant person, a prominent person persecutes me.

Friend

Narru, king of the gods, who created mankind,

And majestic Zulummar, who pinched off the clay for them,

And goddess Mami, the queen who fashioned them,

Gave twisted speech to the human race.

With lies, and not truth, they endowed them forever.

Solemnly they speak favorably of a rich man,

"He is a king," they say, "riches should be his,"

But they treat a poor man like a thief,

They have only bad to say of him and plot his murder,

Making him suffer every evil like a criminal, because he has no … [text uncertain].

Terrifyingly they bring him to his end, and extinguish him like glowing coals.

Sufferer

…I have gone about the square of my city unobtrusively,

My voice was not raised, my speech was kept low.

I did not raise my head, but looked at the ground,

I did not worship even as a slave in the company of my associates.

May the god who has abandoned me give help,

May the goddess who has [forsaken me] show mercy,

The shepherd, the sun of the people, pastures (his flock) as a god should.

AP® History Reasoning Skills

Comparison *In what ways do Amos and the Babylonian Sufferer have similar complaints against their respective upper classes?*

Comparison *Do the Babylonian gods seem to be less directly or more directly involved in human affairs than the Israelite deity?*

Source: Excerpts from the Hebrew Bible quoted by permission. NETS Bible copyright © 1996–2006 by Biblical Studies Press, L.L.C. www.bible.org. All rights reserved. Excerpts from Babylonian document: Pritchard, James, *Ancient Near Eastern Texts Relating to the Old Testament.* © 1969 by Princeton University Press. Reprinted by permission of Princeton University Press.

The Phoenicians developed earlier Canaanite models into an "alphabetic" system of writing with about two dozen symbols, in which each symbol represented a sound. (The Phoenicians represented only consonants, leaving the vowel sounds to be inferred by the reader. The Greeks later added symbols for vowel sounds, creating the first truly alphabetic system of writing—see Chapter 5.) Little Phoenician writing survives, however, probably because scribes used perishable papyrus.

Before 1000 BCE Byblos was the most important Phoenician city-state. It was a distribution center for cedar timber from the slopes of Mount Lebanon and for papyrus from Egypt. King Hiram, who came to power in 969 BCE, was responsible for Tyre's rise to prominence. According to the Hebrew Bible, he formed a close alliance with the Israelite king Solomon and provided skilled Phoenician craftsmen and cedar wood for building the Temple in Jerusalem. In return, Tyre gained access to silver, food, and trade routes to the east and south. In the 800s BCE Tyre took control of nearby Sidon and dominated the Mediterranean coastal trade.

Located on an offshore island, Tyre was practically impregnable. It had two harbors connected by a canal, a large marketplace, a magnificent palace complex with treasury and archives, and temples to the gods Melqart (**MEL-kahrt**) and Astarte (**uh-STAHR-tee**). Some of its 30,000 inhabitants lived in suburbs on the mainland. Its one weakness was its dependence on the mainland for food and fresh water.

Little is known about the internal affairs of Tyre and other Phoenician cities. The names of a series of kings are preserved, and the scant evidence suggests that the political arena was dominated by leading merchant families. Between the ninth and seventh centuries BCE the Phoenician city-states contended with Assyrian aggression, followed in the sixth century BCE by the expansion of the Neo-Babylonian kingdom and later the Persian Empire (see Chapter 5). The Phoenician city-states preserved their autonomy by playing the great powers off against one another when possible and by accepting a subordinate relationship to a distant master when necessary.

3-5b Expansion into the Mediterranean

After 900 BCE Tyre turned its attention westward, establishing colonies on Cyprus, a copper-rich island 100 miles (161 kilometers) from the Syrian coast (see Map 3.4). By 700 BCE a string of settlements in the western Mediterranean formed a "Phoenician triangle" composed of the North African coast from western Libya to Morocco; the south and southeast coast of Spain, including Gades (**GAH-days**) (modern Cadiz [**kuh-DEEZ**]) on the Straits of Gibraltar, controlling passage between the Mediterranean and the Atlantic Ocean; and the islands of Sardinia, Sicily, and Malta off the coast of Italy (see Map 3.5). Many settlements were situated on promontories or offshore islands in imitation of Tyre. The Phoenician trading network spanned the entire Mediterranean.

Frequent and destructive Assyrian invasions of Syria-Palestine and the lack of arable land to feed a swelling population probably motivated Tyrian expansion. Overseas settlement provided an outlet for excess population, new sources of trade goods, and new trading partners. Tyre maintained its autonomy until 701 BCE by paying tribute to the Assyrian kings. In that year it finally fell to an Assyrian army that stripped it of much of its territory and population, allowing Sidon to become the leading city in Phoenicia.

3-5c Carthage's Commercial Empire

Historians know far more about **Carthage** and the other Phoenician colonies in the western Mediterranean than they do about the Phoenician homeland. Much of this comes from Greek and Roman reports of their wars with the western Phoenician communities. For example, the account of the origins of Carthage that begins this chapter comes from Roman sources but probably is based on a Carthaginian original. Archaeological excavation has roughly confirmed the city's traditional foundation date of 814 BCE. The new settlement grew rapidly and soon dominated other Phoenician colonies in the west.

Located just outside the present-day city of Tunis in Tunisia, on a promontory jutting into the Mediterranean, Carthage stretched between the original hilltop citadel and a double harbor. The inner harbor could accommodate 220 warships. A watchtower allowed surveillance of the surrounding area, and high walls made it impossible to see in from the outside. The outer commercial harbor was filled with docks for merchant ships and shipyards. In case of attack, the harbor could be closed off by a huge iron chain.

Carthage City located in present-day Tunisia, founded by Phoenicians ca. 800 BCE, it became a major commercial center and naval power in the western Mediterranean until defeated by Rome in the third century BCE.

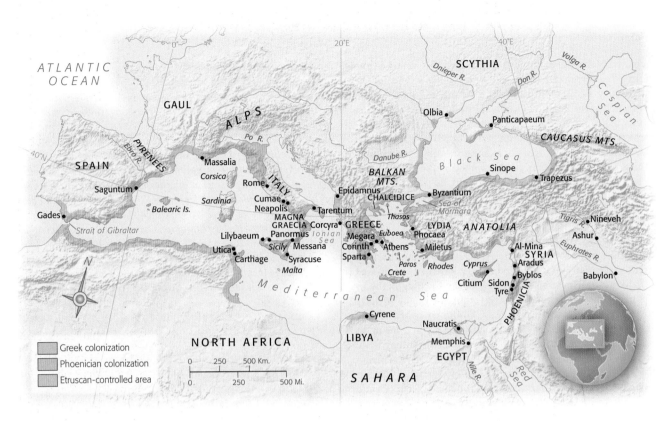

MAP 3.5   Colonization of the Mediterranean   In the ninth century BCE, the Phoenicians of Lebanon began to explore and colonize parts of the western Mediterranean, including the coast of North Africa, southern and eastern Spain, and the islands of Sicily and Sardinia. The Phoenicians were primarily interested in access to valuable raw materials and trading opportunities.

Why did the Phoenicians colonize certain areas of the Mediterranean and not others?

Government offices ringed a large central square where magistrates heard legal cases outdoors. The inner city was a maze of narrow, winding streets, multistory apartment buildings, and sacred enclosures. Farther out was a sprawling suburban district where the wealthy built spacious villas amid fields and vegetable gardens. This entire urban complex was enclosed by a wall 22 miles (35 kilometers) in length. At the most critical point—the 2½-mile-wide (4-kilometer) isthmus connecting the promontory to the mainland—the wall was over 40 feet (13 meters) high and 30 feet (10 meters) thick and had high watchtowers.

With a population of roughly 400,000, Carthage was one of the largest cities in the world by 500 BCE. The population was ethnically diverse, including people of Phoenician stock, indigenous peoples ancestral to modern-day Berbers, and immigrants from other Mediterranean lands as well as sub-Saharan Africa. The Phoenicians readily intermarried with other peoples.

Each year two "judges" were elected from upper-class families to serve as heads of state and carry out administrative and judicial functions. The real seat of power was the Senate, where members of the leading merchant families, who sat for life, directed the affairs of the state. An inner circle of thirty or so senators made the crucial decisions. The leadership occasionally convened an Assembly of the citizens to elect public officials or vote on important issues, particularly when they were divided or wanted to stir up popular enthusiasm for some venture.

There is little evidence at Carthage of the kind of social and political unrest that plagued Greece and Rome. A merchant aristocracy (unlike an aristocracy of birth) was not a closed group, and a climate of economic and social mobility allowed newly successful families and individuals to push their way into the circle of influential citizens. Insofar as everyone benefited from the riches of empire, the masses were usually ready to defer to those who made prosperity possible.

Carthaginian power rested on its navy, which dominated the western Mediterranean for centuries. Phoenician towns provided a network of friendly ports. The Carthaginian fleet consisted of fast, maneuverable galleys (warships propelled by oars). Each bore a sturdy, pointed

AP® Exam Tip
Analyze the economic role of cities as centers of production and commerce.

For centuries the Carthaginians dominated the waters of the western Mediterranean (until their defeat by Rome in the third century BCE). Controlling the Straits of Gibraltar and the entrance to the Atlantic Ocean, they endeavored quite successfully to keep their rivals, the Greeks, who were also founding colonies and seeking commercial opportunities in the western Mediterranean, from breaching the straits and entering the great western ocean. At the same time, the Carthaginians founded a number of settlements on the north African coast outside the straits and explored the Spanish, French, and English coasts to the north and the west African coast to the south.

A fascinating and illuminating record of one of these voyages of discovery along the west African coast has survived indirectly (see Map 3.6). The account must have been composed originally in the Phoenician language of the Carthaginians by the expedition commander, Hanno, who is thought to have lived in the sixth or fifth century BCE, and inscribed on the wall of a temple at Carthage, but it has come down to us in an abridged Greek translation of the fifth or fourth century BCE. This very short document is the longest surviving Phoenician text, ironic in light of the fact that we owe our alphabet (used in this book) to the Phoenician alphabet as adapted by Greeks and Romans. It would be 2,000 years before Portuguese explorers next described this region of west Africa.

Hanno tells us that his mission was to found several settlements outside the straits, on the coast of present-day Morocco:

This is the account of Hanno, king of Carthage [probably a "Judge," the term used for the highest-ranking public officials at Carthage], about his voyage to the Libyan [a Greek term for the African continent] lands beyond the Pillars of Herakles [the Greek term for the Straits of Gibraltar], which he also set up in the shrine of Kronos [a Greek god, probably equated with the chief Carthaginian deity, Ba'al Hammon].

The Carthaginians ordered Hanno to sail out of the Pillars of Herakles and found a number of...cities. He set sail with sixty fifty-oared ships, about thirty thousand men and women, food and other equipment.

After sailing beyond the Pillars for two days, we founded our first city, called Thymiaterion. Below it was a large plain...

Subsequently they founded six more towns, presumably leaving behind substantial numbers of settlers and supplies, and befriended the Lixites, a group of nomadic cattle-herders.

Beyond them, hostile Ethiopians [a Greek term, meaning "burnt faces," used for dark-skinned peoples] occupied a land full of wild animals. It was surrounded by...great mountains.... According to the Lixites, strange people dwell among these mountains: cave men who run faster than horses.... We arrived at the end of the bay, which was overhung by some very great mountains, crowded with savages clad in animals' skins. By throwing stones, they prevented us from disembarking and drove us away. Leaving from there, we arrived at another large, broad river teeming with crocodiles and hippopotamuses.... From there we sailed to the south for twelve days. We remained close to the coast, which was entirely inhabited by Ethiopians, who fled from us when we approached.... Sailing around the mountains for two days, we came to an immense expanse of sea beyond which, on the landward side, was a plain. During the night we observed big and small fires everywhere flaming up at intervals.

Continuing south for five more days, they reached a great bay with a large island.

Here we disembarked. In daytime, we could see nothing but the forest, but during the night, we noticed many fires alight and heard the sound of flutes, the beating of cymbals and tom-toms, and the shouts of a multitude. We grew afraid and our diviners advised us to leave this island. Quickly, we sailed away, passing along a fiery coast full of incense. Large torrents of fire emptied into the sea, and the land was inaccessible because of the heat. Quickly and in fear, we sailed away from that place. Sailing on for four days, we saw the coast by night full of flames. In the middle was a big flame, taller than the others and apparently rising to the stars. By day, this turned out to be a very high mountain, which was called Chariot of the Gods. Sailing thence along the torrents of fire, we arrived after three days at a bay called Horn of the South. In this gulf was an island, resembling the first, with a lagoon, within which was another island, full of savages. Most of them were women with hairy bodies, whom our interpreters called "gorillas." Although we chased them, we could not catch any males: they all escaped, being good climbers who defended themselves with stones. However, we caught three women, who refused to follow those who carried them off, biting and clawing them. So we killed and flayed them and brought their skins back to Carthage. For we did not sail any further, because our provisions were running short. [1]

---

[1]See *www.livius.org/articles/person/hanno-1-the-navigator/hanno-1-the-navigator-2/.*

ram in front that could pierce the hull of an enemy vessel below the water line, while marines (soldiers aboard a ship) fired weapons. Innovations in the placement of benches and oars eventually made room for as many as 170 rowers. The Phoenicians and their Greek rivals set the standard for naval technology in this era.

Carthaginian foreign policy, reflecting the economic interests of the dominant merchant class, focused on protecting the sea lanes, gaining access to raw materials, and

The Carthaginians tell us that they trade with a race of men who live in a part of Libya beyond the Pillars of Herakles. On reaching this country, they unload their goods, arrange them tidily along the beach, and then, returning to their boats, raise a smoke. Seeing the smoke, the natives come down to the beach, place on the ground a certain quantity of gold in exchange for the goods, and go off again to a distance. The Carthaginians then come ashore and take a look at the gold; and if they think it presents a fair price for their wares, they collect it and go away; if, on the other hand, it seems too little, they go back aboard and wait, and the natives come and add to the gold until they are satisfied. There is perfect honesty on both sides; the Carthaginians never touch the gold until it equals in value what they have offered for sale, and the natives never touch the goods until the gold has been taken away.[2]

This method of "silent barter" between peoples who cannot understand each other's languages is interesting in its own right, but the passage also suggests that Hanno and the Carthaginians were well aware that west Africa was a potential source of gold and were eager to open up trade with the region.

Some scholars maintain that Hanno may have reached as far south as Gabon. However, modern scholarship has run into difficulties trying to match Hanno's account to the realities of African geography. Some experts have suggested that the entire account is fictional, but a more likely explanation is that, when the account was made public, distances and geographical features were purposely corrupted so that it could not be used as a guide by commercial rivals like the Greeks. Some of the more terrifying elements in the story—torrents of fire pouring into the sea (perhaps volcanoes?), strange lights, wild savages, and so on—may also have been invented or exaggerated to scare off anyone from attempting to retrace the route to an abundant source of gold.

Questions for Analysis

1. What were the several purposes of Hanno's expedition?

2. How have scholars explained the difficulties they have encountered in matching Hanno's account to the real geography of the West African coast?

3. How were the Carthaginians able to engage in trade with West Africans without the two sides being able to understand each other's languages?

MAP 3.6   The Voyage of Hanno the Carthaginian

Note that Hanno seems to regard the "Gorillas" as some form of savage humans. When naturalists discovered African gorillas in the nineteenth century CE, they labeled them with the term derived from our ancient text.

Hanno is vague about the purpose of the later stages of the voyage, but the fifth century BCE Greek historian Herodotus, perhaps based on traditions about Hanno's voyage, may provide the key:

---

[2]Herodotus 4.196; tr. Aubrey de Selincourt.

fostering trade. Indeed, Carthage claimed the waters of the western Mediterranean as its own (see Environment & Technology: The West African Voyage of Hanno the Carthaginian). Foreign merchants were free to sail to Carthage to market their goods, but if they tried to operate elsewhere on their own, they risked having their ships sunk by the Carthaginian navy. Treaties between Carthage and other states included formal recognition of this maritime commercial monopoly.

The archaeological record provides few clues about the commodities traded by the Carthaginians. These may have included perishable goods—foodstuffs, textiles, animal skins, slaves—and raw metals whose Carthaginian origin would not be evident. Carthaginian ships carried goods manufactured elsewhere, and products brought to Carthage by foreign traders were re-exported.

There is also evidence for trade with sub-Saharan Africa. Hanno (**HA-noe**), a Carthaginian captain of the sixth or fifth century BCE, claimed to have sailed through the Straits of Gibraltar into the Atlantic Ocean and to have explored the West African coast (see Map 3.6). Other Carthaginians explored the Atlantic coast of Spain and France and secured control of an important source of tin in the "Tin Islands," probably Cornwall in southwestern England.

3-5d War and Religion

The Carthaginian state did not directly rule a large territory. A belt of fertile land in north-eastern Tunisia, owned by Carthaginians but worked by native peasants and imported slaves, provided a secure food supply. Beyond this core area the Carthaginians ruled most of their "empire" indirectly and allowed other Phoenician communities in the western Mediterranean to remain independent. These Phoenician communities looked to Carthage for military protection and followed its lead in foreign policy. Only Sardinia and southern Spain were put under the direct control of a Carthaginian governor and garrison, presumably to safeguard their agricultural, metal, and manpower resources.

Carthage's focus on trade may explain the unusual fact that citizens were not required to serve in the army: they were of more value in other capacities, such as trading activities and the navy. Since the indigenous North African population was not politically or militarily well organized, Carthage had little to fear close to home. When Carthage was drawn into a series of wars with the Greeks and Romans from the fifth through third centuries BCE, it relied on mercenaries from the most warlike peoples in its dominions or from neighboring areas. These well-paid mercenaries were under the command of Carthaginian officers; generals were chosen by the Senate and kept in office for as long as they were needed. In contrast to most ancient states, the Carthaginians separated military command from civilian government.

Like the deities of Mesopotamia (see Chapter 2), the gods of the Carthaginians—chief among them Baal Hammon (**BAHL ha-MOHN**), a male storm-god, and Tanit (**TAH-nit**), a female fertility figure—were powerful and capricious entities who had to be appeased by anxious worshipers. Roman sources report that members of the Carthaginian elite would sacrifice their own male children in times of crisis. Excavations at Carthage and other western Phoenician towns have turned up *tophets* (**TOE-fet**)— walled enclosures where thousands of small, sealed urns containing the burned bones of children lay buried. Originally practiced by the upper classes, child sacrifice became more common and involved broader elements of the population after 400 BCE.

Plutarch (**PLOO-tawrk**), a Greek who lived around 100 CE, long after the demise of Carthage, wrote the following on the basis of earlier sources:

> *The Carthaginians are a hard and gloomy people, submissive to their rulers and harsh to their subjects, running to extremes of cowardice in times of fear and of cruelty in times of anger; they keep obstinately to their decisions, are austere, and care little for amusement or the graces of life.*[3]

AP® Exam Tip

How have religions, belief systems, philosophies, and ideologies affected the political, economic, and social development of societies?

Section Review

- Following the upheavals ca. 1200 BCE, Canaanite communities on the coast of Lebanon adopted the city-state political form and turned to seaborne commerce and new kinds of manufacture for their survival.

- In the tenth century BCE, Tyre, located on a practically impregnable offshore island and led by a king and merchant aristocracy, became the dominant Phoenician state.

- A string of settlements in the western Mediterranean formed a "Phoenician triangle" comprising the coasts of North Africa and Spain and islands off the coast of Italy.

- Carthage, founded in present-day Tunisia a little before 800 BCE, led the coalition of Phoenician communities in the western Mediterranean.

- Carthaginian power rested on its navy, which enforced a Carthaginian commercial monopoly in the western Mediterranean. For land warfare, Carthage relied on mercenaries from the most war-like peoples in the region, under the command of Carthaginian officers.

- The religion of the Carthaginians, which included the sacrifice of children in times of crisis, was perceived as different and despicable by their Greek and Roman rivals.

---

[3] Plutarch, Moralia, 799 D, trans. B. H. Warmington, *Carthage* (Harmondsworth, UK: Penguin, 1960), 163.

▶ The Tophet of Carthage
Here, from the seventh to second centuries BCE, the cremated bodies of sacrificed children were buried. Archaeological excavation has confirmed the claim in ancient sources that the Carthaginians sacrificed children to their gods at times of crisis. Stone markers, decorated with magical signs and symbols of divinities as well as family names, were placed over ceramic urns containing the ashes and charred bones of one or more infants or, occasionally, older children.
JTB MEDIA CREATION, Inc/Alamy Stock Photo

We should not take the hostile opinions of Greek and Roman sources at face value. Still, it is clear that the Carthaginians were perceived as different and that cultural barriers, leading to misunderstanding and prejudice, played a significant role in the conflicts among these peoples of the ancient Mediterranean. In Chapter 6 we follow the protracted and bloody struggle between Rome and Carthage for control of the western Mediterranean.

3-6 Failure and Transformation, 750–550 BCE

Between 750 and 550 BCE, what factors prompted the transformation of the ancient Middle East?

The extension of Assyrian power over the entire Middle East had enormous consequences for all the peoples of the region. In 721 BCE the Assyrians destroyed the northern kingdom of Israel and deported a substantial portion of the population, and for over a century the southern kingdom of Judah faced relentless pressure. Assyrian threats and demands for tribute spurred the Phoenicians to explore and colonize the western Mediterranean. Tyre's fall to the Assyrians in 701 BCE accelerated the decline of the Phoenician homeland, but the western colonies, especially Carthage, flourished. Even Egypt, for so long impregnable behind its desert barriers, fell to Assyrian invaders in the mid-seventh century BCE. Southern Mesopotamia was reduced to a protectorate, with Babylon alternately razed and rebuilt by Assyrian kings of differing dispositions. Urartu and Elam, Assyria's nearby rivals, were destroyed.

By 650 BCE Assyria stood supreme in western Asia. But the arms race with Urartu, the frequent expensive campaigns, and the protection of lengthy borders had sapped Assyrian resources. Assyrian brutality and exploitation aroused the hatred of conquered peoples. At the same time, changes in the ethnic composition of the army and the population of the homeland had reduced popular support for the Assyrian state.

Two new political entities spearheaded resistance to Assyria. First, Babylonia had been revived by the Neo-Babylonian, or Chaldaean **(chal-DEE-uhn)**, dynasty (the Chaldaeans had infiltrated southern Mesopotamia around 1000 BCE). Second, the Medes **(MEED)**, an Iranian people, were extending their kingdom on the Iranian Plateau in the seventh

Section Review

- The extension of Assyrian power over the entire Middle East had enormous consequences for all the peoples of the region.

- The costs of frequent military campaigns, the hatred of conquered peoples aroused by Assyrian brutality, and changes in the ethnic composition of the army and the population of the homeland weakened the Assyrian state.

- The Neo-Babylonians and the Medes of northwest Iran launched a series of attacks on the Assyrian homeland that destroyed the chief cities by 612 BCE and led to the depopulation of northern Mesopotamia.

- The Neo-Babylonian kingdom took over much of the territory of the Assyrian Empire and fostered a cultural renaissance.

century BCE. The two powers launched a series of attacks on the Assyrian homeland that destroyed the chief cities by 612 BCE. The destruction systematically carried out by the victorious attackers led to the depopulation of northern Mesopotamia.

The Medes took over the Assyrian homeland and the northern plain as far as eastern Anatolia, but most of the territory of the old empire fell to the **Neo-Babylonian kingdom** (626–539 BCE), thanks to the energetic campaigns of kings Nabopolassar (**NAB-oh-poe-lass-uhr**) (r. 625–605 BCE) and Nebuchadnezzar (r. 604–562 BCE). Babylonia underwent a cultural renaissance. The city of Babylon was enlarged and adorned, becoming the greatest metropolis of the world in the sixth century BCE. Old cults were revived, temples rebuilt, festivals resurrected. The related pursuits of mathematics, astronomy, and astrology reached new heights.

3-7 Conclusion

The Late Bronze Age in the Middle East was a "cosmopolitan" era of shared lifestyles and technologies. Patterns of culture that had originated long before in Egypt and Mesopotamia persisted into this era. Peoples such as the Amorites, Kassites, and Chaldaeans, who migrated into the Tigris-Euphrates plain, were largely assimilated into the Sumerian-Semitic cultural tradition, adopting its language, religious beliefs, political and social institutions, and forms of artistic expression. Similarly, the Hyksos, who migrated into the Nile Delta and controlled much of Egypt for a time, adopted the ancient ways of Egypt. When the founders of the New Kingdom finally ended Hyksos domination, they reinstituted the united monarchy and the religious and cultural traditions of earlier eras.

The Late Bronze Age expansion of commerce and communication stimulated the emergence of new civilizations, including those of the Minoans and Mycenaean Greeks in the Aegean Sea. These new civilizations borrowed heavily from the technologies and cultural practices of Mesopotamia and Egypt, creating dynamic syntheses of imported and indigenous elements.

Ultimately, the very interdependence of the societies of the Middle East and eastern Mediterranean made them vulnerable to the destructions and disorder of the decades around 1200 BCE. The entire region slipped into a "Dark Age" of isolation, stagnation, and decline that lasted several centuries. The early centuries after 1000 BCE saw a resurgence of political organization and international commerce, as well as the spread of technologies and ideas. The Assyrians created an empire of unprecedented size and diversity through superior organization and military technology, and they maintained it through terror and deportations of subject peoples.

Neo-Babylonian kingdom Under the Chaldaeans (nomadic kinship groups that settled in southern Mesopotamia in the early first millennium BCE), Babylon again became a major political and cultural center in the seventh and sixth centuries BCE. After participating in the destruction of Assyrian power, the monarchs Nabopolassar and Nebuchadnezzar took over the southern portion of the Assyrian domains.

The Israelites began as nomadic pastoralists and then settled permanently in Canaan. Conflict with the Philistines forced them to adopt a more complex political structure, and under the monarchy Israelite society grew more urban and economically stratified. While the long, slow evolution of the Israelites from wandering groups of herders to an agriculturally based monarchy followed a common pattern in ancient western Asia, the religious and ethical concepts that they formulated were unique and have had a powerful impact on world history.

After the upheavals of the Late Bronze Age, the Phoenician city-states along the coast of Lebanon flourished. Under pressure from the Neo-Assyrian Empire, the Phoenicians, with Tyre in the lead, began spreading westward into the Mediterranean. Carthage became the most important city outside the Phoenician homeland. Ruled by leading merchant families, it extended its commercial empire throughout the western Mediterranean, maintaining power through naval superiority.

The far-reaching expansion of the Assyrian Empire was the most important factor in the transformation of the ancient Middle East. The Assyrians destroyed many older states and, directly or indirectly, displaced large numbers of people. Their brutality, as well as the population shifts that resulted from their deportations, undercut support for their state. The Chaldaeans and Medes led resistance to Assyrian rule. After the swift collapse of Assyria, the Chaldaeans expanded the Neo-Babylonian kingdom, enlarged the city of Babylon, and presided over a cultural renaissance.

Key Terms

Iron Age p. 51	**Mycenae** p. 59	**Library of Ashurbanipal** p. 64	**Diaspora** p. 68
Hittites p. 52	**shaft graves** p. 59	**Israel** p. 64	**Phoenicians** p. 69
Hatshepsut p. 54	**Linear B** p. 59	**Hebrew Bible** p. 64	**Carthage** p. 72
Akhenaten p. 55	**Neo-Assyrian Empire** p. 61	**First Temple** p. 67	**Neo-Babylonian kingdom** p. 78
Ramesses II p. 56	**mass deportation** p. 63	**monotheism** p. 68	
Minoan p. 57			

Review Questions

1. What factors both enabled the prosperity and technological advances of the complex societies of the Late Bronze Age (later second millennium BCE) in western Asia and the eastern Mediterranean, and contributed to their fall around 1200 BCE?

2. How did the Assyrians of northern Mesopotamia create the largest empire in history up to that time, and how did Assyrian aggression and exploitation impact other peoples in western Asia?

3. What was the role of the Phoenicians in exploring, founding settlements, and expanding trade and communication throughout the lands surrounding the Mediterranean Sea and beyond?

 MindTap® is a fully online, personalized learning experience built upon Cengage Learning content. MindTap® combines student learning tools–readings, multimedia, activities, and assessments–into a singular Learning Path that guides students through the course and helps students develop the critical thinking, analysis, and communication skills that are essential to academic and professional success.

Multiple-Choice Questions

Questions 1–3 refer to the image below.

▲ **Part of a basalt slab depicting Hittite warriors, ninth century BCE.**
DEA/M. SEEMULLER/Getty Images

1. The image presents evidence of which of the following reasons for the dominance in Anatolia of the Hittites, ca. 1500 BCE?

   (A) They were able to spread due to a strong bureaucracy that enabled them to control their large population.

   (B) They were able to utilize the natural resources of the region both for commerce and to provide a military advantage.

   (C) They were ruled over by a succession of strong kings, and they were able to create an advanced, highly urbanized society.

   (D) They took advantage of a peaceful period to create a network of city-states where trade flourished.

2. As the Hittites pictured expanded across Anatolia,

   (A) They became a religiously controlled theocracy where priests held much of the political power.

   (B) They created a culturally rich environment where art and architecture flourished.

   (C) They made an alliance with Greek city-states to seek protection of its eastern borders.

   (D) They had greater access to resources and experienced growing populations.

3. What was a common characteristic of both the Hittite and the Assyrian Empires?

   (A) They were both dominated by similar monotheistic belief systems.

   (B) They were both characterized by a population that was mainly urban and heavily reliant on trade.

   (C) They both originated with pastoralist groups who utilized new types of weapons and modes of transport.

   (D) They were both tolerant of other belief systems and cultures, which enabled them to rule over diverse populations.

Questions 4–6 refer to the image below.

▲ **Detail of an amphora from Thebes** Amphora from Kadmeion of Thebes (Greece), Detail: an inscription in Linear B, Mycenaean Civilization, late 14th Century BC/DE AGOSTINI EDITORE/Bridgeman Images

4. The amphora can be used as evidence to illustrate which of the following?

   (A) The people of the Mycenaean civilization were pastoralists who relied on an animal-based diet.

   (B) The Mycenaean civilization used a script based on the hieroglyphs of the Egyptians.

   (C) The Mycenaean civilization developed a system of record keeping that was needed in trade.

   (D) Most people in the Mycenaean civilization were expert at pot making, and their pottery was valued throughout Greece.

5. In addition to pottery like that pictured, some of the Mycenaean graves found in southern Greece contain jewelry, weapons, and utensils. These artifacts could support which of the following assertions?

(A) There was an even distribution of power between men and women.

(B) As specialized labor developed, new social hierarchies were established.

(C) Most of the people in the Mycenaean civilization were involved in agriculture.

(D) There was little social movement in the hierarchy of the Mycenaean civilization.

6. What can archaeologists who have found amber jewelry in Syria and Greek pottery in parts of the Middle East assert?

(A) The people of the Mediterranean were primarily agriculturalists.

(B) There was a strict social hierarchy based on wealth in the Mediterranean region.

(C) Trade expanded in this period and became increasingly interregional.

(D) Specialized labor became common in urban areas in the Mediterranean region.

Questions 7–10 refer to the passage below.

"7 . . . David captured the fortress of Zion—which is the City of David.

9 David then took up residence in the fortress and called it the City of David. He built up the area around it, from the terraces inward.

10 And he became more and more powerful, because the Lord God Almighty was with him.

11 Now Hiram king of Tyre sent envoys to David, along with cedar logs and carpenters and stonemasons, and they built a palace for David.

12 Then David knew that the Lord had established him as king over Israel and had exalted his kingdom for the sake of his people, Israel."

Bible, II Samuel, 5: 7–12

7. The passage above best supports which of the following statements concerning the ways King David established his control of the kingdom?

(A) King David forbid the construction of magnificent buildings out of fear of invasion.

(B) King David relied heavily on slave labor for his construction projects.

(C) King David utilized a powerful military to help gain power over the people of Israel.

(D) King David asserted that he was divinely chosen to rule over his nation

8. According to the passage, which of the following best describes the economic system of Israel?

(A) Israel used a barter system that allowed trade without a need for coinage.

(B) Israel's economy was dependent on coerced labor.

(C) Israel cooperated in trade agreements with neighboring regions to obtain needed materials.

(D) Israel's economy was highly regulated and controlled directly by the central government.

9. A historian could use the passage above and knowledge of history to infer which of the following about the unification of the Israelite state under King David's son, Solomon?

(A) A powerful army that ensured the security of its borders was essential to unity.

(B) Economic strength was provided by flourishing agriculture, creating a commonality.

(C) A series of powerful leaders imposed strict hierarchical laws to create order.

(D) Unified Israelite culture was based on a code of laws and a common language.

10. What was the most important influence of the Israelite state on later periods of growth?

(A) The architectural style used in the temple in Jerusalem was copied throughout the Middle East.

(B) Hebrew monotheism influenced other major religions such as Christianity and Islam.

(C) The alphabet used by the Israelites was the base of other alphabets in the Mediterranean region.

(D) Jerusalem's role as a major trading hub in the Middle East lasted for centuries.

Short-Answer Questions

"As to Hezekiah, the Jew, he did not submit to my yoke, I laid siege to 46 of his strong cities, walled forts and to the countless small villages in their vicinity, and conquered them by means of well-stamped earth-ramps, and battering-rams brought thus near to the walls combined with the attack by foot soldiers, using mines, breeches as well as sapper work. I drove out of them 200,150 people, young and old, male and female, horses, mules, donkeys, camels, big and small cattle beyond counting, and considered them booty. Himself I made a prisoner in Jerusalem, his royal residence, like a bird in a cage. I surrounded him with earthwork in order to molest those who were leaving his city's gate."

From an account by an Assyrian king, Sennacherib, who captured the city of Jerusalem in 701 BCE

1. Use the passage above and your knowledge of world history to answer all parts of the question that follows.

(A) Identify ONE method of expansion used by empires in this time period.

(B) Explain ONE way empires remained the same throughout this time period.

(C) Explain ONE way the expansion of empires caused changes in this time period.

2. Answer all parts of the question that follows.

(A) Identify ONE way that literature or art affected political, economic, or social institutions in the period 8000 BCE to 600 BCE.

(B) Explain ONE way that belief systems affected political institutions in the period 8000 BCE to 600 BCE.

(C) Explain ONE way that belief systems affected economic or social institutions in the period 8000 BCE to 600 BCE.

New Civilizations Outside the West Asian Core Area, 2300 BCE–350 CE

4

CHAPTER OUTLINE

AP® Framework Terms

Yellow (Huang He) River Valley (Shang)
Sub-Saharan Africa
Confucianism
Confucius
Emperor Wu (Wudi)
Daoism
Ancestor veneration

Overarching Questions

1 How and to what extent have environmental factors, disease, and technology affected patterns of human migration and settlement over time? (ENV)

2 How and why have religions, belief systems, philosophies, and ideologies originated, developed and spread as a result of expanding communication and exchange networks? (CUL)

3 How have cross-cultural interactions resulted in the diffusion of culture, technologies, and scientific knowledge? (CUL)

4 How have different forms of governance been constructed and maintained over time? (SB)

5 How have distinctions based on kinship, ethnicity, class, gender, and race influenced the development and transformation of social hierarchies? (SOC)

Around 2200 BCE an Egyptian official named Harkhuf (**HAHR-koof**) set out from Aswan (**AS-wahn**), on the southern boundary of Egypt, for a place called Yam, far to the south in the land that later came to be called Nubia. He brought gifts from the Egyptian pharaoh for the ruler of Yam, and he returned home with 300 donkeys loaded with incense, ebony, ivory, and other exotic products from tropical Africa. Despite the diplomatic fiction of exchanging gifts, we should probably regard Harkhuf as a brave and enterprising merchant. He returned with something so special that the eight-year-old boy pharaoh, Pepi II, could not contain his excitement. He wrote:

> Come north to the residence at once! Hurry and bring with you this pygmy whom you brought from the land of the horizon-dwellers live, hale, and healthy, for the dances of the god, to gladden the heart, to delight the heart of king Neferkare [Pepi] who lives forever! When he goes down with you into the ship, get worthy men to be around him on deck, lest he fall into the water! When he lies down at night, get worthy men to lie around him in his tent. Inspect ten times at night! My majesty desires to see this pygmy more than the gifts of the mine-land and of Punt![1]

[1] Quoted in Miriam Lichtheim, ed., *Ancient Egyptian Literature: A Book of Readings* (Berkeley, CA: University of California Press, 1978).

▲ **Wall Painting of Nubians Arriving in Egypt with Rings and Bags of Gold, Fourteenth Century BCE**
This image decorated the tomb of an Egyptian administrator in Nubia. Erich Lessing/Art Resource, NY

Scholars identify Yam with Kerma, later the capital of the kingdom of Nubia, on the upper Nile in modern Sudan. For Egyptians, Nubia was a wild and dangerous place. Yet it was developing a more complex political organization, and this illustration demonstrates how vibrant the commerce and cultural interaction between Nubia and Egypt would later become.

In this chapter we discuss other parts of the world outside the core area in western Asia that has been central to this point: East Asia, sub-Saharan Africa, the Eurasian steppes, and continental Europe. These societies emerged later than those in Mesopotamia, Egypt, and the Indus Valley and in more varied ecological conditions—sometimes independently, sometimes under the influence of older centers. Whereas the older river-valley civilizations were largely self-sufficient, many of the new civilizations discussed in the previous chapter and in this chapter were shaped by networks of long-distance trade. In the second millennium BCE a civilization based on irrigation agriculture arose in the valley of the Yellow River and its tributaries in northern China. In the same epoch, in Nubia (southern Egypt and northern Sudan), the first complex society in tropical Africa continued to develop from the roots observed earlier by Harkhuf. The first millennium BCE also witnessed the rise of a new kind of nomadism on the Eurasian steppes and the spread of Celtic peoples across much of continental Europe. These societies represent a variety of responses to different environmental and historical circumstances. However, they have certain features in common and collectively point to a distinct stage in the development of human societies. ●

4-1 Early China, 2000–221 BCE

How did early Chinese rulers use religion to justify and strengthen their power?

On the eastern edge of the vast Eurasian landmass, Neolithic cultures developed as early as 8000 BCE. A more complex civilization evolved in the second and first millennia BCE. Under the Shang and Zhou dynasties, many of the elements of classical Chinese civilization emerged and spread across East Asia. As in Mesopotamia, Egypt, and the Indus Valley, the rise of cities, specialization of labor, bureaucratic government, writing, and other advanced technologies depended on the exploitation of a great river system—the Yellow River (Huang He [**hwahng-HUH**]) and its tributaries—to support intensive agriculture.

4-1a Geography and Resources

China is isolated by formidable natural barriers: the Himalaya (**him-uh-LAY-uh**) mountain range on the southwest; the Pamir (**pah-MEER**) and Tian Mountains and the Takla Makan (**TAH-kluh muh-KAHN**) Desert on the west; and the Gobi (**GO-bee**) Desert and the treeless, grassy hills and plains of the Mongolian steppe to the northwest and north (see Map 4.1). To the east lies the vast Pacific Ocean. Although China's separation was not total—trade goods, people, and ideas moved back and forth between China, India, and Central Asia—in many respects its development was distinctive.

AP® Exam Tip
How have different types of societies adapted to and affected the environment as they settled?

Most of East Asia is covered with mountains, making overland travel and transport difficult. The great river systems of eastern China, however—the Yellow and the Yangzi (**yang-zuh**) Rivers and their tributaries—facilitate east–west movement. In the eastern river valleys dense populations practiced intensive agriculture; on the steppe lands of Mongolia, the deserts and oases of Xinjiang (**shin-jyahng**), and the high plateau of Tibet sparser populations lived largely by herding. The climate zones of East Asia range from the dry, subarctic reaches of Manchuria in the north to the lush, subtropical forests of the south, and a rich variety of plant and animal life are adapted to these zones.

Within the eastern agricultural zone, the north and the south have quite different environments. Each region developed distinctive patterns for land use, the kinds of crops grown, and the organization of agricultural labor. The monsoons that affect India and Southeast Asia (see Chapter 2) drench southern China with heavy rainfall in the summer, the most beneficial time for agriculture. In northern China rainfall is much more erratic. As in Mesopotamia and the Indus Valley, Chinese civilization developed in relatively adverse conditions on the northern plains, a demanding environment that stimulated important technologies and political traditions as well as the philosophical and religious views that became hallmarks of Chinese civilization. By the third century CE, however, the gradual flow of population toward the warmer southern lands caused the political and intellectual center to move south.

The eastern river valleys and North China Plain contained timber, scattered deposits of metals, and, above all, potentially productive land. Winds blowing from Central Asia deposit a yellowish-brown dust called **loess** (**less**) (these particles suspended in the water give the Yellow River its distinctive hue and name). Over the ages a thick mantle of soil has accumulated that is extremely fertile and soft enough to be worked with wooden digging sticks.

In this landscape, agriculture required the coordinated efforts of large numbers of people. Forests had to be cleared. Earthen dikes were constructed to protect nearby fields from recurrent floods on the Yellow River. To cope with the periodic droughts, reservoirs were dug to store river water and rainfall. Retaining walls partitioned the hillsides into flat arable terraces.

The staple crops in the northern region were millet, a grain indigenous to China, and wheat, which had spread to East Asia from the Middle East. Rice, which requires a warmer climate, prospered in the Yangzi River Valley. The cultivation of rice required a great outlay of labor. Rice paddies—the fields where rice is grown—must be flat and surrounded by water channels to bring and lead away water according to a precise schedule. Seedlings sprout in a nursery and are transplanted to the paddy, which is then flooded. Flooding eliminates weeds and rival plants and supports microscopic organisms that keep the soil fertile. When the crop is ripe, the paddy is drained; the rice stalks are harvested with a sickle; and the edible kernels are separated out. The reward for this effort is a harvest that can feed more people per cultivated acre than any other grain, which explains why the south eventually became more populous than the north.

4-1b The Late Neolithic: Artifacts and Legends

Archaeological evidence shows that the Neolithic population of China grew millet, raised pigs and chickens, and used stone tools. Workers made pottery on a wheel and fired it in high-temperature kilns. Some also pioneered the production of silk cloth, first raising silkworms on the leaves of mulberry trees, then carefully unraveling their cocoons to produce silk thread. They

loess A fine, light silt deposited by wind and water. It constitutes the fertile soil of the Yellow River Valley in northern China.

CHRONOLOGY

	China	Nubia	Celtic Europe	Eurasian Steppes
2500 BCE	8000–2000 BCE Neolithic cultures	4500 BCE Early agriculture in Nubia		
2000 BCE	2000 BCE Bronze metallurgy 1750–1045 BCE Shang dynasty	2200 BCE Harkhuf's expeditions to Yam 1750 BCE Rise of kingdom of Kush based on Kerma		
1500 BCE		1500 BCE Egyptian conquest of Nubia		
1000 BCE	1045–256 BCE Zhou dynasty 600 BCE Iron metallurgy	1000 BCE Decline of Egyptian control in Nubia 750 BCE Rise of kingdom based on Napata 712–660 BCE Nubian kings rule Egypt	1000 BCE Origin of Celtic culture in Central Europe	1000 BCE Initial development of pastoral nomadism 700 BCE Scythians drive out Cimmerians and settle area north of Black Sea
500 BCE	551–479 BCE Life of Confucius 356–338 BCE Lord Shang brings Legalist reforms to Qin state	300 BCE–350 CE. Kingdom of Meroë	500 BCE Celtic elites trade for Mediterranean goods 500–300 BCE Migrations across Europe 390 BCE Celts sack Rome	440 BCE Greek historian Herodotus reports on nomadic Scythians 300 BCE Ruler of Chinese state of Zhao equips troops like nomad horsemen 100 BCE Chinese historian Sima Qian describes Xiongnu nomads

built walls of pounded earth by hammering the soil inside temporary wooden frames until it became hard as cement. By 2000 BCE the Chinese had begun to make bronze (a thousand years after the beginnings of bronze-working in the Middle East).

In later times legends depicted the early rulers of China, starting with the Yellow Emperor, as ideal and benevolent masters in a tranquil Golden Age. They were followed by a dynasty called Xia (**shah**), which was in turn succeeded by the **Shang** (**shahng**) dynasty. Since scholars are uncertain about the historical reality of the Xia, Chinese history really begins with the rise of the Shang.

4-1c The Shang Period, 1766–1045 BCE

Little is known about how the Shang rose to dominance around 1766 BCE, since written documents only appear toward the end of Shang rule. These documents are the so-called oracle bones, the shoulder bones of cattle and the bottom shells of turtles employed by Shang rulers to obtain information from ancestral spirits and gods (see Environment & Technology: Divination in Ancient Societies). The writing on the oracle bones concerns the king, his court, weather and its impact on agriculture, warfare against enemies, and religious practices, with little about other aspects of Shang society. The same limitations apply to the archaeological record, primarily treasure-filled tombs of the Shang ruling class.

The earliest known oracle bone inscriptions date to the thirteenth century BCE, but the system was already so sophisticated that some scholars believe writing in China could be considerably older. In the Shang writing system the several hundred characters (written symbols) were originally pictures of objects that become simplified over time, with each character representing a one-syllable word for an object or idea. It is likely that only a small number of people at court used this system. Nevertheless, the Shang writing system is the ancestor of the systems still used in China and elsewhere in East Asia today. Later Chinese writing developed thousands of more complex characters that often provide information about the meaning of the word and its sound.

AP® Exam Tip
Know the Shang Dynasty as an example of a foundational civilization.

Shang The dominant people in the earliest Chinese dynasty for which we have written records (ca. 1766–1045 BCE).

Scholars have reconstructed the major features of Shang religion from the oracle bones. The supreme god, Di (**dee**), who resides in the sky and unleashes the power of storms, is felt to be distant and unconcerned with the fate of humans, and cannot be approached directly. When people die, their spirits survive in the same supernatural sphere as Di and other gods of nature. These ancestral spirits, organized in a heavenly hierarchy that mirrors the social hierarchy on earth, can intervene in human affairs. The Shang ruler has direct access to his more recent ancestors, who have access to earlier generations, who can, in turn, intercede with Di. Thus the ruler is the crucial link between Heaven and earth, using his unrivaled access to higher powers to promote agricultural productivity and protect his people from natural and man-made disasters. This belief was an extremely effective rationale for authoritarian rule.

The king was often on the road, traveling to the courts of his subordinates to reinforce their loyalty, but it is uncertain how much territory in the North China Plain was effectively controlled by the Shang. Excavations at sites elsewhere in China show artistic and technological traditions so different that they are probably the products of independent groups. Both the lack of writing elsewhere in early China and the Han-era conception that China had always been unified obscure from us the probable ethnic, linguistic, and cultural diversity of early China.

The Shang elite were a warrior class reveling in warfare, hunting, exchanging gifts, feasting, and drinking. They fought with bronze weapons and rode into battle on horse-drawn chariots, a technology that originated in western Asia. Frequent military campaigns provided these warriors with a theater for brave achievements and yielded considerable plunder. Many prisoners of war were taken in these campaigns and made into slaves and sacrificial victims.

Excavated tombs of Shang royal and elite families, primarily from the vicinity of Anyang (**ahn-yahng**) (see Map 4.1), contain large quantities of valuable objects made of metal, jade, bone, ivory, shell, and stone, including musical instruments, jewelry, mirrors, weapons, and bronze vessels. These vessels, intricately decorated with stylized depictions of real and imaginary animals, were used to make offerings to ancestral spirits. Possession of bronze objects was a sign of status and authority. The tombs also contain the bodies of family members, servants, and prisoners of war who were killed at the time of the burial. It appears that the objects and people were intended to serve the main occupant of the tomb in the afterlife.

Shang cities are not well preserved in the archaeological record, partly because of the climate of northern China and partly because of the perishable building materials used. With stone in short supply, cities were protected by massive walls of pounded earth, and buildings were constructed with wooden posts and dried mud. A number of sites appear to have served at different times as centers of political control and religion, with palaces, administrative buildings and storehouses, royal tombs, shrines of gods and ancestors, and houses of the nobility. The common people lived in agricultural villages outside these centers.

AP® Exam Tip
How have social categories, roles, and practices been maintained or challenged over time?

◀ **Shang Period Bronze Vessel**   Vessels such as this large wine jar were used in rituals by the Shang ruling class to make contact with their ancestors. As both the source and the proof of the elite's authority, these vessels were often buried in Shang tombs. The complex shapes and elaborate decorations testify to the artisans' skill. Covered ritual 'Fang-yi' wine vessel with 'Tao-tie' motif, Shang Dynasty (cast bronze with grey patina), Chinese School, (12th century B.C.)/Arthur M. Sackler Museum, Harvard University Art Museums, USA/Bequest of Grenville L. Winthrop/The Bridgeman Art Library

4-1d The Zhou Period, 1045–221 BCE

In the mid-eleventh century BCE the Shang were overthrown by the **Zhou (joe)**, whose homeland lay several hundred miles to the west, in the valley of the Wei **(way)** River. While the ethnic origin of the Zhou is unclear (their traditions acknowledged that their ancestors had lived for generations among the western "barbarians"), they took over many elements of Shang culture. The Zhou line of kings was the longest lasting and most revered of all dynasties in Chinese history. The two founders were Wen, a vassal ruler who, after being held prisoner for a time by his Shang overlord, initiated a rebellion of disaffected Shang subjects; and his son, Wu, who mounted a successful attack on the Shang capital and was enthroned as the first ruler of the new dynasty.

Wu justified his achievement in a manner that became the norm throughout subsequent Chinese history. Claiming that the last Shang ruler was depraved and tyrannical, neglecting to honor gods and ancestors and killing and abusing his subjects, he invoked the highest Zhou deity, Tian **(tyehn)** ("Heaven"), who was more compassionate than the aloof Di of the Shang. Wu declared that Heaven granted authority and legitimacy to a ruler as long as he looked out for the welfare of his subjects; the monarch, accordingly, was called the "Son of Heaven." The proof of divine favor was the prosperity and stability of the kingdom. But if the ruler persistently failed in these duties and neglected the warning signs of flood, famine, invasion, or other disasters, Heaven could withdraw this "Mandate" and transfer it to another, more worthy ruler and family.

Zhou The people and dynasty that took over the dominant position in north China from the Shang and created the concept of the Mandate of Heaven to justify their rule. The Zhou era, particularly the vigorous early period (1045–771 BCE), was remembered in Chinese tradition as a time of prosperity and benevolent rule.

MAP 4.1   China in the Shang and Zhou Periods, 1750–221 BCE The Shang dynasty arose in the second millennium BCE in the floodplain of the Yellow River. While southern China benefits from the monsoon rains, northern China depends on irrigation. As population increased, the Han Chinese migrated from their eastern homeland to other parts of China, carrying with them their technologies and cultural practices. Other ethnic groups predominated in more outlying regions, and the nomadic peoples of the northwest constantly challenged Chinese authority.

What were the different environmental conditions in the plains of the Yellow River and Yangzi River that led to dependence on different crops and different ways of organizing agricultural labor?

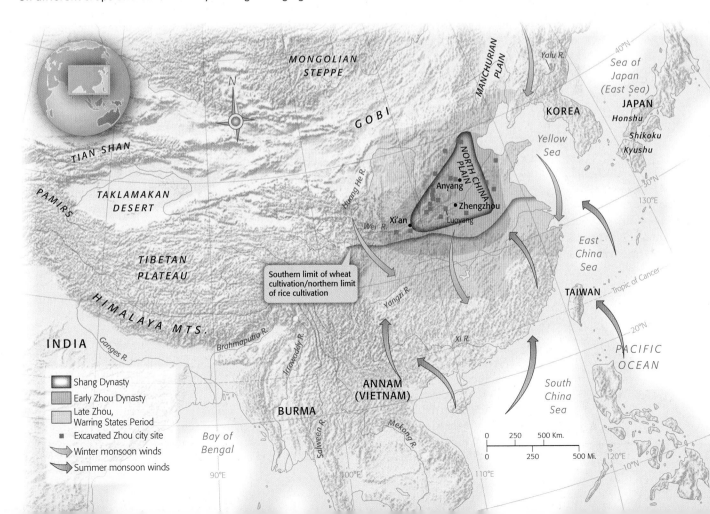

Many ancient peoples believed that the gods controlled the forces of nature and shaped destinies. Starting from this premise, they practiced various techniques of divination—the interpretation of phenomena in the natural world as signs of the gods' will and intentions. Through divination the ancients sought to communicate with the gods and thereby anticipate—even influence—the future.

The Shang ruling class in China frequently sought information from ancestors and other higher powers. The Shang monarch himself, with the help of religious experts, often functioned as the intermediary, since he had access to his own ancestors, who had a high ranking in the hierarchy of the spirit world. Chief among the tools of divination were oracle bones. Holes were first drilled in the shoulder bone of an ox or the bottom shell of a turtle to weaken it, and a red-hot pointed stick was applied, causing the bone or shell to crack. The cracks were then "read" by skilled interpreters as answers, on the part of the ancestor who was being consulted, to whatever questions had been asked. The questions, answers, and, often, confirmation of the accuracy of the prediction were subsequently incised on the shell or bone, providing a permanent record of matters of importance to the ruler, such as imminent weather, the yield of the upcoming harvest, the health of the king and his family, the proper performance of rituals, the prospects of military campaigns and hunting expeditions, and the mood of powerful royal ancestors and other divine forces. Tens of thousands of oracle bones survive as a major source of information about Shang life.

In Mesopotamia in the third and second millennia BCE the most important type of divination involved close inspection of the form, size, and markings of the organs of sacrificed animals. Archaeologists have found models of sheeps' livers labeled with explanations of the meaning of various features. Two other techniques of divination were following the trail of smoke from

burning incense and examining the patterns that resulted when oil was thrown on water.

From about 2000 BCE Mesopotamian diviners also foretold the future from their observation of the movements of the sun, moon, planets, stars, and constellations. In the centuries after 1000 BCE celestial omens were the most important source of predictions about the future, and specialists maintained precise records of astronomical events. Mesopotamian mathematics, essential for calculations of the movements of celestial bodies, was the most sophisticated in the ancient Middle East. Astrology, with its division of the sky into the twelve segments of the zodiac and its use of the position of the stars and planets to predict an individual's destiny, developed out of long-standing Mesopotamian attention to the movements of celestial objects. Horoscopes—charts with calculations and predictions based on an individual's date of birth—have been found from shortly before 400 BCE.

Greeks and Romans frequently used oracles or divination before making decisions. Most famous among the many oracle sites in Greece was Delphi, in a stunning location overlooking the Gulf of Corinth, where advice was sought from the god Apollo. A private individual or the official envoy from a Greek community, after leaving the customary gift for the god and entering the temple, had his question conveyed to the priestess, who fell into a trance (recent geological studies have discovered that the temple lay directly above a fissure, and scholars speculate that a gas rising up into the chamber may have put the priestess into an intoxicated state) and delivered a wild utterance that was then "translated" and written down by the priests who administered the shrine. Information and advice from the god at Delphi helped Greek communities choose where to place new settlements during the centuries of colonization throughout the Mediterranean and Black Seas, and Delphic priests may have collected information from the many

Mandate of Heaven Chinese religious and political ideology developed by the Zhou, according to which it was the prerogative of Heaven, the chief deity, to grant power to the ruler of China and to take away that power if the ruler failed to conduct himself justly and in the best interests of his subjects.

This theory of the **Mandate of Heaven**, which validated the institution of monarchy by connecting the religious and political spheres, served as the foundation of Chinese political thought for 3,000 years.

Much more is known about the early centuries of Zhou rule (the Western Zhou Period, 1045–771 BCE) than the preceding Shang era because of the survival of written texts, above all the *Book of Documents*, a collection of decrees, letters, and other historical and pseudo-historical (some allegedly written by the early emperors of legend) records, and the *Book of Songs*, an anthology of 305 poems, ballads, and folksongs that illuminate the lives of rulers, nobles, and peasants. Additionally, members of the Zhou elite recorded their careers and cited honors received from the rulers in bronze inscriptions.

To consolidate his power, King Wu distributed territories to his relatives and allies, which they were to administer and profit from so long as they remained loyal to him. These regional rulers then apportioned pieces of their holdings to their supporters, creating a pyramidal structure of political, social, and economic relations often referred to as "feudal," borrowing terminology from the European Middle Ages.

When Wu died, his son and heir, Cheng (**chung**), was too young to assume full powers, and for a time the kingdom was run by his uncles, especially the Duke of Zhou. The Duke of Zhou is one of the most famous figures in early Chinese history, in large part because the philosopher Confucius later celebrated him as the ideal administrator who selflessly served as regent for his

travelers who came their way and then dispensed it by means of oracles.

Greek and Roman sources report on practices of divination among the Celts. Predicting the future is one of the many religious functions attributed to the Druids, as well as to a specialized group of "seers." Among their methods was careful observation of the flight patterns of birds and of the appearance of sacrificial offerings. In Ireland a ritual specialist ate the meat of a freshly killed bull, lay down to sleep on the bull's hide, and then had prophetic dreams. The most startling form of Celtic divination is described by the geographer Strabo:

The Romans put a stop to [the] customs . . . connected with sacrifice and divination, as they were in conflict with our own ways: for example, they would strike a man who had been consecrated for sacrifice in the back with a sword, and make prophecies based on his death-spasms.

Such horrifying reports were used by the Romans to justify the conquest of Celtic peoples in order to "civilize" them.

Little is known about the divinatory practices of early American peoples. The Olmec produced polished stone mirrors whose concave surfaces gave off reflected images that were thought to emanate from a supernatural realm. In later Mesoamerican

▲ **Chinese Divination Shell** After inscribing questions on a bone or shell, the diviner applied a red-hot point and interpreted the resulting cracks as a divine response. Courtesy of the Institute of History and Philology, Academia Sinica

societies women threw maize kernels onto the surface of water-filled basins and noted the patterns by which they floated or sank. By this means they ascertained information useful to the family, such as the cause and cure of illness, the right time for agricultural tasks or marriage, and favorable names for newborn children.

It may seem surprising that divination is being treated here as a form of technology. Most modern people would regard such interpretations of patterns in everyday phenomena as mere superstition. However, for ancient peoples who believed that the gods directly controlled events in the natural world, divination amounted to the application of these principles of causation to the socially beneficial task of acquiring information about the future. These techniques were usually known only to a class of experts whose special training and knowledge gave them high status in their society.

Questions for Analysis

1. For ancient peoples, what was the underlying logic of seeing events in the natural world as messages from gods and spirits?

2. In what sense was divination, in all its many forms, a kind of technology?

3. What are some of the ways we in the contemporary world seek information about the future?

young nephew at a delicate time for the new dynasty, then dutifully returned power as soon as the lawful ruler came of age.

The early Zhou rulers constructed a new capital city in their homeland (near modern Xi'an), and other urban centers developed in succeeding centuries. Cities were laid out on a grid plan aligned with the north polar star, with gates in the fortification walls opening to the cardinal directions and major buildings facing south. This was in keeping with an already ancient concern, known as *feng shui* (fung shway) ("wind and water"), to orient structures so that they would be in a harmonious relationship with the terrain; the forces of wind, water, and sunlight; and the invisible energy perceived to be flowing through the natural world.

Alongside the new primacy of the Zhou deity Tian and continuation of religious practices inherited from the Shang era, new forms of divination developed. One increasingly popular method involved throwing down a handful of long and short stalks of the milfoil or yarrow plant and interpreting the patterns they formed. Over time a multilayered text was compiled, called the *Book of Changes*, that explained in detail the meanings of each of the sixty-four standard patterns formed by the stalks. In later ages this practice and the accompanying text also came to be used as a vehicle for self-examination and contemplation of the workings of the world.

The *Book of Songs* provides extraordinary glimpses into the lives, activities, and feelings of a diverse cross-section of early Chinese people—elite and common, male and female, urban and rural. We can glean much from these poems about the situation of women in early China. Some

AP® Exam Tip

Identify and explain several institutions created by rulers to organize their subjects.

describe men and women choosing each other and engaging in sex outside of marriage. Other poems tell of arranged marriages in which the young woman anxiously leaves home and birth family behind and journeys to the household of an unknown husband and new family. One poem describes the different ways that infant boys and girls were welcomed into an aristocratic family. The male was received like a little prince: placed on a bed, swaddled in expensive robes, and given a jade scepter to play with as a symbol of his future authority; the female was placed on the floor and given the weight from a weaving loom to indicate her future obligations of subservience and household labor.

Over the period from the eleventh to eighth centuries BCE the power of the Zhou monarch gradually eroded, largely because of the feudal division of territory and power. In 771 BCE the Zhou capital was attacked by a coalition of enemies, and the dynasty withdrew to a base farther east, at Luoyang (**LWOE-yahng**). This change ushers in the Eastern Zhou Period (770–221 BCE), a long era in which the Zhou monarchs remained as figureheads, given only nominal allegiance by the rulers of many virtually independent states scattered across northern and central China.

The first part of the Eastern Zhou era is called the Spring and Autumn Period (770–481 BCE) because of the survival of a text, the *Spring and Autumn Annals*, that provides a spare historical record of events in the small eastern state of Lu. Later writers added commentaries that fleshed out this skeletal record. The states of this era were frequently at odds with one another and employed various tactics to protect themselves and advance their interests, including diplomatic initiatives, shifting alliances, and coups and assassinations as well as conventional warfare. The overall trend was gradual consolidation into a smaller number of larger and more powerful states.

Warfare was a persistent feature of the period, and there were important transformations in the character and technology of war. In the Shang and early Zhou periods, warfare largely had been conducted by members of the elite, who rode in chariots, treated battle as an opportunity for displays of skill and courage, and adhered to a code of heroic conduct. But in the high-stakes conflicts of the Eastern Zhou era, there was a shift to much larger armies made up of conscripted farmers who fought bloody infantry battles, unconstrained by noble etiquette, in which large numbers were slaughtered. Some men undertook the study of war and composed handbooks, such as Sunzi's *Art of War*. Sunzi (**soon-zuh**) approaches war as a chess game in which the successful general employs deception, intuits the energy potential inherent in the landscape, and psychologically manipulates both friend and foe. The best victories are achieved without fighting so that one can incorporate the unimpaired resources of the other side.

Technological advances also impacted warfare. In the last centuries of the Zhou, the Chinese learned from the nomadic peoples of the northern steppes to put fighters on horseback. By 600 BCE iron began to replace bronze as the primary metal for tools and weapons. There is mounting evidence that ironworking also came to China from the nomadic peoples of the northwest. Metalworkers in China were the first in the world to forge steel by removing carbon during the iron-smelting process.

Another significant development was the increasing size and complexity of the governments that administered Chinese states. Rulers ordered the careful recording of the population, the land, and its agricultural products so that the government could compel peasants to donate labor for public works projects (digging and maintaining irrigation channels and building roads, defensive walls, and palaces), conscript them into the army, and collect taxes. Skilled officials supervised the expanding bureaucracies of scribes, accountants, and surveyors and advised the rulers on various matters. Thus there arose a class of educated and ambitious men who traveled from state to state offering their services to the rulers—and their theories of ideal government.

AP® Exam Tip
Understand how pastoralists acted as developers and disseminators of new weapons and modes of transportation that transformed warfare in agrarian civilizations.

4-1e Confucianism, Daoism, and Chinese Society

The Eastern Zhou era, despite being plagued by political fragmentation, frequent warfare, and anxious uncertainty, was also a time of great cultural development. The two most influential "philosophical" systems of Chinese civilization—Confucianism and Daoism—had their roots in this period, though they would be further developed and adapted to changing circumstances in later times.

Kongzi (**kohng-zuh**) (551–479 BCE), known in the West by the Latin form of his name, **Confucius**, withdrew from public life after unsuccessful efforts to find employment as an official and adviser to several rulers of the day. He attracted a circle of students to whom he presented his wide-ranging ideas on morality, conduct, and government. His sayings were handed down orally by several generations of disciples before being compiled in written form as the *Analects* (see Diversity & Dominance: Human Nature and Good Government in the *Analects* of Confucius and the Legalist Writings of Han Fei). This work, along with a set of earlier texts that were believed (probably wrongly) to have been edited by Confucius—the *Book of Documents*, the *Book of Songs*, the *Book of Changes*, and the *Spring and Autumn Annals*—became the core texts of Confucianism.

Confucius drew upon traditional institutions and values but gave them new shape and meaning. He looked back to the early Zhou period as a Golden Age of wise rulers and benevolent government, models to which the people of his own "broken" society should return. He also placed great importance on the "rituals," or forms of behavior, that guide people in their daily interactions with one another, since these promote harmony in human relations.

For Confucius the family was the fundamental component of society, and the ways in which family members regulated their conduct in the home prepared them to serve as subjects of the state. Each person had his or her place and duties in a hierarchical order that was determined by age and gender. The "filiality" of children to parents, which included obedience, reverence, and love, had its analogue in the devotion of subjects to the ruler. Another fundamental virtue for Confucius was *ren* (**ruhn**), sometimes translated as "humaneness," which traditionally meant the feelings between family members and was now expanded into a universal ideal of benevolence and compassion that would, ideally, pervade every activity. Confucianism placed immense value on the practical task of making society function smoothly at every level. It provided a philosophical and ethical framework for conducting one's life and understanding one's place in the world. But it was not a religion. While Confucius urged respect for gods, ancestors, and religious traditions, he felt that such supernatural matters were unknowable.

Confucius's ideas were little known in his own time, but his teachings were preserved by his followers and gradually spread to a wider audience. Some disciples took Confucianism in new directions. Mengzi (**muhng-zuh**) (known in the West as Mencius, 371–289 BCE), who did much to popularize Confucian ideas in his age, believed in the essential goodness of all human beings and argued that, if people were shown the right way by virtuous leaders, they would voluntarily do the right thing. Xunzi (**shoon-zuh**) (ca. 310–210 BCE), on the other hand, concluded that people had to be compelled and taught to make appropriate choices. (This approach led to the development of a school of thought called Legalism, discussed later in this chapter.) As we shall see in Chapter 6, in the era of the emperors a revised Confucianism became the dominant political philosophy and the core of the educational system for government officials.

If Confucianism emphasized social engagement, its great rival, **Daoism** (**DOW-ism**), urged withdrawal from the empty formalities, rigid hierarchy, and distractions of Chinese society. Laozi (**low-zuh**) is regarded as the originator of Daoism, although virtually nothing is known about him, and some scholars doubt his existence. Laozi is credited with the foundational text of Daoism, the *Classic of the Way of Virtue*, a difficult book full of ambiguity and paradox, beautiful poetic images, and tantalizing hints of "truths" that cannot be adequately explained with words. It raises questions about whether the material world in which we operate is real or a kind of dream that blocks us from perceiving a higher reality. It argues that education, knowledge, and rational analysis are obstacles to understanding and that we would be better off cultivating our senses and trusting our intuitions. The primal world of the distant past was happy and blessed before civilization and "knowledge" corrupted it. The Daoist sage strives to lead a tranquil existence by retreating from the stresses and obligations of a chaotic society. He avoids useless struggles, making himself soft and malleable so that the forces that buffet people can flow harmlessly around him. He chooses not to "act" because such action almost always leads to a different outcome from the one desired, whereas inaction may bring the desired outcome. And he has no fear of death because, for all we know, death may be merely a transformation to another plane of existence. In the end, in a world that is always changing and lacks any absolute morality or meaning, all that matters is the individual's fundamental understanding of, and accommodation to, the *Dao*, the "path" or pattern of nature.

AP® Exam Tip Understand the core beliefs of Confucianism and analyze its impact on Chinese society over time.

AP® Exam Tip Explain how Daoism influenced the development of Chinese culture.

Confucius Western name for the Chinese philosopher Kongzi (551–479 BCE). His doctrine of duty and public service had a great influence on subsequent Chinese thought and served as a code of conduct for government officials.

Daoism Chinese school of thought, originating in the Warring States Period with Laozi. Daoism offered an alternative to the Confucian emphasis on hierarchy and duty.

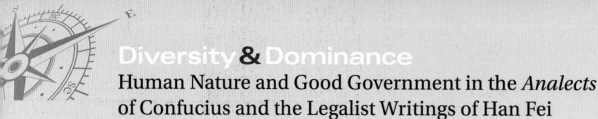
While monarchy (the rule of one man) was the standard form of government in ancient China and was rarely challenged, political theorists and philosophers thought a great deal about the qualities of the ideal ruler, his relationship to his subjects, and the means by which he controlled them. These considerations about how to govern people were inevitably molded by fundamental assumptions about the nature of human beings. In the Warring States Period, as the major states struggled desperately with one another for survival and expansion, such discussions took on a special urgency, and the Confucians and Legalists came to represent two powerful, and largely contradictory, points of view.

The Analects are a collection of sayings of Confucius, probably compiled and written down several generations after he lived, though some elements may have been added even later. They cover a wide range of matters, including ethics, government, education, music, and rituals. Taken as a whole, they are a guide to living an honorable, virtuous, useful, and satisfying life. While subject to reinterpretation according to the circumstances of the times, Confucian principles have had a great influence on Chinese values and behavior ever since.

Han Fei (280–233 BCE), who was, ironically, at one time the student of a Confucian teacher, became a Legalist writer and political adviser to the ruler of the ambitious state of Qin. Eventually he lost out in a power struggle at court and was forced to kill himself.

The following selections illuminate the profound disagreements between Confucians and Legalists over the essential nature of human beings and how the ruler should conduct himself in order to most effectively govern his subjects and protect his kingdom.

Confucius

4:5 Confucius said: "Riches and honors are what all men desire. But if they cannot be attained in accordance with the *dao* [the way] they should not be kept. Poverty and low status are what all men hate. But if they cannot be avoided while staying in accordance with the *dao*, you should not avoid them. If a Superior Man departs from *ren* [humaneness], how can he be worthy of that name? A Superior Man never leaves *ren* for even the time of a single meal. In moments of haste he acts according to it. In times of difficulty or confusion he acts according to it."

16:8 Confucius said: "The Superior Man stands in awe of three things: (1) He is in awe of the decree of Heaven. (2) He is in awe of great men. (3) He is in awe of the words of the sages. The inferior man does not know the decree of Heaven; takes great men lightly and laughs at the words of the sages."

4:14 Confucius said: "I don't worry about not having a good position; I worry about the means I use to gain position. I don't worry about being unknown; I seek to be known in the right way."

7:15 Confucius said: "I can live with coarse rice to eat, water for drink and my arm as a pillow and still be happy. Wealth and honors that one possesses in the midst of injustice are like floating clouds."

13:6 Confucius said: "When you have gotten your own life straightened out, things will go well without your giving orders. But if your own life isn't straightened out, even if you give orders, no one will follow them."

12:2 Zhonggong asked about the meaning of *ren*. The Master said: "Go out of your home as if you were receiving an important guest. Employ the people as if you were assisting at a great ceremony. What you don't want done to yourself, don't do to others. Live in your town without stirring up resentments, and live in your household without stirring up resentments."

1:5 Confucius said: "If you would govern a state of a thousand chariots (a small-to-middle-size state), you must pay strict attention to business, be true to your word, be economical in expenditure and love the people. You should use them according to the seasons."

2:3 Confucius said: "If you govern the people legalistically and control them by punishment, they will avoid crime, but have no personal sense of shame. If you govern them by means of virtue and control them with propriety, they will gain their own sense of shame, and thus correct themselves."

12:7 Zigong asked about government. The Master said, "Enough food, enough weapons and the confidence of the people." Zigong said, "Suppose you had no alternative but to give up one of these three, which one would be let go of first?" The Master said, "Weapons." Zigong said, "What if you had to give up one of the remaining two, which one would it be?" The Master said, "Food. From ancient times, death has come to all men, but a people without confidence in its rulers will not stand."

Daoism, like Confucianism, would continue to evolve for many centuries, adapting to changes in Chinese society and incorporating many elements of traditional religion, mysticism, and magic. Although Daoism and Confucianism may appear to be thoroughly at odds regarding the relationship of the individual and the larger society, many Chinese through the ages have drawn on both traditions, and it has been said that the typical Chinese scholar-official was a Confucian in his work and public life but a Daoist in the privacy of his study.

12:19 Ji Kang Zi asked Confucius about government saying: "Suppose I were to kill the unjust, in order to advance the just. Would that be all right?"

Confucius replied: "In doing government, what is the need of killing? If you desire good, the people will be good. The nature of the Superior Man is like the wind, the nature of the inferior man is like the grass. When the wind blows over the grass, it always bends."

2:19 The Duke of Ai asked: "How can I make the people follow me?" Confucius replied: "Advance the upright and set aside the crooked, and the people will follow you. Advance the crooked and set aside the upright, and the people will not follow you."

2:20 Ji Kang Zi asked: "How can I make the people reverent and loyal, so they will work positively for me?" Confucius said, "Approach them with dignity, and they will be reverent. Be filial and compassionate and they will be loyal. Promote the able and teach the incompetent, and they will work positively for you."

Han Fei

Past and present have different customs; new and old adopt different measures. To try to use the ways of a generous and lenient government to rule the people of a critical age is like trying to drive a runaway horse without using reins or whips. This is the misfortune that ignorance invites. . . .

Humaneness [ren] may make one shed tears and be reluctant to apply penalties, but law makes it clear that such penalties must be applied. The ancient kings allowed law to be supreme and did not give in to their tearful longings. Hence it is obvious that humaneness cannot be used to achieve order in the state. . . .

The best rewards are those that are generous and predictable, so that the people may profit by them. The best penalties are those that are severe and inescapable, so that the people will fear them. The best laws are those that are uniform and inflexible, so that the people can understand them. . . .

Hardly ten men of true integrity and good faith can be found today, and yet the offices of the state number in the hundreds. . . . Therefore the way of the enlightened ruler is to unify the laws instead of seeking for wise men, to lay down firm policies instead of longing for men of good faith. . . .

When a sage rules the state, he does not depend on people's doing good of themselves; he sees to it that they are not allowed to do what is bad. If he depends on people's doing good of themselves, then within his borders he can count fewer than ten instances of success. But if he sees to it that they are not allowed

to do what is bad, then the whole state can be brought to a uniform level of order. Those who rule must employ measures that will be effective with the majority and discard those that will be effective with only a few. Therefore they devote themselves not to virtue but to law. . . .

When the Confucians of the present time counsel rulers, they do not praise those measures that will bring order today, but talk only of the achievements of the men who brought order in the past. . . . No ruler with proper standards will tolerate them. Therefore the enlightened ruler works with facts and discards useless theories. He does not talk about deeds of humaneness and rightness, and he does not listen to the words of scholars. . . .

Nowadays, those who do not understand how to govern invariably say, "You must win the hearts of the people!". . . The reason you cannot rely on the wisdom of the people is that they have the minds of little children. If the child's head is not shaved, its sores will spread; and if its boil is not lanced, it will become sicker than ever . . . for it does not understand that the little pain it suffers now will bring great benefit later. . . .

Now, the ruler presses the people to till the land and open up new pastures so as to increase their means of livelihood, and yet they consider him harsh; he draws up a penal code and makes the punishments more severe in order to put a stop to evil, and yet the people consider him stern. . . . He makes certain that everyone within his borders understands warfare and sees to it that there are no private exemptions from military service; he unites the strength of the state and fights fiercely in order to take its enemies captive, and yet the people consider him violent. . . . [These] types of undertaking all ensure order and safety to the state, and yet the people do not have sense enough to rejoice in them.

AP® History Reasoning Skills

Comparison *What conclusions can be drawn from these passages regarding Confucian and Legalist views about the intrinsic nature of human beings and the interactions between rulers and subjects?*

Contextualization *To what extent did the Qin dynasty reflect the characteristics of an ideal ruler as put forth by Han Fei?*

Sources: Confucius selections from "The Analects of Confucius," translated by A. Charles Muller, from *www.acmuller.net/con-dao/analects.html*. Reprinted by permission of Charles Muller. Passages from "The Five Vermin," from Han Fei Tzu, translated by Burton Watson. Copyright (c) 1964 Columbia University Press. Reprinted with permission of the publisher.

The classical Chinese patterns of family and property took shape in the later Zhou period. The kinship structures of the Shang and early Zhou periods, based on the *clan* (a relatively large group of related families), gave way to the three-generation family of grandparents, parents, and children as the fundamental social unit. Fathers had absolute authority over women and children, arranged marriages for their offspring, and could sell the labor of family members. Only men could conduct rituals and make offerings to the ancestors, though women helped maintain the household's ancestral shrines. A man was limited to one wife but was permitted additional sexual partners, who had the lower status of concubines. A man whose wife died had a duty to remarry in order to produce male heirs to keep alive the cult of the ancestors, whereas women were discouraged from remarrying.

In Chinese tradition the concept of **yin/yang** represented the complementary nature of male and female roles in the natural order. The male principle (yang) was equated with the sun: active, bright, and shining; the female principle (yin) corresponded to the moon: passive, shaded, and reflective. Male toughness was balanced by female gentleness, male action and initiative by female endurance and need for completion, and male leadership by female supportiveness. In its earliest form, the theory considered yin and yang as equal and alternately dominant, like night and day, creating balance in the world. However, as a result of the changing role of women in the Zhou period and the pervasive influence of Confucian ideology, the male principle came to be seen as superior to the female.

4-1f The Warring States Period, 481–221 BCE

The second half of the Eastern Zhou era is conventionally called the Warring States Period (480–221 BCE) because the scale and intensity of rivalry and warfare between the states accelerated. More successful states conquered and absorbed less capable rivals, and by the beginning of the third century BCE only seven major states remained. Each state sought security by any and all means: building walls to protect its borders; putting into the field the largest possible armies; experimenting with military organization, tactics, and technology; and devising new techniques of administration to produce the greatest revenues. Some wars were fought against non-Chinese peoples living on the margins of the states' territories or even in enclaves within the states. In addition to self-defense, the aim of these campaigns was often to increase the territory available for agriculture, since cultivated land was, ultimately, the source of wealth and manpower. The conquered peoples assimilated over time, becoming Chinese in language and culture.

yin/yang In Chinese belief, complementary factors that help to maintain the equilibrium of the world. Yang is associated with masculine, light, and active qualities; yin with feminine, dark, and passive qualities.

The most innovative of all the states of this era was Qin (**chin**), on the western edge of the "Central States" (the term used for the Chinese lands of north and central China). Coming from the same Wei River Valley frontier region as the Zhou long before, and exposed to barbarian influences and attacks, the Qin rulers commanded a nation of hardy farmers and employed them in large, well-trained armies. The very vulnerability of their circumstances may have inspired the Qin rulers of the fourth and third centuries BCE to take great risks, for they were

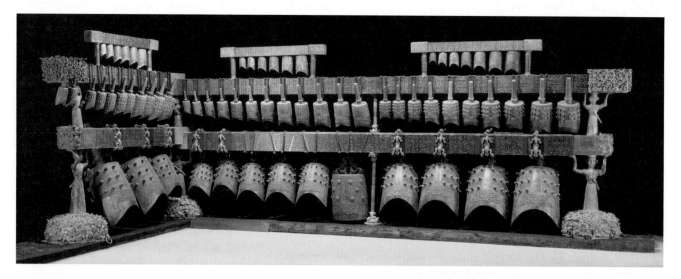

▲ **Chinese Bronze Bells**   This set of sixty-five bells was discovered in the tomb of Marquis Yi, the ruler of one of the warring states in the fifth century BCE. Bells in different sizes were central components of ancient Chinese "orchestras." In the Eastern Zhou era, each state had its own distinctive set of instruments, an assertion of independence and local pride. Martha Avery/Corbis Historical/Getty Images

the first to put into practice the philosophy and methods of the Legalist school of political theorists.

In the mid-fourth century BCE Lord Shang was put in charge of the Qin government. He maintained that the Confucians were mistaken in looking to an idealized past for solutions and naive in thinking that the ruler should worry about his subjects' opinions. In Lord Shang's view, the ruler should trust his own judgment and employ whatever means are necessary to compel obedience and good behavior in his subjects. In the end, Legalists were willing to sacrifice individual freedom to guarantee the security and prosperity of the state. To strengthen the ruler, Lord Shang moved to weaken the Qin nobility, sending out centrally appointed district governors, abolishing many of the privileges of the nobility, and breaking up large estates by requiring property to be divided equally among the surviving sons. Although he eventually became entangled in bitter intrigue at court and was killed in 338 BCE, the Qin rulers of the third century BCE continued to employ Legalist advisers and pursue Legalist policies, and, as we shall see in Chapter 6, they converted the advantages gained from this approach into a position of unprecedented power.

Section Review

- The challenges of engaging in agriculture in the varied environments of East Asia led to the formation of complex, hierarchical societies.

- The Shang and Zhou rulers of early China developed religious ideologies (oracle bone divination, Mandate of Heaven theory) that justified monarchic systems of government.

- The feudal organization of the Zhou state led, over time, to the weakening of the monarch's authority and the rise of many essentially independent states.

- The rivalry and conflict of Chinese states in the later Zhou era led to the rise of bureaucracies, administrative experts, and more deadly forms of warfare.

- This era also saw the rise and rivalry of major philosophical systems: Confucianism, Daoism, and Legalism.

- Although yin/yang theory regarded the female and male principles as interdependent, men were dominant in the family, and the influence of Confucianism led to a reduction in women's status and rights.

4-2 Nubia, 2300 BCE–350 CE

How did the technological and cultural influences of Egypt and sub-Saharan Africa affect the formation of Nubia?

Since the first century BCE the name *Nubia* has been applied to a 1,000-mile (1,600-kilometer) stretch of the Nile Valley lying between Aswan and Khartoum (**kahr-TOOM**) and straddling the southern part of the modern nation of Egypt and the northern part of Sudan (see Map 4.2). Nubia is the only continuously inhabited territory connecting sub-Saharan Africa (the lands south of the Sahara Desert) with North Africa. For thousands of years it has served as a corridor for trade between tropical Africa and the Mediterranean. Nubia was richly endowed with natural resources such as gold, copper, and semiprecious stones.

Nubia's location and natural wealth, along with Egypt's hunger for Nubian gold, explain the early rise of a civilization with a complex political organization, social stratification, metallurgy, monumental building, and writing. Scholars have moved away from the traditional view that Nubian civilization simply imitated Egypt, and they now emphasize the mutually beneficial interactions between Egypt and Nubia and the growing evidence that Nubian culture also drew on influences from sub-Saharan Africa.

4-2a Early Cultures and Egyptian Domination, 2300–1100 BCE

The central geographical feature of Nubia, as of Egypt, is the Nile River. This part of the Nile flows through a landscape of rocky desert, grassland, and fertile plain. River irrigation was essential for agriculture in a climate that was severely hot and, in the north, nearly without rainfall. Six cataracts, barriers formed by large boulders and rapids, obstructed boat traffic. Boats operating between the cataracts and caravans skirting the river made travel and trade possible.

In the fifth millennium BCE bands of people in northern Nubia made the transition from seminomadic hunting and gathering to a settled life based on grain agriculture and cattle herding. From this time on, the majority of the population lived in agricultural villages alongside the river. Even before 3000 BCE Egyptian craftsmen worked in ivory and in ebony wood—products of tropical Africa that came through Nubia.

AP® Exam Tip
Know about expanding trade networks such as that between Egypt and Nubia.

Kush An Egyptian name for Nubia, the region alongside the Nile River south of Egypt, where an indigenous kingdom with its own distinctive institutions and cultural traditions arose beginning in the early second millennium BCE.

Nubia enters the historical record around 2300 BCE in Old Kingdom Egyptian accounts of trade missions to southern lands. At that time Aswan, just north of the First Cataract, was the southern limit of Egyptian control. As we saw with the journey of Harkhuf at the beginning of this chapter, Egyptian officials stationed there led donkey caravans south in search of gold, incense, ebony, ivory, slaves, and exotic animals from tropical Africa. This was dangerous work, requiring delicate negotiations with local Nubian chiefs to secure protection, but it brought substantial rewards to those who succeeded.

During the Middle Kingdom (ca. 2040–1640 BCE), Egypt adopted a more aggressive stance toward Nubia. Seeking to control the gold mines in the desert east of the Nile and to cut out the Nubian middlemen who drove up the cost of luxury goods from the tropics, the Egyptians erected a string of mud-brick forts on islands and riverbanks south of the Second Cataract. The forts regulated the flow of trade goods and protected the southern frontier of Egypt against Nubians and nomadic raiders from the desert. There seem to have been peaceable relations but little interaction between the Egyptian garrisons and the indigenous population of northern Nubia, which continued to practice its age-old farming and herding ways.

Farther south, where the Nile makes a great U-shaped turn in the fertile plain of the Dongola Reach (see Map 4.2), a more complex political entity was evolving from the chiefdoms of the third millennium BCE. The Egyptians gave the name **Kush** to the kingdom whose capital was located at Kerma, one of the earliest urbanized centers in tropical Africa. Beginning around 1750 BCE the kings of Kush built fortification walls and monumental structures of mud brick. The dozens or even hundreds of servants and wives sacrificed for burial with the kings, as well as the rich objects found in their tombs, testify to the wealth and power of the rulers of Kush and imply a belief in an afterlife in which attendants and possessions would be useful. Kushite craftsmen were skilled in metalworking, whether for weapons or jewelry, and produced high-quality pottery.

During the expansionist New Kingdom (ca. 1532–1070 BCE), the Egyptians penetrated more deeply into Nubia (see Chapter 3). They destroyed Kush and its capital (recent archaeological excavations have shown that the Egyptians constructed a new town and palace complex a half-mile north of the abandoned native city) and extended their frontier to the Fourth Cataract. A high-ranking Egyptian official called "Overseer of Southern Lands" or "King's Son of Kush" ruled Nubia from a new administrative center at Napata (**nah-PAH-tuh**), near Gebel Barkal (**JEB-uhl BAHR-kahl**), the "Holy Mountain," believed to be the home of a local god. Exploiting the mines of Nubia, Egypt supplied gold to the states of the Middle East. Fatalities were high among native workers in the brutal desert climate, and the army had to ward off attacks from desert nomads.

Five hundred years of Egyptian domination in Nubia left many marks. The Egyptian government imposed Egyptian culture on the native population. Children from elite families were brought to the Egyptian royal court to guarantee the good behavior of their relatives in Nubia; they absorbed Egyptian language, culture, and religion, which they later carried home with them. Other Nubians served as

MAP 4.2 Ancient Nubia The land route alongside the Nile River as it flows through Nubia has long served as a corridor connecting sub-Saharan Africa with North Africa. Centuries of Egyptian occupation, as well as time spent in Egypt by Nubian hostages, mercenaries, and merchants, led to a marked Egyptian cultural influence in Nubia. Adapted from Map 15 from *The Historical Atlas of Africa*, ed. by J. F. Ajyi and Michael Crowder.

Why is Nubia the only continuously inhabited land linking sub-Saharan and North Africa?

◄ **Nubian Gods** This relief from the wall of a Nubian temple at Naqa shows the Nubian royal family in the presence of the Egyptian deities Amun and Horus and the indigenous lion-god, Apedemak. Nubian culture borrowed from both Egypt and sub-Saharan Africa.

INTERFOTO/Alamy Stock Photo

archers in the Egyptian armed forces. The manufactured goods that they brought back to Nubia have been found in their graves. The Nubians built towns on the Egyptian model and erected stone temples to Egyptian gods, particularly Amon. The frequent depiction of Amon with the head of a ram may reflect a blending of the chief Egyptian god with a Nubian ram deity.

4-2b The Kingdom of Meroë, 800 BCE–350 CE

Egypt's weakness after 1200 BCE led to the collapse of its authority in Nubia. In the eighth century BCE a powerful new native kingdom emerged in southern Nubia. Its history can be divided into two parts. During the early period, between the eighth and fourth centuries BCE, Napata, the former Egyptian headquarters, was the primary center. During the later period, from the fourth century BCE to the fourth century CE, the center was farther south, at **Meroë** (**MER-oh-ee**), near the Sixth Cataract.

For half a century, from around 712 to 660 BCE, the kings of Nubia ruled all of Egypt as the Twenty-fifth Dynasty, conducting themselves in the age-old manner of Egyptian rulers. They were addressed by royal titles, depicted in traditional costume, and buried according to Egyptian custom. However, they kept their Nubian names and were depicted with the physical features of sub-Saharan Africans. They also inaugurated an artistic and cultural renaissance, building on a monumental scale for the first time in centuries and reinvigorating Egyptian art, architecture, and religion. The Nubian kings resided at Memphis, the Old Kingdom capital, while Thebes, the New Kingdom capital, was the residence of a celibate female member of the king's family who was titled "God's Wife of Amon."

The Nubian dynasty made a disastrous mistake in 701 BCE when it offered help to local rulers in Palestine who were struggling against the Assyrian Empire. The Assyrians retaliated by invading Egypt and driving the Nubian monarchs back to their southern domain by 660 BCE. Napata again became the chief royal residence and religious center of the kingdom. However, Egyptian cultural influences remained strong. Court documents continued to be written in Egyptian hieroglyphs, and the mummified remains of the rulers were buried in modestly sized sandstone pyramids along with hundreds of shawabti (**shuh-WAB-tee**) figurines.

By the fourth century BCE the center of gravity had shifted south to Meroë, perhaps because Meroë was better situated for agriculture and trade, the economic mainstays of the Nubian kingdom. As a result, sub-Saharan cultural patterns gradually replaced Egyptian ones. Egyptian hieroglyphs gave way to a new set of symbols, still essentially undeciphered, for writing the Meroitic language. People continued to worship Amon as well as Isis, an Egyptian goddess

AP® Exam Tip
Understand gender roles in early civilizations and explain the development and impact of patriarchy.

Meroë Capital of a flourishing kingdom in southern Nubia from the fourth century BCE to the fourth century CE. In this period Nubian culture shows more independence from Egypt and greater influence from sub-Saharan Africa.

Section Review

- Nubia's natural wealth and location on the trade route between Egypt and sub-Saharan Africa, along with Egypt's hunger for Nubian gold, explain the early rise of a complex civilization there.

- During long periods of Egyptian domination, as well as a period in which Nubian rulers controlled Egypt, Nubian culture and technology were strongly influenced by Egyptian practices.

- During the Meroitic period, Nubia came under stronger cultural influences stemming from sub-Saharan Africa, as seen in the prominent role of queens.

- The city of Meroë was large and impressive, with monumental palaces, temples, and boulevards. It controlled agriculture and trade and was a center of metallurgy.

- Nubia's collapse in the early fourth century CE was due to shifting trade routes and attacks by desert nomads.

connected to fertility and sexuality, but those deities had to share the stage with Nubian deities like the lion-god Apedemak. Meroitic art combined Egyptian, Greco-Roman, and indigenous traditions.

Women of the royal family played an important role in Meroitic politics, another reflection of the influence of sub-Saharan Africa. In their matrilineal system the king was succeeded by the son of his sister. Nubian queens sometimes ruled by themselves and sometimes in partnership with their husbands, playing a part in warfare, diplomacy, and the building of temples and pyramid tombs. They are depicted in scenes reserved for male rulers in Egyptian imagery, smiting enemies in battle and being suckled by the mother-goddess Isis.

Meroë was a huge city for its time, more than a square mile in area, dominating fertile grasslands and converging trade routes. Great reservoirs were dug to catch precious rainfall, and the city was a major center for iron smelting. Although much of the city is still buried under the sand, in 2002 archaeologists, using a magnetometer to detect buried structures, discovered a large palace. The Temple of Amon was approached by an avenue lined with stone rams, and the walled precinct of the "Royal City" was filled with palaces, temples, and administrative buildings. The ruler, who may have been regarded as divine, was assisted by a professional class of officials, priests, and army officers.

Meroë collapsed in the early fourth century CE, overrun by nomads from the western desert who had become more mobile because of the arrival of the camel in North Africa. It had already been weakened when profitable commerce with the Roman Empire was diverted to the Red Sea and to the rising kingdom of Aksum (**AHK-soom**) (in present-day Ethiopia). Thus the end of the Meroitic kingdom was as closely linked to Nubia's role in long-distance commerce as its beginning.

4-3 Pastoral Nomads of the Eurasian Steppes, 1000–100 BCE

How was the rise of steppe nomadism dependent on interactions with settled agricultural peoples, and what new challenges did the nomads pose to farming societies?

4-3a Early Nomadism

Nomads (from a Greek word meaning "wanderers") are people who do not have a single, settled place of residence, but rather move from one temporary encampment to another, usually as a strategy for feeding themselves. For most of human history people were nomadic hunter-gatherers, moving about in search of wild plants they could harvest and animals they could kill. It was only with the Agricultural Revolutions—the domestication of plants and animals—beginning around 10,000 years ago that human groups were able to settle in one place, build permanent homes, acquire more possessions, and create more complex societies (see Chapter 1).

The domestication of herd animals, such as sheep, goats, and cattle, made possible a new kind of nomadism in which people lived off the products of their animals, consuming meat and milk and other dairy products, clothing themselves with hair and hides, and utilizing animal manure to fuel fires. We have already seen several examples of nomadic peoples, initially living on the fringes of the settled, agricultural areas in early western Asia and, in some cases, eventually settling down and assimilating to the cultures of the more advanced agricultural peoples—the Amorites who migrated into southern Mesopotamia and founded Babylon in the early second millennium BCE (see Chapter 2); the Aramaeans who settled in Syria-Palestine

nomads People without permanent, fixed places of residence, whose way of life and means of subsistence require them to periodically migrate, often with their herds of domesticated animals, to a familiar series of temporary seasonal encampments.

and whose language, Aramaic, became widespread in that region; and the early Israelites, whose migratory lifestyle was remembered in the traditions about the patriarchs Abraham, Isaac, and Jacob (see Chapter 3). Many scholars believe that the proto-Indo-Europeans, speakers of the language or languages ancestral to the large family of Indo-European languages found across much of Europe and Asia, were nomadic herders who migrated from an original homeland north of the Black and Caspian Seas beginning in the third millennium BCE They are believed to have first domesticated horses, which enhanced their ability to herd other animals (see Chapter 1).

4-3b Steppe Nomads

Our concern here is with a new kind of pastoral nomadism that arose across the vast Eurasian Steppes in the first millennium BCE. **Steppe**—a word of Russian origin—is used to describe an ecological zone characterized by treeless, grass- and shrub-covered plains and marked by a relatively arid climate with too little precipitation for agriculture and radical extremes of temperature from summer to winter and day to night. The Eurasian Steppes extend from Hungary in eastern Europe across Ukraine and southern Russia, Central Asia, Mongolia, and southern Siberia (see Map 4.3). The peoples who occupied these lands became horse-riding

steppe An ecological region of grass- and shrub-covered plains that is treeless and too arid for agriculture.

MAP 4.3 **Pastoral Nomads of the Eurasian Steppes** This map shows the vast steppes of Eurasia, arid grasslands extending from Hungary to Manchuria, and the nomadic pastoralist peoples who grazed their herds there. Steppe nomads sometimes traded with settled peoples, sometimes raided, forcing neighboring states like China to either buy them off or develop cavalry forces to fight them. Several of these groups, including Parthians, Scythians, and Yuezhi, migrated south to agricultural lands and created powerful states.

What tended to happen along the frontier between lands occupied by pastoral nomads and agriculturalists?

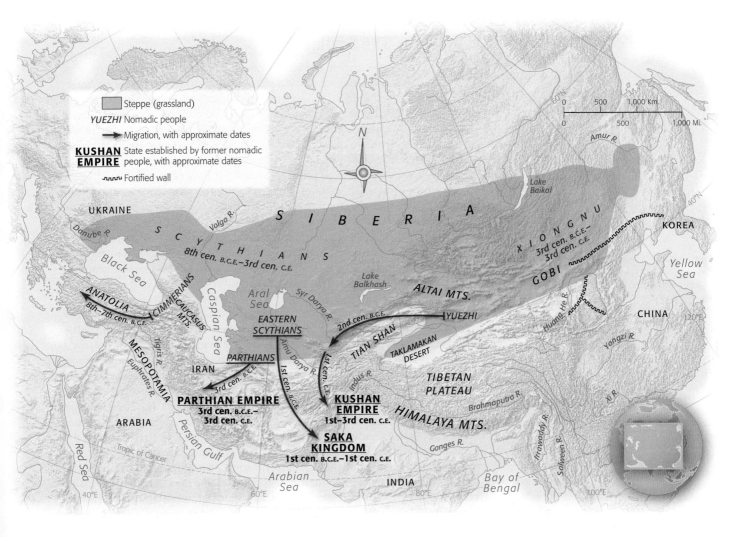

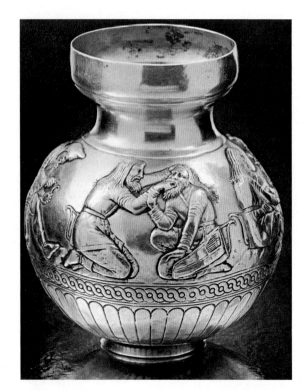

▲ **Scythian Vase**   This gold or electrum vase, found in a burial mound in the Crimea from the fourth century BCE, depicts a dentist at work. Both Scythian men are bearded and long-haired, wearing the trousers of horse-riding nomads and a bow case. The skilled artist may have been a Greek living in a Black Sea colony. INDIVISION CHARMET/State Hermitage Museum, St. Petersburg, Russia/Bridgeman Images

Herodotus Heir to the technique of *historia* ("investigation/research") developed by Greeks in the late archaic period. He came from a Greek community in Anatolia and traveled extensively, collecting information in western Asia and the Mediterranean lands. He traced the antecedents and chronicled the wars between the Greek city-states and the Persian Empire, thus originating the Western tradition of historical writing.

Scythians Term used by the ancient Greeks for the nomadic peoples living on the steppe north of the Black and Caspian Seas.

warriors, driving their herds to seasonal camping grounds and being careful not to overexploit pastures and water sources to the point that they could not recover and be used again. They didn't wander randomly, but rather operated within certain territorial bounds worked out with other groups. Normally they relocated to familiar encampments appropriate to their needs in different seasons. The success of this way of life also depended on a symbiotic interaction of the nomads with settled agricultural peoples, often by trading animal products (live animals, meat, hides, wool, cheese) for agricultural products and manufactured goods (metalwork and textiles), sometimes by raiding and stealing.

Because they lacked the technology of writing, we know relatively little about these peoples and must depend on the information provided by archaeology and the accounts of nomads in the records of literate ancient peoples. Greek and Roman texts tell us something about the peoples on the western range of the steppes, while Chinese sources inform us about the peoples of the eastern side. While there were, no doubt, significant ethnic and linguistic differences among these peoples, they shared many features of technology, culture, and political and social organization, due, in large part, to their mobility and the speed with which objects and ideas could move across this open landscape. Indeed, the steppe was the conduit by which products, such as wheat, and technologies, including bronze and iron metalworking, chariots, and cavalry warfare, traveled from western and Central Asia to East Asia.

4-3c The Scythians

While the origins of pastoral nomadism on the steppe are shrouded in the mists of prehistory, a picture begins to emerge in the centuries just after 1000 BCE. The first Greek historian, **Herodotus** (fifth century BCE), devoted many pages to an account of the Scythian lands and peoples. The Greeks used the term **Scythian** in a very broad and general way to describe peoples living to the north and east of their Aegean homeland: the lands north of the Black and Caspian Seas, or present-day Ukraine and southern Russia. While the Greeks lumped together various peoples who probably would not have regarded themselves as belonging to the same ethnic group, the Scythians were, according to most experts, speakers of languages belonging to the Iranian subgroup of the Indo-European language family. Because Greeks had established colonies around the coasts of the Black Sea, Herodotus was able to travel in this region, and his report, based primarily on information derived from Greek traders who traveled far inland and Scythian natives who interacted with the Greeks, is generally reliable. Some scholars have suggested that Herodotus is also employing the Scythians as a "mirror," emphasizing how different they were in lifestyle, culture, and values from the Greeks as an indirect way of highlighting aspects of Greek civilization.

For Herodotus, the fundamental quality of the Scythians was that they were nomads, people without cities or permanent homes who migrated with their herds of sheep, goats, and cattle and their prized horses, transporting their few possessions and living in carts. They belonged to tribal kinship groups ruled by kings. They are depicted as exceedingly warlike and savage; their chief god is equated with the Greek god of war, Ares, and they are said to drink the blood of their enemies, to cut off their enemies' heads as trophies, and to make goblets out of the skulls and napkins and coats from the skins. They had no images of the gods, no shrines and no altars, and employed a sacrificial ritual quite different from that of the Greeks that sometimes included human sacrifice. When their kings died, they were accompanied in the grave by murdered servants, guards, and horses. In an amusing passage, Herodotus betrays his puzzlement at how they threw brush (presumably cannabis, the plant source for marijuana) on a fire and appeared to be drunk, and how they cleaned their bodies by cavorting in cannabis steam baths. Herodotus also makes clear that not all Scythians were strictly nomadic; some engaged in a mixed pastoral and agricultural economy, and some (perhaps influenced by the nearby Greek settlers) were settled agriculturalists. These observations reinforce the idea that nomadic pastoralists required some form of access to agricultural peoples and the food and goods that they produced.

Herodotus then describes what he sees as the disastrous attempt of the Persian king Darius to invade the lands of the Scythians at the end of the sixth century BCE. Because the Scythians lacked permanent settlements and cultivated fields, there were no obvious targets for the Persians to attack and hold hostage. And because the nomads were exceedingly mobile, they were able to move away from the invaders, drawing them ever further into unknown territory and practicing a "scorched earth" policy of burning the grass and destroying the wells. They clearly felt that there was no shame in retreating, and when, at one point, the Persians were finally drawn up for battle with a contingent of Scythian troops, a hare darted across an open space and all the Scythians took off in pursuit of it. At this point, the Persian king realized that the Scythians were toying with him, and it was all he could do to make a successful escape home with part of his army. Herodotus is obviously taking pleasure at the discomfiture of the powerful Persians, and he may misunderstand Darius's purpose in the invasion—to drive the Scythians far from Persian-controlled lands. Nevertheless, he has brilliantly illustrated the unique difficulties that nomads presented to even powerful ancient states and empires, many of whom found it cheaper to just buy off the nomads by giving them "gifts" in return for not attacking.

4-3d China and the Nomads

Chinese sources provide glimpses of the nomadic peoples living at the other end of the Eurasian Steppes, and these accounts usually match up very closely with those of Herodotus and other Greek and Roman sources, proving the relative cultural and technological uniformity of the Eurasian steppe nomads. Again, it appears that an economy based on pastoral nomadism was taking shape on the steppes in central and eastern Asia in the early first millennium BCE. As the Chinese states of the Spring and Autumn and Warring States periods came under increasing pressure from raiding by swift-moving, horseborne warriors, they began to build walls along their northern frontiers to keep the raiders out, and in the late fourth century BCE the forward-thinking ruler of the state of Zhao took the unprecedented step of outfitting some of his troops with trousers and mounting them on horseback.

Our fullest Chinese account of the northern nomads comes from **Sima Qian (Sih-muh Chyen)** (ca. 100 BCE), who in many ways corresponds to Herodotus as "the father of history" in East Asia. Like Herodotus, he may have been using his description of the Xiongnu (**Shawng-noo**) nomads to highlight characteristic aspects of Chinese civilization. Sima Qian served at the court of the Han emperor Wu and therefore had access to records in the imperial archives and earlier historical texts, as well as some experience traveling on official business among the barbarians.

Sima Qian reports that the Xiongnu had no cities, no fixed dwellings, no agriculture, and no writing. They migrated with their herds to pastures and sources of water. They were trained as warriors from an early age, and for this reason the young and fit were given preference over the old and useless. Though tough and warlike by nature, they felt no shame in retreating when necessary. Their armies lacked discipline and order, and they largely fought for their own personal gain. They swooped in like birds and vanished just as quickly, and they cut off the heads of their vanquished enemies. As with the Scythians, human sacrifice was a component of royal funerals. In Sima Qian's account, a former Chinese official who has defected to the nomads points out that, unlike the Chinese, their lives are simple and unencumbered by excessive rules, rituals, or bureaucracy. Again, the Xiongnu either controlled or were allied to groups that practiced agriculture, which gave them access to items they could not produce themselves. Many scholars believe that the Xiongnu and several other nomadic peoples on the East Asian steppe spoke Turkic languages, while the Yuezhi (**Yweh-juhr**), located further west, spoke an Indo-European language.

In addition to information from ancient texts like those of Herodotus and Sima Qian, archaeological excavation has illuminated our understanding of the culture of pastoral nomads. Because of the lack of permanent settlements, the primary targets of archaeology have been the large burial mounds of the elite. In a number of cases the permafrost of Siberia has preserved materials, such as textiles, that normally do not survive in the archaeological record. The art of the nomads—mainly golden jewelry, horse fittings, and colorful carpets and other textiles—is beautiful to the modern eye, with its emphasis on animals, real and fantastic, often shown in combat

Sima Qian Chief astrologer for the Han dynasty emperor Wu. He composed a monumental history of China from its legendary origins to his own time and is regarded as the Chinese "father of history."

Section Review

- Humans were all nomadic until the Agricultural Revolutions, but the domestication of animals made possible the rise of a new form of pastoral nomadism.

- After 1000 BCE pastoral nomads dominated the vast Eurasian Steppes but still needed goods produced by farming peoples, which they obtained by trading or raiding.

- Our information about the ancient steppe nomads comes primarily from archaeology and the accounts of Greek, Roman, and Chinese texts.

- The toughness and mobility of nomadic peoples posed a major challenge to states and empires.

and in twisting, interlocked poses that conform gracefully to the surface on which they are displayed.

As we will see in subsequent chapters, the nomadic pastoralists of the steppe were, at the least, a constant nuisance to the sedentary agricultural peoples living on their borders. Under normal circumstances the relatively small, fractious tribal groups were as prone to fight each other as to raid the lands and possessions of the farmers in neighboring areas. However, from time to time they united in great confederacies under charismatic leaders, and then they presented a serious military threat even to great states and empires. The Han Chinese emperors would be at war for centuries with the Xiongnu; the Parthians would take over Iran and much of Mesopotamia and become Rome's only great-power rival (see Chapter 6); the late Roman Empire would be hard-pressed by Avars and Huns; and in the medieval period the Mongols and several Turkic peoples would overrun most of Asia (see Chapter 13). While nomadism has become increasingly rare in the industrialized and urbanized modern world, it has been estimated that 30 to 40 million people still practice this ancient way of life, primarily in Central Asia and the West African Sahel region.

4-4 Celtic Europe, 1000–50 BCE

What were the causes behind the spread of Celtic peoples across much of continental Europe, and the later retreat of Celtic cultures to the western edge of the continent?

The southern peninsulas of Europe—present-day Spain, Italy, and Greece—share in the mild climate of all the Mediterranean lands and are separated from "continental" Europe to the north by high mountains (the Pyrenees and Alps). Consequently, the history of southern Europe in antiquity is primarily connected to that of the Mediterranean and Middle East, at least until the Roman conquests north of the Alps (see Chapters 3, 5, and 6).

Continental Europe (including the modern nations of France, Germany, Switzerland, Austria, the Czech Republic, Slovakia, Hungary, Poland, and Romania—see Map 4.4)—was well suited to agriculture and herding. It contained broad plains with good soil and had a temperate climate with cold winters, warm summers, and ample rainfall. It was well endowed with natural resources such as timber and metals, and large, navigable rivers facilitated travel and trade.

Humans had lived in this part of Europe for many thousands of years (see Chapter 1), but their lack of any system of writing severely limits our knowledge of the earliest inhabitants. Around 500 BCE, as Celtic peoples spread from their original homeland across a substantial portion of Europe, they came into contact with the literate societies of the Mediterranean and thereby entered the historical record. Information about the early **Celts** (kelts) comes from the archaeological record, the accounts of Greek and Roman travelers and conquerors, and the oral traditions of Celtic Wales and Ireland that were written down during the European Middle Ages.

4-4a The Spread of the Celts

The term *Celtic* refers to a branch of the large Indo-European family of languages found throughout Europe and in western and southern Asia. Scholars link the Celtic language group to archaeological remains first appearing in parts of present-day Germany, Austria, and the Czech Republic after 1000 BCE (see Map 4.4). Many early Celts lived in or near hill-forts—lofty natural locations made more defensible by earthwork fortifications. By 500 BCE Celtic elites were trading with Mediterranean societies for crafted goods and wine. This contact may have stimulated the new styles of Celtic manufacture and art that appeared at this time.

Celts Peoples sharing common linguistic and cultural features that originated in central Europe in the first half of the first millennium BCE.

MAP 4.4 The Celtic Peoples Celtic civilization originated in central Europe in the early part of the first millennium BCE. Around 500 BCE Celtic peoples began to migrate, making Celtic civilization the dominant cultural style in Europe north of the Alps. The Celts' interactions with the peoples of the Mediterranean, including Greeks and Romans, involved both warfare and trade. Adapted from M. Grant, *Atlas of Classical History*, 5th ed. (New York, NY: Oxford University Press, 1994).

What factors lay behind the migrations of Celtic groups north, west, and south, beginning around 500 BCE? Why didn't they migrate eastward?

These new cultural features coincided with a period in which Celtic groups migrated to many parts of Europe. The motives behind these population movements, the precise timing, and the manner in which they were carried out are not well understood. Celts occupied nearly all of France and much of Britain and Ireland, and they merged with indigenous peoples to create the Celtiberian culture of northern Spain. Other Celtic groups overran northern Italy (they sacked Rome in 390 BCE), raided into central Greece, and settled in central Anatolia (modern Turkey). By 300 BCE Celtic peoples were spread across Europe north of the Alps, from present-day Hungary to Spain and Ireland. Their traces remain in many place names in Europe today.

These widely diffused Celtic groups shared elements of language and culture, but there was no Celtic "nation," for they were divided into hundreds of small, loosely organized kinship groups. In the past scholars built up a generic picture of Celtic society derived largely from the observations of Greek and Roman writers. Current scholarship is focusing attention on the differences as much as the similarities among Celtic peoples. It is unlikely that the ancient Celts identified themselves as belonging to anything akin to our modern conception of "Celtic civilization."

Greek and Roman writers were struck by the appearance of male Celts—their burly size, long red hair, shaggy mustaches, and loud, deep voices—and by their strange apparel, trousers (usually an indication of horse-riding peoples), and twisted gold neck collars. Particularly terrifying were the warriors who fought naked and made trophies of the heads of defeated enemies. Surviving accounts describe the Celts as wildly fond of war, courageous, childishly impulsive and emotional, fond of boasting and exaggeration, yet quick-witted and eager to learn.

▲ **Celtic Hill-Fort in England** Hundreds of these fortresses have been found across Europe. They served as centers of administration, gathering points for Celtic armies, manufacturing centers, storage depots for food and trade goods, and places of refuge. The natural defense offered by a hill could be improved, as here, by the construction of ditches and earthwork walls. Particularly effective was the so-called Gallic Wall, made of a combination of earth, stone, and timber to create both strength and enough flexibility to absorb the pounding from siege engines. Crown copyright. EH

4-4b Celtic Society

One of the best sources of information about Celtic society is the account of the Roman general Gaius Julius Caesar, who conquered Gaul (present-day France) between 58 and 51 BCE. Many Celtic groups in Gaul had once been ruled by kings, but by the time of the Roman invasion they periodically chose public officials, perhaps under Greek and Roman influence.

Celtic society was divided into an elite class of warriors, professional groups of priests and bards (singers of poems about glorious deeds of the past), and commoners. The warriors owned land and flocks of cattle and sheep and monopolized both wealth and power. The common people labored on their land. The Celts built houses (usually round in Britain, rectangular in France) out of wattle and daub—a wooden framework filled in with clay and straw—with thatched straw roofs. Several such houses belonging to related families might be surrounded by a wooden fence for protection.

The warriors of Welsh and Irish legend reflect a stage of political and social development less complex than that of the Celts in Gaul. They raided one another's flocks, reveled in drunken feasts, and engaged in contests of strength and wit. At banquets warriors would fight to the death just to claim the choicest cut of the meat, the "hero's portion."

Druids, the Celtic priests in Gaul and Britain, formed a well-organized fraternity that performed religious, judicial, and educational functions. Trainees spent years memorizing prayers, secret rituals, legal precedents, and other traditions. The priesthood was the one Celtic institution that crossed tribal lines. The Druids sometimes headed off warfare between feuding groups and served as judges in cases involving Celts from different groups. In the first century CE the Roman government attempted to stamp out the Druids, probably because of concern that they might serve as a rallying point for Celtic opposition to Roman rule and also because of their involvement in human sacrifices.

The Celts supported large populations by tilling the heavy but fertile soils of continental Europe. Their metallurgical skills probably surpassed those of the Mediterranean peoples. Celts on the Atlantic shore of France built sturdy ships that braved ocean conditions, and they developed extensive trade networks along Europe's large, navigable rivers. One lucrative commodity was tin, which Celtic traders from southwest England brought to Greek buyers in southern France. By the first century BCE some hill-forts were evolving into urban centers.

Women's lives were focused on childrearing, food production, and some crafts. Their situation was superior to that of women in the Middle East and in the Greek and Roman Mediterranean. Greek and Roman sources depict Celtic women as strong and proud. Welsh and Irish tales portray clever, self-assured women who sit at banquets with their husbands and engage in witty conversation. Marriage was a partnership to which both parties contributed property. Each had the right to inherit the estate if the other died. Celtic women also had greater freedom in their sexual relations than did their southern counterparts.

Tombs of elite women have yielded rich collections of clothing, jewelry, and furniture for use in the next world. Daughters of the elite were married to leading members of other tribes to create alliances. When the Romans invaded Celtic Britain in the first century CE, they sometimes were opposed by Celtic tribes headed by queens, although some experts see this as an abnormal circumstance created by the Roman invasion itself.

Druids The class of religious experts who conducted rituals and preserved sacred lore among some ancient Celtic peoples.

4-4c **Belief and Knowledge**

Historians know the names of more than 400 Celtic gods and goddesses, mostly associated with particular localities or kinship groups. More widely revered deities included Lug (**loog**), the god of light, crafts, and inventions; the horse-goddess Epona (**eh-POH-nuh**); and the horned god Cernunnos (**KURN-you-nuhs**). "The Mothers," three goddesses depicted together holding symbols of abundance, probably played a part in a fertility cult. Halloween and May Day preserve the ancient Celtic holidays of Samhain (**SAH-win**) and Beltaine (**BEHL-tayn**), respectively, which took place at key moments in the agricultural cycle.

The early Celts did not build temples but instead worshiped wherever they felt the presence of divinity—at springs, groves, and hilltops. At the sources of the Seine and Marne Rivers in France, archaeologists have found huge caches of wooden statues thrown into the water by worshipers.

The burial of elite members of early Celtic society in wagons filled with extensive grave goods suggests belief in some sort of afterlife. In Irish and Welsh legends, heroes and gods pass back and forth between the natural and supernatural worlds much more readily than in the mythology of many other cultures, and magical occurrences are commonplace. Celtic priests set forth a doctrine of *reincarnation*—the rebirth of the soul in a new body.

The Roman conquest from the second century BCE to the first century CE of Spain, southern Britain, France, and parts of central Europe curtailed the evolution of Celtic society, as the peoples in these lands were largely assimilated to Roman ways (see Chapter 6). As a result, the inhabitants of modern Spain and France speak languages that are descended from Latin. From the third century CE on, Germanic invaders weakened the Celts still further, and the English language has a Germanic base. Only on the western fringes of the European continent—in Brittany (northwest France), Wales, Scotland, and Ireland—did Celtic peoples maintain their language, art, and culture into modern times.

4-5 **Conclusion**

Environment and Organization

The civilizations of early China, Nubia, the Eurasian Steppes, and the Celts emerged in very different ecological contexts in widely separated parts of the Eastern Hemisphere, and the patterns of organization, technology, behavior, and belief that they developed were, in large part, responses to the challenges and opportunities of those environments.

In the North China Plain, as in the river-valley civilizations of Mesopotamia and Egypt, the presence of great, flood-prone rivers and the lack of dependable rainfall led to the formation of powerful institutions capable of organizing large numbers of people to dig and maintain irrigation channels and build dikes. An authoritarian central government has been a recurring feature of Chinese history from at least as early as the Shang monarchy.

▲ **Dying Celtic Warrior** Life-sized Roman marble statue of a Celtic warrior, slumped on the ground and perishing from a wound. Some Celtic warriors fought naked. Note also his hair, smeared with lime to make it stiff, the metal torque around his neck, and the battle horn at his feet. Scala/Art Resource, NY

Section Review

- Around 500 BCE Celtic-speaking peoples from central Europe began to spread across much of "continental" Europe.

- Most of what we know about the ancient Celts comes from archaeological discoveries and the written reports of Greek and Roman observers, who depict them as impulsive and fond of war.

- Celts lived in relatively small kinship (tribal) groups that were dominated by warrior elites. Hill-forts served as places of assembly and refuges.

- The Celts worshiped many gods in natural settings. The Druids, a priestly class in Gaul (France) and Britain, played a major role in religion, education, and inter-tribal legal matters.

- The Roman Empire's conquest of Celtic lands, followed later by Germanic invasions, pushed Celtic language and culture to the western edge of the European continent.

AP® Exam Tip
Recognize the persistence of shamanism, animism, and ancestor veneration throughout history.

In Nubia, the initial impetus for the formation of a strong state was the need for protection from desert nomads and from the Egyptian rulers who coveted Nubian gold and other resources. Control of these resources and of the trade route between sub-Saharan Africa and the north, as well as the agricultural surplus to feed administrators and specialists in the urban centers, made the rulers and elites of Kerma, Napata, and Meroë wealthy and powerful.

Pastoral nomads found ways to exploit the challenging environment of the Eurasian Steppes. The very nature of their lifestyle, based on migrating with their herds of domesticated animals to seasonal camping grounds, meant that they had no permanent settlements and maintained small, kinship-based groups. Thus, under normal circumstances, their political organization was relatively simple. However, in moments of crisis or when a charismatic military leader came to the fore, they could unite in formidable confederacies.

The Celtic peoples of continental Europe never developed a strong state. They occupied fertile lands with adequate rainfall for agriculture, grazing territory for flocks, and timber for fuel and construction. Kinship groups dominated by warrior elites and controlling compact territories were the usual form of organization. The Celtic elites of central Europe initially traded for luxury goods with the Mediterranean; when they began to expand into lands to the west and south after 500 BCE, they came into even closer contact with Mediterranean peoples. Eventually many Celtic groups were incorporated into the Roman Empire.

Religion and Power

In these, as in most human societies, the elites used religion to bolster their position. The Shang rulers of China were indispensable intermediaries between their kingdom and powerful and protective ancestors and gods. Bronze vessels were used to make offerings to ancestral spirits, and divination by means of oracle bones delivered information of value to the ruler and kingdom. Their Zhou successors developed the concept of the ruler as divine Son of Heaven who ruled in accord with the Mandate of Heaven.

In its religious practices, as in other spheres, the civilization that developed in Nubia was powerfully influenced by its interactions with the more complex and technologically advanced neighboring society in Egypt. Nubian rulers built temples and pyramid tombs on the Egyptian model, but they also synthesized Egyptian and indigenous gods, beliefs, and rituals.

While not much is known about the religious beliefs and practices of the steppe nomads, their mobility and lack of permanent settlements may account for the fact that they didn't build monumental religious shrines. Greco-Roman and Chinese accounts report, and archaeology confirms, that they sacrificed animals, and sometimes human victims, to their gods. The elaborate goods found in elite burials imply belief in an afterlife, and shamans were able to make contact with the gods and the dead.

Among the Celtic peoples of Gaul and Britain, the Druids constituted an elite class of priests who performed vital religious, legal, and educational functions. However, the Celts did not construct temples and ceremonial centers, and instead worshiped hundreds of gods and goddesses in natural surroundings, where they felt the presence of divinity.

A Tale of Two Hemispheres

This chapter has moved beyond the core area of the two oldest complex human societies (Mesopotamia and Egypt) and the neighboring peoples who came under their cultural influence, to focus on East Asia, sub-Saharan Africa, continental Europe, and the vast steppe region linking Europe and Central and East Asia. It thus continues the discussion of the rise of complex societies in the Eastern Hemisphere.

The societies in the other half of the world, the Western Hemisphere, are discussed in Chapter 8. These civilizations—the Olmec in Mesoamerica and Chavín in South America—while contemporary with the societies featured in this chapter, emerged several millennia later than the earliest complex societies in the Eastern Hemisphere. Scholars have debated why powerful civilizations appeared many centuries later in the Western Hemisphere than in the Eastern Hemisphere, and recent theories have focused on environmental differences. The Eastern Hemisphere was home to a far larger number of wild plant and animal species that were particularly well suited to domestication. In addition, the natural east–west axis of the huge landmass of

Europe and Asia allowed for the relatively rapid spread of domesticated plants and animals to climatically similar zones along the same latitudes. Settled agriculture led to population growth, more complex political and social organization, and increased technological sophistication. In the Americas, by contrast, there were fewer wild plant and animal species that could be domesticated, and the north–south axis of the continents made it more difficult for domesticated species to spread because of variations in climate at different latitudes. As a result, the processes that foster the development of complex societies evolved somewhat more slowly.

Key Terms

loess p. 82	**Confucius** p. 89	**Meroë** p. 95	**Scythians** p. 98
Shang p. 83	**Daoism** p. 89	**nomads** p. 96	**Sima Qian** p. 99
Zhou p. 85	**yin/yang** p. 92	**steppe** p. 97	**Celts** p. 100
Mandate of Heaven p. 86	**Kush** p. 94	**Herodotus** p. 98	**Druids** p. 102

Review Questions

1. How does the evolution of early Chinese civilization differ from that of the river-valley civilizations covered in Chapter 2?

2. How do geography, environment, and resources shape the economic, political, and social development of all four civilizations covered in this chapter?

3. How does economic and cultural interdependence on neighboring peoples influence Nubian, steppe nomad, and Celtic civilizations?

 MindTap® is a fully online, personalized learning experience built upon Cengage Learning content. MindTap® combines student learning tools–readings, multimedia, activities, and assessments–into a singular Learning Path that guides students through the course and helps students develop the critical thinking, analysis, and communication skills that are essential to academic and professional success.

Material Culture
Wine and Beer in the Ancient World

The most prized beverages of ancient peoples were wine and beer. Sediments found in jars excavated at a site in northwest Iran prove that techniques for the manufacture of wine were known as early as the sixth millennium BCE. Beer dates back at least as far as the fourth millennium BCE. Archaeological excavations have brought to light the equipment used in preparing, transporting, serving, and imbibing these beverages.

In Egypt and Mesopotamia, beer, made from wheat or barley by an elaborate process, was the staple drink of both the elite and the common people. Women prepared beer for the family in their homes, and breweries produced large quantities for sale. Because the production process left chaff floating on the surface of the liquid, various means were employed to filter this out. Sculptures on Mesopotamian stone reliefs and seals show several drinkers drawing on straws immersed in a large bowl. Archaeologists have found examples of the perforated metal cones that fit over the submerged ends of the straws and filtered the liquid beer drawn through them.

The sharing of beer from a common vessel by several people probably was seen as creating a bond of friendship among the participants. Archaeologists have also found individual beer

◀ **Dionysus in the Vineyard**
This Greek vase of the late sixth century BCE depicts Dionysus, the god of wine. Carrying a large kantharos or drinking vessel, he is enveloped by vines carrying bunches of ripe grapes and accompanied by several Satyrs (mythical creatures combining human features with those of goats or horses) and his human bride Ariadne. Greek drinking paraphernalia often depicted Dionysus and elements of his mythology and cult. DEA/G. DAGLI ORTI/Getty Images

"mugs" resembling a modern watering can: closed bowls with a perforated spout to filter the chaff and a semicircular channel carrying the liquid into the drinker's mouth.

In Greece, Rome, and other Mediterranean lands, where the climate was suitable for cultivating grape vines, wine was the preferred beverage. Vines were prepared in February and periodically pinched and pruned. The full-grown grapes were picked in September and then crushed—with a winepress or by people trampling on them—to produce a liquid that was sealed in casks for fermentation. The new vintage was sampled the following February. Exuberant religious festivals marked key moments in the cycle. Initially expensive and therefore confined to the wealthy and for religious ceremonies, in later antiquity wine became available to a wider spectrum of people. Unlike beer, which requires refrigeration, wine can be stored for a long time in sealed containers and thus could be transported and traded across ancient lands. The usual containers for wine were long, conical pottery jars, which the Greeks called *amphoras*.

The Greeks, who normally mixed wine with water (and thought it scandalous that Persians drank undiluted wine), developed an elaborate array of vessels, made of pottery, metal, and glass, to facilitate mixing, serving, and drinking the precious liquid (see the photo on the facing page). *Kraters* were large mixing bowls into which the wine and water were poured. The *hydria* was used to carry water, and a heater could be used to warm the water when that was desired. Another special vessel could be used to chill the wine by immersion in cold water. Ladles and elegantly narrow vessels with spouts were used to pour the concoction into the drinkers' cups. The most popular shapes for individual drinking vessels were a shallow bowl with two handles, called a *kylix*, and the *kantharos*, a large, deep, two-handled cup. Another popular implement in Greece and western Asia was the *rhyton*, a horn-shaped vessel that tapered into the head and forepaws of an animal with a small hole at the base. The drinker would fill the horn, holding his thumb over the hole until he was ready to drink or pour, then move his thumb and release a thin stream of wine that appeared to be coming out of the animal's mouth.

The drinking equipment belonging to wealthy Greeks was often decorated with representations of the god of wine, Dionysus, holding a kantharos and surrounded by a dense tangle of vines and grape clusters. His entourage included the half-human, half-horse-or-goat Satyrs and the Maenads, literally "crazy women," female worshipers who drank wine and engaged in frenzied dancing until they reached an ecstatic state and sensed the powerful presence of the god.

Greeks, Romans, and other Mediterranean peoples used wine for more conventional religious ceremonies, pouring libations on the ground or on the altar as an offering to the gods. It was also used as a disinfectant and painkiller or as an ingredient in various medicines. Above all, wine was featured at the banquets and drinking parties that forged and deepened social bonds. In the Greek world, the *symposion* (meaning "drinking together") was held after the meal. The host presided over the affair, making the crucial decision about the proportion of water to wine, suggesting topics of conversation, and trying to keep some semblance of order. There might also be entertainment in the form of musicians, dancers, and acrobats.

In early China, magnificent bronze vessels whose surfaces were covered with abstract designs and representations of otherworldly animals were used in elaborate ceremonies at ancestral shrines (see illustration "Shang Period Bronze Vessel," Section 4-1c). The vessels contained offerings of wine and food for the spirits of the family's ancestors, who were imagined to still need and enjoy sustenance in the afterlife. The treasured bronze vessels were often buried with their owners so that they could continue to employ them after death. In later periods, as the ancestral sacrifices became less important, beautiful bronze vessels, as well as their ceramic counterparts, became part of the equipment at the banquets of the well-to-do.

Questions for Analysis

1. What social benefits arise from drinking together?
2. How does wine serve religious purposes?
3. What evidence is there that collective drinking was practiced by the privileged social classes?

Issues in World History
Animal Domestication

Because the earliest domestication of plants and animals took place long before the existence of written records, we cannot be sure how and when humans first learned to plant crops and make use of tamed animals. Historians usually link the two processes as part of an Agricultural Revolution, but they were not necessarily connected.

The domestication of plants is much better understood than the domestication of animals. Foraging bands of humans primarily lived on wild seeds, fruits, and tubers. Eventually some humans tried planting seeds and tubers, favoring varieties that they particularly liked, and a variety that may have been rare in the wild became more common. When such a variety suited human needs, usually by having more food value or being easier to grow or process, people stopped collecting the wild types and relied on farming and further developing their new domestic type.

In the case of animals, the basis of selection to suit human needs is less apparent. Experts looking at ancient bones and images interpret changes in hair color, horn shape, and other visible features as indicators of domestication. But these visible changes did not generally serve human purposes. It is usually assumed that animals were domesticated for their meat, but even this is questionable. Dogs, which may have become domestic tens of thousands of years before any other species, were not eaten in most cultures, and cats, which became domestic much later, were eaten even less often. As for the uses most commonly associated with domestic animals, some of the most important, such as milking cows, shearing sheep, and harnessing oxen and horses to pull plows and vehicles, first appeared hundreds and even thousands of years after domestication.

Cattle, sheep, and goats became domestic around 10,000 years ago in the Middle East and North Africa. Coincidentally, wheat and barley were being domesticated at roughly the same time in the same general area. This is the main reason historians generally conclude that plant and animal domestication are

▲ **Nomadic Pastoralists on the Eurasian Steppe** The domestication of animals engendered a new form of nomadism, enabling certain populations to live in the treeless grasslands of the steppe and move with their animals and portable dwellings to a sequence of water sources and grazing grounds. Paul Harris/Getty Images

closely related. Yet other major meat animals, such as chickens, which originated as jungle fowl in Southeast Asia, and pigs, which probably became domestic separately in several parts of North Africa, Europe, and Asia, have no agreed-upon association with early plant domestication. Nor is plant domestication connected with the horses and camels that became domestic in western Asia and the donkeys that became domestic in the Sahara region around 6,000 years ago. Moreover, though the wild forebears of these species were probably eaten, the domestic forms were usually not used for meat.

In the Middle East humans may have originally kept wild sheep, goats, and cattle for food, though wild cattle were large and dangerous and must have been hard to control. It is questionable whether, in the earliest stages, keeping these animals captive for food would have been more productive than hunting. It is even more questionable whether the humans who kept animals for this purpose had any reason to anticipate that life in captivity would cause them to become domestic.

Human motivations for domesticating animals can be better assessed after a consideration of the physical changes involved in going from wild to domestic. Genetically transmitted tameness, defined as the ability to live with and accept handling by humans, lies at the core of the domestication process. In separate experiments with wild rats and foxes in the twentieth century, scientists found that wild individuals with strong fight-or-flight tendencies reproduce poorly in captivity, whereas individuals with the lowest adrenaline levels have the most offspring in captivity. In the wild, the same low level of excitability would have made these individuals vulnerable to predators and kept their reproduction rate down. However, early humans probably preferred the animals that seemed the tamest and destroyed those that were most wild. In the rat and fox experiments, after twenty generations or so, the surviving animals were born with much smaller adrenal glands and greatly reduced fight-or-flight reactions. Since adrenaline production normally increases in the transition to adulthood, many of the low-adrenaline animals also retained juvenile characteristics, such as floppy ears and pushed-in snouts, both indicators of domestication.

Historians disagree about whether animal domestication was a deliberate process or the unanticipated outcome of keeping animals for other purposes. Some assume that domestication was an understood and reproducible process. Others argue that, since a twenty-generation time span for wild cattle and other large quadrupeds would have amounted to several human lifetimes, it is unlikely that the people who ended up with domestic cows had any recollection of how the process started. This would also rule out the possibility that people who had unwittingly domesticated one species would have attempted to repeat the process with other species, since they did not know what they and their ancestors had done to produce genetically transmitted tameness.

Historians who assume that domestication was an understood and reproducible process tend to conclude that humans domesticated every species that could be domesticated. This is unlikely. Twentieth-century efforts to domesticate bison, eland, and elk have not fully succeeded, but they have generally not been maintained for as long as twenty generations. Rats and foxes have more rapid reproduction rates, and the experiments with them succeeded.

Animal domestication is probably best studied on a case-by-case basis as an unintended result of other processes. In some instances, sacrifice probably played a key role. Religious traditions of animal sacrifice rarely utilize, and sometimes prohibit, the ritual killing of wild animals. It is reasonable to suppose that the practice of capturing wild animals and holding them for sacrifice eventually led to the appearance of genetically transmitted tameness as an unplanned result.

Horses and camels were domesticated relatively late, and most likely not for meat consumption. The societies within which these animals first appeared as domestic species already had domestic sheep, goats, and cattle for meat, and they used oxen to carry loads and pull plows and carts. Horses, camels, and later reindeer may represent successful experiments with substituting one draft animal for another, with genetically transmitted tameness an unexpected consequence of separating animals trained for riding or pulling carts from their wilder kin.

Once human societies had developed the full range of uses of domestic animals—meat, eggs, milk, fiber, labor, transport—the likelihood of domesticating more species diminished. In the absence of concrete knowledge of how domestication had occurred, it was usually easier for people to move domestic livestock to new locations than to attempt to develop new domestic species. Domestic animals accompanied human groups wherever they ventured, and this practice triggered enormous environmental changes as domestic animals, and their human keepers, competed with wild species for food and living space.

Questions for Analysis

1. What are the reasons for thinking that domestication of animals may be less closely related to the beginnings of agriculture than was formerly believed?

2. What motives may have led humans to domesticate animals?

3. How has domestication changed the physical appearance and behavior of animals, when compared to their wild ancestors?

AP® REVIEW QUESTIONS FOR CHAPTER 4

Multiple-Choice Questions

Questions 1–3 refer to the passage below.

"Come north to the residence at once! Hurry and bring with you this pygmy whom you brought from the land of the horizon-dwellers live, hale, and healthy, for the dances of the god, to gladden the heart, to delight the heart of king Neferkare who lives forever! When he goes down with you into the ship, get worthy men to be around him on deck, lest he fall into the water! When he lies down at night, get worthy (20) men to lie around him in his tent. Inspect ten times at night! My majesty desires to see this pygmy more than the gifts of the mine-land and of Punt!"

Pharaoh Pepi II in a letter to an Egyptian official who was travelling back to Egypt from Nubia, ca. 2280 BCE

1. Which of the following best describes the economic characteristics of Nubia, ca. 2200 BCE?

   (A) The Nubian economy was primarily nomadic, with few farmers or herdsmen.

   (B) Nubia had a thriving economy in which the military played an important role.

   (C) Nubia participated in regional trade with the neighboring areas.

   (D) The Nubian economy relied heavily on the state's participation.

2. How did the relationship between Nubia and Egypt change from the time period described in the excerpt and the Middle Kingdom time (2000–1640 BCE)?

   (A) Egyptians attempted to control trade with Nubia by preventing Nubian traders from traveling freely into and out of Egypt.

   (B) Nubian aggression led to armed invasions by Egyptian forces.

   (C) Nomads from the desert region of Nubia began to increasingly invade Egypt, leading to Egyptian economic decline.

   (D) Nubia dominated Egypt during this period and imposed its cultural beliefs and religion on the Egyptian people.

3. How did later Nubian Meroitic society challenge the traditional patriarchal society represented by the Egyptian pharaoh?

   (A) Women became the primary leaders in trade, controlling economic success.

   (B) Matriarchal households allowed women to dominate the home and city.

   (C) In the Meroitic matrilineal system, the king was succeeded by the son of his sister.

   (D) The mother-goddess, Isis, became the Warrior Goddess of Meroë.

Questions 4–7 refer to the passages below.

"The Master said, 'Lead them by means of regulations and keep order among them through punishments, and the people will evade them and will lack any sense of shame. Lead them through moral force and keep order among them through rites, and they will have a sense of shame and will also correct themselves.'"

Confucian Analect, ca. 400 BCE

"Humaneness may make one shed tears and be reluctant to apply penalties, but law makes it clear that such penalties must be applied. The ancient kings allowed law to be supreme and did not give in to their tearful longings. Hence it is obvious that humaneness cannot be used to achieve order in the state."

Han Fei, *The Five Vermin*, 240 BCE

What is softest in the world

Overcomes what is hardest in the world.

No-thing penetrates where there is no space.

Thus I know that in doing nothing there is advantage.

Laozi, *Daodejing*, ca. 400 BCE

4. Which of the following statements best compares the first two views of governance in the passages?

   (A) Both Confucius and Han Fei believed that rulers needed to set strict rules with strict punishment for their kingdoms to maintain order.

   (B) Han Fei was more concerned than Confucius about the need for compassion in governance.

   (C) Confucius believed the key to good leadership was for the ruler to be harsh, whereas Han Fei advocated the importance of empathy.

   (D) Confucius believed government rested on the inherent morality of mankind, whereas Han Fei promoted strict and forceful control.

5. In addition to the philosophies of Confucius and Han Fei, another belief system known as Daoism emerged. Daoism emphasized

   (A) the importance of filial piety and respect for elders.

   (B) the equality of citizens and the importance of gender parity.

   (C) the importance of following a strict, ascetic lifestyle of study and knowledge.

   (D) the importance of malleability and tranquility to follow the natural way.

6. As the population steadily grew, what was the political situation in China at the time of Confucius, Han Fei, and Laozi?

   (A) China was enjoying an era of wealth and prosperity.

   (B) China was controlled by a powerful dynasty that was constantly expanding the realm.

   (C) China was politically fragmented and plagued with frequent warfare over land control.

   (D) China was controlled by a group of invaders from Central Asia.

7. When the Shang dynasty of China was overthrown by the Zhou dynasty in the mid-eleventh century, the coup d'état was justified by the Mandate of Heaven, which is best described by which of the following statements?

   (A) Heaven invested power in monarchs who showed military might.

   (B) Heaven granted authority to a ruler who was just and took care of the people, and Heaven could withdraw this authority if the ruler failed.

   (C) Rulers had the right to use religion to unify the nation.

   (D) Rulers needed to be able to convince their subjects of their divine power.

Questions 8–10 refer to the map on page 97.

8. The spread of pastoral nomads across the steppes of Eurasia shown on the map was caused by

   (A) the need to respond to climatic changes that limited the extent of the nomadic range.

   (B) the ever-present need to find pastures on the sparse grasslands of the steppe region.

   (C) seasonal rains that caused flooding and posed a problem for the herds.

   (D) pressure from invading peoples that forced the nomads to leave.

9. During the spread of nomadic peoples indicated on the map, relationships with the settled agriculturalists were established that are best described by which of the following?

   (A) The nomads relied on the agriculturalists for animal products and most of their staple food.

   (B) The nomads perpetually raided the agriculturalists for food and weapons.

   (C) The nomads had a symbiotic relationship with the settled people involving trade.

   (D) The nomads needed to constantly replenish their populations because of death from disease.

10. What difficulties would a historian encounter when studying the early pastoral nomads identified on the map?

   (A) Historians are too far removed from the time to understand the relationships of nomadic people.

   (B) Historians impose the values of their own civilized societies when evaluating pastoral nomads.

   (C) Historians' study of modern pastoral nomads may not reliably convey an accurate sense of ancient people.

   (D) Historians have difficulty because the nomads did not have written records.

Short-Answer Questions

1. Answer all parts of the question that follows.

   (A) Describe ONE way Chinese philosophies influenced social behavior.

   (B) Describe ANOTHER way Chinese philosophies influenced social behavior.

   (C) Explain ONE way that Chinese philosophies were reflected in cultural achievements.

2. Answer all parts of the question that follows.

   (A) Describe ONE way technology was used to enhance culture in the Afro-Eurasian region during the second and first millennium BCE.

   (B) Describe ONE way that technology was used for territorial gain in the Afro-Eurasian region during the second and first millennium BCE.

   (C) Explain ONE way that technology was transferred across regions during the second and first millennium BCE.

PART II

The Formation of New Cultural Communities, 1000 BCE–400 CE

▲ **Map of the Roman World, ca. 250 CE** The Peutinger Table, drawn on a 22-foot-long manuscript of the twelfth century CE, is ultimately derived from a map of the world as known to inhabitants of the Roman Empire ca. 100 CE. This portion depicts (from top to bottom) southern Russia, Greece on the left, Anatolia on the right, the island of Crete, and the north coast of Africa. The main purpose appears to have been to show roads and distances, and sizes and geographical relationships of places are often distorted. DeA Picture Library/Art Resource, NY

From 1000 BCE to 400 CE, river-valley civilizations changed dramatically as the scale of human activities increased. New centers of power arose with new political structures, social organization, and economic activity. At the same time, these civilizations were moving in new intellectual, artistic, and spiritual directions.

Improvements in technology, along with the expansion of agriculture and trade, led to population increases, the spread of cities, the growth of new social classes, and the diffusion of religious ideas and artistic styles. Accessible systems of writing spurred new thought, literature, and scientific endeavor, creating cultural zones unified by common traditions that would greatly impact subsequent ages.

In many places, iron replaced bronze in weapons, tools, and utensils. Iron tools aided in the clearing of extensive forests around the Mediterranean, in India, and in eastern China, while iron weapons gave an advantage to the armies of Greece, Rome, and imperial China. In the Americas, progress in metallurgy was slower, with copper usage originating in the Andes and reaching Mesoamerica after 500 CE. ●

Environment	Culture	State Building	Economics	Social Structure
• Interaction between environment and settlement	• Origins, beliefs, development, economic/social/political impact, and spread of major religions, philosophies, and belief systems (Christianity, Hinduism, Buddhism, Confucianism, Daoism, and Vedic [Hinduism])	• Evolution of forms of governance	• Impact of technology on economic production and globalization (weapons/maritime technology).	• Impact of kinship, ethnicity, class, gender, and race on social hierarchies (patriarchy)
• Impact of migration, population, and urbanization on environment	• Effect of cross-cultural interactions on diffusion of technology and scientific knowledge	• Impact of economic, social, cultural, and geographical factors on state building, expansion, and dissolution	• Causes/effects of economic strategies of different states and empires	• Impact of ideologies, philosophies, and religions on social hierarchies (Confucianism, Christianity, caste systems)
• Interaction between environment and development of technology, industrialization, transportation, and exchange/communication networks	• Reflection of society in the arts (monumental architecture)	• Influence of internal/external political factors on state building, expansion, and dissolution (conquest of Jewish states)	• Development of modes and locations of production/commerce over time (administrative cities)	• Challenges and confirmations of legal systems, colonialism, nationalism, and independence movements on class, gender, and racial hierarchies over time (Greco-Roman legal system)
• Impact of environmental factors, disease, and technology on migration and settlement.		• Role of cities and trade on the expansion and dissolution of empires	• Development of labor systems (patriarchy, slavery, *corvée* labor)	• Interaction between specialized labor systems and social hierarchy
		• Relationship between states and state-less societies or non-state actors (Xiongnu, Huns)	• Relationship between ideologies, values, and institutions and economic systems (spread of religions)	• Maintenance or challenge to social categories, roles, and practices (Monasticism, Imperial societies)
			• Interaction between local, regional, and global economic systems	

Key Concept 1.3

- How did geography and environment affect the foundation of the Olmec (Mesoamerican) and Chavín (South American) civilizations?
- How did culture play a significant role in unifying states through laws, language, literature, religions, myths, and monumental art? (monumental architecture, Zoroastrianism, Vedic religion, Christianity, Hinduism, Buddhism)

Key Concept 2.1

- How did codification and development of religious traditions provide a bond among people and an ethical code to live by? (Sanskrit, Vedic religions, Hinduism, Brahmin, dharma, reincarnation, caste system)
- How did new belief systems and cultural traditions emerge and spread, asserting universal truths? (Buddhism, Ashoka, Christianity, Jesus of Nazareth, Emperor Constantine, Greco-Roman philosophy)
- How did belief systems both reinforce existing social structures and offer new roles and status to some men and women? (monastic life)
- How were other religious and cultural traditions continued and in some cases incorporated into major religious traditions?

Key Concept 2.2

- How did rulers imposing political unity on areas that had previously been competing states help the number and size of some empires grow dramatically? (Persian Empire, Qin/Han Empires, Mauryan/Gupta Empires, Hellenistic/Roman Empires, Meso and North American Empires)
- What new techniques of imperial administration did these empires and states develop?
- What unique social and economic dimensions developed in imperial societies in Afro-Eurasia and the Americas?
- What difficulties did the Roman, Han, Persian, Mauryan, and Gupta empires encounter that eventually led to their decline, collapse, and transformation into successor empires or states?

5

Greece and Iran, 1000–30 BCE

AP® Framework Terms

Zoroastrianism
Persian Empire
Greco-Roman traditions
Hellenistic Empire
Roman Empire
Greco-Roman philosophy
Mediterranean sea lanes

Overarching Questions

1 How and why have religions, belief systems, philosophies, and ideologies originated, developed, and spread as a result of expanding communication and exchange networks? (CUL)

2 In what ways do the arts reflect the innovation, adaptation, and creativity of specific societies? (CUL)

3 How and why have economic, social, cultural, and geographic factors influenced the process of state building, expansion, and dissolution? (SB)

4 How have economic systems and the development of ideologies, values, and institutions influenced each other? (ECON)

5 How have political, economic, cultural, and demographic factors affected social structures? (SOC)

The Greek historian Herodotus (**heh-ROD-uh-tuhs**) (ca. 485–425 BCE) describes a famine on the island of Thera in the Aegean Sea in the seventh century BCE that caused the desperate inhabitants to send out a detachment of young men to found a new settlement called Cyrene on the coast of North Africa (modern Libya). This is one of our best descriptions of the process by which Greeks spread from their homeland to many parts of the Mediterranean and Black Seas between the eighth and sixth centuries BCE, carrying their language, technology, and culture with them. Cyrene became a populous and prosperous city-state, largely thanks to its exports of silphium—a plant valued for its medicinal properties—as seen on this painted cup with an image of Arcesilas, the ruler of Cyrene, supervising the weighing and transport of the product.

In the 520s BCE Greek Cyrene quietly submitted to the Persian king Cambyses (**kam-BIE-sees**) in one of the more peaceful encounters of the city-states of Greece with the Persian

Empire. This event reminds us that the Persian Empire (and the Hellenistic Greek kingdoms that succeeded it) brought together, in eastern Europe, western Asia, and northwest Africa, peoples and cultural systems that had little direct contact previously, thereby stimulating new cultural syntheses. The claim has often been made that the rivalry and wars of Greeks and Persians from the sixth to fourth centuries BCE were the first act of a drama that has continued intermittently ever since: the clash of the civilizations of East and West, of two peoples and two ways of life that were fundamentally different and almost certain to come into conflict. Some see current tensions between the United States and Middle Eastern states, such as Syria, Iran, Iraq, and Afghanistan, and nongovernmental agents, such as Al Qaeda and ISIS, as the latest manifestation of this age-old conflict.

Ironically, Greeks and Persians had more in common than they realized. Both spoke languages belonging to the same Indo-European language family found throughout Europe and western and southern Asia. Many scholars believe that all the ancient peoples who spoke languages belonging to this family inherited fundamental cultural traits, forms of social organization, and religious outlooks from their shared past. ●

▲ **Painted Cup of Arcesilas of Cyrene** The ruler of this Greek community in North Africa supervises the weighing and export of silphium, a valuable medicinal plant. Greek cup depicting Arcesilas II, King of Cyrene (c.560–550 BC) watching the weighing and loading of silphium, copy of a 6th century BC original (colour litho), French School, (19th century) / Bibliotheque Nationale, Paris, France / Archives Charmet / The Bridgeman Art Library

5-1 Ancient Iran, 1000–500 BCE

How did the Persian Empire rise from its Iranian homeland and succeed in controlling vast territories and diverse cultures?

Iran, the "land of the Aryans," links western Asia with southern and Central Asia, and its history has been marked by this mediating position (see Map 5.1). In the sixth century BCE the vigorous Persians of southwest Iran created the largest empire the world had yet seen. Heirs to the long legacy of Mesopotamian culture, they introduced distinctly Iranian elements and developed new forms of political and economic organization in western Asia.

Relatively little written material from within the Persian Empire has survived, so we are forced to view it, in large part, through the eyes of the ancient Greeks—outsiders who were ignorant at best, often hostile, and interested primarily in events that affected themselves. (Iranian groups and individuals are known in the Western world by Greek approximations of their names; thus these familiar forms are used here, with the original Iranian names given in parentheses.) This Greek perspective leaves us less informed about developments in the central and eastern portions of the Persian Empire. Nevertheless, recent archaeological discoveries and close analysis of the limited written material from within the empire can supplement and correct the perspective of the Greek sources.

5-1a Geography and Resources

Iran is bounded by the Zagros (**ZUHG-roes**) Mountains to the west, the Caucasus (**KAW-kuh-suhs**) Mountains and Caspian Sea to the northwest and north, the mountains of Afghanistan and the desert of Baluchistan (**buh-loo-chi-STAN**) to the east and southeast, and the Persian Gulf to the southwest. The northeast is less protected by natural boundaries, and from that direction Iran was open to attacks by the nomads of Central Asia.

The fundamental topographical features of Iran are high mountains at the edges, salt deserts in the interior depressions, and mountain streams draining into interior salt lakes and marshes. Ancient Iran never had a dense population. The best-watered and most populous parts of the country lie to the north and west; aridity increases and population decreases as one moves south and east. On the interior plateau, oasis settlements sprang up beside streams or springs. The Great Salt Desert, which covers most of eastern Iran, and Baluchistan in the southeast corner were extremely inhospitable. Scattered settlements in the narrow plains beside the Persian Gulf were cut off from the interior plateau by mountain barriers.

In the first millennium BCE irrigation enabled people to move down from the mountain valleys and open the plains to agriculture. To prevent evaporation of precious water in the hot, dry climate, they devised underground irrigation channels. Constructing and maintaining these channels and the vertical shafts that provided access to them was labor-intensive. Normally, local leaders oversaw the expansion of the network in each district. Activity accelerated when a strong central authority organized large numbers of laborers. Even so, human survival depended on a delicate ecological balance, and a buildup of salt in the soil or a falling water table sometimes forced the abandonment of settlements.

Iran's mineral resources—copper, tin, iron, gold, and silver—were exploited on a limited scale in antiquity. Mountain slopes, more heavily wooded than they are now, provided fuel and materials for building and crafts. Because this austere land could not generate much of an agricultural surplus, objects of trade tended to be minerals and crafted goods such as textiles and carpets.

MAP 5.1   The Persian Empire Between 550 and 522 BCE   The Persians of southwest Iran, under their first two kings, Cyrus and Cambyses, conquered each of the major states of western Asia—Media, Babylonia, Lydia, and Egypt. The third king, Darius I, extended the boundaries of the empire as far as the Indus Valley to the east and the European shore of the Black Sea to the west. The first major setback came when the fourth king, Xerxes, failed in his invasion of Greece in 480 BCE. The Persian Empire was considerably larger than its predecessor, the Assyrian Empire. For their empire, the Persian rulers developed a system of provinces, governors, regular tribute, and communication by means of royal roads and couriers that allowed for efficient operations for two centuries.

If, as has recently been argued, the Persians had higher regard for peoples who lived nearest to them, how would they have viewed the Greeks?

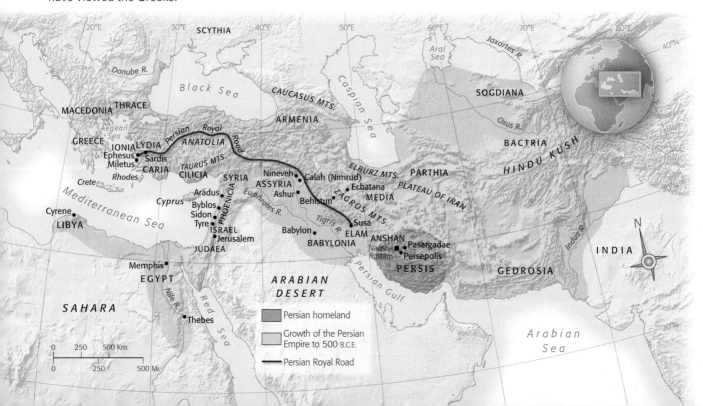

N
he
E
S

CHRONOLOGY

	Greece and the Hellenistic World	Persian Empire
1000 BCE	1150–800 BCE Greece's "Dark Age"	ca. 1000 BCE Persians settle in southwest Iran
800 BCE	ca. 800 BCE Resumption of Greek contact with eastern Mediterranean 800–480 BCE Greece's Archaic period ca. 750–550 BCE Era of colonization ca. 700 BCE Beginning of hoplite warfare ca. 650–500 BCE Era of tyrants	
600 BCE	594 BCE Solon reforms laws at Athens 546–510 BCE Pisistratus and sons hold tyranny at Athens	550 BCE Cyrus overthrows Medes 550–530 BCE Reign of Cyrus 546 BCE Cyrus conquers Lydia 539 BCE Cyrus takes control of Babylonia 530–522 BCE Reign of Cambyses; conquest of Egypt 522–486 BCE Reign of Darius
500 BCE	499–494 BCE Ionian Greeks rebel against Persia 490 BCE Athenians check Persian punitive expedition at Marathon 480–323 BCE Greece's Classical period 477 BCE Athens becomes leader of Delian League 461–429 BCE Pericles dominant at Athens; Athens completes evolution to democracy 431–404 BCE Peloponnesian War	480–479 BCE Xerxes's invasion of Greece
400 BCE	399 BCE Trial and execution of Socrates 359 BCE Philip II becomes king of Macedonia 338 BCE Philip takes control of Greece	387 BCE King's Peace makes Persia arbiter of Greek affairs 334–323 BCE Alexander the Great defeats Persia and creates huge empire 323–30 BCE Hellenistic period
300 BCE	ca. 300 BCE Foundation of the Museum in Alexandria 200 BCE First Roman intervention in the Hellenistic East	
100 BCE	30 BCE Roman annexation of Egypt, the last Hellenistic kingdom	

5-1b The Rise of the Persian Empire

In antiquity many groups of people, whom historians refer to collectively as "Iranians" because they spoke related languages and shared certain cultural features, spread across western and Central Asia—an area comprising not only the modern state of Iran but also Turkmenistan, Afghanistan, and Pakistan. Several of these groups arrived in western Iran near the end of the second millennium BCE. The first to achieve a complex level of political organization were the Medes (*Mada* in Iranian). They settled in the northwest and came under the influence of the ancient centers in Mesopotamia and Urartu (modern Armenia and northeast Turkey). The Medes played a major role in the destruction of the Assyrian Empire in the late seventh century BCE. According to Greek sources, Median kings extended their control westward across Assyria into Anatolia (modern Turkey) and also southeast toward the Persian Gulf, a region occupied by another Iranian people, the Persians (*Parsa*). However, some scholars doubt the Greek testimony about a well-organized Median kingdom controlling such extensive territories.

The Persian rulers—called Achaemenids (**a-KEY-muh-nid**) because they traced their lineage back to an ancestor named Achaemenes—cemented their relationship with the Median court through marriage. **Cyrus** (*Kurush*), the son of a Persian chieftain and a Median princess, united the various Persian tribes and overthrew the Median monarch around 550 BCE. His victory should perhaps be seen less as a conquest than as an alteration of the relations between groups, for Cyrus placed both Medes and Persians in positions of responsibility and retained the framework of Median rule. The differences between these two Iranian peoples were not great, and the Greeks could not readily tell them apart.

AP® Exam Tip
Be familiar with the Persian Empire, especially how it grew and created unity within an expanding empire.

Cyrus Founder of the Achaemenid Persian Empire. Between 550 and 530 BCE he conquered Media, Lydia, and Babylon. Revered in the traditions of both Iran and the subject peoples, he employed Persians and Medes in his administration and respected the institutions and beliefs of subject peoples.

The early inhabitants of western Iran had a patriarchal family organization: the male head of the household had nearly absolute authority over family members. Society was divided into three social and occupational classes—warriors, priests, and peasants—with warriors being the dominant element. A landowning aristocracy, they took pleasure in hunting, fighting, and gardening. The king was the most illustrious member of this group. The priests, or Magi (*magush*), were ritual specialists who supervised the proper performance of sacrifices. The common people—peasants—were primarily village-based farmers and shepherds.

Over the course of two decades the energetic Cyrus (r. 550–530 BCE) redrew the map of western Asia. In 546 BCE he defeated the kingdom of Lydia, and all Anatolia, including the Greek city-states on the western coast, came under Persian control. In 539 BCE he swept into Mesopotamia and overthrew the Neo-Babylonian dynasty that had ruled since the decline of Assyrian power (see Chapter 3). A skillful propagandist, Cyrus showed respect to the Babylonian priesthood and native traditions.

After Cyrus lost his life in 530 BCE while campaigning against nomadic Iranians in the northeast, his son Cambyses (*Kambujiya*, r. 530–522 BCE) set his sights on Egypt, the last of the great ancient kingdoms of the Middle East. After the Persians prevailed in a series of bloody battles, they sent exploratory expeditions south to Nubia and west to Libya. Greek sources depict Cambyses as a cruel and impious madman, but contemporary documents from Egypt show him operating in the same practical vein as his father, cultivating local priests and notables and respecting native traditions.

When Cambyses died in 522 BCE, a Persian nobleman distantly related to the royal family, **Darius I (duh-RIE-uhs)** (*Darayavaush*), seized the throne. His success in crushing many early challenges to his rule testifies to his skill, energy, and ruthlessness. From this reign forward, Medes played a lesser role, and the most important posts went to members of leading Persian families. Darius (r. 522–486 BCE) extended Persian control eastward as far as the Indus Valley and westward into Europe, where he bridged the Danube River and chased the nomadic Scythian (**SITH-ee-uhn**) peoples north of the Black Sea. The Persians erected a string of forts in Thrace (modern-day northeast Greece and Bulgaria) and by 500 BCE were on the doorstep of Greece. Darius also promoted the development of maritime routes. He dispatched a fleet to explore the waters from the Indus Delta to the Red Sea, and he completed a canal linking the Red Sea with the Nile.

Darius I Third ruler of the Persian Empire (r. 522–486 BCE). He crushed the widespread initial resistance to his rule and gave major government posts to Persians rather than to Medes. He established a system of provinces and tribute, began construction of Persepolis, and expanded Persian control in the east (Pakistan) and west (northern Greece).

▶ **Gold Model of Four-Horse Chariot from the Eastern Achaemenid Empire** This model is part of the Oxus Treasure, a cache of gold and silver objects discovered in Tajikistan. Seated on a bench next to the chariot driver, the main figure wears a long robe, a hood, and a torque around his neck, the garb of a Persian noble. It is uncertain whether this model was a child's toy or a votive offering to a deity. Erich Lessing/Art Resource, NY

5-1c Imperial Organization

The empire of Darius I was the largest the world had yet seen (see Map 5.1). Stretching from eastern Europe and Libya to Pakistan, from southern Russia to Sudan, it encompassed multiple ethnic groups and many forms of social and political organization. Darius can rightly be considered a second founder of the Persian Empire, after Cyrus, because he created a new organizational structure that was maintained throughout the remaining two centuries of the empire's existence.

Darius divided the empire into about twenty provinces, each under the supervision of a Persian **satrap** (**SAY-trap**), or governor, who was often related or connected by marriage to the royal family. The satrap's court was a miniature version of the royal court. The tendency for the position of satrap to become hereditary meant that satraps' families lived in the province governed by their head, acquired knowledge about local conditions, and formed connections with the local elite. The farther a province was from the center of the empire, the more autonomy the satrap had, because slow communications made it impractical to refer most matters to the central administration.

One of the satrap's most important duties was to collect and send tribute to the king. Darius prescribed how much precious metal each province was to contribute annually. Some of it was disbursed for necessary expenditures, but most was hoarded. As precious metal was taken out of circulation, the price of gold and silver rose, and provinces found it increasingly difficult to meet their quotas. Evidence from Babylonia indicates a gradual economic decline setting in by the fourth century BCE. The increasing burden of taxation and official corruption may have inadvertently caused the economic downturn.

Well-maintained and patrolled royal roads connected the outlying provinces to the heart of the empire. Way stations were built at intervals to receive important travelers and couriers carrying official correspondence. Military garrisons controlled strategic points, such as mountain passes, river crossings, and important urban centers.

The king had numerous wives and children. Women of the royal family could become pawns in the struggle for power, as when Darius strengthened his claim to the throne by marrying two daughters and a granddaughter of Cyrus. Greek sources portray Persian queens as vicious intriguers, poisoning rival wives and plotting to win the throne for their sons. However, a recent study suggests that the Greek stereotype misrepresents the important role played by Persian women in protecting family members and mediating conflicts.[1] Both Greek sources and documents within the empire reveal that Persian elite women were politically influential, possessed substantial property, traveled, and were prominent on public occasions.

The king and his court moved with the seasons, living in luxurious tents on the road and in palaces in the ancient capitals of Mesopotamia and Iran. Besides the royal family, the king's large entourage included several other groups: (1) the sons of Persian aristocrats, who were educated at court and also served as hostages for their parents' good behavior; (2) many noblemen, who were expected to attend on the king when they were not otherwise engaged; (3) the central administration, including officials and employees of the treasury, secretariat, and archives; (4) the royal bodyguard; and (5) countless courtiers and slaves. Long gone were the simple days when the king hunted and caroused with his warrior companions. Inspired by Mesopotamian conceptions of monarchy, the king of Persia had become an aloof figure of majesty and splendor: "The Great King, King of Kings, King in Persia, King of countries." He referred to everyone, even the Persian nobility, as "my slaves," and anyone who approached him had to bow down before him.

The king owned vast tracts of land throughout the empire. Some of it he gave to his supporters. Donations called "bow land," "horse land," and "chariot land" in Babylonian documents obliged the recipient to provide the corresponding form of military service. Scattered around the empire were gardens, orchards, and hunting preserves belonging to the king and high nobility. The *paradayadam* (meaning "walled enclosure"—the term has come into English as *paradise*), a green oasis in an arid landscape, advertised the prosperity that the king could bring to those who loyally served him. One scholar has recently made a strong case that the "paradises" may even have been intended to give glimpses of the perfection of the world at the time of Creation that the empire was endeavoring to restore.[2]

AP® Exam Tip

Identify, explain, and give examples of imperial organization from the various empires of this time period.

satrap The governor of a province in the Achaemenid Persian Empire, often a relative of the king. He was responsible for protection of the province and for forwarding tribute to the central administration. Satraps in outlying provinces enjoyed considerable autonomy.

---

[1] M. Brosius, *Women in Ancient Persia, 559–331 B.C.* (Oxford and New York: Oxford University Press, 1996).

[2] B. Lincoln, *Religion, Empire, and Torture: The Case of Achaemenian Persia, with a Postscript on Abu Ghraib* (Chicago, IL: University of Chicago Press, 2007).

Surviving administrative records from the Persian homeland reveal how the complex tasks of administration were managed. Government officials distributed food and other essential commodities to large numbers of workers of many different nationalities. Some of these workers may have been prisoners of war brought to the center of the empire to work on construction projects, maintain and expand the irrigation network, and farm the royal estates. Workers were divided into groups of men, women, and children. Women received less than men of equivalent status, but pregnant women and women with babies received additional support. Men and women performing skilled jobs received more than their unskilled counterparts. Administrators were provided with authorizations to requisition food and other necessities while traveling on official business.

The central administration was not based in the Persian homeland but closer to the geographical center of the empire, in Elam and Mesopotamia, where it could employ the trained administrators and scribes of those ancient civilizations. The administrative center of the empire was Susa, the ancient capital of Elam, in southwest Iran near the present-day border with Iraq. It was to Susa that Greeks and others went with requests and messages for the king. A party of Greek ambassadors would need at least three months to make the journey. Additional time spent waiting for an audience with the Persian king, delays due to weather, and the duration of the return trip probably kept the ambassadors away from home a year or more.

However, on certain occasions the kings returned to one special place back in the homeland. Darius began construction of a ceremonial capital at **Persepolis (per-SEH-poe-lis)** (*Parsa*). An artificial platform was erected, and on it were built a series of palaces, audience halls, treasury buildings, and barracks. Here, too, Darius and his son Xerxes (**ZERK-sees**), who completed the project, were inspired by Mesopotamian traditions, for the great Assyrian kings had created new fortress-cities as advertisements of their wealth and power.

5-1d Ideology and Religion

Darius's approach to governing can be seen in the luxuriant relief sculpture that covers the foundations, walls, and stairwells of the buildings at Persepolis. Representatives of all the peoples of the empire—recognizable by their distinctive hair, beards, dress, hats, and footwear—are depicted bringing gifts to the king. In this exercise in what today we would call public relations or propaganda, Darius crafted a vision of an empire of vast extent and abundant resources in which all the subject peoples willingly cooperate. On his tomb Darius subtly contrasted the character of his rule with that of the Assyrian Empire, the Persians' predecessors in these lands (see Chapter 3). Where Assyrian kings had gloried in their power and depicted subjects staggering under the weight of a giant platform that supported the throne, Darius's artists showed erect subjects shouldering the burden willingly and without strain.

What actually took place at Persepolis? This opulent retreat in the homeland was the scene of events of special significance for the king and his people: the New Year's Festival, coronation, marriage, death, and burial. The kings from Darius on were buried in elaborate tombs cut into the cliffs at nearby Naqsh-i Rustam (**NUHK-shee ROOS-tuhm**).

Another perspective on what the Persian monarchy claimed to stand for is provided by several dozen royal inscriptions that have survived. At Naqsh-i Rustam, Darius makes the following claim:

> Ahuramazda (**ah-HOOR-uh-MAZZ-duh**) [the chief deity], when he saw this earth in commotion, thereafter bestowed it upon me, made me king. . . . By the favor of Ahuramazda I put it down in its place. . . . I am of such a sort that I am a friend to right, I am not a friend to wrong. It is not my desire that the weak man should have wrong done to him by the mighty; nor is that my desire, that the mighty man should have wrong done to him by the weak.[3]

Zoroastrianism A religion originating in ancient Iran that became the official religion of the Achaemenids. It centered on a single benevolent deity, Ahuramazda, who engaged in a struggle with demonic forces before prevailing and restoring a pristine world. It emphasized truth-telling, purity, and reverence for nature.

Persepolis A complex of palaces, reception halls, and treasury buildings erected by the Persian kings Darius I and Xerxes in the Persian homeland. It is believed that the New Year's festival was celebrated here, as well as the coronations, weddings, and funerals of the Persian kings, who were buried in cliff-tombs nearby.

The royal inscriptions and the artwork at Persepolis and elsewhere are certainly propaganda, but that does not mean they lack validity. To be effective, propaganda must be predicated on the moral values, political principles, and religious beliefs that are familiar and acceptable in a society, and thus it can provide us with a window on those views.

As this inscription also makes clear, behind Darius and the empire stands the will of god. Ahuramazda made Darius king, giving him a mandate to bring order to a world in turmoil and ensure that all people be treated justly. Ahuramazda is the great god of a religion called **Zoroastrianism (zo-roe-ASS-tree-uh-niz-uhm)**, and it is probable that Darius and his successors were Zoroastrians.

[3]Quoted in R. G. Kent, *Old Persian: Grammar, Texts, Lexicon*, 2d ed. (New Haven, CT: American Oriental Society, 1953), 138, 140.

▲ **Sculpted Images on a Stairwell at Persepolis, ca. 500 BCE** Persepolis, in the Persian homeland, was built by Darius I and his son Xerxes, and it was used for ceremonies of special importance to the Persian king and people—coronations, royal weddings, funerals, and the New Year's Festival. Relief images like these on the stone foundations, walls, and stairways, representing members of the court and embassies bringing gifts, broadcast a vision of the grandeur and harmony of the Persian Empire. arazu/Shutterstock.com

The origins of this religion are shrouded in uncertainty. The *Gathas*, hymns in an archaic Iranian dialect, are said to be the work of Zoroaster (**zo-roe-ASS-ter**) (*Zarathushtra*), who probably lived in eastern Iran sometime between 1700 and 500 BCE. He revealed that the world had been created by Ahuramazda, "the wise lord," but its original state of perfection and unity had been badly damaged by the attacks of Angra Mainyu (**ANG-ruh MINE-yoo**), "the hostile spirit," backed by a host of demons. The struggle between good and evil plays out over thousands of years, with good ultimately destined to prevail. Humanity is a participant in this cosmic struggle, and individuals are rewarded or punished in the afterlife for their actions in life.

Darius has brilliantly joined the moral theology of Zoroastrianism to political ideology. In essence, he is claiming that the divinely ordained mission of the empire is to bring all the scattered peoples of the world back together again under a regime of justice and thereby to restore the perfection of creation.

In keeping with this Zoroastrian worldview, the Persians were sensitive to the beauties of nature and venerated beneficent elements, such as water, which was not to be polluted by human excretion, and fire, which was worshiped at fire altars. Corpses were exposed to wild beasts and the elements to prevent them from putrefying in the earth or tainting the sanctity of fire. Persians were also expected to keep promises and tell the truth. In his inscriptions Darius castigated evildoers as followers of "the Lie."

Zoroastrianism was one of the great religions of the ancient world. It preached belief in one supreme deity, held humans to a high ethical standard, and promised salvation. It traveled across western Asia with the advance of the

Section Review

- The Medes and the Persians of western Iran created complex societies in the seventh and sixth centuries BCE under Mesopotamian influence.

- Cyrus, the founder of the Achaemenid Persian Empire, conquered most of western Asia, while his son Cambyses captured Egypt.

- Darius was a second founder of the empire, creating new systems for administration and collection of tribute.

- The king and his large entourage moved among several imperial centers: Susa was the administrative capital, and Persepolis in the homeland was the site of royal ceremonials.

- Darius was a brilliant propagandist, adapting Zoroastrian religious teachings to create an ideology justifying the empire.

- Zoroastrianism was one of the great religions of the ancient world, holding people to a high ethical standard, and may have influenced Judaism and Christianity.

Persian Empire, and it may have exerted a major influence on Judaism and thus, indirectly, on Christianity. God and the Devil, Heaven and Hell, reward and punishment in the afterlife, and the Messiah and the End of Time all appear to be legacies of this profound belief system. Because of the accidents of history—the fall of the Achaemenid Persian Empire in the later fourth century BCE and the Islamic conquest of Iran in the seventh century CE (see Chapter 9)—Zoroastrianism has all but disappeared, except among a relatively small number of Parsees, as Zoroastrians are now called, in Iran and India.

5-2 The Rise of the Greeks, 1000–500 BCE

What were the most distinctive elements of Greek civilization, and how and why did they evolve in the Archaic and Classical periods?

Because Greece was a relatively resource-poor region, the cultural developments of the first millennium BCE were only possible because the Greeks had access to raw materials and markets abroad. Greek merchants, mercenaries, and travelers were in contact with other peoples and brought home foreign goods and ideas. Under the pressure of population, poverty, war, or political crisis, Greeks settled in other parts of the Mediterranean and Black Sea, bringing their language and culture and influencing other societies. Encounters with the different practices and beliefs of other peoples stimulated the formation of a Greek identity and sparked interest in geography, ethnography, and history. A two-century-long rivalry with the Persian Empire helped shape the destinies of the Greek city-states.

5-2a Geography and Resources

Greece is part of an ecological zone encompassing the Mediterranean Sea and the lands surrounding it (see Map 3.5). This zone is bounded by the Atlantic Ocean to the west, the several ranges of the Alps to the north, the Syrian Desert to the east, and the Sahara to the south. The lands lying within this zone have a similar climate, a similar sequence of seasons, and similar plants and animals. In summer a weather front near the entrance of the Mediterranean impedes the passage of storms from the Atlantic, allowing hot, dry air from the Sahara to creep up over the region. In winter the front dissolves and ocean storms roll in, bringing waves, wind, and cold. It was relatively easy for people to migrate to new homes within this ecological zone without altering familiar cultural practices and means of livelihood.

Greek civilization arose in the lands bordering the Aegean Sea: the Greek mainland, the Aegean islands, and the western coast of Anatolia (see Map 5.2). Southern Greece is a dry and rocky land with small plains separated by low mountain ranges. No navigable rivers ease travel or the transport of commodities. The small islands dotting the Aegean were inhabited from early times. People could sail from Greece to Anatolia almost without losing sight of land. The sea was always a connector, not a barrier. From about 1000 BCE Greeks began settling on the western edge of Anatolia. Broad and fertile river valleys near the coast made Ionia, as the ancient Greeks called this region, a comfortable place.

Greek farmers depended on rainfall to water their crops. The limited arable land, thin topsoil, and sparse rainfall in the south could not sustain large populations. Farmers planted grain (mostly barley, which was hardier than wheat) in the flat plain, olive trees at the edge of the plain, and grapevines on the terraced lower slopes of the foothills. Sheep and goats grazed in the hills during the growing season. In northern Greece, where the rainfall is greater and the land opens out into broad plains, cattle and horses were more abundant. These lands had few metal deposits and little timber, but both building stone, including fine marble, and clay for the potter were abundant.

The Greek mainland has a deeply pitted coastline with many natural harbors. A combination of circumstances—the difficulty of overland transport, the availability of good anchorages, and the need to import metals, timber, and grain—drew the Greeks to the sea. They obtained timber from the northern Aegean, gold and iron from Anatolia, copper from Cyprus, tin from the western Mediterranean, and grain from the Black Sea, Egypt, and Sicily. Sea transport was much cheaper and faster than overland transport. Thus, some Greeks reluctantly embarked upon the sea in their small, frail ships, hugging the coastline or island-hopping where possible.

MAP 5.2   Ancient Greece By the early first millennium BCE Greek-speaking peoples were dispersed throughout the Aegean region, occupying the Greek mainland, most of the islands, and the western coast of Anatolia. The rough landscape of central and southern Greece, with small plains separated by ranges of mountains, and the many islands in the Aegean favored the rise of hundreds of small, independent communities. The presence of adequate rainfall meant that agriculture was organized on the basis of self-sufficient family farms. As a result of the limited natural resources of this region, the Greeks had to resort to sea travel and trade with other lands in the Mediterranean to acquire metals and other vital raw materials.

How does this map help to explain why warfare between early Greek city-states was so frequent?

5-2b The Emergence of the Polis

The first flowering of Greek culture in the Mycenaean civilization of the second millennium BCE, described in Chapter 3, was largely an adaptation to the Greek terrain of the imported institutions of Middle Eastern palace-dominated states. For several centuries after the destruction of the Mycenaean palace-states, Greece lapsed into a "Dark Age" (ca. 1150–800 BCE), a time of depopulation, poverty, and backwardness that left few traces in the archaeological record.

During the Dark Age, the Greeks were largely isolated from the rest of the world. The importation of raw materials, especially metals, had been the chief source of Mycenaean prosperity. Lack of access to resources lay behind the poverty of the Dark Age. With fewer people to feed, the land was largely given over to grazing animals. Although there was continuity of language,

AP® Exam Tip
Identify the location of Greek city-states and colonies and understand the role of geography in the political development of classical Greek civilization.

AP® Exam Tip
Understand the distinctive features of trade routes such as the Mediterranean sea lanes.

religion, and other aspects of culture, there was a sharp break with the authoritarian Mycenaean political structure and centralized control of the economy. This opened the way for the development of new political, social, and economic forms rooted in the Greek environment.

The isolation of Greece ended by 800 BCE when Phoenician ships began to visit the Aegean (see Chapter 3), inaugurating what scholars term the "Archaic" period of Greek history (ca. 800–480 BCE). Soon Greek ships were also plying the waters of the Mediterranean in search of raw materials, trade opportunities, and fertile farmland.

New ideas arrived from the east, such as the depiction of naturalistic human and animal figures and imaginative mythical beasts on painted pottery. The most auspicious gift of the Phoenicians was a writing system. The Phoenicians used twenty-two symbols to represent the consonants in their language, leaving the vowel sounds to be inferred by the reader. To represent Greek vowel sounds, the Greeks utilized some of the Phoenician symbols for which there were no equivalent sounds in the Greek language. This was the first true alphabet, a system of writing that fully represents the sounds of spoken language. An alphabet offers tremendous advantages over systems of writing such as cuneiform and hieroglyphics, whose signs represent entire words or syllables. Because cuneiform and hieroglyphics required years of training and the memorization of hundreds of signs, they were known only by a scribal class whose elevated social position stemmed from their mastery of the technology. With an alphabet only a few dozen signs are required, and people can learn to read and write in a relatively short period of time.

Some scholars maintain that the Greeks first used alphabetic writing for economic purposes, such as to keep inventories of a merchant's wares. Others propose that it was created to preserve the oral epics so important to the Greeks. Whatever its first use, the Greeks soon applied the new technology to new forms of literature, law codes, religious dedications, and epitaphs on gravestones. This does not mean, however, that Greek society immediately became literate in the modern sense. For many centuries, Greece remained a primarily oral culture: people used storytelling, rituals, and performances to preserve and transmit information. Many of the distinctive intellectual and artistic creations of Greek civilization, such as theatrical drama, philosophical dialogues, and political and courtroom oratory, resulted from the dynamic interaction of speaking and writing.

The early Archaic period saw a veritable explosion of population. Studies of cemeteries in the vicinity of Athens show a dramatic population increase (perhaps fivefold or more) during the eighth century BCE. This was probably due, in part, to more intensive use of the land, as farming replaced herding and families began to work previously unused land on the margins of the plains. The accompanying shift to a diet based on bread and vegetables rather than meat may have increased fertility and lifespan. Another factor was increasing prosperity based on the importation of food and raw materials. Rising population density caused villages to merge and become urban centers. Freed from agricultural tasks, some members of the society were able to develop specialized skills in other areas, such as crafts and commerce.

polis The Greek term for a city-state, an urban center and the agricultural territory under its control. It was the characteristic form of political organization in southern and central Greece in the Archaic and Classical periods. Of the hundreds of city-states in the Mediterranean and Black Sea regions settled by Greeks, some were oligarchic, others democratic, depending on the powers delegated to the Council and the Assembly.

Greece at this time consisted of hundreds of independent political entities, reflecting the facts of Greek geography—small plains separated by mountain barriers. The Greek **polis** (**POE-lis**) (usually translated "city-state") consisted of an urban center and the rural territory it controlled. City-states came in various sizes, with populations as small as several thousand or as large as several hundred thousand in the case of Athens.

Most urban centers had certain characteristic features. A hilltop *acropolis* (**uh-KRAW-poe-lis**) ("top of the city") offered refuge in an emergency. The town spread out around the base of this fortified high point. An *agora* (**ah-go-RAH**) ("gathering place") was an open area where citizens came together to ratify decisions of their leaders or to assemble with their weapons before military ventures. Government buildings were located there, but the agora developed into a marketplace as well, since vendors everywhere set out their wares wherever crowds gather. Fortified walls surrounded the urban center; but as the population expanded, new buildings went up beyond the perimeter.

City and country were not as sharply distinguished as they are today. The urban center depended on its agricultural hinterland to provide food, and many people living within the walls of the city worked on nearby farms during the day. Unlike the dependent workers on the estates of Mesopotamia, the rural populations of the Greek city-states were free members of the community.

hoplites A heavily armored Greek infantryman of the Archaic and Classical periods who fought in the close-packed phalanx formation. Hoplite armies—militias composed of middle- and upper-class citizens supplying their own equipment—were for centuries superior to all other military forces.

Each polis was fiercely jealous of its independence and suspicious of its neighbors, leading to frequent conflict. By the early seventh century BCE the Greeks had developed a new kind of warfare, waged by **hoplites** (**HAWP-lite**)—heavily armored infantrymen who fought in close formation. Protected by a helmet, a breastplate, and leg guards, each hoplite held a round shield

▲ **The Acropolis at Athens**   This steep, defensible plateau jutting up from the Attic Plain served as a Mycenaean fortress in the second millennium BCE, and the site of Athens has been continuously occupied since that time. In the mid-sixth century BCE the tyrant Pisistratus built a temple to Athena, the patron goddess of the community. It was destroyed by the Persians when they invaded Greece in 480 BCE. The Acropolis was left in ruins for three decades as a reminder of what the Athenians sacrificed in defense of Greek freedom, but in the 440s BCE Pericles initiated a building program, using funds from the naval empire that Athens headed. These construction projects, including a new temple to Athena—the Parthenon—brought glory to the city and popularity to Pericles and to the new democracy that he championed.   robertharding/Alamy Stock Photo

over his own left side and the right side of the man next to him and brandished a thrusting spear, keeping a sword in reserve. The key to victory was maintaining the cohesion of one's own formation while breaking open the enemy's line. Most of the casualties were suffered by the defeated army in flight.

There was a close relationship between hoplite warfare and agriculture. Greek states were defended by armies of private citizens—mostly farmers—called up for brief periods of crisis, rather than by a professional class of soldiers. Although this kind of fighting called for strength to bear the weapons and armor, as well as courage to stand one's ground in battle, no special training was needed. Campaigns took place when farmers were available, in the windows of time between major tasks in the agricultural cycle. When a hoplite army marched into the fields of another community, the enraged farmers of that community, who had toiled to develop their land and buildings, rarely refused the challenge. Though brutal and terrifying, the clash of two hoplite lines provided a quick decision. Battles rarely lasted more than a few hours, and the survivors could promptly return home to tend their farms.

The expanding population soon surpassed the capacity of the small plains, and many communities sent excess population abroad to establish independent "colonies" in distant lands (see the story at the beginning of this chapter). Not every colonist left willingly. Sources tell of people being chosen by lot and forbidden to return on pain of death. Others, seeing an opportunity to escape from poverty, avoid the constraints of family, or find adventure, voluntarily sought their fortunes on the frontier. After obtaining the approval of the god Apollo from his sanctuary at Delphi, the colonists departed, carrying fire from the communal hearth of the "mother-city," a symbol of the kinship and religious ties that would connect the two communities. They settled by the sea in the vicinity of a hill or other natural refuge. The "founder," a prominent member of the mother-city, allotted parcels of land and drafted laws for the new community. In some cases the indigenous population was driven away or reduced to semiservile status; in other cases there was intermarriage between colonists and natives.

A wave of colonization from the mid-eighth through mid-sixth centuries BCE spread Greek culture far beyond the land of its origins. New settlements sprang up in the northern Aegean area, around the Black Sea, and on the Libyan coast of North Africa. In southern Italy and on the island of Sicily (see Map 3.5) another Greek core area was established. Greek colonists were able to transplant their entire way of life because of the general similarity in climate and ecology in the Mediterranean lands.

The Greeks began to use the term *Hellenes* (**HELL-leans**) (*Graeci* is what the Romans later called them) to distinguish themselves from *barbaroi* (the root of the English word *barbarian*). Interaction with new peoples and exposure to their different practices made the Greeks aware of the factors that bound them together: their language, religion, and lifestyle. It also introduced them to new ideas and technologies. Developments first appearing in the colonial world traveled back to the Greek homeland—urban planning, new forms of political organization, and new intellectual currents.

Coinage was invented in the early sixth century BCE, probably in Lydia (western Anatolia), and soon spread throughout the Greek world and beyond. A coin was a piece of metal whose weight and purity, and thus value, were guaranteed by the state. Silver, gold, bronze, and other metals were attractive choices for a medium of exchange: sufficiently rare to be valuable, relatively lightweight and portable, virtually indestructible, and therefore permanent. Prior to the invention of coinage, people weighed out quantities of metal in exchange for items they wanted to buy. Coinage allowed for more rapid exchanges of goods as well as for more efficient record keeping and storage of wealth. It stimulated trade and increased the total wealth of the society. Even so, international commerce could still be confusing because different states used different weight standards that had to be reconciled, just as people have to exchange currencies when traveling today.

By reducing surplus population, colonization helped relieve pressures within Archaic Greek communities. Nevertheless, this was an era of political instability. Kings ruled the Dark Age societies depicted in Homer's *Iliad* and *Odyssey*, but at some point councils composed of the heads of noble families superseded the kings. This aristocracy derived its wealth and power from ownership of large tracts of land. Peasant families worked this land, occupying small plots and handing over a portion of the crop to the owner. Debt-slaves, who had borrowed money or seed from the lord and lost their freedom when unable to repay the loan, also worked the land. Also living in a typical community were free peasants, who owned small farms, and urban-based craftsmen and merchants, who began to constitute a "middle class."

In the mid-seventh and sixth centuries BCE in one city-state after another, a **tyrant**—a person who seized and held power in violation of the normal political traditions of the community—gained control. Greek tyrants were often disgruntled or ambitious members of the aristocracy who were backed by the emerging middle class. New opportunities for economic advancement and the declining cost of metals meant that more and more men could acquire arms and serve as hoplite soldiers in the local militias. These individuals must have demanded increased political rights as the price of their support for the tyrant.

Ultimately, the tyrants were unwitting catalysts in an evolving political process. Some were able to pass their positions on to their sons, but eventually the tyrant-family was ejected. Authority in the community developed along one of two lines: toward oligarchy (**OLL-ih-gahr-key**), the exercise of political privilege by the wealthier members of society, or toward **democracy**, the exercise of political power by all free adult males.

Greek religion encompassed a wide range of cults and beliefs. The ancestors of the Greeks brought a collection of sky-gods with them when they entered the Greek peninsula at the end of the third millennium BCE. Male gods predominated, but several female deities had important roles. Some gods represented forces in nature: for example, Zeus sent storms and lightning, and Poseidon was master of the sea and earthquakes. The two great epic poems of Homer, the *Iliad* and *Odyssey*, which Greek schoolboys memorized and professional performers recited, put a distinctive stamp on the personalities of these deities. The Homeric gods were *anthropomorphic* (**an-thruh-puh-MORE-fik**)—that is, conceived as human-like in appearance (though taller, more beautiful, and far more powerful than mere mortals) and human-like in their displays of emotion. Indeed, the chief difference between them and human beings was humans' mortality.

Worship of the gods at state-sponsored festivals was as much an expression of civic identity as of personal piety. **Sacrifice**, the central ritual of Greek religion, was performed at altars in front of the temples that the Greeks built to be the gods' places of residence. Greeks gave their gods gifts, often as humble as a small cake or a cup of wine poured on the ground, in the hope that the

---

AP® Exam Tip
Understand the way that Greco-Roman religious and philosophical traditions emphasized logic, empirical observation, and scientific investigation to offer diverse perspectives on social and political developments.

tyrant The term the Greeks used to describe someone who seized and held power in violation of the normal procedures and traditions of the community. Tyrants appeared in many Greek city-states in the seventh and sixth centuries BCE, often taking advantage of the disaffection of the emerging middle class and, by weakening the old elite, unwittingly contributing to the evolution of democracy.

democracy System of government in which all "citizens" (however defined) have equal political and legal rights, privileges, and protections, as in the Greek city-state of Athens in the fifth and fourth centuries BCE.

sacrifice A gift given to a deity, often with the aim of creating a relationship, gaining favor, and obligating the god to provide some benefit to the sacrificer, sometimes in order to sustain the deity and thereby guarantee the continuing vitality of the natural world.

gods would favor and protect them. In more spectacular forms of sacrifice, a group of people would kill one or more animals, spray the altar with the victim's blood, burn parts of its body so that the aroma would ascend to the gods on high, and enjoy a rare feast of meat.

Greek individuals and communities sought advice or predictions about the future from oracles—sacred sites where they believed the gods communicated with humans. Especially prestigious was the oracle of Apollo at Delphi in central Greece. Petitioners left gifts in the treasuries, and the god responded to their questions through his priestess, who gave forth obscure utterances that were translated into more intelligible messages by the professional priests attached to the sanctuary (an exception to the rule that the Greeks—unlike the Egyptians, Mesopotamians, and other ancient peoples—did not develop a caste of religious professionals). As was mentioned earlier, many Greek communities that sent out colonies during the Archaic period first consulted the god at Delphi. It is likely that the priests at Delphi, eager to boost the reputation of their oracle, gathered geographical information from visitors coming to Delphi from many places and used this information to help guide prospective colonists.

Because most Greeks were farmers, a popular form of worship was the fertility cult, in which members worshiped and sought to enhance the productive forces in nature (usually conceived as female deities). This kind of popular religion is often hidden from modern view because of our dependence on literary texts privileging the values of an educated, urban elite.

5-2c New Intellectual Currents

The changes taking place in Greece in the Archaic period—new technologies, increasing prosperity, and social and political development—led to innovations in intellectual outlook and artistic expression. One distinctive feature of the period was a growing emphasis on the uniqueness and rights of the individual.

We see clear signs of individualism in the new lyric poetry—short verses in which the subject matter is intensely personal, drawn from the experience of the poet and expressing his or her feelings (see Diversity & Dominance: Poetry and Society in Early China and Greece). Archilochus (**ahr-KIL-uh-kuhs**), a soldier and poet living in the first half of the seventh century BCE, made a surprising admission:

> Some barbarian is waving my shield, since I was obliged to leave that perfectly good piece of equipment behind under a bush. But I got away, so what does it matter? Let the shield go; I can buy another one equally good.[4]

Here Archilochus is poking fun at the heroic ideal that regarded dishonor as worse than death. In challenging traditional values and expressing personal views, lyric poets paved the way for the modern Western conception of poetry.

Some daring thinkers rejected traditional religious conceptions and sought rational explanations for events in nature. For example, in the sixth century BCE Xenophanes (**zeh-NOFF-uh-nees**) called into question the kind of gods that Homer had popularized.

> But if cattle and horses or lions had hands, or were able to draw with their hands and do the works that men can do, horses would draw the forms of the gods like horses, and cattle like cattle, and they would make their bodies such as they each had themselves.[5]

These early philosophers were primarily concerned with how the world was created, what it is made of, and why changes occur. Some postulated various combinations of earth, air, fire, and water as the primal elements that combine or dissolve to form the numerous substances found in nature. One advanced the theory that the world is composed of microscopic atoms (from a Greek word meaning "indivisible") moving through the void of space, colliding randomly and combining in various ways to form many substances. This model, in some respects startlingly similar to modern atomic theory, was essentially a lucky intuition, but it attests to the sophistication of these thinkers. Most of these thinkers came from Ionia and southern Italy, where Greeks were in close contact with non-Greek peoples. The shock of encountering different ideas may have stimulated new lines of inquiry.

---

[4]R. Lattimore, *Greek Lyrics*, 2d ed. (Chicago, IL: University of Chicago Press, 1960), 2.

[5]G. S. Kirk and J. E. Raven, *The Presocratic Philosophers: A Critical History with a Selection of Texts* (Cambridge, UK: Cambridge University Press, 1957), 169.

Poetry and Society in Early China and Greece

While they are rarely treated together, the contemporaneous civilizations of early China (Zhou dynasty—see Chapter 4) and Greece of the Archaic and Classical periods (ca. 800–323 BCE) exhibit many similarities. For instance, both were politically fragmented into many small, independent states, and both witnessed the formation of seminal technologies, values, and literary and artistic forms in eras of political instability and incessant warfare. Of course, there is no question of the influence of one civilization on the other here. They were unaware of each other's existence since the distances were too great and there was no direct trade or travel between them. However, looking at the similarities and differences between early Greece and China provides a good opportunity to gauge the value of comparative history. Where we find similarities, they have to be credited to independent parallel development. And where we find differences, they provide insights into fundamental differences in institutions, values, and worldviews that still separate East Asian and Western civilizations in our times. In other words, comparative approaches set the two civilizations in dialogue and force us to confront the reasons why they developed differently.

We have an excellent opportunity to observe and compare everyday life and values in the societies of early China and Greece through their poetry. The vast majority of ancient Chinese and Greek people were not literate. They were oralists, who learned information by hearing it, preserved it by memorizing it, and passed it on by telling it. Because the majority of people in ancient China and Greece operated in this way, it is legitimate to regard these cultures as operating primarily by the mechanisms of orality, even though some small percentage of people—primarily educated, upper-class males—were literate and utilized the technology of writing. In oral societies, valuable information can most easily be preserved by putting it in poetic form because poetry is more easily remembered than prose. What constitutes poetry may vary from language to language, but it usually involves some form of fixed meter or rhythm, and it is this structure that makes poetry easily memorized.

The Chinese *Book of Songs* is a complete text containing 305 poems composed between the eleventh and seventh centuries BCE, that is, during the first half of the Zhou Dynasty. In every case the creators of the poems are anonymous. Some of the poems emanate from the Zhou court and relate myth and history about the ruling dynasty, while others illuminate court ceremonial, ancestor worship, and other aspects of the lives of the elite. However, many of the poems appear to be essentially folk songs, created by a wide cross-section of Chinese society, men and women, higher and lower classes, and thereby providing a rich source of information about everyday life, including courtship and marriage, love affairs and rejections, the laments of soldiers far away from home, the yearly round of activities on agricultural estates, and the corruption of officials and general failures of government.

Greek lyric poetry survives only in fragments, that is, quotations from later writers whose texts have survived to our times, or the occasional piece of papyrus unearthed in Egypt. Thus, the task of interpretation is complicated by our ignorance about a given poem's context, the collection of which it may have been a part, and we often can't even be sure whether we have a whole poem or merely a piece. In most cases the name of the poet

is known, and they are, with a few exceptions, educated, elite males. The subject matter thus tends to be things of interest to that group—warfare, politics, drinking parties, love affairs, and athletics.

Let us look at how Chinese and Greek poets portrayed their feelings when abandoned or ignored by someone they love:

Wild and windy was the day;
You looked at me and laughed,
But the jest was cruel, and the laughter mocking.
My heart within is sore.

There was a great sandstorm that day;
Kindly you made as though to come,
Yet neither came nor went away.
Long, long my thoughts.

A great wind and darkness;
Day after day it is dark.
I lie awake, cannot sleep,
And gasp with longing.

Dreary, dreary the gloom;
The thunder growls.
I lie awake, cannot sleep,
And am destroyed with longing.

(Book of Songs 30)

Like the very gods in my sight is he who
sits where he can look in your eyes, who listens
close to you, to hear the soft voice, its sweetness
murmur in love and

laughter, all for him. But it breaks my spirit;
underneath my breast all the heart is shaken.
Let me only glance where you are, the voice dies,
I can say nothing,

but my lips are stricken to silence, under-
neath my skin the tenuous flame suffuses;
nothing shows in front of my eyes, my ears are
muted in thunder.

And the sweat breaks running upon me, fever
shakes my body, paler I turn than grass is;
I can feel that I have been changed, I feel that
death has come near me.

(Sappho of Lesbos, fragment 31)

Both poems represent the voice of a woman. The Greek poem is attributed to the magnificent poet Sappho, who lived on the Aegean island of Lesbos ca. 600 BCE, while the Chinese poet is anonymous. In neither case can we be sure whether we are hearing the voice and experience of a real person or that of a literary persona, a fictional but realistic character, as in many love songs today. Both poems tell of unrequited love, and both describe the physical symptoms of the suffering lover. Both poets use images from nature as analogues for human emotion. In the Chinese case, the phenomena of actual weather mirror the moods of the lover, whereas the Greek poet employs flame and thunder as metaphors. The Chinese poem has a more formal structure—each stanza reports a natural event, a human event, and the feeling that results, and certain lines echo earlier lines. The emotion, while painful, is restrained. The Greek poem has a looser structure and more spontaneous feel, in which the emotion fairly gushes forth. Indeed, one might say that for the Chinese woman love has led to sadness, but for the Greek woman it threatens madness. Finally, the Greek poem relates the desire of one woman for another, and one finds frequent reference in the Greek tradition to both heterosexual and homosexual love, described in very similar ways. The Chinese poems are exclusively about heterosexual love.

Next, we get a glimpse of how Chinese and Greek soldiers thought about war:

> We bring out our carts
> On to those pasture-grounds.
> From where the Sun of Heaven is
> Orders have come that we are to be here.
> The grooms are told
> To get the carts loaded up.
> The kings's service brings many hardships
> It makes swift calls upon us.
>
> We bring out our carts
> On to those outskirts.
> Here we set up the standards,
> There we raise the ox-tail banners,
> The falcon-banner, and the standards
> That flutter, flutter.
> Our sad hearts are very anxious;
> The grooms are worn out.
>
> The king has ordered Nan-zhong
> To go and build a fort on the frontier.
> To bring out the great concourse of chariots,
> With dragon banners and standards so bright.
> The Son of Heaven has ordered us
> To build a fort on that frontier.
> Terrible is Nan-zhong;
> The Xian-yun are undone.
>
> Long ago, when we started,
> The wine-millet and cooking-millet were in flower.
> Now that we are on the march again
> Snow falls upon the mire.
> The king's service brings many hardships.
> We have no time to rest or bide.
> We do indeed long to return;
> But we fear the writing on the tablets…
>
> (Book of Songs 168)

> … For no man ever proves himself a good man in war
> unless he can endure to face the blood and the slaughter,
> go close against the enemy and fight with his hands.
> Here is courage, mankind's finest possession, here is
> the noblest prize that a young man can endeavor to win,
> and it is a good thing his city and all the people share with him
> when a man plants his feet and stands in the foremost spears
> relentlessly, all thought of foul flight completely forgotten,
> and has well trained his heart to be steadfast and to endure,
> and with words encourages the man who is stationed beside him.
> Here is a man who proves himself to be valiant in war.
> With a sudden rush he turns to fight the rugged battalions

> of the enemy, and sustains the beating waves of assault.
> And he who so falls among the champions and loses his sweet life,
> so blessing with honor his city, his father, and all his people,
> with wounds in his chest, where the spear that he was facing
>   has transfixed
> that massive guard of his shield, and gone through his breast-
>   plate as well,
> why, such a man is lamented alike by the young and the elders,
> and all his city goes into mourning and grieves for his loss…
> But if he escapes the doom of death, the destroyer of bodies,
> and wins his battle, and bright renown for the work of his spear,
> all men give place to him alike, the youth and the elders,
> and much joy comes his way before he goes down to the dead.
>
> (Tyrtaeus of Sparta, fragment 12)

The Chinese poem epitomizes a virtual genre of poetry, one that persists right through the imperial period, in which soldiers complain about long terms of service on distant frontiers. All is done on the orders of the king, everyone lives in fear of the king, and all glory for the victory over the barbarian Xianyun people goes to the king and his designated general Nan-zhong. The soldier-narrator presents himself as a passive figure, a witness and a victim to whom things happen. Again, the poem has a repetitive formal structure, with each stanza reporting an activity and concluding with how the narrator and others react emotionally. While there is a quality of pageantry in the description of the force as it sets out, and, perhaps, some pride in the military victory, there is no room for heroism in a world where only the king has any sort of choice, and the overall tone is one of sadness and quiet resignation.

The Greek poem is attributed to Tyrtaeus, and is generally regarded as an exhortation to Spartan soldiers during a bloody and difficult time, the uprising of the Messenians against their Spartan masters in the mid-seventh century BCE. This poem is all about the heroism required of soldiers in war. The Spartan warrior is an active agent—he has a choice about whether to take risks and display heroism. And he gets credit for his choice, great respect and satisfaction should he survive the battle, and, in any case, eternal glory in the memory of his family and fellow-citizens. Greek soldiers are "citizens" in their city-states, that is, they have both rights and obligations as members of a community, whereas Chinese soldiers are merely "subjects" of their ruler. The stark differences in tone and message between the Chinese and Greek poems about war also relate to the fact that, whereas for Greek civilization the heroic epics of Homer were foundational, so far as is known ancient China did not develop a genre of heroic literature.

AP® History Reasoning Skills

Comparison *How do the similarities and differences between the Chinese and Greek poems reflect the social and political institutions of the two societies?*

Contextualization *What factors of Chinese and Greek society support the role of the individual in society exemplified by the excerpts?*

Sources: Tyrtaeus, Fragment 12 translation from *Greek Lyrics*, ed. Richmond Lattimore (Chicago, IL: University of Chicago Press). Copyright © 1949, 1960 by The University of Chicago.

◀ **Oracular Sanctuary of Apollo at Delphi** View of the theater and foundations of the Temple of Apollo. Located in a spectacular setting above the Gulf of Corinth, the zig-zag path that visitors ascended was lined with stone treasure-houses where individuals or communities seeking information about the future left their gifts for the god. The Pythia, a priestess housed in the temple, delivered the god's cryptic response, which was then put into more intelligible form by the professional priests attached to the sanctuary. funkyfood London–Paul Williams/Alamy Stock Photo

In Ionia in the sixth century BCE, a group of men referred to as *logographers* (**loe-GOG-ruff-er**) ("writers of prose accounts"), taking advantage of the nearly infinite capacity of writing to store information, gathered data on a wide range of topics, including *ethnography* (description of foreign people's physical characteristics and cultural practices), the geography of unfamiliar lands, foundation stories of important cities, and the origins of famous Greek families. They were the first to write in *prose*—the language of everyday speech—rather than poetry, which had long facilitated the memorization essential in an oral society. *Historia*, "investigation/research," was the Greek term for the method they used to collect, sort, and select information. An important successor to these early researchers was **Herodotus** (ca. 485–425 BCE), who published his *Histories* in the later fifth century BCE. Early parts of the work are filled with the geographic and ethnographic reports, legends, and marvels dear to the logographers, but in later sections Herodotus focuses on the great event of the previous generation: the wars between the Greeks and the Persian Empire.

Herodotus declared his new conception of his mission in the first lines of the book:

> I, Herodotus of Halicarnassus, am here setting forth my history, that time may not draw the color from what man has brought into being, nor those great and wonderful deeds, manifested by both Greeks and barbarians, fail of their report, and, together with all this, the reason why they fought one another.[6]

In seeking to discover *why* Greeks and Persians came to blows, Herodotus became a historian, directing the all-purpose techniques of *historia* to the narrower service of *history* in the modern sense. For this achievement he is known as the "father of history."

5-2d **Athens and Sparta**

The two preeminent Greek city-states of the late Archaic and Classical periods were Athens and Sparta. The different character of these communities underscores the potential for diversity in human societies, even those arising in similar environmental and cultural contexts.

The ancestors of the Spartans migrated into the Peloponnese (**PELL-uh-puh-neze**), the southernmost part of the Greek mainland, around 1000 BCE. For a time Sparta followed a typical path of development, participating in trade and fostering the arts. Then in the seventh century BCE something altered the character of the Spartan state. Like many other parts of Greece, the Spartan community was feeling the effects of increasing population and a shortage of arable land. However, instead of sending out colonists, the Spartans invaded the fertile plain of neighboring

Herodotus Heir to the technique of *historia* ("investigation/research") developed by Greeks in the late Archaic period. He came from a Greek community in Anatolia and traveled extensively, collecting information in western Asia and the Mediterranean lands. He traced the antecedents and chronicled the wars between the Greek city-states and the Persian Empire, thus originating the Western tradition of historical writing.

[6]Herodotus, *The History*, trans. David Grene (Chicago, IL: University of Chicago Press, 1988), 33. (Herodotus 1.1)

Messenia (see Map 5.2). They took over Messenia and reduced the native population to the status of helots (**HELL-ut**), or state-owned serfs, who became the most abused and exploited population on the Greek mainland.

Fear of a helot uprising led to the evolution of the unique Spartan way of life. The Spartan state became a military camp in a permanent state of preparedness. Territory in Messenia and Laconia (the Spartan homeland) was divided into several thousand lots and assigned to Spartan citizens. Helots worked the land and turned over a portion of what they grew to their Spartan masters, who were freed from food production and able to spend their lives in military training and service.

The Spartan soldier was the best in Greece, and the professional Spartan army was superior to the citizen militias of other Greek states. The Spartans, however, paid a huge personal price for their military readiness. At age seven, boys were taken from their families and put into barracks, where they were toughened by severe discipline, beatings, and deprivation. A Spartan male's whole life was subordinated to the needs of the state. Sparta essentially stopped the clock, declining to participate in the economic, political, and cultural renaissance taking place in the Archaic Greek world. There were no longer any poets or artists at Sparta. To maintain equality among citizens, precious metals and coinage were banned, and Spartans were forbidden to engage in commerce. The fifth-century BCE Athenian historian Thucydides (**thoo-SID-ih-dees**) remarked that in his day Sparta appeared to be little more than a large village and that no future observer of the ruins of the site would be able to guess its power.

The Spartans, practicing a foreign policy that was cautious and isolationist, cultivated a mystique by rarely putting their reputation to the test. Reluctant to march far from home for fear of a helot uprising, the Spartans maintained regional peace through the Peloponnesian League, a system of alliances between Sparta and its neighbors.

In comparison with other Greek city-states, Athens possessed an unusually large and populous territory: the entire region of Attica, containing a number of moderately fertile plains and well suited for cultivation of olive trees. In addition to the urban center of Athens, located 5 miles (8 kilometers) from the sea where the sheer-sided Acropolis towered above the plain, the peninsula was dotted with villages and a few larger towns.

In 594 BCE, however, Athens was on the verge of civil war, and a respected member of the elite class, Solon, was appointed lawgiver and granted extraordinary powers. Solon divided Athenian citizens into four classes based on the annual yield of their farms. Those in the top three classes could hold state offices. Members of the lowest class, with little or no property, could participate in meetings of the Assembly. This arrangement, which made political rights a function of wealth, was far from democratic, but it broke the monopoly on power of a small circle of aristocratic families. Solon also abolished the practice of enslaving individuals for failure to repay their debts, thereby guaranteeing the freedom of Athenian citizens.

Nevertheless, political turmoil continued until 546 BCE, when an aristocrat named Pisistratus (**pie-SIS-truh-tuhs**) seized power. To strengthen his position and weaken the aristocracy, the tyrant enticed the largely rural population to identify with the urban center of Athens, where he was the dominant figure. He undertook a number of monumental building projects, including a Temple of Athena on the Acropolis. He also instituted or expanded several major festivals that drew people to Athens for religious processions, performances of plays, and athletic and poetic competitions.

Pisistratus passed the tyranny on to his sons, but with Spartan assistance the Athenians turned the tyrant-family out in the last decade of the sixth century BCE. In the 460s and 450s BCE **Pericles** (**PER-eh-kleez**) and his political allies took the last steps in the evolution of Athenian democracy, transferring all power to popular organs of government: the Assembly, Council of 500, and People's Courts. Men of moderate or little means now could participate fully in the

Pericles Aristocratic leader who guided the Athenian state through the transformation to full participatory democracy for all male citizens, supervised construction of the Parthenon and other grand public edifices on the Acropolis, and pursued a policy of imperial expansion that led to the Peloponnesian War. He formulated a strategy of attrition but died from the plague early in the war.

Section Review

- In the resource-poor Greek Aegean, prosperity and advancement depended on seaborne trade for metals and other vital materials.

- Hundreds of independent city-states existed in the fragmented Greek landscape. Rainfall-based agriculture allowed the land to be worked by independent farmers who were free citizens of their communities.

- Rapidly expanding population led to urbanization and to colonization, the migration of Greeks to new settlements around the Mediterranean and Black Seas.

- The rise of a middle class and the dependence of communities on a hoplite militia led to political unrest and an extension of political rights to more people.

- The Greeks created the first true alphabetic writing system, but Greece long remained a primarily oral society. New ideas challenged traditional notions, leading to individualism, science, and history.

- Sparta and Athens, though part of the same Greek civilization, evolved politically in different directions: Sparta toward a military oligarchy, Athens to democracy.

political process, being selected by lot to fill even the highest offices and being paid for public service so they could take time off from their work. The focal point of Athenian political life became the Assembly of all citizens. Several times a month proposals were debated, decisions were made openly, and any citizen could speak to the issues of the day.

During this century and a half of internal political evolution, Athens' economic clout and international reputation rose steadily. From the time of Pisistratus, Athenian exports, especially olive oil, became increasingly prominent all around the Mediterranean, crowding out the products of other Greek commercial powerhouses such as Corinth (see Map 5.2). Extensive trade increased the numbers and wealth of the middle class and helps explain why Athens took the path of increasing democratization.

5-3 The Struggle of Persia and Greece, 546–323 BCE

How did the Persian Wars and their aftermath affect the politics and culture of ancient Greece and Iran?

For many Greeks of the fifth and fourth centuries BCE, Persia was the great enemy and the wars with Persia were crucial events. The Persians probably were more concerned about threats farther east. Nevertheless, the encounters of Greeks and Persians over a period of two centuries were of profound importance for the history of the eastern Mediterranean and western Asia.

5-3a Early Encounters

Cyrus's conquest of Lydia in 546 BCE led to the subjugation of the Greek cities on the Anatolian seacoast. In the years that followed, local groups or individuals who collaborated with the Persian government ruled their home cities with minimal Persian interference. All this changed when the Ionian Revolt, a great uprising of Greeks and other subject peoples on the western frontier, broke out in 499 BCE. The Persians needed five years and a massive infusion of troops and resources to stamp out the insurrection.

The failed revolt led to the **Persian Wars**—two Persian attacks on Greece in the early fifth century BCE. In 490 BCE Darius dispatched a force to punish Eretria (**er-EH-tree-uh**) and Athens, two mainland states that had aided the Ionian rebels. Eretria was betrayed to the Persians, and the survivors were marched off to permanent exile in southwest Iran. The Athenians probably would have suffered a similar fate if their hoplites had not defeated the more numerous but lighter-armed Persian troops in a sharp engagement at Marathon, 26 miles (42 kilometers) from Athens.

In 480 BCE Darius's son and successor, Xerxes (*Khshayarsha*, r. 486–465 BCE), set out with a huge invasionary force consisting of the Persian army, contingents from all the peoples of the empire, and a large fleet of ships drawn from maritime subjects. Crossing the narrow Hellespont strait, Persian forces descended into central and southern Greece (see Map 5.2). Xerxes sent messengers ahead to most Greek states, demanding "earth and water"—tokens of submission.

Many Greek communities acknowledged Persian overlordship. But an alliance of southern Greek states bent on resistance was formed under the leadership of the Spartans. This Hellenic League initially failed to halt the Persian advance. At the pass of Thermopylae (**thuhr-MOP-uh-lee**) in central Greece, 300 Spartans and their king gave their lives to buy time for their allies to escape. However, after the city of Athens had been sacked, the Persian navy was lured into the narrow straits of nearby Salamis (**SAH-lah-miss**), sacrificing their advantage in numbers and maneuverability, and suffered a devastating defeat. The following spring (479 BCE), the Persian land army was routed at Plataea (**pluh-TEE-uh**), and the immediate threat to Greece receded. A number of factors account for the outcome: the Persians' difficulty in supplying their very large army in a distant land; their tactical error at Salamis; the superiority of heavily armed Greek hoplite soldiers over lighter-armed Asiatic infantry; and the tenacity of people defending their homeland and liberty.

The Greeks then went on the offensive. The Athenians' stubborn refusal to submit, despite the capture and destruction of their city, and the vital role played by the Athenian navy, which made up half the allied fleet, had earned the city-state a large measure of respect. The next phase of the war—driving the Persians away from the Aegean and liberating Greek states still under

Persian Wars Conflicts between Greek city-states and the Persian Empire, ranging from the Ionian Revolt (499–494 BCE) through Darius's punitive expedition that failed at Marathon (490 BCE) and the defeat of Xerxes's massive invasion of Greece by the Spartan-led Hellenic League (480–479 BCE). This first major setback for Persian arms launched the Greeks into their period of greatest cultural productivity. Herodotus chronicled these events in the first "history" in the Western tradition.

▲ **Replica of Ancient Greek Trireme** Greek warships had a metal-tipped ram in front to pierce the hulls of enemy vessels and a pair of steering rudders in the rear. Though equipped with masts and sails, in battle these warships were propelled by 170 rowers. This modern, full-size replica, manned by international volunteer crews, is helping scholars to determine attainable speeds and maneuvering techniques. Replica of the trireme 'Olympia' at sea (photo)/Private Collection/Photo © Mike Andrews/Photo © Mike Andrews/Bridgeman Images

Persian control—was naval. Thus Athens replaced land-based, isolationist Sparta as leader of the campaign against Persia. In 477 BCE the Delian **(DEE-lih-yuhn)** League was formed. Initially a voluntary alliance of Greek states to prosecute the war against Persia, in less than twenty years Athenian-led League forces swept the Persians from the waters of the eastern Mediterranean and freed all Greek communities except those in distant Cyprus (see Map 3.5).

5-3b The Height of Athenian Power

The Classical period of Greek history (480–323 BCE) begins with the successful defense of the Greek homeland. Ironically, the Athenians, who had played such a crucial role, exploited these events to become an imperial power. A string of successful campaigns and the passage of time led many of their complacent Greek allies to contribute money instead of military forces. The Athenians used the money to build up and staff their navy. Eventually they saw the other members of the Delian League as their subjects and demanded annual monetary contributions and other signs of submission. States that deserted the League were brought back by force, stripped of their defenses, and subordinated to Athens.

Athens' mastery of naval technology transformed Greek warfare and politics and brought great power and wealth to Athens itself. Unlike commercial ships, whose stable, round-bodied hulls were propelled by a single square sail, military vessels could not risk depending on the wind. By the late sixth century BCE the **trireme (TRY-reem)**, a sleek, fast vessel powered by 170 rowers, had become the premier warship. Athenian crews, by constant practice, became the best in the eastern Mediterranean, able to reach speeds of 7 knots and perform complex maneuvers.

The effectiveness of the Athenian navy had significant consequences at home and abroad. The emergence at Athens of a democratic system in which each male citizen had an equal share is connected to the new primacy of the fleet. Hoplites, who had to provide their own armor and weapons, were members of the middle and upper classes. Rowers, in contrast, came from the lower classes, but because they were the source of Athens' power, they could insist on full rights.

The navy allowed Athens to project its power farther than would be possible with a hoplite militia, which could be kept in arms for only short periods of time. In previous Greek wars, the victorious state normally could not occupy a defeated neighbor permanently and was satisfied with booty and, perhaps, minor adjustments to boundary lines. Athens was able to continually dominate and exploit other, weaker communities in an unprecedented way.

AP® Exam Tip

Explain the core ideas of Greek philosophy and identify examples of how those beliefs and values influenced art and architecture.

trireme Greek and Phoenician warship of the fifth and fourth centuries BCE. It was sleek and light, powered by 170 oars arranged in three vertical tiers. Manned by skilled sailors, it was capable of short bursts of speed and complex maneuvers.

Athens used its power to promote its economic interests. Its port, Piraeus (**pih-RAY-uhs**), became the most important commercial center in the eastern Mediterranean. The money collected from the subject states helped subsidize the increasingly expensive Athenian democracy as well as the construction of beautiful buildings on the Acropolis, including the majestic new temple of Athena, the Parthenon. The Athenian leader Pericles redistributed the profits of empire to the many Athenians working on the construction and decoration of these monuments and gained extraordinary popularity.

Other cultural achievements were supported indirectly by the profits of empire. Wealthy Athenians paid the production costs of the tragedies and comedies performed at state festivals, and the most creative artists and thinkers in the Greek world were drawn to Athens. Traveling teachers called *Sophists* ("wise men") provided instruction in logic and public speaking to pupils who could afford their fees. The new discipline of *rhetoric*—the construction of attractive and persuasive arguments—gave those with training and quick wits a great advantage in politics and the courts.

These new intellectual currents came together in 399 BCE when the philosopher **Socrates** (ca. 470–399 BCE) was brought to trial. A sculptor by trade, Socrates spent most of his time in the company of young men who enjoyed conversing with him and observing him deflate the pretensions of those who thought themselves wise. He wryly commented that he knew one more thing than everyone else: that he knew nothing. At his trial, Socrates easily disposed of the charges of corrupting the youth and not believing in the gods of the city. He argued that the real basis of the hostility he faced was twofold: (1) he was being held responsible for the actions of several of his aristocratic students who had tried to overthrow the Athenian democracy and (2) he was being blamed for the controversial teachings of the Sophists, which were widely believed to contradict traditional religious beliefs and undermine morality.

In Athenian trials, juries of hundreds of citizens decided guilt and punishment, often motivated more by emotion than by legal principles. The vote that found Socrates guilty was close. But his lack of contrition in the penalty phase—he proposed that he be rewarded for his services to the state—led the jury to condemn him to death by drinking hemlock. Socrates's disciples regarded his execution as a martyrdom, and smart young men such as Plato withdrew from public life and dedicated themselves to the philosophical pursuit of knowledge and truth.

This period witnesses an important stage in the transition from orality to literacy. Socrates himself wrote nothing, preferring to converse with people. His student Plato (ca. 428–347 BCE) may represent the first truly literate generation that gained much knowledge from books and habitually wrote down their thoughts. On the outskirts of Athens Plato founded the Academy, where young men could pursue a course of higher education. Yet even Plato retained traces of the orality of the world in which he had grown up. He wrote dialogues—an oral form—in which his protagonist, Socrates, uses the "Socratic method" of question and answer to reach a deeper understanding of values such as justice, excellence, and wisdom. Plato refused to write down the most advanced stages of the philosophical and spiritual training that took place at his Academy. He believed that full apprehension of a higher reality, of which our own sensible world is but a pale reflection, could be entrusted only to "initiates" who had completed the earlier stages.

The third of the great classical philosophers, Aristotle (384–322 BCE), came from Stagira in the northern Aegean. After several decades of study at Plato's Academy, he was chosen by the king of Macedonia, Philip II, who had a high regard for Greek culture, to tutor his son Alexander. Later, Aristotle returned to Athens to found his own school, the Lyceum. Of a very different temperament than the mystical Plato, Aristotle collected and categorized a vast array of knowledge. He lectured and wrote about politics, philosophy, ethics, logic, poetry, rhetoric, physics, astronomy, meteorology, zoology, and psychology, laying the foundations for many modern disciplines.

5-3c **Inequality in Classical Greece**

Athens, the inspiration for the concept of democracy in the Western tradition, was a democracy only for the relatively small percentage of inhabitants who were citizens—free adult males of pure Athenian ancestry. Excluding women, children, slaves, and foreigners, this group amounted to 30,000 or 40,000 people out of a total population of approximately 300,000—only 10 or 15 percent.

Socrates Athenian philosopher (ca. 470–399 BCE) who shifted the emphasis of philosophical investigation from questions of natural science to ethics and human behavior. He attracted young disciples from elite families but made enemies by revealing the ignorance and pretensions of others, actions that culminated in his trial and execution by the Athenian state.

▶ **Vase Painting Depicting Women at an Athenian Fountain House, ca. 520 BCE**   Paintings on Greek vases provide the most vivid pictorial record of ancient Greek life. The subject matter usually reflects the interests of the aristocratic males who purchased the vases—warfare, athletics, mythology, drinking parties—but sometimes we are given glimpses into the lives of women and the working classes. These women are presumably domestic servants sent to fetch water for the household from the public fountain. The large water jars they are filling are like the one on which this scene is depicted. Scala / Art Resource, NY

Slaves, mostly of foreign origin, constituted perhaps one-third of the population of Attica in the fifth and fourth centuries BCE, and the average Athenian family owned one or more. Slaves were needed to run the shop or work on the farm while the master attended meetings of the Assembly or served on one of the boards that oversaw the day-to-day activities of the state. The slave was a "living piece of property," required to do any work, submit to any sexual acts, and receive any punishments the owner ordained. Most Greek slaves were domestic servants, often working on the same tasks as the master or mistress. Close daily contact between owners and slaves meant that a relationship often developed, making it hard for slave owners to deny the essential humanity of their slaves. Still, Aristotle rationalized the institution of slavery by arguing that *barbaroi* (non-Greeks) lacked the capacity to reason and thus were better off under the direction of rational Greek owners.

The position of women varied across Greek communities. The women of Sparta, who were expected to bear and raise strong children, were encouraged to exercise, and they enjoyed a level of public visibility and outspokenness that shocked other Greeks. Athens may have been at the opposite extreme as regards the confinement and suppression of women. Ironically, the exploitation of women in Athens, as of slaves, made possible the high degree of freedom enjoyed by men in the democratic state. Greek men justified the confinement of women by claiming that they were naturally promiscuous and likely to introduce other men's children into the household.

Athenian marriages were unequal affairs. A new husband might be thirty, reasonably well educated, a veteran of war, and experienced in business and politics. Under law he had nearly absolute authority over the members of his household. He arranged his marriage with the parents of his prospective wife, who was likely to be a teenager brought up with no formal education and only minimal training in weaving, cooking, and household management. Coming into the home of a husband she hardly knew, she had no political rights and limited legal protection. The primary function of marriage was to produce children, preferably male. It is likely that many more girls than boys were victims of *infanticide*—the killing through exposure of unwanted children.

Husbands and wives had limited contact. The man spent the day outdoors attending to work or political responsibilities; he dined with male friends at night; and usually he slept alone in the men's quarters (see Material Culture: Wine and Beer in the Ancient World). The woman stayed home to cook, clean, raise the children, and supervise the servants, going out only to attend funerals and religious rituals and to make discreet visits to female relatives. During the three-day Thesmophoria (**thes-moe-FOE-ree-uh**) festival, the women of Athens lived together and managed their own affairs in a great encampment, carrying out mysterious rituals to enhance the fertility of the land. The appearance of assertive women on the Athenian stage is also suggestive. Although the plays were written by men and probably reflect a male fear of strong women, the playwrights must have had models in their mothers, sisters, and wives.

The inequality of men and women posed obstacles to creating a "meaningful relationship" between the sexes. To find his intellectual and emotional equal, a man often looked to other men. Bisexuality was common in ancient Greece, as much a product of the social structure as of biological inclinations. A common pattern was that of an older man wooing a youth, in the process mentoring him and initiating him into the community of adult males.

AP® Exam Tip
Identify and explain how classical belief systems reinforced existing social structures and production methods.

AP® Exam Tip
Understand the role of patriarchy in shaping gender and family relations in the imperial societies in this time period.

5-3d Failure of the City-State and Triumph of the Macedonians

The emergence of Athens as an imperial power in the half century after the Persian invasion aroused the suspicions of other Greek states and led to open hostilities between former allies. In 431 BCE the **Peloponnesian War** broke out, a nightmarish struggle between the Athenian and Spartan alliance systems that involved most of the Greek world.

This war was unlike any previous Greek war, as the Athenians used their naval power to insulate themselves from the dangers of a siege by land. In midcentury they had built three long walls connecting the city with the port of Piraeus and the adjacent shoreline. When the war began, Pericles, devising an unprecedented strategy, refused to engage the Spartan-led armies that invaded Attica each year, knowing that, as long as Athens controlled the sea lanes and was able to provision itself, the enemy hoplites must soon return to their farms and the city could not be starved into submission.

The Peloponnesian War dragged on for nearly three decades with great loss of life and squandering of resources. It sapped the morale of all Greece and ended only with the surrender of Athens after defeat in a naval battle in 404 BCE. Because the Persian Empire had bankrolled the construction of ships by the Spartan alliance, Sparta finally was able to take the conflict into Athens' own element, the sea.

The victorious Spartans, who had entered the war championing "the freedom of the Greeks," took over Athens' overseas empire until their own increasingly high-handed behavior aroused the opposition of other city-states. Indeed, the fourth century BCE was a time of nearly continuous skirmishing among Greek states. The independent polis, from one point of view the glory of Greek culture, was also fundamentally flawed because it fostered rivalry, fear, and warfare among neighboring communities.

Internal conflict in the Greek world allowed the Persians to recoup old losses. By the terms of the King's Peace of 387 BCE, to which most of the states of war-weary Greece subscribed, all of western Asia, including the Greek communities of the Anatolian seacoast, were conceded to Persia. The Persian king became the guarantor of a status quo that kept the Greeks divided and weak. Luckily for the Greeks, rebellions in Egypt, Cyprus, and Phoenicia as well as intrigues among some of the satraps in the western provinces diverted Persian attention from thoughts of another Greek invasion.

Meanwhile, in northern Greece developments were taking place that would irrevocably alter the balance of power. Philip II (r. 359–336 BCE) transformed his previously backward kingdom of Macedonia into the premier military power in the Greek world. (Although southern Greeks had long doubted the "Greekness" of the rough and rowdy Macedonians, many modern scholars regard their language and culture as Greek at base, though much influenced by contact with non-Greek neighbors.) Philip made a number of improvements to the traditional hoplite formation. He increased the striking power and mobility of his force by equipping soldiers with longer thrusting spears and less armor. Because horses thrived in the broad plains of the north, he experimented with the coordinated use of infantry and cavalry. His engineers also developed new kinds of siege equipment, including the first *catapults*—machines using the power of twisted cords to hurl arrows or stones great distances. For the first time it became possible to storm a fortified city rather than wait for starvation to take effect.

In 338 BCE Philip defeated a coalition of southern states and established the Confederacy of Corinth as an instrument for controlling the Greek city-states. Philip had himself appointed military commander for a planned all-Greek campaign against Persia, and his generals established a bridgehead on the Asiatic side of the Hellespont. Philip apparently was following the advice of Greek thinkers who had pondered the lessons of the Persian Wars of the fifth century BCE and urged a crusade against the national enemy as a means of unifying their quarrelsome countrymen.

We will never know how far Philip's ambitions extended, for an assassin killed him in 336 BCE. When **Alexander** (356–323 BCE), his son and heir, crossed into Asia in 334 BCE, his avowed purpose was to exact revenge for Xerxes's invasion a century and half before. He defeated the Persian forces of King Darius III (r. 336–330 BCE) in three pitched battles in Anatolia and Mesopotamia, and he ultimately campaigned as far as the Punjab region of modern Pakistan. After more than two centuries of domination in the Middle East, the Achaemenid Persian Empire had fallen.

Alexander the Great, as he came to be called, maintained the framework of Persian administration in the lands he conquered, recognizing that it was well adapted to local circumstances and familiar to the subject peoples. At first, he replaced Persian officials with his own Macedonian and Greek comrades. To control strategic points in his expanding empire, he established a series of Greek-style cities, beginning with Alexandria in Egypt, and settled wounded and aged former

Peloponnesian War A protracted (431–404 BCE) and costly conflict between the Athenian and Spartan alliance systems that convulsed most of the Greek world. The war was largely a consequence of Athenian imperialism. Possession of a naval empire allowed Athens to fight a war of attrition, but ultimately Sparta prevailed because of Athenian errors and Persian financial support.

Alexander King of Macedonia in northern Greece. Between 334 and 323 BCE he conquered the Persian Empire, reached the Indus Valley, founded many Greek-style cities, and spread Greek culture across the Middle East. Later known as Alexander the Great.

soldiers in them. After his decisive victory in northern Mesopotamia (331 BCE), he began to experiment with leaving cooperative Persian officials in place. He also admitted some Persians and other Iranians into his army and the circle of his courtiers, and he adopted elements of Persian dress and court ceremonial. Finally, he married several Iranian women who had useful royal or aristocratic connections, and he pressed his leading subordinates to do the same.

Scholars have reached widely varying conclusions about why Alexander adopted these policies, which were fiercely resented by the Macedonian nobility. Alexander may have operated from a combination of pragmatic and idealistic motives. He set off on his Asian campaign with visions of glory, booty, and revenge. But the farther east he traveled, the more he began to see himself as the legitimate successor of the Persian king (a claim facilitated by the death of Darius III at the hands of subordinates). Besides recognizing that he had responsibilities to all the diverse peoples who fell under his control, he also may have realized the difficulty of holding down so vast an empire by brute force and without the cooperation of important elements among the conquered peoples. In this, he was following the example of the Achaemenids.

Section Review

- The unsuccessful revolt of Greek city-states in western Anatolia led to two Persian attacks on Greece in the early fifth century BCE.

- An ambitious Athens took control of a naval empire in the Aegean. The wealth brought in by the empire subsidized Athenian democracy and culture.

- Ironically, Athenian male citizens were freed up to participate in government and politics by restricting the rights and exploiting the labor of slaves and women.

- The Spartans and their allies, frightened by the growing power of Athens, initiated the lengthy Peloponnesian War but were only able to win with Persian help.

- In the mid-fourth century BCE, Philip II made Macedonia into a military power and forcibly united the Greek city-states.

- His son Alexander the Great conquered and took over the Persian Empire.

5-4 The Hellenistic Synthesis, 323–30 BCE

How did Greeks and non-Greeks interact and develop new cultural syntheses during the Hellenistic Age?

Alexander died suddenly in 323 BCE at the age of thirty-two, with no clear plan for the succession. This event ushered in a half century of chaos as the most ambitious and ruthless of his officers struggled for control of the vast empire. When the dust cleared, the empire had been broken up into three major kingdoms, each ruled by a Macedonian dynasty—the Seleucid (**sih-LOO-sid**), Ptolemaic (**tawl-uh-MAY-ik**), and Antigonid (**an-TIG-uh-nid**) kingdoms (see Map 5.3). Each kingdom faced a unique set of circumstances, and although they frequently were at odds with one another, a rough balance of power prevented any one from gaining the upper hand and enabled smaller states to survive by playing off the great powers.

Historians call the epoch ushered in by Alexander the "**Hellenistic Age**" (323–30 BCE) because the lands in northeastern Africa and western Asia that came under Greek rule became "Hellenized"—that is, powerfully influenced by Greek culture. This was a period of large kingdoms with heterogeneous populations, great cities, powerful rulers, pervasive bureaucracies, and vast disparities in wealth—a far cry from the small, homogeneous, independent city-states of Archaic and Classical Greece. It was a cosmopolitan age of long-distance trade and communications, which saw the rise of new institutions like libraries and universities, new kinds of scholarship and science, and the cultivation of sophisticated tastes in art and literature.

The Seleucids, who took over the bulk of Alexander's conquests, faced the greatest challenges. The Indus Valley and Afghanistan soon split off, and over the course of the third and second centuries BCE Iran was lost to the Parthians. From their capital at Syrian Antioch (**AN-tee-awk**), the Seleucid monarchs controlled Mesopotamia, Syria, and parts of Anatolia. Their sprawling territories were open to attack from many directions, and, like the Persians before them, they had to deal with many ethnic groups organized under various political and social forms. In the countryside, where most of the native peoples resided, the Seleucids largely maintained the Persian administrative system. They also continued Alexander's policy of founding Greek-style cities throughout their domains. These cities served as administrative centers and were also used to attract colonists from Greece, since the Seleucids needed Greek soldiers, engineers, and administrators.

The dynasty of the **Ptolemies** (**TAWL-uh-meze**) ruled Egypt and sometimes laid claim to adjacent Syria-Palestine. The people of Egypt belonged to only one ethnic group and were easily controlled because the vast majority were farmers in villages alongside the Nile. The Ptolemies

AP® Exam Tip
Be familiar with how unity was imposed on the diverse Hellenistic empire in this time period.

Ptolemies The Macedonian dynasty, descended from one of Alexander the Great's officers, that ruled Egypt for three centuries (323–30 BCE). From their magnificent capital at Alexandria on the Mediterranean coast, the Ptolemies largely took over the system created by Egyptian pharaohs to extract the wealth of the land, rewarding Greeks and Hellenized non-Greeks serving in the military and administration.

Hellenistic Age Historians' term for the era, usually dated 323–30 BCE, in which Greek culture spread across western Asia and northeastern Africa after the conquests of Alexander the Great. The period ended with the fall of the last major Hellenistic kingdom to Rome, but Greek cultural influence persisted until the spread of Islam in the seventh century CE.

▲ **Life on the Nile in Hellenistic Egypt** This scene is part of a floor mosaic, from a first century BCE sanctuary in Italy, depicting a panoramic view of life on the Nile. Hippos, crocodiles, and other Egyptian wildlife and plants, as well as Egyptian- and Greek-style buildings, reflect an exotic view of life in the countryside enjoyed by urban Ptolemaic and Roman viewers. Here we see an oar-powered warship, a commercial sailing vessel, and several small rowboats, as well as people involved in various everyday activities. Italy, Lazio, Palestrina, Sanctuary at Praeneste, Mosaic work depicting a sailing scene along the Nile/DE AGOSTINI EDITORE/Bridgeman Images

essentially perfected an administrative structure devised by the Egyptian pharaohs to extract the surplus wealth of this populous and productive land. The Egyptian economy was centrally planned and highly controlled. Vast revenues poured into the royal treasury from rents (the king owned most of the land), taxes of all sorts, and royal monopolies on olive oil, salt, papyrus, and other key commodities.

The Ptolemies ruled from **Alexandria**, the first of the new cities laid out by Alexander himself. Whereas Memphis and Thebes, the capitals of ancient Egypt, had been located upriver, Alexandria was situated where the westernmost branch of the Nile runs into the Mediterranean Sea, linking Egypt and the Mediterranean world. In the language of the bureaucracy, Alexandria was technically "beside Egypt" rather than in it, as if to emphasize the gulf between rulers and subjects.

The Ptolemies also encouraged the immigration of Greeks from the homeland and, in return for their skills and collaboration in the military or civil administration, gave them land and a privileged position in the new society. But the Ptolemies did not plant Greek-style cities throughout the Egyptian countryside. Only the last Ptolemy, Queen Cleopatra (r. 51–30 BCE), even bothered to learn the language of her Egyptian subjects. Periodic insurrections in the countryside were signs of the Egyptians' growing resentment of the Greeks' exploitation and arrogance.

Alexandria City on the Mediterranean coast of Egypt founded by Alexander. It became the capital of the Hellenistic kingdom of the Ptolemies. It contained the famous Library and the Museum, a center for leading scientific and literary figures. Its merchants engaged in trade with areas bordering the Mediterranean Sea and the Indian Ocean.

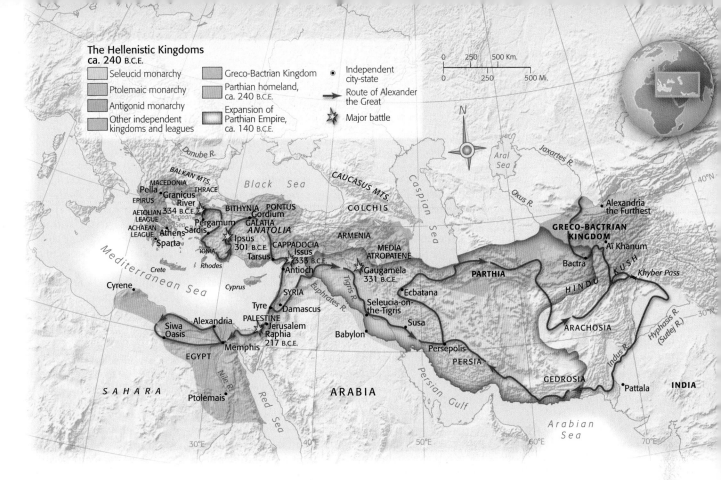

MAP 5.3   Hellenistic Civilization   After the death of Alexander the Great in 323 BCE, his vast empire soon split apart into a number of large and small political entities. A Macedonian dynasty was established on each continent: the Antigonids ruled the Macedonian homeland and tried with varying success to extend their control over southern Greece; the Ptolemies ruled Egypt; and the Seleucids inherited the majority of Alexander's conquests in Asia, though they lost control of the eastern portions because of the rise of the Parthians of Iran in the third and second centuries BCE. This period saw Greeks migrating in large numbers from their overcrowded homeland to serve as a privileged class of soldiers and administrators on the new frontiers, where they replicated the lifestyle of the city-state.

How did their geographical circumstances create different challenges and opportunities for the rulers of the three major Hellenistic kingdoms?

The Antigonid dynasty ruled a compact and ethnically homogeneous kingdom in the Macedonian homeland and northern Greece. Garrisons at strong-points gave the Antigonids a toehold in central and southern Greece, and the shadow of Macedonian intervention always hung over the south. The southern states met the threat by banding together into confederations, such as the Achaean (**uh-KEY-uhn**) League in the Peloponnese, in which member-states maintained local autonomy but pooled resources and military power.

Athens and Sparta, the two leading cities of the Classical period, stood out from these confederations. The Spartans clung to the myth of their own invincibility and made a number of heroic but futile stands against Macedonian armies. Athens, which held a special place in the hearts of all Greeks because of the artistic and literary accomplishments of the fifth century BCE, pursued a policy of neutrality. The city became a large museum, filled with the relics and memories of a glorious past, as well as a university town that attracted the children of the well-to-do from all over the Mediterranean and western Asia.

In an age of cities, the greatest city of all was Alexandria, with a population of nearly half a million. At its heart was the royal compound, containing the palace and administrative buildings, as well as the magnificent Mausoleum of Alexander. (The first Ptolemy had stolen the body of Alexander on its way back to Macedonia for burial, seeking legitimacy for his dynasty by claiming the blessing of the great conqueror, who was declared to be a god.) Two harbors linked the commerce of the Mediterranean with the Red Sea and Indian Ocean. A great lighthouse—the first of its kind, a multistory tower with a fiery beacon visible at a distance of 30 miles (48 kilometers)—was one of the wonders of the ancient world.

AP® Exam Tip
Explain how and why economic, social, cultural, and geographical factors have influenced the process of state building and expansion.

Long before the advent of writing, people studied the appearance and movement of objects in the sky and used this information for a variety of purposes. Ancient hunters, herders, and farmers all coordinated their activities with the cycle of seasons during the year so that they could follow the migrations of prey, find appropriate pastures for domestic animals, and perform vital agricultural tasks.

Ancient farmers drew on an intimate knowledge of the night sky. Hesiod (**HEE-see-uhd**), who lived around 700 BCE, composed a poem called *Works and Days* describing the annual cycle of tasks on a Greek farm. How did the ancient Greeks, with no clocks, calendars, or newspapers, know where they were in the cycle of the year? They oriented themselves by close observation of natural phenomena such as the movements of planets, stars, and constellations in the night sky. Hesiod gives the following advice for determining the proper times for planting and harvesting grain:

Pleiades rising in the dawning sky, Harvest is nigh.
Pleiades setting in the waning night, Plowing is right.

The Pleiades (**PLEE-uh-dees**) are a cluster of seven stars visible to the naked eye. The ancient Greeks observed that individual stars, clusters, and constellations moved from east to west during the night and appeared in different parts of the sky at different times of the year. (In fact, the apparent movement of the stars is due to the earth's rotation on its axis and orbit around the sun against a background of unmoving stars.) Hesiod is telling his audience that, when the Pleiades appear above the eastern horizon just before the light of the rising sun makes all the other stars invisible (in May on the modern calendar), a sensible farmer will cut down his grain crop. Some months later (in our September), when the Pleiades dip below the western horizon just before sunrise, it is time to plow the fields and plant seeds for the next year's harvest.

Farmers such as Hesiod were primarily concerned with the seasons of the year. However, there was also a need to divide the year up into smaller units. The moon, so easily visible in the night sky and with clear phases, offered the unit of the month. Unfortunately, the lunar and solar cycles do not fit comfortably together, since twelve lunar months falls eleven days short of the solar cycle of a 365-day year. Ancient peoples wrestled with ways of reconciling the two cycles, and the months of varying lengths and leap years in our present-day calendar are the legacy of this dilemma.

The complex societies that arose from the fourth millennium BCE onward had additional needs for information derived from astronomical observation, and these needs reflected the distinctive characteristics of those societies. In ancient Egypt an administrative calendar was essential for record keeping and the regular collection of taxes by the government. The Egyptians discovered that a calendar based on lunar months could be kept in harmony with the solar year by inserting an extra month five times over a nineteen-year cycle. They also learned from experience that the flooding of the Nile River—so vital for Egyptian agriculture—happened at the time when Sirius, the brightest star in the sky, rose above the eastern horizon just before the sun came up.

In the second millennium BCE, the Babylonians began to make and record very precise naked-eye observations of the movements of the sun, the moon, and the visible planets, of occasional eclipses, and of other unusual celestial occurrences. Believing that the phenomena they saw in the sky sometimes contained messages and warnings of disaster, the rulers supported specialists who observed, recorded, and interpreted these "signs" from the gods. Using a sophisticated system of mathematical notation, they figured out the regularities of certain cycles and were able to predict future occurrences of eclipses and the movements of the planets.

Alexandria gained further luster from its famous Library, with several hundred thousand volumes, and from its Museum, or "House of the Muses" (divinities who presided over the arts and sciences), a research institution supporting the work of the greatest poets, philosophers, doctors, and scientists of the day. These well-funded institutions made possible significant advances in sciences such as mathematics, medicine, and astronomy (see Environment & Technology: Ancient Astronomy).

Greek residents of Alexandria enjoyed citizenship in a Greek-style polis with an Assembly, a Council, and officials who dealt with local affairs. Public baths and shaded arcades offered places to relax and socialize with friends. Old plays were revived in the theaters, and musical performances and demonstrations of oratory took place in the concert halls. Gymnasia, besides providing facilities for exercise, were where young men of the privileged classes were schooled in athletics, music, and literature. Jews had their own civic government, officials, and law courts and predominated in two of the five main residential districts. Other quarters were filled with the sights, sounds, and smells of ethnic groups from Syria, Anatolia, and the Egyptian countryside.

In all the Hellenistic states, ambitious members of the indigenous populations learned the Greek language and adopted elements of Greek lifestyle, since this put them in a position to become part of the privileged and wealthy ruling class. For the ancient Greeks, to be Greek was primarily a matter of language and lifestyle rather than physical traits. In the Hellenistic Age there was a spontaneous synthesis of Greek and indigenous ways. Egyptians migrated to Alexandria, and Greeks and Egyptians intermarried in the villages of the countryside. Greeks

▲ **Tower of the Winds, Athens, Second Century BCE**   Designed in the Hellenistic period by the astronomer Andronicus of Cyrrhus, the eight sides are decorated with images of the eight directional winds. Sundials on the exterior showed the time of day, and a water-driven mechanism inside the tower revealed the hours, days, and phases of the moon.   De Agostini/Getty Images

Whereas Babylonian science observed and recorded data, Greek philosophers tried to figure out why the heavenly bodies moved as they did and what the actual structure of the *kosmos* (Greek for an "orderly arrangement") was. Aristotle pointed out that because the earth's shadow, as seen on the face of the moon during a lunar eclipse, was curved, the earth must be a sphere. Eratosthenes (**eh-ruh-TOSS-thih-nees**) made a surprisingly accurate calculation of the circumference of the earth. Aristarchus (**ah-ris-TAWR-kiss**) calculated the distances and relative sizes of the moon and sun. He also argued against the prevailing notion that the earth was the center of the universe, asserting that the earth and other planets revolved around the sun. Other Greek theorists pictured the earth as a sphere at the center of a set of concentric spheres that rotated, carrying along the seven visible "planets"—the moon, Mercury, Venus, the sun, Mars, Jupiter, and Saturn—with the outermost ring containing the stars that maintain a fixed position relative to one another.

As a result of the conquests of Alexander the Great, Mesopotamia came under Greek control and Greek astronomers gained access to the many centuries of accumulated records of Babylonian observers. This more precise information allowed Greek thinkers to further refine their models for the structure and movement of celestial objects. The Greek conception of the universe, in the form set down by the second-century CE astronomer Claudius Ptolemy, became the basis of scientific thinking about these matters for the next 1,400 years in the Islamic Middle East and Christian Europe.

Questions for Analysis

1. Why did ancient farmers like Hesiod pay close attention to the night sky?

2. How did ancient peoples deal with the discrepancies created by the different lengths of solar and lunar calendars, and what traces of their solutions are found in our modern calendar?

3. Why did the Babylonians keep careful records of the movement of objects in the sky, and what did Greek astronomers do with this data?

Source: From *Hesiod: Works and Days and Theogony,* trans. by Stanley Lombardo. Copyright © 1993. Reprinted by permission of Hackett Publishing Company.

living amid the monuments and descendants of the ancient civilizations of Egypt and western Asia were exposed to the mathematical and astronomical wisdom of Mesopotamia, the elaborate mortuary rituals of Egypt, and the many attractions of foreign religious cults. With little official planning or blessing, stemming for the most part from the day-to-day experiences and actions of ordinary people, a great multicultural experiment unfolded as Greek and Middle Eastern cultural traits clashed and merged.

5-5 Conclusion

Profound changes took place in the lands of the eastern Mediterranean and western Asia in the first millennium BCE, with Persians and Greeks playing pivotal roles. Let us compare the impacts of these two peoples and assess the broad significance of these centuries.

The empire of the Achaemenid Persians was the largest empire yet to appear in the world, encompassing a wide variety of landscapes, peoples, and social, political, and

Section Review

- In the Hellenistic Age, Greeks controlled western Asia and northwest Africa. Greek culture would have a strong influence in this region for a thousand years.

- Alexander's empire was broken up into three major successor kingdoms in Europe, Asia, and Africa, each with its own unique challenges.

- Alexandria in Egypt, capital of the Ptolemies, was the greatest city in the world. It had a large and diverse population and was a center of commerce for the Mediterranean Sea and Indian Ocean.

- The Ptolemies created the greatest library of antiquity and the Museum, a center of research fostering advances in scholarship, science, technology, and medicine.

- Ambitious and elite members of indigenous peoples learned Greek and adopted a Greek lifestyle in order to be part of the privileged ruling class, while Greeks borrowed from the ancient heritages of Egypt and Mesopotamia.

economic systems. How did the Persians control this diverse collection of lands for more than two centuries? The answer did not lie entirely in brute force. The Persian government demonstrated flexibility and tolerance in its handling of the laws, customs, and beliefs of subject peoples. Persian administration, superimposed on top of local structures, left a considerable role for native institutions.

The Persians also displayed a flair for public relations. Their brand of Zoroastrian religion underlined the authority of the king as the appointee of god, champion of justice, and defender of world order against evil and destructive forces. In their art and inscriptions, the Persian kings broadcast an image of a benevolent empire in which the dependent peoples gladly contributed to the welfare of the realm.

Western Asia underwent significant changes in the period of Persian supremacy. By imposing a uniform superstructure of law and administration and by providing security and stability, the Persian government fostered prosperity, at least for some. It also organized labor on a large scale to construct an expanded water distribution network and work the extensive estates of the Persian royal family and nobility.

Most difficult to assess is the cultural impact of Persian rule. A new synthesis of the long-dominant culture of Mesopotamia with Iranian elements is most visible in the art, architecture, and inscriptions of the Persian monarchs. The Zoroastrian religion may have spread across the empire and influenced other religious traditions, such as Judaism, but Zoroastrianism does not appear to have had broad, popular appeal. The Persian administration relied heavily on the scribes and written languages of its Mesopotamian, Syrian, and Egyptian subjects, and literacy remained the preserve of a small, professional class. Thus the Persian language does not seem to have been widely adopted by inhabitants of the empire.

Nearly two centuries of trouble with the Greeks on their western frontier vexed the Persians, but they were primarily concerned with the security of their eastern and northeastern frontiers, where they were vulnerable to attack by the nomads of Central Asia. The technological differences between Greece and Persia were not great. The only significant difference was the hoplite arms and military formation used by the Greeks, which often allowed them to prevail over the Persians. The Persian king's response in the later fifth and fourth centuries BCE was to hire Greek mercenaries to employ hoplite tactics for his benefit.

Alexander's conquests brought changes to the Greek world almost as radical as those experienced by the Persians. Greeks spilled out into the sprawling new frontiers in northeastern Africa and western Asia, and the independent city-state became inconsequential in a world of large kingdoms. The centuries of Greek domination had a far more pervasive cultural impact on the Middle East than did the Persian period. Whereas Alexander had been inclined to preserve the Persian administrative apparatus, leaving native institutions and personnel in place, his successors relied almost exclusively on a privileged class of Greek soldiers, officers, and administrators.

Equally significant were the foundation of Greek-style cities, which exerted a powerful cultural influence on important elements of the native populations and a system of easily learned alphabetic Greek writing, which led to more widespread literacy and more effective dissemination of information. The result was that the Greeks had a profound impact on the peoples and lands of the Middle East, and Hellenism persisted as a cultural force for a thousand years. And even after Islam spread over this region in the seventh century CE, it absorbed and maintained elements of the Hellenistic legacy (see Chapter 10).

Key Terms

Cyrus p. 115	polis p. 122	Herodotus p. 128	Peloponnesian War p. 134
Darius I p. 116	hoplite p. 122	Pericles p. 129	Alexander p. 134
satrap p. 117	tyrant p. 124	Persian Wars p. 130	Hellenistic Age p. 135
Persepolis p. 118	democracy p. 124	trireme p. 131	Ptolemies p. 135
Zoroastrianism p. 118	sacrifice p. 124	Socrates p. 132	Alexandria p. 136

Review Questions

1. What methods of administration and control for an empire of unprecedented size and diversity were created by the Achaemenid Persians and largely adopted by their Hellenistic Greek (and eventually Roman) successors?

2. How did the more than two-century-long conflict of the Greek city-states with the superpower Persian Empire shape the evolution of Greek civilization?

3. How was the freedom of some Greeks made possible by the suppression of the freedom of others?

4. In the Hellenistic world, with its scattering of Greek cities across a sea of indigenous peoples of northeast Africa and western Asia, which non-Greek groups had the greatest exposure to Greek culture, and what were their motivations to Hellenize, that is, to embrace elements of Greek language and culture?

 MINDTAP From Cengage

MindTap® is a fully online, personalized learning experience built upon Cengage Learning content. MindTap® combines student learning tools—readings, multimedia, activities, and assessments—into a singular Learning Path that guides students through the course and helps students develop the critical thinking, analysis, and communication skills that are essential to academic and professional success.

AP® REVIEW QUESTIONS FOR CHAPTER 5

Multiple-Choice Questions

Questions 1–3 refer to the map below.

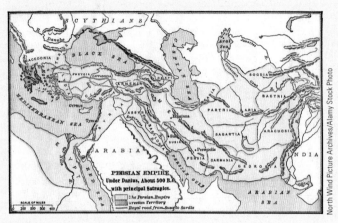

North Wind Picture Archives/Alamy Stock Photo

1. King Darius divided the Persian Empire shown on the map into provinces because they

   (A) reflected the importance of each area based on its size.

   (B) allowed local governors to rule independently.

   (C) were used for local government and to provide tributes.

   (D) were designed purely for military purposes.

2. The location of the Persian Empire in an arid region resulted in

   (A) massive dam-building on major rivers.

   (B) an economy that was based on mineral production rather than agriculture.

   (C) mass migration into neighboring Bactria and Macedonia.

   (D) construction of subterranean irrigation channels.

3. Which of the following was a major difference between Ancient Greece and Ancient Persia that can be inferred from the map?

   (A) Greece was more politically unified than Persia.

   (B) Greek trade was mainly maritime while Persian trade was mainly overland.

   (C) Greece was more mountainous than Persia.

   (D) Greek society was more patriarchal than Persian.

Questions 4–6 refer to the passages below.

"By the grace of Ahuramazda am I king; Ahuramazda has granted me my kingdom.... Within these lands, whosoever was friend, him I have surely protected; whosoever was hostile, him I have utterly destroyed.... What a man does or performs, according to his ability, by that I become satisfied with him ... and I give much to loyal men."

> A proclamation from Darius, carved into a cliff in northwest Iran, ca. 500 BCE

"It is true that we are called a democracy, for the administration is in the hands of the many and not the few. But while the law secures equal justice to all alike in their private disputes, the claim of excellence is also recognized; and when a citizen is in any way distinguished, he is preferred to the public service, not as a matter of privilege, but as the reward of merit."

> A funeral oration given by Pericles, the leader of Athens, ca. 1450 BCE

4. What is the most important difference between the types of political organization advocated by Darius and Pericles?

   (A) Darius is dictatorial over the Persians, while Pericles believes in the equality of all Athenians.

   (B) Darius believes all Persians should be rewarded, while Pericles believes only certain Athenians deserve benefits.

   (C) Darius believes he has a divine right to rule, whereas Pericles was chosen by the citizens.

   (D) Darius is less committed than Pericles to the concept of loyalty to the state.

5. Why is Pericles's speech *not* a true reflection of Athenian politics at the time when he came to power?

   (A) Athens was run by an oligarchy of rich landowners.

   (B) Pericles had seized power and was ruling as a despot.

   (C) Pericles had been appointed by the winning side in a bloody civil war.

   (D) Only certain male citizens could vote in Athens.

6. Which statement best analyzes why Pericles and Darius governed their states in different ways?

   (A) The Greeks were more united than the Persians so their leadership could be more *laissez-faire*.

   (B) The social equality between Athenians created a system where rights could be equally shared, whereas Persia was more socially stratified.

   (C) The democratic nature of Athens was only possible because of its small size, whereas the Persian Empire was larger and more populous.

   (D) The constant threat of warfare in Greece made the Greeks think more militantly, while the lasting peace in Persia supported peace.

Questions 7–10 refer to the passage below.

"The classical civilizations began to emerge as early as the mid-sixth century B.C.E., with the appearance of the Achaemenid dynasty in Persia. Both the volume of cross-cultural trade and the intensity of cross-cultural interactions increased particularly during Hellenistic times, as classical civilizations in Persia and the Mediterranean basin engaged each other politically, militarily, economically, and culturally. Prominent venues of cross-cultural interaction were the many cities."

Jerry H. Bentley, "Cross-Cultural Interaction and Periodization in World History," 1996

7. Which of the following could be construed as a foundational cause for the increasing cross-cultural interactions discussed in the passage?

    (A) There was an increase in the number of religions practiced throughout Eurasia.

    (B) The conflicts that plagued Eurasia eventually led to increased isolation allowing the rest of the world to trade.

    (C) There was cultural homogeneity in both the Mediterranean basin and in Southwest Asia.

    (D) The introduction of coinage made trade easier, leading to increased exchange and record keeping.

8. An example of cross-cultural interaction is how the Greeks acquired their writing and record-keeping system from

    (A) Indo-European invasions.

    (B) trade with the Phoenicians.

    (C) expansion into Persian-occupied Thrace.

    (D) Mycenaean pottery.

9. Which of the following is an example of the cross-cultural exchanges referenced in the passage?

    (A) Vedic beliefs developing from Christianity

    (B) Greek religion as a codification of tribal beliefs

    (C) The impact of Zoroastrianism on Judaism

    (D) The complete lack of Macedonian religious beliefs

10. One example of cross-cultural interactions that supports the claims made in the excerpt is

    (A) Classical Greek design of the Acropolis and Pantheon

    (B) Alexander the Great's marriages to Iranian women to solidify political alliances

    (C) Athenian view of themselves as the defenders of the Greek homeland

    (D) The length of the Peloponnesian War

Short-Answer Questions

1. Answer all parts of the question that follows.

    (A) Identify ONE similarity between Athens and Sparta between 1000 BCE and 300 BCE.

    (B) Identify ONE difference between Athens and Sparta between 1000 BCE and 300 BCE.

    (C) Identify and explain ONE cause for a difference in development between Athens and Sparta between 1000 BCE and 300 BCE.

"[Alexander] began to adapt his own style of living more closely to that of the country and tried to reconcile Asiatic and Macedonian customs: he believed that if the two traditions could be blended his authority would be more securely established when he was far away. . . . For this reason he selected thirty thousand boys and gave orders that they should be taught to speak the Greek language and to use Macedonian weapons. . . . His marriage to Roxane was a love match . . . but it also played a great part in furthering his policy of reconciliation. The (Persians) were encouraged by the feeling of partnership which their alliance created, and they were completely won over by Alexander's moderation and courtesy."

Plutarch, *The Age of Alexander*, 75 CE

2. Use the passage above and your knowledge of world history to answer all parts of the question that follows.

    (A) Identify ONE method Alexander of Macedon used to establish control over the regions he conquered.

    (B) Identify ONE method Alexander of Macedon used to maintain control over the regions he conquered.

    (C) Explain ONE effect of Alexander of Macedon's control over the regions he conquered.

6

An Age of Empires: Rome and Han China, 753 BCE–330 CE

CHAPTER OUTLINE

6-1 Rome's Creation of a Mediterranean Empire, 753 BCE–330 CE

6-2 The Origins of Imperial China, 221 BCE–220 CE

6-3 Conclusion

➤ **DIVERSITY & DOMINANCE**
Socioeconomic Mobility: Winners and Losers in Imperial Rome and Han China

➤ **ENVIRONMENT & TECHNOLOGY**
Ancient Glass

AP® Framework Terms

Roman Empire
Christianity
Jesus of Nazareth
Syncretism
Emperor Constantine
Qin Empire
Han Empire
Eurasian Silk Road

AP® Exam Tip

Comparisons of Han China and Rome are frequent on the AP® World History exam.

Overarching Questions

1 How and why have religions, belief systems, philosophies, and ideologies originated, developed, and spread as a result of expanding communication and exchange networks? (CUL)

2 How have religions, belief systems, philosophies, and ideologies affected the political, economic, and social development of societies? (CUL)

3 How and why have economic, social, cultural, and geographic factors influenced the process of state building, expansion, and dissolution? (SB)

4 How have internal and external political factors influenced the process of state building, expansion, and dissolution? (SB)

5 How have social categories, roles, and practices been maintained or challenged over time? (SOC)

According to Chinese sources, in the year 166 CE a group of travelers identifying themselves as envoys from Andun, the king of distant Da Qin, arrived at the court of the Chinese emperor Huan, one of the Han dynasty rulers. Andun was Marcus Aurelius Antoninus, the emperor of Rome. As far as we know, these travelers were the first "Romans" to reach China, although they probably were residents of one of the eastern provinces of the Roman Empire, and they probably stretched the truth in claiming to be official representatives of the Roman emperor. More likely they were merchants hoping to set up a profitable trading arrangement at the source of the silk so highly prized in the West (see Environment & Technology: Ancient Glass). Chinese officials, however, were in no position to disprove their claim, since there was no direct contact between the Roman and Chinese Empires.

We do not know what became of these travelers, and their mission apparently did not lead to more regular contact between the empires. Even so, the episode raises some interesting points. First, the last centuries BCE and the first centuries CE saw the emergence of two manifestations of a new kind of empire. Second, Rome and China were linked by far-flung international trading networks encompassing the entire Eastern Hemisphere, and they were dimly aware of each other's existence.

The Roman Empire encompassed all the lands surrounding the Mediterranean Sea as well as sizable portions of continental Europe and the Middle East. The Han Empire stretched from the Pacific Ocean to the oases of Central Asia. The

▲ **Dancing Girl Wearing Silk Garment, Second–Third Century CE** This Roman mosaic depicts a musician accompanying a dancer who is wearing a sheer garment of silk imported from China. Scala / Art Resource, NY

largest empires the world had yet seen, they succeeded in centralizing control to a greater degree than earlier empires; their cultural impact on the lands and peoples they dominated was more pervasive; and they were remarkably stable and lasted for many centuries.

Thousands of miles separated Rome and Han China; neither influenced the other. Why did two such unprecedented political entities flourish at the same time? And why did they develop roughly similar solutions to certain problems? Historians have put forth theories stressing supposedly common factors—such as climate change and the pressure of nomadic peoples from Central Asia on the Roman and Chinese frontiers—but no theory has won general support. ●

6-1 Rome's Creation of a Mediterranean Empire, 753 BCE–330 CE

How did Rome create and maintain its vast Mediterranean empire?

Rome's central location contributed to its success in unifying Italy and then all the lands ringing the Mediterranean Sea (see Map 6.1). The middle of three peninsulas that jut from the European landmass into the Mediterranean, the boot-shaped Italian peninsula and the large island of Sicily constitute a natural bridge almost linking Europe and North Africa. Italy was a crossroads in the Mediterranean, and Rome was a crossroads within Italy. Rome lay at the midpoint of the peninsula, about 15 miles (24 kilometers) from the western coast, where a north–south road intersected an east–west river route. The Tiber River on one side and a double ring of seven hills on the other afforded natural protection to the site.

Italy is a land of hills and mountains. The Apennine range runs along its length like a spine, separating the eastern and western coastal plains, while the arc of the Alps shields it on the north. Many of Italy's rivers are navigable, and passes through the Apennines and through the snow-capped Alps allowed merchants and armies to travel overland. The mild Mediterranean climate affords a long growing season and conditions suitable for a wide variety of crops. The hillsides, largely denuded of cover today, were well forested in ancient times, providing timber for construction and fuel. The region of Etruria in the northwest was rich in iron and other metals.

Even though as much as 75 percent of the total area of the Italian peninsula is hilly, there is still ample arable land in the coastal plains and river valleys. Much of this land has extremely fertile volcanic soil and sustained a much larger population than was possible in Greece. While expanding within Italy, the Roman state created effective mechanisms for tapping the human resources of the countryside.

6-1a A Republic of Farmers, 753–31 BCE

Popular legend maintained that Romulus was cast adrift on the Tiber River as a baby, was nursed by a she-wolf, and founded the city of Rome in 753 BCE. Archaeological research, however, shows that the Palatine Hill was occupied as early as 1000 BCE. The merging of several hilltop communities to form an urban nucleus, made possible by the draining of a swamp on the site of the future Roman Forum (civic center), took place shortly before 600 BCE. The Latin speech and cultural patterns of the inhabitants of the site were typical of the indigenous population of most of the peninsula. However, tradition remembered Etruscan immigrants arriving in the seventh century BCE (the Etruscans, from the region north of Rome, were linguistically and culturally different and more technologically advanced than other peoples in Italy), and Rome came to pride itself on offering refuge to exiles and outcasts.

Agriculture was the essential economic activity in the early Roman state, and land was the basis of wealth. As a consequence, social status, political privilege, and fundamental values were related to land ownership. Most early Romans were self-sufficient farmers who owned small plots of land. A small number of families managed to acquire large tracts of land. The heads of these wealthy families were members of the Senate—a "Council of Elders" that played a dominant role in the politics of the Roman state. According to tradition, there were seven kings of Rome between 753 and 507 BCE. The first was Romulus; the last was the tyrannical Tarquinius Superbus. In 507 BCE members of the senatorial class, led by Brutus "the Liberator," deposed Tarquinius Superbus and instituted a *res publica*, a "public possession," or republic.

The **Republic**, which lasted from 507 to 31 BCE, was not a democracy in the modern sense. Sovereign power resided in an Assembly of the male citizens where the votes of the wealthy classes counted for more than the votes of poor citizens. Each year a slate of officials was chosen, with members of the elite competing vigorously to hold offices in a prescribed order. The culmination of a political career was to be selected as one of the two consuls who presided for a year over meetings of the Senate and Assembly and commanded the army on military campaigns.

The real center of power was the **Senate**. Technically an advisory council, first to the kings and later to the annually changing Republican officials, the Senate increasingly made policy and governed. Senators nominated their sons for public offices and filled Senate vacancies from the ranks of former officials. This self-perpetuating body, whose members served for life, brought together the state's wealth, influence, and political and military experience.

The inequalities in Roman society led to periodic conflict between the elite (called "patricians" [puh-TRISH-uhn]) and the majority of the population (called "plebeians" [pluh-BEE-uhn]), a struggle known as the Conflict of the Orders. On several occasions the plebeians refused to work or fight, and even physically withdrew from the city, in order to pressure the elite to make political concessions. One result was publication of the laws on twelve stone tablets ca. 450 BCE, which served as a check on arbitrary decisions by judicial officials. Another important reform was the creation of new officials, the tribunes (**TRIH-byoon**), who were drawn from the nonelite classes and who could veto, or block, actions of the Assembly or officials that threatened the interests of the lower orders. The elite, though forced to give in on key points, found ways to blunt the reforms, in large part by bringing the plebeian leadership into an expanded elite.

The basic unit of Roman society was the family, made up of the several living generations of family members plus domestic slaves. The oldest living male, the *paterfamilias*, exercised

AP® Exam Tip
Understand how classical empires used administrative institutions to organize their subjects, and be able to explain several examples of those institutions.

Republic The period from 507 to 31 BCE, during which Rome was largely governed by the aristocratic Roman Senate.

Senate A council whose members were the heads of wealthy, landowning families. Originally an advisory body to the early kings, in the era of the Roman Republic the Senate effectively governed the Roman state and the growing empire. Under Senate leadership, Rome conquered an empire of unprecedented extent in the lands surrounding the Mediterranean Sea.

CHRONOLOGY

	Rome	China
1000 BCE	1000 BCE First settlement on site of Rome	
500 BCE	507 BCE Establishment of the Republic	480–221 BCE Warring States Period
300 BCE	290 BCE Defeat of tribes of Samnium gives Romans control of Italy 264–202 BCE Wars against Carthage guarantee Roman control of western Mediterranean	221 BCE Qin emperor unites eastern China
200 BCE	200–146 BCE Wars against Hellenistic kingdoms lead to control of eastern Mediterranean	202 BCE Han dynasty succeeds Qin 140–87 BCE Emperor Wu expands the Han Empire 109–91 BCE Sima Qian writes history of China
100 BCE	88–31 BCE Civil wars and failure of the Republic 31 BCE–14 CE Augustus establishes the Principate	9–23 CE Wang Mang usurps throne 25 CE Han capital transferred from Chang'an to Luoyang
50 CE	45–58 CE Paul spreads Christianity in the eastern Mediterranean	99 CE Ban Zhao composes "Lessons for Women"
200 CE	235–284 CE Third-Century Crisis	220 CE Fall of Han dynasty
300 CE	324 CE Constantine moves capital to Constantinople	

absolute authority over other family members. More generally, important male members of the society possessed *auctoritas*, a quality that elicited obedience from their inferiors.

Complex ties of obligation, such as the **patron–client relationship**, bound together individuals of different classes. Clients sought the help and protection of patrons, men of wealth and influence. A patron provided legal advice and representation, physical protection, and loans of money in tough times. In turn, the client was expected to follow his patron into battle, work on his land, and support him in the political arena. Throngs of clients awaited their patrons in the morning and accompanied them to the Forum for the day's business. Especially large retinues brought great prestige. Middle-class clients of aristocrats might be patrons of poorer men. In Rome inequality was accepted, institutionalized, and turned into a system of mutual benefits and obligations.

Historical sources rarely report the activities of Roman women, largely because they played no public role, and nearly all our information pertains to the upper classes. In early Rome, a woman was like a child in the eyes of the law. She started out under the absolute authority of her paterfamilias, and when she married, she came under the jurisdiction of the paterfamilias of her husband's family. Unable to own property or represent herself in legal proceedings, she depended on a male guardian to protect her interests.

Despite these limitations, Roman women were less constrained than their Greek counterparts (see Chapter 5). Over time they gained greater personal protection and economic freedom; for instance, some employed a form of marriage that left a woman under the jurisdiction of her father and independent after his death. There are many stories of strong women with great influence on their husbands or sons who helped shape Roman history. From the first century BCE on, Roman poets confess their love for educated and outspoken women.

Early Romans believed in invisible forces known as *numina*. Vesta, the living, pulsating energy of fire, dwelled in the hearth. Janus guarded the door. The Penates watched over food stored in the cupboard. Other deities resided in nearby hills, caves, grottoes, and springs. Romans made small offerings of cakes and liquids to win the favor of these spirits. Certain gods had larger spheres of operation—for example, Jupiter was the god of the sky, and Mars initially was a god of agriculture as well as war.

The Romans labored to maintain the *pax deorum* ("peace of the gods"), a covenant between the gods and the Roman state. Boards of priests drawn from the aristocracy performed sacrifices and other rituals to win the gods' favor. In return, the gods were expected to support the undertakings of the Roman state.

When the Romans came into contact with the Greeks of southern Italy (see Chapter 5), they equated their major deities with Greek gods—for example, Jupiter with Greek Zeus, Mars with Greek Ares—and they took over the myths attached to those gods.

patron–client relationship In ancient Rome, a fundamental social relationship in which the patron—a wealthy and powerful individual—provided legal and economic protection and assistance to clients, men of lesser status and means, and in return the clients supported the political careers and economic interests of their patron.

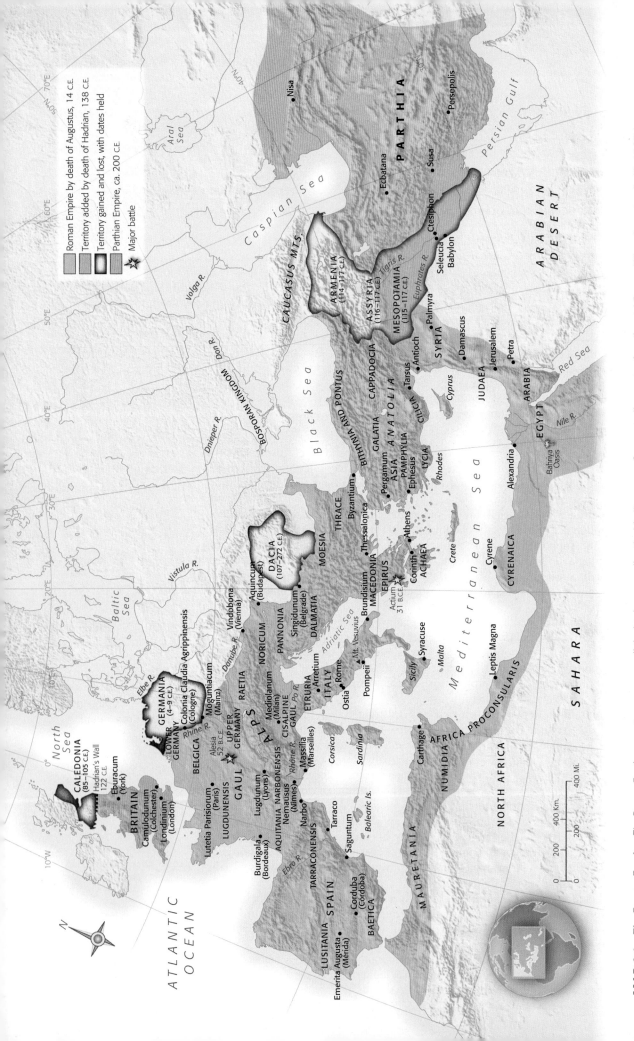

MAP 6.1   The Roman Empire The Roman Empire came to encompass all the lands surrounding the Mediterranean Sea, as well as parts of continental Europe. When Augustus died in 14 CE, he left instructions to his successors not to expand beyond the limits he had set, but Claudius invaded southern Britain in the mid-first century and the soldier-emperor Trajan added Romania early in the second century. Deserts and seas provided solid natural boundaries, but the long and vulnerable river border in central and eastern Europe would eventually prove expensive to defend and vulnerable to invasion by Germanic and Central Asian peoples.

In what ways did the expansion of Roman rule into continental Europe, the eastern Mediterranean and parts of western Asia complicate the task of administering the empire?

Legend

- Roman Empire by death of Augustus, 14 CE.
- Territory added by death of Hadrian, 138 CE.
- Territory gained and lost, with dates held
- Parthian Empire, ca. 200 C.E.
- ★ Major battle

▶ **Statue of a Roman Carrying Busts of His Ancestors, First Century BCE**   Roman society was extremely conscious of status, and the status of an elite Roman family was determined in large part by the public achievements of ancestors and living members. A visitor to a Roman home found portraits of distinguished ancestors in the entry hall, along with labels listing the offices they held. Portrait heads were carried in funeral processions. Alinari/Art Resource, NY

6-1b Expansion in Italy and the Mediterranean

Around 500 BCE Rome was a relatively unimportant city-state in central Italy. Three and a half centuries later, Rome was the center of a huge empire encompassing virtually all the lands surrounding the Mediterranean Sea. Expansion began slowly and then picked up momentum, reaching a peak in the third and second centuries BCE. Some scholars attribute this expansion to the greed and aggressiveness of a people fond of war. Others observe that the structure of the Roman state encouraged war, because the two consuls had only one year in office in which to gain military glory. The Romans invariably claimed that they were only defending themselves. The pattern was that the Romans, feeling insecure, expanded the territory under their control in order to provide a buffer against attack. However, each new conquest became vulnerable and led to further expansion.

The chief instrument of Roman expansion was the army. All male citizens owning a specified amount of land were subject to service. The Roman soldiers' equipment—body armor, shield, spear, and sword—was not far different from that of Greek hoplites, but the Roman battle line was more flexible than the phalanx, being subdivided into units that could maneuver independently. Roman armies were famous for their training and discipline. One observer noted that a Greek army would lazily seek a naturally defended hilltop to camp for the night, but a Roman army would always laboriously fortify an identical camp in the plain.

Rome's conquest of Italy was sparked by friction between the hill tribes of the Apennines, who drove their herds to seasonal grazing grounds, and the farmers of the coastal plains. In the fifth century BCE Rome led a league of central Italian cities organized for defense against the hill tribes. On several occasions in the fourth century BCE the Romans protected the wealthy and sophisticated cities of Campania, the region on the Bay of Naples possessing the richest farmland in Italy. By 290 BCE, in the course of three wars with the Samnite tribes of central Italy, the Romans had extended their "protection" over nearly the entire peninsula.

Unlike the Greeks, who were reluctant to share the privileges of citizenship with outsiders, the Romans often granted some or all of the political, legal, and economic privileges of Roman citizenship to conquered populations. They co-opted the most influential people in the conquered communities and made Rome's interests their interests. Rome demanded soldiers from its Italian subjects, and a seemingly inexhaustible reservoir of manpower was a key element of its military success. In a number of crucial wars, Rome was able to endure higher casualties than the enemy and to prevail by sheer numbers.

Between 264 and 202 BCE Rome fought two protracted and bloody wars against the Carthaginians, those energetic descendants of Phoenicians from Lebanon who had settled in present-day Tunisia and dominated the commerce of the western Mediterranean (see Chapter 3). The Roman state emerged as the unchallenged master of the western Mediterranean and acquired its first overseas provinces in Sicily, Sardinia, and Spain (see Map 6.1). Between 200 and 146 BCE a series of wars pitted the Roman state against the major Hellenistic kingdoms in the eastern Mediterranean. The Romans were at first reluctant to occupy such distant territories and withdrew their troops at the conclusion of several wars. But when the settlements that they imposed failed to take root—often because Rome's "friends" in the Greek world did not understand that they were expected to be deferential and obedient clients to their Roman patron—the frustrated Roman government took over direct administration of these lands. The conquest of the Celtic peoples of Gaul (modern France; see Chapter 4) by Rome's most brilliant general, Gaius Julius Caesar, between 59 and 51 BCE led to Rome's first territorial acquisitions in Europe's heartland.

AP® Exam Tip
Be able to discuss how classical empires grew in this time period and how they created political unity within the expanding empires.

◀ **Scene from Trajan's Column, Rome, ca. 113 CE** The Roman emperor Trajan erected a marble column 125 feet (38 meters) in height to commemorate his triumphant campaign in Dacia (modern Romania). The relief carving, which snakes around the column for 656 feet (200 meters), illustrates numerous episodes of the conquest and provides a detailed pictorial record of the equipment and practices of the Roman army in the field. This panel depicts soldiers building a fort. De Agostini Picture Library / G. Dagli Orti / Bridgeman Images

At first the Romans resisted extending their system of governance and citizenship rights to the distant provinces. Indigenous elite groups willing to collaborate with the Romans were given considerable autonomy, including responsibility for local administration and tax collection. Every year a senator who recently had held a high office was dispatched to each province to serve as governor. Accompanied by a small retinue of friends and relations who served as advisers and deputies, he was responsible for defending the province against outside attack and internal disruption, overseeing the collection of taxes and other revenues due Rome, and deciding legal cases.

Over time, this system of provincial administration proved inadequate. Officials were chosen because of their political connections and often lacked competence. Yearly changes of governor meant that incumbents had little time to gain experience or make local contacts. Although many governors were honest, some unscrupulously extorted huge sums of money from the provincial populace. While governing an ever-larger Mediterranean empire, the Romans were still relying on the institutions and attitudes that developed when Rome was merely a city-state.

6-1c The Failure of the Republic

Rome's success in creating a vast empire unleashed forces that eventually destroyed the Republican system of government. The frequent wars and territorial expansion of the third and second centuries BCE produced profound changes in the Italian landscape. Most of the wealth generated by the conquest and control of new provinces ended up in the hands of the upper classes. Italian farmers were away from home on military service for long periods of time, and while they were away, investors took over their farms by purchase, deception, or intimidation. The small, self-sufficient farms of the Italian countryside, whose peasant owners had been the backbone of the Roman legions, were replaced by *latifundia*, literally "broad estates," or ranches.

The owners of these large estates grazed herds of cattle or grew crops—such as grapes for wine—that brought in big profits, rather than growing wheat, the staple food of ancient Italy. As a result, the population in the burgeoning cities of Italy became dependent on expensive imported grain. Meanwhile, the cheap slave labor provided by prisoners of war made it hard for peasants who had lost their farms to find work in the countryside (see Diversity & Dominance: Socioeconomic Mobility: Winners and Losers in Imperial Rome and Han China). When they moved to Rome and other cities, they found no work there either, and they lived in dire poverty. The growing urban masses, idle and prone to riot, would play a major role in the political struggles of the late Republic.

One consequence of the decline of peasant farmers in Italy was a shortage of men who owned the property required for military service. At the end of the second century BCE Gaius Marius—a "new man," as the Romans called politically active individuals who did not belong to the traditional ruling class—accepted into his legions poor, propertyless men and promised them farms upon retirement from military service. These troops became devoted to Marius and helped him get elected to an unprecedented (and illegal) six consulships.

Between 88 and 31 BCE, a series of ambitious individuals—Sulla, Pompey, Julius Caesar, Mark Antony, and Octavian—commanded armies more loyal to them than to the state. Their use of Roman troops to increase their personal power led to bloody civil wars. The city of Rome was taken by force on several occasions, and victorious commanders executed opponents and controlled the state.

AP® Exam Tip
Explain the administrative difficulties faced by the Roman Republic that led to its decline and its development into the Roman Principate.

6-1d The Roman Principate, 31 BCE–330 CE

Julius Caesar's grandnephew and heir, Octavian (63 BCE–14 CE), eliminated all rivals by 31 BCE and carefully set about refashioning the Roman system of government. He maintained the forms of the Republic—the offices, honors, and privileges of the senatorial class—but fundamentally altered the realities of power. A military dictator in fact, he never called himself king or emperor, claiming merely to be *princeps*, "first among equals," in a restored Republic. Thus, the period following the Republic is called the **Principate**.

Augustus, one of the many honorific titles that the Senate gave Octavian, connotes prosperity and piety, and it became the name by which he is best known to posterity. Augustus's patience and intuitive grasp of human nature enabled him to manipulate all the groups in Roman society. When he died in 14 CE, after forty-five years of carefully veiled rule, few could remember the Republic. During his reign Egypt and parts of the Middle East and central Europe were added to the empire, leaving only the southern half of Britain and modern Romania to be added later.

Augustus allied himself with the **equites (EH-kwee-tays)**, the class of well-to-do Italian merchants and landowners second in wealth and social status to the senatorial class. This body of competent and self-assured individuals became the core of a new, paid civil service that helped run the Roman Empire. At last Rome had a governmental bureaucracy up to the task of managing a large empire with considerable honesty, consistency, and efficiency.

So popular was Augustus when he died that four members of his family succeeded to the position of "emperor" (as we call it) despite serious personal and political shortcomings. However, because of Augustus's calculated ambiguity about his role, the position of emperor was never automatically regarded as hereditary, and after the mid-first century CE other families obtained the post. In theory the early emperors were affirmed by the Senate; in reality they were chosen by the armies. By the second century CE a series of very capable emperors instituted a new mechanism of succession: each adopted a mature man of proven ability as his son and trained him as his successor.

While Augustus had felt it important to appeal to Republican traditions and conceal the source and extent of his power, this became less necessary over time, and later emperors exercised their authority more overtly. In imitation of Alexander the Great and the Hellenistic kings, many Roman emperors were officially deified (regarded as gods) after death. A cult of the living emperor developed as a way to increase the loyalty of subjects.

During the Republic a body of laws had developed, including decrees of the Senate, bills passed in the Assembly, and the practices of public officials who heard cases. In the later Republic legal experts began to analyze laws and legal procedures to determine the underlying principles; then they applied these principles to the creation of new laws required by a changing society. These experts were less lawyers in the modern sense than teachers, though they were sometimes consulted by officials or the parties to legal actions.

During the Principate the emperor became a major source of new laws. Roman law was studied and codified with a new intensity by the class of legal experts, and their interpretations often had the force of law. The basic divisions of Roman law—persons, things, and actions—reveal the importance of property and the rights of individuals in Roman eyes. The culmination of this long process of development and interpretation of the law was the sixth-century CE Digest of Justinian. Roman law has remained the foundation of European law to this day.

6-1e An Urban Empire

The Roman Empire of the first three centuries CE was an "urban" empire. This does not mean that most people lived in cities. Perhaps 80 percent of the 50 to 60 million people in the empire engaged in agriculture and lived in villages or isolated farms. The empire, however, was administered through a network of towns and cities, and the urban populace benefited most.

Numerous towns had several thousand inhabitants, while a few major cities had several hundred thousand. Rome itself had approximately a million residents. The largest cities strained the technological capabilities of the ancients; providing adequate food and water and removing sewage were always problems.

In Rome the upper classes lived in elegant townhouses on one of the hills. The house was centered around an *atrium*, a rectangular courtyard with an open skylight that let in light and rainwater for drinking and washing. Surrounding the atrium were a large dining room for

AP® Exam Tip
Compare the administrative institutions of the Roman Republic with the administrative institutions of the Roman Principate.

Principate A term used to characterize Roman government in the first three centuries CE, based on the ambiguous title princeps ("first citizen") adopted by Augustus to conceal his military dictatorship.

Augustus Honorific name of Octavian, founder of the Roman Principate, the military dictatorship that replaced the failing rule of the Roman Senate. After defeating all rivals, between 31 BCE and 14 CE he laid the groundwork for several centuries of stability and prosperity in the Roman Empire.

equites In ancient Italy, prosperous landowners second in wealth and status to the senatorial aristocracy. The Roman emperors allied with this group to counterbalance the influence of the old aristocracy and used the equites to staff the imperial civil service.

Socioeconomic Mobility: Winners and Losers in Imperial Rome and Han China

Throughout human history, most people have been born into societies in which there was little opportunity or likelihood that they could significantly improve their social or economic circumstances. However, in complex and urbanized civilizations like imperial Rome or Han China, economic advancement (which is generally linked to a higher social status) is more achievable for various reasons, including conditions of peace and stability favorable to commerce brought by the imperial power, the construction of roads over which goods can be conveyed, increased wealth and higher standards of living for many, the presence of large numbers of potential customers in urban centers, and innovative technologies for producing high-quality products. However, two further points need to be made. First, in situations of open economic competition, there are losers as well as winners. And, second, the existence of new forms of wealth and its acquisition by new groups of people tends to destabilize and threaten traditional institutions and values. We are fortunate in having texts from early imperial Rome and Han China that illustrate these processes from the vantage point of "the losers."

Juvenal wrote poetic satires at Rome in the late first and early second centuries CE. Of course satire, by its very nature, exaggerates, but to be effective and funny it has to be based on something real. The main speaker in Juvenal's Third Satire is a friend of the poet named Umbricius, who has decided to abandon the ever more dangerous and frustrating city of Rome for a quieter town on the Bay of Naples.

…'There is no room in the city
for respectable skills,' he said, 'and no reward for one's efforts.
Today my means are less than yesterday; come tomorrow,
the little left will be further reduced…
What can I do in Rome? I can't tell lies; if a book
is bad I cannot praise it and beg for a copy; the stars
in their courses mean nothing to me; I'm neither willing nor able

to promise a father's death; I've never studied the innards
of frogs; I leave it to others to carry instructions and presents
to a young bride from her lover; none will get help from me
in a theft; that's why I never appear on a governor's staff;…
Who, these days, inspires affection except an accomplice—one
whose conscience boils and seethes with unspeakable secrets?…
I shan't mince words. My fellow Romans, I cannot put up with
a city of Greeks…
They make for the Esquiline, or the willow's Hill, intent on
    becoming
the vital organs and eventual masters of our leading houses.
Nimble wits, a reckless nerve, and a ready tongue…
What of the fact that the nation excels in flattery, praising
the talk of an ignorant patron, the looks of one who is ugly…
the whole country's a play. You chuckle, he shakes with a louder
guffaw; he weeps if he spots a tear in the eye of his patron,
yet he feels no grief; on a winter's day if you ask for a brazier,
he dons a wrap; if you say 'I'm warm,' he starts to perspire.
So we aren't on equal terms; he always has the advantage
who night and day alike is able to take his expression
from another's face, to throw up his hands and cheer if his patron
produces an echoing belch or pees in a good straight line…
There's no room here for any Roman…
That same man, moreover, provides a cause and occasion
for universal amusement if his cloak is ripped and muddy,
if his toga is a little stained, and one of his shoes gapes open…
Of all that luckless poverty involves, nothing is harsher
than the fact that it makes people funny.'

Umbricius complains about the difficulty that educated, middle-class Romans like Juvenal and himself have in finding gainful employment and making a decent living. They cannot compete with the swarms of "Greeks" (by which he means people from the Greek-speaking eastern Mediterranean, which would include Greeks proper, Anatolians, Syrians, and Egyp-

dinner and drinking parties, an interior garden, a kitchen, and possibly a private bath. Bedrooms were on the upper level. The floors were decorated with pebble mosaics, and the walls and ceilings were covered with frescoes (paintings done directly on wet plaster) of mythological scenes or outdoor vistas, giving a sense of openness in the absence of windows. The typical aristocrat also owned a number of villas in the Italian countryside to which the family could retreat to escape the pressures of city life.

The poor lived in crowded slums in the low-lying parts of the city. Damp, dark, and smelly, with few furnishings, these wooden tenements were susceptible to frequent fires. Fortunately, Romans could spend much of the day outdoors, working, shopping, eating, and socializing.

The cities, towns, and even the ramshackle settlements that sprang up on the edge of frontier forts were miniature replicas of the capital city in political organization and physical layout. A town council and two annually elected officials drawn from the local elite ran regional affairs with considerable autonomy. This "municipal aristocracy" imitated the manners and conduct of Roman senators, enhancing their status by endowing their communities with attractive elements of Roman urban life—civic buildings, temples, gardens, baths, theaters, amphitheaters—and putting on games and public entertainments.

In the countryside hard work and drudgery were relieved by occasional holidays and village festivals and by the everyday pleasures of sex, family, and conversation. Rural people had to fend for themselves in dealing with bandits, wild animals, and other hazards of country life.

tians), who are such accomplished actors, flatterers, and liars that they ingratiate themselves with the rich and powerful and get all the good jobs and contracts. The real Romans, who have too much dignity to stoop to this level, are left on the outside looking in. As they descend into poverty in a city in which the cost of lodging, food, and everything else is exorbitantly high, they are scorned and humiliated.

We see in this poem a resurgence of long-standing Roman prejudice toward the Greeks. Ironically, the presence of so many Easterners in Rome is a product of the empire, both because large numbers of prisoners of war initially serving as slaves in Italy gained their freedom and Roman citizenship, and because the capital city was a magnet attracting the most able and ambitious people in the empire to come to Rome to make their fortune.

A striking Han Chinese parallel to Juvenal's Third Satire can be found in an essay on friendship written by Wang Fu. He lived in the first half of the second century CE and never obtained an official post, leading him to complain that the system was not operating with fairness.

People compete to flatter and to get close to those who are wealthy and prominent.... People are also quick to snub those who are poor and humble.... If a person makes friends with the rich and prominent, he will gain the benefits of influential recommendations for advancement in office and the advantages of generous presents and other emoluments. But if he makes friends with the poor and humble, he will lose money either from giving them handouts or from unrepaid loans.... This is the reason that crafty, calculating individuals can worm their way up the official ladder while ordinary scholars slip ever more into obscurity. Unless the realm has a brilliant ruler, there may be no one to discern this.... Alas! The gentlemen of today speak nobly but act basely. Their words are upright, but their hearts are false. Their actions do not reflect their words, and their words are out of harmony with their thoughts.... In their lofty

speeches they refer to virtuous and righteous persons as being worthy. But when they actually recommend people for office, they consider only such requirements as influence and prominence. If a man is just an obscure scholar, even if he possesses the virtue of Yan Hui and Min Ziqian, even if he is modest and diligent, even if he has the ability of Yi Yin and Lu Shang, even if he is filled with the most devoted compassion for the people, he is clearly not going to be employed in this world.

As Wang Fu sees it, men of ambition focused all their attention on cultivating the rich and powerful in order to get the recommendations that led to official appointments, and in the process they ignored their real friends, whereas men of talent who could not or would not play this game were overlooked and scorned for their poverty. While appointment to public office was supposed to be meritocratic, based, first, on knowledge of the classic Confucian texts as determined by an exam and then by performance in office, Wang Fu's essay makes clear that what mattered most was connections to powerful people and the recommendations those people made to their peers in the government.

AP® History Reasoning Skills

Comparison *In what ways were traditional institutions and values challenged by the increased socioeconomic mobility in both Imperial Rome and Han China?*

Continuity and Change Over Time *To what extent did the definition of success change with the development of complex, urbanized civilizations in Imperial Rome and Han China?*

Sources: First selection translated by Niall Rudd in *Juvenal, The Satires* (Oxford, UK: Oxford University Press, 1992). Second selection translated by Lily Hwa, in Patricia Buckley Ebrey (ed.), *Chinese Civilization, A Sourcebook*, 2d ed. (New York, NY: Free Press, 1993).

They had little direct contact with the Roman government other than occasional run-ins with bullying soldiers and the dreaded arrival of the tax collector.

The concentration of land ownership in ever fewer hands was temporarily reversed by the distribution of farms to veteran soldiers during the civil wars of the late Republic, but it resumed in the era of the emperors. However, after the era of conquest ended in the early second century CE, slaves were no longer plentiful or inexpensive, and landowners needed a new source of labor. "Tenant farmers" cultivated plots of land in return for a portion of their crops. The landowners lived in the cities and hired foremen to manage their estates. Thus wealth was concentrated in the cities but was based on the productivity of rural laborers.

Some urban dwellers got rich from manufacture and trade. Commerce was greatly enhanced by the thousands of miles of well-built roads and by the **pax romana** ("Roman peace"), the safety and stability guaranteed by Roman might. Grain, meat, vegetables, and other bulk food-stuffs usually were exchanged locally because transportation was expensive and many products spoiled quickly. However, the city of Rome imported massive quantities of grain from Sicily and Egypt to feed its huge population, and special naval squadrons performed this vital task.

Glass, metalwork, delicate pottery, and other fine manufactured products were exported throughout the empire. The centers of production, originally located in Italy, moved into the provinces as knowledge of the necessary skills spread. Other merchants traded in luxury items from far beyond the boundaries of the empire, especially silk from China and spices from India and Arabia (see Environment & Technology: Ancient Glass).

pax romana Literally, "Roman peace," it connoted the stability and prosperity that Roman rule brought to the lands of the Roman Empire in the first two centuries CE. The movement of people and trade goods along Roman roads and safe seas allowed for the spread of cultural practices, technologies, and religious ideas.

▲ **Street in Pompeii, with Mt. Vesuvius in Background** The bustling town of Pompeii on the Bay of Naples was buried in ash by the eruption of Mt. Vesuvius in 79 CE. Archaeologists have unearthed the streets, stores, and houses of this typical Roman town. Note the raised sidewalks and crossing stones that enabled pedestrians to avoid the hazards and filth posed by carts and animals in the roadway. Douglas Scott/Alamy Stock Photo

Roman armies stationed on the frontiers were a large market that promoted the prosperity of border provinces. The revenues collected by the central government transferred wealth from the rich interior provinces like Gaul (France) and Egypt, first to Rome to support the emperor and the central government, then to the frontier provinces to subsidize the armies.

Romanization—the spread of the Latin language and Roman way of life—was strongest in the western provinces, whereas Greek language and culture, a legacy of the Hellenistic kingdoms, predominated in the eastern Mediterranean (see Chapter 5). Modern Portuguese, Spanish, French, Italian, and Romanian evolved from the Latin language. The Roman government did not force Romanization; many provincials chose to adopt Latin and the cultural habits that went with it. There were advantages to speaking Latin and wearing a *toga* (the traditional cloak worn by Roman male citizens), just as people in today's developing nations see advantages in moving to the city, learning English, and wearing Western clothing. Latin facilitated dealings with the Roman administration and helped merchants get contracts to supply the military. Many also were drawn to the aura of success surrounding the language and culture of the dominant people.

The empire gradually granted Roman citizenship, with its privileges, legal protections, and exemptions from some types of taxation, to people living outside Italy. Men who completed a twenty-six-year term of service in the native military units that backed up the Roman legions were granted citizenship and could pass this coveted status on to their descendants. Emperors made grants of citizenship to individuals or entire communities as rewards for good service. Finally, in 212 CE the emperor Caracalla granted citizenship to all free, adult, male inhabitants of the empire.

The gradual extension of citizenship mirrored the empire's transformation from an Italian dominion into a commonwealth of peoples. As early as the first century CE some of the leading literary and intellectual figures came from the provinces. By the second century even the emperors hailed from Spain, Gaul, and North Africa.

Romanization The process by which the Latin language and Roman culture became dominant in the western provinces. Indigenous peoples in the provinces often chose to Romanize because of the political and economic advantages that it brought, as well as the allure of Roman success.

▲ **Roman Aqueduct near Tarragona, Spain** The growth of towns and cities challenged Roman officials to provide an adequate supply of water. Aqueducts channeled water from a source, sometimes many miles away, to an urban complex using only the force of gravity. To bring an aqueduct from high ground into the city, Roman engineers designed long, continuous rows of arches that maintained a steady downhill slope. Scholars sometimes can roughly estimate the population of an ancient city by calculating the amount of water that was available to it. Lenar Musin/Shutterstock

6-1f The Rise of Christianity

During this period of general peace and prosperity, events were taking place in the East that, though little noted at the moment, would be of great historical significance. The Jewish homeland of Judaea (see Chapter 3), roughly equivalent to present-day Israel, came under direct Roman rule in 6 CE. Over the next half century Roman governors insensitive to the Jewish belief in one god provoked opposition to Roman rule. Many waited for the arrival of the Messiah, the "Anointed One," a military leader who would drive out the Romans and liberate the Jewish people.

This is the context for the career of **Jesus**, a young Jewish carpenter from the Galilee region in northern Israel. Since the portrait of Jesus found in the New Testament largely reflects the viewpoint of followers a half century after his death, it is difficult to determine the motives and teachings of the historical Jesus. Some experts believe that he was essentially a rabbi, or teacher. Offended by Jewish religious and political leaders' excessive concern with money and power and by the perfunctory nature of mainstream Jewish religious practice in his time, he prescribed a return to the personal faith and spirituality of an earlier age. Others stress his connections to the apocalyptic fervor found in certain circles of Judaism, such as John the Baptist and the community that authored the Dead Sea Scrolls. They view Jesus as a fiery prophet who urged people to prepare themselves for the imminent end of the world and God's ushering-in of a blessed new age. Still others see him as a political revolutionary, upset by the downtrodden condition of the peasants in the countryside and the poor in the cities, who determined to drive out the Roman occupiers and their collaborators among the Jewish elite.

Whatever the real nature of his mission, the charismatic Jesus eventually attracted the attention of the Jewish authorities in Jerusalem, who regarded popular reformers as potential troublemakers. They turned him over to the Roman governor, Pontius Pilate. Jesus was imprisoned, condemned, and executed by crucifixion, a punishment usually reserved for common criminals. After his death his followers, the Apostles, sought to spread his teachings among their fellow Jews and persuade them that he was the Messiah and had been resurrected (returned from death to life).

AP® Exam Tip
Understand the core beliefs of Christianity and explain how Christianity spread through the Roman empire and other parts of Afro-Eurasia.

Jesus A Jew from Galilee in northern Israel who sought to reform Jewish beliefs and practices. He was executed as a revolutionary by the Romans. Hailed as the Messiah and son of God by his followers, he became the central figure in Christianity, a belief system that developed in the centuries after his death.

Glass was a highly prized commodity in antiquity. While glass was manufactured in various places in the Eastern Hemisphere, glass production reached unparalleled heights of technological and aesthetic sophistication in the Roman Empire of the early centuries CE. It was also widely available and had many uses. The Chinese, who did not acquire this level of glass technology for another fifteen centuries, eagerly imported Roman glass. The story of this commodity illuminates the far-reaching commercial conduits that linked the empires at either end of the hemisphere.

Glassmaking originated in the Middle East in the third millennium BCE, with the earliest products being beads. By the mid-second millennium BCE the first hollow vessels were being produced in Egypt and Mesopotamia. The primary ingredient in glass is silica, usually in the form of sand, which is compounded with soda (sodium carbonate) to reduce the temperature at which the sand melts and then stabilized by calcium, which may already exist naturally in the sand as limestone particles. Early glass production was an expensive procedure, requiring access to soda and the ability to achieve high temperatures. Raw strips of glass were wrapped around a metal and clay core and heated until the strips fused. When the core was removed, the glass object was small and thick-walled. These expensive containers, used to hold perfume or other precious liquids, were only available to the rich and powerful.

A major breakthrough occurred in the late first century BCE or early first century CE with the discovery of techniques for glassblowing, that is, inflating the glass while it is in liquid form. Blown glass vessels use far less glass, have thinner walls,

and can be formed into a wide variety of shapes. A variation of the technique involved blowing into preformed molds. This technological breakthrough probably occurred along the eastern coast of the Mediterranean, at that time part of the Roman Empire. The glass industry of that era had two components. First, raw glass was produced in bulk in the eastern Mediterranean, since the major source of soda was in Egypt, and larger furnaces were developed that could produce huge glass slabs weighing many tons. Second, the raw glass was then exported to workshops throughout the empire and melted down again to produce finished objects. Glass became affordable for many more people.

A peculiarity of glass is that it can be recycled. Both archaeological evidence (e.g., shipwrecks) and texts reveal that broken glass was collected, melted back into raw glass, and turned into new objects.

Early glass was usually brightly colored (color comes from minerals introduced into the glass compound), probably in imitation of gemstones. But Romans of the first century CE developed a taste for clear, uncolored glass that imitated highly prized rock crystal. Glass was used not only for beads and dishware but also for mosaic tiles, and there was early experimentation with flat window glass. Many techniques were developed for decorating glass objects, including enameling (melting a thin layer of glass powder onto an object), creating a cameo effect by superimposing opaque glass forms on the body of a glass vessel, incising, and embedding gold foil between layers of glass.

Paul A Jew from the Greek city of Tarsus in Anatolia, he initially persecuted the followers of Jesus but, after receiving a revelation on the road to Syrian Damascus, became a Christian. Taking advantage of his Hellenized background and Roman citizenship, he traveled throughout Syria-Palestine, Anatolia, and Greece, preaching the new religion and establishing churches. Finding his greatest success among pagans ("gentiles"), he began the process by which Christianity separated from Judaism.

Paul, a Jew from the Greek city of Tarsus in southeast Anatolia, converted to the new creed. Between 45 and 58 CE he threw his enormous talent and energy into spreading the word. Traveling throughout Syria-Palestine, Anatolia, and Greece, he became increasingly frustrated with the refusal of most Jews to accept that Jesus was the Messiah and had ushered in a new age. Many Jews, on the other hand, were appalled by the failure of the followers of Jesus to maintain traditional Jewish practices. Discovering a spiritual hunger among many non-Jews, Paul redirected his efforts toward them and set up a string of Christian (from the Greek name *christos*, meaning "anointed one," given to Jesus by his followers) communities in the eastern Mediterranean.

Paul's career exemplifies the cosmopolitan nature of the Roman Empire. Speaking both Greek and Aramaic, he moved comfortably between the Greco-Roman and Jewish worlds. He used Roman roads, depended on the peace guaranteed by Roman arms, called on his Roman citizenship to protect him from the arbitrary action of local authorities, and moved from city to city in his quest for converts. In 66 CE long-building tensions in Roman Judaea erupted into a full-scale revolt that lasted until 73. One of the casualties of the Roman reconquest of Judaea was the Jerusalem-based Christian community, which focused on converting the Jews. This left the field clear for Paul's non-Jewish converts, and Christianity began to diverge more and more from its Jewish roots.

For more than two centuries, the sect grew slowly but steadily. Many of the first converts were from disenfranchised groups—women, slaves, the urban poor. They received respect not accorded them in the larger society and obtained positions of responsibility when the members of early Christian communities democratically elected their leaders. However, as the religious movement grew and prospered, it developed a hierarchy of priests and bishops and became subject to bitter disputes over theological doctrine (see Chapter 11).

As monotheists forbidden to worship other gods, early Christians were persecuted by Roman officials, who regarded their refusal to worship the emperor as a sign of disloyalty. Despite occasional government-sponsored persecution and spontaneous mob attacks, or perhaps because of them, the young Christian movement continued to gain strength and attract

▲ Roman Glass The discovery of the technique of glassblowing by the first century CE allowed Roman craftsmen to create elegant, thin-walled vessels in varied shapes and sizes. The color comes from trace elements in the sand from which the glass was made. www.BibleLandPictures.com/Alamy Stock Photo

Glass manufacturing came considerably later to East Asia than to western Asia and the Mediterranean. The earliest Chinese glass dates to the fifth century BCE and was initially used to make "eye beads," imitations of beads imported from western Asia that were composed of several layers of glass that had the appearance of an eye. The first vessels were produced during the Han period. The Chinese did not pursue the possibilities of glass to the same extent as their Roman counterparts. They seem to have used it as a less expensive alternative to jade, producing imitations of such jade objects as a special kind of disk placed in the grave of the dead and suits of scale armor, and they preferred jade-like shades of green.

Not possessing the technology of glassblowing, the ancient Chinese valued the elegant and diverse shapes of Roman glassware. One text claims that Emperor Wu (second century BCE) sent agents to the "Southern Sea" (probably India or Southeast Asia) to acquire glass, and Roman texts specify glass as an important component in the Indian Ocean trade (see Chapter 9). Roman glass, which can be distinguished from locally made glass by analysis of its chemical composition, is found in Chinese tombs of the Han era.

The author Petronius tells a story (which we should not necessarily believe) that reveals the admiration, even awe, in which this material was held. A man secured an audience with the Emperor Tiberius and proceeded to show off his remarkable invention—glass that was unbreakable—by dashing a vessel to the ground without consequence. The astute emperor immediately ordered the inventor to be executed, arguing that such a substance would reduce the value of the gold and silver in his treasury.

Questions for Analysis

1. In what ways did the invention of glassblowing change the cost, availability, and uses of glass?
2. Why did the Chinese in the era of the Han dynasty import glass from the distant Roman Empire?
3. What factors conditioned Roman and Chinese tastes for particular colors of glass?

converts. By the late third century CE its adherents were a sizable minority within the Roman Empire and included many educated and prosperous people with posts in the local and imperial governments.

The expansion of Christianity should be seen as part of a broader religious tendency. In the Hellenistic and Roman periods, a number of cults gained popularity by claiming to provide secret information about the nature of life and death and promising a blessed afterlife to their adherents. Arising in the eastern Mediterranean, they spread throughout the Greco-Roman lands in response to a growing spiritual and intellectual hunger not satisfied by traditional pagan practices. These included the worship of the mother-goddess Cybele in Anatolia, the Egyptian goddess Isis, and the Iranian sun-god Mithra. As we shall see, the ultimate victory of Christianity over these rivals had as much to do with historical circumstances as with its spiritual appeal.

6-1g Technology and Transformation

The relative safety and ease of travel brought by Roman arms and roads enabled merchants to sell their wares and early Christians to spread their faith. Surviving remnants of roads, fortification walls, aqueducts, and buildings testify to the engineering expertise of the ancient Romans. Using the labor of military personnel was one of the ways in which the Roman government kept large numbers of soldiers busy in peacetime. Some of the best engineers also served with the army, building bridges, siege works, and ballistic weapons that hurled stones and shafts.

Among the technological achievements of the Romans was the use of arches, which allow even distribution of great weights without thick supporting walls. With the invention of concrete—a mixture of lime powder, sand, and water that could be poured into molds—the Romans could create vast vaulted and domed interior spaces, unlike the rectilinear pillar-and-post construction of the Greeks. A third achievement was the **aqueduct**—a long elevated or

AP® Exam Tip
Understand the influence of technology on the growth of large political structures.

aqueduct A conduit, either elevated or underground, that used gravity to carry water from a source to a location—usually a city—that needed it. The Romans built many aqueducts in a period of substantial urbanization.

underground conduit that carried water from a source to an urban center using only the force of gravity. Made of large cut stones closely fitted and held together by mortar, aqueducts were elevated atop walls or bridges, making it difficult for unauthorized parties to tap the water line for their own use. Sections of aqueduct that crossed rivers presented the same construction challenges as bridges. Roman engineers lowered prefabricated wooden cofferdams—large, hollow cylinders—into the riverbed and pumped out the water so workers could descend and construct cement piers to support the arched segments of the bridge. When an aqueduct reached the outskirts of a city, the water flowed into a reservoir, where it was stored. Pipes connected the reservoir to public fountains and the houses of the rich in different parts of the city.

Defending borders that stretched for thousands of miles was a major challenge. Augustus advised against further expanding the empire because the costs of administering and defending subsequent acquisitions would be greater than the revenues. The Roman army was then reorganized and redeployed to reflect the shift from an offensive to a defensive strategy. At most points the empire was protected by mountains, deserts, and seas. But the lengthy Rhine and Danube river frontiers in Germany and central Europe were vulnerable, guarded only by a string of forts with small garrisons adequate for dealing with raiders. On particularly desolate frontiers, such as in Britain and North Africa, the Romans built long walls to keep out intruders.

Most of Rome's neighbors were less technologically advanced and more loosely organized and so did not pose a serious threat to the security of the empire. The one exception was the Parthian kingdom, heir to the Mesopotamian and Persian Empires, which controlled the lands on the eastern frontier (today's Iran and Iraq). For centuries Rome and Parthia engaged in a rivalry that sapped both sides without any significant territorial gain by either party.

The Roman state prospered for two and a half centuries after Augustus's reforms, but in the third century CE cracks in the edifice became visible. Historians use the term "**Third-Century Crisis**" to refer to the period from 235 to 284 CE, when political, military, and economic problems beset and nearly destroyed the Roman Empire. The most visible symptom of the crisis was the frequent change of rulers: twenty or more men claimed the office of emperor during this period. Most reigned for only a few months or years before being overthrown by rivals or killed by their own troops. Germanic tribesmen on the Rhine/Danube frontier took advantage of the frequent civil wars and periods of anarchy to raid deep into the empire. For the first time in centuries, Roman cities began to erect walls for protection. Several regions, feeling that the central government was not adequately protecting them, broke away and turned power over to a leader who promised to put their interests first.

These crises had a devastating impact on the empire's economy. Buying the loyalty of the armies and defending the increasingly permeable frontiers drained the treasury. The unending demands of the central government for more tax revenues, as well as the interruption of commerce by fighting, eroded the towns' prosperity. Shortsighted emperors, desperate for cash, secretly reduced the amount of precious metal in coins and pocketed the excess. The public quickly caught on, and the devalued coinage became less and less acceptable in the marketplace. The empire reverted to a barter economy, a far less efficient system that further curtailed large-scale and long-distance commerce.

The municipal aristocracy, once the most vital and public-spirited class in the empire, was slowly crushed out of existence. As town councilors, its members were personally liable for shortfalls in taxes owed to the state. The decline in trade eroded their wealth, and many began to evade their civic duties and even went into hiding.

Population shifted out of the cities and into the countryside. Many sought employment and protection from both raiders and government officials on the estates of wealthy and powerful country landowners. The shrinking of cities and movement of the population to the country estates were the first steps in a demographic shift toward the social and economic structures of the European Middle Ages—roughly seven hundred years during which wealthy rural lords dominated a peasant population tied to the land (see Chapter 11).

Just when things looked bleakest, one man pulled the empire back from the brink of disaster. Like many rulers of that age, Diocletian came from one of the eastern European provinces most vulnerable to invasion. A commoner by birth, he had risen through the ranks of the army and gained power in 284. The proof of his success is that he ruled for more than twenty years and died in bed.

Diocletian implemented radical reforms that saved the Roman state by transforming it. To halt inflation (the process by which prices rise as money becomes worth less), Diocletian issued an edict specifying the maximum prices for various commodities and services. He froze many

AP® Exam Tip
Understand how both internal and external factors contributed to the dissolution of classical states like the Roman Principate.

AP® Exam Tip
Understand the role Emperor Constantine played in the support and spread of Christianity.

Third-Century Crisis
Historians' term for the political, military, and economic turmoil that beset the Roman Empire during much of the third century CE: frequent changes of ruler, civil wars, barbarian invasions, decline of urban centers, and near-destruction of long-distance commerce and the monetary economy. After 284 CE Diocletian restored order by making fundamental changes.

people into professions regarded as essential and required them to train their sons to succeed them. This unprecedented government regulation of prices and vocations had unforeseen consequences. A "black market" arose among buyers and sellers who ignored the government's price controls (and threats to impose the death penalty on violators). Many inhabitants of the empire began to see the government as an oppressive entity that no longer deserved their loyalty.

When Diocletian resigned in 305, the old divisiveness reemerged as various claimants battled for the throne. The eventual winner was **Constantine** (r. 306–337), who reunited the entire empire under his sole rule by 324.

In 312 Constantine won a key battle at the Milvian Bridge near Rome. He later claimed that he had seen a cross—the sign of the Christian God—superimposed on the sun before the battle. Believing that the Christian God had helped him achieve the victory, in the following year Constantine issued the Edict of Milan, ending the persecution of Christianity and guaranteeing freedom of worship to Christians and all others. Throughout his reign he supported the Christian church, although he tolerated other beliefs as well. Historians disagree about whether Constantine was spiritually motivated or pragmatically seeking to unify the peoples of the empire under a single religion. In either case, his embrace of Christianity was of tremendous significance. Large numbers of people began to convert when they saw that Christians seeking political office or government favors had clear advantages over non-Christians.

In 324 Constantine transferred the imperial capital from Rome to Byzantium, an ancient Greek city on the Bosporus (**BAHS-puhr-uhs**) strait leading from the Mediterranean into the Black Sea. The city was renamed Constantinople (**cahn-stan-tih-NO-pul**), "City of Constantine." This move both reflected and accelerated changes already taking place. Constantinople was closer than Rome to the most-threatened borders in eastern Europe (see Map 6.1). The urban centers and middle class in the eastern half of the empire had better withstood the Third-Century Crisis than those in the western half. In addition, more educated people and more Christians were living in the eastern provinces.

The conversion of Constantine and the transfer of the imperial capital are sometimes seen as the end of Roman history. But many of the important changes that culminated during Constantine's reign had their roots in events of the previous two centuries, and the Roman Empire as a whole survived for at least another century. The eastern, or Byzantine, portion of the empire (discussed in Chapter 11) survived Constantine by more than a thousand years. Nevertheless, the Roman Empire of the fourth and fifth centuries CE was fundamentally different from the earlier empire, and it is convenient to see Constantine's reign as the beginning of a new epoch.

Section Review

- Rome's central location in Italy and the Mediterranean, and its ability to draw on the manpower resources of Italy, were important factors in its rise to empire.

- Early Rome was ruled by kings, but the Republic, inaugurated shortly before 500 BCE, was guided by the Senate, a council of the heads of wealthy families.

- Roman expansion, first in Italy, then throughout the Mediterranean, was due to several factors: the ambition and desire for glory of its leaders, weaker states appealing to Rome for protection, and Roman fear of others' aggression.

- Within Italy, and later in the overseas provinces, Rome co-opted the elites of subject peoples and extended its citizenship. Many subjects in the western provinces adopted the Latin language and Roman lifestyle.

- The civil wars that brought down the Republic were fought by armies more loyal to their leaders than to the state.

- Augustus developed a new system of government, the Principate, and while claiming to restore the Republic, he really created a military dictatorship.

- The Third-Century Crisis almost destroyed Rome, but Diocletian and Constantine saved the empire by transforming it.

- Christianity originated in the turbulent province of Judaea in the first century CE, and despite official and spontaneous persecution, it grew steadily. Constantine's embrace of Christianity in the early fourth century CE made it virtually the official religion of the empire.

6-2 The Origins of Imperial China, 221 BCE–220 CE

How did imperial China evolve under the Qin and Han dynasties?

The early history of China (described in Chapter 4) was characterized by the fragmentation that geography and political circumstances dictated. The Shang (ca. 1750–1045 BCE) and Western Zhou (1045–771 BCE) dynasties ruled over a compact zone in northeastern China. The last few centuries of nominal Zhou rule—the Warring States Period—saw frequent hostilities among a multitude of small states with somewhat different languages and cultures.

Constantine Roman emperor (r. 306–337). After reuniting the Roman Empire, he moved the capital to Constantinople and made Christianity a favored religion.

In the second half of the third century BCE one of the warring states—the **Qin (chin)** state of the Wei **(way)** River Valley—rapidly conquered its rivals and created China's first empire (221–206 BCE). Built at great cost in human lives and labor, the Qin Empire barely survived the death of its founder, **Shi Huangdi (shih wahng-dee)**. Power soon passed to a new dynasty, the **Han**, which ruled China from 202 BCE to 220 CE (see Map 6.2). Thus began the long history of imperial China—a tradition of political and cultural unity and continuity that lasted into the early twentieth century and still has meaning for the very different China of our time.

6-2a The Qin Unification of China, 221–206 BCE

From the mid-third century BCE, Qin began to methodically conquer and incorporate the other Chinese states, and by 221 BCE it had unified northern and central China in the first Chinese "empire." The name *China*, by which this land is known in the Western world, is probably derived from *Qin*. Qin emerged as the ultimate winner because of a combination of factors: the toughness and military preparedness of a frontier state long accustomed to defending itself against "barbarian" neighbors, the wholehearted adoption of severe Legalist methods for exploiting the natural and human resources of the kingdom (see Chapter 4), and the surpassing ambition of a ruthless and energetic young king.

The Qin monarch, Zheng **(jahng)**, came to the throne at the age of thirteen in 246 BCE. Guided by a circle of Legalist advisers, he launched a series of wars of conquest. After defeating the last of his rivals in 221 BCE, he gave himself a title that symbolized the new state of affairs—Shi Huangdi, or "First Emperor"—and claimed that his dynasty would last 10,000 generations.

The new regime eliminated rival centers of authority. Its first target was the land-owning aristocracy of the conquered states and the system on which aristocratic wealth and power had been based. The Qin government abolished *primogeniture*, the right of the eldest son to inherit all the landed property, requiring estates to be broken up and passed on to several heirs. A new, centrally controlled administrative structure was put in place, with district officials appointed by the king and watched over by his agents.

The Qin government's commitment to standardization helped create a unified Chinese civilization. A code of law, in force throughout the empire, applied punishments evenhandedly to all members of society. The Qin also imposed standardized weights and measures, a single coinage, a common system of writing, and even a specified axle-length for carts so that they would create a single set of ruts in the road.

Li Si **(lee suh)**, the Legalist prime minister, persuaded Shi Huangdi that the scholars (primarily Confucian rivals of the Legalists; see Chapter 4) were subverting the goals of the regime. The Legalists viewed Confucian expectations of benevolent and nonviolent conduct from rulers as an intolerable check on the government's absolute power. Furthermore, the Confucians' appeal to the past impeded the new order being created by the Qin. A crackdown on the scholars ensued in which many Confucian books were publicly burned and many scholars brutally executed.

Shi Huangdi was determined to secure the northern border against nomadic raids on Chinese territory. Pastoralists and farmers had always exchanged goods on the frontier. Herders sought food and crafted goods produced by farmers and townsfolk, and farmers depended on the herders for animals and animal products. Sometimes, however, nomads raided the settled lands and took what they needed. For centuries the Chinese kingdoms had struggled with these tough, horse-riding warriors, building long walls along the frontier to keep them away from vulnerable farmlands (see Chapter 4). Shortly before the Qin unification of China, several states had begun to train soldiers on horseback to contend with the mobile nomads.

Shi Huangdi sent a large force to drive the nomads far north. His generals succeeded momentarily, extending Chinese territory beyond the great northern loop of the Yellow River. They also connected and extended earlier walls to create a continuous fortification, the ancestor of the Great Wall of China. A recent study concludes that, contrary to the common belief that the purpose of the wall was defensive—to keep the "barbarians" out of China—its primary function was offensive, to take in newly captured territory, to which large numbers of Chinese peasants were now dispatched and ordered to begin cultivation.[1]

Qin A people and state in the Wei River Valley of eastern China that conquered rival states and created the first Chinese empire (221–206 BCE). The Qin ruler, Shi Huangdi, standardized many features of Chinese society and ruthlessly marshaled subjects for military and construction projects, engendering hostility that led to the fall of his dynasty shortly after his death. The Qin framework was largely taken over by the succeeding Han dynasty.

Shi Huangdi Founder of the short-lived Qin dynasty and creator of the Chinese Empire (r. 221–210 BCE). He is remembered for his ruthless conquests of rival states, standardization of practices, and forcible organization of labor for military and engineering tasks. His tomb, with its army of life-size terracotta soldiers, has been partially excavated.

Han A term used to designate (1) the ethnic Chinese people who originated in the Yellow River Valley and spread throughout regions of China suitable for agriculture, and (2) the dynasty of emperors who ruled from 202 BCE to 220 CE.

---

[1]Nicola Di Cosmo, *Ancient China and Its Enemies: The Rise of Nomadic Power in East Asian History* (Cambridge, UK: Cambridge University Press, 2002), 155–158.

Shi Huangdi's attack on the nomads had an unanticipated consequence. The threat to their way of life created by the Chinese invasion drove the normally fragmented and quarreling nomad groups to unite in a great confederacy under the dynamic leadership of Maodun (**mow-doon**). This **Xiongnu (SHE-OONG-noo)** Confederacy would pose a huge military threat to China for centuries, with frequent wars and high costs in lives and resources.

Needing many people to serve in the armies, construct roads and walls on the frontiers, and build new cities, palaces, and a monumental tomb for the ruler, the Qin government instituted an oppressive program of compulsory military and labor services and relocated large numbers of people. The recent discovery of a manual of Qin laws used by an administrator, with pre-scriptions less extreme than expected, suggests that the sins of the Qin may have been exaggerated by later sources. Nevertheless, the widespread uprisings that broke out after the death of Shi Huangdi attest to the harsh nature of the Qin regime.

When Shi Huangdi died in 210 BCE, several officials schemed with one of his sons to place him on the throne. The First Emperor was buried in a monumental tomb whose layout mirrored the geography of China, and the tomb was covered with a great mound of earth. Nearby

AP® Exam Tip

Analyze the importance of frontier security for each empire in the time period.

Xiongnu A confederation of nomadic peoples living beyond the northwest frontier of ancient China. Chinese rulers tried a variety of defenses and stratagems to ward off these "barbarians," as they called them, and finally succeeded in dispersing the Xiongnu in the first century CE.

MAP 6.2 Han China The Qin and Han rulers of northeast China extended their control over all of eastern China and extensive territories to the west. A series of walls in the north and northwest, built to check the incursions of nomadic peoples from the steppes, were joined together to form the ancestor of the present-day Great Wall of China. An extensive network of roads connecting towns, cities, and frontier forts promoted rapid communication and facilitated trade. The Silk Road carried China's most treasured products to Central, South, and West Asia and the Mediterranean lands.

Which geographical and ecological features helped to define the limits of the Han empire, and how does one account for the anomalous extension of Han control into the far northwest?

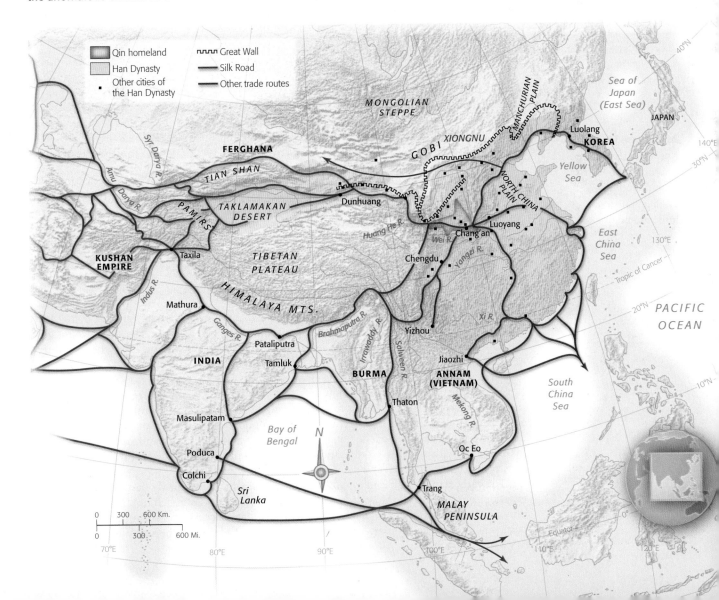

▲ **Terra-Cotta Soldiers from the Tomb of Shi Huangdi, "First Emperor" of China, Late Third Century BCE** Near the monumental tomb that he built for himself, the First Emperor filled a huge underground chamber with more than seven thousand life-size baked-clay statues of soldiers. The terra-cotta army was unearthed in the 1970s. incamerastock/Alamy Stock Photo

AP® Exam Tip
Know the pattern of growth of the Han Empire and how political unity was imposed by rulers.

were buried life-size sculptures of seven thousand soldiers to guard him in the afterlife, a more humane alternative to the human sacrifices of earlier eras. This *terra-cotta* (baked clay) army was discovered in the 1970s CE, but the burial mound remains unexcavated.

The new emperor proved to be weak. Uprisings broke out on many fronts, reflecting both the resentment of the old aristocracies that had been deprived of wealth and privilege and the anger of the commoners against excessive compulsory labor, forced relocations, and heavy taxation. By 206 BCE Qin rule had been broken—the "ten-thousand-generation dynasty" had lasted only fifteen years. Nevertheless, the most important achievements of the Qin, the unification of China and the creation of a single, widely dispersed Chinese style of civilization, would endure.

6-2b The Long Reign of the Han, 202 BCE–220 CE

Despite the overthrow of the Qin, fighting continued among various rebel groups. In 202 BCE Liu Bang (**le-oo bahng**) prevailed and inaugurated a new dynasty, the Han, that would govern China for more than four centuries (202 BCE–220 CE). The Han created the machinery and ideology of imperial government that would prevail for two millennia, and Chinese people today refer to themselves ethnically as "Han."

The new emperor, generally known by the throne name **Gaozu** (**gow-zoo**), came from a modest background. Stories stress his peasant qualities: fondness for drink, blunt speech, and easy manner. Gaozu and his successors courted popularity and consolidated their rule by denouncing the harshness of the Qin and renouncing many Qin laws. In reality, however, they maintained—with sensible modifications—many Legalist-inspired institutions of the Qin to control far-flung territories and diverse populations.

The early Han rulers faced tough challenges. China had been badly damaged by the harsh exactions of the Qin and the widespread fighting in the period of rebellions. Because the economy needed time to recover, Gaozu and his immediate successors had to be frugal, keeping costs down to reduce taxes and undertaking measures to improve the state of agriculture. For

Gaozu The throne name of Liu Bang, one of the rebel leaders who brought down the Qin and founded the Han dynasty in 202 BCE.

instance, during prosperous times the government collected and stored surplus grain that could be sold at reasonable prices in times of shortage.

Gaozu reverted to the traditional feudal grants the Qin had abolished. The eastern parts of China were parceled out to relatives and major supporters, while the rest was divided into "commanderies" directly controlled by the central government. Over the next few reigns, these fiefs were reabsorbed by the Han court as rebellions or deaths of the rulers provided the opportunity.

When Gaozu marched north to confront a Xiongnu incursion, he and his troops were trapped, and he had to negotiate a safe passage home for his army. Realizing the inferiority of Han troops and the limited funds for a military buildup, he adopted a policy of appeasing the Xiongnu. This essentially meant buying them off by dispatching annual "gifts" of rice, silk, and wine, as well as marrying a Han princess to the Xiongnu ruler.

While the throne passed to a young child when Gaozu died in 195 BCE, real power lay with Gaozu's formidable wife, Empress Lü **(lyew)**. Throughout the Han era, empresses played a key role in determining which of the many sons (the emperors had multiple wives and concubines) would succeed to the throne, and they often chose minors or weak figures whom they and their male relatives could control. Under such circumstances Wu came to the throne as a teenager in 141 BCE. The deaths of his grandmother and uncle soon opened the way for him to rule in his own right, and thus began one of the longest and most eventful reigns in the history of the dynasty (141–87 BCE).

We know much about the personality and policies of this emperor because of **Sima Qian (sih-muh chyehn)** (ca. 145–85 BCE), who created the definitive form of historical writing in China. Serving as "chief astrologer" at the Han court, Sima Qian was castrated by Wu for defending a disgraced general. He therefore presents a generally negative view, portraying Wu as being manipulated by religious charlatans promising him magical powers, immortality, and séances with the dead. Reading his account critically, however, one could also conclude that Wu used religious pageantry to boost his own power.

Indeed, Wu did much to increase the power of the emperor. He launched military operations south as far as northern Vietnam and north into Manchuria and North Korea. He abandoned the policy of appeasing the Xiongnu, concluding that this approach had failed since the nomads still made periodic attacks on the northern frontier. Wu built up his military, especially the cavalry, and went on the offensive. Thus began decades of bitter, costly fighting between China and the Xiongnu. In the long run Wu and his successors prevailed, and by the mid-first century CE the Xiongnu Confederacy had disintegrated, though nomad groups still threatened Chinese lands.

Wu dispatched forces to explore and conquer territories northwest of the Chinese heartland, essentially modern Gansu and Xinjiang **(SHIN-jyahng)**. His goals were to improve access to large numbers of horses for his expanding cavalry and to pressure the Xiongnu on their western flank. Thus began the incorporation of this region into greater China. This expansion also brought new economic opportunities, laying the foundations for the Silk Road over which silk and other lucrative trade goods would be carried to Central, southern, and western Asia (see Chapter 9).

The military buildup and frequent wars with the Xiongnu were expensive, forcing Wu to find new revenues. One solution was government monopolies on several high-profit commodities: salt, iron, and alcoholic beverages. These measures were highly controversial.

Another momentous development was the adoption of Confucianism—modified to meet the circumstances of the era—as the official ideology of the imperial system. A university was opened on the outskirts of the capital city, Chang'an **(chahng-ahn)**, and local officials were ordered to send a certain number of promising students from their districts each year. For 2,000 years Chinese government would depend on scholar-officials promoted for their performance

▲ **Gold Belt Buckle, Xiongnu, Second Century BCE**   The Xiongnu, herders in the lands north of China, shared the artistic conventions of nomadic peoples across the steppes of Asia and eastern Europe, such as this fluid, twisting representation of the animals on which they depended for their livelihood. Shi Huangdi's military incursion into their pasturelands in the late third century BCE catalyzed the formation of the Xiongnu Confederacy, whose horse-riding warriors challenged the Chinese for centuries.   The Metropolitan Museum of Art/Art Resource, NY

AP® Exam Tip

Emperor Wu was also known as Wudi. Know how Wudi, a disciple of Confucius, used Confucianism to promote social harmony throughout China.

AP® Exam Tip

Explain the role of land and water trade routes as the basis for economic and cultural exchanges in Afro-Eurasia.

Sima Qian Chief astrologer for the Han dynasty emperor Wu. He composed a monumental history of China from its legendary origins to his own time and is regarded as the Chinese "father of history."

on exams probing their knowledge of Confucian texts. This alliance of Confucians and the imperial government, fraught with tensions, required compromises on both sides. The Confucians gained access to employment and power but had to accommodate ethical principles to the reality of far-from-perfect rulers. The emperors won the backing and services of a class of competent, educated people but had to deal with the Confucians' expectation that rulers should model ethical behavior and their insistence on giving often unwelcome advice.

6-2c Chinese Society

The Chinese government periodically conducted a census of inhabitants, and the results for 2 CE revealed 12 million households and 60 million people. Then, as now, the vast majority lived in the eastern river-valley regions where intensive agriculture could support a dense population.

The fundamental unit was the family, including not only the living but all previous generations. The Chinese believed that their ancestors, whose spirits resided eternally in the supernatural sphere of the gods, maintained an interest in the fortunes of living family members; therefore, descendants consulted, appeased, and venerated the ancestors. Each generation must produce sons to perpetuate the family and maintain the ancestor cult that provided a kind of immortality to the deceased. In earlier times multiple generations and groups of families lived together, but by the imperial era independent nuclear families were the norm.

Within the family was a clear-cut hierarchy headed by the oldest male. Each person had a place and responsibilities, based on gender, age, and relationship to other family members, and people saw themselves as part of an interdependent unit rather than as individual agents. Parents' authority over children did not end with the passing of childhood, and parents occasionally took mature children to court for disobedience. The family inculcated the basic values of Chinese society: loyalty, obedience to authority, respect for elders and ancestors, and concern for honor and appropriate conduct. Because the hierarchy in the state mirrored the hierarchy in the family—peasants, soldiers, administrators, and rulers all made distinctive contributions to the welfare of society—these same attitudes carried over into the relationship between individuals and the state.

Traditional beliefs about conduct appropriate for women are preserved in a biography of the mother of the Confucian philosopher Mencius (Mengzi):

> A woman's duties are to cook the five grains, heat the wine, look after her parents-in-law, make clothes, and that is all! . . . [She] has no ambition to manage affairs outside the house. . . . She must follow the "three submissions." When she is young, she must submit to her parents. After her marriage, she must submit to her husband. When she is widowed, she must submit to her son.[2]

In reality, a woman's status depended on her "location" within various social institutions. Women of the royal family, such as wives of the emperor or queen-mothers, could be influential political figures. A young bride, whose marriage had been arranged by her parents, would go to live with her husband's family, where she was, initially, a stranger who had to prove herself. Mothers-in-law had authority over their sons' wives, and mothers, sisters, and wives competed for influence with the men of the household and a larger share of the family's resources.

"Lessons for Women," written at the end of the first century CE by Ban Zhao (**bahn jow**), illuminates the unresolved tensions in Han society's attitudes toward women. Instructing her own daughters on how to conduct themselves as proper women, Zhao urges them to conform to traditional expectations by obeying males, maintaining their husbands' households, performing domestic chores, and raising the children. Yet she also makes an impassioned plea for the education of girls and urges husbands to respect and not beat their wives.

People lived in various milieus—cities, rural villages and farms, or military camps on the frontiers—and their activities and the quality of their lives were shaped by these contexts. From 202 BCE to 25 CE—the period of the Early, or Western, Han—the capital was at **Chang'an** (modern Xi'an [**shee-ahn**]), in the Wei River Valley, an ancient seat of power from which the Zhou and Qin dynasties had emerged. Protected by a ring of hills but with ready access to the

AP® Exam Tip
Be familiar with ways the social structure was reinforced through ancestor veneration and the impact of belief systems on gender roles.

Chang'an City in the Wei River Valley on the western edge of the North China Plain. It became the capital of the early Han Empire. Its main features were imitated in the cities and towns that sprang up throughout the Han Empire.

[2]Patricia Buckley Ebrey, ed., *Chinese Civilization and Society: A Sourcebook* (New York, NY: Free Press, 1981), 33–34.

fertile plain, Chang'an was surrounded by a wall of pounded earth and brick 15 miles (24 kilometers) in circumference. In 2 CE its population was 246,000. Part of the city was carefully planned. Broad thoroughfares running north and south intersected with others running east and west. High walls protected the palaces, administrative offices, barracks, and storehouses of the imperial compound, to which access was restricted. Temples and marketplaces were scattered about the civic center. Chang'an became a model of urban planning, its main features imitated in cities and towns throughout China (it is estimated that between 10 and 30 percent of the population lived in urban centers). From 25 to 220 CE the Later, or Eastern, Han established its base farther east, in the more centrally located Luoyang (**LWOE-yahng**).

Han literature describes the appearance of the capitals and the activities taking place in the palace complexes, public areas, and residential streets. Moralizing writers criticized the excesses of the elite. Living in multistory houses, wearing fine silks, traveling in ornate horse-drawn carriages, well-to-do officials and merchants devoted their leisure time to art and literature, occult religious practices, elegant banquets, and various entertainments—music and dance, juggling and acrobatics, dog and horse races, and cock and tiger fights. In stark contrast, the common people inhabited a sprawling warren of alleys, living in dwellings packed "as closely as the teeth of a comb."

While the upper echelons of scholar-officials resided in the capital, lower-level bureaucrats were scattered throughout smaller cities and towns serving as headquarters for regional governments. These scholar-officials shared a common Confucian culture and ideology. Exempt from taxes and compulsory military or labor services, they led comfortable lives by the standards of the time. While the granting of government jobs on the basis of performance on the exams theoretically should have given everyone an equal chance, in reality the sons of officials had distinct advantages in obtaining the requisite education in classical texts. Thus the scholar-officials became a self-perpetuating, privileged class. The Han depended on local officials for day-to-day administration of their far-flung territories. They collected taxes, regulated conscription for the army and labor projects, provided protection, and settled disputes.

Merchant families were also based in the cities, and some became very wealthy. However, ancient Chinese society viewed merchants with suspicion, accusing them of greedily driving prices up through speculation and being parasites who lived off the work of others. Advisers to the emperors periodically blamed merchants for the economic ills of China and proposed harsh measures, such as banning them and their children from holding government posts.

The Western Han state required two years of military service from able-bodied males, but by the Eastern Han period the military was staffed by professional soldiers. Large numbers of Chinese men spent long periods away from home in distant frontier posts, building walls and forts, keeping an eye on barbarian neighbors, fighting when necessary, and growing crops to support themselves. Poems written by soldiers complain of rough conditions in the camps, tyrannical officers, and the dangers of confrontations with enemy forces, but above all they are homesick, missing and worrying about aged parents and vulnerable wives and children.

▲ **Silk Burial Banner from Mawangdui** This banner was placed on the coffin containing the mummified body of Lady Dai, wife of the ruler of a dependent kingdom in southern China, in the mid-second century BCE. The lower and upper portions depict the Underworld and Heaven, while the middle register shows the deceased and her family offering sacrifices to help her soul ascend to Heaven. Martha Avery/Getty Images

6-2d New Forms of Thought and Belief

The Han period was rich in intellectual developments, thanks to the relative prosperity of the era, the growth of urban centers, and state support of scholars. In their leisure time scholar-officials read and wrote in a range of genres, including poetry, philosophy, history, and technical subjects.

The Chinese had been preserving historical records since the early Zhou period. However, Sima Qian, the aforementioned "chief astrologer" of Emperor Wu, is regarded as "the father of history" in China, both because he created an organizational framework that became the standard for subsequent historical writing and because he sought the causes of events. Sima's monumental history, covering 2,500 years from legendary early emperors to his own time, was organized in a very different way from Western historical writing. It was divided into five parts: dynastic histories, accounts of noble families, biographies of important individuals and groups (such as Confucian scholars, assassins, barbarian peoples), a chart of historical events, and essays on special topics such as the calendar, astrology, and religious ceremonies. The same event may be narrated in more than one section, sometimes in a different way, inviting the reader to compare and interpret the differences. Sima may have utilized this approach to offer carefully veiled interpretations of past and present. Historians and other scholars in Han China had the advantage, as compared to their Western counterparts, of being employed by the government, but the disadvantage of having to limit their criticism of that government.

There were advances in science and technology. Widespread belief in astrology engendered astronomical observation of planets, stars, and other celestial objects. The watermill, which harnessed the power of running water to turn a grindstone, was used in China long before it appeared in Europe. The development of a horse collar that did not constrict breathing allowed Chinese horses to pull heavier loads than European horses. The Chinese first made paper, perhaps as early as the second century BCE, replacing the awkward bamboo strips of earlier eras. Improvements in military technology included horse-breeding techniques to supply the cavalry and a reliable crossbow trigger. One clever inventor even created an early seismometer to register earthquakes and indicate the direction where the event took place.

The Qin and Han built thousands of miles of roads—comparable in scale to the roads of the Roman Empire—to connect parts of the empire and move armies quickly. They also built a network of canals connecting the river systems of northern and southern China, at first for military purposes but eventually for transporting commercial goods as well. Ultimately, a network of waterways permitted continuous transport of goods between the latitudes of Beijing and Guangzhou (Canton), a distance of 1,250 miles (2,012 kilometers). Some of these canals are still in use.

Chinese religion encompassed a wide spectrum of beliefs. Like the early Romans, the Chinese believed that divinity resided within nature. Most people believed in ghosts and spirits. The state maintained shrines to the lords of rain, wind, and soil, as well as to certain great rivers and high mountains. Sima Qian devoted an essay to the connection between religion and power, showing how emperors used ancient ceremonies and new-fangled cults to secure their authority. Daoism (see Chapter 4) became popular with the common people, incorporating an array of mystical and magical practices, including *alchemy* (the art of turning common materials into precious metals such as gold) and the search for potions that would impart immortality. Because Daoism questioned tradition and rejected the hierarchy and rules of the Confucian elite classes, charismatic Daoist teachers led several popular uprisings in the unsettled last decades of the Han dynasty.

AP® Exam Tip
Explain how religions such as Buddhism were transformed as they spread.

Perhaps as early as the first century CE Buddhism (**BOOD-izm**) began to trickle into China. Originating in northern India in the fifth century BCE (see Chapter 7), it slowly spread through South Asia and into Central Asia, carried by merchants on the Silk Road. Certain aspects of Buddhism fit comfortably with Chinese values: reverence for classic texts was also a feature of Confucianism, and the emphasis on severing attachments to material goods and pleasures found echoes in Daoism. But in other ways the Chinese were initially put off by Buddhist practices. The fact that Buddhist monks withdrew from their families to live in monasteries, shaved off their hair, and abstained from sex and procreation of children was repugnant to traditional Chinese values, which emphasized the importance of family ties, the body as an inviolable gift from parents, and the need to produce children to maintain the ancestor cult. Gradually Buddhism gained acceptance and was reshaped to fit the Chinese context, a process accelerated by the non-Chinese dynasties that dominated the north after the fall of the Han.

6-2e Decline of the Han

A break in the long sequence of Han rulers occurred early in the first century CE when an ambitious official named Wang Mang (**wahng mahng**) seized power (9–23 CE). The new ruler implemented major reforms to address serious economic problems and to cement his popularity with the common people, including limiting the size of the estates of the rich and giving the surplus land to landless peasants. However, a cataclysmic flood that changed the course of the Yellow River caused large numbers of deaths and economic losses. Members of the Han family and other elements of the elite resisted their loss of status and property, and widespread poverty engendered a popular uprising of the "Red Eyebrows," as the insurgents were called. Wang Mang was besieged in his palace and killed, and a member of the Han royal family was soon installed as emperor. In 25 CE Guangwu, founder of the Eastern Han dynasty, moved the capital east to Luoyang.

The dynasty continued for another two centuries, but the imperial court was frequently plagued by weak leadership and court intrigue, with royal spouses and their families jockeying for power behind immature or ineffectual monarchs. Poems from this period complain of corrupt officials, unchecked attacks by barbarians, uprisings of desperate and hungry peasants, the spread of banditry, widespread poverty, and despair.

Several factors contributed to the fall of the Han. Continuous military vigilance along the frontier burdened Han finances and exacerbated the economic troubles of later Han times. Despite the earnest efforts of Qin and early Han emperors to reduce the power and wealth of the aristocracy and turn land over to a free peasantry, by the end of the first century BCE nobles and successful merchants again controlled huge tracts of land. Many peasants sought their protection against the demands of the imperial government, which was thereby deprived of tax revenues and manpower. The Eastern Han rulers abandoned the system of military conscription and were forced to hire more and more foreign soldiers and officers, men willing to serve for pay but not necessarily loyal to the Han state. By the end of the second century the empire was convulsed by civil wars, and in 220 CE, with the former empire broken up into three kingdoms ruled by warlords, the last Han emperor was forced to abdicate.

With the fall of the Han, China entered a period of political fragmentation that lasted until the rise of the Sui **(sway)** and Tang **(tahng)** dynasties in the late sixth and early seventh centuries CE, a story we take up in Chapter 12. In this period the north was dominated by a series of barbarian peoples who combined elements of their own practices with the foundation of Chinese culture. Many ethnic Chinese migrated south into the Yangzi Valley, where Chinese rulers prevailed, and in this era the center of gravity of both the population and Chinese culture shifted to the south.

Section Review

- The tough, disciplined frontier kingdom of Qin conquered all rival kingdoms and unified China by 221 BCE. The First Emperor and his Legalist advisers imposed standardization in many spheres and compelled the labor of many people.

- The Qin attack on the northern nomads led to the formation of the formidable Xiongnu Confederacy, which long posed a military threat to China.

- The Han dynasty added to the Qin foundation, creating fundamental patterns of imperial government that lasted for two millennia.

- Emperor Wu went on the offensive against the nomads, extended Chinese control in the northwest, and began to use Confucian scholars as government officials.

- The family, with its strict hierarchy, roles for each member, and values of deference and obedience, prepared citizens for their obligations to the state.

- The layout, buildings, and activities in the capital city, Chang'an, were replicated in cities and towns across China. Regional administration was based on this network of urban centers.

- The Han era saw major intellectual and technological developments, as well as the arrival of Buddhism in China.

- The fall of the Han dynasty early in the third century CE was followed by the takeover of the northern plain by barbarian peoples. Many Chinese fled south to the Yangzi River Valley, which became the new center of gravity for Chinese civilization.

6-3 Conclusion

Both the Roman Empire and the first Chinese empire arose from relatively small states that, because of their discipline and military toughness, were initially able to subdue their neighbors. Ultimately they unified widespread territories under strong central governments.

Agriculture was the fundamental economic activity and source of wealth. Government revenues primarily derived from a percentage of the annual harvest. Both empires depended initially on sturdy independent farmers pressed into military service or other forms of compulsory labor, though later they came to rely on professional troops. Conflicts over who owned the land and how it was used were at the heart of political and social turmoil. The autocratic rulers of the Roman and Chinese states secured their positions by breaking the power of the old aristocratic families, seizing their excess land, and giving land to small farmers. The later reversal of this process, when wealthy noblemen again gained control of vast tracts of land and reduced the peasants to dependent tenant farmers, signaled the erosion of state authority.

Both empires spread out from an ethnically homogeneous core to encompass widespread territories containing diverse ecosystems, populations, and ways of life. Both brought those regions a cultural unity that has persisted, at least in part, to the present day. This development involved far more than military conquest and political domination. As the population of the core areas outstripped available resources, Italian and Han settlers moved into new regions, bringing their languages, beliefs, customs, and technologies. Many people in the conquered lands were attracted to the culture of the ruler nation and chose to adopt these practices and attach themselves to a "winning cause." Both empires found similar solutions to the problems of administering far-flung territories and large populations in an age when communication depended on men on horseback or on foot. The central government had to delegate considerable autonomy to local officials based in the cities and towns—in the Roman case local elites, in China officials dispatched by the central administration. In both empires a kind of civil service developed, staffed by educated and capable members of a prosperous middle class.

Technologies that facilitated imperial control also fostered cultural unification and improvements in the general standard of living. Roads built to expedite the movement of troops became the highways of commerce and the spread of imperial culture. A network of cities and towns linked the parts of the empire, providing local administrative bases, promoting commerce, and radiating imperial culture into the surrounding countryside. The majority of the population still resided in the countryside, but those living in urban centers enjoyed most of the advantages of empire. Cities and towns modeled themselves on the capital cities of Rome and Chang'an. Travelers found the same types of buildings and public spaces, and similar features of urban life, in outlying regions that they had seen in the capital.

The empires of Rome and Han China faced similar problems of defense: long borders located far from the administrative center and aggressive neighbors who coveted their prosperity. Both had to build walls and maintain chains of forts and garrisons to protect against incursions. The cost of frontier defense was staggering and eventually eroded the economic prosperity of the two empires. As imperial governments demanded more taxes and services from the hard-pressed civilian population, they lost the loyalty of their own people, many of whom sought protection on the estates of powerful rural landowners. As rough neighbors gradually learned the skills that had given the empires an initial advantage and were able to close the "technology gap," the Roman and Han governments eventually came to rely on soldiers hired from the same "barbarian" peoples who were pressing on the frontiers. Eventually, both empires were so weakened that their borders were overrun and their central governments collapsed. Ironically, the newly dominant immigrant groups were so deeply influenced by imperial culture that they maintained it to the best of their abilities.

In referring to the eventual failure of these two empires, we are brought up against important differences that led to contrasting long-term outcomes. In China the imperial model was revived in subsequent eras, but the lands of the western Roman Empire never again achieved the same level of unification. Several interrelated factors account for the different outcomes.

First, these cultures had different attitudes about the relationship of individuals to the state. In China the individual was more deeply embedded in the larger social group. The Chinese family—with its emphasis on a precisely defined hierarchy, unquestioning obedience, and solemn rituals of deference to elders and ancestors—served as the model for society and the state. Moreover, Confucianism, which sanctified hierarchy and provided a code of conduct for public officials, arose long before the imperial system and could be revived and tailored to fit changing political circumstances. Although the Roman family had its own hierarchy and traditions of obedience, the cult of ancestors was not as strong as among the Chinese, and the family was not the organizational model for Roman society and the Roman state. Also, there was no Roman equivalent of Confucianism—no ideology of political organization and social conduct that could survive the dissolution of the Roman state.

Another difference was that opportunities for economic and social mobility were greater in the Roman Empire than in ancient China. Whereas the merchant class in China was frequently disparaged and constrained by the government, the absence of government interference in the Roman Empire resulted in greater economic mobility and a thriving and influential middle class in the towns and cities. The Roman army, because it was composed of professional soldiers in service for decades and constituted a distinct and increasingly privileged group, frequently played a decisive role in political conflict. In China, on the other hand, the army was long drawn from draftees who served for two years and was much less likely to take the initiative in struggles for power.

Although Roman emperors tried to create an ideology to bolster their position, they were hampered by the persistence of Republican traditions and the ambiguities about the position of emperor deliberately cultivated by Augustus. As a result, Roman rulers were likely to be chosen by the army or by the Senate; the dynastic principle never took deep root; and the cult of the emperor had little spiritual content. This stands in sharp contrast to the unambiguous Chinese belief that the emperor was the divine Son of Heaven, with a mandate to rule and privileged access to the beneficent power of the royal ancestors. Thus, in the lands that had once constituted the western part of the Roman Empire, there was no compelling basis for reviving the position of emperor and the territorial claims of empire in later ages.

Finally, Christianity, with its insistence on monotheism and one doctrine of truth, negated the Roman emperor's pretensions to divinity and was unwilling to compromise with pagan beliefs. The spread of Christianity through the provinces during the Late Roman Empire, and the decline of the western half of the empire in the fifth century CE (see Chapter 11), constituted an irreversible break with the past. On the other hand, Buddhism, which came to China in the early centuries CE and flourished in the post-Han era (see Chapter 12), was more easily reconciled with traditional Chinese values and beliefs.

Key Terms

Republic p. 144

Senate p. 144

patron–client
   relationship p. 145

Principate p. 149

Augustus p. 149

equites p. 149

pax romana p. 151

Romanization p. 152

Jesus p. 153

Paul p. 154

aqueduct p. 155

Third-Century Crisis p. 156

Constantine p. 157

Qin p. 158

Shi Huangdi p. 158

Han p. 158

Xiongnu p. 159

Gaozu p. 160

Sima Qian p. 161

Chang'an p. 162

Review Questions

1. What were the most important similarities and differences between these two empires, and what do the similarities and differences tell us about the circumstances and the character of each?

2. How do the different emphases on the "individual" and the "community" seen in Greek and pre-imperial Chinese civilization (see Chapters 4 and 5) continue into the Roman and early imperial Chinese eras?

3. Why was there greater political continuity for several thousand years in Chinese civilization than in the lands of western Europe that were once part of the Roman empire?

 MindTap® is a fully online, personalized learning experience built upon Cengage Learning content. MindTap® combines student learning tools–readings, multimedia, activities, and assessments–into a singular Learning Path that guides students through the course and helps students develop the critical thinking, analysis, and communication skills that are essential to academic and professional success.

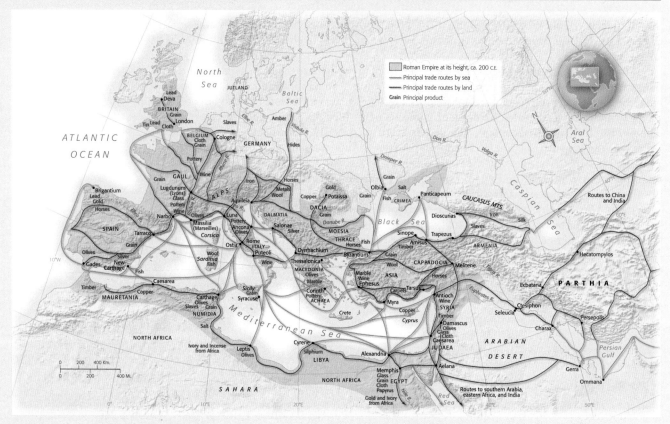

Trade Routes of the Roman Empire

Multiple-Choice Questions

Questions 1–3 refer to the map above.

1. According to the map, which of the following statements best describes the first two centuries CE in the Roman Empire (or Roman Principate)?

   (A) Roman transregional trade involved mainly agricultural items.

   (B) There was little trade outside of the European part of the Roman Empire.

   (C) A period of stability allowed for the spread of goods by road and sea.

   (D) Overland trade was limited due to the impregnable terrain of Europe.

2. What led to Rome becoming the dominant power in the Mediterranean region shown on the map?

   (A) Roman agriculture could flourish as the climate of the Mediterranean region allowed for a wide variety of crops.

   (B) Rome was situated at the western end of the Silk Roads and thus profited from trading with the East.

   (C) Rome made alliances with other groups in the Mediterranean region and became the leading political force.

   (D) Rome was ideally situated on a peninsula that was located in the middle of a vibrant trading zone.

3. The development of which technological advancement in both the Roman Empire and in Han China facilitated the increase in trade evident on the map?

   (A) Extensive road networks

   (B) Paper money and "flying cash"

   (C) A series of aqueducts and canals

   (D) An understanding of latitude

Questions 4–6 refer to the passage below.

"Can anyone be so indifferent or idle as not to care to know by what means, and under what kind of polity, almost the whole inhabited world was conquered and brought under the dominion of the single city of Rome, and that too within a period of not quite fifty-three years? [220–167 BCE] Or who again can be so completely absorbed in other subjects of contemplation or study, as to think any of them superior in importance to the accurate understanding of an event for which the past affords no precedent. . . . Nearly the whole inhabited world was reduced by them to obedience: and they left behind them an empire not to be paralleled in the past or rivaled in the future."

Polybius, *The Histories*, ca. 200 BCE

4. What was the chief device enabling Roman expansion in the third and second centuries BCE?

   (A) Vibrant administrative capabilities that were advantageous in a large empire

(B) A powerful military that was mobile and well disciplined

(C) A unifying language and culture that promoted harmonious social interactions

(D) Economic strength that encouraged the development of nationalism

5. Which of the following describes a strategy used by the Roman Republic to govern relations with ethnically and culturally dissimilar groups as it grew and expanded its boundaries?

(A) The Romans used centralized governments and granted citizenship to conquered people to ensure their loyalty.

(B) The Romans enslaved the majority of males in the regions they conquered to prevent rebellions.

(C) So they could be aware of dissidence, the Romans forced most conquered people to migrate onto the Roman peninsula.

(D) Roman soldiers were ordered to marry local women in the conquered areas to create cultural harmony.

6. Which of the following is a way the expansion described by Polybius eventually led to the fall of the Roman Republic?

(A) Drought and disease caused the loss of crops and the soldiers could no longer be fed

(B) Small farmers mobilized for military service lost their farms, leading to a shortage in those with the property required for military service.

(C) Overproduction of wheat caused a drop in prices, which left Rome unable to finance the legions

(D) Upper class refusal to share the wealth of the empire resulted in soldiers refusing to follow orders.

Questions 7–10 refer to the passages below.

"Let a woman be composed in demeanor and upright in bearing in the service of her husband. Let her live in purity and quietness [of spirit] and keep watch over herself. Let her not love gossip and silly laughter. . . .

In womanly behavior there are four things [to be considered]: womanly virtue, womanly speech, womanly appearance, and womanly work. . . . To guard carefully her chastity, to control circumspectly her behavior, in every motion to exhibit modesty, and to model each act on the best usage: this may be called womanly virtue."

Ban Zhao, excerpts from *Admonitions for Women*, ca. 100 CE

"There appears to be hardly any worthwhile argument for women of full age being in tutela [*under* guardianship]. The common belief, that because of their instability of judgement they are often deceived and that it is only fair to have them controlled by the authority of tutors, seems more specious [erroneous] than true. For women of full age manage their affairs themselves."

Gaius, a celebrated Roman jurist, ca. 170 CE

7. According to Ban Zhao,

(A) the main duty of a woman was to be beautiful.

(B) women should marry young and receive no education.

(C) women should conform to society's norms and act demurely.

(D) a husband had the right to beat his wife if she deserved it.

8. The traditional beliefs that governed the behavior of women during the Han dynasty reflected the moral values of which of the following?

(A) Daoism

(B) Legalism

(C) Mohism

(D) Confucianism

9. The excerpt from Gaius implies that in the Roman Empire, women

(A) have achieved equality with men and are free to enter all public places.

(B) are given very few rights due to their weak nature.

(C) have a level of autonomy in their lives when they reach adulthood.

(D) are gradually losing their rights.

10. Which of these comparisons concerning gender roles in classical societies is *most* correct?

(A) Women in both Han China and the Roman Empire were rising in the social hierarchy.

(B) Women in both Han China and the Roman Empire faced significant restrictions from the patriarchal nature of their societies.

(C) Women in Han China had more autonomy in economic affairs than women in the Roman Empire.

(D) Women in Han China were restricted because of Buddhist practices while women in the Roman Empire were restricted due to Christianity.

Short-Answer Questions

1. Answer all parts of the question that follows.

(A) Identify ONE political or cultural legacy of the Roman Empire.

(B) Identify ANOTHER political or cultural legacy of the Roman Empire.

(C) Explain ONE method used by the Roman Empire to establish control.

2. Answer all parts of the question that follows.

(A) Identify ONE similarity between the decline of the Roman Empire and that of the Han Empire.

(B) Identify ONE difference between the decline of the Roman Empire and that of the Han Empire.

(C) Explain ONE long-term result of the decline of the Roman Empire and the decline of the Han Empire.

7

India and Southeast Asia, 1500 BCE–1025 CE

CHAPTER OUTLINE

7-1 Foundations of Indian Civilization, 1500 BCE–300 CE

7-2 Imperial Expansion and Collapse, 324 BCE–650 CE

7-3 Southeast Asia, 50–1025 CE

7-4 Conclusion

➤ **ENVIRONMENT & TECHNOLOGY**
Indian Mathematics

➤ **DIVERSITY & DOMINANCE**
Relations Between Women and Men in the *Kama Sutra* and the *Arthashastra*

Overarching Questions

1 How and why have religions, belief systems, philosophies, and ideologies originated, developed, and spread as a result of expanding communication and exchange networks? (CUL)

2 How have religions, belief systems, philosophies, and ideologies affected the political, economic, and social development of societies? (CUL)

3 How have different forms of governance been constructed and maintained over time? (SB)

4 How have internal and external political factors influenced the process of state building, expansion, and dissolution? (SB)

5 To what extent have different ideologies, philosophies, and religions affected social hierarchies? (SOC)

▼ **Temple of Minakshi at Madurai** At the annual Chittarai Festival, the citizens of this city in south India celebrate the wedding of their local patron goddess, Minakshi, to the high god Shiva. robertharding/Alamy Stock Photo

In the *Bhagavad-Gita* (**BUH-guh-vahd GEE-tuh**), the most renowned Indian sacred text, the legendary warrior Arjuna (**AHR-joo-nuh**) rides out in his chariot to the open space between two armies preparing for battle. Torn between his social duty to fight for his family's claim to the throne and his conscience, which balks at the prospect of killing relatives, friends, and former teachers in the enemy camp, Arjuna slumps down in his chariot and refuses to fight. But his driver, the god Krishna (**KRISH-nuh**) in disguise, persuades him, in a carefully structured dialogue, both of the necessity to fulfill his duty as a warrior and of the proper frame of mind for performing these acts. In the climactic moment of the dialogue Krishna endows Arjuna with a "divine eye" and permits him to see the true appearance of God:

> It was a multiform, wondrous vision,
> with countless mouths and eyes
> and celestial ornaments,
> Everywhere was boundless divinity
> containing all astonishing things,
> wearing divine garlands and garments,
> anointed with divine perfume.
> If the light of a thousand suns
> were to rise in the sky at once,
> it would be like the light
> of that great spirit.
> Arjuna saw all the universe
> in its many ways and parts,
> standing as one in the body
> of the god of gods.[1]

In all of world literature, this is one of the most compelling attempts to depict the nature of deity. Graphic images emphasize the vastness, diversity, and multiplicity of the god, but in the end we learn that Krishna is the organizing principle behind all creation, that behind diversity and multiplicity lies a higher unity.

This is an apt metaphor for Indian civilization. The enormous variety of the Indian landscape is mirrored in the patchwork of ethnic and linguistic groups that occupy it, the political fragmentation that has marked most of Indian history, the elaborate hierarchy of social groups into which the Indian population is divided, and the thousands of deities who are worshiped at innumerable holy places that dot the subcontinent. Yet, in the end, one can speak of an Indian civilization united by shared views and values. The photograph shows a temple in the city of Madurai in southern India. Here the ten-day Chittarai Festival, the most important religious event of the year in that district, celebrates the wedding of a local goddess, Minakshi, and the great Hindu god Shiva, symbolizing the reconciliation of local and national deities, southern and northern cultural practices, and male and female potentialities.

This chapter surveys the history of South and Southeast Asia from approximately 1500 BCE to 1025 CE, highlighting the evolution of defining features of Indian

---

[1]Barbara Stoler Miller, *The Bhagavad-Gita: Krishna's Counsel in Time of War* (New York, NY: Bantam, 1986), 98–99.

civilization. Considerable attention is given to Indian religious conceptions, due both to religion's profound role in shaping Indian society and the sources of information available to historians. For reasons that are explained below, writing came late to India, and ancient Indians did not develop the same kind of historical consciousness as other peoples of antiquity and took little interest in recording specific historical events. ●

7-1 Foundations of Indian Civilization, 1500 BCE–300 CE

What historical forces led to the development of complex social groupings in ancient India?

India is called a *subcontinent* because it is a large—roughly 2,000 miles (3,200 kilometers) in both length and breadth—and physically isolated landmass. It is set off from the rest of Asia to the north by the Himalayas (**him-uh-LAY-uhs**), the highest mountains on the planet, and by the Indian Ocean on its eastern, southern, and western sides (see Map 7.1). The most permeable frontier, used by invaders and migrating peoples, lies to the northwest, but people using this corridor must cross the mountain barrier of the Hindu Kush (**HIHN-doo KOOSH**) via the Khyber [**KIE-ber**] Pass and the Thar (**tahr**) Desert east of the Indus River.

7-1a The Indian Subcontinent

The subcontinent—which encompasses the modern nations of Pakistan, Nepal, Bhutan, Bangladesh, India, and the adjacent island of Sri Lanka—divides into three distinct topographical zones. The mountainous northern zone contains the heavily forested foothills and high meadows on the edge of the Hindu Kush and Himalaya ranges. Next come the great basins of the Indus and Ganges (**GAHN-jeez**) Rivers. Originating in the snow-clad Tibetan mountains to the north, these rivers have repeatedly overflowed their banks and deposited layer on layer of silt, creating large alluvial plains. Northern India is divided from the third zone, the peninsula proper, by the Vindhya range and the Deccan (**de-KAN**), an arid, rocky plateau. The tropical coastal strip of Kerala (Malabar) in the west, the Coromandel Coast in the east with its web of rivers descending from the central plateau, the flatlands of Tamil Nadu on the southern tip of the peninsula, and the island of Sri Lanka often have followed paths of political and cultural development separate from those of northern India.

The northern rim of mountains shelters the subcontinent from cold Arctic winds and gives it a subtropical climate. The most dramatic source of moisture is the **monsoon** (seasonal wind). The Indian Ocean is slow to warm or cool, while the vast landmass of Asia swings between seasonal extremes of heat and cold. The temperature difference between water and land acts like a bellows, producing a great wind. The southwest monsoon begins in June, absorbing huge amounts of moisture from the Indian Ocean and dropping it over a swath of India that encompasses the rain forest belt on the western coast and the Ganges Basin. Three harvests a year are possible in some places. Rice is grown in the moist, flat Ganges Delta (modern Bengal). Elsewhere the staples are wheat, barley, and millet. The Indus Valley, in contrast, gets little precipitation (see Chapter 2), and agriculture requires extensive irrigation.

Although invasions and migrations usually came by land through the northwest corridor, the ocean has not been a barrier to travel and trade. Mariners learned to ride the monsoon winds across open waters from northeast to southwest in January and to make the return voyage in July. Ships sailed west across the Arabian Sea to the Persian Gulf, the southern coast of Arabia, and East Africa, and east across the Bay of Bengal to Indochina and Indonesia (see Chapter 9).

Many characteristic features of later Indian civilization may derive from the Indus Valley civilization of the third and early second millennia BCE, but proof is hard to come by because writing from that period has not yet been deciphered. That society, with its advanced social organization and technology, succumbed around 1900 BCE to some kind of environmental crisis (see Chapter 2).

AP® Exam Tip
Describe the elements of Indian Ocean trade routes during this time period.

monsoon Seasonal winds in the Indian Ocean caused by the differences in temperature between the rapidly heating and cooling landmasses of Africa and Asia and the slowly changing ocean waters. These strong and predictable winds have long been ridden across the open sea by sailors, and the large amounts of rainfall that they deposit on parts of India, Southeast Asia, and China allow for the cultivation of several crops a year.

Vedas Early Indian sacred "knowledge"—the literal meaning of the term—long preserved and communicated orally by Brahmin priests and eventually written down. These religious texts, including the thousand poetic hymns to various deities contained in the Rig Veda, are our main source of information about the Vedic period (ca. 1500–500 BCE).

CHRONOLOGY

	India	Southeast Asia
2000 BCE		ca. 2000 BCE Swidden agriculture ca. 1600 BCE Beginning of migrations from mainland Southeast Asia to islands in Pacific and Indian Oceans
1500 BCE	ca. 1500 BCE Migration of Indo-European peoples into northwest India	
1000 BCE	ca. 1000 BCE Indo-European groups move into the Ganges Plain	
500 BCE	ca. 500 BCE Siddhartha Gautama founds Buddhism; Mahavira founds Jainism 324 BCE Chandragupta Maurya becomes king of Magadha and lays foundation for Mauryan Empire 273–232 BCE Reign of Ashoka 184 BCE Fall of Mauryan Empire	
1 CE	320 CE Chandra Gupta establishes Gupta Empire	ca. 50–560 CE Funan dominates southern Indochina and the Isthmus of Kra
500 CE	550 CE Collapse of Gupta Empire 606–647 CE Reign of Harsha Vardhana	ca. 500 CE Trade route develops through Strait of Malacca 683 CE Rise of Srivijaya in Sumatra 770–825 CE Construction of Borobodur in Java
1000 CE		1025 CE Chola attack on Palembang and decline of Srivijaya

7-1b The Vedic Age

Historians call the period from 1500 to 500 BCE the Vedic Age, after the **Vedas** (**VAY-duhs**), religious texts that are our main source of information about the period. The foundations for Indian civilization were laid in the Vedic Age. Most historians believe that new groups of people—animal-herding warriors speaking Indo-European languages—migrated into northwest India around 1500 BCE. Some argue for a much earlier Indo-European presence in this region in conjunction with the spread of agriculture. In any case, in the mid-second millennium BCE northern India entered a new historical period associated with the dominance of Indo-European groups.

After the collapse of the Indus Valley civilization there was no central authority to direct irrigation efforts, and the region became home to kinship groups that depended mostly on their herds of cattle for sustenance. These societies were patriarchal, with the father dominating the family as the king ruled the tribe. Members of the warrior class boasted of their martial skill and courage, relished combat, celebrated with lavish feasts of beef and rounds of heavy drinking, and filled their leisure time with chariot racing and gambling.

After 1000 BCE some groups migrated east into the Ganges Plain. New technologies made this advance possible. Iron tools—harder than bronze and able to hold a sharper edge—allowed settlers to fell trees and work the newly cleared land with plows pulled by oxen. The soil of the Ganges Plain was fertile, well watered by the annual monsoon, and able to sustain two or three crops a year. As in Greece at roughly the same time (see Chapter 5), the use of iron tools to open new land for agriculture must have led to a significant increase in population.

Stories about this era, not written down until much later but long preserved by memorization and oral recitation, speak of bitter warfare between two groups of people: the Aryas, relatively light-skinned speakers of Indo-European languages, and the Dasas, dark-skinned speakers of Dravidian languages. It is possible that some Dasas were absorbed into Arya populations and that elites from both groups merged. For the most part, however, Aryas pushed the Dasas south into central and southern India, where their descendants still live. Today Indo-European languages are primarily spoken in northern India, while Dravidian speech prevails in the south.

AP® Exam Tip
Understand the relationship between the Vedic religions and Hinduism.

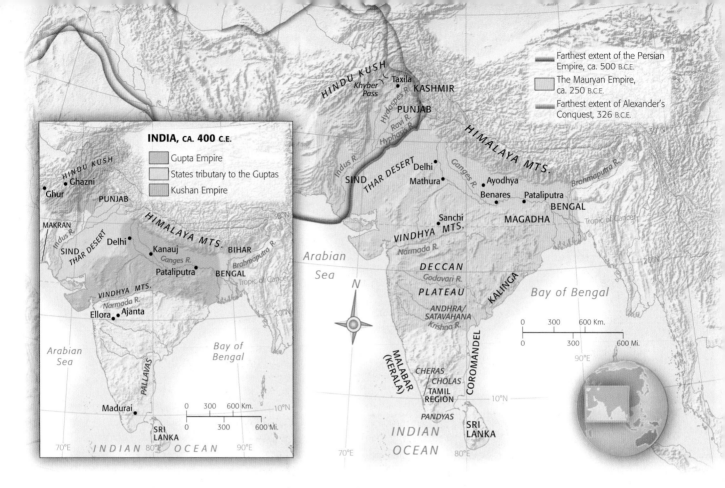

MAP 7.1 Ancient India Mountains and ocean largely separate the Indian subcontinent from the rest of Asia. Migrations and invasions usually came through the Khyber Pass in the northwest. Seaborne commerce with western Asia, Southeast Asia, and East Asia often flourished. Peoples speaking Indo-European languages migrated into the broad valleys of the Indus and Ganges Rivers in the north. Dravidian-speaking peoples remained the dominant population in the south. The diversity of the Indian landscape, the multiplicity of ethnic groups, and the primary identification of people with their class and caste lie behind the division into many small states that has characterized much of Indian political history.

Why was the earlier Maurya empire able to control more extensive territories than the later Gupta empire, and why was neither empire able to dominate the southern part of the subcontinent?

Skin color has been a persistent concern of Indian society and is one of the bases for its historically sharp internal divisions. Over time there evolved a system of **varna**—literally "color," though the word came to indicate something akin to "class." Individuals were born into one of four classes: *Brahmin*, comprising priests and scholars; *Kshatriya* (**kshuh-TREE-yuh**), warriors and officials; *Vaishya* (**VIESH-yuh**), merchants, artisans, and landowners; or *Shudra* (**SHOOD-ra**), peasants and laborers. The designation *Shudra* may have originally been reserved for Dasas, who were given the menial jobs in society. Indeed, the very term *dasa* came to mean "slave." Eventually a fifth group was marked off: the Untouchables. They were excluded from the class system, and members of the other groups literally avoided them because of the demeaning or polluting work to which they were relegated—such as leather tanning, which involved touching dead animals, and sweeping away ashes of the dead after cremations.

People at the top of the social pyramid could explain why this hierarchy existed. According to one creation myth, a primordial creature named Purusha allowed itself to be sacrificed. From its mouth sprang the class of Brahmin priests, the embodiment of intellect and knowledge. From its arms came the Kshatriya warrior class, from its thighs the Vaishya landowners and merchants, and from its feet the Shudra workers.

The varna system was just one of the mechanisms developed to regulate relations between different groups. Within the broad class divisions, the population was further subdivided into numerous **jati**, or birth groups (sometimes called *castes*, from a Portuguese term meaning "breed"). Each jati had its proper occupation, duties, and rituals. Individuals who belonged to a given jati lived with members of their group, married within the group, and ate only with members of the group. Elaborate rules governed their interactions with members of other groups. Members of higher-status groups feared pollution from contact with lower-caste individuals and had to undergo elaborate rituals of purification to remove any taint.

varna/jati Two categories of social identity of great importance in Indian history. *Varna* are the four major social divisions: the Brahmin priest class, the Kshatriya warrior/administrator class, the Vaishya merchant/farmer class, and the Shudra laborer class. Within the system of varna are many *jati*, regional groups of people who have a common occupational sphere and who marry, eat, and generally interact with other members of their group.

AP® Exam Tip
Understand the role of the brahmin and the teachings about dharma and reincarnation as they contributed to the social and political roles of the caste system in India.

The class and caste systems came to be connected to a widespread belief in reincarnation. The Brahmin priests taught that every living creature had an immortal essence: the *atman*, or "breath." Separated from the body at death, the atman was later reborn in another body. Whether the new body was that of an insect, an animal, or a human depended on the **karma**, or deeds, of the atman in its previous incarnations. People who lived exemplary lives would be reborn into the higher classes. Those who misbehaved would be punished in the next life by being relegated to a lower class or even a lower life-form. The underlying message was: You are where you deserve to be, and the only way to improve your lot in the next cycle of existence is to accept your current station and its attendant duties.

The dominant deities in Vedic religion were male and associated with the heavens. To release the dawn, Indra, god of war and master of the thunderbolt, daily slew the demon encasing the universe. Varuna, lord of the sky, maintained universal order and dispensed justice. Agni, the force of fire, consumed the sacrifice and bridged the spheres of gods and humans.

Sacrifice—the dedication to a god of a valued possession, often a living creature—was the essential ritual. The purpose of these offerings was to invigorate the gods and thereby sustain their creative powers and promote stability in the world.

Brahmin priests controlled the sacrifices, for only they knew the rituals and prayers. The *Rig Veda*, a collection of more than a thousand poetic hymns to various deities, and the *Brahmanas*, detailed prose descriptions of procedures for ritual and sacrifice, were collections of priestly lore couched in the Sanskrit language of the Arya upper classes. This information was handed down orally from one generation of priests to the next. The priests' "knowledge" (the term *veda* means just that) was the basis of their economic well-being. They were amply rewarded for officiating at sacrifices, and their knowledge gave them social and political power because they were the indispensable intermediaries between gods and humans. Some scholars hypothesize that the Brahmins resisted the introduction of writing in order to preserve their control of sacred knowledge. This might explain why writing came into widespread use in India later than in other societies of equivalent complexity. However, we may be unaware of earlier uses of writing because it involved perishable materials that have not survived in the archaeological record.

It is difficult to uncover the experiences of women in early India. Limited evidence indicates that women in the Vedic period studied sacred lore, composed religious hymns, and participated in the sacrificial ritual. They could own property and usually did not marry until reaching their middle or late teens. Strong and resourceful women appear in the Indian epic poems originating in this era.

The sharp internal divisions and complex hierarchy of Indian society served important social functions. They provided each individual with a clear identity and role and offered the benefits of group solidarity and support. Moreover, there is evidence that groups sometimes were able to upgrade their status. Thus the elaborate system of divisions was not static and provided a mechanism for working out social tensions. Many of these features have persisted into modern times.

7-1c Challenges to the Old Order: Jainism and Buddhism

After 700 BCE various forms of reaction against Brahmin power and privilege emerged. People who objected to the rigid hierarchy of classes and castes or the community's demands on the individual could retreat to the nearby forest that still covered much of ancient India. These wild places symbolized freedom from societal constraints.

Certain charismatic individuals who abandoned their town or village and moved to the forest attracted bands of followers. Calling into question the priests' exclusive claims to wisdom and the necessity of Vedic chants and sacrifices, they offered an alternate path to salvation: the individual pursuit of insight into the nature of the self and the universe through physical and mental discipline (*yoga*), special dietary practices, and meditation. They taught that by distancing oneself from desire for the things of this world, one could achieve **moksha**, or "liberation." This release from the cycle of reincarnations and union with the divine force that animates the universe sometimes was likened to "a deep, dreamless sleep." The *Upanishads* (**ooh-PAH-nee-shad**)—a collection of more than 100 mystical dialogues between teachers and disciples—reflect this questioning of the foundations of Vedic religion.

karma In Indian tradition, the residue of deeds performed in past and present lives that adheres to a "spirit" and determines what form it will assume in its next life cycle. The doctrines of *karma* and reincarnation were used by the elite in ancient India to encourage people to accept their social position and do their duty.

moksha The Hindu concept of the spirit's "liberation" from the endless cycle of rebirths. There are various avenues—such as physical discipline, meditation, and acts of devotion to the gods—by which the spirit can distance itself from desire for the things of this world and be merged with the divine force that animates the universe.

AP® Exam Tip
Know the core beliefs of Buddhism and understand Buddhism's relationship to the Vedic beliefs.

The most serious threat to Vedic religion and Brahmin prerogatives came from two new religions that emerged around this time: Jainism and Buddhism. Mahavira (540–468 BCE) was known to his followers as Jina, "the Conqueror," from which is derived *Jainism* (**JINE-iz-uhm**), the belief system that he established. Emphasizing the holiness of the life force animating all living creatures, Mahavira and his followers practiced strict nonviolence. They wore masks to prevent accidentally inhaling small insects, and they carefully brushed off a seat before sitting down. Those who gave themselves over completely to Jainism practiced extreme asceticism and nudity, ate only what they were given by others, and eventually starved themselves to death. Less zealous Jainists, restricted from agricultural work by the injunction against killing, were city dwellers engaged in commerce and banking.

Far more significant for Indian and world history was the rise of Buddhism. So many stories were told about Siddhartha Gautama (563–483 BCE), known as the **Buddha**, "the Enlightened One," that it is difficult to separate fact from legend. He came from a Kshatriya family of the Sakyas, a people in the foothills of the Himalayas. As a young man he enjoyed the princely life-style to which he had been born, but at some point he abandoned family and privilege to become a wandering ascetic. After six years of self-deprivation, he came to regard asceticism as no more likely to produce spiritual insight than the luxury of his previous life, and he decided to adhere to a "Middle Path" of moderation. Sitting under a tree in a deer park near Benares on the Ganges River, he gained a sudden and profound insight into the true nature of reality, which he set forth as "Four Noble Truths": (1) life is suffering; (2) suffering arises from desire; (3) the solution to suffering lies in curbing desire; and (4) desire can be curbed if a person follows the "Eightfold Path" of right views, aspirations, speech, conduct, livelihood, effort, mindfulness, and meditation. Rising up, the Buddha preached his First Sermon, a central text of Buddhism, and set into motion the "Wheel of the Law." He soon attracted followers, some of whom took vows of celibacy, nonviolence, and poverty.

Buddha An Indian prince named Siddhartha Gautama who renounced his wealth and social position to search for truth. After becoming "enlightened" (the meaning of Buddha), he enunciated the principles of Buddhism, which evolved and spread throughout India and to Southeast, East, and Central Asia.

▲ **Carved Stone Gateway Leading to the Great Stupa at Sanchi** Pilgrims traveled long distances to visit stupas, mounds containing relics of the Buddha. The complex at Sanchi, in central India, was begun by King Ashoka in the third century BCE, though the gates probably date to the first century CE. This relief shows a royal procession bringing the remains of the Buddha to the city of Kushinagara. De Agostini Picture Lib. / G. Nimatallah/akg-images

In its original form, Buddhism centered on the individual. Although not quite rejecting the existence of gods, it denied their usefulness to a person seeking enlightenment. What mattered was living one's life with moderation, in order to minimize desire and suffering, and searching for spiritual truth through self-discipline and meditation. The ultimate reward was *nirvana*, literally "snuffing out the flame." With nirvana came release from the cycle of reincarnations and achievement of a state of perpetual tranquility. The Vedic tradition emphasized the eternal survival of the atman, the "breath" or nonmaterial essence of the individual. In contrast, Buddhism regarded the individual as a composite without any soul-like component that survived upon entering nirvana.

When the Buddha died, he left no final instructions, instead urging his disciples to "be their own lamp." As the Buddha's message— contained in philosophical discourses memorized by his followers—spread throughout India and into Central, Southeast, and East Asia, its very success began to subvert the individualistic and essentially atheistic tenets of the founder. Buddhist monasteries were established, and a hierarchy of Buddhist monks and nuns came into being. Worshipers erected *stupas* (**STOO-puh**) (large earthen mounds symbolizing the universe) over relics

▲ **Sculpture of the Buddha, Second or Third Century CE**   This depiction of the Buddha, seated beneath the bodhi tree at the moment he achieves enlightenment, is from Gandhara in the northwest. It displays the influence of Greek artistic styles emanating from Greek settlements established in that region by Alexander the Great.
Peter Horree/Alamy Stock Photo

of the cremated founder. Believers began to worship the Buddha himself as a god. Many Buddhists also revered *bodhisattvas* (**boe-dih-SUT-vuh**), saintly men and women who had achieved enlightenment and were on the threshold of nirvana but chose to be reborn into mortal bodies to help others along the path to salvation.

The makers of early pictorial images refused to show the Buddha as a living person and represented him only indirectly, through symbols such as his footprints, his begging bowl, or the tree under which he achieved enlightenment, as if to emphasize his achievement of a state of nonexistence. From the second century CE, however, statues of the Buddha and bodhisattvas began to proliferate, done in native sculptural styles and in a style that showed the influence of the Greek settlements established in Bactria (modern Afghanistan) by Alexander the Great (see Chapter 5). A schism emerged within Buddhism. Devotees of **Mahayana** (**mah-huh-YAH-nuh**) ("Great Vehicle") **Buddhism** embraced the popular new features, while practitioners of **Theravada** (**there-uh-VAH-duh**) ("Teachings of the Elders") **Buddhism** followed most of the original teachings of the founder.

7-1d The Evolution of Hinduism

Challenged by new, spiritually satisfying, and egalitarian movements, Vedic religion made important adjustments, evolving into **Hinduism**, the religion of hundreds of millions of people in South Asia today. The foundation of Hinduism is the Vedic religion of the Arya peoples of northern India. But Hinduism also incorporated elements drawn from the Dravidian cultures of the south, such as an emphasis on intense devotion to the deity and the prominence of fertility rituals. Also present are elements of Buddhism.

The process by which Vedic religion was transformed into Hinduism by the fourth century CE is largely hidden from us. The Brahmin priests maintained their high social status and influence. But sacrifice, though still part of traditional worship, was less central, and there was more opportunity for direct contact between gods and individual worshipers.

The gods were altered, both in identity and in their relationships with humanity. Two formerly minor deities, Vishnu (**VIHSH-noo**) and Shiva (**SHEE-vuh**), became preeminent. Hinduism emphasized the worshiper's personal devotion to a particular deity, usually Vishnu, Shiva, or

Mahayana Buddhism
"Great Vehicle" branch of Buddhism followed in China, Japan, and Central Asia. The focus is on reverence for Buddha and for bodhisattvas, enlightened persons who have postponed nirvana to help others attain enlightenment.

Theravada Buddhism
"Teachings of the Elders" branch of Buddhism followed in Sri Lanka and much of Southeast Asia. Theravada remains close to the original principles set forth by the Buddha; it downplays the importance of gods and emphasizes austerity and the individual's search for enlightenment.

Hinduism A general term for a wide variety of beliefs and ritual practices that have developed in the Indian subcontinent since antiquity. Hinduism has roots in ancient Vedic, Buddhist, and south Indian religious concepts and practices. It spread along the trade routes to Southeast Asia.

Devi (**DEH-vee**) ("the Goddess"). Both Shiva and Devi appear to be derived from the Dravidian tradition, in which fertility cults and female deities played a prominent role. Vishnu, who has a clear Arya pedigree, remains more popular in northern India, while Shiva is dominant in the Dravidian south. These gods can appear in many guises. They are identified by various cult names and are represented by a complex symbolism of stories, companion animals, birds, and objects.

Vishnu, the preserver, is a benevolent deity who helps his devotees in time of need. Hindus believe that whenever demonic forces threaten the cosmic order, Vishnu appears on earth in one of a series of *avataras*, or incarnations. Among his incarnations are the legendary hero Rama, the popular cowherd-god Krishna, and the Buddha (a clear attempt to co-opt the rival religion's founder). Shiva, who lives in ascetic isolation on Mount Kailasa in the Himalayas, is a more ambivalent figure. He represents both creation and destruction, for both are part of a single, cyclical process. He often is represented performing dance steps that symbolize the acts of creation and destruction. Devi manifests herself in various ways—as a full-bodied mother-goddess who promotes fertility and procreation, as the docile and loving wife Parvati, and as the frightening deity who, under the name Kali or Durga, lets loose a torrent of violence and destruction.

The multiplicity of gods (330 million according to one tradition), sects, and local practices within Hinduism is dazzling, reflecting the ethnic, linguistic, and cultural diversity of India. Yet within this variety there is unity. Ultimately, all the gods and spirits are seen as manifestations of a single divine force that pervades the universe. This sense of underlying unity is expressed in texts, such as the passage from the *Bhagavad-Gita* quoted at the beginning of this chapter; in the different potentials of women represented in the various manifestations of Devi; and in composite statues that are split down the middle—half Shiva, half Vishnu—as if to say that they are complementary aspects of one cosmic principle.

Hinduism offers the worshiper a variety of ways to approach god and obtain divine favor—through special knowledge of sacred truths, mental and physical discipline, or extraordinary devotion to the deity. Worship centers on the temples, which range from humble village shrines to magnificent, richly decorated stone edifices built under royal patronage. Beautifully proportioned statues in which the deity may take up temporary residence are adored and beseeched by

▲ **Hindu Temple at Khajuraho**　This sandstone temple of the Hindu deity Shiva, representing the celestial mountain of the gods, was erected at Khajuraho, in central India, around 1000 CE, but it reflects the architectural symbolism of Hindu temples developed in the Gupta period. Worshipers made their way through several rooms to the image of the deity, located in the innermost "womb-chamber" directly beneath the tallest tower. JeremyRichards/Shutterstock.com

▲ **Vishnu Rescuing the Earth Goddess, Fifth Century CE**   This sculpture, carved into the rock wall of a cave at Udayagiri in eastern India, depicts Vishnu in his incarnation as a boar rescuing the Earth Goddess from the vast ocean. As the god treads triumphantly on a subdued snake demon and the joyful goddess clings to his snout, a chorus of gods and sages applaud the miracle. Borromeo/Art Resource, NY

eager worshipers. A common form of worship is *puja*, service to the deity, which can take the form of bathing, clothing, or feeding the statue. Potent blessings are conferred on the man or woman who glimpses the divine image.

Pilgrimage to famous shrines and attendance at festivals offer worshipers additional opportunities to show devotion. The entire Indian subcontinent is dotted with sacred places where worshipers can directly sense and benefit from the inherent power of divinity. Mountains, caves, and certain trees, plants, and rocks are enveloped in an aura of mystery and sanctity. Hindus consider the Ganges River especially sacred, and each year millions of devoted worshipers bathe in its waters and receive their restorative and purifying power. The habit of pilgrimage has promoted contact and the exchange of ideas among people from different parts of India and has helped create a broad Hindu identity and the concept of India as a single civilization, despite enduring political fragmentation.

Religious duties may vary, depending not only on the worshiper's social standing and gender but also his or her stage of life. A young man from one of the three highest classes undergoes a ritual rebirth through the ceremony of the sacred thread, marking the attainment of manhood and readiness to receive religious knowledge. From this point, the ideal life cycle passes through four stages: (1) the young man becomes a student and studies the sacred texts; (2) he then becomes a householder, marries, has children, and acquires material wealth; (3) when his grandchildren are born, he gives up home and family and becomes a forest dweller, meditating on the nature and meaning of existence; (4) he abandons his personal identity altogether and

Section Review

● The Aryas, pastoralist warriors, migrated into the Indus River Valley ca. 1500 BCE and the Ganges Plain after 1000 BCE, driving the Dasas into the southern part of the peninsula.

● The system of classes and castes, a mechanism for regulating the interactions of different groups, was linked to the concept of reincarnation and used to justify the power of the higher classes.

● Brahmin domination was challenged by new religions—Jainism and Buddhism.

● Theravada Buddhism remained close to the ideas of the founder, but Mahayana Buddhism developed gods, saints, monasteries, and shrines.

● Hinduism, created from a Vedic base but including Dravidian and Buddhist elements, preserved Brahmin status and privilege but allowed worshipers to make direct contact with the supernatural.

● Behind the diversity and multiplicity of Indian religion lies an ultimate unity.

becomes a wandering ascetic awaiting death. In the course of a virtuous life he has fulfilled first his duties to society and then his duties to himself, so that by the end he is so disconnected from the world that he can achieve *moksha* (liberation).

The successful transformation of a religion based on Vedic antecedents and the ultimate victory of Hinduism over Buddhism—Buddhism was driven from the land of its birth, though it maintains deep roots in Central, East, and Southeast Asia (see Chapters 9 and 11)—are remarkable phenomena. Hinduism responded to the needs of people for personal deities with whom they could establish direct connections. The austerity of Buddhism in its most authentic form, its denial of the importance of gods, and its expectation that individuals find their own path to enlightenment may have demanded too much of ordinary people. The very features that made Mahayana Buddhism more accessible to the populace—gods, saints, and myths—also made it more easily absorbed into the vast social and cultural fabric of Hinduism.

7-2 Imperial Expansion and Collapse, 324 BCE–650 CE

How, in the face of powerful forces that tended to keep India fragmented, did two great empires—the Mauryan Empire of the fourth to second centuries BCE and the Gupta Empire of the fourth to sixth centuries CE—succeed in unifying much of India?

Political unity in India, on those rare occasions when it has been achieved, has not lasted long. A number of factors have contributed to India's habitual political fragmentation. Different terrains called forth varied forms of organization and economic activity, and peoples occupying diverse zones differed in language and cultural practices. Perhaps the most significant barrier to political unity lay in the complex social hierarchy. Individuals identified themselves primarily in terms of their class and caste; allegiance to a higher political authority was secondary.

Despite these divisive factors, two empires arose in the Ganges Plain in antiquity: the Mauryan (**MORE-yuhn**) Empire of the fourth to second centuries BCE and the Gupta (**GOOP-tuh**) Empire of the fourth to sixth centuries CE. Each extended political control over much of the subcontinent and fostered the formation of a common Indian civilization.

7-2a The Mauryan Empire, 324–184 BCE

Around 600 BCE independent kinship groups and states dotted the landscape of north India. The kingdom of Magadha, in eastern India south of the Ganges (see Map 7.1), began to play an increasingly influential role, however, thanks to wealth based on agriculture, iron mines, and its strategic location astride the trade routes of the eastern Ganges Basin. In the late fourth century BCE Chandragupta Maurya (**MORE-yuh**), a young man from the Vaishya or Shudra class, gained control of Magadha and expanded it into the **Mauryan Empire**—India's first centralized empire. He may have been inspired by the example of Alexander the Great, who had followed up his conquest of the Persian Empire with a foray into the Punjab (northern Pakistan) in 326 BCE (see Chapter 5). Chandragupta (r. 324–301 BCE) and his successors Bindusara (r. 301–273 BCE) and Ashoka (r. 273–232 BCE) extended Mauryan control over the entire subcontinent except the southern tip. Not until the height of the Mughal Empire of the seventeenth century CE was so much of India again under the control of a single government.

Tradition holds that Kautilya, a crafty elderly Brahmin, guided Chandragupta in his conquests and consolidation of power. Kautilya is said to have written a surviving treatise on government, the *Arthashastra* (**ahr-thuh-SHAHS-truh**). Although recent studies have shown that the *Arthashastra* in its present form is a product of the third century CE, its core text may well go back to Kautilya. This coldly pragmatic guide to political success and survival advocates the so-called *mandala* (**man-DAH-luh**) (circle) theory of foreign policy: "My enemy's enemy is my friend." It also presents schemes for enforcing and increasing the collection of tax revenues, and it prescribes the use of spies to keep watch on everyone in the kingdom.

A tax equivalent to as much as one-fourth the value of the harvest supported the Mauryan kings and government. Other revenues came from tolls on trade; government monopolies on

AP® Exam Tip
Know the location of the Mauryan and Gupta empires and how they employed political control.

Mauryan Empire The first state to unify most of the Indian subcontinent. It was founded by Chandragupta Maurya in 324 BCE and survived until 184 BCE. From its capital at Pataliputra in the Ganges Valley it grew wealthy from taxes on agriculture, iron mining, and control of trade routes.

mining, liquor sales, and the manufacture of weapons; and fees charged to those using the irrigation network. Close relatives and associates of the king governed administrative districts based on traditional ethnic boundaries. A large imperial army—with infantry, cavalry, and chariot divisions and the fearsome new element of war elephants—further secured power. Standard coinage issued throughout the empire was used to pay government and military personnel and promote trade.

The Mauryan capital was at Pataliputra (modern Patna), where five tributaries join the Ganges. Surrounded by rivers and further protected by a timber wall and moat, the city extended along the riverbank for 8 miles (13 kilometers). Busy and crowded (the population has been estimated at 270,000), it was governed by six committees with responsibility for manufacturing, trade, sales, taxes, the welfare of foreigners, and the registration of births and deaths.

Ashoka, Chandragupta's grandson, is an outstanding figure in early Indian history. At the beginning of his reign he engaged in military campaigns that extended the boundaries of the empire. During his conquest of Kalinga, a coastal region southeast of Magadha, hundreds of thousands of people were killed, wounded, or deported. Overwhelmed by the brutality of this victory, the young monarch became a convert to Buddhism and preached nonviolence, morality, moderation, and religious tolerance in both government and private life.

Ashoka publicized this program by inscribing edicts on great rocks and polished pillars of sandstone scattered throughout his enormous empire. Among the inscriptions that have survived—they constitute the earliest decipherable Indian writing—is the following:

> For a long time in the past, for many hundreds of years have increased the sacrificial slaughter of animals, violence toward creatures, unfilial conduct toward kinsmen, improper conduct toward Brahmins and ascetics. Now with the practice of morality by King [Ashoka], the sound of war drums has become the call to morality. . . . You [government officials] are appointed to rule over thousands of human beings in the expectation that you will win the affection of all men. All men are my children. Just as I desire that my children will fare well and be happy in this world and the next, I desire the same for all men. . . . King [Ashoka] . . . desires that there should be the growth of the essential spirit of morality or holiness among all sects. . . . There should not be glorification of one's own sect and denunciation of the sect of others for little or no reason. For all the sects are worthy of reverence for one reason or another.[2]

Ashoka, however, was not naive. Despite his commitment to peaceful means, he reminded potential transgressors that "the king, remorseful as he is, has the strength to punish the wrong-doers who do not repent."

7-2b Commerce and Culture in an Era of Political Fragmentation

The Mauryan Empire prospered for a time after Ashoka's death in 232 BCE. Then, weakened by dynastic disputes and the expense of maintaining a large army and administrative bureaucracy, it collapsed from the pressure of attacks in the northwest in 184 BCE. Five hundred years passed before another indigenous state exercised control over northern India.

In the meantime, a series of foreign powers dominated the northwest, present-day Afghanistan and Pakistan, and extended their influence east and south. The first was the Greco-Bactrian kingdom (180–50 BCE), descended from troops and settlers left in Afghanistan by Alexander the Great. Greek influence is evident in the art of this period and in the designs of coins. Occupation by two nomadic groups from Central Asia followed, resulting from large-scale movements of peoples set off by the pressure of Han Chinese forces on the Xiongnu (see Chapter 6). The Shakas, an Iranian people driven southwest along the mountain barrier of the Pamirs and Himalayas, were dominant from 50 BCE to 50 CE. They were followed by the Kushans (**KOO-shahn**), originally from Xinjiang in northwest China, who were preeminent from 50 to 240 CE. At its height the Kushan kingdom controlled much of present-day Uzbekistan, Afghanistan, Pakistan, and northwest India, fostering trade and prosperity by connecting to both the overland Silk Road and Arabian seaports (see Chapter 9). The eastern Ganges region reverted to a patchwork of small principalities, as it had been before the Mauryan era.

Despite political fragmentation in the five centuries after the Mauryan collapse, there were many signs of economic, cultural, and intellectual vitality. The network of roads and towns that had sprung up under the Mauryans fostered lively commerce within the subcontinent, and India

AP® Exam Tip
Be familiar with the role played by Emperor Ashoka in the spread of Buddhism.

AP® Exam Tip
Identify and explain the technological innovations that facilitated long-distance trade in this time period.

Ashoka Third ruler of the Mauryan Empire in India (r. 273–232 BCE). He converted to Buddhism and broadcast his precepts on inscribed stones and pillars, the earliest surviving Indian writing.

---

[2]B. G. Gokhale, *Asoka Maurya* (New York, NY: Twayne, 1966), 152–153, 156–157, 160.

was at the heart of international land and sea trade routes that linked China, Southeast Asia, Central Asia, the Middle East, East Africa, and the lands of the Mediterranean. The growth of crafts (metalwork, cloth making and dying, jewelry, perfume, glass, stone and terra-cotta sculpture), the increasing use of coins, and the development of local and long-distance commerce fostered the expansion and prosperity of urban centers. In the absence of a strong central authority, guilds of merchants and artisans became politically powerful in the towns. They were wealthy patrons of culture and endowed the religious sects to which they adhered—particularly Buddhism and Jainism—with richly decorated temples and monuments.

During the last centuries BCE and first centuries CE the two greatest Indian epics, the *Ramayana* (**ruh-muh-YAH-nuh**) and the *Mahabharata* (**muh-huh-BAH-ruh-tuh**), based on oral predecessors dating back many centuries, achieved their final form. The events that both epics describe are said to have occurred several million years in the past, but the political forms, social organization, and other elements of cultural context—proud kings, beautiful queens, wars among kinship groups, heroic conduct, and chivalric values—seem to reflect the conditions of the early Vedic period, when Arya warrior societies were moving onto the Ganges Plain.

The vast pageant of the *Mahabharata* (it is eight times the length of the Greek *Iliad* and *Odyssey* combined) tells the story of two sets of cousins, the Pandavas and Kauravas, whose quarrel over succession to the throne leads them to a cataclysmic battle at the field of Kurukshetra. The battle is so destructive on all sides that the eventual winner, Yudhishthira, is reluctant to accept the fruits of so tragic a victory.

The *Bhagavad-Gita*, quoted at the beginning of this chapter, is a self-contained (and perhaps originally separate) episode set in the midst of those events. The great hero Arjuna, at first reluctant to fight his own kinsmen, is tutored by the god Krishna and learns the necessity of fulfilling his duty as a warrior. Death means nothing in a universe in which souls will be reborn again and again. The climactic moment comes when Krishna reveals his true appearance—awesome and overwhelmingly powerful—and his identity as Time itself, the force behind all creation and destruction. The *Bhagavad-Gita* offers an attractive resolution to the tension in Indian civilization between duty to society and duty to one's own soul. Disciplined action—that is, action taken without regard for any personal benefits that might derive from it—is a form of service to the gods and will be rewarded by release from the cycle of rebirths.

This era also saw significant advances in science and linguistics. Indian doctors had a wide knowledge of herbal remedies. Panini (late fourth century BCE) undertook a detailed analysis of Sanskrit word forms and grammar. His work led to the standardization of Sanskrit, arresting its natural development and turning it into a formal, literary, and administrative language. *Prakrits*—popular dialects—emerged to become the ancestors of the modern Indo-European languages of northern and central India.

This period of political fragmentation in the north also saw the rise of the Satavahana dynasty (also called Andhra) in the Deccan Plateau from the second century BCE to the early third century CE (see Map 7.1). Elements of north Indian technology and culture—including iron metallurgy, rice-paddy agriculture, urbanization, writing, coinage, and Brahmin religious authority—spread throughout central India, and indigenous kinship groups were absorbed into the Hindu system of class and caste.

In the southernmost parts of the peninsula were the three **Tamil kingdoms** of Cholas, Pandyas, and Cheras. While in frequent conflict with one another and experiencing periods of ascendancy and decline, they persisted in one form or another for over 2,000 years. The period from the third century BCE to the third century CE was a "classical" period of great literary and artistic productivity. Under the patronage of the Pandya kings and the intellectual leadership of an academy of 500 authors, works of literature on a wide range of topics—grammatical treatises, collections of ethical proverbs, epics, and short poems about love, war, wealth, and the beauty of nature—were produced, and music, dance, and drama were performed.

7-2c The Gupta Empire, 320–550 CE

In the early fourth century CE, following the decline of the Kushan and Satavahana regimes in northern and central India, a new imperial entity took shape in the north. Like its Mauryan predecessor, the **Gupta Empire** emerged from the Ganges Plain and had its capital at Pataliputra. The founder, consciously modeling himself on the first Mauryan king, called himself Chandra Gupta (r. 320–335). The monarchs of this dynasty never controlled territories as extensive as those

Mahabharata A vast epic chronicling the events leading up to a cataclysmic battle between related kinship groups in early India. It includes the *Bhagavad-Gita*.

Bhagavad-Gita The most important work of Indian sacred literature, a dialogue between the great warrior Arjuna and the god Krishna on duty and the fate of the spirit.

Tamil kingdoms The kingdoms of southern India, inhabited primarily by speakers of Dravidian languages, developed in partial isolation, and somewhat differently, from the Arya north. They produced epics, poetry, and performance arts. Elements of Tamil religious beliefs were merged into the Hindu synthesis.

Gupta Empire A powerful Indian state based, like its Mauryan predecessor, on a capital at Pataliputra in the Ganges Valley. It controlled most of the Indian subcontinent through a combination of military force and its prestige as a center of sophisticated culture.

of the Mauryans. Nevertheless, over the fifteen-year reign of Chandra Gupta and the forty-year reigns of his three successors—the war-loving Samudra Gupta, Chandra Gupta II, a famed patron of artists and scholars, and Kumara Gupta—Gupta power and influence reached across northern and central India, west to Punjab and east to Bengal, north to Kashmir, and south into the Deccan Plateau (see Map 7.1).

This new empire enjoyed the same strategic advantages as its Mauryan predecessor, sitting astride important trade routes, exploiting the agricultural productivity of the Ganges Plain, and controlling nearby iron deposits. Although similar methods for raising revenue and administering broad territories were adopted, Gupta control was never as effectively centralized as Mauryan authority, and the Gupta administrative bureaucracy and intelligence network were smaller and less pervasive. A standing army, whose strength lay in the excellent horsemanship (learned from the nomadic Kushans) and skill with bow and arrow of its cavalry, maintained tight control and taxation in the core of the empire. Governors, whose position often passed from father to son, had a freer hand in the more outlying areas. Distant subordinate kingdoms and areas inhabited by kinship groups made annual donations of tribute, and garrisons were stationed at key frontier points. At the local level, villages were managed by a headman and council of elders, while the guilds of artisans and merchants had important administrative roles in the cities.

Limited in its ability to enforce its will on outlying areas, the empire found ways to "persuade" others to follow its lead. One medium of persuasion was the splendor, beauty, and orderliness of life at the capital and royal court. The Gupta Empire is a good example of a **theater-state**." A constant round of solemn rituals, dramatic ceremonies, and exciting cultural events was a potent advertisement for the benefits of association with the empire. The center collected luxury goods and profits from trade and redistributed them to dependents through the exchange of gifts and other means. Subordinate princes gained prestige by emulating the Gupta center on whatever scale they could manage, and they maintained close ties through visits, gifts, and marriages to the Gupta royal family.

Astronomers, mathematicians, and other scientists received royal support. Indian mathematicians invented the concept of zero and developed the "Arabic" numerals and system of place-value notation used in most parts of the world today (see Environment & Technology: Indian Mathematics). The Gupta monarchs also supported poets and dramatists and the compilation of law codes and grammatical texts.

Because of the moist climate of the Ganges Plain, few archaeological remains from the Gupta era have survived. An eyewitness account, however, provides valuable information about Pataliputra, the capital city. A Chinese Buddhist monk named Faxian **(fah-shee-en)** made a pilgrimage to the homeland of his faith around 400 CE and left a record of his journey:

> *The royal palace and halls in the midst of the city, which exist now as of old, were all made by spirits which [King Ashoka] employed, and which piled up the stones, reared the walls and gates, and executed the elegant carving and inlaid sculpture-work—in a way which no human hands of this world could accomplish. . . . By the side of the stupa of Ashoka, there has been made a Mahayana [Buddhist] monastery, very grand and beautiful; there is also a Hinayana [Theravada] one; the two together containing six hundred or seven hundred monks. The rules of demeanor and the scholastic arrangements in them are worthy of observation.*[3]

There was a decline in the status of women in this period (see Diversity & Dominance: Relations Between Women and Men in the *Kama Sutra* and the *Arthashastra*). As in Mesopotamia, Greece, and China, several factors—urbanization, increasingly complex political and social structures, and the emergence of a nonagricultural middle class that placed high value on the acquisition and inheritance of property—led to a loss of women's rights and an increase in male control over women's behavior.

Women in India lost the right to own or inherit property. They were also barred from studying sacred texts and participating in sacrificial rituals. In many respects, they were treated as equivalent to the lowest class, the Shudra. A woman was expected to obey first her father, then her husband, and finally her sons. Girls were married at an increasingly early age, sometimes as young as six or seven. This practice meant that the prospective husband could be sure of his wife's

AP® Exam Tip
Understand the role of ideologies, philosophies, and religions on social hierarchies and gender roles.

theater-state Historians' term for a state that acquires prestige and power by developing attractive cultural forms and staging elaborate public ceremonies (as well as redistributing valuable resources) to attract and bind subjects to the center. Examples include the Gupta Empire in India and Srivijaya in Southeast Asia.

[3]James Legge, *The Travels of Fa-hien: Fa-hien's Record of Buddhistic Kingdoms* (Delhi: Oriental Publishers, 1971), 77–79.

Environment & Technology
Indian Mathematics

The so-called Arabic numerals used in most parts of the world today were developed in India. The Indian system of place-value notation was far more efficient than the unwieldy numerical systems of Egyptians, Greeks, and Romans, and the invention of zero was a profound intellectual achievement. This system is used even more widely than the alphabet derived from the Phoenicians (see Chapter 3) and is, in one sense, the only truly global language.

In its fully developed form the Indian method of arithmetic notation employed a base-ten system. It had separate columns for ones, tens, hundreds, and so forth, as well as a zero sign to indicate the absence of units in a given column. This system makes possible the economical expression of even very large numbers. It also allows for the performance of calculations not possible in a system like the numerals of the Romans, where any real calculation had to be done mentally or on a counting board.

A series of early Indian inscriptions using the numerals from 1 to 9 are deeds of property given to religious institutions by kings or other wealthy individuals. They were incised in the Sanskrit language on copper plates. The earliest known example has a date equivalent to 595 CE. A sign for zero is attested by the eighth century, but textual evidence leads to the inference that a place-value system and the zero concept were already known in the fifth century.

This Indian system spread to the Middle East, Southeast Asia, and East Asia by the seventh century. Other peoples quickly recognized its capabilities and adopted it, sometimes using indigenous symbols. Europe received the new technology somewhat later. Gerbert of Aurillac, a French Christian monk, spent time in Spain between 967 and 970, where he was exposed to the mathematics of the Arabs. A great scholar and teacher who eventually became Pope Sylvester II (r. 999–1003), he spread word of the "Arabic" system in the Christian West.

Knowledge of the Indian system of mathematical notation eventually spread throughout Europe, partly through the use of a mechanical calculating device—an improved version of the Roman counting board, with counters inscribed with variants of the Indian numeral forms. Because the counters could be turned sideways or upside down, at first there was considerable variation in the forms. But by the twelfth century they had become standardized into forms close to those in use today. As the capabilities of the place-value system for calculations became clear, the counting board fell into disuse. This led to the adoption of the zero sign—not necessary on the counting board, where a column could be left empty—by the twelfth century. Leonardo Fibonacci, a thirteenth-century CE Italian who

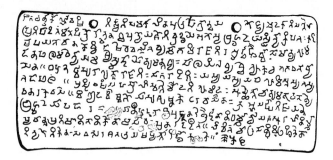

▲ **Copper Plate with Indian Numerals** This property deed from western India shows an early form of the symbol system for numbers that spread to the Middle East and Europe and today is used all over the world. Facsimile by Georges Ifrah. Reproduced by permission of Georges Ifrah

learned algebra in Muslim North Africa and employed the Arabic numeral system in his mathematical treatise, gave additional impetus to the movement to discard the traditional system of Roman numerals.

Why was this marvelous system of mathematical notation invented in ancient India? The answer may lie in the way its range and versatility correspond to elements of Indian cosmology. The Indians conceived of immense spans of time—trillions of years (far exceeding current scientific estimates of the age of the universe as approximately 14 billion years)—during which innumerable universes like our own were created, existed for a finite time, then were destroyed. In one popular creation myth, Vishnu is slumbering on the coils of a giant serpent at the bottom of the ocean, and worlds are being created and destroyed as he exhales and inhales. In Indian thought our world, like others, has existed for a series of epochs lasting more than 4 million years, yet the period of its existence is but a brief and insignificant moment in the vast sweep of time. The Indians developed a number system that allowed them to express concepts of this magnitude.

Questions for Analysis

1. In what ways was the Indian system of mathematics superior to other, earlier systems?

2. When and how did the Indian system reach Europe, and why do we refer to our numbers as "Arabic numerals?"

3. Why might a mathematical system capable of economically expressing and manipulating very large numbers have originated in India?

AP® Exam Tip

Analyze the importance of monastic communities in offering new status to some men and women. Be able to provide specific examples.

virginity and, by bringing her up in his own household, could train her to suit his purposes. The most extreme form of control took place in parts of India where a widow was expected to cremate herself on her husband's funeral pyre. This ritual, called *sati* (**suh-TEE**), was seen as a way of keeping a woman "pure." Women who declined to make this ultimate gesture of devotion were forbidden to remarry, shunned socially, and given little opportunity to earn a living.

Some women escaped male control by entering a Jainist or Buddhist religious community. Status also gave women more freedom. Women who belonged to powerful families and

▶ **Wall Painting from the Caves at Ajanta, Sixth Century CE** During and after the Gupta period, natural caves in the Deccan were turned into shrines decorated with sculpture and painting. This painting reflects members of different castes and ethnic groups. SEF/Art Resource, NY

courtesans trained in poetry and music as well as the ways of providing sexual pleasure had high social standing and sometimes gave money for the erection of religious shrines.

The Mauryans had been Buddhists, but the Gupta monarchs were Hindus. They revived ancient Vedic practices to bring an aura of sanctity to their position. This period also saw a reassertion of the importance of class and caste and the influence of Brahmin priests. In return for the religious validation of their rule given by the Brahmins, the Guptas gave the priests extensive grants of land. The Brahmins became wealthy from the revenues, which they collected directly from the peasants, and they even exercised administrative and judicial authority over the villages in their domains. Nevertheless, it was an era of religious tolerance. The Gupta kings were patrons for Hindu, Buddhist, and Jain endeavors. Buddhist monasteries with hundreds or even thousands of monks and nuns in residence flourished in the cities, and a Buddhist university was established at Nalanda. Northern India was the destination of Buddhist pilgrims from Southeast and East Asia, traveling to visit the birthplace of their faith.

The classic form of the Hindu temple evolved during the Gupta era. Sitting atop a raised platform surmounted by high towers, the temple was patterned on the sacred mountain or palace in which the gods of mythology resided and represented the inherent order of the universe. From an exterior courtyard worshipers approached the central shrine, where the statue of the deity stood. Paintings or sculptured depictions of gods and mythical events covered the walls of the best-endowed sanctuaries. Cave-temples carved out of rock were also richly adorned with frescoes or sculpture.

The vibrant commerce of the previous era continued into the Gupta period, with artisan guilds playing an influential role in the economic, political, and religious life of the towns. The Guptas sought control of the ports on the Arabian Sea but saw a decline in trade with the weakened Roman Empire. In compensation, trade with Southeast and East Asia was on the rise.

AP® Exam Tip
Understand how art and architecture reflected the values of religions and belief systems.

The ancient Indians articulated three broad areas of human concern: dharma—the realm of religious and moral behavior; artha—the acquisition of wealth and property; and kama—the pursuit of pleasure. The Kama Sutra, *which means "Treatise on Pleasure," while best known in the West for its detailed descriptions of erotic activities, is actually far more than a sex manual. It addresses, in a very broad sense, the relations between women and men in ancient Indian society, providing valuable information about the activities of men and women, the psychology of relationships, the forms of courtship and marriage, the household responsibilities of married women, appropriate behavior, and much more. The author of this text, Vatsyayana, lived in the third century CE.*

When a girl of the same caste, and a virgin, is married in accordance with the precepts of Holy Writ, the results of such a union are the acquisition of Dharma and Artha, offspring, affinity, increase of friends, and untarnished love. For this reason a man should fix his affections upon a girl who is of good family, whose parents are alive, and who is three years or more younger than himself. She should be born of a highly respectable family, possessed of wealth, well connected, and with many relations and friends. She should also be beautiful, of a good disposition, with lucky marks on her body, and with good hair, nails, teeth, ears, eyes and breasts, neither more nor less than they ought to be, and no one of them entirely wanting, and not troubled with a sickly body. . . . But at all events, says Ghotakamukha [an earlier writer], a girl who has been already joined with others (i.e., no longer a maiden) should never be loved, for it would be reproachable to do such a thing.

Now in order to bring about a marriage with such a girl as described above, the parents and relations of the man should exert themselves, as also such friends on both sides as may be desired to assist in the matter. These friends should bring to the notice of the girl's parents the faults, both present and future, of all the other men that may wish to marry her, and should at the same time extol even to exaggeration all the excellencies, ancestral and paternal, of their friend, so as to endear him to them. . . . Others again should rouse the jealousy of the girl's mother by telling her that their friend has a chance of getting from some other quarter even a better girl than hers.

A girl should be taken as a wife, as also given in marriage, when fortune, signs, omens, and the words of others are favourable, for, says Ghotakamukha, a man should not marry at any time he likes. A girl who is asleep, crying, or gone out of the house when sought in marriage, or who is betrothed to another, should not be married. The following also should be avoided:

- One who is kept concealed
- One who has an ill-sounding name
- One who has her nose depressed
- One who has her nostril turned up
- One who is formed like a male
- One who is bent down
- One who has crooked thighs
- One who has a projecting forehead
- One who has a bald head
- One who does not like purity
- One who has been polluted by another
- One who is disfigured in any way
- One who has fully arrived at puberty
- One who is a friend
- One who is a younger sister
- One who is a Varshakari [prone to extreme perspiration]

But some authors say that prosperity is gained only by marrying that girl to whom one becomes attached, and that therefore no other girl but the one who is loved should be married by anyone. . . .

A virtuous woman, who has affection for her husband, should act in conformity with his wishes as if he were a divine being, and with his consent should take upon herself the whole care of his family. She should keep the whole house well cleaned, and arrange flowers of various kinds in different parts of it, and make the floor smooth and polished so as to give the whole a neat and becoming appearance. She should surround the house with a garden, and place ready in it all the materials required for the morning, noon and evening sacrifices. Moreover she should herself revere the sanctuary of the Household Gods. . . .

As regards meals, she should always consider what her husband likes and dislikes and what things are good for him, and what are injurious to him. When she hears the sounds of his footsteps coming home she should at once get up and be ready to

Adventurous merchants from the ports of eastern and southern India made the sea voyage to the Malay (**muh-LAY**) Peninsula and islands of Indonesia to exchange Indian cotton cloth, ivory, metalwork, and animals for Chinese silk or Indonesian spices. The overland Silk Road from China was also in operation but was vulnerable to disruption by Central Asian nomads (see Chapter 9).

By the later fifth century CE the Gupta Empire was coming under pressure from the Huns, nomadic invaders from the steppes of Central Asia who poured into the northwest corridor. Defense of this distant frontier region eventually exhausted the imperial treasury, and the empire collapsed by 550.

do whatever he may command her, and either order her female servant to wash his feet, or wash them herself. When going anywhere with her husband, she should put on her ornaments, and without his consent she should not either give or accept invitations, or attend marriages and sacrifices, or sit in the company of female friends, or visit the temples of the Gods. And if she wants to engage in any kind of games or sports, she should not do it against his will. In the same way she should always sit down after him, and get up before him, and should never awaken him when he is asleep.

The core of the Arthashastra, *which means "Science of Wealth," may have been composed in the later third century BCE by Kautilya, an adviser to the first Mauryan ruler, Chandragupta, but the text as we have it includes later additions. While the* Arthashastra *is primarily concerned with how the ruler may gain and keep power, it includes prescriptions on other aspects of life, including the kinds of problems that may threaten or destroy marriages.*

If a woman either brings forth no live children, or has no male issue, or is barren, her husband shall wait for eight years before marrying another. If she bears only a dead child, he has to wait for ten years. If she brings forth only females, he has to wait for twelve years. Then, if he is desirous to have sons, he may marry another. . . . If a husband either is of bad character, or is long gone abroad, or has become a traitor to his king, or is likely to endanger the life of his wife, or has fallen from his caste, or has lost virility, he may be abandoned by his wife. . . .

Women of refractive natures shall not be taught manners by using such expressions as "You, half-naked!; you, fully-naked; you, cripple; you, fatherless; you, motherless." Nor shall she be given more than three beats, either with a bamboo bark or with a rope or with the palm of the hand, on her hips. . . .

A woman who hates her husband, who has passed the period of seven turns of her menses, and who loves another, shall immediately return to her husband both the endowment and jewelry she has received from him, and allow him to lie down with another woman. A man, hating his wife, shall allow her to take shelter in the house of a beggar woman, or of her lawful guardians or of her kinsmen. . . . A woman, hating her husband, cannot divorce her husband against his will. Nor can a man divorce his wife against her will. But from mutual enmity divorce may be obtained. . . .

If a woman engages herself in amorous sports, or drinking in the face of an order to the contrary, she shall be fined three panas. She shall pay a fine of six panas for going out at daytime to sports or to see a woman or spectacles. She shall pay a fine of twelve panas if she goes out to see another man or for sports. For the same offences committed at night the fines shall be doubled. If a woman goes out while the husband is asleep or intoxicated, or if she shuts the door of the house against her husband, she shall be fined twelve panas. If a woman keeps him out of the house at night, she shall pay double the above fine. If a man and a woman make signs to each other with a view to sensual enjoyment, or carry on secret conversation for the same purpose, the woman shall pay a fine of twenty-four panas and the man double that amount. . . . For holding conversation in suspicious places, whips may be substituted for fines. In the center of the village, an outcaste person may whip such women five times on each of the sides of their body. . . .

A Kshatriya who commits adultery with an unguarded Brahman woman shall be punished with the highest amercement; a Vaishya doing the same shall be deprived of the whole of his property; and a Shudra shall be burnt alive wound round in mats. . . . A man who commits adultery with a woman of low caste shall be banished, with prescribed marks branded on his forehead, or shall be degraded to the same caste. A Shudra or an outcaste who commits adultery with a woman of low caste shall be put to death, while the woman shall have her ears and nose cut off.

AP® History Reasoning Skills

Comparison *In what ways are the expectations for women, as laid out in the Kama Sutra, both similar to and different from the roles of women in China or Rome at the same time?*

Contextualization *In light of the prescriptions for how a married woman should treat her husband, in what ways do you think the nature of the relationship described here between a husband and wife might differ from modern-day understandings of marriage?*

Sources: First selection from Sir Richard Burton and F. F. Arbuthnot, *The Kama Sutra of Vatsyayana* (1883), sections III.1, III.4, III.5, IV.1, found at *www.sacredtexts.com/sex/kama/index.htm.* Second selection from R. Shamasastry, *Kautilya's Arthashastra,* 2d ed. (1923), sections III.2, III.3, IV.13, from Internet Indian History Sourcebook at *www.fordham.edu/halsall/india/kautilya2.html.*

The early seventh century saw a brief revival of imperial unity. Harsha Vardhana (r. 606–647), ruler of the region around Delhi, extended his power over the northern plain and moved his capital to Kanauj on the Ganges River. By this time cities and commerce were in decline, much of the land had been given as grants to Brahmin priests and government officials, and the administration was decentralized, depending on the allegiance of largely autonomous vassal rulers. In many respects the situation was parallel to that of the later Roman Empire in Europe (see Chapter 6), as India moved toward a more feudal social and economic structure. After Harsha's death, northern India reverted to its customary state of political fragmentation

Section Review

- The Mauryan Empire, founded in the late fourth century BCE by Chandragupta Maurya, eventually controlled most of the subcontinent.

- King Ashoka, a convert to Buddhism, inscribed stones and pillars with a call to nonviolence, moderation, and religious toleration.

- After the Mauryan fall in 184 BCE, foreign occupiers—Indo-Greeks, Shakas, and Kushans—controlled the northwest.

- Despite political fragmentation, commerce and culture thrived.

- A renaissance of art and literature occurred in the Tamil kingdoms of south India between the third century BCE and the third century CE.

- The Gupta Empire, while not as extensive as the Mauryan Empire, fostered scholarship, science, and the arts from the fourth to sixth centuries CE.

and remained divided until the Islamic invasions of the eleventh and twelfth centuries (see Chapter 15).

During and after the centuries of Gupta ascendancy and decline in the north, the Deccan Plateau and the southern part of the peninsula followed an independent path. In this region, where the landscape is segmented by mountains, rocky plateaus, tropical forests, and sharply cut river courses, there were many small centers of power. From the sixth to twelfth centuries, the Pallavas, Chalukyas, and other warrior dynasties collected tribute and plundered as far as their strength permitted, storing their wealth in urban fortresses. These rulers sought legitimacy and fame as patrons of religion and culture, and much of the distinguished art and architecture of the period were produced in the kingdoms of the south. Many elements of northern Indian religion and culture spread in the south, including the class and caste system, Brahmin religious authority, and worship of Vishnu and Shiva. These kingdoms also served as the conduit through which Indian religion and culture reached Southeast Asia.

7-3 Southeast Asia, 50–1025 CE

How did a number of states in Southeast Asia become wealthy and powerful by exploiting their position on the trade routes between China and India?

Southeast Asia consists of three geographical zones: the Indochina mainland, the Malay Peninsula, and thousands of islands extending on an east–west axis far out into the Pacific Ocean (see Map 7.2). Encompassing a vast area of land and water, this region is now occupied by the countries of Myanmar (myahn-MAH) (Burma), Thailand, Laos, Cambodia, Vietnam, Malaysia, Singapore, Indonesia, Brunei (broo-NIE), and the Philippines. Poised between the ancient centers of China and India, Southeast Asia has been influenced by the cultures of both civilizations. The region first rose to prominence and prosperity because of its intermediate role in the trade exchanges between southern and eastern Asia.

The strategic importance of Southeast Asia is enhanced by the region's natural resources. This is a geologically active zone; the islands are the tops of a chain of volcanoes. Lying along the equator, Southeast Asia has a tropical climate. The temperature hovers around 80°F (30°C), and the monsoon winds provide dependable rainfall throughout the year. Thanks to several growing cycles each year, the region is capable of supporting a large human population. The most fertile agricultural lands lie along the floodplains of the largest silt-bearing rivers or contain rich volcanic soil deposited by ancient eruptions.

7-3a Early Civilization

Rain forest covers much of Southeast Asia. As early as 2000 BCE people in this region practiced *swidden agriculture*, clearing land for farming by cutting and burning the vegetation. The cleared land was farmed for several growing seasons. When the soil was exhausted, the farmers abandoned the patch, allowing the forest to reclaim it, while they cleared and cultivated other nearby fields in similar fashion. Rice was the staple food—labor-intensive (see Chapter 4) but able to support a large population. A number of plant and animal species spread from Southeast Asia to other regions, including rice, soybeans, sugar cane, yams, bananas, coconuts, chickens, and pigs.

The Malay peoples who became the dominant population in this region were the product of several waves of migration from southern China beginning around 3000 BCE. Some indigenous peoples merged with the Malay newcomers; others retreated to remote mountain and forest zones. Subsequently (beginning, perhaps, around 1600 BCE), rising population and disputes within communities prompted streams of people to leave the Southeast Asian mainland for the

MAP 7.2 **Southeast Asia** Southeast Asia's position between the ancient centers of civilization in India and China had a major impact on its history. In the first millennium CE a series of powerful and wealthy states arose in the region by gaining control of major trade routes: first Funan, based in southern Vietnam, Cambodia, and the Malay Peninsula, then Srivijaya on the island of Sumatra, then smaller states on the island of Java. Shifting trade routes led to the rise and fall of the various centers.

The challenge for merchant vessels was to pass from the Indian Ocean to the South China Sea, or vice versa. How did the movement of the main route from the Isthmus of Kra to the Malacca and Sunda Straits affect the rise of different centers?

islands. By the first millennium BCE Southeast Asians had developed impressive navigational skills. They knew how to ride the monsoon winds and interpret the patterns of swells, winds, clouds, and bird and sea life. Over a period of several thousand years groups of Malay peoples in large, double outrigger canoes spread out across the Pacific and Indian Oceans—half the circumference of the earth—to settle thousands of islands.

The inhabitants of Southeast Asia clustered along riverbanks or in fertile volcanic plains. Their fields and villages were never far from the rain forest, with its wild animals and numerous plant species. Forest trees provided fruit, wood, and spices, and the shallow waters surrounding the islands teemed with fish. This region was also an early center of metallurgy. Metalsmiths heated copper and tin ore to the right temperature for producing and shaping bronze implements by using hollow bamboo tubes to funnel oxygen to the furnace.

Northern Indochina, by its geographic proximity, was vulnerable to Chinese pressure and cultural influences, and it was under Chinese political control for a thousand years (111 BCE–939 CE). Farther south, larger states emerged in the early centuries CE in response to two powerful forces: commerce and Hindu-Buddhist culture.

Southeast Asia was situated along the trade routes that merchants used to carry Chinese silk westward to India and the Mediterranean. The movements of nomadic peoples had disrupted the old land route across Central Asia, but Indian demand for silk was increasing—both for domestic use and for transshipment to satisfy the fast-growing luxury market in the Roman Empire. Gradually merchants extended this exchange network to include goods from Southeast Asia, such as aromatic woods, resins, and cinnamon, pepper, cloves, nutmeg, and other spices. Southeast Asian centers rose to prominence by serving this trade network and controlling key points.

The other force leading to the rise of larger political entities was the influence of Hindu-Buddhist culture imported from India. Commerce brought Indian merchants and sailors into the ports of Southeast Asia. As Buddhism spread, Southeast Asia became a way station for Indian missionaries and East Asian pilgrims going to and coming from the birthplace of their faith.

AP® Exam Tip
Explain how Buddhism changed over time as it spread throughout Southeast Asia.

Shrewd Malay rulers looked to Indian traditions as a rich source of ideas and prestige. They borrowed Sanskrit terms such as *maharaja* (**mah-huh-RAH-juh**) (great king), utilized Indian models of bureaucracy, ceremonial practices, and forms of artistic representation, and employed priests, administrators, and scribes skilled in Sanskrit writing to expedite government business. Their special connection to powerful gods and higher knowledge raised them above their rivals.

However, the Southeast Asian kingdoms were not just passive recipients of Indian culture. They took what was useful to them and synthesized it with indigenous beliefs, values, and institutions—for example, local concepts of chiefship, ancestor worship, and forms of oaths. Moreover, they trained their own people in the new ways, so that the bureaucracy contained both foreign experts and native disciples. The whole process amounted to a cultural dialogue between India and Southeast Asia in which both were active participants.

The first major Southeast Asian center, called "**Funan**" (**FOO-nahn**) by Chinese visitors, flourished between the first and sixth centuries CE (see Map 7.2), with its capital at the modern site of Oc-Eo in southern Vietnam. Funan occupied the delta of the Mekong (**MAY-kawng**) River, a "rice bowl" capable of supporting a large population, and its rulers mobilized large numbers of laborers to dig irrigation channels and prevent destructive floods. By extending its control over most of southern Indochina and the Malay Peninsula, Funan was able to dominate the trade route from India to China. The route began in the ports of northeast India, crossed the Bay of Bengal, proceeded by land over the Isthmus of Kra on the Malay Peninsula, and then continued across the South China Sea (see Map 7.2). Indian merchants found that offloading their goods from ships and carrying them across the narrow strip of land was safer than making the 1,000-mile (1,600-kilometer) voyage around the Malay Peninsula—a dangerous trip marked by treacherous currents, rocky shoals, and pirates. Once the portage across the isthmus was finished, the merchants needed food and lodging while waiting for the monsoon winds to shift so they could make the last leg of the voyage to China by sea. Funan stockpiled food and provided security for those engaged in this trade—in return for customs duties and other fees.

Chinese observers have left reports of the prosperity and sophistication of Funan, emphasizing the presence of walled cities, palaces, archives, systems of taxation, and state-organized agriculture. Nevertheless, Funan declined in the sixth century. The most likely explanation is that international trade routes changed and Funan no longer held a strategic position.

Funan An early complex society in Southeast Asia between the first and sixth centuries CE. Centered in the rich rice-growing region of southern Vietnam, it controlled the passage of trade across the Malaysian isthmus.

Srivijaya A state based on the Indonesian island of Sumatra between the seventh and eleventh centuries CE. It amassed wealth and power by a combination of selective adaptation of Indian technologies and concepts, control of the lucrative trade routes between India and China, and skillful showmanship and diplomacy in holding together a disparate realm of inland and coastal territories.

7-3b The Srivijayan Kingdom

By the sixth century a new, all-sea route had developed. Merchants and travelers from south India and Sri Lanka now sailed through the Strait of Malacca (between the west side of the Malay Peninsula and the northeast coast of the island of Sumatra) and into the South China Sea. Although presenting both human and navigational hazards, the new route significantly shortened the journey.

A new center of power, **Srivijaya** (**sree-vih-JUH-yuh**)—Sanskrit for "Great Conquest"—dominated the new southerly route by 683 CE. The capital of the Srivijayan kingdom was at modern-day Palembang in southeastern Sumatra, 50 miles (80 kilometers) up the broad and navigable Musi River, with a good natural harbor. The kingdom was well situated to control the southern part of the Malay Peninsula, Sumatra, parts of Java and Borneo, and the Malacca (**muh-LAH-kuh**) and Sunda straits—vital passageways for shipping (see Map 7.2).

The Srivijayan kingdom gained ascendancy over its rivals and assumed control of the international trade route by fusing four distinct ecological zones into an interdependent network. The core area was the productive agricultural plain along the Musi River. The king and his clerks, judges, and tax collectors controlled this zone directly. Control was less direct over the second zone, the upland regions of Sumatra's

◀ **Srivijaya-Style Stupa in Thailand, Eighth Century CE**   This brick and mortar shrine at Chaiya shows that the influence of Srivijaya reached far into the Southeast Asian mainland.   Michael Freeman/Getty Images

▲ **Aerial View of the Buddhist Monument at Borobodur, Java** This great monument of volcanic stone is more than 300 feet (90 meters) in length and over 100 feet (30 meters) high. Pilgrims made a 3-mile-long (nearly 5-kilometer-long) winding ascent through ten levels intended to represent the ideal Buddhist journey from ignorance to enlightenment. Numerous sculptured reliefs depicting Buddhist legends provide glimpses of daily life in early Java. robertharding/Alamy Stock Photo

interior, with its commercially valuable forest products. Local rulers there were bound to the center by oaths of loyalty, elaborate court ceremonies, and the sharing of profits from trade. The third zone consisted of river ports that had been Srivijaya's main rivals. They were conquered and controlled thanks to an alliance between Srivijaya and neighboring sea nomads, pirates who served as a Srivijayan navy in return for a steady income.

The fourth zone was a fertile "rice bowl" on the central plain of the nearby island of Java— a region so productive, because of its volcanic soil, that it houses and feeds the majority of the population of present-day Indonesia. Srivijayan monarchs maintained alliances, cemented by intermarriage, with several ruling dynasties in this region, and the Srivijayan kings claimed descent from the main Javanese dynasty. These arrangements gave Srivijaya access to large quantities of foodstuffs that people living in the capital and merchants and sailors visiting the various ports needed.

The kings of Srivijaya who constructed and maintained this complex network of social, political, and economic relationships were men of energy and skill. Although their authority depended in part on force, it owed more to diplomatic and even theatrical talents. Like the Gupta monarchy, Srivijaya was a theater-state, securing its preeminence and binding dependents by its sheer splendor and its ability to attract labor, talent, and luxury products. The court was the scene of ceremonies designed to dazzle observers and reinforce an image of wealth, power, and sanctity. Subordinate rulers took oaths of loyalty carrying dire threats of punishment for violations, and in their home locales they imitated the splendid ceremonials of the capital.

The Srivijayan king, drawing upon Buddhist conceptions, presented himself as a bodhisattva, one who had achieved enlightenment and utilized his precious insights for the betterment of his subjects. The king was believed to have magical powers, controlling powerful forces of fertility associated with the rivers in flood and mediating between the spiritually potent realms of the mountains and the sea. He was also said to be so wealthy that he deposited bricks of gold in the river estuary to appease the local gods, and a hillside near town was covered with silver

Section Review

- Climate and resources enabled Southeast Asia to support large human populations.

- Located on the trade and pilgrimage routes between China and India, Southeast Asia came under strong Hindu and Buddhist influence.

- Shrewd rulers used Indian knowledge and personnel to enhance their power and prestige.

- Funan rose to prominence between the first and sixth centuries CE by controlling the trade route across the Malay Peninsula.

- The Srivijayan kingdom flourished between the seventh and eleventh centuries CE and dominated the new international trade route through the Strait of Malacca.

and gold images of the Buddha. The gold originated in East or West Africa and came to Southeast Asia through trade with the Muslim world (see Chapter 9).

The kings built and patronized Buddhist monasteries and schools. In central Java local dynasties allied with Srivijaya built magnificent temple complexes to advertise their glory. The most famous of these, **Borobodur (booh-roe-boe-DOOR)**, built between 770 and 825 CE, was the largest human construction in the Southern Hemisphere.

The kings of Srivijaya carried out this marvelous balancing act for centuries. But the system was vulnerable to shifts in the pattern of international trade. Some such change must have contributed to the decline of Srivijaya in the eleventh century, even though the immediate cause was a destructive raid on the capital Palembang by forces of the Chola kingdom of southeast India in 1025 CE.

After the decline of Srivijaya, leadership passed to new, vigorous kingdoms on the eastern end of Java, and the maritime realm of Southeast Asia remained prosperous and connected to international trade networks. Through the ages Europeans remained dimly aware of this region as a source of spices and other luxury items. Some four centuries after the decline of Srivijaya, an Italian navigator serving under the flag of Spain—Christopher Columbus—sailed westward across the Atlantic Ocean, seeking to establish a direct route to the fabled "Indies" from which the spices came.

7-4 Conclusion

This chapter traces the emergence of complex societies in India and Southeast Asia between the second millennium BCE and the first millennium CE. Because of migrations, trade, and the spread of belief systems, an Indian style of civilization spread throughout the subcontinent and adjoining regions and eventually made its way to the mainland and island chains of Southeast Asia. In this period were laid cultural foundations that in large measure still endure.

The development and spread of belief systems—Vedism, Buddhism, Jainism, and Hinduism—have a central place in this chapter because nearly all the sources of information are religious. A museum visitor examining artifacts from ancient Mesopotamia, Egypt, the Greco-Roman Mediterranean, and China will find many objects of a religious nature. Only the Indian artifacts, however, will be almost exclusively from the religious sphere.

Writing came later to India than to other parts of the Eastern Hemisphere, for reasons particular to the Indian situation. Like Indian artifacts, most ancient Indian texts are of a religious nature. Ancient Indians did not develop a historical consciousness and generate historiographic texts like their Israelite, Greek, and Chinese contemporaries, primarily because they held a strikingly different view of time. The distinctive Indian conception—of vast epochs in which universes are created and destroyed again and again and the essential spirit of living creatures is reincarnated repeatedly—made the particulars of any brief moment seem relatively insignificant.

The tension between divisive and unifying forces can be seen in many aspects of Indian life. Political and social division has been the norm throughout much of the history of India, a consequence of the topographical and environmental diversity of the subcontinent and the complex mix of ethnic and linguistic groups inhabiting it. The elaborate structure of classes and castes was a response to this diversity—an attempt to organize the population and position individuals within an accepted hierarchy, as well as to regulate group interactions. Strong central governments, such as those of the Mauryan and Gupta kings, gained ascendancy for a time and promoted prosperity and development. They rose to dominance by gaining control of metal resources and important trade routes, developing effective military and administrative institutions, and creating cultural forms that inspired admiration and emulation. However, as in archaic Greece and Warring States China, the periods of fragmentation and multiple small centers of power seemed as economically and intellectually dynamic as the periods of unity.

Borobodur A massive stone monument on the Indonesian island of Java, erected by the Sailendra kings around 800 CE. The winding ascent through ten levels, decorated with rich relief carving, is a Buddhist allegory for the progressive stages of enlightenment.

Many distinctive social and intellectual features of Indian civilization—the class and caste system, models of kingship and statecraft, and Vedic, Jainist, and Buddhist belief systems—originated in the great river valleys of the north, where descendants of Indo-European immigrants predominated. Hinduism then embraced elements drawn from the Dravidian cultures of the south as well as from Buddhism. The capacity of the Hindu tradition to assimilate a wide range of popular beliefs facilitated the spread of a common Indian civilization across the subcontinent, although there was, and is, considerable variation from one region to another.

Key Terms

monsoon p. 170	**Buddha** p. 174	**Ashoka** p. 179	**theater-state** p. 181
Vedas p. 170	**Mahayana Buddhism** p. 175	*Mahabharata* p. 180	**Funan** p. 188
varna/jati p. 172	**Theravada Buddhism** p. 175	*Bhagavad-Gita* p. 180	**Srivijaya** p. 188
karma p. 173	**Hinduism** p. 175	**Tamil kingdoms** p. 180	**Borobodur** p. 190
moksha p. 173	**Mauryan Empire** p. 178	**Gupta Empire** p. 180	

Review Questions

1. Why might civilizations, such as that of ancient India, be more innotive and culturally productive in times of political fragmentation than in times of unification?

2. Why and how was the Hindu religion that evolved from Vedism able to overcome the challenges posed by Buddhism and Jainism, whereas Greco-Roman paganism could not ultimately prevail against Christianity?

3. How did certain Southeast Asian rulers use Indian institutions, religions, and technologies to surpass their indigenous rivals?

 MindTap® is a fully online, personalized learning experience built upon Cengage Learning content. MindTap® combines student learning tools–readings, multimedia, activities, and assessments–into a singular Learning Path that guides students through the course and helps students develop the critical thinking, analysis, and communication skills that are essential to academic and professional success.

Multiple-Choice Questions

Questions 1–4 refer to the passages below.

"Matthew, Chapter 4

[23] And Jesus went about all Galilee, teaching in their synagogues, and preaching the gospel of the kingdom, and healing all manner of sickness and all manner of disease among the people.

[24] And his fame went throughout all Syria: and they brought unto him all sick people that were taken with divers diseases and torments, and those which were possessed with devils, and those which were lunatick, and those that had the palsy; and he healed them.

Matthew, Chapter 5

[1] And seeing the multitudes, he went up into a mountain: and when he was set, his disciples came unto him:

[2] And he opened his mouth, and taught them, saying,

[3] Blessed are the poor in spirit: for theirs is the kingdom of heaven . . .

[5] Blessed are the meek: for they shall inherit the earth.

[6] Blessed are they which do hunger and thirst after righteousness: for they shall be filled . . .

[10] Blessed are they which are persecuted for righteousness' sake: for theirs is the kingdom of heaven."

The Gospel of Matthew from the *King James Bible*

"'The Tathagata' [a being who has reached Nirvana], the Buddha continued, 'does not seek salvation in austerities, but neither does he, for that reason, indulge in worldly pleasures, nor live in abundance. The Tathagata has found the middle path.

There are two extremes, which the man who has given up the world ought not to follow—the habitual practice, on the one hand, of self-indulgence which is unworthy, vain and fit only for the worldly-minded and the habitual practice, on the other hand, of self-mortification, which is painful, useless and unprofitable.

Neither abstinence from fish or flesh, nor going naked, nor shaving the head, nor wearing matted hair, nor dressing in a rough garment, nor covering oneself with dirt, nor sacrificing to Agni, will cleanse a man who is not free from delusions.'"

An account of the Buddha's sermon at Benares

1. Which of the following statements best describes Christianity as presented in the excerpt?

    (A) Jesus preached the importance of equality between the genders.

    (B) Jesus supported violence if it enabled salvation.

    (C) Jesus believed that salvation could be found through prayer alone.

    (D) Jesus taught the importance of humility and compassion.

2. In the passage above, the Buddha advocated

    (A) that his followers abstain from the pursuit of knowledge.

    (B) that his followers choose to live in a moderate fashion.

    (C) that his followers abstain from eating the flesh of animals or fish.

    (D) that his followers go naked or dress in simple clothes.

3. Both Christianity and Buddhism challenged the traditional Vedic religion by emphasizing what?

    (A) The value of wealth to achieve goals.

    (B) The role of social class in defining individual worth.

    (C) The importance of the individual over preordained life circumstances.

    (D) The impotence of the individual in the face of the gods.

4. Which of the following comparisons is most accurate?

    (A) Both Christianity and Buddhism asserted universal truths and promised salvation.

    (B) Christianity was more popular than Buddhism and became more widespread in East Asia.

    (C) The religions of Christianity and Buddhism were virtually identical in their effect on society in South Asia.

    (D) Both Christianity and Buddhism focused on reincarnation after death.

Questions 5–7 refer to the image below.

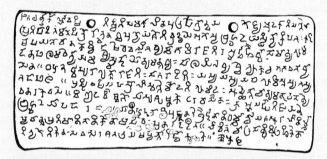

▲ **A property deed on a copper plate showing Indian numerals.** Facsimile by Georges Ifrah. Reproduced by permission of Georges Ifrah.

5. The copper plate can be used to deduce which of the following?

    (A) The role of regional agriculture in the economy that existed in South Asia during the Gupta Empire

    (B) The advantage of using an alphabetic system rather than pictographs to control a large empire

    (C) The advanced literacy that existed in South Asia in the first century CE

    (D) The existence of elaborate legal systems and bureaucracies using alpha-numeric communication

6. The Indian system of numerals shown on the copper plate was transmitted to other parts of Eurasia by the seventh century CE through

  (A) attacks by Indian warriors.

  (B) traders and academics.

  (C) the spread of Hinduism.

  (D) the Hellenistic invaders.

7. The transmission to other regions of the Indian numerals shown in the illustration is most similar to

  (A) the spread of Mahayana Buddhism into East Asia.

  (B) the transmission of Greek philosophies into the Roman Empire.

  (C) the assimilation of the Phoenician alphabet by the Hebrews and Greeks.

  (D) the integration of Buddhism into the Srivijayan Kingdom of Thailand.

Questions 8–10 refer to the image below.

▲ **A seated Buddha from Borobudur, Indonesia, ca. 825 CE.**

Malherbe Marcel/AGE Fotostock

8. The image including a depiction of Buddha best demonstrates which of the following regarding Southeast Asian culture in the first century CE?

  (A) There was a syncretic blending of cultures in the region as outside influences mixed with indigenous styles.

  (B) Buddhism was the dominant force in the region after the development of the Mahayana version of the belief system.

  (C) The rulers of the Srivijayan Kingdom used Buddhism as a means to glorify their realm.

  (D) The climate of Southeast Asia was conducive to the rapid growth of population, which resulted in cultural uniformity.

9. The region of Southeast Asia where the image is found was a vibrant cultural hub in the first century CE for which of the following reasons?

  (A) It was invaded by several different groups from both South and East Asia.

  (B) It was a tributary state of the Han Empire, and therefore adopted several competing philosophies.

  (C) It was a region through which traders passed as they moved from the Indian Ocean and East Asia.

  (D) Its Muslim rulers embraced the ideas of tolerance that were central to Islam.

10. The presence in this region of images of Buddha covered in gold that originated in East or West Africa can be used to support which of the following claims?

  (A) Land and water routes became the basis for interregional trade in the Eastern Hemisphere.

  (B) Muslim traders would only trade with fellow Muslim nations in this region.

  (C) Buddhists in this region highly prized material wealth despite earlier teachings.

  (D) Muslim traders used material goods to sway Buddhist followers away from their original beliefs.

Short-Answer Questions

"Day and night woman must be kept in dependence by the males (of) their (families), and, if they attach themselves to sensual enjoyments, they must be kept under ones control.

Her father protects (her) in childhood, her husband protects (her) in youth, and her sons protect (her) in old age; a woman is never fit for independence.

Reprehensible is the father who gives not (his daughter in marriage) at the proper time; reprehensible is the husband who approaches not (his wife in due season), and reprehensible is the son who does not protect his mother after her husband has died.

Women must particularly be guarded against evil inclinations, however trifling (they may appear); for, if they are not guarded, they will bring sorrow on two families."

The Law Book of Manu, Chapter IX, ca. 200 CE

1. Use the passage above and your knowledge of world history to answer all parts of the question that follows.

  (A) Identify ONE way women's rights were restricted in South Asia during the Gupta Empire not mentioned in the passage above.

  (B) Explain ONE reason why women's rights were restricted in South Asia during the Gupta Empire.

  (C) Explain ONE similarity in the rights of women in South Asia and the rights of women in another classical empire between 1000 BCE and 400 CE.

2. Answer all parts of the question that follows.

  (A) Identify ONE example of long-distance migration in the regions of South and Southeast Asia before 600 CE.

  (B) Explain ONE way technology enabled long-distance migration in the regions of South and Southeast Asia before 600 CE.

  (C) Explain ONE effect of long-distance migration in the regions of South and Southeast Asia before 600 CE.

8

Peoples and Civilizations of the Americas, from 1200 BCE

AP® Framework Terms

Olmec civilization (Mesoamerica)
Chavín civilization (Andean South America)
Shamanism
Teotihuacan
Mayan city-states
Andean South America: Moche
North America: Chaco, Cahokia

Overarching Questions

1 How and to what extent have environmental factors, disease, and technology affected patterns of human migration and settlement over time? (ENV)

2 In what ways do the arts reflect innovation, adaptation, and creativity of specific societies? (CUL)

3 How have different forms of governance been constructed and maintained over time? (SB)

4 How have societies with states and state-less societies interacted over time? (SB)

5 How have distinctions based on kinship, ethnicity, class, gender, and race influenced the development and transformations of social hierarchies? (SOC)

The ancient Mesoamerican civilization of the Maya (**MY-ah**) developed a complex written language that enabled scribes like the one in this illustration to record the important actions of rulers and military events. Recent translations give us a glimpse into the life of a Maya princess. In late August 682 CE the Maya princess Lady Wac-Chanil-Ahau (**wac-cha-NEEL-ah-HOW**) (sometimes translated as Six Sky) walked down the steps from her family's residence and mounted a litter decorated with rich textiles and animal skins. As the procession exited from the urban center of Dos Pilas (**dohs PEE-las**), her military escort spread out through the fields and woods to prevent ambush by enemies. Lady Wac-Chanil-Ahau's destination was the Maya city of Naranjo (**na-RAHN-hoe**), where she was to marry a powerful nobleman. Her father had arranged her marriage to reestablish the royal dynasty of Naranjo, a dynasty eliminated when Caracol, the region's major military power, had conquered that city. For her father, Lady Wac-Chanil-Ahau's passage to Naranjo and marriage represented an opportunity to forge a powerful military

▲ **Maya Scribe** Maya scribes used a complex writing system to record religious concepts and memorialize the actions of their kings. An artisan painted this picture of a scribe on a ceramic plate. Justin Kerr

alliance that could resist Caracol. For us, the story of Lady Wac-Chanil-Ahau illuminates the importance of marriage and lineage to the political life of the classic-period Maya.

Lady Wac-Chanil-Ahau effectively ruled Naranjo even leading successful military campaigns until her son, K'ak Tiliw Chan Chaak (**kahk tee-lew CHAN cha-ahk**), ascended the throne of Naranjo as a five-year-old in 693 CE. Building on his mother's achievements, K'ak Tiliw Chan Chaak proved to be a careful diplomat and formidable warrior during his long reign. He was also a prodigious builder, leaving behind an expanded and beautified capital as part of his legacy. Mindful of the importance of his mother and her lineage from Dos Pilas, he erected numerous *steles* (carved stone monuments) that celebrated her life.[1]

The world of Wac-Chanil-Ahau was challenged by warfare and by dynastic crisis as population increased and as the competition for resources among Maya kingdoms grew more violent. In this environment the rise of Caracol undermined long-standing commercial and political relations in much of southern Mesoamerica and led to more than a century of conflict. Eventually, the dynasty created at Naranjo by the heirs of Lady Wac-Chanil-Ahau militarily challenged Caracol and its ally Tikal. But, despite a shared culture and religion, the ruling lineages of the great Maya cities remained divided by dynastic ambitions and experienced nearly continuous conflict, never successfully forging a regional political structure capable of maintaining regional peace.

As the story of Lady Wac-Chanil-Ahau's marriage and her role in the development of a Maya dynasty suggests, the peoples of the Americas were in constant competition

[1]This summary closely follows the historical narrative and translation of names offered by Linda Schele and David Freidel in *A Forest of Kings: The Untold Story of the Ancient Maya* (New York: Morrow, 1990), 182–186.

for resources. Members of hereditary elites organized their societies to meet these challenges, even as their ambition for greater power predictably ignited new conflicts. No single set of political institutions or technologies worked in every environment, and enormous cultural diversity existed in the ancient Americas. In Mesoamerica (most of Mexico and Central America) and in the Andean region of South America, Amerindian peoples developed an extraordinarily productive and diversified agriculture. They also built great cities that rivaled the capitals of the Chinese and Roman Empires in size and beauty. The Olmec of Mesoamerica and Chavín (**cha-VEEN**) of the Andes were among the earliest civilizations of the Americas. In other regions of the hemisphere, indigenous peoples adapted combinations of hunting and agriculture to maintain a wide variety of settlement patterns, political forms, and cultural traditions. Despite differences, all the cultures and civilizations of the Americas experienced cycles of expansion and contraction as they struggled with the challenges of environmental change, population growth, and war. ●

8-1 Formative Civilizations of the Olmec and Chavín, 1200–200 BCE

How did Olmec and Chavín cultures influence later Mesoamerican and Andean civilizations?

AP® Exam Tip
Understand how core civilizations, such as Olmec and Chavín in the Americas, adapted to and affected their environments over time.

The domestication of new plant varieties, especially potatoes, corn, beans, squash, and sweet potatoes, and a limited development of trade helped promote social stratification and the beginnings of urbanization in both Mesoamerica and the Andes. By 2000 BCE a number of urban centers had begun to project their political and cultural power over neighboring territories, but very few of these early urban places had populations in excess of 2,500. Two of the hemisphere's most impressive cultural traditions, the Olmec of Mesoamerica (Mexico and northern Central America) and Chavín of the mountainous Andean region of South America, developed from these humble origins around 1200 BCE. Before their eclipse before 200 BCE, each had established a cultural legacy that would persist for more than a thousand years.

8-1a The Mesoamerican Olmec, 1200–400 BCE

Mesoamerica is a region of great geographic and climatic diversity. It is extremely active geologically, experiencing both earthquakes and volcanic eruptions. Mountain ranges break the region into microenvironments, including the temperate climates of the Valley of Mexico and the Guatemalan highlands, the tropical forests of the Petén and Gulf of Mexico coast, the rain forest of the southern Yucatán and Belize, and the drier scrub forest of the northern Yucatán (see Map 8.1).

Olmec The first Mesoamerican civilization. Between ca. 1200 and 400 BCE, the Olmec people of central Mexico created a vibrant civilization that included intensive agriculture, wide-ranging trade, ceremonial centers, and monumental construction. The Olmec had great cultural influence on later Mesoamerican societies, passing on artistic styles, religious imagery, sophisticated astronomical observation for the construction of calendars, and a ritual ball game.

Within each of these ecological niches, Amerindian peoples developed specialized technologies that exploited indigenous plants and animals, as well as minerals like obsidian, quartz, and jade. The ability of farmers to produce dependable surpluses of maize, beans, squash, and other locally domesticated plants permitted the first stages of craft specialization and urbanization. Eventually, human contacts across environmental boundaries led to trade and cultural exchange with emerging centers across the region and ultimately with Central and South America. Enhanced trade, increasing agricultural productivity, and rising population created the conditions for urbanization and social stratification.

Scholars refer to the period 1500 BCE to 200 CE in Mesoamerica as the preclassic period. The most important civilization in this period was the **Olmec**, which flourished between 1200 and 400 BCE near the tropical Atlantic coast of Mexico (see Map 8.1). This location allowed the Olmec access to rare shells and other coastal products, like stingray spines, infused with religious

CHRONOLOGY

	Mesoamerica	Northern Peoples	Andean Region
	Before 5000 BCE Domestication of maize, beans, and squash		Before 5000 BCE Domestication of potato, quinoa, manioc, and llama
5000 BCE	Before 2000 BCE Early urbanization	Before 2000 BCE Domestication of squash and seed crops like sunflower	Before 2000 BCE Early urbanization
2000 BCE	1200 BCE Beginning of Olmec civilization	By 1000 BCE Introduction of maize cultivation in desert southwest from Mesoamerica	2000 BCE Metallurgy; domestication of sweet potato
1000 BCE			900 BCE Beginning of Chavín civilization
500 BCE	400 BCE End of Olmec civilization		200 BCE End of Chavín civilization
100 CE	100 First stage of Teotihuacan temple complex 200 Maya early classic period begins	100–400 Hopewell culture in Ohio River Valley 100–200 Introduction of maize agriculture among mound builders	200 Moche begin to dominate Peruvian coast
500 CE	450 Teotihuacan dominates central Mexico 750 Teotihuacan destroyed 800–900 Maya classic-era cities abandoned 968 Toltec capital of Tula founded	700 beginnings of Anasazi culture in Four Corners region 800 beginnings of Mississippian culture	500–1000 Tiwanaku and Wari control Andean highlands 700 End of Moche domination 900 Chimú begin to dominate Peruvian coast
1000 CE	1175 Tula destroyed	1050–1250 Cahokia reaches peak population	1150 Anasazi center of Pueblo Bonito abandoned; other Anasazi centers enter crisis after 1200
1500 CE	Until 1300 Culhuacán and Cholula continue Toltec tradition	Around 1200 Abandonment of major Anasazi centers	1470s End of Chimú domination

significance and facilitated cultural exchanges with other peoples. It is unclear whether Olmec urban centers were rival city-states or were united by a centralized political authority, but scholars agree that San Lorenzo (1200–900 BCE), with a population of between 10,000 to 18,000, was the largest and most important Olmec center. San Lorenzo's cultural influence ultimately extended south and west to the Pacific coast of Central America and north to central Mexico, suggesting its ability to project political and military power. Also founded around 1200 BCE, La Venta (**LA BEN-tah**) became the preeminent Olmec center when San Lorenzo was abandoned or destroyed around 900 BCE. After La Venta's collapse around 600 BCE, Tres Zapotes (**TRACE zah-POE-tace**) survived as the largest Olmec center, although it was much smaller than either of its predecessors.

San Lorenzo and other Olmec cities served primarily as religious centers. The urban elite's power grew with the development of persuasive religious ideologies and compelling religious rituals that helped organize and subordinate neighboring rural populations. As a result, urban centers were dominated by religious architecture that included pyramids, monumental mounds, and raised platforms. Constructed by thousands of laborers recruited in surrounding agricultural zones, the massive urban architecture was embellished with religious symbols tied to an official cult. The elite dominated collective religious life and built their residences on raised platforms located near the most sacred ritual spaces, asserting a legitimacy derived from association with the gods.

The Olmec were polytheistic, and most of their deities had both male and female natures. The motifs found on ceramics, sculptures, and buildings also show that the Olmec blended human and animal characteristics in representations of gods. Rulers were especially associated with the jaguar. Priests and shamans who foretold the future, cured the sick, and led collective rituals claimed the ability to make direct contact with supernatural powers by transforming themselves into powerful animals, such as crocodiles, snakes, and sharks. These transformative powers were

MAP 8.1 Olmec and Chavín Civilizations The regions of Mesoamerica (most of modern Mexico and Central America) and the Andean high-lands of South America have hosted impressive civilizations since early times. The civilizations of the Olmec and Chavín were the originating civilizations of these two regions, providing the foundations of architecture, city planning, and religion.

Did their proximity to the Atlantic and Pacific coasts influence the development of Olmec and Chavín cultures, respectively?

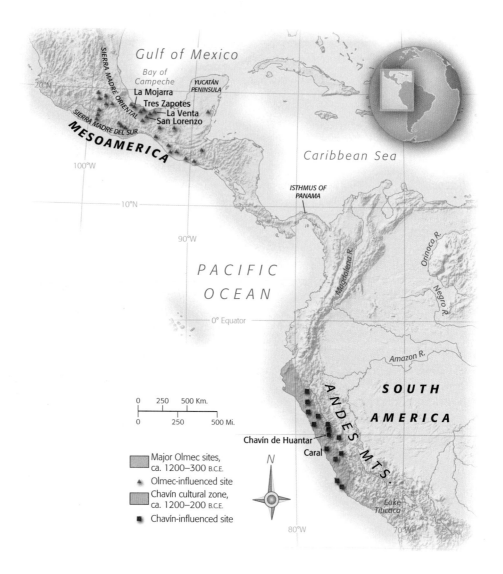

also associated with a ball game played with a solid rubber ball in banked courts located near the center of temple precincts. Versions of this ball game survived until the arrival of Europeans in the sixteenth century.

Olmec religious practice included the close observation of the heavens, and all their major ceremonial centers were laid out in alignment with the paths of certain stars. This concern for astronomic observation led to the development of an accurate calendar that was used to predict seasonal rains and guide the annual cycle of planting and harvesting. The Olmec also developed a form of writing (as yet undeciphered) that scholars believe influenced later innovations among the Maya.

Little is known about Olmec political structure, but it seems likely that the rise of major urban centers coincided with the appearance of a form of kingship that combined religious and secular roles. Rulers and their close kin came to be associated with the gods through bloodletting ceremonies and human sacrifice and through the staging of elaborate rituals that brought together urban and rural populations. The authority of the rulers is suggested by a series of colossal carved stone heads discovered buried near the major urban centers, especially San Lorenzo. These heads, some as large as 11 feet (3.4 meters) high, are the best-known monuments of Olmec culture. Archaeologists believe that they were carved to memorialize individual rulers. Some were depicted wearing the padded helmet used as protection in the sacred ball game.

The first stage of urbanization was tied to the exploitation of products like salt, cacao (chocolate beans), and clay used for ceramics. Control of these resources led to the development of commerce in specialized crafts, such as jewelry manufactured for elites using shells from

▶ **Olmec Head** Giant heads sculpted from basalt are a widely recognized legacy of Olmec culture. Sixteen heads have been found, the largest approximately 11 feet (3.4 meters) tall. Experts in Olmec archaeology believe the heads are portraits of individual rulers, warriors, or ballplayers. photoshooter2015/Shutterstock.com

the coast. In the largest urban centers, skilled artisans were full-time residents who decorated buildings with religious carvings and sculptures. They also produced high-quality crafts, such as exquisite carved jade figurines, necklaces, and ceremonial obsidian knives and axes. The diffusion of these Olmec products among distant locations suggests the existence of a specialized class of merchants.

The mounting wealth and power of the elite and the growing populations of Olmec cities depended on a bargain struck with the much larger populations of the surrounding countryside. The rural masses provided the labor that constructed the pyramids, platforms, and ball courts of the urban centers as well as the food that sustained urban populations, but they also received benefits. As a relief from their routines of heavy labor, they participated in the awe-inspiring ceremonies at San Lorenzo and other centers. Here the official cult directed by the elite explained human origins as well as unforeseen natural events and helped to guide collective life as well as providing spectacles. It also provided practical benefits to the rural masses. The elite used its authority to organize labor to dig drainage canals and construct the raised fields that allowed the expansion of agriculture into wetlands, thus augmenting food production.

Ultimately, every major Olmec center was abandoned, monuments defaced and buried, and buildings destroyed. Even the large carved portrait heads were dragged from the centers, defaced, and buried. Archaeologists interpret these events differently; some see them as evidence of internal upheavals or military attacks by neighboring peoples, whereas others suggest that they were rituals associated with the death or overthrow of a ruler or evidence of internal social conflict. Regardless of the causes for Olmec decline, the influence of this civilization endured for centuries after the abandonment of the chief urban centers. Every subsequent Mesoamerican civilization utilized the rich legacy of Olmec material culture, technology, religious belief and ritual, political organization, art, architecture, and sports.

8-1b Early South American Civilization: Chavín, 900–200 BCE

Geography and environment played a critical role in the development of human society in the Andes. The region's diverse environments—a mountainous core, arid coastal plain, and dense interior tropical forests—challenged human populations, encouraging the development of

AP® Exam Tip
Be familiar with developing trade routes in the Americas and how food crops and technology diffused across the continents.

Chavín The first major urban civilization in South America (900–250 BCE). Its capital, Chavín de Huantar, was located high in the Andes Mountains of Peru. Chavín became politically and economically dominant in a densely populated region that included two distinct ecological zones, the Peruvian coastal plain and the Andean foothills.

llama A hoofed animal indigenous to the Andes Mountains in South America. It was the only domesticated beast of burden in the Americas before the arrival of Europeans. It provided meat and wool. The use of llamas to transport goods made possible specialized production and trade among people living in different ecological zones and fostered the integration of these zones by Chavín and later Andean states.

specialized regional production as well as social institutions and cultural values that facilitated interregional exchanges and shared labor responsibilities.

Scholars use the term *Early Horizon* for the period 900 BCE to 200 CE in Andean history. The earliest urban centers in this region were villages of a few hundred people built along the coastal plain or in the foothills near the coast, where an abundance of fish and mollusks provided a dependable food supply. The later introduction of corn (maize) cultivation from Mesoamerica increased the food supplies of the coast and interior foothills, allowing greater levels of urbanization. Trade between the peoples of the coastal region and Andean foothills also led to the exchange of ceremonial practices, religious motifs, and aesthetic ideas.

Between 900 and 250 BCE Chavín dominated a densely populated region that included large areas of the Peruvian coastal plain and Andean foothills. The capital city of Chavín de Huantar **(cha-BEAN day WAHN-tar)** was located at 10,300 feet (3,139 meters) in the eastern range of the Andes north of the modern city of Lima (see Map 8.1). Its location facilitated exchanges among ecologically distinct zones, linking the coastal fishermen and shell artisans to inland producers of the local grain *quinoa* **(KEEN-wha)**, maize, and potatoes as well as to the llama herders in high mountain valleys and tropical producers of coca on the eastern flank of the Andes. At this time coca was chewed, producing only a mild narcotic effect.

The development of these trade networks led to reciprocal labor obligations that permitted the construction and maintenance of roads, bridges, temples, palaces, and large irrigation and drainage projects, as well as textile production. These reciprocal labor obligations were organized initially by groups of related families who held land communally and claimed descent from a common ancestor. Group members thought of themselves as brothers and sisters and were obliged to aid one another. In the time of Chavín these groups were organized collectively by the state to provide labor to build temples, elite residences, and irrigation works.

Llamas, first bred in the mountainous interior of Peru, were the only domesticated beasts of burden in the Americas, and they played an important role in the economic integration of the Andean region. Llamas provided meat and wool and decreased the labor needed to transport goods. A single driver could control ten to thirty animals, each carrying up to 70 pounds (32 kilograms), while a human porter could carry only about 50 pounds (22.5 kilograms). By moving goods from one ecological zone to another, llamas promoted specialization of production and increased trade. Thus they were crucial to Chavín's development, not unlike the camel in the evolution of trans-Saharan trade (see Chapter 9).

Class distinctions appear to have increased in this period. Modern scholars see evidence that a powerful chief or king dominated Chavín's politics, while a class of priests directed religious life. The most common decorative motif in sculpture, pottery, and textiles was a jaguar-man similar in conception and imagery to the contemporary Olmec symbol. In both civilizations this powerful predator provided an enduring image of religious authority.

Chavín housed a large complex of multilevel platforms made of packed earth or rubble and faced with cut stone or *adobe* (sun-dried brick made of clay and straw). Small buildings used for ritual purposes or as elite residences were built on these platforms. Nearly all the structures were decorated with relief carvings of serpents, condors, jaguars, or human forms. The largest building at Chavín de Huantar measured 250 feet (76 meters) on each side and rose to a height of 50 feet (15 meters). Its hollow interior contained narrow galleries and small rooms that may have been used as burial places for the remains of royal ancestors.

Metallurgy in the Western Hemisphere was first developed in the Andean region around 2000 BCE. The later introduction of metallurgy in Mesoamerica, like the appearance of maize agriculture in the Andes, suggests sustained maritime trade and cultural contacts between the two regions. Archaeological investigations of Chavín de Huantar have uncovered remarkable silver, gold, and gold alloy

Section Review

- Well before 3000 BCE newly domesticated plants, new technologies, and trade led to greater social stratification and the beginnings of urbanization in Mesoamerica and the Andean region of South America.

- The Olmec of Mesoamerica (1200–400 BCE) and the Chavín civilization (900–250 BCE) in the Andes each coordinated exchanges of goods between different ecological zones. Their cultural imageries and urban architectural styles were widely emulated and persisted long afterward.

- Ruling elites residing in urban centers staged elaborate religious ceremonies designed to impress subjects and enhance their own prestige.

- Olmec urban centers were probably ruled by kings, who were depicted in giant stone heads. Olmec shamans communicated with the spirit world, supervised the calendar, and created a system of writing.

- Chavín utilized llamas, the only domesticated beasts of burden in the hemisphere, to transport goods between regions.

ornaments that represent a clear advance over earlier technologies. Improvements in both the manufacture and decoration of textiles are also associated with the rise of Chavín.

Excavations of graves reveal that superior-quality textiles as well as gold crowns, breastplates, and jewelry were used to distinguish rulers from commoners. These rich objects, the quality and abundance of pottery, and the monumental architecture of the major centers all indicate the presence of highly skilled artisans. The enormous scale of the capital and the dispersal of Chavín's pottery styles, religious motifs, and architectural forms over a wide area suggest that Chavín imposed political and economic control over its neighbors by military force. Most scholars believe, however, that, as in the case of the Olmec civilization, Chavín's influence depended more on its development of an attractive religious belief system and related rituals.

There is no convincing evidence, like defaced buildings or broken images, that the eclipse of Chavín (unlike the destruction and abandonment of the Olmec centers) was associated with conquest or rebellion. However, recent investigations have suggested that increased warfare throughout the region disrupted Chavín's trade and undermined the authority of the governing elite. Regardless of what caused the collapse of this powerful culture, the technologies, material culture, statecraft, architecture, and urban planning associated with Chavín influenced the later civilizations of the Andean region for centuries.

8-2 Classic-Era Culture and Society in Mesoamerica, 200–900

What were the most important shared characteristics of Mesoamerican cultures in the classic period?

Between about 200 and 900 CE the peoples of Mesoamerica entered a period of remarkable cultural creativity. Despite enduring differences in language and the absence of regional political integration, Mesoamericans were unified by similarities in material culture, religious beliefs and practices, and social structures first forged in the Olmec era. Building on this legacy, the peoples of the area that is now Central America and south and central Mexico developed new forms of political organization, made great strides in astronomy and mathematics, and improved the productivity of their agriculture. Archaeologists call this mix of achievements the classic period. During this period, a growing population traded a greater variety of products over longer distances, and social hierarchies became more complex. Great cities were constructed that served as centers of political life and as arenas of religious ritual and spiritual experience, not unlike classic-era Greek city-states (see Chapter 5). These political and cultural innovations did not result from the introduction of new technologies. Instead, the achievements of the classic era depended on the ability of increasingly powerful elites to organize and command growing numbers of laborers and soldiers.

8-2a Teotihuacan

Located about 30 miles (48 kilometers) northeast of modern Mexico City, **Teotihuacan (teh-o-tee-WAH-kahn)** (100–750 CE) was one of Mesoamerica's most important classic-period civilizations (see Map 8.3). At the height of its power around 450 CE, it was the largest city in the Americas. With between 125,000 and 150,000 inhabitants, it was larger than all but a small number of contemporary European and Asian cities.

The city center was dominated by religious architecture that was situated to align with nearby sacred mountains and with the movement of the stars. The people of Teotihuacan recognized and worshiped many gods and lesser spirits. Enormous pyramids and more than twenty smaller temples devoted to these gods were arranged along a central avenue. The largest pyramids were dedicated to the Sun and the Moon and to Quetzalcoatl **(kate-zahl-CO-ah-tal)**, the feathered serpent, a culture-god believed to be the originator of agriculture and the arts. Murals suggest that another pair of powerful gods, the storm-god Tlaloc and a powerful female god associated with fertility, were also central figures in the city's religious life. Like the earlier Olmec, Teotihuacan's population practiced human sacrifice, demonstrated by the discovery of more than a hundred sacrificial victims during the modern excavation of the temple of Quetzalcoatl.

AP® Exam Tip
Understand how Teotihuacan and Mayan city-states exemplified expanding empires and how political unity was imposed.

Teotihuacan A powerful city-state in central Mexico (100–750 CE). Its population was more than 125,000 at its peak in 450 CE.

Scholars believe that residents viewed sacrifice as a sacred duty to the gods and as essential to the well-being of society.

The rapid growth in urban population at Teotihuacan initially resulted from a series of nearby volcanic eruptions that disrupted agriculture and forced rural villagers to relocate to the city. Later, as the city elite increased their power, they forced additional farm families from the smaller villages in the region to relocate closer to the urban core. The elite organized these new labor resources to bring marginal lands into production, drain swamps, construct irrigation canals, and build terraces into hillsides. They also expanded the use of **chinampas (chee-NAM-pahs)**, sometimes called "floating gardens." These were narrow artificial islands constructed along lakeshores or in marshes by heaping lake muck and waste material on beds of reeds and anchoring them to the shore. Chinampas permitted year-round agriculture—because of subsurface irrigation and resistance to frost—and thus played a crucial role in sustaining the region's growing population.

The city's role as a religious center and commercial power provided both divine approval of and a material basis for the elite's increased wealth and status. Members of the elite controlled the government, tax collection, and commerce. Their rich and ornate clothing, their abundant diet, and their large, well-made residences signaled the wealth and power of aristocratic families. Temple and palace murals make clear the authority and great prestige of the priestly class as well. Teotihuacan's wealth and religious influence drew pilgrims from distant regions, and many became permanent residents. Many Maya city-states, like the powerful Tikal, were closely tied to Teotihuacan and borrowed elements of religious ritual and symbolism.

There is no clear evidence that individual rulers or a ruling dynasty gained overarching political power. In fact, some scholars suggest that allied elite families or weak kings who were the puppets of these powerful families ruled Teotihuacan. While the absence of walls and other defensive structures before 500 CE suggests that Teotihuacan enjoyed relative peace during its

chinampas Raised fields constructed along lakeshores in Mesoamerica to increase agricultural yields.

early development, archaeological evidence reveals that the city elite did create a powerful military to protect long-distance trade and to compel peasant agriculturalists to transfer their surplus production to the city. Unlike later postclassic civilizations, however, Teotihuacan was not an imperial state controlled by a king and military elite.

By 500 CE the urban population had declined to about 40,000 and the city's residents had begun to build defensive walls. Surviving murals as well as skeletal evidence indicates that Teotihuacan's final century was violent. Scholars believe that the elite had mismanaged resources and then divided into competing factions that stimulated class conflict and the breakdown of public order. In the final stage of collapse around 750 CE the most important temples in the city center were destroyed and religious images defaced. Elite palaces were also systematically pulled down or burned and many of their residents killed. Regardless of the causes, the eclipse of Teotihuacan was felt throughout Mexico and into Central America, as long-established trading routes and cultural contacts disappeared.

8-2b The Maya

During Teotihuacan's ascendancy in the north, the **Maya** developed an impressive civilization in the region that today includes Guatemala, Honduras, Belize, and southern Mexico (see Map 8.2). Given the difficulties imposed by a tropical climate and fragile soils, the cultural and architectural achievements of the Maya were remarkable. Although they shared a single culture, the Maya never created a single, unified state led by a single monarch. Instead, rival kingdoms, often called city-states, led by hereditary rulers struggled with each other for regional dominance, much like the Mycenaean-era Greeks (see Chapter 5).

Today Maya farmers prepare their fields by cutting down small trees and brush and then burning the dead vegetation to fertilize the land. Such swidden agriculture (also called *shifting agriculture* or *slash-and-burn agriculture*) can produce high yields for a few years. However, it uses up the soil's nutrients, eventually forcing farmers to move to more fertile land. The high population levels of the Maya classic period (200–900 CE) required more intensive forms of agriculture. Maya living near the major urban centers achieved high agricultural yields by draining swamps and building elevated fields. They used irrigation in areas with long dry seasons, and they terraced hillsides in the cooler highlands. Maya agriculturists also managed nearby forests, favoring the growth of the trees and shrubs that were most useful to them, as well as promoting the conservation of deer and other animals they hunted for food.

During the classic period, Maya city-states proliferated. The most powerful cities controlled groups of smaller dependent cities and a broad agricultural zone by building impressive temples and by creating rituals that linked the power of kings and royal lineages to the gods. Open plazas were surrounded by high pyramids and by elaborately decorated palaces often built on high ground or on constructed mounds. The effect was to awe the masses drawn from agricultural zones to urban centers for religious and political rituals.

The Maya loved decoration. Carved stone decoration painted in bright colors covered nearly all public buildings. Religious allegories, depictions of gods, the genealogies of rulers, and important historical events were the most common motifs. The Maya also erected beautifully carved altars and stone monoliths near major temples. As was true throughout the Western Hemisphere, this rich legacy of monumental architecture was constructed without the aid of wheels—no pulleys, wheelbarrows, or carts—or metal tools. Masses of men and women aided only by levers and stone tools cut and carried construction materials and lifted them into place.

Maya Mesoamerican civilization concentrated in Mexico's Yucatán Peninsula and in Guatemala and Honduras but never unified into a single empire. Major contributions were in mathematics, astronomy, and development of the calendar.

MAP 8.2   Maya Civilization, 250–1400 CE The Maya never created an integrated and unified imperial state. Instead, Maya civilization developed as a complex network of independent city-states.

Would the geographical location of major classic-era Maya sites help to promote this culture's influence throughout Mesoamerica?

▲ **The Great Plaza at Tikal**   The impressive architectural and artistic achievements of the classic-era Maya are still visible in the ruins of Tikal, in modern Guatemala. Maya centers provided a dramatic setting for the rituals that dominated public life. Construction of Tikal began before 150 BCE; the city was abandoned about 900 CE. A ball court and residences for the elite were part of the Great Plaza.   Daniel Loncarevic/Shutterstock.com

AP® Exam Tip
Compare the political organizations of the Mesoamerican, Andean American, and North American civilizations with those of classical Afro-Eurasian civilizations.

The Maya divided the cosmos into three layers connected along a vertical axis that traced the course of the sun. The earthly arena of human existence held an intermediate position between the heavens, conceptualized as a sky-monster, and a dark underworld. The Maya believed that a sacred tree rose through the three layers; its roots were in the underworld, and its branches reached into the heavens. The temple precincts of Maya cities physically represented essential elements of this religious cosmology. The pyramids were sacred mountains reaching to the heavens. The doorways at the top of the pyramids were portals to the underworld.

Rulers and other members of the elite served both priestly and political functions. They decorated their bodies with paint and tattoos and wore elaborate costumes of textiles, animal skins, and feathers to project both secular power and divine sanction. These lords communicated directly with the supernatural residents of the other worlds and with deified royal ancestors through bloodletting rituals and hallucinogenic trances.

The Maya infused warfare with religious meaning and celebrated it in elaborate rituals. Battle scenes and the depiction of the torture and sacrifice of captives were frequent decorative themes. Typically, Maya military forces fought to secure captives rather than territory. The king, his kinsmen, and other ranking nobles actively participated in war. Elite warriors, if captured, were nearly always sacrificed; captured commoners were more likely to be forced to labor for their captors.

Few women directly ruled Maya kingdoms, but Maya women of the ruling lineages did play important political and religious roles. The consorts of male rulers participated in bloodletting rituals and in other important public ceremonies, and their noble blood helped legitimate the power of their husbands. Although Maya society was *patrilineal* (tracing descent in the male line), there is clear evidence that some male rulers traced their lineages *bilaterally* (in both the male and female lines). Others, like Lady Wac-Chanil-Ahau's son discussed earlier, emphasized the female line if it was of higher political status. Little is known about the lives of poorer women, but scholars believe that women played a central role in the religious rituals of the

Of all the cultures of pre-Columbian America, only the Maya produced a written literature that has survived to the modern era. The literary legacy of the Maya was inscribed on stone monuments, ceramics, jade, shell, and bone. Books of bark paper were the original and most common medium of Maya scribes, but only four of these books have survived to today.

The historical and literary importance of the written record of the Maya has been recognized only recently. In the early nineteenth century, visitors to southern Mexico and Guatemala began to record and decipher the symbols they found on stone monuments. By the end of the nineteenth century, the Maya

system of numbers and the Maya calendar were decoded, but the written record remained undeciphered.

Not until the 1960s did scholars recognize that Maya writing reflects spoken language by having a set word order. Because of the work of modern scholars we now know that Maya writing was capable of capturing the rich meaning of spoken language.

Maya scribes could use signs that represented sounds or signs that represented whole words. *Jaguar* (*balam* in Maya) could be written by using the head of this big cat in symbolic form. Because there were other large cats in the Maya region, scribes commonly added a pronunciation cue like a prefix or suffix to the front or back of the symbol to clarify meaning. In this case they might affix the syllable sign *ba* to the front of the jaguar head or the syllable sign *ma* to the end. Because no other Maya word for feline began with *ba* or ended with *ma*, the reader knew to pronounce the word as *balam* for "jaguar." Alternatively, because the last vowel was not sounded, *balam* could be written with three syllable signs: *ba la ma*.

These signs were expressed in a rich and varied array of stylized forms, much like illustrated European medieval texts, that make translation difficult. But these stylistic devices helped convey meaning. Readers detected meaning not only in what the text "said" but also in how and where the text was written.

The work of Maya scribes was not intended as mass communication, since few Maya could read these texts. Instead, as two of the most respected experts in this field explain, "Writing was a sacred proposition that had the capacity to capture the order of the cosmos, to inform history, to give form to ritual, and to transform the profane material of everyday life into the supernatural."

Questions for Analysis

1. Which Amerindian culture produced a written language?

2. Without an alphabet, how did native scribes write?

3. When did modern scholars learn to read these ancient texts?

balam

ba-balam

balam-ma

ba-balam-ma

ba-la-m(a)

▲ **Maya Glyphs** The Maya developed a sophisticated written language expressed in stylized images (glyphs) conceptually similar to Egyptian hieroglyphics.

Source: Text and illustration based on Linda Schele and David Freidel, *A Forest of Kings: The Untold Story of the Ancient Maya* (New York, NY: William Morrow & Co., 1990).

home and some were healers and shamans. Women were essential to the household economy, the maintenance of essential garden plots and weaving, and in the management of family life.

Building on earlier Olmec achievements, the Maya made important contributions to the development of the Mesoamerican calendar and to mathematics and writing. Time was a central concern, and the Maya developed an accurate calendar system that identified each day by three separate dating systems. The Maya calendar tracked a cycle of ritual activities (260 days divided into thirteen months of twenty days). A second calendar tracked the solar year (365 days divided into eighteen months of twenty days, plus five unfavorable days at the end of the year). The Maya believed that the very survival of humanity was threatened every fifty-two years when the two calendars coincided. Alone among Mesoamerican peoples, the Maya also maintained a continuous "long count" calendar, which began with creation in 3114 BCE.

Maya mathematics and writing provided the foundations for both the calendars and the astronomical observations on which they were based. Their system of mathematics incorporated

Section Review

- Teotihuacan, one of the largest Mesoamerican cities, was ruled by elites who used religious rituals and military power to legitimize their authority over the many agriculturalists who worked the surrounding fields.

- Teotihuacan's impressive urban architecture, complex agriculture, and extensive trade made it a dominating cultural presence throughout Mesoamerica. Its collapse around 750 CE resulted from conflicts within the elite and resource mismanagement.

- The Maya shared a single culture but never created a single, unified state. Instead they developed numerous powerful city-states. Each city, filled with highly decorated monumental architecture, was a religious and political center for the surrounding region.

- Religious architecture dominated the centers of Teotihuacan and Maya cities. Many gods were worshiped, and religious ritual, including human sacrifice, organized collective life.

- The Maya devised an elaborate calendar system, the mathematical concept of zero, and writing.

- After centuries of expansion, the power of the Maya cities declined due to an intensified struggle for resources, leading to class conflict and large-scale warfare.

the concept of the zero and place value but had limited notational signs. Maya writing was a form of hieroglyphic inscription that signified whole words or concepts as well as phonetic cues or syllables (see Environment & Technology: The Maya Writing System). Scribes recorded aspects of public life, religious belief, and the biographies of rulers and their ancestors in books, on pottery, and on the stone columns and monumental buildings of the urban centers. In this sense every Maya city was a sacred text.

Between 800 and 900 CE the Maya abandoned many of their major urban centers. Many cities were destroyed by violence, although a small number of classic-period centers survived for centuries. Decades of urban decline, social conflict, and increased levels of warfare preceded this collapse in many areas. The collapse of Teotihuacan around 750 had certainly contributed to this decline by disrupting long-distance trade in ritual goods and may also have undermined the legitimacy of Maya rulers who maintained ties to that distant cultural center. Certainly, rising regional population, climatic change, and environmental degradation undermined the fragile agricultural system that sustained Maya cities long before the collapse. But it was the growing scale and destructiveness of warfare that finally undermined the political legitimacy of ruling lineages and disrupted the web of economic relationships that tied rural agriculturalists to Maya cities.

▼ **The Mesoamerican Ball Game** From Guatemala to Arizona, archaeologists have found evidence of an ancient ball game played with a solid rubber ball on slope-sided courts shaped like a capital *T*. Among the Maya the game was associated with a creation myth and thus had deep religious meaning. Evidence suggests that some players were sacrificed. This illustration shows the impressive ball court at the great postclassic Maya city of Chichen Itza near modern Merida, Mexico. You can see hoops or rings placed vertically on the two walls. Players drove the solid rubber ball to carom off the walls and along the court without using their hands or feet. They commonly wore protective pads around their waists. Bryan Mullennix World View/Alamy Stock Photo

8-3 The Postclassic Period in Mesoamerica, 900–1300

What role did warfare play in the postclassic period of Mesoamerica?

The division between the classic and postclassic periods is somewhat arbitrary. Not only is there no single explanation for the collapse of Teotihuacan and the abandonment of many Maya urban centers, but these events occurred over a period of more than a century and a half. While many smaller polities survived from the classic to postclassic period, it is clear that the Mesoamerican world went through a deep crisis that took centuries of adjustment to resolve, leading ultimately to the appearance of powerful new urban centers of culture and politics. Two of these, Tula and Cholula, had been deeply influenced by the great classic-era center of Teotihuacan before its eclipse around 750 CE (see Map 8.3).

Mesoamerican population expanded in the postclassic period. At the same time long-distance trade intensified, linking the producers of high-value goods like obsidian, cloth, and metal products to fast-growing cities. Resulting pressures on resources and competition for commercial advantage led to political instability and to increased levels of warfare. The governing elites of major postclassic states, especially the Toltecs, responded to these harsh realities by increasing the size of their armies and by developing political institutions that facilitated their control of large and culturally diverse territories acquired through conquest.

8-3a The Toltecs

While modern archaeology has revealed the civilizations of the Maya and Teotihuacan in previously unimaginable detail, the history of the **Toltecs** (**TOLL-teks**) remains in dispute. The Aztecs, the dominant late postclassic civilization (see Chapter 15), regarded the Toltecs as powerful and influential predecessors, much as the Romans regarded the Greeks. They erroneously believed that the Toltecs were the source of nearly all important cultural achievements. As one Aztec source later recalled:

> In truth [the Toltecs] invented all the precious and marvelous things. . . . All that now exists was their discovery. . . . And these Toltecs were very wise; they were thinkers, for they originated the year count, the day count. All their discoveries formed the book for interpreting dreams. . . . And so wise were they [that] they understood the stars which were in the heavens.[2]

In fact, all these contributions to Mesoamerican culture were in place long before Toltec power spread across central Mexico. Some scholars speculate that the Toltecs were originally a satellite population that Teotihuacan had placed on the northern frontier to protect against the incursions of nomadic peoples. Regardless of their origins, it is clear that Toltec culture was deeply influenced by Teotihuacan, including its preservation of the religious architecture and rituals associated with the feathered serpent god, Quetzalcoatl. The Toltecs also utilized agricultural technologies, like irrigation and terraced hillsides, so important to Teotihuacan's development.

In the more violent era that followed the collapse of Teotihuacan and many Maya city-states, the Toltecs created a state that depended directly on military power. This dependence was illustrated by the use of violent images, like impaled skulls, in the decoration of their chief public buildings. The Toltecs' influence ultimately extended to distant Central America from their political capital at Tula (**TOO-la**), founded in 968 CE north of modern Mexico City. At its peak Tula covered 5.4 square miles (14 square kilometers) and had a population of approximately 60,000. The massive architecture of the city center featured impressive statues of warriors and serpents, colonnaded patios, raised stone platforms, and numerous temples.

Like the earlier Teotihuacan, Tula and its subject dependencies had a multiethnic character that hosted distinct cultural and language communities. The apex of Toltec power also coincided with the development of an alliance with another multiethnic state with historic ties to Teotihuacan located to the south, Culhuacán (**kool whah KHAN**). The exact nature of this alliance

AP® Exam Tip
Define the characteristics of given time periods (e.g., the classical period) and compare with what came before and what followed.

AP® Exam Tip
Understand the role of cross-cultural interactions in the diffusion of cultural traditions and innovations.

Toltecs Powerful postclassic state in central Mexico (900–1175 CE) that influenced much of Mesoamerica. Aztecs later claimed ties to this civilization.

2From the Florentine Codex, quoted in Inga Clendinnen, *Aztecs* (New York, NY: Cambridge University Press, 1991), 213.

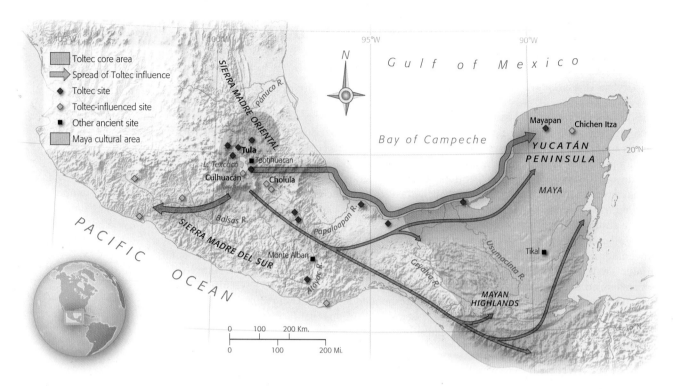

MAP 8.3 **Postclassic Mesoamerica** From their capital, Tula, the Toltecs exercised political and cultural influence across a vast region.
Was the character and geographic breadth of Toltec political and cultural influence similar to that of earlier Teotihuacan?

is unclear, but the presence of Toltec groups in Culhuacán is undeniable. Together the two cities benefited from a military alliance and from networks of tribute and trade established throughout the central Mexican region.

To understand the end of Toltec power, historians rely primarily on written sources from the era of the Spanish conquest, including accounts told to Catholic priests by native informants. According to most of these sources, two chieftains or kings shared power at Tula, and this division of responsibility eventually led to conflict and crisis that weakened Toltec power. Sometime around 1150 CE a struggle between elite groups identified with rival religious cults led to violent clashes within Toltec society and encouraged attacks by rival states. Legends that survived among the Aztecs claimed that Topiltzin (**tow-PEELT-zeen**)—one of the two rulers and a priest of the cult of Quetzalcoatl—and his followers were forced into exile in the east, "the land of the rising sun." One of the ancient texts relates these events in the following manner:

Thereupon he [Topiltzin] looked toward Tula, and then wept. . . . And when he had done these things . . . he went to reach the seacoast. Then he fashioned a raft of serpents. When he had arranged the raft, he placed himself as if it were his boat. Then he set off across the sea.[3]

Some scholars used this Aztec tale to suggest a Toltec conquest of the Maya region, an argument fortified by similarities in decorative motifs, architecture, and urban planning at Tula and at the Maya postclassic center of Chichen Itza (**CHEECH-ehn EET-zah**) in the Yucatán. Scholars now dispute this story, suggesting instead that these regions

Section Review

- In the postclassic era, large, professional militaries allowed Mesoamerican elites to create empires through conquest, resulting in increasingly hierarchical societies.

- The Toltecs used military conquest and political alliances to create a powerful empire with its capital at Tula. Their influence spread across central Mexico.

- The architecture of Tula was decorated with militaristic themes and images of human sacrifice, indicating the increased violence of the postclassic period.

- Tula, Culhuacán, and Cholula were ethnically and religiously diverse cities as well as centers of long-distance trade.

- After the collapse of the Toltec capital Tula in the twelfth century, elements of Toltec culture and religious practice survived in Culhuacán and Cholula.

[3]Quoted in Nigel Davies, *The Toltec Heritage: From the Fall of Tula to the Rise of Tenochtitlán* (Norman, OK: University of Oklahoma Press, 1980), 3.

were linked by long-term cultural exchanges, not by Toltec conquest.

Nevertheless, it is clear that Tula and the Toltec state entered a period of steep decline after 1150 CE that included internal power struggles and an external military threat from the north. The historical Topiltzin was closely linked to the fate of Tula, but his story was more complex than that indicated by Aztec legend. His father Mixcoatl (**mish-coh-AHT-til**) was a Toltec military leader active in Culhuacán and in Cholula, where another satellite Toltec population resided. Topiltzin was probably born in Culhuacán, not Tula. Some oral histories taken down by Spanish priests centuries after the events claim he attempted to save the beleaguered Toltec capital of Tula, but he ultimately failed and retired from power around 1175. While disaster then befell the once-dominant Toltec capital of Tula, an independent Toltec legacy survived until at least 1300 CE in Culhuacán and in nearby Cholula, both serving as centers of the cult of Quetzalcoatl that had probably originated in Teotihuacan.

▲ **Tula**   The capital of the Toltecs was dominated by massive public architecture like these massive carved stone figures.   DEA/G. DAGLI ORTI/Getty Images

8-3b Cholula

Located near the modern Mexican city of Puebla, Cholula developed at about the same time as Teotihuacan. It was situated to serve as a trade center and religious pilgrimage destination linking the Valley of Mexico with Maya regions to the southeast and with the Mixtec peoples of Monte Alban to the southwest in Oaxaca. Among the largest cities of postclassic Mesoamerica, Cholula had a large culturally and linguistically diverse population, including a large Toltec community. Cholula's original ties to the Toltecs are unclear, but sometime after 1000 CE the resident Toltec population appealed to Culhuacán for military assistance and gained the upper hand. While the ultimate fate of this vulnerable Toltec community is not known, Cholula survived as an important regional power until the Spanish conquest, thus connecting the legacies of both Teotihuacan and the Toltecs to the later rise of the powerful Aztec Empire (see Chapter 15).

8-4 Northern Peoples

In what ways did Mesoamerica influence the cultural centers in North America?

By the end of the classic period in Mesoamerica, around 900 CE, important cultural centers had appeared in the southwestern desert region and along the Ohio and Mississippi River Valleys of what is now the United States (see Map 8.4). The peoples of the Southwest benefited from the early introduction of maize and other Mesoamerican cultigens before 1000 BCE. The resulting improvement to agricultural productivity led before 500 CE to rising population, the beginnings of urbanization, and increased social stratification. Maize cultivation slowly moved north and east along Amerindian trade routes until it appeared among the native peoples of the Ohio Valley sometime after 200 CE, approximately a thousand years after its first introduction north of the Rio Grande. It had become the region's chief staple crop after 800. Once widely adopted this useful crop accelerated the development of large population centers and new political institutions.

The two distinct ecological regions evolved different cultural and political traditions. The Anasazi (**ah-nah-SAH-zee**) and their neighbors in the Southwest maintained a relatively egalitarian social structure and retained collective forms of political organization based on kinship and age. The mound builders of the eastern river valleys evolved more hierarchical political institutions, which subordinated groups of small towns and villages to a political center ruled by a hereditary chief who wielded both secular and religious authority.

AP® Exam Tip
Be familiar with the Chaco and Cahokia civilizations in North America and understand how they built political unity.

8-4a **Southwestern Desert Cultures**

Around 300 BCE in what is today Arizona, contacts between local peoples and Mesoamerica led
to the introduction of agriculture based on irrigation. Because irrigation allowed the planting
of two maize crops per year, the population grew and settled village life soon appeared. Of all
the southwestern cultures, the Hohokam of the Salt and Gila River Valleys show the strongest
Mesoamerican influence. Hohokam sites have platform mounds and ball courts similar to those
of Mesoamerica. Hohokam pottery, clay figurines, cast copper bells, and turquoise mosaics also
reflect this influence. By 1000 CE the Hohokam had constructed an elaborate irrigation system.
Hohokam agricultural and ceramic technology then spread over to neighboring peoples, but it
was the Anasazi to the north who left the most vivid legacy of these desert cultures.

Archaeologists use **Anasazi**, a Navajo word meaning "ancient ones," to identify a number of
dispersed, though similar, desert cultures located in what is now the Four Corners region of
Arizona, New Mexico, Colorado, and Utah (see Map 8.4). In the centuries before 700 CE the
Anasazi developed an economy based on the three key Mesoamerican domesticates—maize,

**MAP 8.4   Culture Areas of
North America** In each of the
large ecological regions of North
America, native peoples evolved
distinctive cultures and technologies. Here the Anasazi of the arid
Southwest and the mound-building
cultures of the Ohio and Mississippi
River Valleys are highlighted.

What Mesoamerican agricultural technology and domesticated crop played a role in
the development of all three
North American indigenous
cultures?

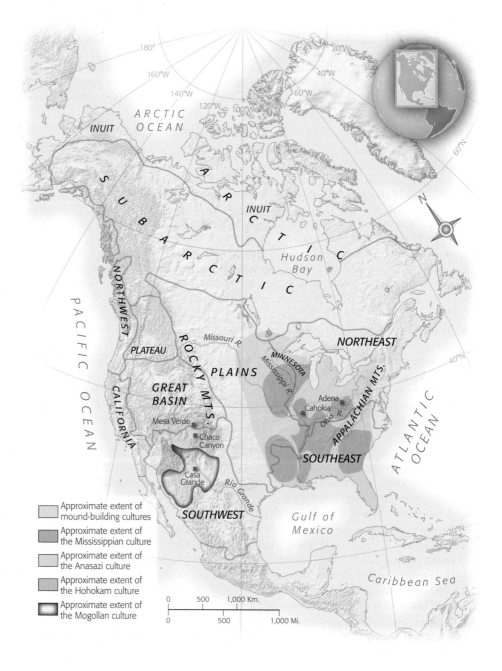

▲ **Mesa Verde Cliff Dwelling** Located in southern Colorado, the Anasazi cliff dwellings of the Mesa Verde region hosted a population of about 7,000 in 1250 CE. The construction of housing complexes and religious buildings in the area's large caves was prompted by increased warfare in the region. kravka/Shutterstock.com

beans, and squash. As irrigation and other technologies increased their productivity, they formed larger villages and evolved a much more complex cultural life centered on underground buildings called *kivas*. They produced pottery decorated with geometric patterns, learned to weave cotton cloth, and, after 900 CE, began to construct large multistory residential and ritual centers.

One of the largest Anasazi communities was located in Chaco Canyon in what is now northwestern New Mexico. There were twelve towns in the canyon and surrounding mesas, suggesting a regional population of 15,000. Pueblo Bonito (founded in 919 CE) had more than 650 rooms arranged in a four-story block of residences and storage rooms; it also had thirty-eight kivas, including a great kiva more than 65 feet (19 meters) in diameter. Hunting, trade, and the need to maintain irrigation works often drew men away from the village. Women shared in agricultural tasks, were specialists in many crafts, and were responsible for food preparation and childcare. At Chaco Canyon the high-quality construction, the size and number of kivas, and the system of roads linking the canyon to outlying towns all suggest that Pueblo Bonito and its nearest neighbors exerted political and cultural dominance over a large region.

As had been the case with the Olmec center of San Lorenzo and Chavín de Huantar in Peru nearly a thousand years earlier, Pueblo Bonito's ascendancy depended on its identity as a sacred site and on the elaboration of an intense cycle of religious rituals that attracted pilgrims from distant locations.

Early archaeologists suggested that the Chaco Canyon culture originated as a colonial appendage of Mesoamerica, but the archaeological record provides little evidence for this theory. Merchants from Chaco did provide Toltec-period peoples of northern Mexico with turquoise in exchange for shell jewelry, copper bells, macaws, and trumpets, but these exchanges occurred late in Chaco's development. More importantly, the signature elements of Mesoamerican cultural influence, such as pyramid-shaped mounds and ball courts, are missing at Chaco.

The abandonment of the major sites in Chaco Canyon in the twelfth century most likely resulted from climate change and the resulting long drought that undermined the culture's fragile agricultural economy. Nevertheless, the Anasazi continued to inhabit cliff dwellings in the Four Corners region for more than a century after the abandonment of Chaco Canyon, with major centers at Mesa Verde in present-day Colorado and at Canyon de Chelly and Kiet Siel in

AP® Exam Tip Understand the role of trade and communication networks in promoting the growth of new trading cities such as Cahokia.

Anasazi Important culture of what is now the southwest United States (700–1300 CE). Centered on Chaco Canyon in New Mexico and Mesa Verde in Colorado, the Anasazi culture built multistory residences and worshiped in subterranean buildings called *kivas*.

Arizona. The construction of these settlements in large natural caves high above valley floors suggests that these surviving settlements were threatened by increased levels of warfare, probably provoked by population pressure on the region's limited arable land.

8-4b Mound Builders: The Hopewell and Mississippian Cultures

From around 100 CE the Hopewell culture spread through the Ohio River Valley. Hopewell peoples constructed large villages and monumental earthworks. Once established, their influence spread west to Illinois, Michigan, and Wisconsin, east to New York and Ontario, and south to Alabama, Louisiana, Mississippi, and even Florida (see Map 8.4). For the necessities of daily life the Hopewell depended on hunting and gathering and on a limited agriculture. They are an early example of a North American **chiefdom**—populations as large as 10,000 and rule by a hereditary chief who exercised both religious and secular responsibilities. Chiefs organized periodic rituals of feasting and gift giving to link diverse kinship groups and guarantee access to specialized crops and craft goods. They also managed long-distance trade for luxury goods and additional food supplies.

The largest Hopewell towns in the Ohio River Valley had several thousand inhabitants and served as ceremonial and political centers. Large mounds built to house burials and serve as platforms for religious rituals dominated major Hopewell centers. Some mounds were oriented to reflect sunrise and moonrise patterns. The abandonment of major sites around 400 CE marked the decline of Hopewell culture.

Hopewell influenced the development of the Mississippian culture (800–1500 CE). As in the case of the Anasazi, some experts have suggested that contacts with Mesoamerica influenced early Mississippian culture, but there is no convincing evidence to support this theory. It is true that maize, beans, and squash, all first domesticated in Mesoamerica, were crucial to the urbanized Mississippian culture. But these plants and related technologies were most likely acquired via trade with intervening cultures.

The development of urbanized Mississippian chiefdoms resulted instead from the accumulated effects of small increases in agricultural productivity and the expansion of trade networks. An improved economy led to population growth, the building of cities, and social stratification. The largest towns shared a common urban plan based on a central plaza surrounded by large platform mounds.

chiefdom Form of political organization with rule by a hereditary leader who held power over a collection of villages and towns. Less powerful than kingdoms and empires, chiefdoms were based on gift giving and commercial links.

The Mississippian culture reached its highest stage of evolution at the great urban center of Cahokia, located near the modern city of East St. Louis, Illinois (see Map 8.4). Cahokia, like Chavín de Huantar, the chief Olmec cities, and contemporary Pueblo Bonito of the Anasazi served as a religious center and pilgrimage site. Subordinated rural populations were organized by the Cahokia elite through obligations of tribute, shared labor, and ritual. At the center of this site was the largest mound constructed in North America, a terraced structure 100 feet (30 meters) high and 1,037 by 790 feet (316 by 241 meters) at the base. Chunkey, a game played by throwing spears at a stone disk rolled along the ground, attracted visitors from great distances. This game, infused with religious meaning and accompanied by gambling, helped establish Cahokia's cultural influence over a large region and was used by the elite to organize tribute payments and labor for the construction of massive public works. It was therefore similar in influence to the Mesoamerican ball game first developed by the Olmec.

In this hierarchical society, commoners lived on the periphery of the ceremonial center where elite housing and temples were located. At its height in about 1200 CE, Cahokia had a population of approximately 20,000—about the same as some of the postclassic Maya cities.

Cahokia controlled surrounding agricultural lands and a large number of secondary towns. Its political and economic influence depended on its location near the confluence of the Missouri, Mississippi, and Illinois Rivers, a location that facilitated commercial exchanges as far away as the coasts of the Atlantic and the Gulf of Mexico. Traders brought seashells,

Section Review

- Transfer of irrigation and corn agriculture from Mesoamerica stimulated the development of Hohokam and Anasazi cultures.

- The Anasazi concentrated in the Four Corners region of the southwestern United States, especially in Chaco Canyon, where they built cities with underground kivas.

- Hopewell culture, organized around chiefdoms in the Ohio River Valley, was based on long-distance trade and religious ritual life centered on large mounds.

- The political organization, trade practices, and mound building of Hopewell were continued by the Mississippian culture, with its largest city, Cahokia, at the site of East St. Louis.

- Environmental changes probably undermined both Anasazi and Mississippian cultures.

copper, mica, and flint to the city, where they were used in manufacture of ritual goods and tools. Burial evidence suggests that the rulers of Cahokia were rich and powerful. In one burial more than fifty young female and male retainers were sacrificed to accompany a ruler after death.

The construction of defensive walls around the ceremonial center and elite residences after 1250 CE provides some evidence that the decline and eventual abandonment of Cahokia were tied to the effects of military defeat or civil war, as had been true in Teotihuacan. There is also evidence that climate change and a series of destructive floods played a role in this great city's decline. Population pressures, exacerbated by environmental degradation caused by deforestation and more intensive farming practices, also undermined Cahokia's viability. Beginning in the thirteenth century Cahokia lost control of many of its dependencies and, as a result, the city's population fell precipitously. Despite its collapse, smaller Mississippian centers that preserved elements of Cahokian culture continued to flourish in the Southeast of the present-day United States until the arrival of Europeans.

8-5 Andean Civilizations, 200–1400

How did the Amerindian peoples of the Andean area adapt to their environment and produce socially complex and politically advanced societies?

AP® Exam Tip
Compare the ways various civilizations used technology to adapt to their environment and adapt the environment to their needs.

The Andean region of South America was an unlikely environment for the development of rich and powerful civilizations (see Map 8.5). Much of the region's mountainous zone is at altitudes that seem too high for agriculture and human habitation. Along the Pacific coast an arid climate posed a difficult challenge to the development of agriculture. To the east of the Andes Mountains, the hot and humid tropical environment of the Amazon headwaters also offered formidable obstacles to the organization of complex societies. Yet the Amerindian peoples of the Andean area produced some of the most socially complex and politically advanced societies of the Western Hemisphere. The very harshness of the environment compelled the development of productive and reliable agricultural technologies and attached them to a complex fabric of administrative structures and social relationships that became the central features of Andean civilization.

8-5a Cultural Response to Environmental Challenge

From the time of Chavín all of the great Andean civilizations succeeded in connecting the distinctive resources of the coastal region, with its abundant fisheries and irrigated maize fields, to the mountainous interior with its herds of llamas and rich mix of grains and tubers. Both regions faced significant environmental challenges. Droughts and shifting sands that clogged irrigation works periodically

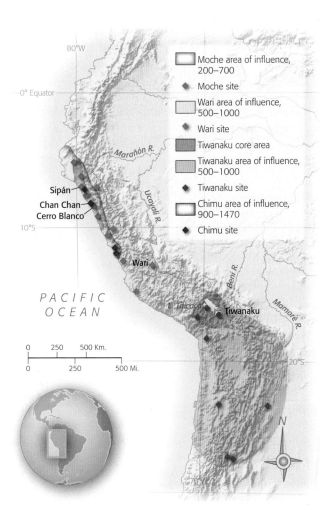

MAP 8.5 Andean Civilizations, 200 BCE–1532 CE In response to these difficult environmental challenges, Andean peoples evolved complex social and technological adaptations. Irrigation systems, the domestication of the llama, metallurgy, and shared labor obligations helped provide a firm economic foundation for powerful, centralized states.

What advantages did Andean civilizations gain by serving as points of exchange between the coast and mountainous regions?

overwhelmed the coastal region's fields, and the mountainous interior presented enormous environmental challenges, since it averaged between 250 and 300 frosts per year.

The development of compensating technologies required an accurate calendar to time planting and harvests and the domestication of frost-resistant varieties of potatoes and grains. Native peoples learned to practice dispersed farming at different altitudes to reduce risks from frosts, and they terraced hillsides to create micro environments within a single area. They also discovered how to use the cold, dry climate to produce freeze-dried vegetable and meat products that prevented famine when crops failed. The domestication of the llama and alpaca also proved crucial, providing meat, wool, and long-distance transportation that linked coastal and mountain economies.

It was the clan, or **ayllu (aye-YOU)**, that provided the foundation for Andean cultural achievement. Members of an ayllu held land communally. Ayllu members thought of each other as brothers and sisters and were obligated to aid each other in tasks that required more labor than a single household could provide. These reciprocal obligations provided the model for the organization of labor and the distribution of goods at every level of Andean society. Just as individuals and families were expected to provide labor to kinsmen, ayllus were collectively expected to provide labor and goods to their rulers.

With the development of territorial states ruled by hereditary aristocracies and kings after 1000 BCE, these obligations were organized on a larger scale. The **mita (MEET-ah)** was a rotational labor draft that organized members of ayllus to work the fields and care for the llama and alpaca herds owned by religious establishments, the royal court, and the aristocracy. Mita laborers built and maintained roads, bridges, temples, palaces, and large irrigation and drainage projects. They also produced textiles and goods essential to ritual life, such as beer made from maize and *coca* (dried leaves chewed as a stimulant and now also the source of the narcotic cocaine).

The ayllu was intimately tied to a uniquely Andean system of production and exchange. Because the region's mountain ranges created a multitude of small ecological areas with specialized resources, each community sought to control a variety of environments so as to guarantee access to essential goods. Coastal regions produced maize, fish, and cotton. Mountain valleys contributed quinoa (the local grain) as well as potatoes and other tubers. Higher elevations contributed the wool and meat of llamas and alpacas, and the Amazonian region provided coca and fruits. Ayllus sent out colonists to exploit the resources of these distinct ecological niches, retaining the loyalty of the colonists by arranging marriages and by coming together for rituals. Historians commonly refer to this system of controlled exchange across ecological boundaries as vertical integration, or verticality.

▲ **Moche Warrior** The Moche of ancient Peru were among the most accomplished ceramic artists of the Americas. Moche potters produced representations of gods and spirits, scenes of daily life, and portrait vases of important people. This warrior is armed with a mace, shield, and protective helmet. D Alderman/Alamy Stock Photo

AP® Exam Tip
Be familiar with the Moche civilization in Andean South America, and pay specific attention to its political structure.

ayllu Andean lineage group or kin-based community.

mita Andean labor system based on shared obligations to help kinsmen and work on behalf of rulers or religious organizations.

Moche Civilization of the north coast of Peru (200–700 CE). An important Andean civilization that built extensive irrigation networks as well as impressive urban centers dominated by brick temples.

8-5b The Early Intermediate Period Moche

Scholars of the Andes call the period 200 to 600 CE the Early Intermediate period. The **Moche (MO-che)** were among the most influential and powerful Andean civilizations of this period, dominating the north coastal region of Peru. While they did not establish a formal empire or create unified political structures ruled by a single monarch, they did exercise authority over a broad geographic region. The most powerful of the Moche urban centers, such as Cerro Blanco located near the modern Peruvian city of Trujillo (see Map 8.5), first established hegemony over neighboring towns and villages and then extended political and economic control over more distant neighbors militarily. Key to this expansion was the elaboration of a potent religious ideology that tied hereditary rulers to the gods through elaborate religious rituals in the major Moche cities.

Archaeological evidence indicates that the Moche cultivated maize, quinoa, beans, manioc, and sweet potatoes with the aid of massive irrigation works, a complex network of canals and aqueducts that connected fields with water sources as far away as 75 miles (121 kilometers). Moche rulers forced commoners and subject peoples to build and maintain these hydraulic works. The Moche also relied on large herds of alpacas and llamas to transport goods across the region's difficult terrain. Their wool, along with cotton provided by farmers, provided the raw material for the thriving Moche textile production.

Evidence from surviving murals and decorated ceramics suggests that Moche society was highly stratified and theocratic. Wealth and power were concentrated, along with political control, in the hands of priests and military leaders. The military conquest of neighboring regions reinforced this hierarchy. Because the elite constructed their residences atop large platforms at Moche ceremonial centers, the powerful literally looked down on the commoners whose labor supported them. Moche burial practices reflected these deep social distinctions. A recent excavation in the Lambeyeque Valley discovered the tomb of a warrior-priest buried with a rich treasure of gold, silver, and copper jewelry, textiles, feather ornaments, and shells (see Diversity & Dominance: Burials as Historical Texts). A group of retainers and servants had been executed and then buried with this powerful man in order to serve him in the afterlife.

Most commoners, on the other hand, devoted their time to subsistence farming and to the payment of labor dues owed to their ayllu and to the elite. Both men and women were involved in agriculture, care of llama herds, and the household economy. They lived with their families in one-room buildings clustered in the outlying areas of cities and in surrounding agricultural zones.

The high quality of Moche textiles, ceramics, and metallurgy indicates the presence of numerous skilled artisans. Women had a special role in the production of textiles, and even elite women devoted time to weaving. Moche culture developed a brilliant representational art. Craftsmen produced highly individualized portrait vases and decorated other ceramics with representations of myths and rituals. They were also accomplished metalsmiths, producing beautiful gold and silver religious objects and jewelry for elite adornment. Metallurgy served more

◀ **The Ritual Center of Tiwanaku** During the Middle Horizon period Tiwanaku was one of the most impressive cities in the Andean region. The ritual center was characterized by beautiful stone construction, sunken plazas, and by large carved stone representations of the gods. Paulo Afonso/Shutterstock.com

Efforts to reveal the history of the Americas before the arrival of Europeans depend on the work of archaeologists. The burials of rulers and other members of elites can be viewed as historical texts that describe how textiles, precious metals, beautifully decorated ceramics, and other commodities were used to reinforce the political and cultural power of ruling lineages. In public, members of the elite were always surrounded by the most desirable goods and rarest products as well as by elaborate rituals and ceremonies. The effect was to create an aura of god-like power. The material elements of political and cultural power were also integrated into the experience of death and burial as members of the elite were sent into the afterlife.

The first photograph is of an excavated Moche tomb in Sipán, Peru. The Moche (200–ca. 700 CE) were one of the most important of the pre-Inka civilizations of the Andean region, masters of metallurgy, ceramics, and textiles. The excavations at Sipán revealed a "warrior-priest" buried with an amazing array of gold, silver, and gilded copper ornaments, jewels, rich textiles, and ceramics. The Sipán tombs are the richest archaeological excavation site ever discovered in the Western Hemisphere. Buried nearby were five human sacrifices, two women, perhaps wives or concubines, two male servants, and a warrior. Three of these victims—the warrior, one woman, and a male servant—are each missing a foot, perhaps amputated to guarantee their continued faithfulness to the deceased ruler in the afterlife.

The second photograph shows the excavation of a classic-era (200–ca. 800 CE) Maya burial at Río Azul in Guatemala. After death this elite male was laid out on a carved wooden platform and cotton mattress and his body was painted with decorations. Mourners covered his body in rich textiles and surrounded him with valuable goods. These included a necklace of individual stones carved in the shape of heads, perhaps a symbol of his prowess in battle, and high-quality ceramics, some filled with foods consumed by the elite like cacao. The careful preparation of the burial chamber had required the work of numerous artisans and laborers, as was the case in the burial of the Moche warrior-priest. In death, as in life, these early American civilizations acknowledged the high status, political power, and religious authority of their elites.

AP® History Reasoning Skills

Contextualization *What can a detailed examination of each burial site reveal about the society in which it was created?*

Nathan Benn/Corbis Historical/Getty Images

George Mobley/NGS Image Collection

▲ **Burials Reveal Ancient Civilizations** (*Left*) Buried around 300 CE, this Moche warrior-priest was buried amid rich tribute at Sipán in Peru. Buried nearby were the bodies of retainers or kinsmen probably sacrificed to accompany this powerful man. (*Right*) Similarly, the burial of a member of the Maya elite at Río Azul in northern Guatemala indicates the care taken to surround the powerful with fine ceramics, jewelry, and other valuable goods.

practical ends as well: artisans produced a range of tools made of heavy copper and copper alloy for agricultural and military purposes.

The archaeological record makes clear that the rapid decline of major Moche centers coincided with a succession of natural disasters in the sixth century as well as with long-term climate changes. A thirty-year drought expanded the area of coastal sand dunes during the sixth century, and powerful winds pushed sand onto fragile agricultural lands, overwhelming the irrigation system. As the land dried, periodic heavy rains caused erosion that damaged fields and weakened the economy that had sustained ceremonial and residential centers. Despite massive efforts to keep the irrigation canals open using forced labor and despite the construction of new urban centers in less vulnerable valleys to the north, Moche civilization never fully recovered. In the eighth century, the rise of a new military power, the Wari (see below), also contributed to the disappearance of the Moche by putting pressure on trade routes that linked the coastal region with the highlands.

8-5c Tiwanaku and Wari

Between 500 and 1000 CE, what Andean scholars call the Middle Horizon period, two powerful civilizations dominated the highlands. The ruins of **Tiwanaku** (**tee-wah-NA-coo**) (see Map 8.5) stand at nearly 13,000 feet (3,962 meters) near Lake Titicaca in modern Bolivia. Tiwanaku's expansion depended on the adoption of technologies that increased agricultural productivity. Modern excavations provide the outline of vast drainage projects that reclaimed nearly 200,000 acres (80,000 hectares) of rich lakeside marshes for agriculture. This system of raised fields and ditches permitted intensive cultivation similar to that achieved by the use of chinampas in Mesoamerica. Fish from the nearby lake and llamas added protein to a diet largely dependent on potatoes and grains. Llamas were also crucial for the maintenance of long-distance trade relationships that brought in corn, coca, tropical fruits, and medicinal plants. The resulting abundance permitted a dense cycle of feasting and religious observance that fueled the rise of a powerful elite.

Tiwanaku was distinguished by the scale of its urban construction and by the high quality of its stone masonry. Thousands of laborers were mobilized to cut and move the large stones used to construct large terraced pyramids, sunken plazas, walled enclosures, and a reservoir. Despite a limited metallurgy that produced only tools of copper alloy, Tiwanaku's artisans built large structures of finely cut stone that required little mortar to fit the blocks. They also produced gigantic human statuary. The largest example, a stern figure with a military bearing, was cut from a single block of stone that measured 24 feet (7 meters) high. These sacred constructions were oriented to reflect celestial cycles and distant Andean peaks infused with religious significance. Collectively, they provided an awe-inspiring setting for the religious rituals that legitimized the city's control of distant territories and peoples and for the elite's domination of society.

Archaeological evidence suggests that Tiwanaku at its height around 800 CE had a full-time population of around 60,000, including communities attracted from distant regions by the city's religious rituals and trade. It is clear that Tiwanaku was a highly stratified society ruled by hereditary elite. This elite initially organized and controlled the ayllus of the surrounding region, but, as their military power grew, eventually utilized drafted labor from conquered and incorporated populations as well. As Tiwanaku's power and wealth grew, thousands of skilled craftsmen constantly expanded and embellished the ceremonial architecture and produced the metal goods, textiles, and pottery consumed by the elite. Military conquests and the establishment of distant colonial populations provided dependable supplies of more exotic products from ecologically distinct zones, such as colorful shells, gold and copper, and fine textiles.

Sometime after 1000 CE urban Tiwanaku was abandoned. While the exact cause is uncertain, we know the eclipse of this great civilization took a long time. There is evidence that years of severe drought led to precipitous population loss and to the breakdown of the long-distance trade in elite goods. This period was associated with the destruction of monumental effigies and other religious symbols, suggesting that worsening material conditions undermined the legitimacy of the elite.

The contemporary site of **Wari** (**WAH-ree**) was located about 450 miles (751 kilometers) to the northwest of Tiwanaku, near the modern Peruvian city of Ayacucho. Wari clearly shared elements of the culture and technology of Tiwanaku, but the exact nature of the relationship between these civilizations remains unclear. Some scholars argue that Wari began as a

Tiwanaku Name of capital city and empire centered on the region near Lake Titicaca in modern Bolivia (500–1000 CE).

dependency of Tiwanaku, while others suggest that they were joint capitals of a single empire. Most now argue that Wari was a distinct culture that evolved a politically centralized state and powerful military. Recent research indicates an aggressive imperial expansion lubricated by captive-taking and human sacrifice.

Urban Wari was larger than Tiwanaku, measuring nearly 4 square miles (10 square kilometers). A massive wall surrounded the city center, which was dominated by a large temple and multifamily housing for elites and artisans. Housing for commoners was located in a sprawling suburban zone. The small scale of its monumental architecture relative to Tiwanaku and the near absence of cut stone masonry in public and private buildings suggest either the weakness of the elite or the absence of specialized construction crafts compared with other Andean centers. A distinctive Wari ceramic style allows experts to trace Wari's influence to the coastal area and to the northern highlands. This expansion occurred at a time of climate change and increasing warfare throughout the Andes that led ultimately to the eclipse of both Tiwanaku and Wari after 1000 CE. In the centuries that followed the collapse of these two powerful centers, the Andean highlands experienced increased levels of violence, as evidenced by the construction of numerous fortifications by the smaller polities and villages that now contended for power.

8-5d Chimú

On the north coast of Peru in the region previously dominated by the Moche, a powerful new imperial state appeared after 900 CE, the period called Late Intermediate (1000–1476 CE) in Andean history. The **Chimú** Empire, or Chimor, with its capital of Chan Chan, eventually controlled more than 600 miles (966 kilometers) of the Pacific coast from Ecuador in the north to central Peru. Building upon the legacy of the Moche who earlier controlled this area, the Chimú depended on the abundant production of an irrigated agricultural hinterland and on the labor provided by conquered dependencies.

While the grandeur of Wari and Tiwanaku can still be seen in surviving monumental stone architecture, the once-great city of Chan Chan, built from adobe, has been much diminished by a thousand years of erosion. Nevertheless, the imperial character of the city remains clear. Nine large residential compounds dominated the urban nucleus. Each one is believed to have housed a ruler and his family during his life and then become the ruler's mausoleum upon his death. With each succession the new ruler would be forced to organize the labor and materials necessary to construct a new palace compound. In addition to the family residence of the ruler, each compound contained a U-shaped room used for official functions and numerous smaller rooms used to store food and other tribute items sent from dependent jurisdictions. This system depended ultimately on a potent military and a series of conquests that only ended in the fifteenth century with the appearance of a more powerful military rival, the Inka (see Chapter 15).

While Chan Chan was the center of imperial government and hosted a large aristocratic population in addition to the reigning family, there was little urban planning. Elite residential compounds were separated by high walls from the humble habitations of commoners dispersed across the city. Chan Chan served primarily as the residential precinct of the elite and those who provided the elite with luxury goods like gold jewelry and high-quality textiles and pottery, rather than as a religious or even commercial center. These patterns were repeated on a modest scale in the regional political capitals that organized the labor necessary to maintain irrigation works and collect the tribute that sustained Chan Chan.

Both the urban architecture and the organization of labor expressed the profound social and economic distance that separated royalty and populace. With a population of only 25,000 to 30,000 at its peak, we know the massive Chimú capital city was built and maintained by labor tributes imposed on dependent rural populations. As the city grew, the construction of large structures like palaces and

Wari Andean civilization culturally linked to Tiwanaku, perhaps beginning as a colony of Tiwanaku.

Chimú A powerful civilization, also called Kingdom of Chimor, that developed on the northern coast of Peru from about 1200 to its conquest by an expanding Inka empire in the 1470s. Its capital city was Chan Chan.

Section Review

- Andean societies developed by devising solutions to problems posed by their complex environment of arid coastlands, cold highlands, and tropical forests.

- The ayllu and mita provided the social base for Andean economic and political organization.

- The Moche developed a powerful state based on irrigated agriculture, exchange between ecological regions, and a powerful religious elite.

- The construction of canals and the development of raised field agriculture made possible the rise of the religious and political center of Tiwanaku.

- Both Tiwanaku and Wari used their powerful militaries to extend their power over large regions and create long-distance networks of trade.

- The Chimú created a powerful new empire in the region previously dominated by the Moche.

religious monuments was subdivided into multiple small tasks assigned to parties of tribute workers from distinct regions who made their own adobe bricks.

The Chimú Empire (Chimor) survived for over four centuries in the difficult arid environment of the Peruvian coast, expanding the scale of Moche irrigation works by developing a larger, more efficient bureaucracy that could organize thousands of conscripted laborers for ever more ambitious irrigation tasks. As this empire expanded, the improved agricultural productivity that resulted from these projects compensated dependent peoples for their labor and for their loss of autonomy. Unlike earlier Andean civilizations, the Chimú did not collapse because of environmental catastrophe or social unrest. Instead, in the 1470s, they fell victim to the rapid imperial expansion of the militarily powerful Inka, who then freely borrowed and adapted Chimú's technologies and political institutions to serve their own imperial ambitions.

8-6 Conclusion

The Toltec Empire and Cholula of Mesoamerica and Chimor of the Andean region were all powerful states that depended on religious practices, technologies, political institutions, and social forms that had developed over nearly 2,000 years. In some cases crucial elements of political life, culture, and economy originated in the era of the Olmec and Chavín. Despite these continuities, rising populations and competition for resources led inevitably to new cycles of violence in both regions. The survival of these states ultimately depended on the power of their armies as much as on the productivity of their economies or the wisdom of their rulers.

Mesoamerica and the Andean region were environmentally challenging regions where a succession of native states found ways to produce and distribute products from distinct ecological regions as well as ways to organize ethnically diverse populations into coherent polities. From the beginning rulers in both regions legitimized their authority religiously, serving as priestly intermediaries with the gods or claiming direct descent from them. The major cities of every important civilization from the time of the Olmec and Chavín to 1400 CE operated as religious as well as political centers. Their urban cores were dominated by monumental religious architecture decorated with symbols connecting elites to the gods through creation myths. Dense cycles of religious ritual conducted by priests and rulers in elaborate costumes legitimized the power of cities over the countryside and habituated rural populations to the transfer of goods and labor that made the achievements of these civilizations possible.

With the important exception of metallurgy developed in the Andes and transferred to Mesoamerica after 500 CE, technology developed slowly in the Americas after the era of the Olmec and Chavín. The dominant powers of each successive era—Teotihuacan and the Moche and, ultimately, the Toltecs and Cholula and Chimú—all depended on the mobilization of ever-larger workforces to meet environmental challenges and support growing urbanization, rather than on innovative technologies. The construction of irrigation canals, raised fields, terraced hillsides, and, in the case of Mesoamerica, chinampas multiplied agricultural productivity, subsidized craft specialization, and, through trade, overcame environmental constraints, but all these technologies were in place for nearly a thousand years before the Toltec, Cholula, and Chimú periods. The growing size of cities, the mounting power of government, and the expanding scale of empire all depended on the refinement of ancient technologies and the mobilization of ever-larger workforces.

There were important differences between Mesoamerica and the Andean region. Mesoamerican cultures developed elementary markets to distribute specialized regional production, although the forced payment of goods as tribute remained important to sustain cities like Toltec Tula. In the postclassic period standardized quantities of cacao beans, metal goods, and cloth were being used as money in these markets. In the Andes reciprocal labor obligations and the managed exchange relationships of ayllus were used to allocate goods. There were important regional political differences as well. In Mesoamerica the Toltecs imposed tribute obligations on defeated peoples but left local hereditary elites in place. The Chimú of the Andes, in contrast, created a more centralized imperial administrative structure managed by a trained bureaucracy and used compulsory labor obligations to produce and distribute goods.

We can find similar patterns in North America. The transfer of agricultural technology, such as irrigation, from Mesoamerica, with its dependence on corn, beans, and squash, influenced the mound-building cultures of the Ohio and Mississippi River Valleys and the desert cultures of the

Southwest. In the desert region of what is now the Southwest of the United States, the Anasazi and other peoples also utilized irrigated agriculture, a technology crucial to both Mesoamerican and Andean cultures. Both the desert and mound-building cultures of North America experienced cycles when powerful new political centers expanded the territories they controlled and consolidated their power until overwhelmed by environmental challenges or displaced by military rivals.

Beginning in the eleventh century the Toltec Empire weakened. The ultimate collapse of Tula left Culhuacán and Cholula as heirs of a much-diminished Toltec presence in central Mexico. Chimor persisted until the fifteenth century, when it also lost momentum and was militarily overwhelmed by the rising Inka Empire around 1470. Great civilizations in both Mesoamerica and the Andean region had risen and then been overwhelmed in earlier epochs as well, as had the major powers of the Four Corners desert region and the Ohio and Mississippi River Valleys. In all these cases, a long period of cultural and political adjustment led eventually to the creation of new indigenous institutions, the adoption of new technologies, and the appearance of new centers of power in new locations. With the appearance of the Aztec and Inka Empires in the fourteenth century, America would experience its final cycle of autonomous indigenous crisis and adjustment. At the end of that century the future of Amerindian peoples would become linked to the cultures of the Old World (see Chapter 15).

Key Terms

Olmec p. 194	chinampas p. 200	chiefdom p. 210	Tiwanaku p. 215
Chavín p. 198	Maya p. 201	ayllu p. 212	Wari p. 216
llama p. 198	Toltecs p. 205	mita p. 212	Chimú p. 216
Teotihuacan p. 199	Anasazi p. 209	Moche p. 212	

Review Questions

1. How did Amerindian cultures use technologies and cultural practices to adapt to environmental challenges in Mesoamerica and the Andean region?

2. Were there important cultural and political similarities among all the Amerindian peoples of the hemisphere?

3. Did belief systems and the elaboration of religious ritual play a role in the development of the most important Amerindian urban centers in the Americas?

 MINDTAP From Cengage

MindTap® is a fully online, personalized learning experience built upon Cengage Learning content. MindTap® combines student learning tools—readings, multimedia, activities, and assessments—into a singular Learning Path that guides students through the course and helps students develop the critical thinking, analysis, and communication skills that are essential to academic and professional success.

Material Culture
Bells, Gongs, and Drums

Thunder, the roar of surf, the gusting of wind—these were the loudest sounds normally heard in prehistoric communities. Other natural sounds were quieter: birdsong, insect whines, the occasional animal bark, grunt, or snuffle. The loudest sounds humans made for themselves were probably shouts, cries, and the pounding of wood and stone. Some loud sounds, such as thunderclaps or the braying of donkeys and the crowing of roosters, gave rise to strong feelings. Thunder seemed to be of supernatural origin, the cockcrow was associated with dawn, and the braying of donkeys, at least in the imaginations of ancient peoples in Egypt and western Asia, was a token of death and the underworld.

When humans devised their own ways of producing loud sounds, they often used them in religious rituals or as symbols of high social rank. Drums were undoubtedly the first man-made devices for making loud sounds. Though the date of 6000 BCE is often given for the first drums, the generally poor preservation of wood and skin in archaeological sites makes it likely that they were in use much earlier but left no identifiable remains. Drumming retained its great ceremonial and political importance in sub-Saharan Africa and pre-Columbian America down to the modern era.

Bells and gongs, the latter either flat metal disks or upward-opening bowls, come much later. Bronze made from copper and tin, the preferred metal for these instruments, does not appear in western Asian archaeological sites before 3000 BCE. Bronze in China is almost as early, and it shows up somewhat later in tin-rich Southeast Asia.

Magnificent bronze drums were made and exported from Vietnam after 1000 BCE. But bells were more important than drums in early Chinese culture. By the late first millennium BCE, court ceremonies and musical performers utilized sets of tuned bells covering five octaves. Some could produce two separate notes, depending on where they were struck. Gongs appeared in China around 500 CE and spread from there to Southeast Asia, where they still play a central role in Indonesian percussion orchestras. Centuries later, when Buddhism spread in East Asia, bells became an essential part of Buddhist worship.

Though tin bronze may have originated in western Asia, large bells were not greatly used in ancient Egypt and Mesopotamia or in Greco-Roman antiquity. Following Jewish precedent, early Christian communities in Egypt and Syria summoned their congregations with trumpets. Around the sixth century CE, rhythmic pounding with a mallet on a long piece of wood or metal called a "semantron" superseded trumpet calls in Eastern Orthodox churches. This device is still used in some Russian Orthodox monasteries.

▶ **Bell Pavilion in Nara, Japan** The Bell Pavilion at the Todai-ji Temple in Nara houses the biggest bell in Japan, cast in 752. Like all wooden buildings in Japan, the pavilion itself has been rebuilt several times, most recently in 1966–1967.

Christian churches may have used bells as early as 500 CE, but evidence of bell use becomes strong only a century later, mostly in connection with Irish churches. The Latin word *clocca*, from which English *clock* derives, comes from the Irish word *clog*, meaning "bell." More than sixty early Irish bells still survive, the earliest made of iron, with bronze becoming the preferred metal by 900 CE.

Early Protestant claims that Catholic ceremonies for blessing bells were superstitious may reflect the fact that many rural communities did attribute supernatural powers to bells. As late as the eighteenth century many French villagers believed that they could ward off crop-damaging hail by ringing their church bell. At the end of the century, such beliefs contributed to villages defying the demand of the secular French Republic that all bells be melted down and the metal recast as cannon. Well into the nineteenth century, France witnessed many struggles between secular and religious officials—mayors and priests—for control of the village bell.

Some bells have gained symbolic importance more recently. In 1871 the New York Stock Exchange adopted a Chinese gong to signal its daily opening and closing in place of the traditional gavel. In 1903 a bell replaced the gong, but the "opening bell" became a media event only in 1995, when guests ranging from corporate executives and foreign dignitaries to basketball star LeBron James, actress Sarah Jessica Parker, and scourge of the universe Darth Vader were invited to mount the podium and perform the ceremony.

Questions for Analysis

1. What comparison can you make between the sound environment of a modern city and that of the preindustrial countryside?

2. What makes the sound of a bell, gong, or drum more impressive than an equally loud automobile alarm or steam whistle?

3. Do drums have a greater or smaller emotional impact than bells and gongs?

Vanni / Art Resource, NY

Issues in World History
Oral Societies and the Consequences of Literacy

The availability of written documents is a key factor used by historians to divide human prehistory from history. When we can read what people of the past thought and said about their lives, we begin to understand their cultures, institutions, values, and beliefs in ways that are not possible based only on the material remains unearthed by archaeologists.

Literacy and nonliteracy are not absolute alternatives. Personal literacy ranges from illiteracy through many shades of *partial literacy* (the ability to write one's name or to read simple texts with difficulty) to the fluent ability to read that is possessed by anyone reading this textbook. And there are degrees of societal literacy, ranging from nonliteracy through so-called craft literacy—in which a small specialized elite uses writing for limited purposes, such as administrative record keeping—up to the near-universal literacy and the use of writing for innumerable purposes that is the norm in the developed world in our times.

The vast majority of human beings of the last 5,000 to 6,000 years, even those living in societies that possessed the technology of writing, were not themselves literate. If most people in a society rely on the spoken word and memory, that culture is essentially "oral" even if some members know how to write. The differences between oral and literate cultures are immense, affecting not only the kinds of knowledge that are valued and the forms in which information is preserved, but also the very use of language, the categories for conceptualizing the world, and ultimately the hard-wiring of the individual human brain (now recognized by neuroscientists to be strongly influenced by individual experience and mental activity).

Ancient Greece of the Archaic and Classical periods (ca. 800–323 BCE) offers a particularly instructive case study because we can observe the process by which writing was introduced into an oral society as well as the far-reaching consequences. The Greeks of the Dark Age and early Archaic period lived in a purely oral society; all knowledge was preserved in human memory and passed on by telling it to others. The *Iliad* and the *Odyssey* (ca. 700 BCE), Homer's epic poems, reflect this state of affairs. Scholars recognize that the creator of these poems was an oral poet, almost certainly not literate, who had heard and memorized the poems of predecessors and retold them his own way. The poems are treasuries of information that this society regarded as useful—events of the past; the conduct expected of warriors, kings, noblewomen, and servants; how to perform a sacrifice, build a raft, put on armor, and entertain guests; and much more.

Embedding this information in a story and using the colorful language, fixed phrases, and predictable rhythm of poetry made it easier for poet and audience to remember vast amounts of material. The early Greek poets, drawing on their strong memories, skill with words, and talent for dramatic performance, developed highly specialized techniques to assist them in memorizing and presenting their tales. They played a vital role in the preservation and transmission of information and thus enjoyed a relatively high social standing and comfortable standard of living. Analogous groups can be found in many other oral cultures of the past, including the bards of medieval Celtic lands, Norse *skalds*, west African *griots*, and the tribal historians of Native American peoples.

Nevertheless, human memory, however cleverly trained and well practiced, can only do so much. Oral societies must be extremely selective about what information to preserve in the limited storage medium of human memory, and they are slow to give up old information to make way for new.

Sometime in the eighth century BCE the Greeks borrowed the system of writing used by the Phoenicians of Lebanon and, in adapting it to their language, created the first purely alphabetic writing, employing several dozen symbols to express the sounds of speech. The Greek alphabet, although relatively simple to learn as compared to the large and cumbersome sets of symbols in such craft literacy systems as cuneiform, hieroglyphics, or Linear B, was probably known at first only to a small number of people and used for restricted purposes. Scholars believe that it may have taken three or four centuries for knowledge of reading and writing to spread to large numbers of Greeks and for the written word to become the primary storage medium for the accumulated knowledge of Greek civilization. Throughout that time Greece was still primarily an oral society, even though some Greeks, mostly highly educated members of the upper classes, were beginning to write down poems, scientific speculations, stories about the past, philosophic musings, and the laws of their communities.

It is no accident that some of the most important intellectual and artistic achievements of the Greeks, including early science, history, drama, and rhetoric, developed in the period when oral and literate ways existed side by side. Scholars have persuasively argued that writing, by opening up a virtually limitless capacity to store information, released the human mind from the hard discipline of memorization and ended the need to be so painfully selective about what was preserved. This made previously unimaginable innovation and experimentation possible. The Greeks began to organize and categorize information in linear ways, perhaps inspired by the linear sequence of the alphabet; and they began to engage in abstract thinking now that it was no longer necessary to put everything in a story format. We can observe changes in the Greek language as it developed a vocabulary full of abstract nouns, accompanied by increasingly complex sentence structure now that the reader had time to go back over the text.

Nevertheless, all the developments associated with literacy were shaped by the deeply rooted oral habits of Greek culture. It is often said that Plato (ca. 429–347 BCE) and his contemporaries of the later Classical Period may have been the first generation of Greeks who learned much of what they knew from books. Even so, Plato was a disciple of the philosopher Socrates, who wrote nothing, and Plato employed the oral form of the dialogue, a dramatized sequence of questions and answers, to convey his ideas in written form.

The transition from orality to literacy met stiff resistance in some quarters. Groups whose position in the oral culture was based on the special knowledge only they possessed—members of the elite who judged disputes, priests who knew the time-honored formulas and rituals for appeasing the gods, oral poets who preserved and performed the stories of a heroic past—resented the consequences of literacy. They did what they could to inflame the common people's suspicions of the impiety of literate men who sought scientific explanations for phenomena, such as lightning and eclipses, that had traditionally been attributed to the will and action of the gods. The elite attacked the so-called Sophists, or "wise men," who charged fees to teach what they claimed were the skills necessary for success, accusing them of subverting traditional morals and corrupting the young.

Other societies, ancient and modern, offer parallel examples of these processes. Oral "specialists" in antiquity, including the Brahmin priests of India and the Celtic Druids, preserved in memory valuable religious information about how to win the favor of the gods. These groups jealously guarded their knowledge because it was the basis of their livelihood and social standing. In their determination to select and to maintain control over those who received this knowledge, they resisted committing it to writing, even after that technology was available. The ways in which oral authorities feel threatened by writing and resist it can be seen in the following quotation from a twentieth-century CE "griot," an oral rememberer and teller of the past in Mali in West Africa:

> We griots are depositories of the knowledge of the past. . . . Other peoples use writing to record the past, but this invention has killed the faculty of memory among them. They do not feel the past anymore, for writing lacks the warmth of the human voice. With them everybody thinks he knows, whereas learning should be a secret. . . . What paltry learning is that which is congealed in dumb books! . . . For generations we have passed on the history of kings from father to son. The narrative was passed on to me without alteration, for I received it free from all untruth.[1]

This point of view is hard for us to grasp, living as we do in an intensely literate society in which the written word is often felt to be more authoritative and objective than the spoken word. It is important, in striving to understand societies of the past, not to superimpose our assumptions on them and to appreciate the complex interplay of oral and literate patterns in many of them.

Questions for Analysis

1. In oral societies (i.e., societies without writing or where writing is known only by a small minority), what methods are used to preserve information?

2. With the adoption of writing, what new possibilities become available for the preservation of information, the development of new intellectual and artistic activities, and even changes in how people use language and conceptualize the world?

3. In light of the profound impacts of the technology of writing on ancient Greek civilization, what might be the impacts on our contemporary civilization of the "information technology revolution" we are currently experiencing?

---

[1]D. T. Niane, *Sundiata: An Epic of Old Mali* (Harlow, UK: Longman, 1986), 41.

Multiple-Choice Questions

Questions 1–4 refer to the image below.

▲ **Remains of Teotihuacan in Central Mexico, Built ca. 450 CE.**

Gordon Galbraith/Shutterstock.com

1. Which of the following descriptions of Teotihuacan can be posited, using the image as evidence?

   (A) The city was built in a region where droughts were common.

   (B) Religious rituals were an important element of city life.

   (C) The city was destroyed by an invasion of neighboring tribes.

   (D) The city was a vital trade center for the region's goods.

2. By examining the remains of Teotihuacan, historians can assert

   (A) there was a strictly patriarchal structure in the Mesoamerican city-state.

   (B) Only a very small number of people actually lived in the city compared to European cities of the same time period.

   (C) the center of the large city was dominated by religious architecture.

   (D) natural resources in Mesoamerica were sparse so rulers needed to demand tribute from nearby groups.

3. Teotihuacan can be compared to Chang'an in Han China in which of the following ways?

   (A) Both cities were centers of democratic administrations ruled over by elected officials.

   (B) Both cities served as centers of trade, religious rituals, and political administration.

   (C) Both cities had massive religious architecture where the people worshipped many gods.

   (D) Both cities had massive walls to provide protection against nomadic tribes.

4. The role of Teotihuacan evidenced by the image enabled

   (A) lesser recognized religious sites outside the city to arise as contrasting choices.

   (B) increased democratic power for the agricultural families who provided the food necessary to sustain the city.

   (C) the establishment of a long-term ruling family resulting in a hereditary monarchy.

   (D) increased power and wealth for the elite families and priests.

Questions 5–7 refer to the image below.

▲ **Detail from a Maya Calendar, ca. 500 CE.** David Pedre/Getty Images

5. An examination of the Mayan calendar provided could be used by a historian to support which of the following claims?

   (A) The Maya were a primitive people who did not have a writing system.

   (B) The Maya system of writing was designed to support only the elite in society.

   (C) The Maya were able to plan the planting and harvesting of crops based on the seasons.

   (D) The Maya had a singular shared state that united all the people of the Yucatan region.

6. Which of the following is most correct when referring to Maya texts such as the calendar above?

(A) They were created by scribes and read regularly by the literate urban population.

(B) They are rare and have never been decoded.

(C) They were not intended for widespread communication because few could read them.

(D) They were usually written by the female priests who lived in the temple complexes.

7. The Maya city-states prospered and their power increased as

(A) the Maya rulers set up rival kingdoms led by hereditary rulers in the Mesoamerican region.

(B) large-scale migration from the Teotihuacan city-state increased the size of the Maya population.

(C) the Maya were successful in defeating the Mexica army in a series of violent battles.

(D) groups that the Maya conquered were given full citizenship and encouraged to fight for the Maya.

Questions 8–10 refer to the passage below.

"This Province is in the form of a circle, surrounded on all sides by lofty and rugged mountains; its level surface comprises an area of about seventy leagues in circumference, including two lakes that overspread nearly the whole valley, being navigated by boats more than fifty leagues round. One of these lakes contains fresh and the other, which is the larger of the two, salt water. On one side of the lakes, in the middle of the valley, a range of highlands divides them from one another, with the exception of a narrow strait which lies between the highlands and the lofty sierras. This strait is a bow-shot wide, and connects the two lakes; and by this means a trade is carried on between the cities and other settlements on the lakes in canoes without the necessity of traveling by land....

There are all kinds of green vegetables, especially onions, leeks, garlic, water cresses, nasturtium, borage, sorrel, artichokes, and golden thistle; fruits also of numerous descriptions, amongst which are cherries and plums, similar to those in Spain; honey and wax from bees, and from the stalks of maize, which are as sweet as the sugar-cane; honey is also extracted from the plant called maguey, which is superior to sweet or new wine; from the same plant they extract sugar and wine, which they also sell."

> A description of Tenochtitlan by Hernan Cortés, excerpted from *Second Letter to Charles V*, 1520

8. Which of the following best characterizes the economy of the Tenochtitlan region described in the excerpt?

(A) A network of powerful states used Tenochtitlan as an *entrepôt* for long-distance trade.

(B) The region had a vibrant economy based on agricultural products centered in the markets of the city.

(C) The region had a primitive economy that used a barter system.

(D) The manufacturing of textiles was a key component of the region's economic system.

9. What can be asserted from Cortés's account about the region of Mesoamerica where Tenochtitlan was located?

(A) The environment presented challenges that human innovation overcame.

(B) The location of the city made it impregnable to invasion.

(C) The greed of the conquistadors is evident in their desire to take over this region.

(D) The region is arid and inhospitable.

10. Which of the following best describes the point of view of Hernan Cortés concerning the Mexica culture?

(A) He was dismissive of the culture as he believed his Spanish culture was superior.

(B) He was empathetic to the Mexica, who he considered a mighty nation.

(C) He was threatened by the might of the Mexica and reluctant to advance into the region.

(D) He was impressed with the culture of the Mexica people.

Short-Answer Questions

1. Answer all parts of the question that follows.

(A) Identify ONE cultural similarity between Meso-american and South American civilizations in the Classical Era, 200–900 CE.

(B) Explain ONE political similarity between Meso-american and South American civilizations in the Classical Era, 200–900 CE.

(C) Explain ONE economic similarity between Meso-american and South American civilizations in the Classical Era, 200–900 CE.

2. Answer all parts of the question that follows.

(A) Identify ONE way civilizations in the Americas adapted to their environment in the Classical Era, 200–900 CE.

(B) Explain ONE way civilizations in the Americas changed their environment in the Classical Era, 200–900 CE.

(C) Explain ANOTHER way civilizations in the Americas changed their environment in the Classical Era, 200–900 CE.

PART III

Growth and Interaction of Cultural Communities, 300 BCE–1200 CE

▲ **Christian World Map from Muslim Spain**   The east is shown at the top of the map with Adam and Eve in the Garden of Eden. Next to them is the holy city of Jerusalem represented by an arched gate suggestive of Andalusian architecture. Alexandria is below the bend of the Nile River at Adam's feet. The Mediterranean Sea is vertical with rectangular islands, and the red stripe to the right is the Red Sea and Indian Ocean. Werner Forman/Universal Images Group/Getty Images

The time period from 300 BCE to 1200 CE was one of vast increases in interactions between settlements. Traders, migrating peoples, and missionaries moved products, technologies, and ideas across long-distance trade networks such as the Silk Roads, Saharan caravan routes, and Indian Ocean sea lanes.

In Africa, Bantu peoples spread iron-working and farming techniques through much of sub-Saharan Africa during migrations, helping foster a distinctive African culture. Inspired by the Prophet Muhammad, conquering Arabs established Muslim rule from Spain to India, laying the foundation for new culture.

In Asia, missionaries and pilgrims helped Buddhism interact with older philosophies and religions to produce distinctive cultural patterns as it spread from India throughout East and Southeast Asia. Simultaneously, the Tang Empire spread Chinese culture and technologies throughout Inner and East Asia.

In Europe, Christian beliefs became enmeshed with political and social structures as Western Europe struggled between royal and church authority, while the Byzantine east and Kievan Russia developed similar but distinctive unions of religious and imperial. The Crusades reconnected Western Europe with the lands of the east. ●

Environment	Culture	State Building	Economics	Social Structure
• Interaction between environment and settlement	• Origins, beliefs, development, economic/social/political impact, and spread of major religions, philosophies, and belief systems (Islam, Neoconfucianism)	• Changes in functions/institutions of governance over time (Imperial cities)	• Causes/effects of economic strategies of different types of communities, states, and empires (impact of trade routes)	• Impact of kinship, ethnicity, class, gender, and race on social hierarchies
• Impact of environmental factors, disease, and technology on migration and settlement	• Effect of cross-cultural interactions on diffusion of technology and scientific knowledge (Silk Road, Trans-Saharan trade, Indian Ocean, Mediterranean Sea)	• Impact of economic, social, cultural, and geographical factors on state building, expansion, and dissolution (decline of Roman, Han)	• Development and change of modes and locations of production over time (roads, currency)	• Impact of ideologies, philosophies, and religions on social hierarchies
• Impact of migration, population, and urbanization on environment	• Reflection and impact of society in the arts (Imperial cities, public performances)	• Impact of internal/external political factors on state building, expansion, and dissolution	• Development and change of labor systems over time (serfdom, feudalism)	• Interaction between specialized labor systems and social hierarchy (feudalism)
• Interaction between environment and development of technology, industrialization, transportation, and exchange/communication networks	• Impact of expanding exchange networks on transregional culture such as music, literature, and visual art	• Political/economic interaction between state and nonstate actors (peasant revolts – Byzantine, Chinese, Arab expansion, interregional trade networks)	• Influence of trade on development of ideologies, values, and institutions on each other (spread of Buddhism, Christianity, Islam via trade routes)	• Maintenance or challenge to social categories, roles, and practices
			• Influence and impact of local, regional, and global economic systems and exchange networks on each other	• Extent to which migrations changed social structures in both sending and receiving societies (diasporic communities – traders)

Key Concept 2.1

- As contacts between regions intensified, how did belief systems both reinforce existing social structures and offer new roles and status to some men and women?
- How were some other religious and cultural traditions incorporated into major religious traditions?

Key Concept 2.2

- What kinds of new techniques of imperial administration did states and empires develop? How were some of these new techniques based off of successes of earlier political forms?
- How did unique social and economic dimensions develop in imperial societies in Afro-Eurasia?
- What political, cultural, and administrative difficulties led to the decline and collapse of the Roman, Han, and Persian empires?

Key Concept 2.3

- What led to land and water routes becoming the basis for interregional trade, communication, and exchange networks in the Eastern Hemisphere?
- How did new technologies facilitate long-distance communication and exchange?
- How did the intensification of trade networks increase cross-cultural exchange in nonmaterial goods (e.g., technology, religious and cultural belief systems, literature, scientific knowledge, domesticated animals, crops, or pathogens)?

Key Concept 3.1

- How did developments in technology and commercial practices lead to increased trade and expand the range of trade networks?
- How did the movement of people cause environmental and linguistic effects?
- How did the intensification of trade networks increase cross-cultural exchange?

Key Concept 3.2

- How did the collapse of empires result in both reconstituted and new state forms?
- How did interregional conflicts between states and empires encourage technological and cultural transfers? (specific focus on Tang China/Abbasid Caliphate and Crusades)

Key Concept 3.3

- How did innovations stimulate agricultural and industrial production?
- How did developing trade contribute to the growth and decline of cities?
- How did religion and other trade-diffused cultural ideas affect labor, gender relations, and family life?

9
Networks of Communication and Exchange, 300 BCE–1100 CE

CHAPTER OUTLINE

AP® Framework Terms

Indian Ocean maritime system
Eurasian Silk Road
Trans-Saharan caravan routes
Monsoon winds
Bantu
Iron

Overarching Questions

1 How and why have religions, belief systems, philosophies, and ideologies originated, developed, and spread as a result of expanding communication and exchange networks? (CUL)

2 How have cross-cultural interactions resulted in the diffusion of culture, technologies, and scientific knowledge? (CUL)

3 How have local, regional, and global economic systems and exchange networks influenced each other over time? (ECON)

4 How have political, economic, cultural, and demographic factors affected social structures? (SOC)

nspired by the tradition of the Silk Road, a Chinese poet named Po Zhuyi (**boh joo-yee**) nostalgically wrote:

Iranian whirling girl, Iranian whirling girl—
Her heart answers to the strings,
Her hands answer to the drums.
At the sound of the strings and drums, she raises her arms,
Like whirling snowflakes tossed about, she turns in her twirling dance.
Iranian whirling girl,
You came from Sogdiana (**sog-dee-A-nuh**).
In vain did you labor to come east more than ten thousand tricents.
For in the central plains there were already some who could do the Iranian whirl,
And in a contest of wonderful abilities, you would not be their equal.[1]

The western part of Central Asia, the region around Samarkand (**SAM-mar-kand**) and Bukhara (**boh-CAR-ruh**)

<hr>

[1]From *The Columbia Anthology of Traditional Chinese Literature*, edited and translated by Victor H. Mair. Copyright © 1994 Columbia University Press. Reprinted with permission of the publisher.

▲ **Indian Ocean Sailing Vessel** Ships like this one, in a rock carving on the Buddhist temple of Borobodur in Java, probably carried colonists from Indonesia to Madagascar. Kimberley Coole/Getty Images

known in the eighth century CE as Sogdiana, was 2,500 miles (4,000 kilometers) from the Chinese capital of Chang'an **(chahng-ahn)**. Caravans took more than four months to trek across the mostly unsettled deserts, mountains, and grasslands.

The Silk Road connecting China and the Middle East across Central Asia fostered the exchange of agricultural goods, manufactured products, and ideas. Musicians and dancing girls traveled, too—as did camel pullers, merchants, monks, and pilgrims. The Silk Road was not just a means of bringing peoples and parts of the world into contact; it was also a social system.

With every expansion of territory, the growing wealth of temples, kings, and emperors enticed traders to venture ever farther afield for precious goods. For the most part, the customers were wealthy elites. But the new products, agricultural and industrial processes, and foreign ideas and customs these long-distance traders brought with them sometimes affected an entire society.

Travelers and traders seldom owned much land or wielded political power. Socially isolated (sometimes by law) and secretive because any talk about markets, products, routes, and travel conditions could help their competitors, they nevertheless contributed more to drawing the world together than did all but a few kings and emperors.

This chapter examines the social systems and historical impact of exchange networks that developed between 300 BCE and 1100 CE in Europe, Asia, and Africa. The Silk Road and the Indian Ocean maritime system illustrate the nature of long-distance trade in this era.

Trading networks were not the only medium for the spread of new ideas, products, and customs. This chapter compares developments along trade routes with folk migration by looking at the beginnings of contact across the Sahara and the simultaneous spread of Bantu-speaking peoples within sub-Saharan Africa. Chapter 6 discussed a third pattern of cultural contact and exchange, that taking place with the beginning of Christian missionary activity in the Roman Empire. This chapter further explores the process by examining the spread of Buddhism in Asia and Christianity in Africa and Asia. ●

9-1 The Silk Road

What factors contributed to the growth of trade along the Silk Road?

AP® Exam Tip
Understand the factors that shaped the distinctive features of long-distance trade routes and their role in the growth of cities and the diffusion of technology, culture, and disease.

Archaeology and linguistic studies show that the peoples of Central Asia engaged in long-distance movement and exchange from at least 3000 BCE. By Roman times Europeans had become captivated by the idea of a trade route linking the lands of the Mediterranean with China by way of Mesopotamia, Iran, and Central Asia. The **Silk Road**, as it came to be called in later times, experienced several periods of heavy use (see Map 9.1). The first began around 100 BCE.

9-1a Iranians and Chinese

The Seleucid kings who succeeded to the eastern parts of Alexander the Great's empire in the third century BCE focused their energies on Mesopotamia and Syria. This allowed an Iranian nomadic leader to establish an independent kingdom in northeastern Iran. The **Parthians**, a people originally from east of the Caspian Sea, had become a major force by 247 BCE. They left few written sources, and recurring wars with Greeks and Romans to the west prevented travelers from the Mediterranean region from gaining firm knowledge of their kingdom. It seems likely, however, that they helped foster the Silk Road by being located on the threshold of Central Asia and sharing customs with steppe nomads farther to the east.

In 128 BCE a Chinese general named Zhang Jian (**jahng jee-en**) made his first exploratory journey across the deserts and mountains of Central Asia on behalf of Emperor Wu of the Han dynasty. After crossing the broad and desolate Tarim Basin north of Tibet, he reached the fertile valley of Ferghana (**fer-GAH-nuh**) and for the first time encountered westward-flowing rivers. There he found horse breeders whose animals far outclassed any horses he had seen. Later Chinese historians looked on General Zhang, who ultimately led eighteen expeditions, as the originator of overland trade with the western lands, and they credited him with personally introducing a whole garden of new plants and trees to China.

Long-distance travel suited the people of the steppes more than the Chinese. The populations of Ferghana and neighboring regions included many nomads who followed their herds and lived in round portable dwellings, sometimes carried on wagons (see Environment & Technology: Nomad Homes). Their migrations had little to do with trade, but they provided pack animals and controlled transit across their lands. The trading demands that brought the Silk Road into being were Chinese eagerness for western products, especially horses, and on the western end, the organized Parthian state, which had captured the flourishing markets of Mesopotamia from the Seleucids and maintained relations with other markets in India.

Silk Road Caravan routes connecting China and the Middle East across Central Asia and Iran.

Parthians Iranian ruling dynasty between ca. 250 BCE and 226 CE.

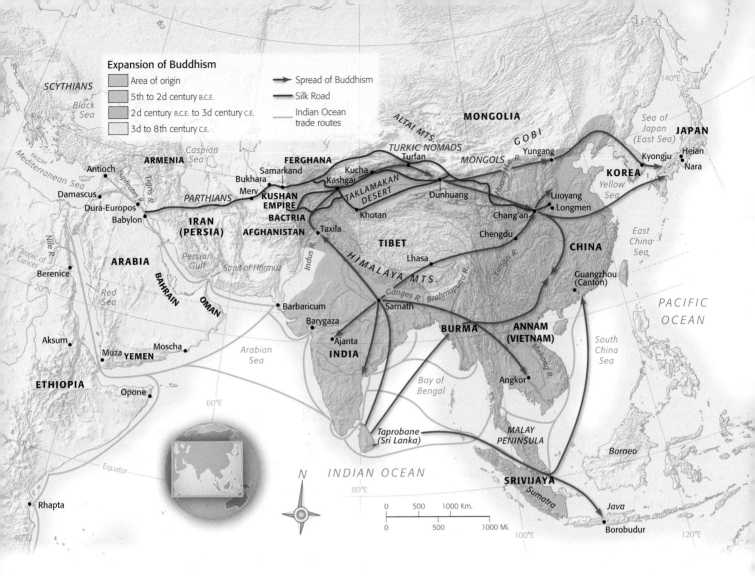

MAP 9.1 Asian Trade and Communication Routes The overland Silk Road was vulnerable to political disruption, but it was much shorter than the maritime route from the South China Sea to the Red Sea, and ships were more expensive than pack animals. Moreover, China's political centers were in the north.

How did seaports differ from caravan cities as sites of cultural interaction?

9-1b Silk and New Crops

By 100 BCE, Greeks could buy Chinese silk from Parthian traders in Mesopotamian border entrepôts. Yet caravans also bought and sold goods along the way in prosperous Central Asian cities like Samarkand and Bukhara. These cities grew and flourished, often under the rule of local princes.

General Zhang definitely seems to have brought two plants to China: alfalfa and wine grapes. The former provided the best fodder for horses. In addition, Chinese farmers adopted pistachios, walnuts, pomegranates, sesame, coriander, spinach, and other new crops. Chinese artisans and physicians made good use of other trade products, such as jasmine oil, oak galls (used in tanning animal hides, dyeing, and making ink), sal ammoniac (for medicines), copper oxides, zinc, and precious stones. Some of these commodities may have entered China by way of Indian Ocean merchants.

Traders going west from China carried new fruits such as peaches and apricots, which the Romans mistakenly attributed to other eastern lands, calling them Persian plums and Armenian plums, respectively. They also carried cinnamon, ginger, and other spices that could not be grown in the West.

All nomads use dwelling designs that are adapted to either occasional or frequent assembly and reassembly and to locally available materials. Native American peoples in the Great Plains region of the United States, for example, construct tall conical homes called *teepees* or *tipis*. They cover a framework of long poles covered with animal skins, leaving a hole at the top to allow smoke to escape. Since saplings suitable for fashioning long poles are often hard to find, both poles and skins are transported to the next campsite for reassembly.

Somalis in east Africa do the same, but make domed tents with the framing poles bent in semicircles. The awkward poles are tied to camel saddles for transportation from place to place. Nomads in the Saharan, Arabian, and Iranian deserts erect wide, low tents of woven wool using short poles and guylines. In still other regions, such as equatorial Africa and Southeast Asia where poles, reeds, and palm fronds are readily available, huts do not need to be disassembled and transported because they can be re-built at every site.

Transportation is also unnecessary for the Inuit and other Arctic groups that built temporary dwellings out of packed snow blocks. *Igloo*, or *iglu*, is a general word for dwelling, but it is commonly used for snow homes in particular. The architecture of the domed structures is skillfully designed to transmit the weight of the blocks downward onto the lower blocks without any need for a framework or for external buttressing.

The Turkic and Mongol peoples of Central Asia form the only nomadic culture that mounts some of their homes on wheels. This reflects a history of cultural expansion eastward from the lowlands of southern Ukraine north of the Black Sea. Strong arguments have been made for Ukraine being the land of origin of wagons using wheels that rotate independently. This design was an offshoot of the original wheel design in which wheels were fixed solidly on the ends of their axles and the whole assembly rotated as a unit.

While copper miners in Hungary and adjacent parts of central Europe probably pushed the first ore-cars, which could not turn corners, along the trenches of copper mines, the Ukrainian versions functioned more flexibly, though sharp curves were still a challenge, and could be used as mobile homes. The Scythians of the mid-first millennium BCE were the first nomadic people known by name to have traversed the Central Asian plains in mobile homes; historians ascribe a similar lifestyle to a series of later nomadic groups down to the nineteenth century. The dwellings were originally arched like an American covered wagon, but they evolved into cylindrical structures that bent in toward the top like teepees. These were called *yurt* in Turkish and *ger* in Mongolian.

Though groups using mobile homes are properly described as horse nomads because of their huge herds and fearsome cavalry, they also kept large numbers of oxen for pulling their dwellings. At some point, probably in the last 500 years, a yurt design that had collapsed framing poles, latticed side supports, and felt coverings for loading on camelback replaced most of the homes on wheels.

Compared with other nomadic cultures elsewhere in the world, the wheel-using peoples of Central Asia maintained a more elaborate standard of material life in their encampments. A single royal pavilion or commander's yurt might be accompanied by 200 carts and wagons bearing furnishings, decorative fabrics, and objects of value.

Questions for Analysis

1. How does caring for flocks and herds affect the living conditions of nomads?

2. Does migration from one campsite to another contribute to or detract from healthy and comfortable living?

3. Why didn't all nomadic groups live in wagons?

◀ **Yurt in Turkmenistan** This circular dwelling, called a yurt in Turkish and a ger in Mongolian, is typical of the traditional homes of Central Asian nomads from Ukraine to Mongolia. It has a structure of poles that bend inward above the level of the doorway and a wooden or reed lattice that goes around their vertical portions. Felt mats cover the walls and roof, and a cloth curtain forms a door. These structures could be mounted on wheeled carts or wagons and lowered to the ground at a new campsite, or else disassembled and carried by pack camels.
Historical image collection by
Bildagentur-online / Alamy Stock Photo

CHRONOLOGY

	Silk Road	Indian Ocean Trade	Saharan Trade
500 BCE			500 BCE–ca. 1000 CE Bantu migrations
	247 BCE Parthian rule begins in Iran		
			ca. 200 BCE Camel nomads in southern Sahara
	128 BCE General Zhang Jian reaches Ferghana		
	100 BCE–300 CE Kushans rule northern Afghanistan and Sogdiana		
			46 BCE First mention of camels in northern Sahara
1 CE	1st century CE First evidence of the stirrup	1st century CE Periplus of the Erythraean Sea; Indonesian migration to Madagascar	
300 CE	ca. 400 CE Buddhist pilgrim Faxian travels Silk Road		ca. 300 CE Beginning of camel nomadism in northern Sahara

9-1c Nomadism in Central and Inner Asia

The Silk Road could not have functioned without pastoral nomads to provide animals, animal handlers, and protection. Descriptions of steppe nomads known as Scythians appear in the history of the Greek writer Herodotus in the sixth century BCE. He portrays them as superb riders, herdsmen, and hunters living in Central Asia, the lands to the north of the Black and Caspian Seas. Moving regularly and efficiently with flocks and herds of enormous size prevented overgrazing. Though the Scythians were fearsome horse archers, their homes, which were made of felt spread over a lightweight framework, were transported on two- or four-wheeled wagons drawn by oxen.

Nomads were not unfamiliar with agriculture or unwilling to use products grown by farmers, but their ideal was self-sufficiency. Since their wanderings with their herds normally took them far from any farming region, self-sufficiency dictated foods they could provide for themselves—primarily meat and milk—and clothing made from felt, leather, and furs. Women oversaw the breeding and birthing of livestock and the preparation of skins. They were also responsible for relocating the portable dwellings (see Environment & Technology: Nomad Homes).

Nomads were most dependent on settled regions for the bronze or iron used in bridles, stirrups, cart fittings, and weapons. They acquired metal implements in trade and reworked them to suit their purposes. Scythians in the Ukraine worked extensively with iron as early as the fourth century BCE, and Turkic-speaking peoples had large ironworking stations south of the Altai Mountains in western Mongolia in the 600s CE. Steppe nomads situated near settled areas also traded wool, leather, and horses for wood, silk, tea, vegetables, and grain.

AP® Exam Tip
Explain how environmental knowledge and technological developments facilitated the growth of long-distance overland trade during this time period.

9-1d The Impact of the Silk Road

As trade became a more important part of Central Asian life, the Iranian-speaking peoples increasingly settled in trading cities and surrounding farm villages. By the sixth century CE, nomads originally from the Altai Mountains farther east had

▶ **Iranian Rider on Silk Road Camel** Glazed ceramic figurines of camels and horses are found in many Inner Asian burials of the Tang period. Most of the camel riders, like this one, have beards and big noses stereotyping people from Central Asia far to the west. Soft pointed caps first appear in images of Scythians living north of Iran. The absence of a saddle and the rider's diminutive size suggest a humorous caricature. Werner Forman/Universal Images Group/Getty Images

Section Review

- The rise of the Parthian kingdom helped foster the Silk Road to meet European demand for Chinese silk and Chinese demand for horses.

- General Zhang first discovered Ferghana and then led expeditions that established the route from China through Central Asia.

- Central Asian nomads facilitated the movement of goods through their lands by providing animals and protection.

- Central Asian trading cities grew as a result of Silk Road trade.

- In addition to silk, agricultural products traveled both ways along the Silk Road.

spread across the steppes and become the dominant pastoral group. These peoples spoke Turkic languages unrelated to the Iranian tongues. The nomads continued to live in the round, portable felt huts called *yurts*, or in Mongolia *gers*, that can still occasionally be seen in Central Asia, but prosperous individuals, both Turks and Iranians, built stately homes decorated with brightly colored wall paintings. The paintings show people wearing Chinese silks and Iranian brocades and riding on richly outfitted horses and two-humped camels. They also indicate an avid interest in Buddhism (discussed later in this chapter), which competed with Nestorian Christianity, Manichaeism, and Zoroastrianism in a lively and inquiring intellectual milieu.

Missionary influences exemplify the impact of foreign customs and beliefs on the peoples along the Silk Road. Military technology affords an example of the opposite phenomenon, steppe customs radiating into foreign lands. Chariot warfare and the use of mounted bowmen originated in Central Asia and spread eastward and westward through military campaigns and folk migrations that began in the second millennium BCE and recurred throughout the period of the Silk Road.

9-1e Warriors and Missionaries

AP® Exam Tip
Explain how religions, belief systems, philosophies, and ideologies developed and spread as a result of expanding communication and exchange networks.

Evidence of the **stirrup**, one of the most important inventions, comes first from the Kushan people who ruled northern Afghanistan in approximately the first century CE. At first a solid bar, then a loop of leather to support the rider's big toe, and finally a device of leather and metal or wood supporting the ball of the foot, the stirrup gave riders far greater stability in the saddle—which itself was in all likelihood an earlier Central Asian invention.

Using stirrups, a mounted warrior could supplement his bow and arrow with a long lance and charge his enemy at a gallop without fear that the impact of his attack would push him off his mount. Far to the west, the stirrup made possible the armored knights who dominated the battlefields of Europe (see Chapter 10), and it contributed to the superiority of the Tang cavalry in China (see Chapter 11).

9-2 The Indian Ocean Maritime System

How did geography affect Indian Ocean trade routes?

AP® Exam Tip
Understand how Indian Ocean sea trade developed and changed over time.

While a land route was established in Central Asia, a multilingual, multiethnic society of seafarers established the **Indian Ocean Maritime System**, a trade network across the Indian Ocean and the South China Sea. These people left few records and seldom played a visible part in the rise and fall of kingdoms and empires, but they forged increasingly strong economic and social ties between the coastal lands of East Africa, southern Arabia, the Persian Gulf, India, Southeast Asia, and southern China.

This trade took place in three distinct regions: (1) in the South China Sea, Chinese and Malays (including Indonesians) dominated trade; (2) from the east coast of India to the islands of Southeast Asia, Indians and Malays were the main traders; and (3) from the west coast of India to the Persian Gulf and the east coast of Africa, merchants and sailors were predominantly Persians and Arabs. However, Chinese and Malay sailors could and did voyage to East Africa, and Arab and Persian traders reached southern China.

stirrup Device for securing a horseman's feet, enabling him to wield weapons more effectively. First evidence of the use of stirrups was among the Kushan people of northern Afghanistan in approximately the first century CE.

Indian Ocean Maritime System In premodern times, a network of seaports, trade routes, and maritime culture linking countries on the rim of the Indian Ocean from Africa to Indonesia.

9-2a Sailors' Tales

From the time of Herodotus in the fifth century BCE, Greek writers regaled their readers with stories of marvelous voyages down the Red Sea into the Indian Ocean or around Africa from the west. Most often, they attributed such trips to the Phoenicians, the most fearless of Mediterranean seafarers. Occasionally a Greek appears. One such was Hippalus, a Greek ship's pilot who was said to have discovered the seasonal monsoon winds that facilitate sailing across the Indian Ocean (see Diversity & Dominance: Travel Accounts of Africa and India).

Of course, the regular, seasonal alternation of steady winds could not have remained unnoticed for thousands of years, waiting for an alert Greek to happen along. The great voyages and discoveries made before written records became common should surely be attributed to the peoples who lived around the Indian Ocean rather than to interlopers from the Mediterranean Sea. The story of Hippalus resembles the Chinese story of General Zhang Jian, whose role in opening trade with Central Asia overshadows the anonymous contributions made by the indigenous peoples. The Chinese may indeed have learned from General Zhang and the Greeks from Hippalus, but other people played important roles anonymously.

9-2b **Ship Design**

The ships used in the Indian Ocean differed from those used in the west. Whereas Mediterranean sailors of the time of Alexander used square sails and long banks of oars to maneuver among the sea's many islands and small harbors, Indian Ocean vessels relied on roughly triangular lateen sails and normally did without oars in running before the wind on long ocean stretches. Mediterranean shipbuilders nailed their vessels together. The planks of Indian Ocean ships were pierced, tied together with palm fiber, and caulked with bitumen. Mediterranean sailors rarely ventured out of sight of land. Indian Ocean sailors, thanks to the monsoon winds, could cover long reaches entirely at sea.

These technological differences prove that the world of the Indian Ocean developed differently than the world of the Mediterranean Sea, where the Phoenicians and Greeks established colonies that maintained contact with their home cities (see Chapters 4 and 5). The traders of the Indian Ocean, where distances were greater and contacts less frequent, seldom retained political ties with their homelands. The colonies they established were sometimes socially distinctive but rarely independent of the local political powers.

> **AP® Exam Tip**
> Be able to explain how environmental knowledge and technological advancements led to the expansion and intensification of long-distance trade routes.

9-2c **Origins of Contact and Trade**

By 2000 BCE Sumerian records indicate regular trade between Mesopotamia, the islands of the Persian Gulf, Oman, and the Indus Valley. However, this early trading contact broke off, and later Mesopotamian trade references mention East Africa more often than India.

A similarly early chapter in Indian Ocean history concerns migrations from Southeast Asia to Madagascar, the world's fourth largest island, situated off the southeastern coast of Africa. About 2,000 years ago, people from one of the many Indonesian islands of Southeast Asia established themselves in that forested, mountainous land 6,000 miles (9,500 kilometers) from home. They could not possibly have carried enough supplies for a direct voyage across the Indian Ocean, so their route must have touched the coasts of India and southern Arabia. No physical remains of their journeys have been discovered, however.

9-2d **Indonesians in Madagascar**

Apparently, the sailing canoes of these people plied the seas along the increasingly familiar route for several hundred years. Settlers farmed the new land and entered into relations with Africans who found their way across the 250-mile-wide (400-kilometer-wide) Mozambique (**moe-zam-BEEK**) Channel around the fifth century CE. Descendants of the seafarers preserved the language of their homeland and some of its culture, such as the cultivation of bananas, yams, and other native Southeast Asian plants. These food crops spread to mainland Africa. But the memory of their distant origins gradually faded, not to be recovered until modern times, when scholars unraveled the linguistic link between the two lands.

9-2e **The Impact of Indian Ocean Trade**

The demand for products from the coastal lands inspired mariners to persist in their long ocean voyages. Africa produced exotic animals, wood, and ivory. Since ivory also came from India, Mesopotamia, and North Africa, the extent of African ivory exports cannot be determined. The highlands of northern Somalia and southern Arabia grew the scrubby trees whose aromatic resins were valued as frankincense and myrrh. Pearls abounded in the Persian Gulf, and evidence of ancient copper mines has been found in Oman in southeastern Arabia. India shipped spices and manufactured goods, and more spices came from Southeast Asia, along with manufactured items, particularly pottery, obtained in trade with China. In sum, the Indian Ocean trading region had a great

The most revealing description of ancient trade in the Indian Ocean and of the human diversity and economic forces shaping the Indian Ocean trading system is found in The Periplus of the Erythraean Sea, *a sailing itinerary (*periplus *in Greek) that was composed in the first century CE by an unknown Greco-Egyptian merchant. It highlights the diversity of peoples and products from the Red Sea to the Bay of Bengal. Historians believe that the descriptions of market towns were based on firsthand experience. The following passages deal with East Africa and the coastal lands of the Indian subcontinent (see Maps 9.1 and 9.2).*

Of the designated ports on the Erythraean Sea [Indian Ocean], and the market-towns around it, the first is the Egyptian port of Mussel Harbor. To those sailing down from that place, on the right hand . . . there is Berenice. The harbors of both are at the [southern] boundary of Egypt. . . .

On the right-hand coast next below Berenice is the country of the Berbers. Along the shore are the Fish-Eaters, living in scattered caves in the narrow valleys. Further inland are the Berbers, and beyond them the Wild-flesh-Eaters and Calf-Eaters, each tribe governed by its chief; and behind them, further inland, in the country towards the west, there lies a city called Meroe.

Below the Calf-Eaters there is a little market-town on the shore . . . called Ptolemais of the Hunts, from which the hunters started for the interior under the dynasty of the Ptolemies. . . . But the place has no harbor and is reached only by small boats. . . .

Beyond this place, the coast trending toward the south, there is the Market and Cape of Spices, an abrupt promontory, at the very end of the Berber coast toward the east. . . . A sign of an approaching storm . . . is that the deep water becomes more turbid and changes its color. When this happens they all run to a large promontory called Tabae, which offers safe shelter. . . .

Beyond Tabae [lies] . . . another market-town called Opone. . . . [I]n it the greatest quantity of cinnamon is produced . . . and slaves of the better sort, which are brought to Egypt in increasing numbers. . . .

[Ships also come] from the places across this sea, from . . . Barygaza, bringing to these . . . market-towns the products of their own places; wheat, rice, clarified butter, sesame oil, cotton cloth . . . and honey from the reed called sacchari [sugar cane]. Some make the voyage especially to these market-towns, and others exchange their cargoes while sailing along the coast. This country is not subject to a King, but each market-town is ruled by its separate chief.

Beyond Opone, the shore trending more toward the south . . . this coast [the Somali region of Azania, or East Africa] is destitute of harbors . . . until the Pyralax islands [Zanzibar]. . . . [A] little to the south of south-west . . . is the island Menuthias [Madagascar], about three hundred stadia from the mainland, low and wooded, in which there are rivers and many kinds of birds and the mountain-tortoise. There are no wild beasts except the crocodiles; but there they do not attack men. In this place there are sewed boats, and canoes hollowed from single logs. . . .

Two days' sail beyond, there lies the very last market-town of the continent of Azania, which is called Rhapta [Dar es-Salaam]; which has its name from the sewed boats (rhapton ploiarion) . . . ; in which there is ivory in great quantity, and tortoise-shell. Along this coast live men of piratical habits, very great in stature, and under separate chiefs for each place. . . .

And these markets of Azania are the very last of the continent that stretches down on the right hand from Berenice; for beyond these places the unexplored ocean curves around toward the west, and running along by the regions to the south of Aethiopia and Libya and Africa, it mingles with the western sea. . . .

Now the whole country of India has very many rivers, and very great ebb and flow of the tides. . . . But about Barygaza [Broach] it is much greater, so that the bottom is suddenly seen, and now parts of the dry land are sea, and now it is dry where ships were sailing just before; and the rivers, under the inrush of the flood tide, when the whole force of the sea is directed against them, are driven upwards more strongly against their natural current. . . .

The country inland from Barygaza is inhabited by numerous tribes. . . . Above these is the very warlike nation of the Bactrians, who are under their own king. And Alexander, setting out from these parts, penetrated to the Ganges. . . . [T]o the present day ancient drachmae are current in Barygaza, coming from this country, bearing inscriptions in Greek letters, and the devices of those who reigned after Alexander. . . .

Inland from this place and to the east, is the city called Ozene [Ujjain]. . . . [F]rom this place are brought down all things needed for the welfare of the country about Barygaza, and many things for our trade: agate and carnelian, Indian muslins. . . .

There are imported into this market-town wine, Italian preferred, also Laodicean and Arabian; copper, tin, and lead; coral and topaz; thin clothing and inferior sorts of all kinds . . . gold and silver coin, on which there is a profit when exchanged for the money of the country. . . . And for the King there are brought into those places very costly vessels of silver, singing boys, beautiful maidens for the harem, fine wines, thin clothing

---

AP® Exam Tip

Be able to provide multiple examples of cultural exchange that resulted from long-distance trade.

variety of highly valued products. Given the long distances and the comparative lack of islands, however, the volume of trade there was undoubtedly much lower than in the Mediterranean Sea.

9-2f Incense, Ivory, and Pottery

The culture of the Indian Ocean ports was often isolated from the hinterlands, particularly in the west. The coasts of the Arabian peninsula, the African side of the Red Sea, southern Iran, and northern India (today's Pakistan) were mostly barren desert. Ports in all these areas tended to be small, and many suffered from meager supplies of fresh water. Farther south in India, the monsoon provided ample water, but steep mountains cut off the coastal plain from the interior of

of the finest weaves, and the choicest ointments. There are exported from these places [spices], ivory, agate and carnelian . . . cotton cloth of all kinds, silk cloth. . . .

Beyond Barygaza the adjoining coast [of western India] extends in a straight line from north to south. . . . The inland country back from the coast toward the east comprises many desert regions and great mountains; and all kinds of wild beasts—leopards, tigers, elephants, enormous serpents, hyenas, and baboons of many sorts; and many populous nations, as far as the Ganges. . . .

This whole voyage as above described . . . they used to make in small vessels, sailing close around the shores of the gulfs; and Hippalus was the pilot who by observing the location of the ports and the conditions of the sea, first discovered how to lay his course straight across the ocean. . . .

About the following region, the course trending toward the east, lying out at sea toward the west is the island Palaesimundu, called by the ancients Taprobane [Sri Lanka]. . . . It produces pearls, transparent stones, muslins, and tortoiseshell. . . .

Beyond this, the course trending toward the north, there are many barbarous tribes, among whom are the Cirrhadae, a race of men with flattened noses, very savage; another tribe, the Bargysi; and the Horse-faces and the Long-faces, who are said to be cannibals.

After these, the course turns toward the east again, and sailing with the ocean to the right and the shore remaining beyond to the left, Ganges comes into view. . . . And just opposite this river there is an island in the ocean, the last part of the inhabited world toward the east, under the rising sun itself; it is called Chryse; and it has the best tortoise-shell of all the places on the Erythraean Sea.

After this region under the very north, the sea outside ending in a land called This, there is a very great inland city called Thinae, from which raw silk and silk yarn and silk cloth are brought on foot. . . . But the land of This is not easy of access; few men come from there, and seldom.

The Chinese traveler Xuanzang (600–664) journeyed across Central Asia to India, making pilgrimage to Buddhist holy places and searching for Sanskrit scriptures to take back to China with him. His descriptions of the places he visited reflect his interests. The following passages come from his description of India.

Towns and Buildings

The towns and villages have inner gates; the walls are wide and high; the streets and lanes are tortuous, and the roads winding. The thoroughfares are dirty and the stalls arranged on both sides of the road with appropriate signs. Butchers, fishers, dancers, executioners, and scavengers, and so on, have their abodes without the city. In coming and going these persons are bound to keep on the left side of the road till they arrive at their homes. Their houses are surrounded by low walls, and form the suburbs. The earth being soft and muddy, the walls of the town are mostly built of brick or tiles. The towers on the walls are constructed of wood or bamboo; the houses have balconies and belvederes, which are made of wood, with a coating of lime or mortar, and covered with tiles. The different buildings have the same form as those in China: rushes, or dry branches, or tiles, or boards are used for covering them. The walls are covered with lime and mud, mixed with cow's dung for purity. At different seasons they scatter flowers about. Such are some of their different customs.

Dress and Appearance

Their clothing is not cut or fashioned; they mostly affect fresh white garments; they esteem little those of mixed color or ornamented. The men wind their garments round their middle, then gather them under the armpits, and let them fall down across the body, hanging to the right. The robes of the women fall down to the ground; they completely cover their shoulders. They wear a little knot of hair on their crowns, and let the rest of their hair fall loose. Some of the men cut off their moustaches, and have other odd customs. . . . In North India, where the air is cold, they wear short and close-fitting garments. . . . The dress and ornaments worn by the nonbelievers [i.e., non-Buddhists] are varied and mixed. Some wear peacocks' feathers; some wear as ornaments necklaces made of skull bones; some have no clothing, but go naked; some wear leaf or bark garments; some pull out their hair and cut off their moustaches; others have bushy whiskers and their hair braided on the top of their heads. The costume is not uniform, and the color, whether red or white, not constant.

AP® History Reasoning Skills

Comparison *In what ways do the perspectives of a trader and a religious pilgrim allow you to compare trade in Africa and India?*

Contextualization *In what ways does each narrative show the influence of the country from which its author comes?*

Source: Samuel Beal, *Buddhist Records of the Western World, Translated from the Chinese of Hiuen Tsiang (A.D. 629)* (London, UK: Trubner and Company, 1884; reprint Delhi: Oriental Books Reprint Corporation, 1969), 73–76.

the country. Thus few ports between Zanzibar and Sri Lanka had substantial inland populations within easy reach. The head of the Persian Gulf was one exception: Shipborne trade was possible from the port of Apologus (later called Ubulla, the precursor of modern Basra) as far north as Babylon and, from the eighth century CE, nearby Baghdad.

9-2g Western Ports

Eastern India, the Malay Peninsula, and Indonesia afforded more hospitable and densely populated shores with easier access to inland populations. Though the fishers, sailors, and traders of the western Indian Ocean system supplied a long series of kingdoms and empires, none of these

Section Review

- The Indian Ocean Maritime System grew from the voyages of diverse seafaring traders.

- The system originated in early Mesopotamian trade routes and the migrations of Southeast Asian peoples to Madagascar.

- Unlike the Mediterranean, the Indian Ocean developed no network of colonies with home ties, but traders intermarried with indigenous peoples to create distinct cultures.

- Trade in a broad range of goods flourished.

consumer societies became primarily maritime in orientation, as the Greeks and Phoenicians did in the Mediterranean. In contrast, seaborne trade and influence seem to have been important even to the earliest states of Southeast Asia.

9-2h Eastern Ports

In coastal areas throughout the Indian Ocean system, small groups of seafarers sometimes had a significant social impact despite their usual lack of political power. Women seldom accompanied the men on long sea voyages, so sailors and merchants often married local women in port cities. The families thus established were bilingual and bicultural. As in many other situations in world history, women played a crucial though not well-documented role as mediators between cultures. Not only did they raise their children to be more cosmopolitan than children from inland regions, but they also introduced the men to customs and attitudes that they carried with them when they returned to sea. As a consequence, the designation of specific seafarers as Persian, Arab, Indian, or Malay often conceals mixed heritages and a rich cultural diversity.

9-3 Routes Across the Sahara

Why did trade begin across the Sahara Desert?

The windswept Sahara, a desert stretching from the Red Sea to the Atlantic Ocean and broken only by the Nile River, isolates sub-Saharan Africa from the Mediterranean world (see Map 9.2). The current dryness of the Sahara dates only to about 2500 BCE. The period of drying-out that preceded that date lasted twenty-five centuries and encompassed several cultural changes. To begin with, travel between a slowly shrinking number of grassy areas was comparatively easy. However, by 300 BCE, scarcity of water was restricting travel to a few difficult routes initially known only to desert nomads. Trade over **trans-Saharan caravan routes**, at first only a trickle, eventually expanded into a significant stream.

9-3a Early Saharan Cultures

Sprawling sand dunes, sandy plains, and vast expanses of exposed rock make up most of the great desert. Stark mountains and rugged highland areas separate its northern and southern portions. The cliffs and caves of these highlands, the last spots where water and grassland could be found as the climate changed, preserve rock paintings and engravings that constitute the primary evidence for early Saharan history.

9-3b Rock Paintings

Though dating is difficult, what appear to be the earliest images, left by hunters in much wetter times, include elephants, giraffes, rhinoceroses, crocodiles, and other animals that have long been extinct in the region. Overlaps in the artwork indicate that the hunting societies were gradually joined by new cultures based on cattle breeding and well adapted to the sparse grazing that remained. Domestic cattle probably originated separately in northern Africa, western Asia, and southern Pakistan. They certainly reached the Sahara before it became completely dry. The beautiful paintings of cattle and scenes of daily life seen in the Saharan rock art depict pastoral societies that bear little similarity to any in western Asia. The people seem physically akin to today's West Africans, and the customs depicted, such as dancing and wearing masks, as well as the breeds of cattle, particularly those with piebald coloring (splotches of black and white), strongly suggest later societies to the south of the Sahara. These factors support the hypothesis that some southern cultural patterns originated in the Sahara when it was still moist.

Overlaps in artwork also show that horse herders succeeded the cattle herders. The rock art changes dramatically in style, from the superb realism of the cattle pictures to sketchier images that are often strongly geometric. Moreover, the horses are frequently shown drawing light chariots.

trans-Saharan caravan routes Trading network linking North Africa with sub-Saharan Africa across the Sahara.

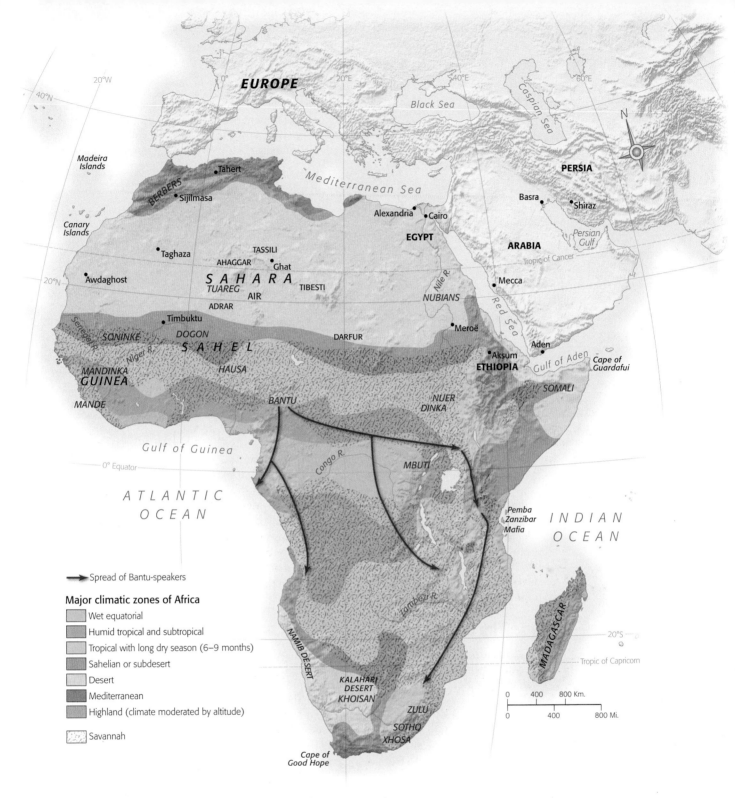

MAP 9.2   Africa and the Trans-Saharan Trade Routes The Sahara and the surrounding oceans isolated most of Africa from foreign contact before 1000 CE. The Nile Valley, a few trading points on the east coast, and limited transdesert trade provided exceptions to this rule; but the dominant forms of sub-Saharan African culture originated far to the west, north of the Gulf of Guinea.

Why were plant and cultural exchanges across the Sahara less productive sources of change in Europe and Africa than those along the Silk Road?

According to the most common theory, intrepid charioteers from the Mediterranean shore drove their flimsy vehicles across the desert and established societies in the few remaining grassy areas of the central Saharan highlands. Some scholars suggest possible chariot routes that refugees from the collapse of the Mycenaean and Minoan civilizations of Greece and Crete (see Chapter 4) might have followed deep into the desert around the twelfth century BCE. However, no archaeological evidence of actual chariot use in the Sahara has been discovered, and it is difficult to imagine

▲ **Cattle Herders in Saharan Rock Art** These paintings represent the most artistically accomplished type of Saharan art. Herding societies of modern times living in the Sahel region south of the Sahara strongly resemble the society depicted here. Henri Lhote

large numbers of refugees from the politically chaotic Mediterranean region driving chariots into a waterless, trackless desert in search of a new homeland somewhere to the south.

As with the cattle herders, therefore, the identity of the Saharan horse breeders and the source of their passion for drawing chariots remain a mystery. Only with the coming of the camel is it possible to make firm connections with the Saharan nomads of today through the depiction of objects and geometric patterns still used by the veiled, blue-robed Tuareg (**TWAH-reg**) people of the highlands in southern Algeria, Niger, and Mali.

9-3c **The Coming of the Camel**

Some historians maintain that the Romans inaugurated an important trans-Saharan trade, but they lack firm archaeological evidence. More plausibly, Saharan trade relates to the spread of camel domestication. Supporting evidence comes from rock art, where overlaps of images imply that camel riders in desert costume constitute the latest Saharan population. The camel-oriented images are decidedly the crudest to be found in the region.

The first mention of camels in North Africa comes in a Latin text of 46 BCE. Since the native camels of Africa probably died out before the era of domestication, the domestic animals most likely reached the Sahara from Arabia, probably by way of Egypt in the first millennium BCE. They could have been adopted by peoples farther and farther to the west, from one central Saharan highland to the next, only much later spreading northward and coming to the attention of the Romans. Camel herding made it easier for people to move away from the Saharan highlands and roam the deep desert.

9-3d **Trade Across the Sahara**

Linkage between two different trading systems, one in the south, the other in the north, developed slowly. Southern traders concentrated on supplying salt from large deposits in the southern desert to the peoples of sub-Saharan Africa. Traders from the equatorial forest zone brought forest products, such as *kola nuts* (a condiment and source of caffeine) and edible palm oil, to trading centers near the desert's southern fringe. Each received the products they needed in their homelands from the other, or from the farming peoples of the **Sahel (SAH-hel)**—literally "the coast" in Arabic, the southern borderlands of the Sahara (see Map 9.2). Middlemen who were native to the Sahel played an important role in this trade, but precise historical details are lacking.

Sahel Belt south of the Sahara; literally "coastland" in Arabic.

In the north, Roman colonists supplied Italy with agricultural products, primarily wheat and olives. Surviving mosaic pavements depicting scenes from daily life show that people living on the farms and in the towns of the interior consumed Roman manufactured goods and shared Roman styles. This northern pattern began to change only in the third century CE with the decline of the Roman Empire, the abandonment of many Roman farms, the growth of nomadism, and a lessening of trade across the Mediterranean.

Section Review

- Rock paintings show that early Saharan cultures included hunting societies and, in isolated areas, groups of cattle breeders.

- Later, horse and camel herders joined these groups.

- Camel-riding nomads most likely pioneered the trans-Saharan trade routes, linking North African and sub-Saharan trade networks.

9-4 Sub-Saharan Africa

What accounts for the substantial degree of cultural unity in Africa south of the Sahara?

The Indian Ocean network and later trade across the Sahara provided **sub-Saharan Africa**, the portion of Africa south of the Sahara, with a few external contacts. The most important African network of cultural exchange from 300 BCE to 1100 CE, however, arose within the region and took the form of folk migration. These migrations and exchanges put in place enduring characteristics of African culture.

9-4a A Challenging Geography

Many geographic obstacles impede access to and movement within sub-Saharan Africa (see Map 9.2). The Sahara, the Atlantic and Indian Oceans, and the Red Sea form the boundaries of the region. With the exception of the Nile, a ribbon of green traversing the Sahara from south to north, the major river systems empty into oceans: the Senegal, Niger, and Zaire (**zah-EER**) Rivers empty into the Atlantic, and the Zambezi River empties into the Mozambique Channel of the Indian Ocean. Rapids limit the use of these rivers for navigation.

Stretching over 50 degrees of latitude, sub-Saharan Africa encompasses dramatically different environments. A 4,000-mile (6,500-kilometer) trek from the southern edge of the Sahara to the Cape of Good Hope would take a traveler from the flat, semiarid **steppes** of the Sahel region to tropical **savanna** covered by long grasses and scattered forest, and then to **tropical rain forest** on the lower Niger and in the Zaire Basin. The rain forest gives way to another broad expanse of savanna, followed by more steppe and desert, and finally by a region of temperate highlands at the southern extremity, located as far south of the equator as Greece and Sicily are to its north. East–west travel is comparatively easy in the steppe and savanna regions—a caravan from Senegal to the Red Sea would have traversed a distance comparable to that of the Silk Road—but difficult in the equatorial rain-forest belt and across the mountains and deep rift valleys that abut the rain forest to the east and separate East from West Africa.

9-4b The Development of Cultural Unity

Cultural heritages shared by the educated elites within each region of the world—heritages that some anthropologists call "**great traditions**"—typically include a written language, common legal and belief systems, ethical codes, and other intellectual attitudes. They loom large in written records as traditions that rise above the diversity of local customs and beliefs commonly distinguished as "**small traditions**".

By the year 1 CE sub-Saharan Africa had become a distinct cultural region, though one not shaped by imperial conquest or characterized by a shared elite culture, a "great tradition." The cultural unity of sub-Saharan Africa rested on similar characteristics shared to varying degrees by many popular cultures, or "small traditions." These had developed during the region's long period of isolation from the rest of the world after the drying-up of the Sahara and had been refined, renewed, and interwoven by repeated episodes of migration and social interaction. Historians know little about this complex prehistory beyond what archaeology indicates for the beginnings of ironworking (see below) and the spread of domesticated grains, such as pearl millet (from Mali) and teff (from Ethiopia), around the third millennium BCE. Thus, to a greater degree than

sub-Saharan Africa Portion of the African continent lying south of the Sahara.

steppes An ecological region of grass- and shrub-covered plains that is treeless and too arid for agriculture.

savanna Tropical or subtropical grassland, either treeless or with occasional clumps of trees. Most extensive in sub-Saharan Africa but also present in South America.

tropical rain forest High-precipitation forest zones of the Americas, Africa, and Asia lying between the Tropic of Cancer and the Tropic of Capricorn.

"great traditions" Historians' term for a literate, well-institutionalized complex of religious and social beliefs and practices adhered to by diverse societies over a broad geographical area.

"small traditions" Historians' term for a localized, usually nonliterate, set of customs and beliefs adhered to by a single society, often in conjunction with a "great tradition."

in other regions, they call on anthropological descriptions, oral history, and comparatively late records of various "small traditions" to reconstruct the broad outlines of cultural formation.

9-4c Economies and Social Practices

Sub-Saharan Africa's cultural unity is less immediately apparent than its diversity. By one estimate, Africa is home to 2,000 distinct languages, many corresponding to social and belief systems endowed with distinctive rituals and cosmologies. There are likewise numerous food production systems, ranging from hunting and gathering—very differently carried out by the Mbuti (**m-BOO-tee**) Pygmies of the equatorial rain forest and the Khoisan (**KOI-sahn**) peoples of the southwestern deserts—to the cultivation of bananas, yams, and other root crops in forest clearings and of sorghum, originally from Egypt, and millet in the savanna lands. Pastoral societies, particularly those depending on cattle, display somewhat less diversity across the Sahel and savanna belt from Senegal to Kenya. Equatorial regions have distinctive breeds of dwarf goats that are resistant to tsetse fly infection.

Sub-Saharan Africa covered a larger and more diverse area than any other cultural region in the first millennium CE and had a lower overall population density. Thus societies and polities had ample room to form and reform, and a substantial amount of space separated different groups. The contacts that did occur did not last long enough to produce rigid cultural uniformity.

9-4d An Isolated World

In addition, for centuries external conquerors could not penetrate the region's natural barriers and impose a uniform culture. The Egyptians occupied Nubia, and some traces of Egyptian influence appear in Saharan rock art farther west, but the Nile cataracts and the vast swampland in the Nile's upper reaches blocked movement farther south. The Romans sent expeditions against pastoral peoples living in the Libyan Sahara but could not incorporate them into the Roman world. Not until the nineteenth century did outsiders gain control of the continent and begin the process of establishing a more or less uniform culture—that of European imperialism.

9-4e African Cultural Characteristics

European travelers who got to know the sub-Saharan region well in the nineteenth and twentieth centuries observed broad commonalities underlying African life and culture. In agriculture, the common technique was cultivation by hoe and digging stick. Plows were never used despite an abundance of cattle in the Sahel. Musically, different groups of Africans played many instruments, especially types of drums, but common features, particularly in rhythm, gave African music as a whole a distinctive character. Music played an important role in social rituals, as did dancing and wearing masks, which often showed great artistry in their design.

African kingdoms varied, but kingship displayed common features, most notably the ritual isolation of the king himself. Fixed social categories—age groupings, kinship divisions, distinct gender roles and relations, and occupational groupings—also show resemblances from one region to another, even in societies too small to organize themselves into kingdoms. Though not hierarchical, these categories played a role similar to the divisions between noble, commoner, and slave prevalent where kings ruled.

9-4f Migration from an Expanding Desert

Some historians hypothesize that these common cultural features emanated from the peoples who once occupied the southern Sahara. In Paleolithic times, periods of dryness alternated with periods of wetness as the Ice Age that locked up much of the world's fresh water in glaciers and icecaps came and went. When European glaciers receded with the waning of the Ice Age, a storm belt brought increased wetness to the Saharan region. Rushing rivers scoured deep canyons. Now filled with fine sand, those canyons are easily visible on flights over the southern parts of the desert. As the glaciers receded farther, the storm belt moved northward to Europe, and dryness set in gradually after 5000 BCE. As a consequence, runs the hypothesis, the region's population migrated southward, becoming increasingly concentrated in the Sahel, which may have been the initial incubation center for Pan-African cultural patterns.

Increasing dryness and the resulting difficulty in supporting the population would have driven some people out of this core into more sparsely settled lands to the east, west, and south. In a parallel development farther to the east, migration away from the growing aridity of the desert seems to have contributed to the settling of the Nile Valley and the emergence of the Old Kingdom of Egypt (see Chapter 2). The archaeological site of Nabta Playa in the totally barren desert west of the Nile in southern Egypt marks a stage in this process. Originally cattle herders around a lake in the tenth millennium BCE, the local population had developed large villages with deep wells, sorghum and millet cultivation, and sheep and goat herding by the seventh millennium. The fifth millennium witnessed their construction of an astronomically oriented ring of stones 2,000 years older than Stonehenge, along with a cattle cult featuring animals buried in stone-built chambers. The excavators see a likely connection between that cult and later cattle worship in dynastic Egypt.

9-4g The Advent of Iron and the Bantu Migrations

Archaeology confirms that agriculture had become common between the equator and the Sahara by the early second millennium BCE. It then spread southward, displacing hunting and gathering as a way of life. Moreover, botanical evidence indicates that banana trees, probably introduced to southeastern Africa from Southeast Asia, made their way north and west, retracing in the opposite direction the presumed migration routes of early agriculturists.

Traces of copper mining appear in the Sahara from the early first millennium BCE. Copper appears in the Niger Valley somewhat later and in the Central African copper belt after 400 CE. Most important of all, iron smelting began in northern sub-Saharan Africa in the early first millennium CE and spread southward from there.

9-4h Early Metalworking

Many historians believe that the secret of smelting iron, which requires very high temperatures, was discovered only once, by the Hittites of Anatolia (modern Turkey) around 1500 BCE (see Chapter 4). If that is the case, it is hard to explain how iron smelting reached sub-Saharan Africa. The earliest evidence of ironworking from the kingdom of Meroë, situated on the upper

AP® Exam Tip
Explain the role of Bantu speakers in the diffusion of technology (such as iron usage), language, and agricultural techniques throughout sub-Saharan Africa, and analyze the environmental impact of that diffusion.

▲ **Stone Circle at Nabta Playa** One of the world's oldest assemblages of large stones, this array in the Sahara Desert west of the Nile River dates to roughly 6000 BCE. It was probably constructed by a cattle-herding society living in the region before it had attained maximum dryness. The purpose of the circle may have been to mark star positions at key points in the annual calendar. Mike P Shepherd/Alamy Stock Photo

Section Review

- An environmentally diverse region, sub-Saharan Africa includes many barriers to travel and communication.

- Sub-Saharan Africa achieved a cultural unity of similar "small traditions."

- Shared characteristics include agricultural methods, approaches to music, forms of kingship, and fixed social categories.

- The likely mechanism of this unity was the Bantu migrations, which were also responsible for the spread of iron smelting throughout sub-Saharan Africa.

Nile and in cultural contact with Egypt, is no earlier than the evidence from West Africa (northern Nigeria). Even less plausible than the Nile Valley as a route of technological diffusion is the idea of a spread southward from Phoenician settlements in North Africa, since archaeological evidence has failed to substantiate the vague Greek and Latin accounts of Phoenician excursions to the south.

A more plausible scenario focuses on Africans' discovering for themselves how to smelt iron. Some historians suggest that they might have done so while firing pottery in kilns. No firm evidence exists to prove or disprove this theory.

Linguistic analysis provides the strongest evidence of extensive contacts among sub-Saharan Africans in the first millennium CE—and offers suggestions about the spread of iron. More than 300 languages spoken south of the equator belong to the branch of the Niger-Congo family known as **Bantu**, after the word meaning "people" in most of the languages.

9-4i Linguistic Relations

AP® Exam Tip
Understand how migrations and commercial contacts led to the diffusion of languages throughout a region and the emergence of new languages.

The distribution of the Bantu languages both north and south of the equator is consistent with a divergence beginning in the first millennium BCE. By comparing core words common to most of the languages, linguists have drawn some conclusions about the original Bantu-speakers, whom they call "proto-Bantu." These people engaged in fishing, using canoes, nets, lines, and hooks. They lived in permanent villages on the edge of the rain forest, where they grew yams and grains and harvested wild palm nuts from which they pressed oil. They possessed domesticated goats, dogs, and perhaps other animals. They made pottery and cloth. Linguists surmise that the proto-Bantu homeland was near the modern boundary of Nigeria and Cameroon.

Because the presumed home of the proto-Bantu lies near the known sites of early iron smelting, migration by Bantu-speakers seems a likely mechanism for the southward spread of iron. The migrants probably used iron axes and hoes to hack out forest clearings and plant crops. According to this scenario, their actions would have established an economic basis for new societies capable of sustaining much denser populations than could earlier societies dependent on hunting and gathering alone. Thus the period from 500 BCE to 1000 CE saw a substantial transfer of Bantu traditions and practices southward, eastward, and westward and their transformation, through intermingling with preexisting societies, into Pan-African traditions and practices.

9-5 The Spread of Ideas

Why do some goods and ideas travel more easily than others?

Ideas, like social customs, religious attitudes, and artistic styles, can spread along trade routes and through folk migrations. In both cases, documenting the dissemination of ideas, particularly in preliterate societies, poses a difficult historical problem.

9-5a Ideas and Material Evidence

Historians know about some ideas only through the survival of written sources. Other ideas do not depend on writing but are inherent in material objects studied by archaeologists and anthropologists. Customs surrounding the eating of pork are a case in point. Scholars disagree about whether pigs became domestic in only one place, from which the practice of pig keeping spread elsewhere, or whether several peoples hit on the same idea at different times and in different places.

9-5b Domestic Pigs

Bantu Collective name of a large group of sub-Saharan African languages and of the peoples speaking these languages.

Southeast Asia was an important early center of pig domestication. Anthropological studies tell us that the eating of pork became highly ritualized in this area and that it was sometimes allowed only on ceremonial occasions. On the other side of the Indian Ocean, wild swine were common in the Nile swamps of ancient Egypt. There, too, pigs took on a sacred role, being associated with the evil god Set, and eating them was prohibited. The biblical prohibition on the Israelites' eating pork, echoed later by the Muslims, probably came from Egypt in the second millennium BCE.

In a third locale in eastern Iran, an archaeological site dating from the third millennium BCE provides evidence of another religious taboo relating to pork. Although the area around the site was swampy and home to many wild pigs, not a single pig bone has been found. Yet small pig figurines seem to have been used as symbolic religious offerings, and the later Iranian religion associates the boar with an important god.

What accounts for the apparent connection between domestic pigs and religion in these far-flung areas? There is no way of knowing. It has been hypothesized that pigs were first domesticated in Southeast Asia by people who had no herd animals—sheep, goats, cattle, or horses—and who relied on fish for most of their animal protein. The pig therefore became a special animal to them. The practice of pig herding, along with religious beliefs and rituals associated with the consumption of pork, could conceivably have spread from Southeast Asia along the maritime routes of the Indian Ocean, eventually reaching Iran and Egypt. But no evidence survives to support this hypothesis. In this case, therefore, material evidence can only hint at the spread of religious ideas, leaving the door open for other explanations.

A more certain example of objects' indicating the spread of an idea is the practice of hammering a carved die onto a piece of precious metal and using the resulting coin as a medium of exchange. From its origin in the Lydian kingdom in Anatolia in the first millennium BCE (see Chapter 5), the idea of trading by means of struck coinage spread rapidly to Europe, North Africa, and India. Was the low-value copper coinage of China, made by pouring molten metal into a mold, also inspired by this practice from far away? It may have been, but it might also derive from indigenous Chinese metalworking.

AP® Exam Tip
Explain the role of certain state practices, such as the minting of coins, in facilitating commercial growth in this time period.

9-5c The Spread of Buddhism

While material objects associated with religious beliefs and rituals are important indicators of the spread of spiritual ideas, written sources deal with the spread of today's major religions. Buddhism grew to become, with Christianity and Islam (see Chapter 9), one of the most popular and widespread religions in the world. In all three cases, the religious ideas spread without dependency on a single ethnic or kinship group.

9-5d Two Kings: Ashoka and Kanishka

King Ashoka, the Mauryan ruler of India, and Kanishka, the greatest king of the Kushans of northern Afghanistan, promoted Buddhism between the third century BCE and the second century CE. However, monks, missionaries, and pilgrims who crisscrossed India, followed the Silk Road, or took ships on the Indian Ocean brought the Buddha's teachings to Southeast Asia, China, Korea, and ultimately Japan (see Map 9.1).

The Chinese pilgrim Faxian (**fah-shee-en**) (who died between 418 and 423 CE) left a written account of his travels. Faxian began his trip in the company of a Chinese envoy to an unspecified ruler or people in Central Asia. After traveling from one Buddhist site to another across Afghanistan and India, he reached Sri Lanka, a Buddhist land, where he lived for two years. He then embarked for China on a merchant ship with two hundred men aboard. A storm drove the ship to Java, which he chose not to describe since it was Hindu rather than Buddhist. After five months ashore, Faxian finally reached China on another ship.

Less reliable accounts make reference to missionaries traveling to Syria, Egypt, and Macedonia, as well as to Southeast Asia. One of Ashoka's sons allegedly led a band of missionaries to Sri Lanka. Later, his sister brought a company of nuns there, along with a branch of the sacred Bo tree under which the Buddha had received enlightenment. At the same time, there are reports of other monks traveling to Burma, Thailand, and Sumatra. Ashoka's missionaries may also have reached Tibet by way of trade routes across the Himalayas.

The different lands that received the story and teachings of the Buddha preserved or adapted them in different ways. Theravada Buddhism, "Teachings of the Elder," was centered in Sri Lanka. Holding closely to the Buddha's earliest teachings, it maintained that the goal of religion, available only to monks, is *nirvana*, the total absence of suffering and the end of the cycle of rebirth (see Chapter 7). This teaching contrasted with Mahayana, or "Great Vehicle" Buddhism, in later centuries the dominant form of the religion in East Asia, which stressed the goal of becoming

AP® Exam Tip
Be familiar with how the growing exchange networks led to travelers who wrote about their travels and spread cultural knowledge.

AP® Exam Tip
Compare the diffusion of Buddhism with that of Christianity.

◀ **Stele of Aksum**   This 70-foot (21-meter) stone is the tallest remnant of a field of *steles*, or standing stones, marking the tombs of Aksumite kings. The carvings of doors, windows, and beam ends imitate common features of Aksumite architecture, suggesting that each stele symbolized a multistory royal palace. The largest steles date from the fourth century CE.   Matej Hudovernik/Shutterstock.com

Armenia One of the earliest Christian kingdoms, situated in eastern Anatolia and the western Caucasus and occupied by speakers of the Armenian language.

Ethiopia East African highland nation lying east of the Nile River.

Section Review

- Material evidence can only offer hints about the spread of some ideas; it cannot completely explain the connection between pigs and religion and the use of coins in different parts of the world.

- Material and documentary evidence show the spread of Buddhism from India along the land and sea trade routes to elsewhere in Asia, with some areas adopting Theravada Buddhism and others Mahayana Buddhism.

- Christianity spread through a combination of trade and imperial politics, with significant Christian societies emerging in Armenia and Ethiopia.

a *bodhisattva*, a person who attains nirvana but chooses to remain in human company to help and guide others.

9-5e The Spread of Christianity

The post-Roman development of Christianity in Europe is discussed in Chapter 10. The Christian faith enjoyed an earlier spread in Asia and Africa before its confrontation with Islam (described in Chapter 9). Jerusalem in Palestine, Antioch in Syria, and Alexandria in Egypt became centers of Christian authority soon after the crucifixion, but the spread of Christianity to Armenia and Ethiopia illustrates the connections between religion, trade, and imperial politics.

Situated in eastern Anatolia (modern Turkey), **Armenia** served recurrently as a battleground between Iranian states to the south and east and Mediterranean states to the west. Each imperial power wanted to control this region so close to the frontier where Silk Road traders met their Mediterranean counterparts. In Parthian times, Armenia's kings favored Zoroastrianism. The invention of an Armenian alphabet in the early fifth century opened the way to a wider spread of Christianity. The Iranians did not give up domination easily, but within a century the Armenian Apostolic Church had become the center of Armenian cultural life.

Far to the south Christians similarly sought to outflank Iran. The Christian emperors in Constantinople (see Chapter 6) sent missionaries along the Red Sea trade route to seek converts in Yemen and **Ethiopia**. In the fourth century CE a Syrian philosopher traveling with two young relatives sailed to India. On the way back the ship docked at a Red Sea port occupied by Ethiopians from the prosperous kingdom of Aksum. Being then at odds with the Romans, the Ethiopians killed everyone on board except the two boys, Aedisius—who later narrated this story—and Frumentius. Impressed by their learning, the king made the former his cupbearer and the latter his treasurer and secretary.

When the king died, his wife urged Frumentius to govern Aksum on her behalf and that of her infant son, Ezana. As regent, Frumentius sought out Roman Christians among the merchants who visited the country and helped them establish Christian communities. When he became king, Ezana, who may have become a Christian, permitted Aedisius and Frumentius to return to Syria. The patriarch of Alexandria, on learning about the progress of Christianity in Aksum, elevated Frumentius to the rank of bishop, though he had not previously been a clergyman, and sent him back to Ethiopia as the first leader of its church.

The spread of Christianity into Nubia, the land south of Egypt along the Nile River, proceeded from Ethiopia rather than Egypt. Politically and economically, Ethiopia became a power at the western end of the Indian Ocean trading system, occasionally even extending its influence across the Red Sea and asserting itself in Yemen (see Map 9.1).

9-6 **Conclusion**

Exchange facilitated by the early long-distance trading systems differed in many ways from the ebb and flow of culture, language, and custom that folk migrations brought about. Transportable goods and livestock and ideas about new technologies and agricultural products sometimes worked great changes on the landscape and in people's lives. But nothing resembling the commonality of African cultural features observed south of the Sahara can be attributed to the societies involved in the Silk Road, Indian Ocean, or trans-Saharan exchanges. Few people were directly involved in these complex social systems of travel and trade compared with the populations with whom they were brought into contact, and their lifestyles as pastoral nomads or seafarers isolated them still more. Communities of traders contributed to this isolation by their reluctance to share knowledge with people who might become commercial competitors.

The Bantu, however, if current theories are correct, spread far and wide in sub-Saharan Africa with the deliberate intent of settling and implanting a lifestyle based on iron implements and agriculture. The metallurgical skills and agricultural techniques they brought with them permitted much denser habitation and helped ensure that the languages of the immigrants would supplant those of their hunting-and-gathering predecessors. Where the trading systems encouraged diversity by introducing new products and ideas, the Bantu migrations brought a degree of cultural dominance that strongly affected later African history.

An apparent exception to the generalization that trading systems have less impact than folk migrations on patterns of dominance lies in the intangible area of ideas. Christianity and Buddhism both spread along trade routes, at least to some degree. Each instance of spread, however, gave rise to new forms of cultural diversity even as overall doctrinal unity made these religions dominant. As "great traditions," the new faiths based on conversion linked priests, monks, nuns, and religious scholars across vast distances. However, these same religions merged with myriad "small traditions" to provide for the social and spiritual needs of peoples living in many lands under widely varying circumstances.

Key Terms

Silk Road p. 226	trans-Saharan caravan	savanna p. 237	Armenia p. 242
Parthians p. 226	routes p. 234	tropical rain forest p. 237	Ethiopia p. 242
stirrup p. 230	Sahel p. 236	"great traditions" p. 237	
Indian Ocean Maritime	sub-Saharan Africa p. 237	"small traditions" p. 237	
System p. 230	steppes p. 237	Bantu p. 240	

Review Questions

1. Does the history of cultural interactions become more or less understandable when empires, states, and political personalities are not at the center of the narrative as they have been in earlier chapters?

2. How does the spread of the Bantu peoples compare with the spread of the Indo-European peoples in the second millennium BCE?

3. Is money essential to long-distance trade, or does exchanging goods for goods produce more significant results in the long run?

 MindTap® is a fully online, personalized learning experience built upon Cengage Learning content. MindTap® combines student learning tools—readings, multimedia, activities, and assessments—into a singular Learning Path that guides students through the course and helps students develop the critical thinking, analysis, and communication skills that are essential to academic and professional success.

AP® REVIEW QUESTIONS FOR CHAPTER 9

Multiple-Choice Questions
Questions 1–4 refer to Map 9.1 on page 227.

1. By the sixth century CE, the increasingly important overland Silk Roads shown on the map were important to trade because they

   (A) provided transportation through an extensive region of homogeneous cultures that existed in Eurasia at the time.

   (B) expanded the geographical range of trade routes by providing a shorter route for goods than the maritime routes previously available.

   (C) created opportunities for overland challenge to Parthian control of Central Asian deserts.

   (D) opened the door for political unification of China.

2. Which of the following transportation technology improvements enabled the increased level of trade across Central Asia along the Silk Roads?

   (A) The invention of the wheel in Mesopotamia

   (B) The development of the chariot in Syria

   (C) The improvement in saddles and stirrups in Afghanistan

   (D) The development of paved roads based on the Roman model

3. Which of the following was an important motivation for the principal trade pattern on the Eurasian Silk Roads?

   (A) Traders carrying mainly agricultural products west from China to Mesopotamia and Rome

   (B) European demand for horses from the steppes of Central Asia and Chinese spices

   (C) Merchants, desiring control, using their goods to wield political power in multiple principalities along the Silk Roads

   (D) Growing demand for luxury goods in Afro-Eurasia and expansion of the Chinese and Persian production of these goods

4. Between 600 and 1450 CE, increased trade along the Eurasian Silk Roads indicated on the map led to

   (A) innovations in transport and the growth of influential trading cities.

   (B) large-scale migration of populations searching for economic advantages.

   (C) an increased number of pastoralists on the Central Asian steppes.

   (D) an increased literacy rate among both Chinese and Turkic peoples.

Questions 5–7 refer to the passage below.

"There is great abundance of pepper and also of ginger, besides cinnamon in plenty and other spices . . . and coconuts. Buckrams [cloth] are made here of the loveliest and most delicate texture in the world. In return, when merchants come here from overseas, they load their ships with brass, which they use as ballast, cloth of gold and silk, sandal, gold, silver, cloves, spikenard and other such spices that are not produced here. . . . Goods are exported to many parts. Those that go to Aden are carried thence to Alexandria."

Marco Polo's description of the southeastern coast of India in the late twelfth century

5. What does the list of varied goods in Marco Polo's account tell historians about the Indian Ocean during the twelfth century?

   (A) Indian Ocean trade was dominated by Indian merchants.

   (B) Indian Ocean trade routes linked states throughout the entire region.

   (C) Trade was more intense across the Indian Ocean than along the Eurasian Silk roads.

   (D) Most of the trade across the Indian Ocean involved spices.

6. What made a traveler's descriptions, like those of Marco Polo, of particular importance?

   (A) No Europeans had ever ventured into the Asian continent in the twelfth century.

   (B) Most of the previous reports about Asian lands had been made by Christian missionaries.

   (C) Most people of the time had very limited knowledge and understanding of foreign lands.

   (D) The printing press made the reports immediately accessible.

7. Which of the following was a social impact of the Indian Ocean trade described by Marco Polo?

   (A) Extreme political power was granted to seafarers due to their economic importance.

   (B) Due to the primarily male sea trade, women became the center of the social hierarchy and gained more rights than in other areas.

   (C) The need for greater literacy was emphasized, as many wanted to be able to read the travelers' tales.

   (D) Increasingly cosmopolitan children were brought up as a bridge between their local mother's culture and their sailor merchant father's culture.

Questions 8–10 refer to the image below.

▲ **Illustration of tribal blacksmith workers, Unyamwezi region, Tanzania, 1864.** Marzolino/Shutterstock.com

8. Historians could use the image provided to support which of the following assertions about sub-Saharan African life?

(A) The civilization that existed in this region of sub-Saharan Africa was primitive and had no effective weapons.

(B) The Bantu migrations and their introduction of iron to sub-Saharan Africa had a significant environmental impact.

(C) There was a centralized government administration that was capable of organizing labor.

(D) Climate was unpredictable and there was a need for large-scale food production using plows.

9. In addition to the study of objects like those in the image, what other element supports the archeological study of the impact of the Bantu migrations?

(A) Farming technology such as the plow allowing the creation of villages in arid regions

(B) Divergent rhythms and sounds in music indicating a slow transfer of European impact

(C) Common core words that demonstrate a linguistic similarity throughout the area

(D) Increasing aridity from the destruction of the landscape by the Bantu migrants

10. Why is it particularly difficult for historians to understand the early cultures of sub-Saharan Africa?

(A) Sub-Saharan Africa has an oral tradition and there are no written records of its ancient history.

(B) There were very few human settlements in Africa before the eighteenth century.

(C) Invasions by Muslims after 600 CE destroyed most records of earlier periods.

(D) Sub-Saharan African cultures did not fully develop until the nineteenth century when the region was changed by European imperialism.

Short-Answer Questions

"This is the great country of the Western Ocean [Indian Ocean]. . . . In the fifth year of the Yongle period the court ordered the principal envoy, the grand eunuch Zheng He, and others to deliver an imperial mandate to the king of this country . . . The people are very honest and trustworthy. Their appearance is smart, fine, and distinguished. . . . Foreign ships from every place come there; and the king of the country also sends a chief and a writer to watch the sales; thereupon they collect the duty and pay it to the authorities."

Ma Huan, a high-level member of Zheng He's staff, *The Overall Survey of the Ocean Shores*, ca. 1433

1. Use the passage above and your knowledge of world history to answer all parts of the question that follows.

(A) Identify ONE development in technology or environmental understanding that led to the intensification of trade in the Indian Ocean region between 600 CE and 1450 CE.

(B) Explain ONE reason for the intensification of trade in the Indian Ocean region between 600 CE and 1450 CE.

(C) Explain ONE result of the intensification of trade in the Indian Ocean region between 600 CE and 1450 CE.

2. Answer all parts of the question that follows.

(A) Identify ONE individual responsible for the spread of Buddhism or Christianity before 1100 CE.

(B) Explain ONE similarity in the spread of Buddhism and the spread of Christianity before 1100 CE.

(C) Explain ONE difference in the spread of Buddhism and the spread of Christianity before 1100 CE.

The Sasanid Empire and the Rise of Islam, 200–1200

10

CHAPTER OUTLINE

10-1 The Sasanid Empire, 224–651

10-2 The Origins of Islam

10-3 The Rise and Fall of the Caliphate, 632–1258

10-4 Islamic Civilization

10-5 Conclusion

➤ **DIVERSITY & DOMINANCE**
Becoming Muslim

➤ **ENVIRONMENT & TECHNOLOGY**
Chemistry

AP® Framework Terms

Rice
Cotton
Textiles
Islam
Prophet Muhammad
Arabian peninsula
Sufis

Overarching Questions

1 How and why have religions, belief systems, philosophies, and ideologies originated, developed, and spread as a result of expanding communication and exchange networks? (CUL)

2 How and why have economic, social, cultural, and geographic factors influenced the process of state building, expansion, and dissolution? (SB)

3 How have societies with states and state-less societies interacted over time? (SB)

4 How have economic systems and the development of ideologies, values, and institutions influenced each other? (ECON)

5 To what extent have different ideologies, philosophies, and religions affected social hierarchies? (SOC)

Knowledge of papermaking, which spread from China to the Middle East after Arab conquests in the seventh century CE established an Islamic caliphate stretching from Spain to Central Asia, provided a medium that was superior to papyrus and parchment and well suited to a variety of purposes. Maps, miniature paintings, and, of course, books became increasingly common and inexpensive. With cheaper books came bookstores, and one of the most informative manuscripts of the period of the Islamic caliphate is a *Fihrist*, or descriptive catalogue, of the books sold at one bookstore in Baghdad.

Abu al-Faraj Muhammad al-Nadim, a man with good connections at the caliph's court, compiled the catalogue, though his father probably founded the bookstore. Its latest entry dates to ca. 990, al-Nadim's death date. Superbly educated, al-Nadim wrote such well-informed comments on books and authors that his catalogue presents a detailed survey of the intellectual world of Baghdad.

▲ **Baghdad Bookstore** With the advent of papermaking, manufacturing books became increasingly common and inexpensive. As a result, bookstores also became more common. Notice how books are shelved on their sides in wall cubicles. akg-images

The first of the *Fihrist*'s ten books deals with Arabic language and sacred scriptures: the Quran, the Torah, and the Gospel. The second covers Arabic grammar, and the third writings from people connected with the caliph's court: historians, government officials, singers, jesters, and the ruler's boon companions. *Al-Nadim* means "book companion," so it is assumed that he knew this milieu well. After dealing with Arabic poetry, Muslim sects, and Islamic law in Books 3 through 6, he comes to Greek philosophy, science, and medicine in Book 7.

Most things we would find today in a bookstore are relegated to the final three chapters. Book 8 divides into three sections, the first being "Story Tellers and Stories." Here he lists a Persian book called *A Thousand Stories*, which in translation became *The Arabian Nights*. Al-Nadim's version no longer survives. The collection we have today comes from a manuscript written 500 years later.

Then come books about "Exorcists, Jugglers, and Magicians," followed by "Miscellaneous Subjects and Fables." These include books on "Freckles, Twitching, Moles, and Shoulders," "Horsemanship, Bearing of Arms, the Implements of War," "Veterinary Surgery," "Birds of Prey, Sport with Them and Medical Care of Them," "Interpretation of Dreams," "Perfume," "Cooked Food," "Poisons," and "Amulets and Charms."

Non-Muslim sects and foreign lands—India, Indochina, and China—fill Book 9, leaving Book 10 for a few final notes on philosophers not mentioned previously.

Altogether, the thousands of titles and authors commented on by al-Nadim provide both a panorama of what interested book buyers in tenth-century Baghdad and a saddening picture of how profound the loss of knowledge has been since that glorious era. ●

10-1 The Sasanid Empire, 224–651

How did the traditions and religious views of pre-Islamic peoples become integrated into the culture shaped by Islam?

The rise in the third century of a new Iranian state, the **(SAH-suh-nid) Sasanid Empire**, continued the old rivalry between Rome and the Parthians along the Euphrates frontier. However, behind this facade of continuity, a social and economic transformation took place that set the stage for a new and powerful religiopolitical movement: Islam.

10-1a Politics and Society

Sasanid Empire Iranian empire, established around 224, with a capital in Ctesiphon, Mesopotamia. The Sasanid emperors established Zoroastrianism as the state religion. Islamic Arab armies overthrew the empire around 651.

Ardashir, whose dynasty takes its name from an ancestor named Sasan, defeated the Parthians around 224 and established the Sasanid kingdom. To the west, the new rulers confronted the Romans, whom later historians frequently refer to as the Byzantines after about 330. Along their desert Euphrates frontier, the Sasanids subsidized nomadic Arab chieftains to protect their empire from invasion (the Byzantines did the same with Arabs on their Jordanian desert frontier). Arab pastoralists farther to the south remained isolated and independent. The rival empires launched numerous attacks on each other across that frontier between the 340s and 628. In times of peace, however, exchange between the empires flourished, allowing goods transported over the Silk Road to enter the zone of Mediterranean trade.

The mountains and plateaus of Iran proper formed the Sasanids' political hinterland, often ruled by the cousins of the *shah* (king) or by powerful families descending from the pre-Sasanid Parthian nobility. Cities there were small walled communities that served more as military strong-points than as centers of population and production. Society revolved around a local aristocracy that lived on rural estates and cultivated the arts of hunting, feasting, and war just like the warriors described in the sagas of ancient kings and heroes sung at their banquets.

Despite the dominance of powerful aristocratic families, long-lasting political fragmentation of the medieval European variety did not develop (see Chapter 11). Also, although many nomads lived in the mountain and desert regions, no folk migration took place comparable to that of

◀ **Sasanid Silver Plate with Gold Decoration** The Sasanid aristocracy, based in the countryside, invested part of its wealth in silver plates and vessels. This image of a Sasanid king hunting on horseback also reflects a favorite aristocratic pastime. 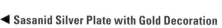 Erich Lessing/Art Resource, NY

CHRONOLOGY

	The Arab Lands	Iran and Central Asia
200	570–632 Life of the Prophet Muhammad	224–651 Sasanid Empire
600	634 Conquests of Iraq and Syria commence 639–642 Conquest of Egypt by Arabs 656–661 Ali caliph; first civil war 661–750 Umayyad Caliphate rules from Damascus	
700	711 Berbers and Arabs invade Spain from North Africa 750 Beginning of Abbasid Caliphate 755 Umayyad state established in Spain 776–809 Caliphate of Harun al-Rashid	711 Arabs capture Sind in India 747 Abbasid revolt begins in Khurasan
800	835–892 Abbasid capital moved from Baghdad to Samarra	875 Independent Samanid state founded in Bukhara
900	909 Fatimids seize North Africa, found Shi'ite Caliphate 929 Abd al-Rahman III declares himself caliph in Córdoba 945 Shi'ite Buyids take control in Baghdad 969 Fatimids conquer Egypt	945 Buyids from northern Iran take control of Abbasid Caliphate
1000	1055 Seljuk Turks take control in Baghdad 1099 First Crusade captures Jerusalem 1171 Fall of Fatimid Egypt 1187 Saladin recaptures Jerusalem 1250 Mamluks control Egypt 1258 Mongols sack Baghdad and end Abbasid Caliphate 1260 Mamluks defeat Mongols at Ain Jalut	1036 Beginning of Turkish Seljuk rule in Khurasan

the Germanic peoples who defeated Roman armies and established kingdoms in formerly Roman territory from about the third century CE onward. The Sasanid and Byzantine Empires generally maintained central control of imperial finances and military power and found effective ways of integrating frontier peoples as mercenaries or caravaneers.

The Silk Road brought new products to Mesopotamia, some of which became part of the agricultural landscape. Sasanid farmers pioneered in planting sugar cane, rice, citrus trees, eggplants, and other crops adopted from India and China. Although the acreage devoted to new crops increased slowly, these products became important consumption and trade items during the succeeding Islamic period.

10-1b Religion and Empire

The Sasanids established their Zoroastrian faith (see Chapter 5), which the Parthians had not particularly stressed, as a state religion similar to Christianity in the Byzantine Empire (see Chapter 11), though other faiths may have competed effectively in eastern Iran. The proclamation of Christianity and Zoroastrianism as official faiths marked the fresh emergence of religion as an instrument of politics both within and between the empires, setting a precedent for the subsequent rise of Islam as the focus of a political empire.

Both Zoroastrianism and Christianity practiced intolerance. A late-third-century inscription in Iran boasts of the persecutions of Christians, Jews, and Buddhists carried out by the Zoroastrian high priest. Yet sizable Christian and Jewish communities remained, especially in Mesopotamia. Similarly, from the fourth century onward, councils of Christian bishops declared many theological beliefs heretical—so unacceptable that they were un-Christian.

Christians then became pawns in the political rivalry with the Byzantines and were sometimes persecuted, sometimes patronized, by the Sasanid kings. In 431 a council of bishops called by the Byzantine emperor declared the Nestorian Christians heretics for over-emphasizing the humanness of Christ. The Nestorians believed that human characteristics and divinity coexisted in Jesus and that Mary was not the mother of God, as many other Christians maintained, but the mother of the human Jesus. After the bishops' ruling, the

AP® Exam Tip
Understand the influence of Zoroastrianism on Judaism, Christianity, and Islam.

Section Review

- Originating in southern Iran, the Sasanids overthrew the Parthians and continued their predecessors' rivalry with Rome.

- Sasanid farmers pioneered the cultivation of Silk Road crops.

- Sasanid kings made Zoroastrianism the state religion, and other religions, particularly Christianity, experienced both toleration and persecution.

- Silk Road trade encouraged movements of peoples in Iran and Central Asia, as well as the exchange of religious ideas and military technology.

Nestorians sought refuge under the Sasanid shah and eventually extended their missionary activities along the Central Asian trade routes.

In the third century a preacher named Mani founded a new religion in Mesopotamia: Manichaeism. Mani preached a dualist faith—a struggle between Good and Evil—theologically derived from Zoroastrianism. Although at first he enjoyed the favor of the shah, he and many of his followers were martyred in 276. However, his religion survived and spread widely. Nestorian missionaries in Central Asia competed with Manichaean missionaries for converts. In later centuries, the term *Manichaean* was applied to all sorts of beliefs about a cosmic struggle between Good and Evil.

The Arabs became enmeshed in this web of religious conflict. The border protectors subsidized by the Byzantines adopted a Monophysite theology, which emphasized Christ's divine nature; the allies of the Sasanids, the Nestorian faith. Through them, knowledge of Christianity penetrated deeper into the Arabian peninsula during the fifth and sixth centuries.

Religion permeated all aspects of community life. Most subjects of the Byzantine emperors and Sasanid shahs identified themselves first and foremost as members of a religious community. Their schools and law courts were religious. They looked on priests, monks, rabbis, and the Zoroastrian *mobads* (priests officiating in fire temples) as moral guides in daily life. Most books discussed religious subjects. In some areas, religious leaders represented their flocks even in such secular matters as tax collection.

10-2 The Origins of Islam

How did the Muslim community of the time of Muhammad differ from the society that developed after the Arab conquests?

The Arabs of 600 CE lived exclusively in the Arabian peninsula and on the desert fringes of Syria, Jordan, and Iraq. Along their Euphrates frontier, the Sasanids subsidized nomadic Arab chieftains to protect their empire from invasion. The Byzantines did the same with Arabs on their Jordanian frontier. Arab pastoralists farther to the south remained isolated and independent, seldom engaging the attention of the shahs and emperors. It was in these interior Arabian lands that the religion of Islam took form.

10-2a The Arabian Peninsula Before Muhammad

AP® Exam Tip

Explain the significance of caravans and caravanserai in facilitating long-distance trade.

Throughout history more people living on the Arabian peninsula have subsisted as farmers than as pastoral nomads. Farming villages supported the comparatively dense population of Yemen, where abundant rainfall waters the highlands during the spring monsoon. Small inlets along the southern coast favored fishing and trading communities. The enormous sea of sand known as the "Empty Quarter" isolated many southern regions from the Arabian interior. In the seventh century, most people in southern Arabia knew more about Africa, India, and the Persian Gulf than about the forbidding interior and the scattered camel- and sheep-herding nomads who lived there.

The Arab pastoralists inhabiting the desert between Syria and Mesopotamia supplied camels and guides and played a significant role as merchants and organizers of caravans. The militarily efficient North Arabian camel saddle, developed around the third century BCE, provided another key to Arab prosperity. Since it seated the rider atop the animal's hump instead of behind it as the South Arabian saddle did, the new device enabled Arabs to strike down on opponents with swords and spears rather than trying to shoot them with bows and arrows. This helped the Arabs take control of the caravan trade in their territories and thereby become so important as suppliers of animal power, even in agricultural districts, that wheeled vehicles—mostly ox carts and horse-drawn chariots—had all but disappeared by the sixth century CE.

Caravan trading provided a rare link among peoples. Nomads derived income from providing camels, guides, and safe passage to merchants bringing the primary product of the south,

MAP 10.1 **Early Expansion of Muslim Rule** Arab conquests of the first Islamic century brought vast territory under Muslim rule, but conversion to Islam proceeded slowly. In most areas outside the Arabian peninsula, the only region where Arabic was then spoken, conversion did not accelerate until the third century after the conquest.

How does the expansion of Muslim rule compare with the earlier spread of Christianity?

the aromatic resins frankincense and myrrh, to northern customers. Return caravans brought manufactured products from Mesopotamia and Syria.

Arabs who accompanied the caravans became familiar with the cultures and lifestyles of the Sasanid and Byzantine Empires, and many of those who pastured their herds on the imperial frontiers adopted one form or another of Christianity. Even in the interior deserts, Semitic polytheism, with its worship of natural forces and celestial bodies, began to encounter more sophisticated religions.

Mecca, a late-blooming caravan city, occupies a barren mountain valley halfway between Yemen and Syria and somewhat inland from the Red Sea coast (see Map 10.1). A nomadic kin group known as the Quraysh **(koo-RAYSH)** settled in Mecca in the fifth century and assumed control of trade. Mecca rapidly achieved a measure of prosperity, partly because it was too far from Byzantine Syria, Sasanid Iraq, and Ethiopian-controlled Yemen for them to attack it.

A cubical shrine with idols inside called the Ka'ba **(KAH-buh)**, a holy well called Zamzam, and a sacred precinct surrounding the two wherein killing was prohibited contributed to the emergence of Mecca as a pilgrimage site. Some Meccans associated the shrine with stories known to Jews and Christians. They regarded Abraham (Ibrahim in Arabic) as the builder of the Ka'ba, and they identified a site outside Mecca as the location where God asked Abraham to sacrifice his son. The son was not Isaac (Ishaq in Arabic), the son of Sarah, but Ishmael (Isma'il in Arabic), the son of Hagar, cited in the Bible as the forefather of the Arabs.

10-2b **Muhammad in Mecca and Medina**

Born in Mecca in 570, **Muhammad** grew up an orphan in the house of his uncle. He engaged in trade and married a Quraysh widow named Khadija **(kah-DEE-juh)**, whose caravan interests he superintended. Their son died in childhood, but several daughters survived. Around 610 Muhammad began meditating at night in the mountainous terrain around Mecca. During one night

AP® Exam Tip
Be familiar with the way diasporic merchant communities along long-distance trade routes led to cultural exchange.

Mecca City in western Arabia; birthplace of the Prophet Muhammad and ritual center of the Islamic religion.

Muhammad Arab prophet (570–632 CE); founder of religion of Islam.

AP® Exam Tip
Know the core beliefs of Islam and be able to explain its diffusion and impact throughout the Arabian peninsula and Afro-Eurasia.

vigil, known to later tradition as the "Night of Power and Excellence," a being whom Muhammad later understood to be the angel Gabriel (Jibra'il in Arabic) spoke to him:

> *Proclaim! In the name of your Lord who created. Created man from a clot of congealed blood. Proclaim! And your Lord is the Most Bountiful. He who has taught by the pen. Taught man that which he knew not.*[1]

For three years Muhammad shared this and subsequent revelations only with close friends and family members. This period culminated in his conviction that he was hearing the words of God (Allah [**AH-luh**] in Arabic). Khadija, his uncle's son Ali, his friend Abu Bakr (**ah-boo BAK-uhr**), and others close to him shared this conviction. The revelations continued until Muhammad's death in 632.

Like most people of the time, including Christians and Jews, the Arabs believed in unseen spirits: gods, demonic *shaitans*, and desert spirits called *jinns* who were thought to possess seers and poets. Therefore, when Muhammad recited his rhymed revelations in public, many people believed he was inspired by an unseen spirit, even if it was not, as Muhammad asserted, the one true god.

Muhammad's earliest revelations called on people to witness that one god had created the universe and everything in it, including themselves. At the end of time, their souls would be judged, their sins balanced against their good deeds. The blameless would go to paradise; the sinful would taste hellfire:

> *By the night as it conceals the light;*
> *By the day as it appears in glory;*
> *By the mystery of the creation of male and female;*
> *Verily, the ends ye strive for are diverse.*
> *So he who gives in charity and fears God,*
> *And in all sincerity testifies to the best,*
> *We will indeed make smooth for him the path to Bliss.*
> *But he who is a greedy miser and thinks himself self-sufficient,*
> *And gives the lie to the best,*
> *We will indeed make smooth for him the path to misery.*[2]

The revelation called all people to submit to God and accept Muhammad as the last of his messengers. Doing so made one a **Muslim**, meaning one who makes "submission," **Islam**, to the will of God.

Because earlier messengers mentioned in the revelations included Noah, Moses, and Jesus, Muhammad's hearers connected his message with Judaism and Christianity, religions they were already familiar with. Yet his revelations charged the Jews and Christians with being negligent in preserving God's revealed word. Thus, even though they identified Abraham/Ibrahim, whom Muslims consider the first Muslim, as the builder of the Ka'ba, which superseded Jerusalem as the focus of Muslim prayer in 624, Muhammad's followers considered his revelation more perfect than the Bible because it had not gone through an editing process.

Some scholars maintain that Muhammad appealed especially to people distressed over wealth replacing kinship as the most important aspect of social relations and over neglect of orphans and other powerless people. Most Muslims, however, put less emphasis on a social message than on the power and beauty of Muhammad's recitations.

Mecca's leaders feared that accepting Muhammad as the sole agent of the one true God would threaten their power and prosperity. They pressured his kin to disavow him and persecuted the weakest of his followers. Stymied by this hostility, Muhammad and his followers fled Mecca in 622 to take up residence in the agricultural community of **Medina** 215 miles (346 kilometers) to the north. This hijra (**HIJ-ruh**) marks the beginning of the Muslim calendar.

10-2c Formation of the Umma

Prior to the hijra, Medinan representatives had met with Muhammad and agreed to accept and protect him and his followers because they saw him as an inspired leader who could calm their perpetual feuding. Together, the Meccan migrants and major groups in Medina bound

Muslim An adherent of the Islamic religion; a person who "submits" (in Arabic, Islam means "submission") to the will of God.

Islam Religion expounded by the Prophet Muhammad on the basis of his reception of divine revelations, which were collected after his death into the Quran. In the tradition of Judaism and Christianity, and sharing much of their lore, Islam calls on all people to recognize one creator god—Allah—who rewards or punishes believers after death according to how they led their lives.

Medina City in western Arabia to which the Prophet Muhammad and his followers emigrated in 622 to escape persecution in Mecca.

---

[1]Quran, Sura 96, verses 1–5.

[2]Quran, Sura 92, verses 1–10.

themselves into a single **umma** (**UM-muh**), a community defined by acceptance of Islam and of Muhammad as the "Messenger of God," his most common title. Partly because three Jewish kin groups chose to retain their own faith, the direction of prayer was changed from Jerusalem toward the Ka'ba in Mecca, now thought of as the "House of God."

Having left their Meccan kin groups, the immigrants in Medina felt vulnerable. During the last decade of his life, Muhammad took active responsibility for his umma. Fresh revelations provided a framework for regulating social and legal affairs and stirred the Muslims to fight against the still-unbelieving city of Mecca. At various points during the war, Muhammad charged the Jewish kin groups, whom he had initially hoped would recognize him as God's messenger, with disloyalty, and he finally expelled or eliminated them. The sporadic war, largely conducted by raiding and negotiating with desert nomads, sapped Mecca's strength and convinced many Meccans that God favored Muhammad. In 630 Mecca surrendered, and Muhammad and his followers made the pilgrimage to the Ka'ba unhindered.

Muhammad stayed in Medina, which had grown into a bustling city-state. Delegations came to him from all over Arabia and returned home with believers who could teach about Islam and collect alms. Muhammad's mission to bring God's message to humanity had brought him unchallenged control of a state that was coming to dominate the Arabian peninsula.

10-2d Succession to Muhammad

In 632, after a brief illness, Muhammad died. Within twenty-four hours a group of Medinan leaders, along with three of Muhammad's close friends, determined that Abu Bakr, one of the earliest believers and the father of Muhammad's favorite wife A'isha (**AH-ee-shah**), should succeed him. They called him the *khalifa* (**kah-LEE-fuh**), or "successor," the English version of which is *caliph*. But calling Abu Bakr a successor did not clarify his powers. Everyone knew that neither Abu Bakr nor anyone else could receive revelations, and they likewise knew that Muhammad's revelations made no provision for succession or for any government purpose beyond maintaining the umma.

Abu Bakr continued and confirmed Muhammad's religious practices, notably the so-called Five Pillars of Islam: (1) avowal that there is only one god and Muhammad is his messenger, (2) prayer five times a day, (3) fasting during the lunar month of Ramadan, (4) paying alms, and (5) making the pilgrimage to Mecca at least once during one's lifetime. He also reestablished and expanded Muslim authority over Arabia's communities, some of which had abandoned their allegiance to Medina or followed various would-be prophets. Muslim armies fought hard to confirm the authority of the newborn **caliphate**. In the process, some fighting spilled over into non-Arab areas in Iraq.

Reportedly, Abu Bakr ordered the men who had written down Muhammad's revelations to collect them in a book. Hitherto written haphazardly on pieces of leather or bone, these now became a single document gathered into chapters. Muslims believe the **Quran** (**kuh-RAHN**), or the Recitation, acquired its final form around the year 650. They see it not as the words of Muhammad but as the unalterable word of God. Theologically, it compares not so much to the Bible, a book written by many hands over many centuries, as to the person of Jesus Christ, whom Christians consider an earthly manifestation of God.

Though united in accepting God's will, the umma soon disagreed over the succession to the caliphate. When rebels assassinated the third caliph, Uthman (**ooth-MAHN**), in 656, and the assassins nominated Ali, Muhammad's first cousin and the husband of his daughter Fatima, to succeed him, civil war broke out. Ali had been passed over three times previously, even though many people considered him to be the Prophet's natural heir. Those who believed Ali was the Prophet's heir came to be known as **Shi'ites**, after the Arabic term *Shi'at Ali* ("Party of Ali").

When Ali accepted the nomination to be caliph, two of Muhammad's close companions and his favorite wife A'isha challenged him. Ali defeated them in the Battle of the Camel (656), so called because the fighting raged around the camel on which A'isha was seated in an enclosed woman's saddle.

After the battle, the governor of Syria, Mu'awiya (**moo-AH-we-yuh**), a kinsman of the slain Uthman from the Umayya clan of the Quraysh, renewed the challenge. Inconclusive battle gave way to arbitration. The arbitrators decided that Uthman, whom his assassins considered corrupt, had not deserved death and that Ali had erred in accepting the caliphate. Ali rejected these findings, but before fighting could resume, one of his own supporters killed him for agreeing to

umma The community of all Muslims. A major innovation against the background of seventh-century Arabia, where traditionally kinship rather than faith had determined membership in a community.

caliphate Office established in succession to the Prophet Muhammad, to rule the Islamic empire; also the name of that empire.

Quran Book composed of divine revelations made to the Prophet Muhammad between around 610 and his death in 632; the sacred text of the religion of Islam.

Shi'ites Muslims belonging to the branch of Islam believing that God vests leadership of the community in a descendant of Muhammad's son-in-law Ali. Shi'ism is the state religion of Iran.

Section Review

- Islam emerged among the nomadic pastoralists and caravan traders of the Arabian peninsula.

- Mecca grew as a caravan city and pilgrimage site identified with Jewish and Christian stories.

- Muhammad experienced revelations that called people to submit to God's will.

- Facing hostility in Mecca, Muhammad and his followers fled to Medina, where they formed the umma.

- As caliph succeeding Muhammad, Abu Bakr confirmed the Five Pillars of Islam and ordered the composition of the Quran.

- Civil war within the umma resulted in the Sunni/Shi'ite division and the foundation of the Umayyad Caliphate.

the arbitration. Mu'awiya offered Ali's son Hasan a dignified retirement and thus emerged as caliph in 661.

Mu'awiya chose his own son, Yazid, to succeed him, thereby instituting the **Umayyad (oo-MY-ad) Caliphate**. When Hasan's brother Husayn revolted in 680 to reestablish the right of Ali's family to rule, Yazid ordered Husayn and his family killed. Sympathy for Husayn's martyrdom helped transform Shi'ism from a political movement into a religious sect.

Several variations in Shi'ite belief developed, but Shi'ites all agree that Ali was the rightful successor to Muhammad and that God's choice as Imam, leader of the Muslim community, has always been one or another of Ali's descendants. They see the caliphal office as more secular than religious. Because the Shi'ites seldom held power, their religious feelings came to focus on outpourings of sympathy for Husayn and other martyrs and on messianic dreams that one of their Imams would someday triumph.

Those Muslims who supported the first three caliphs gradually came to be called "People of Tradition and Community"—in Arabic, *Ahl al-Sunna wa'l-Jama'a*, **Sunnis** for short. Sunnis consider the caliphs to be Imams. As for Ali's followers who had abhorred his acceptance of arbitration, they evolved into small and rebellious Kharijite sects (from *kharaja*, meaning "to secede or rebel") claiming righteousness for themselves alone. These three divisions of Islam, the last now quite minor, still survive.

10-3 The Rise and Fall of the Caliphate, 632–1258

Was the Baghdad caliphate really the high point of Muslim civilization?

The Islamic caliphate built on the conquests the Arabs carried out after Muhammad's death gave birth to a dynamic and creative religious society. By the late 800s, however, one piece after another of this huge realm broke away. Yet the idea of a caliphate, however unrealistic, remains today a touchstone of Sunni belief in the unity of the umma and has proved effective as a political rallying point.

Sunni Islam never gave a single person the power to define true belief, expel heretics, and discipline clergy. Thus, unlike Christian popes and patriarchs, the caliphs had little basis for reestablishing their universal authority once they lost political and military power. Thus some current beliefs about a caliph's authority are recently invented.

10-3a The Islamic Conquests, 634–711

Arab conquests outside Arabia began under the second caliph, Umar (r. 634–644). Arab armies wrenched Syria (636) and Egypt (639–642) away from the Byzantine Empire and defeated the last Sasanid shah, Yazdigird III (r. 632–651). After a decade-long lull, expansion began again. Tunisia fell and became the governing center from which was organized, in 711, the conquest of Spain by an Arab-led army mostly composed of Berbers from North Africa. In the same year, Sind—the southern Indus Valley in today's Pakistan—succumbed to invaders from Iraq. The Muslim dominion remained roughly stable in size for three centuries until conquest began anew in the eleventh century. India and Anatolia then experienced invasions while sub-Saharan Africa and other regions saw Islam expand peacefully by trade and conversion.

Muhammad's close companions, men of political and economic sophistication inspired by his charisma, guided the conquests. The social structure and hardy nature of Arab society lent itself to flexible military operations; and the authority of Medina, reconfirmed during the caliphate of Abu Bakr, ensured obedience.

AP® Exam Tip Understand both the Umayyad and Abbasid methods of political control.

Umayyad Caliphate First hereditary dynasty of Muslim caliphs (661 to 750). From their capital at Damascus, the Umayyads ruled an empire that extended from Spain to India. Overthrown by the Abbasid Caliphate.

Sunnis Muslims belonging to branch of Islam believing that the community should select its own leadership. The majority religion in most Islamic countries.

The decision made during Umar's caliphate to prohibit Arabs from assuming ownership of conquered territory proved important. Umar tied army service, with its regular pay and windfalls of booty, to residence in military camps—two in Iraq (Kufa and Basra), one in Egypt (Fustat), and one in Tunisia (Qairawan). East of Iraq, Arabs settled around small garrison towns at strategic locations and in one large garrison at Marv in present-day Turkmenistan. This policy kept the armies together and ready for action and preserved normal life in the countryside, where some three-fourths of the population lived. Only a tiny proportion of the Syrian, Egyptian, Iranian, and Iraqi populations understood the Arabic language.

The million or so Arabs who participated in the conquests over several generations constituted a small, self-isolated ruling minority living on the taxes paid by a vastly larger non-Arab, non-Muslim subject population. The Arabs had little material incentive to encourage conversion, and there is no evidence of coherent missionary efforts to spread Islam during the conquest period (see Diversity & Dominance: Becoming Muslim).

10-3b The Umayyad and Early Abbasid Caliphates, 661–850

The Umayyad caliphs presided over an Arab realm rather than a religious empire. Ruling from Damascus, their armies consisted almost entirely of Muslim Arabs. Sasanid and Byzantine administrative practices continued in force. Only gradually did the caliphs replace non-Muslim secretaries and tax officials with Muslims and introduce Arabic as the language of government. Distinctively Muslim silver and gold coins introduced at the end of the seventh century symbolized the new order. Henceforward, silver dirhams and gold dinars bearing Arabic religious phrases circulated in monetary exchanges from Morocco to the frontiers of China.

The Umayyad dynasty fell in 750 after a decade of growing unrest. Converts to Islam numbered no more than 10 percent of the indigenous population, but they were still important because of the comparatively small number of Arab warriors. These converts resented Arab social domination. In addition, non-Syrian Arabs envied Syria's domination of caliphal affairs, and pious Muslims looked askance at the secular and even irreligious behavior of some caliphs. Finally, Shi'ites and Kharijites attacked the Umayyad family's legitimacy as Imams, launching a number of rebellions.

In 750 one rebellion, begun in 747 in the region of Khurasan (**kor-uh-SAHN**) in what is today northeastern Iran, overthrew the last Umayyad caliph, though one family member escaped to Spain to found an Umayyad principality there in 755. Many Shi'ites supported the rebellion, thinking they were fighting for the family of Ali. As it turned out, the family of Abbas, one of Muhammad's uncles, controlled the secret organization that coordinated the revolt. Upon victory they established the **Abbasid (ah-BASS-id) Caliphate**. Some of the Abbasid caliphs who ruled after 750 befriended their relatives in Ali's family, and one even flirted with transferring the caliphate to them. The Abbasid family, however, held on to the caliphate until 1258, when Mongol invaders killed the last of them in Baghdad (see Chapter 13).

Initially, the Abbasid dynasty made a fine show of leadership and piety. Theology and religious law became preoccupations at court and among a growing community of scholars devoted to interpreting the Quran, collecting the sayings of the Prophet, and compiling Arabic grammar. (In recent years, some Western scholars have maintained that the Quran, the sayings of the Prophet, and the biography of the Prophet were all composed around this time to provide a foundation myth for the regime. This reinterpretation of Islamic origins has not been generally accepted either in the scholarly community or among Muslims.) Some caliphs sponsored ambitious projects to translate great works of Greek, Persian, and Indian thought into Arabic.

With its roots among the semi-Persianized Arabs of Khurasan, the new dynasty gradually adopted the ceremonies and customs of the Sasanid shahs. Government grew increasingly complex in Baghdad, the newly built capital city on the Tigris River. As more non-Arabs converted to Islam, the ruling elite became more cosmopolitan. Greek, Iranian, Central Asian, and African cultural currents met in the capital and gave rise to an abundance of literary works, a process facilitated by the introduction of papermaking from China. Arab poets neglected the traditional odes extolling life in the desert and wrote instead wine songs (despite Islam's prohibition of alcohol) or poems in praise of their patrons.

The translation of Aristotle into Arabic, the founding of the main currents of theology and law, and the splendor of the Abbasid court—reflected in stories of *The Arabian Nights*

AP® Exam Tip
Describe the political changes within the Islamic world during this time period.

Abbasid Caliphate
Descendants of the Prophet Muhammad's uncle, Abbas, the Abbasids overthrew the Umayyad Caliphate and ruled an Islamic empire from their capital in Baghdad (founded 762) from 750 to 1258.

set in the time of the caliph Harun al-Rashid (hah-ROON al–rah-SHEED) (r. 776–809)—in some respects warrant calling the early Abbasid period a "golden age." Yet the refinement of Baghdad culture only slowly made its way into the provinces. Egypt remained predominantly Christian and Coptic-speaking in the early Abbasid period. Iran never adopted Arabic as a spoken tongue. Most of Berber-speaking North Africa rebelled and freed itself of direct caliphal rule after 740.

Gradual conversion to Islam among the conquered population accelerated in the second quarter of the ninth century. Social discrimination against non-Arab converts gradually faded, and the Arabs themselves—at least those living in cosmopolitan urban settings—lost their previously strong attachment to kinship and ethnic identity.

10-3c Political Fragmentation, 850–1050

Abbasid decline became evident in the second half of the ninth century as conversion to Islam accelerated (see Map 10.2). No government ruling so vast an empire could hold power easily. Caravans traveled only 20 miles (32 kilometers) a day, and the couriers of the caliphal post system usually did not exceed 100 miles (160 kilometers) a day. News of frontier revolts took weeks to reach Baghdad. Military responses might take months.

During the first two Islamic centuries, revolts against Muslim rule had been a concern. The Muslim umma had therefore clung together, despite the long distances. But with the growing conversion of the population to Islam, fears that Islamic dominion might be overthrown faded. Once they became the overwhelming majority, Muslims realized that a highly centralized empire did not necessarily serve the interests of all the people.

By the middle of the ninth century, revolts targeting Arab or Muslim domination gave way to movements within the Islamic community concentrating on seizure of territory and formation of principalities. None of the states carved out of the Abbasid Caliphate after that time repudiated or even threatened Islam. They did, however, cut the flow of tax revenues to Baghdad, thereby increasing local prosperity.

Increasingly starved for funds by breakaway provinces and by an unexplained fall in revenues from Iraq itself, the caliphate experienced a crisis in the late ninth century. Distrusting generals and troops from outlying areas, the caliphs purchased Turkic slaves, **mamluks** (MAM-luke), from Central Asia and established them as a standing army. Well trained and hardy, the Turks proved an effective but expensive military force. When the government could not pay them, the mamluks took it on themselves to seat and unseat caliphs, a process made easier by the construction of a new capital at Samarra, north of Baghdad on the Tigris River.

The Turks dominated Samarra without interference from an unruly Baghdad populace that regarded them as rude and high-handed. However, the money and effort that went into the huge city, which was occupied only from 835 to 892, further sapped the caliphs' financial strength and deflected labor from more productive pursuits.

In 945, after several attempts to find a strongman to save it, the Abbasid Caliphate fell under the control of rude mountain warriors from Daylam in northern Iran. Led by the Shi'ite Buyid (BOO-yid) family, they conquered western Iran as well as Iraq. Each Buyid commander ruled his own principality. After two centuries of glory, the sun began to set on Baghdad. The Abbasid caliph remained, but the Buyid princes controlled him. Being Shi'ites, the Buyids had no special reverence for the Sunni caliph. The Shi'ite teachings they followed held that the twelfth and last Imam had disappeared around 873 and would return as a messiah only at the end of time. Thus they had no Shi'ite Imam to defer to and retained the caliph only to help control their predominantly Sunni subjects.

Dynamic growth in outlying provinces paralleled the caliphate's gradual loss of temporal power. In the east in 875, the dynasty of the Samanids (sah-MAN-id), one of several Iranian families to achieve independence, established a glittering court in Bukhara, a major city on the Silk Road (see Map 10.2). Samanid princes patronized literature and learning, but the language they favored was Persian written in Arabic letters. For the first time, a non-Arabic literature rose to challenge the eminence of Arabic within the Islamic world.

In the west, the Berber revolts against Arab rule led to the appearance after 740 of the city-states of Sijilmasa (sih-jil-MAS-suh) and Tahert (TAH-hert) on the northern fringe of the Sahara. The Kharijite beliefs of these states' rulers interfered with their east–west overland trade and led them to develop the first regular trade across the Sahara desert (see Chapter 9).

AP® Exam Tip
Explain the changes and continuities of coerced labor systems (such as slavery) over time.

mamluks Under the Islamic system of military slavery, Turkic military slaves formed an important part of the armed forces of the Abbasid Caliphate of the ninth and tenth centuries. Mamluks eventually founded their own state, ruling Egypt and Syria (1250–1517).

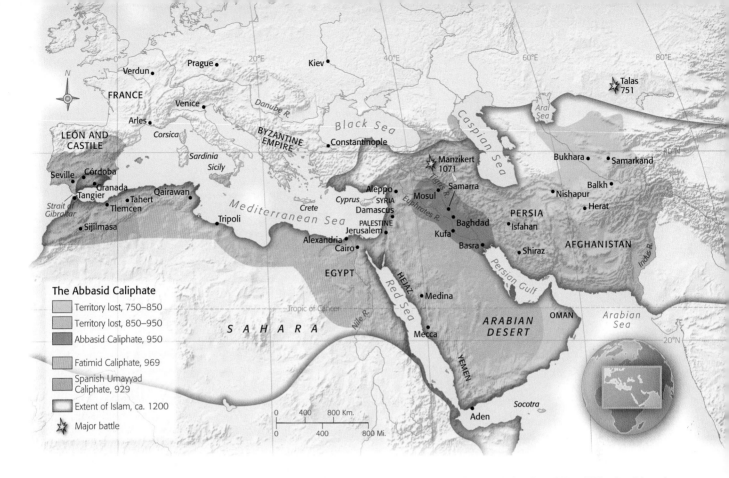

MAP 10.2 Rise and Fall of the Abbasid Caliphate Though Abbasid rulers occupied the caliphal seat in Iraq from 750 to 1258, when Mongol armies destroyed Baghdad, real political power waned sharply and steadily after 850. The rival caliphates of the Fatimids (909–1171) and Spanish Umayyads (929–976) were comparatively short-lived.

How does the fragmentation of the Abbasid Caliphate compare with that of the Roman Empire?

Once traders looked to the desert, they discovered that Berber speakers in the southern Sahara were already carrying salt from the desert into the Sahel region. The northern traders found that they could trade salt for gold by providing the southern nomads, who controlled the salt sources but had little use for gold, with more useful products, such as copper and manufactured goods. Sijilmasa and Tahert became wealthy cities, the former minting gold coins that circulated as far away as Egypt and Syria.

The earliest known sub-Saharan beneficiary of the new exchange system was the kingdom of **Ghana (GAH-nuh)**. It first appears in an Arabic text of the late eighth century as the "land of gold." Few details survive about the early years of this realm, which was established by the **Soninke (soh-NIN-kay)** people and covered parts of Mali, Mauritania, and Senegal, but it prospered until 1076, when it was conquered by nomads from the desert. It was one of the first lands outside the orbit of the caliphate to experience a gradual and peaceful conversion to Islam.

The North African city-states lost their independence after the Fatimid **(FAH-tuh-mid)** dynasty, whose members claimed (perhaps falsely) to be Shi'ite Imams descended from Ali, established itself in Tunisia in 909. After consolidating their hold on northwest Africa, the Fatimids culminated their rise to power by conquering Egypt in 969. Claiming the title of caliph in a direct challenge to the Abbasids, the Fatimid rulers governed from a palace complex outside the old conquest-era garrison city of Fustat **(fuss-TAHT)**. They named the complex Cairo. For the first time Egypt became a major cultural, intellectual, and political center of Islam. The abundance of Fatimid gold coinage, now channeled to Egypt from West Africa, made the Fatimids an economic power in the Mediterranean.

Cut off from the rest of the Islamic world by the Strait of Gibraltar and, from 740 onward, by independent city-states in Morocco and Algeria, Umayyad Spain developed a distinctive Islamic culture blending Roman, Germanic, and Jewish traditions with those of the Arabs and Berbers. Historians disagree on how rapidly and completely the Spanish population converted to Islam. If we assume a process similar to that in the eastern regions, it seems likely that the most rapid surge in Islamization occurred in the middle of the tenth century.

Ghana First known kingdom in sub-Saharan West Africa between the sixth and thirteenth centuries CE. Also the modern West African country once known as the Gold Coast.

▲ **Mosque of Ibn Tulun in Fustat** Completed in 877, this mosque symbolized Egypt becoming for the first time a quasi-independent province under its governor. The kiosk in the center of the courtyard contains fountains for washing before prayer. Before its restoration in the thirteenth century, the mosque had a spiral minaret and a door to an adjoining governor's palace. robertharding/Alamy Stock Photo

As in the east, governing cities symbolized the Islamic presence in al-Andalus, as the Muslims called their Iberian territories. Córdoba, Seville, Toledo, and other cities grew substantially, becoming much larger and richer than contemporary cities in neighboring France. Converts to Islam and their descendants, unconverted Arabic-speaking Christians, and Jews joined with the comparatively few descendants of Arab settlers to create new architectural and literary styles. In the countryside, where the Berbers preferred to settle, a fusion of preexisting agricultural technologies with new crops, notably citrus fruits, and irrigation techniques from the east gave Spain the most diverse and sophisticated agricultural economy in Europe.

The rulers of al-Andalus took the title *caliph* only in 929, when Abd al-Rahman **(AHB-d al–ruh-MAHN)** III (r. 912–961) did so in response to a similar declaration by the recently established (909) Fatimid ruler in Tunisia. By the century's end, however, this caliphate encountered challenges from breakaway movements that eventually splintered al-Andalus into a number of small states. Political decay did not impede cultural growth. Some of the greatest writers and thinkers in Jewish history worked in Muslim Spain in the eleventh and twelfth centuries, sometimes writing in Arabic, sometimes in Hebrew. Judah Halevi (1075–1141) composed exquisite poetry and explored questions of religious philosophy. Maimonides (1135–1204) made a major compilation of Judaic law and expounded on Aristotelian philosophy. At the same time, Islamic thought in Spain attained its loftiest peaks in Ibn Hazm's (994–1064) treatises on love and other subjects, the Aristotelian philosophical writings of Ibn Rushd **(IB-uhn RUSHED)** (1126–1198, known in Latin as Averroës [**uh-VERR-oh-eez**]) and Ibn Tufayl **(IB-uhn too-FILE)** (d. 1185), and the mystic speculations of Ibn al-Arabi **(IB-uhn ahl–AH-rah-bee)** (1165–1240). Christians, too, shared in the intellectual and cultural dynamism of al-Andalus. Translations from Arabic to Latin made during this period had a profound effect on the later intellectual development of western Europe (see Chapter 11).

The Samanids, Fatimids, and Spanish Umayyads, three of many regional principalities, represent the political diversity and awakening of local awareness that coincided with Abbasid decline. Yet drawing and redrawing political boundaries did not result in the rigid division of the

Islamic world into kingdoms. Religious and cultural developments, particularly the rise in cities of a social group of religious scholars known as the **ulama (oo-leh-MAH)**—Arabic for "people with (religious) knowledge"—worked against any permanent division of the Islamic umma.

10-3d Assault from Within and Without, 1050–1258

The role played by Turkish mamluks in the decline of Abbasid power established an enduring stereotype of the Turk as a ferocious, unsophisticated warrior. This image gained strength in 1036 when the Seljuk **(sel-JOOK)** family established a Turkish Muslim state based on nomadic power. Taking the Arabic title *Sultan*, meaning "power," and the revived Persian title *Shahan-shah*, or King of Kings, the Seljuk ruler Tughril **(TOOG-ruhl)** Beg created a kingdom that stretched from northern Afghanistan to Baghdad, which he occupied in 1055. After a century under the thumb of the Shi'ite Buyids, the Abbasid caliph breathed easier under the slightly lighter thumb of the Sunni Turks. The Seljuks pressed on into Syria and Anatolia, administering a lethal blow to Byzantine power at the Battle of Manzikert **(MANZ-ih-kuhrt)** in 1071. The Byzantine army fell back on Constantinople, leaving Anatolia open to Turkish occupation.

Under Turkish rule, which coincided with a severe climatic cooling that reduced harvests in Iran, Iraq, and eastern Anatolia, cities shrank as pastoralists overran their agricultural hinterlands. Irrigation works suffered from lack of maintenance in the unsettled countryside. Tax revenues fell. Quarreling twelfth-century princes fought over cities, but few Turks participated in urban cultural and religious life. The gulf between a religiously based urban society and the

AP® Exam Tip
Understand the patterns of urban revival and decline in this time period.

ulama Muslim religious scholars. From the ninth century onward, the primary interpreters of Islamic law and the social core of Muslim urban societies.

▲ **Tomb of the Samanids in Bukhara** This early-tenth-century structure has the basic layout of a Zoroastrian fire temple: a dome on top of a cube. However, geometric ornamentation in baked brick marks it as an early masterpiece of Islamic architecture. The Samanid family achieved independence as rulers of northeastern Iran and western Central Asia in the tenth century. Bridgeman-Giraudon/Art Resource, NY

▲ **Spanish Muslim Textile of the Twelfth Century** This fragment of woven silk, featuring peacocks and Arabic writing, is one of the finest examples of Islamic weaving. The cotton industry flourished in the early Islamic centuries, but silk remained a highly valued product. Some fabrics were treasured in Christian Europe. Werner Forman / HIP / The Image Works

culture and personnel of the government deepened. When factional riots broke out between Sunnis and Shi'ites, or between rival schools of Sunni law, rulers generally remained aloof, even as destruction and loss of life mounted.

By the early twelfth century, unrepaired damage from floods, fires, and civil disorder had reduced old Baghdad on the west side of the Tigris to ruins. The withering of Baghdad reflected a broader environmental problem: the collapse of the canal system on which agriculture in the Tigris and Euphrates Valley depended. For millennia a center of world civilization, Mesopotamia underwent substantial population loss and never again regained its geographical importance.

The Turks alone cannot be blamed for the demographic and economic misfortunes of Iran and Iraq. Too-robust urbanization, spurred largely by a boom in Iranian cotton production, resulted in strained food resources when the climate deteriorated after 1000. Baghdad, a city with a torrid climate today, experienced heavy winter snowfalls that killed date trees. In addition, the growing practice of paying soldiers and courtiers with land grants led to absentee landlords using agents to collect taxes. These agents gouged villagers to meet their quotas and took little interest in improving production, thus intensifying the agricultural crisis.

Internecine feuding was preoccupying the Seljuk family when the first Christian Crusaders reached the Holy Land and captured Jerusalem in 1099 (see Chapter 11). Though charged with the stuff of romance, the Crusades had little lasting impact on the Islamic lands. The four Crusader principalities of Edessa, Antioch, Tripoli, and Jerusalem simply became pawns in the shifting pattern of politics already in place. Newly arrived knights eagerly attacked the Muslim enemy, whom they called "Saracens" **(SAR-uh-suhn)**; but veteran Crusaders recognized that practicing diplomacy and seeking partners of convenience among rival Muslim princes offered a sounder strategy.

The Muslims finally unified to face the European enemy in the mid-twelfth century. Nur al-Din ibn Zangi **(NOOR uhd–DEEN ib-uhn ZAN-gee)** established a strong state based in Damascus and sent an army to terminate the Fatimid Caliphate in Egypt. A nephew of the Kurdish commander of that expedition, Salah-al-Din, known in the West as Saladin, took advantage of Nur al-Din's timely death to seize power and unify Egypt and Syria. The Fatimid dynasty fell in 1171. In 1187 Saladin recaptured Jerusalem from the Europeans. He then took the title Khadim al-Haramain **(KAH-dim al-ha-ra-MAYN)**, literally "Servant of the Two Holy Places," meaning Mecca and Medina, in a challenge to the caliph's claim to be the paramount Sunni potentate. Revitalizing the pilgrimage became a core concern for later rulers in Egypt and Syria, particularly after the termination of the Baghdad caliphate in 1258. Today the King of Saudi Arabia, who is not a caliph, bears the same title.

Saladin's descendants fought off subsequent Crusades. After one such battle, however, in 1250, Turkish mamluk troops seized control of the government in Cairo, ending Saladin's dynasty. In 1260 these mamluks rode east to confront a new invading force. At the Battle of Ain Jalut **(ine jah-LOOT)** (Spring of Goliath) in Syria, they met and defeated an army of Mongols from Central Asia (see Chapter 13), thus stemming an invasion that had begun several decades before and legitimizing their claim to dominion over Egypt and Syria.

During the ensuing Mamluk period a succession of slave-soldier sultans ruled Egypt and Syria until 1517. Fear of new Mongol attacks receded after 1300, but by then the new ruling system had become fixed. Young Turkish or Circassian slaves, the latter from the eastern end of the Black Sea, were imported from non-Muslim lands, raised in training barracks, and converted to Islam. Owing loyalty to the Mamluk officers who purchased them, they formed a military class that was socially disconnected from the Arabic-speaking native population.

The Mongol invasions, especially their destruction of the Abbasid Caliphate in Baghdad in 1258, shocked the world of Islam. The Mamluk sultan enthroned a relative of the last Baghdad caliph in Cairo, but the Egyptian Abbasids were mere puppets serving Mamluk interests. From Iraq eastward, non-Muslim rule lasted for much of the thirteenth century. Although the Mongols left few ethnic or linguistic traces in these lands, their initial destruction of cities and slaughter of civilian populations, their diversion of Silk Road trade from Baghdad to more northerly routes ending at Black Sea ports, and their casual disregard, even after conversion to Islam, for Muslim religious life and urban culture hastened currents of change already under way.

10-4 Islamic Civilization

How did regional diversity affect the development of Islamic civilization?

Though increasingly unsettled in its political dimension and subject to economic disruptions caused by war, the ever-expanding Islamic world underwent a fruitful evolution in law, social structure, and religious expression. Religious conversion and urbanization reinforced each other to create a distinct Islamic civilization. The immense geographical and human diversity of the Muslim lands allowed many "small traditions" to coexist with the developing "great tradition" of Islam.

10-4a Law and Dogma

The Shari'a, the law of Islam, provides the foundation of Islamic civilization. Yet aside from certain Quranic verses conveying specific divine ordinances—most pertaining to personal and family matters—Islam had no legal system in the time of Muhammad. Arab custom and the Prophet's own authority offered the only guidance. After Muhammad died, the umma tried to follow his example. This became harder and harder to do, however, as those who knew Muhammad best passed away and many Arabs found themselves living in far-off lands. Non-Arab converts to Islam, who at first tried to follow Arab customs they had little familiarity with, had an even harder time.

Islam slowly developed laws to govern social and religious life. The full sense of Islamic civilization, however, goes well beyond the basic Five Pillars mentioned earlier. Some Muslim thinkers felt that the reasoned consideration of a mature man offered the best resolution of issues not covered by Quranic revelation. Others argued for the *sunna*, or tradition, of the Prophet as the best guide. To understand the sunna, they collected and studied thousands of reports, called **hadith (hah-DEETH)**, purporting to convey the precise words or deeds of Muhammad. It became customary to precede each hadith with a chain of oral authorities leading back to the person who had direct acquaintance with the Prophet.

Many hadith dealt with ritual matters, such as how to wash before prayer. Others provided answers to legal questions not covered by Quranic revelation or suggested principles for deciding such matters. By the eleventh century most legal thinkers had accepted the idea that Muhammad's personal behavior provided the best role model and that the hadith constituted the most authoritative basis for law after the Quran itself.

Yet the hadith posed a problem because the tens of thousands of anecdotes included both genuine and invented reports, the latter sometimes politically motivated, as well as stories derived from non-Muslim religious traditions. Only a specialist could hope to separate a sound from a weak tradition. As the hadith grew in importance, so did the branch of learning devoted to their analysis. Scholars discarded thousands for having faulty chains of authority. The most reliable they collected into books that gradually achieved authoritative status. Sunnis placed six books in this category; Shi'ites, four.

As it gradually evolved, the Shari'a embodied a vision of an umma in which all subscribed to the same moral values and political and ethnic distinctions lost importance. Every Muslim ruler was expected to abide by and enforce the religious law. In practice, this expectation often lost out in the hurly-burly of political life. But the Shari'a proved an important basis for an urban lifestyle that varied surprisingly little from Morocco to India.

Section Review

- By 711, Arab armies had conquered an empire stretching from Sind in the east to Spain in the west.

- The Umayyad caliphs ruled an ethnic empire; they governed from Damascus using Sasanid and Byzantine administrative methods.

- The Umayyads fell to rebels who established the Abbasid Caliphate at Baghdad, while surviving Umayyads fled to Spain.

- Influenced by Persian culture, the Abbasids presided over significant spiritual, intellectual, and artistic activity.

- Abbasid decline led to fragmentation of the caliphate into independent states, but the Islamic umma remained intact.

- Political divisions continued as successor states to the former caliphate fell, replaced by Seljuk Turk, Crusader, Mamluk, and Mongol states.

AP® Exam Tip
Explain how the expansion of the Islamic empire incorporated new peoples and understand the impact of expansion on trade and communication.

hadith A tradition relating the words or deeds of the Prophet Muhammad; next to the Quran, the most important basis for Islamic law.

10-4b **Converts and Cities**

Conversion to Islam, more the outcome of people's learning about the new rulers' religion than an escape from the tax on non-Muslims, as some scholars have suggested, helped spur urbanization. Conversion did not require extensive knowledge of the faith. To become a Muslim, a person simply stated, in the presence of a Muslim: "There is no God but God, and Muhammad is the Messenger of God."

Few converts spoke Arabic, and fewer could read the Quran. Many converts knew no more of the Quran than the verses they memorized for daily prayers. Muhammad had established no priesthood to define and spread the faith. Thus new converts, whether Arab or non-Arab, faced the problem of finding out for themselves what Islam was about and how they should act as Muslims. This meant spending time with Muslims, learning their language, and imitating their practices.

In many areas, conversion involved migrating to an Arab governing center. The alternative, converting to Islam but remaining in one's home community, was difficult because religion had become the main component of social identity in Byzantine and Sasanid times. Converts to Islam thus encountered discrimination if they stayed in their Christian, Jewish, or Zoroastrian communities. Migration both averted discrimination and took advantage of the economic opportunities opened up by tax revenues flowing into the Arab governing centers.

The Arab military settlements of Kufa and Basra in Iraq blossomed into cities and became important centers for Muslim cultural activities. As conversion rapidly spread in the mid-ninth century, urbanization accelerated in other regions, most visibly in Iran, where most cities previously had been quite small. Nishapur in the northeast grew from fewer than 20,000 pre-Islamic inhabitants to between 100,000 and 200,000 by the year 1000. Other Iranian cities experienced similar growth. In Iraq, Baghdad and Mosul joined Kufa and Basra as major cities. In Syria, Aleppo and Damascus flourished under Muslim rule. Fustat in Egypt developed into Cairo, one

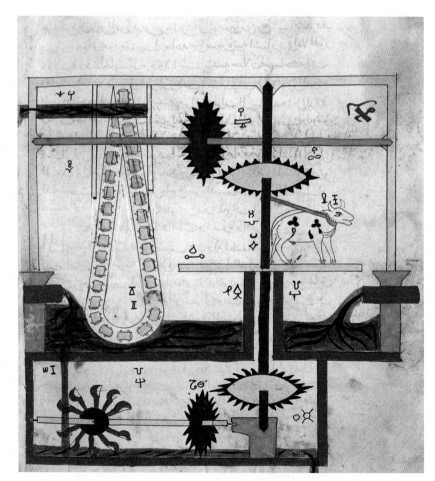

▶ **Model of a Water-Lifting Device** The artist's effort to render a three-dimensional construction in two dimensions shows a talent for schematic drawing. The cow is a dummy in this automaton. Actual power comes from the cupped blades of a waterwheel in a river, concealed in the red box at the bottom of the picture. DEA / G. DAGLI ORTI/ De Agostini/Getty Images

of the largest and greatest Islamic cities. The primarily Christian patriarchal cities of Jerusalem, Antioch, and Alexandria, not being Muslim governing centers, shrank and stagnated.

Conversion-related migration meant that cities became heavily Muslim before the country-side did. This reinforced the urban orientation deriving from the fact that Muhammad and his first followers came from the commercial city of Mecca. Mosques in large cities served both as ritual centers and as places for learning and social activities.

Islam colored all aspects of urban social life. Initially the new Muslims imitated Arab dress and customs, particularly favoring plain linen or cotton over the silk brocade of the non-Muslim Iranian elite, and emulated people they regarded as particularly pious. In the absence of a central religious authority, local variations developed in the way people practiced Islam and in the hadith they attributed to the Prophet. This gave the rapidly growing religion the flexibility to accommodate many different social situations.

By the tenth century, urban growth was affecting the countryside by expanding the consumer market. Citrus fruits, rice, and sugar cane, introduced by the Sasanids, increased in acreage and spread to new areas. Cotton became a major crop in Iran and elsewhere and stimulated textile production. Irrigation works expanded. Abundant coinage facilitated a flourishing intercity and long-distance trade that provided regular links between isolated districts and integrated the pastoral nomads, who provided pack animals, into the region's economy. Trade encouraged the manufacture of cloth, metal goods, and pottery.

Science and technology also flourished (see Environment & Technology: Chemistry). Building on Hellenistic traditions and their own observations and experience, Muslim doctors and astronomers developed skills and theories far in advance of their European counterparts. Working in Egypt in the eleventh century, mathematician and physicist Ibn al-Haytham **(IB-uhn al–HY–tham)** wrote more than a hundred works. Among other things, he determined that the Milky Way lies far beyond Earth's atmosphere, proved that light travels from a seen object to the eye and not the reverse, and explained why the Sun and Moon appear larger on the horizon than overhead.

AP® Exam Tip
Identify examples of crops that diffused throughout the Eastern Hemisphere under the Islamic empire.

▲ **Women Playing Chess in Muslim Spain** As shown in this thirteenth-century miniature, women in their own quarters, without men present, wore whatever clothes and jewels they liked. Notice the henna decorating the hands of the woman in the middle. The woman on the left, probably a slave, plays an oud. Album / Art Resource, NY

Islam, Christianity, and Buddhism enjoyed great success in gaining believers over long stretches of time and place. Writing the history of that success poses problems, however, especially in their earliest moments. Each religious tradition has assembled a mass of often inconsistent or exaggerated traditions regarding how they won over their first believers, most often focusing on individual preachers, missionaries, and scripture translators whom they credit with bringing the faith to this or that people. Some individual conversion stories are also cited, usually concerning intellectuals or saintly individuals who told their stories to followers,

Details about how conversion came about for ordinary individuals are rare, however. This is particularly true of Islam, which achieved political dominion long before the non-Arab mass of the Caliph's subjects joined the faith of the rulers. For the earliest period, what those stories say speaks less to some particular doctrinal or ritual appeal that Islam had than to the particular circumstances of the convert.

Military matters are important, but not, as was once commonly believed, because of Muslim armies offering vanquished peoples a choice between conversion or the sword.

Of a commander in the army of the defeated Sasanid shah it is reported:

"When he saw the appearance of Islam and the glory of its people, and that Sus [an Iranian city] had been conquered, and the continuous flow of supplies to [the Arab commander] Abu Musa, he sent a message to him: 'We would like to enter with you in your religion so that we may fight your Iranian enemies with you.'"

Of an Iranian notable named Sul:

"Sul said to [the Arab commander] Yazid ibn al-Muhallab at the time Jurjan [in Iran] was conquered: 'Is there in Islam someone more illustrious than you at whose hands I might convert to Islam?' Yazid replied: 'Yes, Sulaiman ibn Abd al-Malik [Umayyad caliph ruling 715–717].' Sul said: 'Then dispatch me to him so I can convert to Islam at his hands,' So he did. When Sul arrived, he said to Sulaiman what he had said to Yazid. Then Sulaiman said: 'There is not now among the Muslims anyone more illustrious than I, but the tomb of the Messenger of God . . . is moreso.' 'Then I shall convert to Islam there,' said Sul. So Sulaiman sent him to Medina, and he converted to Islam at that tomb. The he returned to Yazid ibn al-Muhallab and became his companion and managed his expenditures until Salma ibn Abd al-Malik killed him on the day of al-Aqr when he killed Yazid ibn al-Muhallab."

Enslaved prisoners-of-war converted to gain their freedom. Of one eminent Muslim citizen of the city of Isfahan it is reported:

"His father . . . was from Burkhuwar, from the village of Falumiya. His grandfather had been taken prisoner by the Dailamis [marauders from northern Iran]. Then the troops of [the Arab general] Abu Musa engaged the Dailamis and took them prisoner along with the prisoners already with them. [His grandfather] fell in the lot [of prisoners] distributed [as booty] to the warriors of the Murra ibn Hamdan kin group. So he converted to Islam with them and settled in Kufa [in Iraq]. After a long time he returned to his country and his estate, which was still remaining."

Another founder of a major Muslim family in Isfahan:

"Mushkan was originally from Isfahan. When captivity was imminent, his mother took her son, who had earrings in his ears, and placed him in the house of a weaver so that he would not be recognized. For he was entitled Prince . . . . So he was taken prisoner from the house of that weaver and it was afterwards said that he was his son."

Stories may also reflect specific rich and influential targets for conversion:

"Abd Allah [a non-Arab partly of Turkish origin who died in 797] came to Nishapur [in northeastern Iran] and lived on Isa [Jesus] street. He used to see a striking young man ride by. He was the son of Isa ibn Masarjis." [The name Masarjis should be understood as Mar Sergius, or Bishop Sergius, and the street was probably named for him.] "Abd Allah discovered that the young man was a Christian so he called him to Islam, and his prayer was answered. The young man adopted the name Abu Ali al-Hasan, and in the next generation the Masarjis family became one of the leading families of Nishapur. Abu Ali's son was able to loan a million silver coins to the city's governor, Abd Allah b. Tahir."

Occasionally there is a broad, but not necessarily believable, claim of mass conversion:

"Abu Ja'far al-Thumi is the one who called the people of Gilan [in northern Iran] to Islam, and they converted at his hands. All of those among the Gilanis who are on the path of the Sunna are his followers."

10-4c Women and Islam

Women seldom traveled. Those living in rural areas worked in the fields and tended animals. Urban women, particularly members of the elite, lived in seclusion and did not leave their homes without covering themselves. Seclusion of women and veiling in public already existed in Byzantine and Sasanid times. Through interpretation of specific verses from the Quran, these practices now became fixtures of Muslim social life. Although women sometimes became literate and studied with relatives, they did so away from the gaze of unrelated men, and while they played influential roles within the family, public roles were generally barred. Only slave women could

By the beginning of the fourth Islamic century, 150 to 200 years after these stories, conversion was occurring so rapidly that unscrupulous tricksters pretended to be brand new converts in order to solicit welcoming gifts from local Muslim communities. Evidence of religion by this time focused on scriptures. A poem specifying the activities of a guild of beggars, street entertainers, and tricksters includes the following two:

"And of our [guild] is every qanna', who recites volubly from the Gospel and the Warning . . . A qanna' is the person who recites the Torah and the Gospel and leads people to believe that he was formerly a Jew or Christian, but has converted to Islam."

"And the one who claims to be a convert from the People of the Book (qanwana) . . . A qanwana is the person who says 'my father was a Christian and my mother was a Jew. The Prophet . . . appeared to me in a dream and said, "don't be deluded any longer by the faiths of your parents; follow my religion!" So I became a Muslim."

The rarest type of story raises questions as to how much new converts knew about Islamic belief and the contents of the Quran. The following narrative deals with a man named Abu Taiba Isa [Jesus] who founded one of the leading Muslim families in the Iranian city of Jurjan:

"The story of Dinar, the grandfather of Abu Taiba Isa, is that he was a rural landowner from Marv [in Turkmenistan]. He was taken prisoner during [a] raid on Khurasan . . . and fell into the part of the booty that went to a man named Ja'far b. Khirfash. . . . He lived with him for a time, and [Ja'far] manumitted him. Ja'far died without any heir other than Dinar, so [Dinar] took possession of [Ja'far's] wealth. Then he married and a son Sulaiman [Solomon] was born to him . . . Sulaiman left Marv for Juzjanan [in Afghanistan] and settled. There he married a woman named Talha, and she bore him a son Musa [Moses]. . . . Later, while pregnant with Abu Taiba Isa, she had a dream: a chain dangled down from the sky to the earth where a group of people was standing. They jumped at it to grab it, but they couldn't reach it. Then her son, who was in her womb, jumped [and on his third jump] he caught it. As if it were a dust cloud it lifted, and [her husband] Sulaiman was wrapped up in its folds and raised into the sky. After this happened, she told her dream to her husband. He said to her: 'If your dream is true, you will give birth to a virtuous son . . . and I shall be granted martyrdom, if God wills.'

"Later, the people of Juzjanan were struck by famine and a cessation of heavy rains. They went out in the desert to pray for rain,

and it rained. It became known in the city that God had granted them rain through Sulaiman. The people came to him and blessed him. But a governor . . . denied this and threw Sulaiman in jail. Then the people of the city became angry . . . They expelled their governor from the city and freed Sulaiman from prison. They said to . . . their governor, 'You have oppressed a man through whom God has granted us rain and imprisoned him . . .' So he promised he would not repeat such an action, and they took him back as their governor.

"Immediately Sulaiman went out on a raid with ten of his young men. . . . He encountered one of the Turks and they fell into battle. He and nine of his followers were killed. One was left, and brought the news back to [his] wife and son.

Sulaiman's wife Talha stayed in Juz[ja]nan until Abu Taiba reached puberty. When it was a Friday and he was free from school, he used to hide from his mother so she couldn't see him. She condemned this activity and followed him one Friday until he came to a thicket. There he stood and performed devotions. So she returned home, When it was evening and her son came home, she said to him: 'I saw your place, and I am frightened for you because there might be a lion in the thicket. I will not permit you to go there.' He replied: 'Since you know my place, there is no need for me to go there.' And after that he performed his devotions in the courtyard.

When he reached the age of reason, [Abu Taiba] went away to seek knowledge. . . . He encountered the army of Yazid ibn al-Muhallab [d. 720] and met in it [the saintly ascetic] Kurz ibn Wabra. He became his companion up until the army conquered Gorgan. He marked out the place for his house in Gorgan and settled there."

These passages raise so many questions: Was Abu Taiba's mother actually a Christian? Were the people who revered his father Sulaiman Muslims? Why are Abu Taiba's youthful actions called "devotions" instead of "prayers"?

AP® History Reasoning Skills

Comparison *How did conversion to Islam differ from conversion to Christianity or Buddhism? How were conversions similar?*

Sources: Richard W. Bulliet, "Conversion Stories in Early Islam," in Michael Gervers and Ramzi Jibran Bikhazi, eds., *Conversion and Continuity: Indigenous Christian Communities in Islamic Lands Eighth to Eighteenth Centuries* (Papers in Mediaeval Studies 9) (Toronto, ON: Pontifical Institute of Mediaeval Studies, 1990), 123–133; Richard W. Bulliet, *Islam: The View from the Edge* (New York, NY: Columbia University Press, 1994), 47–53.

perform before unrelated men as musicians and dancers. A man could have sexual relations with as many slave concubines as he pleased, in addition to marrying as many as four wives.

Muslim women fared better legally under Islamic law than did Christian and Jewish women under their respective religious codes. Because Islamic law guaranteed daughters a share in inheritance equal to half that of a son, the majority of urban women inherited some amount of money or real estate. This remained their private property to keep or sell. Muslim law put the financial burden of supporting a family exclusively on the husband, who could not legally compel his wife to help out.

AP® Exam Tip
Evaluate the extent to which ideologies, philosophies, and religions affected social hierarchies, such as the role of women in Islamic societies.

Women could also remarry if their husbands divorced them, and they received a cash payment upon divorce. Although a man could divorce his wife without stating a cause, a woman could initiate divorce under specified conditions. Women could also practice birth control. They could testify in court, although their testimony counted as half that of a man. They could go on pilgrimage. Nevertheless, a misogynistic tone sometimes appears in Islamic writings. One saying attributed to the Prophet observed: "I was raised up to heaven and saw that most of its denizens were poor people; I was raised into the hellfire and saw that most of its denizens were women."[3]

In the absence of writings by women about women from this period, the status of women must be deduced from the writings of men. Two episodes involving the Prophet's wife A'isha, the daughter of Abu Bakr, provide examples of how Muslim men appraised women in society. Only eighteen when Muhammad died, A'isha lived for another fifty years. Early reports stress her status as Muhammad's favorite, the only virgin he married and the only wife to see the angel Gabriel. These reports emanate from A'isha herself, who was an abundant source of hadith. As a fourteen-year-old she had become separated from a caravan and rejoined it only after traveling through the night with a man who found her alone in the desert. Gossips accused her of being untrue to the Prophet, but a revelation from God proved her innocence. The second event was her participation in the Battle of the Camel, fought to derail Ali's caliphate. These two episodes came to epitomize what Muslim men feared most about women: sexual infidelity and meddling in politics. Even though the earliest literature dealing with A'isha stresses her position as Muhammad's favorite, his first wife, Khadija, and his daughter, Ali's wife Fatima, eventually surpassed A'isha as ideal women. Both appear as model wives and mothers with no suspicion of sexual irregularity or political manipulation.

10-4d Marginal Communities

As the seclusion of women became commonplace in urban Muslim society, some writers extolled homosexual relationships, partly because a male lover could appear in public or go on a journey. Although Islam deplored homosexuality, one ruler wrote a book advising his son to follow moderation in all things and thus share his affections equally between men and women. Another ruler and his slave-boy became models of perfect love in the verses of mystic poets.

AP® Exam Tip
Explain how and why labor systems (including slavery) developed and changed over time.

Islam allowed slavery but forbade Muslims from enslaving other Muslims or so-called People of the Book—Jews, Christians, and Zoroastrians, who revered holy books respected by the Muslims. Being enslaved as a prisoner of war, a fate that befell many women captured in the camps of defeated armies, constituted an exception. Later centuries saw a constant flow of slaves into Islamic territory from Africa and Central Asia. A hereditary slave society, however, did not develop. Usually slaves converted to Islam, and many masters then freed them as an act of piety. The offspring of slave women and Muslim men were born free.

10-4e The Recentering of Islam

Early Islam centered on the caliphate, the political expression of the unity of the umma. No formal organization or hierarchy, however, directed the process of conversion. Thus there emerged a multitude of local Islamic communities so disconnected from each other that numerous competing interpretations of the developing religion arose. Inevitably, the centrality of the caliphate diminished (see Map 10.2). The appearance of rival caliphates in Tunisia and Córdoba accentuated the problem of decentralization.

The rise of the ulama as community leaders did not prevent growing fragmentation because the ulama themselves divided into contentious factions. During the twelfth century factionalism began to abate, and new socioreligious institutions, including a revitalized pilgrimage to Mecca, emerged to provide the umma with a different sort of religious center. These new developments stemmed in part from an exodus of religious scholars from Iran in response to economic and political disintegration during the late eleventh and twelfth centuries. The flow of Iranians to the Arab lands and to newly conquered territories in India and Anatolia increased after the Mongol invasion.

[3]Richard W. Bulliet, *Islam: The View from the Edge* (New York, NY: Columbia University Press, 1994), 87.

Environment & Technology
Chemistry

Muslim scientists developed sophisticated chemical processes and used them to produce a broad range of goods, including glazes for pottery, rosewater (the distilled essence of roses), hard soap, gunpowder, and various types of glass. The words *chemistry* and *alchemy* are both related to the Arabic term for these activities, *al-kimiya*, and many chemical processes passed from the Muslim world to Europe.

Distillation was used at Baku in Azerbaijan to produce a light flammable liquid called "white *naft*," roughly equivalent to kerosene, from crude oil. Special military units wearing fire-resistant clothing were trained to use white *naft* as an incendiary weapon. Flaming liquids, whose exact composition is still uncertain, could be put into pots and thrown, placed in containers attached to arrows, or pumped from a tube.

Questions for Analysis

1. How did easy access to crude oil contribute to the chemical undertakings of medieval Muslim societies?

2. Why in the age of the Caliphate were oil products like kerosene not widely used for heating, light, and cooking in place of vegetable oil and charcoal?

3. Why do so many Arabic words for chemicals and chemical processes show up in European languages?

◄ **Islamic Glassware** This glass bottle from Syria shows the skill of Muslim chemists and artisans in producing clear, transparent glass. The scratched decoration reflects the Muslim taste for geometric design. Collection of The Corning Museum of Glass, 68.1.1

Fully versed in Arabic as well as their native Persian, immigrant scholars were warmly received. They brought with them a view of religion developed in Iran's urban centers. A type of religious college, the *madrasa* (**MAH-dras-uh**), gained sudden popularity outside Iran, where madrasas had been known since the tenth century. Scores of madrasas, many founded by local rulers, appeared throughout the Islamic world. In the fourteenth century, Mecca became a major educational center for the first time since Muhammad's generation.

Iranians also contributed to the growth of mystic groups known as *Sufi* brotherhoods in the twelfth and thirteenth centuries. The doctrines and rituals of certain Sufis spread from city to city, giving rise to the first geographically extensive Islamic religious organizations. Sufi doctrines varied, but a quest for a sense of union with God through rituals and training was a common aspiration. Sufism had begun in early Islamic times and had doubtless benefited from the ideas and beliefs of people from religions with mystic traditions who converted to Islam.

The early Sufis had been saintly individuals given to ecstatic and poetic utterances and wonder-working. They

▶ **Quran Page Printed from a Woodblock** Printing from woodblocks or tin plates existed in Islamic lands between approximately 800 and 1400. Most prints were narrow amulets designed to be rolled and worn around the neck in cylindrical cases. Less valued than handwritten amulets, many prints came from Banu Sasan con men. Why block-printing had so little effect on society in general and eventually disappeared is unknown.

Reproduced by kind permission of the Syndics of Cambridge University Library, Michaelides (charta) E.32

Section Review

- The foundation of Islamic civilization is the Shari'a, which is derived from the Quran and hadith.

- Urbanization and religious conversion reinforced each other and prompted the expansion of agriculture, trade, science, and technology.

- Women in general enjoyed relatively high status under Islamic law, though urban women tended to live in seclusion.

- Islamic attitudes toward homosexuality were ambivalent, and slavery was an accepted and continuous practice.

- Migrations of Iranian scholars centered Islam on the madrasa and contributed to the rise of Sufism.

attracted disciples but did not try to organize them. The growth of brotherhoods, a less ecstatic form of Sufism, set a tone for society in general. It soon became common for most Muslim men, particularly in the cities, to belong to at least one brotherhood.

A sense of the social climate the Sufi brotherhoods fostered can be gained from a twelfth-century manual:

Every limb has its own special ethics.... The ethics of the tongue. The tongue should always be busy in reciting God's names (dhikr) and in saying good things of the brethren, praying for them, and giving them counsel.... The ethics of hearing. One should not listen to indecencies and slander.... The ethics of sight. One should lower one's eyes in order not to see forbidden things.[4]

Special dispensations allowed people who merely wanted to emulate the Sufis and enjoy their company to follow less demanding rules:

It is allowed by way of dispensation to possess an estate or to rely on a regular income. The Sufis' rule in this matter is that one should not use all of it for himself, but should dedicate this to public charities and should take from it only enough for one year for himself and his family....

There is a dispensation allowing one to watch all kinds of amusement. This is, however, limited by the rule: What you are forbidden from doing, you are also forbidden from watching.[5]

Some Sufi brotherhoods spread in the countryside, and local shrines and pilgrimages to the tombs of Muhammad's descendants and saintly Sufis became popular.

10-5 Conclusion

The Sasanid Empire that held sway in Iran and Iraq from the third to the seventh century resembled the contemporary realm of the eastern Roman emperors ruling from Constantinople. Both states forged strong relations between the ruler and the dominant religion, Zoroastrianism in the former empire, Christianity in the latter. Priestly hierarchies paralleled state administrative structures, and the citizenry came to think of themselves more as members of a faith community than as subjects of a ruler. This gave rise to conflict among religious sects and also raised the possibility of the founder of a new religion commanding both political and religious loyalty on an unprecedented scale. This possibility was realized in the career of the prophet Muhammad in the seventh century.

Islam culminated the trend toward identity based on religion. The concept of the umma united all Muslims in a universal community embracing enormous diversity of language, appearance, and social custom. Though Muslim communities adapted to local "small traditions," by the twelfth century a religious scholar could travel anywhere in the Islamic world and blend easily into the local Muslim community.

By the ninth century, the forces of conversion and urbanization fostered social and religious experimentation in urban settings. From the eleventh century onward, political disruption, the spread of pastoral nomadism, and climatic deterioration slowed this early economic and technological dynamism. Muslim communities then turned to new religious institutions, such as the madrasas and Sufi brotherhoods, to create the flexible and durable community structures that carried Islam into new regions and protected ordinary believers from capricious political rule.

---

[4]Abu Najib al-Suhrawardi, *A Sufi Rule for Novices*, trans. Menahem Milson (Cambridge, MA: Harvard University Press, 1975), 45–58.

[5]Ibid., 73–82.

Key Terms

Sasanid Empire p. 246	**Medina** p. 250	**Umayyad Caliphate** p. 252	**ulama** p. 257
Mecca p. 249	**umma** p. 251	**Sunnis** p. 252	**hadith** p. 259
Muhammad p. 249	**caliphate** p. 251	**Abbasid Caliphate** p. 253	
Muslim p. 250	**Quran** p. 251	**mamluks** p. 254	
Islam p. 250	**Shi'ites** p. 251	**Ghana** p. 255	

Review Questions

1. What are the main differences between Judaism, Christianity, and Islam, all stemming from common, though not identical, scriptural foundations?

2. Are comparisons with the imperial structures of Rome and Han China useful for understanding the Islamic Caliphate?

3. How does everyday life in the Muslim world before 1000 resemble Middle Eastern societies of the pre-Roman era?

 MINDTAP From Cengage   MindTap® is a fully online, personalized learning experience built upon Cengage Learning content. MindTap® combines student learning tools—readings, multimedia, activities, and assessments—into a singular Learning Path that guides students through the course and helps students develop the critical thinking, analysis, and communication skills that are essential to academic and professional success.

AP® REVIEW QUESTIONS FOR CHAPTER 10

Multiple-Choice Questions

Questions 1–3 refer to the passage below.

"This divine writ [the Qur'an]—let there be no doubt about it—is [meant to be] a guidance for all the God-conscious who believe in [the existence of] that which is beyond the reach of human perception, and are constant in prayer, and spend on others out of what We provide for them as sustenance; and who believe in that which has been bestowed from on high upon thee, [O Prophet,] as well as in that which was bestowed before thy time. . . . Verily, those who have attained to faith, as well as those who follow the Jewish faith, and the Christians . . . —all who believe in God and the Last Day and do righteous deeds—shall have their reward with their Sustainer [God]; and no fear need they have, and neither shall they grieve."

Qur'an, Surah 2

1. According to the passage from the Qur'an, the Prophet Muhammad

    (A) was the only one to be ever chosen to spread the message from God.

    (B) received the message after a prolonged period of meditation.

    (C) recognized the faith of those who were considered "People of the Book."

    (D) received the message and was granted immortality on the night he was visited by God's herald.

2. According to the passage, the religion of Islam, expounded by the Prophet Muhammad, was intended as

    (A) a codification of existing cultural beliefs and practices on the Arabian Peninsula.

    (B) an introduction of the Nestorian faith by merchants into the Arabian region.

    (C) an Arab interpretation of Hellenistic philosophies that had spread after the campaigns of Alexander of Macedon.

    (D) an all-encompassing guide to how life should be lived in order to achieve salvation.

3. How did the religion of Islam affect political and economic institutions in the areas where it spread during the Umayyad and Abbasid Caliphates?

    (A) Sharia law provided a political foundation and Muslim traders exchanged goods throughout the region.

    (B) The Islamic region was politically fragmented and the Arabs who traded were the only unifying force.

    (C) There was no political unification or extensive trade due to the conflict between Sunni and Shia Muslims.

    (D) Continuous political domination by the Arab majority created a unified area that produced a platform for long-distance trade.

Questions 4–6 refer to the passage below.

"These men were some of those who took extreme pains to study the ancient sciences, for the sake of which they gave generously what was required, taxing themselves with fatigue. They dispatched to the Byzantine country men who sent scientific manuscripts back to them.

They hired translators from various districts and kept them in attendance for many years, so that they brought to light wonders of learning. The sciences in which they were most interested were geometry, mechanics, dynamics, music and astronomy."

Muslim scholar Ibn al-Nadim's description of a group who studied in Baghdad during the Abbasid era, ca. 980

4. The scientific and mathematical learning that flourished during the Abbasid Caliphate was aided by

    (A) the translation of Greco-Roman classical works into Arabic.

    (B) state sponsorship of visiting experts from neighboring regions.

    (C) the wealth of mathematical research that had accrued during the Umayyad Caliphate.

    (D) Shi'ite domination of the caliphate and of the places of learning.

5. What does the passage indicate about the political situation that existed at the time in the Abbasid Caliphate?

    (A) A rivalry existed between the Abbasid Caliphate and the remains of the Umayyad Caliphate in Spain.

    (B) The Abbasid Caliphate was politically divided between Arab and non-Arab families.

    (C) A level of diplomacy existed between the Abbasid Caliphate and its Christian neighbors.

    (D) The Abbasid Caliphate was ruled by an autocratic caliph who dominated both political and cultural life.

6. Which of the following best describes the changes in the Islamic community by the tenth century as described in the passage?

    (A) The Turkic Mamluks created a new caliphate and ruled from Damascus.

    (B) The Samanid dynasty of Iran swept into power.

    (C) The Abbasid Caliphate began to weaken politically and several new states were created.

    (D) The majority Sunni population rose up and created their own state.

Questions 7–10 refer to the passages below.

"There is a share for men and a share for women from what is left by parents . . . a legal share.

Allah commands you as regards your children's (inheritance); to the male, a portion equal to that of two females . . .

Men are the protectors and maintainers of women, because Allah has made one of them to excel the other, and because they spend (support them) from their means. Therefore the righteous women are devoutly obedient and guard in the husband's absence what Allah orders them to guard. As to those women on whose part you see ill-conduct, admonish them, (next), refuse to share their beds, (and last) beat them, but if they return to obedience, seek not against them means (of annoyance)."

> Laws concerning women from the "Surah An-Nisa"
> section of the Qur'an

"If any man die and leave no sons, if the father and mother survive, they shall inherit [but if they are dead] and he leave brothers or sisters, they shall inherit. . . . But if there are none, the sisters of the father shall inherit.

But of Salic [clan] land no portion of the inheritance shall come to a woman: but the whole inheritance of the land shall come to the male sex.

If anyone have hit a free woman who is pregnant and she dies, he shall be sentenced to 28000 dinars, which make 700 shillings."

> Laws concerning women from the *Lex Salica*, a
> body of laws codified at the time of King Clovis
> of the Carolingian Empire, ca. 500

7. According to the passage from the Qur'an
   (A) men and women are equal in the eyes of Allah.
   (B) women have very few rights in Muslim society.
   (C) it is a woman's role to take care of her husband and sons.
   (D) men should provide for and protect women.

8. The role of men as described in the above passage from the Qur'an is one reason for which of the following cultural developments?
   (A) Women's inability to remarry if divorced by their husbands
   (B) Seclusion of women from public society and veiling when leaving the private sphere
   (C) Increased transfer to a matrilineal society in the late Abbasid Caliphate
   (D) Extreme polygamy in the Umayyad empire, with men taking up to 30 legal wives

9. Based on the passages above, which of the following comparisons is most correct concerning women in the Muslim-controlled Middle East and in the Christian west between 600 and 1450?
   (A) Women had fewer legal rights in the Middle East than in Europe.

   (B) Women's rights were restricted in both regions by a patriarchal social structure.
   (C) Women exercised less power in both regions than in previous periods.
   (D) Christian women in Europe and Muslim women in the Middle East had equivalent legal rights counterparts.

10. Historians have difficulty creating accurate descriptions of the gender structures of societies ca. 1000 because
    (A) few written accounts remain from the period.
    (B) of the scarcity of writings by women.
    (C) most of the source material concerns religious rather than secular matters.
    (D) there is no comparative evidence from the earlier historical period.

Short-Answer Questions

> "Baghdad is a hive of bees in which much honey is produced."
> Quote from a Spanish traveler who visited
> the city during the Abbasid Caliphate

"Baghdad was a veritable City of Palaces, not made of stucco and mortar, but of marble. The buildings were usually of several stories. The palaces and mansions were lavishly gilded and decorated, and hung with beautiful tapestry and hangings of brocade or silk. The rooms were lightly and tastefully furnished with luxurious divans, costly tables, unique Chinese vases and gold and silver ornaments. . . . The mosques of the city were at once vast in size and remarkably beautiful. There were also in Baghdad numerous colleges of learning, hospitals, infirmaries for both sexes, and lunatic asylums."

> Yaqut al-Musta'simi, ca. 1280

1. Use the passages above and your knowledge of world history to answer all parts of the question that follows.
   (A) Identify ONE example of the cultural achievements of the Abbasid Caliphate.
   (B) Explain ONE reason for the cultural achievements of the Abbasid Caliphate.
   (C) Explain the long-term importance of the cultural achievements of the Abbasid Caliphate.

2. Use Map 10.1 on page 249 and your knowledge of world history to answer all parts of the question that follows.
   (A) Identify ONE similarity between the expansion of Muslim rule and the expansion of Christianity by 1200.
   (B) Explain ONE method that enabled Muslim rule to expand by 1200.
   (C) Explain ONE ADDITIONAL method that enabled Muslim rule to expand by 1200.

11 Christian Societies Emerge in Europe, 600–1200

CHAPTER OUTLINE

AP® Framework Terms

Patriarchy
Monasticism
Feudalism
Serfdom
Byzantine Empire
Crusades

Overarching Questions

1 How and to what extent have migration, population, and urbanization affected the environment over time? (ENV)

2 In what ways do the arts reflect innovation, adaptation, and creativity of specific societies? (CUL)

3 How and why have economic, social, cultural, and geographic factors influenced the process of state building, expansion, and dissolution? (SB)

4 How have different labor systems developed and changed? (ECON)

5 To what extent have different ideologies, philosophies, and religions affected social hierarchies? (SOC)

Christmas Day in 800 found Charles, king of the Franks, in Rome instead of at his palace at Aachen in northwestern Germany. At six-foot-three, Charles towered over the average man of his time, and his royal career had been equally gargantuan. Crowned king in his mid-twenties in 768, he had crisscrossed Europe for three decades, waging war on Muslim invaders from Spain, Avar **(ah-vahr)** invaders from Hungary, and a number of German princes.

Charles had subdued many enemies and had become protector of the papacy. So not all historians believe the eyewitness report of his secretary and biographer that Charles was surprised when, as the king rose from his prayers, Pope Leo III placed a new crown on his head. "Life and victory to Charles the August, crowned by God the great and pacific Emperor of the Romans," proclaimed the pope.[1] Then, amid the cheers of the crowd, he humbly knelt before the new emperor.

Charlemagne (SHAHR-leh-mane) (from Latin *Carolus magnus*, "Charles the Great") was the first in western Europe to bear the title *emperor* in over 300 years. Rome's decline and Charlemagne's rise marked a shift of focus for Europe—away from the Mediterranean and toward the north and west. German custom and Christian piety

---

[1]Lewis G. M. Thorpe, *Two Lives of Charlemagne* (Harmondsworth, UK: Penguin, 1969).

▲ **Boatbuilding Scene from the Bayeaux Tapestry** Eleventh-century shipwrights prepare vessels for William of Normandy's invasion of England. Musee de la Tapisserie, Bayeux, France / With special authorisation of the City of Bayeux / Bridgeman Images

transformed the Roman heritage to create a new civilization. While the memory of Greek and Roman philosophy faded, Irish monks preaching in Latin became important intellectual influences in some parts of Europe. Urban life continued the decline that had begun in the later days of the Roman Empire. Historians originally called this era "**medieval**," literally "middle age," because it comes between the era of Greco-Roman civilization and the intellectual, artistic, and economic changes of the Renaissance in the fourteenth century; but research has uncovered many aspects of medieval culture that are as rich and creative as those that came earlier and later.

Charlemagne was not the only ruler in Europe to claim the title emperor. Another emperor held sway in the Greek-speaking east, where Rome's political and legal heritage continued. The Eastern Roman Empire was often called the **Byzantine Empire** after the seventh century, and it was known to the Muslims as Rum (**room**). While western Europeans lived amid the ruins of empire, the Byzantines maintained and reinterpreted Roman traditions. The authority of the Byzantine emperors blended with the influence of the Christian church to form a cultural synthesis that helped shape the emerging kingdom of **Kievan Russia**. Byzantium's centuries-long conflict with Islam helped spur the crusading passion that overtook western Europe in the eleventh century.

The comparison between western and eastern Europe appears paradoxical. Byzantium inherited a robust and self-confident late Roman society and economy, while western Europe could not achieve political unity and suffered severe economic decline. Yet by 1200 western Europe was showing renewed vitality and flexing its military muscles, while Byzantium was showing signs of decline and military weakness. As we explore the causes and consequences of these different historical paths, we must remember that the emergence of Christian Europe included both developments. ●

Charlemagne King of the Franks (r. 768–814); emperor (r. 800–814). Through a series of military conquests he established the Carolingian Empire, which encompassed all of Gaul and parts of Germany and Italy. Though illiterate himself, he sponsored a brief intellectual revival.

medieval Literally "middle age," a term that historians of Europe use for the period around 500 to 1500, signifying its intermediate point between Greco-Roman antiquity and the Renaissance.

Byzantine Empire Historians' name for the eastern portion of the Roman Empire from the fourth century onward, taken from "Byzantium," an early name for Constantinople, the Byzantine capital city. The empire fell to the Ottomans in 1453.

Kievan Russia State established at Kiev in Ukraine around 880 by Scandinavian adventurers asserting authority over a mostly Slavic farming population.

11-1 The Byzantine Empire, 600–1200

How did the Byzantine Empire maintain Roman imperial traditions in the east?

The Byzantine emperors established Christianity as their official religion (see Chapter 6). They also represented a continuation of Roman imperial rule and tradition that was largely absent in the kingdoms that succeeded Rome in the west. Whereas only provincial forms of Roman law survived in the west, Byzantium inherited imperial law intact. Combining the imperial role with political oversight over the Christian church, the emperors made a comfortable transition into the role of all-powerful Christian monarchs. The Byzantine drama, however, played on a steadily shrinking stage. Territorial losses and almost constant military pressure from north and south deprived the empire of long periods of peace.

11-1a An Empire Beleaguered

Having a single ruler endowed with supreme legal and religious authority prevented the breakup of the Eastern Empire into petty principalities, but a series of territorial losses sapped the empire's strength. Between 634 and 650, Arab armies destroyed the Sasanid Empire and captured Byzantine Egypt, Syria, and Tunisia (see Chapter 10). Islam posed a religious as well as a political challenge. By the end of the twelfth century, some two-thirds of the Christians in these former Byzantine territories had adopted the Muslim faith (see Map 11.1).

The loss of such populous and prosperous provinces shook the empire and reduced its power. Although it had largely recovered and reorganized militarily by the tenth century, it never regained the lost lands. Crusaders from western Europe established short-lived Christian principalities at the eastern end of the Mediterranean Sea at the very end of the eleventh century, but the Byzantines found them almost as hostile as the Muslims (see Section 11-6 The Crusades). Eventually the empire succumbed to Muslim conquest in 1453.

The later Byzantine emperors faced new enemies in the north and south. Following the wave of Germanic migrations (see Chapter 6), Slavic and Turkic peoples appeared on the northern frontiers as part of centuries-long and poorly understood population migrations in Eurasian steppe lands. Other Turks led by the Seljuk family became the primary foe in the south (see Chapter 10).

schism A formal split within a religious community.

At the same time, relations with the popes and princes of western Europe steadily worsened. In the mid-ninth century the patriarchs of Constantinople (**cahn-stan-tih-NO-pul**) had challenged the territorial jurisdiction of the popes of Rome and some of the practices of the Latin Church. These arguments worsened over time and in 1054 culminated in a formal **schism** (**SKIZ-uhm**) between the Latin Church and the Orthodox Church—a break that has been only partially mended.

11-1b Society and Urban Life

Imperial authority and urban prosperity in the eastern provinces of the Late Roman Empire initially sheltered Byzantium from many of the economic reverses and population losses suffered by western Europe. However, the two regions shared a common demographic crisis during a sixth-century epidemic of bubonic plague known as "the plague of Justinian," named after the

◀ **Byzantine Church from a Twelfth-Century Manuscript**
The upper portion shows the church facade and domes. The lower portion shows the interior with a mosaic of Christ enthroned at the altar end. World History Archive/World History Archive/Superstock

CHRONOLOGY

	Western Europe	Eastern Europe
600	711 Muslim conquest of Spain 732 Battle of Tours	634–650 Muslims conquer Byzantine provinces of Syria, Egypt, and Tunisia
800	800 Coronation of Charlemagne 843 Treaty of Verdun divides Carolingian Empire among Charlemagne's grandsons 910 Monastery of Cluny founded 962 Beginning of Holy Roman Empire	ca. 880 Varangians take control of Kiev 980 Vladimir becomes grand prince of Kievan Russia
1000	1054 Formal schism between Latin and Orthodox Churches 1066 Normans under William the Conqueror invade England 1076–1078 Climax of investiture controversy 1095 Pope Urban II preaches First Crusade	1081–1118 Alexius Comnenus rules Byzantine Empire, calls for western military aid against Muslims
1200		1204 Western knights sack Constantinople in Fourth Crusade

emperor who ruled from 527 to 565. A similar though gradual and less pronounced social transformation set in around the seventh century, possibly sparked by further epidemics and the loss of Egypt and Syria to the Muslims. Formal histories tell us little, but popular narratives of saints' lives show a transition from stories about educated saints hailing from cities to stories about saints who originated as peasants. In many areas, barter replaced money transactions; some cities declined in population and wealth; and the traditional class of local urban notables nearly disappeared.

As the urban elite class shrank, the importance of high-ranking aristocrats at the imperial court and of rural landowners increased. Power organized by family began to rival power from class-based officeholding. By the end of the eleventh century, a family-based military aristocracy had emerged. Of Byzantine emperor Alexius Comnenus (**uh-LEX-see-uhs kom-NAY-nuhs**) (r. 1081–1118) it was said: "He considered himself not a ruler, but a lord, conceiving and calling the empire his own house."[2] The situation of women changed, too. Although earlier Roman family life was centered on a legally all-powerful father, women had enjoyed comparative freedom in public. After the seventh century women increasingly found themselves confined to the home. Some sources indicate that when they went out, they concealed their faces behind veils. The only men they socialized with were family members. Paradoxically, however, from 1028 to 1056 women ruled the Byzantine Empire alongside their husbands. These social changes and the apparent increase in the seclusion of women resemble simultaneous developments in neighboring Islamic countries, but historians have not uncovered any firm linkage between them.

Economically, the Byzantine emperors continued the Late Roman inclination to set prices, organize grain shipments to the capital, and monopolize trade in luxury goods like Tyrian purple cloth. Such government intervention may have slowed technological development and economic innovation. So long as merchants and pilgrims hastened to Constantinople from all points of the compass, aristocrats could buy rare and costly goods. Just as the provisioning and physical improvement of Rome overshadowed the development of other cities at the height of the Roman Empire, so other Byzantine cities suffered from the intense focus on Constantinople. In the countryside, Byzantine farmers continued to use slow oxcarts and light scratch plows, which were efficient for many, but not all, soil types, long after farmers in western Europe had begun to adopt more efficient techniques (discussed later in this chapter).

AP® Exam Tip
Understand how diffusion of the bubonic plague along trade routes and other factors led to urban decline in this time period.

AP® Exam Tip
Explain how distinctions based on class and gender influenced the development and transformation of social hierarchies.

[2]A. P. Kazhdan and Ann Wharton Epstein, *Change in Byzantine Culture in the Eleventh and Twelfth Centuries* (Berkeley, CA: University of California Press, 1985), 71.

AP® Exam Tip
Explain how
Byzantine expansion
facilitated trade and
communication.

Because Byzantium's Roman inheritance remained so much more intact than western Europe's, few people recognized the slow deterioration. Gradually, however, pilgrims and visitors from the west saw the reality beyond the awe-inspiring, incense-filled domes of cathedrals and beneath the glitter and silken garments of the royal court. An eleventh-century French visitor wrote:

> *The city itself [Constantinople] is squalid and fetid and in many places harmed by permanent darkness, for the wealthy overshadow the streets with buildings and leave these dirty, dark places to the poor and to travelers; there murders and robberies and other crimes which love the darkness are committed. Moreover, since people live lawlessly in this city, which has as many lords as rich men and almost as many thieves as poor men, a criminal knows neither fear nor shame, because crime is not punished by law and never entirely comes to light. In every respect she exceeds moderation; for, just as she surpasses other cities in wealth, so too, does she surpass them in vice.*[3]

---

[3]Ibid., 248.

MAP 11.1   **The Spread of Christianity**   By the early eighth century, Christian areas around the southern Mediterranean from northern Syria to northern Spain, accounting for most of the Christian population, had fallen under Muslim rule; the slow process of conversion to Islam had begun. This change accentuated the importance of the patriarchs of Constantinople, the popes in Rome, and the later converting regions of northern and eastern Europe.

Why did early Islam spread mainly in Christian lands?

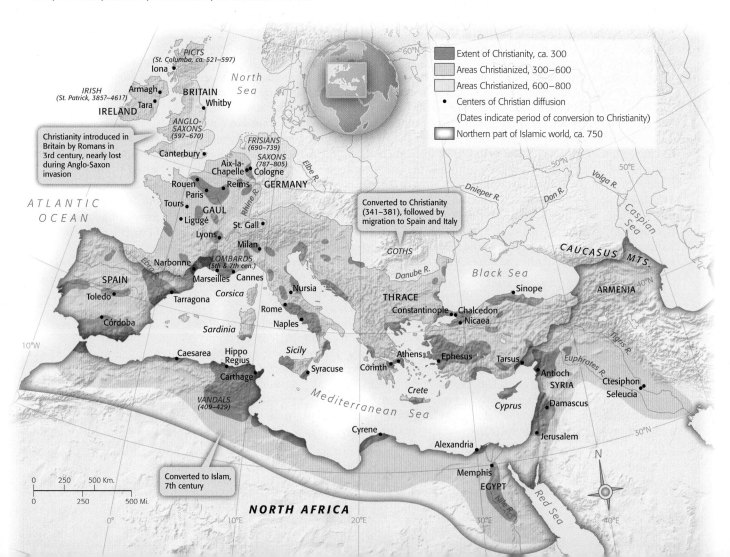

A Byzantine contemporary, Anna Comnena, the brilliant daughter of Emperor Alexius Comnenus, expressed the view from the other side. She scornfully described a prominent churchman and philosopher who happened to be from Italy: "Italos … was unable with his barbaric, stupid temperament to grasp the profound truths of philosophy; even in the act of learning he utterly rejected the teacher's guiding hand, and full of temerity and barbaric folly, [believed] even before study that he excelled all others."[4]

11-1c Cultural Achievements

Though the greatest Byzantine architectural monument, Constantinople's Hagia Sophia (**AH-yah SOH-fee-uh**) ("Sacred Wisdom") cathedral, dates to the reign of Justinian, artistic creativity continually manifested itself in the design and ornamentation of other churches and monasteries. Justinian also ordered the collection of all Roman imperial edicts in a massive law code known as the *Corpus Juris Civilis*, or Body of Civil Law. Byzantine religious art, featuring stiff but arresting images of holy figures against gold backgrounds, strongly influenced painting in western Europe down to the thirteenth century, and Byzantine musical traditions strongly affected the chanting employed in medieval Latin churches.

Another important Byzantine achievement dates to the empire's long period of political decline. In the ninth century brothers named Cyril and Methodius embarked on a highly successful mission to the Slavs of Moravia (part of the modern Czech Republic). They preached in the local language, and their followers perfected a writing system, called Cyrillic (**sih-RIL-ik**), that came to be used by Slavic Christians adhering to the Orthodox—that is, Byzantine—rite. Their careers also mark the beginning of a competition between the Greek and Latin forms of Christianity for the allegiance of the Slavs. The use today of the Cyrillic alphabet among the Russians and other Slavic peoples of Orthodox Christian faith, and of the Roman alphabet among the Poles, Czechs, and Croatians, testifies to this competition (see Section 11-4 Kievan Russia).

Section Review

- Unlike the Western Roman Empire, the Eastern Roman Empire retained its unity and became the Byzantine Empire, headed by an emperor who held both political and religious power.
- A schism split the Orthodox Church from the Catholic Church in the west.
- The Byzantine Empire suffered territorial losses, and its urban centers gradually declined.
- The culture of the Byzantine Empire made many important aesthetic contributions to the art of Europe.
- Byzantine missionaries spread their faith and the Cyrillic alphabet into eastern Europe.

AP® Exam Tip
Be able to compare the spread of religion and culture along trade networks.

11-2 Early Medieval Europe, 600–1000

How did the culture of early medieval Europe develop in the absence of imperial rule?

The disappearance of the imperial legal framework that had persisted to the final days of the Western Roman Empire (see Chapter 6) and the rise of various kings, nobles, and chieftains changed the legal and political landscape of western Europe. In region after region, the family-based traditions of the Germanic peoples, which often fit local conditions better than previous practices, supplanted the edicts of the Roman emperors (see Map 11.2).

Fear and physical insecurity led communities to seek the protection of local strongmen. In places where looters and pillagers might appear at any moment, a local lord with a castle at which peasants could take refuge counted for more than a distant king. Dependency of weak people on strong people became a hallmark of the post-Roman period in western Europe.

11-2a The Time of Insecurity

In 711 a frontier raiding party of Arabs and Berbers, acting under the authority of the Umayyad caliph in Syria, crossed the Strait of Gibraltar and overturned the kingdom of the Visigoths in Spain (see Chapter 10). The disunited Europeans could not stop them from consolidating their hold on the Iberian Peninsula. After pushing the remaining Christian chieftains into the northern mountains, the Muslims moved on to France. They occupied much of the southern coast and penetrated as far north as Tours, less than 150 miles (240 kilometers) from the English Channel, before Charlemagne's grandfather, Charles Martel, stopped their most advanced raiding party in 732.

---

[4]Ibid., 255.

MAP 11.2 Germanic Kingdoms Prior to Islam Though German kings asserted authority over most of western Europe, German-speaking peoples were most numerous east of the Rhine River. In most other areas, Celtic languages—for example, Breton on this map—or languages derived from Latin predominated. Though the Germanic Anglo-Saxon tongue increasingly supplanted Welsh and Scottish in Britain, the absolute number of Germanic settlers seems to have been fairly limited.

In what ways is it misleading to characterize a kingdom with a German ruling family as "Germanic"?

Military effectiveness was the key element in the rise of the Carolingian (**kah-roe-LIN-gee-uhn**) family (from Latin *Carolus*, "Charles"), first as protectors of the *Frankish* (French) kings, then as kings themselves under Charlemagne's father Pepin (r. 751–768), and finally, under Charlemagne, as emperors. At the peak of Charlemagne's power, the Carolingian Empire encompassed all of Gaul and parts of Germany and Italy, with the pope ruling part of the latter. When Charlemagne's son, Louis the Pious, died, the Germanic tradition of dividing property among male heirs led to the Treaty of Verdun (843), which split the empire into three parts. French-speaking in the west (France) and middle (Burgundy) and German-speaking in the east (Germany), the three regions never reunited. Nevertheless, the Carolingian economic system based on landed wealth and a brief intellectual revival sponsored personally by Charlemagne—though he himself was illiterate—provided a common heritage.

A new threat to western Europe appeared in 793, when the Vikings, sea raiders from Scandinavia, attacked and plundered a monastery on the English coast, the first of hundreds of such raids. Local sources from France, the British Isles, and Muslim Spain attest to widespread dread of Viking warriors descending from multi-oared, dragon-prowed boats to pillage monasteries, villages, and towns. Viking shipbuilders made versatile vessels that could brave the stormy North Atlantic and also maneuver up rivers to attack inland towns. As we shall see, in the ninth century raiders from Denmark and Norway harried the British and French coasts while *Varangians* (**va-RAN-gee-anz**) (Swedes) pursued raiding and trading interests, and eventually the building of kingdoms, along the rivers of eastern Europe and Russia. Although many Viking raiders sought booty and slaves, in the 800s and 900s Viking captains organized the settlement of Iceland, Greenland, and, around the year 1000, Vinland on the northern tip of Newfoundland.

Vikings, long settled on lands they had seized in Normandy (in northwestern France), organized the most important and ambitious expeditions in terms of numbers of men and horses and long-lasting impact. William the Conqueror, the duke of Normandy, invaded England in 1066 and brought Anglo-Saxon domination of the island to an end. Other Normans (from "north men") attacked Muslim Sicily in the 1060s and, after thirty years of fighting, permanently severed it from the Muslim world.

AP® Exam Tip
Viking boats are a good example of a technological innovation that helped spur expansion.

11-2b A Self-Sufficient Economy

Archaeology and records kept by Christian monasteries and convents reveal a profound economic transformation that accompanied the new Germanic political order. The new rulers cared little for the urban-based civilization of the Romans, which accordingly shrank in importance. Though the pace of change differed from region to region, most cities lost population, in some cases becoming villages. Roman roads fell into disuse and disrepair. Small thatched houses sprang up beside abandoned villas, and public buildings made of marble became dilapidated in the absence of the laborers, money, and civic leadership needed to maintain them. Paying for purchases in coin largely gave way to bartering goods and services.

Trade across the Mediterranean did not entirely stop after the Muslim conquests. Archaeological investigations of sunken ships show a continuation of contact, but more with North African ports than with Egypt and Syria. Nevertheless, most of western Europe came to rely on meager local resources. These resources, moreover, underwent redistribution.

Roman centralization had channeled the wealth and production of the empire to the capital, which in turn radiated Roman cultural styles and tastes to the provinces. As Roman governors were replaced by Germanic territorial lords, who found the riches of their own culture more appealing than those of Rome, local self-sufficiency became more important. The decline of literacy and other aspects of Roman life made room for the growth of Germanic cultural traditions.

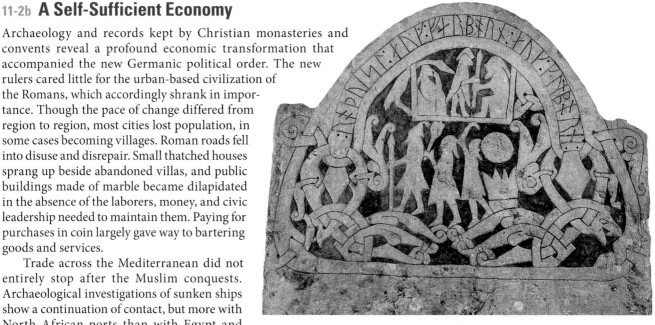

▲ **Viking Runestone** Pre-Christian symbols and myths from northern Europe appear on stones like this one from Sweden. An inscription containing names written in the runic alphabet had elaborately intertwined ornaments at the ends, a feature that reappears in the Christian *Book of Kells* (see Section 11-3b Monasticism). The scene at the top is thought to depict Odin, the chief god of the Vikings. Werner Forman / Art Resource, NY

The diet in the northern countries featured beer, lard or butter, and bread made of barley, rye, or wheat, all supplemented by pork from herds of swine fed on forest acorns and beechnuts, and by game from the same forests. Nobles ate better than peasants, but even the peasant diet was reasonably balanced. The Roman diet based on wheat, wine, and olive oil persisted in the south. The average western European of the ninth century was probably better nourished than his or her descendants 300 years later, when population was increasing and the nobility monopolized the resources of the forests.

In both north and south, self-sufficient farming estates known as **manors** became the primary centers of agricultural production. Fear of attack led many common farmers in the most vulnerable regions to give their lands to large landowners in return for political and physical protection. The warfare and instability of the post-Roman centuries made unprotected country houses especially vulnerable to pillaging. Isolated by poor communications and lack of organized government, landowners depended on their own resources for survival. Many became warriors or maintained a force of armed men. Others swore allegiance to landowners who had armed forces to protect them.

A well-appointed manor possessed fields, gardens, grazing lands, fishponds, a mill, a church, workshops for making farm and household implements, and a village where the farmers dependent on the lord of the manor lived. Depending on local conditions, protection ranged from a ditch and wooden stockade to a stone wall surrounding a fortified *keep* (a stone building). Fortification tended to increase until the twelfth century, when stronger monarchies made it less necessary.

Manor life reflected personal status. Nobles and their families exercised almost unlimited power over the **serfs**—agricultural workers who belonged to the manor, tilled its fields, and owed other dues and obligations. Serfs could not leave the manor where they were born and attach themselves to another lord. Most peasants in England, France, and western Germany were unfree serfs in the tenth and eleventh centuries. However, in Bordeaux (**bore-DOE**), Saxony, and a few

AP® Exam Tip
Explain how and why labor systems (such as serfdom) have developed and changed over time.

manors In medieval Europe, a large, self-sufficient landholding consisting of the lord's residence (manor house), outbuildings, peasant village, and surrounding land.

serfs In medieval Europe, an agricultural laborer legally bound to a lord's property and obligated to perform set services for the lord.

other regions, free peasantry survived based on the egalitarian social structure of the Germanic peoples during their period of migration. Outright slavery, the mainstay of the Roman economy (see Chapter 6), diminished as more and more peasants became serfs in return for a lord's protection. At the same time, the enslavement of prisoners to row galleys and carry out ambitious Roman construction projects became less important as an object of warfare.

11-2c **Early Medieval Society in the West**

Europe's reversion to a self-sufficient economy limited the freedom and potential for personal achievement of most people, but an emerging class of nobles reaped great benefits. During the Germanic migrations and later among the Vikings of Scandinavia, men regularly answered the call to arms issued by war chiefs, to whom they swore allegiance. All warriors shared in the booty gained from raiding. As settlement enhanced the importance of agricultural tasks, laying down the plow and picking up the sword at the chieftain's call became harder.

Those who, out of loyalty or desire for adventure, continued to join the war parties included a growing number of horsemen. Mounted warriors became the central force of the Carolingian army. At first, fighting from horseback did not make a person either a nobleman or a landowner. By the tenth century, however, nearly constant warfare to protect land rights or support the claims of a lord brought about a gradual transformation in the status of the mounted warrior, which led, at different rates in different areas, to landholding becoming almost inseparable from military service.

In trying to understand long-standing traditions of landholding and obligation, lawyers in the sixteenth century and later simplified thousands of individual agreements into a neat system they called "feudalism," from Latin *feodum*, meaning a land awarded for military service. It became common to refer to medieval Europe as a "feudal society" in which kings and lords gave land to "vassals" in return for sworn military support. By analyzing original records, more recent historians have discovered this to be an oversimplification. Relations between landholders and serfs and between lords and vassals differed too much from one place to another, and from one time to another, to fit together in anything resembling a regular system.

The German foes of the Roman legions had equipped themselves with helmets, shields, and swords, spears, or throwing axes. Some rode horses, but most fought on foot. Before the invention of the stirrup by Central Asian pastoralists in approximately the first century CE, horsemen had gripped their mounts with their legs and fought with bows and arrows, throwing javelins, stabbing spears, and swords. Stirrups allowed a rider to stand in the saddle, lean forward, and absorb the impact when his lance struck an enemy at full gallop. This type of warfare required grain-fed horses, "chargers," that were larger and heavier than the small, grass-fed animals of the Central Asian nomads, though smaller and lighter than the draft horses bred in later times for hauling heavy loads. Thus agricultural Europe rather than the grassy steppes produced the charges of armored lancers that came to dominate the battlefield.

By the eleventh century, the knight, called by different terms in different places, had emerged as the central figure in medieval warfare. He wore an open-faced helmet and a long linen shirt, or hauberk (**HAW-berk**), studded with small metal disks (see Environment & Technology: Iron Production). A century later, knightly equipment commonly included a visored helmet that covered the head and neck and a hauberk of chain mail.

Each increase in armor for knight and horse entailed a greater financial outlay. Since land was the basis of wealth, a knight needed financial support from land revenues. Accordingly, kings began to reward armed service with grants of land from their own property. Lesser nobles with extensive properties built their own military retinues the same way.

A grant of land in return for a pledge to provide military service was often called a **fief**. At first, kings granted fiefs to their noble followers, known as **vassals**, on a temporary basis. By the tenth century, most fiefs could be inherited as long as the specified military service continued to be provided. Though patterns varied greatly, the association of landholding with military service made the medieval society of western Europe quite different from the contemporary city-based societies of the Islamic world.

Kings and lords might be able to command the service of their vassals for only part of the year. Vassals could hold land from several different lords and owe loyalty to each one. Moreover, the allegiance that a vassal owed to one lord could entail military service to that lord's master in time of need.

A "typical" medieval realm—actual practices varied between and within realms—consisted of lands directly owned by a king or a count and administered by his royal officers. The king's

fief In medieval Europe, land granted in return for a sworn oath to provide specified military service.

vassals In medieval Europe, a sworn supporter of a king or lord committed to rendering specified military service to that king or lord.

◀ **Offa King of Mercia supervises church construction** Ruling in central England from 757 to 796, Offa strongly supported Christianity. Yet one of the rare gold coins to survive from his reign is inexplicably an Islamic dinar from Baghdad with "Offa Rex" stamped on it. This depiction from about 1250 shows workers using a hand barrow in climbing a ladder alongside another worker using a wheelbarrow. Wheelbarrows were common in China after the second century CE, but seem to have been unknown in Europe before the thirteenth century. Matthew (c.1200-59)/TRINITY COLLEGE LIBRARY DUBLIN/The Board of Trinity College, Dublin, Ireland/Bridgeman Images

or count's major vassals held and administered other lands, often the greater portion, in return for military service. These vassals, in turn, granted land to their own vassals.

The lord of a manor provided local governance and justice, direct royal government being quite limited. The king had few financial resources and seldom exercised legal jurisdiction at a local level. Members of the clergy, as well as the extensive agricultural lands owned by monasteries and nunneries, fell under the jurisdiction of the church, which further limited the reach and authority of the monarch.

Noblewomen became enmeshed in this tangle of obligations as heiresses and as candidates for marriage. A man who married the widow or daughter of a lord with no sons could gain control of that lord's property. Marriage alliances affected entire kingdoms. Noble daughters and sons had little say in marriage matters; issues of land, power, and military service took precedence. Noblemen guarded the women in their families as closely as their other valuables.

Nevertheless, women could own land. A noblewoman sometimes administered her husband's estates when he was away at war. Non-noble women usually worked alongside their menfolk, performing agricultural tasks such as raking and stacking hay, shearing sheep, and picking vegetables. As artisans, women spun, wove, and sewed clothing. The Bayeux (**bay-YUH**) Tapestry, a piece of embroidery 230 feet (70 meters) long and 20 inches (51 centimeters) wide depicting William the Conqueror's invasion of England in 1066, was designed and executed entirely by women, though historians do not agree on who those women were.

Section Review

- In the west, German kingdoms divided territory seized from Rome, and German lifestyles gradually replaced Roman ones.

- Raids by warrior peoples, including Muslims and Vikings, forced an emphasis on warfare.

- The Carolingians created an empire that was later split into three realms.

- Society focused on rural villages and estates—manors—rather than cities.

- Rulers and nobles granted land to vassals in return for military service, thus creating the armed knight.

Despite the collapse of the Roman economy, ironworking expanded throughout Europe. The iron swords of the Germans outperformed traditional Roman weapons, which became obsolete. The spreading use of armor also increased the demand for iron. Archaeologists have found extensive evidence of iron smelting well beyond the frontiers of the Roman Empire. Helg Island in a lake near Stockholm, Sweden, had a large walled settlement that relied entirely on iron trading. Discoveries of a Buddha from India and a christening spoon from Egypt, both datable to the sixth century CE, indicate the range of these trade contacts. At Zelechovice in the Czech Republic, the remains of fifty "slag-pit" furnaces have been dated to the ninth century.

Most iron smelting was done on a small scale. Ore containing iron oxide was shoveled onto a charcoal fire in an open-air hearth pit. The carbon in the charcoal combined with the oxygen in the ore to form carbon dioxide gas, leaving behind a soft glowing lump of iron called a "bloom." This bloom was then pounded on a stone to remove the remaining impurities, like sand and clay, before being turned over to the blacksmith for fabricating into swords or armor.

During the post-Roman centuries, smelters learned to build walls around the hearth pits and then to put domes and chimneys on them. The resulting "slag-pit" furnaces produced greater amounts of iron. They also consumed great amounts of wood. Twelve pounds of charcoal, made from about 25 pounds of wood, were needed to produce 1 pound of bloom iron, and about 3 pounds of useless slag. Though bellows were developed to force oxygen into the fire, temperatures in slag-pit furnaces never became high enough to produce molten metal.

Questions for Analysis

1. If an iron smelter converted ore into rods and plates, what did a blacksmith do?

2. Why did iron replace bronze for most purposes?

3. How did the deep familiarity of the Germanic peoples with iron mining and smelting contribute to their gaining the upper hand over the Roman Empire?

◀ **Iron Smelting**   Two bellows blowing alternately provide a constant stream of air to the furnace. The man on the right pounds the bloom into bars or plates that a blacksmith will reheat and shape.   Sloane 3983 fol.5 Blacksmiths at work, from 'Liber Astrologiae' (vellum), Netherlandish School, (14th century)/British Library, London, UK/British Library Board. All Rights Reserved/ The Bridgeman Art Library

11-3 The Western Church

What role did the Western Church play in the politics and culture of Europe?

Just as the Christian populations in eastern Europe followed the religious guidance of the patriarch of Constantinople appointed by the Byzantine emperor, so the pope commanded similar authority over church affairs in western Europe. And just as missionaries in the east spread Christianity among the Slavs, so missionaries in the west added territory to Christendom with forays into the British Isles and the lands of the Germans. Throughout the period covered by this chapter, Christian society was emerging and changing in both areas.

In the west, Roman nobles lost control of the **papacy**—the office of the pope—and it became a more powerful international office after the tenth century. Councils of bishops—which normally set rules, called *canons*, to regulate the priests and *laypeople* (men and women who were not members of the clergy) under their jurisdiction—became increasingly responsive to papal direction.

Nevertheless, regional disagreements over church regulations, shortages of educated and trained clergy, difficult communications, political disorder, and the general insecurity of the

papacy The central administration of the Roman Catholic Church, of which the pope is the head.

period posed formidable obstacles to unifying church standards and practices (see Diversity & Dominance: The Struggle for Christian Morality). Clerics in some parts of western Europe were still issuing prohibitions against the worship of rivers, trees, and mountains as late as the eleventh century. Church problems included lingering polytheism, lax enforcement of prohibitions against marriage of clergy, *nepotism* (giving preferment to one's close kin), and *simony* (selling ecclesiastical appointments, often to people who were not members of the clergy). The persistence of the papacy in asserting its legal jurisdiction over clergy, combating polytheism and heretical beliefs, and calling on secular rulers to recognize the pope's authority, including unpopular rulings like a ban on first-cousin marriage, constituted a rare force for unity and order in a time of disunity and chaos.

11-3a Politics and the Church

In politically fragmented western Europe, the pope needed allies. Like his son, Charlemagne's father Pepin was a strong supporter of the papacy. The relationship between kings and popes was tense, however, since both thought of themselves as ultimate authorities. In 962 the pope crowned the first "Holy Roman Emperor" (Charlemagne never held this full title). This designation of a secular political authority as the guardian of general Christian interests proved more apparent than real. Essentially a loose confederation of German princes who named one of their own to the highest office, the early **Holy Roman Empire** had little influence west of the Rhine River.

Although the pope crowned the early Holy Roman Emperors, this did not confer absolute political superiority, for the law of the church (known as canon law because each law was called a canon) gave the pope exclusive legal jurisdiction over all clergy and church property wherever located. Nevertheless, since bishops who held land as vassals owed military support or other services and dues to kings and princes, the secular rulers argued that they should have the power to appoint those bishops because that was the only way to guarantee fulfillment of their duties as vassals. The popes disagreed.

In the eleventh century, this conflict over the control of ecclesiastical appointments came to a head. Hildebrand (**HILL-de-brand**), an Italian monk, capped a career of reorganizing church finances when the *cardinals* (a group of senior bishops) meeting in Rome selected him to be Pope Gregory VII in 1073. His personal notion of the papacy (preserved among his letters) represented an extreme position, stating among other claims that

- *The pope can be judged by no one;*
- *The Roman church has never erred and never will err till the end of time;*
- *The pope alone can depose and restore bishops;*
- *He alone can call general councils and authorize canon law;*
- *He can depose emperors;*
- *He can absolve subjects from their allegiance;*
- *All princes should kiss his feet.*[5]

Such claims antagonized lords and monarchs, who had become accustomed to *investing*—that is, conferring a ring and a staff as symbols of authority on bishops and abbots in their domains. Historians apply the term **investiture controversy** to the medieval struggle between the church and the lay lords to control ecclesiastical appointments; the term also refers to the broader conflict of popes versus emperors and kings. When Holy Roman Emperor Henry IV defied Gregory's reforms, Gregory excommunicated him in 1076, thereby cutting him off from church rituals. Stung by the resulting decline in his influence, Henry stood barefoot in the snow for three days outside a castle in northern Italy waiting for Gregory, a guest there, to receive him. Henry's formal act of penance induced Gregory to forgive him and restore him to the church; but the reconciliation, an apparent victory for the pope, did not last. In 1078 Gregory declared Henry deposed. The emperor then forced Gregory to flee from Rome to Salerno, where he died two years later.

The struggle between the popes and the emperors continued until 1122, when a compromise was reached at Worms, a town in Germany. In the Concordat of Worms, Emperor Henry V renounced his right to choose bishops and abbots or bestow spiritual symbols upon them. In return, Pope Calixtus II permitted the emperor to invest papally appointed bishops and abbots with any lay rights or obligations before their spiritual consecration. Such compromises did not fully solve the problem, but they reduced tensions between the two sides.

AP® Exam Tip
Understand the importance of the adaptation of religious institutions to traditional sources of power during this time period.

Holy Roman Empire Loose federation of mostly German states and principalities, headed by an emperor elected by the princes. It lasted from 962 to 1806.

investiture controversy Dispute between the popes and the Holy Roman Emperors over who held ultimate authority over bishops in imperial lands.

---

[5]R. W. Southern, *Western Society and the Church in the Middle Ages* (Harmondsworth, UK: Penguin, 1970), 102.

Ireland

The medieval church believed that Christians could be absolved of their sins by performing public or private penalties, or acts of humiliation. Priests listened to the believers confess their sins and then set the nature and duration of the penance. Books called penitentials guided the priests by stipulating the appropriate penance for specific sins. These books varied over time and tended to reflect local conditions. One of the earliest is attributed to Saint Patrick, who began his missionary work in Ireland in 432. The selections below deal not just with penalties for sin but also with efforts to impose church discipline on priests.

- There shall be no wandering cleric in a parish.
- If any cleric, from sexton [church caretaker] to priest, is seen without a tunic, and does not cover the shame and nakedness of his body; and if his hair is not shaven according to the Roman custom, and if his wife goes about with her head unveiled, he shall be alike despised by laymen and separated from the Church.
- A monk and a virgin, the one from one place, the other from another, shall not dwell together in the same inn, nor travel in the same carriage from village to village, nor continually hold conversation with each other.
- It is not permitted to the Church to accept alms from pagans.
- A Christian who believes that there is a vampire in the world, that is to say, a witch, is to be anathematized [condemned by the Church]; whoever lays that reputation upon a living being, shall not be received into the Church until he revokes with his own voice the crime that he has committed and accordingly does penance with all diligence.
- A Christian who defrauds anyone with respect to a debt in the manner of the pagans, shall be excommunicated [barred from Christian society] until he pays the debt.

England and Southern Germany

Boniface (ca. 675–754), a widely esteemed bishop of the southern German city of Mainz, began life with the name Winfrid in Anglo-Saxon Britain. After working as a missionary in Frisia in the Netherlands, he devoted the bulk of his life to establishing Christianity and respect for Christian law and morality in southern Germany. His letters reflect his passion for reforming personal behavior along Christian lines.

Boniface to Pope Zacharias, 742

We must confess, our father and lord, that after we learned from messengers that your predecessor in the apostolate [i.e., papacy], Gregory of reverend memory … had been set free from the prison of the body and had passed on to God, nothing gave us greater joy or happiness than the knowledge that the Supreme Arbiter had appointed your fatherly clemency to administer the canon law and to govern the Apostolic See.…

Some of the ignorant common people, Alemanians, Bavarians, and Franks, hearing that many of the offenses prohibited by us are practiced in the city of Rome, imagine that they are allowed by the priests there and reproach us for causing them to incur blame in their own lives. They say that on the first day of January year after year, in the city of Rome and in the neighborhood of St. Peter's church by day or night, they have seen bands of singers parading the streets in pagan fashion, shouting and chanting sacrilegious songs and loading tables with food day and night, while no one in his own house is willing to lend his neighbor fire or tools or any other convenience. They say also that they have seen there women with amulets and bracelets of heathen fashion on their arms and legs, offering them for sale to willing buyers.…

Boniface and Other Bishops to King Ethelbald of Mercia (a Saxon Kingdom in England), 746–747

We have heard that you are very liberal in almsgiving, and congratulate you thereon.… We have heard also that you repress robbery and wrongdoing, perjury, and rapine with a strong hand, and that you have established peace within your kingdom.…

But amidst all this, one evil report as to the manner of life of Your Grace has come to our hearing, which has greatly grieved us and which we would wish were not true. We have learned from many sources that you have never taken to yourself a lawful wife.… If you had willed to do this for the sake of chastity and abstinence … we should rejoice, for that is not worthy of blame but rather of praise.

Assertions of royal authority triggered other conflicts as well. Though barely twenty when he became king of England in 1154, Henry II, a great-grandson of William the Conqueror, instituted reforms designed to strengthen the power of the Crown and weaken the nobility. He appointed traveling justices to enforce his laws and made juries, a holdover from traditional Germanic law, into powerful legal instruments. He also established the principle that criminal acts violated the "king's peace" and should be tried and punished in accordance with charges brought by the Crown instead of in response to charges brought by victims.

Henry had a harder time controlling the church. His closest friend and chancellor, or chief administrator, Thomas à Becket (ca. 1118–1170), lived the grand and luxurious life of a courtier. In 1162 Henry persuaded Becket to become a priest and assume the position

But if, as many say—but which God forbid!—you have neither taken a lawful spouse nor observed chastity for God's sake but, moved by desire, have ded your good name before God and man by the crime of adulterous lust, then we are greatly grieved because this is a sin in the sight of God and is the ruin of your fair fame among men.

And now, what is worse, our informants say that these atrocious crimes are committed in convents with holy nuns and virgins consecrated to God, and this, beyond all doubt, doubles the offense....

Northern Germany and Scandinavia

Adam of Bremen's History of the Archbishops of Hamburg-Bremen consists of four sections. The third is devoted to the Archbishop Adalbert, whose death in 1072 stirred Adam to write. References to classical poets, the lives of saints, and royal documents show that Adam, a churchman, had a solid education and access to many sources, including conversations with kings and nobles.

This remarkable man [i.e., Archbishop Adalbert] may ... be extolled with praise of every kind in that he was noble, handsome, wise, eloquent, chaste, temperate. All these qualities he comprised in himself and others besides, such as one is wont to attach to the outer man: that he was rich, that he was successful, that he was glorious, that he was influential. All these things were his in abundance. Moreover, in respect of the mission to the heathen, which is the first duty of the Church at Hamburg, no one so vigorous could ever be found....

As soon as the metropolitan [i.e., Archbishop Adalbert] had entered upon his episcopate [i.e., position as bishop], he sent legates to the kings of the north in the interest of friendship. There were also dispersed throughout all Denmark and Norway and Sweden and to the ends of the earth admonitory letters in which he exhorted the bishops and priests living in those parts ... fearlessly to forward the conversion of the pagans.... [One Danish king] forgot the heavenly King as things prospered with him and married a blood relative from Sweden. This mightily displeased the lord archbishop, who sent legates to the rash king, rebuking him severely for his sin, and who stated finally that if he did not come to his senses, he would have to be cut off with the sword of excommunication. Beside himself with rage, the king then threatened to ravage and destroy the whole diocese of Hamburg. Unperturbed by these threats, our archbishop, reproving and entreating, remained firm, until at length the Danish tyrant was prevailed upon by letters from the pope to give his cousin a bill of divorce....

In Norway ... King Harold surpassed all the madness of tyrants in his savage wildness. Many churches were destroyed by that man; many Christians were tortured to death by him. But he was a mighty man and renowned for the victories he had previously won in many wars with barbarians in Greece and in the Scythian regions [i.e., while assisting the Byzantine empress Zoë fight the Seljuk Turks]. After he came into his fatherland, however, he never ceased from warfare; he was the thunderbolt of the north.... And so, as he ruled over many nations, he was odious to all on account of his greed and cruelty. He also gave himself up to the magic arts and, wretched man that he was, did not heed the fact that his most saintly brother [i.e., Saint Olaf, one of Harold's predecessors] had eradicated such illusions from the realm and striven even unto death for the adoption of the precepts of Christianity.

Across the Elbe [i.e., east of the river Hamburg is on] and in Slavia our affairs were still meeting with great success. For Gottschalk ... married a daughter of the Danish king and so thoroughly subdued the Slavs that they feared him like a king, offered to pay tribute, and asked for peace with subjection. Under these circumstances our Church at Hamburg enjoyed peace, and Slavia abounded in priests and churches....

AP® History Reasoning Skills

Causation *In what ways did key historical events lead to the increased role of the Christian church in European society?*

Contextualization *How do the religious ideas in the passage address the political and economic authority of a Christian kingdom?*

Sources: Excerpts from John T. McNeill and Helena M. Gamer, *Medieval Handbooks of Penance* (New York, NY: Columbia University Press, 1938), 77–78; *The Letters of Saint Boniface*, trans. Ephraim Emerton (New York, NY: Columbia University Press, 2000), 56, 59–60, 103–105; and *History of the Archbishops of Hamburg-Bremen*, trans. Francis J. Tschan (New York, NY: Columbia University Press, 1959 [new ed. 2002]), 114–133.

of archbishop of Canterbury, the highest church office in England. Becket agreed but cautioned that from then on he would act solely in the interest of the church if it came into conflict with the Crown. When Henry sought to try clerics accused of crimes in royal instead of ecclesiastical courts, Archbishop Thomas, now leading an austere and pious life, resisted.

In 1170 four of Henry's knights, knowing that the king desired Becket's death, murdered the archbishop in Canterbury Cathedral. Their crime backfired, and an outpouring of sympathy caused Canterbury to become a major pilgrimage center. In 1173 the pope declared the martyred Becket a saint. Henry allowed himself to be publicly whipped twice in penance for the crime, but his authority had been badly damaged.

◀ **Illustrated Manuscript from Monastic Library** This page from the *Book of Kells*, written around 800 in Ireland, combines an icon-like image of a gospel writer with complex interwoven patterns in the margin that derive from the pre-Christian art of northern Europe. Note the evangelist's blonde hair. Trinity College Library Dublin/The Bridgeman Art Library

Henry II's conflict with Thomas à Becket, like the Concordat of Worms, yielded no clear victor. The problem of competing legal traditions made political life in western Europe more complicated than in Byzantium or the lands of Islam (see Chapter 10). Feudal law, rooted in Germanic custom, gave supreme power to the king. Canon law, based on Roman precedent, visualized a single hierarchical legal institution with jurisdiction over all of Western Christendom. In the eleventh century Roman imperial law, contained in the *Corpus Juris Civilis* (see Section 11–1c Cultural Achievements) and made known by influential scholars, added a third tradition.

11-3b Monasticism

Monasticism featured prominently in the religious life of almost all medieval Christian lands. The origins of group monasticism lay in the eastern lands of the Roman Empire. Pre-Christian practices such as celibacy, continual devotion to prayer, and living apart from society (alone or in small groups) came together in Christian form in Egypt.

The most important form of monasticism in western Europe, however, involved groups of monks or nuns living together in organized communities. The person most responsible for introducing this originally Egyptian practice in the Latin west was Benedict of Nursia (ca. 480–547) in Italy. Benedict began his pious career as a hermit in a cave but eventually organized several monasteries, each headed by an abbot. In the seventh century monasteries based on his model spread far beyond Italy. The Rule Benedict wrote to govern the monks' behavior envisions a balanced life of devotion and work, along with obligations of celibacy, poverty, and obedience to the abbot. Those who lived by this or other monastic rules became *regular clergy*, in contrast to *secular clergy*, priests who lived in society instead of in seclusion and did not follow a formal code of regulations. The Rule of Benedict was the starting point for most forms of western European monastic life and remains in force today in Benedictine monasteries.

Though monks and *nuns*, women who lived by monastic rules in convents, made up a small percentage of the total population, their secluded way of life reinforced the separation of religious affairs from ordinary politics and economics. Monasteries followed Jesus's axiom to "render unto Caesar what is Caesar's and unto God what is God's" better than the many town-based bishops who behaved like lords.

Although some rulers, like Charlemagne, encouraged scholarship at court, many illiterate lay nobles interested themselves only in warfare and hunting. Thus it was monasteries that preserved literacy and learning in the early medieval period. Monks (less often nuns) saw copying manuscripts and even writing books as a religious calling, and monastic scribes preserved many ancient Latin works that would otherwise have disappeared. The survival of Greek works depended more on Byzantine and Muslim scribes in the east.

Monasteries and convents served other functions as well. A few planted Christianity in new lands, as Irish monks did in parts of Germany. Most serviced the needs of travelers, organized agricultural production on their lands, and took in infants abandoned by their parents. Convents provided refuge for widows and other women who lacked male protection in the harsh medieval

AP® Exam Tip Explain how the monastic life both reinforced existing social structures and offered new roles to some men and women.

Monasticism Living in a religious community apart from secular society and adhering to a rule stipulating chastity, obedience, and poverty. It was a prominent element of medieval Christianity and Buddhism. Monasteries were the primary centers of learning and literacy in medieval Europe.

world or who desired a spiritual life. These religious houses presented problems of oversight to the church, however. A bishop might have authority over an abbot or *abbess* (head of a convent), but he could not exercise constant vigilance over what went on behind monastery walls.

The failure of some abbots to maintain monastic discipline led to the growth of a reform movement centered on the Benedictine abbey of Cluny (**KLOO-nee**) in eastern France. Founded in 910 by William the Pious, the first duke of Aquitaine, who completely freed it of lay authority, Cluny gained similar freedom from the local bishop a century later. Its abbots pursued a vigorous campaign, eventually in alliance with reforming popes like Gregory VII, to improve monastic discipline and administration. A magnificent new abbey church symbolized Cluny's claims to eminence. With later additions, it became the largest church in the world.

At the peak of Cluny's influence, nearly a thousand Benedictine abbeys and *priories* (lower-level monastic houses) in various countries accepted the authority of its abbot. Whereas the Benedictine Rule had presumed that each monastery would be independent, the Cluniac reformers stipulated that every abbot and every *prior* (head of a priory) be appointed by the abbot of Cluny and have personal experience of the religious life of Cluny. Monastic reform also gained new impetus in the second half of the twelfth century with the rapid rise of the Cistercian order, which emphasized a life of asceticism and poverty. These movements set the pattern for the monasteries, cathedral clergy, and preaching friars that would dominate ecclesiastical life in the thirteenth century.

Section Review

- Christianity in western Europe focused on the pope in Rome, but conflict with Holy Roman Emperors led to the investiture controversy.

- Likewise, conflict grew between Henry of England and the archbishop Thomas à Becket, leading to Becket's martyrdom.

- One religious constant was life in monasteries; Benedict of Nursia founded the Benedictine Rule, and later the need for greater discipline over monks and nuns led to the founding of Cluny, a center of monastic reform.

- Monasteries provided many charitable services and preserved learning.

11-4 Kievan Russia, 900–1200

What was the significance of the adoption of Orthodox Christianity by Kievan Russia?

Though Latin and Orthodox Christendom followed different paths in later centuries, which of them had a more promising future was not apparent in 900. The Poles and other Slavic peoples living in the north eventually accepted the Christianity of Rome as taught by German priests and missionaries. The Serbs and other southern Slavs took their faith from Constantinople.

The conversion of Kievan Russia, farther to the east, shows how economics, politics, and religious life were closely intertwined. The choice of orthodoxy over Catholicism had important consequences for later European history.

11-4a The Rise of the Kievan Empire

The territory between the Black and Caspian Seas in the south and the Baltic and White Seas in the north divides into a series of east-west zones. Frozen tundra in the far north gives way to a cold forest zone, then to a more temperate forest, then to a mix of forest and steppe grasslands, and finally to grassland only. Several navigable rivers, including the Volga, the Dnieper (**d-NYEP-er**), and the Don, run from north to south across these zones.

Early historical sources reflect repeated linguistic and territorial changes, seemingly under pressure from poorly understood population migrations. Most of the Germanic peoples, along with some Iranian and west Slavic peoples, migrated into eastern Europe from Ukraine and Russia in Roman times. The peoples who remained behind spoke eastern Slavic languages, except in the far north and south: Finns and related peoples lived in the former region, Turkic-speakers in the latter.

Forest dwellers, farmers, and steppe nomads complemented each other economically. Nomads traded animals for the farmers' grain; and honey, wax, and furs from the forests became important exchange items. Traders could travel east and west by steppe caravan (see Chapters 9 and 13), or they could use boats on the rivers to move north and south.

AP® Exam Tip
Compare the expansion and impact of various trade networks during this time period.

Hoards containing thousands of Byzantine and Islamic coins buried in Poland and on islands in the Baltic Sea where fairs were held attest to the trading activity of *Varangians* (Swedish vikings) who sailed across the Baltic and down Russia's rivers. The Varangians exchanged forest products and slaves for manufactured goods and coins, which they may have used as jewelry rather than as money, at markets controlled by the Khazar Turks, a powerful kingdom centered around the mouth of the Volga River.

Historians debate the early meaning of the word *Rus* (from which *Russia* is derived), but at some point it came to refer to Slavic-speaking peoples ruled by Varangians. Unlike western European lords, the Varangian princes and their *druzhina* (military retainers) lived in cities, while the Slavs farmed. The princes occupied themselves with trade and fending off enemies. The Rus of the city of Kiev (**KEE-yev**), which was taken over by Varangians around 880, controlled trade on the Dnieper River and dealt more with Byzantium than with the Muslim world because the Dnieper flows into the Black Sea. The Rus of Novgorod (**NOHV-goh-rod**) played the same role on the Volga. The semilegendary account of the Kievan Rus conversion to Christianity must be seen against this background.

In 980 Vladimir (**VLAD-ih-mir**) I, a ruler of Novgorod who had fallen from power, returned from exile to Kiev with a band of Varangians and made himself the grand prince of Kievan Russia (see Map 11.3). Though his grandmother Olga had been a Christian, Vladimir

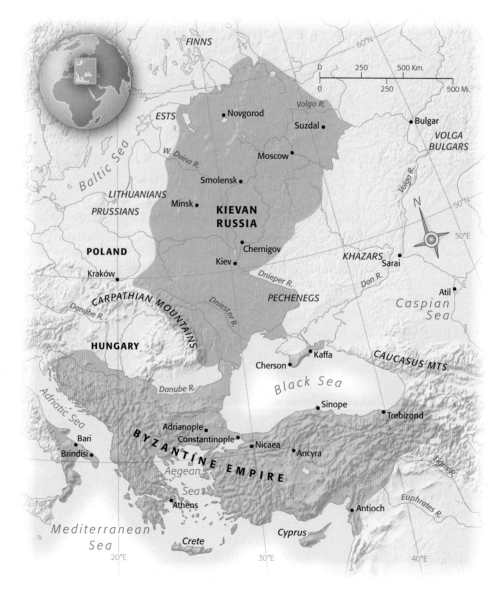

MAP 11.3   Kievan Russia and the Byzantine Empire in the Eleventh Century By the mid-eleventh century, the princes of Kievan Russia had brought all the eastern Slavs under their rule. The loss of Egypt, Syria, and Tunisia to Arab invaders in the seventh to eighth century had turned Byzantium from a far-flung empire into a fairly compact state. From then on the Byzantine rulers looked to the Balkans and Kievan Russia as the primary arena for extending their political and religious influence.

How did the four different writing systems of the tenth century—Roman, Greek, Cyrillic, and Arabic—reinforce cultural divisions?

▶ **Cathedral of Saint Dmitry in Vladimir**   Built between 1193 and 1197, this Russian Orthodox cathedral shows Byzantine influence. The three-arch facade, small dome, and symmetrical Greek Cross floor plan strongly resemble features of the Byzantine church shown on page 250. akg-images / RIA Nowosti

built a temple on Kiev's heights and placed there the statues of the six gods his Slavic subjects worshiped. The earliest Russian chronicle reports that Vladimir and his advisers decided against Islam as the official religion because of its ban on alcohol, rejected Judaism (the religion to which the Khazars had converted) because they thought that a truly powerful god would not have let the ancient Jewish kingdom be destroyed, and even spoke with German emissaries advocating Latin Christianity. Why Vladimir chose Orthodox Christianity over the Latin version is not precisely known. The magnificence of Constantinople seems to have been a consideration. After visiting Byzantine churches, his agents reported: "We knew not whether we were in heaven or on earth, for on earth there is no such splendor of [sic] such beauty, and we are at a loss how to describe it. We know only that God dwells there among men, and their service is finer than the ceremonies of other nations."[6]

After choosing a reluctant bride from the Byzantine imperial family, Vladimir converted to Orthodox Christianity, probably in 988, and opened his lands to Orthodox clerics and missionaries. The patriarch of Constantinople appointed a *metropolitan* (chief bishop) at Kiev to govern ecclesiastical affairs; churches arose in Kiev, one of them on the ruins of Vladimir's earlier hilltop temple; and writing was introduced, using the Cyrillic alphabet devised earlier for the western Slavs. This extension of Orthodox Christendom northward provided a barrier against the eastward expansion of Latin Christianity. Kiev became firmly oriented toward trade with Byzantium and turned its back on the Muslim world, though the Volga trade continued through Novgorod.

Struggles within the ruling family and with other enemies, most notably the steppe peoples of the south, marked the later political history of Kievan Russia. But down to the time of the Mongols in the thirteenth century (see Chapter 13), the state remained and served as an instrument for the Christianization of the eastern Slavs.

11-4b Society and Culture

The manorial agricultural system of western Europe never developed in Kievan Russia because its political power derived from trade rather than from landholding. Farmers practiced shifting cultivation of their own lands. They would burn a section of forest, then lightly scratch the ash-strewn surface with a plow. When fertility waned, they would move to another section of forest. Poor land and a short growing season in the most northerly latitudes made food scarce. Living on their own estates, the druzhina evolved from infantry into cavalry and focused their efforts more on horse breeding than on agriculture.

Large cities like Kiev and Novgorod may have reached between 30,000 and 50,000 people—roughly the size of contemporary London or Paris, but far smaller than Constantinople or major Muslim metropolises like Baghdad and Nishapur. Many cities amounted to little more than fortified trading posts. Yet they served as centers for the development of crafts, some, such as glassmaking, based on skills imported from Byzantium. Artisans enjoyed higher status in society than peasant farmers. Construction relied on wood from the forests, although Christianity brought the building of stone cathedrals and churches on the Byzantine model.

Christianity penetrated the general population slowly. Several polytheist uprisings occurred in the eleventh century, particularly in times of famine, and passive resistance led some groups to reject Christian burial and persist in cremating the dead and keeping the bones of the deceased

[6]S. A. Zenkovsky, ed., *Medieval Russia's Epics, Chronicles, and Tales* (New York, NY: New American Library, 1974), 67.

Section Review

- Power in Kievan Russia depended on trade rather than agriculture; thus there was no manorial system, and lords ruled from cities.

- Varangian traders established political dominion over Slavic peoples.

- The cities of Kiev and Novgorod provided the nucleus of Russian principalities.

- The Kievan ruler Vladimir I made Orthodox Christianity the official religion in Kievan Russia, though it penetrated the population slowly.

- Kievan cities reflected some aspects of Byzantine culture, especially in crafts such as glassmaking.

in urns. Women continued to use polytheist designs on their clothing and bracelets, and as late as the twelfth century they were still turning to polytheist priests for charms to cure sick children. Traditional Slavic marriage practices involving casual and polygamous relations particularly scandalized the clergy.

Christianity eventually triumphed, and its success led to increasing church engagement in political and economic affairs. In the twelfth century, Christian clergy became involved in government administration, some of them collecting fees and taxes related to trade. Direct and indirect revenue from trade provided the rulers with the money they needed to pay their soldiers. The rule of law also spread as Kievan Russia experienced its peak of culture and prosperity in the century before the Mongol invasion of 1237.

11-5 Western Europe Revives, 1000–1200

How did Mediterranean trade help revive western Europe?

Between 1000 and 1200 western Europe slowly emerged from nearly seven centuries of subsistence economy—in which most people who worked on the land could meet only their basic needs for food, clothing, and shelter. With the climate distinctly warmer than in previous centuries, population and agricultural production climbed, and a growing food surplus found its way to town markets, speeding the return of a money-based economy and providing support for larger numbers of craftspeople, construction workers, and traders.

Historians have attributed western Europe's revival to population growth spurred by new technologies and to the appearance in Italy and Flanders, on the coast of the North Sea, of self-governing cities devoted primarily to seaborne trade. For monarchs, the changes facilitated improvements in central administration, greater control over vassals, and consolidation of realms on the way to becoming stronger kingdoms.

11-5a The Role of Technology

AP® Exam Tip
Identify and explain technological innovations (such as the horse collar) that resulted in increased agricultural production.

A lack of concrete evidence confirming the spread of technological innovations frustrates efforts to relate the exact course of Europe's revival to technological change. Nevertheless, most historians agree that technology played a significant role in the near doubling of the population of western Europe between 1000 and 1200. The population of England seems to have risen from 1.1 million in 1086 to 1.9 million in 1200, and the population of the territory of modern France seems to have risen from 5.2 million to 9.2 million over the same period.

Examples that illustrate the difficulty of drawing historical conclusions from scattered evidence of technological change were a new type of plow and the use of efficient draft harnesses for pulling wagons. The Roman plow, which farmers in southern Europe and Byzantium continued to use, scratched shallow grooves, as was appropriate for loose, dry Mediterranean soils. The new plow cut deep into the soil with a knife-like blade, while a curved board mounted behind the blade lifted the cut layer and turned it over. This made it possible to farm the heavy, wet clays of the northern river valleys. Pulling the new plow took more energy, which could mean harnessing several teams of oxen or horses.

Horses plowed faster than oxen but were more delicate. Iron horseshoes, which were widely adopted in this period, helped protect their feet, but like the plow itself, they added to the farmer's expenses. Roman horse harnesses, inefficiently modeled on the yoke used for oxen, put such pressure on the animal's neck that a horse pulling a heavy load risked strangulation. A mystery surrounds the adoption of more efficient designs. The **horse collar**, which moves the point of traction from the animal's throat to its shoulders, first appeared around 800 in a miniature painting, and it is shown clearly as a harness for plow horses in the Bayeux Tapestry, embroidered after 1066. The breast-strap harness, which is not as well adapted for the heaviest work but was preferred in southern Europe, seems to have appeared around 500. In both cases, linguists have tried to trace key technical terms to Chinese or Turko-Mongol words and have argued for technological diffusion across Eurasia. Yet third-century Roman farmers in Tunisia and Libya used both types of harness to hitch horses and camels to plows and carts. This technology, which is still employed in Tunisia, appears clearly on Roman bas-reliefs and lamps; but there is no more concrete evidence of its movement northward into Europe than there is of similar harnessing moving across Asia. Thus the question of where efficient harnessing came from and whether it began in 500 or in 800, or was known even earlier but not extensively used, cannot be easily resolved.

Hinging on this problem is the question of when and why landowners in northern Europe began to use teams of horses to pull plows through moist, fertile river-valley soils that were too heavy for teams of oxen. Horses moved faster but cost more, particularly after the population increase raised the prices of the grain needed to feed them. Thus, it is difficult to say that one technology was always better: although agricultural surpluses did grow and better plowing did play a role in this growth, areas that continued to use oxen and even old-style plows seem to have shared in the general population growth of the period.

11-5b Cities and the Rebirth of the Trade

Independent cities governed and defended by communes appeared first in Italy and Flanders and then elsewhere. Communes were groups of leading citizens who banded together to defend their cities and demand the privilege of self-government from their lay or ecclesiastical lord. Lords who granted such privileges benefited from the commune's economic dynamism. Lacking extensive farmlands, these cities turned to manufacturing and trade, which they encouraged through the laws they enacted. Laws making serfs free once they came into the city, for example, attracted many workers from the countryside. Cities in Italy that had shrunk within walls built by the Romans now pressed against those walls, forcing the construction of new ones. Pisa built a new wall in 1000 and expanded it in 1156. Other twelfth-century cities that built new walls include Florence, Brescia (**BREH-shee-uh**), Pavia, and Siena (**see-EN-uh**).

The city of Venice was organized by settlers on a group of islands at the northern end of the Adriatic Sea that had been largely uninhabited in Roman times. In the eleventh century it became the dominant sea power in the Adriatic and competed with Pisa and Genoa, its rivals on the western side of Italy, for leadership in the trade with Muslim ports in North Africa and the eastern Mediterranean. A somewhat later merchant's list mentions trade in some 3,000 "spices" (including dyestuffs, textile fibers, and raw materials), some of them products of Muslim lands and some coming via the Silk Road or the Indian Ocean Maritime System (see Chapter 9). Among them were eleven types of alum (for dyeing), eleven types of wax, eight types of cotton, four types of indigo, five types of ginger, four types of paper, and fifteen types of sugar, along with cloves, caraway, tamarind, and fresh oranges. By the time of the Crusades (see below), maritime commerce throughout the Mediterranean had come to depend heavily on ships from Genoa, Venice, and Pisa. At the same time, the climate-driven decline of agriculture in Iran and Iraq, which became colder while Europe enjoyed unusual warmth, caused more and more trade from the Indian Ocean and Asia to flow through Egypt and Syria.

Ghent, Bruges (**broozh**), and Ypres (**EEP-r**) in Flanders rivaled the Italian cities in prosperity, trade, and industry. Enjoying comparable independence based on privileges granted by the counts of Flanders, these cities centralized the fishing and wool trades of the North Sea region. Around 1200 raw wool from England began to be woven into woolen cloth for a very large market.

More abundant coinage also signaled the upturn in economic activity. In the ninth and tenth centuries most gold coins had come from Muslim lands and the Byzantine Empire. Being worth too much for most trading purposes, they seldom reached Germany, France, and England, where the widely imitated Carolingian silver penny sufficed. With the economic revival of the twelfth century, however, minting of silver coins began in Scandinavia, Poland, and other outlying regions, and in the following century the reinvigoration of Mediterranean trade made possible a new and abundant gold coinage.

AP® Exam Tip
Identify and explain factors that contributed to urban revival in this time period.

horse collar Harnessing method that increased the efficiency of horses by shifting the point of traction from the animal's neck to the shoulders; its adoption favors the spread of horse-drawn plows and vehicles.

Section Review

- Western Europe became more dynamic after 1000.

- Population grew, and cities expanded both in area and commercial activity, with some cities gaining independence from religious and lay authorities.

- New technologies, such as better plows and horse collars, probably contributed to the economic revival, though how they arrived is unclear.

- Northern Italy and Flanders took the lead as maritime trading centers.

- Gold coinage reappeared after centuries of disuse.

11-6 The Crusades, 1095–1204

What were the origins and impact of the Crusades?

Western European revival coincided with and contributed to the **Crusades**, a series of religiously inspired Christian military campaigns against Muslims in the eastern Mediterranean that dominated the politics of Europe from 1095 to 1204 (see Chapter 10 and Map 11.4). Four great expeditions, the last redirected against the Byzantines and resulting in the Latin capture of Constantinople, constituted the region's largest military undertakings since the fall of Rome. As a result of the Crusades, noble courts and burgeoning cities in western Europe consumed more goods from the east. This set the stage for the later adoption of ideas, artistic styles, and industrial processes from Byzantium and the lands of Islam.

11-6a The Roots of the Crusades

Several social and economic currents of the eleventh century contributed to the Crusades. First, reforming leaders of the Latin Church, seeking to soften the war-like tone of society, popularized the Truce of God. This movement limited fighting between Christian lords by specifying times of truce, such as during *Lent* (the forty days before Easter) and on Sundays. Many knights welcomed a religiously approved alternative to fighting other Christians. Second, ambitious rulers, like the Norman chieftains who invaded England and Sicily, were looking for new lands to conquer. Nobles, particularly younger sons in areas where the oldest son inherited everything, were hungry for land and titles to maintain their status. Third, Italian merchants wanted to increase trade in the eastern Mediterranean and acquire trading posts in Muslim territory. However, without the rivalry between popes and kings already discussed, and without the desire of the church to demonstrate political authority over western Christendom, the Crusades might never have occurred.

Several factors focused attention on the Holy Land, which had been under Muslim rule for four centuries. **Pilgrimages** played an important role in European religious life. In western Europe, pilgrims traveled under royal protection, with a few in their number actually being tramps, thieves, beggars, peddlers, and merchants for whom pilgrimage was a safe way of traveling. Genuinely pious pilgrims often journeyed to visit the old churches and sacred relics preserved in Rome or Constantinople. The most intrepid went to Jerusalem, Antioch, and other cities under Muslim control to fulfill a vow or to atone for a sin.

Knights who followed a popular pilgrimage route across northern Spain to pray at the shrine of Santiago de Compostela learned of the expanding efforts of Christian kings to dislodge the Muslims. The Umayyad Caliphate in al-Andalus had broken up in the eleventh century, leaving its smaller successor states prey to Christian attacks from the north (see Chapter 10). This was the beginning of a movement of reconquest that culminated in 1492 with the surrender of the last Muslim kingdom. The word *crusade*, taken from Latin *crux* for "cross," was first used in Spain. Stories also circulated of the war conducted by seafaring Normans against the Muslims in Sicily, whom they finally defeated in the 1090s after thirty years of fighting.

The tales of pilgrims returning from Palestine further induced both churchmen and nobles to consider the Muslims a proper target for Christian militancy. Muslim rulers, who had controlled Jerusalem, Antioch, and Alexandria since the seventh century, generally tolerated and protected Christian pilgrims. But after 1071, when a Seljuk army defeated the Byzantine emperor at the Battle of Manzikert (see Chapter 10), Turkish nomads spread throughout the region, and security along the pilgrimage route through Anatolia, already none too good, deteriorated further. The decline of Byzantine power threatened ancient centers of Christianity, such as Ephesus in Anatolia, previously under imperial control.

Despite the theological differences between the Orthodox and Roman churches, the Byzantine emperor Alexius Comnenus asked the pope and western European rulers to help him confront the Muslim threat and reconquer what the Christians termed the "Holy Land," the early centers of Christianity in Palestine and Syria. Pope Urban II responded; at the Council of Clermont in 1095, he addressed a huge crowd of people gathered in a field and called on them, as Christians, to stop fighting one another and go to the Holy Land to fight Muslims.

"God wills it!" exclaimed voices in the crowd. People cut cloth into crosses and sewed them on their shirts to symbolize their willingness to march on Jerusalem. Thus began the holy war

Crusades (1095–1204) Armed pilgrimages to the Holy Land by Christians determined to recover Jerusalem from Muslim rule. The Crusades brought an end to western Europe's centuries of intellectual and cultural isolation

pilgrimages Journey to a sacred shrine by Christians seeking to show their piety, fulfill vows, or gain absolution for sins. Other religions also have pilgrimage traditions, such as the Muslim pilgrimage to Mecca and the pilgrimages made by early Chinese Buddhists to India in search of sacred Buddhist writings.

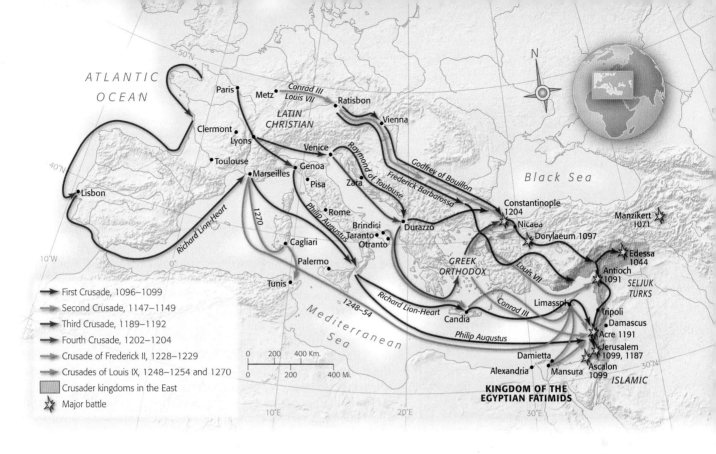

MAP 11.4 The Crusades The first two Crusades proceeded overland through Byzantine territory. The Third Crusade included contingents under the French and English kings, Philip Augustus and Richard Lion-Heart, that traveled by sea, and a contingent under the Holy Roman Emperor Frederick Barbarossa that took the overland route. Frederick died in southern Anatolia. Later Crusades were mostly seaborne, with Sicily, Crete, and Cyprus playing important roles.

What comparisons can be made between the Crusades and the Arab conquests in the name of Islam in the seventh century?

now known as the "First Crusade." People at the time more often used the word *peregrinatio*, "pilgrimage." Urban promised to free Crusaders who had committed sins from their normal penance, or acts of atonement, the usual reward for peaceful pilgrims to Jerusalem.

The First Crusade captured Jerusalem in 1099 and established four Crusader principalities, the most important being the Latin Kingdom of Jerusalem. The next two expeditions strove with diminishing success to protect these gains. Muslim forces retook Jerusalem in 1187. By the time of the Fourth Crusade in 1204, the original religious ardor had so diminished that the commanders agreed, at the urging of the Venetians, to sack Constantinople first to help pay the cost of transporting the army by Venetian ship.

11-6b The Impact of the Crusades

Exposure to Muslim culture in Spain, Sicily, Mediterranean seaports, and the Crusader principalities established in the Holy Land made many Europeans aware of things lacking in their own lives. Borrowings from Muslim society occurred gradually and are not always easy to date, but Europeans eventually learned how to manufacture pasta, paper, sugar, cotton cloth, colored glass, and many other items that had formerly been imported. Arabic translations of and commentaries on Greek philosophical, scientific, and medical works, and equally important original works by Arabs and Iranians, provided a vital stimulus to European thought.

Some works were brought directly into the Latin world through the conquests of Sicily, parts of Spain and the Holy Land, and Constantinople (for Greek texts). Others were rendered into Latin by translators who worked in parts of Spain that continued under Muslim rule. Generations passed before all these works were studied and understood, but they eventually transformed the intellectual world of the western Europeans, who previously had had little familiarity with Greek writings. The works of Aristotle and the Muslim commentaries on them were of particular importance to theologians, but Muslim writers like Avicenna (Ibn Sina) (980–1037) were of parallel importance in medicine.

AP® Exam Tip
Explain how interregional contact between Muslims and Christians during the Crusades encouraged technological and cultural transfers.

◀ **Armored Knights in Battle** This painting from around 1135 shows the armament of knights at the time of the Crusades. Chain mail, a helmet, and a shield carried on the left side protect the rider. The lance carried underarm and the sword are the primary weapons. Notice that riders about to make contact with lances have their legs straight and braced in the stirrups, while riders with swords and in flight have bent legs.

Pierpont Morgan Library/Art Resource, NY

Changes affecting the lifestyle of the nobles took place more quickly. Eleanor of Aquitaine (1122?–1204), one of the most influential women of the crusading era, accompanied her husband, King Louis VII of France, on the Second Crusade (1147–1149). The court life of her uncle Raymond, ruler of the Crusader principality of Antioch, particularly appealed to her. After her return to France, a lack of male offspring led to an annulment of her marriage with Louis, and in 1151 she married Henry of Anjou, who inherited the throne of England as Henry II three years later. Eleanor's sons—Richard Lion-Heart, famed in romance as the chivalrous foe of Saladin during the Third Crusade (1189–1192), and John—rebelled against their father but eventually succeeded him as kings of England.

In Aquitaine, a powerful duchy in southern France, Eleanor maintained her own court for a time. The poet-singers called *troubadours* who enjoyed her favor made her court a center for new music based on the idea of "courtly love," an idealization of feminine beauty and grace that influenced later European ideas of romance. Thousands of troubadour melodies survive in manuscripts, and some show the influence of the poetry styles then current in Muslim Spain. The favorite troubadour instrument, moreover, was the *lute*, a guitarlike instrument with a bulging belly whose design and name (Arabic *al-ud*) come from Muslim Spain. In centuries to come the lute would become the mainstay of Renaissance music in Italy.

Section Review

- The Crusades began because of the Truce of God, which asked Christians to stop fighting one another, and hunger for land and trade.

- Pilgrimages to the Holy Land brought attention to that area, and Pope Urban's sermon initiated the Crusader effort.

- The Crusaders captured Jerusalem and established four principalities.

- Muslim counterattacks provoked additional Crusades, and as energy flagged the Crusaders sacked Constantinople.

- The cultural contact with Muslim lands brought to Europe Muslim interpretations of ancient Greek learning and stimulated other changes in European thought and society.

- Eleanor of Aquitaine, the spouse and later the mother of crusading monarchs, promoted the culture of courtly love.

11-7 Conclusion

The legacy of Roman rule affected eastern and western Europe in different ways. Byzantium inherited the grandeur, pomp, and legal supremacy of the imperial office and merged it with leadership of the Christian church. Although it guarded its shrinking frontiers against foreign invasion, it gradually contracted around Constantinople, its imperial capital, as more and more territory was lost. By contrast, no Roman core survived in the west. The Germanic peoples overwhelmed the legions guarding the frontiers and established kingdoms based on their own traditions. The law of the king and the law of the church did not echo each other. Yet memories of Roman grandeur and territorial unity resurfaced with the idea of a Holy Roman Empire, however unworkable that empire proved to be.

The competition between the Orthodox and Catholic forms of Christianity complicated the role of religion in the emergence of medieval European society and culture. The Byzantine Empire, constructed on a Roman political and legal heritage that had largely passed away in the west, was generally more prosperous than the Germanic kingdoms of western Europe, and its arts and culture were initially more sophisticated. Furthermore, Byzantine society became deeply Christian well before a comparable degree of Christianization had been reached in western Europe. Yet despite their success in transmitting their version of Christianity and imperial rule to Kievan Russia, and in the process erecting a barrier between the Orthodox Russians and the Catholic Slavs to their west, the Byzantines failed to demonstrate the dynamism and ferment that characterized both the Europeans to their west and the Muslims to their south. Byzantine armies played only a supporting role in the Crusades, and the emperors lost their capital and their power, at least temporarily, to western Crusaders in 1204.

Technology and commerce deepened the political and religious gulf between the two Christian zones. Changes in military techniques in western Europe increased battlefield effectiveness, while new agricultural technologies accompanied population increases that revitalized urban life and contributed to the crusading movement by making the nobility hunger for new lands. At the same time, the need to import food for growing urban populations contributed to the growth of maritime commerce in the Mediterranean and North Seas. Culture and manufacturing benefited greatly from the increased pace of communication and exchange. Lacking parallel developments of a similar scale, the Byzantine Empire steadily lost the dynamism of its early centuries and by the end of the period had clearly fallen behind western Europe in prosperity and cultural innovation.

Key Terms

Charlemagne p. 269

medieval p. 269

Byzantine Empire p. 269

Kievan Russia p. 269

schism p. 270

manor p. 275

serf p. 275

fief p. 276

vassal p. 276

papacy p. 278

Holy Roman Empire
p. 279

investiture controversy
p. 279

monasticism p. 282

horse collar p. 287

Crusades p. 288

pilgrimage p. 288

Review Questions

1. How does the survival of Roman values and practices after the fall of the western empire compare with the survival of Greek values and practices after the death of Alexander the Great?

2. Did climate and water resources play as important a role in medieval European history as they did in the ancient Middle East?

3. Was the impact of Germanic and Slavic folk migrations of greater or less importance than the role of Central Asian Turko-Mongolian nomads?

 MINDTAP From Cengage

MindTap® is a fully online, personalized learning experience built upon Cengage Learning content. MindTap® combines student learning tools—readings, multimedia, activities, and assessments—into a singular Learning Path that guides students through the course and helps students develop the critical thinking, analysis, and communication skills that are essential to academic and professional success.

AP® REVIEW QUESTIONS FOR CHAPTER 11

Multiple-Choice Questions

Questions 1–3 refer to the passage below.

"We must confess, our father and lord, that after we learned from messengers that your predecessor in the apostolate [papacy], Gregory of reverend memory…had been set free from the prison of the body and had passed on to God, nothing gave us greater joy or happiness than the knowledge that the Supreme Arbiter had appointed your fatherly clemency to administer the canon law and to govern the Apostolic See…

Some of the ignorant common people, Alemanians, Bavarians, and Franks, hearing that many of the offenses prohibited by us are practiced in the city of Rome imagine that they are allowed by the priests there and reproach us for causing them to incur blame in their own lives. They say that on the first day of January, year after year, in the city of Rome and in the neighborhood of St. Peter's church by day or night, they have seen bands of singers parading the streets in pagan fashion, shouting and chanting sacrilegious songs and loading tables with food day and night, while no one in his own house is willing to lend his neighbor fire or tools or any other convenience. They say also that they have seen there women with amulets and bracelets of heathen fashion on their arms and legs, offering them for sale to willing buyers."

> Boniface, an esteemed bishop of the Southern German city of Mainz in a letter to Pope Zacharias, 742 CE

1. Boniface's letter to the Pope indicates that one of the most central bases of power for guiding peasant lives and actions in Medieval Europe was

   (A) personal preference.

   (B) military might.

   (C) church authority.

   (D) the patriarch of the family.

2. Which of the following is a way that the monastic system helped to address the "ignorance" Boniface refers to in his letter?

   (A) Literate monks made up a large and growing portion of the general population and thereby increased literacy rates.

   (B) Monastic scribes preserved many ancient Latin works, helping diffuse literary tradition where Christianity spread.

   (C) Monks and nuns encouraged peasants to give of their personal effects, gathering large sums of wealth that were used to build public libraries.

   (D) The written word was seen as a challenge to Papal authority, so most books were collected and sent to the Vatican.

3. Boniface's words reflect the connection between religion and governing in Europe. Which of the following best describes how this compares to the relationship between religion and politics in the Caliphates?

   (A) Religion played a strong role in the Caliphates' political tradition, but was only a social element in Western Europe.

   (B) Religion was only minimally important to political decisions in the Caliphates, whereas in Europe religion was all-encompassing.

   (C) Tension between political power and religious tradition made political life in Western Europe more complicated than in the Caliphates.

   (D) Neither the Caliphates nor Western Europe experienced much tension between politics and religion in this time period.

Questions 4–7 refer to the passage below.

"We command moreover that no man shall leave his lord without just cause, nor should any one receive him, except in such a way as was customary in the time of our predecessors.
And we wish you to know that we want to grant right to our faithful subjects and we do not wish to do anything to them against reason. Similarly we admonish you and the rest of our faithful subjects that you grant right to your men and do not act against reason toward them.

And we will that the man of each one of us in whosoever zkingdom he is, shall go with his lord against the enemy, or in his other needs unless there shall have been such an invasion of the kingdom as is called a *landwer*, so that the whole people of that kingdom shall go together to repel it."

> Capitulary [ordinance] made by Emperor Charles the Bald (Charles II) in 847 at Mersen [Meerssen], Holland

4. Emperor Charles the Bald's ordinance presents elements of expectations associated with which of the following?

   (A) Patriarchy

   (B) Monarchy

   (C) Legalism

   (D) Feudalism

5. In return for the security granted by such an agreement, the "free man" was expected to

   (A) provide military service to his lord.

   (B) pay monetary taxes to the lord or king.

   (C) become a servant in the lord's household.

   (D) give up most of his rights.

6. Because of agreements like the one cited in the passage, there was a profound economic transformation in many parts of Western Europe as

   (A) cities flourished due to increased trade.

   (B) urbanization led to a decrease in agricultural productivity.

   (C) the urban-based civilization established by the Romans collapsed.

   (D) wealth and trade were often centered on the capital city.

7. What political development resulted from the creation of agreements like the one made at Mersen?

   (A) Absolute monarchies developed in most parts of Western Europe.

   (B) Kings came to have fewer financial resources and seldom exercised local jurisdiction.

   (C) The power of the Church was usurped by that of local lords.

   (D) Warfare decreased as strong militaries emerged in many regions.

Questions 8–10 refer to the map on page 289.

8. According to the map, the First Crusade

   (A) showed European unity by stemming from multiple points of origin.

   (B) faced little opposition until the crusaders reached Jerusalem.

   (C) lacked support, resulting in a large loss of life and little success.

   (D) was disorganized and lacked adequate leadership.

9. Which of the following was an unintended outcome of the Crusades?

   (A) The creation of a unified Europe under a single ruler

   (B) The spread of Islam throughout Western Europe by returning crusaders

   (C) The transfer of Arab translations of Greek medical texts to Western Europe

   (D) The fall of the Islamic Caliphates and expansion of Catholicism to the Middle East

10. What was the most important long-term impact of the Crusades on Western Europe?

    (A) The spread of Christianity into the Eastern Mediterranean region brought vast wealth to Europe.

    (B) The power of popes increased while the political force of kings was weakened.

    (C) The agrarian economy of Europe was disrupted and rioting broke out in many areas.

    (D) The contact with Muslim lands created demand for luxury goods and stimulated development of trade networks.

Short-Answer Questions

"The country of Fu-lin [Byzantium]. . . . The towns and the country districts are each under the jurisdiction of a *shou-ling* [chief]. Twice a year, during the summer and autumn, they must offer money and cloth. In their criminal decisions they distinguish between great and small offences. Light offences are punished by several tens of blows with the bamboo; heavy offences with up to 200 blows; capital punishment is administered by putting the culprit into a feather bag which is thrown into the sea. They are not bent on making war to neighboring countries, and in the case of small difficulties try to settle matters by correspondence; but when important interests are at stake they will also send out an army. They cast gold and silver coins without holes, however. . . . The people are forbidden to counterfeit the coin. During the sixth year of Yuan-yu [1091] they sent two embassies [to China], and their king was presented, by imperial order, with 200 pieces of cloth, pairs of white gold vases, and clothing with gold bound in a girdle."

From the *Sung-shih (History of the Song)*,
written late thirteenth century

"The inhabitants are just in their dealings, and in the trade there are not two prices. Cereals are always cheap, and the budget is well supplied. When the envoys of neighboring countries arrive at their furthest frontier they are driven by post to the royal capital and, on arrival, are presented with golden money."

MǎDuānlín, a historian of the Song dynasty,
written late thirteenth century

1. Use the passages above and your knowledge of world history to answer all parts of the question that follows.

   (A) Identify ONE example of cross-cultural interactions between the Byzantine Empire and Eurasia.

   (B) Explain ONE political characteristic of the Byzantine Empire.

   (C) Explain ONE economic characteristic of the Byzantine Empire.

2. Answer all parts of the question that follows.

   (A) Identify ONE economic or cultural difference between Russia and feudal Europe between 1000 and 1200.

   (B) Explain ONE economic similarity between Russia and feudal Europe between 1000 and 1200.

   (C) Explain ONE cultural similarity between Russia and feudal Europe between 1000 and 1200.

12 Central and East Asia, 400–1200

AP® Framework Terms

Confucianism
Neo-Confucianism
Compass
Grand Canal
Sui dynasty
Tang dynasty
Song dynasty
Japanese feudalism

Overarching Questions

1 How have religions, belief systems, philosophies, and ideologies affected the political, economic, and social development of societies? (CUL)

2 How and why have economic, social, cultural, and geographic factors influenced the process of state building, expansion, and dissolution? (SB)

3 How have internal and external political factors influenced the process of state building, expansion, and dissolution? (SB)

4 How have economic systems and the development of ideologies, values, and institutions influenced each other? (ECON)

5 How have distinctions based on kinship, ethnicity, class, gender, and race influenced the development and transformation of social hierarchies? (SOC)

The powerful and expansive Tang Empire (618–907) ended four centuries of rule by short-lived and competing states that had brought turmoil to China after the fall of the Han Empire in 220 CE (see Chapter 6). Tang rule also encouraged the spread of Buddhism, brought by missionaries from India and by Chinese pilgrims returning with sacred Sanskrit texts. The Tang left an indelible mark on the Chinese imagination long after it, too, fell.

According to surviving memoirs, people watched shadow plays and puppet shows, listened to music and scholarly lectures, or took in less edifying spectacles like wrestling and bear baiting in the urban entertainment quarters that flourished in southern China under the succeeding Song (**soong**) Empire. From the 1170s onward, singer-storytellers spun long romantic narratives that alternated prose passages with sung verse.

Master Tung's *Western Chamber Romance* stood out for its literary quality. In 184 prose passages and 5,263 lines of verse the narrator tells of a love affair between Chang, a young Confucian scholar, and Ying-ying, a ravishing damsel. Secondary characters include Ying-ying's shrewd and worldly mother, a general who practices just and efficient administration, and a fighting monk named Fa-ts'ung (**fa-soong**). The romance is based on *The Story of Ying-ying* by Tang period author Yüan Chen (**you-ahn shen**) (779–831).

◀ **Going Up the River** Song cities hummed with commercial and industrial activity, much of it concentrated on the rivers and canals linking the capital Kaifeng to the provinces. This detail from *Going Upriver at the Qingming [Spring] Festival* shows a tiny portion of the scroll painting's panorama. Painted by Zhang Zeduan sometime before 1125, its depiction of daily life makes it an important source of information on working people. Before open shop fronts and tea houses a camel caravan departs, donkey carts are unloaded, a scholar rides loftily (if gingerly) on horseback, and women of wealth go by enclosed sedan-chairs. "Going Up the River at the Qingming (Spring) Festival" by Zhang Zeduan/Werner Forman Archive/The Bridgeman Art Library

As the tale begins, the abbot of a Buddhist monastery responds to Chang's request to rent him a study, singing:

Sir, you're wrong to offer me rent.
We Buddhists and Confucians are of one family.
As things stand, I can't give you
A place in our dormitory,
But you're welcome to stay
In one of the guest apartments.

As soon as Chang spies Ying-ying, who lives there with her mother, thoughts of studying flee his mind. Romance takes a detour, however, when bandits attack the monastery. A prose passage explains:

During the T'ang dynasty, troops were stationed in the P'u prefecture. The year of our story, the commander of the garrison, Marshal Hun, died. . . . A subordinate general rebelled with five thousand soldiers. They pillaged and plundered the P'u area. How do I know this to be true? It is corroborated by *The Ballad of the True Story of Ying-ying*.

As the monks dither, one of them lifts his robe to reveal his "three-foot consecrated sword."

[Prose] Who was this monk? He was none other than Fa-ts'ung. . . . When he was young he took great pleasure in archery, fencing, hunting, and often sneaked into foreign states to steal. He was fierce and courageous. When his parents died, it suddenly became clear to him that the way of the world was frivolous and trivial, so he became a monk in the Temple of Universal Salvation . . . .

[Song] He didn't know how to read sutras;
He didn't know how to follow rituals;
He was neither pure nor chaste
But indomitably courageous . . . .[1]

[1]*Master Tung's Western Chamber Romance*, trans. Li-li Ch'en (New York, NY: Columbia University Press, 1994), 22, 42–43, 45–46.

Amidst the love story, the ribaldry, and the derring-do, the author implants historical vignettes that mingle fact and fiction. Sophisticates of the Song era, living a life of ease, enjoyed these romanticized portrayals of Tang society.

The Tang Empire became a model for emerging regimes on the Korean Peninsula, in northeast Asia, on the Japanese islands, and, to a certain extent, in continental Southeast Asia. But the formation of an East Asian cultural zone did not occur in isolation. Travelers from as far as India and Persia traveled to Tang China, bringing with them their native religions, artistic tastes, popular entertainments, technologies, and cuisine. Foreigners worked in the Tang bureaucracy, served in the military, and maintained close ties to the royal family.

The Song Empire that eventually succeeded the Tang Empire never approached the Tang's dominance over East Asia, nor was it as globally connected. However, it was extraordinarily productive and advanced in terms of technology, economy, and government. The sustainable boom in population during the Song Dynasty that fostered urbanization and the expansion of domestic markets and international trade played a major role in these developments. However, these were not simply Chinese achievements; newly introduced rice varieties from Southeast Asia triggered a Song agricultural revolution. ●

12-1 The Sui and Tang Empires, 581–755

What is the importance of Inner and Central Asia as a region of interchange during the Tang period?

After centuries of fragmentation, China was reunified under the Sui (**sway**) dynasty, father and son rulers who held power from 581 until Turks from Central Asia defeated the son in 615. He was assassinated three years later, and the Tang filled the political vacuum.

The small kingdoms of northern China and Central Asia that had come and gone during the period between the Han and the Sui had structured themselves around a variety of political ideas and institutions. Some favored the Chinese tradition, with an emperor, a bureaucracy using the Chinese language exclusively, and a Confucian state philosophy (see Chapter 6). Others reflected Tibetan, Turkic, or other regional cultures and depended on Buddhism to legitimate their rule. Throughout the period the relationship between northern China and the deserts and steppes of Central Asia remained a central focus of political life, a key commercial linkage, and a source of new ideas and practices.

Though northern China constituted the Sui heartland, population centers along the Yangzi (**yahng-zeh**) River in the south grew steadily and pointed to what would be the future direction of Chinese expansion. To facilitate communication and trade with the south, the Sui built the 1,100-mile (1,771-kilometer) **Grand Canal** linking the Yellow River with the Yangzi, and they also constructed irrigation systems in the Yangzi Valley. On their northern frontier, the Sui also improved the Great Wall, the barrier against nomadic incursions that had been gradually constructed by several earlier states.

Sui military ambition, which extended to Korea and Vietnam as well as Central Asia, required high levels of organization and mustering of resources—manpower, livestock, wood, iron, and food supplies. The same was true of their massive public works projects. These burdens proved more than the Sui could sustain. Overextension compounded the political dilemma stemming from the military defeat and subsequent assassination of the second Sui emperor. These circumstances opened the way for another strong leader to establish a new state.

In 618 the powerful Li family took advantage of Sui disorder to carve out an empire of similar scale and ambition. They adopted the dynastic name Tang (see Map 12.1). The brilliant emperor **Li Shimin** (**lee shir-meen**) (r. 626–649) extended his power primarily westward into Central

AP® Exam Tip
Explain how state-sponsored infrastructure like the Grand Canal facilitated commercial growth.

Grand Canal The 1,100-mile (1,771-kilometer) waterway linking the Yellow and the Yangzi Rivers. It was begun in the Han period and completed during the Sui Empire.

Li Shimin One of the founders of the Tang Empire and its second emperor (r. 626–649). He led the expansion of the empire into Central Asia.

	Central Asia	China	Northeast and Southeast Asia	Japan
200		220–589 China disunited 581–618 Sui unification	313–668 Three Korean kingdoms: Koguryŏ, Paekche, Silla	
600	751 Battle of Talas River	618 Tang Empire founded 626–649 Li Shimin reign 690–705 Wu Zhao reign 755–763 An Lushan rebellion	668 Silla victory in Korea	645–655 Taika era 710–784 Nara as capital 752 "Eye-opening" ceremony 794 Heian era
800		840 Suppression of Buddhism 879–881 Huang Chao rebellion 907 End of Tang Empire 960 Song Empire founded	916 Liao Empire founded 918 Koryo founded: Korean Peninsula unified 936 Annam becomes Dai Viet (northern Vietnam)	866–1180 Fujiwara influence
1000	1038–1227 Tanggut state on China's north west frontier	1127–1279 Southern Song period	1115 Jin Empire founded	ca. 1000 *The Tale of Genji*
1200				1185 Kamakura Shogunate founded

Asia. Though he and succeeding **Tang** rulers retained many Sui governing practices, they avoided overcentralization by allowing local nobles, gentry, officials, and religious establishments to exercise significant power (see Diversity & Dominance: Law and Society in China and Japan).

The Tang emperors and nobility descended from the Turkic elites that built small states in northern China after the Han, as well as from Chinese officials and settlers who had moved there. They appreciated the pastoral nomadic culture of Central Asia (see Chapter 9) as well as Chinese traditions. Some of the most impressive works of Tang art are large pottery figurines of the horses and two-humped camels used along the Silk Road, brilliantly colored with glazes devised by Chinese potters. In warfare, the Tang combined Chinese weapons—the crossbow and armored infantrymen—with Central Asian expertise in horsemanship and the use of iron stirrups. At their peak, from about 650 to 751, when they were defeated in Central Asia (present-day Kyrgyzstan) by an Arab Muslim army at the Battle of the Talas River, the Tang armies were a formidable force.

12-1a Chang'an: Metropolis at the Center of East Asia

Much of the global interaction in China during the Sui and Tang dynasties occurred in the capital Chang'an (**chahng-ahn**), named in honor of the old Han capital. With a population of nearly 2 million, Chang'an and its surrounding suburbs constituted the largest metropolitan area in the world at the time. Its gridlike layout, with its palace located in the north Pole Star position to reflect the celestial order, was imitated by Korean and Japanese capitals.

Chang'an became the center of what is often called the **tributary system**, a type of political relationship dating from Han times by which independent countries acknowledged the Chinese emperor's supremacy. Each tributary state sent regular embassies to the capital to pay tribute. As symbols of China's political supremacy, these embassies sometimes meant more to the Chinese than to the tribute-payers, who might have seen them more as a means of accessing the vast Chinese market.

More than simply a political center, Chang'an was also the premier study-abroad destination in Asia. Rulers sent intellectuals to learn *statecraft*, the techniques of running a government, to bring back to their home governments. Nestorian Christian churches and even Jewish communities existed in Chang'an, as did many Daoist and Buddhist temples and monasteries. Monks from Korea and Japan could study with Chinese Buddhists and with Indian masters who taught there in Sanskrit. The diverse population also included Central Asian, Arab, and Persian merchants who became long-time residents of the city. So many Iranians lived in Chang'an, for example, that the government established a special office just to address Iranian–Tang affairs.

AP® Exam Tip Consider the technological and cultural exchanges that were facilitated by trade between the Tang and the Abbasid empires.

Tang Empire Empire unifying China and part of Central Asia, founded 618 and ended 907. The Tang emperors presided over a magnificent court at their capital, Chang'an.

tributary system A system in which, from the time of the Han Empire, countries in East and Southeast Asia not under the direct control of empires based in China nevertheless enrolled as tributary states, acknowledging the superiority of the emperors in China in exchange for trading rights or strategic alliances.

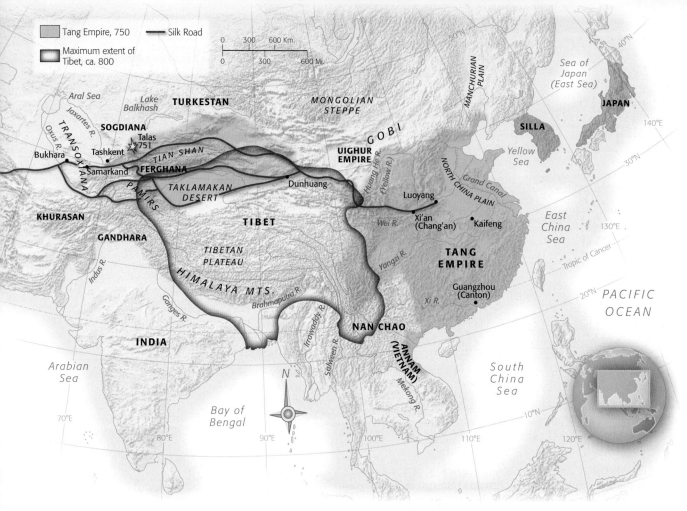

MAP 12.1 **The Tang Empire in Central and Eastern Asia, 750** For over a century the Tang Empire controlled China and a very large part of Central Asia. The defeat of Tang armies in 751 by a force of Arabs, Turks, and Tibetans at the Talas River in present-day Kyrgyzstan ended Tang westward expansion. To the south the Tang dominated Annam. Japan and the Silla kingdom in Korea were leading tributary states of the Tang.

Which posed a greater geographic threat to the Tang, Tibet or the Arabs occupying Iran?

AP® Exam Tip

Understand the reasons for the spread of major religions such as Buddhism.

12-1b Buddhism and the Tang Empire

State cults based on Buddhism had flourished in Central Asia and north China since the fall of the Han, and the Tang rulers followed these Central Asian precedents in their political use of Buddhism. Some interpretations of Buddhist doctrine accorded kings and emperors the spiritual function of welding humankind into a harmonious Buddhist society. Protecting spirits were believed to help the ruler govern and prevent harm from coming to his people.

Mahayana **mah-HAH-YAH-nah** or "Great Vehicle," Buddhism predominated. Mahayana fostered faith in enlightened beings—*bodhisattvas*—who postpone nirvana (see Chapter 7) to help others achieve enlightenment. This permitted the absorption of local gods and goddesses into Mahayana sainthood and thereby made conversion more attractive to the common people. Mahayana also encouraged translating Buddhist scripture into local languages, and it accepted religious practices not based on written texts. The tremendous reach of Mahayana views, which proved adaptable to different societies and classes of people, invigorated travel, language learning, and cultural exchange.

Early Tang princes competing for political influence enlisted monastic leaders to pray for them, preach on their behalf, counsel aristocrats to support them, and—perhaps most important—contribute monastic wealth to their war chests. In return, the monasteries received tax exemptions, land privileges, and gifts.

As the Tang Empire expanded westward through Central Asia, contacts with Afghanistan and India increased, and so did the complexity of Buddhist influence throughout China. The Mahayana network connecting Central Asia and China intersected a vigorous commercial world in which material goods and cultural influences mixed. Though Buddhism and Confucianism proved attractive to many different peoples, regional cultures and identities remained strong, just as regional commitments to Tibetan, Uighur (**WEE-ger**), and other languages and writing systems coexisted with the widespread use of written Chinese. Textiles reflected Persian, Korean, and Vietnamese styles, while influences from every part of Asia appeared in sports, music, and painting. Many historians characterize the Tang Empire as "cosmopolitan" because of its breadth and diversity.

12-1c Upheavals and Repression, 750–879

The later years of the Tang Empire saw increasing turmoil as a result of conflict with Tibetans and Turkic Uighurs. One result was a backlash against "foreigners," which to Confucians included Buddhists. The Tang elites came to see Buddhism as undermining the Confucian idea of the family as the model for the state. Confucian scholar Han Yu (768–824) spoke powerfully for a return to traditional Confucian practices. In "Memorial on the Bone of Buddha," written to the emperor in 819 on the occasion of ceremonies to receive a bone of the Buddha in the imperial palace, he scornfully disparages the Buddha and his followers:

> Now Buddha was a man of the barbarians who did not speak the language of China and wore clothes of a different fashion. His sayings did not concern the ways of our ancient kings, nor did his manner of dress conform to their laws. He understood neither the duties that bind sovereign and subject nor the affections of father and son. If he were still alive today and came to our court by order of his ruler, Your Majesty might condescend to receive him, but . . . he would then be escorted to the borders of the state, dismissed, and not allowed to delude the masses. How then, when he has long been dead, could his rotten bones, the foul and unlucky remains of his body, be rightly admitted to the palace? Confucius said, "Respect spiritual beings, while keeping at a distance from them."[2]

Buddhism was also attacked for encouraging women in politics. Wu Zhao (**woo jow**), a woman who had married into the imperial family, seized control of the government in 690 and declared herself emperor. She based her legitimacy on claiming to be a bodhisattva, an enlightened soul who had chosen to remain on earth to lead others to salvation. She also favored Buddhists and Daoists over Confucians in her court and government.

---

[2]Theodore de Bary, ed., *Sources of Chinese Tradition*, vol. 1, 2nd ed. (New York, NY: Columbia University Press, 1999), 584.

▶ **Iron Stirrups** This bas-relief from the tomb of Li Shimin depicts the type of horse on which the Tang armies conquered China and Central Asia. Saddles with high supports in front and back, breastplates, and *cruppers* (straps beneath the tail that help keep the saddle in place) point to the importance of high speeds and quick maneuvering. Central Asian horsemen had iron stirrups available from the time of the Huns (fifth century). Earlier stirrups were of leather or wood. Stirrups could support the weight of shielded and well-armed soldiers rising in the saddle to shoot arrows or use lances. Horse figures, relief from Emperor T'ai Tsung's tomb in Hsi-An (Shensi), Chinese civilization, 7th century/ De Agostini Picture Library/The Bridgeman Art Library

The Tang law code, compiled in the early seventh century, served as the basis for the Tang legal system and as a model for later dynastic law codes. It combined the centralized authority of the imperial government, as visualized in the legalist tradition dating back to Han times, with Confucian concern for status distinctions and personal relationships. Like contemporary approaches to law in Christian Europe and the Islamic world, it did not fully distinguish between government as a structure of domination and law as an echo of religious and moral values.

Following a Preface, 502 articles, each with several parts, are divided into twelve books. Each article contains a basic ordinance with commentary, subcommentary, and sometimes additional questions. Excerpts from a single article from Book 1, General Principles, follow.

The Ten Abominations

Text: The first is called plotting rebellion.

Subcommentary: The *Gongyang* **GON-gwang** *Commentary* states: "The ruler or parent has no harborers [of plots]. If he does have such harborers, he must put them to death." This means that if there are those who harbor rebellious hearts that would harm the ruler or father, he must then put them to death.

The king occupies the most honorable position and receives Heaven's precious decrees. Like Heaven and Earth, he acts to shelter and support, thus serving as the father and mother of the masses. As his children, as his subjects, they must be loyal and filial. Should they dare to cherish wickedness and have rebellious hearts, however, they will run counter to Heaven's constancy and violate human principle. Therefore, this is called plotting rebellion.

Text: The second is called plotting great sedition.

Subcommentary: This type of person breaks laws and destroys order, is against traditional norms, and goes contrary to virtue . . . .

Commentary: Plotting great sedition means to plot to destroy the ancestral temples, tombs, or palaces of the reigning house.

Text: The third is called plotting treason.

Subcommentary: The kindness of father and mother is like "great heaven, illimitable." . . . Let one's heart be like the [raucous] *xiao* bird or the *jing* beast, and then love and respect both cease. Those whose relationship is within the five degrees of mourning are the closest of kin. For them to kill each other is the extreme abomination and the utmost in rebellion, destroying and casting aside human principles. Therefore this is called contumacy.

Commentary: Contumacy means to beat or plot to kill [without actually killing] one's paternal grandparents or parents; or to kill one's paternal uncles or their wives, or one's elder brothers or sisters, or one's maternal grandparents, or one's husband, or one's husband's paternal grandparents, or his parents . . . .

Text: The fifth is called depravity.

Subcommentary: This article describes those who are cruel and malicious and who turn their backs on morality. Therefore it is called depravity.

Commentary: Depravity means to kill three members of a single household who have not committed a capital crime, or to dismember someone . . . .

Commentary: The offense also includes the making or keeping of poison or sorcery.

Subcommentary: This means to prepare the poison oneself, or to keep it, or to give it to others in order to harm people. But if the preparation of the poison is not yet completed, this offense does not come under the ten abominations. As to sorcery, there are a great many methods, not all of which can be described.

Text: The tenth is called incest.

Subcommentary: The *Zuo Commentary* states: "The woman has her husband's house; the man has his wife's chamber; and there

Later Confucian writers expressed contempt for Wu Zhao and other powerful women, such as the concubine Yang Guifei (**yahng gway-fay**). Bo Zhuyi (**baw joo-ee**), in his poem "Everlasting Remorse," lamented the influence of women at the Tang court, which had caused "the hearts of fathers and mothers everywhere not to value the birth of boys, but the birth of girls."[3] Confucian elites heaped every possible charge on prominent women who offended them, accusing Emperor Wu of grotesque tortures and murders, including tossing the dismembered but still living bodies of enemies into wine vats and cauldrons. They blamed Yang Guifei for the outbreak of the An Lushan rebellion in 755 (see later in this chapter).

Serious historians dismiss the stories about Wu Zhao as stereotypical characterizations of "evil" rulers. *Eunuchs* (castrated palace servants) charged by historians with controlling Chang'an and the Tang court and publicly executing rival bureaucrats represent a similar stereotype. In fact, Wu seems to have ruled effectively and was not deposed until 705, when extreme old age (eighty-plus) incapacitated her. Nevertheless, traditional Chinese historians commonly describe unorthodox rulers and all-powerful women as evil, so the truth about Wu will never be known.

[3]Quoted in David Lattimore, "Allusion in T'ang Poetry," in *Perspectives on the T'ang*, eds. Arthur F. Wright and David Twitchett (New Haven, CT: Yale University Press, 1973), 436.

must be no defilement on either side." If this is changed, then there is incest. If one behaves like birds and beasts and introduces licentious associates into one's family, the rules of morality are confused. Therefore this is called incest.

Commentary: This section includes having illicit sexual intercourse with relatives who are of the fourth degree of mourning or closer . . . .

In Japan during the same period, there appeared a set of governing principles attributed to Prince Shotoku (573–621) called the "Seventeen-Article Constitution." These principles, which continued to influence Japanese government for many centuries, reflect Confucian ideals even though the prince was himself a devout Buddhist. The complete text of five of these principles follows:

I

Harmony is to be valued, and contentiousness avoided. All men are inclined to partisanship and few are truly discerning. Hence there are some who disobey their lords and fathers and who maintain feuds with the neighboring villages. But when those above are harmonious and those below are conciliatory and there is con cord in the discussion of all matters, the disposition of affairs comes about naturally. Then what is there that cannot be accomplished?

VIII

Let ministers and functionaries attend the courts early in the morning, and retire late. The business of the state does not admit of remissness, and the whole day is hardly enough for its accomplishment. If, therefore, the attendance at court is late, emergencies cannot be met; if officials retire soon, the work cannot be completed.

IX

Trustworthiness is the foundation of right. In everything let there be trustworthiness, for in this there surely consists the

good and the bad, success and failure. If the lord and the vassal trust one another, what is there which cannot be accomplished? If the lord and the vassal do not trust one another, everything without exception ends in failure.

XIII

Let all persons entrusted with office attend equally to their functions. Owing to their illness or to their being sent on missions, their work may sometimes be neglected. But whenever they become able to attend to business, let them be as accommodating as if they had cognizance of it from before and not hinder public affairs on the score of their not having had to do with them.

XVII

Matters should not be decided by one person alone. They should be discussed with many others. In small matters, of less consequence, many others need not be consulted. It is only in considering weighty matters, where there is a suspicion that they might miscarry, that many others should be involved in debate and discussion so as to arrive at a reasonable conclusion.

AP® History Reasoning Skills

Contextualization *How could the society for which the text is written lead to differing formats (a law code versus a constitution)?*

Comparison *How is the Confucian concern for family relations, duty, and social status manifested differently in the Chinese and Japanese documents?*

Sources: First selection from Johnson Wallace, *The Tang Code*, Vol. I. Copyright © 1979 Princeton University Press. Reprinted by permission of Princeton University Press. Second selection from *Sources of Japanese Tradition*, Vol. 1, 2nd ed., by Columbia University Press. Reprinted with permission of the publisher.

Even Chinese gentry living in safe and prosperous localities associated Buddhism with social ills. People who worried about "barbarians" ruining their society pointed to Buddhism as evidence of the foreign evil, since it had such strong roots in Central Asia and Tibet. Moreover, because Buddhists shunned earthly ties, monks and nuns severed relations with the secular world in search of enlightenment. They paid no taxes, served in no army. They deprived their families of advantageous marriage alliances and denied descendants to their ancestors. The Confucian elites saw all this as threatening to the family and to the family estates that underlay the Tang economic and political structure.

By the ninth century, hundreds of thousands of people had entered tax-exempt Buddhist institutions. In 840 the government moved to crush the monasteries whose tax exemption had allowed them to accumulate land, serfs, and

Section Review

- After the period of disunity following the fall of the Han, China was united under the Sui, followed by the Tang with its founder Li Shimin.

- Tang culture was based on both Central Asian nomadic culture and war expertise and Chinese tradition.

- The Tang Empire, along with the rival Uighur and Tibetan states, experienced political problems that steadily weakened it.

- In China, this turmoil resulted in a backlash against foreign and female cultural influences and especially Buddhism, as Tang elites led a neo-Confucian reaction.

- The Tang fell due to a combination of destabilizing forces.

◀ **Tang Horsewoman** This ceramic tomb figurine from the far northwest, a region populated largely by Turkic-speaking peoples, is unusual in being painted rather than glazed. The woman's costume suggests that she is of high rank, but not Chinese. Note the difference between the rider's light, toe-only stirrup and the full iron military stirrup shown in the Iron Stirrups illustration in Section 12-1c. Panorama Media/AGE Fotostock

precious objects, often as gifts. Within five years 4,600 temples had been destroyed. Now an enormous amount of land and 150,000 workers were returned to the tax rolls. Buddhist centers like the cave monasteries at Dunhuang were protected by local warlords loyal to Buddhist rulers in Central Asia. Nevertheless, China's cultural heritage suffered a great loss in the dissolution of the monasteries. Some sculptures and grottoes survived only in defaced form. Wooden temples and facades sheltering great stone carvings burned to the ground. Monasteries became legal again in later times, but Buddhism never recovered the influence of early Tang times.

12-1d The End of the Tang Empire, 879–907

The campaigns of expansion in the seventh century had left the empire dependent on local military commanders and a complex tax collection system. Reverses like the Battle of the Talas River in 751, where Arabs halted Chinese expansion into Central Asia, led to military demoralization and underfunding. In 755 An Lushan, a Tang general on the northeast frontier, led about 200,000 soldiers in rebellion. The emperor fled Chang'an and executed his favorite concubine, Yang Guifei, who was rumored to be An Lushan's lover. The rebellion lasted for eight years and resulted in new powers for the provincial military governors who helped suppress it. Even so, Chang'an never recovered, and during the eighth century, its decline symbolized Tang's waning influence over satellite states in Korea and Japan, which could no longer turn to China for support or inspiration.

A disgruntled member of the gentry, Huang Chao (**wang show**), led the most devastating uprising between 879 and 881. Despite his ruthless treatment of the villages he controlled, his rebellion attracted poor farmers and tenants who could not protect themselves from local bosses and oppressive landlords, or who simply did not know where else to turn in the deepening chaos. The new hatred of "barbarians" spurred the rebels to murder thousands of foreign residents in Guangzhou (Canton) and Beijing (**bay-jeeng**).

Local warlords finally wiped out the rebels, but Tang society did not find peace. Refugees, migrant workers, and homeless people became common sights. Residents of northern China fled to the southern frontiers as groups from Central Asia moved into localities in the north. Though Tang emperors continued in Chang'an until a warlord terminated their line in 907, they never regained power after Huang Chao's rebellion.

12-2 China and Its Rivals

What were the effects of the fracturing of power in Central Asia and China?

In the aftermath of the Tang, three new states emerged and competed to inherit its legacy (see Map 12.2). The Liao (**lee-OW**) Empire of the Khitan (**kee-THAN**) people, pastoral nomads related to the Mongols living on the northeastern frontier, established their rule in the north. They centered their government on several cities, but the emperors preferred life in nomad encampments. On the Central Asian frontier in northwestern China, the Minyak people (cousins of the Tibetans) established a state they called Tanggut (1038–1227) (**TAHNG-gut**) to show their connection with the fallen empire. The third state, the Chinese-speaking **Song Empire**, came into being in 960 in central China.

Song Empire Empire in central and southern China (960–1126) while the Liao people controlled the north. Also empire in southern China (1127–1279; the "Southern Song") while the Jin people controlled the north. Distinguished for its advances in technology, medicine, astronomy, and mathematics.

These states embodied the political ambitions of peoples with different religious and philosophical systems—Mahayana Buddhism among the Liao, Tibetan Buddhism among the Tangguts, and Confucianism among the Song. Cut off from Central Asia, the Song used advanced seafaring and sailing technologies to forge maritime connections with other states in East, West, and Southeast Asia. The Song elite shared the late Tang dislike of "barbaric" or "foreign" influences as they tried to cope with multiple enemies that heavily taxed their military capacities. Meanwhile, Korea, Japan, and some Southeast Asian states strengthened political and cultural ties with China.

12-2a The Liao and Jin Challenge

The Liao Empire of the Khitan people extended from Siberia to Central Asia. Variations on Khitan became the name for China in these distant regions: "Kitai" for the Mongols, "Khitai" for the Russians, and "Cathay" for Italian merchants like Marco Polo who reported on China in Europe (see Chapter 13).

The Liao rulers prided themselves on their pastoral traditions as horse and cattle breeders, which were the continuing source of their military might, and they made no attempt to create a single elite culture. Instead, they encouraged Chinese elites to use their own language, study their own classics, and see the emperor through Confucian eyes. And they encouraged other peoples to use their own languages and see the emperor as a champion of Buddhism or as a nomadic chieftain. On balance, Buddhism far outweighed Confucianism in this and other northern states, where rulers depended on their roles as bodhisattvas or as Buddhist kings to legitimate power. Liao rule lasted from 916 to 1125.

The Liao Empire was the most powerful East Asian empire at the time, with the region's largest army. A truce concluded in 1005 required the Song emperor to pay the Liao great quantities of cash and silk annually. A century later, the Song tired of paying tribute and secretly allied with the Jurchens of northeastern Asia, who also resented Liao rule. In 1115 the Jurchens first destroyed the Liao capital in Mongolia and proclaimed their own empire, the Jin (see Map 12.2), and then turned on the Song.

The Jurchens grew rice, millet, and wheat, but they also spent a good deal of time hunting, fishing, and tending livestock. Using Khitan military arts and political organization, they

AP® Exam Tip
Explain the changes and continuities in Chinese society as it transitioned from one dynasty to the next in this time period.

▼ **Buddhist Cave Painting at Dunhuang** Hundreds of caves dating to the period when Buddhism enjoyed popularity and government favor in China survive in Gansu province, which was beyond the reach of the Tang rulers when they turned against Buddhism. This cave, dated to the period 565–576, depicts the historical Buddha flanked by bodhisattvas. Scenes of the Buddha preaching appear on the wall to the left. Zhang Peng/LightRocket/Getty Images

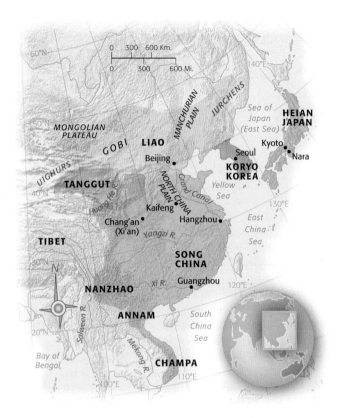

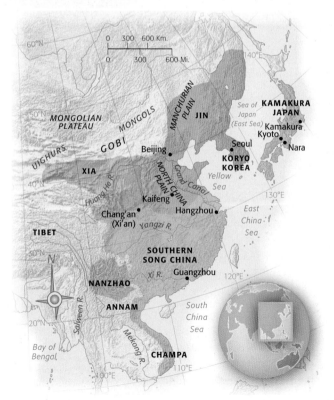

MAP 12.2 Liao and Song Empires, ca. 1100 The states of Liao in the north and Song in the south generally ceased open hostilities after a treaty in 1005 stabilized the border and imposed an annual payment on Song China.

How do this map and Map 12.3 strengthen the notion that Chinese civilization migrated over time from north to south?

became formidable enemies in an all-out campaign against the Song in 1127, laying siege to the Song capital, Kaifeng (**kie-fuhng**), and capturing the Song emperor. Within a few years the Song withdrew south of the Yellow River and established a new capital at Hangzhou (**hahng-jo**), leaving central as well as northern China in Jurchen control (see Map 12.3). Annual payments to the Jin Empire staved off further warfare. Historians generally refer to this period as the "Southern Song" (1127–1279).

12-2b Song Industries

The Southern Song came closer to initiating an industrial revolution than any other premodern state. Many Song advances in technology, medicine, astronomy, and mathematics originated in Tang times, sometimes reaching China from distant places. Song officials, scholars, and businessmen adapted this Tang lore to meet their military, agricultural, and administrative needs.

Song mathematicians introduced the use of fractions, first employing them to describe the phases of the moon. From lunar observations, Song astronomers constructed a very precise calendar and, alone among the world's astronomers, noted the explosion of the Crab Nebula in 1054. Song inventors drew on their knowledge of celestial coordinates, particularly the Pole Star, to refine compass design. The magnetic compass, an earlier Chinese invention, shrank in size in Song times and gained a fixed pivot point for the needle. With a protective glass cover, the compass now became suitable for seafaring, a use first attested in 1090.

Development of the seaworthy compass coincided with new techniques in building China's main oceangoing ship, the **junk**. A stern-mounted rudder improved the steering of the large ship in uneasy seas, and watertight bulkheads helped keep it afloat in emergencies. The shipwrights of the Persian Gulf soon copied these features in their ship designs.

Because they needed iron and steel to make weapons for their army of 1.25 million men, the Song rulers fought their northern rivals for control of mines in north China. Production of coal and iron soared. By the end of the eleventh century, cast iron production reached about 125,000 tons (113,700 metric tons) annually, putting it on a

MAP 12.3 Jin and Southern Song Empires, ca. 1200 After 1127 Song abandoned its northern territories to Jin. The Southern Song continued the policy of annual payments—to Jin rather than Liao—and maintained high military preparedness to prevent further invasions.

How did the shrinkage of Song territory contribute to the independent development of Korea and Japan?

par with the output of eighteenth-century Britain. Engineers became skilled at high-temperature metallurgy using enormous bellows, often driven by water wheels, to superheat the molten ore. Military engineers used iron to buttress defensive works because it was impervious to fire or concussion. Armorers mass-produced body armor. Iron construction also appeared in bridges and small buildings. Mass-production techniques for bronze and ceramics in use in China for nearly 2,000 years were adapted to iron casting and assembly.

To counter cavalry assaults, the Song experimented with **gunpowder**, which they initially used to propel clusters of flaming arrows. During the wars against the Jurchens in the 1100s, the Song introduced a new and terrifying weapon. Shells launched from Song fortifications exploded in the midst of the enemy, blowing out iron shrapnel and dismembering men and horses. The short range of these shells limited them to defensive uses.

12-2c Economy and Society in Song China

In a warlike era, Song elite culture idealized civil pursuits. Socially, the civil man outranked the military man. Private academies, designed to train young men for the official examinations, became influential in culture and politics. New interpretations of Confucian teachings became so important and influential that the term **neo-Confucianism** is used for Song and later versions of Confucian thought.

Zhu Xi (**jew she**) (1130–1200), the most important early neo-Confucian thinker, wrote in reaction to the many centuries during which Buddhism and Daoism had overshadowed the precepts of Confucius. He and others worked out a systematic approach to cosmology that focused on the central conception that human nature is moral, rational, and essentially good. To combat the Buddhist dismissal of worldly affairs as a transitory distraction, they reemphasized individual moral and social responsibility. Their human ideal was the *sage*, a person who could preserve mental stability and serenity while dealing conscientiously with troubling social problems. Whereas earlier Confucian thinkers had written about sage kings and political leaders, the neo-Confucians espoused the spiritual idea of universal sagehood, a state that could be achieved through proper study of thenew Confucian principles and cosmology.

Popular Buddhist sects also persisted during the Song, demonstrating that anti-Buddhist feelings were not as ferocious as Confucian polemics against Buddhism might suggest. Some Buddhists elaborated on Tang-era folk practices derived from India and Tibet. The best known, Chan Buddhism (known as **Zen** in Japan and as Son in Korea), asserted that mental discipline alone could win salvation.

Meditation, a key Chan practice that was employed by Confucians as well as Buddhists, afforded prospective officials relief from studying for civil service examinations, which continued into the Song from the Tang period. Unlike the ancient Han policy of hiring and promoting on the basis of recommendations, Song-style examinations involved a large bureaucracy. Test questions, which changed each time the examinations were given, often related to economic management or foreign policy even though they were always based on Confucian classics.

Hereditary class distinctions meant less than they had in Tang times, when noble lineages played a greater role in the structure of power. The new system recruited the most talented men, whatever their origin. Yet men from wealthy families enjoyed an advantage. Preparation for the tests consumed so much time that peasant boys could rarely compete.

Success in the examinations brought good marriage prospects, the chance for a high salary, and enormous prestige. Failure could bankrupt a family and ruin a man both socially and psychologically. This put great pressure on candidates, who spent days writing essays in tiny, dim, airless examination cells.

During the Song era, a technical change from woodblock to an early form of **movable type** made printing cheaper. To promote its ideological goals, the Song government authorized the mass production of test preparation books in the years before 1000. Although a man had to be literate to read the preparation books and basic education was still rare, a growing number of candidates entered the Song bureaucracy without noble, gentry, or elite backgrounds.

The availability of printed books changed country life as well, since landlords gained access to expert advice on planting and irrigation techniques, harvesting, tree cultivation, threshing, and weaving. Landlords frequently gathered their tenants and workers to show them illustrated texts and explain their meaning. New agricultural land was developed south of the Yangtze River, and iron implements such as plows and rakes, first used in the Tang era, were adapted to southern wet-rice cultivation.

AP® Exam Tip
Explain how Chinese technological innovations in this time period impacted society at home and abroad.

junk A very large flat-bottom sailing ship produced in the Tang, Song, and Ming Empires, specially designed for long-distance commercial travel.

gunpowder A mixture of saltpeter, sulfur, and charcoal, in various proportions. The formula, brought to China in the 400s or 500s, was first used to make fumigators to keep away insect pests and evil spirits. In later centuries it was used to make explosives and grenades and to propel cannonballs, shot, and bullets.

Zen The Japanese word for a branch of Mahayana Buddhism based on highly disciplined meditation. It is known in Sanskrit as *dhyana*, in Chinese as *Chan*, and in Korean as *Son*.

movable type Type in which each individual character is cast on a separate piece of metal. It eventually replaced woodblock printing, allowing for the arrangement of individual letters and other characters on a page, rather than requiring the carving of entire pages at a time. Although China had an early form of moveable type in the eleventh century, Koreans invented durable, metal moveable type in the thirteenth century that may have influenced later print technology in China.

neo-Confucianism Term used to describe new approaches to understanding classic Confucian texts that became the basic ruling philosophy of China from the Song period to the twentieth century.

◄ **Su Song's Astronomical Clock** This gigantic clock built at Kaifeng between 1088 and 1092 combined mathematics, astronomy, and calendar-making with skillful engineering. The team overseen by Su Song placed an armillary sphere on the observation platform and linked it with chains to the water-driven central mechanism shown in the cutaway view. The water wheel also rotated the Buddha statues in the multistory pagoda the spectators are looking at. Other devices displayed the time of day, the month, and the year. From Joseph Needham's *Science and Civilisation in China, Vol 4* (Cambridge, UK: Cambridge University Press, 1962). After the original diagram in Su Song's treatise *Xinyi Xiangfayao*, 1092.

The growing profitability of agriculture interested ambitious members of the gentry. Still a frontier for Chinese settlers under the Tang, the south saw increasing concentration of land in the hands of a few wealthy families. In the process, the indigenous inhabitants of the region, related to the modern-day populations of Malaysia, Thailand, and Laos, retreated into the mountains or southward toward Vietnam.

During the 1100s the total population of the Chinese territories, spurred by prosperity, rose above 100 million. The leading Song cities had fewer than a million inhabitants but were still among the largest cities in the world. Health and crowding posed problems in the Song capitals. Multistory wooden apartment houses fronted on narrow streets—sometimes only 4 or 5 feet (1.2 to 1.5 meters) wide—that were clogged by peddlers or families spending time outdoors. The crush of people called for new techniques in waste management, water supply, and firefighting (see Environment & Technology: East Asian Transportation).

In Hangzhou engineers diverted the nearby river to flow through the city, flushing away waste and pollutants. Arab and European travelers who had firsthand experience with the Song capital, and who were sensitive to urban conditions in their own societies, expressed amazement at Hangzhou's amenities: restaurants, parks, bookstores, wine shops, tea houses, theaters, and various entertainments.

The idea of credit, originating in the robust long-distance trade of the Tang period, spread widely under the Song. Intercity or interregional credit—what the Song called "flying money"—depended on the acceptance of guarantees that the paper could be redeemed for coinage at another location. The public accepted the practice because credit networks tended to be managed by families, so that brothers and cousins were usually honoring each other's certificates.

"Flying money" certificates differed from government-issued paper money, which the Song pioneered. In some years, military expenditures consumed 80 percent of the government budget. The state responded to this financial pressure by distributing paper money. But this made inflation so severe that by the beginning of the 1100s paper money was trading for only 1 percent of its face value. Eventually the government withdrew paper money and instead imposed new taxes, sold monopolies, and offered financial incentives to merchants.

Hard-pressed for the revenue needed to maintain the army, canals, roads, waterworks, and other state functions, the government finally resorted to *tax farming*, selling the rights to tax collection to private individuals. Tax farmers made their profit by collecting the maximum amount and sending an agreed-upon smaller sum to the government. This meant exorbitant rates for taxable services, such as tolls, and much heavier tax burdens on the common people.

Rapid economic growth undermined the remaining government monopolies and the traditional strict regulation of business. Now merchants and artisans as well as gentry and officials could make fortunes. With land no longer the only source of wealth, the traditional social hierarchy common to the agricultural economy weakened, while cities, commerce, consumption, and the use

Chinese transportation practices in the twelfth century come to life in a panorama of a bustling city executed by the famous artist Zhang Zeduan (1085–1145 CE), titled "Along the River During the Qingming Festival," a detail from which appears earlier at the beginning of this chapter is a 17-foot-long scroll painting that contains more detail about everyday urban life than any painting or drawing from Europe, the Middle East, or India in that period. If it portrays street life in truthful fashion, then China was probably the most advanced country in the world in transportation technology.

In addition to pedestrians, store-keepers, and artisans, it depicts four two-humped pack camels, eleven pack mules or donkeys, seventeen human porters, ten *palanquins* (sedan chairs) carried on the shoulders of other porters, nine wheelbarrows, eight mule or ox carts, and a wheelwright's workplace showing artisans assembling a large spoked wheel. River traffic includes twenty highly detailed boats, some with masts that could be lowered to pass under bridges.

Some of the carts are quite elaborate, but none are drawn by horses or resemble the grand military and civilian chariots of the pre-Han and Han era. A few civilian men ride horses with attendants on foot, and one woman sits sideways on a horse being led by a man. There are no four-wheeled vehicles. Porters carrying burdens and palanquins, along with the many boat workers, far outnumber pack and draft animals.

Wheelbarrow pushers and pullers predominate in the area of wheeled vehicles. Unlike wheelbarrows in medieval Europe whose operators had to lift half the load centered behind the wheel, Song wheelbarrows balance immense loads directly over the axle of their single wheel. This greatly reduced the lifting burden of the operator and allowed him to concentrate on pushing. One to three donkeys or mules might assist by pulling on ropes. Wheelbarrows of this efficient variety remained the mainstay of Chinese land transport down to the nineteenth century.

By contrast with China, Japan made no use of wheelbarrows and largely shunned all wheeled vehicles down to the middle of the nineteenth century. Wheeled shrines pushed or pulled by devotees appeared at festivals, and ox carts were occasionally utilized at seaports, but cross-country road traffic was entirely by pack animal, riding animal, and human porters and palanquin carriers. Why the Japanese, who found value in so many Chinese practices, ignored Chinese transport technology is unknown.

Questions for Analysis

1. What made four-wheeled vehicles less desirable then two-wheeled carts?

2. Why might European visitors have failed to bring home with them the idea of the Chinese-style wheelbarrow?

3. What advantages did palanquins offer to people who had the means to hire their porters?

▲ **Chinese Wheelbarrow from Song Dynasty** Since the weight of the load is balanced over a single wheel of large diameter, the two men do not lift much weight, and the donkey does most of the pulling. The operators' primary functions are to keep the wheelbarrow from tipping to the right or to the left and to steer it around corners and obstacles. Power to move forward was sometimes assisted by a square sail mounted on a mast rising over the wheel. akg-images/Pictures From History

Section Review

- Several rival states replaced the fallen Tang Empire, and the close relations between Central Asia and East Asia ended.

- The Liao and Jin Empires encouraged culturally diverse societies and confronted Song China with formidable military threats.

- The Song Empire of central and southern China built upon Tang achievements in technology and science and promoted civil ideals.

- Under the Song, print culture developed, urban populations rose, commercial activity grew through innovation, and women were subordinated to men.

of money and credit boomed. Urban life reflected the elite's growing taste for fine fabrics, porcelain, exotic foods, large houses, and exquisite paintings and books.

In conjunction with the backlash against Buddhism and revival of Confucianism that began under the Tang and intensified under the Song, women experienced subordination, legal disenfranchisement, and social restriction. Merchants spent long periods away from home, and many maintained several wives in different locations. Frequently they depended on wives to manage their homes and even their businesses in their absence. But though women took on responsibility for the management of their husbands' property, their own property rights suffered legal erosion. Under Song law, a woman's property automatically passed to her husband, and women could not remarry if their husbands divorced them or died.

The subordination of women proved compatible with Confucianism, and it became fashionable to educate girls just enough to read simplified versions of Confucian philosophy that emphasized the lowly role of women. Modest education made these young women more desirable as companions for the sons of gentry or noble families and as literate mothers in lower-ranking families aspiring to improve their status. Poet Li Qingzhao (**lee CHING-jow**) (1083–1141) acknowledged and made fun of her unusual status as a highly celebrated female writer:

> Although I've studied poetry for thirty years
> I try to keep my mouth shut and avoid reputation.
> Now who is this nosy gentleman talking about my poetry
> Like Yang Ching-chih (**yahng SHING-she**)
> Who spoke of Hsiang Ssu (**sang sue**) everywhere he went.[4]

Her reference is to a hermit poet of the ninth century who was continually and extravagantly praised by a court official, Yang Ching-chih.

Female foot-binding first appeared among slave dancers at the Tang court, but it did not become widespread until the Song period. The bindings forced the toes under and toward the heel, so that the bones eventually broke and the woman could not walk on her own. In noble and gentry families, foot-binding began between ages five and seven. In less wealthy families, girls worked until they were older, so foot-binding began only in a girl's teens.

---

[4]Quoted at "Women's Early Music, Art, Poetry," music.acu.edu/ www/iawm/pages/reference/tzusongs.html.

◀ **Song River Transport** This seventeenth-century painting shows the emperor Huizong (r. 1100–1126), in red, supervising the ceremonial transfer of pierced stones and a tree. The purpose of their transfer is unknown. Note the differences between the workshop at lower left and the residence at lower right where women, children, and even a pet dog are enjoying life outside the enclosed courtyard. Emperor Hui Tsung (r.1100-26) transporting pierced stones and strange shaped trees, from a History of the Emperors of China (colour on silk), Chinese School, (17th century)/Bibliotheque Nationale, Paris, France/Bridgeman Images

◀ **Female Musicians** A group of entertainers from a Song period copy of a lost Tang painting titled "Night Revels of Han Xizai." The emperor ordered the painter to document the lifestyle of a man who preferred music, dance, and poetry to accepting appointment as prime minister. The mood of genteel indulgence appealed to Song-era elites. Chinese women were not veiled, but foot-binding became common under the Song. The Night Revelry of Han Xizai, by Gu Hongzhong the court painter sent by his suspicious monarch to spy on Han and to make a record of Han's licentious behaviour/ Werner Forman Archive/The Bridgeman Art Library

Many literate men condemned the maiming of innocent girls and the general uselessness of foot-binding. Nevertheless, bound feet became a status symbol. By 1200 a woman with unbound feet had become undesirable in elite circles, and mothers of elite status, or aspiring to such status, almost without exception bound their daughters' feet. They knew that girls with unbound feet faced rejection. Working women and the indigenous peoples of the south, where northern practices took a longer time to penetrate, did not practice foot-binding. Consequently they enjoyed considerably more mobility and economic independence than did elite Chinese women.

12-3 New Kingdoms in East Asia

How did East Asia develop between the fall of the Tang and 1200?

The best possibilities for expanding the Confucian worldview of the Song lay with newly emerging kingdoms to the east and south. Korea, Japan, and Vietnam, like Song China, devoted great effort to the cultivation of rice. This practice fit well with Confucian social ideas, as tending the young rice plants, irrigating the rice paddies, and managing the harvest required coordination among many village and kin groups and rewarded hierarchy, obedience, and self-discipline.

Confucianism also justified using agricultural profits to support the education, safety, and comfort of the literate elite. In each of these new kingdoms Song civilization melded with indigenous cultural and historical traditions to create a distinctive synthesis.

12-3a Chinese Influences

Korea, Japan, and Vietnam had first centralized power under ruling houses in the early Tang period, and their state ideologies continued to resemble that of the early Tang, when Buddhism and Confucianism seemed compatible. Government offices went to noble families and did not depend on passing examinations on Confucian texts. Landowning and agriculture remained the major sources of income, and landowners faced no challenges from a merchant class or urban elite.

Nevertheless, learned men prized literacy in classical Chinese and a good knowledge of Confucian texts. Though formal education was available to only a small number of people, the ruling and landholding elites sought to instill Confucian ideals of hierarchy and harmony among the general population (see Diversity & Dominance: Law and Society in China and Japan).

12-3b Korea

Knowledge of Korea, Japan, and Vietnam comes initially from early Chinese officials and travelers. When the Qin Empire established its first colony in the Korean peninsula in the third century BCE, Chinese bureaucrats began documenting Korean history and customs. Han writers noted the horse breeding, strong hereditary elites, and **shamanism** (belief in the ability of certain individuals to contact ancestors and the invisible spirit world) of Korea's small kingdoms. But Korea quickly absorbed Confucianism and Buddhism.

Mountainous in the east and north, Korea was heavily forested until modern times. The land that can be cultivated (less than 20 percent) lies mostly in the south, where a warm climate and monsoon rains support two crops per year. Population movements from Manchuria, Mongolia, and Siberia to the north and to Japan in the south promoted the spread of languages that were very different from Chinese but distantly related to the Turkic tongues of Central Asia.

In the early 500s the dominant landholding families made inherited status—the "bone ranks"—permanent in Silla (**SILL-ah** or **SHILL-ah**), a kingdom in the southeast of the peninsula. In the early 660s, Silla defeated the southwestern kingdom of Paekche, which had played a major role as a maritime power in transmitting Chinese culture to Japan. Then in 668 the northern Koguryŏ kingdom came to an end after prolonged conflict with the Sui and Tang. Koguryo was so influential in Northeast Asia that the Liao and Jin Empires, and subsequent Korean kingdoms, claimed to inherit its legacy.

Supported by the Tang, Silla now took control of much of the Korean peninsula. The Silla rulers imitated Tang government and examined officials on the Confucian classics. They also sent Buddhist monks to China. But the intellectual exchange was not one-directional: writings by the monk Wonhyo, known as the "Korean Commentary," greatly influenced Buddhism in China. The fall of the Tang in the early 900s coincided with Silla's collapse and enabled the ruling house of **Koryo** (**KAW-ree-oh**), from which the modern name "Korea" derives, to rule a united peninsula for the next three centuries. Threatened constantly by the Liao and then the Jin in northern China, Koryo maintained amicable relations with Song China in the south. The Koryo kings supported Buddhism and made superb printed editions of Buddhist texts.

The oldest surviving woodblock print in Chinese characters comes from Korea in the middle 700s. Commonly used during the Tang period, woodblock printing required great technical skill. A calligrapher would write the text on thin paper, which would then be pasted upside down on a block of wood. Once wetted, the characters showed through from the back, and an artisan would carve away the wooden surface surrounding each character. A fresh block had to be carved for each printed page. Korean artisans developed their own advances in printing, including experiments with movable type. By Song times, Korean experiments reached China, where further improvements led to metal or porcelain type from which texts could be printed cheaply.

12-3c Japan

Japan consists of four main islands and many smaller ones stretching in an arc from as far south as Georgia to as far north as Maine. The nearest point of contact with the Asian mainland lies 100 miles away in southern Korea. In early times Japan was even more mountainous and heavily forested than Korea, with only 11 percent of its land area suitable for cultivation. Mild winters and monsoon rains supported the earliest population centers on the coastlands of the Inland Sea between Honshu and Shikoku Islands. The first rulers to extend their power broadly in the fourth and fifth centuries CE were based in the Yamato River Basin on the Kinai Plain at the eastern end of the sea.

The first Chinese description of Japan, dating from the fourth century, tells of an island at the eastern edge of the world that is divided into hundreds of small communities, with the largest one, called Yamatai, ruled over by a shamaness named Himiko or Pimiko. The location of the

shamanism The practice of identifying special individuals (shamans) who will interact with spirits for the benefit of the community. Characteristic of the Korean kingdoms of the early medieval period and of early societies of Central Asia.

Koryo Korean kingdom founded in 918 and destroyed by a Mongol invasion in 1259.

early Yamatai kingdom remains a source of debate and fascination in Japan, but archeological finds point to frequent interaction with China and Korea.

In the mid-600s the Yamatai rulers, acting on knowledge gained from Korean contacts and embassies to Chang'an sent by five different kings, implemented the Taika (**TIE-kah**) and other reforms, giving this regime the key features of Tang government. A legal code, an official variety of Confucianism, and an official reverence for Buddhism blended with the local recognition of indigenous and immigrant chieftains as territorial administrators. Within a century, a centralized government with a complex system of law had emerged, as attested by a massive history in the Confucian style.

Women from the aristocracy became royal consorts and thereby linked their kinsmen with the royal court. At the death of her husband in 592, Suiko, a woman from the immigrant aristocratic family of Soga, became empress. She occupied the throne until 628, enjoying a longer reign than any other ruler down to the nineteenth century. Asuka, her capital, saw a flowering of Buddhist art, and her nephew Shotoku opened relations with Sui China and is credited with promulgating a "Constitution" in 604 that had lasting influence on Japan's governing philosophy (see Diversity and Dominance: Law and Society in China and Japan).

The Japanese mastered Chinese building techniques so well that Nara (**NAH-rah**) (710–784) and Kyoto (794–1868), Japan's early capitals, provide invaluable evidence of the wooden architecture long since vanished from China. During the eighth century Japan in some ways surpassed China in Buddhist studies. In 752 dignitaries from all over Mahayana Buddhist Asia gathered at the enormous Todaiji temple, near Nara, to celebrate the "eye-opening" of the "Great Buddha" statue.

Though the Japanese adopted Chinese building styles and some street plans, Japanese cities were built without walls. One reason was that central Japan was not plagued by constant warfare. Also, the Confucian Mandate of Heaven, which justified dynastic changes, played no role in legitimating Japanese government. The *tenno*, or "heavenly sovereign"—often called "emperor" in English—belonged to a family believed to have ruled Japan since the beginning of history. The dynasty never changed. A prime minister and the leaders of the native religion, in later times called Shinto, the "way of the gods," exercised real control.

By 750 the government in Nara had reached its zenith. During the Nara and Early Heian periods, the rulers expanded their fledgling regime outward from central Japan. They did this by sending an army led by a "barbarian-subduing generalissimo," the shogun, into regions on the peripheries of the Japanese islands. The court extended Japanese rice-growing culture into the territory of the Hayato people of southern Kyushu and into northeastern Honshu, where the Emishi, a mixed indigenous population, practiced slash-and-burn agriculture. A collection of poems dating from the eighth century, called *Ten Thousand Leaves*, records the hopes and fears of those engaged in expanding the sovereign's contact with China, the Korean peninsula, and Japanese islands distant from the capital city:

> A frontier-guard when I set out, Oh what turmoil there was! Of the work my wife should do,
> I said not a word and came away.[5]

In 794 the central government moved to Kyoto, usually called by its ancient name, Heian (**hay-ahn**). Legally centralized government lasted there until 1185, though power became decentralized toward the end. In Kyoto members of the **Fujiwara** (**foo-jee-WAH-rah**) clan—a family of priests, bureaucrats, and warriors who had succeeded the Soga clan in influence—controlled power and protected the emperor. Fujiwara dominance favored men of Confucian learning over the generally illiterate warriors, and noblemen of the Fujiwara period read the Chinese classics and appreciated painting and poetry.

Gradually, however, the Fujiwara nobles began to entrust responsibility for local government, policing, and tax collection to their warriors, who were known as *samurai*, literally "one who serves." Though often of humble origins, a small number of these warriors had achieved wealth and power by the late 1000s. By the middle 1100s the nobility had lost control, and civil war between rival warrior clans engulfed the capital.

---

[5]The Manyōshū: The Nippon Gakujutsu Shinkokai translation of *One Thousand Poems*, p. 254. Copyright © 1965 Columbia University Press. Reprinted with permission of the publisher.

AP® Exam Tip
Evaluate the ways that China influenced its neighbors like Korea and Japan.

Fujiwara Aristocratic family that dominated the Japanese imperial court between the ninth and twelfth centuries.

Like other East Asian states influenced by Confucianism, the elite families of Fujiwara Japan did not encourage education for women. The hero of the celebrated Japanese novel about Fujiwara court culture, *The Tale of Genji*, written around the year 1000 and often regarded as the world's first novel, remarks: "Women should have a general knowledge of several subjects, but it gives a bad impression if they show themselves to be attached to a particular branch of learning."[6] However, within the marriage politics of the day, having interesting and talented women helped the Fujiwara draw the monarch's attention to their own women rather than those of other families.

Fujiwara noblewomen lived in near-total isolation, generally spending their time on cultural pursuits and the study of Buddhism. To communicate with their families or among themselves, they depended on writing. The simplified syllabic script that they used represented the Japanese language in its fully inflected form (the Chinese classical script used by Fujiwara men could not do so).

Sei Shonagon (**SAY SHOH-nah-gohn**), a lady attending one of the royal consorts, composed her *Pillow Book* between 996 and 1021. Most likely named for being kept by the author's pillow so she could jot down occasional thoughts, this famous work begins:

▲ Silla Warrior   This ewer—the projection in front is the pour spout—reflects Korea's early use of cavalry. Horses were probably introduced to Japan by way of Korea.   DeA Picture Library/Art Resource, NY

Spring is best at dawn as gradually the hilltops lighten, while the light grows brighter until there are purple-tinged clouds trailing through the sky.

Summer is best at night. That goes without saying when there is a full moon. But when fireflies flit here and there in a dark sky, that too is wonderful. It is even wonderful when it is raining.[7]

AP® Exam Tip
Compare the development of Japanese feudalism with feudalism in western Europe.

Military clans acquired increasing importance during the period 1156–1185, when warfare between rival families culminated in the establishment of the **Kamakura (kah-mah-KOO-rah) Shogunate** in eastern Honshu, far from the old religious and political center at Kyoto. The standing of the Fujiwara family fell as nobles and the emperor hurried to accommodate the new warlords. *The Tale of the Heike*, an anonymously composed thirteenth-century epic account of the clan war, reflects a Buddhist appreciation of the impermanence of worldly things, a view that became common among the new warrior class. This class eventually absorbed some of the Fujiwara aristocratic values, but the monopoly of power by nonmilitary civil elite had come to an end.

12-3d Vietnam

Kamakura Shogunate The first of Japan's decentralized military governments (1185–1333).

Not until Tang times did the relationship between Vietnam and China become close enough for economic and cultural interchange to play an important role. Occupying the coastal regions east of the mountainous spine of mainland Southeast Asia, Vietnam's economic and political life centered on two fertile river valleys, the Red River in the north and the Mekong (**may-KONG**) in the south. The rice-based agriculture of Vietnam made the region well suited for integration with southern China. In both regions the wet climate and hilly terrain demanded expertise in irrigation.

Early Vietnamese peoples may have preceded the Chinese in using draft animals in farming and working with metal. But in Tang and Song times the elites of Annam (**ahn-nahm**)—as the Chinese called early Vietnam—adopted Confucian bureaucratic training, Mahayana Buddhism, and other aspects of Chinese culture, and Annamese elites continued to rule in the Tang style after that dynasty's fall. In 936 Annam assumed the name Dai Viet (**die vee-yet**) and maintained good relations with Song China as an independent country.

Section Review

- Korea, Japan, and Vietnam adapted Chinese cultural and political models, including the Tang blend of Confucianism and Buddhism.

- In all three cultures, landowning and agriculture remained the principal source of wealth.

- The Korean peninsula, which was split into three rival kingdoms, became unified under the founder of the Koryo kingdom.

- In Japan, a warrior aristocracy in Kamakura gradually arose beginning in the twelfth century to rule alongside the court nobles and emperor who resided in Kyoto.

- Modern-day Vietnam was originally split into several kingdoms that featured a unique blend of the culture and politics of China and Southeast Asian states.

[6]Quoted in Ivan Morris, *The World of the Shining Prince: Court Life in Ancient Japan* (New York, NY: Penguin Books, 1979), 221–222.

[7]Quoted in Ivan Morris, trans., *The Pillow Book of Sei Shonagon* (New York, NY: Columbia University Press, 1991), section 1.

▲ **Imperial Palace in Kyoto** The first version of the palace was built in the eighth century 1.2 miles (2 kilometers) away from the current site. The Kyoto palace complex was the primary residence of the Japanese emperors until the middle of the nineteenth century, when the imperial capital moved to Tokyo. Being built of wood with cypress-bark roofing, the buildings have been repeatedly ravaged by fire, but each restoration has utilized traditional materials in an effort to preserve the historical forms. The latest rebuilding took place in 1855. The palace complex includes gardens and numerous buildings in a variety of styles particular to different periods in its history. Christian Kober/Alamy

Champa, located in what is now southern Vietnam, rivaled the Dai Viet state. The cultures of India and the Malay Peninsula strongly influenced Champa through maritime networks of trade and communication. During the Tang period, Champa fought with Dai Viet, but both kingdoms cooperated with the less threatening Song. Among the tribute gifts brought to the Song court by Champa emissaries was **Champa rice** (originally from India). Chinese farmers soon made use of this fast-maturing variety to improve their yields of this essential crop.

Vietnam shared the general Confucian interest in hierarchy, but attitudes toward women, like those in Korea and Japan, differed from the Chinese model. None of the societies adopted foot-binding. In Korea strong family alliances that functioned like political and economic organizations allowed women a role in negotiating and disposing of property. Before the adoption of Confucianism, Annamese women had enjoyed higher status than women in China, perhaps because both women and men participated in wet-rice cultivation. The Trung sisters of Vietnam, who lived in the first century CE and led local farmers to create a small, short-lived revolutionary state in resistance against the Han Empire, still serve as national symbols in Vietnam and as local heroes in southern China.

12-4 **Conclusion**

The Tang Empire put into place a solid system of travel, trade, and communications that allowed cultural and economic influences to move quickly from Central Asia to Japan. In addition, diversity within the empire produced great wealth and new ideas. Eventually, however, tensions among rival groups weakened the political structure and led to great violence and misery.

The post-Tang fragmentation permitted regional cultures to emerge that experimented with and often improved on Tang military, architectural, and scientific technologies. In northern and Central Asia, these refinements included state ideologies based on Buddhism, bureaucratic practices based on Chinese traditions, and military techniques combining nomadic horsemanship and strategies with Chinese armaments and weapons. In Song China, the spread of Tang

Champa rice Quick-maturing rice that can allow two harvests in one growing season. Originally introduced into Champa from India, it was later sent to China as a tribute gift by the Champa state.

technological knowledge resulted in the privatization of commerce, major advances in technology and industry, increased productivity in agriculture, and deeper exploration of ideas relating to time, cosmology, and mathematics.

The brilliant achievements of the Song period came from mutually reinforcing developments in economy and technology. Without the rampant warfare and exploitation of the economy in the mid to late Tang period, the Song economy, though much smaller than its predecessor, showed great productivity, circulating goods and money throughout East Asia and stimulating the economies of neighbors.

Korea, Japan, and Vietnam developed distinct social, economic, and political systems. Buddhism became the preferred religion in all three regions, but Chinese influences, largely deriving from a universal esteem for Confucian thought and writings, put down deep roots. All of these societies made advances in agricultural technology and productivity and raised their literacy rates as printing spread. In the absence of a land border with China, Japan retained greater political independence than Korea and Vietnam. The culture of its imperial center reached a high level of refinement, but the political system was ultimately based on a warrior aristocracy.

Key Terms

Grand Canal p. 294	Song Empire p. 300	Zen p. 303	Fujiwara p. 309
Li Shimin p. 294	junk p. 303	movable type p. 303	Kamakura Shogunate p. 310
Tang Empire p. 295	gunpowder p. 303	shamanism p. 308	Champa rice p. 311
tributary system p. 295	neo-Confucianism p. 303	Koryo p. 308	

Review Questions

1. Can the division between northern and southern China be compared with the division between the Western Roman Empire (capital Rome) and the Eastern Roman Empire (Byzantium) in the fourth and fifth centuries CE?

2. What are the similarities and differences between the early historical development of the Japanese islands and of the British Isles at the opposite end of the Eurasian landmass?

3. How does Confucianism compare with Islam and Christianity as a unifying political philosophy?

 MindTap® is a fully online personalized learning experience built upon Cengage Learning content. MindTap® combines student learning tools–readings, multimedia, activities, and assessments–into a singular Learning Path that guides students through the course and helps students develop the critical thinking, analysis, and communication skills that are essential to academic and professional success.

Material Culture
Salt

Though sodium chloride, or table salt, is one of the world's most abundant chemicals, its abundance in some areas and scarcity in others has frequently given it an important role in economic history. Here are some examples.

Outcroppings of rock salt known as salt licks play a nutritional role in the lives of many wild mammals. Prehistoric human hunters sought game at these natural animal gathering places, and some scholars believe that human provision of salt played an important role in domesticating some species.

Trade in salt from the southern regions of the Sahara Desert is described as early as the ninth century CE, but it is probably much older because the Saharan deposits formed an important nutritional source for salt-poor sub-Saharan Africa. The legendary exchange of salt for equivalent quantities of gold symbolizes this commercial importance. Bilma, an oasis town in eastern Niger, still produces salt that is distributed by means of camel caravans trekking across the sand dunes of the Ténéré Desert.

In ancient Rome, a strong-smelling sauce known as *garum* became a cooking staple and an important export item. *Garum* was made by crushing cut up fish, with their entrails, in a small amount of brine. The salt prevented the sauce from spoiling. For common people, using *garum* was a way of avoiding the tax on salt.

Early in the fourteenth century CE a Flemish fisherman devised a method of preserving herring, a small fish. After the head and certain internal organs were removed, enzymes from the pancreas began to digest the flesh and make it tender. Then the fish were packed with salt in casks. Salted herring and its raw materials, salt and herring, became mainstays of the commerce of Scotland, northern Germany, and in particular the Netherlands. A Dutch proverb maintains that the city of Amsterdam was built on herring casks.

In France, a salt tax known as the *gabelle* became a permanent part of royal revenues in the late fourteenth century CE. Everyone over the age of eight was forced to buy a minimum amount of salt every week at a price fixed by the government. Most of the salt was produced by evaporating seawater, but inland provinces in the east exploited salt marshes. Popular resentment against the tax contributed to the French Revolution in 1789. A year later the *gabelle* was canceled.

In nineteenth-century China, where the salt tax had been a mainstay of government revenues since the Tang dynasty, *brine* (saltwater) wells around the western city of Zigong became the basis for one of the country's most prosperous industries. The family-based trusts that extracted the salt from as deep as 3,000 feet were comparable in capital accumulation, management skill, and technological innovation to contemporary European corporations.

In 1930 the British monopoly on salt production in India became the center of a peaceful protest led by Mahatma Gandhi. With seventy-eight followers he marched 240 miles to the seacoast, where the protestors picked up a small lump of salt, thereby breaking the law against private harvesting of salt. Though many were imprisoned, the Salt March became an important model of civil disobedience.

Though salt naturally brings a taste to mind, its historic role relates more to its chemical properties. Salt in water passes easily through the membranes that surround the cells of plants and animals. After a period of time, the moisture within the cell acquires the chemical properties of the salty moisture on the outside. Pieces of pork transform into ham, cucumbers and other vegetables become pickles, and sturgeon eggs become caviar. Since high concentrations of salt kill bacteria, salted foods can be transported and stored for long periods without spoiling or becoming dangerous to eat.

Producing salt from seawater and other sources of brine requires evaporation or boiling. But salt is also available in solid form and can be mined. Cities like Salzburg (literally "Salt Town") in Austria have grown up around salt mines. Underground layers of salt, sometimes hundreds of feet thick, are the residue of dried-up prehistoric seas or oceans. In addition to being processed for consumption, rock salt is used on icy roads. Since saltwater freezes at a lower temperature than fresh water, salt deposited on snow or ice causes melting.

Questions for Analysis

1. Why did salt become such an important trade product?
2. Why would a tax on salt be easy to administer?
3. How many uses of salt can you think of?

◄ **Camel Caravan Carrying Salt in West Africa**   Natural salt deposits, such as those at Bilma in the southern Sahara Desert in Niger, have time and again become the bases for extensive regional and international trade. Transporting the salt can be a challenge, however. Camel transport made salt trading an integral part of the trade between the Saharan region and the agricultural countries of West Africa. In northern Europe the salt springs at Lüneburg near Hamburg, Germany, fed into a maritime trading network throughout the Baltic and North Sea region. Coastal lands could extract salt from seawater by evaporation, though in colder climates, such as Japan, boiling was needed to supplement the power of natural sunlight and heat. VOLKMAR K. WENTZEL/National Geographic Creative

Religious conversion has two meanings that often get confused. The term can refer to the inner transformation an individual may feel on joining a new religious community or becoming revitalized in his or her religious belief. Conversions of this sort are often sudden and deeply emotional. In historical terms, they may be important when they transform the lives of prominent individuals.

In its other meaning, religious conversion refers to a change in the religious identity of an entire population, or a large portion of a population. This generally occurs slowly and is hard to trace in historical documents. As a result, historians have sometimes used superficial indicators to trace the spread of a religion. Doing so can result in misleading conclusions, such as considering the spread of the Islamic faith to be the result of forced conversion by Arab conquerors, or taking the routes traveled by Christian or Buddhist missionaries as evidence that the people they encountered adopted their spiritual message, or assuming that a king or chieftain's adherence to a new religion immediately resulted in a religious change among subjects or followers.

In addition to being difficult to document, religious conversion in the broad societal sense has followed different patterns according to changing circumstances of time and place. Historians have devised several models to explain the different conversion patterns. According to one model, religious labels in a society change quickly, through mass baptism, for example, but devotional practices remain largely the same. Evidence for this can be found in the continuation of old religious customs among people who identify themselves as belonging to a new religion. Another model sees religious change as primarily a function of economic benefit or escape from persecution. Taking this approach makes it difficult to explain the endurance of certain religious communities in the face of hardship and discrimination. Nevertheless, most historians pay attention to economic advantage in their assessments of mass conversion. A third model associates a society's religious conversion with its desire to adopt a more sophisticated way of life, by shifting, for example, from a religion that does not use written texts to one that does.

One final conceptual approach to explaining the process of mass religious change draws on the quantitative models of innovation diffusion that were originally developed to analyze the spread of new technologies in the twentieth century. According to this approach, new ideas, whether in the material or religious realm, depend on the spread of information. A few early adopters—missionaries, pilgrims, or conquerors, perhaps—spread word of the new faith to the people they come in contact with, some of whom follow their example and convert. Those converts in turn spread the word to others, and a chain reaction picks up speed in what might be called a bandwagon effect. The period of bandwagon conversion tapers off when the number of people who have not yet been offered an opportunity to convert diminishes. The entire process can be graphed as a logistic or S-shaped curve. Figure 1, the graph of conversion to Islam in Iran based on changes from Persian (non-Islamic) to Arabic (Islamic) names in family genealogies, shows such a curve over a period of almost four centuries.

In societies that were largely illiterate, like those in which Buddhism, Christianity, and Islam slowly achieved spiritual dominance, information spread primarily by word of mouth. The proponents of the new religious views did not always speak the same language as the people they hoped to bring into the faith. Under these circumstances, significant conversion, that is, conversion that involved some understanding of the new religion, as opposed to forced baptism or imposed mouthing of a profession of faith, must surely have started with fairly small numbers.

Language was crucial. Chinese pilgrims undertook lengthy travels to visit early Buddhist sites in India. There they acquired Sanskrit texts, which they translated into Chinese. These translations became the core texts of Chinese Buddhism. In early Christendom, the presence of bilingual (Greek-Aramaic) Jewish communities in the eastern parts of the Roman Empire facilitated the early spread of the religion beyond its Aramaic-speaking homeland. By contrast, Arabic, the language of Islam, was spoken only in the Arabian peninsula and the desert borderlands that extended northward from Arabia between Syria, Jordan, and Iraq. This initial impediment to the spread of knowledge about Islam dissolved only when intermarriage with non-Muslim, non-Arab women, many of them taken captive and distributed as booty during the conquests, produced bilingual offspring. Bilingual preachers of the Christian faith were similarly needed in the Celtic, Germanic, and Slavic language areas of western and eastern Europe.

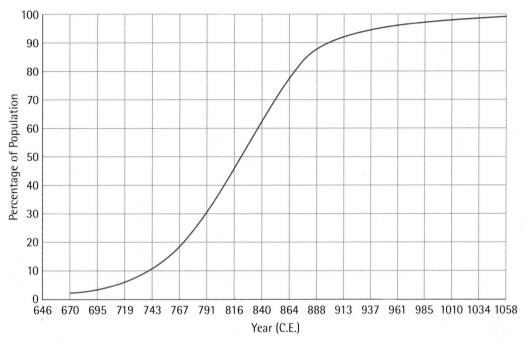

FIGURE 1   Conversion to Islam in Iran

This slow process of information diffusion, which varied from region to region, made changing demands on religious leaders and institutions. When a faith was professed primarily by a ruler, his army, and his dependents, religious leaders gave the highest priority to servicing the needs of the ruling minority and perhaps discrediting, denigrating, or exterminating the practices of the majority. Once a few centuries had passed and the new faith had become the religion of the great majority of the population, religious leaders turned to establishing popular institutions and reaching out to the common people. Historical interpretation can benefit from knowing where a society is in a long-term process of conversion.

These various models reinforce the importance of distinguishing between emotional individual conversion experiences and broad changes in a society's religious identity. New converts are commonly thought of as especially zealous in their faith, and that description is often apt in instances of individual conversion experiences. It is less appropriate, however, to broader episodes of conversion. In a conversion wave that starts slowly, builds momentum in the bandwagon phase, and then tapers off, the first individuals to convert are likely to be more spiritually motivated than those who join the movement toward its end. Religious growth depends as much on making the faith attractive to late converts as to ecstatic early converts.

Questions for Analysis

1. Can the innovation diffusion concept be useful in thinking about the spread of nonreligious attitudes like Hellenism and Confucianism or, in modern times, Marxism and secularism?

2. How might conversion to a brand new faith, such as Islam in seventh-century Arabia or Mormonism, differ from conversion to a long-established faith with an elaborate church organization?

3. What assumptions about the spread of a faith do we make when we characterize an entire country in religious terms, such as being Christian or Buddhist?

Source: Richard W. Bulliet, *Conversion to Islam in the Medieval Period* (Cambridge, MA: Harvard University Press, 1979), 23. Copyright by the President and Fellows of Harvard College.

AP® REVIEW QUESTIONS FOR CHAPTER 12

Multiple-Choice Questions

Questions 1–3 refer to Map 12.1 on page 296.

1. The best explanation for the extent of the area under Tang control is that the Tang

   (A) extended their control of China from the south after the fall of the Sui dynasty.

   (B) economy relied heavily on trade along the lucrative Silk Roads.

   (C) wanted to gain control of the Central Asian steppes to gain tributary states.

   (D) were unable to control the Tibetan region because of heavy opposition.

2. The change in the volume of trade that took place during the Tang era led to

   (A) a greater syncretism between the cultures of East and Central Asia.

   (B) the stagnation of agricultural innovations in an increasingly urban-based economy.

   (C) significant improvements in existing transportation technologies.

   (D) more maritime contact with the Indian Ocean.

3. Based on the map, which of the following examples of art or architecture would most help historians correctly analyze the Tang Dynasty's cultural foundations?

   (A) Characteristic blue and white porcelain that reflects the marine connections of the dynasty

   (B) Large pagoda-like structures that imitate the architectural form of the Buddhist roots of the Tang

   (C) Small figurines that mirror those of the Tang's trading partner to the east, the Sassanid Empire

   (D) Large pottery figurines of horses and camels that display the dynasty's appreciation of pastoral nomads

Questions 4–7 refer to the passage below.

"Your servant begs leave to say that Buddhism is no more than a cult of the barbarian peoples, which spread to China in the time of the Latter Han. It did not exist here in ancient times. . . . When Emperor Gaozu [first emperor of the Tang] received the throne from the House of Sui, he deliberated upon the suppression of Buddhism. But at that time the various officials, being of small worth and knowledge, were unable fully to comprehend the ways of the ancient kings and the exigencies of past and present, and so could not implement the wisdom of the emperor and rescue the age from corruption. Thus the matter came to naught, to your servant's constant regret.

. . . Now Buddha was a man of the barbarians who did not speak the language of China and wore clothes of a different fashion. His sayings did not concern the ways of our ancient kings, nor did his manner of dress conform to their laws. He understood neither the duties that bind sovereign and subject nor the affections of father and son."

"Memorial on the Bone of the Buddha," a message to Emperor Xianzong of the Tang dynasty by Han Yu, 819

4. This passage demonstrates which of the following views of the later Tang dynasty on the cultural nature of earlier dynasties?

   (A) The late Tang praised the cultural diffusion that had occurred with the introduction of Buddhism.

   (B) The late Tang believed that the previous belief system of Daoism was preferable to any other.

   (C) The late Tang criticized the poor decisions made by earlier administrations concerning philosophies.

   (D) The late Tang admired how the early Tang rulers dealt harshly with barbaric religions like Buddhism.

5. By examining the message to the emperor, a historian can determine that

   (A) there were large communities of migrants in Tang China.

   (B) contact with other regions had led to cross-cultural interactions.

   (C) the Tang dynasty began with the violent overthrow of the Sui.

   (D) minorities were responsible for much of the economic prosperity of the time.

6. Which of the following Tang period innovations significantly encouraged the growth of the interregional trade that originally brought Buddhism to China?

   (A) Government issued paper money, which created significant inflation by the beginning of the Song period

   (B) Intercity or interregional credit, later called "flying money," during the Song period, which were often essentially among families

   (C) Banking houses allowing a few wealthy families to essentially control all interregional trade

   (D) Monopolistic corporations that issued bills of trade and allowed for complete control of merchant movement

7. With the fall of the Tang dynasty a new era began, as the Song elite introduced a new interpretation of traditional beliefs called neo-Confucianism, which

   (A) absorbed the inward focus of Buddhism and emphasized personal development.

   (B) increased the importance of women in Chinese society.

   (C) disregarded moral and social responsibility.

   (D) reasserted the primary importance of social and political order over individual cultivation.

Questions 8–10 refer to the passage below.

"When the point of a needle is rubbed with the lodestone, then the sharp end always points south, but some needles point to the north. I supposed that the natures of the stones are not all alike. Just so, at the summer solstice the deer shed their horns, and at the winter solstice the elks do so. Since the south and the north are two opposites, there must be a fundamental difference between them. This has not yet been investigated deeply enough."

"The Director asked me about the shapes of the sun and moon; whether they were like balls or (flat) fans. If they were like balls they would surely obstruct each other when they met. I replied that these celestial bodies were certainly like balls. How do we know this? By the waxing and waning of the moon."

Explanations from an 11th-century book, *Meng Xi Bi Tan* ["Dream Pool Essays"]

8. Based on the first paragraph, science during the Song dynasty was most likely

   (A) invigorated through the translation of Greek and Arabic scientific manuscripts.

   (B) based on careful inquiry about the physical and natural world.

   (C) based mainly on superstition and traditional thought.

   (D) mainly concerned with medicine and the study of herbal remedies.

9. Which of the following is a Song dynasty innovation that along with the compass described in the passage led to the growth of interregional trade?

   (A) The Astrolabe, a star reading device that facilitated navigation on the high seas

   (B) The Junk, a large, ocean-going ship that allowed for better steering and easier transit of rough seas

   (C) Iron, a metal that allowed armor and protection of merchants traveling along the Silk Road

   (D) Iron stirrups, which allowed riders to stay on horses and avoid nomad attacks

10. Based on the passage above, which of the following could be concluded concerning the Song dynasty?

   (A) With the flourishing of the Silk Roads, the Song dynasty was an era of economic plenty.

   (B) The Song dynasty welcomed travelers from the west and the knowledge they shared.

   (C) The Song dynasty was more dominant and globally connected than the earlier Tang.

   (D) The Song dynasty was a period of intellectual curiosity that led to lasting achievements.

Short-Answer Questions

"Women leave their families to marry, and the husband is the master of the household [they marry into]. . . . The husband is to be firm, the wife soft; conjugal affections follow from this. While at home, the two of you should treat each other with the formality and reserve of a guest. Listen carefully to and obey whatever your husband tells you.

When [your] sons go out to school, they seek instruction from a teacher who teaches them proper [ritual] form and etiquette, how to chant poetry, how to write essays. . . . Daughters remain behind in the women's quarters and should not be allowed to go out very often. . . . Teach them sewing, cooking, and etiquette."

Song Ruozhao, *Analects for Women*, written during Tang dynasty, ca. 780

1. Use the passage above and your knowledge of world history to answer all parts of the question that follows.

   (A) Identify ONE restriction on women in China between 600 and 1200.

   (B) Explain ONE accusation against women in the Tang dynasty (618–907).

   (C) Explain ONE reason for restrictions on women in China after the Tang dynasty (907–1200).

2. Answer all parts of the question that follows.

   (A) Identify ONE cultural interchange between China and Korea between 400 and 1200.

   (B) Explain ONE cultural similarity between China and Japan between 400 and 1200.

   (C) Explain ONE political difference between China and Japan between 400 and 1200.

PART IV

Interregional Patterns of Culture and Contact, 1200–1550

▲ **Martin Waldseemüller's Map of the World** This map, published in 1507 and included in a German geography book titled *Cosmographiae Introductio*, marks the first usage of the name *America*, placed one-third of the way from the bottom of the New World's southern continent. After Amerigho (original spelling) Vespucci sailed twice to the New World as a navigator in 1499 and 1501, he wrote letters that misled the author of this map into thinking that Vespucci, and not Columbus, had been the first to land on the mainland. "I do not see what right any one would have to object to calling this part after Americus, who discovered it and who is a man of intelligence, [and so to name it] Amerige, that is, the Land of Americus, or America: since both Europa and Asia got their names from women." Library of Congress

Chinggis Khan's conquests made Mongolia the center of an administrative and trading system linking Europe, the Middle East, Russia, and East Asia. Some lands flourished while others groaned under the tax burdens and physical devastation. Societies that escaped conquest felt the Mongol impact through the need for defense planning and in accelerated processes of urbanization, technological development, and political centralization stimulated by fear of Mongol attack.

By 1500, a new Chinese empire, the Ming, was expanding its influence in Southeast Asia. The Ottomans had overthrown the Byzantine Empire, and Europe's Christian monarchs, victorious over Muslim enemies, were laying the foundations of new overseas empires.

As overland trade faded, Eurasians took to the seas. Although the long-distance voyages of China's Zheng He were spectacular, they lacked long-term results. In contrast, within twenty-five years of Christopher Columbus's arrival in the Americas, a Portuguese ship had sailed around the world. Exposure to the achievements, wealth, and resources of the Americas, sub-Saharan Africa, and Asia guaranteed the further expansion of European exploration and maritime power. ●

Environment	Culture	State Building	Economics	Social Structures
• Impact of environmental factors, disease, and technology on migration and settlement (bubonic plague)	• Origins, beliefs, development, economic/social/political impact, and spread of major religions, philosophies, and belief systems	• Changes and continuities of the creation and maintenance of forms, functions, and institutions of governance	• Causes/effects of economic strategies of different types of communities, states, and empires (Mongol)	• Impact of kinship, ethnicity, class, gender, and race on social hierarchies
• Impact of migration, population, and urbanization on environment	• Effect of cross-cultural interactions on diffusion of technology and scientific knowledge	• Impact of economic, social, cultural, and geographical factors on state building, expansion, and dissolution	• Development and change of labor systems over time (mit'a)	• Impact of ideologies, philosophies, and religions on social hierarchies
• Interaction between environment and development of technology, industrialization, transportation, and exchange/communication networks (Grand Canal, compass, astrolabe)		• Interactions between societies with states and state-less societies (Mongol expansion, Aztec/Mexica)	• Influence of trade on development of ideologies, values, and institutions on each other	• Influence and impact of political, economic, cultural, and demographic factors on social structures
		• Political/economic interactions between states and non-state actors	• Influence and impact of local, regional, and global economic systems and exchange networks on each other (Silk Road, Indian Ocean trade, roads, trade cities)	

Key Concept 3.1

- How did improved transportation technologies and commercial practices lead to an increased trade of goods and ideas and expand the geographical range of existing trade networks?
- How did the movement of peoples cause environmental and linguistic effects?
- How were cross-cultural exchanges fostered by the intensification of existing (or the creation of new) networks of trade and communication?
- How did crops and pathogens, including epidemic diseases like the bubonic plague, travel along trade routes?

Key Concept 3.2

- How did the collapse of empires result in new imperial states and political systems?
- How did interregional contacts and conflicts between states and empires encourage technological and cultural transfers? (specific focus on the Mongol Empire and Zheng He's exploration)

Key Concept 3.3

- How did innovations and the developing trade of foreign luxury goods affect production?
- How did developing trade contribute to the growth and decline of cities?
- How did religion and other trade-diffused ideas affect labor, gender relations, and family life?

Key Concept 4.1

- How did developing global trade bring both prosperity and challenges to existing trade routes?
- How did technological developments in cartography and navigation build on previous knowledge and facilitate remarkable transoceanic travel and trade?
- What was the impact of new transoceanic maritime reconnaissance in this period?

13 Mongol Eurasia and Its Aftermath, 1200–1500

AP® Framework Terms

Astrolabe
Mongol Khanates
Silk Road
Admiral Zheng He
Neo-Confucianism

Overarching Questions

1 How and to what extent have environmental factors, disease, and technology affected patterns of human migration and settlement over time? (ENV)

2 How and why have religions, belief systems, philosophies, and ideologies originated, developed, and spread as a result of expanding communication and exchange networks? (CUL)

3 How have cross-cultural interactions resulted in the diffusion of culture, technologies, and scientific knowledge? (CUL)

4 How and why have economic, social, cultural, and geographic factors influenced the process of state building, expansion, and dissolution? (SB)

5 How have local, regional, and global economic systems and exchange networks influenced each other over time? (ECON)

When Temüjin (**TEM-uh-jin**) was a boy, a rival group murdered his father. Temüjin's mother tried to shelter him, but she could not find a safe haven. At fifteen Temüjin sought refuge with the leader of the Keraits (**keh-rates**), a warring confederation whose people spoke Turkic and respected both Christianity and Buddhism. Temüjin learned the importance of religious tolerance, the necessity of dealing harshly with enemies, and the variety of Inner Asia's cultural and economic traditions.

In 1206 the **Mongols** and their allies acknowledged Temüjin as **Chinggis Khan (CHING-iz KAHN)** (also known as Genghis), or "supreme leader." His advisers spoke many languages and belonged to different religions. His death-bed speech, which cannot be literally true even though a contemporary recorded it, captures the strategy behind Mongol success: "If you want to retain your possessions and conquer your enemies, you must make your subjects submit willingly and unite your diverse energies to a single end."[1] By implementing this strategy, Chinggis Khan became the most famous conqueror in history, initiating an expansion of Mongol dominion that by 1250 stretched from Poland to northern China.

---

[1]Quotation adapted from Desmond Martin, *Chingis Khan and His Conquest of North China* (Baltimore, MD: The John Hopkins Press, 1950), 303.

▲ **Defending Japan** Japanese warriors board Mongol warships with swords to prevent the landing of the invasion force in 1281.
The Granger Collection, New York

Scholars today stress the positive developments that transpired under Mongol rule. European and Asian sources of the time, however, vilify the Mongols as agents of death, suffering, and conflagration, a still-common viewpoint based on reliable accounts of horrible massacres.

The tremendous extent of the Mongol Empire promoted the movement of people and ideas from one end of Eurasia to the other. Trade routes improved, markets expanded, and the demand for products grew. Trade on the Silk Road, which had declined with the fall of the Tang Empire (see Chapter 12), revived.

Between 1218 and about 1350 in western Eurasia and down to 1368 in China, the Mongols focused on specific economic and strategic interests, usually permitting local cultures to survive and develop. In some regions, local reactions to Mongol domination sowed seeds of regional and ethnic identity that blossomed in the period of Mongol decline. Regions as widely separated as Russia, Iran, China, Korea, and Japan benefited from the Mongol stimulation of economic and cultural exchange and also found in their opposition to the Mongols new bases for political consolidation and affirmation of cultural difference. ●

13-1 The Rise of the Mongols, 1200–1260

What accounts for the magnitude and speed of the Mongol conquests?

The Mongol Empire owed much of its success to the cultural institutions and political traditions of the Eurasian *steppes* (prairies) and deserts. The pastoral way of life known as **nomadism** gives rise to imperial expansion only occasionally, and historians disagree about what triggers these episodes. In the case of the Mongols, a precise assessment of the personal contributions of Chinggis Khan and his successors remains uncertain.

Mongols A people of this name is mentioned as early as the records of the Tang Empire, living as nomads in northeastern Eurasia. After 1206 they established an enormous empire under Chinggis Khan, linking western and eastern Eurasia.

Chinggis Khan The title of Temüjin when he ruled the Mongols (1206–1227). It means the "oceanic" or "universal leader." Chinggis Khan was the founder of the Mongol Empire.

nomadism A way of life, forced by a scarcity of resources, in which groups of people continually or seasonally migrate to find pastures and water.

319

13-1a **Nomadism in Central Asia**

The pastoral nomads of the Eurasian steppes played an on-again, off-again role in European, Middle Eastern, and Chinese history for hundreds of years before the rise of the Mongols (see Chapter 9). The Mongol way of life probably did not differ materially from that of those earlier peoples (see Diversity & Dominance: The Secret History of the Mongols). Traditional accounts maintain that the Mongols put their infants on goats to accustom them to riding. Moving regularly and efficiently with flocks and herds, with some homes carried on wheeled vehicles, required firm decision making. The independence of individual Mongols and their families made this decision making public, with many voices being heard. A council made up of representatives from powerful families ratified the decisions of the leader, the *khan*. Yet people who disagreed with a decision could strike out on their own. Even during military campaigns, warriors moved with their families and possessions.

Menial work in camps fell to slaves—either prisoners of war or people who sought refuge in slavery to escape starvation. Weak groups secured land rights and protection from strong groups by providing them with slaves, livestock, weapons, silk, or cash. More powerful groups, such as Chinggis Khan's extended family and descendants, lived almost entirely off tribute, so they spent less time and fewer resources on herding and more on warfare designed to secure greater tribute.

Leading families combined resources and solidified intergroup alliances through arranged marriages and acts of allegiance, a process that helped generate political federations. Marriages were arranged in childhood—in Temüjin's case, at the age of eight—and children thus became pawns of diplomacy. Women from prestigious families could wield power in negotiation and management, though they ran the risk of assassination or execution just like men.

The wives and mothers of Mongol rulers traditionally managed state affairs during the interregnum between a ruler's death and the selection of a successor. Princes and heads of ministries treated such regents with great deference and obeyed their commands without question. Since a female regent could not herself succeed to the position of khan, her political machinations usually focused on gaining the succession for a son or other male relative.

Families often included believers in two or more religions, most commonly Buddhism or Islam. Virtually all Mongols observed the practices of traditional shamanism, rituals in which special individuals were believed to visit and influence the supernatural world. Whatever their faith, the Mongols believed in world rulership by a khan who, with the aid of his shamans, could speak to and for an ultimate god, represented as Sky or Heaven. This universal ruler transcended particular cultures and dominated them all.

13-1b **The Mongol Conquests, 1215–1283**

Shortly after his acclamation in 1206, Chinggis initiated two decades of Mongol aggression. By 1209 he had cowed the Tanggut (**TAHNG-gut**) rulers of northwest China, and in 1215 he captured the Jin capital of Yanjing, today known as Beijing (**bay-jeeng**). He turned westward in 1219 with an invasion of Khwarezm (**kaw-REZM**), a state east of the Caspian Sea that included much of Iran. After 1221, when most of Iran had fallen, Chinggis left the command of most campaigns to subordinate generals.

Ögödei (**ERG-uh-day**), Chinggis's son, became the Great Khan in 1227 after his father's death (see Figure 13.1). He completed the destruction of the Tanggut and the Jin and put their territories under Mongol governors. By 1234 he controlled most of northern China and was threatening the Southern Song (see Chapter 12). Two years later Chinggis's grandson Batu (**BAH-too**) (d. 1255) attacked Russian territories, took control of the towns along the Volga (**VOHL-gah**) River, and conquered Kievan Russia, Moscow, Poland, and Hungary in a five-year campaign. Only the death of Ögödei in 1241, which caused a suspension of campaigning, saved Europe from graver damage. With Chinggis's grandson güyük (**gi-yik**) installed as the new Great Khan, the conquests resumed. In the Middle East a Mongol army sacked Baghdad in 1258 and executed the last Abbasid caliph (see Chapter 10).

CHRONOLOGY	Mongolia and China	Central Asia and Middle East	Russia	Korea, Japan, and Southeast Asia
1200	1206 Temüjin chosen Chinggis Khan of the Mongols 1227 Death of Chinggis Khan 1227–1241 Reign of Great Khan Ögödei 1234 Mongols conquer northern China 1271 Founding of Yuan Empire 1279 Mongol conquest of Southern Song	1219–1223 First Mongol attacks in Iran 1258 Mongols sack Baghdad and kill the caliph 1260 Mamluks defeat Il-khans at Ain Jalut 1295 Il-khan Ghazan converts to Islam	1221–1223 First Mongol attacks on Russia 1240 Mongols sack Kiev 1242 Alexander Nevskii defeats Teutonic Knights 1260 War between Il-khans and Golden Horde	1258 Mongols conquer Koryo rulers in Korea 1274, 1281 Mongols attack Japan 1283 Yuan invades Champa 1293 Yuan attacks Java
1300	1368 Ming Empire founded	1349 End of Il-khan rule ca. 1350 Egypt infected by plague 1370–1405 Reign of Timur	1346 Plague outbreak at Kaffa	1333–1338 End of Kamakura Shogunate in Japan, beginning of Ashikaga 1392 Founding of Choson dynasty in Korea
1400	1403–1424 Reign of Yongle 1405–1433 Voyages of Zheng He	1402 Timur defeats Ottoman sultan 1453 Ottomans capture Constantinople	1462–1505 Ivan III establishes authority as tsar. Moscow emerges as major political center.	1471–1500 Dai Viet conquers Champa

Chinggis Khan's original objective had probably been collecting tribute, but the success of the Mongol conquests created a new situation. Ögödei unquestionably sought to rule a united empire based at his capital, Karakorum (**kah-rah-KOR-um**), and until his death he controlled the subordinate Mongol do-mains: the Golden Horde in Russia and the Chagatai (**JAH-guh-die**) domains in Central Asia (see Map 13.1). After Ögödei's death, however, family unity began to unravel; when Khubilai (**KOO-bih-lie**) declared himself Great Khan in 1260, the descendants of Chinggis's son Chagatai (d. 1242) and other branches of the family refused to accept him. As Karakorum was destroyed in the en-suing fighting, Khubilai transferred his court to the old Jin capital now renamed Bei-jing. In 1271 he declared himself founder of the **Yuan Empire**.

Chagatai's descendants continued to dominate Central Asia and enjoyed close rela-tions with the region's Turkic-speaking nomads. This, plus a continuing hatred of Khubilai, contributed to Central Asia becoming an independent Mongol center and to the spread of Islam there.

After the Yuan destroyed the Southern Song (see Chapter 12) in 1279, Mongol troops attacked Dai Viet—now northern Vietnam—and in 1283 invaded the kingdom of Champa in southern Vietnam. When the initially successful Mongols suffered a defeat, Khubilai was so infuriated that he postponed an invasion of Japan to focus on the Vietnamese kingdoms. In 1287, the Vietnamese troops, under the command of Tran Hung Dao, Vietnam's most famous military hero, defeated the Mongol forces in a final battle. A plan to invade Java by sea also failed, as did two invasions of Japan in 1274 and 1281.

The Mongols seldom outnumbered their enemies, but they were extraordinary riders and utilized superior bows. The Central Asian bow, made by laminating layers of wood, leather,

Yuan Empire Empire created in China and Siberia by Khubilai Khan.

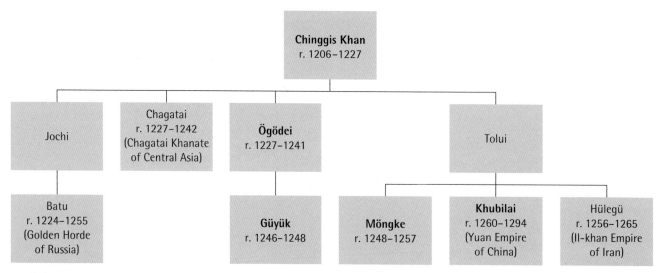

FIGURE 13.1 **Mongol Rulers, 1206–1260** The names of the Great Khans are shown in bold type. Those who founded the regional khanates are listed with their dates of rule. Cengage Learning

and bone, could shoot one-third farther (and was correspondingly more difficult to pull) than the bows used by sedentary enemies.

Rarely did an archer expend all of the five dozen arrows in his quiver. As the battle opened, arrows shot from a distance decimated enemy marksmen. Then the Mongols charged the enemy's infantry to fight with sword, lance, javelin, and mace. The Mongol cavalry met its match only at the Battle of Ain Jalut (**ine jah-LOOT**), where an under-strength force confronted Turkic-speaking Mamluks whose war techniques mirrored their own (see Chapter 10).

The Mongols also fired flaming arrows and hurled enormous projectiles—sometimes flaming—from catapults. The first Mongol catapults, built on Chinese models, transported easily but had short range and poor accuracy. During western campaigns in Central Asia, however, the Mongols encountered a design that again was half as powerful. They used it to hammer the cities of Iran and Iraq.

Cities that resisted faced siege and annihilation. Surrender was the only option. The slaughter the Mongols inflicted on Balkh (**bahlk**) (in present-day northern Afghanistan) and other cities spread terror and caused other cities to surrender. Each conquered area contributed men to the "Mongol" armies. In the Middle East, on the western fringe of their empire, a few Mongol officers commanded armies of recently recruited Turks and Iranians.

13-1c Overland Trade and Disease

Commercial integration under Mongol rule affected all parts of the empire. Like earlier nomad elites, Mongol nobles had the exclusive right to wear silk, almost all of which came from China. New styles

◀ **Passport** The Mongol Empire facilitated the movement of products, merchants, and diplomats over long distances. Travelers frequently encountered new languages, laws, and customs. The *paisa* (from a Chinese word for "Card" or "sign"), with its inscription in Mongolian, proclaimed that the traveler had the ruler's permission to travel through the region. Europeans later adopted the practice, thus making the *paisa* the ancestor of modern passports. The Metropolitan Museum of Art/Image Source/Art Resource, NY

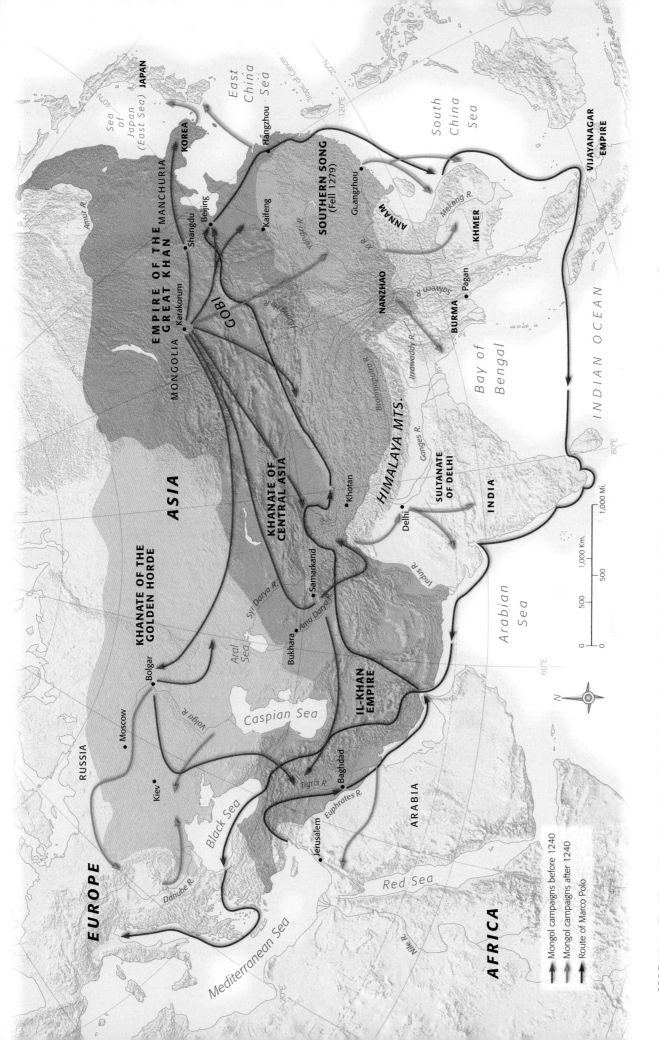

MAP 13.1   The Mongol Domains in Eurasia in 1300   After the death of Chinggis Khan in 1227, his empire was divided among his sons and grandsons. Son Ögödei succeeded Chinggis as Great Khan. Grandson Khubilai expanded the domain of the Great Khan into southern China by 1279. Grandson Hülegü was the first Il-khan in the Middle East. Grandson Batu founded the Khanate of the Golden Horde in southern Russia. Son Chagatai ruled the Chagatai Khanate in Central Asia.

Given the enormous expanse of Central Asia, how could a centralized government expect to control distant provinces?

Written in Mongolian within a few decades after Chinggis Khan's death and embodying the Mongolian oral poetry tradition, The Secret History of the Mongols survives only in a Chinese translation made after the Yuan dynasty had fallen to the Ming. Other descriptions of Mongol life come from non-Mongol sources and reflect the mixed attitudes of different peoples who were threatened by the Mongols or absorbed into their empire. This text uniquely evokes Chinggis Khan.

Packed as it is with personal names and verbatim speeches, The Secret History challenges historians who seek to explain the rise of the Mongols. It may reflect, however, the ruling style of the great conqueror who valued those who served him and put a premium on rational organization. The following excerpt deals with his household guard (slash marks indicate line breaks in the English blank verse translation):

Once the sun has set/ any person found near the palace tent will be seized by the nightguard,/ held through the night and questioned the next morning./ When one company changes place with another/ the nightguards coming in will present their passes and take their place, and the nightguards being relieved will present their passes and leave./ The nightguards who lie around the outside of the tent and guard the door will cut in two any person who tries to enter the tent at night./ Then Chinggis Khan spoke to his original seventy nightguard and made this decree:/ "My senior nightguard,/ on cloudy nights/ you lay around this tent of mine with its smoke hole/ and allowed me to sleep in quiet and peace./ I've gained my throne because of you./ My happy nightguard,/ on starry nights/ you lay around my palace tent/ and within its walls I had nothing to fear./ I've reached my high throne because of you./ My true-hearted nightguard,/ in the howling snowstorms/ you stood in the shivering cold,/ in the pouring rain with no rest,/ laying around this lattice framed tent/ and knowing you're there my heart's been at peace./ The joy of sitting in this throne I owe to you,/ my trusted nightguards. .../

"Let my sons who will sit on this throne after I'm gone/ not forget how well these people have served me./ Never give them cause to complain/ and take care of all their needs./ These ten thousand guards will be like my guardian spirits/ bringing luck and happiness to my house.

William of Rubruck, a Franciscan friar, journeyed to the court of the Great Khan Mönke in 1253–1255 after living for some period of time in crusader territory in the Middle East. He carried a letter from the French king, Louis IX (ruled 1226–1270), asking that the friar and a companion be allowed to stay with the Mongols, preach Christianity, and comfort German prisoners. William never made contact with the Germans, but his highly personal observations on Mongol life fascinated European readers and supply some of the context of The Secret History.

The dwelling in which they sleep is based on a hoop of interlaced branches, and its supports are made of branches, converging at the top around a smaller hoop, from which projects a neck like a chimney. They cover it with white felt: quite often they also smear the felt with chalk or white clay and ground bones to make it gleam whiter, or sometimes they blacken it. . . .

The married women make themselves very fine wagons. … One rich Mo'al [i.e., Mongol] or Tartar has easily a hundred or two hundred such wagons with chests. Baatu has twenty-six wives, each of whom has a large dwelling, not counting the other, smaller ones placed behind the large one, which are chambers, as it were, where the maids live: to each of these dwellings belong a good two hundred wagons.

The History of the World-Conqueror by the Iranian historian 'Ata-Malik Juvaini, who worked for the Mongols in Iran, was written in elegant Persian during the 1250s. It combines a glorification of the Mongol rulers with an unflinching picture of the cruelties and devastation inflicted by their conquests.

He [i.e., Chingiz-Khan] paid great attention to the chase and used to say that the hunting of wild beasts was a proper occupation for the commanders of armies; and that instruction and training therein was incumbent on warriors and men-at-arms. … For a month, or two, or three [the soldiers form] a hunting ring and drive the game slowly and gradually before them, taking care lest any escape from the ring. … Finally, when the ring has been contracted to a diameter of two or three parasangs [approximately 7 to 10 miles] they bind ropes together and cast felts over them; while the troops come to a halt all around the ring, standing shoulder to shoulder.

AP® Exam Tip
Understand the continued diffusion of corps and pathogens along trade routes.

and huge quantities of silk flowed westward to feed the luxury trade in the Middle East and Europe. Artistic motifs from Japan and Tibet reached as far as England and Morocco. Porcelain, another eastern luxury, became important in trade and strongly influenced later tastes in the Islamic world.

Merchants encountered ambassadors, scholars, and missionaries over the long routes to the Mongol courts. Some of the resulting travel literature, like the account of the Venetian Marco

When the ring has been so much contracted that the wild beasts are unable to stir, first the Khan rides in together with some of his retinue; then after he has wearied of the sport, they dismount upon high ground in the center … to watch the princes likewise entering the ring, and after them, in due order, the *noyans* [chiefs], the commanders and the troops … When nothing is left of the game but a few wounded and emaciated stragglers, old men and greybeards humbly approach the Khan, offer up prayers for his well-being and intercede for the lives of the remaining animals …

Now war—with its killing, counting of the slain and sparing of the survivors—is after the same fashion, and indeed analogous in every detail, because all that is left in the neighborhood of the battlefield are a few broken-down wretches.

Hu Szu-hui, a physician of Chinese-Turkic family background, presented the Yuan emperor in 1330 with a manual entitled Proper and Essential Things for the Emperor's Food and Drink. *His work reflects both the meat-heavy diet of the steppes and traditional Chinese concern with good nutrition.*

Foods That Cure Various Illnesses [60 entries]

Donkey's Head Gruel

It cures apoplexy-vertigo, debility of hand and foot, annoying pain of extremities, and trouble in speaking:

Black donkey's head (one; remove hair and wash clean), black pepper (two measures), tsaoko cardamom (two measures). Cook ingredients until overcooked. Add the five spices in fermented black bean juice. Flavor with the spices. Flavor evenly. Eat on an empty stomach.

Fox Meat Gruel

It cures infantile convulsion, epilepsy, spiritual confusion, indistinct speech, and inappropriate singing and laughing:

Fox meat. (The quantity does not matter. Include organ meat.) [To] ingredient add the five spices according to the regular method. Cook until over-cooked. When done eat on an empty stomach.

Bear Meat Gruel

It cures the various winds, foot numbness-insensitivity, and five flaccidities, tendon and muscle spasms:

Bear meat (one measure). [To] ingredient add the five spices in fermented black beans. [Add] onions and sauce. Cook. When done eat on an empty stomach.

Foodstuffs That Mutually Conflict [55 entries]

Horse meat cannot be eaten together with granary rice.
Horse meat cannot be eaten with cocklebur. It can be eaten with ginger.
Pork cannot be eaten together with beef.
Sheep's liver cannot be eaten together with pepper. It wounds the heart.
Hare meat cannot be eaten together with ginger.
Beef cannot be eaten together with chestnuts.
Mare's milk cannot be eaten together with fish hash. It produces obstruction of the bowels.
Venison cannot be eaten together with catfish.
Beef stomach cannot be eaten together with dog meat. Quail meat cannot be eaten together with pork. The face will turn black.
Pheasant eggs cannot be eaten together with onions. It produces vermin.
Meat of sparrows cannot be eaten together with plums. Eggs cannot be eaten together with turtle meat.

AP® History Reasoning Skills

Contextualization *What can each of the three passages (Franciscan Friar, Persian working in the Mongol court, or Chinese physician) reveal about the society in which it was written?*

Comparison *On which society (Europe, China, or Persia) does it seem the Mongols had the greatest impact?*

Sources: Paul Kahn, *The Secret History of the Mongols: The Origin of Chinghis Khan* (San Francisco: North Point Press, 1984), 143–145; *The Mission of Friar William of Rubruck: His Journey to the Court of the Great Khan Mönke* 1253–1255, trans. Peter Jackson (Indianapolis, IN: Hackett, 2009), 73–74; Ata-Malik Juvani, *Genghis Khan: The History of the World-Conqueror*, trans. John Andrew Boyle (Seattle: University of Washington Press, 1997); 27–29; Paul D. Buell and Eugene N. Anderson, *A Soup for the Qan* (London: Routledge, 2000), 428–429, 438–440.

Polo (**mar-koe POE-loe**) (1254–1324), freely mixed the fantastic with the factual. Stories of immense wealth stimulated a European ambition to find easier routes to Asia.

Exchange also spread disease. In the mid-thirteenth century, marmots and other rodents became infected and passed their disease to dogs and people. Though other diseases contributed to the mortality of the resulting pandemic, **bubonic plague**, which probably originated in Central Asia, was certainly involved. An alternative theory sees southern China as the point of origin,

bubonic plague A bacterial disease of fleas that can be transmitted by flea bites to rodents and humans; humans in late stages of the illness can spread the bacteria by coughing. Because of its very high mortality rate and the difficulty of preventing its spread, major outbreaks have created crises in many parts of the world.

Section Review

- The society of the nomadic Mongols functioned through kinship and tribute ties, in which women often played important roles.

- Chinggis Khan began the period of Mongol conquest to win tribute from Eurasian kingdoms.

- His successors turned to territorial rule, yet internal politics split the empire into smaller ones in China and Central Asia.

- The Mongols won territory through superior battle tactics and integrated it into a vast overland commercial network.

- That network allowed the bubonic plague and other diseases to spread across Asia into Europe.

but the great distances involved and the unusually cold winters experienced in China from 1344 to 1353, which would have impeded the reproduction of fleas, indicate otherwise. Plague incapacitated the Mongol army during its assault on the city of Kaffa (**KAH-fah**) in Crimea (**cry-MEE-ah**) in 1346. They withdrew, but the plague remained. From Kaffa flea-infested rats reached Europe and Egypt by ship (see Chapter 14).

Typhus, influenza, and smallpox traveled the same route. The combination of these and other diseases created the "great pandemic" of 1347–1352 and caused deaths far in excess of what the Mongol armies inflicted. Epidemics like this one were exacerbated by the environmental devastation caused by the Mongol conquest. The Mongols destroyed dams, irrigation channels, farmland, and crops; they also cut down trees that helped keep the desert at bay, with the effect of turning large portions of China into steppe.

13-2 The Mongols and Islam, 1260–1500

How did Mongol expansion and Islam affect each other?

From the perspective of Mongol imperial history, the issue of which branches of the family adopted Islam and which did not mostly concerns political rivalries. From the standpoint of Islamic history, however, recovery from the devastation that culminated in the destruction of the Abbasid Caliphate in Baghdad in 1258 attests to the vitality of the faith and the ability of Muslims to overcome adversity. Within fifty years of its darkest hour, Islam reemerged as a potent ideological and political force.

13-2a Mongol Rivalry

By 1260 the **Il-khan** (**IL-con**) state, established by Chinggis's grandson Hülegü, controlled Iran, Azerbaijan, Mesopotamia, and parts of Armenia. North of the Caspian Sea the Mongols who had conquered southern Russia established the capital of their Khanate of the **Golden Horde** (also called the Kipchak [**KIP-chahk**] Khanate) at Sarai (**sah-RYE**) on the Volga River. Like the Il-khans, they ruled an indigenous, mostly Turkic-speaking, Muslim population.

Some members of the Mongol imperial family professed Islam before the Mongol assault on the Middle East, and Turkic Muslims served the family in various capacities. Hülegü himself, though a Buddhist, had a trusted Shi'ite adviser and granted privileges to the Shi'ites. However, the Mongols under Hülegü's command came only slowly to Islam.

Islamic doctrines clashed with Mongol ways. Muslims abhorred the Mongols' worship of Buddhist and shamanist idols. Furthermore, Mongol law specified slaughtering animals without spilling blood, which involved opening the chest and stopping the heart. This horrified Muslims, who were forbidden to consume blood and slaughtered animals by slitting their throats and draining the blood.

Islam became a point of inter-Mongol tension when Batu's successor as leader of the Golden Horde declared himself a Muslim. He swore to avenge the murder of the Abbasid caliph and laid claim to the Caucasus—the mountains between the Black and Caspian Seas—which the Il-khans also claimed (see Map 13.2).

Some European leaders believed that if they helped the non-Muslim Il-khans repel the Golden Horde from the Caucasus, the Il-khans would help them relieve Muslim pressure on the Crusader principalities in Syria, Lebanon, and Palestine (see Chapter 10). This resulted in a brief correspondence between the Il-khan court and Pope Nicholas IV (r. 1288–1292) and a diplomatic mission that sent two Christian Turks to western Europe as Il-khan ambassadors in the late 1200s. The Golden Horde responded by seeking an alliance with the Muslim Mamluks in Egypt (see Chapter 10) against both the Crusaders and the Il-khans. These complicated efforts extended the life of the Crusader principalities, but the Mamluks finally ended their existence in the fifteenth century.

Il-khan A "secondary" or "peripheral" khan based in Persia. The Il-khans' khanate was founded by Hülegü, a grandson of Chinggis Khan, and was based at Tabriz in the Iranian province of Azerbaijan. It controlled much of Iran and Iraq.

Golden Horde Mongol khanate founded by Chinggis Khan's grandson Batu. It was based in southern Russia and quickly adopted both the Turkic language and Islam. Also known as the Kipchak Horde.

Before the Europeans' diplomatic efforts could bear fruit, a new Il-khan ruler, Ghazan (gaz-ZAHN) (1271–1304), declared himself a Muslim in 1295. Conflicting indications of Sunni and Shi'ite affiliation, such as divergent coin inscriptions, indicate that Ghazan had a casual attitude toward theological matters. It is similarly unclear whether the Muslim Turkic nomads who served in his army were Shi'ite or Sunni.

AP® Exam Tip
Consider the impact of Mongol expansion on different regions of Eurasia.

13-2b Islam and the State

The Il-khans gradually came to appreciate the traditional urban culture of the Muslim territories they ruled. Nevertheless, they used tax farming, a fiscal method developed earlier in the Middle East, to extract maximum wealth from their subjects. The government sold tax-collecting contracts to small partnerships, mostly consisting of merchants who might also finance caravans, small industries, or military expeditions. Whoever offered to collect the most revenue for the government won the contracts. They could collect by whatever methods they chose and keep anything in excess of the contracted amount.

Tax farming initially lowered administrative costs; but over the long term, the extortions of the tax farmers drove many landowners into debt and servitude. Agricultural productivity declined, making it hard to supply the army. So the government resorted to taking land to grow its own grain. Like property held by religious trusts, this land paid no taxes. Thus the tax base shrank even as the demands of the army and the Mongol nobility continued to grow.

Ghazan faced many economic problems. Citing Islam's humane values, he promised to reduce taxes. But the need for revenue kept the decrease from becoming permanent. The Chinese practice of printing paper money had been tried unsuccessfully by a predecessor. Now it was tried again. The experiment, to which the Il-khan's subjects responded negatively, pushed the economy into a depression that lasted beyond the end of the Il-khan state in 1349. Mongol nobles competed among themselves for the decreasing revenues, and fighting among Mongol factions destabilized the government.

While the Golden Horde and the Il-khan Empire quarreled, a new power was emerging in the Central Asian Khanate of Chagatai (see Map 13.1). The leader **Timur (TEE-moor)**, known to Europeans as Tamerlane, maneuvered himself into command of the Chagatai forces and launched campaigns into western Eurasia, apparently seeing himself as a new Chinggis Khan. By ethnic background he was a Turk with only an in-law relationship to the family of the Mongol conqueror. This prevented him from assuming the title *khan*, but not from sacking the Muslim sultanate of Delhi in northern India in 1398 or defeating the sultan of the rising Ottoman Empire in Anatolia in 1402. He was reportedly preparing to march on China when he died in 1405. However, Timur's descendants could not hold the empire together.

13-2c Culture and Science in Islamic Eurasia

The Il-khans and Timurids (descendants of Timur) presided over a brilliant cultural flowering in Iran, Afghanistan, and Central Asia based on blending Iranian and Chinese artistic trends and cultural practices. The dominant cultural tendencies were Muslim, however. Timur died before he could reunite Iran and China, but by transplanting Middle Eastern scholars, artists, and craftsmen to his capital, Samar-kand, he fostered the cultural achievements of his descendants.

The historian Juvaini (joo-VINE-nee) (d. 1283), who recorded Chinggis Khan's deathbed speech cited at the beginning of this chapter, came from the city of Balkh, which the Mongols had devastated in 1221. His family switched their allegiance to the Mongols, and both Juvaini and his older brother assumed high government posts. The Il-khan Hülegü, seeking to immortalize and justify his conquests, enthusiastically supported Juvaini's writing of the first comprehensive narrative of Chinggis Khan's empire.

Juvaini combined a florid style with historical objectivity, often criticizing the Mongols. This approach served as an inspiration to **Rashid al-Din (ra-SHEED ad-DEEN)**, Ghazan's prime minister, when he attempted the first history of the world. Rashid al-Din's work included the earliest known general history of Europe, derived from conversations with European monks, and a detailed description of China based on information from an important Chinese Muslim official stationed in Iran. The miniature paintings that accompanied some copies of Rashid al-Din's work included depictions of European and Chinese people and events and reflected the artistic traditions of both cultures. The Chinese compositional techniques helped inaugurate the greatest period of Islamic miniature painting under the Timurids.

AP® Exam Tip
Consider how interregional contact encouraged technological and cultural exchange across the Mongol empire.

Timur Member of a prominent family of the Mongols' Chagatai Khanate, Timur through conquest gained control over much of Central Asia and Iran. He consolidated the status of Sunni Islam as orthodox, and his descendants, the Timurids, maintained his empire for nearly a century and founded the Mughal Empire in India.

Rashid al-Din Adviser to the Il-khan ruler Ghazan, who converted to Islam on Rashid's advice.

Rashid al-Din traveled widely and collaborated with administrators from other parts of the far-flung Mongol dominions. His idea that government should be in accord with the moral principles of the majority of the population buttressed Ghazan's adherence to Islam. Administratively, however, Ghazan did not restrict himself to Muslim precedents but employed financial and monetary techniques that roughly resembled those used in Russia and China.

Under the Timurids, the tradition of the Il-khan historians continued. After conquering Damascus, Timur himself met there with the greatest historian of the age, Ibn Khaldun (**ee-bin hal-DOON**) (1332–1406), a Tunisian. In a scene reminiscent of Ghazan's answering Rashid al-Din's questions on the history of the Mongols, Timur and Ibn Khaldun exchanged historical, philosophical, and geographical viewpoints. Like Chinggis, Timur saw himself as a world conqueror. At their capitals of Samarkand and Herat (in western Afghanistan), later Timurid rulers sponsored historical writing in both Persian and Chagatai Turkish.

A Shi'ite scholar named **Nasir al-Din Tusi** (**nah-SEER ad-DEEN TOO-si**) represents the beginning of Mongol interest in the scientific traditions of the Muslim lands. Nasir al-Din may have joined the entourage of Hülegü during a campaign in 1256 against the Assassins, a Shi'ite religious sect derived from the Fatimid dynasty in Egypt and at odds with his more mainstream Shi'ite views (see Chapter 10). Although Nasir al-Din wrote on history, poetry, ethics, and religion, he made his most outstanding contributions in mathematics and cosmology. Following Omar Khayyam (**oh-mar kie-YAM**) (1038?–1131), a poet and mathematician of the Seljuk (**SEL-jook**)

MAP 13.2   Western Eurasia in the 1300s Ghazan's conversion to Islam in 1295 upset the delicate balance of power in Mongol domains. European leaders abandoned their hope of finding an Il-khan ally against the Muslim defenders in Palestine, while an alliance between the Mamluks and the Golden Horde kept the Il-khans from advancing west. This helped the Europeans retain their lands in Palestine and Syria.

How much of the medieval Caliphate ended up under Mongol or Timurid control?

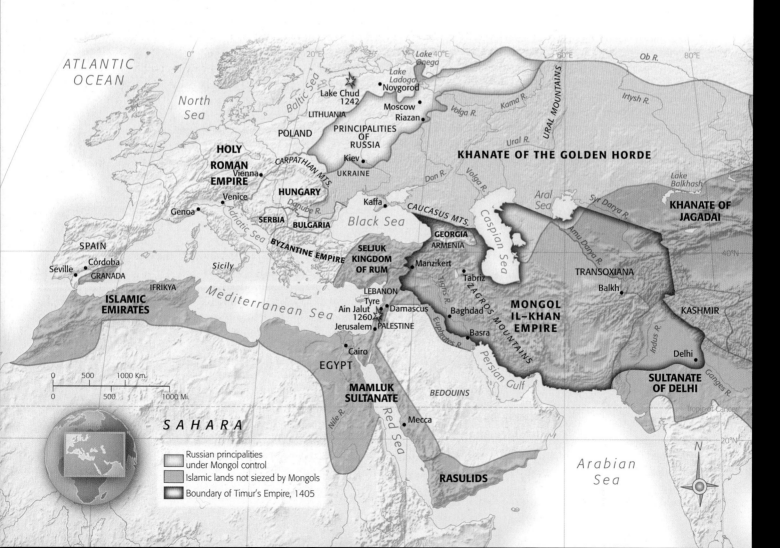

Robert Harding Picture Library Ltd/Alamy

▲ **Tomb of Timur in Samarkand**   The turquoise tiles that cover the dome are typical of Timurid architectural decoration. Timur's family ornamented his capital with an enormous mosque, three large religious colleges facing inward on three sides of an open plaza, and a lane of brilliantly tiled Timurid family tombs in the midst of a cemetery. Timur brought craftsmen to Samarkand from the lands he conquered to build these magnificent structures.

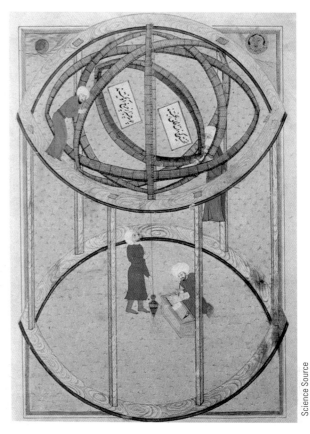

Science Source

▲ **Astronomy and Engineering**   Observational astronomy went hand in hand not only with mathematics and calendrical science but also with engineering as the construction of platforms, instruments for celestial measurement, and armillary spheres became more sophisticated. This manual in Persian, completed in the 1500s but illustrating activities of the Il-khan period, illustrates the use of a plumb line with an enormous armillary sphere.

period, he laid new foundations for algebra and trigonometry. Some followers working at an observatory built for Nasir al-Din at Maragheh **(mah-RAH-gah)**, near the Il-khan capital of Tabriz, used the new mathematical techniques to reach a better understanding of celestial orbits.

Nasir al-Din's work led to major contributions in astronomy that had worldwide influence. Observational astronomy and calendar-making had engaged the interest of earlier Central Asian rulers, particularly the Uighurs **(WEE-ger)** and the Seljuks. Under the Il-khans, the astronomers of Maragheh excelled in predicting eclipses, and astrolabes, armillary spheres, three-dimensional quadrants, and other instruments acquired new precision. The remarkably accurate eclipse predictions and tables prepared by Il-khan and Timurid astronomers reached the hostile Mamluk lands in Arabic translation; Byzantine monks took them to Constantinople and translated them into Greek; Christian scholars working in Muslim Spain rendered them into Latin; and in India the sultan of Delhi ordered Sanskrit versions of them.

Following one of these routes, the mathematical tables and geometric models of lunar motion devised by one of Nasir al-Din's students somehow became known to Nicholas Copernicus (1473–1543), a Polish monk and astronomer (see Chapter 14). Copernicus adopted this lunar model as his own, virtually without revision, and then proposed it as the proper model for planetary movement as well—but with the planets circling the sun.

The Great Khan Khubilai (discussed later in this chapter) summoned a team of Iranians to Beijing to build an observatory for him. Timur's grandson Ulugh Beg **(oo-loog bek)** (1394–1449),

AP® Exam Tip
Recognize the importance of the diffusion of scientific and technological developments (such as the astrolabe and compass) on the Islamic world.

Nasir al-Din Tusi Persian mathematician and cosmologist whose academy near Tabriz provided the model for the movement of the planets that helped to inspire the Copernican model of the solar system.

Section Review

- For the Mongols of the Il-khan and Golden Horde states, Islam became a matter of political rivalry.

- In the Il-khan state Islamic values struggled with economic needs, and the resulting unrest left it open to invasions by Golden Horde Mongols.

- At the same time, Timur took control of the Chagatai territory and began his own imperial conquests.

- Under the Il-khans and Timurids, Iran and Central Asia experienced a flowering of Islamic culture.

- These rulers fostered great achievements in historical writing, literature, art, mathematics, and astronomy.

whose avocation was astronomy, constructed a great observatory in Samarkand and actively participated in compiling observational tables that were later translated into Latin and used by European astronomers.

A further advance made under Ulugh Beg came from mathematician Ghiyas al-Din Jamshid al-Kashi (**gee-YASS ad-DIN jam-SHEED al-KAH-shee**), who noted that Chinese astronomers had long used one ten-thousandth of a day as a unit in calculating the occurrence of a new moon. This seems to have inspired him to employ decimal notation, by which quantities less than one could be represented by a marker to show place. Al-Kashi's proposed value for *pi* (π) was far more precise than any previously calculated. This innovation arrived in Europe by way of Constantinople, where a Greek translation of al-Kashi's work appeared in the fifteenth century.

13-3 Regional Responses in Western Eurasia

What benefits resulted from the integration of Eurasia into the Mongol Empire?

Safe, reliable overland trade benefited Mongol ruling centers and commercial cities along the Silk Road. But the countryside, ravaged by conquest, sporadic violence, and heavy taxes, suffered terribly. As Mongol control weakened, regional forces in Russia, eastern Europe, and Anatolia reasserted themselves. Sometimes this meant collaborating with the Mongols. At other times it meant using local ethnic or religious traditions to resist or roll back Mongol influence.

13-3a Russia and Rule from Afar

The Golden Horde, established after Chinggis's grandson Batu defeated a combined Russian and Kipchak (a Turkic people) army in 1223, started as a unified state but gradually lost unity as some districts crystallized into smaller khanates. The White Horde, for instance, ruled much of southeastern Russia in the fifteenth century, and the Crimean khanate on the northern shore of the Black Sea succumbed to Russian power only in 1783.

East-west routes across the steppe and north-south routes along the rivers of Russia and Ukraine (**you-CRANE**) conferred importance on certain trading *entrepôts* (places where goods are stored and from which they are distributed), as they had under Kievan Russia (see Chapter 11). The Golden Horde capital (Old) Sarai, just north of where the Volga flows into the Caspian Sea (see Map 13.1), ruled its Russian domains to the north and east from afar. To facilitate control, it granted privileges to the Orthodox Church, which then helped reconcile the Russian people to their distant masters.

The politics of language played a role in subsequent history. Old Church Slavonic, an ecclesiastical language, revived; but Russian steadily acquired greater importance and eventually became the dominant written language. Russian scholars shunned Byzantine Greek, previously the main written tongue, even after the Golden Horde permitted renewed contacts with Constantinople. The Golden Horde enlisted Russian princes to act as their agents, primarily as tax collectors and census takers.

The flow of silver and gold into Mongol hands starved the local economy of precious metal. Like the Il-khans, the Golden Horde attempted to introduce paper money as a response to the currency shortage. The unsuccessful experiment left such a vivid memory that the Russian word for money (*denga* [**DENG-ah**]) comes from the Mongolian word for the stamp (*tamga* [**TAHM-gah**]) used to create paper currency. In reality, commerce depended more on direct exchange of goods than on currency transactions.

Alexander Nevskii Prince of Novgorod (r. 1236–1263). He submitted to the invading Mongols in 1240 and received recognition as the leader of the Russian princes under the Golden Horde.

Alexander Nevskii (**nih-EFF-skee**) (ca. 1220–1263), the prince of Novgorod, persuaded some fellow princes to submit to the Mongols. In return, the Mongols favored both Novgorod and the emerging town of Moscow, ruled by Alexander's son Daniel. As these towns eclipsed Kiev (earlier devastated by the Mongols) as political, cultural, and economic centers, they drew people northward to open new agricultural land far from the Mongol steppes. Decentralization continued in the 1300s, with Moscow very gradually becoming Russia's dominant political center.

In appraising the Mongol era, some historians stress Mongol destructiveness and brutality in tax collecting. Ukraine, a fertile and well-populated region in the late Kievan period (1000–1230), suffered severe population loss from these sources. Isolated from developments to the west, Russia and parts of eastern Europe are portrayed as suffering under the "Mongol yoke."

Other historians point out that even before the Mongols struck, Kiev had declined economically (simultaneously with Iran and eastern Anatolia because of climate change) and ceased to mint coins. Yet the Russian territories regularly paid the heavy Mongol taxes in silver, indicating both economic surpluses and an ability to convert goods into cash. The burdensome taxes stemmed less from the Mongols than from their tax collectors, Russian princes who often exempted their own lands and shifted the load to the peasants.

As for Russia's cultural isolation, skeptics observe that before the Mongol invasion, the powerful and constructive role played by the Orthodox Church oriented Russia primarily toward Byzantium (see Chapter 11). This situation discouraged but did not eliminate contacts with western Europe. But repeated wars with the expanding Catholic principality of Lithuania on Russia's western border discouraged extensive relations.

The traditional structure of local government survived Mongol rule, as did the Russian princely families, who continued to battle among themselves for dominance. The Mongols merely added a new player to those struggles.

In the late 1400s Ivan (**ee-VAHN**) III, the prince of Moscow (r. 1462–1505), established himself as an autocratic ruler. Before Ivan, the title **tsar** (from *caesar*), of Byzantine origin, applied only to foreign rulers, whether the emperors of Byzantium or the Turkic khans of the steppe. Ivan's use of the title probably represents an effort to establish a basis for legitimate rule with the decline of the Golden Horde and the disappearance in 1453 of the Byzantine Empire.

AP® Exam Tip
Analyze the changes and continuities in the lands conquered by the Mongols.

tsar From Latin caesar, this Russian title for a monarch was first used in reference to a Russian ruler by Ivan III (r. 1462–1505).

13-3b New States in Eastern Europe and Anatolia

Anatolia and parts of Europe responded dynamically to the Mongol challenges. Raised in Sicily, the Holy Roman Emperor Frederick II (r. 1212–1250) appreciated Muslim culture and did not recoil from negotiating with Muslims. When the pope threatened to excommunicate him unless he waged a crusade, Frederick nominally regained Jerusalem through a flimsy treaty with the Mamluk sultan in Egypt. Dissatisfied, the pope continued to quarrel with the emperor, leaving Hungary, Poland, and Lithuania to deal with the Mongol onslaught on their own. Many princes capitulated and went to (Old) Sarai to offer their submission to Batu.

However, the Teutonic (**two-TOHN-ik**) Knights resisted. This German-speaking order of Christian warriors, originally organized in the Holy Land, sought to Christianize the pagan populations of northern Europe and colonize their territories with German settlers. They also fought against other Christians. To protect Slav territory, Alexander Nevskii joined the Mongols in fighting the Teutonic Knights and their Finnish allies. The latter suffered a catastrophe in 1242, when many broke through an icy northern lake and drowned. This event destroyed the power of the Knights, and the northern Crusades virtually ceased.

The "Mongol" armies encountered by the Europeans consisted mostly of Turks, Chinese, Iranians, a few Europeans, and at least one Englishman, who went to crusade in the Middle East but joined the Mongols and served in Hungary. But most commanders were Mongol.

Initial wild theories describing the Mongols as coming from Hell or from caves where Alexander the Great

akg-images/RIA Nowosti

▶ **Transformation of the Kremlin** Like other northern Europeans, the Russians preferred to build in wood, which was easy to handle and comfortable to live in. But they fortified important political centers with stone ramparts. In the 1300s, the city of Moscow emerged as a new capital, and its old wooden palace, the Kremlin, was gradually transformed into a stone structure.

Section Review

- Mongol conquest devastated Kievan Russia, but the Russian language achieved greater importance, and many Russian traditions survived.

- Mongol conquest prompted decentralization of Russian power away from Kiev, but the Golden Horde's decline set the stage for the rise of Russian autocracy.

- The decline of Mongol power and Byzantine weakness enabled the rise of Lithuania and Serbia in eastern Europe and of the Ottoman Empire in Anatolia.

confined the mythical monsters of antiquity gradually yielded to a more sophisticated understanding as European embassies to Mongol courts returned with reliable intelligence. In some quarters terror gave way to appreciation. Europeans learned about diplomatic passports, coal mining, movable type, high-temperature metallurgy, higher mathematics, gunpowder, and, in the fourteenth century, the casting and use of bronze cannon. Yet with the outbreak of bubonic plague in the late 1340s (see Chapter 14), the memory of Mongol terror helped ignite religious speculation that God might again be punishing the Christians.

In the fourteenth century several regions, most notably Lithuania (**lith-oo-WAY-nee-ah**), escaped the Mongol grip. When Russia fell to the Mongols, Lithuania had experienced an unprecedented centralization and military strengthening. Like Alexander Nevskii, the Lithuanian leaders maintained their independence by cooperating with the Mongols. In the late 1300s Lithuania capitalized on its privileged position to dominate Poland and ended the Teutonic Knights' hope of regaining power.

In the Balkans independent kingdoms separated themselves from the chaos of the Byzantine Empire and thrived amidst the political uncertainties of the Mongol period. The Serbian king Stephen Dushan (ca. 1308–1355) proved the most effective leader. Seizing power from his father in 1331, he took advantage of Byzantine weakness to turn the archbishop of Serbia into an independent patriarch. In 1346 the patriarch crowned him "tsar and autocrat of the Serbs, Greeks, Bulgarians, and Albanians," a title that fairly represents the wide extent of his rule. As in the case of Timur, however, his kingdom declined after his death in 1355 and disappeared entirely after a defeat by the Ottomans at the battle of Kosovo in 1389.

The Turkic nomads whose descendants established the **Ottoman Empire** came to Anatolia in the same wave of Turkic migrations as the Seljuks (see Chapter 10). Though Il-khan influence was strong in eastern Anatolia, a number of small Turkic principalities emerged in the west. The Ottoman principality was situated in the northwest, close to the Sea of Marmara. This not only put them in a position to cross into Europe and take part in the dynastic struggles of the declining Byzantine state, but it also attracted Muslim religious warriors who wished to do battle with Christians on the frontiers. The defeat of the Ottoman sultan by Timur in 1402 was only a temporary setback. In 1453 Sultan Mehmet II captured Constantinople and brought the Byzantine Empire to an end.

The Ottoman sultans, like the rulers of Russia, Lithuania, and Serbia, seized opportunities that arose with the decay of Mongol power. The powerful states they created put strong emphasis on religious and linguistic identity, factors that the Mongols themselves did not stress. As we shall see, Mongol rule stimulated similar reactions in the lands of East and Southeast Asia.

13-4 Mongol Domination in China, 1271–1368

How did Mongol rule in China foster cultural and scientific exchange?

After conquering northern China in the 1230s, Great Khan Ögödei told a Confucian adviser that he planned to turn the heavily populated North China Plain into a pasture for livestock. The adviser reacted calmly but argued that taxing the cities and villages would bring greater wealth. The Great Khan agreed, but he imposed an oppressive tax-farming system instead of the fixed-rate method traditional to China.

The Chinese suffered under this system during the early years, but the Yuan Empire, established by Chinggis Khan's grandson Khubilai in 1271, also brought benefits: secure trade routes; exchange of experts between eastern and western Eurasia; and transmission of information, ideas, and skills.

13-4a The Yuan Empire, 1271–1368

The Yuan sought a fruitful synthesis of the Mongol and Chinese traditions. **Khubilai Khan** gave his oldest son a Chinese name and had Confucianists participate in the boy's education. In public announcements and the crafting of laws, he took Confucian conventions into consideration.

Ottoman Empire Islamic state founded by Osman in northwestern Anatolia around 1300. After the fall of the Byzantine Empire, the Ottoman Empire was based at Constantinople (today Istanbul) from 1453 to 1922. It encompassed lands in the Middle East, North Africa, the Caucasus, and eastern Europe.

Buddhist and Daoist leaders who visited the Great Khan came away believing that they had all but convinced him of their beliefs.

Buddhist priests from Tibet called **lamas (LAH-mah)** became popular with some Mongol rulers. Their idea of a militant universal ruler bringing the whole world under control of the Buddha and thus pushing it nearer to salvation mirrored an ancient Central Asian idea of universal rulership.

Beijing, the Yuan capital, became the center of cultural and economic life. Karakorum had been geographically remote, but Beijing served as the eastern terminus of caravan routes that began near Tabriz, the Il-khan capital, and (Old) Sarai, the Golden Horde capital. A horseback courier system utilizing hundreds of stations maintained communications along routes that were generally safe for travelers. Ambassadors and merchants arriving in Beijing found a city that was much more Chinese in character than Karakorum had been.

Called Great Capital (Dadu) or City of the Khan (*khan-balikh* [**kahn-BAL-ik**], Marco Polo's "Cambaluc"), Khubilai's capital included the Forbidden City, a closed imperial complex with wide streets and a network of linked lakes and artificial islands. In summer, Khubilai practiced riding and shooting at a palace and park in Inner Mongolia. This was Shangdu (**shahng-DOO**), the "Xanadu" (**ZAH-nah-doo**) with its "stately pleasure dome" celebrated by English poet Samuel Taylor Coleridge.

Before the arrival of the Mongols, three separate states with different languages, writing systems, forms of government, and elite cultures competed in China (see Chapter 12), The Tanggut and Jin Empires controlled the north, and the Southern Song controlled most of the area south of the Yellow River. The Great Khans destroyed all three and encouraged the restoration or preservation of many features of Chinese government and society.

The Mongol-ruled Yuan state was cosmopolitan, attracting many non-Chinese who helped the Mongols govern China. By law, Mongols ranked highest. Below them came Central Asians and Middle Easterners, then northern Chinese, and finally southern Chinese. This ranking reflected a hierarchy of functions. The Mongols were the empire's warriors, the Central Asians and Middle Easterners its census takers and tax collectors. The northern Chinese outranked the southern Chinese because they came under Mongol control almost two generations earlier.

Though Khubilai included some "Confucians" (under the Yuan, a formal and hereditary status) in government, their position compared poorly with pre-Mongol times. The Confucians disparaged merchants, many of whom were from the Middle East or Central Asia, and physicians, whom they regarded as mere technicians or Daoist mystics. But the Yuan encouraged doctors and began the process of integrating Chinese medical approaches with those contained in Muslim and Hellenistic sources.

A Muslim governor from Central Asia, Sayyid Ajall Shams al-Din (**SAY-id a-JELL Shams ad-DEEN**), exemplifies a non-Chinese person who helped the Mongols rule and yet still promoted Confucian culture. The Mongols appointed him governor of Yunnan (**YOON-nahn**), their newly acquired territory in the southwest that became a key transit area for trade between Tibet, Burma, the Vietnamese kingdoms, and China. Some scholars have called this area the Southwest Silk Road. Shams al-Din walked a fine line between connecting Yun-nan with the imperial center and relying upon native chieftains to stabilize the area. Moreover, he promoted Confucian education, dress, and rituals and built schools and Confucian temples. Yunnan, once considered only a periphery to earlier Chinese rulers, became an integral part of China under the Mongol rule and remains so to the present.

Like the Il-khans, the Yuan rulers stressed census taking and tax collecting. Persian, Arab, and Uighur administrators staffed the offices of taxation and finance, and Muslim scholars worked at calendar-making and astronomy. The Mongols organized all of China into provinces. Central appointment of provincial governors, tax collectors, and garrison commanders marked a radical change by systematizing control in all parts of the country.

Many cities seem to have prospered: in north China by being on the caravan routes; in the interior by being on the Grand Canal; and along the coast by participation in maritime grain shipments from south China. The reintegration of East Asia (though not Japan) with the overland Eurasian trade, which had lapsed with the fall of the Tang (see Chapter 12), stimulated the urban economies.

With merchants a privileged group, life in the cities changed. So few government posts were open to the old Chinese elite that families that had previously spent fortunes on educating sons for government service sought other opportunities. Many gentry families chose commerce. Corporations—investor groups that behaved as single commercial and legal units and

AP® Exam Tip
Consider how the Mongol Empire could be seen as a turning point in Eurasian history. What changed and what stayed the same before and after this point?

Khubilai Khan Last of the Mongol Great Khans (r. 1260–1294) and founder of the Yuan Empire.

lamas In Tibetan Buddhism, a teacher.

Beijing China's northern capital, first used as an imperial capital in 906 and now the capital of the People's Republic of China.

shared the risk of doing business—handled most economic activities, starting with financing caravans and expanding into tax farming and lending money to the Mongol aristocracy. Central Asians and Middle Easterners headed most corporations in the early Yuan period; but as Chinese bought shares, many acquired mixed membership, or even complete Chinese ownership.

The agricultural base, damaged by war, overtaxation, and the passage of armies, could not satisfy the financial needs of the Mongol aristocracy. Following earlier precedent, the imperial government made up the shortfall with paper money. But people doubted the value of the notes, which were unsecured. Copper coinage partially offset the failure of the paper currency. During the Song, exports of copper to Japan, where the metal was scarce, had caused a severe shortage in China, leading to a rise in the value of copper in relation to silver. By cutting off trade with Japan, the Mongols intentionally or unintentionally stabilized the value of copper coins.

As city life increasingly catered to the tastes of merchants instead of scholars, many gentry families moved from their traditional homes in the countryside to engage in urban commerce. Specialized shops selling clothing, grape wine, furniture, and religiously butchered meats became common. Teahouses offered sing-song girls, drum singers, operas, and other entertainments previously considered coarse. Writers published works in the style of everyday speech. And the increasing influence of the northern, Mongolian-influenced Chinese language, often called Mandarin in the West, resulted in lasting linguistic change.

Cottage industries linked to the urban economies dotted the countryside, where 90 percent of the people lived. Some villages cultivated mulberry trees and cotton using dams, water wheels, and irrigation systems patterned in part on Middle Eastern models. Treatises on planting, harvesting, threshing, and butchering were published. One technological innovator, Huang Dao Po **(hwahng DOW poh)**, brought knowledge of cotton growing, spinning, and weaving from her native Hainan Island to the fertile Yangzi Delta.

Yet on the whole, the countryside did poorly during the Yuan period. Initially, the Mongol princes evicted many farmers and subjected the rest to brutal tax collection. By the time the Yuan shifted to lighter taxes and encouragement of farming at the end of the 1200s, it was too late. Servitude or homelessness had overtaken many farmers. Neglect of dams and dikes caused disastrous flooding, particularly on the Yellow River.

According to Song records from before the Mongol conquest and the Ming census taken after their overthrow—each, of course, subject to inaccuracy or exaggeration—China's population may have shrunk by 40 percent during eighty years of Mongol rule, with many localities in northern China losing up to five-sixths of their inhabitants. Scholars have suggested several causes: prolonged warfare, rural distress causing people to resort to female infanticide, epidemics, a southward flight of refugees, and flooding on the Yellow River. The last helps explain why losses in the north exceeded those in the south and why the population along the Yangzi River markedly increased.

Section Review

- The Great Khans reunified China, expanded its borders, and fostered a synthesis of ideas and cultural traditions.

- Khubilai Khan made Beijing the capital of the Yuan Empire and presided over a social hierarchy with Mongols at the top and southern Chinese at the bottom.

- Mongol rule systematized government, but cities benefited more from Mongol policies than did the countryside.

- China's population shrank as a result of Mongol conquest and rule.

- Mongol-protected trade routes encouraged a steady exchange of scientific and cultural ideas.

- Internal strife weakened the Yuan Empire, which fell to the Ming in 1368, but many Mongols remained in China.

13-4b **The Fall of the Yuan Empire**

In the 1340s strife broke out among the Mongol princes, and within twenty years farmer rebellions and inter-Mongol feuds engulfed the land. Amidst the chaos, in 1368 a charismatic Chinese leader, Zhu Yuanzhang **(JOO yuwen-JAHNG)**, mounted a campaign that destroyed the Yuan Empire and brought China under control of his new empire, the Ming. Many Mongols—as well as the Muslims, Jews, and Christians who had come with them—remained in China. Most of their descendants took Chinese names and became part of the diverse cultural world of China.

Many other Mongols, however, had never moved out of their home territories in Mongolia. Now they welcomed back refugees from the Yuan collapse. Though Turkic peoples were becoming predominant in the steppe regions in the west, including territories still ruled by descendants of Chinggis Khan, Mongols continued to pre-dominate in Central Asia the steppe regions bordering on Mongolia. Some Mongol groups adopted Islam; others favored Tibetan Buddhism. But religious affiliation proved less important than Mongol identity in fostering a renewed sense of unity.

The Ming thus fell short of dominating all the Mongols. The Mongols of Central Asia paid tribute to the extent that doing so facilitated their trade. Other Mongols, however, remained a continuing threat on the northern Ming frontier.

13-5 The Early Ming Empire, 1368–1500

In what ways did the Ming Empire continue or discontinue Mongol practices?

Historians of China, like historians of Russia and Iran, divide over the overall impact of the Mongol era. Since the **Ming Empire** reestablished many practices that are seen as purely Chinese, it receives praise from people who ascribe central importance to Chinese traditions. On the other hand, historians who look upon the Mongol era as a pivotal historical moment when communication across the vast interior of Eurasia served to bring east and west together sometimes see the inward-looking Ming as less productive than the Yuan.

13-5a Ming China on a Mongol Foundation

Zhu Yuanzhang, a former monk, soldier, and bandit, had watched his parents and other family members die of famine and disease, conditions he blamed on Mongol misrule. During the Yuan Empire's chaotic last decades, he vanquished rival rebels and assumed imperial power under the name Hongwu (r. 1368–1398).

Hongwu moved the capital to Nanjing **(nahn-JING)** ("southern capital") on the Yangzi River, turning away from the Mongol's Beijing ("northern capital"; see Map 13.3). Though Zhu Yuanzhang the rebel had espoused a radical Buddhist belief in a coming age of salvation, once in power he used Confucianism to depict the emperor as the champion of civilization and virtue.

Hongwu choked off relations with Central Asia and the Middle East and imposed strict limits on imports and foreign visitors. Silver replaced paper money for tax payments and commerce. These practices, illustrative of an anti-Mongol ideology, proved as economically unwise as some of the Yuan economic policies and did not last. Eventually, the Ming government came to resemble the Yuan. Ming rulers retained the provincial structure and continued to observe the hereditary professional categories of the Yuan period. Muslims made calendars and astronomical calculations at a new observatory at Nanjing, a replica of Khubilai's at Beijing. The Mongol calendar continued in use.

Continuities with the Yuan became more evident after an imperial prince seized power through a coup d'état to rule as the emperor **Yongle (yoong-LAW)** (r. 1403–1424). Yongle returned the capital to Beijing and enlarged and improved Khubilai's Forbidden City, which now acquired its present features: moats, orange-red outer walls, golden roofs, and marble bridges. He intended this combination fortress, religious site, bureaucratic center, and imperial residential park to overshadow Nanjing, and it survives today as China's most imposing traditional architectural complex.

Yongle also restored commercial links with the Middle East. Because hostile Mongols still controlled much of the caravan route, Yongle explored maritime connections. In Southeast Asia, Vietnam became a Ming province as the early emperors continued the Mongol program of aggression. This focus on the southern frontier helped inspire the naval expeditions of the trusted imperial eunuch **Zheng He (jehng huh)** from 1405 to 1433.

A Muslim eunuch whose father and grandfather had made the pilgrimage to Mecca, Zheng He had a good knowledge of the Middle East; and his religion eased relations with the states of the Indian subcontinent, where he directed his first three voyages. Subsequent expeditions reached Hormuz on the Persian Gulf, sailed the southern coast of Arabia and the Horn of Africa (modern Somalia), and possibly reached as far south as the Strait of Madagascar. Recent suggestions that his ships reached Egypt, the Mediterranean, and the Western Hemisphere lack concrete evidence.

On early voyages Zheng He visited long-established Chinese merchant communities in Southeast Asia to cement their allegiance to the Ming Empire and collect taxes. When a community on the island of Sumatra resisted, he slaughtered the men to set an example. The expeditions added some fifty new tributary states to the Ming imperial universe, but trade did not increase as dramatically. Sporadic embassies reached Beijing from rulers in India, the Middle East, Africa, and Southeast Asia. During one visit the ruler of Brunei **(broo-NYE)** died and

Ming Empire Empire based in China that Zhu Yuanzhang established after the overthrow of the Yuan Empire. The Ming emperor Yongle sponsored the building of the Forbidden City and the voyages of Zheng He. The later years of the Ming saw a slowdown in technological development and economic decline.

Yongle The third emperor of the Ming Empire (r. 1403–1424). He sponsored the building of the Forbidden City, a huge encyclopedia project, the expeditions of Zheng He, and the reopening of China's borders to trade and travel.

Zheng He An imperial eunuch and Muslim, entrusted by the Ming emperor Yongle with a series of state voyages that took his gigantic ships through the Indian Ocean, from Southeast Asia to Africa.

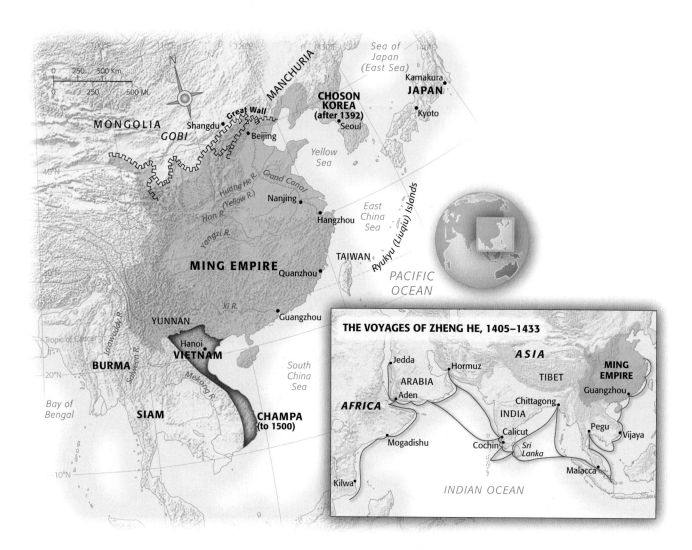

MAP 13.3 **The Ming Empire and Its Allies, 1368–1500** The Ming Empire controlled China but had a hostile relationship with peoples in Mongolia and Inner Asia who had been under the rule of the Mongol Yuan emperors. Mongol attempts at conquest by sea were continued by the Ming mariner Zheng He. Between 1405 and 1433 he sailed to Southeast Asia and then beyond, to India, the Persian Gulf, and East Africa.

How do the voyages of Zheng He compare with those of Columbus?

AP® Exam Tip

Explain how interregional contact encouraged technological and cultural transfers during Chinese maritime activities led by Zheng He.

received a grand burial at the Chinese capital. The expeditions stopped in the 1430s after the deaths of Yongle and Zheng He.

Why did the Chinese not develop seafaring for commercial and military gain? Contemporaries considered the voyages a personal project of Yongle, an upstart ruler who had always sought to prove his worthiness. Building the Forbidden City in Beijing and sponsoring gigantic encyclopedia projects might be taken to reflect a similar character. Yongle may also have been emulating Khubilai Khan's sea expeditions against Japan and Southeast Asia. This would fit with the rumor spread by Yongle's political enemies that he was actually a Mongol.

A less speculative approach starts with the fact that the new commercial opportunities fell short of expectations, despite bringing foreign nations into the Ming orbit. In the meantime, Japanese coastal piracy intensified, and Mongol threats in the north and west grew. The human and financial demands of fortifying the north, redesigning and strengthening Beijing, and outfitting campaigns against the Mongols ultimately took priority over the quest for maritime empire.

13-5b Technology and Population

The Ming government limited mining, partly to maintain the value of metal coins and partly to tax the industry. As a consequence, metal implements became more expensive for farmers. Techniques for making the high-quality bronze and steel used for weapons also declined. Japan

▶ **Examination Cells** Students taking examinations on the Confucian classics to gain admission to the class of officials occupied these cells for 24 to 72 hours, depending on the level they were attempting. In the city of Guangdong there were 7,500 cells in long rows. Candidates were identified only by number, and their essays were rewritten to prevent their handwriting being recognized. Approximately 5 percent of the candidates passed the examination.

Vanni Archive/Art Resource, NY

quickly surpassed China in the production of extremely high-quality swords.

After the death of Emperor Yongle in 1424, shipbuilding skills deteriorated, and few advances occurred in printing, timekeeping, and agricultural technology. Agricultural production peaked around the mid-1400s and remained level for more than a century. New weaving techniques did appear, but technological development in this field had peaked by 1500.

Reactivation of the examination system for recruiting government officials (see Chapter 12) drew large numbers of ambitious men into a renewed study of the Confucian classics. This shift reduced the vitality of commerce, where they had previously been employed, just as population growth was creating a labor surplus. Records indicating a growth from 60 million at the end of the Yuan period in 1368 to nearly 100 million by 1400 may not be entirely reliable, but rapid population growth encouraged the production of staples—wheat, millet, and barley in the north and rice in the south—at the expense of commercial crops such as cotton that had stimulated many technological innovations under the Song. Staple crops yielded lower profits, which further discouraged capital improvements. New foods, such as sweet potatoes, became available but were little adopted. At the same time, population growth in southern and central China caused deforestation and raised the price of wood.

Against the Mongol horsemen in the north the Ming used scattershot mortars and explosive canisters. They even used a few cannon, which they knew about from contacts with the Middle East and later with Europeans (see Environment & Technology: From Gunpowder to Guns). Fearing a loss of technological secrets, the government censored the chapters on gunpowder and guns in early Ming encyclopedias. Shipyards and ports shut down to avoid contact with Japanese pirates and to prevent Chinese from migrating to Southeast Asia.

A technology gap with Korea and Japan opened up nevertheless. When superior steel was needed, supplies came from Japan. Korea moved ahead of China in the design and production of firearms and ships, in printing techniques, and in the sciences of weather prediction and calendar-making. The desire to tap the wealthy Ming market spurred some of these advances.

13-5c The Ming Achievement

In the late 1300s and the 1400s the wealth and consumerism of the early Ming stimulated high achievement in literature, the decorative arts, and painting. The plain writing of the Yuan period had produced some of the world's earliest novels. This genre flourished under the Ming. *Water Margin*, which originated in the raucous drum-song performances

AP® Exam Tip
Explain the diffusion and impact of printing and gunpowder technology during this era.

Section Review

- The first Ming emperor, Hongwu, based his policies on an anti-Mongol ideology, but the Ming government came to adopt Yuan practices.

- Yongle reestablished international commerce and sent Zheng He to explore maritime connections to the Middle East.

- Technological innovation continued, but with less frequent advances and reduced output, and some techniques became guarded secrets.

- The Ming reestablished the Confucian examination system, reducing the vitality of commerce.

- The greatest Ming achievements were in literature, the arts, and porcelain production.

Long before the invention of guns, gunpowder was used in China and Korea to excavate mines, build canals, and channel irrigation. Alchemists in China used related formulas to make noxious gas pellets to paralyze enemies and expel evil spirits. A more realistic benefit was eliminating disease-carrying insects, a critical aid to the colonization of malarial regions in China and Southeast Asia. The Mongol Empire staged fireworks displays on ceremonial occasions, delighting European visitors to Karakorum who saw them for the first time.

Anecdotal evidence in Chinese records gives credit for the introduction of gunpowder to a Sogdian Buddhist monk of the 500s. The monk described the wondrous alchemical transformation of elements produced by a combination of charcoal and saltpeter. In this connection he also mentioned sulfur. The distillation of *naphtha*, a light, flammable derivative of oil or coal, seems also to have been first developed in Central Asia, the earliest evidence coming from the Gandhara region (in modern Pakistan).

By the eleventh century, the Chinese had developed flame-throwers powered by burning naphtha, sulfur, or gunpowder in a long tube. These weapons intimidated and injured foot soldiers and horses and also set fire to thatched roofs in hostile villages and, occasionally, the rigging of enemy ships.

In their long struggle against the Mongols, the Song learned to enrich saltpeter to increase the amount of nitrate in gunpowder. This produced forceful explosions rather than jets of fire. Launched from catapults, gunpowder-filled canisters could rupture fortifications and inflict mass casualties. Explosives hurled from a distance could sink or burn ships.

The Song also experimented with firing projectiles from metal gun barrels. The earliest gun barrels were broad and squat and were transported on special wagons to their emplacements. The mouths of the barrels projected saltpeter mixed with scatter-shot minerals. The Chinese and then the Koreans adapted gunpowder to shooting masses of arrows—sometimes flaming—at enemy fortifications.

In 1280 weapons makers of the Yuan Empire produced the first device featuring a projectile that completely filled the mouth of the cannon and thus concentrated the explosive force. The Yuan used cast bronze for the barrel and iron for the cannonball. The new weapon shot farther and more accurately, and was much more destructive, than the earlier Song devices.

Knowledge of the cannon and cannonball moved westward across Eurasia. By the end of the thirteenth century cannon were being produced in the Middle East. By 1327 small, squat cannon called "bombards" were being used in Europe.

Questions for Analysis

1. What might have been the disadvantages of using gunpowder in battle?
2. Since the Mongol rulers used fireworks displays, why didn't their armies use gunpowder weapons during their century of imperial domination in Eurasia?
3. Why did post-Song China not continue to be the innovation leader in cannon development?

Wubeizhi ('On Warfare') (woodblock print), Chinese School/British Library, London, UK/The Bridgeman Art Library

▲ **Launching Flaming Arrows** Song soldiers used gunpowder to launch flaming arrows.

loosely related to Chinese opera, features dashing Chinese bandits who struggle against Mongol rule. Many authors had a hand in the final print version.

Luo Guanzhong (**law gwahn-joong**), one of the authors of *Water Margin*, is also credited with *Romance of the Three Kingdoms*, based on a much older series of stories that in some ways resemble the Arthurian legends. It describes the attempts of an upright but doomed war leader and his followers to restore the Han Empire of ancient times and resist the power of the cynical but brilliant villain. *Romance of the Three Kingdoms* and *Water Margin* express the militant but joyous pro-China sentiment of the early Ming era and remain among the most appreciated Chinese fictional works.

Probably the best-known product of Ming technological advance was porcelain. The imperial ceramic works at Jingdezhen (**JING-deh-JUHN**) experimented with new production techniques and new ways of organizing and rationalizing workers. "Ming ware," a blue-on-white style developed in the 1400s from Indian, Central Asian, and Middle Eastern motifs, became especially prized. Other Ming goods in high demand included furniture, lacquered screens, and silk, all of which found ready markets in Southeast Asia and the Pacific, India, the Middle East, and East Africa.

13-6 Centralization and Militarism in East Asia, 1200–1500

What are some of the similarities and differences in how Korea and Japan responded to the Mongol threat?

Korea, Japan, and the Vietnamese kingdoms, the other major states of East Asia, were all affected by confrontation with the Mongols, but with differing results. Japan and northern Vietnam escaped Mongol conquest but changed in response to the Mongol threat, becoming more effective and expansive regimes with enhanced commitments to independence.

As for Korea, just as the Ming stressed Chinese traditions and identity in the aftermath of Yuan rule, so Mongol domination contributed to revitalized interest in Korea's own language and history. The Mongols conquered Korea after a difficult war, and though Korea suffered socially and economically under Mongol rule, members of the elite associated closely with the Yuan Empire. After the fall of the Yuan, merchants continued the international connections established in the Mongol period, while Korean armies consolidated a new kingdom and fended off pirates.

AP® Exam Tip
Keep track of the influence of Chinese culture on the surrounding areas such as Korea, Japan, and Vietnam.

13-6a Korea from the Mongols to the Choson Dynasty, 1231–1500

Korea was the answer to the Mongol search for coastal areas from which to launch naval expeditions and choke off the sea trade of their adversaries. By the time the Mongols attacked in 1231, the Choe family had assumed the role of military commander and protector of the Koryo (**KAW-ree-oh**) king (not unlike the shoguns of Japan). Four generations of Choe-led tyranny and years of defensive war left a ravaged countryside, exhausted armies, and burned treasure. The Choe's refusal to sue for peace, or emerge from their capital on Kanghwa Island to drive the Mongols from the Korean peninsula, led to widespread hardship among the populace and frustration among military men and nobles alike. The last of the Choe tyrants was killed by his underlings in 1258. Soon afterward the king surrendered to the Mongols and became a subject monarch by linking his family to the Great Khan by marriage.

By the mid-1300s the Koryo kings were of mostly Mongol descent and favored Mongol dress, customs, and language. The kings, their families, and their entourages often traveled between China and Korea, thus exposing Korea to the philosophical and artistic styles of Yuan China: neo-Confucianism, Chan Buddhism (called Son in Korea), and celadon (light green) pottery.

Mongol control broke down centuries of comparative isolation. Cotton was introduced in southern Korea; gunpowder came into use; and the art of calendar-making stimulated astronomical observation and mathematics. Avenues of advancement opened for Korean scholars willing to learn Mongolian, landowners willing to open their lands to falconry and grazing, and merchants servicing the new royal exchanges with Beijing. These developments contributed to the rise of a new landed and educated class.

When the Yuan Empire fell in 1368, the Koryo ruling family remained loyal to the Mongols until a rebellious general, Yi Songgye (**YEE SONG-gye**), forced it to recognize the new Ming Empire. In 1392, Yi Songgye established a new kingdom called **Choson** (**cho-sun**) with a capital in Seoul and sought to reestablish a distinctive Korean identity. Like Russia and Ming China, the Choson regime publicly rejected the period of Mongol domination. Yet the Choson government continued to employ Mongol-style land surveys, taxation in kind, and military garrison techniques.

Choson The Choson dynasty ruled Korea from the fall of the Koryo kingdom to the colonization of Korea by Japan.

▲ **Movable Type** The improvement of cast bronze tiles, each showing a single character, eliminated the need to cast or carve whole pages. Individual tiles—the ones shown are Korean—could be moved from page frame to page frame and gave an even and pleasing appearance. All parts of East Asia eventually adopted this form of printing for cheap, popular books. In the mid-1400s Korea also experimented with a fully phonetic form of writing, which in combination with movable type allowed Koreans unprecedented levels of literacy and access to printed works. SSPL/The Image Works

Like the Ming emperors, the Choson kings revived the study of the Confucian classics, an activity that required knowledge of Chinese and showed the dedication of the state to learning. This revival may have led to a key technological breakthrough in printing technology.

Koreans had begun using Chinese woodblock printing in the 700s. This technology worked well in China, where a large number of buyers wanted copies of a comparatively small number of texts. But in Korea, the comparatively few literate men had interests in a wide range of texts. Movable wooden or ceramic type appeared in Korea in the early thirteenth century and may have been invented there, but the texts were frequently inaccurate and difficult to read. In the 1400s Choson printers, working directly with the king, developed a reliable device to anchor the pieces of type to the printing plate. By replacing the old beeswax adhesive with solid copper frames, they improved the legibility of the printed page, and high-volume, accurate production became possible. Combined with the phonetic *han'gul* (**HAHN-goor**) writing system, this printing technology laid the foundation for a high literacy rate in Korea.

Choson publications told readers how to produce and use fertilizer, transplant rice seedlings, and engineer reservoirs. Building on Eurasian knowledge imported by the Mongols and introduced under the Koryo, Choson scholars developed a meteorological science of their own. They invented or redesigned instruments to measure wind speed and rainfall and perfected a calendar based on minute comparisons of the Chinese and Islamic systems.

In agriculture, farmers expanded the cultivation of cash crops, the reverse of what was happening in Ming China. Cotton, the primary crop, enjoyed such high value that the state accepted it for tax payments. The Choson army used cotton uniforms, and cotton became the favored fabric of the Korean elite. With cotton gins and spinning wheels powered by water, Korea advanced more rapidly than China in mechanization and began to export considerable amounts of cotton to China and Japan.

Although both the Yuan and the Ming withheld the formula for gunpowder from the Korean government, Korean officials acquired the information by subterfuge. By the later 1300s they had mounted cannon on ships that patrolled against pirates and used gunpowder-driven arrow launchers against enemy personnel and the rigging of enemy ships. Combined with skills in armoring ships, these techniques made the small Choson navy a formidable defense force.

13-6b Political Transformation in Japan, 1274–1500

Having secured Korea, the Mongols looked toward Japan, a target they could easily reach from Korea. Their first 30,000-man invasion force in 1274 included Mongol cavalry and archers and sailors from Korea and northeastern Asia. Its weaponry included light catapults and incendiary and explosive projectiles of Chinese manufacture. The Mongol forces landed successfully and decimated the Japanese cavalry, but a great storm on Hakata (**HAH-kah-tah**) Bay on the north side of Kyushu (**KYOO-shoo**) Island (see Map 13.4) prevented the establishment of a beachhead and forced the Mongols to sail back to Korea.

The invasion hastened social and political changes that were already under way. Under the Kamakura (**kah-mah-KOO-rah**) Shogunate established in 1185—another powerful family actually exercised control—the *shogun*, or military leader, distributed land and privileges to his followers. In return they paid him tribute and supplied him with soldiers. This stable, but decentralized, system depended on balancing the power of regional warlords. Lords in the north and east of Japan's main island were remote from those in the south and west. Beyond devotion to the emperor and the shogun, little united them until the terrifying Mongol threat materialized.

After the return of his fleet, Khubilai sent envoys to Japan demanding submission. Japanese leaders executed them and prepared for war. The shogun then took steps to centralize his military government, effectively increasing the influence of warlords from the south and west of Honshu (Japan's main island) and from the island of Kyushu, where invasion seemed most likely. These local commanders acted under the shogun's orders.

Military planners studied Mongol tactics and retrained and outfitted Japanese warriors for defense against advanced weaponry, while farm laborers drafted from all over the country constructed defensive fortifications. This effort demanded, for the first time, a national system to move resources toward western points rather than toward the imperial or shogunal centers to the east.

The Mongols attacked again in 1281. They brought 140,000 warriors, including many non-Mongols, as well as thousands of horses, in hundreds of ships. However, the wall the Japanese had built to cut off Hakata Bay from the mainland deprived the Mongol forces of a reliable landing point. Japanese swordsmen rowed out and boarded the Mongol ships lingering offshore. Their superb steel swords shocked the invaders, while an epidemic decimated the Mongol troops. After a prolonged standoff, a typhoon struck and sank perhaps half of the Mongol ships. The remainder sailed away, never again to harass Japan. Religious institutions later claimed that their prayers for help brought a "divine wind"—*kamikaze* (**kah-me-kah-zay**)—that drove away the Mongols.

Nevertheless, the Mongol threat continued to influence Japanese development. Prior to his death in 1294, Khubilai had in mind a third invasion. Although his successors did not carry through with it, the shoguns did not know that the Mongols had given up the idea and rebuilt coastal defenses well into the fourteenth century, helping to consolidate the social position of Japan's warrior elite and stimulating the development of a national infrastructure for trade and communication. But the Kamakura Shogunate, based on regionally collected and regionally dispersed revenues, suffered financial strain in trying to pay for centralized road and defense systems.

Between 1333 and 1338 the emperor Go-Daigo (**go-DIE-go**) broke the centuries-old tradition of imperial seclusion and aloofness from government and tried to reclaim power from the shoguns. This effort ignited a civil war that destroyed the Kamakura system. In 1338, with the Mongol threat waning, the **Ashikaga** (**ah-shee-KAH-gah**) **Shogunate** took control at the imperial center of Kyoto.

Under the new shogunate, provincial warlords enjoyed renewed independence. Around their imposing castles, they sponsored the development of market towns, religious institutions, and schools, while the application of technologies imported in earlier periods, including water wheels, improved plows, and Champa rice, increased agricultural productivity.

Growing wealth and relative peace stimulated artistic creativity, mostly reflecting Zen Buddhist beliefs held by the warrior elite. In the simple elegance of architecture and gardens, in the contemplative landscapes of artists, and in the eerie, stylized performances of the Noh theater, the aesthetic code of Zen became established in the Ashikaga era.

Despite the technological advancement, artistic productivity, and rapid urbanization of this period, competition among warlords and their followers led to regional wars. By the late 1400s these conflicts resulted in the near destruction of the warlords. The great Onin War in 1477 left Kyoto devastated and the Ashikaga Shogunate a central government in name only. Ambitious but low-ranking warriors, some with links to trade with the continent, began to scramble for control of the provinces.

After the fall of the Yuan in 1368 Japan resumed overseas trade, exporting raw materials and swords, as well as folding fans, invented in Japan during the period of isolation. Japan's primary imports from China were books and porcelain. The volatile political environment in Japan gave rise to partnerships between warlords and local merchants. All worked to strengthen their own towns and treasuries through overseas commerce or, sometimes, through piracy.

MAP 13.4   Korea and Japan, 1200–1500 The proximity of Korea and northern China to Japan gave the Mongols the opportunity to launch enormous fleets against the Kamakura Shogunate, which controlled most of the three islands (Honshu, Shikoku, and Kyushu) of central Japan.

What is the implication of Japan and Korea insisting today on naming the sea between them differently: Sea of Japan for the Japanese and Eastern Sea for the Koreans?

kamikaze The "divine wind," which the Japanese credited with blowing Mongol invaders away from their shores in 1281.

Ashikaga (ah-shee-KAH-gah) Shogunate The second of Japan's military governments headed by a *shogun* (a military ruler). Sometimes called the Muromachi Shogunate.

13-6c The Emergence of Vietnam, 1200–1500

Before the first Mongol attack in 1257, the states of Dai Viet (northern Vietnam) and Champa (southern Vietnam) had clashed frequently. Dai Viet (once called Annam) looked toward China and had once been subject to the Tang. Chinese political ideas, social philosophies, dress, religion, and language heavily influenced its official culture. Champa related more closely to the trading networks of the Indian Ocean, and its official culture was strongly influenced by Indian religion, language, architecture, and dress. Champa's relationship with China depended in part on how close its enemy, Dai Viet, was to China at any particular time. During the Song period Dai Viet was neither formally subject to China nor particularly threatening to Champa militarily, so Champa inaugurated a trade and tribute relationship with China that spread fast-ripening Champa rice throughout East Asia. The Mongols exacted tribute from both Dai Viet and Champa until the fall of the Yuan Empire in 1368. Mongol political and military ambitions were mostly focused elsewhere, however, which minimized their impact on Vietnamese politics and culture. The two Vietnamese kingdoms soon resumed their warfare. When Dai Viet moved its army to reinforce its southern border, Ming troops occupied the capital, Hanoi, and installed a puppet government. Almost thirty years elapsed before Dai Viet regained independence and resumed a tributary status. By then the Ming were turning to meet Mongol challenges to their north. In a series of ruthless campaigns, Dai Viet terminated Champa's independence, and by 1500 the ancestor of the modern state of Vietnam had been born.

The new state still relied on Confucian bureaucratic government and an examination system, but some practices differed from those in China. The Vietnamese legal code, for example, preserved group landowning and decision making within the villages, as well as women's property rights. Both developments probably had roots in an early rural culture based on the growing of rice in wet paddies; by this time the Dai Viet kingdom considered them distinctive features of its own culture.

Section Review

- Mongol conquest devastated Korea, but Mongol rule opened it to new ideas and technologies.

- The Choson dynasty succeeded the Koryo and fostered local identity while encouraging economic expansion and technological innovation.

- In Japan, the Mongol threat forced military and organizational innovations, but the expense of these defenses weakened the Kamakura Shogunate.

- Go-Daigo's failed attempt to reassert imperial power resulted in the rise of the Ashikaga Shogunate.

- The warring states of Vietnam avoided Mongol conquest but paid tribute to the Yuan Empire.

- After the Ming withdrawal, Dai Viet conquered Champa, establishing a unified state on both Confucian and local practices.

13-7 **Conclusion**

Despite their brutality and devastation, the Mongol conquests brought a degree of unity to the lands between China and Europe that had never before been known. Nomadic mobility and expertise in military technology contributed to communication across vast spaces and initially, at least, an often-callous disregard for the welfare of farmers, as manifested in oppressive tax policies. By contrast, trade received active Mongol stimulation through the protection of routes and encouragement of industrial production.

The Mongols ruled with an unprecedented openness, employing talented people irrespective of their linguistic, ethnic, or religious affiliations. As a consequence, the period of comparative Mongol unity, which lasted less than a century, saw a remarkable exchange of ideas, techniques, and products across the breadth of Eurasia. Chinese gunpowder spurred the development of Ottoman and European cannon, while Muslim astronomers introduced new instruments and mathematical techniques to Chinese observatories.

However, rule over dozens of restive peoples could not endure. Where Mongol military enterprise reached its limit of expansion, it stimulated local aspirations for independence. Division and hostility among branches of Chinggis Khan's family—between the Yuan in China and the Chagatai in Central Asia or between the Golden Horde in Russia and the Il-khans in Iran—provided opportunities for achieving these aspirations. The Russians gained freedom from Mongol domination in western Eurasia, and the general political disruption and uncertainty of the Mongol era assisted the emergence of the Lithuanian, Serbian, and Ottoman states.

In the east, China, Korea, and Dai Viet similarly found renewed political identity in the aftermath of Mongol rule. The invasions expanded China's boundaries as never before, and they have changed little since. A resurgence of native Chinese culture blossomed in the following Ming dynasty. At the same time, Japan fought off two Mongol invasions and transformed its internal political and cultural identity in the process. In every case, the reality or threat of Mongol attack and domination encouraged centralization of government, improvement of military techniques, and renewed stress on local cultural identity. Thus, in retrospect, despite its traditional association with death and destruction, the Mongol period appears as a watershed, establishing new connections between widespread parts of Eurasia and leading to the development of strong, assertive, and culturally creative regional states.

Key Terms

Mongols p. 319
Chinggis Khan p. 319
nomadism p. 319
Yuan Empire p. 321
bubonic plague p. 325
Il-khan p. 326

Golden Horde p. 326
Timur p. 327
Rashid al-Din p. 327
Nasir al-Din Tusi p. 329
Alexander Nevskii p. 330
tsar p. 331

Ottoman Empire p. 332
Khubilai Khan p. 333
lama p. 333
Beijing p. 333
Ming Empire p. 335
Yongle p. 335

Zheng He p. 335
Choson p. 339
kamikaze p. 341
Ashikaga Shogunate p.341

Review Questions

1. Which conqueror changed world history more, Alexander the Great or Chinggis Khan?

2. How does the role of Turks in the Mongol armies compare with that of the Germans in the Roman armies?

3. In comparing the history of Vietnam and Japan, how should one evaluate the importance of trade and contact with other lands?

 MindTap® is a fully online, personalized learning experience built upon Cengage Learning content. MindTap® combines student learning tools—readings, multimedia, activities, and assessments—into a singular Learning Path that guides students through the course and helps students develop the critical thinking, analysis, and communication skills that are essential to academic and professional success.

AP® REVIEW QUESTIONS FOR CHAPTER 13

Multiple-Choice Questions

Questions 1–4 refer to Map 13.1 on page 323.

1. Which of the following statements is best supported by the map?

   (A) The Mongol Empire was isolated from Europe and Asia.

   (B) Trade flourished with the expansion of the Mongol Empire.

   (C) There were no trade routes in Africa or Northern Europe.

   (D) The Mongol Empire controlled trade in all of South and East Asia.

2. Which of the following consequences of economic interactions does the map illustrate?

   (A) The movement and transfer of goods promoted the growth of powerful trading cities like Krakatoum.

   (B) The passage of goods along trade routes mainly remained within a single region like the Khanate of Central Asia.

   (C) Increased trade required merchants to know only one geographical environment well.

   (D) Travelers followed no specific path, but traveled mainly by sea from one region to another.

3. Mongols actively facilitated trade

   (A) through the unification of Central Asia and the enforcement of peace.

   (B) by collecting tribute from the regions that they controlled.

   (C) by taking on the role of merchants on the steppes of Central Asia.

   (D) by constructing roads and bridges on the Silk Roads.

4. As the Mongol Empire expanded, significant technological transfers occurred between the Mongols and the vanquished peoples, including

   (A) the Chinese acceptance of Mongolian carts.

   (B) the Mongol use of gunpowder technologies.

   (C) the Mongol adoption of Indian metallurgy.

   (D) the Russian use of Chinese silk making.

Questions 5–7 refer to the passage below.

"It is the duty of the women to drive the carts, get the dwellings on and off them, milk the cows, make butter and *gruit* (sour curd) and to dress and sew skins, which they do with a thread made of tendons. . . .

The men make bows and arrows, manufacture stirrups and bits, make saddles, do the carpentering on (the framework of) their dwellings and the carts; they take care of the horses, milk the mares, churn the *cosmos* or mare's milk, make the skins in which it is put; they also look after the camels and load them. Both sexes look after the sheep and goats, sometimes the men, other times the women, milking them.

As to their justice you must know that when two men fight together no one dares interfere, even a father dare not aid a son; but he who has the worst of it may appeal to the court of the lord, and if anyone touches him after the appeal, he is put to death. . . . When one is accused by a number of persons, they torture him so that he confesses. They punish homicide with capital punishment, and also co-habiting with a woman not one's own. . . . They also punish with death grand larceny, but as for petty thefts, such as that of a sheep, so long as one has not repeatedly been taken in the act, they beat him cruelly, and if they administer a hundred blows they must use a hundred sticks."

> From a report on the Mongols, sent to King Louis IX of France, by William of Rubruck, 1253–1255

5. Which of the following assertions is best supported by the account of William of Rubruck?

   (A) Mongol gender balance was unclear, with few identifications of gender-specific roles.

   (B) Mongol women were completely confined from social interaction, operating in a separate sphere from their husbands.

   (C) Mongol men exemplified the patriarchal system by restricting the roles wives were allowed to play.

   (D) Mongol women exercised more power and influence within their society than most Western women.

6. The description of gender roles in the account of William of Rubruck best supports which of the following conclusions about the evolution of Mongol social structure in the thirteenth century?

   (A) The social hierarchy was changed by interaction with cultures that the Mongols encountered.

(B) The apparent equality of Mongol men and women was indicative of the incursion of Nestorian Christianity into the empire.

(C) Influence from conquered peoples and other cultures had little effect in changing women's roles in Mongol society.

(D) As the Mongols became more sophisticated, gender roles became more defined.

7. Which of the following statements about governance and legal code in the Mongol empire is most correct?

(A) The Mongol law code was used to establish a concept of fair society in the same way as Hammurabi's Code of the Babylonian Empire.

(B) The Mongol Empire was a lawless society where might was more important than justice.

(C) Mongol justice was governed by the social standing of the individual who committed a crime.

(D) All important legal judgments were made by the clan leader, who controlled the group affairs.

Questions 8–10 refer to Map 13.3 on page 336.

8. Which of the following best explains why Admiral Zheng He was sent on a series of voyages during the Ming Empire?

(A) The Ming were trying to spread Chinese culture and language into South Asia.

(B) The Ming were attempting to control the Indian Ocean region through military might.

(C) The Ming were trying to find trade routes that avoided the Mongols in Central Asia.

(D) The Ming were hoping to find areas where the excess Chinese population could be settled.

9. Which of the following was a long-term effect of the voyages of Zheng He?

(A) Chinese literary, creative, and cultural traditions were fostered in Southeast Asia.

(B) Chinese ships were used as models for the Spanish galleons of the fifteenth century.

(C) Regular contact with India introduced Hinduism, which became a major religion in southern China.

(D) The expense of the voyages led to peasant unrest and the overthrow of the Ming dynasty.

10. What is the connection between the voyages of Zheng He and later developments in Chinese history?

(A) The Mongol Yuan dynasty was a period of cultural advance when Buddhism became dominant.

(B) China's population grew as it benefitted from the introduction of Central Asian crops.

(C) The expansion of the Yuan allowed China to establish tributary relationships with states overseas.

(D) The Mongol culture became a driving force in Chinese society and political organization.

Short-Answer Questions

"Genghis Khan divided his Tartars by captains of ten, captains of a hundred, and captains of a thousand, and over ten millenaries, or captains of a thousand, he placed one colonel, and over one whole army he authorized two or three chiefs, but so that all should be under one of the said chiefs. When they join battle against any other nation, unless they do all consent to retreat, every man who deserts is put to death. . . . Moreover they are required to have these weapons: two long bows or one good one at least, three quivers full of arrows, and one axe, and ropes to draw engines of war. But the richer have single-edged swords, with sharp points, and somewhat crooked. They have also armed horses, with their shoulders and breasts protected; they have helmets and coats of mail. Some of them have jackets for their horses, made of leather artificially doubled or trebled, shaped upon their bodies."

Friar John of Plano Carpini, *History of the Mongols*, ca. 1245

1. Use the passage above and your knowledge of world history to answer all parts of the question that follows.

(A) Identify ONE reason for the expansion of the Mongol Empire.

(B) Explain ONE positive result of the expansion of the Mongol Empire.

(C) Explain ONE negative result of the expansion of the Mongol Empire.

2. Answer all parts of the question that follows.

(A) Identify ONE cultural achievement of the Ming dynasty between 1368 and 1500.

(B) Explain ONE political achievement of the Ming dynasty between 1368 and 1500.

(C) Explain ONE challenge to the Ming dynasty between 1368 and 1500.

14 Latin Europe, 1200–1500

AP® Framework Terms

Hanseatic League
Guild
Bubonic plague/Black Death
Serf
Crusades
Ottoman Empire

Overarching Questions

1 How have religions, belief systems, philosophies, and ideologies affected the political, economic, and social development of societies? (CUL)

2 In what ways do the arts reflect innovation, adaptation, and creativity of specific societies? (CUL)

3 How and why have economic, social, cultural, and geographic factors influenced the process of state building, expansion, and dissolution? (SB)

4 How have different labor systems developed and changed over time? (ECON)

5 How have political, economic, cultural, and demographic factors affected social structures? (SOC)

n the summer of 1454, a year after the Ottoman Turks captured the Greek Christian city of Constantinople, Aeneas Sylvius Piccolomini (**uh-NEE-uhs SIL-vee-uhs pee-kuh-lo-MEE-nee**), destined in four years to become pope, expressed doubts as to whether anyone could persuade the rulers of Christian Europe to take up a new crusade against the Muslims: "Christendom has no head whom all will obey—neither the pope nor the emperor receives his due."

At the time, the Christian states thought more of fighting each other. French and English armies had been battling for over a century; the German emperor presided over dozens of states but did not really control them; and the numerous kingdoms and principalities of Spain and Italy could not unite. The Catholic rulers of Hungary, Poland, and Lithuania, on the front line against the Muslim Ottomans, seemed very far away from the western monarchs. With only slight exaggeration, Aeneas Sylvius moaned, "Every city has its own king, and there are as many princes as there are households." He attributed this lack of unity to European preoccupation with personal welfare and material gain. Both pessimism about human nature and materialism had increased during the previous century, after a devastating plague had carried off a third of Europe's population.

Yet despite all these divisions, disasters, and wars, historians now see the period from 1200 to 1500 (Europe's Late Middle Ages) as a time of unusual progress. Prosperous cities adorned with splendid architecture, institutions

▲ **Burying Victims of the Black Death**   This scene from Tournai, Flanders, captures the magnitude of the plague. Snark/Art Resource, NY

of higher learning, and cultural achievements counterbalanced the avarice and greed that Aeneas Sylvius lamented. While frequent wars caused havoc and destruction, they also promoted the development of military technology and more unified monarchies.

Although their Muslim and Byzantine neighbors commonly called Catholic Europeans "Franks," they ordinarily referred to themselves as "Latins," underscoring their allegiance to the Roman Catholic Church and the Latin language used in its rituals. ●

14-1 Rural Growth and Crisis

How well did inhabitants of Latin Europe, rich and poor, urban and rural, deal with their natural environment?

Between 1200 and 1500, the countries of western Europe brought more land under cultivation using new farming techniques and made greater use of machinery and mechanical forms of energy. Yet for the nine out of ten people who lived in the countryside, hard labor brought meager returns, and famine, epidemics, and war struck often. After the devastation of the Black Death between 1347 and 1351, social changes speeded up by peasant revolts released many persons from serfdom and brought some improvements to rural life.

By contrast, eastern Europe, a region of vast open spaces and sparse population, saw an increase in serfdom. Faced with a labor shortage, nobles agreed to force farm workers to till their lands.

14-1a Peasants, Population, and Plague

In 1200, most western Europeans lived as serfs tilling the soil on large estates owned by the nobility and the church (see Chapter 11). They owed their lord both a share of their harvests and numerous labor services. These obligations combined with inefficient farming practices meant that peasants received meager returns for their hard work. Even with numerous religious holidays, peasants labored some fifty-four hours a week, more than half the time in support of the

AP® Exam Tip
Compare the use of religion and belief systems to reinforce patriarchy in states throughout Afro-Eurasia during this time period.

local nobility. Each noble family, housed in its stone castle, required the labor of fifteen to thirty peasant families living in one-room thatched cottages containing little furniture and no luxuries.

Scenes of rural life show both men and women at work in the fields, but equality of labor did not mean equality at home. In the peasant's hut as elsewhere in medieval Europe, women were subordinate to men. The influential theologian Thomas Aquinas (**uh-KWY-nuhs**) (1225–1274) spoke for his age when he argued that although both men and women were created in God's image, there was a sense in which "the image of God is found in man, and not in woman: for man is the beginning and end of woman; as God is the beginning and end of every creature."[1]

Rural poverty resulted partly from rapid population growth. In 1200, China's population may have exceeded Europe's by two to one; by 1300, the population of each was about 80 million. China's population fell because of the Mongol conquest (see Chapter 13), while Europe's more than doubled between 1100 and 1445. Some historians believe the reviving economy stimulated the increase. Others argue that severe epidemics were few, and warmer-than-usual temperatures after 950, once referred to by climate historians as the Medieval Warm Period but now called the Medieval Climatic Anomaly in view of the chilling of the Middle East, reduced mortality from starvation and exposure.

More people required more productive farming and new agricultural settlements. One widespread new technique, the **three-field system**, replaced the custom of leaving half the land fallow (uncultivated) every year to regain its fertility. Farmers grew crops on two-thirds of their land each year, alternating wheat and rye with oats, barley, or legumes. The third field was left fallow. The oats restored nitrogen to the depleted soil and produced feed for plow horses as well as people. In much of Europe, however, farmers continued to let half of their land lie fallow and use oxen (less efficient but cheaper to maintain than horses) to pull their plows.

Population growth also encouraged new agricultural settlements. In the twelfth and thirteenth centuries, large numbers of Germans migrated into the fertile lands east of the Elbe River from the Baltic Sea in the north to Transylvania (part of modern Romania) in the south. The Order of Teutonic Knights, founded in the Holy Land but given a (temporary) European base of operations by the king of Hungary, slaughtered or drove away native inhabitants who had not yet adopted Christianity. During the thirteenth century, they conquered, resettled, and administered a vast area along the Baltic that later became Prussia (see Map 14.2).

Draining swamps and clearing forests also brought new land under cultivation. But as population continued to rise, some people had to farm lands with poor soils or vulnerability to flooding, frost, or drought. Average crop yields fell accordingly after 1250, and more people lived at the edge of starvation. According to one historian, "By 1300, almost every child born in western Europe faced the probability of extreme hunger at least once or twice during his expected 30 to 35 years of life."[2] One unusually cold spell at the end of the Medieval Climatic Anomaly produced the Great Famine of 1315–1317, which affected much of Europe north of the Alps.

The **Black Death** reversed the population growth. This terrible plague probably originated in Central

---

[1]Quoted in Marina Warner, *Alone of All Her Sex: The Myth and Cult of the Virgin Mary* (New York, NY: Random House, 1983), 179.

[2]Harry Miskimin, *The Economy of the Early Renaissance, 1300–1460* (Englewood Cliffs, NJ: Prentice Hall, 1969), 26–27.

AP® Exam Tip
Consider the impact of agricultural production increase due to technological innovations such as the three-field system.

three-field system A rotational system for agriculture in which two fields grow food crops and one lies fallow. It gradually replaced the two-field system in medieval Europe.

Black Death An outbreak of bubonic plague that spread across Asia, North Africa, and Europe in the mid-fourteenth century, carrying off vast numbers of persons.

Kharbine-Tapabor/The Art Archive at Art Resource, NY

◀ **Rural French Peasants** Many scenes of peasant life in winter are visible in this small painting by the Flemish Limbourg brothers from the 1410s. Above the snow-covered beehives one man chops firewood, while another drives a donkey loaded with firewood to a little village. At the lower right a woman, blowing on her frozen fingers, heads past the huddled sheep and hungry birds to join other women warming themselves in the cottage (whose outer wall the artists have cut away).

CHRONOLOGY

	Technology and Environment	Culture	Politics and Society
1200	1200s Widespread use of crossbows and windmills	1210s Teutonic Knights, Franciscans, Dominicans	1200s Champagne fairs flourish 1204 Fourth Crusade
			1215 Magna Carta issued
		1225–1274 Philosopher-monk Thomas Aquinas	
1300		1300–1500 Rise of universities	
	1315–1317 Great Famine	1313–1375 Giovanni Boccaccio, humanist writer	1337 Start of Hundred Years' War
	1347–1351 Black Death ca. 1350 Growing deforestation	ca. 1390–1441 Jan van Eyck, painter	1381 Wat Tyler's Rebellion
1400	1400s Cannon and hand-held firearms in use		1415 Portuguese take Ceuta 1431 Joan of Arc burned
		1452–1519 Leonardo da Vinci, artist	
	1454 Gutenberg Bible 1476 Coach introduced into western Europe from Hungary	1492 Expulsion of Jews from Spain	1453 End of Hundred-Years' War; Ottomans take Constantinople 1492 Fall of Muslim state of Granada

Asia and spread westward with the Mongol armies or with traders carrying loads infested with infected fleas (see Chapter 13). In 1346, the Mongols attacked the city of Kaffa (**KAH-fah**) on the Black Sea; a year later, Genoese (**JEN-oh-eez**) traders in Kaffa carried the disease to Italy and southern France. For two years, the Black Death spread across Europe, in some places carrying off two-thirds of the population. Average losses in western Europe amounted to one in three.

Victims developed boils the size of eggs in their groins and armpits, black blotches on their skin, foul body odors, and severe pain. In most cases, death came within a few days. Town officials closed their gates to people from infected areas and burned the victims' possessions. Such measures helped to spare some communities but could not halt the advance of the disease (see Map 14.1). Bubonic plague, the primary form of the Black Death, spreads from person to person and through the bites of fleas infesting the fur of certain rats. Even if the medieval doctors had understood the source of the disease, eliminating the rats that thrived on urban refuse would have been difficult.

The plague brought home to people how sudden and unexpected death could be. Some people became more religious, giving money to the church or lashing themselves with iron-tipped whips to atone for their sins. Others chose reckless enjoyment, spending their money on fancy clothes, feasts, and drinking.

Periodic returns of plague made recovery from population losses slow and uneven. Europe's population in 1400 equaled that in 1200. Not until after 1500 did it rise above its preplague level.

14-1b Social Rebellion

In addition to its demographic and psychological effects, the Black Death triggered social changes in western Europe. Workers who survived demanded higher pay for their services. When authorities tried to freeze wages at the old levels, peasants rose up against wealthy nobles and churchmen. During a widespread revolt in France in 1358, known as the Jacquerie, peasants looted castles and killed dozens of persons. In a large revolt in England in 1381 led by Wat Tyler, an estimated 50,000 peasants and craftsmen invaded London, calling for an end to serfdom and obligations to landowners and murdering the archbishop of Canterbury and other officials. Authorities put down these rebellions with great bloodshed and cruelty, but they could not stave off the higher wages and other social changes the rebels demanded.

Serfdom practically disappeared in western Europe as peasants bought their freedom or ran away. Some English landowners who could no longer hire enough fieldworkers began pasturing sheep for their wool. Others grew crops that required less care or made greater use of plow

AP® Exam Tip
Explain why the global plague pandemic was an important factor in the decline of urban areas during this period.

AP® Exam Tip
Understand the causes and consequences of peasant revolts throughout Afro-Eurasia.

horses and laborsaving tools. Because the plague had not killed livestock and game, survivors had abundant meat and leather. Thus, the welfare of the rural population generally improved after the Black Death, though the gap between rich and poor remained wide.

In urban areas, employers raised wages to attract workers. Guilds (discussed later in this chapter) shortened the period of apprenticeship. Competition within crafts also became more common. Although the overall economy shrank with the decline in population, per capita production actually rose.

14-1c **Mills and Mines**

AP® Exam Tip
Compare European economic developments with similar processes in other regions.

Mining, primarily in Germany and east-central Europe, and metalworking and craft mechanization everywhere expanded so greatly in the centuries before 1500 that some historians speak of an "industrial revolution" in medieval Europe. This is too strong a term, but the landscape fairly bristled with mechanical devices. Mills powered by water or wind ground grain, sawed logs, crushed olives, operated bellows, and pounded linen rags for making paper.

Watermills multiplied at a faster rate than the population. In 1086, 5,600 watermills flanked England's many rivers. After 1200, mills spread rapidly across the European mainland. By the early fourteenth century, entrepreneurs had crammed sixty-eight watermills into a 1-mile section of the Seine (sen) River in Paris. Undershot wheels that depended on the river flowing beneath them were less efficient than overshot wheels where water channeled to fall over the top of the wheel combined the force of gravity with the water's current. Windmills multiplied in comparatively dry lands like Spain and in northern Europe, where water wheels froze in winter.

MAP 14.1   The Black Death in Fourteenth-Century Europe Spreading out of Inner Asia along the routes opened by Mongol expansion, the plague reached the Black Sea port of Kaffa in 1346. This map documents its deadly progress year by year from there into the Mediterranean and north and east across the face of Europe.

Why did God's wrath strike most people as a better explanation for the Black Death than contagion?

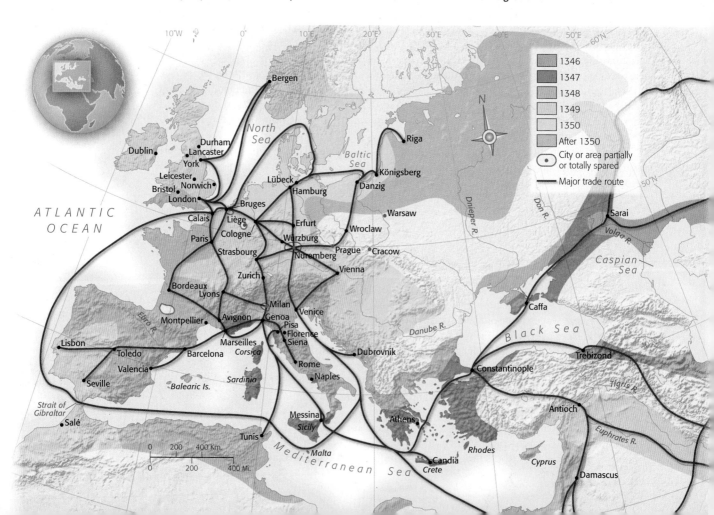

Designs for water mills dated back to Roman times, and the Islamic world, which inherited Hellenistic technologies, knew both water wheels and windmills. However, European-style heavy investment in water or wind power made no sense in Muslim lands because animal power from oxen and camels was so much cheaper where arid and semi-arid wastes provided virtually free grazing. There comparatively cheap and simple single-animal mills and irrigation devices predominated. In Europe, by contrast, where grain farmers grew both human food and animal fodder, population growth increased the cost of animal energy, and of horsepower in particular. One result was that the family name *Miller* became very important in European languages but was rarely used in Arabic, Persian, or Turkish.

Owners invested heavily in building wind and water mills, but since nature furnished the energy to run them for free, they returned great profits. While individuals or monasteries constructed some mills, most were built by groups of investors. Rich millers often aroused the jealousy of their neighbors. In his *Canterbury Tales*, English poet Geoffrey Chaucer (ca. 1340–1400) captured their unsavory reputation by portraying a miller as "a master-hand at stealing grain" by pushing down on the balance scale with his thumb.[3]

Waterpower aided the great expansion of iron making. Water powered the stamping mills that pulverized iron ore, the lifting devices that drained water from deep mines, and the bellows (first documented in the West in 1323) that raised temperatures to the point where liquid iron could be poured into molds. Blast furnaces producing high-quality iron are documented from 1380.

In addition to iron mines in many countries, new silver, lead, and copper mines in Austria and Hungary supplied metal for coins, church bells, cannon, and statues. Techniques of deep mining developed in central Europe spread west in the latter part of the fifteenth century. The first wooden rails for moving ore cars in the mines appeared around 1500. A building boom stimulated stone quarrying in France during the eleventh, twelfth, and thirteenth centuries.

Industrial growth changed the landscape. Towns grew outward and new ones were founded, dams and canals changed the flow of rivers, and quarries and mines scarred the hillsides. Urban *tanneries* (factories that cured and processed leather), the runoff from slaughterhouses, and human waste polluted streams. England's Parliament enacted the first recorded antipollution law in 1388, but enforcement proved difficult.

Deforestation accelerated. Trees provided timber for buildings and ships; tanneries stripped bark to make acid for tanning leather; and many forests gave way to farmland. The glass and iron industries used great quantities of charcoal, made by controlled burning of oak or other hardwood. A single iron furnace could consume all the trees within five-eighths of a mile (1 kilometer) in just forty days. Consequently, the later Middle Ages saw the end of many of western Europe's once-dense forests, except in places where powerful landowners established hunting preserves. Central and eastern Europe, being more lightly populated, experienced less environmental degradation.

Section Review

- Population growth stimulated improved farming methods and agricultural expansion, but peasant life did not significantly improve.

- Famine and the Black Death reversed the population growth and resulted in social change throughout Europe.

- Improved mill designs and other technology stimulated further industrial growth, which, in turn, changed the landscape.

AP® Exam Tip
Understand how humans continued to impact their environment during this time period.

14-2 Urban Revival

What social and economic factors led to the growth of cities in late medieval Europe?

In the tenth century, no town in Latin Europe could compete in size, wealth, or comfort with the cities of Byzantium and Islam. Yet by the later Middle Ages, the Mediterranean, Baltic, and Atlantic coasts boasted wealthy port cities, as did some major rivers draining into these seas. Some Byzantine and Muslim cities still exceeded those of the West in size, but not in commercial, cultural, and administrative dynamism, as marked by impressive new churches, guild halls, and residences.

AP® Exam Tip
Be able to discuss the role and function of trade centers, such as European trade cities.

[3]Quotations here and later in the chapter are from Geoffrey Chaucer, *The Canterbury Tales*, trans. Nevill Coghill (New York, NY: Penguin Books, 1952), 25, 29, 32.

14-2a **Trading Cities**

Most urban growth after 1200 resulted from manufacturing and trade, both between cities and their hinterlands and over long distances. Northern Italy particularly benefited from maritime trade with the port cities of the eastern Mediterranean and, through them, the markets of the Indian Ocean and East Asia. In northern Europe, commercial cities in the county of Flanders (roughly today's Belgium) and around the Baltic Sea profited from regional networks and from overland and sea routes to the Mediterranean.

A Venetian-inspired assault in 1204 against the city of Constantinople, misleadingly named the "Fourth Crusade," temporarily eliminated Byzantine control of the passage between the Mediterranean and the Black Sea and thereby allowed Venice to seize Crete and expand its trading colonies around the Black Sea. Another boon to Italian trade came from the westward expansion of the Mongol Empire, which eliminated middlemen by opening trade routes from the Mediterranean to China that went north of the Caspian Sea instead of through Iran and Iraq (see Chapter 13).

When Mongol decline interrupted the caravan trade in the fourteenth century, Venetian merchants purchased eastern silks and spices brought by other middlemen to Constantinople, Damascus, and Cairo. Three times a year, Venice dispatched convoys of two or three galleys, with sixty oarsmen each, capable of bringing back 2,000 tons of goods.

The sea trade of Genoa on northern Italy's west coast probably equaled that of Venice. Genoese merchants established colonies in the western and eastern Mediterranean and around the Black Sea. In northern Europe, an association of trading cities known as the **Hanseatic (han-see-AT-ik) League** traded extensively in the Baltic, including the coasts of Prussia, newly conquered by German knights. Their merchants ranged eastward to Novgorod in Russia and westward across the North Sea to London.

In the late thirteenth century, Genoese galleys from the Mediterranean and Hanseatic ships from the Baltic were converging on the trading and manufacturing cities in Flanders. Artisans in the Flemish towns of Bruges (**broozh**), Ghent (**gent** [**hard *g* as in *get***]), and Ypres (**EE-pruh**) transformed raw wool from England into a fine cloth that was softer and smoother than the coarse "homespuns" from simple village looms. Dyed in vivid hues, these Flemish textiles appealed to wealthy Europeans, who also appreciated fine textiles from Asia.

Along the overland route connecting Flanders and northern Italy, important trading fairs developed in the Champagne (**sham-PAHN-yuh**) region of Burgundy. The Champagne fairs began as regional markets, exchanging manufactured goods, livestock, and farm produce once or twice a year. When the king of France gained control of Champagne at the end of the twelfth century, royal guarantees of safe conduct to merchants turned these markets into international fairs that were important for currency exchange and other financial transactions as well. A century

AP® Exam Tip
Explain how trading organizations such as the Hanseatic League facilitated commercial growth.

Hanseatic League An economic and defensive alliance of the free towns in northern Germany, founded about 1241 and most powerful in the fourteenth century.

Flemish Weaver (engraving), English School, (19th century) / Private Collection / Look and Learn / The Bridgeman Art Library

◀ **Flemish Weavers, Ypres** The spread of textile weaving gave employment to many people in the Netherlands. The city of Ypres in Flanders (now northern Belgium) was an important textile center in the thirteenth century. This drawing from a fourteenth-century manuscript shows a man and a woman weaving cloth on a horizontal loom.

later, fifteen Italian cities had permanent consulates in Champagne to represent the interests of their citizens. During the fourteenth century, the large volume of trade made it cheaper to ship Flemish woolens around Spain to Italy by sea than to pack them overland on animal backs. Champagne's fairs consequently lost some international trade, but they remained important as regional markets.

In the late thirteenth century, the English monarchy raised taxes on exports of raw wool, making cloth manufacture in England more profitable than in Flanders. Flemish specialists crossed the English Channel and introduced the spinning wheel, perhaps invented in India, and other devices to England. Annual raw wool exports fell from 35,000 sacks of wool at the beginning of the fourteenth century to 8,000 in the mid-fifteenth century, while English wool cloth production rose from 4,000 pieces just before 1350 to 54,000 a century later.

Florence also replaced Flemish imports with its own woolens industry financed by local banking families. In 1338, Florence manufactured 80,000 pieces of cloth, while importing only 10,000. Elsewhere in northern Italy a new industry appeared to manufacture cotton cloth, which had previously been imported across the Mediterranean. These changes in the textile industry show how competition promoted the spread of manufacturing and encouraged new specialties. Other Italian industries that grew on the basis of techniques borrowed from the Muslim world were papermaking, glassblowing, ceramics, and sugar refining.

In the fifteenth century, Venice surpassed its European rivals in the volume of its trade in the Mediterranean as well as across the Alps into central Europe. Its craftspeople manufactured luxury goods once obtainable only from eastern sources, including cotton and sugar grown with slave labor on the islands of Crete, Cyprus, and Sicily. This enterprise later became the model for the slave-based sugar economy of the New World (see Chapter 16). Exports of Italian and northern European woolens to the eastern Mediterranean also rose. In the space of a few centuries, western European cities had used the eastern trade to increase their prosperity and then reduce their dependence on eastern goods.

14-2b Civic Life

Most northern Italian and German cities were independent states, much like the port cities of the Indian Ocean Basin (see Chapter 15). Other European cities held royal charters exempting them from the authority of local nobles. Their autonomy enabled them to adapt to changing market conditions more quickly than cities controlled by imperial authorities, as in China and the Islamic world. Since anyone who lived in a chartered city for over a year could claim freedom, urban life promoted social mobility.

Europe's Jews mostly lived in cities. Spain had the largest communities because of the tolerance of earlier Muslim rulers, but there were also sizable populations as far east as Magdeburg in Prussia. Commercial cities generally welcomed Jews with manufacturing and business skills. Despite official protection by certain Christian princes and kings, however, Jews endured violent religious persecutions or expulsions in times of crisis, such as during the Black Death (see *Diversity & Dominance: Persecution and Protection of Jews, 1272–1349*). In 1492, the Spanish monarchs expelled all Jews in the name of religious and ethnic purity. Only the papal city of Rome left its Jews undisturbed throughout the centuries before 1500.

Within most towns and cities, powerful associations known as guilds dominated civic life. **Guilds** brought together craft specialists, such as silversmiths, or merchants working in a particular trade, to regulate business practices and set prices. Guilds also trained apprentices and promoted members' interests with the city government. By denying membership to outsiders and Jews, guilds protected the interests of families that already belonged to them. They also perpetuated male dominance of most skilled jobs.

Nevertheless, in a few places, women could join guilds either on their own or as the wives, widows, or daughters of male guild members. Large numbers of poor women also toiled in non-guild jobs in urban textile industries and in the food and beverage trades, generally receiving lower wages than men.

Some women advanced socially through marriage to wealthy men. One of Chaucer's *Canterbury Tales* concerns a woman from Bath, a city in southern England, who became wealthy by marrying a succession of old men for their money (and then two other husbands for love), "aside from other company in youth." She was also a skilled weaver, Chaucer says: "In making cloth she showed so great a bent, / She bettered those of Ypres and of Ghent."

AP® Exam Tip Compare Jewish merchant communities in the Mediterranean with other diasporic merchant communities in Afro-Eurasia.

Guilds In medieval Europe, an association of men (rarely women), such as merchants, artisans, or professors, who worked in a particular trade and banded together to promote their economic and political interests. Guilds were also important in other societies, such as the Ottoman and Safavid Empires.

Because they did not belong to the dominant Latin Christian faith, Jews suffered from periodic discrimination and persecution. For the most part, religious and secular authorities tried to curb such anti-Semitism. Jews, after all, were useful citizens who worshiped the same God as their Christian neighbors. Still, it was hard to know where to draw the line between justifiable and unjustifiable discrimination. The famous reviser of Catholic theology, St. Thomas Aquinas, made one such distinction in his Summa Theologica *with regard to attempts at forced conversion.*

Now, the practice of the Church never held that the children of Jews should be baptized against the will of their parents…. Therefore, it seems dangerous to bring forward this new view, that contrary to the previously established custom of the Church, the children of Jews should be baptized against the will of their parents.

There are two reasons for this position. One stems from danger to faith. For, if children without the use of reason were to receive baptism, then after reaching maturity they could easily be persuaded by their parents to relinquish what they had received in ignorance. This would tend to do harm to the faith.

The second reason is that it is opposed to natural justice … it [is] a matter of natural right that a son, before he has the use of reason, is under the care of his father. Hence, it would be against natural justice for the boy, before he has the use of reason, to be removed from the care of his parents, or for anything to be arranged for him against the will of his parents.

The "new view" Aquinas opposed was much in the air, for in 1272 Pope Gregory X issued a decree condemning forced baptism. The pope's decree reviews the history of papal protection given to the Jews, starting with a quotation from Pope Gregory I dating from 598, and decrees two new protections of Jews' legal rights.

Even as it is not allowed to the Jews in their assemblies presumptuously to undertake for themselves more than that which is permitted them by law, even so they ought not to suffer any disadvantage in those [privileges] which have been granted them.

Although they prefer to persist in their stubbornness rather than to recognize the words of their prophets and the mysteries of the Scriptures, and thus to arrive at a knowledge of Christian faith and salvation; nevertheless, inasmuch as they have made an appeal for our protection and help, we therefore admit their petition and offer them the shield of our protection through the clemency of Christian piety. In so doing we follow in the footsteps of our predecessors of happy memory, the popes of Rome—Calixtus, Eugene, Alexander, Clement, Celestine, Innocent, and Honorius.

We decree moreover that no Christian shall compel them or any one of their group to come to baptism unwillingly. But if any one of them shall take refuge of his own accord with Christians, because of conviction, then, after his intention will have been made manifest, he shall be made a Christian without any intrigue. For indeed that person who is known to come to Christian baptism not freely, but unwillingly, is not believed to possess the Christian faith.

Moreover, no Christian shall presume to seize, imprison, wound, torture, mutilate, kill, or inflict violence on them; furthermore no one shall presume, except by judicial action of the authorities of the country, to change the good customs in the land where they live for the purpose of taking their money or goods from them or from others.

In addition, no one shall disturb them in any way during the celebration of their festivals, whether by day or by night, with clubs or stones or anything else. Also no one shall exact any compulsory service of them unless it be that which they have been accustomed to render in previous times.

Inasmuch as the Jews are not able to bear witness against the Christians, we decree furthermore that the testimony of Christians against Jews shall not be valid unless there is among these Christians some Jew who is there for the purpose of offering testimony.

Since it occasionally happens that some Christians lose their Christian children, the Jews are accused by their enemies of secretly carrying off and killing these same Christian children, and of making sacrifices of the heart and blood of these very children. It happens, too, that the parents of these children, or some other Christian enemies of these Jews, secretly hide these very children in order that they may be able to injure these Jews, and in order that they may be able to extort from them a certain amount of money by redeeming them from their straits.

And most falsely do these Christians claim that the Jews have secretly and furtively carried away these children and killed them, and that the Jews offer sacrifice from the heart and the blood of these children, since their law in this matter precisely and expressly forbids Jews to sacrifice, eat, or drink the blood, or eat the flesh of animals having claws. This has been demonstrated many times at our court by Jews converted to the

AP® Exam Tip

Understand the continued diversification of labor including free peasant agriculture, craft production, and guild organization.

By the fifteenth century, a new class of wealthy merchant-bankers was operating on a vast scale and specializing in money changing and loans and making investments on behalf of other parties. Merchants great and small used their services. They also handled the financial transactions of ecclesiastical and secular officials and arranged for the transmission to the pope of funds known as Peter's pence, a collection taken up annually in every church in Latin Europe. Princes

Christian faith: nevertheless very many Jews are often seized and detained unjustly because of this.

We decree, therefore, that Christians need not be obeyed against Jews in such a case or situation of this type, and we order that Jews seized under such a silly pretext be freed from imprisonment, and that they shall not be arrested henceforth on such a miserable pretext, unless—which we do not believe—they be caught in the commission of the crime. We decree that no Christian shall stir up anything against them, but that they should be maintained in that status and position in which they were from the time of our predecessors, from antiquity till now.

We decree, in order to stop the wickedness and avarice of bad men, that no one shall dare to devastate or to destroy a cemetery of the Jews or to dig up human bodies for the sake of getting money [by holding them for ransom]. Moreover, if anyone, after having known the content of this decree, should—which we hope will not happen—attempt audaciously to act contrary to it, then let him suffer punishment in his rank and position, or let him be punished by the penalty of excommunication, unless he makes amends for his boldness by proper recompense. Moreover, we wish that only those Jews who have not attempted to contrive anything toward the destruction of the Christian faith be fortified by the support of such protection....

Despite such decrees, violence against Jews might burst out when fears and emotions were running high. This selection is from the official chronicles of the upper-Rhineland towns.

In the year 1349 there occurred the greatest epidemic that ever happened. Death went from one end of the earth to the other, on that side and this side of the [Mediterranean] sea, and it was greater among the Saracens [Muslims] than among the Christians. In some lands everyone died so that no one was left. Ships were also found on the sea laden with wares; the crew had all died and no one guided the ship. The Bishop of Marseilles and priests and monks and more than half of all the people there died with them. In other kingdoms and cities so many people perished that it would be horrible to describe. The pope at Avignon stopped all sessions of court, locked himself in a room, allowed no one to approach him and had a fire burning before him all the time. And from what this epidemic came, all wise teachers and physicians could only say that it was God's will. And the plague was now here, so it was in other places, and lasted more than a whole year. This epidemic also came to Strasbourg in the summer of the above mentioned year, and it is estimated about sixteen thousand people died.

In the matter of this plague the Jews throughout the world were reviled and accused in all lands of having caused it through the poison which they are said to have put into the water and the wells—that is what they were accused of—and for this reason the Jews were burnt all the way from the Mediterranean into Germany, but not in Avignon, for the pope protected them there.

Nevertheless they tortured a number of Jews in Berne and Zofingen who admitted they had put poison into many wells, and they found the poison in the wells. Thereupon they burnt the Jews in many towns and wrote of this affair to Strasbourg, Freibourg, and Basel in order that they too should burn their Jews.... The deputies of the city of Strasbourg were asked what they were going to do with their Jews. They answered and said that they knew no evil of them. Then ... there was a great indignation and clamor against the deputies from Strasbourg. So finally the Bishop and the lords and the Imperial Cities agreed to do away with the Jews. The result was that they were burnt in many cities, and wherever they were expelled they were caught by the peasants and stabbed to death or drowned....

On Saturday—that was St. Valentine's Day—they burnt the Jews on a wooden platform in their cemetery. There were about two thousand people of them. Those who wanted to baptize themselves were spared. Many small children were taken out of the fire and baptized against the will of their fathers and mothers. And everything that was owed to the Jews was cancelled, and the Jews had to surrender all pledges and notes that they had taken for debts. The council, however, took the cash that the Jews possessed and divided it among the working-men proportionately. The money was indeed the thing that killed the Jews. If they had been poor and if the feudal lords had not been in debt to them, they would not have been burnt.

AP® History Reasoning Skills

Continuity and Change Over Time *In what ways are today's conflicts between majority groups and minority groups the same as and different from those in medieval Europe?*

Comparison *What factors account for the difference between the views of Christian leaders and the Christian masses?*

Source: First selection source is Pocket Books, a division of Simon & Schuster, Inc., and the Vernon & Janet Bourke Living Trust from *The Pocket Aquinas*, edited with translations by Vernon G. Bourke. Copyright © 1960 by Washington Square Press. Copyright renewed © 1988 by Simon & Schuster, Inc. Second and third selections from Jacob R. Marcus, ed., *The Jew in the Medieval World: A Source Book*, 315–1791 (Cincinnati, OH: Union of American Hebrew Congregations, 1938), 152–154, 45–47. Reprinted with permission of the Hebrew Union College Press, Cincinnati.

and kings supported their wars and lavish courts with credit. Some merchant-bankers even developed their own news services, gathering information on any topic that could affect business.

Florentine financiers offered checking accounts, organized private shareholding companies (the forerunners of modern corporations), and improved bookkeeping techniques. In the fifteenth century, the Medici (**MED-ih-chee**) family of Florence operated banks in Italy, Flanders, and London. Medicis also controlled the government of Florence and commissioned artworks.

AP® Exam Tip
Explain how the development of credit and monetization contributed to the growth of interregional trade.

Section Review

- After 1200, most cities grew through manufacture and trade, particularly those of northern Italy, Flanders, and the Baltic coast.

- Expanding trade and technological innovation ultimately reduced Europe's dependence on eastern goods.

- Cities fostered social mobility, but civic life was dominated by guilds, wealthy merchants, and bankers.

- Most urban residents lived in squalor without the amenities of Islamic Middle Eastern cities.

- Gothic cathedrals became signs of special civic pride and prestige in European cities.

The Fuggers (**FOOG-uhrz**) of Augsburg, who had ten times the Medici bank's lending capital, topped Europe's banking fraternity by 1500. Beginning as cloth merchants under Jacob "the Rich" (1459–1525), the family's many activities included the trade in Hungarian copper, essential for casting cannon.

Since Latin Christians generally considered charging interest (*usury*) sinful, Jews predominated in moneylending. Nevertheless, Christian bankers devised ways to get around the condemnation of usury. Some borrowers repaid loans in a different currency at a rate of exchange favorable to the lender. Others added to their repayment a "gift" for the lender. For example, in 1501, church officials agreed to repay a Fugger loan of 6,000 gold ducats in five months along with a "gift" of 400 ducats, amounting to an effective interest rate of 16 percent a year. In fact, the return was less since the church failed to repay the loan on time.

Yet most residents of European cities suffered poverty and ill health. European cities generally lacked civic amenities such as public baths and water supply systems that had existed in Roman times and still survived in Islamic lands.

14-2c Gothic Cathedrals

Master builders and stone masons counted among the skilled people in greatest demand. Though cities competed with one another in the magnificence of their guild halls and town halls, **Gothic cathedrals**, first appearing about 1140 in France, cost the most and brought the greatest prestige. The pointed, or Gothic, arch—replacing the older round, or Romanesque, arch—signaled the new design. External (flying) buttresses stabilizing the high, thin, stone columns below the arches constituted another distinctive feature. This design enabled master builders to push the Gothic cathedrals to great heights and fill the outside walls between the arches with giant windows depicting religious scenes in brilliantly colored stained glass (see Environment & Technology: Stained-Glass Windows). During the next four centuries, interior heights soared ever higher and walls became dazzling curtains of stained glass.

The men who designed and built the cathedrals had little or no formal education and limited understanding of the mathematical principles of civil engineering. Master masons

Gothic cathedrals Large churches originating in twelfth-century France; built in an architectural style featuring pointed arches, tall vaults and spires, flying buttresses, and large stained-glass windows.

◀ **Cathedral at Autun in Eastern France** Begun around 1120 and sufficiently completed to receive the relics of St. Lazaire in 1146, this cathedral reflected Romanesque architectural design and artistic taste. In the fifteenth century a rebuilding program changed the cathedral's external appearance from Romanesque to Gothic, but the images above the west portal survive in their original form. Carved by a sculptor named Gislebertus between 1130 and 1135, they depict the Last Judgment, with Christ enthroned between the saved souls on his right and those condemned to Hell on his left. The sharply angular figures are typical of Romanesque style. Scenes like these taught important religious messages to illiterate worshipers.

Scala/Art Resource, NY

Manufactured glass, as opposed to natural obsidian, is so common a substance in modern times that little thought is given to the fact that it was unknown, poorly developed, or little used for much of the world down to recent centuries. Glass-free or nearly glass-free regions included the pre-Columbian Western Hemisphere, China, Japan, and sub-Saharan Africa. In some places where it was known, such as India, it commonly took the form of highly valued glass beads. Glass beads often became choice trade items in glass-free regions.

In Roman times elegant glass objects such as vials and bottles, often multicolored, were a valued manufacture. However, these were for the most part opaque. In the days of the Caliphate, Muslim chemists discovered ways of making glass transparent, or nearly so. Mamluk period mosque lamps were highly transparent and beautifully decorated with painted designs and calligraphy. Colored glass, however, was not of high priority.

Byzantine glassmakers manufactured clear and semi-clear glass similar to what was being made by their Muslim neighbors. They also produced colorful, but generally opaque, bits of flat glass that were fitted together to compose mosaic pictures. It is supposed that Byzantine artisans fleeing from the sack of Constantinople by crusaders in 1204 brought their skills to Venice, which subsequently became the major European center for glass production.

France was favored with good sands for glassmaking and supplies of the metallic powders mixed with the melted glass to impart bright colors. This made it the optimum center for the production of the stained-glass windows that were the glory of Gothic cathedrals. One scholar writes:

In the philosophical literature of the time … no attributes are used more frequently to describe visual beauty than "lucid," "luminous," "clear." This aesthetic preference is vividly reflected in the decorative arts … with their obvious delight in glittering objects, shiny materials, and polished surfaces. The development of the stained glass window, impelled by the astonishing idea of replacing

▲ **Stained Glass Window from Chartres Cathedral** Bible stories depicted in stained glass taught illiterate worshippers the fundamentals of their faith. Here the nativity of Jesus (lower right) is accompanied by the three Magi (upper right), angels telling shepherds of the event (upper left), and an angel announcing to Mary that she will bear a child (lower left). World History Archive / Alamy Stock Photo

opaque walls by transparent ones, reflects the same taste. And in the great sanctuaries of the twelfth and thirteenth centuries luminosity is a feature demanded and singled out for praise by contemporaries.

Questions for Analysis

1. Why were glass beads so desirable as trade items?
2. Why was transparency not universally sought after by glass makers?
3. Transparency aside, do glass and pottery generally supply the same human needs?

Source: Otto von Simson, *The Gothic Cathedral* (Princeton, NJ: Princeton University Press, 1956), 50–51.

sometimes miscalculated, causing parts of some overly ambitious cathedrals to collapse. The record-high choir vault of Beauvais Cathedral, for instance—154 feet (47 meters) in height—came tumbling down in 1284. But as builders gained experience and invented novel solutions to their problems, success rose from the rubble of their mistakes. The cathedral spire in Strasbourg reached 466 feet (142 meters) into the air—as high as a forty-story building. Such heights were unsurpassed until the nineteenth century.

14-3 Learning, Literature, and the Renaissance

What factors were responsible for the promotion of learning and the arts in Latin Europe?

Throughout the Middle Ages, people in western Europe lived amid reminders of the achievements of the Romans. They wrote and worshiped in a version of their language, traveled their roads, and obeyed some of their laws. The vestments and robes of popes, kings, and emperors followed the designs of Roman officials. Yet the learning of Greco-Roman antiquity virtually disappeared outside of Byzantium and the Muslim world.

14-3a The Renaissance

A small revival of learning at the court of Charlemagne in the ninth century was followed by a larger *renaissance* (rebirth) in the twelfth century, when cities became centers of intellectual and artistic life. The universities established across Latin Europe after 1200 contributed to this cultural revival. In the mid-fourteenth century, the pace of intellectual and artistic life quickened in what is often called the **Renaissance**, which began in northern Italy and later spread to northern and eastern Europe. Some Italian authors saw the Italian Renaissance as a sharp break with an age of darkness.

Before 1100, Byzantine and Islamic scholarship generally surpassed scholarship in Latin Europe. But when Latin Christians wrested southern Italy from the Byzantines and Sicily and Toledo from the Muslims in the eleventh century, they acquired many manuscripts of Greek and Arabic works. These included works by Plato and Aristotle (**AR-ih-stah-tahl**) and Greek treatises on medicine, mathematics, and geography, as well as scientific and philosophical writings by Muslim writers. Latin translations of Iranian philosopher Ibn Sina (**IB-uhn SEE-nah**) (980–1037), known in the West as Avicenna (**av-uh-SEN-uh**), had great influence because of their sophisticated blend of Aristotelian and Islamic philosophy. Jewish scholars contributed significantly to the translation and explication of Arabic and other manuscripts.

In a related development, the thirteenth century saw the foundation of two new religious orders, the Dominicans and the Franciscans. Living according to a rule but not confined to monasteries, these friars brought preaching to the common people and carried the Christian message abroad as missionaries. Some of their most talented members taught in the independent colleges that arose after 1200. Though some aspects of these institutions may derive from institutions of higher Islamic learning called *madrasas* that proliferated after 1100 (see Chapter 10), Latin Europe innovated the idea of **universities** as degree-granting corporations imparting both religious and nonreligious learning.

Between 1300 and 1500, sixty universities, from St. Andrews in Scotland to Krakow and Prague in eastern Europe, joined the twenty established before that time. Students banded together to start some of them; guilds of professors founded others. Teaching guilds, like crafts guilds, set standards for the profession, trained apprentices and masters, and defended their professional interests.

Universities set curricula and instituted final examinations for degrees. Students who passed the exams that ended their apprenticeship received a "license" to teach, while those who completed longer training and defended a masterwork of scholarship became "masters" and "doctors." The University of Paris gradually absorbed the city's various colleges, but the colleges of Oxford and Cambridge remained independent, self-governing organizations.

Since all universities used Latin, students and masters moved freely across political and linguistic borders, seeking the courses and professors they wanted. Some universities offered specialized training. Legal training centered on Bologna in Italy (**buh-LOHN-yuh**); Montpellier in southern France and Salerno in Sicily focused on medicine; Paris and Oxford excelled in theology.

Some topics, such as astronomy, were studied outside the university. Both Greek and Arabic traditions presumed that the planets traced circular orbits around the earth, the circle being a perfect geometrical figure. Celestial observations did not always fit this presumption, however. Fifteenth-century astronomers in both Europe and the lands of Islam theorized explanations for the observational deviations. At the very end of the fifteenth century, Polish-German astronomer Nicolaus Copernicus (**co-PER-ni-cus**), basing his ideas mainly on the Greek Ptolemy but also aware of more recent writings in Arabic, hit on the idea of planets orbiting the sun instead of the earth. His work, finally published as he lay dying of a stroke in 1543, would pose a challenge to the church's assumption that the earth was the center of God's universe.

Though the new learning sometimes raised inconvenient questions, students aspiring to ecclesiastical careers, and their professors, conferred special prominence on theology, seen as the "queen of the sciences" encompassing all true knowledge. Hence, thirteenth-century theologians sought to synthesize the rediscovered philosophical works of Aristotle and the commentaries of Avicenna with the Bible's rerevealed truth. These efforts to synthesize reason and faith were known as **scholasticism** (**skoh-LAS-tih-sizm**).

Thomas Aquinas, a Dominican theology professor at the University of Paris, wrote the most notable scholastic work, the *Summa Theologica* (**SOOM-uh thee-uh-LOH-jih-kuh**), between 1267 and 1273. Although his exposition of Christian belief organized on Aristotelian principles came to be accepted as a masterly demonstration of the reasonableness of Christianity, scholasticism upset many traditional thinkers. Some church authorities tried to ban Aristotle from the

Renaissance A period of intense artistic and intellectual activity, said to be a "rebirth" of Greco-Roman culture. Usually divided into an Italian Renaissance, from roughly the mid-fourteenth to mid-fifteenth century, and a Northern (trans-Alpine) Renaissance, from roughly the early fifteenth to early seventeenth century.

universities Degree-granting institutions of higher learning. Those that appeared in Latin Europe from about 1200 onward became the model of all modern universities.

scholasticism A philosophical and theological system, associated with Thomas Aquinas, devised to reconcile Aristotelian philosophy and Roman Catholic theology in the thirteenth century.

curriculum. However, the considerable freedom of medieval universities from both secular and religious authorities enabled the new ideas to prevail over the fears of church administrators.

14-3b Humanists and Printers

This period also saw important literary contributions. The Italian Dante Alighieri (**DAHN-tay ah-lee-GYEH-ree**) (1265–1321) completed a long, elegant poem, the *Divine Comedy*, shortly before his death. This supreme expression of medieval preoccupations tells the allegorical story of Dante's journey through the nine circles of Hell and the seven terraces of Purgatory, followed by his entry into Paradise. The Roman poet Virgil guides him through Hell and Purgatory; Beatrice, a woman he had loved from afar since childhood and whose death inspired the poem, guides him to Paradise.

The *Divine Comedy* foreshadows the literary fashions of the later Italian Renaissance. Like Dante, later Italian writers made use of Greco-Roman classical themes and mythology and sometimes courted a broader audience by writing not in Latin but in their local language (Dante used the vernacular spoken in Tuscany [**TUS-kuh-nee**]).

Poet Geoffrey Chaucer (ca. 1343–1400), many of whose works show the influence of Dante, wrote in vernacular English. The *Canterbury Tales*, a lengthy poem written in the last dozen years of his life, contains often humorous and earthy tales told by fictional pilgrims on their way to the shrine of Thomas à Becket in Canterbury (see Chapter 11). They present a vivid cross-section of medieval people and attitudes.

Dante influenced the literary movement of the **humanists** that began in his native Florence in the mid-fourteenth century. The term refers to their interest in grammar, rhetoric, poetry, history, and moral philosophy (ethics)—subjects known collectively as the humanities, an ancient discipline. With the brash exaggeration characteristic of new intellectual fashions, humanist writers like poet Francesco Petrarch (**fran-CHES-koh PAY-trahrk**) (1304–1374) and poet and storyteller Giovanni Boccaccio (**jo-VAH-nee boh-KAH-chee-oh**) (1313–1375) proclaimed a revival of a Greco-Roman tradition they felt had for centuries lain buried under the rubble of post-Roman decay.

This idea of a rebirth of learning dismisses too readily the monastic and university scholars who for centuries had been recovering all sorts of Greco-Roman learning, as well as writers like Dante (whom the humanists revered), who anticipated humanist interests by a generation. Yet

humanists European scholars, writers, and teachers associated with the study of the humanities (grammar, rhetoric, poetry, history, languages, and moral philosophy), influential in the fifteenth century and later.

◄ **Dante's Divine Comedy**
This fifteenth-century painting by Domenico di Michelino shows Dante holding a copy of the *Divine Comedy*. Hell is depicted to the poet's right and the terraces of Purgatory behind him, surmounted by the earthly and heavenly Paradise. The city of Florence, with its recently completed cathedral, appears to Dante's left.

aka-images/Rabatti–Domingie

The Art Archive

◀ **A French Printshop, 1537** A workman operates the "press," quite literally a screw device that presses the paper to the inked type. The man behind the pressman uses soft pads to ink the type before a new sheet is inserted. A book results when the sheets are folded and then sewn together. The man on the right is selecting pieces of type from a compartmented box and placing them in a frame for printing.

the humanists had a great impact as educators, advisers, and reformers. Their greatest influence came in reforming secondary education. They introduced a curriculum centered on the languages and literature of Greco-Roman antiquity, which they felt provided intellectual discipline, moral lessons, and refined tastes. This curriculum dominated European secondary schools well into the twentieth century.

Many humanists tried to duplicate the elegance of classical Latin and (to a lesser extent) Greek, which they revered as the pinnacle of learning, beauty, and wisdom. Boccaccio gained fame with his vernacular writings, which resemble Dante's, and especially for the *Decameron*, an earthy work that has much in common with Chaucer's boisterous tales. Under Petrarch's influence, however, Boccaccio turned to writing in classical Latin.

As humanist scholars mastered Latin and Greek, they turned their language skills to restoring the original texts of Greco-Roman writers and of the Bible. By comparing different manuscripts, they eliminated errors introduced by generations of copyists. To aid in this task, Pope Nicholas V (r. 1447–1455) created the Vatican Library, buying scrolls of Greco-Roman writings and paying to have accurate copies and translations made. Working independently, the Dutch scholar Erasmus **(uh-RAZ-muhs)** of Rotterdam (ca. 1466–1536) produced a critical edition of the New Testament in Greek. Erasmus corrected many errors and mistranslations in the Latin text that had been in general use throughout the Middle Ages. Later, this humanist priest and theologian wrote—in classical Latin—influential moral guides, including the *Enchiridion militis christiani* (*The Manual of the Christian Knight*, 1503) and *The Education of a Christian Prince* (1515).

The influence of the humanists grew as the new technology of printing made their critical editions of ancient texts, literary works, and moral guides more available. The Chinese and the Arabs used carved woodblocks for printing, and block-printed playing cards circulated in Europe before 1450, but after that date three European improvements revolutionized printing: (1) movable pieces of type consisting of individual letters, independently invented in Korea (see Chapter 12); (2) walnut oil–based ink suitable for printing on paper without smearing; and (3) the **printing press**, a mechanical device that pressed sheets of paper onto inked type.

Johann Gutenberg **(yoh-HAHN GOO-ten-burg)** (ca. 1394–1468) of Mainz led the way. The Gutenberg Bible of 1454, the first book in the West printed from movable type, exhibited a beauty and craftsmanship testifying to the printer's years of experimentation. Humanists worked closely with the printers, who spread the new techniques to Italy and France. Erasmus did editing and proofreading for Italian scholar-printer Aldo Manuzio (1449–1515) in Venice. Manuzio's press published many critical editions of classical Latin and Greek texts.

printing press A mechanical device for transferring text or graphics from a woodblock or type to paper using ink. Presses using movable type first appeared in Europe in about 1450.

Scala/Art Resource, NY

◀ **Michelangelo's Tomb Statue of Lorenzo de' Medici** The greatest of the Medici bankers, Lorenzo governed Florence during the height of the Renaissance. At the time of his death in 1492 he had fallen under the influence of Girolamo Savonarola, a stern, moralistic priest who felt that art and morals had departed too far from proper Christianity. Nevertheless, the Roman armor and pensive expression of this statue epitomize the antique revival and dedication to thought associated with the term *Renaissance*.

By 1500, at least 10 million printed volumes flowed from presses in 238 European towns, launching a revolution that affected students, scholars, and a growing literate population. These readers consumed unorthodox political and religious tracts along with ancient texts.

14-3c Renaissance Artists

Although the artists of the fourteenth and fifteenth centuries continued to depict biblical subjects, the Greco-Roman revival led some, especially in Italy, to portray ancient deities and myths. Another popular trend involved scenes of daily life.

Neither theme was entirely new, however. Renaissance art, like Renaissance scholarship, owed a debt to earlier generations. Italian painters of the fifteenth century credited the Florentine painter Giotto (**JAW-toh**) (ca. 1267–1337) with single-handedly reviving the "lost art of painting." In religious scenes, Giotto replaced the stiff, staring figures of the Byzantine style, which were intended to overawe viewers, with more natural and human portraits with whose depictions of grief and love viewers could identify. Rather than floating on backgrounds of gold leaf, his saints inhabit earthly landscapes.

North of the Alps, Flemish painter Jan van Eyck (**yahn vahn IKE**) (ca. 1390–1441) mixed his pigments with linseed oil in place of the egg yolk of earlier centuries. Oil paints dried more slowly and gave pictures a superior luster. Italian painters quickly copied van Eyck's technique, though his own masterfully realistic paintings on religious and domestic themes remained distinctive.

Leonardo da Vinci (**lay-own-AHR-doh dah-VIN-chee**) (1452–1519) used oil paints for his *Mona Lisa*. Renaissance artists like Leonardo worked in many media, including bronze sculptures and *frescos* (painting on wet plaster) like *The Last Supper*. Leonardo's notebooks also contain imaginative designs for airplanes, submarines, and tanks. His younger contemporary Michelangelo (**my-kuhl-AN-juh-low**) (1472–1564) painted frescoes of biblical scenes on the ceiling of the Sistine Chapel in the Vatican, sculpted statues of David and Moses, and designed the dome for a new Saint Peter's Basilica in Rome.

The patronage of wealthy and educated merchants and prelates underlay the artistic blossoming in the cities of northern Italy and Flanders. Florentine banker Cosimo de' Medici (1389–1464) and his grandson Lorenzo (1449–1492), known as "the Magnificent," spent immense sums on paintings, sculpture, and public buildings. In Rome, the papacy (**PAY-puh-see**) launched a building program that culminated in the construction of the new Saint Peter's Basilica and a residence for the pope.

These scholarly and artistic achievements exemplify the innovation and striving for excellence of the late Middle Ages. The new literary themes and artistic styles of this period had lasting influence on Western culture. But the innovations in the organization of universities, in printing, and in scientific thought had wider implications, for they were later adopted by cultures all over the world.

Section Review

- Greco-Roman learning returned to Latin Europe through a series of revivals that culminated with the Renaissance.

- An infusion of Greek and Islamic scholarship during the eleventh century helped to prompt the revival of the twelfth and thirteenth centuries.

- Colleges and universities grew, with theology as the preeminent discipline.

- Foreshadowed by Dante, humanism—with its focus on classical languages, literature, ethics, and education—emerged in Italy.

- The influence of the humanists spread through the new print technology.

- Renaissance artists enlarged the thematic and technical resources of painting, sculpture, and architecture.

14-4 Political and Military Transformations

What social, political, and military developments contributed to the rise of European nations in this period?

Stronger and more unified states and armies developed in western Europe in parallel with the economic and cultural revivals (see Map 14.2). Crusades against Muslim states brought consolidation to Spain and Portugal. In Italy and Germany, however, political power remained in the hands of small states and loose alliances. Farther to the east, Lithuania, dynastically linked to Poland, became one of Europe's largest states, while Hungary confronted the Ottoman Empire.

AP® Exam Tip
Be able to explain how feudalism functioned as a social and political structure in medieval Europe. Also, be able to compare European feudalism to feudalism in Japan.

Spread of Latin Christendom

- In 1000 C.E.
- Added 1000–1200
- Lost 1000–1200; regained 1200–1500
- Added 1200–1500
- Lost 1200–1500
- Mixed Latin and Orthodox population
- English holdings, 1360
- Boundary of the Holy Roman Empire

MAP 14.2 Europe in 1453 This year marked the end of the Hundred Years' War between France and England and the fall of the Byzantine capital city of Constantinople to the Ottoman Turks. Muslim advances into southeastern Europe were offset by the Latin Christian reconquests of Islamic holdings in southern Italy and the Iberian Peninsula.

In religious terms, what does a term like *Latin Christendom* actually signify?

▶ **Cannon Deployed in Siege of a City** This miniature painting from around 1470 shows the earliest phase of putting cannon on wheels for use in the field. It is doubtful that these small bombards, one with a double barrel, did much damage to the city's walls. For their conquest of Constantinople in 1453 the Ottomans used cannon so large that sixty oxen were needed to move them to the battlefield.

From a miniature by Loyset Liedet in an illuminated manuscript (c. 1470) of the *Histoire de Charles Martel*

14-4a Monarchs, Nobles, and the Church

Thirteenth-century states continued early medieval state structures (see Chapter 11). Hereditary monarchs topped the political pyramid, but modest treasuries and the rights of nobles and the church limited their powers. Powerful noblemen who controlled vast estates had an important voice in matters of state. The church guarded closely its traditional rights and independence. Towns, too, had acquired rights and privileges. Towns in Flanders, the Hanseatic League, and Italy approached independence from royal interference. In theory the ruler's noble vassals owed military service in time of war. In practice, vassals sought to limit the monarch's power.

In the year 1200, knights still formed the backbone of western European armies, but changes in weaponry brought this into question. Improved crossbows could shoot metal-tipped arrows with enough force to pierce helmets and light body armor. Professional crossbowmen, hired for wages, became increasingly common and much feared. Indeed, a church council in 1139 outlawed the crossbow—ineffectively—as being too deadly for use against Christians. The arrival in Europe of firearms based on the Chinese invention of gunpowder (see Chapter 13) further transformed the medieval army, first on the Ottoman frontier and then farther west.

The church also resisted royal control. In 1302, the outraged Pope Boniface VIII (r. 1294–1303) asserted that divine law made the papacy superior to "every human creature," including monarchs. King Philip "the Fair" of France (r. 1285–1314) responded by sending an army to arrest the pope, a chastisement that hastened Pope Boniface's death. Philip then engineered the election of a French pope, who established a new papal residence at Avignon (**ah-vee-NYON**) in southern France in 1309.

A succession of French-dominated popes residing in Avignon improved church discipline but at the price of compromising their neutrality in the eyes of other rulers. The **Great Western Schism** between 1378 and 1415 saw rival papal claimants at Avignon and Rome vying for Christian loyalties. The papacy eventually regained its independence and returned to Rome, but the long crisis broke the pope's ability to challenge the rising power of monarchs like Philip, who had used the dispute to persuade his nobles to grant him a new tax.

The English monarchy wielded more centralized power as a result of consolidation that took place after the Norman conquest of 1066. Between 1200 and 1400, the Anglo-Norman kings incorporated Wales and reasserted control over most of Ireland. Nevertheless, under King John (r. 1199–1216), royal power suffered a severe setback. Forced to acknowledge the pope as his overlord in 1213, he lost his bid to reassert claims to Aquitaine in southern France the following year

Great Western Schism
A division in the Latin (Western) Christian Church between 1378 and 1415, when rival claimants to the papacy existed in Rome and Avignon.

and then yielded to his nobles by signing the Magna Carta in 1215. This "Great Charter" affirmed that monarchs were subject to established law, confirmed the independence of the church and the city of London, and guaranteed the nobles' hereditary rights.

14-4b The Hundred Years' War

The conflict between the king of France and his vassals known as the **Hundred Years' War** (1337–1453) grew out of a marriage alliance. Marriage between Princess Isabella of France and King Edward II of England (r. 1307–1327) should have ensured the king's loyalty, as a vassal who had inherited French lands from his Norman ancestors. However, when the French royal line produced no other sons, Isabella's son, King Edward III of England (r. 1327–1377), laid claim to the French throne in 1337.

Early in the war, hired Italian crossbowmen reinforced the French cavalry, but the English longbow proved superior. Adopted from the Welsh, the 6-foot (1.8-meter) longbow could shoot farther and more rapidly than the crossbow. Its arrows could not pierce armor, but concentrated volleys found gaps in the knights' defenses or struck their less-protected horses. Heavier and more encompassing armor provided a defense but limited a knight's movements. Once pulled off his steed by a foot soldier armed with a *pike* (hooked pole), he could not get up.

Later in the Hundred Years' War, firearms gained prominence. The first cannon scared the horses with smoke and noise but did little damage. As they grew larger, however, they proved effective in battering the walls of castles and towns. The first artillery use against the French, at the Battle of Agincourt (1415), gave the English an important victory.

Faced with a young French peasant woman called Joan of Arc, subsequent English gains stalled. Acting, she believed, on God's instructions, she put on armor and rallied the French troops to defeat the English in 1429. Shortly afterward, she fell into English hands, and in 1431 she was tried by English churchmen and burned at the stake as a witch.

In the final battles, French cannon demolished the walls of once-secure castles held by the English and their allies. Armies now depended less on knights and more on bowmen, pikemen, musketeers, and artillerymen.

14-4c New Monarchies in France and England

The war proved a watershed in the rise of **new monarchies** in France and England, centralized states with fixed "national" boundaries and stronger representative institutions. English monarchs after 1453 consolidated control over territory within the British Isles, though the Scots defended their independence. The French monarchs also turned to consolidating control over powerful noble families in Burgundy and Brittany.

The new monarchies needed a way to finance their full-time armies. Some nobles agreed to money payments in place of military service and to additional taxes in time of war. For example, in 1439 and 1445, Charles VII of France (r. 1422–1461) successfully levied a new tax on his vassals' land. This not only paid the costs of the war with England but also provided the monarchy a financial base for the next 350 years.

Merchants' taxes also provided revenues. Taxes on the English wool trade, begun by King Edward III, paid most of the costs of the Hundred Years' War. Some rulers taxed Jewish merchants or extorted large contributions from wealthy towns. Individual merchants sometimes curried royal favor with loans. The fifteenth-century French merchant Jacques Coeur (**cur**) gained many social and financial benefits for himself and his family by lending money to French courtiers, but his debtors accused him of murder and had his fortune confiscated.

In the west, the church provided a third source of revenue through voluntary contributions to support a war. English and French monarchs won the right to appoint important church officials in their realms in the fifteenth century. In the east, religion became increasingly a political issue as Catholic Lithuania fought a series of wars with Orthodox Russia with little concern for which faith the common people adhered to.

The shift in power to the monarchs and away from the nobility and the church did not deprive nobles of their social position and roles as government officials and military officers. Moreover, the kings of England and France in 1500 had to deal with representative institutions that had not existed in 1200. The English Parliament proved a permanent check on royal

Hundred Years' War Series of campaigns over control of the throne of France, involving English and French royal families and French noble families.

new monarchies Historians' term for the monarchies in France, England, and Spain from 1450 to 1600. The centralization of royal power was increasing within more or less fixed territorial limits.

power: the House of Lords contained the great nobles and church officials; and the House of Commons represented the towns and the leading citizens of the counties. In France, the Estates General, a similar but less effective representative body, represented the church, the nobles, and the towns.

14-4d Iberian Unification

Spain and Portugal's **reconquest of Iberia** from Muslim rule expanded the boundaries of Latin Christianity. The knights who pushed the borders of their kingdoms southward furthered both Christianity and their own interests. The spoils of victory included irrigated farmland, rich cities, and ports on the Mediterranean Sea and Atlantic Ocean. Serving God, growing rich, and living off the labor of others became a way of life for the Iberian nobility.

The reconquest took several centuries. In 1085 Toledo fell and became a Christian outpost. In 1147 English Crusaders bound for the Holy Land helped take Lisbon, which then displaced the older city of Oporto (meaning "the port"), from which Portugal took its name, as both capital and the kingdom's leading city. After a Christian victory in 1212 broke the back of Muslim power, the reconquest accelerated. Within decades, Portuguese and Castilian forces captured the prosperous cities of Córdova (1236) and Seville (1248) and drove the Muslims from the southwestern region known as Algarve (**ahl-GAHRV**) ("the west" in Arabic). Only the small kingdom of Granada hugging the Mediterranean coast remained in Muslim hands.

By incorporating Algarve in 1249, Portugal attained its modern territorial limits. After a pause to colonize, forcibly Christianize, and consolidate this land, Portugal took the crusade to North Africa. In 1415, Portuguese knights seized the port of Ceuta (**say-OO-tuh**) in Morocco, where they learned more about the Saharan caravan trade in gold and slaves. During the next few decades, Portuguese mariners sailed down the Atlantic coast of Africa seeking access to this trade and contact with a rumored African Christian king (see Chapter 16).

Elsewhere in Iberia, the reconquest continued. Princess Isabella of Castile married Prince Ferdinand of Aragon in 1469. A decade later, when they inherited their respective thrones, the two kingdoms united to become Spain. Their conquest of Granada in 1492 secured the final piece of Muslim territory for the new kingdom.

Ferdinand and Isabella sponsored the first voyage of Christopher Columbus in 1492 (see Chapter 16). In a third momentous event of that year, the monarchs expelled the Jews from their kingdoms. Attempts to convert or expel the remaining Muslims led to a revolt at the end of 1499 that lasted until 1501, and in 1502 the Spanish rulers expelled the last Muslims. Portugal expelled the Jews in 1496, including 100,000 refugees from Spain. For some time afterward

AP® Exam Tip
Understand how the interactions of major religions affected political, social, and cultural interactions in this time period.

reconquest of Iberia
Beginning in the eleventh century, military campaigns by various Iberian Christian states to recapture territory taken by Muslims. In 1492 the last Muslim ruler was defeated, and Spain and Portugal emerged as united kingdoms.

◄ **Hussite Style Battle Wagon**
Hussite wagons carried many soldiers, but this woodcut makes their functions clear. The shoulder cannon would have taken so long to reload that the soldiers with the bow, the crossbow, and the flail, a kind of long-handled hinged club, were needed to keep the enemy away during the interval. The sickles on the wheels and spikes protecting the front of the horses offered protection when the wagon was in motion. Woodcut "De re militari" by Roberto Valturio. Verona, 1472/Alamy

Section Review

- Between 1200 and 1500, monarchs, nobles, and the church struggled over political power.

- Tensions between the French monarchy and the papacy resulted in the Great Western Schism.

- In England, royal power was checked by the papacy and nobility, the latter imposing the Magna Carta on King John.

- The Hundred Years' War between the French monarchy and its vassals introduced new military technologies.

- The war also stimulated the rise of the new centralized monarchies of England and France.

- Spain and Portugal continued the reconquest of Muslim Iberia, a process completed by Ferdinand and Isabella.

- As Muslim territory in Iberia shrank, the rising Ottoman Empire took over much of southeastern Europe.

the Spanish Inquisition, a tribunal established by the two monarchs, exerted itself in identifying and punishing Jews, called Marranos, and Muslims, called Moriscos, who had nominally converted to Christianity but secretly retained their old, forbidden faiths.

14-4e The Ottoman Frontier

As Islam receded in the west, it advanced in the east as the Ottoman Empire (see Chapter 13) inflicted defeat after defeat on the Christian Balkan kingdoms. The Ottoman military was balanced between cavalry archers, primarily Turks, and slave infantrymen armed with hand-held firearms.

Slave soldiery had a long history in Islamic lands (see Chapter 10), but the conquest of the Balkans in the late fourteenth century gave the Ottomans access to a new military resource: Christian prisoners of war enslaved and converted to Islam. These "new troops," called *yeni cheri* in Turkish and *janissaries* (**JAN-i-say-ree**) in English, gave the Ottomans unusual military flexibility. Not coming from a nomadic background like the Turks, they readily accepted the idea of fighting on foot and learning to use guns, which at that time were still too heavy and awkward for a horseman to load and fire. The janissaries lived in barracks and trained all year round. The process of selection for janissary training changed early in the fifteenth century. The new system, called the *devshirme*, imposed a regular levy of male children on Christian villages in the Balkans. Selected children were placed with Turkish families to learn their language and then sent to Istanbul for instruction in Islam, military training, and, for the most talented, opportunities to become senior military commanders and heads of government departments. The Christian European contest between nobles, monarchs, and church authorities scarcely existed in the Ottoman realm.

14-4f Christian Responses

On the Christian side of the frontier, military commanders in Hungary and Bohemia made military innovations of their own, sometimes to fight other Christians. Small cannons were placed in heavy wagons along with archers and pikemen and acting tactically with larger cannon mounted on wheels. A wagon circle called a "laager" offered superior mobile defense. The battlefield effectiveness of these weapons attracted such attention in western Europe that words from Czech and Hungarian, like *howitzer* (a type of artillery), *pistol*, and *coach* were almost universally adopted.

Coach, a word derived from a Hungarian village waystation named Koç, signified a men's passenger vehicle. Male aristocrats, who had for centuries traveled only by horseback, could fight in battle wagons and took to riding in coaches in peacetime. This stylish new vehicle set off a "carriage revolution"—"carriage" in English is synonymous with "coach"—that greatly transformed European transport as interest in coaches spread westward from Hungary.

14-5 Conclusion

Ecologically, the peoples of Latin Europe harnessed the power of wind and water and mined and refined their mineral wealth at the cost of localized pollution and deforestation. However, inability to improve food production and distribution in response to population growth created a demographic crisis that climaxed with the Black Death that devastated Europe in the mid-fourteenth century.

Politically, basic features of the modern European state began to emerge. Frequent wars caused kingdoms of moderate size to develop exceptional military strength. The ruling class, seeing economic strength as the twin of political power, promoted the activities of commercial cities and taxed their profits.

Culturally, autonomous universities and printing supported the advance of knowledge, while art and architecture reached unsurpassed peaks in the Renaissance. Late medieval society also displayed a fundamental fascination with tools and techniques, many of them acquired from the Muslim world or farther east. European success, however, depended just as much on strong motives for expansion. From the eleventh century onward, population pressure, religious zeal, economic enterprise, and intellectual curiosity drove an expansion of territory and resources that took the Crusaders to the Holy Land, merchants to the eastern Mediterranean and Black Seas, German settlers across the Elbe River, and Iberian Christians into the Muslim south.

Key Terms

three-field system p.346
Black Death p. 346
Hanseatic League p. 350
guild p. 351

Gothic cathedrals p. 354
Renaissance
  (European) p. 356
universities p. 356

scholasticism p. 356
humanists (Renaissance)
  p. 357
printing press p. 358

Great Western Schism p. 361
Hundred Years' War p. 362
new monarchies p. 362
reconquest of Iberia p. 363

Review Questions

1. Why did the military targets of the crusading era, the Holy Land and the Arab world more generally, fade in importance in the strategic thinking of late medieval European kingdoms?

2. Which encourages military innovation more, unity within a powerful empire or constant warfare among small states?

3. How does late medieval Latin Christendom compare with the Abbasid Caliphate in its period of fragmentation after 850 CE?

 MindTap® is a fully online, personalized learning experience built upon Cengage Learning content. MindTap® combines student learning tools—readings, multimedia, activities, and assessments—into a singular Learning Path that guides students through the course and helps students develop the critical thinking, analysis, and communication skills that are essential to academic and professional success.

Multiple-Choice Questions

Questions 1–4 refer to the passage below.

"Tell, O Sicily, and ye, the many islands of the sea, the judgements of God. Confess, O Genoa, what thou hast done, since we of Genoa and Venice are compelled to make God's chastisement manifest. Alas! Our ships enter the port, but of a thousand sailors hardly ten are spared. We reach our homes; our kindred and our neighbors come from all parts to visit us. Woe to us for we cast at them the darts of death! Whilst we spoke to them, whilst they embraced us and kissed us, we scattered the poison from our lips. Going back to their homes, they in turn soon infected their whole families, who in three days succumbed, and were buried in one common grave. Priests and doctors visiting the sick returned from their duties ill, and soon were numbered with the dead. O death! Cruel, bitter, impious death! Which thus breaks the bonds of affection and divides father and mother, brother and sister, son and wife. Lamenting our misery, we feared to fly, yet we dared not remain."

> Gabriele de' Mussi, a notary from Piacenza, from an account of the plague in Kaffa and Sicily, 1348

1. The passage best illustrates which of the following situations in Italy in the mid-1300s?

   (A) The beginning of the Renaissance and a revival of classical learning

   (B) The results of interactions along trade routes

   (C) The inability of religious leaders to unite the people

   (D) The powerlessness of the leaders of Florence to maintain order

2. What effect did the outbreak of the plague mentioned in the passage have on the inhabitants of southern Europe?

   (A) Most people stopped believing in God as they witnessed the destruction of their cities.

   (B) The plague impacted people of all social classes because of their increasing interconnectedness.

   (C) Most of the deaths occurred in rural areas so many moved into cities for protection.

   (D) Knowledge of the causes of the plague increased as doctors studied those who were infected.

3. Which of the following was a social response to the effects of the plague referred to in the passage?

   (A) Highly effective rebellions against landowners

   (B) The rise of the power of Christian banking families in major cities

   (C) The increased power of monarchies in Western Europe

   (D) The end of serfdom as peasants bought their freedom or ran away

4. What was a long-term consequence of the epidemic that affected Eurasia in the mid-fourteenth century?

   (A) Mongol control of Central Asia and Eastern Europe ended.

   (B) The trend of population growth was reversed.

   (C) Faith in religion as a means of salvation ended.

   (D) A prolonged war broke out between England and France.

Questions 5–7 refer to the illustration below.

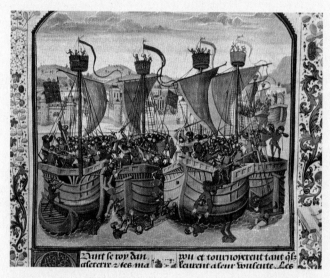

▲ **A miniature of the Battle of Sluis from Jean Froissart's Chronicles, fourteenth century.** De Agostini Picture Library/Getty Images

5. This image of a naval battle during the Hundred Years War provides evidence of

   (A) how the political power of the Church increasingly overshadowed royal power.

   (B) the way feudal systems increased because of the need for protection.

   (C) the increase in conflict as rival European monarchs sought to create centralized states.

   (D) the cosmopolitan nature of Europe created by increased trading among states.

6. The Hundred Years War changed the economic systems in England and France as it helped bring about

   (A) the need for professional armies that had to be funded by monetary taxation.

   (B) an increase in the wool trade between England and Flanders.

   (C) an increase in the importance of agriculture in both the English and French economies.

   (D) the end of the labor system of serfdom.

7. In what way did the restructuring of political control as a result of the Hundred Years War lead to socioeconomic changes?

(A) Women lost their land rights and became more financially dependent on their husbands.

(B) Land-owning nobles increased their control over the social rights of their tenant farmers.

(C) Peasants became more powerful as they were granted new political rights.

(D) The community and financial control of the nobility and the Church diminished.

Questions 8–10 refer to the illustration below.

▲ The September panel from the Cycle of the Months fresco, Trento, Italy, fifteenth century. DEA/G. DAGLI ORTI/Getty Images

8. Which of the following is an assessment of social structure in fifteenth-century Europe that is supported by the fresco panel?

(A) Foreign migrations changed the social structures of both rural and urban areas.

(B) Social class hierarchies continued to have a heavy impact on social structures in rural areas.

(C) Labor specialization led to the breakdown of social barriers throughout Europe.

(D) The rights of women improved as they gained more political rights.

9. During the late Middle Ages in Europe, art such as the fresco above was often a result of which of the following?

(A) Knights who returned from battle and desired beauty as an escape

(B) Church leaders who saw art as an expression of their love for God

(C) Government taxes on increasing merchant profits being used to fund the arts

(D) Individual artists who had made their fortune at a young age

10. Which of the following was not a factor that contributed to urban revival in Europe in the time period of the fresco?

(A) A decrease in trading fairs and trade cities, leaving a few large cities

(B) The availability of safe and reliable transportation

(C) The rise of global commerce across land and sea routes.

(D) Warmer temperatures between the years 800 and 1300, which increased agricultural productivity

Short-Answer Questions

1. Answer all parts of the question that follows.

(A) Identify ONE technological innovation that led to the expansion of long-distance trade routes between 600 and 1450.

(B) Explain ONE way commercial innovation led to the expansion of long-distance trade routes between 600 and 1450.

(C) Explain ONE result of the increase in long-distance trade routes between 600 and 1450.

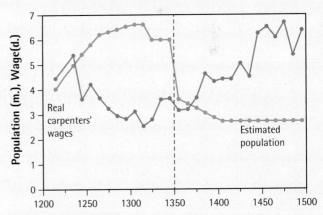

▲ Graph of population levels and carpenters' wages in England between 1200 and 1500.

2. Use the graph above and your knowledge of world history to answer all parts of the question that follows.

(A) Identify ONE cause of demographic change in Europe between 1200 and 1500.

(B) Explain the impact of ONE result of demographic change in Europe between 1200 and 1500.

(C) Explain the impact of ONE ADDITIONAL result of demographic change in Europe between 1200 and 1500.

15
Southern Empires, Southern Seas, 1200–1500

CHAPTER OUTLINE

15-1 Tropical Africa and Asia

15-2 New Islamic Empires

15-3 Indian Ocean Trade

15-4 Social and Cultural Change

15-5 The Western Hemisphere

15-6 Conclusion

➤ **DIVERSITY & DOMINANCE**
Justice and Kingship

➤ **ENVIRONMENT & TECHNOLOGY**
The Indian Ocean Dhow

AP® Framework Terms

Indian Ocean sea lanes
Monsoon winds
Inka road system
Mexica (Aztecs)
Inkas
Inka road system
Mit'a

AP® Exam Tip

Compare the importance of the accounts of interregional travelers within Afro-Eurasia who wrote about their encounters with other cultures.

Overarching Questions

1 How have environmental factors shaped the development of diverse technologies, industrialization, transportation methods, and exchange and communication networks? (ENV)

2 How and why have religions, belief systems, philosophies, and ideologies originated, developed, and spread as a result of expanding communication and exchange networks? (CUL)

3 How and why have economic, social, cultural, and geographic factors influenced the process of state building, expansion, and dissolution? (SB)

4 How have economic systems and the development of ideologies, values, and institutions influenced each other? (ECON)

5 How have social categories, roles, and practices been maintained or challenged over time? (SOC)

Sultan Abu Bakr **(a-BOO BAK-uhr)** customarily offered hospitality to distinguished visitors to his city of Mogadishu, an Indian Ocean port on the northeast coast of Africa. In 1331, he provided food and lodging for Muhammad ibn Abdullah **Ibn Battuta (IB-uhn ba-TOO-tuh)** (1304–1369), a young Muslim scholar from Morocco who had set out to explore the Islamic world. With a pilgrimage to Mecca and travel throughout the Middle East behind him, Ibn Battuta was touring the trading cities of the Red Sea and East Africa. Subsequent travels took him to Central Asia and India, China and Southeast Asia, Muslim Spain, and sub-Saharan West Africa. Recounting some 75,000 miles (120,000 kilometers) of travel over twenty-nine years, Ibn Battuta's journal provides invaluable information on these lands.

Hospitality being considered a noble virtue among Muslims, regardless of physical and cultural differences, the reception at Mogadishu mirrored that at other cities. Ibn Battuta noted that Sultan Abu Bakr had skin darker than his own and spoke a different native language (Somali), but as brothers in faith, they prayed together at Friday

◀ **East African Pastoralists**
Herding large and small livestock has long been a way of life in drier parts of the tropics. Nigel Pavitt/Getty Images

services, where the sultan greeted his foreign guest in Arabic, the common language of the Islamic world: "You are heartily welcome, and you have honored our land and given us pleasure." When Sultan Abu Bakr and his jurists heard and decided cases after the mosque service, they used the religious law familiar in all Muslim lands.

Islam aside, the most basic links among the diverse peoples of Africa and southern Asia derived from the tropical environment itself. A network of overland and maritime routes joined their lands, providing avenues for the spread of beliefs and technologies, as well as goods. Ibn Battuta sailed with merchants down the coast of East Africa and joined trading caravans across the Sahara from Morocco to West Africa. His path to India followed overland trade routes, and a merchant ship carried him on to China.

The tropics of the Western Hemisphere lay beyond even Ibn Battuta's prodigious itinerary. Nevertheless, their environmental features resembled those of tropical Africa and Asia and they witnessed the rise of the impressive empires of the Aztecs and Inkas. ●

15-1 **Tropical Africa and Asia**

How did environmental differences shape cultural differences in tropical Africa and Asia?

The tropical regions of Africa and Asia shared environmental similarities, but they differed markedly in the extent of their interactions with other parts of the world (see Chapter 9). The western regions of Africa were semi-isolated by the Atlantic Ocean and Sahara Desert, while Africa's east coast was in maritime contact with the lands bordering the Indian Ocean. India had long been affected by overland routes through Afghanistan to the Middle East and Central Asia, and it in turn influenced cultural developments in both mainland and island Southeast Asia.

15-1a **Tropical Environments**

Because of the angle of the earth's axis, the sun's rays warm the **tropics** year-round. The equator marks the center of the tropical zone, the Tropic of Cancer and Tropic of Capricorn its outer limits, each circling the globe at 23.5 degrees north or south latitude. This makes the tropical zone approximately 3,200 miles extending from north to south.

Ibn Battuta Moroccan Muslim scholar, the most widely traveled individual of his time. He wrote a detailed account of his visits to Islamic lands from China to Spain and the western Sudan.

tropics Equatorial region between the Tropic of Cancer and the Tropic of Capricorn. It is characterized by generally warm or hot temperatures year-round, though much variation exists due to altitude and other factors. Temperate zones north and south of the tropics generally have a winter season.

Africa and South America lie mostly within the tropics, as do southern Arabia, most of India, both mainland and island Southeast Asia, and Australia (see Map 15.1). Thirty-six percent of the world's land area lies in the tropics, but eighty percent of the southern hemisphere is occupied by oceans. This means that the sea distances between landmasses south of the Tropic of Capricorn are vastly greater than those within or north of the northern tropics. Unlike the Eastern Hemisphere, in the Western Hemisphere the regions that produced the earliest civilizations, Mesoamerica and the Andes and Pacific coastal desert of South America, lay in the tropics (see Chapter 8).

Lacking seasonal variation from hot and cold seasons experienced in temperate lands, the rainy and dry seasons of the Afro-Asian tropics derive from atmospheric patterns and the surrounding oceans. The effect of the earth's rotation on the atmosphere causes winds to move generally from east to west in the tropics and from west to east farther to the north and south. In the north, the winds from the west are called Trade Winds; in the south they are called the Roaring Forties.

Rainfall patterns reflect wind directions, the effect of high mountain ranges, and temperature differences between sea and land. The lofty Andes Mountains, for example, block moist air blowing from the Amazon region, and this creates the world's driest deserts along the western coast of South America in Chile and Peru. Cold ocean currents along the same Pacific coast make for some of the world's most abundant fisheries. Variations in water temperature, called the *El Niño effect*, can temporarily change this pattern and distort world climate patterns

Because moist, storm-producing air masses with low atmospheric pressure move away from high pressure masses, a permanent high-pressure air mass over the South Atlantic delivers heavy rainfall to the western coast of Africa during much of the year. However, in December and January, large high-pressure zones over northern Africa and Arabia produce a southward movement of drier air that limits the inland penetration of the moist ocean winds.

In the lands around the Indian Ocean, the rainy and dry seasons reflect the influence of alternating winds known as **monsoons**. A gigantic high-pressure zone over the Himalaya **(him-AH-la-yuh)** Mountains that peaks from December to March produces southern Asia's dry season by forcing strong ocean winds in the western Indian Ocean to blow toward southward and westward toward Africa (see Map 15.1). This is the northeast monsoon. Between April and August, a low-pressure zone over India reverses the process by drawing moist oceanic air from the south and west to form the southwest monsoon. This brings southern Asia the heavy rains of its wet season, usually called the monsoon season.

Areas with the heaviest rainfall—the broad belt along the equator in coastal West Africa and West-Central Africa, parts of coastal India, and Southeast Asia—have dense rain forests. Lighter rains produce other forest patterns. The English word *jungle* comes from an Indian word for the tangled undergrowth in the forests that once covered most of tropical India.

The northern edge of the tropic zone rarely sees rain at all. The world's largest desert, the Sahara, stretches across northern Africa and continues eastward across Arabia, southern Iran and Pakistan, and northwest India. Northern Mexico and the Southwest of the United States experience similar dryness. The corresponding desert at the edge of the Tropic of Capricorn in the south encompasses southwestern Africa and Australia. Large areas of tropical India, Africa, and South America lie between the deserts and rain forests and experience moderate rainy seasons. These lands range from fairly wet woodlands to the much drier grasslands characteristic of much of East Africa.

Altitude produces other climatic variations. Thin atmospheres at high altitudes hold less heat than atmospheres at lower elevations. Snow covers some of the volcanic peaks of eastern Africa all or part of the year. The snowcapped Himalayas that form India's northern frontier rise so high that they block cold air from moving south and thus give northern India a more tropical climate than its latitude would suggest. The plateaus of inland Africa and the Deccan **(DEK-uhn)** Plateau of central India also enjoy cooler temperatures than the coastal plains.

monsoon Seasonal winds in the Indian Ocean caused by the seasonal impact of high and low pressure over India and in the Himalaya Mountains. These strong and predictable winds have long been ridden across the open sea by sailors, and the large amounts of rainfall that they deposit on parts of India, Southeast Asia, and southern China allow for the cultivation of several crops a year.

15-1b Human Ecosystems

A careful observer touring the tropics in 1200 would have noticed many differences in societies deriving from their particular ecosystems—that is, from how human groups used the plants, animals, and other resources of their physical environments. These systems varied greatly in the density of population they could support.

CHRONOLOGY

	Tropical Africa	Tropical Asia	Western Hemisphere
1200	1230s Mali Empire founded 1270 Solomonic dynasty in Ethiopia founded	1206 Delhi Sultanate founded in India 1298 Delhi Sultanate annexes Gujarat	
1300	1324–1325 Mansa Musa's pilgrimage to Mecca	1398 Timur sacks Delhi; Delhi Sultanate declines	1325 Aztec capital Tenochtitlan founded
1400	1400s Great Zimbabwe at its peak 1433 Tuareg retake Timbuktu; Mali declines		1430s Inka expansion begins
1500		1500 Port of Malacca at its peak	1500–1525 Inka conquer Ecuador 1502 Moctezuma II crowned Aztec ruler

Some peoples continued to rely primarily on hunting, fishing, and gathering and lived in small, mobile groups. For Pygmy (**PIG-mee**) hunters in the dense forests of Central Africa, small size permitted pursuit of prey through dense undergrowth. Hunting also prevailed among some inland groups in Borneo, New Guinea, and the Philippines. A Portuguese expedition led by Vasco da Gama visited the arid coast of southwestern Africa in 1497 and saw there a healthy group of people feeding themselves on "the flesh of seals, whales, and gazelles, and the roots of wild plants." Fishing, which was common along all the major lakes and rivers as well as in the oceans, could be combined with farming or with ocean trade, particularly in Southeast Asia.

Herding provided sustenance in areas too arid for agriculture. Pastoralists consumed milk and sometimes blood from their herds but did not eat a lot of meat since their animals were of greater value to them alive than dead. The deserts of northern Africa and Arabia had small populations that ranged widely with their camels, goats, and donkeys. Some, like the Tuareg (**TWAH-reg**) of the western Sahara, proved invaluable as caravan guides because of their intimate knowledge of the desert. Along the Sahara's southern edge the cattle-herding Fulani (**foo-LAH-nee**) gradually extended their range and by 1500 had spread throughout the western and central Sudan. Other cattle herders lived on either side of the Nile in Sudan and in Somalia.

Pastoral groups in India were less numerous and located mostly in the northwestern deserts. South and Southeast Asia, being generally wetter than tropical Africa outside the rain-forest zone, did not favor pastoralism but did allow for intensive cultivation. High yields supported dense populations. In 1200, over 100 million people lived in South and Southeast Asia, more than four-fifths of them on the fertile Indian mainland. Though a little less than the population of China, this was triple the number of people living in all of Africa and nearly double the number in Europe.

Rice cultivation dominated in the fertile Ganges Plain of northeast India, mainland Southeast Asia, and southern China. In drier areas, farmers grew grains—wheat, sorghum, and millet—and legumes such as peas and beans whose ripening cycles matched the pattern of the rainy and dry seasons. Tree crops, such as kola nuts in West Africa, coconuts in Southeast Asia, and bananas everywhere, made major contributions to the diet, as did yams and other root crops characteristic of rain-forest clearings.

The spread of farming, including the transfer to Africa of Indo-Malayan bananas and root crops like cocoyams, also known as taro, and yams, fit well into the natural environment. In most of sub-Saharan Africa and much of Southeast Asia, extensive rather than intensive cultivation prevailed. Instead of enriching fields with manure and vegetable compost so they could be cultivated year after year, farmers abandoned fields when the natural fertility of the soil fell and cleared new fields. Ashes from the brush, grasses, and tree limbs they cut down

AP® Exam Tip
Be able to identify several examples of crops (such as bananas and rice) that diffused along trade routes throughout Afro-Eurasia.

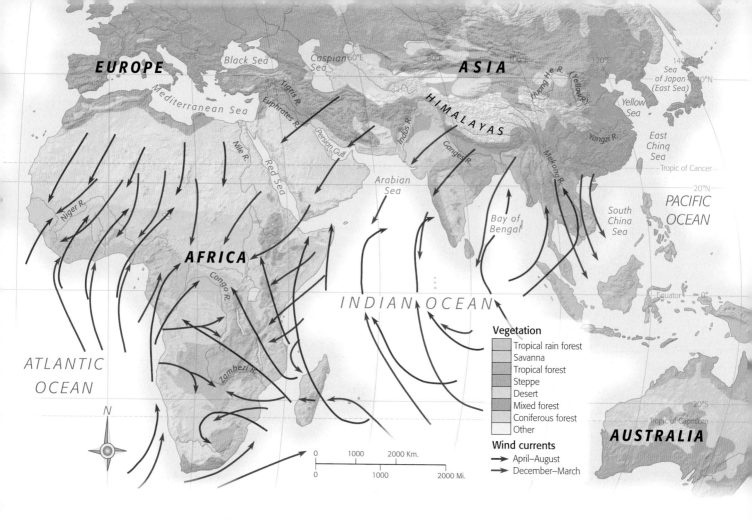

MAP 15.1   Africa and the Indian Ocean Basin: Physical Characteristics Seasonal wind patterns control rainfall in the tropics and produce the different tropical vegetation zones to which human societies have adapted over thousands of years. Wind patterns have also dominated sea travel in the Indian Ocean.

How does the complexity of tropical wind and weather systems compare with those of Eurasia?

and burned boosted the new fields' fertility. Shifting to new land every few years made efficient use of labor in areas with comparatively poor soils and abundant space.

15-1c **Water Systems and Irrigation**

Though the inland delta of the Niger River in West Africa received naturally fertilizing annual floods and could grow rice for sale to the trading cities along the Niger bend, many tropical farmers in India and Southeast Asia had to bring water to their crops. Conserving some of the monsoon rainfall for use during the dry season helped in Vietnam, Java, Malaya, and Burma (now Myanmar), which had terraced hillsides with special water-control systems for growing rice. Villagers in southeast India built stone and earthen dams across rivers to store

◀ **King and Queen of Ife**   This copper-alloy work shows the royal couple of the Yoruba kingdom of Ife, the oldest and most sacred of the Yoruba kingdoms of southwestern Nigeria. The casting dates to the period between 1100 and 1500, except for the reconstruction of the male's face, the original of which shattered in 1957 when the road builder who found it accidentally struck it with his pick.   Andre Held Collection/akg-images

water for gradual release through elaborate irrigation canals. Similar dam and canal systems supplied water farther north.

As had been true since the first river-valley civilizations (see Chapter 2), governments built and controlled the largest irrigation systems. The **Delhi (DEL-ee) Sultanate** (1206–1526) in northern India developed extensive new water-control systems. One large reservoir that supplied Delhi in the first quarter of the thirteenth century had fields of sugar cane, cucumbers, and melons planted along its rim as the water level fell during the dry season. Irrigation canals built in the Ganges Plain in the fourteenth century remained unsurpassed for 500 years. Such systems made it possible to grow crops throughout the year.

Since the tenth century, the island of Ceylon (ancient Serandip; modern Sri Lanka [**sree LAHNG-kuh**]) off India's southern tip possessed the world's greatest concentration of irrigation reservoirs and canals. These facilities supported the population of a large Sinhalese-speaking (**sin-huh-LEEZ**) kingdom in arid northern Ceylon. In Southeast Asia, another impressive system of reservoirs and canals served Cambodia's capital city, Angkor (**ANG-kor**).

Between 1250 and 1400, however, the irrigation complex in Ceylon fell into ruin when invaders from southern India disrupted the Sinhalese government. As a result, malaria spread by mosquitoes breeding in the irrigation canals ravaged the population. In the fifteenth century, the great Cambodian system fell into ruin when the government that maintained it collapsed. No subsequent governments ever rebuilt either system.

The vulnerability of complex irrigation systems constructed by powerful governments contrasts with village-based irrigation systems. Invasion and natural calamity might damage the latter, but they usually bounced back because they depended on local initiative and simpler technologies.

15-1d Mineral Resources

Throughout the tropics, ironworking provided the hoes, axes, and knives farmers used to clear and cultivate their fields. Between 1200 and 1500, the rain forests of coastal West Africa and Southeast Asia opened up for farming. Iron also supplied spear and arrow points, needles, and nails. Indian armorers became known for forging strong and beautiful swords. In Africa, many people attributed magical powers to iron smelters and blacksmiths.

The Copperbelt of southeastern Africa came into prominence during the fourteenth and fifteenth centuries. Smelters cast the metal into large X-shaped *ingots* (metal castings) that local coppersmiths worked into wire and decorative objects.

A mining town in the western Sudan visited by Ibn Battuta produced two sizes of copper bars that served as currency in place of coins. Coppersmiths in the West African city of Ife (now in southern Nigeria) cast highly realistic copper and *brass* (an alloy of copper and zinc) statues and heads that now rank as masterpieces of world art. They utilized the "lost-wax" method, in which molten metal melts a thin layer of wax sandwiched between clay forms, replacing the "lost" wax with hard metal.

African gold moved in quantity across the Sahara and into the Indian Ocean and Red Sea trades. Some came from streambeds along the upper Niger River and farther south in modern Ghana (**GAH-nuh**). Far to the south, beyond the Zambezi (**zam-BEE-zee**) River (in modern Zimbabwe [**zim-BAHB-way**]), archaeologists have discovered thousands of mineshafts, dating from 1200, that were sunk up to 100 feet (30 meters) into the ground to get at gold ores. Although panning for gold remained important in the streams descending from the mountains of northern India, the gold and silver mines in India seem to have been exhausted by this period. Thus, Indians imported considerable quantities of gold for jewelry and temple decoration from Iran and the Ottoman Empire as well as from Southeast Asia and Africa.

Delhi Sultanate
Centralized Indian empire of varying extent, created by Muslim invaders.

Section Review

- The environment of tropical Africa and Asia is governed by wind patterns across oceans and the rainfall that they bring.

- Deserts and rain forests mark the extreme climate variations in these regions, while mountain ranges produce further variations.

- Depending on the regional environment, people fed themselves mainly through hunting and gathering, herding, or farming.

- In West Africa, India, and Southeast Asia, human societies depended on river and irrigation systems of varying complexity.

- Iron, copper, and gold were central to the local economies and long-distance trade systems of tropical Africa and Asia.

15-2 New Islamic Empires

Under what circumstances did the first Islamic empires arise in Africa and India?

Paradoxically, given the Mongol destruction of the Baghdad caliphate in 1258 (see Chapter 13), the territorial expansion of Islam between 1200 and 1500 exceeded the territorial conquests of the Arabs in the seventh century. Historians have paid more attention to the Ottoman conquests of the same period because their adversaries were Europeans (see Chapter 14), but most of the expansion took place in the Muslim south in Africa, South Asia, and Southeast Asia.

The empires of Mali in West Africa and Delhi in northern India formed the largest and richest tropical states during Islam's second period of expansion. Both utilized administrative and military systems introduced from the Islamic heartland. Yet **Mali**, an indigenous African dynasty, grew out of the peaceful influence of Muslim merchants and scholars, while the Delhi Sultanate was founded and ruled by invading Turkish and Afghan Muslims.

15-2a Mali in the Western Sudan

Muslim rule in North Africa beginning in the seventh century (see Chapter 10) greatly stimulated trade across the Sahara. In the centuries that followed, the faith of Muhammad spread slowly to the lands south of the desert, which the Arabs called the *bilad al-sudan* (**bih-LAD uhs-soo-DAN**), "land of the blacks."

Muslim Berbers invading out of the desert in 1076 caused the collapse of Ghana, the empire that preceded Mali in the western Sudan (see Chapter 10). Takrur (**TAHK-roor**), a kingdom on the Atlantic coast whose ruler had become the first sub-Saharan ruler to adopt Islam in the 1030s, allied with the invaders but remained a small state when after their Berber allies turned their attention to interests in Morocco and Spain and away from the sub-Saharan region. Farther east, a truce that had endured since 652 between Christian Nubia along the Nile and Muslim Egypt fell apart in the thirteenth century as the Mamluks of Cairo (see Chapter 10) made repeated attacks. The small Christian kingdoms weakened and fell over the next two centuries, but Christian Ethiopia successfully withstood Muslim advances.

In general, however, Islam's spread south of the Sahara followed a pattern of gradual and peaceful conversion. The expansion of commercial contacts in the western Sudan and on the East African coast greatly promoted the conversion process.

Shortly after 1200, Takrur expanded under King Sumanguru (**soo-muhn-GOO-roo**), only to suffer a major defeat some thirty years later at the hands of Sundiata (**soon-JAH-tuh**), the upstart leader of the Malinke (**muh-LING-kay**) people. Though both leaders professed Islam, Malinke legends recall their battles as duels between powerful magicians, suggesting how much old beliefs mingled with new. Sumanguru could reportedly appear and disappear at will, assume dozens of shapes, and catch arrows in midflight. Sundiata defeated Sumanguru's much larger forces through superior military maneuvers and by wounding his adversary with a special arrow that robbed him of his magical powers. Other victories followed and the Mali Empire was born (see Map 15.2).

Sundiata's empire depended on a well-developed agricultural base and control of the regional and trans-Saharan trade routes, as had Ghana before it. Mali, however, controlled a greater area than Ghana, including not only the core trading area of the upper Niger but also the gold fields of the Niger headwaters to the southwest. More-over, its rulers fostered the spread of Islam among the empire's political and trading elites. Control of the gold and copper trades and contacts with North African Muslim traders gave Mali unprecedented prosperity.

Under the ruler **Mansa Kankan Musa** (**MAHN-suh KAHN-kahn MOO-suh**) (r. 1312–1337), the empire's reputation for wealth spread far and wide. Mansa Musa's pilgrimage to Mecca in 1324–1325 fulfilled his personal duty as a Muslim and at the same time put on display his exceptional wealth. He traveled with a large entourage. Besides his senior wife and 500 of her ladies in waiting and their slaves, one account says there were also 60,000 porters and a vast caravan of camels carrying supplies and provisions. For purchases and gifts, he brought along eighty packages of gold, each weighing 122 ounces (3.8 kilograms). In addition, 500 slaves each carried a golden staff. Mansa Musa dispersed so many gifts when he passed through Cairo that the value of gold was depressed for years. Obviously the days were past when caravan merchants could trade gold for an equal weight of salt because the value of the precious metal on the north side of the Sahara was not known on the south side (see Material Culture: Salt in Chapter 12).

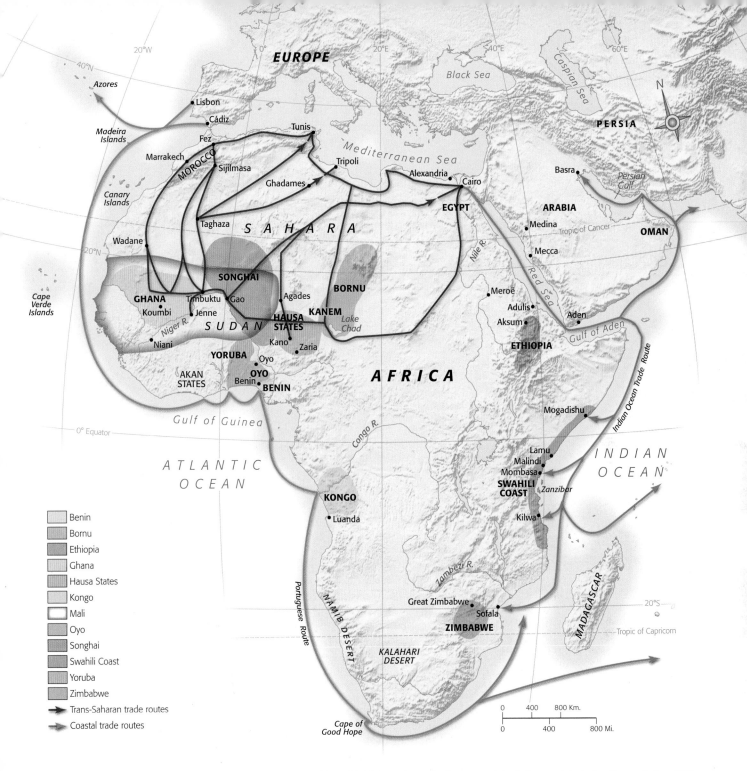

MAP 15.2 Africa, 1200–1500 Many African states had beneficial links to the trade that crossed the Sahara and the Indian Ocean. Before 1500, sub-Saharan Africa's external ties were primarily with the Islamic world.

How does this map, drawn mostly from Arabic and European sources, contribute to the old cliché that the interior of Africa constituted a Dark Continent?

Two centuries after its founding, Mali began to disintegrate. Mansa Suleiman inherited the kingdom from his brother Mansa Musa and hosted Ibn Battuta, but his successors could not prevent rebellions breaking out among the diverse peoples subjected to Malinke rule. Other groups attacked from without. The desert Tuareg retook their city of Timbuktu (**tim-buk-TOO**) in 1433. By 1500, the rulers of Mali had dominion over little more than the Malinke heartland.

The cities of the upper Niger survived Mali's collapse, but some trade and intellectual life moved east to the central Sudan. Shortly after 1450, the rulers of several Hausa city-states officially adopted Islam. These states took on importance as manufacturing and trading centers,

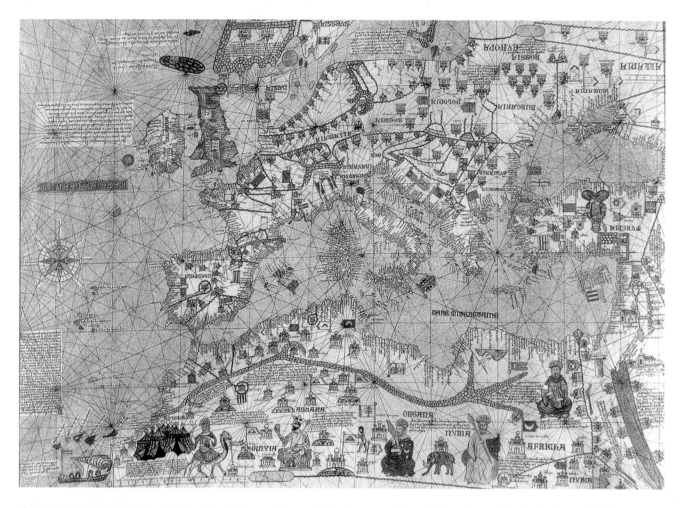

▲ **Map of the Western Sudan (1375)** A Jewish geographer on the Mediterranean island of Majorca drew this lavish map in 1375, incorporating all that was known in Europe about the rest of the world. This portion of the Catalan Atlas shows a North African trader approaching the king of Mali, who holds a gold nugget in one hand and a golden scepter in the other. A caption identifies the black ruler as Mansa Musa, "the richest and noblest king in all the land." Why is the camel rider shown coming from the west instead of from the east? Catalan Atlas: Detail of North Africa and Europe, by Abraham and Jafunda Cresques, 1375, Spanish School (14th century)/Bibliotheque Nationale, Paris, France/Index/Bridgeman Images

becoming famous for cotton textiles and leatherworking. The central Sudanic state of Kanem-Bornu **(KAH-nuhm–BOR-noo)** also expanded in the late fifteenth century from the ancient kingdom of Kanem, whose rulers had accepted Islam in about 1085. At its peak around 1250, Kanem had absorbed the state of Bornu south and west of Lake Chad and gained control of routes crossing the central Sahara. As Kanem-Bornu's armies conquered new territories, they also spread the rule of Islam.

15-2b The Delhi Sultanate in India

Having long ago lost the defensive unity of the Gupta Empire (see Chapter 7), the divided states of northwest India fell prey to raids by the powerful sultan Mahmud **(mah-MOOD)** based in Ghazna, Afghanistan, beginning in the early eleventh century. Repeated campaigns by successive rulers led to a series of Afghan and Turkic dynasties ruling from the city of Delhi from 1206 to 1526. One partisan Muslim chronicler wrote: "The city [Delhi] and its vicinity was freed from idols and idol-worship, and in the sanctuaries of the images of the [Hindu] Gods, mosques were raised by the worshippers of one God."[1] Turkish adventurers from Central Asia flocked to join the invading armies, overwhelming the small Indian states, which were often at war with one another.

---

[1] Hasan Nizami, Taju-l Ma-asir, in Henry M. Elliot, *The History of India as Told by Its Own Historians*, ed. John Dowson (London, UK: Trübner and Co., 1869–1871), 2:219.

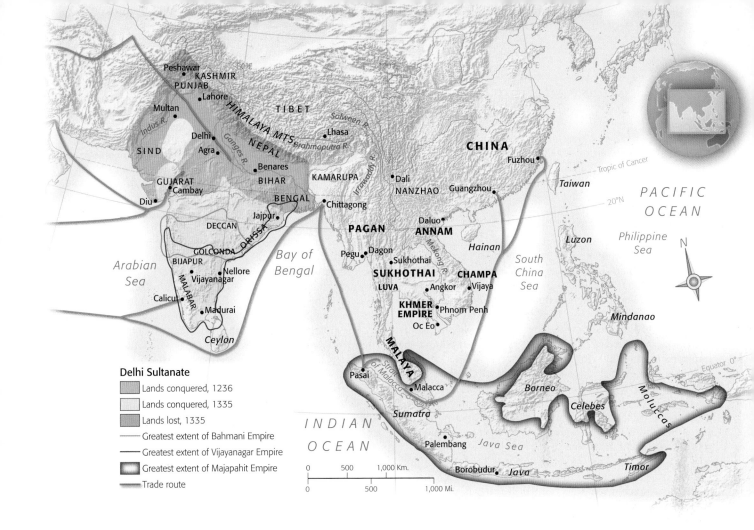

MAP 15.3 South and Southeast Asia, 1200–1500 The rise of new empires and the expansion of maritime trade reshaped the lives of many tropical Asians.

Why had continuous sea contact with India's west coast failed to establish Muslim states before the invasions from Afghanistan in the eleventh and twelfth centuries, yet ultimately proved effective in spreading Islam to island Southeast Asia?

Between 1206 and 1236, the Muslim invaders extended their rule over the Hindu princes and chiefs in much of northern India. Sultan Iltutmish (**il-TOOT-mish**) (r. 1211–1236) consolidated the conquest in a series of military expeditions that made his realm the largest in India (see Map 15.3). The caliphate in Baghdad, soon to be extinguished by the Mongols, officially recognized the Delhi Sultanate as a Muslim realm. Incorporating north India into the Islamic world marked the beginning of the invaders' transformation from brutal conquerors to somewhat more benign rulers. Though doctrinally opposed to idol worship, they granted the Hindus freedom from persecution in return for paying the *jizya*, a tax required of Jews and Christians.

Iltutmish astonished his ministers by passing over his weak and pleasure-seeking sons and designating as his heir his beloved and talented daughter Raziya (**RAH-zee-uh**). He reportedly said, "My sons are devoted to the pleasures of youth: no one of them is qualified to be king. . . . There is no one more competent to guide the State than my daughter." Her brother, who was given to riding his elephant through the bazaar and showering the crowds with coins, ruled ineptly for seven months before the ministers relented and put Raziya on the throne.

A chronicler who knew her explained why this able ruler lasted less than four years (r. 1236–1240):

> *Sultan Raziya was a great monarch. She was wise, just, and generous, a benefactor to her kingdom, a dispenser of justice, the protector of her subjects, and the leader of her armies. She was endowed with all the qualities befitting a king, but she was not born of the right sex, and so in the estimation of men all these virtues were worthless. May God have mercy upon her!*[2]

[2]Minhaju-s Siraj, Tabakat-i Nasiri, in ibid., 2:332–333.

Ibn Battuta wrote vivid descriptions of the powerful men who dominated the Muslim states he visited. Although his accounts are explicitly about the rulers, they also raise important issues about rulers' relations with their subjects. The following account of Sultan Muhammad ibn Tughluq of Delhi may be read as a treatise on the rights and duties of rulers and ways in which individual personalities shaped diverse governing styles.

Muhammad is a man who, above all others, is fond of making presents and shedding blood. There may always be seen at his gate some poor person becoming rich, or some living one condemned to death. His generous and brave actions, and his cruel and violent deeds, have obtained notoriety among the people. In spite of this, he is the most humble of men, and the one who exhibits the greatest equity. The ceremonies of religion are dear to his ears, and he is very severe in respect of prayer and the punishment which follows its neglect. . . .

When drought prevailed throughout India and Sind, . . . the Sultan gave orders that provisions for six months should be supplied to all the inhabitants of Delhi from the royal granaries. . . . The officers of justice made registers of the people of the different streets, and these being sent up, each person received sufficient provisions to last him for six months.

The Sultan, notwithstanding all I have said about his humility, his justice, his kindness to the poor, and his boundless generosity, was much given to bloodshed. It rarely happened that the corpse of some one who had been killed was not seen at the gate of his palace. I have often seen men killed and their bodies left there. One day I went to his palace and my horse shied. I looked before me, and I saw a white heap on the ground, and when I asked what it was, one of my companions said it was the trunk of a man cut into three pieces. The sovereign punished little faults like great ones, and spared neither the learned, the religious, nor the noble. Every day hundreds of individuals were brought chained into his hall of audience; their hands tied to their necks and their feet bound together. Some of them were killed, and others were tortured, or well beaten. . . .

The Sultan has a brother named Masud Khan, [who] was one of the handsomest fellows I have ever seen. The king suspected him of intending to rebel, so he questioned him, and, under fear of the torture, Masud confessed the charge. Indeed,

every one who denies charges of this nature, which the Sultan brings against him, is put to the torture, and most people prefer death to being tortured. The Sultan had his brother's head cut off in the palace, and the corpse, according to custom, was left neglected for three days in the same place. The mother of Masud had been stoned two years before in the same place on a charge of debauchery or adultery. . . .

One of the most serious charges against this Sultan is that he forced all the inhabitants of Delhi to leave their homes. [After] the people of Delhi wrote letters full of insults and invectives against [him,] the Sultan . . . decided to ruin Delhi, so he purchased all the houses and inns from the inhabitants, paid them the price, and then ordered them to remove to Daulatabad. . . .

The greater part of the inhabitants departed, but [h]is slaves found two men in the streets: one was paralyzed, the other blind. They were brought before the sovereign, who ordered the paralytic to be shot away from a *manjanik* [catapult], and the blind man to be dragged from Delhi to Daulatabad, a journey of forty days' distance. The poor wretch fell to pieces during the journey, and only one of his legs reached Daulatabad. All of the inhabitants of Delhi left; they abandoned their baggage and their merchandize, and the city remained a perfect desert.

A person in whom I felt confidence assured me that the Sultan mounted one evening upon the roof of his palace, and, casting his eyes over the city of Delhi, in which there was neither fire, smoke, nor light, he said, "Now my heart is satisfied, and my feelings are appeased.". . . When we entered this capital, we found it in the state which has been described. It was empty, abandoned, and had but a small population.

An epic poem revered as a great Hindu masterpiece in the Tamil language of southern India portrays kingship and justice as qualities far removed from those Ibn Battuta connects with Islamic law. In The Tale of the Anklet, *Kannaki and Kovalan, a couple from Pukar near India's southern tip, marry and separate when Kovalan becomes infatuated with a dancing girl. He recognizes his fault and the couple gets back together. To restart their home life, Kovalan takes his wife's golden anklet to sell in the marketplace. The royal goldsmith, who has stolen the queen's anklet, sees an opportunity to escape his guilt and denounces Kovalan to the king as the thief. The king promptly orders Kovalan's execution.*

Doing her best to prove herself a proper king, Raziya dressed like a man and led her troops atop an elephant. In the end, however, the Turkish chiefs imprisoned her; she escaped, but was killed by a robber soon afterward.

After a half century of stagnation and rebellion, the ruthless but efficient policies of Sultan Ala-ud-din Khalji (**uh-LAH–uh–DEEN KAL-jee**) (r. 1296–1316) increased control over the empire's outlying provinces. Successful frontier raids and high taxes filled his treasury, wage and price controls in Delhi kept down the cost of maintaining a large army, and a network of spies stifled intrigue. When a Mongol threat from Central Asia eased, Ala-ud-din's forces marched southward, capturing the rich trading state of **Gujarat** (**goo-juh-RAHT**) in 1298 and then briefly seizing the southern tip of the Indian peninsula.

Sultan Muhammad ibn Tughluq (**TOOG-look**) (r. 1325–1351) (see Diversity & Dominance: Justice and Kingship) enlarged the sultanate to its greatest extent at the expense of the independent Indian states but balanced his aggressive policy with religious toleration. He even attended Hindu religious festivals. However, his successor, Firuz Shah (**fuh-ROOZ shah**) (r. 1351–1388), alienated powerful Hindus by taxing the Brahmin elite. Muslim chroniclers praised him for constructing forty mosques, thirty colleges, and a hundred hospitals.

Gujarat Region of western India famous for trade and manufacturing; the inhabitants are called Gujaratis.

The distraught widow Kannaki goes to the king and says:

"O king with tinkling anklets! Born in Pukar
As the son of Macattuvan, a merchant prince
Of untarnished fame, Kovalan came to Maturai
For a living, driven by his karma. When he was here
To sell my anklet, he was murdered.
I am his wife: Kannaki is my name."
The king said:
    O divine woman! It is not unjust
To kill a thief. You should know it is the king's duty."
Kannaki of the shining ornaments replied:
"O lord of Korkai who does not dispense justice
Impartially! You should know that my golden anklet
Screams with gems."
    Said the king: "Woman
With a sweet voice! What you have said is true.
Our anklet is filled with pearls. Give me yours."
She gave it, and it was placed before the king.
Her precious anklet she broke open,
And a gem leaped into the king's face.
He saw the gem. His parasol rolled,
His sceptre bent, and he spoke up:
"Am I a king? I listened to the words of a goldsmith!
I alone am the thief! Through my error
I have failed to protect my people
Of the southern kingdom. Let my life crumble in the dust.
He fell down in a swoon. His great queen
Shuddered in confusion, and said:
    "There is no refuge
For a woman who has lost her husband."
    That woman
Of soft words touched her husband's feet and died.

. . . .

In a rage [Kannaki] cried out:
    "Men and women
Of Maturai of the four temples! O gods in heaven
And ascetics, listen! I curse this city. Its king erred
In killing the man I loved. Blameless am I!"
She wrenched off her left breast with her hand,
And grief-stricken went round the city of Maturai
Three times. And with a curse she hurled
Her fair breast on its pleasant street.
Before Kannaki, who had cursed, appeared Agni,
The god of fire, in the guise of a brahman,
Blue in color, with a red tuft and milkwhite teeth.
He said:
    "Virtuous woman! Long ago I was told
To burn this city the day you are wronged.
Who shall now live in it?"
    Kannaki, the golden vine,
Was in a rage, and ordered the god of fire:
"Brahmans, good men, cows, chaste women,
The old and children—spare these. Go
After the wicked."
    Fire and smoke smothered the city
Of Maturai of the king with the lofty chariot

AP® History Reasoning Skills

Comparison *How do the standards of royal justice in the two excerpts compare?*

Sources: First selection from Henry M. Elliot, *The History of India as Told by Its Own Historians* (London, UK: Trübner and Co., 1869–1871) 3: 611–614. Second selection from *The Tale of an Anklet: An Epic of South India. The Cilappatikaram of Ilanko Atikal*, trans. R. Parthasarathy (New York, NY: Columbia University Press, 1993), 188–189, 193–194.

A small minority in a giant land, the Delhi sultans relied on force to keep their subjects submissive, on military reprisals to put down rebellion, and on pillage and high taxes to sustain the ruling elite in luxury and power. The sultanate never escaped the disadvantage of foreign origins and alien religious identity, but some sultans did incorporate a few Hindus into their administrations, and some members of the Muslim elite married women from prominent Hindu families, though the brides had to convert to Islam.

Personal and religious rivalries within the Muslim elite, along with Hindu discontent, threatened the Delhi Sultanate whenever it showed weakness and finally hastened its end. In the mid-fourteenth century, Muslim nobles challenged the sultan's dominion and established the independent Bahmani **(bah-MAHN-ee)** kingdom (1347–1482) on the Deccan Plateau. Defending against the southward push of Bahmani armies, the Hindu states of south India united to form the Vijayanagar **(vee-JAY-yah-nah-GAR)** Empire (1336–1565), which at its height controlled rich trading ports on both coasts of south India and held Ceylon as a tributary state.

Hindu Vijayanagar and the Muslim Bahmani state turned a blind eye to religious differences when doing so favored their interests. Bahmani rulers sought to balance Muslim domination by incorporating Hindu leaders into the government, marrying Hindu wives, and appointing

▶ **Dijinguere Ber Mosque in Timbuktu** Built almost entirely of earth and organic materials, this fourteenth-century mosque can accommodate 2,000 worshipers. Mansa Kankan Musa, the most famous ruler of the Mali Empire, is said to have paid Abu Ishaq al-Sahili, a native of Granada in Muslim Spain, 200 kilograms of gold for designing this masterful combination of Islamic and African traditions. nik wheeler/Getty Images

Section Review

- Islam spread into western sub-Saharan Africa usually by peaceful conversion through trading contacts.

- Founded by Sundiata, Mali depended on agriculture and control of trade routes, and Islam spread among its elites.

- Mali reached its height under Mansa Kankan Musa but declined after the death of his successor, and power shifted eastward.

- Muslim invaders from Afghanistan conquered much of Hindu northern India to establish the Delhi Sultanate.

- The sultanate grew to encompass most of India; the sultans ruled through force, pillage, and heavy taxation.

- Though efficient, the sultanate suffered from internal struggles and fell under pressure from rival states and invaders.

Brahmins to high offices. Vijayanagar rulers hired Muslim horsemen and archers to strengthen their military forces and formed an alliance with the Muslim-ruled state of Gujarat.

By 1351, when all of south India had cast off Delhi's rule, much of north India rose in rebellion. In the east, Bengal broke away from the sultanate in 1338. In the west, Gujarat regained its independence by 1390. The weakening of Delhi's central authority tempted fresh Mongol interest in the area. In 1398, the Turko-Mongol leader Timur (see Chapter 13) captured the city of Delhi. When his armies withdrew the next year with vast quantities of loot and tens of thousands of captives, the largest city in southern Asia lay empty and in ruins. The Delhi Sultanate never recovered.

For all its shortcomings, the Delhi Sultanate triggered the development of centralized political authority in India. Prime ministers and provincial governors serving under the sultans established a bureaucracy, improved food production, promoted trade, and put in circulation a common coinage. Despite the many conflicts that Muslim conquest and rule provoked, Islam gradually acquired a permanent place in South Asia.

15-3 Indian Ocean Trade

How did cultural and ecological differences promote trade, and in turn how did trade and other contacts promote state growth and the spread of Islam?

When the collapse of the Mongol Empire in the fourteenth century disrupted overland routes across Central Asia, the Indian Ocean assumed greater strategic importance in tying together the peoples of Eurasia and Africa. Between 1200 and 1500, the volume of trade in the Indian Ocean increased. The Indian Ocean routes also facilitated the spread of Islam.

15-3a Monsoon Mariners

AP® Exam Tip
Explain how new maritime technologies and advanced knowledge of monsoon winds stimulated exchanges along maritime routes.

The prosperity of Islamic and Mongol empires in Asia, cities in Europe, and new kingdoms in Africa and Southeast Asia stimulated and contributed to the vitality of the Indian Ocean network. The demand for luxuries—precious metals and jewels, rare spices, fine textiles, and other manufactures—rose. Larger ships made shipments of bulk cargoes of ordinary cotton textiles, pepper, food grains (rice, wheat, barley), timber, horses, and other goods profitable. Some goods were transported from one end of this trading network to the other, but few ships or crews made a complete circuit. Instead, the Indian Ocean trade divided into two legs: from the Middle East across the Arabian Sea to India and from India across the Bay of Bengal to Southeast Asia (see Map 15.4).

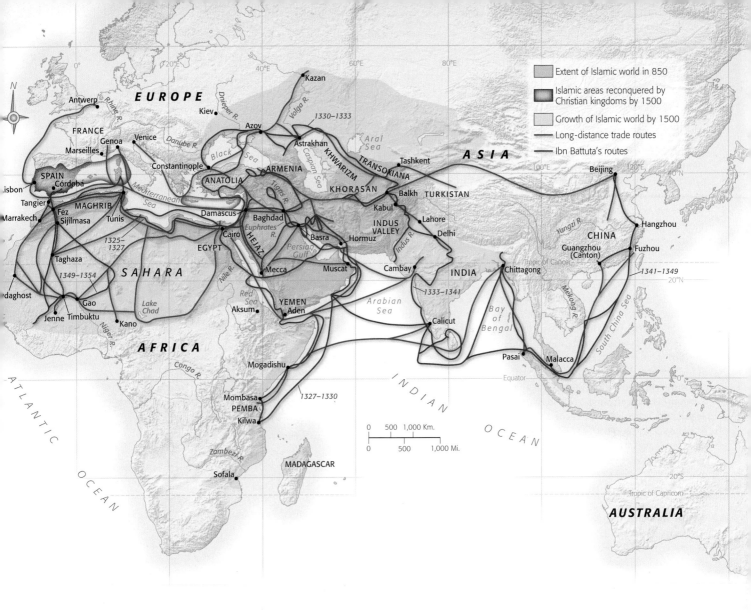

MAP 15.4 Arteries of Trade and Travel in the Islamic World, to 1500 Ibn Battuta's journeys across Africa and Asia made use of land and sea routes along which Muslim traders and the Islamic faith had long traveled.

Why might Ibn Battuta have traveled through China outside the Muslim world but not through Europe?

Shipyards in ports on the Malabar Coast (southwestern India) and in the Persian Gulf built large numbers of **dhows (dow)**, the characteristic cargo and passenger ships of the Arabian Sea. They grew from an average capacity of 100 tons in 1200 to 400 tons in 1500. This was about half the capacity of the largest European ships. On a typical expedition, a dhow might sail west from India to Arabia and Africa on the northeast monsoon winds (December to March) and return on the southwest monsoons (April to August). Small dhows kept the coast in sight. Relying on the stars to guide them, skilled pilots steered large vessels by the quicker route straight across the water. A large dhow could sail from the Red Sea to mainland Southeast Asia in two to four months, but few did so. Eastbound cargoes and passengers from dhows reaching India were likely to be transferred to junks, which dominated the eastern half of the Indian Ocean and the South China Sea (see Environment & Technology: The Indian Ocean Dhow).

Junks—the largest, most technologically advanced, and most seaworthy vessels of the ra— appeared first in China and spread as a part of Chinese overseas culture. Enormous nails held together hulls of heavy spruce or fir planks, in contrast with dhows, whose planks were sewn together with palm fiber. Below the deck, watertight compartments minimized flooding in case of damage to the ship's hull. The largest junks reportedly had twelve sails made of bamboo strips woven into mats and stiffened with battens. They carried a crew of a thousand men, including four hundred soldiers. A large junk might accommodate a hundred passenger cabins and a cargo

dhows Characteristic cargo and passenger ships of the Arabian Sea.

The sailing vessels that crossed the Indian Ocean shared the diversity of that trading area. The name by which we know them, *dhow*, comes from the Swahili language of the East African coast. The planks of teak from which their hulls were constructed were hewn from the tropical forests of south India and Southeast Asia. Their pilots, who navigated by stars at night, may have employed techniques that pastoral nomads had used to find their way across deserts. Some pilots used a magnetic compass, which originated in China.

Dhows came in various sizes and designs, but all had two distinctive features in common. The first was hull construction. The hulls of dhows consisted of planks that were sewn together, not nailed. Cord made of fiber from the husk of coconuts or other materials was passed through rows of holes drilled in the planks. Because cord is weaker than nails, outsiders considered this shipbuilding technique strange. Marco Polo fancifully suggested that it indicated sailors' fear that large ocean magnets would pull any nails out of their ships. Better explanations observe that pliant sewn hulls were cheaper to build than rigid nailed hulls and were less likely to be damaged if the ships ran aground.

The second distinctive feature of dhows was their sails made of palm leaves or cloth. Triangular or nearly triangular—some had a very short leading edge—were suspended from a single boom that crossed a vertical mast at an angle so sharp that its top end extended higher than the mast. Such sails could be turned to catch the wind better than the square sails that were common in the Mediterranean Sea.

Sewn hulls and lateen sails had appeared centuries earlier, but two innovations appeared between 1200 and 1500. The first was borrowed from China, a rudder positioned in the middle of the ship's *stern* (rear end). This replaced the large side oar that formerly had controlled steering. Second, shipbuilders increased the size of dhows to accommodate bulkier cargoes.

European mariners adopted many of the dhow's features after they began to venture into the Indian Ocean.

▲ **Dhow** This modern model shows the vessel's main features.
Science & Society Picture Library/Getty Images

Questions for Analysis

1. Why were Indian Ocean vessels so different from those used by the ancient Egyptians, Greeks, and Romans?
2. Why were dhows not equipped with multiple oars as Mediterranean war vessels were?
3. Did the lateen sail limit the size of dhows?

AP® Exam Tip
Understand the changes and continuities in the Indian Ocean trading network during this time period, and be able to explain the role of Muslim merchant communities in facilitating this trade.

Swahili Coast East African shores of the Indian Ocean between the Horn of Africa and the Zambezi River; from the Arabic sawahil, meaning "shores."

of over 1,000 tons. Junks dominated China's foreign shipping to Southeast Asia and India, but the Chinese did not control all of the junks that plied these waters. During the fifteenth century, similar vessels were launched from shipyards in Bengal and Southeast Asia to be sailed by local crews.

Decentralized and cooperative commercial interests, rather than political authorities, connected the several regions that participated in the Indian Ocean trade. The **Swahili (swah-HEE-lee) Coast** supplied ivory, wood, and gold from inland areas of Africa, while ports around the Arabian peninsula supplied horses, incense, and manufactured goods transshipped from the Mediterranean region. Merchants in the cities of coastal India received goods from east and west, sold some locally, passed others along, and added Indian goods, particularly cotton cloth, to the trade. The Strait of Malacca (**meh-LAK-eh**), between the eastern end of the Indian Ocean and the South China Sea, provided a meeting point for trade from Southeast Asia, China, and the Indian Ocean. In each region, certain ports functioned as giant emporia, consolidating goods from smaller ports and inland areas for transport across the seas.

15-3b Africa: The Swahili Coast and Zimbabwe

Trade expanded steadily along the East African coast from about 1250, giving rise to between thirty and forty separate city-states by 1500. After 1200, masonry buildings as much as four stories high replaced mud and thatch dwellings, and archaeological findings include Chinese porcelain, Indian glass beads, and other exotic goods. Coastal and island peoples shared a common culture and a language built on African grammar and vocabulary but enriched with many Arabic and Persian terms and written in Arabic script. In time, these people became known as "Swahili," from the Arabic word *sawahil* (**suh-WAH-hil**), meaning "shores."

What attracted the Arab and Iranian merchants whom oral traditions associate with the Swahili Coast's commercial expansion? By the late fifteenth century, the major port of Kilwa, described by Ibn Battuta as "one of the most beautiful and well-constructed towns in the world," was annually exporting a ton of gold mined by inland Africans much farther south. Much of it came from or passed through a powerful state on the plateau south of the Zambezi River. At its peak in about 1400, its capital city, now known as **Great Zimbabwe**, occupied 193 acres (78 hectares) and had some 18,000 inhabitants.

Between about 1250 and 1450, local African craftsmen built stone structures for Great Zimbabwe's rulers, priests, and wealthy citizens. The largest structure, an enclosure the size and shape of a large football stadium with walls of unmortared stone 17 feet (5 meters) thick and 32 feet (10 meters) high, served as the king's court. A large conical stone tower was among the many buildings inside the walls.

▲ **Royal Enclosure, Great Zimbabwe**   Inside these oval stone walls the rulers of the trading state of Great Zimbabwe lived. Forced to enter the enclosure through a narrow corridor between two high walls, visitors were meant to be awestruck.

As in Mali, mixed farming and cattle herding provided the economic basis of the Great Zimbabwe state, but long-distance trade brought added wealth. Trade began regionally with copper ingots from the upper Zambezi Valley, salt, and local manufactures. Gold exports to the coast expanded in the fourteenth and fifteenth centuries and brought Zimbabwe to its peak. However, historians suspect that the city's residents depleted nearby forests for firewood while their cattle overgrazed surrounding grasslands. The resulting ecological crisis hastened the empire's decline in the fifteenth century.

15-3c Arabia: Aden and the Red Sea

The city **Aden** (**ADD-en**) near the southwestern tip of the Arabian peninsula had a double advantage in the Indian Ocean trade. Monsoon winds brought enough rainfall to supply drinking water to a large population and grow grain for export, and its location made it a convenient stopover for trade with India, the Persian Gulf, East Africa, and Egypt. Aden's merchants dealt in cotton cloth and beads from India; spices from Southeast Asia; horses from Arabia and Ethiopia; pearls from the Red Sea; manufactured luxuries from Cairo; slaves, gold, and ivory from Ethiopia; and grain, opium, and dyes from Aden's own hinterland.

Common commercial interests generally promoted good relations among the different religions and cultures of this region. For example, in the mid-thirteenth century, a wealthy Jew from Aden named Yosef settled in Christian Ethiopia, where he acted as an adviser. South Arabia had been trading with neighboring parts of Africa since before the time of King Solomon of Israel. The dynasty that ruled Ethiopia after 1270 boasted (legendary) descent from Solomon and the Queen of Sheba from across the Red Sea. Ethiopia's Solomonic dynasty greatly increased trade through the Red Sea port of Zeila (**ZAY-luh**), including slaves, amber, and animal pelts, which went to Aden and on to other destinations.

Friction sometimes arose, however. In the late fifteenth century, Ethiopia's territorial expansion and efforts to increase control over the trade provoked conflicts with Muslims who ruled the coastal states of the Red Sea.

15-3d India: Gujarat and the Malabar Coast

The state of Gujarat in western India prospered from the expanding trade of the Arabian Sea and the rise of the Delhi Sultanate. Blessed with a rich agricultural hinterland and a long coastline, Gujarat attracted new trade after the Mongol destruction of Baghdad in 1258 disrupted the

Great Zimbabwe City, now in ruins (in the modern African country of Zimbabwe), whose many stone structures were built between about 1250 and 1450, when it was a trading center and the capital of a large state.

Aden Port city in the modern south Arabian country of Yemen. It has been a major trading center in the Indian Ocean since ancient times.

northern land routes. Despite the violence of its forced incorporation into the Delhi Sultanate in 1298, Gujarat prospered from increased commercial interaction with Delhi's ruling class. Independent again after 1390, the Muslim rulers of Gujarat extended their control over neighboring Hindu states and regained their preeminent position in the Indian Ocean trade.

Gujaratis exported cotton textiles and indigo to the Middle East and Europe in return for gold and silver. They also shipped cotton cloth, carnelian beads, and foodstuffs to the Swahili Coast in exchange for ebony, slaves, ivory, and gold. During the fifteenth century, Gujarat's trade zone expanded eastward to the Strait of Malacca. There Gujarati merchants helped spread the Islamic faith among East Indian traders, some of whom even imported specially carved gravestones from Gujarat.

Unlike Kilwa and Aden, Gujarat manufactured goods for trade. According to thirteenth-century Venetian traveler Marco Polo, Gujarat's leatherworkers dressed enough skins in a year to fill several ships to Arabia and other places. They made sleeping mats for export to the Middle East "in red and blue leather, exquisitely inlaid with figures of birds and beasts, and skillfully embroidered with gold and silver wire," as well as leather cushions embroidered in gold.

Later observers compared the Gujarati city of Cambay (modern name Khambhat) with cities in Flanders and northern Italy (see Chapter 14) in the scale, craftsmanship, and diversity of its textile industries. Cotton, linen, and silk cloth, along with carpets and quilts, found a large market in Europe, Africa, the Middle East, and Southeast Asia. Cambay also produced polished gemstones, gold jewelry, carved ivory, stone beads, and both pearls and mother of pearl. At the height of its prosperity in the fifteenth century, its well-laid-out streets and open places boasted fine stone houses with tiled roofs. Although Muslim residents controlled most Gujarati overseas trade, its Hindu merchant caste profited so much from related commercial activities that their wealth and luxurious lives became the envy of other Indians.

More southerly cities on the well-watered western coast of India, called the Mala-bar Coast, imitated Gujarat's success. Calicut (**KAL-ih-cut**) (modern name Kozhikode) and other coastal cities prospered from locally woven cotton textiles and locally grown grains and spices. They also served as clearinghouses for the long-distance trade of the Indian Ocean. The Zamorin (**ZAH-much-ruhn**) (ruler) of Calicut presided over a loose federation of its Hindu rulers that united the coastal region, but steep mountains known as the Western Ghats cut the coast off from the inland areas on the Deccan Plateau. As in eastern Africa and Arabia, rulers generally tolerated religious and ethnic groups who contributed to commercial profits. Most trading activity lay in the hands of Muslims, many originally from Iran and Arabia, who intermarried with local Indian Muslims. Jewish merchants also operated from Malabar's trading cities.

Section Review

- Traversed by dhows and junks, the maritime trade network of the Indian Ocean tied together peoples of Asia, Africa, and Europe.

- Decentralized commercial interests rose throughout the network, including the Swahili city-states that exported African gold from Great Zimbabwe.

- Aden dealt in a variety of goods from Africa, Arabia, and Southeast Asia and traded with Zeila on the Red Sea.

- Despite political turmoil, the cities of Gujarat and the Malabar Coast prospered through agriculture, manufacture, and trade.

- Through astute alliances, Malacca grew into the predominant emporium of South-east Asia.

15-3e Southeast Asia

At the eastern end of the Indian Ocean, the Strait of Malacca between the Malay Peninsula and the island of Sumatra provided the principal passage into the South China Sea (see Map 15.3). As trade increased in the fourteenth and fifteenth centuries, this commercial choke point became the site of political rivalry.

The mainland kingdom of Siam controlled most of the upper Malay Peninsula, while the Java-based kingdom of Majapahit (**mah-jah-PAH-heet**) extended its dominion over the lower Malay Peninsula and much of Sumatra. Majapahit, however, could not suppress a nest of Chinese pirates based at the Sumatran city of Palembang (**pah-lem-BONG**) who preyed on ships sailing through the strait. In 1407, a fleet from China commanded by the admiral Zheng He (see Chapter 13) smashed the pirates' power and took their chief back home for trial.

Majapahit, weakened by internal struggles, could not take advantage of China's intervention, making the chief beneficiary the newer port of **Malacca** (or Melaka), which dominated the narrowest part of the strait. Under a prince from Palembang, Malacca had grown from an obscure fishing village into an important port through a series of astute alliances. Nominally subject to the king of Siam, Malacca also secured an alliance with China that was sealed by the visit of the imperial fleet in 1407. The conversion of an early ruler from Hinduism to Islam helped promote trade with Muslim merchants from Gujarat and elsewhere. Merchants also appreciated Malacca's security and low taxes.

Malacca served not just as a meeting point but also as an emporium for Southeast Asian products: rubies and musk from Burma, tin from Malaya, gold from Sumatra, cloves and nutmeg from the Moluccas (or Spice Islands, as Europeans later dubbed them). Shortly after 1500, when Malacca was at its height, one resident counted eighty-four languages spoken among the merchants gathered there, who came from as far away as Turkey, Ethiopia, and the Swahili Coast. Four officials administered the foreign merchant communities: one for the Gujaratis, one for other Indians and Burmese, one for Southeast Asians, and one for the Chinese and Japanese. Malacca's wealth and its cosmopolitan residents set the standard for luxury in Malaya for centuries to come.

AP® Exam Tip
Be able to explain the importance of port cities in the Indian Ocean trading network.

15-4 Social and Cultural Change

What social and cultural changes are reflected in the history of peoples living in tropical Africa and Asia during this period?

State growth, commercial expansion, and the spread of Islam between 1200 and 1500 led to changes in the society and cultural life of numerous peoples. Muslim political and commercial elites grew in numbers and power, and religious agents sought converts both within and beyond the boundaries of Muslim states. Yet Africa and India saw many and diverse instances of local art traditions, rituals, and even theological doctrines being combined with those of Islam to form syncretic religious formations, often in the guise of Sufi brotherhoods, reminiscent of the syncretism of the Hellenistic period (see Chapter 5).

15-4a Architecture, Learning, and Religion

Social and cultural changes typically affected cities more than rural areas. As travelers often observed, wealthy merchants and ruling elites spent lavishly on mansions, palaces, and places of worship while the lives of common people were less affected. Most mosques, local pilgrimage sites, and Sufi shrines surviving from this period blend older traditions and new influences. African Muslims produced Middle Eastern mosque designs in local building materials: sun-baked clay reinforced by wooden crossbeams in the western Sudan, masonry using blocks of coral on the Swahili Coast. Hindu temple architecture influenced, and sometimes provided material for, Muslim places of worship not only in newly Islamized regions like Gujarat, but also in older Muslim lands like Afghanistan and Iran that South Asian artisans were free to travel to once their homelands came under Muslim rule.

The congregational mosque at Cambay, built in 1325, utilized pillars, porches, and arches taken from sacked Hindu and Jain (**jine**) temples. The congregational mosque erected at the Gujarati capital of Ahmadabad (**AH-muhd-ah-bahd**) in 1423 had the open courtyard typical of mosques everywhere, but the surrounding verandas incorporated many Gujarati details and architectural conventions.

Mosques, churches, and temples were centers of education as well as prayer and ritual. Muslims promoted literacy among their sons (and sometimes their daughters) so that they could read sacred texts. In some lands south of the Sahara, Ethiopia excepted, Islam provided the first exposure to literate culture. In much of South Asia, literacy in Indo-European languages like Sanskrit and Dravidian languages like Tamil had been established many centuries before. Even there, however, a migration of Arabic and Persian vocabulary into local languages produced significant changes. Scholars adapted the Arabic alphabet to write local languages like Hausa in Mali and numerous tongues in the Malay Peninsula and island Southeast Asia.

Malacca Port city in the modern Southeast Asian country of Malaysia, founded about 1400 as a trading center on the Strait of Malacca.

Persian became the court language of the Delhi sultanate, but **Urdu (ER-doo)**, a Persian-influenced form of the local Hindustani tongue of northern India, eventually became an important literary language written in Arabic characters. Muslims also introduced paper into their new lands. Although this was an improvement over palm leaves and other fragile materials, tropical humidity and insect life nevertheless made preservation of written knowledge difficult.

Muslim scholars everywhere studied the Quran along with Islamic law and theology. A few demonstrated a high level of interest in mathematics, medicine, science, and philosophy, partly derived from ancient Greek writings translated into Arabic (see Chapter 10). In sixteenth-century **Timbuktu** (see Map 15.2), over 150 schools taught the Quran while leading clerics taught advanced classes in mosques or homes. Books imported from North Africa brought high prices. Al-Hajj Ahmed, a scholar who died in Timbuktu in 1536, possessed some 700 volumes, an unusually large library for that time. In Southeast Asia, Malacca became a center of Islamic learning from which scholars spread Islam throughout the region. Some of the most influential scholars made the pilgrimage to Mecca and studied there before returning home to teach others. Other important centers of learning developed in Muslim India, particularly in Delhi, the capital.

Even in lands seized by conquest, Muslim rulers seldom required conversion. Example and persuasion by merchants and Sufis proved more effective in winning new believers. Muslim domination of long-distance trade assisted the adoption of Islam. Commercial transactions could take place across religious boundaries, but the common code of morality and law that Islam provided encouraged trust and drew many local merchants to Islam. From the major trading centers along the Swahili Coast, in the Sudan, in coastal India, and in Southeast Asia, Islam's influence spread along regional trade routes.

Islam also spread among rural peoples, such as the pastoral Fulani of West Africa and the Somali of northeastern Africa. In Bengal, Muslim religious figures working for state officials oversaw the conversion of jungle into rice paddies and thereby gained converts among the people who came to work the land and inhabit the new villages. At first the new converts melded Islamic beliefs with Hindu traditions, seeing Muhammad, for example, as a manifestation of the god Vishnu. Over time, how-ever, more standard versions of Islam gained headway.

Marriage also played a role. Single Muslim men traveling to and settling in tropical Africa and Asia often married local women. Their children grew up in the paternal faith because Islamic doctrine specified the transmission of religious identity in the male line. Some wealthy men had dozens of children from up to four wives and additional slave concubines. Servants and slaves in such households normally professed Islam.

In India, Muslim invasions eliminated the last strongholds of long-declining Buddhism, including, in 1196, the great Buddhist center of study at Nalanda **(nuh-LAN-duh)** in Bihar **(bee-HAHR)**. Its manuscripts were burned and thousands of monks killed or driven into exile in Nepal and Tibet. With Buddhism reduced to a minor faith in the land of its birth, Islam emerged as India's second most important religion. Islam displaced Hinduism as the elite religion in most of maritime Southeast Asia and slowly supplanted a variety of local cults. In mainland Southeast Asia, Buddhism and Islam vied for supremacy, with Islam prevailing in the south and Buddhism prevailing farther north in Thailand, Cambodia, and Burma (Myanmar).

15-4b Social and Gender Distinctions

A growth in slavery accompanied the rising prosperity of the elites. Military campaigns in India, according to Islamic sources, reduced hundreds of thousands of Hindu "infidels" to slavery. Delhi overflowed with slaves. Sultan Ala-ud-din reportedly owned 50,000 and Firuz Shah 180,000, including 12,000 skilled artisans. Sultan Tughluq sent 100 male slaves and 100 female slaves as a gift to the emperor of China in return for a similar gift.

When African awareness of the value of gold in Mediterranean lands cut into the profitability of trans-Saharan trade, Mali and Bornu revived the trade by sending increasing numbers of slaves across the Sahara to North Africa. The expanding Ethiopian Empire regularly sent captives for sale to Aden traders at Zeila. Many *eunuchs* (castrated males) were included in this trade. According to modern estimates, Saharan and Red Sea traders sold about 2.5 million enslaved Africans between 1200 and 1500. African slaves from the Swahili Coast played conspicuous roles in the navies, armies, and administrations of some Indian states, especially in the fifteenth century. A few African slaves even reached China, where a source from about 1225 says rich families preferred gatekeepers with bodies "black as lacquer." Later Chinese paintings show Portuguese ships manned almost entirely by African seamen.

AP® Exam Tip
Identify and explain examples of cross-cultural exchanges that occurred as a result of networks of trade and communication in Afro-Eurasia.

Urdu A Persian-influenced literary form of Hindi written in Arabic characters and used as a literary language since the 1300s.

Timbuktu City on the Niger River in the modern country of Mali. It was founded by the Tuareg as a seasonal camp sometime after 1000. As part of the Mali Empire, Timbuktu became a major terminus of the trans-Saharan trade and a center of Islamic learning.

With "free" labor abundant and cheap, few slaves worked as farmers. In some places, hereditary castes of slaves dominated certain trades and military units. Indeed, the rulers of the Delhi Sultanate included a number of mamluks, or Turkic military slaves (see Chapter 10). A slave general in the western Sudan named Askia Muhammad seized control of the Songhai Empire (Mali's successor) in 1493. Less fortunate slaves, like the men and women who mined copper in Mali, did hard menial work.

Wealthy households used many slave servants. Eunuchs guarded the harems of wealthy Muslims, but women predominated as household slaves, serving also as entertainers and concubines. Some rich men aspired to having a concubine from every part of the world. One of Firuz Shah's nobles reportedly had 2,000 harem slaves, including women from Turkey and China.

Hindu legal digests and commentaries suggest that the position of Hindu women may have improved somewhat compared to earlier periods. The ancient practice of *sati* (**suh-TEE**)—that is, of a devout upper-caste widow throwing herself on her husband's funeral pyre—remained a meritorious act strongly approved by social custom. But Ibn Battuta makes it clear that sati was strictly optional. Since the Hindu commentaries devote considerable attention to the rights of widows without sons to inherit their husbands' estates, one may even conclude that sati was exceptional.

Indian parents still gave their daughters in marriage before the age of puberty, but consummation of the marriage took place only when the young woman was ready. Wives faced far stricter rules of fidelity and chastity than their husbands and could be abandoned for any serious breach. But other offenses against law and custom usually brought lighter penalties than for men. A woman's male master—father, husband, or owner—determined her status. Women seldom played active roles in commerce, ad-ministration, or religion. Differences between Muslims and Hindus on matters relating to gender were not as great as the formal religious texts of the two religious traditions would suggest. South Asian tradition tended to outweigh Muslim practices imported from Arabia and Persia.

African Islam showed similar compromises with local tradition in the area of gender. In Mali's capital, Ibn Battuta was appalled that Muslim women both free and slave did not completely cover their bodies and veil their faces when appearing in public. He considered their nakedness an offense to women's (and men's) modesty. Elsewhere in Mali, he berated a Muslim merchant from Morocco for permitting his wife to sit on a couch and chat with her male friend. The husband replied, "The association of women with men is agreeable to us and part of good manners, to which no suspicion attaches." Ibn Battuta refused to visit the merchant again.

Besides childrearing, women involved themselves with food preparation and, when not prohibited by religious restrictions, brewing. In many parts of Africa, women commonly made beer from grains or bananas. These mildly alcoholic beverages played an important part in male rituals of hospitality and relaxation.

Throughout tropical Africa and Asia, women did much of the farm work. They also toted home heavy loads of food, firewood, and water balanced on their heads. Other common female activities included making clay pots for cooking and storage and making clothing. In India, the spinning wheel, possibly a local invention, sped up the process of making thread for weaving and thus reduced the cost. Women typically spun at home, leaving weaving to men. In West Africa, women often sold agricultural products, pottery, and other craftwork in the markets.

Section Review

- Social and cultural life changed as a result of state formation, commercial expansion, and the spread of Islam.
- These changes mostly affected cities, where elites financed building programs, fostering hybrid styles of religious architecture.
- Islam spread mainly through peaceful adaptation and promoted education and scholarship.
- With rising prosperity came the expansion of slavery.
- The position of Indian women seems to have improved, and the spread of Islam did not mean adoption of Arab gender customs.

AP® Exam Tip
Explain how social categories, roles, and practices have been maintained and challenged over time.

15-5 The Western Hemisphere

What were the key differences between societies in Africa and Asia and the empires of the Aztecs and Inkas?

Though isolated from the Eastern Hemisphere by oceans that were not crossed until the end of the fifteenth century, the tropical regions of the Western Hemisphere shared many of the climatic characteristics of the Old World tropics (see earlier in this chapter). However, the region's two most powerful urbanized empires, the Aztec of Mexico and the Inka of Peru, developed at altitudes above 7,000 feet, thus experiencing lower average rainfall and temperature than is common across the tropics. They also differed in being themselves centers of civilization rather than subsidiary to dominating political and economic powers located in temperate lands to the north or south.

Mesoamerica, including lowland heavily forested areas, had witnessed a series of urbanized societies—such as the Olmec, Maya, and Toltecs—from the second millennium BCE onward, and the mountains and coastal deserts of the Andean region had an equally long sequence, including Moche, Tiwanaku, Wari, and Chimu (see Chapter 8). City building was less common in most other parts of the Western Hemisphere, though North America had areas of urbanization in the Southwest and the Ohio River valley. This suggests that most other indigenous American peoples subsisted at more basic levels as hunters and gatherers or village agriculturalists, but new archaeological discoveries in the Amazon basin may change this perception.

15-5a Mesoamerica: The Aztecs

The Mexica (**meh-SHE-ca**) were among the northern peoples who pushed into central Mexico in the wake of the Toltec collapse (see Chapter 8). As their power grew through political alliances and military conquest, they created a Mexica-dominated regional power called the Aztec Empire (see Map 15.5). At the time of their arrival the Mexica were organized as an **altepetl** (**al-TEH-peh-tel**), an ethnic state led by a tlatoani (**tlah-toh-AHN-ee**) or ruler. The altepetl, the common political building block across the region, directed the collective religious, social, and political obligations of the ethnic group. A group of **calpolli** (**cal-POH-yee**), each with up to a hundred families, served as the foundation of the altepetl, controlling land allocation, tax collection, and local religious life.

In their new environment the Mexica began to adopt the political and social practices that they found among the urbanized agriculturalists of the valley. At first, they served their more powerful neighbors as serfs and mercenaries. As their strength grew, they relocated to small islands near the shore of Lake Texcoco, and around 1325 CE they began the construction of their twin capitals, **Tenochtitlan** (**teh-noch-TIT-lan**) and Tlatelolco (**tla-teh-LOHL-coh**) (together the foundation for modern Mexico City).

Military successes allowed the Mexica to seize control of additional agricultural land along the lakeshore and to forge military alliances with neighboring altepetl. Once these more complex political and economic arrangements were in place, the Mexica-dominated alliance became the Aztec Empire (see Map 15.5). With increased economic independence, greater political security, and territorial expansion, the **Aztecs** transformed their political organization by introducing a monarchical system similar to that found in more powerful neighboring states and selecting a ruling dynasty with ties to the Toltecs (see Chapter 8). A council of powerful aristocrats selected new rulers from among male members of the ruling lineage. Once selected, the ruler had to renegotiate the submission of tribute dependencies and then demonstrate his divine mandate by undertaking a new round of military conquests. For the Aztecs war was infused with religious meaning, providing the ruler with legitimacy and increasing the prestige of successful warriors.

The Aztecs succeeded in developing a remarkable urban landscape. The population of Tenochtitlan and Tlatelolco combined with that of the cities and towns of the surrounding lakeshore was approximately 500,000 by 1500 CE. Three causeways connected this island capital to the lakeshore. Planners laid out the urban center as a grid where canals and streets intersected at right angles to facilitate the movement of people and goods.

Although warfare gave increased power and privilege to males, women held substantial power and exercised broad influence in Aztec society. The roles of women and men were clearly distinguished, but women were held in high esteem. Scholars call this "gender complementarity." Following the birth of a boy, his umbilical cord was buried on the battlefield and he was given implements to signal his occupation or his role as a warrior. In the case of a girl, her umbilical cord was buried near the hearth and she was given weaving implements and female clothing. Women dominated the household and the markets, and they also served as teachers and priestesses. They were also seen as the founders of lineages, including the royal line.

Aztec military successes and territorial expansion allowed the warrior elite to seize land and peasant labor as spoils of war. In time, the royal family and the highest-ranking members of the

AP® Exam Tip
Compare the imperial system created by the Aztecs with other imperial systems used in the Americas and Afro-Eurasia.

altepetl An ethnic state in ancient Mesoamerica, the common political building block of that region.

calpolli A group of up to a hundred families that served as a social building block of an altepetl in ancient Mesoamerica.

Tenochtitlan Capital of the Aztec Empire, located on an island in Lake Texcoco. Its population was about 125,000 on the eve of Spanish conquest. Mexico City was constructed on its ruins.

Aztecs Also known as Mexica, the Aztecs created a powerful empire in central Mexico (1325–1521 CE). They forced defeated peoples to provide goods and labor as a tax.

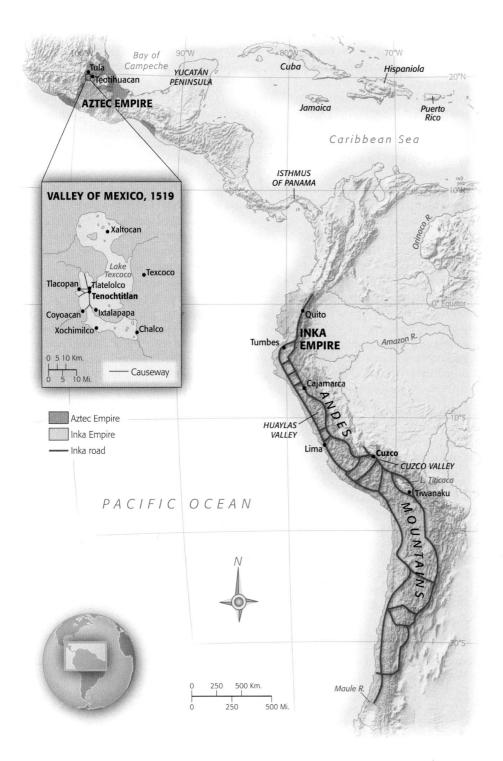

MAP 15.5 Major Mesoamerican Civilizations, 1000 BCE–1519 CE The Aztec Empire in 1518 was based on military conquest. The Aztec capital of Tenochtitlan was located near the classic era's largest city, Teotihuacan, and Tula, capital city of the postclassic Toltecs.

How did a near absence of islands affect contacts between developed areas on the Pacific coast, as opposed to the Caribbean region?

aristocracy possessed extensive estates that were cultivated by slaves and landless commoners. The lower classes received some material rewards from imperial expansion but lost most of their ability to influence or control decisions. Some commoners were able to achieve a degree of social mobility through success on the battlefield.

However, by 1500 CE great inequalities in wealth and privilege characterized Aztec society. One of the Spaniards who participated in the conquest of the Aztec Empire remembered his first meeting with the Aztec ruler Moctezuma (**mock-teh-ZU-ma**) II (r. 1502–1520): "Many great lords walked before the great Montezuma [Moctezuma II], sweeping the ground on which he was to tread and laying down cloaks so that his feet should not touch the earth. Not one of these chieftains dared look him in the face."[3] While commoners lived in small dwellings and ate a limited diet of staples, members of the nobility lived in large, well-constructed, two-story houses and consumed a diet rich in animal protein.

A specialized class of merchants controlled long-distance trade. Given the absence of draft animals and wheeled vehicles, lightweight and valuable products like gold, jewels, feathered garments, cacao beans, and animal skins dominated this commerce. Merchants also provided essential political and military intelligence for the Aztec elite. But although merchants became wealthy and powerful as the Aztecs expanded their empire, they were denied the privileges of the high nobility, which was jealous of its power.

The Aztec state met the challenge of feeding an urban population of approximately 150,000 by efficiently organizing the labor of the calpolli and of additional laborers sent by defeated peoples to expand agricultural land. Aztec *chinampas* (artificial island gardens) contributed maize, fruits, and vegetables to the markets of Tenochtitlan. The imposition of a **tribute system** on conquered peoples also helped relieve some of the pressure of Tenochtitlan's growing population. Unlike the tribute system of Tang China, where tribute had a more symbolic character (see Chapter 12), one-quarter of the Aztec capital's food requirement was satisfied by tribute payments of maize, beans, and other foods sent by nearby political dependencies.

Like commerce throughout the Mesoamerican world, Aztec commerce was carried on without money and credit. Barter was facilitated by the use of cacao beans, quills filled with gold, and cotton cloth as standard units of value to compensate for differences in the value of bartered goods. Aztec expansion facilitated the integration of producers and consumers in the central Mexican economy. Hernán Cortés (1485–1547), the Spanish adventurer who eventually conquered the Aztecs, expressed his admiration for the abundance of the Aztec marketplace:

> One square in particular is twice as big as that of Salamanca and completely surrounded by arcades where there are daily more than sixty thousand folk buying and selling. Every kind of merchandise such as may be met with in every land is for sale.... There is nothing to be found in all the land which is not sold in these markets, for over and above what I have mentioned there are so many and such various things that on account of their very number ... I cannot detail them.[4]

Religious rituals dominated public life in Tenochtitlan. Like the other cultures of the Mesoamerican world, the Aztecs worshiped a large number of gods. Most of these gods had a dual nature—both male and female. The chief god of the Mexica was Huitzilopochtli (**wheat-zeel-oh-POSHT-lee**) or southern hummingbird. Originally associated with war, the Aztecs later identified this god with the Sun. Tenochtitlan was architecturally dominated by a great twin temple devoted to Huitzilopochtli and Tlaloc, the storm-god, symbolizing the two bases of the Aztec economy: war and agriculture.

15-5b **The Andes: The Inka**

In little more than a hundred years, the **Inka** developed a vast imperial state, which they called "Land of Four Corners." By 1525 the empire had a population of more than 6 million and stretched from the Maule River in Chile to northern Ecuador, conquered between 1500 and 1525, and from the Pacific coast across the Andes to the upper Amazon and, in the south, into Argentina (see Map 15.5).

In the early fifteenth century the Inka had been one of many competing military powers in the southern highlands, an area of limited political significance after the collapse of Wari (see Chapter 8). Centered in the valley of Cuzco, the Inka were initially organized as a chiefdom based on reciprocal gift giving and the redistribution of food and textiles. Strong and resourceful leaders consolidated political authority in the 1430s and undertook an ambitious campaign of military expansion.

The Inka state, like earlier highland powers, utilized traditional Andean social customs and economic practices. Tiwanaku had relied in part on the use of colonists to provide supplies of

AP® Exam Tip
Understand and compare the role and importance of coerced labor systems, such as the *mit'a*.

tribute system A system in which defeated peoples were forced to pay a tax in the form of goods and labor. This forced transfer of food, cloth, and other goods subsidized the development of large cities. An important component of the Aztec and Inka economies.

Inka Also called the Inca, largest and most powerful Andean empire. Controlled the Pacific coast of South America from Ecuador to Chile from its capital of Cuzco.

---

[3]Bernal Díaz del Castillo, *The Conquest of New Spain*, trans. J. M. Cohen (London, UK: Penguin Books, 1963), 217.

[4]Hernando Cortés, *Five Letters, 1519–1526*, trans. J. Bayard Morris (New York, NY: Norton, 1991), 87.

resources from distant, ecologically distinct zones. The Inka built on this legacy by conquering additional distant territories and increasing the scale of forced exchanges. Crucial to this process was the development of a large military. Unlike the peoples of Mesoamerica, who distributed specialized goods through markets and tribute relationships, Andean peoples used state power to broaden and expand the vertical exchange system that had permitted self-governing extended family groups called *ayllus* to exploit a range of ecological niches (see Chapter 8). Like earlier highland civilizations, the Inka were pastoralists, and their prosperity and military strength depended on vast herds of llamas and alpacas, which provided food and clothing as well as transport for goods. They gained access to corn, cotton, and other goods from the coastal region via forced exchanges.

Collective efforts by *mita* labor, a system of forced service to the ruler (see Chapter 8), made the Inka Empire possible. Cuzco, the imperial capital, and the provincial cities, the royal court, the imperial armies, and the state's religious cults all rested on this foundation. The mita system also created the material surplus that provided the bare necessities for the old, weak, and ill of Inka society. Each ayllu contributed approximately one-seventh of its adult male population to meet these collective obligations. These draft laborers served as soldiers, construction workers, craftsmen, and runners to carry messages along post roads. They also drained swamps, terraced mountainsides, filled in valley floors, built and maintained irrigation works, and built storage facilities and roads. Inka laborers constructed 13,000 miles (20,930 kilometers) of road, facilitating military troop movements, administration, and trade.

▲ **Inka Tunic** Andean weavers produced beautiful textiles from cotton and from the wool of llamas and alpacas. The Inka inherited this rich craft tradition and produced some of the world's most remarkable textiles. The quality and design of each garment indicated the weaver's rank and power in this society. This tunic was an outer garment for a powerful male. Werner Forman/Universal Images Group/Getty Images

The hereditary chiefs of ayllus, a group that included women, carried out local administrative and judicial functions. As the Inka expanded, they generally left local rulers in place. By doing so they risked rebellion, but they controlled these risks by means of a thinly veiled system of hostage taking and the use of military garrisons. The rulers of defeated regions were required to send their heirs to live at the Inka royal court in Cuzco. Inka leaders even required that defeated peoples send representations of important local gods to Cuzco to be included in the imperial pantheon. These measures promoted imperial integration while at the same time provided hostages to ensure the good behavior of subject peoples.

Conquests magnified the authority of the Inka ruler and led to the creation of an imperial bureaucracy drawn from among his kinsmen. The royal family claimed descent from the Sun, the primary Inka god. Members of the royal family lived in palaces maintained by armies of servants, and their lives were dominated by political and religious rituals that helped legitimize their authority. Among the many obligations associated with kingship was the requirement to extend imperial boundaries by warfare. Thus each new ruler began his reign with conquest.

Tenochtitlan, the Aztec capital, had a population of about 150,000 in 1520. At the height of Inka power in 1530, Cuzco had a population of less than 30,000. Nevertheless, Cuzco was a remarkable place. The Inka were highly skilled stone craftsmen and constructed their most impressive buildings of carefully cut stones fitted together without mortar. Planners laid the city out in the shape of a giant *puma* (a mountain lion). At the city center were the palaces of rulers as well as the major temples. The richest was the Temple of the Sun, its interior lined with sheets of gold and its patio decorated with golden representations of llamas and corn. The ruler made every effort to awe and intimidate visitors and residents alike with a nearly continuous series of rituals, feasts, and sacrifices. Sacrifices of textiles, animals, and other goods sent as tribute dominated

AP® Exam Tip
Understand how the Inka road system demonstrates how commercial growth was facilitated by state practices.

Section Review

- The Western Hemisphere tropics, unlike the temperate zones, were major centers of civilization.

- The Aztecs used conquest, trade, and an extensive irrigation system to build a mighty empire.

- Religion and sacrifice played an important role in Aztec life.

- The Inka relied on forced labor, conquest, and an extensive road system to hold together a diverse empire.

- Vertical exchange of highland products for lowland products benefited everyone in the empire.

AP® Exam Tip
Be able to explain several different systems of record keeping and where they originated.

the city's calendar. The destruction of these valuable commodities, and a small number of human sacrifices, helped give the impression of splendor and sumptuous abundance that appeared to demonstrate the ruler's claimed descent from the Sun.

Inka cultural achievement rested on the strong foundation of earlier Andean civilizations. We know that astronomical observation was a central concern of the priestly class, as in Mesoamerica. The collective achievements of Andean peoples were accomplished with a limited record-keeping system adapted from earlier Andean civilizations. Administrators used knotted colored cords, called **khipus** (**KEE-pooz**), for public administration, population counts, and tribute obligations. Inka weaving and metallurgy, also based on earlier regional development, was more advanced than in Mesoamerica. Inka craftsmen produced utilitarian tools and weapons of copper and bronze as well as decorative objects of gold and silver. Inka women produced textiles of extraordinary beauty from cotton and the wool of llamas and alpacas.

Although the Inka did not introduce new technologies, they increased economic output and added to the region's prosperity. The conquest of large populations in environmentally distinct regions allowed the Inka to multiply the yields produced by the traditional exchanges between distinct ecological niches. This expansion of imperial economic and political power was purchased at the cost of reduced equality and diminished local autonomy. Members of the imperial elite, living in richly decorated palaces in Cuzco and other urban centers, were increasingly distant from the masses of Inka society. Even members of the provincial nobility were held at arm's length from the royal court, while commoners could be executed if they dared to look directly at the ruler's face.

After only a century of regional dominance, the Inka Empire faced a crisis in 1525. The death of the ruler Huayna Capac at the conclusion of the conquest of Ecuador initiated a bloody struggle for the throne. The rivalry of two sons compelled both the professional military and the hereditary Inka elite to choose sides. Civil war was the result. Regionalism and ethnic diversity had always posed a threat to the empire. Now civil war weakened the imperial state and ignited the resentments of conquered peoples on the eve of the arrival of Europeans.

15.6 Conclusion

Tropical Africa and Asia contained 40 percent of the world's population and over a quarter of its habitable land. Between 1200 and 1500, commercial, political, and cultural currents drew the region's peoples closer together. The Indian Ocean became the world's most important and richest trading area; the Delhi Sultanate brought the greatest political unity to India since the decline of the Guptas; and Mali extended the political and trading role pioneered by Ghana in the western Sudan. Trade and empire followed closely the enlargement of Islam's presence and the accompanying diversification of Islamic customs.

Yet many social and cultural practices remained stable. Most tropical Africans and Asians never ventured far outside the rural communities where their families had lived for generations. Their lives followed the patterns of agricultural or pastoral life, the cycle of religious observations, traditional occupational and kinship divisions, and the individual's passage through the stages of life from childhood to elder status. Village communities proved remarkably hardy. They might be ravaged by natural disaster or pillaged by advancing armies, but over time most recovered. Empires and kingdoms rose and fell, but village life endured.

In the Western Hemisphere the powerful empires of the Aztecs and Inka rose in Mesoamerica and the Andean region, respectively. Each was heir to a series of preceding cultures in their area, but they had in common an unprecedented territorial extent. Warfare and religious rituals were hallmarks of both empires, and their success depended on the economic subordination of conquered peoples as well as specialized production in a variety of environmentally distinct regions. The Aztecs excelled at irrigation and trade, the Inka at labor organization and road building.

khipus System of knotted colored cords used by preliterate Andean peoples to transmit information.

Key Terms

Ibn Battuta p. 367	Gujarat p. 376	Urdu p. 384	tribute system p. 388
tropics p. 367	dhows p. 379	Timbuktu p. 384	Inka p. 388
monsoon p. 368	Swahili Coast p. 380	altepetl p. 386	khipus p. 390
Delhi Sultanate p. 371	Great Zimbabwe p. 381	calpolli p. 386	
Mali p. 372	Aden p. 381	Tenochtitlan p. 386	
Mansa Kankan Musa p. 372	Malacca p. 383	Aztecs p. 386	

Review Questions

1. How does the vacationer's stereotype of "tropical" meaning sunshine, relaxation, and unchanging lifestyles compare with the reality of the tropics?

2. Why might the Western Hemisphere tropics have developed as centers of imperial power while the Eastern Hemisphere tropics rarely did so?

3. How does the Indian Ocean differ from the Mediterranean Sea or South China Sea as a trading zone?

 MINDTAP From Cengage   MindTap® is a fully online, personalized learning experience built upon Cengage Learning content. MindTap® combines student learning tools–readings, multimedia, activities, and assessments–into a singular Learning Path that guides students through the course and helps students develop the critical thinking, analysis, and communication skills that are essential to academic and professional success.

AP® REVIEW QUESTIONS FOR CHAPTER 15

Multiple-Choice Questions

Questions 1–3 refer to the passage below.

"The people of Dhufar are traders and have no other means of livelihood. When a ship arrives from India, the sultan's slaves go out to meet it in little boats, taking a full set of robes for the owner and captain, as well as for the kirani, the ship's accountant. . . . Everyone on board is granted hospitality for three days; when the three days are up, they are fed in the sultan's residence. The people do this in order to win the friendship of the ship-owners. They [the Indians] wear cotton clothes imported from India, fastening a length of cloth around their waist in place of trousers.... They manufacture silk, cotton and linen cloth of excellent quality."

> Ibn Battuta's description of Dhufar, on the coast of the Arabian Peninsula, now in Oman, 1331

1. Which of the following statements can be best corroborated by Ibn Battuta's report from the Arabian Peninsula?

   (A) Indian merchants dominated trade in the region.

   (B) A thriving economy of trade and cross-cultural exchange existed in the region.

   (C) Ship owners were considered the most important members of society.

   (D) The people of Dhufar were poor in comparison to the Indian sailors.

2. Ibn Battuta's account demonstrates the importance of which of the following in Indian Ocean society?

   (A) The remnants of earlier society navigational technology

   (B) The textile manufacturing industry of India and China

   (C) The social hierarchy that existed on the Arabian Peninsula

   (D) The role of married women in Arab society

3. Letters like the one above demonstrate which of the following about the exchange of knowledge in the growing trade networks?

   (A) Only economic records of trade can be relied upon to provide unbiased accounts.

   (B) Illiterate societies turned to art and architecture to communicate shared values.

   (C) Systematic governmental control made sure reports were favorable to all parties.

   (D) The increasing number of traveler reports helped facilitate global knowledge about other regions.

Questions 4–7 refer to the passage below.

"The houses of Timbuktu are huts made of clay-covered wattles with thatched roofs. In the center of the city is a temple built of stone and mortar, built by an architect named Granata, and in addition there is a large palace, constructed by the same architect, where the king lives. The shops of the artisans, the merchants, and especially weavers of cotton cloth are very numerous. Fabrics are also imported from Europe to Timbuktu, borne by Berber merchants.

The women of the city maintain the custom of veiling their faces, except for the slaves who sell all the foodstuffs. The inhabitants are very rich, especially the strangers who have settled in the country.

Grain and animals are abundant, so that the consumption of milk and butter is considerable. But salt is in very short supply because it is carried here from Taghaza, some 500 miles from Timbuktu. I happened to be in this city at a time when a load of salt sold for eighty ducats."

> Leo Africanus, a diplomat from al-Andalus, Spain, describes Timbuktu, ca. 1510, from his book, *Description of Africa*

4. What can be ascertained about Timbuktu in the early sixteenth century from the description of Leo Africanus?

    (A) The city was an important trading center.

    (B) Islam was the most important religion in Timbuktu.

    (C) There were many female slaves in Timbuktu.

    (D) The diet of the people of Timbuktu was limited.

5. Which of the following best describes the sociodemographic characteristics of Timbuktu in the early sixteenth century?

    (A) There were more slaves than there were artisans in the city.

    (B) Traders had settled in diasporic communities in parts of the city.

    (C) Most people lived in the center of the city close to the palace.

    (D) Women played a merely domestic role in Timbuktu.

6. Which of the following is a reasonable explanation for the spread of Islam to West African cities like Timbuktu?

    (A) Muslim missionaries established Muslim monasteries and convents in major cities.

    (B) Slaves traded to Mali brought their religion and transferred it to their owners.

    (C) Mansa Musa promised a share of his extreme wealth to anyone who converted.

    (D) Traders and Muslim Berbers brought Islam with them to commercial contacts beyond the Sahara Desert.

7. Which of the following is an evidence of cross-cultural exchange similar to that found in Timbuktu in the period between 1200 and 1500?

    (A) The development of African-inspired musical tones in northern Europe

    (B) The development of Urdu, which combined Arabic characters with local Hindustani language in Delhi

    (C) The introduction of new crops such as potatoes from the Americas to the Sahel region

    (D) Significant increase in European religious influence along the west coast of Africa

Questions 8–10 refer to map on the next page.

8. By examining the map, what can a historian ascertain about the Indian Ocean region, ca. 1500?

    (A) There was limited knowledge of the region's contact with Asia's interior.

    (B) Trade was flourishing and powerful trading cities had developed.

    (C) The greatest threat to trade in the region came from wild animals.

    (D) Arabs dominated the commerce of the region due to their superior technology.

9. Which of the following was true of those conducting Indian Ocean trade by the early 1500s?

    (A) Traders no longer used the monsoon winds when crossing the Indian Ocean, but focused entirely on midocean currents.

    (B) Long-distance trade was dominated by merchants who shared the same culture and remained within specific regional spheres.

    (C) Trade was hindered by the lack of understanding of ocean currents and navigation, making all transportation short distance and limited.

    (D) Marine commerce was conducted by traders from multiple regions, making the area a center for cultural exchange.

10. How was trade in the Indian Ocean in the period from 1200 to 1500 similar to that of the land trade through the Silk Roads?

    (A) The trade relied heavily on slavery and other coercive labor systems.

    (B) Epidemics carried on ships constantly ravaged both the Swahili Coast and India.

    (C) The trade was mainly in luxury goods such as gold, ivory, and spices.

    (D) Trade remained hazardous due to environmental disasters, pirates, and political instability.

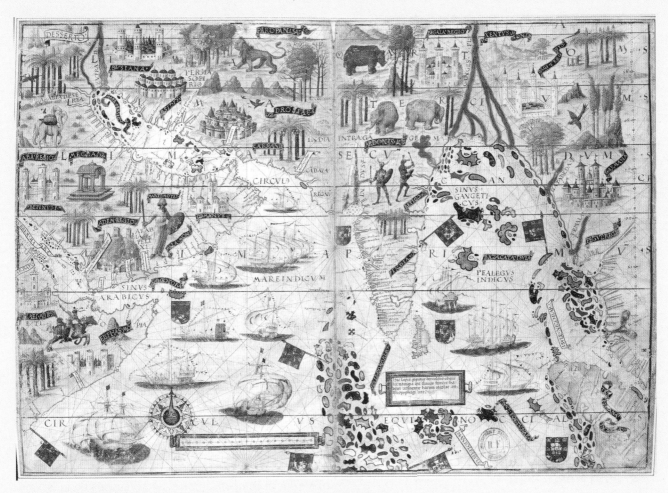

▲ **A map from the Portuguese Miller Atlas, ca. 1519, showing the Indian Ocean.** The Print Collector/Alamy Stock Photo

Short-Answer Questions

1. Use the image below and your knowledge of world history to answer all parts of the question that follows.

   (A) Identify ONE impact of gender on the Aztec way of life.

   (B) Explain ONE way the Aztec rose to power in Mesoamerica in the fourteenth century.

   (C) Explain ONE way the Inka rose to power in the Andes in the fifteeenth century.

2. Answer all parts of the question that follows.

   (A) Identify ONE specific example of the spread of Islam in sub-Saharan Africa between 1200 and 1500.

   (B) Explain ONE reason for the spread of Islam in sub-Saharan Africa between 1200 and 1500.

   (C) Explain ONE result of the spread of Islam in sub-Saharan Africa between 1200 and 1500.

◀ **An Aztec feast, from *History of the Indies* by Diego Durán, 1579.** DEA/G. DAGLI ORTI/Getty Images

16

The Maritime Revolution, to 1550

AP® Framework Terms

Polynesian peoples
Portuguese maritime technology
Compass
Astrolabe
First Columbian voyage (Spain)
North Atlantic fishing
Silver

Overarching Questions

1 How and to what extent have environmental factors, disease, and technology affected patterns of human migration and settlement over time? (ENV)

2 How have cross-cultural interactions resulted in the diffusion of culture, technologies, and scientific knowledge? (CUL)

3 How and why have economic, social, cultural, and geographic factors influenced the process of state building, expansion, and dissolution? (SB)

4 How have local, regional, and global economic systems and exchange networks influenced each other over time? (ECON)

5 How have social categories, roles, and practices been maintained or challenged over time? (SOC)

I n 1511 young Ferdinand Magellan sailed from Europe around the southern tip of Africa and eastward across the Indian Ocean as a member of the first Portuguese expedition to explore the East Indies (maritime Southeast Asia). Eight years later, this time in the service of Spain, he led an expedition that sought to reach the East Indies by sailing westward. By the middle of 1521 Magellan's expedition had achieved its goal by sailing across the Atlantic, rounding the southern tip of South America, and crossing the Pacific Ocean—but at a high price.

Of the five ships that had set out from Spain in 1519, only three made the long passage across the vast Pacific. During this long voyage, dozens of sailors died from starvation and disease. Magellan survived numerous mutinies during his voyage, but died in battle on April 27, 1521, while aiding the forces of a Philippine ruler who had promised to become a Christian.

To consolidate their dwindling resources, the expedition's survivors burned the least seaworthy of their remaining three

▲ **Ferdinand Magellan Navigating the Straits Connecting the Atlantic and Pacific Oceans** This late-sixteenth-century print uses fanciful representations of native peoples and creatures to embellish Magellan's circumnavigation of the globe. INTERFOTO/Alamy Stock Photo

ships and consolidated men and supplies. In the end only the *Victoria* made it across the Indian Ocean and back to Europe. Nevertheless, the *Victoria's* return to Spain on September 8, 1522, was a crowning example of Europeans' determination to make themselves masters of the oceans. A century of daring and dangerous voyages backed by the Portuguese crown had opened new routes through the South Atlantic to Africa, Brazil, and the rich trade of the Indian Ocean. Rival voyages sponsored by Spain since 1492 opened new contacts with the American continents. A maritime revolution was under way that would change the course of history.

This new maritime era marked the end of a long period when Asia had initiated most overland and maritime expansion. Asia had previously been the source of the world's most useful new technologies as well as the most influential systems of belief. Asia was also home to the world's most powerful states and the richest trading networks. The success of Iberian voyages of exploration in the following century would redirect the world's center of power, wealth, and innovation from Asia to the West.

This maritime revolution broadened and deepened contacts, alliances, and conflicts across ancient cultural boundaries. Some of these contacts would prove disastrous for entire populations: Amerindians, for instance, suffered conquest, colonization, and a rapid decline in numbers. And sometimes the results were mixed: Asians and Africans found both risks and opportunities in their new relations with Europe. ●

16-1 **Global Maritime Expansion Before 1450**

What were the objectives and major accomplishments of the voyages of exploration undertaken by Chinese, Polynesians, and other non-Western peoples?

Since ancient times travel across the world's seas and oceans had been one of the great challenges to technological ingenuity. Ships had to be sturdy enough to survive heavy winds and seas, and pilots had to learn how to cross featureless expanses of water to reach their destinations. In time, ships, sails, and navigational techniques perfected in the more protected seas were adapted to open oceans.

However complex and expensive the new technologies and regardless of the dangers of these long-distance voyages, the rewards of sea travel and commerce made them worthwhile. Ships could move goods and people more profitably than any form of overland travel then possible. Crossing unknown waters, finding new lands, developing new markets, discovering new commodities, and establishing new settlements attracted adventurers from every continent. By 1450 daring mariners had discovered and settled most of the islands of the Pacific, the Atlantic, and the Indian Ocean, but no one had yet crossed the Pacific in either direction. Even the smaller Atlantic remained a barrier to contact between the Americas, Europe, and Africa. The inhabitants of Australia were also nearly cut off from contact with the rest of humanity. All this was about to change.

16-1a **The Indian Ocean**

AP® Exam Tip
Understand the connection between migrations and the diffusion of cultural elements.

The archipelagos and coastal regions of Southeast Asia were connected in networks of trade and cultural exchange from an early date. While the region was divided politically, culturally, and religiously, the languages of Malaysia, Indonesia, and the Philippines—as well as coastal regions of Thailand, southern Vietnam, Cambodia, and Hainan, China—all originated from a common Austronesian linguistic root. Scholars often use the term *Malayo Indonesians* or *Malay* to describe the early peoples of this maritime realm.

The region's sailors were highly skilled navigators as well as innovative shipbuilders and sail makers who, in addition to their own achievements, influenced later Chinese and Arab maritime advances. Around 350 they discovered two direct sea routes between Sri Lanka and the South China Sea through the Straits of Malacca and Sunda, thus opening a profitable link to China's silk markets. They were also the first to use the seasonal monsoon winds of the Indian Ocean to extend their voyages for thousands of miles, ultimately reaching East Africa and settling in Madagascar.

By the first century CE the mariners and merchants of India and Southeast Asia were trading across the region for spices, gold, and aromatic woods, even sending spices as far west as Rome through Mediterranean intermediaries (see Chapter 7). Their success attracted African, Arab, and Chinese mariners and merchants into the region, creating a large, integrated, and highly profitable market in the centuries that followed. By 1000 the dhows (**dow**) of Arabs and Africans, as well as Malay *jongs* and Chinese junks, came together in the region's harbors for commerce.

The rise of medieval Islam (see Chapter 10) gave Indian Ocean trade an important boost. The great Muslim cities of the Middle East provided a demand for valuable commodities, and networks of Muslim traders were active across the region. These traders shared a common language, ethic, and law and actively spread their religion to distant trading cities. By 1400 there were Muslim trading communities all around the Indian Ocean. Chinese merchant communities were present as well.

Indian Ocean traders largely operated outside the control of the empires and states they served, but in East Asia imperial China's rulers were growing more and more interested in these wealthy ports of trade. In 1368 the Ming dynasty overthrew Mongol rule and began to reestablish China's predominance and prestige abroad. Having restored Chinese power and influence in East Asia, the Ming moved to establish direct contacts with the peoples around the Indian Ocean, extending their authority into Vietnam through conquest and sending out seven imperial fleets between 1405 and 1433 (see Chapter 13). The enormous size of these expeditions was far

CHRONOLOGY

	Pacific Ocean	Atlantic Ocean	Indian Ocean
1400	300 BCE–1000 CE Polynesian settlement of Pacific islands By 1000 Sporadic Polynesian contacts with American mainland 1200–1300 Polynesian societies in Hawaii, Tonga, and elsewhere develop clear class structures with hereditary chiefs	770–1200 Viking voyages 1300s European settlement of Madeira, Azores, Canaries Early 1300s Mali voyages 1418–1460 Voyages of Henry the Navigator 1440s First slaves from West Africa sent to Europe 1482 Portuguese at Gold Coast and Kongo 1486 Portuguese at Benin 1488 Bartolomeu Dias reaches Indian Ocean 1492 Columbus reaches Caribbean 1492–1500 Spanish conquer Hispaniola 1493 Columbus returns to Caribbean (second voyage) 1498 Columbus reaches mainland of South America (third voyage)	350–1000 Development and integration of Southeast Asian maritime markets 1405–1433 Voyages of Zheng He 1497–1498 Vasco da Gama reaches India
1500		1500 Cabral reaches Brazil	1505 Portuguese bombard Swahili Coast cities 1510 Portuguese take Goa 1511 Portuguese take Malacca
	1519–1522 Magellan expedition	1519–1521 Cortés conquers Aztec Empire 1531–1533 Pizarro conquers Inka Empire 1536 Rebellion of Manco Inka in Peru	1515 Portuguese take Hormuz 1535 Portuguese take Diu 1538 Portuguese defeat Ottoman fleet 1539 Portuguese aid Ethiopia

larger than needed for exploration or promoting trade alone. While the Ming sought to inspire awe of their power and achievements, there were three occasions when military force was used to achieve objectives, including the defeat and capture of the king of Ceylon (now Sri Lanka). While curiosity about this prosperous region may have been a motive for these expeditions, the ports visited by the fleets were major commercial centers and some already had trade relationships with China.

The scale of the Ming expeditions to the Indian Ocean Basin reflects imperial China's resources and ambitions. The first consisted of sixty-two specially built "treasure ships," large Chinese junks each about 300 feet long by 150 feet wide (90 by 45 meters). There were also at least a hundred smaller vessels. Each treasure ship had nine masts, twelve sails, many decks, and a carrying capacity of 3,000 tons (six times the capacity of Columbus's entire fleet). One expedition carried over 27,000 crew and passengers, including infantry and cavalry troops. The ships were armed with small cannon, but in most Chinese sea battles arrows from highly accurate crossbows dominated the fighting.

Admiral **Zheng He (jung huh)** (1371–1435) commanded seven key expeditions, but additional fleets were organized and dispatched as well. A Chinese Muslim with ancestral connections to the Persian Gulf, Zheng was a fitting emissary to the increasingly Muslim-dominated Indian Ocean Basin. The expeditions carried other Arabic-speaking Chinese as interpreters like Ma Huan (see Diversity & Dominance: Understanding Cross-Cultural Encounters). He recorded local customs and beliefs in a journal, observing new flora and fauna and noting exotic

Zheng He An imperial eunuch and Muslim, entrusted by the Ming emperor Yongle with a series of state voyages that took his gigantic ships through the Indian Ocean, from Southeast Asia to Africa.

▲ **Chinese Junk**   This modern drawing shows how much larger one of Zheng He's ships was in relationship to one of Vasco da Gama's vessels. Watertight interior bulkheads increased the seaworthiness of these junks. Sails made of pleated bamboo matting hung from the junk's masts, and a stern rudder provided steering. European ships of exploration, though smaller, were faster and more maneuverable.
Gregory A. Harlin/National Geographic Stock

AP® Exam Tip
Understand the
importance of
innovations in ship
design in the expansion
of interregional trade.

animals such as the black panther of Malaya and the tapir of Sumatra. In India he described the division of the coastal population into five classes, which correspond to the four Hindu varna and a separate Muslim class. He also recorded that traders in the rich Indian trading port of Calicut (**KAL-ih-kut**) could perform error-free calculations by counting on their fingers and toes rather than using the Chinese abacus. After his return, Ma Huan went on tour in China, telling of these exotic places and "how far the majestic virtue of [China's] imperial dynasty extended."[1]

The Chinese "treasure ships" carried rich silks and other valuable goods intended as gifts for distant rulers. In return some of those rulers returned with the fleet to visit the Chinese court while others sent gifts to the Ming emperor. Although the main purpose of these exchanges was diplomatic, they also stimulated trade between China and its southern neighbors. Interest in new contacts was not limited to the Chinese.

At least three trading cities on the Swahili (**swah-HEE-lee**) Coast of East Africa sent delegations to China between 1415 and 1416. The delegates from one of them, Malindi, presented the emperor of China with a giraffe, creating quite a stir among normally reserved imperial officials. These African delegations may have encouraged more contacts because the next three of Zheng's voyages reached the African coast. Unfortunately, no documents record how Africans and Chinese reacted to each other during these historic meetings between 1417 and 1433, but it appears that China's lavish gifts stimulated the Swahili market for silk and porcelain.

Had the Ming court wished to promote trade for the profit of its merchants, Chinese fleets might have come to play a dominant role in Indian Ocean trade. But some high Chinese officials opposed increased contact with peoples whom they regarded as barbarians incapable of making contributions to China. Such opposition caused a suspension in the voyages from 1424 to 1431. The final Chinese expedition sailed between 1432 and 1433.

---

[1]Ma Huan, *Ying-yai Sheng-lan: "The Overall Survey of the Ocean's Shores,"* ed. Feng Ch'eng-Chün, trans. J. V. G. Mills (Cambridge, UK: Cambridge University Press, 1970), 180.

While later Ming emperors would focus their attention on internal matters, long-established Chinese merchant communities continued as major participants in Indian Ocean trade, contributing to the rapid growth of prosperous commercial *entrepôts* (**ON-truh-pohs**) (places where goods are stored or deposited and from which they are distributed) throughout the region. As the sultan of one of the most prosperous trade centers, Melaka (in modern Malaysia), described the era in 1468, "We have learned that to master the blue oceans people must engage in commerce and trade. All the lands within the seas are united in one body. Life has never been so affluent in preceding generations as it is today."[2]

16-1b The Pacific Ocean

Around 3000 BCE seafaring peoples from Southeast Asia reached the island of New Guinea. Sustained contact between these Austronesian-speaking migrants and the island's original population accelerated agricultural development and led to a population expansion that propelled migration to and settlement of nearby islands. The descendants of these peoples, called Lapita by archaeologists, eventually forged a new cultural identity as they colonized the island chains of Melanesia (**mel-uh-NEE-zhuh**). Lapita settlers finally arrived as settlers in Tonga, Fiji, and Samoa between 1000 and 800 BCE.

By 500 BCE a linguistically and culturally distinct Polynesian culture began to emerge from this Lapita origin. Over the following centuries Polynesian peoples would prove to be among the world's most adventurous long-distance voyagers. While the dates for Polynesian discovery and colonization of the remote islands of the Pacific are still debated, their mastery of long-distance maritime exploration in an era when European sailors still feared to stray far from shore is undeniable. Flourishing Polynesian populations pushed east from Tonga, Samoa, and Fiji to colonize the Marquesas (**mar-KAY-suhs**) and the Cook and Society archipelagos sometime before 800 CE.

Polynesians soon launched a second wave of discovery and settlement. Samoa and Tonga provided most of the voyagers and settlers but some voyages sailed from the Marquesas as well. Eventually, these voyages led to the peopling of the most remote areas of the Pacific. Polynesians established settlements on the Hawaiian Islands, roughly 2,300 miles (3,701 kilometers) from the Marquesas and 2,566 miles (4,114 kilometers) from Samoa, around 800 CE. Risky long-distance voyages were soon organized to the southeast and southwest from the Polynesian heartland.

While Polynesian society and political life was generally organized around villages controlled by hereditary chiefs, the Tongan polity established control of the entire archipelago by around 1000 CE and, as a result, had the resources to project its power over long distances. Despite these Tongan advantages, sailing and navigational skills were broadly distributed across this cultural area and Polynesian seafarers from Tahiti and the Marquesas often mixed fishing and regional trading voyages with longer distance exploratory voyages and colonizing ventures.

Recent radiocarbon measurements have forced us to revise the timeline for the discovery and settlement of the island groups furthest from the Polynesian homelands of Tonga and Samoa after 1000 CE. Polynesian colonists, most likely setting off from the Marquesas, settled Easter Island, 2,275 miles (3,662 kilometers) away around 1200 CE. Scientists estimate that around this same time Polynesian settlers also arrived in New Zealand having sailed from the Cook and Society Islands 2,009 miles (3,233 kilometers) away.[3] More impressive still, Polynesian voyagers also made periodic contact with the mainland of South America after 1000 CE, passing on the domesticated Asian chicken and returning home with the sweet potato, an American domesticate that soon became a staple throughout the Pacific region. Contacts were maintained among these distant colonies and the Polynesian homeland, with the possible exceptions of Easter Island and New Zealand, until around 1400 CE when these links were ruptured, an event that accelerated the development of distinct regional cultures and dialects.

AP® Exam Tip
Understand the environmental impact of Polynesian peoples who cultivated transplanted foods and domesticated animals as they moved to new islands.

---

[2]Quotation in Craig A. Lockard, "'The Sea Common to All': Maritime Frontiers, Port Cities, and Chinese Traders in the Southeast Asian Age of Commerce, ca. 1400–1750," *Journal of World History* 21, no. 2 (2010): 228.

[3] The estimates for the Polynesian settlement of the Pacific islands used here follow closely the radiocarbon-based research reported in Terry L. Hunt and Carl P. Lipo, "Late Colonization of Easter Island," *Science*, 311:5767 (March 17, 2006), 1603–1606.

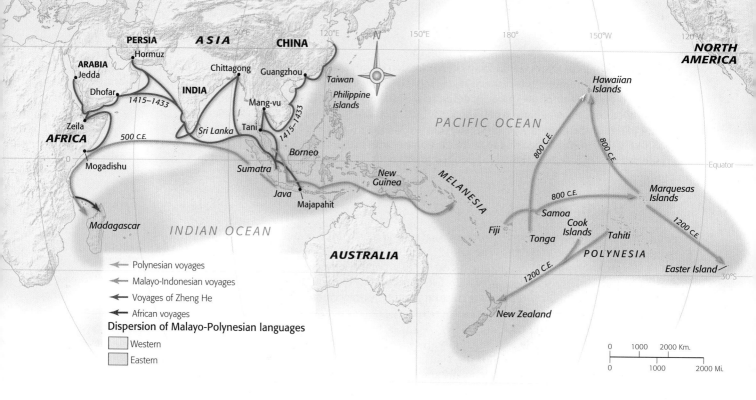

MAP 16.1   Exploration and Settlement in the Indian and Pacific Oceans Before 1500 Over many centuries, mariners originating in Southeast Asia gradually colonized the islands of the Pacific and Indian Oceans. The Chinese voyages led by Zheng He in the fifteenth century were lavish official expeditions.

How did the organization and objectives of Zheng He's voyages differ from those of the Polynesians?

Both DNA evidence and linguistic evidence make clear that the Polynesian settlement of the islands of the eastern Pacific was largely the result of purposeful voyages and not the result of accidental drifting, although storms could have forced some outrigger canoes hundreds of miles off course as a part of this larger experience of adventure and discovery. Following voyages of reconnaissance, Polynesian mariners carried colonizing expeditions in fleets of large double-hulled canoes that relied on scores of paddlers as well as sails. Their largest canoes reached 120 feet (37 meters) in length and carried crews of up to fifty. A wide platform connected the two hulls of these crafts and permitted the transportation of animals and plants crucial to the success of distant and isolated settlements. Long-range expeditions included both men and women and sometimes children. DNA evidence from New Zealand, for example, indicates that the original settlers of New Zealand included one hundred women. The Voyagers carried the staples of Polynesian diet with them: pigs, dogs, and chickens as well as domesticated plants such as taro, bananas, yams, and breadfruit. They also unintentionally carried rats that thrived in the virgin territories of the Pacific. The success of these voyages depended upon reliably navigating across thousands of miles of ocean using careful observation of the currents, stars, and flocks of birds as the crews searched for evidence of land (see Map 16.1). Without a doubt many lives were lost along the way.

While all Polynesian societies descended from the same originating culture and all began with the same tools and the same farming and fishing technologies, significant differences in the geography and climate of the islands they came to inhabit and the isolation of the most distant, like Easter Island and Hawaii, led inexorably to the development of unique societies. Most Polynesian communities depended on farming and fishing, but the intensity of these practices depended on local conditions. In Hawaii, for example, low-lying native forests were converted to farmland using controlled burns, and fishponds were built to increase fish yields. As a result, the Polynesian communities of this archipelago thrived into the era of European expansion.

The most hierarchical social structures and political systems among Polynesians developed in the Hawaiian and Tongan archipelagos, where powerful hereditary chiefs controlled the lives of commoners and managed resources. In these locations, as well as in New Zealand, competition among chiefs led to violence and chronic warfare. On Easter Island, the most isolated of the Polynesian colonies, the combination of population growth, deforestation, and soil erosion intensified this competition, leading ultimately to a brutal cycle of warfare that drastically reduced the population.

16-1c The Atlantic Ocean

The Vikings were the greatest mariners of the Atlantic in the early Middle Ages. These northern European raiders used their small, open ships to attack Europe's coastal settlements for several centuries. Like the Polynesians, the Vikings used their knowledge of the heavens and the seas rather than maps and other navigational devices to find their way over long distances.

The Vikings first settled Iceland in 770 and established a colony on Greenland in 982. By accident one group of Viking voyagers sighted North America in 986. Fifteen years later Leif Ericsson established a short-lived Viking settlement on the island of Newfoundland, which he called Vinland. When the earth's climate cooled after 1200 (see Issues in World History: Climate and Population to 1500), the northern settlements in Greenland went into decline and the Vikings abandoned Vinland.

Some southern Europeans applied maritime skills acquired in the Mediterranean and along the North Atlantic coast to explore to the south. Genoese and Portuguese expeditions pushed into the Atlantic in the fourteenth century, eventually exploring and settling the islands of Madeira (**muh-DEER-uh**), the Azores (**A-zorz**), and the Canaries.

There is some evidence of African voyages of exploration in this period. The celebrated Syrian geographer al-Umari (1301–1349) relates that when Mansa Kankan Musa (**MAHN-suh KAHN-kahn MOO-suh**), the ruler of the West African empire of Mali, passed through Egypt on his lavish pilgrimage to Mecca in 1324, he told of voyages into the Atlantic undertaken by his predecessor, Mansa Muhammad. According to this source, Muhammad had sent out 400 vessels with men and supplies, telling them, "Do not return until you have reached the other side of the ocean or if you have exhausted your food or water." After a long time one canoe returned, reporting that the others were lost in a "violent current in the middle of the sea." Muhammad himself then set out at the head of a second, even larger, expedition, from which no one returned.

In the Americas, early Amerindian voyagers from the Caribbean coast of South America colonized the West Indies. By the year 1000 Amerindians known as the **Arawak** (**AR-uh-wahk**) (also called Taino) had pushed North following the small islands of the Lesser Antilles (Barbados, Martinique, and Guadeloupe) to the Greater Antilles (Cuba, Hispaniola, Jamaica, and Puerto Rico) as well as to the Bahamas (see Map 16.2). The Carib followed the same route in later centuries, and by the late fifteenth century they had overrun most Arawak settlements in the Lesser Antilles and were raiding parts of the Greater Antilles. Both Arawak and Carib peoples also made contact with the North American mainland.

The transfer of maize cultivation to South America after its domestication in Mesoamerica is suggestive of an early chain of contacts among Amerindian peoples, including the use of small boats along the Pacific coast. In the centuries after 100 CE there were significant ongoing maritime contacts between Pacific coast populations in South America and Mesoamerica. Mariners carried pottery, copper, gold and silver jewelry, and textiles from the coast of Ecuador north in two-masted, balsa wood rafts that measured up to 36 feet (11 meters) in length. Rafts of this size could carry more than 20 metric tons of cargo and ten or more crew members. Travel north was facilitated by the favorable winds and currents of the Pacific, but these craft had the capacity to make the return trip carrying cargos of sacred spondylus shells, although sailing southward against the wind added many months to the voyage. One important result of these contacts was the introduction of metallurgy to Mesoamerica after 500.

Arawak Amerindian peoples who inhabited the Greater Antilles of the Caribbean at the time of Columbus.

Section Review

- Polynesians explored and settled the eastern Pacific from the Marquesas to Hawaii, New Zealand, and Easter Island.

- The Indian Ocean became a center of commerce and cultural exchange. Between 1405 and 1433 Chinese Admiral Zheng He's seven expeditions established contacts with South Asian and African peoples.

- Vikings, Amerindians, and Africans also pursued long-distance explorations and settlements.

MAP 16.2   Middle America to 1533   Maritime contacts led to the settlement of the islands of the Greater and Lesser Antilles by South American peoples and to the dissemination of important technologies like metallurgy and maize agriculture along the Pacific coast. The arrival of Europeans in 1492 led to conquest and colonization.

How did the geography of the Western Hemisphere give direction to the spread of technologies and contacts among cultures?

16-2 European Expansion, 1400–1550

In this era of long-distance exploration, did Europeans have any special advantages over other cultural regions?

While the pace and intensity of maritime contacts increased in many parts of the world before 1450, the epic sea voyages sponsored by the Iberian kingdoms of Portugal and Spain are of special interest because they began a maritime revolution that profoundly altered the course of world history. The Portuguese and Spanish expeditions ended the isolation of the Americas and increased the volume of global interaction.

Iberian overseas expansion was the product of two related phenomena. First, Iberian rulers had strong economic, religious, and political motives to expand their influence. And second, improvements in maritime and military technologies gave Iberians the means to master treacherous and unfamiliar ocean environments, seize control of existing maritime trade routes, and conquer new lands.

16-2a **Motives for Exploration**

While the ambitions and adventurous personalities of the rulers of Portugal and Spain led them to sponsor voyages of exploration in the fifteenth century, these voyages built upon four trends evident in Latin Europe since about the year 1000: (1) the revival of urban life and trade, (2) the unique alliance between merchants and rulers in Europe, (3) a struggle with Islamic powers for dominance of the Mediterranean that mixed religious motives with the desire for trade, and (4) growing intellectual curiosity about the outside world.

By 1450 the city-states of northern Italy had well-established trade links to northern Europe, the Indian Ocean, and the Black Sea, and their merchant princes had also sponsored an intellectual and artistic Renaissance. The Italian trading states of Venice and Genoa also maintained profitable commercial ties in the Mediterranean that depended on alliances with Muslims and gave their merchants privileged access to lucrative trade from the East. Even after the expansion of the Ottoman Empire disrupted their trade to the East, these cities did not take the lead in exploring the Atlantic. However, many individual Italians played leading roles in the Atlantic explorations.

In contrast, the history and geography of the Iberian kingdoms led them in a different direction. Muslim invaders from North Africa had conquered most of Iberia in the eighth century. Centuries of warfare between Christians and Muslims followed, and by 1250 the Iberian kingdoms of Portugal, Castile, and Aragon had reconquered all of Iberia except the southern Muslim kingdom of Granada (see Chapter 14). The dynastic marriage of Isabel of Castile and Ferdinand of Aragon in 1469 facilitated the conquest of Granada in 1492 and promoted the development of a more centralized and powerful Spanish government, sixteenth-century Europe's most powerful state.

The long wars with Muslim rivals created a legacy of Christian militancy that influenced the overseas ventures of both Portugal and Spain. But the Iberian rulers and their adventurous subjects also sought material returns. With only a modest share of the Mediterranean trade, they were much more willing than the Italian trading states to seek new routes to the rich trade of Africa and Asia via the Atlantic. Both kingdoms participated in the shipbuilding and the gunpowder revolutions that were under way in Atlantic Europe, and both were especially open to new geographical knowledge.

AP® Exam Tip
Explain the effects of European exploration on different parts of the world.

16-2b **Portuguese Voyages**

Portugal's decision to invest significant resources in new exploration rested on its well-established Atlantic fishing industry and a history of anti-Muslim warfare. When the Muslim government of Morocco in northwestern Africa showed weakness in the fifteenth century, the Portuguese attacked, conquering the city of Ceuta (**say-OO-tuh**) in 1415. The capture of this rich North African city gave the Portuguese better intelligence of the caravans bringing gold and slaves to Ceuta from African states south of the Sahara. Militarily unable to push inland and gain direct access to the gold trade, the Portuguese sought contact with the gold producers by sailing down the African coast.

Prince Henry (1394–1460), third son of the king of Portugal, had led the attack on Ceuta. Because he devoted the rest of his life to promoting exploration, he is known as **Henry the Navigator**. His official biographer highlighted Henry's religious motives for exploration—converting Africans to Christianity, making contact with Christian rulers in Africa, and launching joint crusades with them against the Ottomans. But Prince Henry also wished to discover new places and stimulate profitable new commercial links. Early explorations focused on Africa, but gaining access to India's riches soon became the central objective of Portuguese explorers. While called "the Navigator," Henry himself never ventured far from home. Instead, he sponsored the study of navigation at Sagres (**SAH-gresh**), building on the pioneering efforts of Italian merchants and fourteenth-century Jewish cartographers. His agents collected geographical information from sailors and travelers and fostered new expeditions to explore the Atlantic. Henry's efforts established permanent contact with the Atlantic islands of Madeira in 1418 and the Azores in 1439.

AP® Exam Tip
Understand how the development of maritime technology and navigational skills by the Portuguese led to increased exploration and contact with West Africa.

Henry the Navigator
Portuguese prince who promoted the study of navigation and directed voyages of exploration down the western coast of Africa in the fifteenth century.

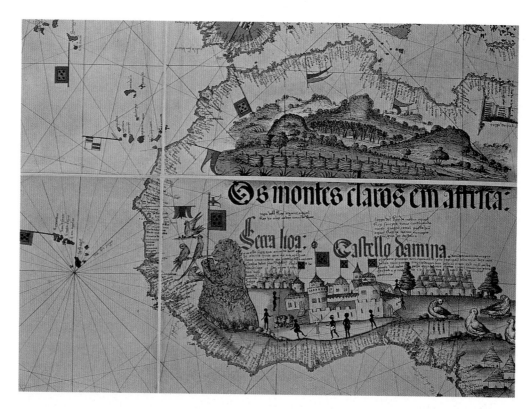

▲ **Portuguese Map of Western Africa, 1502** This map shows in great detail a section of African coastline that Portuguese explorers charted and named in the fifteenth century. The cartographer illustrated the African interior, which was almost completely unknown to Europeans, with drawings of birds and views of coastal sights: Sierra Leone (Serra lioa), named for a mountain shaped like a lion, and the Portuguese Castle of the Mine (Castello damina) on the Gold Coast. akg-images

AP® Exam Tip
Identify examples of innovations in ship design and explain how these innovations contributed to European transoceanic travel.

Henry's staff also improved navigational instruments that had been first developed elsewhere. These instruments included the magnetic compass, first developed in China, and the astrolabe, an instrument of Arab or Greek invention that enabled mariners to determine their location at sea by measuring the position of the sun or the stars in the night sky. Even with such instruments, however, voyages still depended on the skill and experience of navigators.

Portuguese mariners also developed vessels appropriate for voyages of long-distance exploration. Neither the galleys in use in the Mediterranean, powered by both sails and large numbers of oarsmen, nor the three-masted ships of northern Europe with their square sails proved adequate for the Atlantic. The large crews of the galleys could not carry enough supplies for long voyages and the square-rigged northern vessels had trouble sailing at an angle to the wind. Instead, the voyages of exploration made use of a new vessel, the **caravel** (**KAR-uh-vel**), that was much smaller than either the largest European ships or the Chinese junks Zheng used to explore the Indian Ocean. Their size permitted them to enter shallow coastal waters and explore upriver, but they were strong enough to weather ocean storms. They could be equipped with triangular lateen sails that could take the wind on either side for enhanced maneuverability or fitted with square Atlantic sails for greater speed in a following wind. The addition of small cannon made them good fighting ships as well. The caravels' economy, speed, agility, and power justified a contemporary's claim that they were "the best ships that sailed the seas."[4]

Pioneering captains had to overcome the common fear that South Atlantic waters were boiling hot or contained ocean currents that would prevent any ship entering them from ever returning home. It took Prince Henry fourteen years—from 1420 to 1434—to coax an expedition

caravel A small, highly maneuverable three-masted ship used by the Portuguese and Spanish in the exploration of the Atlantic.

---

[4]Alvise da Cadamosto in *The Voyages of Cadamosto and Other Documents*, ed. and trans. G. R. Crone (London, UK: Hakluyt Society, 1937), 2.

to venture beyond southern Morocco (see Map 16.3). It would ultimately take the Portuguese four decades to cover the 1,500 miles (2,400 kilometers) from Lisbon to Sierra Leone (**see-ER-uh lee-OWN**); it then took only three additional decades to explore the remaining 4,000 miles (6,400 kilometers) to the southern tip of the African continent. With experience, navigators learned how to return home speedily by sailing northwest into the Atlantic to the latitude of the Azores, where they could pick up prevailing westerly winds. The knowledge that ocean winds tend to form large circular patterns helped later explorers discover many other ocean routes.

During the 1440s Portuguese raids on the northwest coast of Africa and the Canary Islands began to return with slaves, finding a profitable market in an Iberia still recovering from the population losses of the Black Plague. The total number of Africans captured or purchased on voyages exceeded 80,000 by the end of the century and rose steadily thereafter. However, the gold trade quickly became more important once the Portuguese contacted the trading networks that flourished in West Africa and reached across the Sahara. By 1457 enough African gold was coming back to Portugal for the kingdom to issue a new gold coin called the *cruzado* (crusader), another reminder of how deeply the Portuguese entwined religious and secular motives.

While the Portuguese crown continued to sponsor voyages, the growing participation of private commercial interests accelerated the pace of exploration. In 1469 a prominent Lisbon merchant named Fernão Gomes purchased from the Crown the privilege of exploring 350 miles (550 kilometers) of African coast in return for a trade monopoly. He discovered the uninhabited island of São Tomé (**sow toh-MAY**) located on the equator and converted it to a major producer of sugar dependent on the labor of slaves imported from the African mainland. In the next century the island would serve as a model for the sugar plantations of Brazil and the Caribbean. Gomes also explored the **Gold Coast**, which became the headquarters of Portugal's West African trade.

The desire to find a passage around Africa to the rich spice trade of the Indian Ocean spurred the final thrust down the African coast. In 1488 **Bartolomeu Dias** became the first Portuguese explorer to round the southern tip of Africa and enter the Indian Ocean. This achievement was followed up by **Vasco da Gama** who sailed around Africa and reached India in 1497–1498 (see Environment & Technology: Vasco da Gama's Fleet). Then, in 1500, ships on the way to India under the command of Pedro Alvares Cabral (**kah-BRAHL**) sailed too far west and reached the South American mainland. This discovery established Portugal's claim to Brazil, which would become one of the Western Hemisphere's richest colonies. The gamble that Prince Henry had begun eight decades earlier was about to pay off handsomely.

16-2c Spanish Voyages

In contrast to the persistence and planning behind Portugal's century-long exploration of the South Atlantic, haste and blind luck lay behind Spain's early maritime expansion. Throughout most of the fifteenth century, the Spanish kingdoms were preoccupied with internal affairs: completion of the reconquest of southern Iberia from the Muslims; consolidation of the territories of Isabel and Ferdinand; and the conversion or expulsion of religious minorities. As a result, the Portuguese had already found a new route to the Indian Ocean by the time the Spanish monarchs were ready to turn to overseas exploration.

The leader of the Spanish overseas mission was **Christopher Columbus** (1451–1506), a Genoese mariner who gained experience with Portuguese voyages to the African coast. His four voyages between 1492 and 1504 established the existence of a vast new world across the Atlantic, a land mass with tens of millions of inhabitants and an enormous diversity of languages and cultures that few in "old world" Eurasia and Africa had ever anticipated. But Columbus refused to accept that he had found unknown new continents and peoples, insisting instead that he had found a shorter route to the Indian Ocean.

As a young man Columbus gained considerable experience in the South Atlantic while sailing with Portuguese explorations of the African coast, but he had become convinced there was a shorter way to reach the riches of the East than the route around Africa. By his reckoning (based on a serious misreading of a ninth-century Arab authority), the Canaries were a mere 2,400 nautical miles (4,450 kilometers) from Japan. The actual distance was five times as far.

Columbus proposed to reach Asia by sailing west, but Portuguese authorities twice rejected his plan. Columbus first proposed his expedition to Castile's able ruler Queen Isabel in 1486, but was rejected. In 1492 his persistence was finally rewarded when the queen and her husband, King Ferdinand of Aragon, agreed to fund a modest expedition.

Gold Coast Region of the Atlantic coast of West Africa occupied by modern Ghana; named for its gold exports to Europe from the 1470s onward.

Bartolomeu Dias Portuguese explorer who in 1488 led the first expedition to sail around the southern tip of Africa from the Atlantic and sight the Indian Ocean.

Vasco da Gama Portuguese explorer. In 1497–1498 he led the first naval expedition from Europe to sail to India, opening an important commercial sea route.

Christopher Columbus Genoese mariner who in the service of Spain led four expeditions across the Atlantic, reestablishing contact between the peoples of the Americas and the Old World and opening the way to Spanish conquest and colonization.

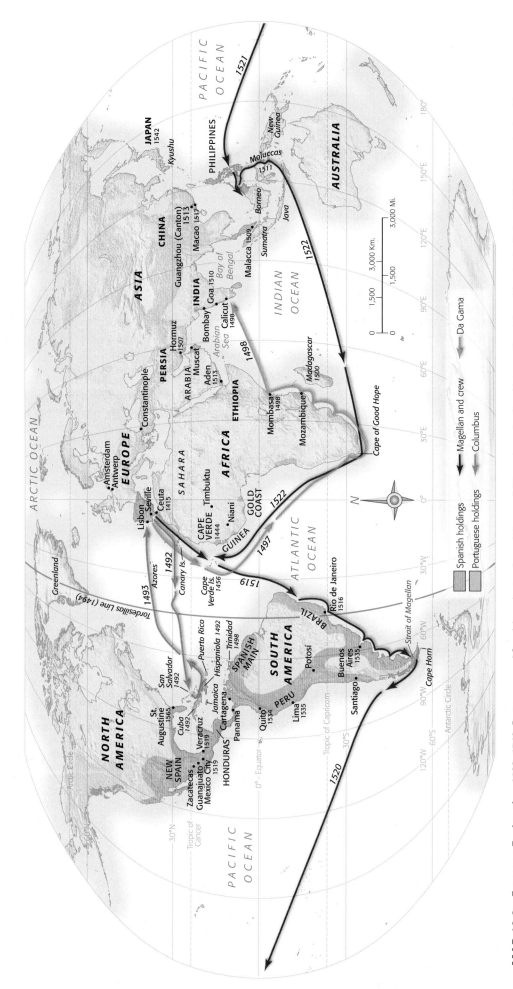

MAP 16.3 **European Exploration, 1420–1542** Portuguese and Spanish explorers showed the possibility and practicality of intercontinental maritime trade. Before 1540 European trade with Africa and Asia was much more important than that with the Americas, but after the Spanish conquest of the Aztec and Inka Empires, transatlantic trade increased dramatically. Notice the Tordesillas line, which in theory separated the Spanish and Portuguese spheres of activity.

What are the most important geographic differences between the Portuguese and Spanish empires as represented in this map?

The four small ships that sailed for India from Lisbon in June 1497 may seem a puny fleet compared to the sixty-two Chinese vessels that Zheng He had led into the Indian Ocean ninety-five years earlier. But given the fact that China had a hundred times as many people as Portugal, Vasco da Gama's fleet represented at least as great a proportional commitment of resources. In any event, the Portuguese expedition had a far greater impact on the course of history. Having achieved its key aims, the Chinese throne sent out no more expeditions after 1433. Although da Gama's ships seemed more odd than awesome to Indian Ocean observers, that modest fleet began a revolution in global relations.

Portugal spared no expense in ensuring that the fleet would make it to India and back. Craftsmen built extra strength into the hulls to withstand the powerful storms that Dias had encountered in 1488 at the tip of Africa. Small enough to be able to navigate shallow harbors and rivers the expedition might encounter, the ships were crammed with casks and barrels of water, wine, oil, flour, meat, and vegetables far in excess of what was required even on a voyage that would take the better part of a year. Arms and ammunition were also in abundance.

Three of da Gama's ships were rigged with square sails on two masts for speed and a lateen sail on the third mast. The fourth vessel was a caravel with lateen sails. Each ship carried three sets of spare sails and plenty of extra rigging so as to be able to repair any damages due to storms. The Crusaders' red crosses on the sails signaled one of the expedition's motives.

The captains and crew—Portugal's most talented and experienced—received extra pay and other rewards for their service. Yet there was no expectation that the unprecedented sums spent on this expedition would bring any immediate return. According to a contemporary chronicle, the only prompt return the Portuguese monarch received was "the knowledge that some part of Ethiopia and the beginning of Lower India had been discovered." However, the scale and care of the preparations suggest that the Portuguese expected the expedition to open up profitable trade to the Indian Ocean. And so it did.

▲ **Vasco da Gama's Flagship**   This vessel carried the Portuguese captain on his second expedition to India in 1505.   The Pierpont Morgan Library / Art Resource, NY

Questions for Analysis

1. Why did the Portuguese voyages have a greater long-term impact than the earlier voyages of the Chinese?

2. What technological innovations aided the success of Vasco da Gama?

3. What was the chief objective of the Portuguese fleet?

Columbus recorded in his log that he and his crew of ninety men "departed Friday the third day of August of the year 1492" toward "the regions of India." Their mission, the royal contract stated, was "to discover and acquire certain islands and mainland in the Ocean Sea." He carried letters of introduction from the Spanish sovereigns to Eastern rulers, including one to the "Grand Khan" (meaning the Chinese emperor), and brought along an Arabic interpreter to facilitate communication with the peoples of eastern Asia. The expedition traveled in three small ships, the *Santa María*, the *Niña*, and the *Pinta*. The *Niña* and the *Pinta* were caravels.

Unfavorable headwinds had impeded other attempts to explore the Atlantic west of the Azores, but Columbus chose a southern route because he had learned in his service with the Portuguese of west-blowing winds in the latitudes of the Canaries. In October 1492 the expedition reached the islands of the Caribbean. Columbus insisted on calling the inhabitants "Indians" because he believed that the islands were part of the East Indies. His second voyage to the Caribbean in 1493 did nothing to change his mind. Even when, two months after Vasco da Gama reached India in 1498, Columbus first sighted the mainland of South America on his third voyage, he stubbornly insisted it was part of Asia. But by then other Europeans were convinced that he had discovered islands and continents previously unknown to the Old World. Amerigo Vespucci's explorations, first on behalf of Spain and then for Portugal, led mapmakers to name the new continents "America" after him, rather than "Columbia" after Columbus.

AP® Exam Tip
Understand how Spanish sponsorship of Columbian and subsequent voyages in the Atlantic and Pacific oceans dramatically increased European interest in transoceanic travel and trade.

Section Review

- Portugal and Spain initiated oversees explorations to expand Christianity and gain new markets.

- Portugal, aided by Prince Henry the Navigator, created a trading empire in Africa and the Indian Ocean.

- Columbus first revealed the Americas to Europe, and other Spanish explorers reached Asia by crossing the Pacific.

To prevent disputes arising from their efforts to exploit their new discoveries and spread Christianity, Spain and Portugal agreed to split the world between them. The Treaty of Tordesillas (**tor-duh-SEE-yuhs**), negotiated by the pope in 1494, drew an imaginary line down the middle of the North Atlantic Ocean. The treaty allocated lands east of the line in Africa and southern Asia to Portugal; lands to the west in the Americas were reserved for Spain. Cabral's discovery of Brazil, however, gave Portugal a valid claim to the part of South America located east of the line.

Where would Spain's and Portugal's spheres of influence divide in the East? Given Europeans' ignorance of the earth's true size in 1494, it was not clear whether the Moluccas (**muh-LOO-kuhz**), whose valuable spices had been a goal of the earlier Iberian voyages, were on Portugal's or Spain's side of the Tordesillas line. The size of the Pacific Ocean would determine the boundary. In the end, the Moluccas turned out to lie well within Portugal's sphere, as Spain formally acknowledged in 1529.

In 1519 **Ferdinand Magellan** (ca. 1480–1521) began his expedition to complete Columbus's interrupted westward voyage by sailing around the Americas and across the Pacific. Despite his death during this voyage on behalf of the king of Spain, Magellan was considered the first person to encircle the globe because a decade earlier he had sailed from Europe to the East Indies as part of an expedition sponsored by his native Portugal. His two voyages took him across the Tordesillas line, through the separate spheres claimed by Portugal and Spain, and established the basis for Spanish colonization of the Philippines after 1564.

Although Columbus failed to find a new route to the East, the consequences of his voyages for European expansion were momentous. Those who followed in his wake laid the basis for Spain's large colonial empire in the Americas and for the empires of other European nations. In turn, these empires promoted the growth of a major new trading network whose importance rivaled and eventually surpassed the Indian Ocean network. Both the eastward and the westward voyages of exploration marked a tremendous expansion of Europe's role in world history.

16-3 Encounters with Europe, 1450–1550

What explains the different nature of Europe's interactions with Africa, India, and the Americas?

AP® Exam Tip
Explain the changes and continuities in the practice of slavery in Africa during this time period.

European actions alone did not determine the global consequences of these new contacts. The ways in which Africans, Asians, and Amerindians perceived these visitors and interacted with them influenced developments as well. Everywhere indigenous peoples evaluated the Europeans as potential allies or enemies, and everywhere Europeans attempted to maximize their economic advantage by inserting themselves into existing commercial and geopolitical arrangements. In general, Europeans made slow progress in establishing colonies and asserting political influence in Africa and Asia, even while profiting from new commercial ties. In the Americas, however, Spain, Portugal, and later other European powers moved rapidly to create colonial empires. In this case the long isolation of the Amerindians from the rest of the world made them more vulnerable to the diseases that these outsiders introduced, limiting their potential for resistance and facilitating European settlement.

16-3a Western Africa

Many along the West African coast were eager for trade with the Portuguese, since it offered new markets for exports and access to imports cheaper than those transported overland from the Mediterranean. This was evident along the Gold Coast of West Africa, first visited by the Portuguese in 1471. Miners in the hinterland had long sold their gold to traders, who took it to trading cities along the southern edge of the Sahara, where it was sold to traders who had crossed the desert from North Africa. Recognizing that they might get more favorable terms from the new visitors from the sea, coastal Africans were ready to negotiate with the royal representative of Portugal who arrived in 1482 to seek permission to erect a trading fort.

Ferdinand Magellan
Portuguese-born navigator who led the Spanish expedition of 1519–1522 that was the first to sail around the world.

This Portuguese noble and his officers (likely including the young Christopher Columbus, who had entered Portuguese service in 1476) were eager to make a proper impression. They dressed in their best clothes, erected and decorated a reception platform, celebrated a Catholic Mass, and signaled the start of negotiations with trumpets, tambourines, and drums. The African king, Caramansa, staged his entrance with equal ceremony, arriving with a large retinue of attendants and musicians. Through an African interpreter, the two leaders exchanged flowery speeches pledging goodwill and mutual benefit. Caramansa then gave permission for a small trading fort, assured, he said, by the appearance of the Portuguese that they were honorable persons, unlike the "few, foul, and vile" Portuguese visitors who had arrived in the previous decade.

Neither side made a show of force, but the Africans' upper hand was evident in Caramansa's warning that he and his people would move away, depriving their fort of food and trade, if the Portuguese acted aggressively. Trade at the post of Saint George of the Mine (later called Elmina) enriched both sides. The Portuguese crown had soon purchased gold equal to one-tenth of the world's total production at the time. In return, Africans received large quantities of goods that Portuguese ships brought from Asia, Europe, and other parts of Africa.

After a century of aggressive expansion, the kingdom of Benin in the Niger Delta was near the peak of its power when it first encountered the Portuguese. Its *oba* (king) presided over an elaborate bureaucracy from a spacious palace in his large capital city, also known as Benin. In response to a Portuguese visit in 1486, the oba sent an ambassador to Portugal to learn more about these strangers. He then established a royal monopoly on trade with the Portuguese, selling pepper and ivory tusks (for export to Portugal) as well as stone beads, textiles, and prisoners of war (for resale as slaves at Elmina). In return, Portuguese merchants provided Benin with copper and brass, fine textiles, glass beads, and a horse for the king to use in royal processions. In the early sixteenth century, as the demand for slaves for the Portuguese sugar plantations on the nearby island of São Tomé grew, the oba first raised the price of slaves and then imposed restrictions that limited their sale.

Early contacts generally involved a mix of commercial, military, and religious exchanges. Some African rulers appreciated the advantage of European firearms over spears and arrows in conflicts with their enemies and actively sought them in trade. Because African religious practices were generally not exclusive, coastal rulers were also willing to test the value of the Christian beliefs and rituals promoted by the Portuguese. The rulers of Benin and Kongo, the two largest coastal kingdoms, accepted both Portuguese missionaries and soldiers as allies in battle to test the efficacy of the Christian religion and European weaponry.

However, Portuguese efforts to persuade the king and nobles of Benin to accept the Catholic faith ultimately failed. Early kings showed some interest, but after 1538 rulers declined to receive more missionaries. They also closed the market in male slaves for the rest of the sixteenth century. We do not know why Benin chose to limit its contacts with the Portuguese, but the result makes clear that these rulers retained the power to control their interactions with Europeans.

Farther south, on the lower Congo River, relations between the kingdom of Kongo and the Portuguese began similarly but had a very different outcome. Like the oba of Benin, the manikongo (**mah-NEE-KONG-goh**) (king of Kongo) sent delegates to Portugal, established a royal monopoly on trade with the Portuguese, and expressed interest in Christian teachings. Deeply impressed with the new religion, the royal family made Catholicism the kingdom's official faith. But Kongo, lacking ivory and pepper, had less to trade than Benin. To acquire the goods offered by the Portuguese and to pay the costs of the missionaries, it had to sell more and more slaves.

Soon the manikongo began to lose his royal monopoly over the slave trade. In 1526 the Christian manikongo, Afonso I (r. 1506–ca. 1540), wrote to his royal "brother," the king of

▲ **Bronze Figure of Benin Nobleman**   Bronze plaque (c. 1600) from royal palace of the oba or king of Benin. Nobleman wears a helmet, coral necklace, embroidered skirt, and anklets.   Denver Art Museum

AP® Exam Tip
Understand the importance of Christianity's continued diffusion from the previous time period.

Portugal, begging for his help in stopping the trade because unauthorized Kongolese were kidnapping and selling people, even members of good families. Alfonso's appeals for help received no reply from Portugal, whose interests were now concentrated in the Indian Ocean. Soon the effects of rebellion and the relocation of the slave trade from his kingdom to the south weakened the manikongo's authority, leading to political instability.

16-3b Eastern Africa

Different still were the reactions of the Muslim rulers of the coastal trading states of eastern Africa. As Vasco da Gama's fleet sailed up the coast in 1498, most rulers gave the Portuguese a cool reception, suspicious of the intentions of visitors who painted Crusaders' crosses on their sails. But the ruler of one of the ports, Malindi, seeing the Portuguese as potential allies who could help him expand the city's trading position, provided da Gama with a pilot to guide him to India. The initial suspicions of the other rulers were proven correct seven years later when a Portuguese war fleet bombarded and looted most of the coastal cities of eastern Africa in the name of Christianity and commerce, while sparing Malindi.

When Portugal initiated the long series of voyages that led them into the Indian Ocean, many hoped that their efforts would lead to an alliance with a mythological African Christian prince, Prestor John, who they hoped still resisted the expansion of Islam (see Diversity & Dominance: Understanding Cross-Cultural Encounters). They were thinking of Christian Ethiopia. Once the Portuguese arrived, the rulers of this eastern African state did see the potential benefit in an alliance against their threatening Muslim neighbors. In the fourteenth and early fifteenth centuries, Ethiopia had faced increasing conflict with Muslim states along the Red Sea. Emboldened by the rise of the Ottoman Turks, who had conquered Egypt in 1517 and launched a major fleet in the Indian Ocean to counter the Portuguese, the talented warlord of the Muslim state of Adal, located at the Horn of Africa, launched a furious assault on Ethiopia. Adal's decisive victory in 1529 reduced the Christian kingdom to a precarious state. At that point Ethiopia's contacts with the Portuguese became crucial.

For decades, delegations from Portugal and Ethiopia had explored a possible alliance based on their mutual adherence to Christianity. A key figure was Queen Helena of Ethiopia, who acted as regent for her young sons after her husband's death in 1478. In 1509 Helena sent a letter to "our very dear and well-beloved brother," the king of Portugal, along with a gift of two tiny crucifixes said to be made of wood from the cross on which Christ had been crucified in Jerusalem. In her letter she proposed an alliance between her army and Portugal's fleet against the Turks; however, Helena's death in 1522 occurred before the alliance could be arranged. Ethiopia's situation then grew more desperate.

Finally, in 1539, when another female ruler was holding what was left of the empire together, a small Portuguese force commanded by Vasco da Gama's son Christopher arrived to aid Ethiopia. With Portuguese help the Ethiopians renewed their struggle. While Muslim forces captured and tortured to death Christopher da Gama, their attack failed when their own leader was mortally wounded in battle. Portuguese aid had helped the Ethiopian kingdom save itself from extinction, but a permanent alliance faltered because Ethiopian rulers refused to transfer their Christian affiliation from the patriarch of Alexandria to the Latin patriarch of Rome (the pope) as the Portuguese insisted.

As these examples illustrate, African encounters with the Portuguese before 1550 varied considerably, as much because of the strategies and leadership of particular African states as because of Portuguese policies. Africans and Portuguese might become royal brothers, bitter opponents, or partners in a mutually profitable trade, but Europeans remained a minor presence in most of Africa in 1550. By then the Portuguese had become far more interested in the Indian Ocean trade.

16-3c Indian Ocean States

Vasco da Gama did not make a great impression on the citizens of Calicut when he arrived on the Malabar Coast of India in May 1498. Da Gama's four small ships were far less imposing than the Chinese fleets that had called at Calicut sixty-five years earlier and no larger than many of the dhows that filled the harbor of this rich and important trading city. The *samorin* (ruler) of

▲ **Portuguese in India**   In the sixteenth century Portuguese merchant fleets and military forces entered the Indian Ocean Basin. Many remained to work as administrators and traders. This Indo-Portuguese drawing from about 1540 shows a Portuguese man speaking to an Indian woman, perhaps making a proposal of marriage.   Album/Art Resource, NY

Calicut and his Muslim officials showed only mild interest in the Portuguese as new trading partners, since the gifts brought by da Gama had provoked derisive laughter. The twelve pieces of fairly ordinary striped cloth, four scarlet hoods, six hats, and six wash basins he presented had seemed inferior goods to those accustomed to the luxuries of the Indian Ocean trade. When da Gama tried to defend his gifts as those of an explorer, not a rich merchant, the samorin cut him short, asking whether he had come to discover men or stones: "If he had come to discover men, as he said, why had he brought nothing?"

Coastal rulers soon discovered that the Portuguese had no intention of remaining poor competitors in the rich trade of the Indian Ocean. Upon da Gama's return to Portugal in 1499, the jubilant King Manuel styled himself "Lord of the Conquest, Navigation, and Commerce of Ethiopia, Arabia, Persia, and India," thus setting forth the ambitious scope of his plans. Previously the Indian Ocean had been an open sea, used by merchants (and pirates) of all the surrounding coasts. Now the Portuguese crown intended to make it a Portuguese sea, the private property of Portugal alone.

The ability of little Portugal to assert control over the Indian Ocean reflected the superiority of its ships and weapons relative to those employed by native authorities who relied on lightly armed merchant dhows. After a Portuguese fleet of eighty-one ships and some 7,000 men bombarded Swahili Coast cities in 1505, Indian ports were the next targets. Goa, on the west coast of India, fell to a well-armed fleet in 1510 and became the base from which the Portuguese menaced

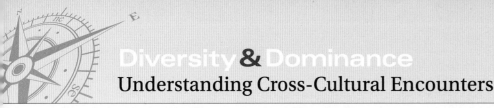
Limited and fragile trade relations linked Asia, Africa, and Europe before 1400. In the next century the development of new maritime routes expanded trade opportunities while also initiating a new, more violent era in which powerful states sought to control distant markets. Long isolated, the Americas were drawn into this expanding orbit after 1492. Religious objectives and human curiosity drove these new connections, as did strategic needs and commercial ambitions. Europe's seafaring nations, especially Portugal and Spain, benefitted the most from this first stage of global economic integration.

Historians trying to understand this important era rely on surviving documents generated by governments as well as on the memoirs, diaries, and letters produced by individual participants. While firsthand accounts from the fifteenth century are commonly filled with fanciful, inaccurate information and distorted by cultural biases when examined from our modern perspective, they also reveal the aspirations, ambitions, and values of the societies that underwrote the long-distance commercial ventures and military expeditions that established a new era in human history.

The first document presented here was written by Ma Huan (c. 1380–1460), a Muslim translator who accompanied the great Chinese admiral Zheng He on three of his seven expeditions to Southeast Asia and the Indian Ocean. Eighteen years after his final voyage in 1433 Ma Huan published his memoir, The Overall Survey of the Ocean's Shores. *In the selection below, Ma Huan describes Ku-Li (Calicut, India, now called Kozhikode), the fabulously wealthy Indian port famous for its exports of pepper and other spices.*

As China retreated from these ambitious and costly efforts in the following decades, Portuguese ships pushed into the Atlantic, exploring south along the African coast. Finally, in 1498, a Portuguese fleet commanded by Vasco da Gama (c. 1469–1524) arrived in Calicut, India. Da Gama's key objective was gaining access to the rich markets of Asia and the valuable spice trade. Since Portugal, like other southern European nations, militarily feared the Muslim powers of the Mediterranean, he also sought to find potential military allies. His sponsors believed that a Christian kingdom under the leadership of a semi-mythological figure, Prester John, had survived the military expansion of Muslim power. Portugal hoped to forge a military alliance with this kingdom to fight the Muslims. Years later da Gama's son Christopher would die fighting in defense of the Christian kingdom of Ethiopia.

The selection from his journal below describes his experience on the coast of Mozambique in East Africa. Unlike the voyages of Zheng He to Calicut and the Malabar coast eight decades earlier, da Gama's arrival in the Indian Ocean would lead eventually to the creation of a long-enduring colonial empire.

Ma Huan on Calicut

"The great country of the Western Ocean" is precisely this country. In the fifth year of the [Yongle period] the court ordered the principal envoy the grand eunuch Zheng He and others to deliver an imperial mandate to the king of this country and to bestow on him a patent conferring a title of honour, and the grant of a silver seal, also to promote all the chiefs and award them hats and girdles [ornate court costumes] of various grades....

The majority of the people in the country all profess the Muslim religion. There are twenty or thirty temples of worship, and once in seven days they go to worship. When the day arrives, the whole family fast and bathe, and attend to nothing else. In the *ssu* [9:00 to 11:00 A.M.] and *wu* [11:00 A.M. to 1:00 P.M.] periods,

AP® Exam Tip
Understand how the increased use of gunpowder weapons and armed trade was critical to imperial expansion.

the trading cities of Gujarat **(goo-juh-RAHT)** to the north and Calicut and other Malabar Coast cities to the south. The Portuguese also took the port of Hormuz, controlling entry to the Persian Gulf, in 1515, but Aden, at the entrance to the Red Sea, successfully resisted their attack. The addition of the Gujarati port of Diu in 1535 consolidated Portuguese dominance of the western Indian Ocean.

Meanwhile, Portuguese explorers had reconnoitered the Bay of Bengal and the waters farther east. The city of Malacca **(muh-LAH-kuh)** on the strait between the Malay Peninsula and Sumatra became the focus of their attention. During the fifteenth century Malacca had become an important commercial destination for merchants from China, Japan, India, the Southeast Asian mainland, and the Moluccas. Among the city's more than 100,000 residents an early Portuguese visitor counted eighty-four different languages, including those of merchants from as far west as Cairo, Ethiopia, and the Swahili Coast of East Africa. Many non-Muslim residents of the city supported letting the Portuguese join its cosmopolitan trading community, perhaps hoping to offset the growing power of Muslim traders. In 1511, however, the Portuguese seized this strategic trading center outright with a force of a thousand fighting men, including 300 mercenaries recruited in southern India.

Force was not always necessary. On the China coast, local officials and merchants interested in profitable new trade with the Portuguese persuaded the imperial government to allow the Portuguese to establish a trading post at Macao **(muh-COW)** in 1557. From their base at Macao, Portuguese ships came to nearly monopolize trade between China and Japan.

the menfolk, old and young, go to the temple to worship. When the *wei* [1:00 to 3:00 P.M.] period arrives, they disperse and return home; thereupon they carry on with their trading, and transact their household affairs. The people are very honest and trustworthy. Their appearance is smart, fine and distinguished.…

As to pepper: the inhabitants of the mountainous countryside have established gardens, and it is extensively cultivated. When the period of the tenth moon arrives, the pepper ripens; and it is collected, dried in the sun, and sold. Of course, big pepper-collectors come and collect it, and take it up to the official storehouse to be stored; if there is a buyer, an official gives permission for the sale; the duty is calculated according to the amount of the purchase price and is paid to the authorities. Each one *po-ho* [local unit of measure] is sold for two hundred gold coins.

The Che-ti [local merchant class] mostly purchase all kinds of precious stones and pearls, and they manufacture coral beads and other such things.

Foreign ships from every place come there; and the king of the country also sends a chief and a writer and others to watch the sales; thereupon they collect the duty and pay it to the authorities.

Vasco da Gama on Mozambique

The people of this country are of a ruddy complexion and well made. They are Mohameddans [Muslims], and their language is the same as that of the Moors. Their dresses are of fine linen or cotton stuffs, with variously colored stripes, and of rich and elaborate workmanship. They all wear *toucas* [hats] with borders of silk embroidered in gold. They are merchants, and have transactions with white Moors [Arabs], four of whose vessels were at the time in port, laden with gold,

silver, cloves, pepper, ginger, and silver rings, as also with quantities of pearls, jewels, and rubies, all of which articles are used by the people of this country. We understood them to say that all these, with the exception of gold, were brought thither by these Moors; that further on, where we were going to, they abounded, and that precious stones, pearls, and spices were so plentiful that there was no need to purchase them as they could be collected in baskets. All this we learned through a sailor the captain had with him, and who, having formerly been a prisoner among the Moors, understood their language.…

We were told, moreover, that Prester John resided not far from this place; that he held many cities along the coast, and that the inhabitants of those cities were great merchants and owned big ships. The residence of Prester was said to be far in the interior, and could be reached only on the back of camels. These Moors had also brought hither two Christian captives from India. This information, and many other things which we heard, rendered us so happy that we cried with joy, and prayed God to grant us health, so that we might behold what we so much desired.

AP® History Reasoning Skills

Comparison *Though they come from very different societies, what similarities can be found in the selections from Ma Huan and Vasco da Gama?*

Contextualization *What can be inferred about religion in Mozambique and Calicut from the excerpts provided?*

Source: Peter C. Mancall, ed., *Travel Narratives from the Age of Discovery: An Anthology* (New York, NY: Oxford University Press, 2006), 62–63, 120, 122, 124.

In the Indian Ocean, the Portuguese used their control of major port cities and their naval superiority to enforce an ever larger trading monopoly. As their power grew, they required all spices, as well as goods carried between major ports like Goa and Macao, to be carried in Portuguese ships. In addition, the Portuguese tried to control and tax other Indian Ocean trade by requiring all merchant ships entering and leaving one of their ports to carry a Portuguese passport and pay customs duties. Portuguese patrols seized vessels that attempted to avoid these monopolies, confiscated their cargoes, and either killed the captain and crew or sentenced them to forced labor.

Reactions to this power grab varied. Like the emperors of China, the Mughal (**MOO-gahl**) emperors of India largely ignored Portugal's maritime intrusions, seeing their interests as maintaining control over their vast land possessions. The Ottomans responded more aggressively, supporting Egypt against the Christian intruders with a large fleet and 15,000 men between 1501 and 1509. Then, having absorbed Egypt into their empire, the Ottomans sent another large expedition against the Portuguese in 1538. Both expeditions failed because Ottoman galleys were no match for the faster, better-armed Portuguese vessels in the open ocean. However, the Ottomans continued to exercise control over the Red Sea and Persian Gulf.

The smaller trading states of the region were less capable of challenging Portuguese domination head-on, since rivalries among them impeded the formation of a common front. Some chose to cooperate with the Portuguese to maintain their prosperity and security. Others engaged in evasion and resistance. Two examples illustrate the range of responses among Indian Ocean peoples.

The merchants of Calicut put up some of the most sustained resistance. In retaliation, the Portuguese embargoed all trade with Aden, Calicut's principal trading partner, and centered their trade on the rival port of Cochin, which had once been a dependency of Calicut. Some Calicut merchants became adept at evading Portuguese naval patrols, but the price of resistance was the shrinking of Calicut's commercial importance as Cochin gradually became the major pepper-exporting port on the Malabar Coast.

The traders and rulers of the state of Gujarat farther north had less success in keeping the Portuguese at bay. At first they resisted Portuguese attempts at monopoly and in 1509 joined Egypt's failed effort to sweep the Portuguese from the Arabian Sea. But in 1535, finding his state at a military disadvantage due to Mughal attacks, the ruler of Gujarat made the fateful decision to allow the Portuguese to build a fort at Diu in return for their support. Once established, the Portuguese gradually extended their control, so that by midcentury they were licensing and taxing all Gujarati ships. Even after the Mughals (who were Muslims) took control of Gujarat in 1572, the Mughal emperor Akbar permitted the Portuguese to continue their maritime monopoly in return for allowing one of his ships to carry pilgrims to Mecca each year without paying the Portuguese any fee.

The Portuguese never gained complete control of the Indian Ocean trade, but their naval supremacy allowed them to dominate key ports and trade routes during the sixteenth century. The resulting profits from spices and other luxury goods had a dramatic effect. The Portuguese were now able to break the pepper monopoly long held by Venice and Genoa, who both depended on Egyptian middlemen, by selling at much lower prices. They were also able to fund a more aggressive colonization of Brazil.

In both Asia and Africa the consequences flowing from these events were startling. Asian and East African traders were now at the mercy of Portuguese warships, but their individual responses affected their fates. Some were devastated. Others prospered by meeting Portuguese demands or evading their patrols. Because the Portuguese sought to control trade routes, not occupy large territories, Portugal had little impact on the Asian and African mainlands, in sharp contrast to what was occurring in the Americas.

AP® Exam Tip
Describe how Europeans were able to establish trading post empires in Africa and Asia as well as the impact those empires had in states in the interior of those continents.

16-3d The Americas

In contrast to the trading empires the Portuguese created in Africa and Asia, the Spanish established a vast territorial empire in the Americas. This outcome had little to do with differences between the two kingdoms, even though Spain had a much larger population and greater resources. The Spanish and Portuguese monarchies had similar motives for expansion and used identical ships and weapons. Rather, the isolation of the Amerindian peoples made their responses to outside contacts different from those of African and Indian Ocean peoples. Isolation slowed the development of metallurgy and other militarily useful technologies in the Americas and also made these large populations exceptionally susceptible to new diseases introduced by Europeans. It was the spread of deadly new diseases, especially smallpox, among Amerindians after 1518 that weakened their ability to resist and facilitated Spanish and Portuguese occupation and settlement.

The first Amerindians to encounter Columbus were the Arawak of Hispaniola (modern Haiti and the Dominican Republic) in the Greater Antilles and the Bahamas to the north (see Map 16.2). They cultivated *maize* (corn), *cassava* (a tuber), sweet potatoes, and hot peppers, as well as cotton and tobacco. Although the islands did not have large gold deposits and, unlike West Africans, the Arawak had not previously traded gold over long distances, the natives were skilled at working gold. While the Arawak at first extended a cautious welcome to the Spanish, they soon learned to tell exaggerated stories about gold deposits in other places to persuade them to move on.

When Columbus made his second trip to Hispaniola in 1493, he brought several hundred settlers who hoped to make their fortune, as well as missionaries who were eager to persuade the Amerindians to accept Christianity. The bad behavior of the settlers, including forced labor and sexual assaults on native women, provoked the Arawak to rebel in 1495. In this and later conflicts, steel swords, horses, and body armor led to Spanish victories and the slaughter of thousands. Thousands more were forced to labor for the Spanish and a smaller group were sent back to Spain as slaves. Meanwhile, cattle, pigs, and goats introduced by the settlers devoured the Arawak's food crops, eventually causing deaths from famine and disease. A governor appointed by the Spanish crown in 1502 institutionalized these demands by dividing the surviving Arawak on Hispaniola among his allies as laborers.

The actions of the Spanish in the Antilles imitated Spanish actions and motives during the wars against the Muslims in Spain in previous centuries: they sought to serve God by defeating nonbelievers and placing them under Christian control—and to become rich in the process. Individual **conquistadors (kon-KEY-stuh-dor)** (conquerors) extended that pattern around the Caribbean as gold and indigenous labor became scarce on Hispaniola. New expeditions searched for gold and Amerindian laborers across the Caribbean region, capturing thousands of Amerindians and relocating them to Hispaniola as slaves. The island of Borinquen (Puerto Rico) was conquered and settled in 1508 and Cuba between 1510 and 1511.

Following two failed expeditions to Mexico, Governor Diego Velázquez of Cuba appointed an ambitious and ruthless nobleman, **Hernán Cortés (kor-TEZ)** (1485–1547), to undertake a new effort. Cortés left Cuba in 1519 with 600 fighting men, including many who had sailed with the earlier expeditions, and most of the island's stock of weapons and horses. After demonstrating his military skills in a series of battles with the Maya, Cortés learned of the rich Aztec Empire in central Mexico.

The Aztecs (also called Mexica) had conquered their vast empire only during the previous century and a half, and many subject peoples were ready to embrace the Spanish as allies. These subject peoples resented the tribute payments, forced labor, and large-scale human sacrifices demanded by the Aztecs. The Aztecs also had powerful native enemies, including the Tlaxcalans **(thlash-KAH-lans)**, who became crucial allies of Cortés. Like the peoples of Africa and Asia when confronted by Europeans, Amerindian peoples, such as the Tlaxcalans of Mexico, calculated as best they could the potential benefit or threat represented by these strange visitors. Individual Amerindians made similar calculations. Malintzin **(mah-LEENT-zeen)** (also called Malinche), a native woman given to Cortés shortly after his arrival in the Maya region, became his translator, key source of intelligence, and mistress. As military allies and as individuals, Amerindians proved crucial to Spanish success.

While the emperor **Moctezuma II (mock-teh-ZOO-ma)** (r. 1502–1520) hesitated to use force and attempted diplomacy instead, Cortés pushed toward the Aztec capital of Tenochtitlan **(teh-noch-TIT-lan)**. Spanish forces used firearms, cavalry tactics, and steel swords to great advantage in battles along their route. In the end Moctezuma agreed to welcome the Spaniards now supported by many thousands of Amerindian allies into Tenochtitlan. As they approached his island capital, the emperor went out in a great procession, dressed in his finery, to welcome Cortés.

Despite Cortés's initial pledge that he came in friendship, Moctezuma was quickly imprisoned. The Spanish looted his treasury, interfered with the city's religious rituals, and eventually massacred hundreds during a festival. These actions provoked a mass rebellion directed against both the Spanish and Moctezuma. During the Spaniards' desperate escape, the Aztecs killed half the Spanish force as well as 4,000 of Cortés's native allies. In the confusion Moctezuma was killed, most likely by the Spanish.

The survivors, strengthened by Spanish reinforcements and aided by the Tlaxcalans, renewed their attack and captured Tenochtitlan in 1521. Because the Spanish believed the Aztecs had hidden treasure, Cortés ordered the brutal torture of the captured ruler Cuauhtemoc. Four years later the Spanish executed Cuauhtemoc. Their victory was aided by a smallpox epidemic that killed more of the city's defenders than did the fighting. One source remembered that the disease "spread over the people as a great destruction." Many Amerindians as well as Europeans blamed the devastating spread of this disease on supernatural forces. Cortés and other Spanish leaders then led expeditions to the north and south accompanied by the Tlaxcalans and other indigenous allies. Everywhere epidemic disease, especially smallpox, helped crush indigenous resistance.

Spanish settlers in Panama had heard tales of rich and powerful civilizations to the south even before the conquest of the Aztecs. During the previous century the Inka had built a vast empire along the Pacific coast of South America (see Chapter 15). As the empire expanded through conquest, the Inka enforced new labor demands and taxes and even exiled rebellious populations from their lands.

About 1525 the Inka ruler Huayna Capac **(WHY-nah KAH-pak)** died in Quito, where he had led a successful military campaign. Two of his sons then fought for the throne. In the end **Atahuallpa (ah-tuh-WAHL-puh)** (r. 1531–1533), the candidate of the northern army, defeated Huascar, the candidate of the royal court at Cuzco. As a result, the Inka military was decimated

AP® Exam Tip Consider the role disease played in the Columbian Exchange both here and in North America.

conquistadors Early-sixteenth-century Spanish adventurers who conquered Mexico, Central America, and Peru.

Hernán Cortés Spanish explorer and conquistador who led the conquest of Aztec Mexico in 1519–1521 for Spain.

Moctezuma II Aztec emperor who died while in custody of the Spanish conquistador Hernán Cortés.

Atahuallpa Last ruling Inka emperor of Peru. He was executed by the Spanish.

▲ **Coronation of Emperor Moctezuma**   This painting by an unnamed Aztec artist depicts the Aztec ruler's coronation. Moctezuma, his nose pierced by a bone, receives the crown from a prince in the palace at Tenochtitlan.   Fol.152v The Crowning of Montezuma II (1466-1520) the Last Mexican Emperor in 1502, 1579 (vellum)/Duran, Diego (16th century)/Biblioteca Nacional, Madrid, Spain/Bridgeman Images

Francisco Pizarro Spanish explorer who led the conquest of the Inka Empire of Peru in 1531–1533.

and the empire's political leadership weakened by the violence; at this critical time **Francisco Pizarro (pih-ZAHR-oh)** (ca. 1478–1541) and his force of 180 men, thirty-seven horses, and two cannon entered the region.

Pizarro had come to the Americas in 1502 at the age of twenty-five to seek his fortune and had participated in the conquest of Hispaniola and in Balboa's expedition across the Isthmus of Panama to the Pacific. In the 1520s he gambled his fortune to finance the exploration of the Pacific south of the equator, where he learned of the riches of the Inka. With a license from the king of Spain, he set out from Panama in 1531 to conquer them.

Having seen signs of the civil war after landing, Pizarro arranged to meet the Inka emperor, Atahuallpa, near the Andean city of Cajamarca **(kah-hah-MAHR-kah)** in November 1532. With supreme boldness and brutality, Pizarro's small band of armed men attacked Atahuallpa and his followers as they entered an enclosed courtyard. Though surrounded by an Inka army of at least 40,000, the Spaniards were able to use their cannon to create confusion while their swords brought down thousands of the emperor's lightly armed retainers and servants. Pizarro now replicated Peru Cortés's strategy by capturing the Inka ruler.

CONQVISTA CORTALE·LA·CAVESA·A ŠVALDA·INGA·VMATACVCHV

◀ **The Execution of Inka Ruler Atahuallpa**   Felipe Guaman Poma de Ayala, a native Andean from the area of Huamanga in Peru, drew this representation of the execution. While Pizarro sentenced Atahuallpa to death by strangulation, not beheading, Guaman Poma's illustration forcefully made the point that Spain had imposed an arbitrary and violent government on the Andean people.   The Execution of the Inca King Atahualpa (woodcut), Poma de Ayala, Felipe Huaman (1526–1613). Private Collection/Bridgeman Images

Atahuallpa, seeking to guard his authority, quickly ordered the execution of his imprisoned brother Huascar. He also attempted to purchase his freedom. Having noted the glee with which the Spaniards seized gold and silver, Atahuallpa offered a ransom he thought would satisfy even the greediest among them: rooms filled to shoulder height with gold and silver. The Inka paid the ransom of 13,400 pounds (6,000 kilograms) of gold and 26,000 pounds (12,000 kilograms) of silver, but the Spaniards still executed Atahuallpa. With the unity of the Inka Empire already battered by the civil war and the death of the ruler, the Spanish occupied Cuzco, the capital city.

Nevertheless, Manco Inka, whom the Spanish had placed on the throne following the execution of his brother Atahuallpa, led a massive native rebellion in 1536. Although defeated by the Spanish, Manco Inka and his followers retreated to the interior and created a much-reduced independent kingdom that survived until 1572. The victorious Spaniards, now determined to settle their own rivalries, initiated a bloody civil war fueled by greed and jealousy. Before peace was established, this struggle took the lives of Francisco Pizarro and most of the other prominent conquistadors. Incited by the fabulous wealth of the Aztecs and Inka, conquistadors now extended their exploration and conquest of South and North America, dreaming of new treasures to loot.

Section Review

- African kingdoms reacted in various ways to the opportunities and threats created by the arrival of the Portuguese, but only Kongo embraced Christianity and accepted a large Portuguese military presence in the sixteenth century.

- However, the Portuguese used military force to consolidate a trade empire in the Indian Ocean.

- After the Spanish occupied the Caribbean, Cortés led an expedition that conquered the Aztecs, weakened by epidemic.

- The Spanish under Pizarro conquered the Inka Empire, already suffering from civil war, and then fell on each other, but surviving conquistadors continued to explore the Americas.

16-4 Conclusion

The voyages of exploration undertaken by the Malays, Chinese, and Polynesians pursued diverse objectives. Malay voyagers were crucial participants in the development of the rich and varied commerce of Southeast Asia and initiated connections between these markets and Arabia and Africa. The great voyages of the Chinese in the early fifteenth century were motivated by an interest in trade, curiosity, and the desire to project imperial power. For the Polynesians, exploration opened the opportunity to both project power and demonstrate expertise while at the same time settling satellite populations that would relieve population pressures. The Vikings, Africans, and Amerindians all undertook long-distance explorations as well, although with fewer lasting consequences.

The projection of European influence between 1450 and 1550 was in some ways similar to that of other cultural regions in that it expanded commercial linkages, increased cross-cultural contacts, and served the ambitions of political leaders. But the result of their voyages proved to be a major turning point in world history. European explorers opened new long-distance trade routes across the world's three major oceans, for the first time establishing regular contact among all the continents. As a result, a new balance of power arose in parts of Atlantic Africa, the Indian Ocean, and the Americas.

The rapid expansion of European empires and the projection of European military power around the world would have seemed unlikely in 1492. No European power matched the military and economic strength of China, and few could rival the Ottomans. Spain lacked strong national institutions, and Portugal had a small population; both had limited economic resources. Because of these limitations, the monarchs of Spain and Portugal allowed their subjects greater initiative as they engaged distant cultures.

The pace and character of European expansion in Africa and Asia were different than in the Americas. In Africa local rulers were initially able to limit European military power to coastal outposts and to control European trade. Only in the Kongo were the Portuguese able to project their power inland. In the Indian Ocean there were mature markets and specialized production for distant consumers when Europeans arrived. Here Portuguese (and later Dutch and British) naval power allowed Europeans to harvest large profits and influence regional commercial patterns, but most native populations continued to enjoy effective autonomy for centuries.

In the Americas, however, the terrible effects of epidemic disease and the destructiveness of the conquest led to the rapid creation of European settlements and the subordination of the surviving indigenous population. Europeans also reacted to the loss of native population by initiating the African slave trade. While the Spanish and Portuguese found few long-distance markets and little large-scale production of goods that they could export profitably to Europe, These American colonies would eventually enrich Europe with the wealth gained from the production of gold, silver, and sugar and other products. Europe's economy would grow dramatically as the Americas were transformed by new technologies, new plants and animals, new languages and beliefs, and by the imposition of oppressive new forms of forced labor, such as slavery.

Key Terms

Zheng He p. 395	**Gold Coast** p. 403	**Ferdinand Magellan** p. 406	**Atahuallpa** p. 413
Arawak p. 399	**Bartolomeu Dias** p. 403	**conquistadors** p. 413	**Francisco Pizarro** p. 414
Henry the Navigator p. 401	**Vasco da Gama** p. 403	**Hernán Cortés** p. 413	
caravel p. 402	**Christopher Columbus** p. 403	**Moctezuma II** p. 413	

Review Questions

1. How would Portugal's growing power in Africa and Asia and Spain's control of a large Western Hemisphere empire serve as foundations for later European global power?

2. What influence would the enormous profits extracted from distant colonies likely have on European economic development?

3. What were key effects of this global transfer of wealth on Europe and on colonized regions?

 MindTap® is a fully online, personalized learning experience built upon Cengage Learning content. MindTap® combines student learning tools—readings, multimedia, activities, and assessments—into a singular Learning Path that guides students through the course and helps students develop the critical thinking, analysis, and communication skills that are essential to academic and professional success.

Material Culture
Head Coverings

Covering the head is one of the most universal of human cultural characteristics. It is also one of the most common ways of signaling social status. Examples can be drawn from every part of the world, from earliest times down to the modern era. In premodern Chinese society, the color and design of a man's cap indicated his rank as clearly as the insignia on military head coverings does today. In most European societies in the seventeenth and eighteenth centuries, men and frequently women of the higher social orders wore wigs, a practice that still survives in the costume of British judges.

Head coverings were particularly important for royalty. From ancient Egypt, where the earliest Pharaonic crowns symbolized the union of the northern and southern parts of the Nile Valley, down to the twentieth century and the jewel-studded crown of the shah of Iran, each land developed its own distinctive royal headdress. This also held true for Native American societies in pre-Columbian times and for African and Polynesian societies. In some societies, such as Sasanid Iran and the Ottoman Empire in what is today Turkey, each ruler's crown or turban had a distinctive design that symbolized his rule.

Head coverings have also played significant roles in religion. In Orthodox Judaism, for example, men wear hats or skullcaps and married women wear wigs as signs of acceptance of God's laws. In Islam, head coverings for women, borrowed from pre-Islamic practice in the Middle East, have become politically controversial in recent years; but prior to the twentieth century it was considered equally improper for a Muslim man to go bareheaded.

Wearing no hat at all was usually a characteristic of slaves or of the poorest elements in society. But it could also signify a deliberate desire to be regarded as humble. Sumerian priests,

▲ **Muslim Head Coverings** The man standing before a governor in this thirteenth-century miniature painting wears a simple skullcap indicating his low social status. The two attendants wear turbans, but the governor's turban is built into a high, conical shape. The folds and tails of turbans signified not only rank, but also place of origin. To this day, men from western Afghanistan wear tightly wound white turbans with long tails whereas men from eastern Afghanistan wear loose colorful turbans. Abu Zayd standing before the governor of Ramba in Baghdad, Arabic miniature, 1237 /DE AGOSTINI EDITORE/Bridgeman Images

Buddhist monks and nuns, and certain Sufis in the Muslim world shaved their heads clean. In Europe, early Christian monks and priests shaved the crown of their heads in the Roman Catholic tradition. This form of tonsure competed with and eventually superseded an Irish Catholic practice of shaving the front of the head. Yet head shaving did not always signify humility. Japanese samurai, or warriors, also shaved the front of their heads.

Head coverings for women, as well as wigs and hairdressing styles, sometimes show greater diversity than those for men. This has been particularly true in societies where women of high status mix with men on public occasions. A magnificent wig, hat, or coiffure under these circumstances might speak as much for the social rank of the woman's husband as for her own.

Given this long history of distinctive head coverings, the abandonment of both men's and women's hats in the second half of the twentieth century marked a major turning point in the history of symbolism. Around the world, the hat-making industry has greatly contracted. In China, Egypt, India, France, or Brazil, headwear no longer provides a clear indication of rank or status. Dignitaries typically pose for group photographs with no hats on at all. Aside from conservative religious groups, the head coverings that remain most often indicate occupations: military, police, construction, athletics, and so on.

The reasons for this change are unclear. The spread of democracy and decline of aristocracy may have contributed to it, but hats have become equally uncommon in dictatorships. A more likely cause is the worldwide role of news photographs, movies, and other pictorial media. The media developed in Europe and the United States tend to take Western customs as normal and exoticize non-Western styles as "native costumes." People everywhere have thus felt pressure to switch to Western styles, including bareheadedness, to fit into the image of the modern world.

Questions for Analysis

1. What might covering the head, or removing a head cover, signify in America today?

2. How desirable is it to be able to distinguish a person's job or social position by looking at his or her head covering?

3. What does wearing a baseball cap convey?

Issues in World History
Climate and Population to 1500

During the millennia before 1500, human populations expanded in three momentous surges. The first occurred after 50,000 BCE when humans emigrated from their African homeland to all of the inhabitable continents. After that, the global population remained steady for several millennia. During the second expansion, between about 5000 and 500 BCE, world population rose from about 5 million to 100 million as agricultural societies spread around the world (see Figure 1) and as experimentation increased plant and animal domestications. Following this dissemination of agricultural technologies, population growth then slowed again for several centuries before a third surge took world population to over 350 million by 1200 CE (Figure 2 shows the population in China and Europe).

For a long time, historians tended to attribute these population surges to cultural and technological advances. Indeed, a great many changes in culture and technology are associated with adaptation to different climates and food supplies in the first surge and with the domestication of plants and animals in the second. However, historians have not found a cultural or technological change to explain the third surge, nor can they explain why human creativity would have stagnated for long periods between the surges. Something else must have been at work.

Recently historians have begun to pay more attention to the impact of long-term variations in global climate. By examining ice cores drilled out of glaciers, scientists have been able to compile dependable records for thousands of years of climate change. The comparative width of tree rings from ancient forests has provided additional data on periods of favorable and unfavorable growth. Such evidence shows that cycles of population growth or stagnation have a strong correlation with changes in global climate.

Historians now believe that global temperatures were above normal for extended periods from the late 1100s to the late 1200s CE. In the temperate lands where most of the world's people lived, these above-normal temperatures meant longer growing seasons, more bountiful harvests, and thus more reliable food supplies. The ways in which societies responded to these medieval periods of higher temperatures are as important as the climate change itself, but it is unlikely that human agency alone would have produced the medieval population surge. One notable example of the complexity of human responses was that of the Vikings, who increased the size and range of their settlements in the North Atlantic, contributing to general population growth, although their raiding also caused death and destruction in a broad geographic area.

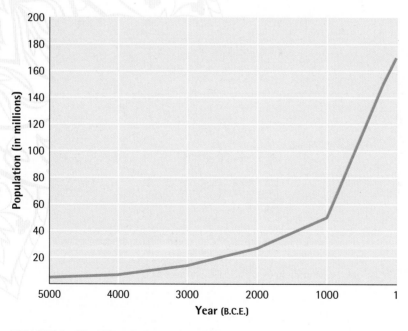

FIGURE 1   World Population, 5000–1 BCE

Some of the complexities involved in the interaction of human agency, climate, and other natural factors are also evident in the demographic changes that followed the medieval warm period. During the 1200s the Mongol invasions caused death and disruption of agriculture across Eurasia. As a result, China's population, which had been over 100 million in 1200, had declined by a third or more by 1300. While the Mongol invasions did not cause harm west of Russia, climate changes in the 1300s resulted in population losses in Europe. Unusually heavy rains caused crop failures and a prolonged famine in northern Europe from 1315 to 1319.

The freer movement of merchants within the Mongol Empire also facilitated the spread of deadly diseases across Eurasia, culminating in the great pandemic known as the Black Death in Europe. The demographic recovery that the relative peace following the Mongol consolidation of power in China was reversed by epidemics. The even larger population losses in Europe from plague may have been affected by an unrelated decrease in global temperatures, dropping to their lowest point in many millennia between 1350 and 1375. After 1400 improving economic conditions enabled population to recover more rapidly in Europe than in China, where the conditions of rural life remained harsh.

Because many other historical circumstances interact with changing weather patterns, historians have a long way to go in deciphering the role of climate in history. Nevertheless, it is a factor that can no longer be ignored as is made clear by modern climate science. Shrinking polar ice caps and glaciers, rising average temperature across the globe, and rising coastal water levels all indicate that human societies will have to make significant adjustments in the coming decades. Projections suggest that some inhabited regions, especially island nations in the Pacific and Indian Ocean, will likely be abandoned. While international agreements have committed nations to climate policies that should slow climate change, powerful companies continue to resist rather than face diminished profits and developing nations fear climate policy may prevent their economic development to the advantage of the world's richest nations. The question is whether national and corporate self-interests undermine the planet's future.

Questions for Analysis

1. What is the best explanation for the surge in human population between 5000 and 500 BCE?

2. How did climate change promote population growth between 1000 and 1300 BCE?

3. What caused the decline in the populations of China and Europe after 1300 CE?

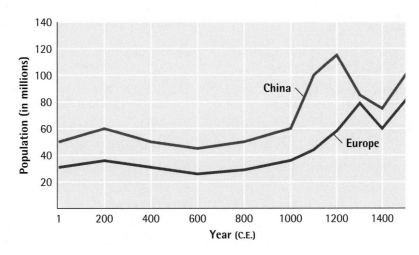

FIGURE 2 Population in China and Europe, 1–1500 CE

Multiple-Choice Questions

Questions 1–4 refer to the passage below.

"In the island . . . called *Hispana*, there are very lofty and beautiful mountains, great farms, groves and fields, most fertile both for cultivation and for pasturage, and well adapted for constructing buildings. The convenience of the harbors in this island, and the excellence of the rivers . . . surpass human belief. . . . Besides, this *Hispana* abounds in various kinds of species, gold and metals. The inhabitants . . . are all, as I said before, unprovided with any sort of iron, and they are destitute of arms. . . . They manifest the greatest affection towards all of us, exchanging valuable things for trifles, content with the very least thing or nothing at all. . . . I gave them many beautiful and pleasing things, which I had brought with me, for no return whatever, in order to win their affection, and that they might become Christians and inclined to love our King and Queen and Princes and all the people of Spain; and that they might be eager to search for and gather and give to us what they abound in and we greatly need."

> Excerpt from a letter written by Christopher Columbus in 1493, announcing his discoveries to King Ferdinand and Queen Isabella, after his first transatlantic voyage

1. According to the argument presented in the passage above, which of the following was a cause for continued exploration of the New World?

   (A) The passage across the Atlantic was easily achieved as the winds are generally favorable.

   (B) The desire for a favorable balance of trade for the Spanish in the Americas

   (C) The plants and animals found in the Americas surpassed those of Spain in variety and size.

   (D) The need to convert native Amerindians to Christianity in order to prevent the spread of Islam

2. The voyages of Columbus in 1492 led directly to a period characterized by

   (A) the expansion of control by the most warlike states of the Americas.

   (B) Amerindians attempting to flee the Americas in the face of European aggression.

   (C) increased European interest in transoceanic travel and trade.

   (D) incursions by dominant Amerindian tribes into tributary states.

3. Competition for trade routes and state rivalries increased in the latter part of the fifteenth century and eventually led to

   (A) open hostilities between the nations of the Iberian Peninsula.

   (B) a treaty between the Spanish and the Portuguese that divided rights to newly explored territories.

   (C) an increased cooperation between the Catholic Church and the monarchies of Western Europe.

   (D) an alliance between the French and the Spanish to counter Portuguese territorial gains.

4. Which of the following was a long-term consequence of the voyage described in the passage above?

   (A) Native people embraced colonization, assimilating quickly into European society.

   (B) Chattel slavery increased as natives proved unsuitable for work on sugar plantations that spread across the region.

   (C) European powers waged war over possessions in the Americas, with natives taking sides in European conflicts.

   (D) Lack of immediate financial gain led European leaders to postpone continued exploration until the late 1500s.

Questions 5–7 refer to the map on the next page.

5. The detailed map of the coast of West Africa made by Portuguese cartographers indicates that

   (A) the Portuguese had in-depth knowledge of the topography and cultures of Africa's interior.

   (B) the Portuguese were competing with the Spanish in gaining mastery of the Atlantic Ocean.

   (C) Portuguese cartographers built on previous technical knowledge from earlier times.

   (D) Portuguese scientists had a clear understanding of the size of the earth and the measurements of longitude and latitude.

▲ **Portuguese Map of Western Africa, 1502**   This map shows in great detail a section of African coastline that Portuguese explorers charted and named in the fifteenth century. The cartographer illustrated the African interior, which was almost completely unknown to Europeans, with drawings of birds and views of coastal sights: Sierra Leone (Serra lioa), named for a mountain shaped like a lion, and the Portuguese Castle of the Mine (Castello damina) on the Gold Coast. akg-images

6. What was the immediate early effect of the Portuguese development of maritime technology and navigation?

(A) Portugal became the most prominent European imperial nation in the early sixteenth century.

(B) Portugal developed an exploitive relationship with West Africa based on slaves and gold.

(C) Portuguese engineers built the largest and most navigable vessels of the age.

(D) Portuguese ships dominated both the Indian and Pacific Oceans.

7. Which of the following is an accurate comparison of the Portuguese and Spanish voyages of exploration?

(A) Portuguese exploration was typically thoughtfully planned and executed, whereas Spanish exploration was hastier and based on luck.

(B) Where Spanish exploration was dedicated entirely to spreading religion, the Portuguese were focused on developing economic might.

(C) The Portuguese had to steal most of the naval technology they used from the Spanish, leading to a slower participation in Atlantic exploration.

(D) The Spanish saw no purpose to exploration of the New World, and instead focused mainly on development of African ports.

Questions 8–10 refer to the passage below.

"You should also know that behind this Cauo Bianco on the land, is a place called Hoden, which is about six days inland by camel. This place is . . . frequented by Arabs, and is a market where the caravans arrive from Timbuktu, and from other places in the land of the Blacks, on their way to our nearer Barbary. . . . They are Muhammadans, and very hostile to Christians.

. . . the crown prince, [Henry the Navigator] has leased this island to Christians [for ten years], so that no one can enter the bay to trade with the Arabs save those who hold the license. They have dwellings on the island and factories where they buy and sell with the said Arabs who come to the coast to trade for merchandise of various kinds, such as woolen cloths, cotton, silver, and "alchezeli," that is, cloaks, carpets, and similar articles and above all, corn, for they are always short of food. They give in exchange slaves whom the Arabs bring from the land of the Blacks, and gold. The crown prince therefore caused a castle to be built on the island to protect this trade forever. For this reason, Portuguese caravels are coming and going all the year to this island."

A report by Venetian explorer Alvise da Cadamosto who helped the Portuguese chart coastal Senegal and Gambia for them in two voyages, ca. 1455

8. An examination of the report above supports which of the following assertions?

(A) The economy of West Africa was undeveloped before the arrival of the Portuguese in the fifteenth century.

(B) There were no threats to the dominance of Portuguese expansion in West Africa.

(C) Existing regional patterns of trade continued to thrive alongside the new arrivals.

(D) People of this part of West Africa had converted to Islam for economic reasons.

9. After reading the report, what conclusion could a historian make about slavery in West Africa at this time?

(A) Slavery was a tradition that was already established when Europeans arrived.

(B) Most of the African slaves were women and were used for domestic work.

(C) Arab traders treated the slaves harshly because of their ethnocentricity.

(D) The growth of the plantation economy increased the demand for slaves in the Americas.

10. As the Portuguese expanded their economic interests in West Africa, which of the following occurred?

(A) West African gold flooded the European markets and became the main force behind a worldwide expansion of trade.

(B) The Atlantic system evolved and created an increase in trade and interactions between Africa, America, and Europe.

(C) The Portuguese created colonies in the region and controlled most of the area between the Gulf of Guinea and the Sahara.

(D) Christianity flourished in Africa, causing mass conversion among the Arab traders.

Short-Answer Questions

"When we had ascended to the summit of the temple, we observed on the platform as we passed, the large stones whereon were placed the victims who were to be sacrificed. Here was a great figure which resembled a dragon, and much blood fresh spilt."

An account of the capital city Tenochtitlán, by Díaz del Castillo, who accompanied Hernán Cortés in the conquest of the Aztec Empire, from *The True History of the Conquest of New Spain*, 1568

"Should you fail to comply [convert], or delay maliciously in so doing, we assure you that with the help of God we shall use force against you, declaring war upon you from all sides and with all possible means, and we shall bind you to the yoke of the Church and of Their Highnesses; we shall enslave your persons, wives and sons, sell you or dispose of you as the King sees fit; we shall seize your possessions and harm you as much as we can as disobedient and resisting vassals."

A letter from King Ferdinand of Castile to the Arawak of the Caribbean, 1490s

1. Use the passages above and your knowledge of world history to answer all parts of the question that follows.

(A) Identify ONE religious belief or practice in Mesoamerica before the arrival of the Europeans.

(B) Explain ONE change to religious beliefs and practices in Mesoamerica after the arrival of the Europeans.

(C) Explain ONE continuity in religious beliefs and practices in Mesoamerica after the arrival of the Europeans.

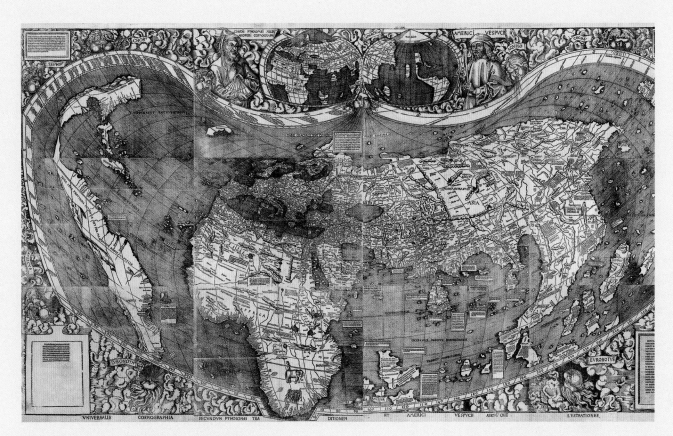

▲ A map of the world by Martin Waldseemuller, 1507

2. Use the map above and your knowledge of world history to answer all parts of the question that follows.

(A) Identify ONE technological development that allowed for the connections between the Eastern and Western hemispheres shown on the map.

(B) Explain ONE demographic result of the connections between the Eastern and Western hemispheres shown on the map.

(C) Explain ONE economic result of the connections between the Eastern and Western hemispheres shown on the map.

PART V

The Globe Encompassed, 1500-1750

▲ Map of the World, ca. 1595
After Ferdinand Magellan, the next explorer to circumnavigate the world was Sir Francis Drake (ca. 1540—1596). Departing with five ships in 1577, Drake nonetheless completed the majority of his voyage in a single ship, the *Golden Hind*, returning to England in 1580. This hand-colored engraving by Jodocus Hondius shows his route. Supported by Queen Elizabeth and other investors, Drake raided Spanish ships and colonial ports and returned with great riches. Unlike Magellan, he traveled far northward before crossing the Pacific, harboring for several weeks near San Francisco Bay and making friendly contact with the native peoples there. Drake later played a decisive role in England's victory against the Spanish Armada in 1588. Library of Congress

Between 1500 and 1750, the world witnessed a tremendous increase in exchange systems. Long-distance sea routes facilitated global trade, ended the isolation of the Americas, and complemented the growth of established land routes. Domesticated animals and crops, as well as diseases, were exchanged between the Old World and the Americas, creating demand and facilitating the establishment of large, prosperous European empires. Labor shortages led to the introduction of enslaved Africans. Europe itself experienced religious change as the Protestant Reformation broke the hegemony of the Catholic Church and allowed the rise of new global players such as the Dutch.

Asians and Africans generally retained control of their lands and participated freely in overseas trade, with the most important changes owing more to internal forces (such as Japan's new governmental focus on economic development and resistance to foreign influence) than to European actions. In northern Eurasia, Russia and China acquired vast new territories and populations. The Islamic world saw the dramatic expansion of the Ottoman Empire and the establishment of the Safavid and Mughal Empires. ●

Environment	Culture	State Building	Economics	Social Structures
• Impact of environmental factors, disease, technology on migration. (Little Ice Age, colonization)	• Origins, beliefs, development, economic/social/political impact, and spread of major religions, philosophies, and belief systems. (Reformation)	• Changes and continuities of the creation and maintenance of forms, functions, and institutions of governance.	• Causes/effects of economic strategies of different types of communities, states, and empires. (Columbian Exchange, Gunpowder Empires)	• Impact of kinship, ethnicity, class, gender, and race on social hierarchies
• Impact of migration, population, and urbanization on environment.	• Effect of cross-cultural interactions on diffusion of technology and scientific knowledge. (Cartography)	• Impact of economic, social, cultural, and geographical factors on state building, expansion, and dissolution. (Mercantilism, joint-stock company)	• Development and change of modes and locations of production over time.	• Challenges and confirmations of legal systems, colonialism, nationalism, and independence movements on class, gender, and racial hierarchies over time. (Columbian Exchange)
• Interaction between environment and development of technology, industrialization, transportation, and exchange/communication networks. (Columbian Exchange)	• Reflection and impact of society in the arts	• Impact of internal/external political factors on state building, expansion, and dissolution	• Development and change of labor systems over time. (Atlantic world, African slavery)	• Interaction between specialized labor systems and social hierarchy. (African slavery, Atlantic world)
		• Interaction between societies with states and state-less societies	• Influence and impact of local, regional, and global economic systems and exchange networks on each other. (Mercantilism, joint-stock companies)	• Maintenance or challenge to social categories, roles, and practices
		• Political/economic interaction between state and nonstate actors. (Globalization)		• Impact of political, economic, cultural, and demographic factors on social structures. (Confucian rituals)

Key Concept 4.1

- How were the technological developments that made transoceanic trade and travel possible both new developments and continuations of earlier knowledge?
- How did established commercial practices and the newly developing transoceanic trade routes both continue the development of regional markets in Afro-Eurasia and create a new flow of silver from the Americas to Asia?
- How did the Columbian Exchange dramatically alter both the old and new worlds?
- How did increasing and intensified connections lead to the spread and reform of existing religions and the creation of syncretic belief systems and practices?
- How did government funding and merchant profits lead to increased literacy and funding for the visual and performing arts?

Key Concept 4.2

- How did the Little Ice Age lead to significant changes in agricultural practices and settlement patterns in the Northern Hemisphere?
- How did the growing global demand for raw materials and finished products lead to and respond to changes in agriculture and labor?
- How did the overwhelming global changes lead to restructuring of the ethnic, racial, and gender hierarchies?

Key Concept 4.3

- What methods did rulers use to legitimize and consolidate their power?
- How did gunpowder, cannons, and armed trade support imperial expansion?
- What major challenges did state consolidation and expansion face?

17 Transformations in Europe, 1500–1750

AP® Framework Terms

Little Ice Age
Mercantilism
Joint-stock companies

Overarching Questions

1 How and to what extent have migration, population, and urbanization affected the environment over time? (ENV)

2 How have religions, belief systems, philosophies, and ideologies affected the political, economic, and social development of societies? (CUL)

3 How have scientific and technological innovations affected religions, belief systems, philosophies, and ideologies over time? (CUL)

4 How have internal and external political factors influenced the process of state building, expansion, and dissolution? (SB)

5 How have social categories, roles, and practices been maintained or challenged over time? (SOC)

In the late sixteenth century Dutch cities grew rich from long-distance trade routes that linked them to traditional markets of the Baltic and Mediterranean and to the newly opened markets of South Asia, Africa, and the Americas. Prosperity allowed the households of Dutch merchants, ship owners, and even artisans to consume luxuries with an extravagance previously limited to the nobility. These newly rich commoners built substantial houses, wore rich clothing, and developed a taste for the exotic goods of distant lands.

By the 1570s tulips had been introduced from the Ottoman lands and were avidly collected by Dutch enthusiasts. Scarce and expensive, owning tulips became a sign of sophistication and wealth. The collectors and botanists who originally purchased tulips were joined by thousands of eager consumers who recognized potential profit in a rare commodity. After prices surged upward in the 1620s they then accelerated in the 1630s, as a speculative market developed and ownership of tulip bulbs became a form of investment. Confident that prices would continue upward, individuals and partnerships paid extravagant amounts for bulbs, believing that they would profit from future resale. Between December 1636 and February 1637, for example, one of the most popular tulip varieties increased twelve times in value, becoming a speculative "bubble." At the peak of this frenzy the rarest bulbs sold for three times the annual income of a skilled carpenter. Then, in February 1637, the tulip market crashed as panicked investors rushed to unload their bulbs. If some had been made rich in this extraordinary trade, many of those who entered the market at the height of Tulipmania and paid peak prices were financially ruined.

▲ The End of the Tulip Bubble The growth of Europe's economy accelerated with the development of commodity and stock markets. While crucial to capital formation and investment, these early markets created the conditions for speculative bubbles. Seventeenth-century Holland experienced one of the most unusual when tulip prices surged to unsustainable levels and then crashed. In this painting an officer protects an exceptional tulip while his men trample less valuable tulips in an attempt to maintain prices by reducing the number of plants available for sale. The Walters Art Museum

While speculative bubbles roiled European economies throughout the early modern period, Europe steadily grew richer and more powerful. The voyages of exploration and conquests of distant lands in the fifteenth and sixteenth centuries (see Chapter 16) had initiated a dramatic commercial expansion. Greater opportunities and accumulating wealth contributed to the growth of manufacturing and to the introduction of commercial and financial innovations such as stock markets, commercial insurance, and expanded property right protections. This was also an era of dramatic social and cultural change, as cities grew in power relative to the countryside and wealthy merchants, investors, and manufacturers grew in power relative to Europe's hereditary nobility.

During this period Europe also developed powerful and efficient armies and governments that established states elsewhere in the world feared, envied, and sometimes imitated. The global balance of power was shifting slowly in Europe's favor. At the beginning of this era, the Ottomans threatened Europe, but by 1750, as the remaining chapters of

Part V detail, Europeans had brought much of the world under their control. No single nation was responsible for this success. Early in this period the Dutch eclipsed the pioneering Portuguese and Spanish; then in the eighteenth century the English and French bested the Dutch.

This was also a period of dynamic cultural change. At the beginning of this era a single Christian tradition dominated western Europe. By its end secular political institutions and economic interests had grown stronger, while Catholic and new Protestant churches were weakened by religious wars. Equally influential was the challenge to Christianity's long domination of European intellectual life posed by the Scientific Revolution and the first stages of the Enlightenment.

The years from 1500 to 1750 were not simply an age of progress for Europe. For many, the ferocious competition of European armies, merchants, and ideas was a wrenching experience. The growth of powerful nation-states extracted a terrible price in death and destruction, and the Reformation brought widespread religious persecution and religious warfare as well as greater individual choice in religion. Women's fortunes remained closely tied to their social class, and few gained equality with men. The expanding economy benefited members of the emerging merchant elite and their political allies, but in an era of rising prices Europe's urban and rural poor struggled to survive. ●

17-1 Culture and Ideas

How did the interplay of traditional beliefs and revolutionary ideas influence the cultural history of early modern Europe?

During the Reformation, theological controversies shattered the religious unity of the Latin Church and contributed to long and violent wars. While the influence of classical ideas from Greco-Roman antiquity increased among better-educated Europeans during the Renaissance (see Chapter 14), bold thinkers began to challenge the authority of both established religion and the Greco-Roman past. Emphasizing the careful observation of the physical universe and a reliance on evidence, they introduced new ideas about the motion of the planets and the natural world, encouraging others to challenge traditional social and political systems. Once in place, these new ideas would influence revolutionary political and social movements in the period after 1750. The transformative impact of these challenges to long-standing religious and intellectual beliefs was multiplied by the technology of the printing press and expanded European literacy.

17-1a Early Reformation

papacy The central administration of the Roman Catholic Church, of which the pope is the head.

Renaissance (European) A period of intense artistic and intellectual activity, said to be a "rebirth" of classic Greco-Roman culture. Usually divided into an Italian Renaissance, from roughly the mid-fourteenth to mid-fifteenth century, and a Northern (trans-Alpine) Renaissance, from roughly the early fifteenth to early seventeenth century.

In 1500 the **papacy**, the central government of Latin Christianity, held an unrivaled position as Europe's preeminent religious and intellectual authority, even though lax clerical standards and corruption were endemic. Recovered from a period when competing popes supported by rival secular rulers disputed control of the church, popes now exercised greater power, which was funded by larger donations and by income from the church's enormous real estate holdings. The construction of fifty-four new churches and other buildings in Rome demonstrated the church's wealth and power and showcased the artistic **Renaissance** then under way. The church leadership intended the size and splendor of the magnificent new Saint Peter's Basilica in Rome to glorify God, display the skill of Renaissance artists and builders, and enhance the standing of the papacy, but the vast expense of its construction and rich decoration also caused scandal.

CHRONOLOGY

	Politics, Economy, and Culture	Environment and Technology	Warfare
1500	1500s Spain's golden century		1526–1571 Ottoman attack on Hapsburg Empire
	1519 Protestant Reformation begins		1546–1555 German Wars of Religion
	1540s Scientific Revolution begins		1562–1598 French Wars of Religion
	1545 Catholic Reformation begins		1566–1648 Netherlands Revolt
	Late 1500s Witch-hunts increase	1590s Dutch develop flyboats; Little Ice Age begins	
1600	1600s Holland's golden century	1600s Growing depletion of forests	1618–1648 Thirty Years' War
	1611 First stock exchange built in Amsterdam	1609 Galileo's astronomical telescope	1642–1649 English Civil War
	1636–1637 Tulip bubble in Netherlands	1682 Canal du Midi completed	1652–1678 Anglo-Dutch Wars
			1667–1697 Wars of Louis XIV
			1683–1697 Ottoman wars
1700	1700s The Enlightenment begins		1701–1714 War of the Spanish Succession
	1719–1720 Mississippi Company bubble in France	1750 English mine nearly 5 million tons of coal a year	
	1720 South Sea Company bubble in England	1755 Lisbon earthquake	

The skillful overseer of the design and financing of Saint Peter's Basilica was Pope Leo X (r. 1513–1521), a member of the wealthy Medici (**MED-ih-chee**) family of Florence, famous for its patronage of the arts. Pope Leo's artistic taste was superb and his personal life free from scandal, but he was more a man of action than a spiritual leader. During his papacy the church aggressively raised funds through the sale of **indulgences**—a forgiveness of the punishment due for past sins.

A young professor of sacred scripture, Martin Luther (1483–1546), saw this practice and other excesses as intolerably corrupt. As the result of a powerful religious experience, Luther had forsaken money and marriage for a monastic life of prayer, self-denial, and study. In his religious quest, he found personal consolation in a passage in Saint Paul's Epistle stating that salvation resulted from religious faith, not from "doing certain things." That passage led Luther to object to the way preachers emphasized giving money to the church more than they emphasized faith. He wrote to Pope Leo to complain of this abuse and challenged the preachers to a debate on the theology of indulgences.

This theological dispute was also a contest between two strong-willed men. Largely ignoring the theological objections, Pope Leo regarded Luther's letter as a challenge to papal power and moved to silence him. During a debate in 1519, a papal representative led Luther into open disagreement with church doctrines, for which the papacy

indulgences The forgiveness of the punishment due for past sins, granted by the Catholic Church authorities as a reward for a pious act. Martin Luther's protest against the sale of indulgences is often seen as touching off the Protestant Reformation.

▶ **Martin Luther (1483–1546)** This portrait of Martin Luther was painted by Lucas Cranach in 1529. As a young professor of sacred scripture, Luther rejected essential teachings and practices of the Catholic Church. His rupture with the pope and the church hierarchy helped ignite the Protestant Reformation and led to a long period of religious war in Europe. Everett Historical/Shutterstock.com

condemned him. Blocked in his effort to reform the church from within, Luther burned the papal *bull* (document) of condemnation, rejected the pope's authority, and began the movement known as the **Protestant Reformation**.

Accusing those whom he called "Romanists" (Roman Catholics) of relying on "good works," Luther insisted that the only way to salvation was through faith in Jesus Christ. He further declared that Christian belief should be based on the word of God in the Bible and on Christian tradition, not on the authority of the pope. Luther's effective use of the printing press to spread his ideas won him the support of powerful Germans, who responded to his nationalist portrayal of an Italian pope seeking to beautify Rome with German funds.

Luther's denunciation of the ostentation and corruption of the church led others to call for a return to what they saw as uncorrupted Christian practices and beliefs. John Calvin (1509–1564), a well-educated Frenchman who left the study of law for theology after experiencing a religious conversion, became one of the most influential Protestant leaders. Although Calvin agreed with Luther's emphasis on faith over works, he denied that human faith alone could merit salvation. Salvation, Calvin believed, was a gift God gave to those He "predestined." Calvin also went farther than Luther in curtailing the power of the clerical hierarchy and in simplifying religious rituals. Calvinist congregations elected their own governing committees and created regional and national *synods* (councils) to regulate doctrinal issues. Calvinists also displayed simplicity in personal dress, life, and worship, avoiding ostentatious living while stripping churches of statues, most musical instruments, stained-glass windows, incense, and vestments.

The Reformers appealed to genuine religious sentiments, but their successes and failures were also influenced by local political and economic conditions. It was no coincidence that the German-born Luther had his greatest success among German speakers and linguistically related Scandinavians. Nor was it surprising that peasants and urban laborers sometimes defied their masters by adopting a different faith. Protestants were no more inclined than Roman Catholics to question male dominance in the church and the family, but most Protestants rejected the medieval tradition of celibate priests and nuns and advocated Christian marriage for all adults.

17-1b The Counter-Reformation and the Politics of Religion

Shaken by the intensity of the Protestant attack, the Catholic Church initiated a campaign of internal reforms. An influential church council met in Trent in northern Italy in 1545. Disrupted by political events and an outbreak of typhus, the council was relocated to Bologna in 1547, but a dispute between the pope and Charles V (1500–1558), the Holy Roman Emperor, made progress difficult. On the insistence of the Emperor, the council reassembled in Trent in 1551 but lasted less than seven months. The final sessions met between January 1562 and December 1563. Despite these interruptions, the council distinguished Catholic doctrines from what its members saw as Protestant "errors" and reaffirmed the supremacy of the pope. It also reaffirmed traditional teaching, including salvation through both faith and good works, the importance of oral confession and penance, and the authority of ecclesiastical authorities in interpreting Scriptures. Bishops allied with the pope dominated the council and limited efforts to reform practices that Luther had condemned as corrupt. Seeking to address unpopular practices condemned by Protestants, the council called for bishops to reside in their dioceses and for dioceses to maintain a theological seminary to train priests.

The creation in 1540 of a new religious order, the Society of Jesus, or "Jesuits," by Spanish nobleman Ignatius of Loyola (1491–1556) was among the most important events of the **Catholic Reformation** (also called the Counter-Reformation). Well-educated Jesuits helped stem the Protestant tide by their teaching and preaching (see Map 17.1), and they gained converts through missions in Asia, Africa, and the Americas (see Chapters 18 and 21).

Given the complexity and intensity stirred by the Protestant Reformation, it is not surprising that both sides persecuted and sometimes executed those with differing views. Bitter "wars of religion" would continue in parts of western Europe until 1648. The rulers of Spain and France were the chief defenders of the Catholic tradition against these Protestant challenges.

Charles V, both Holy Roman Emperor and King of Spain, and his son, King Philip II of Spain (1527—1598), were the key political and military architects of the Counter-Reformation. To confront the Protestant threat in northern Europe, Charles V dialed back his campaign against the Ottoman Empire and North African Muslim states in the Mediterranean and sent large armies to central Europe and the low countries. As a result, Spain's enormous windfall of Western

AP® Exam Tip
Compare the diversity within Christianity created by the Reformation with the divisions that occurred in other religions, such as Islam and Buddhism.

Protestant Reformation
Religious reform movement begun within the Latin Christian Church in 1519. It resulted in the "protesters" forming several new Christian denominations, including the Lutheran and Reformed Churches and the Church of England.

Catholic Reformation
Religious reform movement within the Latin Christian Church, begun in response to the Protestant Reformation. Commonly called the Counter Reformation, it clarified Catholic theology and reformed clerical training and discipline.

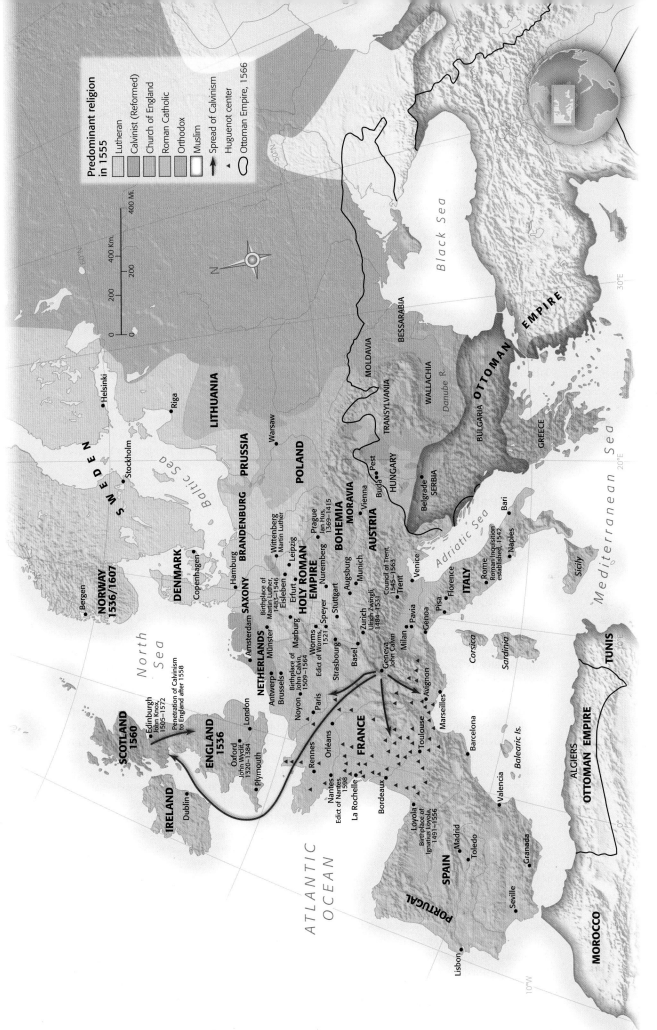

MAP 17.1 Religious Reformation in Europe The Reformation brought greater religious freedom but also led to religious conflict and persecution. In many places the Reformation accelerated the trend toward state control of religion and added religious differences to the motives for wars among Europeans.

Have the boundaries that separated Protestantism and Catholicism in 1555 survived into our era?

Predominant religion in 1555

- Lutheran
- Calvinist (Reformed)
- Church of England
- Roman Catholic
- Orthodox
- Muslim

↑ Spread of Calvinism

▲ Huguenot center

◯ Ottoman Empire, 1566

---

400 Mi.
400 Km.
200
0

N

ATLANTIC OCEAN

North Sea

Baltic Sea

NORWAY 1536/1607

Bergen

SWEDEN

Stockholm

Helsinki

DENMARK

Copenhagen

Riga

LITHUANIA

PRUSSIA

Warsaw

POLAND

BRANDENBURG

Hamburg

Amsterdam

NETHERLANDS

Münster

Antwerp

Brussels

SAXONY

Birthplace of Martin Luther, 1483–1546

Eisleben

Wittenberg Martin Luther

Leipzig

Erfurt

HOLY ROMAN EMPIRE

Birthplace of John Calvin, 1509–1564

Noyon

Marburg

Worms Edict of Worms, 1521

Speyer

Nuremberg

Stuttgart

Augsburg

Munich

Vienna

AUSTRIA

Prague Jan Hus, 1369–1415

BOHEMIA

MORAVIA

HUNGARY

Buda Pest

Belgrade

SERBIA

TRANSYLVANIA

WALLACHIA

MOLDAVIA

BESSARABIA

BULGARIA

OTTOMAN EMPIRE

GREECE

Black Sea

Danube R.

Adriatic Sea

Strasbourg

Basel

Zurich Ulrich Zwingli, 1484–1531

Geneva John Calvin

Milan

Pavia

Genoa

Venice

Council of Trent 1545–1563

Trent

Pisa

Florence

ITALY

Rome Roman Inquisition established, 1542

Naples

Bari

Sardinia

Corsica

Sicily

Mediterranean Sea

SCOTLAND 1560

Edinburgh John Knox, 1505–1572

Penetration of Calvinism to England after 1558

ENGLAND 1536

Oxford John Wyclif, 1320–1384

London

Plymouth

IRELAND

Dublin

Rennes

Orléans

Paris

Nantes Edict of Nantes, 1598

La Rochelle

Bordeaux

FRANCE

Toulouse

Avignon

Marseilles

Barcelona

Balearic Is.

Valencia

Loyola Birthplace of Ignatius Loyola, 1491–1556

Madrid

Toledo

Granada

Seville

SPAIN

PORTUGAL

Lisbon

MOROCCO

TUNIS

ALGIERS

OTTOMAN EMPIRE

Hemisphere bullion (see Chapters 16 and 18) went to subsidize this new military commitment rather than to develop its economy. Philip II continued his father's policies to their disastrous ends: the destruction of the Spanish Armada in 1588 and the recognition of effective Dutch independence in 1609.

In France the Calvinist opponents of the Valois dynasty gained the military advantage in the French Wars of Religion (1562–1598), but, in the interest of national unity, their leader Prince Henry of Navarre ultimately accepted the Catholic faith when he ruled as Henry IV of France. In pursuit of their objective of a union of church and state, Henry IV, his son King Louis XIII, and his grandson King Louis XIV supported the Catholic Church. Ultimately, Louis XIV revoked the Edict of Nantes **(nahnt)** by which his grandfather had granted religious freedom to his Protestant supporters in 1598.

In England King Henry VIII (r. 1509–1547) had initially been a strong defender of the papacy against Lutheran criticism. But when Henry failed to obtain a papal annulment of his marriage to Catherine of Aragon, who had not furnished him with a male heir, he challenged the papacy's authority over the English church. Despite the pope's opposition, the English archbishop of Canterbury annulled Henry's marriage in 1533 and then Parliament made the king head of an autonomous Church of England.

Like many Protestant rulers, Henry used this controversy to strengthen his authority and fatten his pocketbook by closing monasteries and convents and seizing their lands. He gave some land to his powerful allies and used profits from selling other land to pay for his new navy. While the king's power had grown at the expense of the Catholic Church, religious belief and practice were changing also. The new Anglican Church distanced itself from Catholic ritual and theology, but English Puritans (Calvinists who wanted to "purify" the church of all Catholic practices and beliefs) sought more. In 1603 they petitioned the first Stuart king, James I, to weaken the hierarchy by eliminating bishops.

17-1c Local Religion, Traditional Culture, and Witch-Hunts

In both the Protestant north and the Catholic south the institutions that enforced religious orthodoxy were strongest in urban places and weakest in villages and small towns. In these settings, local religion commonly blended the rituals and beliefs of the established churches with local folk customs, pre-Christian beliefs, ancient curing practices, love magic, and the casting of spells. The vigor of these local religious traditions ebbed and flowed in response to the strength of national and regional religious institutions as well as to the experience of economic dislocations, famine, and epidemic. The widespread **witch-hunts** that Protestants and Catholics undertook in early modern Europe were linked to this widespread belief in white and black magic. Yet, these beliefs and fears would not have had such deadly consequences if many educated and powerful city dwellers did not believe in the Devil's power to affect society broadly.

Prevailing European ideas about the natural world blended two distinct traditions. One was an enduring belief in magic and spirits passed down orally from pre-Christian times. The second was the biblical teachings of the Christian and Jewish Scriptures, broadcast by traditional religious authorities and supplemented by growing numbers of religious texts and commentaries published in French, English, and German languages as well as in traditional Latin. For most Europeans, Christian teachings about miracles, saints, and devils coincided easily with beliefs about magic, sorcery, and witchcraft rooted in the distant past.

It was widely assumed that some men and women possessed special powers derived from occult knowledge or, in some cases, from a compact with the Devil. In its benign version, it was assumed that these practitioners could heal the sick, cause love to flourish, or guarantee good fortune. They could also solve disputes with masters or employers or punish enemies. The malevolent version was practiced by witches and warlocks who could cause infertility, illness, or death of loved ones and neighbors, cause crops or businesses to fail, or even provoke epidemics or droughts, sometimes in association with the Devil. While some theologians and jurists questioned the intellectual and religious underpinnings of these assumptions before the mid-sixteenth century, many European civil and ecclesiastical courts would continue to arrest and punish witches until the last decades of the seventeenth century.

The attribution of human triumphs and tragedies to supernatural causes persisted among Europeans long after the end of the witch hysteria. When an earthquake destroyed much of Lisbon, Portugal's capital city, in November 1755, for example, both educated and uneducated

AP® Exam Tip
Explain the changes and continuities in how European rulers used religion to legitimize their rule throughout time.

AP® Exam Tip
Understand how traditional beliefs and major religions combined to create syncretic belief systems and practices.

witch-hunts The pursuit of people suspected of witch-craft, especially in northern Europe in the late sixteenth and seventeenth centuries.

◀ **Death of Three Women Accused of Witchcraft** This sixteenth-century woodcut shows the execution by burning alive of three women accused of witchcraft in October 1555 in Derneburg, Germany. Everett Historical/Shutterstock.com

people saw the event as a punishment sent by God. A Jesuit stated that it was "scandalous to pretend that the earthquake was just a natural event." An English Protestant leader agreed, comparing Lisbon's fate with that of Sodom, the city that God destroyed because of the sinfulness of its citizens, according to the Hebrew Bible.

The extraordinary fear of witches that swept across Europe in the late sixteenth and seventeenth centuries was powerful testimony to the endurance of these beliefs among commoners and the governing class alike. The initial wave of mass witch-hunts began in Protestant regions of Germany in the last decades of the sixteenth century. They continued, and in some areas accelerated, during the period of the Catholic Counter-Reformation. Before this hysteria ended, Catholic and Protestant authorities had collectively tried approximately 100,000 people and executed 60,000—some three-fourths of them women—for practicing witchcraft. The scale of these trials and the numbers of executions could not have happened without the active participation of rulers and judicial authorities. In German city-states like Wü;rzburg and Bamberg, for example, local princes condoned and promoted the trials, thus contributing to hundreds of deaths, including scores of children, in the 1620s and 1630s.

Trial records make it clear that both the accusers and the accused believed that it was possible for angry, jealous, and evil individuals to use black magic in concert with the Devil to cause injury to others. Many, in fact, appear to have willingly admitted to having occult powers and even to consorting with the Devil, but some educated Europeans of this period wondered if these individuals were mentally unbalanced or simply old and senile. Clearly the common use of judicial torture by religious and secular authorities explains why so many of the accused witches confessed.

While the trials and executions transcended both national and religious boundaries, there were significant differences in regional and national practice, even among nations with similar religious traditions. While England's population was roughly five times larger than Scotland's, roughly three times as many witches were executed by the Scots, 120 in the two-year period 1661–1662 alone. The relatively strong Catholic states of France and Spain also had low numbers of executions relative to the German states. In Spain the Inquisition limited arrests of suspected witches based solely on accusations as early as 1526. The judges of the Parlement of Paris mandated appeals of convictions for witchcraft and began to overturn many before the wave of executions crested in northern Europe in the 1620s. Similarly, the more egalitarian and less centralized government of Holland also limited trials and executions. The death toll was highest in German states like Würzburg and Bamberg, which executed 900 and 600, respectively, between 1626 and 1631. Sweden hosted one of the last mass campaigns of extirpation, executing seventy-one convicted witches on a single day in 1675. Even in Orthodox Russia, far from the center of this hysteria, ninety-nine were accused of witchcraft and ten were burned at the stake between 1622 and 1700.

While no single reason can explain the rise in witchcraft accusations and executions in early modern Europe, it is important to recall that these events coincided with a period of rising social tensions, growing rural poverty, and environmental crises. They also coincided with the mass violence of the wars of the Reformation period. While far from being a bizarre aberration, witch-hunts also reflected the tension between popular beliefs and practices and the ambitions of aggressive new religious and political institutions. The Reformation's focus on the Devil—the enemy of God—as the source of evil and the Catholic Counter-Reformation's effort to enforce orthodoxy on recalcitrant rural populations helped to propel the brutal persecutions of this period. In the eighteenth century the era of witchcraft persecutions effectively came to an end. The underlying beliefs were no longer credible among increasingly skeptical judges and rulers influenced by the era's new ideas, while central governments were stronger and less willing to allow popular passions to sway the local administration of justice.

17-1d The Scientific Revolution

Europe's intellectual environment proved to be as tumultuous and unstable as its religious institutions and political organization in the early modern period. At the beginning of the period the writings of classic antiquity and the Bible were the most trusted guides to the natural world. The greatest authority on physics was Aristotle (384–322 BCE), a Greek philosopher who taught that the surface of the earth was composed of two heavy elements, earth and water. The atmosphere was made up of two lighter elements, air and fire, which floated above the ground. Higher still were the sun, moon, planets, and stars, which, according to Aristotelian physics, were so light and pure that they floated in crystalline spheres. This division between the ponderous, heavy earth and airy, celestial bodies accorded perfectly with the orthodox insistence that all heavenly bodies revolved around the earth.

Beginning in the sixteenth century, however, European understandings of the natural world were transformed by a new form of scientific inquiry that emphasized experimentation, careful observation, and mathematical calculations. While this period is often called the **Scientific Revolution,** many of the most influential intellectuals were committed Christians (both Catholic and Protestant) who sought to use science to reinforce religious beliefs. Nevertheless, as this movement gained momentum, and as the convincing results of the experimental method accumulated, European intellectual life became more and more secular and independent.

Nicholas Copernicus (1473–1543), a Polish monk and mathematician, helped initiate the new era when he proposed that the sun, not the earth, as taught by both religious and classical authorities, was the center of the universe (see Chapter 14). To escape anticipated controversies with church authorities, Copernicus delayed the publication of his heliocentric (sun-centered) theory until the end of his life. Once disseminated, his assertion that the sun, not the earth, was at the center of the universe began a revolution in the way human beings understood the structure of the heavens.

Other astronomers, including the Danish Tycho Brahe (1546–1601) and his German assistant Johannes Kepler (1571–1630), strengthened and improved on Copernicus's model, showing that planets actually move in elliptical, not circular, orbits. The most brilliant of the Copernicans was the Italian Galileo Galilei (**gal-uh-LAY-oh gal-uh-LAY-ee**) (1564–1642). In 1609 Galileo built a telescope through which he could look more closely at the heavens, thus confirming empirically the speculations of other astronomers.

At first, those supporting the heliocentric universe faced formidable resistance because they directly challenged the intellectual synthesis of classical and biblical authorities. Many intellectual and religious leaders sought to suppress the new ideas. Most Protestant leaders, following the lead of Martin Luther, condemned the heliocentric universe as contrary to the Bible. Catholic authorities did not react immediately, but, when they did act, they proved more effective in suppressing the new scientific discoveries.

Copernicus died before his book was classified as heretical by Catholic authorities in 1616 and placed on the index of prohibited books. Despite this condemnation, his discoveries helped lead to a more accurate calendar issued in 1582 by Pope Gregory XIII and still used today. Galileo's empirical demonstration of the heliocentric theory led ultimately to a confrontation with the Inquisition. Galileo argued that the Bible was an inspired text, but, when science had established a demonstrable fact, religious authorities should reinterpret the Bible to coincide with the evidence, since it could not be God's intention to mislead. Despite the controversial nature of his opinions,

Scientific Revolution The intellectual movement in Europe, initially associated with planetary motion and other aspects of physics, that by the seventeenth century had laid the groundwork for modern science.

he continued to publish, pressing for a reliance on physical evidence and accurate measurement. Ordered before the Inquisition in 1633, Galileo was confined and shown the instruments of torture. Under intense pressure, Galileo agreed to recite and then sign a formal renunciation of his research. An apparent victory for tradition, this action put the Catholic Church in untenable opposition to a key early achievement of the new science.

Despite opposition from religious and secular authorities, printed books spread the new scientific ideas across Europe. Among the most influential intellectuals was French philosopher and mathematician René Descartes (1595–1650), who furthered the development of physics and calculus when he demonstrated the usefulness of algebra to geometry. After hearing of Galileo's condemnation by the Inquisition in 1633, however, Descartes decided to delay publishing a potentially controversial work on optics and astronomy. In England, another intellectual, Robert Boyle (1627–1691), advocated tirelessly for the usefulness of the experimental method. One of the founders of modern chemistry, he developed an effective vacuum pump and demonstrated that air was necessary for the transmission of sound. He was also among the first to publish the details of experiments, including his failures. Boyle along with others became an enthusiastic missionary of mechanical science and played a key role in the 1662 founding of the Royal Society to promote science. Its motto is "Nullius in Verba" or "Nothing in Words," a demand that science should be based on experiments alone.

Another Englishman, mathematician Isaac Newton (1642–1727), began his work in optics and mathematics, building on the work of Boyle and Descartes. He later carried Galileo's demonstration that the heavens and earth share a common physics to its logical conclusion by formulating mathematical laws that governed all physical objects. His Law of Gravity and his role in developing the calculus made him the most famous and influential man of his era, serving as president of the Royal Society from 1703 until his death.

As late as 1700 most religious and intellectual leaders continued to view the new science with suspicion or hostility because it challenged long-established ways of thought. Yet most of the principal pioneers of the Scientific Revolution, including the Catholics Galileo and Descartes as well as the Protestant Boyle, were convinced that scientific discoveries and revealed religion could be reconciled. However, by showing that the Aristotelians and biblical writers held ideas about the natural world that were unsupportable in the face of scientific discovery, these pioneers opened the door to others who used reason and logic to challenge a broader range of unquestioned traditions and superstitions. The world of ideas was forever changed.

◀ **Trial of Galileo Galilei in Rome in 1633** Galileo was summoned to Rome by the Inquisition to defend his scientific conclusion that the sun, not the earth, was the center of the universe. He was interrogated for 18 days by Church authorities, despite his fragile health. Following this ordeal he was threatened with torture and then sentenced to prison. Under duress Galileo abjured the results of his scientific research and was confined to house arrest until his death in 1642.
Everett Historical/Shutterstock.com

Section Review

- Outraged by corrupt church practices, reformers like Luther and Calvin challenged papal authority and traditional Catholic theology.

- In response to the Protestant reformers, the Catholic Church launched a Counter-Reformation.

- Both Protestants and Catholics, seeking to enforce orthodoxy, sanctioned widespread witch-hunts.

- The thinkers of the Scientific Revolution challenged traditional biblical and Aristotelian conceptions of the cosmos.

- The advances in science prompted Enlightenment thinkers to question many conventional ideas and practices.

AP® Exam Tip
Make note of Enlightenment ideas, and keep track of their long-term effects.

17-1e The Early Enlightenment

Advances in scientific thought inspired some to question the reasonableness of everything from agricultural methods to laws, religion, and social hierarchies. They believed that they could apply the scientific method to analyze economics, politics, and social organization in order to devise the best policies. This enthusiasm for an open and critical examination of human society energized a movement known as the **Enlightenment**. Like the Scientific Revolution, this movement was the work of a few "enlightened" individuals, who often faced bitter opposition from the political and religious establishments. Leading Enlightenment thinkers became accustomed to having their books burned or banned, and many spent long periods in exile to escape persecution.

Influences besides the Scientific Revolution affected the Enlightenment. The religious warfare and intolerance associated with the struggle between Catholicism and Protestantism undermined the moral authority of religion for many, and the efforts of church authorities to impugn the breakthroughs of science also pushed European intellectuals in a secular direction. The popular bigotry manifested in the brutal treatment of suspected witches also shocked many thoughtful people. Leading French thinker François-Marie d'Arouet, better known by his pen name Voltaire (1694–1778), declared: "No opinion is worth burning your neighbor for."

Although many circumstances shaped "enlightened" thinking, new scientific methods and discoveries provided the clearest model for changing European society. Accused of defamation by a powerful French aristocrat, Voltaire fled to England, where he met many leading scientists as well as intellectual luminaries like Alexander Pope and Jonathan Swift. When he returned to France, he became a leading advocate for Newtonian physics in opposition to his countryman Descartes. In his publications Voltaire linked the prestige of the newly ascendant scientific method with his generation's mounting political and social concerns in these terms: "It would be very peculiar that all nature, all the planets, should obey eternal laws" but a human being, "in contempt of these laws, could act as he pleased solely according to his caprice." English poet Alexander Pope (1688–1774) made a similar point in verse: "Nature and Nature's laws lay hidden in night; / God said, 'Let Newton be' and all was light."

The Enlightenment was more a frame of mind than a coherent movement. Individuals who embraced it drew inspiration from different sources and promoted different agendas. Its proponents were clearer about what they disliked than about what changes were necessary. Some idealists thought an "enlightened" society could function with the mechanical orderliness of planets spinning in their orbits, but most reformers focused on smaller, less ambitious objectives. Nearly all were optimistic that—at least in the long run—their discoveries would improve human beliefs and institutions. This faith in progress would help foster the political and social revolutions that transformed the Atlantic world after 1750, as Chapter 23 recounts.

While the Catholic Church and many Protestant clergymen opposed the Enlightenment, European monarchs selectively endorsed new ideas. Monarchs, ambitious to increase their power, found anticlerical intellectuals useful allies against church power and wealth. More predictably, monarchs and their reforming advisers discovered in the Enlightenment's demand for more rational and predictable policies a justification for the expansion of royal authority and the imposition of more efficient tax systems. Europe in 1750 was a place where political and religious divisions, growing literacy, and the printing press made it possible for these controversial and exciting new ideas to thrive despite opposition from ancient and powerful institutions.

Enlightenment
A philosophical movement in eighteenth-century Europe that fostered the belief that one could reform society by discovering rational laws that governed social behavior and were just as scientific as the laws of physics.

17-2 Social and Economic Life

There were large and important differences in the social structures of the major European nations, but there were many shared characteristics as well. European society was dominated by a small number of noble families who enjoyed privileged access to high offices in the church, government, and military and, in most cases, exemption from taxation. Below them was a much larger class of prosperous commoners that included many clergy, bureaucrats, professionals, and

◀ **The Fishwife, 1672** Women were essential partners in most Dutch family businesses. This scene by Dutch artist Adriaen van Ostade shows a woman preparing fish for retail sale. The Fishwife, 1672 (Oil On Canvas)/ Ostade, Adriaen Jansz. Van (1610-85)/Rijksmuseum, Amsterdam, The Netherlands/Bridgeman Images

military officers as well as merchants, some artisans, and rural landowners. The vast majority of Europe's men and women were very poor. Laborers, journeymen, apprentices, and rural laborers struggled to earn their daily bread and often faced unemployment and privation. The poorest members of society lived truly desperate lives, surviving only through guile, begging, or crime. Women remained subordinated to men.

Some social mobility did occur, however, particularly in the middle. The principal engine of social change was an economy stimulated by long-distance trade and by access to the gold and silver of the Americas. Because cities enjoyed the benefits of this expansion disproportionally, they were the principal arenas of new opportunity and social mobility.

17-2a The Bourgeoisie

Europe's cities grew in response to expanding trade and rising commercial profits. In 1500 Paris was the only northern European city with over 100,000 inhabitants. By 1700 both Paris and London had populations over 500,000, and eleven other European cities contained over 100,000 people.

Urban wealth came from manufacturing and finance, but especially from trade, both within Europe and overseas. The French called the urban class that dominated these activities the **bourgeoisie (boor-zwah-ZEE)** (burghers, town dwellers). Members of the bourgeoisie devoted long hours to their businesses and poured much of their profits back into them or into new ventures. Even so, most had enough money to live comfortably in large houses, and some had servants. In the seventeenth and eighteenth centuries wealthier consumers could buy exotic luxuries imported from the far corners of the earth—Caribbean and Brazilian sugar and rum, Mexican chocolate, Virginia tobacco, North American furs, East Indian cotton textiles and spices, and Chinese tea and porcelain.

The Netherlands provides one of the best examples of this new bourgeois reality. The Dutch Republic was the most egalitarian European country in the early modern period. While it retained a nobility, wealthy commoners dominated its economy and politics. Manufacturers and craftsmen turned out a great variety of goods in their factories and workshops. The highly successful

AP® Exam Tip
Explain how the power of political and economic elites fluctuated as they faced new challenges to their position in society.

bourgeoisie In early modern Europe, the class of well-off town dwellers whose wealth came from manufacturing, finance, commerce, and allied professions.

textile industry concentrated on the profitable weaving, finishing, and printing of cloth, leaving spinning to low-paid workers elsewhere. Along with fine woolens and linens, the Dutch also made cheaper textiles for mass markets. Factories in Holland refined West Indian sugar, brewed beer made from Baltic grain, cut Virginian tobacco, and made imitations of Chinese ceramics (see Environment & Technology: East Asian Porcelain in Chapter 21). Free from the censorship and religious persecution imposed by political and religious authorities elsewhere, Holland's intellectuals were active in the Scientific Revolution and early Enlightenment, and its printers published books in many languages, including manuals with the latest advances in machinery, metallurgy, agriculture, and other technical areas. For a small nation that lacked timber and other natural resources, this was a remarkable achievement.

With a population of 200,000 in 1700, Amsterdam was Holland's largest city and Europe's major port. The Dutch developed huge commercial fleets that dominated sea trade in Europe and overseas. Around 1600 they introduced new ship designs, including the *fluit* or "flyboat," a large-capacity cargo ship that was inexpensive to build and required only a small crew. As their trade with distant markets developed they introduced another successful type of merchant ship, the heavily armed "East Indiaman," that helped the Dutch establish their supremacy in the Indian Ocean, supplanting Portugal (see Chapter 16). By one estimate, the Dutch conducted more than half of all the oceangoing commercial shipping in the world in the seventeenth century (for details, see Chapters 20 and 21). Dutch improvements in mapmaking supported these distant commercial connections (see Environment & Technology: Mapping the World).

Amsterdam also served as Europe's financial center. Seventeenth-century Dutch banks had such a reputation for security that wealthy individuals and governments from all over western Europe entrusted them with their money. Dutch banks in turn invested these funds in real estate, loaned money to factory owners and governments, and provided capital for commercial operations overseas.

Individuals seeking higher returns than those provided by banks could purchase shares in a **joint-stock company**, a sixteenth-century forerunner of the modern corporation. Individuals bought and sold shares in specialized financial markets called **stock exchanges**, an Italian innovation transferred to the cities of northwestern Europe in the sixteenth century. The lively Amsterdam Exchange, begun as an outdoor market around 1530, moved into impressive new quarters in 1611. It remained Europe's greatest stock market in the seventeenth and eighteenth centuries.

The Dutch government played a direct role in this process by pioneering the creation of monopoly commercial enterprises like the Dutch East and West India Companies, which were granted monopolies for trade with the East and West Indies (see Diversity & Dominance: Commercial Expansion and Risk). France and England soon chartered monopoly trading companies of their own. These companies then sold shares to individuals to raise large sums for overseas enterprises while spreading the risks (and profits) among many investors (see Chapter 19). In this same era insurance companies were developed to insure long-distance voyages against loss; by 1700, purchasing insurance had become standard commercial practice.

Governments also sought to promote trade by investing in infrastructure. The Dutch built numerous canals to speed transport, lower costs, and drain the lowlands for agriculture. Other governments financed canals as well, including systems of locks to raise barges up over hills. One of the most important was the 150-mile (240-kilometer) Canal du Midi built by the French government between 1661 and 1682 to link the Atlantic and the Mediterranean.

After 1650 the Dutch faced growing competition from the English, who were developing their own close association between business and government. With government support, the English merchant fleet doubled between 1660 and 1700, and foreign trade rose by 50 percent. As a result, state revenue from customs duties tripled, supporting the growth of the navy. In a series of wars (1652–1678) the English government used this new naval might to break Dutch dominance in overseas trade and to extend England's colonial empire.

Some successful members of the bourgeoisie in England and France chose to use their wealth to raise their social status. By retiring from their businesses and buying country estates, they could become members of the **gentry**. They loaned money to impoverished peasants and to members of the nobility and in time increased their land ownership. Some sought aristocratic husbands for their daughters. The old nobility found such alliances attractive because of the large dowries that the bourgeoisie provided. Even in colonial settings, a small number of affluent and ambitious families purchased titles of nobility. While this kind of social mobility satisfied the desire for elevated status in hierarchical societies, it also removed the capital of the most successful bourgeoisie families from commerce and production.

AP® Exam Tip
Understand the role of mercantilism and joint-stock companies in financing exploration and competing in global trade in both domestic and colonial economies.

joint-stock company A business, often backed by a government charter, that sold shares to individuals to raise money for its trading enterprises and to spread the risks (and profits) among many investors.

stock exchange A place where shares in a company or business enterprise are bought and sold.

gentry The class of landholding families in England below the aristocracy.

17-2b **Peasants and Laborers**

Serfdom, which bound men and women to land owned by a local lord, had begun to decline in Europe after the great plague of the mid-fourteenth century. As population recovered in western Europe, an increased competition for work exerted a downward pressure on wages, reducing the usefulness of serfdom and other forms of forced labor to landowners. While there had been a brief expansion of slavery in southern Europe with the introduction of African slaves around 1500, Europeans shipped nearly all African slaves to the Americas after 1600. In eastern Europe, on the other hand, forced labor endured. Large-scale landowners in Russia and elsewhere who produced grains for growing urban markets continued to rely on the bound labor of serfs to ensure their profits.

There is much truth in the argument that western Europe continued to depend on unfree labor but kept it at a distance in its colonies rather than at home (see Chapters 18 and 19). In any event, legal freedom did little to make a peasant's life safer and more secure. The efficiency of European agriculture had improved little since 1300. As a result, bad years brought famine; good ones provided only small surpluses. Indeed, the material conditions experienced by the poor in western Europe may have worsened between 1500 and 1750 as the result of warfare, environmental degradation, and economic contractions. Europeans also felt the adverse effects of a century of relatively cool climate that began in the 1590s. During this **Little Ice Age** average temperatures fell only a few degrees, but the effects were startling (see Issues in World History: Climate and Population to 1500 in Chapter 16).

By 1700 the introduction of high-yielding new crops from the Americas were helping Europe's rural poor avoid starvation. Once grown only as famine foods, potatoes and *maize* (corn) became staples for the rural poor in the eighteenth century. Potatoes sustained life in northeastern and central Europe and in Ireland, while poor peasants in Italy subsisted on maize. The irony is that all of these lands were major exporters of wheat, but the laborers who planted and harvested this crop were so poor they could not afford to eat it.

Other rural residents made their livings as miners, lumberjacks, and charcoal makers. The expanding iron industry in England provided work for all three, but the high consumption of wood fuel caused serious **deforestation**. One early-seventeenth-century observer lamented: "Within man's memory, it was held impossible to have any want of wood in England. But . . . at present, through the great consuming of wood . . . and the neglect of planting of woods, there is a great scarcity of wood throughout the whole kingdom."[1] Eventually, the high price of wood and charcoal encouraged smelters to use coal as an alternative fuel. England's coal mining increased twelvefold, from 210,000 tons in 1550 to 2,500,000 tons in 1700 and to nearly 5 million tons by 1750.

France was more heavily forested than England, but increasing deforestation prompted Jean Baptiste Colbert, France's minister of finance, to predict that "France will perish for lack of wood." In Sweden and Russia, where wood fueled the furnaces of iron foundries, deforestation became an economic threat by the late eighteenth century as iron production rose.

Even in the prosperous Dutch towns, half of the population lived in acute poverty. Authorities estimated that permanent city residents who were too poor to tax, what was called the "deserving poor," made up 10 to 20 percent of the population. That calculation did not include the large numbers of "unworthy poor"—recent migrants from impoverished rural areas, peddlers traveling from place to place, and beggars (many with horrible deformities and illnesses) who tried to survive on charity. The pervasive poverty of rural and urban Europe shocked those who were not hardened to it. In about 1580 the mayor of the French city of Bordeaux (**bor-DOH**) asked a group of visiting Amerindian chiefs what impressed them most about European cities. The chiefs are said to have expressed astonishment at the disparity between fat, well-fed people and the poor, half-starved men and women in rags. Why, the visitors wondered, did the poor not grab the rich by the throat or set fire to their homes?[2]

In fact, this widespread misery provoked many rebellions in early modern Europe. For example, in 1525 peasant rebels in the Alps attacked both nobles and the clergy as representatives of the privileged and landowning classes. They had no love for merchants either, whom they denounced for lending at interest and charging high prices. Rebellions multiplied across Europe as rural conditions worsened. In southwestern France alone some 450 uprisings occurred between 1590 and 1715, many of them set off by food shortages and tax increases. A rebellion in

AP® Exam Tip
Explain both the short- and long-term effects of the Little Ice Age.

AP® Exam Tip
Understand the demographic, biological, and environmental effects of the Columbian Exchange.

Little Ice Age A century-long period of cool climate that began in the 1590s. Its ill effects on agriculture in northern Europe were notable.

deforestation The removal of trees faster than forests can replace themselves.

---

[1]Quoted by Carlo M. Cipolla, "Introduction," *The Fontana Economic History of Europe*, vol. 2, *The Sixteenth and Seventeenth Centuries* (Glasgow, UK: Collins/Fontana Books, 1976), 11–12.

[2]Michel de Montaigne, *Essais* (1588), ch. 31, "Des Cannibales."

Environment & Technology
Mapping the World

In 1602 in China Jesuit missionary Matteo Ricci printed an elaborate map of the world. Working from maps produced in Europe and incorporating the latest knowledge gathered by European maritime explorers, Ricci introduced two changes to make the map more appealing to his Chinese hosts. He labeled it in Chinese characters, and he split his map down the middle of the Atlantic so that China lay in the center. This version pleased the Chinese elite, who considered China the "Middle Kingdom" surrounded by lesser states. A copy of Ricci's map in six large panels adorned the emperor's Beijing palace.

The stunningly beautiful maps and globes of sixteenth-century Europe were the most complete, detailed, and useful representations of the earth that any society had ever produced. The best mapmaker of the century was Gerhard Kremer, who is remembered as Mercator (the merchant) because his maps were so useful to European ocean traders. By incorporating the latest discoveries and scientific measurements, Mercator could depict the outlines of the major continents in painstaking detail, even if their interiors were still largely unknown to outsiders.

To represent the spherical globe on a flat map, Mercator drew the lines of longitude as parallel lines. Because such lines actually meet at the poles, Mercator's projection greatly exaggerated the size of every landmass and body of water distant from the equator. However, Mercator's rendering offered a very practical advantage: sailors could plot their course by drawing a straight line between their point of departure and their destination. Because of this useful feature, the Mercator projection of the world remained in common use until quite recently. To some extent, its popularity came from the exaggerated size this projection gave to Europe. Like the Chinese, Europeans liked to think of themselves as at the center of things. Europeans also understood their true geographical position better than people in any other part of the world.

Questions for Analysis

1. If Matteo Ricci placed China at the center of his world map, is it likely that contemporary European maps, even modern maps, are just as "political" in their orientation?

2. What decisions made by Gerhard Kremer, aka Mercator, survive in modern maps?

3. Why was mapmaking such an important part of this era?

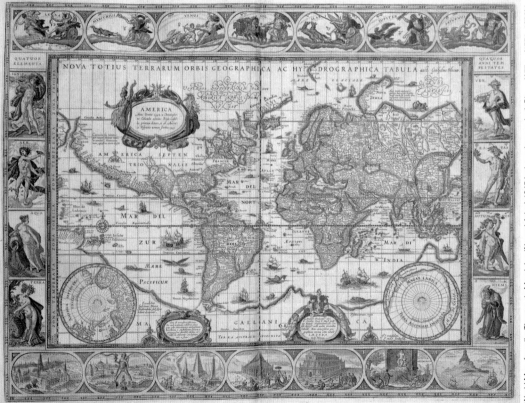

World Map, from 'Le Theatre du Monde' or 'Nouvel Atlas', 1645 (coloured engraving), Blaeu, Willem (1571–1638)/ Bibliotheque des Arts Decoratifs, Paris, France/Archives Charmet/The Bridgeman Art Library

▲ **Dutch World Map, 1641**   It is easy to see why the Chinese would not have liked to see their empire at the far right edge of this widely printed map. Besides the distortions caused by the Mercator projection, geographical ignorance exaggerates the size of North America and Antarctica.

southern France in 1670 began when a mob of townswomen attacked the tax collector. It quickly spread to the country, where peasant leaders cried, "Death to the people's oppressors!" Authorities dealt severely with such revolts once suppressed, executing or maiming their leaders.

17-2c Women and the Family

Women's social and economic status was closely tied to that of their husbands. In some nations a woman could inherit a throne (see Table 17.1 for examples)—in the absence of a male heir. These rare exceptions do not negate the rule that women everywhere ranked below men, but one should also not forget that class and wealth defined a woman's position in life more than her sex. The wife or daughter of a rich man, for example, though often closely confined, had a materially better life than any poor man. Sometimes a single woman might secure a position of responsibility, as in the case of women from good families who headed convents in Catholic countries. But while unmarried women were routinely controlled by fathers and married women controlled by husbands, some widows independently controlled substantial properties and other assets.

In contrast to the arranged marriages that prevailed in much of the rest of the world, young men and women in early modern Europe often chose their own spouses, but privileged families were much more likely to arrange marriages than poor ones. Royal and noble families carefully plotted the suitability of their children's marriages in furthering family interests. Bourgeois parents were less likely to force their children into arranged marriages, but the fact that nearly all found spouses within their own social class strongly suggests that the bourgeoisie promoted marriages that advanced their social aspirations or furthered their business interests.

Europeans also married later than people in other cultural regions. Sons often put off marriage until they could live on their own. Many young women also had to work—helping their parents, as domestic servants, or in some other capacity—to save money for the dowry expected by potential husbands. A *dowry* was the money and household goods—the amount varied by social class—that enabled a young couple to begin marriage independent of their parents. As a result, the typical groom in western and central Europe could not hope to marry before his late twenties, and his bride would be a few years younger—in contrast to the rest of the world, where people usually married in their teens.

Besides enabling young people to be independent of their parents, the late age of marriage in early modern Europe also held down the birthrate and thus limited family size. Even so, about one-tenth of urban births were to unmarried women, often servants. Many mothers, unable to provide for these infants, left them on the doorsteps of churches, convents, or rich households to be raised as "orphans." Many neglected children perished; and many young women newly arrived in Europe's fast-growing cities from the countryside were forced into brothels or begging by their poverty.

Section Review

- Early modern European society was more fluid than it appeared, with an expanding economy and improved education promoting some mobility.

- The urban bourgeoisie created much of Europe's wealth through trade, manufacture, finance, and technological innovation.

- Monarchs sought alliances with the bourgeoisie, whose wealth afforded them political and social advancement as well as revenue.

- Oppressed by economic and environmental trends, peasants and laborers generally lived in poverty, and their misery often provoked rebellion.

- Although women remained subordinate to men, class and wealth were the main determinants of their positions in life.

AP® Exam Tip
Explain the changes and continuities to gender and family roles in Europe during this time period.

17-3 Political Innovations

How did differing policies in the areas of religion, foreign relations, and economics determine the very different experiences of early modern European states?

The monarchs of early modern Europe occupied the apex of the social order, were arbitrators of the intellectual and religious conflicts of their day, and exercised important influence on the economies of their realms. Many European monarchs introduced reforms that achieved a higher degree of political centralization and order in this era, but their ambitions and rivalries could also provoke destructive and costly conflicts. In some cases, civil and international conflicts forced monarchs to find common ground with potential enemies or introduce political innovations that strengthened their nations. During this period, political leadership in Europe passed from Spain to the Netherlands and then to England and France.

In the early modern period, European merchants deepened their engagement with distant markets in Asia, Africa, and the Americas. This first globalization of production and trade led to important economic innovations in Europe like joint-stock companies and stock markets, which allowed merchants to spread speculative risks broadly among investors. Profits from this deepening trade with distant markets became important to Europe's economies in the sixteenth century, leading national governments in the seventeenth century to embrace a new economic theory, mercantilism, that defined national well-being as the expansion of exports and the maintenance of a positive balance of trade. To ensure these objectives, European governments participated fully in the expansion of trade in this period, founding colonies, augmenting navies to defend shipping lanes, and, ultimately, promoting the interests of merchant investors by granting monopoly commercial rights.

All of Europe's major colonial powers—England, France, Spain, Portugal, and Holland—experimented with monopoly trading companies. The Dutch were early innovators, chartering the East India Company in 1609 and then the West India Company in 1621. Trade in the shares of this company helped make Amsterdam Europe's financial capital. The preface to the charter of the West India Company follows.

JUNE 3, 1621

The States-General of the United Netherlands, to all who shall see these Presents, or hear them read, Greeting.

Be it known, that we knowing the prosperity of these countries, and the welfare of their inhabitants depends principally on navigation and trade, which in all former times by the said Countries were carried on happily, and with a great blessing to all countries and kingdoms; and desiring that the aforesaid inhabitants should not only be preserved in their former navigation, traffic, and trade, but also that their trade may be encreased as much as possible in special conformity to the treaties, alliances, leagues and covenants for traffic and navigation formerly made with other princes, republics and people, which we give them to understand must be in all parts punctually kept and adhered to: And we find by experience, that without the common help, assistance, and interposition of a General Company, the people designed from hence for those parts cannot be profitably protected and mantained in their great risque from pirates, extortion and otherwise, which will happen in so very long a voyage. We have, therefore, and for several other important reasons and considerations as thereunto moving, with mature deliberation of counsel, and for highly necessary causes, found it good, that the navigation, trade, and commerce, in the parts of the West-Indies, and Africa, and other places hereafter described, should not henceforth be carried on any otherwise than by the common united strength of the merchants and inhabitants of these countries; and for that end there shall be erected one General Company, which we out of special regard to their common well-being, and to keep and preserve the inhabitants of those places in good trade and welfare, will maintain and strengthen with our Help, Favour and assistance as far as the present state and condition of this Country will admit: and moreover furnish them with a proper Charter, and with the following Priveleges and Exemptions, to wit, That for the Term of four and twenty Years, none of the Natives or Inhabitants of these countries shall be permitted to sail to or from the said lands, or to traffic on the coast and countries of Africa from the Tropic of Cancer to the Cape of Good Hope, nor in the countries of America, or the West-Indies … but in the Name of this United Company of these United Netherlands. And whoever shall presume without the consent of this Company, to sail or to traffic in any of the Places within the aforesaid Limits granted to this Company, he shall forfeit the ships and the goods which shall be found for sale upon the aforesaid coasts and lands; the which being actually seized by the aforesaid Company, shall be by them kept for their own Benefit and Behoof. And in case such ships or goods shall

17-3a State Development

There was a great deal of political diversity in early modern Europe. City-states and principalities abounded, either independently or bound together in federations, of which the **Holy Roman Empire** of the German heartland was the most notable example. There were also a small number of republics. At the same time a number of strong monarchies emerged and developed cohesive national identities.

Holy Roman Empire
Loose federation of mostly German states and principalities, headed by an emperor elected by the princes. It lasted from 962 to 1806.

Habsburg A powerful European royal family that provided many Holy Roman Emperors, founded the Austrian (later Austro-Hungarian) Empire, and ruled sixteenth- and seventeenth-century Spain.

Dynastic ambitions and historical circumstances combined to favor and then block the creation of an integrated European empire in the early sixteenth century. Electors of the Holy Roman Empire chose Charles V (r. 1519–1556) to be emperor in 1519. Like his predecessors for three generations, Charles belonged to the powerful **Habsburg (HABZ-berg)** family of Austria. Three years earlier he had inherited the kingdoms of Castile and Aragon, becoming the first monarch of Spain as Charles I. With these vast resources (see Map 17.2), Charles sought to turn back the advance of Islam on Europe's Mediterranean flank while contending with France for dominance of Italy. Charles and his allies did stop the Ottomans at the gates of Vienna in 1529, but the Ottoman Empire as well as North African Muslim states continued to attack his territories in Italy and Spain, supported at times by the Christian king Francis I of France, who was more interested in defeating Charles's ambitions than in defending Christian Europe.

be sold either in other countries or havens they may touch at, the owners and partners must be fined for the value of those ships and goods: Except only, that they who before the date of this charter, shall have sailed or been sent out of these or any other countries, to any of the aforesaid coasts, shall be able to continue their trade for the sale of their goods, and cosine back again, or otherwise, until the expiration of this charter, if they have had any before, and not longer: Provided, that after the first of July sixteen hundred and twenty one, the day and time of this charters commencing, no person shall be able to send any ships or goods to the places comprehended in this charter, although that before the date hereof, this Company was not finally incorporated: But shall provide therein as is becoming, against those who knowingly by fraud endeavour to frustrate our intention herein for the public good: Provided that the salt trade at Ponte del Re may be continued according to the conditions and instructions by us already given, or that may be given respecting it, any thing in this charter to the contrary notwithstanding.

In 1664 the English author Thomas Mun (1571–1641) published a ringing endorsement of mercantilism in London, arguing that the promotion of foreign trade was the true source of national strength and prosperity. He also set out an ambitious list of skills necessary to a merchant operating in foreign trade, including knowledge of foreign weights and measures, the exchange values of foreign currencies, and shipping rates, as well as knowledge of navigation and foreign languages.

England's Treasure By Foreign Trade (first published in 1664)

Although a Kingdom may be Enriched by Gifts received, or by Purchase taken from some other Nations, yet these are things uncertain and of small Consideration when they happen. The ordinary means therefore to encrease our Wealth and Treasure is by Foreign Trade, wherein wee must ever observe this Rule; to sell more to Strangers yearly than wee consume of theirs in value. For suppose that when theis Kingdom is pletifully served with the Cloth, Lead, Tin, Iron, Fish and other native commodities, we doe yearly export the Overplus to Foreign Countries to the Value of Twenty-two hundred thousand pounds; by which means we are enabled beyond the Seas to buy and bring in foreign wares for our use and Consumptions, to the value of Twenty Hundred Thousand Pounds; By this Order duly kept in our Trading, we may rest assured that the Kingdom shall be Enriched Yearly Two Hundred Thousand Pounds, which must be brought to us in so much Treasure; because that part of our stock which is not returned to us in Wares must necessarily be brought home in Treasure. . . .

Behold then the true Form and Worth of Foreign Trade, which is *The great Revenue of the King, The honour of the Kingdom, The Noble Profession of the Merchant, The School of our Arts, The supply of our Want, The employments of our Poor, The improvement of our Lands, The Nursery of our Mariners, The walls of the Kingdoms, The Means of our Treasure, The Sinews of our Wars, The Terror of our Enemies* [italicized in original]. For all which great and weighty Reasons, do so many well-governed States highly Countenance the Profession, and carefully cherish the Action, not only with Policy to encrease it, but also with Power to Protect it from all foreign Injuries; because they know it is a Principal in Reason of State to Maintain and Defend that which doth Support them and their Estates.

AP® History Reasoning Skills

Causation *In what ways did the development of maritime technology lead to the creation of the West India Company in 1621?*

Contextualization *Based on the excerpts, what were the objectives of mercantilism in this time period?*

Sources: Charter of Privileges and Exemptions the Dutch West India Company published with the permission of The Avalon Project, Lillian Goldman Law Library, Yale Law School. Excerpt from Thomas Mun, *England's Treasure by Foreign Trade* (London, UK: printed and sold by J. Morphew, 1713), 5–6, 87.

With the beginning of the Reformation, Charles redirected his attention as well as significant military and financial resources northward in support of the Counter-Reformation. Charles's defense of Catholic doctrine in the imperial Diet (assembly) was opposed by German princes swayed by Luther's appeals to German nationalism. These disputes led to open warfare in 1546 (the German Wars of Religion). Even though Charles could rely on the great wealth transferred to Spain from the conquests of Mexico and Peru (see Chapter 18), these costly and destructive religious wars drained his treasury and limited his ability to defeat the territorial ambitions of the Ottomans in the Mediterranean.

In the end the ambitions of Charles V were overwhelmed by the scale of his challenges, despite his enormous resources. In the Peace of Augsburg (1555) he recognized the right of German princes to choose whether Catholicism or Lutheranism would prevail in their particular states. He also accepted that Protestant princes would keep any church lands they had seized. This triumph of religious diversity ended Charles's political ambitions and put off German political unification for three centuries. In poor health and exhausted by his efforts, Charles decided to abdicate both the Holy Roman and Spanish thrones and retire to a monastery in 1556.

Charles V's son, Philip II, inherited his father's European territories in the low countries and Italy. He also inherited the throne of Spain with its rich American empire. Philip married Mary I of England and was recognized as her co-ruler, but her death without producing an heir in

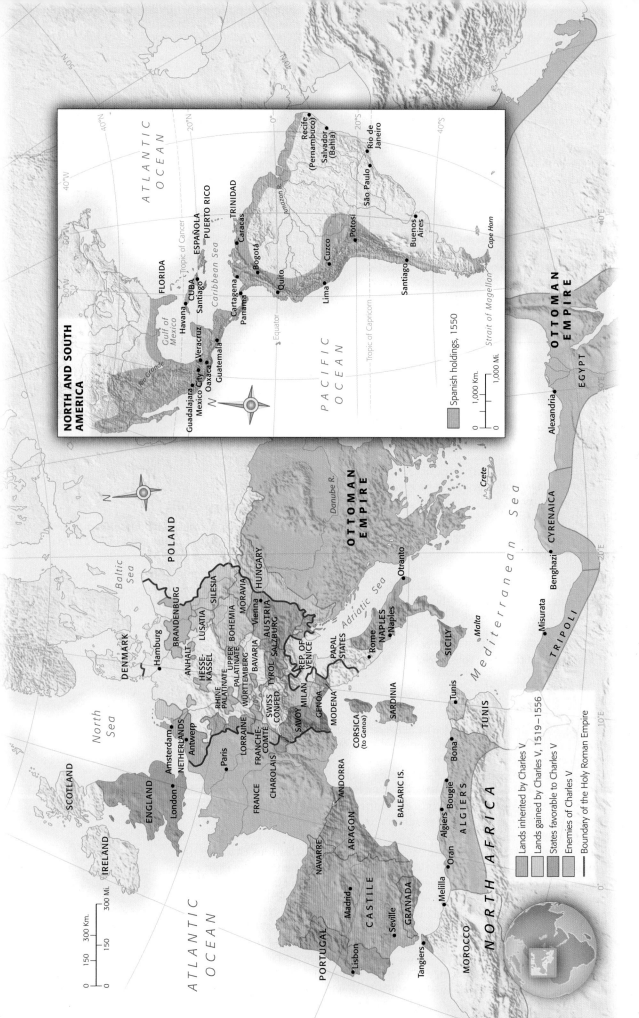

MAP 17.2   The European Empire of Charles V Charles was Europe's most powerful monarch, ruling Spain from 1516 and the Holy Roman Empire from 1519 to his abdication in 1556. The map inset shows his extensive holdings in the Americas, but not those in Asia.

Given the vast territory and cultural diversity of the empire of Charles V, was peace possible?

1558 and the ascension of Elizabeth I permanently ended the dynastic connection of Spain and England. In 1580 Philip inherited the throne of Portugal as well, adding Brazil and Portuguese colonies in Africa and Asia to his Spanish possessions. Ruler of sixteenth-century Europe's mightiest state, Philip II aggressively pursued the geopolitical policies that had thwarted his father.

Charles V's decision to simultaneously fight both Protestantism and the Muslim Ottoman Empire created a crushing debt burden for Philip II. Nevertheless, Philip committed to expensive land wars in the Low Countries and Italy as well as to large naval campaigns against England and the Ottomans. In the end, these wars squandered the great wealth flowing through Iberian ports from the colonial empire, leading to four bankruptcies during his reign. Philip's ambitious military campaigns also increased his dependence on the Spanish nobility, which directed his military forces. While Spain's aristocracy made up only 3 percent of the population, it controlled 97 percent of the land in 1600 and was exempt from most taxes. The nation's poor commoners, on the other hand, faced high sales taxes on manufacturing and commerce.

While Philip's forces had established Spanish domination of the Italian Peninsula and gained important naval victories against the Ottomans in the Mediterranean, he failed to defeat the Protestant rebels of the Netherlands and suffered a crushing naval reversal in his effort to invade England in 1588. In the end, Philip's wars consumed the great wealth of his empire, leaving Spain unprepared to maintain its early domination of the Atlantic when faced by sustained challenges from the Dutch, English, and French.

American bullion shipments dramatically increased the money supply in Europe. In Spain the effects of the resulting inflation (rising prices) made the nation's products uncompetitive, so that goods manufactured in France, Italy, or other European countries were cheaper than goods made in Spain. In this distorted market, Spanish guilds and merchants lost ground while the pace of technological innovation and commercial expansion grew across northern Europe. By 1700 most goods imported into Spain's colonies were of foreign origin. A Spanish saying captured the problem: "American silver was like rain on the roof—it poured down and washed away."

Philip's effort to seal Spain off from the Protestant Reformation and the intellectual tumult of the Scientific Revolution also imposed economic costs. He ordered the borders closed to all foreign publications not licensed by the Catholic Church and commanded all Spanish students to leave foreign universities and return home. Spain had long suffered from the negative intellectual and economic effects of the expulsions of Jews and Muslims ordered by Ferdinand and Isabel, and now Philip's commitment to the Counter-Reformation further isolated the nation's intellectuals from the debates and innovations of the era.

Despite Spain's problems, its rulers, like those of France and England, enjoyed some success promoting national political unification and religious unity. The most successful rulers reduced the autonomy of the church and the nobility by making them part of a unified national structure with the monarch at its head. The imposition of royal power over religious institutions in the sixteenth century was stormy, but the eventual outcome was clear. Bringing the nobles and other powerful interests into a centralized political system would take longer and led to more diverse outcomes.

17-3b The Monarchies of England and France

Over the course of the seventeenth century, the monarchs of England and France faced intense conflicts with powerful rivals. Religion was never absent as an issue in these struggles, but the very different constitutional outcomes that these struggles produced in England and France proved to be of greater significance in the long run.

To evade any check on his power, King Charles I of England (see Table 17.1) ruled for eleven years without summoning Parliament, his kingdom's representative body. Lacking Parliament's consent to new taxes, he raised funds by coercing "loans" from wealthy subjects and by applying existing tax laws more broadly. In 1640 a rebellion in Scotland forced him to summon Parliament to approve new taxes to pay for an army. Noblemen and churchmen sat in the House of Lords while representatives from towns and counties sat in the House of Commons. Before it would authorize new taxes, Parliament insisted on strict guarantees that the king would never again ignore the body's traditional rights. Unwilling to accept this limitation to his authority, King Charles refused and attempted to arrest his critics in the House of Commons in 1642, plunging the kingdom into the **English Civil War**.

Religious division helped fuel this struggle. Although a nominal Protestant, Charles I was married to a Catholic and favored forms of Anglican organization and ritual closest to Catholic

AP® Exam Tip
Be able to give a couple of examples of how different rulers displayed political power. Be able to compare displays of political power in different civilizations.

English Civil War (1642–1649) A conflict over royal versus parliamentary rights, caused by King Charles I's arrest of his parliamentary critics and ending with his execution in 1649. Its outcome checked the growth of royal absolutism and, with the Glorious Revolution of 1688 and the English Bill of Rights of 1689, ensured that England would be a constitutional monarchy.

TABLE 17.1 Rulers in Early Modern Western Europe

Spain	France	England/Great Britain
Habsburg Dynasty	**Valois Dynasty**	**Tudor Dynasty**
Charles I (King of Spain 1516–1556), also known as Charles V (Holy Roman Emperor 1519–1556)	Francis I (1515–1547)	Henry VIII (1509–1547)
Philip II (1556–1598)	Henry II (1547–1559)	Edward VI (1547–1553)
	Francis II (1559–1560)	Mary I (1553–1558)
	Charles IX (1560–1574)	Elizabeth I (1558–1603)
	Henry III (1574–1589)	
	Bourbon Dynasty	**Stuart Dynasty**
Philip III (1598–1621)	Henry IV (1589–1610)[a]	James I (1603–1625)
Philip IV (1621–1665)	Louis XIII (1610–1643	Charles I (1625–1649)[a,b]
	Louis XIV (1643–1715)	(Puritan Republic, 1649–1660)
Charles II (1665–1700)		Charles II (1660–1685)
		James II (1685–1688)[b]
		William III (1689–1702)
		and Mary II (1689–1694)
		Anne (1702–1714)
Bourbon Dynasty		**Hanoverian Dynasty**
Philip V (1700–1746)		
Ferdinand VI (1746–1759)		George I (1714–1727)
	Louis XV (1715–1774)	George II (1727–1760)

[a]Died a violent death.
[b]Was overthrown.

practice, despite a 1605 Catholic plot to blow up his father, King James I. Dissenting Protestants, especially the Puritans, resisted, fearing the re-establishment of the Catholic Church and a bloody repression of their beliefs. As the disagreement between the king and Parliament sharpened after 1640, these religious tensions infused the contest between the king and his Parliamentary enemies. Parliament charged that the king had fallen under the influence of "Jesuited Papists" and arrested and executed the king's ally the Archbishop of Canterbury, William Laud.

Militarily defeated in 1648, Charles refused to compromise. A year later a "Rump" Parliament purged of his supporters ordered his execution. Parliament then replaced the monarchy with a republic led by the victorious Puritan general Oliver Cromwell, who ruled as Protector General until his death in 1658. Cromwell expanded England's presence overseas and imposed firm control over Ireland and Scotland, but he was also unwilling to share power with Parliament. With his death, Parliament restored the Stuart line in the person of the executed king's son, Charles II (r. 1660–1685). James II (r. 1685–1688), his brother, then inherited the throne, but he provoked new conflict by again refusing to respect Parliament's rights and by baptizing his heir as a Roman Catholic. The leaders of Parliament forced him from the throne and into exile in the bloodless Glorious Revolution of 1688. James was replaced by the joint rule of Mary, his daughter, and her husband William of Orange who was Chief Magistrate of the Netherlands as well as James II's nephew. The Bill of Rights of 1689 formalized this new constitutional order by requiring the king to call Parliament frequently to consent to changes in laws or to raise an army in peacetime. Another law reaffirmed the official status of the Church of England but extended religious toleration to dissenting Puritans. Britain exited this tumultuous period with the power of the monarchy reduced and the power of Parliament, still an unrepresentative institution, increased. Similarly, many dissenting Protestant denominations gained greater independence, but other groups, including Catholics and Unitarians, continued to face religious discrimination.

In France the Estates General, like the English Parliament, represented the traditional rights of the clergy, the nobility, and the towns (i.e., the bourgeoisie). The Estates General was able to

AP® Exam Tip
Understand how rulers continued to use religious ideas, art, and monumental architecture to legitimize their rule just as they did in the early days of civilization.

assert its rights during the sixteenth-century French Wars of Religion, when the monarchy was weak. Thereafter France's Bourbon monarchs generally ruled without calling it into session. They put off financial crises by more efficient tax collection, by selling appointments to high government offices, and by borrowing, but by 1700 French debt levels challenged traditional fiscal practices. While some historians have used the term *absolutism* to describe the power of French monarchs in this era, even the most powerful of them, Louis XIV, carefully negotiated his policies with both the nobility and city authorities. While the king's power grew, long-established ways of governing like the sale of offices and reliance on patronage networks and personal relationships continued to frame decision making.

Louis XIV moved his court to a gigantic new palace at **Versailles (vuhr-SIGH)** in 1682. Capable of housing 10,000 people and surrounded by elaborately landscaped grounds and parks, the palace became an effective symbol of growing royal grandeur and power. The relocation of the court to this splendid palace created an arena where the high nobility and ecclesiastical hierarchy more intensely interacted with the monarch in a dense cycle of rituals and ceremonies that emphasized royal power.

Most contemporary European rulers admired and imitated the centralized powers and apparent absolutist authority of the French monarch. The checks and balances of the English model were more admired in later times and gained a favorable press with the beginnings of the Enlightenment. In his influential *Second Treatise of Civil Government* (1690), for example, English political philosopher John Locke (1632–1704) disputed monarchial claims to absolute authority by divine right, arguing that rulers derived their authority from the consent of the governed and were subject to the law. If monarchs overstepped the law, Locke asserted, citizens had the right and the duty to rebel. The consequences of this idea are considered in Chapter 23.

17-3c Warfare and Diplomacy

In addition to the civil wars that afflicted the Holy Roman Empire, France, and England, European states fought numerous international conflicts, provoked in part by efforts to protect or extend colonial empires. As a result, the major European nations were nearly always at war in this period (see the Chronology at the beginning of the chapter). As the geographic scope of warfare and the size of armies and navies grew, monarchs expended ever-larger sums of money and caused widespread devastation and death. The worst of the international conflicts, the Thirty Years' War (1618–1648), caused long-lasting depopulation and economic decline in much of the Holy Roman Empire.

These wars led to dramatic improvements in the organization, skill, and weaponry of European armed forces, making them among the most powerful in the world. The numbers of men in arms increased steadily throughout the early modern period. French forces, for example, grew from eighty-eight regiments of infantry and seventy-two of cavalry in 1691 to 238 regiments of infantry and ninety-four of cavalry in 1714. Even smaller European states built up impressive armies. Sweden, for example, with under a million people, had one of the finest and best-armed military forces in the seventeenth century, and Prussia, though it had fewer than 2 million inhabitants in 1700, boasted a large, well-disciplined army that made it one of Europe's major powers.

Larger armies required more effective command structures. But although some progress was made, the officer corps of the major powers continued to rely on the nobility, and patronage, rather than skill, was the basis for promotion and advancement. Training and battlefield control were marginally improved through more frequent drilling for professional troops and the introduction of new signaling techniques, but battlefields remained chaotic. Fortifications were expanded and improved in Europe and in colonial possessions, and even Spain, facing a deep fiscal crisis, borrowed vast sums to fortify Havana and Cartagena in the Americas. Paying for larger and better-armed fleets proved similarly expensive, but in the face of an intensifying competition for colonial wealth that stretched from the East Indies to the Caribbean and South Atlantic, no great power could afford to cut back.

Safe from the threat of direct invasion, only England among major European powers did not maintain a standing army. Its power depended on its navy. England's rise as a sea power had begun under King Henry VIII, who spent heavily on ships and promoted a domestic iron industry to supply cannon. The Royal Navy also copied innovative ship designs from

AP® Exam Tip
Understand the use of military professionals to maintain centralized control.

Versailles The huge palace built for French king Louis XIV south of Paris. The palace symbolized both French power and the triumph of royal authority over the French nobility.

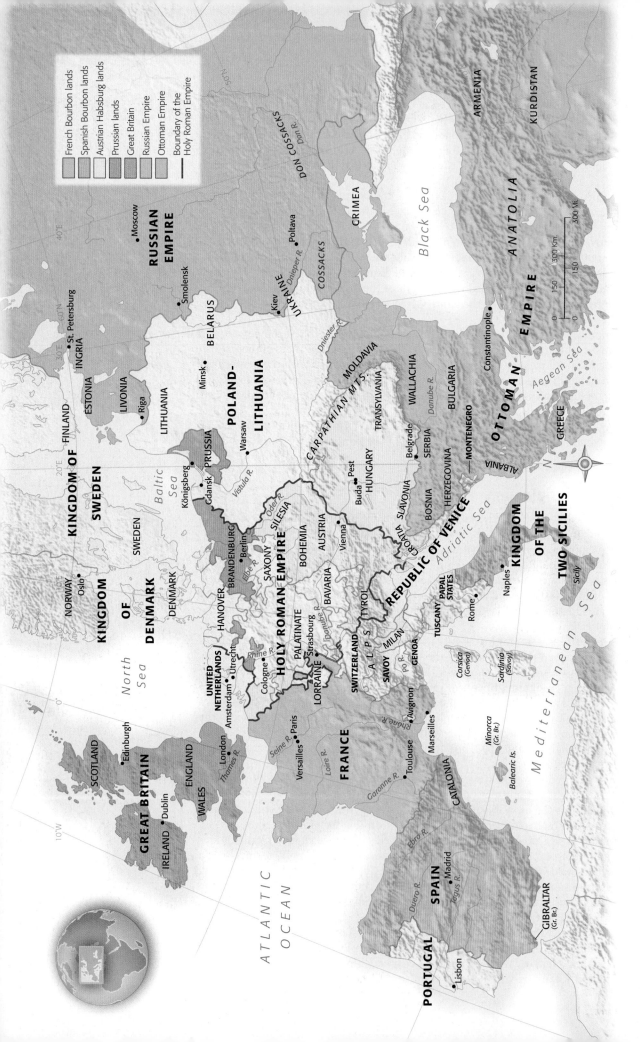

MAP 17.3   Europe in 1740 By the middle of the eighteenth century the great powers of Europe were France, the Austrian Empire, Great Britain, Prussia, and Russia. Spain, the Holy Roman Empire, and the Ottoman Empire were far weaker in 1740 than they had been two centuries earlier.

What were the most important political and territorial changes in Europe represented in Maps 17.2 and 17.3.

the Dutch in the second half of the seventeenth century. The crushing defeat of the Spanish Armada in 1588 by Henry's daughter, Elizabeth I, demonstrated the usefulness of these decisions and accelerated Spain's decline under Philip II. By the early eighteenth century, the Royal Navy had surpassed the rival French fleet in numbers. Now more secure, England merged with Scotland in 1706 to become Great Britain. It then annexed Ireland and built a North American empire.

As nations built up their strength, they also acted to preserve a **balance of power**. Although France was Europe's most powerful state, coalitions of the other great powers frustrated Louis XIV's efforts to expand its borders. In a series of costly eighteenth-century wars beginning with the War of the Spanish Succession (1701–1714), the combination of Britain's naval strength and the land armies of Austria and Prussia blocked French expansionist efforts and prevented the Bourbons from uniting the thrones of France and Spain (see Map 17.3).

17-3d **Paying the Piper**

European nations struggled to pay these heavy military costs while at the same time funding expanded bureaucracies, infrastructure improvements, and the growing extravagance of monarchs, but the obstacles were formidable. Governments collected taxes indirectly using **tax farmers**, private individuals who paid a flat rate to the government, typically less than 50 percent of the estimated tax obligation, for the right to collect the tax. This system allowed governments to avoid creating expensive new bureaucracies, but it also guaranteed corruption

balance of power The policy in international relations by which, beginning in the eighteenth century, the major European states acted together to prevent any one of them from becoming too powerful.

▲ **Versailles**   Constructed during the reign of Louis XIV of France, the palace of Versailles could house 10,000 people. Surrounded by elaborately landscaped grounds and parks, the palace became an effective symbol of royal absolutism. Perspective view of the Chateau, Gardens and Park of Versailles seen from the Avenue de Paris, 1668 (oil on canvas)/Patel, Pierre (1605-76)/Chateau de Versailles, France/Bridgeman Images

and limited revenue growth. The tax exemptions enjoyed by the nobility and clergy were among the greatest obstacles to increasing revenues, since these sectors controlled most of Europe's wealth. In the case of France and Spain, this situation led to the imposition of regressive new taxes on peasants and on commerce. Desperate governments were therefore attracted to dangerous short-term fiscal expedients that included currency debasement and cynical defaults on debts like Philip II's four bankruptcies.

It was inevitable that the success of early capitalism's innovations—joint-stock companies and stock markets—would draw the attention of governments thwarted by the tax intransigence of the elite. While these elites resisted taxation, they often found irresistible largely unregulated and highly speculative financial novelties, such as the stock of monopoly commercial enterprises and government bonds. The results were spectacularly visible in two nearly simultaneous speculative bubbles associated with the French Mississippi Company and the English South Sea Company.

After debasing the value of the nation's silver and gold coinage, the French government granted a license to create a bank to a fugitive Scottish nobleman, John Law, in 1716. The bank was allowed to issue paper money based on the promise to exchange these bills at face value for silver or gold coin. To everyone's surprise, the notes issued by Law's bank not only maintained their value but were preferred to coin for many transactions. As a result, the value of shares in the bank increased dramatically. Then in 1717 the French government allowed Law to create a monopoly company to develop French colonial territories along the Mississippi River, a region erroneously believed to have rich mines. The value of the initial share offering soared and was supplemented by issues of additional shares that also quickly increased in value. In the midst of the bubble, prices for shares could increase 10 to 20 percent in the course of a few hours. Stories of once-poor servants buying mansions and marrying their children into noble families abounded.

As the frenzy for shares mounted, the French government used Law's bank to print more paper money. After all, it was much easier to print money than to collect taxes. The bank's apparent success fed a speculative bubble in Mississippi Company shares as well, even though the company never earned a profit. Then, in 1720, fears that the bank no longer had the resources to exchange coin for its paper bills put pressure on the entire edifice. Even though Law got the government to first discount gold and silver coin against the paper currency and then to restrict individual possession of coin, a nervous French public hoarded coins and avoided paper currency. This situation led to the panicked selling of shares in both the bank and the Mississippi Company. As huge amounts of paper wealth disappeared in a matter of days, Law was forced to run for his life, leaving the French government to face once again its structural fiscal crisis.

In the English example, the English lord treasurer created the South Sea Company and granted it exclusive rights to trade with the Spanish colonies in the Americas in 1711. While the company issued stock that traded freely in the nation's nascent stock market, it was primarily a scheme to reduce the government's huge wartime debt. Holders of these debts were forced by statute to accept shares in the company to replace government debt obligations. Once in possession of the government bonds, the company borrowed new funds based on the supposed security of government debt. To individual investors, the South Sea Company seemed a profitable investment because it enjoyed both large annual interest payments from the government and a monopoly right to trade slaves to the Spanish colonies. In 1719, with news from Paris of the fast-rising share values of the French Mississippi Company on everyone's lips, the British government used the company to transform another £30,000,000 in debt into shares. When South Sea shares issued at £300 rose to £325, the company issued more stock, even though the company had almost no income from its commercial ventures.

In January 1720 share prices reached £1,050 before the inevitable crash dropped prices to £128 and thousands of investors found themselves ruined. Among the investors was scientist Isaac Newton, who said, "I can calculate the motions of the heavenly bodies but not the madness of people." While financial markets would eventually recover from these crashes and grow stronger still, the governments of France and Britain would now be forced to pay their bills by imposing taxes on reluctant citizens (see Chapter 23).

The rise of the Netherlands as an economic power stemmed from very different policies. The Spanish crown had acquired these resource-poor but commercially successful provinces as part of Charles V's inheritance. The decision of his son, King Philip II, to impose Spain's ruinous sales tax and to enforce Catholic orthodoxy drove the Dutch to revolt in 1566 and again

AP® Exam Tip
Understand how tax farming was used to generate revenue for territorial expansion.

tax farmers A system for collecting taxes and other state revenues from the population. Under this system, the state transfers the right of collection to private individuals or to groups of merchants called tax farmers in exchange for a guaranteed fee. Tax farmers accumulated great wealth since the taxes and charges they collected generally exceeded two or three times the amount they paid to the treasury.

▲ **The Spanish Armada** King Philip II of Spain sent a massive fleet against England in 1588. England's defeat of the Spanish fleet weakened Spain and began England's rise to naval dominance. DEA/G. DAGLI ORTI/De Agostini/Getty Images

in 1572. If successful, those measures would have discouraged business and driven away the Calvinists, Jews, and others who were essential to Dutch prosperity. The Dutch fought with skill and ingenuity, raising and training an army and a navy that were among the most effective in Europe. Unable to bear the military costs any longer, Spain accepted a truce that recognized autonomy in the northern Netherlands in 1609. Finally, in 1648, the independence of the seven United Provinces of the Free Netherlands (their full name) became final.

Rather than being ruined by the long war, the Netherlands emerged as the world's greatest trading nation (see Diversity & Dominance: Commercial Expansion and Risk). This economic success owed much to a decentralized government. During the long struggle against Spain, the provinces united around the prince of Orange, their sovereign, who served as commander-in-chief of the armed forces. But in economic matters each province was free to pursue its own interests. The most successful was the maritime province of Holland, which grew rich by favoring commercial interests.

After 1650 the Dutch faced growing competition from the English, who were developing their own close association of business and government. In a series of wars (1652–1678) England used its naval might to break Dutch dominance in overseas trade and extend its own colonial empire. With government support, the English merchant fleet doubled

Section Review

- Greater political centralization enabled early modern monarchs to exert increased influence on economic, religious, and social life.

- While the Holy Roman Empire fragmented along religious and political lines, Spain, France, and England achieved greater centralization and religious unity.

- Spain enforced Catholic unity through the Inquisition and France through Bourbon policy, while in England the church became an arm of royal power.

- In both England and France, monarchs struggled with rivals over the limits of royal authority.

- Armies grew larger and more sophisticated while European powers strove to maintain a balance of power.

- High military costs drove the European powers to attempt a variety of tax and financial policies, the most successful being those of England and the Netherlands.

between 1660 and 1700, and foreign trade rose by 50 percent. As a result, state revenue from customs duties tripled. During the eighteenth century Britain's trading position strengthened still more.

The debts run up by the Anglo-Dutch Wars helped persuade the English monarchy to greatly enlarge the government's role in managing the economy. Instead of continuing to use tax farmers, the government increased revenues by taxing the formerly exempt landed estates of the aristocrats and by collecting taxes directly. To secure cash quickly for warfare and other emergencies and to reduce the burden of debts from earlier wars, England imitated the Dutch by creating a central bank that could issue long-term loans at low rates.

The French government also developed its national economy, especially under royal adviser Jean Baptiste Colbert. He streamlined tax collection, promoted French manufacturing and shipping by imposing taxes on foreign goods, and improved transportation within France itself. Yet the power of the wealthy aristocrats kept the French government from following England's lead in taxing wealthy landowners, collecting taxes directly, and securing low-cost loans. Nor did France succeed in managing its debt as efficiently as England. (The role of governments in promoting overseas trade is also discussed in Chapter 19.)

17-4 Conclusion

Early modern Europe witnessed the weakening of the Catholic Church and the Protestant Reformation. Rejecting the authority of the pope and criticizing the institution of indulgences, Luther insisted on the moral primacy of faith over deeds; Calvin went further, holding that salvation was predestined by God. The pioneers of the Scientific Revolution such as Copernicus and Newton showed that they could explain the workings of the physical universe in natural terms. These scientists did not see any conflict between science and religion, but they paved the way for the more secular thinkers of the Enlightenment, who believed that human reason was capable of—and responsible for—discovering the laws that govern social behavior. By the end of this period, European intellectual life was no longer closely controlled by religious authorities.

Thanks to foreign and domestic trade, European cities in this period experienced rapid growth and the rise of a wealthy commercial class. It was also an era of growing speculative risk and market bubbles like Tulipmania and the Mississippi Company and South Sea bubbles. The Netherlands in particular prospered from expanded manufacturing and trade. With the formation of joint-stock companies and a powerful stock market, Amsterdam became Europe's major port and financial center. For peasants and laborers, however, life did not improve much, although serfdom was all but ended in western Europe. Rural poverty, coupled with the exemption from taxation enjoyed by wealthy landowners, sparked numerous armed rebellions. Women were dependent on their families' and husbands' wealth or lack of it and were barred from attending schools or joining guilds and professions.

Differing policies in the areas of religion, foreign relations, and economics explain the different histories of Europe's early modern states. Charles V, unable to reconcile the diverse interests of his Catholic and Protestant territories and their powerful local rulers, failed to create a unified Holy Roman Empire. Henry VIII, having failed to win an annulment of his marriage to Catherine of Aragon, severed all ties with the pope and led Parliament to accept him as head of the Church of England. Power struggles in England in the seventeenth century ultimately led to the execution of a king and a stronger Parliament, while in contemporary France a stronger monarchy emerged, symbolized by Louis XIV's construction of the palace at Versailles. Spain was Europe's mightiest state in the sixteenth century, but its failure to suppress the Netherlands Revolt and the costs of other wars led to bankruptcy and decline, despite its continued control of a vast empire.

The growth of English naval power led to the defeat of the Dutch in the Anglo-Dutch Wars and of France in the early eighteenth century when it attempted to expand its own empire through a union with Spain. Unlike Spain and France, which maintained aristocrats' traditional exemption from taxation, England began to tax their estates, and this policy—together with the establishment of direct taxation and the creation of a central bank from which it could secure low-cost loans—gave England a stronger financial foundation than its rivals enjoyed.

Key Terms

papacy p. 426

Renaissance (European)
    p. 426

indulgence p. 427

Protestant Reformation
    p. 428

Catholic Reformation p. 428

witch-hunt p. 430

Scientific Revolution p. 432

Enlightenment p. 434

bourgeoisie p. 435

joint-stock company p. 436

stock exchange p. 436

gentry p. 436

Little Ice Age p. 437

deforestation p. 437

Holy Roman Empire p. 440

Habsburg p. 440

English Civil War p. 443

Versailles p. 445

balance of power p. 447

tax farmer p. 448

Review Questions

Analyze the larger developments and continuities within and across chapters.

1. What were the key changes introduced into European intellectual life by the Renaissance and early Enlightenment?

2. What were the most important economic innovations in the period and what nations were chiefly responsible?

3. What were the reasons for the violence afflicting Europe in this era?

 MINDTAP From Cengage   MindTap® is a fully online, personalized learning experience built upon Cengage Learning content. MindTap® combines student learning tools—readings, multimedia, activities, and assessments—into a singular Learning Path that guides students through the course and helps students develop the critical thinking, analysis, and communication skills that are essential to academic and professional success.

Multiple-Choice Questions

Questions 1–3 refer to the passage below.

"The trade of a joint stock company is always managed by a court of directors. This court, indeed, is frequently subject, in many respects, to the control of a general court of proprietors. But the greater part of those proprietors seldom pretend to understand anything of the business of the company, and when the spirit of faction happens not to prevail among them, give themselves no trouble about it, but receive contentedly such half yearly or yearly dividend as the directors think proper to make to them. This total exemption from trouble and from risk, beyond a limited sum, encourages many people to become adventurers in joint stock companies, who would, upon no account, hazard their fortunes in any private copartner [ship]."

Adam Smith explains joint-stock companies
in *Wealth of Nations* (1776)

1. According to Smith, what was the advantage of investing in a joint stock company?

   (A) They tended to be run by experts who could make the wisest decisions on behalf of the stockholders.

   (B) There was no risk associated with joint-stock companies so they were preferable to investments in property.

   (C) The directors were chosen by the stockholders and were therefore accountable to the investors.

   (D) Sharing the risk of investing with a group relieved some of the stress of speculation.

2. What general transformation in the world between 1500 and 1750 might have been a cause of the popularity of Smith's *Wealth of Nations*?

   (A) European financial decisions were increasingly made by autocratic rulers.

   (B) With increased long-distance trade, there were greater opportunities to acquire wealth.

   (C) Europe's hereditary nobility were looking for ways to increase their income as land was seized by the monarchies.

   (D) As European monarchs began to drive back the Ottoman threat, there were financial rewards and opportunities.

3. What earlier economic theory had dominated Western Europe, influencing the creation of joint-stock companies as a way for rulers and investors to profit?

   (A) Mercantilism

   (B) Capitalism

   (C) Market socialism

   (D) Monetarism

Questions 4–6 refer to the passage below.

"The state of monarchy is the supremest thing upon earth. For kings are not only God's lieutenants upon earth, and sit upon God's throne, but even by God himself they are called gods. There be three principal similitudes that illustrate the state of monarchy. [Firstly] In the Scriptures kings are called gods, and so their power after a certain relation compared to the divine power. Kings are also compared to fathers of families, for a king is truly parens patriae [able to make legal decisions], the politic father of his people. And lastly, kings are compared to the head of this microcosm of the body of man."

King James VI [of Scotland] and I [of England],
from a speech to Parliament, 1610

4. In what method commonly used by monarchs in the sixteenth and seventeenth centuries was King James attempting to legitimize his rule with this speech?

   (A) He was establishing his legal right to override the decisions of Parliament.

   (B) He was using his position as the head of the Church of England to validate his control over the people.

   (C) He was showing his compassion for the people of England and thus justifying his role as their king.

   (D) He was using religious doctrine to justify political legitimacy by asserting that he was ruling with the will of God.

5. Which of the following is an example of how another European ruler attempted to reinforce his rule in this period?

   (A) Philip II of Spain sealed off Spain from the threat of Protestantism.

   (B) Charles V of Spain defended Catholic dogma in the Counter-Reformation.

   (C) Louis XIV of France created the gigantic Palace of Versailles near Paris.

   (D) Charles I of England defeated his opponents in the English Civil War.

6. Which of the following would be seen as a challenge to the concept asserted by James I in the speech above?

   (A) Henry VIII's split from the Roman Catholic church

   (B) John Locke's arguments regarding the consent of the governed

   (C) The reinstatement of the Stuart line with the return of Charles II to the throne

   (D) The Bourbon monarch's refusal to call the Estates General

Questions 7–10 refer to the passage below.

"Next to the theologians in happiness are those who commonly call themselves *the religious and monks*. Both are complete misnomers, since most of them stay as far away from religion as possible, and no people are seen more often in public. . . . They cannot read, and so they consider it the height of piety to have no contact with literature. . . . Most of them capitalize on their dirt and poverty by whining for food from door to door. . . . These smooth fellows simply explain that by their very filth, ignorance, boorishness, and insolence they enact the lives of the apostles for us. It is amusing to see how they do everything by rule, almost mathematically. Any slip is sacrilege. Each shoe string must have so many knots and must be of a certain color. . . . They even condemn each other, these professors of apostolic charity, making an extraordinary stir if a habit is belted incorrectly or if its color is a shade too dark. . . . The monks of certain orders recoil in horror from money, as if it were poison, but not from wine or women. They take extreme pains, not in order to be like Christ, but to be unlike each other. They forget that Christ will condemn all of this and will call for a reckoning of that which He has prescribed, namely, charity."

Dutch humanist Desiderius Erasmus,
from *The Praise of Folly*, 1509

7. Erasmus criticizes religious figures by accusing them of

   (A) wasting money by living extravagantly.

   (B) spending their time distributing food rather than praying.

   (C) not following the teachings of Christ by giving to the poor.

   (D) spending their days studying the Bible rather than helping others.

8. What made the words of Erasmus particularly important in the early sixteenth century?

   (A) He was questioning the existing dominance of the Catholic Church.

   (B) He was advocating that priests could reject celibacy and marry.

   (C) He was proposing a new religious sect in Europe.

   (D) He was the first person to use science to attack an institution.

9. What was the global historical context into which Erasmus's *The Praise of Folly* was published?

   (A) Europe was in a period when religion was unimportant in most people's lives.

   (B) A series of plagues in Europe had increased superstition and bigotry.

   (C) Europe was increasingly isolated from the rest of the world due to the threat of the Ottoman Empire.

   (D) Changing patterns of trade intensified connections between groups, leading to the creation of new concepts.

10. Erasmus and other scholars who questioned Roman Catholic Church practices were influential in starting a movement to reform the Church, aided by

    (A) the Ottoman Empire, which looked to weaken Europe.

    (B) the more liberal approach of most Western leaders.

    (C) the new availability of printed materials.

    (D) a series of freethinking popes who questioned Church values.

Short-Answer Questions

1. Answer all parts of the question that follows.

   (A) Identify ONE reason for the increase in warfare in Europe in the sixteenth and seventeenth centuries.

   (B) Explain ONE immediate result of the increase in warfare in Europe in the sixteenth and seventeenth centuries.

   (C) Explain ONE long-term result of the increase in warfare in Europe in the sixteenth and seventeenth centuries.

2. Answer all parts of the question that follows.

   (A) Identify ONE similarity between the Protestant Reformation and the Counter-Reformation.

   (B) Explain ONE difference between the Protestant Reformation and the Counter-Reformation.

   (C) Explain ANOTHER difference between the Protestant Reformation and the Counter-Reformation.

18 The Diversity of American Colonial Societies, 1530–1770

AP® Framework Terms

Columbian Exchange
Smallpox
Measles
Influenza
Mosquitoes
Rats
African slavery

Overarching Questions

1 How and to what extent have environmental factors, disease, and technology affected patterns of human migration and settlement over time? (ENV)

2 How have cross-cultural interactions resulted in the diffusion of culture, technologies, and scientific knowledge? (CUL)

3 How and why have economic, social, cultural, and geographic factors influenced the process of state building, expansion, and dissolution? (SB)

4 What are the causes and effects of economic strategies of different types of communities, states, and empires? (ECON)

5 How have distinctions based on kinship, ethnicity, class, gender, and race influenced the development and transformations of social hierarchies? (SOC)

Shulush Homa—an eighteenth-century Choctaw leader called "Red Shoes" by the English—faced a dilemma. For years he had befriended the French who had moved into the lower Mississippi Valley, protecting their outlying settlements from other native groups and by producing a steady flow of deerskins for trade. In return he received guns and gifts as well as honors previously given only to chiefs. Though born a commoner, he had parlayed his skillful politicking with the French—and the shrewd distribution of the gifts he received—to enhance his position in Choctaw society. Then his fortunes turned. In the course of yet another war between England and France, the English cut off French shipping. Faced with followers unhappy over his sudden inability to supply French guns, Red Shoes forged a dangerous new arrangement with the English that led his former allies, the French, to put a price on his head. His murder in 1747 launched a civil war among the Choctaw. By the end of this conflict both the French colonial population and the Choctaw people had suffered greatly.

The story of Red Shoes reveals a number of themes from the period of European colonization of the Americas. First, although the wars, epidemics, and territorial loss associated with European settlement threatened Amerindians, many adapted the new technologies and new political possibilities to their own purposes and thrived—at least

452

▲ **Choctaw Village in Louisiana at Time of French Colonial Rule**   This scene of village life illustrates the integration of the Choctaw in the colonial economy. The painting places a young African slave and European trade goods in a scene where the Choctaw pursue traditional tasks.   Gift of the estate of Belle J.Bushnell. Courtesy of the Peabody Museum of Archaeology and Ethnology, Havard University, PM# 41-72-10/20(digital file #60741527)

for a time. In the end, though, the best that they could achieve was a holding action. The people of the Old World were coming to dominate the people of the New World.

Second, after centuries of isolation, the political and economic demands of European empires forced the Americas onto the global stage. The influx of Europeans and Africans resulted in a vast biological and cultural transformation, as new plants, animals, diseases, peoples, and technologies fundamentally altered the natural environment. This was not a one-way transfer, however. The technologies and resources of the New World also contributed to profound changes in the Old. Among them, the transfer of American staple crops helped fuel a population spurt in Europe, Asia, and Africa while American riches altered European economic, social, and political relations.

Third, the story of Red Shoes and the Choctaw illustrates the complexity of colonial society, in which Amerindians, Europeans, and Africans all contributed to the creation of new cultures. Although similar processes took place throughout the Americas, the particulars varied from place to place, creating a diverse range of cultures. The society that arose in each colony reflected the colony's mix of native peoples, its connections to the African slave trade, and the characteristics of the European society establishing the colony. As the colonies matured, new concepts of identity developed, and those living in the Americas began to see themselves as distinct. ●

18-1 The Columbian Exchange

How did the Columbian Exchange alter the natural environment of the Americas?

The term **Columbian Exchange** refers to the transfer of peoples, animals, plants, and diseases between the New and Old Worlds. The European invasion and settlement of the Western Hemisphere opened a long era of biological and technological transfers that altered American environments. Within a century of the first European settlement, the domesticated livestock and major agricultural crops of the Old World (the known world before Columbus's voyage) had spread over much of the Americas, and the New World's useful staple crops had enriched the agricultures of Europe, Asia, and Africa. Old World diseases that entered the Americas with European immigrants and African slaves devastated indigenous populations. These dramatic population changes weakened native peoples' capacity for resistance and accelerated the transfer of plants, animals, and related technologies. As a result, the colonies of Spain, Portugal, England, and France became vast arenas of cultural and social experimentation.

18-1a Demographic Changes

Because of their long isolation from other continents (see Chapter 15), the peoples of the New World lacked immunity to diseases introduced from the Old World. As a result, death rates among Amerindian peoples during the epidemics of the early colonial period were very high. The lack of reliable estimates of the Amerindian population at the moment of contact has frustrated efforts to measure the deadly impact of these diseases, but scholars agree that Old World diseases had a terrible effect on native peoples. According to one estimate, the population of central Mexico fell from more than 13 million to approximately 700,000 in the century that followed 1521. In this same period the populations of the Maya and Inka regions declined by nearly 75 percent or more. Brazil's native population fell by more than 50 percent within a century of the arrival of the Portuguese.

Smallpox, which arrived in the Caribbean in 1518, was the deadliest of the early epidemics. In Mexico and Central America, 50 percent or more of the Amerindian population died during the first wave of smallpox epidemics. The disease then spread to South America with equally devastating effects. Measles arrived in the New World in the 1530s and was followed by diphtheria, typhus, influenza, and pulmonary plague. Mortality was often greatest when two or more diseases struck at the same time. Between 1520 and 1521 influenza and other ailments attacked the Cakchiquel of Guatemala. Their chronicle recalls:

> Great was the stench of the dead. After our fathers and grandfathers succumbed, half the people fled to the fields. The dogs and vultures devoured the bodies. . . . So it was that we became orphans, oh my sons! . . . We were born to die![1]

By the mid-seventeenth century malaria and yellow fever were also present in tropical regions of the Americas. The deadliest form of malaria arrived with the African slave trade, ravaging the already reduced native populations and afflicting Europeans as well.

The development of English and French colonies in North America in the seventeenth century led to similar patterns of contagion and mortality. In 1616 and 1617 epidemics nearly exterminated New England's indigenous groups. Epidemics also followed French fur traders as far as Hudson Bay and the Great Lakes. Although there is very little evidence that Europeans consciously used disease as a tool of empire, the deadly results of contact clearly undermined the ability of native peoples to resist settlement.

18-1b Transfer of Plants and Animals

Even as epidemics swept through the indigenous population, the New and the Old Worlds were participating in a vast exchange of plants and animals that radically altered diet and lifestyles in both regions. Settlers brought all the staples of southern European agriculture—such as wheat,

AP® Exam Tip Understand how the Columbian Exchange affected both the Americas and Afro-Eurasia.

Columbian Exchange The exchange of plants, animals, diseases, and technologies between the Americas and the rest of the world following Columbus's voyages.

---

[1]Quoted in Alfred W. Crosby, Jr., *The Columbian Exchange: Biological and Cultural Consequences of 1492* (Westport, CT: Greenwood Press, 1972), 58.

CHRONOLOGY

	Spanish America	Brazil	British America	French America
1500	1518 Smallpox arrives in Caribbean			
	1535 Creation of Viceroyalty of New Spain	1530s Sugar agriculture introduced		1534–1542 Jacques Cartier's voyages to explore Newfoundland and Gulf of St. Lawrence
	1540s Creation of Viceroyalty of Peru	1540–1600 Era of Amerindian slavery		
	1542 New Laws attempt to improve treatment of Amerindians	After 1540 Sugar begins to dominate the economy		
	1545 Silver discovered at Potosí, Bolivia			
1600			1607 Jamestown founded	1608 Quebec founded
	1625 Population of Potosí reaches 120,000	By 1620 African slave trade provides majority of plantation workers	1620 Plymouth founded	
		1630s Quilombo of Palmares founded	1660 Slave population in Virginia begins period of rapid growth	
		1649 First capital of colony established in Salvador da Bahia	1664 English take New York from Dutch	1699 Louisiana founded
1700	1700 Last Habsburg ruler of Spain dies			
	1713 First Bourbon ruler of Spain crowned	1750–1777 Reforms of marquis de Pombal	1754–1763 French and Indian War	1760 English take Canada
	1770s and 1780s Amerindian revolts in Andean region	1775 Creation of Viceroyalty of Brazil with capital in Rio de Janeiro	1759 English defeat French at Quebec	

olives, grapes, and garden vegetables—to the Americas soon after contact. Colonization also introduced African and Asian crops such as rice, bananas, coconuts, breadfruit, and sugar. While natives remained loyal to their traditional staples, they added many foods like citrus fruits, melons, figs, and sugar as well as onions, radishes, and salad greens to their cuisines.

In return the Americas offered the Old World an abundance of useful plants. Maize, potatoes, and manioc revolutionized agriculture and diet in parts of Europe, Africa, and Asia (see Environment & Technology: Natural Disasters and the Caribbean Plantation Economy, in Chapter 19). Many experts assert that the growth of world population after 1700 resulted from the spread of these useful crops, which provided more calories per acre than did most Old World staples. Beans, squash, tomatoes, sweet potatoes, peanuts, chilies, and chocolate also gained widespread acceptance in the Old World. In addition, the New World provided the Old with plants that provided dyes, medicine, varieties of cotton, and tobacco.

The introduction of European livestock had a dramatic impact on New World environments and cultures. Faced with few natural predators, cattle, pigs, horses, and sheep, as well as pests like rats and rabbits, multiplied rapidly in the

AP® Exam Tip
Understand the impact of the Columbian Exchange on the environment.

Section Review

- The creation of Spanish and Portuguese empires in America accelerated global exchanges of peoples, plants, animals, diseases, and technologies.

- Old World diseases decimated New World peoples and made them vulnerable to European expansion, and Old World animals overran the landscape and changed New World practices.

- Both the Old and New Worlds also profited from the introduction of new plants and animals.

◀ **The Columbian Exchange** In this painting an Amerindian woman milks a cow, suggesting how the Columbian Exchange altered native culture and environment. While livestock introduced by Europeans sometimes destroyed the fields of native peoples, cattle, sheep, pigs, and goats also provided food, leather, and wool. Iberfoto/Iberfoto/Superstock

Americas. On the vast plains of southern Brazil, Uruguay, and Argentina, for example, herds of wild cattle and horses exceeded 50 million by 1700.

Where Old World livestock spread most rapidly, environmental changes were dramatic. Many priests and colonial officials noted the destructive impact of marauding livestock on Amerindian agriculturists. The first viceroy of Mexico, Antonio de Mendoza, wrote to the Spanish king: "May your Lordship realize that if cattle are allowed, the Indians will be destroyed." Sheep, which grazed grasses close to the ground, thus promoting erosion, were also an environmental threat.

Yet the viceroy's stark choice misrepresented the complex response of indigenous peoples to these new animals. For example, wild cattle on the plains of South America, northern Mexico, and Texas also provided indigenous peoples with abundant supplies of meat and hides. In the present-day southwestern United States, the Navajo became sheepherders and expert weavers. Even in the centers of European settlement, Amerindians turned European animals to their own advantage by becoming muleteers, cowboys, and sheepherders.

No animal had a more striking effect on the cultures of native peoples than the horse, which increased the efficiency of hunters and the military capacity of warriors on the plains of both North and South America. The horse permitted the Apache, Sioux, Blackfoot, Comanche, Assiniboine, and others to more efficiently hunt the vast herds of buffalo in North America. The horse also revolutionized the cultures of the Mapuche and Pampas peoples in South America.

18-2 Spanish America and Brazil

What role did forced labor play in the main industries of Spanish America and Brazil?

The frontiers of conquest and settlement expanded rapidly. Within 100 years of Columbus's first voyage to the Western Hemisphere, the Spanish Empire in America included most of the islands of the Caribbean and a vast area that stretched from northern Mexico to the plains of the Rio de la Plata region (a region that includes the modern nations of Argentina, Uruguay, and Paraguay). Portuguese settlement developed more slowly, but before the end of the sixteenth century, Portugal had occupied most of the Brazilian coast and laid claim to an enormous region in the South American interior.

Early settlers from Spain and Portugal sought to create colonial societies based on the institutions and customs of their homelands. They viewed society as a vertical hierarchy of estates (classes of society), as uniformly Catholic, and as an arrangement of patriarchal extended-family networks. In the Americas they quickly moved to establish the religious, social, and administrative institutions that were familiar to them.

Despite the imposition of foreign institutions and loss of life caused by epidemics, indigenous peoples exercised a powerful influence on the development of colonial societies. Aztec and Inka elite families sought to protect their traditional privileges and rights through marriage or less formal alliances with Spanish settlers. They also quickly learned to use colonial courts to defend

AP® Exam Tip
Understand the social and economic effects of the American system.

their claims to land. In Spanish and Portuguese colonies, indigenous military allies and laborers proved crucial to the development of European settlements. Nearly everywhere, Amerindian religious beliefs and practices survived beneath the surface of an imposed Christianity. Amerindian languages, cuisines, medical practices, and agricultural techniques also survived the conquest and influenced the development of Latin American culture.

The African slave trade added a third cultural stream to colonial Latin American society. At first, African slaves were concentrated in plantation regions of Brazil and the Caribbean (see Chapter 19), but by the end of the colonial era, Africans and their descendants were living throughout Spanish and Portuguese America, introducing elements of their agricultural practices, music, religious beliefs, cuisine, and social customs to colonial societies.

18-2a State and Church

The Spanish crown moved quickly to curb the independent power of the conquistadors and to establish royal authority over both defeated native populations and European settlers, but geography and technology thwarted this ambition. European officials could not control the distant colonies too closely because it took a ship more than 200 days to make a roundtrip voyage from Spain to Veracruz, Mexico, and much more time to areas of South America like Lima, Peru.

As a result, the highest-ranking Spanish officials in the colonies, the viceroys of New Spain and Peru, enjoyed broad power, but they also faced obstacles to their authority in the vast territories they sought to control. Created in 1535, the Viceroyalty of New Spain, with its capital in Mexico City, included Mexico, the southwest of what is now the United States, Central America, and the islands of the Caribbean. Created five years later, the Viceroyalty of Peru, with its capital in Lima, governed all of Spanish South America (see Map 18.1).

Until the seventeenth century, most colonial officials were born in Spain, but fiscal mismanagement eventually forced the Crown to sell appointments. As a result, local-born members of the colonial elite gained many offices.

In the sixteenth century Portugal concentrated its resources and energies on Asia and Africa. Because early settlers found neither mineral wealth nor rich native empires in Brazil, the Portuguese king was slow to create expensive mechanisms of colonial government in the New World, but mismanagement forced the king to appoint a governor-general in 1549 and make Salvador Brazil's capital. In 1720 the king named the first viceroy of Brazil and then, in 1775, moved the colony's capital to Rio de Janeiro.

The government institutions of the Spanish and Portuguese colonies had a more uniform character and were much more extensive and costly than those later established in North America by France and Great Britain. The enormous wealth produced in Spanish America by silver and gold mines and in Brazil by sugar plantations and, after 1690, gold mines financed these large and intrusive colonial bureaucracies. These institutions made the colonies more responsive to the initiatives of Spanish and Portuguese monarchs, but they also thwarted local economic initiative and political experimentation. More importantly, the heavy tax burden imposed by these two European states drained capital from the colonies, slowing investment and retarding economic growth.

In both Spanish America and Brazil, the Catholic Church became the primary agent for the introduction and transmission of Christian belief as well as European language and culture. The church undertook the conversion of Amerindians, ministered to the spiritual needs of European settlers, and promoted intellectual life through the introduction of the printing press and the founding of schools and universities.

Spain and Portugal justified their American conquests by assuming an obligation to convert native populations to Christianity. This effort to convert America's native peoples expanded Christianity on a scale similar to its earlier expansion in Europe at the time of Constantine in the fourth century. In New Spain alone hundreds of thousands of conversions and baptisms were achieved within a few years of the conquest. However, the small numbers of missionaries limited the quality of indoctrination. One Dominican claimed to the king that the rival Franciscans "have taken and occupied three fourths of the country, though they do not have enough friars for it. . . . In most places they are content to say a mass once a year; consider what sort of indoctrination they give them [natives]!"[2]

AP® Exam Tip
Explain how the increased interaction between hemispheres expanded the spread and reform of existing religions and contributed to religious conflicts and the creation of syncretic belief systems and practices.

---

[2]Fray Andés de Moguer, 1554, quoted in James Lockhart and Enrique Otte, eds., *Letters and People of the Spanish Indies Sixteenth Century* (Cambridge, UK: Cambridge University Press, 1976), 216.

MAP 18.1 **Colonial Latin America in the Eighteenth Century** Spain and Portugal controlled most of the Western Hemisphere in the eighteenth century. In the sixteenth century they had created new administrative jurisdictions—viceroyalties—to defend their respective colonies against European rivals. Taxes assessed on colonial products helped pay for this extension of governmental authority.

Did the territorial scale and geographic diversity of the Spanish colonies and the Portuguese colony of Brazil affect the development of local economies?

▶ **Saint Martín de Porres (1579–1639)** Martín de Porres was the illegitimate son of a Spanish nobleman and a black servant. He entered the Dominican Order in Lima, Peru, where he was known for his generosity, his religious visions, and his ability to heal the sick. In this painting the artist celebrates Martín de Porres's spirituality while representing him doing the type of work presumed to be suitable for a person of mixed descent. Album/Oronoz/Album/Superstock

The Catholic clergy sought to achieve their evangelical ends by first converting members of the Amerindian elites, in the hope that they could persuade others to follow their example. To pursue this objective, Franciscan missionaries in Mexico created a seminary to train members of the indigenous elite to become priests, but they curtailed these idealistic efforts when church authorities discovered that many converts were secretly observing old beliefs and rituals. The trial and punishment of two converted Aztec nobles for heresy in the 1530s and the torture of hundreds of Maya in the 1560s by zealous Franciscan missionaries repelled the church hierarchy and led it to end the violent repression of native religious practice and limit the recruitment of an Amerindian clergy. In Peru a native millenarian movement sought to roll back the Christian evangelical effort in 1564, leading after 1609 to a focused effort by the Catholic Church to eradicate surviving indigenous belief and ritual—an ambition that was never fully realized.

Despite its failures, the Catholic clergy did provide native peoples with some protections against the abuse and exploitation of Spanish settlers. The priest **Bartolomé de Las Casas** (1474–1566) was the most influential defender of the Amerindians in the early colonial period. He arrived in Hispaniola in 1502 as a settler and initially lived from the forced labor of natives. Deeply moved by the deaths of so many Amerindians and by the misdeeds of the Spanish, Las Casas entered the Dominican Order and later became the first bishop of Chiapas, in southern Mexico. For the remainder of his long life Las Casas served as the most-influential advocate for native peoples. His most important achievement was the enactment of the New Laws of 1542—reform legislation that outlawed the enslavement of Amerindians and limited other forms of forced labor.

European clergy had arrived in the Americas with the intention of transmitting Catholic Christian belief and ritual without alteration. The linguistic diversity of Amerindian populations and their geographic dispersal over a vast landscape defeated this ambition. The resulting slow progress and limited success of evangelization led to the appearance of a unique Amerindian Christianity that blended European Christian beliefs with important elements of traditional native cosmology and ritual. The Catholic clergy and most European settlers viewed this evolving mixture as the work of the Devil or as evidence of Amerindian inferiority. Instead, it was one component of the process of cultural borrowing and innovation that contributed to a distinct and original Latin American culture. The importation of millions of enslaved Africans added another rich mix of religious beliefs and practices, including Muslims

After 1600 the terrible loss of Amerindian population caused by epidemics and growing signs of resistance to conversion led the Catholic Church to redirect most of its resources from native regions in the countryside to growing colonial cities and towns with large European populations. One important outcome of this altered mission was the founding of universities and secondary schools and the stimulation of urban intellectual life. Over time, the church became the richest institution in the Spanish colonies, controlling ranches, plantations, and vineyards as well as serving as the society's banker.

Bartolomé de Las Casas First bishop of Chiapas, in southern Mexico. He devoted most of his life to protecting Amerindian peoples from exploitation. His major achievement was the New Laws of 1542, which outlawed the enslavement of Amerindians and limited other forced labor.

AP® Exam Tip
Explain how commercialization and the creation of a global economy were intimately connected to new global circulation of silver from the Americas.

18-2b Colonial Economies

The silver mines of Peru and Mexico and the sugar plantations of Brazil dominated the economic development of colonial Latin America. The mineral wealth of the New World fueled the early development of European capitalism and funded Europe's greatly expanded trade with Asia. Profits produced in these economic centers also promoted the growth of colonial cities, concentrated scarce investment capital and labor resources, and stimulated the development of livestock raising and agriculture in neighboring rural areas (see Map 18.1). Once established, this colonial dependence on mineral and agricultural exports left an enduring social and economic legacy in Latin America.

The Spanish and later the Portuguese produced gold worth millions of pesos, but silver mines in the Spanish colonies generated the most wealth and therefore exercised the greatest economic influence. The first important silver strikes occurred in Mexico in the 1530s and 1540s. In 1545 the Spanish discovered the single richest silver deposit in the Americas at **Potosí** (**poh-toh-SEE**) in Alto Peru (what is now Bolivia). The silver of Alto Peru and Peru dominated the Spanish colonial economy until 1680, when it was surpassed by Mexican silver production. At first, miners extracted silver ore by smelting, a process during which crushed ore, packed with charcoal, was fired in a furnace. But this wasteful use of forest resources led to deforestation near the mining centers. Faced with rising fuel costs, Mexican miners developed an efficient method of chemical extraction that relied on mixing mercury with the silver ore (see Environment & Technology: A Silver Refinery at Potosí, 1700). Silver yields and profits increased with the use of mercury amalgamation, but this process, too, had severe environmental costs, since mercury is a poison that contaminated the environment and sickened the Amerindians forced to work in the mines.

From the time of Columbus, indigenous populations had been compelled to provide labor for European settlers in the Americas. Until the 1540s in Spanish colonies, Spanish authorities divided Amerindians among settlers, who then forced them to provide labor or goods. This form of forced labor was called **encomienda** (**in-co-mee-EN-dah**). As epidemics and mistreatment led to the decline in Amerindian population, reforms such as the New Laws sought to eliminate the encomienda. The discovery of silver, however, led to new forms of compulsory labor. In the mining region of Mexico, where epidemics had reduced Amerindian populations, silver miners came to rely on wage laborers. Peru's Amerindian population survived in larger numbers, allowing the Spanish there to impose a form of labor called the *mita* (**MEE-tah**). Under this system, one-seventh of adult male Amerindians were compelled to work for two to four months each year in mines, farms, or textile factories.

AP® Exam Tip
Understand the important role of a range of coercive labor systems in the Americas in this time period.

As the Amerindian population declined with new epidemics, villages were forced to shorten the period between mita obligations. Instead of serving every seven years, many men returned to the mines after only a year or two. Unwilling to accept mita service and the other tax burdens imposed on Amerindian villages, thousands abandoned traditional agriculture and moved permanently to Spanish mines and farms as paid laborers. The long-term result of these individual decisions weakened Amerindian village life and promoted the assimilation of Amerindians into Spanish-speaking Catholic colonial society.

Before the settlement of Brazil, the Portuguese had already developed sugar plantations using African slave labor on the Atlantic islands of Madeira, the Azores, Cape Verdes, and São Tomé (see Chapter 16). Because of the success of these early experiences, they were able to quickly transfer this profitable form of agriculture to Brazil. After 1540 sugar production expanded rapidly, and by the seventeenth century it dominated the Brazilian economy.

At first the Portuguese sugar planters enslaved Amerindians captured in war or seized from their villages. As a result of the epidemics that raged across Brazil in the sixteenth and seventeenth centuries thousands of Amerindian slaves died, creating a labor shortage. Slave raiders then pushed into the interior, even attacking Amerindian populations in neighboring Spanish colonies.

Amerindian slaves remained an important source of labor and slave raiding a significant business in frontier regions into the eighteenth century. But sugar planters eventually came to rely more on African slaves. While African slaves at first cost much more than Amerindian slaves, planters found them more productive and more resistant to disease. As profits from the plantations increased, imports of African slaves rose from an average of 2,000 per year in the late sixteenth century to approximately 7,000 per year a century later, outstripping the immigration

Potosí Located in what is now Bolivia, one of the richest silver mining centers and most populous cities in colonial Spanish America.

encomienda A grant of authority over a population of Amerindians in the Spanish colonies. It provided the grant holder with a supply of cheap labor and periodic payments of goods by the Amerindians. It obliged the grant holder to Christianize the Amerindians.

Environment & Technology
A Silver Refinery at Potosí, 1700

The silver refineries of Spanish America were among the largest and most heavily capitalized industrial enterprises in the Western Hemisphere during the colonial period, bigger than any mining or industrial site in the British colonies, including the largest sugar mills of the Caribbean. By the middle of the seventeenth century the mines of Potosí, located in Alto Peru (modern Bolivia), had attracted a population of more than 120,000. Tens of thousands were indigenous families forced into long periods of heavy labor at starvation wages. Death rates, especially for those employed deep in the mines, were the highest in the colonial Western Hemisphere.

The accompanying illustration shows a typical refinery (*ingenio*). Aqueducts carried water from large reservoirs on nearby mountainsides to the refineries. The water wheel shown on the right drove two sets of vertical stamps that crushed ore. Each iron-shod stamp was about the size and weight of a telephone pole. Amerindian laborers sorted, dried, and mixed the crushed ore with mercury, a poison that affects the nervous system, and other catalysts to extract the silver. Miners then separated the amalgam using a combination of washing and heating. The end result was a nearly pure ingot of silver that was later assayed and taxed at the mint.

Potosí is located at 13,420 feet (4,090 meters) in the Southern Andes. Silver production at this altitude carried a high environmental cost. Nearby forests were quickly cut down to provide fuel as well as the timbers needed to shore up mine shafts and construct stamping mills and other machinery. This destruction then spread to surrounding areas. Unwanted base metals produced in the refining process poisoned the soil. In addition, the need for tens of thousands of horses, mules, and oxen to drive machinery and transport material led to overgrazing and widespread erosion.

Questions for Analysis

1. What were the human costs associated with this silver mine and refinery?

2. How did this vast mining enterprise threaten the environment?

3. What does the enormous investment in mining and refining silver at Potosí tell us about the Spanish colonial economy?

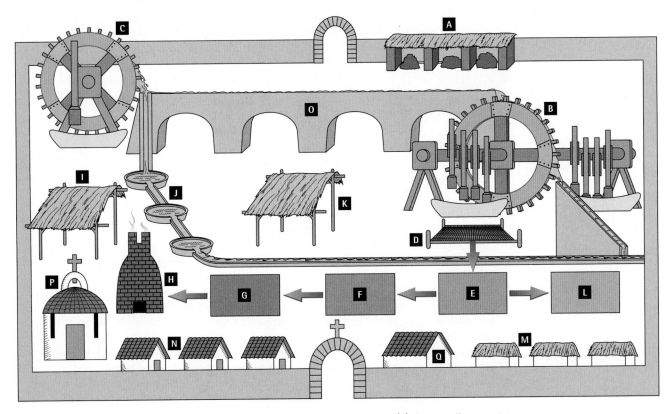

Legend

(A) Storage sheds for ore
(B) Two water-driven stamping mills to crush ore
(C) Additional stamping mill
(D) Screen to sort ore
(E) Ore packed in mixing box
(F) Mercury and catalysts added to ore
(G) Amalgamation occurs
(H) Ore dried in furnace
(I) Mercury removed
(J) Refined ore washed
(K) Ore assayed
(L) Poor quality ore remixed with catalysts
(M) Housing
(N) Offices and sheds
(O) Aquaduct
(P) Chapel
(Q) Mill owner's house

▲ **A Colonial Silver Refinery, 1700** The silver refineries of Spanish America were among the largest industrial establishments in the Western Hemisphere.

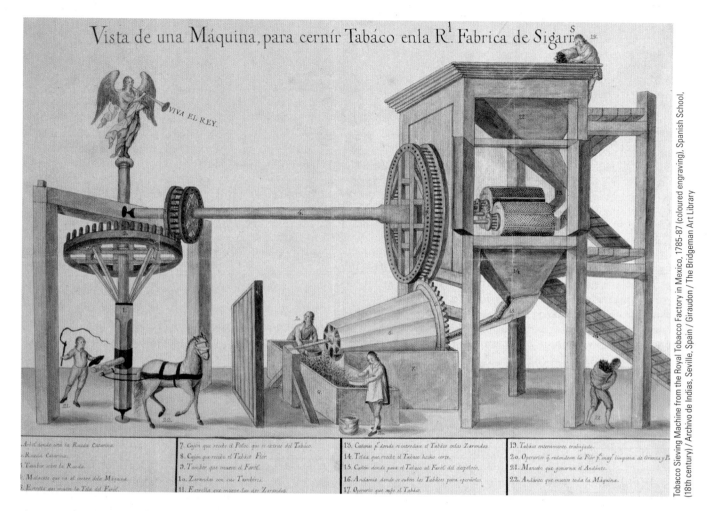

▲ **Tobacco Factory Machinery in Colonial Mexico City**   The tobacco factory in eighteenth-century Mexico City used a horse-driven mechanical shredder to produce snuff and cigarette tobacco.

of free Portuguese settlers. Between 1650 and 1750, for example, nearly five African slaves arrived in Brazil for every free immigrant from Europe.

The mining centers of Mexico and Peru eventually exercised global economic influence. American silver increased the European money supply, promoting commercial expansion and, later, industrialization. Large amounts of silver also flowed to Asia. Both Europe and the Iberian colonies of Latin America ran chronic trade deficits with Asia. As a result, massive amounts of Peruvian and Mexican silver flowed to Asia via Middle Eastern middlemen or across the Pacific to the Spanish colony of the Philippines, where it financed Europe's insatiable appetite for Asian spices, silks, and pottery.

The rich mines of Peru, Bolivia, and Mexico also stimulated urban population growth in the colonies as well as commercial links with distant agricultural and textile producers. Even though located at an inhospitable altitude of 13,420 feet (4,090 meters), the population of the city of Potosí, with 120,000 inhabitants in 1625, was larger than Madrid, Lisbon, or Rome. This rich mining town became the center of a vast regional market that depended on Chilean wheat, Argentine livestock, and Ecuadorian textiles.

The sugar plantations of Brazil played a similar role in integrating the economy of the south Atlantic region. Brazil exchanged sugar, tobacco, and re-exported slaves for *yerba* (Paraguayan tea), hides, livestock, and silver produced in neighboring Spanish colonies. Portugal's increasing openness to British trade also allowed Brazil to become a conduit for an illegal trade between Spanish colonies and Europe. At the end of the seventeenth century, the discovery of gold in Brazil promoted further regional and international economic integration.

18-2c Society in Colonial Latin America

With the exception of some early viceroys, few members of Spain's nobility came to the New World. *Hidalgos* (ee-DAHL-goes)—lesser nobles—were well represented, as were Spanish merchants, artisans, miners, priests, and lawyers. Small numbers of criminals, beggars, and prostitutes also found their way to the colonies. This flow of immigrants from Spain was never large, and Spanish settlers were always a tiny minority in a colonial society numerically dominated by Amerindians and rapidly growing populations of Africans, creoles (whites born in America to European parents), and people of mixed ancestry (see Diversity & Dominance: Race and Ethnicity in the Spanish Colonies: Negotiating Hierarchy).

The most powerful conquistadors and early settlers sought to create a hereditary social and political class comparable to the European nobility. But their systematic abuse of Amerindian communities and the catastrophic effects of the epidemics of the sixteenth century undermined their control of colonial society. With the passage of time colonial officials, the clergy, and the richest merchants came to dominate the social hierarchy. Europeans controlled the highest levels of the church and government as well as commerce, while wealthy American-born creoles exercised a similar role in colonial agriculture and mining. Although tensions between Spaniards and creoles were inevitable, most elite families included both groups.

Before the Europeans arrived in the Americas, the native peoples were members of a large number of distinct cultural and linguistic groups. The effects of conquest and epidemics undermined this rich social and cultural complexity, and the relocation of Amerindian peoples to promote conversion or provide labor further eroded ethnic boundaries among native peoples. Application of the racial label *Indian* by colonial administrators and settlers helped them enforce the tribute and labor demands imposed on native peoples, but it also served to erase the rich cultural diversity that existed among native cultures before the imposition of colonial rule.

Amerindian elites struggled to survive in the new political and economic environments created by military defeat and European settlement. Some sought to protect their positions by forging marriage or less formal relations with colonists. As a result, some indigenous and settler families were tied together by kinship in the decades after conquest, but these links weakened with the passage of time. Hereditary native elites gained some security by becoming essential intermediaries between the indigenous masses and colonial administrators, collecting taxes, recruiting laborers for the mines, and providing military auxiliaries. Despite these efforts, most representatives of the native elite saw their social positions diminished with the passage of time. Indigenous commoners suffered the heaviest burdens. Tribute payments, forced labor obligations, and the loss of traditional land rights were common. European domination dramatically changed the indigenous world by breaking the connections between peoples and places and transforming religious life, marriage practices, diet, and material culture. The survivors of these terrible shocks learned to adapt to the new colonial environment by embracing some elements of the dominant colonial culture or entering the market economies of the cities. They also learned new forms of resistance, like using colonial courts to protect community lands or to resist the abuses of corrupt officials.

Thousands of blacks, many born in Iberia or long resident there, participated in the conquest and settlement of Spanish America. Most of these were slaves; more than 400 slaves participated in the conquests of Peru and Chile alone. In the fluid social environment of the conquest era, many were able to gain their freedom. Juan Valiente escaped from his master in Mexico and then participated in Francisco Pizarro's conquest of the Inka Empire. He later became one of the most prominent early settlers of Chile.

With the opening of a direct slave trade with Africa (for details, see Chapter 19), the cultural character of the black population of colonial Latin America was altered dramatically. While Afro-Iberians spoke Spanish or Portuguese and were Catholic, African slaves arrived in the colonies with different languages, religious beliefs, and cultural practices. European settlers viewed these differences as signs of inferiority that served as a justification for prejudice and discrimination.

A large percentage of slaves imported in the sixteenth century came from West Central Africa, especially the Kingdom of Kongo (see Chapter 16), where they had been exposed to elements of Iberian culture, including religion, language, and technology. The legacy of these shared African cultural elements became enduring components of the colonial cultures of Latin America. But significant differences were present as well, and in regions with large slave majorities, especially the sugar-producing regions of Brazil, these cultural and linguistic barriers often

AP® Exam Tip
Identify and explain several examples of new political and economic elites, such as creoles, that were created in this time period.

AP® Exam Tip
Compare how the Spanish, Portuguese, British, and French treated and exploited different ethnic groups in the Americas.

creoles In colonial Spanish America, term used to describe someone of European descent born in the New World. Elsewhere in the Americas, the term is used to describe all non-native peoples.

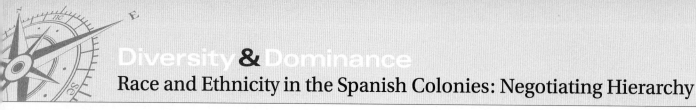
Many European visitors to colonial Latin America were interested in the mixing of Europeans, Amerindians, and Africans in the colonies. Many also commented on the treatment of slaves. The passages that follow allow us to examine these issues in two Spanish colonial societies.

Two young Spanish naval officers and scientists, Jorge Juan and Antonio de Ulloa, arrived in the colonies in 1735 as members of a scientific expedition. They wrote the first selection after visiting the major cities of the Pacific coast of South America and traveling across some of the most difficult terrain in the hemisphere. In addition to their scientific chores, they described architecture, local customs, and the social order. In this section they describe the ethnic mix in Quito, now the capital of Ecuador.

The second selection was published in Lima under the pseudonym Concolorcorvo around 1776. We now know that the author was Alonso Carrío de la Vandera. Born in Spain, he traveled to the colonies as a young man. He served in many minor bureaucratic positions, one of which was the inspection of the postal route between Buenos Aires and Lima. Carrío used his experiences during this long and often uncomfortable trip as the basis of an insightful, and sometimes highly critical, examination of colonial society. The selection that follows describes Córdoba, Argentina.

Juan and Ulloa, as well as Carrío, were perplexed by colonial efforts to create and enforce a racial taxonomy that stipulated and named every possible mixture of European, Amerindian, and African. They were also critical of the vanity and social presumptions of the dominant white population. We are fortunate to have these contemporary descriptions of the diversity of colonial society, but it is important to remember that these authors were clearly rooted in their time and culture and were confident of European superiority. Although they noted many of the abuses suffered by the nonwhite population, their descriptions of these groups often reveal racial bias and the presumption of inferiority.

Quito

This city is very populous, and has, among its inhabitants, some families of high rank and distinction; though their number is but small considering its extent, the poorer class bearing here too great a proportion. The former are the descendants either of the original conquerors, or of presidents, auditors, or other persons of character [high rank], who at different times came over from Spain invested with some lucrative post, and have still preserved their luster, both of wealth and descent, by intermarriages, without intermixing with meaner families though famous for their riches. The commonalty may be divided into four classes; Spaniards or Whites, Mestizos, Indians or Natives, and Negroes, with their progeny.

The name of Spaniard here has a different meaning from that of Chapitone *[sic]* or European, as properly signifying a person descended from a Spaniard without a mixture of blood. Many Mestizos, from the advantage of a fresh complexion, appear to be Spaniards more than those who are so in reality; and from only this fortuitous advantage are accounted as such. The Whites, according to this construction of the word, may be considered as one sixth part of the inhabitants.

The Mestizos are the descendants of Spaniards and Indians. . . . Some are, however, equally tawny with the Indians themselves, though they are distinguished from them by their beards: while others, on the contrary, have so fine a complexion that they might pass for Whites, were it not for some signs which betray them, when viewed attentively. These marks . . . make it very difficult to conceal the fallacy of their complexion. The Mestizos may be reckoned a third part of the inhabitants.

The next class is the Indians, who form about another third; and the others, who are about one sixth, are the Castes [mixed]. These four classes . . . amount to between 50 and 60,000 persons, of all ages, sexes, and ranks. If among these classes the Spaniards, as is natural to think, are the most eminent for riches, rank, and power, it must at the same time be owned, however melancholy the truth may appear, they are in proportion the most poor, miserable and distressed; for they refuse to apply themselves to any mechanic business, considering

AP® Exam Tip

Understand how the growth of plantation economies in the Americas increased the demand for slaves, and be able to give examples of slave resistance.

divided slaves and made resistance more difficult. Over time, elements from many African traditions blended and mixed with European (and in some cases Amerindian) language and beliefs to forge distinct local cultures.

Slave resistance took many forms, including sabotage, malingering, running away, and rebellion. Although many slave rebellions occurred, colonial authorities almost always reestablished control. Groups of runaway slaves, however, were sometimes able to defend themselves for years. In both Spanish America and Brazil, communities of runaways (called *quilombos* [key-LOM-bos] in Brazil and *palenques* [pah-LEN-kays] in Spanish colonies) were common. The largest quilombo was Palmares in Brazil, which survived for nearly ninety years.

Slaves served as skilled artisans, musicians, servants, artists, cowboys, and even soldiers. However, the vast majority were forced to work in export agriculture, sugar, tobacco, indigo, and later coffee. Conditions for slaves were worst on the sugar plantations of Brazil and the Caribbean, where harsh discipline, brutal punishments, and back-breaking labor were common.

it as a disgrace to that quality they so highly value themselves upon, which consists in not being black, brown, or of a copper color. The Mestizos, whose pride is regulated by prudence, readily apply themselves to arts and trades, but chose those of the greatest repute, as painting, sculpture, and the like, leaving the meaner sort to the Indians.

Córdoba

In my computation, there must be within the city and its limited common lands around 500 to 600 [property-owning] residents, but in the principal houses there are a very large number of slaves, most of them [native born blacks] of all conceivable classes, because in this city and in all of Tucumán there is no leniency about granting freedom to any of them.

As I was passing through Córdoba, they were selling 2,000 Negroes, all Creoles from Temporalidades [property confiscated from the Jesuit order in 1767]. . . . Among this multitude of Negroes were many musicians and many of other crafts; they proceeded with the sale by families. I was assured that the nuns of Santa Teresa alone had a group of 300 slaves of both sexes, to whom they give their just ration of meat and dress in the coarse cloth which they make, while these good nuns content themselves with what is left from other ministrations. The number attached to other religious establishments is much smaller, but there is a private home which has 30 or 40, the majority of whom are engaged in various gainful activities. The result is a large number of excellent washerwomen whose accomplishments are valued so highly that they never mend their outer skirts in order that the whiteness of their undergarments may be seen. They do the laundry in the river, in water up to the waist, saying vaingloriously that she who is not soaked cannot wash well. They make ponchos [hand-woven capes], rugs, sashes, and sundries, and especially decorated leather cases which the men sell for 8 reales each, because the hides have no outlet due to the great distance to the port;

the same thing happens on the banks of the Tercero and Cuarto rivers, where they are sold at 2 reales and frequently for less.

The principal men of the city wear very expensive clothes, but this is not true of the women, who are an exception in both Americas and even in the entire world, because they dress decorously in clothing of little cost. They are very tenacious in preserving the customs of their ancestors. They do not permit slaves, or even freedmen who have a mixture of Negro blood, to wear any cloth other than that made in this country, which is quite coarse. I was told recently that a certain bedecked mulatto [woman] who appeared in Córdoba was sent word by the ladies of the city that she should dress according to her station, but since she paid no attention to this reproach, they endured her negligence until one of the ladies, summoning her to her home under some other pretext, had the servants undress her, whip her, burn her finery before her eyes, and dress her in the clothes befitting her class; despite the fact that the [victim] was not lacking in persons to defend her, she disappeared lest the tragedy be repeated.

AP® History Reasoning Skills

Causation *Why did the Spanish feel it necessary to develop the racially based social structure depicted in these passages in their New World colonies? What benefits did white elites receive as a result of these systems?*

Contextualization *What does the humiliation of the mixed-race women in Córdoba reveal about the ideas of race, gender, and class in the Spanish empire?*

Sources: Jorge Juan and Antonio de Ulloa, *A Voyage to South America*, The John Adams translation (abridged), Introduction by Irving A. Leonard (New York, NY: Alfred A. Knopf, 1964), 135–137, copyright © 1964 by Alfred A. Knopf, a division of Random House, Inc.; Concolorcorvo, *El Lazarillo, A Guide for Inexperienced Travelers Between Buenos Aires and Lima, 1773*, translated by Walter D. Kline (Bloomington, IN: Indiana University Press, 1965), 78–80.

Because planters preferred to buy male slaves, there was nearly always a gender imbalance on plantations, proving a significant obstacle to the traditional marriage and family patterns of both Africa and Europe.

Brazil attracted smaller numbers of European immigrants than did Spanish America, and its native populations were smaller and less urbanized. It also came to depend on the African slave as a source of labor earlier than any other American colony. By the early seventeenth century, Africans and their American-born descendants were by far the largest racial group in Brazil. As a result, Brazilian colonial society (unlike Spanish Mexico and Peru) was more influenced by African culture than by Amerindian culture.

Both Spanish and Portuguese law provided for manumission, the granting of freedom to individual slaves, and colonial courts sometimes intervened to protect slaves from the worst physical abuse or to protect married couples from forced separation. The majority of those gaining their liberty had saved money and purchased their own freedom. This meant that manumission

▲ **Painting of Castas**   This is an example of a common genre of colonial Spanish American painting. In the eighteenth century there was increased interest in ethnic mixing, and wealthy colonials as well as some Europeans commissioned sets of paintings that showed a variety of mixed families. The artist typically placed the couples in what he believed was an appropriate setting. In this example, the artist depicted the Amerindian husband with his mestiza (European and Amerindian mixture) wife in an outdoor market where they sold poultry. Colonial usage assigned their child the dismissive racial label *coyote*.   Unknown Mexican artist, De indio y mestiza sale coyote. Reproduced with the permission of the Collection of Jan and Frederick Mayer, Denver

AP® Exam Tip
Be prepared to discuss the racial and ethnic structures of European colonies in the New World.

mestizos The term used by Spanish authorities to describe someone of mixed Amerindian and European descent.

mulattos The term used in Spanish and Portuguese colonies to describe someone of mixed African and European descent.

Section Review

- Colonial governments were created to rule distant colonies.

- The Catholic Church led conversion of Amerindian peoples and spread European cultures and languages.

- Silver mining and sugar production dominated colonial Latin American economies.

- Spanish and Portuguese colonies relied on the forced labor of Amerindians and African slaves.

- New peoples and new cultures resulted from colonial contacts among Amerindians, Europeans, and Africans.

was more about the capacity of individual slaves and slave families to earn income and save than about the generosity of slave owners. Among the minority of slaves to be freed without compensation, household servants were the most likely beneficiaries. Because slave women received more manumissions than men and because any children born to them after this event were legally free, the free black population grew rapidly.

Within a century of settlement, the mixed-descent population was in the majority in many regions. While there were few marriages between Amerindian women and European men, less formal relationships were common. Few European fathers acknowledged their mixed offspring, who were called **mestizos (mess-TEE-zoh)**. Nevertheless, this rapidly expanding group came to occupy a middle position in colonial society, dominating urban artisan trades and small-scale agriculture and ranching. Many members of the elite in frontier regions were mestizos, some proudly asserting their descent from Amerindian noble families. The African slave trade also led to the appearance of new American ethnicities. Individuals of mixed European and African descent—called **mulattos**—came to occupy an intermediate position in the tropics similar to the social position of mestizos in Mesoamerica and the Andean region. In Spanish Mexico and Peru and in Brazil, mixtures of Amerindians and Africans were also common. These mixed-descent groups were called castas (**CAZ-tahs**) in Spanish America.

18-3 English and French Colonies in North America

What were the main similarities and differences among the colonies of Spain, Portugal, England, and France?

The North American empires of England and France had many characteristics in common with the colonial empires of Spain and Portugal (see Map 18.1). The governments of England and France hoped to find easily extracted forms of wealth like gold and silver or great indigenous empires like those of the Aztecs and Inka, but were disappointed. Like the Spanish and Portuguese, English and French settlers responded to native peoples with a mixture of diplomacy and violence. All four colonial empires also imported large numbers of African slaves to spur the economic development of their colonies.

Important differences, however, distinguished North American colonial development from the Latin American model. The English and French colonies were developed nearly a century after Cortés's conquest of Mexico and the initial Portuguese settlement of Brazil. The intervening period had witnessed significant economic and demographic growth in Europe. By the time England and France secured a foothold in the Americas, increased trade had led to greater integration of world cultural regions. Distracted by ventures elsewhere and by increasing military confrontation in Europe, neither England nor France created the large and expensive colonial administrative bureaucracies established by Spain and Portugal. As a result, private companies and powerful private proprietors played a much larger role in the development of English and French colonies. This period had also witnessed the Protestant Reformation, an event that helped frame the character of English and French settlement in the Americas.

When this new wave of European settlers arrived they found hundreds of distinct native peoples living in a great diversity of natural environments. These peoples spoke different languages. Many were organized in villages and towns dependent on agriculture. Others lived in more dispersed settings and relied more intensely on hunting. If compared to the native peoples of Mesoamerica and the Andean region, the native populations of the Atlantic seaboard and the Mississippi and Ohio river valleys were much smaller and more dispersed. This combination of larger flows of European settlers and smaller native populations meant that the economies of the French and English colonies would not rely on the forced labor and tribute payments of native peoples.

18-3a Early English Experiments

England's effort to gain a foothold in the Americas in the late sixteenth century failed, but its effort to establish colonies in the seventeenth century proved more successful. The English relied on private capital to finance settlement and continued to hope that their colonies would become sources of high-value products such as silver, citrus, and wine. English experience in colonizing Ireland after 1566 also influenced these efforts. In Ireland land had been confiscated, cleared of its native population, and offered for sale to English investors. The city of London, English guilds, and wealthy private investors all purchased Irish "plantations" and then recruited "settlers." By 1650 investors had sent nearly 150,000 English and Scottish immigrants, mostly Protestants, to Ireland. Indeed, Ireland attracted six times as many colonists in the early seventeenth century as did New England.

AP® Exam Tip
Compare the characteristics of the various maritime empires established in the Americas by European states.

18-3b The South

In 1606 London investors organized as the Virginia Company took up the challenge of colonizing Virginia. A year later 144 settlers disembarked at Jamestown, an island 30 miles (48 kilometers) up the James River in the Chesapeake Bay region. Additional settlers arrived in 1609. The investors and settlers hoped for immediate profits, but the location was a swampy and unhealthy place where nearly 80 percent of the settlers died in the first fifteen years from disease or Amerindian attacks. In the end the investors recognized that there was no mineral wealth, no passage to Asia, and no docile and exploitable native population. In fact, disease brought by the settlers, most likely influenza, simultaneously decimated the native population. One settler noted that, "few escaped."

In 1624 the English crown dissolved the Virginia Company because of its mismanagement. Freed from the company's commitment to the original location, colonists pushed deeper into the interior and developed a sustainable economy based on furs, timber, and, increasingly, tobacco. The profits from tobacco soon attracted additional immigrants. Along the shoreline of Chesapeake Bay and the rivers that fed it, settlers spread out, developing plantations and farms. Colonial Virginia's dispersed population contrasted with the greater urbanization of Spanish and Portuguese America, where large and powerful cities and networks of secondary towns flourished. No city of any significant size developed in colonial Virginia.

From the beginning, colonists in Latin America had relied on forced labor of Amerindians to develop the region's resources. With the decline in Amerindian populations due to epidemics and mistreatment, colonists turned to the African slave trade, compelling the migration of millions of additional forced laborers. The English settlement of the Chesapeake Bay region added a new system of forced labor to the Western Hemisphere landscape: indentured servitude. **Indentured servants** were racially and religiously indistinguishable from free settlers and eventually accounted for approximately 80 percent of all English immigrants to Virginia and the neighboring colony of Maryland. A young man or woman unable to pay for transportation to the New World accepted an *indenture* (contract) that bound him or her to a term ranging from four to seven years of mandatory labor in return for passage and, at the end of the contract, a small parcel of land, some tools, and clothes.

During the seventeenth century approximately fifteen hundred indentured servants, mostly male, arrived each year (see Chapter 19 for details on the indentured labor system). Planters were more likely to purchase the cheaper limited contracts of indentured servants rather than African slaves during the initial period of high mortality rates. As life expectancy improved, planters began to purchase more slaves because they believed they would earn greater profits from slaves owned for life than from indentured servants bound for short periods of time. As a result, Virginia's slave population grew rapidly, from 950 in 1660 to 120,000 by 1756.

By the 1660s Virginia was administered by a Crown-appointed governor and by representatives of towns meeting together as the **House of Burgesses**. When elected representatives began to meet alone as a deliberative body, they initiated a form of democratic representation that distinguished the English colonies of North America from the colonies of other European powers. Ironically, this expansion in colonial liberties and political rights occurred simultaneously with the dramatic increase in the colony's slave population. The intertwined evolution of American freedom and American slavery gave England's southern colonies a unique and conflicted political character that endured after independence.

English settlement of the Carolinas initially relied on profits from the fur trade. English fur traders pushed into the interior to compete with French trading networks based in New Orleans and Mobile. Native peoples were soon producing over 100,000 deerskins annually to this profitable commerce, but at a high environmental and cultural cost. As Amerindian peoples hunted more intensely, they disrupted the natural balance of animals and plants in southern forests. In 1764 the British official overseeing the native peoples of the southeast estimated that roughly 14,000 Amerindian hunters produced an unsustainable 500,000 deerskins a year. The profits of the fur trade altered Amerindian culture as well, leading villages to place less emphasis on subsistence hunting, fishing, and traditional agriculture. Amerindian life was profoundly altered by deepening dependencies on European products, including firearms, metal tools, textiles, and alcohol.

While increasingly tied to the commerce and culture of the Carolina colony, indigenous peoples were simultaneously being weakened by epidemics, alcoholism, and a rising tide of ethnic conflicts generated by competition for hunting grounds. Conflicts among indigenous peoples—who now had firearms—became more deadly and, as a result, thousands of captured Amerindians were sold as slaves to local colonists, who used them as agricultural workers or exported them to English sugar plantations of the Caribbean. Dissatisfied with the terms of trade imposed by fur traders and angered by this slave trade, Amerindians launched attacks on English settlements in the early 1700s. Their defeat by colonial military forces inevitably led to new seizures of Amerindian land by European settlers. The combined effects of war and epidemic disease drove down the native population and forced many survivors to move into new territories or seek incorporation among native peoples not yet threatened by settlements.

The northern part of the Carolinas, settled from Virginia, followed that colony's mixed economy of tobacco and forest products. Slavery expanded slowly in this region. Charleston and

Indentured servants A migrant to British colonies in the Americas who paid for passage by agreeing to work for a set term ranging from four to seven years.

House of Burgesses Elected assembly in colonial Virginia, created in 1618.

AP® Exam Tip
Compare how the physical environment of the Americas was affected by the introduction of European settlement and agricultural practices.

the interior of South Carolina followed a different path. Settled first by planters from Barbados in 1670, this colony developed an economy based on plantations and slavery in imitation of the colonies of the Caribbean and Brazil. In 1729 North and South Carolina became separate colonies.

Despite an unhealthy climate, the prosperous rice and indigo plantations near Charleston attracted both free immigrants and increasing numbers of African slaves. African slaves had been present from the founding of Charleston and were instrumental in introducing irrigated rice agriculture along the coastal lowlands. They were also crucial to developing plantations of *indigo* (a plant that produced a blue dye) at higher elevations away from the coast. Many slaves were given significant responsibilities. As one planter sending two slaves and their families to a frontier region put it: "[They] are likely young people, well acquainted with Rice & every kind of plantation business, and in short [are] capable of the management of a plantation themselves."[3]

As profits from rice and indigo rose, the importation of African slaves created a black majority in South Carolina. African languages, as well as African religious beliefs and diet, strongly influenced this unique colonial culture. Gullah, a dialect with both African and English roots, evolved as the common idiom of the Carolina coast. Africans played a major role in South Carolina's largest slave uprising, the Stono Rebellion of 1739. Twenty slaves, many of them African Catholics seeking to flee south to Spanish Florida, seized firearms and other weapons and then recruited about a hundred slaves from nearby plantations. Although the colonial militia defeated the rebels and executed many of them, the rebellion shocked slave owners throughout England's southern colonies and led to greater repression.

Colonial South Carolina was the most hierarchical society in British North America. Planters controlled the economy and political life. The richest families maintained impressive households in Charleston, the largest city in the southern colonies, as well as on their plantations in the countryside. Small farmers, cattlemen, artisans, merchants, and fur traders held an intermediate but clearly subordinate social position. Native peoples continued to participate in colonial society but lost ground from the effects of epidemic disease and warfare. As in colonial Latin America, a large mixed population blurred racial and cultural boundaries. On the frontier, the children of white men and Amerindian women held an important place in the fur trade and some of their children rose to positions of authority among the Cherokee, Creek, and Seminole peoples. In the plantation regions and in Charleston, the offspring of white men and black women often held preferred positions within the slave workforce or worked as free craftsmen.

18-3c New England

The colonization of New England by two separate groups of Protestant dissenters, Pilgrims and Puritans, put the settlement of this region on a different course. The **Pilgrims**, who came first, wished to break completely with the Church of England, which they believed was still essentially Catholic (see Chapter 17). As a result, in 1620 approximately 100 settlers—men, women, and children—established the colony of Plymouth on the coast of present-day Massachusetts. Although nearly half of the settlers died during the first winter, the colony survived until 1691, when the larger Massachusetts Bay Colony of the Puritans absorbed Plymouth.

The **Puritans** wished to "purify" the Church of England, not break with it. They wanted to abolish its hierarchy of bishops and priests, free it from governmental interference, and limit membership to people who shared their beliefs. Subjected to increased discrimination in England for their efforts to transform the church, large numbers of Puritans began emigrating from England in 1630.

The Puritan leaders of the Massachusetts Bay Company—the joint-stock company that had received a royal charter to finance the Massachusetts Bay Colony—carried the company charter with them from England to Massachusetts. By bringing the charter, which spelled out company rights and obligations as well as the direction of company government, they limited Crown efforts to control them. By 1643 more than 20,000 Puritans had settled in the Bay Colony.

Immigration to Massachusetts differed from immigration to the Chesapeake and to South Carolina. Most newcomers to Massachusetts arrived with their families. Whereas single males

Pilgrims English Protestant dissenters who established Plymouth Colony in Massachusetts in 1620 to seek religious freedom after having lived briefly in the Netherlands.

Puritans English Protestant dissenters who believed that God predestined souls to heaven or hell before birth. They founded Massachusetts Bay Colony in 1629.

[3]Crosby, *The Columbian Exchange*, 58.

made up 84 percent of Virginia's white population in 1625, Massachusetts had a normal gender balance in its population almost from the beginning. It was also the healthiest of England's colonies. The result was a rapid natural increase in population. The population of Massachusetts quickly became more "American" than the population of southern or Caribbean colonies, whose survival depended on a steady flow of English immigrants and slaves to counter high mortality rates. Massachusetts also was more homogeneous and less hierarchical than either England's southern colonies or the colonies of Spain and Portugal.

Political institutions evolved from the terms of the company charter. Settlers elected a governor and a council of magistrates drawn from the board of directors of the Massachusetts Bay Company. By 1650, disagreements between this council and elected representatives of the towns led to the creation of a lower legislative house that selected its own speaker and developed procedures and rules similar to those of the House of Commons in England. The result was much greater local autonomy and greater local political involvement than in the contemporary colonies of Latin America.

Economically, Massachusetts differed dramatically from the southern colonies. Agriculture met basic needs, but poor soils and harsh climate offered no opportunity to develop cash crops like tobacco or rice. To pay for imported tools, textiles, and other essentials, the colonists needed to discover some profit-making niche in the growing Atlantic market. Fur, timber, and fish provided the initial economic foundation, but New England's economic well-being soon depended on providing commercial and freight services as well as shipbuilding for the dynamic and far-flung Atlantic commercial arena that included the southern colonies, the Caribbean islands, Africa, and Europe.

In Spanish and Portuguese America, heavily capitalized *monopolies* (companies or individuals given exclusive economic privileges) dominated international trade. In New England, by contrast, individual merchants survived by discovering smaller but more sustainable profits in diversified trade across the Atlantic. The colony's commercial success rested on market intelligence, flexibility, and streamlined organization. Urban population growth suggests the success of this development strategy. With 16,000 inhabitants in 1740, Boston, the capital of Massachusetts Bay Colony, was the largest city in British North America.

Lacking a profitable agricultural export like tobacco, New England did not develop the extreme social stratification of the southern plantation colonies. Slaves and indentured servants were present, but in very small numbers. While New England was ruled by the richest colonists and shared the racial attitudes of the southern colonies, it also was the colonial society with fewest differences in wealth and status and with the most uniformly British and Protestant population in the Americas.

18-3d The Middle Atlantic Region

Much of the future success of English-speaking America was rooted in the rapid economic development and remarkable cultural diversity that appeared in the Middle Atlantic colonies. In 1624 the Dutch West India Company established the colony of New Netherland and located its capital on Manhattan Island. Although poorly managed and underfinanced from the start, the colony commanded the potentially profitable and strategically important Hudson River. Dutch merchants established trading relationships with the **Iroquois Confederacy**—an alliance among the Mohawk, Oneida, Onondaga, Cayuga, and Seneca peoples as well as the Tuscarora after 1722—and with other native peoples that gave them access to the rich fur trade of Canada. When confronted by an English military expedition in 1664, the Dutch surrendered without a fight. James, duke of York and later King James II of England, became proprietor of the colony, which was renamed New York.

Tumultuous politics and corrupt public administration characterized colonial New York, but the development of New York City as a commercial and shipping center guaranteed the colony's success. Located at the mouth of the Hudson River, the city played an essential role in connecting the region's grain farmers to the booming markets of the Caribbean and southern Europe. By the early eighteenth century, this colony had a diverse population that included English, Dutch, German, and Swedish settlers as well as a large slave community.

Pennsylvania began as a proprietary colony and as a refuge for Quakers, a persecuted religious minority. Prominent Quaker William Penn secured an enormous grant of territory (nearly the size of England) in 1682 because the English king Charles II was indebted to his father. As

Iroquois Confederacy An alliance of five northeastern Amerindian peoples (six after 1722) that made decisions on military and diplomatic issues through a council of representatives. Allied first with the Dutch and later with the English, the Confederacy dominated the area from western New England to the Great Lakes.

proprietor (owner) of the land, Penn had sole right to establish a government, subject only to the requirement that he provide for an assembly of freemen

Even though Penn quickly lost political control over the settlers, the colony enjoyed remarkable success. By 1700 Pennsylvania had a population of more than 21,000, and Philadelphia, its capital, soon overtook Boston to become the largest city in the British colonies. Healthy climate, excellent land, relatively peaceful relations with native peoples (prompted by Penn's emphasis on negotiation rather than warfare), and access through the port of Philadelphia to exterior markets led to rapid economic and demographic growth.

While both Pennsylvania and South Carolina were grain-exporting colonies, they were very different societies. South Carolina's rice plantations depended on the labor of large numbers of slaves. In Pennsylvania free workers produced the bulk of the colony's grain crops on family farms. As a result, Pennsylvania's economic expansion in the late seventeenth century occurred without reproducing South Carolina's hierarchical and repressive social order. By the early eighteenth century, however, a rich merchant elite was in place and the prosperous city of Philadelphia had a large population of black slaves and freedmen; the fast-growing economy continued to offer opportunities in skilled crafts, trade, and agriculture to free immigrants.

▲ **The Home of Sir William Johnson, British Superintendent for Indian Affairs, Northern District**   As the colonial era drew to a close, the British attempted to limit the cost of colonial defense by negotiating land settlements with native peoples, but the growing tide of western migration doomed these agreements. William Johnson (1715–1774) maintained a fragile peace along the northern frontier by building strong personal relations with influential leaders of the Mohawk and other members of the Iroquois Confederacy. His home in present-day Johnstown, New York, shows the mixed nature of the frontier—the relative opulence of the main house offset by the two defensive blockhouses built for protection. The New York Public Library

18-3e **French America**

Patterns of French colonial settlement more closely resembled those of Spain and Portugal than those of England. The French were committed to missionary activity among Amerindian peoples and emphasized the extraction of natural resources—in this case furs rather than minerals. Between 1534 and 1542 navigator and promoter Jacques Cartier explored the region of Newfoundland and the Gulf of St. Lawrence in three voyages. A contemporary of Cortés and Pizarro, Cartier hoped to find mineral wealth, but the stones he brought back to France turned out to be quartz and iron pyrite, "fool's gold."

The French waited more than fifty years before establishing settlements in North America. Coming to Canada after spending years in the West Indies, Samuel de Champlain founded the colony of **New France** at Quebec **(kwuh-BEC)**, on the banks of the St. Lawrence River, in 1608. This location provided ready access to Amerindian trade routes, but it also compelled French settlers to take sides in the region's ongoing warfare. Champlain allied New France with the Huron and Algonquin peoples, traditional enemies of the powerful Iroquois Confederacy. Although French firearms and armor at first tipped the balance of power to France's native allies, the Iroquois Confederacy proved to be a resourceful and persistent enemy.

The European market for fur, especially beaver, fueled French settlement. Young Frenchmen were sent to live among native peoples to master their languages and customs. These **coureurs de bois (koo-RUHR day BWA),** or "runners of the woods," often began families with indigenous women. Their mixed children, called *métis* **(may-TEES),** helped direct the fur trade. Amerindians actively participated in the trade because they came to depend on the goods they received in exchange for furs—firearms, metal tools, textiles, and alcohol. This change in the material culture of native peoples led to overhunting, which rapidly transformed the environment and led to the depletion of beaver and deer populations. It also increased competition among native peoples for hunting grounds, thus promoting warfare.

New France French colony in North America, with a capital in Quebec, founded 1608. Following military defeat, New France was ceded to the British in 1763.

coureurs de bois French fur traders, many of mixed Amerindian heritage, who lived among and often married with Amerindian peoples of North America.

Frances Anne Hopkins, Shooting the Rapids, Library and Archives Canada, Ref.# C-2774

▲ **Canadian Fur Traders** The fur trade provided the economic foundation of early Canadian settlement. Fur traders were cultural intermediaries. They brought European technologies and products like firearms and machine-made textiles to native peoples and native technologies and products like canoes and furs to European settlers. This canoe with sixteen paddlers was adapted from the native craft by fur traders to transport large cargoes. By the time of the French and Indian War approximately 180,000 beaver pelts were harvested annually.

The proliferation of firearms made indigenous warfare more deadly. The Iroquois Confederacy responded to the increased military strength of France's Algonquin allies by forging commercial and military links with Dutch and later English settlements along the Hudson River. Once armed with firearms, the Iroquois Confederacy nearly eradicated the Huron in 1649 and inflicted a series of humiliating defeats on the French. At the high point of their power in the early 1680s, Iroquois hunters and military forces gained control of much of the Great Lakes region and the Ohio River Valley. A large French military expedition and a relentless attack focused on destroying Iroquois villages and agriculture finally checked Iroquois power in 1701.

In French Canada, the Jesuits led the effort to convert native peoples to Christianity as they had in Brazil and Paraguay. Missionaries mastered native languages, created boarding schools for young boys and girls, and set up model agricultural communities for converted Amerindians. The Jesuits' greatest successes coincided with a destructive wave of epidemics and renewed warfare among native peoples in the 1630s. Eventually, they established churches throughout Huron and Algonquin territories. Nevertheless, native culture persisted. In 1688 a French nun who had devoted her life to instructing Amerindian girls expressed her frustration with the resilience of indigenous culture:

> We have observed that of a hundred [young girls] that have passed through our hands we have scarcely civilized one. . . . When we are least expecting it, they clamber over our wall and go off to run with their kinsmen in the woods, finding more to please them there than in all the amenities of our French house.[4]

Even though the fur trade flourished, population growth was slow. Founded at about the same time as French Canada, Virginia had twenty times more European residents by 1627. Canada's small settler population and the fur trade's dependence on the voluntary participation of Amerindians allowed indigenous peoples to retain greater independence and more control over their traditional lands than was possible in the colonies of Spain, Portugal, or England. Unlike these rival colonial regimes, which sought to transform ancient ways of life or force the transfer of native lands, the French were compelled to treat indigenous peoples as allies and trading partners.

Despite Canada's small population and limited resources, the French aggressively expanded to the west and south. They founded Louisiana in 1699, but by 1708 there were fewer than 300 soldiers, settlers, and slaves in this vast territory. Like Canada, Louisiana depended on the fur trade and on alliances with Amerindian peoples who in turn became dependent on European goods. In 1753 a French official reported a Choctaw leader as saying, "[The French] were the first . . . who made [us] subject to the different needs that [we] can no longer now do without."[5] These contacts were disease vectors as well. One French priest recalled that prior to French settlement the Arkansas people had numbered in the thousands but had been reduced "by war and sickness to almost nothing."[6]

France's North American colonies were threatened by wars between France and England and by the population growth and increasing prosperity of neighboring English colonies. The "French and Indian War" that began in 1754 led to the wider conflict called the Seven Years' War, in 1756–1763, that determined the fate of French Canada (see Map 18.2). England committed a larger military force to the struggle and, despite early defeats, took the French capital of Quebec in 1759. The peace agreement forced France to yield Canada to the English and cede Louisiana to Spain. Amerindian populations

Section Review

- Without Latin America's wealth in silver, gold, and sugar, British North American colonies developed strong regional characters and strong local political traditions.

- British colonies attracted large numbers of free immigrants, but indentured servitude and slavery were crucial to economic development.

- The southern colonies' dependence on forced labor and plantation agriculture led to a society that was more hierarchical and less democratic that those found in the colonies of New England and the Middle Atlantic region.

- With a small population and limited resources, French colonies in North America depended on political and military alliances and commercial relations with native peoples.

- Eventually England defeated France and gained control of North America east of the Mississippi.

---

[4]Quoted in R. Douglas Francis, Richard Jones, and Donald B. Smith, *Origins: Canadian History to Confederation* (Toronto, ON: Holt, Rinehart, and Winston of Canada, 1992), 52.

[5]Quoted in Daniel H. Usner, Jr., *Indians, Settlers and Slaves in a Frontier Exchange Economy: The Lower Mississippi Valley Before 1783*, Institute of Early American History and Culture Series (Chapel Hill, NC: University of North Carolina Press, 1992), 96.

[6]Quoted in Alan Gallay, *The Indian Slave Trade: The Rise of the English Empire in the American South, 1670–1717* (New Haven, CT: Yale University Press, 2002), 112.

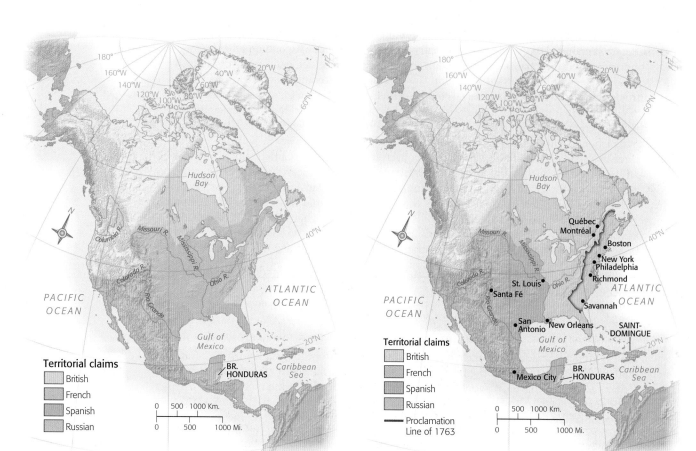

MAP 18.2   European Claims in North America, 1755–1763 The results of the French and Indian War dramatically altered the map of North America. France's losses precipitated conflicts between Amerindian peoples and the rapidly expanding population of the British colonies.

Remembering the key differences in the colonial settlement patterns of the British and French colonies, what would the boundary changes of 1763 mean for the native peoples on North America?

AP® Exam Tip
Understand how state rivalries and competition in trade routes affected state consolidation and expansion.

soon recognized the difference between the English and the French. One Canadian indigenous leader commented to a British officer after the French surrender: "We learn that our lands are to be given away not only to trade thereon but also . . . in full title to various [English] individuals. . . . We have always been a free nation, and now we will become slaves, which would be very difficult to accept after having enjoyed our liberty so long."[7] With the loss of Canada the French concentrated their efforts on their sugar-producing colonies in the Caribbean (see Chapter 19).

18.4 Colonial Expansion and Conflict

What were the effects of the colonial reforms and wars among imperial powers that dominated the Americas during the eighteenth century?

Beginning in the last decades of the seventeenth century, nearly all the European colonies in the Americas experienced economic expansion and population growth. In the next century, the imperial powers responded by strengthening administrative and economic control of their colonies. They also sought to force colonial populations to pay more taxes to help cover the heavy costs of administration and defense. These efforts at reform and restructuring coincided with a series of imperial wars fought along Atlantic trade routes and in the Americas. France's loss of its

---

[7]Quoted in Cornelius J. Jaenen, "French and Native Peoples in New France," in *Interpreting Canada's Past*, ed. J. M. Bumsted, Vol. 1, 2nd ed. (Toronto, ON: Oxford University Press, 1993), 73.

North American colonies in 1763 was one of the most important results of these struggles. Equally significant, colonial populations throughout the Americas became more aware of separate national identities and more aggressive in asserting local interests against the will of distant monarchs.

18-4a Imperial Reform in Spanish America and Brazil

Spain's Habsburg dynasty ended when Charles II died without an heir in 1700 (see Table 17.1). After thirteen years of conflict involving the major European powers, Philip of Bourbon, grandson of Louis XIV of France, gained the Spanish throne. Under Philip V and his heirs, Spain reorganized its administration and tax collection and liberalized colonial trade policies. Spain also created new commercial monopolies and strengthened its navy to protect colonial trade.

For most of the Spanish Empire, the eighteenth century was a period of remarkable economic expansion associated with population growth. Amerindian populations began to recover from the early epidemics; the flow of Spanish immigrants increased; and the slave trade to plantation colonies, like Cuba, was expanded. Mining production increased, with silver production rising steadily into the 1780s. Agricultural exports also expanded, especially exports of tobacco, dyes, hides, chocolate, cotton, and sugar.

The Spanish and Portuguese kings also sought to reduce the power of the Catholic Church while at the same time transferring some church wealth to their treasuries. These efforts led to a succession of confrontations between colonial officials and the church hierarchy. To the kings of Portugal and Spain, the Jesuits symbolized the independent power of the church. In 1759 the Portuguese king expelled this powerful order from his territories, and the Spanish king imitated this decision in 1767. In practice these actions forced many colonial-born Jesuits from their native lands and closed their many schools that had educated the colonial elites.

Bourbon political and fiscal reforms also contributed to a growing sense of colonial grievance by limiting creoles' access to colonial offices and by imposing new taxes and monopolies that transferred more colonial wealth to Spain. Consumer and producer resentment in the colonies led to a series of violent confrontations with Spanish administrators. Many colonials, including members of the elite, resented what they saw as the unilateral overturning of the arrangements and understandings that had governed these societies for centuries. However, the Spanish effort to recruit local elites as military officers to improve imperial defense offered some colonial residents a compensatory opportunity for higher social status and greater responsibility.

In addition to tax rebellions and urban riots, colonial reforms also provoked Amerindian uprisings. In 1780 the Peruvian Amerindian leader José Gabriel Condorcanqui began the largest rebellion. To rally support, he assumed the name of his Inka ancestor Tupac Amaru (**TOO-pack a-MAH-roo**), whom the Spanish executed in 1572. Although a hereditary Quechua leader, **Tupac Amaru II** received his education from the Jesuits and had close ties to the local bishop and other powerful colonial authorities. He was also actively involved in colonial trade. Tupac Amaru II did not clearly state whether he sought only to end local injustices or overthrow Spanish rule, but he clearly sought to redress the grievances of Amerindian communities who suffered from forced labor and from high taxes. As his rebellion spread, he attracted creoles, mestizos, and slaves as well as Amerindians to his cause. After his capture in 1781, the Spanish brutally executed Tupac Amaru II along with his wife and fifteen other family members and allies. Allies and surviving family members continued the rebellion for two years. By the time Spanish authority was firmly reestablished, more than 100,000 lives had been lost and enormous amounts of property destroyed.

Brazil also experienced a similar period of expansion and reform after 1700. Portugal created new administrative positions and gave monopoly companies exclusive rights to little-developed regions. As in Spanish America, a more intrusive colonial government that imposed new taxes led to rebellions and plots, including open warfare in 1707 between local-born "sons of the soil" and "outsiders" in São Paulo. The most aggressive period of reform occurred during the ministry of the marquis of Pombal (1750–1777). The discovery in Brazil of gold in the 1690s and diamonds after 1720 financed the reforms. Brazil's exports of minerals as well as coffee and cotton deepened dependence on the slave trade, and nearly 2 million African slaves were imported in the eighteenth century.

18-4b Reform and Reorganization in British America

England's efforts to reform and reorganize its North American colonies began earlier than the Bourbon initiative in Spanish America. After the period of Cromwell's Puritan Republic (see Chapter 17), the restored Stuart king, Charles II, undertook an ambitious campaign to establish

AP® Exam Tip
Identify and explain several examples of local resistance to state consolidation during this time period.

Tupac Amaru II Member of Inka aristocracy who led a rebellion against Spanish authorities in Peru in 1780–1781. He was captured and executed with his wife and other members of his family.

Sir Henry Chamberlain, Views and Costumes of the City and Neighborhoods of Rio de Janeiro, London, 1822

▲ **Market in Rio de Janeiro**   In many of the cities of colonial Latin America, female slaves and black free women dominated retail markets. In this scene from late colonial Brazil, Afro-Brazilian women sell a variety of foods and crafts.

greater control over the colonies. Between 1651 and 1673 a series of Navigation Acts sought to severely limit colonial trading and colonial production that competed directly with English manufacturers. England also attempted to increase royal control over colonial political life by replacing colonial charters and proprietorships. Because the king viewed the New England colonies as centers of smuggling, he temporarily suspended their elected assemblies while appointing colonial governors and granting them new fiscal and legislative powers.

James II's overthrow in the Glorious Revolution of 1688 (see Chapter 17) ended this confrontation, but not before colonists were provoked to resist and, in some cases, rebel. Colonials overthrew the governors of New York and Massachusetts and removed the Catholic proprietor of Maryland. William and Mary restored relative peace, but these conflicts alerted colonials to the potential aggression of the English government. Colonial politics would remain confrontational until the American Revolution.

Section Review

- In the eighteenth century all European imperial powers sought to establish more effective political control over their colonies and transfer the costs of government and defense to colonial residents.

- Colonial reforms disrupted colonial economic and political accommodations and led to rebellions and other forms of resistance.

During the eighteenth century the English colonies experienced renewed economic growth and attracted a new wave of European immigration, but social divisions were increasingly evident. The colonial population in 1770 was more urban, more clearly divided by class and race, and more vulnerable to economic downturns. Crises were provoked when imperial wars with France and Spain disrupted trade in the Atlantic, increased tax burdens, forced military mobilizations, and provoked frontier conflicts with Amerindians. On the eve of the American Revolution, England defeated France and weakened Spain, but the cost was great. The administrative, military, and tax policies imposed to gain this empire-wide victory had also alienated much of the North American colonial population.

18-5 Conclusion

The New World colonial empires of Spain, Portugal, France, and England had many characteristics in common. All subjugated Amerindian peoples and introduced large numbers of enslaved Africans. Within all four empires European settlement and the introduction of Old World animals and plants also transformed the natural environment. Europeans introduced Old World diseases, such as smallpox, that had a devastating effect on the native populations. Settlers in all four colonial empires applied the technologies of the Old World to the resources of the New, producing mineral and agricultural wealth and exploiting the commercial possibilities of the emerging Atlantic market in ways that accelerated the integration of Europe, Asia, and America.

Each of the New World empires also reflected the distinctive cultural and institutional heritages of its colonizing power. Mineral wealth allowed Spain to develop the most centralized empire, with political and economic power concentrated in great cities like Mexico City and Lima. Portugal and France pursued objectives similar to Spain's, but neither Brazil's agricultural economy, based on sugar, nor France's Canadian fur trade produced the financial resources and levels of centralized control achieved by Spain. Nevertheless, unlike Britain, all three of these Catholic powers were able to impose and enforce significant levels of religious and cultural uniformity in their colonies.

Greater cultural and religious diversity characterized British North America. Immigrants came to the colonies from the British Isles, including all of Britain's religious traditions, as well as from Germany, Sweden, the Netherlands, and France. British colonial government varied somewhat from colony to colony and was much more responsive to local interests. Thus colonists in British North America were better able than those in the areas controlled by Spain, Portugal, and France to respond to changing economic and political circumstances and to influence government policies. Most importantly, the British colonies attracted many more European immigrants than did the other New World colonial empires. Between 1580 and 1760 French colonies received 60,000 European immigrants, Brazil 523,000, and the Spanish colonies 678,000. Within a shorter period—between 1600 and 1760—the British settlements welcomed 746,000. Population in British North America—free and slave combined—had reached an extraordinary 2.5 million by 1775.

Key Terms

Columbian Exchange p. 454
Bartolomé de Las Casas p. 459
Potosí p. 460
encomienda p. 460

creoles p. 463
mestizo p. 466
mulatto p. 466
indentured servant p. 468

House of Burgesses p. 468
Pilgrims p. 469
Puritans p. 469
Iroquois Confederacy p. 470

New France p. 472
coureurs de bois p. 472
Tupac Amaru II p. 475

Review Questions

1. What effects did Amerindian population losses due to epidemics have on European settlement and the African slave trade?

2. Silver mining and sugar agriculture were the two richest economic sectors in the colonial period. What were the key similarities?

3. What were the differences in governance among the colonies of Spain, Portugal, France, and Britain?

 MINDTAP From Cengage — MindTap® is a fully online, personalized learningvw experience built upon Cengage Learning content. MindTap® combines student learning tools–readings, multimedia, activities, and assessments–into a singular Learning Path that guides students through the course and helps students develop the critical thinking, analysis, and communication skills that are essential to academic and professional success.

Multiple-Choice Questions

Questions 1–3 refer to the passage below.

"The Mestizos are the descendants of Spaniards and Indians.... Some are, however, equally tawny with the Indians themselves, though they are distinguished from them by their beards: while others, on the contrary, have so fine a complexion that they might pass for Whites, were it not for some signs which betray them, when viewed attentively. These marks ... make it very difficult to conceal the fallacy of their complexion. The Mestizos may be reckoned a third part of the inhabitants."

> Jorge Juan and Antonio de Ulloa, Spanish naval officers;
> *A Voyage to South America*, 1776

1. Which of the following is an accurate interpretation of the document?

   (A) Spanish colonies strictly enforced segregation laws.

   (B) Europeans only interacted with Amerindians professionally.

   (C) Spaniards made up a majority of the population in South America.

   (D) Intermarriage between Spaniards and Amerindians blurred racial lines.

2. The situation described in the document led to

   (A) a new form of social hierarchy in South America.

   (B) greater freedoms for women of all backgrounds.

   (C) a greater sense of egalitarianism.

   (D) a resurgence of the Inka Empire.

3. Which of the following is one of the reasons for the creation of the Casta system?

   (A) The Spanish focus on silver mining led to a social reward system for those who were most effective in the mines.

   (B) Reliance on coerced labor through the encomienda system required a clearly designated workforce.

   (C) The growth of the plantation system and import of African slaves left Amerindians without a place in the social hierarchy.

   (D) Large numbers of Amerindians descended on Spanish colonies, vastly outnumbering the colonial Spanish.

Questions 4–6 refer to the image below.

▲ **Sugar Plantation in the Americas, Seventeenth Century** Iberfoto/ The Image Works

4. Based on the image above, which of the following is an accurate description of the impact of the sugar industry?

   (A) It provided employment opportunities for European peasants to create wealth and social standing.

   (B) It provided Amerindians with an ability to develop successful business tactics and enter the global trade.

   (C) European agricultural practices in the Americas often required deforestation and other environmental changes to facilitate sugar production.

   (D) Production was so high at such low costs that the global market in sugar plummeted, causing economic despair.

5. Sugar plantations were instrumental to the introduction of African slavery to the Americas because

   (A) only African slaves knew how to successfully grow the sugar.

   (B) disease wiped out large portions of the Amerindian population.

   (C) African slaves were cheaper to obtain than Amerindians who lived deep in the forest.

   (D) the Catholic Church forbade the use of Amerindians as slave labor.

6. The production of sugar was necessary because of which of the following developments?

   (A) Sugar was soon used as a major monetary instrument, similar to salt or silver.

   (B) The Catholic Church saw sugar plantations as a key way to spread religion.

   (C) American foods became staple exports with heavy demand in Europe.

   (D) Sugar spoiled so quickly it had to be constantly resupplied.

Questions 7–10 refer to Map 18.1 on page 458.

7. According to the map, the American colonies were

   (A) lacking environmental diversity.

   (B) completely dominated by the British and French.

   (C) independent soon after colonization.

   (D) used to produce cash crops for export.

8. The establishment of the colonies in the Americas marks the

   (A) end of European involvement in global trade networks.

   (B) beginning of a genuinely global economy.

   (C) dividing of the global economy.

   (D) beginning of land-based empires.

9. Which of the following inferences can be made based on the map?

   (A) Rivalries between European states carried over to the Americas.

   (B) Religious institutions from Europe were short-lived in the Americas.

   (C) Mesoamericans made up the majority of the population in the Americas.

   (D) Most inhabitants lived in the continental interiors of the Americas.

10. The traditional elites of Spain and Portugal were forced to relinquish increasing amounts of power to the viceroys of areas like New Spain and New Peru for which of the following reasons?

    (A) Amerindian support for popular viceroys made them virtually untouchable.

    (B) The New World was so financially beneficial that Old World nobles could not compete with New World viceroys.

    (C) All viceroys were descended from royal blood, and therefore only the King could exercise any control over them.

    (D) Geographical distance made it difficult to exercise control across an ocean voyage taking weeks or months.

Short-Answer Questions

1. Answer all parts of the question that follows.

   (A) Identify ONE item transferred from the New World to the Old World through the Columbian Exchange.

   (B) Explain ONE demographic effect the Columbian Exchange had on the Americas.

   (C) Explain ONE impact (other than demographic) the Columbian Exchange had on the Americas.

▲ **Painting of Castas**   An Amerindian husband with his mestiza (European and Amerindian mixture) wife in an outdoor market where they sold poultry.   Unknown Mexican artist, De indio y mestiza sale coyote. Reproduced with the permission of the Collection of Jan and Frederick Mayer, Denver

2. Use the image above and your knowledge of world history to answer all parts of the question that follows.

   (A) Identify ONE identifier used for people of mixed decent like those in the picture.

   (B) Explain ONE reason Brazilian culture was more heavily influenced by African culture.

   (C) Explain ONE example of slave resistance in the Spanish and Portuguese colonies.

19 The Atlantic System and Africa, 1550–1800

AP® Framework Terms

Atlantic system
Sugar
Plantation system
African slavery
Middle Passage
Mercantilism
Asante (Ashanti)

Overarching Questions

1 How have religions, belief systems, philosophies, and ideologies affected the political, economic, and social development of societies? (CUL)

2 How and why have economic, social, cultural, and geographic factors influenced the process of state building, expansion, and dissolution? (SB)

3 How have local, regional, and global economic systems and exchange networks influenced each other over time? (ECON)

4 How has the development of specialized labor systems interacted with the development of social hierarchies? (ECON)

5 To what extent have legal systems, colonialism, nationalism, and independence movements sustained or challenged class, gender, and racial hierarchies over time? (SOC)

B y the eighteenth century, Europe's Caribbean colonies had collectively become the largest producers of sugar in the world. Across the Caribbean slaves represented about 90 percent of the islands' population and provided nearly all the labor for harvesting and processing sugar cane. The profitable expansion of sugar agriculture in the seventeenth century had opened an expansive new era in the African slave trade. As larger and faster ships carried growing numbers of slaves from Africa, the human cost escalated, as the following example demonstrates.

In 1694 the English ship *Hannibal* called at the West African port of Whydah (**WEE-duh**) to purchase slaves. The king of Whydah invited the ship's captain and officers to his residence, where they negotiated an agreement on the price to be paid for the slaves. The ship's doctor then carefully inspected the naked captives offered for sale to be sure they were of sound body, young, and free of disease. In the end, the *Hannibal* purchased 692 slaves, of whom about a third were women and girls. Once purchased, the slaves were branded with an H (for *Hannibal*) to establish ownership. Loaded on the ship, the crew shackled the men to prevent their escape.

To keep the slaves healthy, the crew fed them twice a day on boiled cornmeal and beans brought from Europe and flavored with hot peppers and palm oil purchased in Africa. Each slave received a pint (half a liter) of water with

▲ **Caribbean Sugar Mill**   Wind power was used to drive the crushing machinery. Once the juice was extracted it was boiled down in the large copper pans housed in the shed next door.   The Crusher Squeezes Juice from the Cane, Antigua, 1823 (print), Clark, William (fl.1823)/British Library, London, UK/British Library Board. All Rights Reserved/The Bridgeman Art Library

every meal. The crew also exercised the slaves every evening by making them "jump and dance for an hour or two to our bagpipe, harp, and fiddle." Despite the incentives and precautions for keeping the cargo alive, deaths were common among the hundreds of people crammed into every corner of a slave ship. The *Hannibal*'s experience was worse than most; it lost 320 slaves and 14 crew members to smallpox and dysentery during its seven-week voyage to Barbados.

As the *Hannibal*'s experience suggests, the Atlantic slave trade took a devastating toll in African lives and was far from a sure-fire money maker for European investors, who in this case lost more than £3,000 on the voyage (approximately $500,000.00 today). Nevertheless, the slave trade and plantation slavery were crucial pieces of a booming new **Atlantic system** that moved goods and wealth, as well as peoples and cultures, around the Atlantic. ●

19-1 **Plantations in the West Indies**

How important was sugar production to the European colonies of the West Indies and to the expansion of the African slave trade?

The West Indies was the first place in the Americas reached by Columbus, and it was also the region of the Americas where native populations collapsed most comprehensively from epidemics. It took a long time to repopulate these islands and forge economic links with other parts of the Atlantic. But after 1650 sugar plantations, African slaves, and European capital made these islands a major center of the Atlantic economy.

AP® Exam Tip
Be able to explain the Atlantic system and how it impacted the world economically, socially, culturally, and demographically.

Atlantic system The network of trading links after 1500 that moved goods, wealth, people, and cultures around the Atlantic Basin.

19-1a Colonization Before 1650

Spanish settlers introduced sugar-cane cultivation into the West Indies shortly after 1500, but these colonies soon fell into neglect as attention shifted to colonizing the Western Hemisphere mainland where rich silver and gold deposits had been revealed. After 1600 the West Indies revived as a focus of colonization, this time by northern Europeans interested in growing tobacco and other crops. In the 1620s and 1630s, English and French colonists settled many islands of the Antilles, driving out small Spanish settlements when necessary. With greater government support, the English colonies prospered, relying initially on tobacco.

Tobacco, a New World leaf long utilized by Amerindians for recreation and medicine, found a ready market among seventeenth-century Europeans. Despite the opposition of individuals like King James I of England, who condemned tobacco smoke as "dangerous to the eye, hateful to the nose, harmful to the brain, and dangerous to the lungs," the habit spread. By 1614 7,000 shops in and around London alone sold tobacco.

The first tobacco colonies suffered from diseases, hurricanes, and attacks by native Caribs and the Spanish (see Environment & Technology: Natural Disasters and the Caribbean Plantation Economy). They also suffered from shortages of supplies from Europe and shortages of labor sufficient to clear land and plant tobacco. The governments of France and England controlled costs by allowing private investors organized as **chartered companies** to develop the colonies in exchange for monopoly control and annual fees. These companies provided passage to the colonies for poor Europeans who were obligated to work three or four years as indentured servants. As a result, the French and English colonial populations grew rapidly in the 1630s and 1640s. By the middle of the century, however, these Caribbean colonies were in crisis due to stiff competition from Virginia tobacco, also cultivated by indentured servants (see Chapter 18). As the English, French, and Dutch colonies of the Caribbean switched from tobacco to sugar cane and from European indentured laborers to the labor of African slaves, profits reached new heights.

The Portuguese first developed sugar plantations that relied on African slaves on islands along the African coast. They later introduced this complex to their American colony, Brazil (see Chapter 18). By 1600 Brazil was the Atlantic world's greatest sugar producer. The Dutch were important participants in the Brazilian sugar business as investors, merchants, and processors.

Dramatic events in Europe overturned this prosperous alliance in the sugar business. Beginning in the 1560s, Dutch Protestants began a rebellion against their Spanish overlords. Then in 1580 the Spanish king Philip II inherited the throne of Portugal (see Chapter 17). As a result, Philip barred the rebellious Dutch from participation in the rich sugar business of Brazil. Decades before formal independence in 1648, the Dutch became militarily and economically strong enough to extend their war against the king of Spain to the coast of Brazil. In 1621 the Dutch government chartered the **Dutch West India Company**, and in 1624 this commercial enterprise led an attack on Brazil's key sugar port, Salvador. The Dutch were soon forced to retreat in the face of local resistance. Then in 1628 a company fleet captured a Spanish treasure convoy in the Caribbean and used some of the windfall to finance an assault on Pernambuco, another one of Brazil's valuable sugar-producing areas. Once established, the Dutch improved the efficiency of the Brazilian sugar industry and also profited from supplying African slaves and European goods to the region.

Once free of Spanish rule in 1640, the reestablished Portuguese crown turned its attention to reasserting its control in Brazil and by 1654 had driven the last of the Dutch from the colony. Some of the expelled planters transferred their capital and knowledge of sugar production to Dutch Caribbean colonies as well as to the English and French islands, modernizing the industry and dramatically expanding exports.

As had been the case in its assault on Brazil, the Dutch West India Company's entry into the African slave trade combined economic and political motives. It seized the important West African trading station of Elmina from the Portuguese in 1638 and then took their port of Luanda (**loo-AHN-duh**) on the Angolan coast in 1641. From these strategic posts in Africa the Dutch shipped slaves to Brazil and the West Indies. Although the Portuguese were able to drive the Dutch out of Angola after a few years, Elmina remained the Dutch West India Company's headquarters in West Africa.

AP® Exam Tip Understand the role of chartered companies in facilitating global and regional trade.

chartered companies Groups of private investors who paid an annual fee to France and England in exchange for a monopoly over trade to the West Indies colonies.

Dutch West India Company Trading company chartered by the Dutch government to conduct its merchants' trade in the Americas and Africa.

CHRONOLOGY

	West Indies	Atlantic	Africa
1500	ca. 1500 Spanish settlers introduce sugarcane cultivation	1611 Amsterdam stock exchange opens	1500–1700 Gold trade predominates 1591 Morocco conquers Songhai
1600	1620s and 1630s English and French colonies in Caribbean 1640s Dutch bring sugar plantation system from Brazil 1655 English take Jamaica 1670s French occupy western half of Hispaniola (modern Haiti)	1621 Dutch West India Company chartered 1654 Dutch expelled from Brazil 1660s English Navigation Acts 1672 Royal African Company chartered 1698 French *Exclusif*	1638 Dutch take Elmina 1680s Rise of Asante
1700	1700 West Indies surpass Brazil in sugar production 1760 Tacky's rebellion in Jamaica	1700 to present Atlantic system flourishing 1713 English receive slave trade monopoly from Spanish Empire	1700–1830 Slave trade predominates 1720s Rise of Dahomey 1730 Oyo makes Dahomey pay tribute

19-1b Sugar and Slaves

The infusion of Dutch expertise and money revived the French colonies of Guadeloupe and Martinique, but the English colony of Barbados best illustrates the dramatic transformation that sugar brought to the seventeenth-century Caribbean. In 1640 Barbados' economy depended largely on tobacco, mostly grown by European settlers, both free and indentured. By the 1680s sugar had become the principal crop and enslaved Africans had become three times as numerous as European settlers. Exporting up to 15,000 tons of sugar a year, Barbados became the wealthiest and most populous of England's American colonies. By 1700 Barbados and other West Indian colonies had collectively surpassed Brazil as the world's principal source of sugar.

This transformation was accomplished at a high environmental cost. Originally covered in tropical forest, Barbados was virtually deforested in a matter of decades. Forests were cut to provide fuel for the refineries and to make more land available for sugar. Widespread deforestation soon led to soil erosion, silted rivers, and fields exhausted of nutrients. As colonists chased the profits associated with sugar production, similar patterns of environmental degradation appeared elsewhere in the Caribbean as well.

The expansion of sugar plantations in the West Indies depended on a sharp increase in the volume of the slave trade from Africa (see Figure 19.1). During the first half of the seventeenth century about 10,000 slaves a year had arrived in the Americas from Africa. Most were destined for Brazil and the mainland Spanish colonies. In the second half of the century the trade averaged 20,000 slaves annually, and more than half were imported by the English, French, and Dutch West Indian colonies. As sugar production surged between 1640 and 1807, more than 4 million slaves were imported into the Caribbean region, ten times the total slave imports of Britain's North American colonies combined.

Cash-short tobacco planters in the seventeenth century preferred indentured Europeans to African slaves because they cost half as much. Thousands of impoverished Europeans, both men and women, were willing to work for little in order to get to the Americas, where they could acquire their own land cheaply at the end of their term of service. However, as the cultivation of sugar spread after

AP® Exam Tip
Be able to compare slavery in the Americas to other labor systems.

Section Review

- England and France relied on private investors organized as chartered companies to develop their Caribbean colonies.

- European colonies in the Caribbean at first depended on tobacco exports but then concentrated on producing sugar, which was more profitable.

- The Dutch helped develop the sugar industry as investors, refiners, slave traders, and disseminators of new technologies.

- European indentured servants provided crucial labor for Caribbean plantations in the early years, but planters switched to African slaves when the flow of indentured laborers was redirected to North America.

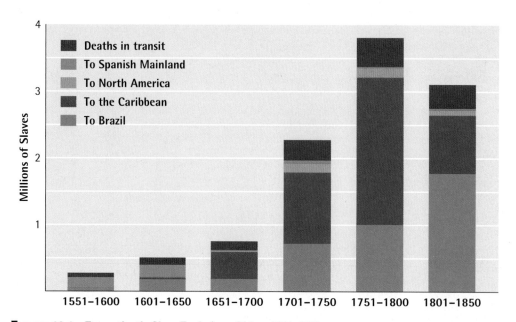

FIGURE 19.1   Transatlantic Slave Trade from Africa, 1551–1850
Source: Data from David Eltis, "The Volume and Structure of the Transatlantic Slave Trade: A Reassessment," *William and Mary Quarterly*, 3rd Series, 58 (2001), tables II and III.

1750, speculators drove land prices in the West Indies so high that former indentured servants could no longer afford to buy land when their labor contracts ended. As a result, poor Europeans chose to indenture themselves in Britain's North American colonies, where cheap land was still available (see Chapter 18). Rather than raise wages to attract European laborers, Caribbean sugar planters switched to African slaves.

Rising sugar prices allowed West Indian sugar planters to afford the higher cost of African slaves. The fact that slaves lived seven years on average after their arrival, while the typical indentured labor contract was for only three or four years, also made slaves a better investment. Dutch, English, and other traders responded to rising labor demands by increasing the flow of slaves to meet the needs of the expanding plantations (see Figure 19.1), but slave prices rose throughout the eighteenth century. These high labor costs were one more factor favoring more efficient large plantations over smaller operations.

19-2 Plantation Life in the Eighteenth Century

What effect did sugar plantations have on the natural environment and on living conditions?

To find more land for sugar plantations, France and England expanded their Caribbean holdings by attacking older Spanish colonies. In 1655 the English seized Jamaica from the Spanish (see Map 18.1). They also took Havana, Cuba, in 1762 and held the city for a year. By the time the occupation ended, English merchants had imported large numbers of slaves and Cuba had begun to switch from tobacco to sugar production. The French seized the western half of the Spanish island of Hispaniola in the 1670s. During the eighteenth century this new French colony of Saint Domingue **(san doh-MANGH)** (present-day Haiti) became the greatest producer of sugar in the Atlantic world, while Jamaica surpassed Barbados as England's most important sugar colony. The technological, environmental, and social transformation of these island colonies illustrates the power of the new Atlantic system.

19-2a Technology and Environment

Sugar production had both an agricultural and an industrial character. On both small farms and large plantations, growing and harvesting sugar cane required only simple tools like spades, hoes, and machetes. Once the cane was cut, however, a more complex and expensive process

▲ **Plantation Scene, Antigua, British West Indies**   The sugar produced at the mill in the background was packed in barrels, carried by carts to the beach, and then transported to the ships that hauled the cargo to Europe. The importance of African labor is evident from the fact that only one white person appears in the painting. British Library Board

was needed to produce sugar. Slaves rushed the cane to mills, where it was crushed and the juice extracted. Lead-lined wooden troughs carried cane juice to a series of large copper kettles where excess water was boiled off, leaving thick syrup. Placed in conical clay molds, the syrup turned to crystallized sugar as it dried. While small refiners relied on small crushing mills powered by animals or even by slave laborers, the largest, most profitable plantations utilized more efficient mills that relied on wind or water power. The economies of scale generated by these large mills meant that over time the more efficient, large-scale producers had lower costs and greater profits, driving many small-scale farmers out of business.

To make the operation more efficient and profitable, investors sought to utilize the costly crushing and refining machinery intensively. As a result, West Indian plantations expanded from an average of around 100 acres (40 hectares) in the seventeenth century to at least twice that size in the eighteenth century. Some plantations were even larger. In 1774 Jamaica's 680 sugar plantations averaged 441 acres (178 hectares), with the largest over 2,000 acres (800 hectares). By this date Jamaica was so specialized in sugar production that this agricultural colony had to import most of its food. Saint Domingue had a comparable number of plantations of smaller average size but generally higher productivity. This French colony was also more diverse in its economy. Although sugar production was paramount, some planters raised provisions for local consumption as well as crops such as coffee and cacao for export.

Sugar agriculture had a mixed environmental record. Some practices were not destructive. Planters powered their mills by water, wind, or animals and fueled their boilers by burning the crushed cane. They fertilized their fields using manure from their livestock. Yet high profits led planters to exploit nature ruthlessly in other ways. Everywhere in the Caribbean, forests were cleared to plant sugar or other export crops. Repeated cultivation of a single crop was also damaging because it removed more nutrients from the soil than animal fertilizer and fallow periods could restore. Instead of rotating sugar with other crops to restore the nutrients

AP® Exam Tip

Explain the trade in cash crops, such as sugar, in the Atlantic system.

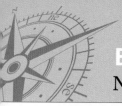

By the middle of the eighteenth century the plantation colonies of the Caribbean were producing prodigious amounts of wealth. The region's most profitable economies were dominated by large sugar plantations and dependent on the labor of slaves. As profits had risen, the importation of African slaves expanded dramatically. Between 1768 and 1786 alone the number of slaves in the British colony of Jamaica increased from 168,900 to 255,700. A similar pattern existed in all the sugar-producing colonies. During this same period, planters across the Caribbean made huge new investments in land and in more productive sugar processing equipment. Despite profits from rising exports, most planters were forced to fund this expansion with borrowed money. While these investments often led to greater profits, heavy debt burdens meant that planters and other investors were vulnerable to any disruption to production.

While the Caribbean economy in this period was powerfully affected by six wars in which British naval forces struggled with French and Spanish rivals for territory and control of trade routes, the impact of hurricanes and other natural disasters proved much more destructive. The Caribbean is an active earthquake zone and European colonies were afflicted by a succession of seismic events in this period. Jamaica is situated on the northern rim of the Caribbean tectonic plate and, in 1692, a powerful earthquake flattened this British colony's major city, Port Royal. Following three destructive shocks that destroyed most of the buildings, the sea receded and then surged back, drowning hundreds of survivors. Jamaica also experienced earthquakes in 1781 and 1812. The Spanish colony of Puerto Rico experienced powerful earthquakes in 1670 and 1787 and Santiago, Cuba, and surrounding areas suffered a devastating quake in 1766. Similarly, the French colony of Saint Domingue (modern Haiti) suffered four earthquakes in less than a century, with the 1751 quake causing the greatest loss of life and property destruction. One witness to this event claimed that "the city of Port-au-Prince was totally destroyed" and another stated "the value of plantations is falling away, and everybody talks of returning to France." The same region suffered from another destructive quake and tsunami in 1770 that claimed more than 500 lives.

Earthquakes could be devastating, but these powerful geological events were typically separated by decades and most destruction occurred within a limited geographic area. The Caribbean hurricane season of the late summer and fall, however, threatened this region annually. While hurricanes also struck the Gulf and Atlantic coasts of North America in this era, they were much more frequent and generally more destructive in the Caribbean. The Spanish colony of Cuba may have experienced the greatest number of hurricanes, with at least ten making landfall between 1750 and 1800, and the French colony of Guadeloupe suffered the greatest loss of life from a single hurricane in 1776 when 6,000 perished.

The prosperous British sugar colony of Jamaica experienced five hurricanes in a seven-year period in the late eighteenth century. The October 1780 hurricane that ravaged a broad swath of the Caribbean proved the most destructive, with more than 500 slaves losing their lives. One survivor of the 1780 hurricane reported to readers in London that "every [sugar] cane, every plantain tree, every fruit-tree, every building [is] entirely blown down." This same storm ravaged Barbados, causing damages of £1,000,000 sterling (roughly £120,000,000 today). Because slaves were housed in the least substantial buildings, they faced the greatest risks, with more than 4,000 slaves killed in Barbados alone.

By the end of the eighteenth century the accumulated effects of hurricanes had played an important role in shaping the society and economy of the Caribbean. In an era without insurance for crops, homes, or sugar refineries, planters attempted to reduce their risk by bending every effort to harvest, process, and ship sugar before the hurricane season began, but this difficult schedule required ideal weather conditions, rapid refining, and the availability of adequate shipping. Since these conditions were

AP® Exam Tip

Understand the environmental impact of the Columbian Exchange.

naturally, planters found it more profitable to clear new lands when yields declined in the old fields. When land was finally exhausted, planters often moved on to new islands. Many of the English who settled Jamaica, for example, had been planters on Barbados. Similarly, the pioneer planters on Saint Domingue came from older French sugar colonies where production had begun to decline. As a result of these environmentally destructive practices, Jamaican sugar production was overtaken by Saint Domingue, which still had virgin land in the second half of the eighteenth century.

In addition to the effects of soil exhaustion and deforestation common on sugar islands, the introduction of non-native animals and cultivated plants also transformed the Caribbean's environment. The Spanish brought cattle, pigs, and horses, which multiplied rapidly. They also introduced new plants. Bananas and plantains introduced from the Canary Islands became food staples in the region, at the same time that sugar and rice, along with native tobacco, became the basis of the plantation economy. Other food crops arrived with the slaves from Africa, including okra, blackeyed peas, yams, grains such as millet and sorghum, and mangoes. Many of these new animals and plants were useful additions to the islands, but they also crowded out indigenous species. The most tragic and dramatic transformation of the West Indies was demographic. Chapter 16 detailed how disease and abuse nearly eliminated the indigenous peoples of the large islands within fifty years of Columbus's first voyage. Far earlier and more completely than in any mainland colony, the West Indies were repeopled from across the Atlantic—first with thousands of free Europeans and then with millions of captive Africans.

seldom present, nearly every planter was forced to absorb the disastrous costs of hurricane damage sooner or later. Following a hurricane, the poorest, most vulnerable planters were often compelled to sell their land and slaves (typically purchased with borrowed money) at depreciated prices. Generally, the richest planters with the largest slaveholdings had the best chance to recover, since they could rebuild quickly and could absorb the steep short-term losses. But even the wealthiest planters were often forced to borrow at high interest rates to make necessary repairs, making them more vulnerable to ruin during the next hurricane season.

Questions for Analysis

1. Did planters respond in different ways to the threats of hurricanes and earthquakes?
2. Did these disasters have long-term effects on the production of sugar?
3. Why were slaves especially vulnerable to these disasters?

Source: This discussion relies in part on Matthew Mulcahy, "Weathering the Storms: Hurricanes and Risk in the British Greater Caribbean," *Business History Review* 78 (2004): 635–663.

▲ **Caribbean Hurricane**   View of town of Léogane in French sugar colony of Saint Domingue (Haiti) during 1791 hurricane. Shipwreck with rescued passengers in foreground. Courtesy of the John Carter Brown Library at Brown University

19-2b Slaves' Lives

During the eighteenth century West Indian plantation colonies were the world's most polarized societies. On most islands 90 percent or more of the inhabitants were slaves. Power resided in the hands of a **plantocracy**, a small number of very rich plantation owners who owned most of the slaves and most of the land. Between the slaves and the masters was a small middle group of estate managers, government officials, artisans, and small farmers, nearly all white. While some free blacks owned property or entered commerce, it is, nevertheless, only a slight simplification to describe eighteenth-century Caribbean society as being made up of a large, abject class of slaves and a small, powerful class of masters.

The profitability of a Caribbean plantation depended on extracting as much work as possible from the slaves, and plantations achieved exceptional productivity through the threat and use of force. Slaves worked long hours in difficult conditions throughout the year, but, when the cane harvest and milling were in full swing, workdays might stretch to eighteen hours or more. As Table 19.1 shows, on a typical Jamaican plantation about 80 percent of the slaves were actively engaged in productive tasks; the only exceptions were infants, the seriously ill, and the very old.

Table 19.1 also illustrates how planters organized slaves by age, sex, and ability. Only 2 or 3 percent of the slaves were house servants. About 70 percent of the ablebodied slaves worked in the fields, most organized in one of three labor gangs. A "great gang," made up of the strongest slaves in the prime of life, did the heaviest work, such as breaking up the soil at the beginning of the

plantocracy In the West Indian colonies, the rich men who owned most of the slaves and most of the land, especially in the eighteenth century.

TABLE 19.1   Slave Occupations on a Jamaican Sugar Plantation, 1788

Occupations and Conditions	Men	Women	Boys and Girls	Total
Field laborers	62	78		140
Tradesmen	29			29
Field drivers	4			4
Field cooks		4		4
Mule-, cattle-, and stablemen	12			12
Watchmen	18			18
Nurse		1		1
Midwife		1		1
Domestics and gardeners		5	3	8
Grass-gang			20	20
Total employed	**125**	**89**	**23**	**237**
Infants			23	23
Invalids (18 with yaws)				32
Absent on roads				5
Superannuated [elderly]				7
Overall total				**304**

Source: From Michael Craton, James Walvin, and David Wright, eds., *Slavery, Abolition and Emancipation*, p. 103. Copyright © 1976. Reprinted by permission of Pearson Education Limited.

planting season. A second gang of youths, elders, and less fit slaves did somewhat lighter work. A "grass gang," composed of children under the supervision of an elderly slave, was responsible for weeding and other simple work, such as collecting grass for the animals. Slaves too old for any field labor tended the toddlers. Women, except when pregnant or briefly after giving birth, were subject to the same brutal labor regime as men. On many plantations they made up the majority of field laborers, even in the great gang doing the heaviest labor. Owners seeking maximum profits even forced nursing mothers to take their babies with them to the fields.

Because the slave trade imported twice as many males as females, men outnumbered women on nearly every Caribbean plantation. As Table 19.1 shows, a little over half of adult males did nongang work. Some tended livestock, and others were skilled craftsmen, such as blacksmiths and carpenters. On most plantations the most important artisan slave was the head boiler, who oversaw the delicate process of reducing the cane sap to crystallized sugar and molasses.

Planters often rewarded skilled slaves with better-quality food and clothing or with time off, but most field slaves were compelled to work without respite by fear of the lash. Slave gangs were led by a privileged male slave, appropriately called the **driver**, whose job was to ensure that the gang completed its work. Since production quotas were high, slaves toiled in the fields from sunup to sunset, except for brief meal breaks. Those who fell behind due to fatigue or illness soon felt the sting of the whip. Planters reserved the most brutal punishments for openly rebellious slaves who refused to work, disobeyed orders, or tried to escape. Floggings, mutilations such as cutting off noses and ears, and beatings were commonly carried out in front of the entire slave population as a form of intimidation. While slaves usually did not work in the fields on Sunday, they could not rest but had to use this time to farm their own provisioning grounds to supplement meager food rations, maintain their dwellings, and do other chores, such as washing and mending their rough clothes.

Except for occasional holidays—including the Christmas-week revels in the British West Indies—there was little time for recreation and relaxation. Slaves might sing in the fields, but singing was simply a way to distract themselves from fatigue and the monotony of the work. There was certainly no time for schooling, nor were masters willing to educate slaves beyond the basic manual skills useful to the plantation.

Time for family life was also inadequate. Although the large proportion of young slaves in plantation colonies ought to have led to a high rate of natural population increase, despite the sex imbalance that resulted from the slave trade, the opposite occurred. Poor nutrition and

AP® Exam Tip
Understand the interplay between growing global demand for goods from the Americas and the growth of slavery in the Americas.

driver A privileged male slave whose job was to ensure that a slave gang did its work on a plantation.

TABLE 19.2 Birth and Death on a Jamaican Sugar Plantation, 1779–1785

| | Born | | | Died | | |
Year	Males	Females	Purchased	Males	Females	Proportion of Deaths
1779	5	2	6	7	5	1 in 26
1780	4	3	—	3	2	1 in 62
1781	2	3	—	4	2	1 in 52
1782	1	3	9	4	5	1 in 35
1783	3	3	—	8	10	1 in 17
1784	2	1	12	9	10	1 in 17
1785	2	3	—	0	3	1 in 99
Total	**19**	**18**	**27**	**35**	**37**	
	Born 37			**Died 72**		

Source: From Michael Craton, James Walvin, and David Wright, eds., *Slavery, Abolition and Emancipation*, p. 105. Copyright © 1976. Reprinted by permission of Pearson Education Limited.

overwork led to lower fertility rates, but high mortality rates for infant slaves also limited population growth. The continuation of heavy fieldwork during the pregnancies of slave women made it difficult to carry a baby to term. Similarly, work demands limited a slave mother's ability to ensure her child's survival. As a result of these conditions, along with disease and accidents from dangerous mill equipment, deaths heavily outnumbered births on West Indian plantations (see Table 19.2). Life expectancy for slaves in nineteenth-century Brazil, for example, was only 23 years of age for males and 25.5 years for females. The figures were probably similar for the eighteenth-century Caribbean. A callous opinion, common among slave owners in the Caribbean and in parts of Brazil, held that it was cheaper to import a youthful new slave from Africa than to raise one to the same age on a plantation.

The harsh conditions of plantation life played a major role in shortening slaves' lives, but the greatest killer was disease. Dysentery caused by contaminated food and water was common. Slaves newly arrived from Africa went through the period of adjustment to a new environment known as **seasoning**, during which one-third, on average, died of unfamiliar diseases. Slaves also suffered from diseases brought with them, including malaria. On the plantation profiled in Table 19.1, for example, more than half of the slaves incapacitated by illness had *yaws*, a painful and debilitating skin disease common in Africa. As a consequence, only slave populations in the healthier temperate zones of North America experienced natural increase.

The combination of high mortality and low fertility among the slaves of the Caribbean plantation colonies led inexorably to an ever-larger African slave trade. Plantation owners had to continually purchase new slaves to replace those who died as well as to expand sugar production. As a result, the majority of slaves on most West Indian plantations were African-born, and African religious beliefs, patterns of speech, styles of dress and adornment, and music were prominent parts of West Indian life.

Given the harsh conditions of their lives, it is not surprising that slaves in the West Indies sought freedom whenever they found an opportunity. Individual slaves often ran away, and sometimes large groups of plantation slaves rose in rebellion against their owners or, less often, against the institution of slavery. On Jamaica alone there were sixteen slave rebellions between 1655 and 1813. In Jamaica in 1760, for example, a slave named Tacky, who had been a chief on the Gold Coast of Africa, led a large rebellion. After his followers broke into a fort and armed themselves, slaves from nearby plantations joined his rebellion. Tacky's followers attacked several plantations, setting them on fire and killing the planter families and white employees. Tacky ultimately died in the fighting, and three of his lieutenants stoically endured cruel deaths by torture as fearful colonial authorities sought to deter others from rebellion.

Because European planters believed that recent arrivals from Africa and slaves with the strongest African heritage were the most likely to lead rebellions, they tried to curtail African cultural traditions. They required slaves to learn the colonial language and discouraged the use of African languages by deliberately mixing slaves from different parts of Africa. In French

AP® Exam Tip
Understand the variety of responses to slavery by the slaves themselves.

seasoning An often difficult period of adjustment to new climates, disease environments, and work routines, such as that experienced by slaves newly arrived in the Americas.

▶ **The Brutal Foundation of Plantation Prosperity** In Caribbean slave societies the punishment of slaves was often conducted in public places in order to intimidate other slaves. In this early nineteenth-century illustration, the slave in the foreground is whipped by two other slaves supervised by his owner. In the background a female slave remains suspended by her wrists from a tree branch after being whipped. Plantation in Surinam, illustration from 'Le Costume Ancien et Moderne' by Jules Ferrario, c.1820 (coloured engraving)/Bramati, G. (19th century)/INDIVISION CHARMET/Bibliotheque des Arts Decoratifs, Paris, France/Bridgeman Images

and Portuguese colonies, slaves were encouraged to adopt Catholic religious practices, though African deities, beliefs, and practices survived, serving as the foundation for modern African-derived religions like Brazilian candomblé and Vodou in Haiti. In the British West Indies, where only Quaker slave owners encouraged Christianity among their slaves before 1800, African-derived religions—like Obeah in Jamaica—flourished, as did African herbal medicine and African beliefs concerning nature spirits and witchcraft.

19-2c Free Whites and Free Blacks

The lives of free men and women were very different from the lives of slaves. In the French colony of Saint Domingue, which had nearly half of all slaves in the Caribbean in the eighteenth century, there were three categories of free people. At the top were wealthy owners of large sugar plantations (the *grands blancs* [**grawn blawnk**], or "great whites"), mostly French nationals, who dominated the economy and society of the island. Second came less-well-off Europeans (*petits blancs* [**pay-TEE blawnk**], or "little whites"). Most served as colonial officials, retail merchants, or small-scale agriculturalists. Nearly all members of both groups owned slaves. Third came the free blacks, many of mixed race. There were almost as many free blacks as free whites in Saint Domingue. While they ranked below whites socially, many free blacks owned property, and a surprising number also owned slaves.

The plantation elite was even more powerful in British colonies. Whereas sugar constituted about half of Saint Domingue's exports, in Jamaica the figure was over 80 percent. Such concentration on sugar production crowded out small cultivators, white or black, and confined most landholding to a few larger owners. At midcentury three-quarters of the farmland in Jamaica belonged to individuals who owned 1,000 acres (400 hectares) or more.

One source estimated that a planter had to invest nearly £20,000 in 1774 (about £2,269,000 or $3,403,000 today) to acquire a medium-size Jamaican plantation of 600 acres (240 hectares). A third of this money went for land on which to grow sugar and food crops, pasture animals, and cut timber and firewood. A quarter of the expense was for the mill and refinery. The largest expense was the purchase of 200 slaves at £40 (about £4,539 or $6,809 today) each. In comparison, the annual wage of an English rural laborer at this time was about £10 (between £1,135 or $1,703 today), approximately one-fourth the price of a slave, and the annual incomes of the ten wealthiest noble families in Britain in 1760 averaged only £20,000 each.

AP® Exam Tip
Explain the changes and continuities to social and political elites throughout history.

Reputedly the richest Englishmen of their time, West Indian planters often translated their wealth into political power and social prestige. The richest planters put their plantations under the direction of local managers while they returned to live in Britain. Between 1730 and 1775 seventy of these absentee planters secured election to the British Parliament, where they formed an influential voting bloc. Planters who continued to reside in the West Indies exercised political power through their control of colonial assemblies.

In most European plantation colonies, it was legally possible for an owner to grant freedom to an individual slave or group of slaves. **Manumission** (the legal grant of freedom by an owner) was more common in Brazil and the Spanish and French colonies than in English colonies. Among English colonies, manumissions were more common in the Caribbean than in North American colonies like South Carolina. While some plantation owners in the Caribbean freed slave women with whom they had had sexual relationships or freed their own children born to slave mothers, the largest group of freed slaves across the Americas had accumulated savings and then purchased their own freedom from their masters. Over time, manumissions led to the development of a large free black population in many colonies. Since the legal condition of children followed that of the mother, slave families often struggled to free women in childbearing years first so that their children would be born free. By the late eighteenth century free blacks made up a large portion of the black populations of Brazil and the French colonies.

Section Review

- Sugar production required larger investments in land, slaves, and machinery than other forms of colonial agriculture.

- Large-scale sugar plantations were more efficient and profitable than smaller plantations.

- Sugar plantations had high environmental costs due to deforestation and soil exhaustion.

- Slaves were closely organized and forced to be productive through the use of harsh punishments.

- Slave populations of the Caribbean experienced high mortality rates and low fertility rates.

- Slaves sought freedom through manumission, flight, or rebellion; some groups of runaways, maroons, forced authorities to recognize their freedom.

Manumission A grant of legal freedom to an individual slave.

◀ **Cudjoe, Leader of the Jamaican Maroons, Negotiates a Peace Treaty** In 1738, after decades of successful resistance to the British, the maroon leader Cudjoe negotiated a peace treaty that recognized the freedom of his runaway followers. Unable to defeat the maroons, the British also granted land and effective self-government to the maroons in exchange for an end to raids on plantations and the promise to return future slave runaways. This illustration from an English periodical provides a crude caricature of the victorious Cudjoe. Everett Historical/Shutterstock.com

As in Brazil and Spanish colonies (see Chapter 18), escaped slaves constituted another part of the free black population. Communities of runaways, called **maroons**, were numerous in Jamaica and Hispaniola as well as in the Guianas **(guy-AHN-uhs)**. Jamaican maroons led by Captain Cudjoe, after withstanding several attacks by the colony's militia, signed a treaty in 1738 that recognized their independence and freedom in return for their cooperation in stopping new runaways and suppressing slave revolts. Unable to win decisive victories, colonial authorities in Spanish, Dutch, and Portuguese colonies signed similar treaties with runaway leaders as well.

19-3 **Creating the Atlantic Economy**

What was the relationship between private investors and European governments in the development of the Atlantic economy?

At once archaic in their cruel system of slavery and oddly modern in their specialization in a single product for export and technological experimentation to improve refining machinery, the West Indian plantation colonies were the bittersweet fruit of a new Atlantic trading system. Changes in the character of Atlantic commerce illustrate the rise of this new system. In the sixteenth century Spanish treasure fleets laden with silver and gold bullion had dominated Atlantic trade. In the late seventeenth and eighteenth centuries the Atlantic trade was dominated by sugar ships returning to Europe from the West Indies and Brazil and by slave ships transporting an average of 250 African captives each to the Americas.

In addition to the plantation system, new economic institutions, new partnerships between private investors and governments in Europe, and new working relationships between European and African merchants created the Atlantic economy. This new trading system is a prime example of how European capitalist relationships were reshaping the world.

19-3a **Capitalism and Mercantilism**

Many of the Spanish and Portuguese voyages of exploration in the fifteenth and sixteenth centuries were government ventures, and both Spain and Portugal tried to restrict the overseas trade of their colonies using royal monopolies (see Chapters 16 and 18). Monopoly control, however, proved both expensive and inefficient. The success of the Atlantic economy in the seventeenth and eighteenth centuries depended much more on private enterprise, which made trade more efficient and profitable and spread risk among a large number of participants. European private investors were attracted to colonial trade by the rich profits generated by New World agriculture and mining, but their success depended on new institutions and the continuation of government protection to reduce the possibility of catastrophic loss.

The growth of the Atlantic economy played an important role in the development of modern **capitalism**. The essence of this economic system was the expansion of credit and the development of large financial institutions—banks, stock exchanges, and chartered trading companies—that enabled merchants and investors to conduct business at great distances from their homes while reducing risks and increasing profits (see Chapter 17). Originally developed for business dealings within Europe, the capitalist system expanded overseas in the seventeenth century, when slow economic growth in Europe led many investors to seek profits in the production and export of colonial products and in satisfying a growing demand for European products in the colonies. Among the Western Hemisphere's exports after 1650, sugar yielded a far higher and more reliable profit than any other cash crop. These profits and the trade they lubricated proved crucial to linking Europe, Africa, and the Americas in the fast-growing Atlantic commercial region.

maroons A slave who ran away from his or her master. Often a member of a community of runaway slaves in the West Indies and South America.

capitalism The economic system of large financial institutions—banks, stock exchanges, investment companies—that first developed in early modern Europe. *Commercial capitalism*, the trading system of the early modern economy, is often distinguished from *industrial capitalism*, the system based on machine production.

Europe reaped a far larger share of the wealth produced in this commercial expansion than American or African participants. Some of these advantages resulted from new institutions that facilitated investment and reduced commercial risks for European merchants, but the ability of powerful European states to compel weaker American and African participants to accept inferior terms of trade also played a key role. Chief among the institutional innovations were private banks, joint-stock companies, speculative markets in commodities and shares, and commercial insurance. It took more than a century for these novelties to take root across the continent, but the earliest adopters, especially the English and Dutch, led the commercial expansion and enjoyed most of the benefits. Spain, Portugal, and France changed more slowly, leaving intrusive state controls of commerce in place until the eighteenth century.

From the fifteenth century, European empires sought to monopolize the profits produced in their colonies by controlling trade and accumulating capital in the form of gold and silver, a system called **mercantilism**. Mercantilist policies strongly discouraged trade with foreign merchants, especially in the colonies, because any balance of trade deficit would be paid in gold or silver. These commercial policies were enforced by customs authorities, navies, and coast guards when necessary to secure exclusive relations. The practical result of these policies was to make European goods imported into American colonies more expensive and the products of colonial planters and other exporters cheaper when purchased by European merchants.

Chartered companies were an important part of mercantilist capitalism. In 1602 the Netherlands gave the Dutch East India Company a monopoly over trade in the Indian Ocean. Private investors who bought shares in the company were amply rewarded when the Dutch East India Company captured control of long-distance trade in the Indian Ocean from the Portuguese (see Chapter 20). As we have seen, the Dutch West India Company, chartered in 1621, sought similar benefits in the Atlantic trade by seizing sugar-producing areas in Brazil and African slaving ports from the Portuguese (see Chapter 17).

These successes inspired other governments to set up their own chartered companies. In 1672 a royal charter placed all English trade with West Africa in the hands of the **Royal African Company** (RAC), which established its headquarters at Cape Coast Castle, just east of Elmina on the Gold Coast. The French government also chartered companies and promoted overseas trade and colonization. Jean Baptiste Colbert (**kohl-BEAR**), King Louis XIV's minister of finance from 1661 to 1683, chartered the French East India and French West India Companies to expel Dutch and English traders from French colonies.

French and English governments also used military force to gain trade advantages in the Americas. For example, restrictions on Dutch access to French and English colonies provoked a series of wars with the Netherlands between 1652 and 1678 (see Chapter 17). The larger English and French navies ultimately defeated the Dutch and drove the Dutch West India Company into bankruptcy. Military and diplomatic pressure also forced Spain after 1713 to grant England and later France monopoly rights to supply slaves to its colonies.

With Dutch competition in the Atlantic reduced, the French and English limited the privileges of their chartered companies. Such new mercantilist policies fostered competition among a nation's own citizens, while using high tariffs and restrictions to exclude foreigners. In the 1660s England passed a series of Navigation Acts that confined trade with its colonies to English ships and cargoes; it later opened trade in Africa to any English subject, claiming that competition would cut the cost of slaves to West Indian planters. The French called their mercantilist legislation, codified in 1698, the *Exclusif* (**ek-skloo-SEEF**), highlighting its exclusionary intentions. Other mercantilist laws sought to protect national manufacturing and agricultural interests from the competition of colonies, imposing prohibitively high taxes on their manufactured goods and products like refined sugar.

As a result of these mercantilist measures, the Atlantic became the most important overseas trading area for Britain, France, and Portugal. The value of imports from West Indian colonies alone accounted for over one-fifth the value of total British imports, while French West Indian colonies played an even larger role in France's overseas trade. Only the Dutch, closed out of much of the American trade, depended more heavily on Asian trade (see Chapter 20). Profits from the Atlantic economy, in turn, promoted further economic expansion and increased the revenues of European governments.

19-3b The Atlantic Circuit

At the heart of this trading system was a clockwise network of sea routes known as the **Atlantic Circuit** (see Map 19.1). The first leg, from Europe to Africa, carried European manufactures—notably metals, hardware, and guns—as well as great quantities of cotton textiles brought from India. While some of these goods were exchanged for West African gold, ivory, timber, and other products, most goods went to purchase slaves, who were then transported across the Atlantic to the plantation colonies in what was known as the **Middle Passage**. On the third leg, plantation goods from the colonies returned to Europe. Each leg carried goods from where they were abundant and relatively cheap to where they were scarce and therefore valuable. Thus, in theory, each

AP® Exam Tip Understand the concept of mercantilism, and be able to explain its role in the development of the Americas.

mercantilism European government policies of the sixteenth, seventeenth, and eighteenth centuries designed to promote overseas trade between a country and its colonies and accumulate precious metals by requiring colonies to trade only with their motherland country. The British system was defined by the Navigation Acts; the French system by regulations collectively known as the *Exclusif*.

Royal African Company A trading company chartered by the English government in 1672 to conduct its merchants' trade on the Atlantic coast of Africa.

Atlantic Circuit The network of trade routes connecting Europe, Africa, and the Americas that underlay the Atlantic system.

Middle Passage The part of the Atlantic Circuit involving the transportation of enslaved Africans across the Atlantic to the Americas.

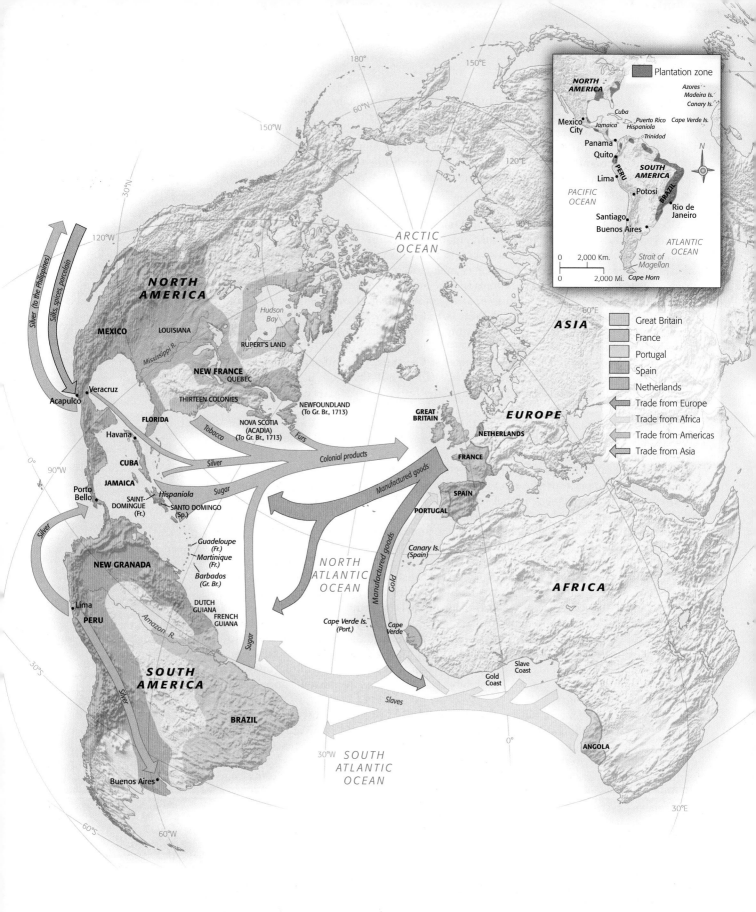

MAP 19.1 **The Atlantic Economy** By 1700 the volume of maritime exchanges among the Atlantic continents had begun to rival the trade of the Indian Ocean Basin. Notice the trade in consumer products, slave labor, precious metals, and other goods. Silver trade to East Asia laid the basis for a Pacific Ocean economy.

Looking at the flow of commodities and slaves as presented in this map, how crucial was the African slave trade to the development of the Atlantic economy?

leg of the Atlantic Circuit could earn profits. In practice, shipwrecks, deaths, piracy, and other risks could turn profit into loss.

The three-sided Atlantic Circuit is only one of many commercial routes that serviced Atlantic trade. Ships making the long voyage from Europe to the Indian Ocean and Asia typically exchanged African gold and American silver for cotton textiles and spices. Merchants then sold these Asian goods in Africa and the Americas as well as in Europe. Many commercial routes were more direct, carrying manufactured goods from Europe or foodstuffs and lumber from New England to the Caribbean. Some Rhode Island and Massachusetts merchants participated in a "Triangular Trade" that carried rum to West Africa, slaves to the West Indies, and molasses and rum back to New England. There was also a considerable two-way trade between Brazil and Angola that exchanged Brazilian tobacco and liquor for slaves. Brazilian tobacco also found its way north as a staple of the Canadian fur trade.

European investment capital, manufactured goods, and shipping dominated the Atlantic system. Europe was also the principal market for American plantation products, products that helped transform European material culture. Before the seventeenth century, sugar was scarce and expensive in Europe and was mostly consumed by the rich. As colonial production increased, prices fell and consumption of sugar in England rose to about 4 pounds (nearly 2 kilograms) per person in 1700. Europeans of modest means spooned sugar into popular new beverages imported from overseas—tea, coffee, and chocolate—to overcome the beverages' natural bitterness. Consumption increased to about 18 pounds (8 kilograms) by the early nineteenth century (well below the American average of about 152 pounds [69 kilograms] a year today).

The flow of sugar to Europe depended on the flow of slaves from Africa (see Map 19.2). The rising volume of the Middle Passage is one measure of the expansion of the Atlantic system. During the 150 years following the arrival of Europeans in the Americas, the slave trade brought some 800,000 Africans across the Atlantic. Volume rose to nearly 7.5 million slaves during the boom in sugar production between 1650 and 1800. By the end of the legal slave trade to the Americas in the nineteenth century, between 12 and 13 million African captives had been forced across the Atlantic. The West Indies, including Cuba, imported nearly 50 percent of this total, while Brazil received nearly a third and North America another 5 percent. The rest went to Spain's mainland colonies (see Figure 19.1).

Seventeenth-century mercantilist policies placed much of the Atlantic slave trade in the hands of chartered companies. During their existence the Dutch West India Company and the English Royal African Company each carried about 100,000 slaves across the Atlantic. In the eighteenth century private English traders from Liverpool and Bristol controlled about 40 percent of the slave trade. The French, operating out of Nantes and Bordeaux, handled about 20 percent and the Dutch only 6 percent. The Portuguese supplying Brazil and other places had nearly 30 percent of the Atlantic slave trade, in contrast to the 3 percent carried in North American ships.

AP® Exam Tip Compare the features of the Atlantic system with other long-distance trade networks during this time period.

▲ **Slave Ship**   This model of the English vessel *Brookes* shows the specially built section of the hold where enslaved Africans were packed together during the Middle Passage. Girls, boys, and women were confined separately. Model of the slave ship 'Brookes' used by William Wilberforce (1759–1833) in the House of Commons to demonstrate conditions on the middle passage, 18th century (wood) (see also 112029, 136291 and 135588)/Wilberforce House, Hull City Museums and Art Galleries, UK/The Bridgeman Art Library

While the volume and duration of the slave trade indicate that it was profitable, the relative value of European goods and African slaves as well as slave prices in American ports determined the profit of individual voyages. Slave traders also had to deliver as many healthy slaves as possible for sale in the plantation colonies, but the terrible conditions on slave ships and the long and treacherous voyages that lasted from six to ten weeks led to high mortalities. Some ships arrived with all of their slaves alive, but large, even catastrophic, losses of life were common (see Figure 19.1). On average, however, slave traders succeeded in lowering mortality during the Middle Passage from about 23 percent on voyages before 1700 to half that in the last half of the eighteenth century, largely a result of using larger and faster ships.

Failed escapes and mutinies contributed to mortality. When opportunities presented themselves (nearness to land, illness among the crew), some enslaved Africans tried to overpower their captors and escape. As result, male slaves were routinely shackled together to prevent escapes while they were still in sight of land or when mutiny was feared while at sea. As an additional precaution, slave traders also commonly confined male slaves below deck during most of the voyage, except during exercise or at mealtimes, when the crew brought them up in small groups under close supervision. In any event, "mutinies" were rarely successful and defeated mutineers were treated with brutality.

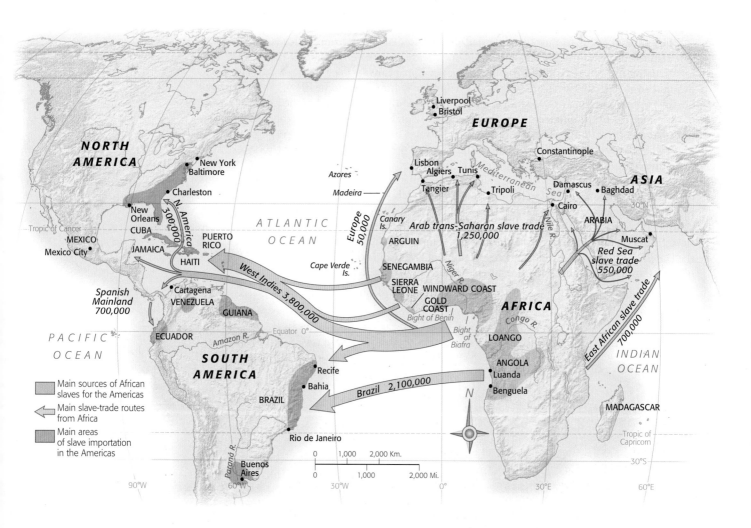

MAP 19.2 The African Slave Trade, 1500–1800 After 1500 a vast new trade in slaves from sub-Saharan Africa to the Americas joined the ongoing slave trade to the Islamic states of North Africa, the Middle East, and India. The West Indies were the major destination of the Atlantic slave trade, followed by Brazil.

Has the slave trade had lasting cultural effects on the societies of the Western Hemisphere?

Mistreatment also contributed to the high mortality of the Middle Passage. Although it was in the interests of the captain and crew to deliver their slave cargo in good condition, slavers used whippings, beatings, and even executions to maintain order. Some slaves developed deep psychological depression, known to contemporaries as "fixed melancholy," and refused to eat. Crews attempted to force-feed these slaves, but some successfully willed themselves to death. The dangers and brutalities of the slave trade were so notorious that many ordinary seamen shunned such work. As a consequence, cruel and brutal officers and crews abounded on slave ships.

Although examples of unspeakable cruelties are common in the records, most deaths in the Middle Passage were the result of disease. Dysentery spread by contaminated food and water caused many deaths. Other slaves died of contagious diseases such as smallpox carried on board by infected slaves or by crew members. These maladies spread quickly in the crowded and unsanitary confines of the ships, claiming the lives of slaves already physically weakened and mentally traumatized by their ordeals. Crew members were exposed to the same epidemics. It is a measure of the callousness of the age, as well as the cheapness of European labor, that over the course of a round-trip voyage from Europe the proportion of crew deaths could be as high as the slave deaths.

Section Review

- Banks, stock markets, and insurance companies helped European nations to develop their colonial empires.

- European nations used mercantilism, a mix of fiscal and trade policies, to monopolize the economic benefits from colonial possessions.

- The Atlantic Circuit was a network of trade networks that connected Europe with Africa and the Western Hemisphere.

- Between 1650 and 1800, 7.5 million African slaves were brought to Europe's American colonies, nine times the number imported in the previous 150 years.

- Conditions on the slave ships were unhealthy and harsh, and mortality rates were high.

19-4 Africa, the Atlantic, and Islam

How did sub-Saharan Africa's expanding contacts in the Atlantic compare with its contacts with the Islamic world?

The Atlantic system took a terrible toll in African lives both during the Middle Passage and under the harsh conditions of plantation slavery. Many thousands of Africans died in the wars that generated the flow of captives and thousands more died while being marched to African ports for sale. The overall effects on Africa of these losses and of other aspects of the slave trade have been the subject of considerable historical debate. It is clear that the trade's impact depended on the intensity and character of different African regions' involvement.

Any assessment of the Atlantic system's effects in Africa must also take into consideration the fact that some Africans profited from the trade by capturing and selling slaves. They chained the slaves or bound them together using forked sticks fastened at the neck for the march to the coast. Once there, captives were bartered to the European slavers for trade goods. The effects on the enslaver were different from the effects on the enslaved. A broader understanding of the Atlantic system's effects in sub-Saharan Africa is facilitated by a comparison with the region's parallel contacts with the Islamic peoples.

19-4a The Gold Coast and the Slave Coast

As Chapter 16 showed, early European visitors to Africa's Atlantic coast were interested more in trading than in colonizing the continent. As the Africa trade mushroomed after 1650, this pattern continued. African kings and merchants sold slaves and other goods at many coastal sites, but the growing slave trade did not lead to substantial European cultural penetration or colonization.

The transition to slave trading was not sudden. Even as slaves were becoming Atlantic Africa's most valuable export, goods such as gold, ivory, and timber remained important. For example, during its eight decades of operation from 1672 to 1752, the English Royal African Company, an important participant in the Atlantic slave trade, made 40 percent of its profits from gold, ivory, and forest products. In some parts of West Africa, such exports other than slaves remained predominant even at the peak of the Atlantic trade.

AP® Exam Tip
Explain the changes and continuities to slavery in Africa during this time period, as well as the demographic impact of the Atlantic slave trade.

African merchants were very discriminating about merchandise they took in exchange for slaves or other goods. A ship that arrived with goods of low quality or not suited to local tastes found it hard to purchase a cargo at a profitable price. European guidebooks to the African trade carefully noted the color and shape of beads, the pattern of textiles, the type of guns, and the sort of metals that were in demand on each section of the coast (see Map 19.3). Although African preferences for merchandise varied, textiles, hardware, and guns were in high demand. Of the goods the English Royal African Company traded in West Africa in the 1680s, over 60 percent were Indian and European textiles and 30 percent were hardware and weaponry. In the eighteenth century, tobacco and rum from the Americas were welcome imports as well.

Both Europeans and Africans sought to drive the best bargain for themselves and sometimes engaged in deceitful practices. The strength of the African bargaining position, however, may be inferred from the fact that as the demand for slaves rose, so too did their price in Africa. In the course of the eighteenth century the value of goods needed to purchase a slave on the Gold Coast doubled and in some places tripled or quadrupled, an effective measure of the rising profitability of American sugar plantations.

African governments on the Gold and Slave Coasts forced Europeans to observe African trading customs and prevented them from taking control of African territory. Rivalry among European nations, each of which established its own trading "castles" along the Gold Coast, also reduced bargaining strength because Africans could shop for better deals among these competitors. In 1700 the head of the Dutch East India Company in West Africa, Willem Bosman (**VIL-uhm boos-MAHN**), bemoaned the fact that, to stay competitive against other European traders, his company had to include large quantities of muskets and gunpowder in the goods it exchanged, thereby adding to Africans' military power.

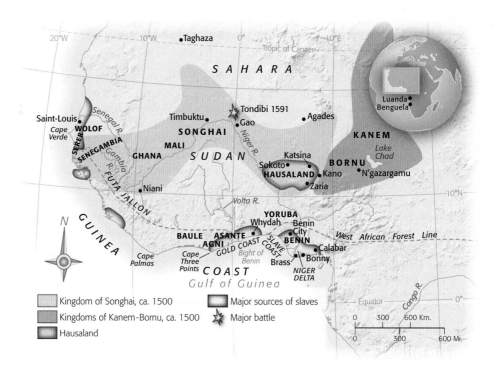

MAP 19.3 West African States and Trade, 1500–1800 The Atlantic and the trans-Saharan trade brought West Africans new goods and promoted the rise of powerful states and trading communities. The Moroccan invasion of Songhai and Portuguese colonization of the Angolan ports of Luanda and Benguela showed the political dangers of such relations.

Is it fair to say that the prospect of greater profit from the slave trade led both European and Islamic powers to expand their influence in Africa?

Bosman also related that his agents had to both pay the local king a substantial customs duty when buying slaves at Whydah and then pay a premium price for the slaves. By African standards, Whydah was a rather small kingdom controlling only the port and its immediate hinterland. In 1727, Dahomey (**dah-HOH-mee**), strengthened militarily by firearms acquired in the slave trade, annexed Whydah.

Two other regional powers, the kingdoms of Oyo (**aw-YOH**) and Asante (**uh-SHAN-tee**), also participated in the Atlantic trade, but neither kingdom was as dependent on it as Dahomey. Overseas trade formed a relatively modest part of the economies of these large and populous states, which maintained extensive overland trade with their northern neighbors and with states across the Sahara. Like the great medieval empires of the western Sudan, Oyo and Asante grew more powerful from external trade but were not dependent on it. In 1730, the Oyo kingdom overran Dahomey, forcing it to pay an annual tribute to keep its independence.

How did African kings and merchants obtain slaves for sale? Bosman dismissed misconceptions prevailing in Europe in his day. "Not a few in our country," he wrote to a friend in 1700, "fondly imagine that parents here sell their children, men their wives, and one brother the other. But those who think so, do deceive themselves; for this never happens on any other account but that of necessity, or some great crime; but most of the slaves that are offered to us are prisoners of war, which are sold by the victors as their booty."[1] His statement confirms other accounts claiming that prisoners of war were the most common source of slaves, but it is harder to prove that capturing slaves for export was a main cause of wars. "Here and there," conclude two respected historians of Africa, "there are indications that captives taken in the later and more peripheral stages of these wars were exported overseas, but it would seem that the main impetus of conquest was only incidentally concerned with the slave-trade."[2]

An early-nineteenth-century king of Asante had a similar view: "I cannot make war to catch slaves in the bush, like a thief. My ancestors never did so. But if I fight a king, and kill him when he is insolent, then certainly I must have his gold, and his slaves, and his people are mine too. Do not the white kings act like this?"[3] English rulers had indeed sentenced seventeenth-century Scottish and Irish prisoners to forced labor in the West Indies. One may imagine that neither African nor European prisoners shared their kings' view that such actions were legitimate.

AP® Exam Tip

Explain how local states (such as the Asante or Ashanti) were able to limit the impact of European trading post empires in Africa.

19-4b The Bight of Biafra and Angola

In the eighteenth century the slave trade expanded eastward to the Bight (**bite**) of Biafra. In contrast to the Gold and Slave Coasts, where strong kingdoms predominated, the densely populated interior of the Bight of Biafra contained no regionally dominant polities. Even so, formidable merchant princes of the coastal ports made European traders give them rich presents.

Using a network of markets and inland trading routes, regional merchants supplied European slave traders at the coast with a mix of debtors, victims of kidnapping, and convicted criminals. As the volume of the Atlantic trade along the Bight of Biafra expanded in the late eighteenth century, some inland markets evolved into giant fairs with different sections specializing in slaves and imported goods. In the 1780s an English ship's doctor reported that African merchants collected slaves at fairs in the interior and that groups of 1,200 to 1,500 enslaved men and women were then sent to the coast from a single fair.[4]

The local context of the Atlantic trade was different south of the Congo estuary at Angola, the greatest source of slaves for the Atlantic trade (see Map 19.2). This was also the one place along Africa's Atlantic coast where a single European nation, Portugal, controlled a significant amount of territory. Except for a brief period when the Dutch exercised control in the seventeenth

---

[1] Willem Bosman, *A New and Accurate Description of Guinea, etc.* (London, 1705), quoted in David Northrup, ed., *The Atlantic Slave Trade* (Lexington, MA: D.C. Heath, 1994), 72.

[2] Roland Oliver and Anthony Atmore, *The African Middle Ages, 1400–1800* (Cambridge, UK: Cambridge University Press, 1981), 100.

[3] King Osei Bonsu, quoted in Northrup, ed., *The Atlantic Slave Trade*, 93.

[4] Alexander Falconbridge, *Account of the Slave Trade on the Coast of Africa* (London, UK: J. Phillips, 1788), 12.

century, Portuguese residents of the main ports of Luanda and Benguela (**ben-GWAY-luh**) served as middlemen between the caravans that arrived from the interior and the ships that crossed from Brazil. From these coastal cities Afro-Portuguese traders guided large caravans of trade goods inland to exchange for slaves at special markets.

Many of the slaves sold at these markets were prisoners of war captured by expanding African states. By the late eighteenth century prisoners captured in wars as distant as 600 to 800 miles (1,000 to 1,300 kilometers) away were carried to the ports for transportation across the Atlantic. Many were victims of wars of expansion fought by the giant federation of Lunda kingdoms. As elsewhere in Africa, prisoners sold as slaves seem to have been a by-product of African wars, rather than the objective of the warring parties.

Research has identified a link between severe eighteenth-century droughts and the development of the Angolan slave trade. Collapsing agricultural production caused by drought drove starving refugees from their homes to better-watered areas controlled by foreign rulers.[5] The powerful African leaders who controlled these neighboring areas gained control of these refugees in return for supplying them with food and water. While these leaders valued refugee children and women as food producers who would quickly assimilate, adult male refugees were seen as more likely to escape or to challenge the ruler's authority. As a result, many male refugees were sold as slaves.

The local rulers benefitting from this booming slave trade used the textiles, weapons, and alcohol they received from European traders as gifts to attract new followers and to cement the loyalty of their established allies. The most successful became heads of powerful new states, stabilizing areas devastated by war and drought and repopulating them with the refugees and prisoners.

Although the organization of Atlantic trade varied from African region to region, it expanded and prospered because both European merchants and African elites benefited. African rulers and merchants exported slaves and other products to obtain foreign goods that made them wealthier and more powerful, and most of the exported slaves were prisoners taken in wars associated with African state growth. But strong African states or powerful merchant communities also proved better able to defend African territory and limit European economic advantages. The Africans who gained from this trade were the rich and powerful few. Many more Africans were losers in the exchanges.

AP® Exam Tip
Be able to give examples of gender and family restructuring that occurred as a result of the African slave trade.

19-4c Africa's European and Islamic Contacts

The ways in which sub-Saharan Africans established new contacts with Europe paralleled their much older pattern of relations with the Islamic world. There were striking similarities in Africa's political, commercial, and cultural interactions with these two external influences between 1500 and 1800, but differences may have been more consequential in influencing the region.

During the three and a half centuries of contact before 1800, Africans ceded very little territory to Europeans. Local African rulers generally kept close tabs on the European trading posts they permitted along the Gold and Slave Coasts and collected lucrative rents and fees. Aside from some uninhabited islands off the Atlantic coast, Europeans established colonial beachheads in only two places, the Portuguese colony of Angola and the Dutch East India Company's Cape Colony at the southern tip of the continent. The Dutch colony was tied to Indian Ocean trade, not to the Atlantic trade and, unlike Angola, did not export slaves. Most of the Cape Colony's 25,750 slaves in 1793 were not Africans; instead, they had been shipped to the colony from Madagascar, South Asia, and the East Indies.

North Africa had become a part of the Islamic world in the first century of Islamic expansion. Sub-Saharan Africans gradually learned of Muslim beliefs and practices from traders who crossed the Sahara from North Africa or who sailed from the Middle East to the Swahili trading cities of East Africa. In the sixteenth century the Islamic Ottoman Empire annexed all of North Africa except Morocco, while Ethiopia lost extensive territory to other Muslim conquerors.

---

[5]Joseph C. Miller, "The Significance of Drought, Disease, and Famine in the Agriculturally Marginal Zones of West-Central Africa," *Journal of African History* 23 (1982): 17–61.

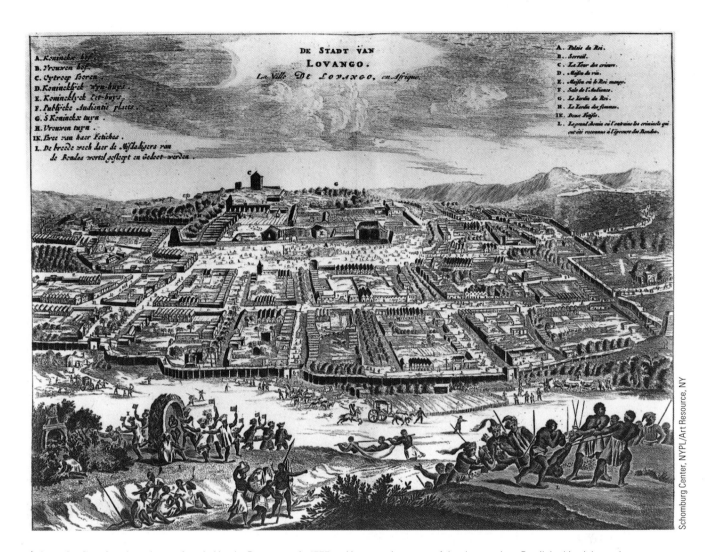

Schomburg Center, NYPL/Art Resource, NY

▲ **Luanda, Angola** Luanda was founded by the Portuguese in 1575 and became the center of the slave trade to Brazil. In this eighteenth-century print the city's warehouses and commercial buildings line the city streets. In the foreground captives are dragged to the port for shipment to the Western Hemisphere.

Until 1590 the Sahara remained an effective buttress against invasion from powerful northern states. The **Songhai** (**song-GAH-ee**) Empire of West Africa challenged the status quo when it pushed its frontier into the Sahara from the south. Ruled by an indigenous Muslim dynasty, Songhai drew its wealth from the trans-Saharan trade (see Map 19.3). This expansion led the kingdom of Morocco to challenge Songhai by sending a military expedition of 4,000 men south across the desert. Although half the invading force perished, the survivors, armed with firearms, defeated Songhai's army of 40,000 in 1591. While Morocco was never able to annex the western Sudan, its forces extracted a massive tribute in slaves and goods from the local population and imposed tolls on trade for the next two centuries.

With Morocco's destruction of Songhai, the **Hausa** trading cities in the central Sudan became the prime destinations for the caravans bringing textiles, hardware, and weapons across the Sahara. The goods the Hausa imported and distributed through their trading networks were similar to those that coastal African traders received from the Atlantic trade, except for the absence of alcohol, prohibited to Muslims. The goods they sent back in return also resembled the major African exports into the Atlantic: gold, textiles and leather goods, and slaves.

Few statistics of the slave trade to the Islamic north exist, but surviving records make clear that the importation of African slaves into Islamic regions was large in scale and sustained for a

Songhai A people, language, kingdom, and empire in western Sudan in West Africa. At its height in the sixteenth century, the Muslim Songhai Empire stretched from the Atlantic to the land of the Hausa and was a major player in the trans-Saharan trade.

Hausa An agricultural and trading people of central Sudan in West Africa. Aside from their brief incorporation into the Songhai Empire, the Hausa city-states remained autonomous until the Sokoto Caliphate conquered them in the early nineteenth century.

▲ **Traders Approaching Timbuktu** As they had done for centuries, traders brought their wares to this ancient desert-edge city. Timbuktu's mosques tower above the ordinary dwellings of the fabled city. Entrance of Heinrich Barth's (1821-65) Caravan into Timbuktu in 1853, from 'Travels and Discoveries in North and Central Africa' by Barth, engraved by Eberhard Emminger (1808-85) published 1857 (colour engraving), Bernatz, Johann Martin (1802-1878) (after)/Bibliotheque Nationale, Paris, France/Archives Charmet/The Bridgeman Art Library

long time, lasting in some places into the second half of the twentieth century. The transatlantic trade, which delivered between 12 and 13 million slaves to the Americas, was significantly larger than the combined Trans Saharan and Indian Ocean trades to Islamic regions. Between 1600 and 1900 slave traders sent about 3,166,000 slaves to Muslim North Africa and the Middle East via various land routes (see Map 19.2). Maritime routes delivered approximately 1,172,000 slaves from sub-Saharan Africa to the Arabian Peninsula and neighboring areas. Another 892,000 slaves were shipped via Indian Ocean routes to markets in Asia Minor, the Indian subcontinent and Persian Gulf region as well as to the Indian Ocean French colonies of Réunion and Mauitius.[6]

In contrast to the plantation slavery of the Americas, most African slaves in the Islamic world served as soldiers and servants. In the late seventeenth and eighteenth centuries Morocco's rulers employed an army of 150,000 African slaves, trusting their loyalty more than that of recruits from their own lands. Moroccans also used slaves on sugar plantations, as servants, and as artisans. Unlike in the Americas, the majority of African slaves in the Islamic world were women who served wealthy households as concubines, servants, and entertainers. The trans-Saharan slave trade also included a much higher proportion of children than the Atlantic trade.

The central Sudanese kingdom of **Bornu** illustrates several aspects of trans-Saharan contacts. Ruled by the same dynasty since the ninth century, this Muslim state had grown and expanded in the sixteenth century as the result of guns imported from the Ottoman Empire. Bornu retained many captives from its wars or sold them as slaves to the north in return for the firearms and horses that underpinned the kingdom's military power. One Bornu king, Mai Ali,

AP® Exam Tip
Compare coerced labor systems around the world.

Bornu A powerful West African kingdom at the southern edge of the Sahara in the central Sudan, which was important in trans-Saharan trade and in the spread of Islam. Also known as Kanem-Bornu, it endured from the ninth century to the end of the nineteenth.

---

[6]These estimates for the volume of the African slave trade follow those offered by David Eltis and David Richardson, *Atlas of the Transatlantic Slave Trade* (New Haven, CT: Yale University Press, 2010), 4–5.

conspicuously displayed his kingdom's new power and wealth while on four pilgrimages to Mecca between 1642 and 1667. On the last, an enormous entourage of slaves—said to number 15,000—accompanied him.

Like Christians of this period, Muslims saw no moral impediment to owning or trading in slaves. Indeed, Islam considered enslaving "pagans" to be a meritorious act because it brought them into the faith. Although Islam forbade the enslavement of Muslims, Muslim rulers in Bornu, Hausaland, and elsewhere were not strict observers of that rule (see Diversity & Dominance: Slavery in West Africa and the Americas).

Sub-Saharan Africans had much longer exposure to Islamic cultural influences than to European cultural influences. Scholars and merchants learned to use the Arabic language to communicate with visiting North Africans and to read the Quran. Islamic beliefs and practices as well as Islamic legal and administrative systems were influential in African trading cities on the southern edge of the Sahara and on the Swahili coast. In some places Islam had extended its influence among rural people, but in 1750 it was still very much an urban religion.

European cultural influence in Africa was more limited. Some coastal Africans had shown an interest in Western Christianity after contacts with the Portuguese, but in the 1700s only Angola had a significant number of Christians. Coastal African traders found it useful to learn European languages, but African languages continued to dominate inland trade routes. A few African merchants sent their sons to Europe to learn European ways. One of these young men, Philip Quaque (**KWAH-kay**), who was educated in England, was ordained as a priest in the Church of England and became the official chaplain of the Cape Coast Castle from 1766 until his death in 1816.

Overall, how different and similar were the material effects of Islam and Europe in sub-Saharan Africa by 1800? While Muslims and Europeans obtained slaves from sub-Saharan Africa, the European trade was larger and the conditions experienced by slaves once disembarked in the Americas were harsher. The Atlantic trade carried about 8 million Africans to the Americas between 1550 and 1800. During this period the Islamic trade to North Africa and the Middle East transported perhaps 2 million African captives. What were the effects on Africa's population? Scholars generally agree on three points: (1) even at the peak of the trade in the 1700s, sub-Saharan Africa's overall population remained very large; (2) localities that contributed heavily to the slave trade, such as lands near the Slave Coast, suffered acute losses; and (3) the ability of a population to recover from losses was related to the proportion of fertile women who were shipped away. The fact that Africans sold fewer women than men into the larger Atlantic trade somewhat reduced the long-term demographic effects of this larger trade.

The slave trade had a mixed impact on sub-Saharan economies. Africans were very particular about what they received in exchange for slaves, and their imports reflected their tastes and needs. The limited volume of manufactured imports could not overwhelm established African weavers, metalworkers, and other producers, and some imported products like textiles and metal bars actually stimulated the local production of tools and clothing. However, while African as well as European states benefited by taxing this trade, most of the economic benefits went to European nations and to their American colonies.

Profits from transporting and selling slaves mostly went to European merchants and ship owners. European manufacturers, like the producers of textiles and metal goods, profited as well. But Europe's American colonies were the major beneficiaries of the African slave trade. With Amerindian population diminished by epidemics and European immigration inadequate to develop American resources, it was the forced labor of African slaves that made possible the enormous wealth produced in a vast region that spread from the Chesapeake to the Río de la Plata. This wealth accelerated the rapid expansion of Western capitalism in the seventeenth and eighteenth centuries, a period that witnessed the political and economic decline of the Ottoman Empire, the dominant state of the Middle East, and other Muslim kingdoms (see Chapter 20).

Section Review

- Powerful rulers and merchants protected African territory from Europeans and imposed control over trade terms.

- Most slaves exported to the Western Hemisphere were prisoners of war.

- African trade and cultural relations with European nations paralleled already established relations with Muslim regions.

- The African slave trade with the Muslim world was smaller than the Atlantic slave trade but lasted longer.

- Most African slaves sent to the Islamic world served as soldiers or servants.

Social diversity was common in Africa, and the domination of masters over slaves was a feature of many societies. Ahmad Baba (1556–1627) was an outstanding Islamic scholar in the city of Timbuktu who came from an old Muslim family of the city. In about 1615 he replied to some questions that had been sent to him. His answers reveal a great deal about the official and unofficial condition of slavery in the Sudan of West Africa, especially in the Hausa states of Kano and Katsina (see Map 19.3).

You asked: What have you to say concerning the slaves imported from the lands of the Sudan whose people are acknowledged to be Muslims, such as Bornu, . . . Kano, Goa, Songhay, Katsina and others among whom Islam is widespread? Is it permissible to possess them [as slaves] or not?

Know—may God grant us and you success—that these lands, as you have stated are Muslim. . . . But close to each of them are lands in which are unbelievers whom the Muslim inhabitants of these lands raid. Some of these unbelievers are under the Muslims' protection and pay them [taxes]. . . . Sometimes there is war between the Muslim sultans of some of these lands and one attacks the other, taking as many prisoners as he can and selling the captive though he is a free-born Muslim. . . . This is a common practice among them in Hausaland; Katsina raids Kano, as do others, though their language is one and their situations parallel; the only difference they recognize among themselves is that so-and-so is a born Muslim and so-and-so is a born unbeliever. . . .

Whoever is taken prisoner in a state of unbelief may become someone's property, whoever he is, as opposed to those who have become Muslims of their own free will . . . and may not be possessed at all.

A little over a century later another African provided information about enslavement practices in the western Sudan. Ayuba Suleiman Diallo (ah-YOO-bah SOO-lay-mahn JAH-loh) *(1701–?), of the state of Bondu some 200 miles from the Gambia River, was enslaved and transported to Maryland, where he was a slave from 1731 to 1733. When an Englishman learned of Ayuba's literacy in Arabic, he recorded his life story, anglicizing his name to Job Solomon. According to the account, slaves in Bondu did much of the hard work, while men of Ayuba's class were free to devote themselves to the study of Islamic texts.*

In February, 1730, Job's father hearing of an English ship at Gambia River, sent him, with two servants to attend him, to sell two Negroes, and to buy paper, and some other necessaries; but desired him not to venture over the river, because the country of the Mandingoes, who are enemies to the people of Futa, lies on the other side. Job not agreeing with Captain Pike (who commanded the ship, lying then at Gambia, in the service of Captain Henry Hunt, brother to Mr. William Hunt, merchant, in Little Tower-street, London) sent back the two servants to acquaint his father with it, and to let him know that he intended to go no farther. Accordingly . . . he crossed the River Gambia, and disposed of his Negroes for some cows. As he was returning home, he stopped for some refreshment at the house of an old acquaintance; and the weather being hot, he hung up his arms in the house, while he refreshed himself. . . . It happened that a company of the Mandingoes, . . . passing by at that time, and observing him unarmed, rushed in, to the number of seven or eight at once, at a back door, and pinioned Job, before he could get his arms, together with his interpreter, who is a slave in Maryland still. They then shaved their heads and beards, which Job and his man resented as the highest indignity; tho' the Mandingoes meant no more by it, than to make them appear like slaves taken in war. On the 27th of February, 1730, they carried them to Captain Pike at Gambia, who purchased them; and on the first of March they were put on board. Soon after Job found means to acquaint Captain Pike that he was the same person that came to trade with him a few days before, and after what manner he had been taken. Upon this Captain Pike gave him free leave to redeem himself and his man; and Job sent to an acquaintance of his father's, near Gambia, who promised to send to Job's father, to inform him of what had happened, that he might take some course to have him set at liberty. But it being a fortnight's [two weeks'] journey between that friend's house and his father's, and the ship sailing in about a week after, Job was brought with the rest of the slaves to Annapolis in Maryland, and delivered to Mr. Vachell Denton. . . .

Mr. Vachell Denton sold Job to one Mr. Tolsey in Kent Island in Maryland, who put him to work in making tobacco; but he was soon convinced that Job had never been used to such labour. He every day showed more and more uneasiness under this exercise, and at last grew sick, being no way able to bear it; so his master was obliged to find easier work for him, and therefore put him to tend the cattle. Job would often leave the cattle, and withdraw into the woods to pray; but a white boy frequently watched him, and whilst he was at his devotion would mock him and throw dirt in his face. This very much disturbed Job, and added considerably to his other misfortunes; all which were increased by his ignorance of the English language, which prevented his complaining, or telling his case to any person about him. Grown in some measure desperate, by reason of his present hardships, he resolved to travel at a venture; thinking he might possibly be taken up by some master, who would use him better, or otherwise meet with some lucky accident, to divert or abate his grief. Accordingly, he travelled thro' the woods, till he came to the County of Kent, upon Delaware Bay. . . . There is a law in force, throughout the [mid-Atlantic] colonies . . . as far as Boston in New England, viz. that any Negroe, or white servant who is not known in the county, or has no pass, may be secured by any person, and kept in the common [jail], till the master of such servant shall fetch him. Therefore Job being able to give no account of himself, was put in prison there.

This happened about the beginning of June 1731, when I, who was attending the courts there, and heard of Job, went with several gentlemen to the [jailer's] house, being a tavern, and desired to see him. He was brought into the tavern to us, but could not speak one word of English. Upon our talking and making signs to him, he wrote a line to two before us, and when he read it, pronounced the words Allah and Mahommed; by which, and his refusing a glass of wine we offered him, we perceived he was a Mahometan [Muslim], but could not imagine of what country he was, or how he got thither; for by his affable carriage, and the easy composure of his countenance, we could perceive he was no common slave.

When Job had been some time confined, an old Negroe man, who lived in that neighborhood, and could speak the Jalloff [Wolof] language, which Job also understood, went to him, and conversed with him. By this Negroe the keeper was informed to whom Job belonged, and what was the cause of his leaving his master. The keeper thereupon wrote to his master, who soon after fetched him home, and was much kinder to him than before; allowing him place to pray in, and in some other conveniences, in order to make his slavery as easy as possible. Yet slavery and confinement was by no means agreeable to Job, who had never been used to it; he therefore wrote a letter in Arabick to his father, acquainting him with his misfortunes, hoping he might yet find means to redeem him. . . . It happened that this letter was seen by James Oglethorpe, Esq. [founder of the colony of Georgia and director of the Royal African Company]; who, according to his usual goodness and generosity, took compassion on Job, and [bought him from his master]; his master being very willing to part with him, as finding him no ways fit for his business.

In spring 1733 Job's benefactors took him to England, teaching him passable English during the voyage, and introduced him to the English gentry. Job attracted such attention that local men took up a collection to buy his freedom and pay his debts, and they also introduced him at the royal court. In 1735 Job returned to Gambia in a Royal African Company ship, richly clothed and accompanied by many gifts.

▲ **Ayuba Suleiman Diallo (1701–?)** Portrait of Ayuba Suleiman Diallo, 1733 (oil on canvas), Hoare, William, of Bath (1707-92)/Private Collection/Photo Christie's Images/The Bridgeman Art Library

AP® History Reasoning Skills

Contextualization *Which aspects of Ayuba Suleiman's experiences of enslavement were normal and which unusual?*

Comparison *How different might Ayuba's experiences of slavery have been had he been sold in Jamaica rather than in Maryland?*

Sources: Hodgkin Thomas, ed., *Nigerian Perspectives: An Historical Anthology*, 2nd ed. (London, UK: Oxford University Press, 1975), 154–156; Thomas Bluett, *Some Memoirs of the Life of Job, the Son of Solomon the High Priest of Boonda in Africa* (London, UK: Richard Ford, 1734), 16–24.

19-5 **Conclusion**

European merchants and investors played a central role in the creation of the Atlantic system. European merchants had expanded trade in the century before Columbus, trading over longer distances and using new credit mechanisms to facilitate transactions. They had engaged the markets of Asia through Muslim middlemen and initiated the first tentative contacts with African markets. By the seventeenth century a more confident and adventurous European investor class was ready to promote colonial production and long-distance trade in a much more aggressive way. The development of banks, stock exchanges, maritime insurance, and chartered companies supported these new ambitions.

The new Atlantic trading system had great importance in world history. In the first phase of their expansion Europeans demonstrated their recently acquired military superiority by conquering and colonizing the Americas and capturing major Indian Ocean trade routes. But the development of the Atlantic system also revealed the ability of Europeans to move beyond capturing the commercial benefits of existing systems in order to create major new trading networks. Beginning in the seventeenth century, the English, Dutch, and French created new colonies in the Caribbean to compete with earlier colonies created by the Spanish and Portuguese (see Chapter 18). While these colonies remained fragile for decades, settlers found ways to profitably produce goods sought by European consumers. Tobacco was the first, but sugar soon supplanted it.

The establishment of plantation societies was not just a matter of replacing native vegetation with alien plants and native peoples with Europeans and Africans. More fundamentally, it made these once-isolated islands part of a dynamic trading system controlled from Europe. The West Indies was not the only place affected. Brazil, large parts of Spanish Central and South America, and the southern region of British North America developed similar linkages, producing sugar, cacao, cotton, coffee, and indigo and depending on slave slave labor.

Despite the central importance of their shared dependence on export markets and African slaves, there were important differences among Europe's American tropical colonies. Only the English experimented with indentured labor on a large scale. But like the colonies of the Portuguese, Dutch, and French, they soon depended on African slave labor. Joint-stock companies and individual investors were crucial to the English colonies. The French entered the process late, but the French state and French monopoly companies quickly developed a massive flow of slaves while securing a profitable home market for the sugar of Saint Domingue and other colonies. After the Dutch attacked but failed to hold Portugal's sugar-producing colony of Brazil and the slave-exporting colony of Angola, they became influential in the transfer of sugar technology and the expansion of the slave trade. While Spain had introduced sugar to the Caribbean and imported African slaves in the early sixteenth century, its most important Caribbean colony, Cuba, only joined the sugar revolution late, becoming the major destination for the slave trade and the major producer of sugar by 1820.

While Africa played an essential role in the Atlantic system, importing trade goods and exporting slaves to the Americas, the Atlantic system dominated Europe's American colonies much more comprehensively. Even at the height of the slave trade in the eighteenth century Africans remained in control of their continent and interacted culturally and politically more with the Islamic world than with the Atlantic.

Sub-Saharan Africa had long-established trade connections with the Islamic world that included the sale of slaves. These trade relationships facilitated the spread of Islam to sub-Saharan Africa and the creation of African Islamic states like Mali and Songhai (see Chapter 15). The volume of the Atlantic trade was much larger than the Islamic slave trade, but the Islamic trade persisted long after European reformers end-ed the Atlantic trade (see Chapter 25). Between 1550 and 1800 four slaves crossed the Atlantic to European colonies for every slave carried across the Sahara. While more males were carried across the Atlantic, the Islamic trade took more women and children, and few slaves in the Islamic region were subjected to the brutal labor conditions of the West Indian plantations.

Key Terms

Atlantic system p. 479	driver p. 486	mercantilism p. 491	Songhai p. 499
chartered companies p. 480	seasoning p. 487	Royal African Company	Hausa p. 499
Dutch West India Company	manumission p. 489	p. 491	Bornu p. 500
p. 480	maroon p. 490	Atlantic Circuit p. 491	
plantocracy p. 485	capitalism p. 490	Middle Passage p. 491	

Review Questions

1. Why did sugar plantations become so dependent on slave labor?

2. How important was the slave trade to the development of the Atlantic commercial system?

3. What were key differences between slavery in the Americas and slavery in Islamic regions?

 MindTap® is a fully online, personalized learning experience built upon Cengage Learning content. MindTap® combines student learning tools—readings, multimedia, activities, and assessments—into a singular Learning Path that guides students through the course and helps students develop the critical thinking, analysis, and communication skills that are essential to academic and professional success.

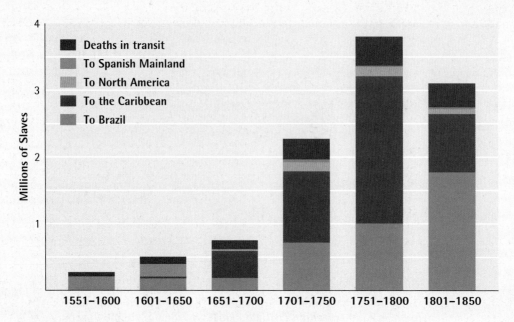

▲ **Transatlantic Slave Trade from Africa, 1551–1850** Source: Data from David Eltis, "The Volume and Structure of the Transatlantic Slave Trade: A Reassessment," William and Mary Quarterly, 3rd Series, 58 (2001), tables II and III.

Multiple-Choice Questions

Questions 1–3 refer to the graph above.

1. The graph supports which of the following assertions?

   (A) The number of slaves transported to the Caribbean remained constant for three centuries.

   (B) A greater number of slaves died in transit to Brazil than to North America.

   (C) Most slaves shipped to North America were men.

   (D) The use of slaves in Brazil increased over time.

2. Which of the following is an explanation for the trend in the graph?

   (A) Greater use of Amerindians in mining operations led to a decreasing need for African slaves.

   (B) Disease killed large numbers of Amerindians, leading to increased demand for African slaves.

   (C) Expansion of plantations in the Caribbean led to increased birth rates and slaves being transported back to Africa.

   (D) Increased urbanization led to a need for more household servants and domestic helpers.

3. Enlightenment ideas in the mid to late 1700s influenced reform movements that challenged existing notions of social relations and could be used to explain what trend in the graph?

   (A) Decrease in slave transport in the early 1800s when slavery was outlawed by some countries

   (B) Lack of transport of slaves to Spanish Mainland from 1650 to the 1700s because Spain was the heart of the Enlightenment

   (C) Decrease in deaths in transit in the early 1800s because Enlightenment thought gave slaves hope and prevented mutiny

   (D) Increase in slave transport to Brazil in the early 1800s because slaves flocked to Brazil to seek religious refuge from Enlightenment thought

Questions 4–6 refer to the passage below.

"Sometimes there is war between the Muslim sultans of some of these lands and one attacks the other, taking as many prisoners as he can and selling the captive though he is a free-born Muslim. . . . This is a common practice among them in Hausaland; Katsina raids Kano, as do others, though their language is one and their situations parallel; the only difference they recognize among themselves is that so-and-so is a born Muslim and so-and-so is a born unbeliever. . . . Whoever is taken prisoner in a state of unbelief may become someone's property, whoever he is, as opposed to those who have become Muslims of their own free will . . . and may not be possessed at all."

Ahmad Baba (1556–1627), Islamic scholar,
Timbuktu, West Africa

4. The passage above supports which of the following statements?

(A) Slavery was a European invention.

(B) Slavery and the slave trade were limited to the African interior.

(C) Slavery was practiced on both sides of the Atlantic.

(D) Slavery occurred only in predominantly Christian regions.

5. The passage above supports which of the following inferences?

(A) Religion both promoted and limited slavery.

(B) Religion rarely influenced the practice of slavery.

(C) Most people became slaves because of their race.

(D) Muslims did not enslave other Muslims.

6. How did slavery in Africa differ from slavery in the Americas during this time period?

(A) Both systems were similar in scale and motivation.

(B) Slavery in the Americas occurred with greater intensity.

(C) African slavery was on a larger scale and scope than slavery in the Americas.

(D) American slave owners refused to take Muslims as slaves.

Questions 7–10 refer to the passage below.

"The specialization by skill and jobs, and the division of labor by age, gender, and condition into crews, shifts and 'gangs,' together with the stress upon punctuality and discipline, are features associated more with industry than agriculture—at least in the sixteenth century."

Sidney W. Mintz, anthropologist, *Sweetness and Power: The Place of Sugar in Modern History*, 1986

7. The passage above supports which of the following facts about slavery?

(A) Planters often rewarded elderly slaves with better-quality food and clothing.

(B) The profitability of plantations depended on extracting as much work as possible through the use of force.

(C) The majority of slaves worked at specialized jobs in the household or in skilled labor shops.

(D) Plantations were structured along an assembly line system, with each slave responsible for only one piece of finished work.

8. According to the passage above, how did sugar plantations differ from labor systems of the previous time period?

(A) Plantations relied on free laborers rather than slaves.

(B) Plantations tended to hire workers with family connections.

(C) Plantations were significantly more regimented than previous systems.

(D) Plantations took greater advantage of female workers than previous systems.

9. Which of the following conclusions is true of the implementation of sugar plantations?

(A) Sugar plantations continued and expanded the use of coercive labor systems in this time period.

(B) Sugar plantations' widespread use resulted in economies that quickly moved toward industrialization.

(C) Sugar plantations supplemented domestic agriculture by producing staple crops.

(D) Sugar plantations struggled to remain profitable during the time period.

10. Slave families often sought to obtain manumission for which individuals first?

(A) Young children so that they would not have to suffer the cruelties of slavery

(B) Women of childbearing age because a child's legal condition followed the mother

(C) Strong young men who could obtain work for wages quickly and free the rest of the family

(D) The elderly who had already worked their whole lives and deserved peace in old age

Short-Answer Questions

1. Answer all parts of the question that follows.

(A) Identify ONE leg of the Atlantic Circuit.

(B) Explain ONE aspect of the relationship between slavery and capitalism.

(C) Explain ONE effect on the world economy of capitalism as practiced in the Atlantic system.

2. Answer all parts of the question that follows.

(A) Identify ONE cause for the expansion of slavery.

(B) Explain ONE effect the expansion of slavery had on the Americas.

(C) Explain ONE effect the expansion of slavery had on Africa.

20 Between Europe and China, 1500–1750

AP® Framework Terms

Mughal Empire
Ottoman Empire
Russian Empire

Overarching Questions

1 How have religions, belief systems, philosophies, and ideologies affected the political, economic, and social development of societies? (CUL)

2 How and why have economic, social, cultural, and geographic factors influenced the process of state building, expansion, and dissolution? (SB)

3 How have internal and external political factors influenced the process of state building, expansion, and dissolution? (SB)

4 How have economic systems and the development of ideologies, values, and institutions influenced each other? (ECON)

5 How have political, economic, cultural, and demographic factors affected social structures? (SOC)

I n 1667, Stenka Razin, the leader of a robber band camped on a tributary of the Don River in southern Russia, pillaged a rich convoy of government and merchant barges on the Volga River and sailed southward toward the trading city of Astrakhan. The city's governor was unable to stop their progress, and they established a new camp by the Caspian Sea at the mouth of the Ural River. From there Razin raided across the sea and down into Iran, defeating both Iranian and Russian armies. In 1670, his forces swollen to 20,000, Razin moved up the Volga, threatening to take Moscow and overthrow the tsar. There a tsarist army finally stopped him, and he was executed the following year.

Razin's followers were Cossacks, people of various ethnic origins who made their way to southern Russia, many of them escaping serfdom in the north, to live as social equals in societies with minimal government and the power to maintain their independence. Modern Russian culture has glorified Razin in music and poetry as a defender of the poor and foe of noble privilege. A famous folksong portrays him sacrificing his bride for the sake of leading his warriors:

So that peace may reign forever
In this band so free and brave
Volga, Volga, Mother Volga
Make this lovely girl a grave.

▲ **Funeral Procession of Suleiman the Magnificent**   Each Ottoman sultan wore a distinctive turban, hence the visible turban representing the body in the hearse.

A less lurid historical understanding of his revolt focuses on the unsettled state of the lands north of the Caspian Sea that had once been the center of the Mongol Golden Horde (see Chapter 13). Muslim Tartars, Buddhist Kalmyks from western Mongolia, and Orthodox Christian Ukrainians and Russians mingled in the sparsely populated frontier between the tsars, the Ottoman sultans, and the Iranian shahs.

But this zone was also becoming a trading nexus. The old Silk Road traversing Central Asia from east to west had faded, but a new axis was in the process of opening, one that linked the Ottoman, Safavid, and Mughal Empires to the south with a growing Russian Empire to the north. Few Russian merchants traveled beyond the tsarist frontiers, but Indian and Armenian traders abounded. Twenty-seven Indians resided on the outskirts of Moscow in 1684, along with various Armenian, Iranian, and Bukharan merchants. Ten times that number lived in Astrakhan, which Ivan IV, "The Terrible," had added to his domains in 1556 and defended against Ottoman attack in 1569.

Russia imported cotton and silk textiles from Iran and India and exported furs, leather goods, walrus tusks, and some woolens. In their business organization, the Indian family firms closely resembled the Italian merchant enterprises of the Renaissance era.

Thus a pattern was set that would last into the twentieth century: while western Europe maintained rigid religious boundaries with very few Muslims living under Christian monarchs, Russia more closely resembled the Muslim empires to its south in tolerating the ethnic and religious diversity that had been a hallmark of Mongol rule. This pattern of various religious groups living together extended into the maritime states of the period as well. ●

20-1 The Ottoman Empire, to 1750

How did the Ottoman Empire rise to power, and what factors contributed to its transformation?

The most durable of the post-Mongol Muslim realms was the **Ottoman Empire**, founded around 1300 (see Map 20.1). By extending Islamic conquests into eastern Europe starting in the late fourteenth century, and by taking Syria and Egypt from the Mamluk rulers in the early sixteenth, the Ottomans seemed to re-create the might of the medieval Islamic caliphate. However, the empire more closely resembled the new centralized monarchies of Europe (see Chapter 17) than any medieval model.

Enduring until 1922, the Ottoman Empire survived several periods of wrenching change, some caused by economic and political problems and others by military innovations. These periods of change reveal the problems faced by the land-based empires situated between Europe and China.

20-1a Expansion and Frontiers

The Ottoman Empire grew from a tiny state in northwestern Anatolia because of three factors: (1) the shrewdness of its founder, Osman (from which the name *Ottoman* comes), and his descendants; (2) control of a strategic link between Europe and Asia on the Dardanelles strait; and (3) the creation of an army that took advantage of the traditional skills of the Turkish cavalryman and the new military possibilities presented by gunpowder.

Ottoman armies attacked Christian enemies in Greece and the Balkans before conquering neighboring Muslim principalities. In 1389 a strong Serbian kingdom was defeated at the Battle of Kosovo (**KO-so-vo**), and by 1402 the sultans ruled much of southeastern Europe and Anatolia. In 1453, Sultan Mehmed II, "the Conqueror," laid siege to Constantinople. His forces used enormous cannon to crush the city's walls, dragged warships over a high hill from the Bosporus strait to the city's inner harbor to get around its sea defenses, and finally overcame the city's land walls with direct infantry assaults. The fall of Constantinople—henceforward commonly known as Istanbul—brought to an end over 1,100 years of Byzantine rule and made the Ottomans seem invincible.

Selim (**seh-LEEM**) I, "the Grim," conquered Egypt and Syria in 1516 and 1517, making the Red Sea the Ottomans' southern frontier. His son, **Suleiman (SOO-lay-man) the Magnificent** (r. 1520–1566), presided over the greatest Ottoman assault on Christian Europe. Seemingly unstoppable, he conquered Belgrade in 1521, expelled the Knights of the Hospital of St. John from the island of Rhodes the following year, and laid siege to Vienna in 1529. Vienna was saved by the need to retreat before the onset of winter more than by military action. Later Ottoman historians looked back on the reign of Suleiman as the period when the imperial system worked to perfection, and they spoke of it as the golden age of Ottoman greatness.

While Ottoman armies pressed deeper and deeper into eastern Europe, the sultans also sought to control the Mediterranean. Between 1453 and 1502, the Ottomans fought the opening rounds of a two-century war with Venice, the most powerful of Italy's commercial city-states. The initial fighting left Venice in control of its lucrative islands like Crete and Cyprus for another century. But it also left Venice a reduced military power compelled to pay tribute to the Ottomans.

In the early sixteenth century, merchants from southern India and Sumatra sent emissaries to Istanbul requesting naval support against the Portuguese. The Ottomans responded vigorously to Portuguese threats close to their territories, such as at Aden at the southern entrance to the Red Sea, and seemed to have a coherent policy for defending Muslim lands bordering the Indian Ocean. By century's end, however, they had pulled back from major maritime commitments outside the Mediterranean Sea. Since eastern luxury products still flowed to Ottoman markets and Portuguese power was territorially limited to fortified coastal points—such as Hormuz at the entrance to the Persian Gulf, Goa in western India, and Malacca in Malaya—it seemed wiser to concentrate the state's resources on defending territory in Europe.

20-1b Central Institutions

By the 1520s, the Ottoman Empire was the most powerful and best-organized state in either Europe or the Islamic world. Its military was balanced between cavalry archers, primarily Turks, and military slaves known as **Janissaries (JAN-nih-say-rees)**.

AP® Exam Tip Compare how the Ottomans expanded their land empire with other empire-building states during this time, such as the Mughal, Russian, and Manchu Empires.

Ottoman Empire Islamic state founded by Osman in northwestern Anatolia around 1300. After the fall of the Byzantine Empire, the Ottoman Empire was based at Istanbul (formerly Constantinople) from 1453 to 1922. It encompassed lands in the Middle East, North Africa, the Caucasus, and eastern Europe.

Suleiman the Magnificent The most illustrious sultan of the Ottoman Empire (r. 1520–1566); also known as Suleiman Kanuni, "The Lawgiver." He significantly expanded the empire in the Balkans and eastern Mediterranean.

Janissaries Infantry, originally of slave origin, armed with firearms and constituting the elite of the Ottoman army from the fifteenth century until the corps was abolished in 1826.

CHRONOLOGY

	Ottoman Empire	Safavid Empire	Mughal Empire	Russia
1500	1516–1517 Selim I conquers Egypt and Syria 1520–1566 Reign of Suleiman the Magnificent; peak of Ottoman Empire 1529 First Ottoman siege of Vienna 1571 Ottoman naval defeat at Lepanto	1502–1524 Shah Ismail establishes Safavid rule in Iran 1587–1629 Reign of Shah Abbas the Great; peak of Safavid Empire	1526 Babur defeats last sultan of Delhi 1556–1605 Akbar rules in Agra; peak of Mughal Empire	1547 Ivan IV adopts title of tsar 1582 Russians conquer Khanate of Sibir
1600	1610 End of Anatolian revolts		1658–1707 Aurangzeb imposes conservative Islamic regime	1613–1645 Rule of Mikhail, the first Romanov tsar 1649 Subordination of serfs complete 1689–1725 Rule of Peter the Great
1700	1730 Janissary revolt begins period of Ottoman conservatism	1722 Afghan invaders topple last Safavid shah 1736–1747 Nadir Shah temporarily reunites Iran, invades India (1739)	1739 Iranians under Nadir Shah sack Delhi	1712 St. Petersburg becomes Russia's capital

▼ **Aya Sofya Mosque in Istanbul**   Originally a Byzantine cathedral, Aya Sofya (in Greek, Hagia Sophia) was transformed into a mosque after 1453, and four minarets were added. It then became a model for subsequent Ottoman mosques. Behind it to the right, the Bosporus strait divides Europe and Asia. To the left, the Golden Horn inlet separates the old city of Istanbul from the newer parts.. The gate to the Ottoman sultan's palace is to the right of the mosque. The pointed tower to the left of the dome is part of the palace. iStock.com/mozcann

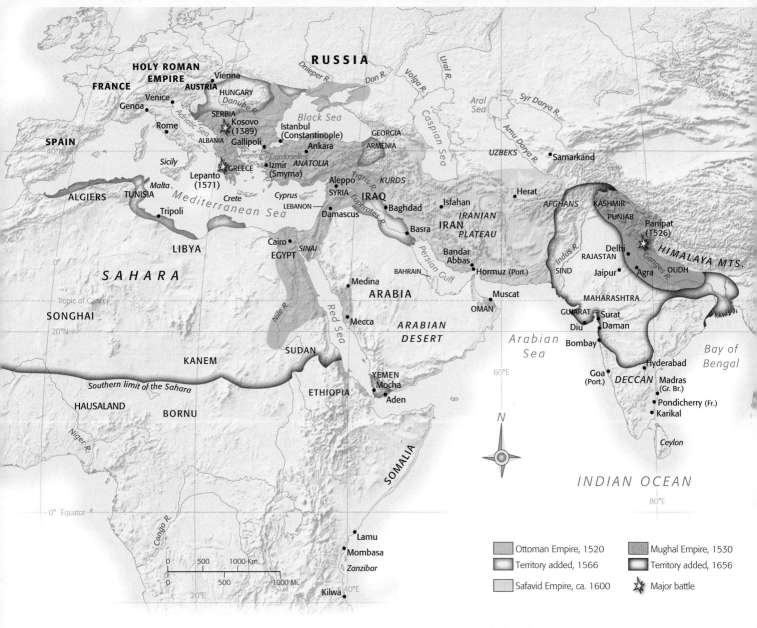

MAP 20.1   Muslim Empires in the Sixteenth and Seventeenth Centuries Iran, a Shi'ite state flanked by Sunni Ottomans on the west and Sunni Mughals on the east, had the least exposure to European influences. Ottoman expansion across the southern Mediterranean Sea intensified European fears of Islam. The areas of strongest Mughal control dictated that Islam's spread into Southeast Asia would be heavily influenced by merchants and religious figures from Gujarat instead of from eastern India.

How did the geographical divide between Sunnis and Shi'ites affect the relations between empires?

Slave soldiery had a long history in Islamic lands, but the conquest of Christian territories in the Balkans in the late fourteenth century gave the Ottomans access to a new military resource. Originating as Christian prisoners of war converted to Islam, these "new troops," called *yeni cheri* in Turkish and *Janissaries* in English, gave the Ottomans unusual military flexibility. Since horseback riding and bowmanship were not part of their cultural backgrounds, they readily accepted the idea of fighting on foot and learning to use guns, which at that time were still too heavy and awkward for a horseman to load and fire. The Janissaries lived in barracks and trained all year round.

The recruitment of Janissaries from prisoners changed early in the fifteenth century. A new system, called the *devshirme*, imposed a levy of male children on Christian villages in the Balkans and occasionally elsewhere. Selected children were placed with Turkish families for language learning and then sent to Istanbul for an education that included instruction in Islam, military training, and, for the top 10 percent, skills that could be used in government administration. Senior military commanders and heads of government departments up to the rank of grand vizier were commonly drawn from among the chosen few who received special training.

The cavalrymen were supported by land grants and administered most rural areas in Anatolia and the Balkans. They maintained order, collected taxes, and reported for each summer's campaign with their horses, retainers, and supplies, all paid for from the taxes they collected. When not campaigning, they stayed at home.

The Ottoman galley-equipped navy was manned by Greek, Turkish, Algerian, and Tunisian sailors, usually under the command of an admiral from one of the North African ports. The balance of the Ottoman land forces brought success to Ottoman arms in recurrent wars with the Safavids of Iran, who were slower to adopt firearms, and in the inexorable conquest of the Balkans. Expansion by sea was less dramatic. A major expedition against Malta in the western Mediterranean failed in 1565. Combined Christian forces also achieved a massive naval victory at the Battle of Lepanto, off Greece, in 1571. But the Ottomans' resources were so extensive that in a year's time they had replaced all of the galleys sunk in that battle.

The Ottoman Empire became cosmopolitan in character. The sophisticated court language, Osmanli **(os-MAHN-lih)** (the Turkish form of *Ottoman*), shared basic grammar and vocabulary with Turkish, but Arabic and Persian elements made it distinct from the Turkish spoken by Anatolia's nomads and villagers. Everyone who served in the military or the bureaucracy and conversed in Osmanli was considered to belong to the *askeri* **(AS-keh-ree)**, or "military," class. Members of this class were exempt from taxes and owed their positions to the sultan.

The Ottomans saw the sultan as providing justice for his "flock of sheep" (*raya* **[RAH-yah]**) and military forces to protect that flock. In return, the raya paid the taxes that supported both the sultan and the military. In reality, the sultan's government remained comparatively isolated from the lives of most subjects. As Islam gradually became the majority religion in some Balkan regions, Islamic law (the Shari'a **[sha-REE-ah]**) conditioned urban institutions and social life (see Diversity & Dominance: Islamic Law and Ottoman Rule). Local customs prevailed among non-Muslims and in many rural areas, and non-Muslims looked to their own religious leaders for guidance in family and spiritual matters.

AP® Exam Tip
Understand the social and political institutions of the Ottoman Empire.

20-1c Crisis of the Military State, 1585–1650

As military technology evolved, cannon and lighter-weight firearms played an ever-larger role on the battlefield. Accordingly, the size of the Janissary corps—and its cost to the government—grew steadily, and the role of the Turkish cavalry diminished. To pay the Janissaries, the sultan started reducing the number of landholding cavalrymen. Revenues previously spent on their living expenses and military equipment went directly into the imperial treasury. Inflation caused by a flood of cheap silver from the New World bankrupted many of the remaining landholders, who were restricted by law to collecting a fixed amount of taxes. Their land was returned to the state. Displaced cavalrymen, armed and unhappy, became a restive element in rural Anatolia.

This complicated situation, exacerbated after 1600 by the climatic deterioration known as the Little Ice Age (see Issues in History: The Little Ice Age), resulted in revolts that devastated Anatolia between 1590 and 1610. Former landholding cavalrymen, short-term soldiers released at the end of the campaign season, peasants overburdened by emergency taxes, and even impoverished students of religion formed bands of marauders. Anatolia experienced the worst of the rebellions and suffered greatly from emigration and the loss of agricultural production. But an increase in banditry, made worse by the government's inability to stem the spread of muskets among the general public, beset other parts of the empire as well.

In the meantime, the Janissaries took advantage of their growing influence to gain relief from prohibitions on their marrying and engaging in business. Janissaries who involved themselves in commerce lessened the burden on the state budget, and married Janissaries who enrolled sons or relatives in the corps made it possible in the seventeenth century for the government to save state funds by abolishing forced recruitment. These savings, however, were more than offset by the increase in the total number of Janissaries and in their steady deterioration as a military force, which necessitated the hiring of more and more supplemental troops.

20-1d Economic Change and Growing Weakness

A very different Ottoman Empire emerged from this crisis. Sultans once had led armies. Now they mostly resided in palaces and had little experience of the real world. The affairs of government were overseen more and more by the chief administrators—the grand viziers.

AP® Exam Tip
Understand the importance of internal challenges to state control, such as uprisings.

Ebu's-Su'ud was the Mufti of Istanbul from 1545 to 1574, serving under the sultans Suleiman the Magnificent (1520–1566) and his son Selim II (1566–1574). Originally one of many city-based religious scholars giving opinions on matters of law, the mufti of Istanbul by Ebu's-Su'ud's time had become the top religious official in the empire and the personal adviser to the sultan on religious and legal matters. The position would later acquire the title Shaikh al-Islam.

Historians debate the degree of independence these muftis had. Since the ruler, as a Muslim, was subject to the Shari'a, the mufti could theoretically veto his policies. On important matters, however, the mufti more often seemed to come up with the answer that best suited the sultan who appointed him. This bias is not apparent in more mundane areas of the law.

The collection of Ebu's-Su'ud's fatwas, or legal opinions, from which the examples below are drawn shows the range of matters that came to his attention. They are also an excellent source for understanding the problems of his time, the relationship between Islamic law and imperial governance, and the means by which the state asserted its dominance over the common people. Some opinions respond directly to questions posed by the sultan. Others are hypothetical, using the names Zeyd, 'Amr, and Hind the way police today use John Doe and Jane Doe. While qadis, or Islamic judges, made findings of fact in specific cases on trial, muftis issued only opinions on matters of law. A qadi as well as a plaintiff or defendant might ask a question of a mufti. Later jurists consulted collections of fatwas for precedents, but the fatwas had no permanent binding power.

On the plan of Selim II to attack the Venetians in Crete in 1570

A land was previously in the realm of Islam. After a while, the abject infidels overran it, destroyed the colleges and mosques, and left them vacant. They filled the pulpits and the galleries with the tokens of infidelity and error, intending to insult the religion of Islam with all kinds of vile deeds, and by spreading their ugly acts to all corners of the earth.

His Excellency the Sultan, the Refuge of Religion, has, as zeal for Islam requires, determined to take the aforementioned land from the possession of the shameful infidels and to annex it to the realm of Islam.

When peace was previously concluded with the other lands in the possession of the said infidels, the aforenamed land was included. An explanation is sought as to whether, in accordance with the pure shari'a, this is an impediment to the Sultan's determining to break the treaty.

Answer: There is no possibility that it could ever be an impediment. For the Sultan of the People of Islam (may God glorify his victories) to make peace with the infidels is legal only when there is a benefit to all Muslims. When there is no benefit, peace is never legal. When a benefit has been seen, and it is then observed to be more beneficial to break it, then to break it becomes absolutely obligatory and binding.

His Excellency [Muhammad] the Apostle of God (may God bless him and give him peace) made a ten-year truce with the Meccan infidels in the sixth year of the Hegira. His Excellency 'Ali (may God ennoble his face) wrote a document that was corroborated and confirmed. Then, in the following year, it was considered more beneficial to break it and, in the eighth year of the Hegira, [the Prophet] attacked [the Meccans], and conquered Mecca the Mighty.

On war against the Shi'ite Muslim Safavids of Iran

Is it licit according to the shari'a to fight the followers of the Safavids? Is the person who kills them a holy warrior, and the person who dies at their hands a martyr?

Answer: Yes, it is a great holy war and a glorious martyrdom.

Assuming that it is licit to fight them, is this simply because of their rebellion and enmity against the [Ottoman] Sultan of the People of Islam, because they drew the sword against the troops of Islam, or what?

Answer: They are both rebels and, from many points of view, infidels.

Can the children of Safavid subjects captured in the Nakhichevan campaign be enslaved?

Answer: No.

The followers of the Safavids are killed by order of the Sultan. If it turns out that some of the prisoners, young and old, are [Christian] Armenian[s], are they set free?

Answer: Yes. So long as the Armenians have not joined the Safavid troops in attacking and fighting against the troops of Islam, it is illegal to take them prisoner.

On the Holy Land

Are all the Arab realms Holy Land, or does it have specific boundaries, and what is the difference between the Holy Land and other lands?

Answer: Syria is certainly called the Holy Land. Jerusalem, Aleppo and its surroundings, and Damascus belong to it.

On land-grants

What lands are private property, and what lands are held by feudal tenure [i.e., assignment in exchange for military service]?

Answer: Plots of land within towns are private property. Their owners may sell them, donate them or convert them to trust. When [the owner] dies, [the land] passes to all the heirs. Lands held by feudal tenure are cultivated lands around villages, whose occupants bear the burden of their services and pay a portion of their [produce in tax]. They cannot sell the land, donate it or convert it to trust. When they die, if they have sons, these have the use [of the land]. Otherwise, the cavalryman gives [it to someone else] by *tapu* [title deed].

On the consumption of coffee

Zeyd drinks coffee to aid concentration or digestion. Is this licit?

Answer: How can anyone consume this reprehensible [substance], which dissolute men drink when engaged in games and debauchery?

The Sultan, the Refuge of Religion, has on many occasions banned coffee-houses. However, a group of ruffians take no notice, but keep coffee-houses for a living. In order to draw the crowds, they take on unbearded apprentices, and have ready instruments of entertainment and play, such as chess and backgammon. The city's rakes, rogues and vagabond boys gather there to consume opium and hashish. On top of this, they drink coffee and, when they are high, engage in games and false sciences, and neglect the prescribed prayers. In law, what should happen to a judge who is able to prevent the said coffee-sellers and drinkers, but does not do so?

Answer: Those who perpetrate these ugly deeds should be prevented and deterred by severe chastisement and long imprisonment. Judges who neglect to deter them should be dismissed.

On matters of theft

How are thieves to be "carefully examined"?

Answer: His Excellency 'Ali (may God ennoble his face) appointed Imam Shuraih as judge. It so happened that, at that time, several people took a Muslim's son to another district. The boy disappeared and, when the people came back, the missing boy's father brought them before Judge Shuraih. [When he brought] a claim [against them on account of the loss of his son], they denied it, saying: "No harm came to him from us." Judge Shuraih thought deeply and was perplexed.

When the man told his tale to His Excellency 'Ali, [the latter] summoned Judge Shuraih and questioned him. When Shuraih said; "Nothing came to light by the shari'a," ['Ali] summoned all the people who had taken the man's son, separated them from one another, and questioned them separately. For each of their stopping places, he asked: "What was the boy wearing in that place? What did you eat? And where did he disappear?" In short, he made each of them give a detailed account, and when their words contradicted each other, each of their statements was written down separately. Then he brought them all together, and when the contradictions became apparent, they were no longer able to deny [their guilt] and confessed to what had happened.

This kind of ingenuity is a requirement of the case. [This fatwa appears to justify investigation of crimes by the state instead of by the qadi. Judging from court records, which contain very few criminal cases, it seems likely that in practice, many criminal cases were dealt with outside the jurisdiction of the qadi's court.]

Zeyd takes 'Amr's donkey without his knowledge and sells it. Is he a thief?

Answer: His hand is not cut off.

Zeyd mounts 'Amr's horse as a courier and loses it. Is compensation necessary?

Answer: Yes.

In which case: What if Zeyd has a Sultanic decree [authorizing him] to take horses for courier service?

Answer: Compensation is required in any case. He was not commanded to lose [the horse]. Even if he were commanded, it is the person who loses it who is liable.

On homicides

Zeyd enters Hind's house and tries to have intercourse forcibly. Since Hind can repel him by no other means, she strikes and wounds him with an axe. If Zeyd dies of the wound, is Hind liable for anything?

Answer: She has performed an act of Holy War [*jihad*].

AP® History Reasoning Skills

Contextualization *What do these fatwas indicate with regard to the balance between practical legal reasoning and religious dictates in the governance of the Ottoman Empire?*

Source: Excerpts from *Ebu's-Su'ud: The Islamic Legal Tradition* by Imber, Colin. Copyright © 1997 Colin Imber, originating publisher Edinburgh University Press. All rights reserved. Used with permission of Stanford University Press, www.sup.org, and Edinburgh University Press, www.euppublishing.com.

▲ **Ottoman Tilework**   Ceramic creations, a centuries-long specialty of Muslim artists, took on new elegance during the Ottoman period. The tomb of Sultan Murad III in the cemetery of Aya Sofya mosque was built in 1599. The tiles were made in Iznik (ancient Nicaea) and feature a tomato red color that is particular to the Ottomans. David Coleman/Alamy Stock Photo

Involvement in business and transmission of corps membership by heredity did not prevent the Janissaries from becoming a powerful faction in urban politics. Tax farming created other new pressures. Tax farmers paid specific taxes, such as customs duties, in advance in return for the privilege of collecting a greater amount from the actual taxpayers.

Rural administration, already disrupted by the rebellions, suffered from the transition to tax farms. The former military landholders had kept order on their lands in order to maintain their incomes. Tax farmers were less likely to live on the land. The imperial government therefore faced greater administrative burdens and came to rely heavily on powerful provincial governors or on wealthy men who purchased lifelong tax collection rights and behaved more or less like private landowners.

Military power slowly ebbed. The ill-trained Janissaries sometimes resorted to hiring substitutes to go on campaign, and the sultans relied on partially trained seasonal recruits and on armies raised by the governors of frontier provinces. A second mighty siege of Vienna failed in 1683, and by the middle of the eighteenth century it was obvious to the Austrians and Russians that the Ottoman Empire was weakening. On the eastern front, however, Ottoman exhaustion after many wars was matched by the demise in 1722 of their perennial adversary, the Safavid state of Iran.

The Ottoman Empire lacked both the wealth and the inclination to match western European economic advances, but it remained much more prosperous than the Russian Empire. While overland trade from the East dwindled as political disorder in Safavid Iran cut deeply into Iranian silk production, new products also came into vogue. Farmers in Greece, Macedonia, Bulgaria, and Anatolia grew mild-flavored, low-nicotine tobacco; and coffee, a Yemeni product, rose from obscurity in the fifteenth century to become the rage first in the Ottoman Empire and then in Europe. By 1770, Muslim merchants trading in the Yemeni port of Mocha (**MOH-kuh**) (literally "the coffee place") were charged 15 percent in duties and fees, while European traders, benefiting from long-standing trade agreements with the Ottoman Empire, paid little more than 3 percent.

Such trade agreements, called *capitulations*, from Latin *capitula*, or "chapter," were first granted as favors by powerful sultans, but they eventually led to European domination of Ottoman seaborne trade. Nevertheless, the Europeans did not control strategic ports in the Mediterranean comparable to Malacca in the Indian Ocean and Hormuz on the Persian Gulf, so their economic power stopped short of colonial settlement or direct control in Ottoman territories.

AP® Exam Tip
Understand how state rivalries challenged state consolidation and expansion.

A few astute Ottoman statesmen observed the growing disarray of the empire and advised the sultans to re-establish the land-grant and devshirme systems of Suleiman's reign. Most people, however, could not perceive the downward course of imperial power, much less the reasons behind it. Far from seeing Europe as the enemy that would eventually dismantle the empire, the Istanbul elite experimented with European clothing and furniture styles and purchased printed books from the empire's first (and short-lived) press. Ottoman historians named the period between 1718 and 1730 when European fashions were in favor the "**Tulip Period**" because of the craze for high-priced tulip bulbs that swept Ottoman ruling circles. The craze echoed a Dutch tulip mania that had begun in the mid-sixteenth century, when the flower was introduced into Holland from Istanbul. The mania peaked in 1636 with particularly rare bulbs going for 2,500 florins apiece—the value of twenty-two oxen.

In 1730, however, gala soirees at which guests watched turtles with candles on their backs wander in the dark through massive tulip beds gave way to a conservative Janissary revolt with strong religious overtones. Sultan Ahmed III abdicated, and the leader of the revolt, Patrona Halil (**pa-TROH-nuh ha-LEEL**), an Albanian former seaman and stoker of the public baths, swaggered around the capital for several months dictating government policies before he was seized and executed.

The Patrona Halil rebellion confirmed the perceptions of a few that the Ottoman Empire was facing severe difficulties. Yet decay at the center spelled benefit elsewhere. In the provinces, ambitious and competent governors, wealthy landholders, urban notables, and nomad chieftains took advantage of the central government's weakness. By the middle of the eighteenth century groups of mamluks had regained a dominant position in Egypt. Though Selim I had defeated the mamluk sultanate in the early sixteenth century, the practice of buying slaves in the Caucasus and training them as soldiers reappeared by the end of the century in several Arab cities. In Baghdad, Janissary commanders and Georgian mamluks competed for power, with the latter emerging triumphant by the mid-eighteenth century.

In Aleppo and Damascus, however, the Janissaries came out on top. Meanwhile, in central Arabia, a puritanical Sunni movement inspired by Muhammad ibn Abd al-Wahhab began a remarkable rise beyond the reach of Ottoman power. Although no region declared full independence, the sultan's power was slipping away, to the advantage of a broad array of lower officials and upstart chieftains in all parts of the empire while the Ottoman economy was reorienting itself toward Europe.

Section Review

- The Ottoman Empire grew through the skill of its founding rulers, control of strategic territory, and military power.

- The empire expanded into southern and eastern Europe, the Middle East, and Africa, reaching its height under Suleiman the Magnificent.

- An initial maritime strategy of confronting the Portuguese in the Indian Ocean faded as the Mediterranean took priority.

- The empire rested on the military led by the sultan, and changes in military structure ultimately weakened the state.

- As the imperial economy reoriented toward Europe, the central government weakened, permitting the rise of local powers.

20-2 The Safavid Empire, 1502–1722

How did the Safavid Empire both resemble and differ from its neighbors?

The **Safavid Empire** of Iran (see Map 20.1) resembled its long-time Ottoman foe in many ways: it initially relied militarily on cavalry paid through land grants, and its population spoke several languages and included many non-Muslims. It also had distinct qualities that to this day set Iran off from its neighbors: it derived part of its legitimacy from the pre-Islamic dynasties of ancient Iran, and it adopted the Shi'ite form of Islam.

20-2a Safavid Society and Religion

The ultimate victor in a complicated struggle for power among Turkish chieftains east of the Ottoman lands was Ismail (**IS-ma-eel**), a boy of Kurdish, Iranian, and Greek ancestry. In 1502, at age sixteen, Ismail proclaimed himself Shah of Iran and declared that from that time forward his realm would be devoted to **Shi'ite** Islam, which revered the family of Muhammad's cousin and son-in-law Ali. Although Ismail's reasons for compelling Iran's conversion to Shi'ism are unknown, the effect of this radical act was to create a deep chasm between Iran and its Sunni

Tulip Period (1718–1730) Last years of the reign of Ottoman sultan Ahmed III, during which European styles and attitudes became briefly popular in Istanbul.

Safavid Empire Iranian kingdom (1502–1722) established by Ismail Safavi, who declared Iran a Shi'ite state.

Shi'ite Muslims belonging to the branch of Islam believing that God vests leadership of the community in a descendant of Muhammad's son-in-law Ali. Shi'ism is the state religion of Iran.

Muslim neighbors. For the first time since its incorporation into the Islamic caliphate in the seventh century, Iran became a truly separate country.

The imposition of Shi'ite belief confirmed differences between Iran and its neighbors that had been long in the making. Persian, written in the Arabic script from the tenth century onward, had emerged as the second language of Islam. Iranian scholars and writers normally read Arabic as well as Persian and sprinkled their writings with Arabic phrases, but their Arab counterparts were much less inclined to learn Persian. After the Mongols destroyed Baghdad, the capital of the Islamic caliphate, in 1258, Iran developed largely on its own, having more extensive contacts with India—where Muslim rulers favored the Persian language—than with the Arabs.

In the post-Mongol period, artistic styles in Iran, Afghanistan, and Central Asia also went their own way. Painted and molded tiles and tile mosaics, often in vivid turquoise blue, became the standard exterior decoration of mosques in Iran but never were used in Syria and Egypt. Persian poets raised verse to peaks of perfection that had no counterpart in Arabic poetry, generally considered to be in a state of decline.

To be sure, Islam itself provided a tradition of belief, learning, and law that crossed ethnic and linguistic borders, but Shah Ismail's imposition of Shi'ism set Iran significantly apart. Shi'ite doctrine says that all temporal rulers, regardless of title, are temporary stand-ins for the **Hidden Imam**, the twelfth descendant of Ali, who disappeared as a child in the ninth century. Some Shi'ite scholars taught the faithful to calmly accept the world as it was and wait quietly for the Hidden Imam's return. Others maintained that they themselves should play a stronger role in political affairs because they were best qualified to know the Hidden Imam's wishes. These two positions, which still play a role in Iranian Shi'ism, enhanced the self-image of religious scholars as independent of imperial authority and stood in the way of their becoming subordinate government functionaries, as happened in the Ottoman Empire.

Shi'ism also affected popular psychology. Annual commemoration of the martyrdom of Imam Husayn (d. 680), Ali's son and third Imam, regularized an emotional outpouring with no parallel in Sunni lands. Day after day for two weeks, preachers recited the woeful tale to crowds of weeping believers, and elaborate street processions, often organized by craft guilds, paraded chanting and self-flagellating men past crowds of reverent onlookers. Of course, Shi'ites elsewhere observed rites of mourning for Imam Husayn, but the impact of these rites was especially great in Iran, where 90 percent of the population was Shi'ite. Over time, the subjects of the Safavid shahs came to feel more than ever a people apart.

Hidden Imam Last in a series of twelve descendants of Muhammad's son-in-law Ali, whom Shi'ites consider divinely appointed leaders of the Muslim community. In occlusion since roughly 873, he is expected to return as a messiah at the end of time.

Shah Abbas I The fifth and most renowned ruler of the Safavid dynasty in Iran (r. 1587–1629). Abbas moved the royal capital to Isfahan in 1598.

20-2b A Tale of Two Cities: Isfahan and Istanbul

Outwardly, Ottoman Istanbul looked quite different from Isfahan (**is-fah-HAHN**), which became Iran's capital in 1598 by decree of **Shah Abbas I** (r. 1587–1629). Built on seven hills beside the narrow Golden Horn inlet,

◀ **Mughal Emperor Jahangir Embracing the Safavid Shah Abbas** Painted by Mughal artist Abu al-Hasan around 1620, this miniature shows the artist's patron, Jahangir, on the right standing on a lion, dominating the diminutive Shah Abbas, standing on a sheep. Though this may accurately reflect Jahangir's view of their relationship, in fact Shah Abbas was a powerful rival for control of Afghanistan, the gateway to India and the meeting point of the lion and the sheep. The globe the monarchs stand on reflects the spread of accurate geographical ideas into the Muslim world.
SuperStock/Glow Images, Inc.

Istanbul boasted a skyline punctuated by the gray stone domes and thin, pointed minarets of the great imperial mosques. The mosques surrounding the royal plaza in Isfahan, in contrast, had unobtrusive minarets and brightly tiled domes. High walls surrounded the sultan's palace in Istanbul. Shah Abbas in Isfahan focused his capital on the giant royal plaza, which was large enough for his army to play polo, and he used an airy palace overlooking the plaza to receive dignitaries and review his troops.

Istanbul's harbor teemed with sailing ships and smaller craft, many of them belonging to a colony of European merchants perched on a hilltop on the other side of the Golden Horn. Isfahan, far from the sea, was only occasionally visited by Europeans. Trade was mostly in the hands of Jews, Hindus and Jains from India, and especially a colony of Armenian Christians brought in by Shah Abbas.

Beneath these superficial differences, the two capitals had much in common. Wheeled vehicles were scarce in hilly Istanbul and nonexistent in Isfahan. Both cities were built for walking and lacked the open spaces common in contemporary European cities. Streets were narrow and irregular. Houses crowded against each other in dead-end lanes. Residents enjoyed their privacy in interior courtyards. Artisans and merchants organized themselves into guilds that had strong social and religious bonds. The shops of each guild adjoined one another in the markets.

Women seldom appeared in public, even in Istanbul's mazelike covered market or in Isfahan's long, serpentine bazaar. At home, the women's quarters—called *anderun* (**an-deh-ROON**), or "interior," in Iran and *harem*, or "forbidden area," in Istanbul—were separate from the public rooms where the men of the family received visitors. In both areas, low cushions, charcoal braziers for warmth, carpets, and small tables constituted most of the furnishings.

The private side of family life has left few traces, but women's society—consisting of wives, children, female servants, and sometimes one or more eunuchs—was not entirely cut off from the outside world. Ottoman court records reveal that women, using male agents, were very active in the urban real estate market. Often they were selling inherited shares of their father's estate, but some both bought and sold real estate on a regular basis and even established religious endowments for pious purposes.

The fact that Islamic law, unlike European codes, permitted a wife to retain her property after marriage gave some women a stake in the general economy and a degree of independence from their spouses. Women also appeared in other types of court cases, where they often testified for themselves, for Islamic courts did not recognize the role of attorney. Although comparable Safavid court records do not survive, historians assume that a parallel situation prevailed in Iran.

AP® Exam Tip
Be able to explain how the Safavid used Shi'ism to help legitimize their rule.

AP® Exam Tip
Evaluate the extent to which different ideologies, philosophies, and religions affected social hierarchies and gender roles.

◀ **Royal Square in Isfahan** Built by the order of Shah Abbas over a period of twenty years starting in 1598, the open space is as long as five football fields (555 by 172 yards). The courtyard of the beautifully tiled royal mosque is in the foreground. The dome of a second mosque halfway down the right side faces a palace on the left with a second story porch for reviewing troops or watching them play polo, those being two of the uses to which the square was put in Safavid times. The entrance to the main bazaar is at the center of the far end.
robertharding/Alamy stock photo

▶ **Ottoman Street Scene** This seventeenth century miniature shows shops in a domed bazaar. The arcade to the left of the passage with the benches shows the entrance to a mosque behind the basin the horse if drinking from and a shop-owner weighing something for a customer. The shops on the right are indoor establishments. DEA/A. DAGLI ORTI/Getty Images

European travelers commented on the veiling of women outside the home, but the norm for both sexes was complete coverage of arms, legs, and hair. Miniature paintings indicate that ordinary female garb consisted of a long, ample dress with a scarf or shawl pulled tight over the forehead to conceal the hair. Lightweight baggy trousers were worn under the dress. This mode of dress differed little from that of men. Poor men wore light trousers, a long shirt, a jacket, and a hat or turban. Wealthier men wore over their trousers ankle-length caftans, often closely fitted around the chest.

Public life was a male domain. Poetry and art, both more elegantly developed in Isfahan than in Istanbul, were as likely to extol the charms of beardless boys as pretty women. Despite religious disapproval of homosexuality, attachments to adolescent boys were neither unusual nor hidden. Women who appeared in public—aside from non-Muslims, the aged, and the very poor—were usually slaves. Miniature paintings frequently depict female dancers, musicians, and even acrobats in attitudes and costumes that range from decorous to decidedly erotic.

Despite social similarities, the overall flavors of Isfahan and Istanbul were not the same. Isfahan had its prosperous Armenian quarter across the river from the city's center, but it was not as cosmopolitan as Istanbul. Shah Abbas located his capital toward the center of his domain away from any unstable frontier. Istanbul, in contrast, was a great seaport and a crossroads located on the straits separating the sultan's European and Asian possessions.

People of all sorts lived or spent time in Istanbul: Venetians, Genoese, Arabs, Turks, Greeks, Armenians, Albanians, Serbs, Jews, Bulgarians, and more. In this respect, Istanbul conveyed the cosmopolitan character of major seaports from Venice to Canton (Guangzhou), though its prosperity rested on the vast reach of the sultan's territories rather than on the voyages of Muslim merchants.

20-2c **Economic Crisis and Political Collapse**

The Safavid Empire's foreign trade rested on the silk fabrics of northern Iran. However, the products that eventually became most powerfully associated with Iran were deep-pile carpets made by knotting colored yarns around stretched warp threads (see Environment & Technology: Persian Rugs). Different cities produced distinctive carpet designs. Women and girls did much of the actual knotting work.

Overall, Iran's manufacturing sector was neither large nor notably productive. Most of the shah's subjects, whether Iranians, Turks, Kurds, or Arabs, lived by subsistence farming or herding. Neither area of activity recorded significant technological advances during the Safavid period.

The Safavids, like the Ottomans, had difficulty finding the money to pay troops armed with firearms. By the end of the sixteenth century, it was evident that a more systematic adoption of cannon and firearms in the Safavid Empire would be needed to hold off the Ottomans and the Uzbeks (**UHZ-bek**) (Turkish rulers who had succeeded the Timurids on Iran's Central Asian frontier; see Map 20.1). Like the Ottoman cavalry a century earlier, warriors from nomadic groups were not inclined to trade their bows for firearms. Shah Abbas responded by establishing a slave corps of year-round soldiers and arming them with guns. The Christian converts to Islam who initially provided the manpower for the new corps were mostly captives taken in raids on Georgia in the Caucasus (**CAW-kuh-suhs**).

In the late sixteenth century, the inflation caused by cheap silver spread into Iran; then overland trade through Safavid territory declined because of mismanagement of the silk monopoly after Shah Abbas's death in 1629. As a result, the later shahs could not afford to pay their army and bureaucracy. Trying to unseat the nomads from their lands to regain control of taxes was more difficult and more disruptive militarily than the piecemeal dismantlement of the land-grant system in the Ottoman Empire. The nomads remained cohesive military forces, and pressure from the center simply caused them to withdraw to their mountain pastures. By 1722, the government had become so weak and commanded so little support from the nomadic groups that an army of marauding Afghans was able to capture Isfahan and effectively end Safavid rule.

Section Review

- The rise of the Shi'ite Safavid Empire completed the long-growing split between Iran and its neighbors.

- Despite significant differences, Istanbul and Isfahan showed some cultural similarities between the Ottoman and Safavid Empires.

- Silks and carpets were important manufactures, but most Safavid subjects made a living by farming or herding.

- High military costs, inflation, and decline of overland trade weakened the state, which fell to Afghan invaders in 1722.

AP® Exam Tip
Explain why the Ottoman, Safavid, and Mughal Empires are referred to as "Gunpowder Empires."

20-3 The Mughal Empire, 1526–1739

How did the Mughal Empire combine Muslim and Hindu elements into an effective state?

What distinguished the Indian empire of the Mughal (**MOH-guhl**) sultans from the empires of the Ottomans and Safavids was the fact that India was a land of Hindus ruled by a Muslim minority. Repeated military campaigns from the early eleventh century onward had established Muslim dominion, but five centuries later the Mughals still had to contend with the Hindus' long-standing resentment. Thus, the challenge facing the Mughals was not just conquering and organizing a large territorial state but also finding a formula for Hindu–Muslim coexistence.

AP® Exam Tip
Consider the development of Sikhism as an example of how the spread of existing religions contributed to the creation of syncretic belief systems and practices.

20-3a Political Foundations

Babur (**BAH-bur**) (1483–1530), the founder of the **Mughal Empire** was a Muslim descendant of both Timur and Chinggis Khan (*Mughal* is Persian for "Mongol"). Invading from Central Asia, Babur defeated the last Muslim sultan of Delhi (**DEL-ee**) in 1526. Babur's grandson **Akbar** (r. 1556–1605), a brilliant but mercurial man, established the central administration of the expanding state. Under him and his three successors—the last of whom died in 1707—all but the southern tip of India fell under Mughal rule, administered first from Agra and then from Delhi.

Akbar granted land revenues to military officers and government officials in return for their service. Grants were called *mansabs* (**MAN-sab**) and their holders *mansabdars* (**man-sab-DAHR**). As in the other Islamic empires, revenue grants were not considered hereditary, and the central government kept careful track of them.

With a population of between 30 and 40 million, a thriving trading economy based on cotton cloth, and a generally efficient administration, India under Akbar was probably the most prosperous empire of the sixteenth century. He and his successors faced few external threats and experienced generally peaceful conditions in their northern Indian heartland.

Mughal Empire Muslim state (1526–1858) exercising dominion over most of India in the sixteenth and seventeenth centuries before political fragmentation caused decline.

Akbar Most illustrious sultan of the Mughal Empire in India (r. 1556–1605). He expanded the empire and pursued a policy of conciliation with Hindus.

mansabs In India, grants of land given in return for service by rulers of the Mughal Empire.

The weaving of flat fabrics by threading woof threads between warp threads stretched on a framework goes back to prehistory in many parts of the world. Making carpets by repeatedly knotting two warp threads together with bits of yarn and then trimming short the protruding tufts, called *pile*, to reveal the weaver's pattern is a rarer technology and one that reached a high level of artistry in Iran and neighboring regions beginning in the fourteenth century CE.

The first known pile carpet was discovered in a fifth-century BCE burial at the Siberian archaeological site of Pazyryk. The design motifs, combined with other archaeological evidence, indicate a Scythian origin for the burial. The Central Asian Scythians were a nomadic people whose remains have been found from the northern side of the Black Sea to the frontiers of Mongolia, which is where Pazyryk is situated.

Since identical technologies rarely come into being independently, it must be assumed that pile carpets were in use in Central Asia for 1,500 years before they became a major manufacture in Iran and Anatolia. It is not surprising, however, that no specimens have survived from this early period since organic materials decay in most climatic conditions. Archaeological examples of early Islamic textiles, for instance, come mostly from bone-dry excavations in Egypt.

It is likely that Central Asian nomads were the primary weavers and users of early pile carpets. The beginnings of the technology in the Middle East proper may possibly be associated with the entry of Turkish nomadic peoples into the region in the eleventh century, a movement that coincided with worsening climatic conditions that devastated the Iranian cotton industry (see Chapter 10). Many carpet designs in later centuries reflect specific nomadic traditions, though urban weavers often explored more adventurous and diverse floral or geometric patterns.

Turkish and Persian carpets appear frequently as luxury imports in European paintings beginning in the fourteenth century. Large quantities of Persian pile carpets date to the Safavid period, beginning in the sixteenth century, and they continue to constitute a major commodity in Iranian trade with Europe down to the present day.

Though independent carpet factories in Iranian cities began with the Safavids, only five out of 1,500 to 2,000 surviving Safavid

▲ **Persian Carpet** Dating to around 1550, this knotted carpet combines several motifs of the Safavid period: flowered borders, fanciful animals in the central area, and a band of calligraphy in yellow cartouches between the two. Large carpets like this were highly prized and many found their way into the export market and eventually into the homes of wealthy Europeans. In Iran, even families of modest means might have carpets in the 3 X 6 foot range. The Print Collector/Alamy Stock Photo

specimens are explicitly dated, which makes the history of the trade difficult to discern. Tabriz, the first Safavid capital in the northeast of Iran, may have had the first factory under royal patronage. Anatolia, the home of most early nomadic supporters of the Safavids, may have preceded Iran in carpet manufacture, and the industry in Mughal India certainly began in imitation of Iran.

The Dutch East India Company marketed Persian carpets throughout the Indian Ocean region. The European trade, dominated by Armenian merchants, was more precarious since it went overland through Ottoman Anatolia, which was often in turmoil because of Safavid-Ottoman wars.

Questions for Analysis

1. What advantages do pile carpets have over flat weaves in terms of usefulness?

2. How is the pile in a modern industrial carpet such as you might find in your home or school secured to its backing?

3. What makes the knotting of carpets compatible with nomadic life?

European trade boomed at the port of Surat in the northwest, but merchants from Multan, today on the Indus River in Pakistan, did more business with Iran and Russia. Lacking a regular navy, the rulers saw the Europeans—after Akbar's time, primarily Dutch and English, the Portuguese having lost most of their Indian ports—less as enemies than as shipmasters whose support could be procured as needed in return for trading privileges.

20-3b Hindus and Muslims

The Mughal state inherited traditions of religious tolerance from both the Islamic caliphate and the Mongols. Seventy percent of the *mansabdars* appointed under Akbar were Muslim soldiers born outside India, but 15 percent were Hindus. Most of the Hindu appointees were warriors from the north called **Rajputs (RAHJ-put)**, one of whom rose to be a powerful revenue minister.

Akbar differed from his Ottoman and Safavid counterparts—Suleiman the Magnificent and Shah Abbas the Great—in his striving for social harmony and not just for territory and revenue. His marriage to a Rajput princess encouraged reconciliation and even intermarriage between Muslims and Hindus. The birth of a son in 1569 ensured that future rulers would have both Muslim and Hindu ancestry.

Akbar ruled that in legal disputes between two Hindus, decisions would be made according to village custom or Hindu law as interpreted by local Hindu scholars, while Shari'a law was for Muslims. Akbar made himself the legal court of last resort.

Akbar also made himself the center of a new "Divine Faith" incorporating Muslim, Hindu, Zoroastrian, Sikh **(sick)**, and Christian beliefs. He liked Sufi ideas, which permeated the religious rituals he instituted at court. To promote serious consideration of his religious doctrines, he personally oversaw, from an elevated catwalk, debates among scholars of all religions assembled in his octagonal audience chamber. When courtiers uttered the Muslim exclamation "Allahu Akbar"—"God is great"—they also understood it in its second grammatical meaning, "God is Akbar."

Akbar's religious views did not survive him, but the court culture he fostered, reflecting a

Rajputs Members of a mainly Hindu warrior caste from northwest India. The Mughal emperors drew most of their Hindu officials from this caste, and Akbar married a Rajput princess.

▶ **Elephants Breaking Bridge of Boats** This illustration of an incident in the life of Akbar illustrates the ability of Mughal miniature painters to depict unconventional action scenes. Because the flow of rivers in India and the Middle East varied greatly from dry season to wet season, boat bridges were much more common than permanent constructions. Akbar Tames the Savage Elephant, Hawa'i, Outside the Red Fort at Agra, miniature from the Akbarnama of Abul Fazl, c.1590 (left hand side of double page miniature, see 4042) (gouache on paper), Basawan and Chatai (fl.1590)/British Museum, London, UK/The Bridgeman Art Librar

Section Review

- Founded by Babur, the Mughal Empire grew under Akbar and his successors to encompass most of India.

- The empire prospered through trade and granted trade privileges to Europeans in exchange for naval support.

- Akbar included both Muslims and Hindus in his government, respected Hindu customs, and strove for religious harmony.

- A hybrid culture flourished, but Aurangzeb practiced Muslim intolerance.

- After Aurangzeb's death, the empire declined through foreign invasion, the rise of regional powers, and European encroachment.

mixture of Muslim and Hindu traditions, flourished until his zealous great-grandson Aurangzeb (**ow-rang-ZEB**) (r. 1658–1707) reinstituted many restrictions on Hindus. Mughal and Rajput miniature paintings reveled in realistic portraits of political figures and depictions of scantily clad women, even though they brought frowns to the faces of pious Muslims, who deplored the representation of human beings. Most of the leading painters were Hindus. In addition to the florid style of Persian verse favored at court, a new taste developed for poetry and prose in the popular language of the Delhi region. The modern descendant of this language is called *Urdu* in Pakistan and *Hindi* in India.

20-3c Central Decay and Regional Challenges

Mughal power did not long survive Aurangzeb's death in 1707. Aurangzeb's additions to Mughal territory in southern India were not all well integrated into the imperial structure, and strong regional powers arose to challenge Mughal military supremacy. A climax came in 1739 when Nadir Shah, a warlord who had seized power in Iran after the fall of the Safavids, invaded the Mughal capital and carried off to Iran the "peacock throne," the priceless jewel-encrusted symbol of Mughal grandeur. Another throne was found for the later Mughals to sit on; but their empire, which survived in name to 1858, was finished.

In 1723, Nizam al-Mulk (**nee-ZAHM al-MULK**), the sultan's powerful vizier, gave up on the central government and established his own nearly independent state at Hyderabad in the eastern Deccan. Other officials bearing the title *nawab* (**nah-WAHB**) became similarly independent in Bengal and Oudh (**OW-ad**) in the northeast, as did the militant Hindu Marathas in the center. In the northwest, simultaneous Iranian and Mughal weakness allowed the Afghans to establish an independent kingdom.

Some of the new regional powers were prosperous and benefited from the removal of the sultan's heavy hand. Linguistic and religious communities, freed from Aurangzeb's religious intolerance, similarly enjoyed greater opportunity for political expression. However, this disintegration of central power favored the intrusion of European adventurers.

In 1741 Joseph François Dupleix (**doo-PLAY**) took over the presidency of the French stronghold of Pondicherry (**pon-dih-CHER-ree**) and began a new phase of European involvement in India. He captured the English trading center of Madras and used his small contingent of European and European-trained Indian troops to become a power broker in southern India. Though offered the title *nawab*, Dupleix preferred to operate behind the scenes, using Indian princes as puppets. His career ended in 1754 when he was called home. Deeply involved in European wars, the French government declined further adventures in India. Dupleix's departure opened the way for the British, whose exploits in India are described in Chapter 26.

20-4 The Russian Empire, 1500–1725

To what extent does Russia's Christianity complicate comparisons with contemporary Muslim states?

Though it was Christian rather than Muslim, the Russian Empire encountered problems and opportunities not unlike the large territorial empires discussed above. Before 1500, the Russian principalities had been dominated by steppe nomads (see Chapter 13). During the next three centuries, however, the rulers of **Muscovy** (**MUSS-koe-vee**), the principality based on Moscow, forged an empire that stretched from eastern Europe across northern Asia and into North America. Moscow lay in the forest zone north of the treeless *steppe* (grasslands) favored by Mongol horse nomads (also known as Tatars or, in western European languages, Tartars).

nawab A Muslim prince allied to British India; technically, a semi-autonomous deputy of the Mughal emperor.

Muscovy Russian principality that emerged gradually during the era of Mongol domination. The Muscovite dynasty ruled without interruption from 1276 to 1598.

The princes of Muscovy led the movement against the Golden Horde and ruthlessly annexed the territories of the neighboring Russian state of Novgorod in 1478. Prince Ivan IV (r. 1533–1584), known as "the Terrible" (meaning the fearsome), pushed Muscovy's conquests south and east at the expense of the Tatar Khanates of Kazan and Astrakhan (see Map 20.2).

Since 1547 the Russian ruler used the title **tsar** (**zahr**) (from the Roman imperial title *caesar*), the term Russians had earlier used for the rulers of the Mongol Empire. The Russian church called Moscow the "third Rome," successor to the Roman Empire's second capital, Constantinople, which had fallen to the Ottoman Turks in 1453.

Yet Russian claims to greatness were exaggerated: in 1600 the empire was poor, backward, and landlocked. Only one seaport—Arkhangelsk near the Arctic circle—connected to the world's oceans. The Crimean Tatars to the south were powerful enough to sack Moscow in 1571, just as Stenka Razin's Cossacks from a nearby region threatened to do a century later. Beyond them, the Ottoman Empire controlled access to the Black Sea, while trade with India had to go through Iran. The kingdoms of Sweden and Poland-Lithuania to the west similarly blocked Russian access to the Baltic Sea.

20-4a The Drive Across Northern Asia

The one route open to expansion, **Siberia**, turned out to be Russia's version of the New World, an immense region of little-known peoples and untapped resources. The Russians and their trading partners particularly prized the soft, dense fur that sables and other forest animals grew to survive the long northern winters. The Strogonovs, a wealthy Russian trading family, led the early Russian exploration of Siberia. The small bands of foragers and reindeer herders already living there could not resist the armed adventurers the Strogonovs hired. Using rifles, their troops destroyed the only political power in the region, the Khanate of Sibir, in 1582. Moving through the dense forests by river, Russian fur trappers reached the Pacific Ocean during the seventeenth century and soon crossed over into Alaska. Russian political control followed more slowly into what was more a frontier zone with widely scattered forts than a province under full control. Beginning in the early seventeenth century the tsars also used Siberia as a penal colony for criminals and political prisoners. In the 1640s Russian settlers began to grow grain in the Amur River Valley east of Mongolia, where they came into contact with Chinese authorities (see Chapter 21).

20-4b Russian Society and Politics to 1725

As the empire expanded, it incorporated people with different languages, religious beliefs, and ethnic identities. Orthodox missionaries strove to Christianize the peoples of Siberia, but among the relatively more populous steppe peoples, Islam prevailed as the dominant religion. Differences in how people outside of cities made their living were equally fundamental. Russians tended to live as farmers and hunters, while the peoples newly incorporated into the empire were either herders and caravan workers or hunters and fishers living along the Siberian rivers.

Diversity arose even among Russian speakers of Orthodox faith. The name **Cossack**, referring to bands of people living on the steppe between Muscovy and the Caspian and Black Seas, probably comes from a Turkic word for a warrior or mercenary soldier. Actually, Cossacks had diverse origins and beliefs, but they all belonged to close-knit bands, fought superbly from the saddle, and terrified both villagers and legal authorities. Cossack allegiances with rulers were temporary; loyalty to the chiefs of their bands was paramount. Cossacks provided most of the soldiers and settlers employed by the Strogonovs, and they founded every major town in Russian Siberia. They also manned the Russian camps on the Amur River. West of the Urals the Cossacks defended Russia against Swedish and Ottoman incursions, but they also preserved their political autonomy (see beginning of this chapter).

The early seventeenth century was a "Time of Troubles" marking the end of the old line of Muscovite rulers. During this era, which coincided with the beginning of the Little Ice Age and a similar period of internal disorder in the Ottoman Empire, Swedish and Polish forces briefly occupied Moscow on separate occasions. Eventually the Russian aristocracy—the boyars (**BOY-ar**)—allowed one of their own, Mikhail Romanov (**ROH-man-off or roh-MAN-off**) (r. 1613–1645), to inaugurate a dynasty that would soon consolidate its own authority while

tsar From Latin *caesar*, this Russian title for a monarch was first used in reference to a Russian ruler by Ivan III (r. 1462–1505).

Siberia The extreme northeastern sector of Asia, including the Kamchatka Peninsula and the present Russian coast of the Arctic Ocean, the Bering Strait, and the Sea of Okhotsk.

Cossack Peoples of the Russian Empire who lived outside the farming villages, often as herders, mercenaries, or outlaws. Cossacks led the conquest of Siberia in the sixteenth and seventeenth centuries.

MAP 20.2 **The Expansion of Russia, 1500–1800** Sweden and Poland initially blocked Russian expansion in Europe, while the Ottoman Empire blocked the southwest. In the sixteenth century, Russia began to expand east, toward Siberia and the Pacific Ocean. By the end of the rule of Catherine the Great in 1796, Russia encompassed all of northern and northeastern Eurasia.

How did the absence of a warm-water seaport hinder Russia's expansion?

successfully competing with neighboring powers. The Romanovs often represented conflicts between Slavic Russians and Turkic steppe peoples as being between Christians and "infidels" or between the civilized and the "barbaric." Despite this rhetoric, there were many similarities between their empire and those of their Muslim neighbors to the south.

As centralized tsarist power rose, the freedom of the peasants who tilled the land in European Russia fell. The Moscovy rulers and early tsars, like the sultans and shahs, rewarded the loyal nobles who dominated the military with grants of land that obliged the local peasants to work for the lords. Law and custom permitted peasants to change masters during a two-week period each year, which encouraged lords to treat their peasants well; but the rising commercialization of agriculture also raised the value of these labor obligations.

Long periods of warfare in the late sixteenth and early seventeenth centuries disrupted peasant life and caused many to flee to the Cossacks or into Siberia. Some who couldn't flee sold themselves into slavery to keep from starving. When peace returned, landlords sought to recover the runaways and bind them more tightly to their land. A law change in 1649 finally transformed the peasants into **serfs** by eliminating the period when they could change masters and ordering runaways to return to their masters.

Like slavery, serfdom was hereditary. In theory the serf was tied to a piece of land, not owned by a master. In practice, strict laws narrowed the difference between serf and slave. In the Russian census of 1795, serfs made up over half the population: landowners made up only 2 percent.

20-4c Peter the Great

The greatest of the Romanovs, Tsar **Peter the Great** (r. 1689–1725), came to the throne a century or so later than the eminent Muslim potentates Suleiman the Magnificent, the Safavid Shah Abbas, and the Mughal sultan Akbar. Whereas Suleiman fought wars with Europeans, and Abbas and Akbar knew them as merchant adventurers, Peter was aware that Europe's wealth and military power had increased enormously during the intervening period. Some Ottoman officials shared this awareness, as evidenced by the vogue for European styles during the "Tulip Period" that coincided with Peter's reign. But no Muslim notable could safely sojourn in Christian Europe long enough to master the new techniques of ruling and acquiring power.

When Peter ascended the throne, there were already hundreds of foreign merchants in Moscow, as there were in Istanbul. Military officers from western Europe, who were paralleled by European converts to Islam in the Ottoman Empire, had already introduced new weapons and techniques, and Italian builders were already influencing church and palace architecture.

Peter accelerated these tendencies in unprecedented fashion. While his half-sister Sophia governed as regent for him and her sickly brother Ivan, he lived on an estate near the foreigners' quarter outside Moscow, where he busied himself gaining practical skills in blacksmithing, carpentry, shipbuilding, and the arts of war. When Princess Sophia tried to take complete control of the government in 1689, Peter rallied enough support to send her to a monastery, secure the abdication of Ivan, and take charge of Russia. He was still in his teens.

To secure a port on the Black Sea, he constructed a small but formidable navy. Describing his wars with the Ottoman Empire as a new crusade to liberate Constantinople from the Muslim sultans, Peter fancied himself the legal protector of Orthodox Christians living under Ottoman rule. His forces seized the port of Azov in 1696 but lost it again in 1713, thus calling a halt to southward expansion.

In the winter of 1697–1698, after his Black Sea campaign, Peter traveled in disguise across Europe to discover how western

AP® Exam Tip
Compare Russian serfdom with other systems of coerced labor, such as slavery.

serfs In medieval Europe, an agricultural laborer legally bound to a lord's property and obligated to perform set services for the lord. In Russia some serfs worked as artisans and in factories; serfdom was not abolished there until 1861.

Peter the Great Russian tsar (r. 1689–1725). He enthusiastically introduced Western languages and technologies to the Russian elite, moving the capital from Moscow to the new city of St. Petersburg.

▶ **Peter the Great** This portrait from his time as a student in Holland in 1697 shows Peter as ruggedly masculine and practical, quite unlike most royal portraits of the day that posed rulers in foppish elegance and haughty majesty. Peter was a popular military leader as well as an autocratic ruler. UniversalImagesGroup/Getty Images

▲ **The Fontanka Canal in St. Petersburg in 1753** The Russian capital continued to grow as a commercial and administrative center. As in Amsterdam, canals were the city's major arteries. On the right is a new summer palace built by Peter's successor. View of the Fontanka River from the grotto and the Guest Palace, etched by Grigory Anikievich Kachalov (1711/12-1759), 1753 (etching with engraving), Makhaev, Mikhail Ivanovich (c.1718-1770) (after)/Hermitage, St. Petersburg, Russia/The Bridgeman Art Library

European societies were becoming so powerful and wealthy. He paid special attention to ships and weapons, even working for a time as a ship's carpenter in the Netherlands. Upon his return to Russia, Peter resolved to expand and reform his vast but backward empire.

In the long and costly Great Northern War (1700–1721), Peter's modernized armies broke Swedish control of the Baltic Sea, making possible more direct contacts between Russia and Europe. This victory forced the European powers to recognize Russia as a major power for the first time, just as the Ottoman Empire was then being viewed as past its prime.

On land captured from Sweden at the eastern end of the Baltic, Peter built St. Petersburg, his window on the West. In 1712 the city became Russia's capital. To demonstrate Russia's new sophistication, Peter ordered architects to build St. Petersburg's houses and public buildings in the baroque style then fashionable in France.

Peter also pushed the Russian elite to imitate European fashions. He personally shaved off his noblemen's long beards to conform to Western styles. To end the traditional seclusion of upper-class Russian women, Peter required officials, military officers, and merchants to bring their wives to the social gatherings he organized in the capital. He also directed the nobles to educate their children.

A decree of 1716 proclaimed that the tsar "is not obliged to answer to anyone in the world for his doings, but possesses power and authority over his kingdom and land, to rule them at his will and pleasure as a Christian ruler." Under this expansive definition of his role, Peter sharply reduced the traditional roles of the boyars in government and the army, brought the Russian Orthodox Church more

Section Review

- Russia grew vastly by colonizing Siberia.
- Lacking seaports, Russia relied on overland trade with European and Muslim neighbors.
- Peter the Great copied western European military and economic techniques but imposed a complete autocracy on his subjects.

firmly under state control, built factories and foundries to provide supplies for the military, increased taxes, and imposed more forced labor on the serfs. Peter was an absolutist ruler of the sort then common in western Europe, but he is equally comparable to the most authoritarian rulers in the contemporary Muslim empires.

20-5 The Maritime Worlds of Islam, 1500–1750

What role does maritime history play in the political and economic life of this period?

As land powers, the Mughal, Safavid, Ottoman, and Russian Empires faced similar problems in the seventeenth and eighteenth centuries. Complex changes in military technology and in the world economy, along with the increasing difficulty of basing an extensive land empire on military forces paid through land grants, affected them all adversely.

AP® Exam Tip

Explain the economic strategies of different types of states and empires.

The new pressures faced by land powers were less important to seafaring countries intent on turning trade networks into maritime empires. Improvements in ship design, navigation accuracy, and the use of cannon gave an ever-increasing edge to European powers competing with local seafaring peoples. Moreover, the development of joint-stock companies, in which many merchants pooled their capital, provided a flexible and efficient financial instrument for exploiting new possibilities. The English East India Company was founded in 1600, the Dutch East India Company in 1602.

Although the Ottomans, Safavids, and Mughals did not effectively contest the growth of Portuguese and then Dutch, English, and French maritime power, the majority of non-European shipbuilders, captains, sailors, and traders were Muslim. The sizable groups of Armenian, Jewish, and Hindu traders remained almost as aloof from the Europeans as the Muslims did. The presence in every port of Muslims following the same legal traditions and practicing their faith in similar ways cemented the Muslims' trading network, and conversion to Islam encouraged the growth of coastal Muslim communities.

Although European missionaries, particularly the Jesuits, tried to extend Christianity into Asia and Africa (see Chapters 16 and 21), most Europeans, the Portuguese excepted, did not treat local converts or the offspring of mixed marriages as full members of their communities. Islam was generally more welcoming. As a consequence, Islam spread extensively into East Africa and Southeast Asia during precisely the same time as rapid European commercial expansion.

20-5a Muslims in Southeast Asia

Historians disagree about the chronology and manner of Islam's spread in Southeast Asia. Arab traders appeared in southern China as early as the eighth century, so Muslims probably reached the East Indies (the island portions of Southeast Asia) at a similarly early date. Nevertheless, the continuing dominance of Indian cultural influences in the area indicates that early Muslim visitors had little impact on local beliefs. Clearer indications of the formation of Muslim communities date from roughly the fourteenth century, with the strongest overseas linkage being to the port of Cambay in India (see Map 20.3) rather than to the Arab world. Islam first took root in port cities and in some royal courts and spread inland only slowly, possibly transmitted by itinerant Sufis.

Although appeals to the Ottoman sultan for support against the Europeans ultimately proved futile, Islam strengthened resistance to Portuguese, Spanish, and Dutch intruders. When the Spaniards conquered the Philippines during the decades following the establishment of their first fort in 1565, they encountered Muslims on the southern island of Mindanao (**min-duh-NOW**) and the nearby Sulu archipelago. They called them "Moros," the Spanish term for their old enemies, the Muslims of North Africa. In the ensuing Moro wars, the Spaniards portrayed the Moros as greedy pirates who raided non-Muslim territories for slaves. In fact, they were political, religious, and commercial competitors whose perseverance enabled them to establish the Sulu Empire based in the southern Philippines, one of the strongest states in Southeast Asia from 1768 to 1848.

Other local kingdoms that looked on Islam as a force to counter the aggressive Christianity of the Europeans included the actively proselytizing Brunei (**BROO-neye**) Sultanate in northern

Borneo and the **Acheh (AH-cheh) Sultanate** in northern Sumatra. At its peak in the early seventeenth century, Acheh succeeded Malacca as the main center of Islamic expansion in Southeast Asia, prospering by trading pepper for cotton cloth from Gujarat in India. Acheh declined after the Dutch seized Malacca from Portugal in 1641.

How well Islam was understood in these Muslim kingdoms is open to question. In Acheh, for example, a series of women ruled between 1641 and 1699. This practice ended when local Muslim scholars obtained a ruling from scholars in Mecca and Medina that Islam did not approve of female rulers. After this ruling, scholarly understandings of Islam gained greater prominence in the East Indies.

Historians have looked at merchants, Sufi preachers, or both as the first propagators of Islam in Southeast Asia. The scholarly vision of Islam, however, took root in the sixteenth century by way of pilgrims returning from years of study in Mecca and Medina. Islam promoted the dissemination of writing in the region. Some of the returning pilgrims wrote in Arabic, others in Malay or Javanese. As Islam continued to spread, *adat* ("custom"), a form of Islam rooted in pre-Muslim religious and social practices, retained its preeminence in rural areas over practices centered on the Shari'a, the religious law. But the royal courts in the port cities began to heed the views of the pilgrim teachers.

20-5b Muslims in Coastal Africa

Muslim rulers also governed the East African ports that the Portuguese began to visit in the fifteenth century (see Map 20.3). People living in the millet and rice lands of the Swahili Coast—from the Arabic *sawahil* (**suh-WAH-hil**), meaning "coasts"—had little contact with those in the dry hinterlands. Throughout this period, the East African lakes region and the highlands of Kenya witnessed unprecedented migration and relocation of peoples because of drought conditions that persisted from the late sixteenth through most of the seventeenth century.

Cooperation among the trading ports of Kilwa, Mombasa, and Malindi was hindered by the thick bush country that separated the cultivated tracts of coastal land and by the fact that the ports competed with one another in the export of ivory, ambergris (**AM-ber-grees**) (a whale by-product used in perfumes), and forest products such as beeswax, copal tree resin, and wood. Kilwa also exported gold. In the eighteenth century slave trading, primarily to Arabian ports but also to India, increased in importance. Because Europeans—the only peoples who kept consistent records of slave-trading activities—played a minor role in this slave trade, few records have survived to indicate its extent. Perhaps the best estimate is that 2.1 million slaves were exported between 1500 and 1890, a little over 12.5 percent of the total traffic in African slaves during that period (see Chapter 19).

Initially, the Portuguese favored the port of Malindi, which caused the decline of Kilwa and Mombasa. Repeatedly plagued by local rebellion, Portuguese power suffered severe blows when the Arabs of **Oman** in southeastern Arabia captured their south Arabian stronghold at Musqat (1650) and then went on to seize Mombasa (1698), which had become the Portuguese capital in East Africa. The Portuguese briefly retook Mombasa but lost control permanently in 1729. From then on, the Portuguese had to content themselves with Mozambique in East Africa and a few remaining ports in India (Goa) and farther east (Macao and Timor).

The Omanis created a maritime empire of their own, one that worked in greater cooperation with the African populations. The Bantu language of the coast, broadened by the absorption of Arabic, Persian, and Portuguese loanwords, developed into **Swahili** (**swah-HEE-lee**), which was spoken throughout the region. Arabs and other Muslims who settled in the region intermarried with local families, giving rise to a mixed population that played an important role in developing a distinctive Swahili culture.

In Northwest Africa the seizure by Portugal and Spain of coastal strong-holds in Morocco provoked a militant response. The Sa'adi family, which claimed descent from the Prophet Muhammad, led a resistance to Portuguese aggression that climaxed in victory at the battle of al-Qasr al-Kabir (Ksar el Kebir) in 1578. The triumphant Moroccan sultan, Ahmad al-Mansur, restored his country's strength and independence. By the early seventeenth century naval expeditions from the port of Salé, referred to in British records as "the Sally Rovers," raided European shipping as far as Britain itself.

Corsairs, or sea raiders, working out of Algerian, Tunisian, and Libyan ports brought the same sort of warfare to the Mediterranean. European governments called these Muslim raiders

Acheh Sultanate Muslim kingdom in northern Sumatra. Main center of Islamic expansion in Southeast Asia in the early seventeenth century, it declined after the Dutch seized Malacca from Portugal in 1641.

Oman Arab state based in Musqat, the main port in the southeast region of the Arabian peninsula. Oman succeeded Portugal as a power in the western Indian Ocean in the eighteenth century.

Swahili Bantu language with Arabic loanwords spoken in coastal regions of East Africa.

MAP 20.3   European Colonization in the Indian Ocean, to 1750 Since Portuguese explorers were the first Europeans to reach India by rounding Africa, Portugal gained a strong foothold in both areas. Rival Spain was barred from colonizing the region by the Treaty of Tordesillas in 1494, which limited Spanish efforts to lands west of a line drawn through the mid-Atlantic Ocean. Extended around the globe, the line provided justification of Spanish colonization in the Philippines. French, British, and Dutch colonies date from after 1600, when joint-stock companies provided a new stimulus for overseas commerce.

How did the absence of habitable land to the south of the Indian Ocean make trade patterns different from those in the Mediterranean Sea?

pirates and slave-takers, and they leveled the same charges against other Muslim mariners in the Persian Gulf and the Sulu Sea. But there was little distinction between the actions of the Muslims and of their European adversaries.

20-5c European Powers in Southern Seas

Through their well-organized Dutch East India Company, the Dutch played a major role in driving the Portuguese from their possessions in the East Indies. Just as the Portuguese had tried to dominate the trade in spices, so the Dutch concentrated at first on the spice-producing islands of Southeast Asia. The Portuguese had seized Malacca, a strategic town on the narrow strait at the

Section Review

- The majority of non-European shipbuilders, captains, sailors, and traders in the Indian Ocean were Muslim.

- A number of local kingdoms in Southeast Asia took on Islam as a force to resist the aggressive Christianity of the Europeans.

- Muslims in coastal Africa intermarried locally, creating a mixed population and helping create a distinctive Swahili culture.

- Over time the successes of European trading companies changed the balance of power in the southern seas, but local merchants never completely disappeared from the commercial scene.

end of the Malay Peninsula, from a local Malay ruler in 1511 (see Chapter 16). The Dutch took it away from them in 1641, leaving Portugal little foothold in the East Indies except the islands of Ambon (**am-BOHN**) and Timor (see Map 20.3).

Although the United Netherlands was one of the least autocratic countries of Europe, the governors-general appointed by the Dutch East India Company deployed almost unlimited powers in their efforts to maintain their trade monopoly. They could even order the execution of their own employees for "smuggling"—that is, trading on their own. Under strong governors-general, the Dutch fought a series of wars against Acheh and other local kingdoms on Sumatra and Java. In 1628 and 1629 their new capital at **Batavia**, now the city of Jakarta on Java, was besieged by a fleet of fifty ships belonging to the sultan of Mataram (**MAH-tah-ram**), a Javanese kingdom. The Dutch held out with difficulty and eventually prevailed when the sultan was unable to get effective help from the English.

In the course of the eighteenth century, the Dutch gradually turned from being middle-men between Southeast Asian producers and European buyers to producing crops in areas they controlled, notably in Java. Javanese teak forests yielded high-quality lumber, and coffee, transplanted from Yemen, grew well in the western hilly regions. In this new phase of colonial export production, Batavia developed from being the headquarters town of a far-flung enterprise to being the administrative capital of a conquered land.

20-6 Conclusion

The complex changes in military technology and economic organization that were under way in smaller European countries in the seventeenth and eighteenth centuries affected the Ottoman, Safavid, and Mughal Empires adversely. Only Russia, by virtue of a single ruler who was able to learn western European techniques firsthand, found success in adopting some of the changes. By western European standards, however, Russia was still a poor and backward country when Peter's reign ended in 1725 while the Muslims ruled rich lands that were ripe for European exploitation.

Improvements in ship design, navigation accuracy, and the use of cannon gave an ever-increasing edge to European powers competing with local sea-faring peoples. In contrast to the age-old Eurasian belief that imperial wealth came from controlling broad expanses of land, western European rulers promoted joint-stock companies and luxuriated in the prosperity gained from their ever-increasing control of Indian Ocean commerce. Eighteenth-century European observers marveled no less at the riches and industry of these eastern lands than at the fundamental weakness of their political and military systems. Yet they persistently underestimated the importance of Islam as a focus of local allegiance and political opposition.

Batavia Fort established around 1619 as headquarters of Dutch East India Company operations in Indonesia; today the city of Jakarta.

Key Terms

Ottoman Empire p. 508	**Shi'ites** p. 515	**Rajputs** p. 521	**serf** p. 525
Suleiman the Magnificent p. 508	**Hidden Imam** p. 516	*nawab* p. 522	**Peter the Great** p. 525
Janissaries p. 508	**Shah Abbas I** p. 516	**Muscovy** p. 522	**Acheh Sultanate** p. 528
Tulip Period p. 515	**Mughal Empire** p. 519	**tsar** p. 523	**Oman** p. 528
Safavid Empire p. 515	**Akbar** p. 519	**Siberia** p. 523	**Swahili** p. 528
	mansabs p. 519	**Cossacks** p. 523	**Batavia** p. 530

Review Questions

1. What importance should be given to the fact that in comparison to the Roman Empire, the traders of the Ottoman, Safavid, and Mughal empires had comparatively limited involvement with seafaring?

2. Did limited geographies and quarrelsome rulers make the monarchies of Western Europe less or more capable of economic and technological advance in comparison with the empires discussed in this chapter?

3. Why did African slavery play a lesser role in the history of the Ottoman, Safavid, Mughal, and Russian empires than it did in the history of Europe and its colonies?

 MindTap® is a fully online, personalized learning experience built upon Cengage Learning content. MindTap® combines student learning tools—readings, multimedia, activities, and assessments—into a singular Learning Path that guides students through the course and helps students develop the critical thinking, analysis, and communication skills that are essential to academic and professional success.

Multiple-Choice Questions
Questions 1–3 refer to the passage below.

On war against the Shi'ite Muslim Safavids of Iran:

Is it licit according to the shari'a to fight the followers of the Safavids? Is the person who kills them a holy warrior, and the person who dies at their hands a martyr?

Answer: Yes, it is a great holy war and a glorious martyrdom.

Assuming that it is licit to fight them, is this simply because of their rebellion and enmity against the [Ottoman] Sultan of the People of Islam, because they drew the sword against the troops of Islam, or what?

Answer: They are both rebels and, from many points of view, infidels.

Can the children of Safavid subjects captured in the Nakhichevan campaign be enslaved?

Answer: No."

A fatwa by Ebu's-Su'ud, Mufti of Istanbul, 1545–1574

1. Based on the passage above, which of the following is an accurate conclusion about religion during this time period?

   (A) Religious communities tended to question the authority of political leaders.

   (B) Religion united regions more than it divided them.

   (C) All religious wars were fought between competing faiths.

   (D) Religious sectarianism in many cases led to violence.

2. Which of the following was true of the Afro-Eurasia area during the time period 1500–1750?

   (A) The increase in interactions between states with varied interpretations of Islam led to increased religious tensions.

   (B) The tensions between the Ottoman and Safavid Empires demonstrated the influence of secularism.

   (C) Most conflicts were between numerous regions with allegiances to competing religions.

   (D) Slavery was no longer a viable institution in most parts of the world during this time period.

3. Which of the following was a factor working against the sectarianism suggested in the passage above?

   (A) Arab merchants competed with Safavid merchants for Indian markets.

   (B) Muslim states utilized the same calendar, spoke Arabic, and worked to facilitate trade.

   (C) The Ottoman and Safavid Empires both had policies concerning religious minorities.

   (D) Neither the Ottomans nor the Safavids revived the office of the caliph.

Questions 4–6 refer to the image below.

▲ **The Taj Majal, Agra, India, Built by Emperor Shah Jahan of the Mughal Empire, 1653** Ivan Vdovin/ullstein bild/The Image Works

4. Based on the image above, built by members of the Mughal Empire, which of the following is an accurate generalization about states during this time period?

   (A) Large-scale architecture was commissioned primarily by merchant elites.

   (B) Architecture was larger and more impressive than in previous time periods.

   (C) Large-scale architecture was used exclusively for religious purposes.

   (D) Rulers used architecture to support their legitimacy as leaders.

5. The Mughal leader, Akbar, differed from his Ottoman and Safavid counterparts in which of the following ways?

   (A) Akbar, unlike the Ottoman and Safavid rulers, enforced religious unity on his people.

   (B) The Ottoman and Safavid rulers expanded the area under their power, while Akbar lost territory during his reign.

   (C) Akbar showed religious tolerance in his desire for social harmony, not just territory or revenue.

   (D) Unlike the Ottoman and Safavid rulers, Akbar was unable to leave power to establish a dynasty, with power transferring away from his family at his death.

6. Which of the following led to the rise of independent states under nawabs in places like Hyderabad, Bengal, and Oudh?

   (A) The imposition of Hinduism on all members of the royal court under Aurangzeb

   (B) Lack of integration of territory and invasion by the same warlord who had seized the Safavid's power

   (C) Aurangzeb's overzealousness in attacking the weakened Safavid empire

   (D) Increasing pressure and interference from Europeans who eventually lured individuals away to claim independence

Questions 7–10 refer to the image below.

▲ **Ottoman Miniature of Janissaries Battling the Knights of St. John in the Siege of Rhodes, 1522** Pictures from History/The Image Works

7. The image above is evidence of Ottoman Empire use of what innovation in military practices?

   (A) The use of professional, full-time soldiers

   (B) The introduction of gunpowder weapons

   (C) The use of siege machines in warfare

   (D) The introduction of iron for making weapons

8. Which of the following best describes the Janissaries?

   (A) The use of elite military forces by rulers to centralize power

   (B) The use of paid citizens to increase recruitment

   (C) The use of bureaucratic institutions to centralize power

   (D) The use of tribute and taxation to raise funds for the state

9. The Ottoman policy for the recruiting of the Janissary demonstrates which of the following situations faced by many states during this time period?

   (A) The need to create religious alternatives for the entire population

   (B) The challenges that come with ruling an ethnically and religiously diverse state

   (C) The lack of suitable laborers for maintaining infrastructure

   (D) The difficulties in maintaining religious orthodoxy within government institutions

10. The *devshirme*, taking male children from certain villages and raising them as an elite, educated fighting force, emphasized the Ottoman Empire attempt to address what?

    (A) The large-scale illiteracy that made the Ottoman Empire extremely poor economically

    (B) A lack of well-trained fighters who were not tied down to the land as part-time farmers

    (C) The adoption of European bureaucratic models while integrating them into traditional Turkish culture

    (D) Creation of a bureaucratic elite while simultaneously decreasing religious diversity

Short-Answer Questions

1. Answer all parts of the question that follows.

   (A) Identify ONE reason the Safavid Empire differed from its Muslim neighbors.

   (B) Explain ONE way the Safavid Empire promoted the centralization of authority under the sultan.

   (C) Explain ONE common threat to central authority in the Ottoman and Safavid Empires.

2. Answer all parts of the question that follows.

   (A) Identify ONE change enacted by Peter the Great to Westernize Russia.

   (B) Explain ONE reason Peter wanted to Westernize Russia.

   (C) Explain ONE continuity with previous Russian rulers during the reign of Peter the Great.

21 East Asia in Global Perspective

AP® Framework Terms

Tokugawa Japan
Silver
Manchu Empire
Qing Empire

Overarching Questions

1 How and to what extent have environmental factors, disease, and technology affected patterns of human migration and settlement over time? (ENV)

2 In what ways do the arts reflect innovation, adaptation, and creativity of specific societies? (CUL)

3 How and why have economic, social, cultural, and geographic factors influenced the process of state building, expansion, and dissolution? (SB)

4 How have internal and external political factors influenced the process of state building, expansion, and dissolution? (SB)

5 How have political, economic, cultural, and demographic factors affected social structures? (SOC)

In the sixteenth century Ming China became a driving force in the first truly global economy, one that joined together Asia, Europe, the Americas, and, to a lesser extent, Africa. To meet China's sky-rocketing demand for silver, European traders imported American silver and in return shipped silk, spices, tea, and other precious goods back to Europe. Christian missionaries joined European merchants as intellectual middlemen in this global interaction.

At century's end, however, from 1592 to 1598, the Imjin War, a conflict surpassed in violence only by the wars of the nineteenth and twentieth centuries, embroiled Korea, Japan, and China. After attempting to conquer China, the Japanese finally returned to their islands, leaving the weakened Ming to face other foes. Korea, the devastated battleground, did not recover for centuries.

In the seventeenth century, **Manchu** armies from Manchuria on China's northeast frontier succeeded where Japan had failed. The Ming emperor had slashed the government payroll to pay the army defending Beijing (**bay-JING**) against the Manchu. Among those losing his job was an apprentice ironworker named Li Zicheng (**lee ZUH-cheng**). By 1630, Li Zicheng had found work as a soldier, but he and his fellow soldiers mutinied when the government failed to provide needed supplies. A natural leader, Li soon headed several thousand Chinese rebels, and in 1635 he and other rebel leaders gained control over much of north-central China.

◀ **Korean Turtle Boats** This painting shows a fleet of Korean warships under the command of Admiral Yi SunShin, who repelled numerous attacks by the Japanese in the last decade of the sixteenth century. Admiral Yi is celebrated for his use of "turtle boats," vessels whose covered decks, possibly made of iron plate, are shown in gray. National Museum of Seoul/Dr. Yushin Yoo

Wedged between the Manchu armies to the north and the rebels south of Beijing, the Ming government tottered. Li Zicheng's forces moved on Beijing, promising an end to Ming abuses and a restoration of peace and prosperity. In April 1644 Li's forces took the city without a fight. The last Ming emperor hanged himself in the palace garden, bringing to an end the dynasty that had ruled China since 1368.

Li's victory was short-lived, however. Preferring the Manchus to an uneducated warlord, the Ming general Wu Sangui and his new northern allies retook Beijing in June. Li's forces scattered, and a year later he was dead, either a suicide or beaten to death by peasants whose food he tried to steal.[1] Now the new masters of China, the Manchus installed their young sovereign as emperor, declared the beginning of a new dynasty called "Qing" (**ching**), and over the next two decades hunted down the last of the Ming loyalists and heirs to the throne.

These centuries may be referred to as the early modern period, a time of greater cultural, commercial, and military connectivity within East Asia. Maritime networks replaced the land-based Silk Road trade. This led to increased presence of Europeans. Some people in China, Korea, and Japan welcomed the European presence, but rulers in Korea and Japan eventually sought to curb foreign influence. Japan and Korea would eventually experience relative peace during the early modern period, while China suffered from large-scale warfare, rebellions, and natural disasters at the beginning and end of the early modern period. Each country, however, at its peak generated commercial and cultural developments that rivaled achievements in Europe. ●

21-1 **East Asia and Europe**

How did the West and East Asia affect each other commercially and intellectually?

In the sixteenth century, European merchant adventurers traveling from Southeast Asia helped build thriving trade networks in East Asia. Because of changes in the Ming fiscal system that required taxes to be paid in cash, China had an urgent demand for silver. Prior to 1500, Japan had supplied much of the foreign silver China needed, as much as 30 percent of the world's total output. This was replaced by American silver, however, mostly from the

Manchu Federation of Northeast Asian peoples who founded the Qing Empire.

---

[1]Adapted from Jonathan D. Spence, *The Search for Modern China* (New York, NY: W.W. Norton, 1990), 21–25.

mines at Potosí in Bolivia (see Chapter 18). European ships transported the bullion with their masters also acting as middlemen in Asian trade routes, sometimes operating as privateers and even pirates.

21-1a Trading Companies and Missionaries

For European merchants, the China trade was second in importance only to the spice trade of Southeast Asia. China's vast population and manufacturing skills drew a steady stream of would-be merchants from western Europe; however, enthusiasm for the trade developed only slowly at the Ming court.

In late 1513 a Portuguese ship reached China but was not permitted to trade. A formal Portuguese embassy in 1517 got bogged down in Chinese protocol and procrastination, and China expelled the Portuguese in 1522. Finally, in 1557, the Portuguese gained permission to trade from a base in Macao (**muh-KOW**) on the southern coast. Spain's China trade was conducted from Manila in the Philippines, where silver-laden galleons arrived from South America. For a time, the Spanish and the Dutch both maintained trading outposts on the island of Taiwan (then called Formosa), but in 1662 they were forced to concede control to the Qing, who for the first time incorporated Taiwan into China.

▲ **Great Pagoda at Kew Gardens** A testament to Europeans' fascination with Chinese culture is the towering Pagoda at the Royal Botanic Gardens in London. Completed in 1762, it was designed by Sir William Chambers as the principal ornament in the pleasure grounds of the White House at Kew, residence of Augusta, the mother of King George III. Martin Vickery/Alamy Stock Photo

By then, the Dutch East India Company (VOC, for Vereenigde Oost-Indische Compagnie) (see Chapter 20) had displaced the Portuguese as the paramount European traders in the Indian Ocean. The Portuguese had tried to dominate the trade in spices by seizing Malacca, a strategic town on the narrow strait at the end of the Malay Peninsula, from a local Malay ruler in 1511. The Dutch took it away from them in 1641, leaving Portugal little foothold in the East Indies except the Islands of Ambon (**am-BOHN**) and Timor.

The governors-general appointed by the VOC deployed almost unlimited authority in their efforts to maintain their trade monopoly. They could even order the execution of their own employees for "smuggling"—that is, trading on their own. Under strong governors-general, the Dutch fought a series of wars against local rulers in Southeast Asia, such as the sultan of a Javanese kingdom called Mataram (**MAH-tah-ram**). Suppressing local rulers, however, was not enough to control the spice trade once other European countries adopted Dutch methods, learned where goods could be acquired, and started to send ships into eastern waters.

In East Asia as well, the VOC established itself as the main European trader. VOC representatives courted official favor in China by acknowledging the moral superiority of the emperor. This meant performing the ritual *kowtow* (in which the visitor knocked his head on the floor while crawling toward the throne) to the Ming emperor.

Along with trade came missionaries. Catholic missionaries accompanied the Portuguese and Spanish merchants to China. While the Franciscans and Dominicans pursued the conversion efforts at the bottom of society, a strategy pioneered in Japan, the Jesuits (members of the Catholic religious order the Society of Jesus) focused on China's intellectual and political elite.

The outstanding Jesuit of late Ming China, Matteo Ricci (**mah-TAY-oh REE-chee**) (1552–1610), became expert in the Chinese language and an accomplished scholar of the Confucian classics. Under Ricci's leadership, the Jesuits adapted Catholicism to Chinese cultural traditions while introducing the Chinese to the latest science and technology from Europe. After 1601 Ricci resided in Beijing on an imperial stipend as a Western scholar. Later Jesuits headed the office of astronomy that issued the official calendar.

CHRONOLOGY

	Korea and Japan	China and Central Asia
1500	1543 First Portuguese contacts with Japan	1517 Portuguese embassy to China
	1592 Japanese invasion of Korea	
1600	1603 Tokugawa Shogunate formed	1601 Matteo Ricci allowed to reside in Beijing
	1633–1639 Japanese edicts close down trade with Europe	1644 Qing conquest of Beijing
		1662–1722 Rule of Emperor Kangxi
		1689 Treaty of Nerchinsk with Russia
		1691 Qing control of Inner Mongolia
1700	1702 Trial of the Forty-Seven Ronin	1736–1796 Rule of Emperor Qianlong
	1792 Russian ships first spotted off the coast of Japan	

Jesuits helped create maps in the European style as practical guides to newly conquered regions and as symbols of Qing dominance. One Chinese emperor, Kangxi, considered introducing the European calendar, but protests from the Confucian elite caused him to drop the plan. When he fell ill with malaria in the 1690s, Jesuit medical treatment (in this case, South American quinine) aided his recovery. Kangxi also ordered the creation of illustrated books in Manchu detailing European anatomical and pharmaceutical knowledge.

To gain converts, the Jesuits made important compromises in their religious teaching. Most importantly, they tolerated Confucian ancestor worship. This excited controversy between the Jesuits and their Catholic rivals in China, the Franciscans and Dominicans, and also between the Jesuits and the pope. In 1690 the disagreement reached a high pitch. Kangxi wrote to Rome supporting the Jesuit position and after further dispute ordered the expulsion of all missionaries who refused to sign a certificate accepting his position. The Jesuit presence in China declined in the eighteenth century, and later Chinese emperors persecuted Christians rather than naming them to high office.

AP® Exam Tip
Consider how the role of Christian missionaries in China supports the argument that the spread of existing religions contributed to the creation of syncretic belief systems and practices.

21-1b Chinese Influences on Europe

The exchange of information between Chinese and Europeans was never one-way. While the Jesuits brought forward new knowledge of anatomy, for example, the Chinese demonstrated an early form of inoculation, called "variolation," that had helped curtail smallpox after the conquest of Beijing. The technique inspired Europeans to develop other vaccines.

Similarly, Jesuit writings about China excited admiration in Europe. The wealthy and the aspiring middle classes demanded Chinese things, or at least "chinoiserie," that is, things that looked Chinese. Silk, porcelain, and tea were avidly sought, along with cloisonné jewelry, jade, lacquered and jeweled room dividers, painted fans, and carved ivory (which originated in Africa and was finished in China). Wallpaper began as an adaptation of the Chinese practice of covering walls with enormous loose-hanging watercolors or calligraphy scrolls. By the mid-1700s special workshops throughout China were producing wallpaper and other items according to the specifications of European merchants. The items were exported to Europe via Canton.

Chinese political philosophy impressed Europeans, too. In the late 1770s poems supposedly written by Emperor Qianlong were translated into French and disseminated in intellectual circles. In these poems the Chinese emperors rule as benevolent despots campaigning against superstition and ignorance, curbing aristocratic excesses, and patronizing science and the arts. This image of a practical, secular, compassionate ruler impressed the French thinker Voltaire, who proclaimed that Chinese emperors were model philosopher-kings and advocated such rulership as a protection against the growth of aristocratic privilege.

AP® Exam Tip
Explain the influence of cultural exchanges between Asia and other regions.

21-1c **Japan and the Europeans**

European contacts with Japan also presented that country with new opportunities and problems. Within thirty years of the arrival of the first Portuguese in 1543, warlords known as *daimyo* (**DIE-mee-oh**) were fighting with Western-style firearms, copied and improved upon by Japanese armorers.

The Japanese welcomed but closely regulated traders from Portugal, Spain, the Netherlands, and England. Aside from a brief boom in porcelain exports in the seventeenth century, few Japanese goods went to Europe, and not much from Europe found a market in Japan. The Japanese sold the Dutch copper and silver, which the Dutch exchanged in China for silks that they then resold in Japan. The Japanese, of course, had their own trade with China.

Portuguese and Spanish merchant ships also brought Catholic missionaries. One of the first, Francis Xavier, a co-founder of the Jesuit Order, went to India in the mid-sixteenth century looking for converts and later traveled throughout Southeast and East Asia. He spent two years in Japan, where he died in 1552, hoping to gain entry to China.

Japanese responses to Xavier and other Jesuits were mixed. Many ordinary Japanese found the new faith deeply meaningful, but the Japanese elite more often opposed it as disruptive and foreign. By 1580 more than 100,000 Japanese had become Christians, and one daimyo gave Jesuit missionaries the port city of Nagasaki (**NAH-guh-SAHK-kee**). In 1613 Date Masamune (**DAH-tay mah-suh-MOO-nay**), the fierce and independent daimyo of northern Honshu (**HOHN-shoo**), sent his own embassy to the Vatican, by way of the Philippines (where there were significant communities of Japanese merchants and pirates) and Mexico City. Some daimyo converts ordered their subjects to become Christians as well.

daimyo Literally, "great name(s)." Japanese warlords and great landowners, whose armed samurai gave them control of the Japanese islands from the eighth to the later nineteenth century. Under the Tokugawa Shogunate they were subordinated to the imperial government.

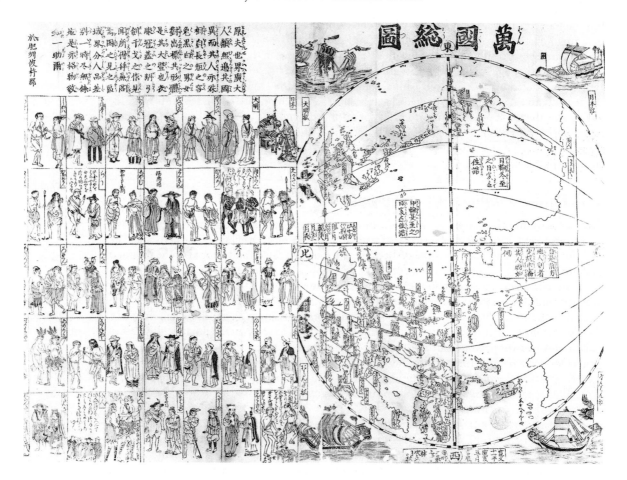

▲ **Comprehensive Map of the Myriad Nations**   Thanks to the "Dutch studies" scholars and to overseas contacts, many Japanese were well informed about the cultures, technologies, and political systems of various parts of the world. This combination map and ethnographic text of 1671 graphically explores the differences among the many peoples living or traveling in Asia. The map of the Pacific hemisphere has the north pole on the left and the south pole on the extreme right of the drawing.   Map of the World, 1671 (woodblock print), Japanese School, (17th century)/Private Collection/Bridgeman Images

By the early seventeenth century there were some 300,000 Japanese Christians and even some Japanese priests. However, suspicions about the intentions of the Europeans turned the shogunal regime against Christianity. A decree issued in 1614 banned Christianity and charged its adherents with seeking to overthrow true doctrine, change the government, and seize the country. Some missionaries left Japan; others worked underground. In 1617 the government began persecutions in earnest, and the beheadings, crucifixions, and forced recantations over the next several decades destroyed almost the entire Christian community. Small groups of Christians practiced their religion in secret, but missionary efforts were generally far less successful than in China, at least until the modern era.

To keep Christianity from resurfacing, a series of decrees issued between 1633 and 1639 sharply curtailed trade with Europe. Europeans who entered the country illegally faced the death penalty, and Japanese subjects were required to produce certificates from Buddhist temples attesting to their religious orthodoxy and loyalty to the regime.

The exclusion of Europe was not total, however. A few Dutch were permitted to reside on a small artificial island in Nagasaki's harbor, and a few Japanese were licensed to supply their needs. What these intermediaries learned about European weapons technology, shipbuilding, mathematics and astronomy, anatomy and medicine, and geography was termed "Dutch studies."

Japanese restrictions on the number of Chinese ships that could trade in Japan were harder to enforce. Regional lords in northern and southern Japan not only pursued overseas trade and piracy but also claimed dominion over islands between Japan and Korea and southward toward Taiwan, including present-day Okinawa. Despite such evasions, the new shogunate achieved substantial success in exercising its authority, keeping most daimyo from forming their own relations with European interests.

> ## Section Review
>
> - European merchants pursued trade contacts with China despite official resistance, and missionaries worked successfully until the eighteenth century.
>
> - The Qing and Europeans engaged in productive exchanges of ideas, and Chinese producers supplied growing European consumer markets.
>
> - The Japanese engaged in regulated trade with Europeans, but rising suspicions caused the Tokugawa to restrict foreign contacts.

21-2 The Imjin War and Japanese Unification

Why did Hideyoshi invade Korea and how did it affect East Asia?

The Imjin War, the largest pre-twentieth-century conflict in East Asian history, had no European involvement. Named in Korean for the year of the water dragon (Imjin), it also has many Chinese names, including "the Korean campaign." In Japan today, it is called "Hideyoshi's invasions." Seven years long (1592–1598), the war had lasting effects in Korea, facilitated the demise of the Ming dynasty in China, and produced bad feelings between Japan and Korea that have lasted down to the present.

Japan changed in three different dimensions between 1500 and 1800: internal and external military conflicts, political growth and strengthening, and expanded commercial and cultural contacts. Along with its relatively homogeneous population and natural boundaries, Japan's smaller size made political unification more achievable than in the great empire of China.

The Ashikaga Shogunate had weakened after the Onin War (see Chapter 13), opening opportunities for daimyo across Japan to fight for land and influence. Warfare among the different daimyo was common, and in the late 1500s it culminated in a prolonged civil war. Each daimyo had a castle town, a small bureaucracy, and a band of warriors, his *samurai*. Daimyo pledged a loose allegiance to the Japanese emperor and to the shogun residing in the capital city of Kyoto (**KYOH-toh**), but neither figure wielded significant political power. Three warlords, often referred to as the "three unifiers," gradually consolidated control over parts of Japan, ending in full unification in the early seventeenth century. First, Oda Nobunaga succeeded in unifying the central part of Japan, including the influential area around Kyoto. When he was betrayed by one of his generals, the second of the unifiers, Hideyoshi Toyotomi, avenged his death, taking control of Nobunaga's forces.

Although born a lowly peasant, Hideyoshi (**HEE-day-YOH-shee**) rose through the warrior ranks and eventually unified the country. Even as he was consolidating his control over Japan, he planned to invade Korea in order to conquer China. In addition, he dispatched retainers to meet officials as far away as the Spanish governor in the Philippines and the

AP® Exam Tip
Explain how rulers in this time period used military professionals to maintain centralized control.

samurai Literally "those who serve," the hereditary military elite of the Tokugawa Shogunate.

◀ **Tokugawa Ieyasu** One of Hideyoshi's allies and last of the "three unifiers." Like many warlords, Ieyasu's formal portrait is done wearing robes appropriate to his court rank, rather than in armor. This attests to the symbolic importance of the court and emperor in Kyoto even after their political power had waned. Portrait of Tokugawa Ieyasu (1543–1616), Japanese, 17th century, Japanese School (17th century)/Private Collection/Bridgeman Images

Portuguese viceroy in Goa (western India), demanding that they submit to him and send tribute. In 1592, buoyed with his progress in unifying Japan, the supremely confident Hideyoshi sent a 160,000-man invasion force to the Asian mainland. Various reasons are given for his decision to invade: to impress domestic rivals, to keep major daimyo busy fighting outside of Japan so they could not rebel, to push out Christian daimyo (who provided a sizable portion of the forces sent to Korea), and to dominate East Asian trade networks. His sights were set on China, however.

Several centuries of peace and court factionalism had left the Koreans ill prepared to handle the battle-tested samurai-led armies. But although the Koreans failed to implement large-scale musket manufacturing or training, a policy that changed after the war began, they did possess cannon. After initial disastrous defeats, what eventually saved them was assistance from the Ming Chinese and their own advanced naval strategy.

While daimyo armies sent to Korea were skilled at land-based fighting, the Japanese navy was unprepared for serious combat. To intercept a portion of the Japanese fleet, Korean admiral Yi Sunshin successfully deployed "turtle ships," highly maneuverable vessels with large cannon and completely covered decks. All told, Yi won some twenty-three consecutive naval battles. On land, the Koreans called upon China for help. Regarding Korea as one of its client states, China obliged. At first the Ming sent only a few thousand troops to Korea, but Hideyoshi's military successes and the fear that his armies might actually reach China convinced the emperor to send more soldiers, eventually totaling some 100,000.

After 1593, the Chinese negotiated a peace with the Japanese, but after a short time Hideyoshi decided that the terms of the peace were inadequate. His forces invaded again in 1597, employing brutal punitive measures as they advanced through the Korean peninsula. However, many daimyo were losing interest in Hideyoshi's dream of defeating China and hoped instead to secure a few provinces in southern Korea for Japan. In poor health, Hideyoshi too grew tired of the war. On his deathbed he gave an order to withdraw all troops from Korea, an order that was followed after his passing in 1598. It still took many years, however, for Japan to conclude peace with Korea. Formal relations did not resume until 1617.

The invasion devastated Korea. In the turmoil after the Japanese withdrawal, the Korean ruling class of nobles laid claim to so much taxpaying land that royal revenues may have fallen by two-thirds. Roughly 80 percent of the arable land was devastated and nearly 20 percent of the population lost, either killed in the fighting or taken as slaves to Japan. Confucian scholars and artisans were included in that number. The occasionally used phrase "pottery wars" refers to the fact that Korean pottery technology, in particular, was so advanced that transplanted Korean specialists transformed Japanese ceramics production in the postwar period.

China also suffered dire consequences. Fighting in Korea depleted the Ming coffers at a time when the empire was also battling peoples to the north. When the emperor established a new tax to recover revenue, protests erupted in the provinces. The battles in Manchuria weakened the Chinese garrisons there, permitting Manchu opposition to consolidate. Manchu forces invaded Korea in the 1620s and eventually compelled Korea to become a tributary state. By 1644 the Manchus would be in possession of Beijing, China's capital.

Section Review

- Following a civil war among the daimyo, Hideyoshi emerged as supreme warlord and invaded Korea as a step toward conquering China.

- Korean naval victories and the dispatch of Chinese armies to Korea blunted the Japanese invasion, which was finally canceled.

- Korea suffered long-lasting devastation from this war.

- The invasion also weakened the Ming dynasty and contributed to its fall.

21-3 Tokugawa Japan and Choson Korea to 1800

What challenges did different social groups face in Tokugawa Japan and Choson Korea?

21-3a Japanese Reunification and Economic Growth

Despite wartime losses, Japan flourished in the postwar era. After Hideyoshi's demise, the last of the three unifiers, Tokugawa Ieyasu (**TOH-koo-GAH-wah ee-ay-YAH-soo**) (1543–1616), asserted his domination over other daimyo and in 1603 established a new military regime known as the **Tokugawa Shogunate**. The shoguns also created a new administrative capital at Edo (**EH-doh**) (now Tokyo). Trade along the well-maintained road between Edo and the imperial capital of Kyoto promoted the development of the Japanese economy and the formation of other trading centers (see Map 21.1).

Although the Tokugawa Shogunate gave Japan more political unity than the islands had seen in centuries, the regionally based daimyo retained a great deal of power and autonomy. Ieyasu and his successors struggled for political centralization, but economic integration proved to be a more important feature of Tokugawa Japan. Because the shoguns required the daimyo to visit Edo frequently, good roads and maritime transport linked the city to the castle towns on three of Japan's four main islands. Commercial traffic developed along these routes, though wheeled vehicles were generally prohibited. Lords received their incomes locally in rice, and they paid their followers in rice. Recipients converted much of this rice into cash, a practice that led to the development of rice exchanges at Edo and at Osaka (**OH-sah-kah**), where merchants speculated in rice prices. By the late seventeenth century Edo was one of the largest cities in the world, with nearly a million inhabitants.

The domestic peace of the Tokugawa era forced the warrior class to adapt to the growing bureaucratic needs of the state. As the samurai became better educated and more attuned to the tastes of the civil elite, they became important customers for merchants dealing in silks, *sake* (**SAH-kay**) (rice wine), fans, porcelain, lacquerware, books, and moneylending. The state attempted—unsuccessfully—to curb the independence of the merchants when the economic well-being of the samurai was threatened by low rice prices or high interest rates.

The 1600s and 1700s were centuries of high achievement in artisanship. Japanese skills in steel making, pottery, and lacquerware were joined by excellence in the production of porcelain (see Environment & Technology: East Asian Porcelain), thanks in no small part to Korean experts brought back to Japan after the invasion of 1592. In the early 1600s manufacturers and merchants amassed enormous family fortunes. Several of the most important industrial and financial enterprises of the twentieth century—for instance, the Mitsui (**MIT-sue-ee**) companies—had their origins in sake breweries of the early Tokugawa period and then branched out into manufacturing, finance, and transport.

Wealthy merchants weakened the Tokugawa policy of controlling commerce by cultivating close alliances with their regional daimyo and, when possible, with the shogun himself. By the end of the 1700s the merchant families of Tokugawa Japan held the key to future modernization and the development of heavy industry.

21-3b Japanese Elite Decline and Social Crisis

During the 1700s population growth put a great strain on the well-developed lands of central Japan. In more remote provinces, where the lords promoted new settlements and agricultural expansion, the rate of economic growth was significantly greater.

Also troubling the Tokugawa government in the 1700s was the shogunate's inability to stabilize rice prices and halt the economic decline of the samurai. The Tokugawa government realized that the rice brokers could manipulate prices and interest rates to enrich themselves at the expense of the samurai, who had to convert their rice allotments into cash. Early Tokugawa laws designed to regulate interest and prices were later supplemented by laws requiring moneylenders to forgive samurai debts. But these laws were not always enforced. By the early 1700s many lords and samurai were dependent on the willingness of merchants to provide credit.

AP® Exam Tip
Consider the daimyo and samurai of Japan as examples of the fluctuating power of political and economic elites.

Tokugawa Shogunate The last of the three shogunates of Japan.

By the 1400s artisans in China, Korea, and Japan were all producing high-quality pottery with lustrous surface glazes. The best-quality pottery, intended for the homes of the wealthy and powerful, was made of pure white clay and covered with a hard translucent glaze. Artisans often added intricate decorations in cobalt blue and other colors. Cheaper pottery found a huge market in East Asia.

Such pottery was also exported to Southeast Asia, the Indian Ocean, East Africa, and the Middle East. Little found its way to Europe before 1600, but imports soared once the Dutch established trading bases in East Asia. Europeans called the high-quality ware "china" or "porcelain." Blue and white designs were especially popular.

One of the great centers of Chinese production was at the large artisan factory at Jingdezhen (**JING-deh-JUHN**). No sooner had the Dutch tapped into this source than the civil wars and Manchu conquests disrupted production in the middle 1600s. Desperate for a substitute source, the Dutch turned to porcelain from Japanese producers at Arita and Imari, near Nagasaki. Despite Japan's restriction of European trade, the Dutch East India Company transported some 190,000 pieces of Japanese ceramicware to the Netherlands between 1653 and 1682.

In addition to a wide range of Asian designs, Chinese and Japanese artisans made all sorts of porcelain for the European market. These included purely decorative pottery birds, vases, and pots as well as utilitarian vessels and dishes intended for table use. The serving dish illustrated here came from dinnerware sets the Japanese made especially for the Dutch East India Company. The VOC logo is the acronym of the company's name in Dutch. It is surrounded by Asian design motifs.

After peace returned in China, the VOC imported tens of thousands of Chinese porcelain pieces a year. The Chinese artisans sometimes produced imitations of Japanese designs that had become popular in Europe. Meanwhile, the Dutch were experimenting with making their own imitations of East Asian porcelain, right down to the Asian motifs and colors that had become so fashionable in Europe.

Questions for Analysis

1. What do people eat off of and serve food from if they don't have ceramic plates and bowls?

2. What connections suit pottery making to processes of mass production?

3. What role did porcelain play in influencing European appreciation of Chinese and Japanese artistic styles?

▲ **Japanese Export Porcelain** Part of a larger set made for the Dutch East India Company. Photograph Courtesy Peabody Essex Museum, #E83830

The legitimacy of the Tokugawa shoguns rested on their ability to reward and protect the interests of the lords and samurai who had supported their rise to power. Moreover, the Tokugawa government, like the governments of China, Korea, and Vietnam, accepted the Confucian idea that agriculture should be the basis of state wealth and that merchants, who were considered morally weak, should occupy lowly positions in society. Tokugawa decentralization, however, not only failed to hinder but actually stimulated the growth of commercial activities.

From the founding of the Tokugawa Shogunate in 1603 until 1800, the economy grew faster than the population. Household amenities and cultural resources that in China appeared only in the cities were common in the Japanese countryside. Despite official disapproval, merchants enjoyed relative freedom and influence in eighteenth-century Japan. They produced a vivid culture of their own, fostering the development of *kabuki* theater, colorful woodblock prints and silk-screened fabrics, and restaurants.

The "Forty-Seven Ronin" (**ROH-neen**) incident of 1701–1703 exemplified the ideological and social crisis of Japan's transformation from a military to a civil society. A senior minister provoked a young daimyo into drawing his sword at the shogun's court. For this offense the young lord was sentenced to commit *seppuku* (**SEP-poo-koo**), the ritual suicide of the samurai. His own followers then became *ronin*, "masterless samurai." Obliged by the traditional code of the warrior to avenge their deceased master, they broke into the house of the senior minister and killed him and others in his household. Then they withdrew to a temple in Edo and notified the shogun of what they had done out of loyalty to their lord and to avenge his death.

A legal debate ensued. To deny the righteousness of the ronin would be to deny samurai values. But to approve their actions would create social chaos, undermine laws against murder, and deny the shogunal government the right to try cases of samurai violence. The shogun ruled that the ronin had to die but would be permitted to die honorably by committing seppuku. Traditional samurai values had to surrender to the supremacy of law. The purity of purpose of the ronin is still celebrated in Japan, but since then Japanese writers, historians, and teachers have recognized that the self-sacrifice of the ronin for the sake of upholding civil law was necessary.

21-3c Choson Korea

Recovery after the Imjin War was hindered by Manchu invasions that lasted until the late 1630s. Even after the Korean king submitted to the new Qing dynasty, factionalism broke out among the officials that turned violent, an on-again, off-again problem throughout the Choson dynasty (1392–1910). Despite these challenges, the Choson dynasty proved to be the longest-lasting state in East Asian history (see Chapter 13). The dominant influence on Korean culture had long been China, to which Korean rulers generally paid tribute. Thus, although the Korean and Japanese languages are closely related, and although Korea had developed its own system of writing in 1443 and made extensive use of printing with movable type from the fifteenth century on, most printing continued to use Chinese characters.

In many ways the Choson dynasty was also a model Confucian state. The government was staffed by men who passed the civil examination system, modeled on the Chinese institution of the same name. But there was one important difference. In theory, if not in practice, anyone could sit for the civil examinations in China, but by the sixteenth century in Choson Korea, one had to be born into the *yangban* (YAHNG-bahn) class to take an examination and work in any position of real influence in government. The yangban, literally "two orders," were a hereditary status group who dominated the civil and military examinations, filling nearly all of the official positions in the national and local governments. Only occasionally was social mobility possible for commoners who tested into the military yangban group, a status typically disdained by the civil yangban. This played a role in stifling recovery from the devastation of war.

The growing influence of Confucianism throughout the Choson dynasty affected attitudes toward women, as it did throughout East Asia. In the previous Koryo period, and early Choson, women were listed in family genealogies alongside their brothers, even after marriage. By the latter part of the Choson dynasty, however, when a woman married, she was removed from her natal family's register. As in China, Confucian teachings discouraged widows from remarrying. Like China and Japan, however, Korean women negotiated Confucian dogma toward women. Women dominated shaman positions, influencing royalty, while some women even became philosophers.

Unlike the majority of commoners, the yangban did not have to pay a household tax, nor did they have to serve in the military (unless they were military yangban). During the Choson period they also owned most of the slaves, which at one point made up nearly 30 percent of the population. In addition to privately owned slaves, local governments also maintained slaves for a variety of clerical and labor jobs. Even Buddhist temples owned slaves. The slave population dropped to about 10 percent in the eighteenth century, when runaway slaves increased and the poor economy meant that most yangban simply hired poor commoners to work in agriculture.

▲ **Woodblock Print of the "Forty-Seven Ronin" Story**   The saga of the Forty-Seven Ronin and the avenging of their fallen leader has fascinated the Japanese public since the event occurred in 1702. This colored woodcut from the Tokugawa period shows members of the group preparing to break into the compound of the court official who occasioned their lord's ritual suicide.   Universal History Archive/Universal Images Group/Getty Images

AP® Exam Tip
Consider the changes and continuities of Chinese influence on Japan and Korea throughout history.

yangban In Koryo and especially Choson Korea, a term for the "two orders," the civil and the military elite families who, by passing government examinations, dominated the Choson Korean bureaucracy and cultural life.

Section Review

- The Tokugawa Shogunate completed the unification of Japan and moved the capital to Edo (Tokyo).

- Economic growth nourished a new merchant-class culture.

- The position of the samurai deteriorated under economic and social pressures.

- The Korean noble class stifled recovery from wartime devastation.

21-4 **From Ming to Qing**

How did China deal with military and political challenges both inside and outside its borders?

The internal and external forces at work in China were different from those in Japan and operated on a much larger scale, but they led in similar directions. By 1800 China had a greatly enhanced empire, an expanding economy, and growing doubts about the importance of European trade and Christianity.

21-4a **Ming Economic Growth, 1500–1644**

The economic and cultural achievements of the early **Ming Empire** (see Chapter 13) continued during the 1500s. But this productive period was followed by many decades of political weakness, warfare, and rural woes until a new dynasty, the Qing from Manchuria, guided China back to peace and prosperity.

European accounts from the early sixteenth century express astonishment at the power, exquisite manufactures, and vast population of Ming China, where cities had long been culturally and commercially vibrant. Many large landowners and absentee landlords lived in town, as did officials, artists, and rich merchants who had purchased ranks or prepared their sons for the examinations. The elite classes had created a brilliant culture in which novels, operas, poetry, porcelain, and painting were all closely interwoven. Catering to these urban elites were many small businesses that prospered through printing, tailoring, running restaurants, or selling paper, ink, ink-stones, and writing brushes. The imperial government operated factories for the production of ceramics and silks, and enormous government complexes at Jingdezhen and elsewhere invented assembly-line techniques and produced large quantities of high-quality ceramics for sale in China and abroad.

Despite these achievements, serious problems developed that left the Ming Empire economically and politically exhausted. There is evidence that the climate changes known as the Little Ice Age in seventeenth-century Europe affected the climate in China as well (see Issues in World History: The Little Ice Age). Annual temperatures dropped, reached a low point around 1645, and remained low until the early 1700s. The resulting agricultural distress and famine fueled large uprisings that hastened the end of the Ming Empire. The devastation caused by these uprisings and the spread of epidemic disease resulted in steep declines in local populations.

The rapid urban growth and business speculation that were part of the burgeoning trading economy also produced problems. Some provinces suffered from price inflation caused by the flood of silver from America. In contrast to the growing involvement of European governments in promoting economic growth, the Ming government pursued some policies that hindered growth. Ming governments persisted, despite earlier failed experiments, in issuing new paper money and copper coinage, even after silver had won the approval of the markets. Corruption compounded government problems. Disorder and inefficiency came to plague the imperial factories, touching off strikes in the late sixteenth and seventeenth centuries. During a labor protest at Jingdezhen in 1601, workers threw themselves into the kilns to protest working conditions.

Yet the urban and industrial sectors of later Ming society fared much better than the agricultural sector. Despite knowledge of new African and American crops gained from European traders, farmers were slow to change their ways. Neither the rice-growing regions in southern China nor the wheat-growing regions in northern China experienced a meaningful increase in productivity under the later Ming. After 1500 economic depression in the countryside, combined with recurring epidemics in central and southern China, kept rural population growth in check.

21-4b **Ming Collapse and the Rise of the Qing**

Environmental, economic, and administrative problems aside, the primary reasons for the fall of the Ming Empire were internal rebellion and threats on the borders. Powerful Mongol federations in the north and west had long exerted pressure on the frontiers. In the late 1500s large numbers of Mongols were unified by their devotion to the Dalai Lama (**DAH-lie LAH-mah**), or universal teacher of Tibetan Buddhism. Building on this spiritual unity, a brilliant leader named Galdan restored Mongolia as a regional military power around 1600. At the same time, the Manchus,

AP® Exam Tip
Explain how the flow of silver from the Americas helped to facilitate a new global circulation of goods and deeply impacted the Chinese economy and culture.

Ming Empire Empire based in China that Zhu Yuanzhang established after the overthrow of the Yuan Empire. The Ming emperor Yongle sponsored the building of the Forbidden City and the voyages of Zheng He. The later years of the Ming saw a slowdown in technological development and economic decline.

an agricultural people who controlled the region north of Korea, grew stronger in the northeast (see chapter opening).

Pirates based in southwest Japan, Okinawa, and Taiwan, many of them Japanese, frequently looted the southeast coast. Ming military resources, concentrated against the Mongols and the Manchus in the north, could not be deployed to defend the coasts. As a result, many southern Chinese migrated to Southeast Asia to profit from the sea-trading networks of the Indian Ocean.

The Imjin War had prompted the Ming to seek the assistance of Manchu troops that then became enemies after the war. With the rebel leader Li Zicheng in possession of Beijing (see the beginning of this chapter) and the emperor dead by his own hand, a Ming general joined forces with the Manchu leaders in the summer of 1644. Instead of restoring the Ming, however, the Manchus claimed China for their own (see Map 21.1) and began a forty-year conquest of the rest of the Ming territories, as well as Taiwan and parts of Mongolia and Central Asia (see Diversity & Dominance: The Manchu Moment: From Ming to Qing).

A Manchu family headed the new **Qing Empire**, and Manchu generals commanded the military forces. But Manchus made up a very small portion of the population. Most Qing officials, soldiers, merchants, and farmers were ethnic Chinese. Like other successful invaders of China, the Qing soon adopted Chinese institutions and policies.

AP® Exam Tip
Compare the challenges faced by the late Ming dynasty with the challenges faced by other dynasties in their decline.

Qing Empire Empire established in China by Manchus who overthrew the Ming Empire in 1644. At various times the Qing also controlled Manchuria, Mongolia, Turkestan, and Tibet. The last Qing emperor was overthrown in 1911.

MAP 21.1   The Qing Empire, 1644–1783 The Qing Empire began in Manchuria and captured north China in 1644. Between 1644 and 1783 the Qing conquered all the former Ming territories and added Taiwan, the lower Amur River basin, Inner Mongolia, eastern Turkestan, and Tibet. The resulting state was more than twice the size of the Ming Empire.

What problems did the Manchu rulers encounter in dealing with the ethnic diversity of the Qing Empire?

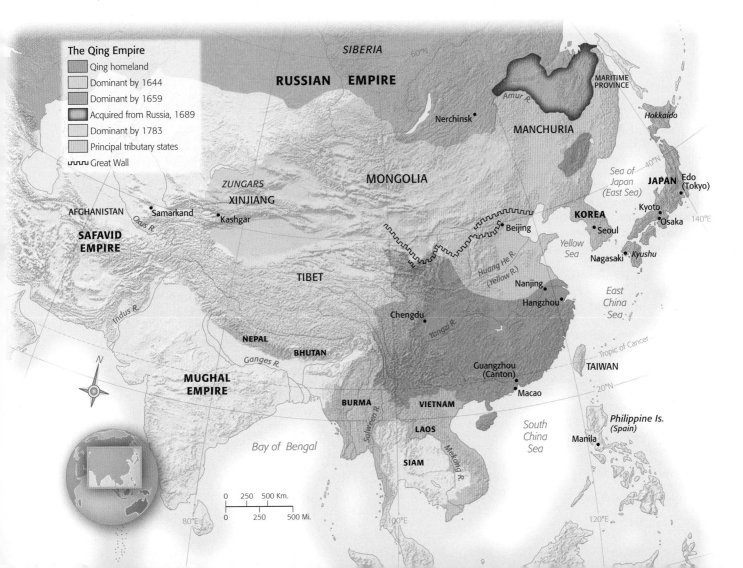

The Manchu elite, like conquerors of other periods, combined enjoyment of the fruits of victory with brutal actions to suppress resistance among their Chinese subjects. The most delicate of sensibilities can be found in the writings of Manchu women close to the Qing court, but in the field masculine brutality held sway until a proper administration was established.

The Qing were not eager for reminders of their brutal takeover to circulate. This rare eyewitness account smuggled out of China reveals not just the violence of the conquest but also the diversity of its impact on men and women, rich and poor.

The account begins in 1645 as rumors of approaching Manchu soldiers spread through Yangzhou, an important city near the juncture of the Yangzi River and the Grand Canal, and the soldiers charged with its defense begin to flee.

Crowds of barefoot and disheveled refugees were flocking into the city. When questioned, they were too distraught to reply. At that point dozens of mounted soldiers in confused waves came surging south looking as though they had given up all hope. Among them appeared a man who turned out to be the commandant himself. It seems he had intended to leave by the east gate but could not because the enemy soldiers outside the wall were drawing too near; he was therefore forced to cut across this part of town to reach the south gate. This is how we first learned for sure that the enemy troops would enter the city. . . .

My house backed against the city wall, and peeping through the chinks in my window, I saw the soldiers on the wall marching south then west, solemn and in step. Although the rain was beating down, it did not seem to disturb them. This reassured me because I gathered that they were well-disciplined units.

. . . For a long time no one came. I retreated again to the back window and found that the regiment on the wall had broken ranks; some soldiers were walking about, others standing still.

All of a sudden I saw some soldiers escorting a group of women dressed in Yangzhou fashion. This was my first real shock. Back in the house, I said to my wife, "Should things go badly when the soldiers enter the city, you may need to end your life."

"Yes," she replied, "Whatever silver we have you should keep. I think we women can stop thinking about life in this world." She gave me all the silver, unable to control her crying. . . .

Soon my younger brother arrived, then my two older brothers. We discussed the situation and I said, "The people who live in our neighborhood are all rich merchants. It will be disastrous if they think we are rich too." I then urged my brothers to brave the rain and quickly take the women by the back route to my older brother's house. His home was situated behind Mr. He's graveyard and was surrounded by the huts of poor families. . . .

The cunning soldiers, suspecting that many people were still hidden, tried to entice them out by posting a placard promising clemency. About fifty to sixty people, half of them women, emerged. My elder brother said, "We four by ourselves will never survive if we run into these vicious soldiers, so we had better join the crowd. Since there are so many of them, escape will be easier. . . ."

The leaders were three Manchu soldiers. They searched my brothers and found all the silver they were carrying, but left me untouched. At that point some women appeared, two of whom called out to me. I recognized them as the concubines of my friend Mr. Zhu Shu and stopped them anxiously. They were disheveled and partly naked, their feet bare and covered with mud up to the ankles. One was holding a girl whom the soldiers hit with a whip and threw into the mud. Then we were immediately driven on. One soldier, sword in hand, took the lead; another drove us from behind with a long spear; and a third walked along on our right and left flanks alternately, making sure no one escaped. In groups of twenty or thirty we were herded along like sheep and cattle. If we faltered we were struck, and some people were even killed on the spot. The women were tied together with long chains around their necks, *like a clumsy string of pearls. Stumbling at every step, they were soon covered with mud. Here and there on the ground lay babies, trampled by people or horses.*

. . . We then entered the house of [a] merchant, . . . which had been taken over by the three soldiers. Another soldier was already there. He had seized several attractive women and was rifling their trunks for fancy silks, which he piled in a heap. Seeing the three soldiers arrive, he laughed and pushed several dozen of us into the back hall. The women he led into a side chamber. . . .

The three soldiers stripped the women of their wet clothing all the way to their underwear, then ordered the seamstress to measure them and give them new garments. The women, thus coerced, had to expose themselves and stand naked. What shame they endured! Once they had changed, the soldiers grabbed them and forced them to join them in eating and drinking, then did whatever they pleased with them, without any regard for decency. . . .

At length, however, there came a soldier of the "Wolf Men" tribe, a vicious-looking man with a head like a mouse and eyes like a hawk. He attempted to abduct my wife. She was obliged to creep forward on all fours, pleading as she had with the others, but to no avail. . . . Just then they ran into a body of mounted soldiers. One of them said a few words to the soldier in Manchu. At this he dropped my wife and departed with them. Barely able to crawl back, she let out a loud sob, every part of her body injured. . . .

Unexpectedly there appeared a handsome looking man of less than thirty, a double-edged sword hung by his side, dressed in Manchu-style hat, red coat, and a pair of black boots. His follower, in a yellow jacket, was also very gallant in appearance. Immediately behind them were several residents of Yangzhou. The young man in red, inspecting me closely, said, "I would judge from your appearance that you are not one of these people. Tell me honestly, what class of person are you?"

I remembered that some people had obtained pardons and others had lost their lives the moment they said that they were poor scholars. So I did not dare come out at once with the truth and instead concocted a story. He pointed to my wife and son and asked who they were, and I told him the truth. "Tomorrow the prince will order that all swords be sheathed and all of you will be spared," he said and then commanded his followers to give us some clothes and an ingot of silver. He also asked me, "How many days have you been without food?"

"Five days," I replied.

"Then come with me," he commanded. Although we only half trusted him, we were afraid to disobey. He led us to a well-stocked house, full of rice, fish, and other provisions. "Treat these four people well," he said to a woman in the house and then left. . . .

[May 2]. Civil administration was established in all the prefectures and counties; proclamations were issued aimed at calming the people, and monks from each temple were ordered to burn corpses. The temples themselves were clogged with women who had taken refuge, many of whom had died of fright or starvation. The "List of Corpses Burned" records more than eight hundred thousand, and this list does not include those who jumped into wells, threw themselves into the river, hanged themselves, were burned to death inside houses, or were carried away by the soldiers.

Decades after the massacre at Yangzhou, Qing court society was ornamented by a number of female poets writing in Manchu. The poetry of Miss Nalan, the youngest daughter of a wealthy Manchu official named Nalan Ming-zhu, was published by her nephew, whose wife Sibo was also a poet. Miss Nalan's poetry captures the atmosphere of northern China where the Manchu court was located.

Freezing Crows
They're waiting for return of spring, this flock of evening crows;
Lingering in the trees they fly about without a pattern.
When spring is back, there is no need for you to stay around:
There will be yellow orioles to grab the finest flowers!

A Peasant Family
Where in this spring breeze will I find Peach Blossom fairyland?
Here in this mountain village where the little birds are chirping.

Now when the peasant has come home, the sun is setting fast—
As darkness falls, a lonely moon shines on the simple door.

Northern Winds
How strong these freezing gales on level plains:
They blow the bitter fleabane from its roots.
With their great noise they shake the brightest sun;
Deliberately they stir up gloomy dusk.
The falling leaves drift through the door in front;
The startled sand disturbs the distant village.
And I recall how standing under flowers
My sleeves once whisked away the warmth of spring.

Sibo, the nephew's wife, following earlier Chinese custom, wrote an essay on instructions for daughters.

Our family has enjoyed the Imperial Grace for several generations, and official appointments have followed one upon the other. Our family status can be called grand indeed! I joined this family at the age of fifteen when I married your father. I served the elder generations and assigned the servants their tasks, so all family affairs were well ordered. But unfortunately your father abandoned us in his middle years and he did not live to see you reach adulthood. . . .

At present your younger brother Ning-xiu already has completed his studies and he also very much follows my teachings. Moreover, His Majesty the Emperor, filled with loving care and concern, has entrusted him with an important post, yet I still do not dare allow him to follow his inclinations and constantly remind him [of his duties]. You, sisters, grew up in the inner apartments and have little experience, so how can I not instruct you? You have to realize that as long as you as daughters live with your parents, you may be forgiven and not punished even if your character is not yet transformed and your behavior not yet perfect. But once you have a husband and become a wife, you will have to prepare the dishes for the ancestral sacrifices and provide for the succeeding generations. In between you, will have to serve your parents-in-law, assist your lord and master, raise your sons and daughters, and command servants and slaves.

AP® History Reasoning Skills

Comparison *What do the women fleeing for their lives have in common with the women living in court? What ethnic differences between Manchus and Chinese are present in these excerpts?*

Sources: From *CHINESE CIVILIZATION: A Sourcebook*, 2nd Edition by Patricia Buckley Ebrey. Copyright © 1981 by The Free Press, a Division of Simon & Schuster, Inc. Copyright © 1993 by Patricia Buckley Ebrey. Reprinted by permission of Simon & Schuster, Inc. All rights reserved. *Two Centuries of Manchu Women Poets: An Anthology.* pp. 40, 42, 46, 47. © 2017. Reprinted with permission of the University of Washington Press.

21-4c **Emperor Kangxi**

The seventeenth and eighteenth centuries—particularly the reigns of the **Kangxi (KAHNG-shee)** (r. 1662–1722) and Qianlong **(chee-YEN-loong)** (r. 1736–1796) emperors—saw renewed economic, military, and cultural achievement in China. Roads and waterworks were repaired, transit taxes lowered, rents and interest rates cut, and incentives established for resettling areas devastated by peasant rebellions. Foreign trade was encouraged. Vietnam, Burma, and Nepal sent embassies to the Qing tribute court and carried the latest Chinese fashions back home. Overland routes from Korea to Central Asia revived.

Kangxi Qing emperor (r. 1662–1722). He oversaw the greatest expansion of the Qing Empire.

Amur River This river valley was a contested frontier between northern China and eastern Russia until the settlement arranged in the Treaty of Nerchinsk (1689).

The Manchu aristocrats who led the conquest of Beijing and north China dominated the first Qing emperor and served as regents for his young son, who was declared emperor in 1662. This child-emperor, Kangxi, sparred politically with the regents until 1669, when at age sixteen he executed the chief regent and thereby gained real control of the government. An intellectual prodigy who had mastered classical Chinese, Manchu, and Mongolian and memorized the Chinese classics, Kangxi guided imperial expansion and maintained stability until his death in 1722.

In the north, the Qing rulers feared an alliance between Galdan's Mongol state and the expanding Russian presence along the **Amur (AH-moor) River**. In the 1680s Qing forces attacked the wooden forts built by hardy Russian scouts on the river's northern bank. Neither empire sent large forces into the Amur territories, so the contest was partly a struggle for the goodwill of the local peoples. The Qing emperor emphasized the importance of treading lightly in the struggle:

Upon reaching the lands of the Evenks and the Dagurs you will send to announce that you have come to hunt deer. Meanwhile, keep a careful record of the distance and go, while hunting, along the northern bank of the Amur until you come by the shortest route to the town of Russian settlement at Albazin. Thoroughly reconnoiter its location and situation. I don't think the Russians will take a chance on attacking you. If they offer you food, accept it and show your gratitude. If they do attack you, don't fight back. In that case, lead your people and withdraw into our own territories.[2]

Qing forces twice attacked Albazin. The Qing were worried about Russian alliances with other frontier peoples, while Russia wished to protect its access to the furs, timber, and metals concentrated in Siberia and Manchuria. The Qing and Russians were also rivals for control of northern Asia's Pacific coast. Seeing little benefit in continued conflict, in 1689 the two empires negotiated the Treaty of Nerchinsk, using Jesuit missionaries as interpreters. The treaty fixed the border along the Amur River and regulated trade across it. Although this was a thinly settled area, the treaty proved important, and the frontier it demarcated has long endured.

The next step was to settle the Mongolian frontier. Kangxi personally led troops in the great campaigns that defeated Galdan, and by 1691 he had brought Inner Mongolia under Qing control.

21-4d **Tea and Diplomacy**

Like the Ming before them, the Qing were reluctant to grant too much access to Europeans. To maintain control over trade, facilitate tax collection, and suppress piracy, the Qing permitted only one market point for each foreign sector. Thus Europeans could trade only at Canton.

This system worked well enough until the late 1700s, when Britain became worried about its massive trade deficit with China. From bases in India and Singapore, British traders moved eastward and by the early 1700s dominated European trading in

▲ **Emperor Kangxi** In a portrait from about 1690, the young Manchu ruler is portrayed as a refined scholar in the Confucian tradition. He was a scholar and had great intellectual curiosity, but this portrait would not suggest that he was also capable of leading troops in battle. Wu Chingteng Xinhua News Agency/Newscom

[2]Adapted from G. V. Melikhov, "Manzhou Penetration into the Basin of the Upper Amur in the 1680s," in *Manzhou Rule in China*, ed. S. L. Tikhvinshii (Moscow: Progress Publishers, 1983).

Canton, displacing the Dutch. The directors of the East India Company (EIC) anticipated limitless profits from China's gigantic markets and advanced technologies.

One product of interest was tea. In medieval and early modern times, tea from China had spread overland to Russia, Central Asia, and the Middle East to become a prized import. Consumers knew it by its northern Chinese name, *cha*—as did the Portuguese. Other western Europeans acquired tea from the sea routes and with it the name used in the Fujian province of coastal China and Taiwan: *te*. In much of Europe, tea competed with chocolate and coffee as a fashionable drink by the mid-1600s.

British tea importers accumulated great fortunes. However, the Qing Empire took payment in silver and rarely bought anything from Britain. With domestic revenues declining in the later 1700s, the Qing government needed the silver and was disinclined to loosen import restrictions. To make matters worse, the EIC had managed its worldwide holdings badly. As it teetered on bankruptcy, its attempts to manipulate Parliament became increasingly intrusive. In 1792 the British government dispatched Lord George Macartney, a well-connected peer with practical experience in Russia and India, to China. Staffed by scientists, artists, and translators as well as guards and diplomats, the **Macartney mission** showed Britain's great interest in the Qing Empire as well as the EIC's desire to revise the trade system.

To fit Chinese traditions, Macartney portrayed himself as a "tribute emissary" come to salute the Qianlong emperor's eightieth birthday. However, he refused to perform the kowtow, though he did agree to bow on one knee as he would to King George III. The Qianlong emperor received Macartney courteously in September 1793 but refused to alter the Canton trading system, open new ports of trade, or allow the British to establish a permanent mission in Beijing. The emperor sent a letter to King George explaining that China had no need to increase its foreign trade, had no use for Britain's ingenious devices and manufactures, and set no value on closer diplomatic ties.

Dutch, French, and Russian missions to achieve what Macartney could not do also failed. European frustration mounted while admiration for China faded. The Qing court would not communicate with foreign envoys or observe the simplest rules of the European diplomatic system. In Macartney's view, China was like a venerable old warship, well maintained and splendid to look at, but obsolete and no longer up to the task.

21-4e Population Growth and Environmental Stress

The Chinese who escorted Macartney and his entourage in 1792–1793 took them through China's prosperous cities and productive farmland. They did not see, however, the economic and environmental decline that had set in during the last decades of the 1700s.

Population growth—a tripling in size since 1500—had intensified demand for food and for more intensive agriculture. With an estimated 350 million people in the late 1700s, China had twice the population of all of Europe. Despite efficient farming and the gradual adoption of New World crops like corn and sweet potatoes, population pressure touched off social and environmental problems. Increased demand for building materials and firewood shrank woodlands. Deforestation, in turn, accelerated wind and water erosion and increased flooding. Dams and dikes were not maintained, and silted-up river channels were not dredged. By the end of the eighteenth century parts of the thousand-year-old Grand Canal linking the rivers of north and south China were nearly unusable, and the towns that bordered it were starved for commerce.

Some interior districts responded to this misery by increasing their output of export goods like tea, cotton, and silk. Some peasants sought seasonal jobs in better-off agricultural areas or worked in low-status jobs such as barge pullers, charcoal burners, or night soil (human waste) carriers. Begging, prostitution, and theft increased in the cities. Rebellions broke out in flood-ravaged central and southwestern China. Indigenous peoples concentrated in the less fertile lands in the south and in the northern and western borderlands of the empire often joined in revolts (see Map 21.2).

AP® Exam Tip
Consider how European trading was limited by the authority of local states.

AP® Exam Tip
Compare the effects of the Columbian Exchange in China with its effects in Europe and Africa.

Macartney mission The unsuccessful attempt by the British Empire to establish diplomatic relations with the Qing Empire.

Section Review

- After the year 1500, financial, environmental, and administrative problems weakened the Ming Empire, and it fell to the Manchus.

- Kangxi expanded the Qing Empire's borders, subdued or contained rival powers, and presided over a flourishing economy and culture.

- The one-sided Qing trading system prompted the Macartney mission and other European embassies to the Qing court, but the Qing refused all requests for more equitable trading conditions.

- By the late eighteenth century, population growth had created social and environmental problems that the Qing could not control.

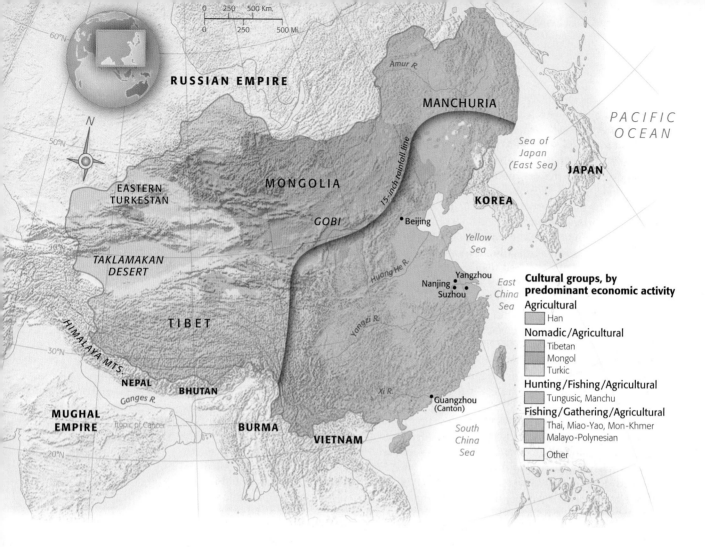

MAP 21.2 Climate and Diversity in the Qing Empire The Qing Empire encompassed different environmental zones, and the climate differences corresponded to population density and cultural divisions. Wetter regions to the east of the 15-inch rainfall line also contained the most densely populated 20 percent of Qing land. The drier, less densely populated 80 percent of the empire was home to the greatest portion of peoples who spoke languages other than Chinese. Many were nomads, fishermen, hunters, and farmers who raised crops other than rice.

Do the advantages of being able to draw on the resources of many different environmental zones outweigh the problems of governing a huge, diverse empire?

The Qing government was not up to controlling its vast empire. It was twice the size of the Ming geographically, but it employed about the same number of officials. The government's dependence on working alliances with local elites had led to widespread corruption and shrinking government revenues. The Qing's spectacular rise had ended, and decline had set in.

21-5 Conclusion

It would be a mistake to think of early modern East Asia as three strictly defined countries filled with people who invariably acted on behalf of their homelands in trade or warfare. During the Imjin War, some Japanese grew tired of fighting in Korea, decided to join the Ming military, and were promoted to high posts by the Chinese. Similarly, some Chinese troops remained in Korea, married local women, and became part of local Korean communities.

Trade and warfare also presented opportunities for groups of people who did not identify with any one country. For example, the Ming–Qing transition and growth in sea trade spurred an increase in piracy during the seventeenth century. The Zheng family dominated piracy in East Asia, defeated the Dutch bases in Taiwan, and eventually worked for the Ming regime to battle the Manchu. The most prominent Zheng pirate-merchant was the half-Japanese, half-Chinese Zheng Chenggong. An enemy of the Qing, he continued to expand the Zheng enterprise and was well known even among Europeans in Asia, who called him Koxinga, the European pronunciation for the name given to him by the Ming loyalists. Even early modern Japanese knew of his exploits through puppet plays. The Zheng also pursued state-building activities, such as establishing an office to collect taxes and regulating trade in the South China Sea.

China is one example of the flourishing of empires in Eurasia between 1500 and 1800. Already a vast empire under the Ming, China doubled in size under the Qing, mostly through westward expansion into less densely populated areas. Like the Russian, Ottoman, and Mughal Empires, it had the strengths and problems of administrative control and tax collection that characterized a large land-based state. The expansion of China incorporated not just new lands but also new peoples. Chinese society had long been diverse, and its geographical, occupational, linguistic, and religious differences grew as the Qing expanded (see Map 21.1). China had also long used Confucian models, imperial customs, and a common system of writing to transcend such differences and to assimilate elites.

Japan was different. Though it was nominally headed by an emperor, real power lay with the successive shoguns. However, Japan lacked a centralizing, common political philosophy like China's Confucianism, which became a common denominator for a wide variety of elites from different cultures, ethnicities, and regions. Tokugawa Japan was similar in size and population to France, the most powerful state of western Europe, but its political system was much more decentralized. As the chapter has shown, Japan's efforts to add colonies on the East Asian mainland failed.

By the late eighteenth century, the weaknesses in China and Japan were becoming more evident to Europeans and would ultimately make these countries vulnerable to Western penetration. China had once led the world in military innovation, including the first uses of gunpowder, but Chinese armies continued to depend on superior numbers and tactics for their success rather than on new technology. Infantrymen armed with guns served alongside others armed with bows and arrows, swords, and spears. The military forces of Japan underwent more innovative changes than those of China and Korea, in part through Western contacts, and in the course of its sixteenth-century wars of unification, Japan produced its own gunpowder revolution. Thereafter, however, it lacked the means to stay abreast of the world's most advanced military technology.

Finally, neither China nor Japan developed navies commensurate with their size and coastlines. Korea had a small but effective navy during the Imjin War, but it could not match China's or Russia's in strength or size. China's defenses against pirates and other sea invaders were left to the small war junks of its maritime provinces, and Japan's naval capacity was similarly decentralized. In 1792, when Russian ships exploring the North Pacific turned toward the Japanese coast, the local daimyo used his own forces to chase them away. All Japanese daimyo understood that they would be on their own if and when foreign incursions increased. As later chapters show, these foreign incursions became reality in the nineteenth century.

Key Terms

Manchu p. 533	Tokugawa Shogunate	Ming Empire p. 542	Amur River p. 546
daimyo p. 536	p. 539	Qing Empire p. 543	Macartney mission p. 547
samurai p. 537	*yangban* p. 541	Kangxi p. 546	

Review Questions

1. What were the crucial differences between Tang China and Ming China?

2. How can the unification of Japan be compared with the almost simultaneous rise of the English monarchy, both being located on islands off the coast of more developed continental states?

3. Does the conquest of China by Manchus bear comparison to the so-called "barbarian" invasions of the Roman Empire?

Material Culture
Four-Wheeled Vehicles

Most modern motor transport is based on the principle of the four-wheeled vehicle. Yet prior to the spread of European technologies and tastes in the age of imperialism, four-wheeled vehicles were rarely seen outside of Europe. The wheeled transport of Central Asia, India, and Southeast Asia was almost exclusively of the two-wheeled cart variety. China made extensive use of single-wheeled wheelbarrows, but wheeled vehicles of any kind were rarely used in Japan and the Middle East.

Economically, the two-wheeled cart was generally superior to the four-wheeled wagon throughout the era of animal-drawn transport. The power a team of oxen or horses could exert did not change with the number of wheels. But each added axle, that is, each additional pair of wheels, increased the friction the animals had to overcome in pulling and also added weight to the vehicle. So even though a wagon might have more space than a cart, the weight that could be loaded was invariably smaller.

Four-wheeled vehicles had the additional disadvantage of being difficult to steer. Paved roads were rare, and rutted dirt tracks made for a bumpy ride unless the wheels were of great diameter. Three feet (1 meter) was a common size. However, such large wheels could not turn very far when the front axle pivoted because they hit the frame of the wagon, and raising the wagon-bed more than 3 feet above the ground to allow them to turn beneath it made the vehicle unstable. Limited to a turning radius of only a few degrees, or more often being constrained by a nonpivoting axle, four-wheeled vehicles could not readily operate in towns and other places where sharp turns were

◀ **Nineteenth-Century Children's Carriage**
This nineteenth-century children's carriage shows the essential changes that defined the coach. The small front wheels turn under the body of the carriage when the front axle pivots in the center. The back wheels are much larger. And the passenger compartment is suspended on springs that run from the front to the back of the vehicle. Erich Lessing/Art Resource, NY

required. Yet making the front wheels smaller so they could turn underneath the wagon-bed made the vehicle difficult to use on rough roads.

Despite these limitations, archaeological evidence shows that both four-wheeled and two-wheeled vehicles were used in Europe, Central Asia, and the Middle East from the fourth millennium BCE onward. By the later days of the Roman Empire, the two-wheeled chariot, formerly the vehicle of warriors, had disappeared, and noblemen had taken to riding horseback. Eventually wagons gave way to carts in Central Asia and disappeared entirely in the Middle East. Yet they continued to be used in Europe.

The reasons for European persistence in an inefficient mode of transport are not clear. However, ancient and medieval images suggest that four-wheeled wagons were used primarily for passengers from the upper classes. More specifically, many images show groups of female passengers. Wagons had advantages as conveyances for elite women. They could easily be enclosed for privacy, and they could hold a noblewoman and her female attendants, thus eliminating the dangers of traveling with only a male driver.

Increased comfort probably played a role in a series of technological improvements that began around the fifteenth century. The word *coach*, of Hungarian origin, signaled the new designs. Pivoting front axles became common, while better paving, particularly in towns, accommodated smaller front wheels. To reduce jolting, the passenger cabin was first suspended on chains or leather straps and later on springs. Efficient harnessing techniques that had first appeared centuries earlier made possible larger teams of animals, heavier vehicles, and faster speeds. And brakes were developed to help manage the heavier loads.

Coach and carriage designs, particularly associated with the upper classes, became more sophisticated over the following centuries. Charles Darwin's grandfather, Erasmus Darwin, was the first to design a steering system of the type used today on automobiles in which each front wheel turns separately while the axle remains fixed. The four-wheeled coach became the basis for steam locomotives and railway carriages, and eventually for the automobile. Other parts of the world adopted European transport designs after European traders and diplomats imported them as symbols of modernity.

However, the question remains: Why did the Europeans stick with inefficient four-wheeled wagons for over 4,000 years when other parts of the world opted exclusively for the two-wheeled alternative? It is unlikely that providing a private traveling compartment for groups of elite women was the sole reason. But the fact that such traveling accommodations became available may offer a technological clue as to why upper-class women in the Middle East, China, India, and other non-European lands were so often prohibited from leaving the house whereas European women enjoyed relatively greater freedom of movement.

Questions for Analysis

1. How might the absence of four-wheeled vehicles have retarded the adoption of automobiles outside of Europe and North America?

2. How might the lighter weight of two-wheeled carts and, in China, one-wheeled wheelbarrows have affected the building of roads?

3. Does the appearance of "woman driver" as a negative stereotype in the 20th century reflect a longer history of gender difference in transportation history?

Issues in World History
The Little Ice Age

Scientific research has revealed that large areas of the globe experienced colder average temperatures from the early fourteenth century to the nineteenth century, a period commonly called the Little Ice Age. The current consensus is that global temperatures averaged about 1° Fahrenheit (0.56° Celsius) cooler than usual, although periods of much colder average temperature have been identified during this period as well. What appears a modest decrease in average temperature had a powerful effect on agricultural production as a succession of shorter and wetter summers led to smaller harvests or, in some cases, to catastrophic harvest failures. Modern scientists now believe that these climate-induced crises were most likely triggered by intense cycles of volcanic activity.

Volcanic eruptions send ash high into the atmosphere, dispersing over large areas of the globe and reducing the amount of solar radiation reaching the earth. Volcanos also emit a large volume of sulfur dioxide, which, once in the stratosphere, turns into sulfuric acid particles that reflect the sun's rays, further cooling temperatures. While the discharge from a single volcano would normally affect climate for two years or less, a succession of eruptions in a compressed period would reinforce and extend these effects by promoting geological changes such as increased glaciation and expanded pack ice. These would cool oceans and suppress temperatures long after the dispersal of the volcanic ash in the atmosphere.

Between 1257 and 1284, four volcanic eruptions in the tropics sent massive clouds of ash into the sky, triggering shorter growing seasons and reducing food production, especially in the Northern Hemisphere. Although farmers tried to adapt by switching to hardier crops and by reducing the size of animal herds, a deep crisis arrived in 1315 when persistent cooler temperatures and heavy rains led to crop failures in Scandinavia, England, Russia, Poland, Germany, and the Low Countries. During this "Great Famine," desperate farmers were forced to eat their seed grain and slaughter draught animals and dairy herds to survive. Large-scale eruptions in 1452 and 1580 again pushed temperatures lower and renewed the cycle of harvest failures.

In 1600, Mount Huanyaputina (**huan-yah-poo-TEE-nuh**) in the Peruvian Andes erupted, sending a dense cloud of volcanic ash into the upper atmosphere and spreading across the globe to screen out sunlight.[1] As a result, the summer of 1601 was the coldest in 200 years in the Northern Hemisphere. Additional downward spikes in temperature resulted from subsequent volcanic eruptions in 1641, 1660, 1783, and 1815.

In the coldest years of the seventeenth century, the growing season in much of Europe was as much as two months shorter than normal, with late frosts repeatedly withering the tender shoots of newly planted crops. Wheat and barley, staple crops across the region, ripened more slowly during cooler summers and were often damaged by early fall frosts. Because the population of the Northern Hemisphere had reached its peak just as this cycle of harvest failures began, the loss of human life, especially among young children and the elderly, was shocking.

Lower temperatures, longer winters with attendant crop failures, malnutrition, and the predictable return of epidemic disease afflicted northern Europe again when summer temperatures registered 2.7° F (1.5° C) lower than normal in 1674 and 1675 and again in 1694 and 1695. In Finland, for example, the cold weather and harvest failures of 1694 and 1695 caused a famine that carried off a quarter to a third of the population. While loss of life caused by crop failures and food shortages was less extreme in southern Europe and Asia Minor, these regions also experienced smaller harvests and higher staple prices repeatedly in the seventeenth century.

Although contemporary accounts and climate measurements are generally scarcer in other parts of the world, there is evidence of significant climate change across the globe. Observations of sunspots in China, Korea, and Japan dropped to zero between 1639 and 1700, suggesting lower average temperatures. Chinese officials reported unusually cool weather on numerous occasions during the seventeenth century. Japan endured its coldest spring of the entire century in 1616 and the Ottoman Empire also experienced unnaturally cold weather along with political turmoil and rural unrest in this same period.

Human populations had developed strategies to survive a single failed harvest by reducing the volume of the harvest sent to market, by drawing on food reserves, or by consuming part of the seed saved for planting the following year. Catastrophes occurred when cold weather or heavy rains damaged crops in two or more successive years. In these cases, the capacity of farmers to recover once temperatures rose was limited because they had reduced seed stores and needed to replenish their herds for food and traction. Farming families suffered greatly when harvests failed, as can be measured by higher mortality rates and falling births. The suffering of the urban poor was commonly intensified by the actions of merchant middlemen who commonly held scarce food supplies away from markets to drive up prices. Transportation

---

[1]Brian Fagan, *The Littlest Ice Age: How Climate Made History, 1300–1850* (New York, NY: Basic Books, 2000).

difficulties due to the cold exacerbated these problems. Since rivers and canals that were normally navigable in winter were frozen solid by the cold and roads were made impassable by snow and mud, food shortfalls could not be efficiently mitigated by the charity of rulers or religious institutions, who in milder weather moved supplies to aid the most desperate populations.

Popular responses to this long era of climate-induced disasters were often violent as afflicted peoples sought scapegoats and punished enemies. Across much of Europe and the Mediterranean region, urban residents rioted to protest scarcities and high bread prices, sometimes attacking merchants or representatives of the governing elite. In the seventeenth century, violence toward religious and ethnic minorities increased, as did the numbers of witch prosecutions. In fact, witch hunts and executions generally occurred in regions most powerfully affected by climate-induced disasters (see Chapter 17). In southern Germany, for example, a destructive hailstorm followed by arctic temperatures led to the arrest, torture, and execution of 900 men and women suspected of witchcraft in 1626. Spasms of witch hysteria occurred in similar circumstances in Scandinavia and Scotland as well following weather-related harvest failures in the middle decades of the seventeenth century.

During this century, religious and political conflicts also roiled many of the world's most powerful states, including England, Spain, China, India, and the Ottoman Empire. They included the Thirty Years War, the civil war in England, the fall of the Ming and ascendance of the Qing in China, and the murder of the Ottoman sultan.

At the end of the eighteenth century, the sun's activity began to return to normal. Volcanic activity remained an important influence on climate, but the incidence of eruptions diminished. The time between El Niño events also lengthened as global temperature rose, contributing to the warming of the Western Hemisphere. As the Little Ice Age subsided, rising average temperatures, milder winters, and larger, more reliable harvests returned. The Thames River, which had frozen repeatedly during the Little Ice Age, froze completely for the last time in 1814. Since 1880 average temperatures have fluctuated narrowly, but have risen recently with the ten warmest years in this long period all recorded since 2000. Scientists identify human alterations to the environment (like destruction of rain forest) and modern technologies (like automobile emissions) as the major contributors to this spike.

Questions for Analysis

1. What were the chief causes of the Little Ice Age?
2. Why did clusters of volcanic eruptions play such an influential role in this period?
3. How can small changes in temperature have such powerful effects on human societies?
4. Might small increases in temperature have similar effects today?

AP® REVIEW QUESTIONS FOR CHAPTER 21

Multiple-Choice Questions

Questions 1–3 refer to the image below.

▲ **Woodblock Print of the "Forty-Seven Ronin" Story** Universal History Archive/Universal Images Group/Getty Images

1. The story of the Ronin in the woodblock print supports which of the following conclusions about the time period?

    (A) There was conflict between the centralizing of authority and traditional values and culture.

    (B) There was new, expanding maritime reconnaissance by European states.

    (C) There was expansion of the plantation systems.

    (D) There was increased participation by peasants in agricultural activity.

2. The tension present in the story illustrates the tension as Japan transitioned

    (A) from established social hierarchy to individual worth based on merit.

    (B) from a monarchy with the Shogun to a series of warlords.

    (C) from a system of warlords to an urban industrial state.

    (D) from a military to a civil society.

3. The challenges faced by Japan, shown in the image above, are most similar to the challenges faced by which of the following leaders in the time period 1450–1750?

    (A) A caliph in the Abbasid Caliphate

    (B) The emperor of the Byzantine Empire

    (C) The emperor of the Han Dynasty

    (D) A feudal king in Europe

Questions 4–6 refer to the map on the next page.

4. Western China's population was sparse for which of the following reasons?

    (A) Vast, uninhabitable areas of swamp and wetlands

    (B) Extensive steppe and desert with limited resources

    (C) Extensive access to fresh water in the interior

    (D) Multiple large urban areas that left little room for agriculture

5. Based on the map, what factor best explains the relationship between patterns of agricultural activity and Han settlement during the eastern Qing period?

    (A) Confucian attitudes toward agriculture

    (B) North–south flowing rivers in eastern China

    (C) Favorable environmental conditions, such as adequate rainfall

    (D) Steppelike conditions

6. Which conclusion can be most effectively drawn from the map and your understanding of world history?

    (A) The Qing dynasty was heavily based in agriculture from the northernmost regions.

    (B) The Qing Empire was dominated by Turkish tribes.

    (C) China acted as a bridge for the spread of Japanese culture.

    (D) Western China was most likely to be influenced by nomadic groups.

Questions 7–10 refer to the passage below.

"There are too many men who claim to be pure scholars and yet are stupid and arrogant; we'd be better off with less talk of moral principle and more practice of it. Even in those who have been the best officials in my reign there are obvious failings . . . one of the worst habits of the great officials, that if they are not recommending their teachers or their friends for office then they recommend their relations. Even among the examiners there are those who are corrupt, those who do not understand basic works, those who asked detailed questions about practical matters of which they know nothing, those who insist entirely on memorization of the Classics and refuse to prescribe essays and put candidates from their own geographical area at the top of the list."

Emperor Kangxi of the Qing Dynasty, *Self-Portrait*, ca. 1690

7. Based on the passage, Emperor Kangxi is concerned that the current condition of the bureaucracy will lead to which of the following?

    (A) The imperial government holding too much power at the expense of the provinces

    (B) The Qing dynasty losing the Mandate of Heaven

    (C) Civil service officials putting too much emphasis on agricultural production and not commerce

    (D) Justification of people's belief in the effectiveness of the Confucian tradition

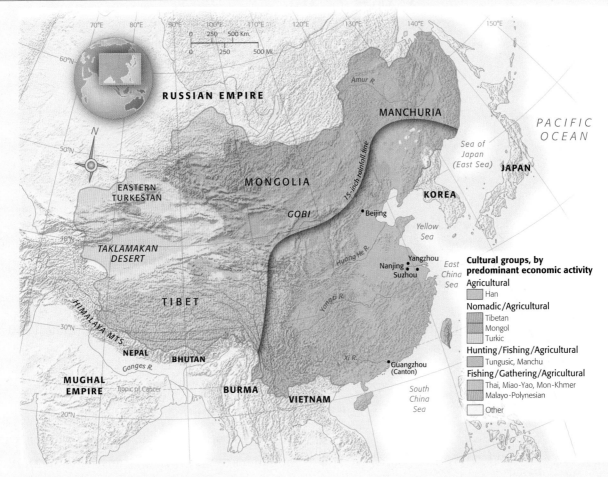

▲ **Climate and Diversity in the Qing Empire**

8. What situation between Emperor Kangxi and the civil service was common to many rulers during the time period?

   (A) Struggles with elites to centralize authority under the ruler

   (B) Dealing with the high cost of border defense

   (C) New religions threatening traditional values

   (D) Peasant rebellions over food shortages

9. Which of the following was a strategy used by Emperor Kangxi and other leaders of the time to address political challenges?

   (A) Harsh legal codes that relied on capital punishment

   (B) Allowing local elites to hold their land tax-free

   (C) Adoption of nationalist ideals to enforce imperial policies

   (D) Replacing military personnel with foreign mercenaries

10. Evidence from the passage could best be used to support which of the following arguments about the time period?

   (A) Leaders faced a variety of internal challenges that threatened their authority.

   (B) Because of internal and external pressures, feudalism dominated governments across Afro-Eurasia.

   (C) Central authorities rejected bureaucratic institutions because of their complexity and predictability.

   (D) Leaders found it was no longer useful to use religion to legitimize their authority over the populace.

Short-Answer Questions

1. Some historians argue that Japan followed extreme isolationist policies in the time period 1450–1750. Use your knowledge of world history to answer all parts of the question that follows.

   (A) Provide ONE piece of evidence challenging the argument of Japan as an isolationist country.

   (B) Provide ANOTHER piece of evidence challenging the argument of Japan as an isolationist country.

   (C) Explain ONE way in which the position that the Tokugawa government was isolationist could be supported.

2. Answer all parts of the question that follows.

   (A) Identify ONE way Europeans tried to establish trade and cultural relations with the Chinese.

   (B) Explain ONE influence China had on Europe as a result of trade.

   (C) Explain ONE effect Europe had on China in this time period.

PART VI

Revolutions Reshape the World, 1750–1870

The late eighteenth and early nineteenth centuries introduced both industrialization and independence revolutions to the Western Hemisphere, transforming political and economic life. The economic, political, and social revolutions that began in the mid-eighteenth century shook the foundations of European culture.

Despite these challenges, European imperialism expanded, with Russia and the United States joining their ranks. After 1900, few parts of the world were able to resist Western imperialism.

◄ **South America 1820s** This map of South America from the 1820s records the comprehensive success of the independence movements. With the exception of the Guyanas, no colonial governments remain. As we examine this map, we are also reminded of the failure of two political experiments designed to hold together geographically and ethnically diverse regions in a single national government. In the northwest is Colombia (also called Gran Colombia), created by the era's greatest revolutionary leader, Simón Bolívar. It quickly broke apart to form the modern nations of Venezuela, Colombia, and Ecuador. The United Provinces of Río de la Plata, located in the southeast, also soon collapsed, giving birth to the nations of Argentina, Paraguay, and Uruguay. Library of Congress

Environment	Culture	State Building	Economics	Social Structures
• Impact of environmental factors, disease, and technology on migration and settlement (Railroads, steamships, telegraph, canals, urbanization)	• Origins, beliefs, development, economic/social/political impact, and spread of major religions, philosophies, and belief systems (Enlightenment)	• Changes and continuities of the creation and maintenance of forms, functions, and institutions of governance (Qing, Ottoman, transoceanic empires)	• Impact of technology on economic production and globalization (Industrial Revolution)	• Impact of kinship, ethnicity, class, gender, and race on social hierarchies (Industrialization, private property)
• Impact of migration, population, and urbanization on environment	• Effect of technological and scientific innovation on religions, belief systems, philosophies, and ideologies over time (Enlightenment)	• Impact of economic, social, cultural, and geographical factors on state building, expansion, and dissolution (Industrial Revolution)	• Causes/effects of economic strategies of different types of communities, states, empires	• Impact of ideologies, philosophies, and religions on social hierarchies (Enlightenment)
• Interaction between environment and development of technology, industrialization, transportation, and exchange/communication networks (Industrial Revolution, sanitation)		• Impact of internal/external political factors on state building, expansion, and dissolution (Enlightenment, capitalism)	• Development and change of modes and locations of production over time (Urbanization, industrialization)	• Interaction between specialized labor systems and social hierarchy (Middle class, working class)
		• Political/economic interaction between state and nonstate actors (Merchants and companies)	• Causes/effects of labor reform movements (Enlightenment, abolition)	
			• Development and change of labor systems over time	
			• Influence and impact of local, regional, and global economic systems and exchange networks on each other (Raw materials, railroads, steamships, canals, telegraph)	

The Industrial Revolution introduced new technologies and patterns of work that made established societies wealthier and more militarily powerful. Western intellectual life became more secular. These years also saw the end of the Atlantic slave trade and later slavery itself, along with the first efforts to improve the status of women.

The Industrial Revolution led to a new wave of imperialism across Africa, Asia, and the Pacific Ocean. The Ottoman and the Qing Empires met this challenge through reform programs that incorporated traditional structures with elements of Western thought, reforms that were echoed in Russia with the abolition of serfdom. ●

Key Concept 5.1

- What factors and developments led to the rise of industrialization?
- What major developments in transportation, communication, and economics made the Industrial Revolution possible?
- How did industrialization reinforce the concept of a single global economy?
- How did industrialization lead to a restructuring of social structures as well as the global economy?

Key Concept 5.2

- How did imperialism, especially the growth of transoceanic empires, influence state formation and contraction around the world?

Key Concept 5.4

- What were the major causes and effects of migration in the increasingly mobile global community?
- How did migration present challenges to existing patterns of living?

22 The Early Industrial Revolution, 1760–1851

AP® Framework Terms

Coal
Iron
Urbanization
Steam engine
Factory system
Adam Smith
Marxism
Capitalism
Railroad
Steamship
Telegraph

Overarching Questions

1 How have religions, belief systems, philosophies, and ideologies affected the political, economic, and social development of societies? (CUL)

2 How and to what extent has technology shaped economic production and globalization over time? (ECON)

3 How have economic systems and the development of ideologies, values, and institutions influenced each other? (ECON)

4 How have local, regional, and global economic systems and exchange networks influenced each other over time? (ECON)

5 How have political, economic, cultural, and demographic factors affected social structures? (SOC)

Manchester was just a small town in northern England in the early eighteenth century. A hundred years later, it had become the fastest-growing city in history. To contemporaries, it was both a marvel and a horror. Prosperous cotton mills were interspersed with squalid workers' housing, built as cheaply as possible. Economist Nassau Senior described these workers' quarters:

> But when I went through their habitations . . . my only wonder was that tolerable health could be maintained by the inmates of such houses. These towns . . . have been erected by small speculators with an utter disregard to everything except immediate profit. . . . In one place we saw a whole street following the course of a ditch, in order to have deeper cellars (cellars for people, not for lumber) without the expense of excavation. Not a house in this street escaped cholera. . . . The streets are unpaved, with a dunghill or a pond in the middle; the houses built back to back, without ventilation or drainage, and whole families occupy each a corner of a cellar or of a garret.[1]

---

[1]Nassau W. Senior, *Letters on the Factory Act, as it affects the cotton manufacture, addressed to the Right Honourable, the President of the Board of Trade*, 2nd ed. (London, UK: Fellows, 1844), 20.

Not everyone deplored the living conditions in the new industrial city. Friedrich Engels, both a factory owner and critic of capitalism, recounted a meeting with a well-to-do citizen:

> One day I walked with one of these middle-class gentlemen into Manchester. I spoke to him about the disgraceful unhealthy slums and drew his attention to the disgusting condition of that part of the town in which the factory workers lived. I declared that I had never seen so badly built a town in my life. He listened patiently and at the corner of the street at which we parted company, he remarked: "And yet there is a great deal of money made here. Good morning, Sir!"[2]

Manchester's rise as a large, industrial city was a result of what historians call the **Industrial Revolution**, the most profound transformation in human life since the beginnings of agriculture. This revolution involved dramatic innovations in manufacturing, mining, transportation, and communications and equally rapid changes in society and commerce, as new relationships between social groups created an environment that was conducive to technical innovation and economic growth. These changes allowed the industrializing countries—first Britain, then western Europe and the United States—to unleash massive increases in production and productivity, exploit the world's natural resources as never before, and transform the environment and human life in unprecedented ways.

Industrialization widened the gap between rich and poor. The people who owned factories and controlled the course of industrial innovations amassed wealth and power over nature as well as over society. While some lived in spectacular luxury, workers, including large numbers of children, worked long hours in dangerous factories, struggled to buy food, and lived crowded together in unsanitary tenements. At the same time, the growing middle classes of industrializing nations grew rapidly, enjoyed fast-improving material conditions, and exercised increased influence in politics and culture.

AP® Exam Tip
The Industrial Revolution and its impact are key components to understanding AP® World History Period 5.

Industrial Revolution The transformation of the economy, the environment, and living conditions, occurring first in England in the eighteenth century, that resulted from the use of steam engines, the mechanization of manufacturing in factories, and innovations in transportation and communication.

---

[2]Friedrich Engels, *Condition of the Working Class in England*, trans. and ed. W. O. Henderson and W. H. Chaloner (Oxford, UK: Blackwell, 1958), 312.

The effect of the Industrial Revolution around the world was also very uneven. The first countries to industrialize grew rich and powerful, facilitating a second great wave of European imperialism in the nineteenth century. In some nations, like Egypt and India, the economic and military power of Europe stifled the tentative beginnings of industrialization. In those parts of Africa, Asia, and Latin America that had not yet begun the transition to industrial production, the European powers and, after 1890, the United States promoted, and in some cases compelled, the development of dependent, primary materials exporting economies to complement their own continued industrialization. The disparity in wealth and power between the industrial and the developing countries that exists today has its origins in the early nineteenth century. ●

22-1 Causes of the Industrial Revolution

What caused the Industrial Revolution?

What caused the Industrial Revolution, and why did it develop so rapidly in England in the eighteenth century? These are two of the great questions of history. The basic preconditions of this momentous event seem to have been population growth that increased demand for goods; an agricultural revolution; the expansion of trade, especially in textiles; and an openness to experimentation and innovation.

22-1a Population Growth

AP® Exam Tip
Identify and explain a variety of factors that led to the rise of industrial production and eventually the Industrial Revolution.

Population growth helped fuel the Industrial Revolution by increasing the demand for goods and by lowering labor costs. Between 1650 and 1850 Europe's population grew from 100 million to 266 million. Simultaneously, Europe became more urban, with the number of city dwellers more than doubling in this same period. This pattern was clearest in England and Wales, where population increased from about 6 million in 1700 to 9 million in 1800 and 18 million by 1850—increases never before experienced in European history. As the pace of manufacturing mounted in the eighteenth century, rural laborers and their families moved to cities in hope of higher earnings and better lives, increasing the political and economic influence of cities.

The growth of population resulted from more widespread resistance to disease and from more abundant and reliable food supplies, thanks to the new crops that originated in the Americas (see Chapter 18). Gradual improvements in income allowed Europeans to marry at earlier ages and have more children. As a result, roughly 40 percent of the population of Britain was under fifteen years of age in the nineteenth century. This high proportion of youths explains the vitality of the British people in that period as well as the widespread use of child labor. This era also witnessed an unprecedented rate of migration. In Britain, agricultural employment fell roughly 50 percent relative to urban employment between 1750 and 1850 as large numbers of country people sought to improve their circumstances by moving to more economically dynamic cities. Similarly, large numbers chose immigration from Ireland to England and, more generally, from Europe to the Americas. Thanks to immigration, the population of the United States rose from 4 million in 1791 to 9.6 million in 1820 and 31.5 million in 1860—faster than in any other part of the world at the time.

22-1b The Agricultural Revolution

agricultural revolution The transformation of farming in the eighteenth century that resulted from the spread of new crops, improvements in cultivation techniques and live-stock breeding, and the consolidation of small holdings into large farms from which tenants and sharecroppers were forcibly expelled. The introduction of mechanical reapers and harvesters accelerated this revolution.

A revolution in farming provided an increased food supply to fast-growing urban populations and at the same time forced many peasants off the land. This **agricultural revolution** had begun long before the eighteenth century. One important aspect was the introduction of new crops like the potato, introduced from South America in the sixteenth century. In the cool and humid regions of Europe, potatoes yielded two or three times more calories per acre than did the traditional crops of wheat, rye, and oats they replaced. Maize (American corn) was also grown across Europe from northern Iberia to the Balkans, adding substantially to the food supply.

CHRONOLOGY

	Technology	Economy, Society, and Politics
1750	1702–1712 Thomas Newcomen builds first steam engine	
	1733 John Kay patented the flying shuttle	
	1759 Josiah Wedgwood opens pottery factory	
	1764 Spinning jenny	
	1769 Richard Arkwright's water frame; James Watt patents steam engine	1776 Adam Smith's *Wealth of Nations*
	1779 First iron bridge	1776–1783 American Revolution
	1785 Samuel Crompton's mule	1789–1799 French Revolution
	1793 Eli Whitney's cotton gin	1792 Mary Wollstonecraft's *A Vindication of the Rights of Woman*
1800	1800 Alessandro Volta's battery	1804–1815 Napoleonic Wars
	1807 Robert Fulton's *North River*	
	1820s Construction of Erie Canal	1820s U.S. cotton industry begins
	1829 *Rocket*, first prize-winning locomotive	1833 Factory Act in Britain
	1837 Wheatstone and Cooke's telegraph; Morse's code	1834 German Zollverein; Robert Owen's Grand National Consolidated Trade Union
	1838 First ships steam across the Atlantic	1847–1848 Irish famine
	1840 *Nemesis* sails to China	1848 Collapse of Chartist movement; revolutions in Europe
	1843 Samuel Morse's Baltimore-to-Washington telegraph	1848 Publication of *Communist Manifesto*
1850	1851 Crystal Palace opens in London	1854 First cotton mill in India

Prosperous landowners with secure titles to their land could afford to bear the risk of trying new methods and new crops. In Great Britain rich landowners "enclosed" the land—that is, consolidated their holdings—and got Parliament to give them title to the commons, lands traditionally shared and used by the rural poor as well as the rich. Once in control of the land, rich landowners drained and improved the soil, bred better livestock, and introduced crop rotation. This "enclosure movement" further impoverished the rural poor by turning tenants and sharecroppers into landless farm laborers dependent on their employers. Large numbers of the rural poor displaced by these measures moved to cities to seek work and many were forced into vagrancy. By the first decade of the nineteenth century, more than 20,000 per year emigrated from the British Isles to North America to seek a better life.

22-1c Trade and Inventiveness

The Industrial Revolution was preceded by a long period of commercial expansion based on growing population and on Europe's much deeper engagement with colonial possessions and with other foreign markets. The innovations of the industrial age came about in part as manufacturers sought to meet increased domestic and foreign demand for textiles and other products through improved efficiency and productivity.

Traditionally, European textiles were produced by skilled artisans organized in guilds using centuries-old technologies. In this system increasing production meant training more artisans, an expensive process that took years. Beginning in the seventeenth century, merchant investors began to relocate some components of textile production away from guild-dominated cities to benefit from lower-cost rural labor, especially during the period between harvesting and planting when agricultural laborers were under-employed. Called proto-industrialization, merchant investors delivered raw materials and supplied simple machinery, like looms and spinning wheels, to the homes of farm families and to rural jobbers who organized groups of laborers.

AP® Exam Tip
Consider the economic changes and continuities in Europe from the previous time period through this one.

In this system the complex tasks associated with artisan production were subdivided into simple procedures that allowed rural workers to quickly gain competence and become productive. Unlike urban artisans, who typically earned daily wages, these proto-industrial workers were only paid for the finished work they produced, thus reducing labor costs. Skilled manufacturers then transformed the spun wool and rough cloth produced by rural laborers into finished goods for domestic and foreign consumers. While proto-industrialization increased cloth production and lowered labor costs, there were chronic problems with quality control and inefficiencies that resulted from the dispersal of production.

In the eighteenth century a dramatic expansion of European commerce with markets in the Americas, Africa, and Asia reinforced the economic effects of the fast-growing European population. Nearly all the European powers profited from plantation colonies in the Americas. As Europeans of even modest means consumed ever-growing quantities of sugar to sweeten their tea, coffee, cocoa, pastries, and candies, the demand for manufactures like porcelain cups and dinnerware increased as well. At the same time planters in the Caribbean imported a steeply rising volume of cotton textiles to clothe themselves and their slaves. Initially, these cotton textiles were imported from Asia, especially India, but, as demand increased, English investors created a domestic cotton textile industry that would become the world's first modern mechanized industry (see discussion of Indian cotton industry later in this chapter).

European governments played a key role in this economic expansion, financing improvements to transportation and promoting foreign trade. Governments across Europe sponsored the expansion of road networks, although maintenance was often inadequate. In Britain local governments' neglect of the roads that served long-distance traffic led to the formation of private "turnpike trusts" that built numerous toll roads. As the volume of commerce increased, canal-building booms occurred in Britain, France, and the low countries in the late eighteenth century. Governments also directly invested in skills and new technologies by creating royal manufacturers that produced fine china, silks, and carpets. Authorities in England, France, Prussia, and Spain, among other European nations, recruited skilled artisans from rival nations, subsidized periodicals that disseminated new technologies, and expanded their navies to better protect foreign trade.

Beginning in the seventeenth century, educated people throughout Europe and the Americas were increasingly fascinated by technology and innovation (see Chapter 17). Across Europe inexpensive periodicals informed the general public of new technologies and scientific discoveries. But it was the multi-volume *Encyclopédie*, published in France over a period of more than twenty years, that most influenced the dissemination of useful technologies by providing detailed diagrams of everything from printing and textile machinery to canal locks and foundry equipment. During the eighteenth century the French, Spanish, and British governments also sought to promote economic growth by sending expeditions around the world to collect plants that could profitably be grown domestically or in their colonies. They all also offered prizes for scientific discoveries, such as determining the longitude of a ship at sea and the accurate measurement of the earth's circumference. It was an era when successful innovators and scientists became celebrities.

22-1d Britain and Continental Europe

AP® Exam Tip
Understand the importance of the diffusion of new methods of production.

Industrialization did not take place everywhere at once. Great Britain took the lead in introducing new technologies and maintained its place as Europe's major industrial power to the end of the nineteenth century. It is useful to divide the British experience into two phases. In the eighteenth century inventors developed machines that multiplied the productive capacities of individual workers, especially in the textile industry. While production increased dramatically, British industry continued to rely on traditional sources of energy, particularly wind, water, and animal power. Then early in the nineteenth century the development of efficient steam engines allowed British entrepreneurs to apply this potent source of energy to industrial machinery.

The technologies associated with both stages of this revolution spread rapidly to continental Europe and the United States. British engineers and skilled machinists were the most active agents in the dissemination of the new technologies. Investors in continental Europe and the United States quickly recognized the advantages of the new technologies and provided high salaries and other inducements to skilled British workers willing to immigrate and introduce the newest technologies. Belgium had the earliest successes in imitating the British industrial model,

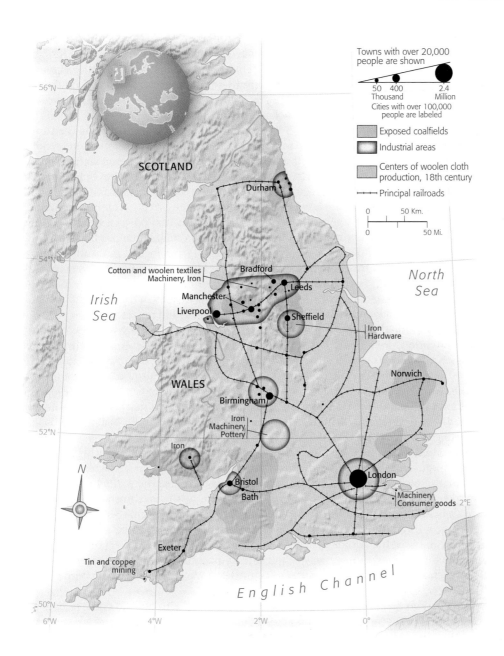

Towns with over 20,000 people are shown

50   400   2.4
Thousand   Million
Cities with over 100,000 people are labeled

Exposed coalfields

Industrial areas

Centers of woolen cloth production, 18th century

Principal railroads

0   50 Km.
0   50 Mi.

SCOTLAND

Durham

Cotton and woolen textiles
Machinery, Iron

Bradford

Leeds

North Sea

Irish Sea

Manchester

Liverpool

Sheffield

Iron
Hardware

WALES

Norwich

Birmingham

Iron
Machinery
Pottery

Iron

London

Bristol
Bath

Machinery
Consumer goods   2°E

N

Exeter

Tin and copper mining

English Channel

MAP 22.1   The Industrial Revolution in Britain, ca. 1850
The first industries arose in northern and western England. These regions had the abundant coal and iron-ore deposits crucial for metallurgy as well as the moist climate and fast-flowing rivers—crucial to the mechanized cotton textile industry.

How important were the location of British coalfields to the later development of Britain's new machine manufacturing centers during the Industrial Revolution?

becoming the continent's most industrialized economy by 1840. While slower to embrace the new technologies, Germany after 1850 became the continent's major producer of coal, iron, and steel. The United States was well established as a major industrial power by 1860, having quickly adopted textile and metallurgical technologies developed first in Great Britain. Despite the efforts of governments to defend their technological advantages, technologies know no borders and are quickly disseminated internationally.

Historians disagree about why Britain played such an important role in the introduction of industrial technologies in the eighteenth and nineteenth centuries, but the influence of some demographic and economic factors seems clear. In a period of growing population, Britain also enjoyed a rising standard of living. Britain's generally higher incomes, relative to most other European nations after 1750, resulted in large part from longer working hours. This combination of a larger and slightly richer population increased demand for the goods produced by the new industries. At the same time, good harvests and a booming overseas trade contributed to the nation's general prosperity and increased the store of capital to invest in innovation in manufacturing.

Britain had a strong craft tradition that employed many thousands of skilled mechanics. As a result, it was already the world's leading exporter of tools, guns, hardware, clocks, and other manufactured goods (see Map 22.1). Britain's mining and metal industries also employed a considerable number of skilled workers with a tradition of experimentation and innovation. British commercial culture was among Europe's most modern, having long enjoyed the benefits of strong banks, joint-stock companies, a stock market, and commercial insurance. In addition, the nation's patent system offered inventors the hope of rich rewards by protecting their intellectual property rights. As the public became aware of early visionaries who became wealthy and respected for their inventions, the enthusiasm for innovation and experimentation spread.

At the dawn of the industrial age, Britain had one of the most fluid societies in Europe. The court was less ostentatious, its aristocracy was less powerful, and the lines separating the social classes were not as sharply drawn as elsewhere in Europe, with the exception of the Netherlands. Compared to France or Spain, the two most important continental powers, British political power was not as centralized or intrusive. While Britain, like its continental neighbors, retained numerous governmental impediments to commercial and technological innovation such as monopoly companies and intrusive trade regulations, some historians argue that this marginally less-regulated environment facilitated experimentation and investment in new technology. As economic growth accelerated, many British commoners grew wealthy in trade and manufacturing and, as a result, society and politics became less hierarchical and more fluid.

While Britain had abundant supplies of coal and iron ore, two key ingredients in the Industrial Revolution, it enjoyed other advantages relative to its competitors. At a time when transportation by land was very costly, Great Britain had good water transportation thanks to its long coastline, navigable rivers, and growing network of canals. It also had a unified internal market with few of the duties and tolls on the movement of goods that had to be paid every few miles in France or Spain. These advantages created a more efficient market and facilitated a growing trade between regions. Britain enjoyed another advantage as well, its ability to compel its colonies to consume British manufactures.

In contrast to Britain, the economies of continental Europe were hampered by high transportation costs, misguided government regulations, and rigid social structures. As a result, attempts to import British techniques and organize factory production elsewhere often foundered for lack of markets or management skills. Nevertheless, British textile machinery was introduced in France and Spain before the French Revolution (see Chapter 23). From then until the end of the Napoleonic wars in 1815, Europe's economies were distorted by the effects of mass military mobilizations and warfare. Although war created opportunities for suppliers of weapons and uniforms, the interruption of trade between Britain and continental Europe slowed the diffusion of new technologies, and the insecurity of countries at war discouraged businessmen from investing in new factories and machinery.

Once revolutions had swept away most of the restrictions of Europe's old regimes, both private investors and European governments acted to import new technologies and adapt them to local conditions. Acutely aware of Britain's head start and the need to stimulate their own industries, continental governments sponsored efforts to imitate or steal British industrial secrets. They recruited British engineers and artisans, created technical schools, and eliminated internal tariff barriers, tolls, and other hindrances to trade. By the 1820s there were several thousand skilled Britons working on the continent, setting up machines, training workers in the new methods, and even starting their own businesses. Following the British model, European governments also encouraged the formation of joint-stock companies and banks to channel private savings into industrial investments. By 1830 the political climate across western Europe had become as favorable to business as Britain's had been a half century earlier. First Belgium and then, after 1850, Germany and France enjoyed industrial booms based on iron, cotton, steam engines, and railroads. Key to the success of Belgium and Germany was the existence of abundant coal and iron-ore deposits. Without plentiful coal for fuel, France retained a more traditional manufacturing economy until the introduction of electricity late in the nineteenth century.

Section Review

- The Industrial Revolution arose from population growth, an agricultural revolution, increased trade, and an interest in innovation.

- Britain industrialized first, thanks to its fluid political structures, transportation infrastructure, inventiveness, and society open to talented and enterprising people.

- Among educated Europeans, practical subjects like business, science, and technology became fashionable.

- On the European continent, the revolutions of 1789–1815 swept away the restrictions of the old aristocratic regimes and allowed for more industrial growth.

22-2 **The Technological Revolution**

What were the key innovations that increased productivity and drove industrialization?

Five innovations spurred industrialization: (1) mass production through the division of labor, (2) new machines and mechanization, (3) a great increase in the manufacture of iron, (4) the steam engine, and (5) the electric telegraph. While the full realization of these innovations occurred first in Great Britain and then spread to the United States and continental Europe in the nineteenth century, China had achieved the first three during the Song dynasty (960–1279). But China did not develop the steam engine or electricity, innovations that dramatically multiplied human productivity. The transformation of Western economies through industrialization depended on the full integration of these new forms of energy with the process of mechanical innovation.

mass production The manufacture of many identical products by the division of labor into many small repetitive tasks. This method was introduced into the manufacture of pottery by Josiah Wedgwood and into the spinning of cotton thread by Richard Arkwright.

Josiah Wedgwood English industrialist whose pottery works first produced fine-quality pottery by industrial methods.

22-2a **Mass Production: Pottery**

The pottery industry offers a good example of **mass production**, the making of many identical items by breaking the process into simple repetitive tasks. Before the mid-eighteenth century, only the wealthy could afford imported Chinese porcelain. Middle-class people used pewter tableware, and the poor ate from wooden or earthenware bowls. Royal manufacturers produced exquisite handmade products for the courts and aristocracy, but their products were much too expensive for mass consumption. As more and more Europeans acquired a taste for tea, cocoa, and coffee, they wanted porcelain that would not spoil the flavor of hot beverages. This demand created opportunities for inventive entrepreneurs.

Britain had many small pottery workshops where craftsmen made a few plates and cups at a time. Much of this activity took place in a part of the Midlands that possessed good clay, coal for firing, and lead for glazing. In 1759, **Josiah Wedgwood**, the son of a potter, started his own pottery business. Today the name *Wedgwood* is associated with expensive, highly decorated china. But Wedgwood's most important

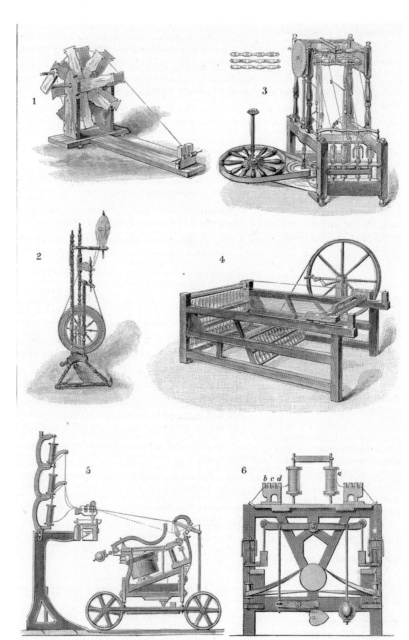

▶ **Development of Spinning Technology** The evolution of spinning technologies. (1) The spinning wheel was still used in Indian textile production into the nineteenth century. (2) The spinning wheel in use in Europe in the seventeenth century. (3) Arkwright's Water Frame (1769) made it possible to spin multiple strong cotton threads and was driven by water power. (4) Hargreaves's Spinning Jenny (1767) allowed a single spinner to produce more thread than twenty individuals using the spinning wheel. (5) Crompton's Mule (1779) combined elements of the Jenny and the water frame to make long, fine cotton yarns suitable for textiles that would compete with India's finest hand-spun production. (6) Danforth's Throstle (1828) was a larger, steam-driven version of the water frame that proved impractical.
Courtesy of Lyman Johnson

Adam Smith (1723–1790), a Scottish philosopher, is famous for his book An Inquiry into the Nature and Causes of the Wealth of Nations, *first published in 1776. It was the first work to explain the economy of a nation as a system. Smith criticized the notion, common in the eighteenth century, that a nation's wealth was synonymous with the amount of gold and silver in the government's coffers (see Chapter 17, Diversity & Dominance: Commercial Expansion and Risk). Instead, he defined wealth as the amount of goods and services produced by a nation's people. By this definition, labor and its products are an essential element in a nation's prosperity.*

In the passage that follows, Smith contrasts two methods of making pins. In one a team of workers divided up the job of making pins and produced a great many every day; in the other pin workers "wrought separately and independently" and produced very few pins per day. It is clear that the division of labor produced more pins per worker per day. But who benefited? Left unsaid is that a pin factory had to be owned and operated by a manufacturer who hired workers and assigned a task to each one.

The illustration shows a pin-maker's workshop in late-eighteenth-century France. Each worker is performing a specific task on a few pins at once, and all the energy comes from human muscles. These are the characteristics of a proto-industrial workshop.

To take an example, therefore, from a very trifling manufacture—but one in which the division of labour has been very often taken notice of—the trade of the pin-maker: a workman not educated to this business (which the division of labour has rendered a distinct trade), nor acquainted with the use of machinery employed in it (to the invention of which the same division of labour has probably given occasion), could scarce, perhaps, with his utmost industry, make one pin in a day, and certainly could not make twenty. But in the way in which this business is now carried on, not only the whole work is a peculiar trade, but it is divided into a number of branches, of which the greater part are likewise peculiar trades. One man draws out the wire, another straights it, a third cuts it, a fourth points it, a fifth grinds it at the top for receiving the head; to make the head requires two or three distinct operations, to put it on, is a peculiar business, to whiten the pins is another; it is even a trade by itself to put them into the paper; and the important business of making a pin is, in this manner, divided into about eighteen distinct operations, which, in some manufactories, are all performed by distinct hands, though in others the same man will sometimes perform two or three of them. I have seen a small manufactory of this kind where ten men only were employed, and where some of them, consequently, performed two or three distinct operations. But though they were very poor, and therefore but indifferently accommodated with the necessary machinery, they could, when they exerted themselves, make among them about twelve pounds of pins in a day.

There are in a pound upwards of four thousand pins of a middling size. Those ten persons, therefore, could make among them upwards of forty-eight thousand pins in a day. Each person, therefore, making a tenth part of forty-eight thousand pins, might be considered as making four thousand eight hundred pins a day. But if they had all wrought separately and independently, and without any of them having been educated to this peculiar business, they certainly could not each of them have made twenty, perhaps not one pin in a day; that is, certainly, not the two hundred and fortieth, perhaps not the four thousand eight hundredth part of what they are at present capable of

division of labor A manufacturing technique that breaks down a craft into many simple and repetitive tasks that can be performed by unskilled workers. Pioneered in the pottery works of Josiah Wedgwood and in other eighteenth-century factories, it greatly increased the productivity of labor and lowered the cost of manufactured goods.

mechanization The application of machinery to manufacturing and other activities. Among the first processes to be mechanized were the spinning of cotton thread and the weaving of cloth in late-eighteenth- and early-nineteenth-century England.

contribution lay in producing ordinary porcelain cheaply by means of the **division of labor** (see Diversity & Dominance: Adam Smith and the Division of Labor).

Wedgwood subdivided the work into simple, repetitive tasks, such as unloading the clay, mixing it, pressing flat pieces, dipping the pieces in glaze, putting handles on cups, packing kilns, and carrying things from one part of his plant to another. To prevent interruptions, he instituted strict discipline among his workers. He substituted the use of molds for the potter's wheel whenever possible, a change that not only saved labor but also created uniform plates and bowls that could be stacked. The end result was that while workers became more productive, they had fewer skills and were paid less.

Wedgwood's interest in applying technology to manufacturing was sparked by his membership in the Lunar Society, a group of businessmen, scientists, and craftsmen that met each month when the moon was full to discuss the practical application of knowledge. In 1782 naturalist Erasmus Darwin encouraged him to purchase a steam engine from Boulton and Watt, a firm founded by two other members of the society. The steam engine that Wedgwood bought to mix clay and grind flint was one of the first to be installed in a factory. The division of labor and new steam-driven machinery allowed Wedgwood to both lower the cost of production and improve quality while at the same time win a greater market share through lower prices.

22-2b Mechanization: The Cotton Industry

The cotton industry, the largest industry in this period, illustrates the role of **mechanization**, the use of machines to do work previously done by hand. Cotton had long been grown in China, India, and the Middle East, where it was spun and woven by hand. The cloth was so much cooler, softer, and cleaner than wool that wealthy Europeans developed a liking for the costly import.

▲ A Pin-Maker's Workshop The man in the middle (Fig. 2) is pulling wire off a spindle (G) and through a series of posts. This ensures that the wire will be perfectly straight. The worker seated on the lower right (Fig. 3) takes the long pieces of straightened wire and cuts them into shorter lengths. The man in the lower left-hand corner (Fig. 5) sharpens twelve to fifteen wires at a time by holding them against a grindstone turned by the worker in Fig. 6. The men in Figs. 4 and 7 put the finishing touches on the points. Other operations—such as forming the wire to the proper thickness, cleaning and coating it with tin, and attaching the heads—are depicted in other engravings in the same encyclopedia. The Pin Factory, plate 2 from Volume IV of the Encyclopedia of Denis Diderot (1713–84) and Jean le Rond d'Alembert (1717–83), 1751–52 (engraving), French School, (18th century) / Private Collection/Bridgeman Images

performing, in consequence of a proper division and combination of their different operations.

AP® History Reasoning Skills

Continuity and Change Over Time *In what ways did Smith's definitions of economic wealth challenge established views of wealth?*

Contextualization *What other examples from the time period could support the advantages of the division of labor?*

Source: Adam Smith, *An Inquiry into the Nature and Causes of the Wealth of Nations*, ed. Edward Gibbon Wakefield (London, UK: Charles Knight and Co., 1843), 7–9.

When the powerful English woolen industry persuaded Parliament to forbid the import of cotton cloth, that prohibition stimulated attempts to import cotton fiber and make the cloth domestically. Here was an opportunity for enterprising inventors to reduce costs through the introduction of laborsaving machinery.

A small innovation in weaving helped initiate a revolution in textile production. In 1733 twenty-nine-year-old English artisan John Kay successfully sought a patent for the wheeled shuttle. The shuttle carried the weft thread back and forth across the loom. By adding wheels, Kay's "flying shuttle" dramatically increased the productivity of weavers and the demand for spun thread. This helped lead, in the 1760s, to a series of inventions that revolutionized the spinning of cotton thread and balanced the textile supply chain. The first was the jenny, invented in 1764, which mechanically drew out the cotton fibers and twisted them into thread. The jenny was simple, cheap to build, and easy for one person to operate. Early models permitted a single worker to spin six or seven threads at once, later ones up to eighty. The thread, however, was soft and irregular and could be used only in combination with linen, a strong yarn derived from the flax plant.

In 1769 **Richard Arkwright** invented another spinning machine that produced thread strong enough to be used without the addition of linen. Arkwright was both a gifted inventor and a successful businessman. His machine was larger and more complex than the jenny and required a source of power such as a water wheel, hence the name "water frame." To obtain the necessary energy, he installed dozens of machines in a building next to a fast-flowing river. The resemblance to a flour mill gave such enterprises the name *cotton mill*. Within a few decades of the introduction of the jenny and water frame, these technologies were imported and adapted to local conditions elsewhere. The skilled mechanics who built British machines served as vectors for this dissemination as they moved to France, Belgium, and the United States to seek higher wages.

AP® Exam Tip
Explain how the development of the factory system impacted labor and social systems.

Richard Arkwright English inventor and entrepreneur who became the wealthiest and most successful textile manufacturer of the early Industrial Revolution. He invented the water frame, a machine that, with minimal human supervision, could spin many strong cotton threads at once.

In 1785 British inventor Samuel Crompton patented a machine that combined the best features of the jenny and the water frame. This device, called the mule, produced a strong thread that was thin enough to be used to make a high-quality cotton cloth called muslin. The mule could make a finer, more even thread than could any human being, and at a lower cost. At last British industry could undersell high-quality handmade cotton cloth from India. With these innovations in place, British cotton output increased tenfold between 1770 and 1790, despite the fact that these large-scale producers still depended on waterpower.

The boom in thread production and the soaring demand for cloth encouraged inventors to mechanize the rest of textile manufacturing. Power looms were perfected after 1815. Other inventions of the period included carding machines, chlorine bleach, and cylindrical presses to print designs on fabric. By the 1830s large textile mills powered by steam engines were performing all the steps necessary to turn raw cotton into printed cloth.

Mechanization offered two advantages: increased productivity for the manufacturer and lower prices for the consumer. Whereas in India it took hand laborers 500 hours to spin a pound of cotton thread, the mule of 1790 could do so in three person-hours, and the self-acting mule—an improved version introduced in 1830—required only eighty minutes. Modern cotton mills needed very few skilled workers, and factory managers often hired children to tend the spinning machines. The same was true of power looms, which gradually replaced handloom weaving: the number of power looms rose from 2,400 in 1813 to 500,000 by 1850. Meanwhile, the price of cloth fell by 90 percent between 1782 and 1812 and kept on dropping. As the unskilled found ready employment and consumers benefitted from lower prices, skilled spinners and handweavers were displaced and impoverished.

The industrialization of Britain made cotton America's most valuable agricultural crop (see Chapter 25). In the 1790s most of Britain's cotton came from India. But in 1793 the American Eli Whitney patented his cotton gin, a simple device that separated the bolls or seedpods from the fiber and made cotton growing economical. This invention permitted the spread of cotton farming into Georgia, then into Alabama, Mississippi, and Louisiana, and finally as far west as Texas. By the late 1850s the southern states were producing a million tons of cotton a year, five-sixths of the world's total and supplying more than 80 percent of Britain's raw material for the booming textile industry. From its foundation, the world's most modern industry, mechanized textile production, depended on the maintenance of the brutal slave regime that produced cotton in the American South. Fears that U.S. cotton production could be ended by slave rebellions and race war led many British textile producers to recommend that Indian cotton imports be increased as an alternative. But expanding Indian exports of raw cotton would depend on depressing India's production of finished textiles.

With the help of British craftsmen who introduced jennies, mules, and power looms, Americans developed their own cotton textile industry in the 1820s. Immigrants from Great Britain played a key role in this process, as did the willingness of American investors to ignore the patent rights of British inventors. By 1840 the United States had 1,200 cotton mills that served the booming domestic market, two-thirds of them in New England. Here again, a rapidly expanding modern industry employing thousands of free workers depended on the slave labor that produced southern cotton.

While the resistance of long-established artisan guilds to the introduction of new technologies slowed technological innovation in the wool textile industry in Britain and elsewhere, machinery adapted from cotton production quickly transformed the spinning of woolen thread by the 1830s. Steam-driven looms soon followed. While displaced skilled workers protested, the momentum was irreversible. In Belgium in 1810, for example, only 5 of the nation's 144 woolen factories were mechanized, but this small number of modern factories generated more than 50 percent of this nation's total production.

22-2c **The Iron Industry**

Iron making was also transformed during the Industrial Revolution. Throughout Eurasia and Africa, iron had long been used for tools, weapons, and household items. During the Song period (960–1279), Chinese forges had produced cast iron in large quantities. Although production declined after the Song, iron continued to be common and inexpensive in China. Wherever iron was produced, however, deforestation eventually drove up the cost of charcoal (used for smelting) and restricted output. Furthermore, iron had to be repeatedly heated and hammered to drive

◀ **Pit Head of a Coal Mine** This is a small coal mine. In the center of this picture stands a Newcomen engine used to pump water from the shaft. The work of hauling coal out of the mine was still done by horses and mules. The smoke coming out of the smokestack is a trademark of the early industrial era. Walker Art Gallery, National Museums Liverpool/The Bridgeman Art Library

out impurities, a difficult, labor-intensive, and costly process. Because of limited wood supplies and the high cost of skilled labor, iron was a rare and valuable metal outside China before the eighteenth century.

A first breakthrough occurred in 1709 when Abraham Darby discovered that *coke* (coal from which the impurities have been cooked out) could be used in place of more expensive charcoal. At first iron produced using coke was of lower quality than charcoal-smelted iron, but it was also much cheaper, for coal was plentiful. In 1784 British inventor Henry Cort found a way to remove some of the impurities in coke-iron by *puddling*—stirring the molten iron with long rods. Cort's process made it possible to produce *wrought iron* (a soft and more malleable form of iron than cast iron) very cheaply. By 1790 four-fifths of Britain's iron was made with coke, while other countries still used charcoal. Coke-iron allowed a great expansion in the size of individual blast furnaces. As a result, Britain's iron production rose fast, from 17,000 tons in 1740 to 3 million tons in 1844, as much as in the rest of the world put together. As in Britain, the existence of large supplies of coal and iron ore allowed a fast pace of industrialization in Belgium and Germany after 1820.

In turn, there seemed no limit to the novel applications for this cheap and useful material. In 1779 Abraham Darby III (grandson of the first Abraham Darby) built a bridge of iron across the Severn River. Then, in 1851, Londoners marveled at the **Crystal Palace**, a huge exhibition hall made entirely of iron and glass. The "Great Exhibition" that showcased the Crystal Palace was a celebration of British industry and power but also included exhibits from the colonies and from other nations.

The availability of cheap iron made the mass production of objects such as guns, hardware, and tools appealing. However, fitting together the parts of these products required a great deal of labor. To reduce labor costs, innovators, like the Americans Eli Whitney (firearms) and Eli Terry (clocks), contributed to the development of standardized interchangeable parts in manufacturing. By the mid-nineteenth century, the use of interchangeable-parts had been widely adopted, including the manufacture of farm equipment and sewing machines. By the 1850s Europeans had begun to call this the "American system of manufactures."

22-2d The Steam Engine

In the history of the world, there had been a number of periods of great technological inventiveness and economic growth. But in all previous cases, the dynamism eventually faltered. The Industrial Revolution, in contrast, has only accelerated. One reason has been increased

AP® Exam Tip Explain the far-reaching effects on global economy, social relations, and culture caused by major developments and innovations in transportation and communication (including railroads, steamships, telegraphs, and canals).

AP® Exam Tip Explain how the steam engine allowed industry to take advantage of new energy resources in fossil fuels, greatly increasing humanity's access to energy.

Crystal Palace Building erected in Hyde Park, London, for the Great Exhibition of 1851. Made of iron and glass, like a gigantic greenhouse, it was a symbol of the industrial age.

▲ **Transatlantic Steamship Race** In 1838, two ships equipped with steam engines, the *Sirius* and the *Great Western*, steamed from England to New York. Although the *Sirius* left a few days earlier, the *Great Western*—shown here arriving in New York harbor—almost caught up with it, arriving just four hours after the *Sirius*. This race inaugurated regular transatlantic steamship service. Science & Society Picture Library/Getty Images

steam engine A machine that turns the energy released by burning fuel into motion. Thomas Newcomen built the first crude but workable steam engine in 1712. James Watt vastly improved his device in the 1760s and 1770s. Steam power was later applied to moving machinery in factories and to powering ships and locomotives.

James Watt Scot who invented the condenser and other improvements that made the steam engine a practical source of power for industry and transportation. The watt, an electrical measurement, is named after him.

interactions between scientists, technicians, and businesspeople. Another has been access to an abundant source of cheap energy, namely fossil fuels. The first machine to transform fossil fuel into mechanical energy was the **steam engine**, a device that set the Industrial Revolution apart from all previous periods of growth and innovation.

Deep-shaft mines were routinely threatened by flooding as they filled with water faster than pumps powered by horses could drain them before the eighteenth century. Then, between 1702 and 1712, Thomas Newcomen developed the first practical steam engine, a crude but effective device that could power pumps to clear water from mines much faster than earlier technologies. The Newcomen engine's voracious appetite for fuel mattered little in coal mines, where fuel was cheap, but it made the engine too costly for other uses. In 1764 another Briton, **James Watt**, a maker of scientific instruments at Glasgow University in Scotland, was asked to repair the university's model Newcomen engine. Watt realized that the engine wasted fuel because the cylinder had to be alternately heated and cooled. He developed a separate condenser—a vessel into which the steam was allowed to escape, leaving the cylinder always hot and the condenser always cold. Watt patented his idea in 1769 and enlisted the help of iron manufacturer Matthew Boulton to turn his invention into a commercial product. Their first engines were sold to pump water out of copper and tin mines, where fuel was too costly for Newcomen engines. Then, in 1781, Watt invented the sun-and-planet gear, which turned the back-and-forth action of the piston into rotary motion. This allowed steam engines to power machinery in flour and cotton mills, pottery manufacturers, and other industries as well. Because there seemed almost no limit to the amount of coal in the ground, steam-generated energy appeared to be an inexhaustible source of power, and steam engines could be used where animal, wind, and water power were lacking. By the 1820s steam engines were powering textile machinery in Belgium and the

United States as well as in Great Britain. In places where coal supplies were limited, like France, the application of steam power to manufacturing developed more slowly.

Inspired by the success of Watt's engine, several inventors put steam engines on boats. The first commercially successful steamboat was Robert Fulton's *North River*, which sailed the Hudson River between New York City and Albany, New York, in 1807. Soon steamboats were launched on the Ohio and the Mississippi Rivers, gateways to the Midwest. By 1830 some 300 steamboats plied the Mississippi and its tributaries. The United States was fast becoming a nation that moved by water in vessels powered by steam.

Oceangoing steam-powered ships were much more difficult to build than river boats because the first steam engines used so much coal that no ship could carry more than a few days' supply. The *Savannah*, which crossed the Atlantic in 1819, for example, was a sailing ship with an auxiliary steam engine that was used for only ninety hours of its twenty-nine-day trip. Engineers soon developed more efficient engines, and in 1838 two steamers, the *Great Western* and the *Sirius*, crossed the Atlantic on steam power alone.

22-2e Railroads

After Watt's patent expired in 1800, inventors experimented with lighter, more powerful high-pressure engines—an idea Watt had rejected as too dangerous. In 1804 Richard Trevithick built an engine that consumed only one-third the coal used by Watt's design and then created several steam-powered vehicles able to travel on roads or rails.

By the 1820s England already had many railways on which horses pulled heavy wagons. In 1829, the owners of the Liverpool and Manchester Railway organized a contest between steam-powered locomotives and horse-drawn wagons. George Stephenson and his son Robert won the contest with their locomotive *Rocket*, which pulled a 20-ton train at up to 30 miles (48 kilometers) per hour. After that triumph, a railroad-building mania swept Britain. In the late 1830s, as passenger traffic soared, entrepreneurs built lines between the major cities and even to small towns. Railroads were far cheaper, faster, and more comfortable than stagecoaches, and millions of people got in the habit of traveling by rail. By 1850, two decades after the success of *Rocket*, Great Britain had 6,087 miles (9,797 kilometers) of railroad line.

The introduction of railroads had their most transformative effects in the United States. By the 1840s, 6,000 miles (9656 kilometers) of track radiated from Boston, New York, Philadelphia, and Baltimore. In the 1850s, 21,000 miles (33,796 kilometers) of additional track were laid, much of it westward across the Appalachians to Memphis, St. Louis, and Chicago. After 1856 the trip from New York to Chicago, which had once taken three weeks by boat and on horseback, could be made in forty-eight hours. This rapid expansion of railroads opened up the Midwest, dispersing the waves of new immigrants, turning the vast prairie into farms to feed the industrial cities of the eastern United States, and creating a vast internal market for manufactures.

Railways also accelerated the industrialization of Europe (see Map 22.2). Belgium, independent since 1830, quickly copied the British railways. In France and Prussia, construction was delayed until the mid-1840s. When it began, however, it not only satisfied the long-standing need for transportation in those countries but also stimulated the iron, machinery, and construction industries. By 1850 Germany had built 3,639 miles (5,856 kilometers) of railroad line and France 1,811 miles (2,915 kilometers).

▲ **Clerkenwell Tunnel**   A nineteenth-century view of a section of the first underground railway opened in London in 1863 by the Metropolitan Railway to carry goods and passengers to developing suburbs. This contemporary image shows how the new technologies of the Industrial Revolution permitted men and women to seek housing at greater distance from their work. It also makes clear how these technologies could dramatically alter the physical environment. Courtesy of Lyman Johnson

AP® Exam Tip

Understand the impact of the steam engine and railroad on trade, transportation, migration, economic development, and imperialism.

Section Review

- A series of technological and organizational innovations transformed manufacturing, transportation, and communication.

- Mechanization, pioneered by Wedgwood, meant that work formerly done by skilled craftsmen was divided into many simple tasks assigned to workers in factories.

- New machines allowed the mass production of cotton yarn and cloth.

- Use of standardized interchangeable parts lowered labor costs and prices.

- The use of coke and new machines made iron cheap and abundant.

- Steam engines provided power for mines, factories, ships, and railroads.

- Electricity found its first practical application in telegraphy.

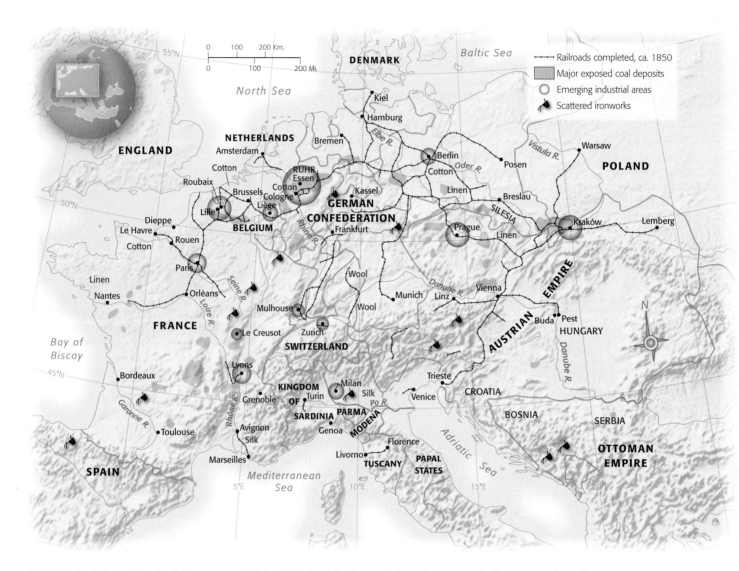

MAP 22.2 **Industrialization in Europe, ca. 1850** In 1850 industrialization was in its early stages on the European continent. The first industrial regions were comparatively close to England and possessed rich coal deposits: Belgium and the Ruhr district of Germany. Politics determined the location of railroads. Notice the star-shaped French network of rail lines emanating from Paris and the lines linking the different parts of the German Confederation.

How important were the developing industrial areas to the location of European railroad lines?

22-2f Communication over Wires

After Italian scientist Alessandro Volta invented the battery in 1800, making it possible to produce an electric current, many inventors tried to apply electricity to communication. The first practical **electric telegraph** systems were developed almost simultaneously in England and America. In 1837 in England Charles Wheatstone and William Cooke introduced a five-wire telegraph, while the American Samuel Morse introduced a code of dots and dashes that could be transmitted with a single wire. Morse convinced the Congress to provide $30,000 (nearly $900,000 in 2015) to "wire" America in 1842 and built a telegraph line connecting Baltimore and Washington, D.C., a year later.

The railroad companies allowed telegraph companies to string wires along the tracks in exchange for the right to send telegrams from station to station announcing the departure and arrival of trains. Such messages made railroads much safer as well as more efficient. By the late 1840s telegraph wires crisscrossed the eastern United States and western Europe. In 1851 the first submarine telegraph cable was laid across the English Channel from England to France (cutting

electric telegraph A device for rapid, long-distance transmission of information over an electric wire. It was introduced in England and North America in the 1830s and 1840s and replaced telegraph systems that utilized visual signals such as semaphores.

the transmission of news from up to four days to a matter of minutes); it was the beginning of a network that eventually connected the entire globe. No longer were communications limited to the speed of a sailing ship, a galloping horse, or a fast-moving train. Together railroads and telegraphs had an enormous economic impact. While railroads could move bulk goods more rapidly and at lower cost than other forms of land transportation, telegraphs dramatically transformed market intelligence by making it possible for producers to keep track of distant consumer needs and prices, thus making markets more efficient and profits more dependable.

22-3 The Impact of the Early Industrial Revolution

What was the impact of these changes on the society and environment of the industrializing countries?

The Industrial Revolution led to profound changes in society, politics, and the economy. At first, the changes were local. Some people became wealthy and built mansions, while others lived in slums with polluted water and air. By the mid-nineteenth century, the worst local effects were being alleviated and cities had become cleaner and healthier. Industrial nations then faced more complex problems: business cycles, labor conflicts, and the environmental degradation of entire regions by mining and industrial pollution. At the global level, industrialization empowered the nations of western Europe and North America to impose themselves on less developed nations.

AP® Exam Tip
Explain how the Industrial Revolution affected economic, social, and political systems.

22-3a The New Industrial Cities

The most dramatic environmental changes brought about by industrialization occurred in urban places. Cities had never before grown so fast. London, one of the largest cities in Europe in 1700 with 500,000 inhabitants, grew to 1,117,000 by 1800 and to 2,685,000 by 1850; it was then the largest city the world had ever known. Manchester, a small town of 20,000 in 1758, reached 303,000 a century later, a fifteen-fold increase. New York City, already 100,000 strong in 1815, reached 600,000 (including Brooklyn) in 1850. In some areas, towns merged and formed megalopolises, such as Greater London, the English Midlands, central Belgium, and the Ruhr district of Germany.

A great deal of money went into the building of fine homes, churches, museums, and theaters in wealthy neighborhoods. Much of the beauty of today's London dates from the time of the Industrial Revolution. Yet, by all accounts, industrial cities grew much too fast, and much of the growth occurred in the poorest neighborhoods. As poor migrants streamed in from the countryside, developers built the cheap, shoddy row houses for them to rent that Nassau Senior described in the chapter opening.

Sudden population growth caused serious urban environmental problems. Town dwellers recently arrived from the country brought country ways with them. People threw their sewage and trash out the windows to be washed down the gutters in the streets. The poor kept pigs and chickens to supplement the meager diet provided from low wages; the rich kept horses for their coaches; and, as a result, pedestrians stepped into the street at their own risk. Air pollution from burning coal, a problem since the sixteenth century, got steadily worse. Many urban dwellers drank water drawn from wells and rivers contaminated by sewage and industrial runoff. The River Irwell, which ran through Manchester, was, in the words of one visitor, "considerably less a river than a flood of liquid manure."[3] "Every day that I live," wrote an American visitor to Manchester, "I thank Heaven that I am not a poor man with a family in England."[4] At the same time, railroads invaded the towns, bringing noise and smoke into densely populated neighborhoods. On the outskirts of cities, railroad yards, sidings, and repair shops covered acres of land, surrounded by miles of warehouses and workers' housing.

AP® Exam Tip
Identify and explain several effects of urbanization during this time period.

---

[3]Quoted in Lewis Mumford, *The City in History* (New York, NY: Harcourt Brace, 1961), 460.

[4]Quoted in F. Roy Willis, *Western Civilization: An Urban Perspective*, vol. II (Lexington, MA: D.C. Heath, 1973), 675.

(Dessin de M. Karl Girardet.)

▲ **Paris Apartment at Night**   This cutaway drawing in a French magazine shows the vertical segregation by social class that prevailed in the 1840s. The lower level is occupied by the *concierge* (the building's caretaker) and her family. The first floor belongs to a wealthy family throwing a party for high-society friends. Middle-class people living on the next floor seem annoyed by the noise coming from below. Above them, a thief has entered an artist's studio. A poor seamstress and her child live in the garret under the roof. When elevators were introduced in the late nineteenth century, people of different income levels were more likely segregated by neighborhoods instead of by floors.   Section of a Parisian building, illustration from 'Le Magasin Pittoresque', engraved by John Quartley (fl.1835–67) 1847 (engraving) (b/w photo), Girardet, Karl (1813–71) (after) / Bibliotheque des Arts Decoratifs, Paris, France / Archives Charmet / The Bridgeman Art Library

Under these conditions, diseases proliferated. To the long list of preindustrial diseases, industrialization added new ailments. Rickets, a bone disease caused by lack of sunshine, became endemic in dark and smoky industrial cities. Steamships brought cholera to Europe from India, causing great epidemics that struck the poorest neighborhoods especially hard. Observers documented the horrors of slum life in vivid detail. Their shocking reports led to municipal reforms, such as garbage removal, water and sewage systems, and parks and schools. These measures began to alleviate the ills of urban life after the mid-nineteenth century.

22-3b Rural Environments

Long before the Industrial Revolution began, practically no wilderness areas were left in Britain and very few in western Europe. Almost every piece of land was covered with fields, forests, or pastures shaped by human activity, or by towns; yet humans continued to alter the environment. As they had been doing for centuries, people cut timber to build ships and houses, to heat homes, and to manufacture bricks, iron, glass, beer, bread, and many other items.

North Americans transformed their environment on a vast scale. Both the Canadian and American governments seized land from native peoples and made it available at low cost to farmers, many of them immigrants, and to logging companies. Settlers viewed forests not as a valuable resource but as a hindrance to development. In their haste to "open up the wilderness," pioneers felled trees and burned them, built houses and abandoned them, and moved on. The cultivation of cotton in the South was especially harmful. Planters cut down forests, grew cotton for a few years until the soil was depleted of nutrients, and then moved west, abandoning the land to scrub pines (see Chapter 25).

In industrializing Europe, raw materials once grown on the land—such as wood, hay, and wool— were replaced by materials found underground, like iron ore and coal, or obtained overseas, like cotton. Across Europe the expansion of coal and iron mining had dramatic and detrimental effects on the environment. As the population increased and land grew scarcer, the cost of growing feed for horses rose, creating incentives to find new, less land-hungry means of transportation. Likewise, as iron became cheaper and wood more expensive, ships and many other objects formerly made of wood began to be made of iron.

22-3c Working Conditions

Industrialization offered new opportunities to some enterprising workers. Carpenters, metalworkers, and machinists were in great demand in a transition dependent on mechanical skills. Some workers became engineers or went into business for themselves. The boldest of these Britons moved to the European continent, the Americas, or India, using their skills to establish new industries.

▲ **An Industrial Canal**   In the late eighteenth and early nineteenth centuries, before railroads were introduced, many canals were constructed in England, continental Europe, and the United States so that barges could transport heavy materials cheaply, such as coal for industrial works and steam engines, stone and bricks for buildings, clay for pottery works, and ores for metal foundries. Canals such as this one, which ran alongside a copper foundry, contributed greatly to Britain's industrial development. Morphart Creation/Shutterstock.com

The successful, however, were a minority. Most industrial jobs required much lower levels of skill than had earlier jobs in artisan production and were repetitive and boring. As mechanization and the factory system matured, the fast-growing workforce depended on a steady flow of unskilled workers from the countryside. Factory work did not vary with the seasons or the time of day but began and ended by the clock. The introduction of gas lighting expanded the working day past sunset (see Environment & Technology: Gas Lighting). Workdays were long, there were few breaks, and foremen watched constantly. Workers who performed one simple task over and over had little sense of achievement or connection to the final product. Industrial accidents were common and could ruin a family dependent on wages. Unlike the artisans they replaced, factory workers had no control over their tools, jobs, or working hours.

Industrial work had a major impact on women and family life as well. Women who could not afford servants had always worked, but mostly within the family: spinning and weaving, sewing hats and clothes, preparing food, washing, and doing a range of other essential household chores. In rural areas, women also did farm work, especially caring for gardens and small animals.

In the early years of industrialization, even where factory work was available, it was never the main occupation of working women. Most young women who sought paid employment became domestic servants in spite of the low pay, drudgery, and risk of sexual abuse by male employers. Women with small children tried hard to find work they could do at home, such as laundry, sewing, embroidery, millinery, or taking in lodgers. Those who worked in factories were concentrated in textile mills because textile work required less strength than metalworking, construction, or hauling. On average, women earned one-third to one-half as much as men. Economist Andrew Ure wrote in 1835: "It is in fact the constant aim and tendency of every improvement in machinery to supersede human labour altogether or to diminish its cost, by

AP® Exam Tip
Explain how and why labor systems have developed over time.

Before the nineteenth century, the night was a dangerous time to be out, and almost everyone went to bed at sundown and got up at dawn. For the managers of industrial establishments, daylight hours were too short, especially in the winter months. They knew that they could keep their factories running after sunset if they had light, but lanterns and candles were costly and dangerous. Wealthy people wanted to light up their homes, and businesses and government offices also needed light as well. While cities had sought to illuminate major thoroughfares since the eighteenth century, most city streets remained dark and dangerous. This situation inspired inventors to look for new ways to produce light.

French engineer Philippe Lebon knew that heating wood to make charcoal produced a flammable gas. In the 1790s he channeled this gas through pipes to illuminate a home and garden. In Britain, engineer William Murdock used the gas released in the process of making coke to light up a house. Moving from these experiments to commercial applications was a long and complicated process, however. Coal gas was smelly and explosive and full of impurities that gave off toxic fumes when it burned. Engineers had to learn ways to extract the gas efficiently, make strong pipes that did not leak, and market the product.

In 1806 Frederick Albert Winsor founded the National Light and Heat Company to produce and distribute gas in London. By 1816, London had 26 miles (42 kilometers) of gas mains bringing gas to several neighborhoods. That same year, Baltimore became the first American city to install gas mains and streetlamps. In the following decades, engineers developed ways of making gas safer and cleaner. They also invented meters to measure the amount of gas consumed and burners that produced a brighter light. As a result of these improvements, the cost of gas dropped to less than a third that of oil lamps of equivalent lighting power. From the 1840s until the early twentieth century, gaslights were installed in homes, businesses, and factories and along streets in the major cities of Europe and America.

The results were astonishing and delighted city dwellers. Mill and factory owners were able to extend the workday and increase production, while shops, restaurants, and other businesses were able to stay open late. Now people could walk the streets in greater safety. Evening illumination also contributed to the tremendous increase in adult education, as working people attended classes after work. Sales of books soared as increasing numbers of people stayed up late reading. Brightly lit cities

▲ **Gas Lighting** For city dwellers, one of the most dramatic improvements brought by industrialization was the introduction of gas lighting. The gas used, a by-product of heating coal to make coke for the iron industry, was distributed in iron pipes throughout the wealthier neighborhoods of big cities. Every evening at dusk, lamplighters went around lighting the street lamps. Mary Evans Picture Library/The Image Works

attracted migrants from the still-dark countryside. Gas lighting had banished the terrors of the night.

Questions for Analysis

1. What were the key stages in utilizing gas to illuminate homes and businesses?
2. How did gas lighting change the workday?
3. How did gas lighting change domestic arrangements?

AP® Exam Tip

Explain how the development of specialized labor systems has interacted with the development of social hierarchies.

substituting the industry of women and children for that of men."[5] Young unmarried women worked to support themselves or to save for marriage. Married women took factory jobs when their husbands' wages were unable to support family life. Mothers of infants faced a hard choice: whether to leave their babies with wet nurses at great expense or bring them to the factory and keep them drugged so they did not disrupt the work patterns. Because husbands and wives increasingly worked in different places and sometimes on different schedules, the Industrial Revolution was in many ways a revolution in family life.

As in preindustrial societies, parents thought children should contribute to their upkeep as soon as they were able to. The first generation of industrial workers brought children as young as five or six with them to the factories and mines, since there were no public schools or daycare

---

[5]Quoted in Joan W. Scott, "The Mechanization of Women's Work," *Scientific American* 247, no. 3 (September 1982): 171.

centers. Many of these children found work at low wages near their parents. Employers sometimes came to prefer child workers because they were cheaper and more docile than adults and because they were better able to tie broken threads or crawl under machines to sweep the dust. In Arkwright's cotton mills, for example, two-thirds of the workers were children. Mine operators used children to pull coal carts along the low passageways from the coal face to the mine shaft. Nearly all these children worked fourteen to sixteen hours a day and were beaten if they made mistakes or fell asleep.

Some manufacturers tried to provide more humane environments. When Francis Cabot Lowell built a cotton mill in Massachusetts, for example, he hired the unmarried daughters of New England farmers, promising them decent wages and housing in dormitories under careful moral supervision. Other manufacturers eager to combine profits with morality followed his example. But soon these early social experiments were overwhelmed by the profit motive, and manufacturers, especially in highly competitive industries, imposed longer hours, harsher working conditions, and lower wages. When young women in New England factories went on strike, the mill owners replaced them with impoverished Irish immigrants willing to accept lower pay and worse conditions.

The cotton boom enriched planters, merchants, and manufacturers and also reinforced and expanded the institution of slavery in the United States. In the 1790s, there were 700,000 slaves of African descent in the United States. As the "Cotton Kingdom" expanded, the number of slaves increased, reaching 3.2 million by 1850, 60 percent located in the cotton region. More slaves were imported before the legal slave trade was ended in 1808 and thousands more were illegally imported later, but natural increase was also important to the growing slave population. While cotton profits soared, the lives of slaves grew more oppressive. Thousands of slave families were broken up by the internal slave trade that moved slaves from tobacco regions to the cotton

▲ **"Love Conquers Fear"** This is a sentimental Victorian drawing of children in a textile mill. Child labor was common in the first half of the nineteenth century, and workers were exposed to dangerous machines and the moving belts that powered them, as well as to dust and dirt. From William Playfair, *The Commercial and Political Atlas*, 1801/Visual Connection Archive

frontier. At the same time, slave states also limited or outlawed manumissions, closing the door on slave families' hopes for freedom. Similarly, European demand for sugar prolonged plantation slavery in the West Indies. Even as the slave trade was attacked by abolitionists, slave labor was used to develop the coffee plantations of southern Brazil. Slavery was not, as white American southerners maintained, a "peculiar institution," a consequence of biological differences or biblical injunctions; it was instead an integral part of both commercial capitalism and the Industrial Revolution.

22-3d Changes in Society

In his novel *Sybil*, or, *The Two Nations*, British politician Benjamin Disraeli (**diz-RAY-lee**) (1804–1881) spoke of "two nations between whom there is no intercourse and no sympathy, who are as ignorant of each other's habits, thoughts, and feelings as if they were dwellers in different zones, or inhabitants of different planets . . . the rich and the poor."[6]

In Britain the worst-off were those who clung to skills or crafts in direct competition with the new mechanized industries, like textiles. The high wages and low productivity of handloom weavers in the 1790s induced inventors to develop power looms. As a result, by 1811 handloom weavers' wages had fallen by a third and by 1832 by two-thirds. Even by working longer hours at reduced compensation, few of these skilled workers could escape unemployment and destitution. While the incomes of workers in mechanized factories did not decline steadily like those of handloom weavers, these workers had little job security and had few opportunities to increase their wages by improving their skill levels. For many factory workers,

AP® Exam Tip
Understand how the Industrial Revolution influenced changes in gender roles.

[6]J. P. T. Bury, *The New Cambridge Modern History*, vol. 10 (Cambridge, UK: Cambridge University Press, 1967), 10.

Section Review

- The Industrial Revolution changed people's lives and the environments in which they lived and worked.

- Cities grew huge and, for most of their inhabitants, unsightly and unhealthy.

- Roads, canals, and railroads crisscrossed open land, changing rural environments.

- Middle-class women were consigned to caring for the home and children, while many working-class women worked long hours at low pay in mines and factories.

- Serious social problems arose, such as unemployment, alcoholism, and the abandonment of children.

especially those newly arrived from rural districts, these harsh conditions, insecurity, and low wages still represented an improvement over their prior employment.

The poor in Britain and across Europe spent nearly all their income on food and shelter. During the war years of 1792 to 1815, the price of food rose much faster than did wages, causing widespread hardship. Then, in the 1820s when wartime shortages ended and the exports of British industrial goods increased, real wages and public health began to improve for working-class families. Prices for food, housing, and clothing fell and wages rose. In this era of relative prosperity even the poor could afford comfortable, washable cotton clothes and underwear. But hard times returned in the "hungry forties." In 1847–1848 the potato crop failed in Ireland. One-quarter of the Irish population died in the resulting famine, and another quarter emigrated to England or North America. As these desperate men and women entered the workforce in their adopted countries, wages fell and employment became less secure.

The real beneficiaries of the early Industrial Revolution were the men and women of the middle class. In Britain, the landowning gentry and merchants had long shared wealth and influence. In the late eighteenth century a new group arose: entrepreneurs whose money came from manufacturing. Most, like Arkwright and Wedgwood, were the sons of middling shopkeepers, craftsmen, or farmers. Their enterprises were usually self-financed, for little capital was needed to start a cotton-spinning or machine-building business. A generation later, in the nineteenth century, some newly rich industrialists bought their way into high society. The integration of successful and wealthy industrialists occurred in western Europe and the United States after 1815 as well.

Before the Industrial Revolution, wives of merchants had often participated in family businesses, and widows occasionally managed sizable businesses on their own. With industrialization came a "cult of domesticity" to justify removing middle-class women from contact with the business world. Instead, the women of this class came to be seen as primarily responsible for the home, the servants, and the education of children as well as managing the family's social life (see Chapter 27). Not all women accepted the logic of being confined to this domestic sphere. Among those actively resisting these changes was Mary Wollstonecraft (1759–1797), who wrote the first feminist manifesto, *Vindication of the Rights of Woman*, in 1792.

While some middle-class people attributed their own success to their efforts and virtues and believed that those who did not succeed had no one but themselves to blame, others actively joined reform efforts to improve education, abolish slavery, protect child workers, modernize poor laws, and reform politics, among other objectives. The moral position of the middle class in the new industrial age mingled condemnation with concern, coupled with feelings of helplessness in the face of terrible social problems, such as drunkenness, prostitution, and child abandonment. Nevertheless, the middle class would become the active center of reform efforts by the middle of the nineteenth century.

22-4 New Economic and Political Ideas

How did the Industrial Revolution influence the rise of new economic and political ideas?

AP® Exam Tip Consider how Enlightenment philosophies applied new ways of understanding and empiricist approaches to both the natural world and human relationships.

The profound changes unleashed by the Industrial Revolution triggered political ferment and ideological conflict. So many wars and revolutions took place during those years that we cannot neatly separate out the consequences of industrialization from the effects of domestic political changes, the Enlightenment's impact on culture, and unrelated economic cycles (see Chapter 23). But it is clear that by undermining social traditions and causing a growing gap between rich and poor, the Industrial Revolution strengthened and focused the competing ideas of laissez faire (**LAY-say fair**) and socialism and sparked workers' organization efforts and protests.

22-4a **Laissez Faire and Its Critics**

The most celebrated exponent of **laissez faire** ("let them do") was Adam Smith (1723–1790), a Scottish economist. In *The Wealth of Nations* (published 1776) Smith argued that if individuals were allowed to seek personal gain, the effect, as though guided by an "invisible hand," would be to increase the general welfare of society. According to Smith, the government should refrain from interfering in business, except to protect private property; it should even allow duty-free trade with foreign countries. By advocating free-market capitalism, Smith was challenging the prevailing economic doctrine, **mercantilism**, which argued that governments should regulate trade in order to maximize their hoard of precious metals, a policy manifested in the monopoly trade companies created by the Dutch, English, and French in the seventeenth century (see Chapters 17 and 19).

Persuaded by Adam Smith's arguments, governments after 1815 dismantled some of their commercial regulations to stimulate trade, but no major power opened its economy to foreign competitors. Even though it was obvious to those advocating trade reform that industrialization was causing widespread misery among the working poor, Britain and other European governments were slower to adjust policies to ameliorate these social ills. Two of Smith's contemporaries, British thinkers Thomas Malthus (1766–1834) and David Ricardo (1772–1832), attempted to explain the poverty they saw without challenging the basic premises of laissez faire. The cause of the workers' plight, they said, was rapid population growth, which outstripped the food supply and led to falling wages. The workers' poverty, they claimed, was as much a result of "natural law" as was the wealth of successful businessmen. For them the only way for the working class to avoid mass famine was to delay marriage and practice self-restraint and sexual abstinence.

Business people in Britain eagerly adopted laissez-faire ideas, derived from Smith and others, that justified their activities and kept the government at bay. But not everyone accepted the grim conclusions of the "dismal science," as economics was then known. British philosopher Jeremy Bentham (1748–1832) believed that it was possible to maximize "the greatest happiness of the greatest number," if only Parliament would study the social problems of the day and pass appropriate legislation. German economist Friedrich List (1789–1846) also rejected laissez faire and free trade as a British trick "to make the rest of the world, like the Hindus, its serfs in all industrial and commercial relations." To protect their "infant industries" from British competition, he argued, the German states had to erect high tariff barriers against imports from Britain. On the European continent, List's ideas helped lead to the formation of the Zollverein (**TSOLL-feh-rine**) in 1834. This was one of the first customs union of most of the German states that reduced tolls and tariffs within the member states while at the same time attempting to control some of the destructive effects of foreign imports, especially British industrial goods.

French social thinkers, moved by sincere concern for the poor, offered a radically new vision of a just civilization. Espousing a philosophy called **positivism**, the count of Saint-Simon (1760–1825) and his disciple Auguste Comte (**COMB-tuh**) (1798–1857) argued that the scientific method could solve social as well as technical problems. They recommended that the poor, guided by scientists and artists, form workers' communities under the protection of benevolent business leaders. These ideas attracted the enthusiastic support of bankers and entrepreneurs, for whom positivism provided a rationale for investing in railroads, canals, and other symbols of modernity. Positivism was most influential in Latin America, where the political elites, especially in Brazil and Mexico, pursued a top-down program of economic development reinforced by harsh police controls and the manipulation of political institutions. The chief tenets of this ideology are emblazed on the Brazilian flag: Order and Progress.

As numerous protest organizations formed across Europe in the wake of the Industrial Revolution, a minority of the working class and those allied with the workers sought to overthrow the new industrial order. Groups calling themselves communists were the most prominent of these radical groups. Two German-born intellectuals, Karl Marx (1818–1883) and his long-time collaborator and benefactor Friedrich Engels (1820–1895), played key roles in formulating this movement's criticism of industrial capitalism. They argued that the concentration of wealth and power associated with industrialization had led to the unbearable oppression of industrial workers (what they called the **proletariat**) and justified revolution. While the monumental work *Das Kapital* (Capital) was Marx's major intellectual achievement, it was *The Communist Manifesto*, published in 1848 with Engels, that proved most influential in spreading his radical critique of capitalism and urging the mobilization of the working class. This short, powerful book argued that history

AP® Exam Tip
Be familiar with the development of capitalism and classical liberalism associated with Adam Smith and John Stuart Mill.

laissez faire The idea that government should refrain from interfering in economic affairs. The classic exposition of laissez-faire principles is Adam Smith's *Wealth of Nations* (1776).

mercantilism European government policies of the sixteenth, seventeenth, and eighteenth centuries designed to promote overseas trade between a country and its colonies and accumulate precious metals by requiring colonies to trade only with their motherland country. The British system was defined by the Navigation Acts, the French system by laws known as the *Exclusif*.

positivism A philosophy developed by the French count of Saint-Simon. Positivists believed that social and economic problems could be solved by the application of the scientific method, leading to continuous progress. Their ideas were popular in France and Latin America in the nineteenth century.

proletariat The class of industrial wage earners who possess neither capital nor the tools of production, unlike the preindustrial artisan class. They, therefore, must earn their living by selling their labor.

was dominated by class struggle and that proletarians would inevitably come together to over-throw the bourgeoisie, the modern class that controlled industry. The book's final words were "Proletarians of all countries unite!"

22-4b Protests and Reforms

AP® Exam Tip
Identify and explain several responses to the spread of global capitalism, such as Marxism.

Workers benefited little from the ideas of these middle-class intellectuals. Instead, they resisted harsh working conditions in their own ways. Periodically, they rioted or went on strike, especially when food prices were high or when downturns in the business cycle left many unemployed. In some places, craftsmen broke into factories and destroyed the new machines that threatened their livelihoods. Such acts of resistance did little to change the nature of industrial work or slow the pace of mechanical innovation.

From the beginnings of the Industrial Revolution workers had resisted the introduction of new technologies. They rightly believed that mechanized production would eliminate their ability to control the pace of production, diminish the value of their skills, and impoverish their families. As early as 1767, disgruntled textile workers mobilized to destroy one of the early textile innovations, James Hargreaves's spinning jenny. Subsequent innovations in both the cotton and woolen industries were also attacked by angry crowds of workers. In 1779, for example, angry workers destroyed nearly every machine driven by waterpower in Blackburn, England. Workers also organized to demand better wages and working conditions. Some contemplated more profound structural changes to society. Workers enlisting in the secret organization United Britons were asked to affirm yes to three questions: Do you desire a total change of the system? Are you willing to risk yourself in a contest to leave posterity free? Are you willing to do all in your power to create the spirit of love and brotherhood and affection among the friends of freedom? The government saw this mobilization as insurrectionary.

Then in 1811 workers in the lace and stocking industries began a campaign of systematic machine breaking. The movement was rooted in the secret workers' organizations already in place in industrial settings. Calling themselves *Luddites* (followers of a fictional Ned Ludd or General Ludd), the protestors attacked more than 100 businesses and destroyed nearly every machine in the district. They also threatened the lives and personal property of factory owners and killed one person. To suppress this movement, the government deployed hundreds of spies and informants as well as sent a military force of 12,000 to the affected region. In 1813 more than twenty Luddites were executed and many more sentenced to transportation and hard labor in Australia. Despite the violence of the repression, workers continued to resist. Three years later, rioters entered a factory at Loughborough (between Manchester and Birmingham), destroyed thirty-seven machines, and set fire to the building. Ten workers were apprehended and eight executed.

Machine breaking and worker mobilizations in France were even more violent. As French entrepreneurs began introducing British industrial technologies in textiles and metallurgy in the late 1770s, workers organized protests against these "foreign" innovations, attacking the British craftsmen installing new technologies and destroying the machines. In the early stages of the French Revolution (see Chapter 23), popular revolutionary sentiment reinforced the resistance of workers to new machinery and undermined the ability of the government to protect factories and machinery. This coincidence of revolutionary political mobilization and the defense of traditional hand crafts meant that French artisans, unlike their English contemporaries, retained control of factory production and France fell decades behind Britain in industrializing.

Mechanization was also resisted in agricultural areas. The effects of enclosure (described earlier in this chapter) and rural population growth combined to force many rural families in Great Britain into poverty. Thousands of tenants and small farmers lost their land, becoming seasonal labors or migrating to industrial cities. This impoverished class of rural workers rose up when wealthy farmers began to introduce mechanical reapers and other machines. Often called the "Captain Swing" riots, rural laborers and many village artisans, such as blacksmiths and wheelwrights, organized against mechanization, setting fires, threatening landlords, demanding higher wages, and breaking machines. This popular movement culminated after 1830 when widespread rural riots forced the British government to mobilize troops and militia in defense of property. Thousands of protestors were arrested and 252 were sentenced to death. In the end, nineteen were executed and the remaining 233 had their sentences commuted to transportation to Australia as convict laborers.

▲ **Captain Swing Riots**   When English landowners introduced reapers and other machines, rural laborers violently resisted by destroying the machines, setting fires, and sometimes attacking the owners and farm managers. The movement was finally repressed by county militias and troops.   Mansell/Getty Images

These violent efforts to block innovation and protect long-established customs in manufacturing and agriculture were superseded by laboring class organizations focused on workplace reform, higher wages, and expanded political rights. Gradually, workers organized to demand universal male suffrage and shorter workdays. In 1834 Robert Owen founded the Grand National Consolidated Trade Union to lobby for an eight-hour workday; it quickly gained half a million members but dissolved a few months later in the face of government prosecutions. A new movement called Chartism arose soon thereafter, led by William Lovett and Fergus O'Connor, that appealed to miners and industrial workers. It demanded universal male suffrage, the secret ballot, salaries for members of Parliament, and annual elections. Chartism collapsed in 1848, but it left a legacy of labor organizing (see Chapter 23). By 1850 the beginnings of the modern union movement were in place in Europe's most industrialized nations.

Eventually, mass movements mobilizing industrial workers persuaded the British Parliament to investigate conditions in factories and mines and initiate some reforms. The Factory Act of 1833 prohibited the employment of children younger than nine in textile mills. It also limited the working hours of children between the ages of nine and thirteen to eight hours a day and of fourteen- to eighteen-year-olds to twelve hours. The Mines Act of 1842 prohibited the employment of women and boys under age ten underground. Belgium and other European nations were slower to introduce workplace reforms. In response to the efforts of workers, the British learned to seek reform through accommodation. On the European continent, in contrast, the revolutions of 1848 revealed widespread discontent with repressive governments but failed to soften the hardships of industrialization (see Chapter 27) until decades later.

Section Review

- Many people sought explanations and proposed solutions for the changes in society and the economy.

- Some economists defended the growing disparities between rich and poor in the name of laissez faire, the free-market idea proposed by Adam Smith that appealed to businesspeople.

- Positivists deplored the hardships caused by industrialization but asserted that they could be ameliorated by technological advances and wise policies.

- Agitation by workers led politicians to investigate the working conditions in mines and factories, especially the work of women and children.

22-5 The Limits of Industrialization Outside the West

How did the Industrial Revolution affect the relations between the industrialized and the nonindustrialized parts of the world?

22-5a Egypt

The spread of the Industrial Revolution in the early nineteenth century transformed the relations of western Europe and North America with the rest of the world. Egypt, strongly influenced by European ideas since the French invasion of 1798, began to industrialize in the early nineteenth century. The driving force was its ruler, **Muhammad Ali** (1769–1849), a man who was to play a major role in the history of the Middle East and East Africa (see Chapters 24 and 26). Muhammad Ali wanted to build up the Egyptian economy and military in order to become less dependent on the Ottoman sultan, his nominal overlord. To do so, he imported advisers and technicians from Europe and built cotton mills, foundries, shipyards, weapons factories, and other industrial enterprises. To pay for all this, he made the peasants grow wheat and cotton, which the government bought at a low price and exported at a profit. He also imposed high tariffs on imported goods to force the pace of industrialization.

Muhammad Ali's efforts fell afoul of the British, who did not want a strong government and modern economy controlling the flow of travelers, goods, and mail across Egypt, the shortest route between Europe and India. When Egypt went to war against the Ottoman Empire in 1839, Britain intervened and forced Muhammad Ali to eliminate all import duties in the name of free trade. Unprotected, Egypt's fledgling industries could not compete with the flood of cheap British products. Thereafter, Egypt exported raw cotton to supply the British textile industry and imported manufactured goods, becoming, as a result, an economic dependency of Britain.

AP® Exam Tip
Understand how the Industrial Revolution shifted various regions' share of global manufacturing.

22-5b India

When European merchants arrived in South Asia in the sixteenth century, Indian cotton textiles held a dominant position in the region's markets. As European powers gained maritime control of the Indian Ocean and south Asia, India's cotton textile production surged. In this expansion, Dutch and British merchants played a leading role in introducing India's cotton textiles to new consumers in Asia as well as in Europe. By the seventeenth century Indian cotton gained wide acceptance in European markets. Because cotton textiles were lighter weight and easier to keep clean than competing linen and wool garments produced by European artisans, demand grew quickly. By the 1650s the finest-quality printed Indian cloth was worn by the powerful and wealthy of Europe and the Americas while less expensive Indian cotton clothed laborers and slaves.

Although the British East India Company (chartered in 1600) maintained trade outposts and forts across Asia, India became the center of its commercial empire and, by the end of the Seven Years War in 1763, the company had established its effective control of Bengal, one of India's most important textile centers. In the following decades the importation of Indian cotton textiles to Britain became a key source of this British company's profits.

This booming trade was opposed by British woolen and linen textile producers who succeeded in imposing tariffs and other duties on Indian textiles. The intention of these "Calico Acts" was to give British producers a chance to produce cotton cloth at competitive prices. But India enjoyed two key advantages: first, it produced raw cotton while Britain had to import its raw material from America and elsewhere and, second, British labor was more than six times more expensive than Indian labor. So, while tariffs and duties provided some protection, the British industry could not compete without lowering labor and raw materials costs. In fact, the importation of Indian textiles increased dramatically during the last three decades of the eighteenth century, despite the tariffs. Indian cotton imports peaked in the 1790s as the first generation of mechanical innovations transformed the production of British cotton cloth. But even though British production costs were falling, a new round of tariffs on Indian textiles were imposed.

Muhammad Ali Leader of Egyptian modernization in the early nineteenth century. He ruled Egypt as an Ottoman governor but had imperial ambitions. His descendants ruled Egypt until overthrown in 1952.

While tariffs helped protect the domestic market for British textile producers, it was the simultaneous mechanical innovations of the Industrial Revolution that ultimately led to the comprehensive decline of the Indian industry. The first stage of British mechanization revolutionized spinning by multiplying the productivity of British workers and lowering the cost of British cotton yarns. This coincided with a massive expansion of American cotton production that reduced the price of raw cotton to British producers. By the 1830s, English yarn made from American cotton and produced by steam-driven machines was cheaper in India than local yarn produced traditionally. As Indian hand weavers switched to these cheap imported yarns to remain competitive, Indian spinners were displaced in large numbers.

Then, with the widespread adoption of steam-driven looms after 1830 in Britain, the cost of machine-made cotton cloth fell steadily, undermining Indian textiles and driving down wages. As British machine-made textiles flooded the Indian market duty-free, many skilled handloom weavers lost employment, although local hand weavers continued to supply India's poor. Because India was a colony, it had no way to protect its domestic textile producers with tariffs or duties as Britain had done 130 years earlier. By the middle of the nineteenth century, the rapidly improving efficiency and the falling prices of mechanized British textile production had prevailed in Britain and in India. Because India's displaced spinners and weavers found few alternatives for employment as their industry contracted in the face of growing imports, most of them became landless peasants, eking out a precarious living.

As a result, India, like other tropical regions, became an exporter of raw materials and an importer of British industrial goods. To hasten this transformation, British entrepreneurs and colonial officials introduced railroads into the subcontinent. The construction of India's railroad network began in the mid-1850s, along with coal mining to fuel the locomotives and the installation of telegraph lines to connect the major cities.

Some Indian entrepreneurs saw opportunities in the atmosphere of change that the British created. In 1854 Bombay merchant Cowasjee Nanabhoy Davar (**cow-AAs-gee Naa-naa-boy Daavar**) imported an engineer, four skilled workers, and several textile machines from Britain and started India's first mechanized textile mill. This was the beginning of India's modern cotton textile industry. Despite many gifted entrepreneurs, however, India's industrialization proceeded at a snail's pace, for the government was in British hands and the British did little to encourage or support Indian industry.

22-5c China

In the eighteenth century the Chinese economy benefited from a long period of relative political stability and from population growth and commercial expansion. During the Qing dynasty, specialized market towns devoted to cotton textiles, silk, and staples developed in east-central China. At the same time, China developed markets in land and labor as well as rudimentary banking and credit mechanisms that facilitated long-distance trade. There were few direct threats to either Chinese borders or Chinese trade. This situation changed as European powers, first the Portuguese and Dutch and then the British and French, established highly militarized commercial presences in Asia. Nevertheless, even as European power grew, China continued to play a major role in the major markets of Asia, maintaining a favorable balance of trade with Europe that was financed by silver from European colonies.

China, however, remained an agrarian empire much less dependent on foreign trade than the major European powers, especially Great Britain. As a result, the Chinese government focused its attention and resources on the production and distribution of food, an effective guarantee of social peace, rather than on trade. While Britain and its European rivals viewed foreign trade as crucial to national well-being and as inherently competitive (see Diversity & Dominance: Commercial Expansion and Risk, in Chapter 17), the Chinese government saw foreign trade as narrowly supplemental to the domestic economy.

With inexpensive and abundant labor, the absence of a true national market, and limited engagement in foreign markets, the Chinese government did not see a clear need to subsidize or promote technology transfers as new machine technologies rapidly transformed the European economy in the first half of the nineteenth century. This situation began to rapidly change when Great Britain, its military transformed by the Industrial Revolution, pressed to reverse the steep trade imbalance long enjoyed by China. Compelled now to recognize the economic and military transformations wrought by industrial innovation in Europe, China faced a succession of internal and foreign threats to stability before its own reforms could begin to take hold.

▲ **A Railroad Bridge Across the Nile**   In the second half of the nineteenth century, industrialized nations, especially Great Britain, sent engineers and equipment to build railroads in less industrialized parts of the world, such as India, South Africa, Latin America, and the Middle East. One such railway connected Cairo and Alexandria in Egypt. Here a railroad bridge crosses the Nile at Benha near the pyramids. Historical/Getty Images

Section Review

- Industrialization gave the newly industrialized nations of the West the power to coerce non-Western societies.

- Britain snuffed out the incipient industrialization in Egypt and India and turned these countries intro producers of raw materials.

- China stagnated and was defeated by Britain and its steam-powered gunboats.

In January 1840 a shipyard in Britain launched a radically new ship. The *Nemesis* had an iron hull, a flat bottom that allowed it to navigate in shallow waters, and a steam engine to power it upriver and against the wind. In November it arrived off the coast of China, heavily armed. Though ships from Europe had been sailing to China for 300 years, the *Nemesis* was the first steam-powered iron gunboat in Asian waters. It was soon joined by other steam-powered warships that collectively established European control of Chinese rivers, bombarding forts and cities and transporting troops and supplies far more quickly than Chinese soldiers could move on foot. With this new weapon, Britain, a small island nation half a world away, was able to defeat the largest and most populated country in the world (see Chapter 24). The cases of Egypt, India, and China show how the demands of Western nations and the military advantage they gained from industrialization led them to interfere in the internal affairs of nonindustrial societies. As we shall see in Chapter 27, this was the start of a new age of Western dominance.

22-6 Conclusion

The Industrial Revolution was the most momentous transformation in history since the beginnings of agriculture. The mechanization of industrial production and the introduction of the steam engine dramatically increased human productivity and lowered the prices of most manufactured goods. Other innovations like railroads and telegraphs increased the speed of transportation and communication, connecting once isolated peoples and cultures. In the century that followed the first wave of innovation, the nations that had embraced and promoted industrialization, Great Britain, Germany, and the United States in particular, grew wealthy and became global powers.

These transformations disrupted long-established institutions and economic relationships while also causing social upheavals and environmental problems. The most successful of the inventors, entrepreneurs, and investors who directed this economic revolution became very wealthy and acquired great influence in political life. At the same time, industrial workers—many of them women and children—often worked in appalling conditions and lived in overcrowded tenements in badly polluted cities. Even in rural settings, mechanization threatened the already difficult circumstances of poor families. While the victors celebrated the fruits of what they called progress, the disadvantaged resisted, organizing protests and, in some cases, turning to violence.

Reacting to the incidents of machine breaking, property destruction, and rioting and to threats of revolution, economists, philosophers, and reformers offered innumerable theories and proposals for reform. Political leaders generally responded with force or the threat of force as workers mobilized and formed unions. Although economic and social reforms were put in place slowly, most industrializing western nations found ways to blunt class antagonisms such as expanding the right to vote, limiting child labor, and, ultimately, legislating minimum wage levels.

Industrialization also had global political consequences. A small number of industrializing nations—first Great Britain, then the nations of western Europe and the United States—grew more powerful and became more willing to impose their will on weaker nations. Those parts of the world that were left behind became, in most cases, political and economic dependencies of these powerful nations.

While the industrialized nations eventually learned to alleviate many of their internal social problems and improve working conditions, the disparity between rich and poor nations persisted for two centuries or more, reinforced in the nineteenth century by a new round of European imperialism in Africa and Asia. The environmental consequences of industrialization have also endured, growing worse as industrialization expanded into new regions and changed from local issues to global threats.

Key Terms

Industrial Revolution p. 557	division of labor p. 564	James Watt p. 568	proletariat p. 577
agricultural revolution p. 558	mechanization p. 564	electric telegraph p. 570	Muhammad Ali p. 580
mass production p. 563	Richard Arkwright p. 565	laissez faire p. 577	
Josiah Wedgwood p. 563	Crystal Palace p. 567	mercantilism p. 577	
	steam engine p. 568	positivism p. 577	

Review Questions

1. What were the reasons that Britain played a leading role in the Industrial Revolution?

2. What were the key changes in the organization of production that resulted from mechanization?

3. How did urban and rural workers respond to the changes introduced by the Industrial Revolution?

Multiple-Choice Questions

Questions 1–3 refer to the image below.

▲ **Railroad Bridge Across the Nile** CORBIS/Getty Images

1. The image supports which of the following conclusions?

   (A) Industrialization's impact was limited to Europe.

   (B) Industrial revolutions occurred in several time periods.

   (C) Industrial technology developed independently in multiple regions.

   (D) Industrialization led to major developments and innovations in transportation.

2. British involvement in Egypt reflects which of the following larger processes in the nineteenth century?

   (A) The closing of the income gap between classes globally

   (B) The use of warfare and diplomacy to expand European influence in Africa

   (C) The use of industrial technology to prevent colonial rebellions

   (D) The decline of cash crops and plantation systems in expanding empires

3. Which of the following was the most likely use of railroads in colonies such as Egypt?

   (A) To promote leisure activities for both Europeans and local populations

   (B) To encourage the building of factories in the colonies

   (C) To give local indigenous populations access to modern travel

   (D) To transport raw materials and military personnel

Questions 4–6 refer to the passage below.

"Many researchers believe that the potato's arrival in northern Europe spelled an end to famine there. (Corn, another American crop, played a similar but smaller role in southern Europe.) More than that, as the historian William H. McNeill has argued, the potato led to empire: 'By feeding rapidly growing populations, [it] permitted a handful of European nations to assert dominion over most of the world between 1750 and 1950.' The potato, in other words, fueled the rise of the West."

Charles C. Mann, "How the Potato Changed the World,"
Smithsonian Magazine, November 2011

4. Which of the following is an argument about industrialization that could be supported by the excerpt?

   (A) The arrival of European crops in the Americas led to a rise in the Amerindian population.

   (B) The encounter between Europe and the Americas was limited to cultural exchanges.

   (C) The arrival of American crops had a significant demographic impact on Europe.

   (D) The Columbian Exchange impacted only the Americas.

5. The expanding population discussed in the excerpt is important in understanding the reason for which of the following aspects of the Industrial Revolution?

   (A) Increasing migration to cities in search of work

   (B) Increasing migration to rural areas to assist in food production

   (C) Increasing use of slavery in mills and factories

   (D) Decreasing immigration to the Americas

6. Which of the following statements about the social impact of industrialization is most correct?

   (A) Industrialization led directly to colonial independence in the time period, and many colonies surpassed their mother countries economically.

   (B) While industrialization led many women to embrace a "cult of domesticity," it led others to begin to challenge gender hierarchies.

   (C) The industrial revolutions reinforced the power of landed elites; however, "city" elites (such as business owners) lost their power.

   (D) American crops led to a politically and economically weaker Europe, while enabling the Americas to throw off the yoke of colonialism.

Questions 7–10 refer to the map below.

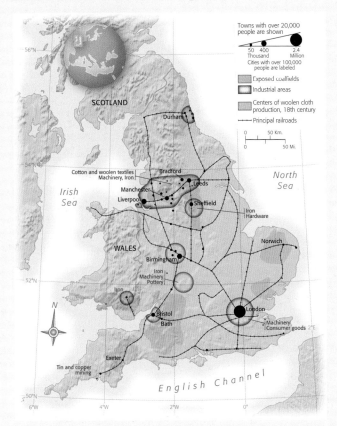

▲ **The Industrial Revolution in Britain, ca. 1850**

7. Based on the map, which of the following was imperative to England's ability to industrialize?

   (A) England's location allowed it to take advantage of continental Europe's natural resources.

   (B) England's forests were still intact and could be used as fuel for factories.

   (C) The development of machines, including steam engines, and England's many natural reserves of coal.

   (D) Most of England's ports had easy access to the Mediterranean trade.

8. Based on the map, a historian could argue that

   (A) even with modern forms of transportation, England had difficulty controlling the economies of its northern regions and Scotland.

   (B) England's role in nineteenth-century industrialization was focused primarily on transporting, not producing, manufactured items.

   (C) England lagged in the industrialization process because of its limited geography.

   (D) England led the industrialization process because of specific environmental advantages.

9. The development of industrial cities like those shown on the map were in part a result of which of the following?

   (A) Specialization of labor and the birth of mass production

   (B) Naval transportation resulting in renewed emphasis on canals

   (C) Significant efforts to clean up cities and make them more habitable

   (D) Migration from the colonies to England in search of work

10. Based on the map provided, industrialization in the eighteenth and nineteenth century had the most significant direct impact on which of the following?

   (A) Rural and farming life

   (B) Communication and transportation

   (C) Religious development and spread

   (D) Legal and bureaucratic institutions

Short-Answer Questions

Question 1 refers to the passage below.

"[T]he trade of the pin-maker: a workman not educated to this business . . . could scarce, perhaps, with his utmost industry, make one pin in a day, and certainly could not make twenty. But in the way in which this business is now carried on . . . but it is divided into a number of branches, of which the greater part are likewise peculiar trades. One man draws out the wire, another straights it, a third cuts it, a fourth points it, a fifth grinds it at the top for receiving the head; to make the head requires two or three distinct operations, to put it on . . . accommodated with the necessary machinery, they could, when they exerted themselves, make among them about twelve pounds of pins in a day."

Adam Smith, *An Inquiry into the Nature and Causes of the Wealth of Nations*, 1776

1. Answer all parts of the question that follows.

   (A) Identify ONE factor that led to the rise of industrial production and eventually the Industrial Revolution.

   (B) Explain ONE way the nature of work changed throughout industrialization.

   (C) Explain ONE way the nature of work remained the same throughout industrialization.

2. Answer all parts of the question that follows.

   (A) Identify ONE location outside of Europe not directly impacted by the rise of the Industrial Revolution.

   (B) Explain ONE way industrialization led to a change in imperialism.

   (C) Explain ONE way locations outside of Europe continued to remain untouched by industrialization.

23 Revolutionary Changes in the Atlantic World, 1750–1850

CHAPTER OUTLINE

AP® Framework Terms

Enlightenment
Natural rights
Social contract
American Declaration of Independence
French Declaration of the Rights of
    Man and the Citizen
American Revolution
Haitian Revolution

Overarching Questions

1 How have religions, belief systems, philosophies, and ideologies affected the political, economic, and social development of societies? (CUL)

2 How have internal and external political factors influenced the process of state building, expansion, and dissolution? (SB)

3 How have economic systems and the development of ideologies, values, and institutions influenced each other? (ECON)

4 How have social categories, roles, and practices been maintained or challenged over time? (SOC)

5 How have political, economic, cultural, and demographic factors affected social structures? (SOC)

I n August 1791 slaves and free blacks began an insurrection in the plantation district of northern Saint Domingue **(san doe-MANG)** (present-day Haiti). During the following decade and a half, Haitian revolutionaries abolished slavery; defeated military forces from Britain and France; and achieved independence.

News and rumors about revolutionary events in France had helped move the island's slave community to rebel. These same events had divided the island's white population into royalists (supporters of France's King Louis XVI) and republicans (who sought an end to monarchy). The large free mixed-race population secured some political rights from the French Assembly but were forced into rebellion by the violent resistance of the slave-owning elite to these reforms.

A black freedman, François Dominique Toussaint, led the insurrection. Taking the name Toussaint L'Ouverture **(too-SAN loo-ver-CHORE)**, he became one of the most remarkable representatives of the revolutionary era. He organized the rebels militarily, negotiated with the island's competing factions and with representatives of Britain and France, and wrote his nation's first constitution. Commonly portrayed as a fiend by slave owners, Toussaint became a towering symbol of resistance to oppression to slaves everywhere.

▲ **Burning of Cap Français, Saint Domingue, in 1793**　In 1791, the slaves of Saint Domingue, France's richest colony, began a rebellion that, after years of struggle, ended slavery and created the Western Hemisphere's second independent nation, Haiti. Burning of the town of Cap-Francais, Saint-Domingue (Haiti), 1795 (colour engraving), French School, (18th century)/Private Collection/Archives Charmet/The Bridgeman Art Library

The Haitian slave rebellion was an important event in the political and cultural transformation of the Western world. Profound changes to the economy, politics, and intellectual life occurred as well. The Industrial Revolution (see Chapter 22) increased manufacturing productivity and led to greater global interdependence, new patterns of consumerism, and altered social structures. At the same time, intellectuals questioned the traditional place of monarchy and religion in Western society. Enriched by the economic dynamism of this period, merchants, professionals, and manufacturers provided an audience for these new intellectual currents as they pressed for a larger political role.

This revolutionary era turned the Western world "upside down." The *ancien régime* **(ahn-see-EN ray-ZHEEM)**, the French term for Europe's old order, rested on medieval principles: politics dominated by powerful monarchs, intellectual and cultural life dominated by religion, and economics dominated by hereditary agricultural elites. In the West's new order, commoners entered political life; science took the place of religion in intellectual life; and economies opened to competition.

This radical transformation did not take place without false starts or setbacks. Imperial powers resisted the loss of colonies; monarchs and nobles struggled to retain their ancient privileges; and church authorities fought against the claims of science. While the liberal and nationalist ideals of the eighteenth-century revolutionary movements were sometimes thwarted in Europe and the Americas, belief in national self-determination and universal suffrage and a passion for social justice continued to animate reformers into the twentieth century. ●

23-1 Prelude to Revolution: The Eighteenth-Century Crisis

How did the costs of imperial wars and the Enlightenment challenge the established authority of monarchs and religion in Europe and the American colonies?

The cost of wars fought among Europe's major powers over colonies and trade helped precipitate the revolutionary era that began in 1775 with the American Revolution. Britain, France, and Spain were the central actors in these global struggles, but other imperial powers participated as well. While these nations had previously fought unpopular and costly wars and paid for them by imposing new taxes, changes in Western intellectual and political environments now produced a much more critical response. Any effort to extend monarchical power or enact new taxes now raised questions about the rights of individuals and the legitimacy of political institutions.

23-1a Colonial Wars and Fiscal Crises

In the seventeenth century competition among European powers became global in character. The newly independent Netherlands attacked the trade routes that linked Spain and Portugal to their American and Asian colonies, even seizing parts of Portugal's colonial empire in Brazil and Angola. Europe's other emerging sea power, Great Britain, also attacked Spanish fleets and seaports in the Americas. These rivalries made the defense of trade routes and distant colonies more expensive and difficult.

The eighteenth century further tested the ability of European powers to pay for their imperial ambitions. As Dutch power ebbed, Britain and France began a long struggle for political preeminence in western Europe and for territory and trade outlets in the Americas and Asia as the older empires of Spain and Portugal struggled to hang on. Nearly all of Europe's great powers participated in the War of the Spanish Succession (1701–1714). A few decades later war between Britain and Spain over smuggling broadened into a generalized European conflict, the War of Austrian Succession (1740–1748). Less than two decades later a frontier conflict between French and British forces and their Amerindian allies then led to a wider struggle, the Seven Years' War (1756–1763). With peace Britain emerged with undisputed control of North America east of the Mississippi River while France had been forced to surrender Canada and its holdings in India.

The enormous cost of these conflicts distinguished them from earlier wars. Traditional taxes collected in traditional ways no longer covered the obligations of governments. While Britain's total annual budget before the Seven Years' War had averaged only £8 million, in 1763 its war debt had reached £137 million and interest payments alone exceeded £5 million. Even as European economies expanded, fiscal crises overtook one European government after another. In an intellectual environment transformed by the Enlightenment, the need for new revenues provoked debate and confrontation within a vastly expanded and more critical public.

23-1b The Enlightenment and the Old Order

The complex and diverse intellectual movement called the **Enlightenment** applied the methods and perspectives of the Scientific Revolution of the seventeenth century to the study of human society as well as to the natural world (see Chapter 17). Some European intellectuals sought to systematize knowledge and organize reference materials. For example, Swedish botanist Carolus Linnaeus (**kar-ROLL-uhs lin-NEE-uhs**) sought to categorize all living organisms, and Samuel Johnson published a comprehensive English dictionary. In France Denis Diderot (**duh-nee DEE-duh-roe**) worked with other thinkers to create a compendium of human knowledge, the thirty-five-volume *Encyclopédie*.

Other thinkers pursued lines of inquiry that more directly challenged long-established religious and political institutions. Some argued that if scientists could understand the laws of nature, then surely similar forms of disciplined investigation might reveal laws of human nature. The most radical wondered whether society and government could be better regulated and more productive if guided by science rather than by hereditary rulers and the church. These new perspectives and the intellectual optimism that fed them helped guide the revolutionary movements of the late eighteenth century.

AP® Exam Tip
Understand how Enlightenment ideas influenced resistance to existing political authority and the expansion of rights in the eighteenth and nineteenth centuries.

Enlightenment A philosophical movement in eighteenth-century Europe that fostered the belief that one could reform society by discovering rational laws that governed social behavior and were just as scientific as the laws of physics.

CHRONOLOGY

	The Americas	Europe
1750	1754–1763 French and Indian War	1756–1763 Seven Years' War
	1770 Boston Massacre	
1775	1776 American Declaration of Independence	1778 Death of Voltaire and Rousseau
	1778 United States alliance with France	
	1781 British surrender at Yorktown	1789 Storming of Bastille begins French Revolution; Declaration of the Rights of Man and the Citizen in France
	1783 Treaty of Paris ends American Revolution	1793–1794 Reign of Terror in France
	1791 Slaves revolt in Saint Domingue (Haiti)	1795–1799 The Directory rules France
	1798 Toussaint L'Ouverture defeats British in Haiti	1799 Napoleon overthrows the Directory
1800	1804 Haitians defeat French invasion and declare independence	1804 Napoleon crowns himself emperor
		1814 Napoleon abdicates; Congress of Vienna opens
		1815 Napoleon defeated at Waterloo
		1830 Greece gains independence; revolution in France overthrows Charles X
		1848 Revolutions in France, Austria, Germany, Hungary, and Italy

English political philosopher John Locke (1632–1704) argued in 1690 that governments were created to protect life, liberty, and property and that the people had a right to rebel when a monarch violated these natural rights. Locke's closely reasoned theory began with the assumption that individual rights were the foundation of civil government. In *The Social Contract*, published in 1762, French-Swiss intellectual Jean-Jacques Rousseau (**zhan-zhock roo-SOE**) (1712–1778) asserted that the will of the people was sacred and that the legitimacy of monarchs depended on the consent of the people. Although both men believed that government rested on the will of the people, Locke emphasized the importance of individual rights secured institutionally while Rousseau, much more distrustful of society and government, envisioned the people acting collectively as a result of their shared historical experience.

All Enlightenment thinkers were not radicals like Rousseau. There was never a uniform program for political and social reform, and the era's intellectuals often disagreed about principles and objectives. While the Enlightenment is commonly associated with hostility toward religion and monarchy, few intellectuals openly expressed republican or atheist sentiments. Even Voltaire, one of the Enlightenment's most critical intellects and great celebrities, believed that Europe's monarchs were the most likely agents of political and economic reform.

Indeed, sympathetic members of the nobility and reforming European monarchs such as Charles III of Spain (r. 1759–1788), Catherine the Great of Russia (r. 1762–1796), and Frederick the Great of Prussia (r. 1740–1786) actively sponsored and promoted the dissemination of new ideas, providing patronage for many intellectuals. They recognized that elements of the Enlightenment buttressed their own efforts to expand royal authority at the expense of religious institutions, the nobility, and regional autonomy. Goals such as the development of national bureaucracies staffed by civil servants selected on merit, the creation of national legal systems, and the modernization of tax systems united many of Europe's monarchs and intellectuals. Monarchs also understood that the era's passion for science and technology held the potential of fattening national treasuries and improving economic performance.

Though willing to embrace reform proposals when they served royal interests, Europe's monarchs moved quickly to suppress or ban radical ideas that promoted republicanism or directly attacked religion. However, too many channels of communication were open to permit a thoroughgoing suppression of ideas. In fact, censorship tended to enhance intellectual reputations, and intellectuals persecuted in their native lands generally found patronage in the courts of foreign rivals.

AP® Exam Tip
Be ready to identify several Enlightenment philosophers and how their ideas were reflected in revolutionary documents.

AP® Exam Tip
Understand the importance of growing demands for women's suffrage and emergent feminism in Europe and the Western Hemisphere.

Many of the major intellectuals of the Enlightenment corresponded with each other as well as with political leaders. This communication led to numerous firsthand contacts among the intellectuals of different nations and helped create a more coherent assault on what they saw as ignorance—beliefs and values associated with the ancien régime and traditional religion. Rousseau had met Scottish philosopher David Hume in Paris. Later, when Rousseau feared arrest in France, Hume helped him seek refuge in Britain. Similarly, Voltaire sought patronage and protection in England and later in Prussia when facing threats in France.

Women were instrumental in the dissemination of these new ideas. In England large numbers of educated middle-class women purchased and discussed books and pamphlets. Some, like Mary Wollstonecraft, were important contributors to intellectual life as writers and commentators, raising by example and in argument the issue of the rights of women. In Paris wealthy women made their homes centers of debate, intellectual speculation, and free inquiry. Their salons brought together philosophers, social critics, artists, members of the aristocracy, and the commercial elite. The salon of Germaine de Staël was a center of political experimentation and argument until she was forced to flee Paris during the Terror (1793).

The intellectual ferment of the era deeply influenced the expanding middle class in Europe and the Western Hemisphere. Members of this class were eager consumers of books and inexpensive newspapers and journals, which were widely available. This broadening of the intellectual audience overwhelmed traditional institutions of censorship. New public venues like the thousands of coffeehouses and teashops located in cities and market towns also became places to discuss scientific discoveries, new technologies, and controversial works on human nature and politics, expanding the Enlightenment's influence beyond the literate minority.

Many European intellectuals were interested in the Americas. Some continued to dismiss the region as barbaric and inferior, but others used idealized accounts of the New World to support their critiques of European society. Many looked to Britain's North American colonies for confirmation of their belief that human nature unconstrained by the corrupted practices of Europe's old order would quickly produce material abundance and social justice. More than any other American, writer and inventor **Benjamin Franklin** came to symbolize the vast potential of America to Europe's intellectuals.

Born in Boston in 1706, the young Franklin trained as a printer. In Philadelphia he succeeded in business and became famous for his *Poor Richard's Almanac*. At forty-two he retired to pursue writing, science, and public affairs. Franklin was instrumental in the creation of the Philadelphia Free Library, the American Philosophical Society, and the University of Pennsylvania. His contributions were both practical and theoretical. The inventor of bifocal glasses, the lightning rod, and an efficient wood-burning stove, he also contributed to scientific knowledge with publications like his 1751 paper, *Experiments and Observations on Electricity*, which won him acclaim from European intellectuals.

Franklin was also an important political figure. He served in many capacities in the colonies and was selected as a delegate to the Continental Congress that issued the Declaration of Independence in 1776. He later became ambassador to Paris, where his achievements, witty conversation, and careful self-promotion made him the symbol of the era. His life seemed to confirm the Enlightenment's most radical objective, the freeing of human potential from the effects of inherited privilege.

As Franklin demonstrates, the Western Hemisphere shared in Europe's intellectual ferment. As the Enlightenment penetrated the New World, intellectuals actively debated the legitimacy of colonialism itself. European efforts to reform colonial policies by unilaterally altering colonial institutions and overturning long-established political practices further radicalized colonial intellectuals. Among peoples compelled to accept the dependence and inferiority explicit in colonial rule, the idea that government authority rested on the consent of the governed would prove explosive.

Many intellectuals resisted the Enlightenment, seeing it as a dangerous assault on the authority of the church and monarchy. This Counter Enlightenment was most influential in France and other Catholic nations. Its adherents emphasized the importance of religious faith to human happiness and social well-being. They also emphasized duty and obligation to the community of believers in opposition to the concern for individual rights and individual fulfillment common in the works of the Enlightenment. Most importantly for the politics of the era, they rejected their enemies' enthusiasm for change and utopianism, reminding their readers of human fallibility and the importance of history and tradition. While the central ideas of the Enlightenment gained

AP® Exam Tip
Consider which groups resisted Enlightenment thinking and what their motives might have been.

Benjamin Franklin
American intellectual, inventor, and politician who helped negotiate French support for the American Revolution.

◀ **Beer Street (1751)** William Hogarth's engraving shows an idealized London street scene where beer drinking is associated with manly strength, good humor, and prosperity. The self-satisfied corpulent figure in the left foreground reads a copy of the king's speech to Parliament. We can imagine him offering a running commentary to his drinking companions as he reads. The New York Public Library

strength across the nineteenth century, the Counter Enlightenment provided ideological support for the era's conservatives and later served as the basis for popular antidemocratic movements.

23-1c Folk Cultures and Popular Protest

While intellectuals and the reforming royal courts of Europe debated the rational and secular enthusiasms of the Enlightenment, most people in Western society remained loyal to competing cultural values grounded in the distant past. Regional folk cultures were rooted in the memory of shared experience and nourished by religious practices that encouraged emotional release. These cultural traditions included coherent expressions of the rights and obligations that connected people with their rulers, a social compact. Authorities who violated these understandings were likely to face violent opposition.

In the eighteenth century, European monarchs sought to increase their authority and to centralize power by reforming tax collection, judicial practice, and public administration. Although monarchs viewed these changes as reforms, common people often saw them as violations of sacred customs and responded with bread riots, tax protests, and attacks on local royal officials. These violent actions sought to preserve custom and precedent rather than overturn traditional authority. In Spain and the Spanish colonies, for example, protesting mobs often expressed love for their monarch while at the same time assaulting his officials and preventing the implementation of his reforms, shouting "Long Live the King! Death to Bad Government!"

Enlightenment-era reformers sought to bring order and discipline to the citizenry by banning or altering numerous popular traditions—such as harvest festivals, religious holidays, and

Section Review

- Wars fought to protect colonies and trade routes overwhelmed the fiscal resources of many European powers.

- European intellectuals applied the methods of scientific inquiry to political and cultural issues during the Enlightenment.

- In the Counter Enlightenment some intellectuals rejected attacks on tradition and religion.

- The effort to create uniform and rational administration provoked popular protest in defense of folk culture and tradition.

country fairs—that enlivened the drudgery of everyday life. These events were popular celebrations of sexuality and individuality as well as opportunities for masked and costumed celebrants to mock the greed, pretension, and foolishness of government officials, the wealthy, and the clergy. Hard drinking, gambling, and blood sports like cockfighting and bearbaiting were popular in preindustrial mass culture as well, but reformers viewed them as corrupt and decadent. As reforming governments undertook to substitute civic rituals, patriotic anniversaries, and institutions of self-improvement for older customs, they often provoked protests and riots.

The efforts of ordinary men and women to resist the growth of government power and the imposition of new cultural forms provide an important political undercurrent to much of the revolutionary agitation and conflict between 1750 and 1850. Spontaneous popular uprisings and protests punctuated nearly every effort at reform in the eighteenth century. But popular protest gained revolutionary potential only when it coincided with ideological division and conflict within the governing class.

23-2 The American Revolution, 1775–1800

What were the direct causes of the American Revolution?

AP® Exam Tip

Examine how the American Revolution reflected Enlightenment ideas and a pursuit of independence and democratic ideals.

In British North America, clumsy efforts to increase colonial taxes to cover rising defense expenditures and to diminish the power of elected colonial legislatures outraged a populace accustomed to local autonomy. Once begun, the American Revolution ushered in a century-long process of political and cultural transformation in Europe and the Americas. By the end of this revolutionary century, constitutions had limited or overturned the authority of monarchs, and religion had lost its dominance of Western intellectual life. At the same time revolutionary changes in manufacturing and commerce replaced the long-established social order determined by birth with a new social ideal emphasizing competition and social mobility.

23-2a Frontiers and Taxes

After defeating the French in 1763, the British government faced two related problems in its North American colonies. As settlers pushed west into Amerindian lands, Britain feared the likelihood of renewed conflict with native peoples and rising military expenses. Already burdened with heavy debts, Britain tried to limit settler pressure on Amerindian lands and to get colonists to shoulder more of the costs of colonial defense and administration.

In the Great Lakes region, the British tried to contain costs by reducing fur prices paid to native hunters and by refusing to continue the French practice of giving gifts and paying rent for frontier forts to Amerindian peoples. But lower fur prices forced native peoples to hunt more aggressively, putting pressure on the environment and endangering some species. The situation got worse as settlers and white trappers pushed across the Appalachians to compete directly with native hunters. The predictable result was renewed violence along the frontier led by Pontiac, an Ottawa chief. His broad alliance of native peoples forged in 1763 drove the British military from some western outposts but failed to dislodge the British from Fort Detroit. Failure led to disaffection among the Amerindian allies and finally to a peace treaty in 1766.

With the outbreak of this conflict the British government reacted by publishing the Proclamation of 1763. This policy established a western limit for settlement, thus undermining the claims of thousands of established white farmers without effectively protecting Amerindian land. No one was satisfied. In 1774 Britain tried again to slow the movement of settlers onto Amerindian lands by annexing western territories to the province of Quebec. Like the 1763 proclamation, this action provoked bitter resentment in the colonies.

In comparison with the French, Spanish, and Portuguese colonies of the Americas, the settlers of the British colonies enjoyed substantial political autonomy, exercising effective local control through elected legislatures and courts. Even as slavery expanded in the southern colonies, free settlers prospered. One measure of this mounting, broadly distributed wealth was the rising tide of imported British consumer goods. While enriching metropolitan producers and merchants, colonial consumption of British cloth, porcelains, tea, and other imports also played a key role in forging a unified colonial material culture that transcended regional economic, social, and even religious differences.

When the British government sought to assert greater political control and force the colonies to pay a much larger share of the costs of defense and governance in the wake of the French and Indian War, colonial settlers used consumer boycotts to great effect. While frontier policies imposed following Pontiac's rebellion led to colonial hostility and suspicion, they did not lead to a breach. British fiscal reforms and new taxes, however, sparked a series of political confrontations that led to political mobilizations and popular protests across the colonies and, ultimately, to rebellion. For example, British regulations imposed in 1764 threatened New England's profitable trade with Spanish and French Caribbean sugar colonies and more effectively policed colonial smuggling. More disruptive still was Britain's outlawing of colonial issues of paper money, a custom made necessary by the colonies' chronic balance-of-payments deficits. Each of these measures was met with protests from colonial legislatures and popular assemblies.

The Stamp Act of 1765—a tax on all legal documents, newspapers, pamphlets, and nearly all printed material—caused especially deep resentment. Propertied colonists, including holders of high office and members of the colonial elite, assumed leading roles in protests and used fiery political language, identifying Britain's rulers as "parricides" and "tyrants" and suggesting that a dependence on British imports threatened traditional liberties. Women from prominent colonial families played a crucial role in organizing boycotts of British goods. For them and for poorer women as well, producing and wearing homespun textiles was increasingly seen as a patriotic obligation. Organizations such as Boston's Sons of Liberty were more confrontational, holding public meetings, intimidating royal officials, and organizing committees to enforce the boycotts. Although this combination of protest and boycott forced the repeal of the Stamp Act, Britain imposed new taxes and duties in 1767. More threatening to colonial peace, Parliament sent British troops to the colonies to quell riots. While the boycotts against the Stamp Act were mostly confined to cities, these new taxes ignited protests across the colonies. Legislatures, town governments, and *ad hoc* committees mobilized the colonists to boycott British goods. One indignant woman expressed her anger to a British officer:

> [T]he most ignorant peasant knows . . . that no man has the right to take their money without their consent. The supposition is ridiculous and absurd, as none but highwaymen and robbers attempt it. Can you, my friend, reconcile it with your own good sense, that a body of men in Great Britain, who have little intercourse with America . . . shall invest themselves with a power to command our lives and properties [?] [1]

British authorities reacted to boycotts and attacks on royal officials by threatening colonial liberties. They dissolved the colonial legislature of Massachusetts and sent two regiments of soldiers to re-establish control of Boston's streets. Popular support for a complete break with Britain grew after March 5, 1770, when British soldiers fired on an angry Boston crowd, killing five civilians. The "Boston Massacre" exposed the naked force on which colonial rule rested and radicalized public opinion throughout the colonies.

Parliament attempted to calm colonial opinion by repealing some taxes and duties, but it stumbled into another crisis when it granted the East India Company a monopoly to import tea to the colonies. This decision raised again the constitutional issue of Parliament's right to tax the colonies. It also provided the perfect target for colonial dissidents seeking to organize protest on a broad scale. Since tea was consumed by nearly everyone, its boycott would potentially unite nearly every class and region. In the heated language of protest, buying and drinking tea was acquiescing to British tyranny. The crisis came to a head when protesters dumped tea worth £10,000 (about £1.2 million or $1.5 million in 2015) into Boston harbor. As news of this act spread, tea was surrendered or, in some cases, seized and burned in innumerable towns and villages across the colonies. Britain responded by appointing a military man, Thomas Gage, as governor of Massachusetts and by closing the port of Boston. British troops now enforced public order in Boston, and public administration was in the hands of a general. This militarization of colonial government undermined Britain's constitutional authority and made rebellion inevitable.

[1]Quoted in Ray Raphael, *A People's History of the American Revolution* (New York, NY: Perennial, 2001), 141.

AP® Exam Tip
Be familiar with the Declaration of Independence and how it reflected the Enlightenment ideals of the American Revolution.

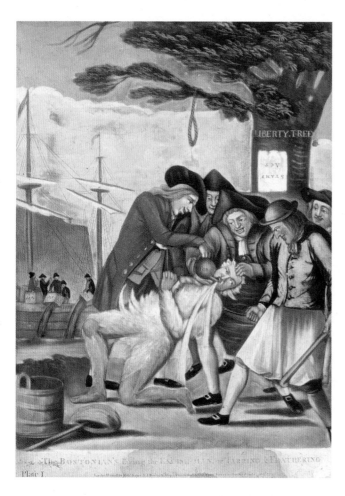

▲ The Tarring and Feathering of a British Official, 1774   British periodicals responded to the rising tide of colonial protest by focusing on mob violence and the breakdown of public order. This illustration portrayed the brutal treatment given John Malcomb, commissioner of customs at Boston. For many in Britain, colonial demands for liberty were little more than an excuse for mob violence. Fotosearch/Getty Images

George Washington Military commander of the American Revolution. He was the first elected president of the United States (1789–1799).

Joseph Brant Mohawk leader who supported the British during the American Revolution.

23-2b The Course of Revolution, 1775–1783

In 1775 representatives from the colonies met in Philadelphia to discuss the situation. Most of the representatives elected to this Continental Congress had been active in the boycotts and protests of the previous decade, and they again used non-importation as a political weapon. But events were moving quickly toward armed confrontation and revolution. Patriot militias had already fought British troops at Lexington and Concord, Massachusetts (see Map 23.1), and few thought compromise possible. The Congress now assumed the powers of government, created a currency, and organized an army led by **George Washington** (1732–1799), a Virginia planter who had served in the French and Indian War.

The angry rhetoric of thousands of street-corner speakers as well as the inflammatory pamphlet *Common Sense*, written by Thomas Paine, a recent immigrant from England living in Virginia, propelled popular support for independence. On July 4, 1776, Congress approved the Declaration of Independence, the document that proved to be the most enduring statement of the revolutionary era's ideology:

> We hold these truths to be self evident: That all men are created equal; that they are endowed by their creator with certain unalienable rights; that among these are life, liberty and the pursuit of happiness; that, to secure these rights, governments are instituted among men, deriving their just powers from the consent of the governed.

The Declaration's affirmation of popular sovereignty and individual rights would influence the language of revolution and popular protest around the world into the modern era.

Great Britain reacted by sending additional military forces to pacify the colonies. By 1778 Britain had 50,000 British troops and 30,000 German mercenaries in the colonies. Despite the existence of a large loyalist community, the British army found it difficult to control the countryside. Although British forces won most of the battles, Washington slowly built a competent Continental army as well as civilian support networks that provided supplies and financial resources.

The British government now ineffectively tried to find a political compromise that would satisfy colonial grievances. But its half-hearted efforts to resolve the conflict over taxes failed, and its offer to roll back the clock and re-establish the administrative arrangements of 1763 made little headway. Overconfidence in its military and poor leadership kept the British from finding a political solution before revolutionary institutions were in place and the armies engaged. By allowing confrontation to occur, the British government lost the opportunity to mobilize and give direction to the large numbers of loyalists and pacifists in the colonies.

Along the Canadian border, both sides solicited Amerindians as allies and feared them as potential enemies. For over a hundred years, members of the powerful Iroquois Confederacy—Mohawk, Oneida, Onondaga, Cayuga, Seneca, and (after 1722) Tuscarora—had protected their traditional lands with a combination of diplomacy and warfare. Just as the American Revolution forced settler families to join the rebels or remain loyal, it divided the Iroquois, who fought on both sides.

The Mohawk proved to be valuable British allies. Their loyalist leader **Joseph Brant** (Thayendanegea [**ta-YEHN-dah-NEY-geh-ah**]) organized Britain's most potent fighting force along the Canadian border. His raids along the northern frontier earned him the title "Monster" Brant, but he was actually a man who moved easily between European and Amerindian cultures. Educated by missionaries, he was fluent in English and helped translate Protestant religious tracts into the Mohawk language. He was friendly with many loyalist families and with British officials and had traveled to London for an audience with George III (r. 1760–1820).

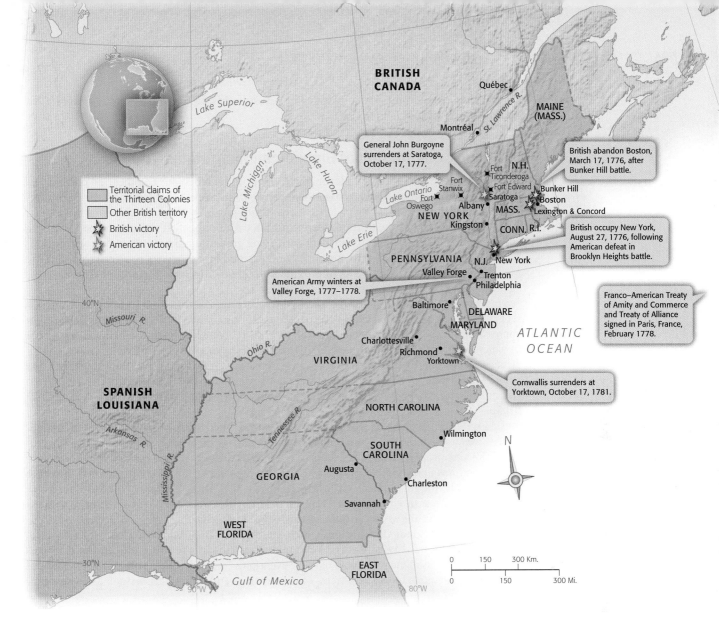

MAP 23.1 **The American Revolutionary War** The British army won most of the major battles, and British troops held most of the major cities. Even so, the American revolutionaries eventually won a comprehensive military and political victory.

Did Britain face significant geographic obstacles in its effort to defeat the revolutionaries?

The defeat in late 1777 of Britain's general John Burgoyne by General Horatio Gates at Saratoga, New York, put the future of the Mohawk at risk. American forces followed this victory with destructive attacks on Iroquois villages that reduced their political and military power. After Britain's defeat, Brant and the Mohawk would join the loyalist exodus to Canada.

The British defeat at Saratoga also convinced France to enter the war as an ally of the United States in 1778. French military help proved crucial, supplying American forces with arms and forcing the British to divert naval and ground forces to defend their colonies in the Caribbean. The French contribution was most obvious in the final battle, fought at Yorktown, Virginia, in 1781 (see Map 23.1). With the American army supported by French soldiers and a large French fleet, General Charles Cornwallis surrendered to Washington as the British military band played "The World Turned Upside-Down."

This victory effectively ended the war, and the Continental Congress sent representatives to the peace conference with instructions to work in tandem with the French government. Believing that France was more concerned with containing British power than with guaranteeing a strong United States, America's peace delegation chose to negotiate directly with Britain and gained a generous settlement. The Treaty of Paris (1783) granted unconditional independence and established generous boundaries for the former colonies. In return the United States promised to repay prewar debts due to British merchants and to allow colonial loyalists who had supported the British to recover property confiscated by patriot forces. In the end, the loyalists were badly treated, and thousands left for Canada.

23-2c The Construction of Republican Institutions, to 1800

Even before the Declaration of Independence, many of the rebellious colonies had created new governments and summoned constitutional conventions to draft formal charters. Europeans were fascinated by the drafting of written constitutions and by their ratifications by popular vote. Many early state constitutions were translated and published in Europe and circulated widely. Remembering colonial conflicts with royal governors, these new state constitutions placed severe limits on executive authority and granted broad powers to elected legislatures. Many also included bills of rights to provide individual citizens with additional protections against tyranny.

It proved more difficult to frame a national constitution. The Second Continental Congress sent the Articles of Confederation—the first constitution of the United States—to the states for approval in 1777, but it was not accepted until 1781. It created a one-house national legislature in which each state had a single vote. While a simple majority of the thirteen states was sufficient to pass minor legislation, nine votes were necessary for declaring war, imposing taxes, and coining or borrowing money. A committee, not a president, exercised executive power. Given the intended weakness of this government, it is remarkable that it organized the defeat of Great Britain.

Many of the most powerful political figures in the United States recognized that the Confederation was unable to enforce unpopular requirements of the peace treaty such as the recognition of loyalist property claims, the payment of prewar debts, and even the payment of military salaries and pensions due veterans. As a result, in September 1786 Virginia invited the other states to discuss the government's failure to deal with trade issues. This assembly called for a new convention to meet in Philadelphia. A rebellion led by Revolutionary War veterans in western Massachusetts gave the assembling delegates a sense of urgency.

The **Constitutional Convention**, which met in May 1787, achieved a nonviolent second American Revolution. With George Washington serving as presiding officer, the delegates pushed aside the announced purpose of the convention—"to render the constitution of the federal government adequate to the exigencies of the union"—and secretly undertook to write a new constitution.

Debate focused on representation, electoral procedures, executive powers, and the relationship between the federal government and the states. The final compromise distributed political power among executive, legislative, and judicial branches and divided authority between the federal government and the states. The chief executive—the president—was to be elected indirectly by "electors" selected by ballot in the states.

Although this constitution created the most democratic government of the era, only a minority of the adult population had full political rights. While some northern states were hostile to slavery, southern leaders successfully protected the institution. Slaves were denied participation in the political process, but slave states were permitted to count three-fifths of the slave population to allocate the number of congressional representatives, thus multiplying the political power of the slave-owning class. Southern delegates also gained a twenty-year continuation of the slave trade to 1808 and a fugitive slave clause that required all states to return runaway slaves to masters.

During the war, women had led prewar boycotts and organized relief and charitable organizations. Some had also served in the military as nurses, and a smaller number had joined the ranks disguised as men. Nevertheless, women were denied political rights in the new republic. Only New Jersey granted the vote to women and free African Americans who met property requirements, but in 1807 the state's lawmakers eliminated these rights.

Constitutional Convention
Meeting in 1787 of the elected representatives of the thirteen original states to write the Constitution of the United States.

Section Review

- Britain tried to prevent new settlements on Amerindian lands and to limit the expense of protecting the frontier.

- New colonial tax and commercial policies provoked colonial protests and boycotts in North America.

- Armed conflict between British troops and colonists led to the calling of the Continental Congress and the Declaration of Independence.

- French military support for the American Revolution proved crucial.

- The American states supported the creation of a new constitution that divided the powers of government.

23-3 The French Revolution, 1789–1815

What were the origins and accomplishments of the French Revolution?

The French Revolution undermined traditional monarchy and hereditary aristocracy as well as the power of the Catholic Church but, unlike the American Revolution, did not create enduring representative institutions or a stable constitutional order. The colonial revolution in North America, however, had not confronted so directly the entrenched privileges of an established church, monarchy, and aristocracy. Among its achievements, the French Revolution expanded mass participation in political life and radicalized the democratic tradition inherited from the English and American experiences. The political passions unleashed by revolutionary events in France also ultimately led to rule by popular demagogues and the dictatorship of Napoleon.

23-3a French Society and Fiscal Crisis

French society was divided in three estates. The clergy, called the First Estate, numbered about 130,000 in a nation of 28 million. The Catholic clergy was organized hierarchically, and priests from noble families held almost all top positions in the church. The church owned about 10 percent of the nation's land and extracted substantial amounts of wealth from the economy in the form of tithes and ecclesiastical fees, but it paid few taxes.

The 300,000 members of the nobility, the Second Estate, controlled about 30 percent of the land and retained ancient rights on much of the rest. Nobles held most high administrative, judicial, military, and church positions. Though barred from some types of commercial activity, nobles were important participants in wholesale trade, banking, manufacturing, and mining. Like the clergy, this estate was hierarchical: important differences in wealth, power, and outlook separated the higher from the lower nobility. In the eighteenth century many wealthy commoners who purchased administrative and judicial offices were permitted to claim noble status.

The Third Estate included everyone else, from wealthy financiers to beggars. The number of propertied and successful commoners grew rapidly in the eighteenth century. Commerce, finance, and manufacturing accounted for much of the wealth of the Third Estate. Wealthy commoners also owned nearly a third of the nation's land. This literate and socially ambitious group supported an expanding publishing industry, subsidized the fine arts, and purchased many of the extravagant new homes built in Paris and other cities.

Artisans, shopkeepers, and small landowners owned property and lived decently when crops were good and prices stable, but by 1780 poor harvests had increased their cost of living and led to a decline in consumer demand for their products. They were rich enough to fear the loss of their property and status and well educated enough to be aware of the growing criticism of the king, but they lacked the means to influence policy.

Poverty was common. Among peasants, who accounted for 80 percent of the French population, family poverty and vulnerability forced young children to seek seasonal work and led many to crime and beggary. Urban poverty was even more common. In 1743, for example, one parish priest estimated that 12,000 of his 15,000 parishioners depended on charity to survive. In Paris and other large French cities the vile living conditions and unhealthy diet of the urban poor were startling to visitors from other European nations. City streets swarmed with beggars and prostitutes. The problem of child abandonment suggests the wretchedness of the French poor: on the eve of the French Revolution French parents gave up at least 40,000 children, mostly infants, per year. Their belief that these children would be adopted was no more than a convenient fiction; in reality the majority died of neglect.

Unable to afford decent housing, obtain steady employment, or protect their children, the poor periodically erupted in violent protest and rage. In the countryside the decisions of the nobility or clergy to increase taxes and other burdens often led to violence. In towns and cities even small increases in the price of bread could spark a riot, since bread prices determined the quality of life of the poor. These explosive episodes, however, were not revolutionary in character; rioters sought immediate relief rather than structural change. That was to change when the Crown tried to solve its fiscal crisis.

The cost of the War of the Austrian Succession (1740–1748) began the crisis. When Louis XV (r. 1715–1774) tried to impose new taxes on the nobility and other privileged groups, widespread

▲ **Parisian Stocking Mender**   The poor lived very difficult lives. This woman uses a discarded wine barrel as a shop where she mends socks. Courtesy of Lyman Johnson

protests erupted. New debt from the Seven Years' War deepened the crisis and compelled the king to impose emergency fiscal measures, but the Parlement of Paris, an appeals court, resisted these measures. Frustrated by these actions, French authorities exiled members of the Parlement and pushed through a series of unpopular fiscal measures.

When the twenty-two-year-old Louis XVI assumed the throne in 1774, he faced a desperate fiscal situation compounded by the growing opposition of French courts to new taxes. In 1774 his chief financial adviser warned that the government could barely afford to operate; as he put it, "the first gunshot [act of war] will drive the state to bankruptcy." Despite this warning, the king decided to support the American Revolution, delaying financial collapse by borrowing enormous sums and disguising the growing debt by fabricating misleading fiscal accounts. By the end of the war, more than half of France's national budget was required to just pay the interest on its debt.

In 1787 the desperate king called an Assembly of Notables to approve a radical and comprehensive reform of economic and fiscal policy. Despite the fact that the king's advisers selected this assembly from the nation's high nobility, the judiciary, and the clergy, these representatives of privilege proved unwilling to support the proposed reforms and new taxes.

23-3b Protest Turns to Revolution, 1789–1792

In frustration, the king dismissed the Notables and attempted to implement reforms on his own, but his effort was met by an increasingly hostile judiciary and by popular demonstrations. The refusal of the elite to grant needed tax concessions forced the king to call the **Estates General**, a customary consultative body representing the three estates that had not met since 1614. The narrow self-interest and greed of the rich—who would not tolerate an increase in their own taxes—rather than the grinding poverty of the common people had created the conditions for revolution.

In late 1788 and early 1789 members of the three estates came together throughout the nation to discuss grievances and elect representatives to meet at Versailles (**vuhr-SIGH**). The Third Estate's representatives were mostly men of substantial property, but some were angry with the king's ministers and inclined to move France toward constitutional monarchy with an elected legislature. Many nobles and members of the clergy sympathized with the reform agenda of the Third Estate, but deep internal divisions over procedural and policy issues limited the power of the First and the Second Estates. Nevertheless, some clergy, and eventually some nobles, joined the debates of the Third Estate, beginning a transition toward an assembly that could claim to represent the entire French nation.

After six weeks of deadlock, the Third Estate, with allies from the other estates, signaled the scale of its ambitions by renaming itself the National Assembly. Fearful of the growing assertiveness of these representatives, the king locked them out of their meeting place. They then moved to an indoor tennis court and pledged to write a constitution. The ascendant ideas of the era, that the people are sovereign and the legitimacy of rulers depends on their fulfilling the people's will, now swept away the king's narrow desire to solve the nation's fiscal crisis. Louis prepared for a confrontation with the National Assembly by moving military forces to Versailles. Before he could act, the people of Paris intervened.

Estates General France's traditional national assembly with representatives of the three estates, or classes, in French society: the clergy, nobility, and commoners. The calling of the Estates General in 1789 led to the French Revolution.

A succession of bad harvests beginning in 1785 had propelled bread prices upward throughout France and provoked an economic depression as demand for nonessential goods collapsed. By the time the Estates General met, nearly a third of the Parisian workforce was unemployed. Hunger and anger marched hand in hand through working-class neighborhoods.

When the people of Paris heard that the king was massing troops in Versailles to arrest the representatives, crowds of common people began to seize arms and mobilize. On July 14, 1789, a crowd attacked the Bastille (**bass-TEEL**), a medieval fortress used as a prison. The futile defense of the Bastille cost ninety-eight lives before its garrison surrendered. Enraged, the attackers hacked the commander to death and then paraded through the city with his head and that of Paris's chief magistrate stuck on pikes.

These events coincided with uprisings by peasants in the country. Peasants sacked manor houses and destroyed documents that recorded their traditional labor and tax obligations. They then refused to pay taxes and dues to landowners and seized common lands. Forced to recognize the fury raging through rural areas, the National Assembly voted to end traditional obligations and the privileges of the nobility and church, essentially ending the feudal system. Having won this victory, peasants ceased their revolt.

These popular uprisings strengthened the hand of the National Assembly in its dealings with the king and led to passage of the **Declaration of the Rights of Man and the Citizen**, which stated the principles for a future constitution. Similarities between the language of this declaration and the U.S. Declaration of Independence resulted in part from the limited participation of Thomas Jefferson, author of the American document, who served as U.S. ambassador to Paris. The French declaration, however, was more sweeping in its language. Among the enumerated natural rights were "liberty, property, security, and resistance to oppression." The Declaration of the Rights of Man and the Citizen also guaranteed free expression of ideas, equality before the law, and representative government.

While delegates debated political issues in Versailles, the economic crisis worsened in Paris. Women employed in the garment industry and small shopkeepers were particularly hard hit. Because the working women of Paris faced high food prices every day as they struggled to feed their families, their anger had a hard edge. Public markets became political arenas where the urban poor met daily in angry assembly. Here the revolutionary link between the material deprivation of the French poor and the political aspirations of the French bourgeoisie was forged.

On October 5, thousands of market women marched the 12 miles (19 kilometers) to Versailles and forced their way into the National Assembly, shouting "the point is that we want bread." The crowd then entered the royal apartments, killed some of the king's guards, and searched for Queen Marie Antoinette (**ann-twah-NET**), whom they hated as a symbol of extravagance. They then forced the royal family to relocate to Paris.

With the king's ability to resist democratic change overcome by the Paris crowd, the National Assembly achieved a radically restructured French society in the next two years. A new constitution dramatically limited monarchical power and abolished the nobility as a hereditary class. Economic reforms swept away monopolies and trade barriers within France. Having renamed itself the Legislative Assembly, legislators then took on the church, seizing its lands to use as collateral for a new paper currency; they also mandated the election of priests and placed them on the public payroll. When the Assembly forced priests to take a loyalty oath, however, many Catholics joined a growing counterrevolutionary movement.

At first, many European monarchs welcomed the weakening of the French king, but by 1791 Austria and Prussia threatened to intervene in support of the monarchy. The Legislative Assembly responded by declaring war. Although the war went badly at first for French forces, people across France responded patriotically to foreign invasions, forming huge new volunteer armies and mobilizing national resources to meet the challenge.

23-3c The Terror, 1793–1794

In this period of national crisis and foreign threat, the French Revolution entered its most radical phase. A failed effort by the king and queen to escape from Paris cost the king his remaining popular support. On August 10, 1792, a crowd invaded his palace in Paris, forcing the king to seek the protection of the Legislative Assembly, which suspended his authority and ordered his imprisonment. These actions helped lead to the formation of a new legislative and executive body, the National Convention. They also created a political environment where competing

AP® Exam Tip

Consider how the Declaration of the Rights of Man and the Citizen reflected the Enlightenment ideals of the French Revolution. Compare this document to the Declaration of Independence.

Declaration of the Rights of Man and the Citizen Statement of fundamental political rights adopted by the French National Assembly at the beginning of the French Revolution.

▶ **Parisians Storm the Bastille** An eyewitness to the storming of the Bastille on July 14, 1789, painted this representation of this epochal event, still celebrated by the French as a national holiday. The Siege of the Bastille, 1789 (gouache on card), Cholat, Claude (18th–19th century) / Musee de la Ville de Paris, Musee Carnavalet, Paris, France / Bridgeman Images

political factions used rumors of plots and conspiracies to justify the use of violence against their rivals and enemies.

Rumors of counterrevolutionary plots also kept working-class neighborhoods in an uproar, and in September a mob surged through the city's prisons, killing nearly half the prisoners. Swept along by popular passion and fear of conspiracy, the newly elected National Convention convicted Louis XVI of treason, sentenced him to death, and proclaimed France a republic. The guillotine ended the king's life in January 1793 (see Environment & Technology: The Guillotine). These events precipitated a wider war with nearly all of Europe's powers allied against France.

The National Convention—the new legislature of the French Republic—convened in September. Almost all its members were from the middle class, and nearly all were **Jacobins (JAK-uh-bin)**—the most uncompromising democrats. Deep political differences, however, separated moderate Jacobins—called "Girondists **(juh-RON-dist)**," after a region in southern France—and radicals known as "the Mountain." Members of the Mountain—so named because their seats were on the highest level in the assembly hall—were more sympathetic than the Girondists to the demands of the Parisian working class and less patient with parliamentary procedure. **Maximilien Robespierre (ROBES-pee-air)**, a young, little-known lawyer deeply influenced by Rousseau's ideas, dominated the Mountain.

With the French economy in crisis and Paris suffering from inflation, high unemployment, and scarcity, Robespierre used the popular press and political clubs to forge an alliance with the volatile Parisian working class. His growing strength in the streets allowed him to purge and execute many of his enemies in the National Convention and to restructure the government. He placed executive power in the hands of the newly formed Committee of Public Safety, which created special courts to seek out and punish enemies of the Revolution.

Among the groups that lost influence were the active feminists of the Parisian middle class and the working-class women who had sought the right to bear arms in defense of the Revolution. These women had provided decisive leadership at crucial times, helping propel the Revolution toward widened suffrage and a more democratic structure. Armed women had actively participated in every confrontation with conservative forces. It is ironic that the National Convention—the revolutionary era's most radical legislative body—chose to repress the militant feminist forces that had prepared the ground for its creation.

Jacobins Radical republicans during the French Revolution. They were led by Maximilien Robespierre from 1793 to 1794.

Maximilien Robespierre Young provincial lawyer who led the most radical phases of the French Revolution. His execution ended the Reign of Terror.

No machine more powerfully symbolizes the revolutionary era than the guillotine. The machine immortalizes Joseph Ignace Guillotin (1738–1814), a physician and member of the French Constituent Assembly. In 1789 Guillotin recommended that executions be made more humane by use of a beheading device. He sought to replace hangings, used for commoners, and beheadings by axe, used for the nobility. Both forms of execution were often conducted with little skill, leading to gruesome and painful deaths. Guillotin believed that a properly designed machine would produce predictable, nearly painless deaths and remove the social distinction between commoners and nobles, seen as embarrassing in a more egalitarian age.

After 1791, execution by beheading became the common sentence for all capital crimes. Another physician, Antoine Louis, secretary of the College of Surgeons, designed the actual machine. Once directed to produce a suitable device, Louis, in many ways a typical technician of his time, systematically examined devices used elsewhere and experimented until satisfied with his results. Praised by contemporaries because it seemed to remove human agency, and therefore the dark desire for revenge, from the death penalty, the guillotine became the physical symbol of the Terror.

Questions for Analysis

1. Did Joseph Ignace Guillotin actually design the guillotine?
2. Why was this device believed to be more humane than earlier forms of execution?
3. How did it become the symbol of the Terror?

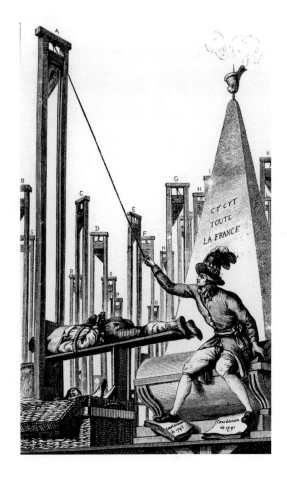

▶ **The Guillotine**   The guillotine, introduced as a more humane and democratic alternative to traditional executions, came to symbolize the arbitrary violence of the French Revolution. In this contemporary cartoon Robespierre, the architect of the Terror, serves as executioner while surrounded by guillotines. Robespierre Guillotining the Executioner having Guillotined all the French People, c.1793 (engraving) (b&w photo)/French School (18th century)/Private Collection/Bridgeman Images

Faced with rebellion in the provinces and foreign invasion, Robespierre and his allies unleashed a period of repression called the Reign of Terror (1793–1794). During the Terror, executions and deaths in prison claimed 40,000 lives while another 300,000 suffered imprisonment. In the Vendée region as many as 170,000 died as the government in Paris asserted control. One general stated, "I crushed the children under the feet of the horses, massacred the women who, at least for these, will not give birth to any more brigands. I do not have a prisoner to reproach me. I have exterminated all."[2]

The revolutionary government also took new actions against the clergy as well, including the provocative measure of forcing priests to marry. Even time was subject to revolutionary change. A new republican calendar created twelve 30-day months divided into 10-day weeks. Sunday, with its Christian meanings, was removed from this revolutionary calendar.

By spring 1794 the Revolution was secure from foreign and domestic enemies, but repression continued. Among the victims were some of Robespierre's closest political collaborators during the Terror. The execution of these former allies prepared the way for Robespierre's own fall by undermining the sense of invulnerability that had secured the loyalty of his remaining partisans. After French victories eliminated the immediate foreign threat in 1794, disaffected members of the Convention voted to arrest Robespierre and then ordered his execution along with that of nearly a hundred of his allies in July.

---

[2]Quoted in David A. Bell, *The First Total War: Napoleon's Europe and the Birth of Warfare as We Know It* (Boston, MA: Houghton Mifflin, 2007), 173.

▶ **Playing Cards from the French Revolution** Even playing cards could be used to attack the aristocracy and Catholic Church. In this pack of cards, "Equality" and "Liberty" replaced kings and queens. New Playing card designs dating from the French Revolution, 1793 (coloured engraving), French School, (18th century)/Private Collection/Archives Charmet/The Bridgeman Art Library

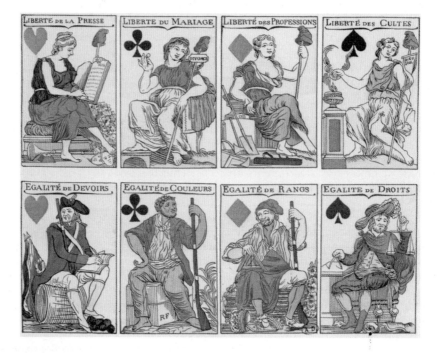

23-3d **Reaction and the Rise of Napoleon, 1795–1815**

Purged of Robespierre's collaborators, the Convention began to undo the radical reforms. It removed emergency economic controls that held down prices and protected the working class. Gone also was toleration for violent popular demonstrations. When the Paris working class rose in protest in 1795, the Convention reacted with overwhelming military force. It also allowed the Catholic Church to regain much of its former influence, but it did not return the church's confiscated wealth. It also put in place a more conservative constitution that protected property, established a voting process that reduced the power of the masses, and created a new executive authority, the Directory.

After losing the election of 1797, the Directory refused to give up power, effectively ending the republican phase of the Revolution. Political authority now depended on coercive force rather than elections. Two years later, a brilliant young general in the French army, **Napoleon Bonaparte** (1769–1821), seized power. Just as the American and French Revolutions had been the start of the modern democratic tradition, the military intervention that brought Napoleon to power in 1799 marked the advent of another modern form of government: popular authoritarianism.

The American and French Revolutions resulted in part from conflicts over representation. If the people were sovereign, what institutions best expressed popular will? In the United States the answer was the expansion of the right to vote and creation of representative institutions. The French Revolution took a different direction with the Reign of Terror. Interventions on the floor of the National Convention by market women and soldiers, the presence of common people at revolutionary tribunals and at public executions, and the expansion of military service were all forms of political communication that temporarily satisfied the French people's desire to influence their government. Napoleon tamed these forms of political expression to organize Europe's first popular dictatorship. He succeeded because his military reputation promised order to a society exhausted by a decade of crisis, turmoil, and bloodshed.

Napoleon sought to realize France's dream of dominating Europe while providing effective protection for persons and property at home. Negotiations with the Catholic Church led to the Concordat of 1801. This agreement gave French Catholics the right to freely practice their religion, but it also recognized the French government's authority to nominate bishops and retain priests on the state payroll. In his comprehensive rewriting of French law, the Civil Code of 1804, Napoleon won the support of the peasantry and the middle class by asserting two basic principles inherited from the moderate first stage of the French Revolution: equality in law and protection of property. Some members of the nobility were won over when Napoleon declared himself emperor and France an empire in 1804. Despite his willingness to make dramatic changes, however, Napoleon continued the denial of political rights for women begun during the Terror. The Civil Code denied women basic political rights and only allowed them to participate in the economy with the guidance and supervision of fathers and husbands.

Napoleon Bonaparte
General who overthrew the French Directory in 1799 and became emperor of the French in 1804. Failed to defeat Great Britain and abdicated in 1814. Returned to power briefly in 1815, he was soon defeated and died in exile.

Germaine de Staël, born Anne-Louise-Germaine Necker in 1766 in Paris, was the daughter of Jacques Necker, a Genevan banker and finance minister of Louis XVI of France. Her mother, Suzanne Curchod, was a clergyman's daughter who established a brilliant salon in Paris that attracted many of the pre-revolutionary period's great intellectuals. In 1786 de Staël married the Swedish ambassador to France and became the Baroness de Staël-Holstein. As a twenty-two-year-old she was already a respected author, having published an influential study of the work of Jean-Jacques Rousseau.

Despite her noble status and her father's close association with the monarchy, de Staël supported the democratizing tendencies in the French Revolution and was regarded by some as a Jacobin. As the revolution radicalized and violence increased, de Staël was protected by her husband's diplomatic status. Nevertheless, she fled France during the Terror. Traveling to England and then the continent, her reputation grew as she published a succession of works on philosophy and literary criticism. She returned to Paris during the Directory and met Napoleon Bonaparte. With his achievement of dictatorial power, de Staël became identified with his opponents.

Bonaparte ordered her banishment from Paris in 1803 and assumed the title of emperor in December 1804. Her exile would last ten years. With the fall of the Bonapartist regime, de Staël attempted to re-establish herself in French intellectual life. Despite her powerful connections across Europe and friendships with figures like Lord Byron, she would remain politically marginalized in Paris to the end of her life in 1817.

The following excerpt provides her penetrating insight into the character of her era's dominant personality, Napoleon Bonaparte. At the end of a turbulent and violent era, Bonaparte had represented himself to the French people as a man uniquely able to solve the nation's enduring political and economic problems. His insatiable ambition, cynicism, self-celebration, cunning, and undeniable political and military skills transformed broad areas of French life. In a remarkable decade he forged a vast continental empire that stretched from Iberia to Russia. This achievement was sustained by the largest military mobilization ever seen. Then, over the next five years, nearly everything he had achieved swept away by military defeat and political miscalculation, leaving as key legacies enormous numbers of military casualties and massive national debt.

As her own life came to an end, de Staël wrote a memoir of this important era. Published posthumously in English in 1818 as Considerations on the Principal Events of the French Revolution, *this multi-volume work has played an influential role in framing our understanding of the Revolution and the rise of Bonaparte.*

It was with this sentiment [a positive opinion], at least, that I saw him for the first time at Paris [in 1797]. I could not find words to reply to him when he came to me to say that he had sought my father at Coppet [her father's hometown in Switzerland], and that he regretted having passed into Switzerland without seeing him. But, when I was a little recovered from the confusion of admiration, a strongly marked sentiment of fear succeeded. Bonaparte,

at that time, had no power; he was even believed to be not a little threatened by the defiant suspicions of the Directory; so that the fear which he inspired was caused only by the singular effect of his person upon nearly all who approached him. I had seen men highly worthy of esteem; I had likewise seen monsters of ferocity: there was nothing in the effect which Bonaparte produced on me that could bring back to my recollection either the one or the other. I soon perceived, in the different opportunities which I had of meeting him during his stay at Paris, that his character could not be defined by the words which we commonly use; he was neither good, nor violent, nor gentle, nor cruel, after the manner of individuals of whom we have any knowledge. Such a being had no fellow, and therefore could neither feel nor excite sympathy: he was more or less than man. His cast of character, his spirit, his language, were stamped with the imprint of an unknown nature—an additional advantage, as we have elsewhere observed, for the subjugation of Frenchmen.

Far from recovering my confidence by seeing Bonaparte more frequently, he constantly intimidated me more and more. I had a confused feeling that no emotion of the heart could act upon him. He regards a human being as an action or a thing, not as a fellow-creature. He does not hate more than he loves; for him nothing exists but himself; all other creatures are ciphers. The force of his will consists in the impossibility of disturbing the calculations of his egoism; he is an able chess-player, and the human race is the opponent to whom he proposes to give checkmate. His successes depend as much on the qualities in which he is deficient as on the talents which he possesses. Neither pity, nor allurement, nor religion, nor attachment to any idea whatsoever could turn him aside from his principal direction. He is for his self-interest what the just man should be for virtue; if the end were good, his perseverance would be noble.

Every time that I heard him speak, I was struck with his superiority; yet it had no similitude to that of men instructed and cultivated by study or society, such as those of whom France and England can furnish examples. But his discourse indicated a fine perception of circumstances, such as the hunter has of his prey. Sometimes he related the political and military events of his life in a very interesting manner; he had even somewhat of Italian imagination in narratives which allowed of gaiety. Yet nothing could triumph over my invincible aversion for what I perceived in him. I felt in his soul a cold sharp-edged sword, which froze the wound that it inflicted; I perceived in his mind a profound irony, from which nothing great or beautiful, not even his own glory, could escape; for he despised the nation whose votes he wished, and no spark of enthusiasm was mingled with his desire of astonishing the human race.

AP® History Reasoning Skills

Causation *What causes Madame de Stael's opinion of Napoleon to change?*

Source: This excerpt from the de Staël memoir is from p. 364 of an anonymous review published in *The British Review and London Critical Journal*, Vol. XII, No. XXIV (November, 1818): 324–367.

▲ **Portrait of Madame de Staël**   Born into a Swiss-French noble family, Germaine de Staël (1766–1817) was an early supporter of the French Revolution. She was twice forced into exile because of her political opinions, first by the Jacobins and then by Napoleon. Her influential publications and travels across Europe made her one of this era's most famous intellectuals. Courtesy of Lyman Johnson

While it re-established order, the Napoleonic system denied or restricted many individual rights. Free speech was limited. Criticism of the government, viewed as subversive, was proscribed, and most opposition newspapers disappeared. Spies and informers directed by the minister of police enforced these draconian policies.

Ultimately, the Napoleonic system depended on the success of French arms (see Map 23.2). From Napoleon's assumption of power until his fall, no single European state could defeat the French military. Austria and Prussia suffered humiliating defeats at his hands and became allies of France. Only Britain, protected by its powerful navy, remained able to thwart Napoleon's plans to dominate Europe.

Desiring to again extend French power to the Americas, Napoleon invaded Portugal in 1807 and Spain in 1808. Despite early French victories, Spanish and Portuguese patriots supported by Great Britain eventually tied down large French armies in a costly conflict. Frustrated by events on the Iberian Peninsula and faced with a faltering economy, Napoleon made the fateful decision to invade Russia. In June 1812 he began his campaign with the largest army ever assembled in Europe, approximately 600,000 men. His army captured Moscow but after five weeks abandoned the city. During the retreat, the brutal Russian winter and attacks by Russian forces destroyed Napoleon's army. A broken and battered remnant of only 30,000 men made it back to France.

After the debacle in Russia, Austria and Prussia deserted Napoleon and entered an alliance with England and Russia against France. Unable to defend Paris, Napoleon abdicated the throne in April 1814 and was exiled to the island of Elba off the coast of Italy. The victorious allies then restored the French monarchy. The following year Napoleon escaped from Elba and returned to France, but an allied army defeated his forces in 1815 at Waterloo, in Belgium. His final exile was on the distant island of St. Helena in the South Atlantic, where he died in 1821.

Among the exiles who returned to Paris in 1814 was the baroness de Staël, Germaine de Staël (b. 1766), the daughter of Jacques Necker, one of Louis XVI's ministers (see Diversity & Dominance: Madame de Staël Remembers Napoleon). An aristocrat and the host of a successful salon in Paris, she was an early supporter of the French Revolution. Madame de Staël remained an influential presence in Paris until the violence of the Jacobin Terror forced her into exile in 1793. She was forced into exile a second time in 1803 by Napoleon who viewed her as a subversive advocate for the political ideals of liberalism. While abroad, she traveled widely, establishing friendships with many of Europe's greatest intellectuals and publishing a series of influential philosophical and literary works.

Madame de Staël finally returned to France following Napoleon's defeat and exile. Despite her intellectual reputation, she was politically isolated until her death in 1817. Her political difficulties foreshadowed the challenges France would face in the nineteenth century. She had been too supportive of the Revolution to be forgiven by the restored French monarchy; she remained too committed to intellectual freedom and political rights to satisfy the radical ambitions of those who sought to renew the revolution; and, she was too committed to representative democracy to please the Bonapartists.

Section Review

- The heavy burden of debt, caused in part by support of the American Revolution, forced Louis XVI to call the Estates General.

- When some members of the nobility and clergy joined the rebellious Third Estate they formed the National Assembly.

- The hungry Parisian masses radicalized the movement for reform by storming the Bastille and forcing the king to move to Paris.

- The Legislative Assembly, led by Robespierre, executed the king and initiated the Terror.

- Exhausted by the violence of the Terror and threatened by foreign enemies, France turned to Napoleon Bonaparte, who dominated Europe until he was defeated in 1814.

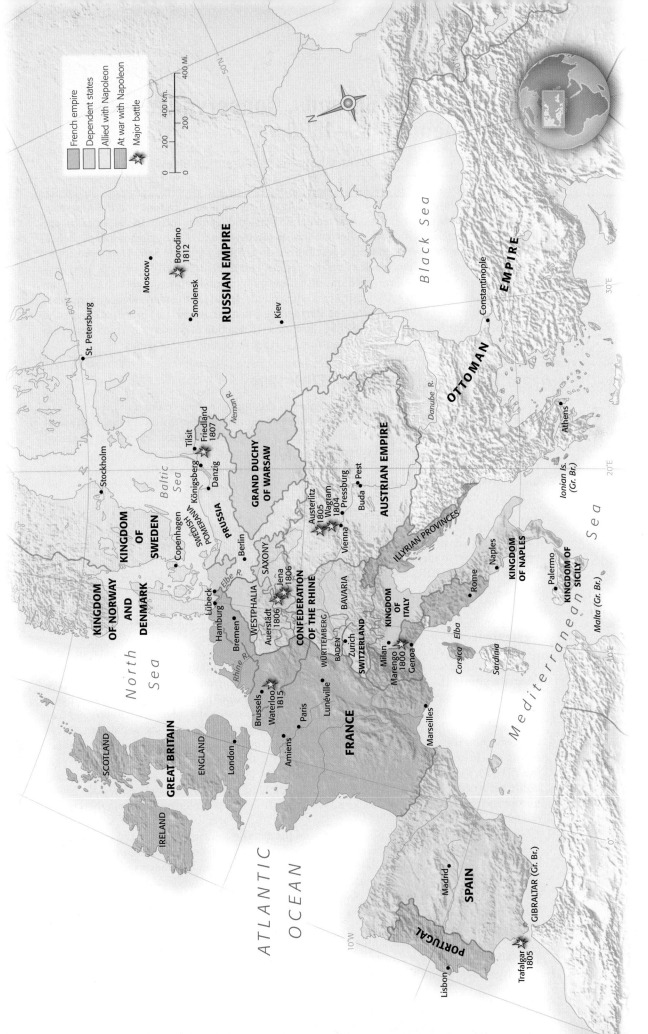

MAP 23.2 Napoleon's Europe, 1810 By 1810 Great Britain was the only remaining European power at war with Napoleon. Because of the loss of the French fleet at the Battle of Trafalgar in 1805, Napoleon was unable to threaten Britain with invasion, and Britain was able to actively assist the resistance movements in Spain and Portugal, thereby helping weaken French power.

Does the very scale of Napoleon's military and diplomatic achievements as shown in this map suggest the reasons for his ultimate defeat?

Legend

- French empire
- Dependent states
- Allied with Napoleon
- At war with Napoleon
- ★ Major battle

Scale: 0 — 200 — 400 Km.
0 — 200 — 400 Mi.

Labels

GREAT BRITAIN
SCOTLAND
ENGLAND
IRELAND
London

ATLANTIC OCEAN

North Sea

KINGDOM OF NORWAY AND DENMARK
Stockholm
Copenhagen

Baltic Sea

KINGDOM OF SWEDEN
St. Petersburg

RUSSIAN EMPIRE
Moscow
Borodino 1812
Smolensk
Kiev

SWEDISH POMERANIA
PRUSSIA
Berlin
Lübeck
Hamburg
Bremen
Königsberg
Danzig
Tilsit
Friedland 1807

GRAND DUCHY OF WARSAW

SAXONY
Jena 1806
Auerstädt 1806
WESTPHALIA
CONFEDERATION OF THE RHINE
BAVARIA
WÜRTTEMBERG
BADEN
Zurich
SWITZERLAND

Elbe R.
Rhine R.
Neman R.

FRANCE
Brussels
Waterloo 1815
Paris
Amiens
Lunéville
Marseilles

AUSTRIAN EMPIRE
Vienna
Austerlitz 1805
Wagram 1804
Pressburg
Buda
Pest
Danube R.

ILLYRIAN PROVINCES

KINGDOM OF ITALY
Milan
Marengo 1800
Genoa
Rome

Corsica
Sardinia
Elba

KINGDOM OF NAPLES
Naples
Palermo
KINGDOM OF SICILY
Malta (Gr. Br.)

Mediterranean Sea

OTTOMAN EMPIRE
Constantinople
Athens
Ionian Is. (Gr. Br.)

Black Sea

SPAIN
Madrid
PORTUGAL
Lisbon
Trafalgar 1805
GIBRALTAR (Gr. Br.)

23-4 Revolution Spreads, Conservatives Respond, 1789–1850

How did revolution in one country help incite revolution elsewhere?

Even as the dictatorship of Napoleon tamed the democratic and populist legacies of the French Revolution, revolutionary ideology was spreading and taking hold in Europe and the Americas. In Europe the French Revolution promoted nationalism and republicanism. In the Americas the legacies of the American and French Revolutions led to a new round of struggles for independence. News of revolutionary events in France destabilized the colonial regime in Saint Domingue (present-day Haiti), a small French colony on the western half of the island of Hispaniola, initiating in 1791 the first successful slave rebellion and adding momentum to efforts to abolish the African slave trade. Similarly, after 1808, frustrations with colonial status led to independence movements in Spain's American colonies and in the Portuguese colony of Brazil. In Europe, however, the spread of revolutionary fervor was met by the concerted reaction of conservative monarchs who formed an alliance committed to extinguishing further revolutionary outbreaks.

23-4a The Haitian Revolution, 1789–1804

In 1789 the French colony of Saint Domingue was among the richest colonies in the Americas. Its production of sugar, cotton, indigo, and coffee accounted for two-thirds of France's tropical imports and generated nearly one-third of all French foreign trade. The plantations that produced this wealth depended on a brutal slave regime. The harsh punishments and poor living conditions experienced by Saint Domingue's slaves were notorious throughout the Caribbean. The resulting high mortality and low fertility rates created an insatiable demand for African slaves. As a result, in 1790 the majority of the colony's 500,000 slaves were African-born.

When news of the meeting of the Estates General arrived on the island in 1789, wealthy planters sent a delegation to Paris to seek more home rule and greater economic freedom for Saint Domingue. That is, they sought more control over the colony's political life and more commercial options in order to increase their profits. The free mixed-race population, the *gens de couleur* (**zhahn deh koo-LUHR**), also sent representatives. Representing a large class of free black planters and urban merchants who owned slaves, they sought political rights and a limit to race discrimination, not an end to slavery. As the French Revolution became more radical, the gens de couleur forged an alliance with sympathetic French radicals, who saw the colony's wealthy planters as royalists and aristocrats.

The political turmoil in France weakened the authority of colonial administrators in Saint Domingue at the same time that the colony experienced crop failures and rising food prices. Given the growing sense of crisis caused by the political vacuum and the local subsistence threats, rich planters, poor whites, and the gens de couleur all pursued their narrow interests, engendering an increasingly bitter and confrontational struggle. Because the colony's large slave population hated the brutal regime that oppressed them and because the growing population of free people of color resented the racial discrimination and political exclusions that beset them, there was no way to limit the violence once the control of the slave owners slipped. When Vincent Ogé (**oh-ZHAY**), a leader of the gens de couleur mission sent to France in hope of gaining political rights, returned to Saint Domingue in 1790, the planters captured him and ordered his brutal torture and execution. The free black and slave populations of the colony soon repaid this cruelty in kind.

By 1791 whites, led by the planter elite, and the gens de couleur were engaged in open warfare. This conflict was transformed when a slave rebellion began on the plantations of the north (see Map 23.3). Rebelling slaves destroyed plantations, killed masters and overseers, and burned crops. A leadership emerged among the rebellious slaves that relied on elements of African political practice and revolutionary ideology from France to mobilize and direct their supporters. With the colony in flames, the French Assembly finally granted political rights to the gens de couleur in April 1792.

The rebellious slaves gained the upper hand under the command of **François Dominique Toussaint L'Ouverture**, a former domestic slave, who organized the rebelling slaves into a disciplined military force. While some French radicals had attacked the institution of slavery from

AP® Exam Tip

Compare the causes, courses, and results of the Haitian, French, and American Revolutions.

AP® Exam Tip

Examine the Haitian Revolution as an example of a successful slave rebellion.

gens de couleur Free men and women of color in Haiti. They sought greater political rights and later supported the Haitian Revolution.

François Dominique Toussaint L'Ouverture Leader of the Haitian Revolution. He freed the slaves and gained effective independence for Haiti despite military interventions by the British and French.

◄ **Haiti's Former Slaves Defend Their Freedom**
In this representation, a veteran army sent by Napoleon to reassert French control in Haiti battles with Haitian forces in a tropical forest. The combination of Haitian resistance and yellow fever defeated the French invasion. Courtesy of Lyman Johnson

the early days of the Revolution, the radical National Convention in Paris only abolished slavery in all French possessions in 1794. This was not narrowly the triumph of idealism over greed. With France at war with Britain and other European powers and Saint Domingue threatened by a British military force, the French government realized that its control of its colony could only be salvaged by acknowledging Toussaint's political and military dominance, in effect, placing the defense of the French colony in the hands of the leader of the slave uprising. This decision resulted more from the French government's internal weakness and its inability to project military power into the Caribbean than from an enduring commitment to the revolutionary transformation of the colony. Legitimized by the French government's decision, Toussaint swept aside his local rivals, defeated the British expeditionary force in 1798, and then led an invasion of the neighboring Spanish colony of Santo Domingo, freeing slaves there. While Toussaint asserted his loyalty to France, he gave the French government no effective role in local affairs.

As reaction overtook revolution in France with the creation of the Directory in 1795, both the abolition of slavery and Toussaint's political position were threatened. When the Directory contemplated the re-establishment of slavery, Toussaint protested:

> *Do they think that men who have been able to enjoy the blessing of liberty will calmly see it snatched away? They supported their chains only so long as they did not know any condition of life more happy than slavery. But today when they have left it, if they had a thousand lives they would sacrifice them all rather than be forced into slavery again.*[3]

When the Directory was replaced by Napoleon Bonaparte in 1799, Toussaint's achievements were directly threatened. In 1802 Napoleon sent a large military force to re-establish both French colonial authority and slavery in Saint Domingue (see Map 23.3), as well as in the nearby French colony of Guadeloupe. At first French forces were successful, capturing Toussaint and sending him to France, where he died in prison. Eventually, however, the French invasion force suffered thousands of losses as a result of a yellow fever epidemic and faced determined resistance of revolutionary armies led by battle-hardened Haitian generals. In 1804 Toussaint's successors declared independence, and the free republic of Haiti joined the United States as the second independent nation in the Western Hemisphere.

---

[3]Quoted in C. L. R. James, *The Black Jacobins*, 2nd ed. (New York, NY: Vintage Books, 1963), 196.

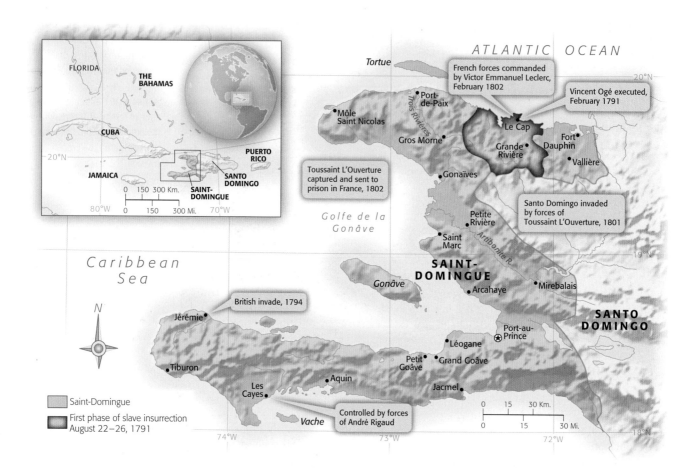

MAP 23.3 **The Haitian Revolution** On their way to achieving an end to slavery and gaining national independence, the Haitian revolutionaries were forced to defeat British and French military interventions as well as the local authority of the slave masters.

Does the geographic location of the French colony of Saint Domingue help explain the influence of the revolution on the institution of slavery in the Western Hemisphere?

23-4b The Congress of Vienna and Conservative Retrenchment, 1815–1820

In 1814–1815 representatives of Britain, Russia, Austria, Prussia, and other European nations met as the **Congress of Vienna** to re-establish political order in Europe. The French Revolution and Napoleon's imperial ambitions had threatened the survival of Europe's old order. The very existence of monarchy and the church had seemed at risk at the height of the revolutionary era. Ancient monarchies had been overturned and dynasties had been replaced with interlopers, often relatives of Napoleon. International borders were redrawn or ignored, while long-established political institutions were threatened or overturned. Responding to more than two decades of revolution and war, the Austrian foreign minister, Prince Klemens von Metternich (**MET-uhr-nik**) (1773–1859), provided key leadership as the victorious allies sought to create a comprehensive peace settlement that would safeguard the conservative order.

The central objective of the Congress of Vienna was to create a strong and stable France as the best guarantee of future peace. To this end it re-established the French monarchy and recognized France's 1792 borders, although most of the victorious allies received some territorial gains. Metternich believed that a strong and stable France had to be offset by a balance of power. Austria, Russia, and Prussia therefore formed a separate alliance to repress revolutionary and nationalist movements that sought to imitate the French Revolution. In 1820 this "Holy Alliance" used military force to defeat liberal revolutions in Spain and Italy. The Holy Alliance also attempted to blunt the force of revolutionary ideas across Europe by repressing republican and nationalist ideas in universities and the press.

Congress of Vienna
Meeting of representatives of European monarchs called to re-establish the old order after the defeat of Napoleon I.

23-4c Nationalism, Reform, and Revolution, 1821–1850

While Metternich's program of conservative retrenchment succeeded in the short term, the powerful ideas associated with liberalism and nationalism remained a vital part of European political life throughout the nineteenth century. Despite the power of the conservative monarchs, popular support for national self-determination and democratic reform grew throughout Europe.

Greece had been under Ottoman control since the fifteenth century. In 1821 Greek patriots launched an independence movement. While Metternich and other conservatives opposed Greek independence, European artists and writers enamored with the cultural legacy of ancient Greece rallied political support for intervention. After years of struggle, Russia, France, and Great Britain combined to force the Ottoman Empire to recognize Greek independence in 1830.

In 1814 the victorious allies placed Louis XVIII, brother of the executed Louis XVI, on the throne of France. Unlike his ancestors, he ruled as a constitutional monarch until his death in 1824, when his brother, the more conservative Charles X, inherited the throne. In 1830 Charles decided to repudiate the constitution, provoking a mass uprising in Paris that forced him to abdicate. The crown then went to the king's cousin, Louis Philippe (**loo-EE fee-LEEP**) (r. 1830–1848), who agreed to accept the French constitution and extended voting privileges.

Revolutionary violence in France had made the British aristocracy and the conservative Tory Party fearful of democracy and mass movements of any kind. In 1815 the British government passed the Corn Laws, which limited the importation of foreign grains. The laws favored the profits of wealthy landowners who produced grain, rather than the needs of the poor who would now be forced to pay more for their bread. When poor consumers organized to overturn these laws, the government out-lawed public meetings and used troops to crush protest in Manchester. Reacting against these policies, English reformers increased the power of the House of Commons, redistributing votes from agricultural to industrial districts and increasing the number of voters by nearly 50 percent. Although the most radical demands of reformers, called Chartists, were defeated, new labor and economic reforms addressing the grievances of workers were put in place (see Chapter 22).

Despite the achievement of Greek independence and limited political reform in France and Great Britain, conservatives continued to hold the upper hand. In 1848 the desire for democratic reform and national self-determination led to upheavals across Europe. The **Revolutions of 1848** began in Paris, where members of the middle class and workers united to overthrow the regime of Louis Philippe and create the Second French Republic. Reformers gave all adult men voting rights, abolished slavery in French colonies, ended the death penalty, and legislated the ten-hour workday. But Parisian workers' demands for programs to reduce unemployment and lower prices provoked conflicts with the middle class, which wanted to protect property rights. When workers rose up against the government, French troops crushed them. Desiring the re-establishment of order, the French elected Louis Napoleon, nephew of the former emperor, president in December 1848. Three years later, he overturned the constitution and, after ruling briefly as dictator, proclaimed himself Emperor Napoleon III.

In 1848 reformers in Hungary, Italy, Bohemia, and elsewhere pressed for greater national self-determination from the Austro-Hungarian Empire. When the monarchy did not meet their demands, students and workers in Vienna took to the streets to force political reforms similar to those sought in Paris. With revolution spreading throughout the empire, Metternich, the symbol of reaction since the Congress of Vienna, fled the capital in disguise. Little lasting change occurred, however, because the new Austrian emperor, Franz Joseph (r. 1848–1916), used Russian military assistance and loyal Austrian troops to re-establish his authority over the protestors.

Similarly, middle-class reformers and workers in Berlin joined forces to force the Prussian king to accept a liberal constitution and seek German unification. But the Constituent Assembly they called to write a constitution and negotiate national integration was diverted to deal with diplomatic conflicts with Austria and Denmark. As a result, the king Frederick William IV (r. 1840–1861) reasserted his authority and thwarted constitutional reform and unification.

Despite their heroism on the barricades of Paris, Vienna, Rome, and Berlin, the revolutionaries of 1848 failed to gain their nationalist and republican objectives. Monarchs retained the support not only of aristocrats but also of

AP® Exam Tip

Be familiar with the rise of nationalism since it is key to understanding later political developments in many parts of the world.

AP® Exam Tip

Identify the goals and outcomes of various forms of revolutionary movements during this time period.

Revolutions of 1848
Democratic and nationalist revolutions that swept across Europe. The monarchy in France was overthrown. In Germany, Austria, Italy, and Hungary the revolutions failed.

Section Review

- The slaves of Saint Domingue, led by Toussaint L'Ouverture, overthrew slavery and gained independence.

- The Congress of Vienna and the Holy Alliance attempted to prevent new revolutionary outbreaks in Europe.

- Nationalism and the desire for democracy led to revolutions in 1830 and 1848, but most failed to achieve their objectives.

▶ **The Revolution of 1830 in Belgium** After the 1830 uprising that overturned the restored monarchy in France, Belgians rose up to declare their independence from Holland. In Poland and Italy, similar uprisings combining nationalism and a desire for self-governance failed. This painting by Baron Gustaf Wappers romantically illustrates the popular nature of the Belgian uprising by bringing to the barricades men, women, and children drawn from both the middle and the working classes. Arterra Picture Library/Alamy Stock Photo

professional militaries, whose enlisted ranks were largely recruited from among peasants who had little sympathy for urban workers. Revolutionary coalitions, in contrast, proved fragile, as when workers' demands for higher wages and labor reform drove their middle-class allies into the arms of the reactionaries.

23-5 Conclusion

The last decades of the eighteenth century began a long period of revolutionary upheaval in the Atlantic world. Costly wars in Europe and along Europe's colonial frontiers in the Americas and Asia helped to provoke change, forcing European monarchs to impose new and unpopular taxes that led to popular protests. The American Revolution initiated these transformations. Having defeated Britain, the citizens of this new American republic created the most democratic government of the time. While full rights were limited and slavery persisted, many Europeans saw this experiment as demonstrating the efficacy of the Enlightenment's most revolutionary political ideas. In the end, however, the compromises over slavery that had made a new Constitution possible in 1787 failed, and, as discussed in Chapter 25, the new nation nearly disintegrated after 1860.

The French Revolution led temporarily to a more radical formulation of representative democracy, but it also led to the violence of the Terror, which cost tens of thousands of lives, the militarization of western Europe, and a destructive cycle of wars. Yet, despite these terrible costs, the French Revolution propelled the idea of democracy and the ideal of equality far beyond the boundaries established by the American Revolution. The Haitian Revolution, set in motion by events in France, not only created the second independent nation of the Western Hemisphere but also delivered a powerful blow to the institution of slavery. In Europe the excesses of the French Revolution and the wars that followed in its wake promoted the political ascent of Napoleon Bonaparte and democracy's modern nemesis, popular authoritarianism.

Each revolution had its own character. The revolutions in France and Haiti proved to be more violent and destructive than the American Revolution. American revolutionaries defeated Great Britain and established independence without overturning a colonial social and political order that depended on slavery in most of the southern colonies. Revolutionaries in France and Haiti faced more strongly entrenched and more powerful oppositions as well as greater social inequalities than American revolutionaries. The resistance of entrenched and privileged elites led inexorably to greater violence. Both French and Haitian revolutionaries also faced powerful foreign interventions that intensified the bloodshed and destructiveness of these revolutions.

The conservative retrenchment that followed the defeat of Napoleon succeeded in the short term. Monarchy, multinational empires, and the established church retained the loyalty of millions of Europeans and could count on the support of many of Europe's wealthiest and most powerful individuals. But liberalism and nationalism continued to stir revolutionary sentiment. The contest between adherents of the old order and partisans of change was to continue well into the nineteenth century. In the end, the nation-state, the Enlightenment legacy of rational inquiry, the popular desire for a wider political participation, and the expansion of secular culture prevailed. This outcome was determined in large measure by the old order's inability to satisfy the demands of new social classes tied to an emerging industrial economy. The narrow confines of a hereditary social system could not contain the material transformations generated by industrial capitalism, and the doctrines of traditional religion could not contain the rapid expansion of scientific learning.

These revolutions began the transformation of Western society, but they did not complete it. Despite the enthusiasm for individual liberty (see Chapter 25) and the language of universal rights that characterized both the American and French Revolutions, slavery endured in the Americas past the mid-1800s. Women and the descendants of African slaves, for example, did not achieve full political rights until the twentieth century. Establishing stable constitutional institutions proved difficult: The United States, France, and Haiti were all forced to abandon their first constitutional experiments. Nevertheless, even though the revolutionary era's achievements often proved imperfect and fragile, the old order that had dominated Europe and the Americas for centuries was mortally wounded.

Key Terms

Enlightenment p. 586
Benjamin Franklin p. 588
George Washington p. 592
Joseph Brant p. 592
Constitutional Convention p. 594

Estates General p. 596
Declaration of the Rights of Man and the Citizen p. 597
Jacobins p. 598

Maximilien Robespierre p. 598
Napoleon Bonaparte p. 600
gens de couleur p. 604

François Dominique Toussaint L'Ouverture p. 604
Congress of Vienna p. 606
Revolutions of 1848 p. 607

Review Questions

1. What were the most significant connections between the Enlightenment and Industrial Revolution and the political revolutions discussed in this chapter?

2. How did the geopolitical rivalry among European powers in the eighteenth century undermine their colonial empires?

3. The revolutionaries of British North America, France, and Saint Domingue all sought "liberty." Did this word have different meanings in each place?

 MindTap® is a fully online, personalized learning experience built upon Cengage Learning content. MindTap® combines student learning tools—readings, multimedia, activities, and assessments—into a singular Learning Path that guides students through the course and helps students develop the critical thinking, analysis, and communication skills that are essential to academic and professional success.

Multiple-Choice Questions

Questions 1–3 refer to the passage below.

"The deprivation of natural, equal, civil, and political rights reduced . . . the lower orders to practice fraud, and the rest to habits of stealing . . . and murders. And why? Because the rich and poor were separated into bands of tyrants and slaves, and the retaliation of slaves is always terrible. . . . Every sacred feeling, moral and divine, has been obliterated, and the dignity of man sullied, by a system of policy and jurisprudence [justice] as repugnant to reason as at variance with humanity.

The only excuse that can be made for the ferocity of the Parisians is then simply to observe that they had not any confidence in the laws."

Mary Wollstonecraft, an early feminist, *An Historical and Moral View of the Origin and Progress of the French Revolution*, 1794

1. In this passage, Wollstonecraft uses which of the following Enlightenment arguments?

   (A) Oppressive regimes are supported by Enlightened philosophy.

   (B) Feudal ties between elites and peasants are necessary for civil society.

   (C) The revolution in France was the result of natural rights abuses.

   (D) The revolution in France was an immoral act against political and religious elites.

2. Wollstonecraft's views on the Parisians could also be applied to what other events in the same time period?

   (A) European elites exercising increased power in the American colonies

   (B) Slave resistance challenging authorities in the Americas

   (C) The increase in religious support for European political legitimacy

   (D) The response of government to early socialist thinkers

3. Which of the following reactions to Wollstonecraft's ideas would most likely come from nobles and church leaders?

   (A) Recognition that natural law is the basis for all legal codes

   (B) Enactment of land reforms to eliminate tensions between the classes

   (C) Encouragement of French society to embrace secularism

   (D) An attempt to maintain authority based on older legal and religious traditions

Questions 4–6 refer to the image below.

▲ **A Revolutionary Frenchwoman kicking down the cathedrals of Paris, late Eighteenth Century** Chronicle/Alamy Stock Photo

4. The tone of this cartoon demonstrates which of the following trend changes during this time period?

   (A) Reactions against the power long held by the Catholic Church

   (B) Celebration of imperial power and traditional social institutions

   (C) Newly developed support for merchant and urban commerce

   (D) Support for increased religious values and leaders

5. *The Declaration of the Rights of Man and the Citizen*, which supported free speech like this cartoon, was modeled after which of the following documents?

   (A) "On the Moral and Political Principles of Domestic Policy"

   (B) Jacobin Charter

   (C) American Declaration of Independence

   (D) The *Gens de Couleur*

6. The ideals expressed in the cartoon support which of the following global trends?

(A) Growing support for sea-based empires in Africa and Asia

(B) Growing acceptance of Enlightenment ideals in Europe and the Americas

(C) Growing acceptance of slavery for the production of cash crops

(D) Growing centralization of authority supported by powerful religious institutions

Questions 7–10 refer to Map 23.3 on page 606.

7. Based on the map, which of the following best explains the context of the Haitian Revolution?

(A) Haiti was an isolated colony with very limited contact with other colonies.

(B) Haiti was an extension of the British mainland.

(C) Haiti was part of a collection of colonies in the Caribbean and Latin America.

(D) The Haitian Revolution set the stage for the French Revolution.

8. Based on the map, which of the following best describes the Haitian Revolution?

(A) The Haitians were fighting multiple imperial powers.

(B) The greatest opposition to the revolution came from land-owning elites in Santo Domingo.

(C) Amerindians carved out a large portion of the colony for themselves.

(D) The United States invaded Haiti several times during the revolution.

9. In what way was the Haitian Revolution similar to other revolutions of the time period?

(A) Revolutions were led by religious elites.

(B) Revolutions facilitated the emergence of independent states.

(C) Revolutions began as movements to support the monarchy.

(D) Revolutions were led by people from the urban working classes.

10. The Haitian Revolution is best understood as a

(A) movement that was fed by Enlightenment thought.

(B) movement that had its roots in religious fanaticism.

(C) movement that rejected the Enlightenment.

(D) slave rebellion that failed to attain its goals.

Short-Answer Questions

1. Historians argue that the Enlightenment had a profound effect on the world in the time period 1750–1900. Use your knowledge of world history to answer all parts of the question that follows.

(A) Provide ONE specific region of the world that was affected by the Enlightenment.

(B) Explain ONE way this region changed as a result of Enlightenment thinking.

(C) Explain ANOTHER way this region changed as a result of Enlightenment thinking.

"It has been said that terror is the principle of despotic government. Does your government therefore resemble despotism? Yes, as the sword that gleams in the hands of the heroes of liberty resembles that with which the henchmen of tyranny are armed. Let the despot govern by terror his brutalized subjects; he is right, as a despot. Subdue by terror the enemies of liberty, and you will be right, as founders of the Republic. The government of the revolution is liberty's despotism against tyranny. Is force made only to protect crime? And is the thunderbolt not destined to strike the heads of the proud?"

Maximilien Robespierre, "On the Moral and Political Principles of Domestic Policy," 1794

2. Use the passage above and your knowledge of world history to answer all parts of the question that follows.

(A) Identify ONE way the French Revolution exemplified Robespierre's argument.

(B) Explain ONE way Robespierre's views differed from those of a supporter of the monarchy.

(C) Explain ONE way Robespierre demonstrates Enlightenment thinking.

24 Land Empires in the Age of Imperialism, 1800–1870

CHAPTER OUTLINE

AP® Framework Terms

Land empires
Ottoman Empire
Russian Empire
Qing Empire

Overarching Questions

1 How have environmental factors shaped the development of diverse technologies, industrialization, transportation methods, and exchange and communication networks? (ENV)

2 How and why have economic, social, cultural, and geographic factors influenced the process of state building, expansion, and dissolution? (SB)

3 How have internal and external political factors influenced the process of state building, expansion, and dissolution? (SB)

4 How have economic systems and the development of ideologies, values, and institutions influenced each other? (ECON)

5 How have political, economic, cultural, and demographic factors affected social structures? (SOC)

During the late 1860s, a little-known warlord named Yaqub Beg unified several Muslim uprisings in Central Asia against a foreign occupier, the Qing Empire. Only a hundred years earlier, in 1759, Qing armies had successfully conquered a vast region of Central Asia and called it Xinjiang, meaning "new territory." Despite attempts to work with local leaders, tensions between locals and Chinese never eased, and the natives rebelled.

Yaqub took full diplomatic advantage of the empires surrounding him. To his south lay India, under the control of an expanding British Empire. To his north was the Russian Empire, Britain's rival in the quest to gain influence in Central Asia. Yaqub sent emissaries to both empires in 1868 and signed commercial treaties in 1872 in exchange for their recognition of his rule over Xinjiang. He even received military support from the distant Ottoman Empire, whose ruler bestowed upon him the title *Commander of the Faithful*. Traditionally a title borne by a caliph, the gift of it to a minor figure indicates a diminished importance for the idea of a caliphate.

For a time it seemed that the Qing might not try to retake Xinjiang. It would be an expensive venture for a government that was looking to spend money modernizing its army and navy. But fears that Russia might take over neighboring Mongolia drove the Chinese back into Xinjiang, and Yaqub's regime collapsed in 1877.

Yaqub's story illustrates the challenges facing Eurasian empires as they over-extended themselves. The largest problems, common to all the agricultural empires of Eurasia, were old and inefficient ways of collecting revenue and centralizing control. While industrializing European economies drawing on the wealth of their overseas

▲ **Trade Warehouse in Guangzhou**   A European merchant enters in the background while Chinese workers pack tea and porcelain.
Manufacture of Porcelain (gouache on paper), Chinese School (19th century)/Peabody Essex Museum, Salem, Massachusetts, USA /The Bridgeman Art Library

colonies increasingly dominated international trade, during the early 1800s rapid population growth and slow agricultural expansion put pressure on much of Eurasia. In addition, earlier military expansion had stretched the resources of imperial treasuries (see Chapter 21), leaving the land-based empires vulnerable to European military pressure. Responses to this pressure varied, with reform and adoption of European practices gaining headway in some lands and tradition being reasserted in others. In the long run, attempts to meet western Europe's economic and political demands produced financial indebtedness to France, Britain, and other Western powers.

This chapter contrasts the experiences of the Qing Empire with those of the Russian and Ottoman Empires. Whereas the Qing opted for resistance, the others made varying attempts to adapt and reform. Russia eventually became part of Europe and shared in many aspects of European culture, while the Ottomans and the Qing became subject to ever-greater imperialist pressure. These different responses raise the question of the role of culture in shaping western Europe's relations with the rest of the world in the nineteenth century. ●

24-1 The Ottoman Empire

What were the benefits and the drawbacks to the Ottoman Empire of the reforms adopted during the Tanzimat period?

During the eighteenth century the central government of the Ottoman Empire lost much of its power to provincial governors, military commanders, ethnic leaders, and bandit chiefs. In several parts of the empire local officials and large landholders tried to increase their independence and divert imperial funds into their own coffers.

A kingdom in Arabia led by the Saud family, following the puritanical and fundamentalist religious views of an eighteenth-century leader named Muhammad ibn Abd al-Wahhab (**moo-HAH-muhd ib-uhn ab-dahl-wa-HAHB**), took control of the holy cities of Mecca and Medina and deprived the sultan of the honor of organizing the annual pilgrimage. Meanwhile, in Egypt, factions of mamluk slave-soldiers purchased as boys in Georgia and nearby parts of the Caucasus and educated for war reasserted their influence. Such soldiers had ruled Egypt between 1260 and 1517, when they were defeated by the Ottomans. Now Ottoman weakness allowed mamluk factions based on a revival of the slave-soldier tradition to re-emerge as local military forces.

For the sultans, the outlook was bleak. At the end of the eighteenth century, the inefficient Janissary corps used the political power it enjoyed in Istanbul to force Sultan Selim III to abandon efforts to train a modern, European-style army. This situation unexpectedly changed when France invaded Egypt.

24-1a Egypt and the Napoleonic Example

Napoleon Bonaparte and an invasion force of 36,000 men and 400 ships invaded Egypt in May 1798. The French quickly defeated the mamluk forces that for several decades had dominated the country under the loose jurisdiction of the Ottoman sultan in Istanbul. Fifteen months later, after being stopped by Ottoman land and British naval forces in an attempted invasion of Syria, Napoleon secretly left Cairo and returned to France. Three months later he seized power and made himself emperor.

Back in Egypt, his generals tried to administer a country that they only poorly understood. Cut off from France by British ships in the Mediterranean, they had little hope of retaining power and agreed to withdraw in 1801. For the second time in three years, a collapse of military power produced a power vacuum in Egypt. The winner of the ensuing contest was **Muhammad Ali** (**moo-HAM-mad AH-lee**), the commander of a contingent of Albanian soldiers sent by the sultan to restore imperial control. By 1805 he had taken the place of the official Ottoman governor, and by 1811 he had dispossessed the mamluks of their lands and privileges.

Muhammad Ali's rise to power coincided with the meteoric career of Emperor Napoleon I. It is not surprising, therefore, that he adopted many French practices in rebuilding the Egyptian state. Militarily, he established special schools for training artillery and cavalry officers, army surgeons, military bandmasters, and others. The curricula of these schools featured European skills and sciences, and Muhammad Ali began to send promising officer trainees to France for education. In 1824 he started a gazette devoted to official affairs, the first newspaper in the Islamic world.

As discussed in Chapter 22, Muhammad Ali built all sorts of factories to outfit his new army. These did not prove efficient enough to survive, but they showed a determination to achieve independence and parity with the European powers.

In the 1830s Muhammad Ali's son Ibrahim invaded Syria and instituted some of the changes already under way in Egypt. The improved quality of the new Egyptian army had been proven during the Greek war of independence (see below), when Ibrahim had commanded an expeditionary force to help the sultan. In response, the sultan embarked on building his own new army in 1826. The two armies clashed when Ibra-him attacked northward into Anatolia in 1839 and defeated the army of his suzerain, the Ottoman sultan. The road to Istanbul seemed open until the European powers intervened and forced a withdrawal to the present-day border between Egypt and Israel.

Muhammad Ali remained Egypt's ruler, under the suzerainty of the sultan, until his death in 1849; his family continued to rule the country until 1952. But his dream of making Egypt a mighty country capable of standing up to Europe faded. What survived was the example he had set for the sultans in Istanbul.

Muhammad Ali Leader of Egyptian modernization in the early nineteenth century. He ruled Egypt as an Ottoman governor but had imperial ambitions. His descendants ruled Egypt until overthrown in 1952.

24-1b Ottoman Reform and the European Model, 1807–1853

At the end of the eighteenth century Sultan Selim (**seh-LEEM**) III (r. 1789–1807), a forward-looking ruler who stayed abreast of events in Europe, introduced reforms to create European-style military units, bring provincial governors under central government control, and standardize taxation. The rise in government expenditures to implement the reforms was supposed to be offset by taxes on selected items, primarily tobacco and coffee.

CHRONOLOGY

	Ottoman Empire	Russian Empire	Qing Empire
1800	1805–1849 Muhammad Ali governs Egypt	1801–1825 Reign of Alexander I	1794–1804 White Lotus Rebellion
	1808–1839 Rule of Mahmud II	1812 Napoleon's retreat from Moscow	
	1826 Janissary corps dissolved	1825 Decembrist revolt	
	1830 Greek independence	1825–1855 Reign of Nicholas I	
	1839 Abdul Mejid begins Tanzimat reforms		
1850	1853–1856 Crimean War	1853–1856 Crimean War	1850–1864 Taiping Rebellion
	1876 First constitution by an Islamic government	1855–1881 Reign of Alexander II	1856–1860 Arrow War
		1861 Emancipation of the serfs	1877 Collapse of Yaqub Beg's revolt in Xinjiang

The reforms failed for political more than economic reasons. The most violent and persistent opposition came from the **Janissary (JAN-nih-say-ree)** military corps (see Chapter 20). In the eighteenth century the Janissaries became a significant political force in Istanbul and in provincial capitals like Damascus and Aleppo. Their interest in preserving special economic privileges made them resist the creation of new military units.

At times, Janissary power produced military uprisings. In the Ottoman territory of **Serbia**, local residents intensely resented the control exercised by Janissary governors. The Orthodox Christians claimed that the Janissaries abused them. In response, Selim threatened to reassign the Janissaries to Istanbul. Suspecting that the sultan wanted to curb their political power, in 1805 the Janissaries revolted and massacred Christians in Serbia. Unable to re-establish central Ottoman rule over Serbia, the sultan had to ask the ruler of Bosnia, a neighboring Balkan province, to join his troops with the peasants of Serbia and suppress the Janissary uprising. The threat of Russian intervention prevented the Ottomans from then disarming the victorious Serbians, so Serbia became effectively independent.

Other opponents of reform included *ulama*, or Muslim religious scholars, who distrusted the secularization of law and taxation that Selim proposed. In the face of widespread rejection of his reforms, Selim suspended his program in 1806. Never-theless, a massive military uprising occurred at Istanbul, and the sultan was deposed and imprisoned. Reform forces recaptured the capital, but not before Selim had been executed. Selim's cousin, Sultan Mahmud **(mah-MOOD)** II (r. 1808–1839), cautiously revived Selim's program, but he realized that reforms needed to be more systematic and imposed more forcefully. The effectiveness of radical reform in Muhammad Ali's Egypt drove this lesson home, as did the insurrection in Greece, during which the Egyptian military performed much better than the main Ottoman army.

Greek independence in 1830 had dramatic international significance. A combination of Greek nationalist organizations and interlopers from Albania sparked the independence movement. Europe's interest in the classical age of Greece and Rome led many Europeans to consider the Greeks' struggle for independence a campaign to re-capture their classical glory from Muslim oppression. Some—including the "mad, bad and dangerous to know" English poet Lord Byron, who lost his life in the war—went to Greece to fight as volunteers. When the combined squadrons of the British, French, and Russian fleets, under orders to observe but not intervene in the war, made an unauthorized attack that sank the Ottoman fleet at the Battle of Navarino, Greek victory was assured (see Map 24.1).

Mahmud II concurred with the pro-Greek Europeans in viewing Ottoman military reversals in Greece as a sign of profound weakness. With popular outrage over the military setbacks strong, the sultan made his move in 1826. First he announced the creation of a new artillery unit, which he had secretly been training. When the Janissaries rose in revolt, as expected, he ordered the new unit to bombard the Janissary barracks. The Janissary corps was officially dissolved.

AP® Exam Tip
Identify and explain several examples of direct resistance within empires, as well as the creation of new states on the peripheries of existing empires.

Janissaries Infantry, originally of slave origin, armed with firearms and constituting the elite of the Ottoman army from the fifteenth century until the corps was abolished in 1826.

Serbia The Ottoman province in the Balkans that rose up against Janissary control in the early 1800s. After World War II the central province of Yugo-slavia. Serb leaders struggled to maintain dominance as the Yugoslav federation dissolved in the 1990s.

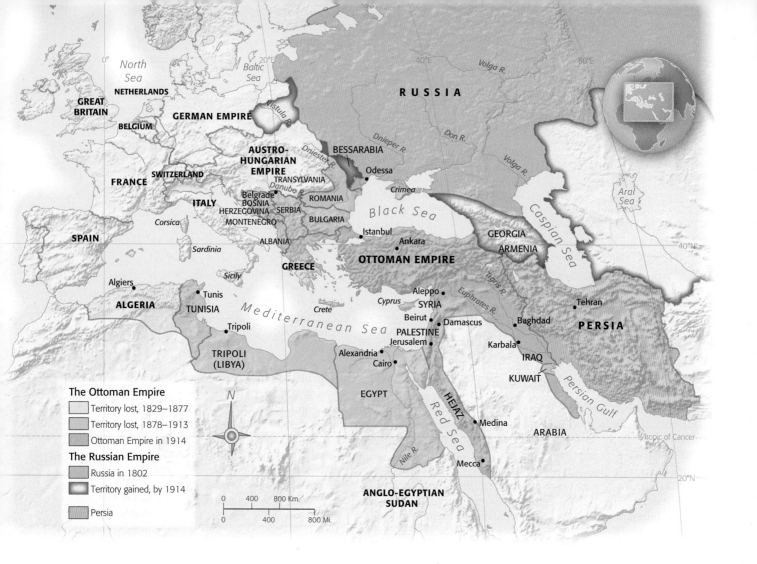

MAP 24.1   The Ottoman and Russian Empires, 1829–1914 At its height the Ottoman Empire controlled most of the perimeter of the Mediterranean Sea. But in the 1800s Ottoman territory shrank as many countries gained their independence. The Black Sea, where the Turkish coast was vulnerable to assault, became a weak spot as Russian naval power grew. Russian challenges to the Ottomans at the eastern end of the Black Sea and to the Persians east and west of the Caspian aroused fears in Europe that Russia was trying to reach the Indian Ocean.

Why did successive Russian rulers express great interest in acquiring naval access to the Mediterranean Sea?

AP® Exam Tip
Compare various reform movements that occurred during this time period.

Tanzimat Restructuring reforms by the nineteenth-century Ottoman rulers, intended to move civil law away from the control of religious elites and make the military and the bureaucracy more efficient.

Like Muhammad Ali, Mahmud felt he could not implement major changes without reducing the political power of the religious elite. He visualized restructuring the bureaucracy and the educational and legal systems, where ulama power was strongest. Before such strong measures could be undertaken, however, Ibrahim attacked from Syria in 1839. Battlefield defeat, the treachery of the rebuilt Ottoman navy in switching sides and supporting Egypt, and the death of Mahmud, all in the same year, left the empire completely dependent on the European powers for survival.

Mahmud's reforming ideas received their widest expression in the **Tanzimat (TAHNZ-ee-MAT)** ("reorganization"), a series of reforms announced by his sixteen-year-old son and successor, Abdul Mejid (**ab-dul meh-JEED**), in 1839 and strongly endorsed by the influential European ambassadors. One proclamation called for public trials and equal protection under the law for all, whether Muslim, Christian, or Jew. It also guaranteed some rights of privacy, equalized the eligibility of men for conscription into the army (a practice copied from Egypt), and provided for a new method of tax collection that legally ended tax farming in the Ottoman Empire. It took many years and strenuous efforts by reforming bureaucrats, known as the "men of the Tanzimat," to give substance to these reforms.

Over time, one legal code after another—commercial, criminal, civil procedure—was introduced to take the place of the corresponding areas of Muslim legal jurisdiction. All the codes were modeled closely on those of Europe. The Shari'a, or Islamic law, gradually became restricted to matters of family law such as marriage and inheritance. As the Shari'a was displaced, job opportunities for the ulama shrank.

European observers praised the reforms for their noble principles and rejection of religious influence. Ottoman citizens were more divided; the Christians and Jews, for whom the Europeans showed the greatest concern, were generally more enthusiastic than the Muslims. Many historians see the Tanzimat as the dawn of modern thought and enlightened government in the Middle East. Others point out that removing the religious elite from influence in government also removed the one remaining check on authoritarian rule.

Like Muhammad Ali, Sultan Mahmud sent military cadets to France and the German states for training. In the 1830s an Ottoman imperial school of military sciences, later transformed into Istanbul University, was established in which instructors from western Europe taught chemistry, engineering, mathematics, and physics in addition to military history. Military education became the model for more general educational reforms. In 1838 the first medical school was established to train army doctors and surgeons. Later, a national system of preparatory schools was created to feed graduates into the military schools. The subjects that were taught and many of the teachers were foreign, raising the issue of whether Turkish should be a language of instruction. Because it was easier to import and use foreign textbooks than to write new ones in Turkish, French became the preferred language in all advanced professional and scientific training. In numerical terms, however, the great majority of students still learned to read and write in Quran schools down to the twentieth century.

In the capital city of Istanbul, the reforms stimulated the growth of a small but cosmopolitan milieu embracing European language and culture. The first Turkish newspaper, a government gazette modeled on that of Muhammad Ali, appeared in 1831. Other newspapers followed, many written in French. Travel to Europe—particularly to England and France—became popular among wealthy Turks. Interest in importing European military, industrial, and communications technology remained strong through the 1800s.

Changes in military practice had unforeseen cultural and social effects. Accepting the European notion that modern weapons and drill required modern military dress, beards were deemed unhygienic and, in artillery units, a fire hazard. Military headgear also became controversial. European military caps, which had leather bills on the front to protect against the glare of the sun, were not acceptable because they interfered with Muslim soldiers' touching their foreheads to the ground in prayer. The compromise was the brimless cap now called the *fez*, which was adopted by the military and then by Ottoman civil officials in the early years of Mahmud II's reign

◀ **Modernized Ottoman Troops** This photograph of a contingent of Imperial Guards in the late nineteenth century shows them equipped and uniformed much like any other European army of the time. The only distinctive feature is the fez, a brimless hat adopted earlier in the century as a symbol of reform. Comparison with the soldiers in the funeral procession of Suleiman the Magnificent (page 489) shows the degree of change from the traditional military uniforms that were still being worn in the eighteenth century. From one of the original photographic album of Sultan Abdul Hamid II, 1842-1918/Library of Congress

The empire's new orientation spread beyond the military. Government ministries that normally recruited from traditional bureaucratic families and relied on on-the-job training were gradually transformed into formal civil services hiring men educated in the new schools. Among self-consciously progressive men, particularly those in government service, European dress became the fashion in the Ottoman cities of the later 1800s, while traditional dress became a symbol of the religious, the rural, and the parochial.

Secularization of the legal code particularly affected non-Muslim Ottoman subjects. Islamic law had required non-Muslims to pay a special head tax that was some-times explained as a substitute for military service. Under the Tanzimat, the tax was abolished and non-Muslims became liable for military service—unless they bought their way out by paying a new military exemption fee. The new law codes gave all male subjects equal access to the civil courts, while the operations of the Islamic law courts shrank. What enhanced the status of non-Muslims most, however, was the strong concern for their welfare consistently expressed by the European powers. The Ottoman Empire became a rich field of operation for Christian missionaries and European supporters of Jewish community life in the Muslim world.

The public rights and political participation granted during the Tanzimat applied specifically to men. Private life, including everything connected to marriage and divorce, remained within the sphere of religious law, and at no time was there a question of political participation or reformed education for women. Indeed, the reforms may have decreased the influence of women. The political changes ran parallel to economic changes that also narrowed women's opportunities.

After silver from the Americas began to flood the empire in the 1600s, workers were increasingly paid in cash rather than in goods, and businesses associated with banking and finance developed. But women were barred from the early industrial labor and the professions, and traditional "woman's work" such as weaving was increasingly mechanized and done by men.

▲ **Interior of the Ottoman Financial Bureau**   This engraving from the eighteenth century depicts the governing style of the Ottoman Empire before the era of westernizing reforms. By the end of the Tanzimat period in 1876, government offices and the costumes of officials looked much more like those in contemporary European capitals.   From Ignatius Mouradgea dOhsson, Tableau General de lEmpire Ottoman, large folio edition, Paris, 17871820, pl. 178, following p. 340

Nevertheless, in the early 1800s women retained considerable power in the management and disposal of their own property, gained mostly through fixed shares of inheritance. After marriage a woman was often pressured to convert her landholdings to cash in order to transfer her personal wealth to her husband's family, with whom she and her husband would reside. However, this was not a requirement, since men were legally obligated to support their families single-handedly. Until the 1820s many wealthy women retained their say in the distribution of property through the creation of charitable trusts for their offspring. Because these trusts were set up in the religious courts, they could be designed to conform to the wishes of family members. Then, in the 1820s and 1830s the secularizing reforms of Mahmud II, which did not always produce happy results, transferred jurisdiction over the charitable trusts from religious courts to the state and undermined women's control over this form of property.

24-1c The Crimean War and Its Aftermath

Since the reign of Peter the Great (r. 1689–1725), the Russian Empire had been attempting to expand southward at the Ottomans' expense (see the section on Russia and Asia). His strongest successor, Catherine the Great (r. 1762–1796), had captured control of the north shore of the Black Sea by 1783, and by 1815 Russia had pried the Georgian region of the Caucasus away from the Ottomans. Moreover, the threat of Russian intervention to protect Serbian Orthodox Christians had prevented the Ottomans from crushing Serbian independence. When Muhammad Ali's Egyptian army invaded Syria in 1833, Russia signed a treaty in support of the Ottomans, whose army was in disarray. In return, the sultan recognized Russia's claim to being the protector of all of the empire's Orthodox subjects. This set the stage for an obscure dispute that resulted in war.

Bowing to British and French pressure, the sultan named France Protector of the Holy Sepulchre in Jerusalem in 1852. Russia protested, but the sultan held firm. So Russia invaded Ottoman territories in what is today Romania, and Britain and France went to war as allies of the sultan. The real causes of the war went beyond church quarrels in Jerusalem and involved diplomatic maneuvering among European powers over whether the Ottoman Empire should continue to exist or, if not, who should take over its territory. The *Eastern Question* was the simple name given to this complex issue. Though the powers, including Russia, had agreed to save the empire in 1839, Britain subsequently became suspicious of Russian ambitions. Prominent anti-Russian politicians in Britain feared that Russia would threaten the British hold on India.

Between 1853 and 1856 the **Crimean (cry-ME-uhn) War** raged in Romania, on the Black Sea, and on the Crimean peninsula. Britain, France, and the Italian kingdom of Sardinia-Piedmont sided with the Ottomans. Britain and France trapped the Russian fleet in the Black Sea, where its commanders decided to sink the ships to protect the approaches to Sevastopol, their main base in Crimea. However, an army largely made up of British and French troops landed and laid siege to the city. Official corruption and lack of railways hampered the Russians' attempts to supply their forces. On the Romanian front, the Ottomans resisted effectively. At Sevastopol, the Russians were outmatched militarily and suffered badly from disease. Tsar Nicholas died as defeat loomed, leaving his successor, Alexander II (r. 1855–1881), to sue for peace when Sevastopol finally fell three months later.

The Crimean War brought significant changes to all the combatants. The tsar and his government, already beset by demands for the reform of serfdom, education, and the military (discussed later), were further discredited. In Britain and France, the conflict was accompanied by massive propaganda campaigns. For the first time newspapers effectively mobilized public support for a war. British press accounts so glamorized British participation that the false impression has lingered that Ottoman troops played a negligible role in the conflict. At the time, however, British and French commanders noted the massive losses among Turkish troops in particular.

▲ **Street Scene in Cairo** This engraving from Edward William Lane's influential travel book, *Account of the Manners and Customs of the Modern Egyptians Written in Egypt During the Years 1833–1835* conveys the image of narrow lanes and small stores that became stock features of European thinking about Middle Eastern cities. From Edward William Lane, The Manners and Customs of the Modern Egyptians (London: J. M. D. & Co. 1860)

AP® Exam Tip
Understand the efforts of land empires (such as Russia) to expand their borders and the impact on neighboring states.

Crimean War Conflict between the Russian and Ottoman Empires fought primarily in the Crimean peninsula. To prevent Russian expansion, Britain and France sent troops to support the Ottomans.

The French press, dominant in Istanbul, promoted a sense of unity between Turkish and French society that continued to influence many aspects of Turkish urban culture.

The larger significance of the Crimean War was that it marked the transition from traditional to modern warfare (see Environment &Technology: The Web of War). All the combatants had previously prided themselves on the use of highly trained cavalry to smash through the front lines of infantry. Cavalry coexisted with firearms until the early 1800s, primarily because early rifles were awkward to load and not very accurate. Cavalry could attack during the intervals between volleys. Then in the 1830s and 1840s percussion caps that did away with pouring gunpowder into the barrel of a musket came into use. In Crimean War battles many cavalry units were destroyed by the rapid fire of rifles that loaded at the breech rather than down the barrel. That was the fate of the famed British Light Brigade, which was sent to relieve an Ottoman unit surrounded by Russian troops.

After the Crimean War, the Ottoman Empire increased its involvement with European commerce. The Ottoman imperial bank was founded in 1840, and a few years later currency reform pegged the value of Ottoman gold coins to the British pound. Sweeping changes in the 1850s expedited the creation of banks, insurance companies, and legal firms throughout the empire. Bustling trade also encouraged a migration from country to city between about 1850 and 1880. Many of the major cities of the empire—Istanbul, Damascus, Beirut, Alexandria, Cairo—expanded. A small but influential urban professional class emerged, as did a considerable class of wage laborers. Other demographic shifts involved refugees from Poland and Hungary, where rivalry between the European powers and the Russian Empire caused political tension and sporadic warfare, and from Georgia and other parts of the Caucasus, where Russian expansion forced many Muslims to emigrate (discussed later).

However, commercial vigor and urbanization could not make up for declining revenues and the chronic insolvency and corruption of the imperial government. From the conclusion of the Crimean War in 1856 on, the Ottoman government became heavily dependent on foreign loans. In return it lowered tariffs to favor European imports and allowed European banks to open in Ottoman cities. Europeans living in Istanbul and other commercial centers enjoyed **extraterritoriality**, the right to be subject to their own laws and exempt from Ottoman jurisdiction.

extraterritoriality The right of foreign residents in a country to live under the laws of their native country and disregard the laws of the host country. In the nineteenth and early twentieth centuries, European and American nationals living in certain areas of Chinese and Ottoman cities were granted this right.

As the result of these measures, imported goods multiplied, but—apart from tobacco and the Turkish opium that American traders took to China to compete against British opium from India—Anatolia produced few exports. As foreign debt grew, so did inflationary trends that left urban populations in a precarious position. By contrast, Egyptian cotton exports soared during the American Civil War, when American cotton exports plummeted; but the profits benefited Muhammad Ali's descendants, who had become the hereditary governors of Egypt, rather than the Ottoman government. The Suez Canal, which was partly financed by cotton profits, opened in 1869, and Cairo was redesigned and beautified. Eventually overexpenditure on these projects plunged Egypt into the same debt crisis that plagued the empire as a whole.

Section Review

- After French withdrawal from Egypt, Muhammad Ali seized control and began a French-influenced modernization program.

- His successors continued the program and attacked the Ottoman Empire, but they were thwarted by the European powers.

- The Greek insurrection, European intervention, and Egyptian attack drove the westernizing reform efforts of Mahmud II and his successors.

- The most comprehensive reform initiative was Abdul Mejid's Tanzimat program.

- The Crimean War marked the transition from traditional to modern warfare and drew the Ottoman Empire into greater involvement with European commerce.

- Declining power and prosperity led to the rise of the Young Ottomans.

The decline of Ottoman power and prosperity had a strong impact on a group of well-educated young urban men who aspired to wealth and influence. They doubted that the empire's rulers and the Tanzimat officials who worked for them would ever stand up to European domination. Though lacking a sophisticated organization, these Young Ottomans (sometimes called Young Turks, though that term properly applies to a later movement) promoted a mixture of liberal ideas derived from Europe, national pride in Ottoman independence, and modernist views of Islam. Prominent Young Ottomans helped draft a constitution that was promulgated in 1876 by a new and as yet untried sultan, Abdul Hamid II. This apparent triumph of liberal reform was short-lived. With war against Russia again threatening in the Balkans in 1877, Abdul Hamid suspended the constitution and the parliament that had been elected that year. Though he ruthlessly opposed further political reforms, the Tanzimat programs of extending modern schooling, utilizing European military practices and advisers, and making the government bureaucracy more orderly continued during his reign.

24-2 The Russian Empire

How did the Russian Empire maintain its status as both a European power and a great Asian land empire?

In 1812, when Napoleon's march on Moscow ended in a disastrous retreat brought on more by what a later tsar called "Generals January and February" than by Russian military action, the European image of Russia changed. Just as Napoleon's withdrawal from Egypt led to Muhammad Ali briefly becoming a political power, so his withdrawal from Russia conferred status on Tsar Alexander I (r. 1801–1825). Conservative Europeans still saw Russia as alien, backward, and oppressive, but they acknowledged its immensity and potential and included the tsar in efforts to suppress revolutionary tendencies throughout Europe.

In several important respects Russia resembled the Ottoman Empire more than the conservative kingdoms of Europe whose autocratic practices it so staunchly supported. Socially dominated by nobles whose country estates were worked by unfree serfs, Russia had almost no middle class. Industry was still at the threshold of development by the standards of the rapidly industrializing European powers, though it was somewhat more dynamic than Ottoman industry. Like Egypt and the Ottoman Empire, Russia engaged in reforms from the top down under Alexander I, but when his conservative brother Nicholas I (r. 1825–1855) succeeded to the throne, iron discipline and suspicion of modern ideas took priority over reform.

AP® Exam Tip
Consider the continuities and changes in land-based empires like Russia and the Ottoman Empire over time.

24-2a Russia and Europe

In 1700 only three Russians out of a hundred lived in cities, two-thirds of them in Moscow alone. By the mid-1800s the town population had grown tenfold, though it still accounted for only 6 percent of the total because the territories of the tsars had grown greatly through wars and colonization (see Chapter 21). These figures demonstrate that, like the Ottoman Empire, Russia was an overwhelmingly agricultural land. However, it had poorer transportation than the Ottoman Empire, since many Ottoman cities were seaports. Both empires encompassed peoples speaking many different languages.

Well-engineered roads did not begin to appear until 1817, and steam navigation commenced on the Volga in 1843. Tsar Nicholas I built the first railroad from St. Petersburg, the Russian capital, to his summer palace in 1837. A few years later his commitment to strict discipline led him to insist that the trunk line from St. Petersburg to Moscow run in a perfectly straight line. American engineers, among them the father of painter James McNeill Whistler, who learned to paint in St. Petersburg, oversaw the laying of track and built locomotive workshops. Industrialization projects depended heavily on foreign expertise. British engineers set up the textile mills that gave woolens and cottons a prominent place among Russia's industries.

Until the late nineteenth century the Russian government's interest in industry was limited. An industrial revolution required educated and independent-minded artisans and entrepreneurs, but Nicholas feared the spread of literacy and modern education—especially anything smacking of liberalism, socialism, or revolution—beyond the minimum needed to train the officer corps and the bureaucracy. He preferred serfs to factory workers, and he paid for imported industrial goods with exports of grain and timber.

Like Egypt and the Ottoman Empire, Russia aspired to Western-style economic development. But when France and Britain entered the Crimean War, they faced a Russian army equipped with obsolete weapons and bogged down by lack of transportation. At a time when European engineers were making major breakthroughs in loading cannon through opening the breech end, muzzle-loading artillery remained the Russian standard.

Yet in some ways Russia bore a closer resemblance to other European countries than the Ottoman Empire did. From the point of view of the French and the British, the Cyrillic alphabet and the Russian Orthodox form of Christianity seemed foreign, but they were not nearly as foreign as the Arabic alphabet and the Muslim faith. Britain and France feared Russia as a rival for power in the east, but they increasingly accepted Tsar Nicholas's view of the Ottoman Empire as "the sick man of Europe," capable of surviving only so long as the European powers permitted.

From the Russian point of view, kinship with western Europe was of questionable value. Westernizers, like the men of the Tanzimat in the Ottoman Empire, put their trust in technical advances and governmental reform. Opposing them were intellectuals known as

The military technologies of the mid-nineteenth century that were used on battlefields in the United States, Russia, India, and China shifted rapidly from one conflict to the next. Faster communications contributed to this dissemination but a new international network of imperialist soldiers played a role as well as they moved from one trouble spot to another.

General Charles Gordon (1833–1885), for instance, was commissioned in the British army in 1852, then served in the Crimean War after Britain entered on the side of the Ottomans. In 1860 he was dispatched to China where he served with British forces during the Arrow War and took part in the sack of Beijing. Afterward, he stayed in China and was seconded to the Qing imperial government until the suppression of the Taipings in 1864, earning himself the nickname "Chinese" Gordon. Gordon later served the ambitious rulers of Egypt as governor of territory along the Nile in the Sudan that they were trying to add to an Egyptian empire. He

▲ **Florence Nightingale During Crimean War**   This 1856 lithograph shows Florence Nightingale supervising nursing care in a hospital in Scutari (ÜskÜdar) across the Bosphorus strait from Istanbul. Though the artist may have exaggerated the neatness and cleanliness of the ward, sanitary measures proved the key to Nightingale's raising of the survival rate of sick and wounded soldiers.   Hospital at Scutari, detail of Florence Nightingale (1820–1910) on the ward, from 'The Seat of War in the East', pub. by Paul & Dominic Colnaghi & Co., 1856 (litho) (detail of 121085)/Simpson, William 'Crimea' (1823–99)/STAPLETON COLLECTION/Private Collection/The Bridgeman Art Library

Slavophiles, who considered the Orthodox faith, the solidity of peasant life, and the tsar's absolute rule to be the proper bases of Russian civilization. After Russia's humiliation in the Crimea, the Slavophile tendency gave rise to **Pan-Slavism**, a militant political doctrine advocating unity of all the Slavic peoples, including those living under Austrian and Ottoman rule.

On the diplomatic front, the tsar's inclusion as a major European ruler contrasted sharply with the sultan's exclusion. However, this did not prevent a powerful sense of Russophobia from developing in the West. Britain in particular saw Russia as a threat to India and despised the subjection of the serfs, who gained their freedom from Tsar Alexander II only in 1861, twenty-seven years after the British had abolished slavery. In addition, the passions generated by the Crimean War and its outcome affected the relations of Russia, Europe, and the Ottoman Empire for the remainder of the nineteenth century.

24-2b Russia and Asia

The Russian drive to the east in the eighteenth century brought the tsar's empire to the Pacific Ocean and the frontiers of China (see Map 21.1) by century's end. In the nineteenth century Russian expansionism focused on the south. There the backwardness of the Russian military did not matter since the peoples they faced were even less industrialized and technologically advanced. In 1860 Russia established a military outpost on the Pacific coast that would eventually grow into the great naval port of Vladivostok, today Russia's most southerly city. In Central Asia the steppe lands of the Kazakh nomads came under Russian control early in the century, setting

Slavophiles Russian intellectuals in the early nineteenth century who favored resisting western European influences and taking pride in the traditional peasant values and institutions of the Slavic people.

Pan-Slavism Movement among Russian intellectuals in the second half of the nineteenth century to identify culturally and politically with the Slavic peoples of eastern Europe.

met his death in 1885 while leading his Egyptian troops, besieged in the city of Khartoum by a Sudanese Sufi leader, Muhammad Ahman ibn Abadallah, who was building a state based on his claim to being the awaited Mahdi, or messiah.

Journalism played an important part in the developing web of telegraph communications that sped orders to and from the battlefields. Readers in London could learn details of dramas occurring in the Crimea or in China within a week of their occurrence. Print and, later, photographic journalism created new "stars" from these war experiences. War correspondents celebrated colorful figures like "Chinese" Gordon and gave readers a feel for what war was like. George W. Cooke, a Special Correspondent for the *Times* of London, covered the war in the Crimea and China and gave a firsthand account of the siege of Sevastopol, the Crimean capital:

Sebastopol [sic] . . . was built for dominion, and not for commerce . . . Its palaces were erected by Russian princes who came south for sunshine, or for the military magnates who were there to plot and execute acts of aggression. We must not forget this as we grope among the ruins . . . these bits of torn Berlin wool work—these crushed rose-coloured bonnets—these fluttering fragments of silk and muslin— these playing-cards and dominoes.

Florence Nightingale became another star. In the wars of the 1800s, the vast majority of deaths resulted from infection or excessive bleeding. Florence Nightingale (1820–1910), while still a young woman, became interested in hospital management and nursing. She went to Prussia and France to study advanced techniques. Before the outbreak of the Crimean War she was credited with bringing about marked improvement in British health care. When the public reacted emotionally to news reports of the suffering wounded soldiers in the Crimea, the British government sent Nightingale to the rescue. Within a year of her arrival the death rate in the military hospitals dropped from 45 percent to under 5 percent. Her techniques for preventing septicemia and dysentery, essentially sanitary measures like washing bed linens after a death and emptying toilet buckets outside, were quickly adopted by those working for and with her. On her return to London, Nightingale established institutes for nursing that soon were recognized around the world for teaching better practices. She herself was lionized by the British public and received the Order of Merit in 1907, three years before her death.

The life of her contemporary, Mary Seacole (1805–1881), undescores the importance of Nightingale's innovations in public hygiene. A Jamaican woman who volunteered to nurse British troops in the Crimean War, Seacole was repeatedly excluded from nursing service by British authorities. She eventually went to Crimea and used her own funds to run a hospital there, bankrupting herself in the process.

The drama of the Crimean War as reported by war correspondents moved the British public to support Seacole after her sacrifices were publicized. She was awarded medals by the British, French, and Turkish governments and today is recognized with her contemporary Florence Nightingale as an innovative field nurse and a champion of public hygiene in peacetime.

Questions for Analysis

1. How did news reporting help rally public support for far-flung imperial military adventures?

2. How did the slowdown in the pace of warfare in Europe between Napole-on's fall in 1815 and the Franco-Prussian War of 1870 affect military careers?

3. Why might war in the Crimea have aroused the feelings of British newspaper readers more than war in China?

Source: George W. Cooke, *Inside Sebastopol, and Experiences in Camp* (London: Chapman and Hall, 1856), 160.

---

the stage for a confrontation with three Uzbek states farther south. They succumbed one by one, beginning in 1865, giving rise to the new province of Turkestan, with its capital at Tashkent in present-day Uzbekistan

In the region of the Caucasus Mountains, the third area of southward expansion, Russia first took over Christian Georgia (1786), Muslim Azerbaijan (**ah-zer-by-JAHN**) (1801), and Christian Armenia (1813) before gobbling up the many small principalities in the heart of the mountains. Between 1829 and 1864 Dagestan, Chechnya (**CHECH-nee-yah**), Abkhazia (**ab-KAH-zee-yah**), and other regions that would one day gain political prominence after the breakup of the Soviet Union became parts of the Russian Empire.

The drive to the south intensified political friction with Russia's new neighbors: Qing China and Japan in the east, Iran on the Central Asian and Caucasus frontiers, and the Ottoman Empire at the eastern end of the Black Sea. In the latter two instances, Muslim refugees from the territories newly absorbed by Russia spread anti-Russian feelings, though some of them brought with them modern skills and ideas gained from exposure to Russian administration and education.

The Russian drive to the south added a new element to the Eastern Question. Many British statesmen and strategists reckoned that a warlike Russia would press on until it had conquered all the lands separating it from British India, a prospect that made them shudder, given India's enormous contribution to Britain's prosperity. The competition that ensued over which power would control southern Central Asia resulted in a standoff in Afghanistan, which became a buffer zone under the control of neither. In Iran, the standoff between the powers helped preserve the weak Qajar dynasty of shahs.

AP® Exam Tip

Compare Russian territorial expansion to that of other nations/ states, such as the United States, that expanded their borders in this time period.

24-2c Cultural Trends

Unlike Egypt and the Ottoman Empire, which began to send students to Europe for training only in the nineteenth century, Russia had been in cultural contact with western Europe since the time of Peter the Great (r. 1689–1725). Members of the Russian court knew Western languages, and the tsars employed officials and advisers from Western countries. Peter had also enlisted the well-educated Ukrainian clerics who headed the Russian Orthodox Church to help spread a Western spirit of education. As a result, Alexander I's reforms met a more positive reception than those of Muhammad Ali and Mahmud II. However, his reforms promised more on paper than they brought about in practice. It took many years to develop a sufficient pool of trained bureaucrats to make the reforms effective.

Ironically, much of the opposition to Alexander's reforms came from well-established families that were not at all unfriendly to Western ideas. Their fear was that the new government bureaucrats, who often came from humbler social origins, would act as agents of imperial tyranny. This fear was realized during the conservative reign of Nicholas I in the same way that the Tanzimat-inspired bureaucracy of the Ottoman Empire served the despotic purposes of Sultan Abdul Hamid II after 1877. Individuals favoring more liberal reforms, including military officers who had served in western Europe, intellectuals who read Western political tracts, and members of Masonic lodges who exchanged views with Freemasons in the West, formed secret societies of opposition. Some placed their highest priority on freeing the serfs; others advocated a constitution and a republican form of government. When Alexander I died in December 1825, confusion over who was to succeed him encouraged a group of reform-minded army officers to try to take over the government and provoke an uprising. This so-called **Decembrist revolt** failed, and many of the participants were severely punished. These events ensured that the new tsar, Nicholas I, would pay little heed to calls for reform over the next thirty years.

The great powers meeting in Paris to settle the Crimean War in 1856 forced Russia to return land to the Ottomans in both Europe and Asia. This humiliation spurred Nicholas's son and successor, Alexander II (r. 1855–1881), to institute major new reforms to reinvigorate the country. The greatest of his reforms was the emancipation of the serfs in 1861. He also authorized new joint-stock companies, projected a railroad network to tie the country together, and modernized the legal and administrative arms of government.

Earlier intellectual and cultural trends flourished under Alexander II. More and more people became involved in intellectual, artistic, and professional life. Most prominent intellectuals received some amount of instruction at Moscow University or some German university. Universities also appeared in provincial cities like Kharkov in Ukraine and Kazan on the Volga River. Student clubs, along with Masonic lodges, became places for discussing new ideas. As Russian scholars and scientists began to achieve recognition for their contributions to European thought, scholarly careers attracted young men from clerical families, who in turn helped stimulate reforms in religious education.

Just as the Tanzimat reforms of the Ottoman Empire preceded the emergence of the Young Ottomans as a new and assertive political and intellectual force in the second half of the nineteenth century, so the initially ineffective reforms of Alexander I set in motion cultural currents that would make Russia a dynamic center of intellectual, artistic, and political life under his nephew Alexander II. Thus, Russia belonged to two different spheres of development. It entered the nineteenth century a recognized force in European politics, but in other ways it resembled the Ottoman Empire. Rulers in both empires instituted reforms, overcame opposition, and increased the power of their governments. These activities stimulated intellectual and political trends that would ultimately work against the absolute rule of tsar and sultan. Yet Russia would eventually develop much closer relations with western Europe and become an arena for every sort of European intellectual, artistic, and political tendency, while the Ottoman Empire would ultimately succumb to European imperialism.

AP® Exam Tip
Consider how the diffusion of Enlightenment thought stimulated discontent with monarchist rule.

Decembrist revolt Abortive attempt by army officers to take control of the Russian government upon the death of Tsar Alexander I in 1825.

Section Review

- Russian society resembled Ottoman society, but Alexander I undertook top-down westernizing reforms.

- Nicholas I's suspicion of Western ideas stalled reform and slowed industrial development.

- Slavophiles opposed westernizers and, after the Crimean War, embraced Pan-Slavism, contributing to Russophobia in the West.

- Russian expansion southward and eastward added vast territories to the empire and caused friction with China, Japan, Iran, and the Ottoman Empire.

- Resistance to Alexander I's bureaucratic reforms sparked the Decembrist revolt, which stiffened Nicholas I's hostility to Western ideas.

- The humiliation of the Crimean War drove Alexander II's reforms, including emancipation of the serfs.

24-3 **The Qing Empire**

How did the impact of European imperialism on China differ from its impact on Russia and the Ottoman Empire?

In 1800 the Qing Empire faced many problems, but no reform movement of the kind initiated by Sultan Selim III emerged in China. The reasons are not difficult to understand. The Qing emperors had skillfully countered Russian strategic and diplomatic moves in the 1600s. Instead of having a Napoleon threatening them with invasion, they enjoyed the admiration of Jesuit priests, who likened them to enlightened philosopher-kings. In 1793, however, a British attempt to establish diplomatic and trade relations—the Macartney mission—turned European opinion against China (see Chapter 21).

China's most serious crises were domestic, not foreign: rebellions by displaced indigenous peoples and the poor, and protests against the injustice of local magistrates. The Qing dealt with these problems by suppressing rebels and dismissing incompetent or untrustworthy officials. They also brushed aside the complaints from European merchants who chafed against the restrictions of the "Canton system" by which the Qing limited and controlled foreign trade.

24-3a **Economic and Social Disorder**

Early Qing successes and territorial expansion sowed the seeds of the domestic and political chaos of the later period. The early emperors encouraged the recovery of farmland, the opening of previously uncultivated areas, and the restoration and expansion of the road and canal systems. These measures expanded the agricultural base and supported a doubling of the population between about 1650 and 1800. Enormous numbers of farmers, merchants, and day laborers migrated in search of less crowded conditions, and a permanent floating population of the unemployed and homeless emerged. By 1800 population strain had caused serious environmental damage in some parts of central and western China.

While farmers tried to cope with agricultural deterioration, other groups vented grievances against the government: minority peoples in central and southwestern China complained about being driven off their lands during the boom of the 1700s; Mongols resented appropriation of their grazing lands and the displacement of their traditional elites. In some regions, village vigilante organizations took over policing and governing functions from Qing officials who had lost control. Growing numbers of people mistrusted the government, suspecting that all officials were corrupt. The increasing presence of foreign merchants and missionaries in Canton and in the Portuguese colony of Macao aggravated discontent in neighboring districts.

In some parts of China the Qing were hated as foreign conquerors and were suspected of sympathy with the Europeans. In 1794 the White Lotus Rebellion—partly inspired by a messianic ideology that predicted the restoration of the Chinese Ming dynasty and the coming of the Buddha—raged across central China and was not suppressed until 1804. It initiated a series of internal conflicts that continued through the 1800s (see discussion of Yaqub Beg's revolt at the beginning of this chapter). Ignited by deepening social instabilities, these movements were sometimes intensified by local ethnic conflicts and by unapproved religions. The ability of some village militias to defend themselves and attack others intensified the conflicts, though the same techniques proved useful to southern coastal populations attempting to fend off British invasion.

AP® Exam Tip Identify and explain the changes and continuities to Qing social policies from the previous time period through this one.

24-3b **The Opium War and Its Aftermath, 1839–1850**

Unlike the Ottomans, the Qing knew little about the enormous fortunes being made in the early 1800s by European and American merchants smuggling opium into China. They did not know that silver gained in this illegal trade was helping finance the industrial transformation of England and the United States. Only slowly did Qing officials become aware of British colonies in India that grew and exported opium, and of the major naval base at Singapore through which British opium reached East Asia.

AP® Exam Tip Consider the influence of outside forces on China in the nineteenth century.

In 1729 the first Qing law banning opium imports was promulgated. By 1800, however, opium smuggling had swelled the annual import level to as many as 4,000 chests. Though British merchants had pioneered this profitable trade, Chinese merchants likewise profited from distributing the drugs. A price war in the early 1820s stemming from competition between British and American importers raised demand so sharply that as many as 30,000 chests were being imported by the 1830s. Addiction spread to people at all levels of Qing society, including high-ranking officials. The Qing emperor and his officials debated whether to legalize and tax opium or to enforce the existing ban more strictly. Having decided to root out the use and importation of opium, in 1839 they sent a high official to Canton to deal with the matter.

Britain considered the ban on opium importation an intolerable limitation on trade, a direct threat to Britain's economic health, and a cause for war. British naval and marine forces arrived on the south China coast in late 1839. The **Opium War** (1839–1842) broke out when negotiations between the Qing official and British representatives reached a stalemate. The war exposed the fact that the traditional, hereditary soldiers of the Qing Empire—the **Bannermen**—were, like the Janissaries of the Ottoman Empire, hopelessly obsolete. As in the Crimean War, the British excelled at sea, where they deployed superior technology. British ships landed marines who pillaged coastal cities and then sailed to new destinations (see Map 24.2). The Qing lacked a navy powerful enough to deal with the British. Thus until they were able to engage the British in prolonged fighting on land, they were unable to defend themselves against British attacks. Even in the land engagements, Qing resources proved woefully inadequate. The British could quickly transport their forces by sea along the coast, whereas Qing troops moved primarily on foot. Moving Qing reinforcements from central to eastern China took more than three months; and when the defense forces arrived, they were exhausted and basically without weapons.

The Bannermen used the few muskets the Qing had imported during the 1700s. The weapons were matchlocks, which required the soldiers to ignite the load of gunpowder in them by hand. Firing the weapons was dangerous, and the canisters of gunpowder that each musketeer carried on his belt were likely to explode if a fire broke out nearby—a frequent occurrence in encounters with British artillery. Most of the Bannermen, however, had no guns at all and fought with swords, knives, spears, and clubs. They were greatly outmatched by the soldiers under British command—many of them Indians—who carried percussioncap rifles, which were far quicker, safer, and more accurate than the matchlocks. In addition, the long-range British artillery could be moved from place to place and proved deadly in the cities and villages of eastern China.

Qing commanders thought that British gunboats rode so low in the water that they could not sail up the Chinese rivers. So they evacuated the coastal areas to counter the British threat. But the British deployed new gunboats for shallow waters and moved without difficulty up the Yangzi River (see Chapter 22).

When the invaders approached Nanjing, the former Ming capital, the Qing decided to negotiate. In 1842 the terms of the **Treaty of Nanking** (the British name for Nanjing) dismantled the old Canton system. The number of **treaty ports**—cities opened to foreign residents—increased from one (Canton) to five (Canton, Xiamen, Fuzhou, Ningbo, and Shanghai [**shahng-hie**]). The island of Hong Kong became a British colony, and British residents in China gained extraterritorial rights. The Qing government agreed to set a low tariff of 5 percent on imports and to pay Britain an indemnity of 21 million ounces of silver as a penalty for having started the war. A supplementary treaty the following year guaranteed **most-favored-nation status** to Britain: any privileges that China granted to another country would be automatically extended to Britain as well. This provision effectively prevented the colonization of China because giving land to one country would have necessitated giving it to all.

With each round of treaties came a new round of privileges for foreigners. In 1860 a new treaty legalized their right to import opium. Later, French treaties established the rights of foreign missionaries to travel in the Chinese countryside and preach their religion. The number of treaty ports grew, too; by 1900 they numbered more than ninety.

The treaty system and the principle of extraterritoriality resulted in the colonization of small pockets of Qing territory, where foreign merchants lived at ease. Greater territorial losses resulted when outlying regions gained independence or were ceded to neighboring countries. Districts north and south of the Amur River in the northeast fell to Russia by treaty in 1858 and 1860; parts of modern Kazakhstan and Kyrgyzstan in the northwest met the same fate in 1864. From

Opium War War between Britain and the Qing Empire that was, in the British view, occasioned by the Qing government's refusal to permit the importation of opium into its territories. The victorious British imposed the one-sided Treaty of Nanking on China.

Bannermen Hereditary military servants of the Qing Empire, in large part descendants of peoples of various origins who had fought for the founders of the empire.

Treaty of Nanking The treaty that concluded the Opium War. It awarded Britain a large indemnity from the Qing Empire, denied the Qing government tariff control over some of its own borders, opened additional ports of residence to Britons, and ceded the island of Hong Kong to Britain.

treaty ports Cities opened to foreign residents as a result of the forced treaties between the Qing Empire and foreign signatories. In the treaty ports, foreigners enjoyed extraterritoriality.

most-favored-nation status A clause in a commercial treaty that awards to any later signatories all the privileges previously granted to the original signatories.

1865 onward the British gradually gained control of territories on China's Indian frontier. In the late 1800s France forced the court of Vietnam to end its tribute relationship to the Qing, while Britain encouraged Tibetan independence.

In Canton, Shanghai, and other coastal cities, Europeans and Americans maintained offices and factories that employed local Chinese as menial laborers. The foreigners built comfortable housing in zones where Chinese were not permitted to live, and they entertained themselves in exclusive restaurants and bars. Around the foreign establishments, gambling and prostitution offered employment to part of the local urban population.

Whether in town or in the countryside, Christian missionaries whose congregations sponsored hospitals, shelters, and soup kitchens or gave stipends to Chinese who attended church enjoyed a good reputation. But just as often the missionaries themselves were regarded

AP® Exam Tip
Understand the concept of economic imperialism and explain several examples of it.

MAP 24.2 Conflicts in the Qing Empire, 1839–1870 In both the Opium War of 1839–1842 and the Arrow War of 1856–1860, the seacoasts saw most of the action. Since the Qing had a weak navy, the well-armed British ships encountered little resistance as they shelled the southern coasts. In inland conflicts, such as the Taiping Rebellion, the opposing armies were massive and slow moving. Battles on land were often prolonged attempts by one side to starve out the other side before making a major assault.

What prevented the Qing Empire from collapsing in the face of so many internal rebellions and foreign impositions?

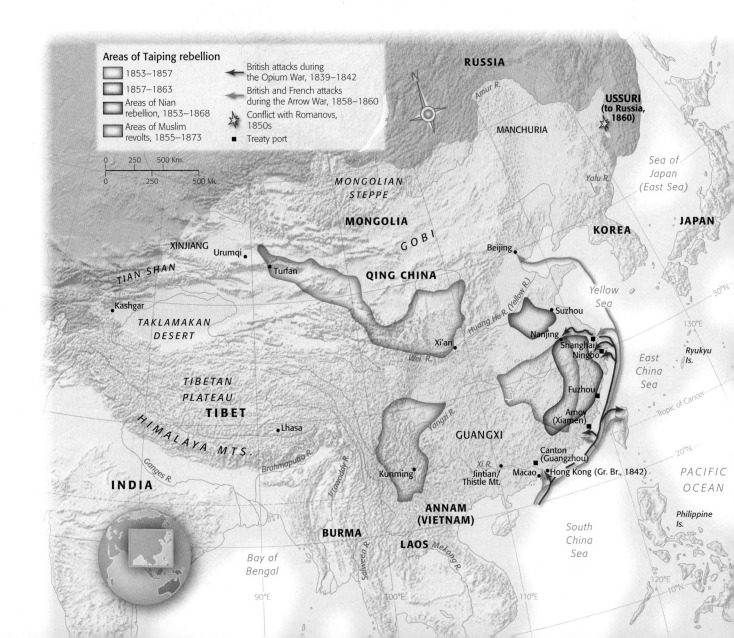

as another evil. They seemed to subvert Confucian beliefs by condemning ancestor worship, pressuring poor families to put their children into Christian orphanages, or fulminating against foot-binding. The growing numbers of foreigners, and their growing privileges, became targets of resentment for a deeply dissatisfied, daily more impoverished, and increasingly militarized society.

24-3c The Taiping Rebellion, 1850–1864

AP® Exam Tip
Compare the Taiping Rebellion with other rebellions influenced by religious ideas, such as the Ghost Dance movement.

The inflammatory mixture of social unhappiness and foreign intrusion exploded in the great civil war usually called the **Taiping (tie-PING). Rebellion** In Guangxi, where the Taiping movement originated, entrenched social problems had been generating disorders for half a century. Agriculture in the region was unstable, and many people made their living from arduous and despised trades such as disposing of human waste, making charcoal, and mining. Ethnic divisions complicated economic distress. The lowliest trades frequently involved a minority group, the Hakkas, and tensions between them and the majority were rising. Problems may have been intensified by sharp fluctuations in the opium trade and reactions to the cultural and economic impact of the Europeans and Americans in Canton.

Hong Xiuquan (**hoong shee-OH-chew-an**), the founder of the Taiping movement, experienced all of these influences. Hong came from a humble Hakka background. After years of study, he competed in the provincial Confucian examinations, hoping for a post in government. He failed the examinations repeatedly, and it appears that he suffered a nervous breakdown in his late thirties. Afterward he spent some time in Canton, where he met both Chinese and American Protestant missionaries, who inspired him with their teachings. Hong had his own interpretation of the Christian message. He saw himself as the younger brother of Jesus, commissioned by God to found a new kingdom on earth and drive the Manchu conquerors, the Qing, out of China. The result would be universal peace. Hong called his new religious movement the "Heavenly Kingdom of Great Peace."

Hong quickly attracted a community of believers, primarily Hakkas like himself. They believed in the prophecy of dreams and claimed they could walk on air. Hong and his rivals for leadership in the movement went in and out of ecstatic trances. They denounced the Manchus as creatures of Satan. News of the sect reached the government, and Qing troops arrived to arrest the Taiping leaders. But the Taipings soundly repelled the imperial troops. Local loyalty to the Taipings spread quickly; their numbers multiplied; and they began to enlarge their domain.

The Taipings relied at first on Hakka sympathy and the charismatic appeal of their religious doctrine to attract followers. But as their numbers and power grew, they altered their methods of preaching and governing, replacing the anti-Chinese appeals used to enlist Hakkas with anti-Manchu rhetoric designed to enlist Chinese. They forced captured villages to join their movement. Once people were absorbed, the Taipings strictly monitored their activities. They also segregated men and women and organized them into work and military teams. Women were forbidden to bind their feet (the Hakkas had never practiced foot-binding) and participated fully in farming and labor. Brigades of women soldiers took the field against Qing forces.

As the movement grew, it began to move toward eastern and northern China (see Map 24.2). Panic preceded the Taipings. Villagers feared being forced into Taiping units, and Confucian elites recoiled in horror from the bizarre ideology of foreign gods, totalitarian rule, and walking, working, warring women. But the huge numbers the Taipings were able to muster overwhelmed attempts at local defense. The tremendous growth in the number of Taiping followers required the movement to establish a permanent base. When the rebel army conquered Nanjing in 1853, the Taiping leaders decided to settle there and make it the capital of the new "Heavenly Kingdom of Great Peace."

Taiping Rebellion
A Christian-inspired rural rebellion that threatened to topple the Qing Empire.

Qing forces attempting to defend north China became more successful as problems of organization and growing numbers slowed Taiping momentum. Increasing Qing military success resulted mainly from the flexibility of the imperial military commanders in the face of an unprecedented challenge. In addition, the military commanders received strong backing from a group of civilian provincial governors who had studied the techniques developed by

▲ **Nanjing Encircled**   For a decade the Taipings held the city of Nanjing as their capital. For years Qing and international troops attempted to break the Taiping hold. By the summer of 1864, Qing forces had built tunnels leading to the foundations of Nanjing's city walls and had planted explosives. The detonation of the explosives signaled the final Qing assault on the rebel capital. As shown here, the common people of the city, along with their starving livestock, were caught in the crossfire. Many of the Taiping leaders escaped the debacle at Nanjing, but nearly all were hunted down and executed. Photo 12/Getty Images

local militia forces for self-defense. Certain provincial governors combined their knowledge of civilian self-defense and local terrain with more efficient organization and the use of modern weaponry. The result was the formation of new military units, in which many of the Bannermen voluntarily served under civilian governors. The Qing court agreed to special taxes to fund the new armies and acknowledged the new combined leadership.

When the Taipings settled into Nanjing, the new Qing armies surrounded the city, hoping to starve out the rebels. The Taipings, however, had provisioned and fortified themselves well. They also had the services of several brilliant young military commanders, who mobilized enormous campaigns in nearby parts of eastern China, scavenging supplies and attempting to break the encirclement of Nanjing. For more than a decade the Taiping leadership remained ensconced at Nanjing, and the "Heavenly Kingdom" endured.

In 1856 Britain and France, freed from their preoccupation with the Crimean War, turned their attention to China. European and American missionaries had visited Nanjing, curious to see what their fellow Christians were up to. Their reports were discouraging. Hong Xiuquan and the other leaders appeared to lead lives of indulgence and abandon, and more than one missionary accused them of homosexual practices. Relieved of the possible accusation of quashing a pious Christian movement, the British and French surveyed the situation.

Though the Taipings were not going to topple the Qing, rebellious Nian ("Bands") in northern China added a new threat in the 1850s. A series of simultaneous large insurrections might indeed destroy the empire. Moreover, since the Qing had not observed all the provisions of the treaties signed after the Opium War, Britain and France were now considering renewing war on the Qing themselves.

In 1856 the British and French launched a series of swift, brutal coastal attacks—a second opium war, called the Arrow War (1856–1860)—that culminated in a British and French invasion of Beijing and the sacking of the Summer Palace in 1860. A new round of treaties punished the Qing for not enacting all the provisions of the Treaty of Nanking. Having secured their principal objective, the British and French forces then joined the Qing campaign against the Taipings. Attempts to coordinate the international forces were sometimes riotous and sometimes tragic, but the injection of European weaponry and money helped quell both the Taiping and the Nian rebellions during the 1860s.

The Taiping Rebellion ranks as the world's bloodiest civil war and the greatest armed conflict before the twentieth century. Estimates of deaths range from 20 million to 30 million. The loss of life came primarily from starvation and disease, for most engagements consisted of surrounding fortified cities and waiting until the enemy forces died, surrendered, or were so weakened that they could be easily defeated. Many sieges continued for months. Reports of people eating grass, leather, hemp, and human flesh were widespread. The dead were rarely buried properly, and epidemic disease was common.

The area of early Taiping fighting was close to the regions of southwest China in which bubonic plague had been lingering for centuries. When the rebellion was suppressed, many Taiping followers sought safety in the highlands of Laos and Vietnam, which soon showed infestation by plague. Within a few years the disease reached Hong Kong. From there it spread to Singapore, San Francisco, Calcutta, and London. In the late 1800s there was intense apprehension over the possibility of a worldwide outbreak, and Chinese immigrants were regarded as likely carriers. This fear became a contributing factor in the passage of discriminatory immigration bans on Chinese in the United States in 1882.

The Taiping Rebellion devastated the agricultural centers of China. Many of the most intensely cultivated regions of central and eastern China were depopulated. Some were still uninhabited decades later, and major portions of the country did not recover until the twentieth century.

Cities, too, were hard hit. Shanghai, a treaty port of modest size before the rebellion, saw its population multiplied many times by the arrival of refugees from war-blasted neighboring provinces. The city then endured months of siege by the Taipings. Major cultural centers in eastern China lost masterpieces of art and architecture; imperial libraries were burned or their collections exposed to the weather; and the printing blocks used to make books were destroyed. While the empire faced the mountainous challenge of dealing with the material and cultural destruction of the war, it also was burdened by a major ecological disaster in the north. The Yellow River changed course in 1855, destroying the southern part

▲ **Street Scene in Guangzhou** This photograph taken in the 1860s by an Englishman shows a comparatively wide market street with signs advertising drugs, cushions, seals, ink, etc. The engraving of a Cairo street scene (page 599) shows a much more exotic stereotype of the orient, complete with a young girl displaying her body while covering her face. Photo by John Thomson/George Eastman House/Getty Images

▲ **Cixi's Allies**   In the 1860s and 1870s, Cixi was a supporter of reform (see Section 24-4d Decentralization at the End of the Qing Empire). In later years she was widely regarded as corrupt and self-centered and as an obstacle to reform. Her greatest allies were the court eunuchs. Introduced to palace life in early China as managers of the imperial harems, eunuchs became powerful political parties at court. The first Qing emperors refused to allow the eunuchs any political influence, but by Cixi's time the eunuchs once again were a political factor.   Tz'u Hsi (1835–1908) Empress Dowager of China, 1903 (b/w photo), French Photographer (20th century)/Private Collection/The Bridgeman Art Library

of impoverished Shandong province with flood and initiating decades of drought along the former riverbed in northern Shandong.

AP® Exam Tip
Explain why land-based empires, such as the Ottoman and Qing Empires, declined during this time period.

24-3d Decentralization at the End of the Qing Empire, 1864–1875

The Qing government emerged from the 1850s with no hope of achieving solvency. The corruption of the 1700s, attempts in the very early 1800s to restore waterworks and roads, and declining yields from land taxes had bankrupted the treasury. By 1850, before the Taiping Rebellion, Qing government expenditures were ten times revenues. The indemnities demanded by Europeans after the Opium and Arrow Wars compounded the problem. Vast stretches of formerly productive rice land were devastated, and the population was dispersed. Refugees pleaded for relief, and the imperial, volunteer, foreign, and mercenary troops that had suppressed the Taipings demanded unpaid wages.

Britain and France became active participants in the period of recovery that followed the rebellion (see Diversity & Dominance: Chinese Responses to Imperialism). To ensure repayment of the debt to Britain, Robert Hart was installed as inspector-general of a newly created Imperial Maritime Customs Service. Britain and the Qing split the revenues he collected. Britons and Americans worked for the Qing government as advisers and ambassadors, attempting to smooth communications between the Qing, Europe, and the United States.

The real work of the recovery, however, was managed by provincial governors who had come to the forefront in the struggle against the Taipings. To prosecute the war, they had won the right to levy their own taxes, raise their own troops, and run their own bureaucracies. These special

The Opium War, followed by the Taiping Rebellion, revealed China's weakness for all to see, but there was no agreement on what should be done to restore its strength. A few provincial officials were able to take effective action, but the competing ideas that were heard at the imperial court tended to cancel each other out.

Feng Guifen, an official and a scholar, came into contact with Westerners defending Shanghai when he took refuge there from the Taipings. The following is from a book of essays he published in 1861.

According to a general geography compiled by an Englishman, the territory of China is eight times that of Russia, ten times that of the United States, one hundred times that of France, and two hundred times that of Great Britain. . . . Yet we are shamefully humiliated by the four nations, not because our climate, soil, or resources are inferior to theirs, but because our people are inferior. . . . Now, our inferiority is not due to our allotment from Heaven [i.e., our inherent nature], but is rather due to ourselves. . . .

Why are the Western nations small and yet strong? Why are we large and yet weak? We must search for the means to become their equal, and that depends solely upon human effort. . . .

We have only one thing to learn from the barbarians, and that is strong ships and effective guns. . . . Funds should be allotted to establish a shipyard and arsenal in each trading port. A few barbarians should be employed, and Chinese who are good in using their minds should be selected to receive instruction so that in turn they may teach many craftsmen. When a piece of work is finished and is as good as that made by the barbarians, the makers should be rewarded with an official *juren* degree and be permitted to participate in the metropolitan examinations on the same basis as other scholars. Those whose products are of superior quality should be rewarded with

the *jinshi* degree [ordinarily conferred in the metropolitan examinations] and be permitted to participate in the palace examinations like others. The workers should be paid double so that they will not quit their jobs.

Our nation's emphasis on civil service examinations has sunk deep into people's minds for a long time. Intelligent and brilliant scholars have exhausted their time and energy in such useless things as the stereotyped examination essays, examination papers, and formal calligraphy. . . . We should now order one-half of them to apply them-selves to the manufacturing of instruments and weapons and to the promotion of physical studies. . . . The intelligence and ingenuity of the Chinese are certainly superior to those of the various barbarians; it is only that hitherto we have not made use of them. When the government above takes delight in something, the people below will pursue it further: their response will be like an echo carried by the wind. There ought to be some people of extraordinary intelligence who can have new ideas and improve on Western methods. At first they may take the foreigners as their teachers and models; then they may come to the same level and be their equals; finally they may move ahead and surpass them. Herein lies the way to self-strengthening.

In 1867 the debate over how to resist foreign military pressure surged through the imperial court. Woren, a Mongol who held the rank of grand secretary, spoke for the conservatives

Mathematics, one of the six arts, should indeed be learned by scholars as indicated in the imperial decree, and it should not be considered an unworthy subject. But according to the viewpoint of your servant, astronomy and mathematics are of very little use. If these subjects are going to be taught by Westerners as regular studies, the damage will be great. . . . Your servant has learned that the way to establish a nation is to lay emphasis on rites and rightness, not on power and

Section Review

- Social unrest grew in Qing China through a combination of discontent among the poor and displaced indigenous peoples and resentment of growing European influence.
- Qing attempts to ban opium imports provoked the Opium War with Britain, which exposed Qing military inferiority.
- The Treaty of Nanking gave extraterritoriality and other privileges to Britain and led to further losses to other Western powers.
- Social resentment and foreign intrusion ignited the Taiping Rebellion, which, after the Arrow War, the Qing quelled with British and French aid.
- The rebellion encouraged epidemics, devastated agriculture, produced overcrowded cities filled with refugees, and coincided with environmental disasters.
- The rebellion and China's recovery afterward resulted in a process of decentralization led by reformist aristocrats.

powers were not entirely canceled when the war ended. Chief among these governors was Zeng Guofan (**zung gwoh-FAN**), who oversaw programs to restore agriculture, communications, education, and publishing, as well as efforts to reform the military and industrialize armaments manufacture.

Like many provincial governors, Zeng preferred to look to the United States rather than to Britain for models and aid. He therefore hired American advisers to run his weapons factories, shipyards, and military academies. He also sponsored a daring program in which promising Chinese boys were sent to Hartford, Connecticut, a center of missionary activity, to learn English, science, mathematics, engineering, and history. They returned to China to assume some of the positions previously held by foreign advisers. Though Zeng was never an advocate of participation in public life by women, his Confucian convictions taught him that educated mothers were more than ever a necessity. He not only encouraged but also partly oversaw

plotting. The fundamental effort lies in the minds of people, not in techniques. Now, if we seek trifling arts and respect barbarians as teachers . . . all that can be accomplished is the training of mathematicians. From ancient down to modern times, your servant has never heard of anyone who could use mathematics to raise the nation from a state of decline or to strengthen it in time of weakness. . . .

Since the conclusion of the peace, Christianity has been prevalent, and half of our ignorant people have been fooled by it. The only thing we can rely on is that our scholars should clearly explain to the people the Confucian tenets, which may be able to sustain the minds of the ignorant populace. Now if these brilliant and talented scholars, who have been trained by the nation and reserved for great future usefulness, have to change from their regular course of study to follow the barbarians, then the correct spirit will not be developed, and accordingly the evil spirit will become stronger. After several years it will end in nothing less than driving the multitudes of the Chinese people into allegiance to the barbarians

The opposing group of ministers who backed the idea of "self-strengthening" responded.

Your ministers have examined the memorial of Woren: the principles he presents are very lofty and the opinion he maintains is very orthodox. Your ministers' point of view was also like that before they began to manage foreign affairs; and yet today they do not presume to insist on such ideas, because of actual difficulties that they cannot help. . .

From the beginning of foreign relations to the present there have been twenty or thirty years. At first the officials inside and outside the capital did not grasp the crux of the matter, and whether they negotiated peace or discussed war, generally these were empty words without effect. . . . Therefore your ministers have pondered a long-term policy and discussed the situation thoroughly with all the provincial officials. Proposals to learn the written and spoken languages of foreign countries, the various methods of making machines, the training of troops with foreign guns, the dispatching of officials to travel in all countries, the investigation of their local customs and social conditions … all these painstaking and special decisions represent nothing other than a struggle for self-strengthening.…

We too are afraid that the people who are learning these things will have no power of discrimination and are likely to be led astray by foreigners, as Woren fears. Therefore we have deliberated and decided that those who participate in these examinations must be persons from regular scholastic channels. It is indeed those students who have read widely and who understand right principles and have their minds set upon upright and grand purposes—and the present situation is just what causes the scholars and officials to feel pain in heart and head—who would certainly be able to lie on faggots and taste gall [i.e., nurse vengeance] in order to encourage each other vigorously to seek the actual achievement of self-strengthening. They are different from those who have vague, easygoing, or indifferent ideas.

AP® History Reasoning Skills

Comparison *How do the Chinese ideas expressed in the passage compare with attitudes toward reform in the Ottoman and Russian Empires?*

Contextualization *How do the views of the writers reflect the traditional examination system they used to achieve their offices?*

Source: Essays of Feng Tuifen published in 1861 in Jiaobinlu kangyi (Personal Protests from the Study of Jiaobin). English translations from Chester Tan, published in Wm. Theodore de Bary and Richard Lafrano, *Sources of Chinese Tradition*, vol. 2, 2nd ed. pp. 235–236, 238–239. Copyright © 2000 Columbia University Press. Reprinted with permission of the publisher.

the advanced classical education of his own daughters. Zeng's death in 1872 deprived the empire of a major force for reform.

The period of recovery marked a fundamental structural change in the Qing Empire. Although the emperors after 1850 were ineffective rulers, a coalition of aristocrats supported the reform and recovery programs. Without their legitimization of the new powers of provincial governors like Zeng Guofan, the empire might have evaporated within a generation. A crucial member of this alliance was Cixi (**TSUH-shee**), who was known as the "Empress Dowager" after the 1880s. Later observers, both Chinese and foreign, reviled her as a monster of corruption and arrogance. But in the 1860s and 1870s Cixi supported the provincial governors, some of whom became so powerful that they were managing Qing foreign policy as well as domestic affairs.

No longer a conquest regime dominated by a Manchu military caste and its Chinese civilian appointees, the empire came under the control of a group of reformist aristocrats and military men, independently powerful civilian governors, and a small number of foreign advisers. The Qing lacked strong, central, unified leadership and could not recover their powers of taxation, legislation, and military command once these had been granted to the provincial governors. From the 1860s forward, the Qing Empire disintegrated into a number of large power zones in which provincial governors handed over leadership to their protégés in a pattern that the Qing court eventually could only ritually legitimate.

AP® Exam Tip
Compare Qing reform efforts with those in the Ottoman and Russian empires.

24-4 Conclusion

The Ottoman, Qing, and Russian Empires shared several characteristics both in their early successes and late-stage challenges. All three maintained a flexible approach when incorporating a diverse group of peoples and cultures into their growing empires. Around the mid-eighteenth century, however, the need to maintain order and increase tax revenues pushed rulers to differentiate groups of people and create stricter hierarchies within each empire, leading to conflict between the minority rulers and the ruled. In addition, population growth that began in the sixteenth century throughout Eurasia, which had been sustainable and beneficial in the expanding territories of Russia and the Qing, eventually became unsupportable. By the nineteenth century, even the Qing Empire, the largest and most advanced Eurasian empire in terms of commercial economy and efficient bureaucratic structures, could no longer effectively deal with the increasing demographic pressures, regional conflict, and political dysfunctions.

Most of the subjects of the Ottoman, Russian, and Qing rulers did not think of European pressure or competition as determining factors in their lives during the first half of the nineteenth century. They continued to live according to the social and economic institutions they inherited from previous generations. By the 1870s, however, the challenge of Europe had become widely recognized. The Crimean War, where European allies achieved a hollow victory for the Ottomans and then pressured the sultan for more reforms, confirmed both Ottoman and Russian military weakness. The Opium War did the same for China. But China, unlike the other empires, was also stricken by rampaging civil war and regional uprisings.

In analyzing the crises of the three empires, historians today stress European economic pressures and observe that all three empires ultimately became insolvent and saw the overthrow of their ruling dynasties. However, at the time what most impressed the Ottomans, Russians, and Chinese was European military superiority, as demonstrated in the Greek war of independence, the Crimean War, and the Opium War. Thus for all three empires, dealing with military emergency took priority over deeper reforms throughout most of the time period of this chapter.

Key Terms

Muhammad Ali p. 612
Janissaries p. 613
Serbia p. 613
Tanzimat p. 614

Crimean War p. 617
extraterritoriality p. 618
Slavophiles p. 620
Pan-Slavism p. 620

Decembrist revolt p. 622
Opium War p. 624
Bannermen p. 624
Treaty of Nanking p. 624

treaty ports p. 624
most-favored-nation status
  p. 624
Taiping Rebellion p. 626

Review Questions

1. Can the spread of modern ideas and technology be compared to the Renaissance in Europe?

2. In view of the decline of Rome and the fragmentation of the Islamic Caliphate, has political control over large expanses of territory always been beneficial to imperial powers?

3. Did religion and political ideology play as important a role in the West's challenges to the Russian, Ottoman, and Qing empires as Christianity and Islam did in the dissolution of the Roman Empire?

MindTap® is a fully online, personalized learning experience built upon Cengage Learning content. MindTap® combines student learning tools—readings, multimedia, activities, and assessments—into a singular Learning Path that guides students through the course and helps students develop the critical thinking, analysis, and communication skills that are essential to academic and professional success.

Multiple-Choice Questions

Questions 1–3 refer to the image below.

▲ **Ironworks, Painting by an Unknown Russian Artist** akg-images/The Image Works

1. The subject matter of the painting provides evidence of which of the following changes in Russian economy in the nineteenth century?

    (A) A continuing effort by the imperial government to promote agriculture

    (B) A slow attempt to shift the focus of the Russian economy to industrialization

    (C) Russian nobles ignoring imperial economic policies to create jobs

    (D) A rejection of Peter the Great's reforms from the eighteenth century

2. Which of the following was true of efforts in Russia like the ones seen in the painting?

    (A) Manors becoming more self-sufficient than in the previous century led to an urban society with no need for agricultural work.

    (B) Growing competition between Russian and Asian artisans helped to spur significant development quickly.

    (C) The government under Alexander I promoted its own state-sponsored vision of industrialization.

    (D) Russia's attempts at expanding its empire into the Americas and Southeast Asia was exceptionally successful.

3. The role of the government in industrial expansion in Russia was most similar to that in

    (A) the Ottoman Empire.

    (B) Britain.

    (C) the United States.

    (D) China.

Questions 4–6 refer to Map 24.1 on page 614.

4. Based on the map, which of the following is an accurate description of the Ottoman Empire leading up to 1900?

    (A) The Ottoman Empire had most of its ports on the Indian Ocean.

    (B) The Ottoman Empire tried to avoid land possessions that included Islamic holy sites.

    (C) The Ottoman Empire attempted to avoid having extensive borders with other Muslim states.

    (D) The Ottoman Empire pursued a policy of expansion, growing dramatically in size.

5. Which of the following was the greatest threat to the stability of the Ottoman Empire?

    (A) The Qing dynasty

    (B) The Russian Empire

    (C) The Italian city-states

    (D) France

6. As was true of other states, the pressures felt by the Ottoman Empire led to which of the following?

(A) Creating a completely land-based empire

(B) Relying on religious elites to maintain state bureaucracies

(C) Attempting to modernize their economies and militaries

(D) Compelling large portions of the population into agrarian jobs

Questions 7–10 refer to the passage below.

"Yet we are shamefully humiliated by the four nations, not because our climate, soil, or resources are inferior to theirs, but because our people are inferior. . . . Now, our inferiority is not due to our allotment from Heaven [i.e., our inherent nature], but is rather due to ourselves. . . . Why are the Western nations small and yet strong? Why are we large and yet weak? We must search for the means to become their equal, and that depends solely upon human effort."

Essays of Feng Guifen, a scholar and official in the Qing dynasty, 1861

7. According to Feng Guifen, what is the source of China's humiliation?

(A) The Qing dynasty is larger but much weaker than the European nations.

(B) The Qing dynasty does not have access to fertile farmland and waterways.

(C) The Qing dynasty rejected its Confucian traditions for European values.

(D) The Qing dynasty persecuted religious and ethnic minorities.

8. Which of the following proved Feng Guifen's view of the Qing Empire correct?

(A) British and French forces assisting the Qing in putting down the Taiping Rebellion.

(B) Britain and France expanding their influence through the Opium Wars.

(C) The Qing dynasty sharing its bureaucratic institutions and Confucian examinations with Western powers.

(D) European powers sharing new technologies with the Qing and profiting off of finished goods.

9. Which of the following actions might Feng Guifen support as a response to European expansion?

(A) Exiling the merchant classes

(B) Eliminating all contact with Western nations

(C) Promoting farming as the primary occupation

(D) Copying and learning industrial techniques from the West

10. Similar to other regions, how did the more traditional segments of the Chinese population react to the presence of the West?

(A) They moved to more remote regions to avoid contact with Westerners.

(B) They used their traditions and belief systems to form resistance movements.

(C) They embraced Western music but not Western dress.

(D) They adopted the religion of the imperialists.

Short-Answer Questions

▲ **Nanjing Encircled**   Universal Images Group/Getty Images

1. Use the image above and your knowledge of world history to answer all parts of the question that follows.

(A) Identify ONE way the painting reflects the change in warfare brought about by industrial-era weapons.

(B) Explain one way tensions and discontent with the Qing Empire developed from 1800 to 1850.

(C) Explain ONE way the Taiping Rebellion caused change in the Qing dynasty after the Rebellion.

2. In the nineteenth century, civilizations looked for ways to adjust to the changes brought about by industrialization. Use your knowledge of world history to answer all parts of the question that follows.

(A) Identify one group that opposed Ottoman Empire reforms.

(B) Explain ONE strategy used by the Ottoman Empire to bring reform.

(C) Explain ONE similarity between the reaction of the Qing and that of the Ottomans to Europe's industrialization.

25

Nation Building and Economic Transformation in the Americas, 1800–1890

AP® Framework Terms

Simón Bolívar
Latin American independence movements
Suffrage
Abolition

Overarching Questions

1 How and to what extent have migration, population, and urbanization affected the environment over time? (ENV)

2 How have religions, belief systems, philosophies, and ideologies affected the political, economic, and social development of societies? (CUL)

3 How have states and state-less societies interacted over time? (SB)

4 How have distinctions based on kinship, ethnicity, class, gender, and race influenced the development and transformations of social hierarchies? (SOC)

5 How have social categories, roles, and practices been maintained or challenged over time? (SOC)

During the nineteenth century the newly independent nations of the Western Hemisphere sought to emulate the rapid economic progress of Europe under the influence of the Industrial Revolution. No technology seemed to represent that progress better than railroads. Everywhere from Argentina to Canada, governments sponsored railroad development. By 1850 there were 9,000 miles (14,480 kilometers) of track in the United States, as much as in the rest of the world. In 1869 the United States finished laying track linking the Atlantic and Pacific coasts. Canada, still a British colony, duplicated this feat in 1886. Latin American nations committed to this technology later than the United States, but railroads there also soon proved important to exports, to new industries, and to political and cultural integration.

Mexico granted the first concession for railroad construction in 1837, but the first significant rail line was only completed in 1873. Few new projects were begun until the presidency of Porfirio Díaz (1876–1880 and 1884–1911), who promoted railroad construction. By the time revolutionaries forced him from office, Mexico had 12,000 miles (19,300 kilometers) of track. Although railroads proved crucial to Mexican economic growth, there was a downside. Foreign investment helped pay for new railroads, but this dependence on foreign capital led to political protests and economic nationalism. Railroad development also had a powerful effect on native peoples, who still controlled large

▲ **The Train Station in Orizaba, Mexico, 1877** In the last decades of the nineteenth century Mexico's political leaders actively promoted economic development. The railroad became the symbol of this ideal. Station at Orizaba, 1878 (colour litho), Castro, Casimior (fl.1878)/Private Collection/The Stapleton Collection/The Bridgeman Art Library

areas of rural Mexico. Because railroads made their lands more valuable, powerful landed families used their political influence to strip this land from indigenous subsistence farmers and use it to produce export crops. As Amerindian villagers lost their traditional lands, the number of rural uprisings increased.

In the nineteenth century the Western Hemisphere experienced radical political and social changes in addition to technological innovations and economic expansion. Brazil and nearly all of Spain's American colonies achieved independence by 1825. As was true in the earlier American and French Revolutions (see Chapter 23), rising nationalism and the ideal of political freedom promoted these changes. Despite the achievement of independence, however, Mexico and other nations in the hemisphere faced foreign interventions and other threats to sovereignty, including regional secessionist movements and civil war.

The new nations of the Western Hemisphere faced difficult questions. If colonies could reject submission to imperial powers, could not internal regions with distinct cultures, social structures, and economies refuse to accept the political authority of newly formed national governments? Would nations born in revolution learn to accept the political strictures of written constitutions—even those they had written themselves? How could the ideals of liberty and freedom expressed in those constitutions be reconciled with the denial of rights to Amerindians, slaves, recent immigrants, and women?

While trying to resolve these political questions, the hemisphere's new nations also attempted to promote economic growth. They imported new technologies like railroads and telegraphs, opened new areas to settlement, and promoted immigration. But the legacy of colonial economic development, with its emphasis on agricultural and mining exports, inhibited efforts to promote diversification and industrialization, just as the legacy of class and racial division thwarted the realization of the independence era's political ideals. ●

25-1 Independence in Latin America, 1800–1830

What were the causes of the revolutions for independence in Latin America?

As the eighteenth century drew to a close, Spain and Portugal held vast colonial possessions in the Western Hemisphere, although their power had declined relative to that of their British and French rivals. Both Iberian empires had reformed their colonial administration and strengthened their military forces in the eighteenth century (see Chapter 18). Despite these efforts, the same economic and political forces that had undermined Britain's rule in its American colonies were present in Spanish America and Brazil.

25-1a Roots of Revolution, to 1810

AP® Exam Tip
Understand how Latin American revolutions fit within the context of revolutions in Period 5.

The great works of the Enlightenment as well as revolutionary documents like the American Declaration of Independence and the French Declaration of the Rights of Man and the Citizen circulated widely in Latin America, but, at the beginning of the nineteenth century, few colonial residents wanted revolutionary change. While colonial elites and middle classes were frustrated by imperial policies and taxes, it was events in Europe that propelled the colonies toward independence. Napoleon's decision to invade Portugal (1807) and Spain (1808), not revolutionary ideas, created a crisis of legitimacy that undermined the authority of colonial officials and ignited Latin America's struggle for independence.

As a French army neared Lisbon in 1808, the Portuguese royal family fled to Brazil protected by a British fleet. Once arrived, King John VI would maintain his court there for over a decade. Napoleon soon forced King Ferdinand VII of Spain to abdicate and placed his own brother, Joseph Bonaparte, on the throne. Spanish patriots fighting against French domination created a new political body, the Junta (**HUN-tah**) Central, to administer the areas they controlled. The junta claimed authority over Spain's colonies, inviting the election of colonial deputies to help draft the nation's first written constitution.

Most residents of colonial Spanish America favored obedience to the Junta Central and many colonies elected deputies to join this constitutional convention, but a vocal minority, including some members of the elite, objected. These dissenters argued that they were subjects of the king, not dependents of the Spanish nation. They wanted to create local juntas in the colonies and govern their own affairs until Ferdinand regained the throne. Spanish loyalists resisted this assertion of local autonomy, provoking armed uprisings. In late 1808 and 1809 popular movements overthrew Spanish colonial officials in Venezuela, Mexico, and Alto Peru (modern Bolivia) and created local juntas. In each case, local Spanish officials quickly reasserted control and punished the leaders, executing many. This harsh repression, however, further polarized public opinion in the colonies and gave rise to a greater sense of a separate American nationality. After 1810 Spanish colonial authorities would face a new round of revolutions now focused on independence.

25-1b Spanish South America, 1810–1825

In Caracas (the capital city of modern Venezuela) a revolutionary junta led by *creoles* (colonial-born whites) declared independence in 1811. Although this group espoused representative democracy, its leaders were landowners who defended slavery and opposed full citizenship for the colony's free black and mixed-race majority. Their aim was to expand their own privileges by eliminating Spaniards from the upper levels of government and the church. The junta's narrow

CHRONOLOGY

	United States and Canada	Mexico and Central America	South America
1800	1789 U.S. Constitution ratified 1803 Louisiana Purchase 1812–1815 War of 1812	1810–1821 Mexican movement for independence	1808 Portuguese royal family arrives in Brazil 1808–1809 Revolutions for independence begin in Spanish South America
1825	1836 Texas gains independence from Mexico 1845 Texas admitted as a state 1848 Women's Rights Convention in Seneca Falls, New York	1846–1848 War between Mexico and the United States 1847–1870 Caste War	1822 Brazil gains independence 1831 Brazil signs treaty with Great Britain to end slave trade; illegal trade continues
1850	1861–1865 Civil War 1867 Creation of Dominion of Canada	1857 Mexico's new constitution limits power of Catholic Church and military 1862–1867 French invade Mexico 1867 Emperor Maximilian executed	1850 Brazilian illegal slave trade suppressed 1865–1870 Argentina, Uruguay, and Brazil wage war against Paraguay
1875	1876 Sioux and allies defeat U.S. Army in Battle of Little Bighorn 1890 "Jim Crow" laws enforce segregation in South 1890s United States becomes world's leading steel producer		1870s Governments of Argentina and Chile begin final campaigns against indigenous peoples 1879–1883 Chile wages war against Peru and Bolivia; telegraph, refrigeration, and barbed wire introduced in Argentina 1888 Abolition of slavery in Brazil

agenda spurred Spanish loyalists to rally thousands of free blacks and slaves to defend the Spanish Empire. Faced with this determined resistance, the revolutionary movement placed overwhelming political authority in the hands of its military leader **Simón Bolívar (see-MOAN bow-LEE-varh)** (1783–1830), who would become the preeminent leader of the independence movement.

The son of wealthy Venezuelan planters, Bolívar had traveled in Europe with a tutor and studied the key works of the Enlightenment. He was a charismatic personality who effectively mobilized political support and held the loyalty of his troops. Defeated on many occasions, Bolívar successfully adapted his objectives and policies to attract new allies and build coalitions. Although initially opposed to the abolition of slavery, for example, he agreed to support emancipation in order to draw slaves and freemen to his cause and to gain military supplies from Haiti. Bolívar was also capable of using harsh methods to ensure victory, proclaiming in 1813 that "any Spaniard who does not . . . work against tyranny in behalf of this just cause will be considered an enemy and punished; as a traitor to the nation, he will inevitably be shot by a firing squad."[1]

Military advantage shifted back and forth between the patriots and loyalists until Bolívar enlisted demobilized English and French veterans of the Napoleonic Wars. Spanish resolve was then fatally weakened by a military revolt in Spain in 1820. The European veterans, hardened by combat, improved the battlefield performance of Bolívar's army, while the revolt in Spain in 1820 forced Ferdinand VII—restored to power in 1814—to accept a constitution that limited the powers of both the monarch and the church. Colonial loyalists who for a decade had fought to maintain the authority of monarch and church viewed these reforms as unacceptably liberal.

With the king's supporters now divided, momentum swung to the patriots. After liberating present-day Venezuela, Colombia, and Ecuador, Bolívar's army entered Peru and Bolivia and defeated the last Spanish armies in 1824. Bolívar and his supporters then attempted to create a broad confederation of the former Spanish colonies. The first steps were the creation of Gran Colombia (now Venezuela, Colombia, and Ecuador) and the unification of Peru and Bolivia, but both of these initiatives had failed by 1830 (see Map 25.1).

AP® Exam Tip
Compare how Bolívar's letter, similar to the American Declaration of Independence and the French Declaration of the Rights of Man and the Citizen, influenced resistance to existing political authority in pursuit of independence and democratic ideals.

Simón Bolívar The most important military leader in the struggle for independence in South America. Born in Venezuela, he led military forces there and in Colombia, Ecuador, Peru, and Bolivia.

---

[1]Quoted in Lyman L. Johnson, "Spanish American Independence and Its Consequences," in *Problems in Modern Latin American History: A Reader*, eds. John Charles Chasteen and Joseph S. Tulchin (Wilmington, DE: Scholarly Resources, 1994), 21.

OREGON COUNTRY
(Joint U.S.-British occupation)

BRITISH NORTH AMERICA (CANADA) (Gr. Br.)

Mississippi R.

New York

Philadelphia
Washington, D.C.

UNITED STATES

Colorado R.

MEXICO 1821

Rio Grande

San Antonio

New Orleans

Charleston

Gulf of Mexico

N

ATLANTIC OCEAN

40°W

40°N

Mexico City

Veracruz

Havana

BAHAMA IS. (Gr. Br.)

HAITI 1804

20°N

CUBA (Spain)

PUERTO RICO (Spain)

BRITISH HONDURAS (Gr. Br.)

GUATEMALA
Guatemala City

JAMAICA (Gr. Br.)

Caribbean Sea

TRINIDAD (Gr. Br.)

UNITED PROVINCES OF CENTRAL AMERICA 1823–1839

Panama

Caracas

BR. GUIANA (Gr. Br.)

VENEZUELA

Magdalena R.

Orinoco R.

DUTCH GUIANA (Neth.)

FRENCH GUIANA (France)

Socorro
Bogotá

GRAN COLOMBIA 1819–1830

Galápagos Islands

Quito
ECUADOR

Amazon R.

Equator 0°

PACIFIC OCEAN

Lima

PERU 1824

EMPIRE OF BRAZIL 1822

Salvador

BOLIVIA 1825
La Paz

Sucre

Paraná R.

20°S

PARAGUAY 1811

Río de Janeiro

São Paulo

CHILE 1817

UNITED PROVINCES OF THE RIO DE LA PLATA 1816

URUGUAY 1828

Valparaíso
Santiago

ARGENTINA
Buenos Aires
Bahía Blanca

Montevideo

PATAGONIA
(Disputed between Argentina and Chile)

Islas Malvinas (Falkland Islands)

80°W

60°W

0   500   1000 Km.
0   500   1000 Mi.

1811 Year independence gained

Colony

MAP 25.1 Latin America by 1830 By 1830 patriot forces had overturned the Spanish and Portuguese Empires of the Western Hemisphere. Regional conflicts, local wars, and foreign interventions challenged the survival of many of these new nations following independence.

What are the key differences between the national boundaries in this map and those that exist today?

Buenos Aires (the capital city of modern Argentina) was the second important center of revolutionary activity in Spanish South America. In Buenos Aires news of French victories in Spain led to the creation of a junta organized by militia commanders, merchants, and ranchers, which overthrew the viceroy in 1810. To deflect the opposition of Spanish loyalists, the junta claimed loyalty to the imprisoned king. Two years after Ferdinand regained the Spanish throne in 1814, junta leaders finally declared independence as the United Provinces of the Río de la Plata.

Patriot leaders in Buenos Aires at first sought to retain control over the territory of the Viceroyalty of Río de la Plata, but Spanish loyalists in Uruguay and Bolivia and a local separatist movement in Paraguay defeated these ambitions. Even within the territory of Argentina, the government in Buenos Aires proven unable to control regional rivalries and political differences. As a result, the region rapidly descended into political chaos and civil war.

A weak succession of juntas, collective presidencies, and dictators lost control over much of the interior of Argentina. But the government in Buenos Aires did manage to recruit and financially support a mixed force of Chileans and Argentines led by José de San Martín (**hoe-SAY deh san mar-TEEN**) (1778–1850), who crossed the Andes Mountains to attack Spanish forces in Chile and Peru. During this campaign San Martín's most effective troops were former slaves, who had gained their freedom by enlisting in the army. After gaining victory in Chile, San Martín pushed on to Peru in 1820, but he failed to gain a clear victory there. Unable to make progress, San Martín surrendered command of patriot forces in Peru to Simón Bolívar, who overcame final Spanish resistance in 1824.

25-1c Mexico, 1810–1823

In 1810 Mexico was Spain's wealthiest and most populous colony. Its silver mines were the richest in the world, and the colony's capital, Mexico City, was larger than any city in Spain. Mexico also had the largest population of Spanish immigrants among the colonies. When news of Napoleon's invasion of Spain reached Mexico, conservative Spaniards in Mexico City overthrew the local viceroy, thinking him too sympathetic to the creoles. This action by Spanish loyalists underlined the new reality: with the king removed from his throne by the French, colonial authority now rested on brute force.

The first stage of the revolution against Spain occurred in central Mexico, where ranchers and farmers had aggressively forced Amerindian communities from their collectively held agricultural lands. Crop failures and epidemics afflicted the region's rural poor, while miners and the urban poor faced higher food prices and rising unemployment as well. With the power of colonial authorities weakened by events in Spain, anger and fear spread through towns and villages in central Mexico.

On September 16, 1810, the parish priest of the small town of Dolores, **Miguel Hidalgo y Costilla** (**mee-GEHL ee-DAHL-go ee cos-TEA-ah**), rang the church bells and attracted a crowd. In a fiery speech he urged the crowd to rise up against the oppression of Spanish officials. Tens of thousands of the rural and urban poor soon joined his movement. While they lacked military discipline and modern weapons, they knew who their oppressors were, the Spanish and colonial-born whites who owned the ranches and mines and forced them to labor at starvation wages. Recognizing the threat posed by the angry masses following Hidalgo, wealthy Mexicans generally supported the Spanish authorities. The military tide quickly turned, and Spanish forces captured and executed Hidalgo in 1811.

The revolution continued under the leadership of another priest, **José María Morelos** (**hoe-SAY mah-REE-ah moh-RAY-los**), a former student of Hidalgo's. A more adept military and political leader than his mentor, Morelos created a formidable fighting force and, in 1813, convened a congress that declared independence and drafted a constitution. Despite these achievements, loyalist forces defeated and then executed Morelos in 1815. Although small numbers of insurgents continued to fight Spanish forces, colonial rule seemed secure in 1820, but news of the military revolt in Spain unsettled the conservative groups who had opposed Hidalgo and Morelos. In 1821 Colonel Agustín de Iturbide (**ah-goos-TEEN deh ee-tur-BEE-deh**) and other local-born loyalist commanders serving Spain forged an alliance with insurgents and then declared Mexico's independence. The conservative origins of Mexico's independence were made clear by the decision of the victors to create a monarchial government and crown Iturbide emperor. In early 1823, however, the army overthrew Iturbide and Mexico became a republic. When Iturbide returned to Mexico from exile in 1824, he was captured and, like Hidalgo and Morelos before him, was executed by a firing squad.

AP® Exam Tip
Compare the role of religion in Mexico's revolution with the role of religion in other revolutions.

Miguel Hidalgo y Costilla
Mexican priest who led the first stage of the Mexican independence war in 1810. He was captured and executed in 1811.

José María Morelos
Mexican priest and former student of Miguel Hidalgo y Costilla, he led the forces fighting for Mexican independence until he was captured and executed in 1815.

◄ **Miguel Hidalgo y Costilla** Padre Miguel Hidalgo y Costilla led the first stage of Mexico's revolution for independence by rallying the rural masses. His defeat, trial, and execution made him one of Mexico's most important political martyrs. Schalkwijk/Art Resource, NY

25-1d Brazil, to 1831

The arrival of the Portuguese royal family in Brazil in 1808 helped maintain the loyalty of the colonial elite even as revolution transformed neighboring Spanish colonies. With Napoleon's defeat in 1814, the Portuguese government called for King John VI to return to Portugal. At first he resisted, but a liberal revolt in Portugal in 1821 forced the king to return to Portugal to protect his family's right to the throne. He left his son Pedro in Brazil as regent.

By this date the Spanish colonies along Brazil's borders had experienced ten years of revolution and civil war, and some, like Argentina and Paraguay, had gained independence. Unable to ignore these struggles, some Brazilians began to re-evaluate Brazil's relationship with Portugal. Many resented their homeland's economic subordination to Portugal, while the arrogance of Portuguese soldiers and bureaucrats led others to talk openly of independence.

Unwilling to return to Portugal and committed to maintaining his family's hold on Brazil, Pedro aligned himself with rising separatist sentiment, and in 1822 declared Brazilian independence. Pedro's decision launched Brazil on a unique political trajectory. Unlike its neighbors, which became constitutional republics, Brazil gained independence as a constitutional monarchy with Pedro I, the son of the king of Portugal, as emperor.

Pedro I was committed to both monarchy and to liberal principles. The Brazilian constitution of 1824 provided for an elected assembly and granted rights to the political opposition, but Pedro made enemies by protecting the Portuguese who remained in Brazil from arrest and seizure of their property. Pedro I also opposed slavery and the slave trade, even though the slave-owning class dominated Brazil. In 1823 he anonymously published an article that characterized slavery as a "cancer eating away at Brazil" (see Diversity & Dominance: The Afro-Brazilian Experience, 1828). His decision in 1831 to ratify a treaty with Great Britain ending Brazilian participation in the slave trade provoked opposition among his nation's most powerful sectors, as did his use of military force to control neighboring Uruguay. As military losses and costs rose, the Brazilian public grew impatient. A vocal minority that sought the creation of a democracy used these issues to rally public opinion against the emperor. Confronted by street demonstrations, Pedro I abdicated the throne in 1831 in favor of his five-year-old son Pedro II. After a nine-year regency, Pedro II assumed full powers as emperor of Brazil and reigned until overthrown by republicans in 1889.

Section Review

- The French invasion of Portugal and Spain created a political crisis in their American colonies that in turn led to independence movements.

- Under the leadership of Simón Bolívar, several South American countries gained independence.

- Mexico gained independence after a long and destructive war.

- Led by the son of the Portuguese king, Brazil gained independence as a monarchy.

25-2 The Problem of Order, 1825–1890

What major political challenges did Western Hemisphere nations face in the nineteenth century?

All the newly independent nations of the Western Hemisphere encountered difficulties establishing stable political institutions. Popular sovereignty found broad support across the hemisphere as all the new nations sought to establish constitutions and elected assemblies. However, this widespread support for constitutional order and for representative government failed to prevent bitter factional conflict, regionalism, and the threats posed by charismatic political leaders and military uprisings.

25-2a Constitutional Experiments

In reaction to what they saw as arbitrary and tyrannical rule by colonial authorities, revolutionary leaders in the United States and Latin America espoused constitutionalism. They believed that the careful description of political powers in written constitutions offered the best protection for individual rights and liberties. In practice, however, many new constitutions proved unworkable. In the United States, George Washington, James Madison, and other leaders became dissatisfied with the first constitution, the Articles of Confederation, and helped write a new constitution. In Latin America few constitutions survived the rough-and-tumble of national politics. For example, Venezuela and Chile ratified and then rejected a combined total of nine constitutions between 1811 and 1833.

AP® Exam Tip
Explore the role of Enlightenment thought on the development of governments in former colonies in the Americas.

Important differences in colonial political experience influenced later political developments in the Americas. The ratification of a new constitution in the United States was the culmination of a long historical process that had begun with the development of English constitutional law and continued under colonial charters. The British colonies provided many opportunities for holding elective offices, and, by the time of independence, citizens had grown accustomed to elections and to the experience of political parties and factions. In contrast, the colonial residents of Portuguese Brazil and Spain's American colonies had almost no experience with elections and representative institutions prior to independence.

Growing enthusiasm for democratic institutions and the desire for effective self-rule led to significant political reform in the Americas, even in regions that remained colonies. British Canada included a number of separate colonies and territories, each with its own government. A provincial governor and appointed advisory council drawn from the local elite dominated political life in each colony, while elected assemblies exercised limited power. The desire to make government more responsive to the will of the assemblies led to armed rebellion in 1837. Britain responded by establishing limited self-rule in each of the Canadian provinces. By the 1860s regional political leaders realized that economic development required a government with a "national" character. Negotiations among Canadian leaders and between them and the British government led to a union of Canadian provinces, the **Confederation of 1867**, and to the creation of the Dominion of Canada with a central government in Ottawa (see Map 25.2).

The path to effective constitutional government was rockier to the south. Because neither Spain nor Portugal had permitted anything like the elected legislatures and municipal governments of colonial British America, the drafters of Latin American constitutions were less constrained by practical political experience. As a result, many of the new Latin American nations experimented with untested political institutions.

Latin American nations found it particularly difficult to define the role of the Catholic Church after independence. In the colonial period the Catholic Church was a religious monopoly that controlled all levels of education and dominated intellectual life, including the right to censor publications and public speech. Many early constitutions aimed to reduce this power by making education secular and by permitting the presence of other religions. The Catholic Church reacted by organizing and financing conservative political movements and, in some places, sponsoring insurrections. Conflicts between liberals who sought the separation of church and state and conservatives who supported the church's traditional powers would dominate political life in many Latin American nations in the nineteenth century.

Limiting the power of the military was another obstacle to the creation of constitutional governments in Latin America. The wars for independence elevated the prestige of military leaders, and, when the wars were over, military commanders seldom proved willing to subordinate themselves to civilian authorities. Frustrated by the chaotic workings of democracy, many citizens saw dictatorships led by the heroes of independence as better protection for their lives and property than constitutional democracy.

25-2b Personalist Leaders

Patriot leaders in both the United States and Latin America gained mass followings during the wars for independence, and some used these followings to gain political power. George Washington's ability to dominate early republican politics in the United States anticipated the later political ascendancy of revolutionary heroes such as Iturbide in Mexico and Bolívar in Gran

Confederation of 1867
Negotiated union of the formerly separate colonial governments of Ontario, Quebec, New Brunswick, and Nova Scotia. This new Dominion of Canada with a central government in Ottawa is seen as the beginning of the Canadian nation.

Brazil was the most important destination for the Atlantic slave trade. From the sixteenth century to the 1850s it imported more than 2 million African slaves. Beginning in the 1820s, Great Britain, Brazil's main trading partner, began to press for an end to the slave trade. British visitors to Brazil became an important source of critical information for those who sought to end the trade.

Robert Walsh, a British clergyman who traveled widely in Brazil in 1828 and 1829, left an account of the complex and unexpected ways that slaves and black freedmen were integrated into Brazilian society.

[At the custom house,] . . . for the first time I saw the Negro population under circumstances so striking to a stranger. The whole labour of bearing and moving burdens is performed by these people, and the state in which they appear is revolting to humanity. Here were a number of beings entirely naked, with the exception of a covering of dirty rags tied about their waists. Their skins, from constant exposure to the weather, had become hard, crusty, and seamed, resembling the coarse black covering of some beast, or like that of an elephant, a wrinkled hide scattered with scanty hairs. On contemplating their persons, you saw them with a physical organization resembling beings of a grade below the rank of man . . . . Some of these beings were yoked to drays, on which they dragged heavy burdens. Some were chained by the necks and legs, and moved with loads thus encumbered. Some followed each other in ranks, with heavy weights on their heads, chattering the most inarticulate and dismal cadence as they moved along. Some were munching young sugarcanes, like beasts of burden eating green provender [animal feed], and some were seen near water, lying on the bare ground among filth and offal, coiled up like dogs, and seeming to expect or require no more comfort or accommodation, exhibiting a state and conformation so un-human, that they not only seemed, but actually were, far below the inferior animals around them. Horses and mules were not employed in this way; they were used only for pleasure, and not for labour. They were seen in the same streets, pampered, spirited, and richly caparisoned, enjoying a state far superior to the negroes, and appearing to look down on the fettered and burdened wretches they were passing, as on beings of an inferior rank in the creation to themselves. . . .

The first impression of all this on my mind, was to shake the conviction I had always felt, of the wrong and hardship inflicted on our black fellow creatures, and that they were only in that state which God and nature had assigned them; that they were the lowest grade of human existence, and the link that connected it with the brute, and that the gradation was so insensible, and their natures so intermingled, that it was impossible to tell where one had terminated and the other commenced; and that it was not surprising that people who contemplated them every day, so formed, so employed, and so degraded, should forget their claims to that rank in the scale of beings in which modern philanthropists are so anxious to place them. I did not at the moment myself recollect, that the white man, made a slave on the coast of Africa, suffers not only a similar mental but physical deterioration from hardships and emaciation, and becomes in time the dull and deformed beast I now saw yoked to a burden.

A few hours only were necessary to correct my first impressions of the negro population, by seeing them under a different aspect. We were attracted by the sound of military music, and found it proceeded from a regiment drawn up in one of the streets. Their colonel had just died, and they attended to form a procession to celebrate his obsequies. They were all of different shades of black, but the majority were negroes. Their equipment was excellent; they wore dark jackets, white pantaloons, and black leather caps and belts, all which, with their arms, were in high order. Their band produced sweet and agreeable music, of the leader's own composition, and the men went through some evolutions with regularity and dexterity. They were only a militia regiment, yet were as well appointed and disciplined as one of our regiments of the line. Here then was the first step in that gradation by which the black population of this country ascend in the scale of humanity; he advances from the state below that of a beast of burden into a military rank, and he shows himself as capable of discipline and improvement as a human being of any other colour.

Our attention was next attracted by negro men and women bearing about a variety of articles for sale; some in baskets, some on boards and cases carried on their heads. They belonged to a class of small shopkeepers, many of whom vend their wares at home, but the greater

---

personalist leaders Political leaders who rely on charisma and their ability to mobilize and direct the masses of citizens outside the authority of constitutions and laws. Nineteenth-century examples include José Antonio Páez of Venezuela and Andrew Jackson of the United States. Twentieth-century examples include Juan Perón of Argentina and Hugo Chávez of Venezuela.

Colombia. In each case, military reputation provided the foundation for personal political power. Washington was distinguished from most other independence-era military leaders by his willingness to surrender power at the end of a term determined by a constitution. More commonly, **personalist leaders** relied on their mass followings rather than on constitutions and laws to govern. In Latin America, a personalist leader who gained and held political power without constitutional sanction was called a *caudillo* (**kouh-DEE-yoh**).

Powerful personal followings allowed **Andrew Jackson** of the United States and **José Antonio Páez** (**hoe-SAY an-TOE-nee-oh PAH-ays**) of Venezuela to challenge constitutional limits to their authority. During the independence wars in Venezuela and Colombia, Páez (1790–1873) was one of Bolívar's most successful generals. Like most of his followers, Páez was uneducated and poor, but his physical strength, courage, and guile made him a natural guerrilla

number send them about in this way, as in itinerant shops. A few of these people were still in a state of bondage, and brought a certain sum every evening to their owners, as the produce of their daily labour. But a large proportion, I was informed, were free, and exercised this little calling on their own account. They were all very neat and clean in their persons, and had a decorum and sense of respectability about them, superior to whites of the same class and calling. All their articles were good in their kind, and neatly kept, and they sold them with simplicity and confidence, neither wishing to take advantage of others, nor suspecting that it would be taken of themselves. I bought some confectionary from one of the females, and I was struck with the modesty and propriety of her manner; she was a young mother, and had with her a neatly dressed child, of which she seemed very fond. I gave it a little comfit [candy-covered nut], and it turned up its dusky countenance to her and then to me, taking my sweetmeat, and at the same time kissing my hand. As yet unacquainted with the coin of the country, I had none that was current about me, and was leaving the articles; but the poor young woman pressed them on me with a ready confidence, repeating in broken Portuguese, *outo tempo.* [sic], I am sorry to say, the "other time" never came, for I could not recognize her person afterwards to discharge her little debt, though I went to the same place for the purpose.

It soon began to grow dark, and I was attracted by a number of persons bearing large lighted wax tapers, like torches, gathering before a house. As I passed by, one was put into my hand by a man who seemed in some authority, and I was requested to fall into a procession that was forming. It was the preparation for a funeral, and on such occasions, I learned that they always request the attendance of a passing stranger, and feel hurt if they are refused. I joined the party, and proceeded with them to a neighbouring church. When we entered we arranged ourselves on each side of a platform which stood near the choir, on which was laid an open coffin, covered with pink silk and gold borders. The funeral service was chanted by a choir of priests, one of whom was a negro, a large comely man, whose jet black visage formed a strong and striking contrast to his white vestments. He seemed to perform his part with a decorum and sense of solemnity, which I did not observe in his brethren. After scattering flowers on the coffin, and fumigating it with incense, they retired, the procession dispersed, and we returned on board. I had been but a few hours on shore, for the first time, and I saw an African negro under four aspects of society; and it appeared to me, that in every one his character depended on the state in which he was placed, and the estimation in which he was held. As a despised slave, he was far lower than other animals of burthen that surrounded him; more miserable in his look, more revolting in his nakedness, more distorted in his person, and apparently more deficient in intellect than the horses and mules that passed him by. Advanced to the grade of a soldier, he was clean and neat in his person, amenable to discipline, expert at his exercises, and showed the port [sic] and being of a white man similarly placed. As a citizen, he was remarkable for the respectability of his appearance, and the decorum of his manners in the rank assigned him; and as a priest, standing in the house of God, appointed to instruct society on their most important interests, and in a grade in which moral and intellectual fitness is required, and a certain degree of superiority is expected, he seemed even more devout in his impressions, and more correct in his manners, than his white associates. I came, therefore, to the irresistible conclusion in my mind, that colour was an accident affecting the surface of a man, and having no more to do with his qualities than his clothes—that God had equally created an African in the image of his person, and equally given him an immortal soul; and that an European had no pretext but his own cupidity, for impiously thrusting his fellow man from that rank in the creation which the Almighty had assigned him, and degrading him below the lot of the brute beasts that perish.

AP® History Reasoning Skills

Continuity and Change Over Time *How do the author's observations about Brazilian slavery challenge and confirm the views introduced in the story of Ayuba Suleiman's experience in Chapter 19?*

Source: Robert Walsh, *Notices of Brazil in 1828 and 1829*, vol. I (London, UK: Frederick Westley and A. H. Davis, 1830), 134–141.

leader and helped him build a powerful political base. Páez described his authority in the following manner: "[The soldiers] resolved to confer on me the supreme command and blindly to obey my will, confident . . . that I was the only one who could save them."[2] Able to count on the personal loyalty of his followers, Páez was seldom willing to accept the constitutional authority of a distant president.

After defeating the Spanish, Bolívar pursued his dream of forging a union of former Spanish colonies modeled on the United States. But he underestimated the strength of nationalist sentiment unleashed by the independence wars. Páez and other Venezuelan leaders resisted the

Andrew Jackson First president of the United States to be born in humble circumstances. He was popular among frontier residents, urban workers, and small farmers. He had a successful political career as judge, general, congressman, senator, and president. After being denied the presidency in 1824 in a controversial election, he won in 1828 and was reelected in 1832.

[2]José Antonio Páez, *Autobiografía del General José Antonio Páez*, vol. 1 (New York, NY: Hallety Breen, 1869), 83.

MAP 25.2 **Dominion of Canada, 1873** Although independence was not yet achieved and settlement remained concentrated along the U.S. border, Canada had established effective political and economic control over its western territories by 1873.

In what ways did the natural environment influence the location of Canada's most populous cities and the Canadian Pacific Railway?

José Antonio Páez Venezuelan soldier who led Simón Bolívar's cavalry force. He became a successful general in the independence wars and built a powerful political base. Unwilling to accept the constitutional authority of Bolívar's government in distant Bogotá, he declared Venezuela's independence from Gran Colombia in 1829.

surrender of their hard-won power to Bolívar's Gran Colombian government in distant Bogotá. When political opponents challenged Bolívar in 1829, Páez declared Venezuela's independence. Merciless to his enemies and indulgent with his followers, Páez ruled the country as president or dictator for the next eighteen years. Despite implementing an economic program favorable to the elite, Páez remained popular with the masses. Even as his personal wealth grew, he took care to present himself as a common man.

Andrew Jackson (1767–1845) was the first U.S. president born in humble circumstances. A self-made man who eventually acquired substantial property and owned over a hundred slaves, Jackson was extremely popular among frontier residents, urban workers, and small farmers. Although he was notorious for his untidy personal life as well as for dueling, his courage, individualism, and willingness to challenge authority helped him attain political success as judge, general, congressman, senator, and president.

During his military career, Jackson proved to be as impatient with civilian authorities as Venezuela's Páez. Widely known because of his victories over the Creek and Seminole Amerindian peoples, he was elevated to the pinnacle of American politics by his celebrated defeat of the British at the Battle of New Orleans in 1815. His invasion of Spanish Florida in 1818 forced the permanent transfer of this territory to the United States a year later. He ran for president in 1824 and received a plurality of the popular votes but failed to win a majority of electoral votes. His followers were embittered when the House of Representatives chose John Quincy Adams as president.

Jackson's followers viewed his landslide election victory in 1828 and reelection in 1832 as the triumph of democracy over entrenched aristocracy. In office Jackson challenged constitutional limits on his authority, increasing presidential power at the expense of Congress and the Supreme Court. Like Páez, Jackson was able to dominate national politics by blending a populist political style that celebrated the virtues and cultural enthusiasms of common people with support for policies that promoted the economic interests of powerful propertied groups.

Personalist leaders were common in both Latin America and the United States in the early decades of the nineteenth century, but Latin America's weaker constitutional tradition, more limited protection of property rights, lower literacy levels, and less-developed communications systems facilitated the ambitions of popular politicians. Once in power, Latin America's personalist leaders often ignored constitutional restraints on their authority and election results seldom determined access to presidential power. As a result, by 1900 every independent Latin American nation had experienced periods of dictatorship.

25-2c The Threat of Regionalism

After independence, national governments in the Western Hemisphere were generally weaker than the colonial governments they replaced. Debates over tariffs, tax and monetary policies, and, in many nations, slavery and the slave trade led some regional elites to attempt secession. Some of the hemisphere's newly independent nations did not survive these struggles, while others lost territories to aggressive neighbors.

In Spanish America all efforts to forge large multistate federations after independence failed. The Viceroyalty of New Spain had included Central America and Mexico, but after independence this union failed when in 1823 local elites broke with Mexico to form the Republic of Central America. A new round of regional disputes and civil wars led to the creation of five separate nations during the 1820s and 1830s. In South America, Bolívar attempted to maintain the colonial unity of Venezuela, Colombia, and Ecuador by creating Gran Colombia with its capital in Bogotá. But even before his death in 1830, Venezuela and Ecuador had become independent states. In the colonial era Argentina, Uruguay, Paraguay, and Bolivia were organized as a single viceroyalty with its capital in Buenos Aires. After the defeat of Spain, the leaders in Paraguay, Uruguay, and Bolivia declared their independence from Argentina.

Regionalism threatened the United States as well. The defense of state and regional interests played an important role in the framing of the U.S. Constitution. Many important constitutional provisions represented compromises forged among competing state and regional leaders. Yet, despite these constitutional compromises, regional rivalries still threatened the nation.

Slavery divided the nation into two separate and competitive societies. A rising tide of immigration to the northern states in the 1830s and 1840s began to move the center of political power away from the South. In response, southern leaders sought to protect slavery by expanding into new territories. They supported the Louisiana Purchase in 1803 (see Map 25.3), which transferred to the United States a vast French territory extending from the Gulf of Mexico to Canada, and the Mexican-American War in 1846, which added nearly half of Mexican territory to the United States. However, this territorial expansion forced a national debate about slavery that contributed to the election of Abraham Lincoln as president in 1860.

Lincoln was committed to checking the spread of slavery, and his election provoked the southern planter elite to choose the dangerous course of secession from the Union. The seceding states formed a new government, the Confederate States of America, known as the Confederacy. Lincoln preserved the Union but at an enormous cost. The U.S. Civil War (1861–1865) was the most destructive conflict in the history of the Western Hemisphere. Up to 750,000 lives were lost before the Confederacy surrendered in 1865. The Union victory led to the abolition of slavery and also transferred national political power to a northern elite committed to industrial expansion and federal support for the construction of railroads and other internal improvements.

Although secession failed, the Confederate States of America were better prepared politically and economically for independence than were the successful secessionist movements that broke up Gran Colombia and other Spanish American federations. The seceding states were richer than any nation in Latin America and the new government's leaders were generally experienced politicians. Nevertheless, the Confederacy failed, in part because of poor timing. The new nations of the Western Hemisphere were most vulnerable to secessionist movements in the early years of their existence; indeed, all the successful secessions occurred shortly after independence. In the case of the United States, an experienced national government legitimated and strengthened by more than seven decades of relative stability and reinforced by dramatic economic and population growth defeated secession, but only with enormous effort.

25-2d Foreign Interventions and Regional Wars

Wars often determined national borders, access to natural resources, and control of markets in the Western Hemisphere. Even after the achievement of independence, Mexico and other Western Hemisphere nations were forced to defend themselves against Europe's great powers.

AP® Exam Tip
Understand how Enlightenment ideas influenced reform movements that challenged existing notions of social relations, such as the abolition of slavery.

MAP 25.3 Territorial Growth of the United States, 1783–1853 The rapid western expansion of the United States resulted from aggressive diplomacy and warfare against Mexico and Amerindian peoples. Railroad development helped integrate the trans-Mississippi west and promote economic expansion.

What does the rapid territorial expansion of the United States in the nineteenth century indicate about the relative political development and economic strength of its two neighbors Canada and Mexico?

Contested national borders and regional rivalries also led to wars between Western Hemisphere nations. By the end of the nineteenth century the United States, Brazil, Argentina, and Chile had all successfully waged wars against their neighbors and established themselves as regional powers.

Within thirty years of independence, the United States fought a second war with England— the War of 1812. The burning of the White House and Capitol by British troops in 1814 symbolized the weakness of the new republic. By the end of the nineteenth century, however, the United States was the hemisphere's greatest military power, and, as a result of its war against Spain in 1898, controlled an empire that reached from the Philippines in the Pacific Ocean to Puerto Rico in the Caribbean (see Chapter 26).

European powers also challenged the sovereignty of the new nations of Latin America. Following independence Argentina faced British and French naval blockades, and British naval forces systematically violated Brazil's territorial waters to stop the importation of slaves. Mexico faced the most serious threats to sovereignty, defeating a weak Spanish invasion in 1829, a French assault on the city of Veracruz in 1838, and a large-scale French invasion in 1862 that sought to install a European monarch.

Mexico also faced a grave threat from the United States. In the 1820s Mexico had encouraged Americans to immigrate to its northern province of Texas. By the early 1830s Americans outnumbered Mexican nationals in Texas and were aggressively challenging Mexican laws such as the prohibition of slavery. An alliance of Mexican liberals and American settlers rebelled in 1835 and gained independence for Texas in 1836. In 1845 the United States made Texas a state, provoking war with Mexico a year later. The surrender of Mexico City in 1848 to American forces compelled Mexico to accept a harsh treaty that forced it to cede vast territories to the United States, including present-day New Mexico, Arizona, and California. In return Mexico received $15 million. When gold was discovered in California in 1848, the magnitude of Mexico's loss became clear.

With the very survival of the nation at stake, Mexico's liberals took power and imposed sweeping reforms, including a new constitution in 1857 that limited the power of the Catholic Church and military. These two powerful institutions and the nation's conservatives then fought a bloody and destructive civil war with the liberals who controlled the government (1858–1861). Rising from humble origins as an impoverished orphan, Amerindian jurist **Benito Juárez (beh-NEE-toh WAH-rez)** assumed the presidency and defeated the conservatives, who then turned to Napoleon III of France for assistance. In 1862, French forces invaded Mexico, forced Juárez to flee Mexico City, and installed the younger brother of the Austrian emperor Franz Joseph I, Archduke Maximilian, as emperor of Mexico. After years of warfare, Juárez drove the French army out of Mexico in 1867, aided by U.S. diplomatic pressure. After capturing Maximilian, Juárez ordered his execution.

This victory over a powerful foreign enemy redeemed a nation humiliated two decades earlier in war with the United States. But the creation of democracy proved more elusive than the protection of Mexican sovereignty. Despite the Mexican constitution's prohibition of presidential re-election, Juárez would serve as president until his death in 1872.

AP® Exam Tip Understand the importance of the United States' expansion of its land borders.

Benito Juárez President of Mexico (1858–1872). Born in poverty in Mexico, he was educated as a lawyer and rose to become chief justice of the Mexican supreme court and then president. He led Mexico's resistance to a French invasion in 1862 and the installation of Maximilian as emperor.

◄ **Execution of Emperor Maximilian of Mexico** This painting by Edouard Manet shows the 1867 execution by firing squad of Maximilian and two of his Mexican generals. The defeat of the French intervention was a great triumph for Mexican patriots led by Benito Juárez.
World History Archive/Alamy Stock Photo

AP® Exam Tip
Understand the role of rising nationalism in the Americas in this time period.

As was clear in the Mexican-American War, wars between Western Hemisphere nations could lead to dramatic territorial changes. Chile established itself as the leading military and economic power on the west coast of South America when it fought two successful wars against an alliance of Peru and Bolivia (1836–1839 and 1879–1883). The second contest, the War of the Pacific, forced Bolivia to cede its only outlet to the sea and Peru to yield rich mining districts to the victorious Chileans.

Argentina and Brazil fought for control of Uruguay in the 1820s, but a military stalemate eventually forced them to recognize Uruguayan independence. Then, in 1865, Argentina and Uruguay joined Brazil to wage war against Paraguay (War of the Triple Alliance). After five years of warfare, Paraguayan dictator Francisco Solano López (**fran-CEES-co so-LAN-oh LOH-pehz**) and more than 20 percent of the nation's population had died. Paraguay then experienced military occupation, loss of territory, and economic penalties.

25-2e Native Peoples and the Nation-State

Relations between the Western Hemisphere's new nation-states and indigenous peoples were shaped by both diplomacy and war. During late colonial times, Spanish, Portuguese, and British colonial governments attempted to restrict the expansion of settlements into territories occupied by Amerindians to prevent costly wars. With independence, the colonial powers' role as mediator and protector ended, leading to the expansion of settlements across the hemisphere and to wars with native peoples in many nations.

In these contests, independent Amerindian peoples posed a significant military challenge to many Western Hemisphere republics. Weakened by civil wars and constitutional crises, new nations were less able to maintain frontier peace than the colonial governments they replaced. After independence Amerindian peoples in Argentina, the United States, Chile, and Mexico succeeded in pushing back frontier settlements. But despite early victories, native military resistance was overcome by 1890 in most of the hemisphere as stronger governments applied larger forces and new weapons to these conflicts.

After the American Revolution, tens of thousands of settlers entered territories previously guaranteed to Amerindians by treaties with Britain. Indigenous leaders responded by forging military alliances with British officials in Canada and with other native peoples. In the Ohio River Valley two Shawnee brothers, **Tecumseh** (**teh-CUM-sah**) and the Prophet (Tenskwatawa), created a broad, well-organized alliance among Amerindian peoples that gained British support. During the War of 1812, American military forces defeated the alliance. Tecumseh died in battle fighting alongside his British allies.

Throughout the 1820s native peoples lost lands to settlers across the Midwest and Southeast. In 1828 the election of Andrew Jackson, a veteran of earlier wars against native peoples, as president brought matters to a head. The Indian Removal Act of 1830 forced the resettlement of the Cherokee, Creek, Choctaw, and other eastern peoples to lands west of the Mississippi River. Nearly half these forced migrants died on this journey, known as the Trail of Tears.

The native peoples of the Great Plains offered formidable resistance to the expansion of white settlement. By the time substantial numbers of white buffalo hunters, cattlemen, and settlers reached the American west, the indigenous peoples were skilled in the use of horses and firearms. These technologies allowed the Sioux, Comanche, Pawnee, Kiowa, and other plains peoples to hunt more efficiently and develop potent military capacities.

After the Civil War, however, a large wave of settlers pushed onto the plains. Buffalo herds were hunted to near extinction and native lands were appropriated by farmers and ranchers. Amerindian resistance to these assaults on their way of life led to four decades of armed conflict with the United States Army. The U.S. government forced the Comanche, who had long dominated the southern plains and who had raided deep into Mexico, to cede their traditional lands in Texas in 1865. The Sioux and their allies held out longer, overwhelming General George Armstrong Custer and the Seventh Cavalry in the Battle of Little Bighorn in 1876, but they were also soon forced to accept reservation life as well. Military campaigns in both the United States and Mexico in the 1870s and 1880s then broke the resistance of the Apache.

The indigenous peoples of Argentina and Chile experienced a similar trajectory of adaptation, resistance, and defeat. Herds of wild cattle provided these peoples with a limitless food supply, and their mastery of the horse increased their military capacities. For a while the natives of Argentina and Chile were able to check the southern expansion of agriculture and ranching.

AP® Exam Tip
Explain several examples of anti-imperial resistance within empires and states.

Tecumseh Shawnee leader who attempted to organize an Amerindian confederacy to prevent the loss of additional territory to American settlers. He became an ally of the British in the War of 1812 and died in battle.

◀ **Navajo Leaders Gathered in Washington to Negotiate**
As settlers pushed west in the nineteenth century, Amerindian peoples were forced to negotiate territorial concessions with the U.S. government. This photo shows Navajo leaders and their Anglo translators in Washington, D.C., in 1874. National Anthropological Archives, Smithsonian Institution, SPC BAE 4420 Vol 6 01007800

Unable to defeat these resourceful enemies, the governments of Argentina and Chile relied on an elaborate system of gift giving and prisoner exchanges to maintain peace on the frontier.

By the 1860s, however, population increase with resulting demands for access to Amerindian lands, political stability, and military modernization allowed Argentina and Chile to take the offensive. In the 1870s the government of Argentina used a large military force armed with modern weapons to crush native resistance on the pampas. In Chile in the 1850s, civil war and an economic depression weakened the central government, and the Mapuches (**mah-POO-chez**) (also called "Araucanians") reclaimed traditional lands by pushing back frontier settlements. By the 1870s, however, Chilean forces armed with new weapons had overwhelmed all Amerindian resistance.

In Chile, Argentina, and the United States, national governments justified military campaigns by demonizing native peoples. Newspaper editorials and the speeches of politicians portrayed Amerindians as brutal and cruel and as obstacles to progress, even though aggression was usually initiated by settlers. In April 1859 a Chilean newspaper commented:

> *The necessity, not only to punish the Araucanian [Mapuche] race, but also to make it impotent to harm us, is well recognized . . . as the only way to rid the country of a million evils. It is well understood that they are odious and prejudicial guests in Chile . . . conciliatory measures have accomplished nothing with this stupid race—the infamy and disgrace of the Chilean nation.[3]*

The author of this racist pronouncement apparently felt no obligation to explain how his nation's original inhabitants had become "guests."

Political divisions and civil wars within the new nations also provided opportunities for some long-pacified native peoples to rebel. In the Yucatán region of Mexico, large landowners forced many Maya (**MY-ah**) communities from traditional agricultural lands, reducing thousands to peonage. Weakened by internal rebellions and by the American

Section Review

- The new nations of the Western Hemisphere, including the United States, found it difficult to establish constitutional governments.

- Charismatic military leaders with large followings, like the populists Andrew Jackson and José Antonio Páez, often took power and challenged constitutional limits on presidential power.

- Secessionist movements and civil wars threatened the survival of many Latin American nations and the United States.

- Wars with foreign powers and with neighboring states endangered the independence and national borders of many Western Hemisphere nations.

- Native peoples throughout the hemisphere tried to defend their territories, but by the end of the nineteenth century, national governments had overcome native resistance.

[3]Quoted in Brian Loveman, *Chile: The Legacy of Hispanic Capitalism* (New York, NY: Oxford University Press, 1979), 170.

invasion, the Mexican government faced a mass rebellion by the Maya in 1847. This well-organized and popular uprising, known as the **Caste War**, nearly returned the Yucatán to native control. Grievances accumulated over more than 300 years led to great violence and property destruction. The end of the war with the United States allowed the government of Mexico to regain control of major towns. Even then, some Maya rebels retreated to unoccupied territories and created an independent state, which they called the "Empire of the Cross." Organized around a mix of traditional beliefs and Christian symbols, this indigenous state resisted Mexican forces until 1870. A few isolated Maya strongholds survived until militarily suppressed in 1901.

25-3 The Challenge of Social and Economic Change

How did economic modernization and the effects of abolition, immigration, and women's rights change the nations of the Western Hemisphere?

During the nineteenth century the newly independent nations of the Western Hemisphere struggled to realize the Enlightenment ideals of freedom and individual liberty that had helped ignite the revolutions for independence. The persistence of slavery and other oppressive colonial-era institutions slowed this process. Nevertheless, by century's end reform movements had ended the slave trade, abolished slavery, expanded voting rights, and facilitated the assimilation of millions of immigrants from Asia and Europe.

Industrialization and integration in the world economy sometimes challenged political stability and social arrangements. While a small number of Western Hemisphere nations embraced industrialization, most remained dependent on the export of agricultural and mining production long after independence. By the end of the century it was clear that the industrializing nations had grown richer than the nations that remained exporters of agricultural products and minerals. All the region's economies, regardless of development path, had become more vulnerable and volatile as a result of greater dependence on foreign markets. Like contemporary movements for social reform, efforts to assert economic sovereignty produced powerful new political forces.

25-3a The Abolition of Slavery

Leaders of the independence movements of the United States and Latin America asserted ideals of universal freedom and citizenship that contrasted sharply with the reality of slavery. Those who sought to end the institution were called **abolitionists**. Despite their efforts, slavery survived in most of the hemisphere until the 1850s. It proved especially difficult to eradicate in regions where the export of plantation products like cotton and sugar was most important—such as the United States, Brazil, and Cuba.

Slavery in the United States was weakened first by the abolition of slavery in some northern states and by the end of the African slave trade in 1808. But the profitable expansion of cotton agriculture after the War of 1812 stalled further progress. In Spanish America tens of thousands of slaves gained freedom by joining the revolutionary armies that fought for independence (see Chapter 23). After independence, most Spanish American republics prohibited the slave trade, but growing international demand for sugar and coffee slowed the achievement of abolition. As prices rose for plantation products, Brazil and Cuba actually increased their imports of slaves even as their neighbors began the gradual abolition of slavery.

During the long struggle to end slavery in the United States, American abolitionists argued that slavery offended Christian morality and the universal rights asserted in the Declaration of Independence. Abolitionist Theodore Weld articulated the religious objection to slavery in 1834:

> *No condition of birth, no shade of color, no mere misfortune of circumstance, can annul the birth-right charter, which God has bequeathed to every being upon whom he has stamped his own image, by making him a free moral agent, and that he who robs his fellow man of this tramples upon right, subverts justice, outrages humanity . . . and sacrilegiously assumes the prerogative of God.*[4]

AP® Exam Tip
Understand how changes in labor systems, such as the abolition of slavery, have changed social structures.

Caste War A rebellion of the Maya people against the government of Mexico in 1847 that nearly returned the Yucatán to Maya rule. Some Maya rebels retreated to unoccupied territories, where they held out until 1901.

abolitionists Men and women who agitated for a complete end to slavery. Abolitionist pressure ended the British transatlantic slave trade in 1808 and slavery in British colonies in 1834. In the United States the activities of abolitionists were one factor leading to the Civil War (1861–1865).

---

[4]Quoted in Bernard Bailyn, David Brion Davis, David Herbert Donald, John L. Thomas, Robert H. Wiebe, and Gordon S. Wood, *The Great Republic: A History of the American People* (Lexington, MA: D.C. Heath, 1981), 398.

Two groups denied full rights under the Constitution—women and free African Americans—played important roles in the abolition of slavery. Women were among the leaders of the American Anti-Slavery Society and produced effective propaganda against slavery. Eventually, thousands of women joined the abolitionist cause. Social conservatives and the defenders of slavery attacked their highly visible public role, leading many women to become public advocates of female suffrage as well. Frederick Douglass, a former slave, was one of the most visible and effective leaders of the abolitionist movement. Some black leaders, believing that peaceful means would fail, pushed the abolitionist movement to accept the inevitability of violence. In 1843 Henry Highland Garnet stirred the National Colored Convention when he demanded, "Brethren, arise, arise, arise! . . . Let every slave in the land do this and the days of slavery are numbered."[5]

In the 1850s the electoral strength of the newly formed Republican Party forced a confrontation between slave and free states. Following the election of Abraham Lincoln in 1860, eleven southern states seceded from the Union. During the Civil War pressure for emancipation rose as tens of thousands of black freemen and escaped slaves joined the Union army. Then, in 1863, in the midst of the Civil War and two years after the abolition of serfdom in Russia (see Chapter 27), Lincoln issued the Emancipation Proclamation, ending slavery in rebel states not occupied by the Union army. In 1865 the Thirteenth Amendment to the Constitution finally abolished slavery completely. But, despite this achievement, most African Americans continued to live in harsh conditions. By the end of the century southern states had instituted "Jim Crow" laws that segregated blacks in public transportation, jobs, and schools, condemning the majority to poverty. The implementation of these laws coincided with increased racial violence that saw an average of fifty African Americans lynched each year.

In Brazil slavery survived for more than two decades after abolition in the United States. Britain, Brazil's major trading partner, pressed for an end to the slave trade after prohibiting this trade to its own colonies in 1807. Despite agreeing to end the trade in 1830, Brazil imported another half-million African slaves illegally before the British navy forced compliance in the 1850s. The Brazilian emperor, Pedro II, and many liberals worked to abolish slavery, but their effort to find a form of gradual emancipation acceptable to slave owners failed.

During Brazil's war with Paraguay (1865–1870), large numbers of slaves joined the Brazilian army in exchange for freedom. Their patriotism and heroism convinced many Brazilians of the injustice of slavery. Educated Brazilians had also come to view slavery as an obstacle to the nation's economic development and as an impediment to democratic reform. As political support for slavery weakened in the 1880s, growing numbers of slaves fled their masters and army officers resisted demands to capture and return the runaways. Brazil finally abolished slavery in 1888. A year later a political rebellion ended the Brazilian monarchy.

The Caribbean received almost 40 percent of all African slaves shipped to the New World. Throughout the region, tiny white minorities lived surrounded by slave and free colored majorities. In the eighteenth century the slave rebellion in Saint Domingue (see Chapter 23) spread terror among slave owners across the Caribbean, convincing slave owners that any effort to overthrow colonial rule would unleash new insurrections. As a result, there was little local support for abolition in the Caribbean. In these colonies abolition would result from decisions made in Europe by imperial governments.

In the Caribbean, as in Brazil and other plantation economies, slaves helped to force abolition by rebelling, running away, and resisting in more subtle ways. Although slave rebellions in Jamaica and Cuba and other Caribbean colonies failed to achieve the success of the Haitian Revolution (1791–1804), they made clear that slaves would never accept their condition.

After 1800, when the profitability of sugar plantations in the British West Indian colonies declined, a coalition of British labor unions, Protestant ministers, and free traders pushed for the abolition of slavery. Britain, the major participant in the eighteenth-century expansion of slavery in the Americas, ended its participation in the slave trade in 1807. It then negotiated treaties with Spain, Brazil, and other importers of slaves to eliminate the slave trade and used its naval forces to force compliance.

Abolition in British colonies occurred in 1834, but "freed" slaves were compelled to remain with former masters as "apprentices." Abuses by planters and resistance to apprenticeship by former slaves led to complete abolition in 1838. A decade later, France abolished slavery in its

---

[5]Quoted in Mary Beth Norton et al., *A People and a Nation: A History of the United States*, 6th ed. (Boston, MA: Houghton Mifflin, 2001), 284.

▲ A Former Brazilian Slave Returns from Military Service
The heroic actions of black freemen and slaves in the Paraguayan War (1865–1870) led many Brazilians to condemn slavery. The original caption for this drawing reads: "On his return from the war in Paraguay: Full of glory, covered with laurels, after having spilled his blood in defense of the fatherland and to free a people from slavery, the volunteer sees his own mother bound and whipped! Awful reality!"
Courtesy Fundacao Biblioteca Nacional Brazil

AP® Exam Tip
Be able to discuss the causes and effects of global migrations in various regions during this time period.

Caribbean colonies. The decision to abolish slavery in the Dutch Empire in 1863 freed 33,000 slaves in Surinam and 12,000 in the Dutch Antilles.

In the Caribbean, slavery lasted longest in Spain's remaining colonies of Cuba and Puerto Rico. Britain used diplomatic pressure and naval force to undermine the slave trade after 1820, but local support for abolition appeared as well. Both Cuba and Puerto Rico had larger white and free colored populations than did the Caribbean colonies of Britain and France, and there was little fear that abolition would lead to the political ascendancy of former slaves. In Puerto Rico, where slaves numbered approximately 30,000, local reformers secured the abolition of slavery in 1873. In Cuba, where there were many more slaves and where slavery was much more important to the economy because of a booming sugar industry, forces supporting independence helped propel the Spanish colonial government toward abolition (see Environment & Technology: Industrializing Sugar Agriculture in Cuba). Beginning in the 1870s, Spain passed a series of laws promoting gradual abolition but requiring long periods of service to former masters. Spain finally abolished slavery in Cuba in 1886.

25-3b Immigration

During the long colonial period free Europeans were a minority among immigrants to the Western Hemisphere. From 1500 to 1760 imported African slaves outnumbered European immigrants in the Western Hemisphere by nearly two to one. Another 4 million African slaves were then imported before the end of the slave trade in the 1850s. After the African slave trade came to an end, millions of Europeans and Asians arrived in the Western Hemisphere as immigrants. This new flood of immigrants in the nineteenth century helped foster the rapid economic growth and territorial occupation of frontier regions in the United States, Canada, Argentina, Chile, and Brazil. By century's end nearly all of the hemisphere's fastest-growing cities (Buenos Aires, Chicago, New York, and São Paulo, for example) had large and diverse immigrant populations. In general, European immigrants avoided the regions that had earlier depended on slavery with their traditions of violence, oppressive labor conditions, and low wages. At the same time, tens of thousands of immigrants from China and India arrived with indenture contracts that directed them to plantation zones in the Caribbean region for a set term. While these indentured workers were not slaves, they were typically required to do brutal manual labor and afforded few legal protections.

Despite this flow of indentured laborers from Asia, Europe provided the majority of immigrants to the Western Hemisphere in the nineteenth century. Initially, most came from western Europe, but after 1870 most immigrants were southern or eastern Europeans. The United States received approximately 600,000 European immigrants in the 1830s, 1.5 million in the 1840s, and then 2.5 million per decade until 1880. In the 1890s an astonishing total of 5.2 million immigrants arrived. Immigration helped push the national population from 39 million in 1871 to 63 million in 1891. Most of these immigrants settled in cities. Chicago, for example, grew from 444,000 in 1870 to 1.7 million in 1900.

European immigration to Latin America also increased dramatically. Combined immigration to Argentina and Brazil rose from under 130,000 in the 1860s to 1.7 million in the 1890s. By 1910, 30 percent of the Argentine population was foreign-born, more than twice the proportion in the U.S. population. Argentina, then a rich exporter of agricultural products, was an extremely attractive destination for European immigrants, receiving more than twice as many immigrants as Canada between 1870 and 1930. Even so, immigration to Canada increased tenfold during this period.

Asian immigration to the Western Hemisphere also increased after 1850. Between 1849 and 1875, approximately 100,000 Chinese immigrants arrived in Peru and another 120,000 entered Cuba. Canada attracted about 50,000 Chinese immigrants in the second half of the century, and the United States received 300,000 Chinese immigrants between 1854 and 1882. India also contributed to the ethnic and cultural transformation of the Western Hemisphere, sending more

◀ **Chinese Funeral in Vancouver, Canada** In the 1890s Vancouver was an important destination for Chinese immigrants. This photo shows how an important element of traditional Chinese culture thrived among the storefronts and streetcar lines of the late-Victorian Canadian city. Vancouver Public Library, Special Collections, VPL #17064

than a half-million immigrants to the Caribbean region. British Guiana alone received 238,000 immigrants, mostly indentured laborers, from the Asian subcontinent.

Despite the obvious economic benefits that accompanied this inflow of people, hostility to immigration mounted in many nations. Nativist political movements argued that it was impossible to integrate large numbers of foreigners into national political cultures. By the end of the century, fear and prejudice led many governments in the Western Hemisphere to limit immigration or to distinguish between "desirable" and "undesirable" immigrants, commonly favoring Europeans over Asians.

Asians faced more obstacles than did Europeans and were more often victims of violence and discrimination. In the 1870s and 1880s anti-Chinese riots erupted in many western cities in the United States. For example, an estimated twenty Chinese were beaten and lynched by a mob in Los Angeles, California, in 1871. Congress responded to this wave of white racism by passing the Chinese Exclusion Act in 1882, which eliminated most Chinese immigration. Similarly, in 1886 popular fears that "inferior races" threatened Canada led that government to impose a head tax, making immigration more difficult for Chinese families. During this same period strong anti-Chinese prejudice surfaced in Peru, Mexico, and Cuba. Japanese immigrants in Brazil and East Indians in the English-speaking Caribbean faced similar prejudices.

European immigrants faced prejudice and discrimination as well. Popular opinion portrayed Italians as criminals or anarchists. In Argentina and the United States, some social scientists argued that Italian immigrants were more violent and less honest than the native-born population. Immigrants from Spain were widely stereotyped in Argentina as miserly and dishonest. Eastern European Jews seeking to escape pogroms and discrimination at home found themselves barred from many educational institutions and professional careers in both the United States and Latin America. Irish, German, Swedish, Polish, and Middle Eastern immigrants were branded with negative stereotypes as well. The justifications for these prejudices were remarkably similar from Canada to Argentina. Immigrants, critics claimed, threatened the well-being of native-born workers by accepting low wages and threatened national culture by resisting assimilation. These prejudiced opinions and the discrimination they always engender remain visible today, as demonstrated by the presidential campaign of Donald Trump, although modern prejudices are now directed at different ethnicities.

Many intellectuals and political leaders wondered if the evolving mix of culturally diverse populations could sustain a common citizenship. This concern led to efforts to compel

AP® Exam Tip
Understand the reaction of receiving societies to immigrants, such as attempts at regulation of immigrants in some states during the nineteenth century.

▶ **Arrest of Labor Activist in Buenos Aires** The labor movement in Buenos Aires grew in numbers and became more radical with the arrival of tens of thousands of Italian and Spanish immigrants. Fearful of socialist and anarchist unions, the government of Argentina used an expanded police force to break strikes. Archivo General de la Nacion, Buenos Aires

immigrants to assimilate. Schools became cultural battlegrounds where language, cultural values, and patriotic attitudes were transmitted to the children of immigrants. Ignoring Canada's large French-speaking population, an English-speaking Canadian reformer commented on recent immigration: "If Canada is to become in a real sense a nation, if our people are to become one people, we must have one language."[6] These fears and prejudices promoted the singing of patriotic songs, the veneration of national flags and other symbols, and the writing of national histories that emphasized patriotism and civic virtue.

25-3c American Cultures

Despite discrimination, immigrants continued to stream into the Western Hemisphere, where they introduced new languages, living arrangements, technologies, and customs. Immigrants also altered politics in many of the hemisphere's nations as they sought to influence government policies and gain access to power. To compensate for their isolation from home, language, and culture, most immigrant groups created ethnically based mutual aid societies, sports and leisure clubs, and neighborhoods. These organizations provided valuable social and economic support for recent arrivals while sometimes worsening the fears of the native-born that immigration posed a threat to national culture. At the same time, shared experiences in their adopted nations as workers, neighbors, or soldiers changed immigrants individually and collectively. The modification of language, customs, values, and behaviors as a result of contact with people from another culture is called **acculturation**.

Immigrants and their children, in turn, made their mark on the cultures of their adopted nations. They learned the language spoken in their adopted countries as fast as possible in order to improve their earning capacity, while words and phrases from their languages entered the vocabularies of their adoptive nations. Languages as diverse as Yiddish and Italian strongly influenced American English, Argentine Spanish, and Brazilian Portuguese. Dietary practices introduced from Europe and Asia altered the cuisine of nearly every American nation. In popular music, the Argentine tango, based on African rhythms, was transformed by new instrumentation and orchestral arrangements brought by Italian immigrants. Mexican ballads blended with English folk music in the U.S. Southwest, and Italian operas played to packed houses in Buenos Aires.

acculturation The adoption of the language, customs, values, and behaviors of host nations by immigrants.

[6]J. S. Woodsworth in 1909, quoted in R. Douglas Francis, Richard Jones, and Donald B. Smith, *Destinies: Canadian History Since Confederation*, 2nd ed. (Toronto, ON: Holt, Rinehart and Winston, 1992), 141.

Union movements and electoral politics in the hemisphere also felt the influence of new arrivals who aggressively sought to influence politics and improve working conditions. The anarchist and socialist beliefs of European immigrants influenced the labor movements of Mexico, Argentina, and the United States. Immigrants also helped form new political movements. Their mutual benevolent societies and less formal ethnic associations pooled resources to help immigrants open businesses, aid the immigration of relatives, or bury family members.

25-3d Women's Rights and the Struggle for Social Justice

In 1848 a group of women angered by their exclusion from an international antislavery meeting issued a call for a conference to discuss women's rights. The resulting **Women's Rights Convention** at Seneca Falls, New York, issued a statement that said, in part, "We hold these truths to be self-evident: that all men and women are equal." While moderates focused on the issues of economic independence and legal rights, increasing numbers of women demanded the right to vote. Others lobbied to provide better conditions for women working outside the home, especially in textile factories. Sarah Grimké responded to criticism of women's activism:

> This has been the language of man since he laid aside the whip as a means to keep woman in subjection. He spares her body, but the war he has waged against her mind, her heart, and her soul, has been no less destructive to her as a moral being. How monstrous is the doctrine that woman is to be dependent on man![7]

AP® Exam Tip
Understand how demands for women's suffrage and emergent feminism challenged political and gender hierarchies.

Progress toward equality between men and women was equally slow in Canada and in Latin America. Canada's first women doctors received their training in the United States because women could not receive medical degrees at home until 1895. Argentina and Uruguay were among the first Latin American nations to provide public education for women, introducing coeducation in the 1870s. Chilean women gained access to some careers in medicine and law in the 1870s, while in Brazil the first women graduated in medicine in 1882. In Argentina the first woman doctor graduated from medical school in 1899.

Throughout the hemisphere more rapid progress occurred in lower-status careers that threatened male economic power less directly, and, by the end of the century, women dominated elementary school teaching. From Canada to Argentina and Chile, the majority of working-class women, although having only limited direct involvement in reform movements, succeeded in transforming gender relations in their daily lives. By the end of the nineteenth century, large numbers of poor women worked outside the home on farms, in markets, and, increasingly, in factories. Many bore full responsibility for providing for their children. Whether men thought women should remain in the home or not, by the end of the century women were unambiguously present in the economy (see also Chapter 27).

There was little progress toward eliminating racial discrimination in the nineteenth century. Blacks were denied the vote throughout the southern United States and were subjected to the indignity of segregation—consigned to separate schools, hotels, restaurants, seats in public transportation, and even water fountains. Racial discrimination against men and women of African descent was also common in Latin America. Unlike the southern states of the United States, however, Latin American nations did not insist on formal racial segregation or permit lynching. Nor did they enforce a strict color line in education or public accommodations. Many men and women of mixed racial background were able to enter the skilled working class or middle class, and some rose to political prominence. Latin Americans tended to view racial identity across a continuum of physical characteristics rather than in the narrow terms of black and white that defined race relations in the United States.

The abolition of slavery in Latin America did not end discrimination. Some leaders of the abolition struggles later organized to promote racial integration. They demanded access to education, the right to vote, and greater economic opportunity, pointing out the economic and political costs of denying full rights to all citizens. Their success depended on effective political organization and on forging alliances with sympathetic white politicians. Black intellectuals also struggled to overturn racist stereotypes. In Brazil, Argentina, and Cuba, as in the United States, political and literary magazines celebrating black cultural achievements became powerful

Women's Rights Convention
An 1848 gathering of women angered by their exclusion from an international anti-slavery meeting. They met at Seneca Falls, New York, to discuss women's rights.

---

[7]Sarah Grimké, "Reply to the Massachusetts Clergy," in *Early American Women: A Documentary History, 1600–1900*, ed. Nancy Woloch (Belmont, CA: Wadsworth, 1992), 343.

weapons in the struggle against racial discrimination. While men and women of African descent continued to experience prejudice and discrimination everywhere in the Americas, successful men and women of mixed descent in Latin America confronted fewer obstacles to advancement than did similar groups in the United States.

25-3e Development and Underdevelopment

While the Atlantic economy experienced three periods of severe economic contraction during the nineteenth century, nearly all the nations of the Western Hemisphere were richer in 1900 than in 1800. The effects of the Industrial Revolution, worldwide population growth, and an increasingly integrated world market combined to stimulate economic expansion (see Environment & Technology: Industrializing Sugar Agriculture in Cuba). Wheat, corn, wool, meats, and nonprecious minerals joined the region's earlier exports of silver, sugar, dyes, coffee, and cotton. The United States was the only Western Hemisphere nation to industrialize, but nearly every government in the hemisphere promoted new industries and technologies. Governments invested in roads, railroads, canals, and telegraph systems to better serve distant markets, while adopting tariff and monetary policies to foster economic diversification and growth. Despite these efforts, by 1900 only three Western Hemisphere nations—the United States, Canada, and Argentina—achieved individual income levels similar to those of western Europe. All three nations had open land, temperate climates, diverse resources, and large inflows of immigrants.

New demands for copper, zinc, lead, coal, and tin unleashed by the Industrial Revolution led to mining booms in the western United States, Mexico, Bolivia, and Chile. The mining companies of the late nineteenth century were heavily capitalized international corporations that could bully governments and buy political favors. By 1900 European and North American corporations owned nearly all the largest mining enterprises in Latin America. Petroleum development, which occurred at the end of the century in Mexico and elsewhere, followed this pattern as well (see the discussion of the Mexican economy during the Díaz dictatorship in Chapter 26).

New technology accelerated economic integration, but the high cost of this technology often increased dependence on foreign capital. Many governments promoted railroads by granting tax benefits, free land, and monopoly rights to both domestic and foreign investors. As a result, by 1890 vast areas of the Great Plains in the United States, the Canadian prairie, the Argentine pampas, and parts of northern Mexico were producing grain and livestock for foreign markets opened by the development of railroads. Steamships also lowered the cost of transportation to distant markets, while the telegraph stimulated expansion by speeding information about the demand for and availability of products.

The simultaneous acquisition of several new technologies could have a dramatic effect on a nation's economy. In Argentina, for example, the railroad, the telegraph, barbed wire, and refrigeration were all introduced in the 1870s and 1880s. Although Argentina had had abundant livestock herds since the colonial period, the distance from Europe's markets prevented Argentine cattle raisers from exporting fresh meat or live animals. Technology overcame these obstacles. The combination of railroads and the telegraph lowered freight costs and improved information about distant markets, steamships shortened the time needed for transatlantic crossings, and refrigerated ships and railcars made it possible to sell meat in distant markets. As land values rose and livestock breeding improved in Argentina, ranchers protected new investments with barbed wire, the first inexpensive fencing available on the nearly treeless plains.

▲ **Lebanon Iron Foundry, Lebanon, Pennsylvania** Modern iron furnace established near iron and coal deposits in 1847. This foundry and many others were connected to regional markets by a turnpike and to the port of Philadelphia and the world beyond by the Union Canal (pictured in foreground) and eventually by railroad. Each of its three furnaces produced about 6 to 8 tons of pig iron per day. This foundry and its neighbors helped make America the world's major producer of iron and steel by the end of the century. Courtesy of Lyman Johnson

Environment & Technology
Industrializing Sugar Agriculture in Cuba

Sugar played a key role in the development of the Western Hemisphere, with the profits of sugar plantations rivalling the vast wealth in silver and gold extracted from Spain's colonial empire. The expansion of sugar agriculture from Brazil to the Caribbean after 1650 was the major driving force in the African slave trade until its effective end in the 1850s. The fact that 70 percent of all African slaves brought to the Americas were distributed to sugar-producing regions is one measure of sugar's influence in the hemisphere. When most of Haiti's sugar plantations were destroyed by revolutionary violence (see Chapter 23), world sugar prices shot upward in the early nineteenth century. Cuban planters jumped into the vacuum, importing tens of thousands of slaves and opening new lands to sugar production. Within two decades, Cuba had become the world's largest sugar producer.

Cuba's sugar industry soon confronted two challenges to its ascendency. Having already ended the slave trade to its own sugar islands in 1807, Great Britain pushed Spain to end the slave trade to Cuba, ultimately using its navy to reduce imports to a trickle. Almost simultaneously, new technologies were introduced in Europe that permitted the profitable extraction of sugar from beets, rather than sugar cane. As a result, labor became more expensive for Cuban planters at the same time that sugar prices fell internationally as global production soared. To remain profitable, the Cuban sugar industry embraced technological innovations that had earlier revolutionized manufacturing.

Planters with the largest estates and the largest numbers of slaves had always enjoyed a competitive advantage over smaller producers because they could afford the most efficient crushing and refining technologies, benefiting from what economists call economies of scale (see Chapter 19). With European beet sugar production driving prices lower, Cuba's large-scale producers displaced their less efficient competitors while at the same opening virgin land to sugar production. Between 1878 and 1900 alone, more than 1.4 million acres of forest were cut down to expand sugar production. As lower prices increased competition and as the volume of sugar production soared in Cuba, the number of sugar producers steadily decreased as the largest estates bought up the smallest, a pattern that neither a destructive revolution (1868–1878) nor the abolition of slavery (1886) could alter.

Concentration was also promoted by the high cost of mechanization. The most heavily capitalized producers imported steam engines to replace the animal traction and water power previously used to crush cane. They also introduced new, more efficient refining technologies. As crushing and refining capacities expanded in these modernized mills, called *centrales* in Spanish, small-scale producers using older technologies were forced to close their expensive and inefficient mills to concentrate on growing sugar cane. Railroad construction multiplied the effects of these innovations, tying distant sugar growers to the mechanized refiners, many of them foreign owned. As had happened in English textile manufacturing during the Industrial Revolution (see Chapter 22), technological innovation in Cuba's sugar industry had concentrated the control of production and wealth in the hands of a new elite. The centrales were truly factories in the fields. As Cuba neared independence in the 1890s, the island's modernized sugar sector consisted of a relatively small number of industrialized refiners and a mass of increasingly vulnerable and dependent cane farmers.

Questions for Analysis

1. What were the two chief threats to the Cuban sugar industry in the last decades of the nineteenth century?

2. What new technologies were introduced to improve the profits of the sugar refineries?

3. Why did the large-scale sugar refiners enjoy a competitive advantage relative to smaller producers?

◀ **Cuban Sugar Refinery Showing Mix of Traditional and Modern Technologies** Sugar cane was delivered to the crushing mill by both ox carts and railroad lines. In the background, steam-driven machinery moves cane to a crusher. Library of Congress

MAP 25.4 **The Expansion of the United States, 1850–1920** The settlement of western territories and their admission as states depended on migration, the exploitation of natural resources, and important new technologies like railroads and telegraphs that facilitated economic and political integration.

Does the density and location of railroad mileage in 1870 and 1920 reflect current population distributions in the United States?

development In the nineteenth and twentieth centuries, the economic process that led to industrialization, urbanization, the rise of a large and prosperous middle class, and heavy investment in education.

underdevelopment The condition experienced by economies that depend on colonial forms of production such as the export of raw materials and plantation crops with low wages and low investment in education.

Growing interdependence and increased competition produced deep structural differences among Western Hemisphere economies by 1900. Two distinct economic tracks became visible. One led to industrialization and prosperity: **development**. The other continued colonial dependence on exporting raw materials and on low-wage industries: **underdevelopment**. By 1900 prosperity was greater and economic development more diversified in English-speaking North America than in the nations of Latin America. With a temperate climate, vast fertile prairies, and an influx of European immigrants, Argentina was the only Latin American nation to approach the prosperity of the United States and Canada in 1900.

Changes in the performance of international markets helped determine the trajectory of Western Hemisphere economies as new nations promoted economic development. At the time that the United States gained independence, the world economy enjoyed rapid growth. With a large merchant fleet, a diversified economy that included some manufacturing, and adequate banking and insurance services, the United States benefited from this expansion. Rapid population growth due in large measure to immigration, high levels of individual wealth, widespread landownership, and relatively high literacy rates also fostered rapid economic development. By 1865 the United States had already established the world's largest railroad network; between then and 1915 railroad mileage multiplied elevenfold (see Map 25.4). Steel production grew rapidly as well, with the United States overtaking world leaders Britain and Germany in the 1890s.

Canada's achievement of greater political autonomy, the Confederation of 1867, coincided with a second period of global economic expansion. Canada also benefited from a special trading relationship with Britain, the world's preeminent industrial nation, and from a rising tide of immigrants after 1850. Nevertheless, some regions within each of these prosperous North American nations—Canada's Maritime Provinces and the southern states of the United States—demonstrated the same patterns of underdevelopment found in Latin America, including greater poverty and low levels of educational attainment.

In contrast, most Latin American nations gained independence in the 1820s when the global economy severely contracted. In the colonial period, Spain and Portugal had promoted the production of agricultural and mining exports in their colonies. After independence these exports faced increased competition. Although these sectors experienced periods of great prosperity in the nineteenth century, they also faced stiff competition and falling prices as new regions began production or competing products captured markets.

The history of the Latin American economies, subject to periodic problems of oversupply and low prices, was one of boom and bust. Many Latin American governments sought to promote exports in the face of increased competition and falling prices by resisting union activity and demands for higher wages and by opening domestic markets to foreign manufactures. The resulting low wages and an abundance of foreign manufactured goods, in turn, undermined efforts to promote domestic industrialization in Latin America.

Weak governments, political instability, and, in some cases, civil war also slowed Latin American economic development. Because Latin America was also dependent on importing foreign capital and technology, Great Britain and, by the end of the century, the United States often imposed unfavorable trade conditions or even intervened militarily to protect their investments. The combined impact of these domestic and international impediments to development became clear when Mexico, Chile, and Argentina failed to achieve high levels of domestic investment in manufacturing late in the nineteenth century, despite a rapid accumulation of wealth derived from traditional exports.

25-3f Altered Environments

Population growth, economic expansion, new technologies, and the introduction of foreign plants and animals dramatically altered American environments in the nineteenth century. Cuba's planters cut down the island's forests in the early nineteenth century to expand sugar production. Growing demand for meat led ranchers to expand livestock-raising into fragile environments in Argentina, Uruguay, southern Brazil, and the southwestern United States later in the century. Other forms of commercial agriculture also threatened the environment. Farmers in South Carolina and Georgia gained a short-term increase in cotton production by abandoning crop rotation after 1870, but this practice quickly led to soil exhaustion and erosion. Similarly, coffee planters in Brazil exhausted soil fertility with a destructive cycle of overplanting followed by expansion onto forest reserves cleared by cutting and burning. The transfers of land from public to private ownership in order to promote livestock-raising and agriculture also altered landscapes. Finally, new technologies had environmental effects. For example, the use of steel plows on North American prairies and Argentine pampas eliminated many native grasses and increased soil erosion.

Rapid urbanization also imposed environmental costs. New York, Chicago, Rio de Janeiro, Buenos Aires, and Mexico City were among the world's fastest-growing cities in the nineteenth century, and governments strained to provide sewers, clean water, and garbage disposal. Timber companies clear-cut large areas of Michigan, Wisconsin, and the Appalachian Mountains in the United States to provide lumber for railroad ties and housing, pulp for paper, and fuel for locomotives and foundries. At the same time, the forest industries of British Honduras (now Belize), Nicaragua, and Guatemala grew rapidly in response to demand in Europe and North America for tropical hardwoods like mahogany. As forests throughout the hemisphere were cleared, animal habitats and native plant species disappeared.

The scale of mining in Nevada, Montana, and California accelerated erosion and pollution. Similar results occurred in other mining areas as well. Nitrate mining and open-pit copper mining in Chile scarred and polluted the environment. The state of Minas Gerais (**ME-nas JER-aize**) in Brazil experienced a series of mining booms that began with gold

AP® Exam Tip
Consider the environmental changes brought about by migrations and the development of industry.

Section Review

- Following independence, American nations eventually abolished the slave trade and slavery.

- After the abolition of slavery, a rush of immigrants from Europe and Asia diversified American nations, though most immigrants faced prejudice.

- The long struggle to achieve women's rights and end racial and ethnic discrimination altered the Western Hemisphere's political culture.

- Although most Western Hemisphere nations were richer in 1900 than in 1800, only Argentina among Latin American nations could match the levels of average wealth found in the United States and Canada; nations and regions dependent on exporting raw materials remained underdeveloped.

- Increased logging, grazing, and mining ruined vast areas of the hemisphere, but minor conservation efforts were under way by the end of the nineteenth century.

in the late seventeenth century and continued with iron ore in the nineteenth. By the end of the nineteenth century, its red soil had been ripped open, its forests were depleted, and erosion was uncontrolled. Similar devastation afflicted parts of Bolivia and Mexico.

By the end of the nineteenth century, small-scale conservation efforts were under way in many nations, and the first national parks and nature reserves were created. In the United States large areas remained undeveloped. In 1872 Yellowstone in Wyoming became the first national park. President Theodore Roosevelt (1901–1909) and naturalist John Muir played major roles in preserving large areas of the western states. Canada created its first national park in Banff in 1885 and expanded it from 10 to 260 square miles (26 to 673 square kilometers) two years later. When confronted with a choice between economic growth and environmental protection, however, the hemisphere's nations embraced growth.

25-4 Conclusion

While the new nations of the Western Hemisphere faced similar challenges in the nineteenth century, they had developed from different colonial traditions. The effort to establish stable constitutional systems proved difficult nearly everywhere. While the constitution of the United States implemented in 1789 endured, conflict over slavery led to the hemisphere's most destructive civil war, threatening the nation's survival. Elsewhere most new constitutions failed within a generation. In Argentina, for example, fifty years passed from the declaration of independence before a stable national government was in place. In many nations, personalist political leaders with large followings, like José Antonio Páez and Andrew Jackson, resisted the constraints of constitutions. Regionalism, ideological confrontations, racial divisions, and conflict with native peoples all threatened political stability as well.

New nations also faced foreign interventions and local wars with regional powers. By 1850 Mexico had lost 50 percent of its territory to the United States and then faced a French invasion in 1862. Bolivia and Peru lost territory to an expansive Chile, while Paraguay lost a disastrous war to an alliance of Argentina, Brazil, and Uruguay. American nations also fought numerous wars with indigenous peoples, finally overwhelming most Amerindian resistance by the 1890s.

The nations of the hemisphere also experienced a series of dramatic social and economic changes in this period. The slave trade and slavery persisted long after independence (see Chapter 19), but after a century of protest and political mobilization, the hemisphere's last slave state, Brazil, freed its slaves in 1888. Slavery left a legacy of racism and discrimination across the Americas. In places where the institution was most important—the plantation regions of Brazil, the Caribbean, and the American South—racial prejudice, discrimination, and persistent low levels of investment in education and internal improvements slowed economic growth and weakened democracy. By 1890 many of the hemisphere's poorest nations or poorest regions within nations were those that had depended on slavery in the colonial and early-national era.

Amerindian populations experienced centuries of exploitation, forced integration in market economies, and compulsory removal to marginal lands. In most of Latin America, Amerindians had been subjected to exploitation for centuries when the Spanish and Portuguese empires finally fell. Once in place, forced labor and other abuses persisted into the twentieth century in nations like Guatemala and Bolivia. With independence, new national governments undertook the pacification of the hemisphere's remaining independent native peoples. By the 1890s nearly all were reduced to reservations or forced onto marginal lands. As a result, Amerindians were, and remain, among the poorest peoples in the hemisphere, suffering oppression, poverty, and disenfranchisement.

Immigration transformed many Western Hemisphere nations. As a general rule, the millions of European immigrants that entered the Western Hemisphere in the nineteenth century avoided regions where slavery dominated or where indigenous populations were compelled to labor. Argentina, Brazil, Canada, and the United States were the most popular destinations, and immigrants to Brazil and the United States avoided the former plantation zones. Instead, hundreds of thousands of Chinese and East Indians, migrating as indentured laborers, were directed to plantation regions, especially in the Caribbean, where they faced racism and discrimination.

Industrialization had a transforming effect on the hemisphere. Wealth, political power, and population were increasingly concentrated in urban areas, and bankers and manufacturers, rather than farmers and plantation owners, increasingly directed national destinies. Industrialization altered the natural environment in dramatic ways. Modern factories consumed huge amounts of raw materials and energy. Copper mines in Chile and Mexico, Cuban sugar plantations, Brazilian coffee plantations, and Canadian lumber companies all left their mark on the natural environment, and all had ties to markets in the United States.

In 1900 nearly every American nation was wealthier, better educated, more democratic, and more populous than at independence. But most of these new nations were also more vulnerable to distant economic forces and more profoundly split between haves and have-nots. The hemisphere was also more clearly divided into a rich north and a poorer south. A small number of nations located in the temperate regions—Canada, the United States, Argentina, and Chile—had become prosperous regional powers relative to their neighbors. While most of the hemisphere's growth continued to depend on the export of agricultural goods and raw materials—sugar, cotton, grains, minerals, and livestock products—the United States had become one of the world's richest industrial nations by 1890.

Key Terms

Simón Bolívar p. 637	**personalist leaders** p. 642	**Caste War** p. 650	**development** p. 658
Miguel Hidalgo y Costilla p. 639	**Andrew Jackson** p. 643	**abolitionists** p. 650	**underdevelopment** p. 658
José María Morelos p. 639	**José Antonio Páez** p. 644	**acculturation** p. 654	
Confederation of 1867 p. 641	**Benito Juárez** p. 647	**Women's Rights Convention** p. 655	
	Tecumseh p. 648		

Review Questions

1. How did the different colonial experiences of Western Hemisphere nations influence their political and economic pathways after independence?

2. How did differences in climate and the natural environment affect the nations of the Western Hemisphere?

3. How did slavery and free immigration affect the Western Hemisphere?

 MindTap® is a fully online, personalized learning experience built upon Cengage Learning content. MindTap® combines student learning tools–readings, multimedia, activities, and assessments–into a singular Learning Path that guides students through the course and helps students develop the critical thinking, analysis, and communication skills that are essential to academic and professional success.

Material Culture
Cotton Clothing

Of all the things that bring us comfort, nothing compares to cotton. For clothes, sheets, and towels, it is the world's favorite textile. And no wonder: cotton is cool next to the skin, can be dyed in bright colors, absorbs moisture, and, unlike other fabrics such as wool, can be washed easily.

The use of cotton for clothing has a long history dating back to 3000 BCE, when it was grown in the Indus River Valley. Originally, the cotton plant was grown and the cloth woven only in India, Mexico, Peru, and a few other places in the tropics. The Maya wove fine textiles from cotton and traded them with other parts of Mesoamerica, while in the Andes region, cotton was commonly mixed with llama wool in textiles. Indian cottons were particularly fine and exported as luxury items to distant markets like China and Rome. Cotton replaced hemp clothing in China in the time of the Mongols and was used extensively

for turbans, pants, and other items of clothing. The Arabs spread cotton growing and weaving to the Middle East and Spain. By the tenth century, it was a major crop in Iran and elsewhere in the region. Many of our names for particular kinds of cotton fabric come from cities in India, like *calico* (from Calicut) or *madras*, or the Middle East, like *damask* (from Damascus) or *muslin* (from Mosul in Iraq).

Around 800 CE, Arab merchants brought cotton cloth to Europe, where it became as precious as silk. Five centuries later Italy developed its own cotton industry. Because of this textile's enormous popularity and high cost, cotton yarn and cloth were the first items to be mass-produced in the Industrial Revolution, with important consequences for India, the American South, and other countries. With the invention of machines like the spinning jenny and the water frame in Britain in the eighteenth

▲ **British Factory Printing Calico Cloth**   In the eighteenth century, calico cloth manufactured in India on hand looms and then printed using wood block enjoyed wide popularity in Asia, Europe and the Americas. By the middle of the nineteenth century British inventors introduced steam-driven machinery that wove and printed high-quality calicos at much lower cost than the traditionally produced Indian competition. Using this price advantage British producers drove Indian cloth from most markets. In this illustration from 1830 we see a British industrial mill producing printed calico cloth.   Calico printing machines powered by belt and shafting through cog wheels from a central energy source (steam or water). Hand-coloured engraving, London, 1834./ UNIVERSAL IMAGES GROUP/Bridgeman Images

century (see Chapter 22), the price of cotton cloth and cotton garments fell dramatically and their markets grew rapidly, expanding across the globe.

Mass production means mass consumption. In the nineteenth century, for the first time, the poor could afford to wear bright, colorful clothes and—even more important—to wash them. Wealthy European families hired seamstresses and tailors who came to the house, took measurements, and returned a few days later with finished clothes. Poorer women sewed clothes for themselves and their families.

Sewing by hand was time-consuming and increasingly costly compared to the declining price of cloth. By the mid-nineteenth century, prosperity and a faster pace of life in Europe and America provided an incentive for inventors to devise a machine that could sew. In 1850, Isaac Singer manufactured the first practical machine for commercial use. A few years later, he designed the "Singer Family Sewing Machine" with an iron stand and a foot-treadle for home use. By 1891 Singer alone had manufactured 10 million machines in the United States and Europe. Some were industrial machines sold to makers of ready-to-wear clothes in the new garment districts. Others were home models, some inexpensive enough for the working class. There were even portable models that seamstresses could take with them to their clients' homes.

The combination of cotton cloth and sewing machines revolutionized clothing. A shirt that took fourteen and a half hours to sew by hand could be made in an hour and a quarter on a machine; an apron could be made in nine minutes instead of an hour and a half. This greater efficiency meant lower prices. Now the poor could afford to own several shirts, skirts, or pants, even underwear. Better-off homemakers subscribed to fashion magazines, bought patterns, and made blouses and dresses, even complicated items like crinolines and hoopskirts, which would once have been too tedious to sew by hand.

Today, the world uses more cotton than any other fiber. China is the largest producer (and consumer) of cotton, followed by the United States, India, and Pakistan. Almost all of the cotton clothing now sold is produced on powerful computerized machines in the developing countries of Asia and Latin America.

Questions for Analysis

1. What advantages did cotton cloth enjoy relative to other natural fabrics?
2. What effect did the Industrial Revolution have on the availability and price of cotton textiles?
3. Why did the sewing machine become so popular so quickly?

Issues in World History
State Power, the Census, and the Question of Identity

Between the American Revolution and the last decades of the nineteenth century, Europe and the Americas were transformed. The ancient power of kings and the authority of religion were eclipsed by muscular new ways of organizing political, economic, and intellectual life. The Western world was vastly different in 1890 than it had been a century earlier. One of the less heralded but enduringly significant changes was the huge expansion of government statistical services.

The rise of the nation-state was associated with the development of modern bureaucratic departments that depended on reliable statistics to measure the nation's achievements and discover its failures. The nation-state, whether democratic or not, mobilized resources on a previously unimaginable scale. Modern states were more powerful and wealthier, and they were also more ambitious and more intrusive in the lives of their citizens. The growth of their power can be seen in the modernization of militaries, the commitment to internal improvements such as railroads, and the growth in state revenues. In recent years, historians have begun to examine a less visible but equally important manifestation of growing state power: census taking.

Governments and religious authorities have counted people since early times. Our best estimates of the Amerindian population of the Western Hemisphere in 1500 rest almost entirely on what were little more than missionaries' guesses about the numbers of people they baptized. Spanish and Portuguese kings were eager to count native populations, since "indios" (adult male Amerindians) were subject to special labor obligations and tribute payments. So, from the mid-sixteenth century onward, imperial officials conducted regular censuses of Amerindians, adapting practices already in place in Europe.

The effort to measure and categorize populations was transformed in the last decades of the eighteenth century when the nature of European governments began to change. The Enlightenment belief that the scientific method could be applied to human society proved to be attractive both to political radicals, like the French revolutionaries, and to reforming monarchs like Maria Theresa of Austria. Enlightenment philosophers had argued that a science of government could remove the inefficiencies and irrationalities that had long subverted the human potential for prosperity and happiness. The French intellectual Condorcet wrote in 1782:

Those sciences, created almost in our own days, the object of which is man himself, the direct goal of which is the happiness of man, will enjoy a progress no less sure than that of the physical sciences . . . . In meditating on the nature of the moral sciences [what we now call the social sciences], one cannot help seeing that, as they are based like the physical sciences on the observation of fact, they must follow the method, acquire a language equally exact and precise, attaining the same degree of certainty.[1]

As confidence in this new "science" grew, the term previously used to describe the development of categories and the collection of numbers concerning society, *political arithmetic*, was abandoned by governments and practitioners in favor of *statistics*, a term that clearly suggests its close ties to the "state." In the nineteenth century the new objectives set out by Condorcet and others led to both the formal university training of statisticians and the creation of government statistical services.

The ambitions of governments in this new era were great. Nation-states self-consciously sought to transform society, sponsoring economic development, education, and improvements in health and welfare. They depended on statistics to measure the effectiveness of their policies and, as a result, were interested in nearly everything. They counted taverns, urban buildings, births and deaths, as well as arrests and convictions. They also counted their populations with a thoroughness never before seen. As statistical reporting became more uniform across Europe and the Americas, governments could measure not only their own progress but also that of their neighbors and rivals.

The revolutionary governments of France modernized the census practices of the overthrown monarchy. They spent much more money, hired many more census takers, and devoted much more energy to training the staff that designed censuses and analyzed results. Great Britain set up an official census in 1801, but it established a special administrative structure only in the 1830s. In the Western Hemisphere nearly every independent nation provided for "scientific" censuses. In the United States the federal constitution required that a census be taken every ten years. Latin American nations, often torn by civil war in the nineteenth century, took censuses less regularly, but even the poorest nations took censuses when they could. It was as if the census itself confirmed the existence of the government, demonstrating its modernity and seriousness.

---

[1]Quoted in James C. Scott, *Seeing like a State. How Certain Schemes to Improve the Human Condition Have Failed* (New Haven, CT: Yale University Press, 1998), 91.

Until recently, historians who relied on these documents in their research on economic performance, issues of race and ethnicity, family life, and fertility and mortality asked few questions about the politics of census design. What could be more objective than rows of numbers? But the advocates of statistics who managed census taking were uninhibited in advertising the usefulness of reliable numbers to the governments that employed them. At the 1860 International Statistical Congress held in London, one speaker said, "I think the true meaning to be attached to 'statistics' is not every collection of figures, but figures collected with the sole purpose of applying the principles deduced from them to questions of importance to the state."[2] The desire to be useful meant that statistics could not be fully objective.

Subjectivity was an unavoidable problem with censuses. Censuses identified citizens and foreign residents by place of residence, sex, age, and family relationships within households as well as profession and literacy. These determinations were sometimes subjective. Modern scholars have demonstrated that census takers also routinely undercounted the poor and those living in rural areas.

Because census takers, as agents of nation-states, were determined to be useful, they were necessarily concerned with issues of nationality and, in the Americas, with race because these characteristics commonly determined political rights and citizenship. The assessment and recording of nationality and race would prove to be among the most politically dubious objectives of the new social sciences.

Nationality had not been a central question for traditional monarchies. For the emerging nation-state, however, nationality was central. A nation's strength was assumed to depend in large measure on the growth of its population, a standard that, once articulated, suggested that the growth of minority populations was potentially dangerous to the state. Who was French? Who was Austrian or Hungarian? European statisticians relied on both *language of use* and *mother tongue* as proxies for *nationality*, the first term being flexible enough to recognize the assimilation of minorities, the second suggesting a more permanent identity based on a person's original language. Both terms forced bilingual populations to simplify their more complex identities. Ethnic minorities, once identified, were sometimes subject to discrimination such as exclusion from military careers or from universities. In parts of Spanish America, *language* was used as a proxy for *race*. Those who spoke Spanish were citizens in the full sense, even if they were indistinguishable from Amerindians in appearance. Those who spoke indigenous languages were "indios" and therefore subject to special taxes and labor obligations and effectively denied the right to vote.

Beyond providing a justification for continuing discrimination, census categories compressed and distorted the complexity and variety of human society to fit the preconceptions of bureaucrats and politicians. Large percentages of the residents of Mexico, Peru, and Bolivia, among other parts of the Americas, were descended from both Europeans and Amerindians and, in the Caribbean region, from Europeans and Africans. Census categories never adequately captured the complexities of these biological and cultural mixtures. We now know that the poor were often identified as "indios" or "blacks" and the better-off were often called something else—"Americanos," "criollos" (creoles), or even whites. Since this process flattened and streamlined the complexities of identity, censuses on their own are not reliable guides to the distribution of ethnicity and race in a population.

In Europe the issue of nationality proved similarly perplexing for census takers and similarly dangerous to those identified as minorities. Linguistic and ethnic minorities had always lived among the politically dominant majorities: Jewish and Polish minorities in areas controlled by German speakers, German speakers among the French, and Serbo-Croatian speakers among Hungarians, for example. The frontiers between these minority populations and their neighbors were always porous and complex. Sexual unions and marriages were common, and two or more generations of a family often lived together in the same household, with the elder members speaking one language and the younger members another. Who was what? In a very real sense, nationality, like race in the Americas, was ultimately fixed by the census process, as the nation-state forced a limited array of politically utilitarian categories onto the rich diversity of ethnicity and culture.

Questions for Analysis

1. Why did governments want to count their populations?
2. What were the problems associated with assessing race and nationality?
3. How did the biases of government officials and census takers influence this process?

[2]This discussion relies heavily on Eliza Johnson (now Ablovatski), "Counting and Categorizing: The Hungarian Gypsy Census of 1893" (M.A. thesis, Columbia University, 1996), especially Chapter III. She quotes from the *Proceedings of the Sixth International Statistical Congress Held in London*, 1860, 379.

Multiple-Choice Questions

Questions 1–3 refer to the passage below.

"[F]or the first time I saw the Negro population under circumstances so striking to a stranger. The whole labour of bearing and moving burdens is performed by these people, and the state in which they appear is revolting to humanity. Here were a number of beings entirely naked, with the exception of a covering of dirty rags tied about their waists. Their skins, from constant exposure to the weather, had become hard, crusty, and seamed, resembling the coarse black covering of some beast, or like that of an elephant, a wrinkled hide scattered with scanty hairs. On contemplating their persons, you saw them with a physical organization resembling beings of a grade below the rank of man. . . . Some of these beings were yoked to drays, on which they dragged heavy burdens. Some were chained by the necks and legs, and moved with loads thus encumbered."

Robert Walsh, British clergyman, *Notices of Brazil in 1828 and 1829*

1. Based on the passage above, which of the following is Walsh describing?

   (A) The large-scale use of slavery in the Americas by European powers

   (B) Traditional slavery in the African interior

   (C) European adoption of Amerindian coercive labor systems

   (D) Impressment of African sailors by European navies

2. The Brazilian Independence movement of 1822, that put Pedro I in power, differed from other independence movements in the Americas in what way?

   (A) It failed to gain any level of independence from Portugal

   (B) It was led by slaves who claimed royal blood for themselves

   (C) It put a member of the ruling family in charge of the newly independent nation

   (D) It was a military coup that was supported by both laborers and the elites

3. Which of the following best describes the way slavery abolition was accomplished in Brazil?

   (A) A slave revolt was led by former slaves who had slowly bought their way to freedom using wages from their work.

   (B) A treaty with England caused public outcry and was one of the causes of the King's overthrow.

   (C) Massive popular support for abolition led to a threat to the King's throne, so he reluctantly agreed to end the slave trade.

   (D) Religious pressure from the Catholic Church and threats of excommunication for all citizens led to political action ending the slave trade.

Questions 4–6 refer to the image below.

▲ Painting of Simón Bolívar and George Washington with Liberty. The caption reads, "Tribute to the two liberators of the New World, Dedicated to the people of America." Mary Evans/The Image Works

4. The relationship between Simón Bolívar and George Washington depicted in the image best illustrates which of the following?

   (A) Both men were celebrated for their religious convictions.

   (B) Both men rejected all class distinctions.

   (C) Elites in the Americas were members of European noble families.

   (D) Latin American nationalists were inspired by the American Revolution.

5. Which of the following best describes the inspiration for both Revolutions referenced in this painting?

   (A) Imperialistic aspirations of new American nation-states

   (B) The Enlightenment

   (C) The Industrial Revolution

   (D) The rise of religious fundamentalism

6. The depictions of Washington and Bolívar in the painting provide evidence of which of the following movements from the time period?

   (A) Marxism's emphasis on economic and political equality

   (B) Growing tensions between the colonies of North and South America

   (C) Social Darwinism's belief that some peoples are inferior to others

   (D) New nationalist identities

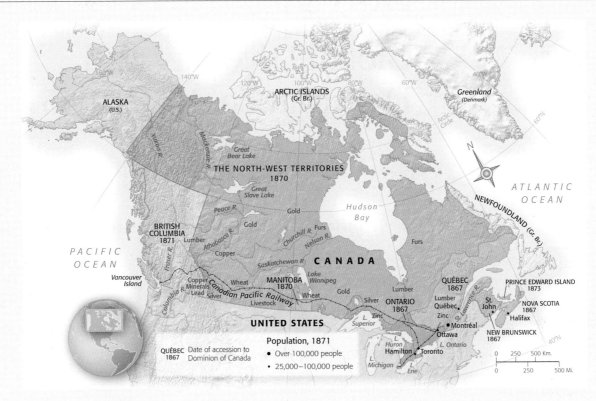

▲ Dominion of Canada, 1873

Questions 7–10 refer to the map above.

7. Based on the map, which of the following most likely encouraged Canadian benefit from the resources displayed on the map?

   (A) Technology allowing individuals to completely master the harsh climate

   (B) Establishment of factories in the Northwest Territories

   (C) Establishment of the Canadian Pacific Railway for transport

   (D) Steamships' ability to plow through ice caps and access Hudson Bay

8. Which of the following is the best explanation for the pattern of development found on the map?

   (A) Development was motivated by military activity.

   (B) Development followed preexisting population centers.

   (C) Development attempted to avoid interference with the United States.

   (D) Development followed natural resources.

9. The relationship between Canada and Great Britain is evidence of which of the following historical patterns from 1750 to 1900?

   (A) Imperial powers used a variety of methods to control and extract resources from their colonial possessions.

   (B) Enlightenment ideals were used to justify economic expansion.

   (C) The influence of nationalist ideals continued to spread to new regions.

   (D) Expansion was fueled by the desire to create a socialist society for workers.

10. Which of the following is the best explanation for the lack of development in the northern portions of Canada?

   (A) Conflicts with the United States and Russia

   (B) Lack of natural resources

   (C) Excessive urban centers

   (D) Environmental obstacles

Short-Answer Questions

1. Answer all parts of the question that follows.

   (A) Identify ONE reason slavery was more important in the Americas compared to Europe until the nineteenth century.

   (B) Explain ONE cause for the end of slavery in many colonies in the Americas by 1900.

   (C) Explain ANOTHER reason for the end of slavery in many colonies in the Americas by 1900.

2. Answer all parts of the question that follows.

   (A) Identify ONE aspect of native people's lives that stayed the same as nation-states developed in the Americas.

   (B) Explain ONE reaction native peoples had to nation-states in the Americas.

   (C) Explain ONE long-term effect government policies had on native peoples in the Americas.

PART VII

Global Diversity and Dominance, 1750–1945

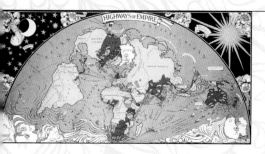

▲ Highways of the Empire
In the late nineteenth century, Europeans believed the world revolved around their subcontinent. World maps printed in Great Britain showed the British Empire in red, with informal dependencies and protectorates in pink. This map, a polar projection with Britain in the exact center, shows the major shipping routes and submarine telegraph cable lines that made London the center of global commerce and finance and ensured the supremacy of the Royal Navy around the world. V&A Images, London/Art Resource, NY

AP® is a trademark registered by the College Board, which is not affiliated with, and does not endorse, this product.

Throughout the early years of the twentieth century, European, U.S., and Japanese colonialism expanded, dividing up the globe through a combination of state-appointed administrations and military involvement built on earlier patterns of business investment. These tensions led to growing conflicts including The Great War and the Russian and Chinese revolutions.

Following the Great War, the capitalist nations of Europe descended into a financial depression, which eventually spread worldwide, while the Soviet Union forced industrialization at breakneck speed. In Germany and Japan, extremists rose to power using military might to solve their countries' grievances. As World War II loomed, India and Latin American nations pushed for independence.

In addition to countless deaths and massive destruction, World War II brought an end to many overseas empires. In the years following the war, India gained its independence from the British Empire, Mao Zedong led the Chinese communists to victory, and Latin American nations challenged foreign involvement. Of all the once great powers, only the United States and the Soviet Union remained to compete for global dominance. ●

Environment	Culture	State Building	Economics	Social Structures
• Impact of environmental factors on the development of diverse technologies, industrialization, transportation methods, and exchange and communication networks	• Origins, beliefs, development, economic/social/political impact, and spread of major religions, philosophies, and belief systems (Imperialism, Social Darwinism, nationalism)	• Changes and continuities of the creation and maintenance of forms, functions, and institutions of governance (Meiji Japan, total wars, communism)	• Causes/effects of economic strategies of different types of communities, states, and empires	• Impact of ideologies, philosophies, and religions on social hierarchies (Anarchism, utopian socialism)
• Interaction between environment and development of technology, industrialization, transportation, and exchange/communication networks	• Effect of technological and scientific innovation on religions, belief systems, philosophies, and ideologies over time (Nationalism)	• Impact of economic, social, cultural, and geographical factors on state building, expansion, and dissolution (Imperialism, Social Darwinism, nationalism)	• Development and change of modes and locations of production over time (Imperialism, fascism)	• Challenges and confirmations of legal systems, colonialism, nationalism, and independence movements on class, gender, and racial hierarchies over time (Anti-imperial resistance, nationalism, anticolonial movements, suffrage)
	• Reflection and impact of society in the arts (Propaganda)	• Impact of internal/external political factors on state building, expansion, and dissolution (Latin American revolutions)	• Causes/effects of labor reform movements	• Maintenance or challenge to social categories, roles and practices (Social Darwinism, feminism)
		• Interaction between states and state-less societies	• Influence of trade on development of ideologies, values, and institutions on each other (Socialism, Marxism, classical liberalism, Social Darwinism, capitalism)	• Impact of political, economic, cultural, and demographic factors on social structures (Independence movements, nationalism)
		• Political/economic interaction between states and non-state actors (Imperialism)		

Key Concept 5.1

- How did a need for raw materials and new markets encourage global trade and a global economy?
- How did the global economy's fluctuations lead to a variety of social, political, and economic results?

Key Concept 5.2

- How did imperialism, especially the growth of transoceanic empires, influence state formation and contraction?
- How were racial ideologies (such as Social Darwinism) used to facilitate and justify imperialism?

Key Concept 5.3

- How did nationalism develop, and how was it useful to government structures and to the creation of new states?
- How did the same ideas that led to rebellion and revolution also lead to growing solidarities across nations?

Key Concept 5.4

- What are the long-term effects of increasingly diverse societies?

Key Concept 6.1

- How did disease and technological developments lead to demographic shifts?

Key Concept 6.2

- How did worldwide conflicts reflect the evolving changes in global power structures?
- How did nationalism and anti-imperialism contribute to the dissolution of empires and restructuring of states?

Key Concept 6.3

- How did different states/nations respond to the social and economic challenges of the twentieth century?

26 Varieties of Imperialism in Africa, India, Southeast Asia, and Latin America, 1750–1914

AP® Framework Terms

Nationalism
Mexican Revolution
Settler colonies
Economic imperialism (neocolonialism)
Anti-imperial resistance

Overarching Questions

1 How have environmental factors shaped the development of diverse technologies, industrialization, transportation methods, and exchange and communication networks? (ENV)

2 How and why have economic, social, cultural, and geographic factors influenced the process of state building, expansion, and dissolution? (SB)

3 How have local, regional, and global economic systems and exchange networks influenced each other over time? (ECON)

4 How have economic systems and the development of ideologies, values, and institutions influenced each other? (ECON)

5 To what extent have legal systems, colonialism, nationalism, and independence movements sustained or challenged class, gender, and racial hierarchies over time? (SOC)

Like many regions that looked to be coherent countries on the maps drawn by imperialism, Algeria was not a unified realm in 1830 when France landed 35,000 troops outside of Algiers. Five days later, at a cost of 6,000 dead and wounded Frenchmen, the *dey* (ruler) of Algiers, an autonomous governor ruling under Ottoman suzerainty, surrendered the city. French nationalists called the invasion a defense of French honor because three years earlier the dey had struck a French diplomat with a fly whisk during an argument over debts lingering from the Napoleonic wars, which had ended more than a decade earlier. Actually the invasion plan had been drawn up in 1808 as part of Napoleon's long-range planning, and in response to businessmen in southern France who sought to acquire new land in North Africa.

The French invasion did not prevent the king of Morocco from claiming dominion over western Algeria, nor did it please the country's five major Sufi brotherhoods, which had earlier staged revolts against Ottoman imperialism. The brotherhood that would prove the hardest for the French to defeat was the Qadiriya, which waged a sixteen-year *jihad* (holy war) that only ended in 1847 with the surrender of its leader Abd al-Qadir.

▲ **Indian Railroad Station, 1866** British India built the largest network of railroads in Asia. People of every social class traveled by train.
An Indian Railway Station, 1854 (engraving) (b/w photo), English School (19th century)/The Illustrated London News Picture Library, London, UK/The Bridgeman Art Library

Abd al-Qadir **(AHB-dahl-KAH-deer)** was only twenty-five when he succeeded his father as head of the brotherhood, but he had spent three years traveling in the Middle East, making the pilgrimage to Mecca, getting to know Qadiriya leaders elsewhere, and studying at famous schools in Tunis and Cairo. He had also observed Muhammad Ali's efforts to build a modern army and industrial economy in Egypt.

Abd al-Qadir relied on an effective network of religious centers (*zawiyas*) that trained judges and administrators and disseminated his vision of an egalitarian society that would observe Islamic law but be dominated by neither Ottoman officials nor French generals. Other Sufi brotherhoods fought separately against the French, but not as successfully.

The French permitted Abd al-Qadir to settle in Damascus after his defeat and pursue a career as an eminent leader of the Muslim community. But his historical image among Arabs is primarily one of resistance to imperialism. Like movements elsewhere opposing imperialist aggression, Abd al-Qadir's Sufi followers could not defeat European firepower. In the long run, however, stories of resistance laid the ideological, if sometimes semilegendary, groundwork for anticolonial movements that would achieve success after World War II.

Defenders of imperialism often cite the benefits of European rule in terms of railroad construction, orderly governance, integration of local production with international trade, and similar economic and administrative factors. But the reputations of leaders like Abd al-Qadir would eventually eclipse the memory of the generals and administrators who oversaw the massive increase in European imperialism starting in the late eighteenth century. ●

26-1 Changes and Exchanges in Africa

How did different African leaders and peoples interact with each other, and how did European nations' relationship to African peoples change during this period?

In the century before 1870, Africa saw dynamic political change and a great expansion of foreign trade. Though some indigenous leaders resisted European imperialism, maps of Africa became increasingly tinted with pink and green, the conventional colors of British and French colonies, respectively. On the economic plane, as the slave trade died under British pressure, trade in other goods grew sharply. Africans produced commodities of use to European industry and consumed large quantities of machine-made textiles and, for those rulers who retained a measure of independence, European firearms.

Zulu A people of modern South Africa whom King Shaka united in 1818.

Afrikaners South Africans descended from Dutch and French settlers of the seventeenth century. Their Great Trek founded new settler colonies in the nineteenth century. Though a minority among South Africans, they held political power after 1910, imposing a system of racial segregation called *apartheid* after 1949.

26-1a Southern Africa

For many centuries the Nguni **(ng-GOO-nee)** peoples had farmed and raised cattle in the fertile coast-lands of southeastern Africa. Faced by drought at the beginning of the nineteenth century, an upstart military leader named Shaka (r. 1818–1828) created the **Zulu** kingdom. Strict military drill and close-combat tactics featuring ox-hide shields and lethal stabbing spears made the Zulu the most powerful and most feared fighters in southern Africa.

Shaka's kingdom expanded by raiding its neighbors, seizing their cattle, and capturing their women and children. Breakaway military bands spread this system of warfare and state building inland to the high plateau country as far north as Lake Victoria (see Map 26.1). As the power and population of these new kingdoms increased, so too did the number of displaced and demoralized refugees around them.

For protection from the Zulu, some neighboring Africans created their own states. The Swazi kingdom consolidated north of the Zulu, and the kingdom of Lesotho **(luh-SOO-too)** grew by attracting refugees to strongholds in southern Africa's highest mountains. Both Lesotho and Swaziland survive as independent states to this day.

Although Shaka ruled for little more than a decade, he left behind a mythic identity as well as a new kingdom. His achievements, however, conflicted with southern Africa's attractiveness to European settlers. The Cape Colony, a Dutch possession that came under British rule after 1806, flourished because of Cape Town's strategic importance as a supply station for ships making the long voyages between Europe and India. With the port city came some 20,000 descendants of Dutch and French settlers who occupied farms and ranches in its hinterland. Despite their European origins, these people thought of themselves as permanent residents of Africa and were beginning to refer to themselves as **Afrikaners (af-rih-KAHN-uhr)**. British governors prohibited extension of the white settler frontier because land grabs invariably led to wars with indigenous Africans. This decision, along with the imposition of laws protecting African rights within Cape Colony (including the emancipation of slaves in 1834), alienated many Afrikaners.

Between 1836 and 1839 parties of Afrikaners embarked on a "Great Trek," leaving British-ruled Cape Colony for the fertile high *veld* (plateau) to the north, region depopulated by two decades of Zulu warfare. The Great Trek laid the foundation for three new settler

▲ **Zulu in Battle Dress, 1838** Elaborate costumes helped impress opponents with the Zulus' strength. Shown here are long-handled spears and thick leather shields. British Library Board/Robana/Art Resource, NY

CHRONOLOGY

	Slavery	Africa	India and Southeast Asia	Latin America
1750			1756 Black Hole of Calcutta 1765 East India Company (EIC) rule of Bengal begins	
1800	1807 Britain outlaws slave trade	1808 Britain takes over Sierra Leone 1809 Sokoto Caliphate founded 1818 Shaka founds Zulu kingdom 1821 Foundation of Liberia	1818 EIC creates Bombay Presidency 1826 EIC annexes Assam and northern Burma 1828 Brahmo Samaj founded	
	1834 Britain frees slaves in its colonies; indentured labor migrations begin 1848 France abolishes slaves in its colonies	1831–1847 Algerians resist French takeover 1836–1839 Afrikaners' Great Trek 1840 Omani sultan moves capital to Zanzibar		
1850	1867 End of Atlantic slave trade	1869 Jaja founds Opobo	1857–1858 Sepoy Rebellion leads to end of EIC rule and Mughal rule 1877 Queen Victoria becomes Empress of India 1885 Indian National Congress formed 1898 Spanish-American War; U.S. takes over Philippines	1876–1910 Porfirio Díaz, dictator of Mexico 1898 Spanish-American War. U.S. takes over Cuba
1900		1899–1902 Boer War 1900s Railroads connect ports to the interior		1910 Mexican Revolution begins 1917 New constitution proclaimed in Mexico

colonies: the Afrikaners' Orange Free State and Transvaal on the high veld and the British colony of Natal on the Indian Ocean coast. Although firearms enabled the settlers to win some important battles against the Zulu and other Africans, they remained a tiny minority surrounded by populous and powerful African kingdoms.

Phenomenal deposits of diamonds, gold, and copper, as along with coal and iron ore, added to the appeal of good pasture and farmland. The discovery of diamonds at Kimberley in 1868 lured thousands of European prospectors as well as Africans looking for work. Great Britain annexed the diamond area in 1871, angering the Afrikaners. Once in the interior, the British defeated the Xhosa (**KOH-sah**) people in 1877 and 1878. Then in 1879 they confronted the militarily powerful Zulu.

The Zulu king Cetshwayo (**set-SHWAH-yo**) resented encirclement by Afrikaners and British, and their proud military tradition led them into a war with the British in 1879. The British lost at Isandhlwana (**ee-sawn-dull-WAH-nuh**), but a few months later the Zulu were in turn defeated. Cetshwayo was sent into exile, and Zulu lands were given to white ranchers.

The already tense relations between the British and the Afrikaners took a turn for the worse when gold was discovered in the Afrikaner republic of Transvaal (**trans-VAHL**) in 1886. Through the gold rush that ensued, the British soon outnumbered the Afrikaners.

Britain's imperial designs in southern Africa were driven in part by the ambition of **Cecil Rhodes** (1853–1902), who once declared that he would "annex the stars" if he could. Rhodes made his fortune in the Kimberley diamond fields and founded De Beers Consolidated, a company

AP® Exam Tip
Understand how global demand for raw goods and precious minerals led to the development of mining centers in Africa and the Americas.

AP® Exam Tip
Be aware that anti-imperial resistance took many forms, including direct resistance within empires (such as the Zulu Uprising) and the creation of new states on the peripheries.

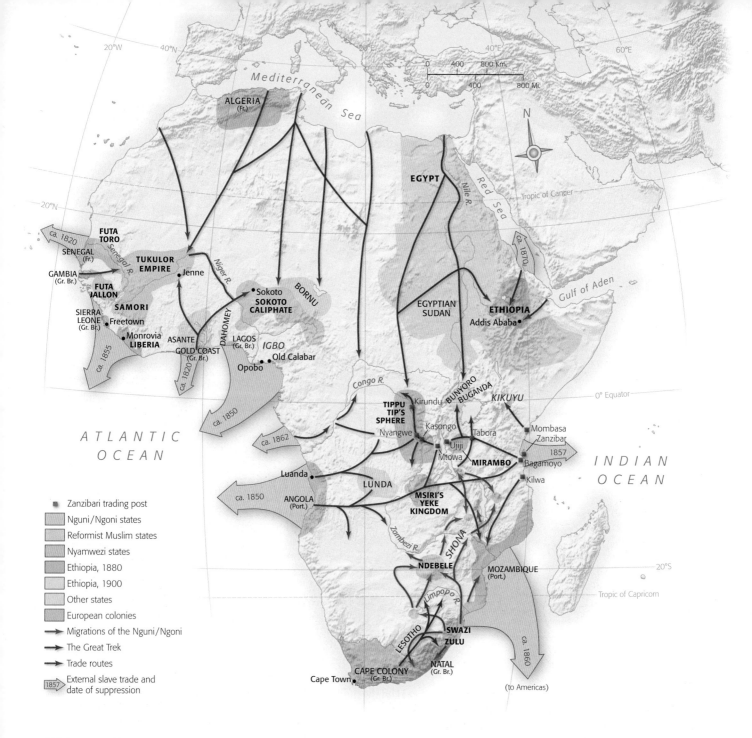

MAP 26.1 Africa in the Nineteenth Century Expanding trade drew much of Africa into global networks, but foreign colonies in 1870 were largely confined to Algeria and southern Africa. Growing trade, Islamic reform movements, and other internal forces created important new states throughout the continent.

What is the geographical relationship between slave exporting regions and resistance to European imperialism?

Cecil Rhodes British entrepreneur and politician involved in the expansion of the British Empire from South Africa into Central Africa. The colonies of Southern Rhodesia (now Zimbabwe) and Northern Rhodesia (now Zambia) were named after him.

that has dominated the world's diamond trade ever since. He then turned to politics. He encouraged the British South Africa Company to push north into Central Africa, where he named two new colonies after himself: Southern Rhodesia (now Zimbabwe) and Northern Rhodesia (now Zambia). The Ndebele (**en-duh-BELL-ay**) and Shona peoples, who inhabited the region, resisted, but the machine guns of the British finally defeated them (see Diversity & Dominance: Two Africans Recall the Arrival of the Europeans).

The inflow of English-speaking whites into the goldfields and diamond mines and British attempts to annex the two Afrikaner (also called Boer) republics, Transvaal and Orange Free State, led to the South African or Boer War, which lasted from 1899 to 1902. At first the Afrikaners had the upper hand. They were highly motivated, possessed modern rifles, and knew the land.

In 1901, however, Great Britain brought in 450,000 troops to crush the Afrikaner armies. Ironically, the Afrikaners' defeat in 1902 led ultimately to victory. Wary of costly commitments overseas, the British expected European settlers in Africa to manage their own affairs, as they were doing in Canada, Australia, and New Zealand. Thus, in 1910 the European settlers created the Union of South Africa, in which the Afrikaners emerged as the dominating element.

Unlike Canada, Australia, and New Zealand, South Africa had a majority of indigenous inhabitants and substantial numbers of Indians and "Cape Coloureds" (people of mixed ancestry). Yet the Europeans were both numerous enough to demand self-rule and powerful enough to deny the vote and other civil rights to the majority. In 1913 the South African parliament passed the Natives Land Act, assigning Africans to reservations and forbidding them to own land elsewhere. This and other racial policies turned South Africa into a land of segregation and oppression.

26-1b West and Equatorial Africa

While Shaka was building his Zulu kingdom, Islamic reform movements were creating another cluster of powerful states in the savannas of West Africa. Islam had long been a force in the politics and cities of this region, but most Muslim rulers had tolerated the older religious practices of their subjects. In the 1770s, however, Muslim scholars began preaching the need to reform Islamic practices. They condemned the accommodations Muslim rulers had made with older traditions and called for a forcible conquest of rural "pagans." Their jihad added new lands where governments enforced Islamic laws and promoted the religion's spread.

The largest of the new Muslim reform movements occurred in the Hausa (**HOW-suh**) states (in northern Nigeria) under the leadership of Usuman dan Fodio (**OO-soo-mahn dahn FOH-dee-oh**)(1745–1817). He charged that the Hausa kings, despite their official profession of Islam, were "undoubtedly unbelievers . . . because they practice polytheistic rituals and turn people away from the path of God." Muslims unhappy with their social or religious position spread the movement to other Hausa states. The successful armies united the conquered Hausa states and neighboring areas under a caliph who ruled from the city of Sokoto.

These new Muslim states became centers of Islamic learning and reform. Schools for training boys in Quranic subjects spread rapidly, and the great library at Sokoto attracted many scholars. Officials permitted non-Muslims within the empire to follow their religions in exchange for paying a special tax, but they suppressed dances and ceremonies associated with traditional religions. The **Sokoto Caliphate** (1809–1906) became the largest state in West Africa since the sixteenth century.

In coastal West Africa, however, the French, who had maintained a foothold in Senegal for centuries, envisioned building a railroad from the upper Senegal River to the upper Niger in order to open the interior to French merchants. This in turn led the French military to undertake the conquest of the interior. Sokoto remained independent, but after 1890 it was embattled both by

▲ **South African Diamond Mine** When diamonds were found in Kimberley, South Africa, in 1868, the discovery precipitated a rush of prospectors from Europe and America. As soon as surface deposits were exhausted, their claims were bought by large companies that could afford the heavy equipment needed to mine deep underground. By the early twentieth century, diamonds came from major industrial mines like the Premier Mine shown here. Gardiner F. Williams/National Geographic Creative

Sokoto Caliphate A large Muslim state founded in 1809 in what is now northern Nigeria.

We know a great deal about the arrival of the Europeans into the interior of Africa from the perspective of the conquerors, but very little about how the events were experienced by Africans. Here are two accounts by African women, one from northern Nigeria whose land was occupied by the British, the other from the Congo Free State, a colony of King Leopold II of Belgium. They show not only how Africans experienced European colonial dominance but also how diverse these African experiences were.

Baba of Karo, a Nigerian Woman, Remembers Her Childhood

When I was a maiden the Europeans first arrived. Ever since we were quite small the *malams* had been saying that the Europeans would come with a thing called a train, they would come with a thing called a motor-car, in them you would go and come back in a trice. They would stop wars, they would repair the world, they would stop oppression and lawlessness, we should live at peace with them. We used to go and sit quietly and listen to the prophecies.

I remember when a European came to Karo on a horse, and some of his foot soldiers went into the town. Everyone came out to look at them, but in Zerewa they didn't see the European. Everyone at Karo ran away—"There's a European, there's a European!"

At that time Yusufu was the king of Karo. He did not like the Europeans, he did not wish them, he would not sign their treaty. Then he say that perforce he would have to agree, so he did. We Habe wanted them to come, it was the Fulani who did not like it. When the Europeans came the Habe saw that if you worked for them they paid you for it, they didn't say, like the Fulani, "Commoner, give me this! Commoner, bring me that!" Yes, the Habe wanted them; they saw no harm in them.

The Europeans said that there were to be no more slaves; if someone said "Slave!" you could complain to the *alkali* who would punish the master who said it, the judge said, "That is what the Europeans have decreed."

The first order said that any slave, if he was younger than you, was your younger brother, if he was older than you was your elder brother—they were all brothers of their master's family. No one used the word "slave" any more. When slavery was stopped, nothing much happened at our *rinji* except that some slaves whom we had bought in the market ran away. Our own father went to his farm and worked, he and his son took up their large hoes; they loaned out their spare farms. Tsoho our father and Kadiri my brother with whom I live now and Babambo worked, they farmed guineacorn and millet and groundnuts and everything; before this they had supervised the slaves' work—now they did their own.

In the old days if the chief liked the look of your daughter he would take her and put her in his house; you could do nothing about it. Now they don't do that.

Ilanga, a Congolese Woman, Recounts Her Capture by Agents of the Congo Free State

. . . we were all busy in the fields hoeing our plantations, for it was the rainy season, and the weeds sprang quickly up, when a runner came to the village saying that a large band of men was coming, that they all wore red caps and blue cloth, and carried guns and long knives, and that many white men were with them, the chief of whom was *Kibalanga* (Michaux). Niendo at once called all the chief men to his house, while the drums were beaten to summon the people to the village. A long consultation was held, and finally we were all told to go quietly to the fields and bring in ground-nuts, plantains, and cassava for the warriors who were coming, and goats and fowl for the white men. The women all went with baskets and filled them, and put them in the road, which was blocked up, so many were there. Niendo then commanded everyone to go and sit quietly in the houses until he gave other orders. This we did, everyone remaining quietly seated while Niendo went up the road with the head men to meet the white

---

neighboring rulers and European encroachment. In 1906 the empire came to an end with France, Britain, and Germany gobbling up various portions.

Farther south, **King Leopold II** of Belgium, following the advice of an American journalist and explorer, **Henry Morton Stanley**, invested his personal fortune in "opening up"—that is, occupying—the Congo Basin, an enormous forested region in the heart of equatorial Africa. With Leopold's money, Stanley returned to Africa from 1879 to 1884 to establish trading posts along the southern bank of the Congo River. At the same time, **Savorgnan de Brazza**, an Italian officer serving in the French army, obtained from an African ruler living on the northern bank a treaty that placed the area under the "protection" of France.

King Leopold II King of Belgium (r. 1865–1909). He was active in encouraging the exploration of Central Africa and became the ruler of the Congo Free State (to 1908).

Henry Morton Stanley British American explorer of Africa, famous for his expeditions in search of Dr. David Livingstone. Stanley helped King Leopold II establish the Congo Free State.

26-1c The Berlin Conference

These events sparked a flurry of diplomatic activity. German chancellor Bismarck called the **Berlin Conference** on Africa of 1884 and 1885. There the major powers agreed that henceforth "effective occupation" would replace the former trading relations between Africans and

chief. We did not know what to think, for most of us feared that so many armed men coming boded evil; but Niendo thought that, by giving presents of much food, he would induce the strangers to pass on without harming us. And so it proved, for the soldiers took the baskets, and were then ordered by the white men to move off through the village. Many of the soldiers looked into the houses and shouted at us words we did not understand. We were glad when they were all gone, for we were much in fear of the white men and the strange warriors, who are known to all the people as being great fighters, bringing war wherever they go. . . .

When the white men and their warriors had gone, we went again to our work, and were hoping that they would not return; but this they did in a very short time. As before, we brought in great heaps of food; but this time *Kibalanga* did not move away directly, but camped near our village, and his soldiers came and stole all our fowl and goats and tore up our cassava; but we did not mind as long as they did not harm us. The next morning it was reported that the white men were going away; but soon after the sun rose over the hill, a large band of soldiers came into the village, and we all went into the houses and sat down. We were not long seated when the soldiers came rushing in shouting, and threatening Niendo with their guns. They rushed into the houses and dragged the people out. Three or four came to our house and caught hold of me, also my husband Oleka and my sister Katinga. We were dragged into the road, and were tied together with cords about our necks, so that we could not escape. We were all crying, for now we knew that we were to be taken away to be slaves. The soldiers beat us with the iron sticks from their guns, and compelled us to march to the camp of *Kibalanga*, who ordered the women to be tied up separately, ten to each cord, and the men in the same way. When we were all collected—and there were many from other villages whom we now saw, and many from Waniendo—the soldiers brought baskets of food for us to carry, in some of which was smoked human flesh (*niama na nitu*).

We then set off marching very quickly. My sister Katinga had her baby in her arms, and was not compelled

to carry a basket; but my husband Oleka was made to carry a goat. We marched until the afternoon, when we camped near a stream, where we were glad to drink, for we were much athirst. We had nothing to eat, for the soldiers would give us nothing, so we lay upon the ground, and at night went to sleep. The next day we continued the march, and when we camped at noon were given some maize and plantains, which were gathered near a village from which the people had run away. So it continued each day until the fifth day, when the soldiers took my sister's baby and threw it in the grass, leaving it to die, and made her carry some cooking pots which they found in the deserted village. On the sixth day we became very weak from lack of food and from constant marching and sleeping in the damp grass, and my husband, who marched behind us with the goat, could not stand up longer, and so he sat down beside the path and refused to walk more. The soldiers beat him, but still he refused to move. Then one of them struck him on the head with the end of his gun, and he fell upon the ground. One of the soldiers caught the goat, while two or three others stuck the long knives they put on the ends of their guns into my husband. I saw the blood spurt out, and then saw him no more, for we passed over the brow of a hill and he was out of sight. Many of the young men were killed the same way, and many babies thrown into the grass to die. A few escaped; but we were so well guarded that it was almost impossible.

AP® History Reasoning Skills

Continuity and Change Over Time *In what ways did the arrival of the Europeans change traditional African life? In what ways did traditional African life remain the same?*

Comparison *How do you explain the difference in views of the white men between these two accounts?*

Sources: From M. F. Smith, ed., *Baba of Karo: A Woman of the Muslim Hausa* (New York: Philosophical Library, 1955), 66–68. Edgar Canisius, *A Campaign Amongst Cannibals* (London: R. A. Everett & Co., 1903), 250–256.

Europeans. Every country with colonial ambitions had to send troops into Africa and participate in the division of the spoils. As a reward for triggering the "scramble" for Africa, Leopold II acquired a personal domain under the name *Congo Free State*, while France and Portugal took most of the rest of equatorial Africa. In this manner, the European powers and King Leopold managed to divide Africa among themselves, at least on paper.

Except in Kenya, Northern Rhodesia, and South Africa, where Europeans found the land and climate to their liking and forced Africans to become squatters, sharecroppers, or ranch hands on land they had farmed for generations, the colonial rulers declared any land that was not farmed to be "vacant" and gave it to private concession companies. In the Gold Coast (now Ghana), British trading companies bought the cocoa grown by African farmers at low prices and resold it for large profits. The interior of French West Africa lagged behind. Although the region could produce cotton, peanuts, and other crops, the difficulties of transportation limited its development before 1914.

Compared to West Africa, equatorial Africa had few inhabitants and little trade. Rather than try to govern these vast territories directly, authorities in the Congo Free State, the French

Savorgnan de Brazza Franco-Italian explorer sent by the French government to claim part of equatorial Africa for France. Founded Brazzaville, capital of the French Congo, in 1880.

Berlin Conference Conference that German chancellor Otto von Bismarck called to set rules for the partition of Africa. It led to the creation of the Congo Free State under King Leopold II of Belgium.

AP® Exam Tip
Consider ways the
Europeans used both
warfare and diplomacy
to extend their empires
in Africa.

Congo, and the Portuguese colonies of Angola and Mozambique awarded huge pieces of land to private concession companies, offering them monopolies on the natural resources and trade of their territories and the right to deploy soldiers and tax the inhabitants. Freed from outside supervision, the companies forced the African inhabitants at gunpoint to produce cash crops and carry them, on their heads or backs, to the nearest railroad or navigable river. The worst abuses took place in the Congo Free State, where a rubber boom made it profitable for private companies to brutalize Africans collecting latex from vines that grew in the forests. After 1906 the British press began publicizing the horrors. The public outcry that followed, coinciding with the end of the rubber boom, convinced the Belgian government to take over Leopold's private empire in 1908.

26-1d Modernization in Egypt and Ethiopia

While colonial states were arising elsewhere, in northeastern Africa Egypt and Ethiopia retained their independence and experimented with **modernization**. Muhammad Ali, who ruled Egypt from 1805 to 1849, began a series of reforms aimed at creating a modern Egypt (see Chapter 24). European pressure sharply curtailed these efforts after 1839, but by the end of his reign Egypt's population had nearly doubled; trade with Europe had expanded by almost 600 percent; and a new class of educated Egyptians was beginning to wield some influence.

Muhammad Ali's grandson Ismail (**is-mah-EEL**) (r. 1863–1879) focused on westernizing Egypt rather than confronting Europe militarily. "My country is no longer in Africa," Ismail declared, "it is in Europe."[1] His efforts increased the number of European advisers in Egypt, as well as Egypt's debts to French and British banks. In the first decade of his reign, revenues increased thirtyfold and exports doubled (largely because of a huge increase in cotton exports during the American Civil War). By 1870 Egypt had a network of new irrigation canals, 800 miles (1,300 kilometers) of railroads, a postal service, and a few dazzling modernization projects in the capital city of Cairo. It also had the **Suez Canal**, which opened in 1869 and immediately affected communications between Europe and Asia.

AP® Exam Tip
Consider ways
that developments
and innovations in
transportation and
communication (such as
railroads, steamships,
and canals) changed
the way goods
were produced and
consumed globally.

Ambitions like the canal and Ismail's dream of an Egyptian empire extending south into Sudan and Ethiopia cost vast sums of money, which the khedives borrowed from European creditors at high interest rates. When the market for Egyptian cotton collapsed after the American Civil War, these debts became a problem. By 1876 foreign debt had risen to £100 million sterling, and the interest payments alone consumed one-third of Egypt's foreign export earnings. To avoid bankruptcy the Egyptian government sold its shares in the Suez Canal to Great Britain and accepted four foreign "commissioners of the debt" to oversee its finances. French and British bankers, still not satisfied, lobbied their governments to secure the loans by stronger measures. In 1878 the two governments obliged Ismail to appoint a Frenchman as minister of public works and a Briton as minister of finance. When high taxes caused hardship and popular discontent, the French and British persuaded the Ottoman sultan to depose Ismail. This foreign intervention provoked a military uprising under Egyptian army colonel Arabi Pasha, which threatened the Suez Canal.

Fearing for their investments, the British sent an army into Egypt in 1882. So important was the Suez Canal to Britain's maritime supremacy that they stayed for seventy years. During those years the British ruled Egypt "indirectly"—that is, they maintained the Egyptian government and the fiction of Egyptian sovereignty but retained real power in their own hands.

Eager to develop Egyptian cotton production, the British brought in engineers and contractors to build the first dam across the Nile, at Aswan in Upper Egypt. When completed in 1902, it captured the annual Nile flood and released its waters throughout the year, allowing farmers to grow two, sometimes three, crops a year. The economic development of Egypt by the British enriched a small elite of landowners and merchants, many of them foreigners. Egyptian peasants got little relief from the heavy taxes collected to pay for their country's crushing foreign debt and the expenses of the British army of occupation. Most Egyptians found British rule more onerous than that of the Ottomans. By the 1890s Egyptian politicians and intellectuals were demanding that the British leave.

modernization The process of reforming political, military, economic, social, and cultural traditions in imitation of the early success of Western societies, usually with no regard for accommodating local traditions in non-Western societies.

Suez Canal Ship canal dug across the isthmus of Suez in Egypt, designed by Ferdinand de Lesseps. It opened to shipping in 1869 and shortened the sea voyage between Europe and Asia. Its strategic importance led to the British occupation of Egypt in 1882.

---

[1] Quoted in P. J. Vatikiotis, *The History of Modern Egypt: From Muhammad Ali to Mubarak*, 4th ed. (Baltimore: Johns Hopkins University Press, 1991), 74.

State building and reform were also under way in Christian Ethiopia. Beginning in the 1840s, Ethiopian rulers purchased modern weapons from European sources and created strong armies loyal to the ruler. Emperor Téwodros (tay-WOH-druhs) II (r. 1833–1868) also encouraged the manufacture of weapons locally. However, his efforts to coerce more technical aid by holding some British officials captive backfired when the British invaded instead. As the British forces advanced, Téwodros committed suicide to avoid being taken prisoner. Satisfied that their honor was avenged, the British withdrew. Téwodros's successor Yohannes (yoh-HAHN-nehs) IV (r. 1872–1889) continued to bring most highland regions under imperial rule. The only large part of ancient Ethiopia that remained outside Emperor Yohannes's rule was the independent Shoa kingdom, ruled by **Menelik II** (MEN-uh-lik) from 1865.

In 1889 Menelik II became emperor of Ethiopia, at a time when his country was threatened by Sudanese Muslims to the west and by France and Italy, which controlled the coast of the Red Sea to the east. As already stated, Ethiopia had been purchasing European and American weapons for many years. When Italians attempted to establish a protectorate over Ethiopia, they found the Ethiopians armed with thousands of rifles and even machine guns and artillery pieces. Although Italy sent 20,000 troops to attack Ethiopia, in 1896 they were defeated at Adowa (AH-do-ah) by a larger and better-trained Ethiopian army.

26-1e Transition from the Slave Trade

The successful slave revolt in Saint Domingue in the 1790s (see Chapter 23) ended slavery in the largest plantation colony in the West Indies. Elsewhere in the Americas, however, slave revolts were brutally repressed. As news of the slave revolts and their repression spread, humanitarians and religious reformers called for an end to the trade. Support for abolition of the trade was found even among Americans wanting to preserve slavery. In 1807 both Great Britain and the United States made importing slaves from Africa illegal for their citizens. Most other Western countries followed suit by 1850, but few enforced abolition with the vigor of the British.

Once the world's greatest slave traders, the British became the most aggressive abolitionists. Britain sent a naval patrol to enforce the ban along the African coast and negotiated treaties allowing the patrol to search other nations' vessels suspected of carrying slaves. Although British patrols captured 1,635 slave ships and liberated over 160,000 enslaved Africans, the trade proved difficult to stop. Cuba and Brazil continued to import huge numbers of slaves, which drove prices up and persuaded some African rulers and merchants to continue to sell slaves and to help foreign slavers evade the British patrols. Because the slave trade moved to other parts of Africa, the transatlantic slave trade did not end until 1867.

AP® Exam Tip
Understand the demographic impact of the slave trade, as well as the effects of its end. Also, consider various forms of coerced labor implemented to fuel the global industrial economy.

▲ Australian Penal Colony   Norfolk Island, a 14-square mile spot of land 877 miles east of the Australian mainland, served as a prison for British convicts deported to Australia from 1788 to 1855. Most prisoners were convicted of non-violent property offenses and on average served three-year terms.   Mary Evans Picture Library/Alamy Stock Photo

Menelik II Emperor of Ethiopia (r. 1889–1911). He enlarged Ethiopia to its present dimensions and defeated an Italian invasion at Adowa (1896).

In exchange for slaves, Africans purchased cloth, metals, and other goods. To continue those imports, Africans expanded their **"legitimate" trade** (exports other than slaves). As the Atlantic slave trade was shut down, they revived old exports or developed new ones. The most successful of the new exports from West Africa was palm oil, used by British manufacturers for soap, candles, and lubricants. Though still a major source of slaves until the mid-1830s, the trading states of the Niger Delta emerged as the premier exporters of palm oil. Coastal African traders bought the palm oil at inland markets and delivered it to European ships at the coast.

The dramatic increase in palm-oil exports—from a few hundred tons at the beginning of the century to tens of thousands of tons by midcentury—altered the social structure of the coastal trading communities. Wealthy coastal traders bought slaves to paddle the giant dugout canoes that transported palm oil from inland markets along the narrow delta creeks to the trading ports. Niger Delta slavery could be as harsh and brutal as slavery on New World plantations, but it offered some slaves a chance to gain wealth and power. Male slaves who supervised canoe fleets were well compensated, and a few even became wealthy enough to take over the leadership of coastal "canoe houses" (companies). The most famous, known as "Jaja" (ca. 1821–1891), rose from canoe slave to become the head of a major canoe house. In 1869, to escape discrimination by free-born Africans, he founded the new port of Opobo, which he ruled as king. In the 1870s Jaja of Opobo was the greatest palm-oil trader in the Niger Delta.

Another effect of the suppression of the slave trade was the spread of Western cultural influences in West Africa. To serve as a base for their anti-slave-trade naval squadron, the British had taken over the small colony of Sierra Leone (**see-AIR-uh lee-OWN**) in 1808. Over the next several years, 130,000 men, women, and children taken from "captured" vessels were liberated in Sierra Leone. Christian missionaries helped settle these **recaptives** in and around Freetown, the capital. Mission churches and schools made many converts among such men and women.

Sierra Leone's schools also produced a number of distinguished graduates. Samuel Adjai Crowther (1808–1891), freed from a slave ship in 1821, became the first Anglican bishop in West Africa in 1864, administering a pioneering diocese along the lower Niger River. James Africanus Horton (1835–1882), the son of slaves liberated in Sierra Leone, became a doctor and the author of many studies of West Africa.

Other Western cultural influences came from people of African birth or descent returning to their ancestral homeland. In 1821, free black Americans founded a settlement that grew into the Republic of Liberia, a place of liberty at a time when slavery was legal and flourishing in the United States. After their emancipation in 1865 other African Americans moved to Liberia. Emma White, a literate black woman from Kentucky, moved from Liberia to Opobo in 1875, where King Jaja employed her to write his commercial correspondence and run a school for his children. Edward Wilmot Blyden (1832–1912), born in the West Indies and proud of his West African parentage, emigrated to Liberia in 1851 and became a professor of Greek, Latin, and Arabic at the fledgling Liberia College.

"legitimate" trade Exports from Africa in the nineteenth century that did not include the newly outlawed slave trade.

recaptives Africans rescued by Britain's Royal Navy from the illegal slave trade of the nineteenth century and restored to free status.

Section Review

- In the south, Shaka established an expansive Zulu kingdom that eventually came in conflict with European settlers.

- Differences between the British and Dutch-descended Afrikaners led to the Boer War, ultimately leaving the defeated Afrikaners in control of a segregated country.

- In the west, Usuman dan Fodio conquered the former Hausa states and formed the Sokoto Caliphate.

- Though the Suez Canal conferred new economic and political importance on Egypt, debts to European bankers led to British occupation; only Ethiopia defeated its European aggressors.

- The abolition of slavery had political consequences and increased the trade of goods like palm oil.

26-1f Secondary Empire in Eastern Africa

When British patrols hampered the slave trade in West Africa, slavers moved to eastern Africa. There the Atlantic slave trade joined an existing trade in slaves to the Islamic world that also was expanding. Two-thirds of the 1.2 million slaves exported from eastern Africa in the nineteenth century went to markets in North Africa and the Middle East; the other third went to plantations in the Americas and to European-controlled Indian Ocean islands.

Slavery also became more prominent within eastern Africa itself. Between 1800 and 1873 Arab and Swahili (**swah-HEE-lee**) owners of clove plantations along the coast purchased some 700,000 slaves to do the hard work of harvesting the spice. The plantations were on Zanzibar Island and in neighboring territories belonging to the Sultanate of

Oman, an Arabian kingdom on the Persian Gulf that had been expanding its control over the East African coast since 1698. The sultan even moved his court to Zanzibar in 1840 to take advantage of the burgeoning trade in cloves. Zanzibar was also an important center of ivory and slave trading until British pressure induced the sultan to ban the export of slaves in 1857 and their import in 1873.

26-2 India Under British Rule

How did Britain secure its hold on India, and what colonial policies led to the beginnings of Indian nationalism?

The might of the Mughal Empire did not long outlast the reign of Aurangzeb, who died in 1707 (see Chapter 20). In 1739 Iranian invaders sacked Delhi and carried off vast amounts of booty. Indian states also took advantage of Mughal weakness to assert their independence. By midcentury, the Maratha (**muh-RAH-tuh**) Confederation, a coalition of states in central India, controlled more land than the Mughals did. Several **nawabs** (**NAH-wab**), a term used for Muslim princes who were nominally deputies of the Mughal emperor, carved out powerful states of their own.

Ambitious young "company men" employed by British, French, and Dutch trading companies used hard bargaining, and hard fighting when necessary, to persuade Indian rulers to allow them to establish coastal trading posts protected by Indian troops known as **sepoys** (**SEE-poy**). In divided India these private armies came to hold the balance of power.

26-2a East India Company

In 1691 Great Britain's East India Company (EIC) had persuaded the nawab of Bengal in northeast India to allow a company trading post at the fishing port of Calcutta. In 1756 a new nawab overran the post and imprisoned a group of EIC men in a cell so small that many died of suffocation. To avenge their deaths in this "Black Hole of Calcutta," a large EIC force from Madras, led by Robert Clive, overthrew the nawab. The weak Mughal emperor was persuaded to acknowledge the East India Company's right to rule Bengal in 1765. By 1788 Calcutta had grown into a city of 250,000.

Bombay was the third major center of British power in India. There, in 1818, the East India Company annexed large territories to form the core of what was called the "Bombay Presidency." This gave the East India Company an empire more populous than western Europe and with fifty times the population of the colonies the British had lost in North America. One goal of the **British raj** (regime) was to remake India on a British model through administrative and social reform, economic development, and the introduction of new technology. Yet the company men— like the Mughals before them—had to temper their interference with Indian social and religious customs lest they provoke rebellion or lose the support of their Indian princely allies.

Another British policy was to substitute private property for India's complex and overlapping patterns of landholding. In Bengal this reform worked to the advantage of large landowners, but in Mysore the peasantry gained. Private ownership made it easier for the state to collect the taxes that were needed to pay for administration, the army, and economic reform.

Such policies of "westernization, Anglicization, and modernization," as they have been called, were only one side of British rule. The other side was the bolstering of "traditions"—both real and newly invented. In the name of tradition, the Indian princes who ruled nearly half of British India were frequently endowed by their British overlords with greater power and splendor and longer tenure than their predecessors had ever had. Likewise, Hindu and Muslim holy men were able to expand their "traditional" power over property and people far beyond what had been the case in earlier times. At the same time, princes, holy men, and other Indians frequently used claims of tradition to resist British rule as well as to turn it to their advantage. The British rulers themselves invented many "traditions"—including elaborate parades and displays—half borrowed from European royal pomp, half from Mughal ceremonies.

The British and Indian elites worked sometimes in close partnership, sometimes in opposition, but always at the expense of the ordinary people of India. Women of every status, members of subordinate Hindu castes, the "untouchables" and "tribals" outside the caste system, and the

AP® Exam Tip
Understand the need for access to raw goods (such as cotton) as motivation for imperialism.

nawab A Muslim prince allied to British India; technically, a semi-autonomous deputy of the Mughal emperor.

sepoy An indigenous soldier in South Asia, especially in the service of the British.

British raj The rule over much of South Asia between 1765 and 1947 by the East India Company and then by a British government.

poor experienced few benefits from the British reforms and much new oppression from the taxes and "traditions" that exalted their superiors' status.

The transformation of British India's economy was also doubled-edged. On the one hand, the raj created many new jobs as a result of the growth of trade and expanded crop production, such as opium in Bengal, largely for export to China (see Chapter 24); coffee in Ceylon; and tea in Assam in northeastern India. On the other hand, competition from cheap cotton goods produced in Britain's industrial mills drove many Indians out of the handicraft textile industry. In the eighteenth century India had been the world's greatest exporter of cotton textiles; in the nineteenth century India increasingly shipped raw cotton to Britain.

During the first half of the nineteenth century, British rulers readily handled isolated local rebellions, but they were concerned about the loyalty of their Indian sepoys. The EIC employed 200,000 sepoys in 1857, along with 38,000 British troops. Armed with modern rifles and disciplined fighting methods, the sepoys had a potential for successful rebellion that other groups lacked.

In the early decades of EIC rule, most sepoys came from Bengal. The Bengali sepoys resented the active recruitment of other ethnic groups into the army after 1848, such as Sikhs (**sick**) from Punjab and Gurkhas from Nepal. In addition, many high-caste Hindus objected to an 1856 law requiring new recruits to be available for service overseas in the growing British empire. Hinduism prohibited ocean travel. Finally, the replacement of the standard military musket by the more accurate Enfield rifle in 1857 required soldiers to use their teeth to tear open the ammunition cartridges, which were greased with animal fat. Hindus were offended by this order if the fat came from cattle, which they considered sacred. Muslims were offended if the fat came from pigs, which they considered unclean.

Although the cartridge-opening procedure was quickly changed, the initial discontent grew into rebellion by Hindu sepoys in May 1857. British troubles mushroomed when Muslim sepoys, peasants, and discontented elites joined in. The rebellion was put down ten months later, but it shook the empire to its core.

Historians have attached different names and meanings to the events of 1857 and 1858. Nineteenth-century British historians labeled it the "**Sepoy Rebellion**" or "Mutiny." Seeing in these events the beginnings of the later movement for independence, some modern Indian historians have termed it the "Revolution of 1857."

26-2b **Political Reform and Industrial Impact**

Regardless of label, the events of 1857–1858 marked a turning point in the history of modern India. In their wake Indians gained a new centralized government, entered a period of rapid economic growth, and began to develop a national consciousness.

In 1858 Britain eliminated the last traces of both Mughal and Company rule. In their place, a new secretary of state for India in London oversaw Indian policy, and a new governor-general in Delhi acted as the British monarch's viceroy. In November 1858 Queen Victoria guaranteed all Indians equal protection of the law and the freedom to practice their religions and social customs; she also assured Indian princes that so long as they were loyal to the queen, British India would respect their control of territories and "their rights, dignity and honour."[2]

British rule continued to emphasize both tradition and reform after 1857. At the top, the British viceroys lived in enormous palaces amid hundreds of servants and gaudy displays of luxury meant to convince Indians that the British viceroys were legitimate successors to the Mughal emperors. They treated the quasi-independent Indian princes with elaborate ceremonial courtesy and maintained them in splendor. When Queen Victoria was proclaimed "Empress of India" in 1877 and periodically thereafter, the viceroys put on great pageants known as **durbars**. At the durbar in Delhi in 1902–1903 to celebrate the coronation of King Edward VII, Viceroy Lord Curzon honored himself with a 101-gun salute and a parade of 34,000 troops in front of 50 princes and 173,000 visitors.

Meanwhile, a powerful and efficient bureaucracy controlled India. Members of the elite **Indian Civil Service** (ICS) held the senior administrative and judicial posts. Numbering only a thousand at the end of the nineteenth century, these men visited the villages in their districts, heard lawsuits and complaints, and passed judgments.

Sepoy Rebellion The revolt of Indian soldiers in 1857 against certain practices that violated religious customs; also known as the *Sepoy Mutiny*.

durbar An elaborate display of political power and wealth in British India in the nineteenth century, ostensibly in imitation of the pageantry of the Mughal Empire.

Indian Civil Service The elite professional class of officials who administered the government of British India. Originally composed exclusively of well-educated British men, it gradually added qualified Indians.

---

[2] Quoted by Bernard S. Cohn, "Representing Authority in Victorian India", in *The Invention of Tradition*, eds. Eric Hobsbawm and Terence Ranger (Cambridge, UK: Cambridge University Press 1983), 165.

▲ **Delhi Durbar, January 1, 1903** The parade of Indian princes on ornately decorated elephants and accompanied by retainers fostered their sense of belonging to the vast empire of India that British rule had created. TopFoto/The Image Works

Recruitment into the ICS was by open examinations. In theory any British subject could take these exams; since they were given in England, however, in practice the system worked to exclude Indians. In 1870 only one Indian was a member of the ICS. Subsequent reforms led to fifty-seven Indian appointments by 1887, but there the process stalled. Working under the ICS were thousands of lesser Indian officials.

The reason qualified Indians were denied entry into the upper administration of their country was the racist contempt most British officials felt for the people they ruled. When he became commander-in-chief of the Indian army in 1892, Lord Kitchener declared:

> It is this consciousness of the inherent superiority of the European which had won for us India. However well educated and clever a native may be, and however brave he may have proved himself, I believe that no rank we can bestow on him would cause him to be considered an equal of the British officer.[3]

After 1857 the government invested millions of pounds sterling in harbors, cities, irrigation canals, and other public works. Forests were felled to make way for tea plantations. Indian farmers were persuaded to grow cotton and jute for export. Engineers built great irrigation systems to alleviate the famines that periodically decimated whole provinces. As a result, India's trade expanded rapidly.

Most of the exports were agricultural commodities: cotton fiber, opium, tea, silk, and sugar. In return India imported manufactured goods from Britain, including machine-made cotton textiles that undercut Indian hand-loom weavers. Some women found jobs at very low pay on

AP® Exam Tip
Compare British colonial processes in South Asia with British colonial processes in other areas of the world.

AP® Exam Tip
Understand the effects of the Industrial Revolution and the spread of capitalism's impact on regions outside of Europe and the United States.

---

[3] James Truslow, *Empire of the Seven Seas: The British Empire 1784–1939* (New York: Charles Scribner's Sons, 2007), 268.

plantations or in the growing cities, where prostitution flourished. Everywhere in India poverty remained the norm.

The Indian government also promoted the introduction of new technologies into India. Earlier in the century there were steamboats on the rivers and a massive program of canal building for irrigation. Beginning in the 1840s a railroad boom gave India its first national transportation network, followed by telegraph lines, and by 1870 India had the fifth largest rail network in the world. Originally designed to serve British commerce, the railroads were owned by British companies, constructed with British rails and equipment, and paid dividends to British investors. Ninety-nine percent of the railroad employees were Indians, but Europeans occupied all the top positions—"like a thin film of oil on top of a glass of water, resting upon but hardly mixing with [those] below," as one official report put it.

Although some Indians opposed the railroads at first because the trains mixed people of different castes, faiths, and sexes, the Indian people took to rail travel with great enthusiasm. Indians rode trains on business, on pilgrimage, and in search of work. In 1870 over 18 million passengers traveled along the network's 4,775 miles (7,685 kilometers) of track, and more than half a million messages were sent up and down the 14,000 miles (22,500 kilometers) of telegraph wires.

But the freer movement of Indian pilgrims and the flood of poor Indians into the cities also promoted the spread of cholera (**KAHL-uhr-uh**), a disease transmitted through water contaminated by human feces. Cholera deaths rose rapidly during the nineteenth century, and eventually the disease spread to Europe. In many Indian minds *kala mari* ("the black death") was a divine punishment for failing to prevent the British takeover. This chastisement also fell heavily on British residents, who died in large numbers. In 1867 officials demonstrated the close connection between cholera and pilgrims who bathed in and drank from sacred pools and rivers. The installation of a new sewerage system and a filtered water supply (1869) in Calcutta dramatically reduced cholera deaths there. Similar measures in Bombay and Madras also led to great reductions, but most Indians lived in small villages where famine and lack of sanitation kept cholera deaths high.

26-2c Indian Nationalism

AP® Exam Tip

The Indian National Congress is a good example of a nationalist movement outside of Europe.

After the failure of the rebellion of 1857 to overthrow British rule, some Indians argued that the only way for Indians to regain control of their destiny was to reduce their country's social and ethnic divisions and promote Pan-Indian nationalism.

Individuals such as Rammohun Roy (1772–1833) had promoted development along these lines a generation earlier. A Western-educated Bengali from a Brahmin family, Roy was a successful administrator for the East India Company and a student of comparative religion. His Brahmo Samaj (**BRAH-moh suh-MAHJ**) (Divine Society), founded in 1828, attracted Indians who sought to reconcile the values of the West with the religious traditions of India. They advocated reforming some Hindu customs, such as the caste system and child marriage, and urged a return to the founding principles of the *Upanishads*, ancient sacred writings of Hinduism. They also backed British efforts to ban practices they found repugnant.

Widow burning (*sati* [**suh-TEE**]) was outlawed in 1829 and slavery in 1843. Reformers sought to correct other abuses of women: prohibitions against widows remarrying were revoked in 1856, and female infanticide was made a crime in 1870.

Although Brahmo Samaj remained influential after the rebellion of 1857, many Indian intellectuals turned to Western secular values and nationalism as the way to reclaim India. In this process the spread of Western education played an important role, a process aided by European and American missionaries. Roy had studied both Indian and Western subjects and helped found the Hindu College in Calcutta in 1816. Other Western-curriculum schools quickly followed, including Bethune College in Calcutta, the first secular school for Indian women, in 1849. India's three universities were established in 1857. In 1870 there were over 24,000 elementary and secondary schools, whose graduates articulated a new Pan-Indian nationalism that transcended regional and religious differences.

Section Review

- Between 1757 and 1857, Britain gained nearly complete control of India.

- The British exploited local traditions and rulers and instituted a colonial government that conferred benefits on those Indians who governed on its behalf while most of the population lived in worsening conditions.

- The Sepoy Rebellion of 1857–1858 prompted reforms and substantial investments in railroads and other public works.

- In response to modernization, Indian nationalism arose in the educated middle class.

Many of the new nationalists came from the Indian middle class, which had prospered from the increase of trade and manufacturing. Educated people resented the obstacles that British rules and prejudices put in the way of their advancement. Hoping to increase their influence and improve their employment opportunities in the Indian government, they convened the first **Indian National Congress** in 1885. The members sought a larger role for Indians in the Civil Service. They also called for reductions in military expenditures, which consumed 40 percent of the government's budget, so that more could be spent on alleviating the poverty of the masses. But although the Indian National Congress promoted unity among the country's religions and social groups, most early members were upper-caste Western-educated Hindus and Parsis. Until it attracted the support of the masses, it could not hope to challenge British rule.

26-3 Southeast Asia and the Pacific

What were the social and cultural effects of imperialism in Asia and the Pacific?

Different parts of Southeast Asia and the Pacific region had differing histories, yet all came under intense imperialist pressure during the nineteenth century. Thomas Stamford Raffles had governed Java from 1811 to 1814, when the politics of Napoleon's wars in Europe allowed the English to displace the Dutch. After a peace treaty in Europe dictated Java's return to the Dutch, Raffles helped establish, in 1824, a new free port at Singapore on the site of a small Malay fishing village with a superb harbor (see Map 26.2). British merchants and Chinese businessmen and laborers soon made Singapore the paramount center of trade and shipping between the Indian Ocean and China. Along with Malacca and other possessions on the strait, Singapore formed the "Straits Settlements," which British India administered until 1867.

British expansion came more quickly in neighboring Burma, which had emerged as a powerful kingdom by 1750. In 1785 Burma tried to annex neighboring territories of Siam (now Thailand) to the east, but a coalition of Thai leaders thwarted Burmese advances by 1802. Burma next attacked Assam to the west, but this provoked a war with British India. After two years of fighting, India annexed Assam in 1826 and occupied two coastal provinces of northern Burma. As the rice and timber trade from these provinces grew important, the occupation became permanent, and in 1852 British India annexed the rest of coastal Burma. The last piece of the country was annexed in 1885, but Thailand remained an independent kingdom.

Indochina fell under French control piece by piece until it was finally subdued in 1895. Similarly, Malaya (now Malaysia) came under British rule in stages during the 1870s and 1880s. In northern Sumatra, however, a region that supplied half the world's production of black pepper, the Dutch fought a ferocious war between 1873 and 1913 against the rulers of Acheh. The Achehnese warriors were inspired, in part, by the mystique of an Islamic jihad, thus creating a tradition of resistance that would continue to resonate throughout the twentieth century.

26-3a Australia

In the once-remote South Pacific, British settlers displaced the indigenous populations of Australia and New Zealand, just as they had done in North America. Portuguese mariners had sighted Australia in the early seventeenth century, but it held little interest for Europeans. However, after English captain James Cook explored New Zealand and the eastern coast of Australia between 1769 and 1778, expanding shipping networks brought in a trickle of visitors and settlers.

When Cook visited, Australia had been the home of about 650,000 hunting-and-gathering people, whose Melanesian (**mel-uh-NEE-zhuhn**) ancestors had settled there some forty thousand years earlier. New Zealand was inhabited by about 250,000 Maori (**MOW-ree [ow as in "cow"]**), who practiced hunting, fishing, and simple forms of agriculture, which their Polynesian ancestors had introduced around 1200. Because of their long isolation from the rest of humanity, the populations of Australia and New Zealand were as vulnerable as the Amerindians had been to unfamiliar diseases introduced by new overseas contacts. By the 1890s, only 93,000 aboriginal Australians and 42,000 Maori survived, and British settler populations outnumbered and dominated the indigenous peoples.

Indian National Congress A movement and political party founded in 1885 to demand greater Indian participation in government. Its membership was middle class, and its demands were modest until World War I. Led after 1920 by Mohandas K. Gandhi, it appealed increasingly to the poor, and it organized mass protests demanding self-government and independence.

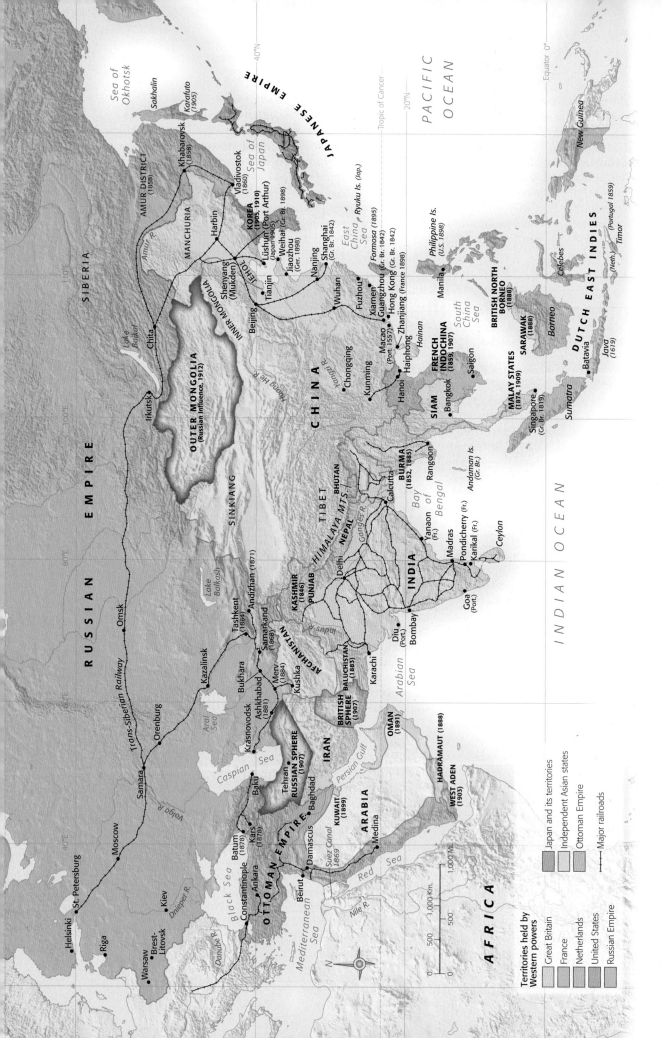

MAP 26.2 Asia in 1914 By 1914, much of Asia was claimed by colonial powers. The southern rim, from the Persian Gulf to the Pacific, was occupied by Great Britain, France, the Netherlands, and the United States. Central Asia had been incorporated into the Russian Empire.

How did the sea-lanes between India and Great Britain contribute to a British fear of Russian expansion?

The first permanent British settlers in Australia were 736 convicts, of whom 188 were women, sent into exile in 1788. Over the next few decades, Australian penal colonies grew slowly and had only slight contact with the indigenous population, whom the British called "Aborigines." However, the discovery of gold in 1851 brought a flood of free European settlers (and some Chinese) and hastened the end of the penal colonies. When the gold rush subsided, government subsidies enabled tens of thousands of British settlers to settle "down under." Though it still took more than three months to reach Australia from Britain, by 1860 Australia had a million immigrants, and the settler population doubled during the next fifteen years.

26-3b New Zealand

British settlers were drawn more slowly to New Zealand. Some of the first were temporary residents along the coast who slaughtered seals and exported pelts to Western countries to be made into men's felt hats. A single ship in 1806 took away 60,000 sealskins. By the early 1820s overhunting had nearly exterminated the seal population. Special ships also hunted sperm whales extensively near New Zealand for their oil, used for lubrication, soap, and lamps; ambergris (**AM-ber-grees**), an ingredient in perfume; and whalebone (actually baleen, feeding bristles made like fingernails of keratin), used as stays in women's corsets. A brief gold rush along with faster ships and subsidized passages attracted more British immigrants after 1860. The colony especially courted women immigrants to offset the preponderance of single men. By the early 1880s this most distant frontier of the British Empire had a settler population of 500,000. Britain encouraged the settlers in Australia and New Zealand to become self-governing, following the 1867 model that had formed the Dominion of Canada out of the diverse and thinly settled colonies of British North America. By gradually turning over governing power to the colonies' inhabitants, Britain satisfied the settlers' desire for greater control over their own territories, muted demands for independence, and made the colonial governments responsible for most of their own expenses.

North American patterns also shaped the indigenous peoples' fate. Aborigines lacked the rights of Australian citizens. The requirement that voters had to be able to read and write English kept Maori from voting in early New Zealand elections, but four seats in the lower house of the legislature were reserved for Maori from 1867 on.

26-3c Hawaii and the Philippines, 1878–1902

The United States was a latecomer in the race for colonial territories. However, by the 1890s it had a fast-growing population and industries that produced more manufactured goods than they could sell at home. This growth contributed to economic depressions in 1893 and 1896 and led merchants and bankers to look to China as an export market. Naval strategist Alfred T. Mahan (**mah-HAHN**) declared: "Whether they will or no, Americans must now begin to look outward. The growing production of the country requires it." Guam, Hawaii, and the Philippines being naval stations on the route to China, expansionist thinkers looked in that direction.

This was not the beginning of American interest in the Pacific. In 1878 the United States obtained the harbor of Pago Pago in Samoa as a coaling and naval station, and in 1887 it secured the use of Pearl Harbor in Hawaii for the same purpose. By 1898 the United States under President William McKinley (1897–1901) had become openly imperialistic and annexed Hawaii as a steppingstone to Asia. As the United States became ever more involved in Asian affairs, Hawaii's strategic location brought an inflow of U.S. military personnel, and its fertile land prompted planters to import laborers from Japan, China, and the Philippines. These immigrants soon outnumbered the native Hawaiians.

While large parts of Asia were falling under colonial domination, the people of the Philippines were chafing under their Spanish rulers. **Emilio Aguinaldo**, leader of a secret society, rose in revolt and proclaimed a republic in 1899. The revolutionaries had a good chance of winning independence, for Spain had its hands full with a revolution in Cuba. Unfortunately for Aguinaldo and his followers, the United States declared war on Spain in April 1898 and quickly overcame Spanish forces in the Philippines and Cuba. After the Spanish defeat, President McKinley realized that a weakened Spain might lose the islands to another imperialist power. Japan,

AP® Exam Tip

Explain the rise of new imperial powers in the Pacific, such as the United States and Japan, in conjunction with the decline of older powers such as Spain and Portugal.

Emilio Aguinaldo Leader of the Filipino independence movement against Spain (1895–1898). He proclaimed the independence of the Philippines in 1899, but his movement was crushed and he was captured by the United States Army in 1901.

◀ **American Troops in the Philippines** The Spanish-American War ended with the United States in control of the Philippines, a land that was already in the grip of an uprising against Spanish rule when the war erupted in Cuba. These soldiers are defending a position near Manila, but Americans continued fighting much longer against Muslim Moros seeking independence on the island of Mindanao to the south. Hulton Archive/Getty Images

Section Review

- Britain, France, and the Netherlands gained economic and political colonial control of Southeast Asia.

- Australia and New Zealand attracted British settlers, whose diseases decimated the native aboriginal and Maori populations.

- The growing economy of the United States led it to pursue economic interests in the Pacific, including Hawaii.

- After a brutal struggle, the Philippines became an American colony.

having recently defeated China in the Sino-Japanese War (1894–1895) and annexed Taiwan (see Chapter 27), was eager to expand its empire. So was Germany, which had taken over parts of New Guinea and Samoa and several Pacific archipelagoes during the 1880s. To forestall them, McKinley purchased the Philippines from Spain for $20 million.

The Filipinos were not eager to trade one master for another. For a while, Aguinaldo cooperated with the Americans in the hope of achieving full independence. When his plan was rejected, he rose up again in 1899 and proclaimed the independence of his country. In spite of protests by anti-imperialists in the United States, the U.S. government decided that its global interests outweighed the interests of the Filipino people. In rebel areas, a U.S. army of occupation tortured prisoners, burned villages and crops, and forced the inhabitants into "reconcentration camps." By the end of the insurrection in 1902, the war had cost the lives of 5,000 Americans and 200,000 Filipinos.

After the insurrection ended, the United States attempted to soften its rule with public works and economic development projects. New buildings went up in the city of Manila; roads, harbors, and railroads were built; and the Philippine economy was tied ever more closely to that of the United States. In 1907 Filipinos were allowed to elect representatives to a legislative assembly, but ultimate authority remained in the hands of a governor appointed by the president of the United States. In 1916 the Philippines were the first U.S. colony to be promised independence, a promise fulfilled only thirty years later.

26-4 Imperialism in Latin America

What were the economic motives behind imperialism in Latin America?

The United States played a lesser role than Britain and other European countries in the economic dominance that characterized imperialism in Central and South America, and business played a more important role than military intervention. But America's imperialist interest in the Philippines mirrored involvement with a Caribbean Spanish possession closer to home.

26-4a American Expansionism and the Spanish-American War, 1898

The United States had long had interests in Cuba, the closest and richest of the Caribbean islands and a Spanish colony. American businesses had invested great sums of money in Cuba's sugar and tobacco industries, and thousands of Cubans had migrated to the United States. In 1895 Cuban nationalist José Martí started a revolution against Spanish rule. American newspapers thrilled readers with lurid stories of Spanish atrocities; businessmen worried about their investments; and politicians demanded that the U.S. government help liberate Cuba.

On February 15, 1898, the U.S. battleship *Maine* accidentally blew up in Havana harbor, killing 266 American sailors. The U.S. government immediately blamed Spain and issued an ultimatum that the Spanish evacuate Cuba. Spain agreed to the ultimatum, but the American press and Congress were eager for war. President McKinley did not restrain them.

The **Spanish-American War** ended quickly. On May 1, 1898, U.S. warships destroyed the Spanish fleet at Manila in the Philippines. Two months later the United States Navy sank the Spanish Atlantic fleet off Santiago, Cuba. By mid-August Spain was suing for peace. U.S. Secretary of State John Hay called it "a splendid little war." The United States purchased the Philippines from Spain but took over Puerto Rico and Guam as war booty. The two islands remain American possessions to this day. Cuba became an independent republic, subject to interference by the United States.

26-4b Economic Imperialism

Latin America won independence from Spain and Portugal in the nineteenth century but did not industrialize. Most Latin American republics, suffering from ideological divisions, unstable governments, and violent upheavals, traded their commodities for foreign manufactured goods and investments and became economically dependent on Great Britain or other foreign countries. A traumatic social revolution and civil war shook Mexico, but even there the region-wide chasm between wealthy landowners and desperately poor peasants persisted.

Latin America's economic potential was huge, for the region could produce many agricultural and mineral products in demand in the industrial countries. What was needed was a means of opening the interior to development. Railroads seemed the perfect answer.

Foreign merchants and bankers along with Latin American landowners and politicians embraced the new technology. Starting in the 1870s, almost every country in Latin America acquired railroads, usually connecting mines or agricultural regions with the nearest port rather than linking up the different parts of the interior. All the equipment and building material came from Britain or the United States. So did the money to build the networks, the engineers who designed and maintained them, and the managers who ran them.

Argentina, a land of rich soil that produced wheat, beef, and hides, gained the longest and best-developed rail network south of the United States. By 1914, 86 per-cent of the railroads in Argentina were owned by British firms; 40 percent of the employees were British; and the official language of the railroads was not Spanish but English. The same was true of mining and industrial enterprises and public utilities throughout Latin America.

In some ways, these countries resembled India and Ireland, which also obtained rail networks in exchange for raw materials and agricultural products. The difference was that the Indians and Irish had little say in the matter because they were under British rule. In Latin America, however, the political elites encouraged foreign companies with generous concessions as the most rapid way to modernize their countries and enrich property owners. Poorer citizens were neither consulted nor allowed to benefit from the railroad boom.

26-4c Revolution and Civil War in Mexico

At the beginning of the twentieth century Mexican society was divided into rich and poor and into populations of Spanish, Indian, and mixed ancestry. A few very wealthy families of Spanish origin, less than 1 percent of the population, owned 85 percent of Mexico's land, mostly in huge *haciendas* (estates). A handful of American and British companies controlled most of Mexico's railroads, silver mines, plantations, and other productive enterprises. At the other end of the

AP® Exam Tip Understand the importance of economic imperialism and neocolonialism.

Spanish-American War War fought in 1898 to expand American imperial possessions. Treaty of Paris ending the conflict confirmed U.S. control of Guam, Puerto Rico, and the Philippines.

social scale were Indians, many of whom did not speak Spanish. *Mestizos* (**mess-TEE-so**), people of mixed Indian and European ancestry, were slightly better off. Most of them were peasants who worked on the haciendas or farmed small communal plots near their ancestral villages.

After independence in 1821 wealthy Mexican families and American companies used bribery and force to acquire millions of acres of good agricultural land from villages in southern Mexico. Peasants lost not only their fields but also their access to firewood and pasture, leaving them little choice but to work on haciendas. To survive, they bought food and other necessities on credit from the landowner's store; eventually, they fell permanently into debt.

For thirty-four years General Porfirio Díaz (**DEE-as**) (1830–1915) had ruled Mexico under the motto "Liberty, Order, Progress." To Díaz "liberty" meant freedom for rich hacienda owners and foreign investors. The government imposed "order" through rigged elections, bribes to Díaz's supporters, and summary justice for those who opposed him. "Progress" meant importing foreign capital, machinery, and technicians to take advantage of Mexico's labor, soil, and natural resources.

During the Díaz years (1876–1910) Mexico City became a showplace with paved streets, streetcar lines, electric street lighting, and public parks. Telegraph and railroad lines connected cities and towns throughout Mexico. But this material progress benefited only a handful of well-connected businessmen and lowered the average Mexican's standard of living.

Though a mestizo himself, Díaz discriminated against the country's nonwhite majority. He and his supporters tried to eradicate what they saw as Mexico's rustic traditions. On many middle- and upper-class tables French cuisine replaced traditional Mexican dishes, and the wealthy traded sombreros and ponchos for European garments. To the educated middle class—the only group with a strong sense of Mexican nationhood—this devaluation of Mexican culture became a symbol of the Díaz regime's failure to defend national interests against foreign influences.

The **Mexican Revolution** was a social revolution that developed haphazardly under ambitious but limited leaders, each representing a different segment of Mexican society. The first was American-educated Francisco I. Madero (1873–1913), the son of a wealthy landowning and mining family. Strongly opposed to Díaz, he called on his fellow citizens to oppose electing him for a sixth term. This sparked a revolution in 1910 and the election of Madero as Díaz's successor. While the Madero presidency was welcomed in some quarters, it was opposed in others. American ambassador Henry Lane Wilson helped General Victoriano Huerta, one of Madero's former supporters, engineer a coup d'état in 1913, and Madero was assassinated after only two years in the presidency. President Woodrow Wilson then disavowed American support of Huerta, recalled Ambassador Wilson, and, as a token of American concern with Mexican unrest, sent United States Marines to seize the port city of Veracruz, which they occupied for six months (see Map 26.3).

The inequities of Mexican society and foreign intervention angered Mexico's middle class and industrial workers. They found leaders in Venustiano Carranza, a landowner, and in Alvaro Obregón (**oh-bray-GAWN**), a schoolteacher. Calling themselves Constitutionalists, Carranza and Obregón organized private armies and overthrew Huerta in 1914. By then, the revolution had spread to the countryside.

Madero's key "popular" ally in 1910–1911 had been **Emiliano Zapata** (**sah-PAH-tah**) (1879–1919), but the two parted ways on the issue of land reform. Himself an Indian farmer, Zapata led a revolt against the haciendas in the mountains of Morelos, south of Mexico City (see Map 26.3). His soldiers were peasants mounted on horseback and armed with pistols and rifles. For several years they periodically came down from the mountains, burned hacienda buildings, and returned land to the Indian villages to which it had once belonged.

Another leader appeared in Chihuahua, a northern state where seventeen individuals owned two-fifths of the land and 95 percent of the people had no land at all. Starting in 1913, **Francisco "Pancho" Villa** (1877–1923)—a former ranch hand, mule driver, and bandit—organized an army of 3,000 men, most of them cowboys, and divided large haciendas into family ranches. After a failed and unexplained attack on the town of Columbus, New Mexico, the U.S. Army sent General John Pershing on a nine-month mission to hunt Villa down. The mission was cut short by American entry into World War I, but, like the occupation of Veracruz, it demonstrated increasing American concern for protecting land and business interests in Mexico.

Zapata and Villa enjoyed tremendous popular support but could never rise above their regional and peasant origins and lead a national revolution. The Constitutionalists had fewer soldiers than Zapata and Villa, but they held the major cities and used the proceeds of oil sales

Mexican Revolution A complicated series of revolts beginning in 1910 aimed at reducing social inequality and establishing constitutional government. A constitution was adopted in 1917.

Emiliano Zapata Revolutionary and leader of peasants in the Mexican Revolution. He mobilized landless peasants in south-central Mexico in an attempt to seize and divide the lands of the wealthy landowners. Though successful for a time, he was ultimately defeated and assassinated.

Francisco "Pancho" Villa A popular leader during the Mexican Revolution. An outlaw in his youth, when the revolution started, he formed a cavalry army in the north of Mexico and fought for the rights of the landless in collaboration with Emiliano Zapata. He was assassinated in 1923.

MAP 26.3 The Mexican Revolution The Mexican Revolution began in two distinct regions of the country. One was the mountainous and densely populated area south of Mexico City, particularly Morelos, homeland of Emiliano Zapata. The other was the dry and thinly populated ranch country of the north, home of Pancho Villa. The fighting that ensued crisscrossed the country along the main railroad lines, shown on the map.

How important was control of the border between Mexico and the United States?

▶ **Mexican Revolution** Emiliano Zapata emerged as revolutionary leader fighting for land reform in his home territory just south of Mexico City. Here his fighters are attacking the forces of General Victoriano Huerta whose assassination of President Madero and usurpation of his office in 1913 touched off open civil war. Pictorial Press Ltd / Alamy Stock Photo

to buy modern weapons. Gradually the Constitutionalists took over most of Mexico. In 1919 they defeated and killed Zapata; Villa was given a large estate to retire to but was assassinated in 1923 after resuming political activity. An estimated 2 million people lost their lives in the civil war, and much of Mexico lay in ruins.

During their struggle to win support against Zapata and Villa, the Constitutionalists adopted many of their rivals' agrarian reforms, such as restoring communal lands to the Indians of Morelos. They also proposed social programs designed to appeal to workers and the middle class. The Constitution of 1917 set out the following principles: a one-term limit on presidential power; economic nationalism (recapturing subsoil rights from foreigners, land reform, and the right of labor to organize); and severe constraints on the church. However, powerful Mexican forces and the United States sought to prevent full implementation of the constitution. By 1928 the Mexican government had made more progress against the church than in the implementation of either political or economic reform.

By the early 1920s a decade of violence had drained the country without resolving the question of who would rule. Carranza, elected president in 1917, did not wish Obregón to succeed him. In response, Obregón allied with two other ambitious leaders and marched on Mexico City. Carranza was killed as he fled. Following the constitution, Obregón served one four-year term as president. He then managed the election of Plutarco Elías Calles (**KAH-yace**), his colleague in the anti-Carranza plot, who served one term with the understanding that Obregón would return to the presidency in 1928. A Catholic militant put a stop to this arrangement by assassinating Obregón before he could take office.

26-4d American Intervention in the Caribbean and Central America, 1901–1914

American intervention in the Western Hemisphere was not limited to Mexico. The nations of the Caribbean and Central America were small and poor, and their corrupt, unstable, and often bankrupt governments offered an open invitation to foreign interference. A government would borrow money to pay for railroads, harbors, electric power, and other symbols of modernity. When it could not repay the loan, the lending banks in Europe or the United States would ask for assistance from their home governments, which sometimes threatened to intervene. To ward off European intervention, the United States sent in the marines on more than one occasion.

Presidents Theodore Roosevelt (1901–1909), William Taft (1909–1913), and Woodrow Wilson (1913–1921) felt impelled to intervene in the region, though they differed sharply on the proper policy the United States should follow toward the small nations to the south. Roosevelt encouraged regimes friendly to the United States; Taft sought to influence them through loans from American banks; and the moralist Wilson tried to impose clean governments by military means.

Having "liberated" Cuba from Spain, in 1901 the United States forced the Cuban government to accept the Platt Amendment, which gave the United States the "right to intervene" to maintain order on the island. The United States used this excuse to occupy Cuba militarily from 1906 to 1909, in 1912, and again from 1917 to 1922. In all but name Cuba became an American protectorate. U.S. troops also occupied the Dominican Republic from 1904 to 1907 and again in 1916, Nicaragua and Honduras in 1912, and Haiti in 1915. They brought sanitation and material progress but no political reforms.

The United States was especially forceful in Panama, which was a province of Colombia. Here the issue was not corruption or debts but a more vital interest. When the United States acquired Hawaii and the Philippines, it recognized the need for a canal that would allow warships to move quickly between the Atlantic and Pacific Oceans. The main obstacle was Colombia, which refused to give the United States a piece of its territory. In 1903 the U.S. government supported a Panamanian rebellion against Colombia and quickly recognized the independence of Panama. In exchange, it obtained the right to build a canal and to occupy a zone 5 miles (8 kilometers) wide on either side of it. Work began in 1904, and the **Panama Canal** opened on August 15, 1914.

Panama Canal Ship canal cut across the isthmus of Panama by United States Army engineers; it opened in 1914. The canal greatly shortened the sea voyage between the east and west coasts of North America. The United States turned the canal over to Panama on January 1, 2000.

Section Review

- The Spanish-American war made Cuba an unofficial American protectorate.

- Britain and the United States invested in railroads and other industrial enterprises throughout Latin America.

- Strong economic and social divisions in Mexico contributed to a revolution involving diverse players.

- After a decade of violence Mexico gained a new constitution.

- Repeated American interventions in the region peaked with the building of the Panama Canal.

26-5 The World Economy and the Global Environment

How did imperialism contribute to the growth and globalization of the world economy?

The nineteenth-century imperialists were not conquerors or empire builders like the Spanish conquistadors. They expressed their good intentions in the clichés of the time: "the conquest of nature," "the annihilation of time and space," "the taming of the wilderness," and "our civilizing mission."

26-5a Expansion of the World Economy

For centuries Europe had been a ready market for spices, sugar, silk, and other imported products. The Industrial Revolution expanded this demand, especially for stimulants such as tea, coffee, and chocolate. The trade in industrial raw materials grew even faster: agricultural products like cotton, jute for bags, palm oil for soap and lubricants, and minerals like diamonds, gold, and copper. Some wild forest products eventually came to be cultivated: timber for buildings and railroad ties, cinchona bark, rubber for rainwear and tires, and gutta-percha (**gut-tah-PER-cha**) (the sap of a Southeast Asian tree) to insulate electric cables.

Economic botany and agricultural science were applied to every promising plant species. European botanists had long collected and classified exotic plants from around the world. In the nineteenth century they founded botanical gardens in Java, India, Mauritius (**maw-REE-shuss**), Ceylon, Jamaica, and other tropical colonies. These gardens not only collected local plants but also transferred commercially valuable plant species from one tropical region to another. Cinchona (**sin-CHO-nah**) (the source of the antimalarial drug quinine), tobacco, sugar, coffee, tea, and other crops were introduced, improved, and vastly expanded in the colonies of Southeast Asia and Indonesia (see Environment & Technology: Imperialism and Tropical Ecology). Cacao and coffee growing spread over large areas of Brazil and Africa; oil-palm plantations were established in Nigeria and the Congo Basin. After 1910, rubber, used to make waterproof garments and bicycle tires, came from plantations in Southeast Asia.

Throughout the tropics, land once covered with forests or devoted to slash-and-burn agriculture was transformed into farms and plantations. In Java and India farmers terraced hillsides, drained swamps, dug wells, and felled trees to obtain arable land and firewood. Colonial rule also fostered population growth. Even in areas not devoted to export crops, growing populations put pressure on the land. For example, the population of Java, an island the size of Pennsylvania, doubled from 16 million in 1870 to over 30 million in 1914.

26-5b Free Trade

By 1870 Britain had added several dozen colonies to the twenty-six colonies it had in 1792. The underlying goal of most British imperial expansion during these decades was

AP® Exam Tip
Understand how the demand for raw goods and markets for finished goods led to a dramatic expansion of the global economy in the nineteenth century.

▲ **A Rubber Plantation** As bicycles and automobiles proliferated in the early twentieth century, the demand for rubber outstripped the supply available from wild rubber trees in the Amazon forest. Rubber grown on plantations in Southeast Asia came on the market from 1910 on. The rubber trees had to be tapped very carefully and on a regular schedule to obtain the latex or sap from which rubber was extracted. In this picture a woman and a boy perform this operation on a plantation in British Malaya. Mary Evans Picture Library/The Image Works

Despite European enthusiasm for botanical research, introducing productive new crops into colonial economies was not always easy. Vanilla, for example, comes from a species of orchid that is native to central Mexico and had been known in Europe since the time of the Spanish conquistador Hernán Cortés. When transplanted into experimental gardens in other tropical regions, the orchid grew readily. But it produced no beans, and hence no vanilla flavoring.

For 300 years Europeans who fancied the taste of vanilla had to rely on Mexican production. Then in 1837 a Belgian botanist named Charles François Antoine Morren discovered that a bee species particular to Mexico played an essential role in pollinating the plants. However, the bees could not survive when introduced to other lands. Morren devised a way of pollinating the vanilla plants by hand, but it proved slow and clumsy in practice and was never commercially adopted.

Four years later, Edmond Albius, a twelve-year-old African slave born and raised on the island of Réunion, a French colony in the Indian Ocean, invented a new method of hand pollination that was quick and efficient. A European scientist sought credit for the discovery, but Albius's master and adoptive father, Ferreol Bellier-Beaumont, defended the boy's claim. Réunion soon became the center of a new industry exporting a tropical commodity that was much in demand, but in time the larger island of Madagascar became the leading non-Mexican producer of vanilla.

As for Albius, after being freed when France outlawed slavery in 1848, he worked as a kitchen servant and then was sentenced to ten years in prison for stealing jewelry. After five years the governor of the colony granted him clemency in recognition of his role in creating the vanilla industry.

The story of Edmond Albius highlights the fact that credit for the development of new or transplanted industrial crops in Europe's tropical colonies belongs not just to European botanists and planters, but also to local farmers who learned to adapt their skills to the new plants. Most of the improvements originating with these non-European workers will never be known, but without their talents and ideas the trans-formation in the global trade in tropical crops that characterized the nineteenth century could scarcely have taken place.

Questions for Analysis

1. What crops in addition to vanilla got transplanted to European colonies in Africa and Asia?

2. Why are the contributions of colonial subjects to the production of new crops so seldom recognized?

3. How does the study of ecology contribute to understanding the economic foundations of imperialism?

▲ **Painting of Vanilla Plant**   The European passion for creating botanical gardens for transplanting trees and flowers from colonial regions was matched by the production of albums of paintings of exotic flora. The long tubular shape of the vanilla blossom shows why it was difficult to pollinate by hand.   Amana Images Inc/Getty Images

trade rather than territory. Most of the new colonies were meant to serve as ports in the growing network of shipping that encircled the globe or as centers of production and distribution for those networks.

This commercial expansion was closely tied to the needs of Britain's growing industrial economy and reflected a new philosophy of overseas trade. Rather than rebuilding the closed mercantilist network of trade with its colonies, Britain sought to trade freely with all parts of the world. Free trade also seemed a wise policy in light of the independence of so many former colonies in the Americas (see Chapter 23).

Whether colonized or not, more and more lands were being drawn into the commercial networks created by British expansion and industrialization. Uncolonized parts of West Africa became major exporters to Britain of vegetable oils and forest products, while areas of eastern Africa free of European control exported the ivory that ended up as piano keys and billiard balls in the homes of the middle and upper classes.

In return for the foodstuffs and industrial raw materials that flowed toward Europe and the United States, the factories of the industrialized nations supplied manufactured goods at very attractive prices. By the mid-nineteenth century a major part of their textile production was destined for overseas markets. Sales of cotton cloth to Africa increased 950 percent from the 1820s to the 1860s. British trade to India grew 350 percent between 1841 and 1870, while India's exports increased 400 percent. Trade with other regions also expanded rapidly. In most cases such trade benefited both sides, but there is no question that the industrial nations were the dominant partners.

26-5c New Labor Migrations

Between 1834 and 1870 many thousands of Indians, Chinese, and Africans went overseas to work, especially on sugar plantations. In the half century after 1870, tens of thousands of Asians and Pacific islanders made similar voyages.

In part these migrations were linked to the end of slavery. After their emancipation in British colonies in 1834, many slaves left the plantations. To compete with sugar plantations in Cuba, Brazil, and the French Caribbean that were still using slave labor, British colonies had to recruit new laborers.

Impoverished Indians seemed one obvious alternative. After planters on Mauritius successfully introduced Indian laborers, the Indian labor trade moved to the British Caribbean in 1838. In 1841 the British government also allowed Caribbean planters to recruit Africans whom British patrols had rescued from slave ships and liberated in Sierra Leone and elsewhere. By 1870 nearly 40,000 Africans had settled in British colonies, along with over a half-million Indians and over 18,000 Chinese. After the French and Dutch abolished slavery in 1848, their colonies also recruited new laborers from Asia and Africa.

Slavery was not abolished in Cuba until 1886, but the rising cost of slaves led the burgeoning sugar plantations to recruit 138,000 new laborers from China between 1847 and 1873. Indentured labor recruits also became the mainstay of new sugar plantations in places that had never known slave labor. After 1850 American planters in Hawaii recruited labor from China and Japan; British planters in Natal (in South Africa) recruited from India; and those in Queensland (in northeastern Australia) relied on laborers from neighboring South Pacific islands.

Larger, faster ships (see Chapter 27) made transporting laborers halfway around the world affordable, though voyages from Asia to the Caribbean still took an average of three months. Despite close regulation and supervision of shipboard conditions, the crowded accommodations encouraged the spread of cholera and other contagious diseases that took many migrants' lives.

All of these laborers served under **contracts of indenture**, which bound them to work for a specified period (usually from five to seven years) in return for free passage to their overseas destination. They were paid a small salary and were provided with housing, clothing, and medical care. Indian indentured laborers also received a free passage home if they worked a second five-year contract. British Caribbean colonies required forty women to be recruited for every hundred men as a way to promote family life. So many Indians chose to stay in Mauritius, Trinidad, British Guiana, and Fiji that they constituted a third or more of the total population of these colonies by the early twentieth century.

AP® Exam Tip
Understand the causes and processes of increased global migration during this time period.

contracts of indenture
A voluntary agreement binding a person to work for a specified period of years in return for free passage to an overseas destination. Before 1800 most indentured servants were Europeans; after 1800 most indentured laborers were Asians.

Section Review

- Industrialization increased demand for food imports and raw materials in Europe, which was met by its worldwide colonies.

- Free trade replaced the earlier focus on complete control of colonial production.

- As slavery ended, laborers were sent from heavily populated countries like India and China to work in European colonies.

- Contracts of indenture provided a framework for this labor migration.

The indentured labor trade reflected the unequal commercial and industrial power of the West, but it was not an entirely one-sided creation. The men and women who signed indentured contracts were trying to improve their lives by emigrating, and many succeeded. For good or ill, more and more of the world's peoples saw their lives being influenced by the existence of Western colonies, Western ships, and Western markets.

26-7 Conclusion

What is the global significance of these complex political and economic changes in southern Asia, Africa, the South Pacific, and Latin America? One perspective stresses the continuing and growing imperialist exploitation of non-Europeans. From another perspective what was most important about this period was not the political and military strength of the Europeans but their growing domination of the world's commerce, especially investment in plantations, railroads, mines, and long-distance ocean shipping. Motives differed somewhat from region to region. Imperialists were drawn to Africa and Southeast Asia by a desire for tropical food-stuffs and industrial raw materials. Land for settlement was the attraction in Australia, New Zealand, and South Africa, as it earlier had been for European settlers in the New World. India and Latin America, having more prosperous middle classes, provided markets for European and American manufactures.

The growing exchanges could be mutually beneficial. As in Europe itself, overseas consumers found industrially produced goods far cheaper and sometimes better than the handicrafts they replaced. Industrialization also created new markets for African and Asian goods, as in the case of palm oil from West Africa or rubber from Malaya. There were also negative impacts, as in the case of weavers thrown out of work in India and the beginnings of deforestation in Southeast Asia.

Imperialist military and commercial strength did not reduce Africa, Asia, Latin America, and the Pacific to mere appendages of Europe. While the balance of power shifted in the Europeans' favor between 1750 and 1914, other cultures were still vibrant and local initiatives often dominant. Islamic reform movements, the rise of the Zulu nation, and the Mexican revolution had greater significance for their respective regions than did Western forces. Despite European power, Latin Americans were still politically in control of their own destinies. Even in India, most people's lives and beliefs maintained continuity with the past.

Key Terms

Zulu p. 670

Afrikaners p. 670

Cecil Rhodes p. 672

Sokoto Caliphate p. 673

King Leopold II p. 674

Henry Morton Stanley p. 674

Savorgnan de Brazza p. 675

Berlin Conference p. 675

modernization p. 676

Suez Canal p. 676

Menelik II p. 677

"legitimate" trade p. 678

recaptives p. 678

nawab p. 679

sepoy p. 679

British raj p. 679

Sepoy Rebellion p. 680

durbar p. 680

Indian Civil Service p. 680

Indian National Congress p. 683

Emilio Aguinaldo p. 685

Spanish-American War p. 687

Mexican Revolution p. 688

Emiliano Zapata p. 688

Francisco "Pancho" Villa p. 688

Panama Canal p. 690

contract of indenture p. 693

Review Questions

1. How does European imperialism in the eighteenth and nineteenth centuries compare to European imperialism in the sixteenth and seventeenth centuries in terms of the shift of wealth from one part of the world to another?

2. Was European imperialism in the eighteenth and nineteenth centuries more or less open to accepting new ideas and lifestyles from imperialized lands than was the Roman Empire or the Abbasid Caliphate?

3. In comparison with other periods of rapid accumulation of imperial power, such as occurred with Alexander the Great, Rome, the Islamic Caliphate, and the Mongol conquests, did the rise of Europe to world domination in the era of imperialism result more from political will or from military power?

MindTap® is a fully online, personalized learning experience built upon Cengage Learning content. MindTap® combines student learning tools—readings, multimedia, activities, and assessments—into a singular Learning Path that guides students through the course and helps students develop the critical thinking, analysis, and communication skills that are essential to academic and professional success.

Multiple-Choice Questions
Questions 1–4 refer to Map 26.1 on page 672.

1. Based on the map, which of the following best describes European imperialism in Africa in the nineteenth century?

   (A) European colonies were mainly limited to coastal regions.

   (B) Europeans made inroads deep into the African interior.

   (C) Most European colonies were limited to southern Africa.

   (D) Most European colonies were limited to Muslim areas alone.

2. Based on the map, how did the British expand their empire in Africa?

   (A) Through access to superior ports

   (B) Through both diplomacy and warfare

   (C) Strong British government support for colonials

   (D) Elimination of native people through disease

3. Which of the following demonstrates continuity from previous time periods as indicated by the map?

   (A) The slave trade continued to dominate the African economy.

   (B) Trade continued across the Sahara.

   (C) Africa continued to conduct most of its trade within the continent.

   (D) Islam continued to dominate Ethiopia.

4. Similar to many other regions in the world during this time period, European colonialism (like that on the map) and other factors led Africa to experience which of the following?

   (A) Intensive industrialization of formerly land-based empires

   (B) Government and nationalist ideals based on Enlightenment ideals

   (C) Disruptions to traditional life leading to mass migrations

   (D) A focus solely on a revived gold and salt trade in the north of the continent

Questions 5–7 refer to the passage below.

"It is this consciousness of the inherent superiority of the European which had won for us India. However well educated and clever a native may be, and however brave he may have proved himself, I believe that no rank we can bestow on him would cause him to be considered an equal of the British officer."

Lord Kitchener, Commander-in-Chief of the Indian army, 1892

5. Based on the passage above, which of the following most likely influenced Lord Kitchener's attitude toward the Indians?

   (A) The solid acceptance of racial hierarchies in the West

   (B) The Enlightenment's emphasis on reason over religious faith

   (C) India's refusal to change its attitudes toward labor and industry

   (D) India's lack of resources that could be exploited in the industrial age

6. The passage above is the direct result of which of the following movements?

   (A) Marxist attitudes toward caste and other forms of social hierarchy

   (B) The change from the colonialism of the previous time period to high imperialism in the nineteenth century

   (C) A continued close relationship between merchants and missionaries

   (D) A continuing movement toward centralized authority in government

7. Which of the following people would most likely disagree with Lord Kitchener's attitudes and have a different view of British imperialism in India?

   (A) A European industrialist

   (B) A member of the British civil service

   (C) A woman of any caste

   (D) An industrial worker

Questions 8–10 refer to the image below.

▲ **Philippine War of Independence, Insurgent Attack, 1899**
Album / Prisma / Superstock

8. Based on the image, the painting depicts which of the following?

   (A) Philippine War of Independence from Spain

   (B) Philippine War of Independence from Britain

   (C) Philippine Civil War

   (D) Philippine War of Independence from the United States

9. The image most strongly supports which of the following arguments:

   (A) Imperialist activities led to resistance and rebellion across the globe.

   (B) Most conflict outside the West was the result of civil war.

   (C) Conflict between Christians and Muslims in the southern Philippines continued to divide the population.

   (D) Conflict was the result of newly formed labor movements from industrial regions.

10. In what way was the Filipino resistance in the image similar to other armed resistance movements from this time period?

    (A) The economic advantages of empire motivated people in many regions.

    (B) Although there was a growth in nationalism, the resistance movement lacked the resources to achieve independence.

    (C) Growing divisions between farmers and industrial workers kept the population from uniting.

    (D) Religious elites preached against the evils of armed resistance and rebellion.

Short-Answer Questions

1. In the time period 1750–1900, much of the world was subject to economic imperialism. Choose TWO of the regions below and answer all parts of the question that follows:

   - South Asia
   - West Africa
   - Southeast Asia and the Pacific

   (A) Identify the economic power that imperialized ONE nation in any of these three regions.

   (B) Explain ONE cause of economic imperialism that was similar between the two regions.

   (C) Explain ONE long-term effect of economic imperialism that was similar for the two regions.

2. Mexico was independent from Spain for nearly 100 years before the Mexican Revolution took place, yet the Revolution was fighting against both changes brought about by independence and problems that had been present for centuries. Based on your knowledge of world history, answer all parts of the question that follows.

   (A) Identify one individual who fought against Diaz's rule in the Mexican Revolution.

   (B) Explain ONE economic or political change in Mexico under Diaz's rule after independence in 1821.

   (C) Explain ONE economic or political continuity in Mexico under Diaz's rule after independence in 1821.

27 The New Power Balance, 1850–1900

CHAPTER OUTLINE

AP® Framework Terms

Railroads
Coal
Steel
Electricity
Chemical industry
Labor unions
Industrial working class
Middle class
Anarchist
Liberalism
Socialism
Nationalism
Marxism
Meiji Japan
Social Darwinism

Overarching Questions

1 How and to what extent have migration, population, and urbanization affected the environment over time? (ENV)

2 How have cross-cultural interactions resulted in the diffusion of culture, technologies, and scientific knowledge? (CUL)

3 How and why have economic, social, cultural, and geographic factors influenced the process of state building, expansion, and dissolution? (SB)

4 How have different labor systems developed and changed over time? (ECON)

5 How have political, economic, cultural, and demographic factors affected social structures? (SOC)

O n July 8, 1853, four American warships, two of them steam-powered, appeared in Edo Bay, close to the capital of Japan. The commander of the fleet, **Commodore Matthew Perry**, delivered a letter to Japanese authorities from the president of the United States, demanding that Japan open its ports to foreign trade. Japan had had contact with Europe since the sixteenth century, when Portuguese mariners and Jesuit missionaries first arrived. The Dutch followed in the seventeenth century. Worried by the disruptive effects of this Western presence, Japan suppressed Christian conversion efforts and then "excluded" European merchants in 1639, although limited contact was permitted at the port of Nagasaki.

While Japan had rejected a similar request delivered by a smaller, less intimidating U.S. naval force in 1845, Perry's modern, well-armed fleet used a series of threatening military maneuvers to make clear the likely violent consequences of any refusal by Japanese authorities to open their markets. When he returned the following year with a larger fleet, the Japanese

▲ **Arrivals from the East**   In 1853, Commodore Matthew Perry's fleet sailed into Edo (now Tokyo) Bay. The first steam-powered warships to appear in Japanese waters caused a sensation among the Japanese. In this print done after the Meiji Restoration, the traditionally dressed local samurai go out to confront the mysterious "black ships."   Glasshouse Images/JT Vintage/Alamy stock photo

agreed to end the exclusion policies that had kept the nation isolated for two and a half centuries. If his display of military force had compelled change, Perry's visit also served to introduce a compelling array of the Industrial Revolution's technological and scientific triumphs to Japan, including a miniature steam railroad, a short telegraph line, and other marvels. For the next twenty years, Japanese society was torn between those who wanted to retreat into isolation and those who wished to embrace the foreign ways and acquire modern machines. For it was now clear that only through industrialization and modernization could Japan escape the fate of other Asian nations, including the great regional power China, who had been forced to accept colonial rule or submit to humiliating trade requirements by European nations or the United States. Japan's rapid transformation into an industrial and military power in the next century was the unforeseen consequence of Perry's mission.

In the late nineteenth century a very small number of states, known as the "Great Powers," dominated the world. Great Britain and France had been recognized as great powers long before the industrial age. Russia achieved this status as a member of the alliance that defeated Napoleon and then began industrializing in the late nineteenth century. Three other emerging powers—Germany, the United States, and Japan—rapidly developed their industrial and military might in the nineteenth century as well. At the dawn of the twentieth century the economic and military ambitions of these potent industrializing powers dramatically altered long-standing political and cultural arrangements globally. Each had extended its territorial reach by establishing new colonies in

Commodore Matthew Perry A navy commander who, on July 8, 1853, became the first foreigner to break through the barriers that had kept Japan isolated from the rest of the world for 250 years.

Africa and Asia and also by creating informal empires where weak local authorities were compelled to grant preferable trade concessions. While rivalries among these powers could lead to conflict and competition, they collectively exercised a worldwide ascendancy never previously witnessed. ●

27-1 New Technologies and the World Economy

What new technologies and industries appeared between 1850 and 1900, and how did they affect the world economy?

The Industrial Revolution marked the beginning of a massive transformation of the world. In the nineteenth century the technologies discussed in Chapter 22—textile mills, railroads, steamships, the telegraph, and others—spread quickly from Britain to other parts of the world. By 1890 Germany and the United States had surpassed Great Britain as the world's leading industrial powers. As industrial modernization expanded and accelerated in the nineteenth century, entirely new technologies, notably electricity and the steel and chemical industries, revolutionized everyday life and transformed the world economy. The motive force behind this second phase of industrialization consisted of potent combinations of business investment, engineering, and science. By the mid-nineteenth century the momentum of industrial research and innovation was reinforced by the creation of numerous engineering schools and research laboratories, first in Germany and then in the United States.

27-1a Railroads

AP® Exam Tip
Consider the impact of major developments and innovations in transportation and communication throughout the Industrial Revolution.

By the mid-nineteenth century, steam engines had become the prime mover of industry and commerce. Nowhere was this more evident than in the spread of **railroads**. By 1850 the first railroads had proved so successful that every industrializing country, and many that aspired to become industrial, began the construction of rail lines. The next fifty years saw a tremendous expansion of the world's rail networks. After a rapid spurt of building new lines, British railroad mileage leveled off in the 1870s at around 20,000 miles (over 32,000 kilometers). France and Germany ultimately built networks larger than Britain's, as did Canada and Russia. The nation with the largest railroad network in 1865, the United States, continued its commitment to this new technology and, by 1917, had increased its mileage eleven times.

Railroads were not confined to the industrialized nations; they could be constructed almost anywhere they would be of value to business or government. That included regions with abundant raw materials or agricultural products, like South Africa, Mexico, and Argentina, or densely populated countries like Egypt. Great Britain built the fourth largest rail network in the world in its largest colony, India, to reinforce its colonial domination and develop new trade opportunities.

European or American engineers and investors built most of the railroads of Africa, Asia, and Latin America and used equipment imported from the West. Japan was the exception. In 1855, barely a year after Commodore Perry's visit, Japanese instrument maker Tanaka Hisashige built a model steam train that he demonstrated to an admiring audience. In the 1870s the Japanese government hired British engineers to build the first full-scale line from Tokyo to Yokohama and then sent them home in the 1880s once they had trained a cadre of Japanese engineers. Within a few years, Japan began manufacturing its own railroad equipment and by 1910 had 7,000 miles (11,200 km) of track.

Railroad development forced the transformation of urban and rural landscapes. Many old cities doubled in size to accommodate railroad stations, sidings, tracks, warehouses, and repair shops. In the countryside, railroads promoted the development of towns and cities established along their rights of way. They also required the construction of bridges, tunnels, and embankments that altered natural environments. The construction of rail lines also promoted the rapid spread of market agriculture, with hundreds of thousands of acres of prairie transformed by the plow in a few decades in the United States, Canada, and Argentina. In early decades, wood-burning steam engines consumed vast amounts of fuel, promoting deforestation in many places. The need for lumber for railroad ties and for the construction of bridges placed additional demands on forest reserves. Technological innovations continued this cycle as, for example,

railroads Networks of iron (later steel) rails on which steam (later electric or diesel) locomotives pulled long trains at high speeds. The first railroads were built in England in the 1830s. Their success caused a railroad-building boom throughout the world that lasted well into the twentieth century.

	Political Events	Social, Cultural, and Technological Events
1850	1853–1854 Commodore Matthew Perry visits Japan	1851 Majority of British population living in cities
		1856 Bessemer converter; first synthetic dye
1860	1860–1870 Unification of Italy	1859 Charles Darwin, *On the Origin of Species*
	1861–1865 American Civil War	1861 Emancipation of serfs (Russia)
	1862–1908 Rule of Empress Dowager Cixi (China)	1866 Alfred Nobel develops dynamite
		1867 Karl Marx, *Das Kapital*
		1866 Transatlantic cable laid
	1868 Meiji Restoration begins modernization drive in Japan	1868–1894 Japan undergoes Western-style industrialization and societal changes
1870	1870–1871 Franco-Prussian War	
	1871 Paris Commune	
	1871 Unification of Germany	
1880		1879 Thomas Edison develops incandescent lamp
1890	1894 Sino-Japanese War	
1900	1900 Boxer Uprising (China)	
	1904–1905 Russo-Japanese War	
	1905 Revolution in Russia	
	1910 Japan annexes Korea	

coal mines were exploited in previously undisturbed agricultural landscapes with the transition to coal-fired engines. While the environmental costs were large, railways accelerated the rate of economic growth as new lands were connected to urban markets and ports, which were, in turn, connected to distant foreign markets by steamships. By the end of the nineteenth century the peoples of the world were more mobile and their economies more intensely linked than at any time in history.

27-1b Steamships and Telegraph Cables

In the mid-nineteenth century, a series of developments radically transformed ocean shipping. First iron, then steel, replaced the wood that had been used for ship construction since ship-building began. Paddle wheels replaced sails and then were replaced by propellers as engineers built more powerful and fuel-efficient engines. The average size of freight-carrying vessels also increased at the same time, growing from an average of 200 tons in 1850 to 7,500 tons in 1900. As both the size of ships and the number of ships grew, coaling stations and ports able to handle large ships were built around the world. For example, Egypt's Suez Canal, constructed in 1869, shortened the distance between Europe and Asia and triggered a massive switch from sail power to steam (see Chapter 26).

These modern shipping lines offered fast, punctual, and reliable service on a fixed schedule for passengers, mail, and perishable freight as the world's fleet of merchant ships grew from 9 million tons in 1850 to 35 million tons in 1910, a progression that can be used as a proxy for growth in the scale of international commerce. The result was falling freight costs and greater commercial integration, changes that benefited not only the exporters of industrial products in Europe and North America but also the Asian, African, and Latin American exporters of agricultural and mining products. Nevertheless, this growing national and regional economic specialization in the nineteenth century concentrated industrial power, leading to today's global inequalities.

At the same time, shipping companies and commercial firms were able to use a new medium of communication, **submarine telegraph cables**, to respond to or anticipate changing conditions in distant markets. As was common with previous infrastructure development, like canals and railroads, the early advancement of this technology depended on the financial support of governments. In this case the French and British governments saw the usefulness of the telegraph for communicating with and controlling distant colonies in Asia and Africa. European businesses, on the other hand, were more interested in laying a cable across the Atlantic to further develop

submarine telegraph cables Insulated copper cables laid along the bottom of a sea or ocean for telegraphic communication. The first short cable was laid across the English Channel in 1851; the first successful transatlantic cable was laid in 1866.

commercial linkages with the Americas. The initial efforts of the 1850s failed, but an improved transatlantic cable was successfully laid in 1866. By the turn of the century, cables connected every country and almost every inhabited island. As they became the indispensable tools of modern shipping and business, the public and the press extolled this "annihilation of time and space."

27-1c The Steel and Chemical Industries

Until the nineteenth century **steel** could be made only in very small quantities by skilled blacksmiths and was reserved for swords, knives, axes, and watch springs. Then came a series of inventions that made it the cheapest and most versatile metal ever known. In the 1850s the American William Kelly and the Englishman Henry Bessemer discovered that air forced through molten pig iron by powerful pumps turned it into steel without additional fuel. Other new processes permitted steel to be made from scrap iron, an increasingly important raw material, and from the phosphoric iron ores common in western Europe. Following these discoveries, steel became cheap and abundant enough to make rails, bridges, ships, and even "tin" cans meant to be used once and thrown away.

The chemical industry followed a similar pattern of innovation. In 1856 the Englishman William Perkin created the first synthetic dye, aniline purple, from coal tar; the next few years were known in Europe as the "mauve decade" from the fashionable synthetic color popular for women's clothes. Industry soon began mass-producing other organic chemicals—compounds containing carbon atoms. Toward the end of the century German chemists synthesized red, violet, blue, brown, and black dyes as well. These bright, long-lasting colors were cheaper to manufacture and could be produced in much greater quantities and at much lower prices than natural dyes. They delighted consumers but ruined the previously-profitable indigo plantations of India and Latin America. Chemistry also made important advances in the manufacture of explosives. The first of these, nitroglycerin, was so dangerous that it could explode if shaken or dropped. In 1866 the Swedish scientist Alfred Nobel found a way to turn nitroglycerin into a stable solid—dynamite. This and other new explosives proved useful in mining and were critical in the construction of railroads and canals. They also enabled the armies and navies of the Great Powers to arm themselves with increasingly accurate and powerful rifles and cannon, thus contributing to the second great wave of imperialism after 1850.

The growing complexity of industrial chemistry made it one of the first fields where science and technology interacted on a daily basis. This development gave a great advantage to Germany, which had the most advanced engineering schools and scientific institutes of the time and whose government funded research and encouraged cooperation between universities and industries. By the end of the nineteenth century, Germany was the world's leading producer of dyes, drugs, synthetic fertilizers, ammonia, and nitrates used in making explosives.

27-1d Environmental Problems

AP® Exam Tip
Provide examples of and evaluate the environmental impact of the Industrial Revolution.

Industrialization and rapid urbanization powerfully affected entire regions such as the English Midlands, the German Ruhr, parts of Pennsylvania in the United States, and the regions around Tokyo and Osaka in Japan. The new steel mills took up as much space as whole towns, belched smoke and particulates, and left behind huge hills of slag and other waste products. Coal-burning steam engines powered the new machine age and, along with mounting domestic coal consumption for cooking and heating, also filled the skies of Manchester, England, and the world's other manufacturing centers with dense smog. One German visitor to Manchester said, "The cloud of coal vapor may be observed from afar. The houses are blackened by it. The river, which flows through Manchester, is so filled with waste dyestuffs that it resembles a dyer's vat."[1]

Rapidly growing urban populations in industrializing European and American cities overwhelmed primitive sanitation systems until the last decades of the nineteenth century. When a drought lowered water levels in Britain's Thames River in 1858, Londoners experienced what they called the "Great Stink" caused by the vast accumulation of untreated human and industrial waste dumped daily into the river over decades. Public outcry led to the construction of a new

steel A form of iron that is both durable and flexible. It was first mass-produced in the 1860s and quickly became the most widely used metal in construction, machinery, and railroad equipment.

---

[1]Quoted in Robert B. Marks, *The Origins of the Modern World: A Global and Environmental Narrative from the Fifteenth to the Twenty-first Century*, 3rd ed. (Boulder, CO: Rowman & Littlefield, 2015), 142.

sewer system that sent the human waste of London further downstream. More threatening still to human beings were pollution-related deadly diseases like typhoid and cholera. By the time the first cholera epidemic subsided in Britain in 1832, 52,000 people had died. The threat continued into the 1840s when roughly 16,000 Londoners were infected a year by typhoid.

The coal smoke of railroad locomotives and other steam engines was a major contributor to air pollution, as were the rapidly developing chemical industries. These same factories also produced tons of toxic effluents that were dumped into rivers. Thus, while industrialization brought vast amounts of new wealth, without environmental regulations it also caused considerable damage to nature and to the health of nearby human populations. Almost universally, it was the poorest populations that suffered the most from these predations.

27-1e Electricity

No innovation of the late nineteenth century changed people's lives as radically as **electricity**. As an energy source, electricity was more flexible and much easier to use than water power or stationary steam engines. At first, producing electric current was so costly that it was used only for electroplating metals and for telegraphy. Then in 1831 the Englishman Michael Faraday showed that the motion of a copper wire through a magnetic field induced an electric current in the wire. Based on this discovery, inventors in the 1870s devised generators that turned mechanical energy into electric current.

Inventors and entrepreneurs now found a host of new applications for electricity. Initially, arc lamps lit up public squares, theaters, and stores, while homes continued to rely on gas lamps, which produced a softer light. Then in 1879 in the United States **Thomas Edison** (1847–1831) developed an incandescent lamp well suited to lighting small rooms. In 1882 Edison created the world's first electrical distribution network in New York City. By the turn of the century electric lighting was rapidly replacing gas lamps in the cities of Europe and North America.

Other uses of electricity quickly appeared. Electric streetcars and subways transported people throughout the cities of Europe and North America. Electric motors replaced steam engines and power belts in factories, increasing productivity and improving workers' safety. Commonly dependent on coal-fired generators, electric energy production from its beginnings was a major contributor to air pollution as well. As demand for electricity grew, engineers supplemented coal-fired generation with hydroelectric plants. The plant at Niagara Falls, on the border between Ontario, Canada, and New York State, produced an incredible 11,000 horsepower when it opened in 1895. At the newly created Imperial College of Engineering in Japan, an Englishman, William Ayrton, became the first professor of electrical engineering anywhere in the world; his Japanese students later went on to found many of that nation's major corporations and government research institutes.

27-1f World Trade and Finance

Improvements in transportation and communication, along with rising world population, led to a tenfold increase in international trade between 1850 and 1913. Europe imported wheat from Canada, the United States, and India, wool from Australia, and beef from Argentina, while it exported coal, railroad equipment, textiles, and machinery to Asia, Africa, and the Americas. Because steamships were much more efficient and faster than sailing ships, the cost of freight dropped dramatically, intensifying long-distance commercial links.

The growth of world trade transformed different parts of the world in different ways. The economies of western Europe and North America, the first to industrialize and the prime beneficiaries, grew more diversified and prosperous. Industries mass-produced consumer goods for a growing number of middle-class and even working-class customers: soap, canned and packaged foods, ready-made clothes, household items, and small luxuries like cosmetics and engravings to decorate middle-class walls. This revolution in consumption occurred at a much slower pace in the developing world and the benefits were more narrowly limited to elites and the urban middle class. These privileged sectors often paid for imported novelties by imposing harsh conditions on the masses who labored in distant plantations and mines.

Even the world's fastest-growing capitalist economies were prey to sudden swings in the business cycle—booms followed by deep depressions, or busts, in which workers lost their jobs and investors lost their fortunes. Because of the close connections among the industrial economies,

AP® Exam Tip
Understand why new methods in the production of steel, chemicals, electricity, and precision machinery are sometimes called a "second Industrial Revolution."

electricity A form of energy used in telegraphy from the 1840s on and for lighting, industrial motors, and railroads beginning in the 1880s.

Thomas Edison American inventor best known for inventing the electric light bulb, acoustic recording on wax cylinders, and motion pictures.

▶ **Paris Lit Up by Electricity, 1900** The electric light bulb was invented in the United States and Britain, but Paris made such extensive use of the new technology that it was nicknamed "City of Lights." To mark the Paris Exposition of 1900, the Eiffel Tower and all the surrounding buildings were illuminated with strings of light bulbs while powerful spotlights swept the sky. aka-images/Newscom

AP® Exam Tip
Explain why some regions benefitted more from the global economy than others.

the collapse of a bank in Austria in 1873 triggered a depression that spread to the United States, causing mass unemployment as 18,000 American businesses failed. Destabilizing worldwide recessions also occurred in the mid-1880s, eventually leading to the Panic of 1893 in the United States, which affected both manufacturing and agriculture and caused unemployment to remain above 10 percent for a decade.

Many contemporaries feared that modern industrial production was growing faster than the capacity of traditional markets to consume goods. This, they believed, led to falling prices and to recession. The only solution, contemporaries assumed, was to expand markets and gain protected access to raw materials. While we now know this analysis was flawed, policymakers in the United States and Europe used these assumptions to justify a new wave of imperialist adventures in Asia, Africa, and Latin America (see Chapter 26). Most of these same powers also put in place high tariffs, but it soon became clear that they could not insulate their economies from the business cycle, for money continued to flow almost unhindered around the world.

One of the main causes of the growing interdependence of the global economy was the financial power of Great Britain, which dominated the flow of trade, finance, and information. In 1900 two-thirds of the world's submarine cables were British owned or passed through Britain, and over half of the world's shipping was British owned. Britain invested one-fourth of its national wealth overseas, much of it in India, the United States, and Argentina. British money financed many of the railroads, harbors, mines, and other big projects outside Europe. While other currencies fluctuated, the pound sterling was as good as gold, and nine-tenths of international transactions used sterling.

Nonindustrial areas were also tied to the world economy as never before. Because many of them produced raw materials that could be replaced by synthetic substitutes (like dyestuffs) or by alternative sources of supply, they were more vulnerable to changes in price and demand than were the industrialized nations. Developing regions that produced sugar, cotton, and dyes all experienced these upsets in the nineteenth century, leading to political instability in many

Section Review

- Industrialization spread throughout the world through trade and new technologies.

- Railroads, almost always financed by Western nations, spread to all continents, changing and enlarging cities and facilitating economic growth.

- Steamships and telegraph cables connected continents and encouraged trade.

- In three new industries—steel, chemicals, and electricity—the United States and Germany surpassed Great Britain.

- World trade boomed in an age of globalization.

cases. Nevertheless, until 1913 the value of exports from the tropical countries generally kept up with the growth of their populations.

27-2 Social Changes

How did the societies of the industrial countries change during this period?

As fast-growing populations swelled Europe's cities to unprecedented size, millions of other Europeans emigrated to the Americas. At the same time, strained relations between industrial employers and workers spawned labor movements and new forms of radical politics. Women as well found their lives dramatically altered by economic and technological change, both in the home and in the public sphere.

AP® Exam Tip
Understand the causes of rapid population growth in both urban and rural areas.

27-2a Population and Migration

The population of Europe grew faster from 1850 to 1914 than ever before or since, almost doubling from 265 million to 468 million. In non-European countries with predominantly white populations—the United States, Canada, Australia, New Zealand, and Argentina—the increase was even greater because of the inflow of European immigrants. There were many reasons for the mass migrations of this period: the Irish famine of 1847–1848; the persecution of Jews in Russia; endemic poverty coupled with population growth in Italy, Spain, Poland, and Scandinavia; and the cultural ties between Great Britain and English-speaking countries overseas. Equally important was the attraction of enhanced opportunities in places like Argentina, Australia, Canada, and the United States—all of which offered cheap land and strong economic growth. The availability to travelers of cheap and rapid steamship and railroad transportation at both ends of immigration pathways also contributed to the scale of this massive population transfer (see Environment & Technology: Railroads and Immigration).

Between 1850 and 1900, on average, over 1 million Europeans migrated overseas every year; then, between 1900 and 1914, the flood rose to over 3 million a year. Over this same fifty-year period the population of the United States and Canada rose from 25 million to 98 million, and the proportion of people of European ancestry in the world's population rose from one-fifth to one-third. Great Britain was the most important source of immigrants by far, but very large numbers of Germans, Italians, and Spaniards joined the swelling ranks of migrants.

Why did the number of Europeans and their descendants overseas jump so dramatically? Much of the increase came from a drop in mortality, as epidemics and starvation became less common. The Irish famine of the 1840s was the last peacetime famine in European history. As farmers plowed up the plains of North America and planted wheat, much of which was shipped to Europe, food supplies increased faster than population while prices dropped. New technologies like canning and refrigeration also made food more abundant year-round, facilitating the export of Argentine beef and mutton to Europe. The diet of Europeans and North Americans also improved as meat, fruits, vegetables, and oils became part of the daily fare of city dwellers in winter as well as in summer.

AP® Exam Tip
Consider the role of migration in population expansion, taking into account both the creation of ethnic enclaves and the impact of transportation technology, making some migration more temporary.

During this period Asians also migrated in large numbers as indentured laborers who were recruited to work on distant plantations, in mines, and on railroads (see Chapter 26). Indians went to Africa, Southeast Asia, and other tropical colonies of Great Britain. Along with Chinese, Indians also emigrated to the East Indies and the Caribbean to work on sugar plantations in places where slavery had been abolished. At the same time, Japanese migrated in large numbers to Brazil and other parts of Latin America. Many Japanese, as well as Chinese and Filipinos, also went to work in agriculture and menial trades in Hawaii and California, where they encountered growing hostility from European Americans.

27-2b Urbanization and Urban Environments

In 1851 Britain became the first nation with a majority of its population living in towns and cities. By 1914, 80 percent of Britain's population was urban, as were 60 percent of the German population and 45 percent of the French. Worldwide urban population grew from 3 percent in 1800 to 14 percent in 1900. At the same time, cities grew to unprecedented size. London grew

Why did so many Europeans emigrate to North America as well as to Argentina and Australia in the late nineteenth and early twentieth centuries? The quick answer is that millions of people longed to escape the poverty or tyranny of their home countries and start new lives in a land of freedom and opportunity. Personal desire alone, however, does not account for the migrations. After all, poverty and tyranny had existed long before the late nineteenth century. Two other factors helped determine when and where people migrated: whether they were allowed to migrate, and whether they were able to.

In the nineteenth century Asians were recruited to build railroads and work on farms and by 1880 roughly 300,000 Chinese had entered the United States. But from the 1890s on, the United States and Canada closed their doors to non-Europeans, so regardless of what they wanted, they could not move to North America. In contrast, emigrants from Europe were admitted almost without restriction until after the First World War.

The ability to travel was a result of improvements in transportation. Until the 1890s most immigrants came from Ireland, England, or Germany—countries with good rail transportation to their seaports and low fares for transport to North America as well as to more-distant destinations like Argentina and Australia by fast steamships. As rail lines were extended into eastern and southern Europe, more and more immigrants from Italy, Austria-Hungary, and Russia joined this flow.

Similarly, until the 1870s most European immigrants to North America settled on the east coast. Then, as the railroads pushed west, more of them settled on farms in the central and western parts of the continent. The power of railroads moved people as much as their desires did. When railroads were built in other attractive destinations for immigrants a similar pattern of dispersal occurred.

Questions for Analysis

1. What factors determined the volume of immigration?
2. How did technological innovations affect this flow?
3. Why were railroads crucial to the immigrant experience in the United States?

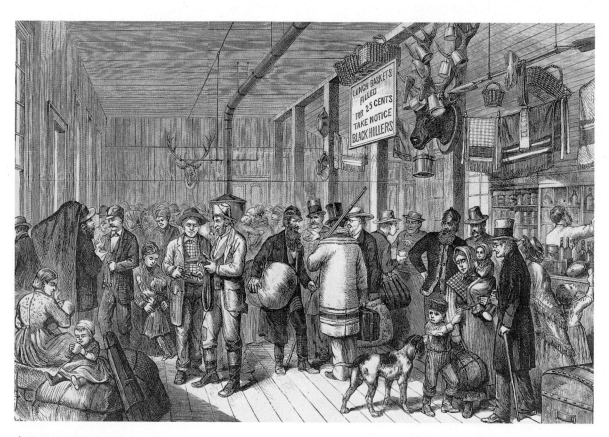

▲ **Emigrant Waiting Room**   The opening of the western region of the United States attracted settlers from the east coast and from Europe. These migrants are waiting for a train to take them to the Black Hills of Dakota during one of the gold rushes of the late nineteenth century. Library of Congress

from 2.7 million in 1850 to 6.6 million in 1900. New York, a small city of 64,000 people in 1800, reached 3.4 million by 1900, more than a fiftyfold increase. In 1800 New York had covered only the southernmost quarter of Manhattan Island, some 3 square miles (nearly 8 square kilometers); by 1900 it covered 150 square miles (390 square kilometers). Similarly, in the English Midlands, in the German Ruhr, and around Tokyo Bay, fast-growing towns fused into one another, filling in the fields and woods that had once separated them.

As cities grew, they changed in character. Newly built railroads not only brought goods into the cities on a predictable schedule but also allowed people to live farther apart. At first, only the well-to-do could afford to commute by train, but, by the end of the century, electric streetcars and subways allowed working-class people to live miles from their workplaces in new suburbs.

In preindustrial and early industrial cities, the poor crowded together in tenements; sanitation was bad; water was often contaminated with sewage; and darkness made life dangerous. Then in the nineteenth century, new urban technologies and the growing powers and responsibilities of governments transformed city life for all but the poorest residents. The most important change was the installation of pipes to bring in clean water and to carry away sewage. At the same time, gas lighting and then electric lighting made cities safer at night. By the turn of the twentieth century municipal governments in Europe and North America provided police and fire protection, sanitation and garbage removal, building and health inspection, public schools, parks, and other amenities unheard of a century earlier.

As sanitation improved, epidemics became rare. For the first time, urban death rates fell below birthrates. The decline in infant mortality was an especially significant indicator of improved hygiene and medical care. Confident that their children would survive infancy, couples began to limit the number of children they had, and ancient scourges like infanticide and child abandonment became less common.

To accommodate the growing population, builders created new neighborhoods, from crowded tenements for the poor to opulent mansions for the newly rich. In the United States urban planners laid out new cities, such as Chicago, on rectangular grids, and middle-class families moved to new developments on the edges of cities, the suburbs. In Paris older neighborhoods with narrow crooked streets and rickety tenements were torn down to make room for broad boulevards and modern apartment buildings. Brilliantly lit by gas and electricity, Paris became a model for city planners from New Delhi to Buenos Aires. The rich continued to live in inner cities that contained the monuments, churches, and palaces of preindustrial times, while many workers often moved to multi-family tenements in the outskirts.

Lower population densities and better transportation divided cities into industrial, commercial, and residential zones occupied by different social classes. Improvements such as public water and sewerage systems, electricity, and streetcars always benefited the wealthy first, then the middle class, and finally the working class. In the complex of urban life, businesses of all kinds arose, and the professions—engineering, accounting, research, journalism, and law, among others—took on increased importance. The new middle class created by the Industrial Revolution imitated the patterns of elites, exhibiting its wealth in fine houses with servants, when possible, and in elegant entertainment.

While urban environments improved in many ways, air quality worsened. Coal, burned to power steam engines and heat buildings, polluted the air, creating unpleasant and sometimes dangerous "pea-soup" fog and coating everything with a film of grimy dust. The thousands of horses that pulled carts and carriages covered the streets with their wastes, causing a terrible stench. The introduction of electricity helped alleviate some of these environmental problems. Electric motors and lamps did not pollute the air, and coal-burning power plants were usually built at a distance from cities. As electric trains and streetcars began replacing horse-drawn trolleys and coal-burning locomotives, cities became cleaner and healthier. However, most of the environmental benefits of electricity were to come in the twentieth century.

27-2c Middle-Class Women's "Separate Sphere"

In English-speaking countries, the period from about 1850 to 1901 is known as the **Victorian Age**. The expression refers not only to the reign of Queen Victoria of England (r. 1837–1901) but also to rules of behavior and to an ideology surrounding the family and relations between men and women. The Victorians contrasted the masculine ideals of strength and courage with the feminine virtues of beauty and kindness, and they idealized the home as a peaceful and loving refuge from the dog-eat-dog world of competitive capitalism.

AP® Exam Tip
Explain the causes and effects of and responses to rapid urbanization.

Victorian Age The reign of Queen Victoria of Great Britain (r. 1837–1901). The term is also used to describe late-nineteenth-century society, with its rigid moral standards and sharply differentiated roles for men and women and for middle-class and working-class people.

AP® Exam Tip
Consider the impact of the Industrial Revolution on gender and family structures.

Victorian morality claimed to be universal, yet it best fit the lives of upper- and middle-class European families. Men and women were thought to belong in **"separate spheres."** Successful businessmen spent their time at work or relaxing in men's clubs. They put their wives in charge of rearing the children, running the household, and spending the family income to enhance the family's social status. The majority of women from the less privileged classes, however, lived constantly with financial pressures. The majority worked outside the home for wages. Others took in laundry or did low-wage piecework, like sewing for garment companies, to supplement household income.

Before electric appliances, maintaining a middle-class home involved enormous amounts of work. Not only were families larger, but middle-class couples entertained often and lavishly. Carrying out these tasks required servants. A family's status and the activities and lifestyle of the "mistress of the house" depended on the availability of servants to help with household tasks. Only families that employed at least one full-time servant were considered middle class.

Toward the turn of the century modern technology began to transform middle-class homes. Modern plumbing eliminated the water pump and the outhouse. Central heating replaced fireplaces, stoves, trips to the basement for coal, and endless dusting. Gas and electricity lit houses and cooked food without soot, smoke, and ashes. In the early twentieth century wealthy families acquired the first vacuum cleaners and washing machines. However, these technological advances did not mean less housework for women. As families acquired new household appliances, they raised their standards of cleanliness, thus demanding just as much labor as before.

The most important duty of middle-class women was raising children. Victorian mothers nursed their own babies and showered their children with love and attention. Even those who could afford governesses remained personally involved in their children's education and upbringing. Girls' education was very different from that of boys. While boys were being prepared for the business world or the professions, girls were taught embroidery, drawing, and music—skills that enhanced their social graces and marriage prospects.

Young middle-class women could work until they got married, but only in genteel places like stores and offices, never in factories. When the typewriter and telephone were introduced into the business world in the 1880s, businessmen found that they could get better work at lower wages from educated young women than from men, and operating these machines then became stereotyped as women's work.

Most professional careers were closed to women, and few universities granted women degrees. In the United States higher education was available to women only at elite colleges in the East and teachers' colleges in the Midwest. European women had fewer opportunities. Before 1914 very few women became doctors, lawyers, or professional musicians. Instead, women were considered well suited to teaching young children and girls—an extension of the duties of Victorian mothers—but only until marriage. A married woman was expected to become pregnant right away and to stay home taking care of her own children rather than other people's.

"separate spheres"
  Nineteenth-century idea in Western societies that men and women, especially of the middle class, should have clearly differentiated roles in society: women as wives, mothers, and homemakers; men as breadwinners and participants in business and politics.

▲ **Separate Spheres in Great Britain**   In the Victorian Age, men and women of the middle and upper classes led largely separate lives. In *Aunt Emily's Visit* (1845), we see women and children at home, tended by a servant. *The Royal Exchange*, meanwhile, was a place for men to transact business.

A home life, no matter how busy, did not satisfy all middle-class women. Some became volunteer nurses or social workers, receiving little or no pay. Others organized as unpaid volunteers to fight prostitution, alcohol, and child labor. By the turn of the century a few women challenged male domination of politics and the law. Suffragists, led in Britain by Emmeline Pankhurst and in the United States by Elizabeth Cady Stanton and Susan B. Anthony, demanded the right to vote. By 1914 U.S. women had won the right to vote in twelve states. British women did not gain the right to vote until 1918.

27-2d Working-Class Women

In the new industrial cities, men and women no longer worked together at home or in the fields, a separation of work and home that affected women even more than men. While working-class women formed a majority of the workers in the modern textile industries and in domestic service, they were also expected to keep homes and raise children. As a result, they led lives of toil and pain. Parents expected girls as young as ten to contribute to the household or earn wages. In Japan, as in Ireland and New England, tenant farmers, squeezed by rising taxes and rents, were forced to send their young daughters to work in textile mills. Others became domestic servants, commonly working sixteen or more hours a day, six and a half days a week, for little more than room and board, usually living in unheated attics or basements. Without appliances, much of their work was physically hard: hauling coal and water up stairs, washing laundry by hand.

Many young women preferred factory work to domestic service because, while still exploited, they avoided some of the humiliation and snobbishness that was predictable when employed as domestic help. Most men and women found employment in industry. Men worked in construction, iron and steel, heavy machinery, or on railroads; women worked in textiles and the clothing trades, extensions of traditional women's household work (see Material Culture: Cotton Clothing in Chapter 25). Appalled by the abuses of women and children in the early years of industrialization, most industrial countries eventually passed protective legislation limiting hours worked or forbidding the employment of women in the hardest and most dangerous occupations, such as mining and foundry work. While the stated intention was to protect women, such legislation reinforced gender divisions in industry, keeping women in low-paid, subordinate positions.

AP® Exam Tip
Explain how demands for women's suffrage and an emergent feminism challenged political and gender hierarchies.

AP® Exam Tip
Explain how urbanization and industrialization led to the development of new social classes, including the middle class and the industrial working class.

◀ **Emmeline Pankhurst Under Arrest** The leader of the British women's suffrage movement frequently called attention to her cause by breaking the law to protest discrimination against women. Here Pankhurst (1858–1938) is being arrested and carried off to jail by the police. Jimmy Sime/Getty Images

Section Review

- As European population grew, millions migrated to other continents.

- Cities grew to enormous size, changing in character and posing difficult housing, sanitation, and environmental problems.

- Middle-class women inhabited a "separate sphere" from men and devoted their lives to their homes and families, but a few fought for equal rights.

- Working-class women, who had to keep a home while earning a living, led hard lives.

Even where women worked alongside men, in factories, for example, they earned only one-third to two-thirds of the wages paid men for similar work.

Except among the well-to-do, married women with children were expected to stay home, even if their husbands did not make enough to support the family. Yet they were expected to contribute to family income. Families who had room to spare, even a bed in a corner of the kitchen, took in boarders. Many women did piecework in addition to home-making such as sewing dresses, making hats or gloves, or weaving baskets. The hardest and worst-paid work was washing other people's clothes. Over-all, many poor women worked at home ten to twelve hours a day and even enlisted the help of their small children, perpetuating child labor practices long outlawed in factories. Without electric lighting and indoor plumbing, even ordinary household duties like cooking and washing remained heavy burdens.

27-3 Socialism and Labor Movements

How did the social consequences of industrialization lead to the rise of socialist and labor movements?

The experience of industrialization combined with the revolutionary ideas and experiences of the late eighteenth century to produce two kinds of mass movements that demanded economic and political reforms: socialism and labor unions. **Socialism** was an ideology developed by radical thinkers who believed that inequality and injustice were the consequences of industrialization and that only strong government regulations, even direct control of industries in some cases, could protect industrial workers from the predatory actions of their employers. **Labor unions** were organizations formed by industrial workers to defend their interests in negotiations with employers. Many grew out of pre-industrial craft organizations like guilds. Unions generally focused their efforts on gaining higher wages and better working conditions, rather than on economic transformation. The socialist and labor movements were never identical. Most of the time they were allies; occasionally they competed for the support of workers.

27-3a Revolutionary Alternatives

The growing wealth and power of industrial elites and the harsh living and working conditions experienced by industrial workers led to the formation of labor unions, the creation of the first government social welfare policies, demands for voting rights, and, for some, the dream of revolutionary transformation. Those seeking a revolution were divided among numerous parties and factions that seldom agreed with each other. Within the diverse and contentious world of left-leaning politics (see Chapter 22 for background), **Karl Marx** (1818–1883) was a formidable theorist of revolution as well as a major contestant for power. Marx shared the Enlightenment's enthusiasm for reason and logic and identified his revolutionary ideal as "scientific socialism." His adherents generally referred to themselves as communists or Marxists. Marx believed that the relentless competition inherent in industrial capitalism would lead ultimately to a social order divided between a wealthy powerful few and a mass of exploited and impoverished workers. This division, once in place, would inevitably lead in Marx's view to revolutions that would end capitalism and create a dictatorship of the proletariat (industrial workers). Once accomplished, this revolution by workers would equitably distribute the material benefits and scientific progress achieved by the Industrial Revolution to society in general. With private property abolished, Marx asserted, the resources of government and industry could be harnessed to end poverty and injustice.

Many of those committed to revolutionary change impatiently rejected Marx's insistence that the mature development of industrial capitalism and the appearance of the modern proletariat were preconditions for revolutionary action and violent resistance to the status quo. They

Socialism A political ideology that originated in Europe in the 1830s. Socialists advocated government protection of workers from exploitation by property owners and government ownership of key industries. This ideology led to the founding of socialist or labor parties throughout Europe in the second half of the nineteenth century.

Labor union An organization of workers in a particular industry or trade, created to defend the interests of members through strikes or direct negotiations with employers.

Karl Marx German journalist and philosopher, founder of the Marxist branch of socialism. He is known especially as author of two books: *Manifesto of the Communist Party* (1848) and *Das Kapital* (Vols. I–III, 1867–1894).

sought redemptive action immediately. Although in broad agreement with Marx's critique of capitalism, his political rivals on the revolutionary left believed that the levels of injustice and inequality already present in industrializing European society justified revolutionary violence right away. Some of these revolutionaries also rejected Marx's belief that his proposed dictatorship of the proletariat, or, indeed, any form of revolutionary government, could avoid recreating the inequality and injustice that already oppressed the poor. Russian intellectual Mikhail Bakunin (1814–1876) argued forcibly that peasants, displaced and unemployed artisans, and other exploited groups also had revolutionary potential and, consequently, that many unindustrialized regions of Europe were already ripe for revolution. Bakunin and his followers also dismissed Marx's faith in a future worker's government as naive: for them government, like capital, was inherently oppressive.

Bakunin exercised a powerful influence over the development of anarchism, the chief revolutionary alternative to communism. Anarchists believed that revolution could be achieved through direct action by individuals and small groups, what they called "propaganda of the deed." One key result of this movement's development was a series of assassinations and bombings that shook the political structures of Europe and the Americas. These attacks included the bombings of the opera (1893) and Corpus Christi celebration (1896) in Spain and the Haymarket bombing in Chicago (1896). They also included the assassinations of President Carnot of France (1894), Prime Minister Cánovas del Castillo of Spain (1897), Empress Elizabeth of Austria (1898), King Umberto of Italy (1900), and President William McKinley of the United States (1901).

The conflict between Marx and Bakunin culminated in 1872 when Bakunin and his adherents were expelled from the revolutionary umbrella organization, the International Workingman's Association. While the followers of Marx forced Bakunin from the center of revolutionary activity, his followers remained a potent source of political violence and working-class mobilization in Italy, Spain, and Argentina well into the twentieth century.

AP® Exam Tip
Examine the reasons for and impacts of workers' organizations, labor unions, and workers' movements that promoted alternative visions of society (such as Marxism).

27-3b Labor Unions and Movements

Since the beginning of the nineteenth century, European workers had united to create "friendly societies" for mutual assistance in times of illness, unemployment, or disability. Unions grew in influence once the laws forbidding workers from striking were abolished in Britain in the 1850s and then in the rest of Europe soon thereafter. Labor unions sought not only better wages but also improved working conditions and insurance against illness, accidents, disability, and old age. These organizations soon spread across Europe and to the Americas. They eventually were organized in Asia and Africa as well. This movement grew slowly because unions required a permanent staff as well as a great deal of money to sustain their members during strikes. Nevertheless, by the end of the century, British labor unions counted 2 million members, and German and American unions had 1 million members each. Once organized, unions became a political force in all democratic countries, advocating for improved wages and working conditions.

Just as labor unions strove to give workers a larger share in the benefits of a capitalist economy, new political parties sought to persuade workers to become part of the existing political system. Beginning in Europe and spreading quickly to the Americas, democratic reform and the campaign against economic injustice were entwined in a common struggle against entrenched privilege. The nineteenth century saw a gradual extension of the right to vote throughout Europe and in both North and South America. Universal male suffrage became law in the United States in 1870, in France and Germany in 1871, in Britain in 1885, and in the rest of Europe soon thereafter. With so many newly enfranchised workers, many socialist politicians hoped to capture seats in their nations' parliaments. Rather than seize power through revolution, these "democratic socialists" expected to obtain concessions from government and eventually even to form a government, rejecting the violent pathway embraced by communists and anarchists.

▲ **Mikhail Bakunin** Anarchist, intellectual, and political rival of Karl Marx. World History Archive/Alamy Stock Photo

Section Review

- Karl Marx and Mikhail Bakunin expected a workers' revolution, but later socialists hoped to gain influence through elections.

- Labor movements and unions worked to improve workers' pay and working conditions.

- Social Democrats believed that political action within electoral politics could improve the conditions of the working class.

Working-class women, burdened with both job and family responsibilities, found little time for politics and were not welcome in the male-dominated trade unions or in radical political parties. A few radicals such as German socialist Rosa Luxemburg and American **anarchist** Emma Goldman became famous but did not have a large following. It was never easy to reconcile the demands of male workers with those of women. In 1889 German socialist Clara Zetkin wrote: "Just as the male worker is subjected by the capitalist, so is the woman [subjected] by the man, and she will always remain in subjugation until she is economically independent. Work is the indispensable condition for economic independence." Six years later, she recognized that the liberation of women would have to await a change in the position of the working class as a whole: "The proletarian woman cannot attain her highest ideal through a movement for the equality of the female sex, she attains salvation only through the fight for the emancipation of labor."[2]

27-4 Nationalism and the Rise of Italy, Germany, and Japan

How was nationalism transformed from a revolutionary to a conservative ideology?

The most influential idea of the nineteenth century was **nationalism**. Whereas individuals had been considered the subjects of a sovereign in the era before the American and French revolutions, eighteenth-century revolutionaries redefined individuals as the citizens of *nations*—a concept identified with a territory, the state that ruled it, and the culture of its people.

27-4a Language and National Identity in Europe Before 1871

Shared language was usually a crucial element in the creation of a shared sense of national identity. It was important both as a way to promote shared experience and historical memory among the people of a nation and as the means of persuasion by which political leaders could inspire their followers to collective action. And the skillful use of shared language was understood to be the key political tool of the new generation of political activists, most of them lawyers, teachers, students, and journalists. Yet language and citizenship seldom coincided perfectly.

The fit between the French nation and the population of French speakers was closer than in most large countries, though some French-speakers lived outside of France and a small minority of French citizens spoke other languages. Italian- and German-speaking peoples, however, were dispersed among many small states in nineteenth-century Europe. Living in the Austrian Empire were peoples who spoke German, Czech, Slovak, Hungarian, Polish, and other languages. Even where people spoke a common language, they were often divided by religion or by institutional identity. The Irish, though English-speaking, were mostly Catholic, whereas the English were primarily Protestant. As nationalists began to insist that the boundaries of states be redrawn to accommodate linguistic, religious, or cultural identities, multiethnic and religiously diverse states like the Austro-Hungarian Empire faced the threat of dissolution or chronic political instability. In Italy and Germany nationalist agitation led to the forging of large new states out of many small ones in 1871. In central and eastern Europe, nationalism led to the breakup of large multiethnic states and the creation of smaller homogeneous ones.

anarchist Revolutionaries who wanted to abolish all private property and governments, usually by violence, and replace them with free associations of groups.

nationalism A political ideology that associates legitimate government with the destiny of a nation—a community defined by a common culture and history as well as by the historic occupation of a specific territory. In the late eighteenth and early nineteenth centuries, nationalism was a force for political mobilization and collective action in western Europe.

[2]Quoted in Bonnie S. Anderson and Judith P. Zinsser, *A History of Their Own: Women in Europe from Prehistory to the Present*, vol. 2 (New York, NY: Harper & Row, 1988), 372, 387.

Until the 1860s nationalism was closely associated with **liberalism**, the revolutionary middle-class ideology associated with the political ideas of the Enlightenment and with the early objectives of the French Revolution. Liberalism asserted the sovereignty of the people, and demanded constitutional government, a national parliament, and freedom of expression (see Chapter 23). Liberals commonly supported free trade and market competition as well. The most famous nationalist of the early nineteenth century was Italian liberal Giuseppe Mazzini (**jew-SEP-pay mots-EE-nee**) (1805–1872), the leader of the failed revolution of 1848 in Italy. Mazzini sought to unify the Italian peninsula into one nation and cooperated with revolutionaries elsewhere to bring nationhood and liberty to all peoples oppressed by tyrants and foreigners. When confronted with the destabilizing energies of liberalism and nationalism the governments of Russia, Prussia, and Austria censored the new ideas and jailed many dissidents but, in the end, they failed to suppress these revolutionary tendencies, which remained a potent political force into the twentieth century.

The revolutions of 1848 convinced conservatives that governments could not forever keep their citizens out of politics and that mass politics, if properly managed by the elite, could strengthen rather than weaken the national governments (see Chapter 23). A new generation of conservative political leaders learned how to preserve the status quo through public education infused with nationalist ideology, universal military service, and colonial conquests, all of which built a sense of national unity while muting class conflict.

27-4b The Unification of Italy, 1860–1870

By the middle of the nineteenth century, popular sentiment was building throughout Italy for national unification. Opposing it were Pope Pius IX, who abhorred everything modern and also directly ruled the Papal States, and Austria, which controlled two Italian provinces, Lombardy and Venetia (see Map 27.1). Three individuals played key roles in the unification of Italy, the prime minister of Piedmont-Sardinia, Count Camillo Benso di Cavour, the intellectual and activist Giuseppe Mazzini, and the man of action Giuseppe Garibaldi. Cavour (1810–1861) saw the geopolitical rivalry between France and Austria as an opportunity to unify Italy. He secretly formed an alliance with France led by Napoleon III and then instigated a war with Austria in 1858. The war was followed by uprisings throughout northern and central Italy in favor of joining Piedmont-Sardinia, a moderate constitutional monarchy under King Victor Emmanuel.

Giuseppe Mazzini (1805–1871) was the leading intellectual among Italian patriots and devoted his life to promoting unification (see Diversity & Dominance: Giuseppe Mazzini on Revolutionary Nationalism). Forced into exile on multiple occasions he pressed other patriots to embrace republicanism as well as unification. He was the founder of the influential organization Young Italy, dedicated to securing "Independence and Liberty." His vision of a united and modern Italy was at odds with Cavour's utilitarian embrace of the Piedmont monarchy. If Mazzini gave this movement its ideals, Garibaldi was the movement's charismatic source of combustion.

While Cavour's conservative, top-down approach to unification prevailed in the north, a more radical approach succeeded in the south. In 1860 the fiery revolutionary **Giuseppe Garibaldi** (**jew-SEP-pay gary-BAHL-dee**) (1807–1882) and a small band of followers landed in Sicily and then in southern Italy, overthrew the Kingdom of the Two Sicilies, and prepared to found a democratic republic. The royalist Cavour, however, took advantage of the unsettled political situation to sideline Garibaldi and transform Piedmont-Sardinia into a new, unified Kingdom of Italy. Unification was completed with the addition of Venetia in 1866 and the Papal States in 1870.

The process of Italian unification illustrates the malleability of nationalism that, in this case, had compromised its radical commitment to republicanism and democracy to achieve national unification under the conservative leadership of King Victor Emmanuel and his conservative supporters, who saw unification as the means to establish a strong centralized government committed to conservative ideals.

27-4c The Unification of Germany, 1866–1871

The unification of most German-speaking people into a single state in 1871 had momentous consequences for the world. Until the 1860s the German-speaking region of central Europe consisted of Prussia, the western half of the Austrian Empire, and numerous smaller states

liberalism A political ideology that emphasizes the civil rights of citizens, representative government, and the protection of private property as well as more economic freedom. This ideology, derived from the Enlightenment, was especially popular among the property-owning middle classes of Europe and North America.

Giuseppe Garibaldi Italian nationalist and revolutionary who conquered Sicily and Naples and added them to a unified Italy in 1860.

MAP 27.1 Unification of Italy, 1860–1870 The unification of Italy was achieved by the expansion of the kingdom of Piedmont-Sardinia, with the help of France.

How long did Italy's unification take, and what Great Power lost territory as a result? Did Piedmont-Sardinia's proximity to France influence unification?

Otto von Bismarck
Chancellor (prime minister) of Prussia from 1862 until 1871, when he became chancellor of Germany. A conservative nationalist, he led Prussia to victory against Austria (1866) and France (1870) and was responsible for the creation of the German Empire in 1871.

(see Map 27.2). Some German nationalists wanted to unite all Germans under the Austrian throne. Others wanted to exclude the Austrian Empire with its many non-Germanic peoples and unite all other German-speaking areas under Prussia. The divisions were also religious: Austria and southwestern Germany were Catholic; Prussia and the northeast were Lutheran. In this context the Prussian state had two advantages: (1) the newly developed industries of the Rhineland, and (2) the first European army to make use of railroads, telegraphs, breechloading rifles, steel artillery, and other products of modern industry.

During the reign of King Wilhelm I (r. 1861–1888), the Prussian government was dominated by a brilliant and authoritarian aristocrat, Chancellor **Otto von Bismarck (UTT-oh von BIS-mark)** (1815–1898). Bismarck was determined to use Prussian industry and German nationalism to make his state the dominant power in Germany. In 1866 Prussia attacked and quickly defeated Austria. To everyone's surprise, Prussia took no Austrian territory. Instead, Prussia and some smaller states formed the North German Confederation, the nucleus of the future Germany. Then in 1870 Bismarck attacked France, still led by Napoleon III. Prussian armies, joined by

MAP 27.2 Unification of Germany, 1866–1871 Germany was united after a series of short, successful wars by the kingdom of Prussia against Austria in 1866 and against France in 1871.

What Prussian neighbors posed the greatest obstacles to unification? Did the successful unification of Germany help lead to the First World War?

---

troops from other German states, used their superior firepower and tactics to achieve a quick victory. "Blood and iron" were the foundation of the new German Empire.

The German spoils of victory included a large indemnity and control over two provinces of France bordering on Germany: Alsace and Lorraine. While the French paid the indemnity easily enough, they resented the loss of their provinces. To the Germans, this region was German because a majority of its inhabitants spoke German. To the French, it was French because most of its inhabitants considered themselves French. These two conflicting definitions of nationalism kept enmity between France and Germany smoldering for decades.

For the French, defeat led to the overthrow of Napoleon III, who had been defeated and captured. With a German army threatening Paris, the imperial government was replaced by the

One of the most potent intellectual and political forces in nineteenth-century Europe and the Americas was nationalism. At its most basic it was a shared pride in the history and accomplishments of one's native people. It was also often an emotional belief in national destiny and a determination to pursue national glory. Wherever peoples shared language, history, and culture but were divided politically and subject to different political institutions and laws, as in Italy and Germany, for example, popular movements supported unification. These desires to create nations organized around shared ethnicity directly threatened many of the long-standing political arrangements that had been created over centuries by the ruling dynasties of Europe.

In the 1830s many young Italians regarded the political divisions imposed on their native land by the Austrian crown, local monarchies, and the pope as intolerable. One of the most important advocates of Italian unification was Giuseppe Mazzini (1805–1872), whose revolutionary activities led to his imprisonment and exile in 1831. While in exile he created the patriot organization Young Italy and continued to urge insurrection. He then returned to Italy from England during the continent-wide revolutionary upheavals of 1848 (see Chapter 23). Although these events seemed to promise the realization of his dreams, a combination of Austrian and French military actions and deep divisions among Italian political leaders led to disappointment. Italy's unification came after 1860 through a military alliance between France and the king of Sardinia, disappointing Mazzini, who was a supporter of democracy and social justice as well as a patriot. While he continued to work for the full emancipation of Italy and for democracy, he refused a seat in the Italian Chamber of Deputies.

Every revolution is the work of a principle that has been accepted as a basis of faith. Whether it invoke nationality, liberty, equality, or religion, it always fulfills itself in the name of a principle, that is to say, of a great truth, which being recognized and approved by the majority of the inhabitants of a country, constitutes a common belief, and sets before the masses a new aim, while authority misrepresents or rejects it. A revolution, violent or peaceful, includes a negation and an affirmation: the negation of an existing order of things, the affirmation of a new order to be substituted for it. A revolution proclaims that the state is rotten; that its machinery no longer meets the needs of the greatest number of the citizens; that its institutions are powerless to direct the general movement; that popular and social thought has passed beyond the vital principle of those institutions; that the new phase in the development of the national faculties finds neither expression nor representation in the official constitution of the country, and that it must therefore create one for itself. This revolution does create. Since its task is to increase, and not diminish the nation's patrimony, it violates neither the truths that the majority possess, nor the rights they hold sacred; but it reorganizes everything on a new basis; it gathers and harmonizes round the new principle all the elements and forces of the country; it gives a unity of direction toward the new aim, to all those tendencies which before were scattered in the pursuit of different aims. Then the revolution has done its work.

We recognize no other meaning in revolution. If a revolution did not imply a general reorganization by virtue of a social principle; if it did not remove a discord in the elements of a state, and place harmony in its stead; if it did not secure a moral unity; so far from declaring ourselves revolutionists, we should believe it our duty to oppose the revolutionary movement with all our power.

Without the purpose hinted at above, there may be riots, and at times victorious insurrections, but no revolutions. You will have changes of men and administration; one caste succeeding to another; one dynastic branch ousting the other. This necessitates retreat; a slow reconstruction of the past, which the insurrection had suddenly destroyed; the gradual re-establishment, under new names, of the old order of things,

French Third Republic. In Paris a potent combination of injured national pride and class resentment led to the creation of a revolutionary Commune committed to resist the Germans as well as the new national government that had surrendered. A war begun by the competing imperial governments of France and Germany was now transformed into a brutal contest between the newly created French Republic supported by the elite and middle class as well as by the provinces and the Paris Commune supported by urban workers and revolutionary socialists. By the time the national government prevailed, both sides had committed hundreds of atrocities and nearly 10,000 Parisians had been killed.

27-4d The West Challenges Japan

In Japan the emperor served a largely religious function and was revered but had no effective political power. Instead, Japan was governed by the Tokugawa Shogunate—a secular government under a military leader, or *shogun*, that had come to power in 1600 (see Chapter 21). Local

which the people had risen to destroy. Societies have such need of unity that if they miss it in insurrection they turn back to a restoration. Then there is a new discontent, a new struggle, a new explosion.

Wherever, in fact, individual rights are exercised without the influence of some great thought that is common to all; where every individual's interests are harmonized by some organization that is directed by a positive ruling principle, and by the consciousness of a common aim, there must be a tendency for some to usurp others' rights. In a society like ours, where a division into classes, call them what you will, still exists in full strength, every right is bound to clash with another right, envious and mistrustful of it; every interest naturally conflicts with an opposing interest: the landlord's with the peasant's; the manufacturer's or capitalist's with the workman's. All through Europe—since equality, however accepted in theory, has been rejected in practice, and the sum of social wealth has accumulated in the hands of a small number of men, while the masses gain but a mere pittance by their relentless toil; it is a cruel irony, it gives inequality a new lease of life, if you establish unrestricted liberty, and tell men they are free, and bid them use their rights.

A social sphere must have its center; a center to the individualists that jostle with each other inside it; a center to all the scattered rays that diffuse and waste their light and heat. The theory that bases the social structure on individual interests cannot supply this center. The absence of a center, or the selection among opposing interests of that which has the most vigorous life, means either anarchy or privilege—that is, either barren strife or the germ of aristocracy, under whatever name it disguises itself, this is the parting of the ways, which it is impossible to avoid.

Is this what we want when we invoke a revolution, since a revolution is indispensable to reorganize our nationality?

. . . We are therefore driven to the sphere of principles. We must revive belief in them, we must fulfill a work of faith. The logic of things demands it. Principles alone are constructive. Ideals are never translated into facts without the general recognition of some strong belief. Great things are never done except by the rejection of individualism and a constant sacrifice of self to the common progress. Self-sacrifice is the sense of duty in action. . . . The individual is sacred; his interests, his rights are inviolable. But to make them the only foundation of the political structure, and tell each individual to win his future with his own unaided strength, is to surrender society and progress to the accidents of chance nature, his social instinct; to plant egotism in the soul; and in the long run impose the dominion of the strong over the weak, of those who have over those who have not. The many futile attempts of the past forty years prove this. . . . If by dint of example you can root in a nation's heart the principle that the French Revolution proclaimed but never carried out, that the State owes every member the means of existence or the chance to work for it, and add a fair definition of existence, you have prepared the triumph of right over privilege; the end of the monopoly of one class over another, and the end of pauperism; for which at present there are only palliatives . . . Christian charity, or cold and brutal maxims like those of the English school of political economists.

When you have raised men's minds to believe in the other principle that society is an association of laborers—and can, thanks to that belief, deduce both in theory and practice all its consequences; you will have no more castes, no more aristocracies, or civil wars, or crisis. You will have a People.

AP® History Reasoning Skills

Causation *According to Mazzini, which aspects of the French Revolution were key to the "triumph of right over privilege"?*

Contextualization *How does the rise of nationalism in Italy or Germany support Mazzini's statement that "a revolution begins with a negation and an affirmation"?*

Source: *The Literature of Italy, 1265–1907*, vol. VI, eds. Rossiter Johnson and Dora K. Ranous, trans. Thomas Okey (New York: The National Alumni, 1907), 296–300, 303, 305.

---

lords, called *daimyos*, were permitted to control their lands and populations with very little interference from the shogunate. In 1603 the shogunate established its capital in the port of Edo (modern Tokyo).

The shogunate slowly expanded commercial and cultural contacts with the outside world in the early decades of the seventeenth century. This included Asian neighbors and a more limited trade with the Dutch, English, and Spanish. At the same time Catholic missionaries created a small community of Japanese converts. These related initiatives culminated in 1615 when Japan sent an official mission across the Pacific to the Spanish colony of New Spain in a Japanese-built ship modeled on Iberian design. The head of the mission then proceeded to Europe and met the Pope as well as secular rulers. While providing some benefits, expanding contacts revealed the shogunate's relative military and economic weaknesses. So, even as Japan sponsored three transpacific voyages, the decision was being made to curtail all foreign contacts.

After 1612 the shogunate had begun an incremental suppression of both Christianity and foreign trade. Converted Christians were first purged from the government. A wave of

AP® Exam Tip
Explain how expansion of U.S. and European influence on Tokugawa Japan led to the emergence of Meiji Japan.

executions of Catholic missionaries and Japanese converts in the 1620s then led to a rebellion that included Christian samurai in the 1630s. Reacting to this turmoil, the shogunate expelled foreigners, limited foreign trade to two small ports, and prohibited foreigners from entering Japan and Japanese from going abroad. They did permit the Dutch to retain a small commercial outpost at Nagasaki and this became Japan's narrow window on the world until Perry's arrival two and half centuries later.

While the penalty for breaking these laws was death, many Japanese ignored them. The most flagrant violators were powerful lords in southern Japan who ran large and very successful pirate or black-market operations and benefited from the decentralization of the political system of the shogunate. But when a genuine foreign threat appeared—as when, in 1792, Russian and British ships were spotted off the Japanese coast—the local lords realized that Japan was too weak and decentralized to resist a foreign invasion. In response, some of these regional lords began to develop their own reformed armies, arsenals, and shipyards. At the same time a small number of Japanese intellectuals experimented with European culture, what they called "Dutch learning."

When Commodore Matthew C. Perry, backed by a powerful fleet, demanded that Japan open its ports to trade in 1853, he precipitated a political crisis. The shogun's advisers advocated capitulation to Perry in an effort to avoid experiencing China's humiliation in the Opium and Arrow Wars. As a result, when Perry returned in 1854, representatives of the shogun indicated their willingness to sign the Treaty of Kanagawa (**KAH-nah-GAH-wah**), modeled on the unequal treaties between China and the Western powers. Angry and disappointed, some provincial governors called for the destruction of the Tokugawa regime and an end to the prohibition of foreigners in Japan.

Hostility to the policies of the shogunate was focused in Satsuma (**SAT-soo-mah**) and Choshu (**CHOE-shoo**), two large domains in southern Japan that had become wealthy and ambitious. Granted some autonomy by their distance from Edo (Tokyo) and benefitting from strong economies and growing populations, they were well placed to topple the archaic old order, but first needed to forge an alliance. When British and French ships shelled the southwestern coasts in 1864 to protest the treatment of foreigners, the action enraged the provincial samurai who rejected the Treaty of Kanagawa imposed by Perry and resented the shogunate's inability to protect the country. In 1867 the leaders of Choshu finally realized that they should stop warring with their rival province, Satsuma, and join forces to lead a rebellion against the shogunate.

27-4e The Meiji Restoration and the Modernization of Japan, 1868–1894

The civil war was intense but brief. In 1868 provincial rebels overthrew the Tokugawa Shogunate and declared the fourteen-year-old emperor Mutsuhito (**moo-tsoo-HEE-toe**) (r. 1868–1912) "restored." The new leaders called their regime the "**Meiji (MAY-gee) Restoration**" after Mutsuhito's reign name (*Meiji* means "enlightened rule"). The "Meiji oligarchs," as the new rulers were known, were extraordinarily talented and far-sighted. Determined to protect their country from Western imperialism, they encouraged Japan's transformation into "a rich country with a strong army" with world-class industries. Though imposed from above, the Meiji Restoration marked as profound a change in Asia as the French Revolution had marked in Europe (see Map 27.3).

The new oligarchs were under no illusion that they could fend off the Westerners without changing their institutions and their society. In the Charter Oath issued in 1868, the young emperor included a prophetic phrase: "Knowledge shall be sought throughout the world and thus shall be strengthened the foundation of the imperial polity." It was to be the motto of a new Japan, which embraced all foreign ideas, institutions, and techniques that could strengthen the nation without ceding control to the foreign agents that facilitated this transformation. The literacy rate in Japan was the highest in Asia at the time, and the oligarchs shrewdly exploited it in their introduction of new educational systems, a conscript army, and new communications. The government was able to establish heavy industry, thanks to decades of industrial development and financing in the provinces in the early 1800s. With a conscript army and a revamped educational system, the oligarchs attempted to create a new citizenry that was literate and competent but also loyal and obedient.

AP® Exam Tip
Explain several examples of state-sponsored visions of industrialization, such as the Meiji reforms.

Meiji Restoration
The political program that followed the destruction of the Tokugawa Shogunate in 1868, in which a collection of young leaders set Japan on the path of political centralization, industrialization, and imperialism.

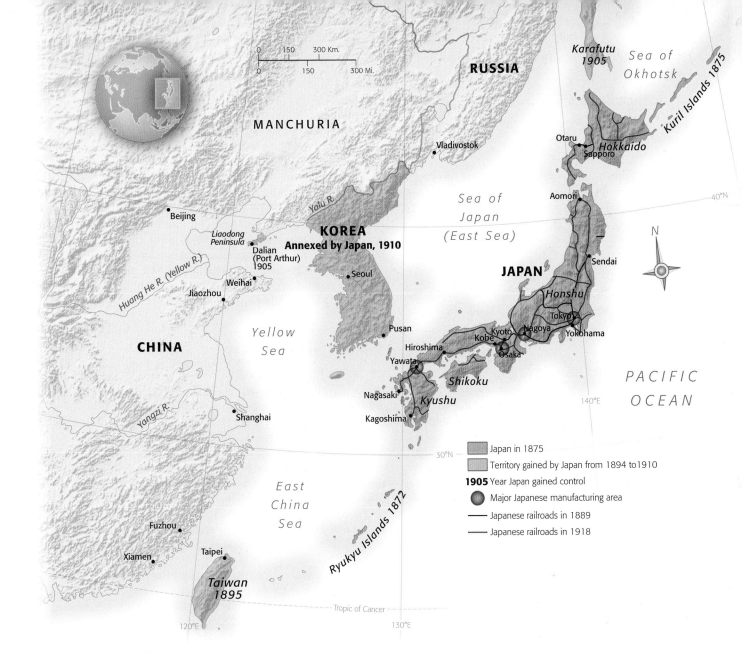

MAP 27.3 Expansion and Modernization of Japan, 1868–1918 As Japan acquired modern industry, it followed the example of the European powers in seeking overseas colonies. This new colonial empire grew at the expense of Japan's neighbors: Taiwan was taken from China in 1895; Karafutu (Sakhalin) was taken from Russia in 1905; and all of Korea became a Japanese colony in 1910.

1. Does the map indicate why naval modernization became a key policy objective in Japan? Did geography help or hinder Japanese modernization?

The Meiji leaders copied the government structure of imperial Germany and modeled the new Japanese navy on the British and the army on the Prussian. They also introduced Western-style postal and telegraph services, railroads and harbor improvements, banking, clocks, and calendars. To learn the secrets of Western strength, they sent hundreds of students to Britain, Germany, and the United States. They also promoted the translation of key scientific and technological research into Japanese. This deep engagement with Europe and the United States led to the popularity of Western-style clothing and hairstyles as well as to Western entertainments like garden parties and formal dances.

The government was especially interested in Western technology. It opened vocational, technical, and agricultural schools, founded four imperial universities, and brought in foreign experts to advise on medicine, science, and engineering. To encourage industrialization, the

Section Review

- Nationalism, the most powerful new ideology of the nineteenth century, defined nations primarily on the basis of language.

- Cavour and Garibaldi helped unify Italy between 1860 and 1870, and Bismarck unified Germany from 1866 to 1871.

- In response to Western intrusion, provincial Japanese lords launched the Meiji Restoration and quickly transformed Japan into a modern industrial nation.

- During this era, the privileged few often misinterpreted Charles Darwin's theory of evolution to justify their control of wealth and power.

government promoted the importation of modern manufacturing machinery in key fields like textiles and railroad equipment. Government direct investment led to rapid growth and Japan quickly became an exporter of cloth and inexpensive consumer goods. These Japanese government-dominated industries exploited their workers ruthlessly, just as the first capitalist industries in Europe and America had done. Under financial pressure, the government eventually sold these enterprises to private investors, mainly large *zaibatsu* (**zye-BOT-soo**), or conglomerates, in 1881, but continued to encourage domestic technological innovation. Thus, carpenter Toyoda Sakichi founded the Toyoda Loom Works (now Toyota Motor Company) in 1906; ten years later he patented the world's most advanced automatic loom.

27-4f Nationalism and Social Darwinism

The Franco-Prussian War of 1870–1871 changed the political climate of Europe, returning France to republicanism and making it more liberal. Germany, Austria-Hungary (as the Austrian Empire had renamed itself in 1867), and Russia remained conservative and mobilized nationalism to help maintain the status quo. The kingdom of Italy completed the unification of the peninsula begun decades earlier.

Nationalism and parliamentary elections made politicians of all parties appeal to public opinion. They were greatly aided by the expansion of the press, especially cheap daily newspapers that sought to increase circulation by publishing sensational articles about overseas conquests and foreign threats. As governments increasingly came to recognize the advantages of an educated population in the competition between states, they opened public schools in every town and admitted women into public-service jobs for the first time. Politicians and journalists appealed to the emotions of the poor, diverting their anger from their employers to foreigners and their votes from socialist to nationalist parties.

In many countries dominant majorities used nationalism to impose their language, religion, or customs on minority populations. The Russian Empire attempted to "Russify" its diverse ethnic populations. The Spanish government made Spanish compulsory in the schools, newspapers, and courts of its Basque- and Catalan-speaking provinces. Similarly, the millions of new immigrants to the United States were pressured to learn English and express patriotic sentiments.

Western culture in the late nineteenth century exalted the powerful over the weak, men over women, rich over poor, Europeans over other races, and humans over nature. Some people attempted to use science to justify and defend the harsh inequalities of gender, ethnicity, and class that were common across Europe and the Americas. One of the most influential scientists of the century, and the one whose ideas were most widely appropriated and willfully misinterpreted, was English biologist Charles Darwin (1809–1882).

In his 1859 book *On the Origin of the Species*, Darwin challenged common assumptions derived from religious beliefs by arguing that the earth was much older than previously believed. Based on years of research of the fossil record and careful observation of nature, he proposed that all forms of life had either evolved in the struggle for survival or become extinct over the course of hundreds of thousands of years. While controversial initially, Darwin's discoveries led to a revolution in the life sciences.

Philosopher Herbert Spencer (1820–1903) and others took up Darwin's ideas of "natural selection" and "survival of the fittest" and applied them superficially to the history of human societies. These "Social Darwinists" developed elaborate pseudo-scientific theories of racial and ethnic differences, claiming that they were the result not of history but of biology. They saw social and racial differences as resulting from natural processes and opposed state intervention to alleviate inequities. Although not based on any research, these ideas gave a scientific-sounding justification for the power of the privileged as well as for imperialism.

AP® Exam Tip

Explain how emerging cultural, religious, and racial ideologies, including Social Darwinism, were used to justify imperialism.

27-5 The Great Powers of Europe, 1871–1900

How did the forces of nationalism affect the major powers of Europe?

After the middle of the century, politicians and journalists discovered that minor incidents involving foreigners could be used to stir up popular indignation against neighboring countries. Military officers, impressed by the awesome power of the weapons that modern industry provided, began to think that their weapons were invincible. As a result, rivalries over colonial territories, ideological differences, and even minor border incidents or trade disagreements contributed to growing international tensions and, ultimately, to war.

27-5a Germany at the Center of Europe

In the final decades of the nineteenth century international relations revolved around Germany because it was located in the center of Europe and had the most powerful army on the European continent. After creating a unified Germany in 1871, Bismarck declared that his country had no further territorial ambitions, and he put his efforts into maintaining the peace in Europe. To isolate France, he forged a loose coalition with Austria-Hungary (defeated by Prussia in 1866) and Russia, the other two conservative monarchical powers. Despite their competing ambitions in the Balkans, he was able to keep his coalition together for twenty years.

Bismarck proved equally adept at strengthening German unity at home. To weaken the influence of middle-class liberals, he extended the vote to all adult men, thereby allowing Socialists supported by the working class to win seats in the *Reichstag* or parliament. By imposing high tariffs on manufactured goods and wheat, he gained the support of both the wealthy industrialists of the Rhineland and the great landowners of eastern Germany, traditional rivals for power. His government supported public and technical education as a means to further stimulate an already impressive industrialization. Bismarck also introduced path-breaking social legislation—medical, unemployment, and disability insurance as well as old-age pensions—long before other industrial countries. Under his leadership, the German people developed a strong sense of national unity and pride in their industrial and military power, sentiments that would help fuel a more aggressive assertion of German power internationally.

In 1888 Wilhelm I was succeeded by his grandson Wilhelm II (r. 1888–1918), an insecure and arrogant man who tried to gain respect by making belligerent speeches. Within two years he had dismissed Chancellor Bismarck and surrounded himself with yes men. He talked about his "global policy" and demanded the creation of a colonial empire in imitation of the French

▲ **Japan's New Army**   After the Meiji Restoration in 1868, the leaders of the new government set out to make Japan "a rich country with a strong army." They modeled the new army on the European armies of the time, with Western-style organization, uniforms, rifles, cannon, and musical instruments. Tsuneo Tamba Collection/The Granger Collection, NY

AP® Exam Tip
Understand the various sources of global conflict in the late nineteenth and early twentieth centuries.

and British. Ruler of the nation with the mightiest army and the largest industrial economy in Europe, he felt that Germany deserved "a place in the sun." This ambition would lead to Great Power rivalries and growing militarization that propelled the world toward World War I.

27-5b The Liberal Powers: France and Great Britain

France, once the dominant nation in Europe, had difficulty reconciling itself to German ascendency after its defeat in the Franco-Prussian War. Though a prosperous country with flourishing agriculture and a large colonial empire, the French republic had some serious weaknesses. France trailed both Great Britain and Germany in the development of modern heavy industry. Also troubling was the fact that France's population was scarcely growing; in 1911 France had only 39 million people compared to Germany's 64 million. In an age when the power of nations was roughly proportional to the size of their armies, France could field an army only two-thirds the size of Germany's.

The French people were also deeply divided over the very nature of the state: factional divisions that had persisted since the era of the French Revolution (see Chapter 23). Some still supported the monarchy or versions of the authoritarianism of Napoleon III while insisting on Catholic domination of religious life and culture. A growing number held republican and anticlerical views. The class divisions made clear in the Paris Commune persisted as well, undermining a unified commitment to the nation. Yet if French political life seemed fragile and frequently in crisis, a long tradition of popular participation in politics and a strong sense of nationhood, reinforced by a fine system of public education, gave the French people a deeper cohesion than appeared on the surface.

Great Britain had a long experience with parliamentary elections and competing parties. The British government alternated smoothly between the Liberal and Conservative Parties, and the income gap between rich and poor gradually narrowed through labor agitation and political reforms. Nevertheless, Britain had problems that grew more apparent as time went on. One was Irish resentment of English rule. Nationalism had strengthened the allegiance of the English, Scots, and Welsh to the British state. But the Irish, excluded from meaningful participation in government because they were Catholic and predominantly poor, saw the British as a foreign occupying force. Some Irish leaders looked to Britain's foreign rivals for support for independence.

Another problem was the British economy. By the last decades of the nineteenth century, Great Britain, the chief engine of industrial innovation for a century, had fallen behind the United States and Germany in such important industries as steel, chemicals, electricity, and textiles. Even in shipbuilding and shipping, Britain's traditional specialty, Germany was fast catching up.

◄ **The Rich and Poor** Despite the impressive economic surge that resulted from European industrialization in the nineteenth century, the continent's cities were still divided by brutal class differences in wealth and political power. In this nineteenth-century painting Russian aristocrats in a sleigh give coins to beggars who plead for assistance. North Wind Picture Archives/Alamy Stock Photo

Britain was also preoccupied with its enormous and fast-growing empire. A source of wealth for investors and the envy of other imperialist nations, the empire was also a constant drain on Britain's finances, for it required Britain to maintain costly fleets of warships and standing armies posted throughout the world. Since many colonies failed to generate the wealth necessary to pay for their own administration and defense, let alone a "profit," the long-term viability of the empire would be put into question by any deep contraction of British economic performance.

For most of the nineteenth century Britain pursued a policy of "splendid isolation." Britain's preoccupation with India led British statesmen to exaggerate the Russian threat to the Ottoman Empire and to the Central Asian approaches to India. Periodic "Russian scares" and Britain's age-old rivalry with France for overseas colonies diverted the attention of British politicians from the rising threat posed by a unified and economically dynamic Germany.

27-5c The Conservative Powers: Russia and Austria-Hungary

The forces of nationalism weakened rather than strengthened Russia and Austria-Hungary. Their populations were far more divided, socially and ethnically, than were the German, French, or British peoples. This vulnerability was made clear by the Austrian Empire's territorial loses in the unification of Italy and Germany.

Nationalism was most divisive in south-central Europe, where many different language groups lived in close proximity. In 1867 the Austrian Empire renamed itself the Austro-Hungarian Empire to appease its Hungarian critics. Although its attempts to promote the cultures of its Slavic-speaking minorities failed to gain their political allegiance, it still thought of itself as a great power and attempted to dominate the Balkans. This strategy irritated Russia, which thought of itself as the protector of Slavic peoples everywhere.

Ethnic diversity also contributed to the instability of imperial Russia. The Polish people rebelled against Russian rule in 1830 and again in 1863–1864. The tsarist empire also included Finland, Estonia, Latvia, Lithuania, and Ukraine; the Caucasus; and the Muslim population of Central Asia conquered between 1865 and 1881. Furthermore, Russia had the largest Jewish population in Europe, and the harshness of its anti-Semitic laws and periodic *pogroms* (massacres) prompted many Jews to flee to America. Given this ethnic complexity, the state's attempts to impose the Russian language on its subjects were divisive instead of unifying.

In 1861 the moderate conservative Tsar Alexander II (r. 1855–1881) emancipated the peasants from serfdom. He did so partly out of a genuine desire to strengthen the bonds between the monarchy and the Russian people, and partly to promote industrialization by enlarging the labor pool. That half-hearted measure, however, only turned serfs into farm workers with few skills and little capital. Though "emancipated," the great majority of Russians had little education, few legal rights, and no say in the government. After Alexander's assassination in 1881, his successors Alexander III (r. 1881–1894) and Nicholas II (r. 1894–1917) reluctantly permitted limited attempts at social change. The Russian commercial middle class was small and had little influence. Industrialization consisted largely of state-sponsored projects, such as railroads, iron foundries, and armament factories, and led to social unrest among urban workers. Wealthy landowning aristocrats continued to dominate the Russian court and administration and blocked most reforms.

The weaknesses in Russia's society and government became glaringly obvious during a war with rapidly industrializing Japan in 1904 and 1905. The fighting took place in Manchuria, a province in northern China far from European Russia, and both armies suffered large losses. Ultimately, the Russian army, which received all its supplies by means of the inefficient Trans-Siberian Railway, was defeated by the better-trained and better-equipped Japanese. When the Russian navy finally arrived in Asian waters in 1905 after its long voyage around Eurasia and Africa, it was destroyed by the Japanese fleet at Tsushima Strait, validating the Meiji commitment to military modernization and establishing Japan as a regional power.

The shock of defeat caused a revolution in 1905 that forced Tsar Nicholas II to grant a constitution and permit

Section Review

- A united Germany, the most powerful state in Europe, became a threat to peace under Wilhelm II.

- France and Great Britain, though liberal democracies, faced difficulties at home and overseas.

- Russia and Austria-Hungary, two conservative empires, failed to adapt their politics to the modernization of their societies.

an elected Duma (parliament). But as soon as he was able to rebuild the army and the police, he reverted to the traditional despotism of his forefathers. In response, small groups of radical intellectuals, angered by the contrast between the wealth of the elite and the poverty of the common people, began plotting the violent overthrow of the tsarist autocracy.

27-6 China, Japan, and the Western Powers

What were the responses of Japan and China to expansion of western economic and military power?

By the nineteenth century, China already had deep commercial and cultural connections with the West that dated from the arrival of the Portuguese and Spanish in Asian waters in the sixteenth century (see Chapter 16). With the growing power of the British in India, Dutch in Indonesia, and French in Southeast Asia, Chinese political and economic vulnerabilities were exposed. Japan initially followed this same path, establishing tentative maritime contacts with the Spanish, Dutch, and British. The Japanese drastically limited contact after 1612 and the archipelago's distance from Europe's Asian colonies and from Europe itself provided some protection from disruptive foreign influences. But, after 1850, China and Japan felt the influence of the Western powers as never before. The Western colonial powers located on China's border demanded access to its economy and demonstrated a willingness to use military force to achieve their objectives. When China attempted to resist, it suffered military defeat as well as grave political and economic consequences. Japan sought to avoid the Chinese experience by embracing Western industrialization and building a strong and modern military.

27-6a China in Turmoil

China had been devastated by the Taiping (**tie-PING**) Rebellion that raged from 1850 to 1864 (see Chapter 24). The French and British took advantage of China's weakness to demand the establishment of treaty ports where they could trade without observing local laws. Unable to resist militarily, China allowed the British to take over customs enforcement and permitted the free import of opium until 1917. In response a Chinese "self-strengthening movement" tried in vain to bring about significant reforms by reducing government expenditures and eliminating corruption. While Meiji reformers in Japan resolutely committed to the transfer of foreign technologies to defend against imperialist aggressions, the **Empress Dowager Cixi** (**TSUH-shee**) (r. 1862–1908) of China sought to reduce foreign influences by opposing railways and other foreign technologies that could carry foreign culture into the interior. The Chinese government did modestly invest in modernization by sending a small number of students overseas to learn new technologies and by setting up a few model factories, but these efforts were handicapped by the government's weak financial resources and by the absence of a modern banking sector. So, without a modern military or a modern economy, Chinese government officials were unable to resist the Westerners outright. Instead, they secretly encouraged crowds to attack and destroy the visible examples of Western technology or attack westernized Chinese. They were thus able to slow the foreign intrusion but, in doing so, they denied themselves the modern tools that might have defended the country against mounting foreign pressure.

27-6b Japan Confronts China

The late nineteenth century marked the high point of European power and arrogance, as the nations of Europe, in a frenzy known as the "New Imperialism," rushed to colonize or economically dominate the last autonomous regions of the world. Yet, at that very moment, two nations outside Europe were establishing themselves as Great Powers. One of them, the United States, was inhabited mainly by people of European origin. Its rise to great-power status had been predicted early in the nineteenth century by the French statesman Alexis de Tocqueville and the nation had been propelled towards industrialization by its Civil War. The other one, Japan, seemed so distant and exotic in 1850 that no European guessed that it would join the ranks of the Great Powers. But Commodore Perry's intrusion had forced the Japan's elite to accept the need for stronger central government, industrialization, and modernization as the only way to avoid China's humiliation

Empress Dowager Cixi
Empress of China and mother of Emperor Guangxi. She put her son under house arrest, supported antiforeign movements, and resisted reforms of the Chinese government and armed forces.

in the Opium War and capitulation to foreign economic domination. By 1867 Japan had committed to industrialization and had already acquired eight steam warships.

As has been true in the rapid development of China in our own times, technology transfers from more developed economies played a key role in Japan's modernization. Missions were sent to Europe and the United States to arrange for the transfer of modern industrial technologies to Japanese industries, including metallurgy, textiles, and railroad rolling stock. Japan's rapid expansion of its railroad network can be used as a proxy for this period of rapid modernization, with mileage increasing from 18 miles to 7,000 miles between 1872 and 1910.

Japan's fast-gathering military strength allowed its leaders to dream of their own conquests. The path to imperialism was laid out by **Yamagata Aritomo**, a leader of the Meiji oligarchs. He believed that to be independent Japan had to define a "sphere of influence" that included Korea, Manchuria, and part of China (see Map 27.3). Unless Japan moved quickly, he believed, European powers would divide these territories among themselves and block Japan's destiny as a world power.

As Japan grew stronger, China was growing weaker. In 1894 the two nations went to war over Korea. The Sino-Japanese War lasted less than six months, with Japan clearly victorious. China was forced to evacuate Korea, cede its control of Taiwan and the Liaodong (**li-AH-oh-dong**) Peninsula, and pay Japan a heavy indemnity. France, Germany, Britain, Russia, and the United States, upset at seeing a newcomer join the ranks of the imperialists, compelled Japan to give up Liaodong in the name of the "territorial integrity" of China. In exchange for their "protection," the Western powers then made China grant them additional territorial and trade concessions, including access to ninety treaty ports.

▲ **Imperialists Dismember China** This period cartoon shows an outraged figure representing China throwing up his hands in horror as England (represented by Queen Victoria), Germany (represented by the Kaiser), Russia (represented by the Tzar), France, and Japan divide Chinese territory among themselves. This cartoon was originally published in January 1898 in the Parisian magazine *Le Petit Journal*. INTERFOTO/Alamy Stock Photo

In 1900 Chinese officials around the Empress Dowager Cixi encouraged a series of antiforeign riots known as the Boxer Uprising. Military forces from the European powers, Japan, and the United States put down the riots and occupied Beijing. Emboldened by China's obvious weakness, Japan and Russia now openly competed for possession of the mineral-rich Chinese province of Manchuria.

Japan's participation in the suppression of the Boxer Uprising demonstrated its military power in East Asia. Then in 1905 Japan surprised the world by defeating Russia in the Russo-Japanese War. By the Treaty of Portsmouth that ended the war, Japan established a protectorate over Korea. In spite of Western attempts to restrict it to the role of junior partner, Japan continued to increase its regional influence. After gaining control of southern Manchuria with its industries and railroads, Japan annexed Korea in 1910, joining the ranks of the world's colonial powers.

Yamagata Aritomo One of the leaders of the Meiji Restoration.

Section Review

- China was weakened by the Taiping Rebellion, a reactionary government under Empress Dowager Cixi, and the demands of the West.

- Japan, in contrast, built up its military and industrial strength and became another imperial power, taking advantage of China's weakness to seize Korea, Taiwan, and southern Manchuria.

27-7 Conclusion

After World War I broke out in 1914, many people, especially in Europe, looked back on the period from 1850 to 1914 as a golden age. For some, and in certain ways, it was. Industrialization was a powerful torrent changing Europe, North America, and East Asia. While shipping and railroads increased their global reach, new technologies—electricity, the steel and chemical industries, and the global telegraph network—contributed to the enrichment and empowerment of the industrial nations.

With these new technologies, memories of the great scourges—famines, wars, and epidemics—faded. Clean water, electric lights, and railways began to improve the lives of city dwellers, even the poor. Municipal services made city life less dangerous and chaotic. Goods from distant lands, even travel to other continents, came within the reach of millions. Middle-class women continued to focus on domestic pursuits and lived in a "separate sphere" from men, but access to education and professional careers initiated a long cycle of change. Many working-class women took jobs in the textile industry, yet their work outside the home paid less than similar jobs held by men and their traditional domestic and childrearing responsibilities continued.

Though Karl Marx predicted an inevitable class struggle between workers and employers as a consequence of industrialization, socialism became more an intellectual current than a revolutionary movement. Workers achieved improvements in wages, job security, and workplace safety through the organization of labor unions, not through revolutions. Nevertheless, labor violence continued unabated across the globe. By the turn of the century, liberal political reforms had taken hold in western Europe. Universal male suffrage became law in the United States in 1870 and in various parts of Europe by the 1880s. At the same time women mobilized in large numbers to demand political rights, an objective not attained in Europe or North America until the twentieth century.

The framework for all these dramatic changes was the nation-state. Until the 1860s nationalism was associated with liberalism, but later generations of conservatives used public education, military service, and colonial conquests to build a sense of national unity. By 1871 both Italy and Germany had become unified states. In Japan, the Meiji Restoration restored power to the emperor and ushered in a period of Western influences and rapid economic growth.

The world economy, international politics, and even cultural and social issues revolved around a handful of countries—the Great Powers—that believed they controlled the destiny of the world. These included the most powerful European nations of the previous century, as well as three newcomers—Germany, the United States, and Japan. The accumulated power and wealth of these nations meant, in practice, that the great majority of the residents of Africa, Asia, and Latin America reciprocally lost political autonomy and opportunities for economic advancement. Despite the creation of vast new amounts of new wealth worldwide due to new technologies and scientific advances, these new benefits were enjoyed only by a small minority of the human race.

Key Terms

Commodore Matthew Perry p. 697	electricity p. 701	Karl Marx p. 708	Meiji Restoration p. 716
railroads p. 698	Thomas Edison p. 701	anarchists p. 710	Empress Dowager Cixi p. 722
submarine telegraph cables p. 699	Victorian Age p. 705	nationalism p. 710	Yamagata Aritomo p. 723
steel p. 700	"separate spheres" p. 706	liberalism p. 711	
	socialism p. 708	Giuseppe Garibaldi p. 711	
	labor union p. 708	Otto von Bismarck p. 712	

Review Questions

1. What new technologies were most important to economic expansion of the second half of the nineteenth century?

2. What were the chief grievances driving demands for enhanced political rights and economic justice in Europe?

3. How did the rising tide of nationalism affect the political boundaries and forms of government in Europe?

4. What were the key differences in the response of China and Japan to the challenge of European imperialism?

MindTap® is a fully online, personalized learning experience built upon Cengage Learning content. MindTap® combines student learning tools—readings, multimedia, activities, and assessments—into a singular Learning Path that guides students through the course and helps students develop the critical thinking, analysis, and communication skills that are essential to academic and professional success.

Multiple-Choice Questions

Questions 1–3 refer to the passage below.

"A social sphere must have its center; a center to the individualists that jostle with each other inside it; a center to all the scattered rays that diffuse and waste their light and heat. The theory that bases the social structure on individual interests cannot supply this center. The absence of a center, or the selection among opposing interests of that which has the most vigorous life, means either anarchy or privilege—that is, either barren strife or the germ of aristocracy, under whatever name it disguises itself, this is the parting of the ways, which it is impossible to avoid.

Is this what we want when we invoke a revolution, since a revolution is indispensable to reorganize our nationality?"

Giuseppe Mazzini, Italian nationalist, nineteenth century

1. According to Mazzini, nationalism is necessary because it

    (A) arouses class loyalties.

    (B) can unite various factions in a society.

    (C) inspires religious devotion.

    (D) grants elites pride of place in society.

2. Which of the following would be an argument against Mazzini's views?

    (A) Filipino resistance to American imperialism

    (B) The Prussian/French tension over Alsace and Lorraine

    (C) Gandhi using nationalism to unite India against the British

    (D) The unification of Germany in the nineteenth century

3. Which segment of society would disagree the most with Mazzini's views?

    (A) Individualists and other modernists

    (B) Farmers and artisans in urban areas

    (C) Merchants and industrialists

    (D) Nobles and other traditional elites

Questions 4–6 refer to the image below.

4. The hair and clothing in the image support which of the following interpretations?

    (A) Japanese culture had been heavily influenced by Western powers

    (B) Japanese culture continued to embrace traditional values and styles

    (C) Japanese culture had shunned any element of fashion that reflected nature

    (D) Japanese industrialization resulted in all citizens dressing alike

5. Mutsuhito's role as emperor of Japan after provincial rebels overthrew the Tokugawa Shogunate was the result of

    (A) a lineage traced back to the Mongols.

    (B) traditional samurai training and battle.

    (C) the Meiji Restoration.

    (D) the ending of World War I.

▲ **The Emperor, Empress, Crown Prince and court ladies on an outing to Asuka Park, c. 1890.** Print by Yōshū Chikanobu

6. Which of the following were changes to Japanese society enacted as part of the attempt to create "a rich country with a strong army" under the Emperor portrayed in the image?

   (A) Emphasis on complete isolation and refusal to trade or interact with the Western world

   (B) A renewed emphasis on state-run industry with severe punishment for individual innovation

   (C) A decrease in literacy rates due to renewed focus on military service

   (D) The founding of imperial universities, technical schools, and agricultural schools

Questions 7–10 refer to the image below.

7. According to the image, the Boxer Rebellion was inspired by which of the following?

   (A) Incursions by steppe nomads

   (B) Industrialization in China

   (C) Western imperialism

   (D) Class conflict

▲ **The Boxer Uprising: The rebellious Boxers put up posters saying "Death to Foreigners."** Leemage/Getty Images

8. Which of the following is an accurate comparison between China's Boxer Rebellion and Japan's Meiji Restoration?

   (A) The Boxers in China rejected modernization while the Meiji in Japan embraced it.

   (B) China's Boxer Rebellion and Japan's Meiji Restoration rejected European industrialization.

   (C) Both movements embraced industrialization and nationalism.

   (D) Both movements followed strict isolationist policies.

9. The Boxer Rebellion and the Meiji Restoration are similar because they both

   (A) wanted to emulate the West.

   (B) were inspired in some ways by nationalism.

   (C) ignored the impact of imperialism.

   (D) promoted their own version of imperialism.

10. Which of the following is a long-term effect of the Boxer Rebellion and similar movements in other regions?

   (A) These regions continued to suffer at the hands of the imperialists.

   (B) Regions outside of Europe suffered from weak economies.

   (C) These rebellions led the way for more successful nationalist movements.

   (D) The rebellions kept these regions from achieving their independence in the twentieth century.

Short-Answer Questions

1. Labor movements grew quickly in the nineteenth century. Based on your knowledge of world history, answer all parts of the question that follows.

   (A) Identify ONE reason for the rise of labor movements.

   (B) Explain ONE way one labor movement addressed social problems.

   (C) Explain ONE effect of labor movements on society.

2. Answer all parts of the question that follows.

   (A) Provide ONE way the experiences of working-class and middle-class women in Europe were similar to each other in the nineteenth and early twentieth centuries.

   (B) Explain ONE way the experience of working-class and middle-class women in Europe differed from each other in the nineteenth and early twentieth centuries.

   (C) Explain ANOTHER way the experience of working-class and middle-class women in Europe differed from each other in the nineteenth and early twentieth centuries.

28 The Crisis of the Imperial Order, 1900–1929

CHAPTER OUTLINE

AP® Framework Terms

World War I
Petroleum
Total war
Communism

Overarching Questions

1 How have religions, belief systems, philosophies, and ideologies affected the political, economic, and social development of societies? (CUL)

2 How and why have economic, social, cultural, and geographic factors influenced the process of state building, expansion, and dissolution? (SB)

3 How have internal and external political factors influenced the process of state building, expansion, and dissolution? (SB)

4 How have economic systems and the development of ideologies, values, and institutions influenced each other? (ECON)

5 To what extent have legal systems, colonialism, nationalism, and independence movements sustained or challenged class, gender, and racial hierarchies over time? (SOC)

On June 28, 1914, Archduke Franz Ferdinand, heir to the throne of Austria-Hungary, was riding in an open carriage through Sarajevo, a city Austria had annexed six years earlier. When the carriage stopped momentarily, Gavrilo Princip, member of a pro-Serbian conspiracy, fired his pistol twice, killing the archduke and his wife.

Those shots ignited a global conflict. All previous wars had caused death and destruction, but they were also marked by heroism and glory. In this new war, four years of bitter fighting produced no true victories, few gains, and no glory, only death for millions of soldiers and dismemberment for three empires. The war became global as the Ottoman Empire fought against Britain and Japan attacked German positions in China. France and Britain involved their empires in the war and brought Africans, Indians, Australians, and Canadians to Europe to fight and labor on the front lines. Finally, in 1917, the United States entered the fray.

In this chapter, we look at the causes, conduct, and consequences of the war in Europe, the Middle East, and Russia. We also discuss the end of the Austro-Hungarian, Tsarist, and Ottoman empires, and postwar upheavals in China and Japan. ●

▲ **Trench Warfare in World War I**   No one anticipated the horrors of trench warfare in which tens of thousands of men excavated positions below ground level while their enemies did the same on the other side of a no-man's-land pockmarked by shell holes, bordered by barbed wire, and swept by machine gun fire. Among innumerable depictions by writers and artists, this one focuses on mud up to the soldiers' knees.   Godong/Alamy Stock Photo

28-1 Origins of the Crisis in Europe and the Middle East

What led to the outbreak of the First World War?

When the twentieth century opened, the world seemed firmly under the control of the great powers (see Chapter 27). The first decade of the twentieth century was a period of relative peace and economic growth in most of the world. Several new technologies—airplanes, automobiles, radio, and cinema—aroused much excitement (see Chapter 30). The great powers were consolidating their colonial conquests of the previous decades, and their alliances were evenly matched. The primary international war of the period, the Russo-Japanese War (1904–1905), ended quickly with a decisive Japanese victory.

However, two major changes undermined the apparent stability. In Europe, tensions mounted as Germany, with its growing industrial and military might, challenged Britain at sea and France in Morocco. And the Ottoman Empire lost territory to nationalistic movements in the Balkans. The resulting power vacuum gradually drew the European powers into a web of hostilities.

28-1a **The Ottoman Empire and the Balkans**

From the fifteenth to the nineteenth centuries the Ottoman Empire was a powerful state, albeit suffering from internal disarray (see Chapter 24). By the late nineteenth century, however, it had fallen behind Europe's most prosperous economically, technologically, and militarily. European statesmen referred to it as the "sick man of Europe."

As the Ottoman Empire weakened, it began losing European provinces: Macedonia in 1902–1903, Bosnia in 1908, Crete in 1909, Albania in 1910. In 1912 Italy conquered Libya, the Ottomans' last foothold in Africa. In the two Balkan Wars of 1912 and 1913 Serbia, Bulgaria, Romania, and Greece chased the Ottomans out of Europe, except for a small enclave around Constantinople.

In reaction, the Turks began to assert themselves against rebellious minorities and meddling foreigners. Many officers in the army, the most Europeanized segment of Turkish society, blamed Sultan Abdul Hamid II (r. 1876–1909) for the decline of the empire. A group known as "Young Turks" plotted to force the sultan to reinstate a stillborn constitution that he had suspended in 1876 before it could have an impact. They alienated other anti-Ottoman groups by advocating centralized rule and the Turkification of ethnic minorities.

In 1909 the parliament, dominated by Young Turks, overthrew Abdul Hamid. The new regime reinvigorated the Tanzimat reform movement that had begun in the early nineteenth century. At the same time, it looked with suspicion on Greek and Armenian minorities. Galvanized by their defeat in the Balkan Wars, the Turks hired a German general to modernize their armed forces. The dangerous mixture of modern armies and nationalism was not limited to the Ottoman Empire, however.

28-1b **Nationalism, Alliances, and Military Strategy**

AP® Exam Tip

Be able to explain how nationalism can function as both a force for unity and division.

The assassination of Franz Ferdinand triggered a chain of events over which military and political leaders lost control. The escalation from royal assassination to global war had causes that went back many years. One was nationalism, which identified citizens with their ethnic group and urged them, when called upon, to kill people they viewed as enemies. Another was the system of alliances and military planning that the great powers had devised to protect themselves from their rivals. A third was Germany's yearning to dominate Europe.

Nationalism united the citizens of France, Britain, Italy, and Germany behind their respective governments and gave them tremendous cohesion and strength of purpose. Only the most powerful feelings could inspire millions of men to march into battle and sustain civilian populations through years of hardship.

Nationalism could also be a dividing force. The Russian, Austro-Hungarian, and Ottoman Empires, large but fragile, contained numerous ethnic and religious minorities. Having repressed some minorities for centuries, the governments could never count on their full support. The very existence of an independent Serbia threatened Austria-Hungary by stirring up the hopes and resentments of its Slavic populations.

Imbued with nationalism, most people viewed war as a crusade for liberty or as long-overdue revenge for past injustices. As memories of the misery and carnage caused by the Napoleonic Wars slowly faded after 1815, revulsion against war gradually weakened. The Crimean War of 1853–1856 and the Franco-Prussian War of 1871 had generated few casualties or long-term consequences. And in the imperialist wars in Africa and Asia (see Chapter 26), Europeans almost always had been victorious at a small cost in money and manpower.

What turned an incident in the Balkans into a great power conflict was the system of alliances. At the center of Europe stood Germany, the most heavily industrialized country in Europe. Its army was the best trained and equipped, and it challenged Great Britain's naval supremacy by building "dreadnoughts"—heavily armed battleships. In 1882 it joined Austria-Hungary and Italy in the Triple Alliance, while France allied itself with Russia. In 1904 Britain and France reached an *entente* (**on-TONT**) ("understanding"), joined by Russia in 1907. Europe was thus divided into two blocs of roughly equal power (see Map 28.1).

The alliance system was cursed by inflexible military planning. In 1914 western and central Europe had highly developed railroad networks but very few motor vehicles, and European armies had grown to include millions of soldiers and reservists. To mobilize these forces and

CHRONOLOGY

	Europe and North America	Middle East	East Asia
1900	1904 British–French entente 1907 British–Russian entente	1909 Young Turks overthrow Sultan Abdul Hamid	1900 Boxer uprising in China 1904–1905 Russo-Japanese War
1910	1912–1913 Balkan Wars 1914 Assassination of Archduke Franz Ferdinand sparks World War I 1916 Battles of Verdun and the Somme 1917 Russian Revolutions; United States enters the war 1918 Armistice ends World War I 1918–1921 Civil war in Russia 1919 Treaty of Versailles	1912 Italy conquers Libya, last Ottoman territory in Africa 1915 British defeat at Gallipoli 1916 Arab Revolt in Arabia 1917 Balfour Declaration 1919–1922 War between Turkey and Greece	1911 Chinese revolutionaries led by Sun Yat-sen overthrow Qing dynasty 1915 Japan presents Twenty-One Demands to China 1919 May Fourth Movement in China
1920	1923–1928 New Economic Policy in Russia	1922 Egypt nominally independent 1923 Mustafa Kemal proclaims Turkey a republic	1927 Guomindang forces occupy Shanghai and expel Communists

transport them to battle would require thousands of trains running on precise schedules. Once under way, a country's mobilization could not be canceled or postponed without causing chaos.

Military planners in France and Germany worked out elaborate railroad timetables to mobilize their respective armies in a few days. Russia, a large country with a limited rail system, needed several weeks to mobilize its forces. Britain, with a tiny volunteer army, had no mobilization plans, and German planners believed that the British would stay out of a war on the European continent. To avoid having to fight France and Russia at the same time, German war planners expected to defeat France in a matter of days, then transport their entire army across Germany to the Russian border by train before Russia could fully mobilize.

On July 28, 1914, Austria-Hungary declared war on Serbia. The declaration of war triggered the mobilization plans of Russia, France, and Germany. On July 29 the Russian government ordered general mobilization to force Austria to back down. On August 1 France ordered general mobilization. Minutes later Germany did likewise. Because of the rigid railroad timetables, war was now automatic.

The Germans planned to wheel through neutral Belgium and invade France from the north. The German General Staff expected France to capitulate before the British could get involved. But on August 3, when German troops entered Belgium, Britain demanded their withdrawal. When Germany refused, Britain declared war on Germany.

Section Review

- As the Ottoman Empire declined, nationalists calling themselves Young Turks tried to create a new Turkish nation.

- Nationalism, competing alliances, and inflexible military plans based on railroads turned an assassination into a cause for war.

28-2 The "Great War" and the Russian Revolutions, 1914–1918

How did the war lead to revolution in Russia?

Throughout Europe, people greeted the outbreak of war with parades and flags, each side expecting a quick victory. German troops marched off shouting, "To Paris!" Spectators in France encouraged their troops with shouts of "Send me the Kaiser's moustache!" German sociologist

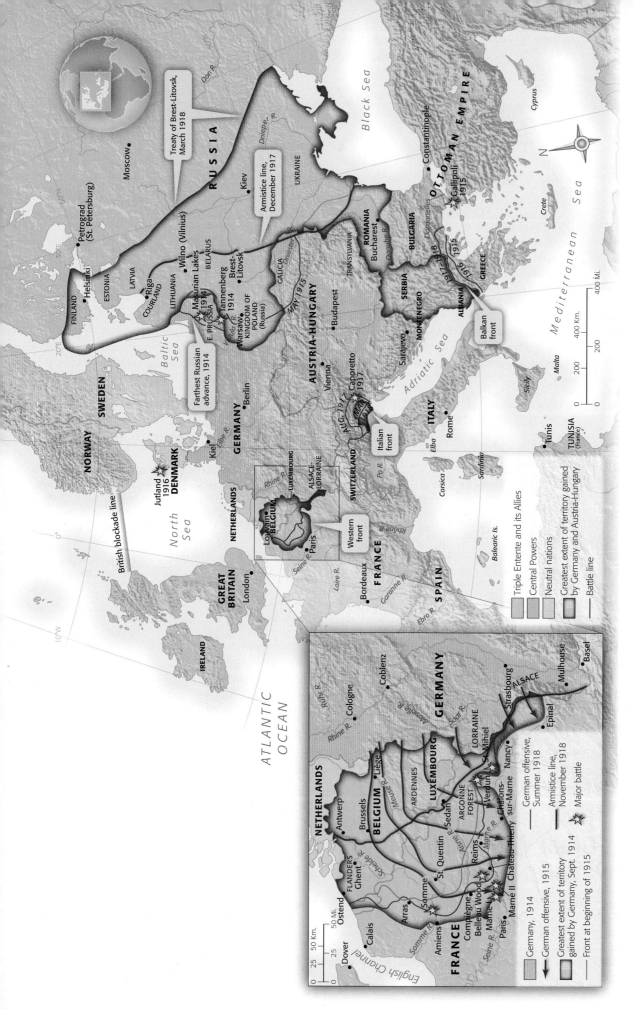

MAP 28.1 **The First World War in Europe** After an initial surge through Belgium into northern France, the German offensive bogged down for four years along the Western Front. To the East, the German armies conquered a large part of Russia during 1917 and early 1918. Despite spectacular victories in the east, Germany lost the war because its armies collapsed along the strategically important Western Front.

How might the war have been affected if Italy had stayed with the Triple Alliance?

Max Weber wrote: "This war, with all its ghastliness, is nevertheless grand and wonderful. It is worth experiencing."[1] When the war began, very few imagined that their side might not win. No one foresaw that everyone would lose.

28-2a Stalemate, 1914–1917

The war that erupted in 1914 was known as the "Great War" until the 1940s, when a far greater one overshadowed it. Its form came as a surprise to all belligerents, from the generals on down. In the classic battles that every officer studied, the advantage always went to the fastest-moving army led by the boldest general. But in 1914 the generals' carefully drawn plans went awry from the start. Believing that a spirited attack would always prevail, French generals hurled their troops, dressed in bright blue-and-red uniforms, against the well-defended German border and suffered a crushing defeat. In battle after battle the much larger German armies defeated the French and the British. By early September the Germans held Belgium and northern France and were fast approaching Paris.

German victory seemed assured. But German troops, who had marched and fought for a month, were exhausted, and their generals wavered. A gap opened between two German armies along the Marne River, into which General Joseph Joffre moved France's last reserves. At the Battle of the Marne (September 5–12, 1914), the Germans were thrown back several miles.

During the next month, both sides spread out until they formed an unbroken line extending over 300 miles (some 500 kilometers) from the North Sea to the border of Switzerland. All along this **Western Front**, the opposing troops prepared their defenses. Their most potent weapons were machine guns, which provided an almost impenetrable defense against advancing infantry but were useless for the offensive because they were too heavy for one man to carry and took too much time to set up.

To escape the deadly streams of bullets, soldiers dug holes in the ground, connected the holes to form shallow trenches, then dug communications trenches to the rear. Within weeks, the battlefields were scarred by lines of trenches several feet deep, their tops protected by sandbags and their floors covered with planks. Trenches were nothing new. What was extraordinary was that the trenches along the entire Western Front were connected, leaving no gaps through which armies could advance (see Map 28.1). How, then, could either side ever hope to win?

For four years, generals on each side again and again ordered their troops to attack. In battle after battle, thousands of young men on one side climbed out of their trenches, raced across the open fields, and were mowed down by enemy machine-gun fire. Hoping to destroy the machine guns, the attacking force would saturate the entrenched enemy lines with artillery barrages. But this tactic alerted the defenders to an impending attack and allowed them to rush in reinforcements and set up new machine guns.

The year 1916 saw the bloodiest and most futile battles of the war. The Germans attacked French forts at Verdun, losing 281,000 men and causing 315,000 French casualties. In retaliation, the British attacked the Germans at the Somme River and suffered 420,000 casualties—60,000 on the first day alone—while the Germans lost 450,000 and the French 200,000.

Warfare had never been waged this way before: mass slaughter in a moonscape of mud, steel, and flesh. Both sides attacked and defended, but neither side could win, for the armies were stalemated by trenches and machine guns. During four years of the bloodiest fighting the world had ever seen, the Western Front moved no more than a few miles one way or another.

At sea, the war was just as inconclusive. As soon as war broke out, the British cut the German overseas telegraph cables, blockaded the coasts of Germany and Austria-Hungary, and set out to capture or sink all enemy ships still at sea. The German High Seas Fleet, built at enormous cost but mostly coal-fueled, seldom left port. Only once, in May 1916, did it confront the oil-fueled and thus more efficient British Grand Fleet. At the Battle of Jutland, off the coast of Denmark, the two fleets lost roughly equal numbers of ships, and the Germans escaped back to their harbors.

In early 1915, in retaliation for the British naval blockade, Germany announced a blockade of Britain by submarines. German submarines attacked every vessel they could. One of their victims

AP® Exam Tip
Understand how new military technology and tactics (such as trench warfare) led to unprecedented levels of wartime casualties.

Western Front A line of trenches and fortifications in World War I that stretched without a break from Switzerland to the North Sea. Scene of most of the fighting between Germany, on the one hand, and France and Britain, on the other.

---

[1]Frank B. Tipton, *A History of Modern Germany since 1815* (Berkeley: University of California Press, 2003), 295.

AP® Exam Tip
Understand why the full mobilization of combatant societies and economies for the war effort during World War I is sometimes called "total war."

AP® Exam Tip
Consider how governments in World War I used a variety of strategies, including political propaganda, art, media, and nationalism, to mobilize populations for the war.

▼ **Women in World War I**   Women played a more important role in World War I than in previous wars. As the armies drafted millions of men, employers hired women for essential war work. This poster extolls the importance of women workers in supplying munitions. Pictorial Press Ltd/Alamy Stock Photo

was the British ocean liner *Lusitania*. The death toll from that attack was 1,198 people, 139 of them Americans. When the United States protested, Germany ceased its submarine campaign, hoping to keep America neutral.

Airplanes were used for reconnaissance and engaged in spectacular but inconsequential dogfights above the trenches (see Environment & Technology: New War, New Tools), introduced on the Western Front in 1915, and killed and wounded attacking soldiers as well as their intended victims, adding to the horror of battle. Primitive tanks aided, but did not cause, the collapse of the German army in the last weeks of the war. Although these weapons were of limited effectiveness in World War I, they offered a preview of future warfare.

28-2b The Home Front and the War Economy

Trench-bound armies demanded ever more weapons, ammunition, and food, so civilians had to work harder, eat less, and pay higher taxes. Textiles, coal, meat, fats, and imported products such as tea and sugar were strictly rationed. Governments gradually imposed stringent controls over all aspects of their economies.

The war economy transformed civilian life. In France and Britain food rations were allocated according to need, improving nutrition among the poor. Unemployment vanished. Thousands of Africans, Indians, and Chinese were recruited for heavy labor in Europe. Employers hired women to fill jobs vacated by men off to war. Some women became streetcar drivers, mail carriers, and police officers. Others found work in the burgeoning government bureaucracies. Many served as doctors, nurses, mechanics, and ambulance drivers in auxiliary military services for the British government after 1917, as the war took its toll of young men. These positions gave thousands of women a sense of participation in the war effort and a taste of personal and financial independence.

German civilians paid an especially high price for the war, for the British naval blockade severed their overseas trade. Wheat flour disappeared, replaced first by rye, then by potatoes and turnips, then by acorns and chestnuts, and finally by sawdust. After the failure of the potato crop in 1916 came the "turnip winter," when people had to survive on 1,000 calories per day, half the normal amount that an active adult needed. Women, children, and the elderly were especially hard hit. Soldiers at the front raided enemy lines to scavenge food.

The war also brought hardships to Europe's African colonies. When the war began, the British and French overran German Togo on the West African coast. The much larger German colonies of Southwest Africa and German Cameroon were conquered in 1915. In German East Africa, the Germans remained undefeated until the end of the war. The Europeans requisitioned foodstuffs, imposed heavy taxes, and forced Africans to grow export crops and sell them at low prices. As Europeans stationed in Africa joined the war, the combination of increased demands on Africans and fewer European officials led to uprisings that lasted for several years. Over a million Africans served in the various armies, and perhaps three times that number were drafted as porters to carry army equipment. Faced with a shortage of young French-men, France drafted Africans into its army, where many fought side by side with Europeans.

One country grew rich during the war: the United States. For two and a half years the United States stayed technically neutral but did a roaring business supplying France and Britain. When the United States entered the war in 1917, businesses engaging in war production made spectacular profits. Civilians were exhorted to help the war effort by investing their savings in war bonds and growing food in backyard "victory gardens." Employment opportunities created by the war played a major role in the migration of African Americans from the rural South to the cities of the North.

Environment & Technology
New War, New Tools

The American Civil War (1860–1865) and the seven-month Franco-Prussian War (1870–1871) were the biggest conflicts between more or less evenly equipped armies in the era following Napoleon's defeat at Waterloo (1815). The Crimean War (1853–1856) was a major conflict, but it pitted a Russian army that had seen few improvements since Napoleon's time against more advanced French and British forces supporting the Ottoman Empire. The Opium Wars, Arrow War, and Taiping Rebellion in China; the Zulu War in South Africa; and other colonial conflicts were even more lopsided in terms of equipment.

World War I introduced a new type of warfare. Rifles were upgraded to machine guns; artillery became heavier and, in the form of tanks, more mobile; and trenches replaced fortress walls that were vulnerable to cannon fire. At sea, the ironclad warships from the American Civil War grew into mammoth dreadnoughts equipped with immense guns. In the air, balloons used for gaining aerial views of battlefield movements shared the sky with primitive warplanes and, occasionally, Zeppelins carrying bombs. All of these developments followed clear nineteenth-century precedents.

Other innovations went beyond guns and explosives and drew on other spheres of endeavor. Germany's chemists, the best in the world, were the first to weaponize poison and disabling gases. Ignoring an international Hague Declaration against "asphyxiating gases" (1899) and a Hague Convention on Land Warfare (1907) that forbade "poison or poisoned weapons," Germany inaugurated gas warfare with greenish chlorine gas in 1915 and added mustard gas to its arsenal in 1917. A French Nobel Prize winner in chemistry responded with phosgene, which was colorless and harder to detect. Britain did not launch its own gas attacks until 1918, and the United States had begun production of its own lethal invention, lewisite, but did not deploy it in battle before the war ended in 1918.

Germany's chemists also developed flamethrowers, though their range of twenty yards and limited fuel supply limited their usefulness. Britain experimented with larger flame projectors but did not find a practical use for them.

Besides weapons and vehicles, including life-saving ambulances, heavy industry provided miles of concertina wire, cylindrical rolls of barbed wire that were strung between upright poles and became a standard obstacle in the no-man's-land between trenches. Germany's Dannert wire was a high-grade, tempered steel version that was hard to cut and did not need poles.

Field telephones improved battlefield communications immensely, though unreeling wire could be a dangerous assignment. Radio was at a more primitive stage but developed rapidly during the war, particularly for naval use. Field sets depended on fragile vacuum tubes, and visible aerials became targets for the enemy.

As for diet, the "iron ration" carried into the field by British soldiers consisted of 1 lb. canned corned beef or Maconochie, a barely edible stew; 12 oz. biscuit; 5/8 oz. tea; 2 oz. sugar; 1/2 oz. salt; 3 oz. cheese; and 1 oz. meat extract (2 cubes.) The German equivalent gave each soldier 250g (8.8 oz) biscuit; 200g (7 oz.) preserved meat or 170g (6 oz.) bacon; 150g (5.3 oz.) preserved vegetables; 25g (9/10 oz.) coffee; and 25g (9/10 oz.) salt.

Even the art world contributed new tools of war. Artist Lucien-Victor Guirand de Scévola, the leader of French camouflage (from Parisian slang *camoufler*, meaning "to disguise") corps, sought to apply cubist principles by using paint and other materials to break up easily identifiable battlefield outlines. One artist, for example, disguised an observation post to look like a tree. British artist Norman Wilkinson came up with "dazzle camouflage," which consisted of painting ships with radically garish geometric patterns that made it difficult for German submarine commanders to tell the speed and direction of ships in convoys.

Questions for Analysis

1. How did changes in warfare reflect economic developments in the late nineteenth century?
2. Why might poison gas have been used despite international prohibitions on its use?
3. Did technology slow down or speed up the pace of war?

▶ **Dazzle Camouflage** Ocean liner painted with dazzle camouflage being used for Atlantic Ocean convoy activities during World War I. The purpose of the camouflage was to confuse submarine commanders looking through a periscope as to the identity, size, speed, and direction of a surface ship. UK: HMT Olympic in dazzle camouflage while in service as a troopship during World War I/PICTURES FROM HISTORY/ Bridgeman Images

MAP 28.2 Territorial Changes in Europe After World War I Although the heaviest fighting took place in western Europe, the territorial changes there were relatively minor. In eastern Europe, in contrast, the changes were enormous. The disintegration of the Austro-Hungarian Empire and the defeat of Russia allowed a belt of new countries to arise, stretching from Finland in the north to Yugoslavia in the south.

How did the Russian Revolution pave the way for redrawing the map of eastern Europe?

28-2c The Ottoman Empire at War

AP® Exam Tip

Explain the role of World War I in the collapse of the Ottoman Empire.

On August 2, 1914, the Turks signed a secret alliance with Germany. In November they joined the fighting, hoping to gain land at Russia's expense. During the campaign in the Caucasus the Turks expelled the Armenians, whom they suspected of being pro-Russian, from their homelands in eastern Anatolia. Hunger and exposure killed hundreds of thousands during the forced march to Syria across the mountains in the winter. Many others were killed by regular and irregular Ottoman military forces, raising the death total to almost genocidal levels.

The Turks also closed the Dardanelles, the strait between the Mediterranean and Black Seas (see Map 28.2). Seeing little hope of victory on the Western Front, Britain tried to open the Dardanelles by landing troops on the nearby Gallipoli Peninsula in 1915. Turkish troops pushed the invaders back into the sea. The British then promised the *emir* (hereditary governor) of Mecca, Hussein ibn Ali, a kingdom of his own if he would lead an Arab revolt against the Turks. In 1916 Hussein rose up and was proclaimed king of Hejaz (**heh-JAHZ**) (western Arabia). His son **Faisal** (**FIE-sahl**) then led an Arab army in support of the British advance from Egypt into Palestine and Syria. The Arab Revolt of 1916 did not affect the struggle in Europe, but it did contribute to the defeat of the Ottoman Empire.

The British made promises to Jews as well as Arabs. For centuries, Jewish minorities in eastern and central Europe had developed a thriving culture despite frequent persecutions. By the early twentieth century a nationalist movement called Zionism, led by **Theodore Herzl**, arose among those who wanted to return to their ancestral homeland in Palestine. Though Palestine had an Arab population, the concept of a Jewish homeland appealed to many Europeans as a humane solution to the problem of European anti-Semitism.

By 1917 Chaim Weizmann (**hi-um VITES-mun**), leader of the British Zionists, had persuaded several British politicians that a Jewish homeland in Palestine should be carved out of the Ottoman Empire and placed under British protection, thereby strengthening the Allied cause. In November, as British armies were advancing on Jerusalem, Foreign Secretary Sir Arthur Balfour wrote:

> *His Majesty's Government view with favor the establishment in Palestine of a national home for the Jewish people and will use their best endeavours to facilitate the achievement of that object, it being clearly understood that nothing shall be done which may prejudice the civil and religious rights of existing non-Jewish communities in Palestine.*[2]

The British did not foresee that this statement, known as the **Balfour Declaration**, would lead to conflicts between Arabs living in Palestine and Jewish settlers.

28-2d Double Revolution in Russia

At the beginning of the war Russia had the largest army in the world, but its generals were incompetent, supplies were lacking, and soldiers were poorly trained and equipped. In August 1914 two Russian armies invaded eastern Germany but were thrown back.

In 1916, after a string of defeats, the Russian army ran out of ammunition and other essential supplies. Soldiers were ordered into battle unarmed and told to pick up the rifles of fallen comrades. Railroads broke down for lack of fuel and parts, and crops rotted in the fields. Civilians faced shortages and widespread hunger. Food and fuel became scarce in the cities. During the bitterly cold winter of 1916–1917, factory workers and housewives lined up in front of grocery stores before dawn to get food. The court of Tsar Nicholas II, however, remained as extravagant and corrupt as ever.

In early March 1917 (February by the old Russian calendar), food ran out in Petrograd (St. Petersburg), the capital. Women staged mass demonstrations. Soldiers mutinied and joined striking workers to form *soviets* (councils) to take over factories and barracks. A few days later the tsar abdicated, and leaders of the parliamentary parties, led by Alexander Kerensky, formed a Provisional Government. Thus began what Russians called the "February Revolution."

Revolutionaries formerly hunted by the tsar's police came out of hiding. Most numerous were the Social Revolutionaries, who advocated the redistribution of land to the peasants. The Mensheviks advocated the electoral politics and reform advocated by European socialists and had a large following among intellectuals and factory workers. The rival **Bolsheviks**, a small but tightly disciplined group of radicals, followed the teachings and tactics of their leader, **Vladimir Lenin** (1870–1924).

Lenin, the son of a government official, became a revolutionary in his teens when his older brother was executed for plotting to kill the tsar. He spent years in exile, first in Siberia and later in Switzerland, where he devoted his full attention to organizing his followers. His goal was to create a party that would lead the revolution rather than wait for it. He explained: "The will of a class is sometimes fulfilled by a dictator. . . . Soviet socialist democracy is not in the least incompatible with individual rule and dictatorship."[3]

In early April 1917 the German government, hoping to destabilize Russia, allowed Lenin to travel from Switzerland to Russia in a sealed railway car. As soon as he arrived in Petrograd,

AP® Exam Tip
Be prepared to explain the globalization of war in the twentieth century.

Faisal Arab prince, leader of the Arab Revolt in World War I. The British made him king of Iraq in 1921, and he reigned under British protection until 1933.

Theodore Herzl Austrian journalist and founder of the Zionist movement urging the creation of a Jewish national homeland in Palestine.

Balfour Declaration Statement issued by Britain's foreign secretary Arthur Balfour in 1917 favoring the establishment of a Jewish national homeland in Palestine.

Bolsheviks Radical Marxist political party founded by Vladimir Lenin in 1903. Under Lenin's leadership, the Bolsheviks seized power in November 1917 during the Russian Revolution.

Vladimir Lenin Leader of the Bolshevik (later Communist) Party. He lived in exile in Switzerland until 1917, then returned to Russia to lead the Bolsheviks to victory during the Russian Revolution and the civil war that followed.

---

[2]Walter Z. Laqueur and Barry Rubin, eds., *The Arab-Israeli Reader: A Documentary History of the Middle East Conflict*, 4th ed. (New York: Penguin Books, 1984), 18.

[3]David Shub, *Lenin: A Biography* (Garden City, NY: Doubleday, 1948), 257.

Section Review

- Europeans greeted the outbreak of war with joy.

- After a month-long German advance into Belgium and France, armies stalemated in a line of trenches along the Western Front, suffering huge casualties but no victory.

- On the home fronts, civilians suffered severe shortages and women entered the workforce, while the United States grew rich on profits from war production.

- The entry of the Ottoman Empire into the war did not tip the balance.

- In the Balfour Declaration, Great Britain promised Jews a "national homeland" in Palestine.

- As Russia weakened, Lenin's Bolsheviks seized power in November 1917.

- Goaded by German submarine warfare, in 1917 the United States entered the war on the Allied side, and Germany began to retreat.

- The war ended on November 11, 1918, with the defeat of Germany.

AP® Exam Tip

Compare the effects of World War I on Russia with the effects of it on the Ottoman Empire.

Woodrow Wilson President of the United States (1913–1921) and a leading figure at the Paris Peace Conference of 1919. He was unable to persuade the U.S. Congress to ratify the Treaty of Versailles or join the League of Nations.

Fourteen Points A peace program presented to the U.S. Congress by President Woodrow Wilson in January 1918. It called for the evacuation of German-occupied lands, the drawing of borders and the settling of territorial disputes by the self-determination of the affected populations, and the founding of an association of nations to preserve the peace and guarantee their territorial integrity. It was rejected by Germany, but it made Wilson the moral leader of the Allies in the last year of World War I.

he announced his program: immediate peace, all power to the soviets, and transfers of land to the peasants and factories to the workers. This plan proved immensely popular among soldiers and workers exhausted by the war.

The next few months witnessed a tug-of-war between the Provisional Government and the various revolutionary factions in Petrograd. When Kerensky ordered another offensive against the Germans, Russian soldiers began to desert by the hundreds of thousands, throwing away their rifles and walking back to their villages. As the Germans advanced, the government lost what little support it had.

Meanwhile, the Bolsheviks were gaining support among the workers of Petrograd and the soldiers and sailors stationed there. On November 6, 1917 (October 24 in the Russian calendar), they rose up and took over the city, calling their action the "October Revolution." Their sudden move surprised rival revolutionary groups that believed, following Marxist theory, that a "socialist" revolution could happen only after many years of "bourgeois" rule. Lenin, more interested in power than in the fine points of Marxist doctrine, overthrew the Provisional Government and arrested Mensheviks, Social Revolutionaries, and other rivals.

Seizing Petrograd was only the first step, for the rest of Russia was in chaos. The Bolsheviks nationalized all private land and ordered the peasants to hand over their crops without compensation. The peasants, having seized their landlords' estates, resisted. In the cities the Bolsheviks took over the factories and drafted the workers into compulsory labor brigades. To enforce his rule Lenin created the Cheka, a secret police force with powers to arrest and execute opponents.

The Bolsheviks also sued for peace with Germany and Austria-Hungary. By the Treaty of Brest-Litovsk, signed on March 3, 1918, Russia lost territories containing a third of its population and wealth. Poland, Finland, and the Baltic states (Estonia, Latvia, and Lithuania) became independent republics. Russian colonies in Central Asia and the Caucasus broke away temporarily.

28-2e The End of the War in Western Europe, 1917–1918

Like many Americans, President **Woodrow Wilson** wanted to stay out of the European conflict. For nearly three years he kept the United States neutral and tried to persuade the belligerents to compromise. But in late 1916 German leaders decided to starve the British into submission by using submarines to sink ships carrying food supplies to Great Britain. The Germans knew that unrestricted submarine warfare was likely to bring the United States into the war, but they were willing to gamble that Britain and France would collapse before the United States could send enough troops to help them.

The submarine campaign resumed on February 1, 1917, and the German gamble failed. The British organized their merchant ships into convoys protected by destroyers, and on April 6 President Wilson asked the United States Congress to declare war on Germany.

In January 1918, President Wilson presented his **Fourteen Points**, a peace plan that called for the German evacuation of occupied lands, the settling of territorial disputes by the decisions of the local populations, and the formation of an association of nations to guarantee the independence and territorial integrity of all states. In response, General Erich von Ludendorff launched a series of surprise attacks that pushed to within 40 miles (64 kilometers) of Paris, but victory eluded him. Meanwhile, every month brought another 250,000 American troops to the front. In August the Allies counterattacked, and the Germans began a retreat that could not be halted.

In late October Ludendorff resigned, and sailors in the German fleet mutinied. Two weeks later, a new German government signed an armistice. At 11:00 A.M. on November 11, the guns on the Western Front went silent.

28-3 Peace and Dislocation in Europe, 1919–1929

What role did the war play in eroding European dominance in the world?

The Great War left Europe in turmoil. Peace Treaty stipulations generated new political tensions and resentments. National economies remained in flux until the mid-1920s. Then, just when peace and prosperity finally seemed at hand, disaster struck in the form of the Great Depression and World War II, which is discussed in Chapter 29.

28-3a The Impact of the War

Between 9 million and 10 million soldiers died in the war. Among the dead were about 2 million Germans, 1.7 million Russians, and 1.7 million Frenchmen. Austria-Hungary lost 1.5 million, the British Empire a million, the Ottoman Empire half a million, Italy 460,000, and the United States 115,000. Perhaps twice that many returned home wounded, gassed, or shell-shocked, many of them handicapped for life.

War and revolution forced almost 2 million Russians, 750,000 Germans, and 400,000 Hungarians to flee their homes. Postwar conflicts also led to the expulsion of hundreds of thousands of Greeks from Anatolia and Muslims from Greece. Many refugees found shelter in France, which welcomed 1.5 million people to bolster its declining population. About 800,000 immigrants reached the United States before immigration laws passed in 1921 and 1924 closed the door to eastern and southern Europeans. Canada, Australia, and New Zealand adopted similar restrictions on immigration. The Latin American republics welcomed European refugees, but their poverty discouraged potential immigrants.

One unexpected by-product of the war was the great influenza epidemic of 1918–1919, which started among soldiers heading for the Western Front. This virulent strain infected almost everyone on earth and killed one person in every forty. Half a million Americans perished in the epidemic—five times as many as died in the war. World-wide, some 20 million people died.

The war also caused serious damage to the environment. No place was ever so completely devastated as the scar across France and Belgium known as the Western Front. The fighting ravaged forests and demolished towns. The earth was gouged by trenches, pitted with craters, and littered with ammunition, broken weapons, chunks of concrete, and the bones of countless soldiers. After the war, it took a decade to clear away the debris, rebuild the towns, and create dozens of military cemeteries with neat rows of crosses stretching for miles.

AP® Exam Tip
Identify and explain the demographic impact of epidemic disease (such as the 1918 influenza epidemic) throughout the twentieth and twenty-first centuries.

28-3b The Peace Treaties

In early 1919 delegates of the victorious powers met in Paris. The defeated powers were kept out until the treaties were ready for signing. Russia was not invited.

From the start, three men dominated the Paris Peace Conference: U.S. president Wilson, British prime minister David Lloyd George, and French premier Georges Clemenceau (**zhorzh cluh-mon-SO**). They ignored the Italians, who had joined the Allies in 1915, and paid even less attention to delegations from smaller European nations. They rejected the Japanese proposal that all races be treated equally. They ignored the Pan-African Congress organized by the African American W. E. B. Du Bois to call attention to the concerns of African peoples around the world. They also ignored the 10,000 would-be attendees that did not represent sovereign states, such as the Arab leader Faisal, the Zionist Chaim Weizmann, and several Armenian delegations. In the

AP® Exam Tip
Evaluate the strengths and weaknesses of new international organizations formed to maintain world peace and facilitate international cooperation.

words of Britain's Foreign Secretary Balfour, they were "three all-powerful, all-ignorant men, sitting there and carving up continents"[4] (see Map 28.3).

Wilson, a high-minded idealist, wanted to apply the principle of self-determination to European affairs, by which he meant creating nations that reflected ethnic or linguistic divisions. He proposed a **League of Nations**, a world organization to safeguard the peace and foster international cooperation. His idealism clashed with the more hardheaded and self-serving nationalism of the Europeans. Lloyd George insisted that Germany pay a heavy indemnity, while Clemenceau wanted Germany to return Alsace and Lorraine, provinces France had lost in the Franco-Prussian War of 1870–1871.

The result was a series of compromises that satisfied no one. The European powers did form a League of Nations, but the U.S. Congress refused to let the United States join. France recovered Alsace and Lorraine but had be content with vague promises of British and American protection if Germany ever rebuilt its army. Britain acquired new territories in Africa and the Middle East but was greatly weakened by human losses and the disruption of its trade.

On June 28, 1919, the German delegates reluctantly signed the **Treaty of Versailles (vuhr-SIGH)**. Germany was forbidden to have an air force and was permitted only a token army and navy. It also gave up a large swath of its eastern territory to a newly reconstituted Poland. The Allies made Germany promise to pay reparations to compensate the victors for their losses, but they did not set a figure or a period of time for payment. A "guilt clause," which was to rankle for years to come, obliged the Germans to accept "responsibility for causing all the loss and damage" of the war. The treaty left Germany humiliated but largely intact. Establishing a peace neither of punishment nor of reconciliation, it was one of the great failures in history.

Meanwhile, the Austro-Hungarian Empire fell apart. New countries appeared in the lands lost by Russia, Germany, and Austria-Hungary: Poland, resurrected after over a century; Czechoslovakia, created from the northern third of Austria-Hungary; and Yugoslavia, combining Serbia and the former south Slav provinces of Austria-Hungary. The new boundaries coincided with the major linguistic groups of eastern Europe, but they all contained disaffected minorities. These small nations were safe only as long as Germany and Russia lay defeated and prostrate.

League of Nations
International organization founded in 1919 to promote world peace and cooperation but greatly weakened by the refusal of the United States to join. It proved ineffectual in stopping aggression by Italy, Japan, and Germany in the 1930s. It was superseded in 1945 by the United Nations, which assumed some of its functions.

Treaty of Versailles The treaty imposed on Germany by France, Great Britain, the United States, and other Allied Powers after World War I. It demanded that Germany dismantle its military and give up some lands to Poland. It was resented by many Germans.

New Economic Policy Policy proclaimed by Vladimir Lenin in 1923 to encourage the revival of the Soviet economy by allowing small private enterprises. Joseph Stalin ended the NEP in 1928 and replaced it with a series of Five-Year Plans.

28-3c Russian Civil War and the New Economic Policy

In December 1918, civil war broke out in Russia. The Communists—as the Bolsheviks called themselves after March 1918—held central Russia, but all the surrounding provinces rose up against them. Counter-revolutionary armies led by former tsarist officers obtained weapons and supplies from the Allies. For three years the two sides burned farms and confiscated crops, causing a famine that claimed 3 million victims, more than had died in Russia in seven years of fighting. By 1921 the Communists had defeated most of their enemies.

Finland, the Baltic states, and Poland remained independent, but the Red Army reconquered other parts of the tsar's empire one by one. In 1922, Ukraine merged with Russia to create the Union of Soviet Socialist Republics (USSR), or Soviet Union. In 1920–1921 the Red Army reconquered the Caucasus and replaced the indigenous leaders with Russians. In 1922 the new Soviet republics of Georgia, Armenia, and Azerbaijan joined the USSR. In this way the Bolsheviks retained control over lands and peoples that had been part of the tsar's empire.

Years of warfare, revolution, and mismanagement had ruined the Russian economy. Factories and railroads had shut down for lack of fuel, raw materials, and parts. Farmland had been devastated and livestock killed, causing hunger in the cities. Finding himself master of a country in ruin, Lenin announced the **New Economic Policy** (NEP) in 1923. It allowed peasants to own land and sell their crops, private merchants to trade, and private workshops to produce goods and sell them on the free market. Only the biggest businesses, such as banks, railroads, and factories, remained under government ownership.

---

[4]David Vital, *A People Apart: The Jews of Europe, 1789–1939* (Oxford, UK: Oxford University Press, 1999), 756.

The relaxation of controls had an immediate effect. Production began to climb, and food and other goods became available. But the NEP brought no change in the ultimate goals of the Communist Party. It merely provided breathing space, what Lenin called "two steps back to advance one step forward." The Communists had every intention of creating a modern industrial economy without private property. This meant investing in heavy industry and electrification and moving farmers to the cities to work in the new industries. It also meant providing food for the urban workers without spending scarce resources to purchase it from the peasants. In other words, it meant making the peasants, the great majority of the Soviet people, pay for the industrialization of Russia. This policy turned them into bitter enemies of the Communists.

When Lenin died in January 1924, his associates jockeyed for power. The leading contenders were Leon Trotsky, commander of the Red Army, and Joseph Stalin, general secretary of the Communist Party. Trotsky had the support of many "Old Bolsheviks" who had joined the party before the revolution. Having spent years in exile, he saw the revolution as a spark that would ignite a world revolution of the working class. Stalin, the only leading Communist who had never lived abroad, insisted that socialism could survive "in one country."

Stalin filled the party bureaucracy with individuals loyal to himself. In 1926–1927 he had Trotsky expelled for "deviation from the party line," and in January 1929 he forced Trotsky to flee the country. Then, as absolute master of the party, he prepared to industrialize the Soviet Union at breakneck speed.

28-3d An Ephemeral Peace

After the enormous sacrifices made during the war, the survivors developed hugely unrealistic expectations and were soon disillusioned. Conservatives in Britain and France longed for a return to the stability of the prewar era—the hierarchy of social classes, prosperous world trade, and European dominance over the rest of the world. Everywhere in the world, people's hopes had been raised by the lofty rhetoric of the war, then dashed by its outcome. In Europe, Germans felt cheated out of a victory that had seemed within their grasp, and Italians were disappointed that their sacrifices had not been rewarded with large territorial gains. Arabs and Indians longed for independence; the Chinese looked for social justice and a lessening of foreign intrusion; and the Japanese hoped to expand their influence in China. In Russia, the Communists were eager to consolidate their power and export their revolution to the rest of the world.

In 1923 Germany suspended reparations payments. In retaliation for the French occupation of the Ruhr, the German government began printing money recklessly, causing the most severe inflation the world had ever seen. Soon German money was worth so little that it took a wheelbarrow full of it to buy a loaf of bread. As Germany teetered on the brink of civil war, radical nationalists tried to overthrow the government. Finally, the German government issued a new currency and promised to resume reparations payments, and the French agreed to withdraw their troops from the Ruhr.

Beginning in 1924 the world enjoyed a few years of calm and prosperity. After the end of the German crisis of 1923, the western European nations became less confrontational, and Germany joined the League of Nations. The vexed issue of reparations also seemed to vanish, as Germany borrowed money from New York banks to make its payments to France and Britain, which used the money to repay their wartime loans from the United States. This triangular flow of money, based on credit, stimulated the rapid recovery of the European economies. France began rebuilding its wartorn northern zone; Germany recovered from its hyperinflation; and a boom began in the United States that was to last for five years.

AP® Exam Tip

Be able to explain how internal and external factors led to the transformation of Russia during the Russian Revolution.

Section Review

- The war caused millions of deaths and injuries and millions of refugees.

- France, Britain, and the United States dominated the Paris Peace Conference, refusing to listen to other voices.

- The United States refused to join the League of Nations, thereby weakening it.

- The Treaty of Versailles humiliated Germany but did not weaken it, thus becoming one of the big failures in history.

- When Austria-Hungary and Russia fell apart, several smaller nations arose in Europe, creating another source of potential conflict.

- After the Bolshevik victory in the Civil War, the Russian economy was in ruins, and Stalin took power.

- After the German hyperinflation of 1923 was resolved, the world economy began to prosper in 1924.

▶ **Lenin the Orator**
The leader of the Bolshevik revolutionaries was a spell-binding orator. Here Lenin is addressing Red Army soldiers in Sverdlov Square, Moscow, in 1920. INTERFOTO/Personalities/Alamy Stock Photo

AP® Exam Tip
Consider how communism is a transnational movement.

While their economies flourished, governments grew more cautious and businesslike. Even the Communists, after Lenin's death, seemed to give up their attempts to spread revolution abroad. Yet neither Germany nor the Soviet Union accepted its borders with the small nations that had arisen between them. In 1922 they signed a secret pact allowing the German army to conduct maneuvers in Russia (in violation of the Versailles treaty) in exchange for German help in building up Russian industry and military potential.

The League of Nations proved adept at resolving numerous technical issues pertaining to health, labor relations, and postal and telegraph communications. Without U.S. participation, however, sanctions against states that violated League rules carried little weight.

28-4 China and Japan: Contrasting Destinies

Why did China and Japan follow such divergent paths in this period?

AP® Exam Tip
Be sure to continue comparing the rise and impacts of nationalism in various countries, including China and Japan.

China and Japan were both subject to Western pressures, but their modern histories have followed opposite paths. China clung much longer than Japan to a traditional social structure and economy, then collapsed into chaos and revolution. Japan experienced reform from above (see Chapter 27), acquiring industry and a powerful military, which it used to take advantage of China's weakness. Their different reactions to the pressures of the West put these two great nations on a collision course.

28-4a Social and Economic Change

China's population—about 400 million in 1900—was the largest of any country in the world and growing fast. In 1900 peasant plots averaged between 1 and 4 acres (less than 2 hectares) apiece, half as large as they had been two generations earlier. Farming methods had not changed in centuries, and landlords and tax collectors took more than half of the harvest. Most Chinese worked incessantly, survived on a diet of grain and vegetables, and spent their lives in fear of floods, bandits, and tax collectors.

Above the peasantry, Chinese society was divided into many groups and strata. Landowners lived off the rents of their tenants. Officials, chosen through an elaborate examination system,

enriched themselves from taxes and the government's monopolies on salt, iron, and other products. Shanghai, China's financial and commercial center, was famous for its wealthy foreigners and its opium addicts, prostitutes, and gangsters.

Although foreign trade represented only a small part of China's economy, contact with the outside world had a tremendous impact on Chinese politics. Young men living in the treaty ports saw no chance for advancement in the old system of examinations and official positions. Some learned foreign ideas in Christian mission schools or abroad. The contrast between the squalor in which most urban residents lived and the luxury of the foreigners' enclaves in the treaty ports sharpened the resentment of educated Chinese.

Japan had few natural resources and very little arable land on which to grow food for its rising population. Typhoons regularly hit its southern regions, and earthquakes periodically shook the country, which lies on the great ring of tectonic fault lines that surround the Pacific Ocean. The Kanto earthquake of 1923 destroyed all of Yokohama and half of Tokyo and killed some 200,000 people.

Japan's population reached 60 million in 1925 and was increasing by a million a year. The crash program of industrialization begun in 1868 by the Meiji oligarchs (see Chapter 27) accelerated during the Great War, when Japan's economy grew four times as fast as western Europe's and eight times faster than China's.

Economic growth aggravated social tensions. The *narikin* ("new rich") affected Western ways and lifestyles that clashed with the austerity of earlier times. In the big cities *mobos* (modern boys) and *mogas* (modern girls) shocked traditionalists with their foreign ways: dancing together, wearing short skirts and tight pants, and behaving like Americans. Students who flirted with dangerous thoughts were called "Marx boys."

The main beneficiaries of prosperity were the *zaibatsu* (**zie-BOT-soo**), or conglomerates, four of which—Mitsubishi, Sumitomo, Yasuda, and Mitsui—controlled most of Japan's industry and commerce. Farmers, who constituted half of the population, remained poor; in desperation some sold their daughters to textile mills or into domestic service. Labor unions were weak and repressed by the police.

Japanese prosperity depended on foreign trade. The country exported silk and light manufactures and imported almost all its fuel, raw materials, machine tools, and even some of its food. Though less at the mercy of the weather than China, Japan was much more vulnerable to swings in the world economy.

28-4b Revolution and War, 1900–1918

In 1900 China's Empress Dowager Cixi (**TSUH-shee**), who had seized power in a palace coup two years earlier, encouraged a secret society, the Righteous Fists, or Boxers, to rise up and expel all the foreigners from China. When the Boxers threatened the foreign legation in Beijing, an international force from the Western powers and Japan captured the city and forced China to pay a huge indemnity. Shocked by these events, many Chinese students became convinced that China needed a revolution to get rid of the Qing dynasty and modernize their country.

When Cixi died in 1908, the Revolutionary Alliance led by **Sun Yat-sen** (**soon yot-SEN**) (1866–1925) prepared to take over. Sun had spent much of his life in Japan, England, and the United States, plotting the overthrow of the Qing dynasty. His ideas were a mixture of nationalism, socialism, and Confucian philosophy. His patriotism, his powerful ambition, and his tenacious spirit attracted a large following.

The military thwarted Sun's plans. After China's defeat in war with Japan in 1895, the government had agreed to equip the army with modern rifles and machine guns. This, combined with the fact that local armies were beholden to warlords rather than to the central government, created a threatening situation for the Qing. When a regional army mutinied in October 1911, **Yuan Shikai** (**you-AHN she-KIE**), the most powerful of the regional generals, refused to defend the Qing. A revolutionary assembly at Nanjing elected Sun Yat-sen president of China in December 1911, but he had no military forces at his command. To avoid a clash with the army, he resigned after a few weeks, and a new national assembly elected Yuan president of the new Chinese republic.

Yuan was an able military leader, but he had no political program. When Sun reorganized his followers into a political party called the **Guomindang** (**gwo-min-dong**) (National People's Party), Yuan quashed every attempt at creating a Western-style government and harassed Sun's followers. Victory in the first round of the struggle to create a new China went to the military.

Meanwhile, the Japanese were quick to join the Allied side in World War I, since they saw the war as an opportunity to advance their interests while the Europeans were occupied elsewhere. They quickly conquered the German colonies in the northern Pacific and on the coast of China, then turned their attention to the rest of China. In 1915 Japan presented China with Twenty-One Demands, which would have turned it into a virtual protectorate. Britain and the United States persuaded Japan to soften the demands but could not prevent it from keeping the German coastal enclaves and extracting railroad and mining concessions at China's expense. In protest, anti-Japanese riots and boycotts broke out throughout China. Thus began a bitter struggle between the two countries that was to last for thirty years.

28-4c Chinese Warlords and the Guomindang, 1919–1929

At the Paris Peace Conference, the great powers accepted Japan's seizure of the German enclaves in China. To many Chinese, this decision was a cruel insult. On May 4, 1919, students demonstrated in front of the Forbidden City of Beijing. Despite a government ban, the May Fourth Movement spread to other parts of China. A new generation was growing up to challenge the old officials, the regional generals, and the foreigners.

Sun Yat-sen tried to make a comeback in Guangzhou (Canton) in the early 1920s. Though not a Communist, he was impressed with the efficiency of Lenin's revolutionary tactics and let

Sun Yat-sen Chinese nationalist revolutionary, founder and leader of the Guomindang until his death. He attempted to create a liberal democratic political movement in China but was thwarted by military leaders.

Yuan Shikai Chinese general and first president of the Chinese Republic (1912–1916). He stood in the way of the democratic movement led by Sun Yat-sen.

Guomindang Nationalist political party founded on democratic principles by Sun Yat-sen in 1912. After 1925, the party was headed by Chiang Kai-shek, who turned it into an increasingly authoritarian movement.

a Soviet adviser reorganize the Guomindang along Leninist lines. He also welcomed members of the newly created Chinese Communist Party into the Guomindang.

When Sun died in 1925, the leadership of his party passed to Jiang Jieshi, known in the West as **Chiang Kai-shek (chang kie-shek)** (1887–1975). An officer and director of the military academy, Chiang trained several hundred young officers who remained loyal to him thereafter. In 1927 he determined to defeat the regional warlords. As his army moved north from its base in Canton, he briefly formed an alliance with the Communists. Once his troops occupied Shanghai, however, he crushed the labor unions and decimated the Communists, whom he considered a threat. He then defeated or co-opted most of the other warlords and established a dictatorship.

Chiang's government issued ambitious plans to build railroads, develop agriculture and industry, and modernize China from the top down. However, his followers were neither competent administrators nor ruthless modernizers. Instead, his government attracted thousands of opportunists whose goals were to "become officials and get rich" by taxing and plundering businesses. In the countryside tax collectors and landowners squeezed the peasants ever harder, even in times of natural disasters. What little money reached the government's coffers went to the military. Thus for twenty years after the fall of the Qing, China remained mired in poverty, subject to corrupt officials and the whims of nature.

Section Review

- Japan prospered during the war and quickly modernized; it also began preying on China.

- When the Qing dynasty ended in 1911, regional general Yuan Shikai took over China and repressed Sun Yat-sen's party, the Guomindang.

- After Sun Yat-sen's death, Chiang Kai-shek established a corrupt military dictatorship.

28-5 The New Middle East

How did the Middle East change as a result of the war?

Having revolted against the Ottoman Empire, many Arabs expected to have a say in negotiations to end the Great War. But the victorious French and British planned to treat the Middle East like a territory open to colonial rule. The result was a legacy of instability that has persisted to this day.

28-5a The Mandate System

At the Paris Peace Conference, France, Britain, Italy, and Japan proposed to divide the former German colonies and the territories of the Ottoman Empire among themselves, but their ambitions clashed with President Wilson's ideal of national self-determination. Eventually, the victors arrived at a compromise solution called the **mandate system**: colonial rulers would administer the territories but would be accountable to the League of Nations for "the material and moral well-being and the social progress of the inhabitants."

Class C Mandates—those with the smallest populations—were treated as colonies by their conquerors. South Africa replaced Germany in Southwest Africa (now Namibia); Britain, Australia, New Zealand, and Japan took over the German islands in the Pacific. Class B Mandates, larger than Class C but still underdeveloped economically, were to be ruled for the benefit of their inhabitants under League of Nations supervision. Most of Germany's African colonies, including Tanganyika, Cameroon, and Togo, fell into this category.

The Arabic-speaking territories of the old Ottoman Empire were Class A Mandates. The League of Nations declared that they had "reached a state of development where their existence as independent nations can be provisionally recognized subject to the rendering of administrative advice and assistance by a Mandatory, until such time as they are able to stand alone." While Arabs interpreted this ambiguous wording as a promise of independence, Britain and France sent troops into the region "for the benefit of its inhabitants." Palestine (divided now into Israel in the west, Jordan in the east, and the Occupied West Bank in between) and Iraq (formerly Mesopotamia) became British mandates; France claimed Syria and Lebanon (see Map 28.3). (See Diversity & Dominance: The Middle East After World War I.)

AP® Exam Tip
Consider the role of the mandate system in the creation of the modern political map of the Middle East.

Chiang Kai-shek Chinese military and political leader. Succeeded Sun Yat-sen as head of the Guomindang in 1925; headed the Chinese government from 1928 to 1949; fought against the Chinese Communists and Japanese invaders. After 1949 he headed the Chinese nationalist government in Taiwan.

mandate system Allocation of former German colonies and Ottoman possessions to the victorious powers after World War I, to be administered under League of Nations supervision.

During the First World War, Entente forces invaded and occupied Palestine, Mesopotamia, and Syria. This raised the question of what to do with these territories after the war. Would they be returned to the Ottoman Empire? Would they simply be added to the colonial empires of Britain and France? Or would they become independent Arab states?

The following documents illustrate the diversity of opinions among various groups planning the postwar settlement: Great Britain, concerned with defeating Germany and maintaining its empire; the United States, basing its policies on lofty principles; and Arab delegates from the Middle East, seeking self-determination.

In the early twentieth century, in response to the rise of anti-Semitism in Europe, a movement called Zionism had arisen among European Jews. Zionists, led by Theodore Herzl, hoped for a return to Israel, the ancestral homeland of the Jewish people. For 2,000 years this land had been a province of various empires—the Roman, Byzantine, Arab, and Ottoman—and was inhabited by Arabic-speaking people, most of whom practiced the Islamic religion.

During the war the British government was receptive to the idea of establishing a Jewish homeland in Palestine. It was motivated by the need to win the war, but it also considered the more distant future. The result was a policy statement, sent by Foreign Secretary Arthur James Balfour to Baron Rothschild, a prominent supporter of the Zionist movement in England. This statement, called the "Balfour Declaration," has haunted the Middle East ever since.

The Balfour Declaration of 1917

Foreign Office
November 2nd, 1917

Dear Lord Rothschild:

I have much pleasure in conveying to you, on behalf of His Majesty's Government, the following declaration of sympathy with Jewish Zionist aspirations which have been submitted to, and approved by, the Cabinet:

His Majesty's Government view with favor the establishment in Palestine of a national home for the Jewish people, and will use their best endeavors to facilitate the achievement of this object, it being clearly understood that nothing shall be done which may prejudice the civil and religious rights of existing non-Jewish communities in Palestine, or the rights and political status enjoyed by Jews in any other country.

I should be grateful if you would bring this declaration to the knowledge of the Zionist Federation.

Yours,
Arthur James Balfour

On January 8, 1918, American president Woodrow Wilson issued his famous Fourteen Points proposal to end the war. Much of his speech was devoted to European affairs or to international relations in general, but two of his fourteen points referred to the Arab world.

Woodrow Wilson's Fourteen Points

What we demand in this war . . . is that the world be made fit and safe to live in; and particularly that it be made safe for every peace-loving nation which, like our own, wishes to live its own life, determine its own institutions, be assured of justice and fair dealing by the other peoples of the world as against force and selfish aggression. All the peoples of the world are in effect partners in this interest, and for our own part we see very clearly that unless justice be done to others it will not be done to us. The programme of the world's peace, therefore, is our programme; and that programme, the only possible programme, as we see it, is this:

XII. The Turkish portions of the present Ottoman Empire should be assured a secure sovereignty, but the other nationalities which are now under Turkish rule should be assured an undoubted security of life and

28-5b The Rise of Modern Turkey

At the end of the war, as the Ottoman Empire teetered on the brink of collapse, France, Britain, and Italy saw an opportunity to expand their empires, and Greece eyed those parts of Anatolia inhabited by Greeks. In 1919 French, British, Italian, and Greek forces occupied Constantinople and parts of Anatolia. By the Treaty of Sèvres (1920) the Allies made the sultan give up most of his lands.

In 1919 Mustafa Kemal had formed a nationalist government in central Anatolia with the backing of fellow army officers. In 1922, after a short but fierce war against invading Greeks, his armies reconquered Anatolia and the area around Constantinople. The victorious Turks forced hundreds of thousands of Greeks from their ancestral homes in Anatolia. In response the Greek government expelled all Muslims from Greece. A Turkish Republic was proclaimed in 1923.

an absolutely unmolested opportunity of autonomous development. . . .

When the war ended, the victorious Allies assembled in Paris to determine, among other things, the fate of the former Arab provinces of the Ottoman Empire. Arab leaders had reason to doubt the intentions of the great powers, especially Britain and France. When the Allies decided to create mandates in the Arab territories on the grounds that the Arab peoples were not ready for independence, Arab leaders expressed their misgivings, as in the following statement.

Memorandum of the General Syrian Congress, July 2, 1919

We the undersigned members of the General Syrian Congress, meeting in Damascus on Wednesday, July 2nd, 1919, made up of representatives from the three Zones, viz., The Southern, Eastern, and Western, provided with credentials and authorizations by the inhabitants of our various districts, Moslems, Christians, and Jews, have agreed upon the following statement of the desires of the people of the country who have elected us. . . .

1. We ask absolutely complete political independence for Syria. . . .

2. Considering the fact that the Arabs inhabiting the Syrian area are not naturally less gifted than other more advanced races and that they are by no means less developed than the Bulgarians, Serbians, Greeks, and Roumanians at the beginning of their independence, we protest against Article 22 of the Covenant of the League of Nations, placing us among the nations in their middle stage of development which stand in need of a mandatory power.

3. . . . relying on the declarations of President Wilson that his object in waging war was to put an end to the ambition of conquest and colonization, . . . and believing that the American Nation is furthest from any thought of colonization and has no political ambition in our country, we will seek the technical and economic assistance from the United States of America, provided that such assistance does not exceed 20 years.

4. In the event of America not finding herself in a position to accept our desire for assistance, we will seek this assistance from Great Britain, also provided that such does not prejudice our complete independence and unity of our country and that the duration of such assistance does not exceed that mentioned in the previous article.

5. We do not acknowledge any right claimed by the French Government in any part whatever of our Syrian country and refuse that she should assist us or have a hand in our country under any circumstances and in any place.

6. We opposed the pretensions of the Zionists to create a Jewish commonwealth in the southern part of Syria, known as Palestine, and oppose Zionist migration to any part of our country; for we do not acknowledge their title but consider them a grave peril to our people from the national, economical, and political points of view. Our Jewish compatriots shall enjoy our common rights and assume our common responsibilities.

AP® History Reasoning Skills

Contextualization *How might the British have justified Balfour's promise both of "a national home for the Jewish people" and "that nothing shall be done which may prejudice the civil and religious rights of existing non-Jewish communities in Palestine"?*

Causation *Why would delegates to the General Syrian Congress object to plans to create mandates in the former Ottoman provinces? Why would they object to the creation of a Jewish commonwealth?*

Sources: The Balfour Declaration, *The Times* (London), November 9, 1917. Memorandum of the General Syrian Congress, *Foreign Relations of the United States: Paris Peace Conference*, vol. 12 (Washington, DC: Government Printing Office, 1919), 780–781.

As a war hero and proclaimed savior of his country, Mustafa Kemal was able to impose wrenching changes on his people. An outspoken modernizer, he was eager to bring Turkey closer to Europe as quickly as possible. He abolished the sultanate, declared Turkey a secular republic, and introduced European laws. In a radical break with Islamic tradition, he suppressed Muslim courts, schools, and religious orders and replaced the Arabic alphabet with the Latin alphabet.

He also attempted to westernize the traditional Turkish family. Women received civil equality, including the right to vote and to be elected to the national assembly. Kemal forbade polygamy and instituted civil marriage and divorce. He even changed people's clothing, strongly discouraging women from veiling their faces, and replacing the fez, a men's hat adopted as a symbol of reform in the nineteenth century, with the European brimmed hat. He ordered everyone to take a family name, choosing the name **Atatürk** ("father of the Turks") for himself. His reforms spread quickly in the cities; but in rural areas, where Islamic traditions remained strong, old ways continued.

Atatürk The founder of modern Turkey. He distinguished himself in the defense of Gallipoli in World War I and expelled a Greek expeditionary army from Anatolia in 1921–1922. He replaced the Ottoman Empire with the Turkish Republic in 1923. As president, he pushed through a radical westernization and reform of Turkish society.

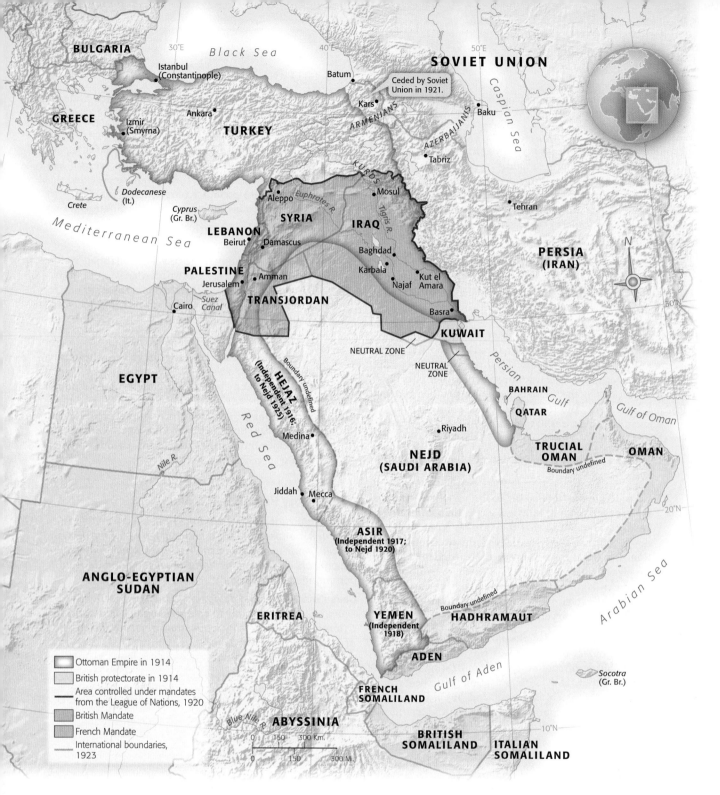

MAP 28.3   Territorial Changes in the Middle East After World War I   The defeat and dismemberment of the Ottoman Empire at the end of World War I resulted in an entirely new political map of the region. The Turkish Republic inherited Anatolia and a small piece of Europe, while the Ottoman Empire's Arab provinces were divided between France and Great Britain. Only Iran and Egypt did not change.

How successful do these territorial changes seem from the viewpoint of today?

28-5c   Arab Lands and the Question of Palestine

Among the Arab people, the thinly disguised colonialism of the mandate system set off protests and rebellions. Arabs viewed the European presence not as liberation from Ottoman oppression, but as foreign occupation, such as fellow Arabs in Algeria, Tunisia, and Morocco were experiencing under French colonialism.

◄ **Mustafa Kemal Atatürk** After World War I, Mustafa Kemal was determined to modernize Turkey on the Western model. Here he is shown wearing a European-style suit and teaching the Latin alphabet. Fotosearch/Getty Images

After World War I, which had left enormous numbers dead from violence and famine, Middle Eastern society underwent dramatic changes. Trucks replaced camel caravans, and landless peasants migrated to the swelling cities. The population of the region is estimated to have bounced back by 50 percent between 1914 and 1939, while that of large cities such as Constantinople, Baghdad, and Cairo doubled.

The urban and mercantile middle class, encouraged by the transformation of Turkey, adopted Western ideas, customs, and styles of housing and clothing. To prepare their sons for jobs in government and business, some families sent them to European secular or mission schools, then to Western colleges in Istanbul, Cairo, or Beirut or to universities abroad. A few women, following American missionary examples, became schoolteachers or nurses. Secular educational opportunities varied widely from Lebanon, where French influence was strong; to Iran, whose first university was established in 1933; to Saudi Arabia, which strongly resisted Western influences.

The region in closest contact with Europe was the Maghrib—Algeria, Tunisia, and Morocco—which the French army considered its private domain. Alongside the old native quarters, the French built modern neighborhoods inhabited mainly by Europeans. France had occupied Algeria since 1830 and had encouraged European immigration. The settlers owned the best lands and monopolized government jobs and businesses, while Arabs and Berbers remained poor and suffered intense discrimination.

The British attempted to control the Middle East with a mixture of bribery and intimidation. They made Faisal, leader of the Arab Revolt, king of Iraq and used aerial bombing of rebellious nomads to enforce their will. In 1931 they reached an agreement with King Faisal's government: official independence for Iraq in exchange for the right to keep two air bases, a military alliance,

AP® Exam Tip
Understand how Zionist Jewish migration to Palestine led to the displacement of Arab Palestinians.

▲ **Kibbutz Ein Harod** One of four settlements established in the Jezreel Valley over a 100-day period in 1921, Ein Harod was part of the effort to drain swamps, suppress malaria, and establish new farms. Initially living in white tents and doing their laundry in steel tubs, the settlers lived lives of hard labor, but one day the famous violinist Jascha Heifetz came to give a concert. Ein Harod, 1921 (b/w photo)/Ben Dov, Yaacov (1882-1968)/ISRAEL MUSEUM, JERUSALEM/ The Israel Museum, Jerusalem, Israel/Bridgeman Images

and an assured flow of petroleum. France, meanwhile, sent thousands of troops to Syria and Lebanon to crush nationalist uprisings.

In Egypt, as in Iraq, the British substituted a phony independence for official colonialism. They declared Egypt independent in 1922 but reserved the right to station troops along the Suez Canal to secure their link with India in the event of war. Most galling to the nationalist Wafd (Delegation [to the Paris peace conference]) Party was the British attempt to remove Egyptian troops from Sudan, a land many Egyptians considered a colony of Egypt. Britain was successful in keeping Egypt in limbo—neither independent nor a colony—thanks to an alliance with King Fuad and conservative Egyptian politicians who feared both secular and religious radicalism.

Before the war, a Jewish minority lived in Palestine, as in other Arab countries. Small numbers of Jews had immigrated to Palestine following their expulsion from Spain in 1492, and a trickle continued into the nineteenth century. As soon as Palestine became a British mandate in 1920, however, many more came from Europe, encouraged by the Balfour Declaration of 1917. Those supporting a socialist version of Zionism established *kibbutzim*, or communal farms, while nonsocialists belonging to the Revisionist wing of the Zionist movement preferred to settle in the cities. But purchases of land by Jewish agencies angered the indigenous Arabs, especially tenant farmers who were evicted to make room for settlers, and in 1920–1921 riots erupted between Jews and Arabs. When far more Jewish immigrants arrived than they had anticipated, the British tried to limit immigration, thereby alienating the Jews without mollifying the Arabs. Increasingly, Jews arrived without papers, smuggled in by

Section Review

- Former Arab provinces of the Ottoman Empire became "mandates" under French or British control.

- Mustafa Kemal Atatürk expelled the Greek minority from Anatolia and founded the Turkish Republic, then pushed it toward secular reform.

- As Middle Eastern society modernized, the Arabs became more politically active but had to endure the mandate system.

- Jewish immigration to Palestine caused growing tensions between Jews, Arabs, and the British.

militant Zionist organizations. In the 1930s the country was torn by strikes and guerrilla warfare that the British could not control. In the process, Britain earned the hatred of both sides.

28-6 Conclusion

In the late 1920s it seemed as though the victors in the Great War might reestablish the prewar prosperity and European dominance of the globe. But the spirit of the 1920s was not real peace; instead, it was the eye of a hurricane. The Great Depression and World War II were in the offing (see Chapter 29).

The Great War caused a major realignment among the nations of the world. France and Britain, the two leading colonial powers, emerged economically weakened despite their victory. The war brought defeat and humiliation to Germany but did not reduce its military or industrial potential. It destroyed the old regime of Russia, leading to civil war and revolution from which the victorious powers sought to isolate themselves. Two other old empires—the Austro-Hungarian and the Ottoman—were divided into many smaller and weaker nations.

Japan took advantage of the European conflict to develop its industries and press its demands on a China weakened by domestic turmoil and social unrest. The United States emerged as the most prosperous and potentially most powerful nation, re-strained only by the isolationist sentiments of many Americans.

In the Middle East, the fall of the Ottoman Empire awakened aspirations of nationhood among the Turkish, Arab, Armenian, and Kurdish inhabitants and Jewish immigrants. These aspirations were thwarted when France and Great Britain succeeded in imposing their rule upon the former Ottoman lands, giving rise to conflicts and bitter enmities.

Key Terms

Western Front p. 731

Faisal p. 735

Theodore Herzl p. 735

Balfour Declaration p. 735

Bolsheviks p. 735

Vladimir Lenin p. 735

Woodrow Wilson p. 736

Fourteen Points p. 736

League of Nations p. 738

Treaty of Versailles p. 738

New Economic Policy p. 738

Sun Yat-sen p. 742

Yuan Shikai p. 742

Guomindang p. 742

Chiang Kai-shek p. 743

mandate system p. 743

Atatürk p. 745

Review Questions

1. Though historians often describe World War I as ushering in a new era after the "long nineteenth century," can an argument be made that the political upheavals stemming from the French Revolution combined with the consolidation of European colonialism made the nineteenth century just as transformative?

2. Where the fragmentation of the Roman Empire and Abbasid Caliphate occurred with little or no change in basic military technology, was technology a decisive factor in the transformations wrought by World War I?

3. Is Lenin the only political figure of the World War I era who might be compared with Alexander the Great, Julius Caesar, Genghis Khan, or Napoleon?

▲ Europe in 1913

Multiple-Choice Questions
Questions 1–3 refer to the map above.

1. Based on the map, which of the following is a reasonable cause to assert for the total war that broke out in Europe in 1914?

   (A) Europe suffered from a lack of industrial development.

   (B) Religious rivalries led to military conflicts.

   (C) Europe had significant difficulties with immigration.

   (D) Europe's biggest powers were part of a complex system of alliances.

2. How does the map support the claim that the Great War was more destructive than previous wars?

   (A) Large numbers of peasants and workers rebelled in western Europe.

   (B) The economies and militaries of Europe were now industrialized.

   (C) A vast number of colonials were brought to Europe to fight for their imperial governments.

   (D) The hand-to-hand combat was intense.

3. Which of the following combatants had industrialized the *least* over the period of time between 1750 and 1914?

(A) England

(B) France

(C) Russia

(D) Germany

Questions 4–6 refer to the image below.

4. Which of the following explains the significance of the photo to the changes in Russia?

(A) Lenin and Trotsky created the first communist government.

(B) The photograph marks the Russian defeat of the Germans.

(C) The unveiling of the statues marks the beginning of Russia's involvement in the Great War.

(D) The event was celebrating the defeat of the United Kingdom.

▲ **Vladimir Ilyich Lenin (left) and Leo Trotsky in Moscow at the unveiling of the monument to Marx and Engels, 1918.** IMAGNO/Votava/The Image Works

5. Which of the following is one of the ways the Communist government under Lenin and Trotsky tried to overcome their main problems in establishing a Marxist government?

(A) Delivering bread and vegetables to peasants across Russia

(B) Increasing military presence at both war fronts

(C) Instituting required higher education to increase literacy and innovation

(D) Nationalizing private land and demanding crops be turned over to the state

6. Which of the following is an accurate comparison between the Russian and the Ottoman Empires at the end of World War I?

(A) Both empires had collapsed due to a combination of internal and external factors.

(B) Both empires had gained land from the war, but suffered internal turmoil.

(C) While the Russians stayed in the war until the end, the Ottomans' early withdrawal helped them survive.

(D) While the Russians lost territory in the war, the Ottomans gained territory and international prestige.

Questions 7–10 refer to the passage below.

"1. We ask absolutely complete political independence for Syria.

. . .

3. Considering the fact that the Arabs inhabiting the Syrian area are not naturally less gifted than other more advanced races and that they are by no means less developed than the Bulgarians, Serbians, Greeks, and Roumanians at the beginning of their independence, we protest against Article 22 of the Covenant of the League of Nations, placing us among the nations in their middle stage of development which stand in need of a mandatory power."

Memorandum of the General Syrian
Congress, July 2, 1919

7. Which of the following can be inferred based on the passage above?

(A) Enlightenment ideals, such as self-determination, had spread beyond Europe and the Americas.

(B) Self-determination was only possible within the secure context of an empire.

(C) Most Syrians in 1919 identified themselves as French nationals.

(D) Arabs were no longer the majority in their own homelands.

8. The memorandum is a direct result of which of the following movements?

   (A) Religious fundamentalism

   (B) Arab industrialization

   (C) Arab nationalism

   (D) Consumerism

9. Which of the following was true of the time period following World War I in which the General Syrian Congress issued this memorandum?

   (A) Woodrow Wilson's Fourteen Points became the defining document supporting nationalism across the Middle East.

   (B) European imperial states like France maintained control of their colonies and in some cases gained territory.

   (C) The Mandate System prevented the expansion of colonialism, but allowed some imperial nations to maintain minor colonies.

   (D) Religion became an insignificant factor as cultures crossed and syncretism melded religions together.

10. Which of the following would be an argument against the claim made in the memorandum?

   (A) The Arab people have a long history of innovation in both politics and technology.

   (B) Arab states in the past found ways to adapt bureaucratic and economic institutions developed by other states.

   (C) Arabs in the region have traditionally been part of empires led by non-Arabs.

   (D) Arabs in Syria rarely engaged in conflict with their Turkish leaders under the Ottoman Empire.

Short-Answer Questions

1. After World War I, there was an attempt to create a Jewish state in the Middle East. Based on your knowledge of world history, answer all parts of the question that follows.

   (A) Identify and explain ONE claim the Zionists of Europe made to support their desire for a Jewish homeland.

   (B) Identify and explain ONE claim the Palestinians made against the Zionist claim.

   (C) Identify and explain ONE reason that a Jewish state was not established after World War I.

2. Based on the map on the next page and your knowledge of world history, answer all parts of the question that follows.

   (A) Provide ONE example of a former German or Ottoman holding that was under a different mandate following World War I.

   (B) Explain ONE reason for the creation of the mandate system in the Middle East.

   (C) Explain ONE effect of the mandate system in the Middle East.

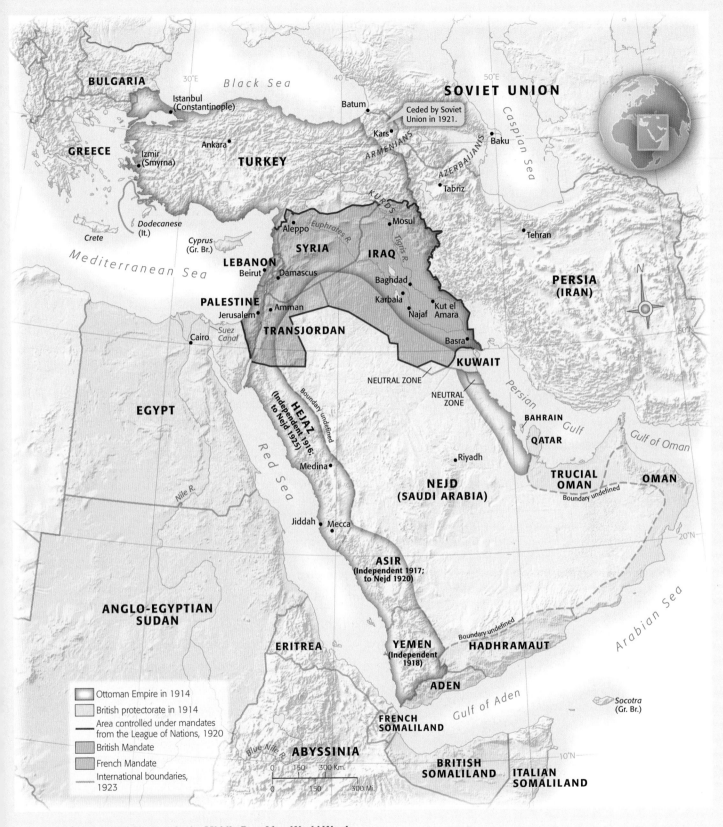

▲ Territorial Changes in the Middle East After World War I

29 The Collapse of the Old Order, 1929–1949

CHAPTER OUTLINE

Overarching Questions

1 How have religions, belief systems, philosophies, and ideologies affected the political, economic, and social development of societies? (CUL)

2 How and why have economic, social, cultural, and geographic factors influenced the process of state building, expansion, and dissolution? (SB)

3 How have internal and external political factors influenced the process of state building, expansion, and dissolution? (SB)

4 How have economic systems and the development of ideologies, values, and institutions influenced each other? (ECON)

5 To what extent have legal systems, colonialism, nationalism, and independence movements sustained or challenged class, gender, and racial hierarchies over time? (SOC)

AP® Framework Terms

Great Depression
World War II
Antibiotics
Total war
Fascism
Communism
Holocaust

Before the First World War Italian poet Filippo Marinetti exalted violence as noble and manly: "We want to glorify war, the world's only hygiene—militarism, deed, destroyer of anarchisms, the beautiful ideas that are death-bringing, and the subordination of women."[1] His friend Gabriele d'Annunzio added: "If it is a crime to incite citizens to violence, I shall boast of this crime."[2] Poets are sometimes more prescient than they imagine.

In the nineteenth century the governments of the great powers were manipulated by politicians through appeals to popular nationalism. Internationally, the world order relied on the maintenance of empires by military or economic means. And the global economy was based on free-market capitalism in which the industrial countries exchanged manufactured goods for the agricultural and mineral products of the nonindustrial world.

After the trauma of World War I the world seemed to return to what U.S. president Warren Harding called "normalcy": prosperity in Europe and America, European colonialism in Asia and Africa, American domination

---

[1]Apollonio Umbro, ed., *Documents of Twentieth Century Art: Futurist Manifestos* (New York: Viking Press, 1973), 23.
[2]Richard F. Hamilton and Holger H. Herwig, *Decisions for War, 1914–1917* (Cambridge, UK: Cambridge University Press, 2004), 199.

▲ **German Dive-Bomber over Eastern Europe** A German Messerschmidt Bf-110 fighter plane attacks a Soviet troop convoy on the Eastern Front.
Universal Images Group/Getty Images

of Latin America, and peace almost everywhere. But in 1929 normalcy vanished. As the Great Depression spread around the world, governments turned against one another in desperate attempts to protect their people's livelihood.

Most survivors of the war had learned to abhor violence. For a few, however, war and domination became a creed, a goal, and a solution to their problems. The Japanese military tried to save their country from the depression by conquering China, which erupted in revolution. In Germany many blamed their troubles on communists and Jews and turned to the Nazis, who promised to save German society by crushing others. In the Soviet Union, Stalin used energetic and murderous means to force his country into a communist version of the Industrial Revolution.

As the old order collapsed, the world was engulfed by a second Great War, one far more global and destructive than the first. Unlike World War I, this was a war of movement in which entire countries were conquered in a matter of weeks. It was also a war of machines: fighter planes and bombers that targeted civilians, tanks, aircraft carriers, and, finally, atomic bombs that obliterated entire cities.

At the end of World War II much of Europe and East Asia lay in ruins, and millions of destitute refugees sought safety in other lands. The colonial powers were either defeated or so weakened that they could no longer prevent their Asian and African subjects from demanding independence. ●

29-1 The Stalin Revolution

How did the Soviet Union change under Stalin, and at what cost?

During the 1920s the Soviet Union recovered from the Revolutions of 1917 and the civil war that followed (see Chapter 28). After Stalin achieved total mastery over this huge nation in 1929, he led it through an economic and social transformation that turned it into a great industrial and military power and intensified both admiration for and fear of communism throughout the world.

29-1a Five-Year Plans

Joseph Stalin Bolshevik revolutionary, head of the Soviet Communist Party after 1924, and dictator of the Soviet Union from 1928 to 1953. He led the Soviet Union with an iron fist, using Five-Year Plans to increase industrial production and terror to crush all opposition.

Five-Year Plans Plans that Joseph Stalin introduced to industrialize the Soviet Union rapidly, beginning in 1928. They set goals for the output of steel, electricity, machinery, and most other products and were enforced by the police powers of the state. They succeeded in making the Soviet Union a major industrial power before World War II.

Joseph Stalin (1879–1953) was the son of a poor shoemaker from the province of Georgia. Before becoming a revolutionary, he studied for the priesthood. Under the name *Stalin* (Russian for "man of steel"), he played a small part in the Revolutions of 1917. He was a hard-working and skillful administrator who rose within the party bureaucracy and filled its upper ranks with men loyal to himself. He then proceeded to make himself absolute dictator and transform Soviet society.

Stalin's ambition was to turn the USSR into an industrial nation. However, industrialization was to serve a different purpose than in other countries. It was not expected to produce consumer goods for a mass market or to enrich individuals. Instead, its aim was to increase the power of the Communist Party domestically and that of the Soviet Union in relation to other countries.

Stalin was determined to prevent a repetition of the humiliating defeat Russia had suffered at the hands of Germany in 1917. His goal was to quintuple the output of electricity and double that of heavy industry—iron, steel, coal, and machinery—in five years. To do so, he devised the first of a series of **Five-Year Plans**. Beginning in October 1928, the Communist Party and government created whole industries and cities from scratch, then trained millions of peasants to work in the new factories, mines, and offices. In every way except actual fighting, Stalin's Russia resembled a nation at war.

Rapid industrialization hastened environmental changes. Hydroelectric dams turned rivers into strings of reservoirs. Roads, canals, and railroad tracks cut the landscape. Forests and grassland were turned into farmland. From an environmental perspective, the Five-Year Plans resembled the transformation that had occurred in the United States and Canada a few decades earlier.

29-1b Collectivization of Agriculture

Since the Soviet Union was still a predominantly agrarian country, the only way to pay for these massive investments, provide the labor, and feed the millions of new industrial workers was to squeeze the peasantry. Stalin therefore proceeded with the most radical social experiment conceived up to that time: the collectivization of agriculture.

Collectivization meant consolidating small private farms into vast collectives and making the farmers work together in commonly owned fields. Each collective was expected to supply the government with a fixed amount of food and distribute what was left among its members. Collectives were to become outdoor factories where food was manufactured through the techniques of mass production and the application of machinery. The purpose of this collectivization was to bring the peasants under government control so they never again could withhold food supplies, as they had done during the Russian civil war of 1918–1921.

When collectivization was announced, the government mounted a massive propaganda campaign and sent party members into the countryside to enlist the farmers' support. At first all seemed to go well, but soon *kulaks*

◀ **The Collectivization of Soviet Agriculture** One of the goals of collectivization was to introduce modern farm machinery. This poster highlights Josef Stalin's personal connection with mechanization. The tractors and operators were assigned to tractor stations, which then supplied them to individual collective farms. Deutsches Plakat Museum, Essen, Germany/Archives Charmet/The Bridgeman Art Library

CHRONOLOGY

	United States, Europe, and North Africa	Asia and the Pacific
1920	1928 Stalin introduces Five-Year Plans and the collectivization of agriculture 1929 Great Depression begins in United States	
1930	1931 Great Depression reaches Europe 1933 Hitler comes to power in Germany	1931 Japanese forces occupy Manchuria 1934–1935 Mao leads Communists on Long March
1935	1936 Hitler invades the Rhineland 1939 (Sept. 1) German forces invade Poland	1937 Japanese troops invade China, conquer coastal provinces; Chiang Kai-shek flees to Sichuan 1937–1938 Japanese troops take Nanjing
1940	1940 (March–April) German forces conquer Denmark, Norway, the Netherlands, and Belgium 1940 (May–June) German forces conquer France 1940 (June–Sept.) Battle of Britain 1941 (June 21) German forces invade USSR 1942–1943 Allies and Germany battle for control of North Africa 1943 Soviet victory in Battle of Stalingrad 1943–1944 Red Army slowly pushes Wehrmacht back to Germany 1944 (June 6) D-day: U.S., British, and Canadian troops land in Normandy	1941 (Dec. 7) Japanese aircraft bomb Pearl Harbor 1942 (Jan.–March) Japanese conquer Thailand, Philippines, Malaya 1942 (June) United States Navy defeats Japan at Battle of Midway 1942-43 Battle of Guadalcanal 1945 Battles of Iwo Jima and Okinawa
1945	1945 (May 7) Germany surrenders	1945 (Aug. 6) United States drops atomic bomb on Hiroshima 1945 (Aug. 14) Japan surrenders 1945–1949 Civil war in China 1949 (Oct. 1) Communists defeat Guomindang; Mao proclaims People's Republic of China

(COO-lock) ("fists"), the better-off peasants, began to resist giving up all their property. When soldiers came to force them into collectives at gunpoint, they burned their crops, smashed their equipment, and slaughtered their livestock. Within a few months they slaughtered half of the Soviet Union's horses and cattle and two-thirds of the sheep and goats. In retaliation, Stalin ruthlessly ordered the "liquidation of kulaks as a class" and incited the poor peasants to attack their wealthier neighbors. Over 8 million kulaks were arrested. Many were executed, and the rest were sent to slave labor camps, where most starved to death.

The peasants who were left had been the least successful before collectivization and proved to be the least competent after. Many were sent to work in factories. The rest were forbidden to leave their farms. With half of their draft animals gone, they could not plant or harvest enough to meet the swelling demands of the cities. Yet government agents took whatever they could find, leaving little or nothing for the farmers themselves. After bad harvests in 1933 and 1934, a famine swept through the countryside, killing some 5 million people, about one in every twenty farmers.

Stalin's second Five-Year Plan, designed to run from 1933 to 1937, was originally intended to produce consumer goods. But when the Nazis took over Germany in 1933 (see below), Stalin changed the plan to emphasize heavy industries that could produce armaments. Between 1927 and 1937 the Soviet output of metals and machines increased fourteen-fold while consumer goods became scarce and food was rationed. After a decade of Stalinism, the Soviet people were more poorly clothed, fed, and housed than they had been before the war.

AP® Exam Tip
Explain how communist states, such as the Soviet Union, often used repressive policies and negative repercussions to control the national economy.

29-1c Terror and Opportunities

The 1930s brought both terror and opportunities to the Soviet people. The forced pace of industrialization, the collectivization of agriculture, and the uprooting of millions of people could be accomplished only under duress. To prevent any possible resistance or rebellion, the NKVD, Stalin's secret police, created a climate of suspicion and fear.

Section Review

- Once in power, Stalin issued Five-Year Plans to accelerate Soviet industrialization.

- When farms were merged into collectives, millions of farmers who resisted were deported and killed; those who were left suffered famine.

- Under the terror, Stalin executed many generals and government officials and sent millions of people to labor camps.

- Stalin's measures subjugated the Russian people but made the Soviet Union the world's third largest industrial power.

AP® Exam Tip

Consider the changes and continuities of twentieth-century Russian/Soviet economic systems.

As early as 1930 Stalin had hundreds of engineers and technicians arrested on trumped-up charges of counterrevolutionary ideas and sabotage. Three years later, he expelled a million members of the Communist Party—one-third of the membership—on similar charges. He then turned on his most trusted associates.

In December 1934 Sergei Kirov, the party boss of Leningrad (now St. Petersburg), was assassinated, perhaps on Stalin's orders. Stalin made a public display of mourning Kirov while blaming others for the crime. He then ordered a series of spectacular purge trials in which he accused most of Lenin's associates of treason. In 1937 he had his eight top generals and many lower officers executed, leaving the Red Army dangerously weakened. Under torture or psychological pressure, almost all the accused confessed to the "crimes" they were charged with.

While "Old Bolsheviks" and high officials were being put on trial, terror spread downward. The government regularly made demands that people could not meet, so everyone was guilty of breaking some regulation or other. People from all walks of life were arrested, some on mere suspicion or because of a false accusation by a jealous coworker or neighbor, some for expressing a doubt or working too hard or not hard enough, some for being related to someone previously arrested, some for no reason at all. Millions of people were sentenced without trials. At the height of the terror, some 8 million were sent to *gulags* (**GOO-log**) (labor camps), where perhaps a million died each year of exposure or malnutrition. To its victims the terror seemed capricious and random. Yet it turned a sullen and resentful people into docile hard-working subjects of the party.

In spite of the fear and hardships, many Soviet citizens supported Stalin's regime. Suddenly, with so many people gone and new industries and cities being built everywhere, there were opportunities for those who remained, especially the poor and the young. Women entered careers and jobs previously closed to them, becoming steelworkers, physicians, and office managers; but they retained their household and childrearing duties, receiving little help from men (see Diversity & Dominance: Women, Family Values, and the Russian Revolution). People who moved to the cities, worked enthusiastically, and asked no questions could hope to rise into the upper ranks of the Communist Party, the military, the government, or the professions—where the privileges and rewards were many.

Stalin's brutal methods helped the Soviet Union industrialize faster than any country had ever done. By the late 1930s the USSR was the world's third largest industrial power, after the United States and Germany. To foreign observers it seemed to be booming with construction projects and labor shortages. Even anti-Communist observers admitted that government planning worked. To millions of Soviet citizens who took pride in the new strength of their country and to many foreigners who contrasted conditions in the Soviet Union with the unemployment and despair in the West, Stalin's achievement seemed worth any price.

29-2 The Depression

What caused the Great Depression, and what effects did it have on the world?

On October 24, 1929—"Black Thursday"—the New York stock market went into a dive. Within days stocks had lost half their value. The fall continued for three years, ruining millions of investors. People with bank accounts rushed to make withdrawals, causing thousands of banks to collapse.

29-2a Economic Crisis

What began as a stock market crash soon turned into the deepest depression in history. As consumers reduced their purchases, businesses cut production, laying off thousands of workers. Female employees were the first laid off on the grounds that men had to support families while women worked only for "pin money." Jobless men deserted their families. Small farmers went bankrupt and lost their land. By mid-1932 the American economy had shrunk by half, and unemployment had risen to an unprecedented 25 percent of the workforce. Many observers thought that free-enterprise capitalism was doomed.

In 1930 the U.S. government, hoping to protect American industries from foreign competition, imposed the Smoot-Hawley tariff, the highest in American history. In retaliation, other countries raised their tariffs in a wave of "beggar thy neighbor" protectionism. The result was crippled export industries and shrinking world trade. While global industrial production declined by 36 percent between 1929 and 1932, world trade dropped by a breathtaking 62 percent.

29-2b Depression in Industrial Nations

By 1931 the depression had spread to Europe. Governments canceled reparations payments and war loans, but it was too late to save the world economy. Though their economies stagnated, France and Britain weathered the depression by making their colonial empires purchase their products rather than the products of other countries. Nations that relied on exports to pay for imported food and fuel suffered much more. In Germany unemployment reached 6 million by 1932, twice as high as in Britain. Half the German population lived in poverty, while those who kept their jobs saw their salaries cut and their living standards fall. In Japan the burden of the depression fell hardest on farmers and fishermen.

This massive economic upheaval had political repercussions. Nationalists everywhere called for autarchy, or independence from the world economy. In the United States Franklin D. Roosevelt was elected president in 1932 on a "New Deal" platform of government programs to stimulate and revitalize the economy. Although the American, British, and French governments intervened in their economies, they remained democratic. In Germany and Japan, as economic grievances worsened long-festering political resentments, radical leaders came to power and turned their nations into military machines, hoping to acquire, by war if necessary, empires large enough to support self-sufficient economies, and at the same time to provide employment in arms factories.

AP® Exam Tip
Explain how the Great Depression led to more active roles for governments in economic life.

◀ **Two Views of the American Way** In this classic photograph, *Life* magazine photographer Margaret Bourke-White captured the contrast between advertisers' view of the ideal American family and the reality of bread lines for the poor. Margaret Bourke-White/Masters/Time Life Pictures/Getty Images

The Bolsheviks were of two minds on the subject of women. They were opposed to bourgeois morality and to the oppression of women, especially working-class women, under capitalism. But what to put in its place?

Alexandra Kollontai was the most outspoken of the Bolsheviks on the subject of women's rights. She advocated the liberation of women, the replacement of housework by communal kitchens and laundries, and divorce on demand. Under socialism, love, sex, and marriage would be entirely equal, reciprocal, and free of economic obligations. Childbearing would be encouraged, but children would be raised communally: "The worker mother . . . must remember that there are henceforth only our children, those of the communist state, the common possession of all workers."

In a lecture she gave at Sverdlov University in 1921, Kollontai declared:

. . . it is important to preserve not only the interests of the woman but also the life of the child, and this is to be done by giving the woman the opportunity to combine labour and maternity. Soviet power tries to create a situation where a woman does not have to cling to a man she has learned to loathe only because she has nowhere else to go with her children, and where a woman alone does not have to fear for her life and the life of her child. In the labour republic it is not the philanthropists with their humiliating charity but the workers and peasants, fellow-creators of the new society, who hasten to help the working woman and strive to lighten the burden of motherhood. . . . I would like to say a few words about . . . the question of abortion, and Soviet Russia's attitude toward it. On 20 November 1920 the labour republic issued a law abolishing the penalties that had been attached to abortion. What is the reason behind this new attitude? Russia after all suffers not from an overproduction of living labour but rather from a lack of it. Russia is thinly, not densely populated. Every unit of labour power is precious. Why then have we declared abortion to be no longer a criminal offence? . . .

Abortion exists and flourishes everywhere, and no laws or punitive measures have succeeded in rooting it out. A way round the law is always found. But "secret help" only cripples women; they become a burden on the labour government, and the size of the labour force is reduced. Abortion, when carried out under proper medical conditions, is less harmful and dangerous, and the woman can get back to work quicker. Soviet power realizes that the need for abortion will only disappear on the one hand when Russia has a broad and developed network of institutions protecting motherhood and providing social education, and on the other hand when women understand that *childbirth is a social obligation*; Soviet power has therefore allowed abortion to be performed openly and in clinical conditions.

Besides the large-scale development of motherhood protection, the task of labour Russia is to strengthen in women the healthy instinct of motherhood, to make motherhood and labour for the collective compatible and thus do away with the need for abortion. This is the approach of the labour republic to the question of abortion, which still faces women in the bourgeois countries in all its magnitude. In these countries women are exhausted by the dual burden of hired labour for capital and motherhood. In Soviet Russia the working woman and peasant woman are helping the Communist Party to

29-2c Depression in Nonindustrial Regions

The depression also spread to Asia, Africa, and Latin America, but very unevenly. In 1930 India erected a wall of import duties to protect its infant industries from foreign competition; its living standards stagnated but did not drop. China was little affected by trade with other countries; its problems were more political than economic.

Countries that depended on exports were hard hit by the depression. Malaya, Indochina, and the Dutch East Indies produced most of the world's natural rubber; when automobile production in the United States and Europe dropped by half, so did imports of rubber, devastating their economies. Egypt, dependent on cotton exports, was also affected, and in the resulting political strife, the government became autocratic and unpopular.

Throughout Latin America unemployment and homelessness increased markedly. The industrialization of Argentina and Brazil was set back a decade or more. Disenchanted with liberal politics, military officers seized power in several Latin American countries (see Chapter 30). Consciously imitating dictatorships emerging in Europe,

Section Review

- The New York stock market crash of 1929 caused business and bank failures and massive unemployment.

- The depression soon spread to all industrial nations, hitting Germany particularly hard.

- Nonindustrial countries, especially those that depended on exports to industrial countries, were also hard hit; only southern Africa was spared.

- In the face of this threat, some countries turned to dictatorship to save their economies.

build a new society and to undermine the old way of life that has enslaved women. As soon as woman is viewed as being essentially a labour unit, the key to the solution of the complex question of maternity can be found.

Fifteen years later Joseph Stalin reversed the Soviet policy on abortion.

The published draft of the law prohibiting abortion and providing material assistance to mothers has provoked a lively reaction throughout the country. It is being heatedly discussed by tens of millions of people and there is no doubt that it will serve as a further strengthening of the Soviet family. . . .

When we speak of strengthening the Soviet family, we are speaking precisely of the struggle against the survivals of a bourgeois attitude towards marriage, women, and children. So-called "free love" and all disorderly sex life are bourgeois through and through, and have nothing to do with either socialist principles or the ethics and standards of conduct of the Soviet citizens. Socialist doctrine shows this, and it is proved by life itself.

The elite of our country, the best of the Soviet youth, are as a rule also excellent family men who dearly love their children. And vice versa: the man who does not take marriage seriously, and abandons his children to the whims of fate, is usually also a bad worker and a poor member of society. . . .

It is impossible even to compare the present state of the family with that which obtained before the Soviet regime—so great has been the improvement towards greater stability and, above all, greater humanity and goodness. The single fact that millions of women have become economically independent and are no longer at the mercy of men's whims, speaks volumes. Compare,

for instance, the modern woman collective farmer who sometimes earns more than her husband, with the pre-revolutionary peasant woman who completely depended on her husband and was a slave in the household. Has not this fundamentally changed family relations, has it not rationalized and strengthened the family? The very motives for setting up a family, for getting married, have changed for the better, have been cleansed of atavistic and barbaric elements. Marriage has ceased to be a matter of sell-and-buy. Nowadays a girl from a collective farm is not given away (or should we say "sold away"?) by her father, for now she is her own mistress, and no one can give her away. She will marry the man she loves. . . .

We alone have all the conditions under which a working woman can fulfill her duties as a citizen and as a mother responsible for the birth and early upbringing of her children.

AP® History Reasoning Skills

Contextualization *To what extent would Soviet society support Kollontai's expectation that women be both workers and mothers without depending on a man?*

Comparison *In what ways are Stalin's and Kollontai's views of the Soviet family similar? In what ways do they differ?*

Sources: First selection from Alexandra Kollontai, "The Labour of Women in the Revolution of the Economy," in *Selected Writings of Alexandra Kollontai*, trans. Alix Holt (Westport, CT: Lawrence Hill & Company, 1978), pp. 148–149. Second selection from Discussion of the Law on Abolition of Legal Abortion, Pravda, Editorials of May 28 and June 9, 1936 (English translation in Rudolf Schlesinger, ed., *Changing Attitudes in Soviet Russia: The Family in the USSR* [London: Routledge & Kegan Paul, 1949], pp. 251–54, 268–69).

they imposed authoritarian control over their economies, hoping to stimulate local industries and curb imports.

Other than the USSR, only southern Africa boomed during the 1930s. As other prices dropped, gold became relatively more valuable. Copper deposits, found in Northern Rhodesia (now Zambia) and the Belgian Congo (now Democratic Republic of the Congo), proved to be cheaper to mine than Chilean copper. But this mining boom benefited only a small number of European and white South African mine owners. For Africans it was a mixed blessing; mining provided jobs and cash wages to men while women stayed behind in the villages, farming, herding, and raising children without their husbands' help.

AP® Exam Tip
Consider how the Great Depression contributed to global conflict and the rise of fascism.

29-3 The Rise of Fascism

How did fascism in Italy and Germany lead to the Second World War?

The Russian Revolution and its Stalinist aftermath frightened property owners in Europe and North America. In western Europe and North America, middle- and upper-income voters took refuge in conservative politics. In southern and central Europe, many blamed ethnic minorities, especially Jews, for troubles that stemmed largely from the burden of war debt. In their yearning

AP® Exam Tip
Be able to explain new forces of nationalism such as fascism and Nazism.

for a mythical past of family farms and small shops, increasing numbers rejected representative government and sought more dramatic solutions.

Radical politicians applied wartime propaganda techniques to appeal to a confused citizenry. They promised to use any means necessary to bring back full employment, stop the spread of communism, and achieve the territorial aspirations that had led to World War I. While defending private property from communism, they borrowed the communist model of politics: a single party and a secret police that ruled by terror and intimidation.

29-3a Mussolini's Italy

The first country to seek radical answers was Italy. World War I, which had never been popular, left thousands of veterans who found neither pride in their victory nor jobs in the postwar economy. Unemployed veterans and violent youths banded together into *fasci di combattimento* (fighting units) to demand action and intimidate politicians. When workers threatened to strike, factory and property owners hired gangs of these *fascisti* to defend them.

Benito Mussolini (1883–1945) had supported Italy's entry into the war. A spellbinding orator, he quickly became the leader of the **Fascist Party**, which glorified warfare and the Italian nation. By 1921 the party had 300,000 members, many of whom used violent methods to repress strikes, intimidate voters, and seize municipal governments. A year later Mussolini threatened to march on Rome if he was not appointed prime minister. The government, composed of timid parliamentarians, gave in.

Mussolini proceeded to install Fascist Party members in all government jobs, crush all opposition parties, and jail anyone who criticized him. The party took over the press, public education, and youth activities and gave employers control over their workers. The Fascists lowered living standards but reduced unemployment and provided social security and public services. They proved to be neither ruthless radicals nor competent administrators.

What Mussolini and the Fascist movement really excelled at was bombastic speeches, spectacular parades, and signs everywhere proclaiming "Il Duce **(eel DOO-chay)** [the Leader] is always right!" Mussolini's genius was to apply the techniques of modern mass communications and advertisement to political life. Movie footage and radio news bulletins galvanized the masses in ways never before done in peacetime. His techniques of whipping up public enthusiasm appealed to other radicals. By the 1930s fascist movements had appeared in most European countries, as well as in Latin America, China, and Japan. Fascism appealed to people who were frightened by rapid change and placed their hopes in charismatic leaders. Of all of Mussolini's imitators, Adolf Hitler was the most sinister.

29-3b Hitler's Germany

Germany had lost the First World War after coming close to winning. Monetary hyperinflation in 1923 wiped out the savings of middle-class families. Less than ten years later the depression caused more unemployment and misery. Millions of Germans blamed Socialists, Communists, Jews, and foreigners for their troubles.

Adolf Hitler (1889–1945) joined the German army in 1914 and was wounded at the front. He later looked back fondly on the clear lines of authority and the camaraderie he had experienced in battle. After the war he used his gifts as an orator to lead a political splinter group called the National Socialist German Workers' Party—**Nazis** for short. While serving a brief jail sentence he wrote *Mein Kampf* **(mine compf)** (*My Struggle*), in which he outlined his goals and beliefs.

When it was published in 1925, *Mein Kampf* attracted little notice. Its ideas seemed so insane that few took it, or its author, seriously. Hitler's ideas went beyond ordinary nationalism. He believed that Germany should annex all German-speaking areas, even those in neighboring countries. He distinguished among a "master race" of Aryans (he meant Germans, Scandinavians, and Britons), a degenerate "Alpine" race of French and Italians, and an inferior race of Russian and eastern European Slavs, fit only to be slaves of the master race. He reserved his most intense hatred for Jews, on whom he blamed every disaster that had befallen Germany, especially the defeat of 1918. He glorified violence and looked forward to a future war in which the "master race" would defeat and subjugate all others.

Hitler's first goal was to reverse the humiliation and repeal the military restrictions of the Treaty of Versailles. Next, he planned to annex all German-speaking territories to a greater

Benito Mussolini Fascist dictator of Italy (1922–1943). He led Italy to conquer Ethiopia (1935), joined Germany in the Axis pact (1936), and allied Italy with Germany in World War II. He was overthrown in 1943 when the Allies invaded Italy.

Fascist Party Italian political party created by Benito Mussolini during World War I. It emphasized aggressive nationalism and was Mussolini's instrument for the creation of a dictatorship in Italy from 1922 to 1943.

Adolf Hitler Born in Austria, Hitler became a radical German nationalist during World War I. He led the National Socialist German Workers' Party—the Nazis—in the 1920s and became dictator of Germany in 1933. He led Europe into World War II.

Nazis German political party led by Adolf Hitler, emphasizing nationalism, racism, and war. When Hitler became chancellor of Germany in 1933, the Nazis became the only legal party and an instrument of Hitler's absolute rule. The party's formal name was National Socialist German Workers' Party.

Germany, then gain *Lebensraum* (**LAY-bens-rowm**) (room to live) at the expense of Poland and the USSR. Finally, he planned to eliminate all Jews from Europe.

From 1924 to 1930 Hitler's followers remained a tiny minority, for most Germans found his ideas too extreme. But when the depression hit, the Nazis gained supporters among the unemployed, who believed their promises of jobs for all, and among property owners frightened by the growing popularity of communists.

In March 1933 Hitler became chancellor of Germany. Once in office, he quickly assumed dictatorial powers. He put Nazis in charge of all government agencies, educational institutions, and professional organizations; banned all other political parties; and threw their leaders into concentration camps. The Nazis deprived Jews of their citizenship and civil rights, prohibited them from marrying "Aryans," ousted them from the professions, and confiscated their property. In August 1934 Hitler proclaimed himself *Führer* (**FEW-rer**) ("leader") and called Germany the "Third Reich," the third German empire after the Holy Roman Empire of medieval times and the German Empire of 1871 to 1918.

The Nazis' economic and social policies were spectacularly effective. The government undertook massive public works projects. Businesses got contracts to manufacture weapons. Women who had entered the workforce were urged to release their jobs to men. By 1936 business was booming; unemployment was at its lowest level since the 1920s; and living standards were rising. Most Germans believed that their economic well-being outweighed the loss of liberty.

AP® Exam Tip

Explain how the Nazi government (sometimes called a "fascist corporatist economy") could be seen as an example of governments taking a more active role in the economy.

29-3c The Road to War, 1933–1939

However, Hitler's goal was not prosperity or popularity, but conquest. As soon as he came to office, he began to build up the armed forces. Meanwhile, he tested the reactions of the other powers through a series of surprise moves followed by protestations of peace.

In 1933 Hitler withdrew Germany from the League of Nations. Two years later he announced that Germany was going to introduce conscription, build up its army, and create an air force—in violation of the Versailles treaty. Neither Britain nor France was willing to risk war by standing up to Germany.

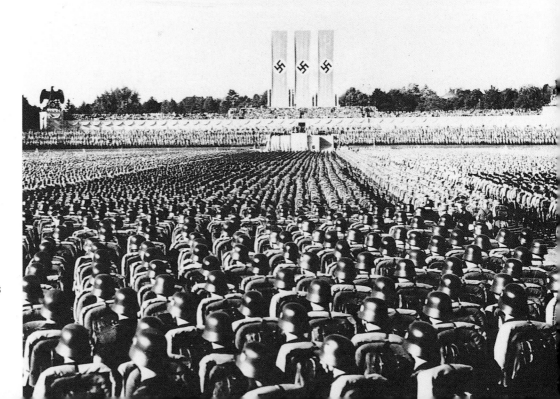

▶ **A Nazi Rally** Hitler organized mass rallies at Nuremberg to whip up popular support for his regime and to indoctrinate young Germans with a martial spirit. Thousands of men in uniform marched in torch-lit parades before Hitler and his top officials. AP Images

Section Review

- The depression gave opportunities to ultranationalist politicians who promised prosperity and order.

- Mussolini, head of the Fascist Party, became dictator of Italy in 1922 and proceeded to quell all opposition.

- After gaining power in 1933, Hitler began to transform the German economy and society and to build up the German armed forces.

- Germany and Italy made aggressive moves that the democracies, fearing another war, did not oppose, but when Germany invaded Poland, Hitler's aggressive objectives were clear.

AP® Exam Tip
Compare Russia under Stalin with Germany under Hitler.

In 1935, emboldened by the weakness of the democracies, Italy invaded Ethiopia, the last independent state in Africa and a member of the League of Nations. The League and the democracies protested, but refused to close the Suez Canal to Italian ships or impose an oil embargo. The following year, when Hitler sent troops into the Rhineland on the borders of France and Belgium, the other powers merely protested.

By 1938 Hitler decided that his rearmament plans were far enough advanced that he could escalate his demands. In March Germany invaded Austria. Most Austrians were German-speakers and accepted the annexation of their country without protest. Then came Czechoslovakia, where a German-speaking minority lived along the German border. Hitler first demanded their autonomy from Czech rule, then their annexation to Germany. Throughout the summer he threatened to go to war. At the Munich Conference of September 1938, the leaders of France, Britain, and Italy gave him everything he wanted without consulting Czechoslovakia. Once again, Hitler learned that aggression paid off.

The weakness of the democracies—now called "appeasement"—had three causes. The first was the deep-seated fear of war among people who had lived through World War I. Unlike the dictators, politicians in the democracies could not ignore their constituents' yearnings for peace. Most people believed that the threat of war might go away if they wished for peace fervently enough. The second cause of appeasement was fear of communism among conservatives, who feared Stalin more than Hitler because Hitler claimed to respect Christianity and private property. The third cause was the very novelty of fascist tactics. Britain's prime minister Neville Chamberlain assumed that political leaders (other than the Bolsheviks) were honorable men and that an agreement was as valid as a business contract. Thus, when Hitler promised to incorporate only German-speaking people into Germany and said he had "no further territorial demands," Chamberlain believed him.

After Munich it was too late to stop Hitler, short of war. Germany and Italy signed an alliance called the Axis, and in March 1939 Germany invaded what was left of Czechoslovakia. Belatedly realizing that Hitler could not be trusted, France and Britain sought Soviet help. Stalin, however, distrusted the "capitalists" as much as they distrusted him. When Hitler offered to divide Poland between Germany and the Soviet Union, Stalin accepted. The Nazi-Soviet Pact of August 23, 1939, freed Hitler from the fear of a two-front war and gave Stalin time to build up his armies. One week later, on September 1, German forces swept into Poland, and the war was on.

29-4 East Asia, 1931–1945

What were the economic reasons behind Japan's invasion of Manchuria?

AP® Exam Tip
Explain the similarities and differences between Japanese and German nationalism.

When the depression hit, the collapse of demand for silk and rice ruined thousands of Japanese farmers; to survive, some even sold their daughters into prostitution, while many poor young men flocked to the military. Ultranationalists resented their country's dependence on foreign trade and what they believed was unnecessary party politics that sullied the righteousness of the divine imperial will. If only Japan had a colonial empire, they thought, it would not be beholden to the rest of the world. But Europeans and Americans had already taken most potential colonies in Asia. Japanese nationalists saw the conquest of China, with its vast population and resources, as the solution to their country's problems.

29-4a The Manchurian Incident of 1931

Meanwhile, in China the Guomindang (**gwo-min-dong**) (see Chapter 28) was becoming stronger and preparing to challenge the Japanese presence in Manchuria, a province rich in coal and iron ore. Junior officers in the Japanese army, frustrated by the caution of their superiors, took action. In September 1931 they blew up part of a railroad track as a pretext for invading the entire province. This invasion was promoted as achieving the "independence" of Manchuria under the name *Manchukuo* (**man-CHEW-coo-oh**), but in reality, Manchukuo remained under Japanese control. Many civilian officials and military leaders back in Tokyo had not approved of the attack, but they soon joined the overwhelmingly positive reaction to the incident by the public, press, and even leftist critics.

The U.S. government condemned the Japanese conquest, and the League of Nations refused to recognize Manchukuo and urged the Japanese to remove their troops from China. Persuaded that the Western powers would not fight, Japan resigned from the League.

During the next few years the Japanese built railways and heavy industries in Manchuria and northeastern China and sped up their rearmament. At home, production was diverted to the military, especially to building warships. The government grew more authoritarian, jailing thousands of dissidents. On several occasions, ultranationalists, many of them junior officers, mutinied or assassinated leading political figures. The mutineers received mild punishments, and generals and admirals sympathetic to their views replaced more moderate civilian politicians.

29-4b The Long March

Until the Japanese seized Manchuria, the Chinese government seemed to be creating conditions for a national recovery. The main challenge to the government of **Chiang Kai-shek** (**chang kie-shek**) came from the Communists. The Chinese Communist Party had been founded in 1921 by a handful of intellectuals and for several years had lived in the shadow of the Guomindang. Its efforts to recruit members among industrial workers came to naught in 1927, when Chiang Kai-shek arrested and executed Communists and labor leaders alike. The few Communists who escaped the mass arrests fled to the remote mountains of Jiangxi (**jang-she**), in southeastern China.

Among them was **Mao Zedong** (**ma-oh zay-dong**) (1893–1976), a farmer's son who had left home to study philosophy. Mao was a man of action whose first impulse was to call for violent effort: "To be able to leap on horseback and to shoot at the same time; to go from battle to battle; to shake the mountains by one's cries, and the colors of the sky by one's roars of anger." In the early 1920s Mao discovered the works of Karl Marx, joined the Communist Party, and soon became one of its leaders.

In Jiangxi Mao began studying conditions among the peasants, in whom Communists had previously shown no interest. He planned to redistribute land from the wealthier to the poorer peasants, thereby gaining adherents for the coming struggle with the Guomindang army. His goal was a complete social revolution from the bottom up. Mao's reliance on the peasantry was a radical departure from Marxist-Leninist ideology, which stressed the backwardness of the peasants and pinned its hopes on industrial workers. Mao therefore had to be careful to cloak his pragmatic tactics in communist rhetoric to allay the suspicions of Stalin and his agents.

Mao was an advocate of women's equality. Before 1927 the Communists had organized the women who worked in Shanghai's textile mills, the most exploited of all Chinese workers. Later, in their mountain stronghold in Jiangxi, they organized women farmers, allowed divorce, and banned arranged marriages and foot-binding. But the party was still run by men whose primary task was warfare.

The Guomindang army pursued the Communists into the mountains, building small forts throughout the countryside. Rather than risk direct confrontations, Mao responded with guerrilla warfare. He harassed the army at its weak points with hit-and-run tactics, relying on the terrain and the support of the peasantry. Whereas government troops often mistreated civilians, Mao insisted that his soldiers help the peasants, pay a fair price for food and supplies, and treat women with respect.

In spite of their good relations with the peasants of Jiangxi, the Communists gradually found themselves encircled by government forces. In 1934 Mao and his followers decided to break out of the southern mountains and trek to Shaanxi (**SHAWN-she**), an even more remote province in northwestern China. The so-called **Long March** took them 6,000 miles (nearly 9,700 kilometers) in one year over desolate mountains and through swamps and deserts, pursued by the army and bombed by Chiang's aircraft. Of the 100,000 Communists who left Jiangxi in October 1934, only 4,000 reached Shaanxi a year later (see Map 29.1). Chiang's government thought it was finally rid of the Communists.

Chiang Kai-shek Chinese military and political leader. Succeeded Sun Yat-sen as head of the Guomindang in 1925; headed the Chinese government from 1928 to 1948; fought against the Chinese Communists and Japanese invaders. After 1949 he headed the Chinese Nationalist government in Taiwan.

Mao Zedong Leader of the Chinese Communist Party (1927–1976). He led the Communists on the Long March (1934–1935) and rebuilt the Communist Party and Red Army during the Japanese occupation of China (1937–1945). After World War II, he led the Communists to victory over the Guomindang. He ordered the Cultural Revolution in 1966.

Long March The 6,000-mile flight of Chinese Communists from southeastern to northwestern China. The Communists, led by Mao Zedong, were pursued by the Chinese army under orders from Chiang Kai-shek. The 4,000 survivors of the march formed the nucleus of a revived Communist movement that defeated the Guomindang after World War II.

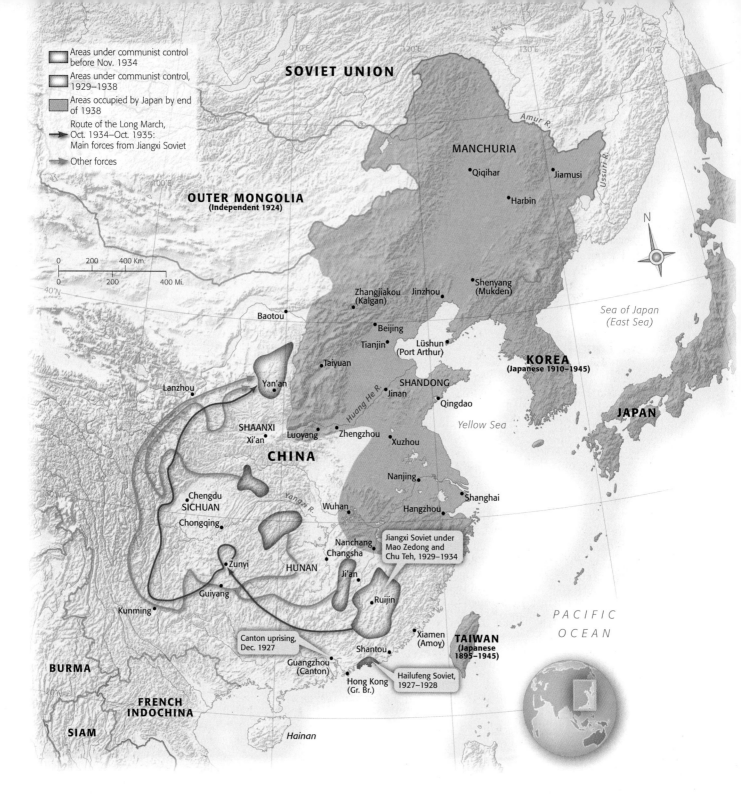

MAP 29.1 **Chinese Communist Movement and the Sino-Japanese War, to 1938** During the 1930s, China was the scene of a three-way war. The Nationalist government attacked and pursued the Communists, who escaped into the mountains of Shaanxi. Meanwhile, Japanese forces, having seized Manchuria in 1931, attacked China in 1937 and quickly conquered its eastern provinces.

What advantage did the Communists gain by trekking to Shaanxi?

29-4c The Sino-Japanese War, 1937–1945

In Japan politicians, senior officers, and business leaders disagreed on how to solve their country's economic problems. Some proposed a quick conquest of China; others advocated war with the Soviet Union. While their superiors hesitated, junior officers took matters into their own hands.

On July 7, 1937, Japanese troops attacked Chinese forces near Beijing. The junior officers who ordered the attack quickly obtained the support of their commanders and then, reluctantly, of the government. Within weeks Japanese troops seized Beijing, Tianjin, Shanghai, and other coastal cities, and the Japanese navy blockaded the entire coast of China.

Once again, the United States and the League of Nations denounced the Japanese aggression. Yet the Western powers were too preoccupied with events in Europe and with their own economic problems to risk a military confrontation in Asia. When the Japanese sank a U.S. gunboat and shelled a British ship on the Yangzi River, the U.S. and British governments expressed righteous indignation but took no action.

Poorly led and armed, the Chinese armies fought bravely but lost every battle. Japanese planes bombed cities while soldiers broke dikes and burned villages, killing thousands of civilians. Within a year Japan controlled the coastal provinces of northern China and the lower Yangzi and Yellow River Valleys, China's richest and most populated regions (see Map 29.1).

In spite of Japanese organizational and fighting skills, the attack on China did not bring victory. The Chinese people continued to resist, either in the army or with the Communist guerrilla forces. As Japan sank deeper into the Chinese quagmire, life became harsher and more repressive for the Japanese people. Taxes rose, food and fuel became scarce, and more and more young men were drafted.

Warfare between the Chinese and Japanese was incredibly violent. In the winter of 1937–1938 Japanese troops took Nanjing, raped 20,000 women, killed roughly 200,000 prisoners and civilians, and looted and burned the city. To slow them down, Chiang ordered the Yellow River dikes blasted open, causing a flood that destroyed 4,000 villages, killed 890,000 people, and made millions homeless. Two years later, when the Communists ordered a massive offensive, the Japanese retaliated with a "kill all, burn all, loot all" campaign, destroying hundreds of villages down to the last person, building, and farm animal.

The Chinese government, led by Chiang Kai-shek, escaped to the mountains of Sichuan in the center of the country. There Chiang built up a huge army, not to fight Japan but to prepare for a future confrontation with the Communists. The army drafted over 3 million men, even though it had only a million rifles and could not provide food or clothing for all its soldiers. The Guomindang raised farmers' taxes, even when famine forced farmers to eat the bark of trees. Such taxes were not enough to support both a large army and the thousands of government officials and hangers-on who had fled to Sichuan. To avoid taxing its wealthy supporters the government printed money, causing inflation, hoarding, and corruption.

From his capital of Yan'an in Shaanxi province, Mao also built up his army and formed a government. Unlike the Guomindang, the Communists listened to the grievances of the peasants, especially the poor, to whom they distributed land confiscated from wealthy landowners. They imposed rigid discipline on their officials and soldiers and tolerated no dissent or criticism from intellectuals. Though they had few weapons, the Communists obtained support and intelligence from farmers in Japanese-occupied territory. They turned military reversals into propaganda victories, presenting themselves as the only group in China that was serious about fighting the Japanese.

Section Review

- Seeing conquest as a solution to its economic problems, in 1931 Japan conquered Manchuria.

- The Chinese government under Chiang Kai-shek fought both the Japanese and the Communists led by Mao Zedong, who fled into the mountains of northern China.

- In 1937, Japanese forces conquered the coastal provinces of China; in the ensuing violent war, however, Japan failed to crush Chinese resistance.

- Chiang Kai-shek fled to the interior and prepared to fight the Communists.

AP® Exam Tip
Understand the Nanjing massacre within the larger context of increased wartime casualties in the twentieth century.

29-5 The Second World War

How was the war fought, and why did Japan and Germany lose?

Many people feared that the Second World War would be a repetition of the First. Instead, it was bigger in every way. It was fought around the world, from Norway to New Guinea and from Hawaii to Egypt, and on every ocean. It killed far more people than World War I, involved all civilians and productive forces, and showed how effectively industry, science, and nationalism could be channeled into mass destruction.

29-5a The War of Movement

In World War II motorized weapons gave back the advantage to the offensive. Opposing forces moved fast, their victories hinging as much on the aggressive spirit of their commanders and the military intelligence they obtained as on numbers of troops and firepower.

The Wehrmacht (**VAIR-mokt**), or German army, set the standard. It not only had tanks, trucks, and fighter planes but had also perfected their combined use in a tactic called *Blitzkrieg* (**BLITS-creeg**) (lightning war): fighter planes scattered enemy troops and disrupted communications, tanks punctured the enemy's defenses, and then, with the help of the infantry, they encircled and captured enemy troops. At sea, both Japan and the United States had developed aircraft carriers that could launch planes against targets hundreds of miles away.

Armies ranged over vast theaters of operations, and countries were conquered in days or weeks. The belligerents mobilized the economies of entire continents, squeezing them for every possible resource. They tried not only to defeat their enemies' armed forces but—by blockades, submarine attacks, and bombing raids—to damage the economies that supported those armed forces. Both sides thought of civilians as legitimate targets.

29-5b War in Europe and North Africa

It took less than a month for the Wehrmacht to conquer Poland (see Map 29.2). Britain and France declared war on Germany but took no military action. Meanwhile, the Soviet Union invaded eastern Poland and the Baltic republics. Although the Poles fought bravely, their infantry and cavalry were no match for German and Russian tanks. During the winter of 1939–1940 Germany and the Western democracies faced each other in what soldiers called a "phony war."

In March 1940 Hitler went on the offensive again, conquering Denmark, Norway, the Netherlands, and Belgium in less than two months. In May he attacked France. Although the French army had as many soldiers, tanks, and aircraft as the Wehrmacht, its morale was low and it quickly collapsed. By the end of June Hitler was master of all of Europe between Russia and Spain.

Germany still had to face Britain. The British had no army to speak of, but they had other assets: the English Channel, the Royal Navy and Air Force, and a tough new prime minister, Winston Churchill. The Germans knew they could invade Britain only by gaining control of the airspace over the Channel, so they launched a massive air attack—the Battle of Britain—lasting from June through September. The attack failed because the Royal Air Force used radar and code-breaking to detect approaching German planes.

Frustrated in the west, Hitler turned his attention eastward, even though it meant fighting a two-front war. So far he had gotten the utmost cooperation from Stalin, who supplied Germany with grain, oil, and strategic raw materials. Yet he had always wanted to conquer Lebensraum in the east and enslave the Slavic peoples who lived there, and he feared that if he waited, Stalin would build a dangerously strong army. In June 1941 Hitler launched the largest attack in history, with 3 million soldiers and thousands of planes and tanks. Within five months the Wehrmacht conquered the Baltic states, Ukraine, and half of European Russia, captured a million prisoners of war, and reached the very gates of Moscow and Leningrad. The USSR seemed on the verge of

▶ **Soviet Tanks at Stalingrad** In the winter of 1942–1943, the Red Army encircled a German army at Stalingrad, a strategic city in southern Russia that marked the furthest eastward advance of the Wehrmacht. The Soviets deployed their new T-34s, the best tanks in the world at the time. Unlike the Germans, Soviet soldiers were equipped with warm winter uniforms with a white outer layer for camouflage in the snow. TASS–Sovfoto

collapse. Then the weather turned cold, machines froze, and the invasion ground to a halt. Like Napoleon, Hitler had ignored the environment of Russia to his peril.

The next spring the Wehrmacht renewed its offensive. It surrounded Leningrad in a siege that was to cost a million lives. Leaving Moscow aside, it turned toward the Caucasus and its oil wells. In August the Germans attacked **Stalingrad** (now Volgograd), the key to the Volga River and the supply of oil. For months German and Soviet soldiers fought over every street and every house. When winter came, the Red Army counterattacked and encircled the city. In February 1943 the remnants of the German army in Stalingrad surrendered. Hitler had lost an army of 200,000 men and his last chance of defeating the Soviet Union and of winning the war (see Map 29.2).

From Europe the war spread to Africa. When France fell in 1940, Mussolini decided that the time had come to realize his imperial ambitions. Italian forces quickly overran British

Stalingrad City in Russia, site of a Red Army victory over the German army in 1942–1943. The Battle of Stalingrad was the turning point in the war between Germany and the Soviet Union. Today it is Volgograd.

MAP 29.2 **World War II in Europe and North Africa** In a series of quick and decisive campaigns from September 1939 to December 1941, German forces overran much of Europe and North Africa. There followed three years of bitter fighting as the Allies slowly pushed the Germans back.

How did the fighting lay the groundwork for postwar Soviet expansion in Europe?

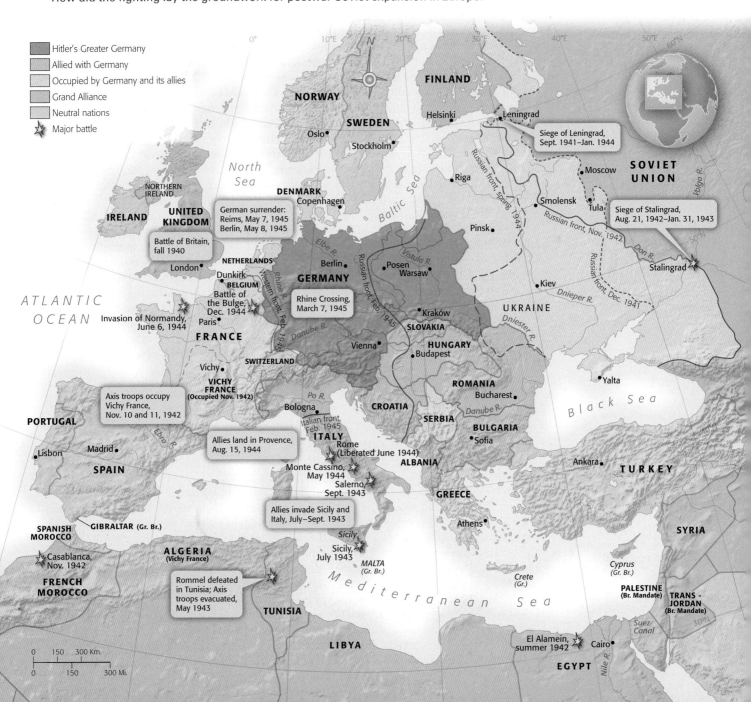

Somaliland, then invaded Egypt. Their victories were ephemeral, however, for when the British counterattacked, Italian resistance crumbled. During 1941 British forces conquered Italian East Africa and invaded Libya as well. The Italian rout in North Africa brought the Germans to their rescue, and during 1942 the German army and the forces of the British Commonwealth seesawed back and forth across the deserts of Libya and Egypt. At **El Alamein** in northern Egypt the British prevailed because they had more weapons and supplies and were better informed about their enemies' plans. The Germans were finally expelled from Africa in May 1943.

29-5c War in Asia and the Pacific

The fall of France and the involvement of Britain and the USSR against Germany presented Japan with the opportunity it had been looking for. Suddenly the European colonies in Southeast Asia, with their abundant oil, rubber, and other strategic materials, seemed ripe for the taking. In July 1941, when the French government, then under German control, allowed Japanese forces to occupy Indochina, the United States stopped shipments of steel, scrap iron, oil, and other products that Japan desperately needed. This left Japan with three alternatives: give up its conquests, as the Americans insisted; face economic ruin; or widen the war. Japan chose war.

Admiral Isoroku Yamamoto, commander of the Japanese fleet, told Prime Minister Fumimaro Konoye: "If I am told to fight regardless of the consequences, I shall run wild for the first six months or a year, but I have utterly no confidence for the second or third year. . . . I hope that you will endeavor to avoid a Japanese-American war." Ignoring his advice, the war cabinet made plans for a surprise attack on the United States Navy, followed by an invasion of Southeast Asia. They knew they could not hope to defeat the United States, but they calculated that the shock of the attack would be so great that isolationist Americans would accept the Japanese conquest of Southeast Asia as readily as they had acquiesced to Hitler's conquests in Europe.

On December 7, 1941, Japanese planes bombed the U.S. naval base at **Pearl Harbor**, sinking or damaging scores of warships but missing the aircraft carriers, which were at sea. Then, in early 1942, the Japanese conquered all of Southeast Asia and the Dutch East Indies. They soon began to confiscate food and raw materials and demand heavy labor from the inhabitants.

Japan's dream of an East Asian empire seemed within reach, for its victories surpassed even Hitler's in Europe. The United States, however, quickly prepared for war. In April 1942 American planes bombed Tokyo. In May the United States Navy defeated a Japanese fleet in the Coral Sea, ending Japanese plans to conquer Australia. A month later, at the **Battle of Midway**, Japan lost four of its six largest aircraft carriers. Without them, Japan faced a long and hopeless war (see Map 29.3).

Nevertheless, driving the Japanese army out of scores of military bases and island fortresses throughout the south Pacific region posed an enormous problem for the United States, which simultaneously had to deploy ships and armies to Europe. Island battles like Guadalcanal, Iwo Jima, and Okinawa did not have as much strategic significance as the siege of Stalingrad or the D-Day invasion (see below), but the losses of American and Japanese lives taxed the endurance of both countries.

29-5d The End of War

After the Battle of Stalingrad the advantage on the Eastern Front shifted to the Soviet Union. By 1943 the Red Army was receiving a growing stream of supplies from factories in Russia and the United States. Slowly at first and then with increasing vigor, it pushed the Wehrmacht back toward Germany.

The Western powers, meanwhile, staged two invasions of Europe. Beginning in July 1943 they captured Sicily and invaded Italy. Italy signed an armistice, but German troops held off the Allied advance for two years. On June 6, 1944—forever after known as D-day—156,000 British, American, and Canadian troops landed on the coast of Normandy in western France—the largest shipborne assault ever staged. Within a week the Allies had more troops in France than Germany did, and by September Germany faced an Allied army of over 2 million men and half a million vehicles.

Although the Red Army was on the eastern border of Germany, ready for the final push, Hitler transferred part of the Wehrmacht westward. Despite overwhelming odds, Germany held out for almost a year, a result of the fighting qualities of its soldiers and the terror inspired by the Nazi regime, which commanded obedience to the end. On May 7, 1945, a week after Hitler committed suicide, German military leaders surrendered.

El Alamein Town in Egypt, site of the victory by Britain's Field Marshal Bernard Montgomery over German forces led by General Erwin Rommel (the "Desert Fox") in 1942–1943.

Pearl Harbor Naval base in Hawaii attacked by Japanese aircraft on December 7, 1941. The sinking of much of the U.S. Pacific Fleet brought the United States into World War II.

Battle of Midway U.S. naval victory over the Japanese fleet in June 1942, in which the Japanese lost four of their best aircraft carriers. It marked a turning point in World War II.

Japan fought on a while longer because the United States had aimed most of its war effort at Germany. Pacific islands that were captured by amphibious landings were turned into air-bases from which to launch bombing raids on Japan's home islands. In June 1944 U.S. bombers began their attacks and American submarines devastated Japanese merchant shipping, cutting the country off from its sources of oil and other raw materials. After May 1945, with Japanese fighters grounded for lack of fuel, U.S. planes began destroying Japanese shipping, industries, and cities at will.

Even as their homeland was being pounded, the Japanese still held strong positions in Asia. Despite its name, "Greater East Asian Co-Prosperity Sphere," the Japanese occupation was harsh and brutal. By 1945 Asians were eager to see the Japanese leave, but not to welcome back the Europeans. Instead, they looked forward to independence (see Chapters 30 and 32).

On August 6, 1945, the United States dropped an atomic bomb on **Hiroshima**, killing some 80,000 people in a flash and leaving about 120,000 more to die in agony from burns and radiation. Three days later another atomic bomb destroyed Nagasaki. On August 14 Emperor Hirohito gave the order to lay down arms. Two weeks later Japanese leaders signed the terms of surrender. The war was officially over.

Hiroshima City in Japan, the first to be destroyed by an atomic bomb, on August 6, 1945. The bombing hastened the end of World War II.

MAP 29.3 World War II in Asia and the Pacific Having conquered much of China between 1937 and 1941, Japanese forces launched a sudden attack on Southeast Asia and the Pacific in late 1941 and early 1942. American forces slowly reconquered the Pacific islands and the Philippines. In August 1945, the atomic bombing of Hiroshima and Nagasaki forced Japan's surrender.

How did the great distance between the United States and Japan affect America's war strategy?

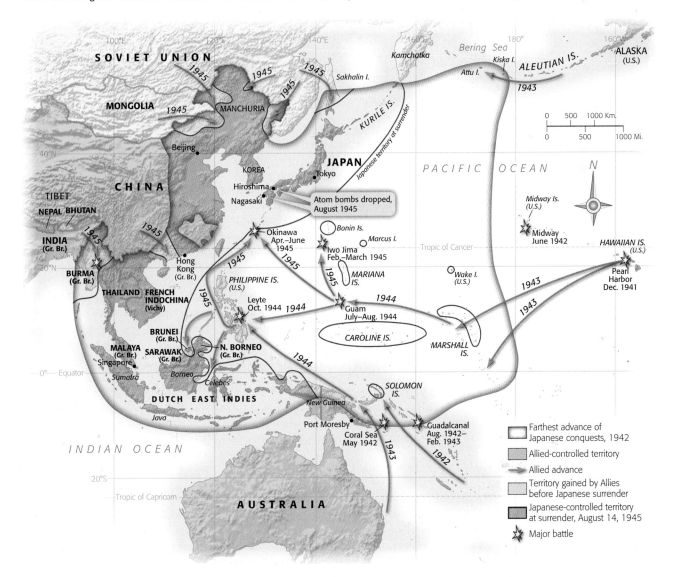

▲ **Hiroshima After the Atomic Bomb** On August 6, 1945, an atomic bomb destroyed the city, killing some 80,000 people. This fire truck, stationed at the Hiroshima Fire Department, is one of the few identifiable objects in the photo. It was located 4,000 feet from ground zero. Bettman/Getty Images

Section Review

- World War II was a war of machines and movement covering entire continents and oceans.

- Hitler's armies quickly overran western Europe, but Hitler failed to defeat Britain by air.

- In 1941 Germany attacked the USSR, but its defeat at Stalingrad in the winter of 1942–1943 sealed its fate.

- After the United States stopped shipments of vital supplies to Japan, in December 1941 Japanese planes bombed Pearl Harbor; a few months later Japan conquered Southeast Asia and Indonesia.

- After mid-1942, however, American forces pushed the Japanese back across the Pacific and began bombing Japan.

- In 1944, on D-day, the Allies landed troops on Normandy beaches and then fought their way a convergence with the Russian army in Germany; meanwhile, two atomic bombs forced Japan to surrender.

- After Japan's defeat, Chiang Kai-shek's army failed from its own ineptness and Mao's Communists took over China.

Were these atomic weapons necessary? At the time, American leaders believed that the conquest of the Japanese homeland would take more than a year and cost the lives of hundreds of thousands of American soldiers. Although some believed the Japanese were determined to fight to the bitter end, others thought they would surrender if they could retain their emperor. Winston Churchill wrote: "It would be a mistake to suppose that the fate of Japan was settled by the atomic bomb. Her defeat was certain before the first bomb fell."[3]

29-5e Collapse of the Guomindang and Communist Victory

The formal Japanese surrender in September 1945 surprised the Guomindang. The United States gave millions of dollars of aid and weapons to the Guomindang, all the while urging "national unity" and a "coalition government" with the Communists. But Chiang used all means available to prepare for a civil war. By late 1945 he had U.S. support, control of China's cities, and an army of 2.7 million, more than twice the size of the Communist forces. But the Guomindang's behavior eroded whatever popular support they had. As they

---

[3]Gar Alperowitz, *Atomic Diplomacy: Hiroshima and Potsdam* (New York: Simon & Schuster, 1965), 176–181 and 236–242.

◄ **Sale of Gold in the Last Days of the Guomindang** This picture was taken by famed French photojournalist Henri Cartier-Bresson in Shanghai just before the arrival of the Communist-led People's Liberation Army in 1949. It shows people desperate to buy gold before their Guomindang currency becomes worthless. Henri Cartier-Bresson/Magnum Photos

moved into formerly Japanese-held territory, they acted like an occupation force. They taxed the people they "liberated" more heavily than the Japanese had, confiscated supplies, and enriched themselves at the expense of the population. Chiang's government printed money so fast that it soon lost all its value. In the countryside the Guomindang's brutality alienated the peasants.

Meanwhile, the Communists obtained Japanese equipment seized by the Soviets in the last weeks of the war and American weapons brought over by deserting Guomindang soldiers. In Manchuria, where they were strongest, they pushed through a radical land reform program, distributing the properties of wealthy landowners among the poorest peasants. In battles against government forces, the higher morale and popular support they enjoyed outweighed the heavy equipment of the Guomindang, whose soldiers began deserting by the thousands.

By 1949 the Guomindang armies were collapsing everywhere, defeated more by their own greed and ineptness than by the Communists. As the Communists advanced, high-ranking members of the Guomindang fled to Taiwan, protected from the mainland by the U.S. Navy. On October 1, 1949, Mao Zedong announced the founding of the People's Republic of China.

29-6 The Character of Warfare

How did science and technology change the nature of warfare?

The war left an enormous death toll. Recent estimates place the figure at close to 60 million deaths, six to eight times more than in World War I. Over half of the dead were civilian victims of massacres, famines, and bombs. The Soviet Union lost between 20 million and 25 million people, more than any other country. China suffered 15 million deaths; Poland lost some 6 million, of whom half were Jewish; the Jewish people lost another 3 million outside Poland. Over 4 million Germans and over 2 million Japanese died. Great Britain lost 400,000 people, and the United States 300,000.

Refugees flooded into many parts of the world. Some 90 million Chinese fled the Japanese advance. In Europe millions fled from the Nazis or the Red Army or were herded back and forth on government orders. Many refugees never returned to their homes.

Belligerents identified not just soldiers but entire peoples as enemies. Some even labeled their own ethnic minorities as "enemies." Another reason for the devastation was the appearance of new technologies that carried destruction deep into enemy territory, far beyond the traditional battlefields. New technologies of warfare and changes in morality formed a lethal combination.

AP® Exam Tip
Consider how
World War II led to the
increased globalization
of science and
technology.

29-6a The Science and Technology of War

As fighting spread around the world, the mobilization of manpower and economies and the mobility of the armed forces grew increasingly crucial, while new aspects of war took on a growing importance. Chemists found ways to make synthetic rubber from coal or oil. Physicists perfected radar, which warned of approaching enemy aircraft and submarines. Cryptanalysts broke enemy codes and were able to penetrate secret military communications. Pharmacologists developed antibiotics that saved the lives of wounded soldiers, who in any earlier war would have died of infections. The war also brought new inventions in media technology (see Environment & Technology: Intelligence and Technology in World War II).

Aircraft development was especially striking. As war approached, German, British, and Japanese aircraft manufacturers developed fast, maneuverable fighter planes. U.S. industry was especially noted for heavy bombers designed to fly in huge formations and drop tons of bombs on enemy cities. Germany responded with radically new designs, including the first jet fighters, low-flying unmanned buzz bombs, and, finally, V-2 missiles against which there was no warning or defense.

Military planners expected scientists to furnish secret weapons that could doom the enemy. In October 1939 President Roosevelt received a letter from physicist Albert Einstein, a Jewish refugee from Nazism, warning of the dangers of nuclear power: "There is no doubt that subatomic energy is available all around us, and that one day man will release and control its almost infinite power. We cannot prevent him from doing so and can only hope that he will not use it exclusively in blowing up his next-door neighbor." Roosevelt placed the vast resources of the U.S. government at the disposal of physicists and engineers. By 1945 they had built two atomic bombs, each one powerful enough to annihilate an entire city.

29-6b Bombing Raids

Since it was very hard to pinpoint individual buildings, especially at night, British air chief marshal Arthur "Bomber" Harris decided that "operations should now be focused on the morale of the enemy civilian population and in particular the industrial workers."

In May 1942, 1,000 British planes dropped incendiary bombs on Cologne, setting fire to the old city. Between July 24 and August 2, 1943, 3,330 British and American planes firebombed Hamburg, killing 50,000 people, mostly women and children. Later raids destroyed Berlin, Dresden, and other German cities. The bombing raids against Germany killed 600,000 people—more than half of them women and children—and injured 800,000, but they failed to break the morale of the German people. German armament production continued to increase until late 1944, and the population remained obedient and hard-working. However, bombing raids against oil depots and synthetic fuel plants almost brought the German war effort to a standstill by early 1945.

Japanese cities were also the targets of American bombing raids. As early as April 1942 sixteen planes launched from an aircraft carrier bombed Tokyo. Later, as American forces captured islands close to Japan, the raids intensified. Their effect was even more devastating than the fire-bombing of German

◄ **U.S. Army Medics and Holocaust Victims** When Allied troops entered the Nazi concentration camps, they found the bodies of thousands of victims of the Holocaust. In Dachau in southern Germany, two U.S. Army medics are overseeing a truckload of corpses to be taken to a burial site. Hulton Deutsch/Getty Images

cities, for Japanese cities were made mostly of wood. In March 1945 bombs set Tokyo ablaze, killing 80,000 people and leaving a million homeless.

29-6c The Holocaust

In World War II, for the first time, more civilians than soldiers were deliberately put to death. The champions in the art of killing defenseless civilians were the Nazis. Their murders were not the accidental by-products of some military goal but a calculated policy of exterminating whole races of people.

AP® Exam Tip
Consider how the twentieth-century rise of extremist groups, such as the Nazis, led to the Holocaust and other attempts to annihilate specific populations.

Their first targets were Jews. Soon after Hitler came to power, he deprived German Jews of their citizenship and legal rights. When eastern Europe fell under Nazi rule, the Nazis herded its large Jewish population into ghettos in the major cities, where many died of starvation and disease. Then, in early 1942, the Nazis decided to carry out Hitler's "final solution to the Jewish problem" by applying modern industrial methods to the slaughter of human beings. Thousands of ordinary German citizens supported and aided the genocide. Every day trainloads of cattle cars arrived at the extermination camps in eastern Europe and disgorged thousands of captives and the corpses of those who had died along the way. The strongest survivors were put to work and fed almost nothing until they died. Women, children, the elderly, and the sick were shoved into gas chambers and asphyxiated with poison gas. **Auschwitz**, the biggest camp, was a giant industrial complex designed to kill up to 12,000 people a day. This mass extermination, now called the **Holocaust** ("burning"), claimed some 6 million Jewish lives.

Besides the Jews, the Nazis also killed 3 million Polish Catholics—especially professionals, army officers, and the educated—in an effort to reduce the Polish people to slavery. They also exterminated homosexuals, Jehovah's Witnesses, Gypsies, the disabled, and the mentally ill—all in the interests of "racial purity." Whenever a German was killed in an occupied country, the Nazis retaliated by burning a village and all its inhabitants. After the invasion of Russia the Wehrmacht was given orders to execute all captured communists, government employees, and officers. They also worked millions of prisoners of war to death or let them die of starvation.

29-6d The Home Front in Europe and Asia

In the First World War there had been a clear distinction between the "front" and the "home front." Not so in World War II, where rapid military movements and air power carried the war into people's homes. For the civilian populations of China, Japan, Southeast Asia, and Europe, the war was far more terrifying than their worst nightmares. Armies swept through the land, confiscating food, fuel, and anything else of value. Bombers and heavy artillery pounded cities into rubble, leaving only the skeletons of buildings, while survivors cowered in cellars. Even when a city was not targeted, air-raid sirens awakened people throughout the night. In countries occupied by the Germans, the police arrested civilians, deporting many to die in concentration camps or to work as slave laborers in armaments factories. Millions fled their homes in terror, losing their families and friends.

The war demanded an enormous and sustained effort from all civilians, but more so in some countries than in others. In 1941, the Soviets dismantled over 1,500 factories and rebuilt them in the Ural Mountains and Siberia, where they soon turned out more tanks and artillery than the Axis.

Half of the ships afloat in 1939 were sunk during the war, but the Allied losses were more than made up for by American shipyards. No Axis and little Japanese shipping survived to 1945. The production of aircraft, trucks, tanks, and other materiel showed a similar imbalance. Although the Axis powers made strenuous efforts to increase their production, they could not compete with the vast outpouring of Soviet and American industry.

The Red Army eventually mobilized 22 million men; Soviet women took over half of all industrial and three-quarters of all agricultural jobs. In the other Allied countries, women also played major roles in the war effort, replacing men in fields, factories, and offices. The Nazis, in contrast, believed that German women should stay home and bear children, and they imported 7 million "guest workers"—a euphemism for captured foreigners.

Auschwitz Nazi extermination camp in Poland, the largest center of mass murder during the Holocaust. Close to a million Jews, Gypsies, Communists, and others were killed there.

Holocaust Nazis' program during World War II to kill people they considered undesirable. Some 6 million Jews perished during the Holocaust, along with millions of Poles, Gypsies, Communists, Socialists, and others.

World War II ushered humanity into the atomic age with the bombing of Hiroshima and Nagasaki. It also marked early steps on the road to the Information Age in which we now live. People had been using radios and telephones for decades, but the technical challenges of keeping such messages secret became matters of life and death. Within Europe, the Axis nations could use hard-wired phone calls that were hard to intercept, but most other combatants relied on radio.

The warring nations assigned thousands of specialists, including linguists, engineers, and mathematicians, to the job of devising code and cipher systems and breaking the systems of their enemies. Successes contributed greatly to military operations. They also laid the groundwork for postwar developments in computers and electronic communications such as today's GPS system.

Ciphers had been in use for centuries. They made messages unreadable by systematically turning plain-text letters into seemingly random strings of letters or numbers, and often mixing up those strings by a second process. The resulting strings could be transmitted by radio, sometimes at high speed or systematically varying frequencies, because the enemy did not know how to decrypt them. Machines did the most sophisticated encipherment during World War II.

Cryptographers at Bletchley Park in Britain achieved the most famous success in decipherment by figuring out how Nazi ciphering machines worked and building their own versions. This required using mathematical models and automated processors to look for recurring patterns in many thousands of intercepts. Mathematician Alan Turing provided the key thinking in this effort, and in the process laid the mathematical basis for the postwar computer industry.

Codes, which substitute one word for another word or group of words, had gained widespread use in telegraphy for a century before the war began. The cost of a telegram was calculated according to the number of words used, so a businessman might use the word "millstone" to tell a partner in another city to "sell 1,000 shares of General Mills." Code words multiplied greatly during the war to conceal place names, weapon names, personal names, and so on. When it was suspected that an enemy had figured out a code, messages could also be used to dupe them into defending the wrong place from attack.

In English, wartime use of abbreviations like CINCPAC (Commander in Chief of the Pacific Fleet) and acronyms like WAC (Women's Army Corps) set a pattern for postwar language developments. Code words for specific military operations were carefully chosen. Winston Churchill, who chose "Overlord" as the codename for the Normandy invasion, wrote in 1943:

> I have crossed out . . . many unsuitable names. Operations in which large numbers of men may lose their lives ought not be described by code-words which imply a boastful or overconfident sentiment, such as "Triumphant," or, conversely, which are calculated to invest a plan with an air of despondency, such as "Wobetide," "Massacre," "Jumble," "Trouble". . . . Proper names are good in this field. The heroes of antiquity, figures from Greek and Roman mythology, the constellations and stars. . . . Care should be taken in all this process.

Other code words, like GI ("government issue") arose out of everyday usage. HF/DF, meaning "high-frequency direction finding," became "huffduff." This did not diminish its significance, however. When radio messages sent by submarines were detected by several listening points, the location of the vessel

29-6e The Home Front in the United States

Safe behind their oceans, Americans felt no bombs, saw no enemy soldiers, had almost no civilian casualties, and suffered fewer military casualties than other countries. The economy went into a prolonged boom after 1940. By 1944 the United States was producing twice as much as all the Axis powers combined. Thanks to huge military orders, jobs were plentiful, bread lines disappeared, and nutrition and health improved. With rationing limiting what civilians could buy, most Americans saved part of their paychecks, laying the basis for a phenomenal postwar consumer boom. Many Americans later looked back on the conflict as the "good war."

World War II also weakened the hold of traditional ideas, as employers recruited women and members of racial minorities to work in jobs once reserved for white men. Six million women entered the labor force during the war, 2.5 million of them in manufacturing jobs previously considered "men's work." In a book titled *Shipyard Diary of a Woman Welder* (1944), Augusta Clawson recalled her experiences in a shipyard in Oregon:

> *The job confirmed my strong conviction—I have stated it before—what exhausts the woman welder is not the work, not the heat, nor the demands upon physical strength. It is the apprehension that arises from inadequate skill and consequent lack of confidence; and this can be overcome by the right kind of training. . . . And so, in spite of the discomforts of climbing, heavy equipment, and heat, I enjoyed the work today because I could do it.*[4]

---

[4]Rosalyn Fraad Baxandall, Linda Gordon, and Susan Reverby, eds., *America's Working Women* (New York: Random House, 1976), 253.

could be quickly determined by huffduff triangulation. Thus, when the German submarine *U-158* broadcast to its home base that it had nothing to report, the three listening posts that picked up the message figured out where it had broadcast from, and a U.S. navy plane flew to that point and sank the vessel before it could dive.

Radar and sonar also provided vital new sources of intelligence. And aerial photography made it possible to survey the effectiveness of bombing raids and see where enemy fortifications were located.

Questions for Analysis

1. What made ciphers and codes especially important in World War II?

2. How have military communication styles, such a using acronyms like WAC and NATO, affected American English?

3. Does the use of code words make communication between speakers of different languages easier or harder?

◄ **"The Enemy Is Listening"**
This warning sign faces a German telephone operator in occupied France. Connecting by means of landlines instead of radio signals gave the Axis an advantage in European operations. Since radio messages could easily be intercepted, they had to be enciphered while telephone communications could use plain speech.
German telecommunication posts in Bretagne, 1941 (b/w photo)/SUEDDEUTSCHE ZEITUNG PHOTO (SECOND ACCOUNT)/Bridgeman Images

Many men opposed women doing work that would take them away from their families. As the labor shortage got worse, however, employers and politicians grudgingly admitted that the government ought to help provide daycare for the children of working mothers. The entry of women into the labor force proved to be one of the most significant consequences of the war.

The war loosened racial bonds as well. Seeking work in war industries, 1.2 million African Americans migrated to the north and west. In the southwest Mexican immigrants took jobs in agriculture and war industries. But no new housing was built to accommodate the influx of migrants to the industrial cities, and many suffered from overcrowding and discrimination. In addition, 112,000 Japanese Americans living on the west coast of the United States were arrested and herded into remote interior internment camps until the war was over, ostensibly to prevent spying and sabotage, but actually because of their race.

29-6f War and the Environment

During the depression, construction and industry had slowed to a crawl, reducing environmental stress. The war reversed this trend, sharply accelerating pressures on the environment.

One reason for the change was the fighting itself. Battles scarred the landscape, leaving behind spent ammunition and damaged equipment. Retreating armies flooded large areas of China and the Netherlands. The bombing of cities left ruins that remained visible for a generation or more.

Section Review

- World War II caused 60 million deaths, most of them civilians, as well as many refugees.

- Scientific technology, especially aircraft design, contributed to the mobility and violence of warfare.

- Allied bombing raids set fire to entire cities in both Europe and Japan.

- In the Holocaust, the Nazis murdered millions of Jews, Poles, Gypsies, and other minorities.

- Industrial economies, especially in the United States and Russia, mobilized civilians to manufacture war materiel.

- A booming American economy provided jobs for women and African Americans.

- Environments in war zones were badly damaged, and construction for the war transformed the environments of many countries.

The main cause of environmental transformation, however, was not the fighting but the economic development that sustained it. The war's half-million aircraft required thousands of air bases, many of them in the Pacific, China, Africa, and other parts of the world that had seldom seen an airplane before. Barracks, shipyards, docks, warehouses, and other military construction sprouted on every continent.

As war industries boomed, so did the demand for raw materials. Mining companies opened new mines and towns in Africa to supply strategic minerals. Latin American countries deprived of manufactured imports began building their own steel mills, factories, and shipyards. In India, China, and Europe, timber felling accelerated far beyond the reproduction rate of trees, replacing forests with denuded land. In a few instances, however, the war was good for the environment. For example, submarine warfare made fishing and whaling so dangerous that fish and whale populations had a few years in which to increase.

29-7 Conclusion

After the Great War ended, the world seemed to return to its prewar state, but it was an illusion. In the Soviet Union, Joseph Stalin was determined to turn his country into a modern industrial state at breakneck speed, regardless of the human cost. Several million people—most of them peasants—died, and millions more were enslaved during the Five-Year Plans and the collectivization of agriculture. By 1941 the USSR was much better prepared for a war with Germany than Russia had been in 1914–1917.

In 1929, after a few years of prosperity, the New York stock market collapsed. Within a few months, the world economy fell into the Great Depression, throwing millions out of work throughout the world. France and Britain survived the depression by making their colonial empires purchase their products. Countries that were dependent on exports, such as Germany and Japan, suffered more until they turned their economies toward arms production. Only the USSR and southern Africa boomed during the 1930s.

In Italy, Mussolini installed Fascist Party members in all government jobs and jailed anyone who criticized him. In Germany, economic collapse led people to entrust their government to Adolf Hitler and his Nazi followers, who quickly set to work establishing a totalitarian government. Nazi Germany's rebuilding of its military and its invasion of Austria and Czechoslovakia were greeted with a policy of appeasement by Western democracies, until finally they could no longer overlook Germany's intentions.

Hard hit by the depression, Japan saw China as a potential colony with resources to help solve its economic problems. In 1931, Japan conquered Manchuria. The United States and the League of Nations protested but did little else. Starting in 1937, a long and brutal war with China became a drain on the Japanese economy and resources. Meanwhile, the Communists, led by Mao Zedong, were slowly gaining support in the Chinese countryside.

The war spread to Europe in 1939 when Germany conquered Poland, then Denmark, Norway, the low countries, and France in 1940. The war turned global in 1941 when Germany invaded the Soviet Union and Japan attacked the United States. In 1943, the Red Army began to push the Germans back. Beginning in June 1944, Anglo-American forces, backed by the overwhelming industrial resources of the United States, drove German forces back from the west. U.S. naval victories in the Pacific and atomic weapons defeated Japan and ended the war in 1945.

The Second World War was by far the deadliest in history. Modern mechanized forces swept across entire nations and oceans. Their targets were not only each other's armed forces, but their civilian populations as well. Though Germany had considerable scientific and technical talent, the war favored the nations with the most heavy industries, namely, the United States and the Soviet Union. The Allies destroyed German and Japanese cities with fire-bombs, and the United States dropped atomic bombs on Hiroshima and Nagasaki. Of the roughly 60 million people who died in the war, most were civilians.

Key Terms

Joseph Stalin p. 752
Five-Year Plans p. 752
Benito Mussolini p. 758
Fascist Party p. 758

Adolf Hitler p. 758
Nazis p. 758
Chiang Kai-shek p. 761
Mao Zedong p. 761

Long March p. 761
Stalingrad p. 765
El Alamein p. 766
Pearl Harbor p. 766

Battle of Midway p. 766
Hiroshima p. 767
Auschwitz p. 771
Holocaust p. 771

Review Questions

1. Given the extent and duration of Napoleon's military campaigns from Egypt in 1798 to Waterloo in 1815, and the related Haitian revolution, could World War II just as well be called World War III? Why or why not?

2. How does Japan's effort to conquer East Asia during World War II compare with Hideyoshi's invasions of Korea and China at the end of the 16th century?

3. How does the effort of Stalin to turn Russia into a great industrial power compare with the reform efforts of Peter the Great and his successors?

MindTap® is a fully online, personalized learning experience built upon Cengage Learning content. MindTap® combines student learning tools–readings, multimedia, activities, and assessments–into a singular Learning Path that guides students through the course and helps students develop the critical thinking, analysis, and communication skills that are essential to academic and professional success.

Multiple-Choice Questions

Questions 1–3 refer to the passage below.

"The fundamental task of the Five-Year Plan was to create such an industry in our country as would be able to re-equip and reorganize, not only the whole of industry, but also transport and agriculture—on the basis of socialism. . . . What are the results of the Five-year Plan in four years in the sphere of industry? . . . We did not have an iron and steel industry, the foundation for the industrialization of the country. Now we have this industry . . . we have abolished unemployment and have relieved the workers of the USSR of its horrors. The same thing must be said in regard to the peasants. They too, have forgotten about the differentiation of the peasants into kulaks and poor peasants, about the exploitation of the poor peasants by the kulaks."

Joseph Stalin, *The Results of the First Five-Year Plan,* 1933

1. Stalin's Five-Year Plans are an example of which of the following?

   (A) Communism tended to create free-market economies.

   (B) Agriculture remained the primary occupation in Stalin's Soviet Union.

   (C) Communist governments in the twentieth century controlled their economies.

   (D) Stalin's plans were meant to increase class diversity.

2. Which of the following is the best explanation for Stalin's policies?

   (A) Marx encouraged states to strengthen religious institutions.

   (B) Marx argued that only agrarian economies could be communist.

   (C) Marxist ideology encouraged consumerism.

   (D) Marxist ideology emphasized industrial life and production.

3. Based on the passage, which of the following best reflects Marxist views concerning class?

   (A) Class distinctions must be crushed.

   (B) A person's status in society is based on education.

   (C) Wealth is a sign of superior intelligence and work ethic.

   (D) Agrarian occupations have the most status.

Questions 4–6 refer to the image at the top of the next column.

4. The photograph of Hiroshima is evidence that

   (A) wars in the twentieth century were similar to those in the nineteenth century.

   (B) infrastructure and civilian populations were legitimate targets.

▲ **Hiroshima after the Atomic Bomb** Bettmann/Getty Images

   (C) atomic bombs were more deadly than conventional bombs.

   (D) modern conflicts were shorter than in previous time periods.

5. Which of the following best explains the image in the photograph?

   (A) Twentieth-century militaries relied on large numbers of personnel.

   (B) Advances in science led to new, more destructive weapons.

   (C) Most destruction in wartime came from internal rebellions.

   (D) The scene was the result of religious fundamentalists.

6. What was a result of the event portrayed in the photograph?

   (A) Atomic weapons changed the nature of global conflict in the Cold War.

   (B) Atomic weapons were limited to only the United States.

   (C) The knowledge and techniques used to build atomic weapons was well known and allowed most nations to build their own weapons.

   (D) Atomic weapons were viewed as a liability and an unwanted expense by most of the leading powers.

Questions 7–10 refer to the map on the next page.

7. Based on the map, which of the following is true?

   (A) World War II affected only isolated regions in Europe, whereas World War I had been total war.

   (B) World War II, like World War I, was affected by alliances between fascist and totalitarian powers.

   (C) World War II's fighting mostly occurred outside of Europe, whereas World War I fighting mainly occurred inside Europe.

   (D) World War II, like World War I, was primarily a naval war in the Mediterranean.

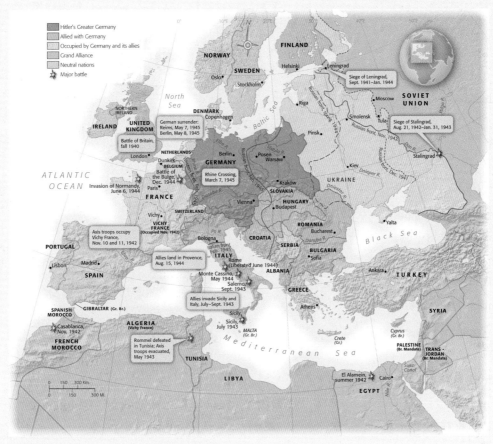

▲ World War II in Europe and North Africa

8. Which of the following best explains why World War II took place in multiple regions?

(A) The combatants were also colonial powers.

(B) European powers had made alliances with African nations.

(C) African nations had declared war on European powers.

(D) Naval power spread the main engagements throughout the Atlantic.

9. The redrawing of the the map after the war ended into "Eastern" and "Western" Europe was a reflection of ideological conflict between

(A) winning states and losing states.

(B) Imperialist and anti-Imperialist.

(C) democracy and Communism.

(D) Muslim and Christian.

10. Which of the following best explains why the Soviet Union was never permanently occupied by either Hitler or Napoleon?

(A) The intensity of the Russian climate

(B) The mountain ranges protecting it from central Europe

(C) The heavy fortifications lining its borders

(D) The attacking nation's lack of military forces

Short-Answer Questions

1. Choose ONE of the following nations and, based on your knowledge of world history, answer all parts of the question that follows.

- The United States
- The Soviet Union
- Germany

(A) Identify ONE effect of the global depression on the chosen country.

(B) Explain ONE action taken by the chosen country to address its economic problems.

(C) Explain an ADDITIONAL action taken by the chosen country to address its economic problems.

2. Based on your knowledge of world history, answer all parts of the question that follows.

(A) Identify ONE way that technology changed warfare in the twentieth century.

(B) Explain ONE long-term effect of this new type of warfare on societies.

(C) Explain ANOTHER long-term effect of this new type of warfare on societies.

30 Revolutions in Living, 1900–1950

AP® Framework Terms

Deforestation
Birth control
Mohandas Gandhi
Partitioning (India/Pakistan)
Great Depression

Overarching Questions

1 In what ways do the arts reflect the innovation, adaptation, and creativity of specific societies? (CUL)

2 How have religions, belief systems, philosophies, and ideologies affected the political, economic, and social development of societies? (CUL)

3 How have states interacted with state-less societies and non-state actors? (SB)

4 To what extent have legal systems, colonialism, nationalism, and independence movements sustained or challenged class, gender, and racial hierarchies over time? (SOC)

5 How have social categories, roles, and practices been maintained or challenged over time? (SOC)

n 1869, three Japanese businessmen—an entrepreneurial former cook, a green grocer, and a wagon builder—responded to government concerns about urban congestion and applied for a license to build a *jinriksha* ("man-power-vehicle"). They described it as "a little seat in the Western style, mounted on wheels so that it can be pulled about. It does not shake as much as the usual cart, and it is easy to turn round. It will not hinder other traffic, and since it can be pulled by one person, it is very cheap."[1] Their first vehicles, which quickly came to be called rickshaws, appeared a year later. A year after that, in 1871, Japan enacted its first patent law, and the three applied for exclusive manufacturing rights. However, so many workshops were by then turning out rickshaws that their application was denied.

An alternative claim of invention arose when an irascible American Baptist missionary named Jonathan Goble petitioned the Tokyo Metropolitan Government to grant him a share of the tax levied on the 30,000 rickshaws then officially registered. He claimed to be the inventor, and a number of Westerners living in Japan supported him, some

---

[1]F. Calvin Parker, *Jonathan Goble of Japan: Marine, Missionary, Maverick* (Lanham, MD: University Press of America, 1990), 222.

▲ **Rickshaw Traffic**   Invented in 1869, the rickshaw transformed urban life in East Asia and the lands bordering on the Indian Ocean. Hung Chung Chih/
Shutterstock

stating that Goble had built the first rickshaw for his ailing wife, and others that he had designed it at the request of a Japanese officer for use in the "imperial pleasure gardens."

The Japanese version of the story, which was reinforced in 1900 by government cash awards to the three businessmen, is highly credible since two-wheeled carts with a similar arrangement of shafts for pulling were in use on Japanese farms and for transporting loads well before European carriages came to be known through the "opening of Japan" in the 1850s (see Chapter 27). Moreover, Japan became the export source for rickshaws throughout Asia and the Indian Ocean region. The Goble story, however, made better sense to Westerners, who had a hard time crediting non-Europeans with inventiveness.

People today often look back and marvel at the incredible material changes their parents and grandparents lived through in the twentieth century. Movies, radio, television, telephones, automobiles, and airplanes all developed during the first half of the century. Norms of daily life rooted in the nineteenth century gave way to new assumptions about many aspects of human life.

Yet many of these assumptions applied more to the industrialized countries of Europe and North America than to those parts of the world that before World War II consisted mostly of imperial possessions or, in the case of Latin America, politically independent countries whose economies were dominated by European or American businesses and investors. Automobiles may have changed dating habits in the United States, but not in China or India, where few private individuals owned cars. Telephones may have put people in easy contact with family and friends in Europe, but not in Africa, where imperialist economic interests saw no profit in stringing copper wire throughout the land.

Changes in the way people lived in the West between 1900 and 1950 are discussed later in this chapter. First we consider how other parts of the world experienced change in more limited ways, often incorporating local cultural traditions that took their societies in distinctive directions. ●

30-1 New Technology Outside the Industrialized World

Why were Europeans and Americans impacted differently from Asians and Africans in regard to technology?

30-1a Urbanization

According to one estimate, Constantinople, the capital of the Byzantine Empire, had a population of 200,000 in 1000 CE and was the only European city to be ranked among the world's ten largest cities. By 1500 Paris had joined Constantinople on the list, and by 1800 so had London. Beijing, the most populous city, then had over 1 million inhabitants, about twice as many as the largest city in 1000.

Industrialization deeply affected population distribution in the course of the nineteenth century. By 1900 all of the world's top ten cities were European or American except for Tokyo. The largest, London, had 6.4 million inhabitants. European dominance waned in the first half of the twentieth century. In 1950 Shanghai, Buenos Aires, Tokyo, and Calcutta (now Kolkata) were on the list, and 12.4 million people resided in the largest city, New York. Today, two European cities, Moscow and Istanbul (formerly Constantinople), make the top ten. Of the rest, four are in China and two in South Asia. Tehran (Iran) and Sao Paulo (Brazil) round out the list. New York is nineteenth. The largest city, Shanghai, has a population of 17.8 million.

In Asia and the Indian Ocean basin, the rickshaw (see chapter opening) contributed to this transformation of urban life just as streetcars had earlier done in Europe and America. Before 1850, Japanese civilians either walked or were carried in plain (*kago*) or fancy (*norimono*) *palanquins*, small seats or cabins suspended from poles carried on the shoulders of bearers. A palanquin required a minimum of two men, or more if the trip was long or the rider wanted to display his or her wealth. The rickshaw cut the expense of personal transport in half and doubled its speed because a rickshaw puller, unlike palanquin bearers, usually ran rather than walked. Rickshaw transport effectively enlarged the area of cities that had previously been scaled for pedestrian access, just as public transport made it possible for Bostonians and Londoners to live away from the city center. Rickshaws also avoided the plague of Western cities: horse manure.

The technical specifications of the first rickshaws have not survived, but the claim that "it does not shake as much as the usual cart" suggests that what made the vehicle a sensational success from the very start was the provision of *leaf springs* (arced steel strips bound at the ends to form an ellipse). The first leaf spring design had been pa-tented in England in 1804 and was probably in use on carriages imported into Japan in the 1850s. Early drawings and photographs of rickshaws consistently show them with leaf springs.

Japanese-made rickshaws stimulated the growth of big Asian cities like Shanghai, Beijing, Singapore, Calcutta, and Bombay and reached across the Indian Ocean to Madagascar and South Africa. Tens of thousands of unskilled workers flocked to these cities to become rickshaw pullers

CHRONOLOGY

	Technology	India	Africa	Latin America
	1869 Rickshaw invented in Japan			
1900	1903 Wright brothers fly first airplane	1905 Viceroy Curzon splits Bengal; mass demonstrations	1900s Railroads connect ports to the interior	
	1907 Bakelite, first plastic, invented	1906 Muslims found All-India Muslim League		
	1912 first feature-length movie in India	1911 British transfer capital from Calcutta to Delhi	1912 African National Congress founded	
	1913 Henry Ford introduces assembly-line production			
	1915–1920 Women gain vote in Norway, Russia, Canada, Germany, Britain, and United States			
1920	1920 Commercial radio begins in United States	1919 Amritsar Massacre	1920s J. E. Casely Hayford organizes political movement in British West Africa	
	1923 Margaret Sanger opens first birth control clinic			
	1925 Commercial radio begins in Japan	1929 Gandhi leads Walk to the Sea		1928 Plutarco Elías Calles founds Mexico's National Revolutionary Party
1930	1932 Empire State Building opens	1930s Gandhi calls for independence; he is repeatedly arrested	1939–1945 A million Africans serve in World War II	1930–1945 Getulio Vargas, dictator of Brazil
	1936 Olympic games in Berlin			1934–1940 Lázaro Cárdenas, president of Mexico
		1939 British bring India into World War II		1938 Cárdenas nationalizes Mexican oil industry; Vargas proclaims Estado Novo in Brazil
1940		1940 Muhammad Ali Jinnah demands a separate nation for Muslims		1943 Juan Perón leads military coup in Argentina
		1947 Partition and independence of India and Pakistan		1946 Perón elected president of Argentina

in the way that European villagers entered the urban economy by way of unskilled manufacturing jobs. Like European mill-hands, rickshaw pullers endured miserable living conditions and occasionally banded together in strikes, particularly in opposition to streetcar companies that threatened their livelihoods. However, streetcars could not deliver passengers directly to their homes or take children safely to school, so the rickshaws survived and evolved into the pedicabs and auto-rickshaws that are still common today.

The rickshaw provides a rare example of an Asian invention transforming urban life in ways unfamiliar to Europeans and Americans. The more frequently told stories focus on Western inventions like railroads and automobiles transforming the non-Western world. Yet even there, the innovations of the Industrial Revolution (see Chapter 22) that imperialist governments and businesses exported to their colonies affected the non-Western world differently than later

AP® Exam Tip
Compare the diffusion of technology from this time period to earlier time periods.

innovations that spread world-wide in the first half of the twentieth century. Whereas railroads and automobiles required steel mills and factories, other new inventions were comparatively inexpensive and adaptable to local customs.

30-1b **Electricity**

Electricity, produced in industrial quantities since the 1890s (see Chapter 27), transformed home life in Europe and North America by attracting private customers. Middle-class homeowners wanted to replace their gas lamps with tungsten filament incandescent bulbs, which improved greatly in brightness and durability between 1904 and World War I. Household items like electric irons, fans, washing machines, and hot plates followed.

Outside of Europe and North America, however, the small size of the middle class made private subscription a poor business model. Electrical generators might be acquired to run factories or light a ruler's palace, but an appliance-oriented lifestyle was slow to develop. Consequently, the foot-operated sewing machine, which had undergone a long development in America and Europe in the nineteenth century, had a wider global spread before World War II than any other appliance. The enormous Japanese electronics company Brother Industries, Ltd. began in 1908 as the Yasui Sewing Machine Company.

30-1c **New Media**

Auguste and Louis Lumière projected the first motion pictures in Paris in 1895. The following year the brothers held demonstrations in Bombay, London, Montreal, New York, and Buenos Aires. Other exhibitors soon showed off the new medium in Johannesburg, Alexandria, and Tokyo. Unlike expensive innovations like automobiles and airplanes, motion pictures could be made cheaply using fairly inexpensive equipment. The idea of moving images appealed just as much to non-European audiences as it did to Europeans.

The first experiments with film in India appeared two years after the Lumières' visit. The first full-length feature, screening in 1912, told the story of a legendary Indian king from the classical Sanskrit epics. Movies also caught on quickly in Japan, which had a tradition of magic lantern displays. Local theatrical traditions like *kabuki* and *bunraku* influenced the style and content of the earliest films just as early European filmmakers concentrated on reproducing stage plays. Japanese films of the silent era were usually accompanied by spoken narration, as were the films the Japanese exported to Formosa (now Taiwan), a Chinese-speaking island that came under Japanese control in 1895.

American and European silent films found ready markets around the world, but non-Western filmmaking flourished in some countries. Moreover, the impact of film was not limited to entertainment. Documentary films and especially newsreels became major sources of information. Filmed news coverage of key political figures like Mahatma Gandhi in India played a major role in their success (see Diversity & Dominance: Gandhi and the New Media), especially after the advent of sound in the late 1920s.

Practical photography began in Europe in 1839, and forty years later an efficient way was developed for printing photographs in newspapers. Photographic images soon became common throughout the world, often as picture postcards. European photographers, however, tended to look upon Asians and Africans, particularly semi-nude women, as exotic subjects and thereby catered to common European assumptions about racial superiority.

Non-European photographers rarely became known outside their home countries. Nevertheless, they produced thousands of images that are now used to reconstruct history. Chinese newspapers and magazines usually published images without naming the photographers. A dozen early photographers became famous in Japan, however, possibly because popular woodblock prints had created an audience for artistic images of everyday scenes. In Iran, the

Auguste and Louis Lumière French inventors of motion pictures whose equipment demonstrations abroad stimulated the growth of cinema around the world.

▲ **Lumière Brothers Camera** In this simple and lightweight early model, turning the crank caused the chain drive to pull the film in front of the lens from a roll suspended above the device. The larger the roll of film (not shown), the longer the resulting movie. Science & Society Picture Library/Getty Images

most avid photographer was the ruler Naser al-Din Shah (r. 1848–1896). Despite Muslim clerical disapproval of making images of human beings, the shah shot some 48,000 pictures, including members of his own family and even nudes and prisoners.

Photography enabled newspapers, magazines, and advertisements to inform even illiterate people about what their country and their fellow citizens looked like, who was ruling them, and how traditional elites and prosperous Europeanized families lived. Thus photography contributed to feelings of national identity and common experience even in lands that were internally divided by language and ethnicity.

Radio had served ships and the military during the Great War as a means of point-to-point telecommunication. After the war, amateurs used surplus radio equipment to talk to one another. The first commercial station began broadcasting in Pittsburgh in 1920. By 1924, 600 stations were broadcasting news, sports, soap operas, and advertising to homes throughout North America. By 1930, 12 million families owned radio receivers. In Europe radio spread more slowly because governments reserved the air-waves for cultural and official programs and taxed radio owners to pay for the service.

Japan followed the North American model of commercial radio. The first AM station began broadcasting in 1925, and by 1941 there were almost fifty stations organized in two networks covering both the home islands and imperial possessions in Formosa (Taiwan), Korea, and Manchuria. Programming increasingly reflected the militarist tendencies of the government, but it also included Japanese and classical Western music, English lessons, exercise programs, and tips for urban gardeners.

Section Review

- Urbanization expanded rapidly in East and South Asia.
- Rickshaws transformed the transportation systems of cities in East Asia, South Asia, and the Indian Ocean littoral.
- Cinema spread rapidly outside Europe and incorporated local performance traditions.
- Photography also spread, both for artistic expression and for newspaper and magazine articles and advertisements.
- Radio developed commercially in Japan, as it did in the United States; but in most European colonies it was controlled by the government.

AP® Exam Tip
Explain the development of increasingly popular global culture during this time period.

▲ **Rural Japan Before World War I** This village scene from Japan reflects the taste for landscapes and ordinary life typical of the earliest photographers in Japan, both European and Japanese. The popularity of such scenes in earlier colored woodcuts may have influenced the choice of such subjects. Royal Photographic Society/Getty Images

Radio development in Shanghai was also robust, with 100,000 receivers in use by 1936. Most were imported, but small local manufacturers contributed to the new fad. British authorities in India and Africa, on the other hand, established central control of radio transmissions and programming. French colonial administrations did likewise.

30-2 New Ways of Living in The Industrialized World

How did new inventions affect daily life in the early twentieth century?

AP® Exam Tip
Understand how World War I's demographic impact went far beyond battlefield casualties.

World War I left a deep imprint on European society and culture. After the war, class and gender distinctions began to fade. Many European aristocrats had died on the battlefields, and with them went their class's long domination of the army, the diplomatic corps, and other elite sectors of society. The United States and Canada with less rigid class structures than European societies felt fewer social changes. Yet on both sides of the Atlantic, engineers, businessmen, lawyers, and other professionals rose to prominence while department stores, banks, insurance companies, and other businesses increased their white-collar workforce. At the same time government administrative jobs expanded in the areas of housing, transportation, schools, public health, and other services. The ambitions and tastes of the rapidly expanding middle class became increasingly evident in the postwar period, while the role of the working class remained about the same.

30-2a Identity

As the centuries-old European distinction between aristocrats and commoners faded in significance, standardized forms of identity became more common. An American passport issued in 1905 was a single 12- by 17-inch piece of paper bearing the seal of the State Department, the secretary of state's signature in facsimile, and in lieu of a photograph, one- or two-word descriptions of the holder's forehead, eyes, nose, mouth, chin, complexion, and facial shape. A Chinese passport of the same period was entirely in Chinese. Crossing international borders became a more complicated process during World War I, and in 1920 the League of Nations held the first of several conferences that standardized the now familiar photograph-and-booklet design.

Prussia in 1910 was the first country to require every automobile operator to have a driver's license, and the practice spread rapidly. In 1913 New Jersey was the first American state to institute such a requirement. These documents eventually became standard proofs of identity in countries that did not issue identity cards to their citizens. Social Security cards began to be issued in the United States in the 1930s, and they too acquired some of the functions of identity cards. In other countries, such as Germany, Great Britain, and Japan, national health system documents served similar functions.

Hereditary titles and listings of noble lineages in reference books like *Burke's Peerage* continued in use among the nobility. However, the idea increasingly spread that a person's identity was tied to his or her name (without title), a photograph, and one or more official numbers issued by government agencies. This idea spread much more slowly outside of Europe and North America.

An additional form of personal identification came forth in 1897 when the world's first fingerprint bureau opened under British auspices in Calcutta (Kolkata). Two Indians, Azizul Haque and Hem Chandra Bose, devised the system of determining every human being's unique identity, but it became known as the Henry System from the name of their British supervisor. Scotland Yard adopted the system in 1901, and the New York Police Department did so in 1906.

AP® Exam Tip
Evaluate the changes in gender roles and both the changes and continuities from previous time periods.

30-2b Women's Lives

Women's lives changed more rapidly in the 1920s than ever before. Although the end of the war saw the end of wartime job opportunities, some women remained in the workforce. The young and wealthy enjoyed more personal freedoms than their mothers had before the war; they drove cars, played sports, traveled alone, and smoked in public. For others, the upheavals of war brought more suffering than liberation. Millions of women had lost their male kin in the war or in the great influenza epidemic. After the war many single women led lives of loneliness and destitution.

In Europe and North America advocates of women's rights had been demanding the vote for women since the 1890s. New Zealand was the only nation to grant women the vote before the twentieth century. Women in Norway were the first to obtain it in Europe, in 1915. Russian women followed in 1917, and Canadians and Germans in 1918. Britain gave women over age thirty the vote in 1918 and later extended it to younger women. The Nineteenth Amendment to the U.S. Constitution granted suffrage to American women in 1920. Women in Turkey began voting in 1934. Everywhere, their influence on politics was less radical than feminists had hoped and conservatives had feared. Even when it did not transform politics and government, however, the right to vote was a potent symbol.

Women were active in many other areas besides the suffrage movement. On both sides of the Atlantic women participated in social reform movements to prevent mistreatment of women and children and of industrial workers. In the United States such reforms were championed by Progressives like Jane Addams (1860–1935), who founded a settlement house in a poor neighborhood and received the Nobel Peace Prize in 1931. In Europe reformers were generally aligned with Socialist or Labour Parties.

Among the most controversial, and eventually most effective, of the reformers were those who advocated contraception, such as the American **Margaret Sanger** (1883–1966). Her campaign brought her into conflict with many authorities, who equated birth control with pornography. Finally, in 1923 she was able to found a birth control clinic in New York. In France, the government prohibited contraception and abortion in 1920 in an effort to increase the birthrate and make up for the loss of so many young men in the war.

30-2c Revolution in the Sciences: The New Physics

The word *progress*, as much associated with extending "modern civilization" to the non-Western world as with technological developments such as railroads and undersea cables, had been a hallmark of most nineteenth-century Euro-American ideologies. After 1900 the word *science* increasingly took its place as a signifier of Western self-esteem. At the end of the nineteenth century, a revolution in physics undermined the old certainties about nature that had already been shaken by Darwinism (see chapter 27). Physicists discovered that atoms, the building blocks of matter, are not indivisible, but consist of far smaller subatomic particles. In 1900 German physicist **Max Planck** (1858–1947) found that atoms emit or absorb energy in discrete amounts called *quanta*.

Few people understood these findings at the time, much less **Albert Einstein's** (1879–1955) pronouncement in 1916 that time, space, energy, and mass are not fixed but are relative to one another. But scientific discovery, punctuated by prestigious Nobel prizes that began to be awarded in 1901, excited pride and wonder in nations that contributed to such advances.

30-2d The New Social Sciences

The new social sciences were more understandable, and thus more unsettling, than the new physics, for they challenged Victorian morality and middle-class values. **Sigmund Freud** (1856–1939), a Viennese physician, developed the technique of psychoanalysis to probe the minds of his patients. His technique uncovered hidden layers of emotion and desire repressed by social restraints. "It is during this [childhood] period of . . . latency that the psychic forces develop which later act as inhibitions on the sexual life, and narrow its direction like dams. These psychic forces are loathing, shame, and moral and esthetic ideal demands,"[2] he declared. Meanwhile, sociologists and anthropologists had begun the empirical study of societies, both Western and non-Western. Before the war French sociologist Emile Durkheim (1858–1917) had come to the then shocking conclusion that "there are no religions that are false. All are true after their own fashion."[3]

[2]Sigmund Freud, *Three Contributions to the Theory of Sex*, trans. A. A. Brill, 2nd ed. (Washington, DC: Nervous and Mental Health Disease Publishing Company, 1920), 40.

[3]Emile Durkheim, *The Elementary Forms of Religious Life*, trans. Karen Elise Fields (New York: Free Press, 1995), 2.

AP® Exam Tip
Evaluate how more effective forms of birth control impacted gender roles.

Margaret Sanger American nurse and author; pioneer in the movement for family planning; organized conferences and established birth control clinics.

Max Planck German physicist who developed quantum theory and was awarded the Nobel Prize for physics in 1918.

Albert Einstein German physicist who developed the theory of relativity, which states that time, space, and mass are relative to each other and not fixed.

Sigmund Freud Austrian psychiatrist, founder of psychoanalysis. He argued that psychological problems were caused by traumas, especially sexual experiences in early childhood, that were repressed in later life. His ideas caused considerable controversy among psychologists and in the general public. Although his views on repressed sexuality are no longer widely accepted, his psychoanalytic methods are still very influential.

If the words *primitive* and *savage* applied to Europeans as well as to other peoples, and if religions were all equally "true," then what remained of the superiority of Western civilization? Cultural relativism, as the new approach to human societies was called, could be as unnerving as relativity in physics; but for many it stimulated a tenacious desire to cling to the old truths.

The arts became a battlefield for confronting traditional values with new images and rhythms. Cubism, an approach to painting and sculpture that sought to go beyond realism and depict many aspects of an image simultaneously, aroused lively debates in the 1910s. A painter like the Spaniard **Pablo Picasso** (1881–1973) changed his nonrealistic style of painting time and again over his long career. Paralleling his audacity in the field of music, Russian composer **Igor Stravinsky** (1882–1971) incorporated so-called primitive rhythms in his ballet *The Rite of Spring*, which debuted in 1913.

The incredible human losses experienced during the Great War shook many artists' and intellectuals' faith in reason and progress. Some poets and artists joined the **Dada** movement, which abandoned rationality and relied instead on intuition, randomness, and nonsense—*dada* stood for the use of meaningless syllables in poetry. Others became Surrealists and produced dreamlike images incorporating what they considered to be symbols of the unconscious mind. Some people accepted the new ideas with enthusiasm. Others condemned and rejected them, particularly in the United States, and clung to the sense of order and faith in progress that had energized Western culture before the war.

30-2e New Technologies and Activities

Some people viewed the sciences with mixed feelings, but new technologies aroused almost universal excitement. In North America even working-class people could afford some of the new products of inventors' ingenuity (see Environment & Technology: New Materials). Mass consumption in Europe lagged behind the United States, particularly after World War II, but science and technology were just as advanced, and public fascination with the latest inventions—the cult of the modern—was just as strong.

Of all the innovations of the time, none attracted public interest more than airplanes. In 1903 two young American mechanics, **Wilbur and Orville Wright**, built the first aircraft that was heavier than air and could be maneuvered in flight. From that moment on, airplanes fascinated people. In 1911 a French pilot flew 6,500 letters from one city in British India to another 8.1 miles (13 kilometers) away, thus inaugurating the first important use of air transport. Military observation and aerial warfare came second. During the Great War the exploits of air aces relieved the tedium of news from the front, but no one anticipated the massive bombing raids of World War II.

The first flight of **KLM Royal Dutch Airlines**, the oldest continuously operating airline, took off in 1920. That year it carried 440 passengers and 22 tons of cargo. Scheduled service to a number of northern European cities soon followed. Its most important service, as an air link to the Dutch East Indies (now Indonesia), began in 1929. Every country with imperial possessions saw international air service as a political necessity. Two of the oldest airlines, however, Qantas in Australia and the German-owned precursor of Avianca in Colombia, functioned entirely outside of Europe.

Health and hygiene were part of the cult of modernity. Advances in medicine—some learned on the battlefield—saved many lives. Wounds were regularly disinfected, and **Marie Curie** (1867–1934), the French discoverer of x-rays, organized radiology vans to help army doctors diagnose fractures during the Great War. Cities built costly water supply and sewage treatment systems. By the 1920s indoor plumbing and flush toilets were becoming common even in working-class neighborhoods.

Interest in cleanliness entered private life. Doctors and home economists bombarded women with warnings and advice on how to banish germs. Soap and appliance manufacturers filled women's magazines with advertisements for products to help keep homes and clothing spotless and meals fresh and wholesome. The decline in infant mortality and improvements in general health and life expectancy in this period owe as much to the cult of cleanliness as to advances in medicine.

Organized baseball leagues arose in America after the Civil War. Football found favor as a college sport around the same time, while basketball originated in 1891 as a YMCA activity. In Britain soccer (football) and rugby leagues formed in the 1880s. All of these sports flourished

---

AP® Exam Tip Consider the globalization of science, technology, and art.

Pablo Picasso Key figure in the movement of modern art away from realistic representation; a founder of cubism and surrealism.

Igor Stravinsky Influential modernist composer known for his experimentation and pulsing rhythms.

Dada Nihilistic movement in poetry and art that began during World War I in reaction to the vast and horrifying loss of life that seemed to make art meaningless.

Wilbur and Orville Wright American bicycle mechanics; the first to build and fly an airplane, at Kitty Hawk, North Carolina, December 7, 1903.

KLM Royal Dutch Airlines Oldest major airline, operating since 1920 in Europe and connecting to the Dutch East Indies in 1929.

Marie Curie Polish-born pioneer in the study of radiation and winner of Nobel Prizes for physics (1903) and chemistry (1911); first female professor at the Sorbonne.

Environment & Technology
New Materials

Nineteenth-century commerce brought many raw materials from European colonies and other faraway places into industrial use. Examples include rubber, a Southeast Asian tree sap called gutta-percha used for electrical insulation, Central Asian camel's hair used for transmission belts, and whale oil for lighting. These exotic materials were valuable, but they did not change the age-old pattern of almost every useful item being manufactured from natural substances.

The first half of the twentieth century saw a revolutionary change in this pattern. Metallurgists and chemists led the way in creating new materials that wrought permanent changes in the look and feel of everyday life. Materials science would go on to become one of the most important areas of technical innovation in later decades.

Though aluminum follows oxygen and silicon as the third most abundant element, it combines so readily with other elements that it was not discovered as a separate element until 1827. Initially as precious as silver, a 2.4-kilogram piece was installed as the capstone of the Washington Monument in 1884. Four years later, however, almost simultaneously in the United States and France, an inexpensive electrolytic method of extracting the metal from bauxite ore was discovered. The light-weight, non-corrosive metal now became available for all manner of uses, from airplanes, beginning with a design by the German Hugo Junkers in 1917, to aluminum foil, which was invented in 1910. And bauxite became an internationally traded commodity.

Stainless steel, made by combining noncorrosive chromium with steel, was invented in 1912, and its many uses accustomed people to thinking of metal industrial products as shiny. Electroplating with chromium came into use in 1924 in Germany and two years later in the United States. The shiny, rust-free metal, which could be deposited as a thin film on either a metallic or plastic base, found numerous uses from musical instruments to automobiles.

Plastics were invented at about the same time. Alexander Parkes invented celluloid, a stable form of explosive guncotton—itself made by soaking fine cotton in sulfuric and nitric acids—and exhibited it at London's Great Exhibition in 1862. The first thermoplastic, hot celluloid could be molded, but it became solid when it cooled. It was used for detachable men's shirt collars, ping-pong balls, and photographic film, and was both fragile and flammable.

Belgian-born Leo Hendrik Baekeland invented Bakelite, a more durable plastic that was also attractive enough to be used for jewelry in 1907. Five years later Swiss chemist Jacques E. Brandenberger, trying to discover a way of waterproofing cloth, experimented with a cellulose-based coating that failed to stick to the cloth and instead peeled off in a clear sheet. Thus was cellophane accidentally invented. In the 1930s an American, Richard Drew, coated cellophane with adhesive and Scotch tape was born.

And there were others: silk-like rayon, 1904; isoprene synthetic rubber, 1909; vinyl, 1926; neoprene synthetic rubber, 1931; plexiglass, 1933; nylon, 1935; Lucite, 1936; fiberglass, 1938—the list goes on, with even more new materials being developed in the later decades of the century.

Questions for Analysis

1. Why do we take for granted a material environment constructed from manufactured substances that did not even exist before 1900?
2. What are the objects we use every day made of?
3. Why did new materials find such broad acceptance?

◀ **Bakelite Jewelry** This pioneering plastic was so attractive that it was made into jewelry. However, its ease of manufacture, hardness, and resistance to electricity, heat, and chemicals suited it to thousands of other uses from clarinets to wire insulation to kitchenware. During World War II it was even considered as a replacement for the copper penny. imageBROKER/Alamy Stock Photo

▲ **First Aluminum Airplane** From the Wright Brothers' first aircraft in 1903 down to the air battles of World War I, wood, cloth, and wire made up the wings and bodies of airplanes. Metals were too heavy for anything but engines and weapons until German manufacturer Hugo Junkers designed the first aluminum flying machine, shown here, in 1917. Museum of Flight Foundation/Getty Images

as spectator activities in the early twentieth century and gave rise to lively press coverage in newspapers. Soccer and rugby, along with the much older sport of cricket, spread readily into Europe's colonies, while baseball found limited favor overseas, primarily in Japan, Cuba, and the Dominican Republic.

Internationally, the upsurge in the role of sports and spectating was closely tied to the revival of the Olympic Games. The ancient Greek games had been discontinued in 393 CE. The inspiration to create a modern form came from **Baron Pierre de Coubertin** (1863–1937), a French educator who was impressed by the sports played at English private schools like Eton and Rugby. He concluded that "organised sport can create moral and social strength."

Coubertin's aristocratic vision of purely amateur international competition came to fruition in Athens in 1896 when fourteen countries, all of them European except Australia and Chile, sent athletes to compete in nonteam sports like tennis, fencing, shooting, cycling, and gymnastics. Women were not included, nor did Coubertin's vision of medals being given for sports-themed art and architecture survive past 1948. The male-only rule was dropped starting with the Paris Olympics of 1900, where women competed in tennis and golf. The role of women increased steadily after that.

Individual excellence was the touchstone of Olympic competition, but nationalistic pride increasingly marked the quadrennial events. The Berlin Olympics of 1936 thus became a showcase for Nazi ideology and spectacle.

30-2f Technology and the Environment

Baron Pierre de Coubertin Founder of the modern Olympic movement, which held its first games in Athens in 1896.

Two new technologies—the skyscraper and the automobile—transformed the urban environment even more radically than the railroad had done. At the end of the nineteenth century architects had begun to design ever-higher buildings using elevators and load-bearing steel frames. Major corporations in Chicago and New York competed to build the most daring buildings in the world, such as New York's fifty-five-story Woolworth Building (1912). A building boom in the late

1920s produced dozens of skyscrapers, culminating with the eighty-six-story Empire State Building in New York in 1932.

European cities restricted the height of buildings to protect their architectural heritage; Paris forbade buildings over 56 feet (17 meters) high. In the 1920s Swiss architect Charles Edouard Jeanneret (1887–1965), known as **Le Corbusier (luh cor-booz-YEH)**, outlined a new approach to architecture that featured simplicity of form, absence of surface ornamentation, easy manufacture, and inexpensive materials such as concrete and glass. Other architects—including the Finn Eero Saarinen, the Germans Ludwig Mies van der Rohe (**LOOD-vig MEES fon der ROW-uh**) and Walter Gropius, and the American Frank Lloyd Wright—also contributed to what became known as the International Style.

Meanwhile, the edges of cities were spreading far into the countryside, thanks to the automobile. The assembly line pioneered by Henry Ford mass-produced vehicles in ever-greater volume and at falling prices. By 1929 Americans owned five-sixths of the world's automobiles, or one car for every five people. Automobiles were praised as the solution to urban pollution; as they replaced carts and carriages, horses disappeared from city streets, as did tons of manure.

The most important environmental effect of automobiles was suburban sprawl. Middle-class families could now live in single-family homes too far apart to be served by public transportation. As middle- and working-class families bought cars, cities acquired rings of automobile suburbs. Los Angeles, the first true automobile city, consisted of suburbs spread over hundreds of square miles and linked together by broad avenues. Many Americans saw Los Angeles as the portent of a glorious future in which everyone would have a car.

European cities that had inherited narrow streets from the premodern past adapted less easily to passenger automobiles. In the countryside, however, high-speed, limited-access expressways, called *autostrada* in Italy and *autobahn* in Germany, became sources of national pride for the regimes of Benito Mussolini and Adolf Hitler. Yet compared with the United States, private automobile ownership remained uncommon.

Technological advances also transformed rural economies. In 1915 Ford introduced a gasoline-powered tractor, and by the mid-1920s these versatile machines began replacing horses. Larger farms profited most from this innovation, while small farmers sold their land and moved to the cities. Tractors and other expensive equipment hastened the transformation of agriculture from family enterprises to larger businesses, or in the USSR to collective farms with state-owned tractor stations (see Chapter 29).

In India, Australia, and the western United States, engineers built dams and canals to irrigate dry lands. Dams offered the added advantage of producing electricity, for which there was a booming demand. The immediate benefits of water control—irrigated land, prevention of floods, and generation of electricity—far outweighed such negative consequences as salt deposits on irrigated fields and harm to wildlife that would eventually emerge.

Section Review

- Government bureaucracies and the middle class grew after World War I, but not the working class.

- In many countries, women gained the right to vote and led reform movements.

- Max Planck and Albert Einstein led a revolution in physics.

- Social scientists like Sigmund Freud undermined the old certainties of European culture by revealing a dark side to human nature.

- After the Wright brothers' first flight, mail delivery and connection with colonies prompted the organization of airlines.

- The cult of cleanliness and spread of sporting activities improved health, with the latter providing new types of spectator entertainment.

- American cities were transformed by skyscrapers, and the automobile led to the creation of suburbs.

30-3 **A New India, 1905–1947**

How was the independence movement in India affected by the new mass media?

Some parts of the non-Western world, such as India, became much more involved in the emerging technologically oriented culture than others, such as sub-Saharan Africa (see below). The consequences of this inequality of access to "modern" developments are still felt today.

Under British rule India acquired railroads, harbors, modern cities, and cotton and steel mills, as well as an active and worldly middle class. The economic transformation of the region awakened in this educated middle class a sense of national dignity that demanded political fulfillment. In response, the British gradually granted India a limited amount of political autonomy

Le Corbusier Professional name of architect Charles-Éduard Jeanneret, who led a modernist movement away from surface decoration and toward form following function.

while maintaining overall control. Religious and communal tensions among the Indian peoples were carefully papered over, and when the British, exhausted by World War II, withdrew in 1947, violent conflicts tore India apart (see Map 30.1).

30-3a The Land and the People

Much of India is fertile land, but it is vulnerable to droughts caused by the periodic failure of the monsoons. When the rains failed from 1896 to 1900, 2 million people died of starvation.

Despite periodic famines, the Indian population grew from 250 million in 1900 to 319 million in 1921 and 389 million in 1941. This growth generated many pressures. Landless young men converged on the cities, exceeding the number of jobs available in the slowly expanding industries. Many of them entered the urban economy as rickshaw pullers. To produce timber for construction and railroad ties and to clear land for tea and rubber plantations, foresters cut down most of the tropical hardwood forests that had covered much of the subcontinent in the nineteenth century. But in spite of deforestation and extensive irrigation, the amount of land

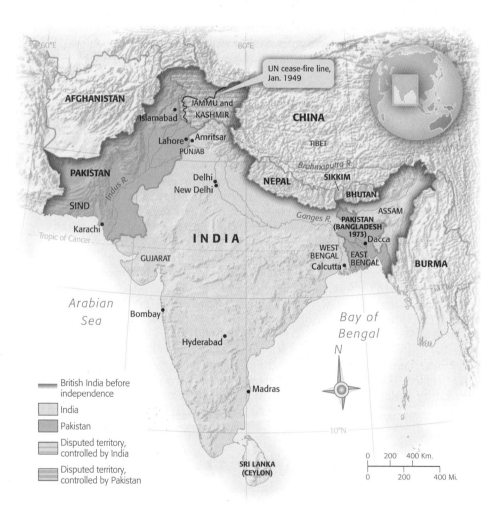

MAP 30.1 The Partition of India, 1947 Before the British, India was divided among many states, ethnic groups, and religions. When the British left in 1947, the subcontinent split along religious lines. The predominantly Muslim regions in the northwest and Muslim East Bengal in the east formed the new nation of Pakistan. The predominantly Hindu center became the Republic of India. Jammu and Kashmir in the northwest remained disputed territories and poisoned relations between the two new countries.

Why is the word India used at one point for a group of principalities, at another for one huge land, and today for the largest country carved out of that huge land?

available to peasant families shrank with each successive generation. Economic development hardly touched the average Indian.

Indians were divided into many classes. Peasants, always the great majority, paid rents to landowners, interest to village moneylenders, and taxes to the government and had little left to improve their land or raise their standard of living. The government protected property owners, from village moneylenders all the way up to the *maharajahs* (mah-huh-RAH-juh) or ruling princes, who owned huge tracts of land. The cities were crowded with craftsmen, traders, and workers of all sorts, most of them very poor. Although the British had banned the burning of Hindu widows on their husbands' funeral pyres, in other respects women's lives changed little under British rule.

Indians also spoke many different languages. As a result of British rule, increasing trade and travel, and newspapers like *The Times of India*, established under that name in 1861, English became the common medium of communication for the Western-educated middle class. This new class of English-speaking bureaucrats, professionals, and merchants was to play a leading role in the independence movement.

The majority of Indians who practiced Hinduism were subdivided into hundreds of castes (*jati*), each affiliated with a particular occupation or kinship group. Hinduism discouraged intermarriage and other social interactions among the castes and with non-Hindus. Until displaced by the British in the eighteenth century, Muslim rulers had dominated northern and central India, and Muslims now constituted one-quarter of the Indian population while forming a majority in the northwest and in eastern Bengal. They felt discriminated against by both British and Hindus.

AP® Exam Tip
Be able to discuss the colonial legacy of imperialism on India and other regions of the world.

30-3b British Rule and Indian Nationalism

Colonial India was ruled by a viceroy appointed by the British government and administered by a few thousand members of the Indian Civil Service. These men, drawn mostly from the English gentry, believed it was their duty to protect the Indian people from the dangers of industrialization and to defend their own positions from Indian nationalists.

As Europeans they admired modern technology. They encouraged railroads, harbors, telegraphs, and other communications technologies, as well as irrigation and plantations, because these increased India's foreign trade and strengthened British control. Yet, they discouraged the cotton and steel industries and limited the training of Indian engineers, to spare India the social upheavals that had accompanied the Industrial Revolution in Europe while protecting British industry from Indian competition.

At the turn of the century most Indians—especially peasants, landowners, and princes—accepted British rule. But the Europeans' racist attitude toward dark-skinned people increasingly offended Indians who had learned English and absorbed English ideas of freedom and representative government, only to discover that racial quotas excluded them from the Indian Civil Service, the officer corps, and prestigious sporting clubs.

In 1885 a small group of English-speaking Hindu professionals founded a political organization called the **Indian National Congress**. For twenty years its members respectfully petitioned the government for access to higher administrative positions and for a voice in official decisions, but they had little influence. Then, in 1905, Viceroy Lord Curzon divided the province of **Bengal** in two to improve the efficiency of its administration. This decision, made without consulting anyone, angered not only educated Indians, who saw it as a way to lessen their influence, but also millions of uneducated Hindu Bengalis, who found themselves outnumbered by Muslims in East Bengal. Soon Bengal was the scene of demonstrations, boycotts of British goods, and even incidents of violence against the British.

In 1906, while the Hindus of Bengal were protesting the partition of their province, Muslims, fearful of Hindu dominance elsewhere in India, founded the **All-India Muslim League**. (Note the English names of these political groups.) The government responded by granting Indians limited voting rights based on wealth. Muslims, however, were on average poorer than Hindus, possibly because many poor and low-caste Hindus had converted to Islam to escape caste discrimination. Taking advantage of these religious divisions, the British instituted separate representation and different voting qualifications for Hindus and Muslims. Then, in 1911, the British transferred the capital of India from Calcutta (Kolkata) to Delhi (**DEL-ee**), the former capital of the Mughal (**MOO-guhl**) emperors. These changes disturbed Indians of all classes and religions

AP® Exam Tip
Identify and explain examples of religious movements, such as that led by Muhammad Ali Jinnah, that challenged colonial rule.

Indian National Congress A movement and political party founded in 1885 to demand greater Indian participation in government. Its membership was middle class, and its demands were modest until World War I. Led after 1920 by Mohandas K. Gandhi, it appealed increasingly to the poor, and it organized mass protests demanding self-government and independence.

Bengal Region of northeastern India. It was the first part of India to be conquered by the British in the eighteenth century and remained the political and economic center of British India throughout the nineteenth century. The 1905 split of the province into predominantly Hindu West Bengal and predominantly Muslim East Bengal (now Bangladesh) sparked anti-British riots.

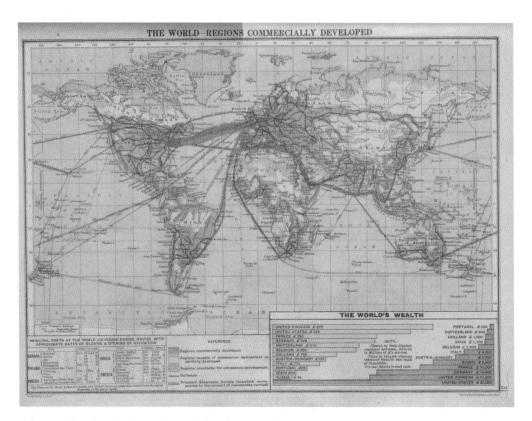

▲ **World Commercial Map, 1920** The primacy of Great Britain in the world of commerce shows up in the table detailing the distribution of the world's wealth and in the steamship lines linking Britain to the United States and to India by way of the Mediterranean. Railroads in South America and Africa were designed to facilitate exports rather than unify the continents. The Peoples Atlas, London Geographical Institute, 1920

and raised their political consciousness. Politics, once primarily the concern of westernized intellectuals, turned into two mass movements: one by Hindus and one by Muslims.

British geologists looked for minerals like coal and manganese that British industry required. However, when the only Indian member of the Indian Geological Service, Pramatha Nath Bose, wanted to prospect for iron ore, he had to resign because the government wanted no part of an Indian steel industry that might compete with British exports. Bose joined forces with Jamsetji Tata, a Bombay textile magnate who decided to produce steel in spite of British opposition. With the help of German and American engineers and equipment, Tata's son Dorabji opened the first steel mill in India in 1911, in a town called Jamshedpur, in honor of his father. Although it produced only a fraction of the steel that India required, Jamshedpur became a powerful symbol of Indian national pride. It also prompted Indian nationalists to ask why a country that could produce its own steel needed foreigners to run its government.

During World War I Indians supported Britain enthusiastically; 1.2 million men volunteered for the army, and millions more voluntarily contributed money to the government. Many expected the British to reward their loyalty with political concessions. Others organized to demand a voice in the government. In 1917, in response to the agitation, the British government announced "the gradual development of self-governing institutions with a view to the progressive realization of responsible government in India as an integral part of the British Empire." This sounded like a promise of self-government, but the timetable was so vague that nationalists denounced it as a devious maneuver to postpone India's independence.

On April 13, 1919, in the city of Amritsar, General Reginald Dyer ordered his troops to fire into a peaceful crowd of some 10,000 demonstrators, killing at least 379 and wounding 1,200. While waves of angry demonstrations swept over India, the British House of Lords voted to approve Dyer's actions, and a fund was raised in appreciation of his services. Indians interpreted these gestures as showing British contempt for their colonial subjects. In the charged atmosphere of the time, the period of gradual accommodation between the British and the Indians came to a close.

All-India Muslim League
Political organization founded in India in 1906 to defend the interests of India's Muslim minority. Led by Muhammad Ali Jinnah, it attempted to negotiate with the Indian National Congress. In 1940, the League began demanding a separate state for Muslims, to be called Pakistan.

30-3c **Mahatma Gandhi and Militant Nonviolence**

For the next twenty years India teetered on the edge of violent uprisings and harsh repression. That it did not succumb was due to **Mohandas K. Gandhi (GAHN-dee)** (1869–1948), a man known to his followers as "Mahatma," the "great soul."

Gandhi began life with every advantage. His family was wealthy enough to send him to England for his education. After his studies he lived in South Africa and practiced law for the small Indian community there. During World War I he returned to India and was one of many Western-educated Hindu intellectuals who joined the Indian National Congress.

Unlike many radical political thinkers of his time, Gandhi denounced the popular ideals of power, struggle, and combat. Instead, inspired by both Hindu and Christian ideals, he preached the saintly virtues of *ahimsa* **(uh-HIM-sah)** (non-violence) and *satyagraha* **(suh-TYAH-gruh-huh)** (the search for truth). He refused to countenance violence among his followers and called off several demonstrations when they turned violent.

In 1921 Gandhi gave up the Western-style suits worn by lawyers and the fine raiment of wealthy Indians and henceforth wore simple peasant garb: a length of home-spun cotton below his waist (*dhoti*) and a shawl to cover his torso. He spoke for the farmers and the outcasts, whom he called *harijan* **(HAH-ree-jahn)**, "children of God." He attracted ever-larger numbers of followers among the poor and the illiterate, who soon began to revere him; and he transformed the cause of Indian independence from an elite movement of the educated into a mass movement with a quasi-religious aura.

Gandhi was a brilliant political tactician and a master of public relations gestures. (see Diversity & Dominance: Gandhi and the Media). In 1929, for instance, he led a few followers on an 80-mile (129-kilometer) walk, camped on a beach, and gathered salt from the sea in a blatant and well-publicized act of civil disregard for the government's monopoly on salt. But he discovered that unleashing the power of popular participation was one thing and controlling its direction was quite another. Within days of his "Walk to the Sea," demonstrations of support broke out all over India, in which the police killed a hundred demonstrators and arrested over 60,000.

Many times during the 1930s Gandhi threatened to fast "unto death," and several times he came close to death, to protest the violence of both the police and his followers and to demand independence. He was repeatedly arrested and spent a total of six years in jail. But every arrest made him more popular. He became a figure of adulation not only in his own country but also in the Western media. In the words of historian Percival Spear, he made the British "uncomfortable in their cherished field of moral rectitude," and he gave Indians the feeling that theirs was the ethically superior cause.

AP® Exam Tip
Be able to explain how Mohandas Gandhi's implementation of nonviolence brought about political change.

Mohandas K. Gandhi
Leader of the Indian independence movement and advocate of nonviolent resistance. After being educated as a lawyer in England, he returned to India and became leader of the Indian National Congress in 1920. He appealed to the poor, led nonviolent demonstrations against British colonial rule, and was jailed many times. Soon after independence he was assassinated for attempting to stop Hindu-Muslim rioting.

◀ **Gandhi's Salt March to the Sea** Mohandas Gandhi, bareheaded and more simply dressed than his followers, led a march of 80 miles to collect sea salt in an act of civil disobedience. News photographs like this played a key role in popularizing his cause and displaying his saintly habits. To his left one man carries a sitar and another has a drum hanging from his shoulder. Dinodia Photos/Alamy Stock Photo

Political figures in many countries made use of radio, newspaper, and newsreel coverage to spread their messages. The Fascists in Italy and the Nazis in Germany used photographs of their uniformed leaders as symbols, filmed their mass rallies, and broadcast their bombastic speeches. But no one showed more skill in using the new media to publicize his movement than Mahatma Gandhi. To identify with the common people of India, he appeared in a plain white loincloth (dhoti) and shawl instead of a uniform. To show the power of civil disobedience, he led his followers in much-photographed marches and demonstrations. Some of his most important speeches were delivered in trial court or to urge people to break the law and then reported in the press.

In 1922, after 2,000 followers of Gandhi's nonviolent movement responded to police gunfire by burning down the police station at Chauri Chaura and killing twenty-two policemen, he was charged with "bringing or attempting to excite disaffection towards His Majesty's Government established by law in British India." Before reading a written statement in which he detailed governmental acts that he considered to be tyrannical, Gandhi said the following.

I would like to state that I entirely endorse the learned Advocate-General's remarks in connection with my humble self. . . . I have no desire whatsoever to conceal from this court the fact that to preach disaffection towards the existing system of Government has become almost a passion with me. . . . I wish to endorse all the blame that the learned Advocate-General has thrown on my shoulders in connection with the Bombay occurrences, Madras occurrences and the Chauri Chaura occurrences. Thinking over these things deeply and sleeping over them night after night, it is impossible for me to dissociate myself from the diabolical crimes of Chauri Chaura or the mad outrages of Bombay. He is quite right when he says, that as a man of responsibility, a man having received a fair share of education, having had a fair share of experience of this world, I should have known the consequences of every one of my acts. I know them. I knew that I was playing with fire. I ran the risk and if I was set free I would still do the same. I have felt

it this morning that I would have failed in my duty, if I did not say what I said here just now.

I wanted to avoid violence. Non-violence is the first article of my faith. It is also the last article of my creed. But I had to make my choice. I had either to submit to a system which I considered had done an irreparable harm to my country, or incur the risk of the mad fury of my people bursting forth when they understood the truth from my lips. I know that my people have sometimes gone mad. I am deeply sorry for it and I am, therefore, here to submit not to a light penalty but to the highest penalty. I do not ask for mercy. I do not plead any extenuating act. I am here, therefore, to invite and cheerfully submit to the highest penalty that can be inflicted upon me for what in law is a deliberate crime, and what appears to me to be the highest duty of a citizen.

In 1930, before embarking on the Salt March, a demonstration of civil disobedience that was heavily covered by newspaper and newsreel reporters, Gandhi delivered the following speech.

In all probability this will be my last speech to you. Even if the Government allow me to march tomorrow morning, this will be my last speech on the sacred banks of the Sabarmati. Possibly these may be the last words of my life here. . . .

From what I have seen and heard during the last fortnight, I am inclined to believe that the stream of civil resisters will flow unbroken. But let there be not a semblance of breach of peace even after all of us have been arrested. We have resolved to utilize all our resources in the pursuit of an exclusively nonviolent struggle. Let no one commit a wrong in anger. This is my hope and prayer. I wish these words of mine reached every nook and corner of the land. My task shall be done if I perish and so do my comrades. . . . Wherever possible, civil disobedience of salt should be started. These laws can be violated in three ways. It is an offence to manufacture salt wherever there are facilities for doing so. The possession and sale of contraband salt, which includes natural salt or salt earth, is also an offence. The purchasers of

30-3d India Moves Toward Independence

AP® Exam Tip

Compare the nationalist independence movement in India to other twentieth-century nationalist independence movements.

In the 1920s, slowly and reluctantly, the British handed over control of "national" areas such as education, the economy, and public works to Indians. They also gradually admitted more Indians into the Civil Service and the officer corps.

In the years before the Second World War, Indian politicians obtained the right to erect high tariff barriers against imports to protect India's infant industries from foreign competition. Behind these barriers, Indian entrepreneurs built plants to manufacture iron and steel, cement, paper, textiles, sugar, and other products. This early industrialization did not provide enough jobs to improve the lives of the Indian peasants or urban poor, but it created a class of wealthy Indian businessmen who supported the Indian National Congress and its demands for independence. Though paying homage to Gandhi, they preferred his designated successor as leader of

such salt will be equally guilty. To carry away the natural salt deposits on the seashore is likewise violation of law. So is the hawking of such salt. In short, you may choose any one or all of these devices to break the salt monopoly.

We are, however, not to be content with this alone. . . . I stress only one condition, namely, let our pledge of truth and non-violence as the only means for the attainment of Swaraj [self-rule] be faithfully kept. For the rest, every one has a free hand. But, that does not give a license to all and sundry to carry on their own responsibility. Wherever there are local leaders, their orders should be obeyed by the people. Where there are no leaders and only a handful of men have faith in the programme, they may do what they can, if they have enough self-confidence. . . .

Much can be done in many other ways besides these. The Liquor and foreign cloth shops can be picketed. We can refuse to pay taxes if we have the requisite strength. The lawyers can give up practice. The public can boycott the law courts by refraining from litigation. Government servants can resign their posts. . . . Let all who are co-operating with the Government in one way or another, be it by paying taxes, keeping titles, or sending children to official schools, etc., withdraw their co-operation in all or as many ways as possible. Then there are women who can stand shoulder to shoulder with men in this struggle.

Gandhi's successor, Jawaharlal Nehru, enjoyed remarkable success as India's first elected prime minister. But his public image was much more conventional. His most famous speech celebrated the granting of India's independence on August 14, 1947.

Long years ago we made a tryst with destiny, and now the time comes when we shall redeem our pledge, not wholly or in full measure, but very substantially. At the stroke of the midnight hour, when the world sleeps, India will awake to life and freedom. A moment comes, which comes but rarely in history, when we step out from the old to the new, when an age ends, and when the soul of a nation, long suppressed, finds utterance. It is fitting that at this solemn moment we take the pledge of dedication to the service of India and her people and to the still larger cause of humanity.

At the dawn of history India started on her unending quest, and trackless centuries are filled with her striving and the grandeur of her success and her failures. Through good and ill fortune alike she has never lost sight of that quest or forgotten the ideals which gave her strength. We end today a period of ill fortune and India discovers herself again. The achievement we celebrate today is but a step, an opening of opportunity, to the greater triumphs and achievements that await us. Are we brave enough and wise enough to grasp this opportunity and accept the challenge of the future? . . .

That future is not one of ease or resting but of incessant striving so that we may fulfill the pledges we have so often taken and the one we shall take today. The service of India means the service of the millions who suffer. It means the ending of poverty and ignorance and disease and inequality of opportunity. The ambition of the greatest man of our generation [i.e., Gandhi] has been to wipe every tear from every eye. That may be beyond us, but as long as there are tears and suffering, so long our work will not be over.

And so we have to labour and to work, and work hard, to give reality to our dreams. Those dreams are for India, but they are also for the world, for all the nations and peoples are too closely knit together today for any one of them to imagine that it can live apart. Peace has been said to be indivisible; so is freedom, so is prosperity now, and so also is disaster in this one world that can no longer be split into isolated fragments. . . .

AP® History Reasoning Skills

Comparison *In what ways does the rhetoric of Gandhi compare with that of Nehru?*

Continuity and Change Over Time *Why did Gandhi's type of movement have so few antecedents? How did it change later world politics?*

Sources: Selected Works of Mahatma Gandhi, Vol. VI: The Voice of Truth, Part I, "Some Famous Speeches," ed. Shriman Narayan Gandhi (1952); Brian McArthur, *Penguin Book of Twentieth Century Speeches* (London: Penguin Viking, 1992), 234–237.

the Indian National Congress, **Jawaharlal Nehru (NAY-roo)** (1889–1964). Unlike Gandhi, Nehru looked forward to creating a modern industrial India.

Congress politicians won regional elections but continued to be excluded from the viceroy's cabinet, the true center of power. When World War II began, Viceroy Lord Linlithgow declared war without consulting a single Indian. The Congress-dominated provincial governments resigned in protest and found that boycotting government office increased their popular support. When the British offered to give India its independence once the war ended, Gandhi demanded full independence immediately. His "Quit India" campaign aroused popular demonstrations against the British and provoked a wave of arrests, including his own. The Second World War divided the Indian people. Most Indian soldiers felt they were fighting to defend their country rather than to support the British Empire. As in World War I, Indians contributed heavily to the Allied war effort, supplying 2 million soldiers and enormous amounts of resources,

Jawaharlal Nehru Indian statesman who succeeded Mohandas K. Gandhi as leader of the Indian National Congress. He negotiated the end of British colonial rule in India and became India's first prime minister (1947–1964).

Section Review

- Under British rule, India's population grew but remained divided by religion and caste.

- The British introduced certain modern technologies but discouraged Indian industry that might compete with British industry.

- British racial policies, brutality, and arrogance awakened a sense of nationhood among educated Indians.

- The Indian National Congress and the All-India Muslim League demanded independence.

- Mahatma Gandhi led the independence movement using nonviolent tactics and turned an upper-class rebellion into one involving all of India.

- Nehru, Gandhi's successor, wanted to modernize India, and the Indian National Congress resisted British rule during World War II.

- When the British left India in 1947, it split into two nations amidst widespread riots and massacres between Hindus and Muslims.

especially the timber needed for emergency construction. A small number of Indians were so anti-British that they joined the Japanese side.

30-3e Partition and Independence

When the war ended, Britain's new Labour Party government prepared for Indian independence, but deep suspicions between Hindus and Muslims complicated the process. The break between the two communities had started in 1937, when the Indian National Congress won provincial elections and refused to share power with the Muslim League. In 1940 the leader of the League, **Muhammad Ali Jinnah (JIH-nah)** (1876–1948), demanded what many Muslims had been dreaming of for years: a country of their own, to be called Pakistan.

As independence approached, talks between Jinnah and Nehru broke down and battle lines were drawn. Violent rioting between Hindus and Muslims broke out. Gandhi's appeals for tolerance and cooperation fell on deaf ears. The British made frantic proposals to keep India united, but their authority was waning fast.

In early 1947 the Indian National Congress accepted the partition of India into two states, one secular but dominated by Hindus, the other Muslim. On August 15 British India gave way to a new India and Pakistan. The Indian National Congress, led by Nehru, formed the first government of India; Jinnah and the Muslim League established a government for the provinces that made up Pakistan.

The rejoicing over independence was marred by violent outbreaks between Muslims and Hindus. In protest against the mounting chaos, Gandhi refused to attend the independence day celebration. Throughout the land, Muslim and Hindu neighbors turned on one another, and armed members of one faith hunted down people of the other faith. Leaving most of their possessions behind, Hindus fled from predominantly Muslim areas, and Muslims fled from Hindu areas. Trainloads of desperate refugees of one faith were attacked and massacred by members of the other or were left stranded in the middle of deserts. Within a few months some 12 million people had abandoned their ancestral homes and a half-million lay dead. In January 1948 Gandhi died too, gunned down by an angry Hindu refugee.

After the sectarian massacres and flights of refugees, Muslims were a minority in all but one state of India. That state was Kashmir, a strategically important region in the foothills of the Himalayas. India annexed Kashmir because the local maharajah was Hindu and because the state held the headwaters of the rivers that irrigated mil-lions of acres of farmland. Most inhabitants would have joined Pakistan if they had been allowed to vote on the matter. The annexation of Kashmir turned India and Pakistan into bitter enemies that fought several wars over the next half century.

30-4 Mexico, Argentina, and Brazil, 1917–1949

Muhammad Ali Jinnah
Indian Muslim politician who founded the state of Pakistan. A lawyer by training, he joined the All-India Muslim League in 1913. As leader of the League from the 1920s on, he negotiated with the British and the Indian National Congress for Muslim participation in Indian politics. From 1940 on, he led the movement for the independence of India's Muslims in a separate state of Pakistan, founded in 1947.

Were economic and technological changes compatible with social justice in Latin America?

Though some parts of the world, notably Latin America, were untouched by the Great War, they still experienced the disruptions and new ways of life of the postwar period. In the early 1920s, after a decade of violence that exhausted all classes (see Chapter 26), the Mexican Revolution lost momentum. President Obregón and his closest associates made all the important decisions, and his successor, Plutarco Elías Calles (**KAH-yace**), founded the National Revolutionary Party, or PNR (the abbreviation of its name in Spanish). The PNR was a forum where all the pressure groups and vested interests—labor, peasants, businessmen, landowners, the military, and others—worked out compromises. The establishment of the PNR gave the Mexican Revolution a second wind.

30-4a The Cárdenas Reforms

Lázaro Cárdenas (**LAH-sah-roe KAHR-dih-nahs**), chosen by Calles to be president in 1934, brought peasants' and workers' organizations into the party, removed generals from government positions, and implemented the reforms promised in the Constitution of 1917.

In 1938 Cárdenas seized the foreign-owned oil industry, which had gained importance with the wartime recognition that modern navies needed petroleum. The American and British oil companies expected their governments to come to their rescue, perhaps with military force. But Mexico and the United States chose to resolve the issue through negotiation, and Mexico retained control of its oil.

30-4b The Transformation of Argentina

Most of Argentina consists of *pampas* (**POM-pus**), flat, fertile land that is easy to till, much like the prairies of the midwestern United States and Canada. At the end of the nineteenth century railroads and refrigerator ships changed Argentina's exports and land use. In the 1920s, European consumers, freed from wartime rationing, savored fresh meat. To safeguard valuable herds, the pampas were divided, cultivated, and fenced with barbed wire. Wheat- and grain-fed beef and mutton replaced the lean free-range cattle of earlier generations. Soon the pampas became one of the world's great centers of wheat and meat production.

Argentina's government represented the interests of the *oligarquía* (**oh-lee-gar-KEE-ah**), a small group of wealthy landowners and exporters. They owned fine homes in Buenos Aires (**BWAY-nos EYE-res**), a city that was built to resemble Paris, traveled frequently to Europe, and spent lavishly. However, they were content to let British companies build Argentina's railroads, processing plants, and public utilities. Argentina imported almost all its manufactured goods from Europe and the United States. So important were British interests in the Argentinean economy that English, not Spanish, was used on the railroads.

30-4c Brazil and Argentina, to 1929

Before the First World War, Brazil produced most of the world's coffee and cacao, grown on vast estates. Natural rubber came from rubber trees growing wild in the Amazon rain forest but had not yet been recognized as a key strategic commodity. Like their Argentinean counterparts, Brazil's elite built palaces in Rio de Janeiro (**REE-oh day zhuh-NAIR-oh**) and even an opera house deep in the Amazon. British companies build railroads, harbors, and other infrastructure and imported most manufactured goods.

Both Argentina and Brazil had small but outspoken middle classes that demanded a share in government and looked to European models. The poor, at the bottom of the social pyramid, were mainly Spanish and Italian immigrants turned landless laborers and meat processors in Argentina or sharecroppers and plantation workers, many descended from slaves, in Brazil.

Rubber exports collapsed after 1912, replaced by cheaper plantation rubber from Southeast Asia. Two years later the outbreak of war put an end to imports from Europe as Britain and France focused all their industries on war production and Germany was cut off entirely. The disruption of the old trade patterns weakened the land-owning class. In Argentina the urban middle class obtained the secret ballot and universal male suffrage in 1916 and elected a liberal politician, **Hipólito Irigoyen** (**ee-POH-lee-toe ee-ree-GO-yen**), as president. To a certain extent, the United States replaced the European countries as suppliers of machinery and consumers of coffee. European immigrants built factories to manufacture textiles and household goods.

The postwar years were a period of prosperity in South America. Trade with Europe resumed; prices for agricultural exports remained high; and both Argentina and Brazil used profits accumulated during the war to industrialize and improve their transportation systems and public utilities. Yet it was also a time of social turmoil, as workers and middle-class professionals demanded the same social reforms and enhanced voice in politics as their European counterparts. In Argentina students' and workers' demonstrations were brutally crushed. In Brazil junior officers faced off several times against the government. Though they accomplished little, these demonstrations laid the groundwork for later reformist movements.

Yet as Argentina and Brazil prospered, new technologies again left them dependent on the advanced industrial countries. Aviation reached Latin America after World War I, when European and American companies such as Aéropostale and Pan American Airways introduced airmail service between cities and linked Latin America with the United States and Europe.

AP® Exam Tip
Describe and provide specific examples of Latin America's role in global affairs in the twentieth century.

Lázaro Cárdenas President of Mexico (1934–1940). He brought major changes to Mexican life by distributing millions of acres of land to the peasants, bringing representatives of workers and farmers into the inner circles of politics, and nationalizing the oil industry.

Hipólito Irigoyen Argentine politician, president of Argentina from 1916 to 1922 and 1928 to 1930. The first president elected by universal male suffrage, he began his presidency as a reformer but later became conservative.

Before and during World War I, radio was used only for point-to-point communications. Transmitters powerful enough to send messages across oceans or continents were complex and expensive, with antennas covering many acres. They used as much electricity as a small town. Right after the war, no Latin American country possessed the knowledge or funds to build its own transmitters. Four powerful radio companies—one British, one French, one German, and one American—formed a cartel to control all radio communications in Latin America. Thus, even as Brazil and Argentina were asserting state control over their railroads and older industries, as Mexico had done with its oil industry, the major industrial countries controlled the diffusion of the newer aviation and radio technologies.

30-4d The Depression and the Vargas Regime in Brazil

The Great Depression (see Chapter 29) hit Latin America as hard as it hit Europe and the United States and proved a more important turning point for the region than either world war. As long-term customers cut back orders, the value of agricultural and mineral exports fell by two-thirds between 1929 and 1932. Argentina and Brazil could no longer afford imported manufactured goods. An imploding economy also undermined their shaky political systems. Like European countries, Argentina and Brazil veered toward authoritarian regimes that promised to solve their economic problems.

In 1930 **Getulio Vargas** (**jay-TOO-lee-oh VAR-gus**) (1883–1954), a state governor, staged a coup and proclaimed himself president of Brazil. He proved to be a masterful politician. He wrote a new constitution that broadened the franchise and limited the president to one term. He also raised import duties and promoted national firms and state-owned enterprises. By 1936 industrial production had doubled, especially in textiles and small manufactures. Under his guidance, Brazil was on its way to becoming an industrial country, as well as a model for other Latin American countries attempting to break away from neo-colonial dependency.

The industrialization of Brazil brought the familiar environmental consequences. Powerful new machines allowed the reopening of old mines and the digging of new ones. Cities grew as poor peasants looking for work arrived from the countryside. In Rio de Janeiro and São Paulo (**sow PAL-oh**), the poor turned steep hillsides and vacant lands into immense *favelas* (**feh-VEL-luhs**) (slums) of makeshift shacks.

The countryside was also transformed. Scrubland was turned into pasture or planted in wheat, corn, and sugar cane. Even the Amazon rain forest—half of the land area of Brazil—was affected. In 1930 American industrialist Henry Ford invested $8 million to clear land along the Tapajós River and prepare it to become the site of the world's largest rubber plantation. Ford encountered opposition from Brazilian workers and politicians; the rubber trees proved vulnerable to diseases; and he had to abandon the project—but not before leaving 3 million acres (1.2 million hectares) denuded of trees.

Although Vargas instituted many reforms favorable to urban workers, he refused to help the millions of landless peasants or challenge the great landowners. In 1938, prohibited by his own constitution from being reelected,

Getulio Vargas Dictator of Brazil from 1930 to 1945 and from 1951 to 1954. Defeated in the presidential election of 1930, he overthrew the government and created Estado Novo ("New State"), a dictatorship that emphasized industrialization and helped the urban poor but did little to alleviate the problems of the peasants.

◀ **Juan and Eva Perón** Juan Perón's presidency of Argentina (1946–1955) relied on his, and especially on his wife Eva's, popularity with the working class. To sustain their popularity, they often organized parades and demonstrations in imitation of the fascist dictators of Europe. This picture shows them riding in a procession in Buenos Aires in 1952. Bettmann/Getty Images

Vargas staged another coup, abolished the constitution, and instituted the Estado Novo (**esh-TAH-doe NO-vo**), or "New State," with himself as supreme leader. He abolished political parties, jailed opposition leaders, and turned Brazil into a fascist state, though one that contributed troops and ships to the Allied war effort once the Second World War broke out.

30-4e Argentina After 1930

Economically, the depression hurt Argentina almost as badly as it hurt Brazil. Politically, however, the consequences were delayed. In 1930 General José Uriburu (**hoe-SAY oo-ree-BOO-roo**) overthrew the popularly elected President Irigoyen. For thirteen years the generals and the oligarchy ruled, doing nothing to lessen the poverty of the workers or the frustrations of the middle class. When World War II broke out, Argentina remained officially neutral.

In 1943 another military revolt flared, this one among junior officers led by Colonel **Juan Perón** (**hoo-AHN pair-OWN**) (1895–1974). The intentions of the rebels were clear:

> *Civilians will never understand the greatness of our ideal; we shall therefore have to eliminate them from the government and give them the only mission which corresponds to them: work and obedience.*[4]

Once in power the officers took over the highest positions in government and business and began to lavish money on military equipment and their own salaries. Their goal, inspired by Nazi victories, was nothing less than the conquest of South America.

As the war turned against the Nazis, the officers saw their popularity collapse. Perón, however, had other plans. Inspired by his charismatic wife **Eva Duarte Perón** (**AY-vuy doo-AR-tay pair-OWN**) (1919–1952), he appealed to the urban workers. Eva Perón became the champion of the *descamisados* (**des-cah-mee-SAH-dohs**), or "shirtless ones," and campaigned tirelessly for social benefits and for the cause of women and children. With his wife's help, Perón won the presidency in 1946 and created a populist dictatorship in imitation of the Vargas regime in Brazil. When Eva died in 1952, however, he lost his political skills (or perhaps they were hers), and soon thereafter was overthrown in yet another military coup.

30-5 Sub-Saharan Africa, 1900–1945

Why was Africa so little involved in the transformations of this era?

In contrast with India and Latin America, sub-Saharan Africa experienced very few of the transformations that marked the first half of the twentieth century. Africa was the last continent to come under European rule (see Chapter 26), and it was still being subjected to the economic and political organizational forces of imperialism when territories that had been colonized longer were already in the beginning stages of political awakening. After World War I Britain, France, Belgium, and South Africa divided Germany's African colonies among themselves. Then in the 1930s Italy invaded Ethiopia. The colonial empires reached their peak shortly before World War II.

Yet it would be a mistake to conclude that developments in Africa would have resembled those elsewhere if imperialism had started sooner. European attitudes toward sub-Saharan African peoples were affected by a long history of racism. One economic theory, for example, "the backward-bending supply curve of labor," maintained that people who were accustomed to living at a bare subsistence level would work fewer hours if their pay was raised above what little was needed to maintain that level. They would prefer to idle their lives away sitting around the village rather than striving to better their standard of living the way European workers theoretically would. This theory was used to stigmatize African workers and justify paying them very low wages.

Section Review

- Lázaro Cárdenas fulfilled some of the promises of the Mexican Revolution and nationalized the oil industry.

- Under its landowning oligarchy, Argentina became a major exporter of beef and wheat and depended on Europeans for its industrial products.

- After World War I, Argentina and Brazil prospered but were still dependent on the United States and Europe for advanced technology.

- Brazil and Argentina suffered greatly from the depression; in the 1930s Vargas's dictatorship modernized Brazil but left the majority in poverty.

- Argentina, under Juan Perón, also industrialized, but his unstable government came to an end in the 1950s.

Juan Perón President of Argentina (1946–1955, 1973–1974). As a military officer, he championed the rights of labor. Aided by his wife Eva Duarte Perón, he was elected president in 1946. He built up Argentinean industry, became very popular among the urban poor, but harmed the economy.

Eva Duarte Perón Wife of Juan Perón and champion of the poor in Argentina. She was a gifted speaker and popular political leader who campaigned to improve the life of the urban poor by founding schools and hospitals and providing other social benefits.

---

[4]George Blankstein, *Perón's Argentina* (Chicago: University of Chicago Press, 1953), 37.

AP® Exam Tip
Compare African interactions with the West in the twentieth century with those from earlier time periods.

30-5a **Colonial Africa: Economic and Social Changes**

Outside of Algeria, Kenya, and South Africa, few Europeans lived in Africa, and they variously spoke Portuguese, Spanish, German, French, English, or Afrikaans. In 1930 Nigeria, with a population of 20 million, was ruled by 386 British officials and by 8,000 policemen and military personnel, of whom 150 were European. Yet even such a small presence stimulated deep social and economic changes.

The colonial powers had built railroads from coastal cities to mines and plantations in the interior to transport raw materials to the industrial world, but few Africans benefited from these changes. Colonial governments took lands from Africans and sold or leased them to European companies or to white settlers. Large European companies dominated wholesale commerce, while Indians, Greeks, and Syrians handled much of the retail trade.

Where land was divided into small farms, some Africans benefited from the boom. Farmers in the Gold Coast (now Ghana [**GAH-nuh**]) profited from the high price of cacao, as did palm oil producers in Nigeria and coffee growers in East Africa. In most of Africa women played a major role in the retail trades, selling cloth, food, pots and pans, and other items in the markets. Many maintained their economic independence and kept their household finances separate from those of their husbands, following a custom that predated the colonial period.

For many Africans, however, economic development meant working in European-owned mines and plantations, often under compulsion. Colonial governments were eager to develop the resources of the territories under their control but would not pay wages high enough to attract workers. Instead, they used their police powers to force Africans to work under harsh conditions for little or no pay. In the 1920s, when the government of French Equatorial Africa decided to build a railroad from Brazzaville to the Atlantic coast, a distance of 312 miles (502 kilometers), it drafted 127,000 men to carve a roadbed across mountains and through rain forests. For lack of food, clothing, and medical care, 20,000 of them died, an average of 64 deaths per mile of track.

Europeans prided themselves on bringing modern health care to Africa; yet before the 1930s other aspects of colonialism actually worsened public health. Migrants and soldiers spread syphilis, gonorrhea, tuberculosis, and malaria. Sleeping sickness and smallpox epidemics raged throughout Central Africa. In recruiting men to work, colonial governments also depleted rural areas of farmers needed to plant and harvest crops. Forced requisitions of food to feed the workers left the remaining populations undernourished and vulnerable to diseases. Not until the 1930s did colonial governments realize the negative consequences of their labor policies and begin to invest in agricultural development and health care for Africans.

▶ **Making Palm Oil**
Oil palms produce two products, a red palm oil squeezed from the pulpy fruit and a yellow palm kernel oil extracted from the fruit's seeds with a simple press. Because it stands up well to heat, it is widely used as a cooking oil and is a major export crop in West Africa and other tropical regions. Eye Ubiquitous/Eye Ubiquitous/Superstock

In 1900 Ibadan (**ee-BAH-dahn**) in Nigeria was the only city in sub-Saharan Africa with more than 100,000 inhabitants; fifty years later, dozens of cities had reached that size. Africans migrated to cities because they offered hope of jobs and excitement and, for a few, the chance to become wealthy.

However, migrations damaged the family life of those involved, for almost all the migrants were men leaving women in the countryside to farm and raise children. Reflecting the colonialists' attitudes, cities built during the colonial period had racially segregated housing, clubs, restaurants, hospitals, and other institutions. Patterns of racial discrimination were most rigid in the white-settler colonies of eastern and southern Africa.

30-5b Religious and Political Changes

Traditional religious belief could not explain the dislocations that foreign rule, migrations, and sudden economic changes brought to the lives of Africans. Many therefore turned to Christianity or Islam.

Christianity was introduced into Africa by Western missionaries, except in Ethiopia, where it was indigenous. It was most successful in West and South Africa, where the European influence was strongest. A major attraction of the Christian denominations was their mission schools, which taught both craft skills and basic literacy, providing access to employment as minor functionaries, teachers, and shopkeepers. These schools educated a new elite, many of whom learned not only skills and literacy but Western political ideas as well. Yet very few students continued their education to the university level. Many Africans accepted Christianity enthusiastically, reading the suffering of their own peoples into the biblical stories of Moses and the parables of Jesus. The churches trained some pupils to become catechists, teachers, and clergymen. Independent Christian churches associated Christian beliefs with radical ideas of racial equality and participation in politics.

Islam spread inland from the East African coast and southward from the Sahel (**SAH-hel**) through the influence and example of Arab and African merchants. Islam also emphasized literacy—in Arabic rather than a European language—and was less disruptive of traditional African customs such as polygamy. In some areas, such as Somalia, Sudan, and Mali, certain Muslim Sufi brotherhoods became associated with resistance to European imperialism.

In Dakar in Senegal and Cape Town in South Africa, small numbers of Africans could obtain secondary education. Even smaller numbers went on to college in Europe or America. Though few in number, they became the leaders of political movements. The contrast between the liberal

◀ **A Quranic School**
In Muslim countries, religious education is centered on learning to read, write, and recite the Quran, the sacred book of the Islamic religion, in the original Arabic. This picture shows boys in a Libyan madrasa (Quranic school) studying writing and religion. Olivier Martel/Getty Images

Section Review

- Colonial rule developed Africa's economies at the expense of its peoples' livelihoods and health.

- Many Africans turned to Christianity or Islam; some, especially those who participated in World War II, began to demand independence.

- The new media were not widely used in Africa.

Blaise Diagne Senegalese political leader. He was the first African elected to the French National Assembly. During World War I, in exchange for promises to give French citizenship to Senegalese, he helped recruit Africans to serve in the French army. After the war, he led a movement to abolish forced labor in Africa.

African National Congress An organization dedicated to obtaining equal voting and civil rights for black inhabitants of South Africa. Founded in 1912 as the South African Native National Congress, it changed its name in 1923. Though it was banned and its leaders were jailed for many years, it eventually helped bring majority rule to South Africa.

Haile Selassie Emperor of Ethiopia (r. 1930–1974) and symbol of African independence. He fought the Italian invasion of his country in 1935 and regained his throne during World War II, when British forces expelled the Italians. He ruled Ethiopia as a traditional autocracy until he was overthrown in 1974.

ideas imparted by Western education and the realities of racial discrimination under colonial rule contributed to the rise of nationalism among educated Africans. In Senegal **Blaise Diagne** (dee-AHN-yuh) agitated for African participation in politics and fair treatment in the French army during World War I, and in the 1920s J. E. Casely Hayford began organizing a movement for greater autonomy in British West Africa. These nationalist movements were inspired by the ideas of Pan-Africanists from America such as W. E. B. Du Bois and Marcus Garvey, who advocated the unity of African peoples around the world, as well as by European ideas of liberty and nationhood. To defend the interests of Africans, Western-educated lawyers and journalists in South Africa founded the **African National Congress** in 1912. Before World War II, however, these nationalist movements were small and had little influence.

The Second World War had a profound effect on the peoples of Africa, even those far removed from the theaters of war. The war brought hardships, such as increased forced labor, inflation, and requisitions of raw materials. Yet it also brought hope. During the campaign to oust the Italians from Ethiopia, Emperor **Haile Selassie** (HI-lee seh-LASS-ee) (r. 1930–1974) led his own troops into Addis Ababa, his capital, and reclaimed his title. A million Africans served as soldiers and carriers in Burma, North Africa, and Europe, where many became aware of Africa's role in helping the Allied war effort. They listened to Allied propaganda in favor of European liberation movements and against Nazi racism and returned to their countries with new and radical ideas.

30-5c Africa and the New Media

South Africa saw the first attempts at radio broadcasting in 1924, but these enjoyed very little success until the South African Broadcasting Corporation was established with monopolistic control over the medium in 1936. Down to World War II it broadcast only in English and Afrikaans. Most efforts in other colonies, such as Mozambique and Kenya, likewise targeted European listeners. The exception was British West Africa—Sierra Leone, Ghana, and Nigeria—where African languages were used. Rather than wireless service, subscribers had loudspeakers in their homes that were connected by wire to the radio station. After 1936 the British authorities generally began to see radio as a medium for reaching Africans who did not understand English.

Africa had almost no cinematic presence prior to World War II, apart from fourteen stereotype-filled Tarzan films made in Hollywood between 1918 and 1949. A few films were made for British and Afrikaner audiences in South Africa, but the French issued a decree in 1934 prohibiting the shooting of movies.

30-6 Conclusion

The First and Second World Wars and the intervening period of economic depression, fascism, and militarism constituted the great dramas of the first half of the twentieth century. But not all parts of the world experienced these convulsions to the same degree. Moreover, these narratives of world war, global depression, and varying regional development do not incorporate the profound changes in ways of living that affected most parts of the world between 1900 and 1950.

While participating in many of these changes, the nonindustrialized nations also had their own technological breakthroughs, such as the rickshaw, and did not use some inventions, such as electricity, in the same way as the West. New media such as cinema and radio were used in different ways as well and sometimes perpetuated themes and images from local cultural sources. At the same time, traditional patterns of village life began to erode as cities grew and urban life, at least for the privileged classes, took on the demeanor and attitudes of Europe. But becoming like Europe did not mean coming to like Europe.

To a much greater degree, the industrialized world experienced a flood of new inventions—automobiles, electric lights, radios, movies, airplanes—that stimulated not only a broader respect for science, but also an expectation that science would continue indefinitely to improve human lives. This was the cult of the modern. Technology even affected the arts, providing new materials for architecture and furniture design, new electronic means of amplifying and distributing music, and an ever-expanding array of tools for making and reproducing images, both still and moving. Yet the devastating human tragedies of war and depression also encouraged currents of nihilism, despair, and questioning of faith.

Imperialism being focused, as always, on benefits for the home country and disdain for native peoples with darker skins, colonial administrators in different parts of the world tried to control the flow of global technological and ideological changes. Having a larger and better-educated middle class than many other non-European lands, India entered more fully into the new ways of living than did sub-Saharan Africa. Latin America, with many European immigrants, was closer economically and ideologically to Europe. Political and cultural independence became a realizable goal in India, where Mahatma Gandhi's nonviolent movement pioneered an entirely new form of political activism. In sub-Saharan Africa, however, European racism and the unwavering favoritism shown to European settlers stifled almost all attempts at change.

Key Terms

Auguste and Louis
  Lumière p. 780
Margaret Sanger p. 783
Max Planck p. 783
Albert Einstein p. 783
Sigmund Freud p. 783
Pablo Picasso p. 784
Igor Stravinsky p. 784
Dada p. 784

Wilbur and Orville
  Wright p. 784
KLM Royal Dutch Airlines
  p. 784
Marie Curie p. 784
Baron Pierre de Coubertin
  p. 786
Le Corbusier p. 787

Indian National Congress
  p. 789
Bengal p. 789
All-India Muslim League
  p. 790
Mohandas K. Gandhi p. 791
Jawaharlal Nehru p. 793
Muhammad Ali Jinnah
  p. 794

Lázaro Cárdenas p. 795
Hipólito Irigoyen p. 795
Getulio Vargas p. 796
Juan Perón p. 797
Eva Duarte Perón p. 797
Blaise Diagne p. 800
African National Congress
  p. 800
Haile Selassie p. 800

Review Questions

1. How does the Indian independence movement and the relations between Great Britain and India compare to the relations between Great Britain and its North American colonies leading up to our Revolutionary War?

2. Which had a greater impact on world history, the Industrial Revolution of the eighteenth and early nineteenth centuries or the coming of commercial electricity and the automobile in the late nineteenth century?

3. How does Latin American dependency on foreign business compare with the relationship of that region's Spanish and Portuguese colonies with the overseas overlords in the sixteenth and seventeenth centuries?

 MINDTAP From Cengage MindTap® is a fully online, personalized learning experience built upon Cengage Learning content. MindTap® combines student learning tools—readings, multimedia, activities, and assessments—into a singular Learning Path that guides students through the course and helps students develop the critical thinking, analysis, and communication skills that are essential to academic and professional success.

Material Culture
Roads

Places where people live and work have paths leading to them. Places where people migrate across grasslands and deserts are poetically called "trackless wastes" because they lack fixed paths. Thus the history of pathways, whether dirt tracks, paved roads, or railway lines, mirrors both the evolution of human activity and changes in the technology of road building and maintenance in relation to varying means of transportation.

Large animals break paths across rough, mountainous, or heavily overgrown territory in seasonal migrations or in search of water, salt, or spots where rivers can be easily crossed. Groups of early humans doubtless took advantage of those paths and broke new ones of their own in lands that they first explored in the process of settling the globe. Ages before the invention of vehicles, therefore, humans established a network of pathways that, in many instances, evolved into roads. Tool-making played an important role in this, both by enabling people to clear away trees and obstacles and by identifying sources of raw materials, such as flint and obsidian for crafting stone tools, as pathway destinations.

Human muscle power for walking, running, and dragging loads shaped this communication network for tens of thousands of years before animal power began to be used, in some regions, around 10,000 years ago. In regions where Neolithic communities created more or less permanent settlements, new paths were created to link the settlements. Animal-drawn sledges were probably the first vehicles, but these would have been used only over short distances. The pack animals that carried loads over longer distances would have used the same paths as humans.

With urban civilization came planned roads and bridges. The Incan road system was as sophisticated as that of the Romans, even though the latter were paved. Stone pavements allowed Rome's legions to march efficiently from one part of their empire to another, as did Incan suspension bridges. Imperial warfare justified paying for and maintaining these networks.

Wheeled vehicles appeared in the fourth millennium BCE, but they did not link easily with the pathways. Some were too steep and included steps. Some had obstructions that a human or a pack animal could maneuver around, but not a cart. Some were not consistently level or wide enough. Thus a distinction arose between foot-paths and vehicular roads.

Paying to build a road suitable for vehicles was always a challenge, particularly when it traversed a series of private properties or separate government jurisdictions. Maintaining the road posed an even greater problem. As traffic increased and vehicles became heavier through improvements in harnessing multiple animal teams, iron-rimmed wheels became increasingly destructive. Hard paving blocks cracked and developed grooves; gravel sprayed to the sides as carriages passed. Except where tolls were required for passage, drivers ignored the damage they were inflicting and moved on while people living by the roadside saw no need to repair a road surface that they had not themselves damaged.

Down to the nineteenth century the designers of wheeled vehicles far surpassed road designers in skill and imagination. Throughout the world most roads were surfaced by dirt or gravel, deeply rutted, dusty in dry weather, and seas of mud when the rains fell. Prosperous towns and cities might lay cobblestones, wooden setts, or bricks; but the idea that cross-country public roads should be a collective responsibility did not fit with most theories of government.

Bad roads were a major problem for inventors tinkering with putting steam engines on wheels. The engines were heavy, and a breakdown caused by a rutted highway could be catastrophic. The solution that emerged in the early nineteenth century involved putting the engine on a mine car and using it to pull a trainload of coal from British coalmines. Miners had been using rails, first wooden and then iron, to move ore within the mines since 1500. A steam railway simply moved this technology into the daylight.

Using rails to control a locomotive's direction raised a new problem, however. The existing road network used by carriages, stagecoaches, and freight wagons had steep hills and sharp curves that rails could not manage. Moreover, rails and rail-beds needed constant maintenance. Hence, it was necessary for railway builders to own the railroad right-of-way.

The network of railroad lines that became the focus of capitalist investment throughout the nineteenth century created a transportation grid that differed in many ways from the historically evolved road system. Cities were redesigned around rail depots and railway yards. Towns that had been well serviced by roads were bypassed by train lines. Rail transport restructured national economies and overturned military plans that had long depended on marching troops to the battlefield.

The spread of the automobile turned attention back to carriage roads. Asphalt and concrete steadily replaced dirt and gravel, and the World War I era saw governments assuming public responsibility for road building and maintenance. The super-highway systems that began with Germany's autobahns in the 1930s combined features of railways and automobile routes. Hills were leveled, turns made more gradual, and controlled exit and entrance points were few and far apart. High speed traffic and long-distance trucking benefited, but many locales languished economically when the route of an interstate passed them by.

As superhighway development pushed through the center of cities, further disruption occurred. Railway stations and the lines of steel that fed them became obsolete while maze-like highway interchanges occupied vast acreage and cut neighborhoods off from one another.

Further revolutions in transport seem to lie in store for the near future. Self-driving vehicles may dramatically change the experience of traveling, affecting everything from the thrill of being fast and reckless to the delight of just driving around instead of entering the address of a specific destination. The movie car chase may become as quaint as the sheriff's posse chasing outlaws on horseback.

Questions for Analysis

1. How did railways reshape urban geography?
2. Is increased speed always a desirable objective in transport design?
3. Since walking and carrying loads satisfied early humans for ten of thousands of years, what prompted them to turn to other modes of transport?

Source: Richard W. Bulliet, *The Wheel: Inventions and Reinventions* (New York: Columbia University Press, 2016).

Issues in World History
Famines and Politics

Human history is filled with tales of famines—times when crops failed, food supplies ran out, and people starved.

Natural Famines

India, dependent on the monsoon rains, has been particularly prone to such calamities, with famines striking two to four times a century, whenever the rains fail for several years in succession. Three times in the eighteenth century famines killed several million people. The nineteenth century was worse, with famines in 1803–1804, 1837–1838, 1868–1870, and 1876–1878. The famine of 1876–1878 also afflicted northern China, causing between 9 and 13 million deaths from hunger and from the diseases of malnutrition. There were even incidents of cannibalism, as starving adults ate starving children.

When drought hit a region, it decimated not only the human population but also the animals they relied on to transport crops or plow the land. When water levels dropped in rivers and canals, food could not be transported by boat to areas where people were starving.

Commercial Famines

That all changed in the nineteenth century. Railroads and steamships could transport foodstuffs quickly across great distances, regardless of the weather. Great Britain, for example, became dependent on imports of wheat and beef. Yet the global death toll from starvation has been far higher since the mid-nineteenth century than ever before. Why?

Consider Ireland. By the early nineteenth century the potato, a crop introduced from the Americas, had become the main source of nutrition for the Irish people. Potatoes grew abundantly and produced more calories per acre than any other crop, allowing the population to increase dramatically.

In 1845 a blight turned the potatoes in the fields black, mushy, and inedible. The harvest was ruined the following year as well. It recovered slightly in 1847 but was bad again in 1848. Tens of thousands died of starvation, while hundreds of thousands died from dysentery, typhus, or cholera. Travelers saw corpses rotting in their hovels or on the sides of roads. Altogether, a million or more people died, while another million emigrated, reducing the population of Ireland by half.

Throughout those years, Ireland exported wheat to England, where people had money to pay for it. Food cost money, and the Irish, poor even before the famines, were destitute and could not afford to buy wheat or bread. The British government was convinced that interfering with the free market would only make things worse. Relief efforts were half-hearted at best; the official responsible for Irish affairs preferred to leave the situation to "the operation of natural causes."

The same held true in India, like Ireland a colony of Great Britain. The drought of 1876–1878 killed over 5 million Indians in the Deccan region, while British officials stood by helpless or indifferent. Part of the problem was transportation. In the 1870s most goods were still transported in bullock carts, but the bullocks starved during the drought. Another obstacle was political. The idea that a government should be responsible for feeding the population was unthinkable at the time. And so, while millions were starving in the Deccan, the Punjab was exporting wheat to Britain.

Over the next twenty years, so-called famine railways were built in the regions historically most affected by the failures of the monsoon. When drought struck again at the end of the century, the railways were ready to transport food to areas that had previously been accessible only by bullock carts. However, the inhabitants of the affected regions had no money with which to buy what little food there was, and the government was still reluctant to interfere with free enterprise. Grain merchants bought all the stocks, hoarded them until the price rose, then used the railways to transport them out of the famine regions to regions where the harvests were better and people had more money.

In the twentieth century, commercial famines became rare as governments realized that they had a responsibility to provide food not only for their own people but also for people in other countries. Yet commercial famines have not entirely disappeared. In 1974, when a catastrophic flood covered half of Bangladesh, the government was too disorganized to distribute its stocks of rice, while merchants bought what they could and exported it to India. Thousands died, and thousands more survived only because of belated shipments of food from donor countries.

Political Famines

To say that governments are responsible for food supplies does not mean that they exercise that responsibility for the good of the people. Some do, but in many instances food is used as a weapon. In the twentieth century global food supplies were always adequate for the population of the world, and transportation was seldom a problem. Yet the century witnessed the most murderous famines ever recorded.

As commercial famines declined, war famines became common. The destruction or requisitioning of crops caused famines in the Russian civil war of 1921–1922, the Japanese occupation of Indochina in 1942–1945, and the Biafran war in Nigeria in 1967–1969.

In 1942 the Japanese army had conquered Burma, a rich rice-producing colony. Food supplies in Bengal, which imported rice from Burma, dropped by 5 percent. As prices began to rise, merchants bought stocks of rice and held them in the hope that prices would continue to increase. Sharecroppers sold their stocks to pay off their debts to landlords and village moneylenders. Meanwhile, the railroads that in peace-time would have carried food from other parts of India were fully occupied with military traffic. By the time Viceroy Lord Wavell ordered the army to transport food to Bengal in October 1943, between 1.5 and 2 million Bengalis had died.

Worst of all were the famines caused by deliberate government policies. The most famous was the famine of 1932–1933 caused by Stalin's collectivization of agriculture. The Communists tried to force the peasants to give up their land and livestock and join collectives, where they could be made to work harder and provide food for the growing cities and industries. When the peasants resisted, their crops were seized. Millions were sent to prison camps, and millions of others died of starvation.

An even worse famine took place in China from 1958 to 1961 during the "Great Leap Forward" (see Chapter 32). Communist Party Chairman Mao Zedong decided to hasten the transformation of China into a communist state by relying not on the expertise of economists and technocrats but on the enthusiasm of the masses. Farms were consolidated into huge communes. Peasants were told to make steel out of household utensils in backyard furnaces. The harvest of 1959 was poor, and later ones were even worse. The amount of grain per person declined from 452 pounds (205 kilograms) in 1957 to 340 pounds (154 kilograms) in 1961. Since the Central Statistical Bureau had been shut down, the central government was unaware of the shortages and demanded ever higher requisitions of food to feed the army and urban and industrial workers and to export to the Soviet Union to pay off China's debts. The amount of food left to the farmers was between one-fifth and one-half of their usual subsistence diet. From 1958 to 1961 between 20 and 30 million Chinese are estimated to have starved or died of the diseases of malnutrition. It was the worst famine in the history of the world. Mao denied its existence.

Nothing quite as horrible has happened since the Great Leap Forward. During the droughts in Africa in the 1970s and 1980s, most people in the affected regions received international food aid. However, to crush rebellions, the governments of Ethiopia and Sudan denied that their people were hungry and prevented food shipments from reaching drought victims.

In the world today, natural disasters are as frequent as ever, and many countries are vulnerable to food shortages. No one now claims that governments have no business providing food to the starving. Though food is not equitably distributed, there is enough for all human beings now, and there will be enough for the foreseeable future. However, humanitarian feelings compete with other political agendas, and the spectre of politically motivated famines still stalks the world.

Questions for Analysis

1. Should international food relief be donated purely on the basis of need, or should political considerations play a role?
2. Should American food supplies go exclusively to foreign countries experiencing famine, or is adequate nutrition a domestic right as well?
3. Should measures other than food donation be imposed by international agencies to fight famine in areas of political unrest?

Multiple-Choice Questions

Questions 1–4 refer to the passage below.

"At the dawn of history India started on her unending quest, and trackless centuries are filled with her striving and the grandeur of her success and her failures. . . . And so we have to labour and to work, and work hard, to give reality to our dreams. Those dreams are for India, but they are also for the world, for all the nations and peoples are too closely knit together today for any one of them to imagine that it can live apart. Peace has been said to be indivisible; so is freedom, so is prosperity now, and so also is disaster in this one world that can no longer be split into isolated fragments."

Jawaharlal Nehru, *Speech Celebrating India's Independence*, 1947

1. In his speech, Nehru is celebrating India's independence from

   (A) economic depression.

   (B) military dictatorship.

   (C) colonial oppression.

   (D) totalitarian regime.

2. Indian independence in 1947 is evidence of which of the following?

   (A) India replaced Great Britain as the most powerful empire in Asia.

   (B) Marxism was widely utilized in South Asia and became the dominant political system for the new nations that emerged after the war.

   (C) Europe lost political influence but remained the dominant economic power in many regions after World War II.

   (D) Global conflict contributed to decolonization in various regions around the world.

3. Nehru's predecessor, Mohandas Gandhi, believed that Indian independence could be gained through

   (A) nonviolent resistance.

   (B) strong isolationist policies.

   (C) the formal British legal system.

   (D) military attacks.

4. Which of the following would be an argument that South Asia did not truly achieve unity after independence?

   (A) The British Empire still controlled much of the Indian Ocean region.

   (B) The colony of India split into multiple nations in 1947.

   (C) Religion remained an important part of life in South Asia.

   (D) Indian democracy was dominated by multiple political parties.

Questions 5–7 refer to the image below.

ETPM1292324   Argentina: August 3, 1952. People of Argentine mourning the death of Eva Peron , pay tribute in a night demonstration before an outsize portrait of the deceased wife of their nation's president . In their hands they hold lighted torches. ©TopFoto/ The Image Works   NOTE: The copyright notice must include "The Image Works" DO NOT SHORTEN THE NAME OF THE COMPANY   ©TopFoto/ The Image Works

▲ **People of Argentina Mourning the Death of Eva Peron, 1952**
TopFoto/The Image Works

5. The photograph above is evidence that the Perons

   (A) were strong allies of the United States.

   (B) were supported primarily by the military.

   (C) were despised by the Catholic Church.

   (D) enjoyed strong populist support.

6. Which of the following best explains the popularity of the Perons?

   (A) Their desire to return Argentina to an agricultural economy

   (B) Their tax policies that favored the wealthy and U.S. corporations

   (C) Their strong support for the working poor

   (D) Their willingness to make Catholicism the official state religion

7. Argentina under the Perons, like many socialist states around the world, attempted to

(A) redistribute land and wealth.

(B) promote the sale of land to international corporations.

(C) encourage the Catholic Church to control education.

(D) support movements to erase national borders.

Questions 8–10 refer to the image below.

▲ **Lumière Brothers Camera** The Art Archive/Musée Français de la Photographie Bievres/Gianni Dagli Orti

8. The movie camera in the photograph led to which of the following?

(A) State control of film throughout the world

(B) A new way to communicate and inform

(C) Use for entertainment only

(D) Limited popularity among the working classes

9. A direct result of the invention of the movie camera was

(A) a contribution to the development of consumerism.

(B) an increase in barriers between linguistic and political groups.

(C) the weakening of national economies.

(D) its replacing all other forms of communication.

10. Which of the following would be an argument against the idea that film created a truly global culture?

(A) Film has been used by religions to spread their beliefs.

(B) Film allowed people all over the world to experience the same ideas and images.

(C) Film was used to promote and strengthen local dialects and culture.

(D) Film was used by Marxists to spread the workers' revolution.

Short-Answer Questions

1. The modern world brought many changes to people's lives. Based on your knowledge of world history, answer all parts of the question that follows with regard to scientific and technological developments.

(A) Describe ONE reason for the increase in innovation in the West in the twentieth century.

(B) Explain ONE effect of new scientific or technological developments on life in the twentieth century.

(C) Explain ANOTHER effect of new scientific or technological developments on life in the twentieth century.

2. Answer all parts of the question that follows.

Choose ONE of the following regions
- South Asia
- Latin America

(A) Identify ONE action or policy used to attain its political goals in the middle of the twentieth century.

(B) Explain ONE way the two regions' political goals were similar.

(C) Explain ONE way the two regions' political goals were different.

PART VIII

Perils and Promises of a Global Community, 1945 to the Present

▲ **Satellite Photograph of the Globe** Photography from space revolutionized mapping, making physical features more important than political boundaries and clearly displaying transient features, such as cloud coverage and storm patterns. In this photograph the distinctive whorl of a tropical storm is visible off the east coast of Japan. More specialized photographic techniques are used to appraise natural resources and environmental problems. Earth Imaging/Getty Images

After World War II, an increasingly interconnected world faced new hopes and fears. The United Nations promoted international cooperation, global trade expanded, and colonies gained independence. Simultaneously, the "Cold War" developed between the United States and the Soviet Union as they competed for global economic and political influence. This tension led to a new round of widespread conflicts, proxy wars, and nuclear stalemate. Terrorism and nuclear proliferation superseded earlier conflicts; the 9/11 attacks by Muslim extremists triggered an American-led "global war on terrorism."

Following World War II, industrialized nations recovered quickly and development continued to spread across the globe. In Africa and other poor regions, however, population growth often offset economic gains. Although the Green Revolution and genetic engineering alleviated much world hunger, industrial growth and automobile use increased pollution. Global warming and other environmental concerns drew international attention.

Globalization affected culture as well, as the Internet and the emergence of English as the global language improved international communication but stimulated fears that cultural diversity could be lost. ●

Environment	Culture	State Building	Economics	Social Structures
• Impact of environmental factors, disease, and technology on migration and settlement (Deforestation)	• Origins, beliefs, development, economic/social/political impact, and spread of major religions, philosophies, and belief systems (Anti-imperialism)	• Changes and continuities of the creation and maintenance of forms, functions, and institutions of governance (Communism, Marxism, state-controlled economies)	• Impact of technology on economic production and globalization	• Impact of kinship, ethnicity, class, gender, and race on social hierarchies
• Impact of migration, population, and urbanization on environment (Green Revolution, global pollution)	• Effect of cross-cultural interactions on diffusion of technology and scientific knowledge (Medical innovation)	• Impact of economic, social, cultural, and geographical factors on state building, expansion, and dissolution (Cold War)	• Causes/effects of economic strategies of different types of communities, states, and empires (Non-Aligned Movement)	• Impact of ideologies, philosophies, and religions on social hierarchies (Nonviolence)
• Interaction between environment and development of technology, industrialization, transportation, and exchange/communication networks	• Effect of technological and scientific innovation on religions, belief systems, philosophies, and ideologies over time (Medical innovation)	• Impact of internal/external political factors on state building, expansion, and dissolution (Anti-imperialism, genocide)	• Development and change of modes and locations of production over time	• Challenges and confirmations of legal systems, colonialism, nationalism, and independence movements on class, gender, and racial hierarchies over time (Postcolonial independence)
	• Reflection and impact of society in the arts (Propaganda, war critiques)	• Interaction between states and state-less societies (Global interdependency)	• Cause/effect of labor reform movement	• Interaction between specialized labor systems and social hierarchies
	• Impact of expanding exchange networks on transregional culture such as music, literature, and visual art (popular culture)	• Political/economic interaction between states and non-state actors	• Influence of trade on development of ideologies, values, and institutions on each other	• Maintenance of or challenges to social categories, roles, and practices (Popular protests)
			• Influence and impact of local, regional, and global economic systems and exchange networks on each other (Oil, nuclear power)	• Impact of political, economic, cultural, and demographic factors on social structures

Key Concept 6.1

- How did advancements in science and technology (including the Green Revolution) spread globally?
- How did human actions affect the environment both positively and negatively?
- How did disease, scientific innovation, and conflict lead to demographic shifts?

Key Concept 6.2

- How did global political order change from the mid-nineteenth century to the mid-twentieth century?
- How did anti-imperialism ideologies contribute to the restructuring of states?
- What demographic and social consequences followed major political changes?
- How did the Cold War redefine the global balance of power?
- How did individuals and groups oppose or intensify conflict in the twentieth century?

Key Concept 6.3

- In what different ways did states respond to the economic challenges of the twentieth century?
- How did states and communities become increasingly interdependent, and how did institutions of global governance contribute to this interdependence?
- How were traditional understandings of race, class, gender, and religion challenged and redefined, especially with regard to education, political participation, and professional roles?
- How have popular and consumer culture become more global?

The Cold War and Decolonization, 1945–1975

31

AP® Framework Terms

Green Revolution
Nuclear power
Oil
Cold War
North Atlantic Treaty Organization (NATO)
Warsaw Pact
Martin Luther King, Jr.
Nelson Mandela
Nonaligned nations

Overarching Questions

1 How have religions, belief systems, philosophies, and ideologies affected the political, economic, and social development of societies? (CUL)

2 How have different forms of governance been constructed and maintained over time and how have functions and institutions of governance changed over time? (SB)

3 How and why have economic, social, cultural, and geographic factors influenced the process of state building, expansion, and dissolution? (SB)

4 How has technology shaped economic production and globalization over time? (ECON)

5 How have local, regional, and global economic systems and exchange networks influenced each other over time? (ECON)

O n January 1, 1959, thirty-two-year-old Fidel Castro entered Havana, Cuba, after having successfully defeated the dictatorship of Fulgencio Batista **(ful-HEHN-see-oh bah-TEES-tah)**. Castro had initiated his revolution in 1953 with an attack on a military barracks, but the attack failed. At his trial, Castro put on a spirited defense that he later published as *History Will Absolve Me*. He proclaimed his objectives as the restoration of Cuban democracy and an ambitious program of social and economic reforms designed to ameliorate the effects of underdevelopment.

On September 26, 1960, Castro addressed the United Nations General Assembly. American resistance to Castro's revolutionary policies had already provoked confrontations. In his speech, Castro offered a broad internationalist and anti-imperialist criticism of the world's developed nations and of the United Nations. He criticized the role of the United Nations in the Congo, suggesting that it had supported Colonel Mobutu Sese Seko, a client of imperialism, rather than Patrice Lumumba, identified by the United States as a dangerous radical. He also strongly supported the independence struggle of the Algerians against the French.

In this speech, Castro outlined an ambitious program of new revolutionary reforms in Cuba, claiming that the United States had supported the Batista dictatorship to protect American investors. Once back in Cuba, Castro

▲ **Fidel Castro Arrives in Havana**   Castro and his supporters overthrew a brutal dictatorship and began the revolutionary transformation of Cuba that led to a confrontation with the United States. Bettmann/Getty Images

pressed ahead with economic reforms that included concentrating power in the hands of his closest allies and nationalizing most American investments. Cuba became a flash point in the Cold War when the United States tried and failed to overthrow Castro in 1961. Castro declared himself to be a socialist and forged an economic and military alliance with the Soviet Union that led in 1962 to the Cuban missile crisis.

The intensity of the Cold War, with its accompanying threat of nuclear destruction, obscured a postwar phenomenon of more enduring importance. The colonial empires were overthrown, and Western power and influence declined in Asia, Africa, and Latin America. The leaders who headed these new nations were sometimes able to use Cold War antagonisms to their own advantage when they forced the Soviet Union and the United States to compete in supplying economic and military assistance. Some, like Castro, became frontline participants in this struggle, but most leaders of emerging nations focused on nation building.

Each former colony had its own history and followed its own route to independence. Thus these new nations had difficulty finding a collective voice in a world increasingly oriented toward two superpowers, the United States and the Soviet Union. Some former colonies sided openly with one or the other, while others banded together in a posture

AP® Exam Tip
Explain the development of the Cold War following World War II.

of neutrality. All spoke with one voice about their need for economic and technical assistance and the obligation of the wealthy nations to satisfy those needs.

Even as the Cold War military rivalry led to extraordinary advances in weaponry and associated technologies, many new nations faced basic problems of educating their citizens, nurturing industry, and escaping the economic constraints imposed by their former imperialist masters. To meet the needs of rapidly growing populations, new national governments in Africa, Asia, and the Middle East rushed to open natural resources to exploitation. In this rush for development, few governments anticipated the environmental consequences of modernization. In most cases deforestation and environmental degradation were the all-too-predictable results. ●

AP® Exam Tip
Consider the new military alliances, such as NATO and the Warsaw Pact, that developed as a result of the Cold War. Explain how these alliances had global impact.

31-1 The Cold War

What were the major threats to world peace during the Cold War?

Since the era of labor unrest that accompanied the Industrial Revolution (see Chapter 25), the political and economic elites of Europe and the United States had viewed the supporters of socialism and communism as threats to free markets and private property. The Russian Revolution as well as the destabilizing economic and political effects of the Great Depression heightened these fears. The wartime alliance between the United States, Great Britain, and the Soviet Union had only temporarily shelved these deeply held antagonisms and fears in order to defeat fascism, rather than resolving them permanently. With the defeat of Germany, however, growing Soviet assertiveness in Europe and communist insurgencies in China and elsewhere confirmed to Western leaders that the threat of worldwide revolution remained their chief challenge.

Western leaders viewed the Soviet Union as the sponsor of world revolution and as the military power most likely to launch a war as destructive and terrible as the one recently ended. As early as 1946 Great Britain's wartime leader, Winston Churchill, said in a speech in Missouri, "From Stettin in the Baltic to Trieste in the Adriatic, an iron curtain has descended across the Continent. . . . I am convinced there is nothing they [the communists] so much admire as strength, and there is nothing for which they have less respect than weakness, especially military weakness." The phrase "**iron curtain**" became a watchword of the **Cold War**, the state of political tension and military rivalry then beginning between the United States and its allies and the Soviet Union and its allies.

In this era of heightened tension, each side viewed every action by its rival a direct existential threat. Fearful of growing Soviet power, the United States and the nations of western Europe established a military alliance in 1949, the **North Atlantic Treaty Organization (NATO)**. The nations of the alliance pledged to treat an attack on any member as an attack on their own territory. Soviet leaders, struggling to recover from the terrible losses sustained in the war against the Axis, responded by creating their own military alliance, the **Warsaw Pact**, to pursue the same objectives in 1955. These treaty commitments meant that any military conflict involving members of the two nuclear-armed alliances would escalate quickly into a generalized war that put the very survival of the human race at risk. The chief effects were to create a decades-long geopolitical stalemate in Europe while relocating armed conflicts over these competing ideological futures to the peripheries of the alliances' spheres of influence in Africa, Asia, and Latin America.

31-1a The United Nations

In 1944 representatives from the United States, Great Britain, the Soviet Union, and China drafted proposals that led to a treaty called the United Nations Charter, ratified on October 24, 1945. Like the earlier League of Nations, the **United Nations** had two main bodies: the General Assembly, with representatives from all member states, and the Security Council, with five permanent members—China (the anticommunist Chinese government based in Taiwan until

iron curtain Winston Churchill's term for the Cold War division between the Soviet-dominated East and the U.S.-dominated West. The term suggested that communist nations were, in effect, prisons.

Cold War The ideological struggle between communism (Soviet Union) and capitalism (United States) for world influence. The Cold War came to an end when the Soviet Union dissolved in 1991.

North Atlantic Treaty Organization (NATO) Organization formed in 1949 as a military alliance of western European and North American states against the Soviet Union and its east European allies.

Warsaw Pact The 1955 treaty binding the Soviet Union and the socialist countries of eastern Europe in an alliance against the North Atlantic Treaty Organization.

United Nations International organization founded in 1945 to promote world peace and cooperation. It replaced the League of Nations.

CHRONOLOGY

	Cold War	Decolonization
1945	1947–1948 Soviet blockade of Berlin 1949 NATO formed	1947 Partition of India 1949 Dutch withdraw from Indonesia

1950	1950–1953 Korean War
	1952 United States detonates first hydrogen bomb
	1954 Jacobo Arbenz over-thrown in Guatemala,
	    supported by CIA
		1954 CIA intervention in Guatemala; defeat at Dienbienphu
		    ends French control of Vietnam

1955	1955 Warsaw Pact created
	1956 Soviet Union suppresses Hungarian revolt
	1957 Soviet Union launches first artificial satellite into
	    earth orbit
		1955 Bandung Conference
		1957 Ghana becomes first British colony in Africa to gain
		    independence
		1959 Triumph of Fidel Castro's revolution in Cuba

1960	1961 East Germany builds Berlin Wall 1961 Bay of Pigs (Cuba) 1962 Cuban missile crisis 1968 Nuclear Non-Proliferation Treaty	1960 Shootings in Sharpeville intensify South African struggle against apartheid; Nigeria becomes independent 1962 Algeria wins independence
1970	1975 Helsinki Accords; end of Vietnam War	1971 Bangladesh secedes from Pakistan

replaced by People's Republic of China in 1971), France, Great Britain, the United States, and the Soviet Union—and seven rotating members. A full-time bureaucracy headed by a Secretary General carried out the organization's day-to-day business and directed agencies focused on specialized international problems—for example, UNICEF (United Nations Children's Emergency Fund), FAO (Food and Agriculture Organization), and UNESCO (United Nations Educational, Scientific and Cultural Organization) (see Environment & Technology: The Green Revolution). Unlike the League of Nations, which required unanimous agreement in both deliberative bodies, the United Nations operated by majority vote, except that the five permanent members of the Security Council had veto power in that chamber.

All signatories to the United Nations Charter renounced war and territorial conquest. Nevertheless, peacekeeping, the sole preserve of the Security Council, became a vexing problem as permanent members exercised their vetoes to protect their allies and interests. Throughout the Cold War the United Nations was seldom able to forestall or quell international conflicts, though from time to time it sent observers or peacekeeping forces to monitor truces or other international agreements.

The decolonization of Africa and Asia greatly swelled the size of the General Assembly, but not the Security Council. Many newly independent countries looked to the United Nations for material assistance and access to a wider political world. While the rivalry of the Security Council's permanent members stymied actions that even indirectly touched on Cold War concerns, the General Assembly became an arena for debates over issues like decolonization and development.

In the early years of the United Nations, General Assembly resolutions carried great weight. An example is a 1947 resolution that sought to divide Palestine into sovereign Jewish and Arab states. Gradually, though, the flood of new members produced a voting majority concerned more with poverty, racial discrimination, and the struggle against imperialism than with the Cold War. As a result, Western powers increasingly disregarded the General Assembly, allowing new countries to have their say but effectively preventing any collective action contrary to their interests.

31-1b Capitalism and Communism

In July 1944, with Allied victory inevitable, economic specialists representing over forty countries met at Bretton Woods, a New Hampshire resort, to devise a new international monetary system. The signatories eventually agreed to fix exchange rates and to create the International Monetary Fund (IMF) and World Bank. The IMF used currency reserves from member nations to finance temporary trade deficits, while the **World Bank** provided funds for reconstructing Europe and helping needy countries after the war.

AP® Exam Tip
Compare the League of Nations and the United Nations.

World Bank A specialized agency of the United Nations that makes loans to countries for economic development, trade promotion, and debt consolidation. Its formal name is the International Bank for Reconstruction and Development.

Environment & Technology
The Green Revolution

Concern about world food supplies appeared with the serious shortages caused by the devastation and trade disruptions of World War II. With the end of the war, feeding the world's fast-growing population provided an immediate challenge to long-established agricultural practices, especially in the developing world. To meet these needs the Food and Agriculture Organization of the United Nations, the Rockefeller Foundation, and the Ford Foundation took leading roles in fostering crop research and agricultural education. In 1966 the International Rice Research Institute (established in 1960–1962) began distributing seeds for an improved rice variety known as IR-8. Crop yields from this and other new varieties, along with improved farming techniques, were initially so impressive, especially in Asia, that a hoped-for new era in agriculture was called the Green Revolution.

After the successful introduction of new rice strains, scientists developed new varieties of corn and wheat. Building on twenty years of Rockefeller-funded research in Mexico, the Centro Internacional de Mejoramiento de Maiz y Trigo (International Center for the Improvement of Maize and Wheat) was established in 1966. This organization soon distributed new varieties of wheat that were resistant to disease and responsive to fertilizer. By 1970 other centers for research on tropical agriculture were established as well.

Despite these advances, experts believed that the success of the Green Revolution required a more comprehensive effort that would mobilize government, foundation, and private-sector resources. The Consultative Group on International Agricultural Research brought together World Bank expertise, private foundations, international organizations, and national foreign aid agencies to undertake worldwide support of efforts to increase food productivity and improve natural resource management. Soon 25 percent of U.S. development assistance and 30 percent of World Bank lending went to agricultural improvements. The combination of innovation and investment led to approximately 2 percent per year in increased agricultural productivity in the 1970s.

Early optimism that these innovations would largely eliminate world hunger has now dissipated. Although crop yields predictably improved as a result of new seeds, improved fertilizers, and irrigation, these improvements were generally too expensive for the poorest farmers to employ. So, enhanced production was easiest to achieve among richer, market-oriented farmers in places with the strongest, best-financed governments. While both Asian and Latin American agriculture became generally more productive, most of the financial benefits were enjoyed by large-scale farmers focused on markets. Small-scale farmers producing mostly subsistence crops were often disadvantaged.

Africa, however, was little affected by these changes, and only today, as Africa faces deepening cycles of famine exacerbated by political instability, is an international effort under way to introduce reforms. Where the Green Revolution's innovations have been the most successful, dependence on patented, costly seed varieties, chemical fertilizers, and irrigation has promoted agricultural consolidation and rewarded large investors, a process that has further impoverished many of the poorest rural residents. This has meant in practice that, as agricultural production has risen, land has been increasingly concentrated in the hands of the rich and the rural poor have been forced to become laborers or migrate to cities.

Questions for Analysis

1. What was the crop improvement that initiated the Green Revolution?
2. Where have the positive effects of these innovations been most visible?
3. Have there been any unforeseen negative consequences from the Green Revolution?

▶ **Miracle Rice** New strains of so-called miracle rice made many nations in South and Southeast Asia self-sufficient in food production. Genetically altered rice is now planted in the Ivory Coast and other African nations. Alexis DUCLOS/Getty Images

AP® Exam Tip
Explain how the Green Revolution and commercial agriculture helped to sustain the earth's growing population.

The Soviet Union attended the Bretton Woods Conference and signed the agreements that went into effect in 1946. But the growing hostility between the Soviet Union and the United States and Britain that would lead to the Cold War undermined cooperation. While the United States held reserves of gold and the rest of the world held reserves of dollars to maintain the stability of the international monetary system, the Soviet Union established a closed monetary system for itself and for allied communist regimes in eastern Europe. In Western countries, supply and demand determined production priorities and prices; in the Soviet command economy, government agencies allocated resources, labor, and goods and even set prices according to governmental priorities, irrespective of market forces.

Many leaders of newly independent states, having won their nation's independence from European colonial powers after years of violent struggle, preferred the Soviet Union's socialist example to the market-oriented capitalism of their former masters. Former colonial powers and the United States sought to promote their own market-based ideas by offering aid packages and technology transfers. In this environment of superpower competition, some developing nations received huge aid packages. Thus, the relative success of economies patterned on Eastern or Western models became part of the Cold War argument. Each side trumpeted the economic successes measured by industrial output, changes in per capita income, and productivity gains associated with their ideological system.

During World War II the U.S. economy escaped the lingering effects of the Great Depression (see Chapter 29) as increased military spending and the military draft raised employment levels and wages. During the war, U.S. factories were converted from the production of consumer goods to weapons. With peace, the pent-up demand for consumer goods led to a period of rapid economic growth and broad prosperity. Europe, still rebuilding from the destruction of the war, at first lagged behind.

World War II had heavily damaged the economy of western Europe. Bombs had flattened cities and destroyed factories, railroads, port facilities, and communication networks. As a result of the war, European populations had lost savings and struggled to find employment. Seeking to forestall the radicalization of European politics and the potential expansion of Soviet influence, the United States decided to financially support the reconstruction of Europe. The **Marshall Plan** and other aid programs provided more than $20 billion to Europe by 1961 (about $158 billion in 2016). European determination backed by American aid spurred recovery, and by 1963 the resurgent European economies had doubled their total 1940 output.

Given that public funds played a crucial role in this process, recovering western European governments sought a greater role in economic management than was common in the United States. In Great Britain, for example, the Labour Party government of the early 1950s nationalized the coal, steel, railroad, and health-care industries. Similarly, the French government nationalized public utilities; the auto, banking, and insurance industries; and parts of the mining industry. These steps provided large infusions of capital for rebuilding and acquiring new technologies and enhanced economic planning.

In 1948 European nations initiated a process of economic cooperation and integration with the creation of the Organisation for European Economic Cooperation (OEEC). They began by cooperating on coal and steel production. Located in disputed border areas, these industries had previously been geopolitical flash points that led to war. With success in these areas, some OEEC countries lowered tariffs with each other to encourage trade. Then in 1957, France, West Germany, Italy, the Netherlands, Belgium, and Luxembourg signed a treaty creating the **European Economic Community**, also known as the **Common Market**. By the 1970s this economic alliance had nearly overtaken the United States in industrial production. Then between 1973 and 1995, Great Britain, Denmark, Greece, Ireland, Spain, Portugal, Finland, Sweden, and Austria joined the alliance, renamed the European Union (EU) in 1993 to reflect growing political integration.

The resulting prosperity brought dramatic changes to the societies of western Europe. Wages increased and social welfare benefits expanded. Governments increased spending on health care, unemployment benefits, old-age pensions, public housing, and grants to poor families, with richer nations like Germany subsidizing the mounting prosperity of poorer nations like Ireland, Spain, Portugal, and Greece. The combination of economic growth and income redistribution raised living standards and fueled demand for consumer goods, leading to the development of a mass consumer society. These benefits would be threatened by the growing health-care and retirement needs of Europe's rapidly aging populations after 2000 (see Chapter 32).

AP® Exam Tip
Compare the economic systems of Western and Eastern bloc states.

Marshall Plan U.S. program to support the reconstruction of western Europe after World War II. By 1961 more than $20 billion in economic aid had been dispersed.

European Economic Community (Common Market) An organization promoting economic unity in Europe, formed in 1957 by consolidation of earlier, more limited, agreements. With the addition of many new nations it became the European Union (EU) in 1993.

The Soviet experience was dramatically different. The rapid economic growth fostered by the Soviet state after 1917 had challenged traditional Western assumptions about economic development and social policy. From the 1920s the Soviet state relied on bureaucratic agencies and political processes to determine the production, distribution, and price of both industrial and agricultural goods as well as natural resources. The government regulated and administered nearly every area of the society, including housing, medical services, retail shops, factories, and the land. Despite many problems and failures, the Soviet state achieved a dramatic expansion in basic industrial production before entering the war.

As in most of western Europe, the economies of the Soviet Union and its eastern European allies were devastated at the end of the Second World War, but they took a different path to reconstruction. The Soviet command economy had enormous natural resources, a large population, and abundant energy at its disposal. It also benefited from the state's large investments in technical and scientific education and heavy industries during the 1930s and war years.

As a result, economic recovery was rapid at first, creating the structural basis for modernization and growth. However, as industrial production throughout the world refocused on consumer goods such as television sets and automobiles rather than coal and steel, the inefficiencies and lack of agility of Soviet bureaucratic control became obvious. By the 1970s the economic gap with the West was undeniable. Soviet industry failed to meet domestic demand for clothing, housing, food, automobiles, and consumer electronics. Worse still, Soviet consumer products were universally uncompetitive with Western products. Similarly, Soviet agricultural production failed to meet even domestic needs, forcing a reliance on imports. More significant still, the Soviet Union fell behind the West in civilian-sector technological innovation, like computers and communication.

31-1c West versus East in Europe and Korea

AP® Exam Tip
Explain how the Cold War created new military alliances such as NATO and the Warsaw Pact.

In Germany, Austria, and Japan, the end of the war meant foreign military occupation and governments controlled by the victors. The Soviet Union initially seemed willing to accept governments in neighboring states that included a mix of parties as long as these governments were not hostile to local communist groups or to the Soviets. In the nations of central and eastern Europe, many remembered the Soviets as enemies of the fascists and were eager to support local communist parties. As relations between the Soviets and the West worsened in the late 1940s, communists gained a series of political victories across eastern and southeastern Europe. In many ways, Soviet leaders were seeking to re-establish traditional Russian spheres of influence as well as buffers between themselves and powerful neighbors. Western leaders saw the emergence of communist regimes in Poland, Czechoslovakia, Hungary, Bulgaria, Romania, Yugoslavia, and Albania, despite their popularity, as a sign of growing Soviet geopolitical aggressiveness.

By 1948 the United States viewed the Soviet Union as an adversary and threat. While the United States had seemed amenable to the Soviet desire for access to the Mediterranean through the Bosporus and Dardanelles straits at war's end, by 1947 it acted to strengthen Turkey and Greece to resist Soviet military pressure as well as defeat local communist political organizations. This decision to hold the line against further Soviet expansion led to the admission of Turkey and Greece to NATO and to the decision to allow West Germany to rearm (see Map 31.1). The Soviets then created the Warsaw Pact in 1955 as a strategic counterweight to NATO.

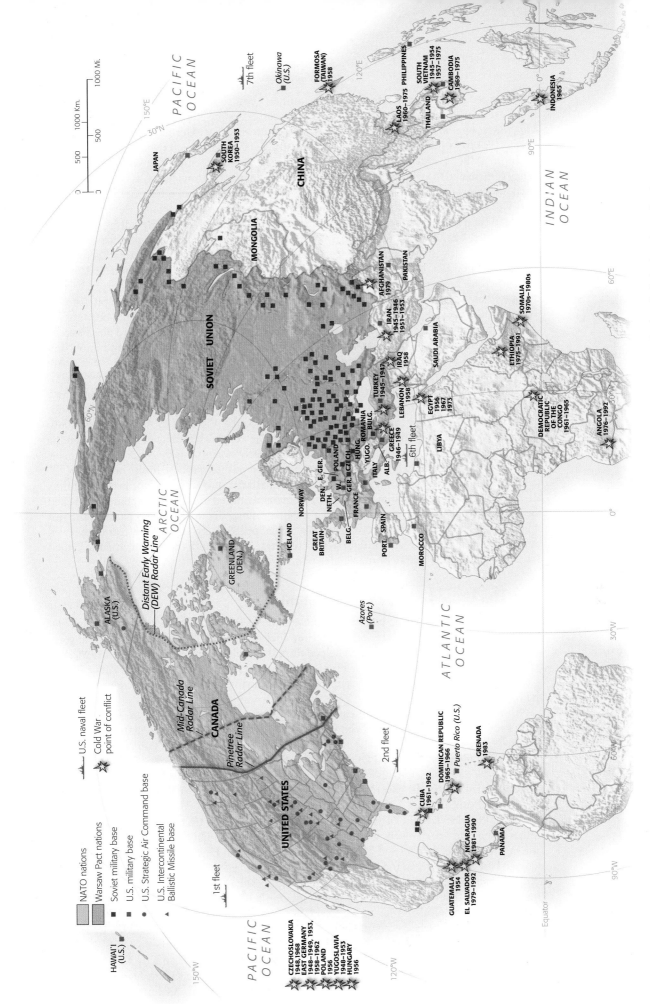

MAP 31.1 Cold War Confrontation A polar projection is shown on this map because Soviet and U.S. strategists planned to attack one another by missile in the polar region, hence the Canadian–American radar lines.

Why were so few of the conflicts of the Cold War period located in the regions where the two alliances directly confronted each other?

NATO nations

Warsaw Pact nations

■ Soviet military base

■ U.S. military base

● U.S. Strategic Air Command base

▲ U.S. Intercontinental Ballistic Missile base

⟶ U.S. naval fleet

✦ Cold War point of conflict

HAWAI'I (U.S.)

CZECHOSLOVAKIA 1948, 1968
EAST GERMANY 1948–1949, 1953, 1958–1962
POLAND 1956
YUGOSLAVIA 1948–1953
HUNGARY 1956

PACIFIC OCEAN

UNITED STATES

1st fleet

2nd fleet

CANADA

Pinetree Radar Line

Mid-Canada Radar Line

Distant Early Warning (DEW) Radar Line

ALASKA (U.S.)

ARCTIC OCEAN

GREENLAND (DEN.)

ICELAND

Azores (Port.)

ATLANTIC OCEAN

GUATEMALA 1954

EL SALVADOR 1979–1992

NICARAGUA 1981–1990

PANAMA

CUBA 1961–1962

DOMINICAN REPUBLIC 1965–1966

Puerto Rico (U.S.)

GRENADA 1983

Equator

6th fleet

SOVIET UNION

MONGOLIA

CHINA

JAPAN

SOUTH KOREA 1950–1953

FORMOSA (TAIWAN) 1958

Okinawa (U.S.)

7th fleet

PACIFIC OCEAN

PHILIPPINES 1945–1975

SOUTH VIETNAM 1945–1954 1957–1975

CAMBODIA 1969–1975

THAILAND

LAOS 1960–1975

INDONESIA 1965

NORWAY

GREAT BRITAIN

DEN.
NETH.
BELG.
W. GER.
FRANCE
E. GER.
POLAND
CZECH.
HUNG.
ROMANIA
YUGO.
BULG.
ITALY
ALB.
GREECE 1946–1949
PORT.
SPAIN

MOROCCO

LIBYA

EGYPT 1956 1967 1973

LEBANON 1958

TURKEY 1945–1947

IRAQ 1958

IRAN 1945–1946 1951–1953

AFGHANISTAN 1979

PAKISTAN

SAUDI ARABIA

SOMALIA 1970s–1980s

ETHIOPIA 1975–1991

DEMOCRATIC REPUBLIC OF THE CONGO 1961–1965

ANGOLA 1976–1992

INDIAN OCEAN

1000 Mi.

1000 Km.

0 500 1000

0 500

30°N

60°N

150°E

120°E

90°E

60°E

30°E

0°

30°W

60°W

90°W

120°W

150°W

Increased hostility did not lead to a direct military confrontation between the two powerful alliances. But the Soviet Union did test Western resolve, first by blockading the British, French, and American zones of Berlin (located in Soviet-controlled East Germany) in 1947–1948 and then in 1961 by building the Berlin Wall to prevent East Germans from fleeing to West Berlin.

In turn, the West tested the East by encouraging divisions within the Warsaw Pact. This policy contributed to an armed anti-Soviet revolt in Hungary that Soviet troops crushed in 1956. Then, in 1968, Soviet troops repressed a peaceful democratic reform effort in Czechoslovakia (now Czech Republic and Slovakia), making clear that, like the West, it would use military force to defend its sphere of influence against internal revolutionary changes. By failing to support either of these challenges to Soviet control, the West effectively accepted the political and ideological boundaries established by the Cold War. In 1968 Leonid Brezhnev, general secretary of the Soviet Union (served 1964–1982), asserted that all communist countries would be defended if they "fell to 'bourgeois forces,'" meaning, in effect, that any country in communist eastern Europe would be invaded if it decided to embrace Western-style democracy and capitalism. By the end of the Second World War, Soviet troops controlled the Korean peninsula north of the thirty-eighth parallel, while American troops controlled the south. When these two powers could not reach an agreement to hold countrywide elections, a communist North Korea and a noncommunist South Korea emerged as competing independent states in 1948. Two years later North Korea invaded South Korea. The United Nations Security Council reacted by calling on its members to come to the defense of South Korea, a vote only possible because the Soviet Union, which had veto power, had boycotted the meeting. In the ensuing **Korean War**, which lasted until 1953, the United States was the primary military ally of South Korea. Victories by American and South Korean forces forced North Korean forces north and the People's Republic of China entered the war in support of North Korea's communist regime, nearly sweeping aside American resistance. But the United States quickly and effectively reacted and pushed Chinese forces north.

Because the United States feared that launching attacks into China might prompt China's ally, the Soviet Union, to retaliate, the conflict remained limited to the Korean peninsula. When the contending armies eventually reached a stalemate along the thirty-eighth parallel, the two sides agreed to a truce but could not agree to a formal peace treaty. As a result, fear of renewed warfare between the two highly militarized Koreas has lingered until the present and the United States has maintained a large military force on the peninsula.

31-1d The United States and Vietnam

AP® Exam Tip

Understand the roles of nationalism and armed struggle in colonial independence movements.

The most important postwar communist movement arose in French Indochina in Southeast Asia. The Vietnamese leader Ho Chi Minh (**hoe chee min**)(1890–1969) had spent several years in France during World War I and had helped form the French Communist Party. In 1930, after training in Moscow, he returned to Vietnam to found the Indochina Communist Party. Forced to take refuge in China while Japan occupied Vietnam during World War II, Ho cooperated with the war effort of the United States.

At war's end the French government was determined to keep its colonial possessions. Ho Chi Minh's nationalist coalition, called the Viet Minh, fought for independence against the French with help from the People's Republic of China. After a brutal struggle, the French stronghold of Dienbienphu (**dee-yen-bee-yen-FOO**) fell in 1954, marking the end of France's colonial enterprise. Ho's victorious Viet Minh forces established a government in Hanoi in the north, while a noncommunist nationalist government led by groups that had supported the French ruled from Saigon in the south.

Under President Dwight D. Eisenhower (served 1953–1961), the United States provided limited military support to the French. Ultimately, Eisenhower decided not to prop up French colonial rule in Vietnam because he and his advisors believed that all European colonial empires were doomed (see Chapter 32) in the era of heightened nationalism that followed the war. After winning independence, communist North Vietnam supported a communist guerrilla movement—the Viet Cong—that took up arms against the anticommunist government of South Vietnam. At issue was the ideological and economic orientation of an independent Vietnam.

While Eisenhower had recognized the anticolonial origins of the struggle led by Ho Chi Minh, President John F. Kennedy (served 1961–1963) saw the conflict more in Cold War terms and embraced a more ambitious and risky set of policy objectives. Kennedy's more fulsome commitment to the South Vietnamese government of President Ngo Dinh Diem (**dee-YEM**) was supported with increased levels of military and development aid. As American force levels

Korean War Conflict that began with North Korea's invasion of South Korea and that came to involve the United Nations (primarily the United States) allying with South Korea and the People's Republic of China allying with North Korea.

◀ **The Vietnamese People at War** American and South Vietnamese troops burned many villages and relocated civilian populations to deprive the enemy of refuges among civilian populations. This policy undermined support for the South Vietnamese government in the countryside. This violent struggle led to an estimated 1.3 to 3.8 million Vietnamese deaths and the destruction of numerous villages and small towns, as is shown in this photo. Dominique BERRETTY/Getty Images

grew, North Vietnam committed its own military forces more directly to the war, relying on material support from the Soviet Union and the Republic of China. Although he knew that the Diem government was corrupt and unpopular, Kennedy feared that a communist victory would encourage communist movements throughout Southeast Asia and alter the Cold War balance of power. He therefore significantly increased the number of American military advisers and also encouraged South Vietnamese military officers to overthrow the corrupt Diem government, leading to Ngo Dinh Diem's assassination in early November 1963.

On November 22, 1963, the unrelated assassination of President Kennedy in Dallas, Texas, elevated Lyndon B. Johnson (served 1963–1969) to the American presidency. Johnson gained congressional support for an unlimited U.S. military deployment that eventually reached 500,000 troops. Because South Vietnam's new rulers proved to be as corrupt and unpopular as the earlier Diem government, many South Vietnamese supported the Viet Cong and Hanoi's drive for national reunification. Despite battlefield success in the **Vietnam War**, the United States failed to achieve a comprehensive victory. In the massive 1968 Tet Offensive, the Viet Cong guerrillas and their North Vietnamese allies gained significant military credibility while suffering significant losses. With a clear victory now unlikely, the antiwar movement in the United States grew in strength (see below).

In 1973 a treaty between North Vietnam and the government of President Richard M. Nixon (served 1969–1974) ended U.S. involvement in the war and promised future elections. Two years later, in violation of the treaty, Viet Cong and North Vietnamese troops overran the South Vietnamese army and captured the southern capital of Saigon, renaming it Ho Chi Minh City. The victors then united the two Vietnams in a single state ruled from the north. Over a million Vietnamese and 58,000 Americans had died during the war. As the victors imposed a new economic and political order, hundreds of thousands of refugees from South Vietnam left for the United States and other Western nations.

While the United States had rationalized its military involvement in South Vietnam as part of its global confrontation with communism, the communist-led government of a newly reunited Vietnam soon found itself at war with its communist neighbors and former allies, rather than with the anticommunist nations of the region. In 1975 communist revolutionaries (the Khmer Rouge) gained power in Cambodia, Vietnam's western neighbor. Not only did this brutal regime led by Pol Pot execute more than 1 million of their fellow citizens, but they also provoked a war with the communist government of Vietnam in 1978. A Vietnamese force of more than 150,000 invaded Cambodia and defeated the Khmer Rouge, setting up an occupation government that lasted a decade. During this occupation, the Vietnamese found themselves facing a

Vietnam War Conflict pitting North Vietnam and South Vietnam communist guerrillas against the South Vietnamese government, aided after 1961 by the United States.

AP® Exam Tip
Consider how individuals like Martin Luther King, Jr. promoted the practice of nonviolence as a way to bring about political change.

resilient guerrilla force that eventually compelled them to withdraw. The Vietnamese invasion of Cambodia also led the Vietnamese into a two-month-long war with the People's Republic of China, which favored the Cambodians. If the region's decades of violence had begun within the frame of Cold War ideological conflict, it had ended after two wars that pitted communist regimes against each other.

President Johnson began his administration committed to a broad program of social reforms and civil rights initiatives, called the Great Society, and was instrumental in passing major civil rights legislation that responded to the heroic campaign for voting rights and integration led by Martin Luther King, Jr. As the commitment of U.S. troops in Vietnam grew, a massive antiwar movement applied the tactics of the civil rights movement to end the war. Growing economic problems and a rising tide of antiwar rallies, soon international in character, undermined support for Johnson, who declined to seek re-election in 1968.

31-1e The Race for Nuclear Supremacy

The terrible devastation of Hiroshima and Nagasaki by atomic weapons (see Chapter 29) framed the strategic decisions in the Korean and Vietnam Wars. The Soviet Union had exploded its first nuclear device in 1949. The United States claimed a new advantage when it exploded a more powerful hydrogen bomb in 1952, but the Soviet Union followed suit less than a year later. As a result, the United States took care not to directly threaten the Soviet Union or China (a nuclear power from 1964) during the Korean or Vietnamese conflicts. But while the Cold War rivals avoided a direct confrontation, the use of threats and the proliferation of small conflicts frightened a world deeply scarred by two world wars.

In 1954 President Eisenhower warned Soviet leaders against attacking western Europe. In response to such an attack, he said, the United States would reduce the Soviet Union to "a smoking, radiating ruin at the end of two hours." A few years later Soviet leader Nikita Khrushchev **(KROOSH-chef)** made an equally stark promise: "We will bury you." He was referring to economic competition, but Americans interpreted the statement to mean literal burial. Rhetoric aside, both men—and their successors—had the capacity to deliver on their threats, and everyone in the world knew that all-out war with nuclear weapons would produce the greatest global devastation in human history.

The Soviet Union's deployment of nuclear missiles to Cuba in 1962 pushed the two sides to the brink of war. Reacting to U.S. efforts to overthrow the Cuban government, Khrushchev and Fidel Castro decided that the deployment of Soviet nuclear weapons in Cuba would force the United States to accept the island's status quo. When the missiles were discovered, the United States declared a naval blockade and prepared to invade Cuba, forcing Khrushchev to remove the missiles. Reciprocally, the United States pledged to respect Cuban sovereignty, in effect agreeing to not invade the island. As frightening as the **Cuban missile crisis** was, the fact that the superpowers chose diplomacy over war gave reason to hope that nuclear weapons might be contained.

AP® Exam Tip
Identify groups and individuals who challenged war, such as the antinuclear movement, and explain their impact.

Fear of a nuclear holocaust produced an international effort to limit proliferation. In 1963 Great Britain, the United States, and the Soviet Union agreed to ban the testing of nuclear weapons in the atmosphere, in space, and under water, thus reducing the danger of radioactive fallout. In 1968 the United States and the Soviet Union together proposed a world treaty against further proliferation, leading ultimately to the Nuclear Non-Proliferation Treaty (NPT) signed by 137 countries. Four additional nations have or are assumed to have nuclear weapons: India, Pakistan, North Korea, and Israel. Only after 1972 did the two superpowers begin the arduous and extremely slow process of negotiating weapons limits.

Cuban missile crisis
Brink-of-war confrontation between the United States and the Soviet Union over the latter's placement of nuclear-armed missiles in Cuba.

The atomic powers France and Britain were economically unable to keep up with the Soviet–American arms race. Instead, they led the European states in an effort to relax tensions. Between 1972 and 1975, the Conference on Security and Cooperation in Europe (CSCE) brought delegates from thirty-seven European states, the United States, and Canada to Helsinki. The Soviet Union's chief objective was European acceptance of the political boundaries of the Warsaw Pact nations as a condition for broad cooperation. In the end, the **Helsinki Accords** affirmed these boundaries (see Chapter 32 for discussion of the collapse of Warsaw Pact) and also called for economic, social, and governmental contacts and for cooperation in humanitarian fields between the rival alliances.

Helsinki Accords Political and human rights agreement signed in Helsinki, Finland, by the Soviet Union and western European countries.

Space exploration was another offshoot of the nuclear arms race. The contest to build larger and more accurate missiles prompted the superpowers to prove their skills in rocketry by launching space satellites. The Soviet Union placed a small *Sputnik* satellite into orbit around the earth in October 1957, and the United States responded with its own satellite three months later. The space race was on, a contest in which accomplishments in space were understood to signify equivalent achievements in the military sphere. In 1969, when Neil A. Armstrong and Edwin E. ("Buzz") Aldrin became the first humans to walk on the moon, America had demonstrated its technological superiority. More recently, the exploration of space has been an arena of cooperation between East and West, with the U.S. and Russia sharing access to the International Space Station. Since ending the Space Shuttle program, American astronauts have traveled to space on board Russian rockets.

Section Review

- The United Nations was created to manage international disputes and facilitate decolonization and development.

- The United States developed the Marshall Plan to aid European recovery from the devastation of World War II.

- The Cold War was a confrontation between two military alliances, NATO and the Warsaw Pact, and two distinct economic systems, capitalism and communism.

- The United States and the Soviet Union avoided a direct conflict, but the Cold War led to wars in Korea and Vietnam.

- The development of nuclear weapons made the Cold War a threat to the survival of the human race and led to nonproliferation treaties.

31-2 Decolonization and Nation Building

How were the experiences of Asia, Africa, and Latin America similar in this period?

After World War I, Germany, Austria-Hungary, and the Ottoman Empire lost their empires, and many colonies and dependencies were transferred to the victors, especially to Great Britain and France. In the two decades following World War II, nearly all remaining colonies gained independence (see Map 31.2). Circumstances differed profoundly from place to place. In some Asian countries, where colonial rule was of long standing, like India, new states possessed viable industries, communications networks, and education systems. In other countries, notably in Africa, decolonized nations faced dire economic problems and disunity resulting from language and ethnic differences.

Most Latin American nations had achieved political independence in the nineteenth century (see Chapter 25). Following World War II, mass political movements in this region focused on the related issue of economic sovereignty—freedom from growing American economic domination—and the desire to end American military interventions. Great Britain and other European nations still retained colonies in the Caribbean after World War II. In the 1960s Barbados, Guyana, Jamaica, and Trinidad Tobago gained independence from Britain, and the smaller British colonies followed in the 1970s and 1980s, as did Surinam, which gained independence from the Netherlands.

Despite their differences, a sense of kinship arose among the nations of Latin America, Africa, and Asia. All shared feelings of excitement and rebirth. As North Americans, Europeans, and the Chinese settled into the exhausting deadlock of the Cold War, visions of independence and national economic development captivated the rest of the world.

AP® Exam Tip
Be prepared to compare different types of independence struggles.

31-2a New Nations in South and Southeast Asia

After partition in 1947, the independent states of India and Pakistan were strikingly dissimilar. Muslim Pakistan defined itself according to religion and quickly fell under the control of military leaders. India, a religiously diverse secular republic led by Prime Minister Jawaharlal Nehru, was much larger and inherited the considerable industrial and educational resources developed by the British, along with a large share of trained civil servants and military officers. Ninety percent of its population was Hindu and most of the rest Muslim.

Adding to the tensions of independence (see Chapter 30) was the decision by the Hindu ruler of the northwestern state Jammu and Kashmir, now commonly called Kashmir, to join India without consulting his overwhelmingly Muslim subjects. As a result, war between India and

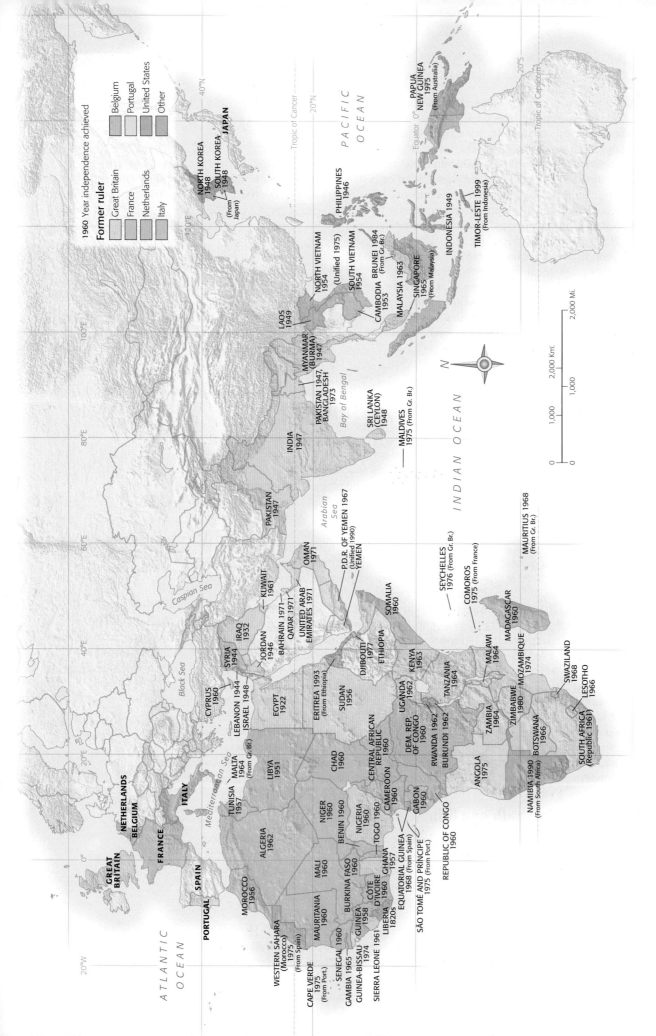

MAP 31.2 Decolonization, 1947–1990 Independence was achieved a decade or so earlier in South and Southeast Asia than in Africa.

What were the key decades in decolonization across the globe?

1960 Year independence achieved

Former ruler

Great Britain	Belgium		
France	Portugal		
Netherlands	United States		
Italy	Other		

GREAT BRITAIN
FRANCE
NETHERLANDS
BELGIUM
ITALY
SPAIN
PORTUGAL

ATLANTIC OCEAN

Mediterranean Sea
Black Sea
Caspian Sea
Arabian Sea
Bay of Bengal
INDIAN OCEAN
PACIFIC OCEAN

Tropic of Cancer
Equator 0°
Tropic of Capricorn

MOROCCO 1956
WESTERN SAHARA 1975 (Morocco) (From Port.)
CAPE VERDE 1975 (From Port.)
MAURITANIA 1960
SENEGAL 1960
GAMBIA 1965
GUINEA-BISSAU 1974
GUINEA 1958
SIERRA LEONE 1961
LIBERIA 1820s
CÔTE D'IVOIRE 1960
GHANA 1957
BURKINA FASO 1960
MALI 1960
NIGER 1960
BENIN 1960
TOGO 1960
NIGERIA 1960
ALGERIA 1962
TUNISIA 1957
MALTA 1964 (From Gr. Br.)
LIBYA 1951
CHAD 1960
EQUATORIAL GUINEA 1968 (From Spain)
SÃO TOMÉ AND PRÍNCIPE 1975 (From Port.)
CAMEROON 1960
GABON 1960
REPUBLIC OF CONGO 1960
CENTRAL AFRICAN REPUBLIC 1960
DEM. REP. OF CONGO 1960
ANGOLA 1975
NAMIBIA 1990 (From South Africa)
BOTSWANA 1966
SOUTH AFRICA (Republic 1961)
ZIMBABWE 1980
MOZAMBIQUE 1974
ZAMBIA 1964
MALAWI 1964
SWAZILAND 1968
LESOTHO 1966
TANZANIA 1964
RWANDA 1962
BURUNDI 1962
UGANDA 1962
KENYA 1963
SOMALIA 1960
ETHIOPIA
DJIBOUTI 1977
SUDAN 1956
ERITREA 1993 (From Ethiopia)
EGYPT 1922
MADAGASCAR 1960
COMOROS 1975 (From France)
SEYCHELLES 1976 (From Gr. Br.)
MAURITIUS 1968 (From Gr. Br.)

CYPRUS 1960
LEBANON 1944
ISRAEL 1948
SYRIA 1944
IRAQ 1932
JORDAN 1946
KUWAIT 1961
BAHRAIN 1971
QATAR 1971
UNITED ARAB EMIRATES 1971
OMAN 1971
P.D.R. OF YEMEN 1967 (Unified 1990) YEMEN

PAKISTAN 1947
INDIA 1947
PAKISTAN 1947
BANGLADESH 1973
SRI LANKA (CEYLON) 1948
MALDIVES 1975 (From Gr. Br.)

NORTH KOREA 1948
SOUTH KOREA 1948
JAPAN
(From Japan)

MYANMAR (BURMA) 1947
LAOS 1949
NORTH VIETNAM 1954 (Unified 1975)
SOUTH VIETNAM 1954
CAMBODIA 1953
MALAYSIA 1963
BRUNEI 1984 (From Gr. Br.)
SINGAPORE 1965 (From Malaysia)
PHILIPPINES 1946
INDONESIA 1949
TIMOR-LESTE 1999 (From Indonesia)
PAPUA NEW GUINEA 1975 (From Australia)

N

0   1,000   2,000 Km.
0   1,000   2,000 Mi.

20°W 0° 20°E 40°E 60°E 80°E 100°E 120°E
40°N 20°N 0° 20°S

Pakistan over Kashmir broke out in 1947 and ended with an uneasy truce. In 1965 war broke out again, this time involving large military forces and the use of air power by both sides. Kashmir has remained a flash point, with significant new clashes in 1999 and 2000.

Despite early predictions that multilingual India might break up into a number of linguistically homogeneous states, most Indians recognized that unity benefited everyone, and the country pursued a generally democratic and socialist line of development. Pakistan, in contrast, did break up. In 1971 the Bengali-speaking eastern section seceded to become the independent country of Bangladesh. During the fighting Indian military forces again struck against Pakistan. Despite their shared political heritage, India, Pakistan, and Bangladesh have found cooperation difficult and have pursued markedly different economic, political, religious, and social paths.

During the war the Japanese supported anti-British Indian nationalists as a way to weaken their enemy; they also encouraged the aspirations of nationalists in the countries they occupied in Southeast Asia. Many Asian nationalists came to see Japanese victories over British, French, and Dutch colonial armies as a demonstration of the political and military capacities of Asian peoples. In the Dutch East Indies, Achmad Sukarno (1901–1970) cooperated with the Japanese in the hope that the Dutch, who had dominated the region economically since the seventeenth century, could be expelled. The Dutch finally negotiated an end to colonial status in 1949, and Sukarno became dictator of the resource-rich but underdeveloped nation of Indonesia. He ruled until 1965, when a military coup ousted him and brutally eliminated the nation's once-powerful Communist Party. The nation's large and prosperous Chinese ethnic community was the target of violence during this period as well, and the new Indonesian government attempted to compel its assimilation, leading to decades of ethnic tension and discrimination.

In 1946 the United States kept its promise of postwar independence for the Philippine Islands but retained close economic ties and leases on military bases, later renegotiated. Britain granted independence to Burma (now Myanmar [my-ahn-MAR]) in 1948 and established the Malay Federation the same year. Singapore, once a member of the federation, became an independent city-state in 1965.

31-2b The Struggle for Independence in Africa

Between 1952 and 1956, France granted independence to Tunisia and Morocco, but it sought to retain Algeria. France had controlled this colony for nearly 150 years and had encouraged Europeans to settle there. By 1950, 10 percent of the Algerian population was of French or other European origin. France also granted political rights to the settler population and asserted the fiction of Algeria's political and economic integration in the French nation. In reality few Algerians benefited from this arrangement, and most resented their continued colonial status.

The Vietnamese military victory over France in 1954 helped provoke a nationalist uprising in Algeria, during which both sides acted brutally. The Algerian revolutionary organization, the Front de Libération National (FLN), was supported by Egypt and other Arab countries who sought the emancipation of all Arab peoples. French colonists considered the country theirs and fought to the bitter end. When Algeria finally won independence in 1962, a flood of angry colonists returned to France. Since few Arabs had received technical training, this departure undermined the economy. Despite harsh feelings left by the war, Algeria retained close and seemingly indissoluble economic ties to France, and Algerians in large numbers emigrated to France in the decades that followed.

Independence was achieved in most of sub-Saharan Africa through negotiation, not revolution. In colonies with significant white settler minorities, however, the path to independence followed the violent experience of Algeria. African nationalists were forced to overcome many obstacles, but they were also able to take advantage of many consequential changes put in place during colonial rule. In the 1950s and 1960s world economic expansion and growing popular support for liberation overcame African worries about potential economic and political problems that might follow independence. Moreover, improvements in medical care and public health had led to rapid population growth in Africa, and the continent's young population embraced the idea of independence.

Western nationalist and egalitarian ideals also helped fuel resistance to colonialism. Most of the leaders of African independence movements were among the most westernized members of these societies. African veterans of Allied armies during World War II had exposure to Allied propaganda that emphasized ideas of popular sovereignty and self-determination. In addition, many leaders were recent graduates of educational institutions created by colonial governments, and a minority had obtained advanced education in Europe and the United States. Nearly all these leaders embraced the idea of majority rule, an ideal inherently subversive in a colonial setting.

African nationalists were able to take advantage of other legacies of colonial rule as well. Schools, labor associations, and the colonial bureaucracy itself proved to be fertile nationalist recruiting centers. Languages introduced by colonial governments were useful in building multiethnic coalitions, while networks of roads and railroads built to promote colonial exports forged new national identities and a new political consciousness.

The young politicians who led the nationalist movements devoted their lives to ridding their homelands of foreign occupation. An example is Kwame Nkrumah (**KWAH-mee nn-KROO-muh**) (1909–1972), who in 1957 became prime minister of Ghana (formerly the Gold Coast), the first British colony in West Africa to achieve independence. After graduating from a Catholic mission school and a government teacher-training college, Nkrumah spent a decade studying philosophy and theology in the United States, where he absorbed ideas about black pride and independence propounded by W. E. B. Du Bois and Marcus Garvey.

During a brief stay in Britain, Nkrumah joined Kenyan nationalist Jomo Kenyatta, a Ph.D. in anthropology, to found an organization devoted to African freedom. In 1947 Nkrumah returned to the Gold Coast to work for independence. The time was right. There was no longer strong public support in Britain for colonialism, and Britain's political leadership was not enthusiastic about investing resources to hold restive colonies. When Nkrumah's party won a decisive election victory in 1951, the British Gold Coast governor appointed him prime minister. Full independence came in 1957. Although Nkrumah remained an effective international spokesman for colonized peoples, he was overthrown in 1966 by a disaffected group of army officers.

Britain soon granted independence to its other West African colonies, including large, populous, and resource-rich Nigeria in 1960. In some British colonies in eastern and southern Africa, however, larger, long-established white settler populations resisted independence. In Kenya a small but influential group of wealthy white coffee planters claimed that a protest movement among the Kikuyu (**kih-KOO-you**) people was proof that Africans were not ready for self-government. The settlers called the movement "Mau Mau," a made-up name meant to evoke an image of primitive savagery. When violence between settlers and anticolonial fighters escalated after 1952, British troops hunted down movement leaders and resettled the Kikuyu in fortified villages. They also declared a state of emergency, banned all African political protest, and imprisoned Kenyatta and other nationalists. Released in 1961, Kenyatta negotiated with the British to write a constitution for an independent Kenya, and in 1964 he was elected the nation's first president. Kenyatta proved to be an effective, though autocratic, ruler, and Kenya benefited from greater stability and prosperity than Ghana and many other former colonies.

African leaders in the sub-Saharan French colonies were more reluctant than their counterparts in British colonies to call for full independence. Promises made during World War II by the Free French movement of General Charles de Gaulle at a conference in Brazzaville, in French Equatorial Africa, seemed to offer these African leaders dramatic changes without actual independence. Dependent on the troops and supplies from French African colonies, de Gaulle had promised Africans a more democratic government, broader suffrage, and greater access to employment in the colonial government. He had also promised better education and health services and an end to many abuses in the colonial system. He had not promised independence, but the politics of postwar colonial self-government ultimately proved irresistible.

◀ **Jomo Kenyatta (1892–1978) and Julius Kambarage Nyerere (1922–1999)** Kenya's newly elected premier, Jomo Kenyatta, is pictured here visiting with the independence hero of Tanzania, Julius Nyerere, in 1966. World History Archive/Alamy Stock Photo

Most Africans elected to office following the postwar French reforms were trained civil servants. Because of the French policy of job rotation, they had typically served in a number of different colonies and thus had a broad regional outlook. They realized that some colonies—such as Ivory Coast, with coffee and cacao exports, fishing, and hardwood forests—had good economic prospects, while others, such as landlocked, desert Niger, did not. Furthermore, they recognized the importance of French public investment in the region—a billion dollars between 1947 and 1956—and their own dependence on colonial civil service salaries. As a result, they generally looked to achieve greater self-government incrementally.

When Charles de Gaulle returned to power in France in 1958, at the height of the Algerian war, he warned that a rush to independence would have costs, saying: "One cannot conceive of both an independent [African] territory and a France which continues to aid it." Ultimately, however, African patriotism prevailed in all of France's West African and Equatorial African colonies. Guinea, under the dynamic leadership of Sékou Touré (**SAY-koo too-RAY**), gained full independence in 1958 and the others in 1960.

Independence in the Belgian Congo was much more chaotic and violent. Contending political and ethnic groups found external allies; some were supported by Cuba and the Soviet Union, while others were supported by the West or by business groups tied to the rich mines. Civil war, the introduction of foreign mercenaries, and the rhetoric of Cold War confrontation roiled the waters and led to a heavy loss of life and great property destruction. In 1965 Mobuto Sese Seko seized power in a military coup that included the assassination of Patrice Lumumba, the nation's first prime minister. Once in power, Mobuto maintained one of the region's most corrupt governments until driven from power in 1997.

The opposition of European settler communities delayed decolonization in southern Africa. While the settler minority tried to defend white supremacy, African-led liberation movements were committed to the creation of nonracial societies and majority rule. In the 1960s African guerrilla movements successfully fought to end Portuguese rule in Angola and Mozambique. Their efforts led to both the overthrow of the antidemocratic government of Portugal in 1974 and independence of the two colonies the following year. After a ten-year fight, European settlers in the British colony of Southern Rhodesia accepted African majority rule in 1980. The new government changed the country's name to Zimbabwe, the name of a great stone city built by Africans long before the arrival of European settlers.

South Africa and neighboring Namibia remained in the hands of European minorities much longer. The large white settler population of South Africa achieved effective independence from Britain in 1961 but kept the black and mixed-race majority in colonial-era subjection, separating the races in a system they called *apartheid* (**a-PART-hite**). Descendents of Dutch and English settlers made up 13 percent of the population but controlled the productive land; the industrial, mining, and commercial enterprises; and the government. Meanwhile, discrimination and segregation in housing, education, and employment confined the lives of people of mixed parentage (10 percent of the population) and South Asians (less than 3 percent).

Indigenous Africans, 74 percent of the population, were subjected to even stricter limitations on housing, freedom of movement, and access to jobs and public facilities. The government created fictional African "homelands" as a way of denying the African majority citizenship and political rights. Not unlike Amerindian reservations, these "homelands" were located in poor regions far from the more dynamic and prosperous urban and industrial areas. Overcrowded and deprived of investment, they were impoverished and lacking in services and opportunities.

The African National Congress (ANC), formed in 1912, led opposition to apartheid (see Diversity & Dominance: Race and the Struggle for Justice in South Africa). After police fired on demonstrators in the African town of Sharpeville in 1960 and banned all peaceful political protest by Africans, a lawyer named Nelson Mandela (1918–2013) organized guerrilla resistance by the ANC. The government sentenced Mandela to life in prison in 1964 and persecuted the ANC, but it was unable to defeat the movement. Facing growing opposition internationally, South Africa freed Mandela from prison in 1990 and began the transition to majority rule (see Chapters 32 and 33).

AP® Exam Tip Consider how individuals such as Nelson Mandela promoted nonviolence as a method of obtaining political change.

31-2c The Quest for Economic Freedom in Latin America

Although Latin America had achieved independence from colonial rule more than a hundred years earlier, European and American economic domination of the region created a semicolonial order (see Chapters 26 and 30). Foreigners controlled Chile's copper, Cuba's sugar, Colombia's

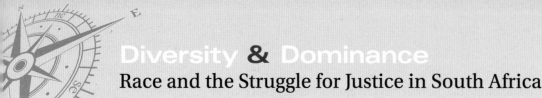
One of South Africa's martyrs in the struggle against apartheid was the thinker and activist Steve Biko (1946–1977). Biko was one of the founders of the Black Consciousness Movement, which focused on the ways in which white settlers had stripped Africans of their freedom. Between 1975 and 1977 police arrested and interrogated him four times. After his arrest in August 1977, the police severely beat him and denied him medical care. His death in police custody caused worldwide outrage. The excerpt below is from his I Write What I Like.

[T]hese are not the people we are concerned with [those who support apartheid]. We are concerned with that curious bunch of nonconformists . . . that [go] under all sorts of names—liberals, leftists etc. These are the people who argue that they are not responsible for white racism and the country's "inhumanity to the black man." These are the people who claim that they too feel the oppression just as acutely as the blacks and therefore should be jointly involved in the black man's struggle for a place under the sun. In short, these are the people who say that they have black souls wrapped up in white skins.

Nowhere is the arrogance of the liberal ideology demonstrated so well as in their insistence that the problems of the country can only be solved by a bilateral approach involving both black and white. This has, by and large, come to be taken in all seriousness as the modus operandi in South Africa by all those who claim they would like a change in the status quo. . . . The integration they talk about is . . . a one-way course, with the whites doing all the talking and the blacks the listening. . . .

Once the various groups within a given community have asserted themselves to the point that mutual respect has to be shown then you have the ingredients for a true and meaningful integration. From this it becomes clear that as long as blacks are suffering from [an] inferiority complex—a result of 300 years of deliberate oppression, denigration and derision—they

will be useless as co-architects of a normal society where man is nothing else but man for his own sake. Hence what is necessary as a prelude to anything else that may come is a very strong grassroots build-up of black consciousness such that blacks can learn to assert themselves and stake their rightful claim.

Thus in adopting the line of a nonracial approach, the liberals are playing their old game. They are claiming a "monopoly on intelligence and moral judgement" and setting the pattern and pace for the realisation of the black man's aspirations. They want to remain in good books with both the black and white worlds. They want to shy away from all forms of "extremisms," condemning "white supremacy" as being just as bad as "Black Power!" They vacillate between the two worlds, verbalising all the complaints of the blacks beautifully while skillfully extracting what suits them from the exclusive pool of white privileges. But ask them for a moment to give a concrete meaningful programme that they intend adopting, then you will see on whose side they really are. Their protests are directed at and appeal to white conscience, everything they do is directed at finally convincing the white electorate that the black man is also a man and that at some future date he should be given a place at the white man's table.

In the following selection Anglican bishop Desmond Tutu (b. 1931) expressed his personal anguish at the death of Steve Biko, summarizing Biko's contributions to the struggle for justice in South Africa. Tutu won the Nobel Peace Prize in 1984 and was named archbishop in 1988. From 1995 to 1998 he chaired the Truth and Reconciliation Commission, which investigated atrocities in South Africa during the years of apartheid. He stated that his objective was to create "a democratic and just society without racial divisions."

When we heard the news "Steve Biko is dead" we were struck numb with disbelief. No, it can't be true! No, it must be a horrible nightmare, and we will awake and

---

coffee, and Guatemala's bananas, leading by the 1930s to growing support for economic nationalism. During the 1930s and 1940s populist political leaders experimented with programs that would constrain foreign investors or, alternatively, promote local efforts to industrialize (see discussion of Getulio Vargas and Juan Perón in Chapter 30).

In Mexico the revolutionary constitution of 1917 began an era of economic nationalism that culminated in the expropriation of foreign oil interests, mostly American, in 1938. The Institutional Revolutionary Party, or PRI (the abbreviation of its name in Spanish), went on to control Mexico until the 1990s, overseeing a period of strong economic expansion during World War II. But a yawning gulf between rich and poor persisted. Although the government dominated important industries like petroleum and restricted foreign investment, rapid population growth, uncontrolled migration to Mexico City and other urban areas, and political corruption undermined efforts to lift the nation's poor. Economic power was concentrated at the top of society, with 2,000 elite families controlling much of the nation's wealth. At the other end of the economic scale were the millions of poor Mexicans struggling to survive. Thwarted by limited opportunities at home, millions of Mexicans migrated to the United States.

Guatemala's situation was more representative of Latin America in 1950. An American corporation, the United Fruit Company, was Guatemala's largest landowner; it also controlled much of the nation's infrastructure, including port facilities and railroads. To limit banana production and keep international prices high, United Fruit kept much of its Guatemalan lands fallow. Jacobo Arbenz Guzmán, elected in 1951, advocated positions broadly similar to those of

AP® Exam Tip

Explain the changes and continuities in the United States' involvement in Latin America during the twentieth century.

find that really it is different—that Steve is alive even if it be in detention. But no, dear friends, he is dead and we are still numb with grief, and groan with anguish "Oh God, where are you? Oh God, do you really care—how can you let this happen to us?"

It all seems such a senseless waste of a wonderfully gifted person, struck down in the bloom of youth, a youthful bloom that some wanted to see blighted. What can be the purpose of such wanton destruction? God, do you really love us? What must we do which we have not done, what must we say which we have not said a thousand times over, oh, for so many years—that all we want is what belongs to all God's children, what belongs as an inalienable right—a place in the sun in our own beloved mother country. Oh God, how long can we go on? How long can we go on appealing for a more just ordering of society where we all, black and white together, count not because of some accident of birth or a biological irrelevance—where all of us black and white count because we are human persons, human persons created in your own image.

God called Steve Biko to be his servant in South Africa—to speak up on behalf of God, declaring what the will of this God must be in a situation such as ours, a situation of evil, injustice, oppression and exploitation. God called him to be the founder father of the Black Consciousness Movement against which we have had tirades and fulminations. It is a movement by which God, through Steve, sought to awaken in the Black person a sense of his intrinsic value and worth as a child of God, not needing to apologise for his existential condition as a black person, calling on blacks to glorify and praise God that he had created them black. Steve, with his brilliant mind that always saw to the heart of things, realised that until blacks asserted their humanity and their personhood, there was not the remotest chance for reconciliation in South Africa. For true reconciliation is a deeply personal matter. It can happen only between persons who assert their own personhood, and who acknowledge and respect that of others. You don't get reconciled to your dog, do you? Steve knew and believed fervently that being pro-black was not the same thing as being anti-white. The Black Consciousness Movement is not a "hate white movement," despite all you may have heard to the contrary. He had a far too profound respect for persons as persons, to want to deal with them under readymade, shopsoiled [sic] categories.

All who met him had this tremendous sense of a warm-hearted man, and as a notable acquaintance of his told me, a man who was utterly indestructible, of massive intellect and yet reticent; quite unshakeable in his commitment to principle and to radical change in South Africa by peaceful means; a man of real reconciliation, truly an instrument of god's peace, unshakeable in his commitment to the liberation of all South Africans, black and white, striving for a more just and more open South Africa.

AP® History Reasoning Skills

Comparison *In what ways do Biko's 1970 essay and Bishop Tutu's eulogy of Biko approach race relations similarly? What differences are apparent?*

Contextualization *What elements of the apartheid movement made Biko's essay necessary?*

Sources: First selection from Steve Biko, *I Write What I Like*, ed. Aelred Stubbs (Chicago, IL: University of Chicago Press, 1978); second selection from Bishop Desmond Tutu, *Crying in the Wilderness: The Struggle for Justice in South Africa*, ed. John Webster (Grand Rapids, MI: William B. Eerdmans Publishing Co., 1982), 61–63.

leaders like Perón of Argentina and Vargas of Brazil (see Chapter 30), who confronted powerful foreign interests. He advocated land reform, which would have transferred these fallow lands to the nation's rural poor. The threatened expropriation angered the United Fruit Company. Simultaneously, Arbenz tried to reduce U.S. political influence, raising fears in Washington that he sought closer ties to the Soviet Union. Reacting to the land reform efforts and to reports that Arbenz was becoming friendly to communism, the U.S. Central Intelligence Agency (CIA), in one of its first major overseas operations, sponsored a takeover by the Guatemalan military in 1954. CIA intervention removed Arbenz, but it also condemned the small and poor nation of Guatemala to decades of governmental instability and a civil war that cost in excess of 200,000 lives.

By the 1950s American companies dominated the Cuban economy. They controlled sugar production, the nation's most important industry, as well as banking, transportation, tourism, and public utilities. The United States was also the most important market for Cuba's exports and the most important source of Cuba's imports. Thus the performance of the U.S. economy largely determined the ebb and flow of Cuban foreign trade. By 1956 sugar accounted for 80 percent of Cuba's exports and 25 percent of Cuba's national income. But demand in the United States dictated keeping only 39 percent of the land owned by the sugar companies in production, while Cuba experienced chronic underemployment. Similarly, immense deposits of nickel in Cuba went untapped because the U.S. government, which owned them, considered them to be a strategic reserve.

While high unemployment and slow growth afflicted the nation, profits went north to the United States or to a small class of wealthy Cubans. Cuba's government was also notoriously

AP® Exam Tip
Understand the influence of socialism and communism in movements to redistribute land and resources in some states during the twentieth century.

Section Review

- Independence in India and Pakistan led to war over Kashmir, which has continued to cause conflict.

- Algeria gained independence from France after a long and violent revolution.

- West African colonies eventually gained independence from Great Britain and France through negotiation, but the Belgian Congo fell under the power of a dictator.

- In southern African colonies, large white settler populations resisted independence, and whites in South Africa instituted the system of segregation called apartheid.

- In Latin American nations economic nationalists sought to reduce or eliminate the economic influence of the United States.

- The CIA interfered forcefully in Guatemala, and its attempt to do the same in Cuba helped lead to the Cuban missile crisis; meanwhile, Castro created a socialist economy.

▲ **Cuban Poster of Ernesto ("Che") Guevara** Che became a leading theorist of communist revolution in Latin America. He was captured and executed in 1967 while leading an insurgency in Bolivia. Barry Lewis/Alamy Stock Photo

corrupt and subservient to the wishes of American interests. As reform-minded young Cubans organized for a national election, Fulgencio Batista, a former military leader and president, illegally seized power in a coup in 1953. Hostility to Batista and anger with the corruption, repression, and foreign economic domination of his government gave rise to the revolution led by Fidel Castro.

Fidel Castro (1927–2016), a young lawyer who had played a prominent role in left-wing politics while at university, led a failed uprising in 1953. Convicted, jailed, and then sent into exile, Castro returned to Cuba in 1956 to establish a successful revolutionary movement in the countryside. His supporters included student groups, labor unions, and adherents of Cuba's traditional parties. When he and his youthful followers took power in 1959, they vowed not to suffer the fate of Arbenz and the Guatemalan reformers. Ernesto ("Che") Guevara **(CHAY guh-VAHR-uh)**, Castro's Argentine-born chief lieutenant who became the main theorist of communist revolution in Latin America, had witnessed the CIA coup in Guatemala firsthand. He and Castro believed that confrontation with the United States was inevitable and moved quickly to remove the existing military leadership and begin revolutionary changes in the economy.

Within a year Castro's government seized and redistributed land, lowered urban rents, and raised wages, effectively transferring 15 percent of the national income from the rich to the poor. Within two years the Castro government had nationalized the property of almost all U.S. corporations in Cuba as well as the wealth of Cuba's elite. To achieve his revolutionary objectives, Castro sought economic support from the Soviet Union. He also consolidated his personal political power, putting aside promises of democratic reform made when fighting Batista.

The United States responded by seeking to destabilize the Cuban economy and undermine the Castro government. These punitive measures by the United States, the nationalization of so much of the economy, and the punishment of Batista supporters caused tens of thousands of Cubans to leave, including some who had opposed Batista. Initially, most emigrants were from wealthy families and the middle class, but when the economic failures of the regime became clear, many poor Cubans fled to the United States or to other Latin American nations.

There is little evidence that Castro was committed to communism before the revolution, but his commitment to break the economic and political power of the United States in Cuba and undertake dramatic social reforms led inevitably to conflict with the United States and to reliance on the Soviet Union. In April 1961, in an attempt to apply the strategy that had removed Arbenz from power in Guatemala, an army of Cuban exiles trained and armed by the CIA landed at the Bay of Pigs in an effort to overthrow Castro. The Cuban army defeated the attempted invasion in a matter of days. The Eisenhower administration had planned the invasion, but the newly elected U.S. president, John F. Kennedy, agreed to carry it out and lived with the embarrassment. This failure helped precipitate the Cuban missile crisis. Fearful of a new invasion, Castro and Khrushchev placed nuclear weapons as well as missiles and bombers in Cuba to forestall an anticipated second attack.

The failure of the Bay of Pigs tarnished the reputation of the United States and the CIA and gave heart to revolutionaries all over Latin America. But the armed revolutionary movements that imitated the tactics and objectives of Cuba's bearded revolutionaries experienced little success. Among the thousands to lose their lives was Che Guevara, captured and executed in 1967 by Bolivian troops trained by the United States. Nevertheless, Castro had demonstrated that revolutionaries could successfully challenge American power and put in place a radical program of economic and social reform in the Western Hemisphere.

31-3 Beyond a Bipolar World

How did the rivalry between the Cold War superpowers affect the rest of the world?

Although no one doubted the dominating role of the East–West superpower rivalry in world affairs, newly independent nations were primarily concerned with domestic and regional issues. Their challenge was to pursue their ends within the bipolar structure of the Cold War—and when possible to take advantage of the East–West rivalry. Where nationalist forces sought to assert political or economic independence, Cold War antagonists provided arms and political support even when the nationalist goals were quite different from those of the supporting superpower. For other nations, the ruinously expensive superpower arms race opened opportunities to expand industries and exports. In short, the superpowers dominated the world but did not control it.

31-3a The Third World

As an early leader of the decolonization movement, Indonesia's President Sukarno was an appropriate figure to host a 1955 meeting of twenty-nine African and Asian countries at Bandung, Indonesia, that proclaimed solidarity among those fighting against colonial rule. This conference marked the beginning of an effort by the many new, poor, mostly non-European nations emerging from colonialism to gain more influence in world affairs. The terms *nonaligned nations* and *Third World*, which became commonplace in the following years, signaled these countries' collective stance toward the rival sides in the Cold War. If the West, led by the United States, and the East, led by the Soviet Union, represented two worlds locked in mortal struggle, the Third World consisted of everyone else.

Leaders of so-called Third World countries preferred the label *nonaligned*, which signaled their independence from Soviet or U.S. control. Leaders in the West noted that the Soviet Union supported many national liberation movements and that the nonaligned movement included communist countries with ties to the Soviet Union such as China and Yugoslavia. As a result, they refused to take the term *nonaligned* seriously. In a polarized world, they saw Sukarno, Nehru, Nkrumah, and Egypt's Gamal Abd al-Nasir (**gah-MAHL AHB-d al–NAH-suhr**) as stalking horses for an ambitious campaign to extend Soviet influence globally. This may have been the view of some Soviet leaders as well, since they were quick to offer military and financial aid to many nonaligned countries.

For the movement's leaders, however, nonalignment was primarily a way to extract money and support from one or both superpowers. By flirting with the Soviet Union or its ally, the People's Republic of China, a country could get weapons, training, and barter agreements that offered an alternative to selling agricultural or mineral products on Western-dominated world markets. The same flirtation might also prompt the United States and its allies to proffer grants and loans, cheap or free surplus grain, and investments in new industries or in infrastructure development.

Nonaligned countries could sometimes play the Cold War rivals against each other. Nasir, who had led a military coup against the Egyptian monarchy in 1952, and his successor Anwar al-Sadat (**al-seh-DAT**) played this game skillfully. The United States offered to build a dam at Aswan (**AS-wahn**), on the Nile River, to increase Egypt's electrical generating and irrigation capacity, but it withdrew the offer when Egypt turned to the Warsaw Pact for armaments in 1956. Worsened relations with the West then led Nasir to nationalize the Suez Canal and the Soviet Union to commit to building the dam at Aswam. Later that same year, Israel, Great Britain, and France allied to invade Egypt, aiming to overthrow Nasir, regain the Suez Canal, and secure Israel from any Egyptian threat. The invasion succeeded militarily, but the United States and the Soviet Union both pressured the invaders to withdraw, thus saving Nasir's government. In 1972 Sadat evicted Soviet military advisers, but a year later he used his Soviet weapons to attack Israel. After he lost that war, he disengaged from the Soviets; he then improved relations with, and sought increased aid from, the United States until his assassination in 1981.

AP® Exam Tip
Explain how the nonaligned movement opposed and promoted alternatives to the existing economic, political, and social orders.

nonaligned nations Developing countries that announced their neutrality in the Cold War.

Third World Term applied to a group of developing countries who professed nonalignment during the Cold War.

► **Prime Minister Jawaharlal Nehru visits with Col. Gamal Abdel Nasser, Premier of Eygypt** India's Jawaharlal Nehru (in white hat) was a central figure in the nonaligned movement, also known as the "Third Force." In 1966 Nehru traveled to meet Nasser in Cairo to try to recruit the Egyptian leader to the nonaligned movement. Keystone Pictures USA/ Alamy Stock Photo

Other nations adopted similar balancing strategies. In each case, local leaders sought to develop their nations' economies and assert or preserve their nations' interests. Manipulating the superpowers was a means toward those ends and implied very little about true ideological orientation of Third World political leaders.

31-3b Japan and China

No countries took more effective advantage of opportunities presented by the superpowers' preoccupations than Japan and China. Japan signed a peace treaty with most of its former enemies in 1951 and regained independence from American occupation the following year. Renouncing militarism and its imperialist past (see Chapter 29), Japan remained on the sidelines throughout the Korean War, although the United States relied on Japanese military bases. Its new constitution, written under American supervision in 1946, allowed only a limited self-defense force, banned the deployment of Japanese troops abroad, and gave the vote to women.

Like the Europeans, the Japanese had suffered high levels of population loss and property destruction in the war. With peace restored, they focused their resources on rebuilding industries and expanding trade. Peace treaties with countries in Southeast Asia specified reparations payable in the form of goods and services, thus reintroducing Japan to that region as a force for economic development rather than as a military occupier. Beginning during the U.S. occupation, Japan had become closely tied to the West by trade and soon benefited from the postwar economic recovery. At the same time, controls placed on Japan by peace conditions kept its military expenditures low during the Cold War, providing an exceptional environment to invest in economic development and infrastructure.

Three industries that took advantage of government aid and new technologies were key to Japan's emergence as an economic superpower after 1975. Electricity was in short supply in 1950, and Tokyo suffered from chronic power outages. Japan responded by constructing a modern, efficient power grid between 1951 and 1970 that produced 60 million kilowatts of electricity. Most of this new capacity came from hydroelectric sources. At the same time steel production and shipbuilding developed rapidly, placing Japan among world leaders in both industries. By the end of the 1970s Japanese industries were competitive with the most advanced industries in the United States.

While Japan benefited from avoiding the heavy defense costs associated with the Cold War, China was at the center of Cold War politics. When Mao Zedong (**maow dzuh-dong**) and the communists defeated the nationalists in 1949 and established the People's Republic of China (PRC), their main ally and source of arms was the Soviet Union. By 1956, however, the PRC and the Soviet Union were beginning to diverge politically, partly in reaction to the Soviet rejection of Stalinism and partly because of China's reluctance to accept the role of subordinate. Mao had his own notions of communism that focused strongly on the peasantry, which the Soviets had ignored in favor of the industrial working class.

Mao's Great Leap Forward in 1958 was intended to propel China into the ranks of world industrial powers by maximizing the output of small-scale, village-level industries and by instituting mass collectivization in agriculture. These untested policies demonstrated Mao's willingness to carry out massive economic and social experiments of his own devising in the face of criticism by the Soviets as well as by traditional economists. By 1962 the revolutionary reforms had failed comprehensively, contributing to an era of famine and privation that cost 20 to 30 million deaths.

In 1966 Mao instituted another radical program, the **Cultural Revolution**, that ordered the mass mobilization of Chinese youth into Red Guard units. His goal was to kindle revolutionary fervor in a new generation to ward off the stagnation and bureaucratization he saw in the Soviet Union, as well as to increase his own power within the Communist Party. Red Guard units criticized and purged teachers, party officials, and intellectuals for "bourgeois values." Executions, beatings, and incarcerations were widespread, leading to a half-million deaths and 3 million purged by 1971. Finally, Mao admitted that attacks on individuals had gotten out of hand and intervened to reestablish order. Mao's wife Jiang Qing (**jyahn ching**) and radical allies dominated the last years of the Cultural Revolution, harshly restricting artistic and intellectual activity.

The rift between the PRC and the Soviet Union allowed U.S. president Richard Nixon (served 1969–1974) to revive relations with China. In 1971 the United States agreed to allow the PRC to join the United Nations and occupy China's permanent seat on the Security Council. This decision necessitated the expulsion from the U.N. of the Chinese nationalist government based on the island of Taiwan, which had previously claimed to be the only legal Chinese authority. The following year, Nixon visited Beijing, initiating a new era of enhanced cooperation between the People's Republic of China and the United States.

31-3c The Middle East

Independence came gradually to the Arab countries of the Middle East. The French Mandate in Syria and Lebanon ended in 1943 and French troops left shortly after World War II. Iraq, Egypt, and Jordan enjoyed nominal independence between the two world wars but remained under indirect British control until the 1950s. Military coups overthrew King Faruq (**fuh-ROOK**) of Egypt in 1952 and King Faisal (**FIE-suhl**) II of Iraq in 1958. King Husayn (**hoo-SANE**) of Jordan dismissed his British military commander in 1956 in response to the Suez crisis, but his poor desert country remained dependent on British and later American financial aid.

Overshadowing all Arab politics, however, was the struggle with Israel, a clear illustration that the superpowers could not control all dangerous international disputes. British policy on Palestine between the wars oscillated between favoring Zionist Jews—who had emigrated to Palestine, encouraged by the Balfour Declaration—and support for the indigenous Palestinian Arabs, who suspected that the Zionists were aiming at an independent state. As more and more Jews sought a safe haven from persecution by the Nazis, Arabs increasingly felt threatened. The Arabs unleashed a guerrilla uprising against the British in 1936, and Jewish groups turned to militant tactics a few years later. Occasionally, Arabs and Jews confronted each other in riots or killings, making it clear that peaceful coexistence in Palestine would be difficult or impossible to achieve.

After the war, under intense pressure to resettle European Jewish refugees, Britain turned the Palestine problem over to the United Nations. In November 1947 the General Assembly voted in favor of partitioning Palestine into two states, one Jewish and one Arab. The Jewish community made plans to declare independence, while the Palestinians, who felt that the proposed land division was unfair to them, took up arms. When Israel declared its independence in May 1948, neighboring Arab countries sent armies to help the Palestinians crush the newborn state.

AP® Exam Tip
Compare Mao's Great Leap Forward with Stalin's Five-Year Plan.

Cultural Revolution (China) Campaign in China ordered by Mao Zedong to purge the Communist Party of his opponents and instill revolutionary values in the younger generation.

► **Chinese Red Guards** During the Cultural Revolution, the Red Guards, young Chinese militants, sought to identify enemies of the Communist Party and Chairman Mao, sometimes labeling their own teachers, parents, and neighbors as enemies of the people. In this photo a victim is forced to wear a dunce cap on which his purported crimes are written. AP Images

Israel militarily prevailed and some 700,000 Palestinians became refugees, finding shelter in United Nations refugee camps in Jordan, Syria, Lebanon, and the Gaza Strip (a bit of coastal land on the Egyptian–Israeli border). The right of these refugees to return home remains a focal point of Arab politics today. In 1967 Israel responded to threatening military moves by Egypt's Nasir by preemptively attacking Egyptian and Syrian air bases. In six days Israel won a smashing victory. When Jordan entered the war, Israel forces took control of Jerusalem, which it had previously split with Jordan, and the West Bank. Acquiring all of Jerusalem satisfied Jews' deep longing to return to their holiest city, but Palestinians continued to regard Jerusalem as their destined capital in any independent government, and Muslims in many countries protested Israeli control of the Dome of the Rock, a revered Islamic shrine located in the city. Israel also occupied the Gaza Strip, the strategic Golan Heights in southern Syria, and the entire Sinai Peninsula (see Map 31.3). These acquisitions resulted in a new wave of Palestinian refugees.

The rival claims to Palestine continued to plague Middle Eastern politics. The Palestine Liberation Organization (PLO), headed by Yasir Arafat (**AR-uh-fat**), waged guerrilla war against Israel, frequently engaging in acts of terrorism. The Israelis were able to blunt or absorb these attacks and launch counter-strikes that likewise involved assassinations and bombings. Though the United States was a firm friend to Israel and the Soviet Union armed most of the Arab states, neither superpower saw the struggle between Zionism and Palestinian nationalism as a vital concern—until oil became a political issue.

The phenomenal concentration of oil wealth in the Middle East—Saudi Arabia, Iran, Iraq, Kuwait, Libya, Qatar, Bahrain, and the United Arab Emirates—was not fully realized until after World War II, when demand for oil rose sharply as civilian economies in Europe, the United States, and Japan recovered and as modern industries spread elsewhere. In 1960, as world demand rose, oil-producing states formed the **Organization of Petroleum Exporting Countries (OPEC)** to promote their collective interest in gaining higher revenues by controlling world production.

Oil politics and the Arab–Israeli conflict intersected in October 1973 during the Yom Kippur War. Surprise attacks by Syria and Egypt threw the Israelis into temporary disarray, but Israel won a clear military victory in the end. Supported by military supplies from the United States, it drove back Syrian forces and trapped an Egyptian army at the Suez Canal's southern end. The United States then arranged a ceasefire and the disengagement of forces. But before that could happen, the Arab oil-producing countries voted to embargo oil shipments to the United States and the Netherlands as punishment for their support of Israel.

AP® Exam Tip
Consider the role of petroleum in raising productivity and increased production of material goods.

Organization of Petroleum Exporting Countries (OPEC) Organization formed in 1960 by oil-producing states to promote their collective interest in generating revenue from oil.

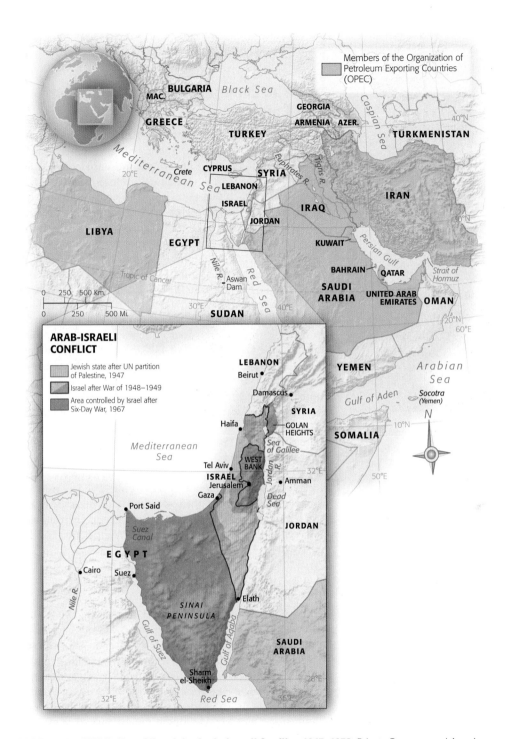

MAP 31.3   Middle East Oil and the Arab–Israeli Conflict, 1947–1973 Private European and American companies had long controlled oil resources. In the 1960s OPEC negotiated agreements for sharing control and eventually establishing national ownership. This set the stage for the use of oil as a weapon in the 1973 Arab-Israeli war as well as for subsequent price increases.

Why did the territorial settlements that followed the wars of 1947, 1967, and 1973 fail to produce a permanent peace between Israel and its Arab neighbors?

The implications of using oil as an economic weapon profoundly disturbed the worldwide oil industry. Prices rose steeply—along with feelings of economic insecurity. In 1974 OPEC responded to the turmoil in the oil market by quadrupling prices, setting the stage for massive transfers of wealth to the oil-producing countries and provoking a feeling of crisis throughout the consuming countries. This was the first time in the modern era that commodity-producers

▲ **Shortage at the Pumps** As gasoline shortages spread across America, prices rose in the late 1970s. Consumers were forced to wait in long lines to fill up their cars with gas. This photo is from Mill Valley, California, in 1974. Bob Kreisel/Alamy Stock Photo

had gained a significant, if temporary, market advantage over the developed industrial economies.

31-3d The Emergence of Environmental Concerns

The Cold War and the massive investments made in postwar economic recovery focused public and governmental attention on technological innovations and enormous projects such as hydroelectric dams and nuclear power stations. Only a few experts warned that untested technologies and industrial expansion were degrading the environment. The superpowers were particularly negligent of the environmental impact of pesticide and herbicide use, automobile exhaust, industrial waste disposal, and radiation.

The wave of student unrest that swept across many parts of the world from 1968 into the 1970s created a new awareness of environmental issues and a new constituency for environmental action. As youth activism grew, governments in the West began to pass new environmental regulations. Among them was the Clean Air Act of 1970. Earth Day, a benchmark of the new awareness, was also first celebrated in 1970, the year in which the United States also established its Environmental Protection Agency.

When oil prices skyrocketed, the problem of finite natural resources became more broadly recognized. Making gasoline engines and home heating systems more fuel efficient and lowering highway speed limits to conserve fuel became matters of national debate in the United States, while poorer countries struggled to find the money to import oil. A widely read 1972 study called *The Limits of Growth* forecast a need to cut back on consumption of natural resources in the twenty-first century. Ecological and environmental problems now vied for public attention with superpower rivalry and Third World nation building.

Section Review

- After decolonization new nations organized the "nonaligned movement" to assert a middle ground between the Cold War rivals.

- After World War II Japan followed the capitalist industrial model while China under Mao tried and failed to industrialize using mass mobilizations and central planning.

- Israel's military victories over its Arab neighbors in 1967 and 1973, while expanding the nation's borders, initiated an enduring cycle of regional tensions and violence between Israelis and Palestinians.

- OPEC's 1973 embargo of oil shipments to nations that supported Israel soon led to steep price increases and a massive redistribution of wealth to oil-producing nations.

- During the 1970s young people provided crucial leadership to a worldwide movement to conserve natural resources and protect the environment.

31-4 Conclusion

The alliance between the Soviet Union and the Western democracies led by the United States did not survive into the post–World War II era. Shortly after the war, both sides began to prepare for a new round of hostilities, establishing competing military alliances and attempting to influence the new governments of nations formerly occupied by the Axis. In the end this confrontation was projected into space, as each side sought to advertise its technological capacity through satellite launches and finally a moon landing.

Each side portrayed this tension as a struggle between irreconcilably different social and economic systems, and each side emphasized the corruption, injustice, and unfairness of its opponent. When Winston Churchill spoke in 1946 of Soviet control of eastern Europe as the imposition of an iron curtain, he suggested that communism and the Soviet system functioned as a prison.

Massive armies armed with increasingly sophisticated weapons, including nuclear weapons far more destructive than those dropped on Japan, defended the boundary that separated the United States and its allies from the Soviet

Union and its allies. This Cold War quickly became global in character as distant civil wars, regional conflicts, and nationalist revolutions were transformed by the support provided by these rivals for global ascendancy.

The desire of colonized peoples to throw off imperial controls and establish independent nations provided many of the era's flash points. The Western nations had defined World War II as a war for freedom and self-determination. The Free French had promised greater autonomy to African colonies, the United States had mobilized nationalist forces to fight against the Japanese in the Philippines and in Vietnam, and Britain also had used forces recruited throughout its empire to fight the war. Once organized and set in motion, these nationalist energies eventually overwhelmed colonial rule. The most powerful force in the postwar era was nationalism, the desire of peoples to control their own destinies.

In Africa, the Middle East, South Asia, and Latin America, this desire to throw off foreign controls led to the creation of scores of new nations by the 1970s. Each nation's struggle had its own character. While in India these passions led to independence, similar sentiments led in China to the overthrow of a government seen as weak and subordinate to foreign powers and to the creation of a communist dictatorship. In much of Africa, the Middle East, and the Caribbean, nationalism overturned colonial rule. In the Middle East the desire for self-government was complicated by the creation of the state of Israel. In Latin America, where most nations had been independent for well over a century, nationalist passions were focused on the desire for economic independence and an end to American military interventions.

The end of Japanese control in Korea and Vietnam led to territorial partitions that separated Soviet-leaning and Western-allied polities. Civil war and foreign interventions soon followed. In both cases the Soviet Union and China supported communist forces. The United States committed large military forces to protect the anticommunist governments, gaining a stalemate in Korea and eventually failing in Vietnam. While these outcomes were mixed for the superpowers, the wars were contained and managed so as to prevent direct engagement and nuclear conflict.

This period also witnessed the beginning of the international environmental movement. Public attention increasingly focused on resource management, pollution, and the preservation of endangered species. In response, the United States and governments in western Europe put in place the first generation of environmental laws. The Clean Air Act in the United States and other measures had an immediate impact, but both policymakers and the public grew aware of ever more serious challenges. The gas crisis of the 1970s gave these efforts a sense of urgency.

Key Terms

iron curtain p. 810	United Nations p. 810	Korean War p. 816	Cultural Revolution (China)
Cold War p. 810	World Bank p. 811	Vietnam War p. 817	p. 829
North Atlantic Treaty	Marshall Plan p. 813	Cuban missile crisis p. 818	Organization of Petroleum
Organization (NATO)	European Economic	Helsinki Accords p. 818	Exporting Countries
p. 810	Community (Common	*nonaligned nations* p. 827	(OPEC) p. 830
Warsaw Pact p. 810	Market) p. 813	*Third World* p. 827	

Review Questions

1. What were the origins of the Cold War?

2. How did the Cold War affect decolonization in the decades that followed World War II?

3. How did the transfer of territories following conflicts between Israel and its neighbors affect the prospects for peace?

 MindTap® is a fully online, personalized learning experience built upon Cengage Learning content. MindTap® combines student learning tools—readings, multimedia, activities, and assessments—into a singular Learning Path that guides students through the course and helps students develop the critical thinking, analysis, and communication skills that are essential to academic and professional success.

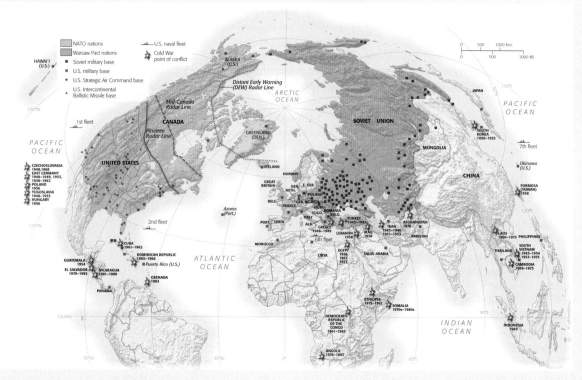

▲ **Cold War Confrontation**

Multiple-Choice Questions

Questions 1–3 refer to the map above.

1. The map demonstrates that the Cold War

  (A) continued the global nature of conflict in the twentieth century.

  (B) differed from other twentieth-century conflicts, which were regional.

  (C) had much in common with conflicts from the previous time period.

  (D) was not an industrialized form of warfare.

2. Which of the following best explains the global nature of the Cold War in the late twentieth century?

  (A) The colonial powers in Europe continued to lead opposing alliances based on new forms of economic colonialism.

  (B) The Cold War was led by newly formed Asian powers that expanded their influence into other regions.

  (C) The United States and the Soviet Union replaced older imperial powers.

  (D) The Cold War intensified conflicts between opposing religious belief systems.

3. Which of the following most likely explains the lack of a foreign military presence in much of Africa and Latin America?

  (A) These regions became formal colonies of a nuclear power.

  (B) These regions were still under the control of their imperial governments from the nineteenth century.

  (C) These regions were not of interest to the United States and the Soviet Union.

  (D) These regions had thrown off their imperial powers and formed new states.

Questions 4–6 refer to the passage below.

"God called Steve Biko to be his servant in South Africa—to speak up on behalf of God, declaring what the will of this God must be in a situation such as ours, a situation of evil, injustice, oppression and exploitation. God called him to be the founder father of the Black Consciousness Movement against which we have had tirades and fulminations. It is a movement by which God, through Steve [Steve Biko], sought to awaken in the Black person a sense of his intrinsic value and worth as a child of God, not needing to apologise for his existential condition as a black person, calling on blacks to glorify and praise God that he had created them black. Steve, with his brilliant mind that always saw to the heart of things, realised that until blacks asserted their humanity and their personhood, there was not the remotest chance for reconciliation in South Africa."

Desmond Tutu, Anglican bishop and winner
of the Noble Peace Prize, 1977

4. Which of the following best describes the theme of Bishop Tutu's writing?

  (A) Races can only exist together in hierarchies.

  (B) Alternatives to the existing social order must be recognized.

(C) Reconciliation between racial groups is impossible.

(D) Imperialist nations will never recognize the harm they have done to others.

5. Bishop Tutu justifies Steve Biko's ideas by

(A) arguing that Biko's ideas are strictly a political movement.

(B) claiming that the races are unable to live together.

(C) using religion to explain the movement and Biko's ideas.

(D) using economic arguments against apartheid.

6. Bishop Tutu and Steve Biko are examples of

(A) a desire to separate race relations and economics into unrelated issues.

(B) a continuation of Social Darwinist views on religion and economics.

(C) the radicalization of religious fundamentalist movements.

(D) opposition to existing social and economic orders in the twentieth century.

Questions 7–10 refer to the image at the top of the next column.

7. The purpose of the poster was most likely to

(A) encourage people to internalize the ideals of the communist revolution.

(B) question Mao's leadership skills.

(C) institute capitalist market reforms.

(D) encourage closer ties with Japan.

8. The spread of communism through posters like this was intended to

(A) encourage peasants to respect national rulers.

(B) unite people across national boundaries.

(C) share the overwhelming victories of communist militaries.

(D) increase the economic impact of communism.

9. The Cultural Revolution in China is an example of which of the following?

(A) Nonviolent actions to achieve political goals

(B) Religious revivalism

(C) Groups sometimes using violence to achieve political goals

(D) Expansion of democratic reforms

10. What was one effect of the Cultural Revolution in China?

(A) A revitalization of the Chinese economy

(B) China becoming more involved in world politics

(C) The suppression of Mao's writings

(D) Stagnation of the Chinese economy

▲ China Cultural Revolution Poster of Chairman Mao (Translation: "The many accomplish great things")
Mary Evans/Grenville Collins/The Image Works

Short-Answer Questions

1. Choose one of the following twentieth-century leaders and, based on your knowledge of world history, answer all parts of the question that follows.

- Nelson Mandela
- Fidel Castro
- Jawaharlal Nehru

(A) Identify ONE reason the chosen leader wanted independence.

(B) Explain ONE strategy used by the chosen leader to attain independence.

(C) Explain ONE challenge the chosen leader faced in building a new state.

2. Answer all parts of the question that follows.

(A) Identify ONE challenge faced by the Middle East in the latter part of the twentieth century.

(B) Explain ONE long-term economic change on the Middle East in the latter part of the twentieth century.

(C) Explain ONE long-term political change in the Middle East in the latter part of the twentieth century.

32

The End of the Cold War and the Challenge of Economic Development and Immigration, 1975–2000

AP® Framework Terms

Internet
Cellular communication
Deforestation
Greenhouse gasses
Genocide
Afghanistan
Cold War
Proxy wars

Overarching Questions

1 How have religions, belief systems, philosophies, and ideologies affected the political, economic, and social development of societies? (CUL)

2 How and why have economic, social, cultural, and geographic factors influenced the process of state building, expansion, and dissolution? (SB)

3 How have internal and external political factors influenced the process of state building, expansion, and dissolution? (SB)

4 How have economic systems and the development of ideologies, values, and institutions influenced each other? (ECON)

5 How have local, regional, and global economic systems and exchange networks influenced each other over time? (ECON)

At the end of the 1970s, China began an ambitious program of economic reforms. Until then, China, with the world's largest population, was a very poor nation. By 1980, China had a gross domestic product (GDP) per capita of approximately $309.00 per year (total goods and services produced divided by population). It lagged far behind the mature industrialized nations of Europe and North America in economic performance, as well as behind more dynamic neighboring nations like Japan and South Korea. Even poor developing nations like Kenya, with a GDP per capita of $642.00, and Bolivia, with a GDP per capita of $696.00, outperformed the Asian giant. Since implementing the reforms, China has experienced rapid economic growth and has become one of the few socialist nations to successfully make the transition to a market-based economy, reaching today a GDP per capita of $8,028.00. Despite this remarkable expansion, millions of Chinese still live in poverty. As is indicated in the opening illustration, ancient technology and poverty can exist in close proximity with modernity and affluence in China and elsewhere. These same problems of poverty and inequality can be found across the globe. In an era of astounding technological change and, until the recession of 2008, spreading prosperity, more than a billion of the world's population still live on less than $1.25 a day.

▲ **Shanghai—Old Meets New** The city of Shanghai is one of the great success stories in a rapidly growing Chinese economy, but its prosperity has left many behind. In this photo a poor man crosses a street in Shanghai's rich, modern commercial district carrying goods in hand-woven baskets balanced on a neck yoke, a technology thousands of years old. Robert Van Der Hilst/ Getty Images

In the first decades of the twenty-first century, population growth continues to outstrip economic resources in many of the nations of the developing world. Since the deep recession that began in 2008, politicians as well as social reformers in the wealthy industrialized nations have criticized the effects of high levels of unemployment, family breakdown, substance abuse, and homelessness. At the start of the twenty-first century, as in the Industrial Revolution (see Chapter 22), an era of relative affluence, increased global economic integration, and rapid technological progress has coincided with problems of social dislocation and mounting inequality. Among the most important events of this period were the emergence of new industrial powers in Asia, the precipitous demise of the Soviet Union and its socialist allies, and the migration of tens of millions of people from poor to rich nations. ●

32-1 Postcolonial Crises and Asian Economic Expansion

How did the Cold War affect economic policies and politics in Latin America, the Middle East, and Asia in the 1970s and 1980s?

Between 1975 and today, wars and revolutions have spread death and destruction through many of the world's least-developed regions. In most cases the origins of conflict were rooted in the experience of colonialism and foreign intervention, but each conflict also had a unique historical character. Throughout these decades of conflict, the two superpowers sought to avoid direct military confrontation while working to gain strategic advantages. The United States and the Soviet Union each supplied arms and financial assistance to nations or insurgent forces hostile to the other. Once linked to superpower rivalries, local conflicts became deadlier. Conflicts where the rival superpowers financed and armed competing factions or parties are called **proxy wars**. Today, long after the collapse of the Soviet Union at the end of the 1980s, an ongoing rivalry between Russia and the United States and its allies has continued to complicate armed conflicts in the Middle East and elsewhere.

In Latin America superpower rivalry transformed limited conflicts over political rights, social justice, and economic policies into a violent cycle of revolution, military dictatorship, and foreign meddling. In Iran and Afghanistan resentment against foreign intrusion and a growing religious hostility to the West's secular culture led to revolutionary transformations. Here again, superpower ambitions and regional political instability helped provoke war and economic decline. These experiences were not universal, however. During this same period some Asian nations experienced rapid economic transformation. Japan emerged as one of the world's leading industrial powers, and a small number of other Asian economies entered the ranks of industrial and commercial powers. Socialist China joined this group of fast-developing Asian nations after initiating market-based economic reforms, becoming the world's second largest economy in 2010.

At the end of the 1980s the Cold War ended with the collapse of the Soviet system in eastern Europe, but the transition to democracy and market economy proved difficult. As both developing and former socialist nations opened their markets to foreign investment and competition, they experienced wrenching social change. Increased globalization coincided with increased inequality in many nations, but some developing nations also attained substantial benefits from rapid technological change and world economic integration.

This period also witnessed a great increase in world population and in levels of international immigration. Population growth and the spread of industrialization had a dramatic impact on the global environment, with every continent feeling the destructive effects of forest depletion, soil erosion, and pollution. Wealthy nations with slow population growth found it easier to respond to these environmental challenges than did poor nations trying to meet the challenge of rapid population growth by expanding their mining and commercial agriculture sectors.

32-1a Revolutions, Repression, and Democratic Reform in Latin America

In the 1970s Latin America entered a dark era of political violence. When revolutionary movements challenged the established order, militaries in many countries overturned constitutional governments and instituted repressive measures. A region of weak democracies in 1960 became a region dominated by military dictatorships with little patience for civil liberties and human rights fifteen years later.

The ongoing confrontation between Fidel Castro of Cuba and the government of the United States (see Chapter 31) helped propel the region toward crisis. The fact that the Cuban communist government survived efforts by the United States to overthrow it energized the revolutionary left throughout Latin America. Fearful that revolution would spread across Latin America, the United States increased support for its political and military allies in that region, training many of the military leaders who led coups during this period.

proxy wars During the Cold War, local or regional wars in which the superpowers pursued their interests by arming, training, and financing local combatants.

CHRONOLOGY

	The Americas	Middle East/Africa	Asia	Eastern Europe
1970	1970 Salvador Allende elected president of Chile			
	1973 Allende overthrown			
	1976 Military takeover in Argentina		1975 Vietnam War ends	
	1979 Sandinistas overthrow Anastasio Somoza in Nicaragua	1979 Shah of Iran overthrown in Islamic Revolution	1979 China begins economic reforms	1978 USSR sends troops to Afghanistan
1980	1983-1990 Democracy returns in Argentina, Brazil, and Chile	1980–1988 Iran-Iraq War	1986 Average Japanese income overtakes income in United States	1985 Mikhail Gorbachev becomes Soviet head of state
	1989 United States invades Panama	1989 USSR withdraws from Afghanistan	1989 Tiananmen Square confrontation	1989 Berlin Wall falls 1989–1991 Communism ends in eastern Europe
1990	1990 Sandinistas defeated in elections in Nicaragua	1990 Iraq invades Kuwait 1991 Persian Gulf War	1990s Japanese recession begins	1990 Reunification of Germany
		1994 Nelson Mandela elected president of South Africa; Tutsi massacred in Rwanda		1992 Yugoslavia disintegrates; Croatia and Slovenia become independent nations
	1998 Election of Hugo Chávez in Venezuela		1997 Asian financial crisis begins	1992–1995 Bosnia crisis

Brazil was the first nation to experience the region-wide conservative reaction to the Cuban Revolution. Claiming that Brazil's civilian political leaders could not protect the nation from communist subversion, the army overthrew the constitutional government of President João Goulart (**ju-wow go-LARHT**) in 1964. Once in power, the military suspended the constitution, outlawed all existing political parties, and exiled former presidents and opposition leaders. Death squads—illegal paramilitary organizations sanctioned by the government—detained, tortured, and executed thousands of citizens. The dictatorship also undertook an ambitious economic program that promoted industrialization through import substitution, using tax and tariff policies to successfully compel foreign-owned companies to increase investment in manufacturing, especially in the auto industry.

This combination of dictatorship, violent repression, and government promotion of industrialization came to be called the "Brazilian Solution." Elements of this "solution" were later imposed across much of the region. In 1970 Chile's newly elected president, **Salvador Allende** (**sal-VAH-dor ah-YEHN-day**), undertook an ambitious program of socialist reforms and nationalized Chile's heavy industry and mines, including the American-owned copper companies that dominated the economy. From the beginning of Allende's presidency the administration of President Richard Nixon (served 1969–1973) sought to undermine the Chilean government. Afflicted by inflation, mass consumer protests, and declining foreign trade, a military uprising led by General Augusto Pinochet (**ah-GOOS-toh pin-oh-CHET**) and supported by the United States overthrew Allende in 1973. President Allende and thousands of Chileans died in the uprising, and thousands more were jailed, tortured, and imprisoned without trial. Once in power Pinochet rolled back Allende's socialist innovations, dramatically reducing state participation in the economy and encouraging foreign investment.

In 1976 Argentina followed Brazil and Chile into dictatorship. Juan Perón had been exiled in 1955 after a military uprising, but with Argentina torn by rising levels of political violence he

AP® Exam Tip
Understand the impact of the development of military dictatorships in the twentieth century.

Salvador Allende Socialist politician elected president of Chile in 1970 and overthrown by the military in 1973. He was killed during the military attack on the presidential palace.

▲ **The Nicaraguan Revolution Overturns Somoza** A revolutionary coalition that included Marxists drove the long-serving dictator Anastasio Somoza from power in 1979. The Somoza family had ruled Nicaragua since the 1930s and maintained a close relationship with the United States. John Giannini/Getty Images

Dirty War War waged by the Argentine military (1976–1983) against leftist groups. Characterized by the use of illegal imprisonment, torture, and executions by the military.

Sandinistas Members of a leftist coalition that overthrew the Nicaraguan dictatorship of Anastasia Somoza in 1979 and attempted to install a socialist economy. The United States financed armed opposition by the Contras. The Sandinistas lost national elections in 1990.

was allowed to return and was then elected president in 1973 (see Chapter 30). Perón had insisted that his third wife, Isabel Martínez de Perón **EES-ah-bell mar-TEEN-ehz deh pair-OWN**), be elected vice president, and she inherited the presidency after his death in 1974. Her weak administration faced a potent leftist guerrilla insurgency, a wave of kidnappings, high inflation, and labor protests. Impatient with the policies of the president, the military seized power and suspended the constitution in 1976. During the next seven years it fought what it called the **Dirty War** against terrorism. More than 10,000 Argentines lost their lives, and thousands of others endured arrest and torture before democracy was restored.

While the left suffered these reverses in South America, a revolutionary movement came to power in Nicaragua in 1979, overthrowing the corrupt dictatorship of Anastasio Somoza. This broad alliance of revolutionaries and reformers called themselves **Sandinistas** (**sahn-din-EES-tahs**). They took their name from Augusto César Sandino, who had led Nicaraguan opposition to a U.S. military intervention between 1927 and 1932. Once in power, the Sandinistas moved leftward, seeking to imitate the command economies of Cuba and the Soviet Union and nationalizing properties owned by members of the Nicaraguan elite and U.S. companies.

U.S. president Jimmy Carter (served 1977–1980) championed human rights in the hemisphere and stopped the flow of U.S. arms to the military regimes with the worst human rights records, like Argentina. Carter also agreed to the re-establishment of Panamanian sovereignty in the Canal Zone at the end of 1999, but his effort to find common ground with the Sandinistas of Nicaragua failed due in large measure to their intransigence.

Carter was defeated in the next election by Ronald Reagan, who was committed to overturning the Nicaraguan Revolution and defeating a revolutionary movement in neighboring El Salvador. With the memory of the Vietnam War still strong (see Chapter 31), the U.S. Congress resisted any use of U.S. combat forces in Nicaragua and El Salvador and put strict limits on military aid. As a result, the Reagan administration tried to roll back the Nicaraguan Revolution through punitive economic measures and the recruitment and arming of a proxy force of anti-Sandinista Nicaraguans, called *Contras* (counter-revolutionaries).

Confident that they were supported by the majority of Nicaraguans and assured that the U.S. Congress was close to cutting off aid to the Contras, the Sandinistas led by Daniel Ortega called for free elections in 1990. But they had miscalculated politically. Exhausted by more than a decade of violence, a majority of Nicaraguan voters rejected the Sandinistas and elected a middle-of-the-road coalition led by Violeta Chamorro (**vee-oh-LET-ah cha-MOR-roe**). Unhappy with corruption and a poor economy, Nicaraguan voters returned Daniel Ortega to the presidency in 2007. He remains in power as of 2017.

In neighboring El Salvador another guerrilla movement, the Farabundo Martí (**fah-rah-BOON-doh mar-TEE**) National Liberation Front, or FMLN (acronym for Spanish name) seemed on the verge of taking power. The Reagan administration responded by providing hundreds of millions of dollars in military assistance and by training units of the El Salvadoran army. The assassination of Archbishop Oscar Romero and other members of the Catholic clergy by death squads tied to the Salvadoran government as well as the murder of thousands of noncombatants by military units trained by the United States undermined this effort and led to the U.S. Congress limiting the role of American soldiers in this nation. However, the electoral defeat of the Sandinistas in Nicaragua and the collapse of the Soviet Union (see below) finally forced the FMLN rebels to negotiate peace, transforming themselves into a left-of-center civilian political party.

During this same period, the violent political confrontation of right and left abated in South America as well. The right-wing military dictatorships established in Brazil, Chile, and Argentina all came to an end between 1983 and 1990, brought down by their own excesses and by popular desires for a return to constitutional government. By 2000, with the Cold War ended, 95 percent of Latin America's population lived again under civilian rule.

At the same time, the influence of the United States grew substantially. The United States had thwarted the left in Nicaragua and El Salvador by funding military proxies. It used its own military in a 1983 invasion of the tiny Caribbean nation of Grenada and again in 1989 to overthrow and arrest dictator General Manuel Noriega (**MAN-wel no-ree-EGG-ah**) of Panama. These actions were powerful reminders to Latin Americans of prior interventions (see Chapter 26), but they also served as reminders of American power at a time when socialism was discredited by the collapse of the Soviet bloc.

From this position of strength, the United States pushed Latin American nations to reform their economies by removing limitations on foreign investment, eliminating many social welfare programs, and reducing public-sector employment (see Chapter 29 for discussion of economic nationalism). Latin American governments responded by selling public-sector industries—like national airlines, manufacturing facilities, and public utilities—to foreign corporations. But popular support for these policies, what Latin Americans called **neoliberalism**, eroded quickly due to political scandals over the terms of these sales of public properties and a slowing world economy. A catastrophic economic and political meltdown in Argentina between 2001 and 2002 contributed to the appearance of a reinvigorated nationalist left in Latin America that sought to roll back neoliberal reforms (see Diversity & Dominance: The Struggle for Women's Rights in an Era of Global Political and Economic Change). Among the most vocal critic of neoliberalism and American influence was Hugo Chávez (**HUGH-go CHA-vez**), elected president of Venezuela in 1998 and serving as the region's chief critic of U.S. policy until his death in 2013. Left-of-center presidents were later elected in Brazil (Luiz Inácio Lula da Silva, 2002), Argentina (Néstor Kirchner, 2003), Bolivia (Evo Morales, 2005), and Ecuador (Rafael Correa, 2007).

32-1b Islamic Revolutions in Iran and Afghanistan

Although the Arab–Israel conflict and the oil crisis (see Chapter 31) concerned both superpowers, the prospect of direct military involvement remained remote. When unexpected crises developed in Iran and Afghanistan, however, significant strategic issues for the superpowers

AP® Exam Tip
Explain the changes and continuities in political economic systems in Latin America during the twentieth and twenty-first centuries.

neoliberalism The term used in Latin America and other developing regions to describe free-market policies that include reducing tariff protection for local industries; the sale of public-sector industries, like national airlines and public utilities, to private investors or foreign corporations; and the reduction of social welfare policies and public-sector employment.

AP® Exam Tip

Explain how a variety of factors, including the Soviet invasion of Afghanistan, led to the end of the Cold War and the collapse of the Soviet Union.

came to the foreground. Both countries adjoined Soviet territory, making Soviet military intervention more likely. Exercising post–Vietnam War caution, the United States reacted with restraint in Iran to avoid military intervention. The Soviet Union chose a bolder and ultimately disastrous course of direct intervention in Afghanistan.

Muhammad Reza Pahlavi (**REH-zah PAH-lah-vee**) succeeded his father as shah of Iran in 1941. In 1953 covert intervention by the U.S. Central Intelligence Agency (CIA) helped the shah retain his throne in the face of a movement to overturn royal power. Even when he finally nationalized the foreign-owned oil industry, the shah continued to enjoy American support. As oil revenues increased following the price increases of the 1970s, the United States encouraged the shah to spend his nation's growing wealth on equipping the Iranian army with modern American weaponry. By the 1970s popular resentment against the ballooning wealth of the elite families that supported the shah and the brutality, inefficiency, malfeasance, and corruption of his government led to mass opposition.

Ayatollah Ruhollah Khomeini (**A-yat-ol-LAH ROOH-ol-LAH ko-MAY-nee**), an exiled Shi'ite (**SHE-ite**) philosopher-cleric who had spent most of his eighty-plus years in religious and academic pursuits, became the leader of the Iranian opposition. Massive protests forced the shah to flee Iran and ended the monarchy in 1979. In the Islamic Republic of Iran, which replaced the monarchy, Ayatollah Khomeini was supreme arbiter of disputes and guarantor of the government's religious legitimacy. He oversaw a parliamentary regime based on European models but imposed religious control over legislation and public behavior. The electoral process was not open to monarchists, communists, and other opposition groups. Shi'ite clerics with little training for government service held many of the highest posts, and stringent measures were taken to combat Western styles and cultural influence. Universities were temporarily closed, and their faculties were purged of secularists and monarchists. Women were compelled to wear modest Islamic garments outside the house, and semi-official vigilante committees policed public morals and cast a pall over entertainment and social life. Many sectors of the Iranian economy were also placed under the direction of clerically controlled foundations, leading to massive capital flight. Clerical mismanagement and inflation have contributed to decades of economic stagnation and isolation in Iran.

President Carter had criticized the shah's repressive regime, but the overthrow of a long-standing ally and the creation of the Islamic Republic were blows to American prestige. The new Iranian regime was anti-Israeli and anti-American. Seeing the United States as a "Great Satan" opposed to Islam, Khomeini fostered Islamic revolutionary movements that threatened the United States and Israel. In November 1979 Iranian radicals seized the U.S. embassy in Tehran and held fifty-two diplomats hostage for 444 days. Americans felt humiliated by their inability to rescue the hostages or negotiate their release.

In the fall of 1980, shortly after negotiations for the release of the hostages began, **Saddam Husain** (**sah-DAHM hoo-SANE**), the ruler of neighboring Iraq, invaded Iran with the intention of toppling the Islamic Republic. His own dictatorial rule rested on a secular, Arab-nationalist philosophy and long-standing friendship with the Soviet Union, which had provided him with advanced weaponry. He feared that the fervor of Iran's revolutionary Shi'ite leaders would infect his own country's Shi'ite majority and threaten his power. The war pitted American weapons in the hands of the Iranians against Soviet weapons in the hands of the Iraqis, but the superpowers avoided overt involvement during eight years of bloodshed. Covertly, however, the United States used Israel to transfer arms to Iran, hoping to gain the release of other American hostages held by radical Islamic groups in Lebanon and to help finance the Contra war against the Sandinista government of Nicaragua. When this deal came to light in 1986, the resulting political scandal intensified American hostility to Iran. Openly tilting toward Iraq, President Reagan sent the United States Navy to the Persian Gulf, ostensibly to protect nonbelligerent shipping. The move helped force Iran to accept a ceasefire in 1988.

Ayatollah Ruhollah Khomeini Shi'ite philosopher and cleric who led the overthrow of the shah of Iran in 1979 and created an Islamic republic.

Saddam Husain (1937–2006) President of Iraq from 1979 until overthrown by an American-led invasion in 2003. Waged war on Iran from 1980 to 1988. His invasion of Kuwait in 1990 was repulsed in the Persian Gulf War in 1991.

While the United States dealt with Iran, the Soviet Union faced even more serious problems in neighboring Afghanistan. In 1978 a Marxist party with a secular agenda seized power. Offended by the new regime's efforts to reform education and grant rights to women, traditional Afghan ethnic and religious leaders led a successful rebellion. The Soviet Union responded by sending its army into Afghanistan to install a communist regime. With the United States, Saudi Arabia, and Pakistan paying, equipping, and training Afghan rebels, the Soviet Union found itself in an unwinnable war like the one the United States had earlier stumbled into in Vietnam. Facing growing economic problems and widespread domestic discontent over the war, Soviet

leaders withdrew their troops in 1989. Three years later rebel groups took control of the entire country and then began to fight among themselves over who should rule. In this chaotic situation a radical Islamic party with close ties to Pakistan, the Taliban, took power in 1996. They installed a harsh religious regime and soon faced armed opposition. The Taliban had received financial support from the Saudi Arabian Osama bin Laden during their rise to power and later provided him with protection as he organized the militant organization al-Qaeda that later attacked the United States on September 11, 2001 (see Chapter 33).

32-1c Asian Transformation

Although Japan has few mineral resources and is dependent on oil imports, the Japanese economy weathered the oil price shocks of the 1970s much better than did the economies of Europe and the United States. In fact, Japan experienced a faster rate of economic growth in the 1970s and 1980s than did any other major developed economy, growing at about 10 percent a year and becoming the world's second largest economy. Average income in Japan also increased rapidly, briefly overtaking that of the United States in the 1980s.

There were major differences between the Japanese and U.S. industrial models. During the American occupation, Japanese industrial conglomerates known as *zaibatsu* (see Chapter 27) were broken up. Although ownership of major industries became less concentrated, business leaders created new industrial alliances to control competition and facilitate the allocation of resources. During the period of dramatic growth there were six major **keiretsu** (**kay-REHT-soo**), each of which included a major bank as well as firms in industry, commerce, and construction tied together in an interlocking ownership structure. There were also minor keiretsu dominated by major industrial corporations, like Toyota.

Tariffs and import regulations inhibiting foreign competition were crucial to the early stages of development of Japan's major industries. These restrictions and Japanese success at exporting manufactured goods through the 1980s produced huge trade surpluses with other nations. Although the United States and the European Community engaged in tough negotiations to try to force open the Japanese market, these efforts had only limited success, and by 1990 Japan's trade surplus with the rest of the world was double that of 1985.

Many experts assumed that Japan's competitive advantages would propel it past the United States as the world's preeminent industrial economy, but during the 1990s Japan entered what would become a more than two-decade-long crisis that dramatically slowed the growth of both

AP® Exam Tip
Be able to explain how governments had a strong role in economic life following World War II.

keiretsu Alliances of corporations and banks that dominate the Japanese economy.

The Struggle for Women's Rights in an Era of Global Political and Economic Change

The struggle for women's rights has been one of the most important social movements of the twentieth and twenty-first centuries. Although we can identify fundamental similarities in objectives across cultural and political boundaries, women in less developed nations are forced to recognize that their objectives and strategies must take into account international inequalities in power and wealth.

In this section Gladys Acosta, a militant Peruvian feminist, discusses her recommended agenda for this struggle in the era after the fall of the Soviet Union and the rise of neoliberalism, the term used in Latin America to identify the free-market economic policies advocated by the United States. Among its chief characteristics are an end to the governmental protections for local industries, a reduction in government social welfare policies (efforts to hold down prices on staples and establish wage minimums, among other policies), a reduction in public-sector employment, a commitment to paying debts to international creditors, and the removal of impediments to foreign investment. Many Latin Americans believe that neoliberalism is a new form of imperialism. While written in the 1990s, this political manifesto deals directly with issues of great relevance today: international indebtedness, the social costs of austerity, and gender inequality.

Neo-Liberalism in Action

When I talk of neo-liberalism, I mean austerity measures, foreign debts, and increased liberties for all those who have the power of money at their disposal and the power of repression over those who make demands. We have now reached a new form of capitalist accumulation. The world's economic system is in a state of change and capital has become more concentrated and centralised. I would not go as far as to say countries don't exist anymore but national identities do certainly play a different role now. . . . If we look at the bare face of neo-liberalism from a woman's point of view, we cannot fail to notice its murderous consequences. . . . At the moment we're experiencing capitalism's greatest ideological offensive. It's all business: everything is bought and sold and everything has its price.

The Consequences of Neo-Liberal Politics

[W]omen play an important role in this ever-more internationalized economy because we represent, as ever, a particularly exploitable workforce. A number of studies have revealed the existence of subcontractor chains who work for

GDP and average income. In the thirty months between January 1990 and July 1992, Japanese stocks and real estate markets lost $2.5 trillion in market value, while the national economy's growth rate fell from 3.1 percent a year to 0.2 percent.

Before the crisis, Japanese real estate and stock markets had become highly overvalued as the nation's huge trade imbalances with the United States and other trading partners flooded the economy with cash and fueled dangerous financial speculation. As the crisis deepened and prices collapsed, the close relationships between industry, government, and banks proved to be a liability, as these powerful institutions acted to prop up inefficient companies and support unsustainable market values. By the end of the 1990s Japan's GDP had suffered a loss greater than that suffered by the United States in the Great Depression, leaving the nation with a crushing debt burden. Despite government efforts to promote recovery with deficit spending, public works projects, and low interest rates, Japan's economy has grown very slowly to the present. In 2010 it lost its position as the world's second largest economy to China.

Other Asian states imitated the Japanese model of development in the 1970s and 1980s. These nations protected new industries from foreign competition while encouraging close alliances among industries and banks. The largest and most successful of them, the Republic of Korea, commonly called South Korea, used a combination of inexpensive labor, strong technical education, and substantial domestic capital reserves to support a massive industrialization effort. Success in heavy industries such as steel and shipbuilding as well as in consumer industries such as automobiles and consumer electronics soon made it a global economic power.

The small nations of Taiwan and Singapore, along with Hong Kong, a British colony until 1997 when it returned to Chinese control, also became industrial and financial powerhouses. As a result of their rapid development, these three economies along with South Korea were called the **Asian Tigers**. While Taiwan suffered a number of political reverses, including the loss of its United Nations seat to the People's Republic of China in 1971 and the withdrawal of diplomatic recognition by the United States, it achieved remarkable economic progress, based in large part on investment in the economy of the People's Republic of China. Hong Kong and Singapore— long-time British colonies with extremely limited natural resources—also enjoyed rapid

AP® Exam Tip
Understand the growth of export-oriented economies in East Asia in this time period. Compare these economies with East Asian economies in earlier time periods.

transnational companies "informally" and mainly employ women. Basically we are dealing with a kind of integration into the world market which often uses our own homes as its outlet. Obviously, this work is badly paid and completely unprotected and has to be done without any of those social rights which were formerly achieved by trade union struggles. . . . As it advances worldwide, this capitalism also encourages the expansion of certain kinds of tourism. A visible increase in prostitution is part of this, whereby women from poor countries are smuggled into large, internationally operated rings which exploit them. The reports of Filipina women traded on the West German market send shivers down our spines. . . .

How the Adoption of Austerity Measures Affects Women's Lives

It is obvious that foreign debt is one of the most inhuman forms of exploitation in our countries when one considers the ratio between work necessary for workers' needs and work producing profit for employers. The experts have already explained how the prevailing exchange and investment structures have created international finance systems which keep whole populations in inhuman conditions. . . . Women in every household are suffering every day as a result of impoverished economies and those who are most exposed to the effects of foreign debt are women.

When it comes to shopping, caring for sick children or the impossibility of meeting their schooling costs, the illusion of "leaving poverty behind" evaporates. Yet the problem is not only of an economic nature because under such circumstances the constant tension leads to grave, often lasting exhaustion. The psychosocial damage is alarming. The adoption of austerity [under neo-liberalism] measures means a curtailment of the state's commitment to social services with a direct effect on women. Daily life becomes hell for them. The lack of even minimal state welfare presents women (and obviously children too) with crushing working days.

AP® History Reasoning Skills

Causation *What has led to the rise of neoliberalism on the lives of female workers?*

Comparison *In what ways do Acosta's views of women and family and the views of Kollontai (Chapter 29) compare?*

Source: From Gladys Acosta, "The View of a Peruvian Militant," in *Compañeras: Voices from the Latin American Women's Movement,* ed. Gaby Küppers (London, UK: Latin American Bureau, 1994). Reprinted with permission of the publisher.

economic development. Both were historically important Asian ports and commercial centers that later developed successful manufacturing, banking, and commercial sectors.

These **newly industrialized economies (NIEs)** shared many characteristics that help explain their rapid industrialization. All had disciplined and hard-working labor forces, and all invested heavily in education. For example, as early as 1980 South Korea had as many engineering graduates as the advanced industrial nations of Germany, Britain, and Sweden combined. All had very high rates of personal saving, about 35 percent of GDP, that was used to fund new technologies, and all emphasized outward-looking export strategies. And, like Japan, all benefited from government sponsorship and protection from foreign competition during development. Despite this momentum, the region was deeply shaken by a financial crisis that began in 1997. Like the recession that afflicted Japan in 1990, a combination of bad loans, weak banks, and the international effects of currency speculation led to a deep regional crisis that was stabilized only by the efforts of the United States, Japan, and international institutions like the International Monetary Fund.

32-1d China Rejoins the World Economy

After Mao Zedong's death in 1976, the Chinese communist leadership began economic reforms that relaxed state control, allowing more initiative and permitting individuals to accumulate wealth. The results were remarkable. Under China's leader **Deng Xiaoping** (**dung shee-yao-ping**) (1904–1997), China permitted foreign investment for the first time since the communists came to power in 1949. Between 1979 and 2014, foreign direct investment in China grew to more than $1.5 trillion as McDonald's, General Motors, Coca-Cola, Airbus, Toyota, and many other foreign companies began doing business. In 2014 foreign direct investment was greater in China than in the United States for the first time, $128 billion to $86 billion. As a result of this pattern, foreign firms now account for roughly 50 percent of China's imports and exports.

By 2010 China had become a major industrial power and the world's most important exporting nation. Despite these changes, state-owned enterprises still employed more than 100 million workers, and most foreign-owned companies were limited to special economic zones.

Asian Tigers Collective name for South Korea, Taiwan, Hong Kong, and Singapore—nations that became economic powers in the 1970s and 1980s.

newly industrialized economies (NIEs) Rapidly growing, new industrial nations of the late twentieth century, including the Asian Tigers.

Deng Xiaoping Communist Party leader who forced Chinese economic reforms after the death of Mao Zedong.

AP® Exam Tip
Explain why some governments, such as China under Deng Xiaoping, began to promote economic liberalization in the late twentieth century.

AP® Exam Tip
Explain how some groups, such as the Tiananmen Square protesters, opposed and promoted alternatives to the existing economic, political, and social orders.

Tiananmen Square Site in Beijing where Chinese students and workers gathered to demand greater political openness in 1989. The demonstration was crushed by Chinese military with great loss of life.

The result was a dual industrial sector—one modern, efficient, and connected to international markets, the other directed by political decisions. While the Chinese have not yet privatized land, by 1990 over 90 percent of China's agricultural land was in the hands of farmers permitted to sell what they produced, but new reforms were slowed by popular opposition to growing inequality among agriculturalists.

In 2010 China became the world's second largest economy, surpassing Japan. The scale of this achievement can be represented by the remarkable growth of China's GDP, the total value of all goods and services produced by the nation. In 1970 China, with a population of nearly 1 billion, had a GDP of $56 billion, roughly half the GDP of Italy ($111 billion), with a population of 55 million people. By 2010 China's GDP had increased eighty-one times, surpassing $4.5 trillion, rising to $11 trillion in 2015. Other developing countries grew substantially in this period as well. India's economy, for example, was larger than China's in 1970 ($66 billion) and increased nineteen times by 2010, to $1.2 trillion. In 2015 it was $2.1 trillion, roughly one-fifth the size of China's.

Despite its enormous achievement, China, with a per capita GDP (GDP divided by national population) as of 2015 of $8,027, has remained substantially poorer than mature industrial economies like the United States and Germany, which have per capita GDPs of $56,115 and $41,313, respectively. However, China is now richer than much of the developing world. Latin America has a per capita GDP of $8,363, the Middle East and North Africa $7,407, sub-Saharan Africa $1,588, and South Asia $1,542. While poverty levels in China have fallen swiftly during this period of rapid development, inequality, especially between rural and urban dwellers, has increased.

The combination of economic reforms, high levels of foreign investment, and technology transfers from developed industrial nations has helped make China one of the world's major industrial powers. As was true earlier with Japan and the Asian Tigers, China's expansion has depended heavily on exports, which accounted for over 40 percent of GDP in 2008, falling to roughly 30 percent by 2017. Success in foreign markets produced a large foreign trade surplus. As was the case with Japan three decades ago, these cash surpluses paid for the government's massive investments in infrastructure, but also promoted speculation in real estate and stocks and propped up a weak banking sector. While the Chinese economy continued to grow at a healthy rate during the worldwide recession that began in 2008, some economists wonder if the speculative excesses can be overcome without a deep contraction similar to that experienced by Japan in the 1990s. The near collapse of China's two major stock markets in 2015–2016, unsustainable real estate values, and rising corporate, government, and household debt levels are all suggestive of future problems.

Deng Xiaoping's strategy of balancing change and continuity avoided some of the social and political costs experienced by Russia and other socialist countries that abruptly embraced capitalism and democracy after the collapse of the Soviet Union (see next section), but he faced a major challenge in 1989. Responding to inflation and to worldwide mass movements in favor of democracy, Chinese students and intellectuals led a series of protests demanding more democracy and an end to corruption. This movement culminated in **Tiananmen (Tee-yehn-ahn-men) Square**, in the heart of Beijing, where hundreds of thousands of protesters gathered and refused to leave. After weeks of standoff, tanks pushed into the square, killing hundreds and arresting thousands. The Communist Party has not faced another direct challenge to its power since then, but growing levels of labor unrest, protests in favor of political rights, corruption scandals, and ethnic confrontations continue to challenge this one-party dictatorship.

Section Review

- During the 1970s and 1980s, political violence grew in Latin America, sponsored in part by U.S. fears of communist subversion.

- The United States opposed revolutionary movements in Nicaragua and El Salvador.

- In the 1990s the United States pushed Latin American nations to introduce neoliberal reforms that opened economies to greater foreign investment.

- A radical anti-American Islamic revolution led by Ayatollah Khomeini triumphed in Iran in 1979 and led to a ten-year war with Iraq.

- The Soviets intervened in Afghanistan in 1979 but failed to defeat local opponents backed by the United States and Pakistan, leading ultimately to Taliban government.

- After three decades of rapid economic growth, Japan entered a deep recession in the 1990s.

- The four Asian Tigers experienced rapid economic growth.

- After Deng Xiaoping reformed and modernized China's economy in 1979, China has experienced three decades of rapid growth.

32-2 The End of the Bipolar World

What forces led to the collapse of the Soviet Union?

After the end of World War II, competition between the alliances led by the United States and the Soviet Union created a bipolar world (see Chapter 31). Every conflict, no matter how local its origins, had the potential of engaging the attention of one or both of the superpowers. The Korean War, decolonization in Africa, the Vietnam War, the Cuban Revolution, and hostilities between Israel and its neighbors all increased tension between the nuclear-armed superpowers. Given this succession of provocations, politics everywhere was dominated by arguments over the relative merits of the competing systems.

Few in 1980 predicted the startling collapse of the Soviet Union. Western observers tended to see communist nations as both more uniform in character and more subservient to the Soviet Union than was true. Long before the 1980s, deep divisions had appeared among communist states. Similarly, nationalism had reappeared as a powerful force among the once-independent nations and ethnic groups brought together within the Soviet Union itself. By the late 1980s these forces threatened the survival of this communist world power.

32-2a Crisis in the Soviet Union

Under U.S. president Ronald Reagan and the Soviet Union's general secretary Leonid Brezhnev (**leh-oh-NEED BREZ-nef**), Cold War rhetoric remained intense. Massive new U.S. investments in armaments placed heavy competitive burdens on a Soviet economy already suffering from shortages and mismanagement. Obsolete industrial plants and centralized planning stifled initiative in the Soviet Union and led to a declining standard of living relative to the West, while the arbitrariness of the bureaucracy, the manipulation of information, and material deprivations created a crisis in morale.

Despite the unpopularity of the war in Afghanistan and growing domestic discontent, Brezhnev refused to modify his unsuccessful policies, but he could not escape criticism. Self-published underground writings (*samizdat* [**sah-meez-DAHT**]) by critics of the regime circulated widely despite government efforts to suppress them. In a series of powerful books, writer Alexander Solzhenitsyn (**sol-zhuh-NEET-sin**) castigated the Soviet system. Although he won a Nobel Prize in literature, Soviet authorities charged him with treason and expelled him in 1974.

By the time **Mikhail Gorbachev** (**GORE-beh-CHOF**) came to power in 1985, weariness with war in Afghanistan, economic decay, and vocal protest had reached critical levels. Casting aside Brezhnev's hard line, Gorbachev authorized major reforms in an attempt to stave off total collapse. His policy of political openness (*glasnost*) permitted criticism of the government and the Communist Party. His policy of **perestroika** (**per-ih-STROY-kuh**) ("restructuring") was an attempt to address long-suppressed economic problems by moving away from central state planning. In 1989 he ended the unpopular war in Afghanistan.

32-2b The Collapse of the Socialist Bloc

In 1980 protests by Polish shipyard workers in the city of Gdansk led to the formation of **Solidarity**, a labor union that grew to 9 million members. The Roman Catholic Church in Poland, strengthened by the elevation of a Pole, Karol Wojtyla (**KAH-rol voy-TIL-ah**), to the papacy as John Paul II in 1978, gave strong moral support to the protest movement.

The Polish communist government imposed martial law in 1981 in response to the growing power of Solidarity and its allies, giving the army effective political control. Seeing Solidarity under tight controls and many of its leaders in prison, the Soviet Union decided not to intervene. But Solidarity remained a potent force with a strong institutional structure and nationally recognized leaders. As Gorbachev loosened political controls in the Soviet Union after 1985, communist leaders elsewhere lost confidence in Soviet resolve, and critics and reformers in Poland and throughout eastern Europe were emboldened.

Beleaguered Warsaw Pact governments vacillated between the relaxation of control and the suppression of dissent. Just as the Catholic clergy in Poland had supported Solidarity, Protestant and Orthodox religious leaders aided the rise of opposition groups elsewhere. This combination

AP® Exam Tip
Explain the factors that contributed to the end of the Cold War and its effect on global politics.

Mikhail Gorbachev Head of the Soviet Union from 1985 to 1991. His liberalization effort improved relations with the West, but he lost power after his reforms led to the collapse of communist governments in eastern Europe.

perestroika Policy of "restructuring" that was the centerpiece of Mikhail Gorbachev's efforts to liberalize communism in the Soviet Union.

Solidarity Polish trade union created in 1980 to protest working conditions and political repression by the Polish communist government allied with the Soviet Union. It began the nationalist opposition to communist rule that led in 1989 to the fall of communism in eastern Europe.

▲ The Fall of the Berlin Wall   The Berlin Wall was the most important symbol of the Cold War. Constructed to keep residents of East Germany from fleeing to the West and defended by armed guards and barbed wire, it was the public face of communism. As the Soviet system fell apart, the residents of East and West Berlin broke down sections of the wall. Régis BOSSU/Corbis via Getty Images

AP® Exam Tip
Explain how the rise of extremist groups in power led to acts of genocide and ethnic violence.

ethnic cleansing Effort to eradicate a people and its culture by means of mass killing and the destruction of historical buildings and cultural materials. Ethnic cleansing was used by all sides in the conflicts that accompanied the disintegration of Yugoslavia in the 1990s.

of nationalism and religion provided a powerful base for opponents of the communist regimes. Communist governments sought to quiet the opposition by turning to the West for trade and financial assistance. They also opened their nations to travelers, ideas, styles, and money from Western countries, all of which accelerated the demand for change, rather than stabilizing the communist regimes.

By the end of 1989 communist governments across eastern Europe had fallen. The dismantling of the Berlin Wall vividly represented this transformation. While communist leaders in Poland, Hungary, Czechoslovakia, and Bulgaria decided that change was inevitable, dictator Nicolae Ceausescu (**nehk-oh-LIE chow-SHES-koo**) of Romania refused to surrender power and was overthrown and executed. The comprehensiveness of these changes became clear in 1990, when the Polish people elected Solidarity leader Lech Walesa (**leck wah-LEN-sah**) as president and the people of Czechoslovakia elected dissident playwright Vaclav Havel (**vah-SLAV hah-VEL**) as president in 1989.

Following the fall of the Berlin Wall, a tidal wave of patriotic enthusiasm swept aside the once-formidable communist government of East Germany. In the chaotic months that followed, East Germans crossed to West Germany in large numbers, and government services in the eastern sector nearly disappeared. The collapse of the East German government led quickly in 1990 to the reunification of Germany.

Soviet leaders knew that similarly powerful nationalist sentiments existed within the Soviet Union as well. The year 1990 brought declarations of independence by Lithuania, Estonia, and Latvia, three small states on the Baltic Sea that the Soviet Union had annexed in 1939. The end of the Soviet Union then came suddenly in 1991 (see Map 32.1). After communist hardliners botched a coup against Gorbachev, disgust with communism boiled over. Boris Yeltsin, the president of the Russian Republic, emerged as the most powerful leader in the country. Russia, the largest republic in the Soviet Union, was effectively taking the place of the disintegrating USSR. In September 1991 the Congress of People's Deputies—the central legislature of the USSR—voted to dissolve the union. Then in December a weak multistate successor with little central control, the Commonwealth of Independent States (CIS), was created and Gorbachev resigned. Facing economic and political challenges, Boris Yeltsin resigned the Russian presidency in January 2000. His successor, Vladimir Putin, still dominates Russia. While efforts to achieve democracy and a modern capitalist economy have stalled, Russia has modernized its military and continued to assert an aggressive foreign policy under Putin.

The ethnic and religious passions that fueled the breakup of the Soviet Union also overwhelmed the Balkan nation of Yugoslavia. In 1991 it dissolved into a morass of separatism and warring ethnic and religious groups. Slovenia and Croatia, the most westerly provinces, both heavily Roman Catholic, became independent states in 1992. The population of Bosnia and Herzegovina was more mixed: 40 percent were Muslims, 30 percent Serbian Orthodox, and 18 percent Catholics. Following the declaration of Bosnian national independence in 1992, the nation's Orthodox Serbs attempted to rid the state of Muslims in a violent process called **ethnic cleansing**. After extensive television coverage of atrocities that included mass murders and wanton property destruction, the United States intervened and eventually brokered a settlement in 1995 that effectively created two ethnically separate political entities.

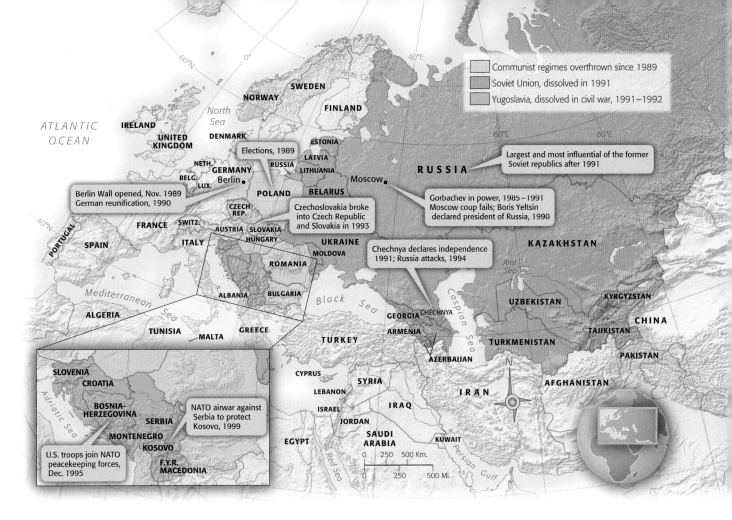

MAP 32.1 **The End of the Soviet Union** When communist hardliners failed to overthrow Gorbachev in 1991, popular anticommunist sentiment swept the Soviet Union. Following Boris Yeltsin's lead in Russia, the republics that constituted the Soviet Union declared their independence.

Why was nationalism a greater threat to the Soviet Union than to NATO?

In 1999 new fighting and a new round of ethnic cleansing occurred in the southernmost Yugoslavian province of Kosovo. Seen by Serbs as their homeland, Kosovo had a predominantly Muslim and Albanian population. When Serbia refused to stop military action, the United States, Britain, and France acted on behalf of NATO by launching an aerial war on Serbian targets in Kosovo and in Serbia itself that forced the withdrawal of Serbian forces from Kosovo. Serbia's president during this violent period, Slobodan Milosevic, was forced from power and turned over to a war crimes tribunal in The Hague, where he died in prison.

32-2c **Africa in the Era of Global Political Change**

Sub-Saharan Africa has experienced political instability, military coups, civil wars, and conflicts over resources since independence. It has also remained among the poorest regions in the world. Southern Africa, however, has seen democratic progress and a steady decline in armed conflicts since 1991. A key change came in South Africa in 1994, when long-time political prisoner Nelson Mandela and his African National Congress (ANC) won the first national elections in which the African majority could participate equally. Also hopeful has been the return to democracy of Nigeria, Africa's most populous state, after decades of military rulers. In 1999, after a succession of military governments, Nigerians elected President Olusegun Obasanjo (**oh-LOO-she-gun oh-BAH-san-jo**) (a former coup leader), and a 2003 vote gave him a second term, despite serious voting irregularities. Similarly, in 2002 Kenyans voted out the Kenya African National Union Party that had held power for thirty-nine years.

Africa was also a scene of ethnic cleansing. In 1994 the political leaders of the Central African nation of Rwanda incited the Hutu people to massacre their Tutsi neighbors. Although

Section Review

- The Cold War ended when growing unrest and criticism led to the collapse of the Soviet Union and allied socialist nations. Mikhail Gorbachev's reform policies accelerated this process.

- The rise of ethnic nationalism and effects of religious divisions led to war and genocide in Yugoslavia.

- South Africa, Nigeria, and Kenya escaped from oppressive conditions, but hundreds of thousands lost their lives in ethnic violence in Rwanda and Congo.

- After Saddam Husain invaded Kuwait, the United States and its allies defeated Iraq in the first Gulf War of 1990.

the major powers had earlier promised to intervene in genocides, they sought to avoid military involvement in Rwanda by not using the word *genocide* to describe the mass slaughter of an ethnic minority. Without foreign intervention, the carnage claimed 750,000 lives, with millions more becoming refugees. Finally, the United States and other powers intervened and the United Nations set up a tribunal to try those responsible for the genocide. In 1998 violence spread from Rwanda to neighboring Congo, where growing opposition and ill health had forced President Joseph Mobutu from office after over three decades of dictatorial misrule. Various peacemaking attempts failed to restore order, and by mid-2003 more than 3 million Congolese had died from disease, malnutrition, and injuries related to the fighting.

32-2d The Persian Gulf War

The Persian Gulf War was the first significant military conflict to occur after the breakup of the Soviet Union and the end of the Cold War. Iraq's ruler, Saddam Husain, had borrowed a great deal of money from neighboring Kuwait and failed to get Kuwait's royal family to reduce this debt. He was also eager to control Kuwait's oil fields. Husain believed that the smaller and militarily weaker nation could be quickly defeated, and he wrongly suspected that the United States would not react. Iraq then invaded Kuwait in August 1990.

The United States decided to use military force to roll back Iraq's invasion. Saudi Arabia, an important ally of the United States and a major oil producer, also supported intervention. With his intention to use force endorsed by the United Nations and with many Islamic nations supporting military action, President George H. W. Bush ordered an attack in early 1991. Iraq's military defeat was both quick and comprehensive, but Bush decided to leave Husain in power. When his rule was challenged by a Shi'ite uprising just months after his defeat, Husain crushed his opponents. The United States imposed various conditions on Iraq that kept tensions high, helping create the conditions for a new, larger war in 2003 (see Chapter 33).

32-3 The Challenge of Population Growth

What explains differences in the rate of population growth among the world's cultural regions?

For most of human history, governments viewed population growth as beneficial, a source of national wealth and power. Since the late eighteenth century, however, many intellectuals and politicians have viewed rising population levels with alarm, fearing that the production of food and other essential resources could not keep up with population growth. Late in the nineteenth century some social critics expressed concern that growing populations would lead ultimately to class and ethnic struggle. By the second half of the twentieth century, fears of population growth were primarily attached to environmental concerns. Are urban sprawl, pollution, and soil erosion the inevitable results of population growth? The questions and debates continue today, but clearly population growth is both a cause and a result of increased global interdependency.

32-3a Demographic Transition

The population of Europe almost doubled between 1850 and 1914, putting enormous pressure on rural land and urban housing and overwhelming fragile public institutions that provided crisis assistance (see Chapter 27). This dramatic growth forced a large wave of European immigrants across the Atlantic, helping to develop the Western Hemisphere and invigorating the Atlantic economy (see Chapter 25). Population growth also contributed to Europe's Industrial Revolution by lowering labor costs and increasing consumer demand.

While some Europeans saw the rapid increase in human population as a blessing, others warned of disaster. The best known of these pessimists was English cleric **Thomas Malthus**, who in 1798 argued that unchecked population growth would outstrip food production. When Malthus looked at Europe's future, he used a prejudiced image of contemporary China to terrify his readers. A visitor to China, he claimed, "will not be surprised that mothers destroy or expose many of their children; that parents sell their daughters for a trifle; . . . and that there should be such a number of robbers. The surprise is that nothing still more dreadful should happen."[1]

The generation that came of age in the years after World War II lived in a world where Malthus seemed to have little relevance. Industrial and agricultural productivity had multiplied supplies of food and other necessities. At the same time, cultural changes associated with expanded female employment, older age at marriage, and more effective family planning had slowed the rate of population increase. By the 1960s Europe and other industrial societies had made the **demographic transition** to lower *fertility rates* (average number of births per woman) and reduced mortality. This meant that populations would age quickly. In the world's most developed nations, for example, median age rose from twenty-nine years in 1950 to thirty-seven years by 2000.

By the late 1970s, the developing world had still not experienced the demographic transition and the global discussion of population growth became highly politicized. Leaders in some developing nations actively promoted large families, arguing that larger populations increased national power. When industrialized nations, mostly white, raised concerns about rapid population growth in Asia, Africa, and Latin America, populist political leaders in these regions responded by asking whether these concerns were racist.

This question exposed the influence of racism in the population debate and temporarily disarmed Western advocates of birth control. However, once the economic shocks of the 1970s and 1980s had revealed the economic vulnerability of poor nations, governments in the developing world jettisoned policies that promoted population growth and began to advocate birth control. Mexico is a good example. In the 1970s the government had encouraged high fertility, and population grew an average of 3 percent per year. In the 1980s Mexico rejected these policies and began to promote birth control, leading by the 1990s to a more manageable annual population growth of 1.7 percent.

---

[1]Quoted in Antony Flew, "Introduction," in Thomas Robert Malthus, *An Essay on the Principle of Population and a Summary View of the Principle of Population* (New York: Penguin Books, 1970), 30.

Thomas Malthus
Eighteenth-century English intellectual who warned that population growth threatened future generations because, in his view, population growth would always outstrip increases in agricultural production.

demographic transition
A change in the rates of population growth. Before the transition, both birthrates and death rates were high, resulting in a slowly growing population; then the death rate dropped but the birthrate remained high, causing a population explosion; finally, after the transition, the birthrate dropped and population growth slowed down. This is the situation today in the wealthiest modern industrial economies.

◀ **Chinese Family-Planning Campaign** To slow population growth, the Chinese government sought to limit parents to a single child, but has relented in the recent past when the economic consequences of a rapidly aging population became clear. Billboards and other forms of mass advertising were an essential part of the original campaign to suppress fertility.
Sally and Richard Greenhill/Alamy Stock Photo

TABLE 32.1 Population for World and Major Areas, 1750–2050

Major Area	Population Size (Millions)						
	1750	1800	1850	1900	1950	2000	2050*
World	791	978	1,262	1,650	2,521	6,055	9,725
Africa	106	107	111	133	221	785	2,478
Asia	502	635	809	947	1,402	3,683	5,267
Europe	163	203	276	408	547	729	707
Latin America and the Caribbean	16	24	38	74	167	519	784
North America	2	7	26	82	172	310	433
Oceania	2	2	2	6	13	30	57

Major Area	Percentage Distribution						
	1750	1800	1850	1900	1950	2000	2050*
World	100	100	100	100	100		100
Africa	13.4	10.9	8.8	8.1	8.8	13.0	25.5
Asia	63.5	64.9	64.1	57.4	55.6	60.8	54.2
Europe	20.6	20.8	21.9	24.7	21.7	12.0	7.3
Latin America and the Caribbean	2.0	2.5	3.0	4.5	6.6	8.6	8.1
North America	0.3	0.7	2.1	5.0	6.8	5.1	4.4
Oceania	0.3	0.2	0.2	0.4	0.5	0.5	0.6

*Estimated

Sources: J. D. Durand, "Historical Estimates of World Population: An Evaluation" (Philadelphia: University of Pennsylvania, Population Studies Center, 1974, mimeographed); United Nations, *The Determinants and Consequences of Population Trends*, vol. 1 (New York: United Nations, 1973); United Nations, *World Population Prospects as Assessed in 1963* (New York: United Nations, 1966); United Nations, *World Population Prospects: The 2015 Revision* (New York: United Nations, 2015); United Nations Population Division, Department of Economic and Social Affairs, *World Population to 2300* (2004), www.un.org/esa/population/publications/longrange2/WorldPop2300final.pdf.

AP® Exam Tip

Consider the role of medical advancements such as antibiotics and of epidemic diseases such as HIV/AIDS on demographics in the twentieth and twenty-first centuries.

World population exploded in the twentieth century, more than doubling between 1950 and 2000 (see Table 32.1). Although the rate of growth has slowed since the 1980s, world population still increases by a number equal to the total population of the United States roughly every three to four years. If fertility had remained constant from the 1990s, with a world average of roughly 2.5 children per woman, population would reach nearly 27 billion in 2100. This will not happen, however, because fertility is declining in most developing nations and is at less than replacement levels in most industrialized countries. In Iran, for example, the average number of children born to each woman dropped from more than six to less than three in the single decade 1986–1996. As a result, most experts estimate a world population in 2050 of around roughly 10 billion.

At the same time, mortality rates have increased in some regions as immigration, commercial expansion, and improved transportation have facilitated the transmission of disease. The rapid spread of HIV/AIDS before the recent development of revolutionary treatments is an example of this phenomenon. Since the beginning of the epidemic 70 million people have been infected with HIV and roughly 35 million have died. Less-developed regions with poorly funded public health institutions and with few resources to invest in prevention and treatment experience the highest rates of infection and the greatest mortality. Of the countries with the highest HIV/AIDS rates, thirty-seven are in Africa, three in Asia, and six in Latin America and the Caribbean. These countries were home to 87 percent of all HIV/AIDS infections. In recent years, prevention programs and much improved drug therapies have slowed both mortality and infection rates, with the greatest successes registered in rich countries with the greatest medical resources. Sub-Saharan Africa, with roughly 70 percent of the world's cases, remains the center of the epidemic in 2016, but the epidemic has persisted in other regions as well, with approximately two million cases found in Latin America and the Caribbean and another one million found in Russia.

32-3b **The Industrialized Nations**

In the developed industrial nations of western Europe and in Japan, fertility levels are so low that population would fall without immigration. Japanese women have an average of 1.4 children, while Italian women have 1.3. Without a dramatic increase in fertility or a greater willingness to accept immigrants, Japan's 2015 population of 127 million will decline to 107 million by 2050. Italy, now receiving large numbers of immigrants from Africa and the Middle East, will still see its population decline from 60 million to 55 million in this same period. By comparison, the average African woman now has 4.7 children. Higher levels of female education and employment, the material values of consumer culture, and access to contraception and abortion explain the low fertility of mature industrial nations. An Italian woman in Bologna, the city with the lowest fertility in the world, put it this way: "I'm an only child and if I could, I'd have more than one child. But most couples I know wait until their 30's to have children. People want to have their own life, they want to have a successful career. When you see life in these terms, children are an impediment."[2]

In industrialized nations life expectancy improved as fertility declined. The combination of abundant food, improved hygiene, and more effective medicines and medical care has lengthened human lives. In 2000 about 20 percent of the population in Europe was age sixty-five or over. By 2050 this proportion will rise to over one-third. Italy soon will have more than twenty adults fifty years old or over for each five-year-old child. Because of higher fertility and greater levels of immigration, the United States is moving in this direction more slowly than western Europe; by 2050 the median age in Europe will be fifty-two, while it will be thirty-nine in the United States.

The combination of falling fertility and rising life expectancy in the industrialized nations presents a challenge very different from the one foreseen by Malthus. These nations generally offer a broad array of social services, including retirement income, medical services, and housing supplements for the elderly. As the number of retirees increases relative to the number of employed people, the cost of these programs are becoming unsustainable, especially in nations with slow rates of economic growth. Economists track this problem by using the PSR (potential support ratio), the ratio of persons fifteen to sixty-four years old (likely workers) to persons sixty-five or older (likely retirees). Between 1950 and 2000 the world's PSR fell from 12 to 9. In mature industrial countries the PSR fell from 8 to 5. By 2050 it will fall to 4 for the world's population and to an unsustainable 2 in mature industrial countries.

32-3c **The Developing Nations**

At current rates, 95 percent of all future population growth will be in developing nations (see Map 32.2 and Table 32.1). A comparison between Europe and Africa illustrates these changes. In 1950 Europe had more than twice the population of Africa. By 1985 Africa's population had drawn even with Europe and, according to United Nations projections, its population will be roughly three times larger than Europe's by 2050.

Rapid population growth continued after 2000 in the developing world even as birthrates fell. Among all developing nations, average birthrates fell from 44 births per thousand inhabitants in 1950 to approximately 22 in 2014. Birthrates fell most steeply in countries experiencing the most rapid economic development. In China the birthrate fell from 42 births per thousand in 1950 to a First World level of 13 in 2014. In this same period birthrates declined from 43 per thousand to 23 in India, another fast-growing economy. Change occurred much more slowly in sub-Saharan Africa, where the birthrates fell from 47 per thousand to 38, and in Muslim countries like Pakistan and Afghanistan, where birthrates declined from 42 to 29 and 53 to 35 per thousand, respectively. The populations of Latin America were also expanding, but at rates much slower than in sub-Saharan Africa and the Muslim nations. In this same period, Latin America's birthrate declined from 43 per thousand in 1950 to 18 in 2014. Regardless of these changes, birthrates remain more than twice as high in the developing world as in the mature industrial nations, with the highest levels in the poorest countries.

---

[2]Population Implosion Worries a Graying Europe," *New York Times*, July 10, 1998.

PAKISTAN

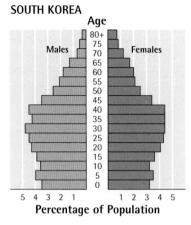

SOUTH KOREA

SWEDEN

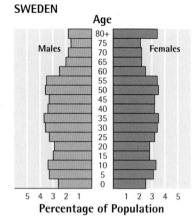

FIGURE 32.1 **Age Structure Comparison of Islamic Nation (Pakistan), Non-Islamic Developing Nation (South Korea), and Developed Nation (Sweden), 2001.** *Source:* U.S. Bureau of the Census, International Database, 2001.

Section Review

- In the twentieth century the developed nations made the demographic transition to low birthrates, while the developing nations began by stressing higher birthrates.

- World population more than doubled between 1950 and 2000.

- In developed nations birthrates fell but longer life expectancy led to slow population growth; in most of the former Soviet Union the combination of low birthrates and limited improvements to life expectancy led to gradually declining populations.

- Developing nations will contribute most of the world's future population growth, despite changing economies and population planning efforts.

- With declining fertility and increasing life expectancy the populations in industrialized nations are growing older rapidly. Developing nations have much younger populations due to declining mortality and high fertility.

32-3d Old and Young Populations

Population pyramids generated by demographers clearly illustrate the profound transformation in human reproductive patterns and life expectancy since World War II. Figure 32.1 shows the 2001 age distributions in Pakistan, South Korea, and Sweden—nations at three different stages of economic development. Sweden is a mature industrial nation. South Korea is rapidly industrializing and has surpassed many European nations in both industrial output and per capita wealth. Pakistan is a poor, traditional Muslim nation with rudimentary industrialization, low educational levels, and little effective family planning.

In 2001 nearly 50 percent of Pakistan's population was under age sixteen. The resulting pressures on the economy have been extraordinary. Every year approximately 150,000 men reach age sixty-five—and another 1.2 million turn sixteen. Pakistan, therefore, has to create more than a million new jobs a year or face growing unemployment and declining wages. Sweden confronts a different problem. Sweden's aging population, growing demand for social welfare benefits, and declining labor pool means that its industries may become less competitive and living standards may decline unless the flow of young immigrants alters the age distribution. In South Korea, a decline in fertility dramatically altered the ratio of children to adults, creating an age distribution similar to that of western Europe.

32-4 Unequal Development and the Movement of Peoples

How does wealth inequality among nations impact international migration patterns?

Two characteristics of the postwar world should now be clear. First, despite decades of experimentation with state-directed economic development, most nations that were poor in 1960 are still poor today. There are notable exceptions. In Asia, first Japan, then the Asian Tigers

(Taiwan, Singapore, South Korea, and Hong Kong), and more recently China have generated high rates of economic growth and are now among the world's most competitive industrial powers. And second, most of the increase in world population since 1950 has occurred in the poorest nations. So, with the rate of population growth overwhelming the pace of economic expansion in the developing world and with birth rates continuing to fall in the developed world, the level of international migration will remain high for the foreseeable future. Political violence in Syria, Libya and elsewhere has contributed to this mass population redistribution in recent years.

Few issues have stirred more controversy than international migration in recent years and in many places this issue has led to the development of nationalist political movements. Even moderate voices have sometimes framed this discussion of immigration as a competition among peoples. Large numbers of legal and illegal immigrants from poor nations with growing populations are entering the developed industrial nations, with the exception of Japan. Large-scale internal migrations within developing countries are a related phenomenon. The movement of impoverished residents from rural areas to the cities of Asia, Africa, and Latin America (see Map 32.2 and Table 32.2) has increased steadily since the 1970s. For millions of the world's poorest people, the experience of internal migration often serves as the first step toward migration abroad.

32-4a The Problem of Inequality

Since 1945 the global economy has expanded more rapidly than at any time in the past. Faster, cheaper communications and enhanced transportation have combined with improvements in industrial and agricultural technologies to create material abundance that would have amazed those who experienced the first Industrial Revolution (see Chapter 22). Despite this remarkable economic expansion, the differences between rich and poor nations remain stark.

The gap between rich and poor nations has grown wider since 1945, although the 2008 recession had a powerful negative effect on many advanced industrial economies, including the United States and European Union. China's spectacular rise as an industrial power since 1980 is a strong indicator that some once-poor countries can modernize and become competitive industrial nations, but growth has moderated there as well in the last few years. Nevertheless, the vast majority of the world's population continues to live in poverty. There are many measures of the relative wealth of nations; GDP per capita measured in U.S. dollars is among the most common.

In 2015 the per capita GDP of Luxembourg was the highest in the world, $101,450; the U.S. figure was $56,116, and the Japanese figure was $32,477, down almost 20 percent since the contraction of the 1990s. The countries of the European Union were generally rich, but some of the former Soviet satellites recently admitted to the European Union have the GDP per capita of developing nations. France and Germany have per capita GDPs of $36,205 and $41,313, respectively. The poorest countries in the European Union, Bulgaria and Romania, have per capita GDPs similar to Russia's ($9,092)—$6,993 and $8,973, respectively.

Many countries in the developing world now approach the poorest tier of European countries in per capita GDP. Per capita GDP for Mexico is $9,005, Brazil $8,538, Chile $13,416, South Africa $5,724, and Gabon $8,266. But many more countries, especially in Asia and Africa, remain very poor: the Philippines, $2,904; India, $1,598; Pakistan, $1,434; Nigeria, $2,640; and Sudan, $2,414. The poorest, like Haiti, Kenya, and Bangladesh, have per capita GDP levels of roughly $1,200.

32-4b Internal Migration: The Growth of Cities

In developing nations migration from rural areas to urban centers increased threefold between 1925 and 1950; the pace of migration then accelerated (see Table 32.2). While slums around the major cities of developing nations are seen as signs of social breakdown and economic failure, life in these urban slums was generally better than life in the countryside. A World Bank study estimated that three out of four rural-to-urban migrants made economic gains. Residents of cities in sub-Saharan Africa, for example, were six times more likely than rural residents to have safe water. An unskilled migrant from the depressed northeast of Brazil could triple his or her income by moving to Rio de Janeiro.

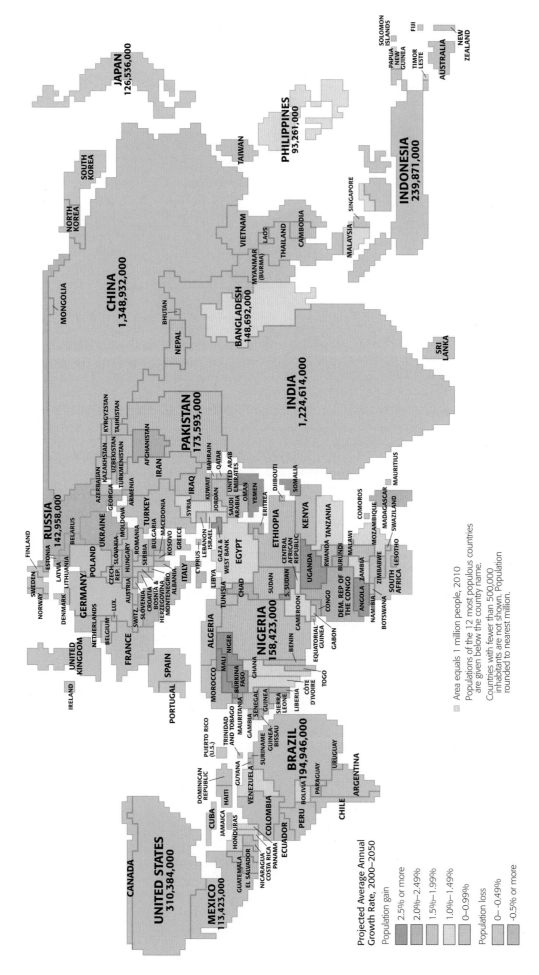

MAP 32.2 World Population Growth Every three years the world's population increases by the equivalent of a nation the size of the United States. Most of this population increase will be in some of the world's poorest nations. By 2050, for example, Pakistan, a nation of only 40 million in 1950, will have the world's third largest population.

What world regions have the fastest-growing and slowest-growing populations?

TABLE 32.2   The World's Largest Cities (Urban Agglomerations of 13 Million or More)

City	1970	City	1990	City	2011	City	2025
1 Tokyo	23.3	1 Tokyo	32.5	1 Tokyo	37.2	1 Tokyo	38.7
2 New York	16.2	2 New York	16.1	2 Delhi	22.7	2 Delhi	32.9
		3 Mexico City	15.3	3 Mexico City	20.4	3 Shanghai	28.4
		4 São Paulo	14.8	4 New York	20.4	4 Mumbai	26.6
		5 Mumbai	12.4	5 Shanghai	20.2	5 Mexico City	24.6
		6 Osaka-Kobe	11.0	6 São Paulo	19.9	6 New York	23.6
		7 Calcutta	10.9	7 Mumbai	19.7	7 São Paulo	23.2
		8 Los Angeles	10.9	8 Beijing	15.6	8 Dhaka	22.9
		9 Seoul	10.5	9 Dhaka	15.4	9 Beijing	22.6
		10 Buenos Aires	10.5	10 Calcutta	14.4	10 Karachi	20.2
				11 Karachi	13.9	11 Lagos	18.9
				12 Buenos Aires	13.5	12 Calcutta	18.7
				13 Los Angeles	13.4	13 Manila	16.3
						14 Los Angeles	15.7
						15 Shenzhen	15.5
						16 Buenos Aires	15.5
						17 Guangzhou	15.5
						18 Istanbul	14.9
						19 Cairo	14.7
						20 Kinshasa	14.5
						21 Chongqing	13.6
						22 Rio de Janeiro	13.6
						23 Bangalore	13.2

Source: United Nations, Economic and Social Affairs, *World Urbanization Prospects: The 2011 Revision Highlights*, 6–7.

As the scale of rural-to-urban migration grew, these benefits became more elusive. In the cities of the developing world basic services have been crumbling under the pressure of rapid population growth. In cities like Mexico City and Manila, which are among the world's largest cities, tens of thousands live in garbage dumps, scavenging for food. In Rio de Janeiro alone an estimated 350,000 abandoned children live in the streets and parks, begging, selling drugs, stealing, and engaging in prostitution to survive. Some nations have tried to relocate migrants back to the countryside. Indonesia, for example, has relocated more than a half-million urban residents since 1969, but its major cities continue to add population.

32-4c Global Migration

After 1950 international levels of migration rose steadily. In the decade 2000-2010 net international migration from poor to rich nations peaked at 3.2 million per year before falling to 2.3 million in recent years. Dramatically rising numbers after 2000 led to increased ethnic and racial tensions in Europe and elsewhere. More recently rising levels of political violence and civil war in places like Iraq, Syria and Afghanistan have dramatically contributed to this migratory flow, causing humanitarian crises in the Middle East and Europe. Political refugees and immigrants have faced murderous violence in Germany; growing anti-immigrant sentiment has strengthened right-wing political movements and led to riots in cities with large immigrant populations in France and Greece; and in the United States anti-immigrant sentiment has led to expanded government efforts to control the southern border and, in 2016, became an issue in the American presidential election.

Immigrants from developing nations have brought host nations many of the same benefits that the great migration of Europeans to the Americas provided a century earlier (see Chapter 25). The United States actively recruited Mexican workers during World War II, and many European nations promoted guest worker programs and other inducements to immigration in the 1960s, when an expanding European economy experienced labor shortages. However, attitudes toward immigrants have changed as the size of immigrant populations have grown, particularly during

AP® Exam Tip
Understand the relationship between imperialism in the previous time period and migration in the twentieth and twenty-first centuries.

▲ **Garbage Dump in Manila, Philippines**   In Third World nations, thousands of poor families live by sorting and selling bottles, aluminum cans, plastic, and newspapers in urban landfills.   Eco Images/Getty Images

periods of economic contraction like the recession that began in 2008. Under intense pressure, native-born workers demanded an end to immigration, seeing immigrants as competitors willing to work for lower wages and less likely to support labor unions.

High fertility among immigrants contributes to these tensions. Most immigrants are young adults who retain the positive attitudes toward early marriage and large families of their native cultures in Latin America, Africa, and the Middle East and, as a result, have higher fertility rates than do native-born populations. Spain provides a useful example. In 2000 Spain had one of the world's lowest fertility rates, 1.2 births per woman. A member of the European Union, its economy was growing and employment opportunities were available to immigrants from Latin America, North Africa, and elsewhere. As a result, Spain briefly became the major immigrant-receiving nation in the European Union, and the immigrant component of Spain's population rose from 2.1 to 14.1 percent by 2010. Because the birthrate of the immigrant population is more than twice as high as that of the native-born population, the effect of this trend has been multiplied, with foreign-born mothers accounting for 20 percent of all births in Spain. Since the beginning of the recession in 2008, immigration to Spain has slowed and birthrates of both native-born and foreign-born have fallen. But even in this altered context, immigrant groups and their Spanish-born children continue to grow as a percentage of the population much faster than the native-born. Similarly, as immigrant populations have increased across Europe and in the United States in the twenty-first century, the resulting cultural conflicts have tested definitions of citizenship and nationality.

Section Review

- As the world economy expanded after World War II, the gap between rich and poor nations grew.

- In the fast-growing nations of the developing world, urban populations have grown as a result of rural-to-urban migration.

- Most of the world's migration is the movement of young men and women from poor nations to rich nations with low birthrates and aging populations.

32-5 Technological and Environmental Change

How has technological change affected the global environment in the recent past?

Technological innovation powered the economic expansion that began after World War II. New technologies increased productivity and disseminated human creativity. They also altered the way people lived, worked, and played. Because most of the economic benefits were initially concentrated in the advanced industrialized nations, technology increased the power of those nations relative to the developing world. This has changed in the last decade with globalization and the rising industrial role of China. Even within developed nations, postwar technological innovations did not benefit all classes, industries, and regions equally. There were losers as well as winners.

Population growth and increased levels of migration and urbanization have intensified environmental threats, as farming acreage, factory production, and the extraction of natural resources all increased dramatically. In the early twenty-first century, the loss of rain forest, soil erosion, global warming, air and water pollution, and extinction of species threatened the quality of life and the survival of human societies. Environmental protection efforts, like the acquisition of new technology, progressed most in rich societies with the greatest economic resources. Pollution and other environmental challenges proliferated in the poorest nations with few resources.

32-5a New Technologies and the World Economy

Nuclear energy, jet engines, radar, and tape recording were among the many World War II developments that later had an impact on consumers' lives. New technology increased industrial productivity, reduced labor requirements, and improved the flow of information that made markets more efficient. The consumer electronics industry rapidly developed new products, changes seen in the music industry's movement from vinyl records to eight-track tapes, CDs, and then MP3 and other digital delivery technologies. Computers became faster, smaller, and less expensive, cell phones were transformed into smartphones, and the speed of news and data transmission accelerated at an unanticipated rate, transforming business, education, and politics globally.

Improvements in existing technologies accounted for much of the developed world's productivity increases during the 1950s and 1960s, as faster, more efficient transportation and communication cut costs and expanded markets. But new technologies were important as well. Governments bore much of the cost of developing and constructing nuclear power plants and sponsored research into new technologies. None has proved more influential in the last four decades than the computer, which has transformed both work and leisure (see Environment & Technology: Connected). The first computers were expensive, large, and slow, and only corporations, governments, and universities could afford them. Each new iteration of computer technology has been smaller, faster, and less expensive. As a result, the serial utilization of desktops, laptops, tablets, and smartphones transformed commerce, education, and government. Today the computational capacity of a 1970s university mainframe computer can be found on the smartphone or tablet of individual university students. The modern smartphone may prove to be the most revolutionary innovation in this ongoing transformation and integration of communication, computation, research, and entertainment.

Computers have also dramatically altered manufacturing. Small dedicated computers now control and monitor machinery in most modern industries. In the developed world, as well as in China and other fast-growing developing economies, factories forced by global competition to improve efficiency and product quality increasingly depend on robots. Japan's early lead in robotics in the 1990s has been reduced as Europe, the United States, and, in recent years, China have all raced to introduce robotics across their economies. While nationalist critics of economic integration and globalization tend to blame unrestricted trade as a threat to local industries and domestic employment, the effect of robotics on factory employment has progressed with little regulation. Take, for example, the American steel industry. Between 1962 and 2005 the industry lost 400,000 workers, but shipments of steel did not decline at all due to enhanced productivity through automation. These technologies are now being employed in white-collar sectors with similar results.

AP® Exam Tip
It is important to understand the effects of new technologies like the Internet and cellular communication on the process of globalization.

The period since World War II witnessed wave after wave of technological innovations. None has had greater impact on the way people work, learn, and live than the computer. Until the 1970s most computing was done on large and expensive mainframe computers. These massive computers were primarily used for data storage and analysis, and the government agencies, universities, and large corporations that owned them controlled access.

Today most computers are in private hands, and most are devoted to communication and information searches and to personal entertainment, a transformation symbolized when the market value of the search engine Google surpassed that of IBM, the key developer of mainframe and PC computing. Before the 1970s few anticipated the technological innovations that revolutionized the computer industry through miniaturization during the last three decades. The key development leading to smaller and cheaper computers was the microprocessor, a silicon chip that contained the computer's brains. Today digital "smart" technologies made possible by this constantly evolving innovation help us manage kitchen appliances, automobiles, fitness routines, personal calendars, household lighting and heating, and a host of other daily activities.

Initially developed to facilitate American defense research in the 1960s, the Internet was the second key to the revolution in communication and publication. It allowed smaller, faster computers and now tablets and smartphones to become research, information, and entertainment portals that could access vast international databases of research, opinion, entertainment, and commerce. Small personal computers and related devices and the World Wide Web have had a revolutionary impact on modern culture, allowing individuals and groups—without the support of governments, corporations, or other powerful institutions—to collect and disseminate information more freely than at any time in the past (see Chapter 33). The disruptive potential of this new forum was indicated in February 2010 when WikiLeaks published more than 250,000 classified U.S. government cables on the Web. Many of the most embarrassing documents were then published by traditional print media. The rise of ISIS (Islamic State of Iraq and Syria, also known as Islamic State of Iraq and the Levant) has also depended in part on the potency of the Web as a political platform and recruitment tool. Donald J. Trump's dependence on Twitter posts in the 2016 presidential campaign is another indication of this technology's political potential.

In the last decade new technologies have permitted the integration of previously distinct devices and technologies. As a result, software and hardware providers now routinely blend the functions and uses of small laptop computers, cellular phones, and MP3 players to provide new business and professional applications and entertainment. Hand-held "convergence devices" evolving from the cellular telephone allow users to make phone calls, send email, search the Internet, read books, play music and videos, find directions, and store digital texts. No corporation has played a more central role in this stage of the computer revolution than Apple, a computer company that has become a major innovator in the smartphone and tablet market. It is now the most valuable corporation in the world. Worth noting is the fact that other representatives of new technology—Google's parent company Alphabet, Microsoft, Facebook, and Amazon—are also at the pinnacle of international corporate wealth and power.

One result of these technological revolutions is the appearance of plugged-in, self-identifying communities in venues like blogs, social media, and chat rooms that transcend or supplement older forms of community based on ethnic, regional, or economic identities. At the same time these innovations have undermined traditional expectations of privacy as corporations and governments routinely follow online activity, dropping targeted advertisements into our online searches and routinely following our physical movements.

◀ **The Connected Crowd**   On the floor of this crowded dance club patrons record the entertainment as well as their own participation on smartphones, transmitting the event simultaneously to friends across the city, nation, and even internationally via Facebook, Instagram, and other social media services.   hurricanehank/ Shutterstock.com

The transnational corporation is the primary agent for these technological changes as well as for the globalization of industrial production. By the twentieth century the growing economic power of corporations in industrialized nations allowed them to invest directly in the mines, plantations, and public utilities of less developed regions. In the post–World War II years many of these companies became truly transnational, having multinational ownership and management. International trade agreements and open markets furthered the process. Ford, Nissan, BMW, Toyota, and other car companies not only produced and sold cars internationally, but their shareholders, workers, and managers also came from numerous nations.

The location of manufacturing plants overseas and the acquisition of corporate operations by foreign buyers rendered such global firms as transnational as the products they sold. In the 1970s and 1980s American brand names like Levi's, Coca-Cola, Marlboro, Gillette, McDonald's, and Kentucky Fried Chicken were global phenomena (see Material Culture: Fast Food). But in time Asian corporate names—Honda, Hitachi, Sony, Sanyo, and Mitsubishi—were blazoned in neon and on giant video screens on the sides of skyscrapers, along with European brands such as Nestlé, Mercedes, Pirelli, and Benetton. Since 1979, China's emergence as a global industrial power has accelerated this process of integration and diffusion. In recent decades major Japanese, American, and European manufacturing giants have located factories that produce automobiles, pharmaceuticals, smartphones, aircraft, and common consumer goods in China to gain access to the Chinese domestic market as well as to lower the price of finished products sold in home markets by utilizing cheaper Chinese labor. One study found that globalization, especially deepening trade with China, had led to the loss of at least 2 million jobs in the United States between 2000 and today.

As transnational manufacturers, agricultural conglomerates, and financial giants became wealthier and more powerful, they increasingly escaped the controls imposed by national governments. If labor costs were too high in Japan, antipollution measures too intrusive in the United States, or taxes too high in Great Britain, transnational companies relocated—or threatened to do so. In 1945, for example, the U.S. textile industry was largely located in low-wage southern right-to-work states (states that inhibit unionization) and dominated the American market while at the same time exporting successfully to foreign markets. As wages in the American South rose and global competition increased, these producers began relocating plants to Puerto Rico in the 1980s and to Mexico after NAFTA went into effect in 1994 (see Chapter 33). Now China is the primary manufacturer of textiles sold in the United States and other developed economies.

32-5b Conserving and Sharing Resources

In the 1960s environmental activists and political leaders began warning about the devastating environmental consequences of population growth, industrialization, natural resource exploitation, and the expansion of agriculture onto marginal lands and forests. Assaults on rain forests, the disappearance of species, and the poisoning of streams and rivers raised public consciousness, as did the depletion and pollution of the world's oceans. Environmental damage occurred both in the advanced industrial economies and in developing nations. The former Soviet Union, where industrial and nuclear wastes were routinely dumped with little concern for environmental consequences, had the worst environmental record.

In the developed world, industrial activity increased much more rapidly than the population grew, and the consumption of energy (coal, electricity, and petroleum) rose proportionally. This pattern is now clear in India, China, and other industrializing nations as well. Indeed, the consumer-driven economic expansion of the post–World War II years became an obstacle to addressing environmental problems, since modern economies depend on a profligate consumption of goods and resources (see Map 32.3). When consumption slows, industrial nations enter a recession, as recently demonstrated in 2008. How could the United States, Germany, Japan, or China change consumption patterns to protect the environment without endangering corporate profits, wages, and employment levels?

Since 1945 population growth has been most dramatic in the developing countries, where environmental pressures have also been extreme. In Brazil, India, and China, for example, the need to expand food production led to rapid deforestation and the extension of farming and grazing onto marginal lands. The results were predictable: erosion and water pollution. These and many other poor nations sought to stimulate industrialization because they believed that the transition from agriculture to manufacturing was the only way to provide for their rapidly growing populations. The argument was compelling: Why should Indians or Brazilians remain poor while Americans, Europeans, and Japanese grew rich?

AP® Exam Tip
Understand the role of transnational corporations in spreading free market principles throughout the world.

AP® Exam Tip
Consider the effects of a globalized consumer society.

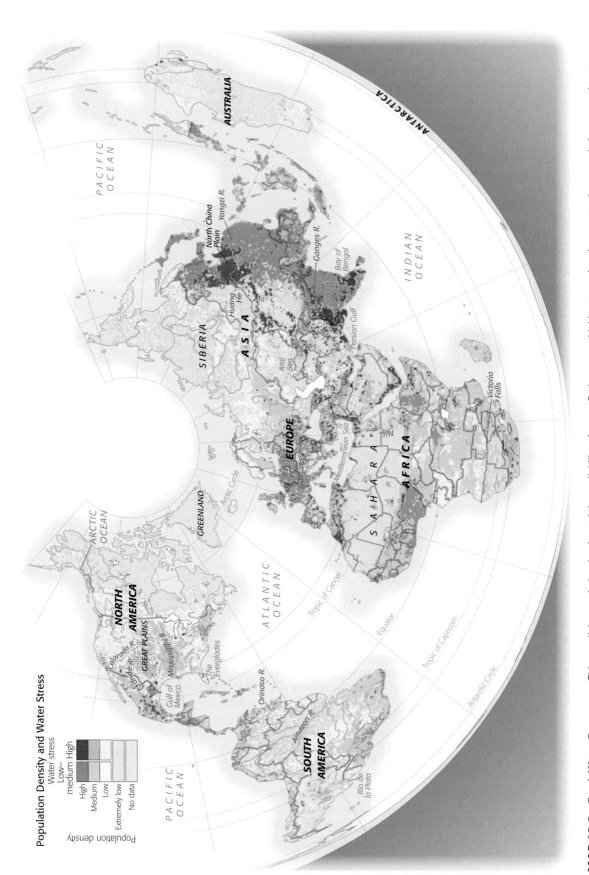

Population Density and Water Stress

Water stress

Low–
medium High

Population density — High, Medium, Low, Extremely low, No data

MAP 32.3 Fresh Water Resources This map links population density and the availability of water. Red areas are highly stressed environments where populations use at least 40 percent or more of available water. Less stressed environments are blue. The deeper the shade of red or blue, the greater the environmental stress. The ongoing effects of global warming on this crucial resource is unknown, but our ability to sustain intense modern agriculture in low-rainfall, high-average-temperature environments will certainly be challenged. *Source:* From "Global Water Stress," National Geographic, September 2002, pp. 14–16. Reprinted by permission of the National Geographic Society.

Which regions are both "highly stressed" and poor?

◀ **Loss of Brazilian Rain Forest** The destruction of large portions of Brazil's virgin rain forest to grow soybeans or raise cattle and other livestock has come to symbolize the growing threat to the environment caused by population growth and economic development. In this photograph we see the scale of environmental destruction. guentermanaus/ Shutterstock.com

32-5c **Responding to Environmental Threats**

Despite the gravity of environmental threats, there were many successful efforts to preserve and protect the environment. The Clean Air Act, the Clean Water Act, and the Endangered Species Act were passed in the United States in the 1970s as part of an environmental effort that included the nations of the European Community and Japan. Grassroots political movements and the media encouraged environmental awareness, and most nations in the developed world enforced strict antipollution laws and sponsored massive recycling efforts. Many also encouraged resource conservation by rewarding energy-efficient factories and manufacturers of fuel-efficient cars and by promoting the use of alternative energy sources such as solar and wind power.

Environmental efforts produced significant results. In western Europe and the United States, air quality improved dramatically. Smog levels in the United States fell nearly a third from 1970 to 2000, even though the number of automobiles increased more than 80 percent. Emissions of lead and sulfur dioxide were down as well. The Great Lakes, Long Island Sound, and Chesapeake Bay were all much cleaner at the beginning of the new century than they had been in 1970.

New technologies made much of the improvement possible; for example, pollution controls on automobiles, planes, and factory smokestacks reduced harmful emissions. At the same time, the desire to preserve the natural environment was growing around the world. In developed nations continued political organization and enhanced awareness of environmental issues seemed likely to lead to step-by-step improvements in environmental policy. In the developing world and most of the former Soviet bloc, however, population pressures and weak governments were major obstacles to effective environmental policies. Since the 1990s the rapid expansion of China's industrial sector as well as industrial growth in other developing nations like India and Brazil has put additional pressure on the environment.

It now seems likely that industrialized nations will have to fund global improvements and that the cost will be high. Slow growth and fiscal crises in the mature industrial economies after the 2008 recession have politicized and slowed the progress of environmental reform. Nevertheless, growing evidence of environmental degradation and global warming have continued to propel popular reform efforts, as when the media drew attention to the precipitous shrinkage of Peru's Andean glaciers and to loss of rain forest in Brazil. Yet, without broad agreement among the rich nations, the economic and political power necessary for environmental protections on

AP® Exam Tip
Understand the environmental impacts of deforestation, desertification, and greenhouse gasses on the debate regarding the nature and causes of climate change.

Section Review

- Improvements in existing technology and new technologies such as the computer have improved manufacturing efficiency and transformed leisure.

- Globalization created a more integrated world economy, connecting producers and consumers from different regions and nations and reducing the ability of a single nation to escape the effects of distant events.

- The environmental movement achieved some successes in developed nations, reducing pollution and improving resource management, but global progress was hindered by a lack of cooperation between developed and developing nations.

a global scale will be very difficult to institute. When representatives from around the world negotiated a far-reaching treaty to reduce greenhouse gases in Kyoto, Japan, in 1997, President George W. Bush refused American participation even though the treaty was affirmed by nearly all other industrial nations. Canada subsequently withdrew from the agreement, and China and other rapidly industrializing nations were largely exempted from the treaty's limits. This agreement, as a result, has had a limited effect on greenhouse gas emissions. More recently, in 2015, world leaders successfully negotiated the Paris Agreement, a broad climate accord to limit the growth of carbon emissions and slow global warming. In 2017 President Donald J. Trump withdrew the United States from this international treaty, despite dire warnings from climate scientists.

32-6 Conclusion

The world was profoundly altered between 1975 and the first decade of the twenty-first century. Both the United States and the Soviet Union feared that every conflict and every regime change represented a potential threat to their strategic interests, and every conflict threatened to provoke confrontation between them. As a result, the superpowers inserted themselves into a succession of civil wars and revolutions. The costs in lives and property were terrible, the gains small. As defense costs escalated, the Soviet system crumbled. By 1991 the Soviet Union and the socialist Warsaw Pact had disappeared, transforming the international stage.

The world was also altered by economic growth and globalization, by population growth and movement, and by technological and environmental change. Led by the postwar recovery of the industrial powers and the remarkable economic expansion of Japan, the Asian Tigers, and more recently China, the world economy grew dramatically until the global recession of 2008. The development and application of new technology contributed significantly to this process. International markets were more open and integrated than at any other time. However, not all the nations of the world benefited from the new wealth and exciting technologies of the postwar era. The capitalist West and a handful of Asian nations grew richer and more powerful, while most of the world's nations remained poor.

Population growth in the developing world was one reason for this divided experience. Despite falling birthrates in many poor countries, most of the world's population growth in recent decades is in developing nations with limited economic growth. Unable to find adequate employment or, in many cases, bare subsistence, people in developing nations have migrated across international borders, hoping to improve their lives. These movements have often provided valuable labor in the factories and farms of the developed world, but they have also provoked cultural, racial, and ethnic tension. Problems of inequality, population growth, and international migration will continue to challenge the global community in the coming decades.

Growing population and the development process have forced marginal lands into production and stimulated the exploitation of new resources. The need to feed a rapidly growing world population has also pressured ocean resources. As the world's population surpassed 6 billion and the populations of the largest cities expanded beyond 20 million, the need to produce and deliver raw materials and finished goods has put tremendous stress on the environment. In the 1990s the rapid development of the Chinese and Indian economies compounded these pressures.

At the same time, new technologies and the wealth produced by economic expansion have allowed the world's richest nations to implement ambitious programs of environmental protection. As a result, pollution produced by automobiles and factories has actually declined in the richest nations. The question that remains is whether rapidly developing nations, such as Brazil, China, and India, will move more quickly than the mature industrial nations did to introduce these new technologies and curtail threats to the environment like global warming.

Key Terms

proxy wars p. 836
Salvador Allende p. 837
Dirty War p. 838
Sandinistas p. 838
neoliberalism p. 839

Ayatollah Ruhollah
  Khomeini p. 840
Saddam Husain p. 840
keiretsu p. 841
Asian Tigers p. 843

newly industrialized
  economies (NIEs) p. 843
Deng Xiaoping p. 843
Tiananmen Square p. 844
Mikhail Gorbachev p. 845
perestroika p. 845

Solidarity p. 845
ethnic cleansing p. 846
Thomas Malthus p. 849
demographic transition
  p. 849

Review Questions

1. Explore the origins and consequences of the large events discussed in the chapter.
2. What was the connection between the Cold War and "proxy wars"?
3. Were there similarities between the economic development of Japan after 1945 and China after 1970?
4. What led to the collapse of the Soviet Union?
5. What are the links between rates of population growth and international immigration?
6. What have been the major consequences of postwar technological change?

 MindTap® is a fully online, personalized learning experience built upon Cengage Learning content. MindTap® combines student learning tools—readings, multimedia, activities, and assessments—into a singular Learning Path that guides students through the course and helps students develop the critical thinking, analysis, and communication skills that are essential to academic and professional success.

AP® REVIEW QUESTIONS FOR CHAPTER 32

Multiple-Choice Questions

Questions 1–3 refer to the passage below.

"It is obvious that foreign debt is one of the most inhuman forms of exploitation in our countries. . . . Women in every household are suffering every day as a result of impoverished economies and those who are most exposed to the effects of foreign debt are women.

When it comes to shopping, caring for sick children or the impossibility of meeting their schooling costs, the illusion of "leaving poverty behind" evaporates. Yet the problem is not only of an economic nature because under such circumstances the constant tension leads to grave, often lasting exhaustion. The psychosocial damage is alarming. The adoption of austerity measures means a curtailment of the state's commitment to social services with a direct effect on women."

Gladys Acosta, "The View of a Peruvian Militant," in *Compañeras: Voices from the Latin American Women's Movement*, 1994

1. The neoliberalism described by Acosta is the direct result of

   (A) the rise of empires in the post–World War II world.

   (B) increased immigration from former colonies to the developed world.

   (C) the end of the Cold War and the spread of free market economies.

   (D) the rise of dictatorships at the end of World War I.

2. Which of the following best reflects Acosta's view?

   (A) Although some people have been hurt by these policies, most of the population has benefited immensely.

   (B) Neoliberalism is a new form of economic imperialism.

   (C) Women and children have benefitted more from the new economy than most other groups.

   (D) Decolonization has protected most former colonies from being further abused by their former mother countries.

3. Which of the following inferences can be substantiated by the passage?

   (A) Although neoliberal policies became more intrusive in local economies, they had little to no effect on home life.

   (B) International organizations were successful in guaranteeing economic opportunities.

   (C) Neoliberalism brought economic and social equality to the developing world.

   (D) New forms of gender hierarchy emerged toward the end of the twentieth century.

Questions 4–7 refer to Map 32.1 on page 847.

4. Which of the following best explains the extent of the Soviet Union prior to 1991?

   (A) Expansion of the Russian Empire in the nineteenth century

   (B) Turkish and Persian expansion into Central Asia

   (C) Peter the Great's Westernization policies

   (D) The rise of international Marxist movements in the late nineteenth century

5. The fall of communist regimes in Eastern Europe led to which of the following?

   (A) The rise of neocommunist governments in the former Warsaw Pact nations

   (B) The expansion of Western power and influence into Eastern Europe

   (C) The formation by Eastern European nations of their own economic union

   (D) The expansion of Russian power into Western Europe

6. The conflicts in the former Yugoslavia were based on which of the following causes?

   (A) Resurgent communist militias

   (B) Lack of economic opportunities

   (C) Ethnic and religious differences

   (D) Access to natural resources

7. Which of the following inferences can be drawn from the breakup of the Soviet Union and its allies depicted on the map?

   (A) The Soviet government succeeded in changing the cultures but not the economies of the various regions within its borders.

   (B) Military actions taken by NATO destabilized the Soviet Union.

   (C) Marxist regimes failed to use art and culture to promote their ideals.

   (D) Regional cultures and religions were more resilient than communist ideals.

Questions 8–10 refer to the table on the next page.

8. Which of the following best explains the most common population changes on the chart from 1900 to 1995?

   (A) The impact of new farming and medical practices

   (B) Devastation and disease from global conflicts

   (C) The spread of communism in multiple world regions

   (D) Warming climates from global climate change

Population for World and Major Areas, 1750-2050

Major Area	Population Size (Millions)						
	1750	1800	1850	1900	1950	2000	2050*
World	791	978	1,262	1,650	2,521	6,055	9,725
Africa	106	107	111	133	221	785	2,478
Asia	502	635	809	947	1,402	3,683	5,267
Europe	163	203	276	408	547	729	707
Latin America and the Caribbean	16	24	38	74	167	519	784
North America	2	7	26	82	172	310	433
Oceania	2	2	2	6	13	30	57

Major Area	Percentage Distribution						
	1750	1800	1850	1900	1950	2000	2050*
World	100	100	100	100	100		100
Africa	13.4	10.9	8.8	8.1	8.8	13.0	25.5
Asia	63.5	64.9	64.1	57.4	55.6	60.8	54.2
Europe	20.6	20.8	21.9	24.7	21.7	12.0	7.3
Latin America and the Caribbean	2.0	2.5	3.0	4.5	6.6	8.6	8.1
North America	0.3	0.7	2.1	5.0	6.8	5.1	4.4
Oceania	0.3	0.2	0.2	0.4	0.5	0.5	0.6

*Estimated

Sources: J. D. Durand, "Historical Estimates of World Population: An Evaluation" (Philadelphia: University of Pennsylvania, Population Studies Center, 1974, mimeographed); United Nations, *The Determinants and Consequences of Population Trends*, vol. 1 (New York: United Nations, 1973); United Nations, *World Population Prospects as Assessed in 1963* (New York: United Nations, 1966); United Nations, *World Population Prospects: The 2015 Revision* (New York: United Nations, 2015); United Nations Population Division, Department of Economic and Social Affairs, *World Population to 2300* (2004), www.un.org/esa/population/publications/longrange2/WorldPop2300final.pdf.

9. Which of the following best explains the population percentage trends in North America and Europe from 1950 to 2050 shown on the chart?

   (A) The spread of infectious diseases such as influenza and HIV

   (B) High mortality rates from global conflicts

   (C) Rising affluence and more effective birth control

   (D) Environmental degradation and famine

10. Families in North America in 2016 had fewer children than their counterparts in the 1950s. Knowing this, what else could account for the change in population from 1950 to 2050?

    (A) Immigration

    (B) Improved farming techniques

    (C) Growth of global trade

    (D) Decline in medical services

Short-Answer Questions

1. Answer all parts of the question that follows.

   (A) Identify ONE cause for the Iranian Revolution.

   (B) Explain ONE way the Iranian Revolution caused a social change.

   (C) Explain ONE way the Iranian Revolution caused a political change.

2. Answer all parts of the question that follows.

   (A) Identify ONE reason China continued to lack economic growth prior to the 1970s.

   (B) Explain ONE way policies put in place by Deng Xiaoping changed the Chinese economy.

   (C) Explain ANOTHER way policies put in place by Deng Xiaoping changed the Chinese economy.

33 Leaving the Twentieth Century

AP® Framework Terms

Globalization
Cultural imperialism
Global popular culture

Overarching Questions

1 How have religions, belief systems, philosophies, and ideologies affected the political, economic, and social development of societies? (CUL)

2 How have expanding exchange networks shaped the emergence of various forms of transregional culture, including music, literature, and visual art? (CUL)

3 How have state and non-state actors interacted economically and politically over time? (SB)

4 How have local, regional, and global economic systems and exchange networks influenced each other over time? (ECON)

5 How have political, economic, cultural, and demographic factors affected social structures? (SOC)

The workday began normally at the World Trade Center in lower Manhattan on the morning of September 11, 2001. The 50,000 people who worked there were making their way to the two 110-story towers. Suddenly, at 8:46 A.M., an American Airlines Boeing 767 with 92 people on board, traveling at a speed of 470 miles (756 kilometers) per hour, crashed into floors 94 to 98 of the north tower, igniting the 10,000 gallons (38,000 liters) of fuel in its tanks. Just before 9:03 A.M. a United Airlines flight with 65 people on board and a similar fuel load hit floors 78 to 84 of the south tower.

As the burning jet fuel engulfed the collision areas, the buildings' occupants struggled through smoke-filled corridors and down dozens of flights of stairs. Many of those trapped above the crash sites used cell phones to say good-bye to loved ones. Rather than endure the flames and fumes, a few jumped to their deaths.

Just before 10:00, temperatures that had risen to 2,300° Fahrenheit (1,260° Celsius) caused the steel girders in the impacted area of the south tower to give way. The collapsing upper floors crushed the floors underneath one by one, engulfing lower Manhattan in a dense cloud of dust. Twenty-eight minutes later the north tower pancaked in a similar manner. Miraculously, most of the buildings' occupants had escaped before the towers collapsed. Besides the people on the planes, nearly 2,600 lost their lives, including some 400 police officers and firefighters helping in the evacuation.

▲ **Watching Financial Markets Fall** After years of economic boom, much of it fueled by inflated housing prices in the United States and ingenious new financial instruments that concealed risk, the world's stock markets fell drastically in 2008–2009. American stocks lost approximately one-third of their value. The banking crisis and resulting unemployment reminded economists of the Great Depression of the 1930s. People in all walks of life, from heads of state, to retirees, to ordinary workers, were forced to reappraise their financial situations. JUSTIN LANE/Newscom/European Pressphoto Agency/ NEW YORK/NEW YORK/UNITED STATES

That same morning another American Airlines jet crashed into the Pentagon, killing all 64 people on board and 125 others inside the military complex near Washington, D.C. Passengers on a fourth plane managed to overpower their hijackers, and the plane crashed in rural Pennsylvania, killing all 45 on board.

The four planes had been hijacked by teams of Middle Eastern men who slit the throats of service and flight personnel and seized control. Of the nineteen hijackers, fifteen were from Saudi Arabia. All had links to an extremist Islamic organization, al-Qaeda **(ahl–KAW-eh-duh)** (the base or foundation), commanded by a rich Saudi named Osama bin Laden **(oo-SAH-mah bin LAH-din)**, who was incensed with American political, military, and cultural influence in the Middle East. The men were educated and well traveled, had lived in the United States, and spoke English. Some had trained as pilots so that they could fly the hijacked aircraft.

The hijackers left few records of their motives, but the acts spoke for themselves. The World Trade Center was a focal point of international business, the Pentagon the headquarters of the American military. The fourth plane was probably meant to hit the Capitol or the White House, the legislative and executive centers of the world's only superpower.

The events of September 11, which became commonly referred to as 9/11, can be understood on many levels. The hijackers and those who sympathized with them saw themselves as engaged in a holy struggle against economic, political, and military institutions they believed to be evil. People directly affected, political leaders around the world, and most television watchers described the attacks as evil deeds against innocent victims.

To understand why the nineteen attackers were heroes to some and terrorists to others, one needs to explore the historical context of global changes at the turn of the millennium and the ideological tensions—religious, political, and economic—they have generated. The unique prominence of the United States in every major aspect of global integration, as well as its support for pro-American governments overseas, also elicits sharply divergent views, including within the United States itself where President Donald J. Trump was elected in 2016 on a platform of transforming America's place in the world, and the world's place in America. ●

33-1 **The Question of Values**

What role do religious beliefs and secular ideologies play in the contemporary world?

People around the world tried to make sense of the increasing violence perpetrated by nonstate organizations like al-Qaeda in terms of their own value systems. With 7 billion people, the world was big enough to include many different approaches, whether religious or secular, local or international, traditional or visionary. Islam stood out, however, as the label most often attached to frightening acts of violence.

33-1a **Faith and Politics**

Religious beliefs had increasingly inspired political actions during the last third of the twentieth century, and the trend intensified in the new century (see Map 33.1). Though for Americans this change reversed a widespread assumption that religion was destined to diminish in importance as global forces brought countries closer and closer together, Western analysts disagreed on the causes of the religious revival.

The birth of the Islamic Republic of Iran in the revolution of 1979 made visible a current of Muslim political assertiveness that had been building for twenty years in several Muslim countries (see Diversity & Dominance: Conflict and Civilization). But by the year 2000 acts of **terrorism** perpetrated by non-Iranian Muslim groups claiming to be acting for religious reasons were capturing the headlines.

33-1b **Terrorism**

Terrorism is a political tactic by which comparatively weak militants use grotesquely inhumane and lethal acts to convince a frightened public that danger is everywhere and their government is incapable of protecting them. Although terrorism has a long history, the instantaneous media links made possible by satellite communications, and the journalistic tradition treating violence as headline news, increased its effectiveness from the 1980s onward.

Bombings, kidnappings, and assassinations made political sense to all sorts of political groups: secular Palestinians confronting Israel; national separatists like the Tamils in Sri Lanka, Basques in Spain, and Chechens in Russia; and Catholic and Protestant extremists in Northern Ireland, to name a few. But Muslim groups gained the lion's share of attention when they targeted the United States and Europe, recruited from Muslim populations all over the world, and made effective use of news coverage and audiovisual communications.

terrorism Political belief that extreme and seemingly random violence will destabilize a government and permit the terrorists to gain political advantage. Though an old technique, terrorism gained prominence in the late twentieth century with the growth of worldwide mass media that, through their news coverage, amplified public fears of terrorist acts.

CHRONOLOGY

	Politics	Economics and Society
2000	2000 Al-Qaeda attacks American destroyer USS *Cole* in Yemen	
2001	2001 George W. Bush becomes president of the United States 2001 Terrorists destroy the World Trade Center and damage the Pentagon on September 11 2001 United States armed forces overthrow Taliban regime in Afghanistan	2001–2003 Terrorist attacks trigger global recession 2001 Shanghai Cooperation Organization formed
2002		2002 Euro currency adopted in twelve European countries
2003	2003 Unfounded fears of weapons of mass destruction lead United States and Britain to invade and occupy Iraq	
2004	2004 Terrorists bomb Spanish trains 2004–2009 Genocidal conflict ongoing in Darfur region of Sudan	2004 Ten new members admitted to European Union
2005	2005 Terrorists bomb London transit system 2005 Mahmoud Ahmedinejad elected president of Iran	
2006	2006 Iraqis elect a government under a new constitution 2006 Hamas movement defeats PLO in Palestinian election 2006 Israel attacks Hezbollah in Lebanon in response to its seizure of Israeli soldiers	
2007	2007 Assassination of Benazir Bhutto deepens political crisis in Pakistan	
2008	2008 Barack Obama elected president of the United States	2008 Collapse of mortgage debt bubble in United States triggers global recession
2012	2012 Barack Obama re-elected president of the United States	
2013	2013 Argentinian becomes Pope Francis I	
2014	2014 Russia seizes Crimea	
2016	2016 Donald Trump elected president of the United States 2016 Abortive coup in Turkey	2016 British vote to leave EU

The political rationale put forward by al-Qaeda, based in Afghanistan, justified *jihad*, or holy war, as a defensive struggle against the United States and the former colonial powers in Europe, the "far enemy," which were seen as essential supports for Muslim monarchies, like Saudi Arabia, and military regimes, like Egypt and Syria, that oppressed their own citizens. If these outsiders were forced to withdraw from the Muslim world, therefore, the oppressive regimes would collapse. The Soviet withdrawal from Afghanistan in 1989 seemed to support this theory. Between 1989 and 2001, when the United States attacked that country in reaction to 9/11, the Afghans sought to govern their own affairs. These efforts led to the rise of an oppressive religious regime known as the Taliban, but the violence of Taliban rule, under whose protective umbrella al-Qaeda took shape, was little worse than that under the earlier Soviet occupation or later American control.

Al-Qaeda's media star and ideological spokesman was **Osama bin Laden**. Born into a wealthy Saudi family and educated as an engineer, bin Laden fought against the Soviet Union in Afghanistan and there recruited and trained a core group of al-Qaeda fighters. Al-Qaeda blew up American embassies in Kenya and Tanzania in 1998, crippled the U.S. Navy destroyer *Cole* during a port call in Yemen in 2000, and then capped everything by the attacks of 9/11. When the "global war on terrorism" declared by President Bush failed to eliminate bin Laden, his mystique grew. Further terrorist attacks—by Indonesians on tourists on the island of Bali in 2002, by North Africans on commuter trains servicing Madrid in 2004, by English-born Muslims on the London transit system in 2005, and by Pakistanis on luxury hotels in Mumbai, India, in 2008—made it clear that the current of violence unleashed by al-Qaeda had become decentralized and that

AP® Exam Tip
Explain how some movements (such as Al-Qaeda) used violence against civilians to achieve political aims.

Osama bin Laden
Saudi-born Muslim extremist who funded the al-Qaeda organization that was responsible for several terrorist attacks, including those on the World Trade Center and the Pentagon in 2001.

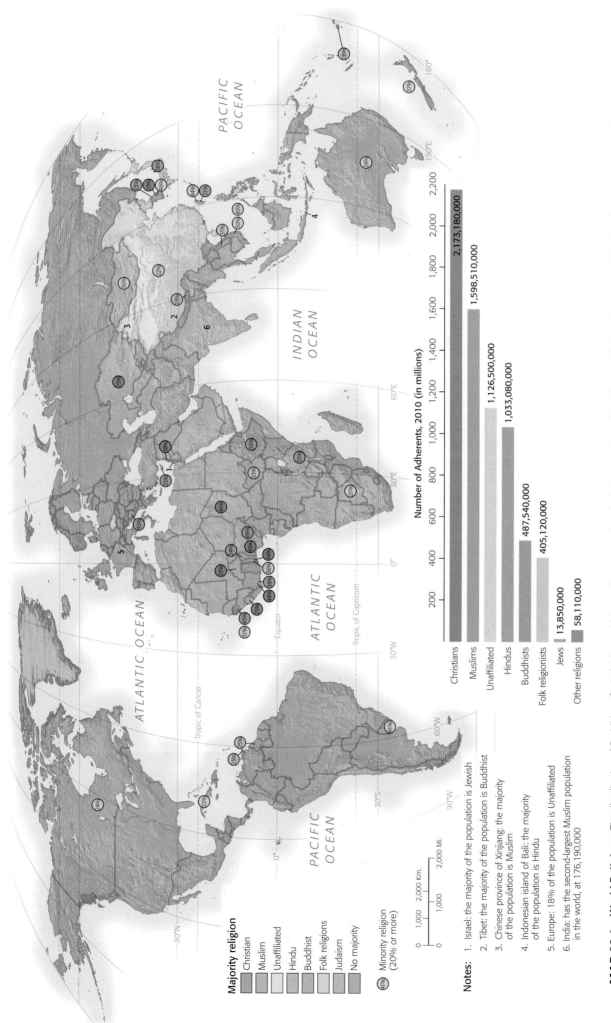

Majority religion

- Christian
- Muslim
- Unaffiliated
- Hindu
- Buddhist
- Folk religions
- Judaism
- No majority

41% Minority religion (20% or more)

Number of Adherents, 2010 (in millions)

Religion	Adherents
Christians	2,173,180,000
Muslims	1,598,510,000
Unaffiliated	1,126,500,000
Hindus	1,033,080,000
Buddhists	487,540,000
Folk religionists	405,120,000
Jews	13,850,000
Other religions	58,110,000

Notes:

1. Israel: the majority of the population is Jewish
2. Tibet: the majority of the population is Buddhist
3. Chinese province of Xinjiang: the majority of the population is Muslim
4. Indonesian island of Bali: the majority of the population is Hindu
5. Europe: 18% of the population is Unaffiliated
6. India: has the second-largest Muslim population in the world, at 176,190,000

MAP 33.1 World Religions The distribution of Buddhism, Christianity, and Islam reflects centuries of missionary efforts. Hinduism and Judaism have expanded primarily through trade and migration. Chinese governments have actively curtailed religious practice. As religion revives as a source of social identity or a rationale for political assertion or mass mobilization, the possibility of religious activism across broad geographic regions becomes greater, as does the likelihood of domestic discord in multireligious states.

Source: Data from Pew Research Center, "The Global Religious Landscape," © 2012, www.pewforum.org/global-religious-landscape.aspx.

How important are differences between Catholic, Orthodox, and Protestant in Christianity, and between Sunni and Shi'ite in Islam?

recruits and cells might no longer be taking orders exclusively from bin Laden. Even after an American commando operation killed bin Laden in his hideout in Pakistan in 2011, affiliates like al-Qaeda in the Arabian Peninsula (AQAP), al-Qaeda in the Islamic Maghreb (AQIM), and Boko Haram continued to operate in Yemen, North Africa (the Maghreb), and West Africa, respectively.

In 2013 an offshoot of al-Qaeda known as the Islamic State of Iraq and Syria (ISIS) or the Islamic State of Iraq and the Levant (ISIL) proclaimed independence from al-Qaeda and announced that a shadowy figure named Abu Bakr al-Baghdadi would henceforth be the *Caliph* (absolute religious ruler) of an Islamic State that would seek the allegiance of Muslims anywhere in the world. Departing from al-Qaeda's justifications of violence based on the far enemy theory, ISIS maintained that it was recreating the original Islamic state of the seventh century and publicized atrocities—including beheadings of captives and wanton destruction of pre-Islamic historical monuments—that horrified the world. Spectacular attacks on civilians in Paris and Brussels in 2016 vaulted ISIS ahead of al-Qaeda as the most alarming perpetrator of violence in the name of Islam. They also demonstrated that flagrant criminality and vigorous recruitment through the use of social media could be successful in attracting fighters even as they outraged world opinion.

33-1c Regime Change in the Muslim World

ISIS took root in the heart of the Arab world because an American invasion of Iraq in 2003, ostensibly in retaliation for the attacks of 9/11, had failed to establish an orderly and effective government there. And a civil war triggered by the "Arab Spring" (see illustration below), a wave of popular anti-regime movements that struck five Arab countries in 2011, continued to wrack Syria.

The Taliban regime's provision of a safe haven for Osama bin Laden and al-Qaeda clearly justified the American invasion of Afghanistan in December 2001. However, the rationale for invading Iraq was less clear. Leading up to the war the American government contended that Iraq was a clear and present danger to the United States because it possessed **weapons of mass destruction** (WMDs): nuclear, chemical, and biological weapons that it might supply to terrorists like bin Laden. When United Nations inspectors failed to find any banned weapons, a split widened between those nations wanting to continue inspections and those, led by the United States, wanting to intervene militarily. Deciding to go it alone, an American-led "coalition of the willing" opened the invasion of Iraq with a spectacular aerial bombardment of Baghdad on March 20, 2003. Twenty-five days later the United States declared that "major fighting" had ended, little realizing that guerrilla insurgency, sectarian violence, and economic devastation would continue for years.

While Iraq fell into a state of turmoil because the coalition army was too small or otherwise poorly equipped to prevent the looting and destruction of government facilities and other lawlessness, a thorough search for WMDs came up empty, and intelligence analyses failed to uncover any evidence that Saddam Husain, Iraq's fallen dictator, had played a role in the 9/11 attacks. American troops finally withdrew from the country in 2010, leaving behind an elected government divided by strong animosity between a Shi'ite majority and a Sunni minority. ISIS, a Sunni organization, took advantage of the turmoil and also attracted Sunni military officers who had been part of Saddam Husain's disbanded army. One-sided government policies favoring the Shi'ites added to the turmoil.

As for Syria, where the Islamic State was centered along the Euphrates River, the "Arab Spring" that toppled the rulers of Tunisia, Libya, Egypt, and Yemen had failed to unseat the ruler Bashar al-Assad. With Russia and Iran supporting the Shi'ite al-Assad and fundamentalist (*salafi*) Sunni Muslims openly or covertly supporting the Islamic State and some smaller resistance groups, chaos reigned in Syria and millions of refugees took the road into exile. The decision by the United States to steer clear of most military operations in Syria that did not specifically target ISIS opened President Barak Obama to political attack as the refugee crisis and civilian death toll swelled and Russian president Vladimir Putin stepped forward as a decisive leader willing to use force to keep Bashar al-Assad in power. Syrian refugees flooding into Europe by way of Turkey exacerbated popular fears of terrorism and immigration there.

weapons of mass destruction Nuclear, chemical, and biological devices that are capable of injuring and killing large numbers of people.

In 1993 Samuel P. Huntington, a professor of government at Harvard University, published "The Clash of Civilizations?" in the journal Foreign Affairs. This article provoked extraordinary debate, particularly after the 9/11 attacks on the World Trade Center and the Pentagon. Some readers deemed it an accurate description of a post–Cold War world in which Islamic countries were destined to conflict violently with the countries of Europe and North America. Others saw it as imprecise in its failure to clarify what a "civilization" is, imperialistic in its unquestioning assumption of Western superiority, and encouraging of anti-Muslim prejudice.

Civilizational identity will be increasingly important in the future, and the world will be shaped in large measure by the interactions among seven or eight major civilizations. These include Western, Confucian, Japanese, Islamic, Hindu, Slavic-Orthodox, Latin American and possibly African civilization. The most important conflicts of the future will occur along the cultural fault lines separating these civilizations from one another.

Why will this be the case?

First, differences among civilizations are not only real; they are basic. Civilizations are differentiated from each other by history, language, culture, tradition and, most important, religion. The people of different civilizations have different views on the relations between God and man, the individual and the group, the citizen and the state, parents and children, husband and wife, as well as differing views of the relative importance of rights and responsibilities, liberty and authority, equality and hierarchy. These differences are the product of centuries. They will not soon disappear. They are far more fundamental than differences among political ideologies and political regimes. Differences do not necessarily mean conflict, and conflict does not necessarily mean violence. Over the centuries, however, differences among civilizations have generated the most prolonged and the most violent conflicts.

Second, the world is becoming a smaller place. The interactions between peoples of different civilizations are increasing; these increasing interactions intensify civilization consciousness and awareness of differences between civilizations and commonalities within civilizations. North African immigration to France generates hostility among Frenchmen and at the same time increased receptivity to immigration by "good" European Catholic Poles. Americans react far more negatively to Japanese investment than to larger investments from Canada and European countries. . . .

Third, the processes of economic modernization and social change throughout the world are separating people from long-standing local identities. They also weaken the nation state as a source of identity. In much of the world religion has moved in to fill this gap, often in the form of movements that are labeled "fundamentalist." Such movements are found in Western Christianity, Judaism, Buddhism and Hinduism, as well as in Islam. In most countries and most religions the people active in fundamentalist movements are young, college-educated, middle-class technicians, professionals and business persons. . . .

As people define their identity in ethnic and religious terms, they are likely to see an "us" versus "them" relation existing between themselves and people of different ethnicity or religion.

The end of ideologically defined states in Eastern Europe and the former Soviet Union permits traditional ethnic identities and animosities to come to the fore. Differences in culture and religion create differences over policy issues, ranging from human rights to immigration to trade and commerce to the environment. . . . Most important, the efforts of the West to promote its values of democracy and liberalism to universal values, to maintain its military predominance and to advance its economic interests engender countering responses from other civilizations. . . .

The interactions between civilizations vary greatly in the extent to which they are likely to be characterized by violence. Economic competition clearly predominates between the American and European subcivilizations of the West and between both of them and Japan. On the Eurasian continent, however, the proliferation of ethnic conflict, epitomized at the extreme in "ethnic cleansing," has not been totally random. It has been most frequent and most violent between groups belonging to different civilizations. In Eurasia the great historic fault lines between civilizations are once more aflame. This is particularly true along the boundaries of the crescent-shaped Islamic bloc of nations from the bulge of Africa to central Asia. Violence also occurs between Muslims, on the one hand, and Orthodox Serbs in the Balkans, Jews in Israel, Hindus in India, Buddhists in Burma and Catholics in the Philippines. Islam has bloody borders.

Rejoinders to Huntington's thesis saw it as a cornerstone of the aggressive policies adopted by the Bush administration after 9/11. As an alternative, they stressed the common values held by peaceful societies and the need for intercultural understanding. Mohammed Khatami, the president of the Islamic Republic of Iran, found support for a more positive framing of the matter when the United Nations, following his proposal, declared 2001 the year of "Dialogue Among Civilizations." Almost simultaneously, the Organization of the Islamic Conference (now called the Organization of Islamic Cooperation), a 57-member international body headquartered in Saudi Arabia and composed of states with large Muslim populations, elaborated upon this concept in the "Tehran Declaration on Dialogue Among Civilizations."

Tehran Declaration on Dialogue Among Civilizations

Praise be to Allah and peace and blessing be upon His prophet and kin and companion.

The representatives of Heads of State and Government of OIC member states . . . [recognizing] the United Nations General Assembly resolution 53/22, designating the year 2001 as the United Nations year of Dialogue among Civilizations;

Guided by the noble Islamic teachings and values [*each of the following principles is accompanied by reference to a verse in the Quran*] on human dignity and equality, tolerance, peace and justice for humankind, and promotion of virtues and proscription of vice and evil;

Drawing upon the Islamic principles of celebration of human diversity, recognition of diversified sources of knowledge, promotion of dialogue and mutual understanding, genuine mutual respect in human interchanges, and encouragement of courteous and civilized discourse based on reason and logic;

Reaffirming the commitment of their Governments to promote dialogue and understanding among various cultures and civilizations, aimed at reaching a global consensus to build a new order for the next millennium founded in faith as well as common moral and ethical values of contemporary civilizations;

Requests the Secretary-General of the OIC to submit this declaration for endorsement to the Chairman of the Eighth Islamic Summit and the 26th Islamic Conference of Foreign Ministers for appropriate action:

A) General principles of dialogue among civilizations
1. Respect for the dignity and equality of all human beings without distinctions of any kind and of nations large and small;
2. Genuine acceptance of cultural diversity as a permanent [quality] of human society and a cherished asset for the advancement and welfare of humanity at large;
3. Mutual respect and tolerance for the views and values of various cultures and civilizations, as well as the right of members of all civilizations to preserve their cultural heritage and values, and rejection of desecration of moral, religious or cultural values, sanctities and sanctuaries;
4. Recognition of diversified sources of knowledge throughout time and space, and the imperative of drawing upon the areas of strengths, richness and wisdom of each civilization in a genuine process of mutual enrichment;
5. Rejection of attempts for cultural domination and imposition as well as doctrines and practices promoting confrontation and clash between civilizations;
6. Search for common grounds between and within various civilizations in order to face common global challenges;
7. Acceptance of cooperation and search for understanding as the appropriate mechanism for the promotion of common universal values as well as for the suppression of global threats;
8. Commitment to participation of all peoples and nations, without any discrimination, in their own domestic as well as global decision-making and value distribution processes;
9. Compliance with principles of justice, equity, peace and solidarity as well as fundamental principles of international law and the United Nations Charter. . . .

A few years later, a joint proposal by the governments of Spain and Turkey received a similar endorsement by the United Nations. This led to the creation of the Alliance of Civilizations. The underlying principles of this organization were expressed in the 2006 report of its "High-Level Group," a body of eminent political, intellectual, and spiritual figures from around the world.

Alliance of Civilizations Report of the High-Level Group

I. Bridging the World's Divides

1.1 Our world is alarmingly out of balance. For many, the last century brought unprecedented progress, prosperity, and freedom. For others, it marked an era of subjugation, humiliation and dispossession. Ours is a world of great inequalities and paradoxes: a world where the income of the planet's three richest people is greater than the combined income of the world's least developed countries; where modern medicine performs daily miracles and yet 3 million people die every year of preventable diseases; where we know more about distant universes than ever before, yet 130 million children have no access to education; where despite the existence of multilateral covenants and institutions, the international community often seems helpless in the face of conflict and genocide. For most of humanity, freedom from want and freedom from fear appear as elusive as ever.

1.2 We also live in an increasingly complex world, where polarized perceptions, fueled by injustice and inequality, often lead to violence and conflict, threatening international stability. Over the past few years, wars, occupation and acts of terror have exacerbated mutual suspicion and fear within and among societies. Some political leaders and sectors of the media, as well as radical groups have exploited this environment, painting mirror images of a world made up of mutually exclusive cultures, religions, or civilizations, historically distinct and destined for confrontation.

1.3 The anxiety and confusion caused by the "clash of civilizations" theory regrettably has distorted the terms of the discourse on the real nature of the predicament the world is facing. The history of relations between cultures is not only one of wars and confrontation. It is also based on centuries of constructive exchanges, cross-fertilization, and peaceful co-existence. Moreover, classifying internally fluid and diverse societies along hard-and-fast lines of civilizations interferes with more illuminating ways of understanding questions of identity, motivation and behavior. Rifts between the powerful and the powerless or the rich and the poor or between different political groups, classes, occupations and nationalities have greater explanatory power than such cultural categories. Indeed, the latter stereotypes only serve to entrench already polarized opinions. Worse, by promoting the misguided view that cultures are set on an unavoidable collision course, they help turn negotiable disputes into seemingly intractable identity-based conflicts that take hold of the popular imagination. It is essential, therefore, to counter the stereotypes and misconceptions that deepen patterns of hostility and mistrust among societies.

AP® History Reasoning Skills

Comparison *How important are culture and religion, as opposed to political ideology or economic inequality, in explaining current world conflicts?*

Continuity and Change Over Time *How have the structure and goals of global interactions both changed and remained the same since the attacks of 9/11?*

Sources: Samuel P. Huntington, "The Clash of Civilizations?" Reprinted by permission of *Foreign Affairs* 72, no. 3 (Summer 1993). Copyright 1993 by the Council on Foreign Relations, Inc. www.ForeignAffairs.com; "The Tehran Declaration on Dialogue Among Civilizations," Organization of the Islamic Conference, www.isesco.org.ma/english/publications/dig/CH11.php; "High-Level Group Report," Alliance of Civilizations, www.unaoc.org/content/view/64/94/lang,english/.

▶ **Arab Spring Demonstrators**
Part of the enormous crowds that unseated the rulers of Egypt, Tunisia, Libya, and Yemen, these women in Cairo's Tahrir Square wear the colorful head scarves that are commonplace in Egypt, sometimes to demonstrate allegiance to Islam and sometimes because they are stylish. AP Images/Khalil Hamra

AP® Exam Tip
Explain how conceptualization of society and culture have changed throughout the twentieth and twenty-first centuries.

33-1d North Korea and Iran

American worries about WMDs were not confined to Iraq. North Korea had an open program to build nuclear weapons, and Iran was suspected of having a covert plan based in part on technological aid secretly transmitted by the head of Pakistan's successful nuclear program. Iran's outspokenly anti-American and anti-Israeli president, Mahmoud Ahmedinejad, elected in 2005, and North Korea's dictators Kim Jong-il (**kim jong-ill**) and after 2011 his son Kim Jong-un presented the United States with difficult challenges. But the invasion option chosen for Iraq, albeit favored by some Bush advisers for Iran, was held in abeyance in favor of diplomatic initiatives. As for North Korea, containment of nuclear threats was a concern for China, South Korea, and Japan as for the United States.

33-1e Hezbollah and Hamas

Iran's challenge to America's hopes for a democratic reshaping of the Middle East took a step forward in 2005 when the Lebanese Shi'ite movement Hezbollah captured 23 out of 128 seats in the Lebanese parliament and in 2006 when the militantly anti-Israeli Hamas movement won an absolute majority of the vote in elections for the Palestine Governing Authority. Both groups were firmly allied with Iran. Attacks launched by Israel against both Hamas and Hezbollah in response to kidnappings of Israeli soldiers in 2006 suggested that Israeli fear of Islamic movements might in the future become more important than Arab world democratization, regardless of American preferences. Hezbollah also followed Iran's lead in sending fighters to Syria in support of Bashar al-Assad.

In 2007 the elected Hamas government succeeded in driving its Palestinian rivals out of the Gaza Strip. During the following months, largely inaccurate rocket barrages launched from there against Israel became a major factor in Israeli politics. The first stages of a planned 403-mile-long security barrier built on the West Bank had almost eliminated attacks by Palestinian suicide bombers, but the rockets provoked public outrage even though the number of casualties was small. At the end of 2008 the Israel Defense Force launched aerial bombardments and ground force incursions in the Gaza Strip that left over a thousand Palestinians dead. However, there was no sign that Hamas had been seriously harmed as a political organization. Indeed, in 2012 a renewed exchange of Hamas rockets and Israeli air strikes showed the persistence of the stalemate in Gaza.

33-1f Muslims and Violence

Elsewhere in the Arab world a rash of popular demonstrations starting at the end of 2010 led to the "Arab Spring," an anti-authoritarian political current that toppled the rulers of Tunisia, Libya, Egypt, and Yemen and plunged Syria into its civil war. Though not the instigators of the demonstrations, previously suppressed Muslim political parties like Egypt's Muslim Brotherhood emerged as the best organized contenders as shaky democratic regimes struggled into being. Tunisia alone, however, emerged from the turmoil with a reasonably democratic government, though one that still fell short in areas like youth employment that had helped trigger the demonstrations. Egypt reverted to military rule when the army overthrew the elected Muslim Brotherhood government.

In trying to explain a current of violence that could strike anywhere in the world but seemed always to center on Muslims, some analysts argued that Islam itself encouraged violence, particularly against non-Muslims. Counterarguments noted that terrorists came from many backgrounds and that the vast majority of Muslims saw their religion as one of peace. Other analysts maintained that rigidly conservative Muslims were blindly opposed to freedom and modernity. The counterargument to them pointed out that al-Qaeda used modern military and propaganda techniques that many of its operatives, like bin Laden himself, received from modern technical educations. A third school of thought argued that the United States instigated al-Qaeda's wrath by policies supporting Israel and stationing troops in Saudi Arabia and that those policies should therefore be reconsidered. Those who disagreed pointed out that despite its support for Israel and Saudi Arabia, the United States had championed the Muslim cause in Bosnia, driven the secular dictator Saddam Husain out of Kuwait, and expressed support for the popular uprisings of the Arab Spring.

After the interventionist attitude of President George W. Bush and the reluctance to get involved of President Obama, America's stance in the Middle East, and vis-à-vis Islam more broadly, remained uncertain when Donald J. Trump became president in 2017 on a platform of vigorous opposition to "radical Islamic terrorism."

33-1g Christians and Jews

As Muslims were rediscovering the political potential of their faith, evangelical Protestants became a powerful conservative political movement in the United States starting with the Moral Majority organization formed during Ronald Reagan's presidential campaign in 1979. Its deep roots in the Republican Party, particularly in state and local government, made evangelical fervor a significant force during the George W. Bush presidency and a major contributor to the election of Donald J. Trump.

Around the world, Catholic conservatives led by Pope John Paul II and Pope Benedict XVI, who succeeded him in 2005, forcefully reiterated politically sensitive teachings: opposition to abortion, homosexuality, marriage of priests, and admission of women to the priesthood. The elevation to the papacy in 2013 of Argentinian Jorge Mario Bergoglio as Pope Francis I, the first from either the Western or the Southern Hemisphere, restored Catholicism's gentler side through a commitment to fighting poverty, but triggered no major changes in controversial areas of dogma.

In Israel, hyperorthodox Jews known as *haredim* played a leading role in the inexorable expansion of Jewish settlements in Palestinian territories captured by Israel in 1967. They vehemently resisted both Israel's dismantling of settlements in Gaza in 2005 and subsequent proposals for withdrawal from the West Bank. The settler movement solidified its political position under Prime Minister Benjamin Netanyahu, Israel's head of government since 2009.

33-1h Universal Rights and Values

AP® Exam Tip
Explain the involvement of global and nongovernmental organizations in the expansion of human rights.

Alongside the growing influence of religion on politics, efforts to promote adherence to universal human rights also expanded. The modern human rights movement grew out of secular statements like the French Declaration of the Rights of Man (1789) and the U.S. Constitution (1788) and Bill of Rights (1791). The **Universal Declaration of Human Rights**, passed by the United

Universal Declaration of Human Rights A 1948 United Nations covenant binding signatory nations to the observance of specified rights.

▶ **Refugees from Civil War in Syria** Though refugees from Afghanistan, Libya, and elsewhere play major roles in a growing world refugee crisis, Syrians have achieved special prominence because many of them travel through Turkey or across the sea to reach havens in Europe. This has intensified long-standing animosity toward Muslims among Europeans who believe they threaten their national cultures. Michael Honegger/Alamy Stock Photo

Nations General Assembly in 1948, culminated this movement by proclaiming itself "a common standard of achievement for all peoples and nations." Its thirty articles condemned slavery, torture, cruel and inhuman punishment, and arbitrary arrest, detention, and exile. The Declaration called for freedom of movement, assembly, and thought. It asserted rights to life, liberty, and security of person; to impartial public trials; and to education, employment, and leisure. The principle of equality was most fully articulated in Article 2:

> Everyone is entitled to all the rights and freedoms set forth in this Declaration, without distinction of any kind, such as race, color, sex, language, religion, or political or other opinion, national or social origin, property, birth or other status.[1]

This passage reflected an international consensus against racism and imperialism and a growing acceptance of the importance of social and economic equality. Most newly independent countries joining the United Nations willingly signed the Declaration because it implicitly condemned Europe's colonial past. The Declaration's principles, however, have too often suffered from neglect under authoritarian regimes.

33-1i **Nongovernmental Organizations**

AP® Exam Tip
Evaluate the role of new international organizations in maintaining world peace and facilitating international cooperation.

nongovernmental organizations (NGOs) Nonprofit international organizations devoted to investigating human rights abuses and providing humanitarian relief.

Besides the official actions of the United Nations and various national governments, individual human rights activists, often working through philanthropic bodies known as **nongovernmental organizations (NGOs)**, have been important forces promoting human rights. Amnesty International, founded in 1961, concentrates on gaining the freedom of people who have been tortured or imprisoned without trial and campaigns against summary executions by government death squads or other gross violations of rights. Arguing that no right is more fundamental than the right to life, other NGOs have devoted themselves to famine relief, refugee assistance, and health care around the world. Médecins Sans Frontières (Doctors Without Borders), founded in 1971, was awarded the Nobel Peace Prize in 1999 for offering medical assistance in scores of crises.

While NGOs often worked in specific countries, other universal goals became enshrined in international agreements that made genocide a crime and promoted environmental protection of the seas, of Antarctica, and of the atmosphere (see Environment & Technology: Global

---

[1]www.un.org/en/universal-declaration-human-rights/

Until the 1980s environmental alarms focused mainly on localized episodes of air and water pollution, exposure to toxic substances, waste management, and the disappearance of wilderness. The development of increasingly powerful computers and complex models of ecological interactions in the 1990s, however, raised awareness of the global scope of certain environmental problems.

Many scientists and policymakers came to perceive global warming, a slow increase in the temperature of the earth's lower atmosphere, as an environmental threat requiring preventive action on an international scale. The warming is caused by a layer of atmospheric gases (carbon dioxide, methane, nitrous oxide, and ozone) that allow solar radiation to reach earth and warm it but that keep infrared energy (heat) from radiating from earth's surface back into space. Called the *greenhouse effect*, this process normally keeps the earth's temperature at a level suitable for life. However, increases in greenhouse-gas emissions—particularly from the burning of fossil fuels in industry and transportation—have added to this insulating atmospheric layer.

Recent events have confirmed predictions of global temperature increases and melting glaciers and icecaps. Greenland glaciers and Arctic Ocean sea ice are melting at record rates, and huge sections of the Antarctic ice shelf are breaking off and floating away. Andean glaciers are shrinking so fast they could disappear in a decade, imperiling water supplies for drinking, irrigation, and hydroelectric production. Drought has affected much of the United States in recent years, and Australia has experienced the "Big Dry," its worst drought in a century.

Despite this evidence, the industrialized countries that produce the most greenhouse gasses have been slow to adopt measures stringent enough to reduce emissions. They cite the negative effects they believe this could have on their economies. Because of these fears, many nations hesitated to sign the 1997 Kyoto Protocol, the first international agreement to impose penalties on countries that failed to cut greenhouse-gas emissions.

Shortly after succeeding George W. Bush as president in 2009, Barack Obama announced to an audience of scientists and citizens concerned with climate matters: "You can be sure that the United States will once again engage vigorously in these negotiations, and help lead the world toward a new era of global cooperation on climate change." Yet when he ran for reelection in 2012, the issue of global warming, which his Republican opponents denied was a real phenomenon, played no role in his campaign. Ironically, a tropical super-storm named Sandy that dealt a devastating blow to New York and New Jersey just before the election seemed to vindicate the prediction that the increased energy in the atmosphere caused by global warming would produce severe weather anomalies around the world.

In 2015 Obama achieved his goal at a Paris conference where all of the world's industrialized nations reached agreement on a United Nations Framework Convention on Climate Change (UNFCCC). Article 2 of the convention sets forth its goals:

(a) Holding the increase in the global average temperature to well below 2 °C above pre-industrial levels and to pursue efforts to limit the temperature increase to 1.5 °C above pre-industrial levels, recognizing that this would significantly reduce the risks and impacts of climate change;

(b) Increasing the ability to adapt to the adverse impacts of climate change and foster climate resilience and low greenhouse gas emissions development, in a manner that does not threaten food production;

(c) Making finance flows consistent with a pathway towards low greenhouse gas emissions and climate-resilient development.

Republican skepticism about global warming prompted President Trump in 2017 to officially withdraw the United States from the convention. Many American states and cities continue to support it, however.

Questions for Analysis

1. Should it be the concern of people today to attack problems that are not expected to become severe for several decades?

2. Do industrialized and nonindustrialized economies share responsibility for climate change?

3. As an environmental problem, is global warming more of a concern than overpopulation, extinction of wild species, or preservation of fresh water supplies?

◀ **Flooding in Bangladesh**　Typhoon-driven floods submerge the low-lying farmlands of Bangladesh with tragic regularity. Any significant rise in the sea level will make parts of the country nearly uninhabitable.　David Greedy/Getty Images

Section Review

- The last third of the twentieth century saw an increase in political action inspired by religious belief.

- Militant Islam has risen in response to authoritarian oppression in many Muslim countries and to the theory that the United States supports such authoritarianism.

- Universal standards of human rights have gained wider acceptance and underlie the work of the United Nations, individual states, and NGOs.

- Concepts of human rights have expanded to address genocide and environmental protection.

- Global debates on women's rights have addressed a variety of economic, political, and social problems but have also involved clashes over cultural values.

Warming). The United States and a few other nations were greatly concerned that such treaties would limit their sovereignty or threaten their national interests. For this reason, the U.S. Congress delayed ratifying the 1949 convention on genocide until 1986. More recently the United States drew widespread criticism for demanding exemption for Americans from the jurisdiction of the International Criminal Court, created in 2002 to try international criminals, and for declaring that "enemy combatants" taken prisoner during the "global war on terrorism" need not be treated in accordance with the Third Geneva Convention (1950) on humane treatment of prisoners of war.

33-1j Women's Rights

The women's rights movement, which began on both sides of the North Atlantic in the nineteenth century, became an important human rights issue in the twentieth century. Rights for women became accepted in Western countries and were enshrined in the constitutions of many nations newly freed from colonial rule. In 1979 the United Nations General Assembly adopted the Convention on the Elimination of All Forms of Discrimination Against Women, and in 1985 the first international conference on the status of women, sponsored by the United Nations Division for the Advancement of Women, was held in Nairobi, Kenya. A second conference in Beijing ten years later added momentum to the movement. By 2012, all but seven UN member countries—Iran, Palau, Somalia, Sudan, South Sudan, Tonga, and the United States—had failed to ratify the convention, though the United States and Palau had signed it without ratification.

Besides highlighting the problems women face around the world, international conferences have also revealed great variety in the views and concerns of women. Feminists from the West, who had been accustomed to dictating the agenda and who had pushed for the liberation of women in other parts of the world, sometimes found themselves accused of having narrow concerns and condescending attitudes. Some non-Western women warned against Western feminists' endorsement of sexual liberation and the deterioration of family life in the West. They found Western feminists' concern with matters such as comfortable clothing misplaced and trivial compared to the issues of poverty and disease.

▶ **Abandoned Housing Development** The bursting of the housing finance bubble brought hundreds of planned development projects to a sudden halt. This picture in Arizona shows sold homes with landscaping, unsold homes without landscaping, and vacant lots. Kristoffer Tripplaar/Alamy Stock Photo

Other cultures came in for their share of criticism. Western women and many secular leaders in Muslim countries protested Islam's requirement that a woman cover her head and wear loose-fitting garments to conceal the shape of her body, practices enforced by law in countries such as Iran and Saudi Arabia. Nevertheless, many outspoken Muslim women voluntarily donned concealing garments as expressions of personal belief, resistance to secular dictatorship, or defense against coarse male behavior.

AP® Exam Tip
Explain gender dynamics in the late twentieth and early twenty-first centuries.

33-2 Globalization and Economic Crisis

What are the main benefits and dangers of growing political, economic, and cultural integration?

The turn of the millennium saw the intensification of **globalization** trends that had been building since the 1970s. These came together in a loose economic pattern known as *neoliberalism* (see Chapter 32). Accelerating trade and travel and new information technologies brought all parts of the world into closer economic, political, and cultural integration and interaction (see Maps 33.2 and 33.3). The collapse of the Soviet Union (see Chapter 31) completed the

globalization The economic, political, and cultural integration and interaction of all parts of the world brought about by increasing trade, travel, and technology.

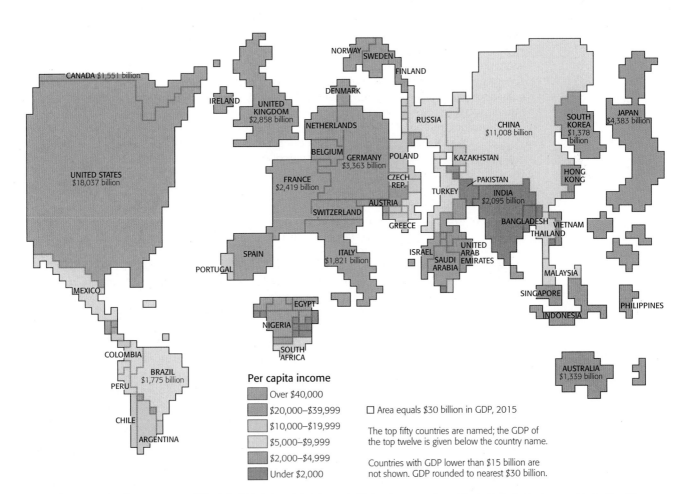

Per capita income
- Over $40,000
- $20,000–$39,999
- $10,000–$19,999
- $5,000–$9,999
- $2,000–$4,999
- Under $2,000

☐ Area equals $30 billion in GDP, 2015

The top fifty countries are named; the GDP of the top twelve is given below the country name.

Countries with GDP lower than $15 billion are not shown. GDP rounded to nearest $30 billion.

MAP 33.2 Global Distribution of Wealth Early industrialization and efficient investment contributed to individual prosperity for the citizens of Japan and Western countries by the 1990s. However, economic dynamism in late-industrializing countries like China and India began to change the world balance of economic power in the early twenty-first century. In nearly all countries the distribution of wealth among individuals varies tremendously, with the gap between rich and poor generally increasing.

Is per capita a good measure of wealth in countries where there is a deep chasm between the wealth of the elite and the incomes of ordinary people?

dissolution of territorial empires that had been under way throughout the twentieth century. As colonies disappeared, autonomous national states (numbering about two hundred) became the norm, and a growing number of them embraced democratic institutions and reduced government controls on private businesses. Selling off government-owned enterprises to private ownership enriched a new class of extremely wealthy transnational investors and managers. The sunny future that seemed in store for democracy and free enterprise exploded in 2008, however, when a massive accumulation of debt in American financial institutions became unsustainable and plunged the world into financial crisis.

33-2a **Global Financial Crisis**

The global financial crisis had complicated roots. During an Asian financial crisis a decade earlier, vast amounts of European and American investment in Thailand, Indonesia, South Korea, and other East Asian countries had created an illusion of great economic dynamism. In 1997, however, the investment boom collapsed, leading to a severe economic downturn. Cautious investors responded by moving their money elsewhere. The United States became a favorite place to invest, helping spur a rapid increase in stock and housing prices and massive growth in the purchase of imported goods. Seeing the value of their houses increasing every year, Americans became wedded to borrowing money with their homes as collateral.

The terrorist attacks of 9/11 shocked the world's financial system. The expansion of trade, global interconnections, and privatization of government enterprises that had gained momentum with the dismantling of socialist economies in the 1990s cooled abruptly in the wake of 9/11. The rate of growth in world trade fell from 13 percent in 2000 to only 1 percent in 2001.

However, money from overseas invested in U.S. markets made it possible for the United States to fight wars in Afghanistan and Iraq while also lowering taxes. The Bush administration deemed it important to encourage business as usual after 9/11 so that al-Qaeda would not think it had seriously injured the United States. The American national debt soared, but the American financial system bounced back from the attacks and people continued to borrow money as if there was no limit on how much their homes were worth.

In 2008 the fevered boom in housing prices collapsed, leaving many homeowners so deeply in debt on their mortgages that they lost their homes. Their mortgages, however, were no longer being held by local banks in the traditional fashion. New and risky lending techniques based on homeowners' assumptions that home prices would continue to rise had caused the bad debts to be distributed throughout the banking system, not just in the United States but around the world. Similar housing speculation occurred in Spain and other countries.

When Lehman Brothers, one of America's foremost financial firms, declared bankruptcy in September, recession turned into catastrophic economic downturn. Stock prices fell, banks teetered on the brink of collapse, and unemployment climbed as employers laid off workers they could no longer afford or did not need to meet falling consumer demand. The effects spread worldwide. Knowledgeable political leaders and economists proclaimed it the worst economic crisis since the Great Depression of the 1930s.

Growth in China and India had resumed quickly after 9/11, and the large populations of these two countries marked them as future economic powers. Their growth increased pressure on world energy supplies. Though the United States continued to consume a quarter of the world's petroleum production, by 2012 it had resumed its position of world's largest producer through the practice of fracking to extract oil from shale deposits.

OPEC's manipulation of world oil prices, combined with political instability in the Middle East, had caused crude oil prices to soar between 1973 and 1985. But aside from those years, the average price of oil remained consistently below $20 per barrel (adjusted for inflation) throughout the second half of the twentieth century. In the year 2000, however, oil prices began a new period of increase caused not by OPEC but by rising demand and confidence in the fevered pace of world economic expansion. By the middle of 2006, the price of a barrel of crude had crept past $70, and in 2008 it spiked to $145 a barrel. This increase fueled ambitious economic programs in producing countries like Russia, Venezuela, Iran, Saudi Arabia, and the sheikhdoms of the Persian Gulf, as well as in the newer OPEC members Ecuador, Nigeria, and Angola. With the financial crisis of 2008, prices fell abruptly, but by 2012 the price per barrel was back in the $90–100 range.

By 2014–2015 a world supply had overtaken world demand. In addition, Saudi Arabia decided to impose financial pain on Iran, a Shi'ite state that it considered a threat to Sunni Islam and Saudi leadership, by increasing production and thereby causing oil prices to drop as precipitously and unexpectedly as they had in 2008. Countries like Venezuela that depended overwhelmingly on oil revenues suffered badly, and Saudi Arabia itself began to face budget deficits.

Unlike the situation in 2008, the prospect of a quick return to high prices seemed dim. The slowing of rapid-growth economies like China's, combined with continuing sluggishness in the United States and European Union (EU), tarnished the vision of neoliberal global transformation and contributed to the reappearance of populist and nationalistic political movements reminiscent of the fascist movements of the Great Depression era.

33-2b Regional Trade Organizations

Regional trade organizations had come into being to promote growth, reduce the economic vulnerability of member states, and, less explicitly, balance American economic dominance. The twenty-seven-member European Union was the most successful (see Map 33.3). The euro, a common currency inaugurated in 2002 and used in twelve member states, competed with the U.S. dollar for investment and banking. However, unequal levels of development among members became a source of crisis in 2009 when the world economic downturn devastated stock markets and increased rates of unemployment. Countries like Greece that had taken on more debt than the revenues produced by their shrinking economies could cover sought assistance from the rest of the EU, but the wealthier countries, led by Germany, proved reluctant to rescue them. Instead, they urged an austerity program of radical cutbacks in public expenditures. These measures increased unemployment, popular discontent, and resentment of immigrants who competed for jobs with native-born citizens. The idea of the euro, a common currency that symbolized Europe's progress toward unity, came into question since countries belonging to the euro zone were not at liberty to devalue their currency and thereby reduce their debt burdens. In 2016 a popular referendum in Britain, which had not adopted the euro, unexpectedly committed the government to withdrawing from the EU. While the terms of this *Brexit* (British exit) remained to be negotiated, concern arose as to whether other EU countries might follow Britain's lead.

Despite the EU's expansion, the North American Free Trade Agreement (NAFTA), which eliminated tariffs among the United States, Canada, and Mexico in 1994, governed the world's largest free-trade zone. Yet heated debate in the United States over illegal immigration across the Mexican border, as well as anti-Hispanic prejudice, limited popular enthusiasm for the agreement. Populist opposition to NAFTA and to immigration from Latin America became a major part of Donald J. Trump's come-from-behind presidential victory in 2016. One of his first acts as president was to authorize building a wall between the United States and Mexico.

The third largest free-trade zone, Mercosur, created by Argentina, Brazil, Paraguay (now suspended), and Uruguay in 1991 and subsequently expanded to include five associate members, visualized a parliament consisting of eighteen representatives from each member state. Other free-trade associations operated in West Africa, southern Africa, Southeast Asia, Central America, the Pacific Basin, and the Caribbean.

The Shanghai Cooperation Organization (SCO) formed in 2001 with China, Russia, and four former Soviet Central Asian republics as members. It originally pursued common security interests, such as combating separatist movements and terrorism, but the accession of India and Pakistan in 2016 and the observer status of Iran, a major oil exporter, and Afghanistan and Mongolia, countries with untapped mineral sources, lent plausibility to the SCO's twenty-year plan for reducing barriers to trade and population movement. Iran, which formally applied for full membership, posed a special problem insofar as both Russia and China were involved in an American-led international campaign to curb its nuclear program. An agreement in 2016 to lift many economic sanctions in return for a 15-year cap on Iranian nuclear expansion eased that problem.

33-2c World Trade Organization

In 1995 the world's major traders established the **World Trade Organization (WTO)**, dedicated to reducing barriers and enforcing international agreements. With the accession of Russia as its 157th member in 2012, the largest economy not to be included was Iran. The WTO had many critics and regularly encountered street protests during its ministerial meetings. Some protesters rallied against neoliberalism and claimed that the organization's idea of free trade enabled low-cost foreign manufacturers to attract business and shrink job opportunities in richer states; others demanded continuing tariff protection for local farmers.

AP® Exam Tip
Identify and explain the impact of several regional trade agreements.

AP® Exam Tip
Discuss the role of global organizations and multinational corporations in the economic system of the modern world.

World Trade Organization (WTO) An international body established in 1995 to foster and bring order to international trade.

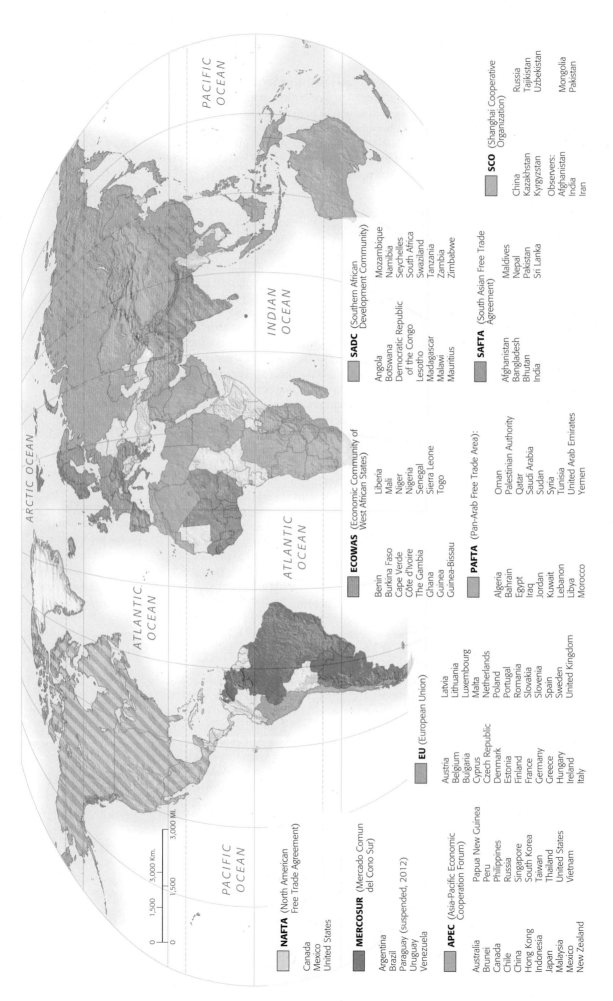

NAFTA (North American Free Trade Agreement)

Canada
Mexico
United States

MERCOSUR (Mercado Comun del Cono Sur)

Argentina
Brazil
Paraguay (suspended, 2012)
Uruguay
Venezuela

APEC (Asia-Pacific Economic Cooperation Forum)

Australia
Brunei
Canada
Chile
China
Hong Kong
Indonesia
Japan
Malaysia
Mexico
New Zealand
Papua New Guinea
Peru
Philippines
Russia
Singapore
South Korea
Taiwan
Thailand
United States
Vietnam

EU (European Union)

Austria
Belgium
Bulgaria
Cyprus
Czech Republic
Denmark
Estonia
Finland
France
Germany
Greece
Hungary
Ireland
Italy
Latvia
Lithuania
Luxembourg
Malta
Netherlands
Poland
Portugal
Romania
Slovakia
Slovenia
Spain
Sweden
United Kingdom

ECOWAS (Economic Community of West African States)

Benin
Burkina Faso
Cape Verde
Côte d'Ivoire
The Gambia
Ghana
Guinea
Guinea-Bissau
Liberia
Mali
Niger
Nigeria
Senegal
Sierra Leone
Togo

SADC (Southern African Development Community)

Angola
Botswana
Democratic Republic of the Congo
Lesotho
Madagascar
Malawi
Mauritius
Mozambique
Namibia
Seychelles
South Africa
Swaziland
Tanzania
Zambia
Zimbabwe

PAFTA (Pan-Arab Free Trade Area):

Algeria
Bahrain
Egypt
Iraq
Jordan
Kuwait
Lebanon
Libya
Morocco
Oman
Palestinian Authority
Qatar
Saudi Arabia
Sudan
Syria
Tunisia
United Arab Emirates
Yemen

SAFTA (South Asian Free Trade Agreement)

Afghanistan
Bangladesh
Bhutan
India
Maldives
Nepal
Pakistan
Sri Lanka

SCO (Shanghai Cooperative Organization)

China
Kazakhstan
Kyrgyzstan
Russia
Tajikistan
Uzbekistan

Observers:
Afghanistan
India
Iran
Mongolia
Pakistan

PACIFIC OCEAN
ARCTIC OCEAN
ATLANTIC OCEAN
ATLANTIC OCEAN
PACIFIC OCEAN
INDIAN OCEAN

0   1,500   3,000 Km.
0   1,500   3,000 Mi.

MAP 33.3   Regional Trade Associations, 2004 International trade and development are major concerns of governments in developed and developing countries. NAFTA, Mercosur, and the EU are free-trade areas. The other associations promote trade and development.

Do regional trade agreements signal increasing globalization or simply formalize linguistic and cultural connections with roots in earlier centuries?

33-2d From Obama to Trump

The sense that Barack Obama had a firm understanding of the financial crisis and the ability to lead the country out of it contributed to his election as president. During the first weeks after he took office in January 2009, he proposed a series of steps, including massive increases in government spending, to improve the economy. Some of the plans bore fruit, such as a rescue of the American automobile industry. Others were stymied after 2010 when Republicans who were concerned about national debt and government budget deficits took over the House of Representatives. The legislative deadlock that ensued curbed administration plans to address unemployment through increased government spending, but Republican sponsorship of tax and governmental budget cuts failed to attract enough voters to prevent Barack Obama from being re-elected in 2012. Economic recovery was slow but steady, though in both the United States and the European Union the trade expansion that globalization had promised at the beginning of the century faded from memory, and the interdependence that had bound the world's economies in a cycle of growth became a dead weight that dragged many countries down.

A growing gap between the very rich and common working folk alarmed both politicians and economists, but only Donald J. Trump, a businessman and television presence, grasped the feeling of abandonment and irrelevance besetting a significant number of Americans. His election to the presidency after a campaign focused on his personality and determination to "Make America Great Again" astonished more than half of Americans that voted for the democratic nominee, Hillary Clinton, and confounded polling organizations that had predicted a democratic victory.

Once inaugurated in 2017 Trump persisted in his vow to make swift changes, and with the Senate and the House of Representatives in Republican hands he had the power to carry his program through. The world then waited to see what he would accomplish in office.

33-2e Globalization and Democracy

The last decades of the twentieth century saw expansions of democratic institutions and personal freedom. People in many countries recognized that elections offered a peaceful way to settle differences among a country's social classes, cultural groups, and regions. Although majority votes could swing from one part of the political spectrum to another, democracies tended to encourage political moderation. Moreover, wars between fully democratic states were extremely rare.

33-2f **Eastern Europe**

The nations of eastern Europe embraced democracy after the fall of the Soviet Union, though some newly democratic states became subject to great mood swings among the electorate. The shift to private ownership of businesses after decades of rigid state control brought riches to a select few, and the removal of trade barriers characteristic of Cold War rivalry opened up new markets and fostered investment from the West.

After 2008, however, rising unemployment and falling exports and stock prices threatened these experiments in free elections and free markets. In Russia, the popular but somewhat authoritarian leader Vladimir Putin followed his country's constitution by stepping down in 2008 after two terms as president. However, he engineered the election of his protégé Dimitri Medvedev as his successor and assumed the office of prime minister himself. This move led some political thinkers to fear a possible return to Soviet-era Russian domination, as did Russia's sudden seizure of the Crimea, a part of Ukraine, in 2014. The mutual admiration between Putin and Trump that became apparent in 2016 made American–Russian relations hard to predict.

33-2g **Democracy in Asia**

Asian democracies proved somewhat more stable. Beginning with free parliamentary elections in 1999, the populous state of Indonesia moved from years of authoritarian and corrupt rule toward more open political institutions. The following years saw a violent independence movement of the Acheh (**ah-CHEH**) district of northern Sumatra, the secession in 2002 of East Timor after years of brutal Indonesian military occupation, terrorist bombings on the island of Bali in 2004, and a devastating earthquake and tsunami in the same year. But democratic elections were regularly held. The losing candidates left office peacefully, and the populace at large accepted the results.

AP® Exam Tip
Understand the spread of democratic institutions following World War II.

Myanmar (formerly Burma), where stifling military governments had held sway since 1962, experienced a rapid move toward democracy after free elections were held in 2010. The following year the military junta was dissolved, and the formerly banned opposition party led by female Nobel Peace Prize winner Aung San Suu Kyi (**owng-SAHN-soo-chi**) gained a significant role in parliament.

In India a major political shift seemed to be at hand in 1998 when the Bharatiya Janata Party (BJP) secured an electoral victory after four decades of Congress Party rule. The success of the BJP came through blatant appeals to Hindu nationalism, the condoning of violence against India's Muslims, and opposition to the social and economic progress of the *Untouchables* (those traditionally confined to the dirtiest jobs). In 2004 the Congress Party returned to power and governmental stability proved strong even in the face of sensational terrorist attacks in Mumbai by Pakistani gunmen in 2008. When the BJP returned to power in 2014, the new Prime Minister, Narendra Modi, committed himself to economic expansion rather than resuming his party's Hindu extremism.

32-2h **Instability in Pakistan and Turkey**

Democracy in Pakistan proved uncertain. President and former military commander Pervez Musharraf's (**pair-VEZ moo-SHAH-ref**) abrupt firing of the country's chief justice, combined with his unpopular support of the Bush administration's war policies, sparked protests and calls for impeachment. He resigned the presidency in 2008. Asif Ali Zardari (**AH-sef AH-lee zar-DAH-ree**), who succeeded him, had inherited the leadership of the majority Pakistan People's Party after the assassination the year before of his charismatic wife Benazir Bhutto, the daughter of a popular earlier prime minister. Zardari faced difficulties forming a strong government because of the growing movement of the Pakistani Taliban to impose their own governance and a rigid Muslim behavioral code in outlying districts, as well as popular opposition to American antiterrorist attacks launched from Afghanistan.

In Turkey, an abortive military coup in 2016 bolstered the popularity of the president, Recep Tayyip Erdogan (**REH-jep TIE-yip ER-do-wan**). Claiming that a Muslim religious movement that he had been close to for most of his political career had engineered the coup, Erdogan imprisoned some 40,000 suspected plotters; fired 100,000 movement members from police force,

▶ Pakistan's Malala Yousafzai Receiving Nobel Peace Prize
At age 17, Malala is the youngest recipient of the prize, which she shared
with India's Kailash Satyarthi. Both campaigned for the rights of children,
particularly for education. When Malala's advocacy of women's education
encountered resistance, religious conservatives attempted to murder her.
That she survived to continue her advocacy and has achieved international
recognition is testimony to the power of her ideas. Nigel Waldron/Getty Images
Entertainment/Getty Images

government, and educational positions; arrested parliament
members representing a Kurdish party; and pushed through
a constitutional change to increase his presidential powers.
These authoritarian actions alarmed many of Turkey's allies
but brought Erdogan closer to Putin in neighboring Russia.

33-2i African Regimes

In sub-Saharan Africa, democracy had mixed results. Nelson
Mandela, the leader of the African National Congress (ANC)
who had become the first postapartheid president of South
Africa in 1994 (see Chapter 31), left office in 1999 and was
succeeded by the deputy president and ANC leader Thabo
Mbeki (**TAA-boh um-BEH-kee**). Mbeki stepped down in 2008
amidst turmoil in the leadership of the ANC. But the democratic system did not seem threatened, even when his successor
Jacob Zuma was charged with corruption.

Elsewhere some elected leaders, such as Robert Mugabe
(**moo-GAH-bay**) in Zimbabwe, used violence and intimidation to hold on to power, and other states, such as Congo, were
plagued with internal revolts and civil wars. Liberians emerged
from fourteen years of civil war in 2003 and two years later
chose Nobel Peace Prize winner Ellen Johnson-Sirleaf (**SUHR-
leef**) to be Africa's first elected female head of state.

In Sudan, the general who had led a military coup in
1989, Omar al-Bashir, became the first sitting head of state
to be charged with genocide and crimes against humanity by
the International Criminal Court in 2009. A festering conflict in Darfur in western Sudan, which had cost hundreds
of thousands of lives and displaced over 2 million people,
was at the heart of the charges. However, a long rebellion in
the south finally came to an end in 2011 with the creation of
a new country with a democratic constitution, the Republic
of South Sudan. Unfortunately, civil unrest resumed in the
new state almost as soon as it came into being.

33-3 Global Culture

How has technology contributed to the process
of global interaction?

Because of changes in electronic technology, today political
and economic events have almost instantaneous impact in
all parts of the world. A global language, a global educational
system, and global forms of artistic expression have all come
into being. Trade, travel, and migration have made a common popular culture unavoidable.

Section Review

- Since the Cold War, global political relations have been
defined largely by economic interconnections.
- To manage economic change, many nations have
joined a variety of trade organizations, and free-trade
policies have caused widespread controversy.
- Global interdependence and rapid economic expansion
and speculation led to a global financial crisis in 2008
that plunged the world into the worst economic slowdown since the Great Depression of the 1930s.
- There has been a general worldwide trend toward
democracy, especially in Asian countries.
- U.S. intervention in Iraq and Afghanistan has shown
that the promotion of democracy by military force
is very difficult, and in the Middle East the Israeli–
Palestinian deadlock and the challenge of Iran stand in
the way of fundamental political change.

AP® Exam Tip
Identify and explain
several examples of
globalized popular and
consumer culture.

33-3a The Media and the Message

The fact that the most pervasive elements of global culture have their origins in the West raised concerns in many quarters about **cultural imperialism**. Critics complained that entertainment conglomerates were flooding the world's movie theaters and television screens with Western images and that goods catering to Western tastes but manufactured in countries with low labor costs, like Bangladesh and Indonesia, were flooding world markets. In this view, global marketing seemed especially insidious in trying to shape a world with a single Western outlook based on capitalist ideology, and at the same time suppressing or devaluing traditional cultures and alternative ideologies. As the leader of the capitalist world, the United States was seen as the primary culprit.

The pace of cultural globalization began to quicken during the economic recovery after World War II. The Hollywood films and American jazz recordings that had become popular in Europe and parts of Asia (see Chapter 30) continued to spread. But the birth of electronic technology opened contacts with large numbers of people who did not have access to movie theaters or phonographs.

The first step was the development of cheap transistor radios that could run on a couple of small batteries. Perfected by American scientists at Bell Telephone Laboratories in 1948, solid-state electronic transistors replaced power-hungry and less reliable electron tubes in radios and other devices. Tube radios, which in some countries required a license to own, had spread worldwide in the decades before the war, but small transistor radios reached parts of the world where homes lacked electricity.

Television, made possible by the electron-scanning gun invented in 1928, became widely available to Western consumers in the 1950s. In poorer parts of the world, TVs were not common until the 1980s and 1990s, after mass production and cheap transistors made sets more affordable. Outside the United States, television broadcasting was usually a government monopoly at first, following the pattern of telegraph and postal service and radio broadcasting. Governments expected news reports and other programming to disseminate a unified national viewpoint.

However, government monopolies eroded as the high cost of television production and the invention of video recording opened up global markets for rebroadcasts of American soap operas, adventure series, and situation comedies. By the 1990s a global network of satellites brought privately owned television broadcasting to even remote areas of the world, and the VCR (videocassette recorder) provided an even greater variety of programs. In the following decade DVD players continued the trend. As a result of wider circulation of programming, people often became familiar with different dialects of English and other languages. People in Portugal who in the 1960s had found it difficult to understand Brazilian Portuguese became avid fans of Brazilian soap operas. And immigrants from Albania and North Africa often arrived in Italy with a command of Italian learned from Italian stations whose signals they could pick up at home.

33-3b Global Communication

CNN (Cable News Network) expanded its international market after becoming the most-viewed and informative news source during the 1991 Persian Gulf War, when it broadcast the coalition aerial assault on Baghdad live. Other 24-hour news broadcasters followed this lead. Some offered fundamentally American viewpoints. Others were independent. Al-Jazeera, based in the Persian Gulf emirate of Qatar, broadcast statements by Osama bin Laden from 2001 onward and offered video footage and interpretation that differed greatly from American coverage of the war in Iraq. Yet during the Arab Spring it gained a reputation for vivid and generally reliable coverage of news events in the Muslim world.

The Internet, a linkage of academic, government, and business computers developed by the U.S. Department of Defense in the 1960s, began to transform world culture in the early years of the twenty-first century. Personal computers proliferated in the 1980s, and with the introduction of the easy-to-use graphic interface of the World Wide Web in 1994, the number of Internet users skyrocketed. Myriad new companies formed to exploit "e-commerce," the commercial dimension of the Internet, and students were soon spending less time studying conventional books and more exploring the Web for information and entertainment. Blogs, or weblogs, offered a vehicle for anyone in the world to place his or her opinions, experiences, and creative efforts before anyone with access to a computer. Easy access to the Internet took a step forward with

cultural imperialism
Domination of one culture over another by a deliberate policy or by economic or technological superiority.

the establishment of "social media" sites like Facebook (2004) and Twitter (2006). Social media played a key role in mustering the massive popular demonstrations of the Arab Spring, and Donald J. Trump used Twitter as his preferred channel of mass communication during the presidential campaign of 2016.

As had happened so often throughout history, technological developments had unanticipated consequences. Although the new telecommunications and entertainment technologies derived disproportionately from American invention, industry, and cultural creativity, Japan and other East Asian nations took the lead in manufacturing and refining consumer electronic devices. Cellular mobile phones became increasingly used for taking and transmitting pictures and connecting to the Internet. Non-Western countries that had adopted telephones late and had limited networks of copper wire benefited most from the improved communication. In 2012 the United States ranked 114th in per capita cellular phone use, sandwiched between the Congo Republic and the Dominican Republic. Qatar topped the list as the country with the highest per capita use.

33-3c The Spread of Popular Culture

For most of history, popular culture consisted of folktales and localized styles of dress, cooking, music, and visual expression (see Issues in World History: Popular Culture—Words of Warning). Only the literate few had full access to the riches of a broader "great tradition," such as Confucianism, Islam, or Buddhism. In modern times, government school systems increased literacy rates but also promoted specifically national values and cultural tastes. Prescribed languages of instruction eroded the use and memory of local languages and traditions. In their place there arose **global popular culture**.

Initially, the content was heavily American. Singer Michael Jackson was almost as well known to the youth of Dar-es-Salaam (Tanzania) and Bangkok (Thailand) as to American fans. Businesses sought out worldwide celebrities like basketball star Michael Jordan and championship golfer Tiger Woods to endorse their products. American television programs, following in the footsteps of American movies, acquired immense followings and inspired local imitations.

But the United States had no monopoly on global popular culture. Latin American soap operas, *telenovelas*, had a vast following in the Americas, eastern Europe, and elsewhere. Mumbai, India, long the world's largest producer of films, made or inspired more films for international audiences, like the 2009 Academy Award–winning *Slumdog Millionaire*. And the martial arts

global popular culture
Popular cultural practices and institutions that have been adopted internationally, such as music, the Internet, television, food, and fashion.

◀ **Japanese Comic Books** After World War II comic magazines emerged as a major form of publication and a distinctive product of culture in Japan. Different series are directed to different age and gender groups. Issued weekly and running to some three hundred pages in black and white, the most popular magazines sell as many copies as do major newsmagazines in the United States. Eye Ubiquitous/Photoshot

filmmakers of Hong Kong saw their style flourish in high-budget international spectaculars like director Ang Lee's *Crouching Tiger, Hidden Dragon* (2000) and the *Matrix* trilogy (1999–2003), which relied heavily on Hong Kong fight choreographers.

33-3d Emerging Global Elite Culture

While the globalization of popular culture has been criticized, cultural links across national and ethnic boundaries at a more elite level have generated little controversy. The end of the Cold War reopened intellectual and cultural contacts between former adversaries, making possible such things as Russian–American collaboration on space missions and extensive business contacts among former rivals. The English language, modern science, and higher education became the key elements of this **global elite culture**.

The emergence of English as the first global language began with the British Empire's introduction of the language to far-flung colonies. After achieving independence in the wake of World War II, most former colonies chose to continue using English as an official language because it provided national unity and a link to the outside world that local languages could not. Countries that chose instead to make a local language official often found the decision counterproductive. Indian nationalists had pushed for Hindi to be India's official language, but they found that students taught in Hindi were unable to compete internationally because of poor knowledge of English. Sri Lanka, which had made Sinhala its official language in 1956, reversed itself after local reporters revealed in 1989 that prominent officials were sending their children to private schools that taught in English.

While similar postcolonial language developments extended the reach of French and Spanish, the use of English as a second language was greatly stimulated by the importance of the United States in world affairs. After the collapse of Soviet domination, students in eastern Europe flocked to study English instead of Russian. Ninety percent of students in Cambodia (a former French colony) chose to study English, even though a Canadian agency offered a sizable cash bonus if they would study French. In the 1990s China made the study of English as a second language nearly universal from junior high school onward.

English has become the language of choice for most international academic conferences, business meetings, and diplomatic gatherings. International organizations that provide equal status to many languages, such as the United Nations and the European Union, often conduct informal committee meetings in English. In cities throughout the world, including in officially anti-American Iran, signs are commonly posted in the local language and in English. Writers from Africa and India have received high honors for novels written in English, as have Arab and Caribbean authors for works written in French. Nevertheless, world literature remains highly diverse in form and language.

33-3e Global Science and University Education

AP® Exam Tip
Understand the importance of the expansion of education in this time period.

By contrast, science and technology have become standardized components of global culture. Though imperialism helped spread the Western disciplines of biology, chemistry, and physics around the world, their importance expanded even further after decolonization as students from newly independent nations sought to compete at an international level. Standardization of scientific terms, weights and measures, computer codes, industrial practices, and even wordless instruction icons underlay the worldwide expansion of commerce.

The third pillar of global elite culture, along with science and globalized languages, is the university. The structure and curricula of modern universities are nearly indistinguishable around the world, making student experiences similar across national boundaries. Instruction in the pure sciences varies little from place to place. Some doctoral science programs in American universities now enroll mostly students from non-Western countries. Standardization is nearly as common in applied sciences such as engineering and medicine and only slightly less so in the social sciences. Although the humanities preserve greater diversity in subject matter and approach, professors and students around the world pay attention to the latest literary theories and topics of historical interest and look to a future of computerized analysis of massive online databases.

New universities, many of them privately funded, have mushroomed in many parts of the world as young people increasingly strive for learning that will improve their employment

global elite culture At the beginning of the twenty-first century, the attitudes and outlook of well-educated, prosperous, Western-oriented people around the world, largely expressed in European languages, especially English.

▲ **Three Gorges Dam on China's Yangzi River** The world's largest hydroelectric facility, completed in 2012, the dam is also designed to improve river shipping and reduce the danger of flooding. However, 1.3 million people were displaced in its construction and many archaeological sites inundated. China/Alamy Stock Photo

opportunities. Some American universities have contributed to this educational expansion by opening branches or research centers in foreign countries.

While university subjects are taught in many languages, instruction in English is spreading rapidly. Because discoveries are often first published in English, advanced students in science, business, and international relations need to know that language to keep up with the latest developments. Many courses in northern European countries have long been offered in English, and elsewhere in Europe courses taught in English have facilitated the EU's efforts to encourage students to study outside their home countries.

33-3f Enduring Cultural Diversity

Although protesters regularly denounce the "Americanization" of the world, a closer look suggests that cultural globalization is more complex. Just as English has spread widely as a second language, so global culture is primarily a second culture that dominates some contexts but does not displace other traditions. From this perspective, American music, fast food, and fashions are more likely to add to a society's options than to displace local culture.

Japan was first to demonstrate that a country with a non-Western culture could industrialize effectively. Individuality was less valued in Japan than the ability of each person to fit into a group, whether as an employee, a member of an athletic team, or a student in a class. Moreover, the Japanese considered it unmannerly to directly contradict, correct, or refuse the request of another person. From a Western point of view, these Japanese customs seemed to discourage individual

AP® Exam Tip
Compare reactions to Westernization in the previous time period to reactions in this time period.

Section Review

- The global pervasiveness of Western culture has provoked charges of U.S. cultural imperialism.

- Technology such as radio, television, and the Internet has played a major role in the spread of Western culture since World War II.

- Technology has also contributed to the emergence of a global popular culture that blends a variety of cultural elements from different countries.

- A global elite culture has also developed combining the English language, science, and higher education.

- Despite globalizing forces, cultural diversity remains strong, if not completely secure.

initiative and personality development and to preserve traditional hierarchies. Japanese women, for example, even though they often worked outside the home, responded only slowly to the American and European feminist advocacy of equality in economic and social relations. However, the Japanese approach to social relations was well suited to an industrial economy. The efficiency, pride in workmanship, and group solidarity of Japanese workers played a major role in transforming Japan from a defeated nation with a demolished industrial base in 1945 to an economic power by the 1980s, but proved less well adapted to the severe economic slowdown that began in the 1990s.

As awareness of the economic impact of Japanese culture and society began to spread, it became apparent that Taiwan and South Korea, along with Singapore and Hong Kong (a British colony before being reunited with China in 1997), were developing dynamic industrial economies of their own. Today India and the People's Republic of China are following the same path without forsaking their national tastes and heritages.

This does not mean that the world's cultural diversity is secure. Every decade a number of minority languages cease to be spoken. Televised national ceremonies or performances for tourists may prevent folk customs and costumes from dying out, but they also tend to devitalize rituals that once had many local variations. While a century ago it was possible to recognize the nationality of people from their clothing and grooming, today most urban men dress the same the world over, although women's clothing shows greater variety. As much as one may regret the disappearance or commercialization of some folkways, most anthropologists would agree that change is characteristic of all healthy cultures. What doesn't change risks extinction.

33-4 Conclusion

Historians often use the term "long nineteenth century" to signify a strong continuity in world political, social, and economic patterns between the end of the nineteenth century and World War I. Whether the twenty-first century is better viewed as having its own distinctive character or as being a prolongation of tendencies rooted in the twentieth century depends on how one weighs the importance of certain events.

The terrorist attacks of 9/11 established terrorism as a worldwide fear and suspicion, if not outright hatred, of Islam and Muslims as a growing popular attitude in some countries. Nothing in the twentieth century bears comparison with the consternation aroused by ISIS, whose atrocities have been publicized around the globe by new means of communication.

The worldwide financial crisis that began in 2008 revealed global linkages between economic transactions that seemed fundamentally local, such as refinancing homes, and the survival of major financial institutions: banks, insurance companies, and accounting firms. The effects of this crisis resembled the Great Depression of the twentieth century, but the underlying causes had more to do with new patterns of investment and electronic communication between financial institutions than with basic matters of supply and demand.

Democracy advanced in some regions of the world as a preferred governing system in the post–Cold War environment, but the memories of colonial exploitation that had fueled so many independence movements became less acute. In many countries, controversies over national and personal identity involved religious debates that had been less important than social class or secular nationalism throughout most of the twentieth century.

At a cultural level, the electronic information age that had begun with the development of computers after World War II encouraged the growth of global cultural attitudes, both popular and elite. The roots of these cultural developments clearly lay in the twentieth century, but the Internet and social media transformed them into something that seemed altogether new.

Key Terms

terrorism   p. 866
Osama bin Laden   p. 867
weapons of mass destruction
   p. 869

Universal Declaration of
   Human Rights   p. 873
nongovernmental organiza-
   tions (NGOs)   p. 874

globalization   p. 877
World Trade Organization
   (WTO)   p. 879
cultural imperialism   p. 884

global popular culture   p. 885
global elite culture   p. 886

Review Questions

1. Is there a clear break between twentieth- and twenty-first-century history?

2. Did either the terrorist attacks of 9/11 or the global financial crisis of 2008 affect the world as strongly as the Great Depression of the 1930s?

3. Can the powerful role played by Western styles, attitudes, and institutions in global culture today be compared with the role of European imperialism in the eighteenth and nineteenth centuries?

 MindTap® is a fully online, personalized learning experience built upon Cengage Learning content. MindTap® combines student learning tools—readings, multimedia, activities, and assessments—into a singular Learning Path that guides students through the course and helps students develop the critical thinking, analysis, and communication skills that are essential to academic and professional success.

Material Culture
Fast Food

Since early times empires and commercial enterprises have moved foods and beverages across borders and cultural boundaries. The list of examples is very long. Sugar, coffee, tea, chocolate, corn, manioc, potatoes, wheat, wine, beer, distilled alcohols, tomatoes, and bananas are a small number of the foods and beverages carried from their origins to new continents and new peoples. In each case, host cultures accepted these additions to their cuisines while at the same time changing their preparation and altering their cultural meanings. Europeans sweetened chocolate, a bitter beverage consumed ritually by the Aztec elite, with sugar and it quickly became a beverage of mass consumption, for example.

In modern industrialized nations fast food has developed to cater to changing needs and habits. Women and men in modern industrial societies marry later or not at all, and families have fewer meals together because of intense school and work schedules. As a result, fast-food outlets have appeared everywhere to meet the needs of this busy, mobile population for cheap and convenient food. In 2006 alone the world market for fast food grew by just under 7 percent, reaching sales of $155 billion.

Increased immigration and travel, as well as greater cultural connectivity promoted by films, television, and the Web, have combined to globalize ideas about food preparation and delivery. McDonald's now operates more than 31,000 restaurants in 119 countries. When a new franchise opened in Kuwait City, the drive-through line was over 10 kilometers (6.2 miles) long. Generally fast-food meals cost the same in every cultural setting. In the United States, one of the richest countries in the world, McDonald's provides low-cost food to the masses, while in Pakistan, one of the poorest, these meals are luxuries. For many in the developing world, fast-food cuisines, restaurant designs, and styles of preparation represent the world of modernity and sophistication, not unlike the enthusiasm in the developed world for Mexican, Thai, or Ethiopian restaurants and cuisines.

▲ **McDonald's Menu Board in India**   McDonald's has adapted its menu in India to reflect the religious mandates of Hinduism; it offers a wide selection of vegetarian and chicken items but no pork or beef.   david pearson/Alamy Stock Photo

Indeed, McDonald's is merely one of numerous examples of fast-food globalization. KFC had 3,200 outlets in China by the end of 2010, surpassing the McDonald's presence in this dynamic economy. Papa John's opened its fortieth outlet in Seoul and its twentieth outlet in Shanghai. Wendy's, Dominos, Cinnabon, and Subway have followed. Current estimates indicate that fast-food restaurants in India have a combined annual income expected to reach $8 billion by 2020; the fast-food market in China is bigger still.

Many condemn this process as Yankee imperialism or as the unwanted homogenization of global culture. Tens of thousands have demonstrated, and some have gone to jail as a result of attacks on these symbols of foreign cultural penetration. Yet, as in earlier examples of unequal cultural exchange, local cultures have found ways to impose their tastes and values on these powerful international businesses. In Singapore McDonald's serves its signature hamburger on rice cakes instead of buns, and in Israel McDonald's established kosher outlets. In Japan McDonald's serves rice cheese balls and a "black" hamburger that is embellished with a squid ink sauce. In India the chain offers the popular McAloo wrap, potato curry in a flour tortilla. KFC, the most successful American chain in China, serves a Beijing duck wrap with spring onions and rice gruel for breakfast. In Saudi Arabia Pizza Hut offers a seafood pizza with shrimp, calamari, crab, and vegetable toppings. In India, with its large vegetarian population, McDonald's, Pizza Hut, and other successful franchises devote as much as 75 percent of their menu to vegetarian foods. In 2012 McDonald's opened its first completely vegetarian outlets in India, where it planned to increase its total number of outlets to 500.

Every society produces a range of products that serve as class and culture markers and as forms of self-expression. In the modern world food helps mark consumers as "traditional" or "sophisticated" and as "rich" or "poor." Both the global success of fast-food companies and the popular protests against them suggest the complexity of these forms of cultural transmission.

Questions for Analysis

1. Why has fast food become so popular in the United States and other developed economies?

2. Are the reasons different in the non-Western world?

3. Have fast-food providers adapted to local tastes in these developing countries?

Historians analyze popular culture in a variety of ways. Material objects, such as farming implements and household decorations, may illuminate the everyday activities of people living at different times and under different circumstances. Visual sources—from fine art, to store signs, to snapshots—are also important, though most artistic images are skewed by the preferences of patrons and by cultural limitations on subject matter. When written works are scarce or unavailable, folktales, nursery rhymes, and other types of lore handed down orally from generation to generation may reflect the tenor of life, though the nature of their transmission makes pinning them down to a particular time and place difficult.

Written sources of a narrative character, as opposed to lists and data sets amenable to quantitative analysis, tend to be of limited use for trying to reconstruct the day-to-day activities of ordinary people. Technical manuals describing agricultural processes, for example, do not necessarily prove that those processes were in use at the time the manual was written because copying from earlier written works was often more common than observing actual activities and because descriptions of innovations often precede their widespread adoption.

The rise of printing both in East Asia and Europe expanded the size of the reading public, particularly when a growing number of authors chose to publish books in local spoken tongues instead of classical languages like Latin, Greek, and even Arabic—to the extent that local spoken dialects of Arabic diverged substantially over the centuries from the standardized written Arabic rooted in the Quran.

Satires and descriptions of carnival-type activities that inverted social conventions, making a poor man or a fool king-for-a-day, for example, give insight into how the literary class perceived the life of common people; but, for the most part, prior to the nineteenth century, there was a deep gulf between book descriptions and the actual lifestyles of the poor and unlettered.

Realism as a literary objective, whether in fiction or newspaper stories, lessened the gulf. Novelists like Charles Dickens (d. 1870), Emile Zola (d. 1902), and Leo Tolstoy (d. 1910) found broad audiences for tales that detailed the social life of the poor as well as the rich. Nevertheless, grim exposés of the miseries of common folk were seldom part of popular culture, which by World War I took the form of songs and jokes performed in music halls, newspaper comic strips, and escapist fiction about poor boys suddenly becoming rich or going off on improbable adventures.

Phonograph records, radio plays, movies, and, from the 1950s on, television shows vaulted popular culture to a much more visible role, partly because they were less ephemeral and could be collected in archives and thereby made available for study. Comic books and magazine advertisements were less widely recognized as elements of popular culture but were important all the same.

As popular culture became more expressive and ubiquitous, many "serious" composers, poets, novelists, and artists became disdainful of "low" tastes and committed to creating works for a shrinking segment of the public that was both well educated and devoted to what was increasingly called "high culture." For historians who want to chronicle the substance of popular culture and its influence on social and political change, or simply to describe the mood the times they are living in, finding linkages between high culture and popular culture constituted a plausible strategy.

Two universally read and admired novels by well-respected serious writers set a pattern for post–World War II popular culture. Aldous Huxley's *Brave New World* published in 1932 and George Orwell's *1984* published in 1949 used the popular genre of science fiction to warn society about dangers facing the world: eugenics and social engineering in the former and fascism and degradation of truth in the latter. Earlier writers of quasi-serious speculative fiction like Jules Verne (d. 1905) and H. G. Wells (d. 1946) had focused more on adventure than on warnings about future dystopia.

The appeal of imminent catastrophe scenarios in popular culture—novels, movies, television, comic books, and computer games—grew slowly but inexorably. Fear of nuclear war and radiation-mutated monsters, clear reactions to the atomic bombs dropped on Hiroshima and Nagasaki, provided the first major theme. Serious nonfiction warning books like Rachel Carson's *Silent Spring* (1962) and Paul Ehrlich's *The Population Bomb* (1968) added environmental pollution and overpopulation to the list of fears for the future, and novels like Michael Crichton's *Andromeda Strain* (1969) and Robin Cook's *Coma* (1977) added medical fears like unstoppable pandemics and criminal organ replacements. Terrorism and visions of catastrophic climate change solidified fear of the future as a fundamental feature of both serious and popular culture.

With the turn of the millennium in the year 2000, many Christians, particularly evangelical Protestants, melded visions of disaster with a belief that the End Times of the world were almost at hand. At the popular culture level, Tim La Haye and Jerry B. Jenkins published the first of their phenomenally popular sixteen-volume series *Left Behind* in 1995. God raises all true Christians to heaven on page one, leaving the rest of the human race to struggle heroically against the Antichrist Secretary General of the United Nations as the apocalypse predicted in the Biblical book of Revelation unfolds.

For Muslims, the year of the Iranian Revolution, 1979, was also the year 1400 of their lunar calendar. This led many to ponder the tradition that at the beginning of every century Allah empowers a Renewer (Arabic mujaddid) to bring the world Muslim community back to the right path. Who the Renewer is might only be seen in retrospect, but Muslims wondered nevertheless whether one or another of the zealots trying by video and social media to stir their brothers and sisters to militant action might be part of Allah's plan.

Historians of the twentieth century have looked to popular culture to help understand why most countries entered World War I with great enthusiasm and World War II with similar enthusiasm on the fascist side, but with great dread on the Allied side. Have several decades of popular culture portraying apocalyptic futures created a fearful mood in the twenty-first century? Fictional catastrophe scenarios ranging from zombie apocalypse at the silly end to deeply considered works of popular writing at the serious end consume the imaginations of novel readers, movie-goers, television viewers, and game players around the world.

Some serious writers resort to science fiction to forge a link with the apocalyptic mindset and thus bring high culture into contact with popular culture. To mention a few, *The Three-Body Problem* (2006), the first volume of a trilogy by China's foremost science fiction writer Cixin Liu, presents a seemingly unending series of world-ending scenarios and rigid political systems, starting during China's Cultural Revolution from 1966 to 1976.

The Water Knife (2005) by Paolo Bacigalupi envisions anarchic chaos overtaking the American Southwest as climate change and exhaustion of the fossil water of the Ogallala Aquifer underlying Nebraska, Kansas, and Texas make urban life virtually impossible.

> People don't actually stay still, you know—when their area is a disaster, they go somewhere else, right? And that's just a natural human impulse. And it's also a natural human impulse for people to sort of hunker down and say 'no, no, this is ours—we've got the good stuff, and we don't want to share.'

Margaret Atwood's *MaddAddam* trilogy (first volume *Oryx and Crake* published in 2003) makes dystopic projections to combine genetic experimentation, climate change, and pandemic disease.

> The people in the chaos cannot learn. They cannot understand what they are doing to the sea and the sky and the plants and the animals. They cannot understand that they are killing them, and that they will end by killing themselves. And there are so many of them, and each one of them is doing part of the killing, whether they know it or not.

And Dave Eggers's *The Circle* (2013) contemplates a chilling dystopia in which everyone is on a Facebook equivalent and under video surveillance all of the time.

> Most people would trade everything they know, everyone they know—they'd trade it all to know they've been seen, and acknowledged, that they might even be remembered. We all know the world is too big for us to be significant. So all we have is the hope of being seen, or heard, even for a moment.

Given the multifaceted bleakness that informs so many of the visions of the future projected by contemporary popular culture, it may not be so surprising that the election of Donald J. Trump was greeted with dismay and trepidation by many people both in America and around the world. History shows that single individuals, all by themselves, cannot bring about either wonderful or dreadful futures. They can, however, capture the mood of a period and build upon it for better or worse.

Questions for Analysis

1. What is the importance of the culture of ordinary people in comparison with that of elite groups?
2. How did technological innovations in the twentieth century change popular culture and the way it is studied?
3. How important is it to think of the future optimistically or pessimistically?

Sources: Paolo Bacigalupi interview by National Public Radio. Retrieved January 2017 from www.npr.org/2015/05/23/408756002/what-if-the-drought-doesnt-end-the-water-knife-is-one-possibility; Margaret Atwood, *Oryx and Crake* (Toronto: McClelland and Stewart, 2003), 291; Dave Eggers, *The Circle* (New York: Knopf, 2013), 490.

Multiple-Choice Questions

Questions 1–4 refer to the passages below.

"On the Eurasian continent, however, the proliferation of ethnic conflict, epitomized at the extreme in 'ethnic cleansing,' has not been totally random. It has been most frequent and most violent between groups belonging to different civilizations. In Eurasia the great historic fault lines between civilizations are once more aflame. This is particularly true along the boundaries of the crescent-shaped Islamic bloc of nations from the bulge of Africa to central Asia. Violence also occurs between Muslims, on the one hand, and Orthodox Serbs in the Balkans, Jews in Israel, Hindus in India, Buddhists in Burma and Catholics in the Philippines. Islam has bloody borders."

> Samuel P. Huntington, a political scientist from the United States, "The Clash of Civilizations?" *Foreign Affairs, 72,* no. 3 (Summer 1993)

"The representatives of Heads of State and Government of OIC member states . . . [recognizing] the United Nations General Assembly resolution 53/22, designating the year 2001 as the United Nations Year of Dialogue among Civilizations; Drawing upon the Islamic principles of celebration of human diversity, recognition of diversified sources of knowledge, promotion of dialogue and mutual understanding, genuine mutual respect in human interchanges, and encouragement of courteous and civilized discourse based on reason and logic; Reaffirming the commitment of their Governments to promote dialogue and understanding among various cultures and civilizations, aimed at reaching a global consensus to build a new order for the next millennium founded in faith as well as common moral and ethical values of contemporary civilizations."

> Mohammed Khatami, president of the Islamic Republic of Iran, "The Tehran Declaration on Dialogue Among Civilizations," Organization of the Islamic Conference, 2001

1. How does Huntington explain the rise in violence in contemporary times?

   (A) Hinduism has grown more violent, especially against Muslim states.

   (B) NATO and other international organizations have continued to destabilize regions dominated by Islam.

   (C) Islam shares borders with other civilizations that follow different religions.

   (D) Ethnic cleansing, not religion, is responsible for most of the violence.

2. Which of the following is evidence in support of Huntington's argument?

   (A) The rise in membership of Hindu nationalist parties in India

   (B) The rise of the Taliban and other fundamentalist Islamic groups

   (C) The spread of NATO and the European Union into Eastern Europe

   (D) The ethnic tensions in Slavic regions

3. How does Khatami's argument differ from Huntington's?

   (A) Khatami asserts that the United Nations is to be held responsible for the violence.

   (B) Khatami suggests commitment to governments interferes with a global peace resulting from religion.

   (C) Khatami believes peace can only be maintained through a moral code based on scientific principles.

   (D) Khatami asserts the essential relationship between civilizations can be one of peace and understanding.

4. Which of the following events supports Khatami's argument?

   (A) Long-standing peace treaties between Israel and Muslim states

   (B) European Union economic sanctions against Russia

   (C) Expansion of multinational corporations providing employment

   (D) The United Nations' monitoring of the development of nuclear technology

Questions 5–7 refer to Map 33.3 on page 880.

5. The map supports which of the following statements concerning the year 2004?

   (A) The world continued to subdivide into smaller, isolated political blocks.

   (B) The nations of the world moved toward regional and transregional trade organizations.

   (C) European and North American trade agreements were more profitable than those in Africa.

   (D) The European Union moved to exclude Eastern Europeans.

6. Which of the following best explains the growing trend on the map?

   (A) The United States and its allies attempting to contain the activities of states that made up the former Soviet Union

   (B) Leaders attempting to maintain centralized control over natural and human resources

   (C) Governments attempting to limit the impact of economic competition

   (D) The spread of free-market economies at the end of the twentieth century

▲ **Demonstrators holding up Facebook logos during the Arab Spring in Rabat, Morocco, March 20, 2011** Adam Tanner/The Image Works

7. Which of the following is evidence of weaknesses with the systems in the map?

   (A) The expansion of the African continent into a single economic market

   (B) The United States banning communist Cuba from NAFTA

   (C) The United Kingdom leaving the European Union

   (D) Russia and China belonging to the same economic organization

Questions 8–10 refer to the image above.

8. The image supports which of the following statements?

   (A) The Internet and social media impact the political process.

   (B) Anticolonial movements continue to use violence to achieve their political goals.

   (C) Demonstrations in the twenty-first century attract large numbers of people but are chaotic and rarely achieve their goals.

   (D) Women are more willing to join protest movements than men.

9. Based on the image, which of the following is evidence of a global consumer culture?

   (A) Electrical wires demonstrating that North African cities have built up their infrastructure

   (B) Women from North Africa wearing blue jeans and using cellphones

   (C) The use of signs and artwork to protest against rulers and despotic governments

   (D) The presence of men in public spaces

10. The image supports which of the following changes from the previous time period?

    (A) Men now dominate both the government and protest movements.

    (B) Religion is used as a way to denounce the impact of modernity on society.

    (C) Women are taking more public roles.

    (D) Mass demonstrations are being led and organized by elites.

Short-Answer Questions

1. Some historians argue that the twentieth and twenty-first centuries have brought greater rights and opportunities to women. Based on your knowledge of world history, answer all parts of the question that follows.

   (A) Identify ONE example of women gaining more political rights than in the previous time period.

   (B) Explain ONE example of women having access to more economic opportunities than in the previous time period.

   (C) Explain ONE example of women continuing to feel the effects of patriarchy.

2. Answer all parts of the question that follows.

   (A) Identify ONE way the global environment has been protected during the period of global population expansion.

   (B) Explain ONE change in the global environment due to human population expansion.

   (C) Explain ANOTHER change in the global environment due to human population expansion.

Glossary

Abbasid Caliphate Descendants of the Prophet Muhammad's uncle, al-Abbas, the Abbasids overthrew the Umayyad Caliphate and ruled an Islamic empire from their capital in Baghdad (founded 762) from 750 to 1258. (*p.* 253)

abolitionists Men and women who agitated for a complete end to slavery. Abolitionist pressure ended the British transatlantic slave trade in 1808 and slavery in British colonies in 1834. In the United States the activities of abolitionists were one factor leading to the Civil War (1861–1865). (*p.* 650)

acculturation The adoption of the language, customs, values, and behaviors of host nations by immigrants. (*p.* 654)

Acheh Sultanate Muslim kingdom in northern Sumatra. Main center of Islamic expansion in Southeast Asia in the early seventeenth century, it declined after the Dutch seized Malacca from Portugal in 1641. (*p.* 528)

Aden Port city in the modern south Arabian country of Yemen. It has been a major trading center in the Indian Ocean since ancient times. (*p.* 381)

Adolf Hitler Born in Austria, Hitler became a radical German nationalist during World War I. He led the National Socialist German Workers' Party—the Nazis—in the 1920s and became dictator of Germany in 1933. He led Europe into World War II. (*p.* 758)

African National Congress An organization dedicated to obtaining equal voting and civil rights for black inhabitants of South Africa. Founded in 1912 as the South African Native National Congress, it changed its name in 1923. Though it was banned and its leaders were jailed for many years, it eventually helped bring majority rule to South Africa. (*p.* 800)

Afrikaners South Africans descended from Dutch and French settlers of the seventeenth century. Their Great Trek founded new settler colonies in the nineteenth century. Though a minority among South Africans, they held political power after 1910, imposing a system of racial segregation called apartheid after 1949. (*p.* 670)

agricultural revolution The transformation of farming in the eighteenth century that resulted from the spread of new crops, improvements in cultivation techniques and livestock breeding, and the consolidation of small holdings into large farms from which tenants and sharecroppers were forcibly expelled. (*pp.* 558, 829)

Agricultural Revolutions The change from food gathering to food production that occurred between about 8000 and 2000 BCE. Also known as the Neolithic Revolution. (*p.* 16)

Akbar Most illustrious sultan of the Mughal Empire in India (r. 1556– 1605). He expanded the empire and pursued a policy of conciliation with Hindus. (*p.* 519)

Akhenaten Egyptian pharaoh (r. 1353–1335 BCE). He built a new capital at Amarna, fostered a new style of naturalistic art, and created a religious revolution by imposing worship of the sun-disk. (*p.* 55)

Albert Einstein German physicist who developed the theory of relativity, which states that time, space, and mass are relative to each other and not fixed. (*p.* 783)

Alexander King of Macedonia in northern Greece. Between 334 and 323 BCE he conquered the Persian Empire, reached the Indus Valley, founded many Greek-style cities, and spread Greek culture across the Middle East. Later known as Alexander the Great. (*p.* 134)

Alexander Nevskii Prince of Novgorod (r. 1236–1263). He submitted to the invading Mongols in 1240 and received recognition as the leader of the Russian princes under the Golden Horde. (*p.* 330)

Alexandria City on the Mediterranean coast of Egypt founded by Alexander. It became the capital of the Hellenistic kingdom of the Ptolemies. It contained the famous Library and the Museum, a center for leading scientific and literary figures. Its merchants engaged in trade with areas bordering the Mediterranean Sea and the Indian Ocean. (*p.* 136)

All-India Muslim League Political organization founded in India in 1906 to defend the interests of India's Muslim minority. Led by Muhammad Ali Jinnah, it attempted to negotiate with the Indian National Congress. In 1940, the League began demanding a separate state for Muslims, to be called Pakistan. (*p.* 790)

altepetl An ethnic state in ancient Mesoamerica, the common political building block of that region. (*p.* 386)

amulet Small charm meant to protect the bearer from evil. Found frequently in archaeological excavations in Mesopotamia and Egypt, amulets reflect the religious practices of the common people. (*p.* 35)

Amur River This river valley was a contested frontier between northern China and eastern Russia until the settlement arranged in the Treaty of Nerchinsk (1689). (*p.* 546)

anarchists Revolutionaries who wanted to abolish all private property and governments, usually by violence, and replace them with free associations of groups. (*p.* 710)

Anasazi Important culture of what is now the southwest United States (700–1300 CE). Centered on Chaco Canyon in New Mexico and Mesa Verde in Colorado, the Anasazi culture built multistory residences and worshiped in subterranean buildings called kivas. (*p.* 209)

Andrew Jackson First president of the United States to be born in humble circumstances. He was popular among frontier residents, urban workers, and small farmers. He had a successful political career as judge, general, congressman, senator, and president. After being denied the presidency in 1824 in a controversial election, he won in 1828 and was reelected in 1832. (*p.* 643)

aqueduct A conduit, either elevated or underground, that used gravity to carry water from a source to a location—usually a city—that needed it. The Romans built many aqueducts in a period of substantial urbanization. (*p.* 155)

Arawak Amerindian peoples who inhabited the Greater Antilles of the Caribbean at the time of Columbus. (*p.* 399)

Armenia One of the earliest Christian kingdoms, situated in eastern Anatolia and the western Caucasus and occupied by speakers of the Armenian language. (*p.* 242)

Ashikaga Shogunate The second of Japan's military governments headed by a shogun (a military ruler). Sometimes called the Muromachi Shogunate. (*p.* 341)

Ashoka Third ruler of the Mauryan Empire in India (r. 273–232 BCE). He converted to Buddhism and broadcast his precepts on inscribed stones and pillars, the earliest surviving Indian writing. (*p.* 179)

Asian Tigers Collective name for South Korea, Taiwan, Hong Kong, and Singapore—nations that became economic powers in the 1970s and 1980s. (*p.* 843)

Atahuallpa Last ruling Inka emperor of Peru. He was executed by the Spanish. (*p.* 413)

Atatürk The founder of modern Turkey. He distinguished himself in the defense of Gallipoli in World War I and expelled a Greek expeditionary army from Anatolia in 1921–1922. He replaced the Ottoman Empire with the Turkish Republic in 1923. As president, he pushed through a radical westernization and reform of Turkish society. (*p.* 745)

Atlantic Circuit The network of trade routes connecting Europe, Africa, and the Americas that underlay the Atlantic system. (*p.* 491)

Atlantic system The network of trading links after 1500 that moved goods, wealth, people, and cultures around the Atlantic Basin. (*p.* 479)

Auguste and Louis Lumière French inventors of motion pictures whose equipment demonstrations abroad stimulated the growth of cinema around the world. (*p.* 780)

Augustus Honorific name of Octavian, founder of the Roman Principate, the military dictatorship that replaced the failing rule of the Roman Senate. After defeating all rivals, between 31 BCE and 14 CE he laid the groundwork for several centuries of stability and prosperity in the Roman Empire. (*p.* 149)

Auschwitz Nazi extermination camp in Poland, the largest center of mass murder during the Holocaust. Close to a million Jews, Gypsies, Communists, and others were killed there. (*p.* 771)

australopithecines The several extinct species of humanlike primates that existed from about 4.5 million years ago to 1.4 million years ago (genus *Australopithecus*). (*p.* 006)

Ayatollah Ruhollah Khomeini Shi'ite philosopher and cleric who led the overthrow of the shah of Iran in 1979 and created an Islamic republic. (*p.* 840)

ayllu Andean lineage group or kin-based community. (*p.* 212)

Aztecs Also known as Mexica, the Aztecs created a powerful empire in central Mexico (1325–1521 CE). They forced defeated peoples to provide goods and labor as a tax. (*p.* 386)

Babylon The largest and most important city in Mesopotamia. It achieved particular eminence as the capital of the Amorite king Hammurabi in the eighteenth century BCE. (*p.* 32)

balance of power The policy in international relations by which, beginning in the eighteenth century, the major European states acted together to prevent any one of them from becoming too powerful. (*p.* 447)

Balfour Declaration Statement issued by Britain's foreign secretary Arthur Balfour in 1917 favoring the establishment of a Jewish national homeland in Palestine. (*p.* 735)

Bannermen Hereditary military servants of the Qing Empire, in large part descendants of peoples of various origins who had fought for the founders of the empire. (*p.* 624)

Bantu Collective name of a large group of sub-Saharan African languages and of the peoples speaking these languages. (*p.* 240)

Baron Pierre de Coubertin Founder of the modern Olympic movement, which held its first games in Athens in 1896. (*p.* 786)

Bartolomé de Las Casas First bishop of Chiapas, in southern Mexico. He devoted most of his life to protecting Amerindian peoples from exploitation. His major achievement was the New Laws of 1542, which outlawed the enslavement of Amerindians and limited other forced labor. (*p.* 459)

Bartolomeu Dias Portuguese explorer who in 1488 led the first expedition to sail around the southern tip of Africa from the Atlantic and sight the Indian Ocean. (*p.* 403)

Batavia Fort established around 1619 as headquarters of Dutch East India Company operations in Indonesia; today the city of Jakarta. (*p.* 530)

Battle of Midway U.S. naval victory over the Japanese fleet in June 1942, in which the Japanese lost four of their best aircraft carriers. It marked a turning point in World War II. (*p.* 766)

Beijing China's northern capital, first used as an imperial capital in 906 and now the capital of the People's Republic of China. (*p.* 333)

Bengal Region of northeastern India. It was the first part of India to be conquered by the British in the eighteenth century and remained the political and economic center of British India throughout the nineteenth century. The 1905 split of the province into predominantly Hindu West Bengal and predominantly Muslim East Bengal (now Bangladesh) sparked anti-British riots. (*p.* 789)

Benito Juárez President of Mexico (1858–1872). Born in poverty in Mexico, he was educated as a lawyer and rose to become chief justice of the Mexican supreme court and then president. He led Mexico's resistance to a French invasion in 1862 and the installation of Maximilian as emperor. (*p.* 647)

Benito Mussolini Fascist dictator of Italy (1922–1943). He led Italy to conquer Ethiopia (1935), joined Germany in the Axis pact (1936), and allied Italy with Germany in World War II. He was overthrown in 1943 when the Allies invaded Italy. (*p.* 758)

Benjamin Franklin American intellectual, inventor, and politician who helped negotiate French support for the American Revolution. (*p.* 588)

Berlin Conference Conference that German chancellor Otto von Bismarck called to set rules for the partition of Africa. It led to the creation of the Congo Free State under King Leopold II of Belgium. (*p.* 675)

Bhagavad-Gita The most important work of Indian sacred literature, a dialogue between the great warrior Arjuna and the god Krishna on duty and the fate of the spirit. (*p.* 180)

bipedalism The ability to walk upright on two legs, characteristic of hominids. (*p.* 006)

Black Death An outbreak of bubonic plague that spread across Asia, North Africa, and Europe in the mid-fourteenth century, carrying off vast numbers of persons. (*p.* 346)

Blaise Diagne Senegalese political leader. He was the first African elected to the French National Assembly. During World War I, in exchange for promises to give French citizenship to Senegalese, he helped recruit Africans to serve in the French army. After the war, he led a movement to abolish forced labor in Africa. (*p.* 800)

Bolsheviks Radical Marxist political party founded by Vladimir Lenin in 1903. Under Lenin's leadership, the Bolsheviks seized power in November 1917 during the Russian Revolution. (*p.* 735)

Bornu A powerful West African kingdom at the southern edge of the Sahara in the central Sudan, which was important in trans-Saharan trade and in the spread of Islam. Also known as Kanem-Bornu, it endured from the ninth century to the end of the nineteenth. (*p.* 500)

Borobodur A massive stone monument on the Indonesian island of Java, erected by the Sailendra kings around 800 CE. The winding ascent through ten levels, decorated with rich relief carving, is a Buddhist allegory for the progressive stages of enlightenment. (*p.* 190)

bourgeoisie In early modern Europe, the class of well-off town dwellers whose wealth came from manufacturing, finance, commerce, and allied professions. (*p.* 435)

British raj The rule over much of South Asia between 1765 and 1947 by the East India Company and then by a British government. (*p.* 679)

bronze An alloy of copper with a small amount of tin (or sometimes arsenic), it is harder and more durable than copper alone. The term *Bronze Age* is applied to the era—the dates of which vary in different parts of the world—when bronze was the primary metal for tools and weapons. (*p.* 38)

bubonic plague A bacterial disease of fleas that can be transmitted by flea bites to rodents and humans; humans in late stages of the illness can spread the bacteria by coughing. Because of its very high mortality rate and the difficulty of preventing its spread, major outbreaks have created crises in many parts of the world. (*p.* 325)

Buddha An Indian prince named Siddhartha Gautama who renounced his wealth and social position to search for truth. After becoming "enlightened" (the meaning of *Buddha*), he enunciated the principles of Buddhism, which evolved and spread throughout India and to Southeast, East, and Central Asia. (*p.* 174)

Byzantine Empire Historians' name for the eastern portion of the Roman Empire from the fourth century onward, taken from "Byzantium," an early name for Constantinople, the Byzantine capital city. The empire fell to the Ottomans in 1453. (*p.* 269)

caliphate Office established in succession to the Prophet Muhammad, to rule the Islamic empire; also the name of that empire. (*p.* 251)

calpolli A group of up to a hundred families that served as a social building block of an altepetl in ancient Mesoamerica. (*p.* 386)

capitalism The economic system of large financial institutions—banks, stock exchanges, investment companies—that first developed in early modern Europe. *Commercial capitalism*, the trading system of the early modern economy, is often distinguished from *industrial capitalism*, the system based on machine production. (*p.* 490)

caravel A small, highly maneuverable three-masted ship used by the Portuguese and Spanish in the exploration of the Atlantic. (*p.* 402)

Carthage City located in present-day Tunisia, founded by Phoenicians ca. 800 BCE. It became a major commercial center and naval power in the western Mediterranean until defeated by Rome in the third century BCE. (*p.* 72)

Caste War A rebellion of the Maya people against the government of Mexico in 1847 that nearly returned the Yucatán to Maya rule. Some Maya rebels retreated to unoccupied territories, where they held out until 1901. (*p.* 650)

Catholic Reformation Religious reform movement within the Latin Christian Church, begun in response to the Protestant Reformation. It clarified Catholic theology and reformed clerical training and discipline. (*p.* 428)

Cecil Rhodes British entrepreneur and politician involved in the expansion of the British Empire from South Africa into Central Africa. The colonies of Southern Rhodesia (now Zimbabwe) and Northern Rhodesia (now Zambia) were named after him. (*p.* 672)

Celts Peoples sharing common linguistic and cultural features that originated in central Europe in the first half of the first millennium BCE. (*p.* 100)

Champa rice Quick-maturing rice that can allow two harvests in one growing season. Originally introduced into Champa from India, it was later sent to China as a tribute gift by the Champa state. (*p.* 311)

Chang'an City in the Wei River Valley in eastern China. It became the capital of the early Han Empire. Its main features were imitated in the cities and towns that sprang up throughout the Han Empire. (*p.* 162)

Charlemagne King of the Franks (r. 768–814); emperor (r. 800–814). Through a series of military conquests he established the Carolingian Empire, which encompassed all of Gaul and parts of Germany and Italy. Though illiterate himself, he sponsored a brief intellectual revival. (*p.* 269)

chartered companies Groups of private investors who paid an annual fee to France and England in exchange for a monopoly over trade to the West Indies colonies. (*p.* 480)

Chavín The first major urban civilization in South America (900– 250 BCE). Its capital, Chavín de Huántar, was located high in the Andes Mountains of Peru. Chavín became politically and economically dominant in a densely populated region that included two distinct ecological zones, the Peruvian coastal plain and the Andean foothills. (*p.* 198)

Chiang Kai-shek Chinese military and political leader. Succeeded Sun Yat-sen as head of the Guomindang in 1925; headed the Chinese government from 1928 to 1948; fought against the Chinese Communists and Japanese invaders. After 1949 he headed the Chinese Nationalist government in Taiwan. (*pp.* 743, 761)

chiefdom Form of political organization with rule by a hereditary leader who held power over a collection of villages and towns. Less powerful than kingdoms and empires, chiefdoms were based on gift giving and commercial links. (*p.* 210)

Chimú A powerful civilization, also called Kingdom of Chimor, that developed on the northern coast of Peru from about 1200 to its conquest by an expanding Inka empire in the 1470s. Its capital city was Chan Chan. (*p.* 216)

chinampas Raised fields constructed along lakeshores in Mesoamerica to increase agricultural yields. (*p.* 200)

Chinggis Khan The title of Temüjin when he ruled the Mongols (1206-1227). It means the "oceanic" or "universal leader." Chinggis Khan was the founder of the Mongol Empire. (*p.* 319)

Choson The Choson dynasty ruled Korea from the fall of the Koryo kingdom to the colonization of Korea by Japan. (*p.* 339)

Christopher Columbus Genoese mariner who in the service of Spain led expeditions across the Atlantic, reestablishing contact between the peoples of the Americas and the Old World and opening the way to Spanish conquest and colonization. (*p.* 403)

city-state A small independent state consisting of an urban center and the surrounding agricultural territory. A characteristic political form in early Mesopotamia, Archaic and Classical Greece, Phoenicia, and early Italy. (*p.* 31)

civilization An ambiguous term often used to denote more complex societies but sometimes used by anthropologists to describe any group of people sharing a set of cultural traits. (*p.* 27)

Cold War The ideological struggle between communism (Soviet Union) and capitalism (United States) for world influence. The Cold War came to an end when the Soviet Union dissolved in 1991. (*p.* 810)

Columbian Exchange The exchange of plants, animals, diseases, and technologies between the Americas and the rest of the world following Columbus's voyages. (*p.* 454)

Commodore Matthew Perry A navy commander who, on July 8, 1853, became the first foreigner to break through the barriers that had kept Japan isolated from the rest of the world for 250 years. (*p.* 697)

Confederation of 1867 Negotiated union of the formerly separate colonial governments of Ontario, Quebec, New Brunswick, and Nova Scotia. This new Dominion of Canada with a central government in Ottawa is seen as the beginning of the Canadian nation. (*p.* 641)

Confucius Western name for the Chinese philosopher Kongzi (551– 479 BCE). His doctrine of duty and public service had a great influence on subsequent Chinese thought and served as a code of conduct for government officials. (*p.* 89)

Congress of Vienna Meeting of representatives of European monarchs called to re-establish the old order after the defeat of Napoleon I. (*p.* 606)

conquistadors Early-sixteenth-century Spanish adventurers who conquered Mexico, Central America, and Peru. (*p.* 413)

Constantine Roman emperor (r. 312–337). After reuniting the Roman Empire, he moved the capital to Constantinople and made Christianity a favored religion. (*p.* 157)

Constitutional Convention Meeting in 1787 of the elected representatives of the thirteen original states to write the Constitution of the United States. (*p.* 594)

contract of indenture A voluntary agreement binding a person to work for a specified period of years in return for free passage to an overseas destination. Before 1800 most indentured servants were Europeans; after 1800 most indentured laborers were Asians. (*p.* 693)

Cossacks Peoples of the Russian Empire who lived outside the farming villages, often as herders, mercenaries, or outlaws. Cossacks led the conquest of Siberia in the sixteenth and seventeenth centuries. (*p.* 523)

coureurs de bois French fur traders, many of mixed Amerindian heritage, who lived among and often married with Amerindian peoples of North America. (*p.* 472)

creoles In colonial Spanish America, term used to describe someone of European descent born in the New World. Elsewhere in the Americas, the term is used to describe all non-native peoples. (*p.* 463)

Crimean War Conflict between the Russian and Ottoman Empires fought primarily in the Crimean Peninsula. To prevent Russian expansion, Britain and France sent troops to support the Ottomans. (*p.* 617)

Crusades (1095–1204) Armed pilgrimages to the Holy Land by Christians determined to recover Jerusalem from Muslim rule. The Crusades brought an end to western Europe's centuries of intellectual and cultural isolation. (*p.* 288)

Crystal Palace Building erected in Hyde Park, London, for the Great Exhibition of 1851. Made of iron and glass, like a gigantic greenhouse, it was a symbol of the industrial age. (*p.* 567)

Cuban missile crisis Brink-of-war confrontation between the United States and the Soviet Union over the latter's placement of nuclear-armed missiles in Cuba. (*p.* 818)

cultural imperialism Domination of one culture over another by a deliberate policy or by economic or technological superiority. (*p.* 884)

Cultural Revolution (China) Campaign in China ordered by Mao Zedong to purge the Communist Party of his opponents and instill revolutionary values in the younger generation. (*p.* 829)

culture Socially transmitted patterns of human action and expression. (*p.* 11)

cuneiform A system of writing in which wedge-shaped symbols represented words or syllables. It originated in Mesopotamia and was used initially for Sumerian and Akkadian but later was adapted to represent other languages of western Asia. Literacy was confined to a relatively small group of administrators and scribes. (*p.* 37)

Cyrus Founder of the Achaemenid Persian Empire. Between 550 and 530 BCE he conquered Media, Lydia, and Babylon. Revered in the traditions of both Iran and the subject peoples, he employed Persians and Medes in his administration and respected the institutions and beliefs of subject peoples. (*p.* 115)

Dada Nihilistic movement in poetry and art that began during World War I in reaction to the vast and horrifying loss of life that seemed to make art meaningless. (*p.* 784)

daimyo Literally, "great name(s)." Japanese warlords and great landowners, whose armed samurai gave them control of the Japanese islands from the eighth to the later nineteenth century. Under the Tokugawa Shogunate they were subordinated to the imperial government. (*p.* 536)

Daoism Chinese school of thought, originating in the Warring States Period with Laozi. Daoism offered an alternative to the Confucian emphasis on hierarchy and duty. (*p.* 89)

Darius I Third ruler of the Persian Empire (r. 522–486 BCE). He crushed the widespread initial resistance to his rule and gave major government posts to Persians rather than to Medes. He established a system of provinces and tribute, began construction of Persepolis, and expanded Persian control in the east (Pakistan) and west (northern Greece). (*p.* 116)

Decembrist revolt Abortive attempt by army officers to take control of the Russian government upon the death of Tsar Alexander I in 1825. (*p.* 622)

Declaration of the Rights of Man and the Citizen Statement of fundamental political rights adopted by the French National Assembly at the beginning of the French Revolution. (*p.* 597)

deforestation The removal of trees faster than forests can replace themselves. (*p.* 437)

Delhi Sultanate Centralized Indian empire of varying extent, created by Muslim invaders. (*p.* 371)

democracy System of government in which all "citizens" (however defined) have equal political and legal rights, privileges, and protections, as in the Greek city-state of Athens in the fifth and fourth centuries BCE. (*p.* 124)

demographic transition A change in the rates of population growth. Before the transition, both birthrates and death rates are high, resulting in a slowly growing population; then the death rate drops but the birthrate remains high, causing a population explosion; finally, the birthrate drops and the population growth slows down. (*p.* 849)

Deng Xiaoping Communist Party leader who forced Chinese economic reforms after the death of Mao Zedong. (*p.* 843)

development In the nineteenth and twentieth centuries, the economic process that led to industrialization, urbanization, the rise of a large and prosperous middle class, and heavy investment in education. (*p.* 658)

dhows Characteristic cargo and passenger ships of the Arabian Sea. (*p.* 379)

Diaspora Greek word meaning "dispersal," used to describe the communities of a given ethnic group living outside their homeland. Jews, for example, spread from Israel to western Asia and Mediterranean lands in antiquity and today can be found throughout the world. (*p.* 68)

Dirty War War waged by the Argentine military (1976–1983) against leftist groups. Characterized by the use of illegal imprisonment, torture, and executions by the military. (*p.* 838)

division of labor A manufacturing technique that breaks down a craft into many simple and repetitive tasks that can be performed by unskilled workers. Pioneered in the pottery works of Josiah Wedgwood and in other eighteenth-century factories, it greatly increased the productivity of labor and lowered the cost of manufactured goods. (*p.* 564)

driver A privileged male slave whose job was to ensure that a slave gang did its work on a plantation. (*p.* 486)

Druids The class of religious experts who conducted rituals and preserved sacred lore among some ancient Celtic peoples. (*p.* 102)

durbar An elaborate display of political power and wealth in British India in the nineteenth century, ostensibly in imitation of the pageantry of the Mughal Empire. (*p.* 680)

Dutch West India Company Trading company chartered by the Dutch government to conduct its merchants' trade in the Americas and Africa. (*p.* 480)

El Alamein Town in Egypt, site of the victory by Britain's Field Marshal Bernard Montgomery over German forces led by General Erwin Rommel (the "Desert Fox") in 1942–1943. (*p.* 766)

electric telegraph A device for rapid, long-distance transmission of information over an electric wire. It was introduced in England and North America in the 1830s and 1840s and replaced telegraph systems that utilized visual signals such as semaphores. (*p.* 570)

electricity A form of energy used in telegraphy from the 1840s on and for lighting, industrial motors, and railroads beginning in the 1880s. (*p.* 701)

Emiliano Zapata Revolutionary and leader of peasants in the Mexican Revolution. He mobilized landless peasants in south-central Mexico in an attempt to seize and divide the lands of the wealthy landowners. Though successful for a time, he was ultimately defeated and assassinated. (*p.* 688)

Emilio Aguinaldo Leader of the Filipino independence movement against Spain (1895–1898). He proclaimed the independence of the Philippines in 1899, but his movement was crushed and he was captured by the United States Army in 1901. (*p.* 685)

Empress Dowager Cixi Empress of China and mother of Emperor Guangxi. She put her son under house arrest, supported antiforeign movements, and resisted reforms of the Chinese government and armed forces. (*p.* 722)

encomienda A grant of authority over a population of Amerindians in the Spanish colonies. It provided the grant holder with a supply of cheap labor and periodic payments of goods by the Amerindians. It obliged the grant holder to Christianize the Amerindians. (*p.* 460)

English Civil War (1642–1649) A conflict over royal versus parliamentary rights, caused by King Charles I's arrest of his parliamentary critics and ending with his execution. Its outcome checked the growth of royal absolutism and, with the Glorious Revolution of 1688 and the English Bill of Rights of 1689, ensured that England would be a constitutional monarchy. (*p.* 443)

Enlightenment A philosophical movement in eighteenth-century Europe that fostered the belief that one could reform society by discovering rational laws that governed social behavior and were just as scientific as the laws of physics. (*pp.* 434, 586)

equites In ancient Italy, prosperous landowners second in wealth and status to the senatorial aristocracy. The Roman emperors allied with this group to counterbalance the influence of the old aristocracy and used the *equites* to staff the imperial civil service. (*p.* 149)

Estates General France's traditional national assembly with representatives of the three estates, or classes, in French society: the clergy, nobility, and commoners. The calling of the Estates General in 1789 led to the French Revolution. (*p.* 596)

Ethiopia East African highland nation lying east of the Nile River. (*p.* 242)

ethnic cleansing Effort to eradicate a people and its culture by means of mass killing and the destruction of historical buildings and cultural materials. Ethnic cleansing was used by both sides of the conflicts that accompanied the disintegration of Yugoslavia in the 1990s. (*p.* 846)

European Economic Community (Common Market) An organization promoting economic unity in Europe, formed in 1957 by consolidation of earlier, more limited, agreements. With the addition of many new nations it became the European Union (EU) in 1993. (*p.* 813)

Eva Duarte Perón Wife of Juan Perón and champion of the poor in Argentina. She was a gifted speaker and popular political leader who campaigned to improve the life of the urban poor by founding schools and hospitals and providing other social benefits. (*p.* 797)

evolution The biological theory that, over time, changes occurring in plants and animals, mainly as a result of natural selection and genetic mutation, result in new species. (*p.* 006)

extraterritoriality The right of foreign residents in a country to live under the laws of their native country and disregard the laws of the host country. In the nineteenth and early twentieth centuries, European and American nationals living in certain areas of Chinese and Ottoman cities were granted this right. (*p.* 618)

Faisal Arab prince, leader of the Arab Revolt in World War I. The British made him king of Iraq in 1921, and he reigned under British protection until 1933. (*p.* 735)

Fascist Party Italian political party created by Benito Mussolini during World War I. It emphasized aggressive nationalism and was Mussolini's instrument for the creation of a dictatorship in Italy from 1922 to 1943. (*p.* 758)

Ferdinand Magellan Portuguese navigator who led the Spanish expedition of 1519–1522 that was the first to sail around the world. (*p.* 406)

fief In medieval Europe, land granted in return for a sworn oath to provide specified military service. (*p.* 276)

First Temple A monumental sanctuary built in Jerusalem by King Solomon in the tenth century BCE to be the religious center for the Israelite god Yahweh. The Temple priesthood conducted sacrifices, received a tithe or percentage of agricultural revenues, and became economically and politically powerful. (*p.* 67)

Five-Year Plans Plans that Joseph Stalin introduced to industrialize the Soviet Union rapidly, beginning in 1928. They set goals for the output of steel, electricity, machinery, and most other products and were enforced by the police powers of the state. They succeeded in making the Soviet Union a major industrial power before World War II. (*p.* 752)

foragers People who support themselves by hunting, fishing, and gathering wild edible plants and insects. (*p.* 13)

Fourteen Points A peace program presented to the U.S. Congress by President Woodrow Wilson in January 1918. It called for the evacuation of German-occupied lands, the drawing of borders and the settling of territorial disputes by the self-determination of the affected populations, and the founding of an association of nations to preserve the peace and guarantee their territorial integrity. It was rejected by Germany, but it made Wilson the moral leader of the Allies in the last year of World War I. (*p.* 736)

Francisco "Pancho" Villa A popular leader during the Mexican Revolution. An outlaw in his youth, when the revolution started, he formed a cavalry army in the north of Mexico and fought for the rights of the landless in collaboration with Emiliano Zapata. He was assassinated in 1923. (*p.* 688)

Francisco Pizarro Spanish explorer who led the conquest of the Inka Empire of Peru in 1531–1533. (*p.* 414)

François Dominique Toussaint L'Ouverture Leader of the Haitian Revolution. He freed the slaves and gained effective independence for Haiti despite military interventions by the British and French. (*p.* 604)

Fujiwara Aristocratic family that dominated the Japanese imperial court between the ninth and twelfth centuries. (*p.* 309)

Funan An early complex society in Southeast Asia between the first and sixth centuries CE. Centered in the rich rice-growing region of southern Vietnam, it controlled the passage of trade across the Malaysian isthmus. (*p.* 188)

Gaozu The throne name of Liu Bang, one of the rebel leaders who brought down the Qin and founded the Han dynasty in 202 BCE. (*p.* 160)

gens de couleur Free men and women of color in Haiti. They sought greater political rights and later supported the Haitian Revolution. (*p.* 604)

gentry The class of landholding families in England below the aristocracy. (*p.* 436)

George Washington Military commander of the American Revolution. He was the first elected president of the United States (1789– 1799). (*p.* 592)

Getulio Vargas Dictator of Brazil from 1930 to 1945 and from 1951 to 1954. Defeated in the presidential election of 1930, he overthrew the government and created Estado Novo ("New State"), a dictatorship that emphasized industrialization and helped the urban poor but did little to alleviate the problems of the peasants. (*p.* 796)

Ghana First known kingdom in sub-Saharan West Africa between the sixth and thirteenth centuries CE. Also the modern West African country once known as the Gold Coast. (*p.* 255)

Giuseppe Garibaldi Italian nationalist and revolutionary who conquered Sicily and Naples and added them to a unified Italy in 1860. (*p.* 711)

global elite culture At the beginning of the twenty-first century, the attitudes and outlook of well-educated, prosperous, Western-oriented people around the world, largely expressed in European languages, especially English. (*p.* 886)

global popular culture Popular cultural practices and institutions that have been adopted internationally, such as music, the Internet, television, food, and fashion. (*p.* 885)

globalization The economic, political, and cultural integration and interaction of all parts of the world brought about by increasing trade, travel, and technology. (*p.* 878)

Gold Coast Region of the Atlantic coast of West Africa occupied by modern Ghana; named for its gold exports to Europe from the 1470s onward. (*p.* 403)

Golden Horde Mongol khanate founded by Chinngis Khan's grandson Batu. It was based in southern Russia and quickly adopted both the Turkic language and Islam. Also known as the Kipchak Horde. (*p.* 326)

Gothic cathedrals Large churches originating in twelfth-century France; built in an architectural style featuring pointed arches, tall vaults and spires, flying buttresses, and large stained-glass windows. (*p.* 354)

Grand Canal The 1,100-mile (1,771-kilometer) waterway linking the Yellow and the Yangzi Rivers. It was begun in the Han period and completed during the Sui Empire. (*p.* 294)

Great Ice Age Geological era that occurred between about 2 million and 11,000 years ago. (*p.* 007)

"great traditions" Historians' term for a literate, well-institutionalized complex of religious and social beliefs and practices adhered to by diverse societies over a broad geographical area. (*p.* 237)

Great Western Schism A division in the Latin (Western) Christian Church between 1378 and 1415, when rival claimants to the papacy existed in Rome and Avignon. (*p.* 361)

Great Zimbabwe City, now in ruins (in the modern African country of Zimbabwe), whose many stone structures were built between about 1250 and 1450, when it was a trading center and the capital of a large state. (*p.* 381)

guild In medieval Europe, an association of men (rarely women), such as merchants, artisans, or professors, who worked in a particular trade and banded together to promote their economic and political interests. Guilds were also important in other societies, such as the Ottoman and Safavid Empires. (*p.* 351)

Gujarat Region of western India famous for trade and manufacturing; the inhabitants are called Gujaratis. (*p.* 376)

gunpowder A mixture of saltpeter, sulfur, and charcoal, in various proportions. The formula, brought to China in the 400s or 500s, was first used to make fumigators to keep away insect pests and evil spirits. In later centuries it was used to make explosives and grenades and to propel cannonballs, shot, and bullets. (*p.* 303)

Guomindang Nationalist political party founded on democratic principles by Sun Yat-sen in 1912. After 1925, the party was headed by Chiang Kai-shek, who turned it into an increasingly authoritarian movement. (*p.* 742)

Gupta Empire A powerful Indian state based, like its Mauryan predecessor, on a capital at Pataliputra in the Ganges Valley. It controlled most of the Indian subcontinent through a combination of military force and its prestige as a center of sophisticated culture. (*p.* 180)

Habsburg A powerful European family that provided many Holy Roman Emperors, founded the Austrian (later Austro-Hungarian) Empire, and ruled sixteenth- and seventeenth-century Spain. (*p.* 440)

hadith A tradition relating the words or deeds of the Prophet Muhammad; next to the Quran, the most important basis for Islamic law. (*p.* 259)

Haile Selassie Emperor of Ethiopia (r. 1930–1974) and symbol of African independence. He fought the Italian invasion of his country in 1935 and regained his throne during World War II, when British forces expelled the Italians. He ruled Ethiopia as a traditional autocracy until he was overthrown in 1974. (*p.* 800)

Hammurabi Amorite ruler of Babylon (r. 1792–1750 BCE). He conquered many city-states in southern and northern Mesopotamia and is best known for a code of laws, inscribed on a black stone pillar, illustrating the principles to be used in legal cases. (*p.* 32)

Han A term used to designate (1) the ethnic Chinese people who originated in the Yellow River Valley and spread throughout regions of China suitable for agriculture and (2) the dynasty of emperors who ruled from 202 BCE to 220 CE. (*p.* 158)

Hanseatic League An economic and defensive alliance of the free towns in northern Germany, founded about 1241 and most powerful in the fourteenth century. (*p.* 350)

Harappa Site of one of the great cities of the Indus Valley civilization of the third millennium BCE. It was located on the northwest frontier of the zone of cultivation (in modern Pakistan). (*p.* 46)

Hatshepsut Queen of Egypt (r. 1473–1458 BCE). She dispatched a naval expedition to Punt (possibly northeast Sudan or Eritrea), the faraway source of myrrh. There is evidence of opposition to a woman as ruler, and after her death her name and image were frequently defaced. (*p.* 54)

Hausa An agricultural and trading people of central Sudan in West Africa. Aside from their brief incorporation into the Songhai Empire, the Hausa city-states remained autonomous until the Sokoto Caliphate conquered them in the early nineteenth century. (*p.* 499)

Hebrew Bible A collection of sacred books containing diverse materials concerning the origins, experiences, beliefs, and practices of the Israelites. Most of the extant text was compiled by members of the priestly class in the fifth century BCE and reflects the concerns and views of this group. (*p.* 64)

Hellenistic Age Historians' term for the era, usually dated 323–30 BCE, in which Greek culture spread across western Asia and northeastern Africa after the conquests of Alexander the Great. The period ended with the fall of the last major Hellenistic kingdom to Rome, but Greek cultural influence persisted until the spread of Islam in the seventh century CE. (*p.* 135)

Helsinki Accords Political and human rights agreement signed in Helsinki, Finland, by the Soviet Union and western European countries. (*p.* 818)

Henry Morton Stanley British American explorer of Africa, famous for his expeditions in search of Dr. David Livingstone. Stanley helped King Leopold II establish the Congo Free State. (*p.* 674)

Henry the Navigator Portuguese prince who promoted the study of navigation and directed voyages of exploration down the western coast of Africa in the fifteenth century. (*p.* 401)

Hernán Cortés Spanish explorer and conquistador who led the conquest of Aztec Mexico in 1519–1521 for Spain. (*p.* 413)

Herodotus Heir to the technique of *historia* ("investigation/research") developed by Greeks in the late Archaic period. He came from a Greek community in Anatolia and traveled extensively, collecting information in western Asia and the Mediterranean lands. He traced the antecedents and chronicled the wars between the Greek city-states and the Persian Empire, thus originating the Western tradition of historical writing. (*p.* 98)

Hidden Imam Last in a series of twelve descendants of Muhammad's son-in-law Ali, whom Shi'ites consider divinely appointed leaders of the Muslim community. In occlusion since roughly 873, he is expected to return as a messiah at the end of time. (*p.* 516)

hieroglyphics A system of writing in which pictorial symbols represented sounds, syllables, or concepts. It was used for official and monumental inscriptions in ancient Egypt. Because of the long period of study required to master this system, literacy in hieroglyphics was confined to a relatively small group of scribes and administrators. (*p.* 41)

Hinduism A general term for a wide variety of beliefs and ritual practices that have developed in the Indian subcontinent since antiquity. Hinduism has roots in ancient Vedic, Buddhist, and south Indian religious concepts and practices. It spread along the trade routes to Southeast Asia. (*p.* 175)

Hipólito Irigoyen Argentine politician, president of Argentina from 1916 to 1922 and 1928 to 1930. The first president elected by universal male suffrage, he began his presidency as a reformer but later became conservative. (*p.* 795)

Hiroshima City in Japan, the first to be destroyed by an atomic bomb, on August 6, 1945. The bombing hastened the end of World War II. (*p.* 767)

history The study of past events and changes in the development, transmission, and transformation of cultural practices. (*p.* 007)

Hittites A people from central Anatolia who established an empire in Anatolia and Syria in the Late Bronze Age. With wealth from the trade in metals and military power based on chariot forces, the Hittites vied with New Kingdom Egypt for control of Syria-Palestine before falling to unidentified attackers ca. 1200 BCE. (*p.* 52)

Holocaust Nazis' program during World War II to kill people they considered undesirable. Some 6 million Jews perished during the Holocaust, along with millions of Poles, Gypsies, Communists, Socialists, and others. (*p.* 771)

Holocene The geological era since the end of the Great Ice Age about 13,000 years ago. (*p.* 12)

Holy Roman Empire Loose federation of mostly German states and principalities, headed by an emperor elected by the princes. It lasted from 962 to 1806. (*pp.* 279, 440)

hominid The biological family that includes humans and human-like primates. (*p.* 006)

Homo erectus An extinct human species. It evolved in Africa about 1.8 million years ago. (*p.* 007)

Homo habilis The first human species (now extinct). It evolved in Africa about 2.3 million years ago. (*p.* 007)

Homo naledi A recently discovered early hominid with a puzzling mix of primitive and more advanced features. (*p.* 008)

Homo sapiens The current human species. It evolved in Africa sometime between 400,000 and 100,000 years ago. (*p.* 008)

hoplite A heavily armored Greek infantryman of the Archaic and Classical periods who fought in the close-packed phalanx formation. Hoplite armies—militias composed of middle- and upper-class citizens supplying their own equipment—were for centuries superior to all other military forces. (*p.* 122)

horse collar Harnessing method that increased the efficiency of horses by shifting the point of traction from the animal's neck to the shoulders; its adoption favors the spread of horse-drawn plows and vehicles. (*p.* 287)

House of Burgesses Elected assembly in colonial Virginia, created in 1618. (*p.* 468)

humanists (Renaissance) European scholars, writers, and teachers associated with the study of the humanities (grammar, rhetoric, poetry, history, languages, and moral philosophy), influential in the fifteenth century and later. (*p.* 357)

Hundred Years' War (1337–1453) Series of campaigns over control of the throne of France, involving English and French royal families and French noble families. (*p.* 362)

Ibn Battuta Moroccan Muslim scholar, the most widely traveled individual of his time. He wrote a detailed account of his visits to Islamic lands from China to Spain and the western Sudan. (*p.* 367)

Igor Stravinsky Influential modernist composer known for his experimentation and pulsing rhythms. (*p.* 784)

Il-khan A "secondary" or "peripheral" khan based in Persia. The Il-khans' khanate was founded by Hülegü, a grandson of Chinggis Khan, and was based at Tabriz in the Iranian province of Azerbaijan. It controlled much of Iran and Iraq. (*p.* 326)

indentured servant A migrant to British colonies in the Americas who paid for passage by agreeing to work for a set term ranging from four to seven years. (*p.* 468)

Indian Civil Service The elite professional class of officials who administered the government of British India. Originally composed exclusively of well-educated British men, it gradually added qualified Indians. (*p.* 680)

Indian National Congress A movement and political party founded in 1885 to demand greater Indian participation in government. Its membership was middle class, and its demands were modest until World War I. Led after 1920 by Mohandas K. Gandhi, it appealed increasingly to the poor, and it organized mass protests demanding self-government and independence. (*p.* 789)

Indian Ocean Maritime System In premodern times, a network of seaports, trade routes, and maritime culture linking countries on the rim of the Indian Ocean from Africa to Indonesia. (*p.* 230)

indulgence The forgiveness of the punishment due for past sins, granted by the Catholic Church authorities as a reward for a pious act. Martin Luther's protest against the sale of indulgences is often seen as touching off the Protestant Reformation. (*p.* 427)

Industrial Revolution The transformation of the economy, the environment, and living conditions, occurring first in England in the eighteenth century, that resulted from the use of steam engines, the mechanization of manufacturing in factories, and innovations in transportation and communication. (*p.* 567)

Inka Largest and most powerful Andean empire. Controlled the Pacific coast of South America from Ecuador to Chile from its capital of Cuzco. (*p.* 388)

investiture controversy Dispute between the popes and the Holy Roman Emperors over who held ultimate authority over bishops in imperial lands. (*p.* 279)

Iron Age Historians' term for the period during which iron was the primary metal for tools and weapons. The advent of iron technology began at different times in different parts of the world. (*p.* 51)

iron curtain Winston Churchill's term for the Cold War division between the Soviet-dominated East and the U.S.-dominated West. (*p.* 810)

Iroquois Confederacy An alliance of five northeastern Amerindian peoples (six after 1722) that made decisions on military and diplomatic issues through a council of representatives. Allied first with the Dutch and later with the English, the Confederacy dominated the area from western New England to the Great Lakes. (*p.* 470)

Islam Religion expounded by the Prophet Muhammad on the basis of his reception of divine revelations, which were collected after his death into the Quran. In the tradition of Judaism and Christianity, and sharing much of their lore, Islam calls on all people to recognize one creator god—Allah—who rewards or punishes believers after death according to how they led their lives. (*p.* 250)

Israel In antiquity, the land between the eastern shore of the Mediterranean and the Jordan River, occupied by the Israelites from the early second millennium BCE. The modern state of Israel was founded in 1948. (*p.* 64)

Jacobins Radical republicans during the French Revolution. They were led by Maximilien Robespierre from 1793 to 1794. (*p.* 598)

James Watt Scot who invented the condenser and other improvements that made the steam engine a practical source of power for industry and transportation. The watt, an electrical measurement, is named after him. (*p.* 568)

Janissaries Infantry, originally of slave origin, armed with firearms and constituting the elite of the Ottoman army from the fifteenth century until the corps was abolished in 1826. (*pp.* 508, 613)

Jawaharlal Nehru Indian statesman who succeeded Mohandas K. Gandhi as leader of the Indian National Congress. He negotiated the end of British colonial rule in India and became India's first prime minister (1947–1964). (*p.* 793)

Jesus A Jew from Galilee in northern Israel who sought to reform Jewish beliefs and practices. He was executed as a revolutionary by the Romans. Hailed as the Messiah and son of God by his followers, he became the central figure in Christianity, a belief system that developed in the centuries after his death. (*p.* 153)

joint-stock company A business, often backed by a government charter, that sold shares to individuals to raise money for its trading enterprises and to spread the risks (and profits) among many investors. (*p.* 436)

José Antonio Páez Venezuelan soldier who led Simón Bolívar's cavalry force. He became a successful general in the war and built a powerful political base. Unwilling to accept the constitutional authority of Bolívar's government in distant Bogotá, he declared Venezuela's independence from Gran Colombia in 1829. (*p.* 644)

José María Morelos Mexican priest and former student of Miguel Hidalgo y Costilla, he led the forces fighting for Mexican independence until he was captured and executed in 1815. (*p.* 639)

Joseph Brant Mohawk leader who supported the British during the American Revolution. (*p.* 592)

Joseph Stalin Bolshevik revolutionary, head of the Soviet Communist Party after 1924, and dictator of the Soviet Union from 1928 to 1953. He led the Soviet Union with an iron fist, using Five-Year Plans to increase industrial production and terror to crush all opposition. (*p.* 752)

Josiah Wedgwood English industrialist whose pottery works first produced fine-quality pottery by industrial methods. (*p.* 563)

Juan Perón President of Argentina (1946–1955, 1973–1974). As a military officer, he championed the rights of labor. Aided by his wife Eva Duarte Perón, he was elected president in 1946. He built up Argentinean industry, became very popular among the urban poor, but harmed the economy. (*p.* 797)

junk A very large flatbottom sailing ship produced in the Tang, Song, and Ming Empires, specially designed for long-distance commercial travel. (*p.* 303)

Kamakura Shogunate The first of Japan's decentralized military governments (1185–1333). (*p.* 310)

kamikaze The "divine wind," which the Japanese credited with blowing Mongol invaders away from their shores in 1281. (*p.* 341)

Kangxi Qing emperor (r. 1662–1722). He oversaw the greatest expansion of the Qing Empire. (*p.* 546)

Karl Marx German journalist and philosopher, founder of the Marxist branch of socialism. He is known for two books: *Manifesto of the Communist Party* (1848) and *Das Kapital* (Vols. I–III, 1867–1894). (*p.* 708)

karma In Indian tradition, the residue of deeds performed in past and present lives that adheres to a "spirit" and determines what form it will assume in its next life cycle. The doctrines of *karma* and reincarnation were used by the elite in ancient India to encourage people to accept their social position and do their duty. (*p.* 173)

keiretsu Alliances of corporations and banks that dominate the Japanese economy. (*p.* 841)

khipus System of knotted colored cords used by preliterate Andean peoples to transmit information. (*p.* 390)

Khubilai Khan Last of the Mongol Great Khans (r. 1260–1294) and founder of the Yuan Empire. (*p.* 333)

Kievan Russia State established at Kiev in Ukraine around 880 by Scandinavian adventurers asserting authority over a mostly Slavic farming population. (*p.* 269)

King Leopold II King of Belgium (r. 1865–1909). He was active in encouraging the exploration of Central Africa and became the ruler of the Congo Free State (to 1908). (*p.* 674)

KLM Royal Dutch Airlines Oldest major airline, operating since 1920 in Europe and connecting to the Dutch East Indies in 1929. (*p.* 784)

Korean War Conflict that began with North Korea's invasion of South Korea and that came to involve the United Nations (primarily the United States) allying with South Korea and the People's Republic of China allying with North Korea. (*p.* 816)

Koryo Korean kingdom founded in 918 and destroyed by a Mongol invasion in 1259. (*p.* 308)

Kush An Egyptian name for Nubia, the region alongside the Nile River south of Egypt, where an indigenous kingdom with its own distinctive institutions and cultural traditions arose beginning in the early second millennium BCE. (*p.* 94)

labor union An organization of workers in a particular industry or trade, created to defend the interests of members through strikes or negotiations with employers. (*p.* 708)

laissez faire The idea that government should refrain from interfering in economic affairs. The classic exposition of laissez-faire principles is Adam Smith's *Wealth of Nations* (1776). (*p.* 577)

lama In Tibetan Buddhism, a teacher. (*p.* 333)

Lázaro Cárdenas President of Mexico (1934–1940). He brought major changes to Mexican life by distributing millions of acres of land to the peasants, bringing representatives of workers and farmers into the inner circles of politics, and nationalizing the oil industry. (*p.* 795)

Le Corbusier Professional name of architect Charles-Éduard Jeanneret, who led a modernist movement away from surface decoration and toward form following function. (*p.* 787)

League of Nations International organization founded in 1919 to promote world peace and cooperation but greatly weakened by the refusal of the United States to join. It proved ineffectual in stopping aggression by Italy, Japan, and Germany in the 1930s, and it was superseded by the United Nations in 1945. (*p.* 738)

"legitimate" trade Exports from Africa in the nineteenth century that did not include the newly outlawed slave trade. (*p.* 678)

Li Shimin One of the founders of the Tang Empire and its second emperor (r. 626–649). He led the expansion of the empire into Central Asia. (*p.* 294)

liberalism A political ideology that emphasizes the civil rights of citizens, representative government, and the protection of private property. This ideology, derived from the Enlightenment, was especially popular among the property-owning middle classes of Europe and North America. (*p.* 711)

Library of Ashurbanipal A large collection of writings drawn from the ancient literary, religious, and scientific traditions of Mesopotamia. It was assembled by the seventh-century BCE Assyrian ruler Ashurbanipal. The many tablets unearthed by archaeologists constitute one of the most important sources of present-day knowledge of the long literary tradition of Mesopotamia. (*p.* 64)

Linear B A set of syllabic symbols, derived from the writing system of Minoan Crete, used in the Mycenaean palaces of the Late Bronze Age to write an early form of Greek. It was used primarily for palace records, and the surviving Linear B tablets provide substantial information about the economic organization of Mycenaean society and tantalizing clues about political, social, and religious institutions. (*p.* 59)

Little Ice Age A century-long period of cool climate that began in the 1590s. Its ill effects on agriculture in northern Europe were notable. (*p.* 437)

llama A hoofed animal indigenous to the Andes Mountains in South America. It was the only domesticated beast of burden in the Americas before the arrival of Europeans. It provided meat and wool. The use of llamas to transport goods made possible specialized production and trade among people living in different ecological zones and fostered the integration of these zones by Chavín and later Andean states. (*p.* 198)

loess A fine, light silt deposited by wind and water. It constitutes the fertile soil of the Yellow River Valley in northern China. (*p.* 82)

Long March The 6,000-mile flight of Chinese Communists from southeastern to northwestern China. The Communists, led by Mao Zedong, were pursued by the Chinese army under orders from Chiang Kai-shek. The 4,000 survivors of the march formed the nucleus of a revived Communist movement that defeated the Guomindang after World War II. (*p.* 761)

ma'at Egyptian term for the concept of divinely created and maintained order in the universe. The divine ruler was the earthly guarantor of this order. (*p.* 40)

Macartney mission The unsuccessful attempt by the British Empire to establish diplomatic relations with the Qing Empire. (*p.* 547)

Mahabharata A vast epic chronicling the events leading up to a cataclysmic battle between related kinship groups in early India. It includes the *Bhagavad-Gita*. (*p.* 180)

Mahayana Buddhism "Great Vehicle" branch of Buddhism followed in China, Japan, and Central Asia. The focus is on reverence for Buddha and for bodhisattvas, enlightened persons who have postponed nirvana to help others attain enlightenment. (*p.* 175)

Malacca Port city in the modern Southeast Asian country of Malaysia, founded about 1400 as a trading center on the Strait of Malacca. (*p.* 383)

Mali Empire created by indigenous Muslims in western Sudan of West Africa from the thirteenth to fifteenth century. It was famous for its role in the trans-Saharan gold trade. (*p.* 372)

mamluks Under the Islamic system of military slavery, Turkic military slaves formed an important part of the armed forces of the Abbasid Caliphate of the ninth and tenth centuries. Mamluks eventually founded their own state, ruling Egypt and Syria (1250–1517). (*p.* 254)

Manchu Federation of Northeast Asian peoples who founded the Qing Empire. (*p.* 533)

Mandate of Heaven Chinese religious and political ideology developed by the Zhou, according to which it was the prerogative of Heaven, the chief deity, to grant power to the ruler of China and to take away that power if the ruler failed to conduct himself justly and in the best interests of his subjects. (*p.* 86)

mandate system Allocation of former German colonies and Ottoman possessions to the victorious powers after World War I, to be administered under League of Nations supervision. (*p.* 743)

manor In medieval Europe, a large, self-sufficient landholding consisting of the lord's residence (manor house), outbuildings, peasant village, and surrounding land. (*p.* 775)

Mansa Kankan Musa Ruler of Mali (r. 1312–1337). His pilgrimage through Egypt to Mecca in 1324–1325 established the empire's reputation for wealth in the Mediterranean world. (*p.* 372)

mansabs In India, grants of land given in return for service by rulers of the Mughal Empire. (*p.* 519)

manumission A grant of legal freedom to an individual slave. (*p.* 489)

Mao Zedong Leader of the Chinese Communist Party (1927–1976). He led the Communists on the Long March (1934–1935) and rebuilt the Communist Party and Red Army during the Japanese occupation of China (1937–1945). After World War II, he led the Communists to victory over the Guomindang. He ordered the Cultural Revolution in 1966. (*p.* 761)

Margaret Sanger American nurse and author; pioneer in the movement for family planning; organized conferences and established birth control clinics. (*p.* 783)

Marie Curie Polish-born pioneer in the study of radiation and winner of Nobel Prizes for physics (1903) and chemistry (1911); first female professor at the Sorbonne. (*p.* 784)

maroon A slave who ran away from his or her master. Often a member of a community of runaway slaves in the West Indies and South America. (*p.* 490)

Marshall Plan U.S. program to support the reconstruction of western Europe after World War II. By 1961 more than $20 billion in economic aid had been dispersed. (*p.* 813)

mass deportation The forcible removal and relocation of large numbers of people or entire populations. The mass deportations practiced by the Assyrian and Persian Empires were meant as a terrifying warning of the consequences of rebellion. They also brought skilled and unskilled labor to the imperial center. (*p.* 63)

mass production The manufacture of many identical products by the division of labor into many small repetitive tasks. This method was introduced into the manufacture of pottery by Josiah Wedgwood and into the spinning of cotton thread by Richard Arkwright. (*p.* 563)

Mauryan Empire The first state to unify most of the Indian subcontinent. It was founded by Chandragupta Maurya in 324 BCE and survived until 184 BCE. From its capital at Pataliputra in the Ganges Valley it grew wealthy from taxes on agriculture, iron mining, and control of trade routes. (*p.* 178)

Max Planck German physicist who developed quantum theory and was awarded the Nobel Prize for physics in 1918. (*p.* 783)

Maximilien Robespierre Young provincial lawyer who led the most radical phases of the French Revolution. His execution ended the Reign of Terror. (*p.* 598)

Maya Mesoamerican civilization concentrated in Mexico's Yucatán Peninsula and in Guatemala and Honduras but never unified into a single empire. Major contributions were in mathematics, astronomy, and development of the calendar. (*p.* 201)

Mecca City in western Arabia; birthplace of the Prophet Muhammad and ritual center of the Islamic religion. (*p.* 249)

mechanization The application of machinery to manufacturing and other activities. Among the first processes to be mechanized were the spinning of cotton thread and the weaving of cloth in late-eighteenth- and early-nineteenth-century England. (*p.* 564)

medieval Literally "middle age," a term that historians of Europe use for the period around 500 to 1500, signifying its intermediate point between Greco-Roman antiquity and the Renaissance. (*p.* 269)

Medina City in western Arabia to which the Prophet Muhammad and his followers emigrated in 622 to escape persecution in Mecca. (*p.* 250)

megaliths Structures and complexes of very large stones constructed for ceremonial and religious purposes in Neolithic times. (*p.* 22)

Meiji Restoration The political program that followed the destruction of the Tokugawa Shogunate in 1868, in which a collection of young leaders set Japan on the path of centralization, industrialization, and imperialism. (*p.* 716)

Memphis The capital of Old Kingdom Egypt, near the head of the Nile Delta. Early rulers were interred in the nearby pyramids. (*p.* 41)

Menelik II Emperor of Ethiopia (r. 1889–1911). He enlarged Ethiopia to its present dimensions and defeated an Italian invasion at Adowa (1896). (*p.* 677)

mercantilism European government policies of the sixteenth, seventeenth, and eighteenth centuries designed to promote overseas trade between a country and its colonies and accumulate precious metals by requiring colonies to trade only with their motherland country. The British system was defined by the Navigation Acts, the French system by laws known as the *Exclusif*. (*p.* 577)

Meroë Capital of a flourishing kingdom in southern Nubia from the fourth century BCE to the fourth century CE. In this period Nubian culture shows more independence from Egypt and the influence of sub-Saharan Africa. (*p.* 95)

mestizo The term used by Spanish authorities to describe someone of mixed Amerindian and European descent. (*p.* 466)

Mexican Revolution A complicated series of revolts beginning in 1910 aimed at reducing social inequality and establishing constitutional government. A constitution was adopted in 1917. (*p.* 688)

Middle Passage The part of the Atlantic Circuit involving the transportation of enslaved Africans across the Atlantic to the Americas. (*p.* 491)

Miguel Hidalgo y Costilla Mexican priest who led the first stage of the Mexican independence war in 1810. He was captured and executed in 1811. (*p.* 639)

Mikhail Gorbachev Head of the Soviet Union from 1985 to 1991. His liberalization effort improved relations with the West, but he lost power after his reforms led to the collapse of communist governments in eastern Europe. (*p.* 845)

Ming Empire Empire based in China that Zhu Yuanzhang established after the overthrow of the Yuan Empire. The Ming emperor Yongle sponsored the building of the Forbidden City and the voyages of Zheng He. The later years of the Ming saw a slowdown in technological development and economic decline. (*pp.* 335, 442)

Minoan Prosperous civilization on the Aegean island of Crete in the second millennium BCE. The Minoans engaged in far-flung commerce around the Mediterranean and exerted powerful cultural influences on the early Greeks. (*p.* 57)

mita Andean labor system based on shared obligations to help kinsmen and work on behalf of rulers or religious organizations. (*p.* 212)

Moche Civilization of north coast of Peru (200–700 CE). An important Andean civilization that built extensive irrigation networks as well as impressive urban centers dominated by brick temples. (*p.* 212)

Moctezuma II Aztec emperor who died while in custody of the Spanish conquistador Hernán Cortés. (*p.* 413)

modernization The process of reforming political, military, economic, social, and cultural traditions in imitation of the early success of Western societies, often without regard for accommodating local traditions in non-Western societies. (*p.* 676)

Mohandas K. Gandhi Leader of the Indian independence movement and advocate of nonviolent resistance. After being educated as a lawyer in England, he returned to India and became leader of the Indian National Congress in 1920. He appealed to the poor, led nonviolent demonstrations against British colonial rule, and was jailed many times. Soon after independence he was assassinated for attempting to stop Hindu–Muslim rioting. (*p.* 791)

Mohenjo-Daro Largest of the cities of the Indus Valley civilization, centrally located in the extensive floodplain of the Indus River in contemporary Pakistan. (*p.* 46)

moksha The Hindu concept of the spirit's "liberation" from the endless cycle of rebirths. There are various avenues—such as physical discipline, meditation, and acts of devotion to the gods—by which the spirit can distance itself from desire for the things of this world and be merged with the divine force that animates the universe. (*p.* 173)

monasticism Living in a religious community apart from secular society and adhering to a rule stipulating chastity, obedience, and poverty. It was a prominent element of medieval Christianity and Buddhism. Monasteries were the primary centers of learning and literacy in medieval Europe. (*p.* 282)

Mongols A people of this name is mentioned as early as the records of the Tang Empire, living as nomads in northern Eurasia. After 1206 they established an enormous empire under Chinggis Khan, linking western and eastern Eurasia. (*p.* 319)

monotheism Belief in the existence of a single divine entity. Some scholars cite the devotion of the Egyptian pharaoh Akhenaten to Aten (sun-disk) and his suppression of traditional gods as the earliest instance. The Israelite worship of Yahweh developed into an exclusive belief in one god, and this concept passed into Christianity and Islam. (*p.* 68)

monsoon Seasonal winds in the Indian Ocean caused by the differences in temperature between the rapidly heating and cooling landmasses of Africa and Asia and the slowly changing ocean waters. These strong and predictable winds have long been ridden across the open sea by sailors, and the large amounts of rainfall that they deposit on parts of India, Southeast Asia, and China allow for the cultivation of several crops a year. (*pp.* 170, 368)

most-favored-nation status A clause in a commercial treaty that awards to any later signatories all the privileges previously granted to the original signatories. (*p.* 624)

movable type Type in which each individual character is cast on a separate piece of metal. It eventually replaced woodblock printing, allowing for the arrangement of individual letters and other characters on a page, rather than requiring the carving of entire pages at a time. Although China had an early form of moveable type in the eleventh century, Koreans invented durable, metal moveable type in the thirteenth century that may have influenced later print technology in China. (*p.* 303)

Mughal Empire Muslim state (1526–1858) exercising dominion over most of India in the sixteenth and seventeenth centuries before political fragmentation caused decline. (*p.* 519)

Muhammad Ali Leader of Egyptian modernization in the early nineteenth century. He ruled Egypt as an Ottoman governor but had imperial ambitions. His descendants ruled Egypt until overthrown in 1952. (*pp.* 580, 612)

Muhammad Ali Jinnah Indian Muslim politician who founded the state of Pakistan. A lawyer by training, he joined the All-India Muslim League in 1913. As leader of the League from the 1920s on, he negotiated with the British and the Indian National Congress for Muslim participation in Indian politics. From 1940 on, he led the movement for the independence of India's Muslims in a separate state of Pakistan, founded in 1947. (*p.* 794)

Muhammad Arab prophet (570–632 CE); founder of religion of Islam. (*p.* 249)

mulatto The term used in Spanish and Portuguese colonies to describe someone of mixed African and European descent. (*p.* 466)

mummy A body preserved by chemical processes or special natural circumstances, often in the belief that the deceased will need it again in the afterlife. (*p.* 44)

Muscovy Russian principality that emerged gradually during the era of Mongol domination. The Muscovite dynasty ruled without interruption from 1276 to 1598. (*p.* 522)

Muslim An adherent of the Islamic religion; a person who "submits" (in Arabic, *Islam* means "submission") to the will of God. (*p.* 250)

Mycenae Site of a fortified palace complex in southern Greece that controlled a Late Bronze Age kingdom. In Homer's epic poems, Mycenae was the base of King Agamemnon, who commanded the Greeks besieging Troy. Contemporary archaeologists call the complex Greek society of the second millennium BCE "Mycenaean." (*p.* 59)

Napoleon Bonaparte General who overthrew the French Directory in 1799 and became emperor of the French in 1804. Failed to defeat Great Britain and abdicated in 1814. Returned to power briefly in 1815 but was defeated and died in exile. (*p.* 600)

Nasir al-Din Tusi Persian mathematician and cosmologist whose academy near Tabriz provided the model for the movement of the planets that helped to inspire the Copernican model of the solar system. (*p.* 329)

nationalism A political ideology that stresses people's membership in a nation—a community defined by a common culture and history as well as by territory. In the late eighteenth and early nineteenth centuries, nationalism was a force for unity in western Europe. In the late nineteenth century it hastened the disintegration of the Austro-Hungarian and Ottoman Empires. In the twentieth century it provided the ideological foundation for scores of independent countries emerging from colonialism. (*p.* 710)

nawab A Muslim prince allied to British India; technically, a semiautonomous deputy of the Mughal emperor. (*pp.* 522, 679)

Nazis German political party led by Adolf Hitler, emphasizing nationalism, racism, and war. When Hitler became chancellor of Germany in 1933, the Nazis became the only legal party and an instrument of Hitler's absolute rule. The party's formal name was National Socialist German Workers' Party. (*p.* 758)

Neo-Assyrian Empire An empire extending from western Iran to Syria-Palestine, conquered by the Assyrians of northern Mesopotamia between the tenth and seventh centuries BCE. They used force and terror and exploited the wealth and labor of their subjects. They also preserved and continued the cultural and scientific developments of Mesopotamian civilization. (*p.* 61)

Neo-Babylonian kingdom Under the Chaldaeans (nomadic kinship groups that settled in southern Mesopotamia in the early first millennium BCE), Babylon again became a major political and cultural center in the seventh and sixth centuries BCE. After participating in the destruction of Assyrian power, the monarchs Nabopolassar and Nebuchadnezzar took over the southern portion of the Assyrian domains. (*p.* 78)

neo-Confucianism Term used to describe new approaches to understanding classic Confucian texts that became the basic ruling philosophy of China from the Song period to the twentieth century. (*p.* 303)

neoliberalism The term used in Latin America and other developing regions to describe free-market policies that include reducing tariff protection for local industries; the sale of public-sector industries, like national airlines and public utilities, to private investors or foreign corporations; and the reduction of social welfare policies and public-sector employment. (*p.* 839)

Neolithic The period of the Stone Age associated with the ancient Agricultural Revolution(s). (*p.* 11)

New Economic Policy Policy proclaimed by Vladimir Lenin in 1923 to encourage the revival of the Soviet economy by allowing small private enterprises. Joseph Stalin ended the NEP in 1928 and replaced it with a series of Five-Year Plans. (*p.* 738)

New France French colony in North America, with a capital in Quebec, founded 1608. Following military defeat, New France was ceded to the British in 1763. (*p.* 472)

new monarchies Historians' term for the monarchies in France, England, and Spain from 1450 to 1600. The centralization of royal power was increasing within more or less fixed territorial limits. (*p.* 362)

newly industrialized economies (NIEs) Rapidly growing, new industrial nations of the late twentieth century, including the Asian Tigers. (*p.* 843)

nomadism A way of life, forced by a scarcity of resources, in which groups of people continually migrate to find pastures and water. (*p.* 319)

nomads People without permanent, fixed places of residence, whose way of life and means of subsistence require them to periodically migrate, often with their herds of domesticated animals, to a familiar series of temporary seasonal encampments. (*p.* 96)

nonaligned nations Developing countries that announced their neutrality in the Cold War. (*p.* 827)

nongovernmental organizations (NGOs) Nonprofit international organizations devoted to investigating human rights abuses and providing humanitarian relief. Two NGOs won the Nobel Peace Prize in the 1990s: International Campaign to Ban Landmines (1997) and Doctors Without Borders (1999). (*p.* 874)

North Atlantic Treaty Organization (NATO) Organization formed in 1949 as a military alliance of western European and North American states against the Soviet Union and its east European allies. (*p.* 810)

Olmec The first Mesoamerican civilization. Between ca. 1200 and 400 BCE, the Olmec people of central Mexico created a vibrant civilization that included intensive agriculture, wide-ranging trade, ceremonial centers, and monumental construction. The Olmec had great cultural influence on later Mesoamerican societies, passing on artistic styles, religious imagery, sophisticated astronomical observation for the construction of calendars, and a ritual ball game. (*p.* 194)

Oman Arab state based in Musqat, the main port in the southeast region of the Arabian peninsula. Oman succeeded Portugal as a power in the western Indian Ocean in the eighteenth century. (*p.* 528)

Opium War War between Britain and the Qing Empire that was, in the British view, occasioned by the Qing government's refusal to permit the importation of opium into its territories. The victorious British imposed the one-sided Treaty of Nanking on China. (*p.* 624)

Organization of Petroleum Exporting Countries (OPEC) Organization formed in 1960 by oil-producing states to promote their collective interest in generating revenue from oil. (*p.* 830)

Osama bin Laden Saudi-born Muslim extremist who funded the al-Qaeda organization that was responsible for several terrorist attacks, including those on the World Trade Center and the Pentagon in 2001. (*p.* 867)

Otto von Bismarck Chancellor (prime minister) of Prussia from 1862 until 1871, when he became chancellor of Germany. A conservative nationalist, he led Prussia to victory against Austria (1866) and France (1870) and was responsible for the creation of the German Empire in 1871. (*p.* 712)

Ottoman Empire Islamic state founded by Osman in northwestern Anatolia around 1300. After the fall of the Byzantine Empire, the Ottoman Empire was based at Istanbul (formerly Constantinople) from 1453 to 1922. It encompassed lands in the Middle East, North Africa, the Caucasus, and eastern Europe. (*pp.* 332, 508)

Pablo Picasso Key figure in the movement of modern art away from realistic representation; a founder of cubism and surrealism. (*p.* 784)

Paleolithic The period of the Stone Age associated with the evolution of humans. (*p.* 11)

Panama Canal Ship canal cut across the isthmus of Panama by United States Army engineers; it opened in 1914. The canal greatly shortened the sea voyage between the east and west coasts of North America. The United States turned the canal over to Panama on January 1, 2000. (*p.* 690)

Pan-Slavism Movement among Russian intellectuals in the second half of the nineteenth century to identify culturally and politically with the Slavic peoples of eastern Europe. (*p.* 620)

papacy The central administration of the Roman Catholic Church, of which the pope is the head. (*pp.* 278, 426)

papyrus A reed that grows along the banks of the Nile River in Egypt. From it was produced a coarse, paper-like writing medium used by the Egyptians and many other peoples in the ancient Mediterranean and Middle East. (*p.* 42)

Parthians Iranian ruling dynasty between ca. 250 BCE and 226 CE. (*p.* 226)

patron–client relationship In ancient Rome, a fundamental social relationship in which the patron—a wealthy and powerful individual—provided legal and economic protection and assistance to clients, men of lesser status and means, and in return the clients supported the political careers and economic interests of their patron. (*p.* 145)

Paul A Jew from the Greek city of Tarsus in Anatolia, he initially persecuted the followers of Jesus but, after receiving a revelation on the road to Syrian Damascus, became a Christian. Taking advantage of his Hellenized background and Roman citizenship, he traveled throughout Syria-Palestine, Anatolia, and Greece, preaching the new religion and establishing churches. Finding his greatest success among pagans ("gentiles"), he began the process by which Christianity separated from Judaism. (*p.* 154)

pax romana Literally, "Roman peace," it connoted the stability and prosperity that Roman rule brought to the lands of the Roman Empire in the first two centuries CE. The movement of people and trade goods along Roman roads and safe seas allowed for the spread of cultural practices, technologies, and religious ideas. (*p.* 151)

Pearl Harbor Naval base in Hawaii attacked by Japanese aircraft on December 7, 1941. The sinking of much of the U.S. Pacific Fleet brought the United States into World War II. (*p.* 766)

Peloponnesian War A protracted (431–404 BCE) and costly conflict between the Athenian and Spartan alliance systems that convulsed most of the Greek world. The war was largely a consequence of Athenian imperialism. Possession of a naval empire allowed Athens to fight a war of attrition, but ultimately Sparta prevailed because of Athenian errors and Persian financial support. (*p.* 134)

perestroika Policy of "restructuring" that was the centerpiece of Mikhail Gorbachev's efforts to liberalize communism in the Soviet Union. (*p.* 845)

Pericles Aristocratic leader who guided the Athenian state through the transformation to full participatory democracy for all male citizens, supervised construction of the Acropolis, and pursued a policy of imperial expansion that led to the Peloponnesian War. He formulated a strategy of attrition but died from the plague early in the war. (*p.* 129)

Persepolis A complex of palaces, reception halls, and treasury buildings erected by the Persian kings Darius I and Xerxes in the Persian homeland. It is believed that the New Year's festival was celebrated here, as well as the coronations, weddings, and funerals of the Persian kings, who were buried in cliff-tombs nearby. (*p.* 118)

Persian Wars Conflicts between Greek city-states and the Persian Empire, ranging from the Ionian Revolt (499–494 BCE) through Darius's punitive expedition that failed at Marathon (490 BCE) and the defeat of Xerxes' massive invasion of Greece by the Spartan-led Hellenic League (480–479 BCE). This first major setback for Persian arms launched the Greeks into their period of greatest cultural productivity. Herodotus chronicled these events in the first "history" in the Western tradition. (*p.* 130)

personalist leaders Political leaders who rely on charisma and their ability to mobilize and direct the masses of citizens outside the authority of constitutions and laws. Nineteenth-century examples include José Antonio Páez of Venezuela and Andrew Jackson of the United States. Twentieth-century examples include Getulio Vargas of Brazil and Juan Perón of Argentina. (*p.* 642)

Peter the Great Russian tsar (r. 1689–1725). He enthusiastically introduced Western languages and technologies to the Russian elite, moving the capital from Moscow to the new city of St. Petersburg. (*p.* 525)

pharaoh The central figure in the ancient Egyptian state. Believed to be an earthly manifestation of the gods, he used his absolute power to maintain the safety and prosperity of Egypt. (*p.* 40)

Phoenicians Semitic-speaking Canaanites living on the coast of modern Lebanon and Syria in the first millennium BCE. From major cities such as Tyre and Sidon, Phoenician merchants and sailors explored the Mediterranean, engaged in widespread commerce, and founded Carthage and other colonies in the western Mediterranean. (*p.* 69)

pilgrimage Journey to a sacred shrine by Christians seeking to show their piety, fulfill vows, or gain absolution for sins. Other religions also have pilgrimage traditions, such as the Muslim pilgrimage to Mecca and the pilgrimages made by early Chinese Buddhists to India in search of sacred Buddhist writings. (*p.* 288)

Pilgrims English Protestant dissenters who established Plymouth Colony in Massachusetts in 1620 to seek religious freedom after having lived briefly in the Netherlands. (*p.* 469)

plantocracy In the West Indian colonies, the rich men who owned most of the slaves and most of the land, especially in the eighteenth century. (*p.* 485)

polis The Greek term for a city-state, an urban center and the agricultural territory under its control. It was the characteristic form of political organization in southern and central Greece in the Archaic and Classical periods. Of the hundreds of city-states in the Mediterranean and Black Sea regions settled by Greeks, some were oligarchic, others democratic, depending on the powers delegated to the Council and the Assembly. (*p.* 122)

positivism A philosophy developed by the French count of Saint Simon. Positivists believed that social and economic problems could be solved by the application of the scientific method, leading to continuous progress. Their ideas became popular in France and Latin America in the nineteenth century. (*p.* 577)

Potosí Located in Bolivia, one of the richest silver mining centers and most populous cities in colonial Spanish America. (*p.* 460)

Principate A term used to characterize Roman government in the first three centuries CE, based on the ambiguous title *princeps* ("first citizen") adopted by Augustus to conceal his military dictatorship. (*p.* 149)

printing press A mechanical device for transferring text or graphics from a woodblock or type to paper using ink. Presses using movable type first appeared in Europe in about 1450. (*p.* 358)

proletariat The class of industrial wage earners who possess neither capital nor the tools of production. They, therefore, must earn their living by selling their labor. (*p.* 577)

Protestant Reformation Religious reform movement within the Latin Christian Church beginning in 1519. It resulted in the "protesters" forming several new Christian denominations, including the Lutheran and Reformed Churches and the Church of England. (*p.* 428)

proxy wars During the Cold War, local or regional wars in which the superpowers armed, trained, and financed the combatants. (*p.* 836)

Ptolemies The Macedonian dynasty, descended from one of Alexander the Great's officers, that ruled Egypt for three centuries (323–30 BCE). From their magnificent capital at Alexandria on the Mediterranean coast, the Ptolemies largely took over the system created by Egyptian pharaohs to extract the wealth of the land, rewarding Greeks and Hellenized non-Greeks serving in the military and administration. (*p.* 135)

Puritans English Protestant dissenters who believed that God predestined souls to heaven or hell before birth. They founded Massachusetts Bay Colony in 1629. (*p.* 469)

pyramid A large, triangular stone monument, used in Egypt and Nubia as a burial place for the king. The largest pyramids, erected during the Old Kingdom near Memphis, reflect the Egyptian belief that the proper and spectacular burial of the divine ruler would guarantee the continued prosperity of the land. (*p.* 40)

Qin A people and state in the Wei River Valley of eastern China that conquered rival states and created the first Chinese empire (221–206 BCE). The Qin ruler, Shi Huangdi, standardized many features of Chinese society and ruthlessly marshaled subjects for military and construction projects, engendering hostility that led to the fall of his dynasty shortly after his death. The Qin framework was largely taken over by the succeeding Han dynasty. (*p.* 158)

Qing Empire Empire established in China by Manchus who overthrew the Ming Empire in 1644. At various times the Qing also controlled Manchuria, Mongolia, Turkestan, and Tibet. The last Qing emperor was overthrown in 1911. (*p.* 543)

Quran Book composed of divine revelations made to the Prophet Muhammad between around 610 and his death in 632; the sacred text of the religion of Islam. (*p.* 251)

railroads Networks of iron (later steel) rails on which steam (later electric or diesel) locomotives pulled long trains at high speeds. The first railroads were built in England in the 1830s. Their success caused a railroad-building boom throughout the world that lasted well into the twentieth century. (*p.* 698)

Rajputs Members of a mainly Hindu warrior caste from northwest India. The Mughal emperors drew most of their Hindu officials from this caste, and Akbar married a Rajput princess. (*p.* 521)

Ramesses II A long-lived ruler of New Kingdom Egypt (r. 1290–1224 BCE). He reached an accommodation with the Hittites of Anatolia after a standoff in battle at Kadesh in Syria. He built on a grand scale throughout Egypt. (*p.* 56)

Rashid al-Din Adviser to the Il-khan ruler Ghazan, who converted to Islam on Rashid's advice. (*p.* 327)

recaptives Africans rescued by Britain's Royal Navy from the illegal slave trade of the nineteenth century and restored to free status. (*p.* 678)

reconquest of Iberia Beginning in the eleventh century, military campaigns by various Iberian Christian states to recapture territory taken by Muslims. In 1492 the last Muslim ruler was defeated, and Spain and Portugal emerged as united kingdoms. (*p.* 363)

Renaissance (European) A period of intense artistic and intellectual activity, said to be a "rebirth" of Greco-Roman culture. Usually divided into an Italian Renaissance, from roughly the mid-fourteenth to mid-fifteenth century, and a Northern (trans-Alpine) Renaissance, from roughly the early fifteenth to early seventeenth century. (*pp.* 356, 426)

Republic The period from 507 to 31 BCE, during which Rome was largely governed by the aristocratic Roman Senate. (*p.* 144)

Revolutions of 1848 Democratic and nationalist revolutions that swept across Europe. The monarchy in France was overthrown. In Germany, Austria, Italy, and Hungary the revolutions failed. (*p.* 607)

Richard Arkwright English inventor and entrepreneur who became the wealthiest and most successful textile manufacturer of the early Industrial Revolution. He invented the water frame, a machine that, with minimal human supervision, could spin many strong cotton threads at once. (*p.* 565)

Romanization The process by which the Latin language and Roman culture became dominant in the western provinces. Indigenous peoples in the provinces often chose to Romanize because of the political and economic advantages that it brought, as well as the allure of Roman success. (*p.* 152)

Royal African Company A trading company chartered by the English government in 1672 to conduct its merchants' trade on the Atlantic coast of Africa. (*p.* 491)

sacrifice A gift given to a deity, often with the aim of creating a relationship, gaining favor, and obligating the god to provide some benefit to the sacrificer, sometimes in order to sustain the deity and thereby guarantee the continuing vitality of the natural world. (*p.* 124)

Saddam Hussein President of Iraq from 1979 until overthrown by an American-led invasion in 2003. Waged war on Iran from 1980 to 1988. His invasion of Kuwait in 1990 was repulsed in the Persian Gulf War in 1991. (*p.* 841)

Safavid Empire Iranian kingdom (1502–1722) established by Ismail Safavi, who declared Iran a Shi'ite state. (*p.* 515)

Sahel Belt south of the Sahara; literally "coastland" in Arabic. (*p.* 236)

Salvador Allende Socialist politician elected president of Chile in 1970 and overthrown by the military in 1973. He died during the military attack. (*p.* 837)

samurai Literally "those who serve," the hereditary military elite of the Tokugawa Shogunate. (*p.* 537)

Sandinistas Members of a leftist coalition that overthrew the Nicaraguan dictatorship of Anastasia Somoza in 1979 and attempted to install a socialist economy. The United States financed armed opposition by the Contras. The Sandinistas lost national elections in 1990. (*p.* 838)

Sargon of Akkad The first Mesopotamian ruler to gain control of multiple city-states, as the Semitic-speaking peoples began to dominate the region. (*p.* 32)

Sasanid Empire Iranian empire, established around 224, with a capital in Ctesiphon, Mesopotamia. The Sasanid emperors established Zoroastrianism as the state religion. Islamic Arab armies overthrew the empire around 651. (*p.* 246)

satrap The governor of a province in the Achaemenid Persian Empire, often a relative of the king. He was responsible for protection of the province and for forwarding tribute to the central administration. Satraps in outlying provinces enjoyed considerable autonomy. (*p.* 117)

savanna Tropical or subtropical grassland, either treeless or with occasional clumps of trees. Most extensive in sub-Saharan Africa but also present in South America. (*p.* 237)

Savorgnan de Brazza Franco-Italian explorer sent by the French government to claim part of equatorial Africa for France. Founded Brazzaville, capital of the French Congo, in 1880. (*p.* 675)

schism A formal split within a religious community. (*p.* 270)

scholasticism A philosophical and theological system, associated with Thomas Aquinas, devised to reconcile Aristotelian philosophy and Roman Catholic theology in the thirteenth century. (*p.* 356)

Scientific Revolution The intellectual movement in Europe, initially associated with planetary motion and other aspects of physics, that by the seventeenth century had laid the groundwork for modern science. (*p.* 432)

scribe In the governments of many ancient societies, a professional position reserved for men who had undergone the lengthy training required to be able to read and write using cuneiform, hieroglyphics, or other early, cumbersome writing systems. (*p.* 34)

Scythians Term used by the ancient Greeks for the nomadic peoples living on the steppe north of the Black and Caspian Seas. (*p.* 98)

seasoning An often difficult period of adjustment to new climates, disease environments, and work routines, such as that experienced by slaves newly arrived in the Americas. (*p.* 487)

Semitic Family of related languages long spoken across parts of western Asia and northern Africa. In antiquity these languages included Hebrew, Aramaic, and Phoenician. The most widespread modern member of the Semitic family is Arabic. (*p.* 30)

Senate A council whose members were the heads of wealthy, land-owning families. Originally an advisory body to the early kings, in the era of the Roman Republic the Senate effectively governed the Roman state and the growing empire. Under Senate leadership, Rome conquered an empire of unprecedented extent in the lands surrounding the Mediterranean Sea. (*p.* 144)

"separate spheres" Nineteenth-century idea in Western societies that men and women, especially of the middle class, should have clearly differentiated roles in society: women as wives, mothers, and homemakers; men as breadwinners and participants in business and politics. (*p.* 706)

sepoy An indigenous soldier in South Asia, especially in the service of the British. (*p.* 679)

Sepoy Rebellion The revolt of Indian soldiers in 1857 against certain practices that violated religious customs; also known as the Sepoy Mutiny. (*p.* 680)

Serbia The Ottoman province in the Balkans that rose up against Janissary control in the early 1800s. After World War II the central province of Yugoslavia. Serb leaders struggled to maintain dominance as the Yugoslav federation dissolved in the 1990s. (*p.* 613)

serf In medieval Europe, an agricultural laborer legally bound to a lord's property and obligated to perform set services for the lord. In Russia some serfs worked as artisans and in factories; serfdom was not abolished there until 1861. (*pp.* 275, 525)

shaft graves A term used for the burial sites of elite members of Mycenaean Greek society in the mid-second millennium BCE. At the bottom of deep shafts lined with stone slabs, the bodies were laid out along with gold and bronze jewelry, implements, weapons, and masks. (*p.* 59)

Shah Abbas I The fifth and most renowned ruler of the Safavid dynasty in Iran (r. 1587-1629). Abbas moved the royal capital to Isfahan in 1598. (*p.* 516)

shamanism The practice of identifying special individuals (shamans) who will interact with spirits for the benefit of the community. Characteristic of the Korean kingdoms of the early medieval period and of early societies of Central Asia. (*p.* 308)

Shang The dominant people in the earliest Chinese dynasty for which we have written records (ca. 1766-1045 BCE). (*p.* 83)

Shi Huangdi Founder of the short-lived Qin dynasty and creator of the Chinese Empire (r. 221-210 BCE). He is remembered for his ruthless conquests of rival states, standardization of practices, and forcible organization of labor for military and engineering tasks. His tomb, with its army of life-size terracotta soldiers, has been partially excavated. (*p.* 158)

Shi'ites Muslims belonging to the branch of Islam believing that God vests leadership of the community in a descendant of Muhammad's son-in-law Ali. Shi'ism is the state religion of Iran. (*pp.* 251, 515)

Siberia The extreme northeastern sector of Asia, including the Kamchatka Peninsula and the present Russian coast of the Arctic Ocean, the Bering Strait, and the Sea of Okhotsk. (*p.* 523)

Sigmund Freud Austrian psychiatrist, founder of psychoanalysis. He argued that psychological problems were caused by traumas, especially sexual experiences in early childhood, that were repressed in later life. His ideas caused considerable controversy among psychologists and in the general public. Although his views on repressed sexuality are no longer widely accepted, his psychoanalytic methods are still very influential. (*p.* 783)

Silk Road Caravan routes connecting China and the Middle East across Central Asia and Iran. (*p.* 226)

Sima Qian Chief astrologer for the Han dynasty emperor Wu. He composed a monumental history of China from its legendary origins to his own time and is regarded as the Chinese "father of history." (*pp.* 99, 161)

Simón Bolívar The most important military leader in the struggle for independence in South America. Born in Venezuela, he led military forces there and in Colombia, Ecuador, Peru, and Bolivia. (*p.* 637)

Slavophiles Russian intellectuals in the early nineteenth century who favored resisting western European influences and taking pride in the traditional peasant values and institutions of the Slavic people. (*p.* 620)

"small traditions" Historians' term for a localized, usually nonliterate, set of customs and beliefs adhered to by a single society, often in conjunction with a "great tradition." (*p.* 237)

socialism A political ideology that originated in Europe in the 1830s. Socialists advocated government protection of workers from exploitation by property owners and government ownership of industries. This ideology led to the founding of socialist or labor parties throughout Europe in the second half of the nineteenth century. (*p.* 708)

Socrates Athenian philosopher (ca. 470-399 BCE) who shifted the emphasis of philosophical investigation from questions of natural science to ethics and human behavior. He attracted young disciples from elite families but made enemies by revealing the ignorance and pretensions of others, actions that culminated in his trial and execution by the Athenian state. (*p.* 132)

Sokoto Caliphate A large Muslim state founded in 1809 in what is now northern Nigeria. (*p.* 673)

Solidarity Polish trade union created in 1980 to protest working conditions and political repression. It began the nationalist opposition to communist rule that led in 1989 to the fall of communism in eastern Europe. (*p.* 845)

Song Empire Empire in central and southern China (960-1126) while the Liao people controlled the north. Empire in southern China (1127-1279; the "Southern Song") while the Jin people controlled the north. Distinguished for its advances in technology, medicine, astronomy, and mathematics. (*p.* 300)

Songhai A people, language, kingdom, and empire in western Sudan in West Africa. At its height in the sixteenth century, the Muslim Songhai Empire stretched from the Atlantic to the land of the Hausa and was a major player in the trans-Saharan trade. (*p.* 499)

Spanish-American War War fought in 1898 to expand American imperial possessions. Treaty of Paris ending the conflict confirmed U.S. control of Guam, Puerto Rico, and the Philippines. (*p.* 687)

Srivijaya A state based on the Indonesian island of Sumatra between the seventh and eleventh centuries CE. It amassed wealth and power by a combination of selective adaptation of Indian technologies and concepts, control of the lucrative trade routes between India and China, and skillful showmanship and diplomacy in holding together a disparate realm of inland and coastal territories. (*p.* 188)

Stalingrad City in Russia, site of a Red Army victory over the German army in 1942–1943. The Battle of Stalingrad was the turning point in the war between Germany and the Soviet Union. Today Volgograd. (*p.* 765)

steam engine A machine that turns the energy released by burning fuel into motion. Thomas Newcomen built the first crude but workable steam engine in 1712. James Watt vastly improved his device in the 1760s and 1770s. Steam power was later applied to moving machinery in factories and to powering ships and locomotives. (*p.* 568)

steel A form of iron that is both durable and flexible. It was first mass-produced in the 1860s and quickly became the most widely used metal in construction, machinery, and railroad equipment. (*p.* 700)

steppe An ecological region of grass- and shrub-covered plains that is treeless and too arid for agriculture. (*p.* 237)

stirrup Device for securing a horseman's feet, enabling him to wield weapons more effectively. First evidence of the use of stirrups was among the Kushan people of northern Afghanistan in approximately the first century CE. (*p.* 230)

stock exchange A place where shares in a company or business enterprise are bought and sold. (*p.* 436)

Stone Age The historical period characterized by the production of tools from stone and other nonmetallic substances. (*p.* 11)

submarine telegraph cables Insulated copper cables laid along the bottom of a sea or ocean for telegraphic communication. The first short cable was laid across the English Channel in 1851; the first successful transatlantic cable was laid in 1866. (*p.* 699)

sub-Saharan Africa Portion of the African continent lying south of the Sahara. (*p.* 237)

Suez Canal Ship canal dug across the isthmus of Suez in Egypt, designed by Ferdinand de Lesseps. It opened to shipping in 1869 and shortened the sea voyage between Europe and Asia. Its strategic importance led to the British occupation of Egypt in 1882. (*p.* 676)

Suleiman the Magnificent The most illustrious sultan of the Ottoman Empire (r. 1520–1566); also known as Suleiman Kanuni, "The Lawgiver." He significantly expanded the empire in the Balkans and eastern Mediterranean. (*p.* 508)

Sumerians The people who dominated southern Mesopotamia through the end of the third millennium BCE. (*p.* 29)

Sun Yat-sen Chinese nationalist revolutionary, founder and leader of the Guomindang until his death. He attempted to create a liberal democratic political movement in China but was thwarted by military leaders. (*p.* 742)

Sunnis Muslims belonging to branch of Islam believing that the community should select its own leadership. The majority religion in most Islamic countries. (*p.* 252)

Swahili Bantu language with Arabic loanwords spoken in coastal regions of East Africa. (*p.* 528)

Swahili Coast East African shores of the Indian Ocean between the Horn of Africa and the Zambezi River; from the Arabic *sawahil*, meaning "shores." (*p.* 380)

Taiping Rebellion A Christian-inspired rural rebellion that threatened to topple the Qing Empire. (*p.* 626)

Tamil kingdoms The kingdoms of southern India, inhabited primarily by speakers of Dravidian languages, which developed in partial isolation, and somewhat differently, from the Arya north. They produced epics, poetry, and performance arts. Elements of Tamil religious beliefs were merged into the Hindu synthesis. (*p.* 180)

Tang Empire Empire unifying China and part of Central Asia, founded 618 and ended 907. The Tang emperors presided over a magnificent court at their capital, Chang'an. (*p.* 295)

Tanzimat Restructuring reforms by the nineteenth-century Ottoman rulers, intended to move civil law away from the control of religious elites and make the military and the bureaucracy more efficient. (*p.* 614)

tax farmer A system for collecting taxes and other state revenues from the population. Under this system, the state transfers the right of collection to private individuals or to groups of merchants called tax farmers in exchange for a guaranteed fee. Tax farmers accumulated great wealth since the taxes and charges they collected generally exceeded by two or three times the amount paid to the treasury. (*p.* 448)

Tecumseh Shawnee leader who attempted to organize an Amerindian confederacy to prevent the loss of additional territory to American settlers. He became an ally of the British in the War of 1812 and died in battle. (*p.* 648)

Tenochtitlan Capital of the Aztec Empire, located on an island in Lake Texcoco. Its population was about 125,000 on the eve of Spanish conquest. Mexico City was constructed on its ruins. (*p.* 386)

Teotihuacan A powerful city-state in central Mexico (100–750 CE). Its population was more than 125,000 at its peak in 450 CE. (*p.* 199)

terrorism Political belief that extreme and seemingly random violence will destabilize a government and permit the terrorists to gain political advantage. Though an old technique, terrorism gained prominence in the late twentieth century with the growth of worldwide mass media that, through their news coverage, amplified public fears of terrorist acts. (*p.* 866)

theater-state Historians' term for a state that acquires prestige and power by developing attractive cultural forms and staging elaborate public ceremonies (as well as redistributing valuable resources) to attract and bind subjects to the center. Examples include the Gupta Empire in India and Srivijaya in Southeast Asia. (*p.* 181)

Thebes Capital city of Egypt and home of the ruling dynasties during the Middle and New Kingdoms. Monarchs were buried across the river in the Valley of the Kings. (*p.* 41)

Theodore Herzl Austrian journalist and founder of the Zionist movement urging the creation of a Jewish national homeland in Palestine. (*p.* 735)

Theravada Buddhism "Way of the Elders" branch of Buddhism followed in Sri Lanka and much of Southeast Asia. Theravada remains close to the original principles set forth by the Buddha; it downplays the importance of gods and emphasizes austerity and the individual's search for enlightenment. (*p.* 175)

Third-Century Crisis Historians' term for the political, military, and economic turmoil that beset the Roman Empire during much of the third century CE: frequent changes of ruler, civil wars, barbarian invasions, decline of urban centers, and near destruction of long-distance commerce and the monetary economy. After 284 CE Diocletian restored order by making fundamental changes. (*p.* 156)

Third World Term applied to a group of developing countries who professed nonalignment during the Cold War. (*p.* 827)

Thomas Edison American inventor best known for inventing the electric light bulb, acoustic recording on wax cylinders, and motion pictures. (*p.* 701)

Thomas Malthus Eighteenth-century English intellectual who warned that population growth threatened future generations because, in his view, population growth would always outstrip increases in agricultural production. (*p.* 849)

three-field system A rotational system for agriculture in which two fields grow food crops and one lies fallow. It gradually replaced the two-field system in medieval Europe. (*p.* 346)

Tiananmen Square Site in Beijing where Chinese students and workers gathered to demand greater political openness in 1989. The demonstration was crushed by Chinese military with great loss of life. (*p.* 844)

Timbuktu City on the Niger River in the modern country of Mali. It was founded by the Tuareg as a seasonal camp sometime after 1000. As part of the Mali Empire, Timbuktu became a major terminus of the trans-Saharan trade and a center of Islamic learning. (*p.* 384)

Timur Member of a prominent family of the Mongols' Chagatai Khanate, Timur through conquest gained control over much of Central Asia and Iran. He consolidated the status of Sunni Islam as orthodox, and his descendants, the Timurids, maintained his empire for nearly a century and founded the Mughal Empire in India. (*p.* 327)

Tiwanaku Name of capital city and empire centered on the region near Lake Titicaca in modern Bolivia (500–1000 CE). (*p.* 215)

Tokugawa Shogunate The last of the three shogunates of Japan. (*p.* 539)

Toltecs Powerful postclassic state in central Mexico (900–1175 CE) that influenced much of Mesoamerica. Aztecs later claimed ties to this civilization. (*p.* 205)

trans-Saharan caravan routes Trading network linking North Africa with sub-Saharan Africa across the Sahara. (*p.* 234)

Treaty of Nanking The treaty that concluded the Opium War. It awarded Britain a large indemnity from the Qing Empire, denied the Qing government tariff control over some of its own borders, opened additional ports of residence to Britons, and ceded the island of Hong Kong to Britain. (*p.* 624)

Treaty of Versailles The treaty imposed on Germany by France, Great Britain, the United States, and other Allied Powers after World War I. It demanded that Germany dismantle its military and give up some lands to Poland. It was resented by many Germans. (*p.* 738)

treaty ports Cities opened to foreign residents as a result of the forced treaties between the Qing Empire and foreign signatories. In the treaty ports, foreigners enjoyed extraterritoriality. (*p.* 624)

tributary system A system in which, from the time of the Han Empire, countries in East and Southeast Asia not under the direct control of empires based in China nevertheless enrolled as tributary states, acknowledging the superiority of the emperors in China in exchange for trading rights or strategic alliances. (*p.* 295)

tribute system A system in which defeated peoples were forced to pay a tax in the form of goods and labor. This forced transfer of food, cloth, and other goods subsidized the development of large cities. An important component of the Aztec and Inka economies. (*p.* 388)

trireme Greek and Phoenician warship of the fifth and fourth centuries BCE. It was sleek and light, powered by 170 oars arranged in three vertical tiers. Manned by skilled sailors, it was capable of short bursts of speed and complex maneuvers. (*p.* 131)

tropical rain forest High-precipitation forest zones of the Americas, Africa, and Asia lying between the Tropic of Cancer and the Tropic of Capricorn. (*p.* 237)

tropics Equatorial region between the Tropic of Cancer and the Tropic of Capricorn. It is characterized by generally warm or hot temperatures year-round, though much variation exists due to altitude and other factors. Temperate zones north and south of the tropics generally have a winter season. (*p.* 367)

tsar (czar) From Latin *caesar*, this Russian title for a monarch was first used in reference to a Russian ruler by Ivan III (r. 1462–1505). (*pp.* 331, 523)

Tulip Period (1718–1730) Last years of the reign of Ottoman sultan Ahmed III, during which European styles and attitudes became briefly popular in Istanbul. (*p.* 515)

Tupac Amaru II Member of Inka aristocracy who led a rebellion against Spanish authorities in Peru in 1780–1781. He was captured and executed with his wife and other members of his family. (*p.* 475)

tyrant The term the Greeks used to describe someone who seized and held power in violation of the normal procedures and traditions of the community. Tyrants appeared in many Greek city-states in the seventh and sixth centuries BCE, often taking advantage of the disaffection of the emerging middle class and, by weakening the old elite, unwittingly contributing to the evolution of democracy. (*p.* 124)

ulama Muslim religious scholars. From the ninth century onward, the primary interpreters of Islamic law and the social core of Muslim urban societies. (*p.* 257)

Umayyad Caliphate First hereditary dynasty of Muslim caliphs (661–750). From their capital at Damascus, the Umayyads ruled an empire that extended from Spain to India. Overthrown by the Abbasid Caliphate. (*p.* 252)

umma The community of all Muslims. A major innovation against the background of seventh-century Arabia, where traditionally kinship rather than faith had determined membership in a community. (*p.* 251)

underdevelopment The condition experienced by economies that depend on colonial forms of production such as the export of raw materials and plantation crops with low wages and low investment in education. (*p.* 658)

United Nations International organization founded in 1945 to promote world peace and cooperation. It replaced the League of Nations. (*p.* 810)

Universal Declaration of Human Rights A 1948 United Nations covenant binding signatory nations to the observance of specified rights. (*p.* 873)

universities Degree-granting institutions of higher learning. Those that appeared in Latin Europe from about 1200 onward became the model of all modern universities. (*p.* 356)

Urdu A Persian-influenced literary form of Hindi written in Arabic characters and used as a literary language since the 1300s. (*p.* 384)

varna/jati Two categories of social identity of great importance in Indian history. *Varna* are the four major social divisions: the Brahmin priest class, the Kshatriya warrior/administrator class, the Vaishya merchant/farmer class, and the Shudra laborer class. Within the system of varna are many *jati*, regional groups of people who have a common occupational sphere and who marry, eat, and generally interact with other members of their group. (*p.* 172)

Vasco da Gama Portuguese explorer. In 1497–1498 he led the first naval expedition from Europe to sail to India, opening an important commercial sea route. (*p.* 403)

vassal In medieval Europe, a sworn supporter of a king or lord committed to rendering specified military service to that king or lord. (*p.* 276)

Vedas Early Indian sacred "knowledge"—the literal meaning of the term—long preserved and communicated orally by Brahmin priests and eventually written down. These religious texts, including the thousand poetic hymns to various deities contained in the *Rig Veda*, are our main source of information about the Vedic period (ca. 1500–500 BCE). (*p.* 170)

Versailles The huge palace built for French king Louis XIV south of Paris. The palace symbolized both French power and the triumph of royal authority over the French nobility. (*p.* 445)

Victorian Age The reign of Queen Victoria of Great Britain (r. 1837– 1901). The term is also used to describe late-nineteenth-century society, with its rigid moral standards and sharply differentiated roles for men and women and for middle-class and working-class people. (*p.* 705)

Vietnam War Conflict pitting North Vietnam and South Vietnam communist guerrillas against the South Vietnamese government, aided after 1961 by the United States. (*p.* 817)

Vladimir Lenin Leader of the Bolshevik (later Communist) Party. He lived in exile in Switzerland until 1917, then returned to Russia to lead the Bolsheviks to victory during the Russian Revolution and the civil war that followed. (*p.* 735)

Wari Andean civilization culturally linked to Tiwanaku, perhaps beginning as a colony of Tiwanaku. (*p.* 216)

Warsaw Pact The 1955 treaty binding the Soviet Union and countries of eastern Europe in an alliance against the North Atlantic Treaty Organization. (*p.* 810)

weapons of mass destruction Nuclear, chemical, and biological devices that are capable of injuring and killing large numbers of people. (*p.* 869)

Western Front A line of trenches and fortifications in World War I that stretched without a break from Switzerland to the North Sea. Scene of most of the fighting between Germany, on the one hand, and France and Britain, on the other. (*p.* 731)

Wilbur and Orville Wright American bicycle mechanics; the first to build and fly an airplane, at Kitty Hawk, North Carolina, on December 7, 1903. (*p.* 784)

witch-hunt The pursuit of people suspected of witchcraft, especially in northern Europe in the late sixteenth and seventeenth centuries. (*p.* 430)

Women's Rights Convention An 1848 gathering of women angered by their exclusion from an international antislavery meeting. They met at Seneca Falls, New York, to discuss women's rights. (*p.* 655)

Woodrow Wilson President of the United States (1913–1921) and the leading figure at the Paris Peace Conference of 1919. He was unable to persuade the U.S. Congress to ratify the Treaty of Versailles or join the League of Nations. (*p.* 736)

World Bank A specialized agency of the United Nations that makes loans to countries for economic development, trade promotion, and debt consolidation. Its formal name is the International Bank for Reconstruction and Development. (*p.* 811)

World Trade Organization (WTO) An international body established in 1995 to foster and bring order to international trade. (*p.* 879)

Xiongnu A confederation of nomadic peoples living beyond the northwest frontier of ancient China. Chinese rulers tried a variety of defenses and stratagems to ward off these "barbarians," as they called them, and finally succeeded in dispersing the Xiongnu in the first century CE. (*p.* 159)

Yamagata Aritomo One of the leaders of the Meiji Restoration. (*p.* 723)

yangban In Koryo and especially Choson Korea, a term for the "two orders," the civil and the military elite families who, by passing government examinations, dominated the Choson Korean bureaucracy and cultural life. (*p.* 541)

yin/yang In Chinese belief, complementary factors that help to maintain the equilibrium of the world. Yang is associated with masculine, light, and active qualities; yin with feminine, dark, and passive qualities. (*p.* 92)

Yongle The third emperor of the Ming Empire (r. 1403–1424). He sponsored the building of the Forbidden City, a huge encyclopedia project, the expeditions of Zheng He, and the reopening of China's borders to trade and travel. (*p.* 335)

Yuan Empire Empire created in China and Siberia by Khubilai Khan. (*p.* 321)

Yuan Shikai Chinese general and first president of the Chinese Republic (1912–1916). He stood in the way of the democratic movement led by Sun Yat-sen. (*p.* 742)

Zen The Japanese word for a branch of Mahayana Buddhism based on highly disciplined meditation. It is known in Sanskrit as *dhyana*, in Chinese as *Chan*, and in Korean as *Son*. (*p.* 303)

Zheng He An imperial eunuch and Muslim, entrusted by the Ming emperor Yongle with a series of state voyages that took his gigantic ships through the Indian Ocean, from Southeast Asia to Africa. (*pp.* 335, 395)

Zhou The people and dynasty that took over the dominant position in north China from the Shang and created the concept of the Mandate of Heaven to justify their rule. The Zhou era, particularly the vigorous early period (1045–771 BCE), was remembered in Chinese tradition as a time of prosperity and benevolent rule. (*p.* 85)

ziggurat A massive pyramidal stepped tower made of mud bricks. It is associated with religious complexes in ancient Mesopotamian cities, but its function is unknown. (*p.* 35)

Zoroastrianism A religion originating in ancient Iran that became the official religion of the Achaemenids. It centered on a single benevolent deity, Ahuramazda, who engaged in a struggle with demonic forces before prevailing and restoring a pristine world. It emphasized truth-telling, purity, and reverence for nature. (*p.* 118)

Zulu A people of modern South Africa whom King Shaka united in 1818. (*p.* 670)

Index

Document-Based Questions (DBQs)

INTRODUCTION

Think of a Document-Based Question (DBQ) as a mini-research paper, or a mini-investigation. In the words of the AP® World History course description book, a DBQ tests your ability "to develop and support an argument using historical source material as evidence."* It is a chance to show that you can interpret documents of all sorts (texts, charts, graphs, photos, and various types of images), question those sources, understand the backgrounds and motivations of their authors, and use the documents to support an argument. The DBQ is a test of your document-reading and analytical skills. In the national exam, the DBQ will focus on one of the history reasoning skills, which will vary with each test; the skills include Causation, Continuity and Change over Time, and Comparison.

These DBQs are designed to be used in conjunction with chapters in *The Earth and Its Peoples* and to give you practice with three of the most crucial and difficult skills: figuring out what exactly the question is asking you to do, writing an acceptable thesis statement, and analyzing documents to support your thesis. Please note that while the DBQ on the exam will only come from periods 3–6 (c. 1450 CE to present), some of these sample DBQs are from periods 1 and 2. Don't be concerned because the important thing is to practice the skills required. With that in mind, the time period of the DBQ shouldn't matter.

The DBQs in this section mirror the format of the AP® World History exam, with seven documents each. Each question is designed to be completed in 60 minutes or less; this time includes a 15-minute reading period.

When working with documents, try following these steps:

---

1. Study the prompt and make sure you know exactly what is being asked. It is a good idea to highlight important words.

---

2. Formulate a thesis that addresses all parts of the question. Before examining the documents, you should be able to identify an argument to be made in response to the question.

---

3. With the prompt in mind, determine the basic content of each document. How can information from the documents support the position you've articulated in your argument?

---

4. Support your thesis with evidence from all, or all but one, of the documents.

---

5. Develop your argument by showing relationships between the documents such as contradiction, corroboration, and/or qualification.

---

6. In your essay, be sure to
   - Provide a general context in which your argument takes place. This might include other topics than the focus of the prompt or, if the question is specific and not global, it might include addressing the prompt topic in other areas of the world.
   - Discuss the intended audience, purpose, historical context, and/or point of view of at least three documents. Who wrote the document? Who was the intended audience? What was the author trying to accomplish? Discussing this information for more than three documents can help add complexity to your argument.
   - Support your argument by using examples beyond those mentioned in or referred to in the documents.
   - Synthesizing your argument into an essay that connects to a broader perspective of events and relates it to a different historical period, a different course theme, or a different field of inquiry, such as government or art history, might add complexity to your essay.

---

* Course and Exam Description, AP® World History, Effective Fall 2017, p. 182. Available online at *www.apcentral.collegeboard.com.*

AP® is a trademark registered by the College Board, which is not affiliated with, and does not endorse, this product.

DBQ 1: The Environment and Ancient Societies (Chapter 1)

Question: Evaluate the extent to which environmental factors influenced ancient societies in Afro-Eurasia.

Document 1

Source: Paleolithic cave painting from Lascaux, southern France, ca. 18000 BCE.

Ruth Hofshi/Alamy Stock Photo

Document 2

Source: Paleolithic tools found in Czechoslovakia.

DEA/A. DAGLI ORTI/Getty Images

Document 3

Source: From the *Epic of Gilgamesh*, Mesopotamian heroic literature, ca. 1700 BCE.

You know the city Shurrupak, it stands on the banks of the Euphrates? That city grew old and the gods that were in it were old. There was Anu, lord of the firmament, their father, and warrior Enlil their counselor, Ninurta (god of irrigation and agriculture) the helper, and Ennugi watcher over canals; and with them also was Ea (god of water and the secret wisdom of sorcery and crafts).

Document 4

Source: Bronze dagger from the Shang dynasty, China, 12th–11th century BCE.

Document 5

Source: *Code of Hammurabi*, compilation of judgments of Mesopotamian legal rulings, ca. 1700 BCE.

53. If a man has neglected to strengthen his bank of the canal, has not strengthened his bank, a breach has opened out itself in his bank, and the waters have carried away the meadow, the man in whose bank the breach has been opened shall render back the grain which he has caused to be lost.

54. If he is not able to render back the grain, one shall give him and his goods for money, and the people of the meadow whose grain the water has carried away shall share it.

55. If a man has opened his runnel to water and has neglected it, and the field of his neighbor the waters have carried away, he shall pay grain like his neighbor.

56. If a man has opened the waters, and the plants of the field of his neighbor the waters have carried away, he shall pay ten *gur* of grain *per gan*.

Document 6

Source: Map of Nile Valley, 2575–1070 BCE.

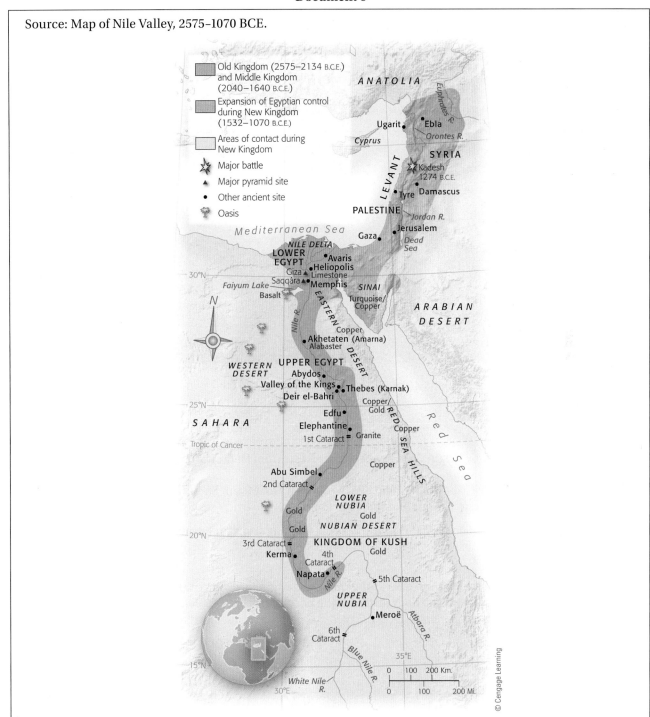

Document 7

Source: *Hymn to the Nile*, ca. 1350–1100 BCE.

Hail to thee, O Nile, that issues from the earth and comes to keep Egypt alive! Hidden in his form of appearance, a darkness by day, to whom minstrels have sung. He that waters the meadows which Recreated, in order to keep every kid alive. He that makes to drink the desert and the place distant from water: that is his dew coming down from heaven.

   When the Nile floods, offering is made to thee, oxen are sacrificed to thee, great oblations are made to thee, birds are fattened for thee, lions are hunted for thee in the desert, fire is provided for thee. And offering is made to every other god, as is done for the Nile, with prime incense, oxen, cattle, birds, and flame.

DBQ 2: Attitudes Toward Social and Economic Relationships (Chapters 2 and 4)

Question: Evaluate the extent to which social and economic relationships fostered change in the imperial societies of Afro-Eurasia in the classical age.

Document 1

Source: Wall relief from the palace of Sennacherib at Ninevah.

Document 2

Source: Hebrew prophet Amos, originally a herdsman, excerpts from Hebrew scriptures, ca. 750 BCE.

4:1 Listen to this message, you women who live like fat cows on Mount Samaria! You oppress the poor; you crush the needy. You say to your husbands, "Bring us more to drink so we can party!" . . .

5:11 Therefore, because you make the poor pay taxes on their crops and exact a grain tax from them, you will not live in the houses you built with chiseled stone, nor will you drink the wine from the fine vineyards you planted.

5:12 Certainly I am aware of your many rebellious acts and your numerous sins. You torment the innocent, you take bribes, and you deny justice to the needy at the city gate.

Document 3

Source: Unnamed Babylonian document, ca. 1000 BCE.

Narru, king of the gods, who created mankind.
And majestic Zulummar, who pinched of the clay for them,
And goddess Mami, the queen who fashioned them.
Gave twisted speech to the human race.
With lies, and not truth, they endowed them forever.
Solemnly the humans speak favorably of a rich man.
"He is kind," they say. "Riches should be his."
But they treat a poor man like a thief.
They have only bad to say of him and plot his murder.
Making him suffer every evil like a criminal.

Document 4

Source: King Darius of Persia, inscription at Behistun in modern-day Iran, ca. 500 BCE.

King Darius says: On this account [the god] Ahuramazda brought me help, and all the other gods, all that there are, because I was not wicked, nor was I a liar, nor was I a tyrant, neither I nor any of my family. I have ruled according to righteousness. Neither to the weak nor to the powerful did I do wrong. Whosoever helped my house, him I favored; he who was hostile, him I destroyed.

Document 5

Source: Vase painting depicting servant women at an Athenian fountain, ca. 520 BCE.

Document 6

Source: Xenophon, an Athenian historian and student of Socrates, ca. 400 BCE.

Why, what knowledge could she have had, Socrates, when I took her for my wife? She was not yet fifteen years old when she came to me, and up to that time she had lived in leading-strings, seeing, hearing and saying as little as possible. If when she came she knew no more than how, when given wool, to turn out a cloak, and had seen only how the spinning is given out to the maids, is not that as much as could be expected?

Document 7

Source: Plautus, a Roman playwright, from his play *Pseudolus*, Act I, Sc. 2, ca. 200 BCE.

Get out, come, out with you, you rascals; kept at a loss, and bought at a loss. Not one of you dreams minding your business, or being a bit of use to me, unless I carry on thus! [He strikes his whip around on all of them.] Never did I see men more like asses than you! Why, your ribs are hardened with the stripes. If one flogs you, he hurts himself the most: [Aside.] Regular whipping posts are they all, and all they do is to pilfer, purloin, prig, plunder, drink, eat, and abscond! Oh! they look decent enough; but they're cheats in their conduct.

DBQ 3: The Role of Women, 600 BCE to 600 CE (Chapters 4 and 5)

Question: Evaluate the impact of attitudes concerning the status of women on social development in the classical age.

Document 1

Source: Passage from *The Laws of Manu*, the most important law book of Hinduism, first century BCE.

In childhood a female must be subject to her father, in youth to her husband; and when her lord is dead, to her sons; a woman must never be independent. Though destitute of virtue, or seeking pleasure (elsewhere), or devoid of good qualities, (yet) a husband must be constantly worshipped as a god by a faithful wife. A virtuous wife who after the death of the husband constantly remains chaste, reaches heaven, though she have no son, just like those chaste men.

Document 2

Source: "Sumangala's Mother," from the *Therigatha*, a collection of songs by Buddhist nuns, 600 BCE.

A woman set free! How free I am, how wonderfully free, from kitchen drudgery. Free from the harsh grip of hunger, and from empty cooking pots, free too of that unscrupulous man, the weaver of sunshades. Calm now, and serene I am, all lust and hatred purged. To the shade of the spreading trees I go and contemplate my happiness.

Document 3

Source: An account of women demonstrating against the Oppian law, from Livy, a Roman historian, 195 BCE.

The law said that no woman might own more than half an ounce of gold nor wear a multicolored dress nor ride in a carriage in the city or in a town within a mile of it, unless there was a religious festival. The tribunes, Marcus and Publius Junius Brutus, were in favor of the Oppian law and said that they would not allow its repeal. Many noble men came forward hoping to persuade or dissuade them; a crowd of men, both supporters and opponents, filled the Capitoline Hill. The matrons, whom neither counsel, nor shame, nor their husbands' orders could keep at home, blockaded every street in the city and every entrance to the Forum. As the men came down to the Forum, the matrons besought them to let them, too, have back the luxuries they enjoyed before, giving their reason that the republic was thriving and that everyone's private wealth was increasing every day. This crowd of women was growing daily, for now they were even gathering from the towns and villages. Twenty years after it was passed, the law was repealed.

Document 4

Source: Speech attributed to Emperor Augustus in Rome, 9 CE.

For is there anything better than a wife who is chaste, domestic, a good house-keeper, a rearer of children; one to gladden you in health, to tend you in sickness; to be your partner in good fortune, to console you in misfortune; to restrain the mad passion of youth, and to temper the unseasonable harshness of old age?

Document 5

Source: Passage from *Admonitions for Women*, by Ban Zhao, 100 CE.

Let a woman retire late to bed, but rise early to her duties; let her not dread tasks by day or by night. Let her not refuse to perform domestic duties whether easy or difficult. That which must be done, let her finish completely, tidily, and systematically. [When a woman follows such rules as these] then she may be said to be industrious.

   Let a woman be composed in demeanor and upright in bearing in the service of her husband.

   Let her live in purity and quietness [of spirit] and keep watch over herself. Let her not love gossip and silly laughter. Let her cleanse, purify, and arrange in order the wine and the food for the offerings to the ancestors. [Observing such principles as these] is what it means to continue the ancestral rites.

Document 6

Source: Detail of a painting from Han China, 100 CE.

Document 7

Source: "The Advantages of Spartan Education and Marriage Customs," by Plutarch, a Greek historian, 75 CE.

Rather it was that Lycurgus took particular care about the women as well as the men. He made the young women exercise their bodies by running and wrestling and throwing the discus and the javelin, so that their offspring would have a sound start by taking root in sound bodies and grow stronger, and the women themselves would be able to use their strength to withstand childbearing and wrestle with labour pains. He freed them from softness and sitting in the shade and all female habits.

DBQ 4: Empire and Trade (Chapters 5 and 6)

Question: Evaluate the extent to which trade affected the development of society in Eurasia in the classical age.

Document 1

Source: Description of Arabia from *Geography*, Book XVI, Chap. iv, by Strabo, a scholar in the Roman republic, ca. 20 CE.

The aromatic country, as I have before said, is divided into four parts. Of aromatics, the frankincense and myrrh are said to be the produce of trees, but cassia the growth of bushes; yet some writers say, that the greater part (of the cassia) is brought from India, and that the best frankincense is that from Persia. . . . Some merchandise is altogether imported into the country, others are not altogether imports, especially as some articles are native products, as gold and silver, and many of the aromatics; but brass and iron, purple garments, styrax, saffron, and costus (white cinnamon), pieces of sculpture, paintings, statues, are not to be procured in the country.

Document 2

Source: Asian trade routes during the Han Empire.

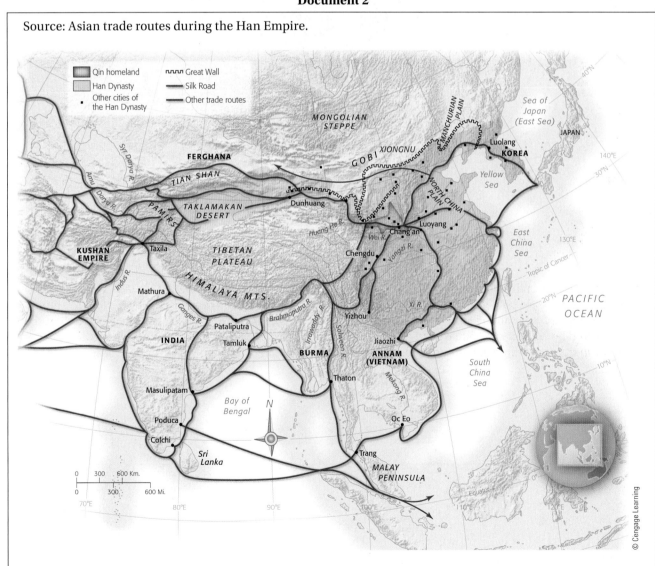

Document 3

Source: Passage on Roman trade with India, from *Natural History*, by Roman scholar Pliny the Elder, 77 CE.

It is appropriate to explain the entire journey from Egypt now that reliable knowledge of it is available for the first time. It is a worthy subject because in no year does India draw off less than fifty million coins from our empire, sending back merchandise that is sold to us at one hundred times its original price. The most advantageous route for those intent on reaching India is to set out from Ocelis. If the west wind is blowing, sailing time is forty days to the first trading station in India.

Document 4

Source: Sculpture of the Buddha, from Gandhara (ancient Afghanistan), second or third century CE.
Seated Buddha in meditation, Greco-Buddhist style, 1st-4th century (bronze), Pakistani School/Lahore Museum, Lahore, Pakistan/Giraudon/The Bridgeman Art Library

Document 5

Source: Indian Ocean sailing itinerary of unknown Greco-Egyptian merchant, first century CE.

Inland from the place and to the east, is the city called Ozene in India. From this place are brought down all things needed for the welfare of the country about Barygaza, and many things for our trade: agate and carnelian, Indian muslins.

There are imported into this market-town, wine, Italian preferred, also Laodicean and Arabian; copper, tin, and lead; coral and topaz; thin clothing and inferior sorts of all kinds, gold and silver coin, on which there is a profit when exchanged for the money of the country. And for the King there are brought into those places very costly vessels of silver, singing boys, beautiful maidens for the harem, fine wines, thin clothing of the finest weaves, and the choicest ointments. There are exported from these places spices, ivory, agate and carnelian, cotton cloth of all kinds, silk cloth.

Document 6

Source: Description of traveling back from India after searching for Buddhist scriptures to take back to China, by the Chinese Buddhist monk Faxian, fifth century CE.

Having obtained the Buddhist scriptures in Sanskrit, Faxian took passage in a large merchant ship, on which there were more than 200 men, and to which was attached by a rope a smaller vessel, as a provision against damage or injury to the large one from the perils of the navigation. After more than ninety days, they arrived at a country called Java-dvipa, where Hinduism is flourishing, while Buddhism is not worth speaking of. After staying there for five months, Faxian again embarked in another large merchant ship, which also had on board more than 200 men.

Document 7

Source: Chinese ceramic figure of Iranian rider on the Silk Road, found in Tang Empire tomb.

DBQ 5: Spread of Islam (Chapter 9)

Question: Evaluate the extent of the impact of Islam's spread from its origins to 1450 CE.

Document 1

Source: Early expansion of Muslim rule.

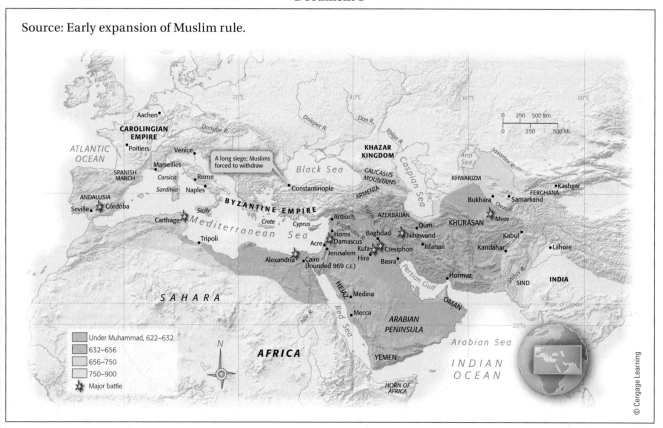

Document 2

Source: Form for Syrian Christians to accept for peace, attributed to Umar, second caliph following the Prophet Muhammad, ca. 637.

This is a writing to Umar from the Christians of *such and such a city*. We will not display the cross upon our churches or display our crosses or our sacred books in the streets of the Muslim or in their marketplaces; that we will strike the clappers in our churches lightly; that we will not recite our services in a loud voice when a Muslim is present; that we will not carry palm-branches or our images in procession in the streets; that at the burial of the dead we will not chant loudly or carry lighted candles in the streets of the Muslims or their marketplaces; that we will not take any slaves who have already been in the possession of Muslims or into their houses; and that we will not strike any Muslim. All this we promise to observe, on behalf of ourselves and our co-religionists, and receive protection from you in exchange; and if we violate any of the conditions of this agreement, then we forfeit your protection and you are at liberty to treat us as enemies and rebels.

Document 3

Source: Tarik, a Muslim leader who led the conquest of Spain, addressing his troops, 711.

The Commander of True Believers, Alwalid, son of Abdalmelik, has chosen you for this attack from among all his Arab warriors; and he promises that you shall become his comrades and shall hold the rank of kings in this country. Such is his confidence in your intrepidity. The one fruit which he desires to obtain from your bravery is that the word of God shall be exalted in this country, and that the true religion shall be established here. The spoils will belong to yourselves.

Document 4

Source: *Travels in Asia and Africa*, by Ibn Battuta, 1325–1354.

I arrived at length at Cairo, mother of cities and seat of Pharaoh the tyrant, mistress of broad regions and fruitful lands, boundless in multitude of buildings, peerless in beauty and splendor, the meeting-place of comer and goer, the halting-place of feeble and mighty, whose throngs surge as the waves of the sea, and can scarce be contained in her for all her size and capacity. It is said that in Cairo there are twelve thousand water-carriers who transport water on camels, and thirty thousand hirers of mules and donkeys, and that on the Nile there are thirty-six thousand boats belonging to the Sultan and his subjects which sail upstream to Upper Egypt and downstream to Alexandria and Damietta, laden with goods and profitable merchandise of all kinds.

Document 5

Source: A report of the Battle of Tours, from the *Chronicle of St. Denis*, 732.

The Muslims planned to go to Tours to destroy the Church of St. Martin, the city, and the whole country. Then came against them the glorious Prince Charles, at the head of his whole force. He drew up his host, and he fought as fiercely as the hungry wolf falls upon the stag. By the grace of Our Lord, he wrought a great slaughter upon the enemies of Christian faith, so that—as history bears witness—he slew in that battle 300,000 men, likewise their king by name Abderrahman.

Document 6

Source: Map of the western Sudan drawn by a Jewish geographer showing a North African merchant approaching Mansa Kankan Musa, the Muslim ruler of Mali, 1375.

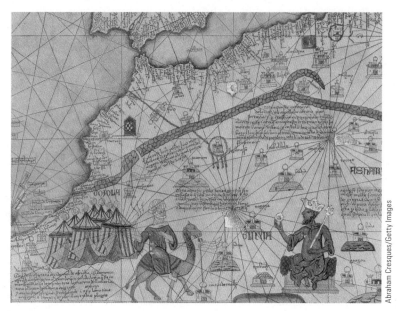

Abraham Cresques/Getty Images

Document 7

Source: Firuz Shah, Muslim sultan of Delhi in India, autobiographical account prepared toward the end of his life, ca. 1380.

The Hindus and idol-worshipers had agreed to pay the money for toleration, and had consented to the poll tax, in return for which they and their families enjoyed security. These people now erected new idol temples in the city and the environs in opposition to the Law of the Prophet which declares that such temples are not to be tolerated. Under Divine guidance I destroyed these edifices, and I killed those leaders of infidelity who seduced others into error, and the lower orders I subjected to stripes and chastisement, until this abuse was entirely abolished.

DBQ 6: Transformations in the Americas and Africa (Chapters 15, 17, and 18)

Question: Evaluate the extent to which the arrival of Europeans led to social transformation of the Americas and Africa from 1492 to 1750.

Document 1

Source: Letter to King Charles V, from Hernán Cortés, leader of the Spanish expedition to conquer the Aztec Empire, 1521.

This great city of Tenochtitlán is built on the salt lake. It has four approaches by means of artificial causeways. The city is as large as Seville or Córdoba. Its streets are very broad and straight. There are bridges, very large, strong, and well-constructed, so that, over many, ten horsemen can ride abreast. The city has many squares where markets are held. There is one square, twice as large as that of Salamanca, all surrounded by arcades, where there are daily more than sixty thousand souls, buying and selling in the service and manners of its people, their fashion of living was almost the same as in Spain, with just as much harmony and order; and considering that these people were barbarous, so cut off from the knowledge of God and other civilized peoples, it is admirable to see to what they attained in every respect.

Document 2

Source: Passage from A *Short Account of the Destruction of the Indies*, written for Charles I of Spain, by Bartolome de las Casas, a Spanish Dominican friar, 1542.

When the Spanish first journeyed there, the indigenous population of the island of Hispaniola stood at some three million; today only two hundred survive. The island of Cuba . . . is now to all intents and purposes uninhabited, and two other large, beautiful and fertile islands, Puerto Rico and Jamaica, have been similarly devastated. Not a living soul remains today on any of the islands of the Bahamas. . . . The native population, which once numbered some five hundred thousand, was wiped out by forcible expatriation to the island of Hispaniola, a policy adopted by the Spaniards in an endeavor to make up losses among the indigenous population of that island. One God-fearing individual was moved to mount an expedition to seek out those who had escaped the Spanish trawl and were still living in the Bahamas and to save their souls by converting them to Christianity, but, by the end of a search lasting three whole years, they had found only the eleven survivors I saw with my own eyes.

Document 3

Source: Illustration by Native American artist showing natives of central Mexico suffering from smallpox, ca. mid-1500s.

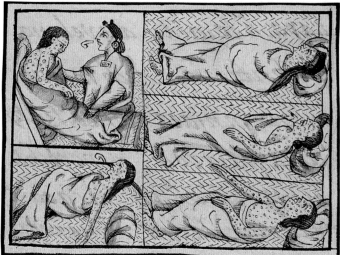

Science Source

Document 4

Source: Letter to King João III of Portugal, from King Afonso of Kongo, a convert to Christianity, 1526.

[I]n our kingdoms there is another great inconvenience which is of little service to God, and this is that many of our people, out of great desire for the wares and things of your kingdoms, which are brought here by your people and in order to satisfy their disordered appetite, seize many of our people, freed and exempt men. And many times noblemen and the sons of noblemen, and our relatives are stolen, and they take them to be sold to the white men who are in our kingdoms and take them hidden or by night, so that they are not recognized. And as soon as they are sold to the white men, they are immediately ironed and branded with fire. And when they are carried off to be embarked, if they are caught by our guards, the whites allege that they have bought them and cannot say from whom, so that it is our duty to do justice and to restore to the free their freedom.

Document 5

Source: *Compendium and Description of the West Indies*, by Antonio Vázquez de Espinosa, a Spanish priest, ca. 1625.

The ore at Potosí silver mine is very rich black flint, and the excavation so extensive that more than 3,000 Indians worked away hard with picks and hammers, breaking up that flint ore; and when they have filled their little sacks, the poor fellows, loaded down with ore, climb up those ladders or rigging, some like masts and others like cables, and so trying and distressing that even an empty-handed man can hardly get up them.

So huge is the wealth that has been taken out of this range since the year 1545, when it was discovered, up to the present year of 1628, that merely from the registered mines, according to most of the accounts in the Spanish royal records, 326 million silver coins have been taken out.

Source: Transatlantic slave trade from Africa.

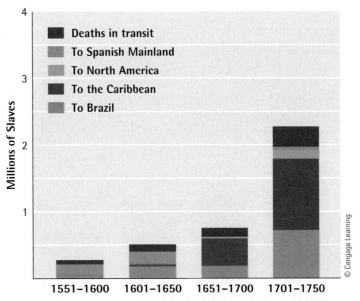

Deaths in transit
To Spanish Mainland
To North America
To the Caribbean
To Brazil

Millions of Slaves

1551–1600 1601–1650 1651–1700 1701–1750

© Cengage Learning

Source: Data from David Eltis, "The Volume and Structure of the Transatlantic Slave Trade: A Reassessment," *William and Mary Quarterly*, 3rd Series, 58 (2001), tables II and III.

Document 7

Source: A description of Quito, Ecuador from *A Voyage to South America*, by Jorge Juan and Antonio de Ulloa, ca. 1735.

The society in Quito, Ecuador is divided into four classes: Spaniards or Whites, Mestizos, Indians or Natives, and Negroes.

Among these classes the Spaniards, as is natural to think, are the most eminent for riches, rank, and power, [but] it must at the same time be owned, however melancholy the truth may appear, they are in proportion the most poor, miserable and distressed; for they refuse to apply themselves to any mechanic business, considering it as a disgrace to that quality they so highly value themselves upon, which consists in not being black, brown, or of a copper color. The Mestizos, whose pride is regulated by prudence, readily apply themselves to arts and trades, but choose those of the greatest repute, as painting, sculpture, and the like, leaving the meaner sort to the Indians.

DBQ 7: Decline of Urban Areas (Chapters 10, 12, and 13)

Question: Evaluate the extent to which outside forces affected the decline of urban areas from 600 to 1450.

Document 1

Source: Account of Viking raids, written by palace officials of French King Louis the Pious, ca. ninth century.

The Danish pirates having made a long sea-voyage (for they had sailed between Spain and Africa) entered the Rhone, where they pillaged many cities and monasteries and established themselves on the island called Camargue. . . . They devastated everything before them as far as the city of Valence. Then, after ravaging all these regions, they returned to the island where they had fixed their habitation. Thence they went on toward Italy, capturing and plundering Pisa and other cities.

Document 2

Source: Passage from *Deeds of the Franks*, a Christian crusader's account of the capture of Jerusalem during the First Crusade, ca. 1100.

The battle raged throughout the day, so that the Temple was covered with their blood. When the pagans had been overcome, our men seized great numbers, both men and women, either killing them or keeping them captive, as they wished. On the roof of the Temple a great number of pagans of both sexes had assembled, and these were taken under the protection of Tancred and Gaston of Beert. Afterward, the army scattered throughout the city and took possession of the gold and silver, the horses and mules, and the houses filled with goods of all kinds.

Document 3

Source: From the *Annals of the Famine of 1315*, by John of Trokelowe, a Benedictine monk and chronicler.

In the year of our Lord 1315, apart from the other hardships with which England was afflicted, hunger grew in the land. . . . Meat and eggs began to run out, capons and fowl could hardly be found, animals died of pest, swine could not be fed because of the excessive price of fodder. A quarter of wheat or beans or peas sold for twenty shillings [In 1313 a quarter of wheat sold for five shillings.], barley for a mark, and oats for ten shillings. . . . The land was so oppressed with want that when the king came to St. Albans on the feast of St. Laurence [August 10] it was hardly possible to find bread on sale to supply his immediate household. . . . Bread did not have its usual nourishing power and strength because the grain was not nourished by the warmth of summer sunshine. Hence those who ate it, even in large quantities, were hungry again after a little while. There can be no doubt that the poor wasted away when even the rich were constantly hungry. . . . Entering the city we consider "them that are consumed with famine" when we see the poor and needy, crushed with hunger, lying stiff and dead in the wards and streets. . . . Four pennies worth of coarse bread was not enough to feed a common man for one day. The usual kinds of meat, suitable for eating, were too scarce; horse meat was precious; plump dogs were stolen. And, according to many reports, men and women in many places secretly ate their own children.

Document 4

Source: Account of the Mongol invasions, from Ibn al-Athir, Arab historian and scholar, ca. 1220.

For these were a people who emerged from the confines of China, and attacked the cities of Turkestan, like Kashghar and Balasaghun, and thence advanced on the cities of Transoxiana, such as Samarqand, Bukhara and the like, taking possession of them, and treating their inhabitants in such wise as we shall mention; and of them one division then passed on into Khurasan, until they had made an end of taking possession, and destroying, and slaying, and plundering, and thence passing on to Ray, Hamadan, and the Highlands, and the cities contained therein, even to the limits of Iraq, whence they marched on the towns of Adharbayjan and Arraniyya, destroying them and slaying most of their inhabitants, of whom none escaped save a small remnant; and all this in less than a year; this is a thing whereof the like has not been heard. And when they had finished with Adharbayjan and Arraniyya, they passed on to Darband-i-Shirwan, and occupied its cities, none of which escaped save the fortress wherein was their King; wherefore they passed by it to the countries of the Lan and the Lakiz and the various nationalities which dwell in that region, and plundered, slew, and destroyed them to the full. And thence they made their way to the lands of Qipchaq, who are the most numerous of the Turks, and slew all such as withstood them, while the survivors fled to the fords and mountain-tops, and abandoned their country, which these Tatars overran. All this they did in the briefest space of time, remaining only for so long as their march required and no more.

Document 5

Source: Account of bubonic plague in Damascus, from Ibn Battuta, Arab traveler, 1348.

I went to Horns and found that the plague had already struck there; about 300 persons died on the day of my arrival. I went to Damascus and arrived on a Thursday; the people had been fasting for three days. . . . The number of deaths among them had risen to 2400 a day. . . . Then we went to Gaza and found most of it deserted because of the number that had died. . . . The qadi told me that only a quarter of the 80 notaries there were left and that the number of deaths had risen to 1100 a day. . . . Then I went to Cairo and was told that during the plague the number of deaths rose to 21,000 a day. I found that all the shaykhs I had known were dead. May God Most High have mercy upon them!

Document 6

Source: Diffusion of bubonic plague in the fourteenth century.

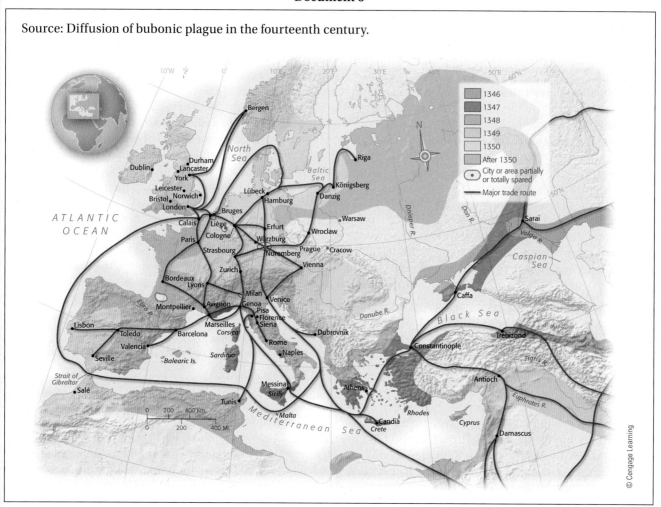

Document 7

Source: Account of the Black Death in Tunis, from Ibn Khaldun, 1347–1348.

Civilization both in the East and the West was visited by a destructive plague which devastated nations and caused populations to vanish. It swallowed up many of the good things of civilization and wiped them out. It overtook the dynasties at the time of their senility, when they had reached the limit of their duration. It lessened their power and curtailed their influence. It weakened their authority. Their situation approached the point of annihilation and dissolution. Civilization decreased with the decrease of mankind. Cities and buildings were laid waste, roads and way-signs were obliterated, settlements and mansions became empty, dynasties and tribes grew weak. The entire inhabited world changed. The East, it seems, was similarly visited, though in accordance with and in proportion to [the East's more affluent] civilization. It was as if the voice of existence in the world had called out for oblivion and restriction, and the world responded to its call.

DBQ 8: Labor Systems from 1500 to 1850 (Chapters 7, 18, and 25)

Question: Evaluate the extent to which labor systems developed in the Americas from 1500 to 1850.

Document 1

Source: Aztec social structure, c. 1400.

Document 2

Source: Speech by Antonio de Montesinos, a Dominican friar in Hispaniola, 1511.

In order to make your sins against the Indians known to you I have come up on this pulpit, I who am a voice of Christ crying in the wilderness of this island, and therefore it behooves you to listen, not with careless attention, but with all your heart and senses, so that you may hear it; for this is going to be the strangest voice that ever you heard, the harshest and hardest and most awful and most dangerous that ever you expected to hear. This voice says that you are in mortal sin, that you live and die in it, for the cruelty and tyranny you use in dealing with these innocent people. Tell me, by what right or justice do you keep these Indians in such a cruel and horrible servitude? On what authority have you waged a detestable war against these people, who dwelt quietly and peacefully on their own land? Why do you keep them so oppressed and weary, not giving them enough to eat, not taking care of them in their illness? For with the excessive work you demand of them they fall ill and die, or rather you kill them with your desire to extract and acquire gold every day. And what care do you take that they should be instructed in religion? Are these not men? Have they not rational souls? Are you not bound to love them as you love yourself?

Document 3

Source: A letter to King Philip II of Spain from Peru, 1559.

[G]reat quantities of gold and silver are no longer found upon the surface of the earth, as they have been in past years; and to penetrate into the bowels of the earth requires greater effort, skill and outlay, and the Spaniards are not willing to do the work themselves, and the natives cannot be forced to do so, because the Emperor has freed them from all obligation of service as soon as they accept the Christian religion. Wherefore it is necessary to acquire negro slaves, who are brought from the coasts of Africa, . . . and these are selling dearer every day, because on account of their natural lack of strength and the change of climate, added to the lack of discretion upon the part of their masters in making them work too hard and giving them too little to eat, they fall sick and the greater part of them die.

Document 4

Source: From the proceedings of the General Court of Colonial Virginia, 1640.

Whereas Hugh Gwyn hath by order from this Board Brought back from Maryland three servants formerly run away from the said Gwyn, the court doth therefore order that the said three servants shall receive the punishment of whipping and to have thirty stripes apiece one called Victor, a Dutchman, the other a Scotchman called James Gregory, shall first serve out their times with their master according to their Indentures, and one whole year apiece after the time of their service is Expired. By their said Indentures in recompense of his Loss sustained by their absence and after that service to their said master is Expired to serve the colony for three whole years apiece, and that the third being a negro named John Punch shall serve his said master or his assigns for the time of his natural Life here or elsewhere.

Document 5

Source: Pamphlet published in London, 1749.

The most approved Judges of the Commercial Interests of these Kingdoms have been of the opinion that our West-Indian and African Trades are the most nationally beneficial of any we carry out. . . . That Traffic alone affords our Planters a constant supply of Negro Servants for the Culture of their Lands in the produce of Sugars, Tobacco, Rice, Rum, Cotton, . . . and all our other Plantation Produce: so that the extensive Employment of our other Shipping in, to and from America, the great Brood of Seamen consequent thereupon, and the daily bread of the most considerable of our British Manufactures, are owing primarily to the Labour of Negroes.

Document 6

Source: Abolition Speech to the British Parliament, by William Wilberforce, 1789.

I must speak of the transit of the slaves in the West Indies. . . . As soon as ever I had arrived thus far in my investigation of the slave trade, I confess to you sir, so enormous so dreadful, so irremediable did its wickedness appear that my own mind was completely made up for the abolition. A trade founded in iniquity, and carried on as this was, must be abolished, let the policy be what it might—let the consequences be what they would, I from this time determined that I would never rest till I had effected its abolition.

Document 7

Source: Excerpt from "Dignity of Labor," in *The Lowell Offering*, a weekly magazine, by Caroline Bean, 1842.

From whence originated the idea, that it was derogatory to a lady's dignity, or a blot upon the female character, to labor? and who was the first to say, sneeringly, "Oh, she works for a living"? Surely, such ideas and expressions ought not to grow on republican soil. The time has been, when ladies of the first rank were accustomed to busy themselves in domestic employment. . . .

Few American fortunes will support a woman who is above the calls of her family; and a man of sense, in choosing a companion to jog with him through all the up-hills and down-hills of life, would sooner choose one who had to work for a living, than one who thought it beneath her to soil her pretty hands with manual labor, although she possessed her thousands. To be able to earn one's own living by laboring with the hands, should be reckoned among female accomplishments; and I hope the time is not far distant when none of my countrywomen will be ashamed to have it known that they are better versed in useful, than they are in ornamental accomplishments.

DBQ 9: Global Interactions (Chapters 12, 19, and 20)

Question: Evaluate the extent of change in attitudes toward global networks of communication and exchange from 1350 to 1750.

Document 1

Source: From *The Rihla [Travels in Asia and Africa]*, by Ibn Battuta, 1355.

We stayed one night in Mombasa, and then pursued our journey to Kilwa, which is a large town on the coast. . . . I was told by a merchant that the town of Sufala lies a fortnight's journey [south] from Kilwa and that gold dust is brought to Sufala from . . . the country of the Limis, which is a month's journey distant from it. Kulwa is a very fine and substantially built town, and all its buildings are of wood. Its inhabitants are constantly engaged in military expeditions, for their country is contiguous to the heathen Zanj.

The sultan at the time of my visit was Abu'l-Muzaffar Hasan, who was noted for his gifts and generosity. He used to devote the fifth part of the booty made on his expeditions to pious and charitable purposes, as is pre-scribed in the Koran, and I have seen him give the clothes off his back to a mendicant who asked him for them.

Document 2

Source: Voyages of the Chinese treasure ships under the command of Zheng He.

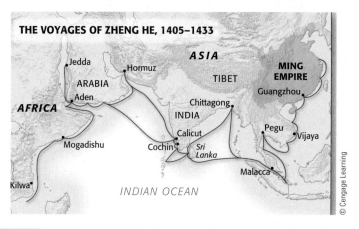

THE VOYAGES OF ZHENG HE, 1405–1433

Document 3

Source: Vasco da Gama's account of his arrival in Calicut, India, 1497.

And the captain-major told him he was the ambassador of a King of Portugal, who was Lord of many countries and the possessor of great wealth of every description, exceeding that of any king of these parts; . . . This, he said, was the reason which induced them to order this country to be discovered, not because they sought for gold or silver, for of this they had such abundance that they needed not what was to be found in this country.

In reply to this the [Indian] king said that he was welcome; that, on his part, he held him as a friend and brother, and would send ambassadors with him to Portugal. . . .

[The next day] the captain-major got ready the following things to be sent to the king, viz., twelve pieces of lambel [heraldry], four scarlet hoods, six hats, four strings of coral, a case containing six wash-hand basins, a case of sugar, two casks of oil, and two of honey. [But] when [messengers] saw the present they laughed at it, saying that it was not a thing to offer to a king, that the poorest merchant from Mecca, or any other part of India, gave more, and that if he wanted to make a present it should be in gold, as the king would not accept such things.

Document 4

Source: Zhang Han, Ming Empire scholar-bureaucrat who was raised in a textile merchant family, ca. 1590.

In the southeast, the various foreigners gain profits from our Chinese goods, and China also gains profits from the foreigners' goods. Trading what we have for what we lack is China's intention in trade. Why shrink from doing so? You might say, "The foreigners frequently invade; the situation is such that we cannot do business with them." But you don't understand that the foreigners will not do without their profits from China, just as we cannot do without our profits from them. Prohibit this, keep them from contact, and how can you avoid their turning to piracy? I maintain that once the maritime markets are opened, the aggressors will cease of their own accord.

Document 5

Source: Journal entry describing a Chinese court scene where Jesuit missionaries were accused of high treason against the Chinese throne, by Matteo Ricci, Italian Jesuit priest of the Roman Catholic Church, ca. 1607.

The Mayor, who was somewhat friendly with the Jesuits, examined the charges of the plaintiffs and the reply of the Jesuit defendants, he took it upon himself to refute the accusers. He said he was fully convinced that these strangers were honest men, and that he knew that there were only two of them in their local residence and not twenty, as had been charged. To this the accusers replied that the Chinese were becoming Christian disciples. To which the Judge replied, "What of it? Why should we be afraid of our own people? Perhaps you are unaware of the fact that Matteo Ricci's company is cultivated by everyone in Beijing and that he is being subsidized by the royal treasury? How dare you who are living outside of the royal city expel men who have permission to live at the royal court! These men have lived here peacefully for twelve years. I command that the Jesuits buy no more large houses, and that the people are not to follow their law."

Document 6

Source: *Closed Country Edict*, by Tokugawa Iemitsu, Japanese shogun, Japan, 1635.

1. Japanese ships are strictly forbidden to leave for foreign countries.
2. No Japanese is permitted to go abroad. If there is anyone who attempts to do so secretly, he must be executed. The ship so involved must be impounded and its owner arrested, and the matter must be reported to the higher authority.
3. If any Japanese returns from overseas after residing there, he must be put to death.
4. If there is any place where the teachings of the Roman Catholic priests are practiced, the two of you must order a thorough investigation.
5. Any informer revealing the whereabouts of the followers of the priests must be rewarded accordingly. If anyone reveals the whereabouts of a high-ranking priest, he must be given one hundred pieces of silver. For those of lower ranks, depending on the deed, the reward must be set accordingly. . . .
8. All incoming ships must be carefully searched for the followers of the priests.

Document 7

Source: *Decree on the Invitation of Foreigners*, from Peter the Great, tsar of Russia, 1702.

We have always tried to maintain internal order, to defend the state against invasion, and in every possible way to improve and to extend trade. With this purpose we have been compelled to make some necessary changes in order that our subjects might more easily gain a knowledge of matters of which they were before ignorant, and become more skillful in their commercial relations. We have therefore given orders for increasing trade with foreigners.

The free exercise of religion of all other sects, although not agreeing with our church, is allowed throughout Russia. We, by the power granted us by the Almighty, shall exercise no compulsion over the consciences of men, and shall gladly allow every Christian to care for his own salvation at his own risk.

DBQ 10: Transforming Social Structure (Chapters 18, 21, 22, 23, and 26)

Question: Evaluate the factors that transformed the social structure in Europe and the Americas from 1750 to 1900.

Document 1

Source: Transatlantic slave trade from Africa, 1750–1850.

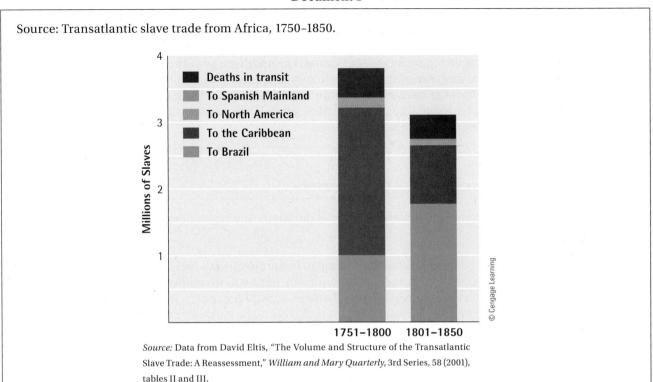

Source: Data from David Eltis, "The Volume and Structure of the Transatlantic Slave Trade: A Reassessment," *William and Mary Quarterly*, 3rd Series, 58 (2001), tables II and III.

Document 2

Source: *Declaration of the Rights of Woman and the Female Citizen*, by Olympe De Gouges, 1791.

Man, are you capable of being just? It is a woman who poses the question; you will not deprive her of that right at least. Tell me, what gives you sovereign empire to oppress my sex? Your strength? Your talents? Observe the Creator in his wisdom; survey in all her grandeur that nature with whom you seem to want to be in harmony, and give me, if you dare, an example of this tyrannical empire. Go back to animals, consult the elements, study plants. . . . Everywhere you will find the [sexes] mingled; everywhere they cooperate in harmonious togetherness in this immortal masterpiece.

Man alone has raised his exceptional circumstances to a principle. Bizarre, blind, bloated with science and degenerated—in a century of enlightenment and wisdom—into the crassest ignorance, he wants to command as a despot a sex which is in full possession of its intellectual faculties; he pretends to enjoy the Revolution and to claim his rights to equality in order to say nothing more about it.

Document 3

Source: *Problems and Progress in Mexico*, by Alexander von Humboldt, a German scientist, ca. 1800.

Mexico is the country of inequality. Nowhere does there exist such a fearful difference in the distribution of fortune, civilization, cultivation of the soil, and population. The interior of the country contains four cities. . . . The central table-land . . . is covered with villages and hamlets like the most cultivated part of Lombardy. To the east and west of this narrow strip succeed tracts of uncultivated ground, on which cannot be found ten or twelve persons to the square league. The capital and several other cities have scientific establishments, which will bear a comparison with those of Europe. The architecture of the public and private edifices, the elegance of the furniture, the equipages, the luxury and dress of the women, the tone of society, all announce a refinement to which the nakedness, ignorance, and vulgarity of the lower people form the most striking contrast. This immense inequality of fortune does not only exist among the caste of whites (Europeans or Creoles), it is even discoverable among the Indians.

Document 4

Source: *The Jamaica Letter*, from Simón Bolívar, leader of the South American independence movement in the 1820s, 1815.

I look upon the present state of America as similar to that of Rome after its fall. We scarcely retain a vestige of what once was; we are, moreover, neither Indian nor European, but a species midway between the legitimate proprietors of this country and the Spanish usurpers. In short, though Americans by birth we derive our rights from Europe, and we have to assert these rights against the rights of the natives, and at the same time we must defend ourselves against the European invaders.

Americans today, and perhaps to a greater extent than ever before, who live within the Spanish system occupy a position in society no better than that of serfs destined for labor. So negative is our existence that I can find nothing comparable in any other civilized society.

Source: Drawing in a French magazine illustrating the social separation in a Paris apartment at night, ca. 1845.

(Dessin de M. Karl Girardet.)

Section of a Parisian building, illustration from 'Le Magasin Pittoresque', engraved by John Quartley (fl.1835-67) 1847 (engraving) (b/w photo), Girardet, Karl (1813–71) (after)/Bibliotheque des Arts Decoratifs, Paris, France/Archives Charmet/The Bridgeman Art Library

Document 6

Source: Interview with Joshua Drake, from the *Sadler Report*, an investigation of conditions in British textile factories, 1832.

Q: Why do you allow your children to go to work at those places where they are ill-treated or over-worked?

A: Necessity compels a man that has children to let them work.

Q: Then you would not allow your children to go to those factories under the present system, if it was not from necessity?

A: No.

Q: Supposing there was a law passed to limit the hours of labor to eight hours a day, or something of that sort, of course you are aware that a manufacturer could not afford to pay them the same wages?

A: No, I do not suppose that they would, but at the same time I would rather have it, and I believe that it would bring me into employ; and if I lost 5pence a day from my children's work, and I got two shillings and six pence myself, it would be better.

Q: You mean to say, that if the manufacturers were to limit the hours of labor, they would employ more people?

A: Yes.

Document 7

Source: A description of industrial Manchester, by Friedrich Engels, 1844.

Passing along a rough bank, among stakes and washing-lines, one penetrates into this chaos of small one-storied, one-roomed huts, in most of which there is no artificial floor; kitchen, living and sleeping-room all in one. In such a hole, scarcely five feet long by six broad, I found two beds—and such bedsteads and beds!—which, with a staircase and chimney-place, exactly filled the room. In several others I found absolutely nothing, while the door stood open, and the inhabitants leaned against it. Everywhere before the doors refuse and offal; that any sort of pavement lay underneath could not be seen but only felt, here and there, with the feet. This whole collection of cattle-sheds for human beings was surrounded on two sides by houses and a factory, and on the third by the river, and besides the narrow stair up the bank, a narrow doorway alone led out into another almost equally ill-built, ill-kept labyrinth of dwellings.

DBQ 11: Imperialist Expansion (Chapters 23, 24, and 25)

Question: Evaluate the extent to which industrialization impacted imperial expansion from 1800 to 1900.

Document 1

Source: Letter addressed to Queen Victoria, from Lin Zexu, Chinese government commissioner sent to Canton to halt British importation of opium, 1839.

I have heard that you are a kind, compassionate monarch. I am sure that you will not do to others what you yourself do not desire. I have also heard that you have instructed every British ship that sails for Canton not to bring any goods to China. The fact that British ships have continued to bring opium to China results per-haps from the impossibility of making a thorough inspection of all of them owing to their large numbers.

I have also heard that the areas under your direct jurisdiction such as London, Scotland, and Ireland do not produce opium; it is produced instead in your Indian possessions such as Bengal, Madras, Patna, and Malwa. In these possessions the English people not only plant opium poppies that grow from one mountain to another but also open factories to manufacture this terrible drug.

May you as ruler check your wicked and sift your vicious people before they come to China, in order to guar-antee the peace of your nation, to show further the sincerity of your politeness and submissiveness, and to let the two countries enjoy together the blessings of peace.

Document 2

Source: *Does Germany Need Colonies? A Political-Economic Reflection*, by Friedrich Fabri, 1879.

It would . . . be advisable for us Germans to learn from the colonial skill of our Anglo-Saxon cousins and begin to emulate them in peaceful competition. When, centuries ago, the German Reich stood at the head of the States of Europe, it was the foremost trading and seagoing power. If the new German Reich wishes to entrench and preserve its regained power for long years to come, then it must regard that power as a cultural mission and must no longer hesitate to resume its colonizing vocation also.

Document 3

Source: Speech to the French Chamber of Deputies, by Jules Ferry, 1884.

In the area of economics, I am placing before you, with the support of some statistics, the considerations that justify the policy of colonial expansion, as seen from the perspective of a need, felt more and more urgently by the industrialized population of Europe and especially the people of our rich and hardworking coun-try of France: the need for outlets [for exports]. . . . Next door Germany is setting up trade barriers; because across the ocean the United States of America have become protectionists, and extreme protectionists at that; because not only are these great markets . . . shrinking, becoming more and more difficult of access, but these great states are beginning to pour into our own markets products not seen there before. . . . Today, as you know, competition, the law of supply and demand, freedom of trade, the effects of speculation, all radiate in a circle that reaches to the ends of the earth.

Document 4

Source: Cartoon "School of Civilization," from the Italian magazine *Il Fischietto*, 1886.

Document 5

Source: Dadabhai Naoroji, an early Indian political and social leader, 1887.

To sum up the whole, the British rule has been: morally, a great blessing; politically, peace and order on one hand, blunders on the other; materially, impoverishment, relieved as far as the railway and other loans go. The natives call the British system "*Sakar ki Churi,*" the knife of sugar. That is to say, there is no oppression, it is all smooth and sweet, but it is the knife, notwithstanding. I mention this that you should know these feelings. Our great misfortune is that you do not know our wants. When you will know our real wishes, I have not the least doubt that you would do justice. The genius and spirit of the British people is fair play and justice.

Document 6

Source: A proclamation of Chinese rebels during the Boxer Rebellion against European imperialism, 1900.

When all the military accomplishments or tactics
Are fully learned,
It will not be difficult to exterminate the "Foreign Devils" then.

Push aside the railway tracks,
Pull out the telephone poles,
Immediately after this destroy the steam[ships].

The great France
Will grow cold and downhearted.
The English and the Russians will certainly disperse.
Let the various "Foreign Devils" all be killed.
May the whole Elegant Empire of the great Qing Dynasty be ever prosperous!

Document 7

Source: "Poor, wicked nineteenth century—Farewell!," by Wilfred Blunt, English poet and writer, 1900.

22nd Dec., 1900. The old century is very nearly out, and leaves the world in a pretty pass, and the British Empire is playing the devil in it as never an empire before on so large a scale. . . . All the nations of Europe are making the same hell upon earth in China, massacring and pillaging and raping in the captured cities as outrageously as in the Middle Ages. The Emperor of Germany gives the word for slaughter and the Pope looks on and approves. In South Africa our troops are burning farms under Kitchener's command. . . . The Americans are spending fifty millions a year on slaughtering the Filipinos; the King of the Belgians has invested his whole fortune on the Congo, where he is brutalizing the Negroes to fill his pockets. . . . The whole white race is reveling openly in violence, as though it had never pretended to be Christian. God's equal curse be on them all! So ends the famous nineteenth century into which we were so proud to have been born.

DBQ 12: Women's Rights (Chapters 28 and 32)

Question: Analyze attitudes concerning women's rights during the twentieth century.

Document 1

Source: Debate in the Syrian Parliament about women's right to vote and hold political office, 1920.

AL-KILANI: We are afraid this question of women's voting will cause social and political unrest. This idea is too premature, and I request that we reject it.

AL JURJIS: . . . I would like to thank Mr. Al-Kilani because I understood from him that he supports the right of women to vote even though he does not think it appropriate for this moment in time! It is true that 98% of our women are ignorant, which is why Al-Kilani made education a requirement.

ZU'AYER: There is no doubt that each and every one of us want[s], desires, and must work to make the woman arrive at a level of advancement where she can take her right. And despite what has been said about the benefit of giving women the right to vote, I still see its approval at this moment does not coincide with the welfare of the nation.

AL-KHATIB: Educated women are few and far between, and we cannot take the exceptions to be the basis of the law, and I beg of you not to undertake a matter that will do greater harm than good.

AL TAWIL: An educated woman is better than a thousand ignorant men, so why would we give men the right to vote and yet deprive educated women from that same right?

THE PRESIDENT: We suggest not dealing with the subject of giving the women the right to vote. Whosoever accepts this raise his hand.

Many hands raised, session concluded.

Document 2

Source: Speech to the Nazi Women's Association, Nuremburg, Germany, by Gertrud Scholtz-Klink, 1935.

I must deal briefly with a question that is constantly brought to our attention, that is, how our present attitude toward life differs from that of the previous women's movement. As a matter of principle, we never have demanded, nor shall we ever demand, equal rights for women with the men of our nation. Instead we shall always make women's special interests dependent upon the needs of our entire nation. All further considerations will follow from this unconditional intertwining of the collective fate of the nation.

Document 3

Source: Early twentieth-century British cartoon, "A Working Man and His Children."

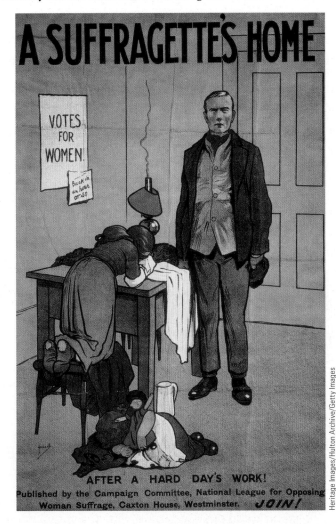

Document 4

Source: Letter to the editor and editorial response printed in official Soviet newspaper *Izvestia* regarding proposed law banning abortion, 1936.

Letter from a Student [K.B.]: "I have read in the press the draft law on the prohibition of abortion, aid to expectant mothers, etc. and cannot remain silent on this matter.

I love children and shall probably have some in four or five years' time. But can I have a child now? Having a child now would mean leaving the Institute [medical school], lagging behind my husband, forgetting everything I have learnt and probably leaving Moscow because there is nowhere to live."

Izvestia's reply: "[K.B.] completely ignored the fact that the government, by widening the network of child-welfare institutions, is easing the mother's task in looking after the child. The main mistake K.B. makes is . . . that she approaches the question as if it were a private matter."

Document 5

Source: "No More Miss America" Brochure, from a feminist group in New York, distributed during the Miss America pageant, 1968.

1. *The Degrading Mindless-Girlie Symbol.* The Pageant contestants epitomize the roles we are all forced to play as women. The parade down the runway blares the metaphor of the county fair, where animals are judged for teeth, fleece, etc. and where the best "specimen" gets the blue ribbon. So are women in our society forced to daily compete for male approval, enslaved by ludicrous "beauty" standards we ourselves are conditioned to take seriously. . . .

9. *Miss America as Dream Equivalent To—?* In this reputed democratic society, where every little boy can grow up to be President, what can every little girl hope to grow up to be? Miss America. That's where it's at. Real power to control our own lives is restricted to men, while women get patronizing pseudo-power, an ermine cloak and a bunch of flowers; men are judged by their actions, women by their appearance.

Document 6

Source: Chinese government billboard encouraging family planning to support the one child policy, 1980s.

Document 7

Source: From *Compañeras: Voices from the Latin American Women's Movement,* a book by Gladys Acosta, Peruvian feminist, 1994.

Gender, the main distinction between all people, is ignored in most philosophical, political, or economic discussions. The reason for this lies partly in the low level of women's participation, but not entirely, because women are not always aware of the system of submission and repression to which we are subjected against our will.

We women play an important role in this ever-more internationalized economy because we represent a particularly exploitable workforce.

Long-Essay Questions (LEQs)

INTRODUCTION

The long-essay question (LEQ) is a chance for you to "demonstrate [your] ability to use historical evidence in crafting a thoughtful historical argument."* You will choose between three comparable long-essay options. Each option will reflect the same history reasoning skill, but will come from different chronological periods and topics. Choose the one you are most comfortable answering. These questions will measure the use of history reasoning skills to explain and analyze significant issues in world history as defined by the thematic learning objectives.

The LEQ is scored using a set of guidelines that assesses how well you are able to apply the history reasoning skills of the Curriculum Framework. On the exam the three options will all emphasize ONE of the following skills: Causation, Continuity and Change over Time, or Comparison. Your essay can receive a maximum of 6 points as scored by an AP® reader. Your classroom teacher may use a different system of grading, but she or he will be looking to see if you demonstrate the same skills as outlined in the framework.

The LEQs in this section mirror the format of the AP® World History exam; you will have 40 minutes to complete your essay.

When writing your LEQs, try following these steps:

1. **Read the prompt carefully and create an outline or graphic organizer**: Underline key words. What is the particular skill that will be assessed? What are some other events that occurred during the same time period? (Try to put the prompt into historical context.) Create an outline or graphic organizer that links your response directly to the prompt.

2. **Write a good thesis** (up to **1 point**): Does the thesis explicitly address all parts of the prompt? Do not simply restate the prompt, but explain how and why you have chosen to make a specific argument. Remember that it is okay for the thesis to consist of multiple sentences.

3. **Provide a historical context for your argument** (up to **1 point**). Consider how your argument relates to broader historical events, developments, or processes. Explain this context for your argument by exploring how the same topic is reflected in other geographical areas (if the prompt is not global), or how other topics add depth.

4. **Use evidence to support your argument** (up to **2 points**): Be sure that your evidence is specific and that it clearly and consistently supports the thesis. Clear linkage between the evidence and the thesis is indicative of a good analytical essay.

5. **Apply the targeted skill being assessed** (Causation, Continuity and Change over Time, or Comparison): Use specific wording and examples that illustrate the history reasoning skill.

6. **Develop the complexity of your argument** (up to **2 points**): Try to demonstrate a complex understanding of the topic throughout your whole essay. This may be done through:
   - Explaining the nuance of an issue by analyzing multiple variables.
   - Explaining both similarity and difference, both continuity AND change, explaining multiple causes, or explaining both causes and effects.
   - Explaining multiple relevant and insightful connections within and across time periods.
   - Confirming the validity of an argument by corroborating multiple perspectives across themes.
   - Qualifying or modifying an argument by taking into account multiple diverse viewpoints.
   - The development of complexity must be demonstrated throughout the whole essay, not in a single phrase or sentence.

---

* Course and Exam Description, AP® World History, Effective Fall 2017, p. 219. Available online at *www.apcentral.collegeboard.com.*

AP® is a trademark registered by the College Board, which is not affiliated with, and does not endorse, this product.

Long-Essay Questions

1. Analyze the extent to which the Neolithic Revolution affected the development of civilization.

2. Evaluate the extent to which civilization developed in one of the following areas from 600 BCE to 600 CE:
   - Rome
   - China
   - India

3. Evaluate the extent to which the spread of Islam affected culture and politics from 600 CE to 1450 CE.

4. Analyze the extent to which increased trade and exchange in the time period of 600 CE to 1450 CE led to cultural changes.

5. Evaluate the difference in impact of the Silk Road with the impact of the Columbian Exchange.

6. Evaluate the extent to which fifteenth-century European exploration changed culture and economic activity around the world.

7. Evaluate the most significant political difference between any two of the below from their inception to 1450 CE.
   - Confucianism
   - Christianity
   - Hinduism

8. Evaluate the degree to which the decline and collapse of the Mongolian and Ottoman Empires were similar.

9. Evaluate the extent to which the Enlightenment impacted culture and politics before 1900.

10. Evaluate the extent to which politics fostered change in the Middle East during the twentieth century.

11. Evaluate the extent of political and economic continuities and changes in China from 1450 to the present.

12. Evaluate the economic and social impacts of imperialism in the late nineteenth and early twentieth centuries.

13. Evaluate whether or not World War II was a transformative event in world history.

14. Evaluate the most significant similarities between India's independence movement and decolonization in Africa.

15. Evaluate the extent of the economic and political impact of globalization from 1945 to the present.